T3-BOE-861

The International Standard Bible Encyclopaedia

M. O. Evans

Managing Editor, International Standard Bible Encyclopaedia

THE INTERNATIONAL STANDARD BIBLE ENCYCLOPAEDIA

JAMES ORR, M.A., D.D., General Editor

JOHN L. NUELSEN, D.D., LL.D.

EDGAR Y. MULLINS, D.D., LL.D.
ASSISTANT EDITORS

MORRIS O. EVANS, D.D., Ph.D., Managing Editor

MELVIN GROVE KYLE, D.D., LL.D., Revising Editor

VOLUME IV
NAARAH—SOCHO

WM. B. EERDMANS PUBLISHING CO.
GRAND RAPIDS, MICH.
1949

Printed in the United States of America
by J. J. Little & Ives Company, New York

NAARAH (נַעֲרָה, *na'ărāh;* B, **αἱ κῶμαι αὐτῶν,** *hai kōmai autōn,* A, **Νααραθά,** *Naarathá;* AV **Naarath**): A town in the territory of Ephraim (Josh **16** 7). It appears as "Naaran" in 1 Ch **7** 28 (B, Νααρνάν, *Naarnán,* A, Νααράν, *Naarán*). *Onom* (s.v. "Noorath") places it 5 Rom miles from Jericho. The name has not been recovered, and no identification is certain. The position would agree with that of *el-'Aujeh,* about 5 miles N.E. of Jericho.

NAARAI, nā'a-rī (נַעֲרַי, *na'ăray*): Son of Ezbai, one of David's heroes (1 Ch **11** 37). In the ‖ passage (2 S **23** 35), he is called "Paarai the Arbite." The true forms of the name and description are uncertain (see Budde, *Richter u. Samuel,* and Curtis, *Chronicles*).

NAARAN, nā'a-ran, **NAARATH,** nā'a-rath (נַעֲרָן, *na'ărān,* נַעֲרָת, *na'ărāth*). See NAARAH.

NAASHON, nā'a-shon, nā-ash'on, **NAASON,** nā'a-son, **NAASSON,** nā-as'on (**Ναασσών,** *Naassōn*): AV Gr form of "Nahshon" (thus RV) (Mt **1** 4; Lk **3** 32).

NAATHUS, nā'a-thus (**Νάαθος,** *Náathos*): One of the sons of Addi who put away his foreign wife (1 Esd **9** 31). It apparently corresponds to "Adna" of Ezr **10** 30, of which it is a transposition. B reads Λάθος, *Láthos,* probably confusing Α and Λ.

NABAL, nā'bal (נָבָל, *nābhāl,* "foolish" or "wicked"; **Ναβάλ,** *Nabál*): A wealthy man of Maon in the highlands of Judah, not far from Hebron, owner of many sheep and goats which he pastured around Carmel in the same district. He was a churlish and wicked man (1 S **25** 2 ff). When David was a fugitive from Saul, he and his followers sought refuge in the wilderness of Paran, near the possessions of Nabal, and protected the latter's flocks and herds from the marauding Bedouin. David felt that some compensation was due him for such services (vs 15 and 25), so, at the time of sheep-shearing—an occasion of great festivities among sheep masters—he sent 10 of his young men to Nabal to solicit gifts of food for himself and his small band of warriors. Nabal not only refused any assistance or presents, but sent back insulting words to David, whereupon the latter, becoming very angry, determined upon the extermination of Nabal and his household and dispatched 400 men to execute his purpose. Abigail, Nabal's wife, a woman of wonderful sagacity and prudence as well as of great beauty, having learned of her husband's conduct and of David's intentions, hurriedly proceeded, with a large supply of provisions, dainties and wine, to meet David and to apologize for her husband's unkind words and niggardliness, and thus succeeded in thwarting the bloody and revengeful plans of Israel's future king. On her return home she found her husband in the midst of a great celebration ("like the feast of a king"), drunken with wine, too intoxicated to realize his narrow escape from the sword of David. On the following morning, when sober, having heard the report of his wife, he was so overcome with fear that he never recovered from the shock, but died 10 days later (vs 36–38). When David heard of his death, he sent for Abigail, who soon afterward became one of his wives. W. W. DAVIES

NABARIAS, nab-a-rī'as (**Ναβαρίας,** *Nabarías,* B, **Ναβαρείας,** *Nabareías*): One of those who stood upon Ezra's left hand as he expounded the Law (1 Esd **9** 44). Esdras (loc. cit.) gives only 6 names, whereas Nehemiah (**8** 4) gives 7. It is probable that the last (Meshullam) of Nehemiah's list is simply dropped and that Nabarias = Hashbaddanah; or it may possibly be a corruption of Zechariah in Nehemiah's list.

NABATAEANS, nab-a-tē'-anz, **NABATHAEANS,** nab-a-thē'anz (**Ναβαταῖοι,** *Nabataíoi;* in 1 Macc **5** 25 ℵ reads **ἀναβάταις οἱ,** *anabátais hoi,* V, **'Αναβαττaίοις,** *Anabattaíois;* AV **Nabathites,** more correctly "Nabataeans"):

1. Locality and Early History

A Sem (Arabian rather than Syrian) tribe whose home in early Hellenistic times was S.E. of Pal, where they had either supplanted or mingled with the Edomites (cf Mal **1** 1–5). In Josephus' day they were so numerous that the territory between the Red Sea and the Euphrates was called Nabatene (*Ant,* I, xii, 4). They extended themselves along the E. of the Jordan with Petra as their capital (Strabo xvi.779; Jos, *Ant,* XIV, i, 4; XVII, iii, 2; *BJ,* I, vi, 2, etc). Their earlier history is shrouded in obscurity. Jerome, *Quaest in Gen* **25** *13,* following the hint of Jos (*Ant,* I, xii, 4), asserts they were identical with the Ishmaelite tribe of Nebaioth, which is possible, though Nebaioth is spelled with ת and Nabataeans with ט. They were apparently the first allies of the Assyrians in their invasions of Edom (cf Mal **1** 1 ff). They were later subdued by Sennacherib (Sayce, *New Light from the Ancient Monuments,* II, 430), but before long regained their independence and resisted Ashurbanipal (Rawlinson, note, ad loc.). According to Alexander Polyhistor (Fr. 18), they were included in the nomadic tribes reduced by David. Their history is more detailed from 312 BC (Diod. Sic. xix), when Antigonus I (Cyclops) sent his general Athenaeus with a force against them in Petra. After an initial advantage, the army of Athenaeus was almost annihilated. Demetrius, the son of Antigonus, was sent against them a few years later, with little success, though he arranged a friendship with them. The first prince mentioned is Aretas I, to whom the high priest Jason fled in 169 BC. They were friendly to the early Maccabees in the anti-Hellenistic struggle, to Judas in 164 BC (1 Macc **5** 25) and to Jonathan in 160 BC (**9** 35).

2. A Strong Kingdom

Toward the end of the 2d cent. BC on the fall of the Ptolemaic and Seleucid Dynasties, the Nabataeans under King Erotimus founded a strong kingdom extending E. of the Jordan (in 110 BC). Conscious now of their own strength, they resented the ambition of the Hasmonean Dynasty—their former allies—and opposed Alexander Jannaeus (96 BC) at the siege of Gaza (Jos, *Ant,* XIII, xiii, 3). A few years later (90 BC) Alexander retaliated by attacking Obedas I, king of the Nabataeans, but suffered a severe defeat E. of the Jordan (Jos, *Ant,* XIII, xiii, 5; *BJ,* I, iv, 4). Antiochus XII of Coele-Syria next led an expedition against the Nabataeans, but was defeated and slain in the battle of Kana (Jos, *Ant,* XIII, xv, 1–2; *BJ,* I, iv, 7–8). Consequently, Aretas III seized Coele-Syria and Damascus and gained another victory over Alexander Jannaeus at Adida (in 85 BC). The Nabataeans, led by Aretas (III ?), espoused the cause of

3. Conflicts

Hyrcanus against Aristobulus, besieged the latter in Jerus and provoked the interference of the Romans, by whom under Scaurus they were defeated (Jos, *Ant,* XIV, i, 4 f; *BJ,* I, vi, 2 f). After the capture of Jerus, Pompey attacked Aretas, but was satisfied with a payment (Jos, ib), and Damascus was added to Syria, though later it appears to have again passed into the hands of Aretas (2 Cor **11** 32). In 55 BC Gabinius led another force against the Nabataeans (Jos, ib). In 47 BC Malchus I assisted Caesar, but in 40 BC refused to assist Herod against the Parthians, thus provoking both the Idumaean Dynasty and the Romans. Antony made a present of part of Malchus' territory to Cleopatra, and the Nabataean kingdom was further humiliated by disastrous defeat in the war against Herod (31 BC).

Under Aretas IV (9 BC—40 AD) the kingdom was recognized by Augustus. This king sided with the Romans against the Jews, and further gained a great victory over Herod Antipas, who had divorced his daughter to marry Herodias. Under King Abias an expedition against Adiabene came to grief. Malchus II (48–71 AD) assisted the Romans in the conquest of Jerus (Jos, *BJ*, III, iv, 2). Rabel (71–106 AD) was the last king of the Nabataeans as a nation. In 106 AD their nationality was broken up by the unwise policy of Trajan, and Arabia, of which Petra was the capital, was made a Rom province by Cornelius Palma, governor of Syria. Otherwise they might have at least contributed to protecting the West against the East. Diodorus (loc. cit.) represents the Nabataeans as a wild nomadic folk, with no agriculture, but with flocks and herds and engaged in considerable trading. Later, however, they seem to have imbibed considerable Aramaean culture, and Aram. became at least the language of their commerce and diplomacy. They were also known as pirates on the Red Sea; they secured the harbor of Elah and the Gulf of 'Aḳaba. They traded between Egypt and Mesopotamia and carried on a lucrative commerce in myrrh, frankincense and costly wares (*KGF*, 4th ed [1901], I, 726–44, with full bibliography).

4. End of the Nation

S. Angus

NABATHITES, nab'a-thīts: AV=RV "Nabathaeans."

NABOTH, nā'both, nā'bōth (נָבוֹת, *nābhōth*, from נוּב, *nūbh*, "a sprout"; **Ναβουθαί**, *Nabouthaí*): The owner of a vineyard contiguous to the palace of King Ahab. The king desired, by purchase or exchange, to add the vineyard to his own grounds. Naboth, however, refused to part on any terms with his paternal inheritance. This refusal made Ahab "heavy and displeased" (1 K **21** 4). Jezebel, the king's wife, then took the matter in hand, and by false accusation on an irrelevant charge procured the death of Naboth by stoning (1 K **21** 7–14). As Ahab was on his way to take possession of the vineyard he met Elijah the prophet, who denounced his vile act and pronounced judgment on king and royal house. A temporary respite was given to Ahab because of a repentant mood (1 K **21** 27–29); but later the blow fell, first upon himself in a conflict with Syria (1 K **22** 34–40); then upon his house through a conspiracy of Jehu, in which Jehoram, Ahab's son, and Jezebel, his wife, were slain (2 K **9** 25–26.30 ff). In both cases the circumstances recalled the foul treatment of Naboth.

Henry Wallace

NABUCHODONOSOR, nab-ū-kō-don'ō-sor (**Ναβουχοδονοσόρ**, *Nabouchodonosór*): LXX and Vulg form of "Nebuchadnezzar" ("Nebuchadrezzar") found in AV of the Apoc in 1 Esd **1** 40. 41.45.48; **2** 10; **5** 7; **6** 26; Ad Est **11** 4; Bar **1** 9.11.12. It is the form used in AV of the Apoc throughout. In RV of Jth and Tob **14** 15, the form "Nebuchadnezzar" is given.

NACON, nā'kon, **THE THRESHING FLOOR OF** (נָכוֹן, *nākhōn;* AV **Nachon**): The place where Uzzah was smitten for putting forth his hand to steady the ark, hence called afterward "Perez-uzzah" (2 S **6** 8); in the ‖ passage (1 Ch **13** 9) we have כִּידֹן, *kīdhon*, and in Jos (*Ant*, VII, iv, 2) Χειδών, *Cheidṓn*. In 1 S **23** 23 the word *nākhōn* occurs, and is tr[d] "of a certainty," m "with the certainty" or "to a set place"; also in 1 S **26** 4 it is tr[d] "of a certainty," m "to a set place." It is uncertain whether in 1 S **6** 6 it is a place-name at all, and no successful attempt has been made to identify either Nacon or Chidon; possibly they are both personal names. E. W. G. Masterman

NACHOR, nā'kor (**Ναχώρ**, *Nachṓr*) AV; Gr form of "Nahor" (thus RV). Grandfather of Abraham (Lk **3** 34).

NADAB, nā'dab (נָדָב, *nādhābh*, "noble"; **Ναδάβ**, *Nadáb*):

(1) Aaron's first-born son (Ex **6** 23; Nu **3** 2; **26** 60; 1 Ch **6** 3 [Heb **5** 29]; **24** 1). He was permitted with Moses, Aaron, the 70 elders, and his brother Abihu to ascend Mt. Sinai and behold the God of Israel (Ex **24** 1.9). He was associated with his father and brothers in the priestly office (Ex **28** 1). Along with Abihu he was guilty of offering "strange fire," and both "died before Jeh" (Lev **10** 1.2; Nu **3** 4; **26** 61). The nature of their offence is far from clear. The word rendered "strange" seems in this connection to mean no more than "unauthorized by the Law" (see זוּר, *zūr*, in *BDB*, and cf Ex **30** 9). The proximity of the prohibition of wine to officiating priests (Lev **10** 8.9) has given rise to the erroneous suggestion of the Midr that the offence of the brothers was drunkenness.

(2) A descendant of Jerahmeel (1 Ch **2** 28.30).

(3) A Gibeonite (1 Ch **8** 30).

(4) Son of Jeroboam I and after him for two years king of Israel (1 K **14** 20; **15** 25). While Nadab was investing Gibbethon, a Phili stronghold, Baasha, who probably was an officer in the army, as throne-robbers usually were, conspired against him, slew him and seized the throne (1 K **15** 27–31). With the assassination of Nadab the dynasty of Jeroboam was extirpated, as foretold by the prophet Ahijah (1 K **14**). This event is typical of the entire history of the Northern Kingdom, characterized by revolutions and counter-revolutions. John A. Lees

NADABATH, nā'da-bath (**Ναδαβάθ**, *Nadabáth;* AV **Nadabatha,** na-dab'a-tha): A city E. of the Jordan from which the wedding party of Jambri were coming when Jonathan and Simon attacked them and slew very many, designing to avenge the murder of their brother John (1 Macc **9** 37 ff). Nebo and Nabathaea have been suggested as identical with Nadabath. Clermont-Ganneau would read *rhabatha*, and identify it with Rabbath-ammon. There is no certainty.

NAGGAI, nag'ī, nag'ā-ī (**Ναγγαί**, *Naggaí;* AV **Nagge**): In Lk **3** 25, the Gr form of the Heb name Nogah (q.v.).

NAHALAL, nā'hal-al (נַהֲלָל, *nahălāl;* B, **Βαιθμάν**, *Baithmán*, A, **Νααλώλ**, *Naalṓl*, and other forms): A city in the territory of Zebulun assigned with its suburbs to the Merarite Levites, out of which the Canaanite inhabitants were not driven (Josh **19** 15, AV [incorrectly] "Nahallal"; **21** 35; Jgs **1** 30, "Nahalol"). In the Talm Jerus (*Meg.*, i.1) it is identified with Mahlul. This name might correspond either with 'Ain Māhil, or with Ma'lūl. The former lies about 3½ miles N.E. of Nazareth on a hill near the eastern boundary of Zebulun. The latter is situated about 3½ miles W. of Nazareth, near the southern border of Zebulun. The change of *n* to *m* is not unusual. W. Ewing

NAHALIEL, na-hā'li-el, na-hal'i-el (נַחֲלִיאֵל, *naḥălī'ēl*, "torrent valley of God"; B, **Μαναήλ,** *Manaēl*, A, **Νααλιήλ,** *Naaliēl*): A place where Israel encamped on the way from Arnon to Jericho, named with Mattanah and Bamoth (Nu **21** 19). *Onom* places it near to the Arnon. It is natural to seek for this "torrent valley" in one of the tributaries of the Arnon. It may be *Wâdy Wāleh*, which drains a wide area to the N.E. of the Arnon; or perhaps *Wâdy Zerḳā Ma'īn* farther to the N.

NAHALLAL, na-hal'al, **NAHALOL,** nā'ha-lol. See Nahalal.

NAHAM, nā'ham (נַחַם, *naḥam*, "comfort"): A Judahite chieftain, father of Keilah the Garmite (1 Ch **4** 19); the passage is obscure.

NAHAMANI, nā-ha-mā'nī, na-ham'a-nī (נַחֲמָנִי, *naḥămānī*, "compassionate"): One of the twelve heads who returned with Zerubbabel (Neh **7** 7). The name is wanting in the ‖ list (Ezr **2** 2). In 1 Esd **5** 8 he is called "Eneneus" (RVm "Enenis").

NAHARAI, nā'ha-rī (נַחֲרַי, *naḥăray*), **NAHARI,** nā'ha-rī (נַחְרַי, *naḥray*): One of David's heroes, Joab's armor-bearer (2 S **23** 37, AV "Nahari"; 1 Ch **11** 39).

NAHASH, nā'hash (נָחָשׁ, *nāḥāsh*, "serpent"; **Ναάς,** *Naás*):

(1) The father of Abigail and Zeruiah, the sisters of David (2 S **17** 25; cf 1 Ch **2** 16). The text in 2 S, where this reference is made, is hopelessly corrupt; for that reason there are various explanations. The rabbis maintain that Nahash is another name for Jesse, David's father. Others think that Nahash was the name of Jesse's wife; but it is not probable that Nahash could have been the name of a woman. Others explain the passage by making Nahash the first husband of Jesse's wife, so that Abigail and Zeruiah were half-sisters to King David.

(2) A king of Ammon, who, at the very beginning of Saul's reign, attacked Jabesh-gilead so successfully, that the inhabitants sued for peace at almost any cost, for they were willing to pay tribute and serve the Ammonites (1 S **11** 1 ff). The harsh king, not satisfied with tribute and slavery, demanded in addition that the right eye of every man should be put out, as "a reproach upon Israel." They were given seven days to comply with these cruel terms. Before the expiration of this time, Saul, the newly anointed king, appeared on the scene with an army which utterly routed the Ammonites (1 S **11** 1 ff), and, according to Jos, killed King Nahash (*Ant*, VI, v, 3).

If the Nahash of 2 S **10** 2 be the same as the king mentioned in 1 S **11**, this statement of Jos cannot be true, for he lived till the early part of David's reign, 40 or more years later. It is, of course, possible that Nahash, the father of Hanun, was a son or grandson of the king defeated at Jabesh-gilead by Saul. There is but little agreement among commentators in regard to this matter. Some writers go so far as to claim that "all passages in which this name [Nahash] is found refer to the same individual."

(3) A resident of Rabbath-ammon, the capital of Ammon (2 S **17** 27). Perhaps the same as Nahash (2), which see. His son Shobi, with other trans-Jordanic chieftains, welcomed David at Mahanaim with sympathy and substantial gifts when the old king was fleeing before his rebel son Absalom. Some believe that Shobi was a brother of Hanun, king of Ammon (2 S **10** 1).

W. W. Davies

NAHATH, nā'hath (נַחַת, *naḥath*):

(1) A grandson of Esau (Gen **36** 13; 1 Ch **1** 37).

(2) A descendant of Levi and ancestor of Samuel (1 Ch **6** 26); also called "Toah" (1 Ch **6** 34) and "Tohu" (1 S **1** 1).

(3) A Levite who, in the time of Hezekiah, assisted in the oversight of "the oblations and the tithes and the dedicated things" (2 Ch **31** 13).

NAHBI, nä'bī (נַחְבִּי, *naḥbī*): The representative of Naphtali among the 12 spies (Nu **13** 14).

NAHOR, nā'hor (נָחוֹר, *nāḥōr;* in the NT **Ναχώρ,** *Nachōr*):

(1) Son of Serug and grandfather of Abraham (Gen **11** 22–25; 1 Ch **1** 26).

(2) Son of Terah and brother of Abraham (Gen **11** 26.27.29; **22** 20.23; **24** 15.24.47; **29** 5; Josh **24** 2).

A city of Nahor is mentioned in Gen **24** 10; the God of Nahor in Gen **31** 53. In AV Josh **24** 2; Lk **3** 34, the name is spelled "Nachor."

NAHSHON, nä'shon (נַחְשׁוֹן, *naḥshōn;* LXX and NT, **Ναασσών,** *Naassṓn*): A descendant of Judah; brother-in-law of Aaron and ancestor of David and of Jesus Christ (Ex **6** 23; Nu **1** 7; 1 Ch **2** 10.11; Ruth **4** 20; Mt **1** 4; Lk **3** 32).

NAHUM, nā'hum (**Ναούμ,** *Naoúm;* AV **Naum**): An ancestor of Jesus in Lk's genealogy, the 9th before Joseph, the husband of Mary (Lk **3** 25).

NAHUM, nā'hum, **THE BOOK OF:**

I. Authorship and Date.—The name Nahum (נַחוּם, *naḥūm;* LXX and NT **Ναούμ,** *Naoúm;* Jos, *Naoúmos*) occurs nowhere else in the OT; in the NT it is found in Lk **3** 25. It is not uncommon in the Mish, and it has been discovered in Phoen inscriptions. It means "consolation," or "consoler," and is therefore, in a sense, symbolical of the message of the book, which is intended to comfort the oppressed and afflicted people of Judah.

1. Name

Of the personal life of Nahum, practically nothing is known. In **1** 1 he is called "the Elkoshite," that is, an inhabitant of Elkosh. Unfortunately, the location of this place is not known. One tradition, which cannot be traced beyond the 16th cent. AD, identifies the home of Nahum with a modern village *Elkush*, or *Alkosh*, not far from the left bank of the Tigris, two days' journey N. of the site of ancient Nineveh. A second tradition, which is at least as old as the days of Jerome, the latter part of the 4th cent., locates Elkosh in Galilee, at a place identified by many with the modern *El-Kauze*, near Ramieh. Others identify the home of the prophet with Capernaum, the name of which means "Village of Nahum." A fourth tradition, which is first found in a collection of traditions

2. Life and Home

entitled "Lives of the Prophets," says "Nahum was from Elkosh, beyond Bet Gabre, of the tribe of Simeon." A place in the S. is more in harmony with the interest the prophet takes in the Southern Kingdom, so that the last-mentioned tradition seems to have much in its favor, but absolute certainty is not attainable.

The Book of Nahum centers around the fall and destruction of Nineveh. Since the capture of the city is represented as still in the future, it seems evident that the prophecies were delivered some time before 607–606 BC, the year in which the city was destroyed. Thus the latest possible date of Nahum's activity is fixed. The earliest possible date also is indicated by internal evidence. In **3** 8 ff the prophet speaks of the capture and destruction of No-amon, the Egyp Thebes, as an accomplished fact. The expedition of Ashurbanipal, king of Assyria, against Egypt, which resulted in the fall of Thebes, occurred about 663 BC. Hence the activity of Nahum must be placed somewhere between 663 and 607.

3. Date

As to the exact period between the two dates there is disagreement among scholars. One thing is made quite clear by the prophecy itself, namely, that at the time the words were spoken or written, Nineveh was passing through some grave crisis. Now we know that during the second half of the 7th cent. BC Assyria was threatened three times: (1) the revolt of Shamash-shumukin of Babylon against his brother, the king of Assyria, 650–648 BC; (2) the invasion of Assyria and threatened attack upon Nineveh by some unknown foe, perhaps the Scythians, about 625 BC; (3) the final attack, which resulted in the fall and destruction of Nineveh in 607–606 BC.

The first crisis does not offer a suitable occasion for Nahum's prophecy, because at that time the city of Nineveh was not in any danger. Little is known concerning the second crisis, and it is not possible either to prove or to disprove that it gave rise to the book. On the other hand, the years immediately preceding the downfall of Nineveh offer a most suitable occasion. The struggle continued for about 2 years. The united forces of the Chaldaeans and Scythians met determined resistance; at last a breach was made in the northeast corner of the wall, the city was taken, pillaged and burned. Judah had suffered much from the proud Assyrian, and it is not difficult to understand how, with the doom of the cruel oppressor imminent, a prophet-patriot might burst into shouts of exultation and triumph over the distress of the cruel foe. "If," says A. B. Davidson, "the distress of Nineveh referred to were the final one, the descriptions of the prophecy would acquire a reality and naturalness which they otherwise want, and the general characteristics of Heb prophecy would be more truly conserved." There seems to be good reason, therefore, for assigning Nahum's activity to a date between 610 and 607 BC.

II. The Book.—Nahum is the prophet of Nineveh's doom. Ch **1** (+**2** 2) contains the decree of Nineveh's destruction. Jeh is a God of vengeance and of mercy (vs 2.3); though He may at times appear slack in punishing iniquity, He will surely punish the sinner. No one can stand before Him in the day of judgment (vs 4–6). Jeh, faithful to those who rely upon Him (ver 7), will be terrible toward His enemies and toward the enemies of His people (ver 8). Judah need not fear: the present enemy is doomed (vs 9–14), which will mean the exaltation of Judah (**1** 15; **2** 2). The army appointed to execute the decree is approaching, ready for battle (**2** 1–4). All efforts to save the city are in vain; it falls (vs 5.6), the queen and her attendants are captured (ver 7), the inhabitants flee (ver 8), the city is sacked and left a desolation (vs 9–13). The destruction of the bloody city is imminent (**3** 1–3); the fate is well deserved and no one will bemoan her (vs 4–7); natural strength and resources will avail nothing (vs 8–11); the soldiers turn cowards and the city will be utterly cut off (vs 12–18); the whole earth will rejoice over the downfall of the cruel oppressor (ver 19).

1. Contents

Opinions concerning the religious significance of the Book of Nahum may differ, but from the standpoint of language and style all students assign to Nahum an exalted place among the prophet-poets of the ancient Hebrews; for all are impressed with the intense force and picturesqueness of his language and style. "Each prophet," says Kirkpatrick, "has his special gift for his particular work. Nahum bears the palm for poetic power. His short book is a Pindaric ode of triumph over the oppressor's fall." So also G. A. Smith: "His language is strong and brilliant; his rhythm rumbles and rolls, leaps and flashes, like the horsemen and chariots he describes."

2. Style

Until recently no doubts were expressed concerning the integrity of the book, but within recent years scholars have, with growing unanimity, denied the originality of **1** 2—**2** 2 (Heb **2** 3), with the exception of **2** 1, which is considered the beginning of Nahum's utterances. This change of opinion is closely bound up with the alleged discovery of distorted remnants of an old alphabetic poem in ch **1** (*HDB*, art. "Nahum"; *Expos*, 1898, 207 ff; *ZATW*, 1901, 225ff; Eiselen, *Minor Prophets*, 422 ff). Now, it is true that in **1** 2–7 traces of alphabetic arrangement may be found, but even here the artistic arrangement is not carried through consistently; in the rest of the chapter the evidence is slight.

3. Integrity

The artificial character of acrostic poetry is generally supposed to point to a late date. Hence those who believe that ch **1** was originally an alphabetic poem consider it an exilic or post-exilic production, which was at a still later date prefixed to the genuine prophecies of Nahum. In support of this view it is pointed out further that the prophecy in ch **1** is vague, while the utterances in chs **2** and **3** are definite and to the point. Some derive support for a late date also from the language and style of the poem.

That difficulties exist in ch **1**, that in some respects it differs from chs **2** and **3**, even the students of the Eng. text can see; and that the Heb text has suffered in transmission is very probable. On the other hand, the presence of an acrostic poem in ch **1** is not beyond doubt. The apparent vagueness is removed, if ch **1** is interpreted as a general introduction to the more specific denunciation in chs **2** and **3**. And a detailed examination shows that in this, as in other cases, the linguistic and stylistic data are indecisive. In view of these facts it may safely be asserted that no convincing argument has been presented against the genuineness of **1** 2—**2** 2. "Therefore," says G. A. Smith, "while it is possible that a later poem has been prefixed to the genuine prophecies of Nahum, and the first ch supplies many provocations to belief in such a theory, this has not been proved, and the able essays of proof have much against them. The question is open."

III. Teaching.—The utterances of Nahum center around a single theme, the destruction of Nineveh. His purpose is to point out the hand of God in the impending fall of the city, and the significance of this catastrophe for the oppressed Hebrews. As a result they contain little direct religious teaching; and what there is of it is confined very largely to the opening vs of ch **1**. These vs emphasize the twofold manifestation of the Divine holiness, the Divine vengeance and the Divine mercy (**1** 2.3). The manifestation of the one results in the destruction of the wicked (**1** 2), the other in the salvation of the oppressed (**1** 15; **2** 2). Faith in Jeh will secure the Divine favor and protection (**1** 7).

1. The Character of Jehovah

2. Nahum's Glee over the Ruin of Nineveh

The fierceness of Nahum, and his glee at the thought of Nineveh's ruin, may not be in accord with the injunction, "Love thine enemy"; but it should be borne in mind that it is not personal hatred that prompts the prophet; he is stirred by a righteous indignation over the outrages committed by Assyria. He considers the sin and overthrow of Nineveh, not merely in their bearing upon the fortunes of Judah, but in their relation to the moral government of the whole world; hence his voice gives utterance to the outraged conscience of humanity.

3. Universality of Jehovah's Rule

While Nahum's message, in its direct teaching, appears to be less spiritual and ethical than that of his predecessors, it sets in a clear light Jeh's sway over the whole universe, and emphasizes the duty of nations as well as of individuals to own His sway and obey His will. This attitude alone will assure permanent peace and prosperity; on the other hand, disobedience to His purpose and disregard of His rule will surely bring calamity and distress. The emphasis of these ethical principles gives to the message of Nahum a unique significance for the present day and generation. "Assyria in his hands," says Kennedy, "becomes an object-lesson to the empires of the modern world, teaching, as an eternal principle of the Divine government of the world, the absolute necessity, for a nation's continued vitality, of that righteousness, personal, civic, and national, which alone exalteth a nation."

4. The Messianic Outlook

In a broad sense, **1** 15 is of Messianic import. The downfall of Nineveh and Assyria prepares the way for the permanent redemption and exaltation of Zion: "the wicked one shall no more pass through thee."

Literature.—Comms. on the Minor Prophets by Ewald, Pusey, Keil, Orelli; G. A. Smith (*Expositor's Bible*); Driver (*New Cent.*); B. A. Davidson, comm. on "Nah," "Hab," "Zeph" (*Cambridge Bible*); A. F. Kirkpatrick, *Doctrine of the Prophets;* Eiselen, *Prophecy and the Prophets;* F. W. Farrar, *Minor Prophets* ("Men of the Bible" series); Driver, *Intro to the Lit. of the OT; HDB*, art. "Nahum"; *EB*, art. "Nahum."

F. C. Eiselen

NAIDUS, nā'i-dus (A, **Νάειδος**, *Náeidos*, B, **Νάαιδος**, *Náaidos*): One of those who had taken "strange wives" (1 Esd **9** 31), apparently = "Benaiah" of Ezr **10** 30, of which it is probably a corruption or the latter part.

NAIL, nāl: (1) As denoting the finger-nail, the Heb word is צִפֹּרֶן, *çippōren* (Dt **21** 12), the captive woman "shall shave her head, and pare her nails." The latter was probably intended to prevent her from marring her beauty by scratching her face, an act of self-mutilation oriental women are repeatedly reported to have committed in the agony of their grief. Aram. טְפַר, *ṭ*[e]*phar* (Dnl **4** 33, "his nails like birds' claws"). (2) As pin or peg (for tents, or driven into the wall) the word is יָתֵד, *yāthēdh* (in Jgs **4** 21 RV, "tent-pin"); in Isa **22** 23, "a nail in a sure place" is a peg firmly driven into the wall on which something is to be hung (ver 24); cf Eccl **12** 11, where the word is *masm*[e]*rōth*, cognate with *maṣmēr* below. (3) For nails of iron (1 Ch **22** 3) and gold (2 Ch **3** 9), and in Isa **41** 7 and Jer **10** 4, the word is מַסְמֵר, *maṣmēr*. (4) In the NT the word is ἧλος, *hēlos*, used of the nails in Christ's hands (Jn **20** 25), and "to nail" in Col **2** 14 ("nailing it to the cross") is προσηλόω, *prosēlóō*.

In a **figurative** sense the word is used of the hard point of a stylus or engraving tool: "The sin of Judah is written with a pen of iron, and with the point [lit. "claw," "nail"] of a diamond: it is graven upon the tablet of their heart, and upon the horns of your altars" (Jer **17** 1). James Orr

NAIN, nā'in (**Ναΐν**, *Naín*): This town is mentioned in Scripture only in connection with the visit of Jesus and the miracle of raising the widow's son from the dead (Lk **7** 11). The name persists to this day, and in the form of *Nein* clings to a small village on the northwestern slope of *Jebel ed-Duhy* ("Hill of Moreh"), the mountain which, since the Middle Ages, has been known as Little Hermon. The modern name of the mountain is derived from *Neby Duhy* whose *wely* crowns the height above the village. There are many ancient remains, proving that the place was once of considerable size. It was never inclosed by a wall, as some have thought from the mention of "the gate." This was probably the opening between the houses by which the road entered the town. Tristram thought he had found traces of an ancient city wall, but this proved to be incorrect. The ancient town perhaps stood somewhat higher on the hill than the present village. In the rocks to the E. are many tombs of antiquity. The site commands a beautiful and extensive view across the plain to Carmel, over the Nazareth hills, and away past Tabor to where the white peak of Hermon glistens in the sun. To the S. are the heights of Gilboa and the uplands of Samaria. The village, once prosperous, has fallen on evil days. It is said that the villagers received such good prices for *simsum* that they cultivated it on a large scale. A sudden drop in the price brought them to ruin, from which, after many years, they have not yet fully recovered.

W. Ewing

NAIOTH, nā'yoth, nī'ōth (נָיוֹת, *nāyōth;* B, **Αὐάθ**, *Auáth*, A, **Ναυιώθ**, *Nauiōth*): This is the name given to a place in Ramah to which David went with Samuel when he fled and escaped from Saul (1 S **19** 18, etc). The term has often been taken as meaning "houses" or "habitations"; but this cannot be justified. There is no certainty as to exactly what the word signified. Clearly, however, it attached to a particular locality in Ramah; and whatever its etymological significance, it denoted a place where the prophets dwelt together. On approaching it in pursuit of David, Saul was overcome by the Spirit of God, and conducted himself like one "possessed," giving rise to the proverb, "Is Saul also among the prophets?" W. Ewing

NAKED, nā'ked, **NAKEDNESS,** nā'ked-nes: "Naked" in the OT represents various derivatives of עוּר, *'ūr*, and עָרָה, *'ārāh*, chiefly עָרוֹם, *'ārōm* (adj.) and עֶרְוָה, *'erwāh* (noun); in the NT the adj. is **γυμνός**, *gumnós*, the noun **γυμνότης**, *gumnótēs*, with vb. **γυμνητεύω**, *gumnēteúō*, in 1 Cor **4** 11. In Ex **32** 25; 2 Ch **28** 19, AV adds פָּרַע, *pāra'*, "break loose," "cast away restraint." Both the Gr and Heb forms mean "without clothing," but in both languages they are used frequently in the sense of "lightly clad" or, simply, "without an outer garment." So, probably, is the meaning in Jn **21** 7—Peter was wearing only the *chitōn* (see Dress); and so perhaps in Mk **14** 51.52 and Mic **1** 8. In Isa **20** 2–4, however, the meaning is lit. (for the "three years" of ver 3 see the comms.). So in Gen **2** 25; **3** 7, where the act of sin is immediately followed by the sense of shame (see Delitzsch, *Bib. Psychology*, and Gunkel, ad loc.). A very common use of "naked" is also "without proper clothing" (Job **22** 6; 1 Cor **4** 11, etc), whence, of course, the expression "clothe the naked." "Nakedness," in addition, is used as a euphemism in 1 S **20** 30. A slightly different euphemistic usage is that of Lev **18** 19, which in Ezk **16** 36.37 is played off against the literal sense (cf Ezk **22** 10; **23** 18.29). The point of Gen **9** 22.23 is a little hard to grasp, but apparently there is here again a euphemism—this time for a particularly horrible act (see the comms. and cf Hab **2** 15). Possibly some of these euphemisms are due to the Massoretes (see OT TEXTS). The Jews objected vigorously to exposure of the body (even athletes insisting on a loin-cloth [cf 2 Macc **4** 12.13]), and compulsory nudity was the extreme of shame and humiliation (Isa **20** 2–4; Lam **1** 8; Hos **2** 3; Nah **3** 5, etc). The relation of this attitude to Israel's high sexual morality needs no explanation. BURTON SCOTT EASTON

NAME, nām (שֵׁם, *shēm;* ὄνομα, *ónoma;* Lat *nomen* [2 Esd **4** 1]; vbs. ὀνομάζω, *onomázo;* Lat *nomino* [2 Esd **5** 26]): A "name" is that by which a person, place or thing is marked and known. In Scripture, names were generally *descriptive* of the person, of his position, of some circumstance affecting him, hope entertained concerning him, etc, so that "the name" often came to stand for the person. In Acts **1** 15; Rev **3** 4, *ónoma* stands for "persons"; cf Nu **26** 53, 55.

I. OT Word and Use.—The word for "name" in the OT is *shēm* (also the name of one of the sons of Noah). The etymology is uncertain, although it may be from *shāmāh* (obs.), "to set a mark"; *shum* is the Aram. form. For the name as descriptive of the person see NAMES. Besides designating persons, the name also stands for fame, renown, reputation, character gained or expressed, etc (Gen **6** 4; 2 S **7** 9.23, etc); it might be an "evil name" (Dt **22** 14.19); the "name" is also equivalent to a "people" or "nation" (which might be "blotted out," i.e. destroyed [Dt **7** 24, etc]); to speak or write "in the name" signified authority (Ex **5** 23; 1 K **21** 8, etc); to "call one's name" over a place or people indicated possession or ownership (2 S **12** 28; Am **9** 12, etc); to act "in the name" was to represent (Dt **25** 6); to be called or known "by name" indicated special individual notice (Ex **31** 2; Isa **43** 1; **45** 3.4). Gen **2** 19.20 even displays a conception of identity between the name and the thing.

1. General

"To name" is sometimes *'āmar*, "to say" (1 S **16** 3); *dābhar*, "to speak" (Gen **23** 16); *nāḳabh*, "to mark out" (Nu **1** 17); *ḳārā'*, "to call" (Gen **48** 16; Isa **61** 6).

2. The Divine Name

Of special interest is the usage with respect to the name of God. (For the various Divine names and their significance see GOD, NAMES OF.) He revealed Himself to Israel through Moses by a *new* name (which was at the same time that of the God of their fathers)—JEHOVAH (q.v.) (*Yahweh*)—the nature of which should be shown by His manifestations on their behalf (Ex **3** 13–16; **15** 2.3). The "name of God was therefore not a mere *word*, but the whole of" the Divine manifestation, the character of God as revealed in His relations to His people and in His dealings with them (Ex **9** 16; Josh **7** 9; **9** 9, etc). The "name of Jeh" was proclaimed to Moses on Mt. Sinai, "Jeh, Jeh, a God merciful and gracious, slow to anger, and abundant in lovingkindness and truth," etc (Ex **34** 6); the name *Jehovah* (so revealed) was (Ex **3** 15) His "memorial Name" (so, often, in ARV; see MEMORIAL). His sole Deity was such an important element in His *name* that Dt **6** 4 f was termed the "Shema" (from *shema'*, "hear," the first word in ver 4), the first article of Israelitish faith, taught to all the children, written on the phylacteries, and still recited as the first act in public and private worship "twice a day by every adult male Jew." Where Jeh is said to *record* His name, or to put His name in a place (or person), some special Divine manifestation is implied, making the place or person sacred to Him (Ex **20** 24; 1 K **8** 16). His "name" was *in* the angel of His Presence (Ex **23** 21); what He does is "for his great name's sake," in fidelity to and vindication of His revealed character and covenant relationship (2 Ch **6** 32; Ps **25** 11); the great things He should do would be "for a name" (Isa **55** 13); He would give His people a new name, "an everlasting name" (Isa **56** 5); to be "called by" the name of Jeh is "to be his people" (2 Ch **7** 14; Isa **43** 7); it implies "protection," etc (Isa **63** 19; Jer **14** 8.9); to "call upon" the name of Jeh was "to worship him" as God (Gen **21** 33; **26** 25, etc); "to confess" His name, to "acknowledge him" (1 K **8** 33.35); to love, trust, act in, etc, "the name," was to love, trust, etc, Jeh Himself (Ps **5** 11; **7** 17). Very frequently, esp. in the Pss and prophecies of Isa and Jer, "the name" of God stands for "God himself"; to "forget his name" was "to depart from him" (Jer **23** 27); "to minister, prophesy, or speak" in His name signified Divine appointment, inspiration, authority (Jer **11** 21; **14** 14.15, etc); we have "swearing by" or "in" the name of Jeh (Dt **6** 13); to take His name "in vain" was to swear falsely (Ex **20** 7; Lev **19** 12); we have "blessing" in His name (Dt **10** 8); "cursing" (2 K **2** 24). In Lev **24** 11, we have the case of one who "blasphemed the Name, and cursed," the penalty for which was death by stoning (vs 13–16). In later Jewish usage (cf Wisd **14** 21) the sacred name Jeh was not pronounced in reading the Scriptures, *'Ădhōnāy* ("my Lord") being substituted for it (the vowels belonging to *'Ădhōnāy* were written with the consonants of the Divine name), hence the frequent term "the Lord" in AV, for which ARV substitutes "Jeh."

II. NT Word and Use.—In the NT *ónoma* has frequently also the significance of denoting the "character," or "work" of the person, e.g. Mt **1** 21, "Thou shalt call his name Jesus; for it is he that shall *save*," etc (Lk **1** 31; **2** 21; **1** 63, "His name is John"; cf the *new* names given to Simon, James and John; Saul's new name of "Paul"). The "name" of God has the same relation to the character of God as in the OT (Mt **6** 9; "Father, glorify thy name," Jn **12** 28); it is manifested by Christ (Jn **17** 26; cf ver 3); the name of Jesus, as manifesting God, takes the place of the name of Jeh in the OT (cf Jas **2** 7 with Jer **14** 9, and see below); to Him is given "the name which is above every name; that in the name of Jesus every knee should bow .... and that every tongue should confess that Jesus Christ is Lord, to the glory of God the Father," Phil **2** 9.10 (cf Isa **45** 23); "It is not the name *Jesus*, but the name *of* Jesus" (Lightfoot), i.e. the name ("Lord") received by Jesus; we have with reference to Jesus simply "the Name" (Acts **5** 41, "worthy to suffer dishonor for the Name"; Jas **5** 14 [probable text, WH], "in the Name"; 3 Jn ver 7, "for the sake of the Name"); the "name of Christ" is equivalent to "Christ himself" (Mt **10** 22; **19** 29); it is the same thing as "his manifestation" (Jn **20** 31); therefore "to believe on his name" is to believe in Him as manifested in His life and work (Jn **1** 12; **2** 23); "in the name of God" means sent by God, as representing Him, with Divine authority (Mt **21** 9; **23** 39); in like manner, we have "prophesying" or "preaching" in the name of *Jesus* (Acts **4** 18; **5** 28). The "name of Jesus" represented His "authority" and "power," e.g. working miracles in His name (Mt **7** 22; Mk **9** 39; Acts **4** 7, 'by what name [or "power"] have ye done this?'), and it is contrasted with casting out evil spirits by some other name or power (Acts **16** 18; **19** 17). The gospel of salvation was to be preached "in his name," by His authority and as making it effectual (Lk **24** 47); sinners were justified "through his name" (Acts **10** 43; 1 Cor **6** 11); sins were forgiven "for his name's sake" (1 Jn **2** 12); men "called upon the name" of Jesus, as they had done on that of Jeh (Acts **9** 14.21 [cf **7** 59]; Rom **10** 13. 14).

1. Character and Work of the Person

"To name the name" of Christ was to belong to Him (2 Tim **2** 19); the calling of His name on the Gentiles signified their acceptance as God's people (Acts **15** 17 [quoted from Am **9** 12]; cf Rom **1** 5); to "hold fast his name" is to be true to Him as made known (Rev **2** 13; **3** 8); to be "gathered together in his name," to "do all things in his name," is as "acknowledging him" (Mt **18** 20; Col **3** 17); "to baptize in" or "into the name" of Jesus Christ (Acts **2** 38; **22** 16, "calling on his name," contrasted with baptizing into one's own name in 1 Cor **1** 13, *eis*) is "to call over them his name" (in the rite), as claiming them for Christ and as their acknowledgment of Him or of faith in Him—becoming His disciples; similarly, to baptize "into [*eis*] the name of the Father, and of the Son, and of the Holy Spirit," represents "dedication to" God as He has been revealed in Christ.

"In the name of" means "as representing" (or as being), e.g. "in the name of a prophet," of "a righteous man," or of "a disciple" (Mt **10** 41.42); to receive a little child "in Christ's name," i.e. as belonging to Him, is to receive Himself (Mt **18** 5; Mk **9** 37; ver 41 to disciples, RV "because ye are Christ's," m "Gr in name that ye are [Christ's]"; Lk **9** 48; cf Mt **18** 20; Mk **13** 6, "Many shall come in my name"; Lk **21** 8).

The significance of the name of Jesus in relation to prayer deserves special notice. To pray in the name of Jesus, to ask anything in His name, according to His promises, "Whatsoever ye shall ask in my name, that will I do" (Jn **14** 13; cf **14** 14; **15** 16; **16** 23); "Hitherto have ye asked nothing in my name: ask . . . . that your joy may be made full" (Jn **16** 24), is not merely to add to our prayers (as is so often unthinkingly done): "we ask all in the name of Jesus," or "through Jesus Christ our Lord," etc, but to pray or ask as His representatives on earth, in His mission and stead, in His spirit and with His aim; it implies union with Christ and abiding in Him, He in us and we in Him. The meaning of the phrase is, "as being one with me even as I am revealed to you." Its two correlatives are "in me" (Jn **6** 56; **14** 20; **15** 4 ff; **16** 33; cf 1 Jn **5** 20), and the Pauline "in Christ" (Westcott, *The Gospel according to St. John*).

2. In Relation to Prayer

W. L. WALKER

NAMES OF GOD. See GOD, NAMES OF.

NAMES, PROPER:

I. THE FORM OF HEBREW NAMES
   1. Various Types
   2. Vocalization
   3. Transposition of Parts
   4. Methods of Abbreviation
II. THE RANGE OF PROPER NAMES
   1. Personal Names
      (1) Not Exclusively Descriptive
      (2) Drawn from a Wide Field
      (3) Influences Leading to Choice
      (4) Popularity of Names: Hard to Determine
   2. Geographical Names
III. CHARACTERISTICS OF BIBLICAL REFERENCES
   1. Derivation of Names Manifest
   2. The Narrator's Only Concern
   3. Allusions Linked with Names

I. Form of Hebrew, or, More Broadly, Semitic, Proper Names.—The Heb proper name consists of a single word, a phrase, or a sentence.

1. Various Types

(1) Where the name is a single word, other than a vb., it may be (*a*) a common noun, concrete, as Barak, "lightning," Tola, "crimson worm," Elon, "oak," Achsah, "anklet," Deborah, "bee"; or abstract, as Uzzah, "strength," Manoah, "rest," Hannah, "grace"; or either abstract or concrete, as Zebul, "habitation"; (*b*) a participle, as Saul, "asked," Zeruiah, "cleft"; (*c*) an adj., as Ikkesh, "perverse," Maharai, "impetuous," Shimei, "famous"; or (*d*) a word that may be either an adj. or an abstract noun according to circumstances. Such are formations after the norm of *ḳaṭṭūl*, as Shammua', which are generally adjs.; and formations by means of the ending *am* or *on*, as Adullam, Zalmon, Gideon, or, with the rejection of the final *n*, Shilo[h] and Solomo[n]. (2) The name may be a phrase, consisting of (*a*) two nouns, as Penuel, "face of God," Samuel, "name of God," Ish-bosheth, "man of shame"; or (*b*) an adj. and a noun, as Jedidiah, "beloved of Jeh"; or (*c*) a preposition and one or more nouns, as Besodeiah, "in the intimacy of Jeh" (Neh **3** 6). (3) When the name is a sentence, the predicate may be (*a*) a noun, the copula being implied, as Abijah, "Jeh is a father," Eliab, "God is a father," Elimelech, "God is king"; or (*b*) an adj., as Tobijah, "Jeh is good" (Zec **6** 10); or (*c*) a participle, as Obed-edom, "Edom is serving"; or (*d*) a finite vb. This last type exhibits five or six varieties: the subject stands before a perfect, as Jonathan, "Jeh hath given," Jehoshaphat, "Jeh hath judged," Eleazar, "God hath helped," Elkanah, "God hath formed"; or before an imperfect, as Eliahba, "God hideth Himself"; or the subject comes after a perfect, as Benaiah, "Jeh hath built," Shephatiah, "Jeh hath judged," Asahel, "God hath made"; or after an imperfect, as Jezreel, "God doth sow." Very often the subject is the pronoun included or implied in the verbal form, as Nathan, "he hath given," Hillel, "he hath praised," Jair, "he enlighteneth," Jephthah, "he openeth." Occasionally the predicate contains an object of the vb., as Shealtiel, "I have asked God" (Ezr **3** 2), or a prepositional phrase, as Hephzibah, "my delight is in her" (2 K **21** 1). The sentence-name is usually a declaration, but it may be an exhortation or a prayer, as Jerubbaal, "let Baal strive," and Hoshea, "save!" (Nu **13** 16), or it may be a question, as Micaiah, "who is like Jeh?" All of the foregoing illustrations have been taken from the Books of Jgs and S, unless otherwise noted.

2. Vocalization

The proper name is treated as one word, whether on analysis it consists of a single word, a phrase, or a sentence; and as such it is subject to the laws of accent and quantity which govern the Heb word. (1) A common noun used as a name undergoes the variations of pronunciation due to the custom of lengthening a short vowel in pause and to the laws which control the aspiration of certain labials, linguals, and palatals. Thus the name Perez, "breach," which appears also as Pharez in AV of the OT, occurs in the Heb text in the four forms *pereç*, *pareç*, *phereç* and *phareç* (Ruth **4** 18; Neh **11** 4.6). (2) In a name consisting of a phrase the normal advance of the accent as usual causes the loss of a pretonic vowel, as is indicated by the suspended letter in J^{e}didiah, "beloved of Jeh"; requires a short vowel in a closed unaccented syllable, as in Mahalăl'el, "praise of God"; allows contraction, as in Bêth-el, "house of God"; and occasions the return of a segholate noun to its primitive form, as in Abdiel, "servant of God," where the vowel *i* is an archaism which has lingered in compound names, but has generally disappeared elsewhere in speech. (3) Names which consist of a sentence are also accented as one word, and the pronunciation is modified accordingly. The synonyms Eliam and Ammiel, "God is a kinsman," not only exhibit the common archaism in the retention of the vowel *i*, but the name Eliām also shows the characteristic lengthening of the vowel in the final accented syllable, so common in nouns. The four forms Eliphelet, Eliphalet, Elpelet and Elpalet, meaning "God is deliverance," represent the variations of the Heb due to the causes already mentioned (1 Ch **3** 8; **14** 5.7; see AV and RV). The requirements regarding the elision and the quantity and quality of vowels, on the shifting of the accent, are also regularly met by the various types of sentence-names in which the predicate is a vb. Thus the personal names *'ĕlīshāmā'* and *'elnāthān* (subject followed by vb. in the perfect); *'elyāḳīm*, *'elyaḥbā'*, and *y^{e}hōyākhīn* (subject and imperfect); *g^{e}dhalyāh*, *y^{e}ḳholyāhū*, *bārakh'ēl*, in which the first vowel is protected by the implied reduplication of the Piel species, *b^{e}nāyāh*, *'ăsāh'ēl*, and *'ăsāh-'ēl*, *'ăsī'ēl*, *ḥăzāh'ēl* and *ḥăzā'ēl* and *p^{e}dhah'ēl* (perfect and subject); *yigdalyāhū*, *yibhn^{e}yāh*, *ya'ăsī'ēl*, *yaḥdī'ēl*, *y^{e}hallel'ēl*, *y^{e}sīmī'ēl* (imperfect and subject); *y^{e}rubba'al* and *yāshobh'ām* (jussive and subject; *ŭ* in sharpened, and *ŏ* in closed, syllable; in Jāshobeam the first long vowel is retained by a secondary accent, marked by metheg); *nāthān* and *yiphtāḥ*, i.e. Jephthah. Ibneiah shows the customary apocopation of the imperfect of Lamedh-he vbs.; and the names Benaiah to Pedahel show the methods of combining the perfect of such vbs. with a following element. The short vowel of the final closed syllable of the imperfect is elided, if the final consonant is permitted to begin the syllable of the next element of the name, as in Jezreel, Jekabzeel, Jerahmeel, Ezekiel, Jehizkiah (see the Heb form of these names); but it is not elided in Ishmael, although the consonant is attached to the following syllable; and elision is avoided, as in Jiphthah-el, by keeping the ultimate and penultimate syllables distinct. Jehucal, a Hophal imperfect, is peculiar in not lengthening the vowel in the accented final syllable, when the vb. is used as a personal name.

3. Transposition of Constituent Parts

When the name was a sentence in Heb, its constituent parts could be transposed without changing the meaning. Thus the father of Bathsheba was called Ammiel, "a kinsman is God," and Eliam, "God is a kinsman" (2 S **11** 3; 1 Ch **3** 5); and similarly, in letters written from Pal to the king of Egypt in the 14th cent. BC, Ilimilki is also called Milkili, the name in either form signifying "God is king." Ahaziah, king of Judah, is called Jehoahaz (cf 2 Ch **21** 17 with **22** 1), a legitimate transposition of the vb. and subject, and meaning in each case, "Jeh hath laid hold."

Not only did transposition take place, but the substitution of a cognate root and even the use of a different part of the vb. also occurred. Thus King Jehoiachin (2 K **24** 6; Jer **52** 31) was known also as Jeconiah (Jer **24** 1; **28** 4) and Coniah (**22** 24.28; **37** 1). The two names Jehoiachin and Jeconiah have exactly the same meaning, "Jeh doth establish"; and Coniah is a synonym, "the establishing of Jeh." The Divine name which begins Jehoiachin is transferred to the end in Jeconiah and Coniah; and the Hiphil imperfect of the vb. *kūn*, which is seen in Jehoiachin, has been replaced by the Qal imperfect of the vb. *kānan* in Jeconiah, and by the construct infinitive of the same species in Coniah. Parallel cases occur in Assyr and Bab lit., among which the two forms of the king's name, Zamama-shum-iddina and Zamama-nadin-shum, exhibit both the transposition of constituent parts and an interchange of preterite and participle.

4. Methods of Abbreviation

Twin forms like Abiner and Abner, Abishalom and Absalom, Elizaphan and Elzaphan, are not the full name and its abbreviation by syncopation, but are merely two variant, equally legitimate, modes of combining the constituent parts. The common methods of shortening were: (1) contraction by the rejection of a weak consonant or the apocopation of a final unaccented vowel, notably illustrated by the Divine name *yᵉhō* at the beginning and *yāhū* at the end of proper names: hence Jehoash became Joash (2 K **12** 1.19), and Amaziahu became Amaziah (2 K **14** 1 Heb text, and 8); (2) abbreviation of composite geographical names by the omission of the generic noun or its equivalent: Jerusalem, which to the Hebrews meant "foundation of peace," was shortened to Salem, "peace" (Ps **76** 2); Kiriath-baal, "city of Baal" (Josh **15** 60), to Baal or Baalah (Josh **15** 9.10; cf 2 S **6** 2); Beeshterah, "house or temple of Astarte," to Ashtaroth; Beth-lebaoth, "house of lionesses," to Lebaoth; Beth-azmaveth to Azmaveth; Beth-rehob to Rehob; Beth-bamoth to Bamoth (M S, l. 27, with Nu **21** 19); Beth-baal-meon to Baal-meon (Nu **32** 38; Josh **13** 17); the same custom existed among the Moabites who spoke of this town indifferently as Beth-baal-meon and Baal-meon (M S, ll. 9, 30); (3) abbreviation by the omission of the Divine name: thus the name of the idolater Micaiah, which means, "who is like Jeh?" (Jgs **17** 1.4 [Heb]), was shortened to Micah, "who is like?" (vs 5.8); and similarly in the case of three other men, namely the prophet (Micaiah, Jer **26** 18 ERV, and Micah, Mic **1** 1), the Levite musician (Neh **12** 35 with **11** 17.22), and the father of Abdon (2 K **22** 12 with 2 Ch **34** 20).

The king of Judah, Yauhazi, as he was known to the Assyrians, i.e. Jehoahaz, "Jeh hath laid hold," is called simply Ahaz, "he hath laid hold," in the Heb records. The town of Jabneel, "God doth cause to be built," was shortened to Jabneh, "he doth cause to be built" (Josh **15** 11; 2 Ch **26** 6; cf 1 Macc **4** 15); Paltiel, "deliverance of God," was curtailed to Palti, "deliverance" (1 S **25** 44; 2 S **3** 15); Abijah, "Jeh is father," to Abi (2 Ch **29** 1 with 2 K **18** 2); and Bamoth-baal, "high places of Baal," to Bamoth (Josh **13** 17 with Nu **21** 19). Abdi, Othni, Uzzi, and not a few other similar names, probably represent curtailment of this sort. The omission of the Divine title has parallels in Assyr and Bab lit.: thus Nabu-nadin-ziri and Nabu-shum-ukin were called Nadinu and Shum-ukin respectively (Dynastic Tablet no. 2, col. iv, 4, 5, with Bab Chron., col. i, 13, 16).

(4) Abbreviation by the elision of the initial consonant, yet so that the remainder is a synonymous name of complete grammatical form. The name of King Hezekiah was written by the Hebrews both *yᵉḥizḳiyāh*, "Jeh doth strengthen," and *ḥizḳiyāh*, "Jeh is strength." The two forms interchange many times in 2 Ch **29**–**33**. Similarly, Jeconiah was shortened to Coniah, as has already been noticed; the name of the town Jekabzeel, "God bringeth together," to Kabzeel, "God's bringing together" (Neh **11** 25 with Josh **15** 21; 2 S **23** 20); Meshelemiah, "Jeh is recompensing," to Shelemiah, "Jeh's recompensing" (1 Ch **26** 1.2 with ver 14); Meshullam, "recompensed," to Shallum, "recompensed" (1 Ch **9** 11; Neh **11** 11 with 1 Ch **6** 12; Ezr **7** 2).

II. The Range of Proper Names.—(1) *Not exclusively descriptive.*—

1. Personal Names

Simonis in his *Onomasticum*, published in 1741, and Gesenius in his *Thesaurus*, issued during the years from 1835 to 1853, endeavored to interpret the proper names as though they were ordinarily intended to characterize the person who bore them. Embarrassed by the theory, Gesenius trd Malchiel by "rex Dei, h. e. a Deo constitutus"; and Simonis trd Malchi-shua by "*regis auxilium*, i.e. auxilium s. salus regi patri praestita"; Ammizabad was rendered by Gesenius "famulus largitoris, h.e. Jehovae," and by Simonis "*populum* (i.e. copiosissimam liberorum turbam) *donavit*"; Gesenius trd Gedaliah "quem *Jehova educavit* vel *roboravit*," Zerahiah "cui Jehova ortum dedit," Jehozadak "quem *Jehova justum fecit*," and Joel "cui *Jehova* est *deus*, i.e. cultor Jehovae"; but Simonis rendered Joel by "*Jehoua* (est) *Deus* . . . . vel (cui) Jehoua Deus (est)." Now Malchiel means "God is king," Malchi-shua "the king, i.e. God, is salvation" (cf Joshua), Ammizabad "the Kinsman hath endowed," Gedaliah "Jeh is great," Zerahiah "Jeh hath risen in splendor," Jehozadak "Jeh is righteous," and Joel, if a compound name, "Jeh is God." A moment's reflection makes clear that these names do not describe the persons who bear them, but in every case speak of God. They emphasize the important facts that personal names might be, and often were, memorial and doctrinal, and that personal names were a part of the ordinary speech of the people, full of meaning and intelligible to all, subject to the phonetic laws of the Hebrews, and obedient to the rules of grammar.

(2) *Drawn from a wide field.*—Parents named their children, and contemporaries dubbed people, from physical and spiritual traits, whether a beauty or a blemish; thus Hophni, "pertaining to the fist," Japhia, "gleaming," Ikkesh, "perverse," Ira, "watchful," Gareb, "rough-skinned," and Hiddai, "joyful." Children were called by the names of natural objects, as Peninnah, "coral," Rimmon, "pomegranate," Tamar, "palm tree," Nahash, "serpent," Eglah, "heifer," Aiah, "bird of prey," and Laish, "lion"; or after kinsfolk or remoter members of the clan, as Absalom's daughter Tamar bore the name of her father's beautiful sister, and as the priest Phinehas took his strange name from the noted Phinehas, who belonged to the same father's house in earlier days. Or the name given to the child furnished a memorial of events in the national history, like Ichabod, "the glory is not" (1 S **4** 21), and probably Obed-edom, "Edom is serving" (cf 1 S **14** 47; **21** 7); or it told of circumstances attending the child's birth, as Saul, "asked," and Elishama, "God hath heard"; or it embodied an article of the parent's creed, as Joab and Abijah, "Jeh is a father," Joel, "Jeh is God"; or it expressed a hope concerning the child or bore witness to a prophecy, as Jedidiah, "beloved of Jeh," and Solomon, "peaceable" (2 S **12** 25; 1 Ch

22 9). Sometimes the name of the tribe or race to which a man belonged became his popular designation, as Cushi, "Cushite." All of these examples have been cited from the records of one period of Israel's history, the times of Samuel and David.

(3) *Influences leading to choice.*—The people in general gathered names for their children freely from all parts of this wide field, but in certain circles influences were at work which tended to restrict the choice to a smaller area. These influences were religious: (*a*) In homes of piety conscious nearness to God on the part of the parents naturally prompted them to bestow religious names upon their children. The name may be without distinct religious mark in its form and meaning, as Ephraim, "double fruitfulness," Manasseh, "making to forget," and yet have been given in acknowledgment of God's grace and be a constant reminder of His goodness (Gen **41** 51.52); or the name may be religious in form, as Shemaiah, "Jeh hath heard," and publicly testify to the parents' gratitude to God. (*b*) The covenant relation, which Jeh entered into with Israel, made the name Jehovah, and that aspect of God's character which is denoted by this name, peculiarly precious to the people of God, and thenceforth the word Jehovah became a favorite element in the personal names of the Israelites, though not, of course, to the exclusion of the great name El, "God." (*c*) Among the kings in the line of David, the consciousness of their formal adoption by Jeh to be His vicegerents on the throne of Israel (2 S **7**; Ps **2**) found expression in the royal names. Jeh, the God of Israel, was acknowledged in the personal name Abijah, borne by the son and successor of Rehoboam. But his was an isolated case, unless the name Asa is an abbreviated form. But with Jehoshaphat, Abijah's grandson, early in the 9th cent., the custom became established. Henceforth it was conventional for the king of Judah to have for his name a sentence with Jeh as its subject. The only exceptions among the 16 successors of Asa on the throne were Manasseh and his son Amon, both of whom were notoriously apostate from Jeh. The full name of Ahaz was Jehoahaz. Josiah's son Shallum as king was known as Jehoahaz; and his brother Eliakim, when placed on the throne by Pharaoh-necoh, was given the name Jehoiakim. (*d*) Akin to the influence exerted by the relation of the kings to the God of Israel, and manifesting almost equal power contemporaneously with it, was the influence of official connection with the sanctuary, either as priests or as subordinate ministers, and it frequently led to the choice of an ecclesiastical name containing the word God or Jeh. During the five centuries and a half, beginning near the close of Solomon's reign and extending to the end of Nehemiah's administration, 22 high priests held office, so far as their names have been preserved in the records. Of these pontiffs 17 bear names which are sentences with Jeh as subject, and another is a sentence with El as subject. The materials for investigation along this line are not complete, as they are in the case of the kings, and ratios derived from them are apt to be erroneous; but evidently the priests of Jeh's temple at Jerus not only recognized the appropriateness for themselves and their families of names possessing a general religious character, but came to favor such as expressly mentioned God, esp. those which mentioned God by His name of Jehovah.

(4) *Popularity of names: hard to determine.*—Until abundant data come to light for all periods of the history, it is precarious to attempt to determine the relative popularity of the various kinds and types of names in any one generation, or to compare period with period with respect to the use or neglect of a particular class of names. For, first, in no period are the names which have been transmitted by the Heb records many as compared with the thousands in use at the time; and, secondly, the records deal with the historical event which was conspicuous at the moment, and rarely mention persons other than the actors in this event.

At one time men and women from the middle class of society are asserting themselves in the national life, and the personal names current in the families of farmers, shopkeepers and soldiers obtain place in the annals; at another time, when the activities of the court are of paramount importance, it is mainly names that were current in official circles which are chronicled; at yet another period, when matters of the national worship engaged the attention of the state, ecclesiastics and laymen from pious families, whose names were quite likely to have a religious meaning, receive mention. Very few names outside of the particular circle concerned are preserved in the records. It is unwarranted, therefore, to draw inferences regarding the relative use of particular names, secular names, for instance, at different periods of the history of Israel, by comparing the number of these names found in a record of political uprisings in the army with the number of similar names in the narrative of an episode which occurred at a later date and in which only priests took part. It is comparing things that differ. It is comparing the number of certain names current in military circles with the number of the same names among ecclesiastics, in order to learn whether these names were more common among the people as a whole in the one period than in the other.

2. Geographical Names

The brine of its waters led the ancient Hebrews to call the Dead Sea the Salt Sea. Bethesda, "house of mercy," received its name from the belief in the healing virtue of its waters; Lebanon, "white," from the snows that cover its crest; Sidon on the Mediterranean Sea and Bethsaida on the Sea of Galilee, from their fisheries; Tyre, from the great rock in the sea on which it was built; the valley of Elah, from the terebinth tree; Luz, from the almond tree; Shittim, from the acacia groves on the eastern terrace of the Jordan valley; and Jericho, from the fragrance of its palms and balsams. The "crags of the wild goats" and En-gedi, "kid spring" (1 S **24** 1.2), were in a desolate, rocky region where the wild goats had their home; Aijalon signifies "place of harts," and Etam denotes a "place of beasts and birds of prey." The hopes of a people and pride in their town were expressed in names like Joppa, "beauty," Tirzah, "pleasantness," Janoah, "rest," Shiloh, "tranquillity," and Salem, "peace." The resemblance of the Sea of Galilee in shape to a harp secured for it its ancient name of Chinnereth. Poetic imagination saw in majestic Mt. Hermon likeness to a soldier's breastplate, and forthwith the mountain was called Serion and Senir. The sanctuary of a deity might give name to a town, hence Beth-dagon, Beth-anath, and Ashtaroth. Sometimes the name of a place commemorated a victory, as rock Oreb, rock Zeeb, and Eben-ezer (Jgs **7** 25; 1 S **7** 12); or enshrined a religious transaction or experience, Beth-el and Beracah (Gen **28** 17–19; 2 Ch **20** 26); or told of a migration, as when colonists gave the name of their native town to their new settlement (Jgs **1** 23–26). Often the name of the founder or other famous inhabitant became attached to a town, and that for various reasons. It was often necessary to distinguish places of the same name from each other by this method; thus certain of the towns called Gibeah became Gibeath-saul and Gibeath-phinehas. The Jebusite stronghold captured by David was named by him the city of David, and was known by this name, as a quarter of Jerus, for many generations (2 S **5** 9; 2 K **16** 20). The practice was common among the Sem contemporaries of Israel, as is illustrated by Dur-sharruken, "Sargonsburg," and Kar-shalmanasharidu, "Shalmaneser's fortress." A town might also be named after the tribe which inhabited it or after the ancestor of the tribe, as Dan (Jgs **18** 29), and possibly under not a few geographical designations a tribal name is hidden, even when the fact has escaped record and is not revealed by the form of the name. In an inquiry after the origin of a geographical designation the first consideration is due to the causes known to be ordinarily at work in giving rise to names of the same aspect as the one under scrutiny; and only when they fail to yield a suitable explanation are less obvious causes worthy of serious attention.

III. Characteristics of Biblical References.—As a rule, Sem words clearly reveal their origin and structure. The Semite might, indeed, err with respect to the particular meaning intended, where a word was current in several significations. Thus the vale of *bākhā'*, mentioned in Ps **84** 7 (Eng. 6), is open to two interpretations: namely, "valley of Baca," so called from the balsam trees in it, and "valley of weeping," as the VSS render the unusual form, regarding it as equivalent to a similar word meaning "weeping." The pl. *b^ekhā'īm*, "mulberry or balsam trees" (2 S **5** 23.24), was understood by Jos to denote a grove known by the name Weepers (*Ant*, VII, iv, 1; cf LXX). In those rare cases where several derivations were possible, the Israelite may not always have known which thought was intended to be embodied in the name which he heard. But he discerned the alternative possibilities; and a parent, in bestowing a name ambiguous in its derivation, might be deliberately taking advantage of its power to be the vehicle for the suggestion and expression of two thoughts (Gen **30** 23.24; Joseph being derivable from both *yāṣaph* and *'āṣaph*).

1. Derivation of Names Manifest

That the object of the Bib. writer was not to make known the derivation of the proper names is clear from cases like Esek, Rehoboth and Ishmael (Gen **16** 11; **26** 20.22): Isaac called the name of the well, Contention, because the herdsmen of Gerar "contended" with him; another well he called Broad Places (roomy places), because Jeh had "made room" for him; and Hagar was directed to name the son that she was about to bear "God doth hear," because Jeh had "heard" her affliction. The narrator's purpose was not to declare that the Heb word for contention, *'ēṣeḳ*, is derived from the Heb vb. for "contend," *'āṣaḳ*, and that the name "God doth hear," *yishmā''ēl*, signifies God doth hear, *yishma' 'ēl*. These derivations and meanings were plain. The purpose was to state the circumstances which led to the choice of the name. There are instances also where no part of the name reappears in the words that state the reason for the use of the name. For example, the name Maher-shalal-hash-baz is not explained by citing the words which compose it. One noun of the composite name appears, indeed, in the exposition of the meaning, but accidentally as it were, and without prominence or significance of position (Isa **8** 3.4). Samuel is a notable example of this method. Hannah called his name Samuel, saying, 'Because of Jeh I asked him' (1 S **1** 20). Simonis, Ewald and Nestle derive the name from *sh^emū^a''ēl*, "heard of God." This etymology would fully satisfy the reason given for the mother's choice of the name; but the suggested derivation is far-fetched, for it is not customary for a Heb word to lose the strong guttural *'ayin*. The guttural was not lost, but was distinctly heard, in Ishmael, where there is the same concurrence of sounds as in *sh^emū^a''ēl*. Kimḥi, on the other hand, suggested that Samuel is a contraction of *shā'ūl mē'ēl*, "asked of God"; and Ewald asserts that this origin is the theory of the narrator (*Lehrbuch der hebräischen Sprache*, 275, n. 3). This is incredible. Such a contraction is "alien to the genius of the Heb language" (Driver, *Text of Samuel*, 13), and the absence of the two consonants *aleph* and *lamedh* before the letter *m* in the midst of the name Samuel would of itself prevent the Semite from imagining such an etymology. The derivation and meaning of Samuel were not obscure. The type was common, and was esp. familiar by reason of the name Peniel, "face of God" (Gen **32** 30f). Samuel means "name of God" (Gesenius). As Jacob, upon his return from Paddan-aram, in fulfilment of his vow erected an altar at Beth-el as a memorial of God's bestowal of the promised blessings and named the place thus consecrated "The God of Beth-el" (Gen **35** 1.3.7), so Hannah having by vow dedicated to Jeh the son for whose birth she was praying, now that her prayer has been answered and the son given, calls him "The name of God" in commemoration of the Giver. The Bib. narrator states the motive which led the mother to choose the name Samuel for her child. In this explanation no part of the name is used. Moreover, the slight assonance between *sh^emū'ēl* and *sh^e'iltīw* in 1 S **1** 20 was unsought, for these words are separated in the Heb text, and the emphasis is placed on the gift's being "from Jeh." The history of the discussion concerning this name shows how far astray criticism has been led by the false theory that the purpose of the narrator was to analyze the name and declare its derivation.

2. The Narrator's Only Concern

Reuben affords evidence to the same effect. The name was known to the early Hebrews in this form exclusively. It is attested by their most ancient literature (Gen **29** 32; **30** 14; Jgs **5** 15.16), by the entire OT, by the Gr tr (A, B and Lucian), by the Tgs, and by the NT (Rev **7** 5). Yet in the 1st cent. Jos, adding a Gr termination, wrote Roubelos; and later the Syr version gave the name as Rûbîl, and the Ethiopic version as Rōbēl and Rūbēl. The late variation is reasonably explained as a softening of the pronunciation, which had come into vogue in certain circles. The liquids, or, to speak particularly regarding Reuben, the liquids *n* and *l*, sometimes interchanged, giving rise to two forms for a word in the same language or in kindred languages (Gesenius, *Thesaurus*, 727; Wright, *Comp. Grammar*, 67; Zimmern, *Vergleichende Grammatik*, § 11*a*). Notwithstanding the evidence furnished by the literature, preference has been given to Reubel as the original form on the ground that "the only plausible explanation of the etymology" given in Gen **29** 32 "is that it is based on the form" *R^e'ūbel* = *R^e'ū ba'al* (Skinner, *Gen*, 386). An exhibition of the etymology was needless, however, and was not the end which the writer had in view. His purpose was to state the occasion for bestowing this particular name upon the child; and in stating it he does full justice to the clear meaning of the good, simple Heb of the name Reuben. The name signifies either "vision of a son" or "Behold ye! a son." In either case the emphatic word is "son." As Hannah, taunted on account of her barrenness, besought God to look on her affliction and give her a man-child (1 S **1** 11), so Leah, using the same words, speaking of the same mercy already shown her, and with the same thought in mind, exclaimed: "Jeh hath looked upon my affliction; for now my husband will love me," and she called the name of her son "Look ye! It's a son" (or, "vision of a son"). A male child was to her a proof of God's regard for her misery, and a guaranty of the future love of her husband for her. Moreover, the name kept the thought constantly before the mind of her husband. Gesenius remarks that Reuben means "properly, 'See ye, a son!' but the sacred writer in Gen **29** 32 explains it as for *rā'āh (rā'ūy) b^e'onyī*, 'provided in my affliction'" (*Lexicon*, *Thesaurus*). This curious specimen of criticism may be regarded as the *reductio ad absurdum* of the hypothesis that the Heb writers intend to give the derivation of the proper names. The result of endeavoring to force the words of the explanation into an intentional etymology compels the assumption that the Heb writer misunderstood one of the simplest phrases of his own language and proposed a contraction impossible in itself and utterly foreign to the principles which underlie Heb speech.

Allusions to proper names are made for the purpose of stating the reason for the bestowal of the name, of pointing out a coincidence between the name and the character or experience of its bearer, or of attaching a prophecy; and it is common to link the allusion with the name by employing the root that underlies the name, or a cog-

3. Allusions Linked with Names

nate root, or some other word that resembles the name in sound: (1) Statement of the reason for the choice of the name: In the case of Simeon, the root of the name is used (Gen **29** 33). Words of this type (with the termination *on*) are formed from nouns and vbs., and have the force of adjs., diminutives, or abstract nouns, and are sometimes used as concrete nouns (Stade, *Lehrbuch der hebräischen Grammatik*, § 296). The Israelite at once recognized the root and formation of the name Simeon, which was a favorite with the Hebrews, and he knew that it could express the abstract idea of hearing. In Gen **29** 33 the narrator is not seeking to impart etymological information; but it is clear that he discerned the derivation when he gave the reason for the choice of this particular name for Leah's second son: "[Leah] said, Because Jeh hath heard that I am hated, he hath therefore given me this son also: and she called his name Simeon." The root of the name is used as a vb. in the statement of the motive. It was convenient and natural to do so, since the vb. *shāma'* was the proper word to express the idea and was one of the most common words in the language. There would be no reason to suppose that identity with the root of the name was intentional, except that care is taken by the narrator in the case of the other sons of Jacob to maintain a similar correspondence. Accordingly, that form of paronomasia is employed where a word is used that is one with the name in derivation, but differs from the name in form and grammatically is a different part of speech.

In the case of Cain a cognate root is used. The name is a segholate noun from the root *ḳūn*, which means "to form," and then specifically to form at the anvil. Cain may accordingly be an abstract noun and denote formation, or a concrete noun denoting a forged weapon, or the agent in the work, namely a smith. In stating the reason for giving this name to the child, it was not feasible to use the vb. *ḳūn*, because of the technical meaning which had become attached to it. To avoid misunderstanding the cognate vb. *ḳānāh* is employed, which has radically the same significance, but is without the technical implications (Gen **4** 1). The result is that kind of paronomasia which exists between words of similar sound and cognate origin, but difference of meaning.

In the case of Noah a root unrelated to the name in origin, but containing a similar sound, is used. The Bib. narrator does not state whether the name Noah is the transliteration of a foreign word or is its tr into Heb; he merely declares that as given it expressed the father's hope that through this child men were to have relief from the ancient curse upon the ground. If the name is Heb, its root may be *nūaḥ*, "rest." At any rate it promptly suggested to the ear of the Hebrew the idea of rest. But the vb. *nūaḥ* is used in Heb, as is the corresponding vb. "rest" in Eng., to express the two ideas of relief and cessation. Lamech did not mean that his son would cause men to cease from work, but that he would secure for them restful relief from toil due to God's curse on account of sin (Gen **5** 29, with a reference to **3** 17–19). The writer does not use the ambiguous word. To avoid ambiguity, yet with a view to preserving assonance with Noah, he employs the vb. *nāḥam*, which has as one of its meanings the sense of comfort and relief.

(2) The indication of a coincidence between the character or experience of a person and his name: Naomi, returning to her home bereaved and in poverty, saw the contrast between her present condition and her name; and she played upon her name by using a word of opposite meaning, saying: 'Call me not Pleasant, call me Bitter; for the Almighty hath dealt very bitterly with me' (Ruth **1** 20). In whatever sense Nabal's name may have been bestowed upon him originally, at any rate his wife saw the correspondence between his name in its ordinary meaning and his conduct toward David, and she played upon it, saying: 'Fool is his name, and folly is with him' (1 S **25** 25). Likewise the agreement between Jacob's character and a meaning that his name has in Heb was seen, and called forth the bitter word-play: 'Is he not rightly named "He supplants"? for he hath supplanted me these two times' (Gen **27** 36). Isaac, so far as the formation is concerned, may be an abstract noun meaning "laughter," or a concrete noun, "laughing one," or a vb. in the imperfect, "he laughs" or "one laughs" (cf Stade, *Lehrbuch der hebräischen Grammatik*, § 259*a*). Whichever specific meaning may have been in the mind of Abraham when he gave the name to his son, yet by reason of its ever speaking of laughter the name was a constant reminder to the parents of the laughter of unbelief with which they had listened to the promise of his birth (Gen **17** 17; **18** 12). But in due time the child of promise has been born. His name, as determined upon, is Isaac. This Sarah knows (**17** 19; **21** 3). Accordingly, the theme with which she greets his advent is laid in her mouth. She plays upon the name Isaac, using the root of the word in various forms, first as a noun and then as a vb., and giving to the vb. a new subject and to the thought a new turn. Instead of the laughter of unbelief, with which the promise was received, 'God,' she says, 'hath prepared for me laughter [of joy], everyone that heareth [of the event] will laugh [with joy] for me' (**21** 6; cf Ps **126** 2).

(3) Attachment of a prophecy to a name: Paronomasia in all of its forms is used for this purpose. A meaning of the name, or a sound heard in it, or a contrast suggested by it may be played upon. In these several ways the prophet Micah plays upon successive names in one paragraph (Mic **1** 10–15). In answer to Abraham's prayer in behalf of Ishmael, a promise is given concerning the lad, which is introduced by a play upon his name: 'As for the boy [named] "God heareth," I have heard thee' (Gen **17** 18.20). To Gad a prophecy is attached in Gen **49** 19. Two cognate roots are employed: *gādhadh*, which underlies the word rendered troop or marauding band, and *gūdh*, which means "to press." In the use not only of the root of the name Gad, but of a different root also that is similar in sound, it is evident that the purpose is simply to play upon the name. The brief oracle is uttered almost exclusively by means of variations in the vocalization of the two roots, producing one of the most successful word-plays in Heb literature.

Judah is a noun corresponding to the Hophal imperfect, and means "thing being praised," "object of praise." In bestowing this name upon her child the mother signified that Jeh was the object of her praise; for she said: "Now will I praise Jeh" (Gen **29** 35). In Gen **49** 8 a prophecy is spoken concerning Judah. The same etymology and meaning are recognized as before, but the application is different. The birth of Judah had made God an object of praise, the great deeds of the tribe of Judah were destined to make that tribe an object of praise. To quote the oracle: ' "Object of praise," thee shall thy brothers praise.' In this difference of reference and in the repetition of the significant word consists the play upon the name.

Dan is played upon in much the same way. The name may be a participle, used as a noun, and be rendered "judge"; but it probably belongs to that numerous class in which the names are vbs. in the perfect, and signifies, "he hath judged." His adoptive mother had called his name Dan, because God had heard her complaint and decided the cause in her favor (Gen **30** 6). In attaching the prophecy, the name is played upon by changing the subject, and, in order to refer to the future, by substituting the imperfect for the perfect of the vb.: ' "He hath judged" shall judge his people, as one of the tribes of Israel' (Gen **49** 16). See also God, Names of; Name.

John D. Davis

NANAEA, na-nē'a (**Ναναία**, *Nanaía*; AV **Nanea**): A female deity worshipped by the Assyrians, Babylonians and Persians and other Asiatic peoples, the Nana or Nanai of the Babylonians, known as "the lady of Babylon." The name means "the undefiled," and probably represented originally the productive powers of Nature (*genetrix*), and as such was the companion of the sun-god. She was identified with Ishtar in Assyria and Ashtoreth in Phoenicia, by the Greeks as Aphrodite (Clem. Alex. *Protr.*, 19), but sometimes as Artemis the huntress (Paus. iii.16.8; Plut. *Artax.* xxvii). Strabo (xv. 733) identifies her with Anaïtis (=Anahita), the Asian Artemis. She was the Venus, but sometimes the Diana, of the Romans. There are many variants of the name: Anaea (Strabo xvi.738), Aneitis (Plut. *Artax.* xxvii), Tanais (Clem. Alex., loc. cit.), also Tanath, sometimes in Phoen inscriptions, Tanata, Anta (Egyp). In 2 Macc **1** 13 ff, a fictitious account is given of the death of Antiochus Epiphanes, in a temple of Nanaea in Persia, by the treachery of Nanaea's priests. The public treasury was often placed in Nanaea's temple; this, Epiphanes was anxious to secure under the pretext of marrying the goddess and receiving the money as a dowry. The priests threw down great stones "like thunderbolts" from above, killed the king and his suite and then cut off their heads. But 1 Macc **6** 1 ff, which is more reliable, gives a different account of the death of Epiphanes after an attempt to rob a rich temple in Elymais. The account of 2 Macc **1** 13 ff must be mere legend, as far as Epiphanes is concerned, but may have been suggested or colored by the story of the death of Antiochus the Great, who met his death while plundering a temple of Belus near Elymais (Strabo xvi.1.18; Diod. Sic. 573; Justin, xxxii.2). The temple of Nanaea referred to in 2 Macc **1** 13 ff may be identified with that of Artemis (Polyb. xxxi.11; Jos, *Ant*, XII, ix, 1) or Aphrodite (Appian, *Syr.* 66; Rawlinson, *Speaker's Comm.*). S. Angus

NAOMI, nā'ō-mī, nȧ-ō'mī, nȧ-ō'mi (נָעֳמִי, *no'ŏmī*, probably = "pleasantness"; LXX B, **Νωεμείν**, *Nōemeín*, A, **Νοεμμεί[ν]**, *Noemmeí[n]*): Wife of Elimelech and mother-in-law of Ruth (Ruth **1** 2—**4** 17). She went with her husband to the land of Moab, and after his death returned to Bethlehem. When greeted on her return, she told the women of the town to call her, not *no'ŏmī* ("pleasantness"), but *mārāh* ("bitterness"), "for," she said, "the Almighty hath dealt very bitterly with me." She advised Ruth in her dealings with Boaz, and afterward nursed their child.

The name may mean "my joy," "my bliss," but is perhaps better explained according to the traditional interpretation as "the pleasant one."

David Francis Roberts

NAPHATH-DOR, nā'fath-dôr (Josh **12** 23 RVm). See Dor.

NAPHISH, nā'fish (נָפִישׁ, *nāphīsh;* **Ναφές**, *Naphés*, D, **Ναφέθ**, *Naphéth*): A son of Ishmael (Gen **25** 15; 1 Ch **1** 31). Naphish, along with other Hagrite clans, was overwhelmingly defeated by the Israelitish tribes on the E. of the Jordan (1 Ch **5** 19, AV "Nephish"). Their descendants are mentioned among the Nethinim by the name "Nephisim," AV and RVm "Nephusim" (Ezr **2** 50); "Nephushesim," AV and RVm "Nephishesim" (Neh **7** 52); "Naphisi" (1 Esd **5** 31).

NAPHISI, naf'i-sī (**Ναφισί**, *Naphisí*, B, **Ναφεισεί**, *Napheiseí*): The name of one of the families which went up out of captivity with Zerubbabel (1 Esd **5** 31) = "Nephushesim" of Neh **7** 52; "Nephisim" of Ezr **2** 50. See Naphish.

NAPHOTH-DOR, nā'foth-dôr (Josh **11** 2 RVm). See Dor.

NAPHTALI, naf'ta-lī (נַפְתָּלִי, *naphtālī;* **Νεφθαλείμ**, *Nephthaleím*):

I. The Patriarch
 1. Name
 2. Circumstances of His Birth
 3. Historical and Traditional Details
II. Tribe of Naphtali
 1. Its Relative Position
 2. Its Location in Palestine
 3. Physical Features
 4. Distinction of the Tribe
 5. Sites and Inhabitants
 6. Labors of Jesus in This District

I. The Patriarch.—The 5th son of Jacob, and the 2d born to him by Rachel's handmaid, Bilhah.

1. Name

He was full brother of Dan (Gen **30** 7 ff). At his birth Rachel is said to have exclaimed, *naphtūlē 'ĕlōhīm niphtaltī*, "wrestlings of God"—i.e. "mighty wrestlings"—"have I wrestled."

2. Circumstances of His Birth

Her sister's fruitfulness was a sore trial to the barren Rachel. By her artifice she had obtained children, the offspring of her maid ranking as her own; and thus her reproach of childlessness was removed. The name N. given to this son was a monument of her victory. She had won the favor and blessing of God as made manifest in the way yearned for by the oriental heart, the birth of sons.

3. Historical and Traditional Details

Personal details regarding the patriarch N. are entirely wanting in Scripture; and the traditions have not much to say about him. According to Tg *Pseudojon*, he was a swift runner. It also tells us that he was one of the 5 brethren whom Joseph chose to represent the family of Jacob in the presence of Pharaoh. He is said to have been 132 years old at his death (Test. XII P, viii, 1, 1). When Jacob and his family moved to Egypt, N. had 4 sons (Gen **46** 24). In Egypt, he died and was buried.

II. Tribe of Naphtali.—When the first census was taken in the wilderness, the tribe numbered

1. Relative Position

53,400 fighting men (Nu **1** 43; **2** 30). At the second census, the numbers had shrunk to 45,400 (Nu **26** 48 ff); but see Numbers. The position of Naphtali in the desert was on the N. of the tabernacle with the standard of the camp of Dan, along with the tribe of Asher (Nu **2** 25 ff). The standard, according to Jewish tradition, was a serpent, or basilisk, with the legend, "Return of Jehovah to the many thousands of Israel" (Tg *Pseudojon* on Nu **2** 25). When the host was on the march, this camp came in the rear (Nu **2** 31). The prince of the tribe at Sinai was Ahira ben Enan (**2** 29). Among the spies the tribe was represented by Nahbi ben Vophsi (**13** 14). Prince Pedahel ben Ammihud was chosen from N. to assist in the division of the land (**34** 28). Toward the end of David's reign the ruler of the tribe was Jeremoth ben Azriel (1 Ch **27** 19). Hiram the Tyrian artificer is described as "the son of a widow of the tribe of N." (1 K **7** 14). But in 2 Ch **2** 14 he is called "the son of a woman of the daughters of Dan." Jgs **5** 15 does not definitely associate Barak with the tribe of Issachar; his residence was at Kedesh (Jgs **4** 6); it is therefore possible that he belonged to the tribe of N.

In the allocation of the land, the lot of N. was the last but one to be drawn (Josh **19** 32–39). The

2. Location in Palestine

boundaries are stated with great fulness. While it is yet impossible to trace them with certainty, the identification of sites in recent years, for which we are mainly indebted to the late Col. Conder, makes possible an approximation. The territory was bounded on the E. by the Sea of

Galilee and the upper reaches of the Jordan. Jos makes it extend to Damascus (*Ant*, V, i, 22); but there is nothing to support this. The southern boundary probably ran from the point where *Wâdy el-Bîreh* enters the Jordan, westward along the northern side of the valley to Mt. Tabor. The western border may have gone up by way of *Ḥaṭṭîn* (Ziddim) and *Yâḳûḳ* (Hukkok) to *Kefr ʿAnân* (Hannathon), bending there to the W., including the land of *er-Râmeh* (Ramah) until it reached the territory of Asher. Running northward again until nearly opposite Tyre, it bent eastward, and once more northward to the *Liṭâny* (Leontes), taking in the larger part of what is called by the Arabs *Belâd Beshârah* and *Belâd es-Shukîf*. Nineteen cities in N. are named in Josh **19** 32 ff. Among them was the famous city of refuge, KEDESH-NAPHTALI (q.v.), on the heights to the W. of the Waters of Merom, where extensive ruins are still to be seen (**20** 7). It, along with Hammoth-dor and Kartan, was assigned to the Gershonite Levites (**21** 23; 1 Ch **6** 76).

The land lying around the springs of the Jordan was included in the lot of N. It is clear that from this part, as well as from the cities named in Jgs **1** 33, N. did not drive out the Canaanites. These the Danites found in possession at the time of their raid. There is no indication that N. resented in any way this incursion of their kindred tribe into their territory (Jgs **18**).

3. Physical Features

The district thus indicated includes much excellent land, both pastoral and arable. There are the broad, rich terraces that rise away to the N. and N.W. of the Sea of Galilee, with the fertile plain of Gennesaret on the seashore. The mountains immediately N. of the sea are rocky and barren; but when this tract is passed, we enter the lofty and spacious lands of upper Galilee, which from time immemorial have been the joy of the peasant farmer. Great breadths there are which in season yield golden harvests. The richly diversified scenery, mountain, hill and valley, is marked by a finer growth of trees than is common in Pal. The terebinth and pine, the olive, mulberry, apricot, fig, pomegranate, orange, lemon and vine are cultivated to good purpose. Water is comparatively plentiful, supplied by many copious springs. It was one of the districts from which Solomon drew provisions, the officer in charge being the king's son-in-law, Ahimaaz (1 K **4** 15).

4. Distinction of the Tribe

The free life of these spacious uplands, which yielded so liberally to the touch of the hand of industry, developed a robust manhood and a wholesome spirit of independence among its inhabitants. According to Jos, who knew them well (*BJ*, III, iii, 2), the country never lacked multitudes of men of courage ready to give a good account of themselves on all occasions of war. Its history, as far as we know it, afforded ample opportunity for the development of warlike qualities. In the struggle with Sisera, N. was found on the high places of the field (Jgs **5** 18). To David's forces at Hebron, N. contributed a thousand captains "and with them with shield and spear thirty and seven thousand" (1 Ch **12** 34). Their position exposed them to the first brunt of attack by enemies from the N.; and in the wars of the kings they bore an important part (1 K **15** 20; 2 K **12** 18; **13** 22); and they were the first on the W. of the Jordan to be carried away captive (2 K **15** 29). See GALILEE.

5. Sites and Inhabitants

The largest town in Mt. Naphtali today is *Ṣafed*, on the heights due N. of the Sea of Galilee, often spoken of as the "city set on a hill." It is built in the form of a horseshoe, open to the N., round the Castle Hill, on which are the ruins of the old fortress of the Templars. This is a position of great strength, which could hardly fail to be occupied in ancient times, although, so far, it cannot be identified with any ancient city. It contains between 20,000 and 30,000 inhabitants. Over against it to the N.W., beyond the deep gorge of

Naphtali: *Ṣafed.*

Wâdy Leimûn, rises *Jebel Jermuk*, the highest mountain in Pal proper (c 4,000 ft.) which may be the scene of the TRANSFIGURATION (q.v.). The inhabitants of *Ṣafed* were massacred by Sultan Bibars in 1266. The city suffered severely from earthquake in 1759; and it shared with Tiberias, also a city of N., the disaster wrought by the earthquake of 1837. It is one of the holy cities of the Jews.

6. Labors of Jesus

In the land of N. Jesus spent a great part of his public life, the land of Gennesaret, Bethsaida, Capernaum and Chorazin all lying within its boundaries (cf Mt **4** 15). W. EWING

NAPHTALI, MOUNT (הַר נַפְתָּלִי, *har naphtālī;* **ἐν τῷ ὄρει τῷ Νεφθαλεί,** *en tō órei tō Nephthaleí*): This was the most northerly of the three divisions of the Western Range, which derived their names from those of the tribes holding chief sway over them—Mt. Judah, Mt. Ephraim, and Mt. Naphtali (Josh **20** 7 AV, RV replaces "Mount" by "the hill country of").

NAPHTHAR, naf′thär (AV): RV "Nephthar."

NAPHTUHIM, naf-tū′him (נַפְתֻּחִים, *naphtūḥīm;* LXX **Νεφθαλείμ,** *Nephthaleím*): A son of Mizraim (Gen **10** 13; 1 Ch **1** 11); but, according to most modern authorities, a district or a dependency of Egypt. Among the many efforts at identification the following deserve notice: Naphtuhim = (1) *Nephthys* (Νέφθυς, *Néphthus*) in the N.E. of Egypt; (2) *Na-ptah*, i.e. the people of Ptah, the dwellers in the neighborhood of Memphis; (3) *Nathu* (according to Herodotus,Ναθῶ, *Nathô*), which occurs in Assurbanipal's Annals as the name of a part of Lower Egypt; (4) Erman (*ZATW*, X, 118), by the change of a letter, reads Petemḥim, which signifies "The Northland"; (5) Spiegelberg sees in the word an old designation of the Delta, and would therefore render the name, "the people of the Delta" (cf Johns, *HDB;* Skinner and Holzinger on *Gen*). JOHN A. LEES

NAPKIN, nap′kin (**σουδάριον,** *soudárion;* Lat *sudarium*): In Lk **19** 20, the cloth in which the "unprofitable servant" wrapped the money of his lord; cf Jn **11** 44; **20** 7; see DRESS, 7; HANDKERCHIEF.

NARCISSUS, när-sis′us (**Νάρκισσος,** *Narkissos*): In Rom **16** 11 St. Paul sends greetings to "them of the household of Narcissus, that are in the Lord." "The last words may suggest that, though only the Christians in this household have a greeting sent to them, there were other members of it with whom the church had relations" (Denney).

Narcissus is a common name, esp. among freedmen and slaves. But, as in the case of Aristobulus, some famous person of this name must be meant. Conybeare and Howson mention two, one the well-known favorite of Claudius, the other a favorite of Nero. The latter, who was put to death by Galba (Dio Cass. lxiv.3), they think to be the Narcissus meant here (*St. Paul*, ch xix). On the other hand, Bishop Lightfoot (*Phil*, 175) holds that "the powerful freedman Narcissus, whose wealth was proverbial [Juv. *Sat.* xiv.329], whose influence with Claudius was unbounded, and who bore a chief part in the intrigues of this reign, alone satisfies this condition." Shortly after the accession of Nero, he had been put to death by Agrippina (Tac. *Ann.* xiii.1; Dio Cass. lx.34) in 54 AD. As this occurred three or four years before the Ep. to the Rom was written, some think another Narcissus is meant. However, as was usual in such cases, his property would be confiscated, and his slaves, becoming the property of the emperor, would swell "Caesar's household" as Narcissiani.

S. F. Hunter

NARD, närd. See Spikenard.

NASBAS, nas′bas (**Νασβᾶς,** *Nasbás*, **א**, **Ναβάδ,** *Nabád*, read by Fritzsche): A name otherwise unknown. It occurs only in Tob **11** 18, "And Achiacharus, and Nasbas his brother's son," came to Tobit's wedding. Opinions are divided as to whether he was "brother's son" of Tobit or Achiacharus. AVm gives the suggestion of Junius, "Achiacharus who is also called Nasbas," thus identifying Nasbas with Achiacharus, which might gain support from **1** 22 where Achiacharus is mentioned as "brother's son" of Tobit. See Achiacharus; Aman. **א** reads "Achiacharus and Nabad his brother's *sons*," which is corrected by another hand to "brother's son" (*ἐξάδελφος, exádelphos*). The Itala gives "*Nabal* avunculus ["maternal uncle"] illius"; the Vulg "*Nabath* consobrini ["cousins"] Tobiae"; Syr "*Laban* his *sister's* son." This person is probably identical with the "Aman" of Tob **14** 10 (see variety of readings under Aman) and the *nephew* in Harris' *Story of Aḥiḳar and His Nephew*.

S. Angus

NASI, nä′sē (B, **Νασεί,** *Naseí*, A, **Νασίθ,** *Nasíth;* AV **Nasith**): The head of one of the families which went up with Zerubbabel (1 Esd **5** 32) = "Neziah" of Ezr **2** 54; Neh **7** 56.

NASOR, nā′sor. See Hazor.

NATHAN, nā′than (נָתָן, *nāthān*, "gift"; **Ναθάν,** *Nathán*): A court prophet in David's reign and a supporter of Solomon at his accession. There are three main incidents in his career as depicted in the OT.

The two ‖ narratives, 2 S **7** 1–17 = 1 Ch **17** 1–15, of which the former is the original, relate how David confided to Nathan his intention to build a house for Jeh's ark. Nathan at first blesses the project, but that same night is given a Divine message, and returns to tell the king that instead of David building a house for Jeh, Jeh will build a house for David: "I will set up thy seed after thee, ... and I will establish his kingdom. . . . . I will be his father, and he shall be my son: if he commit iniquity, I will chasten him with the rod of men" (2 S **7** 12–14). Ver 13 says that "He shall build a house for my name, and I will establish the throne of his kingdom for ever," but this disturbs the one great thought of the passage, which is that God will build a house for David, and which is also the thought in David's prayer (vs 18–29).

1. Nathan and David's Temple-Plans

The word "seed" in ver 12 is collective and so throughout the passage, so that the prophecy does not refer to any individual, but, like Dt **17** 14–20; **18** 15–22, belongs to the group of generic prophecies. Nor is it Messianic, for ver 14 could not be reconciled with the sinlessness of Jesus. The message is rather a promise of the ever-merciful providence of God in dealing with David's family. (See, however, C. A. Briggs, *Messianic Prophecy*, 126 ff.) Budde, who says that the section belongs to the 7th cent. and is certainly preëxilic in the leading thought of the passage, sees in the prophecy something of the idealism of Amos and Hosea, for the prophet teaches that Jeh dwells, not in "a holy place made with hands" (He **9** 11.24), but rather in the life of the nation as represented by the direct succession of Davidic kings. This presents an extension of the teaching of Paul that the very body itself is a sanctuary unto God (1 Cor **6** 19).

2. Nathan and David's Sin

2 S **12** 1–25 narrates Nathan's rebuke of David for his adultery, and for causing the death of Uriah; and then comes an account of the death of Bathsheba's child. In vs 1–15*a*, we have Nathan's parable of the rich man and the poor man's ewe lamb, and the application of it to David's conduct. But several difficulties arise when we ask exactly what Nathan's message to David was: vs 13 f represent the prophet as saying that God has forgiven David but that the child will die, while vs 10–12 speak of a heavy punishment that is to come upon David and his family, and ver 16 does not show any indication of a prophecy as to the child's death. Commentators regard vs 1–15*a* as later in origin than chs **11, 12** in the main, and hold vs 10–12 to be still later than the rest of vs 1–15*a*. Budde omits vs 9*aβ*. 10*abα*.11.12, but regards even the rest of the story as interrupting the connection between **11** 27*b* and **12** 15*b*, and therefore of later date.

3. Nathan and Solomon's Accession

1 K **1** is a part of "one of the best pieces of Heb narrative in our possession" (H. P. Smith, *OT Hist*, 153, n. 2). It narrates the part that Nathan played in the events that led to Solomon's accession. David was getting old and feeble, and the succession had not been settled. When Adonijah, who was probably the eldest son living, gave a banquet to some of his father's state officials, Nathan, who was one of those that had not been invited, incited Bathsheba, Solomon's mother, to remind David of his promise to her that Solomon should succeed to the throne. This she did, and in the middle of her audience with David, Nathan appears with the news of Adonijah's feast and proclamation as king. Solomon is then anointed king by David's command, Nathan being one of his chief supporters. It has been suggested that it is only Nathan who interprets Adonijah's feast as a claim to the throne, but this contradicts ver 5. Yet, whereas in the two sections treated above Nathan is the prophet of Jeh, he is represented in 1 K as an intriguing court politician, planning very cleverly an opportune entrance into David's presence at the very time that Bathsheba has an audience with the king. The ‖ narrative of 1 Ch **28** makes no mention of Nathan, Solomon being there represented as Divinely elected to succeed David.

1 K **4** 5 mentions a Nathan as father of Azariah and Zabud, two of the chief officers of Solomon. He is probably the prophet.

1 Ch **29** 29; 2 Ch **9** 29 refer to "the words" or rather "the acts of Nathan the prophet" as well as those

of Samuel and Gad. "There can be no doubt that these are nothing more than references to the narratives in which Samuel, Nathan and Gad are mentioned in our Books of Samuel" (Curtis on 1 Ch **29** 29). In 2 Ch **29** 25, sanction is claimed for Levitical temple-music as being commanded by God through Nathan and Gad.

Curtis (on 1 Ch **29** 29) observes that Nathan is always called *nābhī'* ("prophet") in S and K and not *rō'eh* or *ḥōzeh*, "seer."

DAVID FRANCIS ROBERTS

NATHAN:

(1) A prophet (2 S **7**; Ps **51**, title). See preceding article.

(2) A son of King David (2 S **5** 14; 1 Ch **3** 5; **14** 4).

(3) Father of Igal, one of David's heroes (2 S **23** 36). In 1 Ch **11** 38, we have "Joel the brother of Nathan"; LXX B has "son" in this ver, but it is impossible to say whether Igal or Joel is the correct name.

(4) A Jerahmeelite (1 Ch **2** 36), whose son is called Zabad, whom some suppose to be the same as Zabud (1 K **4** 5). On this view this Nathan is the same as the prophet (see 1, above).

(5) A companion of Ezra from Babylon (Ezr **8** 16 and 1 Esd **8** 44).

(6) Nathanias (1 Esd **9** 34), one of those who had married foreign wives (Ezr **10** 39).

(7) Name of a family (Zec **12** 12).

DAVID FRANCIS ROBERTS

NATHANAEL, na-than'ā-el (**Ναθαναήλ**, *Nathanaēl*):

(1) One of the "captains over thousands" who furnished the Levites with much cattle for Josiah's Passover (1 Esd **1** 9) = "Nethanel" of 2 Ch **35** 9.

(2) (*Ναθανάηλος*, *Nathanáēlos*, B A om): One of the priests who had married a "strange wife" (1 Esd **9** 22) = "Nethanel" of Ezr **10** 22.

(3) An ancestor of Judith (Jth **8** 1).

(4) One of the Twelve Apostles. See next article.

NATHANAEL (נְתַנְאֵל, *nᵉthan'ēl*, "God has given"; **Ναθαναήλ**, *Nathanaēl*): Nathanael, who was probably a fisherman, belonged to Cana in Galilee (Jn **21** 2). According to the "Genealogies of the Twelve Apostles" (cf Budge, *Contendings of the Apostles*, II, 50), N. was the same as Simon, the son of Cleopas, and was one of the Twelve. He was among those who met and conversed with Jesus during the preaching of John the Baptist at Bethany beyond Jordan (cf Jn **1** 28). From the manner of the invitation extended to him by Philip (Jn **1** 45), it is evident that N. was well versed in ancient Scripture, and that in him also the preaching of John had aroused a certain expectancy. His reply to Philip, "Can any good thing come out of Nazareth?" (Jn **1** 46), was prompted, not by any ill repute of the place, but by its petty insignificance and familiarity in N.'s eyes. To this question Philip made no direct answer, but replied, "Come and see." It was the answer best fitted to the man and the occasion; it appealed to N.'s fair-mindedness and sincerity of purpose. He responded nobly to the call, and on approaching Jesus was received with the words: "Behold, an Israelite indeed, in whom is no guile!" (Jn **1** 47). It was a tribute to that singleness of heart which enabled him to overcome his initial prejudice. The same candor and openness distinguished the after-interview of N. with Jesus, as is evident by his question, "Whence knowest thou me?" (Jn **1** 48). The reply of Jesus was not what he expected. It concerned the time he had spent under the fig tree, kneeling, no doubt, in silent prayer and communion with God, and brought to mind all the sacred hopes and aspirations of that hour. It taught him that here was One who read on the instant the inmost secrets of his heart, and was Himself the ideal for whom he was seeking; and it drew from him the confession, "Rabbi, thou art the Son of God; thou art King of Israel" (Jn **1** 49).

Although N. is mentioned by name only once again in the NT, where he is one of the seven who witnessed the appearance of the risen Jesus at the Sea of Tiberias (Jn **21** 2), it is evident that the connection and companionship of N. with Jesus must have been much closer than those two incidents would lead us to suppose. Accordingly, attempts have been made to identify him with other NT characters, the most commonly accepted being Bartholomew (cf BARTHOLOMEW). The principal arguments in support of this identification are: (1) N. is never mentioned by the synoptists, and Bartholomew is never mentioned by John, who further implies that N. was one of the twelve disciples (cf Jn **20** 24–26; **21** 2); (2) in the Synoptists, Philip is closely connected with Bartholomew (cf lists of the apostles), and in John with N. (cf Jn **1** 45 ff); (3) the fact that most of the other apostles bear two names. Arguments are also adduced to identify him with Simon the Cananaean (cf SIMON). N. has also been identified with Matthew and Matthias (based on the similarity of name-meanings), with John the son of Zebedee, with Stephen, and even with Paul.

C. M. KERR

NATHANIAS, nath-a-nī'as (**Ναθανίας**, *Nathanías*): One of those who put away their foreign wives (1 Esd **9** 34) = "Nathan" of Ezr **10** 39.

NATHAN-MELECH, nā'than-mē'lek (נְתַן־מֶלֶךְ, *nᵉthan-melekh*, "king's gift"): A Judaean official, to whose chamber King Josiah removed "the horses of the sun" (2 K **23** 11). LXX calls him "Nathan, the king's eunuch" (*Ναθὰν βασιλέως τοῦ εὐνούχου*, *Nathán basiléōs toú eunoúchou*).

NATIONS, nā'shunz. See GENTILES; GOIIM; HEATHEN; TABLE OF NATIONS.

NATIVITY, na-tiv'i-ty, **OF MARY, GOSPEL OF THE.** See APOCRYPHAL GOSPELS.

NATURAL, nat'ū-ral, **NATURE,** nā'ṭūr (לֵחַ, *lēaḥ*; **ψυχικός**, *psuchikós*, **φυσικός**, *phusikós*, **φύσις**, *phúsis*):

1. As Used in the OT

"Natural" is the tr of *lēaḥ*, "freshness or vigor" (Dt **34** 7). Of Moses it is said, "His eye was not dim, nor his *natural* force abated."

"Nature" in the sense of a system or constitution does not occur in the OT. The world and men, each individual, were conceived as being the direct creation of a supra-mundane God, and conserved by His power and Spirit. The later conception of "nature" came in through Gr influences.

In the Apoc, we find "nature" in the sense of innate character or constitution (Wisd **7** 20, "the natures [*phúseis*] of living creatures"; **13** 1, "Surely vain are all men by nature" [*phúsei*], 3 Macc **3** 29, "mortal nature" [*phusis*]).

2. As Used in the NT

In the NT "nature" (*phusis*) is frequently found in the latter sense (Rom **1** 26, "against nature"; **2** 14, "by nature"; **2** 27; **11** 24, also "contrary to nature"; 1 Cor **11** 14, "Doth not even nature itself teach you?"; Gal **2** 15; **4** 8; Eph **2** 3; in 2 Pet **1** 4, we have "that ye might be partakers of the divine nature," RVm "or, a"); *phusis* occurs also in Jas **3** 7, "every *kind* of beasts," RVm "Gr nature," also "mankind" (ver 7), RVm "Gr the human nature." "Natural" (Rom **11** 21.24) is the tr of *katá phúsin*, "according to nature." Paul in 1 Cor speaks of "the natural man" (**2** 14, ARVm "or unspiritual, Gr psychical") and of a "natural body" (**15** 44 *bis*), the Gr word being *psuchikos*, "of the soul" (*psuchē*), the animal, natural, principle, as contrasted with what pertains to the higher principle of the spirit (*pneúma*). In 1 Cor **15** 46 the contrast is expressed, "Howbeit that is not first which is spiritual, but that which is natural," ARVm "Gr psychical." The "natural man" is the man in whom the spirit is unquickened, the "natural body" is that corresponding to the psychical or soul-nature, the "spiritual body" that corresponding to the Spirit as the dominant principle of the life. In Jude ver 10, we have *phusikôs*, "naturally," "naturally, as brute beasts," RV "naturally, like the creatures without reason"; *génesis*, "origin," "birth," is tr[d] "natural" (Jas **1** 23, "his natural face," RVm "Gr the face of his birth"); and "nature" (**3** 6, "the course of nature," RV "the wheel of nature," m "or birth") ("wheel" probably means "circle of nature" [the whole creation; see COURSE]); *gnēsiōs*, "genuine" ("true to right nature"), "legitimate," "sincere," is tr[d] "naturally" (Phil **2** 20, "who will naturally care for your state," RV "truly," m "Gr genuinely"). W. L. WALKER

NATURAL FEATURES, fē'ţūrz: As has been pointed out by various authors (cf *HGHL*), the principal physical features of Pal run in N. and S. lines, or rather about from S.S.W. to N.N.E.

The lowland or Shephelah (AV "vale, valley, plain, or low country") includes the maritime plain and the western foothills.

The hill country consists of the mountains of Judaea, and its features are continued northward to the plain of Esdraelon and southward to the Sinaitic peninsula. It is rocky and has very little water. Except for the few fountains, the scanty population depends upon rain water collected during the winter months.

The Arabah (RV) includes the Jordan valley from the Sea of Galilee to the Dead Sea, as well as the depression running from the Dead Sea to the Gulf of Akabah. It is to the latter depression that the name *Wâdi-ul-'Arabah* is now applied by the Arabs. It is bounded on the E. by Mt. Seir or Edom, and on the W. by the mountains of the Sinaitic peninsula. Its highest point, about halfway between the Dead Sea and the Gulf of Akabah, is a few hundred ft. higher than the level of the Mediterranean, but nearly 2,000 ft. above the level of the Dead Sea. From this point the valley slopes southward to the Gulf of Akabah, and northward to the Dead Sea. The lower Jordan valley slopes from about 600 ft. below ocean-level at the Sea of Galilee to about 1,300 ft. below ocean-level at the Dead Sea.

To the E. are **the highlands** of Gilead and Moab rising abruptly from the valley, as does the hill country of Judaea on the W. The country to the

"Up to Jerusalem" from the Good Samaritan's Inn.

E. of the Jordan–Dead Sea–Arabah depression, to the whole of which the name *Ghaur* (*Ghôr*) is applied by the Arabs, is a great table-land sloping gradually to the E. from the sharp edge which overlooks the *Ghaur*. It has no conspicuous peaks. What appear to be peaks when viewed from the *Ghaur* are irregularities of its western contour, which are invisible or appear as slight mounds to the observer who looks westward from any point some miles to the E. Mt. Nebo, for instance, when seen from *Mâdeba* is not readily distinguishable. This is because it really does not rise above the general level of the table-land. The small annual rainfall on the heights near the *Ghaur* diminishes eastward, and the desert begins within from 20 to 40 miles.

Another term much used by OT writers is **South** or Negeb, which embraces the southernmost portion of the promised land, and was never effectively occupied by the Israelites. Its uttermost boundary was the "river of Egypt" (*al-'Arîsh*), and coincides roughly with the present boundary between the Ottoman territory on the E. and the Anglo-Egyp territory of Sinai on the W.

The term **slopes,** *'ăshēdhōth*, AV "springs," occurs in Josh **10** 40, "So Joshua smote all the land, the hill-country . . . . and the lowland, and the slopes, and all their kings"; and again in Josh **12** 7.8, "And Joshua gave it . . . . for a possession according to their divisions; in the hill-country, and in the lowland, and in the Arabah, and in the slopes, and in the wilderness, and in the South." In the former passage, it seems to refer to the foothills which form the eastern or higher part of the lowland or Shephelah. In the latter passage, it might mean the same, or it might mean the descent from the Judaean hills to the *Ghaur*. In Dt **3** 17; **4** 49; Josh **12** 3; **13** 20, we have "the slopes of Pisgah" (*'ashdōth-ha-piṣgāh*, "springs of Pisgah"), which denotes the descent from the heights of Moab to the *Ghaur*. The same word occurs in the sing. in Nu **21** 15, referring to the descent to the Arnon. "Slopes," therefore, does not seem to be a term applied to any particular region.

The wilderness is usually the desert of the wandering, including the central part of the Sinaitic peninsula, but it is by no means always used in this sense, e.g. Josh **8** 15.20.24, where it clearly refers to a region near Ai. "The wilderness" of Mt **4** 1 is thought to be the barren portion of Judaea between Jerus and the Jordan. See CHAMPAIGN; COUNTRY; DESERT; EAST; HILL; LOWLAND; SOUTH.

ALFRED ELY DAY

NATURAL HISTORY, his'tō-ri. See ANIMAL; BOTANY; BIRDS; FISHES; INSECTS; ZOÖLOGY.

NATURAL MAN, THE. See MAN, THE NATURAL.

NATURE. See NATURAL, NATURE.

NAUGHT, nôt, **NAUGHTY,** nô'ti, **NAUGHTINESS,** -nes: In the sense of bad, worthless, worthlessness, the words in AV represent the Heb רַע, *ra'*, changed in RV to "bad" (2 K **2** 19; Prov **20** 14; Jer **24** 2), רֹעַ, *rō^a'*, retained in RV "naughtiness" (1 S **17** 28), הַוָּה, *hawwāh*, rendered in RV in Prov **11** 6 "iniquity," and in **17** 4 "mischievous." In Prov **6** 12, "naughty person," lit. "man of Belial," is in RV "worthless person." In the NT, "superfluity of naughtiness" in Jas **1** 21 (for κακία, *kakía*) becomes in RV "overflowing of wickedness," m "malice," and in Wisd **12** 10 AV's "naughty generation" (πονηρός, *ponērós*) is made into "by birth . . . . evil." JAMES ORR

NAUM, nā'um: AV form, NAHUM (q.v.), the name of an ancestor of Jesus (Lk **3** 25).

NAVE, nāv (1 K **7** 33). See SEA, MOLTEN.

NAVE, nā'vē (**Ναυή**, *Nauē*): Gr form of the Heb proper name "Nun" (so RV), found only in AV of Sir **46** 1.

NAVEL, nā'v'l (שֹׁר, *shōr* [LXX in Prov **3** 8 suggests a different reading, viz. instead of שָׁרֶּךָ, *shorrekhā*, שֵׁרֶךָ, *shērekhā*=שְׁאֵרֶךָ, *sh^e'ērekhā*, "thy flesh"]): The AV translates the Heb *shārīr* in the description of Behemoth (Job **40** 16) by "navel," where modern translators have substituted "muscles"; similarly in the tr of *shōrer* (Cant **7** 2) it has been replaced by "body." There remain two passages of RV where "navel" is retained as the tr of *shōr*. Thus we find the word used, *pars pro toto*, for the whole being: "It [the fear of Jeh] will be health to thy navel, and marrow to thy bones" (Prov **3** 8). The uttermost neglect which a new-born babe can experience is expressed by Ezekiel: "In the day thou wast born thy navel [i.e. umbilical cord] was not cut, neither wast thou washed in water to cleanse thee; thou wast not salted at all, nor swaddled at all" (Ezk **16** 4). H. L. E. LUERING

NAVY, nā'vi. See SHIPS AND BOATS, II, 1, (2).

NAZARENE, naz-a-rēn', naz'a-rēn (**Ναζαρηνός**, *Nazarēnós; Nazōraíos* in Mt, Jn, Acts and Lk): A derivative of Nazareth, the birthplace of Christ. In the NT it has a double meaning: it may be friendly and it may be inimical.

On the lips of Christ's friends and followers, it is an honorable name. Thus Matthew sees in it a fulfilment of the old Isaian prophecy (Isa **11** 1 [Heb]): "That it might be fulfilled which was spoken through the prophets, that he should be called a Nazarene" (Mt **2** 23). According to an overwhelming array of testimony (see Meyer, *Comm.*, in loc.), the name Nazareth is derived from the same √ *nāçar*, found in the text quoted from Isa. We have here undoubtedly to do with a permissible accommodation.

1. An Honorable Title

It is not quite certain that Matthew did not intend, by the use of this word, to refer to the picture of the Messiah, as drawn in Isa **53**, on account of the low estimate in which this place was held (Jn **1** 46). Nor is it permissible, as has been done by Tertullian and Jerome, to substitute the word "Nazarite" for "Nazarene," which in every view of the case is contrary to the patent facts of the life of the Saviour.

Says Meyer, "In giving this prophetic title to the Messiah he entirely disregards the historical meaning of the same (LXX Isa **11** 1, *ánthos*), keeps by the relationship of the name Nazareth to the word *nāçar*, and recognizes by virtue of the same, in that prophetic Messianic name *neçer*, the typical reference to this—that Jesus through His settlement in Nazareth was to become a 'Nazōraios,' a 'Nazarene.'" This name clung to Jesus throughout His entire life. It became His name among the masses: "Jesus of Nazareth passeth by" (Mk **10** 47; Lk **24** 19). Perhaps Matthew, who wrote after the event, may have been influenced in his application of the Isaian prophecy by the very fact that Jesus was popularly thus known. Even in the realm of spirits He was known by this appellation. Evil spirits knew and feared Him, under this name (Mk **1** 24; Lk **4** 34), and the angels of the resurrection morning called Him thus (Mk **16** 6), while Jesus applied the title to Himself (Acts **22** 8). In the light of these facts we do not wonder that the disciples, in their later lives and work, persistently used it (Acts **2** 22; **3** 6; **10** 38).

If His friends knew Him by this name, much more His enemies, and to them it was a title of scorn and derision. Their whole attitude was compressed in that one word of Nathanael, by which he voiced his doubt, "Can any good thing come out of Nazareth?" (Jn **1** 46). In the name "Nazarene," the Jews, who opposed and rejected Christ, poured out all the vials of their antagonism, and the word became a Jewish heritage of bitterness. It is hard to tell whether the appellation, on the lips of evil spirits, signifies dread or hatred (Mk **1** 24; Lk **4** 34). With the gatekeepers of the house of the high priest the case is clear. There it signifies unadulterated scorn (Mt **26** 71; Mk **14** 67). Even in His death the bitter hatred of the priests caused this name to accompany Jesus, for it was at their dictation written above His cross by Pilate (Jn **19** 19). The entire Christian community was called by the leaders of the Jewish people at Jerus, "the sect of the Nazarenes" (Acts **24** 5). If, on the one hand, therefore, the name stands for devotion and love, it is equally certain that on the other side it represented the bitter and undying hatred of His enemies. HENRY E. DOSKER

2. A Title of Scorn

NAZARETH, naz'a-reth (**Ναζαρέτ**, *Nazarét*, **Ναζαρέθ**, *Nazaréth*, and other forms): A town in Galilee, the home of Joseph and the Virgin Mary, and for about 30 years the scene of the Saviour's life (Mt **2** 23; Mk **1** 9; Lk **2** 39.51; **4** 16, etc). He was therefore called Jesus of Nazareth, although His birthplace was Bethlehem; and those who became His disciples were known as Nazarenes. This is the name, with slight modification, used to this day by Moslems for Christians, *Naṣārā*—the sing. being *Naṣrāny*.

1. Notice Confined to the NT

The town is not named in the OT, although the presence of a spring and the convenience of the site make it probable that the place was occupied in old times. Quaresimus learned that the ancient name was *Medina Abiat*, in which we may recognize the Arab. *el-Medīnat el-baiḍah*, "the white town." Built of the white stone supplied by the limestone rocks around, the description is quite accurate. There is a reference in Mish (*Menā-ḥōth*, viii.6) to the "white house of the hill" whence wine for the drink offering was brought. An elegy for the 9th of Ab speaks of a "course" of priests settled in Nazareth. This, however, is based upon an ancient midhrash now lost (Neubauer, *Géogr. du Talm*, 82, 85, 190; Delitzsch, *Ein Tag in Capernaum*, 142). But all this leaves us still in a state of uncertainty.

The ancient town is represented by the modern *en-Nāṣirah*, which is built mainly on the western and northwestern slopes of a hollow among the lower hills of Galilee, just before they sink into the plain of Esdraelon. It lies about midway between the Sea of Galilee and the Mediterranean at Haifa. The road to the plain and the coast goes over the southwestern lip of the hollow; that to Tiberias and Damascus over the heights to the N.E. A rocky gorge breaks down southward, issuing on the plain between two craggy hills. That to the W. is the traditional Hill of Precipitation (Lk **4** 29). This, however, is too far from the city as it must have been in the days of Christ. It is probable that the present town occupies pretty nearly the ancient site; and the scene of that attempt on Jesus' life may have been the cliff, many feet in height, not far from the old synagogue, traces of which are still seen in the western part of the town. There is a good spring under the Greek Orthodox church at the foot of the hill on the N. The water is led in a conduit to the fountain, whither the women and their children go as in old times, to carry home in their jars supplies for domestic use. There is also a tiny spring in the face of the western hill. To the N.W. rises the height on which stands the sanctuary, now in ruins, of *Neby Sa'īn*. From this point a most beautiful and extensive view is obtained, ranging on a clear day from the Mediterranean on the W. to the Mountain of Bashan on the E.; from Upper Galilee and Mt. Hermon on the N. to the uplands of Gilead and Samaria on the S. The whole extent of Esdraelon is seen, that great battlefield, associated with so many heroic exploits in Israel's history, from Carmel and Megiddo to Tabor and Mt. Gilboa.

2. Position and Physical Features

3. Present Inhabitants

There are now some 7,000 inhabitants, mainly Christian, of whom the Greek Orthodox church claims about 3,000. Moslems number about 1,600. There are no Jews. It is the chief market town for the pastoral and agricultural district that lies around it.

4. Labors of Jesus

In Nazareth, Jesus preached His first recorded sermon (Lk **4** 16 ff), when His plainness of speech aroused the homicidal fury of His hearers. "He did not many mighty works there because of their unbelief" (Mt **13** 58). Finding no rest or security in Nazareth, He made His home in Capernaum. The reproach implied in Nathanael's question, "Can any good thing come out of Nazareth?" (Jn **1** 46), has led to much speculation. By ingenious emendation of the text Cheyne would read, "Can the Holy One proceed from Nazareth?" (*EB*, s.v.). Perhaps, however, we should see no more in this than the acquiescence of Nathanael's humble spirit in the lowly estimate of his native province entertained by the leaders of his people in Judaea.

NAZARETH, FROM THE ROAD TO THE PLAIN OF ESDRAELON.

5. Later History

Christians are said to have first settled here in the time of Constantine (Epiphanius), whose mother Helena built the Church of the Annunciation. In crusading times it was the seat of the bishop of Bethsean. It passed into Moslem hands after the disaster to the Crusaders at *Ḥaṭṭîn* (1183). It was destroyed by Sultan Bibars in 1263. In 1620 the Franciscans rebuilt the Church of the Annunciation, and the town rose again from its ruins. Here in 1799 the French general Junot was assailed by the Turks. After his brilliant victory over the Turks at Tabor, Napoleon visited Nazareth. The place suffered some damage in the earthquake of 1837.

Protestant Missions are now represented in Nazareth by agents of the Church Missionary Society, and of the Edinburgh Medical Missionary Society. W. EWING

NAZIRITE, naz′i-rīt (נָזִיר, *nāzīr*, connected with נָדַר, *nādhar*, "to vow"; **ναζείρ**, *nazeír*, **ναζειραῖος**, *nazeiraíos*, as also various words indicating "holiness" or "devotion"; AV **Nazarite,** naz′a-rīt):

1. Antiquity and Origin
2. Conditions of the Vow
3. Initiation
4. Restoration
5. Completion and Release
6. Semi-sacerdotal Character
7. Nazirites for Life
8. Samson's Case
9. Samuel's Case
10. Token of Divine Favor
11. Did Not Form Communities
12. Among Early Christians
13. Parallels among Other Peoples

The root-meaning of the word in Heb as well as the various Gr tr[s] indicates the Nazirite as "a consecrated one" or "a devotee." In the circumstances of an ordinary vow, men consecrated some material possession, but the Nazirite consecrated himself or herself, and took a vow of separation and self-imposed discipline for the purpose of some special service, and the fact of the vow was indicated by special signs of abstinence. The chief OT passages are Jgs **13** 5–7; **16** 17; Nu **6**; Am **2** 11.12; cf Sir **46** 13 (Heb); 1 Macc **3** 49–52.

1. Antiquity and Origin

The question has been raised as to whether the Nazirite vow was of native or foreign origin in Israel. The idea of special separation, however, seems in all ages to have appealed to men of a particular temperament, and we find something of the kind in many countries and always linked with special abstinence of some kind; and from all that is said in the Pent we should infer that the custom was already ancient in Israel and that Mosaism regulated it, bringing it into line with the general system of religious observance and under the cognizance of the Aaronic priests. The critics assign the section dealing with this matter (Nu **6** 1–21) to P, and give it a late date, but there cannot be the least doubt that the institution itself was early. It seems not unlikely that on the settlement in Canaan, when the Israelites, having failed to overcome the native population, began to mix freely with them, the local worship, full of tempting Dionysiac elements, brought forth this religious protest in favor of Israel's ancient and simpler way of living, and as a protection against luxury in settling nomads. It is worthy of note that among the Semites vine-growing and wine-drinking have ever been considered foreign to their traditional nomadic mode of life. It was in this same protest that the Rechabites, who were at least akin to the Nazirites, went still farther in refusing even in Canaan to abandon the nomadic state. See RECHABITES.

2. Conditions of the Vow

The Pent, then, makes provision for the Nazirite vow being taken by either men or women, though the OT does not record a single instance of a female Nazirite. Further, it provides only for the taking of the vow for a limited time, that is, for the case of the "Nazirite of days." No period of duration is mentioned in the OT, but the Mish, in dealing with the subject, prescribes a period of 30 days , while a double period of 60 or even a triple one of 100 days might be entered on. The conditions of Naziritism entailed: (1) the strictest abstinence from wine and from every product of the vine; (2) the keeping of the hair unshorn and the beard untouched by a razor; (3) the prohibition to touch a dead body; and (4) prohibition of unclean food (Jgs **13** 5–7; Nu **6**).

3. Initiation

The ceremonial of initiation is not recorded, the Pent treating it as well known. The Talm tells us that it was only necessary for one to express the wish that he might be a Nazirite. A formal vow was, however, taken; and from the form of renewal of the vow, when by any means it was accidentally broken, we may judge that the head was also shorn on initiation and the hair allowed to grow during the whole period of the vow.

4. Restoration

The accidental violation of the vow just mentioned entailed upon the devotee the beginning of the whole matter anew and the serving of the whole period. This was entered on by the ceremonial of restoration, in the undergoing of which the Nazirite shaved his head, presented two turtle-doves or two young pigeons for sin and burnt offerings, and re-consecrated himself before the priest, further presenting a lamb for a trespass offering (Nu **6** 9-12).

5. Completion and Release

When the period of separation was complete, the ceremonial of release had to be gone through. It consisted of the presentation of burnt, sin and peace offerings with their accompaniments as detailed in Nu **6** 13–21, the shaving of the head and the burning of the hair of the head of separation, after which the Nazirite returned to ordinary life.

6. Semi-sacerdotal Character

The consecration of the Nazirite in some ways resembled that of the priests, and similar words are used of both in Lev **21** 12 and Nu **6** 17, the priest's vow being even designated *nēzer*. It opened up the way for any Israelite to do special service on something like semi-sacerdotal lines. The priest, like the Nazirite, dared not come into contact with the dead (Lev **21** 1), dared not touch wine during the period of service (Lev **10** 9), and, further, long hair was an ancient priestly custom (Ezk **44** 20).

7. Nazirites for Life

The only "Nazirites for life" that we know by name are Samson, Samuel and John the Baptist, but to these Jewish tradition adds Absalom in virtue of his long hair. We know of no one voluntarily taking the vow for life, all the cases recorded being those of parents dedicating their children. In rabbinical times, the father but not the mother might vow for the child, and an interesting case of this kind is mentioned in the dedication of Rabbi Chanena by his father in the presence of Rabban Gamaliel (*Nāzīr*, **29*b***).

8. Samson's Case

Samson is distinctly named a Nazirite in Jgs **13** 7 and **16** 17, but it has been objected that his case does not conform to the regulations in the Pent. It is said that he must have partaken of wine when he made a feast for his friends, but that does not follow and would not be so understood, say, in a Moslem country today. It is further urged that in connection with his fighting he must have come into contact with many dead men, and that he took honey from the carcase of the lion. To us these objections seem hypercritical. Fighting was specially implied in his vow (Jgs **13** 5), and the remains of the lion would be but a dry skeleton and not even so defiling as the ass's jawbone, to which the critics do not object.

9. Samuel's Case

Samuel is nowhere in the OT called a Nazirite, the name being first applied to him in Sir **46** 13 (Heb), but the restrictions of his dedication seem to imply that he was. Wellhausen denies that it is implied in 1 S **1** 11 that he was either a Nathin ("a gift, [one] 'given' unto Jeh"; cf Nu **3** 9; **18** 6) or a Nazirite. In the Heb text the mother's vow mentions only the uncut hair, and first in LXX is there added that he should not drink wine or strong drink, but this is one of the cases where we should not regard silence as final evidence. Rather it is to be regarded that the visible sign only is mentioned, the whole contents of the vow being implied.

10. Token of Divine Favor

It is very likely that Nazirites became numerous in Israel in periods of great religious or political excitement, and in Jgs **5** 2 we may paraphrase, 'For the long-haired champions in Israel.' That they should be raised up was considered a special token of God's favor to Israel, and the tempting of them to break their vow by drinking wine was considered an aggravated sin (Am **2** 11.12). At the time of the captivity they were looked upon as a vanished glory in Israel (Lam **4** 7 m), but they reappeared in later history.

11. Did Not Form Communities

So far as we can discover, there is no indication that they formed guilds or settled communities like the "Sons of the Prophets." In some sense the Essenes may have continued the tradition, and James, the Lord's brother (Euseb., *HE*, II, xxiii, 3, following Hegesippus), and also Banus, tutor of Jos (*Vita*, 2), who is probably the same as the Buni mentioned as a disciple of Jesus in *Ṣanh.* **43*a***, were devotees of a kind resembling Nazirites. Berenice's vow was also manifestly that of the Nazirite (Jos, *BJ*, II, xv, 1).

12. Among Early Christians

The case of John the Baptist is quite certain, and it was probably the means of introducing the custom among the early Christians. It was clearly a Nazirite's vow which Paul took, "having shorn his head in Cenchreae" (Acts **18** 18), and which he completed at Jerus with other Christians similarly placed (Acts **21** 23).

As the expenses of release were heavy for poor men, such were at times aided in this matter by their richer brethren. Thus Agrippa, on his return from Rome, assisted many Nazirites (Jos, *Ant*, XIX, vi, 1), and Paul was also at charges with others (Acts **21** 23).

We come across something of the same kind in many countries, and we find special abstinence always emphasized. Thus we meet with a class of "votaries" as early as the days of Ḥammurabi, and his code devotes quite a number of sections to them. Among other restrictions they were prohibited from even entering a wineshop (*Sect.* **110**).

Then we are familiar with the *Hieródouloi* of the Greeks, and the Vestal Virgins of the Romans.

13. Parallels among Other Peoples

The word *nᵉzīr* also appears in Syr and was applied to the maidens devoted to the service of Belthis. In the East, too, there have always been individuals and societies of ascetics who were practically Nazirites, and the modern dervish in nearly every way resembles him, while it is worthy of record in this connection that the Moslem (an abstainer by creed) while under the vow of pilgrimage neither cuts his hair nor pares his nails till the completion of his vow in Mecca. W. M. CHRISTIE

NEAH, nē'a (הַנֵּעָה, *ha-nē'āh*, "the neah"; **'Αννουά**, *Annouá*): A town in the lot of Zebulun (Josh **19** 13), mentioned along with Gath-hepher and Rimmon. It is possibly identical with "Neiel" (ver 27). No name resembling either of these has yet been recovered, although the district in which the place must be sought is pretty definitely indicated. It may probably have lain to the N. of Rimmon (*Rummāneh*), about 4 miles N.E. of *Ṣeffūriyeh*.

NEAPOLIS, nḗ-ap'ō-lis (**Νεάπολις**, *Neápolis;* WH, *Néa Pólis*): A town on the northern shore of the Aegean, originally belonging to Thrace but later falling within the Rom province of Macedonia. It was the seaport of Philippi, and was the first point in Europe at which Paul and his companions landed; from Troas they had sailed direct to Samothrace, and on the next day reached Neapolis (Acts **16** 11). Paul probably passed through the town again on his second visit to Macedonia (Acts **20** 1), and he certainly must have embarked there on his last journey from Philippi to Troas, which occupied 5 days (Acts **20** 6). The position of Neapolis is a matter of dispute. Some writers have maintained that it lay on the site known as *Eski* (i.e. "Old") *Kavalla* (Cousinéry, *Macédoine*, II, 109 ff), and that upon its destruction in the 6th or 7th cent. AD the inhabitants migrated to the place, about 10 miles to the E., called Christopolis in mediaeval and *Kavalla* in modern times. But the general view, and that which is most consonant with the evidence, both literary and archaeological, places Neapolis at *Kavalla*, which lies on a rocky headland with a spacious harbor on its western side, in which the fleet of Brutus and Cassius was moored at the time of the battle of Philippi (42 BC; Appian *Bell. Civ.* iv.106). The town lay some 10 Rom miles from Philippi, with which it was connected by a road leading over the mountain ridge named Symbolum, which separates the plain of Philippi from the sea.

The date of its foundation is uncertain, but it seems to have been a colony from the island of Thasos, which lay opposite to it (Dio Cassius xlvii.35). It appears (under the name Neopolis, which is also borne on its coins) as a member both of the first and of the second Athenian confederacy, and was highly commended by the Athenians in an extant decree for its loyalty during the Thasian revolt of 411–408 BC (*Inscr. Graec.*, I, Suppl. 51). The chief cult of the city was that of "The Virgin," usually identified with the Gr Artemis. (See Leake, *Travels in Northern Greece*, III, 180; Cousinéry, *Voyage dans la Macédoine*, II, 69 ff, 109 ff; Heuzey and Daumet, *Mission archéol. de Macédoine*, 11 ff.)

M. N. TOD

NEAR, nēr, **NIGH**, nī (chiefly קָרוֹב, *ḳārōbh*, "to draw near," קָרַב, *ḳārabh;* **ἐγγύς**, *eggús*): Used of proximity in place (Gen **19** 20; **45** 10; Ex **13** 17; Ps **22** 11; Jn **3** 23, etc), time (Jer **48** 16; Ezk **7** 7; **30** 3; Mk **13** 28), or kinship (Lev **21** 2; Ruth **3** 12), but also employed of *moral* nearness. Jeh is "nigh" to them that are of a broken heart (Ps **34** 18). God draws nigh to His people, and they to Him (Jas **4** 8). The antithesis is God's "farness" from the wicked.

NEARIAH, nē-a-rī'a (נְעַרְיָה, *nᵉ'aryāh*):
(1) A descendant of David (1 Ch **3** 22 f).
(2) A descendant of Simeon (1 Ch **4** 42).
In both instances LXX reads "Noadiah."

NEBAI, nē'bī, nḗ-bā'i, neb'ā-ī (נֵיבַי, *nēbhay*). See NOBAI.

NEBAIOTH, nḗ-bā'yoth, nḗ-bī'ōth (נְבָיוֹת, נְבָיֹת, *nᵉbhāyōth;* LXX **Ναβαιώθ**, *Nabaiōth*): Firstborn of Ishmael (Gen **25** 13; **28** 9; **36** 3; 1 Ch **1** 29). Isa **60** 7 mentions the tribe Nebaioth with Kedar, with an allusion to its pastoral nature: "the rams of Nebaioth" are to serve the ideal Zion as sacrificial victims. Again associated with Kedar, the name occurs frequently in Assyr inscriptions. The tribe must have had a conspicuous place among the northern Arabs. Jos, followed by Jerome, regarded Nebaioth as identical with the Nabataeans, the great trading community and ally of Rome, whose capital and stronghold was Petra. This view is widely accepted, but the name "Nabataean" is spelled with a *ṭ*, and the interchange of *ṭ* and *t*, although not unparalleled, is unusual. If the name is Arab., it is probably a fem. pl., and in that case could have no connection with the Nabataeans.

A. S. FULTON

NEBALLAT, nḗ-bal'at (נְבַלָּט, *nᵉbhallāṭ;* **Ναβαλλάτ**, *Naballát*): A town occupied by the Benjamites after the exile, named along with Lod and Ono (Neh **11** 34). It is represented by the modern *Beit Nebāla*, 4 miles N.E. of Lydda.

NEBAT, nē'bat (נְבָט, *nᵉbhāṭ*): Father of Jeroboam I (1 K **11** 26, and frequently elsewhere). The name occurs only in the phrase "Jeroboam the son of Nebat," and is evidently intended to distinguish Jeroboam I from the later son of Joash. See JEROBOAM.

NEBO, nē'bō (נְבוֹ, *nᵉbhō;* Assyr *Nabu*): The Bab god of literature and science. In the Bab mythology he is represented as the son and interpreter of Bel-merodach (cf Isa **46** 1; Bel and Nebo there represent Babylon). His own special shrine was at Borsippo. His planet was Mercury. His name enters into Bib. names, as "Nebuchadnezzar," and perhaps "Abed-nego" (Dnl **1** 7, for "Abed-nebo, servant of Nebo"). See BABYLONIA AND ASSYRIA, RELIGION OF.

NEBO (נְבוֹ, *nᵉbhō;* **Ναβαῦ**, *Nabaú*):

(1) This town is named in Nu **32** 3 between Sebam and Beon (which latter evidently represents Baal-meon of ver 38), after Heshbon and Elealeh, as among the cities assigned by Moses to Reuben. It was occupied by the Reubenite clan Bela (1 Ch **5** 8). Here it is named between Aroer and Baal-meon. In their denunciations of wrath against Moab, Isaiah names it along with Medeba (Isa **15** 2) and Jeremiah with Kiriathaim (Jer **48** 1), and again (ver 22) between Dibon and Beth-diblathaim. Mesha (M S) says that by command of Chemosh he went by night against the city, captured it after an assault that lasted from dawn till noon, and put all the inhabitants to death. He dedicated the place to Ashtar-chemosh. Jerome (*Comm.* on Isa **15** 2) tells us that at Nebo was the idol of Chemosh. The site which seems best to meet the requirements of the passages indicated is on the ridge of *Jebel Nebā* to the S.W. of *Ḥesbān*, where ruins of an ancient town bearing the name of *en-Nebā* are found (Buhl, *GAP*, 266).

(2) (נְבוֹ, *nᵉbhō;* B, Ναβοῦ, *Naboú,* A, Ναβώ, *Nabō,* and other forms): Fifty-two descendants of the inhabitants of Nebo returned from exile with Zerubbabel (Ezr **2** 29; Neh **7** 33). The place was in Judah and is named after Bethel and Ai. There is nothing, however, to guide us as to its exact position. It may be represented by either *Beit Nubā*, 12 miles N.W. of Jerus, or *Nuba*, which lies about 4 miles S.S.E of *'Id el-Mā'* (Adullam).

W. Ewing

NEBO, MOUNT (הַר נְבוֹ, *har nᵉbhō;* **Ναβαύ**, *Nabaú*): A mountain in the land of Moab which Moses ascended at the command of God in order that he might see the Land of Promise which he was never to enter. There also he was to die. From the following passages (viz. Nu **33** 47; Dt **32** 49; **34** 1), we gather that it was not far from the plain of Moab in which Israel was encamped; that it was a height standing out to the W. of the mountains of Abarim; that it lay to the E. of Jericho; and that it was a spot from which a wide and comprehensive view of Pal could be obtained. None of these conditions are met by *Jebel 'Aṭṭārūs*, which is too far to the E., and is fully 15 miles S. of a line drawn eastward from Jericho. *Jebel 'Osha*, again, in Mt. Gilead, commands, indeed, an extensive view; but it lies too far to the N., being at least 15 miles N. of a line drawn eastward from Jericho. Both of these sites have had their advocates as claimants for the honor of representing the Bib. Nebo.

The "head" or "top" of Pisgah is evidently identical with Mt. Nebo (Dt **34** 1). After Moses' death he was buried "in the valley in the land of Moab," over against Beth-peor.

The name *Nebā* is found on a ridge which, some 5 miles S.W. of *Ḥesbān* and opposite the northern end of the Dead Sea, runs out to the W. from the

Mt. Nebo from the Spring *'Ain Neba.*

plateau of Moab, "sinking gradually: at first a broad brown field of arable land, then a flat top crowned by a ruined cairn, then a narrower ridge ending in the summit called *Siāghah*, whence the slopes fall steeply on all sides. The name Nebo or Neba [the "knob" or "tumulus"] applies to the flat top with the cairn, and the name *Tal'at eṣ-Ṣufa* to the ascent leading up to the ridge from the N. Thus we have three names which seem to connect the ridge with that whence Moses is related to have viewed the Promised Land, namely, first, Nebo, which is identically the same word as the modern *Neba;* secondly, *Siāghah*, which is radically identical with the Aram. *Se'ath*, the word standing instead of Nebo in the Tg of Onkelos [Nu **32** 3], where it is called the burial place of Moses; thirdly, *Tal'at eṣ-Ṣufa*, which is radically identical with the Heb Zuph (*çūph*), whence Mizpah (*miçpāh*) and Zophim (*çōphīm*). . . . . The name Pisgah is not now known, but the discovery of Zophim [cf Nu **23** 14] confirms the view now generally held, that it is but another title of the Nebo range."

Neither Mt. Hermon nor Dan (*Tell el-Ḳāḍy*) is visible from this point; nor can Zoar be seen; and if the Mediterranean is the hinder sea, it also is invisible. But, as Driver says ("Dt," *ICC*, 419), the terms in Dt **34** 1.3 are hyperbolical, and must be taken as including points filled in by the imagination as well as those actually visible to the eye. Mr. Birch argues in favor of *Tal'at el-Benāt*, whence he believes Dan and Zoar to be visible, while he identifies "the hinder sea" with the Dead Sea (*PEFS*, 1898, 110 ff).

W. Ewing

NEBUCHADNEZZAR, neb-ū-kad-nez'ar, **NEBUCHADREZZAR,** -rez'ar: Nebuchadnezzar, the second king of Babylon of that name, is best known as the king who conquered Judah, destroyed Jerus, and carried the people of the Jews captive to Babylon. Of all the heathen monarchs mentioned by name in the Scriptures, N. is the most prominent and the most important. The prophecies of Jeremiah, Ezekiel, and Daniel, and the last chs of K and Ch centered about his life, and he stands preëminent, along with the Pharaohs of the oppression and the exodus, among the foes of the kingdom of God. The documents which have been discovered in Babylon and elsewhere within the last 75 years have added much to our knowledge of this monarch, and have in general confirmed the Bib. accounts concerning him.

1. His Name

His name is found in two forms in the Bible, Nebuchadnezzar and Nebuchadrezzar. In the LXX he is called Ναβουχοδονοσόρ, *Nabouchodonosór*, and in the Vulg *Nabuchodonosor*. This latter form is found also in the AV Apoc throughout and in RV 1 Esd, Ad Est and Bar, but not Jth or Tob. This change from *r* to *n* which is found in the two writings of the name in the Heb and the Aram. of the Scriptures is a not uncommon one in the Sem languages, as in Burnaburiyash and Burraburiyash, Ben-hadad and Bar-hadad (see Brockelmann's *Comparative Grammar*, 136, 173, 220). It is possible, however, that the form Nebuchadnezzar is the Aram. tr of the Bab Nebuchadrezzar. If we take the name to be compounded of Nabu-kudurri-uṣur in the sense "O Nebo, protect thy servant," then Nabu-kedina-uṣur would be the best tr possible in Aramaic. Such trˢ of proper names are common in the old VSS of the Scriptures and elsewhere. For example, in *WAI*, V, 44, we find 4 columns of proper names of persons giving the Sumerian originals and the Sem trˢ of the same; cf Bar-hadad in Aram. for Heb Ben-hadad. In early Aram. the *ṣ* had not yet become *ṭ* (see Cooke, *Text-Book of North-Sem Inscriptions*, 188 f); so that for anyone who thought that *kudurru* meant "servant," N. would be a perfect tr into Aram. of Nebuchadrezzar.

2. Family

The father of N. was Nabopolassar, probably a Chaldaean prince. His mother is not known by name. The classical historians mention two wives: Amytis, the daughter of Astyages, and Nitocris, the mother of Nabunaid. The monuments mention three sons: Evil-merodach who succeeded him, Marduk-shum-uṣur, and Marduk-nadin-aḥi. A younger brother of N., called Nabu-shum-lishir, is mentioned on a building-inscription tablet from the time of Nabopolassar.

3. Sources of Information

The sources of our information as to the life of N. are about 500 contract tablets dated according to the days, months and years of his reign of 43 years; about 30 building and honorific inscriptions; one historical inscription; and in the books of Jer, Ezk, Dnl, and K. Later sources are Ch, Ezr, and the fragments of Berosus, Menander, Megasthenes, Abydenus, and Alexander Polyhistor, largely as cited by Jos and Eusebius.

From these sources we learn that N. succeeded his father on the throne of Babylon in 604 BC, and reigned till 561 BC. He probably commanded the armies of Babylon from 609 BC. At any rate, he was at the head of the army which defeated Pharaoh-necoh at Carchemish on the Euphrates in 605 BC (see 2 K **23** 31; 2 Ch **35** 20 ff). After having driven Necoh out of Asia and settled the affairs of Syria and Pal, he was suddenly

4. Political History

Boundary Stone of Nebuchadnezzar I.

recalled to Babylon by the death of his father. There he seems quietly to have ascended the throne. In the 4th year of Jehoiakim (or 3d according to the Bab manner of reckoning [Dnl **1** 1]), he came up first against Jerus and carried away part of the vessels of the temple and a few captives of noble lineage. Again, in Jehoiakim's 11th year, he captured Jerus, put Jehoiakim, its king, into chains, and probably killed him. His successor, Jehoiachin, after a three months' reign, was besieged in Jerus, captured, deposed, and carried captive to Babylon, where he remained in captivity 37 years until he was set free by Evil-merodach. In the 9th year of Zedekiah, N. made a 4th expedition against Jerus which he besieged, captured, and destroyed (see Jer **52**). In addition to these wars with Judah, N. carried on a long siege of Tyre, lasting 13 years, from his 7th to his 20th year. He had at least three wars with Egypt. The first culminated in the defeat of Necoh at Carchemish; the second in the withdrawal of Hophra (Apries) from Pal in the 1st year of the siege of Jerus under Zedekiah; and the third saw the armies of N. entering Egypt in triumph and defeating Amasis in N.'s 37th year. In the numerous building and honorific inscriptions of N. he makes no mention by name of his foes or of his battles; but he frequently speaks of foes that he had conquered and of many peoples whom he ruled. Of these peoples he mentions by name the Hittites and others (see Langdon, 148–51). In the *Wâdy-Brissa* inscription, he speaks of a special conquest of Lebanon from some foreign foe who had seized it; but the name of the enemy is not given.

The monuments justify the boast of N.: "Is not this great Babylon that I have built?" (Dnl **4** 30).

5. Buildings, etc

Among these buildings special emphasis is placed by N. upon his temples and shrines to the gods, particularly to Marduk, Nebo and Zarpinat, but also to Shamash, Sin, Gula, Ramman, Mah, and others. He constructed, also, a great new palace and rebuilt an old one of his father's. Besides, he laid out and paved with bricks a great street for the procession of Marduk, and built a number of great walls with moats and moat-walls and gates. He dug several broad, deep canals, and made dams for flooding the country to the N. and S. of Babylon, so as to protect it against the attack of its enemies. He made, also, great bronze bulls and serpents, and adorned his temples and palaces with cedars and gold. Not merely in Babylon itself, but in many of the cities of Babylonia as well, his building operations were carried on, esp. in the line of temples to the gods.

6. Religion, etc

The inscriptions of N. show that he was a very religious man, probably excelling all who had preceded him in the building of temples, in the institution of offerings, and the observance of all the ceremonies connected with the worship of the gods. His larger inscriptions usually contain two hymns and always close with a prayer. Mention is frequently made of the offerings of precious metals, stones and woods, of game, fish, wine, fruit, grain, and other objects acceptable to the gods. It is worthy of note that these offerings differ in character and apparently in purpose from those in use among the Jews. For example, no mention is made in any one of N.'s inscriptions of the pouring out or sprinkling of blood, nor is any reference made to atonement, or to sin.

7. Madness

No reference is made in any of these inscriptions to N.'s insanity. But aside from the fact that we could scarcely expect a man to publish his own calamity, esp. madness, it should be noted that according to Langdon we have but three inscriptions of his written in the period from 580 to 561 BC. If his madness lasted for 7 years, it may have occurred between 580 and 567 BC, or it may have occurred between the Egyp campaign of 567 BC and his death in 561 BC. But, as it is more likely that the "7 times" mentioned in Dnl may have been months, the illness may have been in any year after 580 BC, or even before that for all we know.

8. Miracles, etc

No mention is made on the monuments (1) of the dream of N. recorded in Dnl **2**, or (2) of the image of gold that he set up, or (3) of the fiery furnace from which the three children were delivered (Dnl **3**). As to (1), it may be said, however, that a belief in dreams was so universal among all the ancient peoples, that a single instance of this kind may not have been considered as worthy of special mention. The annals of Ashur-banipal and Nubu-naid and Xerxes give a number of instances of the importance attached to dreams and their interpretation. It is almost certain that N. also believed in them. That the dream recorded in Dnl is not mentioned on the monuments seems less remarkable than that no dream of his is recorded. As to (2) we know that N. made an image of his royal person (*ṣalam sharrutiya*, Langdon, XIX, B, col. x, 6; cf the image of the royal person of Nabopolassar, id, p. 51), and it is certain that the images of the gods were made of wood (id, p. 155), that the images of Nebo and Marduk were conveyed in a bark in the New Year's procession (id, pp. 157, 159, 163, 165) and that there were images of the gods in all the temples (id, *passim*); and that N. worshipped before these images. That N. should have made an image of gold and put it up in the Plain of Dura is entirely in harmony with what we know of his other "pious deeds." (3) As to "the fiery furnace," it is known that Ashurbanipal, king of Assyria, says that his own brother, Shamash-shumukin, was burned in a similar furnace.

The failure of N. to mention any of the particular persons or events recorded in Dnl does not disprove their historicity, any more than his failure to mention the battle of Carchemish, or the siege of Tyre and Jerus, disproves them. The fact is, we have no real historical inscription of N., except one fragment of a few broken lines found in Egypt.

LITERATURE.—T. G. Pinches, *The NT in the Light of the Historical Records and Legends of Assyria and Babylonia;* Stephen Langdon, *Building Inscriptions of the Neo-Babylonian Empire.* See also, Rogers, *History of Babylonia and Assyria;* and McCurdy, *History, Prophecy and the Monuments,* III.

R. DICK WILSON

NEBUSHAZBAN, neb-ū-shaz'ban (נְבוּשַׁזְבָּן, *nebhūshazebhān*=Assyr *Nabusezib-anni,* "Nebo delivers me"; AV **Nebushasban**): An important officer (the *Rab-saris,* "chief captain" or "chief eunuch") of the Bab army, who with Nergal-sharezer and others was appointed to see to the safety of Jeremiah after the taking of Jerus (Jer **39** 13).

NEBUZARADAN, neb-ū-zär-ā'dan, -zär'a-dan (נְבוּזַרְאֲדָן, *nebhūzar'ădhān* = Assyr *Nabu-zara-iddina,* "Nebo has given seed"; **Νεβουζαρδάν,** *Nebouzardán*): Nebuchadnezzar's general at the siege of Jerus (2 K **25** 8.11.20 ‖ Jer **52** 12.15.26; **39** 9.10.11.13). Under the title of "captain of the guard," he commanded the army, and, after the fall of the city, carried out his master's policy with regard to the safety of Jeremiah, the transport of the exiles, and the government of those who were left in the land.

NECHO, NECHOH, nē'kō. See PHARAOH-NECOH.

NECK, nek (צַוָּר, *çawwār,* צַוָּאר, *çawwā'r,* צַוָּרֹן, *çawwārōn,* צַוָּארָה, *çawwā'rāh,* Aram. צַוַּר, *çawwar* [Dnl **5** 7.16.29], עֹרֶף, *'ōreph,* מַפְרֶקֶת, *miphreḳeth* [1 S **4** 18]; **νῶτος,** *nṓtos,* "back" [Bar **2** 33]; occasionally the words גָּרוֹן, *gārōn* [Isa **3** 16; Ezk **16** 11], and גַּרְגְּרוֹת, *gargerōth,* pl. of *gargārāh,* lit. "throat" [Prov **1** 9; **3** 3.22; **6** 21], are trd "neck"): The neck is compared with a tower for beauty (Cant **4** 4; **7** 4) and is decorated with necklaces and chains (Prov **1** 9; **3** 3.22; **6** 21, Heb *gargerōth;* Ezk **16** 11, Heb *gārōn,* "throat"; Dnl **5** 7.16.29, Heb *çawwār*). It is also the part of the body where the yoke, emblem of labor and hardship, dependence and subjection, is borne (Dt **28** 48; Jer **27** 8.11.12; **28** 14; Acts **15** 10). "To shake off the yoke," "to break the yoke," or "to take it off" is expressive of the regaining of independence and liberty, either by one's own endeavors or through help from outside (Gen **27** 40; Isa **10** 27; Jer **28** 11; **30** 8). Certain animals which were not allowed as food (like the firstborn which were not redeemed) were to be killed by having their necks (*'ōreph*) broken (Ex **13** 13; **34** 20); the turtle-doves and young pigeons, which were sacrificed as sin offerings or as burnt offerings, had their heads wrung or pinched off from their necks (Lev **5** 8). In 1 S **4** 18 the Heb word *miphreḳeth* signifies a fracture of the upper part of the spinal column caused by a fall.

It was a military custom of antiquity for the conqueror to place his foot upon the vanquished. This custom, frequently represented in sculpture on many an Egyp temple wall, is referred to in Josh **10** 24; Bar **4** 25 and probably in Rom **16** 20 and Ps **110** 1. St. Paul praises the devotion of Aquila and Priscilla, "who for my life laid down their own necks" (Rom **16** 4). See FOOTSTOOL.

To "fall on the neck" of a person is a very usual mode of salutation in the East (Gen **33** 4; **45** 14; **46** 29; Tob **11** 9.13; Lk **15** 20; Acts **20** 37). In moments of great emotion such salutation is apt to end in weeping on each other's neck.

Readiness for work is expressed by "putting one's neck to the work" (Neh **3** 5). Severe punishment and calamity are said to "reach to the neck" (Isa **8** 8; **30** 28).

The Lord Jesus speaks of certain persons for whom it were better to have had a millstone put around the neck and to have been drowned in the sea. The meaning is that even the most disgraceful death is still preferable to a life of evil influence upon even the little ones of God's household (Mt **18** 6; Mk **9** 42; Lk **17** 2).

To "make the neck stiff," to "harden the neck" indicates obstinacy often mingled with rebellion (Ex **32** 9; **33** 3.5; **34** 9; 2 Ch **30** 8; **36** 13; Neh **9** 16.17.29; Ps **75** 5 [RVm "insolently with a haughty neck"]; Prov **29** 1; Jer **7** 26). Cf σκληροτράχηλος, *sklērotráchēlos,* "stiffnecked" (Acts **7** 51). Similarly Isaiah (**48** 4) speaks of the neck of the obstinate sinner as resembling an iron sinew.

H. L. E. LUERING

NECKLACE, nek'lās (רָבִיד, *rābhīdh,* "chain"): A neck-chain ornament, worn either separately (Ezk **16** 11), or with pendants (Isa **3** 19), such as crescents (Isa **3** 18) or rings (Gen **38** 25); sometimes made of gold (Gen **41** 42; Dnl **5** 29), or of strings of jewels (Cant **1** 10). Even beasts of burden were sometimes so adorned by royalty (Jgs **8** 26). It was considered suggestive of pride (Ps **73** 6) or of filial loyalty (Prov **1** 9). The word does not occur in AV, but such adornments have always been popular in all the Bible lands.

NECO, nē'kō (נְכוֹ, *nekhō* [2 Ch **35** 22; **36** 4]). See PHARAOH-NECOH.

NECODAN, nē-kō'dan. See NEKODA.

NECROMANCY, nek'rō-man-si. See ASTROLOGY, 1; DIVINATION; WITCHCRAFT.

NEDABIAH, ned-a-bī'a (נְדַבְיָה, *nedhabhyāh*): A descendant of David (1 Ch **3** 18).

NEEDLE, nē'd'l (**ῥαφίς,** *rhaphís*): The word "needle" occurs only 3 t, viz. in the reference to Christ's use of the proverb: "It is easier for a camel to go through a needle's eye, than for a rich man to enter into the kingdom of God" (Mt **19** 24; Mk **10** 25; Lk **18** 25). This saying ought to be accepted in the same sense as Mt **23** 24, "Ye blind guides, that strain out the gnat, and swallow the camel!" Christ used them to illustrate absurdities. A rabbinical ‖ is cited, "an elephant through a needle's eye." Some writers have attempted to show that *rhaphis* referred to a small gate of a walled oriental city. No evidence of such a use of the word exists in the terms applied today in Bib. lands to this opening. "Rich man" here has the connotation of a man bound up in his riches. If a man continues to trust in his earthly possessions to save him, it would be absurd for him to expect to share in the spiritual kingdom where dependence upon the King is a first requisite.

The fact that needles are not mentioned elsewhere in the Bible should not be taken to indicate that this instrument was not used. Specimens of bone and metal needles of ancient origin show that they were common household objects. See CAMEL.

JAMES A. PATCH

NEEDLEWORK, nē'd'l-wûrk. See EMBROIDERY.

NEEDY, nēd'i (אֶבְיוֹן, *'ebhyōn*). See Poor.

NEESING, nē'zing (Job **41** 18, AV, ERV "by his neesings a light doth shine," ARV "sneezings"): "Neese" in Elizabethan Eng. (through two distinct derivations) could mean either "sneeze" or "snort," and it is impossible to say which force was intended by the AV editors. The Heb is עֲטִישָׁה, *'ăṭīshāh*, a word found only here, but connected with a Sem √ meaning "sneeze," or, perhaps, "snort." Job **41** 18 is part of the description of the "leviathan" or crocodile. This animal has a habit of inflating himself, and after this he discharges through his nostrils the moist, heated vapor, which sparkles in the sunlight. The act is neither a "sneeze" nor a "snort," but the latter word is sufficiently descriptive. There is no allusion to legendary "fire-spouting" monsters. Cf Job **39** 20; Jer **8** 16.

In the older edd of AV "neesed" is found in 2 K **4** 35: "and the child neesed seven times" (later edd and RV "sneezed"). Burton Scott Easton

NEGEB, neg'eb (הַנֶּגֶב, *ha-neghebh*, "the negeb," or simply, נֶגֶב, *neghebh*, from a √ meaning "to be dry," and therefore in the first instance implying the "dry" or "parched regions," hence in LXX it is usually tr^d ἔρημος, *erēmos*, "desert," also νάγεβ, *nágeb*): As the Negeb lay to the S. of Judah, the word came to be used in the sense of "the South," and is so used in a few passages (e.g. Gen **13** 14) and in such is tr^d λίψ, *líps* (see Geography).

1. Meaning

The Eng. tr is unsuitable in several passages, and likely to lead to confusion. For example, in Gen **13** 1 Abram is represented as going "into the South" when journeying northward from Egypt toward Bethel; in Nu **13** 22 the spies coming from the "wilderness of Zin" toward Hebron are described as coming "by the South," although they were going north. The difficulty in these and many other passages is at once obviated if it is recognized that the Negeb was a geographical term for a definite geographical region, just as Shephelah, lit. "lowland," was the name of another district of Pal. In RV "Negeb" is given in m, but it would make for clearness if it were restored to the text.

2. Description

This "parched" land is generally considered as beginning S. of *ed Dāharīyeb*—the probable site of Debir (q.v.)—and as stretching S. in a series of rolling hills running in a general direction of E. to W. until the actual wilderness begins, a distance of perhaps 70 miles (see Natural Features). To the E. it is bounded by the Dead Sea and the southern Ghor, and to the W. there is no defined boundary before the Mediterranean. It is a land of sparse and scanty springs and small rainfall; in the character of its soil it is a transition from the fertility of Canaan to the wilderness of the desert; it is essentially a pastoral land, where grazing is plentiful in the early months and where camels and goats can sustain life, even through the long summer drought. Today, as through most periods of history, it is a land for the nomad rather than the settled inhabitant, although abundant ruins in many spots testify to better physical conditions at some periods (see I, 5, below). The direction of the valleys E. or W., the general dryness, and the character of the inhabitants have always made it a more or less isolated region without thoroughfare. The great routes pass along the coast to the W. or up the Arabah to the E. It formed an additional barrier to the wilderness beyond it; against all who would lead an army from the S., this southern frontier of Judah was always secure. Israel could not reach the promised land by this route, through the land of the Amalekites (Nu **13** 29; **14** 43–45).

3. OT References

The Negeb was the scene of much of Abram's wanderings (Gen **12** 9; **13** 1.3; **20** 1); it was in this district that Hagar met with the angel (Gen **16** 7.14); Isaac (Gen **24** 62) and Jacob (Gen **37** 1; **46** 5) both dwelt there. Moses sent the spies through this district to the hill country (Nu **13** 17.22); the Amalekites then dwelt there (ver 29) and apparently, too, in some parts of it, the Avvim (Josh **13** 3.4). The inheritance of the children of Simeon, as given in Josh **19** 1–9, was in the Negeb, but in Josh **15** 21–32 these cities are credited to Judah (see Simeon). Achish allotted to David, in response to his request, the city of Ziklag (q.v) in the Negeb (1 S **27** 5 f); the exploits of David were against various parts of this district described as the Negeb of Judah, the Negeb of the Jerahmeelites, and the Negeb of the Kenites, while in 1 S **30** 14 we have mention of the Negeb of the Cherethites and the Negeb of Caleb. To this we may add the Negeb of Arad (Jgs **1** 16). It is impossible to define the districts of these various clans (see separate arts. under these names). The Negeb, together with the "hill-country" and the "Shephelah," was according to Jeremiah (**17** 26; **32** 44; **33** 13) to have renewed prosperity after the captivity of Judah was ended.

4. Later History

When Nebuchadnezzar took Jerus the Edomites sided with the Babylonians (cf Lam **4** 21 f; Ezk **35** 3–15; Ob vs 10–16), and during the absence of the Jews they advanced north and occupied all the Negeb and Southern Judaea as far as Hebron (see Judaea). Here they annoyed the Jews in Maccabean times until Judas expelled them from Southern Judaea (164 BC) and John Hyrcanus conquered their country and compelled them to become Jews (109 BC). It was to one of the cities here—Malatha—that Herod Agrippa withdrew himself (Jos, *Ant*, XVIII, vi, 2).

The palmy days of this district appear to have been during the Byzantine period: the existing ruins, so far as they can be dated at all, belong to this time. Beersheba was an important city with a bishop, and Elusa (mentioned by Ptolemy in the 2d cent.) was the seat of a bishop in the 4th, 5th and 6th cents. After the rise of Mohammedanism the land appears to have lapsed into primitive conditions. Although lawlessness and want of any central control may account for much of the retrogression, yet it is probable that Professor Ellsworth Huntington (loc. cit.) is right in his contention that a change of climate has had much to do with the rise and fall of civilization and settled habitation in this district. The district has long been given over to the nomads, and it is only quite recently that the Turkish policy of planting an official with a small garrison at Beersheba and at *'Aujeh* has produced some slight change in the direction of a settled population and agricultural pursuits.

5. Its Ancient Prosperity

It is clear that in at least two historic periods the Negeb enjoyed a very considerable prosperity. What it may have been in the days of the Patriarchs it is difficult to judge; all we read of them suggests a purely nomadic life similar to the Bedouin of today but with better pasturage. In the division of the land among the tribes mention is made of many cities—the Heb mentions 29 (Josh **15** 21–32; **19** 1–9; 1 Ch **4** 28–33)—and the wealth of cattle evidently was great (cf 1 S **15** 9; **27** 9; **30** 16; 2 Ch **14** 14 f). The condition of things must have been far different from that of recent times.

The extensive ruins at *Bīr es Seba'* (Beersheba) *Khalasa* (Elusa), *Ruheibeh* (Rehoboth, q.v.), *'Aujeh* and other cities, together with the signs of orchards, vineyards and gardens scattered widely around these and other sites, show how comparatively well populated this area was in Byzantine times in particular. Professor Huntington (loc. cit.) concludes from these ruins that the population of the large towns of the Negeb alone at this period must have amounted to between 45,000 and 50,000.

The whole district does not support 1,000 souls today.

LITERATURE.—Robinson, *BR* (1838); Wilton, *The Negeb, or "South Country" of Scripture* (1863); E. H. Palmer, *The Desert of the Exodus*, II (1871); Trumbull, *Kadesh-Barnea* (1884); G. A. Smith, *HGHL*, ch xiii (1894); E. Huntington, *Pal and Its Transformation*, ch vi, etc.

E. W. G. MASTERMAN

NEGINAH, ne-gē'nä (Ps **61** AV, title), **NEGINOTH,** ne-gē'nōth, neg'i-noth (Ps **4** AV, title). See MUSIC; PSALMS.

NEHELAMITE, nē-hel'a-mīt, **THE** (הַנֶּחֱלָמִי, *ha-neḥĕlāmī*): The designation of Shemaiah, a false prophet who opposed Jeremiah (Jer **29** 24.31.32). The word means "dweller of Nehelam," but no such place-name is found in the OT. Its etymology, however, suggests a connection with the Heb *ḥālam*, "to dream," and this has given rise to the rendering of AVm "dreamer."

NEHEMIAH, nē-hē-mī'a, nē-hem-ī'a (נְחֶמְיָה, *neḥemyāh*, "comforted of Jeh"):

1. Family
2. Youth
3. King's Cupbearer
4. Governor of Judaea
5. Death

LITERATURE

Nehemiah, the son of Hacaliah, is the Jewish patriot whose life is recorded in the Bib. work named after him. All that we know about him from contemporary sources is found in this book; and so the readers of this article are referred to the Book of Neh for the best and fullest account of his words and deeds. See EZRA-NEHEMIAH.

1. Family

All that is known of his family is that he was the son of Hacaliah (**1** 1) and that one of his brothers was called Hanani (**1** 2; **7** 2); the latter a man of sufficient character and importance to have been made a ruler of Jerus.

From Neh **10** 1–8 some have inferred that he was a priest, since Nehemiah comes first in the list of names ending with the phrase, "these were the priests." This view is supported by the Syr and Arab. VSS of **10** 1, which read: "Nehemiah the elder, the son of Hananiah the chief of the priests"; and by the Lat Vulg of 2 Macc **1** 21, where he is called "Nehemiah the priest," and possibly by 2 Macc **1** 18, where it is said that Nehemiah "offered sacrifices, after that he had builded the temple and the altar."

The argument based upon Neh **10** 1–8 will fall to the ground, if we change the pointing of the "Seraiah" of the 3d verse and read "its princes," referring back to the princes of ver 1. In this case, Nehemiah and Zedekiah would be the princes; then would come the priests and then the Levites.

Some have thought that he was of the royal line of Judah, inasmuch as he refers to his "fathers' sepulchres" at Jerus (**2** 3). This would be a good argument only if it could be shown that none but kings had sepulchers at Jerus.

It has been argued again that he was of noble lineage because of his position as cupbearer to the king of Persia. To substantiate this argument, it would need to be shown that none but persons of noble birth could serve in this position; but this has not been shown, and cannot be shown.

2. Youth

From the fact that Nehemiah was so grieved at the desolation of the city and sepulchers of his fathers and that he was so jealous for the laws of the God of Judah, we can justly infer that he was brought up by pious parents, who instructed him in the history and law of the Jewish people.

3. Cupbearer of the King

Doubtless because of his probity and ability, he was apparently at an early age appointed by Artaxerxes, king of Persia, to the responsible position of cupbearer to the king. There is now no possible doubt that this king was Artaxerxes, the first of that name, commonly called Longimanus, who ruled over Persia from 464 to 424 BC. The mention of the sons of Sanballat, governor of Samaria, in a letter written to the priests of Jerus in 407 BC, among whom Johanan is esp. named, proves that Sanballat must have ruled in the time of Artaxerxes I rather than in that of Artaxerxes II.

The office of cupbearer was "one of no trifling honor" (Herod. iii.34). It was one of his chief duties to taste the wine for the king to see that it was not poisoned, and he was even admitted to the king while the queen was present (Neh **2** 6). It was on account of this position of close intimacy with the king that Nehemiah was able to obtain his commission as governor of Judaea and the letters and edicts which enabled him to restore the walls of Jerus.

4. Governor of Judaea

The occasion of this commission was as follows: Hanani, the brother of Nehemiah, and other men of Judah came to visit Nehemiah while he was in Susa in the 9th month of the 20th year of Artaxerxes. They reported that the Jews in Jerus were in great affliction and that the wall thereof was broken down and its gates burned with fire. Thereupon he grieved and fasted and prayed to God that he might be granted favor by the king. Having appeared before the latter in the 1st month of the 21st year of Artaxerxes, 444 BC, he was granted permission to go to Jerus to build the city of his fathers' sepulchers, and was given letters to the governors of Syria and Pal and esp. to Asaph, the keeper of the king's forest, ordering him to supply timber for the wall, the fortress, and the temple. He was also appointed governor of the province of which Jerus was the capital.

Armed with these credentials and powers he repaired to Jerus and immediately set about the restoration of the walls, a work in which he was hindered and harassed by Sanballat, the governor of Samaria, and others, some of them Jews dwelling in Jerus. Notwithstanding, he succeeded in his attempt and eventually also in providing gates for the various entrances to the city.

Having accomplished these external renovations, he instituted a number of social reforms. He appointed the officers necessary for better government, caused the people to be instructed in the Law by public readings, and expositions; celebrated the Feast of Tabernacles; and observed a national fast, at which the sins of the people were confessed and a new covenant with Jeh was solemnly confirmed. The people agreed to avoid marriages with the heathen, to keep the Sabbath, and to contribute to the support of the temple. To provide for the safety and prosperity of the city, one out of every ten of the people living outside Jerus was compelled to settle in the city. In all of these reforms he was assisted by Ezra, who had gone up to Jerus in the 7th year of Artaxerxes.

5. Death

Once, or perhaps oftener, during his governorship Nehemiah returned to the king. Nothing is known as to when or where he died. It is certain, however, that he was no longer governor in 407 BC; for at that time according to the Aram. letter written from Elephantine to the priests of Jerus, Bagohi was occupying the position of governor over Judaea. One of the last acts of Nehemiah's government was the chasing away of one of the sons of Joiada, the son of Eliashib, because he had become the son-in-law to Sanballat, the governor of Samaria. As this Joiada was the father of Johanan (Neh **12** 22) who, according to the Aram. papyrus, was high priest in 407 BC, and according to Jos (*Ant*, XI, viii.1) was high priest while Bagohi (Bogoas) was general of Artaxerxes' army, it is certain that Nehemiah was at this time no longer in power. From the 3d of the Sachau papyri, it seems that Bagohi was already governor in 410 BC; and, that at the same time, Dalayah, the son of Sanballat, was governor in Samaria. More definite information on these points is not to be had at present.

LITERATURE.—The only early extra-Bib. data with regard to Nehemiah and the Judaea of his times are to be found: (1) in the Egyp papyri of Elephantine ("Aramäische Papyri und Ostraka aus einer jüdischen Militär-Kolonie zu Elephantine," *Altorientalische Sprachdenkmäler des 5. Jahrhunderts vor Chr.*, Bearbeitet von Eduard Sachau. Leipzig, 1911); (2) in Jos, *Ant*, XI, vi, 6–8; vii, 1, 2; (3) in Ecclus **49** 13, where it is said: "The renown of Nehemiah is glorious; of him who established our waste places and restored our ruins, and set up the gates and bars"; (4) and lastly in 2 Macc **1** 18–36 and **2** 13; in the latter of these passages it speaks of 'the writings and commentaries of Nehemiah; and how he, founding a library, gathered together the acts of the kings and the prophets and of David and the epistles of the kings concerning the holy gifts.'

R. DICK WILSON

NEHEMIAH, BOOK OF. See EZRA-NEHEMIAH.

NEHEMIAS, nē-hē-mī'as: Gr form of Heb *Nehemiah.*

(1) Νεεμίας, *Neemías*, one of the leaders of the return under Zerubbabel (1 Esd **5** 8) = "Nehemiah" of Ezr **2** 2; Neh **7** 7.

(2) Νεεμίας, *Neemías*, B, Ναιμίας, *Naimías*, the prophet Nehemiah (1 Esd **5** 40 where AVm reads "N. who also is Atharias"). Neither Nehemias nor Attharias is found in the ‖ Ezr **2** 63; Neh **7** 65, but הַתִּרְשָׁתָא, *ha-tirshāthā'* = *Tirshatha*, "the governor," by whom Zerubbabel must be intended. Thus the Heb word for "governor" has been converted into a proper name and by some blunder the name Nehemiah inserted, perhaps because he also was known by the title of "governor."

S. ANGUS

NEHILOTH, ne-hil'oth, nē'hi-loth (Ps **5**, title). See MUSIC.

NEHUM, nē'hum (נְחוּם, *neḥūm*): One of the twelve heads of the people who returned with Zerubbabel (Neh **7** 7). In the ‖ passage (Ezr **2** 2), the name appears as REHUM (q.v.), and in 1 Esd **5** 8 as "Roimus."

NEHUSHTA, nē-hush'ta (נְחֻשְׁתָּא, *neḥushtā'*): Mother of King Jehoiachin (2 K **24** 8). She was the daughter of Elnathan of Jerus. After the fall of the city she was exiled with her son and his court (2 K **24** 12; Jer **29** 2).

NEHUSHTAN, nē-hush'tan (נְחֻשְׁתָּן, *neḥushtān;* cf נְחֹשֶׁת, *neḥōsheth*, "brass," and נָחָשׁ, *nāḥāsh*, "serpent"): The word occurs but once, viz. in 2 K **18** 4. In the account there given of the reforms carried out by Hezekiah, it is said that "he brake in pieces the brazen serpent that Moses had made; for unto those days the children of Israel did burn incense to it; and he called it Nehushtan." According to RVm the word means "a piece of brass." If this be correct, the sense of the passage is that Hezekiah not only breaks the brazen serpent in pieces but, suiting the word to the act, scornfully calls it "a [mere] piece of brass." Hezekiah thus takes his place as a true reformer, and as a champion of the purification of the religion of Israel. This is the traditional interpretation of the passage, and fairly represents the Heb text as it now stands.

1. Traditional Interpretation

There are at least three considerations, however, which throw doubt upon this interpretation. In the first place, the word N. is not a common noun, and cannot mean simply "a piece of brass." The point of the Bib. statement is entirely lost by such a construction. It is emphatically a proper noun, and is the special name given to this particular brazen serpent. As such it would be sacred to all worshippers of the brazen serpent, and familiar to all who frequented the Temple. In the second place, it is probable that N. is to be derived from *nāḥāsh*, "serpent," rather than from *neḥōsheth*, "brass," (1) because the Gr VSS, representing a form of the Heb text earlier than MT, suggest this in their transliteration of N. (B, *Nesthaleí;* A, *Nesthán*); (2) because the Heb offers a natural derivation of N. from *nāḥāsh*, "serpent"; and (3) because the name of the image would more probably be based on its form than on the material out of which it was made. In the third place, the reading, "and it was called," which appears in RVm, is decidedly preferable to that in the text. It not only represents the best reading of the Heb, but is confirmed by the similar reading, "and they called it," which appears in the Gr VS referred to above. These readings agree in their indication that N. was the name by which the serpent-image was generally known during the years it was worshipped, rather than an expression used for the first time by Hezekiah on the occasion of its destruction.

2. Derivation: A Proper Noun

Whichever derivation be adopted, however, the word must be construed as a proper name. If it be derived from "brass," then the tr must be, not "a piece of brass," but "The [great] Brass," giving the word a special sense by which it refers unequivocally to the well-known image made of brass. If it be derived from "serpent," then the tr must be, "The [great] Serpent," the word in this case referring in a special sense to the well-known image in serpent form. But the significance of the word probably lies far back of any etymological explanation of it that can now be given. It is not a term that can be adequately explained by reference to verbal roots, but is rather an epitome of the reverence of those who, however mistakenly, looked upon the brazen serpent as a proper object of worship.

In view of the foregoing it may be concluded, (1) that N. was the (sacred) name by which the brazen serpent was known during the years "the children of Israel did burn incense to it"; (2) that the word is derived from *nāḥāsh*, "serpent"; and (3) that it was used in the sense of "The Serpent," *par excellence.* See IMAGES, 6, (2); SERPENT, FIERY.

LINDSAY B. LONGACRE

NEIEL, nē-ī'el (נְעִיאֵל, *ne'ī'ēl;* B, Ἰναήλ, *Inaḗl*, A, Ἀνιήλ, *Aniḗl*): A town on the boundary between Zebulun and Asher mentioned between Jiftah-el and Cabul (Josh **19** 27). It may be the same as Neah (ver 13), but the place is not identified.

NEIGH, nā (צָהַל, *çāhal*, "to cry aloud," "neigh"): Figuratively used to indicate lustful desire (Jer **5** 8; cf **13** 29).

NEIGHBOR, nā'bēr (רֵעַ, *rē a'*, עָמִית, *'āmīth*, "friend," קָרוֹב, *ḳārōbh*, שָׁכֵן, *shākhēn;* ὁ πλησίον, *ho plēsíon*, "near," γείτων, *geítōn*, [cf 2 Macc **6** 8; **9** 25], "inhabitant"; Lat *proximus* [2 Esd **15** 19], *civis* [**9** 45; **10** 2, RVm "townman"]): In the OT, the relationship of neighborhood involves moral and social obligations which are frequently emphasized. These are in the main described in negative rather than positive terms; e.g. there are special injunctions not to bear false witness against a neighbor (Ex **20** 16; Dt **5** 20; Prov **25** 18), or in any way to deal falsely with

1. As Described in the OT

him, defraud him, frame malicious devices or harbor evil thoughts against him (Ex **20** 17; Lev **6** 2; **19** 13; Dt **23** 24 f; Ps **15** 3; **101** 5; Prov **24** 28; Jer **22** 13; Zec **8** 17), or to lead him into shameful conduct (Hab **2** 15), or to wrong him by lying carnally with his wife (Lev **18** 20). But the supreme law that underlies these negative injunctions is stated positively, "Thou shalt love thy neighbor as thyself" (Lev **19** 18). In this verse the term "neighbor" is defined by the expression, "the children of my people." Here, and generally in the OT, the term implies more than mere proximity; it means one related by the bond of nationality, a fellow-countryman, compatriot. Jeh being regarded as a national God, there was no religious bond regulating the conduct of the Hebrews with other nations. Conduct which was prohibited between fellow-Jews was permitted toward a foreigner, e.g. the exaction of interest (Dt **23** 19.20).

In the NT, this limitation of moral obligation to fellow-countrymen is abolished. Christ gives a wider interpretation of the commandment in Lev **19** 18, so as to include in it those outside the tie of nation or kindred. This is definitely done in the parable of the Good Samaritan (Lk **10** 25–37), where, in answer to the question, "Who is my neighbor?" Jesus shows that the relationship is a moral, not a physical one, based not on kinship but on the opportunity and capacity for mutual help. The word represents, not so much a rigid fact, but an ideal which one may or may not realize (ver 36, "Which of these three, thinkest thou, *proved* [lit. *became*, not *was*] neighbor," etc). This larger connotation follows naturally as a corollary to the doctrine of the universal Fatherhood of God. The commandment to love one's neighbor as one's self must not be interpreted as if it implied that we are to hate our enemy (an inference which the Jews were apt to make); human love should be like the Divine, impartial, having all men for its object (Mt **5** 43 ff). Love to one's fellow-men in this broad sense is to be placed side by side with love to God as the essence and sum of human duty (Mt **22** 35–40 ‖ Mk **12** 28–31). Christ's apostles follow His example in giving a central position to the injunction to love one's neighbor as one's self (Jas **2** 8, where it is called the "royal law," i.e. the supreme or governing law; Rom **13** 9; Gal **5** 14).

2. As Described in the NT

D. Miall Edwards

NEKEB, nē′keb: This name occurs only in combination with "Adami" (אֲדָמִי הַנֶּקֶב, *'ădhāmī ha-neḳebh*, "Adami of the pass"); LXX reads the names of two places: καὶ Ἀρμὲ καὶ Νάβωκ, *kaí Armé kaí Nábōk* (B); καὶ Ἀρμαὶ καὶ Νάκεβ, *kaí Armaí kaí Nákeb* (Josh **19** 33), so we should possibly read "Adami and Nekeb." Neubauer says (*Géog. du Talm*, 225) that later the name of Nekeb was Ciyadathah. It may therefore be represented by the modern *Seiyādeh*, not far from *ed-Dāmieh* to the E. of Tabor, about 4 miles S.W. of Tiberias. The name of Nekeb, a town in Galilee, appears in the list of Thothmes III.

NEKODA, nē-kō′da (נְקוֹדָא, *neḳōdhā'*):

(1) Head of a family of Nethinim (Ezr **2** 48; Neh **7** 50; cf 1 Esd **5** 31).

(2) Head of a family which failed to prove its Israelitish descent (Ezr **2** 60; Neh **7** 62; cf 1 Esd **5** 31.37). In the ‖ vs of 1 Esd the names are given thus: Noeba and Nekodan (q.v.).

NEKODAN, nē-kō′dan (Νεκωδάν, *Nekōdán;* RVm "Nekoda"; AV **Necodan**):

(1) Head of a family which returned from exile, but "could not show their families nor their stock" (1 Esd **5** 37) = "Nekoda" of Ezr **2** 60; Neh **7** 62.

(2) See Noeba.

NEMUEL, nem′ū-el, nē-mū′el (נְמוּאֵל, *nemū'ēl*):

(1) A Reubenite, brother of Dathan and Abiram (Nu **26** 9).

(2) A son of Simeon (Nu **26** 12; 1 Ch **4** 24). The name occurs also in the form "Jemuel" (Gen **46** 10; Ex **6** 15). According to Gray (*HPN*), either form is etymologically obscure; but Nemuel is probably correct, for it is easier to account for its corruption into Jemuel than vice versa. The patronymic **Nemuelites** occurs once (Nu **26** 12).

NEMUELITES, nem′ū-el-īts, nē-mū′el-īts (הַנְּמוּאֵלִי, *ha-nemū'ēlī*). See Nemuel, (2).

NEPHEA, nē-fē′a. See Music.

NEPHEG, nē′feg (נֶפֶג, *nephegh*, "sprout," "shoot"):

(1) Son of Izhar, and brother of Korah of the famous trio, Korah, Dathan and Abiram (Ex **6** 21).

(2) A son of David (2 S **5** 15; 1 Ch **3** 7; **14** 6).

NEPHEW, nef′ū, nev′ū. See Relationships, Family.

NEPHI, nē′fī. See Nephthai.

NEPHILIM, nef′i-lim (נְפִלִים, *nephīlīm*): This word, tr[d] "giants" in AV, but retained in RV, is found in two passages of the OT—one in Gen **6** 4, relating to the antediluvians; the other in Nu **13** 33, relating to the sons of Anak in Canaan. In the former place the Nephilim are not necessarily to be identified with the children said to be borne by "the daughters of men" to "the sons of God" (vs 2.4); indeed, they seem to be distinguished from the latter as upon the earth before this unholy commingling took place (see Sons of God). But it is not easy to be certain as to the interpretation of this strange passage. In the second case they clearly represent men of gigantic stature, in comparison with whom the Israelites felt as if they were "grasshoppers." This agrees with Gen **6** 4, "the mighty men that were of old, the men of renown." LXX, therefore, was warranted in translating by *gigantes.*

James Orr

NEPHIS, nē′fis. See Niphis.

NEPHISH, nē′fish, **NEPHISIM,** nē-fī′sim, **NEPHISHESIM,** nē-fish′ē-sim, **NEPHUSIM,** nē-fū-sim (נְפִיסִים, *nephīṣīm*, נְפוּסִים, *nephūṣīm*): The former is the Kethībh (Heb "written") form of the name adopted in RV; the latter the Ḳerē (Heb "read") form, adopted in AV and RVm (Ezr **2** 50). See Naphish; Nephushesim.

NEPHTHAI, nef′thī, nef′thā-ī. See Nephthar.

NEPHTHALIM, nef′tha-lim (Mt **4** 13): The Gr form of Naphtali (q.v.).

NEPHTHAR, nef′thär (Νεφθάρ, *Nephthár;* A and Swete, *Nephthár*, AV and Vulg **Naphthar**), **NEPHTHAI** (Νεφθαί, *Nephthaí*, al. Νεφθαεί, *Nephthaeí*, Fritzsche, Νεφά, *Nephá*, AV and Vulg, following Old Lat, **Nephi;** Swete, following A, gives *Nephthar* twice): According to 2 Macc **1** 19–36, at the time of the captivity the godly priests took of the altar fire of the temple and concealed it "privily in the hollow of a well that was without water," unknown to all. "After many years" (upon the Return), before offering the sacrifices, Nehemiah sent the descendants of the godly priests to fetch the hidden fire. They reported they could find no fire but only "thick water" (ὕδωρ παχύ, *húdōr pachú*), which he commanded them to draw up and sprinkle upon the wood and the sacrifices. After an interval the sun shone forth from behind a cloud and the liquid ignited and consumed the sacrifices. Nehemiah then commanded them to pour (καταχεῖν, *katachein*, al. κατέχειν, *katéchein*, and κατασχεῖν, *kataschein*) the rest of the liquid upon great stones. Another flame sprang up which soon spent itself, "whereas the light from the altar shone still" (RVm, the exact meaning being doubtful). When the king of Persia investigated it, he inclosed the spot as sacred. Nehemiah and his friends called the thick liquid "Nephthar," "which is by interpretation 'cleansing'" (καθαρισμός, *katharismós*), "but most men call it Nephthai."

No satisfactory explanation is to hand of either name, one of which is probably a corruption of the other. And no word exists in the Heb like either of them with the meaning of "cleansing," "purification." The Vulg applies the name to the spot (*hunc locum*), not the thing. The story probably originated in Persia, where *naphtha* was abundant. The ignition of the liquid by the hot rays of the sun and the appearance of the words render it highly probable that it was the inflammable rock-oil *naphtha*, the combustible properties of which were quite familiar to the ancients (Pliny, *NH*, ii. 109; Plutarch, *Alex.* 35; Diosc., i.101; Strabo, *Geogr.* xvi.1, 15); the words then are probably corruptions of what the Greeks termed νάφθα, *náphtha*. Ewald (*Hist.*, V, 163) says: "This is but one of the many stories which sought in later times to enhance the very high sanctity of the Temple, with reference even to its origin." S. ANGUS

NEPHTOAH, nef-tō'a, nef'tō-a (נֶפְתּוֹחַ, *nephtō^ah*, occurs only in the expression מַעְיַן מֵי נ׳, *ma'yan mē n.*, "the fountain of the waters of Nephtoah"; LXX πηγὴ ὕδατος Ναφθώ, *pēgḗ húdatos Naphthō*): This spring was on the border line between Judah and Benjamin (Josh **15** 9; **18** 15). The place is usually identified with *Liftā*, a village about 2 miles N.W. of Jerus, on the east bank of the *Wâdy beit Ḥanīna*. It is a village very conspicuous to the traveler along the high road from Jaffa as he nears Jerus. There are ancient rock-cut tombs and a copious spring which empties itself into a large masonry reservoir. The situation of *Liftā* seems to agree well with the most probable line of boundary between the two tribes; the spring as it is today does not appear to be so abundant as to warrant such an expression as "spring of the waters," but it was, like many such sources, probably considerably more abundant in OT times.

Conder would identify *Liftā* with the ancient ELEPH (q.v.) of Benjamin, and, on the ground that the Talm (see Talm Bab, *Yōmā'* **31***a*) identifies Nephtoah with ETAM (q.v.), he would find the site of Nephtoah at *'Ain 'Atān*, S. of Bethlehem. The Talm is not a sufficiently trustworthy guide when unsupported by other evidence, and the identification creates great difficulty with the boundary line. See *PEF*, III, 18, 43, Sh XVII. E. W. G. MASTERMAN

NEPHUSHESIM, nẹ̄-fush'ē-sim, **NEPHISHESIM**, nē-fish'ē-sim (נְפוּשְׁסִים, *n^ephūsh^eṣīm*, נְפִישְׁסִים, *n^ephīsh^eṣīm*): The former is the K^ethībh (Heb "written") form of the name adopted in RV; the latter the Ḳ^erē (Heb "read") form adopted in AV and RVm (Neh **7** 52). See NAPHISH; NEPHISIM.

NER, nēr (נֵר, *nēr*, "lamp"): Father of Abner (1 S **14** 50 f; **26** 5.14, etc); grandfather of Saul (1 Ch **8** 33). Other references, though adding no further information are 2 S **2** 8.12; **3** 23.25; 28.37; 1 K **2** 5.32, etc.

NEREUS, nē'rūs, nē'rē-us (Νηρεύς, *Nēreús*): The name of a Rom Christian to whom with his sister St. Paul sent greetings (Rom **16** 15). Nereus and the others saluted with him (ver 15) formed a small community or "house church." The name of the sister is not given, but the name Nereis is found on an inscription of this date containing names of the emperor's servants (Lightfoot, *Phil*, 176). Among the *Acta Sanctorum* connected with the early church in Rome are the "Acts of Nereus and Achilleus" which call them chamberlains of Domitilla, the niece of Vespasian, and relate their influence over her in persuading her to remain a virgin. S. F. HUNTER

NERGAL, nâr'gäl (נֵרְגַל, *nēr^eghal*): A Bab deity, identified with the planet Mars, and worshipped at Cutha (cf 2 K **17** 30). See BABYLONIA AND ASSYRIA, RELIGION OF.

NERGAL-SHAREZER, nûr-gal-sha-rē'zar (נֵרְגַל־שַׁרְאֶצֶר, *nēr^eghal-shar'eçer*, Heb form of Assyr *Nergal-sar-uṣur*, "O Nergal, defend the prince"): A Bab officer, the "Rab-mag," associated with Nebushazban in the care of Jeremiah after the fall of Jerus (Jer **39** 3.13). According to Hommel (art. "Babylon," *HDB*) and Sayce (*HDB*, s.v.), Nergal-sharezer is to be identified with Neriglissar who succeeded Evil-merodach on the throne of Babylon (cf Cheyne and Johns, *EB*, s.v.).

NERI, nē'rī (Νηρεί, *Nēreí* [Tisch., Treg., WH], *TR*, Νηρί, *Nērí*; for Heb נֵרִיָּה, *nērīyāh*): The name of an ancestor of Jesus, the grandfather of Zerubbabel (Lk **3** 27). See NERIAH.

NERIAH, nẹ̄-rī'a (נֵרִיָּה, *nērīyāh*, "whose lamp is Jeh"): The father of Seraiah and of Baruch, Jeremiah's friend and secretary (Jer **32** 12.16; **36** 4.8.32; **43** 3). In Bar **1** 1 the Gr form of the name, Νηρ(ε)ίας, *Nēr(e)ías*, is given, and this shortened, Neri, occurs in the genealogy of Jesus Christ.

NERIAS, nẹ̄-rī'as (Νηρ[ε]ίας, *Nēr[e]ías*): The Gr form of Heb *Neriah* found only in Bar **1** 1 as the father of Baruch="Neriah" of Jer **32** 12; **36** 4 ff; **43** 3. To Baruch's brother, Seraiah, the same genealogy is ascribed in Jer **51** 59.

NERO, nē'rō (Νέρων, *Nérōn*):

I. NAME, PARENTAGE AND EARLY TRAINING
II. AGRIPPINA'S AMBITION FOR NERO
Her Nine Measures for Bringing Him to the Throne
III. NERO'S REIGN
1. *Quinquennium Neronis*
2. Poppaea Sabina
3. Poppaea and Tigellinus
4. Burning of Rome
5. Persecution of Christians
6. Conspiracy of Piso
7. Nero in Greece
8. Death of Nero
IV. DOWNFALL AND CHARACTER
1. Seven Causes of Downfall
2. Character
V. "NERO REDIVIVUS"
VI. NERO AND CHRISTIANITY
1. Nero and the NT
2. Neronian Policy and Christianity
LITERATURE

The fifth Rom emperor, b. at Antium December 15, 37 AD, began to reign October 13, 54, d. June 9, 68.

I. Name, Parentage and Early Training.—His name was originally Lucius Domitius Ahenobarbus.

but after his adoption into the Claudian *gens* by the emperor Claudius, he became Nero Claudius Caesar Germanicus. His father was Enaeus Domitius Ahenobarbus ("Brazen-beard"), a man sprung from an illustrious family and of vicious character. His mother was Agrippina the younger, the daughter of Germanicus and the elder Agrippina, sister of the emperor Caius (Caligula) and niece of the emperor Claudius. On the birth of the child, his father predicted, amid the congratulations of his friends, that any offspring of himself and Agrippina could only prove abominable and disastrous for the public (Suet. *Nero* vi: *detestabile et malo publico*). At the age of three the young Domitius lost his father and was robbed of his estates by the rapacity of Caius. In 39 his mother was banished for supposed complicity in a plot against Caius. N. was thus deprived of his mother and at the same time left almost penniless. His aunt, Domitia Lepida, now undertook the care of the boy and placed him with two tutors, a dancer and a barber (Suet. vi). On the accession of Claudius, Agrippina was recalled, and N. was restored to his mother and his patrimony (41 AD).

Nero (Brit. Mus.).

II. Agrippina's Ambition for Nero.—She cared little for her son's moral education, but began immediately to train him for high position. She aimed at nothing less than securing the empire for N. With a view to this she must gain influence over her uncle, the emperor Claudius, who was very susceptible to female charms. At first the path was by no means easy, while the licentious empress, Messalina, was in power. But on the fall and death of Messalina (48 AD)—for which Agrippina may have intrigued—the way seemed opened. With the assistance of the emperor's freedman, Pallas, Agrippina proved the successful candidate for Claudius' affections. She now felt secure to carry out the plans for the elevation of her son: (1) She secured his betrothal to Octavia, the daughter of Claudius, having previously, by the villainy of Vitellius, broken off the engagement between Octavia and Lucius Silanus (ib, xlviii). Later, N. married this unfortunate lady. (2) Vitellius again obliged by securing a modification of Rom law so as to permit a marriage with a brother's (not sister's) daughter, and in 49 Agrippina became empress. (3) In the meantime she had caused Seneca to be recalled from banishment and had intrusted to him the education of N. for imperial purposes. (4) The adoption of her son by Claudius (50 AD). (5) She next secured early honors and titles for N. in order to mark him out as Claudius' successor. (6) She caused Britannicus, Claudius' son, to be kept in the background and treated as a mere child, removing by exile or death suspected supporters of Britannicus. (7) Agrippina was farsighted and anticipated a later secret of Rom imperialism—the influence of the armies in the nomination of emperors. For this cause she took an active interest in military affairs and gave her name to a new colony on the Rhine (modern Cologne). But she did not forget the importance of securing the praetorian guard and Burrus the prefect. (8) She persuaded Claudius to make a will in favor of her son. All was now ready. But Claudius did not like the idea of excluding his son Britannicus from power, and murmurs were heard among the senate and people. Delay might prove fatal to Agrippina's plans, so (9) Claudius must die. The notorious Locusta administered poison in a dish of mushrooms, and Xenophon, Agrippina's physician, thrust a poisoned feather down Claudius' throat on the pretence of helping him to vomit. Burrus then took N. forth and caused him to be proclaimed imperator by the praetorians.

III. Nero's Reign.—Nero's reign falls into three periods, the first of which is the celebrated *quinquennium*, or first 5 years, characterized by good government at home and in the provinces and popularity with both senate and people. Agrippina, having seated her son on the throne, did not purpose to relinquish power herself; she intended to rule along with him. And at first N. was very devoted to her and had given as watchword to the guard, "the best of mothers" (Tac. *Ann.* xiii.2; Suet. ix). This caused a sharp conflict with Seneca and Burrus, who could not tolerate Agrippina's arrogance and unbounded influence over her son. In order to detach him from his mother they encouraged him in an amour with a Gr freedwoman, Acte (Tac. *Ann.* xiii.12). This first blow to Agrippina's influence was soon followed by the dismissal from court of her chief protector Pallas. She now threatened to bring forth Britannicus and present him as the rightful heir to the throne. This cost Britannicus his life, for N., feeling insecure while a son of Claudius lived, compassed his death at a banquet. A hot wine cup was offered Britannicus, and to cool it to taste, cold water was added which had been adulterated with a virulent poison. The victim succumbed immediately. All eyes fastened on N. in suspicion, but he boldly asserted that the death was due to a fit of epilepsy —a disease to which Britannicus had been subject from childhood. Such was the fate of Agrippina's first protégé. She next took up the cause of the despised and ill-treated Octavia, which so incensed her son that he deprived her of her guards and caused her to remove from the palace. Agrippina now disappears for the next few years to come into brief and tragic prominence later. Seneca and Burrus undertook the management of affairs, with results that justified the favorable impression which the first 5 years of N.'s reign made upon the Rom people. Many reforms were initiated, financial, social and legislative. These ministers treated N. to counsels of moderation and justice, dictating a policy which left considerable activity to the senate. But perceiving the bent of his evil nature, they allowed him to indulge in low pleasures and excesses with the most profligate companions, thinking, perhaps, either that the young ruler would in this way prove less harmful to the public, or that, after sowing his wild oats, he would return to the serious business of government. But in both ways they were sorely disappointed, for N., having surrendered himself to the basest appetites, continued to go from excess to excess. He surrounded himself with the most dissolute companions, conspicuous among whom were Salvius Otho and Claudius Senecio.

1. Quinquennium Neronis

2. Poppaea Sabina (58 AD)

The former had a wife as ambitious as she was unprincipled, and endowed, according to Tacitus, with every gift of nature except an "honorable mind." Already divorced before marrying Otho, she was minded to employ Otho merely as a tool to enable her to become N.'s consort. With the appearance of Poppaea Sabina, for such was her name, opens the second period of N.'s reign. She proved his evil star. Under her influence he shook off all restraints, turned a deaf ear to his best advisers and plunged deeper into immorality and crime. She allowed, if not persuaded, N. to give her husband a commission in the distant province of Lusitania. Her jealousy could tolerate no possible rival. She plotted the death of Agrippina to which she easily persuaded N. to consent. This foul crime was planned and carried out with the greatest cunning. Anicetus, admiral of the fleet, undertook to construct a vessel that would sink to order. N. invited his mother to his villa at Baiae at the Quinquatrus celebration. After the banquet she was persuaded to return to Bauli by the vessel prepared. But the plan did not succeed, and Agrippina saved herself by swimming ashore. She pretended to treat the matter as an accident, sending a freedman to N. to inform him of her escape. Anicetus, however, relieved N. of the awkward position by pretending that Agrippina's freedman had dropped a dagger which was considered proof enough of her guilt. Deserted by her friends and slaves except one freedman, she was quickly dispatched by her murderers. N. gave out that she died by suicide (Suet. xxxiv; Tac. *Ann.* cxli–cxlviii).

3. Poppaea and Tigellinus

N. no longer made any secret of taking Poppaea as his mistress, and, under her influence, bid defiance to the best Rom traditions and plunged deeper into dissipation. In 62 AD matters grew much worse by the death of the praetorian prefect, Burrus. Seneca lost in him a powerful ally, and Poppaea gained in one of the new prefects, Sofonius Tigellinus, a powerful ally. She succeeded in causing Seneca to retire from the court. Next she determined to remove Octavia. A charge of adultery was first tried, but as the evidence proved too leaky, N. simply divorced her because of barrenness. Then Anicetus was persuaded to confess adultery with her, and the innocent Octavia was banished to the island of Pandateria, where a little later she was executed at Poppaea's orders and her head brought to her rival (62 AD). Poppaea was now empress, and the next year bore a daughter to N., but the child died when only three months old. Two years later Poppaea herself died during pregnancy, of a cruel kick inflicted by N. in a fit of rage (65 AD). He pronounced a eulogy over her and took a third wife, Statilia Messalina, of whom he had no issue.

N., having by his extravagance exhausted the well-filled treasury of Claudius (as Caius did that of Tiberius), was driven to fill his coffers by confiscations of the estates of rich nobles against whom his creature Tigellinus could trump the slightest plausible charge. But even this did not prevent a financial crisis—the beginning of the bankruptcy of the later Rom empire. The provinces which at first enjoyed good government were now plundered; new and heavy taxes were imposed. Worst of all, the gold and silver coinage was depreciated, and the senate was deprived of the right of copper coinage.

4. Great Fire (July, 64)

This difficulty was much increased by the great fire which was not only destructive to both private and state property, but also necessitated the providing thousands of homeless with shelter, and lowering the price of corn. On July 18, 64, this great conflagration broke out in Circus Maximus. A high wind caused it to spread rapidly over a large portion of the city, sweeping before it ill-built streets of wooden houses. At the end of six days it seemed to be exhausted for lack of material, when another conflagration started in a different quarter of the city. Various exaggerated accounts of the destruction are found in Rom historians: of the 14 city regions 7 were said to have been totally destroyed and 4 partially. N. was at Antium at the time. He hastened back to the city and apparently took every means of arresting the spread of the flames. He superintended in person the work of the fire brigades, often exposing himself to danger. After the fire he threw open his own gardens to the homeless. The catastrophe caused great consternation, and, for whatever reasons, suspicion seemed to fix upon N. Rumor had it that on hearing the Greek verse, "When I am dead let the earth be wrapped in fire," he interrupted, "Nay rather, while I live" (Suet. xxxviii); that he had often deplored the ugliness of the city and wished an opportunity to rebuild it; that he purposely set it on fire in order to find room for his magnificent *Domus Aurea* ("Golden House"); that when the city was burning he gazed upon it from the tower of Maecenas delighted with what he termed "the beauty of the conflagration"; that he recited in actor's costume the sack of Troy (Suet. xxxviii; Tac. *Ann.* xv.38 ff). In spite of all these reports N. must be absolved of the guilt of incendiarism.

5. Persecution of Christians

Such public calamities were generally attributed to the wrath of the gods. In the present case everything was done to appease the offended deity. Yet, in spite of all, suspicion still clung to N. "Wherefore in order to allay the rumor he put forward as guilty [*subdidit reos*], and afflicted with the most exquisite punishments those who were hated for their abominations [*flagitia*] and called 'Christians' by the populace. Christus, from whom the name was derived, was punished by the procurator Pontius Pilatus in the reign of Tiberius. This noxious form of religion [*exitiabilis superstitio*], checked for a time, broke out again not only in Judaea its original home, but also throughout the city [Rome] where all abominations meet and find devotees. Therefore first of all those who confessed [i.e. to being Christians] were arrested, and then as a result of their information a large number [*multitudo ingens*] were implicated [reading *coniuncti*, not *convicti*], not so much on the charge of incendiarism as for hatred of the human race. They died by methods of mockery; some were covered with the skins of wild beasts and then torn by dogs, some were crucified, some were burned as torches to give light at night . . . . whence [after scenes of extreme cruelty] commiseration was stirred for them, although guilty and deserving the worst penalties, for men felt that their destruction was not on account of the public welfare but to gratify the cruelty of one [Nero]" (Tac. *Ann.* xv.44). Such is the earliest account of the first heathen persecution (as well as the first record of the crucifixion by a heathen writer). Tacitus here clearly implies that the Christians were innocent (*subdidit reos*), and that N. employed them simply as scapegoats. Some regard the conclusion of the paragraph as a contradiction to this—"though guilty and deserving the severest punishment" (*adversus sontes et novissima exempla meritos*). But Tacitus means by *sontes* that the Christians were "guilty" from the point of view of the populace, and that they merited extreme punishment also from his own standpoint for other causes, but not for arson. *Fatebantur* does not mean that they confessed to incendiarism, but to being Christians, and *qui fatebantur* means there were some who boldly confessed, while others tried to conceal or perhaps even denied their faith.

But why were the Christians selected as scapegoats? Why not the Jews, who were both numerous and had already offended the Rom government and had been banished in great numbers? Or why not the many followers of the oriental religions, which had proved more than once obnoxious? (1) Poppaea was favorable to Judaism and had certainly enough influence over N.

to protect the Jews; she was regarded by them as a proselyte and is termed by Jos (*Ant*, XX, viii, 11) θεοσεβής, *theosebēs*, "god-fearing." When the populace and N. were seeking victims for revenge, the Jews may have been glad of the opportunity of putting forward the Christians and may have been encouraged in this by Poppaea. Farrar (*Early Days of Christianity*, I, ch iv) sees "in the proselytism of Poppaea, guided by Jewish malice, the only adequate explanation of the first Christian persecution." (2) Closely connected with this was doubtless the observation by the Rom government that Christianity was an independent faith from Judaism. This may first have been brought home to the authorities by the trial of Paul before N., as suggested by Ramsay (*Expos*, July, 1893). Judaism was a recognized and tolerated religion, a *religio licita*, and Christianity when divorced from Judaism became a *religio illicita* and punishable by the state, for Christianity first rose "under the shadow of licensed Judaism" (*sub umbraculo licitae Judaeorum religionis:* Tert. *Apol.*, xxi). (3) As Christianity formed a society apart from Rom society, all kinds of crimes were attributed to its followers, Thyestean feasts, nightly orgies, hostility to temples and images. These *flagitia* seemed summed up in *odium humani generis*, "hatred for the human race." (4) They were easily selected as being so numerous and making most progress in a line opposed to Rom spirit; cf *ingens multitudo* (Tac. *Ann.* xv.44; Clemens Rom., *Cor* **1** 6, πολὺ πλῆθος, *polú plēthos;* cf also "great multitude" of Rev **7** 9; **19** 1). (5) No doubt, too, early Christian enthusiasm was unequivocal in its expressions, esp. in its belief of a final conflagration of the world and its serene faith amid the despair of others.

6. Conspiracy of Piso (65 AD)

In the meantime Tigellinus' tyranny and confiscations to meet N.'s expenses caused deep discontent among the nobles, which culminated in the famous conspiracy at the head of which was C. Calpurnius Piso. The plot was prematurely betrayed by Milichus. An inquisition followed in which the most illustrious victims who perished were Seneca the philosopher, Lucan the poet, Lucan's mother, and later Annaeus Mela, brother of Seneca and father of Lucan, T. Petronius Arbiter, "the glass of fashion." Finally, "N. having butchered so many illustrious men, at last desired to exterminate virtue itself by the death of Thrasea Paetus and Barea Soranus" (Tac. *Ann.* xvi.21 f).

7. Visit to Greece (66 AD)

Having cleared every suspected person out of the way, he abandoned the government in Rome to a freedman Helius, and started on a long visit to Greece (66–68 AD), where he took part in musical contests and games, himself winning prizes from the obsequious Greeks, in return for which N. bestowed upon them "freedom." N. was so un-Roman that he was perfectly at home in Greece, where alone he said he was appreciated by cultured people. In the meantime the revolt of Vindex in Gaul commenced (68 AD), but it was soon quelled by Verginius Rufus on account of its national Gaulic character. Galba of Hither Spain next declared himself *legatus* of the senate and the Rom people. N. was persuaded to return to Rome by Helius; he confiscated Galba's property, but his weakness and hesitancy greatly helped the cause of the latter.

8. Death of Nero

Nymphidius Sabinus, one of the prefects, won over the guard for Galba, by persuading the irresolute emperor to withdraw from Rome and then told the praetorians that N. had deserted them. N. was a coward, both in life and in death. While he had the means of easily crushing Galba, he was revolving plans of despair in his Servilian gardens, whether he should surrender himself to the mercies of the Parthians or to those of Galba; whether Galba would allow him the province of Egypt; whether the public would forgive his past if he showed penitence enough. In his distraction a comforter asked him in the words of Virgil, "Is it then so wretched to die?" He could not summon the courage for suicide, nor could he find one to inflict the blow for him: "Have I then neither friend nor foe?" Phaon a freedman offered him the shelter of his villa a few miles from Rome. Here he prepared for suicide, but with great cowardice. He kept exclaiming, "What an artist I am to perish!" (*Qualis artifex pereo*, Suet. xlix). On learning that he was condemned to a cruel death by the senate, he put the weapon to his throat and was assisted in the fatal blow by Epaphroditus his secretary. A centurion entered pretending he had come to help: "Too late—this is fidelity," were Nero's last words. His remains were laid in the family vault of the Domitii by his two nurses Ecloge and Alexandria and his concubine Acte (Suet. l). Thus perished on July 9, 68 AD the last of the line of Julius Caesar in his 31st year and in the 14th of his reign.

IV. Downfall and Character.—The causes of his downfall were briefly:

1. Seven Causes of Downfall

(1) his lavish expenditure leading to burdensome taxation and financial insecurity; (2) tyranny and cruelty of his favorites; (3) the great fire which brought dissatisfaction to fasten suspicion on N. and the consequent enlargement of his private abode at the expense of the city—esp. the Golden House; (4) the unpopular measure of the extension of Rom franchise to Greece and favored foreigners; (5) the security engendered by the success with which the conspiracy of Piso was crushed; (6) the discovery of another "secret of empire," that an emperor could be created elsewhere than at Rome, that the succession of emperors was not hereditary but rested with the great armies, and (7) the cowardice and weakness which N. displayed in the revolt which led to his death.

His reign is memorable for the activity of Seneca, the great fire, the persecution of Christians, the beginning of the bankruptcy of the later Rom empire, the Armenian disaster of Paetus (62 AD) retrieved by Corbulo and the humiliation of Parthia, the outbreak of the insurrection in Judaea (66 AD), which ended in the destruction of Jerus.

2. Character

Nero ranks with Gaius for folly and vice, while his cruelties recall the worst years of Tiberius. Very effeminate in his tastes, particular about the arrangement of his hair and proud of his voice, his greatest fault was inordinate vanity which courted applause for performances on non-Rom lines. He neglected his high office and degraded Rom *gravitas* by zeal for secondary pursuits. N., like his three predecessors, was very susceptible to female charms. He was licentious in the extreme, even to guilt of that nameless vice of antiquity —love of a male favorite. His cruelty, both directly and through his instruments, made the latter part of his reign as detestable as the *quinquennium* had been golden. He loved the extravagant and luxurious in every exaggerated form. He was a weakling and a coward in his life, and esp. in his death. Of his personal appearance we are told his features were regular and good; the expression of his countenance, however, was somewhat repelling. His frame was ill proportioned—slender legs and big stomach. In later years his face was covered with pimples.

V. "Nero Redivivus."—It seems as if there was something lovable even about this monster, which led a freedman to remain faithful to the last, and his two old nurses and cast-off concubine to care affectionately for his remains, and for a long time there were not wanting hands to strew his grave with spring and autumn flowers and to display his effigy (Suet. lvii). But, whether from the strange circumstances of his death, or the subsequent terrible confusion in the Rom world, or from whatever cause, there soon arose a belief that N. had not really died, but was living somewhere in retirement or had fled among the Parthians, and that he was destined in a short time to return and bring great calamity upon his enemies or the world (*quasi viventis et brevi magno inimicorum malo reversuri:* Suet. lvii). This belief was a force among the Parthians who were ready to take up arms at the report of a pseudo-Nero (Tac. *Hist.* i.2). In the confusion of the year of the four emperors, Greece and Asia were disturbed by the report of the advent of N. (Tac. *Hist.* ii.8), and the historian promises to mention the fortune and attempts of other pseudo-Neros. This belief was taken up by the Jews and amalgamated with their legend of Antichrist. In Asc Isa **4** (1st cent. AD), the Antichrist is clearly identified with N.: "Belial shall appear in the shape of a man, the king of wickedness, the matricide." It occurs again and again in both the Jewish and Christian sections of the Sib Or (**3** 66 ff; **4** 117 f.135 ff; **5** 100 f.136 f.216 f). How far N. was regarded by the Christians as the historical personage of Antichrist is a disputed point. That the common belief of the revival or advent of N. should influence contemporary Christian thought in days of social and political turmoil is highly probable. Bousset (*Comm.*) regards the beast of Rev **13** as Rome, and the smitten head whose "deathstroke was healed" as N., and some scholars take Rev **17** 10 f as referring to N. The "scarlet-colored beast" of **17** 3 may be intended either for the Rom government in general or for N. in particular. That the number 666 (Rev **13** 18) represents in Heb letters the numerical equivalent of *Neron Kesar* is significant, for the Jewish Christians would be familiar with *gēmaṭrīyā'* (the numerical equivalent of names). See NUMBER. Cf Farrar, *Early Days*, ch xxviii, sec. 5. In later times the idea of a twofold Antichrist seems to have arisen—one for the Jews and one for the Gentiles; cf esp. Commodian, *Carm. Apol.* (926): "to us N. became Antichrist, to the Jews the other" (*nobis Nero factus Antichristus, ille Judaeis*). There was an alternate theory that N. had really been killed, but that he would rise again (Sib Or **5** 216 f; Augustine, *De Civ. Dei*, xx.19: *unde nonnulli ipsum resurrecturum et futurum Antichristum suspicantur*).

VI. Nero and Christianity.—The name Nero does not occur in the NT, but he was the Caesar to whom Paul appealed (Acts **25** 11) and at whose tribunal Paul was tried after his first imprisonment. It is quite likely that N. heard Paul's case in person, for the emperor showed much interest in provincial cases. It was during the earlier "golden *quinquennium*" of N.'s reign that Paul addressed his ep. to the Christians at Rome, and probably in the last year of N.'s reign (68 AD) Paul suffered death near the city, though Harnack (*Chronologie*) places his death in the first Neronian persecution of 64. Although the NT gives no hint of a possible visit or sojourn of Peter in Rome, such a sojourn and subsequent martyrdom are highly probable and almost certain from the early persistent tradition, esp. in Clement of Rome, Ignatius and Papias, and later in Tertullian, Clement of Alexandria and the *Liber Pontificalis* (catalogue of popes). His execution at Rome under Nero is practically certain.

1. Nero and the NT

The first persecution to which Christianity was subjected came from the Jews: the *first heathen* persecution took place under N. Up to this time the Rom government had been on friendly terms with Christianity, as Christianity was either not prominent enough to cause any disturbance of society or was confounded by the Romans with Judaism (*sub umbraculo licitae Judaeorum religionis:* Tert. *Apol.*, xxi). Paul, writing to the Christians of the capital, urged them to "be in subjection to the higher powers" as "ordained of God" (Rom **13** 1 ff), and his high estimation of the Rom government as power for the good of society was probably enhanced by his mild captivity at Rome which permitted him to carry on the work of preaching and was terminated by an acquittal on the first trial (accepting the view of a first acquittal and subsequent activity before condemnation at a second trial). But soon, whether because of the trial of Paul, a Rom citizen, at Rome (about 63), or the growing hostility of the Jews, or the increasing numbers and alarming progress of the new religion, the distinction between Christianity and Judaism became apparent to the Rom authorities. If it had not yet been proscribed as a *religio illicita* ("unlicensed religion"), neither had it been admitted as a *religio licita*. Christianity was not in itself as yet a crime; its adherents were not liable to persecution "for the name." According to one view the Neronian persecution was a spasmodic act and an isolated incident in imperial policy: the Christians were on this occasion put forward merely to remove suspicion from N. They were not persecuted either *as Christians* or as incendiaries, but on account of *flagitia* and *odium humani generis*, i.e. Thyestean feasts, Oedipodean incest and nightly orgies were attributed to them, and their withdrawal from society and exclusive manners caused the charge of "hatred for society." The evidence of Tacitus (*Ann.* xv.44) would bear out this view of the Neronian persecution as accidental, isolated, to satisfy the revenge of the mob, confined to Rome and of brief duration. The other view is, however, preferable, as represented by Ramsay (*Church in the Rom Empire*, ch xi) and E. G. Hardy (*Studies in Rom History*, ch iv). Suetonius speaks of the persecution of Christians as a permanent police regulation in a list of other seemingly permanent measures (*Nero* xvi: *afflicti suppliciis Christiani genus hominum superstitionis novae ac maleficae*), which is not inconsistent with the account of Tacitus—who gives the initial step and Suetonius the permanent result. The Christians by these trials, though not convicted of incendiarism, were brought into considerable prominence; their unsocial and exclusive manners, their withdrawal from the duties of state, their active proselytism, together with the charges of immorality, established them in Rom eyes as the enemies of society. Christianity thus became a crime and was banned by the police authorities. Suetonius gives a "brief statement of the permanent administrative principle into which N.'s action ultimately resolved itself" (Ramsay, op. cit., 232). No formal law needed to be passed, the matter could be left with the *prefect* of the city. A trial must be held and the *flagitia* proved before an order for execution, according to Ramsay, but Hardy holds that henceforth the name itself—*nomen ipsum*—was proscribed. A precedent was now established of great importance in the policy of the imperial government toward Christianity (see, further, ROMAN EMPIRE; CHRISTIANITY). There is no reason to suppose that the Neronian persecution of 64 extended beyond Rome to the provinces, though no doubt the attitude of the home government must have had considerable influence with provincial officers. Paul seems to have gone undisturbed, or at least with no unusual obstacles, in his evangelization after his acquittal. The authorities for a general Neronian persecution and formal Neronian laws against Christianity are late; cf Orosius (*Hist.* vii.7, "[Nero] was the first to put to death Christians at Rome and gave orders that they should be subjected *to the same persecution throughout all the provinces*").

2. Neronian Policy and Christianity

LITERATURE.—(*a*) Ancient: Tacitus *Annals* xii–xvi; Suetonius *Nero;* Dio Cassius in *Epit. of Xiphilinus* 61 ff; Zonaras xi. (*b*) Modern: Hermann Schiller, *Geschichte des röm. Kaiserreichs unter der Regierung des Neron* (Berlin, 1872); Merivale, *Hist of the Romans under the Empire;* Ramsay, *Church in the Rom Empire* and *Expos*, 1893; E. G. Hardy, *Christianity and the Rom Government* and *Studies in Rom History;* Mommsen, "Der Religionsfrevel nach röm. Recht," *Histor. Zeitschr.*, 1890; C. F. Arnold, *Die Neronische Christenverfolgung;* Farrar, *Early Days of Christianity;* Baring-Gould, *Tragedy of the Caesars;* G. H. Lewes, "Was Nero a Monster?" in *Cornhill Magazine*, July, 1863; B. W. Henderson, *Life and Principate of the Emperor Nero*, with important bibliography of ancient and modern authorities (London, 1903); Lehmann, *Claudius u. Nero.*

S. ANGUS

NEST (קֵן, *ḳēn;* **νεοσσιά**, *neossiá, nossiá;* in the NT **κατασκήνωσις**, *kataskēnōsis;* Lat *nidus*): A receptacle prepared by a bird for receiving its eggs and young. Nests differ with species. Eagles use a large heap of coarse sticks and twigs on the cleft of a mountain (Job **39** 27 ff; Jer **49** 16; Ob ver 4); hawks prefer trees; vultures, hollow trees or the earth; ravens, big trees; doves and pigeons, trees or rocky crevices (Jer **48** 28); hoopoes, hollow trees; swallows, mud nests under a roof, on cliffs or deserted temples; owls, hollow trees, dark places in ruins or sand burrows (on the *ḳippōz* of Isa **34** 15 see OWL); cranes, storks and herons, either trees (Ps **104** 17) or rushes beside water (storks often choose housetops, as well).

Each nest so follows the building laws of its owner's species that any expert ornithologist can tell from a nest which bird builded it. Early in incubation a bird deserts a nest readily because it hopes to build another in a place not so easily discoverable and where it can deposit more eggs. When the young have progressed until their quickening is perceptible through the thin shells pressed against the breast of the mother, she develops a boldness called by scientists the "brooding fever." In this state the wildest of birds frequently will suffer your touch before deserting the nest. Esp. is this the case if the young are just on the point of emerging. The first Bib. reference to the nest of a bird will be found in Balaam's fourth prophecy in Nu **24** 21: "And he looked on the Kenite, and took up his parable and said, Strong is thy dwelling-place, and thy nest is set in the rock." Here Balaam was thinking of the nest of an eagle, hawk or vulture, placed on solid rock among impregnable crags of mountain tops. The next reference is among the laws for personal conduct in Dt **22** 6: "If a bird's nest chance to be before thee in the way, in any tree or on the ground, with young ones or eggs, and the dam sitting upon the young, or upon the eggs, thou shalt not take the dam with the young." Beyond question this is the earliest law on record for the protection of a brooding bird. It is probable that it was made permissible to take the young, as the law demanded their use, at least in the case of pigeons and doves, for sacrifice. In **29** 18, Job cries,

"Then I said, I shall die in my nest,
And I shall multiply my days as the sand:"

that is, he hoped in his days of prosperity to die in the home he had builded for his wife and children. In Ps **84** 3 David sings,

"Yea, the sparrow hath found her a house,
And the swallow a nest for herself, where she may lay her young,
Even thine altars, O Jeh of hosts,
My King, and my God."

These lines are rich and ripe with meaning, for in those days all the world protected a temple nest, even to the infliction of the death penalty on anyone interfering with it. This was because the bird was supposed to be claiming the protection of the gods. Hebrew, Arab and Egyptian guarded all nests on places of worship. Pagan Rome executed the shoemaker who killed a raven that built on a temple, and Athens took the same revenge on the man who destroyed the nest of a swallow. Isaiah compared the destruction of Assyria to the robbing of a bird's nest: "And my hand hath found as a nest the riches of the peoples; and as one gathereth eggs that are forsaken, have I gathered all the earth: and there was none that moved the wing, or that opened the mouth, or chirped" (Isa **10** 14; cf **16** 2). Matthew quotes Jesus as having said, "The foxes have holes, and the birds of the heaven have nests; but the Son of man hath not where to lay his head" (Mt **8** 20=Lk **9** 58). GENE STRATTON-PORTER

NET. See FISHING; FOWLER.

NETAIM, nā'ta-im, nē'ta-im, nē-tā'im (נְטָעִים, *n^eṭā'īm;* B, **'Αζαείμ,** *Azaeim,* A, **'Αταείμ,** *Ataeim*): In 1 Ch **4** 23 AV reads "those that dwell among plants and hedges," RV "the inhabitants of Netaim and Gederah." The latter may be taken as correct. Gederah was in the Judaean Shephelah. Here also we should seek for Netaim; but no likely identification has yet been suggested.

NETHANEL, nē-than'el, neth'a-nel (נְתַנְאֵל, *n^ethan'ēl,* "God has given"; **Ναθαναήλ,** *Nathanaēl;* AV **Nethaneel,** nē-than'ē-el):

(1) A chief or prince of Issachar (Nu **1** 8; **2** 5; **7** 18.23; **10** 15).

(2) The 4th son of Jesse (1 Ch **2** 14).

(3) One of the trumpet-blowers before the ark when it was brought up from the house of Obed-edom (1 Ch **15** 24).

(4) A Levite scribe, the father of Shemaiah (1 Ch **24** 6).

(5) The 5th son of Obed-edom (1 Ch **26** 4).

(6) One of the princes whom Jehoshaphat sent to teach in the cities of Judah (2 Ch **17** 7).

(7) A Levite who gave cattle for Josiah's Passover (2 Ch **35** 9).

(8) One of the priests who had married foreign wives (Ezr **10** 22; cf 1 Esd **9** 22).

(9) A priest registered under the high priest Joiakim (Neh **12** 21).

(10) A Levite musician who assisted at the dedication of the walls (Neh **12** 36). JOHN A. LEES

NETHANIAH, neth-a-nī'a (נְתַנְיָהוּ, *n^ethanyāhū,* "Jeh has given"; **Ναθανίας,** *Nathanías*):

(1) An Asaphite musician (1 Ch **25** 2.12).

(2) A Levite who accompanied the princes sent by Jehoshaphat to teach in the cities of Judah (2 Ch **17** 8).

(3) The father of Jehudi (Jer **36** 14).

(4) The father of Ishmael, the murderer of Gedaliah (Jer **40** 8.14.15; **41,** 11 t; 2 K **25** 23.25). Some MSS of LXX read here *Maththanías.*

NETHINIM, neth'i-nim (נְתִינִים, *n^ethīnīm,* "given"; **Ναθεινείμ,** *Natheineím;* AV **Nethinims**):

1. Meaning A group of temple-servants (1 Ch **9** 2 and 16 t in Ezr and Neh). The word has always the article, and does not occur in the sing. The LXX translators usually transliterate, but in one passage (1 Ch **9** 2) they render, "the given ones" (*hoi dedoménoi*). The Syr (Pesh) also, in Ezr, Neh, transliterates the word, but in 1 Ch **9** 2 renders it by a word meaning "sojourners." The meaning "given" is suggestive of a state of servitude, and Jos seems to confirm the suggestion by calling the N. "temple-slaves" (*hieródouloi*) (*Ant,* XI, v, 1). It should, however, be noted that another form of this word is employed in the directions regarding the Levites: "Thou shalt *give* the Levites unto Aaron and to his sons: they are wholly *given* unto him on behalf of the children of Israel" (Nu **3** 9; cf also **8** 16.19).

Of the history of the N. in earlier times there are but few and uncertain traces. When Joshua discovered that he had been beguiled

2. History by the Gibeonites into a covenant to let them live, he reduced their tribe to servitude, and declared, "Now therefore ye are cursed, and there shall never fail to be of you bondmen, both hewers of wood and drawers of water for the house of my God" (Josh **9** 23.27). It is no doubt tempting to see in the Gibeonites the earliest N., but another tradition traces their origin to a gift of David and the princes for the service of the Levites (Ezr **8** 20). Their names, too, indicate diversity of origin; for besides being mostly un-Hebrew in aspect, some of them are found elsewhere in the OT as names of non-Israelitish tribes. The Meunim, for example (Ezr **2** 50=Neh **7** 52), are in all likelihood descended from the Meonites or Maonites who are mentioned as harassing Israel (Jgs **10** 12), as in conflict with the Simeonites (1 Ch **4** 41), and as finally overcome by Uzziah (2 Ch **26** 7). The next name in the lists is that of the children of Nephisim. These may be traced to the Hagrite clan of Naphish (Gen **25** 15; 1 Ch **5** 19). In both Ezr and Neh, the list is immediately followed by that of the servants of Solomon, whose duties were similar to, it may be even humbler than, those of the N. These servants of Solomon appear to be descendants of the Canaanites whom Solomon employed in the building of his temple (1 K **5** 15). All these indications are perhaps slight; but they point in the same direction, and warrant the assumption that the N. were originally foreign slaves, mostly prisoners of war, who had from time to time been *given* to the temple by the kings and princes of the nation, and that to them were assigned the lower menial duties of the house of God.

At the time of the return from the exile the N. had come to be regarded as important. Their number was considerable: 392 accom-

3. Post-exilic History panied Zerubbabel at the first Return in 538 BC (Ezr **2** 58=Neh **7** 60). When Ezra, some 80 years later, organized the second Return, he secured a contingent of N. numbering 220 (Ezr **8** 20). In Jerus they enjoyed the same privileges and immunities as the other religious orders, being included by Artaxerxes' letter to Ezra among those who should be exempt from toll, custom and tribute (Ezr **7** 24). A part of the city in Ophel, opposite the Water-gate, was assigned them as an official residence (Neh **3** 26.31), and the situation is certainly appropriate if their duties at all resembled those of the Gibeonites (see Ryle, "Ezra and Nehemiah," in *Cambridge Bible,* Intro, 57). They were also organized into a kind of guild under their own leaders or presidents (Neh **11** 21).

The N. are not again mentioned in Scripture. It is probable that they, with the singers and porters, became gradually incorporated in the general body of Levites; their name passed ere long into a tradition, and became at a later time a butt for the scorn and bitterness of the Talmudic writers against everything that they regarded as un-Jewish.

JOHN A. LEES

NETOPHAH, nē-tō'fa (נְטֹפָה, *neṭōphāh;* LXX **Νετωφά**, *Netōphá*, **Νεφωτά**, *Nephōtá*, and other variants): The birthplace of two of David's heroes, Maharai and Heleb (2 S **23** 28.29), also of Seraiah the son of Tanhumeth the Netophathite, one of the captains who came to offer allegiance to Gedaliah (2 K **25** 23; Jer **40** 8). "The villages of the Netophathites" are mentioned (1 Ch **9** 16) as the dwellings of certain Levites and (Neh **12** 28, AV "Netophathi") of certain "sons of the singers."

The first mention of the place itself is in Ezr **2** 22; Neh **7** 26; 1 Esd **5** 18 (RV "Netophas"), where we have ‖ lists of the exiles returning from Babylon under Zerubbabel; the place is mentioned between Bethlehem and Anathoth and in literary association with other cities in the mountains of Judah, e.g. Gibeon, Kiriath-jearim, Chephereh and Beeroth. In this respect it is most plausible to identify it with NEPHTOAH (q.v.), although the disappearance of the terminal guttural in the latter creates a difficulty. Conder has suggested a site known as *Kh. Umm-Ṭoba*, N.E. of Bethlehem, an ancient site, but not apparently of great importance. *Beit Nettīf*, an important village on a lofty site in the Shephelah near the "Vale of Elah," also appears to have an echo of the name, and indeed may well be the Beth Netophah of the Mish (*Shebhū'ōth*, ix.5; Neubauer, *Géogr.*, 128), but the position does not seem to agree at all with that of the OT Netophah. For *Kh. Umm-Ṭoba* see *PEF*, III, 128; for *Beit Nettīf, PEF*, III, 24; *RBR*, II, 17 f; both Sh XVII.

E. W. G. MASTERMAN

NETOPHAS, nē-tō'fas (B, **Νετέβας**, *Netébas*, A, **Νετωφαέ**, *Netōphaé*): A town named in 1 Esd **5** 18, identical with "Netophah" of Ezr **2** 22; Neh **7** 26.

NETOPHATHI, nē-tof'a-thī, **NETOPHATHITES**, nē-tof'a-thīts. See NETOPHAH.

NETTLES, net''lz: (1) חָרוּל, *ḥārūl* (Job **30** 7; Prov **24** 31; Zeph **2** 9 m, in all, "wild vetches"); the tr "nettles" is due to the supposed derivations of *ḥārūl* from an (obs.) √ חרל, *ḥāral*, meaning "to be sharp" or "stinging," but a tr "thorns" (as in Vulg) would in that case do as well. LXX has φρύγανα ἄγρια, *phrúgana ágria*, "wild brushwood," in Job, and certainly the association with the "saltwort" and the *retm*, "broom," in the passage would best be met by the supposition that it means the low thorny bushes plentiful in association with these plants. "Vetch" is suggested by the Aram., but is very uncertain. (2) קִמּוֹשׂ, *ḳimmōsh* (Isa **34** 13; Hos **9** 6), and pl. קִמְּשֹׂנִים, *ḳimmeshōnīm* (Prov **24** 31), trd (EV) "thorns," because of the tr of *ḥārūl* as "nettles" in the same ver. From Isa **34** 13 *ḳimmōsh* is apparently distinct from thorns, and the tr "nettle" is very probable, as such neglected or deserted places as described in the three references readily become overgrown with nettles in Pal. The common and characteristic Pal nettle is the *Urtica pilulifera*, so called from the globular heads of its flowers.

E. W. G. MASTERMAN

NETWORK, net'wûrk (שְׂבָכָה, *sebhākhāh*): RV in 2 K **25** 17; 2 Ch **4** 13 (also in pl., vs 12.13), for "wreathen work" and "wreath" in AV (of the adornment of the capitals of the pillars of Solomon's temple; see JACHIN AND BOAZ). "Networks" in Isa **19** 9 is in RV correctly rendered "white cloth." In ARV "network" is substituted for "pictures" in AV (Prov **25** 11), "baskets" in ERV, m "filigree work."

NEW, nū, **NEWNESS**, nū'nes (חָדָשׁ, *ḥādhāsh;* **καινός**, *kainós*, **νέος**, *néos*):

1. In the OT

The word commonly trd "new" in the OT is *ḥādhāsh*, "bright," "fresh," "new" (special interest was shown in, and importance attached to, fresh and new things and events); Ex **1** 8; Dt **20** 5; **22** 8; **24** 5; 1 S **6** 7; 2 S **21** 16; Ps **33** 3, "a new song"; Jer **31** 31, "new covenant"; Ezk **11** 19, "a new spirit"; **18** 31, "new heart"; **36** 26, etc; *ḥōdhesh* is "the new moon," "the new-moon day," the first of the lunar month, a festival, then "month" (Gen **29** 14, "a month of days"); it occurs frequently, often trd "month"; we have "new moon" (1 S **20** 5.18.24, etc); *tīrōsh* is "new [sweet] wine" (Neh **10** 39; in Joel **1** 5; **3** 18, it is *'āsīs*, RV "sweet wine"); in Acts **2** 13, "new wine" is *gleúkos*.

Other words in the OT for "new" are *ḥădhath*, Aram. (Ezr **6** 4); *ṭārī*, "fresh" (Jgs **15** 15, RV "a fresh jawbone of an ass"); *berī'āh*, a "creation" (Nu **16** 30, "if Jeh make a new thing," RVm "create a creation"); *bākhar*, "to be first-fruits" (Ezk **47** 12; so RVm); *ḳūm*, "setting," is trd "newly" (Jgs **7** 19); also *miḳḳārōbh*, "recently" (Dt **32** 17, RV "of late"); news is *shemū'āh*, "report," "tidings"; Prov **25** 25, "good news from a far country."

2. In the NT

In the NT "new" (mostly *kainos*, "new," "fresh," "newly made") is an important word. We have the title of the "New Testament" itself, rightly given by ARV as "New Covenant," the designation of "the new dispensation" ushered in through Christ, the writings relating to which the volume contains. We have "new covenant" (*kainos*) in Lk **22** 20, "This cup is the new covenant in my blood" (ERVm "testament"; in Mt **26** 28; Mk **14** 24, "new" is omitted in RV, but in Mt m "many ancient authorities insert new," and in Mk "some ancient authorities"); 1 Cor **11** 25, ERVm "or testament"; 2 Cor **3** 6, ERVm "or testament"; He **8** 8, ERVm "or testament"; in ver 13, "covenant" is supplied (cf He **12** 24, *neos*).

Corresponding to this, we have (2 Cor **5** 17, AV and RV), "The old things have passed away; behold, they are become new"; ib, "If any man is in Christ, he is a new creature," RVm "there is a new creation"; Gal **6** 15, m "or creation," "new man" (Eph **2** 15; **4** 24; Col **3** 10 [*neos*]); "new commandment" (Jn **13** 34); "new doctrine" (Acts **17** 19); "new thing" (**17** 21); "newness of life" (*kainótēs*) (Rom **6** 4); "newness of the spirit" (**7** 6; cf 2 Cor **5** 17); "a new name" (Rev **2** 17; **3** 12); "new heavens and a new earth" (2 Pet **3** 13); "new Jerusalem" (Rev **3** 12; **21** 2); "new song" (Rev **5** 9); cf "new friend" and "new wine" (Sir **9** 10*b*, *c*); *artigénnētos*, "newborn" (1 Pet **2** 2); *prósphatos*, "newly slain," "new" (He **10** 20, RV "a new and living way, through the veil, that is to say, his flesh"; cf Sir **9** 10*a*; Jth **4** 3); "new" is the tr of *neos*, "new," "young" (1 Cor **5** 7; Col **3** 10, "new man"; He **12** 24, "new covenant").

The difference in meaning between *kainos* and *neos*, is, in the main, that *kainos* denotes *new* in respect of *quality*, "the new as set over against that which has seen service, the outworn, the effete, or marred through age"; *neos*, "new [in respect of time], that which has recently come into existence," e.g. *kainón mnēmeíon*, the "new tomb" in which Jesus was laid, was not one recently made, but one in which no other dead had ever lain; the "new covenant," the "new man," etc, may be contemplated under both aspects of *quality* and of *time* (Trench, *Synonyms of the NT*, 209 f).

In Mt **9** 16; Mk **2** 21, *ágnaphos*, "unsmoothed,"

"unfinished," is tr[d] "new," "new cloth," RV "undressed." For "new bottles" (Lk **5** 38 and ||'s), RV has "fresh wine-skins." W. L. WALKER

NEW BIRTH. See REGENERATION.

NEW COMMANDMENT. See BROTHERLY LOVE.

NEW COVENANT. See COVENANT, THE NEW.

NEW EARTH. See ESCHATOLOGY OF THE NT; HEAVENS, NEW.

NEW HEAVENS. See HEAVENS, NEW.

NEW JERUSALEM. See JERUSALEM, NEW; REVELATION OF JOHN.

NEW MAN. See MAN, NEW.

NEW MOON. See MOON, NEW; FASTS AND FEASTS.

NEW TESTAMENT. See BIBLE; CANON OF THE NT; CRITICISM.

NEW TESTAMENT CANON. See CANON OF THE NT.

NEW TESTAMENT LANGUAGE. See LANGUAGE OF THE NT.

NEW TESTAMENT TEXT. See TEXT OF THE NT.

NEW YEAR. See TIME; YEAR.

NEZIAH, nē-zī'a (נְצִיחַ, *n[e]çīaḥ*): The head of a family of Nethinim (Ezr **2** 54; Neh **7** 56), called in 1 Esd **5** 32, "Nasi" (AV and RVm "Nasith").

NEZIB, nē'zib (נְצִיב, *n[e]çībh;* B, **Νασείβ**, *Naseíb*, A, **Νεσίβ**, *Nesíb*): A town in the Judaean Shephelah, mentioned along with Keilah and Mareshah (Josh **15** 43). *Onom* places it 7 miles from Eleutheropolis (*Beit Jibrīn*), on the road to Hebron. It is represented today by *Beit Nasib*, a village with ancient remains some 2 miles S.W. of *Khirbet Kila* (Keilah).

NIBHAZ, nib'haz (נִבְחַז, *nibhḥaz*): Given as the name of an idol of the Avvites, introduced by them into Samaria (2 K **17** 31), but otherwise unknown. The text is supposed to be corrupt.

NIBSHAN, nib'shan (הַנִּבְשָׁן, *ha-nibhshān;* B, **Ναφλαζών**, *Naphlazōn*, A, **Νεβσάν**, *Nebsán*): A city in the Judaean wilderness named between Secacah and the City of Salt (Josh **15** 62). *Onom* knows the place but gives no clue to its identification. The site has not been recovered. Wellhausen suggests the emendation of *nibhshān* to *kibhshān*, "furnace" (*Proleg.*[2], 344).

NICANOR, nī-kā'nor, nī'kā-nôr (**Νικάνωρ**, *Nikánōr*): The son of Patroclus and one of the king's "chief friends" (2 Macc **8** 9), a Syrian general under Antiochus Epiphanes and Demetrius Soter. After the defeat of Seron by Judas, Epiphanes intrusted his chancellor Lysias with the reduction of Judaea (1 Macc **3** 34 ff). Nicanor was one of the three generals commissioned by Lysias—the others being Ptolemy, son of Dorymenes, and Gorgias (**3** 38). The campaign began in 166 BC; the Syrians were defeated at Emmaus (**3** 57 ff), while Gorgias at a later stage gained a victory at Jamnia over a body of Jews who disobeyed Judas (**5** 58). The account given in 2 Macc differs considerably, both in omissions and in additions (2 Macc **8** 9 ff). There Nicanor, not Gorgias, is the chief in command. The battle of Emmaus is not mentioned, but "the thrice-accursed Nicanor," having in overweening pride invited a thousand slavedealers to accompany him to buy the Jewish captives, was humiliated, and his host was destroyed, he himself escaping "like a fugitive slave" to Antioch (2 Macc **8** 34 f). After the death of Epiphanes, Eupator and Lysias (the last two at the hands of Demetrius [1 Macc **7** 2]), Nicanor appears again under King Demetrius in the struggle between Alcimus and Judas. Alcimus, having been seated in the priesthood by Demetrius' officer Bacchides, could not hold it against Judas and the patriots. He appealed again to Demetrius, who this time selected Nicanor, now governor of Cyprus (2 Macc **12** 2) and known for his deadly hatred of the Jews, to settle the dispute and slay Judas (**14** 12 ff; 1 Macc **7** 26 ff). Nicanor was appointed governor of Judaea on this occasion. Again 1 and 2 Macc differ. According to 1 Macc, Nicanor sought in vain to seize Judas by treachery. Then followed the battle of Capharsalama ("village of peace"), in which the Syrians were defeated, though Jos (*Ant*, XII, x, 5) says Judas was defeated. Nicanor retired to Jerus, insulted the priests and threatened the destruction of the temple unless they delivered up Judas. He then retired to Beth-horon to find Judas posted opposite him at Adasa (1 Macc **7** 39 ff), 3½ miles distant. Here on the 13th of the 12th month Adar (March), 161 BC, the Syrians sustained a crushing defeat, Nicanor himself being the first to fall. The Jews cut off his head and proud right hand and hanged them up beside Jerus. For a little while Adasa gave the land of Judah rest. The people ordained to keep this "day of great gladness" year by year—the 13th of Adar, "the day before the day of Mordecai" (Feast of Purim). 2 Macc mentions that Simon, Judas' brother, was worsted in a first engagement (**14** 17), omits the battle of Capharsalama, and represents Nicanor, struck with the manliness of the Jews, as entering into friendly relations with Judas, urging him to marry and lead a quiet life, forgetful of the king's command until Alcimus accused him to Demetrius. The latter peremptorily ordered Nicanor to bring Judas in all haste as prisoner to Antioch (**14** 27). The scene of the final conflict (Adasa) is given only as "in the region of Samaria" (**15** 1). According to this account, it was Judas who ordered the mutilation of Nicanor and in a more gruesome fashion (**15** 30 ff). It is *possible* that the Nicanor, the Cypriarch or governor of Cyprus of 2 Macc **12** 2, is a different person from Nicanor, the son of Patroclus—a view not accepted in the above account. S. ANGUS

NICANOR (**Νικάνωρ**, *Nikánōr*): One of "the seven" chosen to superintend "the daily ministration" of the poor of the Christian community at Jerus (Acts **6** 5). The name is Gr.

NICODEMUS, nik-ō-dē'mus (**Νικόδημος**, *Nikódēmos*): A Pharisee and a "ruler of the Jews," mentioned only by St. John. He (1) interviewed Christ at Jerus and was taught by Him the doctrine of the New Birth (Jn **3** 1–15), (2) defended Him before the Sanhedrin (Jn **7** 50–52), and (3) assisted at His burial (Jn **19** 39–42).

This meeting, which it has been surmised took place in the house of St. John (Jn **3** 1–15), was one of the results of Our Lord's ministry at Jerus during the first Passover (cf Jn **3** 2 with Jn **2** 23). Although N. had been thus won to believe

1. The Interview

in the Divine nature of Christ's mission, his faith was yet very incomplete in that he believed Him to be inspired only after the fashion of the OT prophets. To this faint-hearted faith corresponded his timidity of action, which displayed itself in his coming "by night," lest he should offend his colleagues in the Sanhedrin and the other hostile Jews (ver 2). In answer to the veiled question which the words of N. implied, and to convince him of the inadequacy of mere intellectual belief, Christ proclaimed to him the necessity for a spiritual regeneration: "Except one be born anew, he cannot see the kingdom of God" (ver 3). This was interpreted by N. only in its materialistic sense, and therefore caused him bewilderment and confusion (ver 4). But Christ, as on another occasion when dealing with His questioners on a similar point of doctrine (cf Jn **6** 52.53), answered his perplexity only by repeating His previous statement (ver 5). He then proceeded to give further explanation. The rebirth is not outward but inward, it is not of the body but of the soul (ver 6). Just as God is the real agent in the birth of the body, so also is He the Creator of the New Spirit; and just as no one knoweth whence cometh the wind, or "whither it goeth," yet all can feel its effects who come under its influence, so is it with the rebirth. Only those who have experienced it as a change in themselves, wrought by the Divine Power, are qualified to judge either of its reality or of its effects (vs 7.8). But N., since such experience had not yet been his, remained still unenlightened (ver 9). Christ therefore condemned such blindness in one who yet professed to be a teacher of spiritual things (ver 10), and emphasized the reality in His own life of those truths which He had been expounding (ver 11). With this, Christ returned to the problem underlying the first statement of N. If N. cannot believe in "earthly things," i.e. in the New Birth, which, though coming from above, is yet realized in this world, how can he hope to understand "heavenly things," i.e. the deeper mysteries of God's purpose in sending Christ into the world (ver 12), of Christ's Divine sonship (ver 13), of His relationship to the atonement and the salvation of man (ver 14), and of how a living acceptance of and feeding upon Him is in itself Divine life (ver 15; cf Jn **6** 25–65)?

2. The Defence

The above interview, though apparently fruitless at the time, was not without its effect upon N. At the Feast of Tabernacles, when the Sanhedrin was enraged at Christ's proclamation of Himself as the "living water" (Jn **7** 37.38), N. was emboldened to stand up in His defence. Yet here also he showed his natural timidity. He made no personal testimony of his faith in Christ, but sought rather to defend Him on a point of Jewish law (Jn **7** 50–52; cf Ex **23** 1; Dt **1** 16.17; **17** 6; **19** 15).

3. The Burial

By this open act of reverence N. at last made public profession of his being of the following of Christ. His wealth enabled him to provide the "mixture of myrrh and aloes, about a hundred pounds," with which the body of Jesus was embalmed (Jn **19** 39 ff).

The Gospel of Nicodemus and other apocryphal works narrate that N. gave evidence in favor of Christ at the trial before Pilate, that he was deprived of office and banished from Jerus by the hostile Jews, and that he was baptized by St. Peter and St. John. His remains were said to have been found in a common grave along with those of Gamaliel and St. Stephen.

Nicodemus is a type of the "well-instructed and thoughtful Jew who looked for the consummation of national hope to follow in the line along which he had himself gone, as being a continuation and not a new beginning" (Westcott). The manner in which the Gospel narrative traces the overcoming of his natural timidity and reluctant faith is in itself a beautiful illustration of the working of the Spirit, of how belief in the Son of Man is in truth a new birth, and the entrance into eternal life.

C. M. Kerr

NICODEMUS, GOSPEL OF. See Apocryphal Gospels, III, 3, (*b*).

NICOLAITANS, nik-ō-lā′i-tanz (**Νικολαΐται,** *Nikolaïtai*): A sect or party of evil influence in early Christianity, esp. in the 7 churches of Asia. Their doctrine was similar to that of Balaam, "who taught Balak to cast a stumblingblock before the children of Israel, to eat things sacrificed to idols, and to commit fornication" (Rev **2** 14.15). Their practices were strongly condemned by St. John, who praised the church in Ephesus for "hating their works" (Rev **2** 6), and blamed the church in Pergamum for accepting in some measure their teaching (Rev **2** 15). Except that reference is probably made to their influence in the church at Thyatira also, where their leader was "the woman Jezebel, who calleth herself a prophetess" (Rev **2** 20; cf ver 14), no further direct information regarding them is given in Scripture.

1. The Sect

2. References

Reference to them is frequent in post-apostolic literature. According to Irenaeus (*Adv. Haer.*, i. 26.3; iii.10.7), followed by Hippolytus (*Philos.*, vii.36), they were founded by Nicolaüs, the proselyte of Antioch, who was one of the seven chosen to serve at the tables (Acts **6** 5). Irenaeus, as also Clement of Alexandria (*Strom.*, ii.20), Tertullian and others, unite in condemning their practices in terms similar to those of St. John; and reference is also made to their gnostic tendencies. In explanation of the apparent incongruity of such an immoral sect being founded by one of "good report, full of the Spirit and of wisdom" (cf Acts **6** 3), Simcox argues that their lapse may have been due to reaction from original principles of a too rigid asceticism. A theory, started in comparatively modern times, and based in part on the similarity of meaning of the Gr "Nikolaüs," and the Heb "Balaam," puts forward the view that the two sects referred to under these names were in reality identical. Yet if this were so, it would not have been necessary for St. John to designate them separately.

3. Nicolaitan Controversy

The problem underlying the Nicolaitan controversy, though so little direct mention is made of it in Scripture, was in reality most important, and concerned the whole relation of Christianity to paganism and its usages. The Nicolaitans disobeyed the command issued to the gentile churches, by the apostolic council held at Jerus in 49–50 AD, that they should refrain from the eating of "things sacrificed to idols" (Acts **15** 29). Such a restriction, though seemingly hard, in that it prevented the Christian communities from joining in public festivals, and so brought upon them suspicion and dislike, was yet necessary to prevent a return to a pagan laxity of morals. To this danger the Nicolaitans were themselves a glaring witness, and therefore St. John was justified in condemning them. In writing to the Corinthians, St. Paul gives warning against the same evil practices, basing his arguments on consideration for the weaker brethren (cf 1 Cor **8**).

Literature.—Simcox, "Rev" in the *Cambridge Bible;* H. Cowan in *HDB*, art. "Nicolaitans"; H. B. Swete, *The Apocalypse of St. John*, lxx ff, 27, 28, 37.

C. M. Kerr

NICOLAÜS, nik-ō-lā′us (EV), **NICOLAS,** nik′ō-las (**Νικόλαος,** *Nikólaos*): One of "the seven" chosen to have the oversight of "the daily ministration" to the poor of the church in Jerus (Acts **6** 5). He is called "a proselyte of Antioch"; the other 6 were therefore probably Jews by birth. This is the first recorded case of the admission of a proselyte into office in the Christian church. Some of the church Fathers (Irenaeus, Hippolytus, Pseudo-Tertullian) state that he was the founder of the sect called NICOLAITANS (q.v.) (Rev **2** 15). Other Fathers seem to suggest that this was a vain claim made by this sect in seeking apostolic authority for their opinions. It may be that the opinions of this sect were an antinomian exaggeration of the preaching of Nicolaüs. S. F. HUNTER

NICOPOLIS, ni-kop′ō-lis (**Νικόπολις,** *Nikópolis*): A city in Pal, half-way between Jaffa and Jerus, now called *Ammâs*, mentioned in 1 Macc **3** 40.57 and **9** 50. The earlier city (Emmaus) was burnt by Quintilius Varus, but was rebuilt in 223 AD as Nicopolis.

The Nicopolis, however, to which Paul urges Titus to come (*πρός με εἰς Νικόπολιν, ἐκεῖ γὰρ κέκρικα παραχειμάσαι, prós me eis Nikópolin, ekeí gár kékrika paracheimásai* [Tit **3** 12]) is probably the city of that name situated on the southwest promontory of Epirus. If this view is correct, the statement made by some writers that from *Eastern* Greece (Athens, Thessalonica, Philippi, Corinth) Paul's labors extended to Italy, that he never visited *Western* Greece, requires modification. It is true that we do not hear of his preaching at Patras, Zacynthus, Cephallenia, Corcyra (the modern Corfu), which, as a way-station to and from Sicily, always held preëminence among the Ionian islands; but there can be little doubt that, if his plan of going to Nicopolis was carried out, he desired to evangelize the province of Epirus (as well as Acarnania) in Western Greece. Indeed, it was in this very city of Nicopolis, probably, that he was arrested and taken to Rome for trial—during one of the winters between 64–67 AD.

Nicopolis was situated only a few miles N. of the modern Prevesa, the chief city of Epirus today, the city which the Greeks bombarded in 1912 in the hope of wresting it from the Turks. The ancient city was founded by Augustus, whose camp happened to be pitched there the night before the famous fight with Antony (31 BC). The gulf, called Ambracia in ancient times, is now known as Arta. On the south side was Actium, where the battle was fought. Directly across, only half a mile distant, on the northern promontory, was the encampment of Augustus. To commemorate the victory over his antagonist, the Rom emperor built a city on the exact spot where his army had encamped ("Victory City"). On the hill now called Michalitzi, on the site of his own tent, he built a temple to Neptune and instituted games in honor of Apollo, who was supposed to have helped him in the sea-fight. Nicopolis soon became the metropolis of Epirus, with an autonomous constitution, according to Gr custom. But in the time of the emperor Julian (362) the city had fallen into decay, at least in part. It was plundered by the Goths, restored by Justinian, and finally disappeared entirely in the Middle Ages, so far as the records of history show. One document has *Νικόπολις ἡ νῦν Πρέβεζα, Nikópolis hē nún Prébeza*, "N., which is now Prebeza." In the time of Augustus, however, Nicopolis was a flourishing town. The emperor concentrated here the population of Aetolia and Acarnania, and made the city a leading member of the Amphictyonic Council. There are considerable ruins of the ancient city, including two theaters, a stadium, an aqueduct, etc.

LITERATURE.—Kuhn, *Ueber die Entstehung der Städte der Alten*.

J. E. HARRY

NIGER, nī′jẽr (**Νίγερ,** *Níger*). See SIMEON, (5).

NIGH, nī. See NEAR.

NIGHT, nīt (for the natural usage and the various terms, see DAY AND NIGHT):

Figurative uses: The word "night" (לַיְלָה, *laylāh*, or לַיִל, *layil*) is sometimes used **fig.** in the OT.

1. In the OT

Thus Moses compares the brevity of time, the lapse of a thousand years, to "a watch in the night" (Ps **90** 4). Adversity is depicted by it in such places as Job **35** 10; cf Isa **8** 20; Jer **15** 9. Disappointment and despair are apparently depicted by it in the "burden of Dumah" (Isa **21** 11.12); and spiritual blindness, coming upon the false prophets (Mic **3** 6); again sudden and overwhelming confusion (Am **5** 8; Isa **59** 10 AV, נֶשֶׁף, *nesheph*, "twilight" as in RV).

On the lips of Jesus (Jn **9** 4) it signifies the end of opportunity to labor; repeated in that touching

2. In the NT

little allegory spoken to His disciples when He was called to the grave of Lazarus (Jn **11** 9.10). Paul also uses the figure in reference to the Parousia (Rom **13** 12), where "night" seems to refer to the present aeon and "day" to the aeon to come. He also uses it in 1 Thess **5** 5.7 where the status of the redeemed is depicted by "day," that of the unregenerate by "night," again, as the context shows, in reference to the Parousia. In Rev **21** 25 and **22** 5, the passing of the "night" indicates the realization of that to which the Parousia looked forward, the establishment of the kingdom of God forever. See also Delitzsch, *Iris*, 35. HENRY E. DOSKER

NIGHT-HAWK, nīt′hôk (תַּחְמָס, *taḥmāṣ*, "tachmas"; **γλαύξ,** *glaúx*, but sometimes *strouthós*, and *seirēnos;* Lat *caprimulgus*): The Heb *taḥmāṣ* means "to tear and scratch the face," so that it is very difficult to select the bird intended by its use. Any member of the eagle, vulture, owl or hawk families driven to desperation would "tear and scratch" with the claws and bite in self-defence. The bird is mentioned only in the lists of abominations (see Lev **11** 16; Dt **14** 15). There are three good reasons why the night-hawk or night-jar, more properly, was intended. The lists were sweeping and included almost every common bird unfit for food. Because of its peculiar characteristics it had been made the object of fable and superstition. It fed on wing at night and constantly uttered weird cries. Lastly, it was a fierce fighter when disturbed in brooding or raising its young. Its habit was to lie on its back and fight with beak and claw with such ferocity that it seemed very possible that it would "tear and scratch the face." Some commentators insist that the bird intended was an owl, but for the above reasons the night-jar seems most probable; also several members of the owl family were clearly indicated in the list. See HAWK.

GENE STRATTON-PORTER

NIGHT-MONSTER, nīt′mon-stẽr (לִילִית, *līlīth*, LXX **ὀνοκένταυρος,** *onokentaúros;* Vulg *lamia*):

I. THE ACCEPTED TRANSLATION
   1. Professor Rogers' Statement
   2. Exception to the Statement
II. FOLKLORE IN THE OT
   1. Paucity of References
   2. References in Highly Poetical Passages
   3. The References Allusive
   4. Possibility of Non-mythological Interpretation
   5. The Term *lilith.*

I. The Accepted Translation.—The term "night-monster" is a hypothetical tr of the Heb term לִילִית, *līlīth*, used once only, in Isa **34** 14. The word is tr[d] in AV "screech-owl," m "night monster," RV "night-monster," m "Lilith." The term "night-monster" is also an interpretation, inasmuch as it implies that the Heb word is a Bab loan-word, and that the reference indicates a survival of primitive folklore.

Concerning this weird superstition, and its strange, single appearance in the Book of Isa, Professor Rogers has this to say: "The *lil*, or ghost, was a night-demon of terrible and baleful influence upon men, and only to be cast out with many incantations. The *lil* was attended by a serving maid, the *ardat lili* ("maid of night"), which in the Sem development was transferred into the fem. *lilitu*. It is most curious and interesting to observe that this ghost-demon lived on through the history of the Bab religion, and was carried over into the Heb religion, there to find one single mention in the words of one of the Heb prophets" (*Rel. of Assyria and Babylonia*, 76, 77).

1. Professor Rogers' Statement

Exception is to be taken to this statement, admitting the etymological assumption upon which it rests, that "lilith" is a word in mythology, on the ground that the conception of a night-demon has no place in the religion of the Hebrews as exhibited in the Scriptures. It is certainly worthy of more than passing notice that a conception which is very prominent in the Bab mythology, and is worked out with great fulness of doctrinal and ritualistic detail, has, among the Hebrews, so far receded into the background as to receive but one mention in the Bible, and that a bald citation without detail in a highly poetic passage.

2. Exception to the Statement

The most that can possibly be said, with safety, is that if the passage in Isa is to be taken as a survival of folklore, it is analogous to those survivals of obsolete ideas still to be found in current speech, and in the lit. of the modern world (see LUNATIC). There is no evidence of active participation in this belief, or even of interest in it as such, on the part of the prophetical writer. On the contrary, the nature of the reference implies that the word was used simply to add a picturesque detail to a vivid, imaginative description. All positive evidence of Heb participation in this belief belongs to a later date (see Buxtorf's *Lex.*, s.v. "Talmud").

II. Folklore in the OT.—Attention has been called elsewhere to the meagerness, in the matter of detail, of OT demonology (see DEMON, DEMONOLOGY; COMMUNION WITH DEMONS). A kindred fact of great importance should be briefly noticed here, namely, that the traces of mythology and popular folklore in the Bible are surprisingly faint and indistinct. We have the following set of items in which such traces have been discovered: "Rahab" (רַהַב, *rāhābh*), mentioned in Job **9** 13; **26** 12; Isa **51** 9; "Tanin" (תַּנִּין, *tannīn*), Isa **27** 1; "Leviathan" (לִוְיָתָן, *liwyāthān*), Job **3** 8; Ps **74** 14; Isa **27** 1; Ezk **29** 3; Job **41** *passim;* the "serpent in the sea," in Am **9** 3; "Seirim" (שְׂעִירִים, *se'īrīm*), 2 Ch **11** 15; Lev **17** 7; 2 K **23** 8; Isa **13** 21; **34** 14; "Alukah" (עֲלוּקָה, *'ălūkāh*), Prov **30** 15; "Azazel" (עֲזָאזֵל, *'ăzā'zēl*), Lev **16** 8.10.26; "Lilith" (ut sup.), Isa **34** 14.15.

A review of these passages brings certain very interesting facts to light.

The references are few in number. Rahab is mentioned 3 t; Tanin (in this connection), once; Leviathan, 5 t; the serpent in the sea, once; Seirim, 5 t (twice with reference to idols); Alukah, once; Azazel, 3 t in one ch and in the same connection; Lilith, once.

1. Paucity of References

These references, with the single exception of Azazel to which we shall return a little later, are all in highly poetical passages. On general grounds of common-sense we should not ascribe conscious and deliberate mythology to writers or speakers of the Bible in passages marked by imaginative description and poetic imagery, any more than we should ascribe such beliefs to modern writers under like circumstances. Poetry is the realm of truth and not of matter of fact. In passages of this tenor, mythology may explain the word itself and justify its appropriateness, it does not explain the use of the term or disclose the personal view of the writer.

2. References in Highly Poetical Passages

All these references are in the highest degree allusive. They exhibit no exercise of the mythological fancy and have received no embroidery with details. This is most significant. So far as our specific references are concerned, we are dealing with *petrified mythology*, useful as literary embellishment, but no longer interesting in itself.

3. The References Allusive

Every one of these words is sufficiently obscure in origin and uncertain in meaning to admit the possibility of a non-mythological interpretation; indeed, in several of the parallels a non-mythological use is evident. Bible-Dict. writers are apt to say (e.g. concerning *līlīth*) that there is *no doubt* concerning the mythological reference. The reader may discover for himself that the lexicographers are more cautious (see *BDB*, in loc.). The use of "Rahab" in Job **26** 12 is not mythological for the simple reason that it is **figurative;** the use of "Leviathan" in Isa **27** 1 and Ezk **29** 3 comes under the same category. In Job **40** and **41,** if the identification of behemoth and leviathan with hippopotamus and crocodile be allowed to stand and the mythological significance of the two be admitted, we have the stage where mythology has become a fixed and universal symbolism which can be used to convey truth apart from the belief in it as reality (see LEVIATHAN; "Job," *New Cent. Bible*, p. 335; *Meth. Rev.*, May, 1913, 429 ff). The sea serpent of Am **9** 3 is not necessarily the dragon or *Tiamat*, and the use of the term is merely suggestive. The term *se'īr* is in literal use for "he-goat" (Nu **15** 24, et al.) and is doubtful throughout. Ewald translates it "he-goat" in Isa **34** 14 and "Satyr" in **13** 21. It means lit. "shaggy monster" (Vulg *pilosus*). We do not hesitate on the basis of the evidence to erase "Alukah" (Prov **30** 15, RV "horse-leech," by some tr[d] "vampire") and "Azazel" (Lev **16** 8, etc), interpreted as a "demon of the desert," from the list of mythological words altogether. As ripe a scholar as Perowne ("Prov," *Cambridge Bible*) combats the idea of vampire, and Kellogg ("Lev," *Expositor's Bible*, in loc.) has simply put to rout the mythological-demonic interpretation of Azazel. Even in the case of *līlīth* the derivation is obscure, and the objections urged against the demonic idea by Alexander have not altogether lost their force (see *Comm. on Isa*, in loc.). There is a close balance of probabilities in one direction or the other.

4. Possibility of Non-mythological Interpretation

One further fact with regard to *līlīth* must be considered. The term occurs in a list of creatures, the greater part of which are matter-of-fact animals or birds. A comparative glance at a half-dozen trs of the passage Isa **34** 11–14 will convince any reader

5. The Term *lilith*

that there are a great many obscure and difficult words to be found in the list. Following Delitzsch's tr we have: "pelican," "hedge-hog," "horned-owl," "raven," "wild-dog," "ostrich," "forest-demon" (*seʿīr*), "night-monster." This is a curious mixture of real and imaginary creatures. Alexander acutely observes that there is too much or too little mythology in the passage. One of two conclusions would seem to follow from a list so constructed: Either all these creatures are looked upon as more or less demonic (see Whitehouse, *HDB*, art. "Demon," with which cf W. M. Alexander, *Demonic Possession in the NT*, 16), or, as seems to the present writer far more probable, none in the list is considered otherwise than as supposed literal inhabitants of the wilderness. The writer of Isa **34** 14, who was not constructing a scientific treatise, but using his imagination, has constructed a list in which are combined real and imaginary creatures popularly supposed to inhabit unpeopled solitudes. There still remains a by no means untenable supposition that none of the terms necessarily are mythological in this particular passage.

Louis Matthews Sweet

NIGHT-WATCH, nīt'woch (אַשְׁמוּרָה בַּלַּיְלָה, *'ashmūrah ba-laylāh*, "watch in the night"): One of the three or four divisions of the night. See Watch; Time.

NILE, nīl (Νεῖλος, *Neilos*, meaning not certainly known; perhaps refers to the color of the water, as black or blue. This name does not occur in the Heb of the OT or in the Eng. tr):

On the Bank of the Nile.

A river of North Africa, the great river of Egypt. The name employed in the OT to designate the Nile is in the Heb יְאֹר, *yeʾōr*, Egyp *ăūr*, earlier, *ătūr*, usually trd "river," also occasionally "canals" (Ps **78** 44; Ezk **29** 3 ff). In a general way it means all the water of Egypt. The Nile is also the principal river included in the phrase נַהֲרֵי־כוּשׁ, *nahărē kūsh*, "rivers of Ethiopia" (Isa **18** 1). Poetically the Nile is called יָם, *yām*, "sea" (Job **41** 31; Nah **3** 8; probably Isa **18** 2), but this is not a name of the river. שִׁיחוֹר, *shīḥōr*, not always written fully, has also been interpreted in a mistaken way of the Nile (see Shihor). Likewise נַהַר מִצְרַיִם, *nahar miçrayim*, "brook of Egypt," a border stream in no way connected with the Nile, has sometimes been mistaken for that river. See River of Egypt.

I. The Nile in Physical Geography.—The Nile is formed by the junction of the White Nile and the Blue Nile in lat. 15° 45′ N. and long. 32° 45′ E. The Blue N. rises in the highlands of Abyssinia, lat. 12° 30′ N., long. 35° E., and flows N.W. 850 miles to its junction with the White N. The White N., the principal branch of the N., rises in Victoria Nyanza, a great lake in Central Africa, a few miles N. of the equator, long. 33° E. (more exactly the N. may be said to rise at the headwaters of the Ragera River, a small stream on the other side of the lake, 3° S. of the equator), and flows N. in a tortuous channel, 1,400 miles to its junction with the Blue N. From this junction-point the N. flows N. through Nubia and Egypt 1,900 miles and empties into the Mediterranean Sea, in lat. 32° N., through 2 mouths, the Rosetta, E. of Alexandria, and the Damietta, W. of Port Said. There were formerly 7 mouths scattered along a coast-line of 140 miles.

1. Description

The Nile originated in the Tertiary period and has continued from that time to this, though by the subsidence of the land 220 ft. along the Mediterranean shore in the Pluvial times, the river was very much shortened. Later in the Pluvial times the land rose again and is still rising slowly.

2. Geological Origin

Cultivable Egypt is altogether the product of the N., every particle of the soil having been brought down by the river from the heart of the continent and deposited along the banks and esp. in the delta at the mouth of the river. The banks have risen higher and higher and extended farther and farther back by the deposit of the sediment, until the valley of arable land varies in width in most parts from 3 or 4 miles to 9 or 10 miles. The mouth of the river, after the last elevation of the land in Pluvial times, was at first not far from the lat. of Cairo. From this point northward the river has built up a delta of 140 miles on each side, over which it spreads itself and empties into the sea through its many mouths.

3. The Making of Egypt

The watering of Egypt by the inundation from the N. is the most striking feature of the physical character of that land, and one of the most interesting and remarkable physical phenomena in the world. The inundation is produced by the combination of an indirect and a direct cause. The indirect cause is the rain and melting snow on the equatorial mountains in Central Africa, which maintains steadily a great volume of water in the White N. The direct cause is torrential rains in the highlands of Abyssinia which send down the Blue N. a sudden great increase in the volume of water. The inundation has two periods each year. The first begins about July 15 and continues until near the end of September. After a slight recession, the river again rises early in October in the great inundation. High Nile is in October, 25 to 30 ft., low Nile in June, about 12½ ft. The Nilometer for recording the height of the water of inundation dates from very early times. Old Nilometers are found still *in situ* at Edfu and Assuan. The watering and fertilizing of the land is the immediate effect of the inundation; its ultimate result is that making of Egypt which is still in progress. The settling of the sediment from the water upon the land has raised the surface of the valley about 1 ft. in 300 to 400 years, about 9 to 10 ft. near Cairo since the beginning of the early great temples. The deposit varies greatly at other places. As the deposit of sediment has been upon the bottom of the river, as well as upon the surface of the land, though more slowly, on account of the swiftness of the current, the river also has been lifted up, and thus the inundation has extended farther and farther to the E., and the W., as the level of the valley would permit, depositing the sediment and thus making the cultivable land wider, as well as the soil deeper, year by year. At Heliopolis, a little N. of Cairo, this extension to the E. has been 3 to 4 miles since the building of the great temple there.

4. The Inundation

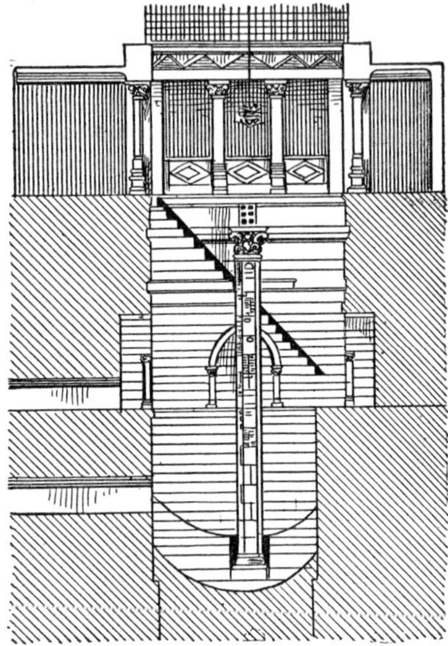

Cross-Section of Nilometer.

At Luxor, about 350 miles farther up the river, where the approach toward the mountains is much steeper, the extension of the good soil to the E. and the W. is inconsiderable.

5. The Infiltration

The ancient Egyptians were right in calling all the waters of Egypt the N., for wherever water is obtained by digging it is simply the N. percolating through the porous soil. This percolation is called the infiltration of the N. It always extends as far on either side of the N. as the level of the water in the river at the time will permit. This infiltration, next to the inundation, is the most important physical phenomenon in Egypt. By means of it much of the irrigation of the land during the dry season is carried on from wells. It has had its influence also in the political and religious changes of the country (cf below).

II. The Nile in History.—Some of the early temples were located near the N., probably because of the deification of the river. The rising of the surface of the land, and at the same time of the bed of the river, from the inundation lifted both Egypt and its great river, but left the temples down at the old level. In time the infiltration of the river from its new higher level reached farther and farther and rose to a higher level until the floor of these old temples was under water even at the time of lowest N., and then gods and goddesses, priests and ceremonial all were driven out. At least two of the greatest temples and most sacred places, Heliopolis and Memphis, had to be abandoned. Probably this fact had as much to do with the downfall of Egypt's religion, as its political disasters and the actual destruction of its temples by eastern invaders. Nature's God had driven out the gods of Nature.

1. The Location of Temples

Some prehistoric burials are found on the higher ground, as at *Kefr 'Amar*. A thousand years of history would be quite sufficient to teach Egyptians that the N. was still making Egypt. Thenceforth, cemeteries were located at the mountains on the eastern and the western boundaries of the valley. Here they continue to this day, for the most part still entirely above the waters of the inundation—and usually above the reach of the infiltration.

2. The Location of Cemeteries

3. Dams in the Nile

The widening of the cultivable land by means of long canals which carried the water from far up the river to levels higher than that of the inundation, farther down the river was practised from very early times. The substitution of dams for long canals was reserved for modern engineering skill. Three great dams have been made: the first a little N. of Cairo, the greatest at Assuan, and the last near Asyut.

4. Famines

Famines in Egypt are always due to failure in the quantity of the waters of inundation. Great famines have not been frequent. The cause of the failure in the water of inundation is now believed to be not so much a lack of the water of inundation from the Blue N. as the choking of the channel of the White N. in the great marsh land of the Sudan by the *sud*, a kind of sedge, sometimes becoming such a tangled mass as to close the channel and impede the flow of the regular volume of water so that the freshet in the Blue N. causes but little inundation at the usual time, and during the rest of the year the N. is so low from the same cause that good irrigation by canals and wells is impossible. A channel through the *sud* is now kept open by the Egyp government.

III. The Nile in Religion.—One of the gods of the Egyp pantheon was Hapi, the Nile. In early times

1. The Nile as a God

it divided the honors with Ra, the sun-god. No wonder it was so. If the Egyptians set out to worship Nature-gods at all, surely then the sun and the Nile first.

2. The Nile in Osirian Myth

The origin of the Osirian myth is still much discussed. Very much evidence, perhaps conclusive evidence, can be adduced to prove that it rose originally from the Nile; that Osiris was first of all the N., then the water of the N., then the soil, the product of the waters of the N., and then Egypt, the N. and all that it produced.

3. The Celestial Nile

Egypt was the Egyptian's little world, and Egypt was the Nile. It was thus quite natural for the Egyptians in considering the celestial world to image it in likeness of their own world with a celestial Nile flowing through it. It is so represented in the mythology, but the conception of the heavens is vague. M. G. Kyle

NIMRAH, nim'ra (נִמְרָה, *nimrāh;* B, Νάμβρα, *Námbra*, A, Ἀμβράμ, *Ambrám*), or **BETH-NIMRAH** (בֵּית נִמְרָה, *bēth nimrāh;* B, Ναμράμ, *Namrám*, A, Ἀμβράν, *Ambrán* [Nu **32** 36], B, Βαιθαναβρά, *Baithanabrá*, A, Βηθαμνά, *Bēthamná* [Josh **13** 27]): These two names evidently refer to the same place; but there is no reason to think, as some have done, from the similarity of the names, that it is identical with Nimrim (q.v.). On the contrary, the indications of the passages cited point to a site E. of the Jordan valley and N. of the Dead Sea. About 11 miles N.E. of the mouth of the Jordan, where *Wâdy Nimrin*, coming down from the eastern up-lands, enters the plain, stands a hill called *Tell Nimrin*, with tombs and certain traces of ancient building. This may be certainly identified with Nimrah and Beth-nimrah; and it corresponds to Bethnambris of *Onom*, which lay 5 Rom miles N. of Livias.

W. Ewing

NIMRIM, nim'rim (מֵי־נִמְרִים, *mē nimrīm;* B, Νεβρείν, *Nebreín*, A, Ἐβρίμ, *Ebrím* [Jer **48** 34], τὸ ὕδωρ τῆς Νιμρείμ, *tó húdōr tēs Nimreím* [Isa **15** 6]): The meaning appears to be "pure" or "wholesome water." The name occurs only in Isa **15** 6 and Jer **48** 34 in oracles against Moab. In each case it is mentioned in association with Zoar and Horonaim. It is therefore probably to be sought to the S.E. of the Dead Sea. *Onom* places a town, Bennamareim, to the N. of Zoar, and identifies it with the OT "Nimrim," as it seems, correctly. The name is still found in *Wâdy Numeireh*, opening on the sea at *Burj Numeirah*, N. of *Ghōr eṣ-Ṣāfiyeh*. The waters of Nimrim may be sought either in *Moiyet Numeirah* or in the spring higher up, where lie the ruins of a town in a well-watered and fruitful district (Buhl, *GAP*, 272). W. Ewing

NIMROD, nim'rod (נִמְרֹד, *nimrōdh;* Νεβρώδ, *Nebrōd*): A descendant of Ham, mentioned in "the generations of the sons of Noah" (Gen **10**; cf 1 Ch **1** 10) as a son of Cush. He established his kingdom "in the land of Shinar," including the cities "Babel, and Erech, and Accad, and Calneh" (ver 10), of which only Babel, or Babylon, and Erech, or Uruk, have been identified with certainty. "The land of Shinar" is the old name for Southern Babylonia, afterward called Chaldaea (*'ereç kasdīm*), and was probably more extensive in territory than the *Šumer* of the inscriptions in the ancient royal title, "King of Shumer and Accad," since Accad is included here in Shinar. Nimrod, like other great kings of Mesopotamian lands, was a mighty hunter, possibly the mightiest and the prototype of them all, since to his name had attached itself the proverb: "Like Nimrod a mighty hunter before Jeh" (ver 9). In the primitive days of Mesopotamia, as also in Pal, wild animals were so numerous that they became a menace to life and property (Ex **23** 29; Lev **26** 22); therefore the king as benefactor and protector of his people hunted these wild beasts. The early conquest of the cities of Babylonia, or their federation into one great kingdom, is here ascribed to Nimrod. Whether the founding and colonization of Assyria (ver 11) are to be ascribed to N. will be determined by the exegesis of the text. EV reads: "Out of that land *he* [i.e. Nimrod] went forth into Assyria, and builded Nineveh," etc, this tr assigning the rise of Assyria to N., and apparently being sustained by Mic **5** 5.6 (cf J. M. P. Smith, "Micah," *ICC*, in loc.); but ARVm renders: "Out of that land went forth *Asshur*, and builded Nineveh," which tr is more accurate exegetically and not in conflict with Mic **5** 6, if in the latter "land of Nimrod" be understood, not as parallel with, but as supplemental to, Assyria, and therefore as Babylon (cf comms. of Cheyne, Pusey, S. Clark, in loc.).

N. has not been identified with any mythical hero or historic king of the inscriptions. Some have sought identification with Gilgamesh, the flood hero of Babylonia (Skinner, Driver, Delitzsch); others with a later Kassite king (Haupt, Hilprecht), which is quite unlikely; but the most admissible correspondence is with Marduk, chief god of Babylon, probably its historic founder, just as Asshur, the god of Assyria, appears in ver 11 as the founder of the Assyr empire (Wellhausen, Price, Sayce). Lack of identification, however, does not necessarily indicate mythical origin of the name. See Astronomy, II, 11; Babylonia and Assyria, Religion of, IV, 7; Merodach; Orion. Edward Mack

NIMSHI, nim'shī (נִמְשִׁי, *nimshī*): The grandfather of Jehu (2 K **9** 2.14). Jehu's usual designation is "son of Nimshi" (1 K **19** 16).

NINEVEH, nin'ē-ve (נִינְוֵה, *nīnᵉwēh;* Νινευή, *Nineuē*, Νινευΐ, *Nineuí;* Gr and Rom writers, Νῖνος, *Nínos*):

I. Beginnings, Name, Position
  1. First Biblical Mention
  2. Etymology of the Name
  3. Position on the Tigris
II. Nineveh and Its Surroundings
  1. Its Walls
  2. Principal Mounds and Gateways
  3. Extent and Population within the Walls
  4. Extent outside the Walls
  5. Calah, Resen and Rehoboth-Ir
  6. Khorsabad
  7. Sherif Khan and Selamieh
  8. Nimroud

I. Beginnings, Name, Position.—The first Bib. mention of Nineveh is in Gen **10** 11, where it is stated that Nimrod (q.v.) or Asshur went out into Assyria, and builded N. and Rehoboth-Ir, and Calah, and Resen between N. and Calah, with the addition, "the same is the great city." Everything indicates that these statements are correct, for N. was certainly at one time under Bab rule, and was at first not governed by Assyr kings, but by *iššakē* or viceroys of Aššur, the old capital. To all appearance N. took its name from the Bab Nina near Lagaš in South Babylonia, on the Euphrates, from which early foundation it was probably colonized. The native name appears as *Ninua* or *Ninâ* (*Ninaa*), written with the character for "water enclosure" with that for "fish" inside, implying a connection between *Ninâ* and the Sem *nūn*, "fish." The Bab Nina was a place where fish were very abundant, and Ištar or Nina, the goddess of the city, was associated with Nin-maḫ, Merodach's spouse, as goddess of reproduction. Fish are also plentiful in the Tigris at *Mosul*, the modern town on the other side of the river, and this may have influenced the choice of the site by the Bab settlers, and the foundation there of the great temple of Ištar or Nina. The date of this foundation is unknown, but it may have taken place about 3000 BC.

1. First Biblical Mention

2. Etymology of the Name

N. lay on the eastern bank of the Tigris, at the point where the Khosr falls into that stream. The outline of the wall is rectangular on the W., but of an irregular shape on the E. The western fortifications run from N.W. to S.E., following, roughly, the course of the river, which now flows about 1,500 yards from the walls, instead of close to them, as anciently.

3. Its Position on the Tigris

II. Nineveh and Its Surroundings.—According to the late G. Smith, the southwestern wall has a length of about 2½ miles, and is joined at its western corner by the northwestern wall, which runs in a northeasterly direction for about 1⅓ miles. The northeastern wall, starting here, runs at first in a southeasterly direction, but turns southward, gradually approaching the southwestern wall, to which, at the end of about 3¼ miles, it is joined by a short wall, facing nearly S., rather more than half a mile long.

1. Its Walls

The principal mounds are Kouyunjik, a little N.E. of the village of *'Amusiyeh*, and Nebi-Yunas, about 1,500 yards to the S.E. Both of these lie just within the S.W. wall. Extensive remains of buildings occupy the fortified area. Numerous openings occur in the walls, many of them ancient, though some seem to have been made after the abandonment of the site. The principal gate on the N.W. was guarded by winged bulls (see Layard, *Monuments of Nineveh*, 2d series, pl. 3; *Nineveh and Babylon*, 120). Other gates gave access to the various commercial roads of the country, those on the E. passing through the curved outworks and the double line of fortifications which protected the northeastern wall from attack on that side, where the Ninevites evidently considered that they had most to fear.

2. Principal Mounds and Gateways

According to G. Smith, the circuit of the inner wall is about 8 miles, and Captain Jones, who made a trigonometrical survey in 1854, estimated that, allotting to each inhabitant 50 sq. yards, the city may have contained 174,000 inhabitants. If the statement in Jon **4** 11, that the city contained 120,000 persons who could not discern between their right hand and their left, be intended to give the number of the city's children only, then the population must have numbered about 600,000, and more than three cities of the same extent would have been needed to contain them. It has therefore been supposed—and that with great probability—that there was a large extension of the city outside its walls. This is not only indicated by Jon **3** 3, where it is described as "an exceeding great city of *three days' journey*" to traverse, but also by the extant ruins, which stretch S.E. along the banks of the Tigris as far as *Nimroud* (Calah), while its northern extension may have been regarded as including Khorsabad.

3. Extent and Population within the Walls

4. Extent outside the Walls

Concerning the positions of two of the cities mentioned with N., namely, Calah and Resen, there can be no doubt, notwithstanding that Resen has not yet been identified—Calah is the modern *Nimroud*, and Resen lay between that site and N. The name Rehoboth-Ir has not yet been found in the inscriptions, but Fried. Delitzsch has suggested that it may be the *rêbit Ninua* of the inscriptions, N.E. of N. If this be the case, the N. of Jonah contained within it all the places in Gen **10** 11.12, and Khorsabad besides.

5. Calah, Resen and Rehoboth-Ir

Taking the outlying ruins from N. to S., we begin with Khorsabad (*Dûr-Šarru-kîn* or *Dûr-Šargina*), 12 miles N.E. of Kouyunjik, the great palace mound of N. proper. Khorsabad is a great inclosure about 2,000 yards square, with the remains of towers and gateways. The palace mound lies on its northwest face, and consists of an extensive platform with the remains of Sargon's palace and its temple, with a *ziqqurat* or temple-tower similar to those at Babylon, Borsippa, Calah and elsewhere. This last still shows traces of the tints symbolical of the 7 planets of which its stages were, seemingly, emblematic. The palace ruins show numerous halls, rooms and passages, many of which were faced with slabs of coarse alabaster, sculptured in relief with military operations, hunting-scenes, mythological figures, etc, while the principal entrances were flanked with the finest winged human-headed bulls which Assyr art has so far revealed. The palace was built about 712 BC, and was probably destroyed by fire when N. fell in 606 BC, sharing the same fate. Some of the slabs and winged bulls are in the Louvre and the British Museum, but most of the antiquarian spoils were lost in the Tigris by the sinking of the rafts upon which they were loaded after being discovered.

6. Khorsabad

Another outlying suburb was probably Tarbiṣu, now represented by the ruins at *Sherif Khan*, about 3 miles N. of Kouyunjik. In this lay a temple—"palace" Sennacherib calls it—dedicated to Nergal. Anciently it must have been a place of some importance, as Esarhaddon seems to have built a palace there, as well as a "seat" for his eldest son, Aššur-banî-âpli. The site of Resen, "between N. and Calah," is thought to be the modern *Selamîeh*, 12 miles S. of N., and 3 miles N. of *Nimroud* (Calah). It is in the form of an irregular inclosure on a high mound overlooking the Tigris, with a surface of about 400 acres.

7. Sherif Khan and Selamîeh

No remains of buildings, sculptures or inscriptions have, however, been found there.

8. Nimroud

After N. itself (Kouyunjik), the ruins known as *Nimroud*, 14 or 15 miles S.E., are the most important. They mark the site of the ancient Calah, and have already been described under that heading (see p. 539). As there stated, the stone-faced temple-tower seems to be referred to by Ovid, and is apparently also mentioned by Xenophon (see Resen). The general tendency of the accumulated references to these sites supports the theory that they were regarded as belonging to N., if not by the Assyrians themselves (who knew well the various municipal districts), at least by the foreigners who had either visited the city or had heard or read descriptions of it.

III. The Palaces at Nineveh Proper.—The palaces at N. were built upon extensive artificial platforms between 30 and 50 ft. high, either of sun-dried brick, as at *Nimroud*, or of earth and rubbish, as at Kouyunjik. It is thought that they were faced with masonry, and that access was gained to them by means of flights of deep steps, or sloping pathways. Naturally it is the plan of the basement floor alone that can at present be traced, any upper stories that may have existed having long since disappeared. The halls and rooms discovered were faced with slabs of alabaster or other stone, often sculptured with bas-reliefs depicting warlike expeditions, the chase, religious ceremonies and divine figures. The depth of the accumulations over these varies from a few inches to about 30 ft., and if the amount in some cases would seem to be excessive, it is thought that this may have been due either to the existence of upper chambers, or to the extra height of the room. The chambers, which are grouped around courtyards, are long and narrow, with small square rooms at the ends. The partition walls vary from 6 to 15 ft. in thickness, and are of sun-dried brick, against which the stone paneling was fixed. As in the case of the Bab temples and palaces, the rooms and halls open into each other, so that, to gain access to those farthest from the courtyard entrance, one or more halls or chambers had to be traversed. No traces of windows have been discovered, and little can therefore be said as to the method of lighting, but the windows were either high up, or light was admitted through openings in the roof.

Entrance to Kouyunjik.

1. The Palace of Sennacherib

The palace of Sennacherib lay in the southeast corner of the platform, and consisted of a courtyard surrounded on all four sides by numerous long halls, and rooms, of which the innermost were capable of being rendered private. It was in this palace that were found the reliefs depicting the siege of Lachish, with the representation of Sennacherib seated on his "standing" throne, while the captives and the spoil of the city passed before him. The grand entrance was flanked by winged bulls facing toward the spectator as he entered. They were in couples, back to back, on each side of the doorway, and between each pair the ancient Bab hero-giant, carrying in one hand the "boomerang," and holding tightly with his left arm a struggling lion (Layard, *Nineveh and Babylon,* 137) was represented, just as at his father Sargon's palace at Khorsabad. The upper part of these imposing figures had been destroyed, but they were so massive, that the distinguished explorer attributed their overthrow not to the act of man, but to some convulsion of Nature.

2. The Palace of Aššur-banî-âpli

In the north of the mound are the ruins of the palace of Aššur-banî-âpli or Assur-bani-pal, discovered by Hormuzd Rassam. His latest plan (*Asshur and the Land of Nimrod,* Cincinnati and New York, 1897, plate facing p. 36) does not give the whole of the structure, much of the building having been destroyed; but the general arrangement of the rooms was upon the traditional lines. The slabs with which they were paneled showed bas-reliefs illustrating the Assyr campaigns against Babylonia, certain Arab tribes, and Elam. As far as they are preserved, the sculptures are wonderfully good, and the whole decorative scheme of the paneled walls, of which, probably, the greater part is forever lost, may be characterized, notwithstanding their defects of perspective and their mannerisms, as nothing less than magnificent. The lion-hunts of the great king, despite the curious treatment of the animals' manes (due to the sculptors' ignorance of the right way to represent hair) are admirable. It would be difficult to improve upon the expressions of fear, rage and suffering on the part of the animals there delineated. The small sculptures showing Aššur-banî-âpli hunting the goat and the wild ass are not less noteworthy, and are executed with great delicacy.

IV. Sennacherib's Description of Nineveh.—In all probability the best description of the city is that

1. The Walls

given by Sennacherib on the cylinder recording his expedition to Tarsus in Cilicia. From ancient times, he says, the circuit of the city had measured 9,300 cubits, and he makes the rather surprising statement that his predecessors had not built either the inner or the outer wall, which, if true, shows how confident they were of their security from attack. He claims to have enlarged the city by 12,515 (cubits). The great defensive wall which he built was called by the Sumerian name of *Bad-imgallabilu-šušu,* which he translates as "the wall whose glory overthrows the enemy." He made the brickwork 40 (cubits) thick, which would probably not greatly exceed the estimate of G. Smith, who reckoned it to have measured about 50 ft. The height of the wall he raised to 180 *tipki*, which, admitting the estimate of Diodorus, should amount to about 100 ft.

2. The Gates—Northwest In this inclosing wall were 15 gates, which he enumerates in full. Three of these were situated in the short northwest wall—the gate of Hadad; the gate of Uru or Hadad of Tarbiṣu (*Sherif Khan*), and the gate of the moon-god Nannar, Sennacherib's own deity. The plans show five openings in the wall on this side, any of which may have been the gate used when going to Tarbiṣu, but that adorned with winged bulls probably furnished the shortest route.

Bas-Relief of Lion-Hunt.

3. The Gates—South and East The gates looking toward the S. and the E. were the Aššur-gate (leading to the old capital); Sennacherib's Ḫalzi-gate; the gate of Šamaš of Gagal, the gate of the god Enlil of Kar-Ninlil, and the "covered gate," which seems to have had the reputation of letting forth the fever-demon. After this are mentioned the Sibaniba-gate, and the gate of Halah in Mesopotamia. This last must have been the extreme northeastern opening, now communicating with the road to Khorsabad, implying that Halah lay in that direction.

4. The Gates—West The gates on the west or river-side of the city were "the gate of Ea, director of my water-springs"; the quay-gate, "bringer of the tribute of my peoples"; the gate of the land of Bari, within which the presents of the Sumuilites entered (brought down by the Tigris from Babylonia, in all probability); the gate of the tribute-palace or armory; and the gate of the god Sar-ur—"altogether 5 gates in the direction of the W." There are about 9 wide openings in the wall on this side, 2 being on each side of the Kouyunjik mound, and 2 on each side of that called Nebi-Yunus. As openings at these points would have endangered the city's safety, these 4 have probably to be eliminated, leaving 2 only N. of Nebi-Yunus, 2 between that and Kouyunjik, and one N. of Kouyunjik. Minor means of exit probably existed at all points where they were regarded as needful.

5. The Outer Wall: the Plantations To the outer wall of the city Sennacherib gave a Sumerian name meaning, "the wall which terrifies the enemy." At a depth of 54 *gar*, the underground water-level, its foundations were laid upon blocks of stone, the object of this great depth being to frustrate undermining. The wall was made "high like a mountain." Above and below the city he laid out plantations, wherein all the sweet-smelling herbs of Heth (Pal and Phoenicia) grew, fruitful beyond those of their homeland. Among them were to be found every kind of mountain-vine, and the plants of all the nations around.

6. The Water-Supply, etc In connection with this, in all probability, he arranged the water-supply, conducting a distant water-course to N. by means of conduits. Being a successful venture, he seems to have watered therewith all the people's orchards, and in winter 1,000 corn fields above and below the city. The force of the increased current in the river Khosr was retarded by the creation of a swamp, and among the reeds which grew there were placed wild fowl, wild swine, and deer(?). Here he repeated his exotic plantations, including trees for wood, cotton (apparently) and seemingly the olive.

7. How the Bas-Reliefs Illustrate the King's Description Sennacherib's bas-reliefs show some of the phases of the work which his cylinder inscriptions describe. We see the winged bulls, which are of colossal dimensions, sometimes lying on their sledges (shaped like boats or Assyr ships), and sometimes standing and supported by scaffolding. The sledges rest upon rollers, and are dragged by armies of captives urged to action by taskmasters with whips. Others force the sledges forward from behind by means of enormous levers whose upper ends are held in position by guy-ropes. Each side has to pull with equal force, for if the higher end of the great lever fell, the side which had pulled too hard suffered in killed and crushed, or at least in bruised, workmen of their number. In the background are the soldiers of the guard, and behind them extensive wooded hills. In other bas-reliefs it is apparently the pleasure-grounds of the palace which are seen. In these the background is an avenue of trees, alternately tall and short, on the banks of a river, whereon are boats, and men riding astride inflated skins, which were much used in those days, as now. On another slab, the great king himself, in his hand-chariot drawn by eunuchs, superintends the work.

How long N. had been the capital of Assyria is unknown. The original capital was Aššur, about 50 miles to the S., and probably this continued to be regarded as the religious and official capital of the country. Aššur-naṣir-âpli seems to have had a

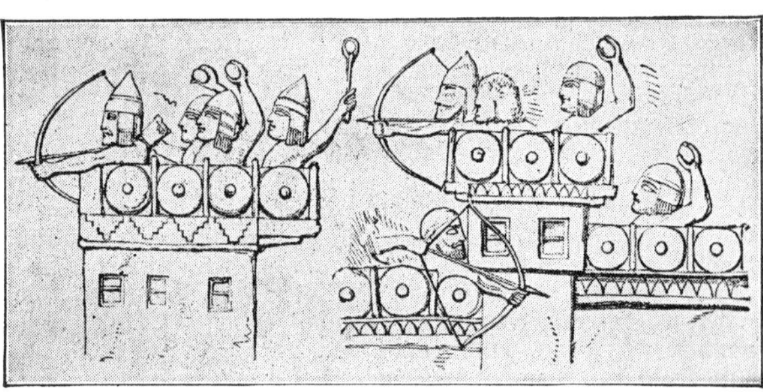

Bas-Relief of Sennacherib Besieging Lachish.
(Brit. Mus.)

8. Nineveh the Later Capital greater liking for Calah (*Nimroud*), and Sargon for Khorsabad, where he had founded a splendid palace. These latter, however, probably never had the importance of N., and attained their position merely on account of the reigning king building a palace and residing there. The period of N.'s supremacy seems to have been from the beginning of the reign of Sennacherib to the end of that of Aššur-banî-âpli, including, probably, the reigns of his successors likewise—a period of about 98 years (704–606 BC).

V. Last Days and Fall of Nineveh.—N., during the centuries of her existence, must have seen many stirring historical events; but the most noteworthy were probably Sennacherib's triumphal entries, including that following the capture of Lachish, the murder of that great conqueror by his sons (the recent theory that he was killed at Babylon needs confirmation), and the ceremonial triumphs of Aššur-banî-âpli—the great and noble Osnappar (Ezr **4** 10). After the reign of Aššur-banî-âpli came his son Aššur-êtil-îlâni, who was succeeded by Sin-šarra-iškun (Saracos), but the history of the country, and also of the city, is practically non-existent during these last two reigns. The Assyr and Bab records are silent with regard to the fall of the city, but Alexander Polyhistor, Abydenus and Syncellus all speak of it. The best account, however, is that of Diodorus Siculus, who refers to a legend that the city could not be taken until the river became its enemy. Arbaces, the Scythian, besieged it, but could not make any impression on it for 2 years. In the 3d year, however, the river (according to Commander Jones, not the Tigris, but the Khosr), being swollen by rains, and very rapid in its current, carried away a portion of the wall, and by this opening the besiegers gained an entrance. The king, recognizing in this the fulfilment of the oracle, gathered together his concubines and eunuchs, and, mounting a funeral pyre which he had caused to be constructed, perished in the flames. This catastrophe is supposed to be referred to in Nah **1** 8: "With an over-running flood he [the Lord] will make a full end of her place [i.e. of N.]," and **2** 6: "The gates of the rivers are opened, and the palace is dissolved." The destruction of the city by fire is probably referred to in **3** 13.15. The picture of the scenes in her streets —the noise of the whip, the rattling wheels, the prancing horses, the bounding chariots (**3** 2 ff), followed by a vivid description of the carnage of the battlefield—is exceedingly striking, and true to their records and their sculptures.

Literature.—The standard books on the discovery and exploration of N. are Layard, *Nineveh and Its Remains* (two vols, 1849); *Nineveh and Babylon* (1853); *Monuments of Nineveh*, 1st and 2d series (plates) (1849 and 1853); and Hormuzd Rassam, *Asshur and the Land of Nimrod* (Cincinnati and New York, 1897).

T. G. Pinches

NINEVEH, LIBRARY OF:

I. The Discovery
II. The Library
III. Writing-Materials
IV. Contents
1. Philology
2. Astronomy and Astrology
3. Religious Texts
4. Law
5. Science
6. Literature
7. History and Chronology
8. Commerce
9. Letters

I. The Discovery.—In the spring of 1850, the workmen of Sir A. H. Layard at Nineveh made an important discovery. In the ruins of the palace of Assur-bani-pal they found a passage which opened into two small chambers leading one into the other. The doorway was guarded on either side by figures of Ea, the god of culture and the inventor of letters, in his robe of fishskin. The walls of the chambers had once been paneled with bas-reliefs, one of which represented a city standing on the shore of a sea that was covered with galleys. Up to the height of a foot or more the floor was piled with clay tablets that had fallen from the shelves on which they had been arranged in order, and the larger number of them was consequently broken. Similar tablets, but in lesser number, were found in the adjoining chambers. After Layard's departure, other tablets were discovered by Mr. Hormuzd Rassam, and then the excavations ceased for many years. The discovery of the Bab version of the account of the Deluge, however, by Mr. George Smith in 1873 led the proprietors of the *Daily Telegraph* to send him to Nineveh in the hope that the missing portions of the story might be found. He had not been excavating there long before he came across a fragment of another version of the story, and then once more the excavations came to an end. Since then expeditions have been sent by the British Museum which have resulted in the recovery of further remains of the ancient library of Nineveh.

II. The Library.—The tablets formed a library in the true sense of the word. Libraries had existed

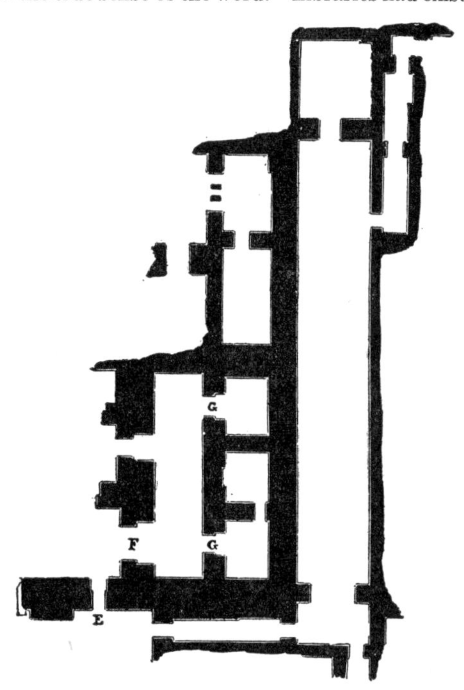

Plan of the Library at Nineveh.

in the cities of Babylonia from a remote date, and the Assyr kings, whose civilization was derived from Babylonia, imitated the example of Babylonia in this as in other respects. The only true book-lover among them, however, was Assur-bani-pal. He was one of the most munificent royal patrons of learning the world has ever seen, and it was to him that the great library of Nineveh owed its existence. New editions were made of older works, and the public and private libraries of Babylonia were ransacked in search of literary treasures.

III. Writing-Materials.—Fortunately for us the ordinary writing-material of the Babylonians and Assyrians was clay. It was more easily procurable than papyrus or parchment, and was specially adapted for the reception of the cuneiform characters. Hence, while the greater part of the old Egyp lit., which was upon papyrus, has perished, that of Babylonia and Assyria has been preserved. In Babylonia the tablets after being inscribed were often merely dried in the sun; in the damper climate of Assyria they were baked in a kiln. As a large amount of text had frequently to be compressed into a small space, the writing is sometimes so minute as to need the assistance of a magnifying glass before it can be read. It is not surprising, therefore, that in the library-chambers of Nineveh Layard found a magnifying lens of crystal, which had been turned on the lathe.

IV. Contents.—The subject-matter of the tablets included all the known branches of knowledge.

1. Philology

Foremost among them are the philological works. The inventors of the cuneiform system of writing had spoken an agglutinative language, called Sumerian, similar to that of the Turks or Finns today; and a considerable part of the early lit. had been written in this language, which to the later Sem Babylonians and Assyrians was what Lat was to the European nations in the Middle Ages. The student was therefore provided with grammars and dictionaries of the two languages, as well as with reading-books and interlinear trs into Assyr of the chief Sumerian texts. Besides this, long lists of the cuneiform characters were drawn up with their phonetic and ideographic values, together with lists of Assyr synonyms, in which, for example, all the equivalents are given of the word "to go." The Assyr lexicographers at times attempted etymologies which are as wide of the mark as similar etymologies given by English lexicographers of a past generation. *Sabattu*, "Sabbath," for instance, is derived from the two Sumerian words, *sa*, "heart," and *bat*, "to end," and so is explained to mean "day of rest for the heart." It is obvious that all this implies an advanced literary culture. People do not begin to compile grammars and dictionaries or to speculate on the origin of words until books and libraries abound and education is widespread.

Inscribed Tablet Impressed with Seals.

2. Astronomy and Astrology

Astronomy occupied a prominent place in Assyr lit., but it was largely mingled with astrology. The Babylonians were the founders of scientific astronomy; they were the first to calculate the dates of lunar and solar eclipses, and to give names to the signs of the Zodiac. Among the contents of the library of Nineveh are reports from the Royal Observatory, relating to the observation of eclipses and the like.

3. Religious Texts

A knowledge of astronomy was needed for the regulation of the calendar, and the calendar was the special care of the priests, as the festivals of the gods and the payment of tithes were dependent upon it. Most of the religious texts went back to the Sumerian period and were accordingly provided with Assyr trs. Some of them were hymns to the gods, others were the rituals used in different temples. There was, moreover, a collection of psalms, as well as numerous mythological texts.

4. Law

The legal lit. was considerable. The earliest law books were in Sumerian, but the great code compiled by Khammurabi, the contemporary of Abraham, was in Sem Babylonian (see ḤAMMURABI). Like English law, Assyro-Babylonian law was case-made, and records of the cases decided from time to time by the judges are numerous.

5. Science

Among scientific works we may class the long lists of animals, birds, fishes, plants and stones, together with geographical treatises, and the pseudo-science of omens. Starting from the belief that where two events followed one another, the first was the cause of the second, an elaborate pseudo-science of augury had been built up, and an enormous lit. arose on the interpretation of dreams, the observation of the liver of animals, etc. Unfortunately Assur-bani-pal had a special predilection for the subject, and the consequence is that his library was filled with works which the Assyriologist would gladly exchange for documents of a more valuable character. Among the scientific works we may also include those on medicine, as well as numerous mathematical tables.

6. Literature

Literature was largely represented, mainly in the form of poems on mythological, religious or historical subjects. Among these the most famous is the epic of the hero Gilgameš in twelve books, the Bab account of the Deluge being introduced as an episode in the eleventh book. Another epic was the story of the great battle between the god Merodach and Tiamat, the dragon of chaos and evil, which includes the story of the creation.

7. History and Chronology

Historical records are very numerous, the Assyrians being distinguished among the nations of antiquity by their historical sense. In Assyria the royal palace took the place of the Bab or Egyp temple; and where the Babylonian or the Egyptian would have left behind him a religious record, the Assyrian adorned his walls with accounts of campaigns and the victories of their royal builders. The dates which are attached to each portion of the narrative, and the care with which the names of petty princes and states are transcribed, give a high idea of the historical precision at which the Assyrians aimed. The Assyr monuments are alone sufficient to show that the historical sense was by no means unknown to the ancient peoples of the East, and when we remember how closely related the Assyrians were to the Hebrews in both race and language, the fact becomes important to the Bib. student. Besides historical texts the library contained also chronological tables and long lists of kings and dynasties with the number of years they reigned. In Babylonia time was marked by officially naming each year after some event that had occurred in the course of it; the more historically-minded Assyrian named the year after a particular official, called *limmu*, who was appointed on each New Year's Day. In Babylonia the chronological system went back to a very remote date. The Babylonians were a commercial people, and for commercial purposes it was necessary to have an exact register of the time.

8. Commerce

The library contained trading documents of various sorts, more esp. contracts, deeds of sale of property and the like. Now and then we meet with the plan of a building. There were also fiscal documents relating to the taxes paid by the cities and provinces of the empire to the imperial treasury.

9. Letters

One department of the library consisted of letters, some of them private, others addressed to the king or to the high officials. Nearly a thousand of these have already been published by Professor Harper.

The clay books, it need hardly be added, were all carefully numbered and catalogued, the Assyr system of docketing and arranging the tablets being at once ingenious and simple. The librarians, consequently, had no difficulty in finding any tablet or series of tablets that might be asked for. We may gather from the inscription attached to the larger works copied from Bab originals as well as to other collections of tablets that the library was open to all "readers." A. H. SAYCE

NINEVITES, nin'ē-vīts (Νινευ[ε]ῖται, *Nineu[e]itai*): Only in Lk **11** 30. The ‖ passage (Mt **12** 41), with Lk **11** 32, has the fuller form, "men of Nineveh," which gives the meaning.

NIPHIS, nī'fis (Νειφεὶς, *Neipheis*, A, Φινεὶς, *Phineis;* AV **Nephis**): Given in 1 Esd **5** 21 m as ="Magbish" of Ezr **2** 30, whose sons are the same in number (156) as those of Niphis, but it would seem rather to be the equivalent of Nebo in ver 29.

NISAN, nī'san (נִיסָן, *nīṣān*): The first month of the Jewish year in which occurred the Passover and which corresponds to April. The month is the same as Abib, which occurs in the Pent. Nisan occurs in Neh **2** 1 and Est **3** 7. It denotes "the month of flowers." See CALENDAR.

NISROCH, nis'rok, niz'rok (נִסְרֹךְ, *niṣrōkh*): The Assyr god in whose temple Sennacherib was worshipping when put to death by his sons (2 K **19** 37; Isa **37** 38). The name is not found elsewhere. Some identify him with Asshur, the national deity. See BABYLONIA AND ASSYRIA, RELIGION OF.

NITRE, nī'tēr (נֶתֶר, *nether;* νίτρον, *nitron*): Nitre as used in AV does not correspond to the present use of that term. Nitre or niter is now applied to sodium or potassium nitrate. The writer has in his collection a specimen of sodium carbonate, called in Arab. *naṭrûn*, which was taken from the extensive deposits in Lower Egypt where it is found as a deposit underneath a layer of common salt. Similar deposits are found in Syria and Asia Minor. This is probably the "nitre" of the Bible. ARV has rendered nitre "lye" in Jer **2** 22, and "soda" in Prov **25** 20. Soda or lye has been used as a cleansing agent from earliest times. It effervesces energetically, when treated with an acid; hence the comparison in Prov **25** 20 of the heavy-hearted man roiled by the sound of singing to the sizzling of soda on which vinegar has been poured. See VINEGAR. JAMES A. PATCH

NO, nō. See NO-AMON.

NOADIAH, nō-a-dī'a (נוֹעַדְיָה, *nō'adhyāh*, "tryst of Jeh"; Νωαδεί, *Noadeí*):

(1) Son of Binnui, one of the Levites to whom Ezra intrusted the gold and silver and sacred vessels which he brought up from Babylon (Ezr **8** 33); also called MOETH (q.v.), son of Sabannus (1 Esd **8** 63).

(2) A prophetess associated with Tobiah and Sanballat in opposition to Nehemiah (Neh **6** 14).

NOAH, nō'a (נֹחַ, *nōaḥ*, "rest"; LXX Νῶε, *Nōe;* Jos, Νῶχος, *Nōchos*): The 10th in descent from Adam in the line of Seth (Gen **5** 28.29). Lamech here seems to derive the word from the √ נָחַם, *nāḥam*, "to comfort," but this is probably a mere play upon the name by Noah's father. The times in which Noah was born were degenerate, and this finds pathetic expression in Lamech's saying at the birth of Noah, "This same shall comfort us in our work and in the toil of our hands, which cometh because of the ground which Jeh hath cursed." Concerning the theory that Noah is the name of a dynasty, like Pharaoh or Caesar, rather than of a single individual, see ANTEDILUVIANS. In his 600th year the degenerate races of mankind were cut off by the Deluge. But 120 years previously (Gen **6** 3) he had been warned of the catastrophe, and according to 1 Pet **3** 20 had been preparing for the event by building the ark (see ARK; DELUGE). In the cuneiform inscriptions Noah corresponds to "Ḥasisadra" (Xisuthrus). After the flood Noah celebrated his deliverance by building an altar and offering sacrifices to Jeh (Gen **8** 20), and was sent forth with God's blessing to be "fruitful, and multiply, and replenish the earth" (Gen **9** 1), as Adam had been sent forth at the beginning (Gen **1** 28). In token of the certainty of God's covenant not to destroy the race again by flood, a rainbow spanned the sky whose reappearance was ever after to be a token of peace. But Noah was not above temptation. In the prosperity which followed, he became drunken from the fruit of the vineyard he had planted. His son Ham irreverently exposed the nakedness of his father, while Shem and Japheth covered it from view (Gen **9** 22.23). The curse upon Canaan the son of Ham was literally fulfilled in subsequent history when Israel took possession of Pal, when Tyre fell before the arms of Alexander, and Carthage surrendered to Rome.

GEORGE FREDERICK WRIGHT

NOAH (נֹעָה, *nō'āh*, "movement"): One of the daughters of Zelophehad (Nu **26** 33; **27** 1; **36** 11; Josh **17** 3 ff).

NOAH, BOOK (APOCALYPSE) OF. See APOCALYPTIC LITERATURE.

NO-AMON, nō-ā'mon (נֹא אָמוֹן, *nō' 'āmōn*, Egyp *nut*, "a city," with the feminine ending *t*, and Amon, proper name of a god, City Amon, i.e. the "City," *par excellence*, of the god Amon; tr[d] in AV "populous No," following the Vulg in a misunderstanding of the word *'āmōn;* RV "No-amon"): Occurs in this form only in Nah **3** 8, but אָמוֹן מִנֹּא, *'āmōn minnō'*, "Amon of No," occurs in Jer **46** 25. Cf also Ezk **30** 14–16, where נֹא, *nō'*, is undoubtedly the same city.

The description of No-amon in Nah **3** 8 seems to be that of a delta city, but יָם, *yām*, "sea," in that passage is used poetically for the Nile, as in Job **41** 31 and in Isa **18** 2. With this difficulty removed, the Egyp etymology of the name leaves no doubt as to the correct identification of the place. The "City Amon" in the days of Nahum, Jeremiah and Ezekiel was Thebes (cf art. "Thebes" in any general encyclopaedia). M. G. KYLE

NOB, nob (נֹב, *nōbh;* B, Νομβά, *Nombá*, A, Νοβά, *Nobá*, and other forms): An ancient priestly town to which David came on his way S. when he fled from Saul at Gibeah (1 S **21** 1). Here he found refuge and succor with Ahimelech. This was observed by Doeg the Edomite, who informed the king, and afterward became the instrument of Saul's savage vengeance on the priests, and on all the inhabitants of the city (ch **22**). The name occurs in Neh **11** 32 in a list of cities, immediately after Anathoth. In Isaiah's ideal account of the Assyrians' march against Jerus, Nob is clearly placed S. of Anathoth. Here, says the prophet, the Assyrian shall shake his hand at the mount of the daughter of Zion, the hill of Jerus. It was a place, therefore, from which the Holy City and the temple were clearly visible.

The district in which the site must be sought is thus very definitely indicated; but within this district no name at all resembling Nob has been discovered, and so no sure identification is yet possible. *'Anāta* (Anathoth) is $2\frac{1}{2}$ miles N.E. of Jerus. Nob therefore lay between that and the city, at a point where the city could be seen, apparently on the great road from the N. Rather more than a mile N. of Jerus rises the ridge *Rās el-Meshārif* (2,665 ft.), over which the road from the N. passes; and here the traveler approaching from that direction obtains his first sight of the city. It is fittingly named "the look-out." Col. Conder states the case for identifying this height with Mt. Scopus where Titus established his camp at the siege of Jerus (*PEFS*, 1874, **111** ff). Immediately S. of the ridge, to the E. of the road, there is a small plateau, S. of which there is a lower ridge, whence the slopes dip into *Wâdy el-Jōz*. This plateau, on which Titus may have sat, is a very probable site for Nob. It quite suits the requirements of Isaiah's narrative, and not less those of David's flight. Gibeah lay not far to the N., and this lay in the most likely path to the S. W. EWING

NOBAH, nō′ba (נֹבַח, *nōbhăh;* B, **Ναβώθ,** *Nabôth,* **Ναβαί,** *Nabaí,* A, **Ναβώθ,** *Nabôth,* **Ναβέθ,** *Nabéth*):

(1) Nobah the Manassite, we are told, "went and took Kenath, and the villages thereof, and called it Nobah, after his own name" (Nu **32** 42). There can be little doubt that the ancient Kenath is represented by the modern *Ḳanawāt*, on the western slope of *Jebel ed-Drūze*, the ancient name having survived that of Nobah.

(2) A city which marked the course of Gideon's pursuit of the Midianites (Jgs **8** 11). It is possible that this may be identical with (1). Cheyne argues in favor of this (*EB*, s.v. "Gideon"). But its mention along with Jogbehah points to a more southerly location. This may have been the original home of the clan Nobah. Some would read, following the Syr in Nu **21** 30, "Nobah which is on the desert," instead of "Nophah which reacheth unto Medeba." No site with a name resembling this has yet been recovered. If it is to be distinguished from Kenath, then probably it will have to be sought somewhere to the N.E. of Rabbath-Ammon (*ʿAmmān*). W. EWING

NOBAI, nō′bī, nob′ā-i (נוֹבַי, *nōbhay,* or נֵיבַי, *nēbhay*): One of those who took part in sealing the covenant (Neh **10** 19).

NOBLE, nō′b'l, **NOBLES,** nō′b'lz, **NOBLEMAN,** nō′b'l-man (חוֹרִים, *ḥōrīm,* אַדִּיר, *'addīr;* **εὐγενής,** *eugenḗs,* **κράτιστος,** *krátistos,* **βασιλικός,** *basilikós*): "Nobles" is the tr of the Heb *ḥōrīm* (occurring only in the pl.), "free-born," "noble" (1 K **21** 8.11; Neh **2** 16; **6** 17, etc); of *'addīr,* "begirded," "mighty," "illustrious" or "noble" (Jgs **5** 13; 2 Ch **23** 20, etc); of *nādhībh,* "liberal," "a noble" (Nu **21** 18; Prov **8** 16, etc).

Other words are *gādhōl,* "great" (Jon **3** 7); *yaḳḳīr,* Aram. "precious" (Ezr **4** 10); *nāghīdh,* "a leader" (Job **29** 10); *partᵉmīm,* "foremost ones" (Est **1** 3; **6** 9); *'ăçīlīm,* "those near," "nobles" (Ex **24** 11); *bārīaḥ,* "fugitive" (Isa **43** 14); *kābhēdh,* "weighty," "honored" (Ps **149** 8); *eugenḗs,* "well born" (Acts **17** 11; 1 Cor **1** 26); *krátistos,* "strongest," "most powerful" (Acts **24** 3; **26** 25).

The Apoc, AV and RV, still further enlarges the list. In RV we have *megistánes,* "great ones" (1 Esd **1** 38; **8** 26, with *éntimos,* "in honor"; Wisd **18** 12). Otherwise RV's uses of "noble," and "nobleness" are for words containing the √ *gen* and referring to birth (cf Wisd **8** 3; 2 Macc **6** 27.31; **12** 42; **14** 42 *bis*). AV's uses are wider (Jth **2** 2, etc).

Nobleman is, in Lk **19** 12, the tr of *eugenḗs ánthrōpos,* "a man well born," and in Jn **4** 46.49 of *basilikos,* "kingly," "belonging to a king," a designation extended to the officers, courtiers, etc, of a king, RVm "king's officer"; he was probably an official, civil or military, of Herod Antipas, who was styled "king" (*basileús*).

For "nobles" (Isa **43** 14), AV "have brought down all their nobles," RV has "I will bring down all of them as fugitives," m "or, as otherwise read, all their nobles even," etc; for "nobles" (Jer **30** 21), "prince"; ERV has "worthies" for "nobles" (Nah **3** 18); RV has "the noble" for "princes" (Prov **17** 26); "nobles" for "princes" (Job **34** 18; Dnl **1** 3), for "Nazarites" (Lam **4** 7, m "Nazirites"); "her nobles" for "his fugitives," m "or, as other otherwise read, fugitives" (Isa **15** 5); ARV has "noble" for "liberal" (Isa **32** 5); for "The nobles held their peace," AVm "The voice of the nobles was hid" (Job **29** 10), RV has "The voice of the nobles was hushed," m "Heb hid"; for "most noble" (Acts **24** 3; **26** 25), "most excellent."

W. L. WALKER

NOD, nod (נוֹד, *nōdh*): The land of Eden, to which Cain migrated after the murder of his brother and his banishment by Jeh (Gen **4** 16). Conjecture is useless as to the region intended. The ideas of China, India, etc, which some have entertained, are groundless. The territory was evidently at some distance, but where is now undiscoverable.

NODAB, nō′dab (נוֹדָב, *nōdhābh;* **Ναδαβαῖοι,** *Nadabaíoi*): A Hagrite clan which, along with Jetur and Naphish, suffered complete defeat at the hands of the trans-Jordanic Israelites (1 Ch **5** 19). It has been suggested that Nodab is a corruption of Kedemah or of Nebaioth, names which are associated with Jetur and Naphish in the lists of Ishmael's sons (Gen **25** 15; 1 Ch **1** 31), but it is difficult to see how even the most careless copyist could so blunder. There is a possible reminiscence of the name in *Nudébe,* a village in the Ḥauran.

NOE, nō′ē (**Νῶε,** *Nōe*): AV of Mt **24** 37.38; Lk **3** 36; **17** 26.27; Tob **4** 12. Gr form of NOAH (q.v.) (thus RV).

NOEBA, nō′ē-ba (**Νοεβά,** *Noebá*): Head of one of the families of temple-servants (1 Esd **5** 31) = "Nekoda" of Ezr **2** 48.

NOGAH, nō′ga (נֹגַהּ, *nōghah,* "splendor"): A son of David born at Jerus (1 Ch **3** 7; **14** 6). In the ∥ list (2 S **5** 14.15) this name is wanting. In its Gr form (**Ναγγαί,** *Naggaí*) it occurs in the genealogy of Jesus (Lk **3** 25).

NOHAH, nō′ha (נוֹחָה, *nōḥāh,* "rest"): The fourth son of Benjamin (1 Ch **8** 2). It is probable that in Jgs **20** 43, instead of "a resting-place" we should read "Nohah," which may have been the settlement of the family.

NOISE, noiz (קוֹל, *ḳōl,* הָמוֹן, *hāmōn,* שָׁאוֹן, *shā'ōn;* **φωνή,** *phōnḗ*): "Noise" is most frequently the tr of *ḳōl,* "voice," "sound," in AV (Ex **20** 18, "the noise of the trumpet," RV "voice"; **32** 17 *bis*.18; Jgs **5** 11, "[they that are delivered] from the noise of the archers," RV "far from the noise," etc, m "because of the voice of"; 1 S **4** 6, etc); *hāmōn,* "noise," "sound" (1 S **14** 19); *rōghez,* "anger," "rage" (Job **37** 2); *rēaʿ,* "outcry" (Job **36** 33); *shā'ōn,* "desolation," "noise" (Isa **24** 8; **25** 5); *tᵉshu'ōth,* "cry," "crying" (Job **36** 29); *pāçaḥ,* "to break forth" (Ps **98** 4); *shāmēaʿ,* "to hear," etc (Josh **6** 10; 1 Ch **15** 28); *phōnē,* "sound," "voice," is trd "noise" (Rev **6** 1, "I heard as it were the noise of thunder," RV "saying as with a voice of thunder"); *rhoizēdón,* "with a hissing or rushing sound" (2 Pet **3** 10, "with a great noise"); *gínetai phōnḗ* (Acts **2** 6, AV "when this was noised abroad," m "when this voice was made," RV "when this sound was heard"); *akoúō,* "to hear"; *dialaléō,* "to talk or speak" throughout, are also trd "noised" (Mk **2** 1; Lk **1** 65). So RV (cf Jth **10** 18, "noised among the tents"). Otherwise in RV Apoc, *thróos,* "confused noise" (Wisd **1** 10); *boḗ,* "outcry" (Jth **14** 19); *ēchos,* "sound" (Wisd **17** 18; cf Sir **40** 13); Lat *vox,* "voice" (2 Esd **5** 7).

For "noise" (Ps **65** 7 *bis*), RV has "roaring"; for "make a noise like the noise of the seas" (Isa **17** 12), "the uproar [m "multitude"] of many peoples, that roar like the roaring of the seas"; for "a voice of noise from the city" (Isa **66** 6), "a voice of tumult from the city"; for "noise" (Jer **10** 22), "voice"; for "a noise" (1 Ch **15** 28), "sounding aloud," "voice" (Ezk **43** 2); for "every battle of the warrior is with confused noise" (Isa **9** 5), "all the armor of the armed man in the tumult," m "every boot of the booted warrior"; for "make a noise," "moan" (Ps **55** 2), "roar" (Isa **17** 12); for "make a loud noise" (Ps **98** 4), "break forth"; for "maketh a noise" (Jer **4** 19), "is disquieted"; for "the noise of his tabernacle" (Job **36** 29), "the thunderings of his pavilion"; for "make any noise with your voice" (Josh **6** 10), "let your voice be heard"; "joyful noise," for "shouting" (Isa **16** 10); for "The Lord on high is mightier than the noise of many waters, yea, than the mighty waves of the sea" (Ps **93** 4), "Above the voices of many waters, the mighty breakers of the sea, Jeh on high is mighty."

W. L. Walker

NOISOME, noi′sum (הַוָּה, *hawwāh*, רַע, *ra‘*; **κακός**, *kakós*): "Noisome" from "annoy" (*annoysome*) has in Bible Eng. the meaning of "evil," "hurtful," not of "offensive" or "loathsome." It is the tr of *hawwāh*, "mischief," "calamity" (Ps **91** 3, "noisome pestilence," RV "deadly"); of *ra‘*, a common word for "evil" (Ezk **14** 15.21), "noisome beasts" (RV "evil"). It occurs also in Job **31** 40 AVm as the tr of *bo'shāh*, "noisome weeds," AV and RV "cockle," m as AVm; of *kakos*, "evil," "bad" (Rev **16** 2), "a noisome and grievous sore." "Noisome" also occurs in Apoc (2 Macc **9** 9) as the tr of *barúnō*, "to make heavy," "oppress," where it seems to have the meaning of "loathsome."

W. L. Walker

NON, non (נוֹן, *nōn*): 1 Ch **7** 27 AV and RVm. See Nun.

NOOMA, nō′ō-ma (**Νοομά**, *Noomá*, B, **'Οομά**, *Oomá*; AV **Ethma**): 1 Esd **9** 35="Nebo" of Ezr **10** 43, of which it is a corruption.

NOON, nōōn, **NOONDAY**, nōōn′dā (צָהֳרַיִם, *çohŏrayim*; **μεσημβρία**, *mesēmbría*): The word means light, splendor, brightness, and hence the brightest part of the day (Gen **43** 16.25; Acts **22** 6). See also Midday; Day and Night; Time.

NOPH, nof (נֹף, *nōph*; in Hos **9** 6 *mōph*): A name for the Egyp city Memphis (so LXX), hence thus rendered in RV (Isa **19** 13; Jer **2** 16; **44** 1; Ezk **30** 13.16). See Memphis.

NOPHAH, nō′fa (נֹפַח, *nōphăh*; LXX does not transliterate): A city mentioned only in Nu **21** 30 (see Nobah). LXX reads *kaí hai gunaíkes éti prosexékausan púr epí Moáb*, "and the women besides [yet] kindled a fire at [against] Moab." The text has evidently suffered corruption.

NORTH, nôrth, **NORTH COUNTRY** (צָפוֹן, *çāphōn*, from √ צָפַן, *çāphan*, "to hide," i.e. "the hidden," "the dark" [Ges.]; **βορρᾶς**, *borrhás*, **βορέας**, *boréas* [Jth **16** 4]; *septentrio* [2 Esd 15 43]): In addition to the many places where "north" occurs merely as a point of the compass, there are several passages in Jer, Ezk and Zeph, where it refers to a particular country, usually Assyria or Babylonia: Jer **3** 18, "They shall come together out of the land of the north to the land that I gave for an inheritance unto your fathers"; Jer **46** 6, "In the north by the river Euphrates have they stumbled and fallen"; Ezk **26** 7, "I will bring upon Tyre Nebuchadrezzar king of Babylon, king of kings, from the north"; Zeph **2** 13, "He will stretch out his hand against the north, and destroy Assyria, and will make Nineveh a desolation."

While the site of Nineveh was N.E. of Jerus, and that of Babylon almost due E., it was not unnatural for them to be referred to as "the north," because the direct desert routes were impracticable, and the roads led first into Northern Syria and then eastward (cf however Gen **29** 1, "Then Jacob went on his journey, and came to the land of the children of the east").

In Ezk **38** 6, we have, "Gomer, and all his hordes; the house of Togarmah in the uttermost parts of the north." It is uncertain what country is here referred to. Some have supposed Armenia (cf Gen **10** 3; 1 Ch **1** 6; Ezk **27** 14).

The north border of the promised land, as outlined in Nu **34** 7–9 and Ezk **47** 15–17, cannot be determined with certainty, because some of the towns named cannot be identified, but it was approximately the latitude of Mt. Hermon, not including Lebanon or Damascus. For **North** (*m^ezārīm*) see Astronomy.

Alfred Ely Day

NORTHEAST, SOUTHEAST: These words occur in Acts **27** 12, "if by any means they could reach Phoenix, and winter there; which is a haven of Crete, looking north-east and south-east." RVm has, "Gr, down the south-west wind and down the north-west wind," which is a lit. tr of the Gr: *eis Phoínika . . . . liména tḗs Krḗtēs bléponta* (looking) *katá líba* (the southwest wind) *kaí katá chōron* (the northwest wind). *Chōros* does not appear to occur except here, but the corresponding Lat *caurus* or *corus* is found in Caesar, Vergil, and other classical authors. AV has "lieth toward the south west and north west." *κατά*, *katá*, with a wind or stream, means, "down the wind or stream," i.e. in the direction that it is blowing or flowing, and this interpretation would indicate a harbor open to the E. If λίψ, *líps*, and χῶρος, *chōros*, are used here as names of directions rather than of winds, we should expect a harbor open to the W. There is good reason for identifying Phoenix (AV "Phenice") with Loutro on the south shore of Crete (*EB*, s.v. "Phenice"), whose harbor is open to the E. See Phoenix.

Alfred Ely Day

NOSE, nōz, **NOSTRILS**, nos′trilz (אַף, *'aph*, "nose," נְחִירַיִם, *n^ehīrayim*, dual of נְחִיר, *n^ehīr*, "nostrils"): The former expression (*'aph* from **'anph*, like Arab. أنف, *'anf*) is often tr^d "face" (which see s.v.) in EV. It is frequently referred to as the organ of breathing, in other words, as the receptacle of the breath or spirit of God: "Jeh . . . . breathed into his nostrils the breath of life; and man became a living soul" (Gen **2** 7; cf **7** 22); "My life is yet whole in me, and the spirit of God is in my nostrils" (Job **27** 3). Therefore a life which depends on so slight a thing as a breath is considered as utterly frail and of no great consequence: "Cease ye from man, whose breath is in his nostrils; for wherein is he to be accounted of?" (Isa **2** 22; cf Wisd **2** 2).

In poetical language such a breath of life is ascribed even to God, esp. with regard to the mighty storm which is thought to proceed from His nostrils (Ex **15** 8; 2 S **22** 9; Ps **18** 8.15).

The phrase, "a smoke in my nose, a fire that burneth all the day" (Isa **65** 5), is equivalent to a perpetual annoyance and cause of irritation. A cruel custom of war, in which the vanquished had their noses and ears cut off by their remorseless conquerors, is alluded to in Ezk **23** 25. As a wild animal is held in check by having his nose pierced and a hook or ring inserted in it (Job **40** 24; **41** 2 [Heb **40** 26]), so this expression is used to indicate the humbling and taming of an obstinate person (2 K **19** 28; Isa **37** 29; cf Ezk **29** 4; **38** 4). But men, and esp. women, had their noses pierced for the wearing of jewelry (Gen **24** 47; Isa **3** 21; Ezk **16** 12). In one passage the meaning is not quite clear, viz. in the enumeration of blemishes which disable a "son of Aaron" from the execution of the priest's office (Lev **21** 18), where EV translates "flat [m "slit"] nose." The Heb word is חָרֻם, *ḥārum*, which is a *hapax legomenon.* It corresponds, however, to the Arab. √ خرما, خرم, *ḥaram, ḥarmān* (*kharam, kharmān*), which means "to open," "to pierce the nose," esp. the bridge of the nose. We may accept this meaning as the one intended in the passage.

Another dark and much discussed passage must still be referred to: "And, lo, they put the branch to their nose" (Ezk **8** 17). The usual explanation (whereof the context gives some valuable hints) is that a rite connected with the worship of Baal (the sun) is here alluded to (see Smend and A. B. Davidson's comms. on the passage). A similar custom is known from Pers sun-worship, where a bunch (*bareçma*) of dates, pomegranates or tamarisks was held to the nose by the worshipper, probably as an attempt to keep the Holy One (sun) from being contaminated by sinful breath (Spiegel, *Eranische Altertümer*, III, 571). Among modern Jews posies of myrtle and other fragrant herbs are held to the nose by the persons attending on the ceremony of circumcision, for the alleged reason of making the sight and smell of blood bearable. Another interpretation of the above passage would understand זְמוֹרָה, *zᵉmōrāh*, in the sense of "male sexual member" (see Gesenius-Buhl, s.v.; Levy, *Nhb. Wörterbuch*, I, 544), and the whole passage as a reference to a sensuous Canaanite rite, such as is perhaps alluded to in Isa **57** 8. In that case the אַפָּם, *'appām*, "their nose," of the MT would have to be considered as *tiḳḳūn ṣōphᵉrīm* (a correction of the scribes) for אַפִּי, *'appī*, "my face." Or read "They cause their stench [*zᵉmōrāthām*] to come up to my face" (Kraetzschmar, ad loc.). See BRANCH.

H. L. E. LUERING

NOSE-JEWELS, nōz-jū'elz, -jōō'elz (נֶזֶם, *nezem* [probably from נָזַם, *nāzam*, "muzzle"], a "nose-ring," or "nose-jewel," so rendered in Isa **3** 21; "jewel in a swine's snout," Prov **11** 22, AVm "ring"; "jewel on thy forehead," Ezk **16** 12, "ring upon thy nose"): In Gen **24** 22, AV rendered incorrectly "earring"; cf ver 47. Indeed, the word had also a more generic meaning of "ring" or "jewelry," whether worn in the nose or not. See Gen **35** 4; Ex **32** 2, where the ornament was worn in the ear. There are several cases without specification, uniformly rendered, without good reason, however, "earring" in AV (Ex **35** 22; Jgs **8** 24. 25; Job **42** 11 ["ring"]; Prov **25** 12; Hos **2** 13 [15]).

The nose-jewel was made of gold or of silver, usually, and worn by many women of the East. It was a ring of from an inch to about three inches (in extreme cases) in diameter, and was passed through the right nostril. Usually there were pendant from the metal ring jewels, beads or coral. Such ornaments are still worn in some parts of the East. See also AMULET; JEWEL.

EDWARD BAGBY POLLARD

NOTABLE, nō'ta-b'l (חָזוּת, *ḥāzūth;* γνωστός, *gnōstós*): "Notable" is the tr of *ḥāzūth*, "conspicuous" (*ḥāzāh*, "to see"), e.g. Dnl **8** 5, "a notable horn," i.e. "conspicuous," AVm "a horn of sight"; ver 8, "notable [horns]"; of *gnōstos*, "known," "knowledge" (Acts **4** 16); of *epísēmos*, "noted," "notable" (Mt **27** 16; in Rom **16** 7, "of note"); of *epiphanḗs*, "very manifest," "illustrious" (cf "Antiochus Epiphanes"); Acts **2** 20, "that great and notable day," quoted from Joel **2** 31; LXX for *yārē'*, "to be feared," AV and RV "terrible" (cf Mal **4** 5); "notable" occurs also in 2 Macc **3** 26 (*ekprepḗs*); **14** 33, RV "for all to see"; **6** 28 (*gennaíos*), "a notable example," RV "noble"; **notably**, only in 2 Macc **14** 31 (*gennaíōs*), "notably prevented," RV "bravely," m "nobly."

W. L. WALKER

NOTE, nōt (חָקַק, *ḥāḳak*, רָשַׁם, *rāsham;* σημειόω, *sēmeióō*, ἐπίσημος, *epísēmos*): "Note" (vb.) is the tr of *ḥāḳak*, "to grave," "to inscribe," etc (Isa **30** 8, "note it in a book," RV "inscribe"); of *rāsham*, "to note down," etc (Dnl **10** 21, RV "inscribed"); of *sēmeioō*, "to put a sign on" (2 Thess **3** 14, "note that man").

"Note" (noun) is the tr of *episēmos*, "marked upon," "distinguished" (Rom **16** 7, "who are of note among the apostles").

"Notes" (musical) occurs in Wisd **19** 18, "notes of a psaltery" (*phthóggos*). W. L. WALKER

NOTHING, nuth'ing (לֹא, *lō'*, לֹא מְאוּמָה, *lō' mᵉ'ūmāh*, etc; μηδείς, *mēdeís*, οὐδείς, *oudeís*): "Nothing" is represented by various words and phrases, often with *lō'*, which is properly a subst. with the meaning of "nothing." Most frequently we have *lō' mᵉ'ūmāh*, "not anything" (Gen **40** 15; Jgs **14** 6).

Other forms are *lō' dhābhār*, "not anything" (Gen **19** 8); *lō'khōl*, "not any[thing]" (Gen **11** 6; Prov **13** 7); *lā'* [Aram.], "no," "nothing" (Dnl **4** 35, "as nothing"); *'ephes*, "end," "cessation" (Isa **34** 12); *biltī*, "without," "save," "not" (Isa **44** 10; Am **3** 4); *'ayin*, "there is not" (Isa **41** 24); once *tōhū*, "emptiness" (Job **6** 18); *bal māh*, "not anything" (Prov **9** 13); *ḥinnām*, "free," "gratis" (2 S **24** 24); *mā'aṭ*, "to make small," "bring to nothing" (Jer **10** 24); *raḳ*, "only" (Gen **26** 29); *lᵉ'al*, "for nothing" (Job **24** 25).

In 2 Macc **7** 12, we have "nothing," adverbially (*en oudení*), "he nothing regarded the pains" (cf 1 K **15** 21); **9** 7 (*oudamṓs*), RV "in no wise"; Wisd **2** 11, "nothing worth" (*áchrēstos*), RV "of no service"; Bar **6** 17.26.

For "nothing" RV has "none" (Ex **23** 26; Joel **2** 3), "never" (Neh **5** 8), "not wherewith" (Prov **22** 27), "vanity and nought" (Isa **41** 29); for "answered nothing" (Mk **15** 5), "no more answered anything"; "answered nothing" in ver 3 is omitted; "anything" for "nothing" (1 Tim **6** 7), "not anything" (Acts **20** 20), "not" (1 Cor **8** 2), "no word" (Lk **1** 37), "not wherewith" (**7** 42); for "to nothing" (Job **6** 18), "up into the waste"; for "it is nothing with" (2 Ch **14** 11), "there is none besides," m "like"; for "lacked nothing" (1 K **4** 27), "let nothing be lacking," for "nothing doubting" (Acts **11** 12), "making no distinction"; for "hoping for nothing again" (Lk **6** 35), "never despairing"; for "are nothing" (Acts **21** 24), "no truth in"; for "nothing shall offend them" (Ps **119** 165), "no occasion of stumbling"; for "bring to nothing" (1 Cor **1** 19), ERV "reject," ARV "bring to nought"; "nothing better" for "no good" (Eccl **3** 12), for "not" (Mt **13** 34, different text), for "no man" (Acts **9** 8), "for nothing," for "free" (Ex **21** 11); "miss nothing" for "not sin" (Job **5** 24), m "shalt not err"; "and shall have nothing" for "and not for himself" (Dnl **9** 26, m "there shall be none belonging to him"). W. L. WALKER

NOUGHT, nôt (חִנָּם, *ḥinnam;* καταργέω, *katargéō*): "Nought" is to be distinguished from "naught" implying "badness" (see NAUGHT). "Nought" in the sense of "nothing," etc, is the tr of *ḥinnām*, "gratis" (Gen **29** 15), and of various other words occurring once only, e.g. *'āwen*, "vanity" (Am **5** 5); *tōhū*, "vacancy," "ruin" (Isa **49** 4); *'epha'*, "nothing" (Isa **41** 24); *nābhēl*, "to fade" (Job **14** 18, m "fadeth away"); *pūr*, "to make void" (Ps **33** 10); *katargeō*, "to make without effect" (1 Cor **1** 28; **2** 6); *oudeis*, "not even one" (Acts **5** 36); *apelegmós*, "refutation" (Acts **19** 27, RV "come into disrepute"); *dōreán*, "without payment" (2 Thess **3** 8, RV "for nought"); *erēmóō*, "to desolate" (Rev **18** 17, RV "made desolate"); *katalúō*, "to loose down" (Acts **5** 38, RV "be overthrown"). In Apoc we have "set at nought" and "come to nought," etc (1 Esd **1** 56; 2 Esd **2** 33; **8** 59).

For "nought" RV has "perish" (Dt **28** 63); for "come to nought" (Job **8** 22), "be no more"; "nought" for "not ought" (Ex **5** 11), for "no might" (Dt **28** 32); for "brought to silence," *bis* (Isa **15** 1), "brought to nought"; ARV "bring to nought" (1 Cor **1** 19) for "bring to nothing" (ERV "reject"); "nought but terror" (Isa **28** 19) for "a vexation only"; "brought to nought" (Isa **16** 4) for "is at an end"; "come to nought" for "taken none effect" (Rom **9** 6); "set at nought" for "despise" (Rom **14** 3).

W. L. Walker

NOURISH, nur'ish (גִּדֵּל, *giddēl*, חִיָּה, *ḥiyyāh*, כִּלְכֵּל, *kilkēl*, רִבָּה, *ribbāh;* **τρέφω**, *tréphō*, **ἀνατρέφω**, *anatréphō*, **ἐκτρέφω**, *ektréphō*, **ἐντρέφω**, *entréphō*): While the word "nourish" was ordinarily an appropriate rendering in the time of the AV, the word has since become much less frequent, and some senses have largely passed out of ordinary use, so that the meaning would now in most cases be better expressed by some other word. *Giddēl* means "to bring up," "rear [children]" (Isa **1** 2, m "made great"; **23** 4; Dnl **1** 5); "cause [a tree] to grow" (Isa **44** 14). *Ḥiyyāh* means "to preserve alive" (with some implication of care) (2 S **12** 3; Isa **7** 21, ARV "keep alive"). *Kilkēl* means "to support," "maintain," "provide for" (esp. with food) (Gen **45** 11; **47** 12; **50** 21). *Ribbāh* means "to bring up," "rear [whelps]," in a **figurative** use (Ezk **19** 2). *Trephō* means "to feed" (transitively) (Acts **12** 20, RV "feed"; Rev **12** 14); "to fatten" (Jas **5** 5, the context indicating an unfavorable meaning). *Anatrephō* is "to bring up," "rear," like *giddēl* (Acts **7** 20.21); *ektrephō* is "to take care of" (Eph **5** 29); *entrephō* means "to bring up in," "train in" (1 Tim **4** 6).

George Ricker Berry

NOVICE, nov'is (**νεόφυτος**, *neóphutos*, "newly planted"): In this sense it is found in LXX of Job **14** 9 and Isa **5** 7. In the NT it occurs once only (1 Tim **3** 6), where it means a person newly planted in the Christian faith, a neophyte, a new convert, one who has recently become a Christian. This term occurs in the list which Paul gives of the qualifications which a Christian bishop must possess. The apostle instructs Timothy, that if any man desires the office of a bishop, he must not be a "novice," must not be newly converted, or recently brought to the faith of Christ "lest he be lifted up with pride, and fall into the condemnation of the devil."

This means that a recent convert runs the very serious risk of being wise in his own eyes, of despising those who are still on the level from which, by his conversion, he has been lifted; and so he becomes puffed up with high ideas of his own importance. He has not yet had time to discover his limitations, he is newly planted, he does not fully understand his true position in the Christian community, he overestimates himself. For these reasons he is peculiarly liable to instability, and to the other weaknesses and sins connected with an inflated opinion of his own powers. His pride is a sure indication of a coming fall. A novice, therefore, must on no account be appointed to the office in question, for he would be sure to bring disgrace upon it.

John Rutherfurd

NUMBER, num'bẽr:

I. Number and Arithmetic.—The system of counting followed by the Hebrews and the Semites generally was the decimal system, which seems to have been suggested by the use of the ten fingers. Heb had separate words only for the first nine units and for ten and its multiples. Of the sexagesimal system, which seems to have been introduced into Babylonia by the Sumerians and which, through its development there, has influenced the measurement of time and space in the western civilized world even to the present day, there is no direct trace in the Bible, although, as will be shown later, there are some possible echoes. The highest number in the Bible described by a single word is 10,000 (*ribbō* or *ribbō'*, *muriás*). The Egyptians, on the other hand, had separate words for 100,000, 1,000,000, 10,000,000. The highest numbers referred to in any way in the Bible are: "a thousand thousand" (1 Ch **22** 14; 2 Ch **14** 9); "thousands of thousands" (Dnl **7** 10; Rev **5** 11); "thousands of ten thousands" (Gen **24** 60); "ten thousand times ten thousand" (Dnl **7** 10; Rev **5** 11); and twice that figure (Rev **9** 16). The excessively high numbers met with in some oriental systems (cf Lubbock, *The Decimal System*, 17 ff) have no parallels in Heb. Fractions were not unknown. We find $\frac{1}{3}$ (2 S **18** 2, etc); $\frac{1}{2}$ (Ex **25** 10.17, etc); $\frac{1}{4}$ (1 S **9** 8); $\frac{1}{5}$ (Gen **47** 24); $\frac{1}{6}$ (Ezk **46** 14); $\frac{1}{10}$ (Ex **16** 36); $\frac{2}{10}$ (Lev **23** 13); $\frac{3}{10}$ (Lev **14** 10), and $\frac{1}{100}$ (Neh **5** 11). Three other fractions are less definitely expressed: $\frac{2}{3}$ by "a double portion," lit. "a double mouthful" (Dt **21** 17; 2 K **2** 9; Zec **13** 8); $\frac{4}{5}$ by "four parts" (Gen **47** 24), and $\frac{9}{10}$ by "nine parts" (Neh **11** 1). Only the simplest rules of arithmetic can be illustrated from the OT. There are examples of addition (Gen **5** 3–31; Nu **1** 20–46); subtraction (Gen **18** 28 ff); multiplication (Lev **25** 8; Nu **3** 46 ff), and division (Nu **31** 27 ff). In Lev **25** 50 ff is what has been said to imply a kind of rule-of-three sum. The old Babylonians had tables of squares and cubes intended no doubt to facilitate the measurement of land (Sayce, *Assyria, Its Princes, Priests and People*, 118; Bezold, *Ninive und Babylon*, 90, 92); and it can scarcely be doubted that the same need led to similar results among the Israelites, but at present there is no evidence. Old Heb arithmetic and mathematics as known to us are of the most elementary kind (Nowack, *HA*, I, 298).

II. Notation of Numbers.—No special signs for the expression of numbers in writing can be proved to have been in use among the Hebrews before the exile. The Siloam Inscription, which is probably the oldest specimen of Heb writing extant (with the exception of the ostraca of Samaria, and perhaps a seal or two and the obscure Gezer tablet), has the numbers written in full. The words used there for 3,200, 1,000 are written as words without any abbreviation. The earlier text of the M S which practically illustrates Heb usage has the numbers 30, 40, 50, 100, 200, 7,000 written out in the same way.

1. By Words

After the exile some of the Jews at any rate employed signs such as were current among the Egyptians, the Aramaeans, and the Phoenicians—an upright line for 1, two such lines for 2, three for 3, and so on, and special signs for 10, 20, 100. It had

2. By Signs

been conjectured that these or similar signs were known to the Jews, but actual proof was not forthcoming until the discovery of Jewish papyri at Assuan and Elephantine in 1904 and 1907. In these texts, ranging from 494 to c 400 BC, the dates are stated, not in words, but in figures of the kind described. We have therefore clear evidence that numerical signs were used by members of a Jewish colony in Upper Egypt in the 5th cent. BC. Now, as the existence of this colony can be traced before 525 BC, it is probable that they used this method of notation also in the preceding century. Conjecture indeed may go as far as its beginning, for it is known that there were Jews in Pathros, that is Upper Egypt, in the last days of Jeremiah (Jer **44** 1.15). Some of the first Jewish settlers in Elephantine may have known the prophet and some of them may have come from Jerus, bringing these signs with them. At present, however, that is pure hypothesis.

3. By Letters

In the notation of the chapters and verses of the Heb Bible and in the expression of dates in Heb books the consonants of the Heb alphabet are employed for figures, i.e. the first ten for 1–10, combinations of these for 11–19, the following eight for 20–90, and the remainder for 100, 200, 300, 400. The letters of the Gr alphabet were used in the same way. The antiquity of this kind of numerical notation cannot at present be ascertained. It is found on Jewish coins which have been dated in the reign of the Maccabean Simon (143–135 BC), but some scholars refer them to a much later period. All students of the Talm are familiar with this way of numbering the pages, or rather the leaves, but its use there is no proof of early date. The numerical use of the Gr letters can be abundantly illustrated. It is met with in many Gr papyri, some of them from the 3d cent. BC (*Hibeh Papyri*, nos. 40–43, etc); on several coins of Herod the Great, and in some MSS of the NT, for instance, a papyrus fragment of Mt (*Oxyrhynchus Pap.*, 2) where 14 is three times represented by *iōta delta* with a line above the letters, and some codices of Rev at **13** 18 where 666 is given by the three letters *chi xi vau* (or *digamma*). It is possible that two of these methods may have been employed side by side in some cases, as in the Punic Sacrificial Tablet of Marseilles, where (l. 6) 150 is expressed first in words, and then by figures.

III. Numbers in OT History.—Students of the historical books of the OT have long been perplexed by the high numbers which are met with in many passages, for example, the number ascribed to the Israelites at the exodus (Ex **12** 37; Nu **11** 21), and on two occasions during the sojourn in the wilderness (Nu **1, 26**)—more than 600,000 adult males, which means a total of two or three millions; the result of David's census 1,300,000 men (2 S **24** 9) or 1,570,000 (1 Ch **21** 5), and the slaughter of half a million in a battle between Judah and Israel (2 Ch **13** 17). There are many other illustrations in the Books of Ch and elsewhere. That some of these high figures are incorrect is beyond reasonable doubt, and is not in the least surprising, for there is ample evidence that the numbers in ancient documents were exceptionally liable to corruption. One of the best known instances is the variation of 1,466 years between the Heb text and the LXX (text of B) as to the interval from the creation of Adam to the birth of Abram. Other striking cases are 1 S **6** 19, where 50,070 ought probably to be 70 (Jos, *Ant*, VI, i, 4); 2 S **15** 7, where 40 years ought to be 4 years; the confusion of 76 and 276 in the MSS of Acts **27** 37, and of 616 and 666 in those of Rev **13** 18. Heb MSS furnish some instructive variations. One of them, no. 109 of Kennicott, reads (Nu **1** 23) 1,050 for 50,000; 50 for 50,000 (**2** 6), and 100 for 100,000 (ver 16). It is easy to see how mistakes may have originated in many cases. The Heb numerals for 30, etc, are the plurals of the units, so that the former, as written, differ from the latter only by the addition of the two letters *yōdh* and *mēm* composing the syllable *-īm*. Now as the *mēm* was often omitted, 3 and 30, 4 and 40, etc, could readily be confused. If signs or letters of the alphabet were made use of, instead of abbreviated words, there would be quite as much room for misunderstanding and error on the part of copyists. The high numbers above referred to as found in Ex and Nu have been ingeniously accounted for by Professor Flinders Petrie (*Researches in Sinai*) in a wholly different way. By understanding *'eleph* not as "thousand," but as "family" or "tent," he reduces the number to 5,550 for the first census, and 5,730 for the second. This figure, however, seems too low, and the method of interpretation, though not impossible, is open to criticism. It is generally admitted that the number as usually read is too high, but the original number has not yet been certainly discovered. When, however, full allowance has been made for the intrusion of numerical errors into the Heb text, it is difficult to resist the belief that, in the Books of Ch, at any rate, there is a marked tendency to exaggeration in this respect. The huge armies again and again ascribed to the little kingdoms of Judah and Israel cannot be reconciled with some of the facts revealed by recent research; with the following, for instance: The army which met the Assyrians at Karkar in 854 BC and which represented 11 states and tribes inclusive of Israel and the kingdom of Damascus, cannot have numbered at the most more than about 75,000 or 80,000 men (*HDB*, 1909, 65*b*), and the Assyr king who reports the battle reckons the whole levy of his country at only 102,000 (*Der alte Orient*, XI, i, 14, note). In view of these figures it is not conceivable that the armies of Israel or Judah could number a million, or even half a million. The contingent from the larger kingdom contributed on the occasion mentioned above consisted of only 10,000 men and 2,000 chariots (*HDB*, ib). The safest conclusion, therefore, seems to be that, while many of the questionable numbers in the present text of the OT are due to copyists, there is a residuum which cannot be so accounted for.

IV. Round Numbers.—The use of definite numerical expressions in an indefinite sense, that is, as round numbers, which is met with in many languages, seems to have been very prevalent in Western Asia from early times to the present day. Sir W. Ramsay (*Thousand and One Churches*, 6) remarks that the modern Turks have 4 typical numbers which are often used in proper names with little or no reference to their exact numerical force —3, 7, 40, 1,001. The Lycaonian district which gives the book its name is called *Bin Bir Kilisse*, "The Thousand and One Churches," although the actual number in the valley is only 28. The modern Persians use 40 in just the same way. "Forty years" with them often means "many years" (Brugsch, cited by König, *Stilistik*, 55). This lax use of numbers, as we think, was probably very frequent among the Israelites and their neighbors. The inscription on the M S supplies a very instructive example. The Israelitish occupation of Medeba by Omri and his son for half the reign of the latter is there reckoned (ll. 7 f) at 40 years. As, according to 1 K **16** 23.29, the period extended to only 23 years at the most, the number 40 must have been used very freely by Mesha's scribe as a round number. It is probably often used in that way in the Bible where it is remarkably frequent, esp. in reference to periods of days or years. The 40 days of the Flood (Gen **7** 4.17), the arrangement of the life of Moses in three periods of 40 years each (Acts **7** 23; Ex **7** 7; Dt **34** 7), the 40 years' rule or reign of Eli (1 S **4** 18), of Saul (Acts **13** 21; cf Jos, *Ant*, VI, xiv, 9), of David (1 K **2** 11), of Solomon (1 K **11** 42) and of Jehoash (2 K **12** 1), the 40 or 80 years of rest (Jgs **3** 11.30; **5** 31; **8** 28), the 40 years of Phili oppression (Jgs **13** 1), the 40 days' challenge of Goliath (1 S **17** 16), the 40 days' fast of Moses (Ex **34** 28), Elijah (1 K **19** 8), and Jesus (Mt **4** 2 and ||), the 40 days before the destruction of Nineveh (Jon **3** 4), and the 40 days before the Ascension (Acts **1** 3), all suggest conventional use, or the influence of that use, for it can hardly be supposed that the number in each of these cases, and in others which might be mentioned, was exactly 40. How it came to be so used is not quite certain, but it may have originated, partly at any rate, in the idea that 40 years constituted a generation or the period at the end of which a man attains maturity, an idea common, it would seem, to the Greeks, the Israelites, and the Arabs. The period of 40 years in the wilderness in the course of which the old Israel died out and a new Israel took its place was a generation (Nu **32** 13, etc). The rabbis long afterward regarded 40 years as the age of understanding, the age when a man reaches his intellectual prime (*Ab*, v, addendum). In the Koran (*Sura* **46**) a man is said to attain his strength when he attains to 40 years, and it was at that age, according to tradition, that Muhammad came forward as a prophet. In this way perhaps 40 came to be used as a round number for an indefinite period with a suggestion of completeness, and then was extended in course of time to things as well as seasons.

Other round numbers are: (1) some of the higher numbers; (2) several numerical phrases. Under (1) come the following numbers. *One hundred*, often of course to be understood literally, but evidently a round number in Gen **26** 12; Lev **26** 8; 2 S **24** 3; Eccl **8** 12; Mt **19** 29 and ||. *A thousand (thousands)*, very often a literal number, but in not a few cases indefinite, e.g. Ex **20** 6 || Dt **5** 10; **7** 9; 1 S **18** 7; Ps **50** 10; **90** 4; **105** 8; Isa **60** 22, etc. *Ten thousand* (Heb *ribbō, ribbōth, rᵉbhābhāh;* Gr *muriás, múrioi*) is also used as a round number as in Lev **26** 8; Dt **32** 30; Cant **5** 10; Mic **6** 7. The yet higher figures, *thousands of thousands*, etc, are, in almost all cases, distinctly hyperbolical round numbers, the most remarkable examples occurring in the apocalyptic books (Dnl **7** 10; Rev **5** 11; **9** 16; Ethiopic En **40** 1). (2) The second group, numerical phrases, consists of a number of expressions in which numbers are used roundly, in some cases to express the idea of fewness. *One or two*, etc: "a day or two" (Ex **21** 21), "an heap, two heaps" (Jgs **15** 16 RVm), "one of a city, and two of a family" (Jer **3** 14), "not once, nor twice," that is "several times" (2 K **6** 10). *Two or three:* "Two or three berries in the [topmost] bough" (Isa **17** 6; cf Hos **6** 2), "Where two or three are gathered together in my name," etc (Mt **18** 20). König refers to Assyr, Syr, and Arab. parallels. *Three or four:* the most noteworthy example is the formula which occurs 8 t in Am (**1** 3.6.9.11.13; **2** 1.4.6), "for three transgressions . . . . yea for four." That the numbers here are round numbers is evident from the fact that the sins enumerated are in most cases neither 3 nor 4. In Prov **30** 15. 18.21.29, on the other hand, where we have the same rhetorical device, *climax ad majus*, 4 is followed by four statements and is therefore to be taken literally. Again, König (ib) points to classical and Arab. parallels. *Four or five:* "Four or five in the outmost branches of a fruitful tree" (Isa **17** 6). *Five or six:* "Thou shouldest have smitten [Syria] five or six times" (2 K **13** 19), an idiom met with also in Am Tab (König, ib). *Six and seven:* "He will deliver thee in six troubles; yea, in seven there shall no evil touch thee" (Job **5** 19). *Seven and eight:* "Seven shepherds, and eight principal men" (Mic **5** 5), that is, "enough and more than enough" (Cheyne); "Give a portion to seven, yea, even unto eight" (Eccl **11** 2). In one remarkable phrase which occurs (with slight variations of form) 24 t in the OT, two Heb words, meaning respectively "yesterday" and "third," are mostly used so as together to express the idea of vague reference to the past. RV renders in a variety of ways: "beforetime" (Gen **31** 2, etc), "aforetime" (Josh **4** 18), "heretofore" (Ex **4** 10, etc), "in time [or "times"] past" (Dt **19** 4.6; 2 S **3** 17, etc).

V. Significant Numbers.—Numerical symbolism, that is, the use of numbers not merely, if at all, with their literal numerical value, or as round numbers, but with symbolic significance, sacred or otherwise, was widespread in the ancient East, esp. in Babylonia and regions more or less influenced by Bab culture which, to a certain extent, included Canaan. It must also be remembered that the ancestors of the Israelites are said to have been of Bab origin and may therefore have transmitted to their descendants the germs at least of numerical symbolism as developed in Babylonia in the age of Hammurabi. Be that as it may, the presence of this use of numbers in the Bible, and that on a large scale, cannot reasonably be doubted, although some writers have gone too far in their speculations on the subject. The numbers which are unmistakably used with more or less symbolic meaning are 7 and its multiples, and 3, 4, 10 and 12.

1. Seven and Its Multiples

By far the most prominent of these is the number 7, which is referred to in one way or another in nearly 600 passages in the Bible, as well as in many passages in the Apoc and the Pseudepigrapha, and later Jewish literature. Of course the number has its usual numerical force in many of these places, but even there not seldom with a glance at its symbolic significance. For the determination of the latter we are not assigned to conjecture. There is clear evidence in the cuneiform texts, which are our earliest authorities, that the Babylonians regarded 7 as the number of totality, of completeness. The Sumerians, from whom the Sem Babylonians seem to have borrowed the idea, equated 7 and "all." The 7-storied towers of Babylonia represented the universe. Seven was the expression of the highest power, the greatest conceivable fulness of force, and therefore was early pressed into the service of religion. It is found in reference to ritual in the age of Gudea, that is perhaps about the middle of the 3d millennium BC. "Seven gods" at the end of an enumeration meant "all the gods" (for these facts and the cuneiform evidence cf Hehn, *Siebenzahl und Sabbath bei den Babyloniern und im AT*, 4 ff). How 7 came to be used in this way can only be glanced at here. The view connecting it with the gods of the 7 planets, which used to be in great favor and still has its advocates, seems to lack ancient proof. Hehn (op. cit., 44 ff) has shown that the number acquired its symbolic meaning long before the earliest time for which that reference can be demonstrated. As this sacred or symbolic use of 7 was not peculiar to the Babylonians and their teachers and neighbors, but was more or less known also in India and China, in classical lands, and among the Celts and the Germans, it probably originated in some fact of common observation, perhaps in the four lunar phases each of which comprises 7 days and a fraction. Conspicuous groups of stars may have helped to deepen the impression, and the fact that 7 is made up of two significant numbers, each, as will be shown, also suggestive of completeness—3 and 4—may have been early noticed and taken into account. The Bib. use of 7 may be conveniently considered under 4 heads: (1) ritual use; (2) historical use; (3) didactic or literary use; (4) apocalyptic use.

(1) *Ritual use of seven.*—The number 7 plays a conspicuous part in a multitude of passages giving rules for worship or purification, or recording ritual actions. The 7th day of the week was holy (see SABBATH). There were 7 days of unleavened bread (Ex **34** 18, etc), and 7 days of the Feast of Tabernacles (Lev **23** 34). The 7th year was the sabbatical year (Ex **21** 2, etc). The Moabite Balak built Balaam on three occasions 7 altars and provided in each case 7 bullocks and 7 rams (Nu **23** 1.14.29). The Mosaic law prescribed 7 he-lambs for several festal offerings (Nu **28** 11.19.27, etc). The 7-fold sprinkling of blood is enjoined in the ritual of the Day of Atonement (Lev **16** 14.19), and elsewhere. Seven-fold sprinkling is also repeatedly mentioned in the rules for the purification of the leper and the leprous house (Lev **14** 7.16.27.51). The leprous Naaman was ordered to bathe 7 times in the Jordan (2 K **5** 10). In cases of real or suspected uncleanness through leprosy, or the presence of a corpse, or for other reasons, 7 days' seclusion was necessary (Lev **12** 2, etc). Circumcision took place after 7 days (Lev **12** 3). An animal must be 7 days old before it could be offered in sacrifice (Ex **22** 30). Three periods of 7 days each are mentioned in the rules for the consecration of priests (Ex **29** 30.35.37). An oath seems to have been in the first instance by 7 holy things (Gen **21** 29 ff and the Heb word for "swear"). The number 7 also entered into the structure of sacred objects, for instance the candlestick or lamp-stand in the tabernacle and the second temple each of which had 7 lights (Nu **8** 2; Zec **4** 2). Many other instances of the ritual use of 7 in the OT and many instructive parallels from Bab texts could be given.

(2) *Historical use of seven.*—The number 7 also figures prominently in a large number of passages which occur in historical narrative, in a way which reminds us of its symbolic significance. The following are some of the most remarkable: Jacob's 7 years' service for Rachel (Gen **29** 20; cf vs 27 f), and his bowing down 7 times to Esau (Gen **33** 3); the 7 years of plenty, and the 7 years of famine (Gen **41** 53 f); Samson's 7 days' marriage feast (Jgs **14** 12 ff; cf Gen **29** 27), 7 locks of hair (Jgs **16** 19), and the 7 withes with which he was bound (vs 7 f); the 7 daughters of Jethro (Ex **2** 16), the 7 sons of Jesse (1 S **16** 10), the 7 sons of Saul (2 S **21** 6), and the 7 sons of Job (Job **1** 2; cf **42** 13); the 7 days' march of the 7 priests blowing 7 trumpets round the walls of Jericho, and the 7-fold march on the 7th day (Josh **6** 8 ff); the 7 ascents of Elijah's servant to the top of Carmel (1 K **18** 43 f); the 7 sneezes of the Shunammitish woman's son (2 K **4** 35); the heating of Nebuchadnezzar's furnace 7 times more than it was wont to be heated (Dnl **3** 19), and the king's madness for 7 times or years (**4** 16.23.25.32); Anna's 7 years of wedded life (Lk **2** 36); the 7 loaves of the 4,000 (Mt **15** 34–36 ‖) and the 7 baskets full of fragments (Mt **15** 37 ‖); the 7 brothers in the conundrum of the Sadducees (Mt **22** 25 ‖); the 7 demons cast out of Mary Magdalene (Mk **16** 9 ‖ Lk **8** 2); the 7 ministers in the church at Jerus (Acts **6** 3 ff), and the 7 sons of Sceva (**19** 14, but the Western text represents them as only 2). The number must no doubt be understood lit. in many of these passages, but even then its symbolic meaning is probably hinted at by the historian. When a man was said to have had 7 sons or daughters, or an action was reported as done or to be done 7 times, whether by design or accident, the number was noted, and its symbolic force remembered. It cannot indeed be regarded in all these cases as a sacred number, but its association with sacred matters which was kept alive among the Jews by the institution of the Sabbath was seldom, if ever, entirely overlooked.

(3) *Didactic or literary use of seven.*—The symbolic use of 7 naturally led to its employment by poets and teachers for the vivid expression of multitude or intensity. This use is sometimes evident, and sometimes latent. (*a*) Evident examples are the 7-fold curse predicted for the murderer of Cain (Gen **4** 15); fleeing 7 ways (Dt **28** 7.25); deliverance from 7 troubles (Job **5** 19); praise of God 7 times a day (Ps **119** 164); 7 abominations (Prov **26** 25; cf **6** 16); silver purified 7 times, that is, thoroughly purified (Ps **12** 6); 7-fold sin; 7-fold repentance, and 7-fold forgiveness (Lk **17** 4; cf Mt **18** 21); 7 evil spirits (Mt **12** 45 ‖ Lk **11** 26). The last of these, as well as the previous reference to the 7 demons cast out of Mary Madgalene reminds us of the 7 spirits of Beliar (XII P, Reuben chs **2** and **3**) and of the 7 evil spirits so often referred to in Bab exorcisms (cf Hehn, op. cit., 26 ff), but it is not safe to connect Our Lord's words with either. The Bab belief may indeed have influenced popular ideas to some extent, but there is no need to find a trace of it in the Gospels. The 7 demons of the latter are sufficiently accounted for by the common symbolic use of 7. For other passages which come under this head cf Dt **28** 7.25; Ruth **4** 15; 1 S **2** 5; Ps **79** 12. (*b*) Examples of latent use of the number 7, of what Zöckler (*RE*[3], "Sieben") calls "latent heptads," are not infrequent. The 7-fold use of the expression "the voice of Jeh" in Ps **29**, which has caused it to be named "The Psalm of the Seven Thunders," and the 7 epithets of the Divine Spirit in Isa **11** 2, cannot be accidental. In both cases the number is intended to point at full-summed completeness. In the NT we have the 7 beatitudes of character (Mt **5** 3–9); the 7 petitions of the Paternoster (Mt **6** 9 f); the 7 parables of the Kingdom in Mt **13**; the 7 woes pronounced on the Pharisees (Mt **23** 13.15.16.23.25.27.29), perhaps the 7 sayings of Jesus, beginning with "I am" (*egō eimi*) in the Fourth Gospel (Jn **6** 35; **8** 12; **10** 7.11; **11** 25; **14** 6; **15** 1), and the 7 disciples at the Lake after the Resurrection (Jn **21** 2). Several groups of 7 are found in the Epp. and in Rev: 7 forms of suffering (Rom **8** 35); 7 gifts or *charismata* (**12** 6–9); 7 attributes of the wisdom that is from above (Jas **3** 17); 7 graces to be added to faith (2 Pet **1** 5 ff); two doxologies each containing 7 words of praise (Rev **5** 12; **7** 12), and 7 classes of men (**6** 15). Other supposed instances of 7-fold grouping in the Fourth Gospel are pointed out by E. A. Abbott (*Johannine Grammar*, 2624 ff), but are of uncertain value.

(4) *Apocalyptic use of seven.*—As might be expected, 7 figures greatly in apocalyptic lit., although it is singularly absent from the apocalyptic portion of Dnl. Later works of this kind, however—the writings bearing the name of Enoch, the Testaments of Reuben and Levi, 2 Esd, etc—supply many illustrations. The doctrine of the 7 heavens which is developed in the Slavonic Enoch and elsewhere and may have been in the first instance of Bab origin is not directly alluded to in the Bible, but probably underlies the apostle's reference to the third heaven (2 Cor **12** 2). In the one apocalyptic writing in the NT, 7 is employed with amazing frequency. We read of 7 churches (**1** 4, etc); 7 golden candlesticks (**1** 12, etc); 7 stars (**1** 16); 7 angels of the churches (**1** 20); 7 lamps of fire (**4** 5); 7 spirits of God (**1** 4; **3** 1; **4** 5); a book with 7 seals (**5** 1); a lamb with 7 horns and 7 eyes (**5** 6); 7 angels with 7 trumpets (**8** 2); 7 thunders (**10** 3); a dragon with 7 heads and 7 diadems (**12** 3); a beast with 7 heads (**13** 1); 7 angels having the 7 last plagues (**15** 1); and 7 golden bowls of the wrath of God (**15** 7) and a scarlet-colored beast with 7 heads (**17** 3) which are 7 mountains (ver 9) and 7 kings (ver 10). The writer, whoever he was, must have had his imagination saturated with the numerical symbolism which had been cultivated in Western Asia for millenniums. There cannot be a shadow of doubt that 7 for him expressed fulness, completeness. As this inquiry will have shown, the significance of the number is practically the same throughout the Bible. Although a little of it may have been rubbed off in the course of ages, the main idea suggested by 7 was never quite lost sight of in Bib. times, and the number is still used in the life and song of the Holy Land and Arabia with at least an echo of its ancient meaning.

The significance of 7 extends to its multiples. *Fourteen*, or twice 7, is possibly symbolic in some cases. The stress laid in the OT on the 14th of the month as the day of the Passover (Ex **12** 6 and 16 other places), and the regulation that 14 lambs were to be offered on each of the 7 days of the Feast of Tabernacles (Nu **29** 13.15) hint at design in the selection of the number, esp. in view of the fact that 7 and 7 occur repeatedly in cuneiform literature—in magical and liturgical texts, and in the formula so often used in the Am Tab: "7 and 7 times at the feet of the king my lord . . . . I prostrate myself." The arrangement of the generations from Abraham to Christ in three groups of 14 each (Mt **1** 17) is probably intentional, so far as the number in each group is concerned. It is doubtful whether the number has any symbolic force in Acts **27** 27; 2 Cor **12** 2; Gal **2** 1. Of course it must be remembered that both the Heb and Gr words for 14 (*'arbā'āh 'āsār; dekatéssares*) suggest that it is made up of 10 and 4, but constant use of 7 in the sense above defined will have influenced the application of its double, at least in some cases.

Forty-nine, or 7×7, occurs in two regulations of the Law. The second of the three great festivals took place on the 50th day after one of the days of unleavened bread (Lev **23** 15 ff), that is, after an interval of 7×7 days; and two years of Jubilee were separated by 7×7 years (Lev **25** 8 ff). The combination is met with also in one of the so-called Penitential Psalms of Babylonia: "Although my sins are 7 times 7, forgive me my sins."

Seven multiplied by ten, or 70, was a very strong

expression of multitude which is met with in a large number of passages in the OT. It occurs of persons: the 70 descendants of Jacob (Ex **1** 5; Dt **10** 22); the 70 elders of Israel (Ex **24** 1.9; Nu **11** 16.24 f); the 70 kings ill treated by Adonibezek (Jgs **1** 7); the 70 sons of Gideon (Jgs **8** 30; **9** 2); the 70 descendants of Abdon who rode on 70 ass-colts (Jgs **12** 14); the 70 sons of Ahab (2 K **10** 1. 6 f); and the 70 idolatrous elders seen by Ezekiel (Ezk **8** 11). It is also used of periods: 70 days of Egyp mourning for Jacob (Gen **50** 3); 70 years of trial (Isa **23** 15.17; Jer **25** 11 f; Dnl **9** 2; Zec **1** 12; **7** 5); the 70 weeks of Daniel (Dnl **9** 24); and the 70 years of human life (Ps **90** 10). Other noticeable uses of 70 are the 70 palm trees of Elim (Ex **15** 27 ‖ Nu **33** 9); the offering of 70 bullocks in the time of Hezekiah (2 Ch **29** 32), and the offering by the heads of the tribes of 12 silver bowls each of 70 shekels (Nu **7** 13 ff). In the NT we have the 70 apostles (Lk **10** 1.17), but the number is uncertain B, D and some VSS reading 72, which is the product, not of 7 and 10, but of 6 and 12. Significant seventies are also met with outside of the Bible. The most noteworthy are the Jewish belief that there were 70 nations outside Israel, with 70 languages, under the care of 70 angels, based perhaps on the list in Gen **10**; the Sanhedrin of about 70 members; the tr of the Pent into Gr by LXX (more exactly 72), and the 70 members of a family in one of the Aram. texts of Sendschirli. This abundant use of 70 must have been largely due to the fact that it was regarded as an intensified 7.

Seventy and seven, or 77, a combination found in the words of Lamech (Gen **4** 24); the number of the princes and elders of Succoth (Jgs **8** 14); and the number of lambs in a memorable sacrifice (Ezr **8** 35), would appeal in the same way to the oriental fancy.

The product of seven and seventy (Gr *hebdomēkontákis heptá*) is met with once in the NT (Mt **18** 22), and in the LXX of the above-quoted Gen **4** 24. Moulton, however (*Gram. of Gr NT Prolegomena*, 98), renders in both passages 70+7; contra, Allen, "Mt," *ICC*, 199. The number is clearly a forceful equivalent of "always."

Seven thousand in 1 K **19** 18 ‖ Rom **11** 4 may be a round number chosen on account of its embodiment of the number 7. In the M S the number of Israelites slain at the capture of the city of Nebo by the Moabites is reckoned at 7,000.

The half of seven seems sometimes to have been regarded as significant. In Dnl **7** 25; **9** 27; **12** 7; Lk **4** 25 ‖ Jas **5** 17; Rev **11** 2; **13** 5 a period of distress is calculated at $3\frac{1}{2}$ years, that is, half the period of sacred completeness.

2. The Number Three

The number *three* seems early to have attracted attention as the number in which beginning, middle and end are most distinctly marked, and to have been therefore regarded as symbolic of a complete and ordered whole. Abundant illustration of its use in this way in Bab theology, ritual and magic is given from the cuneiform texts by Hehn (op. cit., 63 ff), and the hundreds of passages in the Bible in which the number occurs include many where this special significance either lies on the surface or not far beneath it. This is owing in some degree perhaps to Bab influence, but will have been largely due to independent observation of common phenomena—the arithmetical fact mentioned above and familiar trios, such as heaven, earth, and sea (or "the abyss"); morning, noon and night; right, middle, and left, etc. In other words, 3 readily suggested completeness, and was often used with a glance at that meaning in daily life and daily speech. Only a selection from the great mass of Bib. examples can be given here. (1) Three is often found of persons and things sacred or secular, e.g. Noah's 3 sons (Gen **6** 10); Job's 3 daughters (Job **1** 2; **42** 13) and 3 friends (Job **2** 11); Abraham's 3 guests (Gen **18** 2); and Sarah's 3 measures of meal (ver 6; cf Mt **13** 33‖); 3 in military tactics (Jgs **7** 16.20; **9** 43; 1 S **11** 11; **13** 17; Job **1** 17); 3 great feasts (Ex **23** 14); the 3 daily prayers (Ps **55** 17; Dnl **6** 10.13); the 3 night watches (Jgs **7** 19); God's 3-fold call of Samuel (1 S **3** 8); the 3 keepers of the temple threshold (Jer **52** 24); the 3 presidents appointed by Darius (Dnl **6** 2); the 3 temptations (Mt **4** 3. 5 f. 8 f ‖); the 3 prayers in Gethsemane (Mt **26** 39. 42.44 ‖); Peter's 3 denials (Mt **26** 34.75 ‖); the Lord's 3-fold question and 3-fold charge (Jn **21** 15 ff); and the 3-fold vision of the sheet (Acts **10** 16). (2) In a very large number of passages 3 is used of periods of time: 3 days; 3 weeks; 3 months and 3 years. So in Gen **40** 12.13.18; Ex **2** 2; **10** 22 f; 2 S **24** 13; Isa **20** 3; Jon **1** 17; Mt **15** 32; Lk **2** 46; **13** 7; Acts **9** 9; 2 Cor **12** 8. The frequent reference to the resurrection "on the 3d day" or "after 3 days" (Mt **16** 21; **27** 63, etc) may at the same time have glanced at the symbolic use of the number and at the belief common perhaps to the Jews and the Zoroastrians that a corpse was not recognizable after 3 days (for Jewish testimony cf Jn **11** 39; *Y^{e}bhāmōth*, xvi.3; Midr, *Gen*, ch c; *S^{e}māḥōth*, viii; for Pers ideas cf *Expos T*, XVIII, 536). (3) The number 3 is also used in a literary way, sometimes appearing only in the structure. Note as examples the 3-fold benediction of Israel (Nu **6** 24 ff); the Thrice Holy of the seraphim (Isa **6** 3); the 3-fold overturn (Ezk **21** 27 [Heb 32]); the 3-fold refrain of Pss **42, 43** regarded as one psalm (Ps **42** 5.11; **43** 5); the 3 names of God (the Mighty One, God, Jehovah, Josh **22** 22; cf Ps **50** 1); the 3 graces of 1 Cor **13**; the 3 witnesses (1 Jn **5** 8); the frequent use of 3 and 3d in Rev; the description of God as "who is and who was and who is to come" (Rev **1** 4); and 'the Father, the Son, and the Holy Spirit' (Mt **28** 19). In some of these cases 3-fold repetition is a mode of expressing the superlative, and others remind us of the remarkable association of 3 with deity alluded to by Plato and Philo, and illustrated by the triads of Egypt and Babylonia and the Far East. It cannot, however, be proved, or even made probable, that there is any direct connection between any of these triads and the Christian Trinity. All that can be said is, that the same numerical symbolism may have been operative in both cases.

3. The Number Four

The 4 points of the compass and the 4 phases of the moon will have been early noticed, and the former at any rate will have suggested before Bib. times the use of 4 as a symbol of completeness of range, of comprehensive extent. As early as the middle of the 3d millennium BC Bab rulers (followed long afterward by the Assyrians) assumed the title "king of the 4 quarters," meaning that their rule reached in all directions, and an early conqueror claimed to have subdued the 4 quarters. There are not a few illustrations of the use of 4 in some such way in the Bible. The 4 winds (referred to also in the cuneiform texts and the Book of the Dead) are mentioned again and again (Jer **49** 36; Ezk **37** 9), and the 4 quarters or corners (Isa **11** 12; Ezk **7** 2; Rev **20** 8). We read also of the 4 heads of the river of Eden (Gen **2** 10 ff), of 4 horns, 4 smiths, 4 chariots, and horses of 4 colors in the visions of Zechariah (**1** 8 LXX, 18 ff; **6** 1 ff), the chariots being directly connected with the 4 winds; 4 punishments (Jer **15** 3; Ezk **14** 21, the latter with a remarkable Assyr parallel), the 4 kingdoms in Nebuchadnezzar's dream as interpreted (Dnl **2** 37 ff) and Daniel's vision (**7** 3 ff); the 4 living creatures in Ezk (**1** 5 ff; cf **10**), each with 4 faces and 4 wings, and the 4 modeled after them (Rev **4** 6, etc). In most of these cases 4 is clearly symbolical, as in a number of passages in Apoc and Pseudepigrapha. Whether the frequent use of it in the structure of the tabernacle, Solomon's temple, and Ezekiel's temple has anything to do with the symbolic meaning is not clear, but the latter can probably be traced in proverbial and prophetic speech (Prov **30** 15.18.21. 24.29; Am **1** 3.6, etc). The 4 transgressions of the latter represent full-summed iniquity, and the 4-fold grouping in the former suggested the wide sweep of the classification. Perhaps it is not fanciful to find the idea in the 4 sets of hearers of the gospel in the parable of the Sower (Mt **13** 19–23 ||). The rabbis almost certainly had it in mind in their 4-fold grouping of characters in six successive paragraphs (*Ab*, v.16–21) which, however, is of considerably later date.

4. The Number Ten

As the basis of the decimal system, which probably originated in counting with the fingers, 10 has been a significant number in all historical ages. The 10 antediluvian patriarchs (Gen **5**; cf the 10 Bab kings of Berosus, and 10 in early Iranian and far-Eastern myths); the 10 righteous men who would have saved Sodom (Gen **18** 32); the 10 plagues of Egypt; the 10 commandments (Ex **20** 2–17 || Dt **5** 6–21; the 10 commandments found by some in Ex **34** 14–26 are not clearly made out); the 10 servants of Gideon (Jgs **6** 27); the 10 elders who accompanied Boaz (Ruth **4** 2); the 10 virgins of the parable (Mt **25** 1); the 10 pieces of silver (Lk **15** 8); the 10 servants intrusted with 10 pounds (Lk **19** 13 ff), the most capable of whom was placed over 10 cities (ver 17); the 10 days' tribulation predicted for the church of Smyrna (Rev **2** 10); the use of "10 times" in the sense of "many times" (Gen **31** 7; Neh **4** 12; Dnl **1** 20, etc, an idiom met with repeatedly in Am Tab); and the use of 10 in sacred measurements and in the widely diffused custom of tithe, and many other examples show plainly that 10 was a favorite symbolic number suggestive of a rounded total, large or small, according to circumstances. The number played a prominent part in later Jewish life and thought. Ten times was the Tetragrammaton uttered by the high priest on the Day of Atonement; 10 persons must be present at a nuptial benediction; 10 constituted a congregation in the synagogue; 10 was the usual number of a company at the paschal meal, and of a row of comforters of the bereaved. The world was created, said the rabbis, by ten words, and Abraham was visited with 10 temptations (*Ab*, v.1 and 4; several other illustrations are found in the context).

5. The Number Twelve

The 12 months and the 12 signs of the zodiac probably suggested to the old Babylonians the use of 12 as a symbolic or semi-sacred number, but its frequent employment by the Israelites with special meaning cannot at present be proved to have originated in that way, although the idea was favored by both Jos and Philo. So far as we know, Israelitish predilection for 12 was entirely due to the traditional belief that the nation consisted of 12 tribes, a belief, it is true, entertained also by the Arabs or some of them, but with much less intensity and persistence. In Israel the belief was universal and ineradicable. Hence the 12 pillars set up by Moses (Ex **24** 4); the 12 jewels in the high priest's breast-plate (Ex **28** 21); the 12 cakes of shewbread (Lev **24** 5); the 12 rods (Nu **17** 2); the 12 spies (Nu **13**); the 12 stones placed by Joshua in the bed of Jordan (Josh **4** 9); the 12 officers of Solomon (1 K **4** 7); the 12 stones of Elijah's altar (1 K **18** 31); the 12 disciples or apostles (26 t), and several details of apocalyptic imagery (Rev **7** 5 ff; **12** 1; **21** 12.14.16.21; **22** 2; cf also Mt **14** 20 || **19** 28 || **26** 53; Acts **26** 7). The number pointed in the first instance at unity and completeness which had been sanctioned by Divine election, and it retained this significance when applied to the spiritual Israel. Philo indeed calls it a perfect number. Its double in Rev **4** 4, etc, is probably also significant.

6. Other Significant Numbers

Five came readily into the mind as the half of 10. Hence perhaps its use in the parable of the Virgins (Mt **25** 2). It was often employed in literary division, e.g. in the Pent, the Pss, the part of the Hagiographa known as the *Meghillōth*, the Ethiopic Enoch and Mt (**7** 28; **11** 1; **13** 53; **19** 1; **26** 1; cf Sir J. Hawkins, *Horae Synopticae*[2], 163 ff). It seems to have been occasionally suggestive of relative smallness, as in Lev **26** 8, the 5 loaves (Mt **14** 17 ||), 1 Cor **14** 19, and perhaps in Am Tab. It has been remarked (Skinner, "Gen," *ICC*, 483) that the number occurs repeatedly in reference to matters Egyp (Gen **41** 34; **45** 22; **47** 2; Isa **19** 18), but there seems to be no satisfactory explanation. *Sixty:* Although, as was before observed, there is no direct trace in the Bible of the numerical system based on 60, there are a few passages where there may be a distant echo. The 60 cities of Argob (Dt **3** 4; Josh **13** 30; 1 K **4** 13); the 60 mighty men and the 60 queens of Cant **3** 7; **6** 8, the double use of 60 of Rehoboam's harem and family (2 Ch **11** 21), the 3 sacrifices of 60 victims each (Nu **7** 88), and the length of Solomon's temple, 60 cubits (1 K **6** 2 || 2 Ch **3** 3), may perhaps have a remote connection with the Bab use. It must be remembered that the latter was current in Israel and the neighboring regions in the division of the talent into 60 minas. A few passages in the Pseudepigrapha may be similarly interpreted, and the Bab Talm contains, as might be expected, many clear allusions. In the Bible, however, the special use of the number is relatively rare and indirect. *One hundred and ten*, the age attained by Joseph (Gen **50** 22), is significant as the Egyp ideal of longevity (Smith, *DB*[2], 1804 f; Skinner, "Gen," *ICC*, 539 f). *One hundred and fifty-three:* The Gr poet Oppian (c 171 AD) and others are said to have reckoned the number of fishes in the world at this figure (cf Jerome on Ezk **47**), and some scholars find a reference to that belief in Jn **21** 11 in which case the number would be symbolic of comprehensiveness. That is not quite impossible, but the suggestion cannot be safely pressed. Throughout this discussion of significant numbers it must be borne in mind that writers and teachers may often have been influenced by the desire to aid the memory of those they addressed, and may to that end have arranged thoughts and facts in groups of 3, or 4, or 7, or 10, and so on (Sir John Hawkins, *Horae Synopticae*[2], 166 f). They will at the same time have remembered the symbolic force of these numbers, and in some cases, at least, will have used them as round numbers. There are many places in which the round and the symbolic uses of a number cannot be sharply distinguished.

VI. Gematria (*gēmaṭrīyā'*).—A peculiar application of numbers which was in great favor with the later Jews and some of the early Christians and is not absolutely unknown to the Bible, is *Gematria*, that is the use of the letters of a word so as by means of their combined numerical value to express a name, or a witty association of ideas. The term is usually explained as an adaptation of the Gr word *geōmetría*, that is, "geometry," but Dalman (*Wörterbuch*, s.v.) connects it in this application of it with *grammateía*. There is only one clear example in Scripture, the number of the beast which is the number of a man, six hundred sixty and six (Rev **13** 18). If, as most scholars are inclined to believe, a name is intended, the numerical value of the letters composing which adds up to 666, and if it is assumed that the writer thought in Heb or Aram. *Nero Caesar* written with the consonants *nūn*=50, *rēsh*=200, *wāw*=6, *nūn*=50, *ḳōph*=100, *ṣāmekh*=60, *rēsh*=200: total=666, seems to be the best solution. Perhaps the idea suggested by Dr. Milligan that the 3-fold use of 6 which just falls short of 7, the number of sacred completeness, and is therefore a note of imperfection, may have been also in the writer's mind. Some modern scholars find a second instance in Gen **14** 14 and **15** 2. As the numerical value of the consonants which compose *Eliezer* in Heb add up to 318, it has been maintained that the number is not historical, but has been fancifully constructed by means of *gematria* out of the name. This strange idea is not new, for it is found in the Midrash on Gen (ch **43**) in the name of a rabbi who lived c 200 AD, but its antiquity is its greatest merit.

LITERATURE.—In addition to other books referred to in the course of the art.: Hehn, *Siebenzahl und Sabbath bei den Babyloniern und im AT;* König, *Stilistik, Rhetorik, Poetik*, etc, 51–57, and the same writer's art. "Number" in *HDB;* Sir J. Hawkins, *Horae Synopticae*[2], 163–67; Wiener, *Essays in Pentateuchal Criticism*, 155–69; "Number" in *HDB* (1-vol); *EB; Jew Enc;* Smith, *DB;* "Numbers" in *DCG;* "Zahlen" in the Dicts. of Wiener, Riehm[2], Guthe; "Zahlen" and "Sieben" in *RE*[3].

WILLIAM TAYLOR SMITH

NUMBER, GOLDEN. See GOLDEN NUMBER.

NUMBERING. See DAVID; QUIRINIUS.

NUMBERS, num′bẽrz, **BOOK OF:**

I. TITLE AND CONTENTS
  1. Title
  2. Contents
II. LITERARY STRUCTURE
  1. Alleged Grounds of Distribution
  2. Objections to Same
    (1) Hypothesis Unproved
    (2) Written Record Not Impossible
    (3) No Book Ever Thus Constructed
    (4) Inherent Difficulties of Analysis
      (a) The Story of the Spies
      (b) Rebellion of Korah
      (c) Story of Balaam
III. HISTORICAL CREDIBILITY
  1. Seeming Chronological Inaccuracies
    (1) The Second Passover
    (2) The Thirty-seven Years' Chasm
    (3) Fortieth Year
  2. So-called Statistical Errors
    (1) Number of the Fighting Men
    (2) Size of the Congregation
      (a) Multiplication of People
      (b) Exodus in One Day
      (c) Support in Wilderness
      (d) Room at Mt. Sinai
      (e) Slow Conquest of Canaan
    (3) Number of the Firstborn
  3. Alleged Physical Impossibilities
    (1) Duties of the Priests
    (2) Assembling of the Congregation
    (3) Marching of the Host
    (4) Victory over Midian
IV. AUTHORSHIP
  1. Against the Mosaic Authorship
    (1) Alternating Use of Divine Names
    (2) Traces of Late Authorship
  2. For the Mosaic Authorship
    (1) Certain Passages Have the Appearance of Having Been Written by Moses
    (2) Acquaintance with Egyptian Manners and Customs
LITERATURE

I. Title and Contents.—Styled in the Heb Bible בְּמִדְבַּר, *b*[e]*midhbar*, "in the wilderness," from the 5th word in **1** 1, probably because of

1. Title

recording the fortunes of Israel in the Sinaitic desert. The 4th book of the Pent (or of the Hex, according to criticism) was designated Ἀριθμοί, *Arithmoi*, in LXX and *Numeri* in the Vulg, and from this last received its name "Numbers" in the AV, in all 3 evidently because of its reporting the 2 censuses which were taken, the one at Sinai at the beginning and the other on the plains of Moab at the close of the wanderings.

Of the contents the following arrangement will be sufficiently detailed:

2. Contents

(1) Before leaving Sinai, **1** 1—**10** 10 (a period of 19 days, from the 1st to the 20th of the 2d month after the exodus), describing:
  (a) The numbering and ordering of the people, chs **1–4**.
  (b) The cleansing and blessing of the congregation, chs **5, 6**.
  (c) The princes' offerings and the dedication of the altar, chs **7, 8**.
  (d) The observance of a second Passover, **9** 1–14.
  (e) The cloud and the trumpets for the march, **9** 15—**10** 10.
(2) From Sinai to Kadesh, **10** 11—**14** 45 (a period of 10 days, from the 20th to the 30th of the 2d month), narrating:
  (a) The departure from Sinai, **10** 11–35.
  (b) The events at Taberah and Kibroth-hattaavah, ch **11**.
  (c) The rebellion of Miriam and Aaron, ch **12**.
  (d) The mission of the spies, chs **13, 14**.
(3) The wanderings in the desert, chs **15–19** (a period of 37 years, from the end of the 2d to the beginning of the 40th year), recording:
  (a) Sundry laws and the punishment of a Sabbath breaker, ch **15**.
  (b) The rebellion of Korah, ch **16**.
  (c) The budding of Aaron's rod, ch **17**.
  (d) The duties and revenues of the priests and Levites, ch **18**.
  (e) The water of separation for the unclean, ch **19**.
(4) From Kadesh to Moab, chs **20, 21** (a period of 10 months, from the beginning of the 40th year), reciting:
  (a) The story of Balaam, **22** 2—**24** 25.
  (b) The zeal of Phinehas, ch **25**.
  (c) The second census, **26** 1–51.
  (d) Directions for dividing the land, **26** 52—**27** 11.
  (e) Appointment of Moses' successor, **27** 12–23.
  (f) Concerning offerings and vows, chs **28–30**.
  (g) War with Midian, ch **31**.
  (h) Settlement of Reuben and Gad, ch **32**.
  (i) List of camping stations, **33** 1–49.
  (j) Canaan to be cleared of its inhabitants and divided, **33** 50—**34** 29.
  (k) Cities of refuge to be appointed, ch **35**.
  (l) The marriage of heiresses, ch **36**.

II. Literary Structure.—According to modern criticism, the text of Nu, like that of the other books of the Pent (or Hex), instead of being regarded as substantially the work of one writer (whatever may have been his sources of information and whoever may have been its first or latest editor), should be distributed—not always in solid blocks of composition, but frequently in fragments, in sentences, clauses or words, so mysteriously put together that they cannot now with certainty be separated—among three writers, J, E and P with another D (at least in one part)—these writers, individuals and not schools (Gunkel), belonging, respectively: J to the 9th cent. BC (c 830), E to the 8th cent. BC (c 750), P to the 5th cent. BC (c 444), and D to the 7th cent. BC (c 621).

The grounds upon which this distribution is made are principally these: (1) the supposed preferential use of the Divine names, of

1. Alleged Grounds of Distribution

Jeh (Lord) by J, and of Elohim (God) by E and P—a theory, however, which hopelessly breaks down in its application, as Orr (*POT*, ch vii), Eerdmans (*St*, 33 ff) and Wiener (*EPC*, I) have conclusively shown, and as will afterward appear; (2) distinctions in style of composition, which are not always obvious and which, even if they were, would not necessarily imply diversity of authorship unless every author's writing must be uniform and monotonous, whatever his subject may be; and (3) perhaps chiefly a preconceived theory of religious development in Israel, according to which the people in pre-Mosaic times were animists, totemists and polytheists; in Mosaic times and after, henotheists or worshippers of one God, while recognizing the existence of other gods; and latterly, in exilic and post-exilic times, monotheists or worshippers of the one living and true God—which theory, in order to vindicate its plausibility, required the reconstruction of Israel's religious documents in the way above described, but which is now rejected by archaeologists (Delitzsch and A. Jeremias) and by theologians (Orr, Baentsch [though accepting the analysis on other grounds] and König) as not supported by facts.

Without denying that the text-analysis of criticism is on the first blush of it both plausible and attractive and has brought to light valuable information relative to Scripture, or without overlooking the fact that it has behind it the names of eminent scholars and is supported by not a few considerations of weight, one may fairly urge against it the following objections.

2. Objections to Same

(1) *Hypothesis unproved.*—At the best, the theory is an unproved and largely imaginary hypothesis, or series of hypotheses—"hypothesis built on hypothesis" (Orr); and nothing more strikingly reveals this than (*a*) the frequency with which in the text-analysis conjecture ("perhaps" and "probably") takes the place of reasoned proof; (*b*) the arbitrary manner in which the supposed documents are constructed by the critics who, without reason given, and often in violation of their own rules and principles, lift out of J (for instance) every word or clause they consider should belong to E or P, and vice versa every word or clause out of E or P that might suggest that the passage should be assigned to J, at the same time explaining the presence of the inconvenient word or clause in a document to which it did not belong by the careless or deliberate action of a redactor; and (*c*) the failure even thus to construct the documents successfully, most critics admitting that J and E cannot with confidence be separated from each other—Kuenen himself saying that "the attempt to make out a Jehovistic and an Elohistic writer or school of writers by means of the Divine names has led criticism on a wrong way"; and some even denying that P ever existed as a separate document at all, Eerdmans (*St*, 33, 82), in particular, maintaining, as the result of elaborate exegesis, that P could not have been constructed in either exilic or post-exilic times "as an introduction to a legal work."

(2) *Written record not impossible.*—It is impossible to demonstrate that the story of Israel's "wanderings" was not committed to writing by Moses, who certainly was not unacquainted with the art of writing, who had the ability, if any man had, to prepare such a writing, whose interest it was, as the leader of his people, to see that such writing, whether done by himself or by others under his supervision, was accurate, and who besides had been commanded by God to write the journeyings of Israel (**33** 2). To suppose that for 500 years no reliable record of the fortunes of Israel existed, when during these years writing was practised in Egypt and Babylon; and that what was then fixed in written characters was only the tradition that had floated down for 5 cents. from mouth to mouth, is simply to say that little or no dependence can be placed upon the narrative, that while there may be at the bottom of it some grains of fact, the main body of it is fiction. This conclusion will not be readily admitted.

(3) *No book constructed in this way.*—No reliable evidence exists that any book either ancient or modern was ever constructed as, according to criticism, the Pent, and in particular Nu, was. Volumes have indeed been composed by two or more authors, acting in concert, but their contributions have never been intermixed as those of J, E, D and P are declared to have been; nor, when joint authorship has been acknowledged on the title-page, has it been possible for readers confidently to assign to each author his own contribution. And yet, modern criticism, dealing with documents more than 2,000 years old and in a language foreign to the critics—which documents, moreover, exist only in MSS not older than the 10th cent. AD (Buhl, *Canon and Text of the OT*, 28), and the text of which has been fixed not infallibly either as to consonant or vowel—claims that it can tell exactly (or nearly so) what parts, whether paragraphs, sentences, clauses or words, were supplied by J, E, P and D respectively. *Credat Judaeus Apella!*

(4) *Inherent difficulties of analysis.*—The critical theory, besides making of the text of Nu, as of the other books of the Pent, such a patchwork as is unthinkable in any document with ordinary pretension to historical veracity, is burdened with inherent difficulties which make it hard to credit, as the following examples, taken from Nu, will show.

(*a*) The story of the spies: Chs **13** and **14** are thus distributed by Cornill, Driver, Strack and *EB:*

JE, **13** 17*b*–20.22–24.26*b*–31.32*b*.33; **14** 3.4.8.9.11–25.39–45.

P, **13** 1–17*a*.21.25.26*a* (to Paran).32*a*; **14** 1.2 (in the main). 5–7.10.26–38 (in the main).

Kautzsch generally agrees; and Hartford-Battersby in *HDB* professes ability to divide between J and E.

(i) According to this analysis, however, up to the middle of the 5th cent. BC, either JE began at **13** 17*b*, in which case it wanted both the instruction to search the land and the names of the searchers, both of which were subsequently added from P (assuming it to have been a separate document, which is doubtful); or, if JE contained both the instruction and the names, these were supplanted by 1–17*a* from P. As the former of these alternatives is hardly likely, one naturally asks why the opening verses of JE were removed and those of P substituted? And if they were removed, what has become of them? Does not the occurrence of Jeh in 1–17*a*, on the critical principles of some, suggest that this section is the missing paragraph of JE?

(ii) If the JE passages furnish a nearly complete narrative (Driver), why should the late compiler or editor have deemed it necessary to insert two whole verses, 21 and 25, and two halves, 26*a* and 32*a*, if not because without these the original JE narrative would have been incomplete? Ver 21 states in general terms that the spies searched the whole land, proceeding as far N. as Hamath, after which ver 22 mentions that they entered the country from the S. and went up to Hebron and Eshcol, without at all stating an incongruity (Gray) or implying (Driver) that they traveled no farther N. —the reason for specifying the visit to Eshcol being the interesting fact that there the extraordinary cluster of grapes was obtained. Vs 25.26*a* relate quite naturally that the spies returned to Kadesh after 40 days and reported what they had found to Moses and Aaron as well as to all the congregation. Without these verses the narrative would have stated neither how long the land had been searched nor whether Moses and Aaron had received any report from their messengers, although ver 26*b* implies that a report was given to some person or persons unnamed. That Moses and Aaron should not have been named in JE is exceedingly improbable. Ver 32*a* is in no way inconsistent with vs 26*b*–31, which state that the land was flowing with milk and honey. What ver 32*a* adds is an expression of the exaggerated fears of the spies, whose language could not mean that the land was so barren that they would die of starvation, a statement which would have expressly contradicted ver 27 (JE)—in which case why should it have been inserted?—but that, notwithstanding its fruitfulness, the population was continually being wasted by internecine wars and the incursions of surrounding tribes. The starvation theory, moreover, is not supported by the texts (Lev **26** 38; Ezk **36** 13) usually quoted in its behalf.

(iii) To argue (Driver) for two documents because Joshua is not always mentioned along with

Caleb is not strikingly convincing; while if Joshua is not included among the spies in JE, that is obviously because the passages containing his name have been assigned beforehand to P. But if Joshua's name did not occur in JE, why would it have been inserted in the story by a post-exilic writer, when even in Dt **1** 36 Joshua is not expressly named as one of the spies, though again the language in Dt **1** 38 tacitly suggests that both Caleb and Joshua were among the searchers of the land, and that any partition of the text which conveys the impression that Joshua was not among the spies is wrong?

(iv) If the text-analysis is as the critics arrange, how comes it that in JE the name Jeh does not once occur, while all the verses containing it are allocated to P?

(*b*) The rebellion of Korah: Chs **16** and **17** are supposed to be the work of "two, if not three," contributors (Driver, Kautzsch)—the whole story being assigned to P (enlarged by additions about which the text analysts are not unanimous), with the exception of **16** 1*b*.2*a*.12–15.25.26.27*b*–34, which are given to JE, though variations here also are not unknown.

It is admitted that the JE verses, if read continuously, make out a story of Dathan and Abiram as distinguished from Korah and his company; that the motives of Dathan and Abiram probably differed from those of Korah and his company, and that Dathan and Abiram were swallowed up by an earthquake, while the 250 incense-offerers were destroyed by fire. To conclude from this, however, that three or even two narratives have been intermixed is traveling beyond the premises.

(i) If JE contained more about the conspiracy of the Reubenites, Dathan and Abiram, than has been preserved in the verses assigned to it, what has become of the excised verses, if they are not those ascribed to P; and, if they are not, what evidence exists that P's verses are better than the lost verses of JE? And how comes it that in P the Divine name used throughout, with one exception, ver 22, is Jeh, while in JE it occurs only 6 t? (ii) If JE contained only the parts assigned to it and nothing more happened than the Reubenite *émeute*, why should the Korahite rebellion have been added to it 4 cents. later, if that rebellion never happened? (iii) If the Korahite conspiracy did happen, why should it have been omitted in JE, and nothing whispered about it till after the exile? (iv) If the two conspiracies, ecclesiastical (among the princes) and civil (among the laymen), arose contemporaneously, and the conspirators made common cause with one another, in that there was nothing unusual or contrary to experience. (v) If Moses addressed himself now to Korah and again to Dathan and Abiram, why should not the same document say so? (vi) If Dathan and Abiram were engulfed by an earthquake, and the 250 princes were consumed by fire from the tabernacle, even that does not necessitate two documents, since both events might have occurred together. (vii) It is not certain that P (vs 35–43) represents Korah as having been consumed by fire, while JE (vs 31–33) declares he was swallowed up by the earth. At least P (**26** 10) distinctly states that Korah was swallowed up by the earth, and that only the 250 were consumed by fire.

Wherefore, in the face of these considerations, it is not too much to say that the evidence for more documents than one in this story is not convincing.

(*c*) The story of Balaam: Chs **22**–**24** fare more leniently at the hands of analysis, being all left with JE, except **22** 1, which is generously handed over to P. Uncertainty, however, exists as to how to partition ch **22** between J and E. Whether all should be given to E because of the almost uniform use of Elohim rather than of Jeh, with the exception of vs 22–35*a*, which are the property of J because of the use of Jeh (Driver, Kautzsch); or whether some additional verses should not be assigned to J (Cornill, *HDB*), critics are not agreed. As to chs **23** and **24**, authorities hesitate whether to give both to J or to E, or ch **23** to E and ch **24** to J, or both to a late redactor who had access to the two sources—surely an unsatisfactory demonstration in this case at least of the documentary hypothesis. Comment on the use of the Divine names in this story is reserved till later.

Yet, while declining to accept this hypothesis as proved, it is not contended that the materials in Nu are always arranged in chronological order, or that the style of composition is throughout the same, or that the book as it stands has never been revised or edited, but is in every jot and tittle the same as when first constructed. In ch **7**, e.g., the narrative goes back to the 1st day of the 1st month of the 2d year, and in ch **9** to the 1st month of the 2d year, though ch **1** begins with the 1st day of the 2d month of the 2d year. There are also legislative passages interspersed among the historical, and poetical among the prosaic, but diversity of authorship, as already suggested, cannot be inferred from either of these facts unless it is impossible for a writer to be sometimes disorderly in the arrangement of his materials; and for a lawgiver to be also a historian, and for a prose writer occasionally to burst into song. Assertions like these, however, cannot be entertained. Hence any argument for plurality of documents founded on them must be set aside. Nor is it a fair conclusion against the literary unity of the book that its contents are varied in substance and form and have been subjected, as is probable, to revision and even to interpolations, provided always these revisions and interpolations have not changed the meaning of the book. Whether, therefore, the Book of Nu has or has not been compiled from preëxisting documents, it cannot be justly maintained that the text-analysis suggested by the critics has been established, or that the literary unity of Nu has been disproved.

III. Historical Credibility.—Were the narrative in this book written down immediately or soon after the events it records, no reason would exist for challenging its authenticity, unless it could be shown either from the narrative itself or from extraneous sources that the events chronicled were internally improbable, incredible or falsified. Even should it be proved that the text consists of two or more preëxisting documents interwoven with one another, this would not necessarily invalidate its truthfulness, if these documents were practically contemporaneous with the incidents they report, and were not combined in such a way as to distort and misrepresent the occurrences they related. If, however, these preëxisting documents were prepared 500 (JE) or 1,000 (P) years after the incidents they narrate, and were merely a fixing in written characters of traditions previously handed down (JE), or of legislation newly invented and largely imaginary (P), it will not be easy to establish their historical validity. The credibility of this portion of the Pent has been assailed on the alleged ground that it contains chronological inaccuracies, statistical errors and physical impossibilities.

1. Seeming Chronological Inaccuracies

(1) *The second Passover* (**9** *1–5*)—The critical argument is that a contemporary historian would naturally have placed this paragraph before **1** 1. The answer is that possibly he would have done so had his object been to observe strict chronological order, which it manifestly was not (see chs **7** and **9**), and had he when commencing the book deemed it necessary to state that the Israelites had celebrated a second Passover on the legally appointed day, the 14th of the 1st month of the 2d year. This, however, he possibly at first assumed would be understood, and only afterward, when giving the reason for the supplementary Passover, realized that in after years readers might erroneously conclude that this was all the Passover that had been kept in the 2d year. So to obviate any such mistaken inference, he prefixed to his account of the Little Passover, as it is sometimes called, a statement to the effect that the statutory ordinance, the Great Passover, had been observed at the usual time, in the usual way, and that, too, in obedience to the express commandment of Jeh.

(2) *The thirty-seven years' chasm.*—Whether **20** 1 be considered the beginning of the 3d or of the 40th year, in either case a period of 37 years is passed over—in the one case in almost unbroken silence; in the other with scarcely anything of moment recorded save Korah's rebellion and the publication of a few laws concerning offerings to be made when the people reached the land of their habitation. To pronounce the whole book unhistorical because of this long interval of absolute or comparative silence (Bleek) is unreasonable. Most histories on this principle would be cast into the waste-basket. Besides, a historian might have as good reason for passing over as for recording the incidents of any particular period. And this might have been the case with the author of Nu. From the moment sentence of death was passed upon the old generation at Kadesh, till the hour when the new generation started out for Canaan, he may have counted that Israel had practically ceased to be the people of Jeh, or at least that their fortunes formed no part of the history of Jeh's kingdom; and it is noticeable that scarcely had the tribes reassembled at Kadesh in preparation for their onward march than Miriam and Aaron, probably the last of the doomed generation, died. Accordingly, from this point on, the narrative is occupied with the fortunes of the new generation. Whether correct or not, this solution of the 37 years' silence (Kurtz) is preferable to that which suggests (Ewald) that the late compiler, having found it impossible to locate all the traditions he had collected into the closing years of the wanderings, placed the rest of them in the first 2 years, and left the interval a blank—a solution which has not even the merit of being clever and explains nothing. It does not explain why, if the narrator was not writing history, there should have been an interval at all. A romancer would not have missed so splendid an opportunity for exercising his art, would not have left a gap of 37 years unfilled, but like the writers of the apocryphal Gospels would have crowded it with manufactured tales.

On the better theory, not only is the silence explained, but the items inserted are accounted for as well. Though the unbelieving generation had ceased to be the people of Jeh, Aaron had not yet been sentenced to exclusion from the promised land. He was still one of the representatives of the kingdom of Jeh, and Korah's rebellion practically struck a blow at that kingdom. As such it was punished, and the story of its breaking out and suppression was recorded, as a matter that vitally concerned the stability of the kingdom. For a like reason, the legislative sections were included in the narrative. They were Jeh's acts and not the people's. They were statutes and ordinances for the new generation in the new land.

(3) *The fortieth year.*—The events recorded as having taken place between the 1st of the 5th month (the date of Aaron's death) and the 1st of the 11th month (the date of Moses' address) are so numerous and important as to render it impossible, it is said, to maintain the credibility of this portion of the narrative. But (*a*) it is not certain that all the events in this section were finished before Moses began his oration; neither (*b*) is it necessary to hold that they all occurred in succession; while (*c*) until the rapidity with which events followed one another is ascertained, it will not be possible to decide whether or not they could all have been begun and finished within the space of 6 months.

2. So-called Statistical Errors

(1) *Number of the fighting men.*—This, which may be set down roughly at 600,000, has been challenged on two grounds: (*a*) that the number is too large, and (*b*) that the censuses at Sinai and in Moab are too nearly equal.

The first of these objections will be considered in the following section when treating of the size of the congregation. The second will not appear formidable if it be remembered (*a*) that it is neither impossible nor unusual for the population of a country to remain stationary for a long series of years; (*b*) that there was a special fitness in Israel's case that the doomed generation should be replaced by one as nearly as possible equal to that which had perished; (*c*) that had the narrative been invented, it is more than likely that the numbers would have been made either exactly equal or more widely divergent; and (*d*) that so many variations occurring in the strength of the tribes as numbered at Sinai and again in Moab, while the totals so nearly correspond, constitutes a watermark of truthfulness which should not be overlooked.

(2) *The size of the congregation.*—Taking the fighting men at 600,000 and the whole community at 4½ times that number, or about 2½ millions, several difficulties emerge which have led to the suggestion (Eerdmans, Conder, Wiener) that the 600,000 should be reduced (to, say, 6,000), and the entire population to less than 30,000. The following alleged impossibilities are believed to justify this reduction: (*a*) that of 70 families increasing to 2½ millions between the descent into, and the departure from, Egypt; (*b*) that of 2½ millions being led out of Egypt in one day; (*c*) that of obtaining support for so large a multitude with their flocks in the Sinaitic desert; (*d*) that of finding room for them either before the Mount at Sinai, or in the limited territory of Pal; and (*e*) that of the long time it took to conquer Pal if the army was 600,000 strong.

(*a*) Multiplication of people: As to the possibility of 70 souls multiplying in the course of 215 years or 7 generations (to take the shorter interval rather than the longer of 430 years) into 2½ millions of persons giving 600,000 fighting men, that need not be regarded as incredible till the rate of increase in each family is exactly known. Allowing to each of Jacob's grandsons who were married (say 51 out of 53), 4 male descendants (Colenso allows 4½), these would in 7 generations—not in 4 (Colenso)—amount to 835,584, and with surviving fathers and grandfathers added might well reach 900,000, of whom 600,000 might be above 20 years of age. But in point of fact, without definite data about the number of generations, the rates of birth and of mortality in each generation, all calculations are at the best problematical. The most that can be done is to consider whether the narrative mentions any circumstances fitted to explain this large number of fighting men and the great size of the congregation, and then whether the customary objections to the Bib. statement can be satisfactorily set aside.

As for confirmatory circumstances, the Bible expressly states that during the years of the oppression the Hebrews were extraordinarily fruitful, and that this was the reason why Pharaoh became alarmed and issued his edict for the destruction of the male children. The fruitfulness of the Hebrews, however, has been challenged (Eerdmans, *Vorgeschichte Israels*, 78) on the ground that were the births so numerous as this presupposes, two midwives (Ex **1** 15) would not have sufficed for the necessary offices. But if the two to whom Pharaoh spake were the superintendents of the midwives throughout Goshen, to whom the king would hardly address himself individually, or if they were the two officiating in Heliopolis, the statement in Ex **1** 15 will appear natural enough, and not opposed to the statement in Ex **1** 10 that Pharaoh was alarmed at the multiplication of the Hebrews in his land. And, indeed, if the Hebrews were only 30,000 strong, it is not easy to see why the whole might of Egypt could not have kept them in subjection. Then as to the congregation being 2½ millions if the fighting men were 600,000, that corresponds with the proportion which existed among the Helvetii, who had 92,000 men capable of bearing arms out of a population, including children, old men and women, of 368,000 souls (Caesar, *BG*, i, 20). This seems to answer the objection (Eerdmans, *Vorgeschichte Israels*, 78) that the unschooled Oriental is commonly addicted to exaggeration where numbers are concerned.

(*b*) Exodus in one day: The second difficulty would be serious were it necessary to suppose that the Israelites had never heard about their projected journey till the 14th of the 1st month. But the idea of going forth from Egypt must have been before them since the day Moses went to Pharaoh to demand their liberation; and at least 4 days before the 14th they had begun to prepare for departure. In circumstances such as these, with a people thirsting for liberty and only waiting the signal to move, aware also of the hour at which that signal would be given, viz. at midnight, it does not appear so formidable a task as is imagined to get them all assembled in one day at a fore-appointed rendezvous, more esp. as they were not likely to delay or linger in their movements. But how could there have been 2½ millions of fugitives, it is asked (Eerdmans, Wiener), if Pharaoh deemed 600 chariots sufficient for pursuit? The answer is that Pharaoh did not reckon 600 chariots sufficient, but in addition to these, which were "chosen chariots," he took all the chariots of Egypt, his horsemen and his army (Ex **14** 7.9), which were surely adequate to overcome a weaponless crowd, however big it might be. And that it was big, a vast horde indeed, Pharaoh's host implies.

(*c*) Support in wilderness: The supposed difficulty of obtaining support for 2½ millions of people with the flocks and herds in the Sinaitic desert takes for granted that the desert was then as barren a region as it is now, which cannot be proved, and is as little likely to be correct as it would be to argue that Egypt, which was then the granary of the world, was no more fertile than it was 10 years ago, or that the regions in which Babylon and Assyria were situated were as desolate then as they are now. This supposition disregards the fact that Moses fed the flocks of Jethro for 40 years in that same region of Sinai; that when the Israelites passed through it, it was inhabited by several powerful tribes. It overlooks, too, the fact that the flocks and herds of Israel were not necessarily all cooped up in one spot, but were most likely spread abroad in districts where water and vegetation could be found. And it ignores the statement in the narrative that the Israelites were not supplied exclusively by the produce of the desert, but had manna from heaven from the 1st day of the 2d month after leaving Egypt till they reached Canaan. Rationalistic expositors may relegate this statement to the limbo of fable, but unless the supernatural is to be eliminated altogether from the story, this statement must be accorded its full weight. So must the two miraculous supplies of water at Horeb (Ex **17**) and at Kadesh (Nu **20**) be treated. It is sometimes argued that these supplies were quite insufficient for 2½ millions of people with their flocks and herds; and that therefore the congregation could not have been so large. But the narrative in Nu states, and presumably it was the same in Ex, that the smitten rock poured forth its water so copiously and so continuously that 'the people drank abundantly with their flocks.' Wherefore no conclusion can be drawn from this against the reported size of the congregation.

(*d*) Room at Mt. Sinai: As to the impossibility of finding room for 2½ millions of people either before the Mount at Sinai or within the land of Canaan (Conder), few will regard this as self-evident. If the site of their encampment was the Er-Rahab plain (Robinson, Stanley)—though the plain of Sebayeh, admittedly not so roomy, has been mentioned (Ritter, Kurtz, Knobel)—estimates differ as to the sufficiency of accommodation to be found there. Conder gives the dimensions of the plain as 4 sq. miles, which he deems insufficient, forgetting, perhaps, that "its extent is farther increased by lateral valleys receding from the plain itself" (*Forty Days in the Desert*, 73; cf Keil on Ex **19** 1.2). Kalisch, though putting the size of the plain at a smaller figure, adds that "it thus furnished ample tenting ground for the hosts of Israel"—a conclusion accepted by Ebers, Riehm and others. In any case it seems driving literal interpretation to extreme lengths to hold that camping before the Mount necessarily meant that every member of the host required to be in full view of Sinai. As to not finding room in Canaan, it is doubtful if, after the conquest, the remnants of both peoples at any time numbered as many persons as dwelt in Pal during the most flourishing years of the kingdom. It may well be that the whole population of Pal today amounts to only about 600,000 souls; but Pal today under Turkish rule is no proper gauge for judging of Pal under David or even under Joshua.

(*e*) Slow conquest of Canaan: The long time it took to conquer Pal (Eerdmans, *Vorgeschichte Israels*, 78) is no solid argument to prove the unreliable character of the statement about the size of the army, and therefore of the congregation. Every person knows that in actual warfare, victory does not always go with the big battalions; and in this instance the desert-trained warriors allowed themselves to be seduced by the idolatries and immoralities of the Canaanites and forgot to execute the commission with which they had been intrusted, viz. to drive out the Canaanites from the land which had been promised to their fathers. Had they been faithful to Jeh, they would not have taken so long completely to possess the land (Ps **81** 13.14). But if instead of having 600,000 stalwart soldiers they had only possessed 6,000, it is not difficult to see how they could not drive out the Canaanites. The difficulty is to perceive how they could have achieved as much as they did.

(3) *The number of the firstborn.*—That the 22,273 firstborn males from 1 month old and upward (**3** 43) is out of all proportion to the 603,550 men of 20 years old and upward, being much too few, has frequently (Bleek, Bohlen, Colenso and others) been felt as a difficulty, since it practically involves the conclusion that for every firstborn there must have been 40 or 45 males in each family. Various solutions of this difficulty have been offered. The prevalence of polygamy has been suggested (Michaelis, Hävernick). The exclusion of firstborn sons who were married, the inclusion only of the mother's firstborn, and the great fruitfulness of Heb mothers have been called in to surmount the difficulty (Kurtz). But perhaps the best explanation is that only those were counted who were born after the Law was given on the night of the departure from Egypt (Ex **13** 2; Nu **3** 13; **8** 17) (Keil, Delitzsch, Gerlach). It may be urged, of course, that this would require an exceptionally large number of births in the 13 months; but in the exceptionally joyous circumstances of the emancipation this might not have been impossible. In any case, it does not seem reasonable on account of this difficulty, which might vanish were all the facts known, to impeach the historical accuracy of the narrative, even in this particular.

(Note.—In Scotland, with a population of nearly double that of the Israelites, viz. 4,877,648, the marriages in 1909 were 30,092, the lowest on record for 55 years. At this rate the births in Israel during the first 12 months after the exodus might have been 15,046, assuming each marriage to have had issue. As this marriage rate, however, is excessively low for Scotland in normal years, the number of marriages and therefore of births in Israel in the first year after the exodus may well have been twice, if not 3 times, 15,046, i.e. 30,092, or 45,138. Reckoning the half of these as males, viz. 15,046 or 22,569, it does not appear as if the number of the firstborn in the text were quite impossible, on the supposition made.)

3. Alleged Physical Impossibilities

(1) *The duties of the priests.*—These are supposed to have been so onerous that Aaron and his sons could not possibly have performed them. But (*a*) the Levitical laws, though published in the desert, were not necessarily intended to receive full and minute observance there, but only in Canaan. (*b*) In point of fact, as Moses afterward testified (Dt **12** 8), the Levitical laws were not scrupulously kept in the wilderness. (*c*) There is no reason to suppose that the Passover of the 2d year was celebrated otherwise than it had been in Egypt before the exodus, the slaughtering of the lambs being performed by the heads of families. And (*d*) as the Levites were set apart to minister to the tabernacle (Nu **1** 50), they would be able in many ways to assist the priests.

(2) *The assembling of the congregation.*—The assembling of the congregation at the door of the tabernacle (**10** 3.4) has been adduced as another physical impossibility; and no doubt it was if every man, woman and child, or even only every man was expected to be there; but not if the congregation was ordinarily represented by its "renowned" or "called" men, princes of the tribes of their fathers, heads of thousands of Israel (**1** 16). To suppose that anything else was meant is surely not required. When Moses called all Israel and spake unto them (Dt **5** 1; **29** 2), no intelligent person understands that he personally addressed every individual, or spoke so as to be heard by every individual, though what he said was intended for all. An additional difficulty in the way of assembling the congregation, and by implication an argument against the size of the congregation, has been discovered in the two silver trumpets which, it is contended, were too few for summoning so vast a host as 2½ millions of people. But it is not stated in the narrative either (*a*) that it was absolutely necessary that every individual in the camp should hear the sound of the trumpets any more than it was indispensable that Balaam's curse should reëcho to the utmost bounds of Israel (Nu **23** 13), or that a public proclamation by a modern state, though prefaced by means of an "Oyez," should be heard by all within the state or even within its capital; or (*b*) if it was necessary that everyone should hear, that the trumpeters could not move about through the camp but must remain stationary at the tabernacle door; or (*c*) that in the clear air of the desert the sound of the trumpets would not travel farther than in the noisy and murky atmosphere of modern cities; or (*d*) that should occasion arise for more trumpets than two, Moses and his successors were forbidden to make them.

(3) *The marching of the host.*—The marching of the host in four main divisions of about half a million each (**2**; **10** 14–20) has also been pronounced a stumbling-block (Colenso, Eerdmans, Doughty), inasmuch as the procession formed (i.e. if no division began to fall into line till its predecessor had completed its evolutions) would require the whole day for its completion, and would make a column of unprecedented length—of 22 miles (Colenzo), of 600 miles (Doughty)—and would even on the most favorable hypothesis travel only a few miles, when the whole line would again need to reconstruct the camp. The simple statement of this shows its absurdity as an explanation of what actually took place on the march, and indirectly suggests that the narrative may be historical after all, as no romancer of a late age would have risked his reputation by laying down such directions for the march, if they were susceptible of no other explanation than the above. How precisely the march was conducted may be difficult or even impossible to describe in such a way as to obviate all objections. But some considerations may be advanced to show that the march through the desert was neither impossible nor incredible. (*a*) The deploying of the four main divisions into line may have gone on simultaneously, as they were widely apart from each other, on the E. (Judah), on the S. (Reuben), on the W. (Ephraim) and on the N. (Dan). (*b*) There is no ground for thinking that the march would be conducted, at least at first, with the precision of a modern army, or that each division would extend itself to the length of 22 miles. It is more than likely that they would follow their standards as best they could or with such order as could be arranged by their captains. (*c*) If the camps of Judah and Reuben started their preparations together, say at 6 o'clock in the morning (which might be possible), and occupied 4 hours in completing these, they might begin to advance at 10 o'clock and cover 10 miles in another 4 hours, thus bringing them on to 2 PM, after which 4 hours more would enable them to encamp themselves for the night, if that was necessary. The other two divisions falling into line, say at 2 o'clock, would arrive at 6 PM, and by 10 PM would be settled for the night. (*d*) It does not seem certain that every night upon the march they would arrange themselves into a regularly constructed camp; rather it is reasonable to conclude that this would be done only when they had reached a spot where a halt was to be made for some time. (*e*) In any case, in the absence of more details as to how the march was conducted, arithmetical calculations are of little value and are not entitled to discredit the truthfulness of the narrative.

(4) *The victory over Midian.*—This has been objected to on moral grounds which are not now referred to. It is the supposed impossibility of 12,000 Israelites slaying all the male Midianites, capturing all their women and children, including 32,000 virgins, seizing all their cattle and flocks, with all their goods, and burning all their cities and castles without the loss of a single man (**31** 49), which occasions perplexity. Yet Scripture relates several victories of a similar description, as e.g. that of Abraham over the kings of the East (Gen **14** 15), in which, so far as the record goes, no loss was incurred by the patriarch's army; that of Gideon's 300 over the Midianites at a later date (Jgs **7** 22); that of Samson single-handed over 1,000 Philis (Jgs **15** 15); and that of Jehoshaphat at the battle of Tekoa (2 Ch **20** 24), which was won without a blow—all more or less miraculous, no doubt. But in profane history, Tacitus (*Ann.* xiii.39) relates an instance in which the Romans slaughtered all their foes without losing a single man; and Strabo (xvi. 1128) mentions a battle in which 1,000 Arabs were slain by only 2 Romans; while the life of Saladin contains a like statement concerning the issue of a battle (Hävernick, *Intro*, 330). Hence Israel's victory over Midian does not afford sufficient ground for challenging its historic credibility.

IV. Authorship.—Restricting attention to evidence from Nu itself, it may be remarked in a general way that the question of authorship is practically settled by what has been advanced on its literary structure and historical credibility. For, if the materials of the book were substantially the work of one pen (whoever may have been their first collector or last redactor), and if these materials are upon the whole trustworthy, there will be little room to doubt that the original pen was in the hand of a contemporary and eyewitness of the incidents narrated, and that the contemporary and eyewitness was Moses, who need not, however, have set down everything with his own hand, all that is necessary to justify the ascription of the writing to him being that it should have been composed by his authority and under his supervision. In this sense it is believed that indications are not wanting in the book both against and for the Mosaic authorship; and these may now be considered.

1. Against the Mosaic Authorship

(1) *The alternating use of Divine names.*—This usage, after forming so characteristic a feature in Gen and largely disappearing in Ex and Lev, reasserts itself in Nu, and more particularly in the story of Balaam. If chs **23** and **24** can be explained only as late documents pieced together, because of the use of "God" in ch **23** and of "Lord" in ch **24**, then Moses was not their author. But if the varying use of the Divine names is susceptible of explanation on the assumption that the two chapters originally formed one docu-

ment, then most distinctly the claim of Moses to authorship is not debarred. Now whether Balaam was a false or a true prophet, it is clear that he could hope to please Balak only by cursing Israel in the name of Jeh, the Elohim of Israel; and so it is always Jeh he consults or pretends to consult before replying to the messengers of Balak. Four times he did so (**22** 8.19; **23** 3,15); and 3 t it was Elohim who met him (**22** 9.20; **23** 14), while every time it was Jeh who put the word in his mouth. Can any conclusion be fairer than that the historian regarded Elohim and Jeh as the same Divine Being, and represented this as it were by a double emphasis, which showed (*a*) that the Jeh whom Balaam consulted was Elohim or the supreme God, and (*b*) that the God who met Balaam and supplied him with oracles was Israel's Lord? Thus explained, the alternate use of the Divine names does not require the hypothesis of two single documents rolled into one; and indeed the argument from the use of the Divine names is now generally abandoned.

(2) *Traces of late authorship.*—Traces of late authorship are believed to exist in several passages: (*a*) **15** 32–36 seems to imply that the writer was no longer in the wilderness, which may well have been the case, if already he was in the land of Moab. (*b*) **20** 5 suggests, it is said, that the people were then in Canaan. But the language rather conveys the impression that they were not yet come to Canaan; and in point of fact the people were at Kadesh in the wilderness of Zin. (*c*) In **21** 14.15. 17.18.27–30, certain archaic songs are cited as if the people were familiar with them, and the Arnon is mentioned as the border of Moab long before Israel reached the river. But that poets were among the people at the time of the exodus and probably long before, the song of Moses (Ex **15**) shows, and that a Book of the Wars of the Lord was begun to be composed soon after the defeat of Amalek is not an unreasonable hypothesis (Ex **17** 14). As for the statement that "Arnon leaneth upon the borders of Moab," that may have been superfluous as a matter of information to the contemporaries of Moses when they were about to cross the stream (Strack, *Einl*, 25), but it was quite in place in an old prophetic song, as showing that their present position had been long before anticipated and foretold. (*d*) **24** 7, according to criticism, could not have been composed before the rise of the monarchy; and certainly it could not, if prediction of future events is impossible. But if reference to a coming king in Israel was put into Balaam's mouth by the Spirit of God, as the narrator says, then it could easily have been made before the monarchy; and so could (*e*) **24** 17.18 have been written before the reign of David, though the conquest of the Edomites only then began (2 S **8** 14; 1 K **11** 1; 1 Ch **18** 12.13).

Examples such as these show that many, if not most, of the like objections against the Mosaic authorship of this book are capable of at least possible solution; and that Kuenen's caution should not be forgotten: "He who relies upon the impression made by the whole, without interrogation of the parts one by one, repudiates the first principles of all scientific research, and pays homage to superficiality" (*Rel. of Israel*, I, 11).

2. For the Mosaic Authorship

(1) *Certain passages have the appearance of having been written by Moses.*—These are: (*a*) those which bear evidence of having been intended for a people not settled in cities but dwelling in tents and camps, as e.g. chs **1–4**, describing the arrangements for the census and the formation of the camp; **6** 24–26, the high-priestly benediction; **10** 35.36, the orders for the marching and the halting of the host; **10** 1–9, the directions about the silver trumpets; ch **19**, the legislation which obviously presupposes the wilderness as the place for its observance (vs 3.7.9.14). If criticism allows that these and other passages have descended from the Mosaic age, why should it be necessary to seek another author for them than Moses? And if Moses could have composed these passages, a presumption at least is created that the whole book has proceeded from his pen. (*b*) The patriotic songs taken from the Book of the Wars of the Lord (ch **21**), which some critics (Cornill, Kautzsch and others) hold cannot be later than 750 BC, are by equally competent scholars (Bleek, De Wette, E. Meyer, König and others) recognized as parts of Israel's inheritance from the Mosaic age, whensoever they were incorporated in Nu. (*c*) The list of camping stations (ch **33**) is expressly assigned to him. Whether "by the commandment of the Lord" should be connected with the "journeys" (König) or the "writing" makes no difference as to the authorship of this chapter, at least in the sense that it is based on a Mosaic document (Strack). It is true that even if this chapter as it stands was prepared by Moses, that does not amount to conclusive evidence of the Mosaic authorship of the whole book. Yet it creates a presumption in its favor (Drechsler, Keil, Zahn). For why should Moses have been specially enjoined to write so comparatively uninteresting and unprofitable a document as a list of names, many of which are now incapable of identification, if that was all? But if Moses was already writing up a journal or history of the wanderings, whether by his own hand or by means of amanuenses, and whether by express command or without it (not an unreasonable supposition), there was no particular need to record that this was so. If, however, Moses was not thinking of preserving an itinerary, and God for reasons of His own desired that he should do so, then there was need for a special commandment to be given; and need that it should be recorded to explain why Moses incorporated in his book a list of names that in most people's judgment might have been omitted without imperiling the value of the book. Looked at in this way, the order to prepare this itinerary rather strengthens the idea of the Mosaic authorship of the whole book.

(2) *Acquaintance on the part of the author with Egyptian manners and customs.*—This points in the direction of Moses. (*a*) The trial by jealousy (**5** 11–31) may be compared with the tale of Setnau, belonging probably to the 3d cent. BC, but relating to the times of Rameses II, in which Ptahnefer-ka, having found the book which the god Thoth wrote with his own hand, copied it on a piece of papyrus, dissolved the copy in water and drank the solution, with the result that he knew all the book contained (*RP*, IV, 138). (*b*) The consecration of the Levites (**8** 7) resembled the ablutions of the Egyp priests who shaved their heads and bodies every 3d day, bathed twice during the day and twice during the night, and performed a grand ceremony of purification, preparatory to their seasons of fasting, which sometimes lasted from 7 to 40 days and even more (*WAE*, I, 181). (*c*) Uncleanness from contact with the dead (**19** 11) was not unknown to the Egyptians, who required their priests to avoid graves, funerals and funeral feasts (Porphyry, *De Abst.* ii.50, quoted in *Speaker's Comm.*). (*d*) The fish, cucumbers, melons, leeks, onions and garlic referred to in **11** 5 were articles of diet in Egypt (Herod. ii.93). (*e*) The antiquarian statement about Hebron (**13** 22) fits in well with a writer in Mosaic times. "A later writer could have had no authority for making the statement and no possible reason for inventing it" (*Pulpit Comm.* on Nu). On a candid review of all the arguments pro

and con, it is not too much to say that the preponderance of evidence lies on the side of the substantial Mosaicity of the Book of Numbers.

LITERATURE.—Comms. on Nu by Bertheau (ET), Knobel, Keil (ET), Dillmann, Strack, Lange (ET); in *Speaker's Comm.*, *Pulpit Comm.*, *ICC* (Gray); Bib. Intros of De Wette, Hengstenberg, Hävernick, Bleek, König, Strack, Cornill, Driver; in encs, etc, *RE*, *HDB*, *EB*, *Sch-Herz;* critical comms.: Reuss, *Die Geschichte der heiligen Schriften AT;* Kuenen, *The Religion of Israel* (ET); Wellhausen, *Geschichte Israels* and *Prolegomena* (ET); Klostermann, *Der Pentateuch;* Eerdmans, *Alttest. Studien;* Addis, *Documents of Hexateuch; Olford Hexateuch; EPC.*

T. WHITELAW

NUMENIUS, nū-mē'ni-us (**Νουμήνιος,** *Nouménios*): The son of Antiochus, and Antipater were the two ambassadors whom Jonathan sent to the Romans, "to the Spartans, and to other places," after his victory in the plain of Hazor (Galilee) over the princes of Demetrius (1 Macc **12** 1 ff) about 144 BC. Their mission was to confirm and renew the friendship and treaty which had existed from the days of Judas (**8** 17 ff). They were well received and successful, both at Rome (**12** 3 f) and at Sparta (**12** 19 ff; **14** 22 f). After the death of Jonathan, the victories of Simon and the establishment of peace, Simon sent Numenius on a second embassy to Rome (**14** 24), again to confirm the treaty and present a golden shield weighing 1,000 *minae*—apparently just before the popular decree by which Simon was created high priest, leader and captain "for ever" (1 Macc **14** 27 ff), September, 141 BC. The embassy returned in 139 BC, bearing letters from the senate to the kings of Egypt, Syria and "all the countries," confirming the integrity of Jewish territory, and forbidding these kings to disturb the Jews, and requiring them also to surrender any deserters (**14** 15 ff). See also LUCIUS; Schürer, *Gesch. des jüdischen Volkes* (3d and 4th edd), I, 236, 250 f.

S. ANGUS

NÛN, nōōn (נ, ן): The 14th letter of the Heb alphabet; transliterated in this Encyclopaedia as *n*. It came also to be used for the number 50. For name, etc, see ALPHABET.

NUN, nun (נוּן, *nūn*, "fish," derivative meaning "fecundity"): Father of Joshua (referred to thus 29 t) (Ex **33** 11; Nu **11** 28, etc; 1 Ch **7** 27, m "Non"; Sir **46** 1, m "Nave").

NURSE, nûrs, **NURSING,** nûrs'ing: "Nurse" in AV represents two different Heb words: In 8 passages (Gen **24** 59; **35** 8; Ex **2** 7 *bis*.9; 2 K **11** 2; 2 Ch **22** 11; Isa **49** 23) the word—noun or vb.—renders some form of the vb. יָנַק, *yānaḳ*, "to suck." The fem. causative part. of this vb. is commonly used to denote nurse or foster-mother. According to Ex **2** 7 Moses' mother—"a nurse of the Heb women"—became, at Pharaoh's daughter's request, the foster-mother of the foundling. Joash, the son of Ahaziah, was in charge of a nurse until he was 7 years old (2 K **11** 2; 2 Ch **22** 11). But it is obvious that the term was used in a more general way, e.g. of a lady's maid or tire-woman. Rebekah was accompanied by her nurse when she left home to be married (Gen **24** 59; **35** 8). In 5 passages (Nu **11** 12; Ruth **4** 16; 2 S **4** 4; Isa **49** 23; **60** 4 AV) "nurse" represents the Heb word, אָמַן, *'āman*, "to support," "be faithful," "nourish." The part. of this vb. denoted a person who had charge of young children—a guardian or governess. Naomi took charge of Ruth's child "and became nurse unto it" (Ruth **4** 16). In Nu **11** 12 Moses asks whether he has to take charge of the Israelites "as a nursing-father carrieth the sucking child." The same word is found in 2 K **10** 15 (AV "them that brought up," i.e. guardians of the sons of Ahab) and in Est **2** 7 (AV "and he brought up," i.e. he [Mordecai] adopted, his niece). Deutero-Isa uses both terms together (**49** 23) to describe the exalted position of Israel in the future when foreign kings and queens will offer their services and wait upon the chosen people.

In the solitary passage in the NT where "nurse" occurs, it renders the Gr word τροφός, *trophós*. In this case the word does not mean a hired nurse, but a mother who nurses her own children (1 Thess **2** 7).

T. LEWIS

NURTURE, nûr'ṭūr: The word occurs in AV in Eph **6** 4 as the tr of παιδεία, *paideía*, but RV changes to "chastening," and uses "nurture" (vb.) for AV "bring up" (ἐκτρέφω, *ektréphō*) in the first part of the verse. *Paideia* has the idea of training and correction; in RV 2 Esd **8** 12 for Lat *erudio;* and cf AV Wisd **3** 11; Sir **18** 13 (*paideúō*), etc.

NUTS, nuts:

(1) (אֱגוֹז, *'ĕghōz;* **καρύα,** *karúa;* Arab. *jauz*, "the walnut" [Cant **6** 11]): This is certainly the walnut tree, *Juglans regia*, a native of Persia and the Himalayas which flourishes under favorable conditions in all parts of Pal; particularly in the mountains. In such situations it attains the height of from 60 to 90 ft. A grove of such trees affords the most delightful shade.

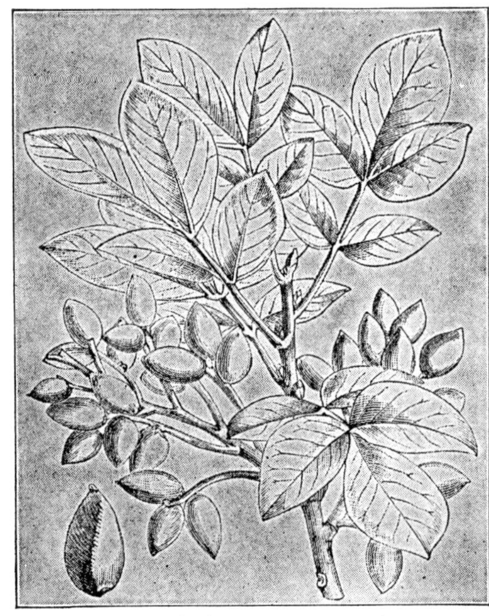
Pistachio Nut (*Pistacia vera*).

(2) (בָּטְנִים, *boṭnīm;* τερέβινθοι, *terébinthoi* [Gen **43** 11, m "pistachio nuts"]): The Heb is perhaps allied to the Arab. *buṭm*, the "terebinth," which is closely allied to the *Pistacia vera*, N.O. *Anacardiaceae*, which produces pistachio nuts. These nuts, known in Arab. as *fistuḳ*, are prime favorites with the people of Pal. They are oblong, ¾ in. long, with green, oily cotyledons. They are eaten raw and are also made into various sweets and confectionery. They are a product of Pal, very likely to be sent as a present to Egypt (Gen **43** 11).

E. W. G. MASTERMAN

NYMPHAS, nim'fas (**Νυμφᾶς,** *Numphás;* Lachmann, Tregelles [m], WH read **Νύμφα,** *Númpha*, the name of a woman [Col **4** 15]): A Christian resident in Laodicea, to whom Paul sends salutations in the ep. which he wrote from Rome to the church in Colossae, the latter city being only a very few miles distant from Laodicea. Indeed, so near were they, that Paul directs that the Ep. to the Col be read also in Laodicea. Nymphas—or if **Nympha** be read, then it is a Christian lady who is meant—was a person of outstanding worth and importance in the church of Laodicea, for he had granted the use of his dwelling-house for the ordinary weekly meetings of the church. The apostle's salutation is a 3-fold one—to the brethren that are in Laodicea, that is to the whole of the Christian community in that city, and to Nymphas, and to the church in his house.

1. A Christian in Laodicea

This fact, that the church met there, also shows that Nymphas was a person of some means, for a very small house could not have accommodated the Christian men and women who gathered together on the first day of every week for the purposes of Christian worship. The church in Laodicea—judging not only from the Ep. to the Eph, which is really Paul's Ep. to the Laodiceans, and which indicates that the church in Laodicea had a numerous membership, but also from what is said of it in Rev **3** 17 AV—must have been large and influential: "Thou sayest, I am rich, and increased with goods, and have need of nothing." The house of Nymphas, therefore, must have possessed a large room or saloon sufficiently commodious to allow the meet ing of a numerous company. Nymphas would be a person both of Christian character and of generous feeling, and of some amount of wealth. Nothing more is known regarding him, as this is the only passage in which he is named.

2. The Church in His House

JOHN RUTHERFURD

O

OABDIUS, ō-ab′di-us (A, **Ὠαβδίος**, *Ōabdíos*, B, **-είος**, *eíos*, Fritzsche, **Ἰωαβδίος**, *Iōabdíos*, om. in AV): One of the sons of Ela who put away their "strange wives" (1 Esd **9** 27) = "Abdi" of Ezr **10** 26.

OAK, ōk: Several Heb words are so tr[d], but there has always been great doubt as to which words should be tr[d] "oak" and which "terebinth." This uncertainty appears in the LXX and all through EV; in recent revisions "terebinth" has been increasingly added in the m. All the Heb words are closely allied and may originally have had simply the meaning of "tree," but it is clear that, when the OT was written, they indicated some special kind of tree.

1. Hebrew Words and References

The words and references are as follows:

(1) אֵלָה, *'ēlāh* (in LXX usually *τερέβινθος*, *terébinthos*, in Vulg *terebinthus*, or, more commonly, *quercus*) (Gen **35** 4; Jgs **6** 11.19; 2 S **18** 9.10.14; 1 K **13** 14; 1 Ch **10** 12; Isa **1** 30; Ezk **6** 13—in all these m "terebinth"). In Isa **6** 13 (AV "teil tree") and Hos **4** 13 (AV "elms") the tr is "terebinths" because of the juxtaposition of *'allōn*, tr[d] "oaks." "Vale of Elah" (m "the Terebinth") is found in 1 S **17** 2.19; **21** 9. The expression in Isa **1** 30, "whose leaf fadeth," is more appropriate to the terebinth than the oak (see below).

(2) אַלָּה, *'allāh* (*terebinthos*, *quercus* [Vulg]), apparently a slight variant for *'ēlāh;* only in Josh **24** 26; Gen **35** 4 (*'ēlāh*) and in Jgs **9** 6 (*'ēlōn*).

(3) אֵלִים or אֵילִים, *'ēlīm*, perhaps pl. of *'ēlāh*, occurs in Isa **1** 29 (m "terebinths"); **57** 5, m "with idols," AV "idols," m "oaks"; **61** 3, "trees"; Ezk **31** 14 (text very doubtful), "height," AVm "upon themselves"; אֵיל, *'ēl*, in El-paran (LXX *terebinthos*) (Gen **14** 6), probably means the "tree" or "terebinth" of Paran. Celsius (*Hierob.* i.34 ff) argues at length that the above words apply well to the TEREBINTH (q.v.) in all the passages in which they occur.

(4) אֵלוֹן, *'ēlōn* (usually *δρῦς*, *drús*, "oak"), in Gen **12** 6; **13** 18; **14** 13; **18** 1; Dt **11** 30; Josh **19** 33; Jgs **4** 11; **9** 6.37; 1 S **10** 3 (AV "plain"); in all these references m has "terebinth" or "terebinths." In Gen **12** 6; Dt **11** 30 we have "oak" or "oaks" "of the teacher" (Moreh); "oak in Zaanannim" in Jgs **4** 11; Josh **19** 33; the "oak of Meonenim," m "the augurs' oak (or, terebinth)" in Jgs **9** 37.

(5) אַלּוֹן, *'allōn* (commonly *δρῦς*, *drús*, or *βάλανος*, *bálanos*), in Gen **35** 8 (cf ver 4); Hos **4** 13; Isa **6** 13, is contrasted with *'ēlāh*, showing that *'allōn* and *'ēlāh* cannot be identical, so no marginal references occur; also in Isa **44** 14; Am **2** 9, but in all other passages, m "terebinth" or "terebinths" occurs. "Oaks of Bashan" occurs in Isa **2** 13; Ezk **27** 6; Zec **11** 2.

If (1) (2) (3) refer esp. to the terebinth, then (4) and (5) are probably correctly tr[d] "oak." If we may judge at all by present conditions, "oaks" of Bashan is far more correct than "terebinths" of Bashan.

2. Varieties of Oak

There are, according to Post (*Flora of Palestine*, 737–41), no less than 9 species of oak (N.O. *Cupuliferae*) in Syria, and he adds to these 12 sub-varieties. Many of these have no interest except to the botanist. The following species are widespread and distinctive: (1) The "Turkey oak," *Quercus cerris*, known in Arab. as *Ballûṭ*, as its name implies, abounds all over European Turkey and Greece and is common in Pal. Under favorable conditions

Oak at Gilead, the Sindeeyan (*Quercus coccifera*).

it attains to great size, reaching as much as 60 ft. in height. It is distinguished by its large sessile acorns with hemispherical cups covered with long, narrow, almost bristly, scales, giving them a mossy aspect. The wood is hard and of fine grain. Galls are common upon its branches.

(2) *Quercus lusitanica* (or *Ballota*), also known in Arab. as *Ballûṭ*, like the last is frequently found dwarfed to a bush, but, when protected, attains a height of 30 ft. or more. The leaves are dentate or crenate and last late into the winter, but are shed before the new twigs are developed. The acorns are solitary or few in cluster, and the cupules are more or less smooth. Galls are common, and a variety of this species is often known as *Q. infectoria*, on account of its liability to infection with galls.

(3) The Valonica oak (*Q. aegolops*), known in Arab. as *Mellûṭ*, has large oblong or ovate deciduous leaves, with deep serrations terminating in a bristle-like point, and very large acorns, globular, thick cupules covered with long reflexed scales. The

cupules, known commercially as valonica, furnish one of the richest of tanning materials.

(4) The Evergreen oak is often classed under the general name "Ilex oak" or Holm (i.e. holly-like) oak. Several varieties are described as occurring in Pal. *Q. ilex* usually has rather a shrublike

"Joshua's Oak"—a Terebinth (Near Abord in Ephraim. Supposed to Be the Largest Tree in Palestine).

growth, with abundant glossy, dark-green leaves, oval in shape and more or less prickly at the margins, though sometimes entire. The cupules of the acorns are woolly. It shows a marked predilection for the neighborhood of the sea. The *Q. coccifera* (with var. *Q. pseudococcifera*) is known in Arab. as *Sindiān*. The leaves, like the last, usually are prickly. The acorns are solitary or twin, and the hemispherical cupules are more or less velvety. On the *Q. coccifera* are found the insects which make the well-known Kermes dye. These evergreen oaks are the common trees at sacred tombs, and the once magnificent, but now dying, "Abraham's oak" at Hebron is one of this species.

Oaks occur in all parts of Pal, in spite of the steady ruthless destruction which has been going on for centuries. All over Carmel, Tabor, around Banias and in the hills to the W. of Nazareth, to mention well-known localities, there are forests of oak; great tracts of country, esp. in Galilee and E. of the Jordan, are covered by a stunted brushwood which, were it not for the wood-cutter, would grow into noble trees. Solitary oaks of magnificent proportions occur in many parts of the land, esp. upon hilltops; such trees are saved from destruction because of their "sacred" character. To bury beneath such a tree has ever been a favorite custom (cf Gen **35** 8; 1 Ch **10** 12). Large trees like these, seen often from great distances, are frequently landmarks (Josh **19** 33) or places of meeting (cf "Oak of Tabor," 1 S **10** 3). The custom of heathen worship beneath oaks or terebinths (Hos **4** 13; Ezk **6** 13, etc) finds its modern counterpart in the cult of the *Wely* in Pal. The oak is sometimes connected with some historical event, as e.g. Abraham's oak of Mamre now shown at Hebron, and "the oak of weeping," *Allon bacuth*, of Gen **35** 8.

3. Oaks in Modern Palestine

E. W. G. Masterman

OAK OF TABOR (אֵלוֹן תָּבוֹר, *'ēlōn tābhōr*): Thus RV in 1 S **10** 3 for AV "plain of Tabor" (RVm "terebinth"). Tabor was famous for its groves of oak, but what "oak" is meant here is not known. Ewald thinks that "Tabor" is a different pronunciation for "Deborah," and connects with Gen **35** 8; but this is not likely. See Oak, 3.

OAR, ōr. See Ships and Boats, II, 2, (3).

OATH, ōth (שְׁבוּעָה, *sh^ebhū'āh*, probably from *shebha'*, "seven," the sacred number, which occurs frequently in the ritual of an oath; **ὅρκος**, *hórkos;* and the stronger word אָלָה, *'ālāh*, by which a curse is actually invoked upon the oath-breaker [LXX **ἀρά**, *ará*]): In Mt **26** 70–74 Peter first denies his Lord simply, then with an oath (*sh^ebhū'āh*), then invokes a curse (*'ālāh*), thus passing through every stage of asseveration.

1. Law Regarding Oaths

The oath is the invoking of a curse upon one's self if one has not spoken the truth (Mt **26** 74), or if one fails to keep a promise (1 S **19** 6; **20** 17; 2 S **15** 21; **19** 23). It played a very important part, not only in lawsuits (Ex **22** 11; Lev **6** 3.5) and state affairs (*Ant*, XV, x, 4), but also in the dealings of everyday life (Gen **24** 37; **50** 5; Jgs **21** 5; 1 K **18** 10; Ezr **10** 5). The Mosaic laws concerning oaths were not meant to limit the widespread custom of making oaths, so much as to impress upon the people the sacredness of an oath, forbidding on the one hand swearing falsely (Ex **20** 7; Lev **19** 12; Zec **8** 17, etc), and on the other swearing by false gods, which latter was considered to be a very dark sin (Jer **12** 16; Am **8** 14). In the Law only two kinds of false swearing are mentioned: false swearing of a witness, and false asseveration upon oath regarding a thing found or received (Lev **5** 1; **6** 2 ff; cf Prov **29** 24). Both required a sin offering (Lev **5** 1 ff). The Talm gives additional rules, and lays down certain punishments for false swearing; in the case of a thing found it states what the false swearer must pay (*Makkōth* **2** 3; *Sh^ebhū'ōth* **8** 3). The Jewish interpretation of the 3d commandment is that it is not concerned with oaths, but rather forbids the use of the name of Jeh in ordinary cases (so Dalman).

2. Forms of Swearing

Swearing in the name of the Lord (Gen **14** 22; Dt **6** 13; Jgs **21** 7; Ruth **1** 17, etc) was a sign of loyalty to Him (Dt **10** 20; Isa **48** 11; Jer **12** 16). We know from Scripture (see above) that swearing by false gods was frequent, and we learn also from the newly discovered Elephantine papyrus that the people not only swore by Jahu (=Jeh) or by the Lord of Heaven, but also among a certain class of other gods, e.g. by Herem-Bethel, and by Isum. In ordinary intercourse it was customary to swear by the life of the person addressed (1 S **1** 26; **20** 3; 2 K **2** 2); by the life of the king (1 S **17** 55; **25** 26; 2 S **11** 11); by one's own head (Mt **5** 36); by the earth (Mt **5** 35); by the heaven (Mt **5** 34; **23** 22); by the angels (*BJ*, II, xvi, 4); by the temple (Mt **23** 16), and by different parts of it (Mt **23** 16); by Jerus (Mt **5** 35; cf *K^ethūbhōth* **2** 9). The oath "by heaven" (Mt **5** 34; **23** 22) is counted by Jesus as the oath in which God's name is invoked. Jesus does not mean that God and heaven are identical, but He desires to rebuke those who paltered with an oath by avoiding a direct mention of a name of God. He teaches that such an oath is a real oath and must be considered as sacredly binding.

Not much is told us as to the ceremonies observed in taking an oath. In patriarchal times he who took the oath put his hand under the thigh of him to whom the oath was taken (Gen **24** 2; **47** 29). The most usual form was to hold up the hand to heaven (Gen **14** 22; Ex **6** 8; Dt **32** 40; Ezk **20** 5). The wife suspected of unfaithfulness, when brought before the priest, had to answer "Amen, Amen" to his adjuration, and this was considered to be an oath on her part (Nu **5** 22). The usual formula of an oath was either: "God is witness betwixt me and thee" (Gen **31** 50), or more commonly: "As Jeh [or God] liveth" (Jgs **8** 19; Ruth **3** 13; 2 S **2** 27; Jer **38** 16), or "Jeh be a true and faithful witness amongst us" (Jer **42** 5). Usually the penalty invoked by the oath was only suggested: "Jeh [or God] do so to me" (Ruth **1** 17; 2 S **3** 9. 35; 1 K **2** 23; 2 K **6** 31); in some cases the punishment was expressly mentioned (Jer **29** 22). Nowack suggests that in general the punishment was not expressly mentioned because of a superstitious fear that the person swearing, although speaking the truth, might draw upon himself some of the punishment by merely mentioning it.

3. The Formula

Philo expresses the desire (ii.194) that the practice of swearing should be discontinued, and the Essenes used no oaths (*BJ*, II, viii, 6; *Ant*, XV, x, 4).

That oaths are permissible to Christians is shown by the example of Our Lord (Mt **26** 63 f), and of Paul (2 Cor **1** 23; Gal **1** 20) and even of God Himself (He **6** 13–18). Consequently when Christ said, "Swear not at all" (Mt **5** 34), He was laying down the principle that the Christian must not have two standards of truth, but that his ordinary speech must be as sacredly true as his oath. In the kingdom of God, where that principle holds sway, oaths become unnecessary.

4. Oaths Permissible

PAUL LEVERTOFF

OBADIAH, ō-ba-dī′a (עֹבַדְיָה, ʿ*ōbhadhyāh*, more fully עֹבַדְיָהוּ, ʿ*ōbhadhyāhū*, "servant of Yahweh"):

(1) The steward or prime minister of Ahab, who did his best to protect the prophets of Jeh against Jezebel's persecution. He met Elijah on his return from Zarephath, and bore to Ahab the news of Elijah's reappearance (1 K **18** 3–16).

(2) The prophet (Ob ver 1). See OBADIAH, BOOK OF.

(3) A descendant of David (1 Ch **3** 21).

(4) A chief of the tribe of Issachar (1 Ch **7** 3).

(5) A descendant of Saul (1 Ch **8** 38; **9** 44).

(6) A Levite descended from Jeduthun (1 Ch **9** 16), identical with Abda (Neh **11** 17).

(7) A chief of the Gadites (1 Ch **12** 9).

(8) A Zebulunite, father of the chief Ishmaiah (1 Ch **27** 19).

(9) One of the princes sent by Jehoshaphat to teach the law in Judah (2 Ch **17** 7).

(10) A Merarite employed by Josiah to oversee the workmen in repairing the temple (2 Ch **34** 12).

(11) The head of a family who went up with Ezra from Babylon (Ezr **8** 9).

(12) One of the men who sealed the covenant with Nehemiah (Neh **10** 5).

(13) A gate-keeper in the days of Nehemiah (Neh **12** 25).

The name "Obadiah" was common in Israel from the days of David to the close of the OT. An ancient Heb seal bears the inscription "Obadiah the servant of the King." JOHN RICHARD SAMPEY

OBADIAH, BOOK OF: Obadiah is the shortest book in the OT. The theme of the book is the destruction of Edom. Consequent upon the overthrow of Edom is the enlargement of the borders of Judah and the establishment of the kingship of Jeh. Thus far all scholars are agreed; but on questions of authorship and date there is wide divergence of opinion.

(1) Jeh summons the nations to the overthrow of proud Edom. The men of Esau will be brought down from their lofty strongholds; their hidden treasures will be rifled; their confederates will turn against them; nor will the wise and the mighty men in Edom be able to avert the crushing calamity (vs 1–9). (2) The overthrow of Edom is due to the violence and cruelty shown toward his brother Jacob. The prophet describes the cruelty and shameless gloating over a brother's calamity, in the form of earnest appeals to Edom not to do the selfish and heartless deeds of which he had been guilty when Jerus was sacked by foreign foes (vs 10–14). (3) The day of the display of Jeh's retributive righteousness upon the nations is near. Edom shall be completely destroyed by the people whom he has tried to uproot, while Israel's captives shall return to take possession of their own land and also to seize and rule the mount of Esau. Thus the kingship of Jeh shall be established (vs 15–21).

1. Contents of the Book

The unity of Ob was first challenged by Eichhorn in 1824, vs 17–21 being regarded by him as an appendix attached to the original exilic prophecy in the time of Alexander Jannaeus (104–78 BC). Ewald thought that an exilic prophet, to whom he ascribed vs 11–14 and 19–21, had made use of an older prophecy by Obadiah in vs 1–10, and in vs 15–18 of material from another older prophet who was contemporary, like Obadiah, with Isaiah. As the years went on, the material assigned to the older oracle was limited by some to vs 1–9 and by others to vs 1–6. Wellhausen assigned to Obadiah vs 1–5.7.10.11.13.14.15*b*, while all else was regarded as a later appendix. Barton's theory of the composition of Ob is thus summed up by Bewer: "Vs 1–6 are a preëxilic oracle of Ob, which was quoted by Jeremiah, and readapted with additions (vs 7–15) by another Obadiah in the early post-exilic days; vs 16–21 form an appendix, probably from Maccabean times" (*ICC*, 5). Bewer's own view is closely akin to Barton's. He thinks that Obadiah, writing in the 5th cent. BC, "quoted vs 1–4 almost, though not quite, literally; that he commented on the older oracle in vs 5–7, partly in the words of the older prophet, partly in his own words, in order to show that it had been fulfilled in his own day; and that in vs 8.9 he quoted once more from the older oracle without any show of literalness." He ascribes to Obadiah vs 10–14 and 15*b*. The appendix consists of two sections, vs 15*a*.16–18 and vs 19–21, possibly by different authors, ver 18 being a quotation from some older prophecy. To the average Bible student all this minute analysis of a brief prophecy must seem hypercritical. He will prefer to read the book as a unity; and in doing so will get the essence of the message it has for the present day.

2. Unity of the Book

Certain preliminary problems require solution before the question of date can be settled.

(1) *Relation of Ob and Jer* ***49***.—(*a*) Did Obadiah quote from Jer? Pusey thus sets forth the impossibility of such a solution: "Out of 16 verses of which the prophecy of Jeremiah against Edom consists, four are identical with those of Obadiah; a fifth embodies a verse of Obadiah's; of the eleven which remain, ten have some turns of expression or idioms, more or fewer, which recur in Jer, either in these prophecies against foreign nations, or in his prophecies generally. Now it would be wholly improbable that a prophet, selecting verses out of the prophecy of Jeremiah, should have selected precisely those which contain none of Jeremiah's characteristic expressions; whereas it perfectly fits in with the supposition that Jeremiah interwove verses of Obadiah with his own prophecy, that in verses so interwoven there is not one expression which occurs elsewhere in Jer" (*Minor Prophets*, I, 347). (*b*) Did Jeremiah quote from Ob? It is almost incredible that the vigorous and well-articulated prophecy in Ob could have been made

3. Date of the Book

by piecing together detached quotations from Jer; but Jeremiah may well have taken from Ob many expressions that fell in with his general purpose. There are difficulties in applying this view to one or two verses, but it has not been disproved by the arguments from meter advanced by Bewer and others. (c) Did both Obadiah and Jeremiah quote from an older oracle? This is the favorite solution among recent scholars, most of whom think that Obadiah preserves the vigor of the original, while Jeremiah quotes with more freedom; but Bewer in *ICC*, after a detailed comparison, thus sums up: "*Our conclusion is that Obadiah quoted in vs 1–9 an older oracle, the original of which is better preserved in Jer **49**.*" The student will do well to get his own first-hand impression from a careful comparison of the two passages. With Ob vs 1–4 cf Jer **49** 14–16; with Ob vs 5.6 cf Jer **49** 9.10*a;* with Ob ver 8 cf Jer **49** 7; with Ob ver 9*a* cf Jer **49** 22*b*. On the whole, the view that Jeremiah, who often quotes from earlier prophets, draws directly from Ob, with free working over of the older prophets, seems still tenable.

(2) *Relation of Ob and Joel.*—There seems to be in Joel **2** 32 (Heb **3** 5) a direct allusion to Ob ver 17. If Joel prophesied during the minority of the boy king Joash (c 830 BC), Obadiah would be, on this hypothesis, the earliest of the writing prophets.

(3) *What capture of Jerus is described in Ob vs 10–14?*—The disaster seems to have been great enough to be called "destruction" (Ob ver 12). Hence most scholars identify the calamity described by Ob with the capture and destruction of Jerus by the Chaldaeans in 587 BC. But it is remarkable, on this hypothesis, that no allusion is made either in Ob or Jer **49** 7–22 to the Chaldaeans or to the destruction of the temple or to the wholesale transportation of the inhabitants of Jerus to Babylonia. We know, however, from Ezk **35** 1–15 and Ps **137** 7 that Edom rejoiced over the final destruction of Jerus by the Chaldaeans in 587 BC, and that they encouraged the destroyers to blot out the holy city. Certain it is that the events of 587 accord remarkably with the language of Ob vs 10–14. Pusey indeed argues from the use of the form of the direct prohibition in Ob vs 12–14 that Edom had not yet committed the sins against which the prophet warns him, and so Jerus was not yet destroyed, when Obadiah wrote. But almost all modern scholars interpret the language of vs 12–14 as referring to what was already past; the prophet "speaks of what the Edomites had actually done as of what they ought not to do." The scholars who regard Obadiah as the first of the writing prophets locate his ministry in Judah during the reign of Jehoram (c 845 BC). Both 2 K and 2 Ch tell of the war of rebellion in the days of Jehoram when Edom, after a fierce struggle, threw off the yoke of Judah (2 K **8** 20–22; 2 Ch **21** 8–10). Shortly after the revolt of Edom, according to 2 Ch **21** 16 f, the Philis and Arabians broke into Judah, "and carried away all the substance that was found in the king's house, and his sons also, and his wives; so that there was never a son left him, save Jehoahaz, the youngest of his sons." Evidently the capital city fell into the hands of the invaders. It was a calamity of no mean proportions.

The advocates of a late date call attention to three points that weaken the case for an early date for Ob: (*a*) The silence of 2 K as to the invasion of the Philis and Arabians. But what motive could the author of Ch have had for inventing the story? (*b*) The absence of any mention of the *destruction* of the city by the Philis and Arabians. It must be acknowledged that the events of 587 BC accord more fully with the description in Ob vs 10–14, though the disaster in the days of Jehoram must have been terrible. (*c*) The silence as to Edom in 2 Ch **21** 16 f. But so also are the historic books silent as to the part that Edom took in the destruction of Jerus in 587. It is true that exilic and post-exilic prophets and psalmists speak in bitter denunciation of the unbrotherly conduct of Edom (Lam **4** 21.22; Ezk **25** 12–14; **35** 1–15; Ps **137** 7; Mal **1** 1–5; cf also Isa **34** and **63** 1–6); but it is also true that the earliest Heb literature bears witness to the keen rivalry between Esau and Jacob (Gen **25** 22 f; **27** 41; Nu **20** 14–21), and one of the earliest of the writing prophets denounces Edom for unnatural cruelty toward his brother (Am **1** 11 f; cf Joel **3** 19 [Heb **4** 19]).

(4) *The style of Ob.*—Most early critics praise the style. Some of the more recent critics argue for different authors on the basis of a marked difference in style within the compass of the twenty-one verses in the little roll. Thus Selbie writes in *HDB:* "There is a difference in style between the two halves of the book, the first being terse, animated, and full of striking figures, while the second is diffuse and marked by poverty of ideas and trite figures." The criticism of the latter part of the book is somewhat exaggerated, though it may be freely granted that the first half is more original and vigorous. The Heb of the book is classic, with scarcely any admixture of Aram. words or constructions. The author may well have lived in the golden age of the Heb language and literature.

(5) *Geographical and historical allusions.*—The references to the different sections and cities in the land of Israel and in the land of Edom are quite intelligible. As to Sepharad (ver 20) there is considerable difference of opinion. Schrader and some others identify it with a Shaparda in Media, mentioned in the annals of Sargon (722–705 BC). Many think of Asia Minor, or a region in Asia Minor mentioned in Pers inscriptions, perhaps Bithynia or Galatia (Sayce). Some think that the mention of "the captives of this host of the children of Israel" and "the captives of Jerus" (ver 20) proves that both the Assyr captivity and the Bab exile were already past. This argument has considerable force; but it is well to remember that Amos, in the first half of the 8th cent., describes wholesale deportations from the land of Israel by men engaged in the slave trade (Am **1** 6–10). The problem of the date of Ob has not been solved to the satisfaction of Bib. students. Our choice must be between a very early date (c 845) and a date shortly after 587, with the scales almost evenly balanced.

4. Interpretation of the Book

Ob is to be interpreted as *prediction* rather than history. In vs 11–14 there are elements of historic description, but vs 1–10 and 15–21 are predictive.

LITERATURE.—Comms.: Caspari, *Der Prophet Obadjah ausgelegt*, 1842; Pusey, *The Minor Prophets*, 1860; Ewald, *Comm. on the Prophets of the OT* (ET), II, 277 ff, 1875; Keil (ET), 1880; T. T. Perowne (in *Cambridge Bible*), 1889; von Orelli (ET), *The Minor Prophets*, 1893; Wellhausen, *Die kleinen Propheten*, 1898; G. A. Smith, *The Book of the Twelve Prophets*, II, 163 ff, 1898; Nowack, *Die kleinen Propheten*, 1903; Marti, *Dodekapropheton*, 1903; Eiselen, *The Minor Prophets*, 1907; Bewer, *ICC*, 1911. Miscellaneous: Kirkpatrick, *Doctrine of the Prophets*, 33 ff; Intros of Driver, Wildeboer, etc; Selbie in *HDB*, III, 577–80; Barton in *JE*, IX, 369–70; Cheyne in *EB*, III, 3455–62; Peckham, *An Intro to the Study of Ob*, 1910; Kent, *Students' OT*, III, 1910.

JOHN RICHARD SAMPEY

OBAL, ō'bal. See EBAL, 1.

OBDIA, ob-dī'a (A, **'Οβδία,** *Obdía*, B, **'Οββειά,** *Hobbeiá*): One of the families of usurping priests (1 Esd **5** 38) = "Habaiah" of Ezr **2** 61; "Hobaiah" of Neh **7** 63.

OBED, ō'bed (עוֹבֵד, עֹבֵד, *'ōbhēdh*, "worshipper"; in the NT Ἰωβήδ, *Iōbēd*):

(1) Son of Boaz and Ruth and grandfather of David (Ruth **4** 17.21.22; 1 Ch **2** 12; Mt **1** 5; Lk **3** 32).

(2) Son of Ephlal and descendant of Sheshan, the Jerahmeelite, through his daughter who was married to Jarha, an Egyp servant of her father's (1 Ch **2** 37.38).

(3) One of David's mighty men (1 Ch **11** 47).

(4) A Korahite doorkeeper, son of Shemaiah, and grandson of Obed-edom (1 Ch **26** 7).

(5) Father of Azariah, one of the centurions who took part with Jehoiada in deposing Queen Athaliah and crowning Joash (2 Ch **23** 1; cf 2 K **11** 1–16).

David Francis Roberts

OBED-EDOM, ō'bed-ē'dom (עֹבֵד־אֱדוֹם [2 Ch **25** 24], עֹבֵד־אֱדֹם [2 S **6** 10; 1 Ch **13** 13.14; **15** 25], but elsewhere without hyphen, *'ōbhēdh-'ĕdhōm*, "servant of [god] Edom"; so W. R. Smith, *Religion of Semites*², 42, and H. P. Smith, *Samuel*, 294 f, though others explain it as="servant of man"): In 2 S **6** 10.11.12; 1 Ch **13** 13.14 a Philistine of Gath and servant of David, who received the Ark of Jeh into his house when David brought it into Jerus from Kiriath-jearim. Because of the sudden death of Uzzah, David was unwilling to proceed with the Ark to his citadel, and it remained three months in the house of Obed-edom, "and Jeh blessed Obed-edom, and all his house" (2 S **6** 11). According to 1 Ch **13** 14 the Ark had a special "house" of its own while there. He is probably the same as the Levite of 1 Ch **15** 25. In 1 Ch **15** 16–21 Obed-edom is a "singer," and in 1 Ch **15** 24 a "doorkeeper," while according to 1 Ch **26** 4-8.15 he is a Korahite doorkeeper, to whose house fell the overseership of the storehouse (ver 15), while 1 Ch **16** 5.38 names him as a "minister before the ark," a member of the house or perhaps guild of Jeduthun (see 2 Ch **25** 24).

Obed-edom is an illustration of the service rendered to Heb religion by foreigners, reminding one of the Simon of Cyrene who bore the cross of Jesus (Mt **27** 32, etc). The Chronicler naturally desired to think that only Levites could discharge such duties as Obed-edom performed, and hence the references to him as a Levite.

David Francis Roberts

OBEDIENCE, ō-bē'di-ens, **OBEY**, ō-bā' (שָׁמַע, *shāma'*; ὑπακοή, *hupakoē*): In its simpler OT meaning the word signifies "to hear," "to listen." It carries with it, however, the ethical significance of hearing with reverence and obedient assent. In the NT a different origin is suggestive of "hearing under" or of subordinating one's self to the person or thing heard, hence, "to obey." There is another NT usage, however, indicating persuasion from, πείθομαι, *peíthomai*.

1. Meaning of Terms

The relation expressed is twofold: first, human, as between master and servant, and particularly between parents and children. "If a man have a stubborn and rebellious son, that will not obey the voice of his father, or the voice of his mother, and, though they chasten him, will not hearken unto them; then shall his father and his mother lay hold on him, and bring him out unto the elders of his city, and unto the gate of his place" (Dt **21** 18.19; cf Prov **15** 20); or between sovereign and subjects, "The foreigners shall submit themselves unto me: as soon as they hear of me, they shall obey me" (2 S **22** 45; 1 Ch **29** 23).

The highest significance of its usage, however, is that of the relation of man to God. Obedience is the supreme test of faith in God and reverence for Him. The OT conception of obedience was vital. It was the one important relationship which must not be broken. While sometimes this relation may have been formal and cold, it nevertheless was the one strong tie which held the people close to God. The significant spiritual relation is expressed by Samuel when he asks the question, "Hath Jeh as great delight in burnt-offerings and sacrifices, as in obeying the voice of Jeh? Behold, to obey is better than sacrifice, and to hearken than the fat of rams" (1 S **15** 22). It was the condition without which no right relation might be sustained to Jeh. This is most clearly stated in the relation between Abraham and Jeh when he is assured "In thy seed shall all the nations of the earth be blessed; because thou hast obeyed my voice" (Gen **22** 18).

2. The OT Conception

In prophetic utterances, future blessing and prosperity were conditioned upon obedience: "If ye be willing and obedient, ye shall eat the good of the land" (Isa **1** 19). After surveying the glories of the Messianic kingdom, the prophet assures the people that "this shall come to pass, if ye will diligently obey the voice of Jeh your God" (Zec **6** 15). On the other hand misfortune, calamity, distress and famine are due to their disobedience and distrust of Jeh. See Disobedience.

This obedience or disobedience was usually related to the specific commands of Jeh as contained in the law, yet they conceived of God as giving commands by other means. Note esp. the rebuke of Samuel to Saul: "Because thou obeyedst not the voice of Jeh, ... therefore hath Jeh done this thing unto thee this day" (1 S **28** 18).

In the NT a higher spiritual and moral relation is sustained than in the OT. The importance of obedience is just as greatly emphasized. Christ Himself is its one great illustration of obedience. He "humbled himself, becoming obedient even unto death, yea, the death of the cross" (Phil **2** 8). By obedience to Him we are through Him made partakers of His salvation (He **5** 9). This act is a supreme test of faith in Christ. Indeed, it is so vitally related that they are in some cases almost synonymous. "Obedience of faith" is a combination used by Paul to express this idea (Rom **1** 5). Peter designates believers in Christ as "children of obedience" (1 Pet **1** 14). Thus it is seen that the test of fellowship with Jeh in the OT is obedience. The bond of union with Christ in the NT is obedience through faith, by which they become identified and the believer becomes a disciple.

3. The NT Conception

Walter G. Clippinger

OBEDIENCE OF CHRIST: The "obedience" (ὑπακοή, *hupakoē*) of Christ is directly mentioned but 3 t in the NT, although many other passages describe or allude to it: "Through the obedience of the one shall the many be made righteous" (Rom **5** 19); "He humbled himself, becoming obedient even unto death, yea, the death of the cross" (Phil **2** 8); "Though he was a Son, yet learned obedience by the things which he suffered" (He **5** 8). In 2 Cor **10** 5, the phrase signifies an attitude *toward* Christ: "every thought into captivity to the obedience of Christ."

His subjection to His parents (Lk **2** 51) was a necessary manifestation of His loving and sinless character, and of His disposition and power to do the right in any situation. His obedience to the moral law in every particular is asserted by the NT writers: "without sin" (He **4** 15); "who knew no sin" (2 Cor **5** 21); "holy, guileless, undefiled, separated from sinners" (He **7** 26), etc; and is affirmed by Himself: "Which of you convicteth me of sin?" (Jn **8** 46); and implicitly conceded by His ene-

1. As an Element of Conduct and Character

mies, since no shadow of accusation against His character appears. Of His ready, loving, joyful, exact and eager obedience to the Father, mention will be made later, but it was His central and most outstanding characteristic, the filial at its highest reach, limitless, "unto death." His usually submissive and law-abiding attitude toward the authorities and the great movements and religious requirements of His day was a part of His loyalty to God, and of the strategy of His campaign, the action of the one who would set an example and wield an influence, as at His baptism: "Thus it becometh us to fulfil all righteousness" (Mt **3** 15); the synagogue worship (Lk **4** 16, "as his custom was"); the incident of the tribute money: "Therefore the sons are free. But, lest we cause them to stumble," etc (Mt **17** 24–27). Early, however, the necessities of His mission as Son of God and institutor of the new dispensation obliged Him frequently to display a judicial antagonism to current prescription and an authoritative superiority to the rulers, and even to important details of the Law, that would in most eyes mark Him as insurgent, and did culminate in the cross, but was the sublimest obedience to the Father, whose authority alone He, as full-grown man, and Son of man, could recognize.

2. Its Christological Bearing

Two Scriptural statements raise an important question as to the inner experience of Jesus. He **5** 8 states that "though he was a Son, yet learned [he] obedience by the things which he suffered" (*émathen aph' hôn épathen tḗn hupakoḗn*); Phil **2** 6.8: "Existing in the form of God . . . . he humbled himself, becoming obedient, even unto death." As Son of God, His will was never out of accord with the Father's will. How then was it necessary to, or could He, *learn* obedience, or *become* obedient? The same question in another form arises from another part of the passage in He **5** 9: "And having been made perfect, he became unto all them that obey him the author [cause] of eternal salvation"; also He **2** 10: "It became him [God] . . . . to make the author [captain] of their salvation perfect through sufferings." How and why should the perfect be *made* perfect? Gethsemane, with which, indeed, He **5** 8 is directly related, presents the same problem. It finds its solution in the conditions of the Redeemer's work and life on earth in the light of His true humanity. Both in His eternal essence and in His human existence, obedience to His Father was His dominant principle, so declared through the prophet-psalmist before His birth: He **10** **7** (Ps **40** 7), "Lo, I am come (in the roll of the book it is written of me) to do thy will, O God." It was His law of life: "I do always the things that are pleasing to him. I do nothing of myself, but as the Father taught me, I speak these things" (Jn **8** 29.28); "I can of myself do nothing. . . . . I seek not mine own will, but the will of him that sent me" (**5** 30). It was the indispensable process of His activity as the "image of the invisible God," the expression of the Deity in terms of the phenomenal and the human. He could be a perfect revelation only by the perfect correspondence in every detail, of will, word and work with the Father's will (Jn **5** 19). Obedience was also His life nourishment and satisfaction (Jn **4** 34). It was the guiding principle which directed the details of His work: "I have power to lay it [life] down, and I have power to take it again. This commandment received I from my Father" (Jn **10** 18); "The Father that sent me, he hath given me a commandment, what I should say, and what I should speak" (Jn **12** 49; cf **14** 31, etc). But in the Incarnation this essential and filial obedience must find expression in human forms according to human demands and processes of development. As true man, obedient disposition on His part must meet the test of voluntary choice under all representative conditions, culminating in that which was supremely hard, and at the limit which should reveal its perfection of extent and strength. It must become hardened, as it were, and confirmed, through a definite obedient act, into obedient human character. The patriot must become the veteran. The Son, obedient on the throne, must exercise the practical virtue of obedience on earth. Gethsemane was the culmination of this process, when in full view of the awful, shameful, horrifying meaning of Calvary, the obedient disposition was crowned, and the obedient Divine-human life reached its highest manifestation, in the great ratification: "Nevertheless, not my will, but thine, be done." But just as Jesus' growth in knowledge was not from error to truth, but from partial knowledge to completer, so His "learning obedience" led Him not from disobedience or debate to submission, but from obedience at the present stage to an obedience at ever deeper and deeper cost. The process was necessary for His complete humanity, in which sense He was "made perfect," complete, by suffering. It was also necessary for His perfection as example and sympathetic High Priest. He must fight the human battles under the human conditions. Having translated obedient aspiration and disposition into obedient action in the face of, and in suffering unto, death, even the death of the cross, He is able to lead the procession of obedient sons of God through every possible trial and surrender. Without this testing of His obedience He could have had the sympathy of clear and accurate knowledge, for He "knew what was in man," but He would have lacked the sympathy of a kindred experience. Lacking this, He would have been for us, and perhaps also in Himself, but an imperfect "captain of our salvation," certainly no "file leader" going before us in the very paths we have to tread, and tempted in all points like as we are, yet without sin. It may be worth noting that He "learned obedience" and was "made perfect" by suffering, not the results of His own sins, as we do largely, but altogether the results of the sins of others.

3. In Its Soteriological Bearings

In Rom **5** 19, in the series of contrasts between sin and salvation ("Not as the trespass, so also is the free gift"), we are told: "For as through the one man's disobedience the many were made sinners, even so through the obedience of the one shall the many be made righteous." Interpreters and theologians, esp. the latter, differ as to whether "obedience" here refers to the specific and supreme act of obedience on the cross, or to the sum total of Christ's incarnate obedience through His whole life; and they have made the distinction between His "passive obedience," yielded on the cross, and His "active obedience" in carrying out without a flaw the Father's will at all times. This distinction is hardly tenable, as the whole Scriptural representation, esp. His own, is that He was never more intensely active than in His death: "I have a baptism to be baptized with; and how am I straitened till it be accomplished" (Lk **12** 50); "I lay down my life, that I may take it again. No one taketh it away from me, but I lay it down of myself. I have power to lay it down, and I have power to take it again" (Jn **10** 17.18). "Who through the eternal Spirit offered himself without blemish unto God" (He **9** 14), indicates the active obedience of one who was both priest and sacrifice. As to the question whether it was the total obedience of Christ, or His death on the cross, that constituted the atonement, and the kindred question whether it was not the spirit of obedience in the act of death, rather than the act itself, that furnished the value of His redemptive work, it might conceivably, though improbably, be said that "the one act of righteousness" through which "the free gift came" was His whole life considered as one act. But these ideas are out of line with the unmistakable trend of Scripture, which everywhere lays principal stress on the death of Christ itself; it is the center and soul of the two ordinances, baptism and the Lord's Supper; it holds first place in the Gospels, not as obedience, but as redemptive suffering and death; it is unmistakably put forth in this light by Christ Himself in His few references to His death: "ransom," "my blood," etc. Paul's teaching everywhere emphasizes the death, and in but two places the obedience; Peter indeed speaks of Christ as an ensample, but leaves as his characteristic thought that Christ "suffered for sins once . . . . put to death in the flesh" (1 Pet **3** 18). In He the center and significance of Christ's whole work is that He "put away sin by the sacrifice of himself" (**9** 26); while John in many places emphasizes the death as atonement: "Unto him that . . . . loosed us from our sins by his blood" (Rev **1** 5), and elsewhere. The Scripture teaching is that "God set [him] forth to be a propitiation, through faith, in his blood" (Rom **3** 25). His lifelong obedience enters in chiefly as making and marking Him the "Lamb without blemish and without spot," who alone could be the atoning sacrifice. If it enters further, it is as the preparation and anticipation of that death, His life so dominated and suffused with the consciousness of the coming sacrifice that it becomes really a part of the death. His obedience at the time of His death could not have been atonement, for it had always existed and had not atoned; but it was the obedience that turned the possibility of atonement into the fact of atonement. He obediently offered up, not His obedience, but Himself. He is set forth as propitiation, not in His obedience, but in His blood, His death, borne as the penalty of sin, in His own body on the tree. The distinction is not one of mere academic theological interest. It involves the whole question of the substitutionary and propitiatory in Christ's redemptive work, which is central, vital and formative, shaping the entire conception of Christianity. The blessed and helpful part which Our Lord's complete and loving obedience plays in the working out of Christian character, by His example and inspiration, must not be underestimated, nor its meaning as indicating the quality of the life which is imparted to the soul which accepts for itself His mediatorial death. These bring the consummation and crown of salvation; they are not its channel, or instrument, or price. See also Atonement.

Literature.—*DCG*, art. "Obedience of Christ"; Denney, *Death of Christ*, esp. pp. 231–33; Champion, *Living Atonement;* Forsythe, *Cruciality of the Cross*, etc; works on the Atonement; Comms., in loc.

Philip Wendell Crannell

OBEISANCE, ō-bā'sans: Is used 9 t in AV in the phrase "made [or did] obeisance" as a rendering of the reflexive form of שָׁחָה (*shāḥāh*), and denotes the bow or curtsey indicative of deference and respect. The same form of the vb. is sometimes trd "to bow one's self" when it expresses the deferential attitude of one person to another (Gen **33** 6.7, etc). Occasionally the vow of homage or fealty to a king on the part of a subject is suggested. In Joseph's dream his brother's sheaves made obeisance to his sheaf (Gen **43** 28; cf also 2 S **15** 5; 2 Ch **24** 17). But in a large number of instances the vb. denotes the prostrate posture of the worshipper in the presence of Deity, and is generally rendered, "to worship" in AV. In all probability this was the original significance of the word (Gen **24** 26, etc). Obeisance (=obedience) originally signified the vow of obedience made by a vassal to his lord or a slave to his master, but in time denoted the act of bowing as a token of respect. T. Lewis

OBELISK, ob'ē-lisk, ob'el-isk: A sacred stone or *maççēbhāh*. For *maççēbhāh* RV has used "pillar" in the text, with "obelisk" in the m in many instances (Ex **23** 24; Lev **26** 1; Dt **12** 3; 1 K **14** 23; Hos **3** 4; **10** 1.2, etc), but not consistently (e.g. Gen **28** 18). See Pillar.

OBETH, ō'beth (Ὠβήθ, *Ōbēth*, B, Οὐβήν, *Oubēn*): One of those who went up with Ezra (1 Esd **8** 32) ="Ebed" of Ezr **8** 6.

OBIL, ō'bil (אוֹבִיל, *'ōbhīl*, "camel driver"): An Ishmaelite who was "over the camels" in David's palace (1 Ch **27** 30).

OBJECT, ob-jekt': Now used only in the sense "to make opposition," but formerly in a variety of meanings derived from the literal sense "to throw against." So with the meaning "to charge with" in Wisd **2** 12, AV "He objecteth to our infamy the transgressing of our education" (RV "layeth to our charge sins against our discipline"), or "to make charges against" in Acts **24** 19, AV "who ought to have been here before thee, and object, if they had ought against me" (RV "and to make accusation").

OBLATION, ob-lā'shun: In Lev and Nu, AV occasionally uses "oblation," but generally "offering," as a rendering of קָרְבָּן, *ḳorbān*—a general term for all kinds of offering, but used only in Ezk, Lev and Nu. RV renders consistently "oblation." In Ezk (also Isa **40** 20), "oblation" renders תְּרוּמָה, *t^erūmāh*, generally trd "heave offering." In some cases (e.g. Isa **1** 13; Dnl **9** 21) "oblation" in AV corresponds to מִנְחָה, *minḥāh*, the ordinary word for "gift," in P "grain offering." See Sacrifice.

OBOTH, ō'both, ō'bōth (אֹבֹת, *'ōbhōth*, "water-bags"): A desert camp of the Israelites, the 3d after leaving Mt. Hor and close to the borders of Moab (Nu **21** 10.11; **33** 43.44). See Wanderings of Israel.

OBSCURITY, ob-skū'ri-ti: In modern Eng. generally denotes a state of very faint but still perceptible illumination, and only when preceded by some such adj. as "total" does it imply the absence of *all* light. In Bib. Eng., however, only the latter meaning is found. So in Isa **29** 18 (אֹפֶל, *'ōphel*, "darkness"); **58** 10; **59** 9 (חֹשֶׁךְ, *ḥōshekh*, "darkness"); Ad Est **11** 8 (γνόφος, *gnóphos*, "darkness"). Cf Prov **20** 20, AV "in obscure darkness," ERV "in the blackest darkness," ARV "in blackness of darkness."

OBSERVE, ob-zûrv' (representing various words, but chiefly שָׁמַר, *shāmar*, "to keep," "to watch," etc): Properly means "to take heed to," as in Isa **42** 20, "Thou seest many things, but thou observest not," and from this sense all the usages of the word in EV can be understood. Most of them, indeed, are quite good modern usage (as "observe a feast," Ex **12** 17, etc; "observe a law," Lev **19** 37, etc), but a few are archaic. So Gen **37** 11, AV "His father observed the saying" (RV "kept the saying in mind"); Hos **13** 7, "As a leopard . . . . will I observe them" (RV "watch"); Jon **2** 8, "observe lying vanities" (RV "regard," but "give heed to" would be clearer; cf Ps **107** 43). Still farther from modern usage is Hos **14** 8, "I have heard him, and observed him" (RV "will regard"; the meaning is "care for"); and Mk **6** 20, "For Herod feared John . . . . and observed him" (RV "kept him safe"). In the last case, the AV editors seem to have used "to observe" as meaning "to give reverence to."

Observation is found in Lk **17** 20, "The kingdom of God cometh not with observation" (*μετὰ παρατηρήσεως, metá paratērēseōs*). The meaning of the Eng. is, "so that it can be observed," but the exact force of the underlying Gr ("visibly"? "so that it can be computed in advance"?) is a matter of extraordinary dispute at the present time. See KINGDOM OF GOD. BURTON SCOTT EASTON

OBSERVER, ob-zûr′vẽr, **OF TIMES.** See DIVINATION.

OBSTINACY, ob′sti-na-si. See HARDENING.

OCCASION, o-kā′zhun: The uses in EV are all modern, but in Jer **2** 24 "occasion" is employed (both in Heb and Eng.) as a euphemism for "time of conception of offspring."

OCCUPY, ok′ū-pī: Is in AV the tr of 7 different words: (1) נָתַן, *nāthan;* (2) סָחַר, *ṣāḥar;* (3) עָרַב, *'ārabh;* (4) עָשָׂה, *'āsāh*, either with or without the added word, מְלָאכָה, *m^e^lā'khāh;* (5) **ἀναπληροῦν,** *anaplēroún;* (6) **περιπατεῖν,** *peripateín;* (7) **πραγματεύειν,** *pragmateúein.* In almost every case the meanings of "to occupy" as used in AV in harmony with the common usage of the time have become obsolete. (1) In Ezk **27** 16.19.22, *nāthan* meant "to trade," and RV reads "traded." (2) From *ṣāḥar,* "to go about," was derived a designation of "merchants" (RV) (Ezk **27** 21). (3) *'Ārabh* (Ezk **27** 9) signifies "to exchange" (ERV and ARVm, but ARV "deal in"). (4) *'āsāh* (Ex **38** 24) means simply "to use" (RV), and the same word in Jgs **16** 11, with *m^e^lā'khāh* ("work") added, signifies that work had been done (RV). (5) In 1 Cor **14** 16, "occupy," the AV rendering of *anaplēroun*, would still be as intelligible to most as RV "fill." (6) "Occupy" in He **13** 9, in the sense of "being taken up with a thing," is the tr (both AV and RV) of *peripatein*, lit. "to walk." Finally (7) *pragmateuein* (Lk **19** 13) is rendered in AV "occupy" in its obsolete sense of "trade" (RV). DAVID FOSTER ESTES

OCCURRENT, o-kur′ent (AV, ERV, 1 K **5** 4): An obsolete form of "occurrence" (so ARV).

OCHIELUS, ō-kī-ē′lus (**'Οχίηλος,** *Ochíēlos*, B, **'Οζιῆλος,** *Oziēlos;* AV **Ochiel**): One of the "captains over thousands" who furnished the Levites with much cattle for Josiah's Passover (1 Esd **1** 9) ="Jeiel" of 2 Ch **35** 9.

OCHRAN, ok′ran (עָכְרָן, *'okhrān*, from *'ākhar*, "trouble"; AV **Ocran**): The father of Pagiel, the prince of the tribe of Asher (Nu **1** 13; **2** 27; **7** 72. 77; **10** 26).

OCHRE, ō′kẽr, **RED** (Isa **44** 13, "He marketh it out with a pencil," m "red ochre," AV "line"; שֶׂרֶד, *seredh*, a word found only here, and of unknown etymology): Designates the implement used by the carpenter to mark the wood after measuring and before cutting. "Red ochre" supposes this to have been a crayon (as does "pencil"), but a scratch-awl is quite as likely. Ochre is a clay colored by an iron compound.

OCIDELUS, os-i-dē′lus, ok-i-dē′lus (A, **'Ωκείδηλος,** *Ōkeídēlos*, B and Swete, **'Ωκαίληδος,** *Ōkaílēdos*, Fritzsche, **'Ωκόδηλος,** *Ōkódēlos;* AV and Fritzsche **Ocodelus**): One of the priests who had married a "strange wife" (1 Esd **9** 22); it stands in the place of "Jozabad" in Ezr **10** 22 of which it is probably a corruption.

OCINA, ō-sī′na, os′i-na, ok′i-na (**'Οκεινά,** *Okeiná*): A town on the Phoen coast S. of Tyre, mentioned only in Jth **2** 28, in the account of the campaign of Holofernes in Syria. The site is unknown, but from the mention of Sidon and Tyre immediately preceding and Jemnaan, Azotus and Ascalon following, it must have been S. of Tyre. One might conjecture that it was Sandalium (Iskanderuna) or *Umm ul-'Awamīd*, but there is nothing in the name to suggest such an identification.

OCRAN, ok′ran. See OCHRAN.

ODED, ō′ded (עוֹדֵד [2 Ch **15**], עֹדֵד [elsewhere], *'ōdhēdh*, "restorer"):

(1) According to 2 Ch **15** 1, he was the father of Azariah who prophesied in the reign of Asa of Judah (c 918–877), but ver 8 makes Oded himself the prophet. The two verses should agree, so we should probably read in ver 8, "the prophecy of Azariah, the son of Oded, the prophet," or else "the prophecy of Azariah the prophet." See AZARIAH.

(2) A prophet of Samaria (2 Ch **28** 9) who lived in the reigns of Pekah, king of the Northern Kingdom, and Ahaz, king of Judah. According to 2 Ch **28,** Oded protested against the enslavement of the captives which Pekah had brought from Judah and Jerus on his return from the Syro-Ephraimitic attack on the Southern Kingdom (735 BC). In this protest he was joined by some of the chiefs of Ephraim, and the captives were well treated. After those who were naked (i.e. those who had scanty clothing; cf the meaning of the word "naked" in Mk **14** 51) had been supplied with clothing from the spoil, and the bruised anointed with oil, the prisoners were escorted to Jericho.

The narrative of ch **28** as a whole does not agree with that of 2 K **15** 37; **16** 5 f, where the allied armies of Rezin of Damascus and Pekah besieged Jerus, but failed to capture it (cf Isa **7** 1–17; **8** 5–8*a*). As Curtis points out (*Chron*, 459, where he compares Ex **21** 2 ff; Lev **25** 29–43; Dt **15** 12–18), wholesale enslavement of their fellow-countrymen was not allowed to the Hebrews, and this fact the passage illustrates. It seems to be a fulfilment in spirit of Isa **61** 1–2, a portion which Our Lord read in the synagogue at Nazareth (Lk **4** 16–20). DAVID FRANCIS ROBERTS

ODES, ōdz, **OF SOLOMON.** See APOCALYPTIC LITERATURE.

ODOLLAM, ō-dol′am (**'Οδολλάμ,** *Odollám*): The Gr form of ADULLAM (q.v.), found only in 2 Macc **12** 38.

ODOMERA, od-ō-mē′ra (**'Οδομηρά,** *Odomērá*, B, **'Οδοαρρής,** *Odoarrēs*, Itala *Odaren;* AV **Odonarkes,** m **Odomarra**): It is not certain whether Odomera was an independent Bedouin chief, perhaps an ally of the Syrians, or an officer of Bacchides. He was defeated by Jonathan in his campaign against Bacchides (1 Macc **9** 66) in 156 BC.

ODOR, ō′dẽr: In the OT the rendering of בֶּשֶׂם, *besem*, "fragrance" (2 Ch **16** 14; Est **2** 12; in Jer **34** 5, RV "burnings"), and of one or two other words; in the NT of ὀσμή, *osmē* (Jn **12** 3; Phil **4** 18; Eph **5** 2 RV); in Rev **5** 8; **18** 13, of θυμίαμα, *thumíama*, where RV (with AVm in former passage) has "incense." See also SAVOR.

OF, ov: (1) In Anglo-Saxon, had the meaning "from," "away from" (as the strengthened form "off" has still), and was not used for genitive or possessive relations, these being expressed by special case-forms. In the Norman period, however, "of" was taken to represent the French *de* (a use well developed by the time of Chaucer), and in the Elizabethan period both senses of "of" were in common use. But after about 1600 the later force of the word became predominant, and in the earlier sense (which is now practically obsolete) it was replaced by other prepositions. In consequence AV (and in some cases RV) contains many uses of "of" that are no longer familiar—most of them, to be sure, causing no difficulty, but there still being a few responsible for real obscurities. (2) Of the uses where "of" signifies "from," the most common obscure passages are those where "of" follows a vb. of hearing. In modern Eng. "hear of" signifies "to gain information about," as it does frequently in AV (Mk **7** 25; Rom **10** 14, etc). But more commonly this use of "of" in AV denotes the source from which the information is derived. So Jn **15** 15, "all things that I have heard of my Father"; Acts **10** 22, "to hear words of thee"; **28** 22, "We desire to hear of thee"; cf 1 Thess **2** 13; 2 Tim **1** 13; **2** 2, etc (similarly Mt **11** 29, "and learn of me"; cf Jn **6** 45). All of these are ambiguous and in modern Eng. give a wrong meaning, so that in most cases (but not Mt **11** 29 or Acts **28** 22) RV substitutes "from." A different example of the same use of "of" is 2 Cor **5** 1, "a building of God" (RV "from"). So Mk **9** 21, "of a child," means "from childhood" ("from a child," RV, is dubious Eng.). A still more obscure passage is Mt **23** 25, "full of extortion and excess." "Full of" elsewhere in AV (and even in the immediate context, Mt **23** 27.28) refers to the *contents*, but here the "of" represents the Gr ἐκ, *ek*, "out of," and denotes the *source*—"The contents of your cup and platter have been purchased from the gains of extortion and excess." RV again substitutes "from," with rather awkward results, but the Gr itself is unduly compressed. In Mk **11** 8, one of the changes made after AV was printed has relieved an obscurity, for where the ed of 1611 read "cut down branches of the trees," the modern edd have "off" (RV "from"). For clear examples of this use of "of," without the obscurities, cf Jth **2** 21, "they went forth of Nineveh"; 2 Macc **4** 34, "forth of the sanctuary"; and, esp., Mt **21** 25, "The baptism of John, whence was it? from heaven, or of men?" Here "from" and "of" represent exactly the same Gr prep., and the change in Eng. is arbitrary (RV writes "from" in both cases). (3) In a weakened sense this use of "of" as "from" was employed rather loosely to connect an act with its source or motive. Such uses are generally clear enough, but the Eng. today seems sometimes rather curious: Mt **18** 13, "rejoiceth more of that sheep" (RV "over"); Ps **99** 8, "vengeance of their inventions" (so AV); 1 Cor **7** 4, "hath not power of her own body" (RV "over"), etc. (4) A very common use of "of" in AV is to designate the agent—a use complicated by the fact that "by" is also employed for the same purpose and the two interchanged freely. So in Lk **9** 7, "all that was done by him . . . . it was said of some . . . . ," the two words are used side by side for the same Gr prep. (RV replaces "of" by "by," but follows a different text in the first part of the verse). Again, most of the examples are clear enough, but there are some obscurities. So in Mt **19** 12, "which were made eunuchs of men," the "of men" is at first sight possessive (RV "by men"). Similarly, 2 Esd **16** 30, "There are left some clusters of them that diligently seek through the vineyard" (RV "by them"). So 1 Cor **14** 24, "He is convinced of all, he is judged of all," is quite misleading (RV "by all" in both cases). Phil **3** 12, AV "I am apprehended of Christ Jesus." seems almost meaningless (RV "by"). (5) In some cases the usage of the older Eng. is not sufficient to explain "of" in AV. So Mt **18** 23, "take account of his servants," is a very poor rendition of "make a reckoning with his servants" (so RV). In Acts **27** 5, the "sea of Cilicia" may have been felt to be the "sea which is off Cilicia" (cf RV), but there are no other instances of this use. In 2 Cor **2** 12, "A door was opened unto me of the Lord" should be "in the Lord" (so RV). 2 S **21** 4, "We will have no silver nor gold of Saul, nor of his house," is very loose, and RV rewrites the verse entirely. In all these cases, AV seems to have looked solely for smooth Eng., without caring much for exactness. In 1 Pet **1** 11, however, "sufferings of Christ" probably yields a correct sense for a difficult phrase in the Gr (so RV, with "unto" in the m), but a paraphrase is needed to give the precise meaning. And, finally, in He **11** 18, the Gr itself is ambiguous and there is no way of deciding whether the prep. employed (πρός, *prós*) means "to" (so RV) or "of" (so AV, RVm; cf He **1** 7, where "of" is necessary).

BURTON SCOTT EASTON

OFFENCE, o-fens', **OFFEND**, o-fend' (מִכְשׁוֹל, *mikhshōl*, אָשָׁם, *'āsham*, חָטָא, *ḥāṭā'*; σκάνδαλον, *skándalon*, σκανδαλίζω, *skandalízō*): "Offend" is either trans or intrans. As trans it is primarily "to strike against," hence "to displease," "to make angry," "to do harm to," "to affront," in Scripture, "to cause to sin"; intrans it is "to sin," "to cause anger," in Scripture, "to be caused to sin." "Offence" is either the cause of anger, displeasure, etc, or a sin. In Scripture we have the special significance of a *stumbling-block*, or cause of falling, sin, etc.

1. OT Usage

In the OT it is frequently the tr of *'āsham*, "to be guilty," "to transgress": Jer **2** 3, RV "shall be held guilty"; **50** 7, RV "not guilty"; Ezk **25** 12, "hath greatly offended"; Hos **4** 15, RVm "become guilty"; **5** 15, "till they acknowledge their offence," RVm "have borne their guilt"; **13** 1, "He offended in Baal," RVm "became guilty"; Hab **1** 11, "He shall pass over, and offend, [imputing] this his power unto his god," RV "Then shall he sweep by [as] a wind, and shall pass over [m "transgress"], and be guilty, [even] he whose might is his god."

In 2 Ch **28** 13, we have *'ashmath 'al*, lit. "the offence against," RV "a trespass [m "or guilt"] against Jeh"; we have also *ḥāṭā'*, "to miss the mark," "to sin," "to err" (Gen **20** 9, RV "sinned against thee"; **40** 1, "offended their lord"; 2 K **18** 14; Jer **37** 18, RV "sinned against thee"); *bāghadh*, "to deal treacherously" (Ps **73** 15, "offend against the generation of thy children," RV "dealt treacherously with"); *ḥābhal*, "to act wickedly" (Job **34** 31); *mikhshōl*, "a stumbling block" (Lev **19** 14; tr[d] in Isa **8** 14, "a rock of offence"; cf Ezk **14** 3; 1 S **25** 31; Ps **119** 165, "nothing shall offend," RV "no occasion of stumbling"; cf Isa **57** 14; Jer **6** 21, etc); *pāsha'*, "to be fractious," "to transgress" (Prov **18** 19, "a brother offended," RVm "injured"). "Offence" is *mikhshōl* (see above, 1 S **25** 31; Isa **8** 14); *ḥēṭ'*, "sin," etc (Eccl **10** 4, "Yielding pacifieth great offences," ARV "Gentleness [ERV "yielding"] allayeth," ARVm "Calmness [ERV "gentleness"] leaveth great sins undone"). "Offender" is *ḥaṭṭā'* (1 K **1** 21, m "Heb sinners"; Isa **29** 21, "that make a man an offender for a word," ARV "that make a man an offender in his cause," m "make men to offend by [their] words," or, "for a word," ERV "in a cause," m "make men to offend by [their] words").

The NT usage of these words deserves special attention. The word most frequently tr[d] "offend" in AV is *skandalizō* (*skandalon*, "offence"), very

2. NT Usage

frequent in the Gospels (Mt **5** 29, "if thy right eye offend thee"; **5** 30; **11** 6; **18** 6, "whoso shall offend one of these little ones"; **13** 41, "all things that offend"; Lk **17** 1, "It is impossible but that offences will come," etc; Rom **14** 21; **16** 17, "Mark them which cause . . . . offences"; 1 Cor **8** 13 *bis*, "if meat make my brother to offend," etc). *Skandalon* is primarily "a trap-stick," "a bent-stick on which the bait is fastened which the animal strikes against and so springs the trap," hence it came to denote a "snare," or anything which one strikes against injuriously (it is LXX for *mōḳēsh*, a "noose" or "snare," Josh **23** 13; 1 S **18** 21); "a stumbling-block" (LXX for *mikhshōl* [see above], Lev **19** 14). For *skandalizō, skandalon*, trd in AV, "offend," "offence," RV gives "cause to stumble," "stumbling-block," etc; thus, Mt **5** 29, "if thy right eye causeth thee to stumble," i.e. "is an occasion for thy falling into sin"; Mt **16** 23, "Thou art a stumbling-block unto me," an occasion of turning aside from the right path; in Mt **26** 31.33 *bis*, "offended" is retained, m 33 *bis*, "Gr caused to stumble" (same word in ver 31); Mk **9** 42, "whosoever shall cause one of these little ones that believe on me to stumble," to fall away from the faith, or fall into sin; Lk **17** 1, "It is impossible but that occasions of stumbling should come; but woe unto him, through whom they come"; in Rom **14** 21; **16** 17; in 1 Cor **8,** Paul's language has the same meaning, and we see how truly he had laid to heart the Saviour's earnest admonitions—"weak brethren" with him answering to the master's "little ones who believe"; Rom **14** 21, "It is good not to eat flesh, nor to drink wine, nor to do anything whereby thy brother stumbleth," i.e. "is led by your example to do that which he cannot do with a good conscience"; ver 20, "It is evil for that man who eateth with offence [*diá proskómmatos*]," so as to place a stumbling-block before his brother, or, rather, 'without the confidence that he is doing right'; cf ver 23, "He that doubteth is condemned if he eat, because he eateth not of faith; and whatsoever is not of faith is sin"; so 1 Cor **8** 13; Rom **16** 17, "Mark them that are causing the divisions and occasions of stumbling, contrary to the doctrine, [m "teaching"] which ye learned" (Is not the "teaching" of Christ Himself implied here?). Everything that would embolden another to do that which would be wrong for him, or that would turn any-one away from the faith, must be carefully avoided, seeking to please, not ourselves, but to care for our brother, "for whom Christ died," "giving no occasion of stumbling [*proskopḗ*] in anything" (2 Cor **6** 3).

Apróskopos, "not causing to stumble," is trd "void of offence" (Acts **24** 16, "a conscience void of offence"; 1 Cor **10** 32, RV "occasion of stumbling"; Phil **1** 10, "void of offence"); *hamartánō*, "to miss the mark," "to sin," "to err," is trd "offended" (Acts **25** 8, RV "sinned"); *hamartía*, "sin," "error" (2 Cor **11** 7, RV "Did I commit a sin?"); *ptaíō*, "to stumble," "fall" (Jas **2** 10; **3** 2 *bis*, "offend," RV "stumble," "stumbleth"); *paráptōma*, "a falling aside or away," is trd "offence" (Rom **4** 25; **5** 15*bis*.16.17.18.20, in each case RV "trespass"); *adikéō*, "to be unrighteous" (Acts **25** 11, RV "wrong-doer," AV "offender").

In Apoc we have "offence" (*skandalon*, Jth **12** 2), RV "I will not eat thereof, lest there be an occasion of stumbling"; "offend" (*hamartanō*, Ecclus **7** 7), RV "sin"; "greatly offended" (*prosochthízō*, **25** 2); "offended" (*skandalizō*, **32** 15), RV "stumble."

W. L. Walker

OFFER, of'ẽr, **OFFERING,** of'ẽr-ing. See Sacrifice.

OFFICE, of'is: In the OT the word is often used in periphrastic renderings, e.g. "minister . . . . in the priest's office," lit. act as priest (Ex **28** 1, etc); "do the office of a midwife," lit. cause or help to give birth (Ex **1** 16). But the word is also used as a rendering of different Heb words, e.g. כֵּן, *kēn*, "pedestal," "place" (Gen **40** 13, AV "place"; **41** 13); עֲבֹדָה, *'ăbhōdhāh*, "labor," "work" (1 Ch **6** 32); פְּקֻדָּה, *pᵉḳuddāh*, "oversight," "charge" (Ps **109** 8); מַעֲמָד, *ma'ămādh*, lit. "standing," e.g. waiting at table (1 Ch **23** 28); מִשְׁמָר, *mishmār*, "charge," observance or service of the temple (Neh **13** 14 AV).

Similarly in the NT the word is used in periphrastic renderings, e.g. priest's office (Lk **1** 8.9); office of a deacon (διακονία, *diakonía*, 1 Tim **3** 10); office of a bishop (ἐπισκοπή, *episkopḗ*, 1 Tim **3** 1). RV uses other renderings, e.g. "ministry" (Rom **11** 13); "serve as deacons" (1 Tim **3** 10). In Acts **1** 20, RV has "office" (m "overseership") for AV "bishoprick."

T. Lewis

OFFICER, of'i-sẽr: In AV the term is employed to render different words denoting various officials, domestic, civil and military, such as סָרִיס, *ṣārīṣ*, "eunuch," "minister of state" (Gen **37** 36); פָּקִיד, *pāḳīdh*, "person in charge," "overseer" (Gen **41** 34); נְצִיב, *nᵉçībh*, "stationed," "garrison," "prefect" (1 K **4** 19); שֹׁטֵר, *shōṭēr*, "scribe" or "secretary" (perhaps arranger or organizer), then any official or overseer. In Est **9** 3 for AV "officers of the king" RV has (more literal) "they that did the king's business."

In the NT "officer" generally corresponds to the Gr word ὑπηρέτης, *hupērétēs*, "servant," or any person in the employ of another. In Mt **5** 25 the term evidently means "bailiff" or exactor of the fine imposed by the magistrate, and corresponds to πράκτωρ, *práktōr*, used in Lk **12** 58.

T. Lewis

OFFICES OF CHRIST. See Christ, Offices of.

OFFSCOURING, of'skour-ing: This strong and expressive word occurs only once in the OT and once in the NT. The weeping prophet uses it as he looks upon his erstwhile fair and holy city, despoiled, defiled, derided by the profane, the enemies of God and of His people (Lam **3** 45, סְחִי, *ṣᵉḥī*). The favored people, whose city lies in heaps and is patrolled by the heathen, are hailed and held up as the scrapings, the offscouring, the offal of the earth. They are humbled to earth, crushed into the dust, carried away to be the slaves of licentious idolaters. The haughty, cruel, cutting boastfulness of the victors covered Israel with contumely.

In 1 Cor **4** 13 the greatest of the apostles reminds the prosperous and self-satisfied Corinthians that they, the apostles, were "made as the filth of the world, the offscouring of all things." In such contempt were they held by the unbelieving world and by false apostles. The strange, strong word (περίψημα, *perípsēma*) should remind us what it cost in former times to be a true servant of Christ.

G. H. Gerberding

OFFSPRING, of'spring. See Children.

OFTEN, of"n (πυκνός, *puknós*, "thick," "close"): An archaic usage for "frequent": "Thine *often* infirmities" (1 Tim **5** 23); cf "by *often* rumination" (Shakespeare, *As You Like It*, IV, i, 18); "The *often* round" (Ben Jonson, *The Forest*, III); "Of wrench'd or broken limb—an *often* chance" (Tennyson, *Gareth and Lynette*).

OG (עוֹג, *'ōgh*; Ὤγ, *Ōg*): King of Bashan, whose territory, embracing 60 cities, was conquered by Moses and the Israelites immediately after the conquest of Sihon, king of the Amorites (Nu **21**

33–35; Dt **3** 1–12). The defeat took place at Edrei, one of the chief of these cities (Nu **21** 33; Josh **12** 4), and Og and his people were "utterly destroyed" (Dt **3** 6). Og is described as the last of the REPHAIM (q.v.), or giant-race of that district, and his giant stature is borne out by what is told in Dt **3** 11 of the dimensions of his "bedstead of iron" (*'eres barzel*), 9 cubits long and 4 broad (13½ ft. by 6 ft.), said to be still preserved at Rabbath of Ammon when the verse describing it was written. It is not, of course, necessary to conclude that Og's own height, though immense, was as great as this. Some, however, prefer to suppose that what is intended is "a sarcophagus of black basalt," which iron-like substance abounds in the Hauran. The conquered territory was subsequently bestowed on the Reubenites, Gadites, and the half-tribe of Manasseh (Nu **32** 33; Dt **3** 12.13). Other references to Og are Dt **1** 4; **4** 47; **31** 4; Josh **2** 10; **9** 10; **13** 12.30). The memory of this great conquest lingered all through the national history (Ps **135** 11; **136** 20). On the conquest, cf Stanley, *Lectures on the History of the Jewish Church*, I, 185–87, and see ARGOB; BASHAN. JAMES ORR

OHAD, ō'had (אֹהַד, *'ōhadh*, meaning unknown): A son of Simeon, mentioned as third in order (Gen **46** 10; Ex **6** 15). The name is not found in the list of Nu **26** 12–14.

OHEL, ō'hel (אֹהֶל, *'ōhel*, "tent"): A son of Zerubbabel (1 Ch **3** 20).

OHOLAH, ō-hō'la (אָהֳלָה, *'ohŏlāh;* AV **Aholah**): The exact meaning is a matter of dispute. As written, it seems to mean a tent-woman, or the woman living in a tent. With a mappik in the last consonant it could mean "her tent." The term is used **symbolically** by Ezekiel to designate Samaria or the kingdom of Israel (Ezk **23** 4.5.36.44). See OHOLIBAH.

OHOLIAB, ō-hō'li-ab (אָהֳלִיאָב, *'ohŏlī'ābh*, "father's tent"; AV **Aholiab**): A Danite artificer, who assisted Bezalel in the construction of the tabernacle and its furniture (Ex **31** 6; **35** 34; **36** 1 f; **38** 23).

OHOLIBAH, ō-hol'i-ba, ō-hō'li-ba (אָהֳלִיבָה, *'ohŏlībhāh*, "tent in her," or "my tent is in her"): An opprobrious and symbolical name given by Ezekiel to Jerus, representing the kingdom of Judah, because of her intrigues and base alliances with Egypt, Assyria and Babylonia, just as the name OHOLAH (q.v.) was given to Samaria or the Northern Kingdom, because of her alliances with Egypt and Assyria. There is a play upon the words in the Heb which cannot be reproduced in Eng. Both Oholah and Oholibah, or Samaria and Jerus, are the daughters of one mother, and wives of Jeh, and both are guilty of religious and political alliance with heathen nations. Idolatry is constantly compared by the Heb prophets to marital unfaithfulness or adultery. W. W. DAVIES

OHOLIBAMAH, ō-hol-i-bā'ma, ō-hol-i-bä'ma (אָהֳלִיבָמָה, *'ohŏlībhāmāh*, "tent of the high place"): (1) One of Esau's wives, and a daughter of Anah the Hivite (Gen **36** 2.5). It is strange that she is not named along with Esau's other wives in either Gen **28** 9 or **26** 30. Various explanations have been given, but none of them is satisfactory. There is probably some error in the text.

(2) An Edomite chief (Gen **36** 41; **1** Ch **1** 52).

OIL, oil (שֶׁמֶן, *shemen;* ἔλαιον, *élaion*):

1. Terms
2. Production and Storage
3. Uses
   (1) As a Commodity of Exchange
   (2) As a Cosmetic
   (3) As a Medicine
   (4) As a Food
   (5) As an Illuminant
   (6) In Religious Rites
      (a) Consecration
      (b) Offerings
      (c) Burials
4. Figurative Uses

1. Terms

Shemen, lit. "fat," corresponds to the common Arab. *senin* of similar meaning, although now applied to boiled butter fat. Another Heb word, *zayith* (*zēth*), "olive," occurs with *shemen* in several passages (Ex **27** 20; **30** 24; Lev **24** 2). The corresponding Arab. *zeit*, a contraction of *zeitun*, which is the name for the olive tree as well as the fruit, is now applied to oils in general, to distinguish them from solid fats. *Zeit* usually means olive oil, unless some qualifying name indicates another oil. A corresponding use was made of *shemen*, and the oil referred to so many times in the Bible was olive oil (except Est **2** 12). Compare this with the Gr ἔλαιον, *élaion*, "oil," a neuter noun from ἐλαία, *elaía*, "olive," the origin of the Eng. word "oil." יִצְהָר, *yiçhār*, lit. "glistening," which occurs less frequently, is used possibly because of the light-giving quality of olive oil, or it may have been used to indicate fresh oil, as the clean, newly pressed oil is bright. מְשַׁח, *m^eshaḥ*, a Chald word, occurs twice: Ezr **6** 9; **7** 22. ἔλαιον, *élaion*, is the NT term.

2. Production

Olive oil has been obtained, from the earliest times, by pressing the fruit in such a way as to filter out the oil and other liquids from the residue. The Scriptural references correspond so nearly to the methods practised in Syria up to the present time, and the presses uncovered by excavators at such sites as Gezer substantiate so well the similarity of these methods, that a description of the oil presses and modes of expression still being employed in Syria will be equally true of those in use in early Israelitish times.

The olives to yield the greatest amount of oil are allowed to ripen, although some oil is expressed from the green fruit. As the olive ripens it turns black. The fruit begins to fall from the trees in September, but the main crop is gathered after the first rains in November. The olives which have not fallen naturally or have not been blown off by the storms are beaten from the trees with long poles (cf Dt **24** 20). The fruit is gathered from the ground into baskets and carried on the heads of the women, or on donkeys to the houses or oil presses. Those carried to the houses are preserved for eating. Those carried to the presses are piled in heaps until fermentation begins. This breaks down the oil cells and causes a more abundant flow of oil. The fruit thus softened may be trod out with the feet (Mic **6** 15)—which is now seldom practised—or crushed in a handmill. Such a mill was uncovered at Gezer beside an oil press. Stone mortars with wooden pestles are also used. Any of these methods crushes the fruit, leaving only the stone unbroken, and yields a purer oil (Ex **27** 20). The method now generally practised of crushing the fruit and kernels with an edgerunner mill probably dates from Rom times. These mills are of crude construction. The stones are cut from native limestone and are turned by horses or mules. Remains of huge stones of this type are found near the old Rom presses in Mt. Lebanon and other districts.

The second step in the preparation of the oil is

the expression. In districts where the olives are plentiful and there is no commercial demand for the oil, the householders crush the fruit in a mortar, mix the crushed mass with water, and after the solid portions have had time to settle, the pure sweet oil is skimmed from the surface of the water.

Ancient Oil Presses (*Land and the Book*).

This method gives a delicious oil, but is wasteful. This is no doubt the beaten oil referred to in connection with religious ceremonials (Ex **27** 20). Usually the crushed fruit is spread in portions on mats of reeds or goats' hair, the corners of which are folded over the mass, and the packets thus formed are piled one upon another between upright supports. These supports were formerly two stone columns or the two sections of a split stone cylinder hollowed out within to receive the mats. Large hollow tree trunks are still similarly used in Syria. A flat stone is next placed on top, and then a heavy log is placed on the pile in such a manner that one end can be fitted into a socket made in a wall or rock in close proximity to the pile. This socket becomes the fulcrum of a large lever of the second class. The lever is worked in the same manner as that used in the wine presses (see Wine Press). These presses are now being almost wholly superseded by hydraulic presses. The juice which runs from the press, consisting of oil, extractive matter and water, is conducted to vats or run into jars and allowed to stand until the oil separates. The oil is then drawn off from the surface, or the watery fluid and sediment is drawn away through a hole near the bottom of the jar, leaving the oil in the container. (For the construction of the ancient oil presses, see *The Excavations of Gezer*, by Macalister.) The oil, after standing for some time to allow further sediment to settle, is stored either in huge earthenware jars holding 100 to 200 gallons, or in underground cisterns (cf 1 Ch **27** 28) holding a much larger quantity. Some of these cisterns in Beirut hold several tons of oil each (2 Ch **11** 11; **32** 28; Neh **13** 5.12; Prov **21** 20). In the homes the oil is kept in small earthen jars of various shapes, usually having spouts by which the oil can be easily poured (1 K **17** 12; 2 K **4** 2). In 1 S **16** 13; 1 K **1** 39, horns of oil are mentioned.

3. Uses

(1) *As a commodity of exchange.*—Olive oil when properly made and stored will keep sweet for years, hence was a good form of merchandise to hold. Oil is still sometimes given in payment (1 K **5** 11; Ezk **27** 17; Hos **12** 1; Lk **16** 6; Rev **18** 13).

(2) *As a cosmetic.*—From earliest times oil was used as a cosmetic, esp. for oiling the limbs and head. Oil used in this way was usually scented (see Ointment). Oil is still used in this manner by the Arabs, principally to keep the skin and scalp soft when traveling in dry desert regions where there is no opportunity to bathe. Sesamé oil has replaced olive oil to some extent for this purpose. Homer, Pliny and other early writers mention its use for external application. Pliny claimed it was used to protect the body against the cold. Many Bib. references indicate the use of oil as a cosmetic (Ex **25** 6; Dt **28** 40; Ruth **3** 3; 2 S **12** 20; **14** 2; Est **2** 12; Ps **23** 5; **92** 10; **104** 15; **141** 5; Ezk **16** 9; Mic **6** 15; Lk **7** 46).

(3) *As a medicine.*—From early Egyp literature down to late Arab. medical works, oil is mentioned as a valuable remedy. Many queer prescriptions contain olive oil as one of their ingredients. The good Samaritan used oil mingled with wine to dress the wounds of the man who fell among robbers (Mk **6** 13; Lk **10** 34.)

(4) *As a food.*—Olive oil replaces butter to a large extent in the diet of the people of the Mediterranean countries. In Bible lands food is fried in it, it is added to stews, and is poured over boiled vegetables, such as beans, peas and lentils, and over salads, sour milk, cheese and other foods as a dressing. A cake is prepared from ordinary bread dough which is smeared with oil and sprinkled with herbs before baking (Lev **2** 4). At times of fasting oriental Christians use only vegetable oils, usually olive oil, for cooking. For Bib. references to the use of oil as food see Nu **11** 8; Dt **7** 13; **14** 23; **32** 13; 1 K **17** 12.14.16; 2 K **4** 2.6.7; 1 Ch **12** 40; 2 Ch **2** 10.15; Ezr **3** 7; Prov **21** 17; Ezk **16** 13.18; Hos **2** 5.8.22; Hag **2** 12; Rev **6** 6.

(5) *As an illuminant.*—Olive oil until recent years was universally used for lighting purposes (see Lamp). In Pal are many homes where a most primitive form of lamp similar to those employed by the Israelites is still in use. The prejudice in favor of the exclusive use of olive oil for lighting holy places is disappearing. Formerly any other illuminant was forbidden (cf Ex **25** 6; **27** 20; **35** 8.14.28; **39** 37; Mt **25** 3.4.8).

(6) *In religious rites.*—(*a*) Consecration of officials or sacred things (Gen **28** 18; **35** 14; Ex **29** 7.21 ff; Lev **2** 1 ff; Nu **4** 9 ff; 1 S **10** 1; **16** 1.13; 2 S **1** 21; 1 K **1** 39; 2 K **9** 1.3.6; Ps **89** 20): This was adopted by the early Christians in their ceremonies (Jas **5** 14), and is still used in the consecration of crowned rulers and church dignitaries. (*b*) Offerings, votive and otherwise: The custom of making offerings of oil to holy places still survives in oriental religions. One may see burning before the shrines along a Syrian roadside or in the churches, small lamps whose supply of oil is kept renewed by pious adherents. In Israelitish times oil was used in the meal offering, in the consecration offerings, offerings of purification from leprosy, etc (Ex **29** 2; **40** 9 ff; Lev **2** 2 ff; Nu **4** 9 ff; Dt **18** 4; 1 Ch **9** 29; 2 Ch **31** 5; Neh **10** 37.39; **13** 5.12; Ezk **16** 18.19; **45**; **46**; Mic **6** 7). (*c*) In connection with the burial of the dead: Egyp papyri mention this use. In the OT no direct mention is made of the custom. Jesus referred to it in connection with His own burial (Mt **26** 12; Mk **14** 3-8; Lk **23** 56; Jn **12** 3-8; **19** 40).

4. Figurative

Abundant oil was a figure of general prosperity (Dt **32** 13; **33** 24; 2 K **18** 32; Job **29** 6; Joel **2** 19.24). Languishing of the oil indicated general famine (Joel **1** 10; Hag **1** 11). Joy is described as the oil of joy (Isa **61** 3), or the oil of gladness (Ps **45** 7; He **1** 9). Ezekiel prophesies that the rivers shall run like oil, i.e. become viscous (Ezk **32** 14). Words of deceit are softer than oil (Ps **55** 21; Prov **5** 3). Cursing becomes a habit with the wicked as readily as oil soaks into bones (Ps **109** 18). Excessive use of oil indicates wastefulness (Prov **21** 17), while the saving of it is a characteristic of the wise (Prov **21** 20). Oil was carried into Egypt, i.e. a treaty was made with that country (Hos **12** 1). JAMES A. PATCH

OIL, ANOINTING (שֶׁמֶן הַמִּשְׁחָה, *shemen ha-mishḥāh*): This holy oil, the composition of which is described in Ex **30** 22–33, was designed for use in the anointing of the tabernacle, its furniture and vessels, the altar and laver, and the priest, that being thus consecrated, they might be "most holy." It was to be "a holy anointing oil" unto Jeh throughout all generations (ver 31). On its uses, cf Ex **37** 29; Lev **8** 12; **10** 7; **21** 10. The care of this holy oil was subsequently entrusted to Eleazar (Nu **4** 16); in later times it seems to have been prepared by the sons of the priests (1 Ch **9** 30). There is a **figurative** allusion to the oil on Aaron's head in Ps **133** 2. See OIL; ANOINTING. JAMES ORR

OIL, BEATEN (Ex **27** 20; Lev **24** 2; Nu **28** 5). See OIL; GOLDEN CANDLESTICK.

OIL, HOLY. See OIL; ANOINTING.

OIL, OLIVE. See OIL; OLIVE TREE.

OIL PRESS. See OIL; WINE PRESS.

OIL-MAKING. See CRAFTS, II, 11.

OIL TREE, oil trē (עֵץ שֶׁמֶן, *'ēç shemen* [Isa **41** 19], m "oleaster," in Neh **8** 15, trd "wild olive," AV "pine"; עֲצֵי שֶׁמֶן, *'ăçē shemen*, in 1 K **6** 23.31.32, trd "olive wood"): The name "oleaster" used to be applied to the wild olive, but now belongs to quite another plant, the silver-berry, *Eleagnus hortensis* (N.O. *Elaeagnaceae*), known in Arab. as *Zeizafān*. It is a pretty shrub with sweet-smelling white flowers and silver-grey-green leaves. It is difficult to see how all the three references can apply to this tree; it will suit the first two, but this small shrub would never supply wood for carpentry work such as that mentioned in 1 K, hence the tr "olive wood." On the other hand, in the reference in Neh **8** 15, olive branches are mentioned just before, so the tr "wild olive" (the difference being too slight) is improbable. Post suggests the tr of *'ēç shemen* by PINE (q.v.), which if accepted would suit all the requirements. E. W. G. MASTERMAN

OINTMENT, oint'ment: The present use of the word "ointment" is to designate a thick unguent of buttery or tallow-like consistency. AV in frequent instances translates *shemen* or *meshaḥ* (see Ex **30** 25) "ointment" where a perfumed oil seemed to be indicated. ARV has consequently substituted the word "oil" in most of the passages. *Merḳāḥāh* is rendered "ointment" once in the OT (Job **41** 31 [Heb **41** 23]). The well-known power of oils and fats to absorb odors was made use of by the ancient perfumers. The composition of the holy anointing oil used in the tabernacle worship is mentioned in Ex **30** 23–25. Olive oil formed the base. This was scented with "flowing myrrh . . . . sweet cinnamon . . . . sweet calamus . . . . and . . . . cassia." The oil was probably mixed with the above ingredients added in a powdered form and heated until the oil had absorbed their odors and then allowed to stand until the insoluble matter settled, when the oil could be decanted. Olive oil, being a non-drying oil which does not thicken readily, yielded an ointment of oily consistency. This is indicated by Ps **133** 2, where it says that the precious oil ran down on Aaron's beard and on the collar of his outer garment. Anyone attempting to make the holy anointing oil would be cut off from his people (Ex **30** 33). The scented oils or ointments were kept in jars or vials (not boxes) made of alabaster. These jars are frequently found as part of the equipment of ancient tombs.

The word trd "ointment" in the NT is μύρον, *múron*, "myrrh." This would indicate that myrrh, an aromatic gum resin, was the substance commonly added to the oil to give it odor. In Lk **7** 46 both kinds of oil are mentioned, and the verse might be paraphrased thus: My head with common oil thou didst not anoint; but she hath anointed my feet with costly scented oil.

For the uses of scented oils or ointments see ANOINTING; OIL. JAMES A. PATCH

OLAMUS, ol'a-mus ('Ωλαμός, *Ōlamós*): One of the Israelites who had taken a "strange wife" (1 Esd **9** 30) = "Meshullam" of Ezr **10** 29.

OLD, ōld. See AGE, OLD.

OLD GATE. See JERUSALEM.

OLD MAN (παλαιός, *palaiós*, "old," "ancient"): A term thrice used by Paul (Rom **6** 6; Eph **4** 22; Col **3** 9) to signify the unrenewed man, the natural man in the corruption of sin, i.e. sinful human nature before conversion and regeneration. It is theologically synonymous with "flesh" (Rom **8** 3–9), which stands, not for bodily organism, but for the whole nature of man (body and soul) turned away from God and devoted to self and earthly things.

The old man is "in the flesh"; the new man "in the Spirit." In the former "the works of the flesh" (Gal **5** 19–21) are manifest; in the latter "the fruit of the Spirit" (vs 22.23). One is "corrupt according to the deceitful lusts"; the other "created in righteousness and true holiness" (Eph **4** 22–24 AV). See also MAN, NATURAL; MAN, NEW. DWIGHT M. PRATT

OLD PROPHET, THE (נָבִיא אֶחָד זָקֵן, *nābhī' 'eḥādh zāḳēn*, "an old prophet" [1 K **13** 11], הַנָּבִיא הַזָּקֵן, *ha-nābhī' ha-zāḳēn*, "the old prophet" [ver 29]):

1. The Narrative

The narrative of 1 K **13** 11–32, in which the old prophet is mentioned, is part of a larger account telling of a visit paid to Bethel by "a man of God" from Judah. The Judaean prophet uttered a curse upon the altar erected there by Jeroboam I. When the king attempted to use force against him, the prophet was saved by Divine intervention; the king then invited him to receive royal hospitality, but he refused because of a command of God to him not to eat or drink there. The Judaean then departed (vs 1–10). An old prophet who lived in Bethel heard of the stranger's words, and went after him and offered him hospitality. This offer too was refused. But when the old prophet resorted to falsehood and pleaded a Divine command on the subject, the Judaean returned with him. While at table the old prophet is given a message to declare that death will follow the southerner's disobedience to the first command. A lion kills him on his way home. The old prophet hears of the death and explains it as due to disobedience to God; he then buries the dead body in his own grave and expresses a wish that he also at death should be buried in the same sepulcher.

2. Critical

There are several difficulties in the text. In ver 11, AV reads "his sons came" instead of "one of his sons came," and tr ver 12*b*: "And his sons shewed the way the man of God went." There is a gap in the MT after the word "table" in ver 20; and ver 23 should be trd, "And it came to pass after he had eaten bread and drunk water, that he saddled for himself the ass, and departed again" (following LXX, B with W. B. Stevenson, *HDB*, III, 594*a*, n.).

Benzinger ("Die Bücher der Könige," *Kurz. Hand-Komm. zum AT*, 91) holds that we have here an example of a midrash, i.e. according to *LOT*, 529, "an imaginative development of a thought or theme suggested by Scripture, esp. a didactic or homiletic exposition or an edifying religious story." 2 Ch **24** 27 refers to a "*midhrāsh* of the book of the kings," and 2 Ch **13** 22 to a "*midhrāsh* of the prophet Iddo." In 2 Ch **9** 29 we have a reference to "the visions of Iddo the seer concerning Jeroboam the son of Nebat." Jos names the Judaean prophet Jadon (*Ant*, VIII, viii, 5), and so some would trace this narrative to the midrash of Iddo, which would be a late Jewish work. There is a trace of late Heb in ver 3, and evidence in several places of a later editing of the original narrative. Kittel and Benzinger think it possible that the section may be based on a historical incident. If the narrative is historical in the main, the mention of Josiah by name in ver 2 may be a later insertion; if not historical, the prophecy there is *ex eventu*, and the whole section a midrash on 2 K **23** 15–20.

3. Central Truths

(1) Several questions are suggested by the narrative, but in putting as well as in answering these questions, it must be remembered that the old prophet himself, as has been pointed out, is not the chief character of the piece. Hence it is a little pointless to ask what became of the old prophet, or whether he was not punished for his falsehood. The passage should be studied, like the parables of Jesus, with an eye on the great central truth, which is, here, that God punishes disobedience even in "a man of God." It is not inconsistent with this to regard the old prophet as an example of "Satan fashioning himself into an angel of light" (2 Cor **11** 14), or of the beast which "had two horns like unto a lamb" (Rev **13** 11).

(2) It must also be remembered that the false prophets of the OT are called prophets in spite of their false prophecies. So here the old prophet in spite of his former lie is given a Divine message to declare that death will follow the other's disobedience.

(3) One other question suggests itself, and demands an answer. Why did the old prophet make the request that at death he should be buried in the same grave as the Judaean (ver 31)? The answer is implied in ver 32, and is more fully given in 2 K **23** 15–20, where King Josiah defiles the graves of the prophets at Bethel. On seeing a "monument" or grave-stone by one of the graves, he inquires what it is, and is told that it marks the grave of the prophet from Judah. Thereupon he orders that his bones be not disturbed. With these the bones of the old prophet escape. Perhaps no clearer instance of a certain kind of meanness exists in the OT. The very man who has been the cause of another's downfall and ruin is base enough to plan his own escape under cover of the virtues of his victim. And the parallels in modern life are many.

David Francis Roberts

OLD TESTAMENT. See Text of the OT.

OLD TESTAMENT CANON. See Canon of the OT.

OLD TESTAMENT LANGUAGES. See Languages of the OT.

OLEASTER, ō-lē-as′tẽr (Isa **41** 19 RVm). See Oil Tree.

OLIVE. See Olive Tree.

OLIVE BERRIES, ber′iz. See Olive Tree.

OLIVE, GRAFTED. See Olive Tree.

OLIVE TREE, ol′iv trē (זַיִת, *zayith*, a word occurring also in Aram., Ethiopic and Arab.; in the last it means "olive oil," and *zaitūn*, "the olive tree"; **ἐλαία**, *elaía*): The olive tree has all through history been one of the most characteristic, most valued and most useful of trees in Pal.

1. The Olive Tree

It is only right that it is the first named "king" of the trees (Jgs **9** 8.9). When the children of Israel came to the land they acquired olive trees which they planted not (Dt **6** 11; cf Josh **24** 13). The cultivation of the olive goes back to the earliest times in Canaan. The frequent references in the Bible, the evidences (see 4 below) from archaeology and the important place the product of this tree has held in the economy of the inhabitants of Syria make it highly probable that this land is the actual home of the cultivated olive. The wild olive is indigenous there. The most fruitful trees are the product of bare and rocky ground (cf Dt **32** 13) situated preferably at no great distance from the sea. The terraced hills of Pal, where the earth lies never many inches above the limestone rocks, the long rainless summer of unbroken sunshine, and the heavy "dews" of the autumn afford conditions which are extraordinarily favorable to at least the indigenous olive.

Typical Grove of Olive Trees at Jerusalem.

The olive, *Olea Europaea* (N.O. *Oleaceae*), is a slow-growing tree, requiring years of patient labor before reaching full fruitfulness. Its growth implies a certain degree of settlement and peace, for a hostile army can in a few days destroy the patient work of two generations. Possibly this may have something to do with its being the emblem of peace. Enemies of a village or of an individual often today carry out revenge by cutting away a ring of bark from the trunks of the olives, thus killing the trees in a few months. The beauty of this tree is referred to in Jer **11** 16; Hos **14** 6, and its fruitfulness in Ps **128** 3. The characteristic olive-green of its foliage, frosted silver below and the twisted and gnarled trunks—often hollow in the center—are some of the most picturesque and constant signs of settled habitations. In some parts of the land large plantations occur: the famous olive grove near Beirūt is 5 miles square; there are also fine, ancient trees in great numbers near Bethlehem.

In starting an **oliveyard** the *fellah* not infrequently plants young wild olive trees which grow plentifully over many parts of the land, or he may grow from cuttings. When the young trees are 3 years old they are grafted from a choice stock and after another three or four years they may commence to bear fruit, but they take quite a decade more before reaching full fruition. Much attention is, however, required. The soil around the trees must be frequently plowed and broken up; water must be conducted to the roots from the earliest rain, and the soil must be freely enriched with a kind of marl known in Arab. as *ḥuwwārāh*. If neglected, the older trees soon send up a great many shoots from the roots all around the parent stem (perhaps the

OLIVE PRESS AT BANIAS NEAR DAN

idea in Ps **128** 3); these must be pruned away, although, should the parent stem decay, some of these may be capable of taking its place. Being, however, from the root, below the original point of grafting, they are of the wild olive type—with smaller, stiffer leaves and prickly stem—and need grafting before they are of use. The olive tree furnishes a wood valuable for many forms of carpentry, and in modern Pal is extensively burnt as fuel.

2. The Fruit

The olive is in flower about May; it produces clusters of small white flowers, springing from the axils of the leaves, which fall as showers to the ground (Job **15** 33). The first olives mature as early as September in some places, but, in the mountain districts, the olive harvest is not till November or even December. Much of the earliest fruit falls to the ground and is left by the owner ungathered until the harvest. The trees are beaten with long sticks (Dt **24** 20), the young folks often climbing into the branches to reach the highest fruit, while the women and older girls gather up the fruit from the ground. The immature fruit left after such an ingathering is described graphically in Isa **17** 6: "There shall be left therein gleanings, as the shaking [m "beating"] of an olive-tree, two or three berries in the top of the uppermost bough, four or five in the outmost branches of a fruitful tree." Such gleanings belonged to the poor (Dt **24** 20), as is the case today. Modern villages in Pal allow the poor of even neighboring villages to glean the olives. The yield of an olive tree is very uncertain; a year of great fruitfulness may be followed by a very scanty crop or by a succession of such.

Olive (*Olea Europaea*).

The olive is an important article of diet in Pal. Some are gathered green and pickled in brine, after slight bruising, and others, the "black" olives, are gathered quite ripe and are either packed in salt or in brine. In both cases the salt modifies the bitter taste. They are eaten with bread.

3. Olive Oil

More important commercially is the oil. This is sometimes extracted in a primitive way by crushing a few berries by hand in the hollow of a stone (cf Ex **27** 20), from which a shallow channel runs for the oil. It is an old custom to tread them by foot (Mic **6** 15). Oil is obtained on a larger scale in one of the many varieties of oil mills. The berries are carried in baskets, by donkeys, to the mill, and they are crushed by heavy weights. A better class of oil can be obtained by collecting the first oil to come off separately, but not much attention is given to this in Pal, and usually the berries are crushed, stones and all, by a circular millstone revolving upright round a central pivot. A plenteous harvest of oil was looked upon as one of God's blessings (Joel **2** 24; **3** 13). That the "labor of the olive" should fail was one of the trials to faith in Jeh (Hab **3** 17). Olive oil is extensively used as food, morsels of bread being dipped into it in eating; also medicinally (Lk **10** 34; Jas **5** 14). In ancient times it was greatly used for anointing the person (Ps **23** 5; Mt **6** 17). In Rome's days of luxury it was a common maxim that a long and pleasant life depended upon two fluids—"wine within and oil without." In modern times this use of oil for the person is replaced by the employment of soap, which in Pal is made from olive oil. In all ages this oil has been used for illumination (Mt **25** 3).

4. Greater Plenty of Olive Trees in Ancient Times

Comparatively plentiful as olive trees are today in Pal, there is abundant evidence that the cultivation was once much more extensive. "The countless rock-cut oil- and wine-presses, both within and without the walls of the city [of Gezer], show that the cultivation of the olive and vine was of much greater importance than it is anywhere in Pal today. . . . . Excessive taxation has made olive culture unprofitable" ("Gezer Mem," *PEF*, II, 23). A further evidence of this is seen today in many now deserted sites which are covered with wild olive trees, descendants of large plantations of the cultivated tree which have quite disappeared.

5. Wild Olives

Many of these spring from the old roots; others are from the fallen drupes. Isolated trees scattered over many parts of the land, esp. in Galilee, are sown by the birds. As a rule the wild olive is but a shrub, with small leaves, a stem more or less prickly, and a small, hard drupe with but little or no oil. That a wild olive branch should be grafted into a fruitful tree would be a proceeding useless and contrary to Nature (Rom **11** 17.24). On the mention of "branches of wild olive" in Neh **8** 15, see OIL TREE.

E. W. G. MASTERMAN

OLIVE, WILD: Figuratively used in Rom **11** 17.24 for the Gentiles, grafted into "the good olive tree" of Israel. See OLIVE TREE.

OLIVE YARD, ol'iv yärd. See OLIVE TREE.

OLIVES, ol'ivz, MOUNT OF (הַר־הַזֵּיתִים, *har ha-zēthīm* [Zec **14** 4], מַעֲלֵה־הַזֵּיתִים, *ma'ălēh ha-zēthīm*, "the ascent of the mount of Olives" [2 S **15** 30, AV "the ascent of (mount) Olivet"]; **τὸ ὄρος τῶν ἐλαιῶν**, *tó óros tōn elaiōn*, "the Mount of Olives" [Mt **21** 1; **24** 3; **26** 30; Mk **11** 1; **13** 3; **14** 26; Lk **19** 37; **22** 39; Jn **8** 1], **τὸ ὄρος τὸ καλούμενον ἐλαιῶν**, *tó óros tó kaloúmenon elaiōn*, "the mount that is called Olivet" [Lk **19** 29; **21** 37; in both references in AV "the mount called (the mount) of Olives"], **τοῦ ἐλαιῶνος**, *toú elaiōnos* [Acts **1** 12, EV "Olivet" lit. "olive garden"]):

1. Names
2. Situation and Extent
3. OT Associations
   (1) David's Escape from Absalom
   (2) The Vision of Ezekiel
   (3) The Vision of Zechariah

4. High Places
5. Olivet and Jesus
6. View of the City from Olivet
7. Churches and Ecclesiastical Traditions

LITERATURE

Olivet comes to us through the Vulg *Olivetum*, "an oliveyard."

1. Names

Jos frequently uses the expression "Mount of Olives" (e.g. *Ant*, VII, ix, 2; XX, viii, 6; *BJ*, V, ii, 3; xii, 2), but later Jewish writings give the name הַר־הַמִּשְׁחָה, *har ha-mishḥāh*, "Mount of Oil"; this occurs in some MSS in 2 K **23** 13, and the common reading הַר־הַמַּשְׁחִית, *har ha-mashḥīth*, "Mount of Corruption," m "destruction," may possibly be a deliberate alteration (see below). In later ages the Mount was termed "the mountain of lights," because here there used to be kindled at one time the first beacon light to announce throughout Jewry the appearance of the new moon.

To the natives of Pal today it is usually known as *Jebel eṭ Ṭûr* ("mountain of the elevation," or "tower"), or, less commonly, as *Jebel Ṭûr ez zait* ("mountain of the elevation of oil"). The name *Jebel ez-zaitûn* ("Mount of Olives") is also well known. Early Arab. writers use the term *Ṭûr Zait*, "Mount of Oil."

2. Situation and Extent

The mountain ridge which lies E. of Jerus leaves the central range near the valley of *Sha'phat* and runs for about 2 miles due S. After culminating in the mountain mass on which lies the "Church of the Ascension," it may be considered as giving off two branches: one lower one, which runs S.S.W., forming the southern side of the Kidron valley, terminating at the *Wādy en Nâr*, and another, higher one, which slopes eastward and terminates a little beyond *el-'Azarēyeh* (modern Bethany). The main ridge is considerably higher than the site of ancient Jerus, and still retains a thick cap of the soft chalky limestone, mixed with flint, known variously as *Nāri* and *Ka'kūli*, which has been entirely denuded over the Jerus site (see JERUSALEM, II, 1). The flints were the cause of a large settlement of paleolithic man which occurred in prehistoric times on the northern end of the ridge, while the soft chalky stone breaks down to form a soil valuable for the cultivation of olives and other trees and shrubs. The one drawback to arboriculture upon this ridge is the strong northwest wind which permanently bends most trees toward the S.E., but affects the sturdy, slow-growing olive less than the quicker-growing pine. The eastern slopes are more sheltered. In respect of wind the Mount of Olives is far more exposed than the site of old Jerus.

The lofty ridge of Olivet is visible from far, a fact now emphasized by the high Russian tower which can be seen for many scores of miles on the E. of the Jordan. The range presents, from such a point of view particularly, a succession of summits. Taking as the northern limit the dip which is crossed by the ancient Anathoth (*'anātā*) road, the most northerly summit is that now crowned by the house and garden of Sir John Gray Hill, 2,690 ft. above sea-level. This is sometimes incorrectly pointed out as Scopus, which lay farther to the N.W. A second sharp dip in the ridge separates this northern summit from the next, a broad plateau now occupied by the great Kaiserin Augusta Victoria Stiftung and grounds. The road makes a sharp descent into a valley which is traversed from W. to E. by an important and ancient road from Jerus, which runs eastward along the *Wādy er Rawābeh*. S. of this dip lies the main mass of the mountain, that known characteristically as the Olivet of ecclesiastical tradition. This mass consists of two principal summits and two subsidiary spurs. The northern of the two main summits is that known as *Karem eṣ Ṣayyād*, "the vineyard of the hunter," and also as "Galilee," or, more correctly, as *Viri Galilaei* (see below, 7). It reaches a height of 2,723 ft. above the Mediterranean and is separated from the southern summit by a narrow neck traversed today by the carriage road. The southern summit, of practically the same elevation, is the traditional "Mount of the Ascension," and for several years has been distinguished by a lofty, though somewhat inartistic, tower erected by the Russians. The two subsidiary spurs referred to above are: (1) a somewhat isolated ridge running S.E., upon which lies the squalid village of *el 'Azarēyeh*—Bethany; (2) a small spur running S., covered with grass, which is known as "the Prophets," on account of a remarkable 4th-cent. Christian tomb found there, which is known as "the tomb of the Prophets"— a spot much venerated by modern Jews.

A further extension of the ridge as *Baṭn el Hawa*, "the belly of the wind," or traditionally as "the Mount of Offence" (cf 1 K **11** 7; 2 K **23** 13), is usually included in the Mount of Olives, but its lower altitude—it is on a level with the temple-platform—and its position S. of the city mark it off as practically a distinct hill. Upon its lower slopes are clustered the houses of *Silwân* (Siloam).

3. OT Associations

The notices of the Mount of Olives in the OT are, considering its nearness to Jerus, remarkably scanty.

(1) David fleeing before his rebellious son Absalom (2 S **15** 16) crossed the Kidron and "went up by the ascent of the mount of Olives, and wept as he went up; and he had his head covered, and went barefoot: and all the people that were with him covered every man his head, and they went up, weeping as they went [ver 30]. . . . . And it came to pass, that, when David was come to the top of the ascent, where he was wont to worship God, [m], behold, Hushai the Archite came to meet him with his coat rent, and earth upon his head [ver 32]. And when David was a little past the top of the ascent, behold, Ziba the servant of Mephibosheth met him, with a couple of asses saddled, and upon them two hundred loaves of bread, and a hundred clusters of raisins, and a hundred of summer fruits, and a bottle of wine" (**16** 1).

It is highly probable that David's route to the wilderness was neither by the much-trodden Anathoth road nor over the summit of the mountain, but by the path running N.E. from the city, which runs between the *Viri Galilaei* hill and that supporting the German Sanatorium and descends into the wilderness by *Wâdy er Rawâbi*. See BAHURIM.

(2) Ezekiel in a vision (**11** 23) saw the glory of Jeh go up from the midst of the city and stand "upon the mountain which is on the east side of the city" (cf **43** 2). In connection with this the Rabbi Janna records the tradition that the *shekhīnāh* stood 3½ years upon Olivet, and preached, saying, "Seek ye the Lord while he may be found, call ye upon him while he is near"—a strange story to come from a Jewish source, suggesting some overt reference to Christ.

(3) In Zec **14** 4 the prophet sees Jeh in that day stand upon the Mount of Olives, "and the Mount of Olives shall be cleft in the midst thereof toward the east and toward the west, and there shall be a very great valley; and half of the mountain shall remove toward the north, and half of it toward the south."

In addition to these direct references, Jewish tradition associates with this mount—this "mount of Corruption"—the rite of the red heifer (Nu **19**); and many authorities consider that this is also the mount referred to in Neh **8** 15, whence the people are directed to fetch olive branches, branches of wild olive, myrtle branches, palm branches and branches of thick trees to make their booths.

4. High Places

It is hardly possible that a spot with such a wide outlook—esp. the marvelous view over the Jordan valley and Dead Sea to the lands of Ammon and Moab—should have been neglected in the days when Sem religion crowned such spots with their sanctuaries. There is OT evidence that there was a "high place" here. In the account of David's flight mention is made of the spot on the summit "where he was wont to worship God" (2 S **15** 32 m). This is certainly a reference to a sanctuary, and there are strong reasons for believing that this place may have been Nob (q.v.) (see 1 S **21** 1; **22** 9.11.19; Neh **11** 32; but esp. Isa **10** 32). This last reference seems to imply a site more commanding in its outlook over the *ancient* city than *Ras el Mushārif* proposed by Driver, one at least as far S. as the Anathoth road, or even that from *Wâdy er Rawābi*. But besides this we have the definite statement (1 K **11** 7): "Then did Solomon build a high place for Chemosh the abomination of Moab, in the mount that is before [i.e. E. of] Jerus, and for Molech the abomination of the children of Ammon," and the further account that the "high places that were before [E. of] Jerus, which were on the right hand [S.] of the mount of corruption [m "destruction"], which Solomon the king of Israel had builded for Ashtoreth the abomination of the Sidonians, and for Chemosh the abomination of Moab, and for Milcom the abomination of the children of Ammon, did the king [Josiah] defile" (2 K **23** 13). That these high places were somewhere upon what is generally recognized as the Mount of Olives, seems clear, and the most probable site is the main mass where are today the Christian sanctuaries, though Graetz and Dean Stanley favor the summit known as *Viri Galilaei*. It is the recognition of this which has kept alive the Jewish name "Mount of Corruption" for this mount to this day. The term *Mons offensionis*, given to the southeastern extension, S. of the city, is merely an ecclesiastical tradidition going back to Quaresmius in the 17th cent., which is repeated by Burckhardt (1823 AD).

5. Olivet and Jesus

More important to us are the NT associations of this sacred spot. In those days the mountain must have been far different from its condition today. Titus in his siege of Jerus destroyed all the timber here as elsewhere in the environs, but before this the hillsides must have been clothed with verdure—oliveyards, fig orchards and palm groves, with myrtle and other shrubs. Here in the fresh breezes and among the thick foliage, Jesus, the country-bred Galilean, must gladly have taken Himself from the noise and closeness of the overcrowded city. It is to the Passion Week, with the exception of Jn **8** 1, that all the incidents belong which are expressly mentioned as occurring on the Mount of Olives; while there would be a special reason at this time in the densely packed city, it is probable that on other occasions also Our Lord preferred to stay outside the walls. Bethany would indeed appear to have been His home in Judaea, as Capernaum was in Galilee. Here we read of Him as staying with Mary and Martha (Lk **10** 38–42); again He comes to Bethany from the wilderness road from Jericho for the raising of Lazarus (Jn **11**), and later He is at a feast, six days before the Passover (Jn **12** 1), at the house of Simon (Mt **26** 6–12; Mk **14** 3–9; Jn **12** 1–9). The Mount of Olives is expressly mentioned in many of the events of the Passion Week. He approached Jerus, "unto Bethphage and Bethany, at the mount of Olives" (Mk **11** 1; Mt **21** 1; Lk **19** 29); over a shoulder of this mount—very probably by the route of the present Jericho carriage road—He made His triumphal entry to the city (Mt **21**; Mk **11**; Lk **19**), and on this road, when probably the full sight of the city first burst into view, He

Mount of Olives from the Golden Gate.

wept over Jerus (Lk **19** 41). During all that week "every day he was teaching in the temple; and every night he went out, and lodged in the mount that is called Olivet" (Lk **21** 37)—the special part of the mount being Bethany (Mt **21** 17; Mk **11** 11). It was on the road from Bethany that He gave the sign of the withering of the fruitless fig tree (Mt **21** 17–19; Mk **11** 12–14.20–24), and "as he sat on the mount of Olives" (Mt **24** 3 f; Mk **13** 3 f) Jesus gave His memorable sermon with the doomed city lying below Him.

On the lower slopes of Olivet, in the Garden of Gethsemane (q.v.), Jesus endured His agony, the betrayal and arrest, while upon one of its higher points—not, as tradition has it, on the inhabited highest summit, but on the secluded eastern slopes "over against Bethany" (Lk **24** 50–52)—He took leave of His disciples (cf Acts **1** 12).

6. View of the City from Olivet

The view of Jerus from the Mount of Olives must ever be one of the most striking impressions which any visitor to Jerus carries away with him. It has been described countless times. It is today a view but of ruin and departed glory compared with that over which Jesus wept. A modern writer with historic imagination has thus graphically sketched the salient features of that sight:

"We are standing on the road from Bethany as it breaks round the Mount of Olives and on looking northwest this is what we see. . . . . There spreads a vast stone stage, almost rectangular, some 400 yds. N. and S. by 300 E. and W., held up above Ophel and the Kidron valley by a high and massive wall, from 50 to 150 ft. and more in height, according to the levels of the rock from which it rises. Deep cloisters surround this platform on the inside of the walls. . . . . Every gate has its watch and other guards patrol the courts. The crowds, which pour through the south gates upon the platform for the most part keep to the right; the exceptions, turning westward, are excommunicated or in mourning. But the crowd are not all Israelites. Numbers of Gentiles mingle with them; there are costumes and colors from all lands. In the cloisters sit teachers with groups of disciples about them. On the open pavement stand the booths of hucksters and money changers; and from the N. sheep and bullocks are being driven toward the Inner Sanctuary. This lies not in the center of the great platform, but in the northwest corner. It is a separately fortified, oblong enclosure; its high walls with their 9 gates rising from a narrow terrace at a slight elevation above the platform and the terrace encompassed by a fence within which none but Israelites may pass. . . . . Upon its higher western end rises a house 'like a lion broad in front and narrow behind.' . . . . From the open porch of this house stone steps descend to a great block of an altar perpetually smoking with sacrifices. . . . . Off the N.W. of the Outer Sanctuary a castle (the Antonia) dominates the whole with its 4 lofty towers. Beyond . . . . the Upper City rises in curved tiers like a theater, while all the lower slopes to the S. are a crowded mass of houses, girded by the eastern wall of the city. Against that crowded background the sanctuary with its high house gleams white and fresh. But the front of the house, glittering with gold plates, is obscured by a column of smoke rising from the altar; and the Priests' Court about the latter is colored by the slaughterers and sacrifices—a splash of red, as our imagination takes it, in the center of the prevailing white. At intervals there are bursts of music; the singing of psalms, the clash of cymbals and a great blare of trumpets, at which the people in their court in the Inner Sanctuary fall down and worship" (extracts from G. A. Smith's *Jerusalem*, II, 518–20).

To the Bible student the NT is the best guide to Olivet; tradition and "sites" only bewilder him.

7. Churches and Ecclesiastical Traditions

Once the main hilltop was a mass of churches. There was the "Church of the Ascension" to mark the spot whereby tradition (contrary to the direct statement of Luke) states that the Ascension occurred; now the site is marked by a small octagonal chapel, built in 1834, which is in the hands of the Moslems. There a "footprint of Christ" is shown in the rock. A large basilica of Helena was built over the place where it was said that Christ taught His disciples. In 1869 the Princess de Latour d'Auvergne, learning that there was a Moslem tradition that this site was at a spot called *el Battaniyeh* south of the summit, here erected a beautiful church known as the Church of the Pater Noster and around the courtyard she had the Lord's Prayer inscribed in 32 languages. When the church was in course of erection certain fragments of old walls and mosaics were found, but, in 1911, as a result of a careful excavation of the site, the foundations of a more extensive mass of old buildings, with some beautiful mosaic in the baptistry, were revealed in the neighborhood; there is little doubt but that these foundations belonged to the actual Basilica of Helena. It is proposed to rebuild the church.

Mention has been made of the name *Viri Galilaei* or Galilee as given to the northern summit of the main mass of Olivet. The name "Mount Galilee" appears to have been first given to this hill early in the 4th cent. and in 1573 AD Rauwolf explains the name by the statement that here was anciently a khan where the Galileans lodged who came up to Jerus. In 1620 Quaresmius applies the names "Galilee" and *Viri Galilaei* to this site and thinks the latter name may be due to its having been the spot where the two angels appeared and addressed the disciples as "Ye men of Galilee" (Acts **1** 11). Attempts have been made, without much success, to maintain that this "Galilee" was the spot which Our Lord intended (Mt **28** 10.16) to indicate to His disciples as the place of meeting.

The Russian inclosure includes a chapel, a lofty tower—from which a magnificent view is obtainable—a hospice and a pleasant pine grove. Between the Russian buildings to the N. and the Church of the Ascension lies the squalid village of *eṭ Ṭûr*, inhabited by a peculiarly turbulent and rapacious crowd of Moslems, who prey upon the passing pilgrims and do much to spoil the sentiment of a visit to this sacred spot. It is possible it may be the original site of Bethphage (q.v.).

Literature.—*PEF*, Memoirs, "Jerusalem" volume; G. A. Smith, *Jerusalem;* Robinson, *BRP*, I, 1838; Stanley, *Sinai and Pal;* Baedeker's *Pal and Syria* (by Socin and Bensinger); Tobler, *Die Siloahquelle und der Oelberg*, 1852; Porter, *Murray's Pal and Syria;* R. Hofmann, *Galilaea auf dem Oelberg*, Leipzig, 1896; Schick, "The Mount of Olives," *PEFS*, 1889, 174–84; Warren, art. "Mount of Olives," in *HDB;* Gauthier, in *EB*, s.v.; Vincent (Père), "The Tombs of the Prophets," *Revue Biblique*, 1901.

E. W. G. Masterman

OLIVET, ol'i-vet. See Olives, Mount of.

OLYMPAS, ō-lim'pas (**Ὀλυμπᾶς**, *Olumpás*): The name of a Rom Christian to whom Paul sent greetings (Rom **16** 15). Olympas is an abbreviated form of Olympiadorus. The joining in one salutation of the Christians mentioned in ver 15 suggests that they formed by themselves a small community in the earliest Rom church.

OLYMPIUS, ō-lim'pi-us (**Ὀλύμπιος**, *Olúmpios*): An epithet of Jupiter or Zeus (q.v.) from Mt. Olympus in Thessaly, where the gods held court presided over by Zeus. Antiochus Epiphanes, "who on God's altars dansed," insulted the Jewish religion by dedicating the temple of Jerus to Jupiter Olympius, 168 BC (2 Macc **6** 2; 1 Macc **1** 54 ff).

OMAERUS, om-a-ē'rus: AV=RV "Ismaerus" (1 Esd **9** 34).

OMAR, ō'mar (אוֹמָר, *'ōmār*, connected perhaps with *'āmar*, "speak"; LXX **Ὠμάν**, *Ōmán*, or **Ὠμάρ**, *Ōmár*): Grandson of Esau and son of Eliphaz in Gen **36** 11; 1 Ch **1** 36; given the title "duke" or "chief" in Gen **36** 15.

OMEGA, ō'me-ga, ō-mē'ga, ō-meg'a. See Alpha and Omega.

OMENS, ō'menz. See Augury; Divination.

OMER, ō'mēr (עֹמֶר, *'ōmer*): A dry measure, the tenth of an ephah, equal to about 7½ pints. See Weights and Measures.

OMNIPOTENCE, om-nip'ō-tens: The noun "omnipotence" is not found in the Eng. Bible, nor any noun exactly corresponding to it in the original Heb or Gr.

1. Terms and Usage

The adj. "omnipotent" occurs in Rev **19** 6 AV; the Gr for this, παντοκράτωρ, *pantokrátōr*, occurs also in 2 Cor **6** 18; Rev **1** 8; **4** 8; **11** 17; **15** 3; **16** 7.14; **19** 15; **21** 22 (in all of which AV and RV render "almighty"). It is also found frequently in LXX, esp. in the rendering of the Divine names Jeh *çebhā'ōth* and *'Ēl Shadday*. In *pantokratōr*, the element of "authority," "sovereignty," side by side with that of "power," makes itself more distinctly felt than it does to the modern ear in "omnipotent," although it is meant to be included in the latter also. Cf further ὁ δύνατος, *ho dúnatos*, in Lk **1** 49.

The formal conception of omnipotence as worked out in theology does not occur in the OT. The substance of the idea is conveyed in various indirect ways.

2. Inherent in OT Names of God

The notion of "strength" is inherent in the OT conception of God from the beginning, being already represented in one of the two Divine names inherited by Israel from ancient Sem religion, the name *'Ēl*. According to one etymology it is also inherent in the other, the name *'Ĕlōhīm*, and in this case the pl. form, by bringing out the fulness of power in God, would mark an approach to the idea of omnipotence. See God, Names of.

In the patriarchal religion the conception of "might" occupies a prominent place, as is indicated by the name characteristic of this period, *'Ēl Shadday;* cf Gen **17** 1; **28** 3; **35** 11; **43** 14; **48** 3; **49** 24.25; Ex **6** 3. This name, however, designates the Divine power as standing in the service of His covenant-relation to the patriarchs, as transcending Nature and overpowering it in the interests of redemption.

Another Divine name which signalizes this attribute is Jeh *çebhā'ōth*, Jeh of Hosts. This name, characteristic of the prophetic period, describes God as the King surrounded and followed by the angelic hosts, and since the might of an oriental king is measured by the splendor of his retinue, as of great, incomparable power, the King Omnipotent (Ps **24** 10; Isa **2** 12; **6** 3.5; **8** 13; Jer **46** 18; Mal **1** 14).

Still another name expressive of the same idea is *'Abhīr*, "Strong One," compounded with Jacob or Israel (Gen **49** 24; Ps **132** 2.5; Isa **1** 24; **49** 26; **60** 16). Further, *'Ēl Gibbōr*, "God-Hero" (Isa **9** 6 [of the Messiah]; cf for the adj. *gibbōr*, Jer **20** 11); and the figurative designation of God as *Çūr*, "Rock," occurring esp. in the address to God in the Psalter (Isa **30** 29, AV "Mighty One"). The specific energy with which the Divine nature operates finds expression also in the name *'Ēl Ḥay*, "Living God," which God bears over against the impotent idols (1 S **17** 26.36; 2 K **19** 4.16; Ps **18** 46; Jer **23** 36; Dnl **6** 20.26 f). An anthropomorphic description of the power of God is in the figures of His "hand," His "arm," His "finger." See God.

3. Other Modes of Expression

Some of the attributes of Jeh have an intimate connection with His omnipotence. Under this head esp. God's nature as Spirit and His holiness come under consideration. The representation of God as Spirit in the OT does not primarily refer to the incorporealness of the Divine nature, but to its inherent energy. The physical element underlying the conception of Spirit is that of air in motion, and in this at first not the invisibility but the force forms the point of comparison. The opposite of "Spirit" in this sense is "flesh," which expresses the weakness and impotence of the creature over against God (Isa **2** 22; **31** 3).

The holiness of God in its earliest and widest sense (not restricted to the ethical sphere) describes the majestic, specifically Divine character of His being, that which evokes in man religious awe. It is not a single attribute coördinated with others, but a peculiar aspect under which all the attributes can be viewed, that which renders them distinct from anything analogous in the creature (1 S **2** 2; Hos **11** 9). In this way holiness becomes closely associated with the power of God, indeed sometimes becomes synonymous with Divine power = omnipotence (Ex **15** 11; Nu **20** 12), and esp. in Ezk, where God's "holy name" is often equivalent to His renown for power, hence interchangeable with His "great name" (Ezk **36** 20–24). The objective Spirit as a distinct hypostasis and the executive of the Godhead on its one side also represents the Divine power (Isa **32** 15; Mt **12** 28; Lk **1** 35; **4** 14; Acts **10** 38; Rom **15** 19; 1 Cor **2** 4).

4. Unlimited Extent of the Divine Power

In all these forms of expression a great and specifically Divine power is predicated of God. Statements in which the absolutely unlimited extent of this power is explicitly affirmed are rare. The reason, however, lies not in any actual restriction placed on this power, but in the concrete practical form of religious thinking which prevents abstract formulation of the principle. The point to be noticed is that no statement is anywhere made exempting aught from the reach of Divine power. Nearest to a general formula come such statements as nothing is "too hard for Jeh" (Gen **18** 14; Jer **32** 17); or "I know that thou canst do everything," or "God . . . . hath done whatever he pleased" (Ps **115** 3; **135** 6), or, negatively, no one "can hinder" God in carrying out His purpose (Isa **43** 13), or God's hand is not "waxed short" (Nu **11** 23); in the NT: "With God all things are possible" (Mt **19** 26; Mk **10** 27; Lk **18** 27); "Nothing is impossible with God" (RV "No word from God shall be void of power," Lk **1** 37). Indirectly the omnipotence of God is implied in the effect ascribed to faith (Mt **17** 20: "Nothing shall be impossible unto you"; Mk **9** 23: "All things are possible to him that believeth"), because faith puts the Divine power at the disposal of the believer. On its subjective side the principle of inexhaustible power finds expression in Isa **40** 28: God is not subject to weariness. Because God is conscious of the unlimited extent of His resources nothing is marvelous in His eyes (Zec **8** 6).

5. Forms of Manifestation

It is chiefly through its forms of manifestation that the distinctive quality of the Divine power which renders it omnipotent becomes apparent. The Divine power operates not merely in single concrete acts, but is comprehensively related to the world as such. Both in Nature and history, in creation and in redemption, it produces and controls and directs everything that comes to pass. Nothing in the realm of actual or conceivable things is withdrawn from it (Am **9** 2.3; Dnl **4** 35); even to the minutest and most recondite sequences of cause and effect it extends and masters all details of reality (Mt **10** 30; Lk **12** 7). There is no accident (1 S **6** 9; cf with ver 12; Prov **16** 33). It need not operate through second causes; it itself underlies all second causes and makes them what they are.

It is creative power producing its effect through a mere word (Gen **1** 3 ff; Dt **8** 3; Ps **33** 9; Rom **4** 17; He **1** 3; **11** 30). Among the prophets, esp. Isaiah emphasizes this manner of the working of the Divine power in its immediateness and suddenness (Isa **9** 8; **17** 13; **18** 4–6; **29** 5). All the processes of Nature are ascribed to the causation of Jeh (Job **5** 9 ff; **9** 5 ff; chs **38** and **39**; Isa **40** 12 ff; Am **4** 13; **5** 8.9; **9** 5.6); esp. God's control of the sea is named as illustrative of this (Ps **65** 7; **104** 9; Isa **50** 2; Jer **5** 22; **31** 35). The OT seldom says "it rains" (Am **4** 7), but usually God causes it to rain (Lev **26** 4; Dt **11** 17; 1 S **12** 17; Job **36** 27; Pss **29** and **65**; Mt **5** 45; Acts **14** 17).

The same is true of the processes of history. God sovereignly disposes, not merely of Israel, but of all other nations, even of the most powerful, e.g. the Assyrians, as His instruments for the accomplishment of His purpose (Am **1—2** 3; **9** 7; Isa **10** 5.15; **28** 2; **45** 1; Jer **25** 9; **27** 6; **43** 10). The prophets ascribe to Jeh not merely relatively greater power than to the gods of the nations, but His power extends into the sphere of the nations, and the heathen gods are ignored in the estimate put upon His might (Isa **31** 3).

Even more than the sphere of Nature and history, that of redemption reveals the Divine omnipotence, from the point of view of the supernatural and miraculous. Thus Ex **15** celebrates the power of Jeh in the wonders of the exodus. It is God's exclusive prerogative to do wonders (Job **5** 9; **9** 10; Ps **72** 18); He alone can make "a new thing" (Nu **16** 30; Isa **43** 19; Jer **31** 22). In the NT the great embodiment of this redemptive omnipotence is the resurrection of believers (Mt **22** 29; Mk **12** 24) and specifically the resurrection of Christ (Rom **4** 17.21.24; Eph **1** 19 ff); but it is evidenced in the whole process of redemption (Mt **19** 26; Mk **10** 27; Rom **8** 31; Eph **3** 7.20; 1 Pet **1** 5; Rev **11** 17).

6. Significance for Biblical Religion

The significance of the idea may be traced along two distinct lines. On the one hand the Divine omnipotence appears as a support of faith. On the other hand it is productive of that specifically religious state of consciousness which Scripture calls "the fear of Jeh." Omnipotence in God is that to which human faith addresses itself. In it lies the ground for assurance that He is able to save, as in His love that He is willing to save (Ps **65** 5.6; **72** 18; **118** 14–16; Eph **3** 20).

As to the other aspect of its significance, the Divine omnipotence in itself, and not merely for soteriological reasons, evokes a specific religious response. This is true, not only of the OT, where the element of the fear of God stands comparatively in the foreground, but remains true also of the NT. Even in Our Lord's teaching the prominence given to the fatherhood and love of God does not preclude that the transcendent majesty of the Divine nature, including omnipotence, is kept in full view and made a potent factor in the cultivation of the religious mind (Mt **6** 9). The beauty of Jesus' teaching on the nature of God consists in this, that He keeps the exaltation of God above every creature and His loving condescension toward the creature in perfect equilibrium and makes them mutually fructified by each other. Religion is more than the inclusion of God in the general altruistic movement of the human mind; it is a devotion at every point colored by the consciousness of that Divine uniqueness in which God's omnipotence occupies a foremost place.

LITERATURE.—Oehler, *Theologie des AT*³, 131, 139 ff; Riehm, *Alttestamentliche Theologie*, 250 ff; Dillmann, *Handbuch der alttestamentlichen Theologie*, 244; Davidson, *OT Theology*, 163 ff; König, *Geschichte der alttestamentlichen Religion*, 127, 135 ff, 391, 475.

GEERHARDUS VOS

OMNIPRESENCE, om-ni-prez'ens: Neither the noun "omnipresence" nor adj. "omnipresent" occurs in Scripture, but the idea that God is everywhere present is throughout presupposed and sometimes explicitly formulated. God's omnipresence is closely related to His omnipotence and omniscience: that He is everywhere enables Him to act everywhere and to know all things, and, conversely, through omnipotent action and omniscient knowledge He has access to all places and all secrets (cf Ps **139**). Thus conceived, the attribute is but the correlate of the monotheistic conception of God as the Infinite Creator, Preserver and Governor of the universe, immanent in His works as well as transcendent above them.

1. Non-Occurrence of the Term in Scripture

The philosophical idea of omnipresence is that of exemption from the limitations of space, subjectively as well as objectively; subjectively, in so far as space, which is a necessary form of all created consciousness in the sphere of sense-perception, is not thus constitutionally inherent in the mind of God; objectively, in so far as the actuality of space-relations in the created world imposes no limit upon the presence and operation of God. This metaphysical conception of transcendence above all space is, of course, foreign to the Bible, which in regard to this, as in regard to the other transcendent attributes, clothes the truth of revelation in popular language, and speaks of exemption from the limitations of space in terms and figures derived from space itself. Thus the very term "omnipresence" in its two component parts "everywhere" and "present" contains a double inadequacy of expression, both the notion of "everywhere" and that of "presence" being spacial concepts. Another point, in regard to which the popular nature of the Scriptural teaching on this subject must be kept in mind, concerns the mode of the Divine omnipresence. In treating the concept philosophically, it is of importance to distinguish between its application to the essence, to the activity, and to the knowledge of God. The Bible does not draw these distinctions in the abstract. Although sometimes it speaks of God's omnipresence with reference to the pervasive immanence of His being, it frequently contents itself with affirming the universal extent of God's power and knowledge (Dt **4** 39; **10** 14; Ps **139** 6–16; Prov **15** 3; Jer **23** 23.24; Am **9** 2).

2. Philosophical and Popular Ideas of Omnipresence

This observation has given rise to the theories of a mere omnipresence of power or omnipresence by an act of will, as distinct from an omnipresence of being. But it is plain that in this antithetical form such a distinction is foreign to the intent of the Bib. statements in question. The writers in these passages content themselves with describing the practical effects of the attribute without reflecting upon the difference between this and its ontological aspect; the latter is neither affirmed nor denied. That no denial of the omnipresence of being is intended may be seen from Jer **23** 24, where in the former half of the verse the omnipresence of ver 23 is expressed in terms of omniscience, while in the latter half the idea finds ontological expression. Similarly, in Ps **139**, cf ver 2 with vs 7 ff, and vs 13 ff. As here, so in other passages the presence of God with His being in all space is explicitly affirmed (1 K **8** 27; 2 Ch **2** 6; Isa **66** 1; Acts **17** 28).

3. Theories Denying Omnipresence of Being

Omnipresence being the correlate of monotheism, the presence of the idea in the earlier parts of the OT is denied by all those who assign the development of monotheism in the OT religion to the prophetic period from the 8th cent. onward. It is undoubtedly true that the earliest narratives speak very anthropomorphically of God's relation to space; they describe Him as coming and going in language such as might be used of a human person. But it does not follow from this that the writers who do so conceive of God's being as circumscribed by space. Where such forms of statement occur, not the presence of God in general, but His visible presence in theophany is referred to. If from the local element entering into the description God's subjection to the limitations of space were inferred, then one might with equal warrant, on the basis of the physical, sensual elements entering into the representation, impute to the writers the view that the Divine nature is corporeal.

4. Denial of the Presence of the Idea in the Earlier Parts of the OT

The theophanic form of appearance does not disclose what God is ontologically in Himself, but merely how He condescends to appear and work for the redemption of His people. It establishes a redemptive and revelatory presence in definite localities, which does not, in the mind of the writer, detract from the Divine omnipresence. Hence, it is not confined to one place; the altars built in recognition of it are in patriarchal history erected in several places and coexist as each and all offering access to the special Divine presence. It is significant that already during the patriarchal period these theophanies and the altars connected with them are confined to the Holy Land. This shows that the idea embodied in them has nothing to do with a crude conception of the Deity as locally circumscribed, but marks the beginning of that gradual restoration of the gracious presence of God to fallen humanity, the completion of which forms the goal of redemption. Thus God is said to dwell in the ark, in the tabernacle, on Mt. Zion (Nu **10** 35; 2 S **6** 2; 2 K **19** 15; Ps **3** 4; **99** 1); in the temple (1 K **8**; Ps **20** 2; **26** 8; **46** 5; **48** 2; Isa **8** 18; Joel **3** 16.21; Am **1** 2); in the Holy Land (1 S **26** 19; Hos **9** 3); in Christ (Jn **1** 14; **2** 19; Col **2** 9); in the church (Jn **14** 23; Rom **8** 9.11; 1 Cor **3** 16; **6** 19; Eph **2** 21.22; **3** 11; 2 Tim **3** 15; He **10** 21; 1 Pet **2** 5); in the eschatological assembly of His people (Rev **21** 3). In the light of the same principle must be interpreted the presence of God in heaven. This also is not to be understood as an ontological presence, but as a presence of specific theocratic manifestation (1 K **8** 27; Ps **2** 4; **11** 4; **33** 13 ff; **104** 3; Isa **6** 1 ff; **63** 15; **66** 1; Hab **2** 20; Mt **5** 34; **6** 9; Acts **7** 48; **17** 28; Eph **1** 20; He **1** 3). How little this is meant to exclude the presence of God elsewhere may be seen from the fact that the two representations, that of God's self-manifestation in heaven and in the earthly sanctuary, occur side by side (1 K **8** 26–53; Ps **20** 2–6; Am **9** 6). It has been alleged that the idea of God's dwelling in heaven marks a comparatively late attainment in the religion of Israel, of which in the pre-prophetic period no trace can as yet be discovered (so Stade, *Bibl. Theol. des AT*, I, 103, 104). There are, however, a number of passages in the Pent bearing witness to the early existence of this belief (Gen **11** 1–9; **19** 24; **21** 17; **22** 11; **28** 12). Jeh comes, according to the belief of the earliest period, with the clouds (Ex **14** 19.20; **19** 9.18; **24** 15; Nu **11** 25; **12** 5). That even in the opinion of the people Jeh's local presence in an earthly sanctuary need not have excluded Him from heaven follows also from the unhesitating belief in His simultaneous presence in a plurality of sanctuaries. If it was not a question of locally circumscribed presence as between sanctuary and sanctuary, it need not have been as between earth and heaven (cf Gunkel, *Gen*, 157).

5. The Special Redemptive and Revelatory Presence of God

Both from a generally religious and from a specifically soteriological point of view the omnipresence of God is of great practical importance for the religious life. In the former respect it contains the guaranty that the actual nearness of God and a real communion with Him may be enjoyed everywhere, even apart from the places hallowed for such purpose by a specific gracious self-manifestation (Ps **139** 5–10). In the other respect the Divine omnipresence assures the believer that God is at hand

6. Religious Significance

to save in every place where from any danger or foe His people need salvation (Isa **43** 2).

LITERATURE.—Oehler, *Theologie des AT*³, 174 ff; Riehm, *Alttestamentliche Theologie*, 262 ff; Dillmann, *Handbuch der alttestamentlichen Theologie*, 246 ff; Davidson, *OT Theology*, 180 ff; König, *Geschichte der alttestamentlichen Religion*, 197 ff.

GEERHARDUS VOS

OMNISCIENCE, om-nish′ens: The term does not occur in Scripture, either in its nominal or in its adjectival form.

1. Words and Usage

In the OT it is expressed in connection with such words as דַּעַת, *da'ath*, בִּינָה, *bīnāh*, תְּבוּנָה, *tebhūnāh*, חָכְמָה, *ḥokhmāh*; also "seeing" and "hearing," "the eye" and "the ear" occur as figures for the knowledge of God, as "arm," "hand," "finger" serve to express His power. In the NT are found γινώσκειν, *ginṓskein*, γνῶσις, *gnṓsis*, εἰδέναι, *eidénai*, σοφία, *sophía*, in the same connections.

2. Tacit Assumption and Explicit Affirmation

Scripture everywhere teaches the absolute universality of the Divine knowledge. In the historical books, although there is no abstract formula, and occasional anthropomorphic references to God's taking knowledge of things occur (Gen **11** 5; **18** 21; Dt **8** 3), none the less the principle is everywhere presupposed in what is related about God's cognizance of the doings of man, about the hearing of prayer, the disclosing of the future (1 S **16** 7; **23** 9–12; 1 K **8** 39; 2 Ch **16** 9). Explicit affirmation of the principle is made in the Psalter, the Prophets, the *ḥokhmāh* literature and in the NT. This is due to the increased internalizing of religion, by which its hidden side, to which the Divine omniscience corresponds, receives greater emphasis (Job **26** 6; **28** 24; **34** 22; Ps **139** 12; **147** 4; Prov **15** 3.11; Isa **40** 26; Acts **1** 24; He **4** 13; Rev **2** 23).

3. Extends to All Spheres

This absolute universality is affirmed with reference to the various categories that comprise within themselves all that is possible or actual. It extends to God's own being, as well as to what exists outside of Him in the created world. God has perfect possession in consciousness of His own being. The unconscious finds no place in Him (Acts **15** 18; 1 Jn **1** 5). Next to Himself God knows the world in its totality. This knowledge extends to small as well as to great affairs (Mt **6** 8.32; **10** 30); to the hidden heart and mind of man as well as to that which is open and manifest (Job **11** 11; **34** 21.23; Ps **14** 2; **17** 2 ff; **33** 13–18; **102** 19 f; **139** 1–4; Prov **5** 21; **15** 3; Isa **29** 15; Jer **17** 10; Am **4** 13; Lk **16** 15; Acts **1** 24; 1 Thess **2** 4; He **4** 13; Rev **2** 23). It extends to all the divisions of time, the past, present and future alike (Job **14** 17; Ps **56** 8; Isa **41** 22–24; **44** 6–8; Jer **1** 5; Hos **13** 12; Mal **3** 16). It embraces that which is contingent from the human viewpoint as well as that which is certain (1 S **23** 9–12; Mt **11** 22.23).

4. Mode of the Divine Knowledge

Scripture brings God's knowledge into connection with His omnipresence. Ps **139** is the clearest expression of this. Omniscience is the omnipresence of cognition (Jer **23** 23 ff). It is also closely related to God's eternity, for the latter makes Him in His knowledge independent of the limitations of time (Isa **43** 8–12). God's creative relation to all that exists is represented as underlying His omniscience (Ps **33** 15; **97** 9; **139** 13; Isa **29** 15). His all-comprehensive purpose forms the basis of His knowledge of all events and developments (Isa **41** 22–27; Am **3** 7).

This, however, does not mean that God's knowledge of things is identical with His creation of them, as has been suggested by Augustine and others. The act of creation, while necessarily connected with the knowledge of that which is to be actual, is not identical with such knowledge or with the purpose on which such knowledge rests, for in God, as well as in man, the intellect and the will are distinct faculties. In the last analysis, God's knowledge of the world has its source in His self-knowledge. The world is a revelation of God. All that is actual or possible in it therefore is a reflection in created form of what exists uncreated in God, and thus the knowledge of the one becomes a reproduction of the knowledge of the other (Acts **17** 27; Rom **1** 20). The Divine knowledge of the world also partakes of the quality of the Divine self-knowledge in this respect, that it is never dormant. God does not depend for embracing the multitude and complexity of the existing world on such mental processes as abstraction and generalization.

The Bible nowhere represents Him as attaining to knowledge by reasoning, but everywhere as simply knowing. From what has been said about the immanent sources of the Divine knowledge, it follows that the latter is not a posteriori derived from its objects, as all human knowledge based on experience is, but is exercised without receptivity or dependence. In knowing, as well as in all other activities of His nature, God is sovereign and self-sufficient. In cognizing the reality of all things He needs not wait upon the things, but draws His knowledge directly from the basis of reality as it lies in Himself. While the two are thus closely connected it is nevertheless of importance to distinguish between God's knowledge of Himself and God's knowledge of the world, and also between His knowledge of the actual and His knowledge of the possible. These distinctions mark off the theistic conception of omniscience from the pantheistic idea regarding it. God is not bound up in His life with the world in such a sense as to have no scope of activity beyond it.

5. God's Omniscience and Human Freewill

Since Scripture includes in the objects of the Divine knowledge also the issue of the exercise of freewill on the part of man, the problem arises, how the contingent character of such decisions and the certainty of the Divine knowledge can coexist. It is true that the knowledge of God and the purposing will of God are distinct, and that not the former but the latter determines the certainty of the outcome. Consequently the Divine omniscience in such cases adds or detracts nothing in regard to the certainty of the event. God's omniscience does not produce but presupposes the certainty by which the problem is raised. At the same time, precisely because omniscience presupposes certainty, it appears to exclude every conception of contingency in the free acts of man, such as would render the latter in their very essence undetermined. The knowledge of the issue must have a fixed point of certainty to terminate upon, if it is to be knowledge at all. Those who make the essence of freedom absolute indeterminateness must, therefore, exempt this class of events from the scope of the Divine omniscience. But this is contrary to all the testimony of Scripture, which distinctly makes God's absolute knowledge extend to such acts (Acts **2** 23). It has been attempted to construe a peculiar form of the Divine knowledge, which would relate to this class of acts specifically, the so-called *scientia media*, to be distinguished from the *scientia necessaria*, which has for its object God Himself, and the *scientia libera* which terminates upon the certainties of the world outside of God, as determined by His freewill. This *scientia media* would then be based on God's foresight of the outcome of the free choice of man. It would involve a knowledge of receptivity, a contribution to the sum total of what God knows derived from observation on His part of the world-process. That is to say, it would be knowledge a posteriori in essence, although not in point of time. It is, however, difficult to see how such a knowledge can be possible in God, when the outcome is psychologically undetermined and undeterminable. The knowledge could originate no sooner than the determination originates through the free decision of man. It would, therefore, necessarily become an a posteriori knowledge in time as well as in essence. The appeal to God's eternity as bringing Him equally near to the future as to the present and enabling Him to see the future decisions of man's free will as though they were present cannot remove this difficulty, for when once the observation and knowledge of God are made dependent on any temporal issue, the Divine eternity itself is thereby virtually denied. Nothing remains but to recognize that God's eternal knowledge of the outcome of the freewill choices of man implies that there enters into these choices, notwithstanding their free character, an element of predetermination, to which the knowledge of God can attach itself.

6. Religious Importance

The Divine omniscience is most important for the religious life. The very essence of religion as communion with God depends on His all-comprehensive cognizance of the life of man at every moment. Hence it is characteristic of the irreligious to deny the omniscience of God (Ps **10** 11.12; **94** 7–9; Isa **29** 15; Jer **23** 23; Ezk **8** 12; **9** 9). Esp. along three lines this fundamental religious importance reveals itself: (*a*) it lends support and comfort when the pious suffer from the misunderstanding and misrepresentation of men; (*b*) it acts as a deterrent to those tempted by sin, esp. secret sin, and becomes a judging principle to all hypocrisy and false security; (*c*) it furnishes the source from which man's desire for self-knowledge can obtain satisfaction (Ps **19** 12; **51** 6; **139** 23.24).

Literature.—Oehler, *Theologie des AT*³, 876; Riehm, *Alttestamentliche Theologie*, 263; Dillmann, *Handbuch der alttestamentlichen Theologie*, 249; Davidson, *OT Theology*, 180 ff.

Geerhardus Vos

OMRI, om′rī (עָמְרִי, *'omrī;* LXX **'Αμβρί,** *Ambrí;* Assyr "Ḥumri" and "Ḥumria"):

(1) The 6th king of Northern Israel, and founder of the IIId Dynasty which reigned for nearly 50 years. Omri reigned 12 years, c 887–876 BC. The historical sources of his reign are contained in 1 K **16** 15–28; **20** 34, the M S, Assyr inscriptions, and in the published accounts of recent excavations in Samaria. In spite of the brief passage given to Omri in the OT, he was one of the most important of the military kings of Northern Israel.

1. His Accession

O. is first mentioned as an officer in the army of Elah, which was engaged in the siege of the Phili town of Gibbethon. While O. was thus engaged, Zimri, another officer of Elah's army, conspired against the king, whom he assassinated in a drunken debauch, exterminating at the same time the remnant of the house of Baasha. The conspiracy evidently lacked the support of the people, for the report that Zimri had usurped the throne no sooner reached the army at Gibbethon, than the people proclaimed O., the more powerful military leader, king over Israel. O. lost not a moment, but leaving Gibbethon in the hands of the Philis, he marched to Tirzah, which he besieged and captured, while Zimri perished in the flames of the palace to which he had set fire with his own hands (1 K **16** 18). O., however, had still another opponent in Tibni the son of Ginath, who laid claim to the throne, and who was supported in his claims by his brother Joram (1 K **16** 22 LXX) and by a large number of the people. Civil war followed this rivalry for the throne, which seems to have lasted for a period of four years (cf 1 K **16** 15, with vs 23 and 29) before O. gained full control.

2. The Founding of Samaria

O.'s military ability is seen from his choice of Samaria as the royal residence and capital of the Northern Kingdom. This step may have been suggested to O. by his own easy conquest of Tirzah, the former capital. Accordingly, he purchased the hill Shomeron of Shemer for two talents of silver, about $4,352.00 in American money. The conical hill, which rose from the surrounding plain to the height of 400 ft., and on the top of which there was room for a large city, was capable of easy defence.

The superior strategic importance of Samaria is evidenced by the sieges it endured repeatedly by the Syrians and Assyrians. It was finally taken by Sargon in 722, after the siege had lasted for 3 years. That the Northern Kingdom endured as long as it did was due largely to the strength of its capital. With the fall of Samaria, the nation fell.

Palace of Omri and Ahab at Samaria.

Recent excavations in Samaria under the direction of Harvard University throw new light upon the ancient capital of Israel. The first results were the uncovering of massive foundation walls of a large building, including a stairway 80 ft. wide. This building, which is Rom in architecture, is supposed to have been a temple, the work of Herod. Under this Rom building was recovered a part of a massive Heb structure, believed to be the palace of O. and Ahab. During the year 1910 the explorations revealed a building covering 1½ acres of ground. Four periods of construction were recognized, which, on archaeological grounds, were tentatively assigned to the reigns of O., Ahab, Jehu, and Jeroboam II. See Samaria and articles by David G. Lyon in *Harvard Theological Review*, IV, 1911; *JBL*, V, xxx, Part I, 1911; *PEFS*, 1911, 79–83.

3. His Foreign Policy

Concerning O.'s foreign policy the OT is silent beyond a single hint contained in 1 K **20** 34. Here we learn that he had to bow before the stronger power of Syria. It is probable that Ben-hadad I besieged Samaria shortly after it was built, for he forced O. to make "streets" in the city for the Syrians. It is probable, too, that at this time Ramoth-gilead was lost to the Syrians. Evidently O. was weakened in his foreign policy at the beginning of his reign by the civil conflict engendered by his accession. However, he showed strength of character in his dealings with foreign powers. At least he regained control over the northern part of Moab, as we learn from the M S. Lines 4–8 tell us that "Omri was king of Israel and afflicted Moab many days because Chemosh was angry with his land. . . . . Omri obtained possession of the land of Medeba and dwelt therein during his days and half the days of his son, forty years."

O. was the first king of Israel to pay tribute to the Assyrians under their king Asurnacirpal III, in 876 BC. From the days of Shalmaneser II (860 BC) down to the time of Sargon (722 BC), Northern Israel was known to the Assyrians as "the land of the house of Omri." On Shalmaneser's black obelisk, Jehu, who overthrew the dynasty of O., is called *Ja'ua abal Ḫumri*, "Jehu son of Omri."

O. entered into an alliance with the Phoenicians by the marriage of his son Ahab to Jezebel, daughter of Ethbaal, king of the Sidonians. This may have been done as protection against the powers from the East, and as such would have seemed to be a wise political move, but it was one fraught with evil for Israel.

4. His Religious Influence and Death

Although O. laid the foundation of a strong kingdom, he failed to impart to it the vitalizing and rejuvenating force of a healthy spiritual religion. The testimony of 1 K **16** 25.26, that he "dealt wickedly above all that were before him," coupled with the reference to "the statutes of Omri" in Mic **6** 16, indicates that he may have had a share in substituting foreign religions for the worship of Jeh, and therefore the unfavorable light in which he is regarded is justified. Upon his death, O. was succeeded upon the throne by his son Ahab, to whom was left the task of shaking off the Syrian yoke, and who went beyond his father in making the Phoen influence along with Baalism of prime importance in Israel, thus leading the nation into the paths that hastened its downfall.

(2) A Benjamite, son of Becher (1 Ch **7** 8).

(3) A Judahite, descendant of Perez, who lived at Jerus (1 Ch **9** 4).

(4) A prince of Issachar in the time of David (1 Ch **27** 18). S. K. MOSIMAN

ON, on (אוֹן, *'ōn;* Egyp *Ăn, Ănt, Ănnū*, probably pronounced *Ăn* only, as this is often all that is written, a "stone" or "stone pillars"): Later called Heliopolis. The name On occurs only in Gen **41** 45. 50; **46** 20. It occurs in one other place in LXX (Ex **1** 11), where On is mentioned with Pithom and Raamses as strong cities which the Israelites built. Heb slaves may have worked upon fortifications here, but certainly did not build the city. On is possibly referred to as עִיר הַהֶרֶס, *'ir ha-hereṣ*, in Isa **19** 18 (see IR-HA-HERES). On may also be mentioned by Jeremiah (**43** 13) under the name Beth-shemesh. Ezekiel speaks of an Aven (אָוֶן, *'āwen*) (Ezk **30** 17), where it is mentioned with Pi-beseth (Bubastis). Aven in this passage is almost certainly the same as On in Gen **41** 45; **46** 20, as the letters of both words are the same in the Heb. Only the placing of the vowel-points makes any difference. If there is a mistake, it is a mistake of the Massoretes, not of the Heb writer.

1. Location and Description

There were two Ons in Egypt: one in Upper Egypt, An-res (Hermonthis); the other in Lower Egypt, An-Meheet (Brugsch, *Geogr. Inschr.*, 254, 255, nos. 1217, *a*, *b*, 1218, 8708, 1225). The latter is the On referred to in the Bible. It lay about 20 miles N. of the site of old Memphis, about 10 miles N.E. of the location of modern Cairo. It has left until this time about 4 sq. miles of ruins within the old walls. Little or nothing remains outside the walls.

On was built at the edge of the desert, which has now retreated some 3 or 4 miles eastward, the result of the rising of the bed of the Nile by sediment from the inundation, and the broadening of the area of infiltration which now carries the water of the Nile that much to the E. The land around On has risen about 10 ft., and the waters of infiltration at the time of lowest Nile are now about 1½ ft. above the floor-level of the temple.

2. History

The history of On is very obscure, yet its very great importance is in no doubt. No clear description of the ancient city or sanctuary has come down to us, but there are so many incidental references, and so much is implied in ancient records, that it stands

Obelisk at On.

out as of the very first importance, both as capital and sanctuary. The city comes from the Ist Dynasty, when it was the seat of government, and indeed must have been founded by the Ist Dynasty or have come down to it from pre-historic time. From the IIId to the VIth Dynasty the seat of government was shifted from On to Memphis, and in the XIIth Dynasty to Diospolis. Throughout these changes On retained its religious importance. It had been the great sanctuary in the time of the Pyramid Texts, the oldest religious texts of Egypt, and judging from the evident great development of the temple of On at the time of the writing of the texts, the city must have antedated them by considerable time (Budge, *Hist of Egypt*, II, 83, 84, 108; Breasted, *Development of Religion and Thought in Egypt*, chs i, ii). The myth of Osiris makes even the charge against Set for the murder of Osiris to have been preferred at Heliopolis (Breasted, op. cit., 34). This certainly implies a very great age for the sanctuary at On. It contained a temple of the sun under the name Ra, the sun, and also Atum, the setting sun, or the sun of the Underworld. There was also a Phoenix Hall and a sacred object called a *ben*, probably a stone, and the origin of the name An, a "stone" or "pillar" (cf Breasted, op. cit., 76, 11, and 71). Though the XIIth Dynasty removed the capital to Diospolis, Usertsen I (Senwesret) of that Dynasty erected a great obelisk at On in front of the entrance to the temple. The situation of this obelisk in the temple-area indicates that the great temple was already more than a half-mile in length as early as the XIIth Dynasty. The mate of this obelisk on the opposite side of the entrance seems not to have been erected until the XVIIIth Dynasty. Its foundations were discovered in 1912 by Petrie. Some scraps of the granite of the obelisk bear inscriptions of Thothmes III. A great Hyksos wall, also discovered by Petrie in 1912, exactly similar to that of the fortified camp at *Tel el Yehudiyeh*, 4 miles N., makes it quite certain that these usurpers between the Old Empire and the New fortified On as the capital once more. The manifest subserviency of the priests of On in the story of Joseph makes it most probable that the old capital at On had already been subjugated in Joseph's time, and that within this old fortification still existing Joseph ruled as prime minister of Egypt. Merenptah in his 5th year began to fortify On. Sheshonk III called himself "divine prince of Annu," and seems to have made On one of the greatest sanctuaries of his long reign. On still figured in Egyp history in the rebellion against Ashurbanipal. The city has been deserted since the Pers invasion of 525 BC. Tradition makes the dwelling-place of Joseph and Mary with the child Jesus, while in Egypt, to have been near Heliopolis.

The exploration of On was attempted by Schiaparelli, but was not carried out, and his work has not been published. In 1912 Petrie began a systematic work of excavation which, it is expected, will continue until the whole city has been examined. The only great discovery of the first season was the Hyksos wall of fortification. Its full import can only be determined by the continuance of the exploration.

M. G. Kyle

ON (אוֹן, *'ōn; Αὐν, Aún*): A Reubenite, son of Peleth, who took part with Dathan and Abiram in their revolt against Moses (Nu **16** 1).

ONAM, ō'nam (אוֹנָם, *'ōnām,* "vigorous"; cf Onan):

(1) "Son" of Shobal "son" of Seir the Horite (Gen **36** 23; 1 Ch **1** 40).

(2) "Son" of Jerahmeel by Atarah; perhaps the name is connected with Onan son of Judah (1 Ch **2** 26.28).

ONAN, ō'nan (אוֹנָן, *'ōnān,* "vigorous"; cf Onam): A "son" of Judah (Gen **38** 4.8–10; **46** 12; Nu **26** 19; 1 Ch **2** 3). "The story of the untimely death of Er and Onan implies that two of the ancient clans of Judah early disappeared" (Curtis, *Chron,* 84). See Skinner, *Gen,* 452, where it is pointed out that in Gen **38** 11 Judah plainly attributes the death of his sons in some way to Tamar herself. The name is allied to Onam.

ONE, wun. See Number.

ONESIMUS, ō-nes'i-mus (Ὀνήσιμος, *Onḗsimos,* lit. "profitable," "helpful" [Col **4** 9; Philem ver 10]):

1. With Paul in Rome

Onesimus was a slave (Philem ver 16) belonging to Philemon who was a wealthy citizen of Colossae, and a prominent member of the church there. O. was still a heathen when he defrauded his master and ran off from Colossae. He found his way to Rome, where evil men tended to flock as to a common center, as Tacitus tells us they did at that period. In Rome he came into contact with Paul, who was then in his own hired house, in military custody.

What brought him into contact with Paul we do not know. It may have been hunger; it may have been the pangs of conscience. He could not forget that his master's house in Colossae was the place where the Christians met in their weekly assemblies for the worship of Christ. Neither could he forget how Philemon had many a time spoken of Paul, to whom he owed his conversion. Now that O. was in Rome—what a strange coincidence—Paul also was in Rome.

The result of their meeting was that O. was converted to Christ, through the instrumentality of the apostle ("my child, whom I have begotten in my bonds," Philem ver 10). His services had been very acceptable to Paul, who would gladly have kept O. with him; but as he could not do this without the knowledge and consent of Philemon, he sent O. back to Colossae, to his master there.

2. Paul's Epistles to Colossae and to Philemon

At the same time Paul wrote to the church in Colossae on other matters, and he intrusted the Ep. to the Col to the joint care of Tychicus and O. The apostle recommends O. to the brethren in Colossae, as a "faithful and beloved brother, who is one of you," and he goes on to say that Tychicus and O. will make known to them all things that have happened to Paul in Rome. Such a commendation would greatly facilitate O.'s return to Colossae.

But Paul does more. He furnishes O. with a letter written by himself to Philemon. Returning to a city where it was well known that he had been neither a Christian nor even an honest man, he needed someone to vouch for the reality of the change which had taken place in his life. And Paul does this for him both in the Ep. to the Col and in that to Philemon.

With what exquisite delicacy is O. introduced! 'Receive him,' says the apostle, 'for he is my own very heart' (Philem ver 12). "The man whom the Colossians had only known hitherto, if they knew him at all, as a worthless runaway slave, is thus commended to them, as no more a slave but a brother, no more dishonest and faithless but trustworthy; no more an object of contempt but of love" (Lightfoot's *Comm. on Col,* 235).

(1) *Onesimus profitable.*—The apostle accordingly begs Philemon to give O. the same reception as he would rejoice to give to himself. The past history of O. had been such as to belie the meaning of his name. He had not been "profitable"—far from it. But already his consistent conduct in Rome and his willing service to Paul there have changed all that; he has been profitable to Paul, and he will be profitable to Philemon too.

(2) *Paul guarantees.*—O. had evidently stolen his master's goods before leaving Colossae, but in regard to that the apostle writes that if he has defrauded Philemon in anything, he becomes his surety. Philemon can regard Paul's handwriting as a bond guaranteeing payment: "Put that to mine account," are his words, "I will repay it." Had Philemon not been a Christian, and had Paul not written this most beautiful letter, O. might well have been afraid to return. In the Rom empire slaves were constantly crucified for smaller offences than those of which he had been guilty. A thief and a runaway had nothing but torture or death to expect.

(3) *The change which Christ makes.*—But now under the sway of Christ all is changed. The master who has been defrauded now owns allegiance to Jesus. The letter, which is delivered to him by his slave, is written by a bound "prisoner of Jesus Christ." The slave too is now a brother in Christ, beloved by Paul: surely he will be beloved by Philemon also. Then Paul intimates that he hopes soon to be set free, and then he will come and visit them in Colossae. Will Philemon receive him into his house as his guest?

(4) *The result.*—It cannot be imagined that this appeal in behalf of O. was in vain. Philemon would do more than Paul asked; and on the apostle's visit to Colossae he would find the warmest welcome, both from Philemon and from Onesimus.

John Rutherfurd

ONESIPHORUS, ō-nē-sif′ō-rus (**Ὀνησίφορος,** *Onēsiphoros,* lit. "profit bringer" [2 Tim **1** 16; **4** 19]): Onesiphorus was a friend of the apostle Paul, who mentions him twice when writing to Timothy. In the former of the two passages where his name occurs, his conduct is contrasted with that of Phygellus and Hermogenes and others—all of whom, like O. himself, were of the province of Asia—from whom Paul might well have expected to receive sympathy and help. These persons had "turned away" from him. O. acted in a different way, for "he oft refreshed me, and was not ashamed of my chain; but, when he was in Rome, he sought me diligently, and found me."

1. The Friend of Paul

O. was one of the Christians of the church in Ephesus; and the second passage, where his name is found, merely sends a message of greeting from Paul, which Timothy in Ephesus is requested to deliver to "the household of O." (AV).

O. then had come from Ephesus to Rome. It was to Paul that the church at Ephesus owed its origin, and it was to him therefore that O. and the Christians there were indebted for all that they knew of Christ. O. gratefully remembered these facts, and having arrived in Rome, and learned that Paul was in prison, he "very diligently" sought for the apostle. But to do this, though it was only his duty, involved much personal danger at that particular time. For the persecution, inaugurated by Nero against the Christians, had raged bitterly; its fury was not yet abated, and this made the profession of the Christian name a matter which involved very great risk of persecution and of death.

2. Visits Paul in Rome

Paul was not the man to think lightly of what his Ephesian friend had done. He remembered too, "in how many things he ministered at Ephesus." And, writing to Timothy, he reminded him that O.'s kindly ministrations at Ephesus were already well known to him, from his residence in Ephesus, and from his position, as minister of the church there.

It should be observed that the ministration of O. at Ephesus was not, as AV gives it, "to me," that is, to Paul himself. "To me" is omitted in RV. What O. had done there was a wide Christian ministry of kindly action; it embraced "many things," which were too well known—for such is the force of the word—to Timothy to require repetition.

The visits which O. paid to Paul in his Rom prison were intensely "refreshing." And it was not once or twice that he thus visited the chained prisoner, but he did so ofttimes.

Though O. had come to Rome, his household had remained in Ephesus; and a last salutation is sent to them by Paul. He could not write again, as he was now ready to be offered, and his execution could not long be delayed. But as he writes, he entertains the kindest feelings toward O. and his household, and he prays that the Lord will give mercy to the household of O.

3. His Household

He also uses these words in regard to O. himself: "The Lord grant unto him to find mercy of the Lord in that day." It is not clear whether O. was living, or whether he had died, before Paul wrote this ep. Different opinions have been held on the subject.

The way in which Paul refers twice to "the household [RV "house"] of Onesiphorus," makes it possible that O. himself had died. If this is so—but certainty is impossible—the apostle's words in regard to him would be a pious wish, which has nothing in common with the abuses which have gathered round the subject of prayers for the dead, a practice which has no foundation in Scripture.

John Rutherfurd

ONIARES, ō-nī′a-rēz, ō-ni-ā′rēz: 1 Macc **12** 19 AV=RV Arius (q.v.).

ONIAS, ō-nī′as (**Ὀνίας,** *Onías*): There were 3 high priests of the name of Onias, and a 4th Onias who did not become a high priest but was known as the builder of the temple of Leontopolis (Jos, *Ant,* XIII, iii, 1–3). Only two persons of the name are mentioned in the Apoc—Onias I and Onias III.

(1) Onias I, according to Jos (*Ant,* XI, viii, 7), the son of Jaddua and father of Simon the Just (ib, XII, ii, 5; Sir **50**), and, according to 1 Macc **12** 7.20, a contemporary of Areus (Arius), king of Sparta, who reigned 309–265 BC (Diod. xx.29). This Onias was the recipient of a friendly letter from Areus of Sparta (1 Macc **12** 7; see MSS readings here, and **12** 20). Jos (*Ant,* XII, iv, 10) represents this letter as written to Onias III, which is an error, for only two Areuses are known, and Areus II reigned about 255 BC and died a child of 8 years (Paus. iii.6.6). The letter—if genuine—exists in two copies (Jos, *Ant,* XII, iv, 10, and 1 Macc **12** 20 ff) (see Schürer, *Hist of the Jewish People,* 4th ed, I, 182 and 237).

(2) Onias III, son of Simon II (Jos, *Ant,* XII, iv, 10), whom he succeeded, and a contemporary of Seleucus IV and Antiochus Epiphanes (2 Macc **3** 1; **4** 7) and father of Onias IV. He was known for his godliness and zeal for the law, yet was on such friendly terms with the Seleucids that Seleucus IV Philopator defrayed the cost of the "services of the sacrifices." He quarreled with Simon the Benjamite, guardian of the temple, about the market buildings (Gr aedileship). Being unable to get the better of Onias and thirsting for revenge, Simon went to Apollonius, governor of Coele-Syria and Phoenicia, and informed him of the "untold sums of money" lodged in the treasury of the temple. The governor told the king, and Seleucus dispatched his chancellor, Heliodorus, to remove the money. Onias remonstrated in vain, pleading for the "deposits of widows and orphans." Heliodorus persisted in the object of his mission. The high priest and the people were in the greatest distress. But when Heliodorus had already entered the temple, "the Sovereign of spirits, and of all authority caused a great apparition," a horse with a terrible rider accompanied by two strong and beautiful young men who scourged and wounded Heliodorus. At the intercession of Onias, his life was spared. Heliodorus advised the king to send on the same errand any enemy or conspirator whom he wished punished. Simon then slandered Onias, and the jealousy having caused bloodshed between their followers, Onias decided to repair in person to the king to intercede for his country. Apparently before a decision was given, Seleucus was assassinated and Epiphanes succeeded (175 BC). Jason, the brother of Onias, having offered the new king larger revenue, secured the priesthood, which he held until he himself was similarly supplanted by Menelaus, Simon's brother (2 Macc **4** 23; Jos, *Ant,* XII, v, 1, says Jason's brother). Menelaus, having stolen golden vessels belonging to the temple to meet his promises made to the king, was sharply reproved by Onias. Menelaus took revenge by persuading Andronicus, the king's deputy, to entice Onias by false promises of friendship from his sanctuary at Daphne and treacherously slay him—an act which caused indignation among both the Jews and the Greeks (2 Macc **4** 34 ff). Jos (*Ant,* XII, v, 1) says that "on the death of Onias the high priest, Antiochus gave the high-priesthood to his brother Jesus [Jason]," but the account of 2 Macc given

above is the more probable. Some see in Dnl **9** 26; **11** 22 reference to Onias III (Schürer, 4th ed, I, 194 ff; III, 144). S. ANGUS

ONIONS, un'yunz (בְּצָלִים, *b^eçālīm;* **κρόμμυον,** *krómmuon*): One of the delicacies of Egypt for which the children of Israel pined in the wilderness (Nu **11** 5). The onion, *allium cepa* (N.O. *Liliaceae*), is known in Arab. as *buṣal* and is cultivated all over Syria and Egypt; it appears to be as much a favorite in the Orient today as ever.

ONLY BEGOTTEN, ōn'li bē-got''n (**μονογενής,** *monogenḗs*): Although the Eng. words are found only 6 t in the NT, the Gr word appears 9 t, and often in the LXX. It is used literally of an only child: "the only son of his mother" (Lk **7** 12); "an only daughter" (**8** 42); "mine only child" (**9** 38); "Isaac . . . . his only begotten" (He **11** 17). In all other places in the NT it refers to Jesus Christ as "the only begotten Son of God" (Jn **1** 14.18; **3** 16.18; 1 Jn **4** 9). In these passages, too, it might be tr[d] as "the only son of God"; for the emphasis seems to be on His uniqueness, rather than on His sonship, though both ideas are certainly present. He is the son of God in a sense in which no others are. "*Monogenḗs* describes the absolutely unique relation of the Son to the Father in His Divine nature; *prōtótokos* describes the relation of the Risen Christ in His glorified humanity to man" (Westcott on He **1** 6). *Christ's uniqueness* as it appears in the above passages consists of two things: (*a*) He reveals the Father: "No man hath seen God at any time; the only begotten Son, who is in the bosom of the Father, he hath declared him" (Jn **1** 18). Men therefore behold His glory, "glory as of the only begotten from the Father" (**1** 14). (*b*) He is the mediator of salvation: "God hath sent his only begotten Son into the world that we might live through him" (1 Jn **4** 9; Jn **3** 16); "He that believeth not [on him] hath been judged already" (Jn **3** 18). Other elements in His uniqueness may be gathered from other passages, as His sinlessness, His authority to forgive sins, His unbroken communion with the Father, and His unique knowledge of Him. To say that it is a uniqueness of nature or essence carries thought no farther, for these terms still need definition, and they can be defined only in terms of His moral consciousness, of His revelation of God, and esp. of His intimate union as Son with the Father (see also BEGOTTEN; PERSON OF CHRIST; SON OF GOD).

The reading "God only begotten" in Jn **1** 18 RVm, though it has strong textual support, is improbable, and can well be explained as due to orthodox zeal, in opposition to adoptionism. See Grimm-Thayer, *Lexicon;* Westcott, ad loc. T. REES

ONO, ō'nō (אוֹנוֹ, *'ōnō;* B, **'Ωνάν,** *Ōnán*, A, **'Ωνώ,** *Ōnṓ*, and other forms): A town mentioned along with Lod as fortified by certain Benjamites (1 Ch **8** 12). The Mish (*'Ărākhīn*, ix.6) says that Joshua fortified it, but there is no such early notice of it in Scripture. It was occupied by Benjamites after the return from exile (Ezr **2** 33; Neh **7** 37; **11** 35). In one of the villages in the plain of Ono, Sanballat and his friends vainly tried to inveigle Nehemiah into a conference (**6** 2). It is represented by the modern *Kefr 'Anā*, which lies to the N.W. of Lydda. In 1 Esd **5** 22, the name appears as "Onus." W. EWING

ONUS, ō'nus. See ONO.

ONYCHA, on'i-ka (שְׁחֵלֶת, *sh^eḥēleth;* cf Arab. سُحَالَة, *suḥâlat*, "filings," "husks"): "Onycha" is a transliteration of the LXX **ὄνυχα,** *ónucha*, acc. of **ὄνυξ,** *ónux*, which means "nail," "claw," "hoof," and also "onyx," a precious stone. The form "onycha" was perhaps chosen to avoid confusion with "onyx," the stone. The Heb *sh^eḥēleth* occurs only in Ex **30** 34 as an ingredient of the sacred incense. It is supposed to denote the horny operculum found in certain species of marine gasteropod molluscs. The operculum is a disk attached to the upper side of the hinder part of the "foot" of the mollusc. When the animal draws itself into its shell, the hinder part of the foot comes last, and the operculum closes the mouth of the shell. The operculum, which may be horny or stony, is absent in some species. The horny opercula when burned emit a peculiar odor, and are still used in combination with other perfumes by the Arab women of Upper Egypt and Nubia. (See Sir S. Baker, *The Nile Tributaries of Abyssinia*, cited by *EB*, s.v. "Onycha.") ALFRED ELY DAY

ONYX, on'iks, ō'niks. See STONES, PRECIOUS.

OPEN, ō'p'n: In the OT represents chiefly פָּתַח, *pāthaḥ*, but also other words, as גָּלָה, *gālāh*, "to uncover"; of the opening of the eyes in vision, etc (thus Balaam, Nu **22** 31; **24** 4; cf Job **33** 16; **36** 10; Ps **119** 18; Jer **32** 11.14). In the NT the usual word is **ἀνοίγω,** *anoígō* (of opening of mouth, eyes, heavens, doors, etc). A peculiar word, **τραχηλίζομαι,** *trachēlízomai* (lit. to have the neck bent back, to be laid bare), is used for "laid open" before God in He **4** 13.

OPEN PLACE: (1) The "open place" of Gen **38** 14 AV, in which Tamar sat, has come from a misunderstanding of the Heb, the translators having taken *b^ephethaḥ 'ēnayim* to mean "in an opening publicly," instead of "in an opening [i.e. a gate] of Enaim" (cf Prov **1** 21 in the Heb). RV has corrected; see ENAIM. (2) In 1 K **22** 10 ‖ 2 Ch **18** 9 RV relates that Ahab and Jehoshaphat sat "each on his throne, arrayed in their robes, in an open place [m "Heb a threshing-floor," AV "a void place"] at the entrance of the gate of Samaria." The Heb here is awkward, and neither the LXX nor the Syr seems to have read the present text in **1** K **22** 10, the former having "in arms, at the gate of Samaria," and the latter "in many-colored garments." Consequently various attempts have been made to emend the text, of which the simplest is the omission of *b^eghōren*, "in an open place." If, however, the text is right—as is not impossible—the open place is a threshing-floor close to the gate. See the commentaries.
BURTON SCOTT EASTON

OPERATION, op-ēr-ā'shun (מַעֲשֶׂה, *ma'ăseh*, "work"; **ἐνέργεια,** *enérgeia*, **ἐνέργημα,** *enérgēma*, "energy"): Twice used in the OT of God's creative work (Ps **28** 4.5; Isa **5** 12). The Holy Spirit's *inworking* and power are manifest in the bestowal of spiritual gifts on individuals and on the church (1 Cor **12** 6 AV), and in the resurrection of Jesus Christ, through which energy or operation of God those dead in sins are, through faith, raised to newness of life (Col **2** 12 AV).

OPHEL, ō'fel (הָעֹפֶל, *ha-'ōphel* [2 Ch **27** 3, **33** 14; Neh **3** 26 f; **11** 21; and without article, Isa **32** 14 and Mic **4** 8; also 2 K **5** 24]):

1. Meaning of Name

There has been considerable divergence of opinion with regard to the meaning of this name. Thus in all the references given above with the art., RV has simply "Ophel," but AV adds in m "the tower"; in Isa **32** 14, "the hill" with m "Ophel," but AV "the forts," m "clifts"; Mic **4** 8, "the hill," m "Heb Ophel," but AV "the stronghold"; 2 K **5** 24, "the hill," m "Heb Ophel," but AV "the tower," m "secret place." It is true that the other occurrences of the word in 1 S **5** 9.12; **6** 5 f, where it is tr[d] "tumors," and Hab **2** 4, where a verbal form is tr[d] "puffed up," seem to imply that one meaning assigned to the root may be that of "swelling." Recently Dr. Burney (*PEF*, January, 1911) has produced strong arguments in favor of Ophel, when used as the name of a locality, meaning "fortress."

2. Three Ophels

Three places are known to have received this name: (1) A certain place on the east hill of Jerus, S. of the temple; to this all the passages quoted above—except one—refer. (2) The "Ophel," tr[d] "hill," situated apparently in Samaria (cf 2 K **5** 3), where Gehazi took his ill-gotten presents from the hands of the servants of Naaman the Syrian. The tr "tower" would suit the sense at least as well. It was some point probably in the wall of Samaria, perhaps the citadel itself. (3) The third reference is not Bib., but on the M S, an inscription of Mesha, king of Moab, contemporary with Omri. He says: "I built ḲRḤH [? Karhah], the wall of *y*[e]*'ārīm*, and the wall of 'Ōphel and I built its gates and I built its towers." In comparing the references to (1) and (3), it is evident that if Ophel means a "hill," it certainly was a fortified hill, and it seems highly probable that it meant some "artificial swelling in a fortification, e.g. a bulging or rounded keep or enceinte" (Burney, loc. cit.). Isa **32** 14 reads, "The palace shall be forsaken; the populous city shall be deserted; the hill [Ophel] and the watch-tower shall be for dens for ever." Here we have palace, city and watch-tower, all the handiwork of the builder. Does it not seem probable that the Ophel belongs to the same category?

3. The Ophel of Jerusalem

The situation of the Ophel of Jerus is very definitely described. It was clearly, from the references (Neh **3** 26.27; 2 Ch **27** 3; **33** 14), on the east hill S. of the temple. Jos states (*BJ*, V, iv, 2) that the eastern wall of the city ran from Siloam "and reaches as far as a certain place which they called Ophlas when it was joined to the eastern cloister of the temple." In *BJ*, V, vi, 1, it states that "John held the temple and the parts thereto adjoining, for a great way, as also 'Ophla,' and the Valley called the 'Valley of the Cedron.'" It is noticeable that this is *not* identical with the "Acra" and "Lower City" which was held by Simon. There is not the slightest ground for applying the name Ophel, as has been so commonly done, to the whole southeastern hill. In the days of Jos, it was a part of the hill immediately S. of the temple walls, but the OT references suit a locality nearer the middle of the southeastern hill. In the art. Zion (q.v.) it is pointed out that that name does not occur (except in reference to the Jebusite city) in the works of the Chronicler, but that "the Ophel," which occurs almost alone in these works, is apparently used for it. Mic **4** 8 m seems to confirm this view: "O tower of the flock, the Ophel of the daughter of Zion." Here the "tower of the flock" may well refer to the shepherd David's stronghold, and the second name appears to be a synonym for the same place.

Ophel then was probably the fortified site which in earlier days had been known as "Zion" or "the City of David." King Jotham "built much" "on the wall of Ophel" (2 Ch **27** 3). King Manasseh "built an outer wall to the city of David, on the west side of Gihon, in the valley, even to the entrance at the fish gate; and he compassed Ophel about with it, and raised it up to a very great height" (2 Ch **33** 14). It was clearly a fortified place of great importance, and its situation must have been so near that of the ancient "Zion" that scarcely any other theory is possible except that it occupied the site of that ancient fortress.

E. W. G. Masterman

OPHIR, ō'fẽr, ō'fir (אוֹפִּיר [Gen **10** 29], אוֹפִר [1 K **10** 11], אֹפִיר, *'ōphīr*): The 11th in order of the sons of Joktan (Gen **10** 29=1 Ch **1** 23). There is a clear reference also to a tribe Ophir (Gen **10** 30). Ophir is the name of a land or city somewhere to the S. or S.E. of Pal for which Solomon's ships along with Phoen vessels set out from Ezion-geber at the head of the Gulf of Aḳabah, returning with great stores of gold, precious stones and "almug"-wood (1 K **9** 28; **10** 11; 2 Ch **9** 10; 1 K **22** 48; 2 Ch **8** 18). We get a fuller list of the wares and also the time taken by the voyage if we assume that the same vessels are referred to in 1 K **10** 22, "Once every three years came the navy of Tarshish, bringing gold, and silver, ivory, and apes, and peacocks." The other products may not have been native to the land of Ophir, but it is certain that the gold at least was produced there. This gold was proverbial for its purity, as is witnessed by many references in the OT (Ps **45** 9; Job **28** 16; Isa **13** 12; 1 Ch **29** 4), and, in Job **22** 24, Ophir is used for fine gold itself. In addition to these notices of Ophir, it is urged that the name occurs also in two passages under the form "Uphaz" (Jer **10** 9; Dnl **10** 5).

1. Scriptural References

2. Geographical Position

At all times the geographical position of Ophir has been a subject of dispute, the claims of three different regions being principally advanced, namely (1) India and the Far East, (2) Africa, (3) Arabia.

(1) *India and the Far East.*—All the wares mentioned are more or less appropriate to India, even including the fuller list of 1 K **10** 22. "Almug"-wood is conjectured to be the Indian sandal-wood. Another argument is based on the resemblance between the LXX form of the word (*Sōpherá*) and the Coptic name for India (*Sophir*). A closer identification is sought with Abhīra, a people dwelling at the mouths of the Indus. Supara, an ancient city on the west coast of India near the modern Goa, is also suggested. Again, according to Wildman, the name denotes a vague extension eastward, perhaps as far as China.

(2) *Africa.*—This country is the greatest gold-producing region of the three. Sofala, a seaport near Mozambique on the east coast of Africa, has been advanced as the site of Ophir, both on linguistic grounds and from the nature of its products, for there all the articles of 1 K **10** 22 could be procured. But Gesenius shows that Sofala is merely the Arab. form of the Heb *sh*[e]*phēlāh*. Interest in this region as the land of Ophir was renewed, however, by Mauch's discovery at Zimbabye of great ruins and signs of old Phoen civilization and worked-out gold mines. According to Bruce (I, 440), a voyage from Sofala to Ezion-geber would have occupied quite three years owing to the monsoons.

(3) *Arabia.*—The claim of Southeastern Arabia as the land of Ophir has on the whole more to support it than that of India or of Africa. The Ophir of Gen **10** 29 beyond doubt belonged to this region, and the search for Ophir in more distant lands can be made only on the precarious assumption that the Ophir of K is not the same as the Ophir of Gen. Of the various products mentioned, the only one which from the OT notices can be regarded as clearly native to Ophir is the gold, and according to Pliny and Strabo the region of Southeastern Arabia bordering on the Persian Gulf was a famous gold-producing country. The other wares were not necessarily produced in Ophir, but were prob-

ably brought there from more distant lands, and thence conveyed by Solomon's merchantmen to Ezion-geber. If the duration of the voyage (3 years) be used as evidence, it favors this location of Ophir as much as that on the east coast of Africa. It seems therefore the least assailable view that Ophir was a district on the Persian Gulf in South-eastern Arabia and served in old time as an emporium of trade between the East and West.

A. S. FULTON

OPHNI, of'nī (הָעָפְנִי, *hā-'ophnī;* **'Αφνή,** *Aphnḗ*): A place in the territory of Benjamin (Josh **18** 24). The modern *Jifneh,* in a fine vale W. of the road to *Nāblus* and 2½ miles N.W. of Bethel, might suit as to position; but the change in the initial letter from *'ain* to *jīm* is not easy. This is the Gophna of the rabbis (cf Jos, *BJ,* III, iii, 5).

OPHRAH, of'ra (עָפְרָה, *'ophrāh;* B, **'Αφρά,** *Aphrá,* A, **'Ιεφραθά,** *Iephrathá,* etc):

(1) A town in the territory allotted to Benjamin named between Parah and Chephar-ammoni (Josh **18** 23). It is mentioned again in 1 S **13** 17. The Philis who were encamped at Michmash sent out marauding bands, one of which went westward, another eastward, down "the valley of Zeboim toward the wilderness"; the third "turned unto the way that leadeth to Ophrah, unto the land of Shual." This must have been northward, as Saul commanded the passage to the S. *Onom* places it 5 Rom miles E. of Bethel. A site which comes near to fulfilling these conditions is *eṭ-Ṭaiyebeh,* which stands on a conical hill some 5 miles N.E. of *Beitīn.* This is possibly identical with "Ephron" (2 Ch **13** 19), and "Ephraim" (Jn **11** 54).

(2) A city in the tribal lot of Manasseh W. of Jordan. It is mentioned only in connection with Gideon, whose native place it was, and with his son Abimelech (Jgs **6** 11, etc). It was, indeed, family property, belonging to Joash the Abiezrite, the father of Gideon. It was apparently not far from the plain of Esdraelon (vs 33 f), so that Gideon and his kinsmen smarted under the near presence of the oppressing Midianites. Manasseh, of course, as bordering on the southern edge of the plain, was in close touch with the invaders. At Ophrah, Gideon reared his altar to Jeh, and made thorough cleansing of the instruments of idolatry. After his great victory, he set up here the golden ephod made from the spoils of the enemy, which proved a snare to himself and to his house (**8** 27). Here he was finally laid to rest. It was at Ophrah that Abimelech, aspiring to the kingdom, put to death upon one stone three score and ten of his brethren, as possible rivals, Jotham alone escaping alive (**9** 5). Apparently the mother of Abimelech belonged to Shechem; this established a relationship with that town, his connection with which does not therefore mean that Ophrah was near it.

No quite satisfactory identification has yet been suggested. Conder (*PEFS,* 1876, 197) quotes the *Samaritan Chronicle* as identifying *Ferata,* which is 6 miles W. of *Nāblus,* with an ancient Ophra, "and the one that suggests itself as most probably identical is Ophrah of the Abiezerite." But this seems too far to the S.

(3) A man of the tribe of Judah, son of Meonothai (1 Ch **4** 14).

W. EWING

OPINION, ō-pin'yun (דֵּעַ, *dē^a',* סְעִפִּים, *ṣe'ippīm*): "Opinion" occurs only 5 t, thrice in Job (**32** 6.10.17) as the tr of *dē^a',* "knowledge," "opinion" (in the address of Elihu), and once of *ṣe'ippīm,* from *ṣā'aph,* "to divide or branch out," hence division or party, unsettled opinion (in the memorable appeal of Elijah, "How long halt ye between two opinions?" 1 K **18** 21, ARV "How long go ye limping between the two sides?"). In Ecclus **3** 24, we have, "For many are deceived by their own vain opinion" (*hupólēpsis,* "a taking up," "a hasty judgment"), RV "The conceit of many hath led them astray."

W. L. WALKER

OPOBALSAMUM, op-o-bal'sa-mum: RVm in Ex **30** 34. See STACTE.

OPPRESSION, o-presh'un: Used in AV to translate a variety of Heb words, all of which, however, agree in the general sense of wrong done by violence to others. There are a few cases where the reference is to the oppression of Israel by foreigners, as by their Egyp masters (Ex **3** 9; Dt **26** 7), or by Syria (2 K **13** 4), or by an unmentioned nation (Isa **30** 20 AVm). In all these cases the Heb original is לַחַץ, *laḥaç.* But in the vast number of cases the reference is to social oppression of one kind or another within Israel's own body. It is frequently the theme of psalmist and prophet and wise man. The poor and weak must have suffered greatly at the hands of the stronger and more fortunate. The word *laḥaç,* various forms of the √ עָשַׁק, *'āshaḳ,* and other words are used by the writers as they express their sorrow and indignation over the wrongs of their afflicted brethren. In his own sorrow, Job remembers the suffering of the oppressed (Job **35** 9; **36** 15); it is a frequent subject of song in the Pss (Ps **12** 5; **42** 9; **43** 2; **44** 24; **55** 3; **119** 134); the preacher observes and reflects upon its prevalence (Eccl **4** 1; **5** 8; **7** 7 AV); the prophets Amos (**3** 9), Isaiah (**5** 7; **59** 13), Jeremiah (**6** 6; **22** 17) and Ezekiel (**22** 7.29) thundered against it. It was exercised toward strangers and also toward the Israelites themselves, and was never wholly overcome. In Jas **2** 6, "oppress" is the rendering of καταδυναστεύω, *katadunasteúō,* "to exercise harsh control over one," "to use one's power against one."

WILLIAM JOSEPH MCGLOTHLIN

OR, ôr: The word is used once for *either* (1 S **26** 10), and is still in poetic use in this sense; as in, "Without *or* wave or wind" (Coleridge); "*Or* the bakke or some bone he breketh in his ȝouthe" (*Piers Plowman* [B], VII, 93; cf *Merchant of Venice,* III, ii, 65). It is also used with "ever" for *before* (Ps **90** 2; Ecclus **18** 19), which ARV substitutes in Eccl **12** 6 (cf vs 1.2); Cant **6** 12; Dnl **6** 24.

ORACLE, or'a-k'l: (1) A Divine utterance delivered to man, usually in answer to a request for guidance. So in 2 S **16** 23 for דָּבָר, *dābhar* ("word," as in RVm). The use in this passage seems to indicate that at an early period oracular utterances were sought from Jeh by the Israelites, but the practice certainly fell into disuse at the rise of prophecy, and there are no illustrations of the means employed (1 S **14** 18.19.36–42, etc, belong rather to DIVINATION [q.v.]). In RVm of such passages as Isa **13** 1, "oracle" is used in the titles of certain special prophecies as a substitute for BURDEN (q.v.) (מַשָּׂא, *massā'*), with considerable advantage (esp. in Lam **2** 14). (2) In heathen temples "oracle" was used for the chamber in which the utterances were delivered (naturally a most sacred part of the structure). This usage, coupled with a mistake in Heb philology (connecting דְּבִיר, *d^{e}bhīr,* "hinder part," with דִּבֵּר, *dibbēr,* "speak"), caused EV to give the title "oracle" to the Most Holy Place of the Temple, in 1 K **6** 5, etc, following the example of Aquila, Symmachus and Vulg. But the title is very unfortunate, as the Most Holy Place had nothing to do with the delivery of oracles, and RV should have corrected (cf Ps **28** 2 m).

(3) In the NT EV employs "oracle" as the tr of λόγιον, *lógion*, "saying," in four places. In all, Divine utterances are meant, specialized in Acts **7** 38 as the Mosaic Law ("living oracles" = "commandments enforced by the living God"), in Rom **3** 2 as the OT in general, and in He **5** 12 as the revelations of Christianity (**6** 2.3). In 1 Pet **4** 11 the meaning is debated, but probably the command is addressed to those favored by a supernatural "gift of speech." Such men must keep their own personality in the background, adding nothing of their own to the inspired message as it comes to them. BURTON SCOTT EASTON

ORACLES, SIBYLLINE, sib'i-līn, -lin. See APOCALYPTIC LITERATURE, V.

ORATOR, or'a-tẽr, **ORATION,** ŏ-rā'shun: The word "orator" occurs twice: (1) As AV rendering of לַחַשׁ, *laḥash;* only Isa **3** 3, "the eloquent orator," AVm "skilful of speech," where RV rightly substitutes "the skilful enchanter." The word *laḥash* is probably a mimetic word meaning "a hiss," "a whisper," and is used in the sense of "incantation," "charm." Hence *nᵉbhōn laḥash* means "skilful in incantation," "expert in magic." See DIVINATION; ENCHANTMENT. (2) As the rendering of ῥήτωρ, *rhḗtōr*, the title applied to Tertullus, who appeared as the advocate of the Jewish accusers of Paul before Felix (Acts **24** 1). The proceedings, as was generally the case in the provincial Rom courts, would probably be conducted in Lat, and under Rom modes of procedure, in which the parties would not be well versed; hence the need of a professional advocate. *Rhḗtōr* is here the equivalent of the older Gr *sunḗgoros*, "the prosecuting counsel," as opposed to the *súndikos*, "the defendant's advocate."

Oration occurs only in Acts **12** 21: "Herod . . . . made an oration unto them" (ἐδημηγόρει πρὸς αὐτούς, *edēmēgórei prós autoús*). The vb. *dēmēgoréō*, "to speak in an assembly" (from *dḗmos*, "people," *agoreúō*, "to harangue"), is often found in classical Gr, generally in a bad sense (Lat *concionari*); here only in the NT. D. MIALL EDWARDS

ORCHARD, ôr'chẽrd: (1) פַּרְדֵּס, *pardēṣ*, from Old Pers, "a walled-in inclosure"; παράδεισος, *parádeisos*, a word in classical Gr applied to the garden of Babylon (Diodorus Siculus xi.10) and to a game park (Xen. *Anab.* i.2, 7). See Neh **2** 8, "forest," m "park"; Cant **4** 13, "orchard," m "paradise" (of pomegranates); Eccl **2** 5, "parks," AV "orchards"; see PARADISE. (2) κῆπος, *kḗpos*, "garden" or "orchard": "a white thorn in an orchard" (Bar **6** 71).

ORDAIN, or-dān', **ORDINATION,** ôr-di-nā'-shun (Lat *ordinare*, "to set in order," "to arrange"; in post-Augustan Lat "to appoint to office"; from *ordo*, gen. *ordinis*, "order," "arrangement"): In AV the vb. "to ordain" renders as many as 35 different words (11 Heb words in the OT, 21 Gr words in Apoc and the NT, and 3 Lat words in Apoc). This is due to the fact that the Eng. word has many shades of meaning (esp. as used in the time AV was made), of which the following are the chief: (1) To set in order, arrange, prepare:

> "All things that we ordainéd festival,
> Turn from their office to black funeral."
> —Shakespeare, *Romeo and Juliet*, IV, v, 84.

This meaning is now obsolete. It is found in AV of Ps **132** 17; Isa **30** 33; He **9** 6 (in each of which cases RV or m substitutes "prepare"); 1 Ch **17** 9 (RV "appoint"); Ps **7** 13 (RV "maketh"); Hab **1** 12 (also RV). (2) To establish, institute, bring into being: "When first this order [i.e. the Garter] was ordained, my Lord" (Shakespeare). So in 1 K **12** 32, "Jeroboam ordained a feast in the 8th month" (ver 33); Nu **28** 6; Ps **8** 2.3; Isa **26** 12; 2 Esd **6** 49 AV (RV "preserve"); Sir **7** 15; Gal **3** 19. (3) To decree, give orders, prescribe:

> "And doth the power that man adores
> Ordain their doom?"
> —Byron.

So Est **9** 27, "The Jews ordained . . . . that they would keep these two days according to the writing thereof"; 1 Esd **6** 34; 2 Esd **7** 17; **8** 14 AV; Tob **1** 6; **8** 7 AV (RV "command"); Ad Est **14** 9; 1 Macc **4** 59; **7** 49; Acts **16** 4; Rom **7** 10 AV; 1 Cor **2** 7; **7** 17; **9** 14; Eph **2** 10 AV. (4) To set apart for an office or duty, appoint, destine: "Being ordained his special governor" (Shakespeare). Frequent in EV. When AV has "ordain" in this sense, RV generally substitutes "appoint"; e.g. "He [Jesus] appointed [AV "ordained"] twelve, that they might be with him" (Mk **3** 14). So 2 Ch **11** 15; Jer **1** 5; Dnl **2** 24; 1 Esd **8** 49; 1 Macc **3** 55; **10** 20; Jn **15** 16; Acts **14** 23; 1 Tim **2** 7; Tit **1** 5; He **5** 1; **8** 3. RV substitutes "formedst" in Wisd **9** 2, "recorded" in Sir **48** 10, "become" in Acts **1** 22, "written of" (m "set forth") in Jude ver 4, but retains "ordain" in the sense of "appoint," "set apart," in 2 K **23** 5; 1 Ch **9** 22; 1 Esd **8** 23; Ad Est **13** 6; Acts **10** 42; **13** 48; **17** 31; Rom **13** 1. (5) To appoint ceremonially to the ministerial or priestly office, to confer holy orders on. This later technical or ecclesiastical sense is never found in EV. The nearest approach is (4) above, but the idea of *formal* or *ceremonial* setting-apart to office (prominent in its modern usage) is never implied in the word.

Ordination: The act of arranging in regular order, esp. the act of investing with ministerial or sacerdotal rank (*ordo*), the setting-apart for an office in the Christian ministry. The word does not occur in EV. The NT throws but little light on the origin of the later ecclesiastical rite of ordination. The 12 disciples were not set apart by any formal act on the part of Jesus. In Mk **3** 14; Jn **15** 16, the AV rendering "ordain" is, in view of its modern usage, misleading; nothing more is implied than an appointment or election. In Jn **20** 21–23, we have indeed a symbolic act of consecration ("He breathed on them"), but "the act is described as one and not repeated. The gift was once for all, not to individuals but to the abiding body" (Westcott, ad loc.). In the Apostolic age there is no trace of the doctrine of an outward rite conferring inward grace, though we have instances of the formal appointment or recognition of those who had already given proof of their spiritual qualification. (1) The Seven were chosen by the brethren as men already "full of the Spirit and of wisdom," and were then "appointed" by the Twelve, who prayed and laid their hands upon them (Acts **6** 1–6). (2) The call of Barnabas and Saul came direct from God (Acts **13** 2, "the work whereunto I have called them"; ver 4, they were "sent forth by the Holy Spirit"). Yet certain prophets and teachers were instructed by the Holy Spirit to "separate" them (i.e. publicly) for their work, which they did by fasting and praying and laying on of hands (ver 3). But it was utterly foreign to Paul's point of view to regard the church's act as *constituting* him an apostle (cf Gal **1** 1). (3) Barnabas and Paul are said to have "ordained," RV "appointed" (χειροτονήσαντες, *cheirotonḗsantes*, "elect," "appoint," without indicating the particular mode of appointment), elders or presbyters in every city with prayers and fasting (Acts **14** 23). So Titus was instructed by Paul to "appoint elders in every city" in Crete (Tit **1** 5). (4) The gift of Timothy for evangelistic work seems to have been formally recognized in two ways: (*a*) by the laying on of the hands of the presbytery (1 Tim **4** 14), (*b*) by the laying on of the hands of Paul himself (2 Tim **1** 6). The words "Lay hands hastily on no man" (1 Tim **5** 22) do not refer to an act of ordination, but probably to the restoration of the penitent. The reference in He **6** 2 is not exclusively to ordination, but to all occasions of laying on of hands (see HANDS, IMPOSITION OF). From the few instances mentioned above (the only ones found in the NT), we infer that it was regarded as advisable that persons holding high office in the church should be publicly recognized in some way, as by laying on of hands, fasting, and public prayer. But no great emphasis was laid on this rite, hence "it can hardly be likely that any essential principle was held to be involved in it" (Hort, *The Christian Ecclesia*, 216). It was regarded as an outward act of approval, a symbolic offering of intercessory prayer, and an emblem of the solidarity of the Christian community, rather than an indispensable channel of grace for the work of the ministry. (For the later ecclesiastical doctrine and rite see Edwin Hatch's valuable art. on "Ordination" in the *Dict. Christian Antiq.*) D. MIALL EDWARDS

ORDER, ôr′dẽr (עָרַךְ, *'ārakh*, "to arrange"; **τάσσειν**, *tássein* [>*diatássein, táxis, tágma*]): "Order" in Bib. phrases may indicate (1) arrangement in rows, (2) sequence in time, (3) classification and organization, (4) likeness or manner, (5) regulation, direction or command, or (6) the declaring of a will. In many passages it is difficult if not impossible to determine from the Eng. text alone in which of these senses the word is used.

The fundamental idea suggested by the Heb, Gr and Eng. words is that of arrangement in rows. Thus

1. Arrangement in Rows

"order" is used in the Bible of arranging wood for an altar (Lev **1** 7; 1 K **18** 33; cf Heb Gen **22** 9; Isa **30** 33); of laying out flax-stalks for drying (Josh **2** 6); of preparing offerings (Lev **1** 8.12; cf **6** 5; Jgs **6** 26); of arranging lamps (Ex **27** 21; **39** 37; Lev **24** 3.4; cf Ps **132** 17); of placing the shewbread on the table (Ex **40** 4.23; Lev **6** 12; **24** 8; 2 Ch **13** 11); of drawing up the battle array (1 Ch **12** 38 [Heb 39, *'ādhar*]); and of arranging weapons in order for battle (Jer **46** 3, ARV "prepare"). As a vb. "to order" in the older VSS usually has the obsolete sense "to arrange" and not the more usual Eng. meanings, "to demand" or "to direct." Thus: "In the tent of meeting shall Aaron order it" (Lev **24** 4, ARV "keep in order"); "Order ye the buckler and shield" (Jer **46** 3; cf Ps **119** 133; Job **23** 4, ARV "set in order"; Jth **2** 16; Wisd **8** 1; **15** 1; Ecclus **2** 6). The Heb *pa'am* (lit. "hoof-beat," "occurrence," "repetition") in the plural conveys the idea of an architectural plan (Ezk **41** 6). Another word, *shālabh*, lit. "to join," in connection with the tabernacle, has in some VSS been tr[d] as including the idea of orderly arrangement (Ex **26** 17). The word "order" standing by itself may mean orderly or proper arrangement (1 Esd **1** 10; Wisd **7** 29; 1 Macc **6** 40; Col **2** 5). Akin to the idea of arranging things in a row is that of arranging words (Job **33** 5; **37** 19; Ps **5** 3), of recounting things in order (Isa **44** 7; Lk **1** 1 AV [*diatassein*]; Lk **1** 3; Acts **11** 4 [*kathexēs*]), of setting forth a legal case (Job **23** 4; **13** 18; cf Ps **50** 21). From the idea of ranging in order for the purpose of comparison the Heb *'ārakh* acquires the meaning "to compare" (Isa **40** 18; Ps **89** 7). This is clearly the meaning of *'ēn 'ărōkh 'ēlekhā* (Ps **40** 5 [Heb 6]), where "They cannot be set in order unto thee" must be interpreted to mean "There is nothing that can be compared unto thee."

As the fundamental meaning of *'ārakh* is arrangement in space, that of *ṣādhar* is order or sequence in

2. Sequence in Time

time. In later Heb *ṣēdher* was used in the sense of "program." In Job **10** 22 *lō' ṣ[e]dhārīm*, absence of regularity, in the description of the uncertain period that follows death probably means "confusion in time." (The LXX [φέγγος, *phéggos*] suggests, in the place of *ṣ[e]dhārīm*, a word for "light," possibly *çohŏrayim*.) In the NT we find "order" used of time in connection with the resurrection of the dead (1 Cor **15** 23 [*tagma*]) and of a succession of places visited (Acts **18** 23 [*kathexēs*]). The phrase "in order unto" (Ps **119** 38) expresses causal sequence and hence purpose.

The idea of classification is present in the Heb *tāḳan*, tr[d] "set in order," with reference to a collec-

3. Classification and Organization

tion of proverbs (Eccl **12** 9). The same stem is used with reference to the arranging of singers before the altar (Heb Ecclus **47** 9). The classification of priests according to their service is spoken of as "ordering" (1 Ch **24** 3.19, Heb *pāḳadh*). Next to the high priests ranked priests of the second order (*mishneh*, 2 K **23** 4; cf **25** 18 ‖ Jer **52** 24). The related concept of organization is present where the Heb *kūn* (lit. "to establish") is tr[d] "order" (Isa **9** 7 AV, "to establish" ARV; Ps **119** 133; 2 Ch **29** 35; cf 1 Macc **16** 14). A similar use of the term "order" is found in the NT in connection with the organization of the affairs of the church (1 Cor **16** 1 [*diatassein*]; Tit **1** 5 [*epidiorthóō*]; 1 Cor **11** 34).

"Order," in the sense of likeness or manner, is used in the phrase "after the order of Melchisedek" to

4. Likeness or Manner

translate the Heb *'al dibh[e]rath*, or rather the archaic form *'al dibh[e]rāthī* (Ps **110** 4), which in other passages is tr[d] "because of" (cf Eccl **3** 18; **7** 14; **8** 2). This well-known phrase is rendered in LXX *katá tḗn táxin*, a tr adopted in He **5** 6.10; **6** 20; **7** 11.17, where the passage from Ps is made the basis of an extended argument, in the course of which "order" is taken in the sense of "likeness" (He **7** 16).

In the sense of regulation, we find "order" as a tr of *mishpāṭ* (which is lit. "the ruling of a *shōphēṭ*,"

5. Regulation, Direction, Command

whether as a judicial decree or legislative act) in connection with the conduct of priests (1 Ch **6** 32 [Heb 17]; 2 Ch **30** 16; cf Lk **1** 8; 1 Esd **1** 6), and with reference to the Nazirite regulations in the story of Samson (Jgs **13** 12, RV "manner"), church services (1 Cor **14** 40) and, in the older Eng. VSS, with reference to other ritual matters (1 Ch **15** 13; **23** 31; 2 Ch **8** 14, ARV "ordinance"). The phrase *'al yadh*, lit. "according to the hand of," tr[d] in Ezr **3** 10; 1 Ch **25** 2*b*.3.6 *bis* in various ways, means "under the direction of," or "under the order of," as tr[d] in the last instance. The modern sense of "command" is suggested here and in several other instances (1 Esd **8** 10; 1 Macc **9** 55). He "that ordereth his conversation aright" (*sām derekh*, Ps **50** 23) is probably one who chooses the right path and directs his steps along it. "Who shall order the battle?" (1 K **20** 14) is corrected in ARV: "Who shall begin the battle?" (cf 2 Ch **13** 3, Heb *'āṣar*, lit. "to bind," hence "to join" or "begin"; cf *proelium committere*).

The phrase "to set one's house in order" (Isa **38** 1 ‖ 2 K **20** 1; 2 S **17** 23), used of Hezekiah and Ahithophel, in contemplation of death, means to give final instructions to one's household or to make one's will. The Heb *çāwāh* used in this phrase is the stem found in the later Heb *çawwā'āh,* "a verbal will" (*Bābhā' Bathrā'* **147***a*, **151***b; BDB*). Great moral weight was attached in Bib. times to the charges laid upon a household by a deceased father or remoter ancestor, not only as to the disposition of property but also as to personal conduct. (Cf the case of the Rechabites, where the same Heb expression is used, *çiwwāh 'ālēnū*, Jer **35** 6.)

6. Declaring of Last Will

NATHAN ISAACS

ORDINANCE, ôr'di-nans: This word generally represents חֻקָּה, *ḥuḳḳāh*, something prescribed, enactment, usually with reference to matters of ritual. In AV the same word is frequently tr[d] by "statute" or "statutes," which is also the rendering of a similar Heb word, viz. חֹק, *ḥōḳ*. RV generally retains "ordinance," but sometimes substitutes "statute" (e.g. Ex **18** 20; Ps **99** 7). In one instance RV renders "set portion" (Ezk **45** 14). The word generally has a religious or ceremonial significance. It is used for instance in connection with the Passover (Ex **12** 43; Nu **9** 14). According to Ex **12** 14, the Passover was "an ordinance for ever," i.e. a permanent institution. In the pl. the word is often employed, along with such terms as commandments, laws, etc, with reference to the different prescriptions of the Deuteronomic and Priestly codes (Dt **6** 1.2; Lev **18** 4).

1. OT Use

In 11 passages (Ex **15** 25; Josh **24** 25; 1 S **30** 25; 2 K **17** 34.37; 2 Ch **33** 8; **35** 13; Ps **119** 91; Isa **58** 2 *bis;* Ezk **11** 20) "ordinance" is the rendering of מִשְׁפָּט, *mishpāṭ*, judgment, decision or sentence by a judge or ruler. In the Book of the Covenant (Ex **20** 22—**23** 33) the term "judgments" denotes civil, as contrasted with ritual, enactments. In 2 K **17** 34 AV employs "manners" and "ordinances" as renderings of this word. In 3 passages (Lev **18** 30; **22** 9; Mal **3** 14) "ordinance" is the tr of מִשְׁמֶרֶת, *mishmereth*, "charge," which RV restores. In one instance (Neh **10** 32) ordinance renders מִצְוָה, *miçwāh*, "commandment," while in Ezr **3** 10 AV the phrase "after the ordinance of David" represents a Heb phrase which lit. means "upon the hands of David," i.e. under the guidance or direction of David.

In the NT, "ordinance" renders different Gr words, viz. (1) δικαίωμα, *dikaíōma*, in Lk **1** 6 and He **9** 1.10. The word means lit. "anything declared right"; but in these passages ceremonial and religious regulation; (2) δόγμα, *dógma*, in Eph **2** 15; Col **2** 14. In the NT this word always means a decree or edict (Acts **17** 7); (3) παράδοσις, *parádosis*, in 1 Cor **11** 2 AV, RV substitutes "traditions"; (4) κτίσις, *ktísis*, "setting up," "institution," in 1 Pet **2** 13. The term is used exclusively of the action of God. Peter implies that institutions, apparently human, such as the family and the state, are of Divine origin. The same doctrine is found in Rom **13** 1.

2. NT Use

T. LEWIS

ORDINANCES OF HEAVEN. See ASTRONOMY, I, 1.

ORDINATION, ôr-di-nā'shun. See ORDAIN, ORDINATION.

OREB, ō'reb (עֹרֵב, עֹרֵב, *'ōrēbh*, "raven," esp. "crow"), and **ZEEB,** zē'eb, zēb (זְאֵב, *ze'ēbh*, "wolf") (Jgs **7** 25; **8** 3; Ps **83** 11, and Isa **10** 26 [Oreb only]): Two Midianite chieftains captured and beheaded by the Ephraimites, who brought their heads to Gideon.

As to the meaning of the two names, both words are found in Arabic. Robertson Smith, *Kinship,* etc (190 ff, 218 ff), says that the use of the names of animals as names of persons is a relic of totemism. But Nöldeke (*ZDMG*, XL, 160 ff) and others hold that such a use shows a desire that those so named should be as disagreeable to their enemies as the plant or animal which the name denoted. Some again (e.g. Stade, *Geschichte*, 189 ff) maintain that the two names here are borrowed from localities and not vice versa, as Jgs **7** 25 implies. If so, we must take the names to be originally two places, apparently in Ephraim, for the words "beyond Jordan" in **7** 25 contradict **8** 4, where it is said that Gideon came to the Jordan and passed over. Moore (*Jgs*, 214) suggests that the two localities were near the junction with the Jordan of the stream that comes from *Wâdy Far'ah*. The construction of the Heb allows of a tr "the rock [called] Oreb," and "the winepress [called] Zeeb."

1. Meaning of Names

The account of a battle here is corroborated by Isa **10** 26, a verse which mentions the "rock of Oreb," and suggests that the great defeat of the Midianites took place there (cf Isa **9** 4). The passage in Isa **10** 24–26 is prose, however, and is said to be late editing (see G. H. Box, *Isa*, 65). In Ps **83** 11 (Heb 12) there is a prayer that God would make the "nobles" among the Psalmist's enemies as Oreb and Zeeb.

2. The Battle of Oreb

DAVID FRANCIS ROBERTS

OREB: In 2 Esd **2** 33 AV for MT. HOREB (q.v.; so RV).

OREN, ō'ren (אֹרֶן, *'ōren;* 'Αράμ, *Arám*, Alex. *Aran*): A son of Jerahmeel, the firstborn of Hezron (1 Ch **2** 25).

ORGAN, ôr'gan. See MUSIC.

ORION, ō-rī'on: A brilliant constellation dedicated to Nimrod or Merodach. See ASTRONOMY, II, 11.

ORNAMENT, ôr'na-ment (עֲדִי, *'ădhī*, "adornment"): In common with all the Orientals, the Hebrews were very fond of wearing ornaments, and their tendency to extravagance of this kind often met with stern prophetic rebuke (Isa **3** 16–24; Ezk **13** 18–20). On this subject, little is said in the NT apart from Jesus' (Lk **7** 25; **12** 23) and James's (**2** 2) invectives against meretricious estimates of moral character. Yet the employment of attractive attire receives sanction in the Divine example of Ezk **16** 10–14.

Ornaments in general would include finely embroidered or decorated fabrics, such as the priest's dress or the high-priestly attire, and the richly wrought veil, girdle and turban used by the wealthier class. But the term may be limited here to the various rings, bracelets and chains made of precious metals and more or less jeweled (cf Jer **2** 32).

These latter, described in detail under their own titles, may be summarized here as finger-rings, particularly prized as seal-rings (Gen **38** 18.25; Jer **22** 24); arm-rings or bracelets (Gen **24** 22; 2 S **1** 10); earrings (Gen **35** 4; Ex **32** 2); nose-rings (Gen **24** 47; Ezk **16** 12); anklets or ankle-chains (Isa **3** 16.18); head-bands or fillets or cauls (referred to in Isa **3** 18 only), and necklaces or neck-chains (Gen **41** 42; Ezk **16** 11).

Figurative: The universal devotion to ornament among the Orientals is the occasion for frequent Bib. allusions to the beauty and splendor of fine jewelry and attire. But everywhere, in Divine injunctions, the emphasis of value is placed upon the beauty of holiness as an inward grace rather than on the attractions of outward ornament (Job

40 10; Ps **110** 3; Joel **2** 13; 1 Tim **2** 9.10; 1 Pet **3** 4). In grievous sorrow, all ornament was to be laid aside in token of mourning (Ex **33** 4–6).

LEONARD W. DOOLAN

ORNAN, ôr′nan (1 Ch **21** 15). See ARAUNAH.

ORPAH, ôr′pä (עָרְפָּה, *'orpāh;* for meaning see below): A Moabitess, wife of Mahlon, son of Elimelech and Naomi. Unlike her sister Ruth she returned to her own people after escorting Naomi on her way to Judah (Ruth **1** 4 ff). Her name is supposed to be derived from the Heb word for "neck" (עֹרֶף, *'ōreph*), and so to mean "stiff-necked" because of her turning back from following her mother-in-law; others take it to mean "gazelle."

ORPHAN, ôr′fan: This word occurs once only in the OT (Lam **5** 3, where it stands for יָתוֹם, *yāthōm,* elsewhere rendered "fatherless," and in LXX always ὀρφανός, *orphanós*); in the Apoc it occurs 3 t (2 Esd **2** 20; Tob **1** 8; 2 Macc **8** 28). There is no clear case where it means the loss of both parents. The Scriptures devote considerable attention to the widow and orphan, and the idea is that the child is fatherless. It is not found in AV of the NT; but the Gr word *orphanos* occurs twice, Jn **14** 18 (AV "comfortless," RV "desolate," m "orphans") and Jas **1** 27 ("fatherless"). See FATHERLESS.

D. MIALL EDWARDS

ORTHOSIA, ôr-thō-sī′a (Ὀρθωσίας, *Orthōsías;* AV **Orthosias**): The city to which Tryphon fled when he escaped from Dora, where he was besieged by Antiochus Sidetes (1 Macc **15** 37). According to Pliny (*NH*, v.17) it lay S. of the river Eleutherus, and N. of the city of Tripolis. The Peutinger Tables place it 12 Rom miles N. of Tripolis and 30 miles S. of Antaradus on the Phoen coast. Porter would place it on the southern bank of *Nahr el-Bārid.*

OSAIAS, ō-zā′yas, ō-sā′yas (Ὠσαίας, *Ōsaías;* B omits): In 1 Esd **8** 48 a corruption of Jeshaiah (cf Ezr **8** 19).

OSEA, ō-zē′a, ō-sē′a: In 2 Esd **13** 40=HOSHEA, king of Israel (q.v.).

OSEAS, ō-zē′as, ō-sē′as: "Osee" in 2 Esd **1** 39; the prophet Hosea.

OSEE, ō′zē, ō′sē (Ὡσηέ, *Hōsēé*): AV in Rom **9** 25; the prophet Hosea (thus RV).

OSHEA, ō-shē′a, ō′shē-a (RV "Hoshea" [Nu **13** 8.16]): The original name of Joshua, the son of Nun, changed by Moses (ver 16) from Hoshea (*hōshē*[a]*'*, "help") to Joshua (*y*[e]*hōshū*[a]*'*, "help of Jeh"). See JOSHUA.

OSNAPPAR, os-nap′ar (Ezr **4** 10). See ASHURBANIPAL.

OSPRAY, os′prā (עָזְנִיָּה, *'oznīyāh;* ἁλιάετος, *haliáetos;* Lat *Pandion haliaetus*): A large hawk preferring a diet of fish. The word is found in the list of abominations only. See Lev **11** 13; Dt **14** 12. The ospray was quite similar in appearance to some of the smaller eagles, and by some it is thought that the short-toed eagle is intended. But the eagle and the gier-eagle had been specified, and on account of the ospray plunging into water for food and having feet bare to the lower leg-joint and plumage of brighter and more distinctive marking, it seems very probable that it was recognized as a distinctive species, and so named separately. Moreover, the ospray was not numerous as were other hawks and eagles. It was a bird that lived almost wholly on fish, and these were not plentiful in the waters of Pal. This would tend to make it a marked bird, so no doubt the tr is correct as it stands, as any hawk that lived on fish would have been barred as an article of diet (see Tristram, *Nat. Hist of the Bible,* 182; also Studers, *Birds of North America,* p. and pl. 16).

GENE STRATTON-PORTER

OSSIFRAGE, os′i-frāj (פֶּרֶס, *pereṣ;* γύψ, *gúps;* Lat *Ossifraga*): The great bearded vulture known as the lammer-geier (Lev **11** 13; Dt **14** 12 AV, RV "gier-eagle"). The Heb name *pereṣ* means "to break." Lat *ossis,* "bone," and *frangere,* "to break," indicate the most noticeable habit of the bird. It is the largest of the vulture family, being 3½ ft. in length and 10 in sweep. It has a white head, black beard on the chin, and the part of the eye commonly called the "white" in most animals, which is visible in but few birds, in this family is pronounced and of a deep angry red, thus giving the bird a formidable appearance. The back is grayish black, the feathers finely penciled, the shaft being white, the median line tawny. The under parts are tawny white and the feet and talons powerful. It differs from the vulture in that it is not a consistent carrion feeder, but prefers to take prey of the size captured by some of the largest eagles. It took its name from the fact that after smaller vultures and eagles had stripped a carcase to the last shred of muscle, the lammergeier then carried the skeleton aloft and dropped it repeatedly until the marrow from the broken bones could be eaten. It is also very fond of tortoise, the meat of which it secures in the same manner. As this bird frequents Southern Europe, it is thought to be the one that mistook the bald head of Aeschylus, the poet, for a stone and let fall on it the tortoise that caused his death. This bird also attacks living prey of the size of lambs, kids and hares. It is not numerous and does not flock, but pairs live in deep gorges and rocky crevices. It builds an enormous nest, deposits one pinkish or yellowish egg, and the young is black. It requires two years to develop the red eyes, finely penciled plumage and white head of the adult bird. It was included among the abominations because of its diet of carrion.

GENE STRATTON-PORTER

OSTRACA, os′tra-ka: The word *ostracon* ("potsherd," Heb *ḥeres*) occurs in Job **2** 8 (LXX), καὶ ἔλαβεν ὄστρακον, *kaí élaben óstrakon,* "and he took him a potsherd." Earthen vessels were in universal use in antiquity (they are twice mentioned in the NT: σκεύη ὀστράκινα, *skeúē ostrákina* [2 Cor **4** 7; 2 Tim **2** 20]), and the broken fragments of them, which could be picked up almost anywhere, were made to serve various purposes. Upon the smoothest of these pieces of unglazed pottery the poorest might write in ink his memoranda, receipts, letters or texts.

A fortunate discovery at Samaria (1910), made among the ruins of Ahab's palace, has brought to light 75 Heb ostraca inscribed with ink, in the Phoen character, with accounts and memoranda relating to private matters and dating probably from the time of Ahab. Their historical contribution, aside from the mention of many names of persons and places, is slender, but for ancient Heb writing and to a less extent for Heb words and forms they are of value, while the fact that in them we possess documents actually penned in Israel in the 9th cent. BC gives them extraordinary interest. The nature of ostraca tends to their preservation under conditions which would quickly destroy parchment,

1. Hebrew Ostraca

skin or papyrus, and this discovery in Pal encourages the hope of further and more significant finds.

2. Greek Ostraca

Gr ostraca in large quantities have been found in Egypt, preserving documents of many kinds, chiefly tax receipts. The texts of some 2,000 of these have been published, principally by Wilcken (*Griechische Ostraka*, 2 vols, 1899), and serve to illustrate in unexpected ways the everyday Gr speech of the

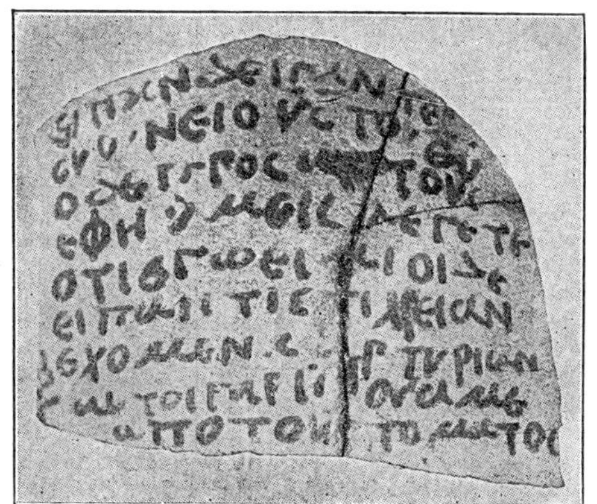

Ostracon with Lk **22** 70f.

common people of Egypt through the Ptolemaic, Rom and Byzantine periods. Like the papyri, they help to throw light on NT syntax and lexicography, as well as on ancient life in general.

3. New Testament Ostraca

It is said that Cleanthes the Stoic, being too poor to buy papyrus, used to write on ostraca, but no remains of classical lit. have been found on the ostraca thus far discovered. In some instances, however, Christian literary texts are preserved upon ostraca. Some years ago Bouriant bought in Upper Egypt 20 ostraca, probably of the 7th cent., inscribed with the Gr text of parts of the Gospels. The ostraca are of different sizes, and preserve among others one long continuous passage (Lk **22** 40–71), which runs over 10 of the pieces. The ostraca contain from 2 to 9 verses each, and cover Mt **27** 31.32; Mk **5** 40.41 (**9** 3); **9** 17.18.22; **15** 21; Lk **12** 13–16; **22** 40–71; Jn **1** 1–9; **1** 14–17; **18** 19–25; **19** 15–17. The texts are in 3 different hands, and attest the interest of the poor in the gospel in the century of the Arab conquest. Another late ostracon has a rough drawing labeled "St. Peter the evangelist," perhaps in allusion to the Gospel of Peter.

4. Coptic Ostraca

Coptic ostraca, too, are numerous, esp. from the Byzantine period, and of even more interest for Christian history than the Greek. A Sa'idic ostracon preserves the pericope on the woman taken in adultery (Jn **7** 53—**8** 11), which is otherwise unattested in the Sa'idic NT. A Christian hymn to Mary, akin to the canticles of Luke, and some Christian letters have been found. The work of W. E. Crum on the Coptic ostraca is of especial importance. See, further, Deissmann, *Light from the Ancient East*, 1910; Lyon, *Harvard Theol. Review*, January, 1911.

EDGAR J. GOODSPEED

OSTRICH, os'trich (יַעֲנָה, *ya'ănāh;* **στρουθός**, *strouthós;* Lat *Struthio camelus*): The largest bird now living. The Heb words *ya'ănāh*, which means "greediness," and *bath ha-ya'ănāh*, "daughter of greediness," are made to refer to the indiscriminate diet of the ostrich, to which bird they apply; and again to the owl, with no applicability. The owl at times has a struggle to swallow whole prey it has taken, but the mere fact that it is a night hunter forever shuts it from the class of greedy and promiscuous feeders. The bodies of owls are proverbially lean like eagles. Neither did the owl frequent several places where older versions of Jer and Isa place it; so the tr[s] are now correctly rendered "ostrich." These birds came into the Bible because of their desert life, the companions they lived among there, and because of their night cries that were guttural, terrifying groans, like the roaring of lions. The birds were brought into many pictures of desolation, because people dreaded their fearful voices. They homed on the trackless deserts that were dreaded by travelers, and when they came feeding on the fringe of the wilderness, they fell into company with vulture, eagle, lion, jackal and adder, and joined their voices with the night hawks and owls. For these reasons no birds were more suitable for drawing strong comparisons from.

1. Physical Peculiarities

They attained a height ranging from 6 to 8 ft., and weighed from 200 to 300 lbs. The head was small with large eyes having powerful vision, and protected by lashes. The neck was long, covered with down, and the windpipe showed, while large bites could be seen to slide down the gullet. The legs were bare, long, and the muscles like steel from the long distances covered in desert travel. The foot was much like the cloven hoof of a beast. The inner toe was 7 in. long, with a clawlike hoof, the outer, smaller with no claw. With its length and strength of leg and the weight of foot it could strike a blow that saved it from attack by beasts smaller than a leopard. The wings were small, the muscles soft and flabby. They would not bear the weight of the bird, but the habit of lifting and beating them proved that this assisted in attaining speed in running (cf Xen. *Anab.* i.5.2,3). The body was

Ostriches.

covered with soft flexible feathers, the wings and tail growing long plumes, for which the bird has been pursued since the beginning of time. These exquisite feathers were first used to decorate the headdress and shields of desert chieftains, then as decorations for royalty, and later for hat and hair ornaments. The badge of the Prince of Wales is three white ostrich plumes. The females are smaller, the colors gray and white, the males a glossy black, the wing and tail plumes white. The ostrich has three physical peculiarities that stagger scientists. It has eyelashes, developed no doubt to protect the eyes from the dust and sand of desert life. On the wings are two plumeless shafts like large porcupine quills. These may be used in resisting attack. It also has a bladder like a mammal, that collects uric acid, the rarest organ ever developed in a feathered creature.

These birds homed on the deserts of Arabia and at the lower end of the great Salt Sea. Here the ostrich left her eggs on the earth and warmed them in the sand. That they were not hard baked was due to the fact that they were covered for protection during the day and brooded through the cooler nights. The eggs average 3 lbs. weight. They have been used for food in the haunts of the ostrich since the records of history began, and their stout shells for drinking-vessels. It is the custom of natives on finding a nest to take a long stick and draw out an egg. If incubation has advanced enough to spoil the eggs for use, the nest is carefully covered and left; if fresh, they are eaten, one egg being sufficient for a small family. No doubt these were the eggs to which Job referred as being tasteless without salt (Job **6** 6). The number of eggs in the nest was due to the fact that the birds were polygamous, one male leading from 2 to 7 females, all of which deposited their eggs in a common nest. When several females wanted to use the nest at the same time, the first one to reach it deposited her egg in it, and the others on the sand close beside. This accounts for the careless habits of the ostrich as to her young. In this communal nest, containing from 2 to 3 dozen eggs, it is impossible for the mother bird to know which of the young is hers. So all of them united in laying the eggs and allowing the father to look after the nest and the young. The bird first appears among the abominations in Lev **11** 16 RV, AV "owl"; Dt **14** 16, RV "little owl," AV "owl." This must have referred to the toughness of grown specimens, since there was nothing offensive in the bird's diet to taint its flesh and the young tender ones were delicious meat. In his agony, Job felt so much an outcast that he cried:

2. Eggs and Care of Young

"I am a brother to jackals,
And a companion to ostriches" (Job **30** 29).

Again he records that the Almighty discoursed to him of the ostrich in the following manner:

"The wings of the ostrich wave proudly;
But are they the pinions and plumage of love?" etc (**39** 13-18).

The ostrich history previously given explains all this passage save the last two verses, the first of which is a reference to the fact that the Arabs thought the ostrich a stupid bird, because, when it had traveled to exhaustion, it hid its head and thought its body safe, and because some of its eggs were found outside the nest. The second was due to a well-known fact that, given a straight course, the ostrich could outrun a horse. The birds could attain and keep up a speed of 60 miles an hour for the greater part of half a day and even longer, hence it was possible to take them only by a system of relay riders (Xen., op. cit.) When Isaiah predicted the fall of Babylon, he used these words: "But wild beasts of the desert shall lie there; and their houses shall be full of doleful creatures; and ostriches shall dwell there, and wild goats shall dance there" (Isa **13** 21). Because this was to be the destruction of a great city, located on the Euphrates River and built by the fertility and prosperity of the country surrounding it, and the ruins those of homes, the bird indicated by every natural condition would be the owl. The wild goats clambering over the ruins would be natural companions and the sneaking wolves—but not the big bird of daytime travel, desert habitation, accustomed to constant pursuit for its plumage. Exactly the same argument applies to the next reference by the same writer (**34** 13). "And the wild beasts of the desert shall meet with the wolves, and the wild goat shall cry to his fellow; yea, the night monster shall settle there, and shall find her a place of rest" (**34** 14). "The beasts of the field shall honor me, the jackals and the ostriches; because I give waters in the wilderness, and rivers in the desert, to give drink to my people, my chosen" (**43** 20). Here we find the ostrich in its natural location, surrounded by creatures that were its daily companions. The next reference also places the bird at home and in customary company: "Therefore the wild beasts of the desert with the wolves shall dwell there, and the ostriches [AV "owls"] shall dwell therein: and it shall be no more inhabited forever; neither shall it be dwelt in from generation to generation" (Jer **50** 39).

3. OT References

"Even the jackals draw out the breast, they give suck to their young ones:
The daughter of my people is become cruel, like the ostriches in the wilderness" (Lam **4** 3).

This reference is made to the supposed cruelty of the ostrich in not raising its young.

Gene Stratton-Porter

OTHNI, oth'nī (עָתְנִי, *'othnī*, meaning unknown): A son of Shemaiah, a Korahite Levite (1 Ch **26** 7).

OTHNIEL, oth'ni-el (עָתְנִיאֵל, *'othnī'ēl*): A hero in Israel, son of Kenaz, Caleb's younger brother. He conquered Kiriath-sepher, later known as Debir, in the territory of Judah in the days of Joshua, and was given the daughter of Caleb, Achsah, to wife as a reward (Josh **15** 17 ‖ Jgs **1** 13). He later smote Cushan-rishathaim, king of Mesopotamia, whom the children of Israel had served 8 years, and thus not only saved the Israelites, but by reviving national sentiment among them (cf *Ant*, V, iv, 3), and reëstablishing government, became the first of those hero-rulers known as "judges." The effects of his victory lasted an entire generation (40 years, Jgs **3** 9-11). He had a son named Hathath (1 Ch **4** 13) and probably another named Meonothai (cf recensio Luciana of LXX, ad loc.). In the days of David we find a family bearing the name of Othniel, from which came Heldai the Metophathite, captain of the twelfth month (1 Ch **27** 15).

Nathan Isaacs

OTHONIAS, oth-ō-nī'as (**'Οθονίας**, *Othonías*): One of those who had taken "strange wives" (1 Esd **9** 28) = "Mattaniah" of Ezr **10** 27.

OUCHES, ouch'ez, -iz (מִשְׁבְּצוֹת, *mishbçōth* [Ex **28** 11.13.14.25; **39** 6.13.16.18]; ARV "settings," but in Ex **39** 13, "inclosings"): The secondary meaning of this now archaic word is the gold or silver setting of a precious stone. In Ex, where it occurs 8 t, it is clear that the gold settings of the engraved stones forming the breast-plate of the high priest are intended; the onyx stones forming the fibula or brooch for holding together the two sides of the breast-plate being said to be "inclosed in ouches [settings] of gold" (Ex **39** 6). Not only were these two onyx or beryl stones so set, but the 12 stones forming the front of the breast-plate were "inclosed in gold in their settings" (Ex **28** 20). The same word occurs in Ps **45** 13, where the king's daughter is said to have her clothing "*inwrought* with gold," i.e. embroidered with gold thread or wire. Ex **39** 3 tells us how this wire was produced. From this fact it may be inferred that the settings of the breast-plate were not solid pieces of gold, but were formed of woven wire wreathed round the stones, in a sort of filigree. See also Stones, Precious.

W. Shaw Caldecott

OUTCAST, out'kast: Represents some form of דָּחָה, *dāḥāh*, or נָדָה, *nādhah*, both meaning "thrust out." In Jer **30** 17 "outcast" means "thrust out of society," "degraded person"; elsewhere it means "exile" (Ps **147** 2; Isa **16** 3 f; Jer **49** 36).

OUTER, out'ẽr: This adj. is used 12 t by Ezekiel of the outside court of the temple. In Mt we find it 3 t (**8** 12; **22** 13; **25** 30) in "outer darkness" (τὸ σκότος τὸ ἐξώτερον, *tó skótos tó exṓteron*), which typifies the utter darkness of the doom of the lost.

OUTGOING, out'gō-ing: In Ps **65** 8, "Thou makest the outgoings of the morning and evening to rejoice," the Heb is מוֹצָא, *mōçā'*. The word (from *yāçā'*, "to go forth") refers to the "going forth" of the sun, and so means "east" (as in Ps **75** 6). The connection of *mōçā'* with "evening" is therefore zeugmatic, but the meaning is clear and there are extra-Bib. parallels (cf "the two Orients"). In Josh **17** 18, AV uses "outgoings" for the Heb תּוֹצָאוֹת, *tōçā'ōth* (also from *yāçā'*), where the meaning is "extremity" (RV "goings out," as in Nu **34** 5, etc). "Outwent" occurs in Mk **6** 33. BURTON SCOTT EASTON

OUTLANDISH, out-land'ish (Neh **13** 26, AV "Him did outlandish women cause to sin"): "Outlandish" in modern Eng. is colloquial only and with the sense "utterly extraordinary," but AV uses it in the lit. meaning "out of the land," "foreign," ERV "strange women," ARV "foreign women," Heb נָכְרִי, *nokhrī*, "foreign."

OUTRAGE, out'rāj, **OUTRAGEOUS,** out-rā'jus: The noun (from the Fr. *outre*+*age*, "that which goes beyond") only in the heading to Ps **10** AV; the adj. in Prov **27** 4, AV and ERV, for שֶׁטֶף, *sheṭeph*, "flood." "Anger is overwhelming" (ARV), is much better.

OUTROADS, out'rōdz (**ἐξοδεύω**, *exodeúō*, "to go forth," "to make a military expedition"; AV and RV in 1 Macc **15** 41, "horsemen . . . . that they might make outroads upon the ways of Judah"; 1 Esd **4** 23, RV "goeth forth to make outroads"): "Outroads" is obsolete, but its opposite, "inroads," is still good Eng.

OUTWARD, out'wẽrd, **MAN** (**ἔξω**, *éxō*, "outside," "without," "out of doors"): The body, subject to decay and death, in distinction from the inner man, the imperishable spiritual life which "is renewed day by day" (2 Cor **4** 16); also the body as the object of worldly thought and pride in external dress and adornment (1 Pet **3** 3). See MAN, NATURAL; MAN, NEW.

OVEN, uv''n. See BREAD; FURNACE.

OVERCHARGE, ō-vẽr-chärj': Lk **21** 34, "lest haply your hearts be overcharged with drunkenness" (βαρύνω, *barúnō*, "burden," here with the force "be occupied with"); 2 Cor **2** 5, AV "that I may not overcharge you" (ἐπιβαρέω, *epibaréō*, "overload"), RV "that I press not too heavily." See CHARGES.

OVERPASS, ō-vẽr-pas': A special tr of the very common vb. עָבַר, *'ābhar*, "to pass over," found in EV of Ps **57** 1 and Isa **26** 20 in the sense "to pass by," and in Jer **5** 28 with the meaning "to overflow."

OVERPLUS, ō'vẽr-plus: Lev **25** 27, for עָדַף, *'ādhaph*, "excess."

OVERSEER, ō-vẽr-sē'ẽr, or -sẽr': One who overlooks, inspects; in the OT from נָצַח, *nāçaḥ* (2 Ch **2** 18; in 2 Ch **34** 13 RV changes to "set forward"), and פָּקַד, *pāḳadh* (Gen **39** 4.5; 2 Ch **34** 12.17; RV has this word for AV "officers" in Gen **41** 34, and for "rulers" in 1 Ch **26** 32); in the NT once for ἐπίσκοπος, *epískopos*, in Acts **20** 28, where RV has "bishops" (m "overseers"; cf 1 Pet **5** 2). See BISHOP.

OWL, oul (בַּת הַיַּעֲנָה, *bath ha-ya'ănāh;* Lat *Ulula*): The name of every nocturnal bird of prey of the N.O. *Striges*. These birds range from the great horned owl of 2 ft. in length, through many subdivisions to the little screech-owl of 5 in. All are characterized by very large heads, many have

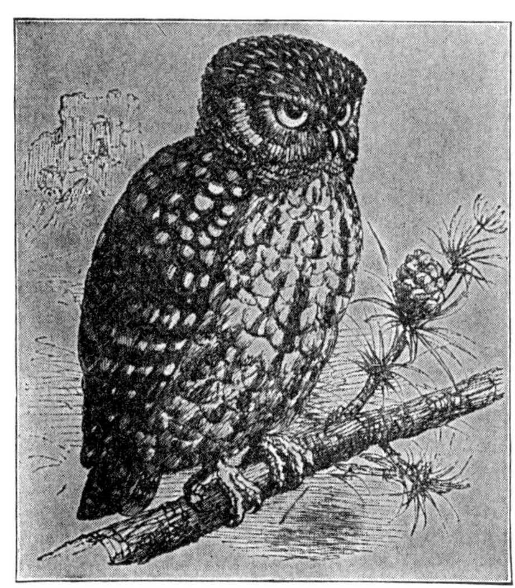

Owl (*Athene meridionalis*).

ear tufts, all have large eyes surrounded by a disk of tiny, stiff, radiating feathers. The remainder of the plumage has no aftershaft. So these birds make the softest flight of any creature traveling on wing. A volume could be written on the eye of the owl, perhaps its most wonderful feature being in the power of the bird to enlarge the iris if it wishes more distinct vision. There is material for another on the prominent and peculiar auditory parts. With almost all owls the feet are so arranged that two toes can be turned forward and two back, thus reinforcing the grip of the bird by an extra toe and giving it unusual strength of foot. All are night-hunters, taking prey to be found at that time, of size according to the strength. The owl was very numerous in the caves, ruined temples and cities, and even in the fertile valleys of Pal. It is given place in the Bible because it was considered unfit for food and because people dreaded the cries of every branch of the numerous family. It appeared often, as most birds, in the early VSS of the Bible; later translators seem to feel that it was used in several places where the ostrich really was intended (see OSTRICH). It would appear to a natural historian that the right bird could be selected by the location, where the text is confusing. The ostrich had a voice that was even more terrifying, when raised in the night, than that of the owl. But it was a bird of the desert, of wide range and traveled only by day. This would confine its habitat to the desert and the greenery where it joined fertile land, but would not bring it in very close touch with civilization. The owl is a bird of ruins, that lay mostly in the heart of rich farming lands, where prosperous cities had been built and then destroyed by enemies. Near these locations the ostrich would be pursued for its plumage, and its nesting conditions did not prevail. The location was strictly the owl's chosen haunt, and it had the voice to fit all the requirements of the text. In the lists of abominations, the original Heb *yanshūph*, derived from a root meaning twilight, is tr[d] "great owl" (see Lev **11** 17 and Dt **14** 16). It is probable that this was a bird about 2 ft. in length, called the eagle-owl. In the same lists the word *kōs* (νυκτικόραξ, *nuktikórax*) refers to ruins, and the bird indicated is specified as the "little owl," that is, smaller than the great owl—about the size of our barn owl. This bird is referred to as the "mother of ruins," and the tr[s] that place it in deserted temples and cities are beyond all doubt correct. *Ḳippōz* (ἐχῖνος, *echinos*) occurs once (Isa **34** 15), and is tr[d] "great owl" in former versions; lately (in ARV) it is changed to "dart-snake" (ERV "arrowsnake"). In this same description *līlīth* (ὀνοκένταυρος, *onokéntauros*), "a specter of night," was formerly screech-owl, now it reads "night monster," which is more confusing and less suggestive. The owls in the lists of abominations (Lev **11** 17.18; Dt **14** 16) are the little owl, the great owl and the horned owl. The only other owl of all those that produced such impressions of desolation in the Books of Isa, Jer, Job and Mic is referred to in Ps **102** 6:

"I am like a pelican of the wilderness;
I am become as an owl of the waste places."

Here it would appear that the bird habitual to the wilderness and the waste places, that certainly would be desert, would be the ostrich—while in any quotation referring to ruins, the owl would be the bird indicated by natural conditions.

GENE STRATTON-PORTER

OWL, GREAT (יַנְשׁוּף, *yanshūph;* LXX ἶβις, *íbis*, or εἶβις, *eíbis*): A member of the Pal species of the family *Strigidae*. The great owl mentioned in the Bible was no doubt their largest specimen of the family, a bird fully 2 ft. in length, full feathered, with unusually large head and long ear tufts. It was a formidable and noble-appearing bird, with resounding voice. It was abundant among the ruins of temples, the tombs of Carmel, the caves of Gennesaret, and among the ruined cities of Southern Judah. It is included in the abomination lists of Lev **11** 17 and Dt **14** 16. See OWL.

GENE STRATTON-PORTER

OWL, LITTLE (כּוֹס, *kōs;* νυκτικόραξ, *nuktikórax;* Lat *Athene meridionalis*): A night bird of prey distinguished by a round head, and extremely large eyes. The little owl is left in RV only in the lists of abominations (see Lev **11** 17; Dt **14** 16). See OWL.

OWL, SCREECH. See NIGHT MONSTER.

OWNER, ōn'ẽr. See SHIPS AND BOATS, III, 2.

OX. See ANTELOPE; CATTLE; WILD OX.

OX, oks (Ὢξ, *Ȫx*): One of the ancestors of Judith (Jth **8** 1). The name is not Heb. Perhaps the Itala *Ozi* and the Syr *Uz* point to the Heb *Uzzi*.

OX-GOAD, oks'gōd. See GOAD.

OZEM, ō'zem (אֹצֶם, *'ōçem*, meaning unknown):
(1) The 6th son of David (1 Ch **2** 15). LXX (Ἄσομ, *Ásom*) and Vulg suggest that the name should be pointed אָצֹם, *'āçōm*.
(2) A "son" of Jerahmeel (1 Ch **2** 25).

OZIAS, ō-zī'as:
(1) (Ὀζείας, *Ozeías*, Ὀζίας, *Ozías*, B *a b*): The son of Micah, a Simeonite, one of the 3 rulers of Bethulia in the days of Judith (Jth **6** 15.16; **7** 23; **8** 9 ff; **10** 6).
(2) (Ὀζείας, *Ozeías*, B and Swete; AV **Ezias** [1 Esd **8** 2], following A, Ἐζίας, *Ezías*): An ancestor of Ezra (1 Esd **8** 2; 2 Esd **1** 2) = "Uzzi" of Ezr **7** 4; 1 Ch **6** 51.
(3) Head of a family of temple-servants who returned with Zerubbabel (1 Esd **5** 31) = "Uzza" of Ezr **2** 49; Neh **7** 51.
(4) Gr form of UZZIAH (q.v.) in Mt **1** 8.9 AV. A king of Judah.

S. ANGUS

OZIEL, ō'zi-el (Ὀζειήλ, *Ozeiḗl*): An ancestor of Judith (Jth **8** 1); another form of the OT name "Uzziel."

OZNI, oz'nī (אָזְנִי, *'oznī*, "my hearing," or "my ear"): A "son" of Gad (Nu **26** 16) = "Ezbon" of Gen **46** 16 (cf 1 Ch **7** 7).

OZNITES, oz'nīts (with the art. הָאָזְנִי, *hā-'oznī* [collective], "the Oznites"): Of the clan of Ozni (Nu **26** 16). See OZNI.

OZORA, ō-zō'ra. See EZORA.

P

PAARAI, pā'a-rī (פַּעֲרַי, *pa'ăray*, "devotee of Peor"): One of David's 37 valiant men (2 S **23** 35). Doubtless the "Naarai" of 1 Ch **11** 37.

PACATIANA, pā-ka-ti-ā'na, pak-a-tī'a-na (Πακατιανή, *Pakatianḗ*): About 295 AD, when the province of Asia was broken up, two new provinces were formed, Phrygia Prima (Pacatiana), of which Laodicea was "the chiefest city" (subscription to 1 Tim AV), and Phrygia Secunda (Salutaris). See PHRYGIA, and *HDB*, III, 865.

PACE, pās (צַעַד, *ça'adh*): A step in 2 S **6** 13, hence about one yard.

PACHON, pā'kon (Παχών, *Pachṓn*): The name of a month mentioned in 3 Macc **6** 38.

PADDAN, pad'an (Gen **48** 7; AV **Padan,** pā-dan). See next article.

PADDAN-ARAM, pad'an-ā'ram or p.-âr'am (פַּדַּן אֲרָם, *paddan 'ărām;* LXX Μεσοποταμία τῆς Συρίας, *Mesopotamía tēs Surías;* AV **Padan-aram**): In Gen **48** 7, Paddan stands alone, but as the LXX, Sam, and Pesh read "Aram" also, it must in this verse have dropped out of the MT. In the time of Abraham, *padanu* occurs on the Bab contract-tablets as a land measure, to which we may compare the Arab. *feddān* or "ox-gang." In the Assyr syllabaries it is the equivalent of *iklu*, "a field," so that Paddan-aram would mean "the field of Aram," and with this we may compare Hos **12** 12 (Heb **12** 13) and the use of the Heb *sādheh* in connection with Moab and Edom (Jgs **5** 4; Ruth **1** 6).

Furthermore, *padanu* and *harranu* are given as synonyms with the meaning of "road."

Paddan-aram occurs only in the PC, but it corresponds to the "Haran" of the older documents. The versions agree in translating both as Mesopotamia, and identify with the home of the patriarchs and the scene of Jacob's exile the district of Haran to the E. of the Upper Euphrates valley. More in harmony with the length of Jacob's flight, as indicated by the time given (Gen **31** 22.23), is Harran-el-ʿAwamid, an ancient site 10 miles to the E. of Damascus, which satisfies all the demands of history. See ARAM. W. M. CHRISTIE

PADDLE, pad''l (יָתֵד, *yāthēdh*): Dt **23** 13 (Heb 14), RVm "shovel."

PADON, pā'don (פָּדוֹן, *pādhōn*, "redemption"): One of the Nethinim (see NETHINIM) who returned with Zerubbabel (Ezr **2** 44; Neh **7** 47); the "Phaleas" of 1 Esd **5** 29 (m "Padon").

PAGIEL, pā'gi-el, pā'ji-el, pa-gī'el (פַּגְעִיאֵל, *paghʿīʼēl*, "God's intervention"): Son of Ocran, of the tribe of Asher, among those enrolled by Moses at the numbering of Israel (Nu **1** 13; **2** 27). When the tabernacle was set up, the heads of the families of Israel "brought their offerings" in rotation, and Pagiel, as prince of his tribe, came on the 11th day (Nu **7** 72). Nu **7** 72–77 describes his offering. In the journeyings of Israel he was "over the host of the tribe of the children of Asher" (Nu **10** 26), and possibly standard-bearer (cf Nu **10** 14.22.25). HENRY WALLACE

PAHATH-MOAB, pā'hath-mō'ab (פַּחַת־מוֹאָב, *paḥath mōʼābh*, "sheik of Moab"; in 1 Esd **5** 11; **8** 31, "Phaath Moab"): A Jewish clan probably named after an ancestor of the above title. Part of the clan returned with Zerubbabel (Ezr **2** 6; cf Neh **7** 11) under two family names, Jeshua and Joab; and a part came back with Ezra (Ezr **8** 4). Hashub, a "son of Pahath-moab," is named among the repairers of both the wall and the "tower of the furnaces" at Jerus (Neh **3** 11). It is the name of one of the signatories "sealing" the "sure covenant" of Neh **9** 38 (Neh **10** 14). Some of the sons of this name had taken "strange wives" (Ezr **10** 30). HENRY WALLACE

PAI, pā'ī (פָּעִי, *pāʿī*; Φογώρ, *Phogôr*): The royal city of Hadad or Hadar, king of Edom (1 Ch **1** 50). The name is given as "Pau" (פָּעוּ, *pāʿū*) in Gen **36** 39. There is no indication of its position. It is not identified.

PAIN, pān (חוּל, *ḥūl*, חִיל, *ḥīl*, חֶבֶל, *ḥēbhel*, חָלָה, *ḥālāh*, חַלְחָלָה, *ḥalḥālāh*, כְּאֵב, *kāʼēbh*, כְּאֵב, *keʼēbh*, מֵצַר, *mēçar*, מַכְאֹב, *makhʼōbh*, עָמָל, *ʿāmāl*, צִיר, *çīr*; βασανίζω, *basanízō*, πόνος, *pónos*, ὠδίν, *ōdín*): These words signifying various forms of bodily or mental suffering are generally tr^d "pain"; 28 out of the 34 passages in which the word is used are in the poetical or prophetical books and refer to conditions of mental disquiet or dismay due to the punishment of personal or national sin. In one instance only is the word used as a historic record of personal physical pain: the case of the wife of Phinehas (1 S **4** 19), but the same word *çīr* is used **figuratively** in Isa **13** 8; **21** 3; Dnl **10** 16, and tr^d "pangs" or "sorrows." In other passages where we have the same comparison of consternation in the presence of God's judgments to the pangs of childbirth, the word used is *ḥēbhel*, as in Isa **66** 7; Jer **13** 21; **22** 23; **49** 24. In some of these and similar passages several synonyms are used in the one verse to intensify the impression, and are tr^d "pain," "pangs," and "sorrows," as in Isa **13** 8.

The word most commonly used by the prophets is some form of *ḥūl* or *ḥīl*, sometimes with the addition "as of a woman in travail," as in Ps **48** 6; Isa **26** 18; Jer **6** 24; **22** 23; Mic **4** 10. This pain is referred to the heart (Ps **55** 4) or to the head (Jer **30** 23; cf vs 5.6). In Ezk **30** 4, it is the penal affliction of Ethiopia, and in ver 16, AV "Sin [Tanis] shall have great pain" (RV "anguish"); in Isa **23** 5 Egypt is sorely pained at the news of the fall of Tyre. Before the invading host of locusts the people are much pained (Joel **2** 6 AV). Pain in the sense of toil and trouble in Jer **12** 13 is the tr of *ḥālāh*, a word more frequently rendered grieving or sickness, as in 1 K **14** 1; Prov **23** 35; Cant **2** 5; Jer **5** 3. The reduplicated form *ḥalḥālāh* is esp. used of a twisting pain usually referred to the loins (Isa **21** 3; Ezk **30** 4.9; Nah **2** 10).

Pain in the original meaning of the word (as it has come down to us through the Old Fr. from the Lat *poena*) as a penalty inflicted for personal sin is expressed by the words *kāʼēbh* or *keʼābh* in Job **14** 22; **15** 20, and in the questioning complaint of the prophet (Jer **15** 18). As a judgment on personal sin pain is also expressed by *makhʼōbh* in Job **33** 19; Jer **51** 8, but this word is used in the sense of afflictions in Isa **53** 3 in the expression "man of sorrows." The Psalmist (Ps **25** 18) praying for deliverance from the afflictions which weighed heavily on him in turn uses the word *ʿāmāl*, and this word which primarily means "toil" or "labor," as in Eccl **1** 3, or "travail," as in Isa **53** 11, is tr^d "painful" in Ps **73** 16, as expressing Asaph's disquiet due to his misunderstanding of the ways of Providence. The "pains of hell" (Ps **116** 3 AV), which got hold of the Psalmist in his sickness, is the rendering of the word *mēçar*; the same word is tr^d "distress" in Ps **118** 5. Most of these words have a primary physical meaning of twisting, rubbing or constricting.

In the NT *ōdín* is tr^d "pain" (of death, RV "pang") in Acts **2** 24. This word is used to express any severe pain, such as that of travail, or (as in Aeschylus, *Chöephori*, 211) the pain of intense apprehension. The vb. from this, √ *ōdunômai*, is used by the Rich Man in the parable to describe his torment (RV "anguish") (Lk **16** 24). The related vb. *sunōdínō* is used in Rom **8** 22 and is tr^d "travailing in pain together." In much the same sense the word is used by Euripides (*Helena*, 727).

In Rev **12** 2 the woman clothed with the sun (*basanizoménē*) was in pain to be delivered; the vb. (*basanízō*) which means "to torture" is used both in Mt **8** 6 in the account of the grievously tormented centurion's servant, and in the description of the laboring of the apostles' boat on the stormy Sea of Galilee (Mt **14** 24). The former of these seems to have been a case of spinal meningitis. This vb. occurs in Thucydides vii.86 (viii.92), where it means "being put to torture." In the two passages in Rev where pain is mentioned the word is *ponos*, the pain which affected those on whom the fifth vial was poured (**16** 10), and in the description of the City of God where there is no more pain (**21** 4). The primary meaning of this word seems to be "toil," as in *Iliad* xxi.525, but it is used by Hippocrates to express disease (*Aphorisma* iv.44).

ALEX. MACALISTER

PAINFULNESS, pān'fo͝ol-nes (μόχθος, *móchthos*): In the summary of his missionary labors in 2 Cor **11** 27 AV, St. Paul uses this word. RV renders it "travail," which probably now expresses its meaning more closely, as in modern usage "painfulness" is usually restricted to the condition of actual soreness or suffering, although we still use "painstaking" in the sense of careful labor. The Gr word is used for toil or excessive anxiety, as in Euripides (*Medea*, 126), where it refers to that care for her children which she had lost in her madness. Tindale uses "painfulness" in 1 Jn **4** 18 as the tr of κόλασις, *kólasis*, which AV renders "torment" and RV "punishment."

ALEX. MACALISTER

PAINT, pānt (from Old Fr. *peinctre*, frequentative of *peindre*, Lat *pingo*, "to paint"): (1) From Heb vb. מָשַׁח, *māshaḥ*, "to smear," "to anoint," "to paint," describing the painting of interiors with vermilion, perhaps resembling lacquer: "ceiled with cedar, and painted with vermilion" (Jer **22** 14). The shields of the Ninevite soldiers were red, presumably painted (Nah **2** 3). (2) From noun פּוּךְ, *pūkh*, "paint," "antimony," "stibium," "black mineral powder," used as a cosmetic, to lend artificial size and fancied beauty to the eye, always spoken of as a meretricious device, indicating light or unworthy character. Jezebel "painted her eyes, and attired her head" (2 K **9** 30, lit. "put *pūkh* into her eyes"). To the harlot city Jerus, Jeremiah (**4** 30) says, "deckest thee . . . . , enlargest thine eyes with paint" (*pūkh*). AV renders "rentest thy face," as if the stain were a cut, or the enlarging done by violence. (3) From vb. כָּחַל, *kāḥal*, "to smear," "to paint." Ezekiel says to Oholah-Oholibah (Judah-Israel), "didst wash thyself, paint [*kāḥal*] thine eyes," as the adulteress prepares herself for her paramour (Ezk **23** 40). The antimony, in an extremely fine powder (Arab. *kuḥl*, from *kāḥal*), is placed in the eye by means of a very fine rod, bodkin, or probe, drawn between the edges of the eyelids. This distends the eye, and also increases its apparent size, the effect being increased by a line of stain drawn from the corner, and by a similar line prolonging the eyebrow. See EYEPAINT; COLOR. PHILIP WENDELL CRANNELL

PAINTING, pān'ting. See CRAFTS, II, 12.

PAIR, pâr: The m of Cant **4** 2 (but not of the ‖ **6** 6) reads, "which are all of them in pairs," while the text has, "whereof every one hath twins." The Heb מַתְאִימוֹת, *math'īmōth*, is from a √ *tā'am*, "be double," and is perhaps susceptible of either meaning. But the description is of sheep, and the m gives no comprehensible figure, while the text points to the exceedingly sleek and healthy appearance. "Pairs" seems to result from confusing the figure with the thing figured—the teeth, where each upper is paired with the corresponding lower.

PALACE, pal'ās: In Heb chiefly אַרְמוֹן, *'armōn*, in RV text tr[d] "castle" in 1 K **16** 18; 2 K **15** 25; בִּירָה, *bīrāh*, הֵיכָל, *hēkhāl*, the same word often rendered "temple"; in Gr αὐλή, *aulē*, in RV tr[d] "court" (Mt **26** 3.58.69; Mk **14** 54.66; Lk **11** 21; Jn **18** 15). On the other hand, "palace" takes the place in RV of AV "common hall" or "judgment hall" (*praitōrion*, Mt **27** 27; Jn **18** 28. 33; **19** 9; Acts **23** 35). See JUDGMENT, HALL OF. A description of Solomon's palace is given in 1 K **7** 1-12 (see TEMPLE). Archaeology has brought to light the remains of great palaces in Egypt, Babylonia, Assyria (Sargon, Sennacherib, Assurbanipal, etc), Susa, etc. See HOUSE.

JAMES ORR

PALAESTRA, PALESTRA, pa-les'tra. See GAMES, II, 3, (*i*).

PALAL, pā'lal (פָּלָל, *pālāl*, "judge"): Son of Uzai, and one of the repairers of the wall (Neh **3** 25).

PALANQUIN, pal-an-kēn': In Cant **3** 9 occurs אַפִּרְיוֹן, *'appiryōn*, a word that has no Sem cognates and is of dubious meaning. In form, however, it resembles the Sanskrit *paryañka*, and still more closely the Gr φορεῖον, *phoreíon*, both of which mean "litter bed." Hence RV "palanquin" (ultimately derived from *paryañka*). The m "car of state" and AV "chariot" are mere guesses.

PALESTINA, pal-es-tī'na (פְּלֶשֶׁת, *p[e]lesheth*): Ex **15** 14; Isa **14** 29.31 AV; changed in RV to PHILISTIA (q.v.).

PALESTINE, pal'es-tīn (פְּלֶשֶׁת, *p[e]lesheth*; Φυλιστιείμ, *Phulistieim*, Ἀλλόφυλοι, *Allóphuloi*; AV Joel **3** 4 [RV "Philistia"], "Palestina"; AV Ex **15** 14; Isa **14** 29.31; cf Ps **60** 8; **83** 7; **87** 4; **108** 9):

I. PHYSICAL CONDITIONS
1. General Geographical Features
2. Water-Supply
3. Geological Conditions
4. Fauna and Flora
5. Climate
6. Rainfall
7. Drought and Famine

II. PALESTINE IN THE PENTATEUCH
1. Places Visited by Abraham
2. Places Visited by Isaac
3. Places Visited by Jacob
4. Mentioned in Connection with Judah
5. Review of Geography of Genesis
6. Exodus and Leviticus
7. Numbers
8. Deuteronomy

III. PALESTINE IN THE HISTORIC BOOKS OF THE OT
1. Book of Joshua
2. Book of Judges
3. Book of Ruth
4. Books of Samuel
5. Books of Kings
6. Post-exilic Historical Books

IV. PALESTINE IN THE POETIC BOOKS OF THE OT
1. Book of Job
2. Book of Psalms
3. Book of Proverbs
4. Song of Songs

V. PALESTINE IN THE PROPHETS
1. Isaiah
2. Jeremiah
3. Ezekiel
4. Minor Prophets

VI. PALESTINE IN THE APOCRYPHA
1. Book of Judith
2. Book of Wisdom
3. 1 Maccabees
4. 2 Maccabees

VII. PALESTINE IN THE NT
1. Synoptic Gospels
2. Fourth Gospel
3. Book of Acts

LITERATURE

The word properly means "Philistia," but appears to be first used in the extended sense, as meaning all the "Land of Israel" or "Holy Land" (Zec **2** 12), by Philo and by Ovid and later Rom authors (Reland, *Pal Illustr.*, I, 38-42).

I. Physical Conditions.—The Bible in general may be said to breathe the air of Pal; and it is here intended to show how important for sound criticism is the consideration of its geography, and of the numerous incidental allusions to the natural features, fauna, flora, cultivation, and climate of the land in which most of the Bible books were written. With the later history and topography of Pal, after 70 AD, we are not here concerned, but a short account of its present physical and geological conditions is needed for our purpose.

1. General Geographical Features

Pal W. of the Jordan, between Dan and Beersheba, has an area of about 6,000 sq. miles, the length from Hermon southward being nearly 150 miles, and the width gradually increasing from 20 miles on the N. to 60 miles on the S. It is thus about the size of Wales, and the height of the Palestinian mountains is about the same as that of the Welsh. E. of the Jordan an area of about 4,000 sq. miles was included in the land of Israel. The general geographical features are familiar to all.

(1) The land is divided by the deep chasm of the Jordan valley—an ancient geological fault continuing in the Dead Sea, where its depth (at the

bottom of the lake) is 2,600 ft. below the Mediterranean.

(2) W. of the valley the mountain ridge, which is a continuation of Lebanon, has very steep slopes on the E. and long spurs on the W., on which side the foothills (Heb *shᵉphēlāh* or "lowland") form a distinct district, widening gradually southward, while between this region and the sea the plains of Sharon and Philistia stretch to the sandhills and low cliffs of a harborless coast.

(3) In Upper Galilee, on the N., the mountain ridge rises to 4,000 ft. above the Mediterranean. Lower Galilee, to the S., includes rounded hills less than 1,000 ft. above the sea, and the triangular plain of Esdraelon drained by the River Kishon between the Gilboa watershed on the E. and the long spur of Carmel on the W.

(4) In Samaria the mountains are extremely rugged, but a small plain near Dothan adjoins that of Esdraelon, and another stretches E. of Shechem, 2,500 ft. above the level of the Jordan valley. In Judaea the main ridge rises toward Hebron and then sinks to the level of the Beersheba plains about 1,000 ft. above the sea. The desert of Judah forms a plateau (500 ft. above sea-level), between this ridge and the Dead Sea, and is throughout barren and waterless; but the mountains—which average about 3,000 ft. above the sea—are full of good springs and suitable for the cultivation of the vine, fig and olive. The richest lands are found in the *shᵉphēlāh* region—esp. in Judaea—and in the corn plains of Esdraelon, Sharon, and Philistia.

(5) E. of the Jordan the plateau of Bashan (averaging 1,500 ft. above the sea) is also a fine corn country. S. of this, Gilead presents a mountain region rising to 3,600 ft. above sea-level at *Jebel Osha'*, and sloping gently on the E. to the desert. The steep western slopes are watered by the Jabbok River, and by many perennial brooks. In North Gilead esp. the wooded hills present some of the most picturesque scenery of the Holy Land. S. of Gilead, the Moab plateau (about 2,700 ft. above sea-level) is now a desert, but is fitted for corn culture, and in places for the vine. A lower shelf or plateau (about 500 to 1,000 ft. above sea-level) intervenes between the main plateau and the Dead Sea cliffs, and answers to the Desert of Judah W. of the lake.

2. Water-Supply

The water-supply of Pal is abundant, except in the desert regions above noticed, which include only a small part of its area. The Jordan runs into the Dead Sea, which has no outlet and which maintains its level solely by evaporation, being consequently very salt; the surface is nearly 1,300 ft. below the Mediterranean, whereas the Sea of Galilee (680 ft. below sea-level) is sweet and full of fish. The Jordan is fed, not only by the snows of Hermon, but by many affluent streams from both sides. There are several streams also in Sharon, including the Crocodile River under Carmel. In the mountains, where the hard dolomite limestone is on the surface, perennial springs are numerous. In the lower hills, where this limestone is covered by a softer chalky stone, the supply depends on wells and cisterns. In the Beersheba plains the water, running under the surface, is reached by scooping shallow pits—esp. those near Gerar, to be noticed later.

3. Geological Conditions

The fertility and cultivation of any country depends mainly on its geological conditions. These are comparatively simple in Pal, and have undergone no change since the age when man first appeared, or since the days of the Heb patriarchs. The country was first upheaved from the ocean in the Eocene age; and, in the subsequent Miocene age, the great crack in the earth's surface occurred, which formed a narrow gulf stretching from that of the *'Akabah* on the S. almost to the foot of Hermon. Further upheaval, accompanied by volcanic outbreaks which covered the plateaus of Golan, Bashan, and Lower Galilee with lava, cut off the Jordan valley from the Red Sea, and formed a long lake, the bottom of which continued to sink on the S. to its present level during the Pleiocene and Pluvial periods, after which—its peculiar fauna having developed meanwhile—the lake gradually dried up, till it was represented only, as it now is, by the swampy *Ḥûleh*, the pear-shaped Sea of Galilee, and the Dead Sea. These changes all occurred long ages before the appearance of man. The beds upheaved include: (1) the Nubian Sandstone (of the Greensand period), which was sheared along the line of the Jordan fault E. of the river, and which only appears on the western slopes of Hermon, Gilead, and Moab; (2) the limestones of the Cretaceous age, including the hard dolomite, and softer beds full of characteristic fossils; (3) the soft Eocene limestone, which appears chiefly on the western spurs and in the foothills, the angle of upheaval being less steep than that of the older main formation. On the shores of the Mediterranean a yet later sandy limestone forms the low cliffs of Sharon. See GEOLOGY OF PALESTINE.

4. Fauna and Flora

As regards fauna, flora and cultivation, it is sufficient here to say that they are still practically the same as described throughout the Bible. The lion and the wild bull (*Bos primigenius*) were exterminated within historic times, but have left their bones in the Jordan gravels, and in caves. The bear has gradually retreated to Hermon and Lebanon. The buffalo has been introduced since the Moslem conquest. Among trees the apple has fallen out of cultivation since the Middle Ages, and the cactus has been introduced; but Pal is still a land of corn, wine and oil, and famous for its fruits. Its trees, shrubs and plants are those noticed in the Bible. Its woods have been thinned in Lower Galilee and Northern Sharon, but on the other hand the copse has often grown over the site of former vineyards and villages, and there is no reason to think that any general desiccation has occurred within the last 40 centuries, such as would affect the rainfall.

5. Climate

The climate of Pal is similar to that of other Mediterranean lands, such as Cyprus, Sicily or Southern Italy; and, in spite of the fevers of mosquito districts in the plains, it is much better than that of the Delta in Egypt, or of Mesopotamia. The summer heat is oppressive only for a few days at a time, when (esp. in May) the dry wind—deficient in ozone—blows from the eastern desert. For most of the season a moisture-laden sea breeze, rising about 10 AM, blows till the evening, and fertilizes all the western slopes of the mountains. In the bare deserts the difference between 90° F. by day and 40° F. by night gives a refreshing cold. With the east wind the temperature rises to 105° F., and the nights are oppressive. In the Jordan valley, in autumn, the shade temperature reaches 120° F. In this season mists cover the mountains and swell the grapes. In winter the snow sometimes lies for several days on the watershed ridge and on the Edomite mountains, but in summer even Hermon is sometimes quite snowless at 9,000 ft. above the sea. There is perhaps no country in which such a range of climate can be found, from the Alpine to the tropical, and none in which the range of fauna and flora is consequently so large, from the European to the African.

6. Rainfall

The rainfall of Pal is between 20 and 30 in. annually, and the rainy season is the same as in other Mediterranean countries. The "former rains" begin with the thunderstorms of November, and the "latter rains" cease with April showers. From December to February—except in years of drought—the rains are heavy. In most years the supply is quite sufficient for purposes of cultivation. The ploughing begins in autumn, and the corn is rarely spoiled by storms in summer. The fruits ripen in autumn and suffer only from the occasional appearance of locust swarms. There appears to be no reason to suppose that climate or rainfall have undergone any change since the times of the Bible; and a consideration of Bible allusions confirms this view.

7. Drought and Famine

Thus the occurrence of drought, and of consequent famine, is mentioned in the OT as occasional in all times (Gen **12** 10; **26** 2; **41** 50; Lev **26** 20; 2 S **21** 1; 1 K **8** 35; Isa **5** 6; Jer **14** 1; Joel **1** 10–12; Hag **1** 11; Zec **14** 17), and droughts are also noticed in the Mish (*Ta'ănīth*, i. 4–7) as occurring in autumn, and even lasting throughout the rainy season till spring. Good rains were a blessing from God, and drought was a sign of His displeasure, in Heb belief (Dt **11** 14; Jer **5** 24; Joel **2** 23). A thunderstorm in harvest time (May) was most unusual (1 S **12** 17.18), yet such a storm does still occur as a very exceptional phenomenon. By "snow in harvest" (Prov **25** 13) we are not to understand a snowstorm, for it is likened to a "faithful messenger," and the reference is to the use of snow for cooling wine, which is still usual at Damascus. The notice of fever on the shores of the Sea of Galilee (Mt **8** 14) shows that this region was as unhealthy as it still is in summer. The decay of irrigation in Sharon may have rendered the plain more malarious than of old, but the identity of the Palestinian flora with that of the Bible indicates that the climate, generally speaking, is unchanged.

II. Palestine in the Pentateuch.—The Book of Gen is full of allusions to sites sacred to the memory of the Heb patriarchs.

1. Places Visited by Abraham

In the time of Abraham the population consisted of tribes, mainly Sem, who came originally from Babylonia, including Canaanites ("lowlanders") between Sidon and Gaza, and in the Jordan valley, and Amorites ("highlanders") in the mountains (Gen **10** 15–19; Nu **13** 29). Their language was akin to Heb, and it is only in Egypt that we read of an interpreter being needed (Gen **42** 23), while excavated remains of seal-cylinders, and other objects, show that the civilization of Pal was similar to that of Babylonia.

(1) *Shechem.*—The first place noticed is the shrine or "station" (*māḳōm*) of Shechem, with the Elon Moreh (LXX "high oak"), where Jacob afterward buried the idols of his wives, and where Joshua set up a stone by the "holy place" (Gen **12** 6; **35** 4; Josh **24** 26). Sam tradition showed the site near *Balâṭa* ("the oak") at the foot of Mt. Gerizim. The "Canaanite was then in the land" (in Abraham's time), but was exterminated (Gen **34** 25) by Jacob's sons. From Shechem Abraham journeyed southward and raised an altar between Bethel (*Beitîn*) and Hai (*Ḥayân*), E. of the town of Luz, the name of which still survives hard-by at the spring of *Lôzeh* (Gen **12** 8; **13** 3; **28** 11.19; **35** 2).

(2) *The Negeb.*—But, on his return from Egypt with large flocks (**12** 16), he settled in the pastoral region, between Beersheba and the western Kadesh (**13** 1; **20** 1), called in Heb the *neghebh*, "dry" country, on the edge of the cultivated lands. From E. of Bethel there is a fine view of the lower Jordan valley, and here Lot "lifted up his eyes" (**13** 10), and chose the rich grass lands of that valley for his flocks. The "cities of the Plain" (*kikkār*) were clearly in this valley, and Sodom must have been near the river, since Lot's journey to Zoar (**19** 22) occupied only an hour or two (vs 15.23) through the plain to the foot of the Moab mountains. These cities are not said to have been visible from near Hebron; but, from the hilltop E. of the city, Abraham could have seen "the smoke of the land" (**19** 28) rising up. The first land owned by him was the garden of Mamre (**13** 18; **18** 1; **23** 19), with the cave-tomb which tradition still points out under the floor of the Hebron mosque. His tent was spread under the "oaks of Mamre" (**18** 1), where his mysterious guests rested "under the tree" (ver 8). One aged oak still survives in the flat ground W. of the city, but this tree is very uncommon in the mountains of Judah. In all these incidental touches we have evidence of the exact knowledge of Pal which distinguishes the story of the patriarchs.

(3) *Campaign of Amraphel.*—Pal appears to have been an outlying province of the empire of Ḥammurabi, king of Babylon in Abraham's time; and the campaign of Amraphel resembled those of later Assyr overlords exacting tribute of petty kings. The route (**14** 5–8) lay through Bashan, Gilead and Moab to Kadesh (probably at Petra), and the return through the desert of Judah to the plains of Jericho. Thus Hebron was not attacked (see ver 13), and the pursuit by Abraham and his Amorite allies led up the Jordan valley to Dan, and thence N. of Damascus (ver 15). The Salem whose king blessed Abraham on his return was thought by the Samaritans, and by Jerome, to be the city near the Jordan valley afterward visited by Jacob (**14** 18; **33** 18); but see JERUSALEM.

(4) *Gerar.*—Abraham returned to the southern plains, and "sojourned in Gerar" (**20** 1), now *Umm Jerrâr*, 7 miles S. of Gaza. The wells which he dug in this valley (**26** 15) were no doubt shallow excavations like those from which the Arabs still obtain the water flowing under the surface in the same vicinity (*SWP*, III, 390), though that at Beersheba (**21** 25–32), to which Isaac added another (**26** 23–25), may have been more permanent. Three masonry wells now exist at *Bîr es Seba'*, but the masonry is modern. The planting of a "tamarisk" at this place (**21** 33) is an interesting touch, since the tree is distinctive of the dry lowlands. From Beersheba Abraham journeyed to "the land of Moriah" (LXX "the high land") to sacrifice Isaac (**22** 2); and the mountain, according to Heb tradition (2 Ch **3** 1), was at Jerus, but according to the Samaritans was Gerizim near the Elon Moreh—a summit which could certainly have been seen "afar off" (ver 4) on "the third day."

2. Places Visited by Isaac

Isaac, living in the same pastoral wilderness, at the western Kadesh (**25** 11) and at Gerar (**26** 2), suffered like his father in a year of drought, and had similar difficulties with the Philis. At Gerar he sowed corn (**26** 12), and the vicinity is still capable of such cultivation. Thence he retreated S.E. to Rehoboth (*Ruḥeibeh*), N. of Kadesh, where ancient wells like those at Beersheba still exist (**26** 22). To Beersheba he finally returned (ver 23).

3. Places Visited by Jacob

When Jacob fled to Haran from Beersheba (**28** 10) he slept at the "place" (or shrine) consecrated by Abraham's altar near Bethel, and—like any modern Arab visitor to a shrine—erected a memorial stone (ver 18), which he renewed twenty years later (**35** 14) when God appeared to him "again" (ver 9).

(1) *Haran to Succoth.*—His return journey from Haran to Gilead raises an interesting question. The distance is about 350 miles from Haran to the Galeed or "witness heap" (**31** 48) at Mizpah—probably *Sûf* in North Gilead. This distance Laban is said to have covered in 7 days (**31** 23), which would be possible for a force mounted on riding camels. But the news of Jacob's flight reached Laban on the 3d day (ver 22), and some time would elapse before he could gather his "brethren." Jacob with his flocks and herds must

have needed 3 weeks for the journey. It is remarkable that the vicinity of Mizpah still presents ancient monuments like the "pillar" (ver 45) round which the "memorial cairn" (*yᵉghar-sāhădhūthā*) was formed. From this place Jacob journeyed to Mahanaim (probably *Maḥmah*), S. of the Jabbok river—a place which afterward became the capital of South Gilead (Gen **32** 1 f; 1 K **4** 14); but, on hearing of the advance of Esau from Edom, he retreated across the river (Gen **32** 22) and then reached Succoth (**33** 17), believed to be *Tell Der'ala*, N. of the stream.

(2) *From the Jordan to Hebron.*—Crossing the Jordan by one of several fords in this vicinity, Jacob approached Shechem by the perennial stream of *Wâdy Fâr'ah*, and camped at Shalem (*Sâlim*) on the east side of the fertile plain which stretches thence to Shechem, and here he bought land of the Hivites (**33** 18–20). We are not told that he dug a well, but the necessity for digging one in a region full of springs can only be explained by Hivite jealousy of water rights, and the well still exists E. of Shechem (cf Jn **4** 5 f), not far from the Elon Moreh where were buried the *tᵉrāphīm* (Gen **35** 4) or "spirits" (Assyr *tarpu*) from Haran (**31** 30) under the oak of Abraham. These no doubt were small images, such as are so often unearthed in Pal. The further progress of Jacob led by Bethel and Bethlehem to Hebron (**35** 6.19.27), but some of his elder sons seem to have remained at Shechem. Thus Joseph was sent later from Hebron (**37** 14) to visit his brethren there, but found them at Dothan.

(3) *Dothan* (**37** 17) lay in a plain on the main trade route from Egypt to Damascus, which crossed the low watershed at this point and led down the valley to Jezreel and over Jordan to Bashan. The "well of the pit" (*SWP*, II, 169) is still shown at *Tell Dothân*, and the Ishmaelites, from Midian and Gilead, chose this easy caravan route (**37** 25.28) for camels laden with the Gilead balm and spices. The plain was fitted for feeding Jacob's flocks. The products of Pal then included also honey, pistachio nuts, and almonds (**43** 11); and a few centuries later we find notice in a text of Thothmes III of honey and balsam, with oil, wine, wheat, spelt, barley and fruits, as rations of the Egyptian troops in Canaan (Brugsch, *Hist Egypt*, I, 332).

The episode of Judah and Tamar is connected with a region in the *Shᵉphēlāh*, or low hills of Judaea.

4. Mentioned in Connection with Judah

Adullam (*'Aîd-el-ma*), Chezib (*'Ain Kezbeh*), and Timnath (*Tibneh*) are not far apart (Gen **38** 1.5.12), the latter being in a pastoral valley where Judah met his "sheep shearers." Tamar sat at "the entrance of Enaim" (cf vs 14.22 ERV) or Enam (Josh **15** 34), perhaps at *Kefr 'Ana*, 6 miles N.W. of Timnath. She was mistaken for a *kᵉdhēshāh*, or votary of Ashtoreth (Gen **38** 15.21), and we know from Ḥammurabi's laws that such votaries were already recognized. The mention of Judah's signet and staff (ver 18) also reminds us of Bab customs as described by Herodotus (i.195), and signet-cylinders of Bab style, and of early date, have been unearthed in Pal at Gezer and elsewhere (cf the "Bab garment," Josh **7** 21).

5. Review of Geography of Genesis

Generally speaking, the geography of Gen presents no difficulties, and shows an intimate knowledge of the country, while the allusions to natural products and to customs are in accord with the results of scientific discovery. Only one difficulty needs notice, where Atad (**50** 10) on the way from Egypt to Hebron is described as "beyond the Jordan." In this case the Assyr language perhaps helps us, for in that tongue *Yaur-danu* means "the great river," and the reference may be to the Nile itself, which is called *Yaur* in Heb (*yᵉ'ōr*) and Assyr alike.

6. Exodus and Leviticus

Ex is concerned with Egypt and the Sinaitic desert, though it may be observed that its simple agricultural laws (chs **21**–**23**), which so often recall those of Ḥammurabi, would have been needed at once on the conquest of Gilead and Bashan, before crossing the Jordan. In Lev (ch **11**) we have a list of animals most of which belong to the desert—as for instance the "coney" or hyrax (Lev **11** 5; Ps **104** 18; Prov **30** 26), but others—such as the swine (Lev **11** 7), the stork and the heron (ver 19)—to the *'Arabah* and the Jordan valley, while the hoopoe (AV "lapwing," ver 19) lives in Gilead and in Western Pal. In Dt (ch **14**) the fallow deer and the roe (ver 5) are now inhabitants of Tabor and Gilead, but the "wild goat" (ibex), "wild ox" (buball), "pygarg" (addax) and "chamois" (wild sheep), are found in the *'Arabah* and in the deserts.

7. Numbers

In Nu the conquest of Eastern Pal is described, and most of the towns mentioned are known (**21** 18–33); the notice of vineyards in Moab (ver 22) agrees with the discovery of ancient rock-cut wine presses near Heshbon (*SEP*, I, 221). The view of Israel, in camp at Shittim by Balaam (**22** 41), standing on the top of Pisgah or Mt. Nebo, has been shown to be possible by the discovery of *Jebel Neba*, where also rude dolmens recalling Balak's altars have been found (*SEP*, I, 202). The plateau of Moab (**32** 3) is described as a "land for cattle," and still supports Arab flocks. The camps in which Israel left their cattle, women and children during the wars, for 6 months, stretched (**33** 49) from Beth-jeshimoth (*Suweimeh*), near the northeastern corner of the Dead Sea over Abel-shittim ("the acacia meadow"—a name it still bears) in a plain watered by several brooks, and having good herbage in spring.

8. Deuteronomy

(1) *Physical allusions.*—The description of the "good land" in Dt (**8** 7) applies in some details with special force to Mt. Gilead, which possesses more perennial streams than Western Pal throughout—"a land of brooks of water, of fountains and springs, flowing forth in valleys and hills"; a land also "of wheat and barley, and vines and fig-trees and pomegranates, a land of olive-trees and honey" is found in Gilead and Bashan. Pal itself is not a mining country, but the words (ver 9), "a land whose stones are iron, and out of whose hills thou mayest dig copper," may be explained by the facts that iron mines existed near Beirût in the 10th cent. AD, and copper mines at Punon N. of Petra in the 4th cent. AD, as described by Jerome (*Onom*, s.v. "Phinōn"). In Dt also (**11** 29; cf **27** 4; Josh **8** 30) Ebal and Gerizim are first noticed, as beside the "oaks of Moreh." Ebal the mountain of curses (3,077 ft. above sea-level) and Gerizim the mountain of blessings (2,850 ft.) are the two highest tops in Samaria, and Shechem lies in a rich valley between them. The first sacred center of Israel was thus established at the place where Abraham built his first altar and Jacob dug his well, where Joseph was buried and where Joshua recognized a holy place at the foot of Gerizim (Josh **24** 26). The last chapters of Dt record the famous Pisgah view from Mt. Nebo (**34** 1–3), which answers in all respects to that from *Jebel Neba*, except as to Dan, and the utmost (or "western") sea, neither of which is visible. Here we should probably read "toward" rather than "to," and there is no other hill above the plains of Shittim whence a better view can be obtained of the Jordan valley, from Zoar to Jericho, of the watershed mountains as far N. as Gilboa and Tabor, and of the slopes of Gilead.

(2) *Archaeology.*—But besides these physical

allusions, the progress of exploration serves to illustrate the archaeology of Dt. Israel was commanded (**12** 3) to overthrow the Can. altars, to break the standing stones which were emblems of superstition, to burn the *'ăshērāh* poles (or artificial trees), and to hew down the graven images. That these commands were obeyed is clear. The rude altars and standing stones are now found only in Moab, and in remote parts of Gilead, Bashan, and Galilee, not reached by the power of reforming kings of Judah. The *'ăshērāh* poles have disappeared, the images are found, only deep under the surface. The carved tablets which remain at Damascus, and in Phoenicia and Syria, representing the gods of Canaan or of the Hittites, have no counterpart in the Holy Land. Again when we read of ancient "landmarks" (Dt **19** 14; Prov **22** 28; **23** 10), we are not to understand a mere boundary stone, but rather one of those monuments common in Babylonia—as early at least as the 12th cent. BC—on which the boundaries of a field are minutely described, the history of its grant by the king detailed, and a curse (cf Dt **27** 17) pronounced against the man who should dare to remove the stone. (See illustration under NEBUCHADNEZZAR.)

III. Palestine in the Historic Books of the OT.—

1. Book of Joshua

Josh is the great geographical book of the OT; and the large majority of the 600 names of places, rivers and mountains in Pal mentioned in the Bible are to be found in this book.

(1) *Topographical accuracy.*—About half of this total of names were known, or were fixed by Dr. Robinson, between 1838 and 1852, and about 150 new sites were discovered (1872–78, 1881–82) in consequence of the 1-in. trigonometrical survey of the country, and were identified by the present writer during this period; a few interesting sites have been added by M. Clermont-Ganneau (Adullam and Gezer), by Rev A. Henderson (Kiriath-jearim), by Rev. W. F. Birch (Zoar at *Tell esh Shâghûr*), and by others. Thus more than three-quarters of the sites have been fixed with more or less certainty, most of them preserving their ancient names. It is impossible to study this topography without seeing that the Bible writers had personal knowledge of the country; and it is incredible that a Heb priest, writing in Babylonia, could have possessed that intimate acquaintance with all parts of the land which is manifest in the geographical chapters of Josh. The towns are enumerated in due order by districts; the tribal boundaries follow natural lines—valleys and mountain ridges—and the character of various regions is correctly indicated. Nor can we suppose that this topography refers to conditions subsequent to the return from captivity, for these were quite different. Simeon had ceased to inhabit the south by the time of David (1 Ch **4** 24), and the lot of Dan was colonized by men of Benjamin after the captivity (**8** 12.13; Neh **11** 34.35). Tirzah is mentioned (Josh **12** 24) in Samaria, whereas the future capital of Omri is not. Ai is said to have been made "a heap for ever" (**8** 28), but was inhabited apparently in Isaiah's time (**10** 28=Aiath) and certainly after the captivity (Ezr **2** 28; Neh **7** 32; **11** 31=Aija). At latest, the topography seems to be that of Solomon's age, though it is remarkable that very few places in Samaria are noticed in the Book of Josh.

(2) *The passage of the Jordan.*—Israel crossed Jordan at the lowest ford E. of Jericho. The river was in flood, swollen by the melting snows of Hermon (Josh **3** 15); the stoppage occurred 20 miles farther up at Adam (*ed-Dâmieh*), the chalky cliffs at a narrow place being probably undermined and falling in, thus damming the stream. A Moslem writer asserts that a similar stoppage occurred in the 13th cent. AD, near the same point. (See JORDAN RIVER.) The first camp was established at Gilgal (*Jilgûlieh*), 3 miles E. of Jericho, and a "circle" of 12 stones was erected. Jericho was not at the mediaeval site (*er Rîḥa*) S. of Gilgal, or at the Herodian site farther W., but at the great spring *'Ain es Sulṭân*, close to the mountains to which the spies escaped (**2** 16). The great mounds were found by Sir C. Warren to consist of sun-dried bricks, and further excavations (see *Mitteil. der deutschen Orient-Gesell.*, December, 1909, No. 41) have revealed little but the remains of houses of various dates.

(3) *Joshua's first campaign.*—The first city in the mountains attacked by Israel was Ai, near *Ḥayân*, 2 miles S. E. of Bethel. It has a deep valley to the N., as described (Josh **8** 22). The fall of Ai and Bethel (ver 17) seems to have resulted in the peaceful occupation of the region between Gibeon and Shechem (**8** 30—**9** 27); but while the Hivites submitted, the Amorites of Jerus and of the S. attacked Gibeon (*el Jîb*) and were driven down the steep pass of Beth-horon (*Beit 'Aûr*) to the plains (**10** 1–11). Joshua's great raid, after this victory, proceeded through the plain to Makkedah, now called *el Mughâr*, from the "cave" (cf **10** 17), and by Libnah to Lachish (*Tell el Ḥesy*), whence he went up to Hebron, and "turned" S. to Debir (*edh Ḍhâherîyeh*), thus subduing the *shᵉphēlāh* of Judah and the southern mountains, though the capital at Jerus was not taken. It is now very generally admitted that the six letters of the Amorite king of Jerus included in Am Tab may refer to this war. The *'Abîri* or *Ḥabiri* are therein noticed as a fierce people from Seir, who "destroyed all the rulers," and who attacked Ajalon, Lachish, Ashkelon, Keilah (on the main road to Hebron) and other places (see EXODUS, THE).

(4) *The second campaign* (**11** 1–14) was against the nations of Galilee; and the Heb victory was gained at "the waters of Merom" (ver 5). There is no sound reason for placing these at the *Ḥûleh* lake; and the swampy Jordan valley was a very unlikely field of battle for the Can. chariots (ver 6). The kings noticed are those of Madon (*Madîn*), Shimron (*Semmunieh*), Dor (possibly *Tell Thorah*), "on the west," and of Hazor (*Ḥazzûr*), all in Lower Galilee. The pursuit was along the coast toward Sidon (ver 8); and Merom may be identical with Shimron-meron (**12** 20), now *Semmunieh*, in which case the "waters" were those of the perennial stream in *Wâdy el Melek*, 3 miles to the N., which flow W. to join the lower part of the Kishon. Shimron-meron was one of the 31 royal cities of Pal W. of the Jordan (**12** 9–24).

The regions left unconquered by Joshua (**13** 2–6) were those afterward conquered by David and Solomon, including the Phili plains, and the Sidonian coast from Mearah (*el Mogheirîyeh*) northward to Aphek (*Afḳa*) in Lebanon, on the border of the Amorite country which lay S. of the "land of the Hittites" (**1** 4). Southern Lebanon, from Gebal (*Jubeil*) and the "entering into Hamath" (the Eleutherus Valley) on the W., to Baal-gad (probably at *'Ain Judeideh* on the northwestern slope of Hermon) was also included in the "land" by David (2 S **8** 6–10). But the whole of Eastern Pal (**13** 7–32), and of Western Pal, excepting the shore plains, was allotted to the 12 tribes. Judah and Joseph (Ephraim and Manasseh), being the strongest, appear to have occupied the mountains and the *shᵉphēlāh*, as far N. as Lower Galilee, before the final allotment.

Thus the lot of Simeon was within that inherited by Judah (**19** 1), and that of Dan seems to have been partly taken from Ephraim, since Joseph's lot originally reached to Gezer (**16** 3); but Benjamin appears to have received its portion early (cf **15** 5–11; **16** 1.2; **18** 11–28). This lot was larger than that of Ephraim, and Benjamin was not then the "smallest of the tribes of Israel" (1 S **9** 21), since the destruction of the tribe did not occur till after the death of Joshua and Eleazar (Jgs **20** 28).

The twelve tribes were distributed in various regions which may here briefly be described. **Reuben** held the Moab plateau to the Arnon (*Wâdy Môjub*) on the S., and to the "river of Gad" (*Wâdy Nâ'aûr*) on the N., thus including part of the Jordan valley close to the Dead Sea. **Gad** held all the W. of Gilead, being separated from the Ammonites by the upper course of the Jabbok. All the rest of the Jordan valley E. of the river was included in this lot. **Manasseh** held Bashan, but the conquest was not completed till later. **Simeon** had the *negheb* plateau S. of Beersheba. **Judah** occupied the mountains S. of Jerus, with the *shephēlāh* to their W., and claimed Philistia S. of Ekron. **Benjamin** had the Jericho plains and the mountains between Jerus and Bethel. The border ran S. of Jerus to Rachel's tomb (1 S **10** 2), and thence W. to Kiriath-jearim (*'Erma*) and Ekron. **Dan** occupied the lower hills W. of Benjamin and Ephraim, and claimed the plain from Ekron to Rakkon (*Tell er Raḳḳeit*) N. of Joppa. **Manasseh** had a large region, corresponding to Samaria, and including Carmel, Sharon and half the Jordan valley, with the mountains N. of Shechem; but this tribe occupied only the hills, and was unable to drive the Canaanites out of the plains (Josh **17** 11.16). **Ephraim** also complained of the smallness of its lot (ver 15), which lay in rugged mountains between Bethel and Shechem, including, however, the corn plateau E. of the latter city. **Issachar** held the plains of Esdraelon and Dothan, with the Jordan valley to the E., but soon became subject to the Canaanites. **Zebulun** had the hills of Lower Galilee, and the coast from Carmel to Accho. **Naphtali** owned the mountains of Upper Galilee, and the rich plateau between Tabor and the Sea of Galilee. **Asher** had the low hills W. of Naphtali, and the narrow shore plains from Accho to Tyre. Thus each tribe possessed a proportion of mountain land fit for cultivation of figs, olives and vines, and of arable land fit for corn. The areas allotted appear to correspond to the density of population that the various regions were fitted to support.

The Levitical cities were fixed in the various tribes as centers for the teaching of Israel (Dt **33** 10), but a Levite was not obliged to live in such a city, and was expected to go with his course annually to the sacred center, before they retreated to Jerus on the disruption of the kingdom (2 Ch **11** 14). The 48 cities (Josh **21** 13–42) include 13 in Judah and Benjamin for the priests, among which Beth-shemesh (1 S **6** 13.15) and Anathoth (1 K **2** 26) are early noticed as Levitical. The other tribes had 3 or 4 such cities each, divided among Kohathites (10), Gershonites (13), and Merarites (12). The six Cities of Refuge were included in the total, and were placed 3 each side of the Jordan in the S., in the center, and in the N., namely Hebron, Shechem and Kedesh on the W., and Bezer (unknown), Ramoth (*Reimûn*) and Golan (probably *Saḥem el Jaulân*) E. of the river. Another less perfect list of these cities, with 4 omissions and 11 minor differences, mostly clerical, is given in **1** Ch **6** 57–81. Each of these cities had "suburbs," or open spaces, extending (Nu **35** 4) about a quarter-mile beyond the wall, while the fields, to about half a mile distant, also belonged to the Levites (Lev **25** 34).

2. Book of Judges

(1) *Early wars.*—In Jgs, the stories of the heroes who successively arose to save Israel from the heathen carry us to every part of the country. "After the death of Joshua" (**1** 1) the Canaanites appear to have recovered power, and to have rebuilt some of the cities which he had ruined. Judah fought the Perizzites ("villagers") at Berek (*Berḳah*) in the lower hills W. of Jerus, and even set fire to that city. Caleb attacked Debir (vs 12–15), which is described (cf Josh **15** 15–19) as lying in a "dry" (AV "south") region, yet with springs not far away. The actual site (*edh Ḍhâherîyeh*) is a village with ancient tombs 12 miles S.W. of Hebron; it has no springs, but about 7 miles to the N.E. there is a perennial stream with "upper and lower springs." As regards the Phili cities (Jgs **1** 18), the LXX reading seems preferable; for the Gr says that Judah "did not take Gaza" nor Ashkelon nor Ekron, which agrees with the failure in conquering the "valley" (ver 19) due to the Canaanites having "chariots of iron." The Can. chariots are often mentioned about this time in the Am Tab and Egyp accounts speak of their being plated with metals. Manasseh, Ephraim, Zebulun, Asher and Naphtali, were equally powerless against cities in the plains (vs 27–33); and Israel began to mingle with the Canaanites, while the tribe of Dan seems never to have really occupied its allotted region, and remained encamped in the borders of Judah till some, at least, of its warriors found a new home under Hermon (**1** 34; **18** 1–30) in the time of Jonathan, the grandson of Moses.

(2) *Defeat of Sisera.*—The oppression of Israel by Jabin II of Hazor, in Lower Galilee, appears to have occurred in the time of Rameses II, who, in his 8th year, conquered Shalem (*Sâlim*, N. of Taanach), Anem (*'Anîn*), Dapur (*Debûrieh*, at the foot of Tabor), with Bethanath (*'Ainitha*) in Upper Galilee (Brugsch, *Hist Egypt*, II, 64). Sisera may have been an Egyp resident at the court of Jabin (Jgs **4** 2); his defeat occurred near the foot of Tabor (ver 14) to which he advanced E. from Harosheth (*el Ḥarathîyeh*) on the edge of the sea plain. His host "perished at Endor" (Ps **83** 9) and in the swampy Kishon (Jgs **5** 21). The site of the Kedesh in "the plain of swamps" (**4** 11) to which he fled is doubtful. Perhaps Kedesh of Issachar (1 Ch **6** 72) is intended at *Tell Ḳadeis*, 3 miles N. of Taanach, for the plain is here swampy in parts. The Can. league of petty kings fought from Taanach to Megiddo (**5** 19), but the old identification of the latter city with the Rom town of Legio (*Lejjûn*) was a mere guess which does not fit with Egyp accounts placing Megiddo near the Jordan. The large site at *Mugedd'a*, in the Valley of Jezreel seems to be more suitable for all the OT as well as for the Egyp accounts (*SWP*, II, 90–99).

(3) *Gideon's victory.*—The subsequent oppression by Midianites and others would seem to have coincided with the troubles which occurred in the 5th year of Minepthah (see EXODUS, THE). Gideon's home (Jgs **6** 11) at Ophrah, in Manasseh, is placed by Sam tradition at *Fer'ata*, 6 miles W. of Shechem, but his victory was won in the Valley of Jezreel (**7** 1–22); the sites of Beth-shittah (*Shaṭṭa*) and Abel-meholah (*'Ain Ḥelweh*) show how Midian fled down this valley and S. along the Jordan plain, crossing the river near Succoth (*Tell Der'ala*) and ascending the slopes of Gilead to Jogbehah (*Jubeiḥah*) and Nobah (**8** 4–11). But Oreb ("the raven") and Zeeb ("the wolf") perished at "the raven's rock" and "the wolf's hollow" (cf **7** 25), W. of the Jordan. It is remarkable (as pointed out by the present author in 1874) that, 3 miles N. of Jericho, a sharp peak is now called "the raven's nest," and a ravine 4 miles farther N. is named "the wolf's hollows." These sites are rather farther S. than might be expected, unless the two chiefs were separated from the fugitives, who followed Zebah and Zalmunna to Gilead. In this episode "Mt. Gilead" (**7** 3) seems to be a clerical error for "Mt. Gilboa," unless the name survives in corrupt form at *'Aîn Jâlûd* ("Goliath's spring"), which is a large pool, usually supposed to be the spring of Harod (**7** 1), where Gideon camped, E. of Jezreel.

The story of Abimelech takes us back to Shechem. He was made king by the "oak of the pillar" (**9** 6), which was no doubt Abraham's oak already noticed; it seems also to be called 'the enchanter's oak' (ver 37), probably from some superstition connected with the burial of the Teraphim under it by Jacob. The place called Beer, to which Jotham fled from Abimelech (ver 21), may have been

Beeroth (*Bîreh*) in the lot of Benjamin. Thebez, the town taken by the latter (ver 50), and where he met his death, is now the village *Ṭûbâs*, 10 miles N.E. of Shechem.

The Ammonite oppression of Israel in Gilead occurred about 300 years after the Heb conquest (**11** 26), and Jephthah the deliverer returned to Mizpah (ver 29), which was probably the present village *Ṣûf* (already noticed), from his exile in the "land of Tob" (vs 3.6). This may have been near *Ṭaiyibeh*, 9 miles S. of Gadara, in the extreme N. of Gilead—a place notable for its ancient dolmens and rude stone monuments, such as occur also at Mizpah. Jephthah's dispute with the men of Ephraim (**12** 1) indicates the northern position of Mizpah. Aroer (**11** 33) is unknown, but lay near Rabbath-ammon (Josh **13** 25; 2 S **24** 5); it is to be distinguished from Aroer (*'Ar'aîr*) in the Arnon ravine, mentioned in Jgs **11** 26.

The scene of Samson's exploits lies in the *shephēlāh* of Judah on the borders of Philistia. His home at Zorah (*Ṣŭr'ah*) was on the hills N. of the Valley of Sorek, and looked down on "the camp of Dan" (**13** 25 m), which had been pitched in that valley near Beth-shemesh. Eshtaol (*Eshu'a*) was less than 2 miles E. of Zorah on the same ridge. Timnath (**14** 1) was only 2 miles W. of Beth-shemesh, at the present ruin *Tibneh*. The region was one of vineyards (ver 5), and the name Sorek (*Sûrîk*) still survives at a ruin 2 miles W. of Zorah. Sorek signified a "choice vine," and a rock-cut wine press exists at the site (*SWP*, III, 126). These 5 places, all close together, were also close to the Phili corn lands (**15** 5) in a region of vines and olives. Samson's place of refuge in the "cleft of the rock of Etam" (see **15** 8) was probably at *Beit 'Aṭâb*, only 5 miles E. of Zorah, but rising with a high knoll above the southern precipices of the gorge which opens into the Valley of Sorek. In this knoll, under the village, is a rock passage now called "the well of refuge" (*Bîr el Ḥasûtah*), which may have been the "cleft" into which Samson "went down." Lehi (ver 9) was apparently in the valley beneath, and the name ("the jaw") may refer to the narrow mouth of the gorge whence, after conference with the Philis, the men of Judah "went down" (ver 11) to the "cleft of the rock of Etam" (*SWP*, III, 83, 137), which was a passage 250 ft. long leading down, under the town, to the spring. All of Samson's story is connected with this one valley (for Delilah also lived in the "Valley of Sorek," **16** 4) excepting his visit to Gaza, where he carried the gates to the 'hill facing Hebron' (**16** 3), traditionally shown (*SWP*, III, 255) at the great mound on the E. side of this town where he died, and where his tomb is (wrongly) shown. Another tomb, close to Zorah, represents a more correct tradition (**16** 31), but the legends of Samson at this village are of modern Christian origin.

The appendix to Jgs includes two stories concerning Levites who both lived in the time of the 2d generation after the Heb conquest (**18** 30; **20** 28), and who both "sojourned" in Bethlehem of Judah (**17** 8; **19** 2), though their proper city was one in Mt. Ephraim. In the first case Jonathan, the grandson of Moses, founded a family of idolatrous priests, setting up Micah's image at Dan (*Tell el Ḳâḍî*) beside the sources of the Jordan, where ancient dolmen altars still exist. This image may have been the cause why Jeroboam afterward established a calf-temple at the same place. It is said to have stood there till the "captivity of the ark" (St. Petersburg MS, Jgs **18** 30), "all the time that the house of God was in Shiloh" (ver 31). From this narrative we learn that the tribe of Dan did not settle in its appointed lot (**18** 1), but pitched in the "camp of Dan," west of Kiriath-jearim (ver 12). This agrees with the former mention of the site (**13** 25) as being near Zorah; and the open valley near Beth-shemesh is visible, through the gorges of Lehi, from the site of Kiriath-jearim at *'Erma*.

(4) *Appendix: Defeat of Benjamin.*—In the 2d episode we trace the journey of the Levite from Bethlehem past Jerus to Gibeah (*Jeba'*), E. of Ramah (*er-Râm*), a distance which could easily be traversed in an afternoon (cf **19** 8–14). Gibeah was no doubt selected as a halting-place by the Levite, because it was a Levitical city. The story of the great crime of the men of Gibeah was well known to Hosea (**9** 9). Israel gathered against them at Mizpah (*Tell en Naṣbeh*) on the watershed, 3 miles to the N.W., and the ark was brought by Phinehas to Bethel (cf **20** 1.31; **18** 26.27), 3 miles N.E. of Mizpah. The defeat of Benjamin occurred where the road to Gibeah leaves the main north road to Bethel (ver 31), W. of Ramah. The survivors fled to the rock Rimmon (*Rummôn*), 3½ miles E. of Bethel, on the edge of the "wilderness" which stretches from this rugged hill toward the Jordan valley. The position of Shiloh, 9 miles N. of this rock, is very accurately described (**21** 19) as being N. of Bethel (*Beitîn*), and E. of the main road, thence to Shechem which passes Lebonah (*Lubban*), a village 3 miles N.W. of *Seilûn* or Shiloh. The "vineyards," in which the maidens of Shiloh used to dance (ver 20) at the Feast of Tabernacles, lay no doubt where vineyards still exist in the little plain S. of this site. It is clear that the writer of these two narratives had an acquaintance with Palestinian topography as exact as that shown throughout Jgs. Nor (if the reading "captivity of the ark" be correct) is there any reason to suppose that they were written after 722 BC.

3. Book of Ruth

The Book of Ruth gives us a vivid picture of Heb life "when the judges ruled" (**1** 1 AV), about a century before the birth of David. Laws as old as Ḥammurabi's age allowed the widow the choice of remaining with the husband's family, or of quitting his house (cf **1** 8). The beating out of gleanings (**2** 17) by women is still a custom which accounts for the rock mortars found so often scooped out on the hillside. The villager still sleeps, as a guard, beside the heap of winnowed corn in the threshing-floor (**3** 7); the head-veil, still worn, could well have been used to carry six measures of barley (ver 15). The courteous salutation of his reapers by Boaz (**2** 4) recalls the common Arab. greeting (*Allah ma'kûm*), "God be with you." But the thin wine (ver 14) is no longer drunk by Moslem peasants, who only "dip" their bread in oil.

4. Books of Samuel

(1) *Samuel.*—The two Books of S present an equally valuable picture of life, and an equally real topography throughout. Samuel's father—a pious Levite (1 Ch **6** 27)—descended from Zuph who had lived at Ephratah (Bethlehem; cf 1 S **9** 4.5), had his house at Ramah (**1** 19) close to Gibeah, and this town (*er-Râm*) was Samuel's home also (**7** 17; **25** 1). The family is described as 'Ramathites, Zuphites of Mt. Ephraim' (**1** 1), but the term "Mt. Ephraim" was not confined to the lot of Ephraim, since it included Bethel and Ramah, in the land of Benjamin (Jgs **4** 5). As a Levite, Elkanah obeyed the law of making annual visits to the central shrine, though this does not seem to have been generally observed in an age when "every man did that which was right in his own eyes" (Jgs **21** 25). The central shrine had been removed by Joshua from Shechem to the remote site of Shiloh (Josh **22** 9), perhaps for greater security, and here the tabernacle (ver 19) was pitched (cf 1 S **2** 22) and remained for 4 centuries till the death

of Eli. The great defeat of Israel, when the ark was captured by the Philis, took place not far from Mizpah (**4** 1), within an easy day's journey from Shiloh (cf ver 12). Ekron, whence it was sent back (**6** 16), was only 12 miles from Beth-shemesh (*'Ain-shems*), where the ark rested on a "great stone" (LXX, ver 18); and Beth-shemesh was only 4 miles W. of Kiriath-jearim (ver 21), which was in the mountains, so that its inhabitants "came down" from "the hill" (**6** 21; **7** 1) to fetch the ark, which abode there for 20 years, till the beginning of Saul's reign (**14** 18), when, after the war, it may have been restored to the tabernacle at Nob, to which place the latter was probably removed after Eli's death, when Shiloh was deserted. The exact site of Nob is not known, but probably (cf Isa **10** 32) it was close to Mizpah, whence the first glimpse of Jerus is caught, and thus near Gibeon, where it was laid up after the massacre of the priests (1 S **21** 1; **22** 9.18; 2 Ch **1** 3), when the ark was again taken to Kiriath-jearim (2 S **6** 2). Mizpah (*Tell en-Naṣbeh*) was the gathering-place of Israel under Samuel; and the "stone of help" (Eben-ezer) was erected, after his victory over the Philis, "between Mizpah and Shen" (1 S **7** 12)—the latter place (see LXX) being probably the same as Jeshanah (*'Ain Sînai*), 6 miles N. of Mizpah which Samuel visited yearly as a judge (ver 16).

(2) *Saul's search.*—The journey of Saul, who, "seeking asses found a kingdom," presents a topography which has often been misunderstood. He started (**9** 4) from Gibeah (*Jeba'*) and went first to the land of Shalisha through Mt. Ephraim. Baal-shalisha (2 K **4** 42) appears to have been the present *Kefr Thilth*, 18 miles N. of Lydda and 24 miles N.W. from Gibeah. Saul then searched the land of Shalim—probably that of Shual (1 S **13** 17), N.E. of Gibeah. Finally he went south beyond the border of Benjamin (**10** 2) to a city in the "land of Zuph," which seems probably to have been Bethlehem, whence (as above remarked) Samuel's family—descendants of Zuph—came originally. If so, it is remarkable that Saul and David were anointed in the same city, one which Samuel visited later (**16** 1.2 ff) to sacrifice, just as he did when meeting Saul (**9** 12), who was probably known to him, since Gibeah and Ramah were only 2 miles apart. Saul's journey home thus naturally lay on the road past Rachel's tomb near Bethlehem, and along the Bethel road (**10** 2.3) to his home at Gibeah (vs 5.10). It is impossible to suppose that Samuel met him at Ramah—a common mistake which creates great confusion in the topography.

(3) *Saul's coronation and first campaign.*—Saul concealed the fact of his anointing (**10** 16) till the lot fell upon him at Mizpah. This public choice by lot has been thought (Wellhausen, *Hist Israel*, 1885, 252) to indicate a double narrative, but to a Hebrew there would not appear to be any discrepancy, since "The lot is cast into the lap; but the whole disposing thereof is of Jeh" (Prov **16** 33). Even at Mizpah he was not fully accepted till his triumph over the Ammonites, when the kingdom was "renewed" at Gilgal (**11** 14). This campaign raises an interesting question of geography. Only 7 days' respite was allowed to the men of Jabesh in Gilead (**11** 3), during which news was sent to Saul at Gibeah, and messengers dispatched "throughout the borders of Israel" (ver 7), while the hosts gathered at Bezek, and reached Jabesh on the 7th or 8th day (vs 8–10) at dawn. Bezek appears to be a different place from that W. of Jerus (Jgs **1** 4) and to have been in the middle of Pal at *Ibzîk*, 14 miles N. of Shechem, and 25 miles W. of Jabesh, which probably lay in *Wâdy Yâbis* in Gilead. The farthest distances for the messengers would not have exceeded 80 miles; and, allowing a day for the news to reach Saul and another for the march from Bezek to Jabesh, there would have been just time for the gathering of Israel at this fairly central meeting-place.

The scene of the victory over the Philis at Michmash is equally real. They had a 'post' in Geba (or Gibeah, **13** 3), or a governor (cf LXX), whom Jonathan slew. They came up to Michmash (*Mukhmâs*) to attack Jonathan's force which held Gibeah, on the southern side of the Michmash valley, hard by. The northern cliff of the great gorge was called Bozez ("shining") in contrast to the southern one (in shadow) which was named Seneh or "thorn" (**14** 4). Jos (*BJ*, V, ii, 2) says that Gibeah of Saul was by "the valley of thorns," and the ravine, flanked by the two precipitous cliffs E. of Michmash, is still called *Wâdy es Suweinît*, or "the valley of little thorn trees." Jonathan climbed the steep slope that leads to a small flat top (1 S **14** 14 AV), and surprised the Phili 'post.' The pursuit was by Bethel to the Valley of Aijalon, down the steep Beth-horon pass (vs 23.31); but it should be noted that there was no "wood" (vs 25.26) on this bare hilly ridge, and the word (cf Cant **5** 1) evidently means "honeycomb." It is also possible that the altar raised by Saul, for fulfilment of the Law (Gen **9** 4; Ex **20** 25), was at Nob where the central shrine was then established.

(4) *David's early life.*—David fed his flocks in the wilderness below Bethlehem, where many a silent and dreadful "Valley of Shadows" (cf Ps **23** 4) might make the stoutest heart fail. The lion crept up from the Jordan valley, and (on another occasion) the bear came down from the rugged mountains above (1 S **17** 34). No bears are now known S. of Hermon, but the numerous references (2 K **2** 24; Isa **59** 11; Hos **13** 8; Prov **17** 12; **28** 15) show that they must have been exterminated, like the lion, in comparatively late times. The victory over Goliath, described in the chapter containing this allusion, occurred in the Valley of Elah near Shochoth (*Shuweikeh*); and this broad valley (*Wâdy es Sunt*) ran into the Phili plain at the probable site of Gath (*Tell es Ṣâfi*) to which the pursuit led (1 S **17** 1.2.52). The watercourse still presents "smooth stones" (ver 40) fit for the sling, which is still used by Arab shepherds; and the valley still has in it fine "terebinths" such as those from which it took its name Elah. The bronze armor of the giant (vs 5.6) indicates an early stage of culture, which is not contradicted by the mention of an iron spearhead (ver 7), since iron is found to have been in use in Pal long before David's time. The curious note (ver 54) as to the head of Goliath being taken "to Jerus" is also capable of explanation. Jerus was not conquered till at least 10 years later, but it was a general practice (as late as the 7th cent. BC in Assyria) to preserve the heads of dead foes by salting them, as was probably done in another case (2 K **10** 7) when the heads of Ahab's sons were sent from Samaria to Jezreel to be exposed at the gate.

David's outlaw life began when he took refuge with Samuel at the "settlements" (Naioth) near Ramah, where the company of prophets lived. He easily met Jonathan near Gibeah, which was only 2 miles E.; and the "stone of departure" ("Ezel," 1 S **20** 19) may have marked the Levitical boundary of that town. Nob also (**21** 1) was, as we have seen, not far off, but Gath (ver 10) was beyond the Heb boundary. Thence David retreated up the Valley of Elah to Adullam (*'Aîd-el-ma*), which stood on a hill W. of this valley near the great turn (southward) of its upper course. An inhabited cave still exists here (cf **22** 1), and the site meets every requirement (*SWP*, III, 311, 347, 361–67). Keilah (**23** 1) is represented by the village *Kîla*, on the east side of the same valley, 3 miles farther up; and Hereth (**22** 5) was also near, but "in Judah" (**23** 3), at the village *Kharâs* on a wooded spur 7 miles N.W. of Hebron. Thence David went "down" (ver 4) to Keilah 2 miles away to the W. As there was no safety for the outlaws, either in Philistia or in Judah, they had to retreat to the wilderness of Ziph (*Tell ez Zîf*), 4 miles S.E. of Hebron. The word "wood" (*ḥōresh*) may more probably be a proper name, represented by the ruin of *Khoreisa*, rather more than a mile S. of Ziph, while the hill Hachilah (ver 19) might be the long spur, over the Jeshimon or desert of Judah, 6 miles E. of Ziph, now called *el Kôla*. Maon (*M'aîn*) lay on the edge of the same desert still farther S., about 8 miles from Hebron. En-gedi (**23** 29; **24** 1.2) was on the precipices by the Dead Sea. The "wild goats" (ibex) still exist here in large droves, and the caves of this desert are still used as folds for sheep in spring (ver 3). The villagers S. of Hebron are indeed remarkable for their large flocks which—by agreement with the nomads—are sent to pasture in the Jeshimon, like those of Nabal, the rich man of Carmel (*Kurmul*), a mile N. of Maon (**25** 2), who refused the customary present to David's band which had protected his shepherds "in the fields" (ver 15) or pastures of the wilderness. In summer David would naturally return to the higher ridge of Hachilah (**26** 1) on the south side of which there is a precipitous gorge (impassable save by a long détour), across which he talked to Saul (ver 13), likening himself (ver 20) to the desert "partridge" still found in this region.

(5) *Defeat and death of Saul.*—The site of Ziklag is doubtful, but it evidently lay in the desert S. of Beersheba (Josh **15** 31; **19** 5; 1 Ch **4** 30; 1 S **27** 6–12), far from Gath, so that King Achish did not know whether David had raided the S. of Judah, or the tribes toward Shur. Saul's power in the mountains was irresistible; and it was for this reason perhaps that his fatal battle with the Philis occurred far N. in the plain near Jezreel. They camped (1 S **28** 4) by the fine spring of Shunem (*Sûlem*), and Saul on Gilboa to the S. The visit to Endor (*Andûr*) was thus a perilous adventure, as Saul must have stolen by night round the Phili host to visit this place N. of Shunem. He returned to the spur of Gilboa on which Jezreel stands (**29** 1), and the spring noticed is a copious supply N. of the village *Zer'în*. Beth-shan (**31** 12) was at the mouth of the valley of Jezreel at *Beisân*, and here the bodies of Saul and his sons were burned by the men of Jabesh-gilead; but, as the bones were preserved (ver 13; 2 S **21** 13), it is possible that the corpses were cremated in pottery jars afterward buried under the tree. Excavations in Pal and in Babylonia show that this was an early practice, not only in the case of infants (as at Gezer, and Taanach), but also of grown men. See PALESTINE (RECENT EXPLORATION). The list of cities to which David sent presents at the time of Saul's death (**30** 26–31) includes those near Ziklag and as far N. as Hebron, thus referring to "all the places where David himself and his men were wont to haunt."

(6) *Wellhausen's theory of a double narrative.*—The study of David's wanderings, it may be noted, and of the climatic conditions in the Jeshimon desert, does not serve to confirm Wellhausen's theory of a double narrative, based on the secret unction and public choice of Saul, on the double visit to Hachilah, and on the fact that the gloomy king had forgotten the name of David's father. The history is not a "pious make-up" without "a word of truth" (Wellhausen, *Hist Israel*, 248–49); and David, as a "youth" of twenty years, may yet have been called a "man of war"; while "transparent artifice" (p. 251) will hardly be recognized by the reader of this genuine chronicle. Nor was there any "Aphek in Sharon" (p. 260), and David did not "amuse himself by going first toward the north" from Gibeah (p. 267); his visit to Ramah does not appear to be a "worthless anachronistic anecdote" (p. 271); and no one who has lived in the terrible Jeshimon could regard the meeting at Hachilah as a "jest" (p. 265). Nor did the hill ("the dusky top") "take its name from the circumstance," but Wellhausen probably means the *Ṣela'ha-maḥl^{e}kōth* ("cliff of slippings" or of "slippings away"), now *Wâdy Malâḳeh* near Maon (cf 1 S **23** 19.24.28), which lay farther S. than Ziph.

(7) *Early years of David's reign.*—David, till the 8th year of his reign, was king of Judah only. The first battle with Saul's son occurred at Gibeon (2 S **2** 13), where the "pool" was no doubt the cave of the great spring at *el Jîb;* the pursuit was by the 'desert Gibeon road' (ver 24) toward the Jordan valley. Gibeon itself was not in a desert, but in a fertile region. Abner then deserted to David, but was murdered at the "well of Sirah" (*'Ain Sârah*) on the road a mile N. of David's capital at Hebron. Nothing more is said about the Philis till David had captured Jerus, when they advanced on the new capital by the valley of Rephaim (**5** 22), which apparently ran from S. of Jerus to join the valley of Elah. If David was then at Adullam ("the hold," ver 17 AV; cf 1 S **22** 5), it is easy to understand how he cut off the Phili retreat (2 S **5** 23), and thus conquered all the hill country to Gezer (ver 25). After this the ark was finally brought from Baale-judah (Kiriath-jearim) to Jerus (**6** 2), and further wars were beyond the limits of Western Pal, in Moab (**8** 2) and in Syria (vs 3–12); but for "Syrians" (ver 13) the more correct reading appears to be Edomites (1 Ch **18** 12), and the "Valley of Salt" was probably S. of the Dead Sea. Another war with the Syrians, aided by Aramaeans from E. of the Euphrates, occurred E. of the Jordan (2 S **10** 16–18), and was followed by the siege of Rabbath-ammon (*'Ammân*), E. of Gilead, where we have notice of the "city of waters" (**12** 27), or lower town by the stream, contrasted, it seems, with the citadel which was on the northern hill.

(8) *Hebrew letter-writing.*—In this connection we find the first notice of a "letter" (**11** 14) as written by David to Joab. Writing is of course noticed as early as the time of Moses when—as we now know—the Canaanites wrote letters on clay tablets in cuneiform script. These, however, were penned by special scribes; and such a scribe is mentioned early (Jgs **8** 14). David himself may have employed a professional writer (cf 2 S **8** 17), while Uriah, who carried his own fate in the letter, was probably unable to read. Even in Isaiah's time the art was not general (Isa **29** 12), though Heb kings could apparently write and read (Dt **17** 18; 2 K **19** 14); to the present day the accomplishment is not general in the East, even in the upper class. It should be noted that the first evidence of the use of an alphabet is found in the early alphabetic Pss, and the oldest dated alphabetic text yet known is later than 900 BC. The script used in the time of Moses may have been cuneiform, which was still employed at Gezer for traders' tablets in 649 BC. The alphabet may have come into use first among Hebrews, through Phoen influence in the time of David; and so far no script except this and the cuneiform has been unearthed in Pal, unless it is to be recognized in signs of the Hittite syllabary at Lachish and Gezer. Another interesting point, as regards Heb civilization in David's time, is the first mention of "mules" (2 S **13** 29; **18** 9; 1 K **1** 33.38), which are unnoticed in the Pent. They are represented as pack animals on an Assyr bas-relief; but, had they been known to Moses, they would probably have been condemned as unclean. The sons of David fled on mules from Baal-hazor (*Tell 'Aṣûr*) "beside Ephraim" (now probably *Ṭaiyibeh*), N. of Bethel, where Absalom murdered Amnon.

(9) *Later years of David's reign.*—On the rebellion of Absalom David retreated to Mahanaim, apparently by the road N. of the Mount of Olives, if the Tg of Jonathan (2 S **16** 5) is correct in placing Bahurim at Almon (*'Almît*), N.E. of Jerus. It is not clear where the "wood of Ephraim," in which Absalom perished, may have been, but it was beyond Jordan in Gilead (**17** 22; **18** 6); and oak woods are more common there than in Western Pal. The latest revolt, after Absalom's death, was in the extreme north at Abel (*Abil*), in Upper Galilee (**20** 14), after which Joab's journey is the last incident to be studied in the Books of S. For census purposes he went E. of the Jordan to Aroer (perhaps the city on the Arnon), to the "river of Gad" (*Wâdy Nâ'aûr*) near Jazer, and through Gilead. Tahtim-hodshi (**24** 6) is believed (on the authority of three Gr MSS) to be a corruption of "the Hittites at Kadesh" (*Ḳades*), the great city on the Orontes (see HITTITES), which lay on the northern boundary of David's dominions, S. of the kingdom of Hamath. Thence Joab returned to Zidon and Tyre, and after visiting all Judah to Beersheba reached Jerus again within 10 months. The acquisition of the temple-site then closes the book.

5. Books of Kings

(1) *Solomon's provinces.*—The Books of K contain also some interesting questions of geography. Solomon's twelve provinces appear to answer very closely to the lots of the twelve tribes described in Josh. They included (1 K **4** 7–19) the following: (*a*) Ephraim, (*b*) Dan, (*c*) Southern Judah (see Josh **12** 17), (*d*) Manasseh, (*e*) Issachar, (*f*) Northern Gilead and Bashan, (*g*) Southern Gilead, (*h*) Naphtali, (*i*) Asher, (*j*) part of Issachar and probably Zebulun (the text is doubtful, for the order of ver 17 differs in LXX), (*k*) Benjamin, (*l*) Reuben. LXX renders the last clause (ver 19), "and one Naseph [i.e. "officer"] in the land of Judah"—probably superior to the other twelve. Solomon's dominions included Philistia and Southern Syria, and stretched along the trade route by Tadmor (Palmyra) to Tiphsah on the Euphrates (vs 21.24; cf **9** 18=Tamar; 2 Ch **8** 4=Tadmor). Another Tiphsah (now *Tafsaḥ*) lay 6 miles S.W. of Shechem (2 K **15** 16). Gezer was presented to Solomon's wife by the Pharaoh (1 K **9** 16).

(2) *Geography of the Northern Kingdom.*—Jeroboam was an Ephraimite (**11** 26) from Zereda, probably *Ṣurdah*, 2 miles N.W. of Bethel, but the LXX reads "Sarira," which might be *Ṣarra*, 1½ miles E. of Shiloh. After the revolt of the ten tribes, "Shishak king of Egypt" (**11** 40; **14** 25) sacked Jerus. His own record, though much damaged, shows that he not only invaded the mountains near Jerus, but that he even conquered part of Galilee. The border between Israel and Judah lay S. of Bethel, where Jeroboam's calf-temple was erected (**12** 29), Ramah (*er-Râm*) being a frontier town with Geba and Mizpah (**15** 17.22); but after the Syrian raid into Galilee (ver 20), the capital of Israel was fixed at Tirzah (ver 21), a place celebrated for its beauty (Cant **6** 4), and perhaps to be placed at *Teiaṣîr*, about 11 miles N.E. of Shechem, in romantic scenery above the Jordan valley. Omri reigned here also for six years (**16** 23) before he built Samaria, which remained the capital till 722 BC. Samaria appears to have been a city at least as large as Jerus, a strong site 5 miles N.W. of Shechem, commanding the trade route to its west. It resisted the Assyrians for 3 years, and when it fell Sargon took away 27,290 captives. Excavations at the site will, it may be hoped, yield results of value not as yet published. See next article.

The wanderings of Elijah extended from Zarephath (*Ṣurafend*), S. of Sidon, to Sinai. The position of the Brook Cherith (**17** 3) where—according to one reading—"the Arabs brought him bread and flesh" (**17** 6) is not known. The site of this great contest with the prophets of the Tyrian Baal is supposed to be at *el Maḥraḳah* ("the place of burning") at the southeastern end of the Carmel ridge. Some early king of Israel perhaps, or one of the

Brook Cherith (Looking N.E.).

judges (cf Dt **33** 19), had built an altar to Jeh above the Kishon (1 K **18** 20.40) at Carmel; but, as the water (ver 33) probably came from the river, it is doubtful whether this altar was on the "top of Carmel," 1,500 ft. above, from which Elijah's servant had full view of the sea (vs 42.43). Elijah must have run before Ahab no less than 15 miles, from the nearest point on Carmel (ver 46) to Jezreel, and the journey of the Shunammite woman to find Elisha (2 K **4** 25) was equally long. The vineyard of Naboth in Jezreel (1 K **21** 1) was perhaps on the east of the city (now *Zer'în*), where rock-cut wine presses exist. In the account of the ascension of Elijah, the expression "went down to Bethel" (2 K **2** 2) is difficult, if he went "from Gilgal" (ver 1). The town intended might be *Jiljilia*, on a high hill 7 miles N. of Bethel. LXX, however, reads "they came."

(3) *Places connected with Elisha.*—The home of Elisha was at Abel-meholah (1 K **19** 16) in the Jordan valley (Jgs **7** 22), probably at *'Ain Ḥelweh*, 10 miles S. of Beth-shan. If we suppose that Ophel (2 K **5** 24 RVm), where he lived, was the present *'Afûleh*, it is not only easy to understand that he would often "pass by" Shunem (which lay between Ophel and Abel-meholah), but also how Naaman might have gone from the palace of Jezreel to Ophel, and thence to the Jordan and back again to Ophel (vs 6.14.24), in the course of a single day in his chariot. The road down the valley of Jezreel was easy, and up it Jehu afterward drove furiously, coming from Ramoth in Gilead, and visible afar off from the wall of Jezreel (**9** 20). The 'top of the ascents' (ver 13), at Ramoth, refers no doubt to the high hill on which this city (now *Reimûn*) stood as a strong fortress on the border between Israel and the Syrians. The flight of Ahaziah of Judah, from Jezreel was apparently N. by Gur (*Ḳâra*), 4 miles W. of Ibleam (*Yebla*), on the road to "the garden house" (*Beit Jenn*), and thence by Megiddo (*Mujedda'*) down the Jordan valley to Jerus (**9** 27.28). Of the rebellion of Moab (2 K **1** 1; **3** 4) it is

enough to point out here that King Mesha's account on the M S agrees with the OT, even in the minute detail that "men of Gad dwelt in Ataroth from of old" (cf Nu **32** 34), though it lay in the lot of Reuben.

6. Post-exilic Historical Books

The topographical notices in the books written after the captivity require but short notice. The Benjamites built up Lod (*Ludd*), Ono (*Kefr 'Ana*) and Aijalon (*Yalo*), which were in the lot of Dan (1 Ch **8** 12; Neh **11** 35), and it is worthy of note that Lod (Lydda) is not to be regarded as a new town simply because not mentioned in the earlier books; for Lod is mentioned (no. 64) with Ono in the lists of Thothmes III, a century before the Heb conquest of Pal. The author of Ch had access to information not to be found elsewhere in the OT. His list of Rehoboam's fortresses (2 Ch **11** 6–10) includes 14 towns, most of which were on the frontiers of the diminished kingdom of Judah, some being noticed (such as Shoco and Adoraim) in the list of Shishak's conquests. He speaks of the "valley of Zephathah" (**14** 10), now *Wâdy Ṣâfieh*, which is otherwise unnoticed, and places it correctly at Mareshah (*Mer'ash*) on the edge of the Phili plain. He is equally clear about the topography in describing the attack on Jehoshaphat by the Ammonites, Moabites and Edomites. They camped at En-gedi (*'Ain Jidi*), and marched W. toward Tekoa (*Teḳu'a*); and the thanksgiving assembly, after the Heb victory, was in the valley of Beracah (2 Ch **20** 1.20.26), which retains its name as *Breikût*, 4 miles W. of Tekoa.

IV. Palestine in the Poetic Books of the OT.—

1. Book of Job

In Job the scene is distinctively Edomite. Uz (Job **1** 1; cf Gen **22** 21 ERV; Jer **25** 20; Lam **4** 21) and Buz (Job **32** 2; cf Gen **22** 21) are the Assyr *Ḥazu* and *Bazu* reached by Esarhaddon in 673 BC S. of Edom. Tema and Sheba (Job **6** 19) are noticed yet earlier, by Tiglath-pileser III, and Sargon, who conquered the Thamudites and Nabataeans. We have also the conjunction of snowy mountains and ice (Job **6** 16) with notice of the desert and the *'Arabah* valley (**24** 5), which could hardly apply to any region except Edom. Again, we have a nomad population dwelling close to a city (**29** 4–7)—perhaps Petra, or *Mâ'an* in Edom. There were mines, not only in the Sinaitic desert, but at Punon in Northern Edom (cf **28** 2–11). The white broom (**30** 4) is distinctive of the deserts of Moab and Edom. The wild ass and the ostrich (**39** 5.13) are now known only in the desert E. of Edom; while the stork (**39** 13 RVm) could have been found only in the *'Arabah*, or in the Jordan valley. The wild ox (**39** 9 RV), or *Bos primigenius*, is now extinct (LXX "unicorn," Nu **23** 22; Dt **33** 17), though its bones occur in Lebanon caves. It was hunted about 1130 BC in Syria by Tiglath-pileser I (cf Ps **29** 6), and is mentioned as late as the time of Isaiah (**34** 7) in connection with Edom; its Heb name (*r^{e'}ēm*) is the Assyr *rimu*, attached to a representation of the beast. As regards the crocodile ("leviathan," **41** 1), it was evidently well known to the writer, who refers to its strong, musky smell (ver 31), and it existed not only in Egypt but in Pal, and is still found in the Crocodile River, N. of Caesarea in Sharon. Behemoth (**40** 15), though commonly supposed to be the hippopotamus, is more probably the elephant (on account of its long tail, its trunk, and its habit of feeding in mountains, vs 17.20.24); and the elephant was known to the Assyrians in the 9th cent. BC, and was found wild in herds on the Euphrates in the 16th cent. BC. The physical allusions in Job seem clearly, as a rule, to point to Edom, as do the geographical names; and though Christian tradition in the 4th cent. AD (St. Silvia, 47) placed Uz in Bashan, the LXX (**42** 18) defines it as lying "on the boundary of Edom and Arabia." None of these allusions serves to fix dates, nor do the peculiarities of the language, though they suggest Aram. and Arab. influences. The mention of Babylonians (**1** 17) (*Kasdim*) as raiders may, however, point to about 600 BC, since they could not have reached Edom except from the N., and did not appear in Pal between the time of Amraphel (who only reached Kadesh-barnea), and of Nebuchadnezzar. It is at least clear (**24** 1–12) that this great poem was written in a time of general anarchy, and of Arab lawlessness.

2. Book of Psalms

In the Pss there are many allusions to the natural phenomena of Pal, but there is very little detailed topography. "The mountain of Bashan" (Ps **68** 15) rises E. of the plateau to 5,700 ft. above sea-level; but Zalmon (ver 14) is an unknown mountain (cf Zalmon, Jgs **9** 48). This Ps might well refer to David's conquest of Damascus (2 S **8** 6), as Ps **72** refers to the time of Solomon, being the last in the original collection of "prayers of David" (ver 20). In Ps **83** (vs 6–8) we find a confederacy of Edom, Ishmael, Moab and the Hagarenes (or "wanderers" E. of Pal; cf 1 Ch **5** 18–22) with Gebal (in Lebanon), Ammon, Amalek, and Tyre, all in alliance with Assyria—a condition which first existed in 732 BC, when Tiglath-pileser III conquered Damascus. The reference to the "northern" ("hidden") tribes points to this date (ver 3), since this conqueror made captives also in Galilee (2 K **15** 29; 1 Ch **5** 26; Isa **9** 1).

3. Book of Proverbs

In Prov the allusions are more peaceful, but not geographical. They refer to agriculture (**3** 10; **11** 26; **12** 11; **25** 13), to trade (**7** 16; **31** 14.24) and to flocks (**27** 23–27). The most remarkable passage (**26** 8) reads literally, "As he that packs a stone into the stone-heap, so is he that giveth honor to a fool." Jerome said that this referred to a superstitious custom; and the erection of stone heaps at graves, or round a pillar (Gen **31** 45.46), is a widely spread and very ancient custom (still preserved by Arabs), each stone being the memorial of a visitor to the spot, who thus honors either a local ghost or demon, or a dead man—a rite which was foolish in the eyes of a Hebrew of the age in which this verse was written (see *Expos T*, VIII, 399, 524).

4. Song of Songs

The geography of Cant is specially important to a right understanding of this bridal ode of the Syrian princess who was Solomon's first bride. It is not confined, as some critics say it is, to the north, but includes the whole of Pal and Syria. The writer names Kedar in North Arabia (**1** 5) and Egypt, whence horses came in Solomon's time (**1** 9; 1 K **10** 28.29). He knows the *henna* (AV "camphire") and the vineyards of En-gedi (**1** 14), where vineyards still existed in the 12th cent. AD. He speaks of the "rose" of Sharon (**2** 1), as well as of Lebanon, with Shenir (Assyr *Saniru*) and Hermon (**4** 8) above Damascus (**7** 4). He notices the pastoral slopes of Gilead (**6** 5), and the brown pool, full of small fish, in the brook below Heshbon (**7** 4), in Moab. The locks of the "peaceful one" (**6** 13, Vulg *pacifica*) are like the thick copses of Carmel; 'the king is caught in the tangles' (**7** 5). See Gallery. She is "beautiful as Tirzah [in Samaria], comely as Jerus, terrible to look at" (**6** 4 AV). She is a garden and a "paradise" ("orchard") of spices in Lebanon, some of which spices (calamus, cinnamon, frankincense and myrrh) have come from far lands (**4** 12–15). Solomon's vineyard—another emblem of the bride—(**1** 6; **8** 11) was in Baal-hamon, which some suppose to be Baal-hermon, still famous for its vineyards. He comes to fetch her from the wilderness (**3** 6); and the dust raised by his followers is like that of the whirlwind pillars which stalk over the dry plains of Bashan in summer. The single word "paradise" (**4** 13 m) is hardly evidence enough to establish late date, since—though used in Pers—its etymology and origin are unknown. The word for "nuts" (Heb *'ĕghōz*) is also not Pers (**6** 11), for the Arab. word جوز, *jauz*, is Sem, and means a "pair," applying to the walnut which abounds in Shechem. The "rose of Sharon" (**2** 1), according to the Tg, was the white "narcissus"; and the Heb word occurs also in Assyr (*ḥabaṣillatu*), as noted by Delitzsch (quoting *WAI*, V, 32, no. 4), referring to a white bulbous plant.

Sharon in spring is covered still with wild narcissi, Arab. *buṣeil* (cf Isa **35** 1.2). There is perhaps no period when such a poem is more likely to have been written than in the time of Solomon, when Israel "dwelt safely, every man under his vine and under his fig-tree" (1 K **4** 25); when the roe and the fallow deer (Cant **2** 17; 1 K **4** 23) abounded; and when merchants (Cant **3** 6) brought "powders" from afar; when also the dominion included Damascus and Southern Lebanon, as well as Western Pal with Gilead and Moab. See also SONG OF SONGS.

V. Palestine in the Prophets.—Isaiah (**1** 8) likens Zion, when the Assyr armies were holding Samaria, Moab and Philistia, to "a booth in a vineyard, a lodge in a garden of cucumbers." He refers no doubt to a "tower" (Mt **21** 33), or platform, such as is to be found beside the rock-cut wine press in the deserted vineyards of Pal; and such as is still built, for the watchman to stand on, in vineyards and vegetable gardens.

1. Isaiah

The chief topographical question (**10** 28–32) refers to the Assyr advance from the north, when the outposts covered the march through Samaria (whether in 732, 722, or 702 BC) to Philistia. They extended on the left wing to Ai (*Ḥayân*), Michmash (*Mukhmâs*), and Geba, S. of the Michmash valley (*Jeba'*), leading to the flight of the villagers, from Ramah (*er-Râm*) and the region of Gibeah—which included Ramah, with Geba (1 S **22** 6) and Migron (1 S **14** 2) or "the precipice." They were alarmed also at Gallim (*Beit Jâla*), and Anathoth (*'Anâta*), near Jerus; yet the advance ceased at Nob (cf Neh **11** 32) where, as before noted, the first glimpse of Zion would be caught if Nob was at or near Mizpah (*Tell en Naṣbeh*), on the main north road leading W. of Ramah.

Another passage refers to the towns of Moab (Isa **15** 1–6), and to Nimrim (*Tell Nimrîn*) and Zoar (*Tell esh Shâghûr*) in the valley of Shittim. The ascent of Luhith (ver 5) is the present *Ṭal'at el Ḥeith*, on the southern slope of Nebo (*Jebel Nebâ*). The curious term "a heifer of three years old" (cf Jer **48** 34 m) is taken from LXX, but might better be rendered "a round place with a group of three" (see EGLATH-SHELISHIYAH). It is noticed with the "high places" of Moab (Isa **15** 2; Jer **48** 35), and probably refers to one of those large and ancient stone circles, surrounding a central group of three rude pillars, which still remain in Moab (*SEP*, **I**, 187, 203,233) near Nebo and Zoar. Sibmah—probably *Sûmieh*, 2 miles S.W. of Heshbon (*Ḥesbân*)—is said to have had vines reaching to Jazer (*Sâ'aûr*, 6 miles to the N.); and rock-cut wine presses still remain at Sibmah (Isa **16** 8; Jer **48** 32). The Bozrah mentioned with Edom (Isa **34** 6; **63** 1; Jer **49** 13.22; Mic **2** 12) is probably *Buṣeirah*, near the southern border of Moab. In the last-cited passage there is a play on the words *baçrāh* ("fortress") and *boçrāh* for "sheepfold."

2. Jeremiah

In Jer (**1** 1), Anathoth (*'Anâta*) is mentioned as a priests' city (cf 1 K **2** 26). The "place" or shrine of Shiloh was deserted (Jer **7** 12), but the town seems still to have been inhabited (**41** 5). The "pit" at Mizpah (vs 6–9) may have been the great rock reservoir S. of *Tell en-Naṣbeh*. The Moabite towns noticed (**48** 1–5.20–24.31–45; **49** 3) with Rabbah (*'Ammân*) have been mentioned as occurring in the parallel passages of Isa. The numerous petty kings in Edom, Moab, Philistia, Phoenicia, and Arabia (**25** 20–24) recall those named in Assyr lists of the same age. Lam **4** 3 recalls Job **39** 14 in attributing to the ostrich want of care for her young, because she endeavors (like other birds) to escape, and thus draws away the hunter from the nest. This verse should not be regarded as showing that the author knew that whales were mammals, since the word "sea-monsters" (AV) is more correctly rendered "jackals" (RV) or "wild beasts."

PILGRIMS BATHING IN THE JORDAN.

3. Ezekiel

In Ezk (ch **27**), Tyre appears as a city with a very widespread trade extending from Asia Minor to Arabia and Egypt, and from Assyria to the isles (or "coasts") of the Mediterranean. The "oaks of Bashan" (**27** 6; Isa **2** 13; Zec **11** 2) are still found in the S.W. of that region near Gilead. Judah and Israel then provided wheat, honey, oil and balm for export as in the time of Jacob. Damascus sent white wool and the wine of Helbon (*Ḥelbôn*), 13 miles N., where fine vineyards still exist. The northern border described (**47** 15–18) is the same that marked that of the dominions of David, running along the Eleutherus River toward Zedad (*Ṣŭdŭd*). It is described also in Nu **34** 8–11 as passing Riblah (*Riblah*) and including Ain (*el 'Ain*), a village on the western slopes of the Anti-Lebanon, E. of Riblah. In this passage (as in Ezk **47** 18) the Hauran (or Bashan plain) is excluded from the land of Israel, the border following the Jordan valley, which seems to point to a date earlier than the time when the Havvoth-jair (Nu **32** 41; Dt **3** 14; Josh

13 30; Jgs **10** 4; 1 K **4** 13; 1 Ch **2** 23), in Gilead and Bashan, were conquered or built—possibly after the death of Joshua. The southern border of the land is described by Ezekiel (**47** 19) as reaching from Kadesh (-barnea)—probably Petra—to Tamar, which seems to be *Tamrah,* 6 miles N.E. of Gaza.

4. Minor Prophets

In the Minor Prophets there are fewer topographical notices. Hosea (**12** 11) speaks of the altars of Gilead and Gilgal as being "as heaps in the furrows of the fields." He perhaps alludes to the large dolmen-fields of this region, which still characterize the country E. of the Jordan. He also perhaps speaks of human sacrifice at Bethel (**13** 2). In Joel (**1** 12) the apple tree (Heb *tappūᵃḥ,* Arab. *tuffâḥ*) is noticed (cf Cant **2** 3.5; **8** 5), and there seems to be no reason to doubt that the apple was cultivated, since el Muḳaddasi mentions "excellent apples" at Jerus in the 10th cent. AD, though it is not now common in Pal. The sycamore fig (Am **7** 14), which was common in the plains and in the *shᵉphēlāh* (1 K **10** 27), grew also near Jericho (Lk **19** 4), where it is still to be found. In Mic (**1** 10–15), a passage which appears to refer to Hezekiah's reconquest of the *shᵉphēlāh* towns and attack on Gaza before 702 BC (2 K **18** 8; 2 Ch **28** 18) gives a list of places and a play on the name of each. They include Gath (*Tell es Ṣâfi*), Saphir (*es Sâfîr*), Lachish (*Tell el-Ḥesy*), Achzib (*'Ain Kezbeh*), and Mareshah (*Mer'ash*): "the glory of Israel shall come even unto Adullam" (*'Aid-el-ma*) perhaps refers to Hezekiah himself (Mic **1** 15). After the captivity Philistia (Zec **9** 5) was still independent. See Philistines. The meaning of the "mourning of Hadadrimmon in the Valley of Megiddon" (Zec **12** 11) is disputed. Jerome (see Reland, *Pal Illustr.*, II, 891) says that the former of these names referred to a town near Jezreel (Maximianopolis, now *Rummâneh,* on the western side of the plain of Esdraelon), but the mourning "for an only son" was probably a rite of the Syrian god called Hadad, or otherwise Rimmon, like the mourning for Tammuz (Ezk **8** 14).

VI. Palestine in the Apocrypha.

1. Book of Judith

—The Book of Jth is regarded by Renan (*Evangiles,* 1877, 29) as a *Haggādhā'* or legend, written in Heb in 74 AD. It is remarkable, however, that its geographical allusions are very correct. Judith was apparently of the tribe of Manasseh (**8** 2.3); and her husband, who bore this name, was buried between Dothaim (*Tell Dothân*) and Balamon (in *Wâdy Belameh*), E. of Dothan. Her home at Bethulia was thus probably at *Mithilieh,* on a high hill (**6** 11.12), 5 miles S.E. of Dothan (*SWP,* II, 156), in the territory of Manasseh. The requirements of the narrative are well met; for this village is supplied only by wells (**7** 13.20), though there are springs at the foot of the hill to the S. (**7** 7.12), while there is a good view over the valley to the N. (**10** 10), and over the plain of Esdraelon to Nazareth and Tabor. Other mountains surround the village (**15** 3). The camp of the invaders reached from Dothan to Belmaim (Balamon) from W. to E., and their rear was at Cyamon (*Tell Ḳeimûn*), at the foot of Carmel. The Babylonians were allied with tribes from Carmel, Gilead and Galilee on the N. with the Samaritans, and with others from Betane (probably Beth-anoth, now *Beit 'Ainûn,* N. of Hebron), Chellus (*Klalash*—the later Elusa—8 miles S.W. of Beersheba), and Kades (*'Ain Ḳadis*) on the way to Egypt. Among Samaritan towns S. of Shechem, Ekrebel (*'Aḳrabeh*) and Chusi (*Kûzah*) are mentioned, with "the brook Mochmur" (*Wâdy el Ḥumr*) rising N. of Ekrebel and running E. into the Jordan.

2. Book of Wisdom

The philosophical Book of Wisd has no references to Pal; and in Ecclus the only allusions are to the palm of En-gaddi (**24** 14), where palms still exist, and to the "rose plant in Jericho" (**24** 14; cf **39** 13; **50** 8); the description of the rose as "growing by the brook in the field" suggests the rhododendron (Tristram, *NHB,* 477), which flourishes near the Jordan and grows to great size beside the brooks of Gilead.

3. 1 Maccabees

Judas Maccabaeus.—The first Book of Macc is a valuable history going down to 135 BC, and its geographical allusions are sometimes important. Modin, the home of Judas Maccabaeus (**2** 15), where his brother Simon erected seven monuments visible from the sea (**9** 19; **13** 25–30), was above the plain in which Cedron (*Katrah,* 5 miles E. of Jamnia) stood (**15** 40.41 **16** 4.9), and is clearly the present village *el Midieh* on the low hills with a sea view, 17 miles from Jerus and 6 miles E. of Lydda, near which latter Eusebius (*Onom* s.v. "Modeim") places Modin. The first victory of Judas (**3** 24) was won at Beth-horon, and the second at Emmaus (*'Amwâs*) by the Valley of Aijalon—the scenes of Joshua's victories also.

The Greeks next attempted to reach Jerus from the S. and were again defeated at Beth-zur (**4** 29), now *Beit-ṣûr,* on the watershed, 15 miles S. of Jerus, where the road runs through a pass. Judas next (after cleansing the temple in 165 BC) marched S. of the Dead Sea, attacking the Edomites at Arabattine (perhaps Akrabbim) and penetrating to the Moab plateau as far N. as Jazar (**5** 3–8). On his return to Judaea the heathen of Gilead and Bashan rose against the Israelites of Tubias (ver 13) or Tob (*Taiyibeh*), and the Phoenicians against the Galilean Hebrews who were, for a time, withdrawn to Jerus until the Hasmoneans won complete independence (**11** 7.59). In the regions of Northern Gilead and Southern Bashan (**5** 26.36.37) Judas conquered Bosor (*Buṣr*), Alema (*Kefr el-ma*), Casphon (*Khisfîn*), Maged (perhaps *el Mejd,* N. of *'Ammân*), and Carnaim (Ashteroth-karnaim), now *Tell 'Ashterah.* The notice of a "brook" at the last-named place (ver 42) is an interesting touch, as a fine stream runs S. from the west side of the town. In 162 BC Judas was defeated at Bathzacharias (**6** 32), now *Beit Skâria,* 9 miles S. of Jerus, but the cause was saved by a revolt in Antioch; and in the next year he defeated Nicanor near Caphar-salama (perhaps *Selmeh,* near Joppa), and slew him at Adasah (*'Adaseh*), 8 miles S.E. of Beth-horon (**7** 31.40.45). The fatal battle in which Judas was killed (**9** 5.15) was fought also near Beth-horon. He camped at Eleasa (*Il'asa*), close by, and defeated the Greeks on his right, driving them to Mt. Azotus (or Beth-zetho, according to Jos [*Ant,* XII, xi, 2]), apparently near *Bîr-ez-Zeit,* 4 miles N.W. of Bethel; but the Greeks on his left surrounded him during this rash pursuit.

On the death of Judas, Bacchides occupied Judaea and fortified the frontier towns (**9** 50.51) on all sides. Simon and Jonathan were driven to the marshes near the Jordan, but in 159 BC the Greeks made peace with Jonathan who returned to Michmash (ver 73) and 7 years later to Jerus (**10** 1.7). Three districts on the southern border of Samaria were then added to Judaea (**10** 30; **11** 34), namely Lydda, Apherema (or Ephraim) now *Ṭaiyibeh,* and Ramathem (*er-Râm*); and Jonathan defeated the Greeks in Philistia (**10** 69; **11** 6). Simon was "captain" from the "Ladder of Tyre" (*Râs en Naḳûrah*), or the pass N. of Accho, to the borders of Egypt (**11** 59); and the Greeks in Upper Galilee were again defeated by Jonathan, who advanced from Gennesaret to the plain of Hazor (*Ḥazzûr*), and pursued them even to Kedesh Naphtali (*Ḳedes*), northward (vs 63.73). He was victorious even to the borders of Hamath, and the Eleutherus River (*Nahr el Kebîr*), N. of Tripolis, and defeated the Arabs, called Zabadeans (probably at *Zebdâny* in Anti-Lebanon), on his way to Damascus (**12** 25. 30.32). He fortified Adida (*Ḥaditheh*) in the *shᵉphēlāh* (ver 38), W. of Jerus, where Simon awaited the Gr usurper Tryphon (**13** 13.20), who attempted to reach Jerus by a long détour to the S. near Adoraim (*Dûra*), but failed on account of the snow in the mountains. After the treacherous capture of Jonathan at Accho, and his death in Gilead (**12** 48; **13** 23), Simon became the ruler of all Pal to Gaza (**13** 43), fortifying Joppa, Gezer and Ashdod (**14** 34) in 140 BC. Five years later he won a final victory at Cedron (*Ḳatrah*), near Jamnia (*Yebnah*), but was murdered at Dok (**16** 15), near Jericho, which site was a small fort at *'Ain Dûk,* a spring N. of the city.

4. 2 Maccabees

The second Book of Macc presents a contrast to the first in which, as we have seen, the geography is easily understood. Thus the site of Caspis with its lake (**12** 13.16) is doubtful. It seems to be placed in Idumaea, and Charax may be the fortress of *Kerak* in Moab (ver 17). Ephron, W. of Ashteroth-karnaim (vs 26.27), is unknown; and Beth-shean is called by its later name Scythopolis (ver 29), as in the LXX (Jgs **1** 27) and in Jos (*Ant,* XII, viii, 5; vi, 1). A curious passage (**13** 4–6) seems to refer to the Pers burial towers (still used by Parsees), one of which appears to have existed at Berea (Aleppo), though this was not a Gr custom. See Asmoneans.

VII. Palestine in the NT.

1. Synoptic Gospels

—We are told that Our Lord was born in "Bethlehem of Judaea"; and the theory of Neubauer, adopted by Grätz, that Bethlehem of Zebulun (Josh **19** 15)—which was the present *Beit-Lahm,* 7 miles N.W. of Nazareth—is to be understood, is based on a mistake. The

Jews expected the Messiah to appear in the home of David (Mic **5** 2); and the Northern Bethlehem was not called "of Nazareth," as asserted by Rix (*Tent and Testament*, 258); this was a conjectural reading by Neubauer (*Géog. du Talm*, 189), but the Talm (Talm Jerus, *Meghillah* **1** 1) calls the place *Bethleḥem-ṣerīdh* (or "of balm"), no doubt from the storax bush (*Styrax officinalis*) or stacte (Ex **30** 34), the Arab. *'abhar*, which still abounds in the oak wood close by.

(1) *Galilean scenery.*—The greater part of the life of Jesus was spent at Nazareth in Zebulun, and the ministry at Capernaum in Naphtali (cf Mt **4** 13–15; Isa **9** 1), with yearly visits to Jerus. The Gospel narratives and the symbolism of the parables constantly recall the characteristic features of Galilean scenery and nature, as they remain unchanged today. The "city set on a hill" (Mt **5** 14) may be seen in any part of Pal; the lilies of the field grow in all its plains; the "foxes have holes" and the sparrows are still eaten; the vineyard with its tower; the good ploughland, amid stony and thorny places, are all still found throughout the Holy Land. But the deep lake surrounded by precipitous cliffs and subject to sudden storms, with its shoals of fish and its naked fishers; the cast nets and drag nets and small heavy boats of the Sea of Galilee, are more distinctive of the Gospels, since the lake is but briefly noticed in the OT.

Traditional Mount of the Precipitation near Nazareth.

(2) Nazareth was a little village in a hill plateau N. of the plain of Esdraelon, and 1,000 ft. above it. The name (Heb *nāçārāh*) may mean "verdant," and it had a fine spring, but it is connected (Mt **2** 23) in the Gospels with the prophecy of the "branch" (*nēçer*, Isa **11** 1) of the house of David. Its population was Hebrew, for it possessed a synagogue (Lk **4** 16). The "brow of the hill whereon their city was built" (**4** 29) is traditionally the "hill of the leap" (*Jebel Ḳafsi*), 2 miles to the S.—a cliff overlooking the plain. Nazareth was not on any great highway; and so obscure was this village that it is unnoticed in the OT, or by Jos, while even a Galilean (Jn **1** 46) could hardly believe that a prophet could come thence. Jerome (*Onom* s.v.) calls it a "village"; but today it is a town with 4,000 Christians and 2,000 Moslems, the former taking their Arab. name (*Naṣârah*) from the home of their Master.

Plowing near Nazareth.

(3) Capernaum (Mt **4** 13; **9** 1) lay on the shore of the Sea of Galilee, apparently (Mt **14** 34; Jn **6** 17) in the little plain of Gennesaret, which stretches for 3 miles on the northwest side of the lake, and which has a breadth of 2 miles. It may have stood on a low cliff (though this is rendered doubtful by the Sin. MS rendering of Mt **11** 23—"Shalt thou be exalted unto heaven?"), and it was a military station where taxes were levied (**9** 9), and possessed a synagogue (Mk **1** 21; Lk **4** 33; Jn **6** 59). Christian tradition, since the 4th cent. AD, has placed the site at *Tell Ḥûm*, where ruins of a synagogue (probably, however, not older than the 2d cent. AD) exist; but this site is not in the plain of Gennesaret, and is more probably *Kephar 'Aḥīm* (Talm Bab, *Menāḥōth* **85***a*). Jewish tradition (*Midhrash Ḳōheleth*, vii.20) connects Capernaum with *mīnīm* or "heretics"—that is to say Christians—whose name may yet linger at *'Ain Minyeh* at the north end of the plain of Gennesaret. Jos states (*BJ*, III, x, 8) that the spring of Capernaum watered this plain, and contained the catfish (*coracinus*) which is still found in *'Ain el Mudawwerah* ("the round spring"), which is the principal source of water in the Gennesaret oasis.

(4) The site of Chorazin (*Kerâzeh*) has never been lost. The ruined village lies about 2¼ miles N. of *Tell Ḥûm* and possesses a synagogue of similar character. Bethsaida ("the house of fishing") is once said to have been in Galilee (Jn **12** 21), and Reland (*Pal Illustr.*, II, 553–55) thought that there were two towns of the name. It is certain that the other notices refer to Bethsaida, called Julias by Herod Philip, which Jos (*Ant*, XVIII, ii, 1; iv, 6; *BJ*, III, x, 7) and Pliny (*NH*, v.15) place E. of the Jordan, near the place where it enters the Sea of Galilee. The site may be at the ruin *ed Dikkeh* ("the platform"), now 2 miles N. of the lake, but probably nearer of old, as the river deposit has increased southward. There are remains of a synagogue here also. The two miracles of feeding the 5,000 and the 4,000 are both described as occurring E. of the Jordan, the former (Lk **9** 10) in the desert (of Golan) "belonging to the city called Bethsaida" (AV). The words (Mk **6** 45 AV), "to go to the other side before unto Bethsaida," may be rendered without any straining of grammar, "to go to the side opposite to Bethsaida." For the disciples are not said to have reached that city; but, after a voyage of at least 3 or 4 miles (Jn **6** 17.19), they arrived near Capernaum, and landed in Gennesaret (Mk **6** 53), about 5 miles S.W. of the Jordan.

(5) The place where the swine rushed down a steep place into the lake (Mt **8** 32; Mk **5** 1; Lk **8** 26) was in the country of the Gerasenes (see Vat. MS), probably at *Ḳersa* on the eastern shore opposite Tiberias, where there is a steep slope to the water. It should be noted that this was in Decapolis (Mk **5** 20), a region of "ten cities" which lay (except Scythopolis) in Southwest Bashan, where a large number of early Gr inscriptions have been found, some of which (e.g. Vogüé-Waddington, nos. 2412, 2413) are as old as the 1st cent. AD. There was evidently a Gr population in this region in the time of Our Lord; and this accounts for the feeding of swine, otherwise distinctive of "a far country" (Lk **15** 13.15); for, while no Hebrew would have tended the unclean beast in Pal, the Greeks were swineherds from the time at least of Homer.

(6) The site of Magadan-Magdala (*Mejdel*) was

on the west shore at the S.W. end of the Gennesaret plain (Mt **15** 39). In Mk **8** 10 we find Dalmanutha instead. Magdala was the Heb *mighdōl* ("tower"), and Dalmanutha may be regarded as the Aram. equivalent (*D^{e}'almānūthā*) meaning "the place of high buildings"; so that there is no necessary discrepancy between the two accounts. From this place Jesus again departed by ship to "the other side," and reached Bethsaida (Mt **16** 5; Mk **8** 13.22), traveling thence up the Jordan valley to Caesarea Philippi (Mt **16** 13; Mk **8** 27), or *Bâniâs*, at the Jordan springs. There can be little doubt that the "high mountain apart" (Mt **17** 1) was Hermon. The very name signifies "separate," applying to its solitary dome; and the sudden formation of cloud on the summit seems to explain the allusion in Lk **9** 34.

(7) Other allusions in the Synoptic Gospels, referring to natural history and customs, include the notice of domestic fowls (Mt **23** 37; **26** 34), which are never mentioned in the OT. They came from Persia, and were introduced probably after 400 BC. The use of manure (Lk **13** 8) is also unnoticed in the OT, but is mentioned in the Mish (*Sh^{e}bī'īth*, ii.2), as is the custom of annually whitening sepulchers (Mt **23** 27; *Sh^{e}ḳālīm*, i.1). The removal of a roof (Mk **2** 4; cf Lk **5** 19) at Capernaum was not difficult, if it resembled those of modern Galilean mud houses, though the Third Gospel speaks of "tiles" which are not now used. Finally, the presence of shepherds with their flocks (Lk **2** 8) is not an indication of the season of the nativity, since they remain with them "in the field" at all times of the year; and the "manger" (Lk **2** 7) may have been (as tradition affirmed even in the 2d cent. AD) in a cave like those which have been found in ruins N. and S. of Hebron (*SWP*, III, 349, 369) and elsewhere in Pal.

2. Fourth Gospel

(1) The topography of the Fourth Gospel is important as indicating the writer's personal knowledge of Pal; for he mentions several places not otherwise noticed in the NT. Beth-abarah (Jn **1** 28, RV "Bethany"; **10** 40), or "the house of the crossing," was "beyond the Jordan." Origen rejected the reading "Bethania," instead of Beth-abarah, common in his time, and still found in the three oldest uncial MSS in the 4th and 5th cents. AD. The place was a day's journey from Cana (cf Jn **1** 29.35.43; **2** 1), which may have been at *'Ain Ḳânâ*, a mile N. of Nazareth. It was two or three days' distance from Bethany near Jerus (Jn **10** 40; **11** 3.6.17), and would thus lie in the upper part of the Jordan valley where, in 1874, the surveyors found a ford well known by the name *'Abârah*, N. of *Beisân*, in the required situation. John, we are told, baptized in "all the region round about the Jordan" (Mt **3** 5), including the waters of "Ænon near to Salim" (Jn **3** 23). There is only one stream which answers to this description, namely that of *Wâdy Fâr'ah*, N.E. of Shechem, on the boundary of Judaea and Samaria, where there is "much water." Ænon would be *'Ainûn*, 4 miles N., and Salim is *Sâlim*, 4 miles S. of this perennial affluent of the Jordan.

(2) The site of Sychar (Sam *Iskar*, Arab. *'Askar*) near Jacob's well (Jn **4** 5.6) lay W. of Salim, and just within the Sam border. The present village is only half a mile N. of the well. Like the preceding sites, it is noticed only in the Fourth Gospel, as is Bethesda, while this Gospel also gives additional indications as to the position of Calvary. The town of Ephraim, "near to the wilderness" (**11** 54), is noticed earlier (2 S **13** 23; cf Ephraim, 2 Ch **13** 19 m), and appears to be the same as Apherema (1 Macc **11** 34), and as Ophrah of Benjamin (Josh **18** 23; 1 S **13** 17). Eusebius (*Onom* s.v.) places it 20 Rom miles N. of Jerus, where the village *Ṭaiyibeh* looks down on the desert of Judah.

3. Book of Acts

In the Book of Acts the only new site, unnoticed before, is that of Antipatris (**23** 31). This stood at the head of the stream (Me-jarkon) which runs thence to the sea N. of Joppa, and it was thus the half-way station between Jerus and the seaside capital at Caesarea. The site is now called *Râs el 'Ain* ("head of the spring"), and a castle, built in the 12th cent., stands above the waters. The old Rom road runs close by (*SWP*, II, 258). Caesarea was a new town, founded by Herod the Great about 20 BC (*SWP*, II, 13–29). It was even larger than Jerus, and had an artificial harbor. Thence we may leave Pal with Paul in 60 AD. The reader must judge whether this study of the country does not serve to vindicate the sincerity and authenticity of Bible narratives in the OT and the NT alike.

LITERATURE.—Though the lit. connected with Pal is enormous, and constantly increasing, the number of really original and scientific sources of knowledge is (as in other cases) not large. Besides the Bible, and Jos, the Mish contains a great deal of valuable information as to the cultivation and civilization of Pal about the 1st and 2d cents. AD. The following 20 works are of primary importance. The *Onomasticon* of Eusebius and Jerome shows intimate acquaintance with Pal in the 4th cent. AD, though the identification of Bible sites is as often wrong as right. The rabbinical geography is discussed by A. Neubauer (*La géographie du Talmud*, 1868), and the scattered notices by Gr and Rom writers were collected by H. Reland (*Palaestina ex monumentis veteribus illustrata*, 2 vols, 1714). The first really scientific account of the country is that of Dr. E. Robinson (*Bib. Researches*, 1838, and *Later Bib. Researches*, 1852; in 3 vols, 1856). *The Survey of Western Pal* (7 vols, 1883) includes the present writer's account of the natural features, topography and surface remains of all ages, written while in command (1872–78) of the 1-inch trigonometric survey. *The Survey of Eastern Pal* (1 vol, 1889) gives his account of Moab and Southern Gilead, as surveyed in 1881–82. The natural history is to be studied in the same series, and in Canon Tristram's *Natural History of the Bible*, 1868. The geology is best given by L. Lartet (*Essai sur la géologie de la Palestine*) and in Professor Hull's *Memoir on the Geol. and Geog. of Arabia Petraea*, etc, 1886. The *Archaeological Researches* of M. Clermont-Ganneau (2 vols, 1896) include his discoveries of Gezer and Adullam. Much information is scattered through the *PEFQ* (1864–1910) and in *ZDPV*. G. Schumacher's *Across the Jordan*, 1885, *Pella*, 1888, and *Northern 'Ajlûn*, 1890, give detailed information for Northeast Pal; and *Lachish*, by Professor Flinders Petrie, is the memoir of the excavations which he began at *Tell el-Ḥesy* (identified in 1874 by the present writer), the full account being in *A Mound of Many Cities* by F. J. Bliss, 1894. Other excavations, at Gath, etc, are described in *Excavations in Pal* (1898–1900), by F. J. Bliss, R. A. S. Macalister, and Professor Wünsch; while the mémoir of his excavations at Gezer (2 vols) has recently been published by Professor Macalister. For those who have not access to these original sources, *The Historical Geography of the Holy Land* by Professor G. A. Smith, 1894, and the essay (300 pp.) by Professor D. F. Buhl (*Geographie des alten Palästina*, 1896) will be found useful. The best guide book to Pal is still that of Baedeker, written by Dr. A. Socin and published in 1876[5], 1912. This author had personal acquaintance with the principal routes of the country. Only standard works of reference have been herein mentioned, to which French, German, American, and British explorers and scholars have alike contributed. See JERUSALEM.

C. R. CONDER

PALESTINE (RECENT EXPLORATION):

Preliminary Consideration

Previous to the last century, almost the entire stock of knowledge concerning ancient Pal, including its races, laws, languages, history and manners, was obtained from Jos and the Bible, with a few brief additional references given by Gr and Rom authors; knowledge concerning modern Pal was limited to the reports of chance travelers. The change has been due largely to the compelling interest taken in sacred history and the "Holy Oracles." This smallest country in the world has aroused the spirit of exploration as no other country has or could. It has largely stimulated many of the investigations carried on in other lands.

I. Era of Preparation.—Much direct information concerning ancient Pal, absolutely essential to the success of modern exploration in that land, has come through discoveries in other countries; but due in many cases to Bib. influence.

1. Outside of Palestine

All the most important Heb and Gr MSS and VSS of the Bible and most of the Jewish Talm and apocryphal and Wisdom books were found outside of Pal. The pictures of its population, cities, fortresses and armies give a color and perspective to its ancient history far more vivid than can be found on any of its own contemporary monuments. The records of Thothmes III (15th cent. BC) describing the capture of Megiddo in the plain of Esdraelon with its vast stores of "chariots wrought with gold," bronze armor, silver and ebony statues, ivory and ebony furniture, etc, and of his further capture of 118 other Can. towns, many of which are well known from the Bible, and from which he takes an enormous tribute of war materials, golden ornaments and golden dishes, "too many to be weighed," find no parallel in any indigenous record—such records even if written having been doomed to perish because of the soil, climate and character of the rocks W. of the Jordan. So c 1400 BC, the Am Tab (discovered in 1887) mention by name many Bib. cities, and give much direct information concerning the political and social conditions at that period, with at least 6 letters from the governor of Jerus, who writes to the Pharaoh news that the Egyp fleet has left the coast, that all the neighboring cities have been lost to Egypt, and that Jerus will be lost unless help can be had quickly against the invasion of the Khabiri. The literature of the XIXth Dynasty contains many Heb names with much information concerning Goshen, Pithom, Canaan, etc, while in one huge stele of Menephtah the Israelites are mentioned by name. Later Egyp Pharaohs give almost equally important knowledge concerning Pal, while the Assyr texts are even more direct. The black obelisk of Shalmaneser II (9th cent.) catalogues and pictures the tribute received from Jehu; almost every king of the 8th cent. tells something of his relations with the rulers of Jerus or Damascus, throwing immense light on local politics, and the later Bab records give vividly the conditions previous to and during the exile, while the edict of Cyrus gives the very decree by virtue of which the Jews could return to their native land. Later discoveries, like the CH at Susa (1901), the Sendjirli and other Aram. texts from Northern Syria (1890, 1908), and the Elephantine papyri, some of which are addressed to the "sons of Sanballat" and describe a temple in Egypt erected to Yahu (Jehovah) in the 5th cent. BC, may not give direct information concerning Pal, but are important to present explorers because of the light thrown upon the laws of Pal in patriarchal times; upon the thought and language of a neighboring Sem community at the time of the Monarchy; upon the religious ritual and festivals of Nehemiah's day, and upon the general wealth and culture of the Jews of the 5th cent.; opening up also for the first time the intimate relations which existed between Jerus and Samaria and the Jews of the Dispersion. So the vast amounts of Gr papyri found recently in the *Fayyûm* not only have preserved the "Logia" and "Lost Gospels" and fragments of Scripture texts, early Christian Egyp ritual, etc, but have given to scholars for the first time contemporaneous examples of the colloquial language which the Jews of Pal were using in the 1st cent. AD, and in which they wrote the "memoirs" of the apostles and the Gospels of Jesus.

2. In Palestine

(1) *Early Christian period.*—At this time, during the first three or four centuries the ancient sites and holy places were identified, giving some valuable information as to the topographical memories of the earlier church. By far the most valuable of these carefully prepared summaries of ancient Bible places, with their modern sites, and the distances between them, was the *Onomasticon* of Eusebius, as it was enlarged by Jerome, which attempted seriously the identification of some 300 holy places, most of these being vitally important for the modern student of the Bible. While some of these identifications were "curiously incorrect" (Bliss) and the distances even at the best only approximate, yet few satisfactory additions were made to the list for 1,500 years; and it was certainly a splendid contribution to Palestinian topography, for the list as a whole has been confirmed by the scientific conclusions of recent investigators.

(2) *Period of cursory observation.*—The earliest traveler who has left a record of his journey into Pal was Sinuhit, who, perhaps a century after Abraham, mentions a number of places known to us from the Bible and describes Canaan as a "land of figs and vines, ... where wine was more plentiful than water, ... honey and oil in abundance . . . . all kinds of fruit upon its trees, barley and spelt in the fields, and cattle beyond number"; each day his table is laden with "bread, wine, cooked flesh and roasted fowl . . . . wild game from the hills and milk in every sort of cooked dish" (Breasted, *Ancient Records*, I, 496). A few other Egyp visitors (1300–1000 BC) add little to our knowledge. The report of the Heb spies (Nu **13**) records important observations, although they can only humorously be called "genuine explorers" (Bliss), and Joshua's list of cities and tribes, although their boundaries are carefully described (chs **13–21**), are naturally excluded from this review.

The record of early Christian travel begins with the Bordeaux Pilgrim (332 AD), and during the next two centuries scores of others write out their observations in the Holy Land, but for 1,000 years there is scarcely a single visitor who looks at the country except through the eyes of the monks. A woman traveler of the 4th cent. reports some interesting facts about the early ritual of the Jerus church and the catechumen teaching, and surprises us by locating Pithom correctly (although the site was totally forgotten and only recovered in 1883), and the *Epitome of Eucherius* (5th cent.) gives a clear description of the holy places in Jerus; but almost the only other significant sign that anyone at this era ever made serious observations of value comes from the very large, fine mosaic of the 5th cent. recently discovered at Madeba, which gives a good impression of ancient Jerus with its buildings, and a careful bird's-eye view of the surrounding country (see below II, 3). By the middle of the 6th cent. the old "Holy Places" were covered by churches, while new ones were manufactured or discovered in dreams, and relics of martyrs' bones began to engross so much attention that no time was left in which to make any ordinary geographical or natural-history observations. A little local color and a few facts in regard to the plan of early churches and the persecution of Christians by Moslems constitute almost the sum total of value to be gathered from the multitude of pilgrims between the 6th and 12th cents. In the 12th cent. John of Würzburg gives a few geographical notes of value; Theoderich notices certain inscriptions and tombs, describes accurately the churches and hospitals he visits, with their pictures and decorations, and outlines intelligently the boundaries of Judaea and the salient features of the mountains encompassing Jerus; the Abbot Daniel notices the wild beasts in the Jordan forests and the customs at church feasts, and his account is important because of the light it throws on conditions in Pal just after its conquest by the Crusaders, while in the 13th cent. Burchard of Mt. Zion makes the earliest known mediaeval map of Pal, mentions over 100 Scripture sites, and shows unexpected interest in the plant and animal life of the country—but this practically exhausts the valuable information from Christian sources in these centuries. The Moslem pilgrims and writers from the 9th to the 15th cents. show far more regard to geographical realities than the Christians. It is a Moslem, Istakhri, who in the 10th cent. makes the first effort at a systematic geography of Pal, and in the 10th and 13th cents., respectively, Muḳaddasi, after 20 years of preparation, and Yāḳūt, in a "vast work," publish observations concerning climate, native customs, geographical divisions, etc, which are yet valuable, while Naṣir-i-Ḳhusran, in the 11th cent., also gave important information concerning Palestinian botany, gave dimensions of buildings and gates, and even noticed to some extent the ancient arches and ruins—though in all these there are pitiful inaccuracies of observation and induction. One of the best Moslem writers thinks the water of Lake Tiberias is not fit to drink because the city sewerage has ceased to flow into it, and Christian writers from the 7th cent. down to modern times continually mention the Jor and Dan as two fountains from which the Jordan rises, and continually report the most absurd stories about the Dead Sea and about its supernatural saltness, never noticing the salt mountain near by and the other simple causes explaining this phenomenon. See DEAD SEA.

In the 14th cent. Marino Sanuto gave a "most complete monograph" (Ritter) of Palestinian geography, his maps being really valuable, though, according to modern standards, quite inaccurate. The Jew, Estoai ben Moses ha-Phorhi, in this same century advanced beyond all Christian writers in a work of "real scientific knowledge" (Bliss), in which he correctly identified Megiddo and other ancient sites, though the value of his work was not recognized for 400 years. The great name of the 15th cent. is that of the Dominican, Father Felix Fabri, who in his large book, *Wanderings in the Holy Land*, was the first to notice monuments and ruins to which no Bib. traditions were attached (Bliss), and who, within a decade of the discovery of America, described most vividly the dangers and miseries of the sea voyages of that era, and in most modern fashion narrated his adventures among the Saracens; yet notwithstanding the literary value of the book and his better method of arranging his materials, Fabri actually explained the saltness of the Dead Sea as due to the sweat which flowed from the skin of the earth! In the 16th cent. travelers showed more interest in native customs, but the false traditional identification of sites was scarcely questioned; the route of travel was always the same, as it was absolutely impossible to get E. of the Jordan, and even a short trip away from the caravan was dangerous.

(3) *Beginning of scientific observation.*—In the 17th cent. Michal Nau, for 30 years a missionary in Pal, De la Roque and Hallifix showed a truly scientific veracity of observation and an increasing accuracy in the recording and verification of their notes, and Maundrell advanced beyond all his predecessors in noticing the antiquities on the seacoast, N. of Beirût; but all of these, though possessing fine qualities as explorers, were forced to travel hastily and limit their study to a very narrow field.

II. Era of Scientific Exploration.—(1) *First trained explorers.*—True scientific exploration opened with the 18th cent., as men began to think of this as itself an important life-work and not merely as a short episode in a life devoted to more serious pursuits.

1. Period of Individual Enterprise

Th. Shaw (1722) carefully fitted himself as a specialist in natural history and physical geography, and scientifically reported a number of new facts, e.g. conditions and results of evaporation, etc, in the Dead Sea. Bishop Pococke (1738) had been well trained, was free from the bondage of tradition, and did for the antiquities of Pal what Maundrell had done for those of Syria, making a large number of successful identifications of sites and contributing much to the general knowledge of Pal. Volney (1783) was a brilliant literary man, in full sympathy with the scientific spirit, who popularized results and made a considerable number of original researches, esp. in the Lebanon. Seetzen (1800–7) and Burckhardt (1810–12) are called by Bliss "veritable pioneers in the exploration of the ruins of Eastern and Southern Pal." The former opened Caesarea Philippi to light, visited a large unexplored district and made important observations in almost every field of knowledge, zoölogy, meteorology, archaeology; the latter, having become an Arab in looks and language, was able to go into many places where no European had ventured, one of his chief triumphs being the discovery of Petra and the scientific location of Mt. Sinai.

(2) *The climax of individual exploration.*—The climax of the era of scientific observation, unassisted by learned societies, was reached by the American clergyman and teacher, Edward Robinson. He spent parts of two years in Pal (1838 and 1852) and in 1856 published 3 vols of *Biblical Researches*. He strictly employed the scientific method, and showed such rare insight that scarcely one of his conclusions has been found incorrect. His knowledge was as extensive as minute, and although he gave, in all, only five months of steady labor to the specific task of exploration, yet in that time he "reconstructed the map of Pal" (Bliss), and his conclusions henceforth "formed the ground work of modern research" (Conder). He studied Jerus, being the first to show that the ancient fragment of an arch (now "Robinson's") had been part of the bridge connecting the temple with Mt. Zion, and was the first to trace with accuracy the windings of the tunnel leading from the Virgin's Fount to the Pool of Siloam. All Judaea, Galilee and Samaria were very well covered by him. He was the first to notice that the ruined building at *Tell Ḥûm* was a synagogue; from the top of one hill he recognized seven Bib. sites which had been lost for at least 1,500 years; he identified correctly at least 160 new sites, almost all being Bib. places. Robinson's results were phenomenal in number and variety, yet necessarily these have been constantly improved upon or added to in each generation since, for no man can cover the entire field or be a specialist in every department. W. M. Thomson in his *LB* (new ed, 1910) and G. E. Post, *Flora of Syria, Pal, and Sinai* (1896), gave a needed popular résumé of the manners, customs and folklore of the people, as these illustrated the Bible, and many books and articles since have added to this material.

In 1848 the United States sent an expedition under Lieutenant Lynch to the Dead Sea, which ascertained the exact width, depth, currents, temperature, etc, and many parties since have added to this knowledge (see e.g. DEAD SEA; and also *PEFS*, 1911, XII, 7). From 1854 to 1862 De Vogüé thoroughly examined the monuments of Central Syria and remained the sole authority on this section down to the American Archaeological Expedition of 1899. Tabler (1845–63) scientifically described Jerus and its environs, and the districts lying between Jaffa and the Jordan, and between Jerus and Bethel. Guérin who studied Pal during periods covering 23 years (1852–75), though limited by lack of funds, covered topographically, with a minuteness never before attempted, almost the whole of Judaea, Samaria and Galilee, gathering also many new records of monuments and inscriptions, the record of which was invaluable because many of these had been completely destroyed before the arrival of the next scientific party. A most sensational discovery was that of Rev. F. Klein in 1868, when he found at Dibon the huge basalt tablet set up by Mesha, king of Moab (9th cent. BC), on which in a language closely resembling the Heb, he gave honor to his god Chemosh by describing his successful revolt against a successor of Omri, the latter being mentioned by name with many well-known Bib. places. In style, thought and language this inscription greatly resembles the early OT records.

With the foundation of the Palestine Exploration Fund (1865) the work of exploration took on an entirely new phase, since in this case, not a single individual, but a large company of specialists entered the work, having behind them sufficient funds for adequate investigation in each necessary line of research, and with the British War Office furnishing its expert Royal Engineers to assist the enterprise.

2. Scientific Coöperative Surface Exploration

Under the auspices of this society during the next 15 years Jerus was explored as never before, and all Western Pal was topographically surveyed (see below); a geological survey (1883–84) of Sinai, *Wâdy 'Arabah* and the Dead Sea, and later of Mt. Seir (1885) was accomplished under Professor Edward Hull; the natural history of the country was treated with great thoroughness by several specialists; Palmer and Drake in the dress of Syrian natives, without servants, risked the dangerous journey through the Desert of the Tih in order to locate so far as possible the route of the Exodus; Clermont-Ganneau, who had previously made the discovery of the Jewish placard from the Temple, forbidding strangers to enter the sacred enclosure, added greatly to archaeological knowledge by gathering and deciphering many ancient inscriptions, uncovering buried cemeteries, rock-cut tombs and other monuments. He also laid down important criteria for the age of stone masonry (yet see *PEFS*, 1897, LXI); identified various sites including Adullam, found the "stone of Bethphage," "Zoheleth," etc, and made innumerable plans of churches, mosques, tombs, etc, and did an incredible amount of other important work. Capt., afterward Col., C. R. Conder did an equally important work, and as the head of the archaeological party could finally report 10,000 place-names as having been gathered, and 172 new Bible sites successfully identified, while the boundaries of the tribes had been practically settled and many vitally important Bible locations for the first time fixed. The excavations in Jerus under the same auspices had meanwhile been carried out as planned. After an introductory examination by Sir Charles Wilson, including some little excavating, Sir Charles Warren (1867–70) and, later, Col. Conder (1872–75) made thorough excavations over a large area, sinking shafts and following ancient walls to a depth of 80–150 ft. They uncovered the Temple-area from its countless tons of débris and traced its approximate outline; examined underground rock chambers; opened ancient streets; discovered many thousand specimens of pottery, glass, tools, etc, from Jewish to Byzantine periods; found the pier in the Tyropœon Valley, where Robinson's arch had rested, and also parts of the ancient bridge; traced the line of several important ancient walls, locating gates and towers, and fixed the date of one wall certainly as of the 8th cent. BC, and probably of the age of Solomon (G. A. Smith), thus accomplishing an epoch-making work upon which all more recent explorers have safely rested—as Maudslay (1875), in his masterly discovery and examination of the Great Scarp, and Guthe (1881), who made fine additional discoveries at Ophel, as well as Warren and Conder in their work afterward (1884), when they published plans of the whole city with its streets, churches, mosques, etc, 25 in. to the mile, which in that direction remains a basis for all later work. See JERUSALEM.

Perhaps, however, the greatest work of all done by this society was the Topographical Survey (1881–86), accomplished for Judaea and Samaria by Col. Conder, and for Galilee by Lord Kitchener, resulting in a great map of Western Pal in 26 sheets, on a scale of an inch to the mile (with several abridged additions), showing all previous identifications of ancient places. These maps, with the seven magnificent vols of memoirs, etc, giving the other scientific work done by the various parties, marked such an epoch-making advance in knowledge that it has been called "the most important contribution to illustrate the Bible since its translation into the vulgar tongue."

In addition to the above the Palestine Exploration Fund established a *Quarterly Statement* and *Society of Biblical Archaeology* from which subscribers could keep in touch with the latest Bib. results, and published large quantities of tr[s] of ancient texts and travels and of books reporting discoveries as these were made. Altogether more advance was made during these 15 years from 1865–80 than in the 15 centuries before.

3. Most Recent Results in Surface Exploration

The next ten years (1880–90) did not furnish as much new material from Pal exploration, but in 1880 the Siloam Inscription (cf 2 K **20** 20; 2 Ch **32** 30) was accidentally found in Jerus, showing the accuracy with which the engineers of Hezekiah's day could, at least occasionally, cut long tunnels through the rock (see also Clermont-Ganneau, *Archaeological Researches*, 313); and in 1881–85 Conder and Schumacher attempted their difficult task of making a scientific topographical map of Eastern Pal. In 1881 H. Clay Trumbull rediscovered and properly described Kadesh-barnea, settling authoritatively its location and thus making it possible to fix previously obscure places mentioned in the account of the Exodus wanderings. Since 1890 continued investigations in small districts not adequately described previously have taken place, new additions to the zoölogical, botanical, geological and meteorological knowledge of Pal have been frequent; studies of irrigation and the water-supply have been made, as well as investigations into the customs, proverbs, folklore, etc, of the Arabs; many districts E. of the Jordan and through Petra down into Sinai have yielded important results, and many discoveries of surface tombs, ossuaries, mosaics, seals and manuscripts have been made in many parts of Pal. This has been done perhaps chiefly by the Palestine Exploration Fund, but much by individuals and some by the newly organized excavation societies (see below). The most surprising discoveries made by this method of surface exploration (a method which can never become completely obsolete) have been the finding at different times of the four Boundary Stones of Gezer (1874, 1881, 1889) by Clermont-Ganneau, and, in 1896, of the very large mosaic at Madeba by Father Cleopas, librarian of the Greek Patriarch.

The latter proved to be part of the pavement of a 6th-cent. basilica and is a "veritable map of Pal," showing its chief cities, the boundaries of the tribes, and esp. the city of Jerus with its walls, gates, chief buildings, including the Church of the Holy Sepulchre, and chief streets, notably one long straight street intersecting the city and lined with colonnades. As Madeba lies near the foot of Mt. Nebo, it is thought the artist may have intended to represent ideally a modern (6th-cent.) vision of Moses. George Adam Smith (*HGHL*, 7th ed, 1901); *Jerusalem* (2 vols, 1910), and E. Huntington, *Pal and Its Transformation* (1911), have given fine studies illustrating the supreme importance of accurate topographical knowledge in order to understand correctly the Bible narratives and the social life and politics of the Hebrews.

III. Era of Scientific Excavation.—(1) *Tell el-Ḥesy* (Palestine Exploration Fund).—Exploration

1. Southern Palestine

must always continue, but excavation is a vast advance. The modern era in Palestinian study begins with Petrie at LACHISH (q.v.) in 1890. Though Renan was actually the first man to put a spade into the soil (1860), yet his results were practically confined to Phoenicia. From Renan's time to 1890 there had been no digging whatever, excepting some narrow but thorough work in Jerus, and a slight tickling of the ground at Jericho and at the so-called Tombs of the Kings. Nothing was more providential than this delay in beginning extensive excavations in Pal, such as had been previously so profitably conducted in Egypt and elsewhere. The results could not have been interpreted even two years earlier, and even when these excavations were commenced, the only man living who could have understood what he found was the man who had been selected to do the work. Nearly two centuries before, a traveler in Pal (Th. Shaw) had suggested the possibility of certain mounds ("tells") being artificial (cf Josh **8** 28; Jer **30** 18); but not even Robinson or Guérin had suspected that these were the cenotaphs of buried cities, but had believed them to be mere natural hills. The greatest hour in the history of exploration in Pal, and perhaps in any land, was that in which on a day in April, 1890, W. M. Flinders Petrie climbed up the side of *Tell el-Ḥesy*, situated on the edge of the Phili plain, c 30 miles S.W. of Jerus, and 17 miles

N.E. from Gaza, and by examining its strata, which had been exposed by the stream cutting down its side, determined before sunset the fact, from pieces of pottery he had seen, that the site marked a city covering 1,000 years of history, the limits of occupation being probably 1500 BC to 500 BC. This ability to date the several occupations of a site without any inscription to assist him was due to the chronological scale of styles of pottery which he had originated earlier and worked out positively for the Gr epochs at Naukratis a year or two before, and for the epochs preceding 1100 BC at *Illahun* in the *Fayyûm* only a month or two before. The potsherds were fortunately very numerous at *Tell el-Ḥesy*, and by the end of his six weeks' work he could date approximately some eight successive occupations of the city, each of these being mutually exclusive in certain important forms of pottery in common use. Given the surface date, depth of accumulation and rate of deposit as shown at Lachish, and a pretty sure estimate of the history of other sites was available. Not only was this pottery scale so brilliantly confirmed and elaborated at *Tell el-Ḥesy* that all excavators since have been able accurately to date the last settlement on a mound almost by walking over it; but by observations of the methods of stone dressing he was able to rectify many former guesses as to the age of buildings and to establish some valuable architectural signs of age. He proved that some of the walls at this site were built by "the same school of masons which built the Temple of Solomon," and also that the Ionic volute, which the Greeks borrowed from the Asiatics, went back in Pal at least to the 10th cent. BC, while on one pilaster he found the architectural motif of the "ram's horn" (cf Ps **118** 27). He also concluded, contrary to former belief, that this mound marked the site of Lachish (Josh **10** 31; 2 K **18** 14), as by a careful examination he found that no other ruins near could fill the known historic conditions of that city, and the inscription found by the next excavator and all more recent research make this conclusion practically sure. Lachish was a great fortress of the ancient world. The Egyp Pharaohs often mention it, and it is represented in a picture on an Assyr monument under which is written, "Sennacherib . . . . receives the spoil of Lachish" (see 2 K **18** 14). It was strategically a strong position, the natural hill rising some 60 ft. above the valley and the fortification which Sennacherib probably attacked being over 10 ft. thick. The débris lay from 50–70 ft. deep on top of the hill. Petrie fixed the directions of the various walls, and settled the approximate dates of each city and of the imported pottery found in several of these. One of the most unexpected things was an iron knife dug up from a stratum indicating a period not far from the time when Israel must have entered Canaan, this being the earliest remnant of iron weapons ever found up to this date (cf Josh **17** 16).

The next two years of scientific digging (1891–92), admirably conducted by Dr. F. G. Bliss on this site, wholly confirmed Petrie's general inductions, though the limits of each occupation were more exactly fixed and the beginning of the oldest city was pushed back to 1700 BC. The work was conducted under the usual dangers, not only from the Bedawîn, but from excessive heat (104° in the shade), from malaria which at one time prostrated 8 of the 9 members of the staff, scarcity of water, which had to be carried 6 miles, and from the sirocco (see my report, *PEFS*, XXI, 160–70 and Petrie's and Bliss's journal, XXI, 219–46; XXIII, 192, etc). He excavated thoroughly one-third of the entire hill, moving nearly a million cubic feet of débris. He found that the wall of the oldest city was nearly 30 ft. thick, that of the next city 17 ft. thick, while the latest wall was thin and weak. The oldest city covered a space 1,300 ft. sq., the latest one only about 200 ft. sq. The oldest pottery had a richer color and higher polish than the later, and this art was indigenous, for at this level no Phoen or Mycenaean styles were found. The late pre-Israelitish period (1550–800 BC) shows such importations and also local Cypriote imitations. In the "Jewish" period (800–300 BC) this influence is lost and the new styles are coarse and ungraceful, such degeneration not being connected with the entrance of Israel into Canaan, as many have supposed, but with a later period, most probably with the desolation which followed the exile of the ten tribes (Bliss and Petrie). In the pre-Israelite cities were found mighty towers, fine bronze implements, such as battle-axes, spearheads, bracelets, pins, needles, etc, a wine and treacle press, one very large building "beautifully symmetrical," a smelting furnace, and finally an inscribed tablet from Zimrida, known previously from the Am Tab to have been governor of Lachish, c 1400 BC. Many Jewish pit ovens were found in the later ruins and large quantities of pottery, some containing potters' marks and others with inscriptions. Clay figures of Astarte, the goddess of fertility, were found in the various layers, one of these being of the unique Cypriote type, with large earrings, and many Egyp figures, symbols and animal forms. See also LACHISH, KIRIATH-SEPHER, and GERAR.

(2) *Excavations in Jerus.*—During 1894–97, notwithstanding the previously good work done in Jerus (see above) and the peculiar embarrassments connected with the attempt to dig in a richly populated town, Dr. Bliss, assisted by an expert architect, succeeded in adding considerably to the sum of knowledge. He excavated over a large area, not only positively confirming former inductions, but discovering the remains of the wall of the empress Eudocia (450 AD), and under this the line of wall which Titus had destroyed, and at a deeper level the wall which surrounded the city in the Herodian age, and deeper yet that which must probably be dated to Hezekiah, and below this a construction "exquisitely dressed, with pointed masonry," which must be either the remains of a wall of Solomon or some other preëxilic fortification not later than the 8th cent. He found gates and anciently paved streets and manholes leading to ancient sewer systems, and many articles of interest, but esp. settled disputed questions concerning important walls and the levels of the ancient hills, thus fixing the exact topography of the ancient city. H. G. Mitchell and others have also carefully examined certain lines of wall, identifying Nehemiah's Dung Gate, etc, and making a new survey of certain parts of underground Jerus, the results of the entire work being a modification of tradition in a few particulars, but confirmatory in most. The important springs and reservoirs, valleys and hills of the ancient Jerus have been certainly identified. It is now settled that modern Jerus "still sits virtually upon her ancient seat and at much the same slope," though not so large as the Jerus of the kings of Judah which certainly extended over the Southwestern Hill. Mt. Zion, contrary to tradition which located it on the Southwestern Hill where the citadel stands, probably lay on the Eastern Hill above the Virgin's Spring (Gihon). On this Eastern Hill at Ophel lay the Temple, and S. of the Temple on the same hill "above Gihon" lay the old Jebusite stronghold (David's City). The ancient altar of burnt offering was almost surely at *es-Sakhra*. The evidence has not been conclusive as to the line of the second wall, so that the site of Golgotha and the Holy Sepulchre cannot certainly

EXCAVATIONS ON SOUTHEASTERN HILL OF JERUSALEM

be determined (see George Adam Smith's exhaustive work, *Jerus*, 2 vols, 1907; Sir Charles Wilson, *Golgotha and the Holy Sepulchre*, 1906; and cf Selah Merrill, *Ancient Jerus*, 1908; C. R. Conder, *City of Jerus*, 1909; P. H. Vincent, *Underground Jerus*, 1911).

(3) *Excavations in the Shephēlah* (Palestine Exploration Fund).—During 1898–1900 important work was done by Bliss and Macalister at 4 sites on the border land between Philistia and Judaea, while five other small mounds were tunneled, but without important results. The four chief sites were *Tell Zakariya*, lying about midway between Jerus and *Tell el-Ḥesy; Tell eṣ Ṣāfi*, 5 miles W. of *Tell Zakariya*, and *Tell Sandaḥannah*, about 10 miles S.; while *Tell ej-Judeideh* lay between *Tell Zakariya* and *Tell Sandaḥannah*. As *Tell ej-Judeideh* was only half-excavated and merely confirmed other results, not being remarkable except for the large quantity of jar inscriptions found (37), we omit further mention of it. (*a*) *Tell Zakariya:* From this height, 1,214 ft. above the sea, almost all Philistia could be seen. A pre-Israelitish town was found under some 20 ft. of débris, containing pre-Israelitish, Jewish and Seleucidan pottery. Many vaulted cisterns, partly hewn from the rock, were found in the lowest level. In later levels Jewish pit ovens were found and inscribed jar-handles with winged Egyp symbols, implements of bronze, iron, bone and stone, and Egyp images of Bes and the Horus eye, etc, besides a strange bronze figure of a woman with a fish's tail which seems to represent Atargatis of Ashkelon. The ancient rampart was strengthened, perhaps in Rehoboam's time, and towers were added in the Seleucidan era. Only half of this site was excavated. (*b*) *Tell eṣ-Ṣāfi:* The camp was pitched near here in the Vale of Elah. From a depth of 21 ft. to the rock, was found the characteristic pre-Israelitish pottery and much imported pottery of the Mycenaean type. A high place was also found here, containing bones of camels, sheep, cows, etc, and several monoliths of soft limestone *in situ*, and near by a jar-burial. In an ancient rubbish heap many fragments of the goddess of fertility were found. Many old Egyp and later Gr relics were also found, and four Bab seals and the usual pottery from Jewish and later periods. With strong probability this site was identified as **Gath.** (*c*) *Tell Sandaḥannah:* This was situated c 1,100 ft. above sea-level. The town covered about 6 acres and was protected by an inner and outer wall and occasional towers. The strongest wall averaged 30 ft. thick. The work done here "was unique in the history of Palestinian excavation" (Bliss). At *Tell el-Ḥesy* only one-third of each stratum was excavated; at *Tell Zakariya* only one-half; at Jerus the work was confined to the enclosures of the temple, a few city walls and a few churches, pools, streets, etc, but at *Tell Sandaḥannah* "we recovered almost an entire town, probably the ancient **Mareshah** [Josh **15** 44], with its inner and outer walls, its gates, streets, lanes, open places, houses, reservoirs, etc" (Bliss). Nearly 400 vessels absolutely intact and unbroken were found. It was a Seleucidan town of the 3d and 2d cent. BC, with no pre-Israelitish remains. The town was built with thin brick, like blocks of soft limestone, set with wide joints and laid in mud with occasionally larger, harder stones chisel-picked. The town was roughly divided into blocks of streets, some of the streets being paved. The houses were lighted from the street and an open court. Very few rooms were perfectly rectangular, while many were of awkward shape. Many closets were found and pit ovens and vaulted cisterns, reached by staircases, as also portions of the old drainage system. The cisterns had plastered floors, and sometimes two heavy coats of plaster on the walls; the houses occasionally had vaulted roofs but usually the ordinary roof of today, made of boards and rushes covered with clay. No religious building was found and no trace of a colonnade, except perhaps a few fragments of ornament. An

Stamped Jar-Handles, Lamp and Iron Implements from Tombs at *Beit Jibrîn.*

enormous columbarium was uncovered (1906 niches). No less than 328 Gr inscriptions were found on the handles of imported wine jars. Under the Seleucidan town was a Jewish town built of rubble, the pottery of the usual kind including stamped jar-handles. An Astarte was found in the Jewish or Gr stratum, as also various animal forms. The Astarte was very curious, about 11 in. high, hollow, wearing a long cloak, but with breasts, body and part of right leg bare, having for headdress a closely fitting sunbonnet with a circular serrated top ornament in front and with seven stars in relief. A most striking find dating from about the 2d cent. AD was that of 16 little human figures bound in fetters of lead, iron, etc, undoubtedly representing "revenge dolls" through which the owners hoped to work magic on enemies, and 49 fragments of magical tablets inscribed in Gr on white limestone, with exorcisms, incantations and imprecations. It ought to be added that the four towns as a whole supplement each other, and positively confirm former results. No royal stamps were found at *Tell el-Ḥesy*, but 77 were found in these 4 sites, in connection with 2- or 4-winged symbols (Egyp scarabaeus or winged sun-disk). Writing-materials (*styli*) were found in all strata, their use being "continuous from the earliest times into the Seleucidan period" (Bliss). From the four towns the evolution of the lamp could be traced from the pre-Israelite, through the Jewish to the Gr period. Some 150 of the labyrinthine rock-cut caves of the district were also examined, some of which must be pre-Christian, as in one of these a million cubic feet of material had been excavated, yet so long ago that all signs of the rubbish had been washed away.

(4) *Painted "Tombs of Marissa."*—In 1902 John P. Peters and Hermann Thiersch discovered at *Beit Jibrîn* (adjoining *Tell Sandaḥannah*) an example of sepulchral art totally different from any other ever found in Pal. It was a tomb containing several chambers built by a Sidonian, the walls being brilliantly painted, showing a bull, panther, serpent, ibex, crocodile with ibis (?) on its back, hunter on horseback, etc, with dated inscriptions, the earliest being 196 BC (see John P. Peters, *Painted Tombs in Necropolis of Marissa*, 1905). The writer (April 18, 1913) found another tomb here of similar character, decorated with grapes, birds, two cocks (life size), etc. Perhaps most conspicuous was a wreath of beautiful flowers with a cross ⊕ in its center. Nothing shows the interrelations of that

age more than this Phoen colony, living in Pal, using the Gr language but employing Egyp and Libyan characteristics freely in their funeral art.

2. Northern Palestine

(1) *Tell Ta'annek* (Austrian government and Vienna Academy).—During short seasons of three years (1902–4) Professor Ernst Sellin of Vienna made a rapid examination of this town (Bib. **Taanach**), situated in the plain of Esdraelon in Northern Pal, on the ancient road between Egypt and

Interior of Tomb at Marissa.

Babylon. Over 100 laborers were employed and digging was carried on simultaneously at several different points on the mound, the record being kept in an unusually systematic way and the official reports being minute and exhaustive. Only a general statement of results can be given, with an indication of the directions in which the "findings" were peculiar. The absence of Phoen and Mycenaean influence upon the pottery in the earliest levels (1000–1600 BC) is just as marked as at other sites, the kind of pottery and the presence of Sem *maççēbhōth* (see IMAGES) in the Jewish periods are just as in previous sites, and the development in mason work and in pottery is identically the same in this first city to be excavated in Northern Pal as in Southern Pal. "The buildings and antiques might be interchanged bodily without any serious confusion of the archaeological history of Pal. . . . . Civilization over all Western Pal is thus shown to have had the same course of development, whether we study it N. or S." (Macalister). This is by far the most important result of this excavation, showing that, notwithstanding divergences in many directions, an equivalent civilization, proving a unity in the dominating race, can be seen over all parts of Pal so far examined. Iron is introduced at the same time (c 1000 BC), and even the toys and pottery decorations are similar, and this continues through all the periods, including the Jewish. Yet foreign intercourse is common, and the idols, even from the earliest period, "show religious syncretism" (Sellin). From almost the oldest layer comes a curious seal cylinder containing both Egyp and Bab features. On one pre-Israelite tablet are pictures of Hadad and Baal. The Astarte cult is not quite as prominent here as in Southern Pal. No figures of the goddess come from the earliest strata, but from 1600 BC to c 900–800 BC they are common; after this they cease. The ordinary type of Astarte found in Babylonia and Cyprus as well as in Pal—with crown, necklace, girdle, anklets, and hands clasped on breasts—is found most frequently; but from the 12th to the 9th cent. other forms appear representing her as naked, with hips abnormally enlarged, to show her power of fecundity. One figure is of a peculiarly foreign type, wearing excessively large earrings, and this is in close connection with one of the most unique discoveries ever made in Pal—a hollow terra cotta Can. or Israelite (2 K **16** 10) altar (800–600 BC), having no bottom but with holes in its walls which admitted air and insured draft when fire was kindled below; in its ornamentation showing a mixture of Bab and Egyp motives, having on its right side winged animals with human heads by the side of which is a man (or boy) struggling with a serpent the jaws of which are widely distended in anger; at its top two ram's (?) horns, and between them a sacrificial bowl in which to receive the "drink offering"; on its front a tree (of life), and on each side of it a rampant ibex. A bronze serpent was found near this altar, as also near the high place at Gezer. Continuous evidence of the gruesome practice of foundation sacrifices, mostly of little children, but in one case of an adult, was found between the 13th and 9th cents. BC, after which they seem to cease. In one house the skeletons of a lady and five children were found, the former with her rings and necklace of gold, five pearls, two scarabs, etc. Many jar-burials of new-born infants, 16 in one place, were found, and, close to this deposit, a rock-hewn altar with a jar of yellow incense (?). Egyp and Bab images were found of different eras and curious little human-looking amulets (as were also found at Lachish) in which the parental parts are prominent, which Sellin and Bliss believe to be "teraphim" (Gen **31** 19.34; but see Driver, *Modern Research*, 57, etc), such as Rachel, being pregnant, took with her to protect her on the hard journey from Haran to Pal (Macalister).

The high place, with one or more steps leading up to it, suggesting "elevation, isolation and mystery" (Vincent), is represented here as in so many other Palestinian ruins, and the evidence shows that it continued long after the entrance of Israel into Canaan. When Israel entered Pal, no break occurred in the civilization, the art development continuing at about the same level; so probably the two races were at about the same culture-level, or else the Hebrew occupation of the land was very gradual. In the 8th cent. there seems to be an indication of the entrance of a different race, which doubtless is due to the Assyr exile. A most interesting discovery was that of the dozen cuneiform tablets found in a terra cotta chest or jar (cf Jer **32** 14) from the pre-Israelite city.

These few letters cannot accurately be called "the first library found in Pal"; but they do prove that libraries were there, since the personal and comparatively unimportant character of some of these notes and their easy and flowing style prove that legal, business and literary documents must have existed. These show that letter-writing was used not only in great questions of state between foreign countries, but in local matters between little contiguous towns, and that while Pal at this period (c 1400 BC) was politically dependent on Egypt, yet Babylonia had maintained its old literary supremacy. One of these letters mentions "the finger of Ashirat," this deity recalling the *'ăshērāh* or sacred post of the OT (see IMAGES); another note is written by Ahi-Yawi, a name which corresponds to Heb Ahijah ("Jeh is Brother"), thus indicating that the form of the Divine name was then known in Canaan, though its meaning (i.e. the essential name; cf Ex **6** 3; **34** 6; Neh **1** 9; Jer **44** 26), may not have been known. Ahi-Yawi invokes upon Ishtar-washur the blessing of the "Lord of the Gods."

On the same level with these letters were found two subterranean cells with a rock-hewn chamber in front and a rock-hewn altar above, and even the ancient drain which is supposed to have conveyed the blood from the altar into the "chamber of the dead" below. It may be added that Dr. Sellin thinks the condition of the various walls of the city is entirely harmonious with the Bible accounts of its history (Josh **12** 21; **17** 11; Jgs **1** 27; **5** 19–21; 1 K **4** 12; **9** 15; 1 Ch **7** 29). So far as the ruins testify, there was no settled city life between c 600 BC and 900 AD, i.e. it became a desolation about the time of the Bab captivity. An Arab castle dates from about the 10th cent. AD.

(2) *Tell el-Mutesellim* (**Megiddo**, Josh **12** 21; Jgs **5** 19; 2 K **9** 27).—This great commercial and military center of Northern Pal was opened to the world in 1903–5 by Dr. Schumacher and his efficient staff, the diggings being conducted under the auspices of His Majesty the Kaiser and the Ger. Pal Society. The mound, about 5 miles N.W. from *Ta'anach*, stood prominently 120 ft. above the plain, the ruins being on a plateau 1,020×750 ft. in area. An average of 70 diggers were employed for the entire time. The débris was over 33 ft. deep, covering some eight mutually excluding populations. The surrounding wall, 30×35 ft. thick, conformed itself to the contour of the town. The excavations reached the virgin rock only at one point; but the oldest stratum uncovered showed a people living in houses, having fire, cooking food and making sacrifices; the next city marked an advance, but the third city, proved by its Egyp remains to go back as far as the 20th cent. BC, showed a splendid and in some directions a surprising civilization, building magnificent city gates (57×36 ft.), large houses and tombs with vaulted roofs, and adorning their persons with fine scarabs of white and green steatite and other jewelry of stone and bronze. It was very rich in colored pottery and little objects such as tools, seals, terra cotta figures and animals, including a bridled horse, and some worked iron is also said to have been found. In one pile of bodies were two children wearing beautiful bronze anklets. The city lying above this begins as early as the 15th cent. BC, as is proved by a scarab of Thothmes III and by other signs, although the scarabs, while Egyp in form, are often foreign in design and execution. Anubis, Bes, Horus and other Egyp figures appear, also 32 scarabs in one pot, much jewelry, including gold ornaments, and some very long, sharp bronze knives. One tomb contained 42 vessels, and one skeleton held 4 gold-mounted scarabs in its hand. One remarkable fragment of pottery contained a colored picture of pre-Israelite warriors with great black beards, carrying shields (?). A most interesting discovery was that of the little copper (bronze?) tripods supporting lamps, on one of which is the figure of a flute-player, being strikingly similar to pictures of Delphic oracles and to representations lately found in Crete (*MNDPV*, 1906, 46). This city was destroyed by a fearful conflagration, and is separated from the next by a heavy stratum of cinders and ashes. The fifth city is remarkable for a splendid palace with walls of stone from 3–5 ft. thick. This city, which probably begins as early as Solomon's time, shows the best masonry. An oval, highly polished seal of jasper on which is engraved a Heb name in script closely resembling the M S, suggests a date for the city, and casts an unexpected light upon the Heb culture of Pal in the days of the monarchy. The seal is equal to the best Egyp or Assyr work, clearly and beautifully engraved, and showing a climax of art. In the center is the Lion (of Judah), mouth wide open, tail erect, body tense. Upon the seal is carved: "To Shema, servant of Jeroboam." This name may possibly not refer to either of the Bib. kings (10th or 8th cent. BC), but the stratum favors this dating. The seal was evidently owned by some Hebrew noble at a prosperous period when some Jeroboam was in power, and so everything is in favor of this being a relic from the court of one of these kings, probably the latter (Kautzsch, *M u. N*, 1904, 81). We have here, in any case, one of the oldest Heb inscriptions known, and one of the most elegant ever engraved (see *MNDPV*, 1906, 33). After seeing it the Sultan took it from the museum into his own private collection. A second seal of lapis lazuli, which Schumacher and Kautzsch date from about the 7th cent. BC, also contains in Old Heb the name "Asaph" (cf *M u. N*, 1906, 334; *MNDPV*, 1904, 147). There are several other remarkable works of art, as e.g. a woman playing the tambourine, wearing an Egyp headdress; several other figures of women besides several Astartes, and esp. a series of six terra cotta heads, one with a prominent Sem nose, another with Egyp characteristics, another quite un-Egyp, with regular features, vivacious eyes, curls falling to her shoulders and garlanded with flowers.

The sixth stratum might well be called the temple-city, for here were found the ruins of a sanctuary built of massive blocks in which remained much of the ceremonial furniture—sacrificial dishes, a beautiful basalt pot with three feet, a plate having a handle in the form of a flower, etc. Seemingly connected with the former town, three religious stones were found covered by a fourth, and one with a pyramidal top; so here several monoliths were found which would naturally be thought of as religious monuments—though, since they have been touched with tools, this is perhaps doubtful (Ex **20** 25). One incense altar, carved out of gray stone, is so beautiful as to be worthy of a modern Gr cathedral. The upper dish rests on a support of carved ornamental leaves painted red, yellow and cobalt blue, in exquisite taste, the colors still as fresh as when first applied. A blacksmith's shop was found in this stratum, containing many tools, including iron plowshares, larger than the bronze ones in the 3d and 4th layers. Allegorical figures were found, which may possibly belong to the former town, representing a man before an altar with his hands raised in adoration, seemingly to a scorpion, above which are a 6-pointed star, crescent moon, etc. Another most wonderful seal of white hard stone is engraved with three lines of symbols, in the first a vulture chasing a rabbit; in the second a conventional palm tree, with winged creatures on each side; in the third a lion springing on an ibex (?) under the crescent moon. Near by was found a cylinder of black jasper, containing hieroglyphs, and much crushed pottery. The 7th city, which was previous to the Gr or Rom eras, shows only a complex of destroyed buildings. After this the place remains unoccupied till the 11th cent. AD, when a poor Arab tower was erected, evidently to protect the passing caravans.

In the cave Umgharet ez-Zuttiyeh a little northwest of the plain of Bethsaida was found by Truville-Petrie, 1927, a prehistoric skull, at least a skull in the prehistoric strata, which has attracted much attention of anthropologists. Whether it represents a race of men, or simply an abnormal skull, cannot be known unless a large number like it be found.

(3) *Tell Ḥûm* (**Capernaum**), *etc.*—In April and May, 1905, the German Oriental Society excavated a Heb synagogue of the Rom era at *Tell Ḥûm*. It was 78 ft. long by 59 ft. wide, was built of beautiful white limestone, almost equal to marble, and was in every way more magnificent than any other yet found in Pal, that in Chorazin being the next finest. Its roof was gable-shaped and it was surprisingly ornamented with fine carvings representing animals, birds, fruits, flowers, etc, though in some cases these ornamentations had been intentionally mutilated. In January, 1907, Macalister and Masterman proved that *Khan Minyeh* was not the ancient Capernaum, as it contained no pottery older than Arab time, thus showing *Tell Ḥûm* to be the ancient site, so that the synagogue just excavated may be the one referred to in Lk **7** 5. At *Samieh*, 6 hours N. of Jerus, two important Can. cemeteries were discovered by the fellahin in 1906, consisting of circular or oval tomb chambers, with roofs roughly dome-shaped, as at Gezer (see below). A large quantity of pottery and bronze objects, much of excellent quality, was found (*Harvard Theol. Rev.*, I, 70–96; Masterman, *Studies in Galilee;* Henson, *Researches in Palestine*). See CAPERNAUM.

Jericho (German Oriental Society).—During 1908–9, Dr. E. Sellin, assisted by a specialist in pottery, (Watzinger) and a professional architect (Langenegger), with the help of over 200 workmen, opened to view this famous Bib. city (Josh **6** 1–24). Jericho was most strategically situated at the eastern gateway of Pal, with an unlimited water-supply in the *'Ain es-Sultan*, having complete control of the great commercial highway across the Jordan and possessing natural provisions in its palm forest (Smith, *HGHL*). It was also set prominently on a hill rising some 40 ft. above

3. Eastern Palestine

Excavations at Jericho.

the plain. The excavations proved that from the earliest historic time these natural advantages had been increased by every possible artifice known to ancient engineers, until it had become a veritable Gibraltar. The oldest city, which was in the form of an irregular ellipse, somewhat egg-shaped, with the point at the S.W., was first surrounded with a rampart following the contour of the hill, a rampart so powerful that it commands the admiration of all military experts who have examined it.

The walls even in their ruins are some 28 ft. high. They were built in three sections: (*a*) a substratum of clay, gravel and small stones, making a deposit upon the rock about 3 or 4 ft. deep, somewhat analogous to modern concrete; (*b*) a rubble wall, 6 to 8 ft. thick, of large stones laid up to a height of 16 ft. upon this conglomerate, the lowest layers of the stone being enormously large; (*c*) upon all this a brick wall over 6 ft. thick, still remaining, in places, 8 ft. high. Not even Megiddo, famous as a military center throughout all the ancient world, shows such workmanship (cf Josh **2** 1; Nu **13** 28). "These were masters in stone work and masonry" (*The Builder*); "Taken as a whole it may justly be regarded as a triumph of engineering skill which a modern builder, under the same conditions, could scarcely excel" (Langenegger); "It is as well done as a brilliant military engineer with the same materials and tools could do today" (Vincent). All the centuries were not able to produce a natural crevice in this fortification. At the N., which was the chief point of danger, and perhaps along other sections also, a second wall was built about 100 ft. inside the first, and almost as strong, while still another defence ("the citadel"), with 265 ft. of frontage, was protected not only by another mighty wall but by a well-constructed glacis. The old pre-Israelite culture in Jericho was exactly similar to that seen in the southern and northern cities, and the idolatry also. In its natural elements Can. civilization was probably superior to that of the Hebrews, but the repugnant and ever-present polytheism and fear of magic led naturally to brutal and impure manifestations. It cannot be doubted that, at least in some cases, the infants buried in jars under the floors represent foundation sacrifices. Some of the pottery is of great excellence, comparing favorably with almost the best examples from Egypt; a number of decorative figures of animals in relief are specially fine; the bronze utensils are also good; esp. notable are the 22 writing-tablets, all ready to be used but not inscribed. Somewhere near the 15th cent. the old fortifications were seriously damaged, but equally powerful ones replaced them. The German experts all believed that a break in the city's history was clearly shown about the time when, according to the pottery, Israel ought to have captured the city, and it was confidently said that the distinctively Can. pottery ceased completely and permanently at this point; but further research has shown that at least a portion of the old town had a practically continuous existence (so Josh **16** 7; Jgs **1** 16; **3** 13; 2 S **10** 5). No complete Israelitish house was preserved, but the Israelitish quarter was located close to the spring and no little furniture of the usual kind was found, including dishes, pots, cornmills, lamps, etc, many iron instruments and terra cotta heads of men and animals. The pottery is quite unlike the old Canaanite, being closely allied to the Gr-Phoen ware of Cyprus. It is noticeable that, as in other Palestinian towns, in the Jewish era, little Bab influence is discernible; the Aegean and Egyp influence is not as marked as in the cities dug up near the Mediterranean coast. One large edifice (60 by 80 ft.) is so like the dwellings of the 7th cent. BC at Sendjirli that "they seem to have been copied from Syrian plans" (Vincent). Absolutely unique was the series of 12 Rhodian jar-handles stamped in Aram., "To Jehovah" (*Yah, Yahu*). Vincent has suggested that as during the monarchy (7th to 6th cent.) "To the King" meant probably "For His Majesty's Service," so in post-exilic time the Divine name meant "For the Temple" (*Rev. biblique*). After the exile the city had about 3 centuries of prosperity; but disappears permanently in the Maccabean era (*MNDPV*, 1907; *MDOG*, 1908–9; *PEFS*, 1910; *Rev. biblique*, 1907–9).

(1) *Jerusalem*.—See above, III, 1, (2).

4. Central Palestine

(2) *Samaria* (Harvard Expedition).—Although the ancient capital of the Northern Kingdom, yet Samaria was centrally located, being 20 miles from the Mediterranean coast and only about 30 miles N. of Jerus. Ancient Samaria was very famous in Israel for its frivolity and wealth, special mention being made of its ointments, instruments of music, luxurious couches, and its "ivory palace" (Am **6** 4–6; 1 K **16** 24). Its history is known so fully that the chronological sequences of the ruins can be determined easily. The citadel and town originated with Omri, c 900 BC (1 K **16** 24); the Temple of Baal and palace were constructions of Ahab (1 K **16** 32; **22** 39); it continued prosperous down to the Assyr exile, 722 BC (1 K **22** to 2 K **17**); Sargon and Esarhaddon established a Bab colony and presumably fortified the town (720–670 BC); Alexander the Great captured it in 331 BC, and established there a Syrio-Maccabean colony; it was destroyed by John Hyrcanus in 109 BC, but rebuilt by Pompey in 60 BC, and again by Herod (30–1 BC). All of these periods are identified in the excavations, Herod's work being easily recognized, and Josephus' description of the town being found correct; the Gr work is equally well defined, so that the lower layers of masonry which contained the characteristic Jewish pottery, and which in every part of the ruin lay immediately under the Bab and Gr buildings, must necessarily be Heb, the relative order of underlying structures thus being "beyond dispute" (Reisner). During 1908–9 George A. Reisner with a staff of specialists, including David G. Lyon of the Harvard Semitic Museum, G. Schumacher, and an expert architect, undertook systematically and thoroughly to excavate this large detached "tell" lying 350 ft. above

the valley and 1,450 ft. above sea-level, its location as the only possible strategic stronghold proving it to be the ancient Samaria. This was a "gigantic enterprise" because of the large village of 800 population (*Sebastiyeh*), and the valuable crops which covered the hill. Some $65,000 were spent during the two seasons, and the work finally ceased before the site was fully excavated. The following statement is an abridgment, in so far as possible in their words, of the official reports of Drs. Reisner and Lyon to the *Harvard Theol. Review:* An average of 285 diggers were employed the first season and from 230–60 the second. Hundreds of Arabian lamps, etc, were found close to the surface, and then nothing more until the Rom ruins. Many fine Rom columns still remained upright, upon the surface of the hill. The road of columns leading to the Forum and ornamental gate (oriented unlike the older gates), the great outer wall "20 stadii in circuit" (Jos), the hippodrome, etc, were all found with inscriptions or coins and pottery of the early Roman Empire. Even the old Rom chariot road leading into the Forum was identified. Adjoining the Forum and connected with it by a wide doorway was a basilica, consisting of a large open stone-paved court surrounded by a colonnade with mosaic floor. An inscription in Greek on an architrave in the courtyard dates this to 12–15 AD. The plan of the Herodian temple consisted of a stairway, a portico, a vestibule and a cella with a corridor on each side. The staircase was about 80 ft. wide, composed of 17 steps beautifully constructed, the steps being quite modern in style, each tread overlapping the next lower by several inches. The roof was arched and the walls very massive and covered with a heavy coat of plaster still retaining traces of color. A few Gr *graffiti* were found near here, and 150 "Rhodian" stamped amphora handles and many fragments of Lat inscriptions. A complete inscription on a large stele proved to be a dedication from some Pannonian soldiers (probably 2d or 3d cent. AD) to "Jupiter Optimus Maximus." Near this was found a torso of heroic size carved in white marble, which is much finer than any ever before discovered in Pal, the work "bringing to mind the Vatican Augustus" (Vincent), though not equal to it. Close to the statue was a Rom altar (presumably Herodian) c 13 by 7 ft., rising in six courses of stone to a height of 6 ft. Beneath the Rom city was a Seleucid town (c 300–108 BC), with its fortifications, gateway, temples, streets, and great public buildings and a complex of private houses, in connection with which was a large bath house, with mosaic floor, hot and cold baths, water closet, etc, which was heated by a furnace. Underneath the Gr walls, which were connected with the well-known red-figured Gr ware of c 400 BC, were brick structures and very thick fortress walls built in receding courses of small stones in the Bab style. In the filling of the construction trench of this Bab wall were found Israelite potsherds and a Heb seal with seemingly Bab peculiarities, and one fragment of a cuneiform tablet. Below these Bab constructions "there is a series of massive walls beautifully built of large limestone blocks founded on rock and forming a part of one great building, which can be no other than the Jewish palace." It consisted of "great open courts surrounded by small rooms, comparable in plan and even in size with the Bab palaces and is certainly royal in size and architecture." Its massive outlines which for the first time reveal to the modern world the masonry of an Israelite palace show that unexpected material resources and technical skill were at the command of the kings of Israel. An even greater discovery was made when on the palace hill was found an alabaster vase inscribed with the cartouche of Osorkon II of Egypt (874–853 BC), Ahab's contemporary; and at the same level, about 75 fragments of pottery, not jar-handles but ostraca, inscribed with records or memorials in ancient Hebrew. The script is Phoen, and according to such experts as Lyon and Driver, practically identical with that of the Siloam Inscription (c 700 BC) and M S (c 850 BC). "The inscriptions are written in ink with a reed pen in an easy flowing hand and show a pleasing contrast to the stiff forms of Phoen inscriptions cut in stone. The graceful curves give evidence of a skill which comes only with long practice" (Lyon). The ink is well preserved, the writing is distinct, the words are divided by dots or strokes, and with two exceptions all the ostraca are dated, the reigning king probably being Ahab. The following samples represent the ordinary memoranda: "In the 11th year. From 'Abi'ezer. For 'Asâ, 'Akhemelek (and) Ba'alâ. From 'Elnathan (?). . . . . In 9th yr. From Yasat. For 'Abino'am. A jar of old wine. . . . . In 11th yr. For Badyo. The vineyard of the Tell." Baal and El form a part of several of the proper names, as also the Heb Divine name, the latter occurring naturally not in its full form, YHWH, but as ordinarily in compounds YW (Lyon, *Harvard Theol. Rev.*, 1911, 136–43; cf Driver, *PEFS*, 1911, 79–83). In a list of 30 proper names all but three have Bib. equivalents. "They are the earliest specimens of Heb writing which have been found, and in amount they exceed by far all known ancient Heb inscriptions; moreover, they are the first Palestinian records of this nature to be found" (see esp. Lyon, op. cit., I, 70–96; II, 102–13; III, 136–38; IV, 136–43; Reisner, ib, III, 248–63; also *Theol. Literaturblatt*, 1911, III, 4; Driver, as above; *MNOP*, 1911, 23–27; *Rev. biblique*, VI, 435–45).

(3) *'Ain Shems* (**Beth-shemesh**, 1 S **6** 1–21; 2 K **14** 11).—In a short but important campaign, during 1911–12, in which from 36 to 167 workmen were employed, Dr. D. Mackenzie uncovered a massive double gate and primitive walls 12–15 ft. high, with mighty bastions, and found in later deposits Egyp images, Syrian Astartes, imported Aegean vases and a remarkable series of inscribed royal jar-handles "dating from the Israelite monarchy" (Vincent), as also what seemed to be an ancient Sem tomb with façade entrance. The proved Cretan relations here are esp. important. The town was suddenly destroyed, probably in the era of Sennacherib (*PEFS*, 1911, LXIX, 172; 1912, XII, 145).

(4) *Gezer* (Palestine Exploration Fund).—*Tell ej-Jezer* occupies a conspicuous position, over 250 ft. above the plain, and 750 ft. above the sea, on a ridge of hills some 20 miles N.W. of Jerus, overlooking the plain toward Jaffa, which is 17 miles distant. It is in plain sight of the two chief trade caravan roads of Southern Pal which it controlled. The ancient Gezer was well known from many references to it on the Egyp records, the names of several governors of Gezer being given in letters dating from c 1400 BC and Menephtah (c 1200 BC) calling himself "Binder of Gezer," etc. The discovery of the boundary stones of Gezer (see above) positively identified it. It was thoroughly excavated by R. A. Stewart Macalister in 1902–5, 1907–9, during which time 10,000 photographs were made of objects found. No explorations have been so long continued on one spot or have brought more unique discoveries or thrown more light upon the development of Palestinian culture and religion, and none have been reported as fully (*Excavations of Gezer*, 1912, 3 vols; *Hist of Civilization in Pal*, 1912). Ten periods are recognized as being distinctly marked in the history of the mound—which broadly

speaking represents the development in all parts of Pal: (*a*) pre-Sem period (c 3000–2500 BC), to the entrance of the first Semites; (*b*) first Sem city (c 2500–1800 BC), to the end of the XIIth Egyp Dynasty; (*c*) second Sem city (c 1800–1400 BC), to the end of the XVIIIth Egyp Dynasty; (*d*) third Sem city (c 1400–1000 BC), to the beginning of the Heb monarchy; (*e*) fourth Sem city (c 1000–550 BC), to the destruction of the monarchy and the Bab exile; (*f*) Pers and Hel period (550–100 BC), to the beginning of the Rom dominion; (*g*) Rom (100 BC–350 AD); (*h*) Byzantine (350–600 AD); (*i*) and (*j*) early and modern Arabian (350 AD to the present). The last four periods have left few important memorials and may be omitted from review.

(*a*) The aboriginal non-Sem inhabitants of Gezer were troglodytes (cf Gen **14** 6) living in the caves which honeycomb this district (cf *ZDPV*, 1909, VI, 12), modifying these only slightly for home purposes. They were a small race 5 ft. 4 in. to 5 ft. 7 in. in height, slender in form, with rather broad heads and thick skulls, who hunted, kept domestic animals (cows, sheep, goats); had fire and cooked food; possessed no metals; made by hand a porous and gritty soft-baked pottery which they decorated with red lines; and were capable of a rude art—the oldest in Pal—in which drawings of various animals are given. They prized certain bars of stone (possibly phallic); they probably offered sacrifices; they certainly cremated their dead, depositing with the ashes a few food vessels. The crematory found was 31 ft. long by 24 wide, and in it the bodies were burned whole, without regard to orientation. Many cup marks in the rocks suggest possible religious rites; in close connection with these markings were certain remains, including bones of swine (cf Lev **11** 7).

(*b*) The Semites who displaced this population were more advanced in civilization, having bronze tools and potter's wheels, with finer and more varied pottery; they were a heavier race, being 5 ft. 7 in. to 5 ft. 11 in. tall, larger-boned, thicker-skulled, and with longer faces. They did not burn but buried their dead carelessly upon the floor of the natural caves. The grave deposits are the same as before; occasionally some beads are found with the body. The former race had surrounded their settlement with a wall 6 ft. high and 8 ft. thick, mostly earth, though faced with selected stones; but this race built a wall of hammered stones, though irregularly cut and laid, the wall being 10 ft. thick, and one gateway being 42 ft. wide, flanked by two towers. While huts were always the common residences (as in later eras), yet some buildings of stone were erected toward the close of this period and one large palace was found, built of stone and having a row of columns down the center, and containing a complex of rooms, including one rectangular hall, 40 ft. long by 25 ft. wide. Most remarkable of all were their works of engineering. They hewed enormous constructions, square, rectangular and circular, out of the soft chalk and limestone rocks, one of which contained 60 chambers, one chamber being 400 by 80 ft. The supreme work, however, was a tunnel which was made c 2000 BC, passing out of use c 1450–1250 BC, and which shows the power of these early Palestinians. It was 200–250 ft. long and consisted of a roadway cut through the hill of rock some 47½ ft. to an imposing archway 23 ft. high and 12 ft. 10 in. broad, which led to a long sloping passage of equal dimensions, with the arch having a vaulted roof and the sides well plumb. This led into a bed of much harder rock, where dimensions were reduced and the workmanship was poorer, but ultimately reached, about 130 ft. below the present surface of the ground, an enormous living spring of such depth that the excavators could not empty it of the soft mud with which it was filled. A well-cut but well-worn and battered stone staircase, over 12 ft. broad, connected the spring with the upper section of the tunnel 94 ft. above. Beyond the spring was a natural cave 80 by 25 ft. Dr. Macalister asks, "Did a Canaanite governor plan and Canaanite workmen execute this vast work? How did the ancient engineers discover the spring?" No one can answer; but certainly the tunnel was designed to bring the entrance of the water passage within the courtyard protected by the palace walls.

Another great reservoir, 57 by 46 ft., at another part of the city was quarried in the rock to a depth of 29½ ft., and below this another one of equal depth but not so large, and narrowing toward the bottom. These were covered with two coats of cement and surrounded by a wall; they would hold 60,000 gals.

(*c*) The second Sem city, built on the ruins of the first, was smaller, but more luxurious. There were fewer buildings but larger rooms. The potter's wheel was worked by the foot. Pottery becomes much finer, the styles and decoration reaching a climax of grace and refinement. Foreign trade begins in this period and almost or quite reaches its culmination. The Hyksos scarabs found here prove that under their rule (XVIth and XVIIth Dynasties) there was close intercourse with Pal, and the multitudes of Egyp articles show that this was also true before and after the Hyksos. The Cretan and the Aegean trade, esp. through Cyprus, introduced new art ideas which soon brought local attempts at imitation. Scribes' implements for writing in wax and clay begin here and are found in all strata hereafter.

Interments in the Second Burial Cave at Gezer.

While the pottery is elaborately painted, it is but little molded. The older "combed" ornament practically disappears, while burnished ornament reaches high-water mark. Animal figures are common, the eyes often being elaborately modeled and stuck on; but it is infantile art. Burials still occur in natural caves, but also in those hewn artificially; the bodies are carelessly deposited on the floor without coffins, generally in a crouching position, and stones are laid around and over them without system. Drink offerings always and food offerings generally are placed with the dead. Scarabs are found with the skeletons, and ornaments of bronze and silver, occasionally gold and beads, and sometimes weapons. Lamps also begin to be deposited, but in small numbers.

(*d*) During this period Menephtah "spoiled Gezer," and Israel established itself in Canaan. The excavations have given no hint of Menephtah's raid, unless it be found in an ivory pectoral bearing his cartouche. About 1400 BC a great wall, 4 ft. thick, was built of large and well-shaped stones and protected later by particularly fine towers, perhaps, as Macalister suggests, by the Pharaoh who captured Gezer and gave it as a dowry to his daughter, wife of King Solomon. A curious fact, which seemingly illustrates Josh **16** 10, is the large increase of the town shortly after the Heb invasion. "The houses are smaller and more crowded and the sacred area of the high place is built over." "There is no indication of an exclusively Israelite population around the city outside" (Macalister, v. Driver, *Modern Research*, 69). That land was taken for building purposes from the old sacred enclosure, and that new ideas in building plans and more heavily fortified buildings were now introduced have been thought to suggest the entrance among the ancient population of another element with different ideas. The finest palace of this period with very thick walls (3–9 ft.) carefully laid out at right angles, and certainly built near "the time of the Heb invasion," was perhaps the residence of Horam (Josh **10** 33). At this period seals begin (10 being found here, as against 28 in the next period, and 31 in the Hellenistic) and also iron tools; the use of the carpenter's compass is proved, the bow drill was probably in use, bronze and iron nails appear (wrought iron being fairly common from c 1000 BC); a cooking-pot of bronze was found, and spoons of shell and bronze; modern methods of making buttons and button holes are finest from this period, pottery buttons being introduced in the next city. One incidental Bible reference to the alliance between Gezer and Lachish (Josh **10** 33) finds unexpected illustration from the fact that a kind of pottery peculiar to Lachish, not having been found in any other of the Southern Palestinian towns, was found at Gezer. The pottery here in general shows the same method of construction as in the 3d stratum, but the decoration and shapes deteriorate, while there is practically no molding. It shows much the same foreign influence as before, the styles being affected from Egypt, Crete, the Aegean, and esp. Cyprus. From this period come 218 scarabs, 68 from the period previous and 93 from the period following. Ornamental colored specimens of imported Egyp glass also occur, clear glass not being found till the next period. Little intercourse is proved with Babylon at this era: as against 16 Bab cylinders found in the previous period, only 4 were found in this and 15 in the next period. There is no marked change in the method of disposing of the dead, but the food vessels are of smaller size and are placed in the graves in great numbers, most of these being broken either through the use of poor vessels because of economy or with the idea of liberating the spirit of the object that it might serve the deceased in the spirit world. Lamps are common now in every tomb but there is a marked decrease in the quantity and value of ornamental objects. Religious emblems occur but rarely. The worship of Astarte (see ASHTORETH), the female consort of Baal, is most popular at this era, terra cotta figures and plaques of this goddess being found in many types and in large numbers. It is suggestive that these grow notably less in the next stratum. It is also notable that primitive idols are certainly often intentionally ugly (Vincent). So to this day Arabs ward off the evil eye.

(*e*) This period, during which almost the entire prophetic lit. was produced, is of peculiar interest. Gezer at this time as at every other period was in general appearance like a modern Arab village, a huge mass of crooked, narrow, airless streets, shut inside a thick wall, with no trace of sanitary conveniences, with huge cisterns in which dead men could lie undetected for centuries, and with no sewers. Even in the Maccabean time the only sewer found ran, not into a cesspool, but into the ground, close to the governor's palace. The mortality was excessively high, few old men being found in the cemeteries, while curvature of the spine, syphilis, brain disease, and esp. broken, unset bones were common. Tweezers, pins and needles, kohl bottles, mirrors, combs, perfume boxes, scrapers (for baths) were common in this stratum and in all that follow it, while we have also here silver earrings, bracelets and other beautiful ornaments with the first sign of clear glass objects; tools also of many kinds of stone, bronze and iron, an iron hoe just like the modern one, and the first known pulley of bronze. The multitude of Heb weights found here have thrown much new light on the weight-standards of Pal (see esp. Macalister, *Gezer*, II, 287–92; E. J. Pilcher, *PEFS*, 1912; A. R. S. Kennedy, *Expos T*, XXIV).

The pottery was poor in quality, clumsy and coarse in shape and ornament, excepting as it was imported, the local Aegean imitations being unworthy. Combed ornament was not common, and the burnished as a rule was limited to random scratches. Multiple lamps became common, and a large variety of styles in small jugs was introduced. The motives of the last period survive, but in a degenerate form. The bird friezes so characteristic of the 3d Sem period disappear. The scarab stamp goes out of use, but the impressions of other seals "now become fairly common as potter's marks." These consist either of simple devices (stars, pentacles, etc) or of names in Old Heb script. These Heb-inscribed stamps were found at many sites and consist of two classes, (i) those containing personal names, such as Azariah, Haggai, Menahem, Shebaniah, etc, (ii) those which are confined to four names, often repeated—Hebron, Socoh, Ziph, Mamshith—in connection with a reference to the king, e.g. "For [or Of] the king of Hebron." These latter date, according to Dr. Macalister's final judgment, from the

Stamped Jar-Handles Excavated at Gezer.

Pers period. He still thinks they represent the names of various potters or potters' guilds in Pal (cf 1 Ch **2, 4, 5,** and see esp. *Bible Side-Lights from Gezer*, 150, etc), but others suppose these names to represent the local measures of capacity, which differed in these various districts; others that these represented different tax-districts where wine jars would be used and bought. At any rate, we certainly have here the work of the king's potters referred to in 1 Ch **4** 23. Another very curious Heb tablet inscription is the so-called Zodiacal Tablet, on which the signs of the Zodiac are figured with certain other symbols which were at first supposed to express some esoteric magical or religious meaning, but which seem only to represent the ancient agricultural year with the proper months indicated for sowing and reaping—being the same as the modern seasons and crops excepting that flax was cultivated anciently. An even more important literary memorial from this period consists of two cuneiform tablets written about three-quarters of a century after the Ten Tribes had been carried to Assyria and foreign colonies had been thrown into Israelite territory. This collapse of the Northern Kingdom was not marked by any local catastrophe, so far as the ruins indicate, any more than the collapse of the Can. kingdom when Israel entered Pal; but soon afterward we find an Assyr colony settled in Gezer "using the Assyr language and letters . . . . and carrying on business with Assyr methods." In one tablet (649 BC), which is a bill of sale for certain property, containing description of the same, appeared the name of the buyer, seals of seller and signature of 12 witnesses, one of whom is the Egyp governor of the new town, another an Assyr noble whose name precedes that of the governor, and still another a Western Asiatic, the others being Assyrian. It is a Hebrew "Nethaniah," who the next year, as the other tablet shows, sells his field, his seal bearing upon it a lunar stellar emblem. Notwithstanding the acknowledged literary work of high quality produced in Pal during this period, no other hint of this is found clear down to the Gr period except in one neo-Bab tablet.

The burials in this period were much as previously, excepting that the caves were smaller and toward the end of the period shelves around the walls received the bodies. In one Sem tomb as many as 150 vessels were found. Quite the most astonishing discovery at this level was that of several tombs which scholars generally agree to be "Philistine." They were not native Canaanite, but certainly Aegean intruders with relations with Crete and Cyprus, such as we would expect the Philis to have (see PHILISTINES). The tombs were oblong or rectangular, covered with large horizontal slabs, each tomb containing but a single body, stretched out with the head to the E. or W. One tomb was that of a girl of 18 with articles of alabaster and silver about her, and wearing a Cretan silver mouth plate; another was a man of

High Place of the Cave-Dwellers at Gezer.

40 with agate seal of Assyr design, a two-handled glass vessel, etc; another was a woman surrounded by handsome ornaments of bronze, lead, silver and gold, with a basalt scarab between her knees. The richest tomb was that of a girl whose head had been severed from the body; with her was a hemispherical bowl, ornamented with rosette and lotus pattern, and a horde of beautiful things. The iron in these tombs was noticeable (cf 1 S **17** 7), and in one tomb were found two ingots of gold, one of these being of the same weight almost to a fraction as that of Achan (Josh **7** 21). The most impressive discovery was the high place. This began as early as 2500–2000 BC, and grew by the addition of monoliths and surrounding buildings up to this era. The eight huge uncut pillars which were found standing in a row, with two others fallen (yet cf Benzinger, *Heb Archaeology*, 320), show us the actual appearance of this ancient worshipping-place so famous in the Bible (Dt **16** 22; 2 K **17** 9.11; **23** 8). The top of one of these monoliths had been worn smooth by kisses; another was an importation, being possibly, as has been suggested, a captured "Aril"; another stone, near by, had a large cavity in its top, nearly 3 ft. long and 2 ft. broad and 1 ft. 2 in. deep, which is differently interpreted as being the block upon which the *'ăshērāh*, so often mentioned in connection with the *maççēbhōth*, may have been erected, or as an altar, or perhaps a laver for ritual ablutions. Inside the sacred enclosure was found a small bronze cobra (2 K **18** 4), and also the entrance to an ancient cave, where probably oracles were given, the excavators finding that this cave was connected with another by a small, secret passage—through which presumably the message was delivered. In the stratum underlying the high place was a cemetery of infants buried in large jars. "That the sacrificed infants were the firstborn, devoted in the temple, is indicated by the fact that none were over a week old" (Macalister). In all the Sem strata bones of children were also found in corners of the houses, the deposits being identical with infant burials in the high place; and examination showed that these were not stillborn children. At least some of the burials under the house thresholds and under the foundation of walls carry with them the mute proofs of this most gruesome practice. In one place the skeleton of an old woman was found in a corner where a hole had been left just large enough for this purpose. A youth of about 18 had been cut in two at the waist and only the upper part of his body deposited. Before the coming into Pal of the Israelites, a lamp began to be placed under the walls and foundations, probably symbolically to take the place of human sacrifice. A lamp and bowl deposit under the threshold, etc, begins in the 3d Sem period, but is rare till the middle of that period. In the 4th Sem period it is common, though not universal; in the Hellenic it almost disappears. Macalister suspects that these bowls held blood or grape juice. In one striking case a bronze figure was found in place of a body. Baskets full of phalli were carried away from the high place. Various types of the Astarte were found at Gezer. When we see the strength and popularity of this religion against which the prophets contended in Canaan, "we are amazed at the survival of this world-religion," and we now see "why Ezra and Nehemiah were forced to raise the 'fence of the law' against this heathenism, which did in fact overthrow all other Sem religions" (George Adam Smith, *PEFS*, 1906, 288).

(*f*) During the Maccabean epoch the people of Gezer built reservoirs (one having a capacity of 4,000,000 gals.), used well-paved rooms, favored complex house plans with pillars, the courtyard becoming less important as compared with the rooms, though domestic fowls were now for the first time introduced. The architectural decorations have

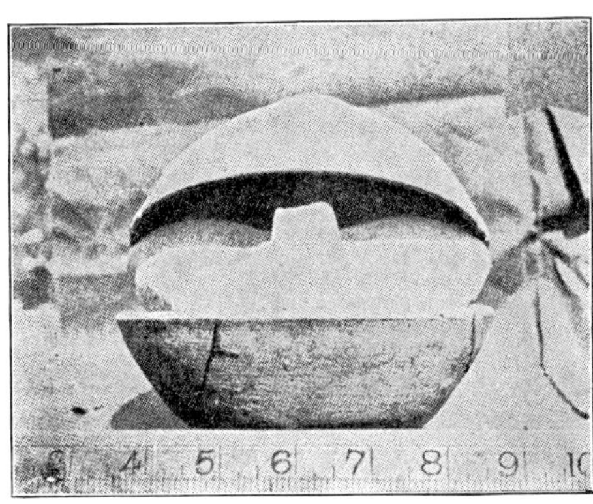

Lamp and Bowls Discovered at Gezer.

all been annihilated (as elsewhere in Pal) excepting a few molded stones and an Ionic volute from a palace, supposed to be that of Simon Maccabaeus because of the references in Jos and because of a scribbled imprecation found in the courtyard: "May fire overtake [?] Simon's palace." This is the only inscription from all these post-exilic centuries, to which so much of the beautiful Bible lit. is ascribed, excepting one grotesque animal figure on which is scrawled a name which looks a little like "Antiochus." Only a few scraps of Gr bowls, some Rhodian jar-handles, a few bronze and iron arrow heads, a few animal figures and a fragment of an Astarte, of doubtful chronology, remain from these four centuries. The potsherds prove that foreign imports continued and that the local potters followed classic models and did excellent work. The ware was always burnt hard; combed ornament and burnishing were out of style; molded ornament was usually confined to the rope design; painted decorations were rare; potter's marks were generally in Gr, though some were in Heb, the letters being of late form, and no names appearing similar to those found in Scripture. The tombs were well-cut square chambers, with shafts hewn in the rock for the bodies, usually nine to each tomb, which were run into them head foremost. The doorways were well cut, the covers almost always being movable flat slabs, though in one case a swinging stone door was found—circular rolling stones or the "false doors" so often found in the Jerus tombs being unknown here. Little shrines were erected above the forecourt or vestibule. When the body decayed, the bones in tombs having these *kūkhīn*, shafts, were collected into ossuaries, the inscriptions on these ossuaries showing clearly the transition from Old Heb to the square character. After the Maccabean time the town was deserted, though a small Christian community lived here in the 4th cent. AD. See also GEZER.

LITERATURE.—Most important recent monographs: Publications of Palestine Exploration Fund, esp. *Survey of Western Pal* (9 vols, 1884); *Survey of Eastern Pal* (2 vols, 1889); "Pal Pilgrim's Text Society's Library" (13 vols) and the books of W. M. Flinders Petrie, F. J. Bliss and R. A. S. Macalister; also Bliss, *Development of Pal Exploration* (1906), and Macalister, *Bible Side-Lights from the Mound of Gezer* (1906); Ernst Sellin, *Tell Ta'annek* (1904); *Eine Nachlese auf dem Tell Ta'annek* (1905); C. Steuernagel, *Tell el-Mutesellim* (1908); Mommert, *Topog. des alten Jerus* (1902–7); H. Guthe, *Bibelatlas* (1911).

Most important periodicals: *PEFS; ZDPV; Mitteilungen und Nachrichten des deutschen Palästina-Vereins; Palästina-Jahrbuch (MNDPV); Revue Biblique.*

Most important general works: L. B. Paton, *Early History of Syria and Pal* (1902); Cuinet, *Syrie, Liban et Pal* (1896–1900); H. V. Hilprecht, *Explorations in Bible Lands during the 19th Cent.* (1903); P. H. Vincent, *Canaan, d'après l'exploration récente* (1907); G. A. Smith, *Jerus* (1908); S. R. Driver, *Modern Research as Illustrating the Bible* (1909).

CAMDEN M. COBERN

PALLU, pal'ū, **PALLUITES,** pal'ū-īts (פַּלּוּא, *pallū'*, "distinguished"): A son of Reuben (Gen **46** 9 ["Phallu"]; Ex **6** 14; Nu **26** 5.8; 1 Ch **5** 3). Perhaps Peleth of Nu **16** 1 is the same. **Palluites,** the patronymic, occurs in Nu **26** 5.

PALM, päm (**OF THE HAND**) (כַּף, *kaph*): The Heb word which is used in a variety of senses (see HAND; PAW) is usually trd "hand" in EV, but the tr "palm" is found in 5 passages of the OT, in 3 of which the Heb text adds the word יָד, *yādh* ("hand," 1 S **5** 4; 2 K **9** 35; Dnl **10** 10). It would properly mean the "hollow hand" (root *kāphaph*, "to bend," "to curve"), which receives or grasps things. It is therefore used in reference to filling the priest's hands with sacrificial portions (Lev **14** 15.26). The palms of the hands of Dagon are mentioned as cut off, when the idol was found mutilated in the presence of the ark of Jeh (1 S **5** 4), from which may be inferred that this idol probably was represented with hands spread out in blessing, as we find in numerous Bab representations of divinities.

In a beautiful metaphor God answers the repentant people of Jerus, who thought Jeh had forgotten and forsaken them: "Behold, I have graven thee upon the palms of my hands" (Isa **49** 16; see also Ecclus **18** 3). Daniel is touched upon the palms of his hands to wake him from sleep (Dnl **10** 10).

In the NT we find the phrase, "to smite with the palms of the hands," as a tr of the Gr vb. ῥαπίζω, *rhapízō* (Mt **26** 67; see also **5** 39 and LXX Hos **11** 4; 1 Esd **4** 30), and, derived from the same vb., ῥάπισμα, *rhápisma*, a blow of the palm on the cheek, etc (Mk **14** 65; Jn **18** 22; **19** 3, where, however, in EV the word "palm" has not been given). The marginal tr "to smite or strike with rods" (Mt **26** 67; Jn **18** 22; **19** 3) and "strokes of rods" (Mk **14** 65 m) does not seem to be applicable to the Gr text of the OT and NT, while it is a frequent meaning of the words in classical language. It would therefore be better to eliminate these marginal additions.

H. L. E. LUERING

PALM TREE, päm'trē (תָּמָר, *tāmār*, same as the Aram. and Ethiopic, but in Arab.="date"; **φοίνιξ,** *phoínix* [Ex **15** 27; Lev **23** 40; Nu **33** 9; Dt **34** 3; Jgs **1** 16; **3** 13; 2 Ch **28** 15; Neh **8** 15; Ps **92** 12; Cant **7** 7 f; Joel **1** 12]; תֹּמֶר, *tōmer*, Deborah "dwelt under the palm-tree" [Jgs **4** 5]; "They are like a palm-tree [m "pillar"], of turned work" [Jer **10** 5]; תִּמֹרָה, *tīmōrāh* [only in pl.], the palm tree as an architectural feature [1 K **6**

1. Palm Trees

Date Palm with Fruit (at Jaffa).

29.32.35; **7** 36; 2 Ch **3** 5; Ezk **40** 16]; Gr only Ecclus **50** 12; Jn **12** 13; Rev **7** 9): The palm, *Phoenix dactylifera* (N.O. *Palmeae*), Arab. *nakhl*, is a tree which from the earliest times has been associated with the Sem peoples. In Arabia the very existence of man depends largely upon its presence, and many authorities consider this to have been its original habitat. It is only natural that such a tree should have been sacred both there and in Assyria in the earliest ages. In Pal the palm leaf appears as an ornament upon pottery as far back as 1800 BC (cf *PEF*, Gezer Mem., II, 172). In Egypt the tall palm stem forms a constant feature in early architecture, and among the Hebrews it was extensively used as a decoration of the temple (1 K **6** 29.32.35; **7** 36; 2 Ch **3** 5). It is a symbol of beauty (Cant **7** 7) and of the righteous man:

"The righteous shall flourish like the palm-tree:
He shall grow like a cedar in Lebanon.
They are planted in the house of Jehovah;
They shall flourish in the courts of our God.
They shall still bring forth fruit in old age;
They shall be full of sap and green" (Ps **92** 12–14).

The palm tree or branch is used extensively on Jewish coinage and most noticeably appears as a symbol of the land upon the celebrated *Judaea Capta* coins of Vespasian. A couple of centuries or so later it forms a prominent architectural feature in the ornamentation of the Galilean synagogues, e.g. at *Tell Ḥûm* (Capernaum). The method of artificial fertilization of the pistillate (female) flowers by means of the staminate (male) flowers appears to have been known in the earliest historic times. Winged figures are depicted on some of the early Assyr sculptures shaking a bunch of the male flowers over the female for the same purpose as the people of modern Gaza ascend the tall trunks of the fruit-bearing palms and tie among the female flowers a bunch of the pollen-bearing male flowers,

In Pal today the palm is much neglected; there are few groves except along the coast, e.g. at the bay of Akka, Jaffa and Gaza; solitary palms occur all over the land in the courtyards of mosques (cf Ps **92** 13) and houses even in the mountains.

2. Their Ancient Abundance in Palestine

Once palms flourished upon the Mount of Olives (Neh **8** 15), and Jericho was long known as the "city of palm-trees" (Dt **34** 3; Jgs **1** 16; **3** 13; 2 Ch **28** 15; Jos, *BJ*, IV, viii, 2–3), but today the only palms are scarce and small; under its name Hazazon-tamar (2 Ch **20** 2), En-gedi would appear to have been as much a place of palms in ancient days as we know it was in later history. A city, too, called Tamar ("date palm") appears to have been somewhere near the southwestern corner of the Dead Sea (Ezk **47** 19; **48** 28). Today the numerous salt-encrusted stumps of wild palm trees washed up all along the shores of the Dead Sea witness to the existence of these trees within recent times in some of the deep valleys around.

Coin of Vespasian Representing Judaea Mourning for Her Captivity.

Branches of palms have been symbolically associated with several different ideas. A palm branch is used in Isa **9** 14; **19** 15 to signify the "head," the highest of the people, as contrasted with the rush, the "tail," or humblest of the people. Palm branches appear from early times to have been associated with rejoicing.

3. Palm Branches

On the first day of the Feast of Tabernacles the Hebrews were commanded to take branches of palms, with other trees, and rejoice before God (Lev **23** 40; cf Neh **8** 15; 2 Macc **10** 7). The palm branch still forms the chief feature of the *lūlābh* carried daily by every pious Jew to the synagogue, during the feast. Later it was connected with the idea of triumph and victory. Simon Maccabaeus entered the Akra at Jerus after its capture, "with thanksgiving, and branches of palm trees, and with harps, and cymbals, and with viols, and hymns, and songs: because there was destroyed a great enemy out of Israel" (1 Macc **13** 51 AV; cf 2 Macc **10** 7). The same idea comes out in the use of palm branches by the multitudes who escorted Jesus to Jerus (Jn **12** 13) and also in the vision of the "great multitude, which no man could number . . . . standing before the . . . . Lamb, arrayed in white robes, and palms in their hands" (Rev **7** 9). Today palms are carried in every Moslem funeral procession and are laid on the new-made grave.

See also TAMAR as a proper name.

E. W. G. MASTERMAN

PALMER-WORM, päm′ẽr-wûrm (גָּזָם, *gāzām;* LXX **κάμπη**, *kámpē* [Am **4** 9; Joel **1** 4; **2** 25]): "Palmer-worm" means "caterpillar," but the insect meant is probably a kind of locust. See INSECT; LOCUST.

PALSY, pôl′zi, **PARALYSIS**, pa-ral′i-sis (**παράλυσις**, *parálusis*): The Eng. word "palsy" is derived from the OFr. *paralesie*, which in Middle Eng. was shortened into *palesie*, the form in which it appears in Wyclif's version. In the 16th cent. it appears as "palsy," the form used in AV. This, however, is seldom used at the present day, the Latinized Gr form "paralysis" being more frequently employed, both in modern literature and in colloquial Eng. "Sick of the palsy" is the tr either of the adj. *paralutikós* or of the part. of the vb. *paralúomai*. The disease is one characterized by extreme loss of the power of motion dependent on some affection either of the motor centers of the brain or of the spinal cord. It is always serious, usually intractable, and generally sudden in onset (1 Macc **9** 55 f). Miraculous cures by Our Lord are related in general terms, as in Mt **4** 24; Acts **8** 7. Aeneas (Acts **9** 33) was probably a paralytic eight years bedridden. Though the Lord addressed the paralytic let down through the roof (Mt **9** 6; Mk **2** 3; Lk **5** 18) as "son," it was not necessarily a proof that he was young, and though He prefaces the cure by declaring the forgiveness of sin, we need not infer that the disease was the result of an evil life, although it may have been. Bennett conjectures that the centurion's palsied servant grievously tormented was suffering from progressive paralysis with respiratory spasms (see PAIN). The subst. *paralusis* is only once used in the LXX in Ezk **21** 10, but here it refers to the loosing of the sword, not to the disease.

ALEX. MACALISTER

PALTI, pal′tī (פַּלְטִי, *palṭī*, "Jeh delivers"):

(1) One of the "searchers" of Canaan sent by Moses (Nu **13** 9), representing Benjamin in the expedition (ver 9).

(2) The man to whom Saul gave Michal, David's wife, after the estrangement (1 S **25** 44). He is "the captain of the people" of 2 Esd **5** 16 ("Paltiel," m "Psaltiel"). In 2 S **3** 15, he is named "Phaltiel" (AV), "Paltiel" (RV), and is there mentioned in connection with David's recovery of Michal.

PALTIEL, pal′ti-el (פַּלְטִיאֵל, *palṭī′ēl*, "God's deliverance"):

(1) A prince of Issachar (Nu **34** 26).

(2) Same as PALTI, (2) (q.v.).

PALTITE, pal′tīt (פַּלְטִי, *palṭī* [as Palti]; LXX B, **Κελωθεί**, *Kelōthei*, A, **Φελλωνεί**, *Phellōneí*): The description occurs but once in this form and is then applied to Helez, one of David's 30 valiant men (2 S **23** 26). Helez' name, however, occurs in 1 Ch **11** 27 and **27** 10 as the "Pelonite." Doubtless there is some confusion of words. The word may be given as a patronymic of Palti, or it may designate a native of the village of Beth-pelet mentioned in Josh **15** 27 and Neh **11** 26 as being in Lower Judah. Helez, however, is described as "of the children of Ephraim" in 1 Ch **27** 10.

PAMPHYLIA, pam-fil′i-a (**Παμφυλία**, *Pamphulía*): A country lying along the southern coast of Asia Minor, bounded on the N. by Pisidia, on the E. by Isauria, on the S. by the Mediterranean Sea, and on the W. by Lycia (Acts **2** 10; **27** 5).

1. Physical Features

In the earliest time Pamphylia was but a narrow strip of low-lying land between the base of the mountains and the sea, scarcely more than 20 miles long and half as wide. A high and imposing range of the Taurus Mountains practically surrounds it upon three sides, and, jutting out into the sea, isolates it from the rest of Asia Minor. Its two rivers, the Cestrus and the Cataractes, are said by ancient writers to have been navigable for several miles inland, but now the greater part of their water is diverted to the fields for irrigating purposes, and the general surface of the country has been constantly changed by the many rapid mountain streams. The level fertile coast land is therefore well watered, and the moist air, which is excessively hot and enervating, has always been laden with fever. Several roads leading from the coast up the steep mountain to the interior existed in ancient times; one of them, called the Kimax or the Ladder, with its broad stair-like steps 2,000 ft. high, may still be seen. Beyond the steps is the high land which was once called "Pisidia," but which the Romans, in 70 AD, made a part of Pamphylia.

2. Importance

Pamphylia, unless in pre-historic times, was never an independent kingdom; it was subject successively to Lydia, Persia, Macedonia, Pergamos and Rome. Because of its comparatively isolated position, civilization there was less developed than in the neighboring countries, and the Asiatic influence was at most times stronger than the Gr. As early as the 5th cent. BC a Gr colony settled there, but the Gr language which was spoken in some of its cities soon became corrupt; the Gr inscriptions, appearing upon the coins of that age, were written in a peculiar character, and before the time of Alexander the Great, Gr ceased to be spoken. Perga then became an important city and the center of the Asiatic religion, of which the Artemis of Perga, locally known as Leto, was the goddess. Coins were struck also in that city. Somewhat later the Gr city of Attalia, which was founded by Attalus III Philadelphus (159–138 BC), rose to importance, and until recent years has been the chief port of entry on the southern coast of Asia Minor. About the beginning of our era, Side became the chief city, and issued a long and beautiful series of coins, possibly to facilitate trade with the pirates who found there a favorable market for their booty. Pamphylia is mentioned as one of the recipients of the "letters" of 1 Macc **15** 23.

3. Introduction of Christianity

Christianity was first introduced to Pamphylia by Paul and Barnabas (Acts **13** 13; **14** 24), but because their stay in the country was brief, or because of the difficulty of communication with the neighboring countries, or because of the Asiatic character of the population, it was slow in being established. See also Attalia; Perga; Side, the chief cities of Pamphylia.

E. J. Banks

PAN: Name of a utensil used in the preparation or the serving of food, and representing several words in the original. Passing over the use of the word in connections like 1 Ch **9** 31, "things baked in pans," where the Heb word *ḥăbhittīm* refers, not to the pan itself, but to the cakes baked in the flat pan or griddle which was called *maḥăbhath* (see below), and the "firepans" (*maḥtāh*) (Ex **27** 3; 1 K **7** 50, etc) which seem to have been used to carry burning coals, we note the following words:

(1) מַחֲבַת, *maḥăbhath*, "pan" AV, "baking-pan" RV, a dish of uncertain shape and size which was used in the preparation of the *minḥāh*, or vegetable offering. See Lev **2** 5; **6** 21; **7** 9; 1 Ch **23** 29. On the basis of Ezk **4** 3 it might be assumed that the pan was rectangular in shape and of good size.

(2) כִּיּוֹר, *kiyyōr*, rendered "pan" in 1 S **2** 14. The same word is used in the phrase, "pan of fire" RV, "hearth of fire" AV (Zec **12** 6); and it is also tr[d] "laver" in the descriptions of the furnishing of tabernacle and temple (Ex **30** 18; 1 K **7** 30, etc). As it held water and was used for boiling meat and the like, it must have been a kind of pot or kettle.

(3) מַשְׂרֵת, *masrēth* (2 S **13** 9). The connection gives no clue as to shape or size except that it must have been small enough to serve food in, and of the proper shape to hold a substance which could be poured out. Some authorities suggest a connection with the root שְׂאֹר, *se'ōr*, "leaven," and think that this pan was like the kneading-trough in shape.

(4) סִיר, *ṣīr*, rendered "pan" in Ex **27** 3 AV, "pot" RV (see Pot).

(5) פָּרוּר, *pārūr*, "pan" in Nu **11** 8 AV, "pot" RV (see Pot).

(6) צַלָּחָה, *çēlāḥāh* (2 Ch **35** 13). Some kind of dish or pot. Slightly different forms of the same root are rendered "cruse" (2 K **2** 20 [*çelōḥīth*]), "dish" (2 K **21** 13 [*çallaḥath*]); and also in RV in Prov **19** 24; **26** 15, instead of the probably incorrect "bosom" of AV.

(7) λέβης, *lébēs*, tr[d] "pan" in 1 Esd **1** 12 AV (RV "cauldron").

(8) τήγανον, *tḗganon*, 2 Macc **7** 3.5, with the vb. τηγανίζω, *tēganízō*, ver 5, is the usual Gr word for "frying-pan," but here a large sheet of metal must be meant (cf 4 Macc **8** 13; **12** 10.20).

Literature.—Whitehouse, *Primer of Hebrew Antiquities*, 76, 77; Benzinger, *Hebräische Archäologie*, 70, 71; Nowack, *Hebräische Archäologie*, I, 144.

Walter R. Betteridge

PANNAG, pan'ag (פַּנַּג, *pannagh*; **κασία**, *kasía*; Ezk **27** 17 m, "Perhaps a kind of confection"): One of the articles of commerce of Judah and Israel. The *kasia* of the LXX is said to be a shrub similar to the laurel. Nothing is known of the nature of pannag. Cheyne (*EB*, 3555) thinks the Heb letters have got misplaced and should be גֶּפֶן, *gephen*, "vine," and he would join to it the דְּבַשׁ, *debhash*, "honey," which follows in the verse, giving a tr "grape honey," the ordinary *dibbs* of Pal—an extremely likely article of commerce. See Honey.

PANOPLY, pan'o-pli: 1 Macc **13** 29 RVm. See Armor.

PAP (שַׁד, *shadh*, שֹׁד, *shōdh*, "breast" [Ezk **23** 21]; **μαστός**, *mastós*, "the breast" [Lk **11** 27; **23** 29; Rev **1** 13]): The Eng. word, which goes back to Middle Eng. "pappe" (see Skeat, *Concise Etymological Dict. of the Eng. Language*, 327) and is now obsolete, has been replaced in RV by "breast." The Heb word signifies the "female breast"; the Gr word has a wider signification, including the male chest.

PAPER, pā'pēr. See Crafts, II, 13; Papyrus; Reed; Writing.

PAPER REEDS, rēdz: In Isa **19** 7 AV (RV "meadows").

PAPHOS, pā'fos: The name of two towns, Old (Παλαιὰ Πάφος, *Palaiá Páphos*, or Παλαίπαφος, *Palaípaphos*) and New Paphos (Νέα Πάφος, *Néa Páphos*), situated at the southwestern extremity of Cyprus.

1. Site

Considerable confusion is caused by the use of the single name Paphos in ancient writers to denote now one, now the other, of these cities. That referred to in Acts **13** 6.13 is strictly called New Paphos (modern *Baffa*), and lay on the coast about a mile S. of the modern *Ktima* and some 10 miles N.W. of the old city. The latter (modern *Kouklia*) is situated on an eminence more than a mile from the sea, on the left bank of the *Diárrizo*, probably the ancient Bocarus.

2. History of Old Paphos

It was founded by Cinyras, the father of Adonis, or, according to another legend, by Aerias, and formed the capital of the most important kingdom in Cyprus except that of Salamis. Its territory embraced a considerable portion of Western Cyprus, extending northward to that of Soli, southward to that of Curium and eastward to the range of Troödus. Among its last kings was Nicocles, who ruled shortly after the death of Alexander the Great. In 310 BC Nicocreon of Salamis, who had been set over the whole of Cyprus by

Ptolemy I of Egypt, was forced to put an end to his life at Paphos for plotting with Antigonus (Diodorus xx. 21, who wrongly gives the name as Nicocles; see *Athenische Mitteilungen*, XXII, 203 ff), and from that time Paphos remained under Egyp rule until the Rom annexation of Cyprus in 58 BC. The growth of New Paphos brought with it the decline of the old city, which was also ruined by successive earthquakes. Yet its temple still retained much of its old fame, and in 69 AD Titus, the future emperor of Rome, turned aside on his journey to Jerus, which he was to capture in the following year, to visit the sacred shrine and to inquire of the priests into the fortune which awaited him (Tacitus *Hist.* ii.2–4; Suetonius *Titus* 5).

3. History of New Paphos

New Paphos, originally the seaport of the old town, was founded, according to tradition, by Agapenor of Arcadia (*Iliad* ii.609; Pausan. viii.5, 2). Its possession of a good harbor secured its prosperity, and it had several rich temples. According to Dio Cassius (liv.23) it was restored by Augustus in 15 BC after a destructive earthquake and received the name Augusta (Gr Sebaste). Under the Rom Empire it was the administrative capital of the island and the seat of the governor. The extant remains all date from this period and include those of public buildings, private houses, city walls and the moles of the harbor.

4. The Temple and Cult

But the chief glory of Paphos and the source of its fame was the local cult, of which the kings and their descendants remained hereditary priests down to the Rom seizure of Cyprus. The goddess, identified with the Gr Aphrodite, who was said to have risen from the sea at Paphos, was in reality a Nature-goddess, closely resembling the Bab Ishtar and the Phoen Astarte, a native deity of Asia Minor and the Aegean Islands. Her cult can be traced back at Paphos to Homeric times (*Odyssey* viii.362) and was repeatedly celebrated by Gr and Lat poets (Aeschylus *Suppl.* 555; Aristoph. *Lys.* 833; Virgil *Aen.* i.415; Horace *Odes* i.19 and 30; iii.26; Statius *Silvae* i.2, 101, etc). The goddess was represented, not by a statue in human form, but by a white conical stone (Max. Tyr. viii.8; Tacitus *Hist.* ii.3; Servius *Ad Aen.* i.724), of which models were on sale for the benefit of pilgrims (Athenaeus xv.18); her worship was sensuous in character and she is referred to by Athanasius as the deification of lust (*Contra Gentes* 9). Excavation has brought to light at Old Paphos a complex of buildings belonging to Rom times and consisting of an open court with chambers or colonnades on three sides and an entrance on the E. only, the whole forming a quadrilateral enclosure with sides about 210 ft. long. In this court may have stood the altar, or altars, of incense (Homer speaks of a single altar, Virgil of "a hundred altars warm with Sabaean frankincense"); no blood might be shed thereon, and although it stood in the open it was "wet by no rain" (Tacitus, l.c.; Pliny, *NH*, ii.210). On the south side are the ruins of another building, possibly an earlier temple, now almost destroyed save for the western wall (*Journal of Hellenic Studies*, IX, 193–224). But the fact that no remains or inscriptions have been found here earlier than the Rom occupation of Cyprus militates against the view that the sanctuary stood at this spot from prehistoric times. Its site may be sought at *Xylino*, a short distance to the N. of *Kouklia* (D. G. Hogarth, *Times*, August 5, 1910), or possibly on the plateau of *Rhantidi*, some 3 miles S.E. of the village, where numerous inscriptions in the old Cyprian syllabic script were found in the summer of 1910 (M. Ohnefalsch-Richter, *Times*, July 29, 1910).

5. The Apostles' Visit

After visiting Salamis and passing through the whole island, about 100 miles in length, Barnabas, Paul and Mark reached Paphos, the residence of the Rom proconsul, Sergius Paulus (for the title see Cyprus). Here too they would doubtless begin by preaching in the synagogue, but the governor—who is probably the same Paulus whose name appears as proconsul in an inscription of Soli (D. G. Hogarth, *Devia Cypria*, 114)—hearing of their mission, sent for them and questioned them on the subject of their preaching. A Jew named Bar-Jesus or Elymas, who, as a Magian or soothsayer, "was with the proconsul," presumably as a member of his suite, used all his powers of persuasion to prevent his patron from giving his adherence to the new faith, and was met by Paul (it is at this point that the name is first introduced) with a scathing denunciation and a sentence of temporary loss of sight. The blindness which at once fell on him produced a deep impression on the mind of the proconsul, who professed his faith in the apostolic teaching. From Paphos, Paul and his companions sailed in a northwesterly direction to Perga in Pamphylia (Acts **13** 6–13).

Paul did not revisit Paphos, but we may feel confident that Barnabas and Mark would return there on their 2d missionary journey (Acts **15** 39). Of the later history of the Paphian church we know little. Tychicus, Paul's companion, is said to have been martyred there, and Jerome tells us that Hilarion sought in the neighborhood of the decayed and almost deserted town the quiet and retirement which he craved (*Vita Hilar.* 42). The *Acta Barnabae* speak of a certain Rhodon, who was attached to the temple service at Old Paphos, as having accepted the Christian faith.

Literature.—Besides the works already referred to, see *Journal of Hellenic Studies*, IX, 175–92 (citation of passages from ancient authors relating to Old Paphos, together with a list of mediaeval and modern authorities), 225–71 (inscriptions and tombs), and the bibliography appended to art. Cyprus.

Marcus N. Tod

PAPYRUS, pa-pī′rus (*Cyperus papyrus;* **βύβλος**, *búblos*, **βίβλος**, *bíblos*, whence **βιβλίον**, *biblíon*, "a roll," **τὰ βιβλία**, *tá biblía*, "the Books" = the Bible):

1. Papyrus Paper
2. Egyptian Papyri
3. Aramaic Papyri
4. Greek Papyri
5. Their Discovery
6. Classical Papyri
7. Septuagint Papyri
8. NT Papyri
9. Theological Papyri
10. Documentary Papyri
11. Contribution to NT Study
12. Chief Collections
13. Coptic, Arabic and Other Papyri

A marsh or water plant, abundant in Egypt in ancient times, serving many purposes in antiquity. The papyrus tuft was the emblem of the Northern Kingdom in Egypt. Like the lotus, it suggested one of the favorite capitals of Egyp architecture. Ropes, sandals, and mats were made from its fibers (see *Odyssey* xxi.391; Herod. ii.37, 69), and bundles of the long, light stalks were bound together into light boats (Isa **18** 2; Breasted, *Hist Egyptians*, 91).

1. Papyrus Paper

Most importantly, from it was made the tough and inexpensive paper which was used from very ancient times in Egypt and which became the common writing-material of the ancient world. The white cellular pith of the long triangular papyrus stalk was stripped of its bark or rind and sliced into thin strips. Two layers of these strips were laid at right angles to each other, pasted together (Pliny says with the aid of Nile water), dried and smoothed. The sheets thus formed were

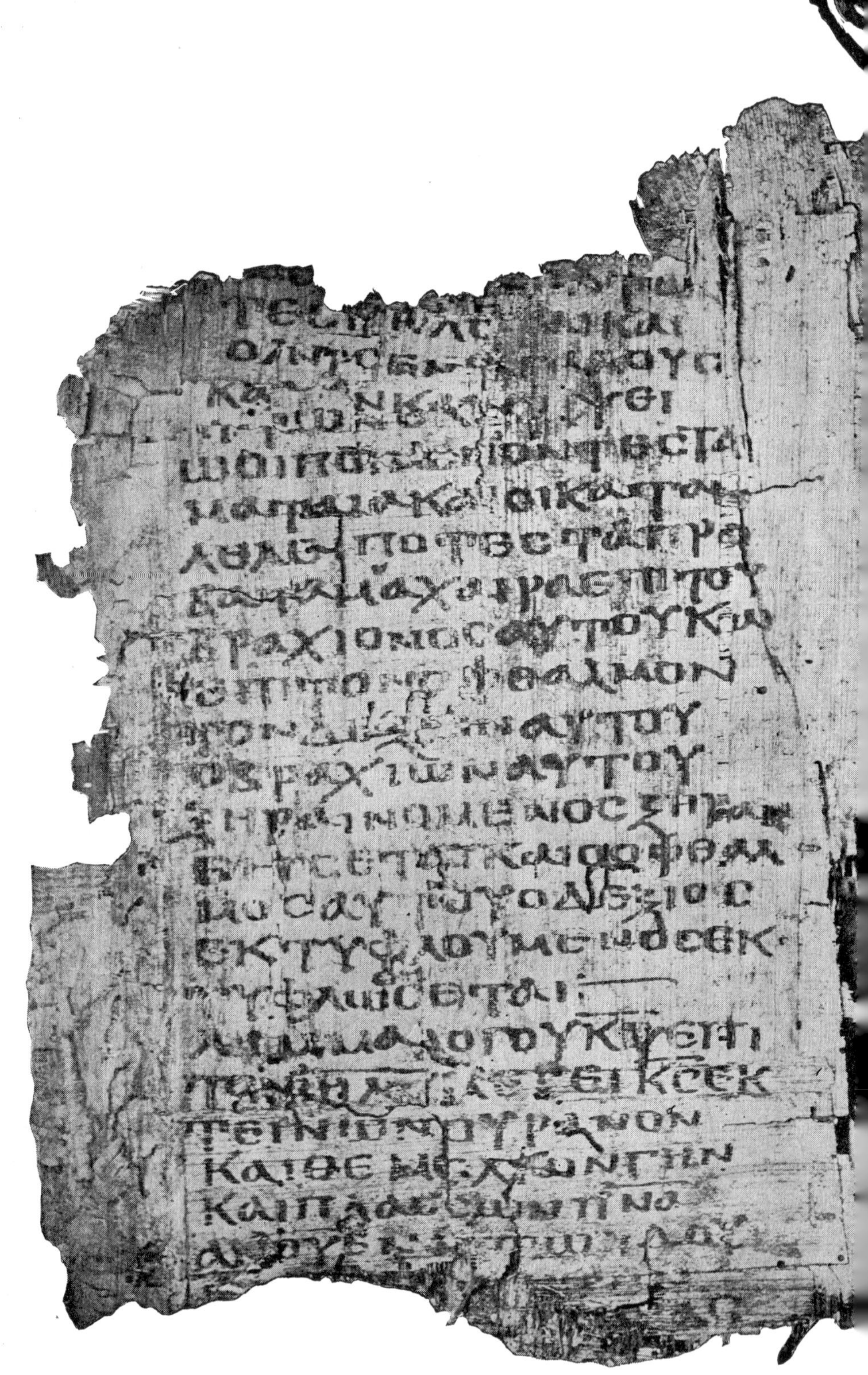

ANCIENT MAN

TS ON PAPYRUS

pasted one to another to form a roll of any length desired. The process and the product are described by Pliny the Elder (*NH*, xiii.11–13).

Egyp papyrus rolls are in existence dating from the 27th cent. BC, and no doubt the manufacture of papyrus had been practised for centuries before. The Egyp rolls were sometimes of great length and were often beautifully decorated with colored vignettes (Book of the Dead). Egyp documents of great historical value have been preserved on these fragile rolls. The Papyrus Ebers of the 16th cent. BC sums up the medical lore of the Egyptians of the time of Amenhotep I. The Papyrus Harris, 133 ft. long, in 117 columns, dates from the middle of the 12th cent. BC and records the benefactions and achievements of Ramses III. For the XIXth, XXth and XXIst dynasties, indeed, papyri are relatively numerous, and their contribution important for Egyp history, life and religion. By the year 1000 BC, papyrus had doubtless come to be used for writing far beyond the limits of Egypt. The Wenamon Papyrus (11th cent.) relates that 500 rolls of papyrus were among the gifts sent from the Delta to the Prince of Biblus, but except in the rarest instances papyri have escaped destruction only in Upper Egypt, where climatic conditions esp. favored their preservation.

2. Egyptian Papyri

Papyrus Antiquorum.

In very recent years (1898, 1904, 1907) several Aram. papyri have been found on the Island of Elephantine, just below the First Cataract, dating from 494 to 400 BC. They show that between 470 and 408 BC a flourishing colony of Jews existed there, doing business under Pers sway, and worshipping their god Yahu, not in a synagogue, but in a temple, in which they offered meal offerings, incense and burnt offerings. In 408, the Egyptians had destroyed their temple at Yeb, and the Jews appealed for redress to the Pers governor. It is well known that some Jews had taken refuge in Egypt in 586 BC, taking the prophet Jeremiah with them, and with some such band of refugees the Yeb colony may have originated, although it may have been much older (cf Jer **44** 1.15; *BW*, XXIX, 1907, 305 ff; XXXI, 448 ff; chief publications by Euting, Sayce and Cowley, and esp. Sachau, *Drei aramäische Papyrusurkunden aus Elephantine*, 2d ed, 1908; *Aramäische Papyrus und Ostraka*, 1911).

3. Aramaic Papyri

With Alexander's conquest of Egypt (332 BC), and the subsequent Ptolemaic dynasty, Greeks came more than ever before into Egypt, and from Gr centers like Alexandria and Arsinoë in the Fayûm the Gr language began to spread. Through the Ptolemaic (323–30 BC), Rom (30 BC–292/93 AD), and Byzantine periods (292/93–640 AD), that is, from the death of Alexander to the Arab conquest, Gr was much used in Upper and Lower Egypt, and Gr papyri from these times are now abundant. The 300 Aphrodito Gr and Coptic papyri published by Bell and Crum (1910) date from 698–722 AD, and show how Gr persisted in the Arab period.

4. Greek Papyri

The first important discovery of Gr papyri made in modern times was among the ruins of Herculaneum, near Naples, where in 1752 in the ruins of the house of a philosopher which had been destroyed and buried by volcanic ashes from Vesuvius (79 AD) a whole library of papyrus rolls was found, quite charred by the heat. With the utmost pains many of these have been unrolled and deciphered, and the first part of them was published in 1793. They consist almost wholly of works of Epicurean philosophy. In 1778 the first discovery of Gr papyri in Egypt was made. In that year some Arabs found 40 or 50 papyrus rolls in an earthen pot, probably in the Fayûm, where Philadelphus settled his Gr veterans. One was purchased by a dealer and found its way into the hands of Cardinal Stefano Borgia; the others were destroyed as of no worth. The Borgia Papyrus was published 10 years later. It was a document of little value, recording the forced labor of certain peasants upon the Nile embankment of a given year.

5. Their Discovery

In 1820 another body of papyri was found by natives, buried, it was said, in an earthen pot, on the site of the Serapeum at Memphis, just above Cairo. These came for the most part from the 2d cent. BC. They fell into various hands, and are now in the museums of London, Paris, Leyden, Rome and Dresden. With them the stream of papyri began to flow steadily into the British and Continental museums. In 1821 an Englishman, Mr. W. J. Bankes, bought an Elephantine roll of the xxivth book of the *Iliad*, the first Gr literary papyrus to be derived from Egypt. The efforts of Mr. Harris and others in 1847–50 brought to England considerable parts of lost orations of Hyperides, new papyri of the xviith book of the *Iliad*, and parts of *Iliad* ii, iii, ix. In 1855 Mariette purchased a fragment of Alcman for the Louvre, and in 1856 Mr. Stobart obtained the funeral oration of Hyperides.

The present period of papyrus recovery dates from 1877, when an immense mass of Gr and other papyri, for the most part documentary, not literary, was found in the Fayûm, on the site of the ancient Arsinoë. The bulk of this collection passed into the hands of Archduke Rainer at Vienna, minor portions of it being secured by the museums of Paris, London, Oxford and Berlin. These belong largely to the Byzantine period. Another great find was made in 1892 in the Fayûm; most of these went to Berlin, some few to the British Museum, Vienna and Geneva. These were mostly of the Rom period.

It will be seen that most of these discoveries were the work of natives, digging about indiscriminately in the hope of finding antiquities to sell to tourists or dealers. By this time, however, the Egypt Exploration Fund had begun its operations in Egypt, and Professor Flinders Petrie was at work there. Digging among Ptolemaic tombs at Gurob in 1889–90, Professor Petrie found many mummies, or mummy-casings, adorned with breast-pieces and sandals made of papyri pasted together. The separation of these was naturally a tedious and delicate task, and the papyri when extricated were often badly damaged or mutilated; but the Petrie papyri, as they were called, were hailed by scholars as the most important found up to that time, for they came for the most part from the 3d cent. BC. Startling acquisitions were made about this time by representatives of the British Museum and the Louvre. The British Museum secured papyri of the lost work of Aristotle on the *Constitution of Athens*, the lost *Mimes* of Herodas, a fragment of an oration of Hyperides, and extensive literary papyri of works already extant; while the Louvre secured the larger part of the *Oration against Athenogenes*, the masterpiece of Hyperides. In 1894 Bernard P. Grenfell, of Oxford, appeared in Egypt, working with Professor Petrie in his excavations, and securing papyri with Mr. Hogarth for England. In that year Petrie and Grenfell obtained from native dealers papyrus rolls, one more than 40 ft. in length, preserving revenue laws of Ptolemy Philadelphus, dated in 259–258 BC. These were published in 1896 by Mr. Grenfell, the first of many important works in this field from his pen.

With Arthur S. Hunt, of Oxford, Mr. Grenfell excavated in 1896–97, at Behnesa, the Rom Oxyrhynchus, and unearthed the greatest mass of Gr papyri of the Rom period thus far found. In 9 large quarto volumes, aggregating 3,000 pages, only a beginning has been made of publishing these Oxyrhynchus texts, which number thousands and are in many cases of great importance. The story of papyrus digging in Egypt since the great find of 1896–97 is largely the record of the work of Grenfell and Hunt. At Tebtunis, in the Fayûm, in 1900, they found a great mass of Ptolemaic papyri, comparable in importance with their great discovery at Oxyrhynchus. One of the most productive sources of papyri at Tebtunis was the crocodile cemetery, in which many mummies of the sacred crocodiles were found rolled in papyrus. Important Ptolemaic texts were found in 1902 at Hibeh, and a later visit to Oxyrhynchus in 1903 produced results almost as astonishing and quite as valuable as those of the first excavations there. The work of Rubensohn at Abusir in 1908 has exceptional interest, as it developed the first considerable body of Alexandrian papyri that has been found. The soil and climate of Alexandria are destructive to papyri, and only to the fact that these had anciently been carried off into the interior as rubbish is their preservation due. Hogarth, Jouguet, Wilcken and other Continental scholars have excavated in Egypt for papyri with varying degrees of success. The papyri are found in graves a few feet below the surface, in house ruins over which sand has drifted, or occasionally in earthen pots buried in the ground. Despite government efforts to stop indiscriminate

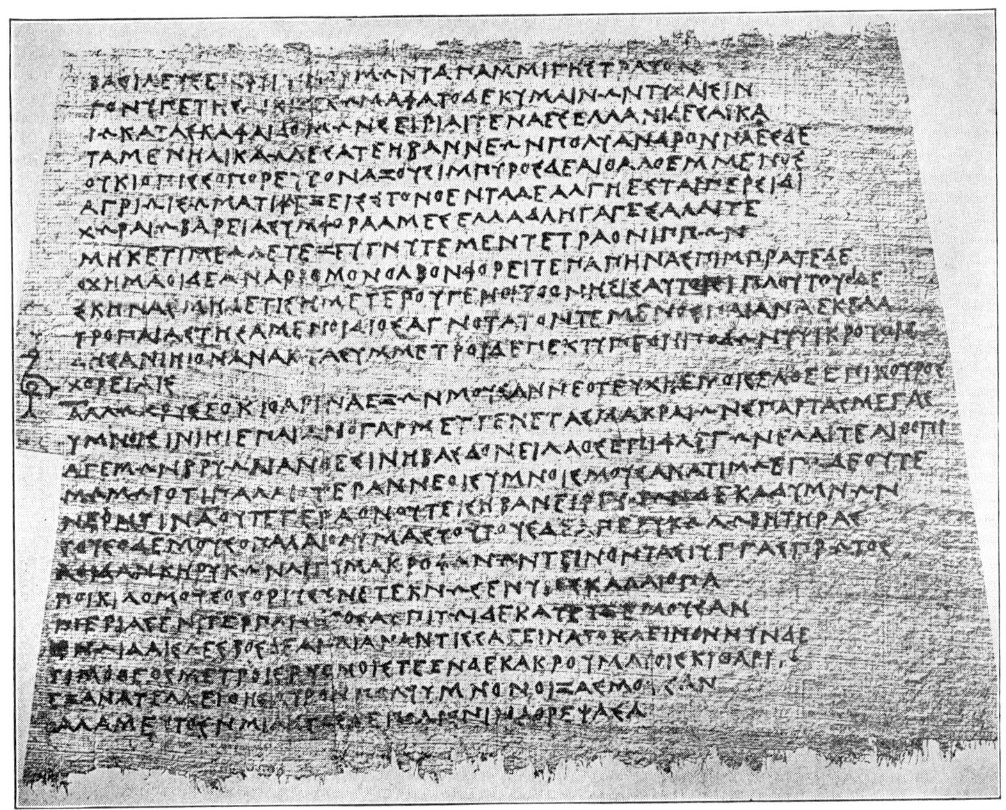

Timotheus Papyrus.

native digging, papyri in considerable quantities have continued to find their way into the hands of native dealers, and thence into English, Continental, and even American collections.

6. Classical Papyri

Thus far upward of 650 literary papyri, great and small, of works other than Bib. have been published. The fact that about one-third of these are Homeric attests the great popularity enjoyed by the Homeric poems in Gr-Rom times. These are now so abundant and extensive as to make an im-

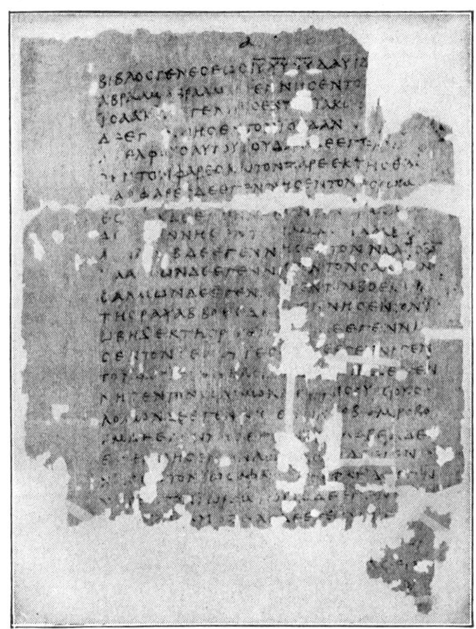

Greek Papyrus Containing Mt **1** 1-9.12.13.14-20.

portant contribution to the Homeric text. Rather less than one-third preserve works of other ancient writers which were already known to us through later copies, mediaeval or modern. Among these are works of Plato, Demosthenes, Isocrates, Thucydides, Euripides, Sophocles, Aeschines, Herodotus and others. Rather more than one-third preserve works, or fragments of works, which have been either quite unknown or, oftener, regarded as lost. Such are portions of Alcman and Sappho, fragments of the comedies of Menander and the iambi of Callimachus, *Mimes* of Herodas, poems of Bacchylides, parts of the lost *Antiope* and *Hypsipyle* of Euripides, Aristotle *On the Constitution of Athens*, the *Persae* of Timotheus (in a papyrus of the 4th cent. BC, probably the oldest Gr book in the world), and six orations, one of them complete, of Hyperides. In 1906 Grenfell and Hunt discovered at Oxyrhynchus the unique papyrus of the lost *Paeans* of Pindar, in 380 fragments, besides the *Hellenica* of Theopompus (or Cratippus?), whose works were believed to have perished.

7. Septuagint Papyri

Of the Gr OT (LXX) more than 20 papyri have been discovered. Perhaps the most important of these is the Berlin Genesis (3d or 4th cent.) (1) in a cursive hand, purchased at Akhmîm in 1906. Other papyri preserving parts of Gen among the Amherst (2), British Museum (3), and Oxyrhynchus (4), papyri date from the 3d or 4th cent. A Bodleian papyrus leaf (5) (7th or 8th cent.) preserves Cant **1** 6–9. An Amherst papyrus (6) (7th cent.) contains Job **1** 21 f; **2** 3. There are several papyri of parts of the Pss. An Amherst papyrus (7) (5th or 6th cent.) has Ps **5** 6–12. Brit. Mus. 37 (Fragmenta Londinensia, 6th or 7th cent.) (8), of thirty leaves, contains Ps **10** 2—**18** 6 and **20** 14—**34** 6. This was purchased in 1836 and is one of the longest of Bib. papyri. Brit. Mus. 230 (9) (3d cent.) preserves Ps **12** 7—**15** 4. A Berlin papyrus (10) contains Ps **40** 26—**41** 4. Oxyrhynchus papyrus 845 (11) (4th or 5th cent.) contains parts of Pss **68, 70**. Another Amherst papyrus (12) (7th cent.) shows parts of Pss **108, 118, 135, 138–140**. There is also a papyrus at Leipzig (13) which contains part of the Pss. Of the Prophets the chief papyrus is the Heidelberg codex (14) (7th cent.), which contains Zec **4** 6—Mal **4** 5. Oxyrhynchus 846 (15) (6th cent.) contains Am **2**. A Rainer papyrus (16) (3d cent.) preserves Isa **38**

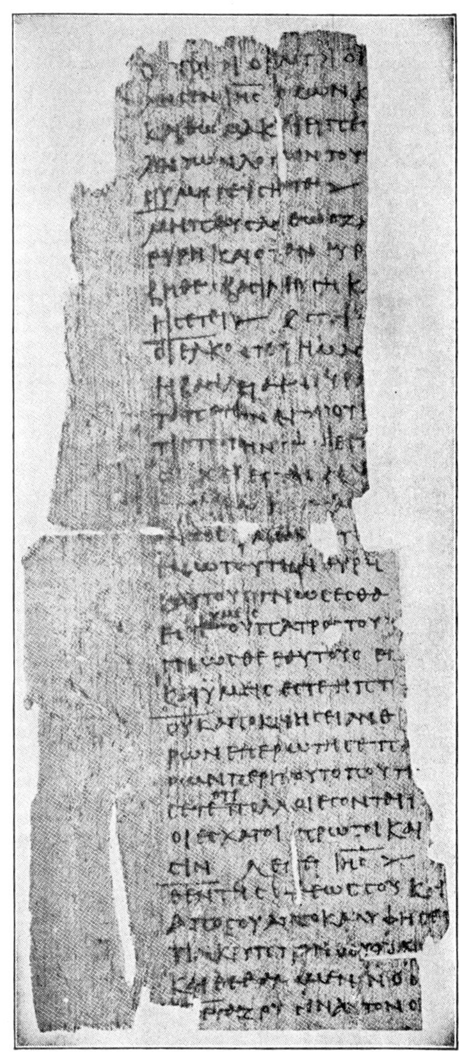

New Sayings of Jesus.

3–5.13–16, and a Bodleian (17) (3d cent.) shows Ezk **5** 12—**6** 3. The Rylands papyri include Dt **2, 3** (18) (4th cent.); Job **1, 5, 6** (19) (6th or 7th cent.); Ps **90** (20) (5th or 6th cent.). Recent Oxyrhynchus volumes supply parts of Ex **21, 22, 40** (21, 22) (3d cent., O.P. 1074, 1075); and of Gen **16** (23) (3d cent., O.P. 1166), and **31** (24) (4th cent., O.P. 1167). The great antiquity of some of these documents gives especial interest to their readings.

8. NT Papyri

Twenty-three papyri containing parts of the Gr NT have thus far been published, nearly half of them coming from Oxyrhynchus (O.P. 2, 208, 209, 402, 657, 1008, 1009, 1078, 1079, 1170, 1171). The pieces range in date from the 3d to the 6th cent. Their locations, dates and contents are:

1. Philadelphia, Pa. 3d or 4th cent. Mt **1** 1–9.12. 13.14–20 (O.P. 2).
2. Florence. 5th or 6th cent. Jn **12** 12–15.
3. Vienna. 6th cent. Lk **7** 36–45; **10** 38–42.
4. Paris. 4th cent. Lk **1** 74–80; **5** 3–8; **5** 30—**6** 4.
5. London. 3d or 4th cent. Jn **1** 23–31.33–41; **20** 11–17.19–25 (O.P. 208).
6. Strassburg. ? cent. Jn **11** 45.
7. Kiew. ? cent. Lk **4** 1.2.
8. Berlin. 4th cent. Acts **4** 31–37; **5** 2–9; **6** 1–6. 8–15.
9. Cambridge, Mass. 4th or 5th cent. 1 Jn **4** 11–13.15–17 (O.P 402).
10. Cambridge, Mass. 4th cent. Rom **1** 1–7 (O.P. 209).
11. St. Petersburg. 5th cent. 1 Cor **1** 17–20; **6** 13. 18; **7** 3.4.10–14.
12. Didlington Hall. 3d or 4th cent. He **1** 1.
13. London. 4th cent. He **2** 14—**5** 5; **10** 8—**11** 13; **11** 28—**12** 17 (O.P. 657). This is the most considerable papyrus of the NT, and doubly important because Codex Vaticanus breaks off with He **9** 14.
14. Sinai. 5th cent. 1 Cor **1** 25–27; **2** 6–8; **3** 8–10.20.
15. Oxford. 4th cent. 1 Cor **7** 18—**8** 4 (O.P. 1008). Phil **3** 9–17; **4** 2–8 (O.P. 1009).
16. Manchester (Rylands). 6th or 7th cent. Rom **12** 3–8.
17. Manchester (Rylands). 3d cent. Tit **1** 11–15; **2** 3–8.
18. Oxford. 4th cent. He **9** 12–19 (O.P. 1078).
19. Oxford. 3d or 4th cent. Rev **1** 4–7 (O.P. 1079).
20. Oxford. 5th cent. Mt **10** 32—**11** 5 (O.P. 1170).
21. Oxford. 3d cent. Jas **2** 19—**3** 2.4–9 (O.P. 1171).
22. Florence. 7th cent. Mt **25** 12–15.20–23.
23. Florence. ? cent. Jn **3** 14–18.31.32.

Berlin Pap. 13,269 (7th cent.) is a liturgical paraphrase of Lk **2** 8–14.

Further details as to nos. 1–14 may be found in Gregory, *Textkritik*, 1084–92, and for nos. 1–23 in Kenyon, *Handbook to Text. Crit.*[2], or Milligan, *NT Documents*, 249–54.

9. Theological Papyri

Among other theological papyri, the Oxyrhynchus Sayings of Jesus (O.P. 1,654), dating from the 2d and 3d cents., are probably the most widely known (see LOGIA). Other Oxyrhynchus pieces preserve parts of the Apocalypse of Baruch (chs **12–14**; 4th or 5th cent.; O.P. 403); the Gospel according to the Hebrews (? in its later form, if at all; 3d cent.; O.P. 655); the Acts of John (4th cent.; O.P. 850, cf 851); the Shepherd of Hermas (3d or 4th cent.; O.P. 404); Irenaeus, *Adv. Haer.*, iii.9 (3d cent.; O.P. 405). Other small fragments of the Shepherd and Ignatius are among the Amherst and Berlin papyri. Early Christian hymns, prayers and letters of interest have also been found.

10. Documentary Papyri

We have spoken thus far only of literary papyri, classical and theological. The overwhelming majority of the papyri found have of course been documentary—private letters, accounts, wills, receipts, contracts, leases, deeds, complaints, petitions, notices, invitations, etc. The value of these contemporary and original documents for the illumination of ancient life can hardly be overestimated. The life of Upper Egypt in Ptolemaic and Rom times is now probably better known to us than that of any other period of history down to recent times. Many papyrus collections have no literary papyri at all, but are rich in documents. Each year brings more of these to light and new volumes of them into print. All this vast and growing body of material contributes to our knowledge of Ptolemaic and imperial times, often in the most intimate ways. Among the most important of these documentary papyri from Ptolemaic times are the revenue laws of Ptolemy Philadelphus (259 BC) and the decrees of Ptolemy Euergetes II, 47 in number (118 BC, 140–139 BC). Very recently (1910) a Hamburg papyrus has supplied the *Constitutio Antoniniana*, by which Rom citizenship was conferred upon the *peregrini* of the empire. The private documents in ways even more important illustrate the life of the common people under Ptolemaic and Rom rule.

11. Contribution to NT Study

It is not necessary to point out the value of all this for Bib. and esp. NT study. The papyri have already made a valuable contribution to textual materials of both OT and NT. For other early Christian lit. their testimony has been of surprising interest (the Oxyrhynchus Logia and Gospel fragments). The discovery of a series of uncial MSS running through six centuries back of the Codex Vaticanus bridges the gap between what were our earliest uncials and the hand of the inscriptions, and puts us in a better position than ever before to fix the dates of uncial MSS. Minuscule or cursive hands, too, so common in NT MSS of the 10th and later cents., appear in a new light when it is seen that such writing was not a late invention arising out of the uncial, but had existed side by side with it from at least the 4th cent. BC, as the ordinary, as distinguished from the literary, or book, hand. See WRITING. The lexical contribution of these documentary papyri, too, is already considerable, and is likely to be very great. Like the NT writings, they reflect the common as distinguished from the literary language of the times, and words which had appeared exceptional or unknown in Gr lit. are now shown to have been in common use. The problems of NT syntax are similarly illuminated. Specific historical notices sometimes light up dark points in the NT, as in a British Museum decree of Gaius Vibius Maximus, prefect of Egypt (104 AD), ordering all who are out of their districts to return to their own homes in view of the approaching census (cf Lk **2** 1–5). Most important of all is the contribution of the papyri to a sympathetic knowledge of ancient life. They constitute a veritable gallery of NT characters. A strong light is sometimes thrown upon the social evils of the time, of which Paul and Juvenal wrote so sternly. The child, the prodigal, the thief, the host with his invitations, the steward with his accounts, the thrifty householder, the soldier on service receiving his viaticum, or retired as a veteran upon his farm, the Jewish money-lender, the husbandman, and the publican, besides people in every domestic relation, we meet at first hand in the papyri which they themselves in many cases have written. The worth of this for the historical interpretation of the NT is very great.

12. Chief Collections

The principal collections of Gr papyri with their editors are Schow, Herculaneum Papyri; Peyron, Turin Papyri; Leemans, Leyden Papyri; Wessely, Rainer and Paris Papyri; Kenyon and Bell, British Museum Papyri; Mahaffy and Smyly, Petrie Papyri; Grenfell and Hunt, Oxyrhynchus, Amherst and Hibeh Papyri (with Hogarth), Fayûm Papyri, and (with Smyly and Goodspeed) Tebtunis Papyri; Hunt, Rylands Papyri; Nicole, Geneva Papyri; Krebs, Wilcken, Viereck, Schubart and others, Berlin Papyri; Meyer, Hamburg and Giessen Papyri; Deissmann, Heidelberg Papyri; Vitelli and Comparetti, Florence Papyri; Mitteis, Leipzig Papyri; Preisigke, Strassburg Papyri; Reinach, Paris Papyri; Jouguet and Lesquier, Lille Papyri; Rubensohn Elephantine Papyri; Maspero, Cairo Papyri; Goodspeed. Cairo and Chicago Papyri. The Munich papyri have been described by Wilcken. Milligan's *Gr Papyri*, Kenyon's *Palaeography of Gr Papyri*, and Deissmann's *Light from the Ancient East* are useful introductions to the general subject. Mayser has prepared a *Grammatik der Ptolemäischen Papyri*.

Coptic, Arab., Heb and Demotic papyri are

numerous; even Lat papyri are found. The Coptic have already made important contributions to early Christian literature. A considerable Coptic fragment of the Acts of Paul, and a Coptic (Akhmîmic) codex of 1 Clement, almost complete, have recently been published by Carl Schmidt. Another much mutilated papyrus of 1 Clement, with James, complete, is at Strassburg. A Coptic text of Prov has been brought to Berlin from the same source which supplied the Clement codex (the White Convent, near Akhmîm); indeed, Bib. papyri in Coptic are fairly numerous, and patristic lit. is being rapidly enriched by such discoveries of Coptic papyri, e.g. the Dt, Jon, Acts papyrus, 1912 (cf *Sahidic NT*, Oxford, 1911).

13. Coptic, Arabic and Other Papyri

Arab. papyri first began to appear from Egypt in 1825, when three Arab. pieces were brought to Paris and published by Silvestre de Sacy. Two others, from the 7th cent., were published by him in 1827. It was not until the great papyrus finds of 1877–78, however, that any considerable number of Arab. papyri found their way into Europe. The chief collections thus far formed are at Vienna (Rainer Collection), Berlin and Cairo. Becker has published the Schott-Reinhardt Arab. papyri at Heidelberg, and Karabacek has worked upon those at Vienna. They belong of course to the period after the Arab. conquest, 640 AD.

EDGAR J. GOODSPEED

PAPYRUS, VESSELS OF. See SHIPS AND BOATS, II, 2, (1).

PARABLE, par'a-b'l:

1. Name
2. Historical Data
3. Christ's Use of Parables
4. Purpose of Christ in Using Parables
5. Interpretation of the Parables
6. Doctrinal Value of the Parables

1. Name

Etymologically the word "parable" (παραβάλλω, *parabállō*) signifies a placing of two or more objects together, usually for the purpose of a comparison. In this widest sense of the term there is practically no difference between parable and simile (see Thayer, *Dict. of NT Gr*, s.v.). This is also what substantially some of Christ's parables amount to, which consist of only one comparison and in a single verse (cf Mt **13** 33.44–46). In the more usual and technical sense of the word, "parable" ordinarily signifies an imaginary story, yet one that in its details could have actually transpired, the purpose of the story being to illustrate and inculcate some higher spiritual truth. These features differentiate it from other and similar figurative narratives as also from actual history. The similarity between the last-mentioned and a parable is sometimes so small that exegetes have differed in the interpretation of certain pericopes. A characteristic example of this uncertainty is the story of Dives and Lazarus in Lk **16** 19–31. The problem is of a serious nature, as those who regard this as actual history are compelled to interpret each and every statement, including too the close proximity of heaven and hell and the possibility of speaking from one place to the other, while those who regard it as a parable can restrict their interpretation to the features that constitute the substance of the story. It differs again from the fable, in so far as the latter is a story that could not actually have occurred (e.g. Jgs **9** 8 ff; 2 K **14** 9; Ezk **17** 2 f). The parable is often described as an extended metaphor. The etymological features of the word, as well as the relation of parables to other and kindred devices of style, are discussed more fully by Ed. Koenig, in *HDB*, III, 660 ff.

2. Historical Data

Although Christ employed the parable as a means of inculcating His message more extensively and more effectively than any other teacher, He did not invent the parable. It was His custom in general to take over from the religious and linguistic world of thought in His own day the materials that He employed to convey the higher and deeper truths of His gospels, giving them a world of meaning they had never before possessed. Thus e.g. every petition of the Lord's Prayer can be duplicated in the Jewish liturgies of the times, yet on Christ's lips these petitions have a significance they never had or could have for the Jews. The term "Word" for the second person in the Godhead is an adaptation from the Logos-idea in contemporaneous religious thought, though not specifically of Philo's. Baptism, regeneration, and kindred expressions of fundamental thoughts in the Christian system, are terms not absolutely new (cf Deutsch, art. "Talmud," *Literary Remains*). The parable was employed both in the OT and in contemporaneous Jewish literature (cf e.g. 2 S **12** 1–4; Isa **5** 1–6; **28** 24–28, and for details see Koenig's art., l.c.). Jewish and other non-Bib. parables are discussed and illustrated by examples in Trench's *Notes on the Parables of Our Lord*, introd. essay, ch iv: "On Other Parables besides Those in the Scriptures."

3. Christ's Use of Parables

The one and only teacher of parables in the NT is Christ Himself. The Epp., although they often employ rhetorical allegories and similes, make absolutely no use of the parable, so common in Christ's pedagogical methods. The distribution of these in the Canonical Gospels is unequal, and they are strictly confined to the three Synoptic Gospels. Mark again has only one peculiar to this book, namely, the Seed Growing in Secret (Mk **4** 26), and he gives only three others that are found also in Mt and Lk, namely the Sower, the Mustard Seed, and the Wicked Husbandman, so that the bulk of the parables are found in the First and the Third Gospels. Two are common to Mt and Lk, namely the Leaven (Mt **13** 33; Lk **13** 21) and the Lost Sheep (Mt **18** 12; Lk **15** 3 ff). Of the remaining parables, 18 are found only in Lk and 10 only in Mt. Lk's 18 include some of the finest, viz. the Two Debtors, the Good Samaritan, the Friend at Midnight, the Rich Fool, the Watchful Servants, the Barren Fig Tree, the Chief Seats, the Great Supper, the Rash Builder, the Rash King, the Lost Coin, the Lost Son, the Unrighteous Steward, the Rich Man and Lazarus, the Unprofitable Servants, the Unrighteous Judge, the Pharisee and Publican, and the Pounds. The 10 peculiar to Mt are the Tares, the Hidden Treasure, the Pearl of Great Price, the Draw Net, the Unmerciful Servant, the Laborers in the Vineyard, the Two Sons, the Marriage of the King's Son, the Ten Virgins, and the Talents. There is some uncertainty as to the exact number of parables we have from Christ, as the Marriage of the King's Son is sometimes regarded as a different recension of the Great Supper, and the Talents of the Pounds. Other numberings are suggested by Trench, Jülicher and others.

4. Purpose of Christ in Using Parables

It is evident from such passages as Mt **13** 10 ff (cf Mk **4** 10; Lk **8** 9) that Christ did not in the beginning of His career employ the parable as a method of teaching, but introduced it later. This took place evidently during the 2d year of His public ministry, and is closely connected with the changes which about that time He made in His attitude toward the people in general. It evidently was Christ's purpose at the outset to win over, if possible, the nation as a whole to His cause and to the gospel; when it appeared that the leaders and the great bulk of the people would not accept Him for what He wanted to be and clung tenaciously to their carnal Messianic ideas and ideals, Christ ceased largely to appeal to the masses, and, by confining His instructions chiefly to His disciples and special friends, saw the necessity of organizing an *ecclesiola in ecclesia*, which was eventually to develop into the world-conquering church. One part of this general withdrawal of Christ from a proclamation of His gospel to the whole nation was this change in His method of teaching and the adoption of the parable. On that subject He leaves no doubt, according to Mt **13** 11 ff; Mk **4** 12; Lk **8** 10. The purpose of the parable is both to reveal and to conceal the truth. It was to serve the first purpose in the case of the disciples, the second in the case of the undeserving Jews. Psychologically this difference, notwithstanding the acknowledged inferiority in the training and education of the disciples, esp. as compared with the scribes and lawyers, is not hard to understand. A simple-minded Christian, who has some understanding of the truth, can readily understand figurative illustrations of this truth, which would be absolute enigmas even to an educated Hindu or Chinaman. The theological problem involved is more difficult. Yet it is evident that we are not dealing with those who have committed the sin against the Holy Ghost, for whom there is no possibility of a return to grace, according to He **6** 4–10; **10** 26 (cf Mt **12** 31.32; Mk **3** 28–30), and who accordingly could no longer be influenced by an appeal of the gospel, and we have rather before us those from whom Christ has determined to withdraw the offer of redemption—whether temporarily or definitely and finally, remaining an open question—according to His policy of not casting pearls before the swine. The proper sense of these passages can be ascertained only when we remember that in Mk **4** 12 and Lk **8** 10, the ἵνα, *hína*, need not express purpose, but that this particle is used here to express mere result only, as is clear too from the passage in Mt **13** 13, where the ὅτι, *hóti*, is found. The word is to be withheld from these people, so that this preaching would not bring about the ordinary results of conversion and forgiveness of sins. Hence Christ now adopts a method of teaching that will hide the truth from all those who have not yet been imbued by it, and this new method is that of the parable.

5. Interpretation of the Parables

The principles for the interpretation of the parables, which are all intended primarily and in the first place for the disciples, are furnished by the nature of the parable itself and by Christ's own method of interpreting some of them. The first and foremost thing to be discovered is the scope or the particular spiritual truth which the parable is intended to convey. Just what this scope is may be stated in so many words, as is done, e.g., by the introductory words to that of the Pharisee and the Publican. Again the scope may be learned from the occasion of the parable, as the question of Peter in Mt **18** 21 gives the scope of the following parable, and the real purpose of the Prodigal Son parable in Lk **15** 11 ff is not the story of this young man himself, but is set over against the murmuring of the Pharisees because Christ received publicans and sinners, in vs 1 and 2, to exemplify the all-forgiving love of the Father. Not the Son but the Father is in the foreground in this parable, which fact is also the connecting link between the two parts. Sometimes the scope can be learned only from an examination of the details of the parable itself and then may be all the more uncertain.

A second principle of the interpretation of the parables is that a sharp distinction must be made between what the older interpreters called the body (*corpus*) and the soul (*anima*) of the story; or, to use other expressions, between the shell or bark (*cortex*) and the marrow (*medulla*). Whatever serves only the purpose of the story is the "ornamentation" of the parable, and does not belong to the substance. The former does not call for interpretation or higher spiritual lesson; the latter does. This distinction between those parts of the parable that are intended to convey spiritual meanings and those which are to be ignored in the interpretation is based on Christ's own interpretation of the so-called *parabolae perfectae*. Christ Himself, in Mt **13** 18 ff, interprets the parable of the Sower, yet a number of data, such as the fact that there are four, and not more or fewer kinds of land, and others, are discarded in this explanation as without meaning. Again in His interpretation of the Tares among the Wheat in Mt **13** 36 ff, a number of details of the original parable are discarded as meaningless.

Just which details are significant and which are meaningless in a parable is often hard, sometimes impossible to determine, as the history of their exegesis amply shows. In general it can be laid down as a rule, that those features which illustrate the scope of the parable belong to its substance, and those which do not, belong to the ornamentation. But even with this rule there remain many exegetical *cruces* or difficulties. Certain, too, it is that not all of the details are capable of interpretation. Some are added of a nature that indeed illustrate the story as a story, but, from the standpoint of Christian morals, are more than objectionable. The Unjust Steward in using his authority to make the bills of the debtors of his master smaller may be a model, in the shrewd use of this world's goods for his purpose, that the Christian may follow in making use of his goods for his purposes, but the action of the steward itself is incapable of defence. Again, the man who finds in somebody else's property a pearl of great price but conceals this fact from the owner of the land and quietly buys this ground may serve as an example to show how much the kingdom of God is worth, but from an ethical standpoint his action cannot be sanctioned. In general, the parable, like all other forms of figurative expression, has a meaning only as far as the *tertium comparationis* goes, that is, the third thing which is common to the two things compared. But all this still leaves a large debatable ground in many parables. In the Laborers in the Vineyard does the "penny" mean anything, or is it an ornament? The history of the debate on this subject is long. In the Prodigal Son do all the details of his sufferings, such as eating the husks intended for swine, have a spiritual meaning?

6. Doctrinal Value of the Parables

The interpreters of former generations laid down the rule, *theologia parabolica non est argumentativa*, i.e. the parables, very rich in mission thoughts, do not furnish a basis for doctrinal argument. Like all figurative expressions and forms of thought, the parables too contain elements of doubt as far as their interpretation is concerned. They illustrate truth but they do not prove or demonstrate truth. *Omnia similia claudicunt*, "all comparisons limp," is applicable here also. No point of doctrine can be established on figurative passages of Scripture, as then all elements of doubt would not be eliminated, this doubt being based on the nature of language itself. The argumentative or doctrinal value of parables is found in this, that they may, in accordance with the analogy of Scripture, illustrate truth already clearly expressed elsewhere. Cf esp. Trench, introd. essay, in *Notes on the Parables of Our Lord*, ch iii, 30–43; and Terry,

Biblical Hermeneutics, Part II, ch vi: "Interpretation of Parables," 188–213, in which work a full bibliography is given. Cf also art. "Parabel" in *RE*.

G. H. SCHODDE

PARACLETE, par'a-klēt:

1. Where Used

This word occurs 5 t in the NT, all in the writings of John. Four instances are in the Gospel and one in the First Ep. In the Gospel the passages are **14** 16.26; **15** 26; **16** 7; in the Ep., **2** 1. "Paraclete" is simply the Gr word transferred into Eng. The tr of the word in EV is "Comforter" in the Gospel, and "Advocate" in the Ep. The Gr word is παράκλητος, *paráklētos*, from the vb. παρακαλέω, *parakaléō*. The word for "Paraclete" is passive in form, and etymologically signifies "called to one's side." The active form of the word is παρακλήτωρ, *paraklḗtōr*, not found in the NT but found in LXX in Job **16** 2 in the pl., and means "comforters," in the saying of Job regarding the "miserable comforters" who came to him in his distress.

2. General Meaning

In general the word signifies (1) a legal advocate, or counsel for defence, (2) an intercessor, (3) a helper, generally. The first, or technical, judicial meaning is that which predominates in classical usage, corresponding to our word "advocate," "counsel," or "attorney." The corresponding Lat word is *advocatus*, "advocate," the word applied to Christ in EV in the tr of the Gr word *paraklētos*, in 1 Jn **2** 1. There is some question whether the tr "Comforter" in the passages of John's Gospel in AV and RV is warranted by the meaning of the word. It is certain that the meaning "comforter" is not the primary signification, as we have seen. It is very probably, however, a secondary meaning of the word, and some of its cognates clearly convey the idea of comfort in certain connections, both in LXX and in the NT (Gen **37** 35; Zec **1** 13; Mt **5** 4; 2 Cor **1** 3.4). In the passage in 2 Cor the word in one form or another is used 5 t and in each means "comfort." In none of these intances, however, do we find the noun "Paraclete," which we are now considering.

3. In the Talmud and Targums

Among Jewish writers the word "Paraclete" came to have a number of meanings. A good deed was called a paraclete or advocate, and a transgression was an accuser. Repentance and good works were called paracletes: "The works of benevolence and mercy done by the people of Israel in this world become agents of peace and intercessors [paracletes] between them and their Father in heaven." The sin offering is a paraclete; the paraclete created by each good deed is called an angel (*Jew Enc*, IX, 514–15, art. "Paraclete").

4. As Employed by Philo

Philo employs the word in several instances. Usually he does not use it in the legal, technical sense. Joseph is represented as bestowing forgiveness on his brethren who had wronged him and declaring that they needed "no one else as paraclete," or intercessor (*De Joseph* c. 40). In his *Life of Moses*, iii.14, is a remarkable passage which indicates Philo's spiritualizing methods of interpreting Scripture as well as reflects his philosophic tendency. At the close of a somewhat elaborate account of the emblematic significance of the vestments of the high priest and their jeweled decorations, his words are: "The twelve stones arranged on the breast in four rows of three stones each, namely, the logeum, being also an emblem of that reason which holds together and regulates the universe. For it was indispensable [ἀναγκαῖον, *anagkaion*] that the man who was consecrated to the Father of the world should have, as a paraclete, his son, the being most perfect in all virtue, to procure the forgiveness of sins, and a supply of unlimited blessings." This is rather a striking verbal or formal parallel to the statement in 1 Jn **2** 1 where Christ is our Advocate with the Father, although of course Philo's conceptions of the Divine "reason" and "son" are by no means the Christian conceptions.

5. The Best Translation

If now we raise the question what is the best tr of the term "Paraclete" in the NT, we have a choice of several words. Let us glance at them in order. The tr "Comforter" contains an element of the meaning of the word as employed in the Gospels, and harmonizes with the usage in connection with its cognates, but it is too narrow in meaning to be an adequate tr. Dr. J. Hastings in an otherwise excellent article on the Paraclete in *HDB* says the Paraclete was not sent to comfort the disciples, since prior to His actual coming and after Christ's promise the disciples' sorrow was turned into joy. Dr. Hastings thinks the Paraclete was sent to cure the unbelief or half-belief of the disciples. But this conceives the idea of comfort in too limited a way. No doubt in the mind of Jesus the comforting aspect of the Spirit's work applied to all their future sorrows and trials, and not merely to comfort for their personal loss in the going of Christ to the Father. Nevertheless there was more in the work of the Paraclete than comfort in sorrow. "Intercessor" comes nearer the root idea of the term and contains an essential part of the meaning. "Advocate" is a closely related word, and is also suggestive of the work of the Spirit. Perhaps there is no Eng. word broad enough to cover all the significance of the word "Paraclete" except the word "Helper." The Spirit helps the disciples in all the above-indicated ways. Of course the objection to this tr is that it is too indefinite. The specific Christian conception is lost in the comprehensiveness of the term. Our conclusion, therefore, is that the term "Paraclete" itself would perhaps be the best designation of the Spirit in the passage in John's Gospel. It would thus become a proper name for the Spirit and the various elements of meaning would come to be associated with the words which are found in the context of the Gospel.

Christianity introduced many new ideas into the world for which current terms were inadequate media of expression. In some cases it is best to adopt the Christian term itself, in our translations, and let the word slowly acquire its own proper significance in our thought and life. If, however, instead of translating we simply transfer the word "Paraclete" as a designation of the Holy Spirit in the Gospel passages, we would need then to translate it in the passage in the Ep. where it refers to Christ. But this would offer no serious difficulty. For fortunately in the Ep. the word may very clearly be tr[d] "Advocate" or "Intercessor."

6. Christ's Use of the Word

We look next at the contents of the word as employed by Jesus in reference to the Holy Spirit. In Jn **14** 16 the Paraclete is promised as one who is to take the place of Jesus. It is declared elsewhere by Jesus that it is expedient that He go away, for unless He go away the Paraclete will not come (Jn **16** 7). Is the Paraclete, then, the successor or the substitute for Christ as He is sometimes called? The answer is that He is both and neither. He is the successor of Christ historically, but not in the sense that Christ ceases to act in the church. He is the substitute for Christ's physical presence, but only in order that He may make vital and actual Christ's spiritual presence. As we have seen, the Paraclete moves only in the range of truths conveyed in and through Christ as the historical manifestation of God. A "Kingdom of the Spirit," therefore, is impossible in the Christian sense, save as the historical Jesus is made the basis of the Spirit's action in history. The promise of Jesus in **14** 18, "I come unto," is parallel and equivalent in meaning with the preceding promise of the Paraclete. The following are given as the specific forms of activity of the Holy Spirit: (1) to show them the things of Christ, (2) to teach them things to come, (3) to teach them all things, (4) to quicken their memories for past teaching, (5) to bear witness to Christ, (6) to dwell in believers, (7) other things shown in the context such as "greater works" than those of Christ (see Jn **14** 16.17), (8) to convict of sin, of righteousness and judgment. It is possible to range the shades of meaning outlined above under these various forms of the Spirit's activity. As Comforter His work would come under (1), (2), (3) and (6); as Advocate and Intercessor under (6), (7), (8); as Helper and Teacher under (1), (2), (3), (4), (5), (6), (7), (8).

The manner of the sending of the Paraclete is of interest. In Jn **14** 16 the Paraclete comes in answer to Christ's prayer. The Father will give the Spirit whom the world cannot receive. In **14** 26 the Father will send the Spirit in Christ's name. Yet in **15** 26 Christ says, "I will send [him] unto you from the Father, even the Spirit of truth," and in **16** 7, "If I go, I will send him unto you." See Holy Spirit.

7. As Applied to Christ

It remains to notice the passage in 1 Jn **2** 1 where the term "Paraclete" is applied to Christ: "If any man sin, we have an Advocate with the Father, Jesus Christ the righteous"; ver 2 reads: "and he is the propitiation for our sins; and not for ours only, but also for the whole world." Here the meaning is quite clear and specific. Jesus Christ the righteous is represented as our Advocate or Intercessor with the Father. His righteousness is set over against our sin. Here the Paraclete, Christ, is He who, on the basis of His propitiatory offering for the sins of men, intercedes for them with God and thus averts from them the penal consequences of their transgressions. The sense in which Paraclete is here applied to Christ is found nowhere in the passages we have cited from the Gospel. The Holy Spirit as Paraclete is Intercessor or Advocate, but not in the sense here indicated. The Spirit as Paraclete convicts the world of sin, of righteousness and judgment. Jesus Christ as Paraclete vindicates believers before God.

Literature.—Grimm-Thayer, *Gr-Eng. Lexicon of the NT;* Cremer, *Biblico-Theol. Lexicon; HDB,* art. "Paraclete"; *DCG,* art. "Paraclete"; *EB,* art. "Paraclete"; *Jew Enc,* art. "Paraclete"; Hare, *Mission of the Comforter;* Pearson, *On the Creed;* Taylor, *Sayings of the Jewish Fathers;* various comms., Westcott, Godet and others. See list of books appended to art. on Holy Spirit.

E. Y. Mullins

PARADISE, par'a-dīs (פַּרְדֵּס, *pardēṣ;* **παράδεισος,** *parádeisos*): A word probably of Pers origin meaning a royal park. See Garden.

1. Origin and Meaning

The word occurs in the Heb Scriptures but 3 t: Cant **4** 13, where it is trd "an orchard"; Neh **2** 8, where it is trd "a forest" (RVm "park"); Eccl **2** 5, where it is in the pl. number (AV "orchards," RV "parks"). But it was early introduced into the Gr language, being made specially familiar by Xenophon upon his return from the expedition of Cyrus the Younger to Babylonia (see *Anab.* i.2, § 7; 4, §9; *Cyrop.* i.3, §14). In LXX the word is of frequent use in translating other terms of kindred significance. The Garden of Eden became "the paradise of pleasure or luxury" (Gen **2** 15; **3** 23; Joel **2** 3). The valley of the Jordan became 'the paradise of God' (Gen **13** 10). In Ezk **31** 8.9, according to LXX, there is no tree in the 'paradise of God' equal to that which in the prophet's vision symbolizes the glory of Assyria. The figures in the first 9 verses of this chapter may well have been suggested by what the prophet had himself seen of parks in the Pers empire.

2. Use in Jewish Literature

In the apocryphal and pseudepigraphical lit. the word is extensively used in a spiritual and symbolic sense, signalizing the place of happiness to be inherited by the righteous in contrast to Gehenna, the place of punishment to which the wicked were to be assigned. In the later Jewish lit. "Sheol" is represented as a place where preliminary rewards and punishments are bestowed previous to the final judgment (see Apocalyptic Literature; Eschatology of the OT; and cf 2 Esd **2** 19; **8** 52). But the representations in this lit. are often vague and conflicting, some holding that there were 4 divisions in Sheol, one for those who were martyred for righteousness' sake, one for sinners who on earth had paid the penalty for their sins, one for the just who had not suffered martyrdom, and one for sinners who had not been punished on earth (En **102** 15). But among the Alexandrian Jews the view prevailed that the separation of the righteous from the wicked took place immediately after death (see Wisd **3** 14; **4** 10; **5** 5.17; Jos, *Ant,* XVIII, i, 3; *BJ,* II, viii, 14). This would seem to be the idea underlying the use of the word in the NT where it occurs only 3 t, and then in a sense remarkably free from sensuous suggestions.

3. Used by Christ

Christ uses the word but once (Lk **23** 43), when He said to the penitent thief, "To-day shalt thou be with me in Paradise" (see Abraham's Bosom [cf Hades]). This was no time to choose words with dialectical precision. The consolation needed by the penitent thief suffering from thirst and agony and shame was such as was symbolized by the popular conception of paradise, which, as held by the Essenes, consisted of "habitations beyond the ocean, in a region that is neither oppressed with storms of rain, or snow, or with intense heat, but that this place is such as is refreshed by the gentle breathing of a west wind, that is perpetually blowing from the ocean" (Jos, *BJ,* II, viii, 11). See Eschatology of the NT.

4. Other Forms and Uses

Nowhere in His public teaching did Christ use the word "Paradise." He does indeed, when speaking in parables, employ the figure of the marriage supper, and of new wine, and elsewhere of Abraham's bosom, and of houses not made by hands, eternal in the heavens; but all these references are in striking contrast to the prevailing sensuous representations of the times (see 2 Esd **2** 19; **8** 52), and such as have been introduced into Mohammedan lit. Likewise St. Paul (2 Cor **12** 4) speaks of having been "caught up into Paradise" where he "heard unspeakable words, which it is not lawful for a man to utter." See Eschatology of the NT. But in ver 2 this is referred to more vaguely as "the third heaven." In Rev **2** 7 it is said to the members of the church at Ephesus who should overcome, "I [will] give to eat of the tree of life, which is in the Paradise of God," where the Eden of Gen **2** 8 is made the symbol of the abode of the righteous, more fully described without the words in the last chapter of the book. The reticence of the sacred writers respecting this subject is in striking contrast to the profuseness and crudity both of rabbinical writers before Christ and of apocryphal writers and Christian commentators at a later time. "Where the true Gospels are most reticent, the mythical are most exuberant" (Perowne). This is esp. noticeable in the Gospel of Nicodemus, the *Acta Philippi,* the writings of Tertullian (*De Idol.* c. 13; *De Anim.* c. 55; Tertullian's treatise *De Paradiso* is lost), Clement of Alexandria (Frag. 51), and John of Damascus (*De Orthod. Fid.,* ii, 11). In modern lit. the conception of Paradise is effectually sublimated and spiritualized in Faber's familiar hymn:

"O Paradise, O Paradise,
I greatly long to see
The special place my dearest Lord
Is destining for me;
Where loyal hearts and true
Stand ever in the light,
All rapture thro' and thro',
In God's most holy sight."

LITERATURE.—The articles in the great Dicts., esp. Herzog, *RE; HDB;* Alger, *Critical History of the Doctrine of a Future Life;* Schodde, *Book of En;* Lightfoot, *Hor. Heb.* on Lk **23** 43; Salmond, *The Christian Doctrine of Immortality,* 346 ff. For a good account of Jewish and patristic speculation on Paradise, see Professor Plumptre's art. in Smith's *DB,* II, 704 ff.

G. F. WRIGHT

PARAH, pā'ra, par'a (הַפָּרָה, *ha-pārāh;* B, **Φαρά,** *Phará,* A, **'Αφάρ,** *Aphár*): A city named as in the territory of Benjamin between Avvim and Ophrah (Josh **18** 23). It may with some confidence be identified with *Fārah* on *Wâdy Fārah,* which runs into *Wâdy Suweinīṭ,* about 3 miles N.E. of *'Anāta.*

PARALYSIS, pa-ral'i-sis, **PARALYTIC,** par-a-lit'ik. See PALSY.

PARAMOUR, par'a-mōōr (פִּלֶּגֶשׁ, *pillegheshׁ,* "a concubine," masc. or fem.): A term applied in Ezk **23** 20 to the male lover, but elsewhere tr[d] "concubine."

PARAN, pā'ran, **EL-PARAN** (פָּארָן, *pā'rān,* אֵיל פָּארָן, *'ēl-pā'rān;* **Φαράν,** *Pharán*):

(1) **El-paran** (Gen **14** 6) was the point farthest S. reached by the kings. LXX renders אֵיל by τερέβινθος, *terébinthos,* and reads, "unto the terebinth of Paran." The evidence is slender, but it is not unreasonable to suppose that this is the place elsewhere (Dt **2** 8; 1 K **9** 26, etc) called Elath or Eloth (איל with fem. termination), a seaport town which gave its name to the Aelanitic Gulf (modern Gulf of *'Aḳaba*), not far from the wilderness of Paran (2).

(2) Many places named in the narrative of the wanderings lay within the **Wilderness of Paran** (Nu **10** 12; **13** 21; **27** 14; cf **13** 3.26, etc). It is identified with the high limestone plateau of *Et-Tih,* stretching from the S.W. of the Dead Sea to Sinai along the west side of the Arabah. This wilderness offered hospitality to Ishmael when driven from his father's tent (Gen **21** 21). Hither also came David when bereaved of Samuel's protection (1 S **25** 1).

(3) **Mount Paran** (Dt **33** 2; Hab **3** 3) may be either *Jebel Maḳrah,* 29 miles S. of *'Ain Ḳadīs* (Kadesh-barnea), and 130 miles N. of Sinai (Palmer, *Desert of the Exodus,* 510); or the higher and more imposing range of mountains W. of the Gulf of *'Aḳaba.* This is the more probable if El-paran is rightly identified with Elath.

(4) Some place named **Paran** would seem to be referred to in Dt **1** 1; but no trace of such a city has yet been found. Paran in 1 K **11** 18 doubtless refers to the district W. of the Arabah.

W. EWING

PARBAR, pär'bär (פַּרְבָּר, *parbār* [1 Ch **26** 18], and פַּרְוָרִים, *parwārīm,* tr[d] "precincts" [AV "suburbs" in 2 K **23** 11]; LXX **φαρουρείμ,** *pharoureím*): In 1 Ch **26** 18 reference is made to the position of the gatekeepers, "for Parbar westward, four at the causeway, and two at Parbar." The word is supposed to be of Pers origin, connected with *Parwâr,* meaning "possessing light," and hence the meaning has been suggested of "colonnade" or "portico," some place open to the light. In the pl. form (2 K **23** 11) the situation of the house of "Nathan-melech" is described, and the tr, "in the colonnades," should, if the above origin is accepted, be more correct than EV. It is difficult to understand the occurrence of a Pers word at this time, and it has been suggested (*EB,* col 3585) that the word is a description of the office of Nathan-melech, *ba-parwārīm* being a misreading for *ba-p[e]rādhīm,* meaning "who was over the mules."

E. W. G. MASTERMAN

PARCEL, pär'sel: Properly "a little part," in Elizabethan Eng. being used in almost any sense. In AV of Gen **33** 19; Josh **24** 32; Ruth **4** 3; 1 Ch **11** 13.14 it is the tr of חֶלְקָה, *ḥelḳāh;* Jn **4** 5 of χωρίον, *chōríon*—both the Gr and Heb words meaning a "piece of land." RV writes "plot" in 1 Ch **11** 13.14, but if the change was needed at all, it should have been made throughout.

PARCHED, pärcht: Four different root words have been tr[d] "parched" in EV:

(1) קָלָה, *ḳālāh,* "roasted." This word is applied to corn or pulse. It is a common practice in Pal and Syria to roast the nearly ripe wheat for eating as a delicacy. A handful of heads of fully developed grain, with the stalks still attached, are gathered and bound together and then, holding the bunch by the lower ends of the stalks, the heads are toasted over a fire of straw or thorn bush. By the time most of the sheaths are blackened the grain is toasted, and, after rubbing off the husks between the hands, is ready to eat (Lev **2** 14). A form of pulse is toasted in the same way and is more sought after than the grain. In the larger towns and cities, venders go about the streets selling bunches of toasted chick-peas. The Bible references, however, are probably to another form of roasted grain. The threshed wheat or pulse is roasted over a fire on an iron pan or on a flat stone, being kept in constant motion with a stirrer until the operation is finished. The grain thus prepared is a marketable article. Parched grain is not now so commonly met with as the pulse, which either roasted or unroasted is called *ḥommoṣ* (from Arab. "to roast" or "parch"). Parched pulse is eaten not only plain, but is often made into confection by coating the seeds with sugar. In Bible times parched wheat or pulse was a common food, even taking the place of bread (Lev **23** 14; Josh **5** 11; Ruth **2** 14). It was a useful food supply for armies, as it required no further cooking (1 S **17** 17). It was frequently included in gifts or hostages (1 S **25** 18; 2 S **17** 28).

(2) חָרֵר, *ḥārēr,* "burned" or "parched" (cf Arab. *ḥariḳ,* "burned"), is used in the sense of dried up or arid in Jer **17** 6.

(3) צִחֵה, *çiḥeh,* is used in Isa **5** 13, AV "dried up," RV "parched"; צְחִיחָה, *ç[e]ḥīḥāh,* in Ps **68** 6, AV "dry," RV "parched."

(4) שָׁרָב, *shārābh,* rendered "parched" in AV, is "glowing" in RV. The word implies the peculiar wavy effect of the air above parched ground, usually accompanied by mirages (cf Arab. *serāb,* "mirage") (Isa **35** 7; **49** 10). In predicting a happy future for Zion the prophet could have chosen no greater contrast than that the hot glowing sands which produce illusive water effects should be changed into real pools. See MIRAGE. JAMES A. PATCH

PARCHED, pärcht, **CORN.** See FOOD.

PARCHMENT, pärch'ment (**μεμβράνα,** *membrána* [2 Tim **4** 13]): The word "parchment," which occurs only once (2 Tim **4** 13), is derived from Lat *pergamena* (Gr Περγαμενή, *Pergamenē*), i.e. pertaining to Pergamum, the name of an ancient city in Asia

Minor where, it is believed, parchment was first used. Parchment is made from the skins of sheep, goats or young calves. The hair and fleshy portions of the skin are removed as in tanning by first soaking in lime and then dehairing, scraping and washing. The skin is then stretched on a frame and treated with powdered chalk, or other absorptive agent, to remove the fatty substances, and is then dried. It is finally given a smooth surface by rubbing with powdered pumice. Parchment was extensively used at the time of the early Christians for scrolls, legal documents, etc, having replaced papyrus for that purpose. It was no doubt used at even a much earlier time. The roll mentioned in Jer **36** may have been of parchment. Scrolls were later replaced by codices of the same material. After the Arabs introduced paper, parchment was still used for centuries for the book bindings. Diplomas printed on "sheepskins," still issued by many universities, represent the survival of an ancient use of parchment. See following article.

JAMES A. PATCH

PARCHMENTS, pärch′ments (**μεμβράναι,** *membránai,* "membranes," "parchments," "vellum"): The skins, chiefly of sheep, lambs, goats and calves, prepared so as to be used for writing on (2 Tim **4** 13).

In Gr and Rom times parchment was much employed as a writing material. "At Rome, in the 1st cent. BC, and the 1st and 2d cents. AD, there is evidence of the use of vellum, but only for notebooks and for rough drafts or inferior copies of literary works. . . . . A fragment of a vellum MS, which may belong to this period, is preserved in Brit. Mus. Add. MS 34,473, consisting of two leaves of Demosthenes, *De Fals. Leg.*, in a small hand, which appears to be of the 2d cent." (F. G. Kenyon in *HDB*, IV, 947).

Paul directs Timothy that, when he comes from Ephesus to Rome, he is to bring "the books, esp. the parchments." These, as well as the "cloak," which is also mentioned, had evidently been "left at Troas with Carpus." What were these parchments? They are distinguished from "the books," which were probably a few choice volumes or rolls, some portions of the Scriptures of the OT, some volumes of the Law of Moses or of the Prophets or of the Pss. Among "the books" there might also be Jewish exegetical works, or heathen writings, with which, as is made evident by references in his Epp., Paul was well acquainted.

The parchments were different from these, and were perhaps notebooks, in which the apostle had, from time to time, written what he had observed and wished to preserve as specially worthy of remembrance, facts which he had gathered in his study of the OT or of other books. These notes may have been the result of many years' reading and study, and he wished Timothy to bring them to him.

Various conjectures have been made in regard to the contents of "the parchments." It has been suggested by Kenyon (*HDB*, III, 673) that they contained the OT in Gr; by Farrar, that the parchments were a diploma of Paul's Rom citizenship; by Bull, that they were his commonplace books; by Latham, that the parchments were a copy of the *Grundschrift* of the Gospels, a volume containing the all-important narrative of the Saviour's life and cross and resurrection. Workman (*Persecution in the Early Church*, 39) writes: "By *tas membranas* I understand the proofs of his citizenship."

Whatever their contents may have been, they were of such value that Paul wished to have them with him in his prison at Rome, so that, if life were spared for even a few weeks or months, the books and parchments might be at hand for reference. Perhaps in the fact that the books and the parchments and the cloak had been left at Troas with Carpus, there may be a hint that his final arrest by the Rom authorities took place at that city, and that it was the suddenness of his arrest that caused him to be unable to carry his books and parchments and the cloak with him. "The police had not even allowed him time to find his overcoat or necessary documents" (Workman, op. cit., 39; see p. 1886, **14**).

Be this as it may, he desired to have them now. His well-disciplined mind, even in the near prospect of death by public execution, could find the most joyous labor in the work of the gospel, wherever his influence reached, and could also find relaxation among "the books, esp. the parchments."

JOHN RUTHERFURD

PARDON, pär′d′n, pär′dun. See FORGIVENESS.

PARE, pâr (**THE NAILS**) (עָשָׂה, *'āsāh,* "to fix," "manipulate"): The word, which in Heb has a very wide range of application, and which is of very frequent occurrence in the Heb Bible, is found in the above meaning in but one passage of EV (Dt **21** 12; see NAIL). In a similar sense it is found in 2 S **19** 24, where it is used to express the dressing of the feet and the trimming of the beard.

PARENT, pâr′ent. See CHILDREN; CRIMES; EDUCATION; FAMILY; PUNISHMENTS.

PARK, pärk (פַּרְדֵּס, *pardēs;* LXX **παράδεισος,** *parádeisos;* cf Arab. فِرْدَوْس, *firdaus*): "I made me gardens and parks," AV "orchards" (Eccl **2** 5); "Asaph the keeper of the king's forest," RVm "park" (Neh **2** 8). The same word occurs in Cant **4** 13, "Thy shoots are an orchard [RVm "paradise"] of pomegranates." According to Liddell and Scott, *paradeisos* occurs first in Xenophon, who always uses it of the parks of Pers kings and noblemen. Like many other quadriliterals the word is undoubtedly of eastern origin. It seems to connote an inclosure. It is used in LXX of the Garden of Eden. Cf Lk **23** 43; 2 Cor **12** 4; Rev **2** 7. See PARADISE.

ALFRED ELY DAY

PARLOR, pär′lẽr: This word in AV, occurring in Jgs **3** 20–25; 1 S **9** 22; 1 Ch **28** 11, is in every instance changed in RV: in Jgs into "upper room," in 1 S into "guest-chamber," in 1 Ch into "chambers," representing as many Heb words. See HOUSE.

PARMASHTA, pär-mash′ta (פַּרְמַשְׁתָּא, *parmashtā';* LXX **Μαρμασιμά,** *Marmasimá,* or **Μαρμασιμνά,** *Marmasimná*): One of the sons of Haman (Est **9** 9).

PARMENAS, pär′mē-nas (**Παρμενᾶς,** *Parmenás*): A Gr name, an abbreviated form of Parmenides. Parmenas was one of "the seven" chosen by the people and appointed by the apostles to superintend the daily distribution to the Christian poor of Jerus (Acts **6** 5). Tradition states that he was martyred at Philippi, in the reign of Trajan, but his name does not appear again in Scripture.

PARNACH, pär′nak (פַּרְנָךְ, *parnākh,* "gifted"): Father of Elizaphan, the prince of Zebulun (Nu **34** 25).

PAROSH, pā′rosh, par′osh (פַּרְעֹשׁ, *par'ōsh,* "flea" [leap]): A family that in part returned under Zerubbabel (Ezr **2** 3; Neh **7** 8), and in part under Ezra (Ezr **8** 3; there spelt "Pharosh," AV). Some of the family had foreign wives (Ezr **10** 25). One descendant, Pedaiah (see PEDAIAH, [3]), helped to rebuild the city walls (Neh **3** 25), and others were among those who "sealed" the covenant of Nehemiah (Neh **10** 1.14). In 1 Esd **5** 9; **8** 30; **9** 26, "Phoros."

PAROUSIA, pa-rōō-zhi-a:

The Second Advent of our Lord has been throughout Christian history a perplexity only less than was His First Advent as an anticipation to the Jews. It will conduce to humility in all to remember how the Jews, while holding tenaciously, and full of ardent hope, to the confident expectancy of the First Advent, yet erred so disastrously concerning the arrangement of the details of that Coming as to lose altogether the vision, when the event had passed by unrecognized by them, so that to-day the Messianic hope of the Jew is but a magnificent headless statue, a broken relic in their museum of history. Hardly less important is it for us to remember that no one yet has ever rightly interpreted prophecy *before its fulfilment;* prophecy is not history written beforehand; it is the dawn that heralds the coming day, but does not reveal it.

Even in this day of high-power critical microscopes, when criticism presumes to settle definitely all questions of history and of literature, alas! the critics are themselves hopelessly divided on this subject of the Second Advent. The earlier ones, like Hengstenberg, thought the millennium began in the Middle Ages and would end in the nineteenth century. Now some twentieth-century criticism, after its evaporating critical method, has resolved the millennium into thin air, and some very definite and explicit prophecy into mere flowers of a perfervid rhetoric.

Yet such a blessed hope as His Coming, however persons may interpret or misinterpret it, must not be passed by in silence as some desire; such silence would, in a little while, lose the hope; anything good or bad will die of neglect. Nor may any persons of serious faith entertain any ideas of the Second Advent which take away, or even obscure, its reality and so resolve it presently into nothingness. So the discussion of the subject here may not be allowed to rove over all the vagaries of opinion, but be limited to a very few of the views entertained. Two principles are in mind according to which the subject is to be given large place in this Revised Edition of the INTERNATIONAL STANDARD BIBLE ENCYCLOPAEDIA:

I. That there is to be a real Parousia, a Second Advent of the Christ, a Personal Appearing, the prophecy of which must not be allowed to evaporate as mere rhetorical phrases.

II. That the order of events at the Parousia may be a legitimate subject of discussion by those who equally hold to the reality of the Personal Appearing.

Beyond the limits of discussion which these two principles bring into view it would not be in keeping with the purpose and spirit of this Encyclopaedia to go; a purpose to avoid speculation and keep to known facts, and a charitable spirit of catholicity which tolerates differences of opinion among those of faith grounded in the Word. In accordance with this, the Postmillennial view and the Premillennial view of a real Advent are here to be presented by men of unquestioned scholarship, of deep piety, and of temperateness of expression and catholicity of spirit. While this may not, in every case, satisfy extremists of either view of the order of events at the Parousia, it will hold before us all *the certainty of His Appearing.*

POSTMILLENNIAL VIEW

I. General Facts concerning Christ's Second Coming.—

1. Certainty of the Second Coming

The doctrine of Christ's Second and Final Coming is distinctly taught and abundantly attested in the NT, though the phrase "Second Coming" is nowhere used in the Bible: Acts **1** 11; 1 Cor **4** 5; 1 Thess **4** 15–17; 2 Thess **1** 10; He **10** 37; Jude 14; Rev **1** 7; **3** 11; **22** 20. Christ is ὁ ἐρχόμενος, *ho, erchómenos* the Coming One, both with reference to His First Coming; Mt **21** 9; Lk **7** 19–20; **19** 38; Jn **3** 31; cf Mal **3** 2; **4** 5, and with respect to His Second Coming: Rev **1** 7; **4** 8; **11** 17. The doctrine concerning Christ's Second Coming occupies a most prominent place in NT teaching.

2. Manner of Christ's Second Coming

While not all passages which treat this paramount event are equally clear, the following facts regarding Christ's Second Advent are indisputably inculcated in the NT: (1) Christ's Second Coming will be *public,* visible to believers and unbelievers alike: Mt **24** 27, 30; **25** 31–46; Lk **17** 24; Acts **1** 9, 11; Rom **2** 5–16; 1 Cor **4** 5; **15** 51–52; 2 Cor **5** 10; Rev **20** 11. (2) It will be *glorious;* for as the First Coming was in humility and weakness, so the Second Coming will be "with power and great glory"; Mt **16** 27; **24** 30; **25** 31; Mk **10** 37; Lk **9** 26; Acts **17** 31; Rom **14** 10; Phil **3** 20; Titus **2** 13. (3) It will be *unexpected,* sudden, and unheralded by special or immediate warnings: Mt **24** 27, 42–44; Mk **13** 35–37; Lk **21** 34–36; 2 Pet **3** 10. (4) Nevertheless, it will be *preceded by definite signs* clearly foretold: universal preaching of the Gospel: Mt **24** 14; Mk **13** 10; Acts **1** 8; apostasy and the coming of the Antichrist: 2 Thess **2** 3–4; 2 Tim **3** 1; 2 Pet **3** 3–4; 1 Jn **4** 1, 3; great calamities on earth: Mt **24**; Mk **13**; Lk **21**. (5) In spite of these signs, which shall be fulfilled in ever increasing number as the Coming approaches, *wicked and unbelieving men will scoff* at the preaching of Christ's Second Coming: 1 Tim **4** 1–3; 2 Pet **3** 3–12, so that when the Lord will come He will not find much faith on earth: Lk **18** 8. (6) It will occur in an *hour unknown* to men and angels, as that hour was unknown to Christ according to His human nature in His state of humiliation: Mt **24** 36–51; **25** 1–12; Mk **13** 32; Lk **21** 34–36; Acts **1** 7; 1 Thess **5** 1–3. All attempts to compute the time are therefore in vain. (7) Yet it is *near at hand:* 1 Jn **2** 18; 1 Pet **4** 7; 1 Cor **10** 11; Jas **5** 8–9. From the teaching of Scriptures there is nothing to prevent the Coming of Christ at any moment.

II. Descriptive Terms of Christ's Second Coming.—

1. Apocalypse

Christ's Second Coming is predicted partly in clear, unmistakable words, and partly by terms, which though synonymous, have peculiar connotations that shed particular light upon the great event. Such terms are, first, "Apocalypse," *apokálupsis,* revelation: 1 Cor **1** 7; 2 Thess **1** 7; 1 Pet **1** 7.13; **4** 13. This expression depicts Christ's appearance in majesty and glory, His "uncovering of glory." In the state of humiliation the Saviour's glory was concealed; on the day of His Second Coming it will be revealed and made manifest to all men: Mt **24** 30.

2. Epiphany

The second term by which Christ's Second Coming is described is "Epiphany," *epiphâneia*, which means manifestation, or appearance: 2 Thess **2** 8; 1 Tim **6** 14; 2 Tim **4** 1, 8; Titus **2** 13. In Hel Gr the word denoted the official arrival of rulers, and in the NT it emphasizes Christ's appearance as the "Coming of the Lord," and stressing His dignity.

3. Parousia

The third term, which is more generally used than the two just named, is *parousîa*, which means presence, or advent: Mt **24** 3, 27, 37, 39; 1 Cor **15** 23; 1 Thess **2** 19; **3** 13; **4** 15; **5** 23; 2 Thess **2** 1, 9; Jas **5** 7, 8; 2 Pet **1** 16; **3** 4, 12; 1 Jn **2** 28. The word is so frequent that it has been taken over into English and so stands for Christ's Second Coming as its official technical term. Like *epiphâneia*, it also denotes the arrival of rulers and reflects the majesty of the Lord at His coming. Sometimes the word simply means "presence": 2 Cor **10** 10; Phil **2** 12; or "coming" in the sense of arrival: 1 Cor **16** 17; 2 Cor **7** 6, 7; Phil **1** 26. In 2 Thess **2** 9 it denotes the coming of Antichrist. In patristic lit it also denotes the Incarnation of the Lord, cf Justin's *Trypho*, XIV. However, also the term *epiphâneia* denotes the Incarnation of the Lord: 2 Tim **1** 10. In every case in the NT where the terms mean the Second Coming of Christ, the text and context suggest the exact meaning.

4. "The Day"

Other descriptive terms are: "Day of God," 2 Pet **3** 12; "Day of the Lord," 1 Thess **5** 2; "Day of the Lord Jesus," and "of Jesus Christ," 1 Cor **1** 8; Phil **1** 6, 10; 2 Pet **3** 10; "That Day," 2 Thess **1** 10; 2 Tim **1** 12, 18; "The Last Day" Jn **6** 39–54; "The Great Day," "The Day of Redemption," "The Day of Wrath," "Day of Judgment," "Day of Revelation," Rom **2** 5; Eph **4** 30; 2 Pet **2** 9; Jude 6; Rev **6** 17. All these terms are fully understood, if interpreted in the sense of the clear passages which foretell Christ's Second Coming in express terms: Mt **25**; Mk **13**; Lk **21**. It is on these passages that the doctrine of Christ's Second Coming must be based, for there our Lord speaks with great clearness.

III. Events connected with Christ's Second Coming.—The events which the Holy Scriptures connect with Christ's Second Coming are:

1. Three Special Events Connected with Christ's Coming

(1) The simultaneous resurrection of all the dead, both good and bad: Dnl **12** 2; Jn **5** 28–29; **6** 40, 44; **11** 24; 1 Cor **15** 23; 1 Thess **4** 16; Rev **20** 11–15. The only passage which seems to contradict the simultaneous resurrection of all the dead is Rev **20** 1–10; this shall be considered later. (2) The Judgment of all men, the good and the bad, the dead and those alive at Christ's Coming: Mt **7** 21, 23; **13** 30–43; **16** 27; **25** 31–46; Acts **17** 31; Rom **2** 5, 16; **14** 10; 1 Cor **3** 12–15; **4** 5; 2 Cor **5** 9–11; 2 Thess **1** 6–10; Jude 15; Rev **1** 7; **20** 11; **21** 1. (3) The general conflagration of the world and the generation of the "new heaven and the new earth": Mt **24** 35; Lk **21** 33; He **1** 11; 2 Pet **3** 7–13; Rev **20** 11; **21** 1.

2. The Judgment

The Judgment is ascribed to the Father: He **10** 30; **12** 23; **13** 4; Jas **4** 11, 12; 1 Pet **1** 17; Rev **14** 7; **20** 11 and perhaps in Jude 14–15. It is ascribed to Christ in Acts **10** 42; 2 Cor **5** 10; 2 Tim **4** 1. In Rom **14** 9–10 the two concepts are interwoven and according to Acts **17** 31; Rom **2** 16 and perhaps Rom **3** 6 God mediates judgment through Christ. In Jn **5** 22 Christ claims for Himself the authority to judge as the Son of Man. These passages are not contradictory, for the Judgment is an "*opus ad extra*," a work of the whole Trinity. But in a special sense according to the Holy Scriptures, Jesus Christ, in both natures, as the God-man will execute the Judgment in His official character as Mediator: Mt **16** 27; **19** 28; **24** 30; Jn **5** 27; Acts **17** 31; Rom **2** 16. In the Judgment Christ will be assisted by all true believers; Mt **19** 28; 1 Cor **6** 2–3, and by the holy angels; Mt **25** 31; 1 Thess **4** 16; 2 Thess **1** 7–8; Jude 14–15, the believers confirming the Judgment, and the angels assembling those who are to be judged and separating them: Mt **13** 41–50; **24** 31; 1 Thess **4** 17.

The *subjects* of Christ's Judgment are the whole race of Adam without exception, but especially the multitude of the condemned: Eccl **11** 9; **12** 14; Mt **11** 22; **12** 36; Rom **2** 5; 1 Cor **4** 5; Jude 15; the communion of believing saints, in as much as their faith and righteousness will be proved by their works; so that properly speaking they will not be brought into judgment: Mt **25** 31–40; **3** 18; Jn **5** 24; Eph **4** 30. In particular, Christ will judge the *deeds* of men: Ps **62** 12; Prov **24** 12; Jer **25** 14; **32** 19; Mt **16** 27; Rom **2** 6; 1 Cor **3** 8; 2 Cor **5** 10; 1 Pet **1** 17; Rev **22** 12. Since every work has its source in unbelief, the crucial question will be that of faith or infidelity: Jn **3** 18; Phil **3** 9. However, not only the actual works, but also the words and secret thoughts and purposes of the heart will appear in Judgment: Mt **12** 36 ff; Rom **2** 16; 1 Cor **4** 5, Eph **5** 11–13; 1 Tim **5** 24 25. While thus in the Judgment the sins of the ungodly will be revealed: Mt **25** 41–46; Jude 6, 14–15; Rev **20** 12, those of the believers will be covered: Isa **43** 25; Jer **31** 34; Ezk **18** 22; Mic **7** 19; for to them Christ will come as the Redeemer: Lk **21** 28; Rom **8** 23; as Savior: Mt **25** 34–36; Jn **14** 3; as Advocate: Rom **8** 34; 1 Jn **2** 1; as Rewarder of the crown: 2 Tim **4** 8; Rev **2** 17.19. As ungodly enemies of Christ, also the evil angels will be judged: Mt **25** 41; 2 Pet **2** 4; Jude 6.

The *norm* by which Christ will judge is His Word: Jn **12** 48; the Law: Rom **2** 12; the Gospel: Rom **2** 16; 2 Thess **1** 8; the books: Rev **20** 12; but this expression is perhaps only a symbol of the omniscience of God.

The *sentence* pronounced upon the ungodly will be eternal damnation: Dnl **12** 2; **5** 22, 29, 30; **8** 12; **13** 42; Mt **25** 41–46; Mk **9** 43, 44; Lk **16** 23; Jn **3** 36; Rom **2** 5; 2 Thess **1** 9; Jude 13; Rev **14** 10, 11; **21** 8. The term "*aionios*" is an emphatic term to express the idea of endless duration: Mt **19** 29; Mk **10** 30; Jn **3** 15; Rom **2** 7; **16** 26; He **9** 14. In Mt **25** 46 the same term is used in a single sentence to define at once the duration of the future happiness of the saints, and the misery of the lost. So also the word "*aidios*" signifies the idea of eternal or never ending, expressing the eternal duration of the Godhead: Rom **1** 20, and the eternal duration of the sufferings of the evil angels and their followers: Mt **25** 41; Jude 6; Rev **20** 10.

To all true *believers* Christ will give eternal life: Mt **5** 8; **12** 43; **19** 28; **25** 21, 31–40; Lk **6** 21; **23** 43; Jn **3** 16; **10** 27, 28; Rom **8** 18; 1 Cor **13** 12; 2 Tim **4** 18; He **13** 14; 1 Jn **3** 2; Rev **2** 10; **14** 13; **21** 4. The most prominent element of the blessedness of heaven is the beatific vision: Ps **17** 15; Mt **5** 8; **18** 10; Jn **17** 24; 1 Jn **3** 2; Rev **22** 4. It is endless reign in communion with God in glory: 1 Tim **6** 19; 2 Tim **2** 12; Rev **22** 14.

3. The End of the World

The *execution* of the sentence by the divine Judge will be followed immediately by the end of the present world, which will be brought about by fire: Ps **102** 26; Isa **34**; Mt **24** 35; 1 Cor **7** 31; 2 Pet **3** 7, 10, and the creation of a new heaven and a new earth: Isa **65** 17; **66** 22; 2 Pet **3** 13;

Rev **21** 1. Whether this prophecy should be interpreted literally or not, cannot be ascertained with certainty. At any rate, the believers will enjoy eternal life with Christ, and this should comfort and inspire them to a joyful hope.

IV. The Proper Use of the Doctrine.—To all believers the doctrine of Christ's Second Coming is a most glorious and comforting revelation. It has been revealed for the very purpose of consoling them in their tribulations and of stimulating them to duty: Lk **21** 28; 1 Cor **1** 7; Phil **3** 20; Col **3** 4, 5; 1 Thess **1** 10; **4** 18; He **9** 28; Jas **5** 7; 2 Pet **3** 12; 1 Jn **3** 2, 3; Rev **22** 20. They should love, watch, wait for, and hasten unto the coming of their Lord: Lk **12** 35, 37; 1 Cor **1** 7, 8; Phil **3** 20; 1 Thess **1** 9.10; 2 Tim **4** 8; 2 Pet **3** 12; Rev **22** 20. There is nothing in the Holy Scriptures which makes the Coming of Christ a cause of fear to them; with unfeigned joy they should await and pray for that great event.

1. The Comfort of the Doctrine

However, to all unbelievers and wicked rejectors of the Gospel, the revelation is a terrible warning. They should be filled with fearful apprehension, and escape the dreadful doom of all the wicked through repentance: Mk **13** 35, 37; Jn **3** 18; 2 Thess **1** 7, 8; 2 Pet **3** 3, 4, 9, 10; Jude 14, 15.

2. The Doctrine a Warning

V. The Doctrine and the Confessions of the Church.—The Christian Church in its official declarations has treated the doctrine of Christ's Second Coming with brevity, but with great clearness, and in this presentation of the doctrine we have followed the official standards of faith. The holy apostles considered the Second Coming of Christ as near at hand: Phil **1** 6; 1 Thess **4** 15; He **10** 25; Jas **5** 8; 1 Pet **1** 5. This expectation is reflected in the Confessions of the Ancient Church:

(1) "From thence He shall come to judge the quick and the dead" (Apostles' Creed).

(2) "And he shall come again with glory to judge both the quick and the dead" (Nicene Creed).

(3) "At whose coming all men shall rise again with their bodies, and shall give account of their own works" (Athanasian Creed).

(4) "They also teach that Christ will appear at the end of the world for judgment, and that He will raise all the dead, and that He will give to the pious elect eternal life and perpetual joy, but condemn wicked men and devils, that they shall be tormented without end. They condemn the Anabaptists, who believe that there will be an end of the future punishment of lost men and devils. And they condemn others who scatter Jewish opinions, to the effect that before the resurrection of the dead the pious will occupy the kingdom of the world, and the wicked be everywhere in subjection" (Augsburg Confession, Part 1, Art. V.17).

(5) "They teach: 1. At the last day shall be a general resurrection of the dead both of the just and of the unjust; 2. All found alive shall be immediately changed; 3. Immediately after the resurrection shall follow the general and final judgment of all angels and men, good and bad; 4. That the date of this day and hour is purposely kept secret by God. In Ques. 53–56, we are further taught that Christ's Second Coming will not occur until the "last day," "the end of the world," and that He will then come "to judge the world in righteousness" (Westminster Confession, chs 32 and 33; Larger Catechism, Ques. 87–89; cf Hodge, *Outline of Theology*, 576).

The Protestant churches of the Reformation, following the ancient Church, thus centered their eschatological hope in the doctrine that Christ would return to judge the quick and the dead, destroy the present world, consign the wicked to eternal punishment, and lead the believers into eternal life. The conception of a millennial reign of Christ on earth was never embodied in the dogma of the Church.

VI. Questions To Be Considered in Connection with Christ's Second Coming.—Bitter controversies have been waged within Christendom on points of belief in connection with the doctrine of Christ's Second Advent. The most prominent of these regards the millennial reign of Christ on earth inculcated on the basis of Rev **20** 1–10. To this day the belief is widely spread and warmly defended that there will be a millennium (a period of a thousand years) with world-wide righteousness, introduced by, or preceding, the sudden, unannounced visible Advent of Christ. The details of the millennial scheme vary greatly, and the statements of the various exponents of the doctrine are often contradictory, so that the whole controversy has caused much confusion among Christian believers.

1. The Millennial Reign of Christ

The following considerations are suggested to assist the Bible student in his search for certainty: (1) The doctrine of a millennial reign of Christ has never been adopted into the official Creed of the Christian Church; on the contrary, the Confessions of the most prominent historical churches have declared themselves against it. (2) The doctrine of Chiliasm or Millenarianism is so hopelessly confused and inconsistent that it can never serve as an article of faith to be accepted by all believers; agreement is lacking even with reference to essential points. (3) The doctrine is not taught in the clear Scripture passages which treat the Second Coming of Christ *ex professo;* and yet these are the passages upon which the Christian must rely for clear information on the subject. (4) The doctrine opposes all those passages which connect Christ's Second Coming immediately: (*a*) with the resurrection of the just and the unjust, so that all the dead, both good and bad, rise at the same time: Dnl **12** 2; Jn **5** 28, 29; 1 Cor **15** 23; 1 Thess **4** 16; Rev **20** 11, 15; (*b*) with the simultaneous judgment of all men, the good and the bad together: Mt **7** 21–23; **13** 30–43; **16** 24, 27; **25** 31–46; Rom **2** 5, 16; 1 Cor **3** 12–15; 2 Cor **5** 9–11; 2 Thess **1** 6–10; Rev **20** 11–15; (*c*) with the general conflagration and the generation of the "new heaven and the new earth": 2 Pet **3** 7–13; Rev **20** 11; **21** 1. All these passages are silent on the millennial reign of Christ and allow no time for such a reign. (*d*) The conception of a millennial reign is evidently Judaic in origin and Judaizing in tendency; manifestly it grew out of the carnal conception of the Jews that Christ's kingdom would be earthly. Cf 2 Esd VII. 28 ff, where the following order of eschatological events appears: A time of final trial, the coming of the Messiah, a war of nations against Him, the descent of the heavenly Jerusalem, the gathering of the dispersed Israelites, the four-hundred-year reign of the Messiah, seven days of silence, the renewal of the world, the general resurrection, and the last Judgment. However, this apocalyptical teaching was not the universal belief of the Jews at the time of Christ. (*e*) The opinion of a millennial reign of Christ is inconsistent with the Scriptural doctrine concerning the nature of Christ's kingdom. The Holy Scriptures teach distinctly that Christ's kingdom is not of the world, but spiritual: Mt **13** 11–44; Jn **18** 36; Rom **14** 17; that regeneration (conversion) is the only means of admission into it: Jn **3** 5–6; that the blessings of the kingdom are purely spiritual, consisting in pardon, peace, sanctification, etc.: Mt **3** 2–11; Col **1** 13, 14; and that Christ's kingdom has already come: Acts **2** 29–36; **3** 13–15; **4** 26–28; **5** 29–31; He **10** 12, 13; Rev **3** 7–12. Hence also the prophecies of the OT, predicting Christ's kingdom, must be regarded as referring to the present dispensation of grace, and not to any future millennial reign of Christ.

Thus it is clear that the scope and purpose of the NT Scriptures is not millenarian. In Mk **1** 15 Christ indeed announces that the kingdom of God is at hand, but He does not speak of any provisory kingdom to be founded by Him. His Second Coming is identical with the Last Judgment; until then the wheat and tares are to grow together. The renewal of the world in Mt **19** 28 is connected with the Final Judgment. Especially at the Last Supper did Christ make the supernatural character of His future kingdom clear to His disciples: Mk **14** 25. St. Paul also pictures the Church as enjoying the fruition of its faith, not upon earth, but in heaven: Phil **3** 20. Also in his other Epistles Paul's trend of teaching is not an earthly hope, but the hope of consummated joy in heaven: 1 Cor **15** 25 ff. If, in spite of all this, the hope of a temporal millennial reign of Christ was early adopted in the Christian Church, though never officially, it was due to the violence of persecution which no doubt suggested a hope so inviting and glorious.

2. Rev 20 1–10

The only passage which seems at first to teach the contrary is Rev **20** 1–10. However, let the Bible student bear in mind that this passage will support the opinion of the millenarian scheme only if it is interpreted with the barest literalness. That caution must be exercised in interpreting this passage is clear from the following facts: (1) It occurs in a book concerning whose canonicity there has been extended dissent; (2) It is found in one of the most figurative books of Scripture; (3) It constitutes only an obscure part in this confessedly obscure book; (4) The literal interpretation contradicts what the Scriptures uniformly teach with reference to the nature of the resurrection body, which is said to be "spiritual," and not "natural" or of "flesh and blood": 1 Cor **15** 44; (5) The passage does not speak of a millennial reign of Christ on earth, and is not connected with the doctrine of Christ's Second Coming; for clearly the scene pictured is one which takes place in heaven, since the text speaks only of "souls."

As the student observes, the passage is therefore one of great difficulty, and so far not a single interpretation of it has met with the approval of all exegetes, since each raises new difficulties. Withal the text is highly obscure, difficult, and perplexing, and therefore too inadequate to base upon it a doctrine or creed.

3. Conversion of the Jews

A third question that has been raised in connection with the doctrine of Christ's Second Coming pertains to the conversion of the Jews. Advocates of the millennial reign of Christ on earth defend with great ardor the doctrine that the Jews will be converted either at the commencement, or during the continuance, of the millennial reign. This opinion is based upon such passages as: Isa **59** 20; Jer **31** 31; Zec **12** 10; **13** 1; Rom **11** 15–29; 2 Cor **3** 15, 16; the last being the most important. However, it is clear that the phrase used in that passage "all Israel" must be restricted according to the custom of Scripture to "a definite number." The literal translation would furnish the incredible view that not a single Israelite would be lost. Certainly the phrase cannot be construed as referring to the "Israel according to the flesh." That would demand the resurrection of all the dead Israelites and the salvation of such reprobates as Saul and Judas. In short, if the phrase "all Israel" is interpreted literally, deductions would have to be made that are inconsistent with clear Scriptural doctrines. But if the phrase is applied to the "Israel according to the spirit," that is, the elect in Israel, who correspond to the "fulness of the Gentiles," the meaning is clear. Paul himself suggests this interpretation by referring to the election in ver. 28: "as touching the election." Paul here as everywhere teaches the Scriptural doctrine that only the elect will be saved: Rom **9** 6–18; **9** 23, 24, 27; **10** 20–21; **11** 4–5. The phrase, "all Israel," then represents the sum total of God's elect. These shall be saved by grace, not during any future millennial age, but in this present dispensation of grace. The ingathering of the elect Jews and the elect Gentiles is taking place now through the preaching of the Gospel. Paul stresses this point by stating that "blindness in part is happened to Israel, until the fulness of the Gentiles be come in. And so all Israel shall be saved"; Rom **11** 25–26. "As the fulness of the Gentiles does not mean each and every nation, for such conversion of the Gentiles to the Church is not to be expected, but only a large number of Gentiles, so the salvation and conversion of the Jews, one and all, is not to be hoped for" (Baldwin). "All Israel" is "the remnant according to the election of grace": Rom **11** 2–5; cf **11** 7: "The election hath obtained it, and the rest were blinded."

4. The Church of Christ on Earth

The hope of Christ's millennial reign on earth is based, no doubt, and perhaps quite unconsciously, upon the earnest desire of every Christian heart for the vindication of Christ's glory and love on earth.

Nevertheless, the Holy Scriptures assure us that the revelation of Christ's glory and love will not come in this dispensation, but at the end of time, when the millions of believers, the sum total of God's elect, will be revealed in glory: Mt **25** 31–40; Rev. **21**. Till that time the Church of Christ will remain a church militant, suffering the same humiliation which Christ endured on earth. All Christians must bear their Master's cross; be hated of all men; be persecuted for Christ's sake, apparently constituting only "a little flock" which fights under the banner of Christ against Satan, the world, and the flesh: Mt **7** 13, 14; **22** 14; **24** 9, 10; Lk **12** 32; Jn **18** 36; Rom **7** 14; Gal **5** 17; Eph **6** 10, 11; 1 Pet **5** 8, 9; 1 Jn **5** 4; Rev **3** 10, 11. Especially shall the last days before Christ's Second Coming be full of tribulation: Mt **24**; Mk **13**; Lk **17** 24–30; **21** 7–19; 1 Tim **4** 1–3; 2 Tim **3** 1–5; **4** 3–5. The Church will be transformed into a church triumphant through Christ's glorious coming: Rev **2** 10; **4** 4; **7** 9; it should therefore center its hope in His triumphant Advent: Phil **3** 20; Rev **22** 17, 20. In this glorious hope it is to find its richest comfort.

5. The Apostles and Christ's Second Coming

Another question that has been considered in connection with Christ's Second Coming is whether the apostles expected Christ's Second Advent during their lifetime. Passages which have been adduced to prove this are: Phil **1** 6; 1 Thess **4** 15; He **10** 25; Jas **5** 8; etc. In all these passages Christ's Second Coming is pictured as near at hand; yet at the same time the holy writers never taught that it would occur in their lifetime, or at any fixed time whatever. During Christ's life they expected that He would establish His kingdom in glory: Lk **24** 21; Acts **1** 6. But in their inspired writings they taught only: (1) That Christ's Coming should be desired; and (2) that since it was uncertain as to time, it should always be regarded as imminent. At the same time they pointed out that certain events were to transpire before Christ's Second Coming, e.g., the Antichristian apostasy: 2 Thess **2** 4. In general, their teachings with respect to the Second Coming are clear and uniform.

The interpretation of Mt **24** and **25** has always caused great difficulties to the Bible student, and many contradictory explanations have been offered on these two chapters, which are believed to answer three different questions: (1) When would the temple and the city be destroyed? (2) What were to be the signs of Christ's Second Coming? (3) When would the end of the world occur? The difficulty in interpreting the chapters arises from the fact that it is hard to separate the portions relating to these several questions, for some of the prophecies manifestly refer to the destruction of Jerusalem and others to the destruction of the world. The interpretation becomes simple, if the student bears in mind that prophecy is epitelesmatic, that is, that it extends from that which is near to that which is far away, not always in logical sequence, but so that the main events of both are put in close proximity. Thus, while Christ speaks of the destruction of Jerusalem, He beholds by the same prophetic glimpse the destruction of the world, and He freely passes from the one to the other, since both are similar. What the Saviour views first is the destruction of Jerusalem, which marks the end of the OT dispensation; from this His view extends to the destruction of the world, the end of the second dispensation. The signs ushering in the two events are quite similar; conditions in both instances are much the same, and therefore also the same warnings are in place. From the one Christian believers are to learn the lessons regarding the other. When the prophecy is interpreted in this manner, most of the difficulties vanish, and the two chapters are seen to agree well with what other Scripture passages say concerning Christ's Coming.

6. Mt 24 and 25

The last question pertains to the prophecy of universal Gospel preaching before Christ's Coming. This the Holy Scriptures assert with great clearness: Mt **24** 14. However, Paul calls attention to the fact that already at his time the Gospel was universally preached: Rom **1** 5, 8; **10** 18; Col **1** 6, 23. Cf Mt **28** 19; Mk **16** 20. Events in church history have shown a steady development of mission work, until today the Gospel of Christ is witnessed in the whole world, and the Gospel age may be said to have appeared. This may be considered as the fulfilment of the Saviour's promise and a sign of the speedy return of the divine Judge. For while the Word is being preached, the other signs are being steadily fulfilled; apostasy increases; love is waxing cold; and the true church of Christ, which is loyal to His Word, is suffering tribulation. There are not more fitting words with which to close this article than the warning of the Saviour: "Watch ye therefore; for ye know not when the master of the house cometh, at even, or at midnight, or at the cock-crowing, or in the morning: Lest coming suddenly He find you sleeping. And what I say unto you, I say unto all, Watch, Mk **14** 35–37.

7. Universal Gospel Preaching

LITERATURE.—For the study of the subject the Bible student may consult the following: Strong, *Systematic Theology*, Vol. III, pp. 1003–15; Hodge, *Outline of Theology*, pp. 566–87; Jacobs, *Summary of Christian Faith*, pp. 504–17; Pieper, *Christliche Dogmatik*, Vol. III, pp. 579–601; Geberding, *When Christ Comes*, pp. 15–43; Evans, *The Great Doctrines of the Bible*, pp. 236–44; W. E. Blackstone, *Jesus Is Coming;* Erdman, *The Return of Christ;* Rall, *Modern Premillennialism and the Christian Hope;* Eaton, *The Millennial Dawn Heresy;* Sheldon, *System of Christian Doctrine*, pp. 559–68; J. A. Seiss, *The Last Times;* A. C. Gaebelein, *The Harmony of the Prophetic Word;* J. M. Gray, *A Text Book on Prophecy;* R. A. Torrey, *The Return of the Lord Jesus;* I. M. Haldeman, *The Return of the Lord Jesus;* H. C. Sheldon, *Studies in Recent Adventism;* J. H. Snowden, *The Coming of the Lord;* Shailer Mathews, *Will Christ Come Again?* F. C. Porter, *Messages of the Apocalyptic Writers;* R. H. Charles, *Eschatology;* W. Bousset, *Die Religion des Judentums;* H. A. Kennedy, *St. Paul's Conception of the Last Things;* S. J. Case, *The Millennial Hope;* Shailer Mathews, *The Messianic Hope in the New Testament;* I. T. Beckwith, *The Apocalypse of John;* S. J. Case, *The Revelation of John;* R. H. Charles, *Exposition of Revelation*, in the International Critical Commentary; cf. also sub "Millennium", *Encyclopaedia Britannica; Hastings' Dictionary of the Bible; The New Schaff-Herzog Encyclopaedia of Religious Knowledge;* also C. A. Briggs, "Origin and History of Premillennialism," *Luth. Quarterly*, Vol. IX; also S. H. Kellogg, *Premillennialism*, Vol. XLV, *Bibliotheca Sacra;* also Reports of Prophetic Conferences: *Premillennial Essays* (New York); *Prophetic Studies* (Chicago); *The Coming and Kingdom of Christ* (Chicago). The literature is immense, and the student must study both sides of the questions with constant attention to Scripture.

JOHN THEODORE MUELLER

PREMILLENNIAL VIEW

I. Terms.—The word Parousia (Gr. παρουσία, lit. "presence") is used in the NT as a technical term to denote the return of Christ in glory at the end of the age. In other connections the word may mean simply "presence" as opposed to absence (2 Cor **10** 10: Phil **1** 26; **2** 12) or the arrival which introduces that presence, as in 1 Cor **16** 17; 2 Cor **7** 6, 7; 2 Thess **2** 9; 2 Pet **3** 12. When applied to Christ, however, the term invariably indicates his Second Coming, or Advent. Mt **24** 3, 27, 37, 39; 1 Cor **15** 23; 1 Thess **2** 19; **3** 13; **4** 15; **5** 23; 2 Thess **2** 1, 8; Jas **5** 7, 8; 2 Pet **1** 16; **3** 4, 12; 1 Jn **2** 28. While the exact phrase Second Coming, or Second Advent, is not found in the NT, the phrase is almost universally employed now to denote the future return of Christ and corresponds to the term Parousia. Synonymous NT expressions are (1) "Apocalypse" (Gr ἀποκάλυψις, *apokálypsis*) "revelation," a term used to express the truth that Christ had withdrawn into the sphere of the unseen and will be revealed in glory. This word is used particularly of the judicial aspect of his Coming, and in references to his enemies (Lk **17** 30; Acts **3** 21; I Cor **1** 7; 2 Thess **1** 7, 8; 1 Pet **1** 13, 20; **5** 4). (2) "Epiphany" (Gr ἐπιφάνεια, *epiphaneia*) "manifestation," used of the Incarnation in 2 Tim **1** 10, but of the Second Coming in 2 Thess **2** 8; 1 Tim **6** 14; 2 Tim **4** 1, 8; Tit **2** 13. Like the word Parousia, this term in Hellenistic Gr. is employed to denote the ceremonial arrival of rulers. (3) "The Day of the Lord," a phrase variously modified as "The Day" (Gr *heméra*), "That Day," "The Day of Jesus Christ." This phrase is associated so specifically with the judgment which follows the Parousia that it is used as a synonym for judgment (cf Acts **19** 38; 1 Cor **4** 3). The phrase occurs Mt **7** 22; **24** 36; Mk **13** 32; Lk **10** 12; **17** 24; **21** 34; Acts **2** 20; Rom **13** 12; 1 Cor **1** 8; **3** 13; **5** 5; 2 Cor **1** 14; Phil **1** 6; **2** 16; 1 Thess **5** 2, 4 (cf vs 5, 8); 2 Thess **2** 2; 2 Tim **1** 12, 18; **4** 8; He **10** 25; 2 Pet **3** 10.

II. Nature of the Event.—The Second Coming of Christ is to be personal, visible, glorious. Much of the language in which it is described is symbolic and apocalyptic; nevertheless it is evident that the term Parousia defines a literal, bodily reappearing of Christ. His coming is to be "on the clouds," "in clouds," "in a cloud," "with great power and glory," and attended by angels (Mt **24** 30; Mk **13** 26; Lk **21** 27; Mt **24** 31; Mk **8** 38; Mk **13** 27; 2 Thess **1** 7). When on trial before the high priest, Christ predicts that His judges shall "see the Son of Man coming on the clouds of heaven" (Mt **26** 64; Mk **14** 62). At His Ascension, angel messengers declare to the disciples "This same Jesus which is taken up from you into heaven, shall so come in like manner as ye have seen him go into heaven" (Acts **1** 11).

Possibly the most complete account is in **1** Thess **4** 16 ff: "For the Lord himself shall descend from heaven with a shout, with the voice of the archangel, and with the trump of God; and the dead in Christ shall rise first. Then we that are alive that are left, shall together with them be caught up in the clouds to meet the Lord in the air. And so shall we be ever with the Lord" (cf 1 Cor **15** 52 RV). The event will break upon the unbelieving world as a sudden surprise, while men are occupied with their earthly affairs, like the Flood in the time of Noah, or the destruction of Sodom in the time of Lot (Lk **17** 26–30; 34). Its coming will be as that of a thief, stealing into the house without warning (Lk **12** 39 ff), or as the arrival of an absent master at an hour when his servants are not expecting him (Lk **12** 42–46). However, when it does occur it will be widely and dazzlingly brilliant, like the lightning-flash which illumes all the heavens (Mt **24** 27; Lk **17** 24); as John declares in the Apocalypse, "Behold he cometh with clouds and every eye shall see him" (Rev **1** 7). The Parousia, therefore, is not to be confused with the spiritual presence of Christ. The latter is also a blessed reality. In His farewell discourse, delivered on the night of his betrayal, Jesus cheered His disciples by His sure word of promise, "I will not leave you comfortless; I will come to you" (Jn **14** 18). This belief in the spiritual coming of Christ, this confidence in his unseen presence, has been the stay and encouragement of His followers through all the ages. Nothing should make us blind to this great truth. We should go forth and work with more gladness and zeal as we remember his words, "Lo, I am with you always" (Mt **28** 20). However, this is distinct from the other glorious reality that some day Christ will reappear, literally, in bodily form, and "when He shall be manifested we shall be like him, for we shall see Him as He is" (1 Jn **3** 2 RV).

So, too, this return is to be distinguished from the promised coming of the Holy Spirit at Pentecost. Both comings are mentioned in the first chapter of the Acts. First, "Ye shall receive power, after that the Holy Ghost is come upon you"; and the second, "this same Jesus shall so come in like manner."

The marvels of Pentecost were rightly attributed to the power of the risen, living, divine Lord; yet long after that memorable day the apostles continued to predict with confidence the fulfilment of this second promise, and to comfort believers by the assurance of the "praise and honor and glory" they should receive at "the appearing of Jesus Christ" (1 Pet **1** 7).

Nor yet was this latter promise fulfilled in the destruction of Jerusalem. It is easy to understand why these two events have been confused, for both were predicted by our Lord in the same prophetic discourse. He combined the descriptions and used the features of the nearer event to color the picture of the more remote. He employed the approaching doom of the sacred city as a type and symbol of the judgments upon His enemies that will attend his visible return. One of these great events, the fall of the city at the hands of Titus, is now in the distant past, but the other is still future, namely, the glorious reappearing of Christ.

Nor should we identify the coming of Christ with the death of a believer. It is true that death may be in some respects but the servant in black livery who ushers us into the presence of the King; "To depart" is "to be with Christ" which for us "is far better" (Phil **1** 23); "to be absent from the body" is "to be at home with the Lord" (2 Cor **5** 8). Yet, death is inseparable from pain and loss and sorrow and separation and anguish and tears. Death is still, in most of his aspects, our enemy; but the coming of Christ is our blessed hope; it is not the same as death. When Christ returns He will raise the dead and will destroy death and will repair all the evil that death has wrought.

Jesus was Himself very careful to distinguish between the death of His followers and His own return. In the closing chapter of his Gospel the Apostle John records the prediction of the death by which Peter was to "glorify God," and the further statement in reference to the "beloved disciple," that possibly he might not die but might live until his Lord returned: "If I will that he tarry till I come, what is that to thee?" (Jn **21** 22). Therefore death and the return of Christ are not identical, but are contrasted events.

More startling than the scenes at Pentecost, more momentous than the fall of Jerusalem, more evident and significant than the indwelling of the Spirit, more to be desired than our departure to be with the Lord, will be the literal, visible return of Christ. Nor does it seem possible to identify this Coming of Christ with the gradual spread of his kingdom, and to regard it as descriptive of this present dispensation which began with Pentecost and will continue until "the kingdoms of this world are become the kingdoms of our Lord and of his Christ" (Rev **11** 15). This ultimate triumph of Christ is absolutely assured; however, the Parousia describes not an era of time, but a distinct event which will bring to its consummation and perfection the glorious kingdom of Christ.

III. Preceding Events.—The time of the Parousia is absolutely unknown. All attempts at determining its date have proved futile and are severely rebuked by the words of Christ (Mt **24** 36). However, certain events are predicted as preceding his return, and immediately before he appears certain signs will be manifest so that his followers will be prepared for his coming and "the day of the Lord" will not "overtake" them "as a thief in the night" (1 Thess **5** 1–4). Supreme among all these precursory movements is the world-wide proclamation of the Gospel (Mt **24** 14).

This preaching is to be no mere superficial heralding of the good news. The process is clearly indicated by the work of the apostles, who sought to establish in every land Christian churches which would be self-supporting and self-propagating, the members of which would take their places in society and in the state, and do everything in their power to purify and strengthen and bless the circles and the communities in which they lived. The work was substantial; its methods were sane and wise. Christians were to be the "salt of the earth"; they were to be the "light of the world." No theory concerning the return of our Lord can be Scriptural which subordinates the preaching of the Gospel to any form of social service, or which on the other hand fails to establish abiding institutions, or to express in human helpfulness the true spirit of Christ.

Still, by whatever processes it may be carried on, the supreme event, the incomparably important condition to be fulfilled before the return of Christ, is the preaching of His Gospel in all the world and unto every creature.

Just how far the evangelization of the world is synonymous with the conversion of the world is a debated question to which no exact answer probably can be given. The New Testament indicates, and modern history is recording, great triumphs of the Gospel. Most readers interpret the words of our Lord as indicating that the influence of this Gospel will permeate all human society, and that Christian institutions will be established throughout all the earth. The number of Christian nations will continue to increase and when the work of conversion has reached its climax among the Gentiles, practically the entire Jewish race will accept Jesus as their

Messiah, either before or at the time of His return: "For I would not, brethren, that ye should be ignorant of this mystery," writes the apostle, "that blindness in part is happened to Israel, until the fulness of the Gentiles be come in. And so all Israel shall be saved" (Rom **11** 25, 26). The present age is to be one of superb missionary effort, and the church of Christ is ever to be a source of blessing to the world (also Mt **23** 39; Lk **13** 35; Acts **1** 6, 7; **3** 19–21).

There is, however, a darker side to the picture. The present age is described as one of mingled good and evil, and its close is to be marked by days of deep darkness just before the dawn of a brighter era. This is plainly indicated by the parables of our Lord, by His definite prophecies and by the writings of the apostles.

For instance, in the parable of the Wheat and the Tares (Mt **13** 24–30) which Jesus Himself interprets (Mt **13** 36–43) He pictures the character of the present age down to its very end; He declares that His truth is to be proclaimed and His followers to be found in all the wide world; yet everywhere, and in their very midst, there will appear "the sons of the evil one"; and this mingled condition will continue during the entire era: "Let both grow together until the harvest" and "the harvest" is the "end of the age"; the time of the return of Christ and of the "judgment"; then "He will gather out of His kingdom all things that cause stumbling, and them that do iniquity, and shall cast them into the furnace of fire. . . . . Then shall the righteous shine forth as the sun in the kingdom of their Father" (Mt **13** 41–43).

Then again when Jesus sends forth His disciples to witness for Him in all the earth, He does not encourage them with any promise of a world-wide conversion previous to His return. On the contrary, He warns them that they will be hated and despised and persecuted even until the end (Mt **10** 1–42).

When in His great prophetic discourses He more particularly describes the character of this entire age and of the events which constitute its close, He insists that wars are not merely to mark its end, but are to characterize this entire era: "And ye shall hear of wars and rumors of wars; see that ye be not troubled: for all these things must come to pass, but the end is not yet." He declares that just before His return there will be on earth a period of unprecedented distress and tribulation, and that "immediately after the tribulation of those days shall the sun be darkened, and the moon shall not give her light, and the stars shall fall from heaven, and the powers of the heavens shall be shaken: and then shall appear the sign of the Son of man in heaven: and then shall all the tribes of the earth mourn, and they shall see the Son of man coming in the clouds of heaven with power and great glory" (Mt **24** 29, 30).

With these predictions of our Lord the teachings of His apostles are in exact accord, both as to the mingled good and evil of the present age and as to the distressful features which characterize its close. When they refer to "the last days," their words are not to be pressed too literally; they sometimes did have those exact days in mind, but frequently they referred to those days as already existing, and always their expressions indicate conditions which they believed would obtain to the very end of the age. That is to say, whenever they began, these "last days" were to continue until the return of the Lord.

These solemn words are not to be regarded lightly, when, for example, Paul declares in his last message: "This know also, that in the last days perilous times shall come. For men shall be lovers of their own selves, covetous, boasters, proud, blasphemers, disobedient to parents, unthankful, unholy, without natural affection, trucebreakers, false accusers, incontinent, fierce, despisers of those that are good, traitors, heady, highminded, lovers of pleasures more than lovers of God; having a form of godliness, but denying the power thereof" (2 Tim **3** 1–5).

In his last message to the Church, Peter warns us that the characteristic error of the false teachers who appear at the end of the age will be the denial of the return of our Lord: "There shall come in the last days scoffers, walking after their own lusts, and saying Where is the promise of His coming?" (2 Pet **3** 3–4).

Amid the dark shadows of these "last times" looms up one sinister figure of imposing power and malevolent purpose, the "Antichrist," the "Beast," the "Man of Sin." Endless have been the speculations concerning this mysterious and malign being. One thing is evident, he is in full career at the time when Christ returns. This career seems to have been made possible by a great apostasy (2 Thess **2** 3), a "falling away" from a true faith in God. Even after the world has been evangelized, apparently out of the very heart of Christendom, steps forth this final embodiment of evil, who will demand for himself divine worship, who will arrogate universal power who will cause immeasurable suffering to the people of God, but "whom the Lord Jesus shall slay with the breath of his mouth, and bring to nought by the manifestation of his coming" (2 Thess **2** 8, RV).

Antiochus Epiphanes and Nero and other cruel tyrants have been types and prophecies of this future "Man of Sin." John tells us that persons of this character, men of this same spirit, real "Antichrists," already existed in his day (1 Jn **2** 18). Paul declared that the "iniquity" which would culminate in the great Apostasy and in the Man of Sin was working in his day, only some "restraining" agency or person prevented for the present that matchless outbreak of "lawlessness" which would call for the personal intervention of the returning Christ. With such definite predictions of events to precede the Parousia, it has been found difficult to reconcile certain teachings of Christ and of Paul. Mt **10** 23 "Ye shall not have gone over the cities of Israel till the Son of man be come," spoken in reference to the rejection of his messengers during the present age, possibly may be an encouragement to faithful service in view of the personal protection of Christ or of His ultimate return. Mt **16** 28 may be a reference to the Transfiguration which was a foregleam of his glorious return, as interpreted by Peter (2 Pet **1** 15–18). Mt **24** 34 "This generation shall not pass, till all these things be fulfilled" may refer to the Destruction of Jerusalem which was being predicted as a type of the Parousia. Whatever the interpretation of these passages, there can be no doubt that the teachings of Christ were to the effect that His return was not to be immediate, but only after the lapse of a considerable period of time. He endeavored to correct the false impression that He would return shortly "Because they thought that the kingdom of God should immediately appear" (Lk **19** 11). His going away was like that of a man "travelling in a far country," who "after a long time" came to reckon with his servants. Before his return, Peter was first to grow old and to suffer martyrdom (Jn **21** 18–23). Jerusalem was to be destroyed and "trodden down of the Gentiles, until the times of the Gentiles" were fulfilled (Lk **21** 24). The Gospel was first to be "preached in all the world for a witness unto all nations" (Mt **24** 14). There was to be a Great Tribulation, more terrible than any the world had ever seen and "immediately after" would be seen "the Son of man coming in the clouds of heaven with power and great glory" (Mt **24** 29, 30). How can these predictions be reconciled with the exhortations to watch for His return (Mt **24** 42–44)? The solution of the difficulty is found in the very fact that the exhortation follows the prediction of events after which His followers were to watch for His Parousia, and further, in that these very events might take place in the lifetime of any generation. The same is true in the case of Paul. He is accused of having been mistaken as to the time of the Parousia and of having changed his mind. The fact is that he believed the Lord might return in his lifetime; he never stated that he would. When he uses the phrase "we that are alive, that are left unto the coming of the Lord," he simply identifies himself with Christians in general and proceeds to state what will be the experience of all believers who are living when the Lord returns. He does not mean to affirm that he will be of that number. If so, in other epistles, he would not have ranked himself among those who are to be raised from the dead (1 Cor **6** 14; 2 Cor **4** 14; Phil **3** 11); and again in other places stated that he was uncertain whether he would be living or not at the time when Christ should come (2 Cor **5** 6–10; Phil **1** 21; **3** 20, 21). Only when, as an old man, in his final imprisonment at Rome, he was assured of his coming martyrdom did he give up the expectation that he might live until his Lord appeared. He then stated definitely that he was to die; but he intimated that Timothy, to whom he is writing, should preach the Gospel and should expect that in his lifetime the Lord possibly might return. Paul did not expect, as he wrote from his dungeon, that the Lord might return at "any moment" and deliver him from death, but he did believe that the coming of Christ might take place in that very generation.

IV. Events to follow.—After the events which are to accompany or to result from the Parousia, the first to be mentioned is the Resurrection of the dead. The Bible plainly teaches that there is to be a resurrection both of the just and of the unjust. Jesus declared that an hour was coming when "all that are in the tombs" should hear His voice and come forth, "they that have done good unto the resurrection of life; and they that have done evil unto the resurrection of judgment" (Jn **5** 28–29). John indicates that possibly these resurrections may be separated in time, as they are distinct in character (Rev. **20** 4–6). However, the whole stress of the NT teaching is laid upon the resurrection of believers, and this event is made prominent as one of the most comforting truths of our Christian faith. In addition to many briefer references, we find that, in the fifteenth of 1 Cor, Paul devotes an entire chapter to this theme.

A careful study shows that the term "resurrection," when applied to the future experience of believers, never refers to the mere persistence of personality, or to the immortality of the soul, or to a spiritual renewal or quickening, but always has reference to the clothing of the spirit with a glorious and an immortal body.

Just what the substance, or nature, of this body is to be, we are not told; only that it is to be like the glorified body of Christ. It is called a "spiritual body"; which does not mean that it is "made out of spirit", but that it is perfectly adapted to the indwelling of the perfected spirit (1 Cor **15** 35–49). Christianity is not a religion which predicts a future state of shadowy, ghostly, and insubstantial felicity; but one in which glorified beings are embodied in physical yet heavenly splendor. It is intimated that there is a relation between the present mortal body and the future body of glory; but in what the identity consists or by what link it is secured, is not made plain.

It is evident, however, that the resurrection is a future event; it does not take place at death, but at the return of Christ. Our loved ones who disappear from our sight pass into heavenly blessedness; their bodies are asleep but not their souls; they are "with Christ", they are "at home with the Lord." There is, however, one degree of glory which they do not yet enjoy. They are now disembodied spirits, but they yet are to be clothed with immortal bodies of celestial splendor. This experience will be theirs at the return of Christ. For "now hath Christ been raised from the dead, the first fruits of them that are asleep. For since by man came death, by man came also the resurrection of the dead. For as in Adam all die, so also in Christ shall all be made alive. But each in his own order: Christ the first fruits; then they that are Christ's at His coming" (1 Cor **15** 20–23).

The return of the Lord also brings a transformation for the living. It is commonly said that "nothing is so sure as death"; there is one thing more sure; it is that one generation of Christians will never die, but will be living when the Lord returns, and at his coming, will pass into glory without dying. "Behold, I tell you a mystery: We all shall not sleep, but we shall all be changed, in a moment, in the twinkling of an eye, at the last trump: for the trumpet shall sound, and the dead shall be raised incorruptible, and we shall be changed. For this corruptible must put on incorruption, and this mortal must put on immortality" (1 Cor **15** 51–53 RV).

However, at the return of Christ, believers are not only to be transfigured, they are to be translated: "For this we say unto you by the word of the Lord, that we that are alive, that are left unto the coming of the Lord, shall in no wise precede them that are fallen asleep. For the Lord himself shall descend from heaven, with a shout, with the voice of the archangel, and with the trump of God: and the dead in Christ shall rise first; then we that are alive, that are left, shall together with them be caught up in the clouds, to meet the Lord in the air; and so shall we ever be with the Lord" (1 Thess **4** 15–17 RV; 1 Cor **15** 51–52; 2 Cor **5** 1–5; Phil **3** 20, 21). There is no support in Scripture for the theory that this Rapture of the Church is to be "secret," that it is imminent, that it may be "at any moment," that it will precede the Apostasy, and Great Tribulation, and indeed will occur "three and half years" or "seven years" before the actual Reappearing of Christ. Paul clearly states to his readers that the day of Christ's coming and of their "gathering together unto him," would not dawn "except the falling away" came first and "the Man of Sin" was revealed (2 Thess **2** 1–3). Then, too, John states (Rev **20** 4–6) that the martyrs who suffer death in the Great Tribulation will have part in the First Resurrection. The Parousia and the First Resurrection must, therefore, follow the Tribulation, and cannot occur before the coming of the Man of Sin.

The return of Christ is also a time when Christians receive their rewards. Only in a popular sense can we speak of the dead as having "gone to their reward." In reality they are still waiting for their rewards, the "crown of life," or the crown of blessedness, which they ultimately are to receive (Jas **1** 12; 1 Pet **5** 4). As Paul himself declared, "henceforth there is laid up for me the crown of righteousness which the Lord, the righteous judge, shall give me at that day; and not to me only, but also to all them that have loved his appearing" (2 Tim **4** 8). We cannot even conjecture the nature of these future rewards, but it would seem that the chief of all is to be that spiritual perfection which will result from a more perfect knowledge of Christ. "It is not yet made manifest what we shall be. We know that, if he shall be manifested, we shall be like him: for we shall see him even as he is" (1 Jn **3** 2 RV).

This matter of rewards, however, suggests a darker side of the doctrine, for there are rewards for the wicked as well as for the good. The coming of Christ introduces the Judgment. This reality is painted for us in colors which make the scene impressive and solemn. We see the picture in which all nations are gathered before the throne of the Son of Man, while some are sent away into everlasting punishment, and others are given a place in the kingdom which has been prepared before the foundation of the world (Mt **25** 31–46). Or, again, we see "a great white throne" and the dead, the small and the great, standing before it, and the books are opened, "and if any was not found written in the book of life he was cast into the lake of fire" (Rev **20** 11–15).

Last of all, but most important of all, the chief issue of the coming of Christ is to be his universal rule. Even the word "judgment" has a brighter meaning. It is used to signify not only "condemnation" but also "righteous rule." The coming of Christ is certain to be followed by the perfected kingdom of God. This kingdom has its heavenly and also its earthly aspects, and the chief reason why Christians should hope and yearn for the return of their Lord is because they believe it will issue in the final and complete fulfilment of that matchless prayer: "Our Father which art in heaven, Hallowed be thy name. Thy kingdom come. Thy will be done in earth, as it is in heaven" (Mt **6** 9–10). Between the present era and the time of the perfected kingdom of God many interpreters introduce the "Millennium," "The Thousand Years," described by John in the twentieth chapter of the Apocalypse.

This obscure and difficult passage of Scripture contains a highly figurative description of a limited time during which Satan is bound, and the nations are at rest, and risen martyrs reign with Christ; but after this "Thousand Years" Satan is loosed and leads the nations of the earth against "the camp of the saints," and "the beloved city"; but his hosts are destroyed by fire from heaven and he is "cast into the lake of fire and brimstone."

All this is full of mystery. These symbols cannot be interpreted with certainty or with confidence. No prediction of such a limited period of peace and blessedness is found elsewhere in the Bible. That the kingdom of God ultimately is to be universal upon earth, both the OT and the NT distinctly affirm, but they nowhere hint that it is to be limited to a "thousand years," and they describe no other age of universal peace which ends in such Satanic rebellion and world-wide war. If, however, such a millennial era is to exist, it must be preceded and not followed by the Parousia. The present age preceding the Parousia is to be one of mingled good and evil. Existing evil will persist and it will reach its supreme embodiment in the Man of Sin whom Christ will destroy at His Coming (2 Thess **2** 7–10). There is no place for a "millennium" before the return of Christ. Probably most of the passages which are supposed to describe this millennial reign should be understood as referring to that perfected kingdom which is yet to fill the world with righteousness and peace, and to which there is to be no end. This kingdom will appear in its completed glory at the Coming of the King (Mt **19** 28; Ps **72** 5, 7, 17; Isa **11** 6; Lk **1** 32; Dnl **7** 14; Acts **3** 19–21; Rom **8** 21–23; He **1** 6, 13; **2** 5–8; 1 Pet **3** 10–13 RV).

V. Significance of the Doctrine.—The fact of the Parousia has been, in all ages of the church, a source of inspiration and cheer. Upon it are based exhortations to purity, fidelity, holiness, hope, and practically all the virtues of a Christian life. At the present day the significance of the doctrine is commonly disregarded. On the other hand, there are those who emphasize the truth out of all proportion to other Christian doctrines. The Parousia must be regarded as the capstone rather than the foundation of the Christian faith. Our Lord did lay great stress upon the duty of watchfulness in view of His promised Coming. He showed that the term must include a main element of real expectancy; yet, he further indicated that this should be as far removed from feverish excitement as from careless disregard. In three notable parables relative to His return, He described to His followers the real character of Christian watchfulness. First of all there is the parable of the Ten Virgins (Mt **25** 1–13), which is designed to teach the spiritual preparation which will be manifested by those who are truly watching for the Coming of Christ. The second parable is that of the servants to whom the Master intrusted certain talents commanding them to use these gifts wisely as they waited for His return (Mt **25** 14–30). Jesus thus taught the obvious lesson that in His absence each one of His followers must be faithful and diligent in the use of every gift and opportunity to speed the Gospel and to advance His cause. Working and watching are not the same, but true watchfulness will always issue in wise and devoted service. Last of all the Master paints the august scene of judgment. It portrays many solemn truths but none is more obvious than this, namely, that those who are really watching for the return of their Lord will be most unceasing in their work of loving sympathy and relief. Surely everyone who is mindful of the predicted return of Christ will be inclined so to live that they can pray fervently and sincerely, "Even so, come, Lord Jesus," "come quickly" (Rev **22** 20). This event will result in the consummation of God's plans for the world.

LITERATURE.—References at close of articles on ESCHATOLOGY, ANTICHRIST, MILLENNIUM, RESURRECTION, JUDGMENT, etc. Commentaries by Alford, Godet, Meyer. Also George N. H. Peters, *The Theocratic Kingdom, Premillennial Essays* of the Prophetic Conference, New York, 1879; Erdman, *The Return of Christ;* Godet, *Studies on the Epistles*, pp. 2–30. S. H. Kellog, *Premillennialism*, Vol. XLV, *Bibliotheca Sacra;* A. C. Gaebelein, *The Harmony of the Prophetic Word;* Rall, *Modern Premillennialism and the Christian Hope;* Loisy, *Gospel and the Church* (Cf his *Evangiles Synoptiques*); Schweitzer, *The Quest of the Historical Jesus.*

CHARLES R. ERDMAN

PARSHANDATHA, pär-shan-dā'tha, pär-shan'-da-tha (פַּרְשַׁנְדָּתָא, *parshandāthā';* LXX **Φαρσάν,** *Pharsán,* or **Φαρσανεστάν,** *Pharsanestán;* perhaps from the Pers *fraçna-data,* "given by prayer"): One of the sons of Haman (Est **9** 7).

PART, pärt: As a vb. is no longer in good use (except in a few special phrases, cf Ruth **1** 17), but is obscure only in Prov **18** 18, where the meaning is "break up their quarrel" (cf 2 S **14** 6). RV has not changed AV's usage, except (strangely) in 1 S **30** 24, where "share" is written. For the noun see PORTION.

PARTHIANS, pär'thi-anz (**Πάρθοι,** *Párthoi*): A people mentioned in Acts **2** 9 only, in connection with other strangers present at Jerus at Pentecost, from which we infer that they were Jews or proselytes from the regions included in the Parthian empire. This empire stretched from the Euphrates to the confines of India and the Oxus, and for centuries was the rival of Rome, and more than once proved her match on the battlefield. The Parthians are not mentioned in the OT, but are frequently in Jos, and they had an important connection with the history of the Jews, on account of the large colonies of the latter in Mesopotamia, and

1. Country and Early History

the interference of the Parthians in the affairs of Judaea, once making it a vassal state.

Parthia proper was a small territory to the S.E. of the Caspian Sea, about 300 miles long by 120 wide, a fertile though mountainous region, bordering on the desert tract of Eastern Persia. The

Parthian Horsemen.
(From the Triumphal Arch of Septimius Severus, Rome.)

origin of the Parthians is rather uncertain, though the prevailing opinion is that they were of Scythic stock or of the great Tartar race. We have no reference to them earlier than the time of Darius the Great, but they were doubtless among the tribes subdued by Cyrus, as they are mentioned by Darius as being in revolt. They seem to have remained faithful to the Persians after that, and submitted to Alexander without resistance.

2. The Seleucid Kings

They next came under the rule of the Seleucid kings of Syria, but revolted about 250 BC, in the reign of Antiochus II (Theos), and gained their independence under the lead of Arsaces I who established the dynasty of the Arsacidae, which continued for nearly 5 centuries. His capital was Hecatompylos, but his reign continued only about 3 years, and his brother Tridates succeeded him as Arsaces II and he consolidated the kingdom. The war between the Seleucids and the Ptolemies freed him from interference from that quarter until 237 BC, when Seleucus II (Callinicus) marched against him, but was completely defeated, and Parthian independence was secured. Artabanus I, who followed him, extended his dominions westward to the Zagros Mountains, but Antiochus III would not permit such an encroachment with impunity, and led an expedition against him, driving him back and even invading his ancestral dominion. But after a struggle of some years the Parthians remained still unsubdued, and the difficulties of the contest led Antiochus to conclude peace with him in which he acknowledged the independence of Parthia. For about a quarter of a century the king of Parthia remained quiet, but Phraates I (181–174 BC) recommenced aggressions on the Seleucid empire which were continued by Mithridates I (174–137), who added to his dominions a part of Bactria, on the E., and Media, Persia and Babylonia on the W. This was a challenge to Demetrius II, of Syria, to whose empire the provinces belonged, and he marched against him with a large force, but was defeated and taken prisoner. He remained in Parthia some years, well treated by Phraates II, whose sister he married, and, when Phraates wished to create a diversion against Antiochus Sidetes, he set Demetrius at liberty and sent him back to Syria. Antiochus was at first successful, as his force of 300,000 men far outnumbered the Parthians, but he was at last defeated and slain in 129 BC and his army destroyed. This was the last attempt of the Seleucid kings to subdue Parthia, and it was acknowledged as the dominant power in Western Asia. But Phraates fell in conflict with the Scyths, whom he called in to aid him in his war with Sidetes, and his successor likewise, and it was only on the accession of Mithridates in 124 BC that these barbarians were checked. The king then turned his attention toward Armenia, which he probably brought under his control, but its king Tigranes recovered its independence and even attacked the Parthians, and took from them two provinces in Mesopotamia.

3. In Contact with Rome

Not long after, the power of Rome came into contact with Armenia and Parthia. In 66 BC when, after subduing Mithridates of Pontus, Pompey came into Syria, Phraates III made an alliance with him against Armenia, but was offended by the way in which he was treated and thought of turning against his ally, but refrained for the time being. It was only a question of time when the two powers would come to blows, for Parthia had become an empire and could ill brook the intrusion of Rome into Western Asia. It was the ambition and greed of Crassus that brought about the clash of Rome and Parthia. When he took the East as his share of the Rom world as apportioned among the triumvirs, he determined to rival Caesar in fame and wealth by subduing Parthia, and advanced across the Euphrates on his ill-fated expedition in 53 BC. The story of his defeat and death and the destruction of the army and loss of the Rom eagles is familiar to all readers of Rom history. It revealed Parthia to the world as the formidable rival of Rome, which she continued to be for nearly 3 centuries. After the death of Crassus, the Parthians crossed the Euphrates and ravaged Northern Syria, but retired the following year without securing any portion of the country, and thus ended the first war with Rome. In 40 BC, after the battle of Philippi, Pacorus, who was then king, invaded Syria a second time and took possession of it together with all Pal, Tyre alone escaping subjection. He set Antigonus on the throne of Judaea, deposing Hyrcanus for the purpose. Syria and Pal remained in the hands of Parthia for 3 years, but the coming of Ventidius gave a new turn to affairs. He drove the Parthians out of Syria, and when they returned the following year, he defeated them again and Pacorus was slain. Parthia had to retire within her own borders and remain on the defensive. Antony's attempt to subdue them proved abortive, and his struggle with Octavian compelled him to relinquish the project. The Parthians were unable to take advantage of the strife in the Rom empire on account of troubles at home. An insurrection led by Tiridates drove the king Phraates IV from the throne, but he recovered it by the aid of the Scyths, and Tiridates took refuge in Syria with the youngest son of the king. Augustus afterward restored him without ransom, and obtained the lost standards of Crassus, and thus peace was established between the rival empires. Each had learned to respect the power of the other, and, although contention arose regarding the suzerainty of Armenia, peace was not seriously disturbed between them for about 130 years, or until the reign of Trajan. Parthia was not at peace with herself, however. Dynastic troubles were frequent, and the reigns of the kings short. Artabanus III, who reigned 16–42 AD, was twice expelled from his kingdom and twice recovered his throne. In his days occurred a terrible massacre of Jewish colonists in Mesopotamia, as narrated by Jos (*Ant*, XVIII, ix). The contest with Rome over Armenia was settled in the days of Nero in a manner satisfactory to both parties, so that peace was not broken for

50 years. The ambition of Trajan led him to disregard the policy inaugurated by Augustus, adhered to, for the most part, by succeeding emperors, not to extend the limits of the empire. After the conquest of Dacia he turned his attention to the East and resolved on the invasion of Parthia. The Parthian king, Chosroës, endeavored to placate Trajan by an embassy bearing presents and proposals of peace, but Trajan rejected them and carried out his purpose. He subdued Armenia, took Upper Mesopotamia, Adiabênê (Assyria), Ctesiphon, the capital, and reached the Pers Gulf, but was obliged to turn back by revolts in his rear and failed to reduce the fortress of Hatra. The conquered provinces were restored, however, by Hadrian, and the Parthians did not retaliate until the reign of Aurelius, when they overran Syria, and in 162 AD Lucius Verus was sent to punish them. In the following year he drove them back and advanced into the heart of the Parthian empire, inflicting the severest blow it had yet received. It was evident that the empire was on the decline, and the Romans did not meet with the resistance they had experienced in former times. Severus and Caracalla both made expeditions into the country, and the latter took the capital and massacred the inhabitants, but after his assassination his successor, Macrinus, fought a three days' battle with the Parthians at Nisibis in which he was worsted and was glad to conclude a peace by paying an indemnity of some £1,500,000 (217 AD).

4. Fall of the Empire

But this was the last achievement of the Parthians. It is evident that Artabanus had suffered severely in his conflict with the Romans, and was unable to put down the revolt of the Persians under the lead of Artaxerxes, who overthrew the Parthian empire and established the dynasty of the Sassanidae in its place (226 AD).

5. Culture

The Parthians were not a cultured people, but displayed a rude magnificence, making use, to some extent, of remains of Gr culture which they found within the regions they seized from the empire of Alexander. They had no native lit., as far as known, but made use of Gr in writing and on their coins. They were familiar with Heb or Syro-Chaldaic, and the later kings had Sem legends on their coins. Jos is said to have written his history of the Jewish War in his native tongue for Parthian readers. In their method of government they seem to have left the different provinces pretty much to themselves, so long as they paid tribute and furnished the necessary contingents.

H. Porter

PARTICULAR, pär-tik'ū-lar, par-tik'ū-lar, **PARTICULARLY**: The adverbial phrase "in particular" occurs twice in AV (1 Cor **12** 27, ἐκ μέρους, *ek mérous*, RV "severally," RVm "each in his part"; and Eph **5** 33, οἱ καθ' ἕνα, *hoi kath' héna*, RV "severally"); in both cases it has the obsolete meaning of "severally," "individually." The advb. "particularly" occurs in the same sense in Acts **21** 19 AV, καθ' ἓν ἕκαστον, *kath' hén hékaston*, RV "one by one," and He **9** 5 AV, κατὰ μέρος, *katá méros*, RV "severally." We have the pl. noun in the sense of "details" in 2 Macc **2** 30: "to be curious in particulars"; **11** 20 (AV "Of the particulars I have given order," RV "I have given order in detail"); and the adj. "particular" in the sense of "special" in the first Prologue to Sirach (AV, Vulg *peculiares;* the whole section omitted in RV).

D. Miall Edwards

PARTITION, pär-tish'un, par-tish'un, **THE MIDDLE WALL OF** (τὸ μεσότοιχον τοῦ φραγμοῦ, *tó mesótoichon toú phragmoú* [Eph **2** 14]): What Paul here asserts is that Christ is our peace, the peace of both Jewish and gentile believers. He has made them both to be one in Himself, and has broken down the middle wall of partition which divided them from one another. Then the apostle regards Jew and Gentile as two, who by a fresh act of creation in Christ are made into one new man. In the former of these similes he refers to an actual wall in the temple at Jerus, beyond which no one was allowed to pass unless he were a Jew, the balustrade or barrier which marked the limit up to which a Gentile might advance but no farther. Curiously, this middle wall of partition had a great deal to do with Paul's arrest and imprisonment, for the multitude of the Jews became infuriated, not merely because of their general hostility to him as an apostle of Christ and a preacher of the gospel for the world, but specially because it was erroneously supposed that he had brought Trophimus the Ephesian past this barrier into the temple (Acts **21** 29), and that he had in this manner profaned the temple (**24** 6), or, as it is put in **21** 28, he had 'brought Greeks into the temple and polluted this holy place.' In the assault which they thereupon made on Paul they violently seized and dragged him out of the temple—dragged him outside the balustrade. The Levites at once shut the gates, to prevent the possibility of any further profanation, and Paul would have been torn in pieces, had not the Rom commander and his soldiers forcibly prevented.

1. The Barrier in the Temple

2. Herod's Temple; Its Divisions; the Courts

In building the temple Herod the Great had inclosed a large area to form the various courts. The temple itself consisted of the two divisions, the Holy Place, entered by the priests every day, and the Holy of Holies into which the high priest entered alone once every year. Immediately outside the temple there was the Court of the Priests, and in it was placed the great altar of burnt offering. Outside of this again was the Court of the Sons of Israel, and beyond this the Court of the Women. The site of the temple itself and the space occupied by the various courts already mentioned formed a raised plateau or platform. "From it you descended at various points down 5 steps and through gates in a lofty wall, to find yourself overlooking another large court—the outer court to which Gentiles, who desired to see something of the glories of the temple and to offer gifts and sacrifices to the God of the Jews, were freely admitted. Farther in than this court they were forbidden, on pain of death, to go. The actual boundary line was not the high wall with its gates, but a low stone barrier about 5 ft. in height, which ran round at the bottom of 14 more steps" (J. Armitage Robinson, D.D., *St. Paul's Ep. to the Eph,* 59; see also Edersheim, *The Temple, Its Ministry and Services as They Were at the Time of Jesus Christ,* 46).

The middle wall of partition was called *ṣōrēgh*, and was built of marble beautifully ornamented.

3. The Court of the Gentiles

The Court of the Gentiles formed the lowest and the outermost inclosure of all the courts of the sanctuary. It was paved with the finest variegated marble. Its name signified that it was open to all, Jews or Gentiles alike. It was very large, and is said by Jewish tradition to have formed a square of 750 ft. It was in this court that the oxen and sheep and the doves for the sacrifices were sold as in a market. It was in this court too that there were the tables of the money-changers, which Christ Himself overthrew when He drove out the sheep and oxen and them that bought and sold in His Father's house. The multitudes assembling in this court must have been very great, esp. on occasions such as the Passover and Pentecost and at the other great feasts, and the din of voices must oftentimes have been most disturbing. As already seen, beyond this court no Gentile might go. See Temple.

In the year 1871, while excavations were being made on the site of the temple by the Palestine Exploration Fund, M. Clermont-Ganneau discovered one of the pillars which Jos describes as having been erected upon the very barrier or middle wall of partition, to which Paul refers. This pillar is now preserved in the Museum at Constantinople and is inscribed with a Gr inscription in capital or uncial letters, which is translated as follows:

NO MAN OF ANOTHER NATION TO
ENTER WITHIN THE FENCE AND
ENCLOSURE ROUND THE TEMPLE,
AND WHOEVER IS CAUGHT WILL
HAVE HIMSELF TO BLAME THAT
HIS DEATH ENSUES

While Paul was writing the Ep. to the Eph at Rome, this barrier in the temple at Jerus was still standing, yet the chained prisoner of Jesus Christ was not afraid to write that Christ had broken down the middle wall of partition, and had thus admitted Gentiles who were far off, strangers and foreigners, to all the privileges of access to God anciently possessed by Israel alone; that separation between Jew and Gentile was done away with forever in Christ.

4. The Throwing Down of the Barrier

If Paul wrote the Ep. to the Eph in 60 or 61 AD, then the actual barrier of stone remained in its position in the Court of the Gentiles not more than some 10 years, for it was thrown down in the burning of the temple by the Rom army. And out of those ruins a fragment has been excavated in our own day, containing the very inscription threatening death to the gentile intruder, and reminding us that it is only in Christ Jesus that we now draw nigh unto God, and that we are thus one body in Christ, one new man. Christ has broken down the middle wall of partition, for He, in His own person, is our peace.

John Rutherfurd

Warning Tablet of Herod's Temple.

PARTRIDGE, pär′trij (קֹרֵא, *ḳōrē′;* Lat *perdix;* LXX, 1 S **26** 20, **νυκτικόραξ**, *nuktikórax*, "owl," Jer **17** 11, **πέρδιξ**, *pérdix*): A bird of the family *Tetraonidae*. The Heb word for this bird, *ḳōrē′*, means "a caller," and the Lat *perdix* is supposed to be an imitation of its cry, and as all other nations base their name for the bird on the Lat, it becomes quite evident that it was originally named in imitation of its call. The commonest partridge of Pal, very numerous in the wilderness and hill country, was a bird almost as large as a pheasant. It had a clear, exquisite cry that attracted attention, esp. in the mating season. The partridge of the wilderness was smaller and of beautifully marked plumage. It made its home around the Dead Sea, in the Wilderness of Judaea and in rocky caverns. Its eggs were creamy white; its cry very similar to its relatives'. The partridge and its eggs were used for food from time immemorial.

The first reference to it is found in 1 S **26** 20: "Now therefore, let not my blood fall to the earth away from the presence of Jeh: for the king of Israel is come out to seek a flea, as when one doth hunt a partridge in the mountains." David in this dialogue with Saul clearly indicates that if he did not hunt the partridge himself, he knew how it was done. The birds were commonly chased up the mountains and stunned or killed with "throw sticks." David knew how deft these birds were at hiding beside logs and under dry leaves colored so like them as to afford splendid protection; how swiftly they could run; what expert dodgers they were; so he compared taking them with catching a flea. The other reference is found in Jer **17** 11: "As the partridge that sitteth on eggs which she hath not laid, so is he that getteth riches, and not by right; in the midst of his days they shall leave him, and at his end he shall be a fool." If this reference is supposed to indicate that partridges are in the habit of brooding on the nest of their kind or of different birds, it fails wholly to take into consideration the history of the bird. Partridges select a location, carefully deposit an egg a day for from 10 to 15 days, sometimes 20, and then brood, so that all the young emerge at one time. But each bird knows and returns to its nest with unfailing regularity. It would require the proverbial "Philadelphia lawyer" to explain this reference to a "partridge sitting on eggs she had not laid." No ornithologist ever could reconcile it to the habits or characteristics of the birds. AV tr[d] these lines, "As the partridge sitteth on eggs, and hatcheth them not." This was easy to explain clearly. The eggs of the partridge were delicious food, and any brooding bird whose nest was discovered after only a few days of incubation did not hatch, because she lost her eggs. Also the eggs frequently fall prey to other birds or small animals. Again, they are at the mercy of the elements, sometimes being spoiled by extremely wet cold weather. Poultry fanciers assert that a heavy thunder storm will spoil chicken eggs when hatching-time is close; the same might be true with eggs of the wild. And almost any wild bird will desert its nest and make its former brooding useless, if the location is visited too frequently by man or beast.

There is also a partridge reference in the Book of Ecclus (**11** 29 ff RV): "Bring not every man into thine house; for many are the plots of the deceitful man. As a decoy partridge in a cage, so is the heart

Partridge.

of a proud man; and as one that is a spy, he looketh upon thy falling. For he lieth in wait to turn things that are good into evil; and in things that are praiseworthy he will lay blame." The reference is to confining a tame partridge in a hidden cage so that its calls would lure many of its family within range of arrows or "throw sticks" used by concealed hunters. Gene Stratton-Porter

PARUAH, pa-rōō'a (פָּרוּחַ, *pārūaḥ*, "blooming"): Father of Jehoshaphat, who was one of Solomon's twelve victualers or providers, and had charge in Issachar of this function (1 K **4** 17).

PARVAIM, pär-vā'im (פַּרְוָיִם, *parwāyim;* LXX **Φαρουαΐμ,** *Pharouaím*): The word occurs only in 2 Ch **3** 6, as the place from which Solomon obtained gold for the decoration of his Temple. A derivation is given from the Sanskrit *pūrva*, "eastern," so that the name might be a vague term for the East (Gesenius, *Thesaurus*, 1125). Whether there was such a place in Arabia is doubtful. *Farwa* in Yemen has been suggested, and also *Sāḳ el Farwain* in Yemamah. Some have considered the name a shortened form of *Ṣᵉpharvāyim* which occurs in the Syr and Tg Jonathan for the "Sephar" of Gen **10** 30. A. S. Fulton

PASACH, pā'sak (פָּסַךְ, *pāṣakh*, "divider"): Son of Japhlet, descendant of Asher (1 Ch **7** 33).

PAS-DAMMIM, pas-dam'im. See Ephes-dammim.

PASEAH, pa-sē'a, pas'ē-a (פָּסֵחַ, *pāṣēaḥ*, "limping"):

(1) A son of Eshton, descendant of Judah (1 Ch **4** 12).

(2) The eponym of a family of Nethinim (Ezr **2** 49; Neh **7** 51, AV "Phaseah" = "Phinoe" (1 Esd **5** 31).

(3) Father of Joiada, who helped to repair the old gate (Neh **3** 6).

PASHHUR, pash'hur, **PASHUR,** pash'ur (פַּשְׁחוּר, *pashḥūr*, "splitter," "cleaver"): The name of several persons difficult to individuate:

(1) A priest, son of Immer, and "chief governor in the house of the Lord" (Jer **20** 1), who persecuted Jeremiah, putting him in "the stocks" hard by the "house of Jeh" in the "gate of Benjamin" (Jer **20** 2). When released, Jeremiah pronounced Divine judgment on him and the people. Future captivity and an exile's death are promised to Pashur whose name he changed from its masterful significance to a cowering one. "Terror on every side" (*māghōr miṣṣābhībh*) is to take the place of "stable strength" (Jer **20** 3 ff).

(2) Son of Melchiah, a prince of Judah, and one of the delegation sent by Zedekiah, the king, to consult Jeremiah (Jer **21** 1). It looks like a larger and later deputation, similarly sent, to which this Pashur belongs, whose record is given in Jer **38** 1–13. Accompanying them was one, Gedaliah, who was a son of (3).

(3) Another Pashur (Jer **38** 1), who may be the person mentioned in 1 Ch **9** 12; Neh **11** 12.

(4) A priest, of those who "sealed" Nehemiah's covenant (Neh **10** 1.3), who may, however, be the same as (5).

(5) The chief of a priestly family called "sons of Pashur" (Ezr **2** 38; **10** 22; Neh **7** 41; 1 Esd **5** 25 ["Phassurus," m "Pashhur"]; **9** 22 ["Phaisur," m "Pashhur"]). Doubtless it is this Pashur, some of whose sons had "strange wives" (Ezr **10** 22). Henry Wallace

PASS, pas, **PASSAGE,** pas'āj, **PASSENGER,** pas'en-jẽr: "To pass" bears different meanings and corresponds to various words in Heb and Gr. It occurs frequently in the phrase "and it came to pass" (lit. and it was). This is simply a Heb idiom linking together the different paragraphs of a continuous narrative. As a rule "pass" renders the Heb word עָבַר, *'ābhar*. This vb. has various meanings, e.g. "to pass over" a stream (Gen **31** 21); "to cross" a boundary (Nu **20** 17); "to pass through," or "traverse," a country (Nu **21** 22); "to pass on" (Gen **18** 5); "to pass away," "cease to exist" (Job **30** 15). The word is used metaphorically, "to pass over," "overstep," "transgress" (Nu **14** 41). In the causative form the vb. is used in the phrase "to cause to pass through fire" (Dt **18** 10; 2 K **16** 3). In AV "pass" sometimes has the force of "surpass," "exceed," e.g. 2 Ch **9** 22, "King Solomon passed all the kings of the earth in riches and wisdom"; cf also Eph **3** 19, "the love of Christ which passeth knowledge," and Phil **4** 7, "the peace of God, which passeth all understanding."

Passage in AV renders מַעֲבָר, *ma'ăbhār*, or מַעְבָּרָה, *ma'ăbhārāh*. The former word denotes (1) the ford of a river (Gen **32** 23 AVm); (2) the pass of a mountain range (1 S **13** 23). In the only other instance of the use of the shorter form (Isa **30** 32 m), AV renders "where the grounded staff shall pass." A more correct tr would be, "and every sweep [or stroke] of the appointed staff." The longer form bears both meanings, viz. "ford" (e.g. Josh **2** 7; Jgs **3** 28, etc) and "pass" (1 S **14** 4; Isa **10** 29). In Josh **22** 11, the rendering 'towards the region opposite the children of Israel' would be more correct than AV, "at the passage of the children of Israel." In EV of Nu **20** 21 "passage" seems to mean "right of way," and renders the infinitive of the Heb vb. In Jer **22** 20 AV the word rendered "passage" should be tr[d] "from Abarim" (as in RV), a mountain range in Moab, N.E. of the Dead Sea.

Passenger in AV means a "passer-by." In Ezk **39** 11.14.15 where the word occurs 4 t in AV, RV translates "them that pass through." T. Lewis

PASSING OF MARY, THE. See Apocryphal Gospels.

PASSION, pash'un, **PASSIONS,** pash'unz: "Passion" is derived from Lat *passio*, which in turn is derived from the vb. *patior*, with the √ *pat*. The Lat words are connected with the Gr √ παθ, *path*, which appears in a large number of derivatives. And in Gr, Lat, and Eng. (with other languages in addition) words connected with this √ *pat, path*, are often susceptible of a great variety of meanings, for which the dicts. must be consulted. For "passion," however, as it appears in EV, only three of these meanings need be considered. (1) Close to what seems to be the primary force of the root is the meaning "suffer," and in this sense "passion" is used in Acts **1** 3, "to whom he also showed himself alive after his passion." This tr is a paraphrase (Gr "after he had suffered"), due to the Vulg (*post passionem suam*), and in Eng. is as old as Wycliff, whom the subsequent EV has followed. This is the only case in AV and RV where "passion" has this meaning, and it can be so used in modern Eng. only when referring (as here) to the sufferings of Christ (cf "Passion play"). (2) "Suffering," when applied to the mind, came to denote the state that is controlled by some emotion, and so "passion" was applied to the emotion itself. This is the meaning of the word in Acts **14** 15, "men of like passions," and Jas **5** 17, "a man of like passions," Gr ὁμοιοπαθής, *homoiopathḗs*; RVm "of like nature" gives the meaning exactly: "men with the same emotions as we." (3) From "emotion" a transition took place to "strong emotion," and this is the normal force of "passion" in modern Eng. AV does not use this meaning, but in RV "passion" in this sense is the tr of πάθος, *páthos*, in its three occurrences: Rom **1** 26 (AV "affection"); Col **3** 5 (AV "inordinate affection"); 1 Thess **4** 5 (AV "lust"). It is used also for two occurrences of πάθημα, *páthēma* (closely allied to *pathos*) in Rom **7** 5 (AV "motions," AVm "passions") and in Gal **5** 24 (AV "affection"). The fixing of the exact force in any of these cases is a delicate problem fully discussed in the comms. In Col **3** 5 only does "passion" stand as an isolated term. The context here perhaps gives the word a slight sexual reference, but this must not be overstressed; the warning probably includes any violent over-emotion that robs a man of his self-control. See AFFECTION; MOTION. BURTON SCOTT EASTON

PASSION, GOSPEL OF THE. See APOCRYPHAL GOSPELS.

PASSOVER, pas'ō-vẽr (פֶּסַח, *peṣaḥ*, from *pāṣaḥ*, "to pass" or "spring over" or "to spare" [Ex **12** 13.23.27; cf Isa **31** 5]. Other conjectures connect the word with the "passing over" into a new year, with Assyr *pašâḫu*, meaning "to placate," with Heb *pāṣah*, meaning "to dance," and even with the skipping motions of a young lamb; Aram. פַּסְחָא, *paṣḥā'*, whence Gr **Πάσχα,** *Páscha;* whence Eng. "paschal." In early Christian centuries folk-etymology connected *páscha* with Gr *páschō*, "to suffer" [see PASSION], and the word was taken to refer to Good Friday rather than the Passover):

1. *Peṣaḥ* and *Maççōth*
2. *Peṣaḥ miçrayim*
3. *Peṣaḥ dōrōth*
4. *Maççōth*
5. The *'Ōmer*
6. Non-traditional Theories
7. The Higher Criticism
8. Historical Celebrations: OT Times
9. Historical Celebrations: NT Times
10. The Jewish Passover

The Passover was the annual Heb festival on the evening of the 14th day of the month of 'Ābhībh or Niṣan, as it was called in later times. It was followed by, and closely connected with, a 7 days' festival of *maççōth*, or unleavened bread, to which the name Passover was also applied by extension (Lev **23** 5). Both were distinctly connected with the Exodus, which, according to tradition, they commemorate; the Passover being in imitation of the last meal in Egypt, eaten in preparation for the journey, while Jeh, passing over the houses of the Hebrews, was slaying the firstborn of Egypt (Ex **12** 12 f; **13** 2.12 ff); the *maççōth* festival being in memory of the first days of the journey during which this bread of haste was eaten (Ex **12** 14–20).

1. *Peṣaḥ* and *Maççōth*

The ordinance of *peṣaḥ miçrayim*, the last meal in Egypt, included the following provisions: (1) the taking of a lamb, or kid without blemish, for each household on the 10th of the month; (2) the killing of the lamb on the 14th at even; (3) the sprinkling of the blood on doorposts and lintels of the houses in which it was to be eaten; (4) the roasting of the lamb with fire, its head with its legs and inwards—the lamb was not to be eaten raw nor sodden (*bāshal*) with water; (5) the eating of unleavened bread and bitter herbs; (6) eating in haste, with loins girded, shoes on the feet, and staff in hand; (7) and remaining in the house until the morning; (8) the burning of all that remained; the Passover could be eaten only during the night (Ex **12** 1–23).

2. *Peṣaḥ miçrayim*

This service was to be observed as an ordinance forever (Ex **12** 14.24), and the night was to be *lēl shimmūrīm*, "a night of vigils," or, at least, "to be much observed" of all the children of Israel throughout their generations (Ex **12** 42). The details, however, of the *peṣaḥ dōrōth*, or later observances of the Passover, seem to have differed slightly from those of the Egyp Passover (Mish, *Peṣāḥīm*, ix.5). Thus it is probable that the victim could be taken from the flock or from the herd (Dt **16** 2; cf Ezk **45** 22). (3), (6) and (7) disappeared entirely, and judging from Dt **16** 7, the prohibition against seething (Heb *bāshal*) was not understood to apply (unless, indeed, the omission of the expression "with water" gives a more general sense to the Heb word *bāshal*, making it include roasting). New details were also added: for example, that the Passover could be sacrificed only at the central sanctuary (Dt **16** 5); that no alien or uncircumcised person, or unclean person could partake thereof, and that one prevented by uncleanness or other cause from celebrating the Passover in season could do so a month later (Nu **9** 9 ff). The singing of the *Hallel* (Pss **113–118**), both while the Passover was being slaughtered and at the meal, and other details were no doubt added from time to time.

3. *Peṣaḥ dōrōth*

Unleavened bread was eaten with the Passover meal, just as with all sacrificial meals of later times (Ex **23** 18; **34** 25; Lev **7** 12), independently perhaps of the fact that the Passover came in such close proximity with the Feast of Unleavened Bread (Ex **12** 8). Jewish tradition distinguishes, at any rate, between the first night and the rest of the festival in that the eating of *maççōth* is an obligation on the first night and optional during the rest of the week (*Peṣāḥīm* **120***a*), although the eating of unleavened bread is commanded in general terms (Ex **12** 15.18; **13** 6.7; **23** 15; **34** 18; Lev **23** 6; Nu **28** 17). The eating of leavened bread is strictly prohibited, however, during the entire week under the penalty of *kārēth*, "excision" (Ex **12** 15.19 f; **13** 3; Dt **16** 3), and this prohibition has been observed traditionally with great care. The 1st and 7th days are holy convocations, days on which no labor could be done except such as was necessary in the preparation of food. The festival of *maççōth* is reckoned as one of the three pilgrimage festivals,

4. *Maççōth*

though strictly the pilgrimage was connected with the Passover portion and the first day of the festival.

During the entire week additional sacrifices were offered in the temple: an offering made by fire and a burnt offering, 2 young bullocks, 1 ram, 7 lambs of the first year without blemish, together with meal offerings and drink offerings and a goat for a sin offering.

5. The 'Ōmer

During the week of the *maççōth* festival comes the beginning of the barley harvest in Pal (*Menāḥōth* **65***b*) which lasts from the end of March in the low Jordan valley to the beginning of May in the elevated portions. The time of the putting-in of the sickle to the standing corn (Dt **16** 9) and of bringing the sheaf of the peace offering is spoken of as the morrow after the Sabbath (Lev **23** 15), that is, according to the Jewish tradition, the day after the first day, or rest-day, of the Passover (*Menā.* **65***b; Meg Ta'an.* **1**; Jos, *Ant*, III, x, 5), and according to Samaritan and Boethusian traditions and the modern Karites the Sunday after the Passover. At this time a wave offering is made of a sheaf, followed by an offering of a lamb with a meal and drink offering, and only thereafter might the new corn be eaten. From this day 7 weeks are counted to fix the date of Pentecost, the celebration connected with the wheat harvest. It is of course perfectly natural for an agricultural people to celebrate the turning-points of the agricultural year in connection with their traditional festivals. Indeed, the Jewish liturgy of today retains in the Passover service the Prayer of Dew (*ṭal*) which grew up in Pal on the basis of the needs of an agricultural people.

6. Non-traditional Theories

Many writers, however, eager to explain the entire festival as originally an agricultural feast (presumably a Canaanitic one, though there is not a shred of evidence that the Canaanites had such a festival), have seized upon the *'ōmer*, or sheaf offering, as the basis of the *ḥagh* (festival), and have attempted to explain the *maççōth* as bread hastily baked in the busy harvest times, or as bread quickly baked from the freshly exempted first-fruits. Wherein these theories are superior to the traditional explanation so consistently adhered to throughout the Pent it is difficult to see. In a similar vein, it has been attempted to connect the Passover with the sacrifice or redemption of the firstborn of man and beast (both institutions being traditionally traced to the judgment on the firstborn of Egypt, as in Ex **13** 11–13; **22** 29.30; **23** 19; **34** 19.20), so as to characterize the Passover as a festival of pastoral origin. Excepting for the multiplication of highly ingenious guesses, very little that is positive has been added to our knowledge of the Passover by this theory.

7. The Higher Criticism

The Pent speaks of the Passover in many contexts and naturally with constantly varying emphasis. Thus in the story of the Exodus it is natural to expect fewer ritual details than in a manual of temple services; again, according to the view here taken, we must distinguish between the *pesaḥ miçrayim* and the *pesaḥ dōrōth*. Nevertheless, great stress is laid on the variations in the several accounts, by certain groups of critics, on the basis of which they seek to support their several theories of the composition of the Pent or Hex. Without entering into this controversy, it will be sufficient here to enumerate and classify all the discrepancies said to exist in the several Passover passages, together with such explanations as have been suggested. These discrepancies, so called, are of three kinds: (1) mere omissions, (2) differences of emphasis, and (3) conflicting statements. The letters, J, E, D, P and H will here be used to designate passages assigned to the various sources by the higher criticism of today merely for the sake of comparison. (1) There is nothing remarkable about the omission of the daily sacrifices from all passages except Lev **23** 8 (H) and Nu **28** 19 (P), nor in the omission of a specific reference to the holy convocation on the first day in the contexts of Dt **16** 8 and Ex **13** 6, nor even in the omission of reference to a central sanctuary in passages other than Dt **16**. Neither can any significance be attached to the fact that the precise day is not specified in Ex **23** (E) where the appointed day is spoken of, and in Lev **23** 15 (H) where the date can be figured out from the date of Pentecost there given. (2) As to emphasis, it is said that the so-called Elohist Covenant (E) (Ex **23**) has no reference to the Passover, as it speaks only of *maççōth* in ver 15, in which this festival is spoken of together with the other *reghālīm* or pilgrimage festivals. The so-called Jehovistic source (J) (Ex **34** 18–21.25) is said to subordinate the Passover to *maççōth*, the great feast of the Jehovistic history (JE) (Ex **12** 21–27.29–36.38.39; **13** 3–16); in Dt (D) the Passover is said to predominate over *maççōth*, while in Lev (P and H) it is said to be of first importance. JE and P emphasize the historical importance of the day. Whether these differences in emphasis mean much more than that the relative amount of attention paid to the paschal sacrifice, as compared with *maççōth*, depends on the context, is of course the fundamental question of the higher criticism; it is not answered by pointing out that the differences of emphasis exist. (3) Of the actual conflicts, we have already seen that the use of the words "flock" and "herd" in Dt and Heb *bāshal* are open to explanation, and also that the use of the *maççōth* at the original Passover is not inconsistent with the historical reason for the feast of *maççōth*—it is not necessary to suppose that *maççōth* were *invented* through the necessity of the Hebrews on their journey. There is, however, one apparent discrepancy in the Bib. narrative that seems to weaken rather than help the position of those critics who would ascribe very late dates to the passages which we have cited: Why does Ezekiel's ideal scheme provide sacrifices for the Passover different from those prescribed in the so-called P ascribed to the same period (Ezk **45** 21)?

8. Historical Celebrations: OT Times

The children of Israel began the keeping of the Passover in its due season according to all its ordinances in the wilderness of Sinai (Nu **9** 5). In the very beginning of their national life in Pal we find them celebrating the Passover under the leadership of Joshua in the plains of Jericho (Josh **5** 10). History records but few later celebrations in Pal, but there are enough intimations to indicate that it was frequently if not regularly observed. Thus Solomon offered sacrifices three times a year upon the altar which he had built to Jeh, at the appointed seasons, including the Feast of Unleavened Bread (1 K **9** 25=2 Ch **8** 13). The later prophets speak of appointed seasons for pilgrimages and sacrifices (cf Isa **1** 12–14), and occasionally perhaps refer to a Passover celebration (cf Isa **30** 29, bearing in mind that the Passover is the only night-feast of which we have any record). In Hezekiah's time the Passover had fallen into such a state of desuetude that neither the priests nor the people were prepared for the king's urgent appeal to observe it. Nevertheless, he was able to bring together a large concourse in Jerus during the 2d month and institute a more joyful observance than any other recorded since the days of Solomon. In the 18th year of King Josiah, however, there was celebrated the most memorable Passover, presumably in the matter of conformity to rule, since the days of the Judges (2 K **23** 21; 2 Ch **35** 1 ff). The continued observance of the feast to the days of the exile is attested by Ezekiel's interest in it (Ezk **45** 18). In post-exilic times it was probably observed more scrupulously than ever before (Ezr **6** 19 ff).

9. Historical Celebrations: NT Times

Further evidence, if any were needed, of the importance of the Passover in the life of the Jews of the second temple is found in the Talm, which devotes to this subject an entire tractate, *Peṣāḥīm*, on which we have both Bab and Pal *gemārā'*. These are devoted to the sacrificial side and to the minutiae of searching out and destroying leaven, what constitutes leaven, and similar questions, instruction in which the children of Israel sought for 30 days before the Passover. Jos speaks of the festival often (*Ant*, II, xiv, 6; III, x, 5; IX, iv, 8; XIV, ii, 2; XVII, ix, 3; *BJ*, II, i, 3; V, iii, 1; VI, ix, 3). Besides repeating the details already explained in the Bible, he tells of the innumerable multitudes that came for the Passover to Jerus out of the country and even from beyond its limits. He estimates that in one year in the days of Cestius, 256,500 lambs were slaughtered and that at least 10 men were counted to each. (This estimate of course includes the regular population of Jerus. But even then it is doubtless exaggerated.) The NT bears testimony, likewise, to the coming of great multitudes to Jerus (Jn **11** 55; cf also **2** 13; **6** 4). At this great festival even the Rom officers released prisoners in recognition of the people's celebration. Travel and other ordinary pursuits were no doubt suspended (cf Acts **12** 3; **20** 6). Naturally the details were impressed on the minds of the people and lent themselves to symbolic and homiletic purposes (cf 1 Cor **5** 7; Jn **19** 34–36, where the paschal lamb is made to typify Jesus; and He **11** 28). The best-known instance of such symbolic use is the institution of the Eucharist on the basis of the paschal meal. Some doubt exists as to whether the Last Supper was the paschal meal or not. According to the Synoptic Gospels, it was (Lk **22** 7; Mt **26** 17; Mk **14** 12); while according to John, the Passover was to be eaten some time following the Last Supper (Jn **18** 28). Various harmonizations of these passages have been suggested, the most ingenious, probably, being on the theory that when the Passover fell on Friday night, the Pharisees ate the meal on Thursday and the Sadducees on Friday, and that Jesus followed the custom of the Pharisees (Chwolson, *Das letzte Passahmal Jesu*, 2d ed, St. Petersburg, 1904). Up to the Nicene Council in the year 325, the church observed Easter on the Jewish Passover. Thereafter it took precautions to separate the two, condemning their confusion as Arianism.

10. The Jewish Passover

After the destruction of the temple the Passover became a home service. The paschal lamb was no longer included. Only the Samaritans have continued this rite to this day. In the Jewish home a roasted bone is placed on the table in memory of the rite, and other articles symbolic of the Passover are placed beside it: such as a roasted egg, said to be in memory of the free-will offering; a sauce called *ḥărōṣeth*, said to resemble the mortar of Egypt; salt water, for the symbolic dipping (cf Mt **26** 23); the bitter herbs and the *maççōth*. The *ṣēdher* (program) is as follows: sanctification; washing of the hands; dipping and dividing the parsley; breaking and setting aside a piece of *maççāh* to be distributed and eaten at the end of the supper; reading of the *haggādhāh shel peṣaḥ*, a poetic narrative of the Exodus, in answer to four questions asked by the youngest child in compliance with the Bib. command found 3 t in Ex and once in Dt, "Thou shalt tell thy son on that day"; washing the hands for eating; grace before eating; tasting the *maççāh;* tasting the bitter herbs; eating of them together; the meal; partaking of the *maççāh* that had been set aside as *'ăphīḳōmēn* or dessert; grace after meat; *Hallel;* request that the service be accepted. Thereafter folk-songs are sung to traditional melodies, and poems recited, many of which have allegorical meanings. A cup of wine is used at the sanctification and another at grace, in addition to which two other cups have been added, the 4 according to the Mish (*Peṣāḥīm* x.1) symbolizing the 4 words employed in Ex **6** 6.7 for the delivery of Israel from Egypt. Instead of eating in haste, as in the Egyp Passover, it is customary to recline or lean at this meal in token of Israel's freedom.

The prohibition against leaven is strictly observed. The searching for hidden leaven on the evening before the Passover and its destruction in the morning have become formal ceremonies for which appropriate blessings and declarations have been included in the liturgy since the days when Aram. was the vernacular of the Jews. As in the case of other festivals, the Jews have doubled the days of holy convocation, and have added a semi-holiday after the last day, the so-called *'iṣṣur ḥagh*, in token of their love for the ordained celebration and their loathness to depart from it.

Nathan Isaacs

PASTOR, pas'tēr (רֹעֶה, *rō'eh;* **ποιμήν**, *poimēn;* lit. a helper, or feeder of the sheep [AV Jer **2** 8; **3** 15; **10** 21; **12** 10; **17** 16; **22** 22; **23** 1.2, and in Eph **4** 11, AV and RV]): Besides the literal sense the word has now a **figurative** meaning and refers to the minister appointed over a congregation. This latter meaning is recognized in the tr of AV. See Ministry.

PASTORAL, pas'tor-al, **EPISTLES, THE:**

The First and Second Epp. to Tim, and the Ep. to Tit form a distinct group among the letters written by Paul, and are now known as the Pastoral Epp. because they were addressed to two Christian ministers. When Timothy and Titus received these epp. they were not acting, as they had previously done, as missionaries or itinerant evangelists, but had been left by Paul in charge of churches; the former having the oversight of the church in Ephesus, and the latter having the care of the churches in the island of Crete. The Pastoral Epp. were written to guide them in the discharge of the duties devolving upon them as Christian pastors. Such is a general description of these epp. In each of them, however, there is a great deal more than is covered or implied by the designation, "Pastoral"—much that is personal, and much also that is concerned with Christian faith and doctrine and practice generally.

I. Genuineness.—In regard to the genuineness of the epp. there is abundant external attestation.

1. External Evidence

Allusions to them are found in the writings of Clement and Polycarp. In the middle of the 2d cent. the epp. were recognized as Pauline in authorship, and were freely quoted.

"Marcion indeed rejected them, and Tatian is supposed to have rejected those to Timothy. But, as Jerome states in the preface to his *Comm. on Tit*, these heretics rejected the epp., not on critical grounds, but merely because they disliked their teaching. He says they used no argument, but merely asserted, This is Paul's, This is not Paul's. It is obvious that men holding such opinions as Marcion and Tatian held, would not willingly ascribe authority to epp. which condemned asceticism. So far, then, as the early church can guarantee to us the authenticity of writings ascribed to Paul, the Pastoral Epp. are guaranteed" (Marcus Dods, *Intro to the NT*, 167).

The external evidence is all in favor of the reception of these epp., which were known not only to Clement and Polycarp, but also to Irenaeus, Tertullian, the author of the Ep. to the churches of Vienne and Lyons, and Theophilus of Antioch. The evidence of Polycarp, who died in 167 AD, is remarkably strong. He says, "The love of money is the beginning of all trouble, knowing . . . . that we brought nothing into the world, neither can carry anything out" (cf 1 Tim **6** 7.10). It would be difficult to overthrow testimony of this nature.

The decision of certain critics to reject the Pastoral Epp. as documents not from the hand of Paul, "is not reached on the external evidence, which is perhaps as early an attestation as can be reasonably expected.

2. Genuineness Questioned

They are included in the Muratorian Canon, and quoted by Irenaeus and later writers as Paul's" (A. S. Peake, *A Critical Intro to the NT*, 60). This admission is satisfactory. In recent times, however, the authenticity of these epp. has been called in question by Schmidt, Schleiermacher, Baur, Renan, and many others. Baur asserted that they were written for the purpose of combating the Gnosticism of the 2d cent., and of defending the church from it by means of ecclesiastical organization, and that the date of their composition was about the year 150 AD.

II. Alleged Difficulties against Pauline Authorship.—Various difficulties have been alleged against the reception of the Pastoral Epp. as Pauline. The chief of these are: (1) the difficulty of finding any place for these letters in the life of Paul, as that is recorded in the Acts and in the Pauline Epp. written before the Pastorals; (2) the fact that there are said to be in them indications of an ecclesiastical organization, and of a development of doctrine, both orthodox and heretical, considerably in advance of the Pauline age; (3) that the language of the epp. is, to a large extent, different from that in the accepted epp.; (4) the "most decisive" of all the arguments against the Pauline authorship—so writes Dr. A. C. McGiffert (*A History of Christianity in the Apostolic Age*, 402)—is that "the Christianity of the Pastoral Epp. is not the Christianity of Paul."

1. Relative to Paul's Experiences

Where can a place be found for these epp., in the life of Paul? The indications of the date of their composition given in the epp. themselves are these.

(1) *Data in 1 Tim.*—In 1 Tim **1** 3 Paul had gone from Ephesus to Macedonia, and had left Timothy in Ephesus in charge of the church there. In the Acts and in the previously written Pauline epp., it is impossible to find such events or such a state of matters as will satisfy these requirements. Paul had previously been in Ephesus, on several occasions. His 1st visit to that city is recorded in Acts **18** 19–21. On that occasion he went from Ephesus, not into Macedonia, but into Syria. His 2d visit was his 3 years' residence in Ephesus, as narrated in Acts **19**; and when he left the city, he had, previous to his own departure from it, already sent Timothy into Macedonia (**19** 22)—a state of matters exactly the reverse of that described in 1 Tim **1** 3. Timothy soon rejoined Paul, and so far was he from being left in Ephesus then, that he was in Paul's company on the remainder of his journey toward Jerus (Acts **20** 4; 2 Cor **1** 1).

No place therefore in Paul's life, previous to his arrest in Jerus, and his first Rom imprisonment, can be found, which satisfies the requirements of the situation described in 1 Tim **1** 3. "It is impossible, unless we assume a second Rom imprisonment, to reconcile the various historical notices which the ep. [2 Tim] contains" (McGiffert, op. cit., 407).

In addition to this, the language used by the apostle at Miletus, when he addressed the elders of the Ephesian church (Acts **20** 30) about the men speaking perverse things, who should arise among them, showed that these false teachers had not made their appearance at that time. There is, for this reason alone, no place for the Pastoral Epp. in Paul's life, previous to his arrest in Jerus. But Paul's life did not end at the termination of his first Rom imprisonment; and this one fact gives ample room to satisfy all the conditions, as these are found in the three Pastorals.

Those who deny the Pauline authorship of these epp. also deny that he was released from what, in this article, is termed his 1st Rom imprisonment. But a denial of this latter statement is an assumption quite unwarranted and unproved. It assumes that Paul was not set free, simply because there is no record of this in the Acts. But the Acts is, on the very face of it, an incomplete or unfinished record; that is, it brings the narrative to a certain point, and then breaks off, evidently for the reason which Sir W. M. Ramsay demonstrates, that Luke meant to write a sequel to that book—a purpose, however, which he was unable, owing to some cause now unknown, to carry into execution. The purpose of the Acts, as Ramsay shows (*St. Paul the Traveller and the Rom Citizen*, 23, 308), is to lead up to the release of Paul, and to show that the Christian faith was not a forbidden or illegal religion, but that the formal impeachment of the apostle before the supreme court of the empire ended in his being set at liberty, and thus there was established the fact that the faith of Jesus Christ was not, at that time, contrary to Rom law. "The Pauline authorship . . . . can be maintained only on the basis of a hypothetical reconstruction, either of an entire period subsequent to the Rom imprisonment, or of the events within some period known to us" (McGiffert, op. cit., 410). The one fact that Paul was set free after his 1st Rom imprisonment gives the environment which fits exactly all the requirements of the Pastoral Epp.

Attention should be directed to the facts and to the conclusion stated in the art. PRAETORIUM (q.v.), Mommsen having shown that the words, "My bonds became manifest in Christ throughout the whole prætorian guard" (Phil **1** 13), mean that at the time when Paul wrote the Ep. to the Phil, the case against him had already come before the supreme court of appeal in Rome, that it had been partly heard, and that the impression made by the prisoner upon his judges was so favorable, that he expected soon to be set free.

The indications to be drawn from other expressions in three of the epp. of the Rom captivity—Phil, Col and Philem—are to the same effect. Thus, writing to the Philippians, he says that he hopes to send Timothy to them, so soon as he sees how matters go with him, and that he trusts in the Lord that he himself will visit them shortly. And again, writing to his friend Philemon in the city of Colossae, he asks him to prepare him a lodging, for he trusts that through the prayers of the Colossians, he will be granted to them.

These anticipations of acquittal and of departure from Rome are remarkable, and do not in any degree coincide with the idea that Paul was not set free but was condemned and put to death at that time. "It is obvious that the importance of the trial is intelligible only if Paul was acquitted. That he was acquitted follows from the Pastoral Epp. with certainty for all who admit their genuineness; while even they who deny their Pauline origin must allow that they imply an early belief in historical details which are not consistent with Paul's journeys before his trial, and must either be pure inventions or events that occurred on later journeys. . . . . If he was acquitted, the issue of the trial was a formal decision by the supreme court of the empire that it was permissible to preach Christianity; the trial, therefore, was really a charter of religious liberty, and therein lies its immense importance. It was indeed overturned by later decisions of the supreme court; but its existence was a highly important fact for the Christians" (Ramsay, op. cit., 308). "That he was acquitted is demanded both by the plan evident in Acts and by other reasons well stated by others" (ib, 360).

It should also be observed that there is the direct and corroborative evidence of Paul's release, afforded by such writers as Cyril of Jerus, Ephrem Syr., Chrysostom and Theodoret, all of whom speak of Paul's going to Spain. Jerome (*Vir. Ill.*, 5) gives it as a matter of personal knowledge that Paul traveled as far as Spain. But there is more important evidence still. In the Muratorian Canon, l. 37, there are the words, "profectionem Pauli ab urbe ad Spaniam proficiscentis" ("the journey of Paul as he journeyed from Rome to Spain"). Clement also in the ep. from the church in Rome to the church in Corinth, which was written not later than the year 96 AD, says in reference to Paul, "Having taught righteousness to the whole world, and having gone to the extremity of the west [*epí tó térma tês dúseōs elthṓn*] and having borne witness before the rulers, so was he released from the world and went to the holy place, being the greatest example of endurance." The words, "having gone to the extremity of the west," should be specially noticed. Clement was in Rome when he wrote this, and, accordingly, the natural import of the words is that Paul went to the limit of the western half of the then known world, or in other words, to the western boundary of the lands bordering the Mediterranean, that is, to Spain.

Now Paul never had been in Spain previous to his arrest in Jerus, but in Rom **15** 24.28 he had twice expressed his intention to go there. These independent testimonies, of Clement and of the Muratorian Canon, of the fact that after Paul's arrest in Jerus he did carry into execution his purpose to visit Spain, are entitled to great weight. They involve, of course, the fact that he was acquitted after his 1st Rom imprisonment.

Having been set free, Paul could not do otherwise than send Timothy to Philippi, and himself also go there, as he had already promised when he wrote to the Philippian church (Phil **2** 19.24). As a matter of course he would also resume his apostolic journeys for the purpose of proclaiming the gospel. There is now ample room in his life for the Pastoral Epp., and they give most interesting details of his further labors. The historical and geographical requirements in 1 Tim are, in this way, easily satisfied. It was no great distance to Ephesus from Philippi and Colossae, where he had promised that he would "come shortly."

(2) *Data in 2 Tim.*—The requirements in 2 Tim are (*a*) that Paul had recently been at Troas, at Corinth, and at Miletus, each of which he mentions (2 Tim **4** 13.20); (*b*) that when he wrote the epp. he was in Rome (**1** 17); (*c*) that he was a prisoner for the cause of the gospel (**1** 8; **2** 9), and had once already appeared before the emperor's supreme court (**4** 16.17); (*d*) that he had then escaped condemnation, but that he had reason to believe that on the next hearing of his case the verdict would be given against him, and that he expected it could not be long till execution took place (**4** 6); (*e*) that he hoped that Timothy would be able to come from Ephesus to see him at Rome before the end (**4** 9.21). These requirements cannot be made to agree or coincide with the first Rom captivity, but they do agree perfectly with the facts of the apostle's release and his subsequent second imprisonment in that city.

(3) *Data in Tit.*—The data given in the Ep. to Tit are (*a*) that Paul had been in Crete, and that Titus had been with him there, and had been left behind in that island, when Paul sailed from its shores, Titus being charged with the oversight of the churches there (Tit **1** 5); and (*b*) that Paul meant to spend the next winter at Nicopolis (**3** 12). It is simply impossible to locate these events in the recorded life of Paul, as that is found in the other epp., and in the Acts. But they agree perfectly with his liberation after his first Rom imprisonment. "As there is then no historical evidence that Paul did not survive the year 64, and as these Pastoral Epp. were recognized as Pauline in the immediately succeeding age, we may legitimately accept them as evidence that Paul did survive the year 64—that he was acquitted, resumed his missionary labors, was again arrested and brought to Rome, and from this second imprisonment wrote the Second Ep. to Tim—his last extant writing" (Dods, *Intro to the NT*, 172).

The second difficulty alleged against the acceptance of these epp. as Pauline is that there are said to exist in them indications of an ecclesiastical organization and of a doctrinal development, both orthodox and heretical, considerably later than those of the Pauline age.

2. Subject-Matter Post-Pauline

(1) The first statement, that the epp. imply an ecclesiastical organization in advance of the time when Paul lived, is one which cannot be maintained in view of the facts disclosed in the epp. themselves. For directions are given to Timothy and to Titus in regard to the moral and other characteristics necessary in those who are to be ordained as bishops, elders, and deacons. In the 2d cent. the outstanding feature of ecclesiastical organization was the development of monarchical episcopacy, but the Pastoral Epp. show a presbyterial administration. The office held by Timothy in Ephesus and by Titus in Crete was, as the epp. themselves show, of a temporary character. The directions which Paul gives to Timothy and Titus in regard to the ordaining of presbyters in every church are in agreement with similar notices found elsewhere in the NT, and do not coincide with the state of church organization as that existed in the 2d cent., the period when, objectors to the genuineness of the epp. assert, they were composed. "Everyone acquainted with ancient literature, particularly the literature of the ancient church, knows that a forger or fabricator of those times could not possibly have avoided anachronisms" (Zahn, *Intro to the NT*, II, 93). But the ecclesiastical arrangements in the Pastoral Epp. coincide in all points with the state of matters as it is found in the church in the time of the apostles, as that is described in the Acts and elsewhere in the NT.

It seems an error to suppose, as has often been done, that these epp. contain the germ of monarchical episcopacy; for the Christian church had already, from the day of Pentecost, existed as a society with special officers for the functions of extension, discipline and administration. The church in the Pastoral Epp. is a visible society, as it always was. Its organization therefore had come to be of the greatest importance, and esp. so in the matter of maintaining and handing down the true faith; the church accordingly is described as "the pillar and stay of the truth" (1 Tim **3** 15 m), that is, the immovable depository of the Divine revelation.

(2) The other statement, that the epp. show a doctrinal development out of harmony with the Pauline age is best viewed by an examination of what the epp. actually say.

In 1 Tim **6** 20, Paul speaks of profane and vain babblings and oppositions of *gnṓsis* (RV "knowledge," AV "science") falsely so called. In Tit **3** 9, he tells Titus to avoid foolish questions and genealogies and contentions and strivings about the law. These phrases have been held to be allusions to the tenets of Marcion, and to those of some of the gnostic sects. There are also other expressions, such as fables and endless genealogies (1 Tim **1** 3.4; **6** 3), words to no profit but the subverting of the hearer (2 Tim **2** 14), foolish and unlearned questions which do gender strifes (2 Tim **2** 23), questions and strifes of words (1 Tim **6** 4.5), discussions which lead to nothing but word-battles and profane babbling. Such are the expressions which Paul uses. These, taken with what is even more clearly stated in the Ep. to the Col, certainly point to an incipient Gnosticism. But had the writer of the Pastoral Epp. been combating the Gnosticism of the 2d cent., it would not have been phrases like these that he would have employed, but others much more definite. Godet, quoted by Dods (*Intro*, 175), writes, "The danger here is of substituting intellectualism in religion for piety of heart and life. Had the writer been a Christian of the 2d cent., trying, under the name of Paul, to stigmatize the gnostic systems, he would certainly have used much stronger expressions to describe their character and influence."

It should be observed that the false teachers described in 2 Tim **3** 6–9.13, as well as in other places in these epp., were persons who taught that the Mosaic Law was binding upon all Christians. They laid stress upon rabbinic myths, upon investigations and disputations about genealogies and specific legal requirements of the OT. What they taught was a form of piously sounding doctrine assuming to be Christian, but which was really rabbinism.

"For a pseudo-Paul in the post-apostolic age—when Christians of Jewish birth had become more and more exceptions in the gentile Christian church—to have invented a description of and vigorously to have opposed the *heterodidáskaloi*, who did not exist in his own age, and who were without parallel in the earlier epp. of Paul, would have been to expose himself to ridicule without apparent purpose or meaning" (Zahn, *Intro*, II, 117). "A comparison of the statements in these epp. about various kinds of false doctrine, and of those portions of the same that deal with the organization and officers of the church, with conditions actually existing in the church, esp. the church of Asia Minor, at the beginning and during the course of the 2d cent., proves, just as clearly as does the external evidence, that they must have been written at latest before the year 100. But they could not have been written during the first two decades after Paul's death, because of the character of the references to persons, facts and conditions in Paul's lifetime and his own personal history, and because of the impossibility on this assumption of discovering a plausible motive for their forgery. Consequently the claim that they are post-Pauline, and contain matter which is un-Pauline, is to be treated with the greatest suspicion" (Zahn, op. cit., II, 118).

3. Difficulty Connected with the Language

The third difficulty alleged against the Pauline authorship of the Pastoral Epp. is connected with the language employed, which is said to be, to a large extent, different from that in the accepted epp. The facts in regard to this matter are that in 1 Tim there are 82 words not found elsewhere in the NT; in 2 Tim there are 53 such words, and in Tit there are 33. But, while the total of such words in the three epp. is 168, this number, large though it appears, may be compared with the words used only once in the other Epp. of Paul. In Rom, 1 Cor, 2 Cor, Gal, Eph, Phil, Col, 1 Thess, 2 Thess and Philem, the words of this description are 627 in number. So nothing can be built upon the fact of the 168 peculiar words in the Pastoral Epp., that can safely be alleged as proof against their Pauline authorship. The special subjects treated in these epp. required adequate language, a requirement and a claim which would not be refused in the case of any ordinary author.

The objections to the Pauline authorship of the Pastorals, based upon the dissimilarity of diction in them and in Eph, Phil and Col, cease to exist when the theory is no longer persisted in, that the nucleus of the Pastoral Epp. was composed during the Rom imprisonment, which, according to this theory ended, not in the apostle's release, but in his execution. The fact that he was writing to intimate and beloved friends, both on personal matters and on the subject of church organization, and on that of incipient Gnosticism, which was troubling the churches of Asia Minor, made it essential that he should, to a large extent, use a different vocabulary.

4. Is There "Another Gospel" in the Pastorals?

The "most decisive" of all the arguments against the Pauline authorship is that "the Christianity of the Pastoral Epp. is not the Christianity of Paul" (McGiffert, *A History of Christianity*, 402). "For the most part," Dr. McGiffert writes, "there is no trace whatever of the great fundamental truth of Paul's gospel—death unto the flesh and life in the Spirit." Now this is not so, for the passages which Dr. McGiffert himself gives in a footnote (2 Tim **1** 9–11; **2** 11 ff; Tit **3** 4–7), as well as other references, do most certainly refer to this very aspect of the gospel. For example, the passage in 2 Tim **2** contains these words, "If we died with him [Christ], we shall also live with him." What is this but the great truth of the union of the Christian believer with Christ? The believer is one with Christ in His death, one with Him now as He lives and reigns. The objection, therefore, which is "most decisive of all," is one which is not true in point of fact. Dr. McGiffert also charges the author of the Pastoral Epp. as being "one who understood by resurrection nothing else than the resurrection of the fleshly body" (p. 430). The body of Our Lord was raised from the dead, but how very unjust this accusation is, is evident from such a passage as 1 Tim **3** 16, "And without controversy great is the mystery of godliness;

He who was manifested in the flesh,
Justified in the Spirit,
Seen of angels,
Preached among the nations,
Believed on in the world,
Received up in glory."

Charges of this nature are unsupported by evidence, and are of the kind on which Dr. A. S. Peake (*A Critical Intro to the NT*, 71) bases his rejection of the Pauline authorship—except for a Pauline nucleus—that he "feels clear." More than an *ipse dixit* of this sort is needed.

The theory that the Pastoral Epp. are based upon genuine letters or notes of Paul to Timothy and Titus is thus advocated by Peake, McGiffert, Moffatt and many others. It bears very hard upon 1 Tim. "In 1 Tim not a single verse can be indicated which clearly bears the stamp of Pauline origin" (Peake, op. cit., 70). "We may fairly conclude then in agreement with many modern scholars that we have here, in the Pastoral Epp., authentic letters of Paul to Timothy and Titus, worked over and enlarged by another hand" (McGiffert, op. cit., 405). In regard to 1 Tim he writes, "It is very likely that there are scattered fragments of the original ep. in 1 Tim, as for instance in ver 23. But it is difficult to find anything which we can be confident was written by Paul" (p. 407).

Dr. McGiffert also alleges that in the Pastoral Epp., the word "faith" "is not employed in its profound Pauline sense, but is used to signify one of the cardinal virtues, along with love, peace, purity, righteousness, sanctification, patience and meekness." One of the Pauline epp., with which he contrasts the Pastorals, is the Ep. to the Gal; and the groundlessness of this charge is evident from Gal **5** 22, where "faith" is included in the list there given of the fruit of the Spirit, along with love, joy, peace, longsuffering, gentleness, goodness, meekness and self-control.

If the Pastoral Epp. are the work of Paul, then, Dr. McGiffert concludes, Paul had given up that form of the gospel which he had held and taught throughout his life, and descended from the lofty religious plane upon which he had always moved, to the level of mere piety and morality (op. cit., 404). But this charge is not just or reasonable, in view of the fact that the apostle is instructing Timothy and Titus how to combat the views and practices of immoral teachers. Or again, in such a passage as 1 Tim **1** 12–17 AV, the author of the ep. has not descended from the lofty plane of faith to that of mere piety and morality, when he writes, "The grace of our Lord was exceeding abundant with faith and love which is in Christ Jesus. This is a faithful saying, and worthy of all acceptation, that Christ Jesus came into the world to save sinners; of whom I am chief."

If such be the "most decisive" objection against the Pauline authorship, the other difficulties, as already seen, need not cause alarm, for they resolve themselves into the equally groundless charges that the historical requirements of the epp. cannot be fitted into any part of Paul's life, and that the doctrine and ecclesiastical organization do not suit the Apostolic age. These objections have been already referred to.

The real difficulty, writes Dr. Peake (*A Critical Intro*, 68), is that "the old energy of thought and expression is gone, and the greater smoothness and continuity in the grammar is a poor compensation for the lack of grip and of continuity in the thought." Dr. Peake well and truly says that this statement does not admit of detailed proof. Lack of grip and lack of continuity of thought are not the characteristics of such passages as 1 Tim **1** 9–17, a passage which will bear comparison with anything in the acknowledged Pauline Epp.; and there are many other similar passages, e.g. Tit **2** 11—**3** 7.

What must be said of the dulness of the intelligence of Christian men and of the Christian church as a whole, if they could thus let themselves be imposed upon by epp. which purported to be Paul's, but which were not written by him at all, but were the enlargement of a Pauline nucleus? Can it be believed that the church of the 2d cent., the church of the martyrs, was in such a state of mental decrepitude as to receive epp. which were spurious, so far as the greater portion of their contents is concerned? And can it be believed that this idea, so recently originated and so destitute of proof, is an adequate explanation of epp. which have been received as Pauline from the earliest times?

When placed side by side with sub-apostolic writings like the *Didache*, Clem. Rom., Polycarp and Ignatius, "it is difficult to resist the idea which returns upon one with almost every sentence that . . . . the Pastorals are astonishingly superior" (Moffatt, *The Historical NT*, 556). Godet, quoted by R. D. Shaw (*The Pauline Epp.*, 441), writes, "When one has had enough of the pious amplifications of Clement of Rome, of the ridiculous inanities of Barnabas, of the general oddities of Ignatius, of the well-meant commonplaces of Polycarp, of the intolerable verbiage of Hermas, and of the nameless platitudes of the *Didache*, and, after this promenade in the first decade of the 2d cent., reverts to our Pastoral Epp., one will measure the distance that separates the least striking products of the apostolic literature from what has been preserved to us as most eminent in the ancient patristic literature."

In the case of some modern critics, the interpolation hypothesis "is their first and last appeal, the easy solution of any difficulty that presents itself to their imaginations. Each writer feels free to give the kaleidoscope a fresh turn, and then records with blissful confidence what are called the latest results. . . . . The whole method postulates that a writer must always preserve the same dull monotone or always confine himself to the same transcendental heights. . . . . He must see and say everything at once; having had his vision and his dream, he must henceforth be like a star and dwell apart. . . . . To be stereotyped is his only salvation. . . . . On such principles there is not a writer of note, and there never has been a man in public life, or a student in the stream of a progressive science, large parts of whose sayings and doings could not be proved to be by some one else" (Shaw, *The Pauline Epp.*, 483).

III. Date and Order.—In regard to the date of these epp., external and internal evidence alike go to show that they belong to practically the same period. The dates of their composition are separated from each other by not more than three or four years; and the dates of each and all of them must be close to the Neronic persecution (64 AD). If Paul was executed 67 AD (see Ramsay, *St. Paul*, 396), there is only a short interval of time between his release in 61 or 62, and his death in 67, that is a period of some 5 or 6 years, during which his later travels took place, and when the Pastoral Epp. were written. "Between the three letters there is an affinity of language, a similarity of thought, and a likeness of errors combated, which prevents our referring any of them to a period much earlier than the others" (Zahn, *Intro*, II, 37).

1. Date of the Epistles

2. Their Order

The order in which they were written must have been 1 Tim, Tit, 2 Tim. It is universally acknowledged that 2 Tim is the very last of Paul's extant epp., and the internal evidence of the other two seems to point out 1 Tim as earlier than Tit.

To sum up, the evidence of the early reception of the Pastoral Epp. as Pauline is very strong. "The confident denial of the genuineness of these letters—which has been made now for several generations more positively than in the case of any other Pauline epp.—has no support from tradition. . . . . Traces of their circulation in the church before Marcion's time are clearer than those which can be found for Rom and 2 Cor" (Zahn, op. cit., II, 85). The internal evidence shows that all three are from the hand of one and the same writer, a writer who makes many personal allusions of a nature which it would be impossible for a forger to invent. It is generally allowed that the personal passages in 2 Tim **1** 15–18; **4** 9–22 are genuine. But if this is so, then it is not possible to cut and carve the epp. into fragments of this kind. Objections dating only a century back are all too feeble to overturn the consistent marks of Pauline authorship found in all three epp., corroborated as this is by their reception in the church, dating from the very earliest period. The Pastoral Epp. may be used with the utmost confidence, as having genuinely come from the hand of Paul.

LITERATURE.—R. D. Shaw, *The Pauline Epp.;* A. S. Peake, *A Critical Intro to the NT;* A. C. McGiffert, *A History of Christianity in the Apostolic Age;* Theodor Zahn, *An Intro to the NT;* Marcus Dods, *Intro to the NT;* Weiss, *Einleitung in das NT* (ET); C. J. Ellicott, *A Critical and Grammatical Comm. on the Pastoral Epp.;* Patrick Fairbairn, *The Pastoral Epp.;* John Ed. Huther, *Critical and Exegetical Handbook of the Epp. of St. Paul to Timothy and Titus;* George Salmon, *A Historical Intro to the Study of the Books of the NT;* James Moffatt, *The Historical NT; Intro to the Lit. of the NT;* Adolf Jülicher, *An Intro to the NT;* Caspar René Gregory, *Canon and Text of the NT.*

The "lives" of Paul may also be consulted, as they contain much that refers to these epp., i.e. those by Conybeare and Howson, Lewin, Farrar and others. See also Ramsay's *St. Paul the Traveller and the Rom Citizen.*

JOHN RUTHERFURD

PASTURAGE, pas′t̬ūr-āj, **PASTURE,** pas′t̬ūr. See SHEEP-TENDING.

PATARA, pat′a-ra (**τὰ Πάταρα,** *tá Pátara*): A coast city of ancient Lycia, from which, according to Acts **21** 1, Paul took a ship for Phoenicia. Because of its excellent harbor, many of the coast trading ships stopped at Patara, which therefore became an important and wealthy port of entry to the towns of the interior. As early as 440 BC autonomous coins were struck there; during the 4th and the 3d cents. the coinage was interrupted, but was again resumed in 168 BC when Patara joined the Lycian league. Ptolemy Philadelphus enlarged the city, and changed its name to Arsinoë in honor of his wife. The city was celebrated not only as a trading center, but esp. for its celebrated oracle of Apollo which is said to have spoken only during the six winter months of the year. Among the ruins there is still to be seen a deep pit with circular steps leading to a seat at the bottom; it is supposed that the pit is the place of the oracle. In the history of early Christianity, Patara took but little part, but it was the home of a bishop, and the birthplace of St. Nicholas, the patron saint of the sailors of the E. Though born at Patara, St. Nicholas was a bishop and saint of Myra, a neighboring Lycian city, and there he is said to have been buried. *Gelemish* is the modern name of the ruin. The walls of the ancient city may still be traced, and the foundations of the temple and castle and other public buildings are visible. The most imposing of the ruins is a triumphal arch bearing the inscription: "Patara the Metropolis of the Lycian Nation." Outside the city walls many sarcophagi may be seen, but the harbor, long ago choked by sand, has been converted into a useless swamp. See also MYRA.

E. J. BANKS

PATE, pāt (קָדְקֹד, *ḳodhḳōdh*): The word usually trd "crown," "crown of the head" (Gen **49** 26; Dt **28** 35; **33** 16.20; 2 S **14** 25; Job **2** 7; Isa **3** 17; Jer **2** 16; **48** 45) and "scalp" (Ps **68** 21) is rendered "pate" in Ps **7** 16 in agreement with earlier Eng. translators since Coverdale: "His mischief shall return upon his own head, and his violence shall come down upon his own pate." The reason for the choice of the word lies evidently in the desire to make the Heb parallelism with "head" (*rō'sh*) apparent. The same object has, however, been achieved differently in another poetical passage (Gen **49** 26 ‖ Dt **33** 16), viz. by the juxtaposition of "head" and "crown of the head."

H. L. E. LUERING

PATH, path, **PATHWAY**, path'wā (אֹרַח, *'ōraḥ*, נְתִיבָה, *n^ethībhāh*, etc; **τρίβος**, *tribos*, **τροχιά**, *trochiá*):

(1) *In the OT*.—In addition to its obvious literal sense (e.g. Gen **49** 17), it has very frequently a **figurative** meaning. (*a*) As applied to man, a course or manner of life: (i) man's outward lot in life, his career or destiny, whether of the just man (Isa **26** 7) or of the ungodly (Job **8** 13); (ii) frequently in an ethical sense, of men's conduct or inward life-purpose, whether it be good or evil (e.g. Prov **2** 15), generally accompanied by a term defining the moral quality of the conduct, either an abstract noun (e.g. "the paths of uprightness," Prov **2** 13; **4** 11; "the paths of justice," Prov **2** 8; Isa **40** 14; "the paths of life," Ps **16** 11; Prov **2** 19), or a concrete adj. or noun (e.g. "crooked paths," Isa **59** 8; "the paths of the righteous," Prov **2** 20; **4** 18). (*b*) The term is also applied to God either (i) of the methods of the Divine Providence, God's dealings with men (Ps **25** 10; **65** 11), or (ii) of the principles and maxims of religion and morality Divinely revealed to man ("Show me thy ways, O Jeh, teach me thy paths," Ps **25** 4; cf Isa **2** 3).

(2) *In the Apoc* we have the "paths" of Wisdom (*tribos*, Bar **3** 21.31); the "path" shown to men by the Law (*semita*, 2 Esd **14** 22); and a man's "paths" (*tribos*, Tob **4** 10).

(3) *In the NT* the word occurs only in Mt **3** 3 and ‖ passages Mk **1** 3; Lk **3** 4 (of the forerunner's work), and in He **12** 13 (in the OT ethical sense).

Pathway occurs in Prov **12** 28 (*derekh n^ethībhāh*) and Wisd **5** 10 (*atrapós*). See WAY.

D. MIALL EDWARDS

PATHEUS, pa-thē'us (**Παθαῖος**, *Pathaios*, **Φαθαῖος**, *Phathaios*): One of the Levites who had married a foreign wife (1 Esd **9** 23) = "Pethahiah" of Ezr **10** 23.

PATHROS, path'ros (פַּתְרוֹס, *pathrōṣ;* Egyp *Pata resii*, the "South land"; LXX **γῆ Παθουρῆς**, *gē Pathourēs*): The Heb form of the Egyp name for Upper Egypt (Isa **11** 11; Jer **44** 1.15; Ezk **29** 14; **30** 14).

PATHRUSIM, path-rōō'sim, path-rū'sim (פַּתְרֻסִי, *pathruṣī*, "an inhabitant of Pathros"; LXX **οἱ Πατροσωνιειμ**, *hoi Patrosōnieim*): The branch of the Egyptians who came from PATHROS (q.v.). They are represented as begotten of Mizraim, "Mizraim begat Zudim . . . . and Pathrusim" (Gen **10** 13 f; 1 Ch **1** 11 f).

PATIENCE, pā'shens (**ὑπομονή**, *hupomonē*, **μακροθυμία**, *makrothumía*): "Patience" implies suffering, enduring or waiting, as a determination of the will and not simply under necessity. As such it is an essential Christian virtue to the exercise of which there are many exhortations. We need to "wait patiently" for God, to endure uncomplainingly the various forms of sufferings, wrongs and evils that we meet with, and to bear patiently injustices which we cannot remedy and provocations we cannot remove.

The word "patience" does not occur in the OT, but we have "patiently" in Ps **40** 1 as the tr of *ḳāwāh*, "to wait," "to expect," which word frequently expresses the idea, esp. that of waiting on God; in Ps **37** 7, "patiently" ("wait patiently") is the tr of *ḥūl*, one of the meanings of which is "to wait" or "to hope for" or "to expect" (cf Job **35** 14); "patient" occurs (Eccl **7** 8) as the tr of *'erekh rūaḥ*, "long of spirit," and (Job **6** 11) "that I should be patient" (*ha'ărīkh nephesh*). Cf "impatient" (Job **21** 4).

"Patience" occurs frequently in the Apoc, esp. in Ecclus, e.g. **2** 14; **16** 13; **17** 24; **41** 2 (*hupomonē*); **5** 11 (*makrothumia*); **29** 8 (*makrothuméō*, RV "long suffering"); in Wisd **2** 19, the Gr word is *anexikakía*.

In the NT *hupomonē* carries in it the ideas of endurance, continuance (Lk **8** 15; **21** 19; Rom **5** 3.4, ARV "stedfastness"; **8** 25, etc).

In all places ARVm has "stedfastness," except Jas **5** 11, where it has "endurance"; *makrothumia* is trd "patience" (He **6** 12; Jas **5** 10); *makrothumeō*, "to bear long" (Mt **18** 26.29; Jas **5** 7; see LONGSUFFERING); the same vb. is trd "be patient" (1 Thess **5** 14, RV "longsuffering"; Jas **5** 7.8, AV and RV "patient"); *makrothúmōs*, "patiently" (Acts **26** 3); *hupoménō* (1 Pet **2** 20); *anexíkakos* is trd "patient" (2 Tim **2** 24, RV, AVm, "forbearing"); *epieikḗs*, "gentle" (1 Tim **3** 3, RV "gentle"); *hupomenō* (Rom **12** 12, "patient in tribulation"). For "the patient waiting for Christ" (2 Thess **3** 5), RV has "the patience of Christ."

Patience is often hard to gain and to maintain, but, in Rom **15** 5, God is called "the God of patience" (ARVm "stedfastness") as being able to grant that grace to those who look to Him and depend on Him for it. It is in reliance on God and acceptance of His will, with trust in His goodness, wisdom and faithfulness, that we are enabled to endure and to hope stedfastly. See also GOD.

W. L. WALKER

PATMOS, pat'mos (**Πάτμος**, *Pátmos;* Ital. San Giovanni di Patino): A Turkish island of the group Sporades, S.W. of Samos, mentioned once in the Bible, Rev **1** 9, "I, John . . . . was in the isle that is called Patmos, for the word of God and the testimony of Jesus" (διὰ τὸν λόγον τοῦ θεοῦ καὶ τὴν μαρτυρίαν Ἰησοῦ, *diá tón lógon toú theoú kaí tēn marturían Iēsoú*). The island is 10 miles long, and about 6 broad along the northern coast. It is for the most part rocky. The highest part is Mt. St. Elias, which rises to a height of over 800 ft. As in Greece, and in the adjacent mainland of Asia Minor, the land is treeless. Near the city of Patmos there is a good harbor. A famous monastery, St. Christodulos, was founded on the island in 1088. Near this is a thriving school, attended by students from all parts of the Archipelago. The population of the island numbers 3,000, almost entirely Gr. The ancient capital was on an isthmus between the inlets of La Scala and Merika. Many ruins can still be seen. The huge walls of Cyclopean masonry, similar to those at Tiryns, attest their great age. In Rom times Patmos was one of the many places to which Rome banished her exiles. In 95 AD, according to a tradition preserved by Irenaeus, Eusebius, Jerome and others, St. John was exiled here—in the 14th year of the reign of Domitian—whence he returned to Ephesus under Nerva (96 AD). The cave in which he is said to have seen his visions is still pointed out to the traveler. Only a small part of the once valuable library in the monastery of St. Christodulos is left. Just 100 years ago (1814) Mr. E. D. Clark purchased here the manuscript of Plato which is now in the Bodleian Library, the celebrated Clarkianus, a parchment written in the year 895, and admittedly the best of all for the 1st of the 2 vols into which the works of Plato were divided for convenience. Patmos is mentioned by Thucydides (iii.33), by Pliny (*NH*, iv.23), and by Strabo (x.5). See also John the Apostle; Revelation of John.

Literature.—Tozer, *The Islands of the Aegean* (1890), 178–95; Walpole, *Turkey* (London, 1820), II, 43; E. D. Clark, *Travels* (London, 1818), VI, 2; Ross, *Reisen* (Stuttgart, 1840), II; Guérin, *Description de l'Ile de Patmos* (Paris, 1856).

J. E. Harry

PATRIARCH, pā'tri-ärk, **PATRIARCHS** (**πατριάρχης**, *patriárchēs*): The word occurs in the NT in application to Abraham (He **7** 4), to the sons of Jacob (Acts **7** 8.9), and to David (Acts **2** 29). In LXX it is used as the equivalent of the head of the fathers' house, or of a tribe (1 Ch **24** 31; **27** 32; 2 Ch **26** 12). Commonly now the term is used of the persons whose names appear in the genealogies and covenant-histories in the periods preceding Moses (Gen **5**, **11**, histories of Noah, Abraham, Isaac, Jacob, etc; cf "patriarchal dispensation"). The problems connected with the longevity ascribed to the patriarchs in the genealogies and narratives in Gen are dealt with in special articles. See Antediluvian Patriarchs; Antediluvians; Genealogy.

James Orr

PATRIARCHS, TESTAMENTS OF THE TWELVE. See Apocalyptic Literature, IV, 1.

PATRIMONY, pat'ri-mō-ni (הָאָבוֹת, *hā-'ābhōth*, "the fathers"): A word occurring once in EV (Dt **18** 8), meaning lit. "the fathers," which, however, is obscure, probably by reason of abbreviation for some phrase, e.g. "house of the fathers." It may indicate "some private source of income possessed by the Levite [who has come up from a country district to the central sanctuary] distinct from what he receives as a priest officiating at the central sanctuary" (Driver, "Dt," *ICC*, in loc.). Beyond this one occurrence of the word the same idea is conveyed often by other words or phrases: "He divided unto them his living" (Lk **15** 13); "Teacher, bid my brother divide the inheritance with me" (Lk **12** 13). Full and specific directions were given in the Law for the division of the patrimony (Nu **27**; Dt **21**, etc) and for its redemption (Ruth **4** 1–12). The idea was frequently used with **figurative** and spiritual application: the land of Canaan was Israel's patrimony, being inherited from Jeh (Ps **105** 11); salvation because of its origin in grace was the believer's patrimony (Gal **3** 26—**4** 7). Contrariwise Israel was Jeh's inheritance (Isa **19** 25; **63** 14; cf Ps **33** 12); and the whole earth is the Messiah's patrimony, inherited from His Eternal Father (Ps **2** 8). See Birthright; Family; Inheritance; Property.

Edward Mack

PATROBAS, pat'rō-bas (**Πατρόβας**, *Patróbas*): The name of a member of the Christian community at Rome to whom Paul sent greetings (Rom **16** 14). The name is an abbreviated form of "Patrobius." There was a wealthy freedman of Nero of the same name who was put to death by Galba (Tac. *Hist.* i.49; ii.95). The Patrobas of St. Paul may have been a dependent of his.

PATROCLUS, pa-trō'klus (**Πάτροκλος**, *Pátroklos*): The father of the Syrian general Nicanor (2 Macc **8** 9).

PATTERN, pat'ērn (תַּבְנִית, *tabhnīth*, "model," מַרְאֶה, *mar'eh*, "a vision" or "view"): The OT words tr[d] "pattern" do not necessarily indicate a drawing such as a modern constructor begins with, or the patterns made from these drawings for the guidance of workmen. In Ex **25** 9.40 the word "idea" or "suggestion" would possibly indicate more distinctly than "pattern" what Moses received in regard to the building of the tabernacle, etc. It is doubtful if any architect's drawing was ever made of the temple. It is not the custom in Pal and Syria today to work from any pattern more concrete than an idea. A man who wants a house calls the builder and says he wants to build so many rooms of such and such dimensions with, for example, a court 10 *drahs* (arm's lengths) wide and 15 *drahs* long, made of sandstone and plastered inside and out. With these meager instructions the builder starts. The details are worked out as the building proceeds. When a piece of iron or brass work is to be made, the customer by gestures with his hands outlines the form the piece should take. "I want it *haik wa haik*" ("thus and thus"), he says, and leaves the metal worker to conceive the exact form. It is probable that directions similar to these were given by David to Solomon. "Then David gave Solomon his son the pattern [his conception] of the porch of the temple," etc (1 Ch **28** 11). The above does not apply to Gr and Rom work in Syria. Their workmen, probably mostly native, were trained to work from models. Williams in the *Architect*, January, 1913, says of the works at Baalbek and Palmyra, "There is a machine-like resemblance betokening slavish copying." At the present time native workmen coming under the influence of foreigners are beginning to work from models and plans, but they show little tendency to create models of their own.

Three Gr words have been tr[d] in the NT: *τύπος*, *túpos*, "type," occurs in Tit **2** 7 and He **8** 5. In the first instance RV reads "ensample." *ὑποτύπωσις*, *hupotúpōsis*, "outline," has been similarly tr[d] in 1 Tim **1** 16, but "pattern" in 2 Tim **1** 13. In He **9** 24 ARV *ἀντίτυπος*, *antítupos*, is rendered "like in pattern." *ὑπόδειγμα*, *hupódeigma*, AV "pattern," is tr[d] in ARV "copy" (He **8** 5), "copies" (He **9** 23). At the time of the tr of AV the word "pattern" meant either the thing to be copied or the copy.

James A. Patch

PAU, pā'ū. See Pai.

PAUL, pôl, **THE APOSTLE:**

I. Sources.—For discussion of the historical value of the Acts of the Apostles see the art. on that subject. It is only necessary to say here that the view of Sir W. M. Ramsay in general is accepted as to the trustworthiness of Luke, whose authorship of the Acts is accepted and proved by Harnack (*Die Apostelgeschichte*, 1908; *The Acts of the Apostles*, tr by Wilkinson, 1909; *Neue Untersuch. zur Ap.*, 1911; *The Date of the Acts and of the Synoptic Gospels*, tr by Wilkinson, 1911). The proof need not be given again. The same hand appears in the "we"-sections and the rest of the book. Even Moffatt (*Intro to the Lit. of the NT*, 311) admits the Lukan authorship though dating it in 100 AD instead of 60–62 AD, against Harnack. The Acts is written independently of the Epp. of Paul, whether early or late, and supplements in a wonderful way the incidental references in the epp., though not without lacunae and difficulties.

1. The Acts

(1) *Pauline authorship.*—See the articles on each ep. for detailed criticism. It is here assumed that the Ep. to the He was not written by Paul, though Pauline in point of view. One cannot stop to prove every statement in an article like this, else a large book would be needed. Criticism is not an infallible science. One can turn easily from the Hatch-Van Manen art. on "Paul" in *EB* (1902) to the Maclean art. on "Paul the Apostle" in the 1-vol *HDB* (1909). Van Manen's part of the one denies all the thirteen, while Maclean says: "We shall, in what follows, without hesitation use the thirteen epp. as genuine." It is certain that Paul wrote more epp., or "letters," as Deissmann (*Light from the Ancient East*, 225) insists on calling all of Paul's epp. Certainly Philem is a mere "letter," but it is difficult to say as much about Rom. Deissmann (*St. Paul*, 22) admits that portions of Rom are like "an epistolary letter." At any rate, when Moffatt (*Intro to the Lit. of the NT*, 64–82) carefully justifies the Pauline authorship of both 1 and 2 Thess, it is clear that the case against them cannot be very strong, esp. as Moffatt stands out against the genuineness of Eph (op. cit., 393) and the Pastoral Epp. (p. 414).

2. The Thirteen Epistles

Bartlet, who was once at a loss to know what to do with the Pastorals on the theory that Paul was not released from the Rom imprisonment (*Apostolic Age*, 1899, 200), is now quite willing to face the new facts set forth by Ramsay (*Expos*, VII, viii–ix, VIII, i), even if it means the admission of a second Rom imprisonment, a view that Bartlet had opposed. He now pleads for "the fresh approach from the side of experience, by men who are in touch with the realities of human nature in all its variety, as well as at home in the historical background of society in the early Rom empire, that has renovated the study of them and taken it out of the old ruts of criticism in which it ha_ _noved for the most part in modern times" (*Expos*, January, 1913, 29). Here Bartlet, again, now eloquently presents the view of common-sense criticism as seen by the practical missionary better than by a life "spent amid the academic associations of a professor's chair," though he pauses to note as an exception Professor P. Gardner's *The Religious Experience of St. Paul* (1912). We may quote Bartlet once more (*Expos*, January, 1913, 30): "In the recovery of a true point of view a vital element has been the newer conception of Paul himself and so of Paulinism. Paul the doctrinaire theologian, or at least the prophet of a one-sided gospel repeated with fanatical uniformity of emphasis under all conditions, has largely given place to Paul the *missionary*, full indeed of inspired insight on the basis of a unique experience, but also of practical instinct, the offspring of sympathy with living men of other types of training. When the Pastorals are viewed anew in the light of this idea, half their difficulties disappear." One need not adopt Deissmann's rather artificial insistence on "letters" rather than "epistles," and his undue depreciation of Paul's intellectual caliber and culture as being more like Amos than Origen (*St. Paul*, 1912, 6), in order to see the force of this contention foı proper understanding of the social environment of Paul. Against Van Manen's "historical Paul" who wrote nothing, he places "the historic Paul" who possibly wrote all thirteen. "There is really no trouble except with the letters to Timothy and Titus, and even there the difficulties are perhaps not quite so great as many of our specialists assume" (*St. Paul*, 15). See Pastoral Epistles. Deissmann denies sharply that Paul was an "obscurantist" who corrupted the gospel of Jesus, "the dregs of doctrinaire study of St. Paul, mostly in the tired brains of gifted amateurs" (p. 4). But A. Schweitzer boldly proclaims that he alone has the key to Paul and Jesus. It is the "exclusively Jewish eschatological" (*Paul and His Interpreters*, 1912, ix) conception of Christ's gospel that furnishes Schweitzer's spring-board (*The Quest of the Historical Jesus*). Thus he will be able to explain "the Hellenization of the gospel" as mediated through Paul. To do that Schweitzer plows his weary way from Grotius to Holtzmann, and finds that they have all wandered into the wilderness. He is positive that his eschatological discovery will rescue Paul and some of his epp. from the ruin wrought by Steck and Van Manen, to whose arguments modern criticism has nothing solid to offer, and the meager negative crumbs offered by Schweitzer ought to be thankfully received (ib, 249).

(2) *Lightfoot's grouping* (cf *Bib. Essays*, 224).—There is doubt as to the position of Gal. Some advocates of the South-Galatian theory make it the very earliest of Paul's Epp., even before the Jerus Conference in Acts **15**. So Emmet, *Comm. on Gal* (1912), ix, who notes (Preface) that his comm. is the first to take this position. But the North-Galatian view still has the weight of authority in spite of Ramsay's powerful advocacy in his various books (see *Hist. Comm. on Gal*), as is shown by Moffatt, *Intro to the Lit. of the NT*, 90 ff. Hence Lightfoot's grouping is still the best to use.

(*a*) First Group: 1 and 2 Thess, from Corinth, 52–53 AD. Harnack's view that 2 Thess is addressed to a Jewish Christian church in Thessalonica while 1 Thess is addressed to a gentile church is accepted by Lake (*Earlier Epp. of St. Paul*, 1911, 83 ff), but Frame (*ICC*, 1912, 54) sees no need for this hypothesis. Milligan is clear that 1 Thess precedes 2 Thess (*Comm.*, 1908, xxxix) and is the earliest of Paul's Epp. (p. xxxvi). The accent on eschatology is in accord with the position of the early disciples in the opening chapters of Acts. They belong to Paul's stay in Corinth recorded in Acts **18**.

(*b*) Second Group: 1 Cor, 2 Cor, Gal, Rom, 55–58 AD. This is the great doctrinal group, the four chief epp. of Baur. They turn about the Judaizing controversy which furnishes the occasion for the expansion of the doctrine of justification by faith in opposition to the legalistic contention of the Judaizing Christians from Jerus (Acts **15** 1–3; Gal **2** 1–10). The dates of these epp. are not perfectly clear. 1 Cor was written shortly before the close of Paul's 3 years' stay at Ephesus (Acts **20** 31; 1 Cor **16** 8; Acts **20** 1 f). 2 Cor was written a few months later while he was in Macedonia (**2** 13; **7** 5.13; **8** 16–24). Rom was written from Corinth (**16** 23; Acts **20** 2 f) and sent by Phoebe of Cenchreae (Rom **16** 1). The integrity of Rom is challenged by some who deny in particular that ch **16** belongs to the ep. Moffatt (*Intro*, 134–38) gives an able, but unconvincing, presentation of the arguments for the addition of the chapter by a later hand. Deissmann (*St. Paul*, 19) calls Rom **16** "a little letter" addressed to the Christians at Ephesus. Von Soden (*Hist of Early Christian Lit.*, 78) easily justifies the presence of Rom **16** in the Ep. to the Rom: "These greetings, moreover, were certainly intended by St. Paul to create bonds of fellowship between the Pauline Christians and the Rom community, and to show that he had not written to them quite exclusively in his own name." A common-sense explanation of Paul's personal ties in Rome is the fact that as the center of the world's life the city drew people thither from all parts of the earth. So today many a man has friends in New York or London who has never been to either city. A much more serious controversy rages as to the integrity of 2 Cor. Semler took 2 Cor **10–13** to be a separate and later ep., because of its difference in tone from 2 Cor **1–9**, but Hausrath put it earlier than chs **1–9**, and made it the letter referred to in **2** 4. He has been followed by many scholars like Schmiedel, Cone, McGiffert, Bacon, Moffatt, Kennedy, Rendall, Peake, Plummer. Von Soden (*Hist of Early Christian Lit.*, 50) accepts the partition-theory of 2 Cor heartily: "It may be shown with the highest degree of probability that this letter has come down to us in 2 Cor **10** 1—**13** 10." But the unity of the ep. on the theory that the change in tone is a climax to the disobedient element of the church is still maintained with force and justice by Klopper, Zahn, Bachmann, Denney, Bernard, A. Robertson, Weiss, Menzies. The place of the writing of Gal turns on its date. Lightfoot (in loc.) argues for Corinth, since it was probably written shortly before Rom. But Moffatt (*Intro*, 102) holds tentatively to Ephesus, soon after Paul's arrival there from Galatia. So he gives the order: Gal, 1 and 2 Cor, Rom. In so much doubt it is well to follow Lightfoot's logical argument. Gal leads naturally to Rom, the one hot and passionate, the other calm and contemplative, but both on the same general theme.

(*c*) Third group: Phil, Philem, Col, Eph. Date 61–63, unless Paul reached Rome several years earlier. This matter depends on the date of the coming of Festus to succeed Felix (Acts **24** 27). It was once thought to be 60 AD beyond any doubt, but the whole matter is now uncertain. See "Chronology," III, 2, (2), below. At any rate these four epp. were written during the first Rom imprisonment, assuming that he was set free.

But it must be noted that quite a respectable group of scholars hold that one or all of these epp. were written from Caesarea (Schultz, Thiersch, Meyer, Hausrath, Sabatier, Reuss, Weiss, Haupt, Spitta, McPherson, Hicks). But the arguments are more specious than convincing. See Hort, *Rom and Eph*, 101–10. There is a growing opinion that Philem, Col and Eph were written from Ephesus during a possible imprisonment in Paul's stay of 3 years there. So Deissmann (*Light from the Ancient East*, 229; *St. Paul*, 16); St. Lisco (*Vincula Sanctorum*, 1900); M. Albertz (*Theol. Studien und Kritiken*, 1910, 551 ff); B. W. Bacon (*Journal of Bib. Lit.*, 1910, 181 ff). The strongest argument for this position is that Paul apparently did not know personally the readers of Eph (**1** 15); cf also Col **1** 4. But this objection need not apply if the so-called Ephesian Ep. was a circular letter and if Paul did not visit Colossae and Laodicea during his 3 years at Ephesus. The theory is more attractive at first than on reflection. It throws this group before Rom—a difficult view to concede.

But even so, the order of these epp. is by no means certain. It is clear that Philem, Col and Eph were sent together. Tychicus was the bearer of Col (**4** 7 f) and Eph (**6** 21 f). Onesimus bore Philem (vs 10.13) and was also the companion of Tychicus to Colossae (Col **4** 9). So these three epp. went together from Rome. It is commonly assumed that Phil was the last of the group of four, and hence later than the other three, because Paul is balancing life and death (Phil **1** 21 ff) and is expecting to be set free (**1** 25), but he has the same expectation of freedom when he writes Philem (ver 22). The absence of Luke (Phil **2** 20) has to be explained on either hypothesis. Moffatt (*Intro*, 159) is dogmatic, "as Phil was certainly the last letter that he wrote," ruling out of court Eph, not to say the later Pastoral Epp. But this conclusion gives Moffatt trouble with the Ep. to the Laodiceans (Col **4** 16) which he can only call "the enigmatic reference" and cannot follow Rutherford (*St. Paul's Epp. to Colossae and Laodicea*, 1908) in identifying the Laodicean Ep. with Eph, as indeed Marcion seems to have done. But the notion that Eph was a circular letter designed for more than one church (hence without personalities) still holds the bulk of modern opinion.

Von Soden (*Hist of Early Christian Lit.*, 294) is as dogmatic as Wrede or Van Manen: "All which has hitherto been said concerning this ep., its form, its content, its ideas, its presuppositions, absolutely excludes the possibility of a Pauline authorship." He admits "verbal echoes of Pauline epp."

Lightfoot puts Phil before the other three because of its doctrinal affinity with the second group in ch **3** as a reminiscence, and because of its anticipation of the Christological controversy with incipient Gnosticism in ch **2**. This great discussion is central in Col and Eph. At any rate, we have thus a consistent and coherent interpretation of the group. Philem, though purely personal, is wondrously vital as a sociological document. Paul is in this group at the height of his powers in his grasp of the Person of Christ.

(*d*) Fourth group: 1 Tim, Tit, 2 Tim. The Pastoral Epp. are still hotly disputed, but there is a growing willingness in Britain and Germany to make a place for them in Paul's life. Von Soden bluntly says: "It is impossible that these epp. as they stand can have been written by St. Paul" (*Hist of Early Christian Lit.*, 310). He finds no room for the heresy here combated, or for the details in Paul's life, or for the linguistic peculiarities in Paul's style. But he sees a "literary nicety"—this group that binds them together and separates them from Paul. Thus tersely he puts the case against the Pauline authorship. So Moffatt argues for the "sub-Pauline environment" and "sub-Pauline atmosphere" of these epp. with the advanced ecclesiasticism (*Intro to the Lit. of the NT*, 410 ff). Wrede thrusts aside the personal details and argues that the epp. give merely the tendency of early Christianity (*Ueber Aufgabe und Methode der Sogen. NT Theologie*, 1897, 357). The Hatch-Van Manen art. in *EB* admits only that "the Pastoral Epp. occupy themselves chiefly with the various affairs of the churches within 'Pauline circles.'"

Moffatt has a vigorous attack on these letters in *EB*, but he "almost entirely ignores the external evidence, while he has nothing to say to the remarkable internal evidence which immediately demands our attention" (Knowling, *Testimony of St. Paul to Christ*, 3d ed, 1911, 129). Moffatt (*Intro to the Lit. of the NT*, 414) holds that the Pastoral Epp. came from one pen, but the personality and motives are very vague to him. The personal details in 2 Tim **1** 14–18; **4** 9–22 are not on a par with those in *The Acts of Paul and Thekla* in the 2d cent. Many critics who reject the Pauline authorship of the Pastoral Epp. admit the personal details in 2 Tim, but it is just in such matters that forgeries are recognizable. To admit these fragments is logically to admit the whole (Maclean in 1-vol *HDB*), as Moffatt sees (*Intro*, 414), however much he seeks to tone down the use of Paul's name as "a Christian form of *suasoriae*," and "a further and inoffensive development of the principle which sought to claim apostolic sanction for the expanding institutions and doctrines of the early church" (ib, 415). The objection against these epp. from differences in diction has been grievously overdone. As a matter of fact, each of the four groups has words peculiar to it, and naturally so. Style is a function of the subject as well as a mark of the man. Besides, style changes with one's growth. It would have been remarkable if all four groups had shown no change in vocabulary and style. The case of Shakespeare is quite pertinent, for the various groups of plays stand more or less apart. The Pastoral Epp. belong to Paul's old age and deal with personal and ecclesiastical matters in a more or less reminiscential way, with less of vehement energy than we get in the earlier epp., but this situation is what one would reasonably expect. The "ecclesiastical organization" argument has been greatly overdone. As a matter of fact, "the organization in the Pastoral Epp. is not apparently advanced one step beyond that of the church in Philippi in 61 AD" (Ramsay, *Expos*, VII, viii, 17). The "gnosis" met by these epp. (1 Tim **6** 20; Tit **1** 14) is not the highly developed type seen in the Ignatian Epp. of the 2d cent. Indeed, Bartlet ("Historic Setting of the Pastoral Epp.," *Expos*, January, 1913, 29) pointedly says that, as a result of Hort's "Judaistic Christianity" and "Christian Ecclesia" and Ramsay's "Historical Comm. on the Epp. of Timothy" (*Expos*, VII, vii, ix, VIII, i), "one feels the subject has been lifted to a new level of reality and that much criticism between Baur and Jülicher is out of date and irrelevant." It is now shown that the Pastoral Epp. are not directed against Gnosticism of advanced type, but even of a more Jewish type (Tit **1** 14) than that in Col. Ramsay (*Expos*, VIII, i, 263) sweeps this stock criticism aside as "from the wrong point of view." It falls to the ground. Lightfoot ("Note on the Heresy Combated in the Pastoral Epp.," *Bib. Essays*, 413) had insisted on the *Jewish* character of the Gnosticism attacked here. As a matter of fact, the main objection to these epp. is that they do not fit into the story in Acts, which breaks off abruptly with Paul in Rome. But it is a false premise to assume that the Pastoral Epp. have to fit into the events in Acts. Harnack turns the objection that Paul in Acts **20** 26 predicted that he would never see the Ephesian elders again into a strong argument for the date of Luke's Gospel before 2 Tim **4** 21 (*The Date of Acts and Synoptic Gospels*, 103). Indeed, he may not have revisited Ephesus after all, but may have seen Timothy at Miletus also (1 Tim **1** 3). Harnack frankly admits the acquittal and release of Paul and thus free play for the Pastoral Epp. Blass (*Acta Apostolorum*, 24) acknowledges the Pastoral Epp. as genuine. So also Findlay, art. "Paul," in *HDB*; Maclean in 1-vol *HDB*; Denney in *Standard BD*. Sanday (*Inspiration*, 364) comments on the strength of the external evidence for the Pastoral Epp. Even Holtzmann (*Einl*[3], 291) appears to admit echoes of the Pastoral Epp. in the Ignatian Epp. Lightfoot (*Bib. Essays*, "Date of the Pastoral Epp.," 399–437) justifies completely the acceptance of the Pauline authorship. Deissmann (*St. Paul*, 15) has a needed word: "The delusion is still current in certain circles that the scientific distinction of a Bible scholar may be estimated in the form of a percentage according to the proportion of his verdicts of spuriousness. . . . . The extant letters of St. Paul have been innocently obliged to endure again a fair share of the martyrdom suffered by the historic St. Paul." See further PASTORAL EPISTLES.

(3) *Paul's conception of his Epp.*—Assuming, therefore, the Pauline authorship of the thirteen epp., we may note that they reveal in a remarkable way the growth in Paul's apprehension of Christ and Christianity, his adaptation to varied situations. his grasp of world-problems and the eternal values of life. Paul wrote other epp., as we know. In 1 Cor **5** 9 there is a clear reference to a letter not now known to us otherwise, earlier than 1 Cor. The use of "every epistle" in 2 Thess **3** 17 naturally implies that Paul had written more than two already. It is not certain to what letter Paul refers in 2 Cor **2** 4—most probably to one between 1 and 2 Cor, though, as already shown, some scholars find that letter in 2 Cor **10–13**. Once more Paul (Col **4** 16) mentions an ep. addressed to the church at Laodicea. This ep. is almost certainly that which we know as Eph. If not, here is another lost ep. Indeed, at least two apocryphal Epp. to the Laodiceans were written to supply this deficiency. As early as 2 Thess **2** 2 forgers were at work to palm off epp. in Paul's name, "or by ep. as from us," to attack and pervert Paul's real views, whom Paul denounces. It was entirely possible that this "nefarious work" would be continued (Gregory, *Canon and Text of the NT*, 1907, 191), though, as Gregory argues, Paul's exposure here would have a tendency to put a stop to it and to put Christians on their guard and to watch for Paul's signature to the epp. as a mark of genuineness (2 Thess **3** 17; 1 Cor **16** 21; Gal **6** 11; Col **4** 18). This was all the more important since Paul evidently dictated his letters to amanuenses, as to Tertius in the case of Rom (**16** 22). In the case of Philem (ver 19), Paul probably wrote the whole letter. We may be sure therefore that, if we had the other genuine letters of Paul, they would occupy the same general standpoint as the thirteen now in our possession. The point to note here is that the four groups of Paul's Epp. fit into the historical background of the Acts as recorded by Luke, barring the fourth group which is later than the events in Acts. Each group meets a specific situation in a definite region or regions, with problems of vital interest. Paul attacks these various problems (theological, ecclesiastical, practical) with marvelous vigor, and applies the eternal principles of the gospel of Christ in such fashion as to furnish a norm for future workers for Christ. It is not necessary to say that he was conscious of that use. Deissmann (*St. Paul*, 12 f) is confident on this point: "That a portion of these confidential letters should be still extant after centuries, St. Paul cannot have intended, nor did it ever occur to him that they would be." Be that as it may, and granted that Paul's Epp. are "survivals, in the sense of the technical language employed by the historical method" (ib, 12), still we must not forget that Paul attached a great deal of importance to his letters and urged obedience to the teachings which they contained: "I adjure you by the Lord that this ep. be read unto all the brethren" (1 Thess **5** 27). This command we find in the very first one preserved to us. Once more note 2 Thess **3** 14: "And if any man obeyeth not our word by this ep., note that man, that ye have no company with him." Evidently therefore Paul does not conceive his epp. as mere incidents in personal correspondence, but authoritative instructions for the Christians to whom they are addressed. In 1 Cor **7** 17, "And so ordain I in all the churches," he puts his epistolary commands on a par with the words of Jesus quoted in the same chapter. Some indeed at Corinth (2 Cor **10** 9 f) took his "letters" as an effort to "terrify" them, a thing that he was afraid to do in person. Paul (ver 11) does not deny the authority of his letters, but claims equal courage when he comes in person (cf 2 Cor **13** 2.10). That Paul expected his letters to be used by more than the one church to which they were addressed is clear from Col **4** 16: "And when this ep. hath been read among you, cause that it be read also in the church of the Laodiceans; and that ye also read the ep. from Laodicea." If the letter to Laodicea is our Eph and a sort of circular letter (cf Gal), that is clear. But it must be noted that Col, undoubtedly a specific letter to Colossae, is likewise to be passed on to Laodicea. It is not always observed that in 1 Cor **1** 2, though the ep. is addressed "unto the church of God which is at Corinth," Paul adds, "with all that call upon the name of our Lord Jesus Christ in every place, their Lord and ours." Philem is, of course, a personal letter, though it deals with a sociological problem of universal interest. The Pastoral Epp. are addressed to two young ministers and have many personal details, as is natural, but the epp. deal far more with the social aspects of church life and the heresies and vices that were threatening the very existence of Christianity in the Rom empire. Paul is eager that Timothy shall follow his teaching (2 Tim **3** 10 ff), and "the same commit thou to faithful men, who shall be able to teach others also" (**2** 2). It is this larger view of the future of Christianity that concerns Paul very keenly. The very conception of his ministry to the Gentiles (Rom **15** 16; Eph **3** 7 ff) led Paul to feel that he had a right to speak to all, "both to Greeks and to Barbarians" (Rom **1** 14), and hence even to Rome (**1** 15 f). It is a mis-

take to limit Paul's Epp. to the local and temporary sphere given them by Deissmann.

(4) *Development in Paul's Epp.*—For Paul's gospel or theology see later. Here we must stress the fact that all four groups of Paul's Epp. are legitimate developments from his fundamental experience of grace as conditioned by his previous training and later work. He met each new problem with the same basal truth that Jesus is the Messiah, the Son of God, revealed to Paul on the way to Damascus. The reality of this great experience must here be assumed (see discussion later). It may be admitted that the Acts does not stand upon the same plane as the Pauline Epp. as a witness concerning Paul's conversion (Fletcher, *The Conversion of St. Paul*, 1910, 5). But even so, the Epp. amply confirm Luke's report of the essential fact that Jesus appeared to Paul in the same sense that He did to the apostles and 500 Christians (1 Cor **15** 4–9). The revelation of Christ to Paul and in Paul (ἐν ἐμοί, *en emoi*, Gal **1** 16) and the specific call connected therewith to preach to the Gentiles gave Paul a place independent of and on a par with the other apostles (**1** 16 f; **2** 1–10). Paul's first preaching (Acts **9** 20) "proclaimed Jesus, that he is the Son of God." This "primitive Paulinism" (Sabatier, *The Apostle Paul*, 1893, 113) lay at the heart of Paul's message in his sermons and speeches in Acts. Professor P. Gardner regards Luke as a "careless" historian ("The Speeches of St. Paul in Acts," *Cambridge Bib. Essays*, 1909, 386), but he quite admits the central place of Paul's conversion, both in the Acts and the Epp. (ib; cf also *The Religious Experience of St. Paul*).

We cannot here trace in detail the growth of Paulinism. Let Wernle speak (*Beginnings of Christianity*, 1903, I, 224) for us: "The decisive factor in the genius of St. Paul's theology was his personal experience, his conversion on the road to Damascus." This fact reappears in each of the groups of the Epp. It is the necessary implication in the apostolic authority claimed in 1 Thess **2** 4–6; 2 Thess **2** 15; **3** 6.14. "We might have claimed authority as apostles of Christ" (1 Thess **2** 6). For the second group we need only refer to 1 Cor **9** 1 f and **15** 1–11, where Paul justifies his gospel by the fact of having seen the risen Jesus. His self-depreciation in ver 9 is amply balanced by the claims in ver 10. See also 2 Cor **10–13** and Gal **1** and **2** for Paul's formal defence of his apostolic authority. The pleasantry in Rom **15** 14 does not displace the claim in **15** 16.23 f. In the third group note the great passage in Phil **3** 12–14, where Paul pointedly alludes to his conversion: "I was laid hold of by Jesus Christ," as giving him the goal of his ambition, "that I may lay hold"; "I count not myself yet to have laid hold." This concentration of effort to come up to Christ's purpose in him is the key to Paul's life and letters, "I press on toward the goal." So the golden cord reappears in Eph **3** 2–13: "How that by revelation was made known unto me the mystery, as I wrote before in few words, whereby, when ye read, ye can perceive my understanding in the mystery of Christ." In the fourth group he still recalls how Christ Jesus took pity on him, the blasphemer, the persecutor, the chief of sinners, and put him into the ministry, "that in me as chief might Jesus Christ show forth all his longsuffering, for an ensample of them that should thereafter believe on him unto eternal life" (1 Tim **1** 16). He kept up the fight to the end (2 Tim **4** 6 f), for the Lord Jesus stood by him (**4** 17), as on the road to Damascus. So the personal note of experience links all the epp. together. They reveal Paul's growing conception of Christ. Paul at the very start perceived that men are redeemed by faith in Jesus as the Saviour from sin through His atoning death, not by works of the Law (Acts **13** 38 f). In the first group there are allusions to the "work of faith and labor of love and patience of hope in our Lord Jesus Christ" (1 Thess **1** 3). He speaks of "election" (**1** 4) and "our gospel" (**1** 5) and the resurrection of Jesus (**1** 10). The Father, Son and Spirit coöperate in the work of salvation (2 Thess **2** 13 f), which includes election, belief, sanctification, glorification. It is not necessary to press the argument for the conception of salvation by faith in Christ, grace as opposed to works, in the second group. It is obviously present in the third and the fourth. We seem forced to the view therefore that Paul's experience was revolutionary, not evolutionary. "If we consider the whole history of Paul as it is disclosed to us in his letters, are we not forced to the conclusion that his was a catastrophic or explosive, rather than a slowly progressive personality?" (Garvie, *Studies of Paul and His Gospel*, 1911, 32). "His gospel was included in his conversion, and it was meditation that made explicit what was thus implicit in his experience" (ib). This is not to say that there was no "spiritual development of St. Paul" (Matheson, 1890). There was, and of the richest kind, but it was a growth of expression in the successive application of the fundamental Christian conception. The accent upon this or that phase of truth at different stages in Paul's career does not necessarily mean that the truth is a new one to him. It may simply be that the occasion has arisen for emphasis and elaboration.

In a broad generalization the first group of the epp. is eschatological, the second soteriological, the third Christological, and the fourth pastoral (Garvie, *Studies of Paul and His Gospel*, 22). But one must not get the notion that Paul did not have a full gospel of salvation in the first group, and did not come to the true motive of the person of Christ as Lord till the second, or understand the pastoral office till the fourth. See emphasis on Paul's work as pastor and preacher in 1 Thess **2** (first group), and the Lordship of Christ also (1 Thess **1** 1.3; 2 Thess **1** 1; **2** 13 f), on a par with the Father.

There was a change of accent in each group on questions of eschatology, but in each one Paul cherishes the hope of the second coming of Christ up to the very end when he speaks of his own death (2 Tim **4** 8.18). Paul has a whole gospel of grace in all his epp., but he presses home the special phase of truth needed at the moment, always with proper balance and modification, though not in the form of a system of doctrine. In the first group he relieves the minds of the Thessalonian Christians from the misapprehension into which they had fallen concerning his position on the immediate coming of Christ. In the second group Paul vindicates the gospel of grace from the legalistic addition of the Judaizers who sought to rob the Gentiles of their freedom by insisting that they become Jews as well as Christians. This ringing battle is echoed in Acts **15** and is the mightiest conflict of Paul's career. We hear echoes of it in Phil **3**, but he had won his contention. In the third group the battle with error has shifted to the province of Asia, esp. the Lycus Valley, where a mystic mixture of Judaism (Essenism) and heathen mystery-religions and philosophies (incipient Gnosticism) was so rife in the 2d cent. (the various forms of Gnosticism which combined with some aspects of Christianity). It is possible also that Mithraism was already a foe of Christianity. The central position and essential deity of Jesus Christ was challenged by these new and world-old heresies, and Paul attacks them with marvelous skill in Col and Eph and works out in detail his teaching concerning the person of Christ with due emphasis on the soteriological aspects of Christ's work and on Christian life. Bruce (*St. Paul's Conception of Christianity*) conceives that Paul gives us his entire conception of Christianity in the four great epp. of the second group, while B. Weiss (*Bib. Theol. of the NT*) sees a more developed doctrine in the third group. He is in his prime in both groups. In the fourth group the same struggle lingers on with variations in Crete and even in Ephesus. The Jewish phase of the heresy is more decided (perhaps Pharisaic), and recalls to some extent the Judaistic controversy in the second group. Paul is older and faces the end, and Christianity has enemies within and without. He turns to young ministers as the hope of the future in the propagation of the gospel of the happy God. The fires have burned lower, and there is less passion and heat. The tone is now fierce, now tender. The style is broken and reminiscent and personal, though not with the rush of torrential emotion in 2 Cor, nor the power of logic in Gal and Rom. Each ep. fits into its niche in the group. Each group falls into proper relation to the stage in Paul's life and justly reveals the changes of thought and feeling in the great apostle. It is essential that one study Paul's Epp. in their actual historical order if one wishes to understand the mind of Paul. Scholars are not agreed, to be sure on this point. They are not agreed on anything, for that matter. See two methods of presenting Paul's Epp. in Robertson, *Chronological NT* (1904), and Moffatt, *Historical NT* (1901).

II. Modern Theories about Paul.—Findlay (*HDB*, "Paul") utters a needed warning when he reminds us that the modern historical and psychological method of study is just as liable to prepossession and prejudice as the older categories of scholastic and dogmatic theology.

1. Criticism Not Infallible

"The focus of the picture may be displaced and its colors falsified by philosophical no less than by ecclesiastical spectacles" (ib). Deissmann (*St. Paul*, 4 f) sympathizes with this protest against the infallibility of modern subjective criticism: "That really and properly is the task of the modern student of St. Paul: to come back from the paper St. Paul of our western libraries, Germanized, dogmatised, modernized, to the historic St. Paul; to penetrate through the 'Paulinism' of our NT theologies to the St. Paul of ancient reality." He admits the thoroughness and the magnitude of the work accomplished in the 19th cent. concerning the literary questions connected with Paul's letters, but it is a "doctrinaire interest" that "has gone farther and farther astray." Deissmann conceives of Paul as a "hero of piety first and foremost," not as a theologian. "As a religious genius St. Paul's outlook is forward into a future of universal history." In this position of Deissmann we see a return to the pre-Baur time. Deissmann would like to get past all the schools of criticism, back to Paul himself.

2. The Tübingen Theory

Baur started the modern critical attitude by his *Pastoralbriefe* (1835, p. 79), in which he remarked that there were only four epp. of Paul (Gal 1 and 2 Cor, Rom) which could be accepted as genuine. In his *Paulus* (1845) he expounded this thesis. He also rejected the Acts. From the four great epp. and from the pseudo-Clementine literature of the 2d cent., Baur argued that Paul and Peter were bitter antagonists. Peter and the other apostles were held fast in the grip of the legalistic conception of Christianity, a sort of Christianized Pharisaism. Paul, when converted, had reacted violently against this view, and became the exponent of gentile freedom. Christianity was divided into two factions, Jewish Christians (Petrinists) and gentile Christians (Paulinists). With this "key" Baur ruled out the other Pauline epp. and Acts as spurious, because they did not show the bitterness of this controversy. He called them "tendency" writings, designed to cover up the strife and to show that peace reigned in the camp. This arbitrary theory cut a wide swath for 50 years, and became a fetich with many scholars, but it is now dead. "It has been seen that it is bad criticism to make a theory on insecure grounds, and then to reject all the literature which contradicts it" (Maclean in 1-vol *HDB*). Ramsay (*The First Christian Cent.*, 1911, 195) contends that the perpetuation of the Baur standpoint in Moffatt's *Intro to the Lit. of the NT* is an anachronism: "We are no longer in the 19th cent. with its negations, but in the 20th cent. with its growing power of insight and the power of belief that springs therefrom." Van Manen (*EB*) calls the Baur view that of the "old guard" of liberal theology in Germany, Switzerland, France, Holland, and, to some extent, in Britain.

3. Protest against Baur's View

But even in Germany the older conservative view of Paul has always had champions. The most consistent of the recent opponents of Baur's views in Germany is Th. Zahn (cf his *Einl in das NT*, 2 vols, 1897–99; *Intro to the NT*, 3 vols, 1910). In Britain the true successor of Lightfoot as the chief antagonist of the Tübingen School is Sir W. M. Ramsay, whose numerous volumes (*Church in the Rom Empire*, 1893; *Cities and Bishoprics of Phrygia*, 1895; *St. Paul the Traveller*, 1896; *Pauline and Other Studies*, 1906; *Cities of St. Paul*, 1908; *Luke the Physician and Other Studies*, 1908; *Pictures of the Apostolic Church*, 1910; *The First Christian Century*, 1911) have given the finishing touches to the overthrow of Baur's contention.

4. Successors to Baur

But even so, already the Baur school had split into two parts. The ablest representatives, like H. J. Holtzmann, Pfleiderer, Harnack, Jülicher, Lipsius, von Soden, were compelled to admit more of Paul's Epp. as genuine than the four principal ones, till there are left practically none to fight over but Eph and the Pastoral Epp. This progress eliminated completely Baur's thesis and approached very nearly to the position of Lightfoot, Ramsay and Zahn. Von Soden (*Early Christian Lit.*, 324) still stands out against 2 Thess, but Harnack has deserted him on that point. But the old narrow view of Baur is gone, and von Soden is eloquent in his enthusiasm for Paul (ib, 119): "As we gaze upon the great literary memorials of the Greeks we may well question whether these Pauline letters are not equal to them—indeed, do not surpass them—in spiritual significance, in psychological depths and loftiness of ideal, above all in the art of complete and forcible expression." The other wing of Baur's school Findlay (*HDB*) calls "ultra-Baurians." It is mainly a Dutch school with Loman and Van Manen as its main exponents, though it has support in Germany from Steck and Völter, and in America from W. B. Smith. These writers do not say that Paul is a myth, but that our sources (Acts and the 13 epp.) are all legendary. It is a relentless carrying of Baur's thesis to a *reductio ad absurdum*. Van Manen (*EB*) says of "the historical Paul" as distinct from "the legendary Paul": "It does not appear that Paul's ideas differed widely from those of the other disciples, or that he had emancipated himself from Judaism or had outgrown the law more than they." When one has disposed of all the evidence he is entirely free to reconstruct the pictures to suit himself. Quite arbitrarily, Van Manen accepts the "we"-sections in Acts as authoritative. But these give glimpses of the *historical* Jesus quite as truly as the Pauline Epp., and should therefore be rejected by advocates of the mythical Jesus. So the pendulum swings back and forth. One school destroys the other, but the fact of Paul's personality remains. "The new start is one of such importance that we must distinguish the pre-Pauline from the post-Pauline Christianity, or, what amounts to the same thing, the Palestinian sect and the world-religion" (Wernle, *Beginnings of Christianity*, I, 159).

5. Appeal to Comparative Religion

In his *Paulus* (1904), Wrede finds the explanation of Paul's theology in late Jewish apocalyptic views and in the oriental mystery-religions. Bousset (*Die Religion des Judenthums im NT Zeitalter*, 1903) seeks to find in the "late Jewish apocalyptic" "conceptions from the Bab and the Irano-Zarathustrian religions" (Schweitzer, *Paul and His Interpreters*, 173). According to Wrede's view, Paul is one of the creators of "Christ" as distinct from the Jesus of history (cf "Jesus or Christ," *HJ*, suppl., January, 1909). "Wrede's object is to overthrow the view predominant in modern theology, that Paul loyally and consistently expounded and developed the theology of Jesus" (J. Weiss, *Paul and Jesus*, 1909, 2). J. Weiss in this book makes a careful reply to Wrede as others have done; cf A. Meyer, *Jesus or Paul* (1909), who concludes (p. 134) dramatically: "Paul—just one who points the way to Jesus and to God!" See also Jülicher, *Paulus und Jesus* (1907); Kaftan, *Jesus und Paulus* (1906); Kölbing, *Die geistige Einwirkung der Person Jesu und Paulus* (1906). The best reply to Wrede's arguments about the mystery-religion is found in articles in the *Expos* for 1912–13 (now in book form) by H. A. A. Kennedy on "St. Paul and the Mystery-Religions." The position of Wrede is carried to its logical conclusion by Drews (*Die Christus-Mythe*, 1909), who makes Paul the creator of Christianity. W. B. Smith (*Der vorchristliche Jesus*, 1906) tries to show that "Jesus" was a pre-Christian myth or god. Schweitzer (*Paul and His Interpreters*, 235) sums the matter up thus: "Drews's thesis is not merely a curiosity; it indicates the natural limit at which the hypothesis advanced by the advocates of comparative religion, when left to its own momentum, finally comes to rest."

6. The Eschatological Interpretation

Schweitzer himself may be accepted as the best exponent of the rigid application of this view to Paul (*Paul and His Interpreters*, 1912) that he had made to Jesus (*The Quest of the Historical Jesus*, 1910). He glories in the ability to answer the absurdities of Steck, Loman and Van Manen and Drews by showing that the eschatological conceptions of Paul in his epp. are primitive, not late, and belong to the 1st cent., not to the 2d (*Paul and His Interpreters*, 249). He thus claims to be the true pupil of Baur, though reaching conclusions utterly different. There is undoubtedly an element of truth in this contention of Schweitzer, but he loses his case, when he insists that nothing but eschatology must be allowed to figure. "The edifice constructed by Baur has fallen," he proclaims (p. viii), but he demands that in its place we allow the "exclusively Jewish-eschatological" (p. ix) interpretation. There he slips, and his theory will go the way of that of Baur. C. Anderson Scott ("Jesus and Paul," *Cambridge Bib. Essays*, 365) admits that Paul has the same eschatological outlook as Jesus, but also the same ethical interest. It is not "either . . . . or," but both in each case. See a complete bibliography of the "Jesus and Paul" controversy in J. G. Machens' paper on "Jesus and Paul" in *Bib. and Theol. Studies* (1912, 547 f). As Ramsay insists, we are now in the 20th cent. of insight and sanity, and Paul has come to his own. Even Wernle (*Beginnings of Christianity*, I, 163) sees that Paul is not the creator of the facts: "He merely transmits historical facts. God—Christ—Paul, such is the order." Saintsbury (*History of Criticism*, 152) says: "It has been the mission of the 19th cent. to prove that everybody's work was written by somebody else, and it will not be the most useless task of the 20th to betake itself to more profitable inquiries."

III. Chronology of Paul's Career.—There is not a single date in the life of Paul that is beyond

1. Schemes

dispute, though several are narrowed to a fine point, and the general course and relative proportion of events are clear enough. Luke gave careful data for the time of the birth of Jesus (Lk **2** 1 f), for the entrance of the Baptist on his ministry (**3** 1 f), and the age of Jesus when He began His work (**3** 23), but he takes no such pains in the Acts with chronology. But we are left with a number of incidental allusions and notes of time which call for some discussion. For fuller treatment see CHRONOLOGY OF THE NT. Garvie (*Life and Teaching of Paul*, 1910, 181) gives a comparative table of the views of Harnack, Turner, Ramsay and Lightfoot for the events from the crucifixion of Christ to the close of Acts. The general scheme is nearly the same, differing from one to four years here and there. Shaw (*The Pauline Epp.*, xi) gives a good chronological scheme. Moffatt (*Intro to the Lit. of the NT*, 62 f) gives the theories of 23 scholars:

Turner, "Chronology," in *HDB;* Neteler, *Untersuchung NT Zeitverhältnisse*, 1894; O. Holtzmann, *NT Zeitgeschichte*, 1895, changed in 2d ed, 1906; Bartlet, *Apostolic Age*, xiii f; Cornely (cf Laurent), *NT Studien;* Harnack, *Chron. d. altchristl. Lit. bis Eusebius*, 233–39; McGiffert, *Apostolic Age*, 164, 172; Zahn, *Intro*, III, 450 f; Ramsay, "The Pauline Chronology," *Pauline and Other Studies*, 345 f; Lightfoot, *Bib. Essays*, 213–33; Wendt, *Acts*, 53–60, Meyer, *Comm.;* Renan, *St. Paul;* Bornemann, *Thess*, 17 f, Meyer, *Comm.;* Clemen, *Paulus*, I, 411; Giffert, *Student's Life of Paul*, 242–59; Weiss, *Intro*, I, 154 f; Sabatier, *Paul*, 13 f; Jülicher, *Einl*[6], 31 f; Findlay, "Paul" in *HDB;* Farrar, *Paul*, Appendix; Belser, *Theol. Quartalschrift;* Steinmann, *Abfassungszeit d. Gal*, 169; Hoennicke, *Die Chronologie des Paulus.*

Let us look at the dates given by ten of this list:

	Turner	Bartlet	Harnack	McGiffert	Zahn	Ramsay	Lightfoot	Clemen	Findlay	Hoennicke
Conversion	35–36	31–32	30	31–32	35	32	34	31	36	33–35
First visit to Jerusalem	38	34–35	33	34–35	38	34	37	34	39	36–38
Second visit to Jerusalem	46	46	44	45	44	45	45	. .	. .	45–46
First missionary tour	47	47	45	before 45	50–51	46–48	48	46	46	49 ?
Conference at Jerusalem	49	49	46–47	45	52	50	51	48	49	50–52
Second missionary tour	49	49	46–47	46	52	50–53	51	49–52	49	. .
Third missionary tour	52	52	50	49	54	53–57	54	53–59	53	. .
Arrest in Jerusalem	56	56	53–54	53	58	57	58	59	57	. .
Arrival in Rome	59	59	56–57	56	61	60	61	62	60	60–62
Death of Paul	64–65	61–62	64	58	66–67	67	67	64	67	. .

This table shows very well the present diversity of opinion on the main points in Paul's life. Before expressing an opinion on the points at issue it is best to examine a few details. Paul himself gives some notes of time. He gives "after 3 years" (Gal **1** 18) as the period between his conversion and first visit to Jerus, though he does not necessarily mean 3 full years. In Gal **2** 1, Paul speaks of another visit to Jerus "after the space of 14 years." Then again Luke quotes him as saying to the Ephesian elders at Miletus that he had spent "3 years" at Ephesus (Acts **20** 31). These periods of time all come before Paul's last visit and arrest in Jerus, and they do not embrace all the time between his conversion and arrest. There is also another note of time in 2 Cor **12** 2, where he speaks in an enigmatic way of experiences of his "14 years" ago from the writing of this ep. from Macedonia on the third tour. This will take him back to Tarsus before coming to Antioch at the request of Barnabas, and so overlaps a bit the other "14" above, and includes the "3 years" at Ephesus. We cannot, therefore, add these figures together for the total. But some light may be obtained from further details from Acts and the Epp.

2. Crucial Points

(1) *The death of Stephen.*—Saul is "a young man" (Acts **7** 58) when this event occurs. Like other young Jews he entered upon his life as a rabbi at the age of thirty. He had probably been thus active several years, esp. as he was now in a position of leadership and may even have been a member of the Sanhedrin (Acts **26** 10). Pontius Pilate was not deposed from his procuratorship till 36 AD, but was in a state of uneasiness for a couple of years. It is more probable, therefore, that the stoning of Stephen would take place after his deposition in the interregnum, or not many years before, when he would be afraid to protest against the lawlessness of the Jewish leaders. He had shown timidity at the death of Jesus, 29 or 30 AD, but some of the forms of law were observed. So nothing decisive is here obtained, though 35 AD seems more probable than 32 or 33.

(2) *The flight from Damascus.*—Paul locates this humiliating experience (2 Cor **11** 32 f) when "the governor under Aretas the king guarded the city of the Damascenes." Aretas the Arabian, and not the Roman, has now control when Paul is writing. The likelihood is that Aretas did not get possession of Damascus till 37 AD, when Tiberius died and was succeeded by Caligula. It is argued by some that the expression "the city of the Damascenes" shows that the city was not under the control of Aretas, but was attacked by a Bedouin chieftain who lay in wait for Paul before the city. That to me seems forced. Jos (*Ant*, XVIII, v, 3; vi, 3) at any rate is silent concerning the authority of Aretas over Damascus from 35–37 AD, but no coins or inscriptions show Rom rule over the city between 35 and 62 AD. Ramsay, however ("The Pauline Chronology," *Pauline and Other Studies*, 364), accepts the view of Marquardt (*Römische Staatsalterth.*, I, 404 f) that it was possible for Aretas to have had possession of Damascus before 37 AD. The flight from Damascus is the same year as the visit to Jerus, Paul's first after his conversion (Acts **9** 26; Gal **1** 18). If we knew the precise year of this event, we could subtract two or three years and reach the date of his conversion. Lightfoot in his *Comm. on Gal* gives 38 as the date of this first visit to Jerus, and 36 as the date of the conversion, taking "after 3 years" in a free way, but in his *Bib. Essays*, 221, he puts the visit in 37 and the conversion in 34, and says "'after 3 years' must mean three whole years, or substantially so." Thus we miss a sure date again.

(3) *The death of Herod Agrippa I.*—Here the point of contact between the Acts (**12** 1-4.19-23) and Jos (*Ant*, XIX, viii) is beyond dispute, since both record and describe in somewhat similar vein the death of this king. Jos says that at the time of his death he had already completed the 3d year of his reign over the whole of Judaea (*Ant*, XIX, viii, 2). He received this dignity soon after Claudius began to reign in 41 AD, so that makes the date 44 AD. He died after the Passover in that year (44), for Peter was imprisoned by him during that feast (Acts **12** 3). But unfortunately Luke sandwiches the narrative about Herod Agrippa in between the visit of Barnabas and Saul to Jerus from Antioch (Acts **11** 29 f) and their return to Antioch (**12** 25). He does not say that the events here recorded were exactly synchronous with this visit, for he says merely "about that time." We are allowed therefore to place this visit before 44 AD or after, just as the facts require. The mention of "elders" in Acts **11** 30 instead of apostles (cf both in **15** 4) may mean that the apostles are absent when the visit is made. After the death of James (**12** 1 f) and release of Peter we note that Peter "went to another place" (**12** 17). But the apostles are back again in Jerus in **15** 4 ff. Lightfoot (*Bib. Essays*, 216) therefore places the visit "at the end of 44, or in 45." Once more we slip the connection and fail to fix a firm date for Paul. It is disputed also whether this 2d visit to Jerus according to Acts (**9** 26; **11** 29 f) is the same as the "again" in Gal **2** 1. Ramsay (*St. Paul the Traveller*, 59) identifies the visit in Gal **2** 1 with that in Acts **11** 29 f, but Lightfoot (*Bib. Essays*, 221) holds that it "must be identified with the third of the Acts" (**15** 4 ff). In Gal **1** and **2** Paul is not recording his visits to Jerus, but showing his independence of the apostles when he met them in Jerus. There is no proof that he saw the apostles on the occasion of the visit in Acts **11** 29 f. The point of Lightfoot is well taken, but we have no point of contact with the outside history for locating more precisely the date of the visit of Gal **2** 1 and Acts **15** 4 ff, except that it was after the first missionary tour of Acts **13** and **14**.

(4) *The first missionary tour.*—Sergius Paulus is proconsul of Cyprus when Barnabas and Saul visit the island (Acts **13** 7). The proconsul Paulus is mentioned in a Gr inscription of Soloi (Hogarth, *Devia Cypria*, 1889, 114) and Lucius Sergius Paulus in *CIL*, VI, 31, 545, but, as no mention of his being proconsul is here made, it is probably earlier than that time. The Soloi inscription bears the date 53 AD, but Sergius Paulus was not proconsul in 51 or 52. Hence he may have been proconsul in 50 or the early part of 51 AD. It could not be later and may have been earlier.

(5) *The first visit to Corinth.*—The point to note here is that Gallio becomes proconsul of Achaia (Acts **18** 12). Paul has been apparently in Corinth a year and six months when Gallio appears on the scene (Acts **18** 11). Aquila and Priscilla had "lately come from Italy" (**18** 2) when Paul arrived there. They had been expelled from Rome by the emperor Claudius (**18** 2). On the arrival of Gallio the Jews at once accuse Paul before him; he refuses to interfere, and Paul stays on for a while and then leaves for Syria with Aquila and Priscilla (**18** 18). Deissmann (*St. Paul*, Appendix, I, "The Proconsulate of L. Junius Gallio") has shown beyond reasonable doubt that Gallio, the brother of Seneca, became proconsul of Achaia about July, 51 AD (or possibly 52). On a stone found at Delphi, Gallio is mentioned as proconsul of Achaia according to the probable restoration of part of the text. But the stone mentions the fact that Claudius had been acclaimed imperator 26 times. By means of another inscription we get the 27th proclamation as

imperator in connection with the dedication of an aqueduct on August 1, 52 AD. So thus the 26th time is before this date, some time in the earlier part of the year. We need not follow in detail the turns of the argument (see Deissmann, op. cit.). Once more we do not get a certain date as to the year. It is either the summer of 51 or 52 AD, when Gallio comes. And Paul has already been in Corinth a year and a half. But the *terminus ad quem* for the close of Paul's two years' stay in Corinth would be the early autumn of 52 AD, and more probably 51 AD. Hence the 2 Thessalonian Epp. cannot be later than this date. Before the close of 52 AD, and probably 51, therefore must come the 2d missionary tour, the conference at Jerus, the first missionary tour, etc. Deissmann is justified in his enthusiasm on this point. He is positive that 51 AD is the date of the arrival of Gallio.

(6) *Paul at Troas according to Acts* ***20*** *6 f.*—On this occasion Luke gives the days and the time of year (Passover). Ramsay figures (*St. Paul the Traveller*, 289 f) that Paul had his closing service at Troas on Sunday evening and the party left early Monday morning. Hence he argues back to the Passover at Philippi and concludes that the days as given by Luke will not fit into 56, 58, or 59 AD, but will suit 57. If he is correct in this matter, then we should have a definite year for the last trip to Jerus. Lewin (*Fasti Sacri*, nos. 1856, 1857) reaches the same conclusion. The conclusion is logical if Luke is exact in his use of days in this passage. Yet Lightfoot insists on 58 AD, but Ramsay has the advantage on this point. See *Pauline and Other Studies*, 352 f.

(7) *Festus succeeding Felix.*—When was Felix recalled? He was appointed procurator in 52 AD (Schürer, *Jewish People in the Time of Christ*, I, ii, 174). He was already ruler "many years" (Acts **24** 10) when Paul appears before him in Caesarea. He holds on "two years" when he is succeeded by Festus (Acts **24** 27). But in the *Chronicle* of Eusebius (Armenian text) it is stated that the recall of Felix took place in the last year of Claudius, or 54 AD. But this is clearly an error, in spite of the support given to it by Harnack (*Chronologie d. Paulus*), since Jos puts most of the rule of Felix in the reign of Nero (*Ant*, XX, viii, 1–9; *BJ*, II, xii, 8–14), not to mention the "many years" of Paul in Acts **24** 10. But the error of Eusebius has now been explained by Erbes in his *Todestage Pauli und Petri*, and is made perfectly clear by Ramsay in *Pauline and Other Studies*, 349 ff. Eusebius overlooked the interregnum of 6 years between the death of Herod Agrippa I in 44 AD and the first year of Herod Agrippa II in 50 AD. Eusebius learned that Festus came in the 10th year of Herod Agrippa II. Counting from 50 AD, that gives us 59 AD as the date of the recall of Felix. This date harmonizes with all the known facts. "The great majority of scholars accept the date 60 for Festus; but they confess that it is only an approximate date, and there is no decisive argument for it" (Ramsay, *Pauline and Other Studies*, 351). For minute discussion of the old arguments see Nash, art. "Paul" in new *Sch-Herz Enc;* Schürer, *Hist of the Jewish People*, I, ii, 182 ff. But if Erbes and Ramsay are correct, we have at last a date that will stand. So then Paul sails for Rome in the late summer of 59 AD and arrives at his destination in the early spring ("had wintered," Acts **28** 11) of 60 AD. He had been "two whole years in his own hired dwelling" (**28** 30) when Luke closes the Acts. On the basis of his release in 63 or early 64 and the journeyings of the Pastoral Epp., Paul's death would come by early summer of 68 before Nero's death, and possibly in 67. On this point see later. We can now count back from 59 AD with reasonable clearness to 57 as the date of Paul's arrest in Jerus. Paul spent at least a year and three months (Acts **19** 8.10) in Ephesus (called in round numbers three years in Acts **20** 31). It took a year for him to reach Jerus, from Pentecost (1 Cor **16** 8) to Pentecost (Acts **20** 16). From the spring of 57 AD we thus get back to the end of 53 as the time of his arrival in Ephesus (Acts **19** 1). We have seen that Gallio came to Corinth in the summer of 51 AD (or 52), after Paul had been there a year and a half (Acts **18** 11), leaving ample time in either case for the journeys from Corinth to Ephesus, to Caesarea, to Jerus apparently (Acts **18** 21 f), and to Ephesus (**19** 1) from the summer of 51 (or 52) we go back two years to the beginning of the 2d missionary tour (Acts **16** 1–6) as 49 (or 50). The Jerus Conference was probably in the same year, and the first missionary tour would come in the two (or three) preceding years 47 and 48 (48–49). The stay at Antioch (Acts **14** 28) may have been of some length. So we come back to the end of 44 or beginning of 45 for the visit to Jerus in Acts **11** 29 f. Before that comes the year in Antioch with Barnabas (**11** 26), the years in Tarsus in Cilicia, the "three years" after the conversion spent mostly in Arabia (Gal **1** 17 f), Paul's first appearance at the death of Stephen (Acts **7** 58). These early dates are more conjectural, but even so the facts seem to indicate 35 AD as the probable year of Saul's conversion. The year of his birth would then be between 1 and 5 AD, probably nearer 1. If so, and if his death was in 67 or 68 AD, his age is well indicated. He was "Paul the Aged" (Philem ver 9) when he wrote to Philemon from Rome in 61–63 AD.

IV. His Equipment.—Ramsay chooses as the title of ch ii, in his *St. Paul the Traveller*, the words "The Origin of St. Paul." It is not possible to explain the work and teaching of Paul without a just conception of the forces that entered into his life. Paul himself is still woefully misunderstood by some. Thus A. Meyer (*Jesus or Paul*, 1909, 119) says: "In spite of all that has been said, there is no doubt that St. Paul, with his peculiar personality, with his tendency to recondite gnostic speculation and rabbinic argument, has heavily encumbered the cause of Christianity. For many simple souls, and for many natures that are otherwise constituted than himself, he has barred the way to the simple Christianity of Jesus." That is a serious charge against the man who claimed to have done more than all the other apostles, and rightly, so far as we can tell (1 Cor **15** 10), and who claimed that his interpretation of Jesus was the only true one (Gal **1** 7–9). Moffatt (*Paul and Paulinism*, 1910, 70) minimizes the effect of Paulinism: "The majority of Paul's distinctive conceptions were either misunderstood, or dropped, or modified, as the case might be, in the course of a few decades." "Paulinism as a whole stood almost as far apart from the Christianity that followed it as from that which preceded it" (ib, 73). "The aim of some scholars seems to be to rob every great thinker of his originality" (Garvie, *Studies of Paul and His Gospel*, 1). Ramsay (*Pauline and Other Studies*, 3 ff) boldly challenges the modern prejudice of some scholars against Paul by asking, "Shall we hear evidence or not?" Every successive age must study afresh the life and work of Paul (ib, 27) if it would understand him. Deissmann (*St. Paul*, 3 f) rightly sees that "St. Paul is spiritually the great power of the apostolic age." Hence "the historian, surveying the beginnings of Christianity, sees St. Paul as first after Jesus." Feine (*Jesus Christus und Paulus*, 1902, 298) claims that Paul grasped the essence of the ministry of Christ "auf das tiefste." I own myself a victim to "the charm of Paul," to use Ramsay's phrase (*Pauline and Other Studies*,

27). In seeking to study "the shaping influences" in Paul's career (Alexander, *The Ethics of St. Paul*, 1910, 27), we shall be in error if we seek to explain everything by heredity and environment and if we deny any influence from these sources. He is what he is because of original endowments, the world of his day, and his experience of Christ Jesus. He had both essential and accidental factors in his equipment (Fairbairn, *Studies in Religion and Theology*, 1910, 469 f). Let us note the chief factors in his religious development.

1. The City of Tarsus

Geography plays an important part in any life. John the Baptist spent his boyhood in the hill country of Judaea in a small town (Lk **1** 39) and then in the wilderness. Jesus spent His boyhood in the town of Nazareth and the country round. Both John and Jesus show fondness for Nature in all its forms. Paul grew up in a great city and spent his life in the great cities of the Rom empire. He makes little use of the beauties of Nature, but he has a keen knowledge of men (cf Robertson, *Epochs in the Life of Paul*, 12). Paul was proud of his great city (Acts **21** 39). He was not merely a resident, but a "citizen" of this distinguished city. This fact shows that Paul's family had not just emigrated from Judaea to Tarsus a few years before his birth, but had been planted in Tarsus as part of a colony with full municipal rights (Ramsay, *St. Paul the Traveller*, 31 f). Tarsus was the capital of Cilicia, then a part of the province of Syria, but it had the title of metropolis and was a free city, *urbs libera* (Pliny, *NH*, v.27). To the ancient Gr the city was his "fatherland" (Ramsay, *Cities of St. Paul*, 1908, 90). Tarsus was situated on the river Cydnus, and in a wide plain with the hill country behind and the snow-covered Taurus Mountains in the distance. It was subject to malaria. Ramsay (ib, 117 ff) from Gen **10** 4 f holds that the early inhabitants were Greeks mingled with Orientals. East and West flowed together here. It was a Rom town also with a Jewish colony (ib, 169 ff), constituting a city tribe to which Paul's family belonged. So then Tarsus was a typical city of the Gr-Rom civilization.

The religions of the times all met there in this great mart of business. But it was one of the great seats of culture also. Strabo (xiv.6.73) even says that "Tarsus surpassed all other universities, such as Alexandria and Athens, in the study of philosophy and educational literature in general." "Its great preëminence," he adds, "consists in this, that the men of learning here are all natives." Accordingly, he and others have made up a long list of distinguished men who flourished at Tarsus in the late autumn of Gr learning: philosophers—of the Academy, of the Epicurean and Stoic schools—poets, grammarians, physicians. At Tarsus, one might say, "you breathed the atmosphere of learning" (Lightfoot, *Bib. Essays*, 205). But Ramsay (*Cities of St. Paul*, 231 f) cautions us not to misunderstand Strabo. It was not even one of the three great universities of the world in point of equipment, fame, students from abroad, or general standing. It was not on a par with Athens and Alexandria, except that "it was rich in what constitutes the true excellence and strength of a university, intense enthusiasm and desire for knowledge among the students and great ability and experience among some at least of the teachers" (ib, 233). Strabo was very fond of Athenodorus, for instance. No students from abroad came to Tarsus, but they went from Tarsus elsewhere. But Philostratus represents Apollonius of Tyana as disgusted with the university and the town, and Dio Chrysostom describes Tarsus as an oriental and non-Hellenic town.

Ramsay speaks of Tarsus in the reign of Augustus as "the one example known in history of a state ruled by a university acting through its successive principals." "It is characteristic of the general tendency of university life in a prosperous and peaceful empire, that the rule of the Tarsian University was marked by a strong reaction toward oligarchy and a curtailment of democracy; that also belongs to the oriental spirit, which was so strong in the city. But the crowning glory of Tarsus, the reason for its undying interest to the whole world, is that it produced the apostle Paul; that it was the one city which was suited by its equipoise between the Asiatic and the Western spirit to mold the character of the great Hellenist Jew; and that it nourished in him a strong source of loyalty and patriotism as the citizen of no mean city" (Ramsay, op. cit., 235). The city gave him a schooling in his social, political, intellectual, moral, and religious life, but in varying degrees, as we shall see. It was because Tarsus was a cosmopolitan city with "an amalgamated society" that it possessed the peculiar suitability "to educate and mold the mind of him who would in due time make the religion of the Jewish race intelligible to the Gr-Rom world" (ib, 88). As a citizen of Tarsus Paul was a citizen of the whole world.

2. Roman Citizenship

It was no idle boast with Paul when he said, "But I am *a Roman* born" (Acts **22** 28). The chief captain might well be "afraid when he knew that he was a Roman, and because he had bound him" (**22** 29). Likewise the magistrates at Philippi "feared when they heard that they were Romans" (Acts **16** 39), and promptly released Paul and Silas and "asked them to go away from the city." "To the Roman his citizenship was his passport in distant lands, his talisman in seasons of difficulties and danger. It shielded him alike from the caprice of municipal law and the injustice of local magistrates" (Lightfoot, *Bib. Essays*, 203). As a citizen of Rome, therefore, Paul stood above the common herd. He ranked with the aristocracy in any provincial town (Ramsay, *St. Paul the Traveller*, 31). He would naturally have a kindly feeling for the Rom government in return for this high privilege and protection. In its pessimism the Rom empire had come to be the world's hope, as seen in the Fourth Eclogue of Virgil (Ramsay, *Cities of St. Paul*, 49). Paul would seize upon the Rom empire as a fit symbol of the kingdom of heaven. "Our citizenship is in heaven" (Phil **3** 20); "Ye are no more strangers and sojourners, but ye are fellow-citizens with the saints" (Eph **2** 19). So he interprets the church in terms of the body politic as well as in terms of the Israelite theocracy (Col **2** 19). "All this shows the deep impression which the Rom institutions made on St. Paul" (Lightfoot, *Bib. Essays*, 205). Ramsay draws a striking parallel under the heading, "Paulinism in the Rom Empire" (*Cities of St. Paul*, 70 ff). "A universal Paulinism and a universal Empire must either coalesce, or the one must destroy the other." It was Paul's knowledge of the Rom empire that gave him his imperialism and statesmanlike grasp of the problems of Christianity in relation to the Rom empire. Paul was a statesman of the highest type, as Ramsay has conclusively shown (*Pauline and Other Studies*, 49–100). Moffatt (*Paul and Paulinism*, 66) does say: "His perspective was not imperialistic," but he shows thereby a curious inability to understand Paul. The vision of Paul saw that the regeneration of the empire could come only through Christianity. Ramsay strikingly shows how the emperor dreaded the spiritual upheaval in Paulinism and fought it steadily till the time of Constantine, when "an official Christianity was victorious, but Pauline Christianity had perished, and Paul was now a mere saint, no longer Paul but St. Paul, forgotten as a man or a teacher, but remembered as a sort of revivification of the old pagan gods" (*Cities of St. Paul*, 78). But, as Ramsay says, "it was not dead; it was only waiting its opportunity; it revived when freedom of thought and freedom of life began to stir in Europe; and it guided and stimulated the Protestants of the Reformation."

Suffer Ramsay once more (*Pauline and Other Studies*, 100): "Barbarism proved too powerful for the Gr-Rom civilization unaided by the new religious bond; and every channel through which that civilization was preserved or interest in it maintained, either is now or has been in some essential part of its course Christian after the Pauline form." Paul would show the Rom genius for organizing the churches established by him. Many of his churches would be in Rom colonies (Antioch in Pisidia, Philippi, Corinth, etc). He would address his most studied ep. to the church in Rome, and Rome would be the goal of his ministry for many years (Findlay, *HDB*). He would show his conversance with Rom law, not merely in knowing how to take advantage of his rights as a citizen, but also in the use of legal terms like "adoption" (Gal **4** 5 f), where the adopted heir becomes son, and heir and son are interchangeable. This was the obsolete Rom law and the Gr law left in force in the provinces (cf Gal **3** 15). But in Rom **8** 16 f the actual revocable Rom law is referred to by which "heirship is now deduced from sonship, whereas in Gal sonship is deduced from heirship; for at Rome a son must be an heir, but an heir need not be a son (cf He **9** 15 ff which presupposes *Rom* law and the revocability of a will)" (Maclean in 1-vol *HDB*). So in Gal **3** 24 the tutor or pedagogue presents a Gr custom preserved by the Romans. This personal guardian of the child (often a slave) led him to school, and was not the guardian of the child's property in Gal **4** 2. See Ramsay, *Gal*, 337–93; Ball, *St. Paul and the Rom Law*, 1901, for further discussion. As a Roman, Paul would have "*nomen* and *praenomen*, probably taken from the Rom officer who gave his family *civitas;* but Luke, a Greek, had no interest in Rom names. Paulus, his *cognomen*, was not determined by his *nomen;* there is no reason to think he was an *Æmilius*" (Ramsay, *St. Paul the Traveller*, 31). It is probable, though not certain, that Paul spoke Latin (see Souter, *Expos*, April, 1911). He was at any rate a "*Roman gentleman*" (Findlay, *HDB*), as is shown by the dignity of his bearing before governors and kings and the respect accorded him by the proconsul Sergius Paulus, the procurator Porcius Festus, and the centurion Julius, whose prisoner he was in the voyage to Rome. His father, as a Rom citizen, probably had some means which may have come to Paul before the appeal to Rome, which was expensive (Ramsay, *St. Paul the Traveller*, 310 ff). Though a prisoner in Rome, he made Rome "his best vantage ground and his adoptive home," and it was here that he rose to "his loftiest conceptions of the nation and destiny of the universal church" (Findlay, *HDB*) as "an ambassador in chains" (Eph **6** 20). As a Rom citizen, according to tradition, he was beheaded with the sword and not subjected to crucifixion, the traditional fate of Simon Peter. He saw the true *pax Romana* to be the peace that passeth all understanding (Phil **4** 7; cf Rostron, *The Christology of St. Paul*, 1912, 19).

3. Hellenism

It is not possible "to specify all the influences that worked on Paul in his youth" (Ramsay, *Cities of St. Paul*, 79). We do not know all the life of the times. But he was subject to all that life in so far as any other Jewish youth was. "He was master of all the education and the opportunities of his time. He turned to his profit and to the advancement of his great purpose all the resources of civilization" (Ramsay, *Pauline and Other Studies*, 285). I heartily agree with this conception of Paul's ability to assimilate the life of his time, but one must not be led astray so far as Schramm who, in 1710, wrote *De stupenda eruditione Pauli* ("On the Stupendous Erudition of Paul"). This is, of course, absurd, as Lightfoot shows (*Bib. Essays*, 206). But we must not forget Paul lived in a Gr city and possessed Gr citizenship also (Ramsay, *St. Paul the Traveller*, 33). Certainly the Gr traits of adaptability, curiosity, alertness, the love of investigation were marked features of his character, and Tarsus afforded wide opportunity for the acquiring of these qualities (*The Ethics of St. Paul*, 39). He learned to speak the vernacular *koinē* like a native and with the ease and swing displayed by no other NT writer save Luke and the author of He. He has a "poet's mastery of language," though with the passion of a soul on fire, rather than with the artificial rules of the rhetoricians of the day (Deissmann, *Light from the Ancient East*, 239 f). Blass (*Die Rhythmen der asianischen und römischen Kunstprosa*, 1905) holds that Paul wrote "rhythmically elaborated artistic prose—a singular instance of the great scholar's having gone astray" (Deissmann, *Light*, etc, 64). But there is evidence that Paul was familiar with the use of the diatribe and other common rhetorical devices, though he was very far from being tinged with Atticism or Asianism. It is certain that Paul did not attend any of the schools of rhetoric and oratory. Heinrici (Vorrede to 1 Cor in Meyer's *Krit. exeget. Komm.*) argues that Paul's methods and expressions conform more nearly to the cynic and Stoic diatribe than to the rabbinical dialectic; cf also Wendland und Kern, *Philo u. d. kynisch-stoische Diatribe*, and Hicks, "St. Paul and Hellenism" in *Stud. Bib.*, IV. How extensive was his acquaintance with Gr lit. is in doubt. Lightfoot says: "There is no ground for saying that St. Paul was a very erudite or highly-cultivated man. An obvious maxim of practical life from Menander (1 Cor **15** 33), a religious sentiment of Cleanthes repeated by Aratus, himself a native of Tarsus (Acts **17** 28), a pungent satire of Epimenides (Tit **1** 12), with possibly a passage here and there which dimly reflects some classical writer, these are very slender grounds on which to build the supposition of vast learning" (*Bib. Essays*, 206); but Lightfoot admits that he obtained directly or indirectly from contact with Gr thought and learning lessons far wider and more useful for his work than a perfect style or a familiar acquaintance with the classical writers of antiquity. Even so, there is no reason to say that he made his few quotations from hearsay and read no Gr books (cf Zahn, *Intro to the NT*, 52). Certainly he knew the Gr OT and the Jewish Apoc and apocalypses in Gr. Garvie is only willing to admit that Paul had such knowledge of Gr lit. and philosophy as any Jew, living among Greeks, might pick up (*Life and Teaching of Paul*, 2), and charges Ramsay with "overstating the influence of the gentile environment on Paul's development" (*Studies of Paul and His Gospel*, 8). Ramsay holds that it is quite "possible that the philosophical school at Tarsus had exercised more influence on Paul than is commonly allowed" (*St. Paul the Traveller*, 354). Tarsus was the home of Athenodorus. It was a stronghold of Stoic thought. "At least five of the most eminent teachers of that philosophy were in the university" (Alexander, *Ethics of St. Paul*, 47). It is not possible to say whether Paul attended these or any lectures at the university, though it is hard to conceive that a brilliant youth like Saul could grow up in Tarsus with no mental stimulus from such a university. Garvie (ib, 6) asks when Paul could have studied at the university of Tarsus. He was probably too young before he went to Jerus to study under Gamaliel. But it is not probable that he remained in Jerus continuously after completing his studies till we see him at the death of Stephen (Acts **7** 58). He may have returned to Tarsus meanwhile and taken such studies. Another possibility is that he took advantage of the years in Tarsus after his conversion (Acts **9** 30; Gal **1** 21) to equip himself better for his mission to the Gentiles to which he had been called. There is no real difficulty on the score of time. The world was saturated with Gr ideas, and Paul could not escape them. He could not escape it unless he was innocent of all culture. Ramsay sees in Paul a love of truth and reality "wholly inconceivable in a more narrow Hebrew, and wholly inexplicable without an education in Gr philosophy" ("St. Paul and Hellenism," *Cities of St. Paul,* 34). Paul exhibited a freedom and universalism that he found in the Gr thought of the time which was not so decayed as some think. For the discussion between Garvie and Ramsay see *Expos,* April and December, 1911. Pfleiderer (*Urchristenthum,* Vorwort, 174–78) finds a "double root" of Paulinism, a Christianized Hellenism and a Christianized Pharisaism. Harnack is more nearly correct in saying that "notwithstanding Paul's Gr culture, his conception of Christianity is, in its deepest ground, independent of Hellenism." The Hellenistic influence on Paul was relative and subordinate (Wendland, *Die hel.-röm. Kultur in ihren Beziehungen zu Judenthum und Christenthum,* 3te Aufl, 1912, 245), but it was real, as Köhler shows (*Zum Verständnis des Apostels Paulus,* 9). He had a "Gr inheritance" beyond a doubt, and it was not all unconscious or subliminal as Rostron argues (*Christology of St. Paul,* 17). It is true that in Athens the Stoics and Epicureans ridiculed Paul as a "picker up of learning's crumbs"—Browning's rendering (*An Epistle*) of σπερμολόγος, *spermológos.* Paul shows a fine scorn of the sophistries and verbal refinements of the mere philosophers and orators in 1 Cor **1** and **2,** but all the same he reveals a real apprehension of the true significance of knowledge and life. Dr. James Adam (*The Religious Teachers of Greece,* 360) shows instances of "the real kinship of thought between Plato and St. Paul." He does not undertake to say how it came about. He has a Platonic expression, τὰ διὰ τοῦ σώματος, *tá diá toú sṓmatos,* in 2 Cor **5** 10, and uses a Stoic and cynic word in 2 Cor **9** 8, αὐτάρκειαν, *autárkeian.* Indeed, there are so many similarities between Paul and Seneca in language and thought that some scholars actually predicate an acquaintance or dependence of the one on the other. It is far more likely that Paul and Seneca drew upon the common phrases of current Stoicism than that Seneca had seen Paul's Epp. or knew him personally. Lightfoot has a classic discussion of the matter in his essay on "St. Paul and Seneca" in the *Comm. on Phil* (see also Carr, "St. Paul's Attitude to Gr Philosophy," *Expos,* V, ix). Alexander finds four Stoic ideas (Divine Immanence, Wisdom, Freedom, Brotherhood) taken and glorified by Paul to do service for Christ (*Ethics of St. Paul,* 49–55). Often Paul uses a Stoic phrase with a Christian content. Lightfoot boldly argues (*Bib. Essays,* 207) that the later Gr lit. was a fitter handmaid for the diffusion of the gospel than the earlier.

Paul as the apostle to the Gr-Rom world had to "understand the bearings of the moral and religious life of Greece as expressed in her literature, and this lesson he could learn more impartially and more fully at Tarsus in the days of her decline than at Athens in the freshness of her glory" (ib). Ramsay waxes bold enough to discuss "the Pauline philosophy of history" (*Cities of St. Paul,* 10–13). I confess to sympathy with this notion and find it in all the Pauline epp., esp. in Rom. Moffatt (*Paul and Paulinism,* 66) finds "a religious philosophy of history" in Rom **9–11,** throbbing with strong personal emotion. Paul rose to the height of the true Christian philosopher, though not a technical philosopher of the schools. Deissmann (*St. Paul,* 53) admits his language assigns him "to an elevated class," and yet he insists that he wrote "large letters" (Gal **6** 11) because he had "the clumsy, awkward writing of a workman's hand deformed by toil" (p. 51). I cannot agree that here Deissmann understands Paul. He makes "the world of St. Paul" on too narrow a scale.

4. The Mystery-Religions

Was Paul influenced by Mithraism? H. A. A. Kennedy has given the subject very careful and thorough treatment in a series of papers in *Expos* for 1912–13, already mentioned (see II, 5, above). His arguments are conclusive on the whole against the wild notions of W. B. Smith, *Der vorchristliche Jesus;* J. M. Robertson, *Pagan Christs;* A. Drews, *Die Christus-Mythe;* and Lublinski, *Die Entstehung des Christentums aus der antiken Kultur.* A magic papyrus about 300 AD has "I adjure thee by the god of the Hebrew Jesu" (ll. 3019 f), but Deissmann (*Light from the Ancient East,* 256) refuses to believe this line genuine: "No Christian, still less a Jew, would have called Jesus 'the god of the Hebrews.'" Clemen (*Primitive Christianity and Its non-Jewish Sources,* 1912, 336) indorses this view of Deissmann and says that in the 1st cent. AD "one cannot speak of non-Jewish influences on Christology." One may dismiss at once the notion that Paul "deified" Jesus into a god and made Him Christ under the influence of pagan myths. Certainly pagan idolatry was forced upon Paul's attention at every turn. It stirred his spirit at Athens to see the city full of idols (Acts **17** 16), and he caught eagerly at the altar to an unknown god to give him an easy introduction to the true God (**17** 23); but no one can read Rom **1** and **2** and believe that Paul was carried away by the philosophy of vain deceit of his time. He does use the words "wisdom" and "mystery" often in 1 Cor, Col, and Eph, and in Phil **4** 12, "I [have] learned the secret," he uses a word employed in the mystic cults of the time. It is quite possible that Paul took up some of the phrases of these mystery-religions and gave them a richer content for his own purposes, as he did with some of the gnostic phraseology (*Plērōma,* "fulness," for instance). But Schweitzer (*Paul and His Interpreters,* 191 f) deals a fatal blow against the notion that the mystery-religions had a formative influence on Paul. He urges, with point, that it is only in the 2d cent. that these cults became widely extended in the Rom empire. The dates and development are obscure, but it "is certain that Paul cannot have known the mystery-religions in the form in which they are known to us, because in this fully developed form they did not exist." Cumont (*Les religions orientales dans le paganisme romain,* 2d ed, 1909 [ET]) insists repeatedly on the difficulties in the way of assuming without proof that Mithraism had any influence on Paul. But in particular it is urged that Paul drew on the "mysteries" for his notions of baptism and the Lord's Supper as having magical effects. Appeal is made to the magical use of the name of Jesus by the strolling Jewish exorcists in Ephesus (Acts **18** 13 ff). Kirsopp Lake (*Earlier Epp. of St. Paul,* 233) holds that at Corinth they all accepted Christianity as a mystery-religion and Jesus as "the Redeemer-God, who had passed through death to life, and offered participation in this new life to those who shared in the mysteries which He offered," viz. baptism and the Lord's Supper. But Kennedy (*Expos,* December, 1912, 548) easily shows how with Paul baptism and the Lord's Supper are not magical sacraments producing new life, but symbolic pictures of death to sin and new life in Christ which the believer has already experienced. The battle is still raging on the subject of the mystery-religions, but it is safe to say that so far nothing more than illustrative material has been shown to be true of Paul's teaching from this source.

There is nothing incongruous in the notion that Paul knew as much about the mystery-religions as he did about incipient Gnosticism. Indeed the two things may have been to some extent combined in some places. A passage in Col **2** 18 has long bothered commentators: "dwelling in the things which he hath seen," or (m) "taking his stand upon the things," etc. Westcott and Hort even suspected an early error in the text, but the same word, ἐμβατεύω, *embateúō*, has been found by Sir W. M. Ramsay as a result of investigations by Makridi Bey, of the Turkish Imperial Museum, in the sanctuary of Apollo at Claros, a town on the Ionian coast. Some of the initiates here record the fact and say that being "enquirers, having been initiated, they *entered*" (*embateúō*). The word is thus used of one who, having been initiated, enters into the life of the initiate (cf *Independent*, 1913, 376). Clearly, then, Paul uses the word in that sense in Col **2** 18.

For further discussion see Jacoby, *Die antiken Mysterienreligionen und das Christentum;* Glover, *Conflict of Religions in the Early Rom Empire;* Reitzenstein, *Die hell. Mysterienreligionen;* Friedländer, *Rom Life and Manners under the Early Empire,* III; Thorburn, *Jesus Christ, Historical or Mythical.*

M. Brückner (*Der sterbende und auferstehende Gottheiland in den orientalischen Religionen und ihr Verhältnis zum Christentum,* 1908) says: "As in Christianity, so in many oriental religions, a belief in the death and resurrection of a Redeemer-God (sometimes as His Son) occupied a central place in the worship and cultus." To this Schweitzer (*Paul and His Interpreters,* 193) replies: "What manipulations the myths and rites of the cults in question must have undergone before this general statement could become possible! Where is there anything about dying and resurrection in Mithra?" There we may leave the matter.

Paul was Gr and Rom, but not "pan-Bab," though he was keenly alive to all the winds of doctrine that blew about him, as we see in Col, Eph, and the Pastoral Epp.

5. Judaism

But he was most of all the Jew, that is, before his conversion. He remained a Jew, even though he learned how to be all things to all men (1 Cor **9** 22). Even though glorying in his mission as apostle to the Gentiles (Eph **3** 8), he yet always put the Jew first in opportunity and peril (Rom **2** 9 f). He loved the Jews almost to the point of death (Rom **9** 3). He was proud of his Jewish lineage and boasted of it (2 Cor **11** 16–22; Acts **22** 3 ff; **26** 4 ff; Phil **3** 4–6). "His religious patriotism flickered up within his Christianity" (Moffatt, *Paul and Paulinism,* 66). Had he not been a Rom citizen with some Gr culture and his rich endowments of mind, he would probably not have been the "chosen vessel" for the work of Christ among the Gentiles (Garvie, *Studies of Paul and His Gospel,* 15). Had he not been the thorough Jew, he could not have mediated Christianity from Jew to Greek. "In the mind of Paul a universalized Hellenism coalesced with a universalized Hebraism" (Ramsay, *Cities of St. Paul,* 43). Ramsay strongly opposes the notion of Harnack and others that Paul can be understood "as purely a Hebrew." So in Paul both Hebraism and Hellenism meet, though Hebraism is the main stock. He is a Jew in the Gr-Rom world and a part of it, not a mere spectator. He is the Hellenistic Jew, not the Aram. Jew of Pal (cf Simon Peter's vision on the house-top at Joppa, for instance). But Paul is not a Hellenizing Jew after the fashion of Jason and Menelaus in the beginning of the Maccabean conflict. Findlay (*HDB*) tersely says: "The *Jew* in him was the foundation of everything that Paul became." But it was not the narrowest type of Judaism in spite of his persecution of the Christians. He belonged to the Judaism of the Dispersion. As a Rom citizen in a Gr city he had departed from the narrowest lines of his people (Ramsay, *Cities of St. Paul,* 47). His Judaism was pure, in fact, as he gives it to us in Phil **3** 5. He was a Jew of the stock of Israel, of the tribe of Benjamin. He was a Hebrew, of the seed of Abraham (2 Cor **11** 22). He shared in full all the covenant blessings and privileges of his people (Rom **9** 1–5), whose crowning glory was, that of them came Jesus the Messiah. He was proud of the piety of his ancestors (2 Tim **1** 3), and made progress as a student of Judaism ahead of his fellows (Gal **1** 14). His ancestry was pure, Hebrew of the Hebrews (Phil **3** 5), and so his family preserved the native Palestinian traditions in Tarsus. His name Saul was a proof of loyalty to the tribe of Benjamin as his cognomen Paul was evidence of his Rom citizenship. In his home he would be taught the law by his mother (cf Gal **1** 14), as was true of Timothy's mother and grandmother (2 Tim **1** 5). In Tarsus he would go to the synagogue also. We know little of his father, save that he was a Rom citizen and so a man of position in Tarsus and possibly of some wealth; that he was a tent-maker and taught his son the same trade, as all Jewish fathers did, whatever their rank in life; that he was a Pharisee and brought up his son as a Pharisee (Acts **23** 6), and that he sent the young Saul to Jerus to study at the feet of Gamaliel (Acts **22** 3). Paul always considered himself a Pharisee as distinct from the Sadducaic scepticism (**23** 6). Many of the Pharisaic doctrines were identical with those of Christianity. That Paul did not consider himself a Pharisee in all respects is shown later by his conflict with the Judaizers (Gal **2**; Acts **15**; 2 Cor **10–13**). Paul says that he was reared as a strict Pharisee (Acts **26** 5), though the school of Gamaliel (grandson of Hillel) was not so hard and narrow as that of Shammai. But all Pharisees were stricter than the Sadducees. So Jerus played an important part in the training of Saul (Acts **22** 3), as Paul recognized. He was known in Jerus as a student. He knew Aram. as well as Gr (and Lat), and could speak in it so as to attract the attention of a Jewish audience (Acts **22** 2). Paul was fortunate in his great teacher Gamaliel, who was liberal enough to encourage the study of Gr lit. But his liberality in defending the apostles against the Sadducees in Acts **5** 34–39 must not be misinterpreted in comparison with the persecuting zeal of his brilliant pupil against Stephen (**7** 58). Stephen had opened war on the Pharisees themselves, and there is no evidence that Gamaliel made a defence of Stephen against the lawless rage of the Sanhedrin. It is common for pupils to go farther than their teachers, but Gamaliel did not come to the rescue. Still Gamaliel helped Saul, who was undoubtedly his most brilliant pupil and probably the hope of his heart for the future of Judaism. Harnack (*History of Dogma,* I, 94) says: "Pharisaism had fulfilled its mission in the world when it produced this man." Unfortunately, Pharisaism did not die; in truth has never died, not even from Christianity. But young Saul was the crowning glory of Pharisaism. An effort has recently been made to restore Pharisaism to its former dignity. Herford (*Pharisaism, Its Aim and Method,* 1912) undertakes to show that the Gospels have slandered Pharisaism, that it was the one hope of the ancient world, etc. He has a chapter on "Pharisaism and Paul," in which he claims that Paul has not attacked the real Pharisaism, but has aimed his blows at an unreal creation of his own brain (p. 222). But, if Paul did not understand Pharisaism, he did not understand anything. He knew not merely the OT in the Heb and the LXX tr, for he quotes from both, though usually from the LXX, but he also knew the Jewish Apoc and apocalypses, as is shown in various ways in his writings (see arts. on these subjects). Schweitzer (*Paul and His Interpreters*) carries too far his idea that Paul and Jesus merely moved in the circle of Jewish eschatology. He makes it explain everything, and that it cannot do. But Paul does show acquaintance with some of these books. See Kennedy, *St. Paul's Conception of the Last Things* (1904), for a sane and adequate discussion of this phase of the subject. Pfleiderer pursues the subject in his *Paulinism*, as does Kabisch in his *Eschatologie*. So Sanday and Headlam use this source in their *Comm. on Rom.* Paul knew Wisd, also, a book from the Jewish-Alexandrian theology with a tinge of Gr philosophy (see Goodrick, *Book of Wisd*, 398–403; cf also Jowett's essay on "St. Paul and Philo" in his *Epp. of St. Paul*). Paul knew how to use allegory (Gal **4** 24) in accord with the method of Philo. So then he knew how to use the Stoic diatribe, the rabbinical diatribe and the Alexandrian allegory. "In his cosmology, angelology, and demonology, as well as eschatology, he remains essentially Jewish" (Garvie, *Studies of Paul and His Gospel*, 17). When he becomes a Christian he will change many of his views, for Christ must become central in his thinking, but his method learned in the rabbinical schools remains with him (Köhler, *Zum Verständnis*, etc, 7). Here, then, is a man with a wonderfully rounded culture. What of his mental gifts?

6. Personal Characteristics

Much as we can learn about the times of Paul (cf Selden, *In the Time of Paul*, 1900, for a brief sketch of Paul's world), we know something of the political structure of the Rom world, the social life of the 1st cent. AD, the religious condition of the age, the moral standards of the time, the intellectual tendencies of the period. New discoveries continue to throw fresh light on the life of the middle and lower classes among whom Paul chiefly labored. And, if Deissmann in his brilliant study (*St. Paul, A Study in Social and Religious History*) has pressed too far the notion that Paul the tent-maker ranks not with Origen, but with Amos the herdman (p. 6, on p. 52 he calls it a mistake "to speak of St. Paul the artisan as a proletarian in the sense which the word usually bears with us"), yet he is right in insisting that Paul is "a religious genius" and "a hero of piety" (p. 6). It is not possible to explain the personality and work of a man like Paul by his past and to refer with precision this or that trait to his Jewish or Gr training (Alexander, *Ethics of St. Paul*, 58). "We must allow something to his native originality" (ib). We are all in a sense the children of the past, but some men have much more the power of initiative than others. Paul is not mere "eclectic patchwork" (Bruce, *St. Paul's Conception of Christ*, 218). Even if Paul was acquainted with Philo, which is not certain, that fact by no means explains his use of Philo, the representative Jew of the Hellenistic age. "Both are Jews of the Dispersion, city-dwellers, with marked cosmopolitan traits. Both live and move in the LXX Bible. Both are capable of ecstatic and mystical experiences, and have many points of contact in detail. And yet they stand in very strong contrast to one another, a contrast which reminds us of the opposition between Seneca and St. Paul. . . . . Philo is a philosopher, St. Paul the fool pours out the vials of his irony upon the wisdom of the world" (Deissmann, *St. Paul*, 110). Deissmann, indeed, cares most for "the living man, Paul, whom we hear speaking and see gesticulating, here playful, gentle as a father, and tenderly coaxing, so as to win the hearts of the infatuated children—there thundering and lightning with the passionate wrath of a Luther, with cutting irony and bitter sarcasm on his lips" (ib, 16 f).

(1) *Personal appearance.*—We have no reliable description of Paul's stature and looks. The Acts of Paul and Thecla (§3) have a protraiture thus: "Baldheaded, bowlegged, strongly built, a man small in size, with meeting eyebrows, with a rather large nose, full of grace, for at times he looked like a man and at times he had the face of an angel," and Ramsay (*Church in the Rom Empire*, 32) adds: "This plain and unflattering account of the apostle's personal appearance seems to embody a very early tradition," and in ch xvi he argues that this story goes back to a document of the 1st cent. We may not agree with all the details, but in some respects it harmonizes with what we gather from Paul's Epp. Findlay (*HDB*) notes that this description is confirmed by "the lifelike and unconventional figure of the Rom ivory diptych, 'supposed to date not later than the 4th cent.'" (Lewin's *Life and Epp. of St. Paul*, Frontispiece, and II, 211). At Lystra the natives took Barnabas for Jupiter and Paul for Hermes, "because he was the chief speaker" (Acts **14** 12), showing that Barnabas had the more impressive appearance, while Paul was his spokesman. In Malta the natives changed their minds in the opposite direction, first thinking Paul a murderer and then a god because he did not die from the bite of the serpent (Acts **28** 4–6). His enemies at Corinth sneered at the weakness of his bodily presence in contrast to the strength of his letters (2 Cor **10** 9 f). The attack was really on the courage of Paul, and he claimed equal boldness when present (vs 11 f), but there was probably also a reflection on the insignificance of his physique. The terrible bodily sufferings which he underwent (2 Cor **11** 23–26) left physical marks (στίγματα, *stigmata*, Gal **6** 17) that may have disfigured him to some extent. Once his illness made him a trial to the Galatians to whom he preached, but they did not scorn him (Gal **4** 14). He felt the frailty of his body as an earthen vessel (2 Cor **4** 7) and as a tabernacle in which he groaned (**5** 4). But the effect of all this weakness was to give him a fresh sense of dependence on Christ and a new influx of Divine power (2 Cor **11** 30; **12** 9). But even if Paul was unprepossessing in appearance and weakened by illness, whether ophthalmia, which is so common in the East (Gal **4** 15), or malaria, or recurrent headache, or epilepsy, he must have had a tough constitution to have endured such hardship to a good old age. He had one infirmity in particular that came upon him at Tarsus (2 Cor **12** 1–9) in connection with the visions and revelations of the Lord then granted him. The affliction seems to have been physical (σκόλοψ τῇ σαρκί, *skólops tē̃ sarkí*, "a stake in the flesh" or "for the flesh"), and it continued with him thereafter as a messenger of Satan to buffet Paul and to keep him humble. Some think that this messenger of Satan was a demon that haunted Paul in his nervous state. Others hold it to be epilepsy or some form of hysteria superinduced by the visions and revelations which he had had. Cf Krenkel, *Beiträge* (pp. 47–125), who argues that the ancients looked with such dread on epilepsy that those who beheld such attacks would "spit out" so as to escape the evil (cf modern "knocking on wood"); cf *qui sputatur morbus* in Plautus (*Captivi*, iii.4, 17). Reference is made to Gal **4** 14, οὐδὲ ἐξεπτύσατε, *oudé exeptúsate*, "nor did ye spit out," as showing that this was the affliction of Paul in Galatia. But epilepsy often affects the mind, and Paul shows no sign of mental weakness, though his enemies charged him with insanity (Acts **26** 24; 2 Cor **5** 13; **12** 11). It is urged in reply that Julius Caesar, Alfred the Great, Peter the Great, and Napoleon all had epilepsy without loss of mental force. It is difficult to think headache or malaria could have excited the disgust indicated in Gal **4** 14, where some trouble with the eyes seems to be indicated. The ministers of Satan (2 Cor **11** 15) do not meet the requirements of the case, nor mere spiritual sins (Luther),

nor struggle with lust (Roman Catholic, *stimulus carnis*). Garvie (*Studies of Paul and His Gospel*, 65, 80) thinks it not unlikely that "it was the recurrence of an old violent temptation," rather than mere bodily disease. "Can there be any doubt that this form of temptation is more likely to assail the man of intense emotion and intense affection, as Paul was?" But enough of what can never be settled. "St. Paul's own scanty hints admonish to caution" (Deissmann, *St. Paul*, 63). It is a blessing for us not to know, since we can all cherish a close bond with Paul. Ramsay (*St. Paul the Traveller*, 37 ff) calls special attention to the look of Paul. He "fastened his eyes on" the man (Acts **13** 9; **14** 9). He argues that Paul had a penetrating, powerful gaze, and hence no eye trouble. He calls attention also to gestures of Paul (Acts **20** 24; **26** 2). There were artists in marble and color at the court of Caesar, but no one of them cared to preserve a likeness of the poor itinerant preacher who turned out to be the chief man of the age (Deissmann, *St. Paul*, 58). "We are like the Christians of Colossae and Laodicea, who had not seen his face in the flesh" (Col **2** 1).

(2) *His natural endowments*.—In respect to his natural endowments we can do much better, for his epp. reveal the mind and soul of the man. He is difficult to comprehend, not because he conceals himself, but because he reveals so much of himself in his epp. He seems to some a man of contradictions. He had a many-sided nature, and his very humanness is in one sense the greatest thing about him. There are "great polar contradictions" in his nature. Deissmann (*St. Paul*, 62 ff) notes his ailing body and his tremendous powers for work, his humility and his self-confidence, his periods of depression and of intoxication with victory, his tenderness and his sternness; he was ardently loved and furiously hated; he was an ancient man of his time, but he is cosmopolitan and modern enough for today. Findlay (*HBD*) adds that he was a man possessed of dialectical power and religious inspiration. He was keenly intellectual and profoundly mystical (cf Campbell, *Paul the Mystic*, 1907). He was a theologian and a man of affairs. He was a man of vision with a supreme task to which he held himself. He was a scholar, a sage, a statesman, a seer, a saint (Garvie, *Studies in Paul and His Gospel*, 68–84). He was a man of heart, of passion, of imagination, of sensibility, of will, of courage, of sincerity, of vivacity, of subtlety, of humor, of adroitness, of tact, of genius for organization, of power for command, of gift of expression, of leadership—"All these qualities and powers went to the making of Jesus Christ's apostle to the nations, the master-builder of the universal church and of Christian theology" (Findlay, *HDB;* see Lock, *St. Paul the Master Builder*, 1905; and M. Jones, *St. Paul the Orator*, 1910).

I cannot agree with Garvie's charge of cowardice (*Life and Teaching of Paul*, 173) in the matter of the purifying rites (Acts **21** 23) and the dividing of the Sanhedrin (**23** 6). The one was a mere matter of prudence in a nonessential detail, the other was justifiable skill in resisting the attack of unscrupulous enemies. One does not understand Paul who does not understand his emotional nature. He was "quick, impetuous, strenuous, impassioned" (Bevan, *St. Paul in the Light of To-day*, 1912, 26). His heart throbs through his epp., and he loves his converts like a mother or a lover (Findlay, *HDB*) rather than a pastor. We feel the surging emotion of his great spirit in 1 Thess, 1 Cor, 2 Cor, Gal, Rom, Phil, 2 Tim in particular. He had the spiritual temperament and reaches his highest flights in his moments of rhapsody. He has elasticity and rebound of spirit, and comes up with the joy of victory in Christ out of the severest trials and disappointments. His ambition is great, but it is to serve Christ his Lord. He is a man of faith and a man of prayer. For him to live is Christ. He has a genius for friendship and binds men to him with hooks of steel—men like Barnabas, Silas, Timothy, Luke, Titus (Speer, *The Man Paul*, 1900, 111 ff). He is not afraid to oppose his friends when it is necessary for the sake of truth, as with Peter (Gal **2** 11 ff) and with Barnabas (Acts **15** 35 ff). "While God made Paul like the other apostles out of the clay whereof ordinary men are fashioned, yet we may say that He took extraordinary pains with his education" (Fairbairn, *Studies in Religion and Theology*, 471). If ever a man, full-blooded and open-eyed, walked the earth, it was Paul. It is a debatable question whether Paul was married or not. He certainly was not when he wrote (1 Cor **7** 7; **9** 5). But, if he was a member of the Sanhedrin when he cast his vote against the disciples (Acts **26** 10), as his language naturally means, then he had been married.

There is in Paul the gift of leadership in a marked degree. He, though young, is already at the head of the opposition to Stephen (Acts **7** 58), and soon drives the disciples out of Jerus.

(3) *His supernatural gifts*.—He had his share of them. He had all the gifts that others could boast of at Corinth, and which he lightly esteemed except that of prophecy (1 Cor **14** 18–29). He had his visions and revelations, but would not tell what he had seen (2 Cor **12** 1–9). He did the signs of an apostle (2 Cor **12** 12–14). He had the power to work miracles (1 Cor **4** 19–21) and to exercise discipline (1 Cor **5** 4 f; 2 Cor **13** 1–3). But what he cared for most of all was the fact that Jesus had appeared to him on the road to Damascus and had called him to the work of preaching to the Gentiles (1 Cor **15** 8).

No other element in the equipment of Paul is comparable in importance to his conversion.

7. Conversion

(1) *Preparation*.—It was sudden, and yet God had led Saul to the state of mind when it could more easily happen. True, Saul was engaged in the very act of persecuting the believers in Jerus. His mind was flushed with the sense of victory. He was not conscious of any lingering doubts about the truth of his position and the justice of his conduct till Jesus abruptly told him that it was hard for him to kick against the goad (Acts **26** 14). Thus suddenly brought to bay, the real truth would flash upon his mind. In later years he tells how he had struggled in vain against the curse of the Law (Rom **7** 7 f). It is probable, though not certain, that Paul here has in mind his experience before his conversion, though the latter part of the chapter may refer to a period later. There is difficulty in either view as to the "body of this death" that made him so wretched (Rom **7** 24). The Christian keeps up the fight against sin in spite of defeat (**7** 23), but he does not feel that he is "carnal, sold under sin" (**7** 14). But when before his conversion did Paul have such intensity of conviction? We can only leave the problem unanswered. His reference to it at least harmonizes with what Jesus said about the goad. The words and death of Stephen and the other disciples may have left a deeper mark than he knew. The question might arise whether after all the Nazarenes were right. His plea for his conduct made in later years was that he was conscientious (Acts **26** 9) and that he did it ignorantly in unbelief (1 Tim **1** 13). He was not wilfully sinning against the full light as he saw it. It will not do to say with Holsten that Saul was half-convinced to join the disciples, and only needed a jolt to turn him over. He was "yet breathing threatening and slaughter against the disciples of the Lord" (Acts **9** 1), and went to the high priest and asked for letters to Damascus demanding the arrest of the disciples there. His temper on the whole is distinctly hostile to Christ, and the struggle against his course was in the subconscious mind. There a volcano had gathered ready to burst out.

It is proper to ask whether Paul had known Jesus in the flesh, but it is not easy to give a categorical reply. It is possible, though hardly likely, that Paul had come to Jerus to study when Jesus as a boy of 12 visited the temple, and so heard Jesus and the doctors. That could be true only in case Paul was born 5 or 6 BC, which is quite unlikely. It is possible again that Paul may have remained in Jerus after his graduation at the school of Gamaliel and so was present in Jerus at the trial and death of Jesus. Some of the ablest of modern scholars hold that Paul knew Jesus in the flesh. It will at once seem strange that we have no express statement to this effect in the letters of Paul, when he shows undoubted knowledge of various events in the life of Christ (cf Wynne, *Fragmentary Records of Jesus of Nazareth*, 1887). It is almost certain, as J. Weiss admits (*Paul and Jesus*, 41), that in 1 Cor **9** 1 Paul refers to the Risen Jesus. The passage in 2 Cor **5** 16 is argued both ways: "Wherefore we henceforth know no man after the flesh: even though we have known Christ after the flesh, yet now we know him so no more." J. Weiss (ib, 41–55) argues strongly for the view that he knew Jesus in the flesh. But in the first clause of the sentence above Paul means by "after the flesh," not acquaintance, but standpoint. It is natural to take it in the same way as applied to Christ. He has changed his viewpoint of Christ and so of all men. Weiss pleads (ib, p. 40), at any rate, that we have no word saying that "Paul had *not* seen Jesus in person." It may be said in reply that the fact that Jesus has to tell Paul who He is (Acts **9** 5) shows that Paul did not have personal acquaintance with Him. But the question may be left in abeyance as not vitally important. He certainly had not understood Jesus, if he knew Him.

(2) *Experience*.—Space does not permit a discussion of this great event of Paul's conversion at all commensurate with its significance. A literature of importance has grown up around it besides the lengthy discussions in the lives and theologies of Paul (see e.g. Lord Lyttleton's famous *Observations on Saul's Conversion*, 1774; Fletcher's *A Study of the Conversion of St. Paul*, 1910; Gardner, *The Religious Experience of St. Paul*, 1911; Maggs, *The Spiritual Experience of St. Paul*). All sorts of theories have been advanced to explain on naturalistic grounds this great experience of Christ in the life of Paul. It has been urged that Paul had an epileptic fit, that he had a sunstroke, that he fell off his horse to the ground, that he had a nightmare, that he was blinded by a flash of lightning, that he imagined that he saw Jesus as a result of his highly wrought nervous state, that he deliberately renounced Judaism because of the growing conviction that the disciples were right. But none of these explanations explains. Mere prejudice against the supernatural, such as is shown by Weinel in his *Paulus*, and by Holsten in his able book (*Zum Evangelium d. Paulus und Petrus*), cannot solve this problem. One must be willing to hear the evidence. There were witnesses of the bright light (Acts **26** 13) and of the sound (**9** 7) which only Paul understood (**22** 9), as he alone beheld Jesus. It is claimed by some that Paul had a trance or subjective vision, and did not see Jesus with his eyes. Denney (*Standard Bible Dict.*) replies that it is not a pertinent objection. Jesus (Jn **21** 1) "manifested" Himself, and Paul says that he "saw" Jesus (1 Cor **9** 1), that Jesus "appeared" (1 Cor **15** 8) to him. Hence it was both subjective and objective. But the reality of the event was as clear to Paul as his own existence. The account is given 3 t in Acts (chs **9, 22, 26**) in substantial agreement, with a few varying details. In ch **9** the historical narrative occurs, in ch **22** Paul's defence before the mob in Jerus is given, and in ch **26** we have the apology before Agrippa. There are no contradictions of moment, save that in ch **26** Jesus Himself is represented as giving directly to Paul the call to the Gentiles while in chs **9** and **22** it is conveyed through Ananias (the fuller and more accurate account). There is no need to notice the apparent contradiction between **9** 7 and **22** 9, for the difference in case in the Gr gives a difference in sense, hearing the sound, with the genitive, and not understanding the sense, with the accusative. Findlay (*HBD*) remarks that the conversion of Paul is a psychological and ethical problem which cannot be accounted for save by Paul's own interpretation of the change wrought in him. He saw Jesus and surrendered to Him.

(3) *Effect on Paul*.—His surrender to Jesus was instantaneous and complete: "What shall I do, Lord?" (Acts **22** 10). He could not see for the glory of that light (**22** 11), but he had already seen "the light of the knowledge of the glory of God in the face of Jesus Christ" (2 Cor **4** 6). The god of this world could blind him no longer. He had seen Jesus, and all else had lost charm for Paul. There is infinite pathos in the picture of the blind Saul led by the hand (Acts **9** 8) into Damascus. All the pride of power is gone, all the lust for vengeance. The fierceness of the name of Saul is well shown in the dread that Ananias has and the protest that he makes to the Lord concerning him (**9** 10–14). Ananias doubtless thought that the Lord had made a strange choice of a vessel to bear the message of Christ to the Gentiles, kings, and the children of Israel (**9** 15), but there was hope in the promise of chastisement to him (**9** 16). So he went, and calls him "Brother Saul." Saul was filled with the Holy Spirit, the scales fell from his eyes, he was baptized. And now what next? What did the world hold in store for the proud scion of Judaism who had renounced power, place, pride for the lowly Nazarene? He dared not go back to Jerus. The Jews in Damascus would have none of him now. Would the disciples receive him? They did. "And he was certain days with the disciples that were at Damascus" (**9** 19). Ananias vouched for him by his vision. Then Saul took his courage in his hands and went boldly into the synagogues and "proclaimed Jesus, that he is the Son of God" (**9** 20). This was a public committal and a proclamation of his new creed. There was tremendous pith and point in this statement from Saul. The Jews were amazed (Acts **9** 21). This is the core of Paul's message as we see in his later ministry (Acts **13**; **17** 3). It rests at bottom on Paul's own experience of grace. "His whole theology is nothing but the explanation of his own conversion" (Stalker, *Life of St. Paul*, 45). We need not argue (Garvie, *Studies of Paul and His Gospel*, 51) that Paul understood at once the full content of the new message, but he had the heart of it right.

V. Work.—There was evidently a tumult in Paul's soul. He had undergone a revolution, both intellectual and spiritual. Before he proceeded farther it was wise to think through the most important implications of the new standpoint. Luke gives no account of this personal phase of Paul's career, but he allows room for it between Acts **9** 21 and 22. It is Paul who tells of his retirement to Arabia (Gal **1** 17 f) to prove his independence of the apostles in Jerus. He did not go to them for instruction or for ecclesiastical authority. He did not adopt the merely traditional view of Jesus as the Messiah. He knew, of course, the Christian contention well enough, for he had answered it often enough. But now his old arguments were gone and he must work his way round to the other side, and be able to put his new gospel with clearness and force. He was done with calling Jesus anathema (1 Cor **12** 3). Henceforth to him Jesus is Lord. We know nothing of Paul's life in Arabia nor in what part of Arabia he was. He may have gone to Mt. Sinai and thought out grace in the atmosphere of law, but that is not necessary. But it is clear that Paul grew in apprehension of the things of Christ during these years, as indeed he grew to the very end. But he did not grow away from the first clear vision of Christ. He claimed that God had revealed His Son in him that he might preach to the Gentiles (Gal **1** 16). He claimed that from the first and to the very last. The undoubted development in Paul's Epp. (see Matheson, *Spiritual Development*

1. Adjustment

of St. Paul, and Sabatier, *The Apostle Paul*) is, however, not a changing view of Christ that nullifies Paul's "original Christian inheritance" (Köhler, *Zum Verständnis des Apostels Paulus*, 13). Pfleiderer (*Influence of the Apostle Paul on the Development of Christianity*, 3d ed, 1897, 217) rejects Col because of the advanced Christology here found. But the Christology of Col is implicit in Paul's first sermon at Damascus. "It is impossible to escape the conclusion that the significance and value of the Cross became clear to him almost simultaneously with the certainty of the resurrection and of the Messiahship of Jesus" (Garvie, *Studies*, etc, 57). The narrow Jew has surrendered to Christ who died for the sins of the world. The universal gospel has taken hold of his mind and heart, and it will work out its logical consequences in Paul. The time in Arabia is not wasted. When he reappears in Damascus (Acts **9** 22) he has "developed faith" (Findlay, *HDB*) and energy that bear instant fruit. He is now the slave of Christ. For him henceforth to live is Christ. He is crucified with Christ. He is in Christ. The union of Paul with Christ is the real key to his life. It is far more than a doctrine about Christ. It is real fellowship with Christ (Deissmann, *St. Paul*, 123). Thus it is that the man who probably never saw Christ in the flesh understands him best (Wernle, *Beginnings of Christianity*, I, 159).

2. Opposition

Saul had "increased the more in strength, and confounded the Jews that dwelt in Damascus, proving that this is the Christ" (Acts **9** 22). Now he not merely "proclaims" as before (**9** 20); he "proves." He does it with such marvelous skill that the Jews are first confounded, then enraged to the point of murder. Their former hero was now their foe. The disciples had learned to run from Saul. They now let him down in a basket through the wall by night and he is gone (Acts **9** 23 ff). This then is the beginning of the active ministry of the man who was called to be a chosen vessel to Gentiles, kings, and Jews. There was no need to go back to the wilderness. He had gotten his bearings clearly now. He had his message and it had his whole heart. He had not avoided Jerus because he despised flesh and blood, but because he had no need of light from the apostles since "the Divine revelation so completely absorbed his interest and attention" (Garvie, *Life and Teaching of Paul*, 33). No door was open as yet among the Gentiles. Sooner or later he must go to Jerus and confer with the leaders there if he was to coöperate with them in the evangelization of the world. Saul knew that he would be an object of suspicion to the disciples in Jerus. That was inevitable in view of the past. It was best to go, but he did not wish to ask any favors of the apostles. Indeed he went in particular "to visit Cephas" (m to "become acquainted with," Gal **1** 18). They knew each other, of course, as opponents. But Saul comes now with the olive branch to his old enemy. He expressly explains (Gal **1** 19) that he saw no other apostle. He did see James, the Lord's brother, who was not one of the Twelve. It seems that at first Peter and James were both afraid of Saul (Acts **9** 26), "not believing that he was a disciple." If a report came 3 years before of the doings at Damascus, they had discounted it. All had been quiet, and now Saul suddenly appears in Jerus in a new rôle. It was, they feared, just a ruse to complete his work of old. But for Barnabas, Saul might not have had that visit of 15 days with Peter. Barnabas was a Hellenist of Cyprus and believed Saul's story and stood by him. Thus he had his opportunity to preach the gospel in Jerus, perhaps in the very synagogues in which he had heard Stephen, and now he is taking Stephen's place and is disputing against the Grecian Jews (Acts **9** 29). He had days of blessed fellowship (**9** 28) with the disciples, till the Grecian Jews sought to kill him as Saul had helped to do to Stephen (**9** 29). It was a repetition of Damascus, but Saul did not wish to run again so soon. He protested to the Lord Jesus, who spoke in a vision to him, and recalls the fate of Stephen, but Jesus bids him go: "For I will send thee forth far hence unto the Gentiles" (Acts **22** 17–21). One martyr like Stephen is enough. So the brethren took him down to Caesarea (Acts **9** 30). It was an ominous beginning for a ministry with so clear a call. Where can he go now?

3. Waiting

They "sent him forth to Tarsus" (Acts **9** 30). Who would welcome him there? At Jerus he apparently avoided Gamaliel and the Sanhedrin. He was with the Christians and preached to the Hellenistic Jews. The Jews regarded him as a turncoat, a renegade Jew. There were apparently no Christians in Tarsus, unless some of the disciples driven from Jerus by Saul himself went that far, as they did go to Antioch (Acts **11** 19 f). But Saul was not idle, for he speaks himself of his activity in the regions of Syria and Cilicia during this "period of obscurity" (Denney, *Standard Bible Dict.*) as a thing known to the churches of Judaea (Gal **1** 21 f). He was not idle then. The way was not yet opened for formal entrance upon the missionary enterprise, but Saul was not the man to do nothing at home because of that. If they would not hear him at Damascus and Jerus, they would in the regions of Syria and Cilicia, his home province. We are left in doubt at first whether Paul preached only to Jews or to Gentiles also. He had the specific call to preach to the Gentiles, and there is no reason why he should not have done so in this province, preaching to the Jews first as he did afterward. He did not have the scruples of Simon Peter to overcome. When he appears at Antioch with Barnabas, he seems to take hold like an old hand at the business. It is quite probable, therefore, that this obscure ministry of some 8 or 10 years may have had more results than we know. Paul apparently felt that he had done his work in that region, for outside of Antioch he gives no time to it except that in starting out on the second tour from Antioch "he went through Syria and Cilicia, confirming the churches" (Acts **15** 41), churches probably the fruit of this early ministry and apparently containing Gentiles also. The letter from the Jerus conference was addressed to "the brethren who are of the Gentiles in Antioch and Syria and Cilicia" (Acts **15** 23). Cilicia was now part of the Rom province of Syria. So then we conclude that Saul had a gentile ministry in this region. "Independently, under no human master, he learned his business as a missionary to the heathen" (Findlay, *HDB*). One can but wonder whether Saul was kindly received at home by his father and mother. They had looked upon him with pride as the possible successor of Gamaliel, and now he is a follower of the despised Nazarene and a preacher of the Cross. It is possible that his own exhortations to fathers not to provoke their children to wrath (Eph **6** 4) may imply that his own father had cast him out at this time. Findlay (*HDB*) argues that Saul would not have remained in this region so long if his home relations had been altogether hostile. It is a severe test of character when the doors close against one. But Saul turned defeat to glorious gain.

Most scholars hold that the ecstatic experience told by Paul in 2 Cor **12** 1–9 took place before he came to Antioch. If we count the years strictly, 14 from 56 AD would bring us to 42 AD. Paul had spent a year in Antioch before going up to Jerus

(Acts **11** 29 f). Findlay (*HDB*) thinks that Paul had the visions before he received the call to come to Antioch. Garvie (*Life and Teaching of Paul*, 41) holds he received the call first. "Such a mood of exaltation would account for the vision to which he refers in 2 Cor **12** 1–4." At any rate he had the vision with its exaltation and the thorn in the flesh with its humiliation before he came to Antioch in response to the invitation of Barnabas. He had undoubtedly had a measure of success in his work in Cilicia and Syria. He had the seal of the Divine blessing on his work among the Gentiles. But there was a pang of disappointment over the attitude of the Jerus church toward his work. He was apparently left alone to his own resources. "Only such a feeling of disappointment can explain the tone of his references to his relations to the apostles (Gal **1** 11–24)" (Garvie, *Life and Teaching of Paul*, 41). There is no bitterness in this tone—but puzzled surprise. It seems that the 12 apostles are more or less absent from Jerus during this period with James the brother of the Lord Jesus as chief elder. A narrow Pharisaic element in the church was active and sought to shape the policy of the church in its attitude toward the Gentiles. This is clear in the treatment of Peter, when he returned to Jerus after the experience at Caesarea with Cornelius (Acts **11** 1–18). There was acquiescence, but with the notion that this was an exceptional case of the Lord's doing. Hence they show concern over the spread of the gospel to the Greeks at Antioch, and send Barnabas to investigate and report (Acts **11** 19–22). Barnabas was a Hellenist, and evidently did not share the narrow views of the Pharisaic party in the church at Jerus (**11** 2), for he was glad (**11** 23 f) of the work in Antioch. Probably mindful of the discipline attempted on Simon Peter, he refrained from going back at once to Jerus. Moreover, he believed in Saul and his work, and thus he gave him his great opportunity at Antioch. They had there a year's blessed work together (**11** 25 ff). So great was the outcome that the disciples received a new name to distinguish them from the Gentiles and the Jews. But the term "Christian" did not become general for a long time. There was then a great Gr church at Antioch, possibly equal in size to the Jewish church in Jerus. The prophecy by Agabus of a famine gave Barnabas and Saul a good excuse for a visit to Jerus with a general collection—"every man according to his ability"—from the Gr church for the relief of the poverty in the Jerus church. Barnabas had assisted generously in a similar strain in the beginning of the work there (Acts **4** 36 f), unless it was a different Barnabas, which is unlikely. This contribution would help the Jerus saints to understand now that the Greeks were really converted. It was apparently successful according to the record in Acts. The apostles seem to have been absent, since only "elders" are mentioned in **11** 30.

4. Opportunity

The incidents in ch **12**, as already noted, are probably not contemporaneous with this visit, but either prior or subsequent to it. However, it is urged by some scholars that this visit is the same as that of Gal **2** 1–10, since Paul would not have omitted it in his list of visits to Jerus. But then Paul is not giving a list of visits, but is only showing his independence of the apostles. If they were absent from Jerus at that time, there would be no occasion to mention it. Besides, Luke in Acts **15** does recount the struggle in Jerus over the problem of gentile liberty. If that question was an issue at the visit in Acts **11** 30, it is quite remarkable that he should have passed it by, esp. if the matter caused as much heat as is manifest in Gal **2**, both in Jerus and Antioch. It is much simpler to understand that in Acts **15** and Gal **2** 1–10 we have the public and the private aspects of the same issue, than to suppose that Luke has slurred the whole matter over in Acts **11** 30. The identification of the visit of Gal **2** with that in Acts **11** 30 makes it possible to place Gal before the conference in Jerus in Acts **15** and implies the correctness of the South-Galatian theory of the destination of the ep. and of the work of Paul, a theory with strong advocates and arguments, but which is by no means established (see below for discussion at more length). So far as we can gather from Luke, Barnabas and Saul returned from Jerus with John Mark (Acts **12** 25), "when they had fulfilled their ministration" with satisfaction. The Pharisaic element was apparently quiescent, and the outlook for the future work among the Gentiles seemed hopeful. Ramsay (*St. Paul the Traveller*, 62 ff) argues strongly for identifying the revelation mentioned in Paul's speech in Acts **22** 20 f with this visit in **11** 30 (**12** 25), rather than with the one in Acts **9** 29 f. There is a textual problem in **12** 25, but I cannot concur in the solution of Ramsay.

5. The First Great Mission Campaign: Acts 13 and 14, 47 and 48 AD

Paul had already preached to the Gentiles in Cilicia and Syria for some 10 years. The work was not new to him. He had had his specific call from Jerus long ago and had answered it. But now an entirely new situation arises. His work had been individual in **Cilicia.** Now the Spirit specifically directs the separation of **Barnabas** and Saul to this work (Acts **13** 2). They were to go together, and they had the sympathy and prayers of a great church. The endorsement was probably not "ordination" in the technical sense, but a farewell service of blessing and good will as the missionaries went forth on the world-campaign (**13** 3). No such unanimous endorsement could have been obtained in Jerus to this great enterprise. It was momentous in its possibilities for Christianity. Hitherto work among the Gentiles had been sporadic and incidental. Now a determined effort was to be made to evangelize a large section of the Rom empire. There is no suggestion that the church at **Antioch** provided funds for this or for the two later campaigns, as the church at Philippi came to do. How that was managed this time we do not know. Some individuals may have helped. Paul had his trade to fall back on, and often had resort to it later. The presence of John Mark "as their attendant" (**13** 5) was probably due to Barnabas, his cousin (Col **4** 10). The visit to **Cyprus,** the home of Barnabas, was natural. There were already some Christians there (Acts **11** 20), and it was near. They preach first in the synagogues of the Jews at **Salamis** (**13** 5). We are left to conjecture as to results there and through the whole island till **Paphos** is reached. There they meet a man of great prominence and intelligence, **Sergius Paulus,** the Rom proconsul, who had been under the spell of a sorcerer with a Jewish name—Elymas Bar-jesus (cf Peter's encounter with Simon Magus in Samaria). In order to win and hold Sergius Paulus, who had become interested in Christianity, Paul has to punish **Bar-jesus** with blindness (**13** 10 ff) in the exercise of that apostolic power which he afterward claimed with such vigor (1 Cor **5** 4 f; 2 Cor **13** 10). He won Sergius Paulus, and this gave him cheer for his work. From now on it is Paul, not Saul, in the record of Luke, perhaps because of this incident, though both names probably belonged to him from the first. Now also Paul steps to the fore ahead of Barnabas, and it is "Paul's company" (**13** 13) that sets sail from Paphos for **Pamphylia.** There is no evidence here of resentment on the part of Barnabas at the leadership of Paul. The whole campaign may have been planned from the start by the Holy Spirit as the course now taken may have been due to Paul's leadership. John Mark deserts at **Perga** and returns to Jerus (his home), not to Antioch (**13** 13). Paul and Barnabas push on to the tablelands of **Pisidia.** Ramsay (*St. Paul the Traveller*, 93) thinks that Paul had malaria down at **Perga** and hence desired to get up into higher land. That is possible. The places mentioned in the rest of the tour are **Antioch** in Pisidia (**13** 14), and **Iconium** (**13** 51), **Lystra** (**14** 8), and **Derbe** (**14** 20), cities of **Lycaonia.** These terms are ethnographic descriptions of the southern divisions of the Rom province of Galatia, the northern portion being Galatia proper or North Galatia. So then Paul and Barnabas are now at work in **South Galatia,** though Luke does not mention that name, using here only the popular designations. The work is wonderfully successful. In these cities, on one of the great Rom roads east and west, Paul is reaching the centers of provincial life as will be his custom. At Antioch Paul is invited to repeat his sermon on the next Sabbath (**13** 42), and Luke records at length the report of this discourse which has the characteristic notes of Paul's gospel as we see it in his epp. Paul may have kept notes of the discourse. There were devout Gentiles at these services. These were the first to be won, and thus a wider circle of Gentiles could be reached. Paul and Barnabas were too successful at Antioch in Pisidia. The jealous Jews opposed, and Paul and Barnabas dramatically turned to the Gentiles (**13** 45 ff). But the Jews reached the city magistrate through the influential women, and Paul and Barnabas were ordered to leave (**13** 50 f). Similar success brings like results in Iconium. At Lystra, before the hostile Jews come, Paul and Barnabas have great success and, because of the healing of the impotent man, are taken as Mercury and Jupiter respectively, and worship is offered them. Paul's address in refusal is a fine plea on the grounds of natural theology (**14** 15–18). The attempt on Paul's life after the Jews came seemed successful. In the band of disciples that "stood round about him," there may have been Timothy, Paul's son in the gospel. From Derbe they retrace their steps to Perga, in order to strengthen the churches with officers, and then sail for Seleucia and Antioch. They make their report to the church at Antioch. It is a wonderful story. The door of faith is now wide open for the Gentiles who have entered in great numbers (**14** 27). No report was sent to Jerus. What will the Pharisaic party do now?

6. The Conflict at Jerusalem Acts 15; Gal 2, 49 AD

The early date of Gal, addressed to these churches of Pisidia and Lycaonia before the Conference in Jerus does not allow time for a second visit there (Gal **4** 13), and requires that the Judaizers from Jerus followed close upon the heels of Paul and Barnabas (Gal **1** 6; **3** 1) in South Galatia. Besides, there is the less likelihood that the matter would have been taken a second time to Jerus (Acts **15** 2 f) if already the question had been settled in Paul's favor (Acts **11** 30). It is strange also that no reference to this previous conference on the same subject is made in Acts **15,** since Peter does refer to his experience at Caesarea (**15** 9) and since James in Acts **21** 25 specifically ("we wrote") mentions the letter of Acts **15** in which full liberty was granted to the Gentiles. Once more, the attack on the position of Paul and Barnabas in Acts **15** 1 is given as a new experience, and hence the sharp dissension and tense feeling. The occasion for the sudden outbreak at Antioch on the part of the self-appointed (Acts **15** 24) regulators of Paul and Barnabas lay in the reports that came to Jerus about the results of this campaign on a large scale among the Gentiles. There was peril to the supremacy of the Jewish element. They had assumed at first, as even Peter did who was not a Judaizer (Acts **10**), that the Gentiles who became disciples would also become Jews. The party of the circumcision had made protest against the conduct of Peter at Caesarea (**11** 1 f) and had reluctantly acquiesced in the plain work of God (**11** 18). They had likewise yielded in the matter of the Greeks at Antioch (**11** 19 ff) by the help of the contribution (**11** 29 f). But they had not agreed to a campaign to Hellenize Christianity. The matter had to stop. So the Judaizers came up to Antioch and laid down the law to Paul and Barnabas. They did not wait for them to come to Jerus. They might not come till it was too late (cf Barnabas in Acts **11**). Paul and Barnabas had not sought the controversy. They had both received specific instructions from the Holy Spirit to make this great campaign among the Gentiles. They would not stultify themselves and destroy the liberty of the Gentiles in Christ by going back and having the Mosaic Law imposed on them by the ceremony of circumcision. They saw at once the gravity of the issue. The very essence of the gospel of grace was involved. Paul had turned away from this yoke of bondage. He would not go back to it nor would he impose it on his converts. The church at Antioch stood by Paul and Barnabas. Paul (Gal **2** 2) says that he had a revelation to go to Jerus with the problem. Luke (Acts **15** 3) says that the church sent them. Surely there is no inconsistency here. It is not difficult to combine the personal narrative in Gal **2** with the public meetings recorded in Acts **15.** We have first the general report by Paul and Barnabas to the church in Jerus (Acts **15** 4 f) to which instant exception was made by the Judaizing element. There seems to have come an adjournment to prepare for the conflict, since in ver 6 Luke says again that "the apostles and the elders were gathered together to consider of this matter." Between these two public meetings we may place the private conference of Paul and Barnabas with Peter, John and James and other teachers (Gal **2** 1–10). In this private conference some of the timid brethren wished to persuade Paul to have Titus, a Gr Christian whom Paul had brought down from Antioch (a live specimen!), offered as a sacrifice to the Judaizers ("false brethren") and circumcised. But Paul stood his ground for the truth of the gospel and was supported by Peter, John and James. They agreed all around for Paul and Barnabas to go on with their work to the Gentiles, and Peter, John and James would push the work among the Jews (a division in sphere of work, like home and foreign missions, not a denominational cleavage). Here, then, for the first time, Paul has had an opportunity to talk the matter over with the apostolic teachers, and they agree. The Judaizers will have no support from the apostles. The battle was really won in their private conference. In the second public meeting (Acts **15** 6–29) all goes smoothly enough. Ample opportunity for free discussion is offered. Then Peter shows how God had used him to preach to the Romans, and how the Jews themselves had to believe on Christ in order to be saved. He opposed putting a yoke on the Gentiles that the Jews could not bear. There was a pause, and then Barnabas and Paul (note the order here: courtesy to Barnabas) spoke again. After another pause, James, the president of the conference, the brother of the Lord Jesus, and a stedfast Jew, spoke. He cited Am **9** 11 f to show that God had long ago promised a blessing to the Gentiles. He suggests liberty to the Gentiles with the prohibition of pollution of idols, of fornication, things strangled, and blood. His ideas are embodied in a unanimous decree which strongly commends "our beloved Barnabas and Paul," and disclaims responsibility for the visit of the Judaizers to Antioch. The Western text omits "things strangled" from the decree. If this is correct, the decree prohibits idolatry, fornication and murder (Wilson, *Origin and Aim of the Acts of the Apostles,* 1912, 55). At any rate, the decision is a tremendous victory for Paul and Barnabas. If the other reading is correct, Jewish feelings about things strangled and blood are to be respected. The decision was received with great joy in Antioch (Acts **15** 30–35).

Some time later Peter appears at Antioch in the fullest fellowship with Paul and Barnabas in their work, and joins them in free social intercourse with the Gentiles, as he had timidly done in the home of Cornelius, till "certain came from James" (Gal **2** 11 f), and probably threatened to have Peter up before the church again (Acts **11** 2) on this matter, claiming that James agreed with them on the subject. This I do not believe was true in the light of Acts **15** 24, where a similar false claim is discredited, since James had agreed with Paul in Jerus (Acts **15** 19 ff; Gal **2** 9 f). The new ground for complaint was that they had not settled the question of social relations with the Gentiles in the Jerus conference and that Peter had exceeded the agreement there reached. Peter quailed before the accusation, "fearing them that were of the circumcision" (Gal **2** 12). To make it worse, "even Barnabas was carried away with their dissimulation" (**2** 13). Under this specious plea Paul was about to lose the fruit of the victory already won, and charged Peter to his face with Judaizing hypocrisy (**2** 11–14). It was a serious crisis. Peter had not changed his convictions, but had once more cowered in an hour of peril. Paul won both Barnabas and Peter to his side and took occasion to show how useless the death of Christ was if men could be saved by mere legalism (**2** 21). But the Judaizers had renewed the war, and they would keep it up and harry the work of Paul all over the world. Paul had the fight of his life upon his hands.

7. The Second Mission Campaign Acts 15 : 36—18 : 22; 1 and 2 Thess, 49–51 (or 52) AD

The impulse to go out again came from Paul. Despite the difference in Gal **2** 13, he wished to go again with Barnabas (Acts **15** 36), but Barnabas insisted on taking along John Mark, which Paul was not willing to do because of his failure to stick to the work at Perga. So they agreed to disagree after "sharp contention" (**15** 39 f). Barnabas went with Mark to Cyprus, while Paul took **Silas,** "being commended by the brethren to the grace of the Lord." Luke follows the career of Paul, and so Barnabas drops out of view (cf later 1 Cor **9** 6). Paul and Silas go "through **Syria** and **Cilicia,** confirming the churches" (Acts **15** 41). They pass through the Cilician gates to **Derbe,** the end of the first tour, and go to **Lystra.** Here they pick up **Timothy,** who more than takes Mark's place in Paul's life. Timothy's mother was a Jewess and his father a Greek. Paul decided therefore to have him circumcised since, as a half-Jew, he would be esp. obnoxious to the Jews. This case differed wholly from that of **Titus,** a Greek, where principle was involved. Here it was a matter merely of expediency. Paul had taken the precaution to bring along the decrees of the Conference at Jerus in case there was need of them. He delivered them to the churches. It has to be noted that in 1 Cor **8–10** and in Rom **14** and **15,** when discussing the question of eating meats offered to idols, Paul does not refer to these decrees, but argues the matter purely from the standpoint of the principles involved. The Judaizers anyhow had not lived up to the agreement, but Paul is here doing his part by the decision. The result of the work was good for the churches (Acts **16** 4).

When we come to Acts **16** 6, we touch a crucial passage in the South-Galatian controversy. Ramsay (*Christianity in the Rom Empire*, chs iii–vi; *Hist and Geography of Asia Minor; St. Paul the Traveller*, chs v, vi, viii, ix; *Expos*, IV, viii, ix, "replies to Chase"; "Galatia," *HDB; Comm. on Gal; The Cities of St. Paul; Expos T*, 1912, 1913) has become by his able advocacy the chief champion of the view that Paul never went to Galatia proper or **North Galatia,** and that he addressed his ep. to **South Galatia,** the churches visited in the first tour. For a careful history of the whole controversy in detail, see Moffatt, *Intro to the Lit. of the NT*, 90–106, who strongly supports the view of Lightfoot, H. J. Holtzmann, Blass, Schürer, Denney, Chase, Mommsen, Steinmann, etc. There are powerful names with Ramsay, like Hausrath, Zahn, Bartlet, Garvie, Weizsäcker, etc. The arguments are too varied and minute for complete presentation here. The present writer sees some very attractive features in the South-Galatian hypothesis, but as a student of language finds himself unable to overcome the syntax of Acts **16** 6. The minor difficulty is the dropping of καί, *kaí*, between "Phrygia" and "Galatic region" by Ramsay. It is by no means certain that this is the idea of Luke. It is more natural to take the terms as distinct and coördinated by *kaí*. In *St. Paul the Traveller*, 212, Ramsay pleads for the aorist of subsequent time, but Moulton (*Prolegomena*, 133) will have none of it. With that I agree. The aorist participle must give something synchronous with or antecedent to the principal verb. In *Expos T* for February, 1913, 220 f, Ramsay comes back to the "construction of **16** 6." He admits that the weight of authority is against the *TR* and in favor of διῆλθον . . . . κωλυθέντες, *diélthon . . . . kōluthéntes*. He now interprets the language thus: "Paul, having in mind at Lystra his plan of going on to Asia from Galatia, was ordered by the Spirit not to preach in Asia. He therefore made a tour through the Phrygio-Galatic region, which he had already influenced so profoundly from end to end (**13** 49)." But there is grave difficulty in accepting this interpretation as a solution of the problem. Ramsay here makes the narrative in ver 6 resumptive and takes us back to the standpoint of ver 1 at Lystra. The proper place for such a forecast was in ver 1, or at most before ver 4, which already seems to mark an advance beyond Lystra to Iconium and Antioch in Pisidia: "and as they went on their way through the cities."

Besides, "the Phrygio-Galatic region" lay between Lystra and Asia, and, according to Ramsay, after the prohibition in Lystra, he went straight on toward Asia. This is certainly very artificial and unlike the usual procedure. According to the other view, Paul had already visited the churches in Lycaonia and Pisidia on his former visit. He wished to go on west into Asia, probably to Ephesus, but was forbidden by the Holy Spirit, and as a result turned northward through Phrygia and the regions of Galatia, using both terms in the ethnographic sense. Paul was already in the province of Galatia at Derbe and Lystra. The matter has many "ins and outs" and cannot be argued further here. It is still in debate, but the present interpretation is in harmony with the narrative in Acts. See also GALATIA; GALATIANS, EPISTLE TO THE.

By this view Paul had not meant to stop in Galatia proper and did so only because of an attack of illness (Gal **4** 13). It is possible that **Luke** may have come to his rescue here. At any rate, he finally pushes on opposite **Mysia** and **Bithynia** in the extreme north and was forbidden by the Spirit from going on into Bithynia. So they came down to **Troas** (Acts **16** 7 f) when Luke ("we," **16** 10) appears on the scene and the Macedonian call comes to Paul. Thus Paul is led out of Asia into **Europe** and carries the gospel successively to **Philippi,** Thessalonica, Beroea, Athens, and Corinth. The gospel is finally planted in the great provinces of Macedonia and Achaia. In Philippi, a Rom colony and military outpost, Paul finds few Jews and has to go out to a prayer-place to find a few Jewish women to whom he can tell the story of Jesus. But he gains a start with Lydia and her household, and soon arouses the hostility of a company of men who were making money out of a poor girl's powers of divination. But before Paul and Silas leave the jail, the jailer is himself converted, and a good church is established. At **Thessalonica** Paul has great success and arouses the jealousy of the Jews who gather a rabble and raise a disturbance and charge it up to Paul. At Philippi appeal was made to prejudice against Jews. At Thessalonica the charge is made that Paul preaches Jesus as a rival king to Caesar. In **Beroea** Paul and Silas have even more success till the Jews come from Thessalonica and drive Paul out again. Timothy, who has come out from Philippi where Luke has remained, and Silas stay in Beroea while Paul hurries on to **Athens** with some of the brethren, who return with the request for Timothy and Silas "to come to him with all speed." Apparently Timothy did come (1 Thess **3** 1 f), but Paul soon sent him back to Thessalonica because of his anxiety about conditions there. Left alone in Athens, Paul's spirit was stirred over the idolatry before his eyes. He preaches in the synagogues and argues with the Stoics and Epicureans in the Agora who make light of his pretensions to philosophy as a "babbler" (Acts **17** 18). But curiosity leads them to invite him to speak on the **Areopagus.** This notable address, all alive to his surroundings, was rather rudely cut short by their indifference and mockery, and Paul left Athens with small results for his work. He goes over to **Corinth,** the great commercial city of the province, rich and with bizarre notions of culture. Paul determined (1 Cor **2** 1–5) to be true to the cross, even after his experience in Athens. He gave them, not the flashy philosophy of the sophists, but the true wisdom of God in simple words, the philosophy of the cross of Christ (1 Cor **1** 17—**3** 4). In Corinth Paul found fellow-helpers in **Aquila and Priscilla,** just expelled from Rome by Claudius. They have the same trade of tent-makers and live together (Acts **18** 1–4), and Paul preached in the synagogues. Paul is cheered by the coming of Timothy and Silas from Thessalonica (**18** 5) with supplies from Philippi, as they had done while in Thessalonica (Phil **4** 15 f). This very success led to opposition, and Paul has to preach in the house of Titus Justus. But the work goes on till Gallio comes and a renewed effort is made to have it stopped, but Gallio declines to interfere and thus practically makes Christianity a *religio licita,* since he treats it as a variety of Judaism. While here, after the arrival of Timothy and Silas, Paul writes the two letters to Thessalonica, the first of his 13 epp. They are probably not very far apart in time, and deal chiefly with a grievous misunderstanding on their part concerning the emphasis placed by him on the Man of Sin and the Second Coming. Paul had felt the power of the empire, and his attention is sharply drawn to the coming conflict between the Rom empire and the kingdom of God. He treats it in terms of apocalyptic eschatology. When he leaves Corinth, it is to go by **Ephesus,** with Aquila and Priscilla whom he leaves there with the promise to return. He goes down to **Caesarea** and "went up and saluted the church" (Acts **18** 22), probably at **Jerus** (fourth visit), and "went down to **Antioch."** If he went to Jerus, it was probably incidental, and nothing of importance happened. He is back once again in Antioch after an absence of some 3 or 4 years.

8. The Third Mission Campaign, Acts 18:23—21:14; 1 and 2 Cor; Gal; Rom, 52 (or 53)-57 (or 58) AD

The stay of Paul at Antioch is described as "some time" (Acts **18** 23). Denney (*Standard Bible Dict.*) conjectures that Paul's brief stay at Jerus (see above) was due to the fact that he found that the Judaizers had organized opposition there against him in the absence of the apostles, and it was so unpleasant that he did not stay. He suggests also that the Judaizers had secured letters of commendation from the church for their emissaries (2 Cor **3** 1) to Corinth and Galatia, who were preaching "another Jesus" of nationalism and narrowness, whom Paul did not preach (Gal **1** 6; 2 Cor **11** 4). Both Denney and Findlay follow Neander, Wieseler, and Sabatier in placing here, before Paul starts out again from Antioch, the visit of certain "from James" (Gal **2** 12), who overpowered Peter for the moment. But I have put this incident as more probably before the disagreement with Barnabas over Mark, and as probably contributing to that breach at the beginning of the second tour. It is not necessary to suppose that the Judaizers remained acquiescent so long.

Paul seems to have set out on the third tour alone —unless Timothy came back with him, of which there is no evidence save that he is with Paul again in **Ephesus** (Acts **19** 22). What became of Silas? Paul "went through the region of **Galatia,** and **Phrygia,** in order, establishing all the disciples" (Acts **18** 23), the opposite order to **16** 6, "through the region of Phrygia and Galatia." According to the North-Galatian view, here followed, he went through the northern part of the province, passing through Galatia proper and Phrygia on his way west to **Ephesus.** Luke adds, "Paul having passed through the upper country came to Ephesus" (**19** 1). The ministry of **Apollos** in Ephesus (**18** 24–28) had taken place before Paul arrived, though Aquila and Priscilla were still on hand. Apollos passed over to Corinth and innocently became the occasion of such strife there (1 Cor **1–4**) that he left and refused to return at Paul's request (1 Cor **16** 12). Paul has a ministry of 3 years, in round numbers, in Ephesus, which is full of excitement and anxiety from the work there and in Corinth. He finds on his arrival some ill-informed disciples of John the Baptist who are ignorant of the chief elements of John's teaching about repentance, Jesus, and the Holy Spirit (Acts **19** 2–7), matters of which Apollos had knowledge, though he learned more from Priscilla and Aquila, but there is no evidence that he was rebaptized as was true of the 12 disciples of John (Robertson, *John the Loyal,* 290–303). The boldness of Paul in Ephesus led in 3 months to his departure from the synagogue to the schoolhouse of Tyrannus, where he preached for 2 years (Acts **19** 8–10) with such power that "all they that dwelt in Asia heard the word of the Lord." It is not strange later to find churches at Colossae and Hierapolis in the Lycus Valley (cf also Rev **1** 11). Paul has a sharp collision with the strolling Jewish exorcists that led to the burning of books of magic by the wholesale (**19** 11–20), another proof of the hold that magic and the mysteries had upon the Orient. Ephesus was the seat of the worship of Diana whose wonderful temple was their pride. A great business in the manufacture of shrines of Diana was carried on here by Demetrius, and "this Paul" had hurt his trade so much that he raised an insurrection under the guise of piety and patriotism and might have killed Paul with the mob, if he could have got hold of him (**19** 23–41). It was with great difficulty that Paul was kept from going to the amphitheater, as it was. But here, as at Corinth, the Rom officer (the town clerk) defended Paul from the rage of his enemies (there the jealous Jews, here the tradesmen whose business suffered). He was apparently very ill anyhow, and came near death (2 Cor **1** 9). All this seems to have hastened his departure from Ephesus sooner than Pentecost, as he had written to the Corinthians (1 Cor **16** 8). His heart was in Corinth because of the discussions there over him and Apollos and Peter, by reason of the agitation of the Judaizers (1 Cor **1** 10–17). The household of Chloe had brought word of this situation to Paul. He had written the church a letter now lost (1 Cor **5** 9). They had written him a letter (1 Cor **7** 1). They sent messengers to Paul (1 Cor **16** 17). He had sent Timothy to them (1 Cor **4** 17; **16** 10), who seems not to have succeeded in quieting the trouble. Paul wrote 1 Cor (spring of 56), and then sent Titus, who was to meet him at Troas and report results (2 Cor **2** 12 f). He may also have written another letter and sent it by Titus (2 Cor **2** 3 f). The sudden departure from Corinth brought Paul to **Troas** ahead of time, but he could not wait for Titus, and so pushed on with a heavy heart into **Macedonia,** where he met him, and he had good and bad news to tell (2 Cor **2** 12 ff; **7** 5–13). The effect on Paul was instantaneous. He rebounded to hope and joy (2 Cor **2** 14 ff) in a glorious defence of the ministry of Jesus (cf Robertson, *The Glory of the Ministry; Paul's Exultation in Preaching)*, with a message of cheer to the majority of the church that had sustained Paul and with instructions (chs **8** and **9**) about the collection for the poor saints in Jerus, which must be pushed to a completion by Titus and two other brethren (possibly also Luke, brother of Titus, and Erastus). Timothy and Erastus had been sent on ahead to Macedonia from Ephesus (Acts **19** 22), and Timothy sends greetings with Paul to the Corinthians in a letter (2 Cor) which Paul now forwards, possibly by Titus. The latter part of the ep. (chs **10–13**) deals with the stubborn minority who still resist the authority of Paul as an apostle. On the proposed treatment of these chapters as a separate ep. see the earlier part of this art. Paul seems to wait a while before going on to Corinth. He wishes the opposition to have time to repent. During this period he probably went round about to **Illyricum** (Rom **15** 19). He spent three months in **Greece** (Acts **20** 2 f), probably the winter of 56 and 57.

We have placed Gal in the early part of this stay in Corinth, though it could have been written while at Ephesus. Rom was certainly written while here, and they both treat the same general theme of justification by faith. Ramsay (*Expos*, February, 1913, 127–45) has at last come to the conclusion that Gal belongs to the date of Acts **15** 1 f. He bases this conclusion chiefly on the "absolute independence" of his apostleship claimed in Gal **1** and **2**, which, he holds, he would not have done after the conference in Acts **15**, which was "a sacrifice of complete independence." This is a curious interpretation, for in Gal **2** 1–10 Paul himself tells of his recognition on terms of equality by Peter, John and James, and of his going to Jerus by "revelation," which was just as much "a sacrifice of complete independence" as we find in Acts **15**. Besides, in 2 Cor **11** 5 and **12** 11 Paul expressly asserts his equality (with all humility) with the very chiefest apostles, and in 1 Cor **15** 10 he claims in so many words to have wrought more than all the apostles. Perhaps messengers from Galatia with the contributions from that region report the havoc wrought there by the Judaizers. Gal is a tremendous plea for the spiritual nature of Christianity as opposed to Jewish ceremonial legalism.

Paul had long had it in mind to go to Rome. It was his plan to do so while at Ephesus (Acts **19** 21) after he had gone to Jerus with the great collection from the churches of Asia, Galatia, Achaia, and Macedonia. He hoped that this collection would have a mollifying effect on the Jerus saints as that from Antioch had (Acts **11** 29 f). He had changed some details in his plans, but not the purpose to go to Jerus and then to Rome. Meanwhile, he writes the longest and most important letter of all to the Romans, in which he gives a fuller statement of his gospel, because they had not heard him preach, save his various personal friends who had gone there from the east (ch **16**). But already the shadow of Jerus is on his heart, and he asks their prayers in his behalf, as he faces his enemies in Jerus (Rom **15** 30–32). He hopes also to go on to Spain (**15** 24), so as to carry the gospel to the farther west also. The statesmanship of Paul comes out now in great clearness. He has in his heart always anxiety for the churches that consumes him (2 Cor **11** 28 f). He was careful to have a committee of the churches go with him to report the collection (2 Cor **8** 19 f). Paul had planned to sail direct for Syria, but a plot on his life in Corinth led him to go by land via Macedonia with his companions (Acts **20** 2–4). He tarried at **Philippi** while the rest went on to Troas. At Philippi Paul is joined again by Luke, who stays with him till Rome is reached. They celebrate the Passover (probably the spring of 57) in Philippi (Acts **20** 6). We cannot follow the details in Acts at **Troas,** the voyage through the beautiful **Archipelago,** to **Miletus.** There Paul took advantage of the stop to send for the elders of Ephesus to whom he gave a wonderful address (Acts **20** 17–38). They change ships at **Patara** for **Phoenicia** and pass to the right of **Cyprus** with its memories of Barnabas and Sergius Paulus and stop at **Tyre,** where Paul is warned not to go on to Jerus. The hostility of the Judaizers to Paul is now common talk everywhere. There is grave peril of a schism in Christianity over the question of gentile liberty, once settled in Jerus, but unsettled by the Judaizers. At **Caesarea** Paul is greeted by **Philip** the evangelist and his four daughters (prophetesses). At Caesarea Paul is warned in dramatic fashion by Agabus (cf Acts **11** 28) not to go on to Jerus (**21** 9 ff), but Paul is more determined than ever to go, even if he die (**20** 13). He had had three premonitions for long (**20** 22 ff), but he will finish his course, cost what it may. He finds a friend at Caesarea in Mnason of Cyprus, an early disciple, who was to be the host of Paul in Jerus (**21** 16).

9. Five Years a Prisoner, Acts 21:17—28:31; Phil; Philem; Col; Eph, 57–62 (or 63) AD

Paul had hoped to reach **Jerus** by Pentecost (Acts **20** 16). He seems to have done so. Luke gives the story of Paul in Jerus, Caesarea, and the voyage to Rome in much detail. He was with him and considered this period of his ministry very important. The welcome from the brethren in Jerus was surprisingly cordial (Acts **21** 17). On the very next day Paul and his party made a formal call on James and all the elders (**21** 18 f), who gave a sympathetic hearing to the narrative of God's dealings with Paul and the Gentiles. He presented the alms (collection) in due form (**24** 17), though some critics have actually suggested that Paul used it to defray the expenses of the appeal to Caesar. Ramsay's notion that he may have fallen heir by now to his portion of his father's estate is quite probable. But the brethren wish to help Paul set himself right before the rank and file of the church in Jerus, who have been imposed upon by the Judaizers who have misrepresented Paul's real position by saying that he urged the Jewish Christians to give up the Mosaic customs (**21** 21). The elders understand Paul and recall the decision of the conference at which freedom was guaranteed to the Gentiles, and they have no wish to disturb that (**21** 25). They only wish Paul to show that he does not object to the Jewish Christians keeping up the Mosaic regulations. They propose that Paul offer sacrifice publicly in the temple and pay the vows of four men, and then all will know the truth (**21** 23 f). Paul does not hesitate to do that (**21** 26 ff). He had kept the Jewish feasts (cf **20** 6) as Jesus had done, and the early disciples in Jerus. He was a Jew. He may have had a vow at Corinth (**18** 18). He saw no inconsistency in a Jew doing thus after becoming a Christian, provided he did not make it obligatory on Gentiles. The real efficacy of the sacrifices lay in the death of Jesus for sin. Garvie (*Life and Teaching of Paul*, 173) calls this act of Paul "scarcely worthy of his courage as a man or his faith in God." I cannot see it in that light. It is a matter of practical wisdom, not of principle. To have refused would have been to say that the charge was true, and it was not. So far as the record goes, this act of Paul accomplished its purpose in setting Paul in a right light before the church in Jerus. It took away this argument from the Judaizers. The trouble that now comes to Paul does not come from the Judaizers, but from "the Jews from Asia" (**21** 27). If it be objected that the Jerus Christians seem to have done nothing to help Paul during his years of imprisonment, it can be said that there was little to be done in a legal way, as the matter was before the Rom courts very soon. The attack on Paul in the temple was while he was doing honor to the temple, engaged in actual worship offering sacrifices. But then Jews from Ephesus hated him so that they imagined that he had Greeks with him in the Jewish court, because they had seen him one day with Trophimus in the city (**21** 27 ff). It is a splendid illustration of the blindness of prejudice and hate. It was absolutely untrue, and the men who raised the hue and cry in the temple against Paul as the desecrator of the holy place and the Law and the people disappear, and are never heard of more (**24** 18 f). But it will take Paul five years or more of the prime of his life to get himself out of the tangled web that will be woven about his head. Peril follows peril. He was almost mobbed, as often before, by the crowd that dragged him out of the temple (**21** 30 f). It would remind Paul of Stephen's fate. When the Rom captain rescued him and had him bound with two chains as a dangerous bandit, and had him carried by the soldiers to save his life, the mob yelled "Away with him" (**21** 36 f), as they had done to Jesus. After the captain, astonished that "Paul the Egyp assassin" can speak Gr, grants him permission to stand on the steps of the tower of Antonia to speak to the mob that clamored for his blood, he held their rapt attention by an address in Aram. (**22** 2) in which he gave a defence of his whole career. This they heard eagerly till he spoke the word "Gentiles," at which they raged more violently than ever (**22** 21 ff). At this the captain has Paul tied with thongs, not understanding his Aram. speech, and is about to scourge him when Paul pleads his Rom citizenship, to the amazement of the centurion (**22** 24 ff). Almost in despair, the captain, wishing to know the charge of the Jews against Paul, brings him before the Sanhedrin. It is a familiar scene to Paul, and it is now their chance for settling old scores. Paul makes a sharp retort in anger to the high priest Ananias, for which he apologizes as if he was so angry that he had not noticed, but he soon divides the Sanhedrin hopelessly on the subject of the resurrection (cf the immunity of the disciples on that issue when Gamaliel scored the Sadducees in Acts **5**). This was turning the tables on his enemies, and was justifiable as war. He claimed to be a Pharisee on this point, as he was still, as opposed to the Sadducees. The result was that Paul had to be rescued from the contending factions, and the captain knew no more than he did before (**23** 1–10). That night "the Lord stood by him" and promised that he would go to Rome (**23** 11). That was a blessed hope. But the troubles of Paul are by no means over. By the skill of his nephew he escaped the murderous plot of 40 Jews who had taken a vow not to eat till they had killed Paul (**23** 12–24). They almost succeeded, but Claudius Lysias sent Paul in haste with a band of soldiers to Caesarea to Felix, the procurator, with a letter in which he claimed to have rescued Paul from the mob, "having learned that he was a Roman" (**23** 26–30). At any rate he was no longer in the clutches of the Jews. Would Rom provincial justice be any better? Felix follows a perfunctory course with Paul and shows some curiosity about Christianity, till Paul makes him tremble with terror, a complete reversal of situations (cf Pilate's meanness before Jesus). But love of money from Paul or the Jews leads Felix to keep Paul a prisoner for two years, though convinced of his innocence, and to hand him over to Festus, his successor, because the Jews might make things worse for him if he released him (ch **24**). The case of the Sanhedrin, who have now made it their own (or at least the Sadducean section), though pleaded by the Rom orator Tertullus, had fallen through as Paul calmly riddled their charges. Festus is at first at a loss how to proceed, but he soon follows the steps of Felix by offering to play into the hands of the Jewish leaders by sending Paul back to Jerus, whereupon Paul abruptly exercises his right of Rom citizenship by appealing to Caesar (**25** 1–12). This way, though a long one, offered the only ray of hope. The appearance of Paul before Agrippa and Bernice was simply by way of entertainment arranged by Festus to relieve his guests of *ennui*, but Paul seized the opportunity to make a powerful appeal to Agrippa that put him in a corner logically, though he wriggled out and declined to endorse Christianity, though confirming Paul's innocence, which Festus also had admitted (**25** 13—**26** 32). Paul was fortunate in the centurion Julius who took him to Rome, for he was kindly disposed to him at the start, and so it was all the way through the most remarkable voyage on record. Luke has surpassed his own record in ch **27**, in which he traces the voyage, stage by stage, with change of ship at **Myra,** delay at **Fair Havens, Crete,** and shipwreck on the island of **Malta.** More is learned about ancient seafaring from this chapter than from any other source (see art. PHOENIX, and Smith, *Voyage and Shipwreck of St. Paul*, 1866). In it all Paul is the hero, both on the ships and in Malta. In the early spring of 60 another ship takes Paul and the other prisoners to **Puteoli.** Thence they go on to **Rome,** and enter by the Appian Way. News of Paul's coming had gone on before (his ep. had come 3 years ago), and he had a hearty welcome. But he is now an imperial prisoner in the hands of Nero. He has more liberty in his own hired house (**28** 16.30), but he is chained always to a Rom soldier, though granted freedom to see his friends and to preach to the soldiers. Paul is anxious to remove any misapprehensions that the Jews in Rome may have about him, and tries to win them to Christ, and with partial success (**28** 17–28). And here Luke leaves him a prisoner for 2 years more, probably because at this point he finishes the Book of Acts. But, as we have seen, during these years in Rome, Paul wrote Phil, Philem, Col, and Eph. He still has the churches on his heart. They send messengers to him, and he writes back to them. The incipient Gnosticism of the East has pressed upon the churches at Colossae and Laodicea, and a new peril confronts Christianity. The Judaizing controversy has died away with these years (cf Phil **3** 1 ff for an echo of it), but the dignity and glory of Jesus are challenged. In the presence of the power of Rome Paul rises to a higher conception than even that of the person of Christ and the glory of the church universal. In due time Paul's case was disposed of and he was once more set free. The Romans were proverbially dilatory. It is doubtful if his enemies ever appeared against him with formal charges.

10. Further Travels

The genuineness of the Pastoral Epp. is here assumed. But for them we should know nothing further, save from a few fragments in the early Christian writings. As it is, some few who accept the Pastoral Epp. seek to place them before 64 AD, so as to allow for Paul's death in that year from the Neronian persecution. In that case, he was not released. There is no space here to argue the question in detail. We can piece together the probable course of events. He had expected when in Corinth last to go on to Spain (Rom **15** 28), but now in Rome his heart turns back to the east again. He longs to see the Philippians (**1** 23 ff) and hopes to see Philemon in Colossae (Philem ver 22). But he may have gone to Spain also, as Clement of Rome seems to imply (Clement ad Cor **5**), and as is stated in the Canon of Muratori. He may have been in Spain when Rome was burned July 19, 64 AD. There is no evidence that Paul went as far as Britain. On his return east he left Titus in Crete (Tit **1** 5). He touched at Miletus when he left Trophimus sick (2 Tim **4** 20) and when he may have met Timothy, if he did not go on to Ephesus (1 Tim **1** 3). He stopped at Troas and apparently expected to come back here, as he left his cloak and books with Carpus (2 Tim **4** 13). He was on his way to Macedonia (1 Tim **1** 3), whence he writes Timothy in 65–67 a letter full of love and counsel for the future. Paul is apprehensive of the grave perils now confronting Christianity. Besides the Judaizers, the Gnostics, the Jews and the Romans, he may have had dim visions of the conflict with the mystery-religions. It was a syncretistic age, and men had itching ears. But Paul is full of sympathy and tender solicitude for Timothy, who must push on the work and get ready for it. Paul expects to spend the winter in Nicopolis (Tit **3** 12), but is apparently still in Macedonia when he writes to Titus a letter on lines similar to those in 1 Tim, only the note is sharper against Judaism of a certain type. We catch another glimpse of Apollos in **3** 13. Paul hits off the Cretans in **1** 10 with a quotation from Epimenides, one of their own poetic prophets.

11. Last Imprisonment and Death in Rome, 68 (or 67) AD

When Paul writes again to Timothy he has had a winter in prison, and has suffered greatly from the cold and does not wish to spend another winter in the Mamertine (probably) prison (2 Tim **4** 13.21). We do not know what the charges now are. They may have been connected with the burning of Rome. There were plenty of informers eager to win favor with Nero. Proof was not now necessary. Christianity is no longer a *religio licita* under the shelter of Judaism. It is now a crime to be a Christian. It is dangerous to be seen with Paul now, and he feels the desertion keenly (2 Tim **1** 15 ff; **4** 10). Only Luke, the beloved physician, is with Paul (**4** 11), and such faithful ones as live in Rome still in hiding (**4** 21). Paul hopes that Timothy may come and bring Mark also (**4** 11). Apparently Timothy did come and was put into prison (He **13** 23). Paul is not afraid. He knows that he will die. He has escaped the mouth of the lion (2 Tim **4** 17), but he will die (**4** 18). The Lord Jesus stood by him, perhaps in visible presence (**4** 17). The tradition is, for now Paul fails us, that Paul, as a Rom citizen, was beheaded on the Ostian Road just outside of Rome. Nero died June, 68 AD, so that Paul was executed before that date, perhaps in the late spring of that year (or 67). Perhaps Luke and Timothy were with him. It is fitting, as Findlay suggests, to let Paul's words in 2 Tim **4** 6–8 serve for his own epitaph. He was ready to go to be with Jesus, as he had long wished to be (Phil **1** 23).

VI. Gospel.—I had purposed to save adequate space for the discussion of Paul's theology, but that is not now possible. A bare sketch must suffice. Something was said (see above on his epp. and equipment) about the development in Paul's conception of Christ and his message about Him. Paul had a gospel which he called his own (Rom **2** 16). I cannot agree with the words of Deissmann (*St. Paul*, 6): "St. Paul the theologian looks backward toward rabbinism. As a religious genius St. Paul's outlook is forward into a future of universal history." He did continue to use some rabbinical methods of argument, but his theology was not rabbinical. And he had a theology. He was the great apostle and missionary to the heathen. He was a Christian statesman with far-seeing vision. He was the loving pastor with the shepherd heart. He was the great martyr for Christ. He was the wonderful preacher of Jesus. But he was also "Paul the theologian" (Garvie, *Life and Teaching of Paul*, ch v). There are two ways of studying his teaching. One is to take it by groups of the epp., the purely historical method, and that has some advantages (cf Sabatier, *The Apostle Paul*). But at bottom Paul has the same message in each group, though with varying emphasis due to special exigencies. The same essential notes occur all through. The more common method, therefore, is to study his gospel topically, using all the epp. for each topic. A measure of historical development may still be observed. Only the chief notes in Paul's gospel can be mentioned here. Even so, one must not turn to his epp. for a complete system of doctrine. The epp. are "occasional letters, *pièces de circonstance*" (Findlay, *HDB*), and they do not profess, not even Rom, to give a full summary of Christian doctrine. They are vital documents that throb with life. There is no theological manual in them. But Paul's gospel is adequately stated repeatedly. Paul's message is Christocentric. Jesus as Messiah he preached at once on his conversion (Acts **9** 20.22). He knew already the current Jewish Messianism to which Jesus did not correspond. The acceptance of Jesus as He was (the facts about Him and teachings) revolutionized his Messianic conceptions, his view of God, and his view of man. "When he takes and uses the Messianic phraseology of his day, he fills it with a meaning new and rich" (Rostron, *Christology of St. Paul*, 31). Paul was not merely a new creature himself, but he had a new outlook: "Wherefore we henceforth know no man after the flesh: even though we have known Christ after the flesh, yet now we know him so no more. Wherefore if any man is in Christ, he is a new creature: the old things are passed away; behold, they are become new. But all things are of God, who reconciled us to himself through Christ, and gave unto us the ministry of reconciliation; to wit, that God was in Christ reconciling the world unto himself, not reckoning unto them their trespasses, and having committed unto us the word of reconciliation" (2 Cor **5** 16–19). Perhaps no single passage in Paul's Epp. tells us more than this one of the change in Paul's theological conceptions wrought by his conversion. His view of Christ as the revealer of God (God in Christ) and the manifestation of love for men (of God, who reconciled us to Himself, reconciling the world to Himself) and the means (through Christ) by whom God is able to forgive our sins ("not reckoning unto them their trespasses") on the basis of the atoning death of Christ ("wherefore"; for this see vs 14 f just before ver 16) with whom the believer has vital union ("in Christ") and who transforms the nature and views of the believer, is here thoroughly characteristic. Paul's passion is Christ (2 Cor **5** 14; Phil **1** 21). To gain Christ (**3** 8), to know Christ (**3** 10), to be found in Christ (**3** 9), to know Christ as the mystery of God (Col **2** 2 f), to be hid with Christ in God (**3** 3)—this with the new Paul is worth while. Thus Paul interprets God and man, by his doctrine of Christ. To him Jesus is Christ and Christ is Jesus. He has no patience with the incipient Cerinthian Gnosticism, nor with the docetic Gnosticism that denied the true humanity of Jesus. The real mystery of God is Christ, not the so-called mystery-religions. Christ has set us free from the bondage of ceremonial legalism. We are free from the curse of the law (Gal **3** 13). Grace is the distinctive word for the gospel (Rom **3**–**5**), but it must lead to sanctification (Rom **6**–**8**), not license (Col **3**). Paul's Christology is both theocentric and anthropocentric, but it is theocentric first. His notion of redemption is the love of God seeking a world lost in sin and finding love's way, the only way consonant with justice, in the atoning sacrifice of Jesus Christ His Son (Rom **3** 21–31). The sinner comes into union with God in Christ by faith in Christ as Redeemer and Lord. Henceforth he lives to God in Christ by the help of the Holy Spirit (Rom **8**; Gal **5**). Paul presents God as

Father of all in one sense (Eph **4** 6), but in a special sense of the believers in Christ (Rom **8** 15 f). Jesus Christ is the Incarnation of the Pre-incarnate Son of God (2 Cor **8** 9; Phil **2** 5–10), who is both God and man (Rom **1** 3 f). With Paul the agent of creation is Jesus (Col **1** 15 f), who is also the head of the church universal (Col **1** 18; Eph **1** 22 f). In the work of Christ Paul gives the central place to the cross (1 Cor **1** 17 f; **2** 2; Col **2** 20; Eph **2** 13–18). Sin is universal in humanity (Rom **1** 18—**3** 20), but the vicarious death of Christ makes redemption possible to all who believe (Rom **3** 21 ff; Gal **3** 6–11). The redeemed constitute the kingdom of God or church universal, with Christ as head. Local bodies (churches) are the chief means for pushing the work of the kingdom. Paul knows two ordinances, both of which present in symbolic form the death of Christ for sin and the pledge of the believer to newness of life in Christ. These ordinances are baptism (Rom **6** 1–11) and the Lord's Supper (1 Cor **11** 17–34). If he knew the mystery-religions, they may have helped him by way of illustration to present his conception of the mystic union with Christ. Paul is animated by the hope of the second coming of Christ, which will be sudden (1 Thess **5** 1–11) and not probably at once (2 Thess **2**), but was to be considered as always imminent (1 Thess **5** 2 ff). Meanwhile, death brings us to Christ, which is a glorious hope to Paul (2 Cor **5** 1–10; Phil **1** 21 ff; 2 Tim **4** 18). But, while Paul was a theologian in the highest and best sense of the term, the best interpreter of Christ to men, he was also an ethical teacher. He did not divorce ethics from religion. He insisted strongly on the spiritual experience of Christ as the beginning and the end of it all, as opposed to mere ritualistic ceremonies which had destroyed the life of Judaism. But all the more Paul demanded the proof of life as opposed to mere profession. See Rom **6–8** in particular. In most of the epp. the doctrinal section is followed by practical exhortations to holy living. Mystic as Paul was, the greatest of all mystics, he was the sanest of moralists and had no patience with hypocrites or licentious pietists or idealists who allowed sentimentalism and emotionalism to take the place of righteousness. His notion of the righteousness demanded by God and given by God included both sanctification and justification. In the end, the sinner who for Christ's sake is treated as righteous must be righteous. Thus the image of God is restored in man by the regenerating work of the Spirit of God (2 Cor **3** 18). Paul sees God in the face of Christ (2 Cor **4** 6), and the vision of Christ brings God to all who see.

LITERATURE.—Out of the vast Pauline lit. the following selections may be mentioned:

(1) General Works: Addis, *Christianity and the Rom Empire*, 1893; Bartlet, *The Apostolic Age*, 1899; Böhlig, *Die Geisteskultur von Tarsos*, 1913; Clemen, *Primitive Christianity and Its Non-Jewish Sources*, 1912; Cumont, *Oriental Religions in Rom Paganism*, 1911; Deissmann, *Light from the Ancient East*, 1910; Dewick, *Primitive Christian Eschatology*, 1912; Döllinger, *Gentile and Jew in the Courts of the Temple of Christ*, tr, 1862; Farrar, *Early Days of Christianity*, 1882, *Darkness and Dawn*, 1893; Ferrero, *Greatness and Decline of Rome*, 1908; Friedländer, *Rom Life and Manners under the Early Empire;* Glover, *Conflict of Religions in the Early Rom Empire*, 1910; Gunkel, *Zum religionsgeschichtlichen Verst. d. NT*, 1903; Hausrath, *Time of the Apostles*, tr; Neander, *Planting and Training of the Christian Church*, tr; McGiffert, *A Hist of Christianity in the Apostolic Age*, 1897; Ramsay, *The Church in the Rom Empire*, 1893, *Cities and Bishoprics of Phrygia*, 1895, *The First Christian Cent.*, 1911; Reitzenstein, *Die hellenistischen Mysterienreligionen*, 1910; Ropes, *The Apostolic Age*, 1906; Schürer, *HJP;* Weizsäcker, *The Apostolic Age in the Christian Church*, 1894–95.

(2) Introductions: E. Burton, *Chron of St. Paul's Epp.;* Clemen, *Die Chron der Paulinischen Briefe*, 1893, *Die Einheitlichkeit der Paulinischen Briefe*, 1894; Findlay, *Epp. of Paul the Apostle*, 1893; Gloag, *Intro to the Pauline Epp.*, 1876; Gregory, *Canon and Text of the NT*, 1900; Hort, *Prolegomena to Rom and Eph*, 1895; Harnack, *The Acts of the Apostles*, 1909, *Date of the Acts and the Synoptic Gospels*, 1911, *History of Early Christian Lit. until Eusebius*, 1897; Holtzmann, *Einleitung*[3], 1892; James, *Genuineness and Authorship of the Pastoral Epp.*, 1906; Jülicher, *Intro to the NT*, 1903; Lake, *Earlier Epp. of St. Paul*, 1911; Moffatt, *Intro to the Lit. of the NT*, 1911; Peake, *Critical Intro to the NT*, 1909; Salmon, *Intro to the NT*, 1892; R. Scott, *Epp. of Paul*, 1909; Shaw, *The Pauline Epp.*, 1903; von Soden, *History of Early Christian Lit.*, 1906; B. Weiss, *Present State of the Inquiry Concerning the Genuineness of Paul's Epp.*, 1897; Zahn, *Intro to the NT*, 1909.

(3) Commentaries: For exegetical comms. on special epp. see special arts. For the ancients see Chrysostom for the Greeks, and Pelagius for the Latins. For the Middle Ages see Thomas Aquinas. For the later time see Beza, Calvin, Colet, Estius, Grotius, Cornelius à Lapide, Wettstein, Bengel. Among the moderns note Alford, Beet (*Rom-Col*), Boise, *Bible for Home and School, Cambridge Bible for Schools, Cambridge Gr Testament, New Cent. Bible;* Drummond, *Epp. of Paul*, Ellicott (all but Rom and 2 Cor), *Expositor's Bible, Expositor's Gr Testament;* Holtzmann, *Hand-Comm. zum NT;* Jowett (1 and 2 Thess, Rom, Gal), Lightfoot (Gal, Phil, Col, Philem and Notes), Lietzmann, *Handbuch zum NT;* Meyer (tr, revised Ger. edd), Zahn, *Kommentar zum NT.*

(4) Lives and Monographs: Albrecht, *Paulus der Apostel Jesu Christi*, 1903; Bacon, *The Story of Paul*, 1904; Bartlet, art. in *Enc Brit*, 11th ed; Baring-Gould, *A Study of St. Paul*, 1897; Baur, *The Apostle Paul*[2], 1845; Bevan, *St. Paul in the Light of Today*, 1912; Bird, *Paul of Tarsus*, 1900; Campbell, *Paul the Mystic*, 1907; Chrysostom, *Homiliae in Laude S. Pauli*, Opera, vol II, ed Montf. (more critically in Field's ed); Clemen, *Paulus*, 1904; Cone, *Paul the Man, the Missionary*, 1898; Cohu, *St. Paul in the Light of Recent Research*, 1910; Conybeare and Howson, *Life and Epp. of St. Paul* (many edd); Deissmann, *St. Paul*, 1912; Drescher, *Das Leben Jesu bei Paulus*, 1900; Drury, *The Prison Ministry of St. Paul*, 1910; Eadie, *Paul the Preacher*, 1859; Farrar, *Life and Work of St. Paul* (various edd); Erbes, *Die Todestage der Apostel Paulus und Petrus*, 1899; Fletcher, *A Study of the Conversion of St. Paul*, 1911; Forbes, *Footsteps of St. Paul in Rome*, 1899; Fouard, *St. Paul and His Mission*, 1894, *Last Years of St. Paul*, 1897; Gardner, *Religious Experience of St. Paul*, 1911; Garvie, *Life and Teaching of St. Paul*, 1909, *Studies of St. Paul and His Gospel*, 1911; Gilbert, *Student's Life of Paul*, 1899; Heim, *Paulus*, 1905; Hönnicke, *Chronologie des Lebens Pauli*, 1904; Iverach, *St. Paul, His Life and Time*, 1890; Johnston, *The Mission of St. Paul to the Rom Empire*, 1909; M. Jones, *St. Paul the Orator*, 1910; Kennedy, *St. Paul and the Mystery-Religions*, 1913; Köhler, *Zum Verständnis d. Apostels Paulus*, 1908; Lewin, *Life and Epp. of St. Paul*, 1875; Lock, *St. Paul the Master Builder*, 1905; Lyttleton, *Observations on Saul's Conversion*, 1774; Myers, *Saint Paul* (various edd); Matheson, *Spiritual Development of St. Paul*, 1891; Means, *St. Paul and the Ante-Nicene Church*, 1903; Noesgen, *Paulus der Apostel der Heiden*, 1908; Paley, *Horae Paulinae*, 1790; Ramsay, *St. Paul the Traveller*, 1896, *Pauline and Other Studies*, 1906, *Cities of St. Paul*, 1908, *Luke the Physician and Other Studies*, 1908, *Pictures of the Apostolic Church*, 1910; Renan, *St. Paul*, 1869; A. T. Robertson, *Epochs in the Life of Paul*, 1909, *The Glory of the Ministry or Paul's Exultation in Preaching*, 1911; Sabatier, *The Apostle Paul*, 1896; Selden, *In the Time of Paul*, 1900; Schweitzer, *St. Paul and His Interpreters*, 1912; Smith, *Voyage and Shipwreck of St. Paul*[4], 1880; Speer, *The Man Paul*, 1900; Stalker, *Life of St. Paul*, 1889; Taylor, *Paul the Missionary*, 1882; Underhill, *Divine Legation of St. Paul*, 1889; Weinel, *Paul* (tr, 1906); Whyte, *The Apostle Paul*, 1903; Wilkinson, *Epic of Saul*, 1891, *Epic of Paul*, 1897; Wrede, *Paulus*[2], 1907 (tr); Wright, *Cities of Paul*, 1907; Wynne, *Fragmentary Records of Jesus of Nazareth by a Contemporary*, 1887.

(5) Teaching: A. B. D. Alexander, *The Ethics of St. Paul*, 1910; S. A. Alexander, *Christianity of St. Paul*, 1899; Anonymous, *The Fifth Gospel*, 1906; R. Allen, *Christology of St. Paul*, 1912; M. Arnold, *St. Paul and Protestantism*, 1897; Ball, *St. Paul and the Rom Law*, 1901; Breitenstein, *Jésus et Paul*, 1908; Bruce, *St. Paul's Conception of Christianity*, 1898; Brückner, *Die Entstehung der Paulinischen Christologie*, 1903; Bultmann, *Der Stil der Paulin. Predigt und die kyn. Diatribe*, 1910; Chadwick, *Social Teaching of St. Paul*, 1907, *Pastoral Teaching of St. Paul*, 1907; M. Dibelius, *Die Geisterwelt im Glauben des Paulus*, 1909; Dickie, *Culture of the Spiritual Life*, 1905; Dickson, *St. Paul's Use of the Terms Flesh and Spirit*, 1883; Du Bose, *Gospel according to St. Paul*, 1907; Dykes, *Gospel according to St. Paul*, 1888; Everett, *Gospel of Paul*, 1893; Feine, *Paul as Theologian* (tr, 1908); Greenough, *Mind of Christ in St. Paul;* Goguel, *L'Apôtre Paul et Jésus Christ*, 1904; Harford, *The Gospel according to St. Paul*, 1912; Hicks, "St. Paul and Hellenism," *Stud. Bibl.*, IV; Holsten, *Das Evangelium des Paulus*, 1898; Jülicher, *Paulus und Jesus*, 1907; Kaftan, *Jesus und Paulus*, 1906; Kennedy, *St. Paul's Conceptions of Last Things*, 1904; Knowling, *Testimony of St. Paul to Christ* (3d ed, 1911); A. Meyer, *Jesus or Paul?* 1909;

Moffatt, *Paul and Paulinism*, 1910; Montet, *Essai sur la christologie de Saint Paul*, 1906; Nägeli, *Der Wortschatz des Apostels Paulus*, 1905; Oehler, *Paulus und Jesus*, 1908; Paterson, *The Pauline Theology*, 1903; Pfleiderer, *Paulinismus*, 1873, *Influence of the Apostle Paul on the Development of Christianity*, 1885; Prat, *La théologie de Saint Paul*, 1907; Ramsay, *The Teaching of St. Paul in Terms of the Present Day*, 1913; Resch, *Paulinismus und die Logia Jesu*, 1904; Rostron, *The Christology of St. Paul*, 1912; Simon, *Die Psychologie des Apostels Paulus*, 1897; Somerville, *St. Paul's Conception of Christ*, 1897; Stevens, *The Pauline Theology*, 1894; Thackeray, *Relation of St. Paul to Contemporary Jewish Thought*, 1900; J. Weiss, *Paul and Jesus*, 1909; *Paul and Justification*, 1913; Williams, *A Plea for a Reconstruction of St. Paul's Doctrine of Justification*, 1912; Wustmann, *Jesus und Paulus*, 1907; Zahn, *Das Gesetz Gottes nach der Lehre des Apostels Paulus*[2], 1892.

A. T Robertson

PAUL, VOYAGE AND SHIPWRECK OF. See Paul the Apostle, V, 9; Phoenix.

PAULINE, pŏl′īn THEOLOGY

I. Preparation.—Paul, the first great Christian theologian was thoroughly prepared in the providence of God for his task of teaching the Gospel to the Gentiles. He was born a Roman citizen. This gave him an assured civil and social status, and he was not slow to avail himself of all the privileges of citizenship whenever necessary (Acts **22** 25–28). His writings show a wide knowledge of Roman law and institutions, and contain many striking illustrations drawn from them.

1. Tarsus

His birth and boyhood in Tarsus, a Greek-speaking city noted for its intellectuality, resulted in his mastery of the Greek language, brought him in contact with Greek culture, gave him an acquaintance with city life that proved useful in after-years, and perhaps afforded him his first impressions of the moral corruption of Paganism which he so graphically describes in Rom **1**. He was born "an Hebrew of the Hebrews," that is of pure Hebrew descent. His parents, though living in a Greek-speaking city, maintained the customs of their native land, reading the Hebrew OT and speaking Aramaic (Phil **3** 5). As his father was a Pharisee (Acts **23** 6; **26** 5) he would be taught from infancy to revere the Law, written and oral, and to follow the rigorous external observances of the Pharasaic rites.

2. Jerusalem

The strict discipline of such a home must have exercised a decided influence on his character and prepared him for more advanced study after he had become a "son of the law." He was destined to be a rabbi and was accordingly sent to Jerusalem to study under the greatest of the Jewish teachers, the tolerant and liberal-minded Gamaliel. At exactly what age he reached Jerusalem, or how long he pursued his studies there, is not known. Certain it is, however, that he made a great reputation as a student of the Law and as an ardent and patriotic devotee of Pharasaism. In his defense before Agrippa he asserts that his manner of life was a matter of common knowledge and that his fellow-citizens could testify, if they would, to his standing as a Pharisee (Acts **26** 4–5; Gal **1** 13–14). Only a hyper-skeptical attitude toward the Acts doubts or denies the early residence and training at Jerusalem.

It is impossible to decide whether or not Paul was personally acquainted with Christ during His earthly ministry. 2 Cor **5** 16 has been pressed into service as proof that he was, but the verse is capable of other interpretations and does not decide the matter.

3. The Persecutor

If he met with Christ before the crucifixion, it is strange that he does not refer to it in the epistles. He may have returned to Tarsus (so some) and been there during Christ's ministry. However that may be, he was in Jerusalem during the debates caused by Stephen's teaching and may himself have been one of those who were both silenced and enraged by "The wisdom and Spirit" with which the martyr spoke. At any rate when Stephen was stoned he took charge of the garments of the executioners, and was not merely consenting to Stephen's death, but giving his hearty approval of it. On the very day of the stoning Saul started on his career of destruction. "He laid waste the church, entering into every house and dragging men and women committed them to prison" (Acts **8** 3). He saw very clearly that the only way to destroy the new creed was utterly to destroy its confessors. Not satisfied with the apparent destruction of the Jerusalem church, he became the official agent of the Sanhedrin to prosecute the work abroad and started for Damascus on his murderous errand. The vigor with which he pursued it seems to indicate that he was utterly untroubled by any qualms of conscience over Stephen's death. In fact he seems to have had the full approval of his conscience until he was divinely arrested (Acts **26** 9; 1 Tim **1** 13). It requires a mighty force to convince any sincere, intense, and excited fanatic that his course is wrong. All that Paul had learned about the Christian teaching and the Christian claim that Jesus the Nazarene was the Messiah and all that he witnessed of Christian fortitude in suffering, even to death, seemed rather to intensify his opposition and render him more determined to exterminate the Christians.

II. Conversion.—The career of the persecutor was checked, however, when he neared Damascus. Three accounts of his conversion are found in the Acts. Hostile criticism has magnified some apparent discrepancies found in them, but the consensus of scholars is that these accounts are true. They all mention the light; the voice saying, "Saul, Saul why persecutest thou me?" his answer, "Who art thou, Lord?" and Christ's reply, "I am Jesus whom thou persecutest." Blinded by the "glory of that light," awed by the vision of Jesus risen and exalted to glory, he exclaims, "What shall I do, Lord?" His submission to Jesus as Lord is instantaneous and complete. Helpless and humbled he is led into Damascus where he finds refuge in the house of Judas. There "he was three days without sight and did neither eat nor drink." All that we really know of him during these three days is the Lord's statement to Ananias, "Behold he prayeth." It requires no effort of the imagination, however, to believe that he experienced an agony of conviction of sin such as sometimes has preceded the conversion of great souls. He had made the personal acquaintance of the risen Lord, and found that he had been persecuting Him in the persons of his followers. His views were revolutionized. In this period of profound conviction, he passed through an experience that seems to be in part described in Rom **7** 7–25, an experience that taught him the fundamental truths of his theology. His theology was born and its type fixed in his conversion experience, and, instead of being something distinct and apart from his religion, it was its essence. It was both his creed and his life.

Various efforts have been made to deny the reality of Paul's miraculous conversion. It has been ascribed to a violent thunder-storm during which, already feeling the pangs of remorse over the death of Stephen, he imagined he saw the Lord in the vivid flash that blinded him, and heard his voice in the thunder; others ascribed it to a sunstroke that rendered him unconscious and left him the victim of hallucinations in which Jesus seemed to appear to him; others hold that the experience was wholly subjective, that Paul saw Jesus in a vision or trance. These and similar rationalistic explanations labor under a twofold difficulty. In the first place, they find nothing in the Acts or Pauline epistles to justify them; and second, like all efforts to explain supernatural events by natural causes they impose a greater strain on human credulity than it is well able to bear. Paul's period of blindness and suspense was brought to a close through the ministrations of Ananias. His sight was restored, he passed too from spiritual darkness into spiritual light, he was filled with the Holy Spirit, made aware of his mission, and baptized into the Christian church (Acts **9** 10–19; **22** 12–16).

III. Teaching.—Immediately he began to preach in the synagogues. "He heralded (the person) Jesus, that he is the Son of God" (Acts **9** 20; cf Mt **16** 16–17; Jn **6** 69; 1 Jn **4** 15), and "confounded the Jews that dwelt at Damascus, proving (by comparison) that this is the Christ" (Acts **9** 22; cf Lk **24**). Paul's profound knowledge of the text of the OT gained during his study with Gamaliel, and illumined now by the Holy Spirit made him a formidable antagonist in debate, and, as in the case of Stephen, stirred up the wrath of the Jews. Paul's life, however, was saved. He was to continue Stephen's work and expand Stephen's teaching. It is immaterial whether we place Paul's stay in Arabia before or after the account of the preaching in Damascus.

1. Christ

The thing of prime importance is the fact that in preaching the divine sonship of Jesus he had struck, apparently, a bolder and fuller note than any heard so far in the apostolic witness. The fact that Jesus was the Son of God was all inclusive. If so, he was invested with all the attributes of divinity and was to be worshiped and obeyed as God. From this basal fact we see his profound and comprehensive Christology developing and expanding until it reaches its fulness in the marvelous statements of the prison letters (Phil **2** 5–11, cf Jn **5** 17–18; Col **1** 15–23, cf Jn **1**; Eph **1** 20–23).

Indeed, from the moment of his conversion, Paul never had any doubts about the Divinity of Christ. This is sometimes denied and the statement made that Paul never directly asserts the Divinity of Christ. With reference to this it is well said (H. L. Goudge, *The Theology of St Paul*, in *A New Commentary on Holy Scripture*) "He speaks of him, as we have seen, as 'God, blessed forever' (Rom **9** 5), no other interpretation of the passage being surely possible, and the same definite ascription of Divinity is probably found in 2 Thess **1** 12 and Titus **2** 13. Equally clear is the language of Col **2** 9, 'in him dwelleth all the fulness of the Godhead bodily' (cf Col **1** 19); and almost equally that of Phil **2** 6, since, whatever the exact shade of meaning which we give to the word 'form' it either asserts our Lord's Divinity or implies it. . . . . St. Paul freely applies language spoken of Jehovah in the OT to the Lord Himself (Rom **10** 12–13; 1 Cor **1** 2; **2** 16; Phil **2** 10–11). He does not indeed assert that the OT language applies to the Lord alone; the words quoted in Phil **2** 10–11 are in Rom **14** **11** applied to the Father. But so fully is the Father found in Christ that such words may be applied to either. Again, we may sin against Christ as we sin against God (1 Cor **8** 12); and tempt Christ as we tempt God (1 Cor **10** 9). The day of Jehovah becomes the day of our Lord Jesus Christ (1 Cor **1** 8, etc); the tribunal of God (Rom **14** 10–12), the tribunal of Christ (2 Cor **5** 10); the kingdom of God (Rom **14** 17), the kingdom of Christ (Eph **5** 5); the church of God (1 Cor **10** 32), the church of Christ (Rom **16** 16); and the spirit of God (1 Cor **2** 11), the spirit of Christ (Rom **8** 9). Indeed . . . . it does not matter whether we speak of the faith which God asks of us as faith in God or as faith in Christ, if only we understand that faith in Christ is itself faith in God and nothing else." God was in Christ reconciling the world unto himself (2 Cor **5** 19; Jn **14** 5–9). He who comes to Christ comes to God.

2. Spirit

At his conversion Paul received "power" (Acts **1** 8; Lk **24** 49) such as the other apostles had received at Pentecost. That is, he was fitted to be an efficient witness to the mission and message of Jesus Christ and endowed with all the extraordinary gifts and qualifications needed to discharge his office of Apostle to the Gentiles (Gal **2** 7–10). Paul, however, does not emphasize the miraculous working of the Spirit so much as His work of promoting holiness and so building up the Church of God.

Like all orthodox Jews he must have believed in the personality and Divinity of the Spirit. Both are certainly revealed in the OT in a manner suited to the pupilage of the Church, but not nearly so fully as in the writings of the NT. At all times "the executive of the Godhead." He appears pre-eminent in the New Dispensation in ministering to the spiritual welfare and prosperity of the Church. In accordance with Christ's own promise he took charge of the Church after the Ascension as Christ's permanent representative. Thus he is called the Spirit of Christ, because he dispenses the blessings of salvation to believers (Rom **8** 9; Jn **3** 34). No NT writer realizes more fully than Paul the nature, presence, and office of the Spirit.

His personality and Divinity are assumed rather than proved. Paul, perhaps in the vividness of his own assurance, felt that these outstanding facts needed no proof. As to personality knowledge is ascribed to the Spirit (1 Cor **2** 10–11); will (1 Cor **12** 11); purpose or thoughts, *phrónēma* (Rom **8** 27); feeling (Rom **15** 30; Eph **4** 30). His activities in applying redemptive blessings to believers involve personality. He is pre-eminently their Paraclete (helper) at all times and in all ways. He leads them, if permitted, in all the affairs of life (Acts **16** 6–7; Rom **8** 14; cf Jn **14** 16–18; **15** 26–27; **16** 13); he teaches the teachers of the Church (1 Cor **2** 13) and indicates their fields of labor (Acts **13** 2); he intercedes (Rom **8** 26); he cries out earnestly (Gal **4** 6). With reference to what mere energy or influence could such language fitly be used? These and numerous other passages impel us to the opinion that Paul was fully persuaded that the Spirit was a person, and wished his readers to believe the same.

Equally evident is his belief in the Divinity of the Spirit. In Acts **28** 25–27 Paul ascribes to the Holy Spirit language that in (Isa **6** 8–10) is ascribed to Him who in (Isa **6** 5) is called the King, Jehovah of hosts. The spirit seems to be identified with Christ in essence, aim, and power in 2 Cor **3** 17. From the very birth of the Christian Church the Divinity of the Spirit was recognized and taught. Peter asserted that Ananias had lied to the Holy Spirit and in doing so had not lied to men but to God (Acts **5** 3–4). Only a few passages need be cited to show that this doctrine permeated Paul's teaching. Many of the passages that teach the personality of the Spirit imply his possession of divine attributes such as omnipresence (1 Cor **12** 13; Rom **8** 9–11); omnipotence (Rom **8** 11; Titus **3** 5); omniscience (1 Cor **2** 10–11), and regenerating power is ascribed to Him in (Rom **8** 2; 1 Cor **6** 11; Titus **3** 5; cf Jn **3** 5–6, 8). In all the Pauline teaching His equality with the Father and Son is either asserted or assumed as in (Eph **2** 18; 2 Cor **13** 14) and at the same time He is distinguished from them. It will be noted that in many of the foregoing passages Paul assumes the doctrine of the Trinity. While he made no formal statement of it, it is manifest that it lay at the very foundation of his theology. It dominates his whole conception of the great plan of man's redemption from sin (See Holy Spirit, Trinity).

By his own personal experience and the guidance of the Spirit Paul came to believe most earnestly in the doctrine of the mystical union, that spiritual, real, intimate, mysterious, and eternal relation with Christ, effected by the Spirit of Christ at the time of regeneration, whereby a mutual indwelling is established between Christ and the quickened soul. Christ is said to dwell in the believer (Rom **8** 9–11; cf Jn **3** 34; Eph **3** 17; Col **1** 27; cf Jn **14** 23) and the believer is said to dwell in Christ (1 Cor **1** 30; 2 Cor **5** 17). While, however, it is a union of persons, it is not a personal union, for believers are not constituted one *person* with Christ but one *mystical body* of which He is the head both of authority and influences (1 Cor **12** 12–27; cf Jn **2** 8).

3. Mystical Union

This union is spiritual; one Spirit fills both Head and members (Rom **8** 9; 1 Cor **6** 17); *real*, "we are members of his body, of his flesh, and of his bones" (Eph **5** 30); *intimate* (1 Cor **3** 10–11; Eph **2** 20–22; **5** 23); *mysterious* (2 Cor **6** 16; Gal **2** 20; **3** 27; Eph **5** 32; Col **2** 12); *eternal* (Rom **8** 38–39). In short, it is a vital union, through which believers share in all the benefits secured by Christ's death and resurrection, in all the merits of his deeds as man's Redeemer as well as in His glorious destiny (Rom **6** 1–10). Hence, it follows that only by union with Christ effected and maintained by the Spirit by means of the word on the Divine side, and by faith on man's can anyone be saved (Eph **2** 8; **3** 17; cf Jn **3** 2–13).

It is a matter of great practical import to remember that Paul's marvelous success as apostle, preacher, pastor, organizer, leader is to be attributed to his ever present consciousness of the personality and presence of the Holy Spirit and his implicit confidence in the Spirit's aid. Some researches as to how far Christians really believe in the Spirit have revealed a tendency, often unconscious, to think of Him as essentially inferior to the Father and the Son and to engage in spiritual duties without any conscious dependence on Him or any effort to secure his aid. "I believe in the Holy Spirit" was not only a part of Paul's theology but a principle of his spiritual life and the real secret of his power with God and man.

In the epistles to the Romans and Galatians Paul develops the doctrine of salvation. In his view men need it imperatively. They need it because of sin.

4. Salvation

(1) *The need, sin.*—Sin in the Pauline theology is not the result of unfavorable environment, nor of a deficiency in education, nor the remains of some brute ancestor that may be eradicated by more exact culture, nor is it due to any deficiency or lapse in the process of evolution. All these explanations are impotent satisfactorily to account for sin's prevalence, power, and moral hideousness. Paul uses many words to express his idea of its *true nature,* and each one of these implies failure to come up to the divine ideal. Sin in his teaching is "missing the mark, an evil deed, transgression, a lapse from uprightness, wrong-doing toward God or man, impiety, impurity, lawlessness, disobedience (to a voice), error, etc" (cf Thayer, Trench). In Rom **1** 18—**3** 20 he convicts both Jews and Gentiles of sin. The whole cosmos has become *hupodikos* "owing satisfaction to God and liable to punishment from Him" (Thayer). It is "guilty before God" (AV) or "under the judgment of God" (Rom **3** 19 ARV). Guilt is often defined as the "*liability* to suffer the penalty of the law." In the administration of human law this is an adequate definition; for though the guilty are *liable* to punishment they often escape; but in the divine government no sin will escape punishment, hence guilt in the Pauline theology is the *obligation* to suffer the penalty of the law, and that penalty is death. To suffer sin to pass unpunished would be to tarnish the justice of God (Rom **1** 18).

But Paul pictures men as corrupt as well as guilty; they are slaves under sin's power. The natural man is its bond slave (Rom **6** 17, 19, 20; **7** 16), the victim of ungovernable passions; guilty, powerless, corrupt he needs a Saviour. This condition of guilt and corruption Paul ascribes to Adam. "Through one man sin entered into the world and death through sin, and so death passed unto all men, for that all sinned." Whether Adam was the exemplary, the efficient, or the judicial cause of the universality of sin and death is not determined by the mere meaning of these words; they simply assert the fact. "One thing is clear Adam was the cause of sin in a sense analogous to that in which Christ is the cause of righteousness" (Hodge on Rom **5** 12–21; cf Jn **12** 32).

(2) *The instrument, the gospel.*—The instrument by which men are rescued from this condition is the "gospel of God," promised through the prophets of the Old Dispensation and proclaimed through the apostles of the New. This gospel was a piece of supernatural information about the incarnation of the Son of God and his mission into this world to save sinners. He came to found a new race. "The last Adam became a life-giving spirit" (1 Cor **15** 45; cf Jn **5** 21; **6** 33, 39, 40, 54, 57). This gospel "concerning Jesus Christ our Lord" is the means or vehicle through which God exercises his saving power; "it is the power of God unto salvation." It has no intrinsic power, but it is exactly suited to accomplish the divine purpose and becomes irresistible when energized by the Spirit of God. Paul's statement that "the gospel is the power of God unto salvation" has been confirmed by the experience of nineteen centuries. Every attempt to substitute anything else for the simple story of the Cross has ended in failure.

(3) *The method, justification.*—The method of saving men revealed in the gospel is by a Divine righteousness. It reveals "a righteousness of God from faith unto faith; as it is written, But the righteous shall live by faith." The meaning of the term "righteousness" here has been a *crux interpretorum.* Paul, say some, means that the gospel reveals the Divine attribute of justice or righteousness, as in (Rom **3** 5, 25, 26). In that case he is made to say that he is not ashamed of the gospel because it reveals God's justice. But tidings of the justice that condemns is not good tidings to a convicted sinner. Others say the "righteousness of God" means the inherent excellence obtained by man's effort in conjunction with the work of the Holy Spirit in the soul. Paul could scarcely have meant this, for he is sure that in his "flesh dwelleth no good thing" (Rom **7** 18). Every view that makes this righteousness human, or partly human, runs contrary to the whole tenor of Paul's teaching (Rom **3** 20, 28; cf Jn **5** 46; Mt **20** 28). Man's

best efforts to save himself, as Paul so thoroughly learned when he was converted, are futile. When he said "not by works done in righteousness (i.e. the best of which man is capable) which we did ourselves, but according to his mercy he saved us through the washing of regeneration and the renewing of the Holy Spirit" (Titus **3** 5), he spoke out of the fulness of his own experience. One who had made such an intense and diligent struggle to gain salvation by his own works, and had succeeded so far as to deem himself alive, and then suddenly found himself subject to death, as Paul did on the Damascus road, is entitled to speak with authority about what kind of righteousness really saves men. He ascribes it to God, because He has procured and provided it (Rom **1** 17; **3** 21, 22). It is not justice, but what justice demands for its own satisfaction (Rom **4** 6, 11; 2 Cor **5** 21; Phil **3** 9). It is found in Christ (Rom **10** 4; 1 Cor **1** 30; 2 Cor **5** 21; Phil **3** 9; cf Mt **5** 17). Its content is Christ's active and passive obedience. It is a righteousness "devised and procured, revealed and given, approved and crowned by God; it includes all God's benefits in Christ to a sinner's salvation" (Bengel). It satisfies all the demands of the law and justice of God and man's deepest need. Provided for us by God in His own Son it is not merely offered to men in the gospel but *given* to them. Christ and His righteousness are God's supreme gifts to men (Rom **5** 8; cf Jn **3** 16; **6** 32, 33). It is the all sufficient ground of man's justification before God (Rom **3** 21–24; **4** 1–8; **10** 1–10; cf Mt **3** 9; **5** 17; **10** 32; Lk **12** 8).

The verb "to justify" is never used by Paul in the sense of "to make righteous," but always with the meaning to "declare righteous." It is a forensic term, and is the act of a judge declaring that the person is just or conformed to the law. "This declaration may be either on the ground of personal or imputed righteousness; or in the language of Paul, of 'the righteousness of the law," or of 'the righteousness of faith.' In the first sense no man can be declared righteous, because all have sinned; in the second sense believers are declared righteous, because they appropriate to themselves the righteousness of Christ" (Gloag, *Pauline Epp*), (2 Cor **5** 18, 19).

(4) *The means, faith.*—Paul emphasizes *faith* as the only means of securing an interest in Christ's righteousness: "Whom God set forth to be a propitiation through faith in his blood" (Rom **3** 25). This faith is more than mere assent to the testimony of the gospel about Christ; it is trust, a personal confidence, or better, a confiding in Christ, yielding one's self to him without recourse, with implicit assurance that He will save us. He is the immediate, God is the ultimate object of it. We come into contact with the Father through the Son: "God was in Christ reconciling the world unto himself."

"Hence also faith is that which unites us to Christ, so that there is a mutual transference of our sins to Him and of His righteousness to us. The believer is regarded as one with Christ. He suffered in Christ, and rose with Him. In Christ he paid the penalty of the law, and in Christ he perfectly fulfilled its requirements. And thus by faith he receives the righteousness of Christ which justifies him before God" (Gloag, *Pauline Epp*).

(5) *Sanctification.*—In the Pauline theology not only is the guilty justified, pardoned, and received into favor (Rom **5** 1), but the sinful is made holy—sanctified. This word is sometimes used in a ceremonial sense, yet ordinarily when used with reference to believers it means to make morally clean or pure (1 Cor **1** 2; cf 1 Cor **6** 11) not merely by consecration to God, but by the infusion of his grace, which frees them from the power and pollution of sin and renews them in knowledge, righteousness, and true holiness (Eph **4** 24; Col **3** 10). Justification is an act done once for all; sanctification is a process, its beginning is synchronous with regeneration, its consummation is at death. "In regeneration the new creature is formed, but, while perfect in all its parts, is small and feeble; in sanctification it grows in all its parts, acquires vigor and activity, and advances toward the full stature of a perfect man in Christ Jesus" (Phil **1** 6).

Sanctification is viewed both as a privilege and a duty. As a privilege it is the subject of prophecy (Ezk **36** 25–27) and prayer (Jn **17** 17). Our Lord interceded that his followers might be sanctified. As a duty it is the work of man (2 Cor **7** 1), not as if he could perfect himself in holiness, but because he can use the means provided him, trusting in divine grace to render them effectual. "Work out your own salvation with fear and trembling; for it is God who worketh in you both to will and to work for his good pleasure" (Phil **2** 12, 13).

In the process of sanctification the understanding undergoes progressive illumination by the Word and Spirit of truth (Eph **1** 17, 18), the will is conformed to the will of God (Rom **12** 1, 2), love to God and man increases (Gal **5** 22; Eph **1** 4, **4** 2, 15, **5** 2; 1 Thess **3** 12, **4** 9; 2 Thess **3** 5), holy principles and practices are strengthened and the influence of the world is weakened (Gal **6** 14); faith grows more vital and vigorous as it gains clearer and fuller apprehension of the truth as it is in Jesus (Rom **1** 8; 2 Cor **10** 15; Col **2** 5, 7; 1 Thess **1** 8; **3** 2, 5, 6, 7, 10; 2 Thess **1** 3), and hope glows with ever increasing lustre as it contemplates the prospect of "eternal life which God, who cannot lie promised before times eternal" (Titus **1** 2).

The work of sanctification extends to the whole man and is ascribed to all the persons of the Trinity. Paul prays God to sanctify the Thessalonians wholly (1 Thess **4** 3; **5** 23). Again, it is ascribed to Jesus Christ (Eph **5** 26–27; Titus **2** 14), and in (1 Cor **6** 11; 2 Thess **2** 13) it is ascribed to the Holy Spirit.

The body shares in this sanctification because it is a "shrine, *nāós*," of the Holy Spirit (1 Cor **6** 19) and a member of Christ (1 Cor **6** 15). In the very nature of the case it is necessary for the sanctification of the whole person that the body be brought under the control of the sanctified soul and used in the service, and for the glory, of God (Rom **6** 13; **12** 1). Finally Paul declares the body is to be raised in glory (1 Cor **15** 43, 44) and "He will change the passing fashion of this body of ours—the body of our temporary humiliation, so as to share the lasting form of His own body—the body of his eternal glory. He will do this by the working of the divine power which enables Him even to bring into subjection to Himself all things alike" (Plummer on *Phil.*). This will mark the glorious consummation of the process of sanctification. Where in all literature is there anything so optimistic, so cheering as Paul's outlook for the Christian? See ESCHATOLOGY.

As sanctification is a duty, man must actively co-operate with the Spirit. First of all by the exercise of faith, which, as it is the means of our justification (Rom **5** 1) and of our union with Christ (Col **2** 7, 12) is also the internal means of our sanctification (Acts **15** 9; **26** 18); because it yields implicit submission to the teachings of Christ as the *rule* of holiness (Acts **20** 32; Rom **6** 17, 18; **15** 4), contemplates the life of the incarnate Christ as its example and encouragement (1 Cor **11** 1), seeks His fellowship and aid in prayer (Eph **6** 18; Phil **4** 6, 7), recognizes all the events of God's providence as purposed for man's spiritual and eternal good (Rom **8** 28), and finds in the sacraments not saviours from sin on the one part, nor mere symbols of Christ's work on the other, but real vehicles of grace, actually putting the believing participant in possession of the blessings they symbolize (Rom **6** 3–5; ,1 Cor **12** 13; 1 Cor **10** 16, 17).

The effort to derive Paul's doctrine of the sacraments from the mystery religions has so far failed of proof (Machen, *Origin of Paul's Religion*, reissued 1928; cf Cumont, *The Mysteries of Mithra;* Angus, *The Mystery Religions and Christianity*). In the very nature of the case a Hebrew of the Hebrews, as Paul was, would not be susceptible to Pagan faiths which, while they may have had some very general and merely external resemblance to Christianity, were so very far removed from its nature, teachings, and effects both upon individuals and society. One might with equal probability say that the persecuted Covenanters adopted their custom of meeting in the mountain caverns, because Macbeth's witches had set such a notable example. Quite a similarity too is found in their respective vocabularies. Such words as "double," "toil," "trouble," "fire," "cauldron" must have been derived from the witches chorus!

While no graces are lacking in the believer, they are not perfected; and though sin is dethroned, it is not destroyed and uses every artifice and effort to regain the throne. The struggle is unceasing and bitter. Paul describes it in Rom **7** so graphically that he must be speaking from his own experience. Perhaps every Christian has to learn at sometime by actual experience the futility of trying to overcome sin by legal obedience in his own strength. "Let any Christian try to become holy by law-keeping in his own might, and he will soon understand experimentally and full well the significance of Rom **7** 14–25. Our sanctification, like our justification, is in the Lord Jesus Christ and by His Holy Spirit. It was to this Paul came at length—'I thank God through Jesus Christ our Lord' " (Rom **8** 1–4).

"But let it be observed further, even after he has found victory through the Lord Jesus, he still says, 'So then, with the mind I myself serve the law of God, but with the flesh the law of sin.' 'Germanicus reigned in the hearts of the Romans, but Tiberius in the provinces' " (W. G. Moorehead, *The Ep to the Romans*).

What Paul learned by experience, as well as by revelation, effectually freed him from the stifling tentacles of legalism, convinced him that "Christ was the end of the law unto righteousness to everyone that believeth" (Rom **10** 4) and made him the herald of a Saviour in whom Greek and Jew, circumcision and uncircumcision, barbarian, Scythian, bondman, freeman (Col **3** 11) found an equal welcome, satisfaction of every spiritual need, and a new and vital bond of brotherhood which erased prejudices racial, educational, social, or ritualistic.

5. Redemption

Redemption sometimes means "deliverance effected through the death of Christ from the retributive wrath of a holy God and the merited penalty of sin" (Rom **3** 24; Eph **1** 7; Col **1** 14, Thayer). When, however, it is distinguished from justification and sanctification it refers not to past deliverance but to the future final deliverance from all evil which will signalize the coming advent of Christ. Such is evidently its meaning in 1 Cor **1** 30, where it is mentioned last in the series of benefits derived from union with Christ. The Holy Spirit is said to be given as an *arrabōn*, an *earnest* or partial payment to assure of the payment of the whole inheritance, and his indwelling assures us of our standing, and secures our final deliverance (Eph **1** 14; **4** 30). Paul paints a graphic picture of this "redemption day" in Rom **8** 18–25. Suffering is to cease and glory is to be revealed; because creation (personified) animate and inanimate, longs for it anxiously, eagerly, persistently. Then, not only the sons of God will be revealed, but their sonship, their condition of full privilege, when everybody will be raised and welcomed by its Redeemer. Then creation will cease to groan, because it will be freed from every trace of feebleness, fraility, and decay, and be restored to its pristine glory. If it was cursed for man's sake, it will surely share in man's deliverance. How far sin affected the earth itself no one knows, but Paul evidently believed it would finally share in some way in the outburst of glory that will greet the manifestation of the redeemer when every trace of sin's reign and stain will be obliterated.

6. Atonement

The doctrine of atonement lies at the very foundation of the Pauline theology. In Rom **3** 25 Christ is called a *hilastērion*—a propitiation or an expiatory sacrifice, "through faith, in His blood." God's enemies are said to be reconciled to Him through the death of His Son and those so reconciled shall be saved by His life (Rom **5** 10). Again it is through Him we received reconciliation (Rom **5** 11). "In 2 Cor **5** 18–20 two arguments are used to prove that God has received us into His favour: first, that He does not impute to men their trespasses; second, that He has deposited the doctrine of reconciliation in the souls of the preachers of the Gospel" (Thayer). In Eph **2** 16 the word translated "reconcile" means complete reconciliation. The same word is used in Col **1** 20–22. Another series of passages emphasizes the value of Christ's blood (His poured out life), so in Acts **20** 28 it is the purchase price of the church; propitiation is by blood (Rom **3** 25); "Divine mercy did not mean indifference to Divine Law" (Moule, Cam Bib, *Rom*). In Eph **1** 7; Col **1** 14 we are said to have redemption through the blood, and the alienated and those once "far off are made nigh by the blood of Christ" (Eph **2** 13). A study of these and many similar passages certainly proves that the doctrine of atonement permeated Paul's teaching and this atonement was necessary not only because of man's sin, but God's own nature. His own justice compelled him to provide a way whereby, in justifying the ungodly, He might honor His own nature and His own law. Again Paul undoubtedly teaches that Christ saves men not by His example, nor His teaching, nor His moral influence, but by His sacrifice; "Christ died for our sins according to the scriptures" (1 Cor **15** 3). On what other theory can we explain the tremendous influence of the apostolic teaching, and indeed the preaching of Christ's vicarious sacrifice in every age since (Jn **10** 15; **15** 13; **1** 29).

7. Church

The Pauline teachings about the Church are of immense practical importance. The early Christian leaders held exalted views about it and the teaching of these fostered popular respect for that society which in 1 Tim **3** 15 is called the house or family of God, the Church of the living God, the pillar (to display) and the ground (or buttress) of the truth, to preserve it. In its first organization it was a representative democracy (Acts **6** 3–6; **15** 22). Christ is the Head of the Church which is His body. He is the source of all authority and spiritual influences (Eph **1** 22, 23; **5** 23; Col **1** 18, 24); the wisdom of God is made known by the Church, and glory is ascribed to God in the Church (Eph **3** 10, 21). Christ is its cornerstone, and it is the family and household of God (Eph **2** 19–22); and Christ provides ministers for it (Eph **4** 11, 12); it is the object of His self-sacrificing love (Eph **5** 25); Christ intends to present it to Himself a spotless Church (Eph **5** 26, 27). It is God's own society for the propagation of saving truth. It is not synonymous with the kingdom; but it is preparing the way for it and may perhaps be rightly considered as the militia of the kingdom sent out with the King's proclamation of pardon and peace for the rebellious. Its aim is reformation through regeneration, by preaching the everlasting Gospel of the Son of God.

Paul's most important relation to the Church was the service which he rendered in his unfolding more fully that Gospel of the Son of God, the development of doctrine. Some critical writers would discredit the writings of Paul and those of John, and indeed nearly all the writers of the Epistles in what they are pleased to call a "back-to-Jesus" movement. Such a critical method is subversive of the whole scheme of revelation; it sets up a subjective criterion which, at last analysis, means simply that "what is not in accord with my philosophy of religion is not revelation." In pursuit of this method even the very words of Christ are subjected to the same criterion to determine which are authentic and which not!

In fact, the development of doctrine found in Paul and other epistolary writers is an integral part of that progress of doctrine which is the final and conclusive test of that divine superintendence which has been named the Inspiration of the Scriptures. Christ himself said that he came but "to fulfill." This fulfilling, bringing out into the open, making more manifest in his personification of the message of Good News, runs all the way from the Protevangelium in Genesis to the mysteries of the Apocalypse.

At the beginning, revelation was a bud of promise, a closed bud, which like a rosebud gave but the faintest glimpse of the beauty and suggestion of the fragrance within. It was revelation in Promise. In the wilderness period this revelation bud opened and was exemplified in a revelation in great Providences, God's moving pictures. Revelation through Prophecy came as the Psalmists and historians and proverbialists and statesmen and prophets compared and discussed and explained, and so the flower was still more unfolded, it was opening to display its glory. Then in Christ there came revelation in Person. He exemplified in Himself, the one highest type of Christian, what had been shown in the ceremonial in the Tabernacle and the Temple. Then in the Acts and the Epistles we have the further unfolding of revelation through Preaching by word and by letter until we have its culmination in the Epistle to the Hebrews and the writings of Paul and John. At last, that which was but a bud of Promise at the beginning had become the full-blown flower of the Gospel. Paul but carries on the teaching of the Baptist when he pointed to Jesus, saying "Behold the Lamb of God," and of our Lord himself when, after partaking of the Passover Lamb, he said, "This is my body," thus announcing that substitutionary atonement which Paul unfolds so fully in his Epistles.

Now this Progress of Doctrine over a period of 1500 years, throughout sixty-six books by some forty different authors in different lands and using different languages, cannot be accounted for except by adequate superintendence. The only adequate superintendence under such conditions is divine superintendence. Thus Paul's progress of doctrine, the great epistolary contribution which he made to the Church, was of a piece with this the final proof of the divineness of the Book. Instead of this progress of doctrine being the condemnation of Paul, the absence of it would put him out of the canon.

For Paul's Eschatology see MAN OF SIN and SECOND THESSALONIANS.

LITERATURE.—Cf. PAUL THE APOSTLE. Conybeare and Howson, *Life and Epp of St. Paul;* Deismann, *St. Paul;* Farrar, *Life and Work of St. Paul;* Glover, *Paul of Tarsus;* Goodwin, *Harmony of the Life of Paul;* Hayes, *Paul and His Epp;* Iverach, *St. Paul, His Life and Times;* A. T. Robertson, *Paul, The Interpreter of Christ;* Sabatier, *The Apostle Paul;* Stalker, *Life of St. Paul;* Taylor, *Paul, The Missionary.* Commentaries:—Abbott, *Eph and Col, ICC;* Gore, *A New Commentary on Holy Scripture; Expositor's Greek Testament;* Gloag, *Acts, Intro to Pauline Epp;* Godet, *Rom;* Hackett, *Acts;* Hodge, *Rom, 1 and 2 Cor, and Eph;* Howson, *Metaphors of St. Paul;* Lightfoot, *Gal, Phil, and Col;* Meyer, *Acts;* Moorehead, *Outline Studies on the Acts and the Epp;* Moule, *Cam Bib on Rom;* Moule, *Cam Bib on Col and Philem;* New Century Bib on *The Pauline Epp;* Plummer, *Phil, 1 and 2 Thess;* A. T. Robertson, *Paul and The Intellectuals, The Ep to the Col;* Sanday and Headlam, *Rom;* Vincent, *Phil and Philem, ICC.* Introductions:—Foakes-Jackson and Smith, *A Brief Bib Hist;* Gregory, *Canon and Text of the NT;* Harnack, *Date of The Acts and the Synoptic Gospels;* McClymont, *NT Criticism;* Nestle, *Textual Criticism of the NT;* Salmon, *Intro to the NT;* Symes, *The Evolution of the NT;* B. Weiss, *Intro to the NT;* Zahn, *Intro to the NT;* General Works:—Angus, *The Mystery Religions and Christianity;* Bruce, *The Providential Order of the World, St. Paul's Conception of Christianity;* Cobern, *The New Archaeological Discoveries;* Cumont, *The Mysteries of Mithra;* Cunningham, *Doctrine of Forgiveness, Vol LX Victoria Institute;* Deissmann, *Light from the Ancient East;* Fairweather, *Jesus and the Greeks;* Friedlander, *Hellenism and Christianity;* Gilbert, *Students' Life of Paul, First Interpreters f Jesus;* Hurst, *Literary Background of the NT;* Kent, *Work and Teachings of the Apostles;* Machen, *Origin of Paul's Religion;* Margolis and Marx, *Hist of the Jewish People;* Moffatt, *Paul and Paulinism;* Patton, *Fundamental Christianity;* Pfleiderer, *The Influence of the Apostle Paul on Christianity;* Purves, *The Apostolic Age;* Ramsay, *St. Paul the Traveller and the Rom Citizen, The Cities of St. Paul, The Teaching of St. Paul in Terms of the Present Day;* Robertson, *Luke the Historian in the Light of Recent Research;* Ropes, *The Apostolic Age;* Schürer, HJP; Snowden, *Making and Meaning of NT;* Uhlhorn, *Conflict of Christianity with Heathenism;* F. Von Schlegel, *Philosophy of Hist.;* John Bailie, *The place of Jesus Christ in Modern Christianity.*

J. H. WEBSTER

PAULUS, pô′lus, **SERGIUS,** sûr′ji-us (**Σέργιος Παῦλος,** *Sérgios Paúlos*): The Rom "proconsul" (RV) or "deputy" (AV) of Cyprus when Paul, along with Barnabas, visited that island on his first missionary journey (Acts **13** 4.7). The official title of Sergius is accurately given in Acts. Cyprus was originally an imperial province, but in 22 BC it was transferred by Augustus to the Senate, and was therefore placed under the administration of proconsuls, as is attested by extant Cyprian coins of the period. When the two missionaries arrived at Paphos, Sergius, who was a "prudent man" (AV) or "man of understanding" (RV), i.e. a man of practical understanding, "sought to hear the word of God" (Acts **13** 7). Bar-Jesus, or Elymas, a sorcerer at the court of Sergius, fearing the influence of the apostles, sought, however, "to turn aside the proconsul from the faith," but was struck with blindness (vs 8–11); and the deputy, "when he saw what was done, believed, being astonished at the teaching of the Lord" (ver 12). The narrative indicates that not only the miracle but also the attention with which Sergius listened to the teaching of Paul (cf ver 7) conduced to his conversion (Bengel). Attempts have been made to trace some connection between the name Sergius Paulus and the fact that Saul is first called Paul in ver 9, but the joint occurrence of the two names is probably to be set down as only a coincidence.

C. M. KERR

PAVEMENT, pāv′ment: In the OT, with the exception of 2 K **16** 17, the Heb word is רִצְפָּה, *riçpāh* (2 Ch **7** 3; Est **1** 6; Ezk **40** 17, etc); in Sir **20** 18 and Bel ver 19 the word is ἔδαφος, *édaphos;* in Jn **19** 13, the name "The Pavement" (λιθόστρωτος, *lithóstrōtos,* "paved with stone") is given to the place outside the Praetorium on which Pilate sat to give judgment upon Jesus. Its Heb (Aram.) equivalent is declared to be GABBATHA (q.v.). The identification of the place is uncertain.

PAVILION, pa-vil′yun: A covered place, booth, tent, in which a person may be kept hid or secret (סֹךְ, *ṣōkh,* Ps **27** 5; סֻכָּה, *ṣukkāh*—the usual term—Ps **31** 20), or otherwise be withdrawn from view

The term is used with reference to God (2 S **22** 12; Ps **18** 11); to kings drinking in privacy (1 K **20** 12.16); RV gives "pavilion" for AV "tabernacle" in Job **36** 29; Isa **4** 6; while in Nu **25** 8 it substitutes this word, with m "alcove," for AV "tent" (*ḳubbāh*), and Jer **43** 10, for "royal pavilion" (*shaphrūr*), reads in m "glittering pavilion."

James Orr

PAW, pô (כַּף, *kaph*, lit. "palm," יָד, *yādh*, lit. "hand"): The former (*kaph*) is applied to the soft paws of animals in contradistinction to the hoofs (Lev **11** 27); the latter is thrice used in 1 S **17** 37: "Jeh that delivered me out of the paw [*yādh*] of the lion, and out of the paw [*yādh*] of the bear, he will deliver me out of the hand [*yādh*] of this Philistine." The vb. "to paw" (חָפַר, *ḥāphar*) is found in the description of the horse: "He paweth [m "they paw"] in the valley, and rejoiceth in his strength: he goeth out to meet the armed men [m "the weapons"]" (Job **39** 21). The word is usually tr[d] "to delve into," "to pry into," "to explore."

H. L. E. Luering

PÊ, pā (פ, פּ, ף): The 17th letter of the Heb alphabet; transliterated in this Encyclopaedia as *p* with daghesh and *ph* (=*f*) without. It came also to be used for the number 80. For name, etc, see Alphabet.

PEACE, pēs (שָׁלוֹם, *shālōm;* εἰρήνη, *eirēnē*): Is a condition of freedom from disturbance, whether outwardly, as of a nation from war or enemies, or inwardly, within the soul. The Heb word is *shālōm* (both adj. and subst.), meaning, primarily, "soundness," "health," but coming also to signify "prosperity," well-being in general, all good in relation to both man and God. In early times, to a people harassed by foes, peace was the primary blessing. In Ps **122** 7, we have "peace" and "prosperity," and in **35** 27; **73** 3, *shālōm* is tr[d] "prosperity." In 2 S **11** 7 AV, David asked of Uriah "how Joab did" (m "of the peace of Joab"), "and how the people did [RV "fared," lit. "of the peace of the people"], and how the war prospered" (lit. "and of the peace [welfare] of the war").

1. In the OT

(1) *Shālōm* was the common friendly greeting, used in asking after the health of anyone; also in farewells (Gen **29** 6, "Is it well with him?" ["Is there *peace* to him?"]; **43** 23, "Peace be to you"; ver 27, "He asked them of their welfare [of their *peace*]"; Jgs **6** 23, "Jeh said unto him, Peace be unto thee"; **18** 15 [AV "saluted him," m "Heb asked him of peace," RV "of his welfare"]; **19** 20, etc). See also Greeting. (2) Peace from enemies (implying prosperity) was the great desire of the nation and was the gift of God to the people if they walked in His ways (Lev **26** 6; Nu **6** 26, "Jeh lift up his countenance upon thee, and give thee peace"; Ps **29** 11; Isa **26** 12, etc). To "die in peace" was greatly to be desired (Gen **15** 15; 1 K **2** 6; 2 Ch **34** 28, etc). (3) Inward peace was the portion of the righteous who trusted in God (Job **22** 21, "Acquaint now thyself with him, and be at peace [*shālam*]"; Ps **4** 8; **85** 8, "He will speak peace unto his people, and to his saints"; **119** 165; Prov **3** 2. 17; Isa **26** 3, "Thou wilt keep him in perfect peace [Heb "peace, peace"], whose mind is stayed on thee; because he trusteth in thee"; Mal **2** 5); also outward peace (Job **5** 23.24; Prov **16** 7, etc). (4) Peace was to be sought and followed by the righteous (Ps **34** 14, "Seek peace, and pursue it"; Zec **8** 16.19, "Love truth and peace"). (5) Peace should be a prominent feature of the Messianic times (Isa **2** 4; **9** 6, "Prince of Peace"; **11** 6; Ezk **34** 25; Mic **4** 2-4; Zec **9** 10).

In the NT, where *eirēnē* has much the same meaning and usage as *shālōm* (for which it is employed in the LXX; cf Lk **19** 42, RV "If thou hadst known .... the things which belong unto peace"), we have still the expectation of "peace" through the coming of the Christ (Lk **1** 74.79; **12** 51) and also its fulfilment in the higher spiritual sense.

2. In the NT

(1) The gospel in Christ is a message of peace from God to men (Lk **2** 14; Acts **10** 36, "preaching .... peace by Jesus Christ"). It is "peace with God through our Lord Jesus Christ," in Rom **5** 1; AV **10** 15; peace between Jew and Gentile (Eph **2** 14.15); an essential element in the spiritual kingdom of God (Rom **14** 17). (2) It is to be cherished and followed by Christians. Jesus exhorted His disciples, "Have salt in yourselves, and be at peace one with another" (Mk **9** 50); Paul exhorts, "Live in peace: and the God of love and peace shall be with you" (2 Cor **13** 11; cf Rom **12** 18; 1 Cor **7** 15). (3) God is therefore "the God of peace," the Author and Giver of all good ("peace" including every blessing) very frequently (e.g. Rom **15** 33; **16** 20; 2 Thess **3** 16, etc, "the Lord of peace"). "Peace from God our Father and the Lord Jesus Christ" is a common apostolic wish or salutation (cf 1 Cor **1** 3; 2 Cor **1** 2, etc). (4) We have also "peace" as a greeting (Mt **10** 13; Lk **10** 5); "a son of peace" (**10** 6) is one worthy of it, in sympathy with it; the Lord's own greeting to His disciples was "Peace be unto you" (Lk **24** 36; Jn **20** 19.21. 26), and ere He left them He gave them specially His blessing of "Peace" (Jn **14** 27); we have also frequently "Go in peace" (Mk **5** 34; Lk **7** 50). In Lk **19** 38, we have "peace in heaven" (in the acclamation of Jesus on His Messianic entry of Jerus). (5) The peace that Christ brought is primarily spiritual peace from and with God, peace in the heart, peace as the disposition or spirit. He said that He did not come "to send peace on the earth, but a sword," referring to the searching nature of His call and the divisions and clearances it would create. But, of course, the spirit of the gospel and of the Christian is one of peace, and it is a Christian duty to seek to bring war and strife everywhere to an end. This is represented as the ultimate result of the gospel and Spirit of Christ; universal and permanent peace can come only as that Spirit rules in men's hearts.

"Peace" in the sense of silence, to hold one's peace, etc, is in the OT generally the tr of *ḥārash*, "to be still, or silent" (Gen **24** 21; **34** 5; Job **11** 3); also of *ḥāshāh*, "to hush," "to be silent" (2 K **2** 3.5; Ps **39** 2), and of other words. In Job **29** 10 ("The nobles held their peace," AV), it is *ḳōl*, "voice."

In the NT we have *siōpáō*, "to be silent," "to cease speaking" (Mt **20** 31; **26** 63; Acts **18** 9, etc); *sigáō*, "to be silent," "not to speak" (Lk **20** 26; Acts **12** 17); *hēsucházō*, "to be quiet" (Lk **14** 4; Acts **11** 18); *phimóō*, "to muzzle or gag" (Mk **1** 25; Lk **4** 35).

In Apoc *eirēnē* is frequent, mostly in the sense of peace from war or strife (Tob **13** 14; Jth **3** 1; Ecclus **13** 18; 1 Macc **5** 54; **6** 49; 2 Macc **14** 6, *eustátheia*="tranquillity").

RV has "peace" for "tongue" (Est **7** 4; Job **6** 24; Am **6** 10; Hab **1** 13); "at peace with me" for "perfect" (Isa **42** 19, m "made perfect" or "recompensed"); "security" instead of "peaceably" and "peace" (Dnl **8** 25; **11** 21.24); "came in peace to the city," for "came to Shalem, a city" (Gen **33** 18); "it was for my peace" instead of "for peace" (Isa **38** 17); "when they are in peace," for "and that which should have been for their welfare" (Ps **69** 22).

W. L. Walker

PEACE OFFERING. See Sacrifice.

PEACEMAKER, pēs′māk-ẽr: Occurs only in the pl. (Mt **5** 9, "Blessed are the peacemakers [*eirēnopoioí*]: for they shall be called sons of God" [who is "the God of peace"]). We have also what seems to be a reflection of this saying in Jas **3** 18, "The fruit of righteousness is sown in peace for [RVm "by"] them that make peace" (*toís poioúsin eirḗnēn*). In classical Gr a "peacemaker" was an ambassador sent to treat of peace. The word in Mt **5** 9 would, perhaps, be better rendered "peace-workers," implying not merely making peace between those who are at variance, but *working* peace as that which is the will of the God of peace for men.

W. L. WALKER

PEACOCK, pē'kok (תֻּכִּיִּים, *tukkīyīm* [pl.]; Lat *Pavo cristatus*): A bird of the genus *Pavo*. Japan is the native home of the plainer peafowl; Siam, Ceylon and India produce the commonest and most gorgeous. The peacock has a bill of moderate size with an arched tip, its cheeks are bare, the eyes not large, but very luminous, a crest of 24 feathers 2 in. long, with naked shafts and broad tips of blue, glancing to green. The neck is not long but proudly arched, the breast full, prominent and of bright blue green, blue predominant. The wings are short and ineffectual, the feathers on them made up of a surprising array of colors. The tail consists of 18 short, stiff, grayish-brown feathers. Next is the lining of the train, of the same color. The glory of this glorious bird lies in its train. It begins on the back between the wings in tiny feathers not over 6 in. in length, and extends backward. The quills have thick shafts of purple and green shades, the eye at the tip of each feather from one-half to 2 in. across, of a deep peculiar blue, surrounded at the lower part by two half-moon-shaped crescents of green. Whether the train lies naturally, or is spread in full glory, each eye shows encircled by a marvel of glancing shades of green, gold, purple, blue and bronze. When this train is spread, it opens like a fan behind the head with its sparkling crest, and above the wondrous blue of the breast. The bird has the power to contract the muscles at the base of the quills and play a peculiar sort of music with them. It loves high places and cries before a storm in notes that are startling to one not familiar with them. The bird can be domesticated and will become friendly enough to take food from the hand. The peahen is smaller than the cock, her neck green, her wings gray, tan and brown—but she has not the gorgeous train. She nests on earth and breeds with difficulty when imported, the young being delicate and tender. The grown birds are hardy when acclimated, and live to old age. By some freak of nature, pure white peacocks are at times produced. Aristophanes mentioned peafowl in his *Birds*, ll. 102, 269. Alexander claimed that he brought them into Greece from the east, but failed to prove his contention. Pliny wrote that Hortensius was the first to serve the birds for food, and that Aufidius Lurco first fattened and sold them in the markets. It was the custom to skin the bird, roast and recover it and send it to the table, the gaudy feathers showing.

The first appearance of the bird in the Bible occurs in a summing-up of the wealth and majesty of Solomon (1 K **10** 22: "For the king had at sea a navy of Tarshish with the navy of Hiram: once every three years came the navy of Tarshish, bringing gold, and silver, ivory, and apes, and peacocks"). (Here LXX translates πελεκητοί [s.c. λίθοι], *pelekētoí* [*líthoi*] = "[stones] carved with an ax.") The same statement is made in 2 Ch **9** 21: "For the king had ships that went to Tarshish with the servants of Huram; once every three years came the ships of Tarshish, bringing gold, and silver, ivory, and apes, and peacocks" (LXX omits). There is no question among scholars and scientists but that these statements are true, as the ships of Solomon are known to have visited the coasts of India and Ceylon, and Tarshish was on the Malabar coast of India, where the native name of the peacock was *tokei*, from which *tukkīyīm* undoubtedly was derived (see GOLD, and *Expos T*, IX, 472). The historian Tennant says that the Heb names for "ivory" and "apes" were also the same as the Tamil. The reference to the small, ineffectual wing of the peacock which scarcely will lift the weight of the body and train, that used to be found in Job, is now applied to the ostrich, and is no doubt correct:

> "The wings of the ostrich wave proudly;
> But are they the pinions and plumage of love?"
> (Job **39** 13).

While the peacock wing seems out of proportion to the size of the bird, it will sustain flight and bear the body to the treetops. The wing of the ostrich is useless for flight. GENE STRATTON-PORTER

PEARL, pûrl. See STONES, PRECIOUS.

PECULIAR, pē̇-kūl'yar: The Lat *peculium* means "private property," so that "peculiar" properly = "pertaining to the individual." In modern Eng. the word has usually degenerated into a half-colloquial form for "extraordinary," but in Bib. Eng. it is a thoroughly dignified term for "esp. one's own"; cf the "peculiar treasure" of the king in Eccl **2** 8 (AV). Hence "peculiar people" (AV Dt **14** 2, etc) means a people esp. possessed by God and particularly prized by Him. The word in the OT (AV Ex **19** 5; Dt **14** 2; **26** 18; Ps **135** 4; Eccl **2** 8) invariably represents סְגֻלָּה, *ṣeghullāh*, "property," an obscure word which LXX usually rendered by the equally obscure περιούσιος, *periousios* (apparently meaning "superabundant"), which in turn is quoted in Tit **2** 14. In Mal **3** 17, however, LXX has περιποίησις, *peripoíēsis*, quoted in 1 Pet **2** 9. ERV in the NT substituted "own possession" in the two occurrences, but in the OT kept "peculiar" and even extended its use (Dt **7** 6; Mal **3** 17) to cover every occurrence of *ṣeghullāh* except in 1 Ch **29** 3 ("treasure"). ARV, on the contrary, has dropped "peculiar" altogether, using "treasure" in 1 Ch **29** 3; Eccl **2** 8, and "own possession" elsewhere. AV also has "peculiar commandments" (ἴδιος, *ídios*, "particular," RV "several") in Wisd **19** 6, and RV has "peculiar" where AV has "special" in Wisd **3** 14 for ἐκλεκτή, *eklektḗ*, "chosen out."

BURTON SCOTT EASTON

PEDAHEL, ped'a-hel, pē̇-dä'el (פְּדַהְאֵל, *pedhah'ēl*, "whom God redeems"): A prince of Naphtali; one of the tribal chiefs who apportioned the land of Canaan (Nu **34** 28; cf ver 17).

PEDAHZUR, pē̇-dä'zur (פְּדָהצוּר, *pedhāhçūr*): Mentioned in Nu **1** 10; **2** 20; **7** 54.59; **10** 23 as the father of Gamaliel, head of the tribe of Manasseh, at the time of the exodus. See *Expos T*, VIII, 555ff.

PEDAIAH, pē̇-dā'ya, pē̇-dī'a (פְּדָיָהוּ, *pedhāyāhū*, "Jeh redeems"):

(1) Father of Joel, who was ruler of Western Manasseh in David's reign (1 Ch **27** 20). Form פְּדָיָה, *pedhāyāh* (see above).

(2) Pedaiah of Rumah (2 K **23** 36), father of Zebudah, Jehoiakim's mother.

(3) A son of Jeconiah (1 Ch **3** 18); in ver 19 the father of Zerubbabel. Pedaiah's brother, Shealtiel, is also called father of Zerubbabel (Ezr **3** 2; but in 1 Ch **3** 17 AV spelled "Salathiel"). There may have been two cousins, or even different individuals may be referred to under Shealtiel and Salathiel respectively.

(4) Another who helped to repair the city wall (Neh **3** 25), of the family of PAROSH (q.v.). Perhaps this is the man who stood by Ezra at the reading of the Law (Neh **8** 4; 1 Esd **9** 44, called "Phaldeus").

(5) A "Levite," appointed one of the treasurers

over the "treasuries" of the Lord's house (Neh **13** 13).

(6) A Benjamite, one of the rulers residing in Jerus under the "return" arrangements (Neh **11** 7).

Henry Wallace

PEDESTAL, ped'es-tal (כֵּן, *kēn*): In two places (1 K **7** 29.31) RV gives this word for AV "base" (in Solomon's "Sea").

PEDIAS, ped'i-as, pē-dī'as (Πεδίας, *Pedías*, A, Παιδείας, *Paideías;* AV by mistake **Pelias**): One of those who had taken "strange wives" (1 Esd **9** 34) = "Bedeiah" of Ezr **10** 35.

PEDIGREE, ped'i-grē (הִתְיַלֵּד, *hithyallēdh*, "to show one's birth"): The Eng. word "pedigree" occurs only once in the Bible, according to the concordance. In Nu **1** 18, it is said: "They declared their pedigrees"; that is, they enrolled or registered themselves according to their family connections. The same idea is expressed frequently, employing a different term in the Heb, by the common phrase of Ch, Ezr and Neh, "to reckon by genealogy," "to give genealogy," etc (cf 1 Ch **7** 5.9; Ezr **2** 62 ff; Neh **7** 64). These last passages indicate the importance of the registered pedigree or genealogy, esp. of the priests in the post-exilic community, for the absence of the list of their pedigrees, or their genealogical records, was sufficient to cause the exclusion from the priesthood of certain enrolled priests.

Walter R. Betteridge

PEEL, pēl, **PILL,** pil: "Pill" (Gen **30** 37.38; Tob **11** 13 [RV "scaled"]) and "peel" (Isa **18** 2.7 [AV and RVm]; Ezk **29** 18 [AV and ERV]) are properly two different words, meaning "to remove the hair" (*pilus*) and "to remove the skin" (*pellis*), but in Elizabethan Eng. the two were confused. In Isa **18** 2.7, the former meaning is implied, as the Heb word here (מָרַט, *māraṭ*) is rendered "pluck off the hair" in Ezr **9** 3; Neh **13** 25; Isa **50** 6. The word, however, may also mean "make smooth" (so RVm) or "bronzed." This last, referring to the dark skins of the Ethiopians, is best here, but in any case AV and RVm are impossible. In the other cases, however, "remove the skin" (cf "scaled," Tob **11** 13 RV) is meant. So in Gen **30** 37.38, Jacob "peels" (so RV) off portions of the bark of his rods, so as to give alternating colors (cf ver 39). And in Ezk **29** 18, the point is Nebuchadrezzar's total failure in his siege of Tyre, although the soldiers had carried burdens until the skin was peeled from their shoulders (cf ARV "worn").

Burton Scott Easton

PEEP, pēp (צָפַף, *çāphaph;* AV Isa **8** 19; **10** 14 [RV "chirp"]): In **10** 14, the word describes the sound made by a nestling bird; in **8** 19, the changed (ventriloquistic?) voice of necromancers uttering sounds that purported to come from the feeble dead. The modern use of "peep" = "look" is found in Sir **21** 23, as the tr of παρακύπτω, *parakúptō:* "A foolish man peepeth in from the door of another man's house."

PEKAH, pē'kä (פֶּקַח, *pekaḥ*, "opening" [of the eyes] [2 K **15** 25–31]; Φάκεε, *Phákee*): Son of Remaliah, and 18th king of Israel.

1. Accession

Pekah murdered his predecessor, Pekahiah, and seized the reins of power (ver 25). His usurpation of the throne is said to have taken place in the 52d year of Uzziah, and his reign to have lasted for 20 years (ver 27). His accession, therefore, may be placed in 748 BC (other chronologies place it later, and make the reign last only a few years).

Pekah came to the throne with the resolution of assisting in forming a league to resist the westward advance of Assyria. The memory of defeat by Assyria at the battle of Karkar in 753, more than 100 years before, had never died out.

2. Attitude of Assyria

Tiglath-pileser III was now ruler of Assyria, and in successive campaigns since 745 had proved himself a resistless conqueror. His lust for battle was not yet satisfied, and the turn of Philistia and Syria was about to come. In 735, a coalition, of which Pekah was a prominent member, was being formed to check his further advance. It comprised the princes of Comagene, Gebal, Hamath, Arvad, Ammon, Moab, Edom, Gaza, Samaria, Syria, and some minor potentates, the list being taken from a roll of the subject-princes who attended a court and paid tribute after the fall of Damascus. Ahaz likewise attended as a voluntary tributary to do homage to Tiglath-pileser (2 K **16** 10).

While the plans of the allies were in course of formation, an obstacle was met with which proved insurmountable by the arts of diplomacy.

3. Judah Recalcitrant

This was the refusal of Ahaz, then on the throne of David, to join the confederacy. Arguments and threats having failed to move him, resort was had to force, and the troops of Samaria and Damascus moved on Jerus (2 K **16** 5). Great alarm was felt at the news of their approach, as seen in the 7th and 8th chapters of Isa. The allies had in view to dispossess Ahaz of his crown, and give it to one of their own number, a son of Tabeel. Isaiah himself was the mainstay of the opposition to their projects. The policy he advocated, by Divine direction, was that of complete neutrality. This he urged with passionate earnestness, but with only partial success. Isaiah (probably) had kept back Ahaz from joining the coalition, but could not prevent him from sending an embassy, laden with gifts to Tiglath-pileser, to secure his intervention. On the news arriving that the Assyrian was on the march, a hasty retreat was made from Jerus, and the blow soon thereafter fell, where Isaiah had predicted, on Rezin and Pekah, and their kingdoms.

The severely concise manner in which the writer of K deals with the later sovereigns of the Northern Kingdom is, in the case of Pekah, supplemented in Ch by further facts as to this campaign of the allies.

4. Chronicles Ancillary to Kings

The Chronicler states that "a great multitude of captives" were taken to Damascus and many others to Samaria. These would be countrymen and women from the outlying districts of Judah, which were ravaged. Those taken to Samaria were, however, returned, unhurt, to Jericho by the advice of the prophet Oded (2 Ch **28** 5–15).

The messengers sent from Jerus to Nineveh appear to have arrived when the army of Tiglath-pileser was already prepared to march.

5. Fall of Damascus; Northern and Eastern Palestine Overrun

The movements of the Assyrians being expedited, they fell upon Damascus before the junction of the allies was accomplished. Rezin was defeated in a decisive battle, and took refuge in his capital, which was closely invested. Another part of the invading army descended on the upper districts of Syria and Samaria. Serious resistance to the veteran troops of the East could hardly be made, and city after city fell. A list of districts and cities that were overrun is given in 2 K **15** 29. It comprises Gilead beyond Jordan—already partly depopulated (1 Ch **5** 26); the tribal division of Naphtali, lying to the W. of the lakes of Galilee and Merom, and all Galilee, as far S. as the plain of Esdraelon and the Valley of Jezreel. Cities particularly mentioned are Ijon (now *'Ayûn*), Abel-beth-maacah (now *'Abi*),

Janoah (now *Yânûn*), Kedesh (now *Kados*) and Hazor (now *Hadîreh*).

These places and territories were not merely attacked and plundered. Their inhabitants were removed, with indescribable loss and suffering, to certain districts in Assyria, given as Halah, Habor, Hara, and both sides of the river Gozan, an affluent of the Euphrates.

6. Deportation of the Inhabitants

The transplantation of these tribes to a home beyond the great river was a new experiment in political geography, devised with the object of welding the whole of Western Asia into a single empire. It was work of immense difficulty and must have taxed the resources of even so great an organizer as Tiglath-pileser. The soldiers who had conquered in the field were, of course, employed to escort the many thousands of prisoners to their new locations. About two-thirds of the Sam kingdom, comprising the districts of Samaria, the two Galilees, and the trans-Jordanic region, was thus denuded of its inhabitants.

7. Death of Pekah

Left with but a third of his kingdom—humbled but still defiant—Pekah was necessarily unpopular with his subjects. In this extremity—the wave of invasion from the N. having spent itself—the usual solution occurred, and a plot was formed by which the assassination of Pekah should be secured, and the assassin should take his place as a satrap of Assyria. A tool was found in the person of Hoshea, whom Tiglath-pileser claims to have appointed to the throne. The Bib. narrative does not do more than record the fact that "Hoshea the son of Elah made a conspiracy against Pekah the son of Remaliah, and smote him, and slew him, and reigned in his stead" (2 K **15** 30). The date given to this act is the 20th year of Jotham. As Jotham's reign lasted but 16 years, this number is evidently an error.

8. References in Isaiah

For the first time, the historian makes no reference to the religious conduct of a king of Israel. The subject was beneath notice. The second section of Isaiah's prophecies (**7** 1—**10** 4) belongs to the reign of Ahaz and thus to the time of Pekah, both of whom are named in it. Pekah is named in **7** 1, and is often, in this and the next chapter, referred to as "the son of Remaliah." His loss of the territorial divisions of Zebulun and Naphtali is referred to in **9** 1, and is followed by a prophecy of their future glory as the earthly home of the Son of Man. The wording of Isa **9** 14 shows that it was written before the fall of Samaria, and that of Isa **10** 9–11 that Damascus and Samaria had both fallen and Jerus was expected to follow. This section of Isaiah may thus be included in the literature of the time of Pekah.

W. Shaw Caldecott

PEKAHIAH, pek-a-hī'a, pē-kä'ya (פְּקַחְיָה, *peḳaḥyāh*, "Jeh hath opened" [the eyes] [2 K **15** 23–26]; Φακεσίας, *Phakesías*, A, Φακείας, *Phakeías*): Son of Menahem, and 17th king of Israel. He is said to have succeeded his father in the "50th year of Azariah" (or Uzziah), a synchronism not free from difficulty if his accession is placed in 750–749 (see Menahem; Uzziah). Most date lower, after 738, when an Assyr inscription makes Menahem pay tribute to Tiglath-pileser (cf 2 K **15** 19–21).

1. Accession

2. Regicide in Israel

Pekahiah came to the throne enveloped in the danger which always accompanies the successor of an exceptionally strong ruler, in a country where there is not a settled law of succession. Within two years of his accession he was foully murdered—the 7th king of Israel who had met his death by violence (the others were Nadab, Elah, Tibni, Jehoram, Zechariah and Shallum). The chief conspirator was Pekah, son of Remaliah, one of his captains, with whom, as agent in the crime, were associated 50 Gileadites. These penetrated into the palace (RV "castle") of the king's house, and put Pekahiah to death, his bodyguards, Argob and Arieh, dying with him. The record, in its close adherence to fact, gives no reason for the king's removal, but it may reasonably be surmised that it was connected with a league which was at this time forming for opposing resistance to the power of Assyria. This league, Pekahiah, preferring his father's policy of tributary vassalage, may have refused to join. If so, the decision cost him his life. The act of treachery and violence is in accordance with all that Hosea tells us of the internal condition of Israel at this time: "They . . . . devour their judges; all their kings are fallen" (Hos **7** 7).

3. Pekahiah's Character

The narrative of Pekahiah's short reign contains but a brief notice of his personal character. Like his predecessors, Pekahiah did not depart from the system of worship introduced by Jeroboam, the son of Nebat, "who made Israel to sin." Despite the denunciations of the prophets of the Northern Kingdom (Am **5** 21–27; Hos **8** 1–6), the worship of the calves remained, till the whole was swept away, a few years later, by the fall of the kingdom.

After Pekahiah's murder, the throne was seized by the regicide Pekah.

W. Shaw Caldecott

PEKOD, pē'kod (פְּקוֹד, *peḳōdh*): A name applied in Jer **50** 21 and Ezk **23** 23 to the Chaldaeans. EVm in the former passage gives the meaning as "visitation."

PELAIAH, pē-lā'ya, pē-lī'a (פְּלָאיָה, *pelā'yāh*):

(1) A son of Elioenai, of the royal house of Judah (1 Ch **3** 24).

(2) A Levite who assisted Ezra by expounding the Law (Neh **8** 7), and was one of those who sealed the covenant with Nehemiah (**10** 10). He is called "Phalias" in 1 Esd **9** 48 (RV).

PELALIAH, pel-a-lī'a (פְּלַלְיָה, *pelalyāh*, "Jeh judges"): A priest, father of Jeroham, one of the "workers" in the Lord's house (Neh **11** 12).

PELATIAH, pel-a-tī'a (פְּלַטְיָה, *pelaṭyāh*, "Jeh delivers"):

(1) One who "sealed" the covenant (Neh **10** 22).

(2) A descendant of Solomon, grandson of Zerubbabel (1 Ch **3** 21).

(3) A Simeonite, one of the captains who cleared out the Amalekites and dwelt on the captured land (1 Ch **4** 42.43).

(4) A prince of the people whom Ezekiel (in Babylon) pictures as 'devising mischief' and giving 'wicked counsel' in Jerus. He is represented as falling dead while Ezekiel prophesies (Ezk **11** 1.13). His name has the ו, *ū*, ending.

PELEG, pē'leg (פֶּלֶג, *pelegh*, "watercourse," "division"): A son of Eber, and brother of Joktan. The derivation of the name is given: "for in his days was the earth divided" (*niphleghāh*) (Gen **10** 25; cf Lk **3** 35, AV "Phalec"). This probably refers to the scattering of the world's population and the confounding of its language recorded in Gen **11** 1–9. In Aram. *pelagh* and Arab. *phalaj* mean "division"; in Heb *pelegh* means "watercourse." The name may really be due to the occupation by this people of some well-watered (furrowed), district (e.g. in Babylonia), for these patronymics represent races, and the derivation in Gen **10** 25 is a later editor's remark.

S. F. Hunter

PELET, pē'let (פֶּלֶט, *pelet*, "deliverance"):
(1) Son of Iahdai (1 Ch **2** 47).
(2) Son of Azmaveth, one of those who resorted to David at Ziklag while he was hiding from Saul (1 Ch **12** 3).

PELETH, pē'leth (פֶּלֶת, *peleth*, "swiftness"):
(1) Father of On, one of the rebels against Moses and Aaron (Nu **16** 1); probably same as PALLU (q.v.).
(2) A descendant of Jerahmeel (1 Ch **2** 33).

PELETHITES, pel'ē-thīts, pē'leth-īts (פְּלֵתִי, *p^elēthī*): A company of David's bodyguard, like the CHERETHITES (q.v.) (2 S **8** 18; **15** 18); probably soldiers of Beth-pelet. See BETH-PELET.

PELIAS, pē-lī'as: AV=RV "Pedias."

PELICAN, pel'i-kan (קָאַת, *ķā'ath;* Lat *Pelecanus onocrotalus* [LXX reads πελεκάν, *pelekán*, in Lev and Pss, but has 3 other readings, that are rather confusing, in the other places]): Any bird of the genus *Pelecanus*. The Heb *ķī'* means "to vomit." The name was applied to the bird because

Pelican (*Pelecanus onocrotalus*).

it swallowed large quantities of fish and then disgorged them to its nestlings. In the performance of this act it pressed the large beak, in the white species, tipped with red, against the crop and slightly lifted the wings. In ancient times, people, seeing this, believed that the bird was puncturing its breast and feeding its young with its blood. From this idea arose the custom of using a pelican with lifted wings in heraldry or as a symbol of Christ and of charity. (See *Fictitious Creatures in Art*, 182–86, London, Chapman and Hall, 1906.) Pal knew a white and a brownish-gray bird, both close to 6 ft. long and having over a 12 ft. sweep of wing. They lived around the Dead Sea, fished beside the Jordan and abounded in greatest numbers in the wildernesses of the Mediterranean shore. The brown pelicans were larger than the white. Each of them had a long beak, peculiar throat pouch and webbed feet. They built large nests, 5 and 6 ft. across, from dead twigs of bushes, and laid two or three eggs. The brown birds deposited a creamy-white egg with a rosy flush; the white, a white egg with bluish tints. The young were naked at first, then covered with down, and remained in the nest until full feathered and able to fly. This compelled the parent birds to feed them for a long time, and they carried such quantities of fish to a nest that the young could not consume all of them and many were dropped on the ground. The tropical sun soon made the location unbearable to mortals. Perching pelicans were the ugliest birds imaginable, but when their immense brown or white bodies swept in a 12 ft. spread across the land and over sea, they made an impressive picture. They are included, with good reason, in the list of abominations (see Lev **11** 18; Dt **14** 17). They are next mentioned in Ps **102** 6:

> "I am like a pelican of the wilderness;
> I am become as an owl of the waste places."

Here David from the depths of affliction likened himself to a pelican as it appears when it perches in the wilderness. See Isa **34** 11: "But the pelican and the porcupine shall possess it; and the owl and the raven shall dwell therein: and he will stretch over it the line of confusion, and the plummet of emptiness." Here the bird is used to complete the picture of desolation that was to prevail after the destruction of Edom. The other reference concerns the destruction of Nineveh and is found in Zeph **2** 14: "And herds shall lie down in the midst of her, all the beasts of the nations: both the pelican and the porcupine shall lodge in the capitals thereof; their voice shall sing in the windows; desolation shall be in the thresholds: for he hath laid bare the cedar-work." GENE STRATTON-PORTER

PELISHTIM, pel'ish-tim, pe-lish'tīm (פְּלִשְׁתִּים, *p^elishtīm* [RVm of Gen **10** 14]). See PHILISTINES.

PELONITE, pel'ō-nīt, pē'lō-nīt, pē-lō'nīt (פְּלוֹנִי, *p^elōnī*, a place-name): Two of David's heroes are thus described: (1) "Helez the Pelonite" (1 Ch **11** 27) (see PALTITE); and (2) "Ahijah the Pelonite" (1 Ch **11** 36).

PEN, (עֵט, *'ēt*, חֶרֶט, *ḥereṭ;* κάλαμος, *kálamos*): The first writing was done on clay, wax, lead or stone tablets by scratching into the material with some hard pointed instrument. For this purpose bodkins of bronze, iron, bone or ivory were used (Job **19** 24; Isa **8** 1; Jer **17** 1). In Jer **17** 1 a diamond is also mentioned as being used for the same purpose. In Jer **36** Baruch, the son of Neriah, declares that he recorded the words of the prophet with ink in the book. In ver 23 it says that the king cut the roll with the penknife (lit. the scribe's knife). This whole scene can best be explained if we consider that Baruch and the king's scribes were in the habit of using reed pens. These pens are made from the hollow jointed stalks of a coarse grass growing in marshy places. The dried reed is cut diagonally with the penknife and the point thus formed is carefully shaved thin to make it flexible and the nib split as in the modern pen. The last operation is the clipping off of the very point so that it becomes a stub pen. The Arab scribe does this by resting the nib on his thumb nail while cutting, so that the cut will be clean and the pen will not scratch. The whole procedure requires considerable skill. The pupil in Heb or Arab. writing learns to make a pen as his first lesson. A scribe carries a sharp knife around with him for keeping his pen in good condition, hence the name penknife. The word used in 3 Jn ver 13 is *kalamos*, "reed," indicating that the pen described above was used in John's time (cf *ķalam*, the common Arab. name for pen). See INK; INK-HORN; WRITING.

Figurative: "Written with a pen of iron," i.e. indelibly (Jer **17** 1). "My tongue is the pen of a ready writer" (Ps **45** 1; cf Jer **36** 18). As the trained writer records a speech, so the Psalmist's tongue impresses or engraves on his hearers' minds what he has conceived.

JAMES A. PATCH

PENCE, pens, **PENNY.** See MONEY.

PENCIL, pen′sil (Isa **44** 13, m "red ochre," AV "line"). See LINE; OCHRE, RED.

PENDANT, pen′dant (from Fr. from Lat *pendeo*, "to hang"): Not in AV. Twice in RV. (1) נְטִיפוֹת, *neṭīphōth* (AV "collars"), ornaments of the Midianites captured by Gideon (Jgs **8** 26). (2) נְטִפוֹת, *neṭiphōth* (AV "chains"), an article of feminine apparel (Isa **3** 19). The reference seems to be (Cheyne, "Isaiah" *Polychrome Bible* [*HDB*, III, 739]) to ear-drops, pearl or gold ornaments resembling a drop of water, fastened, probably, to the lobe of the ear.

PENIEL, pē-nī′el, pen′i-el, pē′ni-el (פְּנִיאֵל, *penī′ēl*, "face of God"; Εἶδος θεοῦ, *Eídos theoú*): This is the form of the name in Gen **32** 30. In the next verse and elsewhere it appears as "Penuel." The name is said to have been given to the place by Jacob after his night of wrestling by the Jabbok, because, as he said, "I have seen God face to face, and my life is preserved." It was a height evidently close by the stream over which Jacob passed in the morning. Some have thought it might be a prominent cliff, the contour of which resembled a human face. Such a cliff on the seashore to the S. of Tripoli was called *theoú prósōpon*, "face of God" (Strabo xvi.2.15 f). In later times a city with a strong tower stood upon it. This lay in the line of Gideon's pursuit of the Midianites. When he returned victorious, he beat down the place because of the churlishness of the inhabitants (Jgs **8** 8.9.17). It was one of the towns "built" or fortified by Jeroboam (1 K **12** 25). Merrill would identify it with *Telūl edh-Dhahab*, "hills of gold," two hills with ruins that betoken great antiquity, and that speak of great strength, on the S. of the Jabbok, about 10 miles E. of Jordan (for description see Merrill, *East of the Jordan*, 390 ff). A difficulty that seems fatal to this identification is that here the banks of the Jabbok are so precipitous as to be impassable. Conder suggests *Jebel 'Osha*. The site was clearly not far from Succoth; but no certainty is yet possible.

W. EWING

PENINNAH, pē-nin′a (פְּנִנָּה, *peninnāh*, "coral," "pearl"): Second wife of Elkanah, father of Samuel (1 S **1** 2.4).

PENKNIFE, pen′nīf (Jer **36** 23). See PEN.

PENNY, pen′i (δηνάριον, *dēnárion;* Lat *denarius* [q.v.]): ARV (Mt **18** 28; **20** 2.9.10.13, etc) renders it by "shilling" except in Mt **22** 19; Mk **12** 15 and Lk **20** 24, where it retains the original term as it refers to a particular coin. See DENARIUS; MONEY.

PENSION, pen′shun (1 Esd **4** 56, AV "and he commanded to give to all that kept the city pensions and wages"; κλῆρος, *klḗros*, "allotted portion," usually [here certainly] of lands [RV "lands"]): Literally means simply "payment," and AV seems to have used the word in order to avoid any specialization of *klḗros*. There is no reference to payment for past services. See LOT.

PENTATEUCH, pen′ta-tūk:

I. TITLE, DIVISION, CONTENTS
II. AUTHORSHIP, COMPOSITION, DATE
  1. The Current Critical Scheme
  2. The Evidence for the Current Critical Scheme
    (1) Astruc's Clue
    (2) Signs of Post-Mosaic Date
    (3) Narrative Discrepancies
    (4) Doublets
    (5) The Laws
    (6) The Argument from Style
    (7) Props of the Development Hypothesis
  3. The Answer to the Critical Analysis
    (1) The Veto of Textual Criticism
    (2) Astruc's Clue Tested
    (3) The Narrative Discrepancies and Signs of Post-Mosaic Date Examined
    (4) The Argument from the Doublets Examined
    (5) The Critical Argument from the Laws
    (6) The Argument from Style
    (7) Perplexities of the Theory
    (8) Signs of Unity
    (9) The Supposed Props of the Development Hypothesis
  4. The Evidence of Date
    (1) The Narrative of Genesis
    (2) Archaeology and Genesis
    (3) The Legal Evidence of Genesis
    (4) The Professedly Mosaic Character of the Legislation
    (5) The Historical Situation Required by P
    (6) The Hierarchical Organization in P
    (7) The Legal Evidence of P
    (8) The Evidence of D
    (9) Later Allusions
    (10) Other Evidence
  5. The Fundamental Improbabilities of the Critical Case
    (1) The Moral and Psychological Issues
    (2) The Historical Improbability
    (3) The Divergence between the Laws and Post-exilic Practice
    (4) The Testimony of Tradition
  6. The Origin and Transmission of the Pentateuch
III. SOME LITERARY POINTS
  1. Style of Legislation
  2. The Narrative
  3. The Covenant
  4. Order and Rhythm
IV. THE PENTATEUCH AS HISTORY
  1. Textual Criticism and History
  2. Hebrew Methods of Expression
  3. Personification and Genealogies
  4. Literary Form
  5. The Sacred Numbers
  6. Habits of Thought
  7. National Coloring
  8. How Far the Pentateuch Is Trustworthy
    (1) Contemporaneous Information
    (2) Character of Our Informants
    (3) Historical Genius of the People
    (4) Good Faith of Deuteronomy
    (5) Nature of the Events Recorded
    (6) External Corroborations
  9. The Pentateuch as Reasoned History
V. THE CHARACTER OF THE PENTATEUCH
  1. Hindu Law Books
  2. Differences
  3. Holiness
  4. The Universal Aspect
  5. The National Aspect
LITERATURE

I. Title, Division, Contents (תּוֹרָה, *tōrāh*, "law" or "teaching").—It has recently been argued that the Heb word is really the Bab *tertu*, "divinely revealed law" (e.g. Sayce, *Churchman*, 1909, 728 ff), but such passages as Lev **14** 54–57; Dt **17** 11 show that the legislator connected it with הוֹרָה, *hōrāh* (from *yārāh*), "to teach." Also called by the Jews חֲמִשָּׁה חוּמְשֵׁי תוֹרָה, *ḥămishshāh ḥūmeshī tōrāh*, "the five-fifths of the law": ὁ νόμος, *ho nómos*, "the Law." The word "Pentateuch" comes from πεντάτευχος, *pentáteuchos*, lit. "5-volumed [sc. book]." The Pent consists of the first five books of the Bible, and forms the first division of the Jewish Canon, and the whole of the Sam Canon. The 5-fold division is certainly old, since it is earlier than the LXX or the Sam Pent. How much older it may be is unknown. It has been thought that the 5-fold division of the Psalter is based on it.

The five books into which the Pent is divided are respectively Gen, Ex, Lev, Nu, and Dt, and the separate arts. should be consulted for information as to their nomenclature.

The work opens with an account of the Creation, and passes to the story of the first human couple. The narrative is carried on partly by genealogies and partly by fuller accounts to Abraham. Then comes a history of Abraham, Isaac and Jacob, the collateral lines of descendants being rapidly dismissed. The story of Joseph is told in detail, and Gen closes with his death. The rest of the Pent covers the oppression of the Israelites in Egypt, their exodus and wanderings, the conquest of the trans-Jordanic lands and the fortunes of the people to the death of Moses. The four concluding books contain masses of legislation mingled with the narrative (for special contents, see arts. on the several books).

II. Authorship, Composition, Date.—The view that Moses was the author of the Pent, with the exception of the concluding vs of Dt, was once held universally. It is still believed by the great mass of Jews and Christians, but in most universities of Northern Europe and North America other theories prevail. An application of what is called "higher" or "documentary criticism" (to distinguish it from lower or textual criticism) has led to the formation of a number of hypotheses. Some of these are very widely held, but unanimity has not been attained, and recent investigations have challenged even the conclusions that are most generally accepted. In the Eng.-speaking countries the vast majority of the critics would regard Driver's *LOT* and Carpenter and Harford-Battersby's *Hexateuch* as fairly representative of their position, but on the Continent of Europe the numerous school that holds some such position is dwindling alike in numbers and influence, while even in Great Britain and America some of the ablest critics are beginning to show signs of being shaken in their allegiance to cardinal points of the higher-critical case. However, at the time of writing, these latter critics have not put forward any fresh formulation of their views, and accordingly the general positions of the works named may be taken as representing with certain qualifications the general critical theory. Some of the chief stadia in the development of this may be mentioned.

1. The Current Critical Scheme

After attention had been drawn by earlier writers to various signs of post-Mosaic date and extraordinary perplexities in the Pent, the first real step toward what its advocates have, till within the last few years, called "the modern position" was taken by J. Astruc (1753). He propounded what Carpenter terms "the clue to the documents," i.e. the difference of the Divine appellations in Gen as a test of authorship. On this view the word *'Ĕlōhīm* ("God") is characteristic of one principal source and the Tetragrammaton, i.e. the Divine name *YHWH* represented by the "Lord" or "God" of AV and RV, shows the presence of another. Despite occasional warnings, this clue was followed in the main for 150 years. It forms the starting-point of the whole current critical development, but the most recent investigations have successfully proved that it is unreliable (see below, 3, [2]). Astruc was followed by Eichhorn (1780), who made a more thorough examination of Gen, indicating numerous differences of style, representation, etc.

Geddes (1792) and Vater (1802–5) extended the method applied to Gen to the other books of the Pent.

In 1798 Ilgen distinguished two Elohists in Gen, but this view did not find followers for some time. The next step of fundamental importance was the assignment of the bulk of Dt to the 7th cent. BC. This was due to De Wette (1806). Hupfeld (1853) again distinguished a second Elohist, and this has been accepted by most critics. Thus there are four main documents at least: D (the bulk of Dt), two Elohists (P and E) and one document (J) that uses the Tetragrammaton in Gen. From 1822 (Bleek) a series of writers maintained that the Book of Josh was compounded from the same documents as the Pent (see Hexateuch).

Two other developments call for notice: (1) there has been a tendency to subdivide these documents further, regarding them as the work of schools rather than of individuals, and resolving them into different strata (P_1, P_2, P_3, etc, J_1, J_2, etc, or in the notation of other writers Jj Je, etc); (2) a particular scheme of dating has found wide acceptance. In the first period of the critical development it was assumed that the principal Elohist (P) was the earliest document. A succession of writers of whom Reuss, Graf, Kuenen and Wellhausen are the most prominent have, however, maintained that this is not the first but the last in point of time and should be referred to the exile or later. On this view the theory is in outline as follows: J and E (so called from their respective Divine appellations)—on the relative dates of which opinions differ—were composed probably during the early monarchy and subsequently combined by a redactor (R^{je}) into a single document JE. In the 7th cent. D, the bulk of Dt, was composed. It was published in the 18th year of Josiah's reign. Later it was combined with JE into JED by a redactor (R^{jed}). P or PC, the last of all (originally the first Elohist, now the PC) incorporated an earlier code of uncertain date which consists in the main of most of Lev 17–26 and is known as the Law of Holiness (H or P^h). P itself is largely post-exilic. Ultimately it was joined with JED by a priestly redactor (R^p) into substantially our present Pent. As already stated, the theory is subject to many minor variations. Moreover, it is admitted that not all its portions are equally well supported. The division of JE into J and E is regarded as less certain than the separation of P. Again, there are variations in the analysis, differences of opinion as to the exact dating of the documents, and so forth. Yet the view just sketched has been held by a very numerous and influential school during recent years, nor is it altogether fair to lay stress on minor divergences of opinion. It is in the abstract conceivable that the main positions might be true, and that yet the data were inadequate to enable all the minor details to be determined with certainty (see Criticism of the Bible).

This theory will hereafter be discussed at length for two reasons: (1) while it is now constantly losing ground, it is still more widely held than any other; and (2) so much of the modern lit. on the OT has been written from this standpoint that no intelligent use can be made of the most ordinary books of reference without some acquaintance with it.

Before 1908 the conservative opposition to the dominant theory had exhibited two separate tendencies. One school of conservatives rejected the scheme *in toto;* the other accepted the analysis with certain modifications, but sought to throw back the dating of the documents. In both these respects it had points of contact with dissentient critics (e.g. Delitzsch, Dillmann, Baudissin, Kittel, Strack, Van Hoonacker), who sought to save for conservatism any spars they could from the general wreckage. The former school of thought was most prominently represented by the late W. H. Green, and J. H. Raven's *OT Intro* may be regarded as a typical modern presentation of their view; the latter esp. by Robertson and Orr. The scheme put forward by the last named has found many adherents. He refuses to regard J and E as two separate documents, holding that we should rather think (as in the case of the ‖ Pss) of two recensions of one document marked by the use of different Divine appellations. The critical P he treats as the work of a supplementer, and thinks it never had an independent existence, while he considers the whole Pent as early. He holds that the work was done by "original composers, working with a common aim, and toward a common end, in contrast with the idea of late irresponsible redactors, combining, altering, manipulating, enlarging at pleasure" (*POT*, 375).

While these were the views held among OT critics, a separate opposition had been growing up among archaeologists. This was of course utilized to the utmost by the conservatives of both wings. In some ways archaeology undoubtedly has confirmed the traditional view as against the critical (see Archaeology and Criticism); but a candid survey leads to the belief that it has not yet dealt a mortal blow, and here again it must be remembered that the critics may justly plead that they must not be judged on mistakes that they made in their earlier investigations or on refutations of the more uncertain portions of their theory, but rather on the main completed result. It may indeed be said with confidence that there are certain topics to which archaeology can never supply any conclusive answer. *If* it be the case that the Pent contains hopelessly contradictory laws, no archaeological discovery can make them anything else; *if* the numbers of the Israelites are original and impossible.

archaeology cannot make them possible. It is fair and right to lay stress on the instances in which archaeology has confirmed the Bible as against the critics; it is neither fair nor right to speak as if archaeology had done what it never purported to do and never could effect.

The year 1908 saw the beginning of a new critical development which makes it very difficult to speak positively of modern critical views. Kuenen has been mentioned as one of the ablest and most eminent of those who brought the Graf-Wellhausen theory into prominence. In that year B. D. Eerdmans, his pupil and successor at Leyden, began the publication of a series of OT studies in which he renounces his allegiance to the line of critics that had extended from Astruc to the publications of our own day, and entered on a series of investigations that were intended to set forth a new critical view. As his labors are not yet complete, it is impossible to present any account of his scheme; but the volumes already published justify certain remarks. Eerdmans has perhaps not converted any member of the Wellhausen school, but he has made many realize that their own scheme is not the only one possible. Thus while a few years ago we were constantly assured that the "main results" of OT criticism were unalterably settled, recent writers adopt a very different tone: e.g. Sellin (1910) says, "We stand in a time of fermentation and transition, and in what follows we present our own opinion merely as the hypothesis which appears to us to be the best founded" (*Einleitung*, 18). By general consent Eerdmans' work contains a number of isolated shrewd remarks to which criticism will have to attend in the future; but it also contains many observations that are demonstrably unsound (for examples see *BS*, 1909, 744–48; 1910, 549–51). His own reconstruction is in many respects so faulty and blurred that it does not seem likely that it will ever secure a large following in its present form. On the other hand he appears to have succeeded in inducing a large number of students in various parts of the world to think along new lines and in this way may exercise a very potent influence on the future course of OT study. His arguments show increasingly numerous signs of his having been influenced by the publications of conservative writers, and it seems certain that criticism will ultimately be driven to recognize the essential soundness of the conservative position. In 1912 Dahse (*TMH*, I) began the publication of a series of volumes attacking the Wellhausen school on textual grounds and propounding a new pericope hypothesis. In his view many phenomena are due to the influence of the pericopes of the synagogue service or the form of the text and not to the causes generally assigned.

The examination of the Graf-Wellhausen theory must now be undertaken, and attention must first be directed to the evidence which is adduced in its support. Why should it be held that the Pent is composed mainly of excerpts from certain documents designated as J and E and P and D? Why is it believed that these documents are of very late date, in one case subsequent to the exile?

2. Evidence for the Current Critical Scheme

(1) *Astruc's clue.*—It has been said above that Astruc propounded the use of the Divine appellations in Gen as a clue to the dissection of that book. This is based on Ex **6** 3, 'And I appeared unto Abraham, unto Isaac, and unto Jacob, as '*El Shadday* [God Almighty]; but by my name *YHWH* I was not known to them.' In numerous passages of Gen this name is represented as known, e.g. **4** 26, where we read of men beginning to call on it in the days of Enosh. The discrepancy here is very obvious, and in the view of the Astruc school can be satisfactorily removed by postulating different sources. This clue, of course, fails after Ex **6** 3, but other difficulties are found, and moreover the sources already distinguished in Gen are, it is claimed, marked by separate styles and other characteristics which enable them to be identified when they occur in the narrative of the later books (see Criticism of the Bible).

(2) *Signs of post-Mosaic date.*—Close inspection of the Pent shows that it contains a number of passages which, it is alleged, could not have proceeded from the pen of Moses in their present form. Probably the most familiar instance is the account of the death of Moses (Dt **34**). Other examples are to be found in seeming allusions to post-Mosaic events, e.g. in Gen **22** we hear of the Mount of the Lord in the land of Moriah; this apparently refers to the Temple Hill, which, however, would not have been so designated before Solomon. So too the list of kings who reigned over Edom "before there reigned any king over the children of Israel" (**36** 31) presumes the existence of the monarchy. The Canaanites who are referred to as being "then in the land" (Gen **12** 6; **13** 7) did not disappear till the time of Solomon, and, accordingly, if this expression means "then still" it cannot antedate his reign. Dt **3** 11 (Og's bedstead) comes unnaturally from one who had vanquished Og but a few weeks previously, while Nu **21** 14 (AV) contains a reference to "the book of the Wars of the Lord" which would hardly have been quoted in this way by a contemporary. Ex **16** 35 refers to the cessation of the manna after the death of Moses. These passages, and more like them, are cited to disprove Mosaic authorship; but the main weight of the critical argument does not rest on them.

(3) *Narrative discrepancies.*—While the Divine appellations form the starting-point, they do not even in Gen constitute the sole test of different documents. On the contrary, there are other narrative discrepancies, antinomies, differences of style, duplicate narratives, etc, adduced to support the critical theory. We must now glance at some of these.

In Gen **21** 14 f Ishmael is a boy who can be carried on his mother's shoulder, but from a comparison of **16** 3.16; **17**, it appears that he must have been 14 when Isaac was born, and, since weaning sometimes occurs at the age of 3 in the East, may have been even as old as 17 when this incident happened. Again, "We all remember the scene (Gen **27**) in which Isaac in extreme old age blesses his sons; we picture him as lying on his deathbed. Do we, however, all realize that according to the chronology of the Book of Gen he must have been thus lying on his deathbed for eighty years (cf **25** 26; **26** 34; **35** 28)? Yet we can only diminish this period by extending proportionately the interval between Esau marrying his Hittite wives (**26** 34) and Rebekah's suggestion to Isaac to send Jacob away, lest he should follow his brother's example (**27** 46); which, from the nature of the case, will not admit of any but slight extension. Keil, however, does so extend it, reducing the period of Isaac's final illness by 43 years, and is conscious of no incongruity in supposing that Rebekah, 30 years after Esau had taken his Hittite wives, should express her fear that Jacob, then aged 77, will do the same" (Driver, *Contemporary Review*, LVII, 221).

An important instance occurs in Nu. According to **33** 38, Aaron died on the 1st day of the 5th month. From Dt **1** 3 it appears that 6 months later Moses delivered his speech in the plains of Moab. Into those 6 months are compressed one month's mourning for Aaron, the Arad campaign, the wandering round by the Red Sea, the campaigns against Sihon and Og, the missions to Balaam and the whole episode of his prophecies, the painful occurrences of Nu **25**, the second census, the appointment of Joshua, the expedition against Midian, besides other events. It is clearly impossible to fit all these into the time.

Other discrepancies are of the most formidable character. Aaron dies now at Mt. Hor (Nu **20** 28; **33** 38), now at Moserah (Dt **10** 6). According to Dt **1**; **2** 1.14, the children of Israel left Kadesh-barnea in the 3d year and never subsequently returned to it, while in Nu they apparently remain there till the journey to Mt. Hor, where Aaron dies in the 40th year. The Tent of Meeting perhaps provides some of the most perplexing of the discrepancies, for while according to the well-known scheme of Ex **25** ff and many other passages, it was a large and heavy erection standing in the midst of the camp, Ex **33** 7–11 provides us with another Tent of Meeting that stood outside the camp at a distance and could be carried by Moses alone. The vbs. used are frequentative, denoting a regular practice, and it is impossible to suppose that after receiving the commands for the Tent of Meeting Moses could have instituted a quite different tent *of the same name*. Joseph again is sold, now by Ishmaelites (Gen **37** 27.28*b*; **39** 1), anon by Midianites (**37** 28*a*.36). Sometimes he is imprisoned in one place, sometimes apparently in another. The story of Korah, Dathan and Abiram in Nu **16** is equally full of difficulty. The enormous numbers of the Israelites given in Nu **1–4,** etc, are in conflict with passages that regard them as very few.

(4) *Doublets.*—Another portion of the critical argument is provided by doublets or duplicate narratives of the same event, e.g. Gen **16** and **21.** These are particularly numerous in Gen, but are not confined to that book. "Twice do quails appear in connection with the daily manna (Nu **11** 4–6.31 ff; Ex **16** 13). Twice does Moses draw water from the rock, when the strife of Israel begets the name Meribah ('strife') (Ex **17** 1–7; Nu **20** 1–13)" (Carpenter, *Hexateuch*, I, 30).

(5) *The laws.*—Most stress is laid on the argument from the laws and their supposed historical setting. By far the most important portions of this are examined in Sanctuary and Priests (q.v.). These subjects form the two main pillars of the Graf-Wellhausen theory, and accordingly the arts. in question must be read as supplementing the present article. An illustration may be taken from the slavery laws. It is claimed that Ex **21** 1–6; Dt **15** 12 ff permit a Hebrew to contract for life slavery after 6 years' service, but that Lev **25** 39–42 takes no notice of this law and enacts the totally different provision that Hebrews may remain in slavery only till the Year of Jubilee. While these different enactments might proceed from the same hand if properly coördinated, it is contended that this is not the case and that the legislator in Lev ignores the legislator in Ex and is in turn ignored by the legislator in Dt, who only knows the law of Ex.

(6) *The argument from style.*—The argument from style is less easy to exemplify shortly, since it depends so largely on an immense mass of details. It is said that each of the sources has certain characteristic phrases which either occur nowhere else or only with very much less frequency. For instance in Gen **1,** where *'Ĕlōhīm* is used throughout, we find the word "create," but this is not employed in **2** 4*b* ff, where the Tetragrammaton occurs. Hence it is argued that this word is peculiarly characteristic of P as contrasted with the other documents, and may be used to prove his presence in e.g. **5** 1 f.

(7) *Props of the development hypothesis.*—While the main supports of the Graf-Wellhausen theory must be sought in the arts. to which reference has been made, it is necessary to mention briefly some other phenomena to which some weight is attached. Jer displays many close resemblances to Dt, and the framework of K is written in a style that has marked similarities to the same book. Ezk again has notable points of contact with P and esp. with H; either he was acquainted with these portions of the Pent or else he must have exercised considerable influence on those who composed them. Lastly the Chronicler is obviously acquainted with the completed Pent. Accordingly, it is claimed that the literature provides a sort of external standard that confirms the historical stages which the different Pentateuchal sources are said to mark. Dt influences Jer and the subsequent literature. It is argued that it would equally have influenced the earlier books, had it then existed. So too the completed Pent should have influenced K as it did Ch, if it had been in existence when the earlier history was composed.

3. Answer to the Critical Analysis

(1) *The veto of textual criticism.*—The first great objection that may be made to the higher criticism is that it starts from the Massoretic text (MT) without investigation. This is not the only text that has come down to us, and in some instances it can be shown that alternative readings that have been preserved are superior to those of the MT. A convincing example occurs in Ex **18.** According to the Heb, Jethro comes to Moses and says "I, thy father-in-law . . . . am come," and *subsequently* Moses goes out to meet his father-in-law. The critics here postulate different sources, but some of the best authorities have preserved a reading which (allowing for ancient differences of orthography) supposes an alteration of a single letter. According to this reading the text told how one (or they) came to Moses and said "Behold thy father-in-law . . . . is come." As the result of this Moses went out and met Jethro. The vast improvement in the sense is self-evident. But in weighing the change other considerations must be borne in mind. Since this is the reading of some of the most ancient authorities, only two views are possible. Either the MT has undergone a corruption of a single letter, or else a redactor made a most improbable cento of two documents which gave a narrative of the most doubtful sense. Fortunately this was followed by textual corruption of so happy a character as to remove the difficulty by the change of a single letter; and this corruption was so widespread that it was accepted as the genuine text by some of our best authorities. There can be little doubt which of these two cases is the more credible, and with the recognition of the textual solution the particular bit of the analysis that depends on this corruption falls to the ground. This instance illustrates one branch of textual criticism; there are others. Sometimes the narrative shows with certainty that in the transmission of the text transpositions have taken place; e.g. the identification of Kadesh shows that it was S. of Hormah. Consequently a march to compass Edom by way of the Red Sea would not bring the Israelites to Hormah. Here there is no reason to doubt that the events narrated are historically true, but there is grave reason to doubt that they happened in the present order of the narrative. Further, Dt gives an account that is parallel to certain passages of Nu; and it confirms those passages, but places the events in a different order. Such difficulties may often be solved by simple transpositions, and when transpositions in the text of Nu are made under the guidance of Dt they have a very different probability from guesses that enjoy no such sanction. Another department of textual criticism deals with the removal of glosses, i.e. notes that have crept into the text. Here the ancient VSS often help us, one or other omitting some words which may be proved from other sources to be a later addition. Thus in Ex **17** 7 the Vulg did not know the expression, "and Meribah" (one word in Heb), and calls the place "Massah" simply. This is confirmed by the fact that Dt habitually calls the place Massah (**6** 16; **9** 22; **33** 8). The true Meribah was Kadesh (Nu **20**) and a glossator has here added this by mistake (see further [4] below). Thus we can say that a scientific textual criticism often opposes a real veto to the higher critical analysis by showing that the arguments rest on late corruptions and by explain-

ing the true origin of the difficulties on which the critics rely.

(2) *Astruc's clue tested.*—Astruc's clue must next be examined. The critical case breaks down with extraordinary frequency. No clean division can be effected, i.e. there are cases where the MT of Gen makes P or E use the Tetragrammaton or J *'Ĕlōhīm*. In some of these cases the critics can suggest no reason; in others they are compelled to assume that the MT is corrupt for no better reason than that it is in conflict with their theory. Again the exigencies of the theory frequently force the analyst to sunder verses or phrases that cannot be understood apart from their present contexts, e.g. in Gen **28** 21 Carpenter assigns the words "and Jeh will be my God" to J while giving the beginning and end of the verse to E; in ch **31,** ver 3 goes to a redactor, though E actually refers to the statement of ver 3 in ver 5; in ch **32,** ver 30 is torn from a J-context and given to E, thus leaving ver 31 (J) unintelligible. When textual criticism is applied, startling facts that entirely shatter the higher critical argument are suddenly revealed. The variants to the Divine appellations in Gen are very numerous, and in some instances the new readings are clearly superior to the MT, even when they substitute *'Ĕlōhīm* for the Tetragrammaton. Thus, in **16** 11, the explanation of the name Ishma*el* requires the word *'Ĕlōhīm*, as the name would otherwise have been Ishma*yah*, and one Heb MS, a recension of the LXX and the Old Lat do in fact preserve the reading *'Ĕlōhīm*. The full facts and arguments cannot be given here, but Professor Schlögl has made an exhaustive examination of the various texts from Gen **1** 1 to Ex **3** 12. Out of a total of 347 occurrences of one or both words in the MT of that passage, there are variants in 196 instances. A very important and detailed discussion, too long to be summarized here, will now be found in *TMH*, I. Wellhausen himself has admitted that the textual evidence constitutes a sore point of the documentary theory (*Expos T*, XX, 563). Again in Ex **6** 3, many of the best authorities read "I was not made known" instead of "I was not known"—a difference of a single letter in Heb. But if this be right, there is comparative evidence to suggest that to the early mind a revelation of his name by a deity meant a great deal more than a mere knowledge of the name, and involved rather a pledge of his power. Lastly the analysis may be tested in yet another way by inquiring whether it fits in with the other data, and when it is discovered (see below 4, [1]) that it involves ascribing, e.g. a passage that cannot be later than the time of Abraham to the period of the kingdom, it becomes certain that the clue and the method are alike misleading (see further *EPC*, ch i; *Expos T*, XX, 378 f, 473–75, 563; *TMH*, I; *PS*, 49–142; *BS*, 1913, 145–74; A. Troelstra, *The Name of God*, *NKZ*, XXIV [1913], 119–48; *Expos*, 1913).

(3) *Narrative discrepancies and signs of post-Mosaic date.*—Septuagintal MSS are providing very illuminating material for dealing with the chronological difficulties. It is well known that the LXX became corrupt and passed through various recensions (see SEPTUAGINT). The original text has not yet been reconstructed, but as the result of the great variety of recensions it happens that our various MSS present a wealth of alternative readings. Some of these show an intrinsic superiority to the corresponding readings of the MT. Take the case of Ishmael's age. We have seen (above, 2, [3]) that although in Gen **21** 14 f he is a boy who can be carried by his mother even after the weaning of Isaac, his father, according to **16** 3.16, was 86 years old at the time of his birth, and, according to ch **17,** 100 years old when Isaac was born. In **17** 25 we find that Ishmael is already 13 a year before Isaac's birth. Now we are familiar with marginal notes that set forth a system of chronology in many printed Eng. Bibles. In this case the Septuagintal variants suggest that something similar is responsible for the difficulty of our Heb. Two MSS, apparently representing a recension, omit the words, "after Abram had dwelt ten years in the land of Canaan" in **16** 3, and again, ver 16, while in **17** 25 there is a variant making Ishmael only 3 years old. If these readings are correct it is easy to see how the difficulty arose. The narrative originally contained mere round numbers, like 100 years old, and these were not intended to be taken literally. A commentator constructed a scheme of chronology which was embodied in marginal notes. Then these crept into the text and such numbers as were in conflict with them were thought to be corrupt and underwent alteration. Thus the 3-year-old Ishmael became 13.

The same MSS that present us with the variants in Gen **16** have also preserved a suggestive reading in **35** 28, one of the passages that are responsible for the inference that according to the text of Gen Isaac lay on his deathbed for 80 years (see above, 2, [3]). According to this Isaac was not 180, but 150 years old when he died. It is easy to see that this is a round number, not to be taken literally, but this is not the only source of the difficulty. In **27** 41, Esau, according to EV, states "The days of mourning for my father are at hand; then will I slay my brother Jacob." This is a perfectly possible rendering of the Heb, but the LXX tr[d] the text differently, and its rendering, while grammatically correct, has the double advantage of avoiding Isaac's long lingering on a deathbed and of presenting Esau's hatred and ferocity far more vividly. It renders, "May the days of mourning for my father approach that I may slay my brother Jacob." Subsequent translators preferred the milder version, but doubtless the LXX has truly apprehended the real sense of the narrative. If we read the ch with this modification, we see Isaac as an old man, not knowing when he may die, performing the equivalent of making his will. It puts no strain on our credulity to suppose that he may have lived 20 or 30 years longer. Such episodes occur constantly in everyday experience. As to the calculations based on **25** 26 and **26** 34, the numbers used are 60 and 40, which, as is well known, were frequently employed by the ancient Hebrews, not as mathematical expressions, but simply to denote unknown or unspecified periods. See NUMBER.

The other chronological difficulty cited above (viz. that there is not room between the date of Aaron's death and the address by Moses in the plains of Moab for all the events assigned to this period by Nu) is met partly by a reading preserved by the Pesh and partly by a series of transpositions. In Nu **33** 38 Pesh reads "first" for "fifth" as the month of Aaron's death, thus recognizing a longer period for the subsequent events. The transpositions, however, which are largely due to the evidence of Dt, solve the most formidable and varied difficulties; e.g. a southerly march from Kadesh no longer conducts the Israelites to Arad in the north, the name Hormah is no longer used (Nu **14** 45) before it is explained (**21** 3), there is no longer an account directly contradicting Dt and making the Israelites spend 38 years at Kadesh immediately after receiving a Divine command to turn "tomorrow" (Nu **14** 25). A full discussion is impossible here and will be found in *EPC*, 114–38. The order of the narrative that emerges as probably original is as follows: Nu **12; 20** 1.14–21; **21** 1–3; **13; 14; 16–18; 20** 2–13.22*a;* **21** 4*b*–9, then some missing vs, bringing the Israelites to the head of the Gulf of Akabah and narrating the turn northward from Elath and Ezion-geber, then **20** 22*b*–29; **21** 4*a*, and some lost words telling of the arrival at the station before Oboth. In Nu **33**, ver 40 is a gloss that is missing in Lagarde's LXX, and vs 36*b*–37*a* should probably come earlier in the chapter than they do at present.

Another example of transposition is afforded by Ex **33** 7–11, the passage relating to the Tent of Meeting which is at present out of place (see above 2, [3]). It is supposed that this is E's idea of the Tabernacle, but that, unlike P, he places it outside the camp and makes Joshua its priest. This latter view is discussed and refuted in PRIESTS, 3, where it is shown that Ex **33** 7 should be rendered "And Moses used to take a [or, the] tent and pitch it *for himself*," etc. As to the theory that this is E's account of the Tabernacle, Ex **18** has been overlooked. This chapter belongs to the same E but refers to the end of the period spent at Horeb, i.e. it is later than **33** 7–11. In vs 13–16 we find Moses sitting with all the people standing about him because they came to inquire of God; i.e. the business which according to ch **33** was transacted in solitude outside the camp was performed within the camp in the midst of the people at a later period. This agrees with P, e.g. Nu **27**. If now we look at the other available clues, it appears that **33** 11 seems to introduce Joshua for the first time. The passage should therefore precede **17** 8–15; **24** 13; **32** 17, where he is already known. Again, if Ex **18** refers to the closing scenes at Horeb (as it clearly does), Ex **24** 14 providing for the temporary transaction of judicial business reads very strangely. It ought to be preceded by some statement of the ordinary course in normal times when Moses was not absent from the camp. Ex **33** 7 ff provides such a statement. The only earlier place to which it can be assigned is after **13** 22, but there it fits the context marvelously, for the statements as to the pillar of cloud in **33** 9 f attach naturally to those in **13** 21 f. With this change all the difficulties disappear. Immediately after leaving Egypt Moses began the practice of carrying a tent outside the camp and trying cases there. This lasted till the construction of the Tabernacle. "And there I will meet with thee, and I will commune with thee" (Ex **25** 22). After its erection the earlier tent was disused, and the court sat at the door of the Tabernacle in the center of the camp (see, further, *EPC*, 93–102, 106 f).

Some other points must be indicated more briefly. In Nu **16** important Septuagintal variants remove the main difficulties by substituting "company of Korah" for "dwelling of Korah, Dathan, and Abiram" in two vs (see *EPC*, 143–46). Similarly in the Joseph-story the perplexities have arisen through corruptions of verses which may still be corrected by the versional evidence (*PS*, 29–48). There is evidence to show that the numbers of the Israelites are probably due to textual corruption (*EPC*, 155–69). Further, there are numerous passages where careful examination has led critics themselves to hold that particular verses are later notes. In this way they dispose of Dt **10** 6 f (Aaron's death, etc), the references to the Israelitish kingdom (Gen **36** 31) and the Canaanites as being "then" in the land (**12** 6; **13** 7), the bedstead of Og (Dt **3** 11) and other passages. In Gen **22**, "the land of Moriah" is unknown to the VSS which present the most diverse readings, of which "the land of the Amorite" is perhaps the most probable; while in ver 14 the LXX, reading the same Heb consonants as MT, translates "In the Mount the Lord was seen." This probably refers to a view that God manifested Himself esp. in the mountains (cf 1 K **20** 23.28) and has no reference whatever to the Temple Hill. The Massoretic pointing is presumably due to a desire to avoid what seemed to be an anthropomorphism (see further *PS*, 19–21). Again, in Nu **21** 14, the LXX knows nothing of "a book of the Wars of Jeh" (see Field, *Hexapla*, ad loc.). It is difficult to tell what the original reading was, esp. as the succeeding words are corrupt in the Heb, but it appears that no genitive followed "wars" and it is doubtful if there was any reference to a "book of wars."

(4) *The argument from the doublets examined.*—The foregoing sections show that the documentary theory often depends on phenomena that were absent from the original Pent. We are now to examine arguments that rest on other foundations. The doublets have been cited, but when we examine the instances more carefully, some curious facts emerge. Gen **16** and **21** are, to all appearance, narratives of different events; so are Ex **17** 1–7 and Nu **20** 1–13 (the drawing of water from rocks). In the latter case the critics after rejecting this divide the passages into 5 different stories, two going to J, two to E and one to P. If the latter also had a Rephidim-narrative (cf Nu **33** 14 P), there were 6 tales. In any case both J and E tell *two* stories each. It is impossible to assign any cogency to the argument that the author of the Pent could not have told two such narratives, if not merely the redactor of the Pent but also J and E could do so. The facts as to the manna stories are similar. As to the flights of quails, it is known that these do in fact occur every year, and the Pent places them at almost exactly a year's interval (see *EPC*, 104 f, 109 f).

(5) *The critical argument from the laws.*—The legal arguments are due to a variety of misconceptions, the washing out of the historical background and the state of the text. Reference must be made to the separate articles (esp. SANCTUARY; PRIESTS). As the slave laws were cited, it may be explained that in ancient Israel as in other communities slavery could arise or slaves be acquired in many ways: e.g. birth, purchase (Gen **14** 14; **17** 12, etc), gift (**20** 14), capture in war (**14** 21; **34** 29), kidnapping (Joseph). The law of Ex and Dt applies *only* to Heb slaves acquired by purchase, not to slaves acquired in any other way, and least of all to those who in the eye of the law were not true slaves. Lev **25** has nothing to do with Heb slaves. It is concerned merely with free Israelites who become insolvent. "If thy brother be waxed poor with thee, and sell himself" it begins (ver 39). Nobody who was already a slave could wax poor and sell himself. The law then provides that these insolvent freemen were not to be treated as slaves. In fact, they were a class of free bondmen, i.e. they were full citizens who were compelled to perform certain duties. A similar class of free bondmen existed in ancient Rome and were called *nexi*. The Egyptians who sold themselves to Pharaoh and became serfs afford another though less apt parallel. In all ancient societies insolvency led to some limitations of freedom, but while in some full slavery ensued, in others a sharp distinction was drawn between the slave and the insolvent freeman (see further *SBL*, 5–11).

(6) *The argument from style.*—Just as this argument is too detailed to be set out in a work like the present, so the answer cannot be given with any degree of fulness. It may be said generally that the argument too frequently neglects differences of subject-matter and other sufficient reasons (such as considerations of euphony and slight variations of meaning) which often provide far more natural reasons for the phenomena observed. Again, the VSS suggest that the Bib. text has been heavily glossed. Thus in many passages where the frequent recurrence of certain words and phrases is

supposed to attest the presence of P, versional evidence seems to show that the expressions in question have been introduced by glossators, and when they are removed the narrative remains unaffected in meaning, but terser and more vigorous and greatly improved as a vehicle of expression. To take a simple instance in Gen **23** 1, "And the life of Sarah was a hundred and seven and twenty years: . . . . *the years of the life of Sarah*," the italicized words were missing in the LXX. When they are removed the meaning is unaltered, but the form of expression is far superior. They are obviously a mere marginal note. Again the critical method is perpetually breaking down. It constantly occurs that redactors have to be called in to remove from a passage attributed to some source expressions that are supposed to be characteristic of another source, and this is habitually done on no other ground than that the theory requires it. One instance must be given. It is claimed that the word "create" is a P-word. It occurs several times in Gen **1** 1—**2** 4*a* and 3 t in Gen **5** 1.2, but in **6** 7 it is found in a J-passage, and some critics therefore assign it to a redactor. Yet J undoubtedly uses the word in Nu **16** 30 and D in Dt **4** 32. On the other hand, P does not use the word *exclusively*, even in Gen **1** 1—**2** 4, the word "make" being employed in **1** 7. 25.26.31; **2** 2, while in **2** 3 both words are combined. Yet all these passages are given unhesitatingly to P.

(7) *Perplexities of the theory.*—The perplexities of the critical hypothesis are very striking, but a detailed discussion is impossible here. Much material will, however, be found in *POT* and *Eerd. St.* A few general statements may be made. The critical analysis repeatedly divides a straightforward narrative into two sets of fragments, neither of which will make sense without the other. A man will go to sleep in one document and wake in another, or a subject will belong to one source and the predicate to another. No intelligible account can be given of the proceedings of the redactors who at one moment slavishly preserve their sources and at another cut them about without any necessity, who now rewrite their material and now leave it untouched. Even in the ranks of the Wellhausen critics chapters will be assigned by one writer to the post-exilic period and by another to the earliest sources (e.g. Gen **14**, pre-Mosaic in the main according to Sellin [1910], post-exilic according to others), and the advent of Eerdmans and Dahse has greatly increased the perplexity. Clue after clue, both stylistic and material, is put forward, to be abandoned silently at some later stage. Circular arguments are extremely common: it is first alleged that some phenomenon is characteristic of a particular source; then passages are referred to that source for no other reason than the presence of that phenomenon; lastly these passages are cited to prove that the phenomenon in question distinguishes the source. Again the theory is compelled to feed on itself; for J, E, P, etc, we have schools of J's, E's, etc, subsisting side by side for centuries, using the same material, employing the same ideas, yet remaining separate in minute stylistic points. This becomes impossible when viewed in the light of the evidences of pre-Mosaic date in parts of Gen (see below 4, [1] to [3]).

(8) *Signs of unity.*—It is often possible to produce very convincing internal evidence of the unity of what the critics sunder. A strong instance of this is to be found when one considers the characters portrayed. The character of Abraham or Laban, Jacob or Moses is essentially unitary. There is but one Abraham, and this would not be so if we really had a cento of different documents representing the results of the labor of various schools during different centuries. Again, there are sometimes literary marks of unity, e.g. in Nu **16**, the effect of rising anger is given to the dialogue by the repetition of "Ye take too much upon you" (vs 3.7), followed by the repetition of "Is it a small thing that" (vs 9.13). This must be the work of a single literary artist (see further *SBL*, 37 f).

(9) *Supposed props of the development hypothesis.*—When we turn to the supposed props of the development hypothesis we see that there is nothing conclusive in the critical argument. Jer and the subsequent lit. certainly exhibit the influence of Dt, but a Book of the Law was admittedly found in Josiah's reign and had lain unread for at any rate some considerable time. Some of its requirements had been in actual operation, e.g. in Naboth's case, while others had become a dead letter. The circumstances of its discovery, the belief in its undoubted Mosaic authenticity and the subsequent course of history led to its greatly influencing contemporary and later writers, but that really proves nothing. Ezk again was steeped in priestly ideas, but it is shown in PRIESTS, 5*b*, how this may be explained. Lastly, Ch certainly knows the whole Pent, but as certainly misinterprets it (see PRIESTS). On the other hand the Pent itself always represents portions of the legislation as being intended to reach the people only through the priestly teaching, and this fully accounts for P's lack of influence on the earlier literature. As to the differences of style within the Pent itself, something is said in III, below. Hence this branch of the critical argument really proves nothing, for the phenomena are susceptible of more than one explanation.

4. Evidence of Date

(1) *The narrative of Genesis.*—Entirely different lines of argument are provided by the abundant internal evidences of date. In Gen **10** 19, we read the phrase "as thou goest toward Sodom and Gomorrah, and Admah and Zeboiim" in a definition of boundary. Such language could only have originated when the places named actually existed. One does not define boundaries by reference to towns that are purely mythical or have been overthrown many centuries previously. The consistent tradition is that these towns were destroyed in the lifetime of Abraham, and the passage therefore cannot be later than his age. But the critics assign it to a late stratum of J, i.e. to a period at least 1,000 years too late. This suggests several comments. First, it may reasonably be asked whether much reliance can be placed on a method which after a century and a half of the closest investigation does not permit its exponents to arrive at results that are correct to within 1,000 years. Secondly, it shows clearly that in the composition of the Pent very old materials were incorporated in their original language. Of the historical importance of this fact more will be said in IV; in this connection we must observe that it throws fresh light on expressions that point to the presence in Gen of sources composed in Pal, e.g. "the sea" for "the West" indicates the probability of a Palestinian source, but once it is proved that we have materials as old as the time of Abraham such expressions do not argue post-Mosaic, but rather pre-Mosaic authorship. Thirdly, the passage demolishes the theory of schools of J's, etc. It cannot seriously be maintained that there was a school of J's writing a particular style marked by the most delicate and subjective criteria subsisting continuously for some 10 or 12 centuries from the time of Abraham onward, side by side with other writers with whom its members never exchanged terms of even such common occurrence as "handmaid."

Gen **10** 19 is not the only passage of this kind.

In **2** 14 we read of the Hiddekel (Tigris) as flowing E. of Aššur, though there is an alternative reading "in front of." If the tr "east" be correct, the passage must antedate the 13th cent. BC, for Aššur, the ancient capital, which was on the west bank of the Tigris, was abandoned at about that date for Kalkhi on the E.

(2) *Archaeology and Genesis.*—Closely connected with the foregoing are cases where Gen has preserved information that is true of a very early time only. Thus in **10** 22 Elam figures as a son of Shem. The historical Elam was, however, an Aryan people. Recently inscriptions have been discovered which show that in very early times Elam really was inhabited by Semites. "The fact," writes Driver, ad loc., "is not one which the writer of this verse is likely to have known." This contention falls to the ground when we find that only three verses off we have material that goes back at least as far as the time of Abraham. After all, the presumption is that the writer stated the fact because he knew it, not in spite of his not knowing it; and that knowledge must be due to the same cause as the noteworthy language of ver 19, i.e. to early date.

This is merely one example of the confirmations of little touches in Gen that are constantly being provided by archaeology. For the detailed facts see the separate arts., e.g. AMRAPHEL; JERUSALEM, and cf IV, below.

From the point of view of the critical question we note (*a*) that such accuracy is a natural mark of authentic early documents, and (*b*) that in view of the arguments already adduced and of the legal evidence to be considered, the most reasonable explanation is to be found in a theory of contemporary authorship.

(3) *The legal evidence of Genesis.*—The legal evidence is perhaps more convincing, for here no theory of late authorship can be devised to evade the natural inference. Correct information as to early names, geography, etc, might be the result of researches by an exilic writer in a Bab library; but early customs that are confirmed by the universal experience of primitive societies, and that point to a stage of development which had long been passed in the Babylonia even of Abraham's day, can be due to but one cause—genuine early sources. The narratives of Gen are certainly not the work of comparative sociologists. Two instances may be cited. The law of homicide shows us two stages that are known to be earlier than the stage attested by Ex **21** 12 ff. In the story of Cain we have one stage; in Gen **9** 6, which does not yet recognize any distinction between murder and other forms of homicide, we have the other.

Our other example shall be the unlimited power of life and death possessed by the head of the family (**38** 24; **42** 37, etc), which has not yet been limited in any way by the jurisdiction of the courts as in Ex-Dt. In both cases comparative historical jurisprudence confirms the Bible account against the critical, which would make e.g. Gen **9** 6 post-exilic, while assigning Ex **21** to a much earlier period. (On the whole subject see further *OP*, 135 ff.)

(4) *The professedly Mosaic character of the legislation.*—Coming now to the four concluding books of the Pent, we must first observe that the legislation everywhere professes to be Mosaic. Perhaps this is not always fully realized. In critical editions of the text the rubrics and an occasional phrase are sometimes assigned to redactors, but the representation of Mosaic date is far too closely interwoven with the matter to be removed by such devices. If e.g. we take such a section as Dt **12,** we shall find it full of such phrases as "for ye are not as yet come to the rest and to the inheritance," etc; "when ye go over Jordan," "the place which the Lord *shall* choose" (AV), etc. It is important to bear this in mind throughout the succeeding discussion.

(5) *The historical situation required by P.*—What do we find if we ignore the Mosaic dress and seek to fit P into any other set of conditions, particularly those of the post-exilic period? The general historical situation gives a clear answer. The Israelites are represented as being so closely concentrated that they will always be able to keep the three pilgrimage festivals. One exception only is contemplated, viz. that ritual uncleanness or a journey may prevent an Israelite from keeping the Passover. Note that in that case he is most certainly to keep it one month later (Nu **9** 10 f). How could this law have been enacted when the great majority of the people were in Babylonia, Egypt, etc, so that attendance at the temple was impossible for them on any occasion whatever? With this exception the entire PC always supposes that the whole people are at all times dwelling within easy reach of the religious center. How strongly this view is embedded in the code may be seen esp. from Lev **17,** which provides that all domestic animals to be slaughtered for food must be brought to the door of the Tent of Meeting. Are we to suppose that somebody deliberately intended such legislation to apply when the Jews were scattered all over the civilized world, or even all over Canaan? If so, it means a total prohibition of animal food for all save the inhabitants of the capital.

In post-exilic days there was no more pressing danger for the religious leaders to combat than intermarriage, but this code, which is supposed to have been written for the express purpose of bringing about their action, goes out of its way to give a fictitious account of a war and incidentally to legalize some such unions (Nu **31** 18). And this chapter also contains a law of booty. What could be more unsuitable? How and where were the Jews to make conquests and capture booty in the days of Ezra?

"Or again, pass to the last chapter of Nu and consider the historical setting. What is the complaint urged by the deputation that waits upon Moses? It is this: If heiresses 'be married to any of the sons of the other tribes of the children of Israel, then shall their inheritance be taken away from the inheritance of our fathers, and shall be added to the inheritance of the tribe whereunto they shall belong.' What a pressing grievance for a legislator to consider and redress when tribes and tribal lots had long since ceased to exist for ever!" (*OP*, 121 f).

Perhaps the most informing of all the discrepancies between P and the post-exilic age is one that explains the freedom of the earlier prophets from its literary influence. According to the constant testimony of the Pent, including P, portions of the law were to reach the people only through priestly teaching (Lev **10** 11; Dt **24** 8; **33** 10, etc). Ezra on the other hand read portions of P to the whole people.

(6) *The hierarchical organization in P.*—Much of what falls under this head is treated in PRIESTS, 2, (*a*), (*b*), and need not be repeated here. The following may be added: "Urim and Thummim were not used after the Exile. In lieu of the simple conditions—a small number of priests and a body of Levites—we find a developed hierarchy, priests, Levites, singers, porters, Nethinim, sons of Solomon's servants. The code that *ex hypothesi* was forged to deal with this state of affairs has no acquaintance with them. The musical services of the temple are as much beyond its line of vision as the worship of the synagogue. Even such an organization as that betrayed by the reference in 1 S **2** 36 to the appointment by the high priest to positions

carrying pecuniary emoluments is far beyond the primitive simplicity of P" (*OP*, 122).

(7) *The legal evidence of P.*—As this subject is technical we can only indicate the line of reasoning. Legal rules may be such as to enable the historical inquirer to say definitely that they belong to an early stage of society. Thus if we find elementary rules relating to the inheritance of a farmer who dies without leaving sons, we know that they cannot be long subsequent to the introduction of individual property in land, unless of course the law has been deliberately altered. It is an everyday occurrence for men to die without leaving sons, and the question what is to happen to their land in such cases must from the nature of the case be raised and settled before very long. When therefore we find such rules in Nu **27**, etc, we know that they are either very old or else represent a deliberate change in the law. The latter is really out of the question, and we are driven back to their antiquity (see further *OP*, 124 ff). Again in Nu **35** we find an elaborate struggle to express a general principle which shall distinguish between two kinds of homicide. The earlier law had regarded all homicide as on the same level (Gen **9**). Now, the human mind only reaches general principles through concrete cases, and other ancient legislations (e.g. the Icelandic) bear witness to the primitive character of the rules of Nu. Thus an expert like Dareste can say confidently that such rules as these are extremely archaic (see further *SBL* and *OP*, *passim*).

(8) *The evidence of D.*—The following may be quoted: "Laws are never issued to regulate a state of things which has passed away ages before, and can by no possibility be revived. What are we to think, then, of a hypothesis which assigns the code of Dt to the reign of Josiah, or shortly before it, when its injunctions to exterminate the Canaanites (**20** 16-18) and the Amalekites (**25** 17-19), who had long since disappeared, would be as utterly out of date as a law in New Jersey at the present time offering a bounty for killing wolves and bears, or a royal proclamation in Great Britain ordering the expulsion of the Danes? A law contemplating foreign conquests (**20** 10-15) would have been absurd when the urgent question was whether Judah could maintain its own existence against the encroachments of Babylon and Egypt. A law discriminating against Ammon and Moab (**23** 3.4), in favor of Edom (vs 7.8), had its warrant in the Mosaic period, but not in the time of the later kings. Jeremiah discriminates precisely the other way, promising a future restoration to Moab (**48** 47) and Ammon (**49** 6), which he denies to Edom (**49** 17.18), who is also to Joel (**3** 19), Ob, and Isa (**63** 1-6), the representative foe of the people of God. . . . . The allusions to Egypt imply familiarity with and recent residence in that land. . . . . And how can a code belong to the time of Josiah, which, while it contemplates the possible selection of a king in the future (Dt **17** 14 ff), nowhere implies an actual regal government, but vests the supreme central authority in a judge and the priesthood (**17** 8-12; **19** 17); which lays special stress on the requirements that the king must be a native and not a foreigner (**17** 15), when the undisputed line of succession had for ages been fixed in the family of David, and that he must not 'cause the people to return to Egypt' (ver 16), as they seemed ready to do on every grievance in the days of Moses (Nu **14** 4), but which no one ever dreamed of doing after they were fairly established in Canaan?" (Green, *Moses and the Prophets*, 63 f). This too may be supplemented by legal evidence (e.g. **22** 26 testifies to the undeveloped intellectual condition of the people). Of JE it is unnecessary to speak, for Ex **21** f are now widely regarded as Mosaic in critical circles. Wellhausen (*Prolegomena*[6], 392, n.) now regards their main elements as pre-Mosaic Canaanitish law.

(9) *Later allusions.*—These are of two kinds. Sometimes we have references to the laws, in other cases we find evidence that they were in operation. (*a*) By postulating redactors evidence can be banished from the Bib. text. Accordingly, reference will only be made to some passages where this procedure is not followed. Ezk **22** 26 clearly knows of a law that dealt with the subjects of P, used its very language (cf Lev **10** 10 f), and like P was to be taught to the people by the priests. Hos **4** 6 also knows of some priestly teaching, which, however, is moral and may therefore be Lev **19**; but in **8** 11-13 he speaks of 10,000 written precepts, and here the context points to ritual. The number and the subject-matter of these precepts alike make it certain that he knew a bulky written law which was not merely identical with Ex **21-23**, and this passage cannot be met by Wellhausen who resorts to the device of translating it with the omission of the important word "write." (*b*) Again, in dealing with institutions the references can often be evaded. It is possible to say, "Yes, this passage knows such and such a law, but this law does not really come into existence with D or P, but was an older law incorporated in these documents." That argument would apply, e.g. to the necessity for two witnesses in the case of Naboth. That is a law of D, but those who assign Dt to the reign of Josiah would assert that it is here merely incorporating older material. Again the allusions sometimes show something that differs in some way from the Pent, and it is often impossible to prove that this was a development. The critics in such cases claim that it represents an earlier stage, and it frequently happens that the data are insufficient either to support or refute this view. "But fortunately there are in P certain institutions of which the critics definitely assert that they are late. Accordingly, references that prove the earlier existence of such institutions have a very different probative value. Thus it is alleged that before the exile there was but one national burnt offering and one national meal offering each day: whereas Nu **28** demands two. Now in 1 K **18** 29.36, we find references to the offering of the evening oblation, but 2 K **3** 20 speaks of 'the time of offering the oblation' in connection with the morning. Therefore these two oblations were actually in existence centuries before the date assigned to P—who, on the critical theory, first introduced them. So 2 K **16** 15 speaks of 'the morning burnt-offering, and the evening meal-offering . . . . with the burnt-offering of all the people of the land, and their meal-offering.' This again gives us the *two* burnt offerings, though, on the hypothesis, they were unknown to preëxilic custom. Similarly in other cases: Jer **32** shows us the land laws in actual operation; Ezekiel is familiar with the Jubilee laws—though, on the critical hypothesis, these did not yet exist. Jeroboam was acquainted with P's date for Tabernacles, though the critics allege that the date was first fixed in the Exile" (*OP*, 132 f).

(10) *Other evidence.*—We can only mention certain other branches of evidence. There is stylistic evidence of early date (see e.g. Lias, *BS*, 1910, 20-46, 299-334). Further, the minute accuracy of the narrative of Ex-Nu to local conditions, etc (noticed below, IV, 8, [6]), affords valuable testimony. It may be said generally that the whole work—laws and narrative—mirrors early conditions, whether we regard intellectual, economic or purely legal development (see further below, IV, and *OP*, *passim*).

(1) *Moral and psychological issues.*—The great fundamental improbabilities of the critical view

have hitherto been kept out of sight in order that the arguments for and against the detailed case might not be prejudiced by other considerations. We must now glance at some of the broader issues. The first that occurs is the moral and psychological incredibility. On theory two great frauds were perpetrated—in each case by men of the loftiest ethical principles. Dt was deliberately written in the form of Mosaic speeches by some person or persons who well knew that their work was not Mosaic. P is a make-up—nothing more. All its references to the wilderness, the camp, the Tent of Meeting, the approaching occupation of Canaan, etc, are so many touches introduced for the purpose of deceiving. There can be no talk of literary convention, for no such convention existed in Israel. The prophets all spoke in their own names, not in the dress of Moses. David introduced a new law of booty in his own name; the Chronicler repeatedly refers temple ordinances to David and Solomon; Samuel introduced a law of the kingdom in his own name. Yet we are asked to believe that these gigantic forgeries were perpetrated without reason or precedent. Is it credible? Consider the principles inculcated, e.g. the Deuteronomic denunciations of false prophets, the prohibition of adding aught to the law, the passionate injunctions to teach children. Can it be believed that men of such principles would have been guilty of such conduct? *Nemo repente fit turpissimus*, says the old maxim; can we suppose that the denunciations of those who prophesy falsely in the name of the Lord proceed from the pen of one who was himself forging in that name? Or can it be that the great majority of Bible readers know so little of truth when they meet it that they cannot detect the ring of unquestionable sincerity in the references of the Deuteronomist to the historical situation? Or can we really believe that documents that originated in such a fashion could have exercised the enormous force for righteousness in the world that these documents have exercised? *Ex nihilo nihil*. Are literary forgeries a suitable parentage for Gen **1** or Lev or Dt? Are the great monotheistic ethical religions of the world, with all they have meant, really rooted in nothing better than folly and fraud?

5. Fundamental Improbabilities of the Critical Case

(2) *The historical improbability.*—A second fundamental consideration is the extraordinary historical improbability that these frauds could have been successfully perpetrated. The narrative in K undoubtedly relates the finding of what was regarded as an authentic work. King and people, priests and prophets must have been entirely deceived if the critical theory be true. It is surely possible that Huldah and Jeremiah were better judges than modern critics. Similarly in the case of P, if e.g. there had been no Levitical cities or no such laws as to tithes and firstlings as were here contemplated, but entirely different provisions on the subjects, how came the people to accept these forgeries so readily? (See further *POT*, 257 f, 294–97.) It is of course quite easy to carry this argument too far. It cannot be doubted that the exile had meant a considerable break in the historical continuity of the national development; but yet once the two views are understood the choice cannot be difficult. On the critical theory elaborate literary forgeries were accepted as genuine ancient laws; on the conservative theory laws were accepted because they were in fact genuine, and interpreted as far as possible to meet the entirely different requirements of the period. This explains both the action of the people and the divergence between preëxilic and post-exilic practice. The laws were the same but the interpretation was different.

(3) *Divergence between the laws and post-exilic practice.*—Thirdly, the entire perversion of the true meaning of the laws in post-exilic times makes the critical theory incredible. Examples have been given (see above, 4, [5], [6], and Priests, *passim*). It must now suffice to take just one instance to make the argument clear. We must suppose that the author of P deliberately provided that if Levites approached the altar both they and the priests should die (Nu **18** 3), because he really desired that they should approach the altar and perform certain services there. We must further suppose that Ezra and the people on reading these provisions at once understood that the legislator meant the exact opposite of what he had said, and proceeded to act accordingly (1 Ch **23** 31). This is only one little example. It is so throughout P. Everybody understands that the Tabernacle is really the second Temple and wilderness conditions post-exilic, and everybody acts accordingly. Can it be contended that this view is credible?

(4) *The testimony of tradition.*—Lastly the uniform testimony of tradition is in favor of Mosaic authenticity—the tradition of Jews, Samaritans and Christians alike. The national consciousness of a people, the convergent belief of Christendom for 18 centuries are not lightly to be put aside. And what is pitted against them? Theories that vary with each fresh exponent, and that take their start from textual corruption, develop through a confusion between an altar and a house, and end in misdating narratives and laws by 8 or 10 centuries! (see above 3 and 4; Sanctuary; Priests).

6. Origin and Transmission of the Pentateuch

If anything at all emerges from the foregoing discussion, it is the impossibility of performing any such analytical feat as the critics attempt. No critical microscope can possibly detect with any reasonable degree of certainty the joins of various sources, even if such sources really exist, and when we find that laws and narratives are constantly misdated by 8 or 10 centuries, we can only admit that no progress at all is possible along the lines that have been followed. On the other hand, certain reasonable results do appear to have been secured, and there are indications of the direction in which we must look for further light.

First, then, the Pent contains various notes by later hands. Sometimes the VSS enable us to detect and remove those notes, but many are pre-versional. Accordingly, it is often impossible to get beyond probable conjectures on which different minds may differ.

Secondly, Gen contains pre-Mosaic elements, but we cannot determine the scope of these or the number and character of the sources employed, or the extent of the author's work.

Thirdly, the whole body of the legislation is (subject only to textual criticism) Mosaic. But the laws of Dt carry with them their framework, the speeches which cannot be severed from them (see *SBL*, II). The speeches of Dt in turn carry with them large portions of the narrative of Ex-Nu which they presuppose. They do not necessarily carry with them such passages as Ex **35–39** or Nu **1–4**, **7**, **26**, but Nu **1–4** contains internal evidence of Mosaic date.

At this point we turn to examine certain textual phenomena that throw light on our problem. It may be said that roughly there are two great classes of textual corruption—that which is due to the ordinary processes of copying, perishing, annotating, etc, and that which is due to a conscious and systematic effort to fix or edit a text. In the case of ancient authors, there comes a time sooner or later when scholarship, realizing the corruption that has taken place, makes a systematic attempt to produce, so far as possible, a correct standard text. Instances that will occur to many are to be found in the work of the Massoretes on the Heb text, that of Origen and others on the LXX, and that of the commission of Peisistratos and subsequently of the Alexandrian critics on Homer. There is evidence that such revisions took place in the case of the Pent. A very important instance is to be found in the chronology of certain portions of Gen of which three different VSS survive, the Massoretic, Sam and Septuagintal. Another instance of even greater consequence for the matter in hand is to be found in Ex **35–39**. It is well known that the LXX preserves an entirely different edition from that of MT (supported in the main by the Sam and other VSS). Some other examples have been noticed incidentally in the preceding discussion; one other that may be proved by further research to possess enormous importance may be mentioned. It appears that in the law of the kingdom (Dt **17**) and some other passages where the Massoretic and Sam texts speak of a hereditary king, the LXX knew nothing of such a person (see further *PS*, 157–68). The superiority of the LXX text in this instance appears to be attested by 1 S, which is unacquainted with any law of the kingdom.

Thus we know of at least three recensions, the M, the Sam and the Sept. While there are many minor readings (in cases of variation through accidental corruption) in which the two last-named agree, it is nevertheless true that in a general way the Sam belongs to the same family as the M, while the LXX in the crucial matters represents a different textual tradition from the other two (see *Expos*, September 1911, 200–219). How is this to be explained? According to the worthless story preserved in the letter of Aristeas the LXX was tr[d] from MSS brought from Jerus at a date long subsequent to the Sam schism. The fact that the LXX preserves a recension so different from both Sam and MT (i.e. from the most authoritative Palestinian tradition of the 5th cent. BC and its lineal descendants) suggests that this part of the story must be rejected. If so, the LXX doubtless represents the text of the Pent prevalent in Egypt and descends from a Heb that separated from the ancestor of the M before the Sam schism. At this point we must recall the fact that in Jer the LXX differs from MT more widely than in any other Bib. book, and the current explanation is that the divergence goes back to the times of Jeremiah, his work having been preserved in two editions, an Egyp and a Bab. We may be sure that if the Jews of Egypt had an edition of Jer, they also had an edition of that law to which Jer refers, and it is probable that the main differences between LXX and MT (with its allies) are due to the two streams of tradition separating from the time of the exile—the Egyp and the Bab. The narrative of the finding of the Book of the Law in the days of Josiah (2 K **22**), which probably refers to Dt only, suggests that its text at that time depended on the single MS found. The phenomena presented by Gen-Nu certainly suggest that they too were at one time dependent on a single damaged MS, and that conscious efforts were made to restore the original order—in some cases at any rate on a wrong principle (see esp. *EPC*, 114–38; *BS*, 1913, 270–90). In view of the great divergences of the LXX in Ex **35–39**, it may be taken as certain that in some instances the editing went to considerable lengths.

Thus the history of the Pent, so far as it can be traced, is briefly as follows: The backbone of the book consists of pre-Mosaic sources in Gen, and Mosaic narratives, speeches and legislation in Ex-Dt. To this, notes, archaeological, historical, explanatory, etc, were added by successive readers. The text at one time depended on a single MS which was damaged, and one or more attempts were made to repair this damage by rearrangement of the material. It may be that some of the narrative chapters, such as Nu **1–4, 7, 26,** were added from a separate source and amplified or rewritten in the course of some such redaction, but on this head nothing certain can be said. Within a period that is attested by the materials that survive, Ex **35–39** underwent one or more such redactions. Slighter redactions attested by Sam and LXX have affected the chronological data, the numbers of the Israelites and some references to post-Mosaic historical events. Further than this it is impossible to go on our present materials.

III. Some Literary Points.—No general estimate of the Pent as literature can or need be attempted. Probably most readers are fully sensible to its literary beauties. Anybody who is not would do well to compare the chapter on Joseph in the Koran (**12**) with the Bib. narrative. A few words must be said of some of the less obvious matters that would naturally fall into a literary discussion, the aim being rather to draw the reader's attention to points that he might overlook.

Of the style of the legislation no sufficient estimate can now be formed, for the first requisite of legal style is that it should be clear and unambiguous to contemporaries, and today no judgment can be offered on that head. There is, however, one feature that is of great interest even now, viz. the prevalence in the main of three different styles, each marked by its special adaptation to the end in view. These styles are (1) mnemonic, (2) oratorical, and (3) procedural. The first is familiar in other early legislations. It is lapidary, terse in the extreme, pregnant, and from time to time marked by a rhythm that must have assisted the retention in the memory. Occasionally we meet with parallelism. This is the style of Ex **21** ff and occasional later passages, such as the judgment in the case of Shelomith's son (Lev **24** 10 ff). No doubt these laws were memorized by the elders.

1. Style of Legislation

Secondly, the legislation of Dt forms part of a speech and was intended for public reading. Accordingly, the laws here take on a distinctly oratorical style. Thirdly, the bulk of the rest of the legislation was intended to remain primarily in the custody of the priests who could certainly write (Nu **6** 23). This was taken into account, and the style is not terse or oratorical, but reasonably full. It was probably very clear to those for whom the laws were meant. There are minor varieties of style but these are the most important. (On the whole subject see esp. *PS*, 170–224.)

What holds good of the laws is also true with certain modifications of the narrative. The style varies with the nature of the subject, occasion and purpose. Thus the itinerary in Nu **33** is intentionally composed in a style which undoubtedly possesses peculiar qualities when chanted to an appropriate tune. The census lists, etc, appear to be written in a formal official manner, and something similar is true of the lists of the spies in Nu **13**. There is no ground for surprise in this. In the ancient world style varied according to the *genre* of the composition to a far greater extent than it does today.

2. The Narrative

A literary form that is peculiar to the Pent deserves special notice, viz. the covenant document as a form of literature. Many peoples have had laws that were attributed to some deity, but it is only here that laws are presented in the form of sworn agreements entered into with certain formalities between the nation and God. The literary result is that certain portions of the Pent are in the form of a sort of deed with properly articulated parts. This deed would have been ratified by oath if made between men, as was the covenant between Jacob and Laban, but in a covenant with God this is inapplicable, and the place of the jurat is in each case taken by a discourse setting forth the rewards and penalties attached by God to observance and breach of the covenant respectively. The covenant conception and the idea that the laws acquire force because they are terms in an agreement *between* God and people, and not merely because they were commanded by God, is one of extraordinary importance in the history of thought and in theology, but we must not through absorption in these aspects of the question fail to notice that the conception found expression in a literary form that is unknown elsewhere and that it provides the key to the comprehension of large sections of the Pent, including almost the whole of Dt (see in detail *SBL*, ch ii).

3. The Covenant

Insufficient attention has been paid to order and rhythm generally. Two great principles must be borne in mind: (1) in really good ancient prose the artist appeals to the ear in many subtle ways, and (2) in all such prose, emphasis and meaning as well as beauty are given to a great extent by the order of the words. The figures of the old Gr rhetoricians play a considerable part. Thus the figure called *kúklos*, "the circle," is sometimes used with great skill. In this the clause or sentence begins and ends with the same word, which denotes alike the sound and the thought. Probably the

4. Order and Rhythm

most effective instance—heightened by the meaning, the shortness and the heavy boom of the word—is to be found in Dt **4** 12, where there is an impressive "circle" with קוֹל, *ḳōl*, "voice"—the emphasis conveyed by the sound being at least as marked as that conveyed by the sense. This is no isolated instance of the figure; cf e.g. in Nu **32** 1, the "circle" with "cattle"; **14** 2 that with "would that we had died." Chiasmus is a favorite figure, and assonances, plays on words, etc, are not uncommon. Such traits often add force as well as beauty to the narrative, as may be seen from instances like Gen **1** 2: תֹהוּ וָבֹהוּ, *tōhū wā-bhōhū*, "waste and void"; **4** 12: נָע וָנָד, *nā' wā-nādh*, "a fugitive and a wanderer"; **9** 6: שֹׁפֵךְ דַּם הָאָדָם בָּאָדָם דָּמוֹ יִשָּׁפֵךְ, *shōphēkh dam hā-'ādhām, bā-'ādhām dāmō, yishshāphēkh*, lit. "shedding blood-of man, by-man his-blood shall-be-shed"; Nu **14** 45: וַיַּכּוּם וַיַּכְּתוּם, *wayyakkūm wayyakkᵉthūm*, "and smote them and beat them down."

The prose of the Pent, except in its more formal and official parts, is closely allied to poetry (cf e.g. the Aeschylean "Sin coucheth at the door" [Gen **4** 7]; "The fountains of the great deep [were] broken up, and the windows of heaven were opened" [**7** 11]; "how I bare you on eagles' wings" [Ex **19** 4]). In the oratorical prose of Dt we find an imagery and a poetical imagination that are not common among great orators. Its rhythm is marked and the arrangement of the words is extraordinarily forcible, esp. in such a chapter as ch **28**. It is difficult to convey any idea of how much the book loses in EV from the changes of order. Occasionally the rendering does observe the point of the original, e.g. in Dt **4** 36: "Out of heaven he made thee to hear his voice," and if we consider how strikingly this contrasts with the flat "He made thee to hear his voice out of heaven," some notion may perhaps be formed of the importance of retaining the order. More frequently, however, the Eng. is false to the emphasis and spirit of the Heb. Sometimes, but not always, this is due to the exigencies of Eng. idiom. This is the cardinal fault of AV, which otherwise excels so greatly.

IV. The Pentateuch as History.—Beyond all doubt, the first duty of any who would use the Pent for historical purposes is to consider the light that textual criticism throws upon it. So many of the impossibilities that are relied upon by those who seek to prove that the book is historically worthless may be removed by the simplest operations of scientific textual criticism, that a neglect of this primary precaution must lead to disastrous consequences.

1. Textual Criticism as History

After all, it is common experience that a man who sets out to produce a history—whether by original composition or compilation—does not intentionally make, e.g., a southward march lead to a point northward of the starting-place, or a woman carry an able-bodied lad of 16 or 17 on her shoulder, or a patriarch linger some 80 years on a deathbed. When such episodes are found, the rudiments of *historical* judgment require that we should first ask whether the text is in order, and if the evidence points to any easy, natural and well-supported solutions of the difficulties, we are not justified in rejecting them without inquiry and denying to the Pent all historical value. It is a priori far more probable that narratives which have come down to us from a date some 3,000 years back may have suffered slightly in transmission than that the Pent was in the first instance the story of a historical wonderland. It is far more reasonable, e.g., to suppose that in a couple of verses of Ex a corruption of two letters (attested by Aquila) has taken place in the MT than that the Pent contains two absolutely inconsistent accounts of the origin of the priesthood (see Priests). Accordingly, the first principle of any scientific use of the Pent for historical purposes must be to take account of textual criticism.

2. Hebrew Methods of Expression

Having discovered as nearly as may be what the author wrote, the next step must be to consider what he meant by it. Here, unfortunately, the modern inquirer is apt to neglect many most necessary precautions. It would be a truism, but for the fact that it is so often disregarded, to say that the whole of a narrative must be carefully read in order to ascertain the author's meaning; e.g. how often we hear that Gen **14** represents Abram as having inflicted a defeat on the enemy with only 318 men (ver 14), whereas from ver 24 (cf ver 13) it appears that in addition to these his allies Aner, Eshcol and Mamre (i.e. as we shall see, the inhabitants of certain localities) had accompanied him! Sometimes the clue to the precise meaning of a story is to be found near the end: e.g. in Josh **22** we do not see clearly what kind of an altar the trans-Jordanic tribes had erected (and consequently why their conduct was open to objection) till ver 28, when we learn that this was an altar of the pattern of the altar of burnt offering, and so bore not the slightest resemblance to such lawful altars as those of Moses and Joshua (see Altar; Sanctuary). Nor is this the only instance in which the methods of expression adopted cause trouble to some modern readers; e.g. the word "all" is sometimes used in a way that apparently presents difficulties to some minds. Thus in Ex **9** 6 it is possible to interpret "all" in the most sweeping sense and then see a contradiction in vs 19.22, etc, which recognize that some cattle still existed. Or again the term may be regarded as limited by ver 3 to all the cattle in the field (see All).

3. Personification and Genealogies

At this point two further idiosyncrasies of the Sem genius must be noted—the habits of personification and the genealogical tendency; e.g. in Nu **20** 12–21, Edom and Israel are personified: "thy brother Israel," "Edom came out against him," etc. Nobody here mistakes the meaning. Similarly with genealogical methods of expression. The Semites spoke of many relationships in a way that is foreign to occidental methods. Thus the Heb for "30 years old" is "son of 30 years." Again we read "He was the father of such as dwell in tents" (Gen **4** 20). These habits (of personification and genealogical expression of relationships) are greatly extended, e.g. "And Canaan begat Zidon his first-born" (**10** 15). Often this leads to no trouble, yet strangely enough men who will grasp these methods when dealing with ch **10** will claim that ch **14** cannot be historical because localities are there personified and grouped in relationships. Yet if we are to estimate the historical value of the narrative, we must surely be willing to apply the same methods to one chapter as to another if the sense appears to demand this. See, further, Genealogies.

4. Literary Form

A further consideration that is not always heeded is the exigency of literary form; e.g. in Gen **24** there occurs a dialogue. Strangely enough, an attack has been made on the historical character of Gen on this ground. It cannot be supposed—so runs the argument—that we have here a literal report of what was said. This entirely ignores the practice of all literary artists. Such passages are to be read as giving a literary presentation of what occurred; they convey a far truer and more vivid idea of what passed than could an actual literal report of the mere words, divorced from the gestures, glances and modulations of the voice that play such an important part in conversation.

5. The Sacred Numbers

Another matter is the influence of the sacred numbers on the text; e.g. in Nu **33** the journeys seem designed to present 40 stations and must not be held to exclude camping at other stations not mentioned; Gen **10** probably contained 70 names in the original text. This is a technical consideration which must be borne in mind, and so, too, must the Heb habit of using certain round numbers to express an unspecified time. When, for instance, we read that somebody was 40 or 60 years old, we are not to take these words literally. "Forty years old" often seems to correspond to "after he had reached man's estate" (see Number).

6. Habits of Thought

Still more important is it to endeavor to appreciate the habits of thought of those for whom the Pent was first intended, and to seek to read it in the light of archaic ideas. One instance must suffice. Of the many explanations of names few are philologically correct. It is certain that Noah is not connected with the Heb for "to comfort" or Moses with "draw out"—even if Egyp princesses spoke Heb. The etymological key will not fit. Yet we must ask ourselves whether the narrator ever thought that it did. In times when names were supposed to have some mystic relation to their bearers they might be conceived as standing also in some mystic relation to events either present or future; it is not clear that the true original meaning of the narratives was not to suggest this in literary form. How far the ancient Hebrews were from regarding names in the same light as we do may be seen from such passages as Ex **23** 20 f; Isa **30** 27; see further *EPC*, 47 ff; see also NAMES, PROPER.

7. National Coloring

The Pent is beyond all doubt an intensely national work. Its outlook is so essentially Israelitish that no reader could fail to notice the fact, and it is therefore unnecessary to cite proofs. Doubtless this has in many instances led to its presenting a view of history with which the contemporary peoples would not have agreed. It is not to be supposed that the exodus was an event of much significance in the Egypt of Moses, however important it may appear to the Egyptians of today; and this suggests two points. On the one hand we must admit that to most contemporaries the Pentateuchal narratives must have seemed out of all perspective; on the other the course of subsequent history has shown that the Mosaic sense of perspective was in reality the true one, however absurd it may have seemed to the nations of his own day. Consequently in using the Pent for historical purposes we must always apply two standards—the contemporary and the historical. In the days of Moses the narrative might often have looked to the outsider like the attempt of the frog in the fable to attain to the size of an ox; for us, with the light of history upon it, the values are very different. The national coloring, the medium through which the events are seen, has proved to be true, and the seemingly insignificant doings of unimportant people have turned out to be events of prime historical importance.

There is another aspect of the national coloring of the Pent to be borne in mind. If ever there was a book which revealed the inmost soul of a people, that book is the Pent. This will be considered in V, below, but for the present we are concerned with its *historical* significance. In estimating actions, motives, laws, policy—all that goes to make history—character is necessarily a factor of the utmost consequence. Now here we have a book that at every point reveals and at the same time grips the national character. Alike in cont nts and in form the legislation is adapted with the utmost nicety to the nature of the people for which it was promulgated.

8. How Far the Pentateuch Is Trustworthy

When due allowance has been made for all the various matters enumerated above, what can be said as to the trustworthiness of the Pentateuchal history? The answer is entirely favorable.

(1) *Contemporaneous information.*—In the first place the discussion as to the dating of the Pent (above, II, 4) has shown that we have in it documents that are in many cases certainly contemporaneous with the matters to which they relate and have been preserved in a form that is substantially original. Thus we have seen that the wording of Gen **10** 19 cannot be later than the age of Abraham and that the legislation of the last four books is Mosaic. Now contemporaneousness is the first essential of credibility.

(2) *Character of our informants.*—Given the fact (guaranteed by the contemporaneousness of the sources) that our informants had the means of providing accurate information if they so desired, we have to ask whether they were truthful and able. As to the ability no doubt is possible; genius is stamped on every page of the Pent. Similarly as to truthfulness. The conscience of the narrators is essentially ethical. This appears of course most strongly in the case of the legislation (cf Lev **19** 11) and the attribution of truthfulness to God (Ex **34** 6), but it may readily be detected throughout; e.g. in Gen **20** 12 the narrative clearly shows that truthfulness was esteemed as a virtue by the ancient Hebrews. Throughout, the faults of the *dramatis personae* are never minimized even when the narrator's sympathy is with them. Nor is there any attempt to belittle the opponents of Israel's heroes. Consider on the one hand the magnanimity of Esau's character and on the other the very glaring light that is thrown on the weaknesses of Jacob, Judah, Aaron. If we are taught to know the Moses who prays, "And if not, blot me, I pray thee, out of thy book which thou hast written" (Ex **32** 32), we are also shown his frequent complaints, and we make acquaintance with the hot-tempered manslayer and the lawgiver who disobeyed his God.

(3) *The historical genius of the people.*—Strangely enough, those who desire to discuss the trustworthiness of the Pent often go far afield to note the habits of other nations and, selecting according to their bias peoples that have a good or a bad reputation in the matter of historical tradition, proceed to argue for or against the Pentateuchal narrative on this basis. Such procedure is alike unjust and unscientific. It is unscientific because the object of the inquirer is to obtain knowledge as to the habits of this people, and in view of the great divergences that may be observed among different races the comparative method is clearly inapplicable; it is unjust because this people is entitled to be judged on its own merits or defects, not on the merits or defects of others. Now it is a bare statement of fact that the Jews possess the historical sense to a preëminent degree. Nobody who surveys their long history and examines their customs and practices to this day can fairly doubt that fact. This is no recent development; it is most convincingly attested by the Pent itself, which here, as elsewhere, faithfully mirrors the spirit of the race. What is the highest guaranty of truth, a guaranty to which unquestioning appeal may be made in the firm assurance that it will carry conviction to all who hear? "Remember the days of old, Consider the years of many generations: Ask thy father and he will show thee; Thine elders, and they will tell thee" (Dt **32** 7). "For ask now of the days that are past, which were before thee, since the day that God created man upon the earth," etc (Dt **4** 32). Conversely, the due handing down of tradition is a religious duty: "And it shall come to pass, when your children shall say unto you, What mean ye by this service? that ye shall say," etc (Ex **12** 26 f). "Only take heed to thyself, and keep thy soul diligently, lest thou forget the things which thine eyes saw, and lest they depart from thy heart all the days of thy life; but make them known unto thy children, and thy children's children" (Dt **4** 9). It is needless to multiply quotations. Enough has been said to show clearly the attitude of this people toward history.

(4) *The good faith of Deuteronomy.*—Closely connected with the preceding is the argument from the very obvious good faith of the speeches in Dt. It is not possible to read the references to events in such a chapter as ch **4** without realizing that the speaker most fully believed the truth of his statements. The most unquestionable sincerity is impressed upon the chapter. The speaker is referring to what he believes with all the faith of which he is

capable. Even for those who doubt the Mosaic authenticity of these speeches there can be no doubt as to the writer's unquestioning acceptance of the historical consciousness of the people. But once the Mosaic authenticity is established the argument becomes overwhelming. How could Moses have spoken to people of an event so impressive and unparalleled as having happened within their own recollection if it had not really occurred?

(5) *Nature of the events recorded.*—Another very important consideration arises from the nature of the events recorded. No nation, it has often been remarked, would gratuitously invent a story of its enslavement to another. The extreme sobriety of the patriarchal narratives, the absence of miracle, the lack of any tendency to display the ancestors of the people as conquerors or great personages, are marks of credibility. Many of the episodes in the Mosaic age are extraordinarily probable. Take the stories of the rebelliousness of the people, of their complaints of the water, the food, and so on: what could be more in accordance with likelihood? On the other hand there is another group of narratives to which the converse argument applies. A Sinai cannot be made part of a nation's consciousness by a clever story-teller or a literary forger. The unparalleled nature of the events narrated was recognized quite as clearly by the ancient Hebrews as it is today (see Dt **4** 32 ff). It is incredible that such a story could have been made up and successfully palmed off on the whole nation. A further point that may be mentioned in this connection is the witness of subsequent history to the truth of the narrative. Such a unique history as that of the Jews, such tremendous consequences as their religion has had on the fortunes of mankind, require for their explanation causal events of sufficient magnitude.

(6) *External corroborations.*—All investigation of evidence depends on a single principle: "The coincidences of the truth are infinite." In other words, a false story will sooner or later become involved in conflict with ascertained facts. The Bib. narrative has been subjected to the most rigorous cross-examination from every point of view for more than a century. Time after time confident assertions have been made that its falsehood has been definitely proved, and in each case the Pent has come out from the test triumphant. The details will for the most part be found enumerated or referred to under the separate articles. Here it must suffice just to refer to a few matters. It was said that the whole local coloring of the Egyp scenes was entirely false, e.g. that the vine did not grow in Egypt. Egyptology has in every instance vindicated the minute accuracy of the Pent, down to even the non-mention of earthenware (in which the discolored Nile waters can be kept clean) in Ex **7** 19 and the very food of the lower classes in Nu **11** 5. It was said that writing was unknown in the days of Moses, but Egyptology and Assyriology have utterly demolished this. The historical character of many of the names has been strengthened by recent discoveries (see e.g. JERUSALEM; AMRAPHEL). From another point of view modern observation of the habits of the quails has shown that the narrative of Nu is minutely accurate and must be the work of an eyewitness. From the ends of the earth there comes confirmation of the details of the evolution of law as depicted in the Pent. Finally it is worth noting that even the details of some of the covenants in Gen are confirmed by historical parallels (*Churchman*, 1908, 17 f).

It is often said that history in the true sense was invented by the Greeks and that the Heb genius was so intent on the Divine guidance that it neglected secondary causes altogether. There is a large measure of truth in this view; but so far as the Pent is concerned it can be greatly overstated.

9. The Pentateuch as Reasoned History

One great criticism that falls to be made is entirely in favor of the Hebrew as against some Greeks, viz. the superior art with which the causes are given. A Thucydides would have stated the reasons that induced Pharaoh to persecute the Israelites, or Abraham and Lot to separate, or Korah, Dathan and Abiram and their followers to rebel; but every reader would have known precisely what he was doing and many who can read the material passages of the Pent with delight would have been totally unable to grapple with his presentation of the narrative. The audience is here more unsophisticated and the material presented in more artistic form. In truth, any historian who sat down to compose a philosophical history of the period covered by the Pent would in many instances be surprised at the lavish material it offered to him. A second criticism is more obvious. The writer clearly had no knowledge of the other side of the case. For example, the secondary causes for the defeat near Hormah are plain enough so far as they are internal to the Israelites—lack of *morale*, discipline and leadership, division of opinion, discouragement produced by the Divine disapproval testified by the absence from the army of Moses and the Ark, and the warnings of the former—but the secondary causes on the side of the Amalekites and Canaanites are entirely omitted. Thus it generally happens that we do not get the same kind of view of the events as might be possible if we could have both sides. Naturally this is largely the case with the work of every historian who tells the story from one side only and is not peculiar to the Pent. Thirdly, the object of the Pent is not merely to inform, but to persuade. It is primarily statesmanship, not literature, and its form is influenced by this fact. Seeking to sway conduct, not to provide a mere philosophical exposition of history, it belongs to a different (and higher) category from the latter, and where it has occasion to use the same material puts it in a different way, e.g. by assigning as motives for obeying laws reasons that the philosophic historian would have advanced as causes for their enactment. To some extent, therefore, an attempt to criticize the Pent from the standpoint of philosophic history is an attempt to express it in terms of something that is incommensurable with it.

V. Character of the Pentateuch.—The following sentences from Maine's *Early Law and Custom* form a suggestive introduction to any consideration of the character of the Pent:

1. Hindu Law Books

"The theory upon which these schools of learned men worked, from the ancient, perhaps very ancient, Apastamba and Gautama to the late Manu and the still later Narada, is perhaps still held by some persons of earnest religious convictions, but in time now buried it affected every walk of thought. The fundamental assumption is that a sacred or inspired lit. being once believed to exist, all knowledge is contained in it. The Hindu way of putting it was, and is, not simply that the Scripture is true, but that everything which is true is contained in the Scripture. . . . . It is to be observed that such a theory, firmly held during the infancy of systematic thought, tends to work itself into fact. As the human mind advances, accumulating observation and accumulating reflection, nascent philosophy and dawning science are read into the sacred literature, while they are at the same time limited by the ruling ideas of its priestly authors. But as the mass of this literature grows through the additions made to it by successive expositors, it gradually specializes itself, and subjects, at first mixed together under vague general conceptions, become separated from one another and isolated. In the history of law the most important early specialization is that which separates what a man ought to *do* from what he ought to *know*. A great part of the religious literature, including the Creation of the Universe, the structure of Heaven, Hell, and the World or Worlds, and the nature of the Gods, falls under the last head, what a man ought to know. Law-books first appear as a subdivision of the first branch, what a man should do. Thus the most ancient books of this class are short manuals of conduct for an Aryan Hindu who would lead a perfect life. They contain much more ritual than law, a great deal more about the impurity caused by touching impure things than about crime, a great deal more about penances than about punishments" (pp. 16–18).

It is impossible not to see the resemblances to the Pent that these sentences suggest. Particularly interesting is the commentary they provide on the attitude of Moses toward knowledge: "The secret things belong unto Jeh our God; but the things that are revealed belong unto us and to our children for ever, that we may do all the words of this law" (Dt **29** 29).

But if the Pent has significant resemblances to other old law books, there are differences that are even more significant.

2. Differences

"By an act that is unparalleled in history a God took to Himself a people by means of a sworn agreement. Some words that are fundamental for our purpose must be quoted from the offer; 'Now, therefore, if ye will obey my voice indeed, and keep my covenant, then ye shall be mine own possession from among all peoples: for all the earth is mine: and ye shall be unto me a kingdom of priests and a holy nation.' The views here expressed dominate the legislation. Holiness—the correlative holiness to which the Israelites must attain because the Lord their God is holy—embraces much that is not germane to our subject, but it also covers the whole field of national and individual righteousness. The duty to God that is laid upon the Israelites in these words is a duty that has practical consequences in every phase of social life. I have already quoted a sentence from Sir Henry Maine in which he speaks of the uniformity with which religion and law are implicated in archaic legislation. There is a stage in human development where life is generally seen whole, and it is to this stage that the Pent belongs. But no other legislation so takes up one department of man's life after another and impresses on them all the relationship of God and people. Perhaps nothing will so clearly bring out my meaning as a statement of some of the more fundamental differences between the Pentateuchal legislation and the old Indian law-books which often provide excellent parallels to it. Those to which I desire to draw particular attention are as follows: The Indian law-books have no idea of national (as distinct from individual) righteousness—a conception that entered the world with the Mosaic legislation and has perhaps not made very much progress there since. There is no personal God: hence His personal interest in righteousness is lacking: hence, too, there can be no relationship between God and people: and while there is a supernatural element in the contemplated results of human actions, there is nothing that can in the slightest degree compare with the Personal Divine intervention that is so often promised in the Pentateuchal laws. The caste system, like Hammurabi's class system, leads to distinctions that are always inequitable. The conception of loving one's neighbour and one's sojourner as oneself are alike lacking. The systematic provisions for poor relief are absent, and the legislation is generally on a lower ethical and moral level, while some of the penalties are distinguished by the most perverted and barbarous cruelty. All these points are embraced in the special relationship of the One God and the peculiar treasure with its resulting need for national and individual holiness" (*PS*, 330 f).

3. Holiness

These sentences indicate some of the most interesting of the distinguishing features of the Pent—its national character, its catholic view of life, its attitude toward the Divine, and some at any rate of its most peculiar teachings. It is worth noting that Judaism, the oldest of the religions which it has influenced, attaches particular importance to one chapter, Lev **19**. The keynote of that chapter is the command: 'Holy shall ye be, for holy am I the Lord your God'—to preserve the order and emphasis of the original words. This has been called the Jew's *imitatio Dei,* though a few moments' reflection shows that the use of the word "imitation" is here inaccurate. Now this book with this teaching has exercised a unique influence on the world's history, for it must be remembered that Judaism, Christianity and Islam spring ultimately from its teachings, and it is impossible to sever it from the history of the "people of the book"—as Mohammed called them. It appears then that it possesses in some unique way both an intensely national and an intensely universal character and a few words must be said as to this.

4. The Universal Aspect

The great literary qualities of the work have undoubtedly been an important factor. All readers have felt the fascination of the stories of Gen. The Jewish character has also counted for much; so again have the moral and ethical doctrines, and the miraculous and unprecedented nature of the events narrated. And yet there is much that might have been thought to militate against the book's obtaining any wide influence. Apart from some phrases about all the families of the earth being blessed (or blessing themselves) in the seed of Abraham, there is very little in its direct teaching to suggest that it was ever intended to be of universal application. Possibly these phrases only mean that other nations will use Israel as a typical example of greatness and happiness and pray that they may attain an equal degree of glory and prosperity. Moreover, the Pent provides for a sacrificial system that has long ceased to exist, and a corpus of jural law that has not been adopted by other peoples. Of its most characteristic requirement—holiness—large elements are rejected by all save its own people. Wherein then lies its universal element? How came this the most intensely national of books to exercise a world-wide and ever-growing influence? The reason lies in the very first sentence: "In the beginning God created the heavens and the earth." This doctrine of the unity of an Almighty God is the answer to our question. Teach that there is a God and One Only All-powerful God, and the book that tells of Him acquires a message to all His creatures.

5. The National Aspect

Of the national character of the work something has already been said. It is remarkable that for its own people it has in very truth contained life and length of days, for it has been in and through that book that the Jews have maintained themselves throughout their unique history. If it be asked wherein the secret of this strength lies, the answer is in the combination of the national and the religious. The course of history must have been entirely different if the Pent had not been the book of the people long before the Jews became the people of the book.

Literature.—The current critical view is set forth in vast numbers of books. The following may be mentioned: *LOT;* Cornill's *Intro to the Canonical Books of the OT;* Carpenter and Harford-Battersby's *Hexateuch* (a 2d ed of the Intro without the text has been published as *The Composition of the Hexateuch*); the vols of the *ICC, Westminster Comms. and Century Bible.* Slightly less thoroughgoing views are put forward in the Ger. Intros of König (1893), Baudissin (1901), Sellin (1910); and Geden, *Outlines of Intro to the Heb Bible* (1909); Kittel, *Scientific Study of the OT* (ET, 1910); *Eerdm. St.* has entirely divergent critical views; *POT; TMH,* I, and W. Möller, *Are the Critics Right?* and *Wider den Bann der Quellenscheidung;* Robertson, *Early Religion of Israel;* Van Hoonacker, *Lieu du culte,* and *Sacerdoce lévitique* are all much more conservative and valuable. J. H. Raven, *OT Intro,* gives a good presentation of the most conservative case. The views taken in this article are represented by *SBL, EPC, OP, PS,* Troelstra, *The Name of God,* and in some matters, *TMH,* I.

Harold M. Wiener

PENTATEUCH, PROBLEM OF (Supplement **1929**).

Any adequate consideration of the problem of the Pent must do two things; must define the exact limits of the problem and present a satisfactory solution. The old law of rhetoric that the first step in argument is to define the terms has never been abrogated, though it has fallen too much into desuetude. Much waste energy of controversy over the problem of the Pent and other Biblical problems of to-day is due to the fact that the disputants are not discussing exactly the same things.

Then any consideration of the problem of the Pent which falls short of a satisfactory solution does not get us on very far. Controversial literature has its uses, but they are rather limited in scope; mere controversy falls short of any constructive helpfulness. A life of controversy, merely slaying giants, may leave the victor master of the field, but with the original problem over which the conflict was waged still unsolved. The archaeological method is a method of facts, it seeks not merely to discuss problems, but to solve them.

I. Delimitation of the Problem.—The archaeologist is in fact a diagnostician; he takes things exactly as he finds them and studies the case from its symptomatological appearances and—as does every diagnostician—especially from its peculiarities. He analyzes and classifies, and when the induction and classification is complete, draws conclusion from the facts and finds no greater value in the conclusion than is shown in the evidence. In fact, he begins by studying the remains *exactly as he finds them*.

So our problem here is the problem of the Pent as it is, especially the problem presented by its striking and puzzling peculiarities. It is a part of the literary remains of antiquity so that to examine it by archaeological methods we must begin on the surface of the Pent as it is. Thus accepting the Pent literature as a finished product we will classify things as they appear and from their interrelation attempt to learn how the Pent came to be in its present form (Kyle, *The Problem of the Pentateuch*, pp. xv–xxi).

Most discussion of the problem of the Pent is concerning its author and its time of composition. It may be conceded that these are the most important questions, but it may be that some other approach will bring us into view of a solution of the problem of author and time of composition more easily. There are several parts of a house more important than the vestibule, yet it is the best way to enter the house. Here we have a remarkable collection of laws both civil and ecclesiastical, an interesting historical narrative, and the biography of a man all mingled together. Indeed the laws are inserted in the narrative in such fashion that they might be entirely lifted out together with here and there an introductory phrase and the narrative and the biography would yet be complete and uninterrupted. Where else in all literature are laws and narrative mingled together in such peculiar fashion?

Then the laws in the Pent seem at times indiscriminately mixed; a law assessing the penalty for criminal conduct coming in the midst of ritual directions for worship, or a rubric is found in the midst of criminal laws. In what other law-book is it so? The laws themselves of whatever kind are also fragmentary; there are some very large groups and again there are little fragments of law turning up unexpectedly in the midst of the story at any point. That is most peculiar; how did it come to be so? Occasionally also laws are repeated at different places both in the laws and in the course of the narrative, sometimes in the same words and sometimes somewhat altered in sense as well as phraseology.

The literary style of the Pent is quite different in different parts. Much use has been made of this at times as evidence of the work of different authors and of the composite character of the Pent, as though that were the only source of variations in style. On the other hand some have resented the very suggestion of differences of style in the Pent as though it were a dangerous concession. The facts need only concern us. Certainly no one can read the Decalogue and the list of judgments following, so judicial and sententious, then read the most verbose description of the decorations of the tabernacle, or directions for the detection of leprosy, and still again the eloquent incitement to patriotism in the speeches of Moses in Dt and say that they are all in the same style! One cannot help exclaiming that they ought not to be in the same style, even though from the same author.

Last of all there are historical peculiarities, not to say discrepancies, which attract attention and demand explanation. Discrepancies are not necessarily contradictions, but they do not "sound together," and call for something to be added to make them harmonize.

Now how did the Pent as it is to-day get into this form? This is the real problem of the Pent. The question is not primarily when? or where? or by whom?, but why? and how? Approaching the subject with these questions, we shall perhaps find at last the answer to when? and where? and by whom?

II. The Solution of the Problem.—A solution by archaeological methods must begin with facts and then, by the closest scrutiny of the facts, learn their significance. Thus it will be shown that the only theory which the archaeological method knows is theory which is the result of research, not mere hypothesis which is only the legitimate instrument of research.

The solution now to be presented arises from a strict application of this archaeological method to the peculiarities of the Law as literary remains of antiquity. It appeared in the course of an original analysis of the materials of the books of the Law. The ultimate result was as unexpected and startling to the author as it may be to anyone who reads it. Unexpectedness is, indeed, one of the marks of real discovery everywhere.

1. Characteristics of the Pent

(1) It very soon appears on investigation that there are in the Pent different kinds of laws. (A) There are various general terms for law or laws, in fact any kind of a law, and these terms are used throughout the books of the Law. *Tōrah*, usually translated "law" is so used 55 times; sometimes of a particular kind of law (Ex **12** 49); sometimes of the Statutes of the ceremonial law (Lev **6** 9, 14; cf Bib Heb, **6** 2, 7). Again this word is used for the whole Law (Dt **1** 5 and many places, cf Heb Concordance). Two other words are used as synonyms for *tōrah*, *dath* (Dt **33** 2), and *ḥōḳ* (Gen **47** 26). *Debārīm*, "words," is used to denote law or laws in Pent 32 times in the intensive sense of "utterances" or "oracles" (Ex **34** 28; Dt **10** 4). *'Imrah*, "word," is also once used in the same sense (Dt **33** 9). *'edhuth*, "testimony," occurs 34 times in the sense of "witness." *Bārīth* is also used for the Law or for a part of it 30 times. Indeed the scriptural idea of all law of God is as a covenant with man, though man does not always respond (Ex **34** 28; Dt **4** 13; **5** 2; **9** 9, 11, 15; cf Wiener, "Studies in Biblical Law," *Bibliotheca Sacra*, July, 1918, 1919). *Miçwōth*, "commandments," any kind of commandment of God, is used in the Law 46 times.

(B) In marked contrast to these general terms for law of any kind are certain words which, by their definitive meanings, clear differentiation, and the exactly discriminating use made of them are shown to be technical terms. It will at once be perceived that this is a departure from the usual way in which the terms for law have been regarded by Pent scholars generally. There is an occasional passing reference to "The Book of Judgments" (*Oxford Hex* I, 111) or the calling of some laws "technical," though no technical use of them is noted (Kautzsch, *Lit of OT*, 30). Sometimes the words which are now found to be technical are used interchangeably (Green, *Unity of Gen*).

The first of these technical terms to be noted is *mĭshpāṭīm*, usually translated "judgments," literally "judgings," i.e. decisions of judges; these fixed by precedent, and approved of God, were written down among the laws of Israel. These are defined in the Heb as laws "one with another," things which were the subject of controversy between two individuals or between an individual and the state. Thus the "judgments" were civil and criminal laws, usually concerning things wrong in themselves, *mala in se*, and were always subject to trial in the courts. Citation of a few of these "judgments" will make clear their character and complete reference to every use of the word in the Law will show it to be uniform. In Ex **21** we have, 2–6, such laws to **23** 19 (for every instance in the Law cf Kyle, *The Problem of the Pent*, Investigation I). Wherever it is said "These are the judgments," such laws and no others are found in the lists given.

Again, *ḥŭḳḳīm*, usually translated "statutes," denotes a very different kind of laws. The Heb word means "directions," from the throwing out of the hand to guide one. Such exactly are the laws called "statutes"; they are directions about things not wrong in themselves, *mala in se*, but only so because of the statute, *mala prohibita*, not matter of controversy "one with another," but matters of mere direction by the statute and usually, and, indeed, especially in the functions of religion. All administration of these laws was, not by the magistrates, but by the priests. Citation of a few of these laws will indicate at once their character. Ex (**25**–**40**) describes the tabernacle and its construction. Lev (**1**–**3** 17) sacrifices. Wherever this title "statutes" is given to a group of laws, such laws, and no others, are found in that group.

Still another technical term, *miçwōth*, "commandments" is used in the Pent. In addition to its general use, already noted, this term has a distinctly technical use specifically to denote the Decalogue. When used in connection with "judgments" and "statutes" as titles for groups of laws it refers always to the Decalogue. When thus used as a title there is always found one or more of the "commandments" in that group of laws. As "judgments" correspond closely to our civil and criminal laws, and the "statutes" to our "statutes" concerning things not *mala in se*, and especially to ecclesiastical laws, so the "commandments" are fundamental law, as the Magna Charta of England or the Constitution of the United States.

It is to be noted concerning all these technical terms that absolute uniformity in use is not necessary in order that a term may be a technical term. It becomes, then, the more interesting, surprising indeed, to find that there are no exceptions to the technical use of these terms, except what has already been noticed, that *miçwōth* has use frequently as a common term, when not used in connection with *mĭshpāṭīm* or *ḥŭḳḳīm*. Wherever it is said these are the "judgments" or the "statutes," only "judgments" or "statutes" will be found there. If it is said these are the "judgments and statutes," then both these kinds of laws will be found in that list, but no "commandments" will be found there. If it is said these are the "judgments" and "commandments," or "statutes" and "commandments," or the "judgments and statutes and commandments," then, in every case, just those kinds of laws mentioned, and all those kinds, and no other will be found in that list. To such extreme of exactness is this usage carried that certain circumlocutions are devised in order to designate peculiar laws. A special law for the establishment of a new "judgment," as in the case of the inheritance of Zelophehad's daughters (Nu **27** 11), or the establishment of cities of refuge (Nu **35** 11–29), is given a special name. Being in character a "judgment" and in enactment a new direction, a "statute," such law is called a "statute of judgment," an exact discrimination in the use of these words and a clear indication that they are technical terms. Another investigation (id, *Problem of the Pent* VI) into the use of these words throughout the Heb Bible discovers that the technical use of these terms continued throughout the period of the Judges, was carried into the time of David and Solomon, but fell into complete neglect in the time of the apostasy, and later, at the reformation and return from exile, was revived to complete use again.

(2) These various *kinds* of laws indicated by technical terms were also put to quite different *uses* according to their character and these various uses naturally resulted in quite different literary forms of expression. The proper use of some laws requires that they be memorized. We teach our children the Ten Commandments and our magistrates need to know the common laws to administer justice without needing to consult lawbooks. So in Israel also. Thus the Decalogue and the Judgments are in mnemonic form. They are brief, terse, expressed in verbs and nouns with hardly ever an adjective or adverb in the Heb.

The statutes were for very different use. The people did not need to be most familiar with them, but were always to be directed by the priests. Moreover they were either new "directions" or, in the case of ritual forms, at least freed from all idolatrous significance and given a new spiritual content. This naturally required a descriptive style, no matter who might be the author. An examination of a few of the statutes, as the directions for the making of the tabernacle (Ex **25**–**40**), the making of the vestments (Ex **28** 6–12), the design of the decorations of the furniture (Ex **25** 31–36) and especially for the detection of leprosy (Lev **13** 28–52) will fully illustrate this.

The speeches of Moses in Dt inevitably call for a hortatory style, regardless of the person of the author. The same judge would naturally give decision from the bench in simple, terse language suited to a judicial decision; if called upon to address a class in a law school on the same subject, would speak in descriptive and explanatory language; and if called to deliver an address still on the same subject on some national holiday, would use impassioned language suited to the occasion. Exactly so the speeches of Moses in Dt, though treating of the same subject material as the words so simply spoken from the mount, or descriptively expounded in the other books of the Law, are now given in all the fervor of the language of impassioned oratory. *If it were not so*, they would appear to be *not authentic*. Thus such change in expression of laws as is often attributed to different authors is naturally demanded by the differing circumstances of the utterance even by the same author.

(3) Now that analysis and classification has been completed, examination and comparison, according to the archaeological method, is in order. The narrative introduction to the Decalogue, to the description of the tabernacle, and to the speeches of

Moses in Dt, naturally belong with those groups of laws. Thus also other groups long or short, so that all the narrative portions may thus be distributed among the groups of the various kinds of Laws. The commandments and the judgments being in the same literary style are thus in any consideration of style to be grouped together.

If now the various groups of commandments and judgments with the narrative portions belonging to them be gathered together, and the groups of statutes with the narrative portions belonging to them be similarly collected, and we note that the speeches of Moses with their appropriate narrative portions make another distinct portion, we have three natural and harmonious segments of the books of the Law from Ex to Dt. The mnemonic laws with their narrative portions, and the descriptive laws and narrative portions, and again Dt as a distinct whole by itself compose other complete and harmonious segments of the books of the Law. But since the mnemonic laws are the commandments and the judgments, and the descriptive laws are the statutes and Dt is always Dt, it appears at once that these two separate divisions of the books of the Law are identical.

(4) The Documentary Theory makes also three general divisions of the material of the Pent. Comparison is at once suggested between the divisions just noted according to *kinds* and *uses* of laws with the divisions according to the Documentary Theory. Here the surprise of the investigations awaits us. The mnemonic laws, the commandments and the judgments with the narrative portions naturally belonging to them, are discovered to be identical with that portion of the Pent which in the Documentary Theory is assigned to the J-E document including those brief portions of J and E still pointed out; the descriptive laws, the statutes, with the narrative portions belonging with them, are exactly the same as the P document inclusive of the portion of that document called H; and Dt is, of course, Dt in each case. This identification is not merely in a general way accurate, but is startlingly exact, with no more variation than the slight margin of phrases or verses occasionally found to be difficult of assignment by either method of partition.

"It is a fundamental principle of the examining and interpreting of evidence that nothing is to be supposed, if the case is made complete by the known evidence without any supposition. These investigations show that the case for the differences of form and style and vocabulary in the Pent is complete without any suppositional element. It is, of course, admitted that no theory or explanation in life and literature, which are never mechanical but always subject to the caprices of human volition, is ever proved simply by the fact that it works; but an explanation that works without calling in the aid of any suppositional element without which it is inadequate, is more probable than one which invokes such aid. Common sense does not take kindly to suppositions when none are needed" (id, *The Problem of the Pent*, Investigation IV with Diagram).

The peculiarities of the Pent have been considered and found already in large part to yield to an explanation by the facts of the Pent itself.

2. Composition of the Pent

The archaeological method is still confronted, however, with the Pent *as it is*, with all its various elements not in the systematic order in which they have been assorted, but presenting all the puzzling peculiarities which we have pointed out, the fragmentariness of the codes, the repetition of laws, and the distribution of all throughout a running narrative. To reconstruct aright the historical events which brought about these strange results is the real problem of the Pent. Was it constructed in this form out of fragmentary materials at hand, long after the events narrated and by persons in nowise connected with them, or did it grow into this form in a journalistic way throughout the journey depicted and the history narrated? The archaeological method requires that we visualize what is required by each of these methods of composition? and so be able to judge which is most in accord with psychological expectations and especially with the *facts of the Pent as it is*.

(1) According to the requirements of the Documentary Theory, the final redactor, or redactors, as many prefer to think, had three important documents which they proceeded to combine into one book. If the process was a long one, it still involved the same actions to produce the Pent as it is, however much the process was drawn out. The documents in hand were the J-E document containing narrative and civil and criminal laws, thus constituting a harmonious and self-consistent document; the P document also containing much narrative and a code of laws or directions of a totally different character from those of the J-E document, religious ritual and directions for the construction of a building for religious purposes, ecclesiastical laws in fact, also forming a complete and self-consistent document; and third, the D document containing a very little introductory narrative and a narrative conclusion, for four great addresses on laws both civil and ecclesiastical, though chiefly the former (cf Welhausen, *Composition des Hexateuchs; The Oxford Hexateuch;* Simpson, *Pentateuchal Criticism*).

The redactors with these various documents before them, took the civil and criminal laws out of the J-E document and the ecclesiastical laws out of the P document and broke them up into, some large and many small, fragments, mixed the fragments together even putting often a fragment from one of these documents into a group of laws taken from the other document, and again repeating some law and writing it in in several different places. They must have done so, *for it is so now*, the result of the final redaction. The narrative portions of both the J-E document and the P document were now broken up into fragments and then pieced together so as to make a continuous narrative, a few connecting phrases being supplied to make complete sense where it was lacking. They must have done so, *for the narrative is so now*, a very complete story. Still the redactors were not satisfied; they still had two documents, not one book. They then broke up the combined laws into fragments, spread out the combined narrative and inserted these fragments of laws in the breaks, writing again a few introductory words where necessary. They must have done *this* also, if it were made from the original J-E and P documents, *for it is so now*. Then they appended the D document to the end of the combined two documents and, presto, the Pent was finished!

Now it may be frankly admitted that it is physically possible that the Pent might have been constructed in this fashion by piecing together fragments which have first been made fragments. Children at their play with paste and scissors often do so. It seems impossible to imagine any person, or any number of persons, making law books in this way. Such a law book could not find acceptance among intelligent people, if indeed, any sane man could prepare such a book.

(2) Let us now try to visualize what the wilderness discloses and see the Pent as a product of the journey. The well-known formula of revelation through Moses was "God spake unto Moses, saying, Speak unto the people." It is evident that Moses was first of all a speaking prophet. This is, in fact, exactly what that wilderness journey required;

writing was well known, but certainly writing materials among these refugees, and still more writing opportunity among shepherds in the wilderness, would be far from adequate for the instruction of so great a multitude. Then no very considerable number of the people could be addressed orally at one time. Besides, the children of Israel were "wanderers (shepherds) in the wilderness." In a land where it takes ten acres to pasture one goat, necessity required that the shepherds should scatter far and wide and not always be around the camp and accessible to Moses' teaching. Only representatives of the tribes were kept at the tabernacle as guards and doubtless changed from time to time. Thus Moses would need to repeat his teachings. Moreover some laws had special need of reiteration. Even a modern preacher has been known to preach more than once on some subjects. Especially is this true of such subjects as Sabbath-keeping, treatment of servants and employees, and honesty and purity of life, and the sacredness of life. It is just such laws that are repeated in the record of the Pent code.

Again it is to be noted that Moses was also a writing prophet. In Ex (**17** 14) we read "And the Lord said unto Moses, Write these things in a book." Eight times in the Pent writing is distinctly mentioned or distinctly implied (*Bible Teacher*, Bib. gains from Egyp explorations Nov, 1901). Whether Moses actually wrote "these things" with his own hand or used scribes as was the common method in Egypt, as it is in our literary and business world today, does not matter. In any case, Moses was also a writing prophet.

Then notices of passing time occur with great frequency in the Pent. "They journeyed from," "they tarried here," "on the morrow." Plainly the books are journalistic in form (Naville, *Schweich Lectures*, 1915, 44). This form is a fact. How did the Pent get into this form? Were things written down from day to day as they happened, or were the books cast into this form artificially and at a later time? The four facts, that "Moses spake unto the people," that he "wrote these things in a book," that what has come to us is in journalistic form, and that Moses was first a speaking prophet and only secondarily a writing prophet put clearly before us the literary method indicated in the wilderness sojourn and which we find in the Pent itself as it now is.

With these facts in mind, it is not difficult to reconstruct the wilderness life and the record of it, and the visualization is just what we see in the Pent. The cloud moved and the tents were struck and these facts were written "in the 'book.'" The cloud rested and tarried and events took place; these were all duly set down in the journal. Moses "spake unto the people, saying!" and what he said in its substance, at least, was written just there in the "book." Sometimes only a few laws were promulgated or discussed, sometimes a long list, but whatever there was the record was made in its place. When the wandering shepherds came in, repetition of important teachings was made and recorded. Thus time went on and the journey went on and the "book" grew until, at last, on the plains of Moab, a great national assembly was held and patriotic addresses delivered and all duly recorded. Moses died and this fact, also, was noted by the scribe quite in accord with the Egyp literary custom, which allowed a man to speak even in the first person on his tombstone. So the journey ended and the journal was complete.

(3) Thus, in the most natural, simple way in exact accord with the conditions of the wilderness life and journey, are all the peculiarities of the composition of the Pent accounted for and that without any suppositions.

What has been said pertains almost wholly to the portion of the Pent in which are embedded the laws.

3. Additional Considerations

Solution of the Problem of the whole of the Pent demands some additional considerations. The narrative preceding the laws, now known as Gen seems to have been prepared, in part at least, from documents handed down from the earliest times, there are sufficient library marks upon it; and certainly in part by direct revelation, for no man was present at creation to leave a record. This book was added as a preface to the books containing the Law; Gen "beginnings." According to the Documentary Theory, Gen is largely in the style of the P document and is distinctly so designated (Kautzsch, *Lit OT*). This is exactly what the style ought to be, for it represents the style of the author of the descriptive portions of the books of the Law. The Decalogue was given of God; the judgments being "judgings," decisions of judges, were in the language of usage; only the narrative and the statutes represent immediately the style of the author of the Pent. Thus it is the descriptive style that we should expect to find and do find in Gen.

The discriminative use of the divine names of which so much has been made in critical discussions is in exact harmony with this solution of the problem of the Pent. Indeed, this discriminative use of the divine names is in common use among ourselves and passes unnoticed, because so perfectly natural. In courts of law the general name for deity, God or the Almighty, is commonly used, but seldom the covenant names, Redeemer, Saviour, Christ. But in ecclesiastical courts, while the general names for deity are sometimes heard, the covenant names are used much more frequently. In like manner, and just as naturally, we find *Elohim* used almost exclusively in the civil and criminal law portions of the Pent, the so-called J-E document, and the name Jehovah used almost exclusively in the statutes, denominated the P document; though in either case, in these ancient documents or in modern law courts, these words are sometimes used interchangeably (cf *Green, Unity of Genesis*).

To this solution of the Problem of the Pent it may plausibly be said: These are but collateral facts of the Documentary Theory, additional "marks," criteria of the various authors: J and E were legal writers and P an ecclesiastical writer. Plausible as it seems, it has no standing in court and that for one reason which excludes all others. An attorney gave several reasons for the absence of his client, and concluded "Finally, your honor, he is dead!" This distinction in the use of technical terms runs all the way through the Law. It is fully observed in Dt. How, on the Documentary Theory would the Deuteronomist observe this distinction? J-E had only civil and criminal laws and could not show such discrimination, for there cannot be distinction without comparison, and the P document, which furnishes the comparison, according to the theory, *was not yet written*. So this witness for the technical law terms as collateral facts of the Documentary Theory needed in court to testify for the Deuteronomist on behalf of that theory, if he were not dead, at least had *not yet begun to live*. Statement of other reasons in reply to this objection is unnecessary.

M. G. Kyle

PENTATEUCH, THE SAMARITAN, sa-mar'i-tan:

I. Knowledge of Samaritan Pentateuch
  1. In Older Times
  2. Revived Knowledge
II. Codices and Script
  1. Nāblûs Roll
  2. The Script
  3. Peculiarities of Writing

The existence of a Sam community in Nāblûs is generally known, and the fact that they have a recension of the Pent which differs in some respects from the Massoretic has been long recognized as important.

I. Knowledge of the Samaritan Pentateuch.—Of the Gr Fathers Origen knew of it and notes two insertions which do not appear in the MT—Nu **13** 1 and **21** 12, drawn from Dt **1** 2 and **2** 18. Eusebius of Caesarea in his *Chronicon* compares the ages of the patriarchs before Abraham in the LXX with those in the Sam Pent and the MT.

1. In Older Times

Samaritan High Priest with Scroll.

Epiphanius is aware that the Samaritans acknowledged the Pent alone as canonical. Cyril of Jerus notes agreement of LXX and Sam in Gen **4** 8. These are the principal evidences of knowledge of this recension among the Gr Fathers. Jerome notes some omissions in the MT and supplies them from Sam. The Talm shows that the Jews retained a knowledge of the Sam Pent longer, and speaks contemptuously of the points in which it differs from the MT. Since the differences observed by the Fathers and the Talmudists are to be seen in the Sam Pent before us, they afford evidence of its authenticity.

2. Revived Knowledge

After nearly a millennium of oblivion the Sam Pent was restored to the knowledge of Christendom by Pietro de la Valle who in 1616 purchased a copy from the Sam community which then existed in Damascus. This copy was presented in 1623 to the Paris Oratory and shortly after published in the Paris Polyglot under the editorship of Morinus, a priest of the Oratory who had been a Protestant. He emphasized the difference between the MT and Sam Pent for argumentative reasons, in order to prove the necessity for the intervention of the church to settle which was Scripture. A fierce controversy resulted, in which various divines, Protestant and Catholic, took part. Since then copies of this recension have multiplied in Europe and America. All of them may be regarded as copies ultimately of the Nāblûs roll. These copies are in the form, not of rolls, but of codices or bound volumes. They are usually written in two columns to the page, one being the Tg or interpretation and this is sometimes in Aramaic and sometimes in Arabic. Some codices show three columns with both Tgs. There are probably nearly 100 of these codices in various libraries in Europe and America. These are all written in the Sam script and differ only by scribal blunders.

II. Codices and Script.—The visitor to the Samaritans is usually shown an ancient roll, but only rarely is the most ancient exhibited, and when so exhibited still more rarely is it in circumstances in which it may be examined. Dr. Mills, who spent three months in the Sam community, was able to make a careful though interrupted study of it. His description (*Nāblûs and the Modern Samaritans*, 312) is that "the roll is of parchment, written in columns, 13 in. deep, and 7½ in. wide. The writing is in a fair hand, rather small; each column contains from 70 to 72 lines, and the whole roll contains 110 columns. The name of the scribe is written in a kind of acrostic, running through these columns, and is found in the Book of Dt. The roll has the appearance of very great antiquity, but is wonderfully well preserved, considering its venerable age. It is worn out and torn in many places and patched with re-written parchment; in many other places, where not torn, the writing is unreadable. It seemed to me that about two-thirds of the original is still readable. The skins of which the roll is composed are of equal size and measure each 25 in. long by 15 in. wide." Dr. Rosen's account on the authority of Kraus (*Zeitschr. der deutsch-morgenl. Gesellsch.*, XVIII, 582) agrees with this, adding that the "breadth of the writing is a line and the space between is similar." Both observers have noted that the parchment has been written only on the "hair" side. It is preserved in a silk covering inclosed in a silver case embossed with arabesque ornaments.

1. The Nāblûs Roll

2. The Script

The reader on opening one of the codices of the Sam Pent recognizes at once the difference of the writing from the characters in an ordinary Heb Bible. The Jews admit that the character in which the Sam Pent is written is older than their square character. It is said in the Talm (*Sanhedhrīn* **21***b*): "The law at first was given to Israel in *'ibhrī* letters and in the holy tongue and again by Ezra in the square [*'ăshūrīth*] character and the Aram. tongue. Israel chose for themselves the *'ăshūrīth* character and the holy tongue: they left to the *hedhyōṭōth* ["uncultured"] the *'ibhrī* character and the Aram. tongue—'the Cuthaeans are the *hedhyōṭōth*,' said Rabbi Ḥasda." When Jewish hatred of the Samaritans, and the contempt of the Pharisees for them are remembered, this admission amounts to a demonstration. The Sam script resembles that on the Maccabean coins, but is not identical with it. It may be regarded as between the square character and the angular, the latter as is seen in the M S and the Siloam inscription. Another intermediate form, that found on the Assouan papyri, owes the differences it presents to having been written with a reed on papyrus. As the chronology of these scripts is of importance we subjoin those principally in question.

Samaritan Name	Hebrew Name	Moabite Stone 850 BC	Siloam 706 BC	Assouan 400 BC	Maccabean 100 BC	Samaritan	Square 200 AD
Alaf	Aleph						א
Bit	Beth						ב
Gaman	Gimel						ג
Dalath	Daleth						ד
I	He						ה
Dai	Vav						ו
Zen	Zain						ז
It	Heth						ח
Tit	Teth						ט
Yud	Yodh						י
Kaf	Kaph						כך
Labad	Lamed						ל
Mim	Mem						מם
Nun	Nun						נן
Simcat	Samech						ס
In	Ain						ע
Fi	Pe						פף
Çade	Çadi						צץ
Ḳof	Koph						ק
Rish	Resh						ר
Shin	Shin						ש
Taf	Tav						ת

Table Showing Script of Semitic Languages.

The study of these alphabets will confirm the statement above made that the Sam alphabet is, in evolution, between the square character and the angular, nearer the latter than the former, while the characters of the Assouan papyri are nearer the former than the latter. Another point to be observed is that the letters which resemble each other in one alphabet do not always resemble in another. We can thus, from comparison of the letters liable to be confused, form a guess as to the script in which the document containing the confusion was written.

In inscriptions the lapidary had no hesitation, irrespective of syllables, in completing in the next line any word for which he had not sufficient room.

3. Peculiarities in Writing

Thus the beginnings and endings of lines were directly under each other, as on the M S. In the papyri the words are not divided, but the scribe was not particular to have the ends of lines directly under each other. The scribe of the square character by use of *literae dilatabiles* secured this without dividing the words. The Samaritan secured this end by wider spacing. The first letter or couple of letters of each line are placed directly under the first letter or letters of the preceding line—so with the last letters—two or three—of the line, while the other words are spread out to fill up the space. The only exception to this is a paragraph ending. Words are separated from each other by dots; sentences by a sign like our colon. The Torah is divided into 966 *ḳisam* or paragraphs. The termination of these is shown by the colon having a dot added to it, thus :. Sometimes this is reinforced by a line and an angle—<. These *ḳisam* are often enumerated on the margin; sometimes, in later MSS in Arab. numerals. A blank space sometimes separates one of these *ḳisam* from the next.

When the scribe wished to inform the reader of his personality and the place where he had written the MS he made use of a peculiar device.

4. The *Tarikh*

In copying he left a space vacant in the middle of a column. The space thus left is every now and then bridged by a single letter. These letters read down the column form words and sentences which convey the information. In the case of the Nāblûs roll this *tarīkh* occurs in Dt and occupies three columns. In this it is said, "I Abishua, son of Pinhas [Phinehas], son of Eleazar, son of Aharun [Aaron] the priest, have written this holy book in the door of the tabernacle of the congregation in Mt. Gerizim in the 13th year of the rule of the children of Israel in the land of Canaan." Most of the codices in the libraries of Europe and America have like information given in a similar manner. This *tarīkh* is usually Heb, but sometimes it is in Sam Aramaic. Falsification of the date merely is practically impossible; the forgery must be the work of the first scribe.

Not only has the difference of script to be considered, but also the different values assigned to the letters. The names given to the letters differ considerably from the Heb, as may be seen above.

5. The Mode of Pronunciation

There are no vowel points or signs of reduplication. Only B and P of the *BGaDH-KPHaTH* letters are aspirated. The most singular peculiarity is that none of the gutturals is pronounced at all—a peculiarity which explains some of the names given to the letters. This characteristic appears all the more striking when it is remembered how prominent gutturals are in Arab., the everyday language of the Samaritans. The first 5 verses of Gen are subjoined according to the Sam pronunciation, as taken down by Petermann (*Versuch einer hebr. Formenlehre*, 161), from the reading of Amram the high priest: *Barashēt bara Eluwēm it ashshamēm wit aareç. Waareç ayata-te'u ube'u waashek al fani . . . . tum uru Eluwem amra, efet al fani ammem waya'mer Eluwēm ya'i or way'ai or wayerē Eluwem it a' or ki tov wayabdel Eluwem bin a'or ubin aashek uyikra Eluwēm la'or yom ula 'ashek ḳara lila. Uyai 'erev uyai beḳar yom a'ad.*

There is no doubt that if the inscription given above is really in the MS it is a forgery written on the skin at the first. Of its falsity

6. The Age of the Nāblûs Roll

also there is no doubt. The Am Tab sent from Canaan and nearly contemporary with the Israelite conquest of the land were impressed with cuneiform characters and the language was Bab. Neglecting the *tarīkh*, we may examine the matter independently and come to certain conclusions. If it is the original from which the other MSS have been copied we are forced to assume a date earlier at least than the 10th cent. AD, which is the date of the earliest Heb MS. The script dates from the Hasmoneans. The reason of this mode of writing being perpetuated in copying the Law must be found in some special sanctity in the document from which the copies were made originally. Dr. Mills seems almost inclined to believe the authenticity of the *tarīkh*. His reasons, however, have been rendered valueless by recent discoveries. Dr. Cowley, on the other hand, would date it somewhere about the 12th cent. AD, or from that to the 14th. With all the respect due to such a scholar we venture to think his view untenable. His hypothesis is that an old MS was found and the *tarīkh* now seen in it was afterward added. That, however, is impossible unless a new skin—the newness of which would be obvious—had been written over and inserted. Even the comparatively slight change implied in turning Ishmael into Israel in the *tarīkh* in the Nāblûs roll necessitates a great adjustment of lines, as the letters of the *tarīkh* must read horizontally as well as perpendicularly. If that change were made, the date would then be approximately 650 AD, much older than Cowley's 12th cent. There is, however, nothing in this to explain the sanctity given to this MS. There is a tradition that the roll was saved from fire, that it leaped out of the fire in the presence of Nebuchadnezzar. If it were found unconsumed when the temple on Mt. Gerizim was burned by John Hyrcanus I, this would account for the veneration in which it is held. It would account also for the stereotyping of the script. The angular script prevailed until near the time of Alexander the Great. In it or in a script akin to it the copy of the Law must have been written which Manasseh, the son-in-law of Sanballat, brought to Samaria. The preservation of such a copy would be ascribed to miracle and the script consecrated.

III. Relation of the Samaritan Recension to the MT and LXX.—While the reader of the Sam

1. Relation to MT: Classification of Differences

Pent will not fail to observe its practical identity with the MT, closer study reveals numerous, if minor, differences. These differences were classified by Gesenius. Besides being illogical, his classification is faulty, as founded on the assumption that the Sam Pent text is the later. The same may be said of Kohn's. We would venture on another classification of these variations, deriving the principle of division from their origin. These variations were due either to (1) accident or (2) intention. (1) The first of these classes arose from the way in which books were multiplied in ancient days. Most commonly one read and a score of scribes, probably slaves, wrote to this dictation. Hence errors might arise (*a*) when from similarity of letters the reader mistook one word for another. (*b*) If the reader's pronunciation was not distinct the scribes might mis-hear and therefore write the word amiss. (*c*) Further, if the reader began a sentence which opened in a way that generally was followed by certain words or phrases, he might inadvertently conclude it, not in the way it was written before him, but in the customary phrase. In the same way the scribe through defective attention might also blunder. Thus the accidental variations may be regarded as due to mistakes of *sight, hearing* and *attention.* (2) Variations due to intention are either (*a*) grammatical, the removal of peculiarities and conforming them to usage, or (*b*) logical, as when a command having been given, the fulfilment is felt to follow as a logical necessity and so is narrated, or, if narrated, is omitted according to the ideas of the scribe; (*c*) doctrinal changes introduced into the text to suit the doctrinal position of one side or other. Questions of propriety also lead to alterations—these may be regarded as quasi-doctrinal.

(1) *Examples of accidental variations.*—(*a*) Due to mistakes of sight: The cause of mistakes of sight is the likeness of differing letters. These, however, differ in different scripts, as may be proved by consideration of the table of alphabets. Some of these mistakes found in connection with the Sam Pent appear to be mistakes due to the resemblance of letters in the Sam script. Most of these are obvious blunders; thus in Gen **19** 32, we have the meaningless *tabhinu* instead of *'ābhīnū,* "our father," from the likeness of ࠕ, *t*, to ࠀ, *a*. In Gen **25** 29 we have *çāzedh* instead of *yāzedh,* "to seethe," because of the likeness of ࠑ, *ç*, to ࠉ, *y* or *i*. These, while in Blayney's transcription of Walton's text, are not in Petermann or the Sam Tg. The above examples are mistakes in Sam MSS, but there are mistakes also in the MT. In Gen **27** 40 the RV rendering is "When thou shalt break loose, thou shalt shake his yoke from off thy neck." This rendering does violence to the sense of both vbs. and results in a tautology. In the Hiphil the first vb. *rūdh* ought to mean "to cause to wander," not "to break loose," and the second vb. *pāraḳ* means "to break," not "to shake off." The Sam has "When thou shalt be mighty, thou shalt break his yoke from off thy neck." The MT mistake may be due to the confounding of ࠀ, *a*, with ࠕ, *t*, and the transposition of ࠃ, *d*, and ࠁ, *b*. The vb. *'ādhar,* "to be strong," is rare and poetic, and so unlikely to suggest itself to reader or scribe. The renderings of the LXX and Pesh indicate confusion. There are numerous cases, however, where the resembling letters are not in the Sam script, but sometimes in the square character and sometimes in the angular. Some characters resemble each other in both, but not in the Samaritan. The cases in which the resemblance is only in letters in the square script may all be ascribed to variation in the MT. Cases involving the confusion of *wāw* and *yōdh* are instances in point. It may be said that every one of the instances of variation which depends on confusion of these letters is due to a blunder of a Jewish scribe, e.g. Gen **25** 13, where the Jewish scribe has written *n^ebhīth* instead of *n^ebhāyōth* (*Nebaioth*) as usual; **36** 5, where the Jewish scribe has *y^e'īsh* instead of *y^e'ūsh* (*Jeush*), as in the Ḳ^erē. In Gen **46** 30, by writing *r^e'ōthī* instead of *rā'īthī,* the Jewish scribe in regard to the same letters has made a blunder which the Sam scribe has avoided. When *d* and *r* are confused, it must not be ascribed to the likeness in the square script, for those letters are alike in the angular also. As the square is admitted to be later than the date of the Sam script, these confusions point to a MS in angular. There are, however, confusions which apply only to letters alike in angular. Thus *binyāmīm,* invariably in the Sam Pent Benjamin, *binyāmīn,* is written *Benjamin;* also in Ex **1** 11 *pithōn* instead of *pithōm,* but *m* and *n* are alike only in the script of the Siloam inscription. In Dt **12** 21, the Sam has לְשַׁכֵּן, *l^eshakkēn,* as the MT has in **12** 11, whereas the MT has לָשׂוּם, *lāsūm.* A study of the alphabets on p. 2314 will show the close resemblance between *wāw* and *kāph* in the Siloam script, as well as the likeness above mentioned between *m* and *n*. This points to the fact that the MSS from which the MT and the Sam were transcribed in some period of their history were written in angular of the type of the Siloam inscription, that is to say of the age of Hezekiah.

(*b*) Variations due to mistakes of hearing: The great mass of these are due to one of two sources, either on the one hand the insertion or omission of *wāw* and *yōdh,* so that the vowel is written *plenum* or the reverse, or, on the other hand, to the mistake of the gutturals. Of the former class of variations there are dozens in every chapter. The latter also is fairly frequent, and is due doubtless to the fact that in the time when the originals of the present MSS were transcribed the gutturals were not pronounced at all. Gen **27** 36 shows א and ה interchanged, ה and ח in Gen **41** 45, ח for ע in Gen **49** 7, and א and ע in Gen **23** 18, in many Sam MSS, but the result is meaningless. This inability to pronounce the gutturals points to a date considerably before the Arab domination. Possibly this avoidance of the gutturals became fashionable during the Rom rule, when the language of law was Lat, a language without gutturals. A parallel instance may be seen in Aquila, who does not transliterate any gutturals. This loss of the gutturals may be connected with the fact that in Assyr *'ālēph* is practically the only guttural. The colonists from Assyria might not unlikely be unable to pronounce the gutturals.

(c) Changes due to deficient attention: Another cause of variation is to be found in reader or scribe not attending sufficiently to the actual word or sentence seen or heard. This is manifested in putting for a word its equivalent. In Gen **26** 31 the Sam has *lᵉrē'ēhū*, "to his friend," instead of as the MT *lᵉ'āḥīw*, "to his brother," and in Ex **2** 10 Sam has *na'ar* for *yeledh* in MT. In such cases it is impossible to determine which represents the original text. We may remark that the assumption of Gesenius and of such Jewish writers as Kohn that the MT is always correct is due to mere prejudice. More important is the occasional interchange of *YHWH* and *'Ĕlōhīm*, as in Gen **28** 4, where Sam has *YHWH* and the MT *'Ĕlōhīm*, and Gen **7** 1 where it has *'Ĕlōhīm* against *YHWH* in the MT. This last instance is the more singular, in that in the 9th verse of the same chapter the MT has *'Ĕlōhīm* and the Sam *YHWH*. Another class of instances which may be due to the same cause is the completion of a sentence by adding a clause or, it may be, dropping it from failure to observe it to be incomplete, as Gen **24** 45. If the MT be the original text, the Sam adds the clause "a little water from thy pitcher"; if the Sam, then the MT has dropped it.

(2) *Changes due to intention.*—(*a*) Grammatical: The variations from the MT most frequently met with in reading the Sam Pent are those necessary to conform the language to the rules of ordinary grammar. In this the Sam frequently coincides with the Ḳᵉrē of the MT. The Kᵉthībh of the MT has no distinction in gender between *hu'* in the 3d personal pronoun sing.—in both masc. and fem. it is *hū'*. The Sam with the Ḳᵉrē corrects this to *hī'*. So with *na'ar*, "a youth"—this is common in the Kᵉthībh, but in the Ḳᵉrē when a young woman is in question the fem. termination is added, and so the Sam writers also. It is a possible supposition that this characteristic of the Torah is late and due to blundering peculiar to the MS from which the Massoretes copied the Kᵉthībh. That it is systematic is against its being due to blunder, and as the latest Heb books maintain distinction of gender, we must regard this as an evidence of antiquity. This is confirmed by another set of variations between the Sam and the MT. There are, in the latter, traces of case-endings which have disappeared in later Heb. These are removed in the Sam. That case terminations have a tendency to disappear is to be seen in Eng. and Fr. The sign of the accusative, *'ēth*, frequently omitted in the MT, is generally supplied in Sam. A short form of the demonstrative pronoun pl. (*'ēl* instead of *'ēllāh*) is restricted to the Pent and 1 Ch **20** 8. The syntax of the cohortative is different in Sam from that in the Massoretic Heb. It is not to be assumed that the Jewish was the only correct or primitive use. There are cases where, with colloquial inexactitude, the MT has joined a pl. noun to a singular vb., and vice versa; these are corrected in Sam. Conjugations which in later Heb have a definite meaning in relation to the root, but are used in the MT of the Torah in quite other senses, are brought in the Sam Pent into harmony with later use. It ought in passing to be noted that these pentateuchal forms do not occur in the Prophets; even in Josh **2** 15 we have the fem. 3d personal pronoun; in Jgs **19** 3 we have *na'ărāh*.

(*b*) Logical: Sometimes the context or the circumstances implied have led to a change on one side or another. This may involve only the change of a word, as in Gen **2** 2, where the Sam has "sixth" instead of "seventh" (MT), in this agreeing with the LXX and Pesh, the Jewish scribe thinking the "sixth day" could only be reckoned ended when the "seventh" had begun. In Gen **4** 8, after the clause, "And Cain talked with [said to] Abel his brother," the Sam, LXX and Pesh add, "Let us go into the field." From the evidence of the VSS, from the natural meaning of the vb. *'āmar*, "to say," not "to speak," from the natural meaning also of the preposition *'el*, "to," not "with" (see Gesenius), it is clear that the MT has dropped the clause and that the Sam represents the true text. If this is not the case, it is a case of logical completion on the part of the Sam. Another instance is the addition to each name in the genealogy in Gen **11** 10–24 of the sum of the years of his life. In the case of the narrative of the plagues of Egypt a whole paragraph is added frequently. What has been commanded Moses and Aaron is repeated as history when they obey.

(*c*) Doctrinal: There are cases in which the text so suits the special views of the Samaritans concerning the sanctity of Gerizim that alteration of the original in that direction may be supposed to be the likeliest explanation. Thus there is inserted at Gen **20** 67 a passage from Dt **27** 2 slightly modified: Gerizim being put for Ebal, the object of the addition being to give the consecration of Gerizim the sanction of the Torah. Kennicott, however, defends the authenticity of this passage as against the MT. Insertion or omission appears to be the result of doctrinal predilection. In Nu **25** 4.5 the Sam harmonizes the command of Jeh with the action of Moses. The passage removed has a bloodthirsty Moloch-like look that might seem difficult to defend. On the other hand, the Jewish hatred of idolatry might express itself in the command to "take all the heads of the people and hang them up before the Lord against the sun," and so might be inserted. There are cases also where the language is altered for reasons of propriety. In these cases the Sam agrees with the Ḳᵉrē of the MT.

These variations are of unequal value as evidences of the relative date of the Sam recension of the Pent. The intentional are for this purpose of little value; they are evidence of the views prevalent in the northern and southern districts of Pal respectively. Only visual blunders are of real importance, and they point to a date about the days of Hezekiah as the time at which the two recensions began to diverge. One thing is obvious, that the Sam, at least as often as the MT, represents the primitive text.

2. Relation of Samaritan Recension to LXX

(1) *Statement of hypotheses.*—The frequency with which the points in which the Sam Pent differs from the MT agree with those in which the LXX also differs has exercised scholars. Castelli asserts that there are a thousand such instances. It may be noted that in one instance, at any rate, a passage in which the Sam and the LXX agree against the MT has the support of the NT. In Gal **3** 17, the apostle Paul, following the Sam and LXX against the MT, makes the "430 years" which terminated with the exodus begin with Abraham. As a rule the attention of Bib. scholars has been so directed to the resemblances between the Sam and the LXX that they have neglected the more numerous points of difference. So impressed have scholars been, esp. when Jews, by these resemblances that they have assumed that the one was dependent on the other. Frankel has maintained that the Sam was trᵈ from the LXX. Against this is the fact that in all their insulting remarks against them the Talmudists never assert that the "Cuthaeans" (Samaritans) got their Torah from the Greeks. Further, even if they only got the Law through Manasseh, the son-in-law of Sanballat, and even if he lived in the time of Alexander the Great, yet this was nearly half a century before the earliest date of the LXX. Again, while there are many evidences in the LXX that it has been trᵈ from Heb, there are none in the Sam that it has been trᵈ from Gr. The converse hypothesis is maintained by Dr. Kohn with all the emphasis of extended type. His hypothesis is that before the LXX was thought of a Gr tr was made from a Sam copy of the Law for the benefit of Samaritans resident in Egypt. The Jews made use of this at first, but when they found it wrong in many points, they purposed a new tr, but were so much influenced by that to which they were accustomed that it was only an improved edition of the Sam which resulted. But it is improbable that the Samaritans, who were few and who had comparatively little intercourse with Egypt, should precede the more numerous Jews with their huge colonies in Egypt, in making a Gr tr. It is further against the Jewish tradition as preserved to us by Jos. It is against the Sam tradition as learned by the present writer from the Sam high priest. According to him, the

Samaritans had no independent tr, beyond the fact that five of the LXX were Samaritan. Had there been any excuse for asserting that the Samaritans were the first translators, that would not have disappeared from their traditions.

(2) *Review of these hypotheses.*—The above unsatisfactory explanations result from deficient observation and unwarranted assumption. That there are many cases where the Sam variations from the MT are identical with those of the LXX is indubitable. It has, however, not been observed by those Jewish scholars that the cases in which the Sam alone or LXX alone, one or other, agrees with the MT against the other, are equally numerous. Besides, there are not a few cases in which all three differ. It ought to be observed that the cases in which the LXX differs from the MT are much more numerous than those in which the Sam differs from it. One has only to compare the Sam, LXX and MT of any half a dozen consecutive chapters in the Pent to prove this. Thus neither is dependent on the others. Further, there is the unwarranted assumption that the MT represents the primitive text of the Law. If the MT is compared with the VSS, it is found that the LXX, despite the misdirected efforts of Origen to harmonize it to the Palestinian text, differs in very many cases from the MT. Theodotion is nearer, but still differs in not a few cases. Jerome is nearer still, though even the text behind the Vulg is not identical with the MT. It follows that the MT is the result of a process which stopped somewhere about the end of the 5th cent. AD. The origin of the MT appears to have been somewhat the result of accident. A MS which had acquired a special sanctity as belonging to a famous rabbi is copied with fastidious accuracy, so that even its blunders are perpetuated. This supplies the Kethībh. Corrections are made from other MSS, and these form the Ḳerē. If our hypothesis as to the age of the Nāblûs roll is correct, it is older than the MT by more than half a millennium, and the MS from which the LXX was trd was nearly a couple of centuries older still. So far then from its being a reasonable assumption that the LXX and Sam differ from the MT only by blundering or wilful corruption on the part of the former, the converse is at least as probable. The conclusion then to which we are led is that of Kennicott (*State of Heb Text Diss.*, II, 164) that the Sam and LXX being independent, "each copy is invaluable—each copy demands our pious veneration and attentive study." It further ought to be observed that though Dr. Kohn points to certain cases where the difference between the MT and the LXX is due to confusion of letters only possible in Sam character, this does not prove the LXX to have been trd from a Sam MS, but that the MSS of the MT used by the LXX were written in that script. Kohn also exhibits the relation of the Sam to the Pesh. While the Pesh sometimes agrees with the Sam where it differs from the MT, more frequently it supports the MT against the Sam.

IV. Bearing on the Pentateuchal Question.—Jos (*Ant*, XI, viii, 2) makes Sanballat contemporary with Alexander the Great, and states that his son-in-law Manasseh came to Samaria and became the high priest. Although it is not said by Jos, it is assumed by critics that he brought the completed Torah with him. This Manasseh is according to Jos the grandson of Eliashib the high priest, the contemporary of Ezra and Nehemiah, and therefore contemporary with Artaxerxes Longimanus. Nehemiah (**13** 28) mentions, without naming him, a grandson of Eliashib, who was son-in-law of Sanballat, whom he chased from him. It is clear that Jos had dropped a century out of his history, and that the migration of Manasseh is to be placed not c 335 BC, but c 435 BC. Ezra is reputed to be, if not the author of the PC in the Pent, at all events its introducer to the Palestinians, and to have edited the whole, so that it assumed the form in which we now have it. But he was the contemporary of Manasseh, and had been, by his denunciation of foreign marriages, the cause of the banishment of Manasseh and his friends. Is it probable that he, Manasseh, would receive as Mosaic the enactments of Ezra, or convey them to Samaria? The date of the introduction of P, the latest portion of the Law, must accordingly be put considerably earlier than it is placed at present. We have seen that there are visual blunders that can be explained only on the assumption that the MS from which the mother Sam roll was copied was written in some variety of angular script. We have seen, further, that the peculiarities suit those of the Siloam inscription executed in the reign of Hezekiah, therefore approximately contemporary with the priest sent by Esarhaddon to Samaria to teach the people "the manner of the God of the land." As Amos and Hosea manifest a knowledge of the whole Pent before the captivity, it would seem that this "Book of the Law" that was "read [Am **4** 5 LXX] without," which would be the source from which the priest sent from Assyria taught as above "the manner of the God of the land," would contain all the portions—J, E, D, and P—of the Law. If so, it did not contain the Book of Josh; notwithstanding the honor they give the conqueror of Canaan, the Samaritans have not retained the book which relates his exploits. This is confirmed by the fact that the archaisms in the MT of the Pent are not found in Josh. It is singular, if the Prophets were before the Law, that in the Law there should be archaisms which are not found in the Prophets. From the way the Divine names are interchanged, as we saw, sometimes *'Ĕlōhīm* in the Sam represents *YHWH* in the MT, sometimes vice versa, it becomes obviously impossible to lay any stress on this. This conclusion is confirmed by the yet greater frequency with which this interchange occurs in the LXX. The result of investigation of the Sam Pent is to throw very considerable doubt on the validity of the critical opinions as to the date, origin and structure of the Pent.

V. Targums and Chronicle.—As above noted, there are two Tgs or interpretations of the Sam Pent, an Aramaic and an Arabic. The Aram. is a dialect related to the Western Aram., in which the Jewish Tgs were written, sometimes called Chaldee. It has in it many strange words, some of which may be due to the language of the Assyr colonists, but many are the result of blunders of copyists ignorant of the language. It is pretty close to the original and is little given to paraphrase. Much the same may be said of the Arab. Tg. It is usually attributed to Abu Said of the 13th cent., but according to Dr. Cowley only revised by him from the Tg of Abulhassan of the 11th cent. There is reference occasionally in the Fathers to a *Samaritikon* which has been taken to mean a Gr version. No indubitable quotations from it survive—what seem to be so being really trs of the text of the Sam recension. There is in Arab. a wordy chronicle called "The Book of Joshua." It has been edited by Juynboll. It may be dated in the 13th cent. More recently a "Book of Joshua" in Heb and written in Sam characters was alleged to be discovered. It is, however, a manifest forgery; the characters in which it is written are very late. It is partly borrowed from the canonical Josh, and partly from the older Sam Book of Joshua with fabulous additions. The Chronicle of Abulfatah is a tolerably accurate account of the history of the Samaritans after Alexander the Great to the 4th cent. AD.

Literature.—The text in the Sam script is found in the polyglots—Paris and London. Walton's text in the London *Polyglot* is transcribed in square characters by Blayney, Oxford, 1790. The Eng. works of importance of recent times are Mills, *Nablus and the Samaritans*, London, 1864; Nutt, *Fragments of a Sam Tg*, London, 1874; Montgomery, *The Samaritans*, Philadelphia, 1907 (this has a very full bibliography which includes articles in periodicals); Iverach Munro, *The Sam Pent and Modern Criticism*, 1911, London. In Germany, Gesenius' dissertation, *De Pentateuchi Samari-*

tani origine, etc, Jena, 1815, has not quite lost its value; Kohn, *De Pentateucho Samaritano*, Leipzig, 1865; Petermann, *Versuch einer hebr. Formenlehre nach der Aussprache der heutigen Samaritaner*, Leipzig, 1868. There are besides arts. on this in the various Bib. Dicts. and Encs. In the numerous religious and theological periodicals there have been arts. on the Sam Pent of varying worth. The Aram. Tg has been transcribed in square characters and edited by Brüll (Frankfort, 1875).

J. E. H. Thomson

PENTECOST, pen'tē-kost: As the name indicates (πεντηκοστή, *pentēkostē*), this second of the great Jewish national festivals was observed on the 50th day, or 7 weeks, from the Paschal Feast, and therefore in the OT it was called "the feast of weeks." It is but once mentioned in the historical books of the OT (2 Ch **8** 12.13), from which reference it is plain, however, that the people of Israel, in Solomon's day, were perfectly familiar with it: "offering according to the commandment of Moses, on the sabbaths, and on the new moons, and on the set feasts, three times in the year, even in the feast of unleavened bread, and in the feast of weeks, and in the feast of tabernacles." The requirements of the three great festivals were then well understood at this time, and their authority was founded in the Mosaic Law and unquestioned. The festival and its ritual were minutely described in this Law. Every male in Israel was on that day required to appear before the Lord at the sanctuary (Ex **34** 22.23). It was the first of the two agrarian festivals of Israel and signified the completion of the barley-harvest (Lev **23** 15.16; Dt **16** 9.10), which had begun at the time of the waving of the first ripe sheaf of the first-fruits (Lev **23** 11). Pentecost, or the Feast of Weeks, therefore fell on the 50th day after this occurrence. The wheat was then also nearly everywhere harvested (Ex **23** 16; **34** 22; Nu **28** 26), and the general character of the festival was that of a harvest-home celebration. The day was observed as a Sabbath day, all labor was suspended, and the people appeared before Jeh to express their gratitude (Lev **23** 21; Nu **28** 26). The central feature of the day was the presentation of two loaves of leavened, salted bread unto the Lord (Lev **23** 17.20; Ex **34** 22; Nu **28** 26; Dt **16** 10). The size of each loaf was fixed by law. It must contain the tenth of an ephah, about three quarts and a half, of the finest wheat flour of the new harvest (Lev **23** 17). Later Jewish writers are very minute in their description of the preparation of these two loaves (Jos, *Ant*, III, x, 6). According to the Mish (*Menāḥōth*, xi.4), the length of the loaf was 7 handbreadths, its width 4, its depth 7 fingers. Lev **23** 18 describes the additional sacrifices required on this occasion. It was a festival of good cheer, a day of joy. Free-will offerings were to be made to the Lord (Dt **16** 10), and it was to be marked by a liberal spirit toward the Levite, the stranger, and orphans and widows (Dt **16** 11.14). Perhaps the command against gleaning harvest-fields has a bearing on this custom (Lev **23** 22).

1. In the OT

The OT does not give it the historical significance which later Jewish writers have ascribed to it. The Israelites were admonished to remember their bondage on that day and to reconsecrate themselves to the Lord (Dt **16** 12), but it does not yet commemorate the giving of the Law at Sinai or the birth of the national existence, in the OT conception (Ex **19**). Philo, Jos, and the earlier Talm are all ignorant of this new meaning which was given to the day in later Jewish history. It originated with the great Jewish rabbi Maimonides and has been copied by Christian writers. And thus a view of the Jewish Pentecost has been originated, which is wholly foreign to the scope of the ancient institution.

2. In the NT

The old Jewish festival obtained a new significance, for the Christian church, by the promised outpouring of the Holy Spirit (Jn **16** 7.13). The incidents of that memorable day, in the history of Christianity, are told in a marvelously vivid and dramatic way in the Acts of the Apostles. The old rendering of *sumplēroústhai* (Acts **2** 1) by "was fully come" was taken by Lightfoot (*Hor. Heb.*) to signify that the Christian Pentecost did not coincide with the Jewish, just as Christ's last meal with His disciples was considered not to have coincided with the Jewish Passover, on Nisan 14. The bearing of the one on the other is obvious; they stand and fall together. RV translates the obnoxious word simply "was now come." Meyer, in his commentary on the Acts, treats this question at length. The tradition of the ancient church placed the first Christian Pentecost on a Sunday. According to John, the Passover that year occurred on Friday, Nisan 14 (**18** 28). But according to Mt, Mk and Lk, the Passover that year occurred on Thursday, Nisan 14, and hence Pentecost fell on Saturday. The Karaites explained the *shabbāth* of Lev **23** 15 as pointing to the Sabbath of the paschal week and therefore always celebrated Pentecost on Sunday. But it is very uncertain whether the custom existed in Christ's day, and moreover it would be impossible to prove that the disciples followed this custom, if it could be proved to have existed. Meyer follows the Johannic reckoning and openly states that the other evangelists made a mistake in their reckoning. No offhand decision is possible, and it is but candid to admit that here we are confronted with one of the knottiest problems in the harmonizing of the Gospels. See Chronology of the NT.

The occurrences of the first pentecostal day after the resurrection of Christ set it apart as a Christian festival and invested it, together with the commemoration of the resurrection, with a new meaning. We will not enter here upon a discussion of the significance of the events of the pentecostal day described in Acts **2**. That is discussed in the article under Tongues (q.v.). The Lutherans, in their endeavor to prove the inherent power of the Word, claim that "the effects then exhibited were due to the Divine power inherent in the words of Christ; and that they had resisted that power up to the day of Pentecost and then yielded to its influence." This is well described as "an incredible hypothesis" (Hodge, *Systematic Theol.*, III, 484). The Holy Spirit descended in answer to the explicit promise of the glorified Lord, and the disciples had been prayerfully waiting for its fulfilment (Acts **1** 4.14). The Spirit came upon them as "a power from on high." God the Holy Spirit proved on Pentecost His personal existence, and the intellects, the hearts, the lives of the apostles were on that day miraculously changed. By that day they were fitted for the arduous work that lay before them. There is some difference of opinion as to what is the significance of Pentecost for the church as an institution. The almost universal opinion among theologians and exegetes is this: that Pentecost marks *the founding of the Christian church as an institution.* This day is said to mark the dividing line between the ministry of the Lord and the ministry of the Spirit. The later Dutch theologians have advanced the idea that the origin of the church, as an institution, is to be found in the establishment of the apostolate, in the selection of the Twelve. Dr. A. Kuyper holds that the church as an institution was founded when the Master selected the Twelve, and that these men were "qualified for their calling by the power of the Holy Spirit." He distinguishes between the *institution* and the *constitution* of the church. Dr. H. Bavinck says: "Christ gathers a church about Himself, rules it directly so long as He is on the earth, and appoints twelve apostles who later on will be His witnesses. The institution of the apostolate is an esp. strong proof of the institutionary character which Christ gave to His church on the earth" (*Geref. Dogm.*, IV, 64).

Whatever we may think of this matter, the fact remains that Pentecost completely changed the apostles, and that the enduement with the Holy Spirit enabled them to become witnesses of the resurrection of Christ as the fundamental fact in historic Christianity, and to extend the church according to Christ's commandment. Jerome has an esp. elegant passage in which Pentecost is compared with the beginning of the Jewish national life on Mt. Sinai (*Ad Tabiol*, § 7): "There is Sinai, here Sion; there the trembling mountain, here the trembling house; there the flaming mountain, here the flaming tongues; there the noisy thunderings, here the sounds of many tongues; there the clangor of the ramshorn, here the notes of the gospel-trumpet." This vivid passage shows the close analogy between the Jewish and Christian Pentecost.

3. Later Christian Observance

In the post-apostolic Christian church Pentecost belonged to the so-called "Semestre Domini," as distinct from the "Semestre Ecclesiae," the church festivals properly so called. As yet there was no trace of Christmas, which began to appear about 360 AD. Easter, the beginning of the pentecostal period, closed the "Quadragesima," or "Lent," the entire period of which had been marked by self-denial and humiliation. On the contrary, the entire pentecostal period, the so-called "Quinquagesima," was marked by joyfulness, daily communion, absence of fasts, standing in prayer, etc. Ascension Day, the 40th day of the period, ushered in the climax of this joyfulness, which burst forth in its fullest volume on Pentecost. It was highly esteemed by the Fathers. Chrysostom calls it "the metropolis of the festivals" (*De Pentec.*, Hom. ii); Gregory of Nazianzen calls it "the day of the Spirit" (*De Pentec.*, Orat. 44). All the Fathers sound its praises. For they fully understood, with the church of the ages, that on that day the dispensation of the Spirit was begun, a dispensation of greater privileges and of a broader horizon and of greater power than had hitherto been vouchsafed to the church of the living God. The festival "Octaves," which, in accordance with the Jewish custom, devoted a whole week to the celebration of the festival, from the 8th cent., gave place to a two days' festival, a custom still preserved by the Roman church and such Protestant bodies as follow the ecclesiastical year. The habit of dressing in white and of seeking baptism on Pentecost gave it the name "Whitsunday," by which it is popularly known all over the world. HENRY E. DOSKER

PENUEL, pē-nū'el, pen'ū-el. See PENIEL.

PENURY, pen'ū-ri (מַחְסוֹר, *maḥṣōr*): In Prov **14** 23, with sense of "poverty," "want": "The talk of the lips tendeth only to penury." In the NT the word in Lk **21** 4 (ὑστέρημα, *hustérēma*) is in RV trd "want" (of the widow's mites).

PEOPLE, pē'p'l: In EV represents something over a dozen Heb and Gr words. Of these, in the OT, עַם, *'am*, is overwhelmingly the most common (some 2,000 t), with לְאוֹם, *le'ōm*, and גּוֹי, *gōy*, next in order; but the various Heb words are used with very little or no difference in force (e.g. Prov **14** 28; but, on the other hand, in Ps **44** contrast vs 12 and 14). Of the changes introduced by RV the only one of significance (cited explicitly in the Preface to ERV) is the frequent use of the pl. "peoples" (strangely avoided in AV except Rev **10** 11; **17** 15), where other nations than Israel are in question. So, for instance, in Ps **67** 4; Isa **55** 4; **60** 2, with the contrast marked in Ps **33** 10 and 12; Ps **77** 14 and 15, etc. In the NT, λάος, *láos*, is the most common word, with ὄχλος, *óchlos*, used almost as often in AV. But in RV the latter word is almost always rendered "multitude," "people" being retained only in Lk **7** 12; Acts **11** 24.26; **19** 26, and in the fixed phrase "the common people" (ὁ πολὺς ὄχλος, *ho polús óchlos*) in Mk **12** 37; Jn **12** 9.12 m (the retention of "people" would have been better in Jn **11** 42, also), with "crowd" (Mt **9** 23. 25; Acts **21** 35). The only special use of "people" that calls for attention is the phrase "people of the land." This may mean simply "inhabitants," as Ezk **12** 19; **33** 2; **39** 13; but in 2 K **11** 14, etc, and the parallel in 2 Ch, it means the people as contrasted with the king, while in Jer **1** 18, etc, and in Ezk **7** 27; **22** 29; **46** 3.9, it means the common people as distinguished from the priests and the aristocracy. A different usage is that for the heathen (Gen **23** 7.12.13; Nu **14** 9) or half-heathen (Ezr **9** 1.2; **10** 2.11; Neh **10** 28-31) inhabitants of Pal. From this last use, the phrase came to be applied by some rabbis to even pure-blooded Jews, if they neglected the observance of the rabbinic traditions (cf Jn **7** 49 AV). For "people of the East" see CHILDREN OF THE EAST.

BURTON SCOTT EASTON

PEOR, pē'or (הַפְּעוֹר, *ha-pe'ōr*; Φογώρ, *Phogṓr*):

(1) A mountain in the land of Moab, the last of the three heights to which Balaam was guided by Balak in order that he might curse Israel (Nu **23** 28). It is placed by *Onom* on the way between Livias and Heshbon, 7 Rom miles from the latter. Buhl would identify it with *Jebel el-Mashaḳḳar*, on which are the ruins of an old town, between *Wâdy A'yūn Mūsa* and *Wâdy Ḥesbān*.

(2) A town in the Judaean uplands added by LXX (Φαγώρ, *Phagṓr*) to the list in Josh **15** 9. It may be identical with *Khirbet Fāghūr* to the S. of Bethlehem.

(3) Peor, in Nu **25** 18; **31** 16; Josh **22** 17, is a Divine name standing for "Baal-peor."

(4) In Gen **36** 39, LXX reads *Phogōr* for "Pau" (MT), which in 1 Ch **1** 50 appears as "Pai."

W. EWING

PERAEA, pē-rē'a (ἡ Περαία, *hē Peraía*, Περαῖος, *Peraíos*, Περαΐτης, *Peraîtēs*): This is not a Scriptural name, but the term used by Jos to denote the district to which the rabbis habitually refer as "the land beyond Jordan." This corresponds to the NT phrase *péran toú Iordánou* (Mt **4** 15; **19** 1, etc). The boundaries of the province are given by Jos (*BJ*, III, iii, 3). In length it reached from Pella in the N. to Machaerus in the S., and in breadth from the Jordan on the W. to the desert on the E. We may take it that the southern boundary was the Arnon. The natural boundary on the N. would be the great gorge of the *Yarmūk*. Gadara, Jos tells us (*BJ*, IV, vii, 3, 6), was capital of the Peraea. But the famous city on the *Yarmūk* was a member of the Decapolis, and so could hardly take that position. More probably Jos referred to a city the ruins of which are found at *Jedūr*—a reminiscence of the ancient name—not far from *es-Salṭ*. The northern Gadara then holding the land on the southern bank of the *Yarmūk*, the northern boundary of the Peraea would run, as Jos says, from Pella eastward. For the description of the country thus indicated see GILEAD, 2.

1. The Country

In the time of the Maccabees the province was mainly gentile, and Judas found it necessary to remove to Judaea the scattered handful of Jews to secure their safety (1 Macc **5** 45). Possibly under

2. History Hyrcanus Jewish influence began to prevail; and before the death of Jannaeus the whole country owned his sway (*HJP*, I, i, 297, 306). At the death of Herod the Great it became part of the tetrarchy of Antipas (*Ant*, XVII, vii, 1). The tetrarch built a city on the site of the ancient Beth-haram (Josh **13** 27) and called it Julias in honor of the emperor's wife (*Ant*, XVIII, ii, 1; *BJ*, II, ix, 1). Here Simon made his abortive rising (*Ant*, XVII, x, 6; *BJ*, II, iv, 2). Claudius placed it under the government of Felix (*BJ*, II, xii, 8). It was finally added to the Rom dominions by Placidus (*BJ*, IV, vii, 3–6). Under the Moslems it became part of the province of Damascus.

Peraea, "the land beyond Jordan," ranked along with Judaea and Galilee as a province of the land of Israel. The people were under the same laws as regarded tithes, marriage and property.

Peraea lay between two gentile provinces on the E., as Samaria between two Jewish provinces on the W. of the Jordan. The fords below *Beisān* and opposite Jericho afforded communication with Galilee and Judaea respectively. Peraea thus formed a link connecting the Jewish provinces, so that the pilgrims from any part might go to Jerus and return without setting foot on gentile soil. And, what was at least of equal importance, they could avoid peril of hurt or indignity which the Samaritans loved to inflict on Jews passing through Samaria (Lk **9** 52f; *Ant*, XX, vi, 1; *Vita*, 52).

It seems probable that Jesus was baptized within the boundaries of the Peraea; and hither He came from the turmoil of Jerus at the Feast of the Dedication (Jn **10** 40). It was the scene of much quiet and profitable intercourse with His disciples (Mt **19**; Mk **10** 1–31; Lk **18** 15–30). These passages are by many thought to refer to the period after His retirement to Ephraim (Jn **11** 54). It was from Peraea that He was summoned by the sisters at Bethany (ver 3).

Peraea furnished in Niger one of the bravest men who fought against the Romans (*BJ*, II, xx, 4; IV, vi, 1). From Bethezob, a village of Peraea, came Mary, whose story is one of the most appalling among the terrible tales of the siege of Jerus (*BJ*, VI, iii, 4). Jos mentions Peraea for the last time (*BJ*, VI, v, 1), as echoing back the doleful groans and outcries that accompanied the destruction of Jerus. W. Ewing

PERAZIM, per'a-zim, pē-rā'zim, **MOUNT** (הַר־פְּרָצִים, *har-p^erāçīm*): "Jeh will rise up as in mount Perazim" (Isa **28** 21). It is usually considered to be identical with Baal-perazim (q.v.), where David obtained a victory over the Philis (2 S **5** 20; 1 Ch **14** 11).

PERDITION, pẽr-dish'un (ἀπώλεια, *apṓleia*, "ruin" or "loss," physical or eternal): The word "perdition" occurs in the Eng. Bible 8 t (Jn **17** 12; Phil **1** 28; 2 Thess **2** 3; 1 Tim **6** 9; He **10** 39; 2 Pet **3** 7; Rev **17** 11.18). In each of these cases it denotes the final state of ruin and punishment which forms the opposite to salvation. The vb. *apollúein*, from which the word is derived, has two meanings: (1) to lose; (2) to destroy. Both of these pass over to the noun, so that *apōleia* comes to signify: (1) loss; (2) ruin, destruction. The former occurs in Mt **26** 8; Mk **14** 4, the latter in the passages cited above. Both meanings had been adopted into the religious terminology of the Scriptures as early as the LXX. "To be lost" in the religious sense may mean "to be missing" and "to be ruined." The former meaning attaches to it in the teaching of Jesus, who compares the lost sinner to the missing coin, the missing sheep, and makes him the object of a seeking activity (Mt **10** 6; **15** 24; **18** 11; Lk **15** 4.6.8.24.32; **19** 10). "To be lost" here signifies to have become estranged from God, to miss realizing the relations which man normally sustains toward Him. It is equivalent to what is theologically called "spiritual death." This conception of "loss" enters also into the description of the eschatological fate of the sinner as assigned in the judgment (Lk **9** 24; **17** 33), which is a loss of life. The other meaning of "ruin" and "destruction" describes the same thing from a different point of view. *Apōleia* being the opposite of *sōtēria*, and *sōtēria* in its technical usage denoting the reclaiming from death unto life, *apōleia* also acquires the specific sense of such ruin and destruction as involves an eternal loss of life (Phil **1** 28; He **10** 39). Perdition in this latter sense is equivalent to what theology calls "eternal death." When in Rev **17** 8.11 it is predicated of "the beast," one of the forms of the world-power, this must be understood on the basis of the OT prophetic representation according to which the coming judgment deals with powers rather than persons.

The Son of Perdition is a name given to Judas (Jn **17** 12) and to the Antichrist (2 Thess **2** 3). This is the well-known Heb idiom by which a person typically embodying a certain trait or character or destiny is called the son of that thing. The name therefore represents Judas and the Antichrist (see Man of Sin) as most irrecoverably and completely devoted to the final *apōleia*. Geerhardus Vos

PERES, pē'rez. See Mene.

PERESH, pē'resh (פֶּרֶשׁ, *peresh*, "dung"): Son of Machir, grandson of Manasseh through his Aramitish concubine (1 Ch **7** 14.16).

PEREZ, pē'rez, **PHAREZ,** fā'rez (פֶּרֶץ, *pereç*, "breach"): One of the twins born to Judah by Tamar, Zerah's brother (Gen **38** 29.30). In AV Mt **1** 3 and Lk **3** 33, he is called "Phares," the name in 1 Esd **5** 5. He is "Pharez" in AV Gen **46** 12; Nu **26** 20.21; Ruth **4** 12.18; 1 Ch **2** 4.5; **4** 1; **9** 4. In AV and RV 1 Ch **27** 3; Neh **11** 4.6, he is "Perez." He is important through the fact that by way of Ruth and Boaz and so through Jesse and David his genealogy comes upward to the Saviour. The patronymic "Pharzite" occurs in Nu **26** 20 AV.

Perezites (Nu **26** 20, AV "Pharzites"). The patronymic of the name Perez.

Henry Wallace

PEREZ-UZZA, pē-rez-uz'za. See Uzza.

PERFECT, pûr'fekt, **PERFECTION,** pẽr-fek'-shun (שָׁלֵם, *shālēm*, תָּמִים, *tāmīm*; τέλειος, *téleios*, τελειότης, *teleiótēs*): "Perfect" in the

1. In the OT OT is the tr of *shālēm*, "finished," "whole," "complete," used (except in Dt **25** 15, "perfect weight") of persons, e.g. a "perfect heart," i.e. wholly or completely devoted to Jeh (1 K **8** 61, etc; 1 Ch **12** 38; Isa **38** 3, etc); *tāmīm*, "complete," "perfect," "sound or unblemished," is also used of persons and of God, His way, and law ("Noah was a just man and perfect," RVm "blameless" [Gen **6** 9]; "As for God, his way is perfect" [Ps **18** 30]; "The law of Jeh is perfect" [Ps **19** 7], etc); *tām*, with the same meaning, occurs only in Job, except twice in Pss (Job **1** 1.8; **2** 3, etc; Ps **37** 37; **64** 4); *kālīl*, "complete," and various other words are tr^d "perfect."

Perfection is the tr of various words so trd once only: *kālīl* (Lam **2** 15); *mikhlāl*, "completeness" (Ps **50** 2); *minleh*, "possession" (Job **15** 29, AV "neither shall he prolong the perfection thereof upon the earth," ARV "neither shall their possessions be extended on the earth," m "their produce bend to the earth"; ERV reverses this text and m); *tikhlāh*, "completeness," or "perfection" (Ps **119** 96); *takhlīth* (twice), "end," "completeness" (Job **11** 7, "Canst thou find out the Almighty unto perfection?" **28** 3, "searcheth out all perfection," AV, RV "to the furthest bound"; cf **26** 10, RV "unto the confines of light and darkness"); *tōm*, "perfect," "completeness" (Isa **47** 9, AV "They shall come upon thee in their perfection," RV "in their full measure"). RVm gives the meaning of "the Urim and the Thummim" (Ex **28** 30, etc) as "the Lights and the Perfections."

2. In the NT

In the NT "perfect" is usually the tr of *teleios*, primarily, "having reached the end," "term," "limit," hence "complete," "full," "perfect" (Mt **5** 48, "Ye therefore shall be perfect, as your heavenly Father is perfect"; Mt **19** 21, "if thou wouldst be perfect"; Eph **4** 13, AV "till we all come . . . . unto a perfect man," RV "full-grown"; Phil **3** 15, "as many as are perfect," ARVm "full-grown"; 1 Cor **2** 6; Col **1** 28, "perfect in Christ"; **4** 12; Jas **3** 2 m, etc).

Other words are *teleióō*, "to perfect," "to end," "complete" (Lk **13** 32, "The third day I am perfected," RVm "end my course"; Jn **17** 23, "perfected into one"; 2 Cor **12** 9; Phil **3** 12, RV "made perfect"; He **2** 10, etc); also *epiteléō*, "to bring through to an end" (2 Cor **7** 1, "perfecting holiness in the fear of God"; Gal **3** 3, "Are ye now made perfect by the flesh?" AV, RV "perfected in the flesh," m "Do ye now make an end in the flesh?"); *katartízō*, "to make quite ready," "to make complete," is trd "perfect," "to perfect" (Mt **21** 16, "perfected praise"; Lk **6** 40, "Every one when he is perfected shall be as his teacher"; 1 Cor **1** 10; 2 Cor **13** 11, "be perfected"; 1 Thess **3** 10; 1 Pet **5** 10, RVm "restore"); *akribôs*, "accurately," "diligently," is trd "perfect" (Lk **1** 3, "having had perfect understanding," RV "having traced . . . . accurately"; Acts **18** 26 AV, RV "more accurately"). We have also *ártios*, "fitted," "perfected" (2 Tim **3** 17, RV "complete"); *plēróō*, "to fill," "to make full" (Rev **3** 2, ARV "perfected," ERV "fulfilled"); *katartismós*, "complete adjustment," "perfecting" (Eph **4** 12, "for the perfecting of the saints").

Perfection is the tr of *katártisis*, "thorough adjustment," "fitness" (2 Cor **13** 9, RV "perfecting"); of *teleíōsis* (He **7** 11); of *teleiótēs* (He **6** 1, RVm "full growth"); it is trd "perfectness" (Col **3** 14); "perfection" in Lk **8** 14 is the tr of *telesphoréō*, "to bear on to completion or perfection." In Apoc "perfect," "perfection," etc, are for the most part the tr of words from *télos*, "the end," e.g. Wisd **4** 13; Ecclus **34** 8; **44** 17; **45** 8, *suntéleia*, "full end"; **24** 28; **50** 11.

RV has "perfect" for "upright" (2 S **22** 24.26 *bis*); for "sound" (Ps **119** 80); for "perform" (Phil **1** 6); for "undefiled" (Ps **119** 1, m "upright in way"); for "perfect peace, and at such a time" (Ezr **7** 12), "perfect and so forth"; for "He maketh my way perfect" (2 S **22** 33), "He guideth the perfect in his way," m "or, 'setteth free.' According to another reading, 'guideth my way in perfectness' "; "shall himself perfect," m "restore," for "make you perfect" (1 Pet **5** 10); "perfecter" for "finisher" (He **12** 2); "perfectly" is omitted in RV (Mt **14** 36); "set your hope perfectly on" for AV "hope to the end for" (1 Pet **1** 13).

3. The Christian Ideal

Perfection is the Christian ideal and aim, but inasmuch as that which God has set before us is infinite—"Ye therefore shall be perfect, as your heavenly Father is perfect" (Mt **5** 48)—absolute perfection must be forever beyond, not only any human, but any finite, being; it is a Divine ideal forever shining before us, calling us upward, and making endless progression possible. As noted above, the perfect man, in the OT phrase, was the man whose heart was truly or wholly devoted to God. Christian perfection must also have its seat in such a heart, but it implies the whole conduct and the whole man, conformed thereto as knowledge grows and opportunity arises, or might be found. There may be, of course, a *relative* perfection, e.g. of the child as a child compared with that of the man. The Christian ought to be continually moving onward toward perfection, looking to Him who is able to "make you perfect in every good thing [or work] to do his will, working in us that which is well-pleasing in his sight, through Jesus Christ; to whom be the glory for ever and ever. Amen" (He **13** 21).

W. L. WALKER

PERFORM, pẽr-fôrm′ (Fr. *parfournir*, "to furnish completely," "to complete," "finish entirely"): In modern Eng., through a mistaken connection with "form," "perform" usually suggests an act in its continuity, while the word properly should emphasize only the completion of the act. AV seems to have used the word in order to convey the proper sense (cf Rom **15** 28; 2 Cor **8** 11; Phil **1** 6, where RV has respectively "accomplish," "complete," "perfect"), but usually with so little justification in the Heb or Gr that "do" would have represented the original even better. RV has rarely changed the word in the OT, and such changes as have been made (Dt **23** 23; Est **1** 15, etc) seem based on no particular principle. In the NT the word has been kept only in Mt **5** 33 and Rom **4** 21, but in neither verse does the Gr accent the completion of the act, in the former case *apodídōmi*, lit. "to give back," in the latter *poiéō*, "to make," "to do," being used.

Performance is found in AV Sir **19** 20 (RV "doing"); 2 Macc **11** 17 (inserted needlessly and omitted by RV); Lk **1** 45 (RV "fulfilment"); 2 Cor **8** 11 (RV "completion").

BURTON SCOTT EASTON

PERFUME, pûr′fūm, pẽr-fūm′, **PERFUMER** (קְטֹרֶת, *ḳᵉṭōreth*, קָטַר, *ḳāṭar*, lit. "incense"): The ancients were fond of sweet perfumes of all kinds (Prov **27** 9), and that characteristic is still esp. true of the people of Bible lands. Perfumed oils were rubbed on the body and feet. At a feast in ancient Egypt a guest was anointed with scented oils, and a sweet-smelling water lily was placed in his hand or suspended on his forehead. In their religious worship the Egyptians were lavish with their incense. Small pellets of dried mixed spices and resins or resinous woods were burned in special censers. In the preparation of bodies for burial, perfumed oils and spices were used. Many Bib. references indicate the widespread use of perfumes. Cant **7** 8 suggests that the breath was purposely scented; clothing as well as the body was perfumed (Ps **45** 8; Cant **3** 6; **4** 11); couches and beds were sprinkled with savory scents (Prov **7** 17); ointments were used in the last rites in honor of the dead (2 Ch **16** 14; Lk **24** 1; Jn **19** 39). The writer has in his collection a lump of prepared spices and resins taken from a tomb dating from the 1st or 2d cent. AD, which was apparently fused and run into the thoracic cavity, since an impression of the ribs has been made on the perfume. Its odor is similar to that of the incense used today, and it perfumes the whole case where it is kept. The above collection also contains a small glass vial in which is a bronze spoon firmly held in some solidified ointment, probably formerly perfumed oil. Perfumes were commonly kept in sealed alabaster jars or cruses (Lk **7** 38). Thousands of these cruses have been unearthed in Pal and Syria.

Perfumes were mixed by persons skilled in the art. In AV these are called "apothecaries" (רַקָּח, *raḳḳāḥ*). The RV "perfumer" is probably a more correct rendering, as the one who did the compounding was not an apothecary in the same sense as is the person now so designated (Ex **30** 25.35; **37** 29; Eccl **10** 1).

Today incense is used in connection with all religious services of the oriental Christian churches. Although there is no direct mention of the uses of incense in the NT, such allusions as Paul's "a sacrifice to God for an odor of a sweet smell" (Eph **5** 2; Phil **4** 18) would seem to indicate that it was used by the early Christians.

The delight of the people of Syria in pleasant odors is recorded in their literature. The attar of roses (from Arab. *'itr*, "a sweet odor") was a well-known product of Damascus. The guest in a modern Syrian home is not literally anointed with oil, but he is often given, soon after he enters, a bunch of aromatic herbs or a sweet-smelling flower to hold and smell. During a considerable portion of the year the country air is laden with the odor of aromatic herbs, such as mint and sage. The Arab. phrase for taking a walk is *shemm el-hawa'*, lit. "smell the air." See INCENSE; OIL; OINTMENT.

JAMES A. PATCH

PERFUME-MAKING. See CRAFTS, II, 14.

PERGA, pûr′ga (**Πέργη**, *Pérgē*): An important city of the ancient province of Pamphylia, situated

1. Location and History

on the river Cestris, 12 miles N.E. of Attalia. According to Acts **13** 13, Paul, Barnabas and John Mark visited the place on their first missionary journey, and 2 years later, according to Acts **14** 24.25, they may have preached there. Though the water of the river Cestris has now been diverted to the fields for irrigating purposes, in ancient times the stream was navigable, and small boats from the sea might reach the city. It is uncertain how ancient Perga is; its walls, still standing, seem to come from the Seleucidan period or from the 3d cent. BC. It remained in the possession of the Seleucid kings until 189 BC, when Rom influence became strong in Asia Minor. A long series of coins, beginning in the 2d cent. BC, continued until 286 AD, and upon them Perga is mentioned as a metropolis. Though the city was never a stronghold of Christianity, it was the bishopric of Western Pamphylia, and several of the early Christians were martyred there. During the 8th cent. under Byzantine rule the city declined; in 1084 Attalia became the metropolis, and Perga rapidly fell to decay. While Attalia was the chief Gr and Christian city of Pamphylia, Perga was the seat of the local Asiatic goddess, who corresponded to Artemis or Diana of the Ephesians, and was locally known as Leto, or the queen of Perga. She is frequently represented on the coins as a huntress, with a bow in her hand, and with sphinxes or stags at her side.

The ruins of Perga are now called Murtana. The walls, which are flanked with towers, show the city

2. The Ruins

to have been quadrangular in shape. Very broad streets, running through the town, and intersecting each other, divided the city into quarters. The sides of the streets were covered with porticos, and along their centers were water channels in which a stream was always flowing. They were covered at short intervals by bridges. Upon the higher ground was the acropolis, where the earliest city was built, but in later times the city extended to the S. of the hill, where one may see the greater part of the ruins. On the acropolis is the platform of a large structure with fragments of several granite columns, probably representing the temple of the goddess Leto; others regard it as the ruin of an early church. At the base of the acropolis are the ruins of an immense theater which seated 13,000 people, the agora, the baths and the stadium. Without the walls many tombs are to be seen. E. J. BANKS

PERGAMOS, pûr′ga-mos, or **PERGAMUM**, pûr′ga-mum (**ἡ Πέργαμος**, *hē Pérgamos*, or **τὸ Πέργαμον**, *tó Pérgamon*): Pergamos, to which the ancient writers also gave the neuter form of the name, was a city of Mysia of the ancient Rom province of Asia, in the Caicus valley, 3 miles from the river, and about 15 miles from the sea. The

1. History

Caicus was navigable for small native craft. Two of the tributaries of the Caicus were the Selinus and the Kteios. The former of these rivers flowed through the city; the latter ran along its walls. On the hill between these two streams the first city stood, and there also stood the acropolis, the chief temples, and the theaters of the later city. The early people of the town were descendants of Gr colonists, and as early as 420 BC they struck coins of their own. Lysimachus, who possessed the town, deposited there 9,000 talents of gold. Upon his death, Philetaerus (283–263 BC) used this wealth to found the independent Gr dynasty of the Attalid kings. The first of this dynasty to bear the title of king was Attalus I (241–197 BC), a nephew of Philetaerus, and not only did he adorn the city with beautiful buildings until it became the most wonderful city of the East, but he added to his kingdom the countries of Mysia, Lydia, Caria, Pamphylia and Phrygia. Eumenes II (197–159 BC) was the most illustrious king of the dynasty, and during his reign the city reached its greatest height. Art and literature were encouraged, and in the city was a library of 200,000 volumes which later Antony gave to Cleopatra. The books were of parchment which was here first used; hence the word "parchment," which is derived from the name of the town P. Of the structures which adorned the city, the most renowned was the altar of Zeus, which was 40 ft. in height, and also one of the wonders of the ancient world. When in 133 BC Attalus III, the last king of the dynasty, died, he gave his kingdom to the Rom government. His son, Aristonicus, however, attempted to seize it for himself, but in 129 he was defeated, and the Rom province of Asia was formed, and P. was made its capital. The term Asia, as here employed, should not be confused with the continent of Asia, nor with Asia Minor. It applied simply to that part of Asia Minor which was then in the possession of the Romans, and formed into the province of which P. was the capital. Upon the establishment of the province of Asia there began a new series of coins struck at P., which continued into the 3d cent. AD. The magnificence of the city continued.

There were beautiful temples to the four great gods Zeus, Dionysus, Athena and Asklepios. To

2. Religions

the temple of the latter, invalids from all parts of Asia flocked, and there, while they were sleeping in the court, the god revealed to the priests and physicians by means of dreams the remedies which were necessary to heal their maladies. Thus opportunities of deception were numerous. There was a school of medicine in connection with the temple. P. was chiefly a religious center of the province. A title which it bore was "Thrice Neokoros," meaning that in the city 3 temples had been built to the Rom emperors, in which the emperors were worshipped as gods. Smyrna, a rival city, was a commercial center, and as it increased in wealth, it gradually became the political center. Later, when it became the capital, P. remained the religious center. As in many of the towns of Asia Minor, there were at P. many Jews, and in 130 BC the people of the city passed a decree in their favor. Many of the Jews were more or less assimilated with the Greeks, even to the extent of bearing Gr names.

Christianity reached P. early, for there one of the Seven Churches of the Book of Rev stood, and there, according to Rev **2** 13, Antipas was martyred; he was the first Christian to be put to death by the Rom state. The same passage speaks of P. as the place "where Satan's throne is," probably referring to the temples in which the Rom emperors were worshipped. During the Byzantine times P. still continued as a religious center, for there a bishop lived. However, the town fell into the hands of the Seljuks in 1304, and in 1336 it was taken by Suleiman, the son of Orkhan, and became Turkish.

3. Christianity

The modern name of the town, which is of considerable size, possessing 15 mosques, is *Bergama*, the Turkish corruption of the ancient name. One of its mosques is the early Byzantine church of St. Sophia. The modern town is built among the ruins of the ancient city, but is far less in extent. From 1879 to 1886 excavations among the ruins were conducted by Herr Humann at the expense of the German government. Among them are still to be seen the base of the altar of Zeus, the friezes of which are now in the Pergamon Museum, Berlin; the theater, the agora, the gymnasium and several temples. In ancient times the city was noted for its ointments, pottery and parchment; at present the chief articles of trade are cotton, wool, opium, valonia, and leather. E. J. Banks

PERIDA, pĕ-rī'da (פְּרִידָא, *p^erīdhā'*, "recluse"): A family of "Solomon's servants" (Neh **7** 57). In Ezr **2** 55, a difference in the Heb spelling gives "Peruda" for the same person, who is also the "Pharida" of 1 Esd **5** 33.

PERIZZITE, per'i-zīt, pe-riz'īt (פְּרִזִּי, *p^erizzī*; **Φερεζαῖος,** *Pherezaíos*): Signifies "a villager," and so corresponds with the Egyp *fellah*. Hence the Perizzite is not included among the sons of Canaan in Gen **10,** and is also coupled with the Canaanite (Gen **13** 7; **34** 30; Jgs **1** 4). We hear, accordingly, of Canaanites and Perizzites at Shechem (Gen **34** 30), at Bezek in Judah (Jgs **1** 4) and, according to the reading of LXX, at Gezer (Josh **16** 10). In Dt **3** 5 and 1 S **6** 18, where AV has "unwalled towns" and "country villages," LXX has "Perizzite," the lit. tr of the Heb being "cities of the Perizzite" or "villager" and "village of the Perizzite." The same expression occurs in Est **9** 19, where it is used of the Jews in Elam. In Josh **17** 15.18, where the Manassites are instructed to take possession of the forest land of Carmel, "Perizzites and Rephaim" are given as the equivalent of "Canaanite." A. H. Sayce

PERJURY, pûr'jū-ri. See Crimes; Oath; Punishments.

PERPETUAL, pĕr-pet'ū-al, **PERPETUALLY,** pĕr-pet'ū-al-i, **PERPETUITY,** pûr-pĕ-tū'i-ti (עוֹלָם, *'ōlām*, נֵצַח, *neçaḥ*, תָּמִיד, *tāmīdh*):

Perpetual is usually the tr of *'ōlām*, properly, "a wrapping up" or "hiding," used often of time indefinitely long, and of eternity when applied to God; hence we have, "for perpetual generations" (Gen **9** 12); "the priesthood by a perpetual statute" (Ex **29** 9; cf **31** 16; Lev **3** 17; **24** 9, etc); "placed the sand for the bound of the sea, by a perpetual decree, that it cannot pass it" (Jer **5** 22, RVm "an everlasting ordinance which it cannot pass"); "sleep a perpetual sleep" (Jer **51** 39.57); "Moab shall be . . . . a perpetual desolation" (Zeph **2** 9), etc; *neçaḥ*, "preëminence," "perpetuity," "eternity" (often tr[d] "for ever," Ps **9** 6), is tr[d] "perpetual" (Ps **74** 3; Jer **15** 18); *nāçaḥ* (part.) (Jer **8** 5); *tāmīdh*, "continuance," generally rendered "continually," but sometimes "perpetual" or "perpetually" (Ex **30** 8; Lev **6** 20).

Perpetually is the rendering of *'adh*, properly "progress," "duration," hence long or indefinite time, eternity (usually in AV rendered "for ever"), in Am **1** 11, "His anger did tear perpetually"; and of *kōl ha-yāmīm*, "all the days" (1 K **9** 3; 2 Ch **7** 16, "my heart shall be there perpetually"; cf Mt **28** 20, *pásas tás hēméras*, lit. "all the days").

Perpetuity occurs in RV of Lev **25** 23.30, "The land shall not be sold in perpetuity," "The house . . . . shall be made sure in perpetuity."

Perpetual is frequent in Apoc, most often as the tr of *aiṓnios* and kindred words, e.g. Jth **13** 20, "a perpetual praise"; Wisd **10** 14, "perpetual glory," RV "eternal"; Ecclus **11** 33, "a perpetual blot," RV "blame for ever"; 1 Macc **6** 44, "a perpetual name," RV "everlasting"; *aénaos*, "ever-flowing," occurs in Wisd **11** 6 (so RV); *endelechḗs*, "constant" (Ecclus **41** 6, "perpetual reproach").

For "perpetual" (Jer **50** 5; Hab **3** 6) RV has "everlasting"; for "the old hatred" (Ezk **25** 15), "perpetual enmity"; for "perpetual desolation" (Jer **25** 12), "desolate for ever," m "Heb 'everlasting desolations.'" W. L. Walker

PERSECUTION, pûr-sĕ-kū'shun (**διωγμός,** *diōgmós* [Mt **13** 21; Mk **4** 17; **10** 30; Acts **8** 1; **13** 50; Rom **8** 35; 2 Cor **12** 10; 2 Thess **1** 4; 2 Tim **3** 11]):

The importance of this subject may be indicated by the fact of the frequency of its occurrence, both in the OT and NT, where in AV the words "persecute," "persecuted," "persecuting" are found no fewer than 53 t, "persecution" 14 t, and "persecutor" 9 t.

It must not be thought that persecution existed only in NT times. In the days of the OT it existed too. In what Jesus said to the Pharisees, He specially referred to the innocent blood which had been shed in those times, and told them that they were showing themselves heirs—to use a legal phrase—to their fathers who had persecuted the righteous, "from the blood of Abel the righteous unto the blood of Zachariah" (Mt **23** 35).

1. Persecution in OT Times

In the period between the close of the OT and the coming of Christ, there was much and protracted suffering endured by the Jews, because of their refusal to embrace idolatry, and of their fidelity to the Mosaic Law and the worship of God. During that time there were many patriots who were true martyrs, and those heroes of faith, the Maccabees, were among those who "know their God . . . . and do exploits" (Dnl **11** 32). 'We have no need of human help,' said Jonathan the Jewish high priest, 'having for our comfort the sacred Scriptures which are in our hands' (1 Macc **12** 9).

2. Between the Testaments

In the Ep. to the He, persecution in the days of the OT is summed up in these words: "Others had trial of mockings and scourgings, yea, moreover of bonds and imprisonment: they were stoned, they were sawn asunder, they were tempted, they were slain with the sword: they went about in sheepskins, in goatskins; being destitute, afflicted, ill-treated (of whom the world was not worthy)" (He **11** 36–38).

3. Foretold by Christ

Coming now to NT times, persecution was frequently foretold by Christ, as certain to come to those who were His true disciples and followers. He forewarned them again and again that it was inevitable. He said that He Himself must suffer it (Mt **16** 21; **17** 22.23; Mk **8** 31).

4. A Test of Discipleship

It would be a test of true discipleship. In the parable of the Sower, He mentions this as one of the causes of defection among those who are Christians in outward appearance only. When affliction or persecution ariseth for the word's sake, immediately the stony-ground hearers are offended (Mk **4** 17).

5. A Means of Blessing

It would be a sure means of gaining a blessing, whenever it came to His loyal followers when they were in the way of well-doing; and He thus speaks of it in two of the Beatitudes, "Blessed are they that have been persecuted for righteousness' sake: for theirs is the kingdom of heaven"; "Blessed are ye when men shall reproach you, and persecute you . . . . for my sake" (Mt **5** 10.11; see also ver 12).

6. Various Forms

It would take different forms, ranging through every possible variety, from false accusation to the infliction of death, beyond which, He pointed out (Mt **10** 28; Lk **12** 4), persecutors are unable to go. The methods of persecution which were employed by the Jews, and also by the heathen against the followers of Christ, were such as these: (1) Men would revile them and would say all manner of evil against them falsely, for Christ's sake (Mt **5** 11). (2) Contempt and disparagement: "Say we not well that thou art a Samaritan, and hast a demon?" (Jn **8** 48); "If they have called the master of the house Beelzebub, how much more them of his household!" (Mt **10** 25). (3) Being, solely on account of their loyalty to Christ, forcibly separated from the company and the society of others, and expelled from the synagogues or other assemblies for the worship of God: "Blessed are ye, when men shall hate you, and when they shall separate you from their company, and reproach you, and cast out your name as evil, for the Son of man's sake" (Lk **6** 22); "They shall put you out of the synagogues" (Jn **16** 2). (4) Illegal arrest and spoliation of goods, and death itself.

All these various methods, used by the persecutor, were foretold, and all came to pass. It was the fear of apprehension and death that led the eleven disciples to forsake Jesus in Gethsemane and to flee for their lives. Jesus often forewarned them of the severity of the persecution which they would need to encounter if they were loyal to Him: "The hour cometh, that whosoever killeth you shall think that he offereth service unto God" (Jn **16** 2); "I send unto you prophets . . . . some of them shall ye kill and crucify; and some of them shall ye scourge in your synagogues, and persecute from city to city" (Mt **23** 34).

7. In the Case of Jesus

In the case of Christ Himself, persecution took the form of attempts to entrap Him in His speech (Mt **22** 15); the questioning of His authority (Mk **11** 28); illegal arrest; the heaping of every insult upon Him as a prisoner; false accusation; and a violent and most cruel death.

8. Instigated by the Jews

After Our Lord's resurrection the first attacks against His disciples came from the high priest and his party. The high-priesthood was then in the hands of the Sadducees, and one reason which moved them to take action of this kind was their 'sore trouble,' because the apostles "proclaimed in Jesus the resurrection from the dead" (Acts **4** 2; **5** 17). The gospel based upon the resurrection of Christ was evidence of the untruth of the chief doctrines held by the Sadducees, for they held that there is no resurrection. But instead of yielding to the evidence of the fact that the resurrection had taken place, they opposed and denied it, and persecuted His disciples. For a time the Pharisees were more moderate in their attitude toward the Christian faith, as is shown in the case of Gamaliel (Acts **5** 34); and on one occasion they were willing even to defend the apostle Paul (Acts **23** 9) on the doctrine of the resurrection. But gradually the whole of the Jewish people became bitter persecutors of the Christians. Thus in the earliest of the Pauline Epp., it is said, "Ye also suffered the same things of your own countrymen, even as they [in Judaea] did of the Jews; who both killed the Lord Jesus and the prophets, and drove out us, and please not God, and are contrary to all men" (1 Thess **2** 14.15).

9. Stephen

Serious persecution of the Christian church began with the case of Stephen (Acts **7** 1–60); and his lawless execution was followed by "a great persecution" directed against the Christians in Jerus. This "great persecution" (Acts **8** 1) scattered the members of the church, who fled in order to avoid bonds and imprisonment and death. At this time Saul signalized himself by his great activity, persecuting "this Way unto the death, binding and delivering into prisons both men and women" (Acts **22** 4).

10. The Apostles James and Peter

By and by one of the apostles was put to death—the first to suffer of "the glorious company of the apostles"—James the brother of John, who was slain with the sword by Herod Agrippa (Acts **12** 2). Peter also was imprisoned, and was delivered only by an angel (**12** 7–11).

11. Gentile Persecution

During the period covered by the Acts there was not much purely gentile persecution: at that time the persecution suffered by the Christian church was chiefly Jewish. There were, however, great dangers and risks encountered by the apostles and by all who proclaimed the gospel then. Thus, at Philippi, Paul and Silas were most cruelly persecuted (Acts **16** 19–40); and, even before that time, Paul and Barnabas had suffered much at Iconium and at Lystra (Acts **14** 5.19). On the whole the Rom authorities were not actively hostile during the greater part of Paul's lifetime. Gallio, for instance, the deputy of Achaia, declined to go into the charge brought by the Jews at Corinth against Paul (Acts **18** 14.15.16). And when Paul had pleaded in his own defence before King Herod Agrippa and the Rom governor Festus, these two judges were agreed in the opinion, "This man doeth nothing worthy of death or of bonds" (Acts **26** 31). Indeed it is evident (see Ramsay, *St. Paul the Traveller and the Rom Citizen*, 308) that the purpose of Paul's trial being recorded at length in the Acts is to establish the fact that the preaching of the gospel was not forbidden by the laws of the Rom empire, but that Christianity was a *religio licita*, a lawful religion.

Christianity, at first, not a forbidden religion.—This legality of the Christian faith was illustrated and enforced by the fact that when Paul's case was heard and decided by the supreme court of appeal at Rome, he was set free and resumed his missionary labors, as these are recorded or referred to in the Pastoral Epp. "One thing, however, is clear from a comparison of Phil with 2 Tim. There had been in the interval a complete change in the policy toward Christianity of the Rom government. This change was due to the great fire of Rome (July, 64). As part of the persecution which then broke out, orders were given for the imprisonment of the Christian leaders. Poppaea, Tigellinus and their Jewish friends were not likely to forget the prisoner of two years before. At the time St. Paul was away from Rome, but steps were instantly taken for his arrest. The apostle was brought back to the city in the autumn or winter of 64. . . . . That he had a trial at all, instead of the summary punishment of his brethren, witnesses to the importance attached by the government to a show of legality in the persecution of the leader" (Workman, *Persecution in the Early Church*, 38). See PASTORAL EPISTLES; PAUL THE APOSTLE.

12. The Neronic Persecution

The legal decisions which were favorable to the Christian faith were soon overturned on the occasion of the great fire in Rome, which occurred in July, 64. The public feeling of resentment broke out against the emperor to such a degree that, to avoid the stigma, just or unjust, of being himself guilty of setting the city on fire, he made the Christians the scapegoats which he thought he needed. Tacitus (*Annals* xv.44) relates all that occurred at that time, and what he says is most interesting, as being one of the very earliest notices found in any profane author, both of the Christian faith, and of Christ Himself.

(1) *Testimony of Tacitus.*—What Tacitus says is that nothing that Nero could do, either in the way of gifts to the populace or in that of sacrifice to the Rom deities, could make the people believe that he was innocent of causing the great fire which had consumed their dwellings. Hence to relieve himself of this infamy he falsely accused the Christians of being guilty of the crime of setting the city on fire. Tacitus uses the strange expression "the persons commonly called Christians who were hated for their enormities." This is an instance of the saying of all manner of evil against them falsely, for Christ's sake. The Christians, whose lives were pure and virtuous and beneficent, were spoken of as being the offscouring of the earth.

(2) *References in 1 Pet.*—The First Ep. of Peter is one of the parts of the NT which seem to make direct reference to the Neronic persecution, and he uses words (1 Pet **4** 12 ff) which may be compared with the narrative of Tacitus: "Beloved, think it not strange concerning the fiery trial among you, which cometh upon you to prove you, as though a strange thing happened unto you: but insomuch as ye are partakers of Christ's sufferings, rejoice. . . . . If ye are reproached for the name of Christ, blessed are ye; because the Spirit of glory and the Spirit of God resteth upon you. For let none of you suffer as a murderer, or a thief, or an evil-doer, or as a meddler in other men's matters: but if a man suffer as a Christian, let him not be ashamed; but let him glorify God in this name. For the time is come for judgment to begin at the house of God. . . . . Wherefore let them also that suffer according to the will of God commit their souls in well-doing unto a faithful Creator."

(3) *Tacitus' narrative.*—How altogether apposite and suitable was this comforting exhortation to the case of those who suffered in the Neronic persecution. The description which Tacitus gives is as follows: "Christus, the founder of that name, was put to death as a criminal by Pontius Pilate, procurator in the reign of Tiberius. But the pernicious superstition, repressed for a time, broke out again not only through Judaea, where the mischief originated, but through the city of Rome also, whither all things horrible and disgraceful flow from all quarters as to a common sink, and where they are encouraged. Accordingly, first, those were seized who confessed they were Christians; next, on their information, a vast multitude were convicted, not so much on the charge of setting the city on fire, as of hating the human race. And in their deaths they were made the subject of sport, for they were covered with the skins of wild beasts and were worried to death by dogs, or nailed to crosses, or set fire to, and when day declined were burned to serve for nocturnal lights. Nero offered his own gardens for that spectacle, and exhibited circus games, indiscriminately mingling with the common people dressed as a charioteer, or else standing in his chariot. Whence a feeling of compassion arose toward the sufferers, though guilty and deserving to be made examples of by capital punishment, because they seemed not to be cut off for the public good, but to be victims to the ferocity of one man." See NERO.

(4) *NT references.*—Three of the books of the NT bear the marks of that most cruel persecution under Nero, the Second Ep. to Timothy, the First Ep. of Peter—already referred to—and the Rev of John. In 2 Tim, Paul speaks of his impending condemnation to death, and the terror inspired by the persecution causes "all" to forsake him when he is brought to public trial (2 Tim **4** 16).

The "fiery trial" is spoken of in 1 Pet, and Christians are exhorted to maintain their faith with patience; they are pleaded with to have their "conversation honest" (1 Pet **2** 12 AV), so that all accusations directed against them may be seen to be untrue, and their sufferings shall then be, not for ill-doing, but only for the name of Christ (**3** 14.16). "This important ep. proves a general persecution (**1** 6; **4** 12.16) in Asia Minor N. of the Taurus (**1** 1; note esp. Bithynia) and elsewhere (**5** 9). The Christians suffer 'for the name,' but not the name alone (**4** 14). They are the objects of vile slanders (**2** 12.15; **3** 14–16; **4** 4.15), as well as of considerable zeal on the part of officials (**5** 8 [Gr **3** 15]). As regards the slanders, the Christians should be circumspect (**2** 15.16; **3** 16.17; **4** 15). The persecution will be short, for the end of all things is at hand (**4** 7.13; **5** 4)" (Workman, *Persecution in the Early Church*, 354).

13. Persecution in Asia

In Rev the apostle John is in "Patmos, for the word of God and the testimony of Jesus" (Rev **1** 9). Persecution has broken out among the Christians in the province of Asia. At Smyrna, there is suffering, imprisonment and prolonged tribulation; but the sufferers are cheered when they are told that if they are faithful unto death, Christ will give them the crown of life (Rev **2** 10). At Pergamum, persecution has already resulted in Antipas, Christ's faithful martyr, being slain (**2** 13). At Ephesus and at Thyatira the Christians are commended for their patience, evidently indicating that there had been persecution (**2** 2.19). At Philadelphia there has been the attempt made to cause the members of the church to deny Christ's name (**3** 8); their patience is also commended, and the hour of temptation is spoken of, which comes to try all the world, but from which Christ promised to keep the faithful Christians in Philadelphia. Strangely enough, there is no distinct mention of persecution having taken place in Sardis or in Laodicea.

14. Rome as Persecutor

As the book proceeds, evidences of persecution are multiplied. In **6** 9, the apostle sees under the altar the souls of them that were slain for the word of God and for the testimony which they held; and those souls are bidden to rest yet for a little season "until their fellow-servants also and their brethren, who should be killed even as they were, should have fulfilled their course" (**6** 11). The meaning is that there is not yet to be an end of suffering for Christ's sake; persecution may continue to be as severe as ever. Cf **20** 4, "I saw the souls of them that had been beheaded for the testimony of Jesus, and for the word of God, and such as worshipped not the beast," for the persecution had raged against all classes indiscriminately, and Rom citizens who were true to Christ had suffered unto death. It is to these that reference is made in the words "had been beheaded," decapitation being reserved as the most honorable form of execution, for Rom citizens only. So terrible does the persecution of Christians by the imperial authorities become, that Rome is "drunken with the blood of the saints, and with the blood of the martyrs of Jesus" (**17** 6; **16** 6; see also **18** 24; **19** 2).

Paul's martyrdom is implied in 2 Tim, throughout the whole ep., and esp. in **4** 6.7.8. The martyrdom of Peter is also implied in Jn **21** 18.19, and in

2 Pet **1** 14. The abiding impression made by these times of persecution upon the mind of the apostle John is also seen in the defiance of the world found throughout his First Ep. (**2** 17; **5** 19), and in the rejoicing over the fall of Babylon, the great persecuting power, as that fall is described in such passages as Rev **14** 8; **15** 2.3; **17** 14; **18** 24.

Following immediately upon the close of the NT, there is another remarkable witness to the continuance of the Rom persecution against the Christian church. This is Pliny, proconsul of Bithynia.

15. Testimony of Pliny, 112 AD

In 111 or 112 AD, he writes to the emperor Trajan a letter in which he describes the growth of the Christian faith. He goes on to say that "many of all ages and of all ranks and even of both sexes are being called into danger, and will continue to be so. In fact the contagion of this superstition is not confined to the cities only, but has spread to the villages and country districts." He proceeds to narrate how the heathen temples had been deserted and the religious rites had been abandoned for so long a time: even the sacrificial food—that is, the flesh of the sacrificial victims—could scarcely find a purchaser.

But Pliny had endeavored to stem the tide of the advancing Christian faith, and he tells the emperor how he had succeeded in bringing back to the heathen worship many professing Christians. That is to say, he had used persecuting measures, and had succeeded in forcing some of the Christians to abandon their faith. He tells the methods he had used. "The method I have observed toward those who have been brought before me as Christians is this. I asked them whether they were Christians. If they admitted it, I repeated the question a second and a third time, and threatened them with punishment. If they persisted I ordered them to be punished. For I did not doubt, whatever the nature of that which they confessed might be, that a contumacious and inflexible obstinacy ought to be punished. There were others also, possessed with the same infatuation, whom, because they were Rom citizens, I ordered to be sent to Rome. But this crime spreading, as is usually the case, while it was actually under legal prosecution, several cases occurred. An anonymous information was laid before me, containing the names of many persons. Those who denied that they were Christians, or that they had ever been so, repeated after me an invocation of the gods, and offered prayer, with wine and incense, to your statue, which I had ordered to be brought in for this very purpose, along with the statues of the gods, and they even reviled the name of Christ; whereas there is no forcing, it is said, those who are really Christians into any of these compliances: I thought it proper to discharge them. Others who were accused by a witness at first confessed themselves Christians, but afterward denied it. Some owned indeed that they had been Christians formerly, but had now, some for several years, and a few above 20 years ago, renounced it. They all worshipped your statue and the images of the gods. . . . . I forbade the meeting of any assemblies, and therefore I judged it to be so much the more necessary to endeavor to extort the real truth by putting to the torture two female slaves, who were called deaconesses, yet I found nothing but an absurd and extravagant superstition."

In Trajan's reply to Pliny he writes, "They [the Christians] ought not to be searched for. If they are brought before you and convicted, they should be punished, but this should be done in such a way, that he who denies that he is a Christian, and when his statement is proved by his invoking our deities, such a person, although suspected for past conduct, must nevertheless be forgiven, because of his repentance."

These letters of Pliny and Trajan treat state-persecution as the standing procedure—and this not a generation after the death of the apostle John. The sufferings and tribulation predicted in Rev **2** 10, and in many other passages, had indeed come to pass. Some of the Christians had denied the name of Christ and had worshipped the images of the emperor and of the idols, but multitudes of them had been faithful unto death, and had received the martyr's crown of life.

16. 2d and 3d Centuries

Speaking generally, persecution of greater or less severity was the normal method employed by the Rom empire against the Christian church during the 2d and the 3d cents. It may be said to have come to an end only about the end of the 3d or the beginning of the 4th cent., when the empire became nominally Christian. When the apostolic period is left, persecution becomes almost the normal state in which the church is found. And persecution, instead of abolishing the name of Christ, as the persecutors vainly imagined they had succeeded in doing, became the means of the growth of the Christian church and of its purity. Both of these important ends, and others too, were secured by the severity of the means employed by the persecuting power of the Rom empire.

Under Trajan's successor, the emperor Hadrian, the lot of the Christians was full of uncertainty: persecution might break out at any moment. At the best Hadrian's régime was only that of unauthorized toleration.

17. Best Emperors the Most Cruel Persecutors

With the exception of such instances as those of Nero and Domitian, there is the surprising fact to notice, that it was not the worst emperors, but the best, who became the most violent persecutors. One reason probably was that the ability of those emperors led them to see that the religion of Christ is really a divisive factor in any kingdom in which civil government and pagan religion are indissolubly bound up together. The more that such a ruler was intent on preserving the unity of the empire, the more would he persecute the Christian faith. Hence among the rulers who were persecutors, there are the names of Antoninus Pius, Marcus Aurelius the philosopher-emperor, and Septimius Severus (died at York, 211 AD).

18. Causes of Persecution

Persecution was no accident, which chanced to happen, but which might not have occurred at all. It was the necessary consequence of the principles embodied in the heathen Rom government, when these came into contact and into conflict with the essential principles of the Christian faith. The reasons for the persecution of the Christian church by the Rom empire were (1) political; (2) on account of the claim which the Christian faith makes, and which it cannot help making, to the exclusive allegiance of the heart and of the life. That loyalty to Christ which the martyrs displayed was believed by the authorities in the state to be incompatible with the duties of a Rom citizen. Patriotism demanded that every citizen should unite in the worship of the emperor, but Christians refused to take part in this worship on any terms, and so they continually lived under the shadow of a great hatred, which always slumbered, and might break out at any time. The claim which the Christian faith made to the absolute and exclusive loyalty of all who obeyed Christ was such that it admitted of no compromise with heathenism. To receive Christ into the pantheon as another divinity, as one of several—this was not the Christian faith. To every loyal follower of Christ compromise with other faiths was an impossibility. An accommodated Christianity would itself have been false to the only true God and Jesus Christ whom He had sent, and would never have conquered the world. To the heathen there were lords many and gods many, but to the Christians there was but one God the Father and one Lord Jesus Christ, the Saviour of the world (1 Cor **8** 5.6). The essential absoluteness of the Christian faith was its strength, but this was also the cause of its being hated.

"By a correct instinct paganisms of all sorts discerned in the infant church their only rival. So, while the new Hercules was yet in the cradle, they sent their snakes to kill him. But Hercules lived to cleanse out the Augean stables" (Workman, op. cit., 88).

"For 200 years, to become a Christian meant the great renunciation, the joining a despised and persecuted sect, the swimming against the tide of popular prejudice, the coming under the ban of the Empire, the possibility at any moment of imprisonment and death under its most fearful forms. For 200 years he that would follow Christ must count the cost, and be prepared to pay the same with his liberty and life. For 200 years the mere profession of Christianity was itself a crime. *Christianus sum* was almost the one plea for which there was no forgiveness, in itself all that was necessary as a 'title' on the back of the condemned. He who made it was allowed neither to present apology, nor call in the aid of a pleader. 'Public hatred,' writes Tertullian, 'asks but one thing, and that not investigation into the crimes charged, but simply the confession of the Christian name.' For the name itself in periods of stress, not a few, meant the rack, the blazing shirt of pitch, the lion, the panther, or in the case of maidens an infamy worse than death" (Workman, 103).

19. 200 Years of Persecution

Service in the Rom army involved, for a Christian, increasing danger in the midst of an organized and aggressive heathenism. Hence arose the persecution of the Christian soldier who refused compliance with the idolatrous ceremonies in which the army engaged, whether those ceremonies were concerned with the worship of the Rom deities or with that of Mithraism. "The invincible saviour," as Mithra was called, had become, at the time when Tertullian and Origen wrote, the special deity of soldiers. Shrines in honor of Mithra were erected through the entire breadth of the Rom empire, from Dacia and Pannonia to the Cheviot Hills in Britain. And woe to the soldier who refused compliance with the religious sacrifices to which the legions gave their adhesion! The Christians in the Rom legions formed no inconsiderable proportion of "the noble army of martyrs," it being easier for the persecuting authorities to detect a Christian in the ranks of the army than elsewhere.

20. Persecution in the Army

In the 2d and 3d cents. Christians were to be found everywhere, for Tertullian, in an oftentimes quoted passage in his *Apology*, writes, "We live beside you in the world, making use of the same forum, market, bath, shop, inn, and all other places of trade. We sail with you, fight shoulder to shoulder, till the soil, and traffic with you"; yet the very existence of Christian faith, and its profession, continued to bring the greatest risks. "With the best will in the world, they remained a peculiar people, who must be prepared at any moment to meet the storm of hatred" (Workman, 189). For them it remained true that in one way or another, hatred on the part of the world inevitably fell to the lot of those who walked in the footsteps of the Master; "All that would live godly in Christ Jesus shall suffer persecution" (2 Tim **3** 12).

21. Tertullian's *Apology*

The strange title, "the third race," probably invented by the heathen, but willingly accepted by the Christians without demur, showed with what a bitter spirit the heathen regarded the faith of Christ. "The first race" was indifferently called the Roman, Greek, or Gentile. "The second race" was the Jews; while "the third race" was the Christian. The cry in the circus of Carthage was *Usque quo genus tertium?* "How long must we endure this third race?"

22. "The Third Race"

But one of the most powerful causes of the hatred entertained by the heathen against the Christians was, that though there were no citizens so loyal as they, yet in every case in which the laws and customs of the empire came into conflict with the will of God, their supreme rule was loyalty to Christ, they must obey God rather than man. To worship Caesar, to offer even one grain of incense on the shrine of Diana, no Christian would ever consent, not even when this minimum of compliance would save life itself.

23. Hatred against Christians

The Rom empire claimed to be a kingdom of universal sway, not only over the bodies and the property of all its subjects, but over their consciences and their souls. It demanded absolute obedience to its supreme lord, that is, to Caesar. This obedience the Christian could not render, for unlimited obedience of body, soul and spirit is due to God alone, the only Lord of the conscience. Hence it was that there arose the antagonism of the government to Christianity, with persecution as the inevitable result.

These results, hatred and persecution, were, in such circumstances, inevitable; they were "the outcome of the fundamental tenet of primitive Christianity, that the Christian ceased to be his own master, ceased to have his old environment, ceased to hold his old connections with the state; in everything he became the bond-servant of Jesus Christ, in everything owing supreme allegiance and fealty to the new empire and the Crucified Head. 'We engage in these conflicts,' said Tertullian, 'as men whose very lives are not our own. We have no master but God'" (Workman, 195).

The persecution inaugurated by the emperor Decius in 250 AD was particularly severe. There was hardly a province in the empire where there were no martyrs; but there were also many who abandoned their faith and rushed to the magistrates to obtain their *libelli*, or certificates that they had offered heathen sacrifice. When the days of persecution were over, these persons usually came with eagerness to seek readmission to the church. It was in the Decian persecution that the great theologian Origen, who was then in his 68th year, suffered the cruel torture of the rack; and from the effects of what he then suffered he died at Tyre in 254.

24. The Decian Persecution

Many *libelli* have been discovered in recent excavations in Egypt. In the *Expos T* for January, 1909, p. 185, Dr. George Milligan gives an example, and prints the Gr text of one of these recently discovered Egyp *libelli*. These *libelli* are most interesting, illustrating as they do the account which Cyprian gives of the way in which some faint-hearted Christians during the Decian persecution obtained certificates—some of these certificates being true to fact, and others false—to the effect that they had sacrificed in the heathen manner. The one which Dr. Milligan gives is as follows: "To those chosen to superintend the sacrifices at the village of Alexander Island, from Aurelius Diogenes, the son of Satabus, of the village of Alexander Island, being about 72 years old, a scar on the right eyebrow. Not only have I always continued sacrificing to the gods, but now also in your presence, in accordance with the decrees, I have sacrificed and poured libations and tasted the offerings, and I request you to countersign my statement. May good fortune attend you. I, Aurelius Diogenes, have made this request."

25. *Libelli*

(2d Hand) "I, Aurelius Syrus, as a participant, have certified Diogenes as sacrificing along with us."

(1st Hand) "The first year of the Emperor Caesar Gaius Messius Quintus Trajan Decius Pius Felix Augustus, Epiph. 2" (= June 25, 250 AD).

Under Valerian the persecution was again very severe, but his successor, Gallienus, issued an edict of toleration, in which he guaranteed freedom of worship to the Christians. Thus Christianity definitely became a *religio licita*, a lawful religion. This freedom from persecution continued until the reign of Diocletian.

The persecution of the Christian church by the empire of Rome came to an end in March, 313 AD, when Constantine issued the document known as the "Edict of Milan," which assured to each individual freedom of religious belief. This document marks an era of the utmost importance in the history of the world. Official Rom persecution had done its worst, and had failed; it was ended now; the Galilean had conquered.

26. The Edict of Milan

The results of persecution were: (1) It raised up witnesses, true witnesses, for the Christian faith. Men and women and even children were among the martyrs whom no cruelties, however refined and protracted, could terrify into denial of their Lord. It is to a large extent owing to persecution that the Christian church possesses the testimony of men like Quadratus and Tertullian and Origen and Cyprian and many others. While those who had adopted the Christian faith in an external and formal manner only generally went back from their profession, the true Christian, as even the Rom proconsul Pliny testifies, could not be made to do this. The same stroke which crushed the straw—such is a saying of Augustine's—separated the pure grain which the Lord had chosen.

27. Results of Persecution

(2) Persecution showed that the Christian faith is immortal even in this world. Of Christ's kingdom there shall be no end. "Hammer away, ye hostile bands, your hammers break, God's altar stands." Pagan Rome, Babylon the Great, as it is called by the apostle John in the Apocalypse, tried hard to destroy the church of Christ; Babylon was drunk with the blood of the saints. God allowed this tyranny to exist for 300 years, and the blood of His children was shed like water. Why was it necessary that the church should have so terrible and so prolonged an experience of suffering? It was in order to convince the world that though the kings of the earth gather themselves against the Lord and against His Christ, yet all that they can do is vain. God is in the midst of Zion; He shall help her, and that right early. The Christian church, as if suspended between heaven and earth, had no need of other help than that of the unseen but Divine hand, which at every moment held it up and kept it from falling. Never was the church more free, never stronger, never more flourishing, never more extensive in its growth, than in the days of persecution.

And what became of the great persecuting power, the Rom empire? It fell before the barbarians. Rome is fallen in its ruins, and its idols are utterly abolished, while the barbarians who overwhelmed the empire have become the nominally Christian nations of modern Europe, and their descendants have carried the Christian faith to America and Australia and Africa and all over the world.

(3) Persecution became, to a large extent, an important means of preserving the true doctrines of the person and of the work of Christ. It was in the ages of persecution that Gnosticism died, though it died slowly. It was in the ages of persecution that Arianism was overthrown. At the Council of Nicea in 325 AD, among those who were present and took part in the discussion and in the decision of the council, there were those who "bore in their bodies the branding-marks of Jesus," who had suffered pain and loss for Christ's sake.

Persecution was followed by these important results, for God in His wisdom had seen fit to permit these evils to happen, in order to change them into permanent good; and thus the wrath of man was overruled to praise God, and to effect more ultimate good, than if the persecutions had not taken place at all. What, in a word, could be more Divine than to curb and restrain and overrule evil itself and change it into good? God lets iniquity do what it pleases, according to its own designs; but in permitting it to move on one side, rather than on another, He overrules it and makes it enter into the order of His providence. So He lets this fury against the Christian faith be kindled in the hearts of persecutors, so that they afflict the saints of the Most High. But the church remains safe, for persecution can work nothing but ultimate good in the hand of God. "The blood of the martyrs is the seed of the church." So said Tertullian, and what he said is true.

Persecution has permanently enriched the history of the church. It has given us the noble heritage of the testimony and the suffering of those whose lives would otherwise have been unrecorded. Their very names as well as their careers would have been unknown had not persecution "dragged them into fame and chased them up to heaven."

Persecution made Christ very near and very precious to those who suffered. Many of the martyrs bore witness, even when in the midst of the most cruel torments, that they felt no pain, but that Christ was with them. Instances to this effect could be multiplied. Persecution made them feel how true Christ's words were, that even as He was not of the world, so they also were not of it. If they had been of the world, the world would love its own, but because Christ had chosen them out of the world, therefore the world hated them. They were not greater than their Lord. If men had persecuted Jesus, they would also persecute His true disciples. But though they were persecuted, they were of good cheer, Christ had overcome the world; He was with them; He enabled them to be faithful unto death. He had promised them the crown of life.

Browning's beautiful lines describe what was a common experience of the martyrs, how Christ "in them" and "with them," "quenched the power of fire," and made them more than conquerors:

"I was some time in being burned,
But at the close a Hand came through
The fire above my head, and drew
My soul to Christ, whom now I see.
Sergius, a brother, writes for me
This testimony on the wall—
For me, I have forgot it all."

JOHN RUTHERFURD

PERSEPOLIS, pẽr-sep′ō-lis (2 Macc **9** 2; **Περσέπολις,** *Persépolis,* **Περσαίπολις,** *Persaípolis,* in Ptolemy **Περσόπολις,** *Persópolis;* original Pers name unknown; Pahlavī *Stakhr,* now *Iṣṭakhr* and *Chihil Minār,* "Forty Turrets"): The ruins of Persepolis lie about 35 miles N.E. of Shīrāz and some 40 miles S. of the ruins of Pasargadae.

1. Location

The magnificent palace of which such striking remains are still visible (*Takht i Jamshīd*) was built by Darius and Xerxes of white marble and black stone. The city was captured, pillaged and burnt by Alexander in 324 BC, most of the inhabitants being massacred or enslaved. Much of the treasure of the Pers kings was found there. Curtius says the palace was never rebuilt. Antiochus Epiphanes (166 BC) tried but failed to plunder the temple (of Anaïtis, Anāhita?) there (2 Macc **9** 2; perhaps this is the incident referred to in 1 Macc **6** 1 ff, and Polyb. xxxi.11). At Persepolis were the sepulchers of the Achaemenian kings (except Cyrus). Long and important inscriptions of Darius and Xerxes are found at Persepolis and the neighboring Naqsh i Rustam, in cuneiform characters and in the Achaemenian Pers, Assyr and neo-Susian tongues (published by Spiegel, Rawlinson and Weisbach). Clitarchus first among Europeans mentions the city. The writer of this article visited it in 1892. Not now inhabited.

2. History

LITERATURE.—Inscriptions (as above), Arrian, Curtius, Polybius, Pliny, Diod. Siculus, mediaeval and modern travelers.

W. ST. CLAIR TISDALL

PERSEUS, pûr′sūs, pûr′sē-us (**Περσεύς,** *Perseús*): In 1 Macc **8** 5 the conquest of "Perseus, king of the Citims" (RV "king of Chittim") was part of the "fame of the Romans" which reached the ears of Judas. This Perseus, the son and successor of Philip III of Macedonia, came to the throne in 178 BC and was the last king of Macedonia. In 171 BC began the war with Rome which ended in his disastrous defeat and capture at Pydna, 168 BC (to which 1 Macc **8** 5 refers), by L. Aemilius Paulus. Macedonia soon became a Rom province. Perseus was led to Rome to grace the triumph of his conqueror, by whose clemency he was spared, and died in captivity at Rome (Polyb. xxix.17; Livy xliv. 40 ff).

Kittim or Chittim, properly of the people of the town of Citium in Cyprus, then signifying Cyprians, and extended by Jewish writers (Gen **10** 4; Nu **24** 24; Isa **23** 1; Jer **2** 10; Ezk **27** 6; Dnl **11** 30; Jos, *Ant*, I, vi) to include the coasts of Greece generally, is here applied to Macedonia. In 1 Macc **1** 1 Macedonia (or Greece) is called "the land of Chittim."

S. ANGUS

PERSEVERANCE, pûr-sē-vẽr′ans: The word occurs only once in AV (Eph **6** 18), where it refers quite simply to persistence in prayer. In theology (esp. in the phrase "final perseverance") the word has come to denote a special persistency, the undying continuance of the new life (manifested in faith and holiness) given by the Spirit of God to man. It is questioned whether such imparted life is (by its nature, or by the law of its impartation) necessarily permanent, indestructible, so that the once regenerate and believing man has the prospect of final glory infallibly assured. This is not the place to trace the history of a great and complex debate. It is more fitting here to point to the problem as connected with that supreme class of truths in which, because of our necessary mental limits, the entire truth can only be apprehended as the unrevealed but certain harmony of seeming contradictions. Scripture on the one hand abounds with assurances of "perseverance" as a fact, and largely intimates that an exulting anticipation of it is the intended experience of the believer (see Jn **10** 28 above all, and cf among other passages Rom **8** 31–37; 1 Pet **1** 8.9). On the other hand, we find frequent and urgent warnings and cautions (see e.g. 1 Cor **8** 11; **9** 27). The teacher dealing with actual cases, as in pastoral work, should be ready to adopt both classes of utterances, each with its proper application; applying the first, e.g., to the true but timid disciple, the latter to the self-confident. Meanwhile Scripture on the whole, by the manner and weight of its positive statements, favors a humble belief of the permanence, in the plan of God, of the once-given new life. It is as if it laid down "perseverance" as the Divine rule for the Christian, while the negative passages came in to caution the man not to deceive himself with appearances, nor to let any belief whatever palliate the guilt and minimize the danger of sin. In the biographies of Scripture, it is noteworthy that no person appears who, at one time certainly a saint, was later certainly a castaway. The awful words of He **6** 4–6; **10** 26.27 appear to deal with cases (such as Balaam's) of much light but no loving life, and so are not precisely in point. Upon the whole subject, it is important to make "the Perseverance of the Saviour" our watchword rather than "the Perseverance of the saint." HANDLEY DUNELM

PERSIA, pûr′sha, -zha (פָּרַס, *pāraṣ;* Περσίς, *Persís;* in Assyr *Parsu, Parsua;* in Achaemenian Pers *Pārsa*, modern *Fārs*): In the Bible (2 Ch **36** 20.22.23; Ezr **1** 1.8; Est **1** 3.14.18; **10** 2; Ezk **27** 10; **38** 5; Dnl **8** 20; **10** 1; **11** 2) this name denotes properly the modern province of Fārs, not the whole Pers empire. The latter was by its people called Airyana, the present Īrān (from the Skt. word *ārya*, "noble"); and even now the Persians never call their country anything but Īrān, never "Persia." The province of Persis lay to the E. of Elam (Susiana), and stretched from the Pers Gulf to the Great Salt Desert, having Carmania on the S.E. Its chief cities were Persepolis and Pasargadae. Along the Pers Gulf the land is low, hot and unhealthy, but it soon begins to rise as one travels inland. Most of the province consists of high and steep mountains and plateaus, with fertile valleys. The table-lands in which lie the modern city of Shīrāz and the ruins of Persepolis and Pasargadae are well watered and productive. Nearer the desert, however, cultivation grows scanty for want of water. Persis was doubtless in early times included in Elam, and its population was then either Semitic or allied to the Accadians, who founded more than one state in the Bab plain. The Āryan Persians seem to have occupied the country in the 8th or 9th cent. BC. W. ST. CLAIR TISDALL

PERSIAN, pûr′shan, -zhan, **LANGUAGE AND LITERATURE (ANCIENT)**:

I. Language (Introductory).—The Pers language, ancient and modern alike, is an Āryan tongue. In its ancient forms it is more closely connected with Vedic Sanskṛit than with any other language except Armenian. Most of its roots are to be found also in Slavonic, Gr, Lat and other tongues of the same stock.

Dialects There were two main dialects in the ancient language of Īrān (*Airyanem*), (1) that of the Persians proper, and (2) that of the Medes. The former is known to us from the inscriptions of the Achaemenian kings, the latter from the Avesta, and a few Median words preserved for us by Herodotus and other Gr writers.

II. Old Persian Inscriptions.—These fall between 550 and 330 BC, and contain about 1,000 lines and 400 words. They are carved upon the rocks in

Part of Rock of Behistān.

a cuneiform character, simplified from that of the neo-Susian, which again comes from the neo-Bab syllabary. In Old Pers inscriptions only 44 characters are employed, of which 7 are ideographs or contractions. The remaining 37 phonetic signs are syllabic, each consisting of an open syllable and not merely of a single letter, except in case of separate vowels. The syllabary, though much simpler than any other cuneiform system, does not quite attain therefore to being an alphabet. It was written from left to right, like the other cuneiform syllabaries. Of Cyrus the Great only one Pers sentence has been found: *Adam Kurush Khshāyathiya Hakhāmanishiya*, "I am Cyrus the King, the Achaemenian." Darius I has left us long inscriptions, at Behistān (Besitūn), Mt. Alvand, Persepolis, Naqsh i Rustam, etc, and one at Suez, the latter mentioning his conquest of Egypt and the construction of the first (?) Suez canal:

Adam niyashtāyam imām yuviyām kañtanaiy hacā Pirāva nāma rauta tya Mudrāyaiy danauvatiy abiy daraya tya hacā Pārsā aiti.

("I commanded to dig this canal from the river named the Nile, which flows through Egypt, to the sea which comes from Persia.")

We have also inscriptions of Xerxes at Persepolis and many short ones of Artaxerxes I, Artaxerxes Mnēmōn, and Artaxerxes Ochus. From them all taken together we learn much concerning the history and the religion of the Achaemenian period.

It is from Achaemenian or Old Pers, and not from the Medic or Avestic, that modern Pers has sprung through Pahlavī and Darī as intermediate stages. This is probably due to the political supremacy which the Persians under the Achaemenides gained over the Medes. The few words in the inscriptions which might otherwise be doubtful can be understood through comparison with Armenian and even with the modern Pers, e.g. *yuviya* in the above inscription is the modern vulgar Pers *jûb*.

III. Medic Dialect.—The Medic dialect is represented in literature by the Avesta or sacred books of the Zoroastrians (Pārsīs). The word *Avesta* does not occur in the book itself and is of uncertain meaning and signification. It is probably the *Abashtā* of *Beh. Inscr.*, IV, 64, and means either (1) an interview, meeting (Skt. *avashtā*, "appearance before a judge"; Av. *ava-stā*, "to stand near"), or (2) a petition (Pahl. *apastān*, "petition"; Arm. *apastan*, "refuge," "asylum"), in either case deriving its name from Zoroaster's drawing near to Ahura Mazda in worship.

1. Ordinary Avestic

Yezdikhast.

This dialect represents a much greater decadence in grammar and vocabulary than does the Old Pers. Many of its consonants and most of its vowels are weakened. Its verbs have almost entirely lost the augment; its declensional system shows extreme confusion. It stands to Old Pers grammatically somewhat as Eng. does to Ger. Its alphabet, consisting of 43 letters, is derived from the Syr (probably the Estrangelā), and is written from right to left. As a specimen of the language of most of the Avesta we give the following extract (*Yasna* LXIV, 15[61]):

Dāidī mōi, yé gãm tashō apasca urvarω̄sca
Ameretātā, haurvātā, Spéništā Mainyū Mazdā,
Tévīshī, utayūiti, Manaǹhā Vōhū, séǹhē.

("Give me, O thou who didst make the bull [earth], and the waters and the plants, immortality, health—O most Bountiful Spirit, Mazda—strength, might, through Vōhu Manō, I say.")

There is a sub-dialect of Medic (Avestic) known as the Gāthā-dialect, from the fact that the *Gāthās*, or "Hymns" (*Yasna* XXVIII–XXXIV, XLII–L, LII), and also the prayers (*Yathā Ahū Vairyō, Ashem Vōhū, Airyamā Ishyō*, and originally *Yēǹhé Hātãm*, and a few scattered passages elsewhere) are composed in it. This represents, speaking generally, an older form of the Avestic. It is probably the old language of Bactria or of Margiana. *Gāthā* I, 2, runs thus:

2. Gāthic

Yé vω̄, Mazdā Ahurā, pairijasāi Vōhū Manaǹhā,
Maibyō dāvōi ahvω̄ (astvatasca hyaṭca manaǹhō)
Āyaptā Ashāṭ hacā, yāiš rapeñtō daidīṭ hvāthrē.

("To me, O Ahura Mazda, who approach you two through Vōhu Manō, grant the benefits from Asha, [those] of both worlds, both of the material [world] and of that which is of the spirit, through which [benefits] may [Asha] place in glory those who please him.")

The meter of the *Gāthās*, like that of the other Avestic poems, is based on the number of syllables in a line, with due regard to the caesura. But the condition of the text is such that there is great difficulty in recovering the original reading with sufficient accuracy to enable us to lay down rules on the subject with any certainty. The first *Gāthā* is composed of strophes of 3 lines each (as above). Each line contains 16 syllables, with a caesura after the 7th foot.

IV. Zoroaster.—Many of the *Gāthās* are generally ascribed to Zoroaster himself, the rest to his earliest disciples. They compose the most ancient part of the Avesta. It is now becoming a matter of very great probability that Zoroaster lived at earliest in the middle of the 7th cent. BC, more probably a century later. The *Artā Vīrāf Nāmak* says that his religion remained pure for 300 years, and connects its corruption with the alleged destruction of much of the Avesta in the palace burned by Alexander at Persepolis, 324 BC. This traditional indication of date is confirmed by other evidence. Zoroaster's prince Vishtāspa (in Gr *Hustáspēs*) bears the same name as the father of Darius I, and was probably the same person. Vishtāspa's queen Hutaosa, who also protected and favored Zoroaster, bears the same name (in Gr *Atóssa*) as Cambyses' sister who afterward married Darius, and probably belonged to the same family. Zoroastrianism comes to the fore under Darius, whereas Cyrus in his inscriptions speaks as a decided polytheist. Hence we conclude that the earliest part of the Avesta belongs to c 550 BC. Of Zoroaster himself we learn much from the Avesta, which traces his genealogy back for 10 generations. It mentions his wife's name (Hvōvi), and tells of his 3 sons and 3 daughters. His first disciple was Frashaoštra, his wife's natural uncle. His own name means "Owner of the yellow camel," and has none of the higher meanings sometimes assigned to it by those who would deny his existence. Tradition says he was born at Ragha (*Raga, Rai*), about $5\frac{1}{2}$ miles S. of the present *Ṭehrān*, though some think his native place was Western Atropatene (*Āẕarbāījān*). Rejected by his own tribe, the Magi, he went to Vishtāspa's court in Bactria. The faith which he taught spread to the Pers court (very naturally, if Vishtāspa was identical with Darius' father) and thence throughout the country. Tradition (*Yasht* XIX, 2, etc) says that the Avesta was revealed to Zoroaster on Mt. Ushi-darena ("intellect-holding") in Sīstān. But it is not the composition of one man or of one age.

1. His Date, etc

Herodotus makes no mention of Zoroaster, but speaks of the Magi (whom he calls a Median tribe [i.101]) as already performing priestly functions. His description of their repetition of charms and theological compositions (i.132) would agree very well with recitation of the *Gāthās* and *Yasna*. Mention of controversies with Gautama, Buddha's disciples (*Yasht* XIII, 16) who probably reached Persia in the 2d cent. BC, is another indication of date. The fact that in both the *Yasna* and the *Vendīdād* heretics (*zañda*) are mentioned who preferred the comm. (*zañd*) on the Avesta to the Avesta itself, is a sign of late date. Names of certain persons found in the Avesta (e.g. Ātare-pāta, a Dastūr who lived under Hormuzd I, 273 AD, and Rāštare-Yagheñti, whom the *Dīnkart* identifies with the chief Mobed of Sapor II, 309–379 AD, Āderpād Mārespand, and who, according to the *Patēt*, §28, "purified" the revelation made to Zoroaster, i.e. revised the text of the earlier parts of the Avesta) enable us to prove that certain portions of the work as we now have it were composed as late as near the end of the 4th cent. of our era. It is said that the text was in confusion in the time of Vologases I (51–78 [?] AD). A recension was then begun, and continued with much zeal by Ardashīr Pāpakān, 226–40 AD. According to Geldner (*Prolegomena*, xlvi) the final recension took place some considerable time after Yezdigird III (overthrown 642 AD). In the times

2. Date of Avesta

of the Sāsānides there were, it is said, 21 *Naskas* or volumes of the Avesta, and the names of these are given in the *Dīnkart* (Book IX). Of these we now possess only one entire *Naska*, the *Vendīdād*, and portions of three others.

3. Divisions of the Present Avesta

The present Avesta is divided into 5 parts: (1) The *Yasna* (√ *yaz*, Skt. *yaj*, "to invoke," "to praise") contains 72 chapters of hymns for use at sacrifices, etc, including the "Older *Yasna*" or *Gāthās*. (2) The *Vispered* (*vīspa*, "every," "all," and *rādha*, "a lord") is divided into 24 chapters in Geldner's edition; it is supplementary to the *Yasna*. (3) The *Vendīdād* (*van+daēva+dāta*, "law for vanquishing the demons") contains 22 chapters. The first chapter contains the Iranian myth about the order in which the provinces of the Iranian world were created by Ahura Mazda. It tells how the Evil Spirit, Aṅrō Mainyuš, created plagues, sins and death, to destroy the good creatures of the Good Spirit. The greater part of the book contains ceremonial laws and formulae, some of them loathsome and all rather petty and superstitious in character. (4) The *Yashts*, 21 in all, are hymns, telling many mythological tales about Mithra, Tishtriya, etc. (5) The *Khorda Avesta* ("Little Avesta") consists of a number of short compositions, hymns, etc, compiled by the Āderpād Mārespand (Ādharpādh Mahraspand, Ātarobāṭ Mānsarspendān) already mentioned, in Sapor II's reign.

Much of the Avesta is said to have been destroyed by the Khalīfah ʽUmar's orders when Persia was conquered by the Arabs after the battle of Nahāvand (642 AD). Certainly ʽUmar ordered the destruction of Pers libraries, as we learn from the *Kashfu'z Ẕunūn* (p. 341).

V. Pahlavī.—Under ancient Pers literature may be classed the *Pahlavī* (*a*) inscriptions of Sapor at *Hājīābād* and elsewhere, (*b*) legends on Sāsānian coins, (*c*) translations of certain parts of the Avesta, made under the Sāsānides for the most part, (*d*) such books as the *Artā Vīrāf Nāmak*, the *Zād Sparam*, *Dīnkart*, *Ōrmazd Yasht*, *Patēt*, *Būndihīshnīh*, etc. These are mostly of religious import. The *Artā Vīrāf Nāmak* gives a description of the visit of the young *dastūr* Artā Vīrāf, to the Zoroastrian heaven. The *Būndihīshnīh* ("creation") tells how Ōrmazd and Ahriman came into being, and treats of the 9,000 years' struggle between them. Pahlavī, as *written* (the so-called *Huzvaresh*), contains an immense number of Aram. words, but the Pers terminations attached to these show that they were *read* as Pers: thus *yehabūnt-ano* is written, and *dāt-ano* ("to give") is read. Pahlavī works that are no longer extant are the sources of the *Vīs o Rāmīn*, *Zarātusht Nāmah*, *Shāhnāmah*, etc.

1. Literature

2. Comparison

In order to understand the relation in which the Pers dialects and stages in the history of the language stand to one another, it may be well to subjoin a list of words in Old Pers, Avestic, Pahlavī and modern Pers. It will be seen that Avestic is not the source of the Āryan part of the present tongue.

Meaning	Avestic	Old Pers	Pahlavī	Mod. Pers
Friend...	*zušta*	*daushtā*	*dōst*	*dūst*
Hand....	*zasta*	*dasta*	*dast*	*dast*
Bactria...	*Bākhdhi*	*Bākhtri*	*Bāhr*	*Balkh*
Straight..	*drva(šta)*†	*duru-va(šta)*	*drust*	*durust*
Greatest .	*mazišta*†	*mathishta*	*mahist*	*mahīn*
Most right ..	*razišta*†	*rāsta*	*rāst*	*rāst*
Abode....	*nmāna* (Gāthic *demāna*)	*māniya*	*mān*	(*mān-dan* "to remain")

† Superlatives

LITERATURE.—Achaemenian inscriptions, Korsowitz, Spiegel, Rawlinson: Geiger and Kuhn (editors), *Grundriss der iranischen Philologie;* Darmesteter, *Études iraniennes;* Spiegel, *Eranische Altertumskunde;* Nöldeke, *Aufsätze zur persischen Geschichte;* W. Geiger, *Ostiranische Kultur im Altertum;* Geldner's ed of Avesta; Professor Browne, *Literary History of Persia;* De Harlez, *Manuel de la langue de l'Avesta, Manuel de la langue Pehlevie,* and *Intro to the Avesta;* Haug, *Book of Artā Vīrāf;* Cook, *Origins of Religion and Language.*

W. ST. CLAIR TISDALL

PERSIAN RELIGION (ANCIENT):

I. Before Zoroaster.—There are clear indications in the Avesta that the religion of the Medes and Persians before Zoroaster's time agreed in most respects with that of the Indian Āryans, and in a less degree with the beliefs of the Āryans in general.

1. Early Āryan Religion

All the Āryan tribes in very ancient times showed great respect for the dead, though they carefully distinguished them from the gods (cf Rig-Veda X, 56, 4). The latter were principally the powers of Nature, the wind, fire, water, the sky, the sun, the earth, and a host of personifications. The procreative powers in Nature, animate and inanimate, seeming to be the source of animal and vegetable life, received adoration, which ultimately led to unspeakable corruption. Herodotus tells us that the Persians in his time worshipped the sun, moon, sky, earth, fire, wind and water (i.131). Offerings to the gods were laid on a mass of pomegranate twigs (*baresman*, Skt. *barhis*), and the flesh of victims was *boiled*, not burnt. Libations of *haoma*-juice were poured out, just as in India the *soma* was the drink of both gods and their worshippers.

2. Avesta and Rig-Veda

A comparison between the spiritual beings mentioned in the Avesta and those spoken of in the Rig-Veda is most instructive in two ways. It shows that the original religion of the Iranians and of the Indian Āryans agreed very closely; and it also enables us to realize the immensity of the reformation wrought by Zoroaster. Many of the names of supernatural beings are practically the same; e.g. Indra (Indra, Andra), Mitra (Mithra), Aryaman (Airyaman), Asura (Ahura), Apām Napāt (Apām Napāt), Tvashṭri (? Tishtrya), Rāma (Rāman), Vāyu (Vāyu), Vāta (Vāta). So are many words of religious import, as Sōma (Haoma), Mantra (Māthra), Hōtra (Zaotar). The Yama of India is the Yima of Persia, and the father of the one is Vivasvat and that of the other Vīvaṅhaṭ, which is the same word with dialectic change. The Holy River of the Avesta, Aredhvī Sūra, the Unstained (Anāhita), is represented by the Sarasvatī, the Gangā (Ganges) and other sacred streams worshipped in India. In Persia Ātar (or Fire) is a son of Ahura Mazda (*Yasna* LXIV, 46–53), as Agni (=Ignis) is of Tvashṭri in the Rig-Veda. Ārmaiti is Ahura Mazda's daughter, as Saraṇyu in the Rig-

Veda is the daughter of Tvashṭṛi, the "Creator." The use of *gomēz* (*bovis urina*) for purification is common to both India and Persia. Though the *soma*-plant is not now the same as the *haoma*, the words are the same, and no doubt they at one time denoted one and the same plant. Many of the myths of the Avesta have a great resemblance to those of the Rig-Veda. This comparison might be extended almost indefinitely.

In another respect also there is an important agreement between the two. Though some 33 deities are adored in the Vedic Hymns, yet, in spite of polytheism and low ideas of the Divine, traces of something higher may be found. Varuṇa, for instance, represents a very lofty conception. In the closest connection with him stands Asura, who is a being of great eminence, and whose sons are the gods, esp. the Ādityas.

Tvashṭṛi again is creator of heaven and earth and of all beings, though his worship was ultimately in Vedic times displaced by that of Indra.

3. The Creator

It is clear then that the Indian Āryans were worshippers of the Creator and that they knew something of Him long before they sank into polytheism. In the Avesta and in the Pers cuneiform inscriptions alike, Ahura Mazda occupies much the same position as Varuṇa, Asura (the same word as Ahura), or Tvashṭṛi in the Rig-Veda, or rather in the ancient belief of which traces are retained in the latter work. Hence, as the Avesta teaches, Zoroaster was not for the first time preaching the existence of Ahura Mazda, but he was rather endeavoring to recall his people to the belief of their ancestors, the doctrine which Ahura Mazda had taught Yima in primeval time in his first revelation (*Vendīdād* II, 1–16,42). The great truth of the existence of the Creator, testified to by tradition, reason and conscience, undoubtedly contributed largely to Zoroaster's success, just as a similar proclamation of the God Most High (*Allāh Ta'ālā'*), worshipped by their ancestors, helped the thoughtful among the Arabs in later years to accept Muḥammad's teaching. The consciousness in each case that the doctrine was not new but very ancient, materially helped men to believe it true.

II. Zoroastrianism.—The reformation wrought by Zoroaster was a great one. He recognized—as Euripides in Greece did later—that "if the gods do aught shameful, they are not gods." Hence he perceived that many of the deities worshipped in Īrān were unworthy of adoration, being evil in character, hostile to all good and therefore to the "All-Wise" Spirit (Ahura Mazda) and to men. Hence his system of dualism, dividing all beings, spiritual or material, into two classes, the creatures of Ahura Mazda and those of the "Destroying Mind" (Aṅrō Mainyuš). So many of the popular deities were evil that Zoroaster used the word *daēva* (the same as *deva*, *deus*, and Aram. *di*) to denote henceforth an *evil* spirit, just as Christianity turned the Gr *daímones* and *daimónia* (words used in a good sense in classical authors) into "demons." Instead of this now degraded word *daēva*, he employed *baga* (Old Pers; Av. *bagha*, Vedic *bhaga*, "distribution," "patron," "lord") for "God."

1. Leading Principle

But it must be remembered that Zoroaster did not teach monotheism. Darius says that "Auramazda and *the other gods that there are*" brought him aid (*Beh. Inscr.*, IV, 60–63), and both he and Xerxes speak of Auramazda as "the greatest of the gods." So, even in the first *Gāthā*, Zoroaster himself invokes Asha, Vōhu-Manō, Ārmaiti, Sraosha, and even Géuš-urvan ("the Soul of the Bull"), as well as Ahura Mazda.

2. Not Monotheistic

(1) *Darius and Xerxes.*—Darius mentions the "clan-gods," but does not name any of them. He and Xerxes ascribe the creation of heaven and earth to Auramazda, and say that the latter, "Who made this earth, who made yon sky, who made man, who made happiness for man," has appointed each of them king. It is "by the grace of Auramazda" (*vashnā Auramazdāha*) that Darius conquers his enemies. But both Artaxerxes Mnēmōn and Artaxerxes Ōchus couple Mithra and Anāhata (Anāhita) with Auramazda (Ahura Mazda) in praying for the protection of the empire.

Ahura Mazda.

(2) *Ahura Mazda.*—In the Avesta, Ahura Mazda is one of the seven Amesha Speñtas or "Bountiful Immortals." He is the father of one of them, Speñta Ārmaiti, who is also his spouse. He is *primus inter pares* among them, their chief, but by no means the only god. Monotheism is distinctly taught in later Zoroastrian works, for instance, in the *Zarātusht-Nāmah*, composed 1278 AD, but it is due to Christian and Islāmic influence.

The modern Zoroastrian view, clearly stated in the *Dasātīr i Āsmānī* and elsewhere, that all the good creatures of Ōrmazd (Ahura Mazda) are entitled to adoration, undoubtedly rests upon the Avesta. There we find, in the first place, the Amesha Speñtas, who occupy in regard to Mazda the same position as do the Vedic Ādityas toward Varuṇa, though *not one* of the Ādityas is identical with any of the Amesha Speñtas.

3. Objects of Worship

The names of these are: (1) Ahura Mazda (otherwise called Speñtō Mainyuš or "Bountiful Mind"); (2) Vōhu Manō ("Good Mind"); (3) Asha Vahišta ("Best Righteousness"); (4) Khshathra Vairya ("Excellent Ruler"); (5) Speñta Ārmaiti ("Bounteous Piety"); (6) Haurvatāt ("Health"); (7) Ameretāt ("Immortality"). Each has a special province: thus Ārmaiti is the general spirit of earth and presides over its fruitfulness. She is the patroness of virtuous matrons. Khshathra is the guardian of metals. Vōhu Manō guards sheep and cattle and introduces to Ahura Mazda the spirits of the just. Next in rank come the Yazatas ("Worshipful Ones"), of whom there are a large number. Three of them, Mithra, Rashnu and Sraosha, preside at the judgment of the dead on the 4th day from death. Rashnu holds the scales in which a man's deeds are weighed. Sraosha guards the soul during the first three nights after death. Airyaman Ishya ("the longed-for comrade") is the protector of mankind, the bestower of peace and happiness. On one occasion (*Vend.*, *Farg.* XXII, 23–29) Ahura Mazda sends his messenger Nairyō Saṅha ("male instructor") to ask his aid against overwhelming odds. Rāman Ḥvāstra, the bosom friend of Mithra, presides over the atmosphere and also gives its taste to food. Mithra is the genius of truth, possessed of 1,000 ears, and riding in a single-wheeled chariot (the sun), while darting golden darts and driving fiery steeds. Tishtrya, identified with the dog-star Sirius, sends rain and is by Ahura Mazda endowed with his own power and dignity (*Yasht* VIII, 52 ff). This is true of Mithra also (*Yasht* X, 1), Ātar ("Fire"), Vāyu ("Air"), Vāta ("Wind"), Verethraghna ("Mars"), Saoka ("Prosperity"), Aršṭāt (genius of Justice), Vāzišta ("Lightning"), Frādatfshu (the guardian of cattle), Berejya (genius of corn),

Cistā and Daēnā ("Knowledge" and "Religion"), who are others of the Yazatas. All these are entitled to worship at the hands of the true adorer of Mazda (Mazdayasna, opposed to Daēvayasna, or worshipper of the demons).

4. Aṅrō Mainyuš and His Creatures

In opposition to the creatures of Ahura Mazda are those of Aṅrō Mainyuš, who is the source of all moral and material evil. The first chapter of the *Vendīdād* tells how he created something bad in opposition to everything good made by Ahura Mazda.

A demon is the adversary of each Amesha Speñta: Aka Manō ("Evil Mind") that of Vōhu Manō, and so in order: Indra (or Andra, "demon of untruthfulness"), Saurva ("evil government"), Nāṅhaithya ("discontent"), Tauru ("who poisons water") and Zairi ("poison"), being antagonistic to the other Bountiful Immortals. Aēshma-Daēva ("Demon of Wrath")—the Asmodeus of Tob **3** 8—is the special foe of Sraosha, the genius of obedience. Apaosha, demon of drought, is the enemy of Tishtrya. Būiti (or Būidhi) teaches men to worship idols, and also causes death. Būshyāsta is the demon of sloth. Vīdhātuš or Astuvidhōtuš causes death by destroying the body. Other evil beings, Drujes, Pairikas, Jainis, Yatus, are so numerous in the later parts of the Avesta that a pious Zoroastrian must have lived in continual dread of their assaults. He had even to conceal the parings of his nails, lest they should be used as darts to his injury by these his spiritual foes.

Combat between King and Evil Spirit.

5. Production v. Destruction

Holiness does not enter into Zoroaster's conception of the Divine nature. This is a point to which attention has not yet been properly directed, though its importance can hardly be exaggerated. The epithet *Speñta*, often applied to Ahura Mazda and mistranslated "Holy," is by the Zoroastrians themselves in Pahlavī rendered *afzūnik*, i.e. "that causes increase." Its √ *span* or *spēn*=Skt. *śvi*, "to swell," "to grow," "to increase." The opposite to this is the term *aṅrō* (*aṅgro*, from √ *aṅgh;* cf Ger. *eng*, "narrow") applied to the Evil Spirit, and denoting "narrowing," "decreasing," "destroying." Hence, as the Destroyer, he is styled *pōurumahrka*, "full of death."

Fertility.—Ahura Mazda and his assistants promote life, fertility in man, beast and plant, agriculture, increase; while Aṅrō Mainyuš and his creatures cause destruction and death. Ātar ("Fire"), also styled *Apām Napāt* ("Offspring of the Waters"), is the vital flame and the male energy in the world; Aredhvī Sūra Anāhita is the female. As a river the latter flows from Mt. Hukairya, a peak in the Elburz Range (*Yasna* LXIV), into the Caspian Sea (Vōurukasha) in the midst of which grows the tree *Hvāpa* ("well watered"), which bears the seeds of all plants. *Anāhita* means "undefiled," but it is applied to purity of *water* (to defile any of the four "elements" was, for later Zoroastrians, a grievous sin) and not to any *moral* purity in the goddess. Her association with Mithra was close, even in Herodotus' time, for he falls into the mistake of saying (i.131) that the Persians called Aphrodite Mithra, when he should have said Anaïtis (Anāhita). Though god of truth and righteousness Mithra is not associated with moral purity (chastity). On the contrary, he was said to fertilize the earth with his rays, as sun-god, and Anāhita as goddess of fruitfulness represented the female principle in conjunction with him. The vileness which led to the identification of Anāhita with the Bab Mylitta was doubtless of later date than Zoroaster's time, yet there was little or nothing in Zoroastrianism to check it. Something similar asserts itself in Armenia, as well as in Irān, and in fact in all Nature-worship everywhere. Associated with this was the form of incest known as next-of-kin marriage (Av. *Ḫvaētva-datha*, Pahl. *Khvētūkdas*), which permitted and encouraged marriages between brothers and sisters.

6. Contest between Ōrmazd and Ahriman

According to later Zoroastrian belief, the contest between Ōrmazd (Ahura Mazda) and Ahriman (Aṅrō Mainyuš), after continuing for 9,000 years, is to be decided in favor of the former only through his possessing foreknowledge and Ahriman's lacking it (*Būnd.*, I). Both came into existence independently in limitless time (Av. *Zrvāna Akarana; Vend.*, *Farg.* XIX, 13; Pahl. *Damān ī Akanārakhōmand, Būnd.*, I), which, personified in the *Vendīdād*, is called "Self-created," and is there by Ahura Mazda's command invoked by Zoroaster in conjunction with Vāyu, the *Air*, the Winds, "the bountiful, beauteous daughter of Ahura Mazda" (Ārmaiti), the Earth, and other objects of worship (loc. cit.). No creature of Ahriman is to be worshipped; hence Indra, though in later Vedic times rising in India to a leading position in the Pantheon, is in the Avesta accounted a fiend, the very impersonation of the Lie which the Avesta so firmly denounces and which Darius mentions as the cause of all the rebellions, which produced so much bloodshed in his time. No virtue was valued so highly as truth in ancient Īrān, as Herodotus agrees with the Avesta in testifying.

7. Ethics

Avestic morality encourages the destruction of all hurtful things, as being of Aṅrō Mainyuš' creation, and the propagation of everything good. Hence agriculture is esp. commended, together with the rearing of cattle and sheep. Somewhat later the whole duty of man was said to consist in good thoughts, good words, good deeds. Fierce opposition to every other religion was enjoined as a religious duty, and, under the Sāsānides esp., this led to fearful and repeated persecutions of Christians throughout the empire.

8. Sacred Thread

The Sacred Thread (Av. *Aiwyāṅhana;* Skt. *Upavītam*, etc, now by the Pārsīs styled the *Kushti*) plays as important a part in Zoroastrianism as in Hindūism. So do charms, *māthras* (Skt. *mantras*), consisting in repetitions of the verses of the Avesta. The latter is even adored.

9. Early Traditions

The first thing created by Ahura Mazda was a Bull, which may represent the earth, and reminds us of the Cow Audhumla in the *Edda* (*Gylfaginning* VI). This was killed by Aṅrō Mainyuš (in a later version, by Mithra). His spirit (*Gēuš Urvan*) went to heaven and became the guardian of cattle.

The first man was Gaya-maretan ("Mortal Life"); hence the phrase *Haca Gayāṭ Marethnaṭ ā Saoshyantāṭ*, "from Gaya-maretan [Gayōmard, Kayomarth] to Saoshyant" (*Yasna* XXVI, 10; *Yasht* XIII, 145), means "from the beginning to the end of the world." From the *Airyanem Vaêjō* ("Āryan germ"), the first home of the Iranians, men were compelled to migrate because Aṅrō Mainyuš so altered the climate that the winter became ten months long and the summer only two. Yima Khshaêta ("Yima the Brilliant," Pers *Jamshīd*), son of Vīvaṅhāṭ, though he twice refused Ahura Mazda's commission to guard his creatures, and though by three lies he lost the "Royal Light" (*Ḥvarenō Kavaêm*) which he originally possessed, was yet directed to prepare a very extensive inclosure (*Vāra*), in which he preserved "the seeds of sheep and cattle, of men, of dogs, of birds, and of red, glowing fires" from some terribly severe winters which came upon the earth (*Vendīdād* II; *Yasht* XIX). The *Būndihīshnīh* tale of a flood differs from this, preserving an independent narrative. Ahura Mazda's law was preached to men within Yima's inclosure.

10. The Earth

The earth consists of seven divisions, called *Karshvares* (cf the Skt. *dvīpas*). Only one of these, Ḥvaniratha, is inhabited by men; the others are separated from it by impassable abysses. Sun, moon, and stars revolve round Mt. Taêra, a peak in the Elburz Mountains (Demāvend?). A later legend says that the Elburz Range surrounds the earth.

11. Heaven and Hell

Each god and man possesses a *fravashi*, which has been compared to a guardian spirit and seems to differ from the soul (*urvan*). After judgment by Mithra, Rashnu and Sraosha, the souls of the dead must cross the *Chinvaṭ*-bridge ("Bridge of the Judge"), which is guarded by two dogs and is narrow and difficult for the unjust, but wide and easy for the just. The righteous man then advances through three Paradises, those of Good Thoughts, Good Words and Good Works (*Humata, Hūkhta, Hvaršta: Yasht* XVI; *Artā Vīrāf Nāmak*, VII–IX), until, led by Sraosha, Ātar, and Vōhu Manō, he finally reaches Ahura Mazda's abode of light and glory, *Garō-nmāna* (in *Gāthās, Gāro-demāna;* Pahl. *Garōtmān*), where Ahura Mazda himself receives him with the words: "Greeting to thee; well hast thou come; from that mortal world hast thou come to this pure, bright place" (*A. V. Nāmak*, XI, 8, 9). But the soul of the wicked man, passing through regions of Evil Thoughts, Evil Words and Evil Deeds, finally reaches a dark and gloomy Hell (*Duzhaṅh*). In later times it was believed that those not yet fit for heaven waited in *Misvānō Gātuš*, an intermediate place where the extra merits of the just were stored up for the benefit of the less fortunate (*Vend., Farg.* XIX). A later name was *Hamistakān*. But De Harlez is of the opinion that this idea was borrowed from mediaeval Christianity.

12. Interment

In primeval times the Persians buried or burned their dead. Zoroastrianism may have introduced the *dakhma* (*Vendīdād, passim*) or Tower of Silence, on which bodies are exposed to be eaten by vultures. Those of which the ruins have been discovered at Al Hibbah are very ancient. But in Herodotus' time it was usual, after permitting the flesh to be devoured by dogs and birds, to cover the bones with wax and bury them (Herod. i.140). This was done to prevent them from coming in contact with and so polluting the earth. The custom of burial is proved by the tombs of the Achaemenian kings near Persepolis, and that of Cyrus, a stone chamber raised high above the ground, at Pasargadae.

13. Worship

Zoroastrianism permits no idol-worship and no temples, fire-altars only being used. These were served by *Ātharvans* or fire-priests, who fed the fire with costly wood and poured into it libations of *haoma*-juice, taking care to cover their mouths with a cloth

Fire Altars.

(*paiti-dhāna*) to keep the sacred fire from being polluted by their breath. Sacrifices were often offered on the tops of the highest mountains under the open sky (Herod. i.132; Xen. *Cyrop.* viii).

14. The Magi

The Magi doubtless owed their monopoly of priestly functions to their being Zoroaster's own tribe. They are not mentioned as priests in the Pers cuneiform inscriptions. Only once does the word "Magus" occur in the Avesta, and then in composition (*Mōghu-ṭbish*, a Magus-hater, *Yasna* LXV, 7). It is not necessary to trace to Bab influence the decay of Zoroastrianism and its degradation in late Achaemenian times. This was at least in large measure due to a revival of the ideas and practices forbidden by Zoroaster, which reassert themselves in some parts of the Avesta, and which afterward gave rise to Mithraism.

15. Eschatology

The Avesta states that, 1,000 years after Zoroaster's death, a prophet named Ukhshyaṭ-ereta will arise from his seed to restore his religion. After another 1,000 years another, Ukhshyaṭ-nemaṅh, will appear for the same purpose. The end of the world will come 1,000 years later. Then a third prophet, Saoshyaṅṭ, will be born, and will usher in the Restoration (*frashō-kereti*) of the world to its primitive happiness and freedom from the evil creatures of Aṅrō Mainyuš. This process will be completed in 57 years, during which 6 other prophets will perform in the other 6 *Karshvares* the work which will here be accomplished by Saoshyaṅṭ. But mention of this Restoration occurs only in very late parts of the Avesta (e.g. *Vend., Farg.* XVIII, 51). It does *not* mean Resurrection, as De Harlez has shown. Later still, something of the kind *was* believed, and in the *Būndihīshnīh* (ch v) and the *Patēt* (§ 28) we have the word *rīstākhīz* (from Av. *irista*, "departed," and *ḥvīs*, "to rise"), which does mean "rising of the dead." But it can hardly be doubted that the doctrine is due to Heb and Christian influence, esp. when we consider

16. Hebrew and Christian Influence

the late and uncertain date of the books in which the idea occurs. Israelites settled in Media in large numbers in or about 730–728 BC under Sargon (2 K **17** 6), long before Zoroaster's birth. It is possible that his reformation may have owed much therefore to Heb influence. See, further, ZOROASTRIANISM.

The idea of virgin birth has been asserted to occur in Zoroastrianism, both with reference to Zoroaster himself and to the last three great prophets of whom mention has been made. This is an error. The Avesta and *all later* Zoroastrian books speak of Zoroaster's birth as quite natural, his father being Pōurushaspa. Nor is virgin birth referred to in the case of Saoshyañt and the rest. (*Mater cuiusque ex iis, sese in lacu quodam lavans, Zoroastris semine illic reposito gravida facta filium pariet: Vend., Farg.* XIX, 4–6; *Yasht* XIII, 128, 142; *Bŭnd.*, XXXII, 8, 9.) Virginity is not highly esteemed in the Avesta, though fornication is condemned.

17. No Virgin Birth

Literature.—Geldner's ed of text of *Avesta;* De Harlez, *Avesta;* Achaemenian Inscriptions; *Sacred Books of the East*, vols IV, XXIII, XXXI; Grassmann, *Wörterbuch zum Rig Veda;* Haug and West, *Artā Virāf Nāmak;* Spiegel, *Einleitung in die trad. Schriften der Parsen; Eranische Altertumskunde;* Darmesteter, *Études iraniennes;* Haug, *Essays on . . . . Religion of Pārsis;* De Harlez, *Manuel du Pehlavi;* Cook, *Origins of Religion and Language.* See also Zoroastrianism.

W. St. Clair Tisdall

PERSIANS, pûr'shanz, -zhanz (פָּרַס, *pāraṣ*, also =Persia, Persis [q.v.]; adj. פַּרְסִי, *parṣī*, Heb, and פַּרְסָי, *parṣay*, Aram.; **Πέρσαι,** *Pérsai*, adj. only in Neh **12** 22; Dnl **6** 28; Achaem. Pers *Pārsa*, name of both country and people; does not occur in Avesta):

The Persians are not mentioned in the Bible until the exilic books (2 Ch **36** 20.22.23; Ezr **1** 1.2.8; **3** 7; Est **1** 19, etc; Dnl **5** 28; **6** 8.12.15.28), being previously included under the Medes (Gen **10** 2), as they were by Thucydides, and even by Xenophon often.

I. Affinity.—Being of the same stock as the Medes they shared the name Āryans (Achaem. *āriya;* Av. *airya;* Skt. *ārya*, "noble"); cf the Naqsh i Rustam Inscription, where Darius I calls himself "a Persian, son of a Persian, an Āryan, of Āryan descent" (ll. 13, 14). Tradition assigns as their earliest known habitat the so-called *Airyanem Vaêjô* ("Āryan germ"), a district between the Jaxartes and the Oxus (*Vendīdād* I), whence they migrated gradually to what was afterward known as Persis (modern *Fārs*), including probably part of Elam.

1. Three Classes The Avesta shows that the Medo-Pers community was divided into 3 classes (*zañtu*): the *Āthravans* or fire-priests, the *Rathaêštars* or charioteers, and the *Vāstryafshuyans* or cattle-rearers (cf the three original Hindū castes, the *Brāhmaṇs*, the *Kshattriyas* and the *Vaišyas*). A 4th class, the artisans or *Hūitis*, came later. But these were classes, not castes.

2. Tribal and Clan Divisions They were also divided into tribes, clans (Achaem. *vith;* Av. *vīs;* cf *vicus*) and families or households (Achaem. *taumā;* Av. *nmāna*). Herodotus (i.125) mentions ten Pers tribes, the chief being the Pasargadae, to which belonged the Achaemenian clan (*φρήτρη, phrētrē*) which included the royal family. This dynasty traced its origin to Achaemenes (*Hakhāmanish*) according to Da-

3. Achaemenian Dynasty rius and Herodotus. The following scheme will serve to show the descent of the line of Pers kings mentioned in the Bible and in secular history up to the time of the fall of the dynasty in 331 BC.

Achaemenes (Hakhāmanish)
Tēispēs (Chaishpish, Šispiš)
- Cyrus
  - Cambyses
    - Cyrus the Great
      - Cambyses
- Ariaramnēs (Ariyārāmnā)
  - Arsamēs (Arshāma)
    - Hystaspēs (Vishtāspa)
      - Darius I
        - Xerxes I (Ahasuerus)
          - Artaxerxes I (Longimanus)
            - Xerxes II
            - Sogdianus
            - Darius II (Nothos, Ōchos)
              - Artaxerxes II (Mnēmōn)
                - Artaxerxes III (Ōchos)
                  - Arsēs
                - (Sisygambis, a daughter)
                  - Darius III (Codomannus) [Neh **12** 22; 1 Macc **1** 1]

II. Civilization.—The Persians had indulged less in luxury than the Medes, until their conquest of Media and other lands under Cyrus

1. Writing the Great gave them the opportunity, which they were not slow to embrace, being famed for their readiness to adopt foreign customs. Writing was introduced from Babylonia through Elam. This cuneiform char-

2. Institutions and Customs acter was afterward superseded by one derived from Syria, from which came the Avestic writing, which, in its corrupt Pahlavī form, lasted until the Arabian conquest imposed the Arab. character on the people. The Achaemenian kings probably borrowed from Babylon and further developed their system of royal posts (Est **8** 14) or messengers (and even the words ἄγγαροι, *ággaroi*, and ἀστάνδαι, *astándai*, used to denote them, are almost certainly Babylonian). Of these men's pace it was said, "No mortal thing is quicker." The custom of showing special honor to the "Benefactors of the King" (Herod. viii.85: ὀροσάγγαι, *orosággai*=Av. *uru*+*sañh*, "widely renowned") is referred to in Est **6** 1.2.3, and that of covering the (head and) face of a criminal condemned to death (with a large black cap) (Est **7** 8.9) occurs in the *Shāhnāmah* also.

(1) *The king* was an arbitrary ruler with unlimited power, the council of seven princes who stood nearest to the throne (Est **1** 14; cf Herod. iii. 70–84) having no share in the government.

(2) *The army.*—As soldiers, the Persians were famous as archers and javelin-throwers; they

Persian Warriors.

were also skilled in the use of the sling, and above all in riding. Boys were taken from the women's into the men's part of the house at the age of 5, and were there trained in "riding, archery and speaking the truth" until 20 years old. In Darius' inscriptions, as well as in the Avesta, lying is regarded as a great crime.

(3) *Marriage.*—The Persians practised polygamy, and marriages between those next of kin were approved of. Pride and garrulity are mentioned as distinctive of the Pers character.

III. History.—Pers history, as known to us, begins with Cyrus the Great. His ancestors, for

1. Cyrus

at least some generations, seem to have been chiefs or "kings" of Anshan, a district in Persia or Elam. Cyrus himself (*WAI*, V, plate 35) gives his genealogy up to and including Tĕispēs, entitling all his ancestors whom he mentions, kings of Anshan. Phraortēs, king of the Medes, is said to have first subjugated the Persians to that kingdom about 97 years before Cyrus (Herod. i.102). Cyrus himself headed his countrymen's revolt against Astyages, who advanced to attack Pasargadae (549 BC). His army mutinied and surrendered him to Cyrus, whom the Greeks held to be his grandson on the mother's side. Cyrus, becoming supreme ruler of both Medes and Persians, advanced to the conquest of Lydia. He defeated and captured Croesus, overran Lydia, and compelled the Greek colonies in Asia Minor to pay tribute (547 BC).

He overthrew the Sute (Bedawīn) across the Tigris the following year, and was then invited by a

2. Capture of Babylon

a large party in Babylonia to come to their help against the usurper Nabunāhid, whose religious zeal had led him to collect as many as possible of the idols from other parts of Babylonia and remove them to Babylon, thereby increasing the sacredness and magnificence of that city but inflicting injury on neighboring and more ancient sanctuaries. Defeating Nabunāhid's army and capturing the king, Cyrus sent his own forces under Gōbryas (Gubaru, Gaubaruva) to take possession of Babylon. This he did in June, 538, "without opposition and without a battle." The citadel, however, where Belshazzar "the king's son" was in command, held out for some months, and was then taken in a night attack in which "the king's son" was slain. Cyrus made Gōbryas viceroy of Chaldaea, and he "appointed governors in Babylonia" (Cyrus' "Annalistic Tablet"). When Gōbryas died within the year, Cyrus' son Cambyses was made viceroy of the country, now become a province of the Pers empire. Cyrus restored the gods to their sanctuaries, and this doubtless led to permission being given to the Jews to return to Jerus, taking with them their sacred vessels, and to rebuild their temple. Cyrus was killed in battle against some frontier tribe (accounts differ where) in 529 BC. His tomb at Murghāb, near the ruins of Pasargadae, is still standing.

Cyrus' son and successor, Cambyses, invaded Egypt and conquered it after a great battle near

3. Cambyses

Pelusium (525 BC). During his absence, a Magian, Gaumāta, who pretended to be Smerdis (Bardiya), Cambyses' murdered brother, seized the throne. Marching against him, Cambyses committed suicide. After a reign of 7 months,

4. Pseudo-Smerdis

the usurper was overthrown and slain by Darius and his 6 brother-nobles (their names in Herod. iii.70 are confirmed with one exception in Darius' Besitūn Inscription, col. iv, 80–86). Darius became king as the heir of Cambyses (521 BC). But

5. Darius I

in nearly every part of the empire rebellions broke out, in most cases headed by real or pretended descendants of the ancient kings of each country. After at least 3 years' struggle Darius' authority was firmly established everywhere. He then divided the empire into satrapies, or provinces (*dahyāva*), of which there were at first 23 (Beh. Inscription, col. i, 13–17), and ultimately at least 29 (Naqsh i Rustam Inscription, 22–30). Over these he placed satraps of noble Pers or Median descent, instead of representatives of their ancient kings. His empire extended from the Indus to the Black Sea, from the Jaxartes to beyond the Nile.

Tomb of Cyrus.

Darius united the latter river with the Red Sea by a canal, the partly obliterated inscription commemorating

6. Darius' Suez Canal

which may perhaps be thus restored and rendered: "I am a Persian; with Persia I seized Egypt. I commanded to dig this canal from the river named the Nile [Pirāva], which flows through Egypt, to this sea which comes from Persia. Then this canal was dug, according as I commanded. And I said, 'Come ye from the Nile through this canal to Persia.'"

Darius' expedition into Scythia, his success in subduing the rebellion among the Asiatic Greeks, his attempts to conquer Greece itself and his overthrow at Marathon (499–490 BC) are part of the history of Greece. A rebellion in Egypt had not been repressed when Darius died in 485 BC.

Xerxes I, who succeeded his father, regained Egypt, but his failure in his attempts to conquer

7. Xerxes I

Greece largely exhausted his empire. In 464 BC he was murdered. His son Artaxerxes I, surnamed "the long-armed," succeeded him, being himself succeeded in 424 BC by his son Xerxes II, who was murdered the following year. This ended the legitimate Achaemenian line, the next king, Darius II (styled *Nothos*, or "bastard," as well as Ōchos), being one of Artaxerxes' illegitimate sons (we pass over Sogdianus' brief reign).

8. Artaxerxes I

Artaxerxes II, Mnēmōn, succeeded his father and left the throne to his son Artaxerxes III, Ōchos. The latter was murdered with all his sons but the youngest, Arsēs, by an Egyp eunuch Bagōas, probably in revenge for Artaxerxes' conduct in Egypt (338 BC). Arsēs was murdered by Bagōas 3 years later, when Darius III,

9. Xerxes II

Codomannus, the son of Sisygambis, daughter of Artaxerxes II, and her husband, a Pers noble, ascended the throne. Darius was completely overthrown by Alexander the Great in the battle of Gaugamela or Arbela, 331 BC, and shortly after fell by an assassin's hand. This ended the Pers empire of the Achaemenides, the whole of the lands composing it becoming part of the empire of Macedon.

10. Later Persian Kings

IV. First Mention in Inscriptions.—Persia (*Parsua*) is first mentioned as a country in an inscription of Rammānu Nirāri III (*WAI*, I, plate 35, no. 1, l. 8), who boasts of having conquered it and other lands (he reigned from 812 to 783 or from 810 to 781 BC).

Literature.—Besides the main authorities mentioned in the text, we learn much from Spiegel, *Die Altpersischen Keilinschriften*, Arrian, Thucydides, Polybius, Strabo, Curtius.

W. St. Clair Tisdall

PERSIS, pûr′sis (**Περσίς**, *Persís*): The name of a female member of the Christian community at Rome, to whom Paul sent greetings (Rom **16** 12). Paul designates her "the beloved, who labored much in the Lord." The name is not found in inscriptions of the imperial household, but it occurs as the name of a freedwoman (*CIL*, VI, 23, 959).

PERSON, pûr′sun, pûr′s'n, **PERSONALITY**, pûr-sun-al′i-ti (**נֶפֶשׁ**, *nephesh*, **אִישׁ**, *'īsh*, **אָדָם**, *'ādhām*, **פָּנִים**, *pānīm;* **πρόσωπον**, *prósōpon*, **ὑπόστασις**, *hupóstasis*): The most frequent word for "person" in the OT is *nephesh*, "soul" (Gen **14** 21, "Give me the persons, and take the goods"; **36** 6, AV "all the persons"; Nu **5** 6, AV "that person," etc); *'īsh*, "a man," "an individual," is also used (Jgs **9** 2, "threescore and ten persons"; 1 S **16** 18, "a comely person," etc); *'ādhām*, "a man," "a human being" (Nu **31** 28, "of the persons, and of the oxen"; Prov **6** 12, "a worthless person," etc); *'ěnōsh*, "a man," "a weak, mortal man," occurs twice (Jgs **9** 4, AV "vain and light persons"; Zeph **3** 4); *ba'al*, "owner," "lord," is once trd "person" (Prov **24** 8, AV "a mischievous person"), and *methīm*, "men," once (Ps **26** 4, AV "vain persons"); *pānīm*, "face," is frequently trd "person" when the reference is to the external appearance, as of persons in high places, rich persons who could favor or bribe, etc, chiefly in the phrases "regarding the person," "accepting the person" (Dt **10** 17; Mal **1** 8).

In the NT *prosōpon*, "face," "countenance," stands in the same connection (Mt **22** 16, "Thou regardest not the person of men"; Gal **2** 6, "God accepteth not man's person"; Acts **10** 34, "God is no respecter of persons"; Rom **2** 11, "there is no respect of persons with God"; Eph **6** 9; Col **3** 25; Jas **2** 1.9); in 2 Cor **1** 11 we have "persons" (*prosōpon*), absol. as in the later Gr, "the gift bestowed . . . . by many persons," the only occurrence in the NT; in **2** 10 *prosōpon* may stand for "presence," as RV "in the presence of Christ," but it might mean "as representing Christ"; in He **1** 3, AV *hupostasis*, "that which lies under," *substratum*, is rendered "person," "the express image of his person," i.e. of God, which RV renders "the very image of his substance," m "the impress of his substance," i.e. the manifestation or expression of the invisible God and Father. "Person" is also frequently supplied as the substantive implied in various adjs., etc, e.g. profane, perjured, vile.

In the Apoc we have *prosōpon* trd "person" (Jth **7** 15, RV "face"; Ecclus **10** 5, etc); the "accepting of persons" is condemned (Wisd **6** 7; Ecclus **4** 22.27; **7** 6; **20** 22, RV "by a foolish countenance"; **35** 13; **42** 1; "With him [God] is no respect of persons," Ecclus **35** 12).

RV has "soul" for "person" (Nu **5** 6), "face" (Jer **52** 25), "man" (Mt **27** 24); "reprobate" for "vile person" (Ps **15** 4), ARV, ERVm "fool" (Isa **32** 5.6); ARV "men of falsehood" for "vain persons" (Ps **26** 4); for "a wicked person," RV has "an evil thing" (Ps **101** 4); "back to thee in his own person" (*autón*, different text) for "again thou therefore receive him" (Philem ver 12); "take away life" for "respect any person" (2 S **14** 14); "with seven others" for "the eighth person" (2 Pet **2** 5); "false swearers" for "perjured persons" (1 Tim **1** 10); "seven thousand persons" for "of men seven thousand" (Rev **11** 13).

Personality is that which constitutes and characterizes *a person*. The word "person" (Lat *persona*) is derived from the mask through which an actor spoke his part (*per-sona*). "From being applied to the mask, it came next to be applied to the actor, then to the character acted, then to any assumed character, then to anyone having any character or station"; lastly, it came to mean an individual, a feeling, thinking and acting being. For full personality there must be self-consciousness, with the capability of free thought and action—self-determination—hence we speak of personal character, personal action, etc. A person is thus a responsible being, while an animal is not. Personality is distinctive of man. The personality is the unit of the entire rational being, perhaps most clearly represented by "the will"; it is that which is deepest in man, belonging, of course, not to the realm of space or the region of the visible, but existing as a spiritual reality in time, with a destiny beyond it. It is the substance (*hupostasis*) of the being, that which underlies all its manifestations; hence the rendering "the express image of his person" in He **1** 3 AV. *Hupostasis* was employed by the early Gr Fathers to express what the Latins intended by *persona;* afterward *prosōpon* was introduced.

Recent psychology has brought into prominence elements in the *subconscious* realm, the relation of which to the personality is obscure. There seems to be more in each individual than is normally expressed in the personal consciousness and action. The real, responsible personality, however, is something which is always *being formed*. The phenomenon of double personality is pathological, as truly the result of brain disease as is insanity.

In the Bible man is throughout regarded as personal, although it was only gradually that the full importance of the individual as distinct from the nation was realized. The use of *prosōpon* for "person" indicates also a more external conception of personality than the modern. With the Hebrews the *nephesh* was the seat of personality, e.g. "Thou wilt not leave my soul [*nephesh*] to Sheol" (Ps **16** 10); "Thou hast brought up my soul from Sheol" (Ps **30** 3). God is also always regarded as *personal* (who has created man in His own image), and although the representations seem often anthropomorphic they are not really such. The Divine personality could only be conceived after the analogy of the human, as far as it could be definitely conceived at all; but God was regarded as transcending, not only the whole of Nature, but all that is human, e.g. "God is not a man, that he should lie" (Nu **23** 19; 1 S **15** 29); "Canst thou by searching find out God?" (Job **11** 7; Isa **40** 28; cf Eccl **3** 11; **8** 17, etc). In the NT the personality of God is, on the warrant of Jesus Himself, conceived after the analogy of human fatherhood, yet as transcending all our human conceptions: "How much more?" (Mt **7** 11); "Who hath known the mind of the Lord? or who hath been his counsellor?" (Rom **11** 34). Man is body, soul and spirit, but God in Himself is Spirit, infinite, perfect, ethical Spirit (Mt **5** 48; Jn **4** 24). He is forever more than all that is created, "For of him, and through him, and unto him, are all things" (Rom **11** 36). The human personality, being spiritual, survives bodily dissolution and in Christ becomes clothed again with a spiritual body (Phil **3** 21; 1 Cor **15** 44).

W. L. Walker

PERSON OF CHRIST:

Method of the Article

It is the purpose of this article to make as clear as possible the conception of the Person of Christ, in the technical sense of that term, which lies on—or, if we prefer to say so, beneath—the pages of the NT. Were it its purpose to trace out the process by which this great mystery has been revealed to men, a beginning would need to be taken from the intimations as to the nature of the person of the Messiah in OT prophecy, and an attempt would require to be made to discriminate the exact contribution of each organ of revelation to our knowledge. And were there added to this a desire to ascertain the progress of the apprehension of this mystery by men, there would be demanded a further inquiry into the exact degree of understanding which was brought to the truth revealed at each stage of its revelation. The magnitudes with which such investigations deal, however, are very minute; and the profit to be derived from them is not, in a case like the present, very great. It is, of course, of importance to know how the person of the Messiah was represented in the predictions of the OT; and it is a matter at least of interest to note, for example, the difficulty experienced by Our Lord's immediate disciples in comprehending all that was involved in His manifestation. But, after all, the constitution of Our Lord's person is a matter of revelation, not of human thought; and it is preeminently a revelation of the NT, not of the OT. And the NT is all the product of a single movement, at a single stage of its development, and therefore presents in its fundamental teaching a common character. The whole of the NT was written within the limits of about half a century; or, if we except the writings of John, within the narrow bounds of a couple of decades; and the entire body of writings which enter into it are so much of a piece that it may be plausibly represented that they all bear the stamp of a single mind. In its fundamental teaching, the NT lends itself, therefore, more readily to what is called dogmatic than to what is called genetic treatment; and we shall penetrate most surely into its essential meaning if we take our start from its clearest and fullest statements, and permit their light to be thrown upon its more incidental allusions. This is peculiarly the case with such a matter as the person of Christ, which is dealt with chiefly incidentally, as a thing already understood by all, and needing only to be alluded to rather than formally expounded. That we may interpret these allusions aright, it is requisite that we should recover from the first the common conception which underlies them all.

I. The Teaching of Paul.—(1) *General drift of passage.*—We begin, then, with the most didactic of the NT writers, the apostle Paul, and with one of the passages in which he most fully intimates his conception of the person of his Lord, Phil **2** 5-9.

1. Phil 2: 5-9

Even here, however, Paul is not formally expounding the doctrine of the Person of Christ; he is only alluding to certain facts concerning His person and action perfectly well known to his readers, in order that he may give point to an adduction of Christ's example. He is exhorting his readers to unselfishness, such unselfishness as esteems others better than ourselves, and looks not only on our own things but also on those of others. Precisely this unselfishness, he declares, was exemplified by Our Lord. He did not look upon His own things but the things of others; that is to say, He did not stand upon His rights, but was willing to forego all that He might justly have claimed for Himself for the good of others. For, says Paul, though, as we all know, in His intrinsic nature He was nothing other than God, yet He did not, as we all know right well, look greedily on His condition of equality with God, but made no account of Himself, taking the form of a servant, being made in the likeness of men; and, being found in fashion as a man, humbled Himself, becoming obedient up to death itself, and that, the death of the cross. The statement is thrown into historical form; it tells the story of Christ's life on earth. But it presents His life on earth as a life in all its elements alien to His intrinsic nature, and assumed only in the performance of an unselfish purpose. On earth He lived as a man, and subjected Himself to the common lot of men. But He was not by nature a man, nor was He in His own nature subject to the fortunes of human life. By nature He was God; and He would have naturally lived as became God—'on an equality with God.' He became man by a voluntary act, 'taking no account of Himself,' and, having become man, He voluntarily lived out His human life under the conditions which the fulfilment of His unselfish purpose imposed on Him.

(2) *Our Lord's intrinsic Deity.*—The terms in which these great affirmations are made deserve the most careful attention. The language in which Our Lord's intrinsic Deity is expressed, for example, is probably as strong as any that could be devised. Paul does not say simply, "He was God." He says, "He was in the form of God," employing a turn of speech which throws emphasis upon Our Lord's possession of the specific quality of God. "Form" is a term which expresses the sum of those char-

acterizing qualities which make a thing the precise thing that it is. Thus, the "form" of a sword (in this case mostly matters of external configuration) is all that makes a given piece of metal specifically a sword, rather than, say, a spade. And "the form of God" is the sum of the characteristics which make the being we call "God," specifically God, rather than some other being—an angel, say, or a man. When Our Lord is said to be in "the form of God," therefore, He is declared, in the most express manner possible, to be all that God is, to possess the whole fulness of attributes which make God God. Paul chooses this manner of expressing himself here instinctively, because, in adducing Our Lord as our example of self-abnegation, his mind is naturally resting, not on the bare fact that He is God, but on the richness and fulness of His being as God. He was all this, yet He did not look on His own things but on those of others.

It should be carefully observed also that in making this great affirmation concerning Our Lord, Paul does not throw it distinctively into the past, as if he were describing a mode of being formerly Our Lord's, indeed, but no longer His because of the action by which He became our example of unselfishness. Our Lord, he says, "being," "existing," "subsisting" "in the form of God"—as it is variously rendered. The rendering proposed by RVm, "being originally," while right in substance, is somewhat misleading. The vb. employed means "strictly 'to be beforehand,' 'to be already' so and so" (Blass, *Grammar of NT Greek*, ET, 244), "to be there and ready," and intimates the existing circumstances, disposition of mind, or, as here, mode of subsistence in which the action to be described takes place. It contains no intimation, however, of the cessation of these circumstances or disposition, or mode of subsistence; and that, the less in a case like the present, where it is cast in a tense (the imperfect) which in no way suggests that the mode of subsistence intimated came to an end in the action described by the succeeding vb. (cf the ||'s, Lk **16** 14.23; **23** 50; Acts **2** 30; **3** 2; 2 Cor **8** 17; **12** 16; Gal **1** 14). Paul is not telling us here, then, what Our Lord was once, but rather what He already was, or, better, what in His intrinsic nature He is; he is not describing a past mode of existence of Our Lord, before the action he is adducing as an example took place—although the mode of existence he describes was Our Lord's mode of existence before this action—so much as painting in the background upon which the action adduced may be thrown up into prominence. He is telling us who and what He is who did these things for us, that we may appreciate how great the things He did for us are.

(3) *No exinanition.*—And here it is important to observe that the whole of the action adduced is thrown up thus against this background—not only its negative description to the effect that Our Lord (although all that God is) did not look greedily on His (consequent) being on an equality with God; but its positive description as well, introduced by the "but . . . ." and that in both of its elements, not merely that to the effect (ver 7) that 'he took no account of himself' (rendered not badly by AV, He "made himself of no reputation"; but quite misleading by RV, He "emptied himself"), but equally that to the effect (ver 8) that "he humbled himself." It is the whole of what Our Lord is described as doing in vs 6–8, that He is described as doing despite His "subsistence in the form of God." So far is Paul from intimating, therefore, that Our Lord laid aside His Deity in entering upon His life on earth, that he rather asserts that He retained His Deity throughout His life on earth, and in the whole course of His humiliation, up to death itself, was consciously ever exercising self-abnegation, living a life which did not by nature belong to Him, which stood in fact in direct contradiction to the life which was naturally His. It is this underlying implication which determines the whole choice of the language in which Our Lord's earthly life is described. It is because it is kept in mind that He still was "in the form of God," that is, that He still had in possession all that body of characterizing qualities by which God is made God, for example, that He is said to have been made, not man, but "in the likeness of man," to have been found, not man, but "in fashion as a man"; and that the wonder of His servanthood and obedience, the mark of servanthood, is thought of as so great. Though He was truly man, He was much more than man; and Paul would not have his readers imagine that He had become merely man. In other words, Paul does not teach that Our Lord was once God but had become instead man; he teaches that though He was God, He had become also man.

An impression that Paul means to imply, that in entering upon His earthly life Our Lord had laid aside His Deity, may be created by a very prevalent misinterpretation of the central clause of his statement—a misinterpretation unfortunately given currency by the rendering of ERV: "counted it not a prize to be on an equality with God, but emptied himself," varied without improvement in ARV to: "counted not the being on an equality with God a thing to be grasped, but emptied himself." The former (negative) member of this clause means just: He did not look greedily upon His being on an equality with God; did not "set supreme store" by it (see Lightfoot on the clause). The latter (positive) member of it, however, cannot mean in antithesis to this, that He therefore "emptied himself," divested Himself of this, His being on an equality with God, much less that He "emptied himself," divested Himself of His Deity ("form of God") itself, of which His being on an equality with God is the manifested consequence. The vb. here rendered "emptied" is in constant use in a metaphorical sense (so only in the NT: Rom **4** 14; 1 Cor **1** 17; **9** 15; 2 Cor **9** 3) and cannot here be taken literally. This is already apparent from the definition of the manner in which the "emptying" is said to have been accomplished, supplied by the modal clause which is at once attached: by "taking the form of a servant." You cannot "empty" by "taking"—*adding*. It is equally apparent, however, from the strength of the emphasis which, by its position, is thrown upon the "himself." We may speak of Our Lord as "*emptying* Himself" of something else, but scarcely, with this strength of emphasis, of His "emptying *Himself*" of something else. This emphatic "Himself," interposed between the preceding clause and the vb. rendered "emptied," builds a barrier over which we cannot climb backward in search of that of which Our Lord emptied Himself. The whole thought is necessarily contained in the two words, "emptied *himself*," in which the word "emptied" must therefore be taken in a sense analogous to that which it bears in the other passages in the NT where it occurs. Paul, in a word, says here nothing more than that Our Lord, who did not look with greedy eyes upon His estate of equality with God, emptied Himself, if the language may be pardoned, of Himself; that is to say, in precise accordance with the exhortation for the enhancement of which His example is adduced, that He did not look on His own things. 'He made no account of Himself,' we may fairly paraphrase the clause; and thus all question of what He emptied Himself of falls away. What Our Lord actually did, according to Paul, is expressed in the following clauses; those now before us express more the moral character of His act. He took "the form of a servant," and so was "made in the likeness of men." But His doing this showed that He did not set overweening store by His state of equality with God, and did not account Himself the sufficient object of all the efforts. He was not self-regarding: He had regard for others. Thus He becomes our supreme example of self-abnegating conduct. See also KENOSIS.

(4) *Our Lord's humanity.*—The language in which the act by which Our Lord showed that He was self-abnegating is described, requires to be taken in its complete meaning. He took "the form of a servant, being made in the likeness of men," says Paul. The term "form" here, of course, bears the same full meaning as in the preceding instance of its occurrence in the phrase "the form of God." It imparts the specific quality, the whole body of characteristics, by which a servant is made what we know as a servant. Our Lord assumed, then, according to Paul, not the mere state or condition or outward appearance of a servant, but the reality; He became an actual "servant" in the world. The act by which He did this is described as a "taking," or, as it has become customary from this description of it to phrase it, as an "assumption." What is meant is that Our Lord took up into His personality a human nature; and therefore it is immediately explained that He took the form of a servant by "being made in the likeness of men." That the apostle does not say, shortly, that He assumed a human nature, is due to the engagement of his mind with the contrast which he wishes to bring out forcibly for the enhancement of his appeal to Our Lord's example, between what Our Lord is by nature and what He was willing to become, not looking on His own things but also on the things of others. This contrast is, no doubt, embodied in the simple opposition of God and man; it is much more pungently expressed in the qualificative terms, "form of God" and "form of a servant." The Lord of the world became a servant in the world; He whose right it was to rule took obedience as His life-characteristic. Naturally therefore Paul employs here a word of quality rather than a word of mere nature; and then defines his meaning in this word of quality by a further epexegetical clause. This further clause—"being made in the likeness of men"—does not throw doubt on the reality of the human nature that was assumed, in contradiction to the emphasis on its reality in the phrase "the form of a servant." It, along with the succeeding clause—"and being found in fashion as a man"—owes its peculiar form, as has already been pointed out, to the vividness of the apostle's consciousness, that he is speaking of one who, though really man, possessing all that makes a man a man, is yet, at the same time, infinitely more than a man, no less than God Himself, in possession of all that makes God God. Christ Jesus is in his view, therefore (as in the view of his readers, for he is not instructing his readers here as to the nature of Christ's person, but reminding them of certain elements in it for the purposes of his exhortation), both God and man, God who has "assumed" man into personal union with Himself, and has in this His assumed manhood lived out a human life on earth.

2. Other Pauline Passages

The elements of Paul's conception of the person of Christ are brought before us in this suggestive passage with unwonted fulness. But they all receive endless illustration from his occasional allusions to them, one or another, throughout his Epp. The leading motive of this passage, for example, reappears quite perfectly in 2 Cor **8** 9, where we are exhorted to imitate the graciousness of Our Lord Jesus Christ, who became for our sakes (emphatic) poor—He who was (again an imperfect participle, and therefore without suggestion of the cessation of the condition described) rich—that we might by His (very emphatic) poverty be made rich. Here the change in Our Lord's condition at a point of time perfectly understood between the writer and his readers is adverted to and assigned to its motive, but no further definition is given of the nature of either condition referred to. We are brought closer to the precise nature of the act by which the change was wrought by such a passage as Gal **4** 4. We read that "When the fulness of the time came, God sent forth his Son, born of a woman, born under the law, that he might redeem them that were under the law." The whole transaction is referred to the Father in fulfilment of His eternal plan of redemption, and it is described specifically as an incarnation: the Son of God is born of a woman—He who is in His own nature the Son of God, abiding with God, is sent forth from God in such a manner as to be born a human being, subject to law. The primary implications are that this was not the beginning of His being; but that before this He was neither a man nor subject to law. But there is no suggestion that on becoming man and subject to law, He ceased to be the Son of God or lost anything intimated by that high designation. The uniqueness of His relation to God as His Son is emphasized in a kindred passage (Rom **8** 3) by the heightening of the designation to that of God's "own Son," and His distinction from other men is intimated in the same passage by the declaration that God sent Him, not in sinful flesh, but only "in the likeness of sinful flesh." The reality of Our Lord's flesh is not thrown into doubt by this turn of speech, but His freedom from the sin which is associated with flesh as it exists in lost humanity is asserted (cf 2 Cor **5** 21). Though true man, therefore (1 Cor **15** 21; Rom **5** 21; Acts **17** 31), He is not without differences from other men; and these differences do not concern merely the condition (as sinful) in which men presently find themselves; but also their very origin: they are from below, He from above—'the first man is from the earth, earthy; the second man is from heaven' (1 Cor **15** 47). This is His peculiarity: He was born of a woman like other men; yet He descended from heaven (cf Eph **4** 9; Jn **3** 13). It is not meant, of course, that already in heaven He was a man; what is meant is that even though man He derives His origin in an exceptional sense from heaven. Paul describes what He was in heaven (but not alone in heaven)—that is to say before He was sent in the likeness of sinful flesh (though not alone before this)—in the great terms of "God's Son," "God's own Son," "the form of God," or yet again in words whose import cannot be mistaken, 'God over all' (Rom **9** 5). In the last cited passage, together with its parallel earlier in the same ep. (Rom **1** 3), the two sides or elements of Our Lord's person are brought into collocation after a fashion that can leave no doubt of Paul's conception of His twofold nature. In the earlier of these passages he tells us that Jesus Christ was born, indeed, of the seed of David according to the flesh, that is, so far as the human side of His being is concerned, but was powerfully marked out as the Son of God according to the Spirit of Holiness, that is, with respect to His higher nature, by the resurrection of the dead, which in a true sense began in His own rising from the dead. In the later of them, he tells us that Christ sprang indeed, as concerns the flesh, that is on the human side of His being, from Israel, but that, despite this earthly origin of His human nature, He yet is and abides (present participle) nothing less than the Supreme God, "God over all [emphatic], blessed forever." Thus Paul teaches us that by His coming forth from God to be born of woman, Our Lord, assuming a human nature to Himself, has, while remaining the Supreme God, become also true and perfect man. Accordingly, in a context in which the resources of language are strained to the utmost to make the exaltation of Our Lord's being clear—in which He is described as the image of the invisible God, whose being antedates all that is created, in whom, through whom and to whom all things have been created, and in whom they all subsist—we are told not only that (naturally) in Him all the fulness dwells (Col **1** 19), but, with complete explication, that 'all the fulness of the Godhead dwells in him bodily' (Col **2** 9); that is to say, the very Deity of God, that which makes God God, in all its completeness, has its permanent home in Our Lord, and that in a "bodily fashion," that is, it is in Him clothed with a body. He who looks upon Jesus Christ sees, no doubt, a body and a man; but as he sees the man clothed with the body, so he sees God Himself, in all the fulness of His Deity, clothed with the humanity. Jesus Christ is therefore God "manifested in the flesh" (1 Tim **3** 16), and His appearance on earth is an "epiphany" (2 Tim **1** 10), which is the technical term for manifestations on earth of a God. Though truly man, He is nevertheless also our "great God" (Tit **2** 13).

II. Teaching of the Epistle to the Hebrews.—The conception of the person of Christ which underlies and finds expression in the Ep. to the He is indistinguishable from that which governs all the allusions to Our Lord in the Epp. of Paul. To the author of this ep. Our Lord is above all else the Son of God in the most eminent sense of that word; and it is the Divine dignity and majesty belonging to Him from His very nature which forms the fundamental feature of the image of Christ which stands before his mind. And yet it is this author who, perhaps above all others of the NT writers, emphasizes the truth of the humanity of Christ, and dwells with most particularity upon the elements of His human nature and experience.

He 2:1 ff

(1) *Background of express Deity.*—The great Christological passage which fills ch **2** of the Ep. to the He rivals in its richness and fulness of detail, and its breadth of implication, that of Phil **2**. It is thrown up against the background of the remarkable exposition of the Divine dignity of the Son which occupies ch **1** (notice the "therefore" of **2** 1). There the Son had been declared to be "the effulgence of his (God's) glory, and the very image of his substance," through whom the universe has been created and by the word of whose power all things are held in being; and His exaltation above the angels, by means of whom the Old Covenant had been inaugurated, is measured by the difference between the designations "ministering spirits" proper to the one, and the Son of God, nay, God itself (**1** 8.9), proper to the other. The purpose of the succeeding statement is to enhance in the thought of the Jewish readers of the ep. the value of the salvation wrought by this Divine Saviour, by removing from their minds the offence they were in danger of taking at His lowly life and shameful death on earth. This earthly humiliation finds its abundant justification, we are told, in the greatness of the end which it sought and attained. By it Our Lord has, with His strong feet, broken out a pathway along which, in Him, sinful man may at length climb up to the high destiny which was promised him when it was declared he should have dominion over all creation. Jesus Christ stooped only to conquer, and He stooped to conquer not for Himself (for He was in His own person no less than God), but for us.

(2) *Completeness of humanity.*—The language in which the humiliation of the Son of God is in the first instance described is derived from the context. The establishment of His Divine majesty in ch **1** had taken the form of an exposition of His infinite exaltation above the angels, the highest of all creatures. His humiliation is described here therefore as being "made a little lower than the angels" (**2** 9). What is meant is simply that He became man; the phraseology is derived from Ps **8** AV, from which had just been cited the declaration that God had made man (despite his insignificance) "but a little lower than the angels," thus crowning him with glory and honor. The adoption of the language of the psalm to describe Our Lord's humiliation has the secondary effect, accordingly, of greatly enlarging the reader's sense of the immensity of the humiliation of the Son of God in becoming man: He descended an infinite distance to reach man's highest conceivable exaltation. As, however, the primary purpose of the adoption of the language is merely to declare that the Son of God became man, so it is shortly afterward explained (**2** 14) as an entering into participation in the blood and flesh which are common to men: "Since then the children are sharers in flesh and blood, he also himself in like manner partook of the same." The voluntariness, the reality, the completeness of the assumption of humanity by the Son of God, are all here emphasized.

The proximate end of Our Lord's assumption of humanity is declared to be that He might die; He was "made a little lower than the angels . . . . because of the suffering of death" (**2** 9); He took part in blood and flesh in order "that through death . . . ." (**2** 14). The Son of God as such could not die; to Him belongs by nature an "indissoluble life" (**7** 16 m). If He was to die, therefore, He must take to Himself another nature to which the experience of death were not impossible (**2** 17). Of course it is not meant that death was desired by Him for its own sake. The purpose of our passage is to save its Jewish readers from the offence of the death of Christ. What they are bidden to observe is, therefore, Jesus, who was made a little lower than the angels because of the suffering of death, 'crowned with glory and honor, that by the grace of God the bitterness of death which he tasted might redound to the benefit of every man' (**2** 9), and the argument is immediately pressed home that it was eminently suitable for God Almighty, in bringing many sons into glory, to make the Captain of their salvation perfect (as a Saviour) by means of suffering. The meaning is that it was only through suffering that these men, being sinners, could be brought into glory. And therefore in the plainer statement of ver 14 we read that Our Lord took part in flesh and blood in order "that through death he might bring to nought him that had the power of death, that is, the devil; and might deliver all them who through fear of death were all their lifetime subject to bondage"; and in the still plainer statement of ver 17 that the ultimate object of His assimilation to men was that He might "make propitiation for the sins of the people." It is for the salvation of sinners that Our Lord has come into the world; but, as that salvation can be wrought only by suffering and death, the proximate end of His assumption of humanity remains that He might die; whatever is more than this gathers around this.

The completeness of Our Lord's assumption of humanity and of His identification of Himself with it receives strong emphasis in this passage. He took part in the flesh and blood which is the common heritage of men, after the same fashion that other men participate in it (**2** 14); and, having thus become a man among men, He shared with other men the ordinary circumstances and fortunes of life, "in all things" (**2** 17). The stress is laid on trials, sufferings, death; but this is due to the actual course in which His life ran—and that it might run in which He became man—and is not exclusive of other human experiences. What is intended is that He became truly a man, and lived a truly human life, subject to all the experiences natural to a man in the particular circumstances in which He lived.

(3) *Continued possession of Deity.*—It is not implied, however, that during this human life—"the days of his flesh" (**5** 7)—He had ceased to be God, or to have at His disposal the attributes which belonged to Him as God. That is already excluded by the representations of ch **1**. The glory of this dispensation consists precisely in the bringing of its revelations directly by the Divine Son rather than by mere prophets (**1** 1), and it was as the effulgence of God's glory and the express image of His substance, upholding the universe by the word of His power, that this Son made purification of sins (**1** 3). Indeed, we are expressly told that even in the days of the flesh, He continued still a Son (**5** 8), and that it was precisely in this that the wonder lay: that though He was and remained (imperfect participle) a Son, He yet learned the obedience He had set Himself to (cf Phil **2** 8) by the things which He suffered. Similarly, we are told not only that, though an Israelite of the tribe of Judah, He possessed "the power of an indissoluble life" (**7** 16 m), but, describing that higher nature which gave Him this power as an "eternal Spirit" (cf "spirit of holiness," Rom **1** 4), that it was through this eternal Spirit that He could offer Himself without blemish unto God, a real and sufficing sacrifice, in contrast with the shadows of the Old Covenant (**9** 14). Though a man, therefore, and truly man, sprung out of Judah (**7** 14), touched with the feeling of human infirmities (**4** 15), and tempted like as we are, He was not altogether like other men. For one thing, He was "without sin" (**4** 15; **7** 26), and, by this characteristic, He was, in every sense of the words, separated from sinners. Despite the completeness of His identification with men, He remained, therefore, even in the days of His flesh different from them and above them.

III. Teaching of Other Epistles.—It is only as we carry this conception of the person of Our Lord with us—the conception of Him as at once our Supreme Lord, to whom our adoration is due, and our fellow in the experiences of a human life—that unity is induced in the multiform allusions to Him throughout, whether the Epp. of Paul or the Ep. to the He, or, indeed, the other epistolary literature of the NT. For in this matter there is no difference between those and these. There are no doubt a few passages in these other letters in which a plurality of the elements of the person of Christ are brought together and given detailed mention. In 1 Pet **3** 18, for instance, the two constitutive elements of His person are spoken of in the contrast, familiar from Paul, of the "flesh" and the "spirit." But ordinarily we meet only with references to this or that element separately. Everywhere Our Lord is spoken of as having lived out His life as a man; but everywhere also He is spoken of with the supreme reverence which is due to God alone, and the very name of God is not withheld from Him. In 1 Pet **1** 11 His preëxistence is taken for granted; in Jas **2** 1 He is identified with the Shekinah, the manifested Jeh—'our Lord Jesus Christ, the Glory'; in Jude ver 4 He is "our only Master [Despot] and Lord"; over and over again He is the Divine Lord who is Jeh (e.g. 1 Pet **2** 3.13; 2 Pet **3** 2.18); in 2 Pet **1** 1, He is roundly called "our God and Saviour." There is nowhere formal inculcation of the entire doctrine of the person of Christ. But everywhere its elements, now one and now another, are presupposed as the common property of writer and readers. It is only in the Epp. of John that this easy and unstudied presupposition of them gives way to pointed insistence upon them.

IV. Teaching of John.—In the circumstances in which he wrote, John found it necessary to insist upon the elements of the person of Our Lord—His true Deity, His true humanity and the unity of His person—in a manner which is more didactic in form than anything we find in the other writings of the NT. The great depository of his teaching on the subject is, of course, the prologue to his Gospel.

1. The Epistles

But it is not merely in this prologue, nor in the Gospel to which it forms a fitting introduction, that these didactic statements are found. The full emphasis of John's witness to the twofold nature of the Lord is brought out, indeed, only by combining what he says in the Gospel and in the Epp. "In the Gospel," remarks Westcott (on Jn **20** 31), "the evangelist shows step by step that the historical Jesus was the Christ, the Son of God (opposed to mere 'flesh'); in the Ep. he reaffirms that the Christ, the Son of God, was true man (opposed to mere 'spirit'; 1 Jn **4** 2)." What John is concerned to show throughout is that it was "the true God" (1 Jn **5** 20) who was "made flesh" (Jn **1** 14); and that this 'only God' (Jn **1** 18, RVm "God only begotten") has truly come "in . . . . flesh" (1 Jn **4** 2). In all the universe there is no other being of whom it can be said that He is God come in flesh (cf 2 Jn ver 7, He that "cometh in the flesh," whose characteristic this is). And of all the marvels which have ever occurred in the marvelous history of the universe, this is the greatest—that 'what was from the beginning' (1 Jn **2** 13.14) has been heard and gazed upon, seen and handled by men (1 Jn **1** 1).

From the point of view from which we now approach it, the prologue to the Gospel of John may be said to fall into three parts. In the first of these, the nature of the Being who became incarnate in the person we know as Jesus Christ is described; in the second, the general nature of the act we call the incarnation; and in the third, the nature of the incarnated person. See JOHANNINE THEOLOGY, III; JOHN, GOSPEL OF, IV, 1, (3), 2.

2. Prologue to the Gospel

(1) *The Being who was incarnated.*—John here calls the person who became incarnate by a name peculiar to himself in the NT—the "Logos" or "Word." According to the predicates which he here applies to Him, he can mean by the "Word" nothing else but God Himself, "considered in His creative, operative, self-revealing, and communicating character," the sum total of what is Divine (C. F. Schmid). In three crisp sentences he declares at the outset His eternal subsistence, His eternal intercommunion with God, His eternal identity with God: 'In the beginning the Word was; and the Word was with God; and the Word was God' (Jn **1** 1). "In the beginning," at that point of time when things first began to be (Gen **1** 1), the Word already "was." He antedates the beginning of all things. And He not merely antedates them, but it is immediately added that He is Himself the creator of all that is: 'All things were made by him, and apart from him was not made one thing that hath been made' (**1** 3). Thus He is taken out of the category of creatures altogether. Accordingly, what is said of Him is not that He was the first of existences to come into being—that 'in the beginning He already had come into being'—but that 'in the beginning, when things began to come into being, He already *was*.' It is express eternity of being that is asserted: "the imperfect tense of the original suggests in this relation, as far as human language can do so, the notion of absolute, supra-temporal existence" (Westcott). This, His eternal subsistence, was not, however, in isolation: "And the Word was with God." The language is pregnant. It is not merely coexistence with God that is asserted, as of two beings standing side by side, united in a local relation, or even in a common conception. What is suggested is an active relation of intercourse. The distinct personality of the Word is therefore not obscurely intimated. From all eternity the Word has been with God as a fellow: He who in the very beginning already "was," "was" also in communion with God. Though He

was thus in some sense a second along with God, He was nevertheless not a separate being from God: "And the Word was"—still the eternal "was"—"God." In some sense distinguishable from God, He was in an equally true sense identical with God. There is but one eternal God; this eternal God, the Word is; in whatever sense we may distinguish Him from the God whom He is "with," He is yet not another than this God, but Himself is this God. The predicate "God" occupies the position of emphasis in this great declaration, and is so placed in the sentence as to be thrown up in sharp contrast with the phrase "with God," as if to prevent inadequate inferences as to the nature of the Word being drawn even momentarily from that phrase. John would have us realize that what the Word was in eternity was not merely God's coeternal fellow, but the eternal God's self.

(2) *The incarnation.*—Now, John tells us that it was this Word, eternal in His subsistence, God's eternal fellow, the eternal God's self, that, as "come in the flesh," was Jesus Christ (1 Jn **4** 2). "And the Word became flesh" (Jn **1** 14), he says. The terms he employs here are not terms of substance, but of personality. The meaning is not that the substance of God was transmuted into that substance which we call "flesh." "The Word" is a personal name of the eternal God; "flesh" is an appropriate designation of humanity in its entirety, with the implications of dependence and weakness. The meaning, then, is simply that He who had just been described as the eternal God became, by a voluntary act in time, a man. The exact nature of the act by which He "became" man lies outside the statement; it was matter of common knowledge between the writer and the reader. The language employed intimates merely that it was a definite act, and that it involved a change in the life-history of the eternal God, here designated "the Word." The whole emphasis falls on the nature of this change in His life-history. He became *flesh.* That is to say, He entered upon a mode of existence in which the experiences that belong to human beings would also be His. The dependence, the weakness, which constitute the very idea of flesh, in contrast with God, would now enter into His personal experience. And it is precisely because these are the connotations of the term "flesh" that John chooses that term here, instead of the more simply denotative term "man." What he means is merely that the eternal God became man. But he elects to say this in the language which throws best up to view what it is to become man. The contrast between the Word as the eternal God and the human nature which He assumed as flesh, is the hinge of the statement. Had the evangelist said (as he does in 1 Jn **4** 2) that the Word 'came in flesh,' it would have been the continuity through the change which would have been most emphasized. When he says rather that the Word became flesh, while the continuity of the personal subject is, of course, intimated, it is the reality and the completeness of the humanity assumed which is made most prominent.

(3) *The incarnated person.*—That in becoming flesh the Word did not cease to be what He was before entering upon this new sphere of experiences, the evangelist does not leave, however, to mere suggestion. The glory of the Word was so far from quenched, in his view, by His becoming flesh, that he gives us at once to understand that it was rather as "trailing clouds of glory" that He came. "And the Word became flesh," he says, and immediately adds: "and dwelt among us (and we beheld his glory, glory as of the only begotten from the Father), full of grace and truth" (**1** 14). The language is colored by reminiscences from the Tabernacle, in which the Glory of God, the Shekinah, dwelt. The flesh of Our Lord became, on its assumption by the Word, the Temple of God on earth (cf Jn **2** 19), and the glory of the Lord filled the house of the Lord. John tells us expressly that this glory was visible, that it was precisely what was appropriate to the Son of God as such. "And we beheld his glory," he says; not divined it, or inferred it, but perceived it. It was open to sight, and the actual object of observation. Jesus Christ was obviously more than man; He was obviously God. His actually observed glory, John tells us further, was a "glory as of the only begotten from the Father." It was unique; nothing like it was ever seen in another. And its uniqueness consisted precisely in its consonance with what the unique Son of God, sent forth from the Father, would naturally have; men recognized and could not but recognize in Jesus Christ the unique Son of God. When this unique Son of God is further described as "full of grace and truth," the elements of His manifested glory are not to be supposed to be exhausted by this description (cf **2** 11). Certain items of it only are singled out for particular mention. The visible glory of the incarnated Word was such a glory as the unique Son of God, sent forth from the Father, who was full of grace and truth, would naturally manifest.

That nothing should be lacking to the declaration of the continuity of all that belongs to the Word as such into this new sphere of existence, and its full manifestation through the veil of His flesh, John adds at the close of his exposition the remarkable sentence: 'As for God, no one has even yet seen him; God only begotten, who is in the bosom of the Father—he hath declared him' (**1** 18 m). It is the incarnate Word which is here called 'only begotten God.' The absence of the article with this designation is doubtless due to its parallelism with the word "God" which stands at the head of the corresponding clause. The effect of its absence is to throw up into emphasis the quality rather than the mere individuality of the person so designated. The adj. "only begotten" conveys the idea, not of derivation and subordination, but of uniqueness and consubstantiality: Jesus is all that God is, and He alone is this. Of this 'only begotten God' it is now declared that He "is"—not "was," the state is not one which has been left behind at the incarnation, but one which continues uninterrupted and unmodified—"into"—not merely "in"—"the bosom of the Father"—that is to say, He continues in the most intimate and complete communion with the Father. Though now incarnate, He is still "with God" in the full sense of the external relation intimated in **1** 1. This being true, He has much more than seen God, and is fully able to "interpret" God to men. Though no one has ever yet seen God, yet he who has seen Jesus Christ, "God only begotten," has seen the Father (cf **14** 9; **12** 45). In this remarkable sentence there is asserted in the most direct manner the full Deity of the incarnate Word, and the continuity of His life as such in His incarnate life; thus He is fitted to be the absolute revelation of God to man.

3. The Gospel

This condensed statement of the whole doctrine of the incarnation is only the prologue to a historical treatise. The historical treatise which it introduces, naturally, is written from the point of view of its prologue. Its object is to present Jesus Christ in His historical manifestation, as obviously the Son of God in flesh. "These are written," the Gospel testifies, "that ye may believe that Jesus is the Christ, the Son of God" (**20** 31); that Jesus who came as a man (**1** 30) was thoroughly known in His human origin (**7** 27), confessed Himself man (**8** 40), and died as a man dies

(**19** 5), was, nevertheless, not only the Messiah, the Sent of God, the fulfiller of all the Divine promises of redemption, but also the very Son of God, that God only begotten, who, abiding in the bosom of the Father, is His sole adequate interpreter. From the beginning of the Gospel onward, this purpose is pursued: Jesus is pictured as ever, while truly man, yet manifesting Himself as equally truly God, until the veil which covered the eyes of His followers was wholly lifted, and He is greeted as both Lord and God (**20** 28). But though it is the prime purpose of this Gospel to exhibit the Divinity of the man Jesus, no obscuration of His manhood is involved. It is the Deity of the man Jesus which is insisted on, but the true manhood of Jesus is as prominent in the representation as in any other portion of the NT. Nor is any effacement of the humiliation of His earthly life involved. For the Son of man to come from heaven was a descent (**3** 13), and the mission which He came to fulfil was a mission of contest and conflict, of suffering and death. He brought His glory with Him (**1** 14), but the glory that was His on earth (**17** 22) was not all the glory which He had had with the Father before the world was, and to which, after His work was done, He should return (**17** 5). Here too the glory of the celestial is one and the glory of the terrestrial is another. In any event, John has no difficulty in presenting the life of Our Lord on earth as the life of God in flesh, and in insisting at once on the glory that belongs to Him as God and on the humiliation which is brought to Him by the flesh. It is distinctly a duplex life which he ascribes to Christ, and he attributes to Him without embarrassment all the powers and modes of activity appropriate on the one hand to Deity and on the other to sinless (Jn **8** 46; cf **14** 30; 1 Jn **3** 5) human nature. In a true sense his portrait of Our Lord is a dramatization of the God-man which he presents to our contemplation in his prologue.

V. Teaching of the Synoptic Gospels.—The same may be said of the other Gospels. They are all dramatizations of the God-man set forth in thetical exposition in the prologue to John's Gospel. The Gospel of Luke, written by a known companion of Paul, gives us in a living narrative the same Jesus who is presupposed in all Paul's allusions to Him. That of Mark, who was also a companion of Paul, as also of Peter, is, as truly as the Gospel of John itself, a presentation of facts in the life of Jesus with a view to making it plain that this was the life of no mere man, human as it was, but of the Son of God Himself. Matthew's Gospel differs from its fellows mainly in the greater richness of Jesus' own testimony to His Deity which it records. What is characteristic of all three is the inextricable interlacing in their narratives of the human and Divine traits which alike marked the life they are depicting. It is possible, by neglecting one series of their representations and attending only to the other, to sift out from them at will the portrait of either a purely Divine or a purely human Jesus. It is impossible to derive from them the portrait of any other than a Divine-human Jesus if we surrender ourselves to their guidance and take off of their pages the portrait they have endeavored to draw. As in their narratives they cursorily suggest now the fulness of His Deity and now the completeness of His humanity and everywhere the unity of His person, they present as real and as forcible a testimony to the constitution of Our Lord's person as uniting in one personal life a truly Divine and a truly human nature, as if they announced this fact in analytical statement. Only on the assumption of this conception of Our Lord's person as underlying and determining their presentation, can unity be given to their representations; while, on this supposition, all their representations fall into their places as elements in one consistent whole. Within the limits of their common presupposition, each Gospel has no doubt its own peculiarities in the distribution of its emphasis. Mark lays particular stress on the Divine power of the man Jesus, as evidence of His supernatural being; and on the irresistible impression of a veritable Son of God, a Divine being walking the earth as a man, which He made upon all with whom He came into contact. Luke places his Gospel by the side of the Ep. to the He in the prominence it gives to the human development of the Divine being whose life on earth it is depicting and to the range of temptation to which He was subjected. Matthew's Gospel is notable chiefly for the heights of the Divine self-consciousness which it uncovers in its report of the words of Him whom it represents as nevertheless the Son of David, the Son of Abraham; heights of Divine self-consciousness which fall in nothing short of those attained in the great utterances preserved for us by John. But amid whatever variety there may exist in the aspects on which each lays his particular emphasis, it is the same Jesus Christ which all three bring before us, a Jesus Christ who is at once God and man and one individual person. If that be not recognized, the whole narrative of the Synoptic Gospels is thrown into confusion; their portrait of Christ becomes an insoluble puzzle; and the mass of details which they present of His life-experiences is transmuted into a mere set of crass contradictions. See also GOSPELS, THE SYNOPTIC.

VI. Teaching of Jesus.—The Gospel narratives not only present us, however, with dramatizations of the God-man, according to their authors' conception of His composite person. They preserve for us also a considerable body of the utterances of Jesus Himself, and this enables us to observe the conception of His person which underlay and found expression in Our Lord's own teaching.

1. The Johannine Jesus

The discourses of Our Lord which have been selected for record by John have been chosen (among other reasons) expressly for the reason that they bear witness to His essential Deity. They are accordingly peculiarly rich in material for forming a judgment of Our Lord's conception of His higher nature. This conception, it is needless to say, is precisely that which John, taught by it, has announced in the prologue to his Gospel, and has illustrated by his Gospel itself, compacted as it is of these discourses. It will not be necessary to present the evidence for this in its fulness. It will be enough to point to a few characteristic passages, in which Our Lord's conception of His higher nature finds esp. clear expression.

(1) *His higher nature.*—That He was of higher than earthly origin and nature, He repeatedly asserts. "Ye are from beneath," he says to the Jews (**8** 23), "I am from above: ye are of this world; I am not of this world" (cf **17** 16). Therefore, He taught that He, the Son of Man, had "descended out of heaven" (**3** 13), where was His true abode. This carried with it, of course, an assertion of preëxistence; and this preëxistence is explicitly affirmed: "What then," He asks, "if ye should behold the Son of man ascending where he was before?" (**6** 62). It is not merely preëxistence, however, but eternal preëxistence which He claims for Himself: "And now, Father," He prays (**17** 5), "glorify thou me with thine own self with the glory which I had with thee before the world was" (cf ver 24); and again, as the most impressive language possible, He declares (**8** 58 AV): "Verily, verily, I say unto you, Before Abraham was, I am," where He claims for Himself the timeless present of eternity as His mode of existence. In the former of these two last-

cited passages, the character of His preëxistent life is intimated; in it He shared the Father's glory from all eternity ("before the world was"); He stood by the Father's side as a companion in His glory. He came forth, when He descended to earth, therefore, not from heaven only, but from the very side of God (**8** 42; **17** 8). Even this, however, does not express the whole truth; He came forth not only from the Father's side where He had shared in the Father's glory; He came forth out of the Father's very being—"I came out from the Father, and am come into the world" (**16** 28; cf **8** 42). "The connection described is inherent and essential, and not that of presence or external fellowship" (Westcott). This prepares us for the great assertion: "I and the Father are one" (**10** 30), from which it is a mere corollary that "He that hath seen me hath seen the Father" (**14** 9; cf **8** 19; **12** 45).

(2) *His humiliation.*—In all these declarations the subject of the affirmation is the actual person speaking: it is of Himself who stood before men and spoke to them that Our Lord makes these immense assertions. Accordingly, when He majestically declared, "I and the Father are" (plurality of persons) "one" (neuter singular, and accordingly singleness of being), the Jews naturally understood Him to be making Himself, the person then speaking to them, God (**10** 33; cf **5** 18; **19** 7). The continued sameness of the person who has been, from all eternity down to this hour, one with God, is therefore fully safeguarded. His earthly life is, however, distinctly represented as a humiliation. Though even on earth He is one with the Father, yet He "descended" to earth; He had come out from the Father and out of God; a glory had been left behind which was yet to be returned to, and His sojourn on earth was therefore to that extent an obscuration of His proper glory. There was a sense, then, in which, because He had "descended," He was no longer equal with the Father. It was in order to justify an assertion of equality with the Father in power (**10** 25.29) that He was led to declare: "I and my Father are one" (**10** 30). But He can also declare "The Father is greater than I" (**14** 28). Obviously this means that there was a sense in which He had ceased to be equal with the Father, because of the humiliation of His present condition, and in so far as this humiliation involved entrance into a status lower than that which belonged to Him by nature. Precisely in what this humiliation consisted can be gathered only from the general implication of many statements. In it He was a "man": 'a man who hath told you the truth, which I have heard from God' (**8** 40), where the contrast with "God" throws the assertion of humanity into emphasis (cf **10** 33). The truth of His human nature is, however, everywhere assumed and endlessly illustrated, rather than explicitly asserted. He possessed a human soul (**12** 27) and bodily parts (flesh and blood, **6** 53 ff; hands and side, **20** 27); and was subject alike to physical affections (weariness, **4** 6, and thirst, **19** 28, suffering and death), and to all the common human emotions—not merely the love of compassion (**13** 34; **14** 21; **15** 8–13), but the love of simple affection which we pour out on "friends" (**11** 11; cf **15** 14.15), indignation (**11** 33.38) and joy (**15** 11; **17** 13). He felt the perturbation produced by strong excitement (**11** 33; **12** 27; **13** 21), the sympathy with suffering which shows itself in tears (**11** 35), the thankfulness which fills the grateful heart (**6** 11.23; **11** 41; **16** 27). Only one human characteristic was alien to Him: He was without sin: "the prince of the world," He declared, "hath nothing in me" (**14** 30; cf **8** 46). Clearly Our Lord, as reported by John, knew Himself to be true God and true man in one indivisible person, the common subject of the qualities which belong to each.

2. The Synoptic Jesus

(1) *His Deity.*—(*a*) Mk **13** 32: The same is true of His self-consciousness as revealed in His sayings recorded by the synoptists. Perhaps no more striking illustration of this could be adduced than the remarkable declaration recorded in Mk **13** 32 (cf Mt **24** 36): 'But of that day or that hour knoweth no one, not even the angels in heaven, nor yet the Son, but the Father.' Here Jesus places Himself, in an ascending scale of being, above "the angels in heaven," that is to say, the highest of all creatures, significantly marked here as supramundane. Accordingly, He presents Himself elsewhere as the Lord of the angels, whose behests they obey: "The Son of man shall send forth his angels, and they shall gather out of his kingdom all things that cause stumbling, and them that do iniquity" (Mt **13** 41), "And he shall send forth his angels with a great sound of a trumpet, and they shall gather together his elect from the four winds, from one end of heaven to the other" (Mt **24** 31; cf **13** 49; **25** 31; Mk **8** 38). Thus the "angels of God" (Lk **12** 8.9; **15** 10) Christ designates as His angels, the "kingdom of God" (Mt **12** 28; **19** 24; **21** 31.43; Mk and Lk often) as His Kingdom, the "elect of God" (Mk **13** 20; Lk **18** 7; cf Rom **8** 33; Col **3** 12; Tit **1** 1) as His elect. He is obviously speaking in Mk **13** 22 out of a Divine self-consciousness: "Only a Divine being can be exalted above angels" (B. Weiss). He therefore designates Himself by His Divine name, "the Son," that is to say, the unique Son of God (**9** 7; **1** 11), to claim to be whom would for a man be blasphemy (Mk **14** 61.64). But though He designates Himself by this Divine name, He is not speaking of what He once was, but of what at the moment of speaking He is: the action of the vb. is present, "knoweth." He is claiming, in other words, the supreme designation of "the Son," with all that is involved in it, for His present self, as He moved among men: He is, not merely was, "the Son." Nevertheless, what He affirms of Himself cannot be affirmed of Himself distinctively as "the Son." For what He affirms of Himself is ignorance—"not even the Son" knows it; and ignorance does not belong to the Divine nature which the term "the Son" connotes. An extreme appearance of contradiction accordingly arises from the use of this terminology, just as it arises when Paul says that the Jews "crucified the Lord of glory" (1 Cor **2** 8), or exhorts the Ephesian elders to "feed the church of God which he purchased with his own blood" (Acts **20** 28 m); or John Keble praises Our Lord for "the blood of souls by Thee redeemed." It was not the Lord of Glory as such who was nailed to the tree, nor have either "God" or "souls" blood to shed.

We know how this apparently contradictory mode of speech has arisen in Keble's case. He is speaking of men who are composite beings, consisting of souls and bodies, and these men come to be designated from one element of their composite personalities, though what is affirmed by them belongs rather to the other; we may speak, therefore, of the "blood of souls" meaning that these "souls," while not having blood as such, yet designate persons who have bodies and therefore blood. We know equally how to account for Paul's apparent contradictions. We know that he conceived of Our Lord as a composite person, uniting in Himself a Divine and a human nature. In Paul's view, therefore, though God as such has no blood, yet Jesus Christ who is God has blood because He is also man. He can justly speak, therefore, when speaking of Jesus Christ, of His blood as the blood of God. When precisely the same phenomenon meets us in Our Lord's speech of Himself, we must presume that it is the outgrowth of precisely the same state of things. When He speaks of "the Son" (who is God) as ignorant, we must understand that He is designating Himself as "the Son" because of His higher nature, and yet has in mind the ignorance of His lower nature; what He means is that the person properly designated "the Son" is ignorant, that is to say with respect to the human nature which is as intimate an element of His personality as is His Deity.

When Our Lord says, then, that "the Son knows not," He becomes as express a witness to the two natures which constitute His person as Paul is when he speaks of the blood of God, or as Keble is a witness to the twofold constitution of a human being when he speaks of souls shedding blood. In this short sentence, thus, Our Lord bears witness to His Divine nature with its supremacy above all creatures, to His human nature with its creaturely limitations, and to the unity of the subject possessed of these two natures.

(*b*) Other passages: Son of Man and Son of God: All these elements of His personality find severally repeated assertions in other utterances of Our Lord recorded in the Synoptics. There is no need to insist here on the elevation of Himself above the kings and prophets of the Old Covenant (Mt **12** 41 ff), above the temple itself (Mt **12** 6), and the ordinances of the Divine Law (Mt **12** 8); or on His accent of authority in both His teaching and action, His great "I say unto you" (Mt **5** 21.22), 'I will; be cleansed' (Mk **1** 41; **2** 5; Lk **7** 14); or on His separation of Himself from men in His relation to God, never including them with Himself in an "Our Father," but consistently speaking distinctively of "my Father" (e.g. Lk **24** 49) and "your Father" (e.g. Mt **5** 16); or on His intimation that He is not merely David's Son but David's Lord, and that a Lord sitting on the right hand of God (Mt **22** 44); or on His parabolic discrimination of Himself a Son and Heir from all "servants" (Mt **21** 33 ff); or even on His ascription to Himself of the purely Divine functions of the forgiveness of sins (Mk **2** 8) and judgment of the world (Mt **25** 31), or of the purely Divine powers of reading the heart (Mk **2** 8; Lk **9** 47), omnipotence (Mt **24** 30; Mk **14** 62) and omnipresence (Mt **18** 20; **28** 10). These things illustrate His constant assumption of the possession of Divine dignity and attributes; the claim itself is more directly made in the two great designations which He currently gave Himself, the Son of Man and the Son of God. The former of these is His favorite self-designation. Derived from Dnl **7** 13.14, it intimates on every occasion of its employment Our Lord's consciousness of being a supramundane being, who has entered into a sphere of earthly life on a high mission, on the accomplishment of which He is to return to His heavenly sphere, whence He shall in due season come back to earth, now, however, in His proper majesty, to gather up the fruits of His work and consummate all things. It is a designation, thus, which implies at once a heavenly preëxistence, a present humiliation, and a future glory; and He proclaims Himself in this future glory no less than the universal King seated on the throne of judgment for quick and dead (Mk **8** 31; Mt **25** 31). The implication of Deity imbedded in the designation, Son of Man, is perhaps more plainly spoken out in the companion designation, Son of God, which Our Lord not only accepts at the hands of others, accepting with it the implication of blasphemy in permitting its application to Himself (Mt **26** 63.65; Mk **14** 61.64; Lk **22** 29.30), but persistently claims for Himself both, in His constant designation of God as His Father in a distinctive sense, and in His less frequent but more pregnant designation of Himself as, by way of eminence, "the Son." That His consciousness of the peculiar relation to God expressed by this designation was not an attainment of His mature spiritual development, but was part of His most intimate consciousness from the beginning, is suggested by the sole glimpse which is given us into His mind as a child (Lk **2** 49). The high significance which the designation bore to Him is revealed to us in two remarkable utterances preserved, the one by both Matthew (**11** 27 ff) and Luke (**10** 22 ff), and the other by Matthew (**28** 19).

(*c*) Mt **11** 27; **28** 19: In the former of these utterances, Our Lord, speaking in the most solemn manner, not only presents Himself, as the Son, as the sole source of knowledge of God and of blessedness for men, but places Himself in a position, not of equality merely, but of absolute reciprocity and interpenetration of knowledge with the Father. "No one," He says, "knoweth the Son, save the Father; neither doth any know the Father, save the Son . . . ." varied in Luke so as to read: "No one knoweth who the Son is, save the Father; and who the Father is, save the Son . . . ." as if the being of the Son were so immense that only God could know it thoroughly; and the knowledge of the Son was so unlimited that He could know God to perfection. The peculiarly pregnant employment here of the terms "Son" and "Father" over against one another is explained to us in the other utterance (Mt **28** 19). It is the resurrected Lord's commission to His disciples. Claiming for Himself all authority in heaven and on earth—which implies the possession of omnipotence—and promising to be with His followers 'alway, even to the end of the world'—which adds the implications of omnipresence and omniscience—He commands them to baptize their converts 'in the name of the Father and of the Son and of the Holy Ghost.' The precise form of the formula must be carefully observed. It does not read: 'In the names' (plural)—as if there were three beings enumerated, each with its distinguishing name. Nor yet: 'In the name of the Father, Son and Holy Ghost,' as if there were one person, going by a threefold name. It reads: 'In the name [singular] of the Father, and of the [article repeated] Son, and of the [article repeated] Holy Ghost,' carefully distinguishing three persons, though uniting them all under one name. The name of God was to the Jews Jeh, and to name the name of Jeh upon them was to make them His. What Jesus did in this great injunction was to command His followers to name the name of God upon their converts, and to announce the name of God which is to be named on their converts in the threefold enumeration of "the Father" and "the Son" and 'the Holy Ghost.' As it is unquestionable that He intended Himself by "the Son," He here places Himself by the side of the Father and the Spirit, as together with them constituting the one God. It is, of course, the Trinity which He is describing; and that is as much as to say that He announces Himself as one of the persons of the Trinity. This is what Jesus, as reported by the Synoptics, understood Himself to be. See TRINITY.

(2) *His humanity.*—In announcing Himself to be God, however, Jesus does not deny that He is man also. If all His speech of Himself rests on His consciousness of a Divine nature, no less does all His speech manifest His consciousness of a human nature. He easily identifies Himself with men (Mt **4** 4; Lk **4** 4), and receives without protest the imputation of humanity (Mt **11** 19; Lk **7** 34). He speaks familiarly of His body (Mt **26** 12.26; Mk **14** 8; **14** 22; Lk **22** 19), and of His bodily parts—His feet and hands (Lk **24** 39), His head and feet (Lk **7** 44–46), His flesh and bones (Lk **24** 39), His blood (Mt **26** 28; Mk **14** 24; Lk **22** 20). We chance to be given indeed a very express affirmation on His part of the reality of His bodily nature; when His disciples were terrified at His appearing before them after His resurrection, supposing Him to be a spirit, He reassures them with the direct declaration: "See my hands and my feet, that it is I myself: handle me, and see; for a spirit hath not flesh and bones, as ye behold me having" (Lk **24** 39). His testimony to His human soul is just as express: "My soul," says He, "is exceeding sorrowful, even unto death" (Mt **26** 38; Mk **14** 34). He speaks of the human dread with which

He looked forward to His approaching death (Lk **12** 50), and expresses in a poignant cry His sense of desolation on the cross (Mt **27** 46; Mk **15** 34). He speaks also of His pity for the weary and hungering people (Mt **15** 32; Mk **8** 2), and of a strong human desire which He felt (Lk **22** 15). Nothing that is human is alien to Him except sin. He never ascribes imperfection to Himself and never betrays consciousness of sin. He recognizes the evil of those about Him (Lk **11** 13; Mt **7** 11; **12** 34. 39; Lk **11** 29), but never identifies Himself with it. It is those who do the will of God with whom He feels kinship (Mt **12** 50), and He offers Himself to the morally sick as a physician (Mt **9** 12). He proposes Himself as an example of the highest virtues (Mt **11** 28 ff) and pronounces him blessed who shall find no occasion of stumbling in Him (Mt **11** 6).

(3) *Unity of the Person.*—These manifestations of a human and Divine consciousness simply stand side by side in the records of Our Lord's self-expression. Neither is suppressed or even qualified by the other. If we attend only to the one class we might suppose Him to proclaim Himself wholly Divine; if only to the other we might equally easily imagine Him to be representing Himself as wholly human. With both together before us we perceive Him alternately speaking out of a Divine and out of a human consciousness; manifesting Himself as all that God is and as all that man is; yet with the most marked unity of consciousness. He, the one Jesus Christ, was to His own apprehension true God and complete man in a unitary personal life.

VII. The Two Natures Everywhere Presupposed.—There underlies, thus, the entire literature of the NT a single, unvarying conception of the constitution of Our Lord's person. From Mt where He is presented as one of the persons of the Holy Trinity (**28** 19)—or if we prefer the chronological order of books, from the Ep. of Jas where He is spoken of as the Glory of God, the Shekinah (**2** 1)—to the Apocalypse where He is represented as declaring that He is the Alpha and the Omega, the First and the Last, the Beginning and the End (**1** 8.17; **22** 13), He is consistently thought of as in His fundamental being just God. At the same time from the Synoptic Gospels, in which He is dramatized as a man walking among men, His human descent carefully recorded, and His sense of dependence on God so emphasized that prayer becomes almost His most characteristic action, to the Epp. of John in which it is made the note of a Christian that He confesses that Jesus Christ has come in flesh (1 Jn **4** 2) and the Apocalypse in which His birth in the tribe of Judah and the house of David (**5** 5; **22** 16), His exemplary life of conflict and victory (**3** 21), His death on the cross (**11** 8) are noted, He is equally consistently thought of as true man. Nevertheless, from the beginning to the end of the whole series of books, while first one and then the other of His two natures comes into repeated prominence, there is never a question of conflict between the two, never any confusion in their relations, never any schism in His unitary personal action; but He is obviously considered and presented as one, composite indeed, but undivided personality. In this state of the case not only may evidence of the constitution of Our Lord's person properly be drawn indifferently from every part of the NT, and passage justly be cited to support and explain passage without reference to the portion of the NT in which it is found, but we should be without justification if we did not employ this common presupposition of the whole body of this literature to illustrate and explain the varied representations which meet us cursorily in its pages, representations which might easily be made to appear mutually contradictory were they not brought into harmony by their relation as natural component parts of this one unitary conception which underlies and gives consistency to them all. There can scarcely be imagined a better proof of the truth of a doctrine than its power completely to harmonize a multitude of statements which without it would present to our view only a mass of confused inconsistencies. A key which perfectly fits a lock of very complicated wards can scarcely fail to be the true key.

VIII. Formulation of the Doctrine.—Meanwhile the wards remain complicated. Even in the case of our own composite structure, of soul and body, familiar as we are with it from our daily experience, the mutual relations of elements so disparate in a single personality remain an unplumbed mystery, and give rise to paradoxical modes of speech which would be misleading, were not their source in our duplex nature well understood. We may read, in careful writers, of souls being left dead on battlefields, and of everybody's immortality. The mysteries of the relations in which the constituent elements in the more complex personality of Our Lord stand to one another are immeasurably greater than in our simpler case. We can never hope to comprehend how the infinite God and a finite humanity can be united in a single person; and it is very easy to go fatally astray in attempting to explain the interactions in the unitary person of natures so diverse from one another. It is not surprising, therefore, that so soon as serious efforts began to be made to give systematic explanations of the Bib. facts as to Our Lord's person, many one-sided and incomplete statements were formulated which required correction and complementing before at length a mode of statement was devised which did full justice to the Bib. data. It was accordingly only after more than a century of controversy, during which nearly every conceivable method of construing and misconstruing the Bib. facts had been proposed and tested, that a formula was framed which successfully guarded the essential data supplied by the Scriptures from destructive misconception. This formula, put together by the Council of Chalcedon, 451 AD, declares it to have always been the doctrine of the church, derived from the Scriptures and Our Lord Himself, that Our Lord Jesus Christ is "truly God and truly man, of a reasonable soul and body; consubstantial with the Father according to the Godhead, and consubstantial with us according to the manhood; in all things like unto us, without sin; begotten before all ages of the Father according to the Godhead, and in these latter days, for us and for our salvation, born of the Virgin Mary, the Mother of God, according to the manhood; one and the same Christ, Son, Lord, Only-begotten, to be acknowledged in two natures inconfusedly, unchangeably, indivisibly, inseparably; the distinction of natures being by no means taken away by the union, but rather the property of each nature being preserved, and concurring in one Person and one subsistence, not parted or divided into two persons, but one and the same Son, and Only-begotten, God, the Word, the Lord Jesus Christ." There is nothing here but a careful statement in systematic form of the pure teaching of the Scriptures; and therefore this statement has stood ever since as the norm of thought and teaching as to the person of the Lord. As such, it has been incorporated, in one form or another, into the creeds of all the great branches of the church; it underlies and gives their form to all the allusions to Christ in the great mass of preaching and song which has accumulated during the centuries; and it has supplied the background of the devotions of the untold multitudes who through the Christian ages have been worshippers of Christ.

LITERATURE.—The appropriate sections in the treatises on the Bib. theology of the NT; also A. B. Bruce, *The Humiliation of Christ*, 2d ed, Edinburgh, 1881; R. L. Ottley, *The Doctrine of the Incarnation*, London, 1896; H. C. Powell, *The Principle of the Incarnation*, London, 1896; Francis J. Hall, *The Kenotic Theory*, New York, 1898; C. A. Briggs, *The Incarnation of the Lord*, New York, 1902; G. S. Streatfeild, *The Self-Interpretation of Jesus Christ*, London, 1906; B. B. Warfield, *The Lord of Glory*, New York, 1907; James Denney, *Jesus and the Gospel*, London, 1909; M. Lepin, *Christ and the Gospel: or, Jesus the Messiah and Son of God*, Philadelphia, 1910; James Stalker, *The Christology of Jesus*, New York, 1899; D. Somerville, *St. Paul's Conception of Christ*, Edinburgh, 1897; E. H. Gifford, *The Incarnation: a Study of Phil 2 5–11*, London, 1897; S. N. Rostron, *The Christology of St. Paul*, London, 1912; E. Digges La Touche, *The Person of Christ in Modern Thoughts*, London, 1912.

[NOTE.—In this art. the author has usually given his own translation of quotations from Scripture, and not that of any particular VS.]

BENJAMIN B. WARFIELD

PERSONALITY. See PERSON.

PERSUADE, pẽr-swād′, **PERSUASION**, pẽr-swā′-zhun: (1) In the older Eng. "persuade" need not mean "convince" (although this is its usual sense in the AV: Mt **27** 20, etc), but may mean only "attempt to convince," "argue with." This is well brought out in Acts **26** 28, where the Gr is lit. "In little thou 'persuadest' [πείθεις, *peítheis*] to make me a Christian." AV took *peitheis* as "convince" ("almost thou persuadest me . . . ."), but this is impossible, and so the RV rendered *peitheis* by "thou wouldest fain." To keep something of the language of AV, "persuasion" was supplied after "little," but it should have been italicized, for it is merely conjectural, as ARVm recognizes by giving "time" as an alternative for "persuasion." The text of the passage, however, is suspected. See ALMOST. Similarly in Acts **13** 43, RV replaces "persuade" by "urge," and the same change should have been made also in 2 K **18** 32 and ||'s. (2) The "popular persuasions" of 1 Esd **5** 73 are "efforts to persuade the people" (uncertain text, however). Acts **19** 8 AV writes "persuading the things" (RV "*as to* the things") for "present the things persuasively." And in Gal **1** 10 (ERV and AV, not in ARV) and 2 Cor **5** 11, there is a half-ironic force in the word: St. Paul's enemies have accused him of using unworthy persuasion in making his conversions.

BURTON SCOTT EASTON

PERUDA, pe-rōō′da (פְּרוּדָא, *peˢrūdhā′*). See PERIDA.

PERVERSE, pẽr-vûrs′: The group "perverse, -ly, -ness," "act perversely" in AV represents nearly 20 Heb words, of which, however, most are derivatives of the stems עָוָה, *'āwāh*, לוּז, *lūz*, עָקַשׁ, *'ākash*. RV has made few changes. In Job **6** 30, RV "mischievous" is better for the *taste* of a thing, and in Isa **59** 3 greater emphasis is gained by RV "wickedness." In Ezk **9** 9, "wresting of judgment" is perhaps too concrete, and "perverseness" is kept in the m (inverted in AV). RVm "headlong" in Nu **22** 32 is over-literal, but in **23** 21 ARVm's "trouble" is a distinct improvement.

PESTILENCE, pes′ti-lens (דֶּבֶר, *debher*; λοιμός, *loimós*): Any sudden fatal epidemic is designated by this word, and in its Bib. use it generally indicates that these are Divine visitations. The word is most frequently used in the prophetic books, and it occurs 25 t in Jer and Ezk, always associated with the sword and famine. In 4 other passages it is combined with noisome or evil beasts, or war. In Am **4** 10 this judgment is compared with the plagues of Egypt, and in Hab **3** 5 it is a concomitant of the march of God from the Arabian mountain. There is the same judicial character associated with pestilence in Ex **5** 3; **9** 15; Lev **26** 25; Nu **14** 12; Dt **28** 21; 2 S **24** 21; 1 Ch **21** 12; Ezk **14** 19.21. In the dedication prayer of Solomon, a special value is besought for such petitions against pestilence as may be presented toward the temple (2 Ch **6** 28). Such a deliverance is promised to those who put their trust in God (Ps **91** 6). Here the pestilence is called noisome, a shortened form of "annoysome," used in the sense of "hateful" or that which causes trouble or distress. In modern Eng. it has acquired the sense of loathsome. "Noisome" is used by Tindale where AV and RV have "hurtful" in 1 Tim **6** 9.

The Lat word *pestilentia* is connected with *pestis*, "the plague," but pestilence is used of any visitation and is not the name of any special disease; *debher* is applied to diseases of cattle and is tr[d] "murrain."

In the NT pestilence is mentioned in Our Lord's eschatological discourse (Mt **24** 7 AV; Lk **21** 11) coupled with famine. The assonance of *loimós* and *limós* in these passages (*loimos* is omitted in the RV passage for Mt) occurs in several classical passages, e.g. Herodotus vii.171. The pestilence is said to walk in darkness (Ps **91** 6) on account of its sudden onset out of obscurity unassociated with any apparent cause.

ALEX. MACALISTER

PESTLE, pes″l (עֱלִי, *'ĕlī*): A rounded implement of wood or stone used for pounding, bruising, or powdering materials in a mortar. Used only in Prov **27** 22. See MORTAR.

PETER, pē′tẽr (**SIMON**, sī′mon):

1. Name and Early Career
2. First Appearance in Gospel History
3. Life-Story
   (1) First Period
   (2) Second Period
4. Character
5. Writings
   (1) First Epistle
   (2) Second Epistle
6. Theology
   (1) Messianic Teaching
   (2) Justification
   (3) Redemption
   (4) Future Life
   (5) Holy Scripture
   (6) Apostasy and Judgment
   (7) Second Coming of Christ

LITERATURE

The data for this article are found chiefly in the four Gospels; in Acts, chs **1–15**; in Gal **1** and **2**; and in the two Epp. of Peter.

1. Name and Early Career

Simon (or Simeon) was the original name of Peter, the son of Jonas (or John), and brother of Andrew, a disciple of John the Baptist, as Peter also may have been. A fisherman by occupation, he was an inhabitant of Bethsaida on the Sea of Galilee, though subsequently he dwelt with his family at Capernaum (Mt **4** 18; **8** 14; **10** 2; **16** 16.17; **17** 25; Mk **1** 16.29.30.36; Lk **5** 3.4. 5.8.10; **22** 31; **24** 34; Jn **1** 40–44).

2. First Appearance in Gospel History

His first appearance in Gospel history is in Jn **1** 35–42, when Andrew, having discovered Jesus to be the Messiah, "first findeth his own brother Simon," and "brought him unto Jesus"; on which occasion it was that the latter, beholding him, said, "Thou shalt be called Cephas," an Aram. surname whose Gr synonym is *Petrós*, or Peter, meaning "a rock" or "stone." At this time also he received his first call to the discipleship of Jesus, although, in common with that of others of the Twelve, this call was twice repeated. See Mt **4** 19; Mk **1** 17; Lk **5** 3 for the second call, and Mt **10** 2; Mk **3** 14.16; Lk **6** 13.14 for the third. Some interpret the second as that when he was chosen to be a constant companion of Jesus, and the third when he was at length selected as an apostle.

The life-story of Peter falls into two parts: first, from his call to the ascension of Christ; secondly, from that event to the close of his earthly career.

3. Life-Story

(1) *The first period* again may be conveniently divided into the events prior to the Passion of Christ and those following. There are about ten of the former: the healing of his wife's mother at Capernaum (Mt **8** 14 ff); the great draught of fishes, and its effect in his self-abasement and surrender of his all to Jesus (Lk **5** 1-11); his call to the apostolic office and his spiritual equipment therefor (Mt **10** 2); his attachment to his Master, as shown in his attempt to walk upon the waves (Mt **14** 28); the same attachment as shown at a certain crisis, in his inquiry "Lord, to whom shall we go?" (Jn **6** 68); his noble confession of Jesus as the Christ, the Son of the living God, and, alas, the rebuke that followed it (Mt **16** 13-23); the exalted privileges he enjoyed with James and John as witness of the raising of Jairus' daughter (Mk **5** 37) and the transfiguration of his Lord (Mt **17** 1-5); and finally, the incident of the tribute money, found only in Mt **17** 24.

The events beginning at the Passion are more easily recalled, because to so large an extent are they found in all the Gospels and about in the same order. They commence with the washing of his feet by the Master at the time of the last Passover, and the two mistakes he made as to the spiritual import of that act (Jn **13** 1-10); the first of his presumptuous boastings as to the strength of his devotion to his Master, and the warning of the latter as to Satan's prospective assault upon him (Lk **22** 31-34), twice repeated before the betrayal in Gethsemane (Mt **26** 31-35); the admission to the garden to behold the Saviour's deepest distress, the charge to watch and pray, and the failure to do so through sleepiness (Mt **26** 36-46); the mistaken courage in severing the ear of Malchus (Jn **18** 10-12); the forsaking of his Lord while the latter was being led away as a prisoner, his following Him afar off, his admission into the high priest's palace, his denial "before them all," his confirmation of it by an oath, his remembrance of the warning when "the Lord turned and looked upon Peter," and his tears of bitterness as he went out (Mt **26** 56-58; Mk **14** 66-72; Lk **22** 54-62; Jn **18** 15-27).

It will be seen that the story of Peter's fall is thus related by all the evangelists, but, to quote another, "None have described it in a more heinous light than Mark; and if, as is generally supposed, that Gospel was reviewed by Peter himself and even written under his direction, this circumstance may be considered as an evidence of his integrity and sincere contrition."

Nothing more is heard of Peter until the morning of the resurrection, when, on the first tidings of the event, he runs with John to see the tomb (Jn **20** 1-10); his name is esp. mentioned to the women by the angel (Mk **16** 7); and on the same day he sees Jesus alive before any of the rest of the Twelve (Lk **24** 34; 1 Cor **15** 5). Subsequently, at the Sea of Tiberias, Peter is given an opportunity for a threefold confession of Jesus whom he had thrice denied, and is once more assigned to the apostolic office; a prediction follows as to the kind of death he should die, and also a command to follow his Lord (Jn **21**).

(2) *The second period*, from the ascension of Christ to the conversion of Paul, is more briefly sketched. After the ascension, of which Peter was doubtless a witness, he "stood up in the midst of the brethren" in the upper room in Jerus to counsel the choice of a successor to Judas (Acts **1** 15-26). On the day of Pentecost he preaches the first gospel sermon (Acts **2**), and later, in company with John, instrumentally heals the lame man, addresses the people in the Temple, is arrested, defends himself before the Sanhedrin and returns to his "own company" (Acts **3**, **4**). He is again arrested and beaten (ch **5**); after a time he is sent by the church at Jerus to communicate the Holy Ghost to the disciples at Samaria (ch **8**). Returning to Jerus (where presumably Paul visits him, Gal **1** 18), he afterward journeys "throughout all parts," heals Aeneas at Lydda, raises Dorcas from the dead at Joppa, sees a vision upon the housetop which influences him to preach the gospel to the gentile centurion at Caesarea, and explains this action before "the apostles and the brethren that were in Judaea" (**9** 32-41; ch **11**).

After a while another persecution arose against the church, and Herod Agrippa, having put James to death, imprisons Peter with the thought of executing him also. Prayer is made by the church on his behalf, however, and miraculous deliverance is given him (ch **12**). Retiring for a while from public attention, he once more comes before us in the church council at Jerus, when the question is to be settled as to whether works are needful to salvation, adding his testimony to that of Paul and Barnabas in favor of justification by faith only (ch **15**).

Subsequently he is found at Antioch, and having fellowship with gentile Christians until "that certain came from James," when "he drew back and separated himself, fearing them that were of the circumcision," for which dissembling Paul "resisted him to the face, because he stood condemned" (Gal **2** 11-14).

Little more is authentically known of Peter, except that he traveled more or less extensively, being accompanied by his wife (1 Cor **9** 5), and that he wrote two epp., the second of which was penned as he approached the end of his life (2 Pet **1** 12-15).

The tradition is that he died a martyr at Rome about 67 AD, when about 75 years old. His Lord and Master had predicted a violent death for him (Jn **21** 18.19), which it is thought came to pass by crucifixion under Nero. It is said that at his own desire he was crucified head downward, feeling himself unworthy to resemble his Master in his death.

It should be observed, however, that the tradition that he visited Rome is only tradition and nothing more, resting as it does partly upon a miscalculation of some of the early Fathers, "who assume that he went to Rome in 42 AD, immediately after his deliverance from prison" (cf Acts **12** 17). Schaff says this "is irreconcilable with the silence of Scripture, and even with the mere fact of Paul's Ep. to the Rom, written in 58, since the latter says not a word of Peter's previous labors in that city, and he himself never built on other men's foundations" (Rom **15** 20; 2 Cor **10** 15.16).

4. His Character

The character of Peter is transparent and easily analyzed, and it is doubtless true that no other "in Scriptural history is drawn for us more clearly or strongly." He has been styled the prince of the apostles, and, indeed, seems to have been their leader on every occasion. He is always named first in every list of them, and was their common spokesman. He was hopeful, bold, confident, courageous, frank, impulsive, energetic, vigorous, strong, and loving, and faithful to his Master notwithstanding his defection prior to the crucifixion. It is true that he was liable to change and inconsistency, and because of his peculiar temperament he sometimes appeared forward and rash. Yet, as another says, "His virtues and faults had their common root in his enthusiastic disposition," and the latter were at length overruled by Divine grace into the most beautiful humility and meekness, as evinced in his two Epp.

The leadership above referred to, however, should not lead to the supposition that he possessed any supremacy over the other apostles, of which there is no proof. Such supremacy was never conferred upon him by his Master, it was never claimed by himself, and was never conceded by his associates. See in this connection Mt **23** 8–12; Acts **15** 13.14; 2 Cor **12** 11; Gal **2** 11.

It is true that when Christ referred to the meaning of his name (Mt **16** 18), He said, "Upon this rock I will build my church," but He did not intend to teach that His church would be built upon Peter, but upon Himself as confessed by Peter in ver 16 of the same chapter. Peter is careful to affirm this in the first of his two Epp. (**2** 4–9). Moreover, when Christ said, "I will give unto thee the keys of the kingdom of heaven," etc (Mt **16** 19), He invested him with no power not possessed in common with his brethren, since they also afterward received the same commission (Mt **18** 18; Jn **20** 23). A key is a badge of power or authority, and, as many Protestant commentators have pointed out, to quote the language of one of them, "the apostolic history explains and limits this trust, for it was Peter who opened the door of the gospel to Israel on the day of Pentecost (Acts **2** 38–42) and to the Gentiles in the house of Cornelius (Acts **10** 34–46)." Some, however, regard this authority as identical with the great commission (Mt **28** 19). See Keys, Power of the.

5. His Writings

The two Epp. of Peter were written presumably late in life, as appears esp. of the Second (**1** 12–15). Both were addressed to the same class of persons, chiefly Jewish Christians scattered abroad in the different provinces of Asia Minor, among whom Paul and his associates had planted the gospel (1 Pet **1** 1.2; 2 Pet **3** 1). The First was written at Babylon (1 Pet **5** 13), doubtless the famous Babylon on the Euphrates, which, though destroyed as a great capital, was still inhabited by a small colony of people, principally Jews (see Weiss, *INT*, II, 150; but see also Peter, First Epistle of).

(1) *First Epistle.*—The theme of the First Ep. seems to be the living hope to which the Christian has been begotten, and the obligations it lays upon him. The living hope is expounded in the earlier part of the first chapter down to ver 13, where the obligations begin to be stated, the first group including hope, godly fear, love to the brethren, and praise (**1** 13—**2** 10).

The writer drops his pen at this point, to take it up again to address those who were suffering persecution for righteousness' sake, upon whom two more obligations are impressed, submission to authority, and testimony to Christ (**2** 11—**4** 6). The third group which concludes the book begins here, dealing with such themes as spiritual hospitality in the use of heavenly gifts, patience in suffering, fidelity in service, and humility in ministering to one another. The letter was sent to the churches "by Silvanus, our faithful brother," the author affirming that his object in writing was to exhort and testify concerning "the true grace of God" (**5** 12).

The genuineness of this First Ep. has never been doubted, except of course by those who in these latter days have doubted everything, but the same cannot be said of the Second. It is not known to whom the latter was intrusted; as a matter of fact it found no place in the catalogues of the NT Scriptures of the 2d and 3d cents. The first church employing it was at Alexandria, but subsequently the church at large became satisfied from internal evidence of its genuineness and inspiration, and when the Canon was pronounced complete in the 4th cent., it was without hesitancy received.

(2) *Second Epistle.*—The Second Ep. claims to have been written by Peter (**1** 1; **3** 1.2), to doubt which would start more serious difficulties than can be alleged against its genuineness, either because of its late admission to the Canon or its supposed diversity of style from Peter's early writing. See Peter, Second Epistle of.

His object is the same in both Epp., to "stir up your sincere mind by putting you in remembrance" (**3** 1). Like Paul in his Second Ep. to Tim, he foresees the apostasy in which the professing church will end, the difference being that Paul speaks of it in its last stage when the laity have become infected (2 Tim **3** 1–5; **4** 3.4), while Peter sees it in its origin as traceable to false teachers (2 Pet **2** 1–3.15–19). As in the First Ep. he wrote to exhort and to testify, so here it is rather to caution and warn. This warning was, as a whole, against falling from grace (**3** 17.18), the enforcement of which warning is contained in **1** 2–11, the ground of it in **1** 12–21, and the occasion of it in the last two chapters. To speak only of the occasion: This, as was stated, was the presence of false teachers (**2** 1), whose eminent success is predicted (**2** 2), whose punishment is certain and dreadful (**2** 3–9), and whose description follows (**2** 10–22). The character of their false teaching (ch **3**) forms one of the most interesting and important features of the Ep., focusing as it does on the Second Coming of Christ.

6. Theology

The theology of Peter offers an interesting field of study because of what may be styled its freshness and variety in comparison with that of Paul and John, who are the great theologians of the NT.

(1) *Messianic teaching.*—In the first place, Peter is unique in his Messianic teaching as indicated in the first part of the Acts, where he is the chief personage, and where for the most part his ministry is confined to Jerus and the Jews. The latter, already in covenant relations with Jeh, had sinned in rejecting Jesus as the Messiah, and Peter's preaching was directed to that point, demanding repentance or a change of mind about Him. The apparent failure of the OT promises concerning the Davidic kingdom (Isa **11** 10–12; Jer **23** 5–8; Ezk **37** 21–28) was explained by the promise that the kingdom would be set up at the return of Christ (Acts **2** 25–31; **15** 14–16); which return, personal and corporeal, and for that purpose, is presented as only awaiting their national repentance (Acts **3** 19–26). See Scofield, *Reference Bible*, at the places named.

(2) *Justification.*—But Peter's special ministry to the circumcision is by no means in conflict with that of Paul to the Gentiles, as demonstrated at the point of transition in Acts **10**. Up until this time the gospel had been offered to the Jews only, but now they have rejected it in the national sense, and "the normal order for the present Christian age" is reached (Acts **13** 44–48). Accordingly, we find Peter, side by side with Paul, affirming the great doctrine of justification by faith only, in the words, "We believe that through the grace of the Lord Jesus Christ we [Jews] shall be saved, even as they [Gentiles]" (Acts **15** 11 AV). Moreover, it is clear from Peter's Second Ep. (**1** 1) that his conception of justification from the Divine as well as the human side is identical with that of Paul, since he speaks of justifying faith as terminating on the righteousness of our God and Saviour Jesus Christ. As we understand it, this is not the righteousness which God *is*, but the righteousness which God *gives* (cf Rom **1** 16.17; **3** 21–25; 2 Cor **5** 20.21).

(3) *Redemption.*—Passing from his oral to his written utterances, Peter is particularly rich in his allusions to the redemptive work of Christ. Limiting ourselves to his First Ep., the election of the individual believer is seen to be the result of the

sprinkling of Christ's blood (**1** 1); his obedience and godly fear are inspired by the sacrifice of the "lamb without blemish and without spot: Who verily was foreordained before the foundation of the world" (**1** 17–20 AV). But most interesting are the manner and the connection in which these sublime truths are sometimes set before the reader. For example, an exhortation to submission on the part of household slaves is the occasion for perhaps the most concise and yet comprehensive interpretation of Christ's vicarious sufferings anywhere in the NT (**2** 18–25, esp. the last two verses; cf also in its context **3** 18–22).

(4) *Future life.*—Next to the redemptive work of Christ, the Petrine teaching about the future life claims attention. The believer has been begotten again unto "a lively [or living] hope" (1 Pet **1** 3); which is "an inheritance" "reserved in heaven" (**1** 4); and associated with "praise, and glory and honor at the revelation [Second Coming] of Jesus Christ" (**1** 7.13; **4** 13; **5** 4.10; 2 Pet **1** 11.16; **3** 13, etc). This "hope" or "inheritance" is so real and so precious as to cause rejoicing even in times of heaviness and trial (1 Pet **1** 6); to stimulate to holiness of living (**1** 13–16); to patience in persecution (**4** 12.13); fidelity in service (**5** 1–4); stedfastness against temptation (**5** 8–10); and growth in grace (2 Pet **1** 10.11). It is a further peculiarity that the apostle always throws the thought of the present suffering forward into the light of the future glory. It is not as though there were merely an allotment of suffering here, and an allotment of glory by and by, with no relation or connection between the two, but the one is seen to be incident to the other (cf 1 Pet **1** 7.11; **4** 13; **5** 1; 2 Pet **3** 12.13). It is this circumstance, added to others, that gives Peter the title of the apostle of hope, as Paul has been called the apostle of faith, and John the apostle of love.

(5) *Holy Scripture.*—Considering their limitations as to space, Peter's Epp. are notable for the emphasis they lay upon the character and authority of the Holy Scriptures. 1 Pet **1** 10–12 teaches a threefold relation of the Holy Spirit to the Holy Word as its Author, its Revealer, and its Teacher or Preacher. The same chapter (vs 22–25) speaks of its life-giving and purifying power as well as its eternal duration. Ch **2** opens with a declaration of its vital relation to the Christian's spiritual growth. In **4** 11, it is shown to be the staple of the Christian's ministry. Practically the whole of the Second Ep. is taken up with the subject. Through the "exceeding great and precious promises" of that Word, Christians become "partakers of the divine nature" (**1** 4 AV); that they may be kept "always in remembrance" is Peter's object in writing (vs 12–15 AV); the facts of that Word rest on the testimony of eyewitnesses (vs 16–18); its origin is altogether Divine (vs 20.21); which is as true of the NT as of the OT (**3** 2); including the Epp. of Paul (vs 15.16).

(6) *Apostasy and judgment.*—This appreciation of the living Word of God finds an antithesis in the solemn warning against apostate teachers and teaching forming the substance of 2 Pet **2** and **3**. The theology here is of judgment. It is swift and "lingereth not" (**2** 1–3); the Judge is He who "spared not" in olden time (vs 4–7); His delay expresses mercy, but He "will come as a thief" (**3** 9.10); the heavens "shall pass away," the earth and its works shall be burned up (ver 10); "What manner of persons ought ye to be in all holy living and godliness?" (ver 11).

(7) *Second Coming of Christ.*—Peter's theology concerning judgment is a further illustration of the Messianic character of his instruction. For example, the Second Coming of Christ of which he speaks in the closing chapter of the Second Ep. is not that aspect of it associated with the translation of His church, and of which Paul treats (1 Thess **4** 13–18), but that pertaining to Israel and the day of Jeh spoken of by the OT prophets (Isa **2** 12–22; Rev **19** 11–21, etc).

LITERATURE.—The history of Peter is treated more or less at length in the intros to the comms. on his Epp., and in works on the life of Christ. But particular reference is made to the following: F. W. Farrar, *Early Days of Christianity*, London, 1882; J. S. Howson, *Studies in the Life of St. Peter*, London, 1883; H. A. Birks, *Life and Character of St. Peter*, London, 1887; W. M. Ramsay, *The Church in the Rom Empire*, London, 1893; Mason Gallagher, *Was Peter Ever at Rome?* Philadelphia, 1895; A. C. McGiffert, *The Apostolic Age*, New York, 1897; W. H. Griffith Thomas, *The Apostle Peter*, London, 1904; G. Matheson, *Representative Men of the NT*, London, 1905; A. J. Southouse, *The Making of Simon Peter*, New York, 1906; A. C. Gaebelein, *The Gospel of Matthew*, New York, 1907; *The Acts of the Apostles*, New York, 1912; Edmundson, *Church in Rome in the 1st Cent.*, 1913; Smith, *The Days of His Flesh*, New York, 1911.

On the theology of Peter, consult the subject in works on Systematic or Bib. Theology, and see also R. W. Dale, *The Atonement*, 97–148, London, 1875; C. A. Briggs, *Messiah of the Apostles*, 21–41, New York, 1895; Scofield, *Reference Bible*, where pertinent.

Among comms. on 1 and 2 Pet may be mentioned: Brown, 3 vols, Edinburgh, 1848–56; Demarest, 2 vols, New York, 1851–65; Leighton, republished, Philadelphia, 1864; Lillie, New York, 1869; G. F. C. Fronmüller, in Lange's *Comm.*, ET, New York, 1874; Plumptre, *Cambridge Bible*, 1883; Spitta, *Der zweite Brief des Petrus*, Halle, 1885; F. B. Meyer, London, 1890; Lumby, *Expositor's Bible*, London, 1894; J. H. Jowett, London, 1905; Bigg, *ICC*, 1901.

JAMES M. GRAY

PETER, APOCALYPSE OF. See APOCRYPHAL GOSPELS, II, 4; LITERATURE, SUB-APOSTOLIC (Intro).

PETER, GOSPEL ACCORDING TO. See APOCRYPHAL GOSPELS; LITERATURE, SUB-APOSTOLIC.

PETER, THE FIRST EPISTLE OF:

Simon Peter was a native of Galilee. He was brought to the Saviour early in His ministry by his brother Andrew (Jn **1** 40.41). His call to the office of apostle is recorded in Mt **10** 1–4; Mk **3** 13–16.

He occupied a distinguished place among the Lord's disciples. In the four lists of the apostles found in the NT his name stands first (Mt **10** 2–4; Mk **3** 16–19; Lk **6** 14–16; Acts **1** 13). He is the chief figure in the first twelve chapters of the Acts. It is Peter that preaches the first Christian sermon (Acts **2**), he that opens the door of the gospel to the gentile world in the house of the Rom soldier, Cornelius, and has the exquisite delight of witnessing scenes closely akin to those of Pentecost at Jerus (Acts **10** 44–47). It was given him to pronounce the solemn sentence on the guilty pair, Ananias and Sapphira, and to rebuke in the power of the Spirit the profane Simon Magus (Acts **5** 1–11; **8** 18–23). In these and the like instances Peter exhibited the authority with which Christ had invested him (Mt **16** 19)—an authority bestowed upon all the disciples (Jn **20** 22.23)—the power to bind and to loose.

Two Epp. are ascribed to Peter. Of the Second

doubt and uncertainty have existed from the early ages to the present. The genuineness and authenticity of the First are above suspicion.

I. Canonicity of 1 Peter.—The proof of its integrity and trustworthiness is ample and altogether satisfactory. It falls into parts: external and internal. The historical attestation to its authority as an apostolic document is abundant. Polycarp, disciple of the apostle John, martyred in 156 AD at 86 or more years of age, refers to the Ep. in unmistakable terms. Irenaeus, a man who may well be said to represent both the East and the West, who was a disciple of Polycarp, quotes it copiously, we are assured. Clement of Alexandria, born c 150 AD, died c 216 AD, cites it many times in his *Stromata*, one passage (**4** 8) being quoted five times by actual count. "The testimony of the early church is summed up by Eusebius (*HE*, III, xxiii, 3). He places it among those writings about which no question was ever raised, no doubt ever entertained by any portion of the catholic church" (Professor Lumby in *Bible Comm.*).

1. External Evidence

The internal evidence in favor of the Ep. is as conclusive as the external. The writer is well acquainted with Our Lord's teaching, and he makes use of it to illustrate and enforce his own. The references he makes to that teaching are many, and they include the four Gospels. He is familiar likewise with the Epp., particularly Jas, Rom, and Eph. But what is esp. noteworthy is the fact that 1 Pet in thought and language stands in close relation with the apostle's discourses as recorded in Acts. By comparing 1 Pet **1** 17 with Acts **10** 34; **1** 21 with **2** 32–36 and **10** 40.41; **2** 7.8 with **4** 10.11; **2** 17 with **10** 28, and **3** 18 with **3** 14, one will perceive how close the parallel between the two is. The inference from these facts appears legitimate, viz. 1 Pet in diction and thought belongs to the same period of time and moves in the same circle of truth as do the other writings of the NT. The writer was an apostle, and he was Simon Peter.

2. Internal Evidence

II. The Address.—Peter writes to the "elect who are sojourners of the Dispersion." James employs the term "Dispersion" to designate believing Hebrews of the Twelve Tribes who lived outside the land (**1** 1). The Jews included in it the whole body of Israelites scattered among the gentile nations (Jn **7** 35). But we must not conclude from this that the Ep. is directed to Christian Jews alone. Gentile believers are by no means excluded, as **1** 14.18.20; **2** 10; **3** 6; **4** 3.4 abundantly attest. Indeed, the gentile element in the churches of Asia Minor largely predominated at the time. The term "sojourners" represents a people away from home, strangers in a strange land; the word is tr[d] "pilgrims" in **2** 11 and He **11** 13—an appropriate name for those who confess that they have here no continuing city, but who seek one to come. While no doubt Peter had believing Israelites in mind when he wrote, for he never forgot that his ministry belonged primarily to the circumcision (Gal **2** 7.8), he did not neglect the more numerous gentile converts, and to these he speaks as earnestly as to the others; and these also were "sojourners."

Three of the four provinces Peter mentions, viz. Pontus, Cappadocia, and Asia, had representatives at the memorable Pentecost in Jerus (Acts **2** 9; 1 Pet **1** 1). Many of these "sojourners of the Dispersion" may have believed the message of the apostle and accepted salvation through Jesus Christ, and returned home to tell the good news to their neighbors and friends. This would form a strong bond of union between them and Peter, and would open the way for him to address them in the familiar and tender manner of the Ep.

Silvanus appears to have been the bearer of the letter to the Christians of Asia Minor: "By Silvanus, our faithful brother, as I account him, I have written unto you briefly" (**5** 12). It is an assumption to assert from these words that Silvanus was employed in the composition of the letter. The statement denotes rather the bearer than the writer or secretary. Silvanus was Paul's companion in the ministry to the Asiatic churches, and since we do not read of him as going with Paul to Jerus or to Rome, it is probable he returned from Corinth (Acts **18** 5) to Asia Minor and labored there. He and Peter met, where no one knows, though not a few think in Rome; as likely a guess perhaps is in Pal. At any rate, Silvanus gave Peter an account of the conditions in the provinces, the afflictions and persecutions of believers, and the deep need they had for sympathy and counsel. He would, accordingly, be of the greatest assistance to the apostle. This seems to account for the peculiarity of language which Peter uses: "By Silvanus, our faithful brother, I have written unto you," as if he had some share in furnishing the contents of the Ep.

Silvanus

III. Place and Time of Composition.—According to **5** 13 the Ep. was written in Babylon. But what place is meant? Two cities having this name were known in apostolic times. One was in Egypt, probably on or near the present site of Cairo, and we are told that it was a "city of no small importance." Epiphanius calls it "great Babylon" (Zahn). The absence, however, of all tradition that would tend to identify this place with the Babylon of the Ep. seems to shut it out of the problem. Babylon on the Euphrates is regarded by many as the place here designated. Jews in considerable numbers still dwelt in Babylon, notwithstanding the massacre of thousands in the reign of Claudius, and the flight of multitudes into other countries. There is much to be said in favor of this city as the place meant, and yet the absence of tradition in its support is a very serious difficulty. A third view regards it as symbolical of Rome. Roman Catholics thus interpret it, and not a few Protestants so understand it. Tradition which runs back into the first half of the 2d cent. appears to favor it, though much uncertainty and obscurity still surround the earliest ages of our era, in spite of the unwearied researches of modern scholars. Papias, bishop of Hierapolis, who lived in the first half of the 2d cent., appears to have had no doubt that Peter was martyred in Rome, and that the Babylon of the Ep. designates the Imperial City. There are very serious objections to this interpretation. One is, that it is totally out of keeping with Peter's manner of writing. Preëminently he is direct and matter-of-fact in his style. The metaphorical language he employs is mostly drawn from the OT, or, if from himself, it is so common of use as to be well understood by all readers. It is altogether improbable that this man, plain of speech almost to bluntness, should interject in the midst of his personal explanations and final salutations such a mystical epithet with no hint of what he means by it, or why he employs such a mode of speech.

1. Babylon: Which?

Besides, there is no evidence that Rome was called Babylon by the Christians until the Book of Rev was published, i.e. c 90–96 AD. But if 1 Pet is dependent on the Apocalypse for this name of Babylon as Rome, Peter could not have been its author, for he died years before that date. The Ep. was written about 64 AD, at the time when persecutions under the infamous Nero were raging, at which time also the apostle himself bore his witness and went to his heavenly home, even as his Master had forewarned him (Jn **21** 18.19). While not unmindful of the great difficulties that beset the view, nevertheless we are inclined to the opinion that the Babylon of **5** 13 is the ancient city on the Euphrates. See PETER (SIMON).

2. Babylon Not Rome

IV. Design.—The apostle had more than one object in view when he addressed the "elect" in Asia Minor. The Lord Jesus had charged him, "Feed my lambs"—"Tend my sheep"—"Feed my sheep" (Jn **21** 15–17). His two Epp. certify how faithfully he obeyed the charge. With loving and tender hand he feeds the lambs and tends the whole flock, warns against foes, guards from danger, and leads them into green pastures and beside still waters. He reminds them of the glorious inheritance they are to possess (**1** 3–9); he exhorts them to walk in the footsteps of the uncomplaining Christ (**2** 20–25); to be compassionate, loving, tender-hearted, humble-minded, and circumspect in their passage through this unfriendly world (**3** 8–12). He sums up the main duties of Christian life in the short but pregnant sentences, "Honor all men. Love the brotherhood. Fear God. Honor the king" (**2** 17). But his supreme object is to comfort and encourage them amid the persecutions and the sufferings to which they were unjustly subjected, and to fortify them against the heavier trials that were impending.

1. Persecution

From the beginning the Christian church was the object of suspicion and of hatred, and many of its adherents had suffered even unto death at the hands of both hostile Jews and fanatical Gentiles. But these afflictions were generally local and sporadic. There were churches of large membership and wide influence which were unmolested (1 Cor **4** 8–10), and which seem to have been able to get fair treatment in heathen courts (1 Cor **6** 1–6). But the condition brought to view in 1 Pet is altogether different. Trials and afflictions of the severest sort assail them, and an enmity and hostility, bent on their destruction, pursue them with tireless energy. The whole Christian body shared in the persecutions (**5** 9). The trial was a surprise (**4** 12), both in its intensity, for Peter calls it "fiery," and for its unexpectedness. The apostle represents it as a savage beast of prey, a roaring lion, prowling about them to seize and devour (**5** 8.9).

A variety of charges were brought against the Christians, but they were calumnies and slanders, without any foundation in fact. They were spoken against as evil-doers (**2** 12—*kakopoiôn; malefici*, Tacitus calls them). Their adversaries railed against them (**3** 9); reviled them (**3** 16); spake evil of them (**4** 4); reproached them for the name of Christ (**4** 14). These are ugly epithets. They show how bitter was the hatred and how intense the hostility felt by the heathen toward the Christians who dwelt among them. If there had been any justification for such antagonism in the character and the conduct of Christ's people, if they were evil-doers, "haters of the human race," to be classed with thieves and murderers and meddlers in other men's matters (**4** 14–16), as they were accused of being and doing, we could understand the fierce opposition which assailed them and the savage purpose to suppress them altogether, but the only ground for the enmity felt against them was the refusal of the Christians to join their heathen neighbors in their idolatries, their feasts, winebibbings, revelings, carousings, lasciviousness and lusts in which once they freely shared (**4** 2–4). The Asian saints had renounced all such wicked practices, had separated themselves from their old companions in riotous living and revolting debaucheries; they were witnesses against their immoralities, and hence became the objects of intense dislike and persecuting animosity. Peter bears testimony to the high character, the purity of life and the self-sacrificing devotion of these believers. In all Asia Minor no better company of men and women could be found than these disciples of Jesus Christ; none more submissive to constituted authority, none more ready to help their fellow-men in their distress and trouble. The head and front of their offending was their separation from the ungodly world about them, and their solemn witness against the awful sins done daily before their eyes.

2. Example of Christ

How mightily does the apostle minister to his suffering friends! He bids them remember the uncomplaining Christ when He was unjustly afflicted by cruel men (**2** 19–25). He tells them how they may effectively put to silence their accusers, and refute the calumnies and the slanders that are so cruelly circulated against them, namely, by living such pure and godly lives, by being so meek, docile, patient, stedfast, true and faithful to God, that none can credit the false accusations (**2** 1–5; **2** 13–17; **3** 8.9.13–17; **5** 6–11).

3. Relation to State

There is little or no evidence in the Ep. that the persecutions were inflicted by imperial authority or that the state was dealing with the Christians as enemies who were dangerous to the peace of society. In the provinces to which the letter was sent there seems to have been complete absence of formal trial and punishment through the courts. Peter does not speak of legal proceedings against the Christians by the magistrates. On the contrary, he urges them to be subject to every ordinance of man for the Lord's sake: whether to the king as supreme; or unto governors, as sent by him for vengeance on evil-doers and for praise to them that do well (**2** 13). They are to honor all men, to honor the king (**2** 17). This submission would scarcely be pressed if the state had already proscribed Christianity and decreed its total suppression. This the imperial government did later on, but there is no evidence furnished by the apostle that in 64 AD—the date of the Ep.—the government formally denounced Christians and determined to annihilate them.

Peter exhorts his fellow-believers to silence their persecutors by their upright conduct (**2** 15); they are thus to put them to shame who falsely accuse them (**3** 16); and they are not to combat evil with evil nor answer reviling with reviling, but contrariwise with blessing (**3** 9). The antagonism here indicated obviously springs from the heathen populace; there is no hint of arraignment before magistrates or subjection to legal proceedings. It is unbelievers who revile and slander and denounce the people of God in the provinces.

Everything in the Ep. points to the time of Nero, 64 AD, and not to the time of Domitian or Trajan, or even Titus. In Rome vast multitudes of Christians were put to death in the most brutal fashion, so Tacitus relates, but the historian asserts that there was a sinister report to the effect that Nero himself instigated the burning of the city (July 19, 64), and "he [Nero] falsely diverted the charge on to a set of people to whom the vulgar gave the name of Christians (or Chrestians), and who were detested for the abominations which they perpetrated." See Nero. Certain facts are clear from Tacitus' statements, viz. that at the time the Christians were well known as a distinct sect; and that they were subjected to the dreadful sufferings inflicted upon them because they were Christians; and the persecutions at the time were instigated by the fear and the brutality of the tyrant. Peter likewise recognizes the fact that believers were disliked and calumniated by their heathen neighbors for the same reason—they were Christians: "If ye are reproached for the name of Christ, blessed are ye" (**4** 14); "But if a man suffer as a Christian, let him not be ashamed; but let him glorify God in this name" (**4** 16). But the imperial government at the time does not appear to have taken formal action for the overthrow of Christianity as a system inimical to the empire. Of course, where direct charges of a criminal nature were made against Christians, judicial inquiry into them would be instituted. But in the Ep. what believers had to endure and suffer were the detraction, the vituperation, the opprobrium and the vile and malignant slanders with which the heathen assailed them.

V. Characteristic Features of the Epistle.—It has certain very distinct marks, some of which may be noticed.

1. Freedom in Structure

It does not observe a close logical sequence in its structure, as those of Paul so prominently display. There is truth in Dean Alford's statement, although perhaps he pushes it rather far: "The link between one idea and another is found, not in any progress of unfolding thought or argument, but in the last word of the foregoing sentence which is taken up and followed out in the new one" (see **1** 5.6.7.9.10, etc). This peculiarity, however, does not interfere with the unity of the ep., it rather adds to it, and it gives to it a vividness which it otherwise might not possess.

2. Hope

It is the ep. of hope. How much it makes of this prime grace! Peter seems never to grow weary of describing it and exalting its radiant beauty and desirableness. He calls it a living hope (**1** 3). It is born by the resurrection of Jesus Christ from the dead, and it calmly awaits the glorious inheritance that soon will be enjoyed. It is a hope that will be perfected at the advent of Christ (**1** 13), and it is set on God, hence cannot fail (**1** 21). With sickly, dying hope we are quite familiar. The device which a certain state (South Carolina) has inscribed on its Great Seal is, *dum spiro spero* ("while I live I hope"). Such a hope may serve for a commonwealth whose existence is limited to this world, but a man needs something more enduring, something imperishable. "It is a fearful thing when a man and his hopes die together" (Leighton). A Christian can confidently write, "when I am dying I hope," for his is a living hope that fills and thrills the future with a blessed reality.

3. Inheritance

The Christian's glorious inheritance (**1** 3–5) is depicted in one of the most comprehensive and suggestive descriptions of the believer's heritage found in the Bible. It is declared to be "incorruptible." The word points to its substance. It is imperishable. In it there is no element of decay. It holds in its heart no germ of death. Like its author, the living God, it is unchangeable and eternal. It is "undefiled." It is not stained by sin nor polluted by crime, either in its acquisition or its possession. Human heritages generally are marred by human wrongs. There is hardly an acre of soil that is not tainted by fraud or violence. The coin that passes from hand to hand is in many instances soiled by guilt. But this of Peter is absolutely pure and holy. It "fadeth not away." It never withers. Ages do not impair its beauty or dim its luster. Its bloom will remain fresh, its fragrance undiminished, forever. Thus our inheritance "is glorious in these respects: it is in its *substance*, incorruptible: in its *purity*, undefiled: in *beauty*, unfading" (Alford).

Now why does the apostle in the very opening of his Ep. give so lofty a place to the saints' inheritance? He does so in order to comfort and encourage his fellow-believers with the consolations of the Lord Himself, that they may bear stedfastly their manifold sufferings and triumph over their weighty afflictions. Hence he writes: "Wherein ye greatly rejoice, though now for a little while, if need be, ye have been put to grief in manifold trials, that the proof of your faith . . . . may be found unto praise and glory and honor at the revelation of Jesus Christ" (**1** 6–9). He lifts their thoughts and their gaze up far above the troubles and distresses around them to Him whose they are, whom they serve, who will by and by crown them with immortal bliss.

4. Testimony of Prophets

The prophets and their study are described in **1** 10.11: "Concerning which salvation the prophets sought and searched diligently, who prophesied of the grace that should come unto you," etc. With Peter and his fellow-apostles the testimony of the prophets was authoritative and final. Where they had a clear word from the OT Scriptures, they felt that every question was settled and controversy was at an end.

(1) *Salvation.*—The burden of the prophetic communications was salvation. The prophets spoke on many subjects; they had to exhort, rebuke and entreat their wayward contemporaries; to denounce sin, to announce judgment on the guilty and to recall them to repentance and reformation. But ever and anon their vision was filled with the future and its blessedness, their voices would swell with rapture as they saw and foretold the great salvation to be brought to the world and the grace that would then so copiously go out unto men; for the Messiah was to appear and to suffer, the just for the unjust, that He might bring us to God.

(2) *Spirit of Christ.*—The prophet's messages were the messages of the Spirit of Christ. It was He who testified beforehand the sufferings of Christ and the glories that should follow. The prophets always disclaim any part in the origination of their messages. They affirm in the most positive and solemn manner that their predictions are not their own, but God's. Hence they are called the Lord's "spokesmen," the Lord's "mouth" (Ex **4** 15.16; **7** 1.2; 2 Pet **1** 21).

(3) *Prophetic study.*—They "sought and searched diligently." These terms are strong and emphatic. They pored over the predictions which the Spirit had revealed through themselves; they scrutinized them with eager and prolonged inquiry. Two points engaged their attention: "What time or what manner of time the Spirit of Christ which was in them did point unto." The first "what" relates to the time of the Messiah's advent; the second "what" to the events and circumstances which would attend His appearing—a fruitful theme, one that engages the inquiry of nobler students—"which things angels desire to look into."

5. The Christian Brotherhood

The Christian brotherhood is described in **2** 9.10: "But ye are an elect race, a royal priesthood, a holy nation, a people for *God's* own possession, that ye may show forth the excellencies of him who called you out of darkness into his marvellous light." The brotherhood is the new Israel. The apostle describes it in terms which were applied to the old Israel, but which include more than the ancient Israel ever realized. The exalted conception is by one who was a strict Jew, the apostle of the circumcision, and who held somewhat closely to the Mosaic institutions to the end of his life. All the more significant on this account is his testimony. The descriptive titles which he here gathers together and places on the brow of the Christian brotherhood are of the most illustrious sort. A distinguished man, a noble, a general, a statesman, will sometimes appear in public with his breast covered with resplendent decorations which mark his rank or his achievements. But such distinctions sink into insignificance alongside of this dazzling cluster. This is the heavenly nobility, the royal family of the Lord of glory, decorated with badges brighter far than ever glittered on the breast of king or emperor. But even in this instance Peter reminds Christians of the glorious destiny awaiting them that they may be strengthened and stimulated to stedfastness and loyalty in the midst of the trials and afflictions to which they are subjected (**2** 11.12)

6. Spirits in Prison

A study of 1 Pet **3** 18–20—"preached unto the spirits in prison"—should here follow in the present cursory review of the characteristic features of the Ep., but anything like an adequate examination of this difficult passage would require more space than could be given it. Suffice it to quote a sentence from Professor Zahn (*NT*, II, 289) with which the writer agrees: "That interpretation of 1 Pet **3** 19 is in all probability correct, according to which a preaching of Christ at the time of the Flood is referred to, i.e. a preaching through Noah, so that Noah is here represented as a preacher of righteousness, as in 2 Pet **2** 5." See PRISON, SPIRITS IN.

VI. Analysis.—A very general analysis of the Ep. is the following:

(1) Christian privileges, **1**—**2** 10.
(2) Christian duties, **2** 11—**4** 11.
(3) Persecutions and trials, **4** 12—**5** 11.
(4) Personal matters and salutations, **5** 12-14.

The chief doctrines of Christianity are found in 1 Pet. The vicarious suffering and death of the Lord Jesus Christ (**2** 24; **3** 18); the new birth (**1** 3.23); redemption by the blood of Christ (**1** 18. 19), faith, hope, patient endurance under unjust suffering, and holiness of life, are all pressed upon Christians with great earnestness and force.

Literature.—Bible Dicts., *DB*, *HDB*, Davis, *DB*, *EB*, *Sch-Herz*, vol VIII; Intros: Westcott, Salmon, Zahn; Vincent, *Word Studies;* Comms.: *Bible Comm.*, *Cambridge Bible for Schools;* Lillie, Jameson, Fausett and Brown, Alford, Bigg, Mayor (on 2 Pet), Johnstone (homiletical), New York, 1888; Hort, 1 Pet **1** 1—**2** 17, New York, 1898.

William G. Moorehead

PETER, THE SECOND EPISTLE OF:

I. External Evidence in Favor of Its Apostolic Authority
   1. Ancient Opinion
   2. Modern Opinion
   3. Dr. Chase's View
II. Internal Evidence in Support of Its Apostolic Authority
   1. Style and Diction
   2. Reason of Dissimilarities
   3. Claim to Petrine Authorship
   4. Christian Earnestness
   5. Relation to Apostles
   6. Autobiographical Allusions
   7. Quoted by Jude
III. Doctrinal Teachings of the Epistle
   1. Saving Knowledge
      (1) Basis
      (2) Growth
      (3) Inerrancy of Sources
   2. The Three Worlds
      (1) The Old World
      (2) The Present World
      (3) The New World

The Second Ep. of Peter comes to us with less historical support of its genuineness than any other book of the NT. In consequence, its right to a place in the Canon is seriously doubted by some and denied by others. There are those who confidently assign it to the Apostolic age and to the apostle whose name it bears in the NT, while there are those who as confidently assign it to post-apostolic times, and repudiate its Petrine authorship. It is not the aim of this article to trace the history of the two opinions indicated above, nor to cite largely the arguments employed in the defence of the Ep., or those in opposition to it; nor to attempt to settle a question which for more than a thousand years the wisest and best men of the Christian church have been unable to settle. Such a procedure would in this case be the height of presumption. What is here attempted is to point out as briefly as may be some of the reasons for doubting its canonicity, on the one hand, and those in its support, on the other.

I. External Evidence in Favor of Its Apostolic Authority.—It must be admitted at the very outset that the evidence is meager. The first writer who mentions it by name is Origen (c 240 AD). In his homily on Josh, he speaks of the two Epp. of Peter. In another place he quotes 2 Pet **1** 4: "partakers of the divine nature," and gives it the name of Scripture. But Origen is careful to say that its authority was questioned: "Peter has left one acknowledged Ep., and perhaps a second, for this is contested." Eusebius, bishop of Caesarea, regarded it with even more suspicion than did Origen, and accordingly he placed it among the disputed books (*Antilegomena*). Jerome knew the scruples which many entertained touching the Ep., but notwithstanding, he included it in his Vulg Version. The main reason for Jerome's uncertainty about it he states to be "difference of style from 1 Pet." He accounts for the difference by supposing that the apostle "made use of two different interpreters." As great teachers and scholars as Origen, Eusebius, and Jerome, e.g. Athanasius, Augustine, Epiphanius, Rufinus and Cyril, received it as genuine. At the Reformation Erasmus rejected 2 Pet; Luther seems to have had no doubt of its genuineness; while Calvin felt some hesitancy because of the "discrepancies between it and the First." In the 4th cent., two church councils (Laodicea, c 372, and Carthage, 397) formally recognized it and placed it in the Canon as equal in authority with the other books of the NT.

1. Ancient Opinion

2. Modern Opinion

The opinion of modern scholars as to references in post-apostolic literature to 2 Pet is not only divided, but in many instances antagonistic. Salmon, Warfield, Zahn and others strongly hold that such references are to be found in the writings of the 2d cent., perhaps in one or two documents of the 1st. They insist with abundant proof in support of their contention that Irenaeus, Justin Martyr, the Shepherd of Hermas, and the *Didache*, and Clement of Rome, were all acquainted with the Ep. and made allusions to it in their writings. Weighing as honestly and as thoroughly as one can the citations made from that literature, one is strongly disposed to accept the evidence as legitimate and conclusive.

3. Dr. Chase's View

On the other side, Professor Chase (*HDB*) has subjected all such references and allusions in the primitive writings to a very keen and searching criticism, and it must be frankly confessed that he has reduced the strength of the evidence and argument very greatly. But Professor Chase himself, from the remains of the ancient literature, and from the internal evidence of the Ep. itself, arrives at the conclusion that 2 Pet is not at all an apostolic document, that it certainly was not written by Peter, nor in the 1st cent. of our era, but about the middle of the 2d cent., say 150 AD. If this view is accepted, we must pronounce the Ep. a forgery, pseudonymous and pseudepigraphic, with no more right to be in the NT than has the Apocalypse of Peter or the romance of the Shepherd of Hermas.

II. Internal Evidence in Support of Its Apostolic Authority.—At first sight, this seems to be not altogether reassuring, but looking deeper into the letter itself we arrive at a satisfactory conclusion. Difference of style between the two Epp. attributed to Peter is given as one prominent reason for questioning the validity of the Second. It is mainly if not entirely on this ground that Jerome, Calvin and others hesitated to receive it. It is noteworthy that in the earlier times objections were not urged because of its relation to Jude—its borrowing from Jude, as is often charged in our days. Its alleged dissimilarity to 1 Pet in diction, structure, and measurably in its contents, explains why it was discredited. Admitting that there is substantial ground for this criticism, nevertheless there are not a few instances in which words rarely found in the other Bib. books are common to the two Epp. Some examples are given in proof: "precious" (1 Pet **1** 7.19; 2 Pet **1** 1) (a compound), occurring often in Rev, not often in other books; "virtue" (1 Pet **2** 9 AVm; 2 Pet **1** 3), found elsewhere only in Phil **4** 8; "supply" (1 Pet **4** 11; 2 Pet **1** 5), rare in other books; "love of brethren" (1 Pet **1** 22; 2 Pet **1** 7 m), only in three places besides; "behold" (1 Pet **2** 12; **3** 2 [verbal form]; 2 Pet **1** 16) (eyewitnesses), not found elsewhere in the NT; "without blemish," "without spot" (1 Pet **1** 19; 2 Pet **3** 14) (order

1. Style and Diction

of words reversed); also positive side (**2** Pet **2** 13), "spots and blemishes"; the words do not occur elsewhere; "ungodly" (1 Pet **4** 18; 2 Pet **2** 5; **3** 7) occurs in but three other places, except Jude, which has it three times.

2. Reason of Dissimilarities

Besides, there are many striking similarities in thought and diction in the two Epp. Two instances are given. In the First the saved are described as the "elect" (**1** 1), and as "called" (**2** 21). In the Second, the two great truths are brought together (**1** 10). Likewise, in both stress is laid upon prophecy (1 Pet **1** 10–12; 2 Pet **1** 19–21). Now, all this tends to prove that the writer of the Second Ep. was well acquainted with the peculiarity of diction employed in the First, and that he made use purposely of its uncommon terms, or, if the Second was written by another than the apostle, he succeeded surprisingly well in imitating his style. The latter alternative does not merit discussion. The differences arise mainly out of the subjects treated in the two, and the design which the writer seems to have kept constantly in view. In the First, he sought to comfort, strengthen and sustain his persecuted brethren; this is his supreme aim. In the Second he is anxious to warn and to shield those whom he addresses as to impending dangers more disastrous and more to be feared than the sufferings inflicted by a hostile world. In the First, judgment had begun at the house of God (**4** 17.18), and believers were to arm, not to resist their persecutors, but for martyrdom (**4** 1). But in the Second, a very different condition of things is brought to view. Ungodly men holding degrading principles and practising shocking immoralities were threatening to invade the Christian brotherhood. Evil of a most vicious sort was detected by the watchful eye of the writer, and he knew full well that if suffered to continue and grow, as assuredly it would, utter ruin for the cause he loved would ensue. Therefore he forewarns and denounces the tendency with the spirit and energy of a prophet of God.

3. Claim to Petrine Authorship

2 Pet opens with the positive statement of Peter's authorship: "Simon ["Symeon," Nestle, Weymouth] Peter, a servant . . . . of Jesus Christ." The insertion of "Symeon," the old Heb name, in the forefront of the document is significant. If a forger had been writing in Peter's name he would have begun his letter almost certainly by copying the First Ep. and simply written, "Peter, an apostle of Jesus Christ." Note also that "servant" is introduced into the Second Ep., but is absent from the First. He designates himself as a servant and apostle of Jesus Christ. "Although several pseudonymous writings appear in early Christian literature, there is no Christian document *of value* written by a forger who uses the name of an apostle" (Dods, *SBD*). If this important statement is accepted at its full worth, it goes far to settle the question of authorship. Both "servant" and "apostle" appear in the opening sentence, and the writer claims both for himself.

4. Christian Earnestness

Furthermore, the writer is distinctively a Christian; he addresses those who "have obtained a like precious faith with us in the righteousness of our God and the Saviour Jesus Christ" (**1** 1). His is the same precious faith which all the saints enjoy; his also the exceeding great and precious promises of God, and he expects with all other believers to be made a partaker of the Divine nature (**1** 3.4). Is it at all probable that one with such a faith and such expectations would deliberately forge the name of Simon Peter, an apostle of Jesus Christ? The writer is unsparing in his denunciations of false teachers, corrupters of others, and perverters of the truth. He instances the fall of the angels, the destruction of Sodom, the rebuke of Balaam, as examples of the doom of those who know the truth and yet live in shameful sin and crime. Would a Christian and servant of Jesus Christ be at all likely to commit in the most flagrant manner the things he so vehemently condemns? If the writer was not the apostle Peter, he was a false teacher, a corrupter of others, and a hypocrite, which seems incredible to us.

Moreover, he associates himself with the other apostles (**3** 2), is in full sympathy with Paul and is acquainted with Paul's Epp. (**3** 15.16), and he holds and teaches the same fundamental truth. An apostolic spirit breathes through this document such as is generally absent from spurious writings and such as a forger does not exhibit. He is anxiously concerned for the purity of the faith and for the holiness and fidelity of believers. He exhorts them to give "diligence that ye may be found in peace, without spot and blameless in his sight," and that they "grow in the grace and knowledge of our Lord and Saviour Jesus Christ" (**3** 14.18). All this and much more of like devout teaching is apostolic in tone and betokens genuineness and reality.

5. Relation to Apostles

6. Auto-biographical Allusions

Still further, the writer appeals to certain facts in the life of Peter that are almost autobiographical. For example, he speaks of "putting off of my tabernacle . . . . even as our Lord Jesus Christ signified unto me" (**1** 13.14). The reference undoubtedly is to Jn **13** 36; **21** 18.19. He claims to have been a witness of the Transfiguration (**1** 16–18). He indirectly claims the inspiration without which true prophecy is impossible (**1** 19–21). He asserts that this is his "second epistle" (**3** 1). This testimony on the part of the writer is personal, emphatic and direct. It reads much like Peter's plain way of speaking of himself at the Council of Jerus, "Ye know that a good while ago God made choice among you, that by my mouth the Gentiles should hear the word of the gospel, and believe" (Acts **15** 7).

7. Quoted by Jude

Once more, Jude appears to quote from 2 Pet (see JUDE). The question of the priority of the two Epp. is by no means settled. Many recent writers give the precedence to Jude, others to Peter. One of the highest authority, Zahn (*NT*, II, 238 ff), argues with great force in support of the view that Peter's is the older and that Jude cites from it. The arguments in favor of this latter belief are here only summarized: (1) Jude cites from writings other than Scripture, as the apocryphal Book of En and perhaps also from the Assumption of Moses. Peter scarcely quotes from any source. The former would be more likely to cite 2 Pet **2**—**3** 3 than the latter from Jude vs 4–16. The resemblance between these two sections of the Epp. is so close that one must have drawn both thoughts and language from the other, or both availed themselves of the same documentary source. Of this latter supposition antiquity furnishes no hint. The differences are as marked as the resemblances, and hence the one who cites from the other is no servile copyist. The real difference between the two is that between prediction and fulfilment. (2) Peter predicts the advent of the "false teachers" (**2** 1). His principal vbs. are in the future tense (**2** 1.2.3.12.13). He employs the present tense indeed in describing the character and the conduct of the libertines (**2** 17.18), but their presence and their disastrous teaching he puts in the future (**2** 13.14). The deadly germs were there when he wrote, the rank growth would speedily follow. Jude, on the contrary, throughout his short letter, speaks of the same corrupters as already come; his objects are present, they are in the midst of the people of God and actively doing their deadly work. (3) Jude twice refers to certain sources of information touching these enemies, with which his readers were acquainted and which were designed to warn them of the danger and keep them from betrayal. The two sources were (*a*) a writing that spoke of "ungodly men, turning the grace of our God into lasciviousness, and denying our only Master and Lord, Jesus Christ," ver 4; (*b*) the prediction of Peter that "in the last days mockers shall come with mockery, walking after their own lusts" (2 Pet **3** 3). Jude urges his readers to remember the words which the apostles of Christ had before spoken, and then he cites this prediction of Peter in almost the exact terms: "In the last time there shall be mockers, walking after their ungodly lusts." He applies the prediction to the libertines then and there practising their unholy deeds: "These are they who make separations, sensual, having not the Spirit." The conclusion is inevitable. Jude quotes from Peter. (4) Chronology gives the priority to Peter. The apostle died between 63–67 AD, probably in 64 AD. The vast majority of recent interpreters date the Ep. of Jude at 75–80 AD. There is no doubt but that it was written after the destruction of Jerus, 70 AD. Accordingly, it is later than Peter's death by from 5 to 10 years. Jude quoted from 2 Pet. This being so, it follows that his Ep. endorses that of Peter as being apostolic and likewise canonical, for he recognizes Peter as an apostle and gifted with the prophetic spirit. See JUDE; PETER (SIMON).

III. Doctrinal Teachings of the Epistle.—Only some of the more important features of the Ep. are here noticed. If all were treated as they deserve to be, this article would expand into the proportions of a commentary.

The key-word of 1 Pet is *Hope;* of 2 Pet *Knowledge.* The apostle gives to this gift of grace a prominent place (**1** 2.3.5.6.8; **2** 20.21; **3** 18). The term he uses is largely in the intensified form, viz. "full knowledge"; that is, knowledge that rests on fact, knowledge that comes to the believer as something supernatural, as being communicated by the Spirit of God, and therefore is true and complete. The grace and peace Peter asks for the saints should issue in the knowledge of God and of Jesus Our Lord, who has granted unto us all things that pertain unto life and godliness through the knowledge of Him (**1** 2.3).

1. Saving Knowledge

(1) *The basis* of saving knowledge rests on the "exceeding great and precious promises" which He has made us, and which become ours by faith in Him. It leads us into acquaintance with the righteousness of God, into the realization of our calling as saints, and of the glorious destiny that awaits them who know and trust God (**1** 2–4 AV).

(2) *The growth* in true knowledge (**1** 5–11): "In your faith supply virtue," etc. He does not ask that faith be supplied, that these believers already had. But starting with faith as the foundation of all, let the other excellencies and virtues be richly and abundantly furnished. The original word for "supply" is derived from the Gr "chorus," in behalf of the members of which the manager supplied all the equipments needed. And Peter appropriating that fact urges Christians to give all diligence to furnish themselves with the gifts and grace he mentions, which are far more needful to the Christian than were the equipments for the ancient chorus. See SUPPLY.

What a magnificent cluster Peter here gives! Each springs out of the other; each is strengthened by the other. "In your faith supply virtue," or fortitude, manliness; and let virtue supply "knowledge." Knowledge by itself tends to puff up. But tempered by the others, by self-control, by patience, by godliness, by love, it becomes one of the most essential and powerful forces in the Christian character. Paul begins his list of the "fruits of the Spirit" with love (Gal **5** 22); Peter ends his with love. It is like a chain, each link holds fast to its fellow and is a part of the whole. It matters little at which end of the chain we begin to count, for the links form a unity, and to touch one is to touch all. God freely gives what we need and all we need; we are to "add all diligence" to supply the need richly.

(3) *Inerrancy of the sources* of saving knowledge (**1** 16–21). The apostle rests his teaching on two trustworthy facts: (*a*) the fact and meaning of the Saviour's Transfiguration; (*b*) the fact of the inspiration of the Holy Spirit. Taken together these two facts invest his teaching with infallible certainty. "For we did not follow cunningly devised fables, when we made known unto you the power and coming of our Lord Jesus Christ, but we were eyewitnesses of his majesty." Pagan mythology, so widely prevailing at the time in Asia Minor, indeed over the whole heathen world, was composed of "myths" (Peter's word) skilfully framed and poetically embellished. Jewish cabalism, and the wild vagaries springing up in the Christian brotherhood itself had no place in the gospel message nor in apostolic teaching. What Peter and his fellow-disciples taught was the very truth of God, for at the Transfiguration they saw the outshining glory of the Son of God, they heard the Divine Voice, they beheld the two visitants from the unseen world, Moses and Elijah. Of the majestic scene they were eyewitnesses. Peter adds, "And we have the word of prophecy made more sure." The Transfiguration has confirmed what the prophets say touching the future and God's purpose to fill the earth with His glory; every word He has spoken is to be made good.

Moreover, the apostle appeals to the inspiration of the prophets in confirmation of his teaching: "No prophecy of scripture is of private interpretation. For no prophecy ever came by the will of man: but men spake from God, being moved by the Holy Spirit." He recognizes this as primary truth, that prophecy is not of one's own origination, nor is it to be tied up to the times of the prophet. The prophecy was brought to him, as it is brought to us. Peter and his fellow-believers did not follow "cunningly devised fables"; they were borne along in their prophetic utterances by the Spirit.

Of course in **3** 5–13, where the three worlds are spoken of, three globes are not meant, but three vast epochs, three enormous periods in earth's history. The apostle divides its history into three clearly defined sections, and mentions some of the characteristic features of each.

2. The Three Worlds

(1) *The old world.*—"The world that then was" (**3** 6): this is his first world. It is the antediluvian world that is meant, the world which the Flood overwhelmed. Scoffers in Peter's time asked, no doubt with a sneer, "Where is the promise of his coming? for, from the day that the fathers fell asleep, all things continue as they were from the beginning of the creation" (**3** 4). This is a surprisingly modern inquiry. Mockers then as now appealed to the continuity of natural processes, and to the inviolability of Nature's laws. Nature keeps her track with unwavering precision. There is no sign of any change; no catastrophe is likely, is possible. The promise of His coming fails. Peter reminds the skeptics that a mighty cataclysm did once overwhelm the world. The Flood drowned every living thing, save those sheltered within the ark. As this is a historical fact, the query of the mockers is foolish.

(2) *The present world.*—Peter's second world is "the heavens that now are, and the earth" (**3** 7). It is the present order of things in sky and earth that is meant. He asserts that this world is "stored up for fire, being reserved against the day of judgment and destruction of ungodly men." The margin reads, "stored with fire," i.e., it contains within itself the agency by which it may be consumed. The world that now is, is held in strict custody, reserved, not for a second deluge, but for fire. The advent of Christ and the judgment are associated in Scripture with fire: "Our God shall come, and shall not keep silence: a fire shall devour before him, and it shall be very tempestuous round about him" (Ps **50** 3 AV; cf Isa **66** 15.16; Dnl **7** 10.11). Nor is the NT silent on this point: "the revelation of the Lord Jesus from heaven with the angels of his power in flaming fire" (2 Thess **1** 7).

Ample materials are stored up in the earth for its consumption by fire. The oils and the gases so inflammable and destructive in their energy can, when it may please God to release these forces, speedily reduce the present order of things to ashes. Peter's language does not signify earth's annihilation, nor its dissolution as an organic body, nor the end of time. He speaks of cosmical convulsions and physical revolutions of both sky and earth, such as shall transform the planet into something glorious and beautiful.

(3) *The new world.*—The third world is this: "But, according to his promise, we look for new heavens and a new earth, wherein dwelleth righteousness" (**3** 13). This is Paradise restored. We have sure ground for the expectancy; the last two chapters of Rev contain the prophetic fulfilment: "And I saw a new heaven and a new earth: for the first heaven and the first earth are passed away; and the sea is no more." The accomplishment of these sublime predictions will involve a fundamental change in the constitution of the globe. Life would be impossible if the sea was no more. But He who made the world can surely recreate it, clearing it of every vestige of sin and misery and imperfection, fitting it for the dwelling of perfect beings and of

His supreme glory. Immanuel will dwell with the holy inhabitants of the new earth and in the new Jerus which is to descend into the glorified planet. John is bidden, "Write, for the predictions are faithful and true; they shall not fail to come to pass."

"Earth, thou grain of sand on the shore of the Universe of God,
On thee has the Lord a great work to complete."

LITERATURE.—See at end of PETER, FIRST EPISTLE OF; PETER (SIMON).

WILLIAM G. MOOREHEAD

PETHAHIAH, peth-a-hī'a (פְּתַחְיָה, *p^ethaḥyāh*, "Jeh opens up"):

(1) Chief of the 19th course of priests (1 Ch **24** 16).

(2) One of the Levites having "foreign wives" (Ezr **10** 23; Neh **9** 5; "Patheus" in 1 Esd **9** 23).

(3) Son of Meshezabeel, descendant of Judah, who was "at the king's hand in all matters concerning the people" (Neh **11** 24).

PETHOR, pē'thor (פְּתוֹר, *p^ethōr;* **Φαθοῦρα,** *Phathoúra,* **Βαθοῦρα,** *Bathoúra*): The dwelling-place of Balaam, situated on "the river" (the Euphrates) (Nu **22** 5). In Dt **23** 4, it is further described as being in Mesopotamia (Aram-naharaim). Pethor is identified with the Pedru(i) of the geographical lists of Thothmes III (c 1500 BC) and the Pitru (Pithru) of the Assyr king Shalmaneser II, who states that in his 3d year (857 BC) he took the city Ana-Aššur-utîr-aṣbat (meaning: "I founded [it] anew for Aššur"), which the Ḫattâa (Hittites) called Pitru. He says that it lay on the farther (western) bank of the Euphrates, by the Sagurru or Sagūra River, the modern *Sajūr*. The importance of Pitru is indicated by the fact that he received there the tribute of the kings of Carchemish, Comagene, Melitene and other districts.

1. Possibly the Assyrian Pitru

As Pitru is about 400 miles from Moab, this meant for Balaam a three or four weeks' journey, but the messengers sent to fetch him, though they had to travel that distance twice, could naturally, by pressing their mounts, have performed it in much less time. Doubt may likewise be entertained as to the identity of Pethor with Pitru by the absence in the latter of the *ô*, which would lead one to expect rather the Assyr form *Pit(h)ūru*. Shalmaneser, however, says that Pitru was the Hittite name, and that may account for it. With regard to the derivation, nothing can at present be said, except that, as a Hittite name, Tomkins (*Records of the Past,* V [London, 1891], 38) has compared the name Pitru with the Pteria of Herodotus i.76 (identified with Boghaz-keui, the great Hittite capital in Cappadocia, anciently called Ḫattu).

2. Difficulties of Identification

T. G. PINCHES

PETHUEL, pē-thū'el (פְּתוּאֵל, *p^ethū'ēl,* "God's opening"): Father of Joel the prophet (Joel **1** 1).

PETITION, pē-tish'un: Used in EV only as a noun, usually as representing the Heb שְׁאֵלָה, *sh^e'ēlāh* (Ps **20** 5, מִשְׁאָלָה, *mish'ālāh*), from the common vb. שָׁאַל, *shā'al,* "to ask." The noun, consequently, has no technical meaning, and may be used indifferently in the active (Est **7** 2) or passive (1 S **1** 27) sense, or for a petition addressed to either God (1 S **1** 17) or man (1 K **2** 16), while in Jgs **8** 24; Job **6** 8; Ps **106** 15, it is rendered simply "request." Otherwise "petition" represents the Aram. בָּעוּ, *bā'ū* (Dnl **6** 7.13), the Gr *αἴτημα, aítēma* (1 Jn **5** 15), and *δέησις, déēsis* (1 Macc **7** 37, RV "supplication"), and the Lat *oratio* (2 Esd **8** 24). BURTON SCOTT EASTON

PETRA, pē'tra. See SELA.

PEULTHAI, pē-ul'thī, **PEULLETHAI,** pē-ul'ē-thī (פְּעֻלְּתַי, *p^e'ull^ethay,* "Jeh's seed"): One of the "porters," 8th son of Obed-edom (1 Ch **26** 5).

PHAATH MOAB, fā'ath mō'ab (A, **Φαὰθ Μωάβ,** *Phaáth Mōáb,* B followed by Swete, **Φθαλειμωάβ,** *Phthaleimōáb* [1 Esd **5** 11]; 1 Esd **8** 31 [AV "Pahath Moab"], B followed by Swete reads **Μααθμωάβ,** *Maathmōáb;* Fritzsche in both places reads **Φαὰθ Μωάβ**): One of the families, part of which, consisting "of the sons of Jesus and Joab 2,812," went up out of captivity with Zerubbabel and Joshua (1 Esd **5** 11), and part of which, viz. "Eliaonias the son of Zaraias and with him 200 men," went up with Ezra (1 Esd **8** 31="Pahath-moab" of Ezr **2** 6; **8** 4; [**10** 30]; and Neh **7** 11 [**3** 11; **10** 14]). As the name of a Jewish clan or family the name Phaath or Pahath Moab presents difficulties of which explanations are offered, though none is convincing. It is generally taken as "ruler of Moab," which may refer to the Israelite conquest of Moab in which this family may have distinguished itself, or it may have arisen from the settlement and incorporation of a Moabite family in Heb territory, or from the settlement of an Israelite family in Moabite territory (cf 1 Ch **4** 22); or it may be the corruption of some unknown word or name. Instances of such corruption are quite common in these apocryphal Heb proper names. See PAHATH-MOAB.

S. ANGUS

PHACARETH, fak'a-reth (**Φακαρέθ,** *Phakaréth,* but B followed by Swete correctly reads **Φ. Σαβειή,** *Sabeiḗ,* together, A followed by AV reading "sons of Sabie," as a distinct family, 1 Esd **5** 34): The same as "Pochereth-hazzebaim" of Ezr **2** 57.

PHAISUR, fā'sur, fā-ī'sur (B, **Φαισούρ,** *Phaisoúr,* A, **Φαισού,** *Phaisoú*): Head of one of the families of priests some of whom had taken "strange wives" (1 Esd **9** 22)="Pashhur" of Ezr **10** 22; styled "Phassurus" in 1 Esd **5** 25.

PHALDEUS, fal-dē'us (A [Fritzsche], **Φαλδαῖος,** *Phaldaíos,* B [Swete], **Φαλαδαῖος,** *Phaladaíos;* AV **Phaldaius**): One of those who stood on Ezra's left hand when he expounded the Law (1 Esd **9** 44)="Pedaiah" of Neh **8** 4.

PHALEAS, fa-lē'as (**Φαλαίας,** *Phalaías*): A family of "temple-servants" who went up with Zerubbabel from Babylon (1 Esd **5** 29)="Padon" of Ezr **2** 44.

PHALEC, fā'lek (**Φαλέκ,** *Phalék,* WH, **Φάλεκ,** *Phálek*): AV; Gr form of "Peleg" (thus RV) (Lk **3** 35).

PHALIAS, fa-lī'as (**Φαλίας,** *Phalías,* A, **Φιάθας,** *Phiáthas;* AV **Biatas,** following Aldine **Βιάτας,** *Biátas*): One of the Levites who read and explained the Law to the multitude (1 Esd **9** 48)="Pelaiah" of Neh **8** 7.

PHALLU, fal'ōō (פַּלּוּא, *pallū'*). See PALLU.

PHALTI, fal'tī (פַּלְטִי, *palṭī*). See PALTI.

PHALTIEL, fal'ti-el (פַּלְטִיאֵל, *palṭī'ēl;* Syr "Psaltiel"; Vulg and AV **Salathiel**): "The captain of the people" who came to Esdras between his first and second vision (2 Esd **5** 16). Fritzsche (*Libri Apoc vet. test.*) reads "Phalthiel." See PALTIEL.

PHANUEL, fan-ū'el, fan'ū-el (פְּנוּאֵל, *p^enū'ēl,* "vision of God"; **Φανουήλ,** *Phanouḗl*): Parent of Anna (Lk **2** 36). See PENIEL.

PHARAKIM, far′a-kim (**Φαρακείμ,** *Pharakeím,* B, **Φαρακέμ,** *Pharakém;* AV **Pharacim**): One of the families of temple-servants who returned with Zerubbabel (1 Esd **5** 31; not found in Ezr or Neh).

PHARAOH, fā′rō, fā′rā-ō (פַּרְעֹה, *par'ōh;* **Φαραώ,** *Pharaō;* Egyp *per aa,* "great house"):

1. Use of Name in Egypt

Many and strange differences of opinion have been expressed concerning the use of this name in Egypt and elsewhere, because of its importance in critical discussions (see below). *EB* says "a name given to all Egyp kings in the Bible"; it also claims that the name could not have been received by the Hebrews before 1000 BC. *HDB* (III, 819) says that a letter was addressed to Amenhotep as "Pharaoh, lord of," etc. According to Winckler's theory of a North Arabian Musri, it was the Hebrews alone in ancient times who adopted the term Pharaoh from the Egyptians, the name not being found even in the Am Tab or anywhere else in cuneiform literature for the king of Egypt. Such a result is obtained according to Winckler's theory by referring every reference in cuneiform to "Pir'u, king of Musri" to the North Arabian country.

Pharaoh.

In Egyp inscriptions the term "Pharaoh" occurs from the Pyramid inscriptions onward. At first it is used with distinct reference to its etymology and not clearly as an independent title. Pharaoh, "great house," like Sublime Porte, was applied first as a metaphor to mean the government. But as in such an absolute monarchy as Egypt the king was the government, Pharaoh was, by a figure of speech, put for the king. Its use in Egypt clearly as a title denoting the ruler, whoever he might be, as Caesar among the Romans, Shah among Persians, and Czar among Russians, belongs to a few dynasties probably beginning with the XVIIIth, and certainly ending not later than the XXIst, when we read of Pharaoh Sheshonk, but the Bible does not speak so, but calls him "Shishak king of Egypt" (1 K **14** 25). This new custom in the use of the title Pharaoh does not appear in the Bible until we have "Pharaoh-necoh." Pharaoh is certainly used in the time of Rameses II, in the "Tale of Two Brothers" (*Records of the Past,* 1st series, II, 137; *Recueil de Travaux,* XXI, 13, l. 1).

2. Significance of Use in the Bible

It appears from the preceding that Bib. writers use this word with historical accuracy for the various periods to which it refers, not only for the time of Necoh and Hophra, but for the time of Rameses II, and use the style of the time of Rameses II for the time of Abraham and Joseph, concerning which we have not certain knowledge of its use in Egypt. It is strongly urged that writers of the 7th or 5th cent. BC would not have been able to make such historical use of this name, while, to a writer at the time of the exodus, it would have been perfectly natural to use Pharaoh for the king without any further name; and historical writers in the time of the prophets in Pal would likewise have used Pharaoh-necoh and Pharaoh Hophra. This evidence is not absolutely conclusive for an early authorship of the Pent and historical books, but is very difficult to set aside for a late authorship (cf Gen **12** 14–20; **41** 14; Ex **1** 11; **3** 11; 1 K **3** 1; **14** 25; 2 K **23** 29; Jer **44** 30; also 1 K **11** 19; 2 K **18** 21; 1 Ch **4** 18).

M. G. Kyle

PHARAOH HOPHRA, hof′ra (פַּרְעֹה חָפְרַע, *par'ōh ḥophra';* **Οὐαφρή,** *Houaphrē*):

1. Sole King, 589–570 BC

He is so called in Scripture (Jer **44** 30); Herodotus calls him Apries (ii.169). He is known on the monuments as Uah 'ab 'ra. He was the son of Psammetichus II, whose Gr mercenaries have left inscriptions upon the rocks of Abu-Sim-bel, and the grandson of Pharaoh-necoh. He reigned alone from 589 BC to 570 BC, and jointly, by compulsion of his people, with his son-in-law Aahmes (Gr *Amasis*) for some years longer. No sooner had he mounted the throne than he yielded to the overtures of Zedekiah of Judah, who thought Hophra's accession a good opportunity for throwing off the yoke of Babylon. So, as Ezekiel says (**17** 15), "he rebelled against him [Nebuchadrezzar] in sending his ambassadors into Egypt, that they might give him horses and much people."

2. Alliance with Zedekiah

Zedekiah had entered into the intrigue against the advice of Jeremiah, and it proved fatal to Zedekiah and the kingdom. Nebuchadrezzar was not slow to punish the disloyalty of his vassal, and in a brief space his armies were beleaguering Jerus. The Egyptians did indeed march to the relief of their allies, and the Chaldaeans drew off their forces from Jerus to meet them. But the Egyptians returned without attempting to meet the Chaldaeans in a pitched battle, and Jerus was taken, the walls broken down and the temple burnt up with fire.

3. Reception of Jeremiah and Jewish Captives

When Jerus had fallen and Nebuchadrezzar's governor, Gedaliah, had been assassinated, the dispirited remnant of Judah, against the advice of Jeremiah, fled into Egypt, carrying the prophet with them. They settled at Tahpanhes, then Daphnae (modern *Tell Defenneh*), now identified with a mound bearing the significant name of *Ḳaçr Bint el Yahudi,* "the palace of the Jew's daughter." Here Pharaoh had a palace, for Jeremiah took great stones and hid them in mortar in the brickwork "which is at the entry of Pharaoh's house at Tahpanhes," and prophesied that Nebuchadrezzar would spread his royal pavilion over them (Jer **43** 8–13). The Pharaoh of that day was Hophra, and when the fortress of Tahpanhes was discovered and cleared in 1886, the open-air platform before the entrance was found. "Here the ceremony described by Jeremiah took place before the chiefs of the fugitives assembled on the platform, and here Nebuchadrezzar spread his royal pavilion. The very nature of the site is precisely applicable to all the events" (Flinders Petrie, *Nebesheh and Defenneh,* 51). It was in 568 BC that the prophecy was fulfilled when Nebuchadrezzar marched into the Delta.

4. Palace at Memphis

More recently, in 1909, in the course of excavations carried on by the British School of Archaeology in Egypt, the palace of King Apries, Pharaoh Hophra, has been discovered on the site of Memphis, the ancient capital of Egypt. Under the grey mud hill, close to the squalid Arab village of *Mitrahenny*, which every tourist passes on the way to *Sakkhara*, had lain for centuries Hophra's magnificent palace, 400 ft. long by 200 ft., with a splendid pylon, an immense court, and stone-lined halls, of which seven have been found intact. With many other objects of value there was found a fitting of a palanquin of solid silver, decorated with a bust of Hathor with a gold face. It is said to be of the finest workmanship of the time of Apries, a relic of the fire, which, Jeremiah predicted at Tahpanhes, the Lord of Hosts was to kindle "in the houses of the gods of Egypt" (Jer **43** 12).

Pharaoh Hophra, as Jeremiah prophesied (**44** 29 f), became the victim of a revolt and was finally strangled.

LITERATURE.—Flinders Petrie, *History of Egypt*, III, 344 f; Wiedemann, *Geschichte von Alt-Aegypten*, 190 ff; Flinders Petrie and J. H. Walker, *Memphis*, I, II ("The Palace of Apries"); Herodotus ii.161–69.

T. NICOL

PHARAOH-NECOH, nē'kō (פַּרְעֹה נְכֹה, *par'ōh nᵉkhōh*, also נְכוֹ, *nᵉkhō*; Νεχαώ, *Nechaō* [2 K **23** 29.33.34; 2 Ch **35** 22; **36** 4, AV **Necho,** RV NECO; Jer **46** 2; 2 Ch **35** 20, AV **Necho,** RV NECO]): Nekau II of the monuments—Gr *Nekōs*—was the 2d king of the XXVIth Dynasty, being the son of Psammetichus I, famous in Gr contemporary history, whose long reign has left so many memorials both in Upper and Lower Egypt (Herod. ii.153, 158, 169). The great event of his reign (610–594 BC) was his expedition across Syria to secure for himself a share in the decaying empire of Assyria. In the days of Esarhaddon and Ashurbanipal, Egypt had been tributary to Assyria, and, when it began to break up, Egypt and other subject kingdoms saw their opportunity to throw off its yoke. Psammetichus had turned back the Scythian hordes which had reached his border on their western march, and now his son Necoh was to make a bold stroke for empire.

1. Pharaoh-Necoh, 610-594 BC

On his expedition toward the East, he had to pass through the territory of Judah, and he desired to have Josiah its king as an ally. Whatever may have been his reasons, Josiah remained loyal to his Assyr suzerain, declined the Egyp alliance, and threw himself across the path of the invader. The opposing armies met on the battlefield of Megiddo, 608 BC, where Josiah was mortally wounded and soon after died amid the lamentations of his people. Necoh marched northward, captured Kadesh, and pressed on to the Euphrates. Not having met an enemy there, he seems to have turned back and established himself for a time at Riblah in Syria. To Riblah he summoned Jehoahaz whom the people had anointed king in room of his father Josiah, deposed him after a brief reign of 3 months, and set his brother Jehoiakim on the throne as the vassal of Egypt. Jehoiakim paid up the tribute of a hundred talents of silver and a talent of gold which Necoh had imposed upon the land, but he recovered it by exactions which he made from the people (2 K **23** 35).

2. Battle of Megiddo, 608 BC

The Egyp monarch still kept some hold upon Syria, and his presence there had attracted the attention of the newly established power at Babylon. The Chaldaeans under Nebuchadrezzar set out for the Euphrates, and, meeting the army of Pharaoh-necoh at Carchemish, inflicted upon him a signal defeat. The Chaldaeans were now undisputed masters of Western Asia, and the sacred historian relates that "the king of Egypt came not again any more out of his land; for the king of Babylon had taken, from the brook of Egypt unto the river Euphrates, all that pertained to the king of Egypt" (2 K **24** 7).

3. Battle of Carchemish, 604 BC

While Pharaoh-necoh II was ambitious to extend his empire, he was bent also upon the commercial development of Egypt. For this he set himself to collect a navy. He had two fleets built, composed of triremes, one of them to navigate the Mediterranean, the other to navigate the Red Sea. In order to secure a combination of his fleets, he conceived the idea of reopening the canal between the Nile and the Red Sea which had been originally constructed by Seti I and Rameses II, two Pharaohs of the days of the Israelite oppression, but had become silted up by desert sands. He excavated this old canal, following the line of the former cutting, and widening it so that two triremes might meet and pass each other in it. According to Herodotus he was obliged to desist from the undertaking in consequence of the mortality among the laborers, and it was left to Darius to complete. He also resolved to try whether it was possible to circumnavigate Africa, and, manning his ships with Phoenician sailors, he sent them forth with instructions to keep the coast of Africa on their right and to return to Egypt by way of the Mediterranean. They succeeded, and, rounding the Cape of Good Hope from the East, anticipated by two millenniums the feat which Vasco da Gama accomplished from the West. The enterprise took more than two years, and the result of it was of no practical value. Herodotus, when he visited Egypt in 450 BC, saw still remaining the docks which Necoh had built for the accommodation of his fleet.

4. Commercial Development of Egypt

LITERATURE.—Flinders Petrie, *History of Egypt*, III, 335 ff; Wiedemann, *Geschichte von Alt-Aegypten*, 179–90; Rawlinson, *Egypt* ("Story of the Nations"), 354 ff; Herodotus ii.158, 159.

T. NICOL

PHARAOH'S DAUGHTER (בַּת־פַּרְעֹה, *bath-par'ōh*): The princess who rescued Moses (Ex **2** 5–10; He **11** 24). This is probably a title as well as an appellation, indicating not only one of the daughters of a Pharaoh, but also some very distinguished rank, thought to be most probably that of the heir to the throne by birth; though she was debarred from reigning by reason of sex, she still possessed the right to entail the scepter and crown to her oldest son. Positive identification of the "Pharaoh's daughter" mentioned in the Bible is not possible yet. All attempts toward identification are, of course, guided by the particular theory of the oppressor accepted. If the Pharaoh of the Oppression was Rameses II, as is most likely, then Pharaoh's daughter was probably the daughter of Seti I, an older sister of Rameses II. If, as many think, the Pharaoh of the Oppression was Thothmes III, then Pharaoh's daughter was some unknown princess. Some have thought she was Hatshepsut, the "Queen Elizabeth of Egypt."

M. G. KYLE

PHARATHON, far'a-thon (Φαραθών, *Pharathōn*): One of the strong cities of Judaea fortified by Bacchides during the Maccabean war (1 Macc **9** 50). LXX reads "Thamnatha-pharathon" as the name of one city. Jos, however (*Ant*, XIII, i, 3), and Syr supply the "and" between them. The name represents a Heb *pir'āthōn*. If it is to be taken strictly as in Judaean territory, it cannot be identified with PIRATHON (q.v.) of Jgs **12** 15. In that case we should probably seek for it with Dr. G. A. Smith in some fortress covering the top of *Wâdy Far'ah*.

W. EWING

PHARES, fā'rēz (Φαρές, *Pharés*): AV; Gr form of "Perez" (thus RV) (Mt **1** 3; Lk **3** 33).

ANCIENT PAINTING OF AN EGYPTIAN PRINCESS

PHAREZ, fā'rēz (AV 1 Esd **5** 9; **8** 30): The same as RV PHOROS (q.v.).

PHARIDA, fa-rī'da (**Φαρειδά**, *Phareidá*, A, **Φαριδά**, *Pharidá*; AV **Pharira**): The clan name of one of the families of "the servants of Solomon" who came up from Babylon with Zerubbabel (1 Esd **5** 33) = "Peruda" of Ezr **2** 55 = "Perida" of Neh **7** 57.

PHARIRA, fa-rī'ra: AV = RV PHARIDA (q.v.).

PHARISEES, far'i-sēz (פְּרוּשִׁים, *perūshīm*; **Φαρισαῖοι**, *Pharisaíoi*):

1. Name and General Character

A prominent sect of the Jews. The earliest notice of them in Jos occurs in connection with Jonathan, the high priest. Immediately after the account of the embassy to the Lacedaemonians, there is subjoined (Jos, *Ant*, XIII, v, 9) an account of the Pharisees, Sadducees and Essenes, therefore implying that then and in this connection they had been prominent, although no notice of any of these parties is to be found that confirms that view. Later (XIII, x, 5), the Pharisees are represented as envious of the success of John Hyrcanus; Eleazar, one of them, insults him at his own table. From the fact that earlier in the history the Assidaeans occupy a similar place to that occupied later by the Pharisees, it may be deduced that the two parties are in a measure one. See HASIDAEANS; ASMONEANS. It would seem that not only the Pharisees, but also the Essenes, were derived from the Assidaeans or *ḥăşīdhīm*.

2. Authorities

In considering the characteristics and doctrines of the Pharisees we are in some difficulty from the nature of our authorities. The writers of the NT assume generally that the character and tenets of the Pharisees are well known to their readers, and only lay stress on the points in which they were in antagonism to Our Lord and His followers. The evidence of Jos, a contemporary and himself a Pharisee, is lessened in value by the fact that he modified his accounts of his people to suit the taste of his Rom masters. The Pharisees, with him, are a philosophic sect, and not an active political party. Their Messianic hopes are not so much as mentioned. Although the Talm was written, both Mish and Gemara, by the descendants of the Pharisees, the fact that the Gemara, from which most of our information is derived, is so late renders the evidence deduced from Talmudic statements of little value. Even the Mish, which came into being only a century after the fall of the Jewish state, shows traces of exaggeration and modification of facts. Still, taking these deficiencies into consideration, we may make a fairly consistent picture of the sect. The name means "separatists," from פָּרַשׁ, *pārash*, "to separate"—those who carefully kept themselves from any legal contamination, distinguishing themselves by their care in such matters from the common people, the *'am hā-'āreç*, who had fewer scruples. Like the Puritans in England during the 17th cent., and the Presbyterians in Scotland during the same period, the Pharisees, although primarily a religious party, became ere long energetically political. They were a closely organized society, all the members of which called each other *ḥăbhērīm*, "neighbors"; this added to the power they had through their influence with the people.

I. History of the Sect.—The Assidaeans (*ḥăşīdhīm*) were at first the most active supporters of Judas Maccabaeus in his struggle for religious freedom. A portion of them rather than fight retired to the desert to escape the tyranny of Epiphanes (1 Macc **2** 27 f). The followers of these in later days became the Essenes. When Judas Maccabaeus cleansed the temple and rededicated it with many sacrifices, it is not expressly said, either in the Books of Macc or by Jos, that he acted as high priest, but the probability is that he did so. This would be a shock to the Assidaean purists, as Judas, though a priest, was not a Zadokite; but his actions would be tolerated at that time on account of the imminent necessity for the work of reconsecration and the eminent services of Judas himself and his family.

1. Associated at First with Hasmoneans, but Later Abandon Them

When Bacchides appeared against Jerus with Alcimus in his camp, this feeling against Judas took shape in receiving the treacherous Alcimus into Jerus and acknowledging him as high priest, a line of action which soon showed that it was fraught with disaster, as Alcimus murdered many of the people. They had to betake themselves anew to Judas, but this desertion was the beginning of a separating gulf which deepened when he made a treaty with the idolatrous Romans. As is not infrequently the case with religious zealots, their valor was associated with a mystic fanaticism. The very idea of alliance with heathen powers was hateful to them, so when Judas began to treat with Rome they deserted him, and he sustained the crushing defeat of Eleasa. Believing themselves the saints of God and therefore His peculiar treasure, they regarded any association with the heathen as faithlessness to Jeh. Their attitude was much that of the Fifth Monarchy men in the time of Cromwell, still more that of the Cameronians in Scotland at the Revolution of 1688 who, because William of Orange was not a "covenanted" king, would have none of him. As the later Hasmoneans became more involved in worldly politics, they became more and more alienated from the strict Assidaeans, yet the successors of Judas Maccabaeus retained their connection with the party in a lukewarm fashion, while the Sadducean sect was gaining in influence.

About this time the change of name seems to have been effected. They began to be called Pharisees, *perūshīm*, instead of *ḥăşīdhīm*—"separatists" instead of saints. A parallel instance is to be found in the religious history of England.

The Puritans of the 17th cent. became in the 19th "Non-conformists." The earliest instance of the Pharisees' intervening in history is that referred to in Jos (*Ant*, XIII, x, 5), where Eleazar, a Pharisee, demanded that John Hyrcanus should lay down the high-priesthood because his mother had been a captive, thus insinuating that he—Hyrcanus—was no true son of Aaron, but the bastard of some nameless heathen to whom his mother had surrendered herself. This unforgivable insult to himself and to the memory of his mother led Hyrcanus to break with the Pharisaic party definitely. He seems to have left them severely alone.

2. Change of Name

The sons of Hyrcanus, esp. Alexander Jannaeus, expressed their hostility in a more active way. Alexander crucified as many as 800 of the Pharisaic party, a proceeding that seems to intimate overt acts of hostility on their part which prompted this action. His whole policy was the aggrandizement of the Jewish state, but his ambition was greater than his military abilities. His repeated failures and defeats confirmed the Pharisees in their opposition to him on religious grounds. He scandalized them by calling himself king, although not of the Davidic line, and further still by adopting the heathen name "Alexander," and having it stamped in Gr characters on his coins. Although a high priest was forbidden to marry a widow, he married the widow of his brother. Still further, he incurred their opposition by abandoning the Pharisaic tradition as to the way in which the libation water was poured out. They retaliated by rousing his people against him and conspiring with the Syrian king. On his deathbed he advised his wife, Alexandra Salome, who succeeded him on the throne, to make peace with the Pharisees. This she did by throwing herself entirely into their hands. On her death a struggle for the possession of the throne and the high-priesthood began between her two sons, John Hyrcanus II and Aristobulus II. The latter, the more able and energetic, had the support of the Sadducees; the former, the elder of the two brothers, had that of the Pharisees. In the first phase of the conflict, Hyrcanus was defeated and compelled to make a disadvantageous peace with his brother, but, urged by Antipater, the Idumaean, he called in Aretas, who inclined the balance at once to the side of Hyrcanus. The Romans were appealed to and they also, moved partly by the astuteness of Antipater, favored Hyrcanus. All this resulted ultimately in the supremacy of the Herodians, who through their subservience to Rome became inimical to the Pharisees and rivals of the Sadducees.

3. Later Fortunes of the Sect

When the NT records open, the Pharisees, who have supreme influence among the people, are also strong, though not predominant, in the Sanhedrin. The Herodians and Sadducees, the one by their alliance with the Rom authorities, and the other by their inherited skill in political intrigue, held the reins of government. If we might believe the Talmudic representation, the Pharisees were in the immense majority in the Sanhedrin; the *nāsī'*, or president, and the *'abh-bēth-dīn*, or vice-president, both were Pharisees. This, however, is to be put to the credit of Talmudic imagination, the relation of which to facts is of the most distant kind.

4. In NT Times

Recently Büchler (*Das grosse Synedrion in Jerus*) has attempted to harmonize these Talmudic fables with the aspect of things appearing in the NT and Jos. He assumes that there were two Sanhedrins, one civil, having to do with matters of government, in which the Sadducees were overwhelmingly predominant, and the other scholastic, in which the Pharisees were equally predominant—the one the Senate of the nation, like the Senate of the United States, the other the Senate of a university, let us say, of Jerus. Although followed by Rabbi Lauterbach in the *Jew Enc*, this attempt cannot be regarded as successful. There is no evidence for this dual Sanhedrin either in the NT or Jos, on the one hand, or in the Talm on the other.

Outside the Sanhedrin the Pharisees are ubiquitous, in Jerus, in Galilee, in Peraea and in the Decapolis, always coming in contact with Jesus. The attempts made by certain recent Jewish writers to exonerate them from the guilt of the condemnation of Our Lord has no foundation; it is contradicted by the NT records, and the attitude of the Talm to Jesus.

The Pharisees appear in the Book of Acts to be in a latent way favorers of the apostles as against the high-priestly party. The personal influence of Gamaliel, which seems commanding, was exercised in their favor. The anti-Christian zeal of Saul the Tarsian, though a Pharisee, may have been to some extent the result of the personal feelings which led him to perpetuate the relations of the earlier period when the two sects were united in common antagonism to the teaching of Christ. He, a Pharisee, offered himself to be employed by the Sadducean high priest (Acts **9** 1.2) to carry on the work of persecution in Damascus. In this action Saul appears to have been in opposition to a large section of the Pharisaic party. The bitter disputes which he and the other younger Pharisees had carried on with Stephen had possibly influenced him.

When Paul, the Christian apostle, was brought before the Sanhedrin at Jerus, the Pharisaic party were numerous in the Council, if they did not even form the majority, and they readily became his defenders against the Sadducees.

5. In Post-apostolic Times

From Jos we learn that with the outbreak of the war with the Romans the Pharisees were thrust into the background by the more fanatical Zealots, Simon ben Gioras and John of Gischala (*BJ*, V, i). The truth behind the Talmudic statements that Gamaliel removed the Sanhedrin to Jabneh and that Johanan ben Zakkai successfully entreated Vespasian to spare the scholars of that city is that the Pharisees in considerable numbers made peace with the Romans. In the Mish we have the evidence of their later labors when the Sanhedrin was removed from Jabneh, ultimately to Tiberias in Galilee. There under the guidance of Jehuda ha-Ḳādhōsh ("the Holy") the Mish was reduced to writing. It may thus be said that Judaism became Pharisaism, and the history of the Jews became that of the Pharisees. In this later period the opposition to Christianity sprang up anew and became embittered, as may be seen in the Talmudic fables concerning Jesus.

II. Doctrines of the Pharisees.—The account given of the doctrines of the Pharisees by Jos is clearly influenced by his desire to parallel the Jewish sects with the Gr philosophical schools. He directs especial attention to the Pharisaic opinion as to fate and free will, since on this point the Stoic and Epicurean sects differed very emphatically. He regards the Pharisaic position as midway between that of the Sadducees, who denied fate altogether and made human freedom absolute, and that of the Essenes that "all things are left in the hand of God." He says "The Pharisees ascribe all things to fate and God, yet allow that to do what is right or the contrary is principally in man's own power, although fate coöperates in every action." It is to be noted that Jos, in giving this statement of views, identifies "fate" with "God," a process that is more plausible in connection with the Lat

1. Josephus' Statements Colored by Greek Ideas

fatum, "something decreed," than in relation to the impersonal *moíra*, or *heimarménē*, of the Greeks. As Jos wrote in Gr and used only the second of these terms, he had no philological inducement to make the identification; the reason must have been the matter of fact. In other words, he shows that the Pharisees believed in a personal God whose will was providence.

2. Conditional Reincarnation

In connection with this was their doctrine of a future life of rewards and punishments. The phrase which Jos uses is a peculiar one: "They think that every soul is immortal; only the souls of good men will pass into another body, but the souls of the evil shall suffer everlasting punishment" (*aïdíā timōríā kolázesthai*). From this it has been deduced that the Pharisees held the transmigration of souls. In our opinion this is a mistake. We believe that really it is an attempt of Jos to state the doctrine of the resurrection of the body in a way that would not shock Hellenic ideas. The Gr contempt for the body made the idea of the resurrection abhorrent, and in this, as in most philosophical matters, the Romans followed the Greeks. It would seem that Jos regarded the Pharisees as maintaining that this resurrection applied only to the righteous. Still even this restriction, though certainly the natural interpretation, is not absolutely necessary. This is confirmed by the corresponding section in the *Antiquities* (XVIII, i, 3): "They also believe . . . . that under the earth there will be rewards or punishments, according as they have lived virtuously or viciously in this life, and the latter are to be detained in an everlasting prison, but that the former shall have power to revive and live again." Jos also declares the Pharisees to be very attentive students of the law of God: "they interpret the law with careful exactitude."

3. NT Presentation of Pharisaic Doctrines

Nothing in the Gospels or the Acts at all militates against any part of this representation, but there is much to fill it out. They believed in angels and spirits (Acts **23** 8). From the connection it is probable that the present activity of such beings was the question in the mind of the writer. In that same sentence belief in the resurrection is ascribed to the Pharisees.

4. Traditions Added to the Law

Another point is that to the bare letter of the Law they added traditions. While the existence of these traditions is referred to in the Gospels, too little is said to enable us to grasp their nature and extent (Mt **15** 2 ff; **16** 5 ff; Mk **7** 1–23). The evangelists only recorded these traditional glosses when they conflicted with the teaching of Christ and were therefore denounced by Him. We find them exemplified in the Mish. The Pharisaic theory of tradition was that these additions to the written law and interpretations of it had been given by Moses to the elders and by them had been transmitted orally down through the ages. The classical passage in the Mish is to be found in *Pirḳē 'Ābhōth:* "Moses received the [oral] Law from Sinai and delivered it to Joshua and Joshua to the elders, and the elders to the prophets and the prophets to the men of the great synagogue." Additions to these traditions were made by prophets by direct inspiration, or by interpretation of the words of the written Law. All this mass, as related above, was reduced to writing by Jehuda ha-Ḳādhōsh in Tiberias, probably about the end of the 2d cent. AD. Jehuda was born, it is said, 135 AD, and died somewhere about 220 AD.

The related doctrines of the immortality of the soul, the resurrection of the body, and the final judgment with its consequent eternal rewards and punishments formed a portion and a valuable portion of this tradition.

5. Traditional Interpretation of the Law by Pharisees

Less valuable, at times burdensome and hurtful, were the minute refinements they introduced into the Law. Sometimes the ingenuity of the Pharisaic doctors was directed to lighten the burden of the precept as in regard to the Sabbath. Thus a person was permitted to go much farther than a Sabbath day's journey if at some time previous he had deposited, within the legal Sabbath day's journey of the place he wished to reach, bread and water; this point was now to be regarded as the limit of his house, and consequently from this all distances were to be ceremonially reckoned (*Jew Enc*, s.v. "Erub"). The great defect of Pharisaism was that it made sin so purely external. An act was right or wrong according as some external condition was present or absent; thus there was a difference in bestowing alms on the Sabbath whether the beggar put his hand within the door of the donor or the donor stretched his hand beyond his own threshold, as may be seen in the first Mish in the Tractate *Shabbāth*. A man did not break the Sabbath rest of his ass, though he rode on it, and hence did not break the Sabbath law, but if he carried a switch with which to expedite the pace of the beast he was guilty, because he had laid a burden upon it.

6. Close Students of the Text of Scripture

Along with these traditions and traditional interpretations, the Pharisees were close students of the sacred text. On the turn of a sentence they suspended many decisions. So much so, that it is said of them later that they suspended mountains from hairs. This is esp. the case with regard to the Sabbath law with its burdensome minutiae. At the same time there was care as to the actual wording of the text of the Law; this has a bearing on textual criticism, even to the present day. A specimen of Pharisaic exegesis which Paul turns against their followers as an *argumentum ad hominem* may be seen in Gal **3** 16: "He saith not, And to seeds, as of many; but as of one, And to thy seed, which is Christ."

(1) *Messianic hopes.*—It is also to be said for them, that they maintained the Messianic hopes of the nation when their rivals were ready to sacrifice everything to the Romans, in order to gain greater political influence for themselves. Their imagination ran riot in the pictures they drew of these future times, but still they aided the faith of the people who were thus in a position to listen to the claims of Christ. They were led by Rabbi Aḳiba in the reign of Hadrian to accept Bar-Cochba about a century after they had rejected Jesus. They were fanatical in their obedience to the Law as they understood it, and died under untold tortures rather than transgress.

(2) *Almsgiving.*—They elevated almsgiving into an equivalent for righteousness. This gave poverty a very different place from what it had in Greece or among the Romans. Learning was honored, although its possessors might be very poor. The story of the early life of Hillel brings this out. He is represented as being so poor as to be unable sometimes to pay the small daily fee which admitted pupils to the rabbinic school, and when this happened, in his eagerness for the Law, he is reported to have listened on the roof to the words of the teachers. This is probably not historically true, but it exhibits the Pharisaic ideal.

III. Organization of the Pharisaic Party.—We have no distinct account of this organization, either in the Gospels, in Jos, or in the Talm. But the close relationship which the members of the sect sustained to each other, their habit of united action as exhibited in the narratives of the NT and of Jos are thus most naturally explained. The Talmudic account of the *ḥăbhērīm* affords confirmation of this. These were persons who primarily associated for the study of the Law and for the better observance of its precepts. No one was admitted to these *ḥă-*

bhūrōth without taking an oath of fidelity to the society and a promise of strict observance of Levitical precepts.

Pharisaic Brotherhoods

One of the elements of their promise has to be noted. The *ḥābhēr* promised not to pay *ma'ăsrōth*, "tithe," or *terūmāh*, "heave offering," to a priest who was not a *ḥābhēr*. They were only permitted to take this oath when their associates in the brotherhood certified to their character. Even then the candidate had to pass through a period of probation of 30 days, according to the "house of Hillel," of a year, according to the "house of Shammai." This latter element, being quite *more Talmudico*, may be regarded as doubtful. Association with any not belonging to the Pharisaic society was put under numerous restrictions. It is at least not improbable that when the lawyer in Lk **10** 29 demanded "Who is my neighbor?" he was minded to restrict the instances of the command in Lev **19** 18 to those who were, like himself, Pharisees. A society which thus had brotherhoods all over Pal and was separated from the rest of the community would naturally wield formidable power when their claims were supported by the esteem of the people at large. It is to be observed that to be a *ḥābhēr* was a purely personal thing, not heritable like priesthood, and women as well as men might be members. In this the Pharisees were like the Christians. In another matter also there was a resemblance between them and the followers of Jesus; they, unlike the Sadducees, were eager to make proselytes. "Ye compass sea and land to make one proselyte" (Mt **23** 15). Many members of Rom society, esp. women, were proselytes, as, for instance, Poppaea Sabina.

IV. Character of the Pharisees.—Because the ideal of the Pharisees was high, and because they reverenced learning and character above wealth and civil rank, they had a tendency to despise those who did not agree with them. We see traces of this in the Gospels; thus Jn **7** 49: "This multitude that knoweth not the law are accursed." The distinction between the Pharisees, the Puritans and the *'am hā-'āreç*, "the people of the land," began with the distinction that had to be kept between the Jews and the Gentiles who had entered the land as colonists or intruders. These would, during the Bab captivity, almost certainly speak Western Aram., and would certainly be heathen and indulge in heathen practices. They were "the people of the land" whom the returning exiles found in possession of Judaea.

1. Pharisees and People of the Land

Mingled with them were the few Jews that had neither been killed nor deported by the Babylonians, nor carried down into Egypt by Johanan, the son of Kareah. As they had conformed in a large measure to the habits of their heathen neighbors and intermarried with them, the stricter Jews, as Ezra and Nehemiah, regarded them as under the same condemnation as the heathen, and shrank from association with them. During the time of Our Lord's life on earth the name was practically restricted to the ignorant Jews whose conformity to the law was on a broader scale than that of the Pharisees. Some have, however, dated the invention of the name later in the days of the Maccabean struggle, when the ceremonial precepts of the Law could with difficulty be observed. Those who were less careful of these were regarded as *'am hā-'āreç*.

2. Arrogance toward Other Jews

The distinction as exhibited in the Talm shows an arrogance on the part of the Pharisaic *ḥābhēr* that must have been galling to those who, though Jews as much as the Pharisees, were not Puritans like them. A *ḥābhēr*, that is a Pharisee, might not eat at the table of a man whose wife was of the *'am hā-'āreç*, even though her husband might be a Pharisee. If he would be a full *ḥābhēr*, a Pharisee must not sell to any of the *'am hā-'āreç* anything that might readily be made unclean. If a woman of the *'am hā-'āreç* was left alone in a room, all that she could touch without moving from her place was unclean. We must, however, bear in mind that the evidence for this is Talmudic, and therefore of but limited historical value.

3. Regulations for the ḥābhēr

4. The NT Account

(1) *Their scrupulosity.*—We find traces of this scrupulosity in the Gospels. The special way in which the ceremonial sanctity of the Pharisees exhibited itself was in tithing, hence the reference to their tithing "mint and anise and cummin" (Mt **23** 23). In the parable of the Pharisee and the Publican, one of the things that the Pharisee plumes himself on is that he gives tithes of all he possesses (Lk **18** 12). He is an example of the Pharisaic arrogance of those "who trusted in themselves that they were righteous and set all others at nought." Their claiming the first seats in feasts and synagogues (Mt **23** 6) was an evidence of the same spirit.

(2) *Their hypocrisy.*—Closely akin to this is the hypocrisy of which the Pharisees were accused by Our Lord. When we call them "hypocrites," we must go back to the primary meaning of the word. They were essentially "actors," *poseurs*. Good men, whose character and spiritual force have impressed themselves on their generation, have often peculiarities of manner and tone which are easily imitated. The very respect in which they are held by their disciples leads those who respect them to adopt unconsciously their mannerisms of voice and deportment. A later generation unconsciously imitates, "acts the part." In a time when religion is persecuted, as in the days of Antiochus Epiphanes, or despised as it was in the Hellenizing times which preceded and succeeded, it would be the duty of religious men not to hide their convictions. The tendency to carry on this public manifestation of religious acts after it had ceased to be protest would be necessarily great. The fact that they gained credit by praying at street corners when the hour of prayer came, and would have lost credit with the people had they not done so, was not recognized by them as lessening the moral worth of the action. Those who, having lived in the period of persecution and contempt, survived in that when religion was held in respect would maintain their earlier practice without any *arrière-pensée*. The succeeding generation, in continuing the practice, consciously "acted." They were *poseurs*. Their hypocrisy was none the less real that it was reached by unconscious stages. Hypocrisy was a new sin, a sin only possible in a spiritual religion, a religion in which morality and worship were closely related. Heathenism, which lay in sacrifices and ceremonies by which the gods could be bribed, or cajoled into favors, had a purely casual connection with morality; its worship was entirely a thing of externals, of acting, "posing." Consequently, a man did not by the most careful attention to the ceremonies of religion produce any presumption in favor of his trustworthiness. There was thus no sinister motive to prompt to religion. The prophets had denounced the insincerity of worship, but even they did not denounce hypocrisy, i.e. religion used as a cloak to hide treachery or dishonesty. Religion had become more spiritual, the connection between morality and worship more intimate by reason of the persecution of the Seleucids.

5. Talmudic Classification of the Pharisees

The Talm to some extent confirms the representation of the Gospels. There were said to be seven classes of Pharisees: (1) the "shoulder" Pharisee, who wears his good deeds on his shoulders and obeys the precept of the Law, not from principle, but from expediency; (2) the "wait-a-little" Pharisee, who begs for time in order to perform a meritorious action; (3) the "bleeding" Pharisee, who in his eagerness to avoid looking on a woman shuts his eyes and so bruises himself to bleeding by stumbling against a wall; (4) the "painted" Pharisee, who advertises his holiness lest any one should touch him so that he should be defiled; (5) the "reckoning" Pharisee, who is always saying "What duty must I do to balance any unpalatable duty which I have neglected?"; (6) the "fearing" Pharisee, whose relation to God is one merely of trembling awe; (7) the Pharisee from "love." In all but the last there was an element of "acting," of hypocrisy. It is to be noted that the Talm denounces ostentation; but unconsciously that root of the error lies in the externality of their righteousness; it commands an avoidance of ostentation which involves equal "posing."

V. Our Lord's Relationship to the Pharisees.—

1. Pharisees' Efforts to Gain Christ to Their Side

The attitude of the Pharisees to Jesus, to begin with, was, as had been their attitude to John, critical. They sent representatives to watch His doings and His sayings and report. They seem to have regarded it as possible that He might unite Himself with them, although, as we think, His affinities rather lay with the Essenes. Gradually their criticism became opposition. This opposition grew in intensity as He disregarded their interpretations of the Sabbatic law, ridiculed their refinements of the law of tithes and the distinctions they introduced into the validity of oaths, and denounced their insincere posing. At first there seems to have been an effort to cajole Him into compliance with their plans. If some of the Pharisees tempted Him to use language which would compromise Him with the people or with the Rom authorities, others invited Him to their tables, which was going far upon the part of a Pharisee toward one not a *ḥābhēr*. Even when He hung on the cross, the taunt with which they greeted Him may have had something of longing, lingering hope in it: "If he be the King of Israel, let him now come down from the cross, and we will believe him" (Mt **27** 42 AV). If He would only give them that sign, then they would acknowledge Him to be the Messiah.

2. Reasons for Pharisaic Hatred of Christ

The opposition of the Pharisees to Jesus was intensified by another reason. They were the democratic party; their whole power lay in the reputation they had with the people for piety. Our Lord denounced them as hypocrites; moreover He had secured a deeper popularity than theirs. At length when cajolery failed to win Him and astute questioning failed to destroy His popularity, they combined with their opponents, the Sadducees, against Him as against a common enemy.

3. Our Lord's Denunciation of the Pharisees

On the other hand, Jesus denounced the Pharisees more than He denounced any other class of the people. This seems strange when we remember that the main body of the religious people, those who looked for the Messiah, belonged to the Pharisees, and His teaching and theirs had a strong external resemblance. It was this external resemblance, united as it was with a profound spiritual difference, which made it incumbent on Jesus to mark Himself off from them. All righteousness with them was external, it lay in meats and drinks and divers washings, in tithing of mint, anise and cummin. He placed religion on a different footing, removed it into another region. With Him it was the heart that must be right with God, not merely the external actions; not only the outside of the cup and platter was to be cleansed, but the inside first of all. It is to be noted that, as observed above, the Pharisees were less antagonistic to the apostles when their Lord had left them. The after-history of Pharisaism has justified Our Lord's condemnation.

LITERATURE.—Histories of Israel: Ewald, V, 365 ff, ET; Herzfeld, III, 354 ff; Jost, I, 197 ff; Grätz, V, 91 ff; Derenbourg, 75–78, 117–44, 452–54; Holtzmann, II, 124 ff; Renan, V, 42 ff; Stanley, III, 376 ff; Cornill, 145 ff, ET; Schürer, II, ii, 4 ff, ET (*GJV*[4], II, 447 ff); Kuenen, III, 233 ff, ET.

Life and Times of Christ: Hausrath, I, 135 ff, ET; Edersheim, I, 310 ff; Lange, I, 302 ff, ET; Farrar, II, 494 ff; Geikie, II, 223 ff; Keim, I, 250 ff; Thomson, *Books Which Influenced Our Lord*, 50 ff; Weiss, I, 285 ff, ET; de Pressensé, 116 ff.

Arts. in Encs, Bible Dicts., Lexicons, etc: Ersch and Gruber, *Allg. Enc* (Daniel); Winer, *Realwörterbuch*; Herzog, *RE*, ed 1 (Reuss), edd 2, 3 (Sieffert); Hamburger, *Realenc.*; Smith's *DB* (Twisleton); Kitto's *Cyclopaedia of Bib. Lit.* (Ginsburg); *HDB* (Eaton); *EB* (Cowley, Prince); Schenkel, *Bibel-Lexicon* (Hausrath); *Jew Enc* (Kohler); *Temple Dict. of the Bible* (Christie); Hastings, *DCG* (Hugh Scott, Mitchell).

Monographs: Wellhausen, Montet, Geiger, Baneth, Müller, Hanne, Davaine, Herford; Weber, *System der altsynagogen Palestinischen Theologie*, 10 ff, 44 ff; Keil, *Bib. Archaeology*, II, 1680; Ryle and James, *Pss of Solomon*, xliv ff; Nicolas, *Doctrines religieuses des juifs*, 48 ff.

J. E. H. THOMSON

PHAROSH, fā'rosh (פַּרְעֹשׁ, *par'ōsh*). See PAROSH.

PHARPAR, fär'par (פַּרְפַּר, *parpar*; LXX B, Ἀφαρφά, *Apharphá*, A, Φαρφαρά, *Pharphará*): A river of Damascus, mentioned in 2 K **5** 12, along with the Abana or Amana. See ABANA.

PHARZITES, fär'zīts (הַפַּרְצִי, *ha-parçī*). See PEREZ.

PHASEAH, fa-sē'a, **PASEAH**, pa-sē'a (פָּסֵחַ, *pāṣēaḥ*, "lame"):

(1) A descendant of Judah, son of Eshton (1 Ch **4** 12).

(2) Name of a family of Nethinim (Ezr **2** 49; Neh **7** 51 [AV "Phaseah"]; "Phinoe" of 1 Esd **5** 31 RV).

(3) Father of Joiada (AV "Jehoiada"), the repairer of the "old gate" in Jerus (Neh **3** 6).

PHASELIS, fa-sē'lis (Φάσηλις, *Phásēlis*): A city of Lycia in Southern Asia Minor, on the seacoast, near the boundary of Pamphylia, to which country some ancient writers have assigned it. Situated on the extreme end of a promontory which projected into the sea, and with high mountains in the rear, it was separated both politically and geographically from the rest of Lycia. Hence it may be understood how it early became the favorite haunt of pirates. Already in the 6th cent. BC, when trade was carried on with Egypt, the city struck coins of its own; upon them the prow and the stern of a war galley were commonly represented The coinage ceased in 466 BC, but it was resumed about 400 BC, when the city again became practically independent. For a time Phaselis was under the control of the Seleucid kings of Syria, but in 190 BC it again regained its independence or continued as a member of the league of Lycian cities (1 Macc **15** 23). Before the beginning of the Christian era it had lost considerable of its earlier importance, yet it was still famed for its temple of Athene in which it was said that the sword of Achilles was preserved, and also for the attar of roses which was produced there. It figures little in early Christian history, yet in Byzantine times it was the residence of a bishop. Its site, now marked by the ruins of the stadium, temples and theater, bears the Turkish name of *Tekir Ova*. See also LYCIA.

E. J. BANKS

PHASIRON, fas'i-ron (A, Φασιρών, *Phasirṓn*, B, Φασειρών, *Phaseirṓn*, V, Φαρισών, *Pharisṓn*): The name of an unknown Arab tribe whom Jonathan overcame in the wilderness near Bethbasi; or possibly the name of an Arab chief (1 Macc **9** 66).

PHASSARON, fas'a-ron: AV=RV PHASSURUS (q.v.).

PHASSURUS, fas-ū'rus, fas'ū-rus (Φάσσουρος, *Phássouros*, B, Φάσσορος, *Phássoros*; AV Phassaron, after Aldine): The name of one of the families which went up from exile with Zerubbabel (1 Esd **5** 25) = "Pashhur" of Ezr **2** 38; Neh **7** 41; according to Ezr and Neh and RV numbering, 1,247; according to AV following A, 1,047.

PHEBE, fē'bē (**Φοίβη,** *Phoíbē*). See Phoebe.

PHENICE, fē-nī'sē. See Phoenicia; Phoenix.

PHENICIA, fē-nish'i-a (**Φοινίκη,** *Phoiníkē*). See Phoenicia.

PHERESITES, fer'ē-sīts: AV = RV "Pherezites" (1 Esd **8** 69; 2 Esd **1** 21) = "Perizzite."

PHEREZITE, fer'ē-zīt: AV form in Jth **5** 16 for RV "Perizzite" and both AV and RV in 2 Esd **1** 21 for "Perizzite"; one of the Canaanitish tribes.

PHI-BESETH, fī'bē-seth, fib'ē-seth (פִּי־בֶסֶת, *pī-bheseth*). See Pi-beseth.

PHICOL, fī'kol (פִּיכֹל, *pīkhōl;* **Φικόλ,** *Phikól;* AV **Phichol**): The captain of the host of the Phili king Abimelech of Gerar (Gen **21** 22; **26** 26).

PHILADELPHIA, fil-a-del'fi-a (**Φιλαδελφία,** *Philadelphía*): A city of ancient Lydia in Asia Minor on the Cogamus River, 105 miles from Smyrna. It stood upon a terrace 650 ft. above the sea. Behind it are the volcanic cliffs to which the Turks have given the name of Devitt, or "inkwells"; on the other side of the city the land is exceedingly fertile, and there was produced a wine of whose excellence the celebrated Rom poet Virgil wrote. Philadelphia is not so ancient as many of the other cities of Asia Minor, for it was founded after 189 BC on one of the highways which led to the interior. Its name was given to it in honor of Attalus II, because of his loyalty to his elder brother, Eumenes II, king of Lydia. Still another name of the city was Decapolis, because it was considered as one of the ten cities of the plain. A third name which it bore during the 1st cent. AD was Neo-kaisaria; it appears upon the coins struck during that period. During the reign of Vespasian, it was called Flavia. Its modern name, *Ala-shehir*, is considered by some to be a corruption of the Turkish words *Allah-shehir*, "the city of God," but more likely it is a name given it from the reddish color of the soil. In addition to all of these names it sometimes bore the title of "Little Athens" because of the magnificence of the temples and other public buildings which adorned it. Philadelphia quickly became an important and wealthy trade center, for as the coast cities declined, it grew in power, and retained its importance even until late Byzantine times. One of the Seven Churches of the Book of Rev (Rev **3** 7 ff) was there, and it was the seat of a bishop. As in most Asia Minor cities, many Jews lived there, and they possessed a synagogue. During the reign of Tiberius the city was destroyed by an earthquake, yet it was quickly rebuilt. Frederick Barbarossa entered it while on his crusade in 1190. Twice, in 1306 and 1324, it was besieged by the Seljuk Turks, but it retained its independence until after 1390, when it was captured by the combined forces of the Turks and Byzantines. In 1403 Tamerlane captured it, and, it is said, built about it a wall of the corpses of his victims.

Ala-shehir is still a Christian town; one-fourth of its modern population is Greek, and a Gr bishop still makes his home there. One of the chief modern industries is a liquorice factory; in the fields about the city the natives dig for the roots. On the terrace upon which the ancient city stood, the ruins of the castle and the walls may still be seen, and among them is pointed out the foundation of the early church. The place may now best be reached by rail from Smyrna. E. J. Banks

PHILARCHES, fi-lär'kēz. See Phylarches.

PHILEMON, fi-lē'mon, fī-lē'mun (**Φιλήμων,** *Philḗmōn*): Among the converts of St. Paul, perhaps while at Ephesus, was one whom he calls a "fellow-worker," Philemon (Philem ver 1). He was probably a man of some means, was celebrated for his hospitality (vs 5–7) and of considerable importance in the ecclesia at Colossae. It was at his house (ver 2) that the Colossian Christians met as a center. It is more than probable that this was a group of the Colossian church rather than the entire ecclesia. His wife was named Apphia (ver 2); and Archippus (ver 2) was no doubt his son. From Col **4** 17 we learn that Archippus held an office of some importance in Colossae, whether he was a presbyter (Abbott, *ICC*), or an evangelist, or perhaps the reader (Zahn), we cannot tell. He is called here (ver 2) St. Paul's "fellow-soldier."

The relation between the apostle and Philemon was so close and intimate that St. Paul does not hesitate to press him, on the basis of it, to forgive his slave, Onesimus, for stealing and for running away. See Philemon, Epistle to.

Tradition makes Philemon the bishop of Colossae (*Apos Const*, vii, 46), and the Gr Martyrology (Menae) for November 22 tells us that he together with his wife and son and Onesimus were martyred by stoning before Androcles, the governor, in the days of Nero. With this the Lat Martyrology agrees (cf Lightfoot, *St. Ignatius*, II, 535). This evidence, however, is unsatisfactory and cannot be trusted as giving unquestionable facts as to Philemon. The only sure information is that in the ep. bearing his name. Charles Smith Lewis

PHILEMON, EPISTLE TO: This most beautiful of all St. Paul's Epp., and the most intensely human, is one of the so-called Captivity Epp. of which Eph, Col, and Phil are the others. Of these four Philippians (q.v.) stands apart, and was written more probably after the other three. These are mutually interdependent, sent by the same bearer to churches of the same district, and under similar conditions.

There is some diversity of opinion as to the place from which the apostle wrote these letters.

1. Place of Writing

Certain scholars (Reuss, Schenkel, Weiss, Holtzmann, Hilgenfeld, Hausrath and Meyer) have urged Caesarea in opposition to the traditional place, Rome. The arguments advanced are first that Onesimus would have been more likely to have escaped to Caesarea than to Rome, as it is nearer Colossae than Rome is, to which we may reply that, though Caesarea is nearer, his chance of escape would have been far greater in the capital than in the provincial city. Again it is said that as Onesimus is not commended in Eph, he had already been left behind at Colossae; against which there are advanced the precarious value of an argument from silence, and the fact that this argument assumes a particular course which the bearers of the letters would follow, viz. through Colossae to Ephesus. A more forcible argument is that which is based on the apostle's expected visit. In Phil **2** 24 we read that he expected to go to Macedonia on his release; in Philem ver 22 we find that he expected to go to Colossae. On the basis of this latter reference it is assumed that he was to the south of Colossae when writing and so at Caesarea. But it is quite as probable that he would go to Colossae through Philippi as the reverse; and it is quite possible that even if he had intended to go direct to Colossae when he wrote to Philemon, events may have come about to cause him to change his plans. The last argument, based on the omission of any reference to the earthquake of which Tacitus (*Ann.* xiv.27) and Eusebius (*Chron.*, Ol, 207) write, is of force as opposed to the Rom origin of the letters only on the assumption that these writers both refer to the same event (by no means sure) and that the epp. were written after that event, and that it was necessary that St. Paul should have mentioned it. If the early chronology be accepted it falls entirely, as Tacitus' earlier date would be after the epp. were written. In addition we have the further facts, favorable to Rome, that St. Paul had no such freedom in Caesarea as he is represented in these epp. as enjoying; that no mention is made of Philip who was in Caesarea and a most important member of that community (Acts **21** 8), and finally that there is no probability that so large a body of disciples and companions could have gathered about the apostle in his earlier and more strict imprisonment, at Caesarea. We may therefore conclude that the Captivity Epp. were written from Rome, and not from Caesarea.

2. Authenticity

The external evidence for the ep. is less extensive than that of some of the other epp., but it is abundantly strong. The play on the word Onesimus which St. Paul himself uses (Philem ver 11) is found in Ignat., *Eph*, ii. This may not mean necessarily a literary connection, but it suggests this. The ep. is known to Tertullian, and through him we know that Marcion accepted it (*Adv. Marc.*, v.21). It is in the list in the Muratorian Fragment (p. 106, l. 27), and is quoted by Origen as Pauline (*Hom. in Jer.*, 19) and placed by Eusebius (*HE*, III, xxv) among the acknowledged books.

It has twice been the object of attack. In the 4th and 5th cents. it was opposed as unworthy of St. Paul's mind and as of no value for edification. This attack was met successfully by Jerome (*Comm. in Philem*, praef.), Chrysostom (*Argum. in Philem*) and Theodore of Mopsuestia (*Spicil. in Solesm*, I, 149), and the ep. was finally established in its earlier firm position. The later attack by Baur was inspired by his desire to break down the corroborative value of Philem to the other Captivity Epp., and has been characterized by Weiss as one of Baur's worst blunders. The suggestions that it is interpolated (Holtzmann), or allegorical (Weizsäcker and Pfleiderer), or based on the letter of Pliny (Ep. IX, 21) to Sabinianus (Steck), are interesting examples of the vagaries of their authors, but "deserve only to be mentioned" (Zahn). In its language, style and argument the letter is clearly Pauline.

3. Date

The date will, as is the case with the other Captivity Epp., depend on the chronology. If the earlier scheme be followed it may be dated about 58, if the later about 63, or 64.

4. Argument

The apostle writes in his own and Timothy's name to his friend PHILEMON (q.v.) in behalf of Onesimus, a runaway slave of the latter. Beginning with his usual thanksgiving, here awakened by the report of Philemon's hospitality, he intercedes for his 'son begotten in his bonds' (ver 10), Onesimus, who though he is Philemon's runaway slave is now "a brother." It is on this ground that the apostle pleads, urging his own age, and friendship for Philemon, and his present bonds. He pleads, however, without belittling Onesimus' wrongdoing, but assuming himself the financial responsibility for the amount of his theft. At the same time the apostle quietly refers to what Philemon really owes him as his father in Christ, and begs that he will not disappoint him in his expectation. He closes with the suggestion that he hopes soon to visit him, and with greetings from his companions in Rome.

5. Value

The charm and beauty of this ep. have been universally recognized. Its value to us as giving a glimpse of St. Paul's attitude toward slavery and his intimacy with a man like Philemon cannot be overestimated. One of the chief elements of value in it is the picture it gives us of a Christian home in the apostolic days; the father and mother well known for their hospitality, the son a man of position and importance in the church, the coming and going of the Christian brethren, and the life of the brotherhood centering about this household.

LITERATURE.—Lightfoot, *Col and Philem;* Vincent, "Phil" and "Philem" (*ICC*); von Soden, *Hand Commentar;* Alexander, in *Speaker's Comm.*

CHARLES SMITH LEWIS

PHILETUS, fi-lē'tus, fī-lē'tus (Φίλητος, *Philētos* [2 Tim **2** 17]):

1. The Nature of His Error

This person is mentioned by Paul, who warns Timothy against him as well as against his associate in error, Hymenaeus. The apostle speaks of Hymenaeus and Philetus as instances of men who were doing most serious injury to the church by their teaching, and by what that teaching resulted in, both in faith and morals. The specific error of these men was that they denied that there would be any bodily resurrection. They treated all Scriptural references to such a state, as figurative or metaphorical. They spiritualized it absolutely, and held that the resurrection was a thing of the past. No resurrection was possible, so they taught, except from ignorance to knowledge, from sin to righteousness. There would be no day when the dead would hear the voice of Christ and come forth out of the grave. The Christian, knowing that Christ was raised from the dead, looked forward to the day when his body should be raised in the likeness of Christ's resurrection. But this

2. How It Overthrew Faith

faith was utterly denied by the teaching of Hymenaeus and Philetus. This teaching of theirs, Paul tells us, had overthrown the faith of some. It would also overthrow Christian faith altogether, for if the dead are not raised, neither is Christ risen from the dead, and "ye are yet in your sins" (1 Cor **15** 17).

The denial of the resurrection of the body, whether of mankind generally or of Christ, is the overthrow of the faith. It leaves nothing to cling to, no living Christ, who saves and leads and comforts His people. The apostle proceeds to say that teaching of this kind "eats as doth a gangrene," and that it increases unto more ungodliness. As a canker or gangrene eats away the flesh, so does such teaching eat away Christian faith. Paul is careful to say, more than once, that the teaching which denies that there will be a resurrection of the dead leads inevitably to "ungodliness" and to "iniquity." See HYMENAEUS.

JOHN RUTHERFURD

PHILIP, fil'ip (Φίλιππος, *Phílippos*, "lover of horses"):

(1) The father of Alexander the Great (1 Macc **1** 1; **6** 2), king of Macedonia in 359–336 BC. His influence for Greece and for mankind in general lay in hastening the decadence of the Gr city-state and in the preparations he left to Alexander for the diffusion throughout the world of the varied phases of Gr intellectual life.

(2) A Phrygian left by Antiochus Epiphanes as governor at Jerus (c 170 BC) and described in 2 Macc **5** 22 as "more barbarous" than Antiochus himself, burning fugitive Jews who had assembled in caves near by "to keep the sabbath day secretly" (2 Macc **6** 11) and taking special measures to check the opposition of Judas Maccabaeus (2 Macc **8** 8). There is some ground for identifying him with—

(3) A friend or foster-brother of Antiochus (2 Macc **9** 29), appointed by Antiochus on his deathbed as regent. Lysias already held the office of regent, having brought up the son of Antiochus from his youth, and on the death of his father set him up as king under the name of Eupator. The accounts of the rivalries of the regents and of the fate of Philip as recorded in 1 Macc **6** 56; 2 Macc **9** 29; Jos, *Ant*, XII, ix, 7, are not easily reconciled.

(4) Philip V, king of Macedonia in 220–179 BC. He is mentioned in 1 Macc **8** 5 as an example of the great power of the Romans with whom Judas Maccabaeus made a league on conditions described (op. cit.). The conflict of Philip with the Romans coincided in time with that of Hannibal, after whose defeat at Zama the Romans were able to give undivided attention to the affairs of Macedonia. Philip was defeated by the Romans under Flaminius, at Cynoscephalae (197 BC), and compelled to accept the terms of the conquerors. He died in 179, and was succeeded by his son Perseus, last king of Macedonia, who lost his crown in his contest with the Romans. See PERSEUS. J. HUTCHISON

PHILIP (Φίλιππος, *Phílippos*): One of the Twelve Apostles. Philip belonged to Bethsaida of Galilee (Jn **1** 44; **12** 21). Along with Andrew and other fellow-townsmen, he had journeyed to Bethany to hear the teaching of John the Baptist, and there he received his first call from Christ, "Follow me" (Jn **1** 43). Like Andrew, Philip immediately won a fresh follower, Nathanael, for Jesus (Jn **1** 45). It is probable that he was present at most of the events recorded of Jesus' return journey from Bethany to Galilee, and that the information relating to these was supplied to St. John by him and St. Andrew (cf ANDREW). His final ordination to the Twelve is recorded in Mt **10** 3; Mk **3** 18; Lk **6** 14; Acts **1** 13. At the feeding of the 5,000, Philip was asked the question by Jesus, "Whence are we to buy bread, that these may eat?" (Jn **6** 5–7). He was appealed to by the Greeks when they desired to interview Jesus at the Passover (Jn **12** 20–33). During the address of Jesus to His disciples after the Last Supper, Philip made the request, "Lord, show us the Father, and it sufficeth us" (Jn **14** 8).

1. NT References

According to the "Genealogies of the Twelve Apostles," Philip was of the house of Zebulun (cf Budge, *Contendings of the Apostles*, II, 50). Clement of Alexandria (*Strom.*, iii.4, 25, and iv.9, 73) gives the tradition identifying him with the unknown disciple who asked permission to go and bury his father ere he followed Jesus (cf Mt **8** 21; Lk **9** 59), and says that he died a natural death. Owing to confusion with Philip the evangelist, there is much obscurity in the accounts of Apoc lit. concerning the earlier missionary activities of Philip the apostle. The "Acts of Philip" tell of a religious controversy between the apostle and a Judaean high priest before the philosophers of Athens. Later Lat documents mention Gaul (Galatia) as his field. As to his sending Joseph of Arimathaea thence to Britain, see JOSEPH OF ARIMATHAEA. The evidence seems conclusive that the latter part of his life was spent in Phrygia. This is supported by Polycrates (bishop of Ephesus in the 2d cent.), who states that he died at Hierapolis, by Theodoret, and by the parts of the *Contendings of the Apostles* dealing with Philip. Thus according to "The Preaching of St. Philip and St. Peter" (cf Budge, *Contendings of the Apostles*, II, 146), Phrygia was assigned to Philip as a mission field by the risen Christ when He appeared to the disciples on the Mount of Olives, and "The Martyrdom of St. Philip in Phrygia" (Budge, II, 156) tells of his preaching, miracles and crucifixion there.

2. Apocryphal References

Philip was regarded in early times as the author of "The Gospel of Philip," a gnostic work of the 2d cent., part of which was preserved by Epiphanius (cf Hennecke, *Neutestamentliche Apokryphen*, 40, 41). See APOCRYPHAL GOSPELS.

As with Andrew, Philip's Gr name implies he had Gr connections, and this is strengthened by the fact that he acted as the spokesman of the Greeks at the Passover. Of a weaker mold than Andrew, he was yet the one to whom the Greeks would first appeal; he himself possessed an inquirer's spirit and could therefore sympathize with their doubts and difficulties. The practical, strong-minded Andrew was naturally the man to win the impetuous, swift-thinking Peter; but the slower Philip, versed in the Scriptures (cf Jn **1** 45), appealed more to the critical Nathanael and the cultured Greeks. Cautious and deliberate himself, and desirous of submitting all truth to the test of sensuous experience (cf Jn **14** 8), he concluded the same criterion would be acceptable to Nathanael also (cf Jn **1** 46). It was the presence of this materialistic trend of mind in Philip that induced Jesus, in order to awaken in His disciple a larger and more spiritual faith, to put the question in Jn **6** 6, seeking "to prove him." This innate diffidence which affected Philip's religious beliefs found expression in his outer life and conduct also. It was not merely modesty, but also a certain lack of self-reliance, that made him turn to Andrew for advice when the Greeks wished to see Jesus. The story of his later life is, however, sufficient to show that he overcame those initial defects in his character, and fulfilled nobly the charge that his risen Lord laid upon him (cf Mt **28** 16–20).

3. Character

C. M. KERR

PHILIP ("tetrarch," Lk **3** 1). See HEROD.

PHILIP, THE EVANGELIST: One of "the seven" chosen to have the oversight of "the daily ministration" of the poor of the Christian community in Jerus (Acts **6** 5). Whether Philip, bearing a Gr name, was a Hellenist, is not known, but his missionary work reveals to us one free from the religious prejudices of the strict Hebrew.

The martyrdom of Stephen was the beginning of a systematic persecution of the church in Jerus, and all except the apostles were scattered over Judaea and Samaria (Acts **8** 1), and even as far as Phoenicia, Cyprus and Antioch (**11** 19). Thus the influence of the new teaching was extended, and a beginning made to the missionary movement. The story of Philip's missionary labors is told in Acts **8** 5 ff. He went to the chief city of Samaria, called Sebaste in honor of Augustus (Gr *Sebastós*). The Samaritans, of mixed Israelitish and gentile blood, had, in consequence of their being rigidly excluded from the Jewish church since the return from exile, built on Mt. Gerizim a rival sanctuary to the temple. To them Philip proclaimed the Christ and wrought signs, with the result that multitudes gave heed, and "were baptized, both men and women." They had been under the influence of a certain sorcerer, Simon, who himself also believed and was baptized, moved, as the sequel proved, by the desire to learn the secret of Philip's ability to perform miracles (see SIMON MAGUS). The apostles (Acts **8** 14) at Jerus sanctioned the admission of Samaritans into the church by sending Peter and John, who not only confirmed the work of Philip, but also themselves preached in many Samaritan villages.

The next incident recorded is the conversion of a Gentile, who was, however, a worshipper of the God of Israel, a eunuch under Candace, queen of the Ethiopians. As he was returning from worshipping in the temple at Jerus, he was met by Philip on the road to Gaza. Philip expounded to him that portion of Isa **53** which he had been reading aloud as he sat in his chariot, and preached unto him Jesus. It is another sign of Philip's insight into the universality of Christianity that he baptized this eunuch who could not have been admitted into full membership in the Jewish church (Dt **23** 1). See ETHIOPIAN EUNUCH.

After this incident Philip went to Azotus (Ashdod), and then traveled north to Caesarea, preaching in the cities on his way. There he settled, for Luke records that Paul and his company abode in the house of Philip, "the evangelist," "one of the seven," for some days (Acts **21** 8 ff). This occurred more than 20 years after the incidents recorded in Acts **8**. Both at this time and during Paul's imprisonment at Caesarea, Luke had the opportunity of hearing about Philip's work from his own lips. Luke records that Philip had 4 daughters who were preachers (Acts **21** 9).

The Jewish rebellion, which finally resulted in the fall of Jerus, drove many Christians out of Pal, and among them Philip and his daughters. One tradition connects Philip and his daughters with Hierapolis in Asia, but in all probability the evangelist is confounded with the apostle. Another tradition represents them as dwelling at Tralles, Philip being the first bishop of the Christian community.

S. F. HUNTER

PHILIP, THE GOSPEL OF. See APOCRYPHAL GOSPELS; PHILIP THE EVANGELIST.

PHILIPPI, fi-lip'ī (**Φίλιπποι**, *Phílippoi*, ethnic **Φιλιππήσιος**, *Philippēsios*, Phil **4** 15): A city of Macedonia, situated in 41° 5′ N. lat. and 24° 16′ E. long. It lay on the Egnatian Road, 33 Rom miles from Amphipolis and 21 from Acontisma, in a plain bounded on the E. and N. by the mountains which lie between the rivers Zygactes and Nestus, on the W. by Mt. Pangaeus, on the S. by the ridge called in antiquity Symbolum, over which ran the road connecting the city with its seaport, NEAPOLIS (q.v.), 9 miles distant. This plain, a considerable part of which is marshy in modern, as in ancient, times, is connected with the basin of the Strymon by the valley of the Angites (Herodotus vii.113), which also bore the names Gangas or Gangites (Appian, *Bell. Civ.* iv.106), the modern *Anghista.* The ancient name of Philippi was Crenides (Strabo vii.331; Diodorus xvi.3, 8; Appian, *Bell. Civ.* iv.105; Stephanus Byz. s.v.), so called after the springs which feed the river and the marsh; but it was refounded by Philip II of Macedon, the father of Alexander the Great, and received his name.

1. Position and Name

Appian (*Bell. Civ.* iv.105) and Harpocration say that Crenides was afterward called Daton, and that this name was changed to Philippi, but this statement is open to question, since Daton, which became proverbial among the Greeks for good fortune, possessed, as Strabo tells us (vii.331 fr. 36), "admirably fertile territory, a lake, rivers, dockyards and productive gold mines," whereas Philippi lies, as we have seen, some 9 miles inland. Many modern authorities, therefore, have placed Daton on the coast at or near the site of Neapolis. On the whole, it seems best to adopt the view of Heuzey (*Mission archéologique*, 35, 62 ff) that Daton was not originally a city, but the whole district which lay immediately to the E. of Mt. Pangaeus, including the Philippian plain and the seacoast about Neapolis. On the site of the old foundation of Crenides, from which the Gr settlers had perhaps been driven out by the Thracians about a century previously, the Thasians in 360 BC founded their colony of Daton with the aid of the exiled Athenian statesman Callistratus, in order to exploit the wealth, both agricultural and mineral, of the neighborhood. To Philip, who ascended the Macedonian throne in 359 BC, the possession of this spot seemed of the utmost importance. Not only is the plain itself well watered and of extraordinary fertility, but a strongly fortified post planted here would secure the natural land-route from Europe to Asia and protect the eastern frontier of Macedonia against Thracian inroads. Above all, the mines of the district might meet his most pressing need, that of an abundant supply of gold. The site was therefore seized in 358, the city was enlarged, strongly fortified, and renamed, the Thasian settlers either driven out or reinforced, and the mines, worked with characteristic energy, produced over 1,000 talents a year (Diodorus xvi.8) and enabled Philip to issue a gold currency which in the West soon superseded the Pers darics (G. F. Hill, *Historical Greek Coins*, 80 ff). The revenue thus obtained was of inestimable value to Philip, who not only used it for the development of the Macedonian army, but also proved himself a master of the art of bribery. His remark is well known that no fortress was impregnable to whose walls an ass laden with gold could be driven. Of the history of Philippi during the next 3 centuries we know practically nothing. Together with the rest of Macedonia, it passed into the Rom hands after the battle of Pydna (168 BC), and fell in the first of the four regions into which the country was then divided (Livy xlv.29). In 146 the whole of Macedonia was formed into a single Rom province. But the mines seem to have been almost, if not quite, exhausted by this time, and Strabo (vii.331 fr. 41) speaks of Philippi as having sunk by the time of Caesar to a "small settlement" (*κατοικία μικρά*, *katoikía mikrá*). In the autumn of 42 BC it witnessed the death-struggle of the Rom republic. Brutus and Cassius, the leaders of the band of conspirators who had assassinated Julius Caesar, were faced by Octavian, who 15 years later became the Emperor Augustus, and Antony. In the first engagement the army of Brutus defeated that of Octavian, while Antony's forces were victorious over those of Cassius, who in despair put an end to his life. Three weeks later the second and decisive conflict took place. Brutus was compelled by his impatient soldiery to give battle, his troops were routed and he himself fell on his own sword. Soon afterward Philippi was made a Rom colony with the title *Colonia Iulia Philippensis.* After the battle of Actium (31 BC) the colony was reinforced, largely by Ital. partisans of Antony who were dispossessed in order to afford allotments for Octavian's veterans (Dio Cassius li.4), and its name was changed to *Colonia Augusta Iulia* (*Victrix*) *Philippensium.* It received the much-coveted *ius Italicum* (*Digest* L. 15, 8, 8), which involved numerous privileges, the chief of which was the immunity of its territory from taxation.

2. History

Coin of Philippi.

In the course of his second missionary journey Paul set sail from Troas, accompanied by Silas (who bears his full name Silvanus in 2 Cor **1** 19; 1 Thess **1** 1; 2 Thess **1** 1), Timothy and Luke, and on the following day reached Neapolis (Acts **16** 11). Thence he journeyed by road to Philippi, first crossing the pass some 1,600 ft. high which leads over the mountain ridge called Symbolum and afterward traversing the Philippian plain. Of his experiences there we have in Acts **16** 12–40 a

3. Paul's First Visit

singularly full and graphic account. On the Sabbath, presumably the first Sabbath after their arrival, the apostle and his companions went out to the bank of the Angites, and there spoke to the women, some of them Jews, others proselytes, who had come together for purposes of worship.

One of these was named Lydia, a Gr proselyte from Thyatira, a city of Lydia in Asia Minor, to the church of which was addressed the message recorded in Rev **2** 18–29. She is described as a "seller of purple" (Acts **16** 14), that is, of woolen fabrics dyed purple, for the manufacture of which her native town was famous. Whether she was the agent in Philippi of some firm in Thyatira or whether she was carrying on her trade independently, we cannot say; her name suggests the possibility that she was a freedwoman, while from the fact that we hear of her household and her house (ver 15; cf ver 40), though no mention is made of her husband, it has been conjectured that she was a widow of some property. She accepted the apostolic message and was baptized with her household (ver 15), and insisted that Paul and his companions should accept her hospitality during the rest of their stay in the city (see further LYDIA).

All seemed to be going well when opposition arose from an unexpected quarter. There was in the town a girl, in all probability a slave, who was reputed to have the power of oracular utterance. Herodotus tells us (vii.111) of an oracle of Dionysus situated among the Thracian tribe of the Satrae, probably not far from Philippi; but there is no reason to connect the soothsaying of this girl with that worship. In any case, her masters reaped a rich harvest from the fee charged for consulting her. Paul, troubled by her repeatedly following him and those with him crying, "These men are bondservants of the Most High God, who proclaim unto you a way of salvation" (Acts **16** 17 m), turned and commanded the spirit in Christ's name to come out of her. The immediate restoration of the girl to a sane and normal condition convinced her masters that all prospect of further gain was gone, and they therefore seized Paul and Silas and dragged them into the forum before the magistrates, probably the *duumviri* who stood at the head of the colony. They accused the apostles of creating disturbance in the city and of advocating customs, the reception and practice of which were illegal for Rom citizens. The rabble of the market-place joined in the attack (ver 22), whereupon the magistrates, accepting without question the accusers' statement that Paul and Silas were Jews (ver 20) and forgetting or ignoring the possibility of their possessing Rom citizenship, ordered them to be scourged by the attendant lictors and afterward to be imprisoned. In the prison they were treated with the utmost rigor; they were confined in the innermost ward, and their feet put in the stocks. About midnight, as they were engaged in praying and singing hymns, while the other prisoners were listening to them, the building was shaken by a severe earthquake which threw open the prison doors. The jailer, who was on the point of taking his own life, reassured by Paul regarding the safety of the prisoners, brought Paul and Silas into his house where he tended their wounds, set food before them, and, after hearing the gospel, was baptized together with his whole household (vs 23–34).

On the morrow the magistrates, thinking that by dismissing from the town those who had been the cause of the previous day's disturbance they could best secure themselves against any repetition of the disorder, sent the lictors to the jailer with orders to release them. Paul refused to accept a dismissal of this kind. As Rom citizens he and Silas were legally exempt from scourging, which was regarded as a degradation (1 Thess **2** 2), and the wrong was aggravated by the publicity of the punishment, the absence of a proper trial and the imprisonment which followed (Acts **16** 37). Doubtless Paul had declared his citizenship when the scourging was inflicted, but in the confusion and excitement of the moment his protest had been unheard or unheeded. Now, however, it produced a deep impression on the magistrates, who came in person to ask Paul and Silas to leave the city. They, after visiting their hostess and encouraging the converts to remain firm in their new faith, set out by the Egnatian Road for Thessalonica (vs 38–40). How long they had stayed in Philippi we are not told, but the fact that the foundations of a strong and flourishing church had been laid and the phrase "for many days" (ver 18) lead us to believe that the time must have been a longer one than appears at first sight. Ramsay (*St. Paul the Traveller*, 226) thinks that Paul left Troas in October, 50 AD, and stayed at Philippi until nearly the end of the year; but this chronology cannot be regarded as certain.

Several points in the narrative of these incidents call for fuller consideration. (1) We may notice, first, the very small part played by Jews and Judaism at Philippi.

There was no synagogue here, as at Salamis in Cyprus (Acts **13** 5), Antioch in Pisidia (**13** 14.43), Iconium (**14** 1), Ephesus (**18** 19.26; **19** 8), Thessalonica (**17** 1), Beroea (**17** 10), Athens (**17** 17) and Corinth (**18** 4). The number of resident Jews was small, their meetings for prayer took place on the river's bank, the worshippers were mostly or wholly women (**16** 13), and among them some, perhaps a majority, were proselytes. Of Jewish converts we hear nothing, nor is there any word of Jews as either inciting or joining the mob which dragged Paul and Silas before the magistrates. Further, the whole tone of the ep. to this church seems to prove that here at least the apostolic teaching was not in danger of being undermined by Judaizers. True, there is one passage (Phil **3** 2–7) in which Paul denounces "the concision," those who had "confidence in the flesh"; but it seems "that in this warning he was thinking of Rome more than of Philippi; and that his indignation was aroused rather by the vexatious antagonism which there thwarted him in his daily work, than by any actual errors already undermining the faith of his distant converts" (Lightfoot).

(2) Even more striking is the prominence of the Rom element in the narrative. We are here not in a Gr or Jewish city, but in one of those Rom colonies which Aulus Gellius describes as "miniatures and pictures of the Rom people" (*Noctes Atticae*, xvi.13).

In the center of the city is the *forum* (ἀγορά, *agorá*, ver 19), and the general term "magistrates" (ἄρχοντες, *árchontes*, EV "rulers," ver 19) is exchanged for the specific title of *praetors* (στρατηγοί, *stratēgoí*, EV "magistrates," vs 20. 22.35.36.38); these officers are attended by lictors (ῥαβδοῦχοι, *rhabdoúchoi*, EV "sergeants," vs 35.38) who bear the *fasces* with which they scourged Paul and Silas (ῥαβδίζω, *rhabdízō*, ver 22). The charge is that of disturbing public order and introducing customs opposed to Rom law (vs 20.21), and Paul's appeal to his Rom *civitas* (ver 37) at once inspired the magistrates with fear for the consequences of their action and made them conciliatory and apologetic (vs 38.39). The title of *praetor* borne by these officials has caused some difficulty. The supreme magistrates of Rom colonies, two in number, were called *duoviri* or *duumviri* (*iuri dicundo*), and that this title was in use at Philippi is proved by three inscriptions (Orelli, No. 3746; Heuzey, *Mission archéologique*, 15, 127). The most probable explanation of the discrepancy is that these magistrates assumed the title of *praetor*, or that it was commonly applied to them, as was certainly the case in some parts of the Rom world (Cicero *De lege agraria* ii.34; Horace *Sat.* i.5, 34; Orelli, No. 3785).

(3) Ramsay (*St. Paul the Traveller*, 200 ff) has brought forward the attractive suggestion that Luke was himself a Philippian, and that he was the "man of Macedonia" who appeared to Paul at Troas with the invitation to enter Macedonia (Acts **16** 9).

In any case, the change from the 3d to the 1st person in ver 10 marks the point at which Luke joined the apostle, and the same criterion leads to the conclusion that Luke remained at Philippi between Paul's first and his third visit to the city (see below). Ramsay's hypothesis would explain (*a*) the fulness and vividness of the narrative of Acts **16** 11–40; (*b*) the emphasis laid on the importance of Philippi (ver 12); and (*c*) the fact that Paul recognized as a Macedonian the man whom he saw in his vision, although there was nothing either in the language, features or dress of Macedonians to mark them out from other Greeks. Yet Luke was clearly not a householder at Philippi (ver 15), and early tradition refers to him as an Antiochene (see, however, Ramsay, op. cit. 389 f).

(4) Much discussion has centered round the description of Philippi given in Acts **16** 12. The reading of ℵ A C, etc, followed by WH, RV, etc, is:

ἥτις ἐστὶν πρώτη τῆς μερίδος Μακεδονίας πόλις κολωνία, *hḗtis estín prṓtē tḗs merídos Makedonías pólis kolōnía*. But it is doubtful whether *Makedonias* is to be taken with the word which precedes or with that which follows, and further the sense derived from the phrase is unsatisfactory. For *prōtē* must mean either (1) first in political importance and rank, or (2) the first which the apostle reached. But the capital of the province was Thessalonica, and if *tēs meridos* be taken to refer to the easternmost of the 4 districts into which Macedonia had been divided in 168 BC (though there is no evidence that that division survived at this time), Amphipolis was its capital and was apparently still its most important city, though destined to be outstripped by Philippi somewhat later. Nor is the other rendering of *prōtē* (adopted, e.g. by Lightfoot) more natural. It supposes that Luke reckoned Neapolis as belonging to Thrace, and the boundary of Macedonia as lying between Philippi and its seaport; moreover, the remark is singularly pointless; the use of *estin* rather than *ḗn* is against this view, nor is *prōtē* found in this sense without any qualifying phrase. Lastly, the *tēs* in its present position is unnatural; in B it is placed after, instead of before, *meridos*, while D (the Bezan reviser) reads κεφαλὴ τῆς Μακεδονίας, *kephalḗ tḗs Makedonías*. Of the emendations which have been suggested, we may notice three: (*a*) for *meridos* Hort has suggested *Pierídos*, "a chief city of Pierian Macedonia"; (*b*) for *prōtē tēs* we may read *prṓtēs*, "which belongs to the first region of Macedonia"; (*c*) *meridos* may be regarded as a later insertion and struck out of the text, in which case the whole phrase will mean, "which is a city of Macedonia of first rank" (though not necessarily *the* first city).

4. Paul's Later Visits

Paul and Silas, then, probably accompanied by Timothy (who, however, is not expressly mentioned in Acts between **16** 1 and **17** 14), left Philippi for Thessalonica, but Luke apparently remained behind, for the "we" of Acts **16** 10–17 does not appear again until **20** 5, when Paul is once more leaving Philippi on his last journey to Jerus. The presence of the evangelist during the intervening 5 years may have had much to do with the strength of the Philippian church and its stedfastness in persecution (2 Cor **8** 2; Phil **1** 29.30). Paul himself did not revisit the city until, in the course of his third missionary journey, he returned to Macedonia, preceded by Timothy and Erastus, after a stay of over 2 years at Ephesus (Acts **19** 22; **20** 1). We are not definitely told that he visited Philippi on this occasion, but of the fact there can be little doubt, and it was probably there that he awaited the coming of Titus (2 Cor **2** 13; **7** 5.6) and wrote his 2d Ep. to the Corinthians (**8** 1 ff; **9** 2–4). After spending 3 months in Greece, whence he intended to return by sea to Syria, he was led by a plot against his life to change his plans and return through Macedonia (Acts **20** 3). The last place at which he stopped before crossing to Asia was Philippi, where he spent the days of unleavened bread, and from (the seaport of) which he sailed in company with Luke to Troas, where seven of his companions were awaiting him (**20** 4–6). It seems likely that Paul paid at least one further visit to Philippi in the interval between his first and second imprisonments. That he hoped to do so, he himself tells us (Phil **2** 24), and the journey to Macedonia mentioned in 1 Tim **1** 3 would probably include a visit to Philippi, while if, as many authorities hold, 2 Tim **4** 13 refers to a later stay at Troas, it may well be connected with a further and final tour in Macedonia. But the intercourse between the apostle and this church of his founding was not limited to these rare visits. During Paul's first stay at Thessalonica he had received gifts of money on two occasions from the Philippian Christians (Phil **4** 16), and their kindness had been repeated after he left Macedonia for Greece (2 Cor **11** 9; Phil **4** 15). Again, during his first imprisonment at Rome the Philippians sent a gift by the hand of one of their number, Epaphroditus (Phil **2** 25; **4** 10.14–19), who remained for some time with the apostle, and finally, after a serious illness which nearly proved fatal (**2** 27), returned home bearing the letter of thanks which has survived, addressed to the Philippian converts by Paul and Timothy (**1** 1). The latter intended to visit the church shortly afterward in order to bring back to the imprisoned apostle an account of its welfare (**2** 19.23), but we do not know whether this plan was actually carried out or not. We cannot, however, doubt that other letters passed between Paul and this church besides the one which is extant, though the only reference to them is a disputed passage of Polycarp's *Epistle to the Philippians* (iii.2), where he speaks of "letters" (ἐπιστολαί, *epistolaí*) as written to them by Paul (but see Lightfoot's note on Phil **3** 1).

5. Later History of the Church

After the death of Paul we hear but little of the church or of the town of Philippi. Early in the 2d cent. Ignatius, bishop of Antioch, was condemned as a Christian and was taken to Rome to be thrown to the wild beasts. After passing through Philadelphia, Smyrna and Troas, he reached Philippi. The Christians there showed him every mark of affection and respect, and after his departure wrote a letter of sympathy to the Antiochene church and another to Polycarp, bishop of Smyrna, requesting him to send them copies of any letters of Ignatius which he possessed. This request Polycarp fulfilled, and at the same time sent a letter to the Philippians full of encouragement, advice and warning. From it we judge that the condition of the church as a whole was satisfactory, though a certain presbyter, Valens, and his wife are severely censured for their avarice which belied their Christian profession. We have a few records of bishops of Philippi, whose names are appended to the decisions of the councils held at Sardica (344 AD), Ephesus (431) and Chalcedon (451), and the see appears to have outlived the city itself and to have lasted down to modern times (Le Quien, *Oriens Christ.*, II, 70; Neale, *Holy Eastern Church*, I, 92). Of the destruction of Philippi no account has come down to us. The name was perpetuated in that of the Turkish hamlet *Felibedjik*, but the site is now uninhabited, the nearest village being that of *Raktcha* among the hills immediately to the N. of the ancient acropolis. This latter and the plain around are covered with ruins, but no systematic excavation has yet been undertaken. Of the extant remains the most striking are portions of the Hellenic and Hellenistic fortification, the scanty vestiges of the theater, the ruin known among the Turks as *Derekler*, "the columns," which perhaps represents the ancient *thermae*, traces of a temple of Silvanus with numerous rock-cut reliefs and inscriptions, and the remains of a triumphal arch (*Kiemer*).

Literature.—The fullest account of the site and antiquities is that of Heuzey and Daumet, *Mission archéologique de Macédoine*, chs i–v and Plan A; Leake, *Travels in Northern Greece*, III, 214–25; Cousinéry, *Voyage dans la Macédoine*, II, 1 ff; Perrot, "Daton. Néapolis. Les ruines de Philippos," in *Revue archéologique*, 1860; and Hackett, in *Bible Union Quarterly*, 1860, may also be consulted. For the Latin inscriptions see *CIL*, III, 1, nos. 633–707; III, Suppl., nos. 7337–7358; for coins, B. V. Head, *Historia Numorum*, 192; *Catalogue of Coins in the British Museum: Macedonia*, etc, 96. For the history of the Philippian church and the narrative of Acts **16** 12–40 see Lightfoot, *St. Paul's Ep. to the Philippians*, 47–65; Ramsay, *St. Paul the Traveller and the Rom Citizen*, 202–26; Conybeare and Howson, *Life and Epp. of St. Paul*, ch ix; Farrar, *Life and Work of St. Paul*, ch xxv; and the standard comms. on the Acts—esp. Blass, *Acta Apostolorum*—and on Philippians.

M. N. Tod

PHILIPPIANS, fi-lip'i-anz, THE EPISTLE TO:

I. Paul and the Church at Philippi
II. Characteristics of the Church at Philippi
III. Characteristics of the Epistle
  1. A Letter
  2. A Letter of Love
  3. A Letter of Joy
  4. Importance Theologically
IV. Genuineness of the Epistle
V. Place, Date and Occasion of Writing
VI. Contents of the Epistle
Literature

I. Paul and the Church at Philippi.—Paul was on his second missionary journey in the year 52 AD. He felt that he was strangely thwarted in many of his plans. He had had a most distressing illness in Galatia. The Spirit would not permit him to preach in Asia, and when he essayed to enter Bithynia the Spirit again would not suffer it. Baffled and perplexed, the apostle with his two companions, Silas and Timothy, went on to the seacoast and stopped in Troas. Here at last his leading became clear. A vision of a man from Macedonia convinced him that it was the will of God that he should preach in the western continent of Europe. The way was opened at once. The winds were favorable. In two days he came to Neapolis. At once he took the broad paved way of the Via Egnatia up to the mountain pass and down on the other side to Philippi, a journey of some 8 miles. There was no synagogue at Philippi, but a little company of Jews gathered for Sabbath worship at "a place of prayer" (προσευχή, *proseuchē*, Acts **16** 13), about a mile to the W. of the city gate on the shore of the river Gangites (see Proseucha). Paul and his companions talked to the women gathered there, and Lydia was converted. Later, a maid with the spirit of divination was exorcised. Paul and Silas were scourged and thrown into prison, an earthquake set them free, the jailer became a believer, the magistrates repented their treatment of men who were Rom citizens and besought them to leave the city (Acts **16** 6–40). Paul had had his first experience of a Rom scourging and of lying in the stocks of a Rom prison here at Philippi, yet he went on his way rejoicing, for a company of disciples had been formed, and he had won the devotion of loyal and loving hearts for himself and his Master (see Philippi). That was worth all the persecution and the pain. The Christians at Philippi seem to have been Paul's favorites among all his converts. He never lost any opportunity of visiting them and refreshing his spirit with their presence in the after-years. Six years later he was resident in Ephesus, and having sent Titus to Corinth with a letter to the Corinthians and being in doubt as to the spirit in which it would be received, he appointed a meeting with Titus in Macedonia, and probably spent the anxious days of his waiting at Philippi. If he met Titus there, he may have written 2 Cor in that city (2 Cor **2** 13; **7** 6). Paul returned to Ephesus, and after the riot in that city he went over again into Macedonia and made his third visit to Philippi. He probably promised the Philippians at this time that he would return to Philippi to celebrate the Easter week with his beloved converts there. He went on into Greece, but in 3 months he was back again, at the festival of the resurrection in the year 58 AD (Acts **20** 2.6). We read in 1 Tim **1** 3 that Paul visited Macedonia after the Rom imprisonment. He enjoyed himself among the Philippians. They were Christians after his own heart. He thanks God for their fellowship from the first day until now (Phil **1** 5). He declares that they are his beloved who have always obeyed, not in his presence only, but much more in his absence (**2** 12). With fond repetition he addresses them as his brethren, beloved and longed for, his joy and crown, his beloved (**4** 1). This was Paul's favorite church, and we can gather from the ep. good reason for this fact.

II. Characteristics of the Church at Philippi.—(1) It seems to be the least Jewish of all the Pauline churches. There were few Jews in Philippi. No Heb names are found in the list of converts in this church mentioned in the NT. The Jewish opponents of Paul seem never to have established themselves in this community. (2) Women seem to be unusually prominent in the history of this church, and this is consistent with what we know concerning the position accorded to woman in Macedonian society. Lydia brings her whole family with her into the church. She must have been a very influential woman, and her own fervor and devotion and generosity and hospitality seem to have been contagious and to have become characteristic of the whole Christian community. Euodia and Syntyche are mentioned in the ep., two women who were fellow-laborers with Paul in the gospel, for both of whom he has great respect, of both of whom he is sure that their names are written in the book of life, but who seem to have differed with each other in some matter of opinion. Paul exhorts them to be of the same mind in the Lord (**4** 2). The prominence of women in the congregation at Philippi or the dominance of Lydia's influence among them may account for the fact that they seem to have been more mindful of Paul's comfort than any of his other converts were. They raised money for Paul's support and forwarded it to him again and again. They were anxious that he should have all that was needful. They were willing to give of their time and their means to that end. There seem to have been no theological differences in their company. That may testify to the fact that the most of them were women. (3) There were splendid men in the church membership too. Some of them were Macedonians and some of them were Rom veterans.

Hausrath declares that the Macedonians represented the "noblest and soundest part of the ancient world. . . . . Here was none of the shuffling and the indecision of the Asiatics, none of the irritable vanity and the uncertain levity of the Gr communities. . . . . They were men of sterner mold than could be found in Asia Minor or languorous Syria. The material was harder to work in, and offered more stubborn resistance; but the work, once done, endured. A new Macedonian phalanx was formed here, a phalanx of Pauline Christians. . . . . Manliness, loyalty, firmness, their characteristics in general history, are equally their characteristics in the history of the Christian church. . . . . They were always true to Paul, always obedient, always helpful" (*Time of the Apostles*, III, 203–4).

Paul rejoiced in them. They were spirits congenial with his own. The Rom veterans had been trained in the Rom wars to hardness and discipline and loyalty. They were Rom citizens and proud of the fact. In the ep. Paul exhorts them to behave as citizens worthy of the gospel of Christ (**1** 27), and he reminds them that though they were proud of their Rom citizenship, as was he, they all had become members of a heavenly commonwealth, citizenship in which was a much greater boon than even the *jus Italicum* had been. In **3** 20 Paul states the fact again, "Our citizenship is in heaven"; and he goes on to remind them that their King is seated there upon the throne and that He is coming again to establish a glorious empire, for He has power to subject all things unto Himself.

It is to these old soldiers and athletes that Paul addresses his military and gymnastic figures of speech. He informs them that the whole praetorian guard had heard of the gospel through his imprisonment at Rome (**1** 13). He sends them greeting from the saints that are in Caesar's household (**4** 22). He prays that he may hear of them that they stand fast like an immovable phalanx, with one soul striving athletically for the faith of the gospel (**1** 27). He knows that they will be fearless and brave, in nothing affrighted by the adversaries (**1** 28). He speaks of his own experience as a wrestling-match, a conflict or contest (**1** 30). He joys in the sacrifice and service of their faith (**2** 17). He calls Epaphroditus not only his fellow-worker but his fellow-soldier (**2** 25). He likens the Christian life to a race in which he presses on toward the goal unto the prize (**3** 14). He asks the Philippians to keep even, soldierly step with him in the Christian walk (**3** 16). These metaphors have their appeal to an athletic and military race, and they bear their testimony to the high regard which Paul had for this type of Christianity and for those in whose lives it was displayed. We do not know the names of many of these men, for only Clement and Epaphroditus are mentioned here; but we gather much concerning their spirit from this ep., and we are as sure as Paul himself that their names are all written in the book of life (**4** 3).

(4) If the constituent elements of the church at Philippi fairly represented the various elements of the population of the city, they must have been cosmopolitan in character. Philippi was an old Macedonian city which had been turned into a Rom colony. It was both Gr and Rom in its characteristics. Christianity had been introduced here by two Jews, who were Rom citizens, and a Jewish son of a gentile father. In the account given of the founding of the church in Acts **16** three converts are mentioned, and one is a Jewish proselyte from Asia, one a native Greek, and one a Rom official. The later converts doubtless represented the same diversity of nationality and the same differences in social position. Yet, apart from those two good women, Euodia and Syntyche, they were all of one mind in the Lord. It is a remarkable proof of the fact that in Christ all racial and social conditions may be brought into harmony and made to live together in peace. (5) They were a very liberal people. They gave themselves to the Lord and to Paul (2 Cor **8** 5), and whenever they could help Paul or further the work of the gospel they gave gladly and willingly and up to the limit of their resources; and then they hypothecated their credit and gave beyond their power (2 Cor **8** 3). Even Paul was astonished at their giving. He declares that they gave out of much affliction and deep poverty, that they abounded in their bounty, and that they were rich only in their liberality (2 Cor **8** 2).

Surely these are unusual encomiums. The Philippians must have been a very unusual people. If the depth of one's consecration and the reality of one's religion are to be measured by the extent to which they affect the disposition of one's material possessions, if one measure of Christian love is to be found in Christian giving, then the Philippians may well stand supreme among the saints in the Pauline churches. Paul seems to have loved them most. He loved them enough to allow them to contribute toward his support. Elsewhere he refused any help of this sort, and stedfastly adhered to his plan of self-support while he was preaching the gospel. He made the single exception in the case of the Philippians. He must have been sure of their affection and of their confidence. Four times they gave Paul pecuniary aid. Twice they sent him their contributions just after he had left them and gone on to Thessalonica (**4** 15.16). When Paul had proceeded to Corinth and was in want during his ministry there his heart was gladdened by the visitation of brethren from Philippi, who supplied the measure of his want (2 Cor **11** 8.9). It was not a first enthusiasm, forgotten as soon as the engaging personality of the apostle was removed from their sight. It was not merely a personal attachment that prompted their gifts. They gave to their own dear apostle, but only that he might minister to others as he had ministered to them. He was their living link with the work in the mission field.

Eleven years passed by, and the Philippians heard that Paul was in prison at Rome and again in need of their help. Eleven years are enough to make quite radical changes in a church membership, but there seems to have been no change in the loyalty or the liberality of the Philippian church in that time. The Philippians hastened to send Epaphroditus to Rome with their contributions and their greetings. It was like a bouquet of fresh flowers in the prison cell. Paul writes this ep. to thank them that their thought for him had blossomed afresh at the first opportunity they had had (**4** 10). No wonder that Paul loved them and was proud of them and made their earnestness and sincerity and affection the standard of comparison with the love of others (2 Cor **8** 8).

III. Characteristics of the Epistle.—It is a *letter*. It is not a treatise, as Rom, He, and 1 Jn are. It is not an encyclical full of general observations and exhortations capable of application at any time and anywhere, as the Ep. to the Eph and the Ep. of James and the Epp. of Peter are. It is a simple letter to personal friends. It has no theological discussions and no rigid outline and no formal development. It rambles along just as any real letter would with personal news and personal feelings and outbursts of personal affection between tried friends. It is the most spontaneous and unaffected of the Pauline Epp. It is more epistolary than any of the others addressed to the churches.

1. A Letter

It is a *letter of love*. All of the other epp. have mixed feelings manifest in them. Sometimes a feeling of grief and of indignation is dominant, as in 2 Cor. Sometimes the uppermost desire of Paul in his writing seems to be the establishment of the truth against the assault of its foes, as in Gal and Rom. Always more or less fault is suggested in the recipients of the warnings and the exhortations Paul feels compelled to write to them. In Philippi alone there is no fault to be found. The only suggestion of such a thing is in the reference to the difference of opinion between Euodia and Syntyche, and while Paul thinks this ought to be harmonized, he does not seem to consider it any very serious menace to the peace of the church. Aside from this Paul has nothing but praise for his beloved brethren and prayer that their love may abound yet more and more in knowledge and all discernment (**1** 9). He is full of thankfulness upon all his remembrance of them (**1** 3). He rejoices in the privilege of being offered upon the sacrifice and service of their faith (**2** 17). The church at Philippi may not have been conspicuous in charisms as the church at Corinth was, but it had the fruits of the Spirit in rich measure. Paul seems to think that it needed only to rejoice in its spiritual possessions and to grow in grace and in the mind of Christ. His heart is full of gratitude and love as he writes. He rejoices as he thinks of them. His peace and his hope are triumphant over present affliction and the prospect of persecution and death. If this is his last will and testament to his beloved church, as Holtzmann calls it, he has nothing to bequeath them but his unqualified benediction. Having loved them from the first, he loves them to the end.

2. A Letter of Love

It is a *letter of joy*. It was Bengel who said, *Summa epistolae: gaudeo, gaudete*, "The sum of the ep. is, I rejoice; rejoice ye." Paul was a man whose spirits were undaunted in any circumstances. He might be scourged in one city and stoned in another and imprisoned in a third and left for dead in a fourth, but as long as he retained consciousness and as soon as he regained consciousness he rejoiced. Nothing could dampen his ardor. Nothing could disturb his peace. In Philippi he had been scourged and cast into the inner prison and his feet had been made fast in the stocks, but at midnight he and Silas were singing hymns of praise to God. He is in prison now in Rome, but he is still rejoicing. Some men would have been discouraged in such circumstances. Wherever Paul had gone his preaching had been despised, and he had been persecuted. The Jews had slandered him and harassed him, and so many of his converts had proved to be fickle and false. The years had gone by and the breach between him and his brethren had widened

3. A Letter of Joy

rather than lessened, and at last they had succeeded in getting him into prison and keeping him there for years. Prison life is never pleasant, and it was far less so in that ancient day than it is now.

Paul was such an ardent spirit. It was more difficult for him to be confined than it would be for a more indolent man. He was a world-missionary, a restless cosmopolite ranging up and down through the continents with the message of the Christ. It was like putting an eagle into a cage to put him into prison. Many eagles mope and die in imprisonment. Paul was not moping. He was writing this Ep. to the Phil and saying to them, "The things which happened unto me have fallen out rather unto the progress of the gospel . . . . therein I rejoice, yea, and will rejoice" (**1** 12.18). His enemies were free to do and to say what they pleased, and they were making the most of the opportunity. He could no longer thwart or hinder them. Some men would have broken out into loud lamentations and complaints. Some men would have worried about the conditions and would have become nervous about the outcome of the cause. The faith of even John the Baptist failed in prison. He could not believe that things were going right if he were not there to attend to them. Paul's faith never wavered. His hope never waned. His joy was inexhaustible and perennial. He was never anxious. Did he hear the sentry's step pacing up and down the corridor before his prison door? It reminded him of the peace of God which passeth all understanding, guarding his heart and his thoughts in Christ Jesus (**4** 7), standing sentry there night and day. The keynote of this ep. is "Rejoice in the Lord always: again I will say, Rejoice" (**4** 4).

Paul is old and worn and in prison, but some 20 t in the course of this short letter to the Philippians he uses the words, joy, rejoice, peace, content, and thanksgiving. It is a letter full of love and full of joy.

4. Importance Theologically

It is of great importance theologically. It is one of the paradoxes to which we become almost accustomed in Paul's writings that this simplest of his letters, most epistolary and most personal throughout, should yet contain the fullest and most important putting of the theology of the incarnation and exaltation that came from his pen. He has only a practical end in view. He is exhorting the Philippians to humility, and he says to them, 'Have the mind which was in Christ who emptied himself and then was exalted' (**2** 5–11). It is the most theological passage in the ep. It is one of the most doctrinally important in the NT. It is Paul's final contribution to the solution of the great mystery of the coming of the Saviour and the economy of salvation. It is his last word, at any length, on this subject. He states plainly the fact of the kenosis, the morale of the redemption, the certainty of the exaltation, and the sure hope of the universal adoration in the end. The most vital truths of Christology are here clearly stated and definitely formulated for all time. Jesus was a real man, not grasping at any of the attributes of Deity which would be inconsistent with real and true humanity, but in whole-hearted surrender of sacrifice submitting to all the disabilities and limitations necessary to the incarnate conditions. He was equal with God, but He emptied Himself of the omnipotence and the omniscience and the omnipresence of His pre-incarnate state, and was found in form as a man, a genuine man obedient to God in all His life. He always maintained that attitude toward God which we ought to maintain and which we can maintain in our humanity, in which He was on an equality with us. We ought to have the mind which was in Christ. He humbled Himself and became obedient. He was obedient through life and obedient unto death, yea, even unto the death of the cross. It is a great passage, setting forth profoundest truths in the tersest manner. It is the crowning revelation concerning Jesus in the Pauline Epp. It represents Paul's most mature thought upon this theme. See KENOSIS.

IV. Genuineness of the Epistle.—The genuineness of the ep. is very generally admitted today. It was in the Canon of Marcion. Its name occurs in the list on the Muratorian Fragment. It is found in both the Pesh and the Old Lat VSS. It is mentioned by Polycarp and quoted in the letter of the churches of Lyons and Vienne, in the Ep. of Diognetus, and in the writings of Irenaeus and Clement of Alexandria. Baur made a determined attack upon its authenticity. He declared that it was not doctrinal and polemical like the other Pauline Epp., but that it was full of shallow imitations of these. He said it had no apparent motive and no connected argument and no depth of thought. He questioned some of the historical data and suspected gnostic influence in certain passages. Bleek said of Baur's arguments that they were partly derived from a perverted interpretation of certain passages in the ep.; they partly rested upon arbitrary historical presuppositions; and some of them were really so weak that it was hard to believe that he could have attached any importance to them himself. It is not surprising that few critics have been found willing to follow Baur's leadership at this point. Biederman, Kneucker, Hinsch, Hitzig, Hoekstra, and Holsten may be mentioned among them. The genuineness of the ep. has been defended by Weizsäcker, Weiss, Pfleiderer, Jülicher, Klöpper, Schenkel, Reuss, Hilgenfeld, Harnack, Holtzmann, Mangold, Lipsius, Renan, Godet, Zahn, Davidson, Lightfoot, Farrar, McGiffert, and practically all of the Eng. writers on the subject. Weizsäcker says that the reasons for attributing the ep. to the apostle Paul are "overwhelming." McGiffert declares: "It is simply inconceivable that anyone else would or could have produced in his name a letter in which no doctrinal or ecclesiastical motive can be discovered, and in which the personal element so largely predominates and the character of the man and the apostle is revealed with so great vividness and fidelity. The ep. deserves to rank alongside of Gal, Cor, and Rom as an undoubted product of Paul's pen, and as a coördinate standard by which to test the genuineness of other and less certain writings" (*The Apostolic Age*, 393). This is the practically unanimous conclusion of modern scholarship.

V. Place, Date and Occasion of Writing.—This is one of the prison epp. (see PHILEMON). Paul makes frequent reference to his bonds (**1** 7.13.14.17). He was for 2 years a prisoner in Caesarea (Acts **24** 27). Paulus and others have thought that the ep. was written during this imprisonment; but the references to the praetorian guard and the members of Caesar's household have led most critics to conclude that the Rom imprisonment was the one to which the ep. refers. Philem, Col and Eph were also written during the Rom imprisonment, and these three form a group by themselves. Phil is evidently separated from them by some interval. Was it written earlier or later than they? Bleek, Lightfoot, Sanday, Hort, Beet and others think that the Ep. to the Phil was written first. We prefer, however, to agree with Zahn, Ramsay, Findlay, Shaw, Vincent, Jülicher, Holtzmann, Weiss, Godet, and others, who argue for the writing of Phil toward the close of the Rom imprisonment.

Their reasons are as follows: (1) We know that some considerable time must have elapsed after Paul's arrival at Rome before he could have written this ep.; for the news of his arrival had been carried to Philippi and a contribution to his needs had been raised among his friends there, and Epaphroditus had carried it to Rome. In Rome, Epaphroditus had become seriously sick and the news of this sickness had been carried back to Philippi and the Philippians had sent back a message of sympathy to him. At least four trips between Rome and Philippi are thus indicated, and there are intervals of greater or less length between them. The distance between the two cities was some 700 miles. Communication was easy by the Appian Way and Trajan's Way to Brundusium and across the narrow straits there to the Egnatian Way, which led directly to Philippi. There were many making the trip at all times, but the journey would occupy a month at least, and the four journeys suggested in the ep. were not in direct succession. (2) Paul says that through him Christ had become known throughout the whole praetorian guard (**1** 13). It must have taken some time for this to become possible. (3) The conditions outside the prison, where Christ was being preached, by some in a spirit of love, and by others in a spirit of faction, cannot be located in the earliest months of Paul's sojourn in Rome (**1** 15–17). They must belong to a time when Christianity had developed in the city and parties had been formed in the church. (4) Luke was well known at Philippi. Yet he sends no salutation to the Philippians in this ep. He would surely have done so if he had been with Paul at the time of its writing. He was with the apostle when he wrote to the Colossians, and so was Demas (Col **4** 14). In this ep. Paul promises to send Timothy to Philippi, and says, "I have no man likeminded, who will care truly for your state" (**2** 20). This must mean that Aristarchus, Demas and Luke were all gone. They had all been with him when he wrote the other epp. (5) His condition as a prisoner seems to have changed for the worse. He had enjoyed comparative liberty for the first 2 years of his imprisonment at Rome, living in his own hired house and accessible to all his friends. He had now been removed, possibly to the guardroom of the praetorian cohort. Here he was in more rigorous confinement, in want and alone. (6) Paul writes as if he thought that his case would be decided soon (**2** 23.24). He seems to be facing his final trial. He is not sure of its outcome. He may die a martyr's death, but he expects to be acquitted and then to be at liberty to do further missionary work. This was not his immediate expectation when he wrote the other epp., and therefore they would seem to be earlier than this. (7) The ep. is addressed to all the saints in Philippi, with the bishops and deacons (**1** 1). These official titles do not occur in any earlier epp., but they are found in the Pastoral Epp., which were written still later. Therefore they link the Ep. to the Phil with the later rather than the earlier epp.

From these indications we conclude that this is the last of Paul's Epp. to the churches. Hilgenfeld calls this the swan song of the great apostle. In it Paul has written his last exhortations and warnings, his last hopes and prayers for his converts to the Christian faith. Its date must be somewhere toward the close of the Rom imprisonment, in the year 63 or 64 AD. Epaphroditus had brought the contribution of the Philippians to Paul in Rome. He had plunged into the work there in rather reckless fashion, risking his life and contracting a malarial fever or some other serious sickness; but his life had been spared in answer to the prayers of Paul and his friends. Now Paul sends him back to Philippi, though he knows that he will be very lonely without him; and he sends with him this letter of acknowledgment of their gift, filled with commendation and encouragement, gratitude and love.

VI. Contents of the Epistle.—The ep. is not capable of any logical analysis. Its succession of thought may be represented as follows: (1) Address (**1** 1.2). (2) Thanksgiving and prayer (**1** 3–11): Paul is thankful for their fellowship and confident of their perfection. He longs for them and prays that their love may be wise to discriminate among the most excellent things and that they may be able to choose the very best, until they are filled with the fruits of righteousness, which are through Jesus Christ, unto the glory and the praise of God. (3) Information concerning his own experience (**1** 12–30): (*a*) His evangelism (vs 12–14): Everything had turned out well. Paul is in prison, but he has been indefatigable in his evangelism. He has been chained to a soldier, but that has given him many an opportunity for personal and private and prolonged conversation. When the people have gathered to hear, the guard has listened perforce; and when the crowd was gone, more than once the soldier has seemed curious and interested and they have talked on about the Christ. Paul has told his experience over and over to these men, and his story has been carried through the whole camp. (*b*) His tolerance (vs 15–18): Not only has the gospel found unexpected furtherance inside the prison walls, but through the whole city the brethren have been emboldened by Paul's success to preach Christ, some through faction and envy and strife, and some through love. Paul rejoices that Christ is preached, whether by his enemies or by his friends. He would much prefer to have the gospel presented as he himself preached it, but he was great-souled and broad-minded enough to tolerate differences of opinion and method among brethren in Christ. "In every way, whether in pretence or in truth, Christ is proclaimed; and therein I rejoice, yea, and will rejoice" (**1** 18). This is one of the noblest utterances of one of the greatest of men. Paul is sorry that everybody does not see things just exactly as he does, but he rejoices if they glorify Christ and would not put the least hindrance in their way. (*c*) His readiness for life or death (vs 19–26): Paul says, Give me liberty or give me death; it will be Christ either way. To live is to work for Christ; to die is to be with Christ. "To me to live is Christ, and to die is gain." Here is Paul's soliloquy in the face of possible martyrdom or further missionary labors.

We are reminded of Hamlet's soliloquy in Shakespeare. "To be or not to be"—that is the question with both Hamlet and Paul. Hamlet weighs evils against evils and chooses the lesser evils in sheer cowardice in the end. Paul weighs blessings against blessings, the blessings of life for Christ and the blessings of death with Christ, and chooses the lesser blessings in pure unselfishness in the end. They both choose life, but the motives of their choice are radically different; and Paul lives with rejoicing while Hamlet lives in despair and in shame. The aged apostle would rather die than live, but he would rather live than die before his work was done.

(*d*) His example (vs 27–30): Paul was a Rom citizen and so were they. He tried to live worthy of his citizenship and so must they. He had a still higher ambition, that he and they might live as citizens worthy of the gospel of Christ. He fought as a good soldier. He stood fast in the faith. He was in nothing affrighted by the adversaries. Let them follow his example. They were engaged in the same conflict. To them it had been granted to believe and to suffer in the behalf of Christ. Their faith was not of themselves; it was the gift of God. Their suffering was not self-chosen; it too was a gift of God. (4) Exhortation to follow the example of Christ (**2** 1–18): Let the Philippians have the mind and spirit of Jesus, and Paul will rejoice to pour out his life as a libation upon the sacrifice and service of their faith. (5) Reasons for sending Timothy and Epaphroditus to them (**2** 19–30). (6) Paul's example (**3** 1–21):

(*a*) In the repudiation of all confidence in the flesh (vs 1–7): There are certain dogs and evil workers who belong to the old Jewish persuasion who glory in the flesh. Paul does not. He glories in Christ Jesus and has no confidence in the flesh. He has much reason to be proud of his past, for he would rank high on his record among them. He was of the stock of Israel, the prince with God. He belonged to the race of those who wrestled with God and got the victory. He was of the tribe of Benjamin, the only one of the patriarchs born in the Chosen Land. The first king of Israel had been chosen from this tribe. It alone had been faithful to the house of David at the time of the Great Schism. It held the place of honor in the militant host of the Israelites (Jgs **5** 14; Hos **5** 8). It was a matter of pride to belong to this singly faithful and signally honored tribe. He was a Hebrew of Hebrews, and he belonged to that sect among the Hebrews that was notorious for its scrupulous observance of all the religious ritual, for its patriotism and zeal, for its piety and devotion. Among these Pharisees he was conspicuous for his enthusiasm. He was the chosen instrument of the Sanhedrin to persecute and annihilate the Christian church. No one could find fault with his legal righteousness. He claimed to be blameless as judged by their standard. That was his record. Who has any better one, in pedigree or in piety? All of these things Paul counts but loss for Christ. (*b*) In the maintenance and pursuit of spiritual perfection (vs 8–16): The word "perfect" is used twice in this paragraph. We read: "Not that I have already obtained, or am already made perfect: but I press on." Many of the authorities quote these words as indicative of Paul's humility in disclaiming any present perfection of character while he avows his purpose to strive on toward perfection as long as he lives. Such an interpretation is wholly aside from Paul's thought. He is not talking about perfection in patience and peace and devotion and character. That perfection he claims for himself and for the Philippians in this paragraph toward the close: "Let us therefore, as many as are perfect, be thus minded." The perfection of which he speaks earlier is the perfection possible in the resurrection life of the saints in bliss. He has not attained unto the resurrection from the dead and is not perfect with the perfection of heaven. That is the goal of his endeavor. He presses on to that mark. In the meantime he maintains that perfection of consecration and of faith that results in present Christian perfection of character and which is the only guaranty of that perfection to be revealed to those who attain unto the resurrection from the dead. (*c*) In heavenly citizenship (vs 17–21): Paul walks with his mind on heavenly things. There are those who mind earthly things. They are enemies of the cross, but he has sworn eternal allegiance to the cross. Their end is perdition, while his end is sure salvation. Their god is the belly, while his goal is the perfection of the spirit. Their glory is in their shame, while his glory is in Christ alone. "Brethren, be ye imitators together of me, and mark them that so walk even as ye have us for an ensample." Then "The Lord . . . . shall fashion anew the body of our humiliation," the body of our earthly pilgrimage, the body that so often fails the racer to the goal and cannot keep up with the desire of his spirit, and will conform it "to the body of his glory," the perfect body of those who have attained to the resurrection of the dead. It is not "our vile body" that is to be changed That gives a false sense in modern Eng. The body is not vile, and the Bible nowhere says that it is. It was

Manichean or neo-Platonic heresy that matter was evil and the body vile. Plotinus blushed that he had a body; Jesus never did. The Christian will honor the body as the temple of the Holy Spirit. It was the vehicle of the incarnation, and he honors it for that. Yet the body prepared for Jesus was the body of His humiliation. It bound Him to the earth. It wearied when He was most anxious to work. It failed Him when He most needed strength. Paul says that our bodies are like the body of Jesus of Nazareth now, and they shall be like the body of our risen Lord in due time.

(7) A series of short exhortations (**4** 1–9): This series ends with the command, "The things which ye both learned and received and heard and saw in me, these things do: and the God of peace shall be with you." All these exhortations, then, are based upon his own conduct and experience and example. They had seen the embodiment of these things in him. They were to be imitators of him in their obedience to them. Therefore as we read them we have side-lights thrown upon the character of the apostle who had taught and preached and practised these things.

What do they tell us concerning the apostle Paul? (*a*) His stedfastness and his love for his friends (ver 1): He had a genius for friendship. He bound his friends to him with cords of steel. They were ready to sacrifice anything for him. The reason for that was that he sacrificed everything for them, and that he had such an overflowing love for them that his love begot love in them. They could depend upon him. (*b*) His sympathy with all good men and all good women and his desire that they live in peace (vs 2.3): The true yoke-fellow mentioned here cannot be identified now. He has been variously named by the critics, as Epaphroditus, Barnabas, Luke, Silas, Timothy, Peter, and Christ. There may be a proper name in the phrase, either Genisius or Syzygus. We are wholly ignorant as to whom Paul meant. (*c*) His constant rejoicing in the Lord (ver 4). (*d*) His sweet reasonableness ("moderation," AV, RV "forbearance," ver 5): So Matthew Arnold translates the Gr noun here. Tindale called it courtesy. It is a combination of forbearance and graciousness, of modesty and courtesy, of consideration and esteem such as was characteristic of Christ. Paul had it. There was a sweet reasonableness about him that made his personality a most winning and attractive one. (*e*) His freedom from anxiety (vs 6.7): Paul's fearless confidence was born on the one hand from his assurance that the Lord was near, and on the other from his faith in prayer. It passed all understanding how Paul was kept from all anxiety. It was the power of prayer that did it. It was the peace of God that did it. It was the Lord at hand who did it. (*f*) His habitual high thinking (ver 8): All that was worthy in the ideals of the Gr philosophers Paul made the staple of his thought. He delighted in things true and honorable and just and pure and lovely and of good report. He knew that virtue was in these things and that all praise belonged to them. He had learned that while his mind was filled with these things he lived in serenity and peace.

(8) Thanks for their gift (**4** 10–20). (9) Salutations (**4** 21.22). (10) Benediction (**4** 23). This is not a theological ep. and therefore it is not an esp. Christological one. Yet we count the name of Christ 42 t in this short letter, and the pronouns referring to Him are many more. Paul cannot write anything without writing about Christ. He ends: "The grace of the Lord Jesus Christ be with your spirit." The spirit of Christ and the grace of Christ are in the entire ep.

LITERATURE:—Works on Introduction: Zahn, Weiss, Jülicher, Salmon, Dods, Bacon, Bennett and Adeney; McClymont, *The NT and Its Writers;* Farrar, *The Messages of the Books;* Fraser, *Synoptical Lectures on Books of the Holy Scripture;* Godet, *Studies on the Epp.* Works on the Pauline Epp.: Findlay, Shaw. Comms.: Lightfoot, Vincent, Weiss, Beet, Ellicott, Haupt, Moule. Devotional studies: Moule, Meyer, Jowett, Noble.

DOREMUS ALMY HAYES

PHILISTIA, fi-lis'ti-a: The country is referred to under various designations in the OT: viz. פְּלֶשֶׁת, *pᵉlesheth* (Philistia) (Ps **60** 8 [Heb 10]; **87** 4), אֶרֶץ פְּלִשְׁתִּים, *'ereç pᵉlishtīm,* "land of the Philistines" (Gen **21** 32.34), גְּלִוֹת הַפְּלִשְׁתִּים, *gᵉlōth ha-pᵉlishtīm;* LXX *gē tōn Phulistieím,* "the regions of the Philistines" (Josh **13** 2). The Egyp monuments have *Puirsatha, Pulsath* (Budge), *Peleset* (Breasted) and *Purasati* (*HGHL*), according to the different voweling of the radicals; the Assyr form is *Palastu* or *Pilistu,* which corresponds very closely to the Egyp and the Heb. The extent of the land is indicated in Josh **13** 2 as being from the Shihor, or Brook of Egypt (RV), to the border of Ekron, northward. The eastern border was along the Judaean foothills on the line of Beth-shemesh (1 S **6** 9) with the sea on the W. It was a very small country, from 25 to 30 miles in length and with an average width of about half the length, but it was fertile, being an extension of the plain of Sharon, except that along the coast high sand dunes encroached upon the cultivated tract. It contained many towns and villages, the most important being the five so often mentioned in Scripture: Gaza, Ashdod, Ashkelon, Gath and Ekron. The population must have been large for the territory, which enabled them to contend successfully with the Israelites, notwithstanding the superiority of position in the hills to the advantage of the latter. H. PORTER

PHILISTIM, fi-lis'tim, fil'is-tim (פְּלִשְׁתִּים, *pᵉlish-tīm* [Gen **10** 14 AV]). See PHILISTINES.

PHILISTINES, fi-lis'tinz, fil'is-tīnz, fil'is-tinz (פְּלִשְׁתִּים, *pᵉlishtīm;* **Φυλιστιείμ,** *Phulistieím,* **ἀλλόφυλοι,** *allóphuloi*):

I. OT Notices.—The Philis were an uncircumcised people inhabiting the shore plain between Gezer and Gaza in Southwestern Pal (see PHILISTIA). The name Pal itself (Heb *pᵉlesheth*) refers to their country.

1. Race and Origin

The word means "migrants," and they came from another country. They are noticed 286 t in the OT, and their country 8 t. The question of their race and origin is of great importance as affecting the genuine character and reliability of the Bible notices. In Gen **10** 14 (1 Ch **1** 12) they are reckoned with other tribes in Mizraim (Egypt) as descendants of Ham, and as cousins of the old inhabitants of Babylonia (ver 6). They are said to be a branch of the Casluhim—an unknown people —or, according to LXX, of the Casmanim, which would mean "shavers of the head"—a custom of the Phoenicians (forbidden to Hebrews as a rule), as known from a picture of the time of Thothmes III in the 16th cent. BC. They are also connected with the Caphtorim or people of Caphtor, whence indeed they are said to have come (Jer **47** 4; Am **9** 7). Caphtor was a "shoreland," but its position is doubtful (see Dt **2** 23); the Caphtorim found an earlier race of Avim living in "enclosures" near Gaza, and destroyed them. In the LXX of this passage (and in Am **9** 7) Cappadocia stands for Caphtor (*Kaphtōr*), and other VSS have the same reading. Cappadocia was known to the Assyrians as *kat-pat-uka* (probably an Akkadian term—"land of the Kati"), and the Kati were a people living in Cilicia and Cappadocia, which region had a Sem population side by side with Mongols (see HITTITES) at least as early as the time of Moses. It is very likely therefore that this reading is correct.

2. Religion

According to the OT and monuments alike, the Philis were a Sem people, and they worshipped two Bab gods, Dagon (1 S **5** 2) and Ashtaroth (**31** 10), both of whom were adored very early in Babylonia, both, however, having names of Akkadian and not of Sem origin. In Sem speech Dagon meant "corn," and was so understood in the time of Philo of Gebal, a Gr-Phoen writer who attributes the art of corn-growing to this deity. But the original name was *Da-gān*, and in Akkadian *da* is "the upper part of a man," and *gān* (Turkish *ḳaan*) probably means "a large fish." The new man deity was well known to the Assyrians, and is represented in connection with Sennacherib's worship of Ea, the sea-god, when he embarked on the Pers Gulf. Thus Dagon was probably a title of Ea ("the water spirit"), called by Berosus Oannes (*u-ḫa-na*, "lord of the fish"), and said to have issued from this same gulf. We consequently read that when the statue of Dagon at Ashdod fell (1 S **5** 4), its head and hands were broken off, and only "the great fish" was left. In 1874 the present writer found a seal near Ashdod representing a bearded god (as in Babylonia) with a fish tail (see DAGON). As to Ashtoreth, who was adored in Philistia itself, her name is derived from the Akkadian Istar ("light maker"), a name for the moon-goddess and—later—for the planet Venus (see ASHTORETH).

3. Individual Philistines Mentioned

The Philis had reached Gerar by the time of Abraham, and it was only in the age of the Hyksos rulers of the Delta that Can. tribes could be described as akin, not only to Babylonians, but also to certain tribes in Egypt, a circumstance which favors the antiquity of the ethnic chapter, Gen **10**. We have 9 Phili names in the OT, all of which seem to be Sem, including Abimelech—"Moloch is my father"—(Gen **20** 2–18; **21** 22–32; **26** 8–11) at Gerar, S.E. of Gaza, Ahuzzath ("possession," Gen **26** 26), and Phicol (of doubtful meaning), with Delilah ("delicate," Jgs **16** 4), Goliath (probably the Bab *galu*, "great"), and Saph (2 S **21** 18), perhaps meaning "increase." These two brothers were sons of Raphah ("the tall"); but Ishbi-benob (ver 16), another of the family, perhaps only means "the dweller in Nob" (*Beit Nûba*, N. of Gezer). The king of Gath in David's time was Achish ("the gift" in Bab), who (1 S **27** 2) was the son of Maoch, "the oppressor." According to LXX, Jonathan killed a Phili named Nasib (1 S **13** 3.4, where AV reads "a garrison"). If this is correct the name (meaning "a pillar") would also be Sem.

4. Title of Ruler and Circumcision

Besides these personal names, and those of the cities of Philistia which are all Sem, we have the title given to Phili lords, *ṣeren*, which LXX renders "satrap" and "ruler," and which probably comes from a Sem root meaning "to command." It constantly applies to the rulers of Gaza, Ashdod, Ashkelon, Gath and Ekron, the 5 chief cities of Philistia. The fact that the Philis were uncircumcised does not prove that they were not a Sem people. Herodotus (ii.104) says that the Phoenicians acknowledged that they took this custom from the Egyptians, and the Arabs according to this passage were still uncircumcised, nor is it known that this was a custom of the Babylonians and Assyrians. The LXX translators of the Pent always render the name *Phulistieím*, and this also is found in 8 passages of Josh and Jgs, but in the later books the name is tr[d] as meaning "strangers" throughout, because they were not the first inhabitants of Philistia.

5. History in the OT to Death of Saul

The Philis conquered the "downs" (*g^elīlōth*, Joel **3** 4) near the seacoast, and were so powerful at the time of the Heb conquest that none of their great towns were taken (Josh **13** 3; Jgs **3** 3). By the time of Samson (about 1158 BC) they appear as oppressors of Israel for 40 years (Jgs **13** 1; **15** 20), having encroached from their plains into the *Sh^ephēlāh* (or low hills) of Judah, at the foot of the mountains. Delilah was a Phili woman, living in the valley of Sorek, close to Samson's home. In the last year of Eli (1 S **4** 1) we find the Philis attacking the mountains near Mizpeh, where they captured the ark. Samuel drove them back and placed his monument of victory between Mizpeh and Jeshanah (Shen; see LXX; 1 S **7** 12) on the mountain ridge of Benjamin. He even regained towns in the *Sh^ephēlāh* as far as Ekron and Gath (ver 14); but at the opening of Saul's reign (**10** 5) the Philis had a "garrison" at Gibeah—or a chief named Hasib according to LXX. They raided from this center (**13** 17–23) in all directions, and prevented the Hebrews from arming themselves, till Jonathan drove them from Michmash (**14** 1–47). David's victory (**17** 2) was won in the Valley of Elah E. of Gath, and the pursuit (ver 52) was as far as Ekron. We here read that the Phili champion wore armor of bronze (vs 4–7), his spear head being of iron. They still invaded the *Sh^ephēlāh* after this defeat, robbing the threshing-floors of Keilah (**23** 1) near Adullam at the foot of the Hebron Mountains (see **23** 27; **24** 1). David's band of outlaws gradually increasing from 400 to 600 men (**22** 2; **27** 2), being driven from the Heb lands, accompanied him to Gath, which is usually placed at *Tell es-Ṣâfi*, at the point where the Valley of Elah enters the Phili plain. It appears that Achish, king of Gath, then ruled as far S. as Ziklag (Josh **15** 31; 1 S **27** 6) in the Beersheba plains; but he was not aware of the direction of David's raids at this distance. Achish supposed David to be committed to his cause (**27** 12), but the Phili lords suspected him and his Heb followers (**29** 3) when going up to Jezreel.

6. History Continued to Time of Ahaz

After they had killed Saul, we hear no more of them till the 8th year of David, when, after taking Jerus, he apparently went down to Adullam (2 S **5** 17) and fell upon them in their rear as they advanced on his capital. He then destroyed their supremacy (**8** 1) as far as Gezer (1 Ch **20** 4), and the whole of Philistia was subject to Solomon (1 K **4** 21), though not long after his death they seem to have held the town of Gibbethon (**15** 27; **16** 15) in the hills of Dan. Hezekiah smote the Philis as far as Gaza (2 K **18** 8) before 702 BC, in which year (according to the Taylor cylinder) Sennacherib made Hezekiah deliver up Padii, king of Ekron, who had been carried prisoner to Jerus. The accounts in Ch refer to David's taking Gath (1 Ch **18** 1), which was recovered later, and again taken by Uzziah (2 Ch **26** 6). The Philis sent gifts to Jehoshaphat (**17** 11), but invaded the *Sh^ephēlāh* (**28** 18) in the time of Ahaz.

7. Later Notices

In this age the "lords" of the 5 cities of Philistia are called "kings," both in the Bible and on Assyr monuments. Isaiah (**2** 6) speaks of Phili superstitions, Ezekiel (**25** 15.16) connects them with the Cherethim on the seacoast. They still held Gath in the time of Amos (**6** 2), and Gaza, Ashdod and Ekron in that of Zephaniah (**2** 5), who again mentions the Cherethim with Philis, as inhabitants of Canaan or the "lowlands." The last notice (Zec **9** 6) still speaks of kings in Ashkelon, Gaza, Ekron and Ashdod at a time when the Ionians had become known in Judah (ver 13); but the Philis are unnoticed by Ezra or Nehemiah, unless we suppose that the "speech of Ashdod" (Neh **13** 24) was their old dialect, which appears—like the language of the Canaanites in general in earlier times—to have resembled that of the Babylonians and Assyrians, and to have thus differed—though Sem—from the Hebrews.

Their further history is embraced in that of the various cities to which reference can be made under the articles pertaining to them.

II. Monumental Notices.—These are of great importance, because they confirm the OT statements from a time at least as early as that of Moses, and down to 670 BC.

1. Palestinian Excavations

Recent excavations at Gezer show the early presence of two races at this Phili city, one being Sem, the other probably Egyp. Scarabs as old as the XIIth Dynasty were found, and in the 15th cent. BC Gezer was

Heads of Philistines.

held by Amenophis III. At Lachish also seals of this king and his queen have been found, with a cuneiform letter to Zimridi, who was ruler of the city under the same Pharaoh. At Gaza a temple was built by Amenophis II. The names of places in Philistia noticed yet earlier by Thothmes III are all Sem, including Joppa, Saphir, Gerar, Gezer, etc. In the Am Tab we have also (about 1480 BC) letters from chiefs subject to Amenophis III at Joppa, Ashkelon, Gezer, Lachish and Keilah which show us a Sem population, not only by the language of these letters, but also by the names of the writers. In the case of Ashkelon esp. the Sem rulers are found to have worshipped Dagon; and, though the name

Philistine Wagons.

"Philistine" does not occur, the race was clearly the same found by the Assyrians in 800 BC in the land of *Palastan* beside the Great Sea. These names include *Yamir-Dagān* ("Dagon sees"), *Dagān-takala* ("Dagon is a protection") and *Yadaya* (the "grateful") at Ashkelon; *Bīa* ("asked for"), son of the woman *Gulata*, at Joppa; *Yabnilu* ("God made"), at Lachish, with *Zimridi*—a name found also in Sabaean Arab.; while, at Gezer, *Yapa'a* represents the Bib. Japhia (Josh **10** 3), and *Milkilu* ("Moloch is king") the Heb Malchiel. Others might be added of the same character, but these examples are enough to show that, in the time of Moses and Joshua, the population of Philistia was the same that is noticed in the OT as early as Abraham's age.

When therefore scholars speak of the Philis as being non-Sem—and probably Aryan—invaders of the country, arriving about 1200 BC, they appear not only to contradict the Bible, but also to contradict the monumental evidence of the earlier existence of Sem Dagon-worshippers at Ashkelon. In this later age Rameses III was attacked, in Egypt, by certain northern tribes who came by sea, and also by land, wasting first the country of the Hittites and Amorites. Among them were the Danau, who were probably Gr Danai. They were exterminated in the Delta, and in the subsequent advance of Rameses III to the Euphrates. On a colored picture they are represented as fair people; and two of the tribes were called *Pūrstau* and *Takarri*, whom Chabas supposed to be Pelasgi (since *l* and *r* are not distinguished in Egyp) and Teucrians. These two tribes wear the same peculiar headdress. Brugsch supposed the former to be Philis (*Geog.*, I, 10), but afterward called them *Purosata* (*Hist Egypt*, II, 148). The inscriptions accompanying the picture on the temple walls say that they came from the north, and "their home was in the land of the Pūrstau, the Takarri," etc. There is thus no reason at all to suppose that they were Philis, nor did they ever settle in Philistia.

2. Egyptian Monuments

The Assyr texts agree with those already mentioned in making the inhabitants of Philistia Semitic. Rimmon-nirari, about 800 BC, was the first Assyr conqueror in *Palastau* ("by the great sea"). In 734 and 727 BC, Tiglath-pileser attacked the *Pilisti*, and mentions a king of Ashkelon named *Mitinti* ("my gift"), and his son *Rukufti* whose name resembles that of the Kenite called Rechab in the OT. The name of the king of Gaza was *Ḥanun*, or "merciful." In 711 BC Sargon took Ashdod, and speaks of its king *Azuri*, whose name recalls the Amorite Aziru, and of *Aḥimiti* ("a brother *is* sent"), and the usurper *Yamanu* ("stedfast"), who fled before him. Sennacherib, in 702 BC, gives the names of cities in Philistia (including Eltekeh and Beneberak near Joppa) which are Sem. He notices *Ṣidḳa* (Zadok) of Ashkelon, and also *Sarludari* ("the Lord be praised"), son of Rukubti in the same city, with *Mitinti* of Ashdod, and *Padii* ("redeeming") of Ekron, while *Ṣil-b'el* ("Baal is a protection") was king of Gaza. In 679 BC Esarhaddon speaks of *Ṣilli-b'el* ("Baal is my protection") of Gaza, with *Mitinti* of Ashkelon, *Ika-samsu* ("the sun-god is manifest") of Ekron, and *Abi-milki* of Ashdod, who bore the ancient Phili name Abimelech. In 670 BC, when Assur-bani-pal set up many tributary kings in Egypt, we find again the name *Sarludari* applied to a ruler of Pelusium, who may have been a Philistine. It is thus abundantly clear that the monumental notices all agree with the OT as to the names and nationality of the Philis, and as to their worship of Baal and Dagon; the conjecture that they were Aryan foreigners, arriving in 1200 BC, is not based on any statement of the monuments, but merely rests on a guess which Brugsch subsequently abandoned. It resembles many other supposed discrepancies between Bib. and contemporary records due to the mistakes of modern commentators.

3. Assyrian Texts

III. The Cretan Theory.—This strange theory, which is apparently of Byzantine origin, would make the Philis come from Crete. It still finds supporters, though it does not rest on any Bib. or monumental evidence. The Cherethim (Ezk **25** 16; Zeph **2** 5) were a Sem people named with the Philis in Canaan. The LXX renders the word *Krētēs* or *Krētoi;* and, about 1770 AD, Michaëlis (*Spicil.*, I, 292–308) argued that this meant "Cretans," and that the Philis therefore came from Caphtor, which must be Crete. The passages, however, refer to Philistia and not to any island, and the LXX translators, as

1. Cherethim and Kretes

we have seen, placed Caphtor in Cappadocia. The Cherethi—in the singular—is mentioned (1 S **30** 14) as a people of Philistia (ver 16), near Ziklag, and their name probably survives at the present town called *Keratîyeh* in the Phili plain.

Yet, many theories are founded on this old idea about the Cherethites. Some suppose that Tacitus confused the Jews with the Philis as having come from Crete; but what he actually says (*Hist.* v.11) is that "the Jews ran away from Crete," and "the inhabitants are named *Idaci* [from Mt. Ida], which, with a barbarous augment, becomes the name of the *Judaei*." This absurd derivation shows at least that Tacitus did not mean the Philis. Stephen of Byzantium said that the god Marna at Gaza was like the Cretan Jove. Probably he had seen the huge statue of a seated Jove found near Gaza, and now at Constantinople, but this is late Gr work, and the name Marna ("our lord") is Sem. Stephen also thought that Minois—the port of Gaza—was named from the Cretan Minos, but it is an Arab. word *Mîneh*, for "harbor," still applying to the same place.

No critical student is likely to prefer these later speculations to our present monumental information, even without reference to the contradiction of the Bible. Yet these blunders have given rise to the supposition that Caphtor is to be identified with a region known to the Egyptians as *Keft*, with inhabitants called *Kefau*. The latter are represented in a tomb of the XVIIIth Dynasty near Thebes. They are youths of brown color, with long black hair, and the same type is found in a Cypriote figure. They are connected with islanders of the "green sea," who may have lived in Arvad or in Cyprus; but there is no evidence in any written statement that they were Cretans, though a figure at Knossos in Crete somewhat resembles them. There are many indications that this figure—painted on the wall of the later palace—is not older than about 500 BC, and the Sidonians had colonies in Crete, where also pottery is found just like that marked by a Phoen inscription in Cyprus. The *Kefau* youths bring vases as presents, and these—in all their details—are exactly the same as those represented in another picture of the time of Thothmes III, the bearers in this case being *Ḥarri* from North Syria, represented with black beards and Sem features. Moreover, on the bilingual inscription called the Decree of Canopus (238 BC), the *Keft* region is said to be "Phoenicia," and the Gr translator naturally knew what was meant by his Egyp colleague. *Keft* in fact is a Sem word for "palm," occurring in Heb (Isa **9** 14; **19** 15), and thus applicable to the "palm"-land, Phoenicia. Thus, even if *Keft* were related to Caphtor, the evidence would place the Phili home on the Phoen shores, and not in Crete. There is indeed no evidence that any European race settled near the coasts of Pal before about 680 BC, when Esarhaddon speaks of Gr kings in Cyprus. The Cretan theory of Michaëlis was a literary conjecture, which has been disproved by the results of exploration in Asia.

2. Caphtor and Keft

IV. David's Guards.—Another strange theory, equally old, represents David as being surrounded with foreign mercenaries—Philis and Carians—as Rameses II employed mercenaries called *Shairtanau* from Asia Minor. The suggestion that the Cherethites were of this race is scarcely worth notice, since the Heb *kāph* is never represented by *sh* in Egyp. David's band of Heb exiles, 400 in number, followed him to Gath where 200 Gittites joined him (2 S **15** 18). In later times his army consisted of "the Cherethi" (*kᵉrēthī*, in sing.) and "the Pelethi" (*pᵉlēthī*), commanded by the Heb leader Benaiah, son of Jehoiada (2 S **8** 18; **15** 18; **20** 7; 1 K **1** 38.44), together with the Gittites under Ittai of Gath. These guards are never said to have been Philis, but "the Cherethi" is supposed to mean one of the Cherethim tribe, and "the Pelethi" to be another name for the Philistine. As regards the Gittites, the fact that they came from Gath does not prove that they were Philis, any more than was David himself because he came back from this city. David calls Ittai an "enemy" and an "exile," but it is probable that he was the same hero, so named (2 S **23** 29), who was the son of Ribai from Gibeah of Benjamin. He had himself not long joined David, being no doubt in exile at Gath, and his tribe at first opposed David, taking the side of their tribesman Saul. Even when Ittai's men joined the Cherethi and Pelethi against Absalom, they were naturally suspected; for David still had enemies (2 S **15** 5–13) among Benjamites of Saul's house. It is also surely impossible to suppose that David would have left the ark in charge of a Phili; and Obed-edom the Gittite (2 S **6** 10) was a Levite, according to a later account (1 Ch **15** 18), bearing a Heb name, meaning perhaps "servant of men," or "humble worshipper." It seems equally unlikely that, in later times, a pious priest like Jehoiada (2 K **11** 4) would have admitted foreign mercenaries into the temple. In this passage they are called *kārī*, as also in 2 S **20** 23, where LXX has *Cherethi*. The suggestion of Wellhausen that they were Carians does not seem probable, as Carians had not even reached Egypt before about 600 BC.

1. The "Cherethi" and the "Pelethi" Not Mercenaries

The real explanation of these various words for soldiers seems simple; and David—being a very popular king—is not likely to have needed foreign mercenaries; while the Philis, whom he had so repeatedly smitten, were very unlikely to have formed trusty guards. The word "Cherethi" (*kᵉrēthī*) means a "smiter" or a "destroyer," and "Pelethi" (*pᵉlēthī*) means "a swift one" or "pursuer." In the time of Joash the temple-guards are called *kārī* (2 K **11** 4.19, Carites), which LXX treats as either sing. or pl., and *rāçīm* or "runners" (see 1 S **22** 17; 1 K **14** 27.28; 2 K **10** 25), these two bodies perhaps answering to the Cherethi and Pelethi of David's time; for *kārī* means "stabber." The term *rāçīm*, or "runners," is however of general application, since Jehu also had troops so called (2 K **10** 25). Evidently we have here two classes of troops—as among the Romans—the heavier regiment of "destroyers," or "stabbers," being armed with swords, daggers or spears; while the "swift ones" or "runners" pursued the defeated foe. Thus in Egypt we find, yet earlier, the ax-man supported by the bow-man in regular regiments; and in Assyria the spear-man with heavy shields defending the bow-man. We have also a picture of the time of Tiglath-pileser II representing an Assyr soldier on a camel. The Pelethi or "pursuers" may have been "runners" on foot, but perhaps more probably mounted on camels, or on horses like the later Assyrians; for in the time of Solomon (1 K **4** 28) horses and riding camels were in use—the former for chariots. It is clear that David's band, leaving the vicinity of Jezreel (1 S **29** 1; **30** 1), could not have reached Ziklag "on the third day" (a distance of 120 miles) on foot; so that the camel corps must have existed even before the death of Saul.

2. Meaning of These Terms

These considerations seem to make it evident that David's guards were native Hebrews, who had been with him as exiles and outlaws at Adullam and Gath, and that the Cherethi or "destroyer" only accidentally had a title like that of the Phili tribe of "destroyers" or Cherethim, who were not Cretans, it would seem, any more than the "stabbers" were Carians.

3. Native Hebrews

4. Review The general result of our inquiry is, that all monumental notices of the Philis agree with the OT statements, which make them to be a Sem people who had already migrated to Philistia by the time of Abraham, while the supposed discrepancies are caused by the mistakes made by a commentator of the 18th cent., and by archaeologists of later times.

LITERATURE—Paton, *Early History of Syria and Pal;* Smith, *HGHL;* Budge, *History of Egypt;* Breasted, *History of Egypt;* Rawlinson, *Ancient Monarchies;* Herodotus with most histories of Egypt, Babylon, and Assyria for the period from the 13th cent. BC to the time of Alexander. Nordtzij, *The Philistines;* Macalister, *Philistines.*

C. R. CONDER

PHILISTINES, LORDS OF THE. See PHILISTIA.

PHILISTINES, SEA OF THE (Ex **23** 31). See MEDITERRANEAN SEA.

PHILO, fī′lō, **JUDÆUS,** jōō-dē′us:

1. His Life
2. Importance of the Period
3. The Task of Philo
4. Changes and New Problems
5. Three Subjects of Inquiry
   (1) The Conception of God
   (2) God's Relation to the World
   (3) Doctrine of Man
6. Philo's Works

LITERATURE

1. His Life Born probably in the first decade of Augustus Caesar, who became emperor in 27 BC. He died possibly in the last years of Claudius (41–54 AD), more likely in the early years of Nero (54–65 AD). We have no exact information about either date. He was a native of Alexandria, Egypt. His relatives were wealthy and prominent, probably sacerdotal, Jews. He received the best Jewish education, and was trained also in gentile learning—grammar, rhetoric, philosophy, geometry, poetry, music. Enjoying ample means, he was enabled to devote his career to scholarship. The Alexandrian Jews wielded great influence in the contemporary Rom empire, and the prominence of Philo's family is attested by the fact that his brother, Alexander Lysimachus, was Alabarch of Alexandria. The single date in Philo's life which we know accurately is connected with their leadership. In the winter of 39–40 AD, he was spokesman of the deputation sent to Rome to protest against imposition of emperor-worship upon fellow-citizens of his faith. The mission failed, Philo, with his two colleagues, meeting rebuff, even insult. It was little likely that Caligula would heed grievances which included specifically dissent from worship of himself. Philo records his distaste for political activity, and, so far as we know, the Rom incident excepted, he devoted himself principally to letters. As a young man probably, he had undertaken a journey to Jerus, almost in the nature of a pilgrimage to the ancient shrine of his religion. He paid a second visit to Rome possibly after 50 AD, at all events, in the reign of Claudius. For the rest, our knowledge of his life is scanty and, sometimes, legendary.

2. Importance of the Period The period covered by his career coincides with one of the most momentous epochs in history. For it witnesses, not only the foundation of the Rom imperial system, but also the beginning of the end of ancient classical civilization in its dominant ideas, and the plantation of Christianity. Preëminently an era of transition, it was marked by significant displacements in culture, the effects of which continue to sway mankind even yet. Minor phenomena aside, three principal movements characterized the time: the Pagan reaction, or reversion to forms of religion that had sufficed the peoples of the Rom empire hitherto—this manifested itself strongly with Augustus, and entered its decline perhaps with the death of Plutarch (c 120 AD); the appearance of Christianity; and what is known as Syncretism, or interfusion between the conceptions of different races, esp. in religion, philosophy and morals—a circumstance which affected the fortunes of Christianity deeply, found its chief exponent in Philo, and maintained itself for several centuries in the theosophical systems of the Gnostics and neo-Platonists. Thus, to understand Philo, and to realize his importance, it is essential to remember the internal spirit of his age. The "universalism" of the Rom empire has been so named because, within the political framework, various peoples and divergent civilizations commingled and came eventually to share something of a common spirit, even of a common language. Philo's prominence as a figure in the world of thought, and as an authority for the general culture of NT times, is out of all proportion to the fragmentary information available about his external career. Contemporary currents, subtle as they were, perplexing as they still remain, met and fused in his person. Hence his value as an index to the temperament of the period cannot well be overrated.

3. The Task of Philo A Jew by nature and nurture, an oriental mystic by accident of residence, a Gr humanist by higher education and professional study, an ally of the Rom governing classes, familiar with their intellectual perspective, Philo is at once rich in suggestion and blurred in outline. Moreover, he addressed himself to two tasks, difficult to weld into a flawless unity. On the one hand, he wrote for educated men in Gr-Rom society, attempting to explain, often to justify, his racial religion before them. The ancient state religion having fallen upon inanition, he enjoyed unusual opportunity to point the merits of the Jewish faith as the "desire of all nations," the panacea of which the need was everywhere felt. On the other hand, he had to confront his orthodox coreligionists, with their separatist traditions and their contempt for paganism in all its works. He tried to persuade them that, after all, Gr thought was not inimical to their cherished doctrines, but, on the contrary, involved similar, almost identical, principles. He thus represented an eclectic standpoint, one in which Gr philosophy blended with historical and dogmatic deductions from the Jewish Scriptures. The result was Philo's peculiar type of theosophy—we cannot call it a system. Taking the OT for text, he applied the "allegorical" method, with curious consequences. He taught that the Scriptures contain two meanings: a "lower" meaning, obvious in the literal statements of the text; and a "higher," or hidden meaning, perceptible to the "initiate" alone. In this way he found it possible to reconcile Gr intellectualism with Jewish belief. Greek thought exhibits the "hidden" meaning; it turns out to be the elucidation of the "allegory" which runs through the OT like a vein of gold. Moses, and the rest, are not merely historical figures, the subjects of such and such vicissitudes, but representative types of reason, righteousness, the virtues, and so forth. The tendency to fusion of this kind was no new thing. It is traceable for some three centuries before Philo, who may be said to complete the process. It had been familiar to the rabbis, and to the Hellenistic philosophers, particularly the Stoics, who applied this method to the Gr poetical myths. Philo reduces it to an expert art, and uses it as an instrument to dissipate all difficulties. He believed himself to be thoroughly true to the OT. But, thanks to his method, he rendered it malleable, and could thus adjust its interpretation to what he considered to be the intellectual necessities of his generation. Nay more, he felt that, when at his best in this process, he became a vehicle of Divine possession. He says, "Through the influence of Divine inspiration I have become excited profoundly . . . . then I have been conscious of a richness of interpretation, an enjoyment of light, a most penetrating sight, a most manifest energy in all that was to be done." Again, "I am irradiated with the light of wisdom," and, "all intellect is a Divine inspiration." Little wonder, then, that we have a strange mixture of philosophy and religion, of rationalism and piety, of clear Gr intellectualism with hazy oriental mysticism. Hence, too, the philosophy of Philo is subordinate to his explanation of the Scriptures, and compromise, rather than logical thinking, marks his leading positions.

4. Changes and New Problems

After the death of Cicero (43 BC) a change, long preparing, asserted itself in ancient thought. Mixture of national, or racial, characteristics was consummated, and thoughtful men, irrespective of race-origin, became persons to each other. A reorganization of standards of ethical judgment was thus rendered inevitable, and Judaism came to interfuse more freely with Gr philosophy as one consequence. While it is true that "reason" preserved its traditional supremacy as *the* means to solve all problems, the nature of the chief quest underwent transformation. The old association of man with Nature gave way to a dualism or opposition between the world-order and another existence lying behind it as its originator or sustainer. The system of Nature having disappointed expectation, thinkers asked how they could escape it, and assure themselves of definite relations with the Divine Being. They sought the desiderated connection within their own souls, but as a distant ideal. This was the problem that confronted Philo, who attacked it from the Jewish side. Now Judaism, like Gr thought, had also experienced a change of heart. Jeh had been the subject of an idealizing process, and tended, like the Stoic deity, to lose specific relation with the world and man. Accordingly, a new religious question was bringing the philosophy and the faith into closer contact. Could they join forces? Philo's consequent embarrassment rooted, not simply in this fresh problem, but in the difficulties inseparable from the adjustment of his available methods and materials. For, while the Jewish Messiah had passed over into the Gr *Logos*, the two systems preserved their separation in no small measure, Philo being the most conspicuous mediator. He was familiar with the mystic, transcendent concept of Deity extracted, thanks to long misinterpretation, from Plato's cosmogonic dialogue, *Timaeus*. Here God was elevated above the world. His conception of the presence, or immanence, of the Deity in the world came from the Stoics. The Jewish religion gave him the doctrine of a righteous (pure) Deity, whose moral inwardness made relations with men possible. Moreover, contemporary angelology and demonology enabled him to devise a scheme whereby the pure Deity could be linked with the gross world, notwithstanding its ineradicable evil. Little wonder, then, that he compassed an amalgamation only, and this in consonance with the theosophical drift of the age. Nevertheless, he counteracted the deistic tendencies of rabbinical speculation by reference to Hellenistic pantheism, and, at the same time, counteracted this pantheism by the inward moralism of his national faith. The logical symmetry of the Gr mind was reinforced by Hebraic religious intuition. The consequence was a ferment rather than a system, but a ferment that cast up the clamant problem in unmistakable fashion. The crux was this: Man must surmount his own fragmentary experience and rise to an absolute Being; but, its absoluteness notwithstanding, this Being must be brought into direct contact with the finite. Philo was unable to reconcile the two demands, because he could not rise above them; but the effort after reconciliation controls all his thought. As a result, he concentrated upon three main subjects of inquiry: (1) the conception of God; (2) the manner of God's relation to the world; (3) human nature.

5. Three Subjects of Inquiry

(1) *Philo's doctrine of God*, like that of the neo-Platonic school, which he heralded, is thoroughly dualistic. No doubt, it is determined largely by certain human analogies. For example, God's existence is necessary for the control of the world, just in the same way as man's mind must exist to furnish the principle of all human action; and, as matter is not self-determined, a principle, analogous to mind, is demanded, to be its first cause. Further, as the permanent soul remains unchanged throughout the vicissitudes of a human life, so, behind the ceaseless play of phenomena, there must reside a self-existent Being. Nevertheless, the human analogy never extends to God in His actual Being. No human traits can attach to the Deity. Language may indicate such parallelism, nay the Scriptures are full of instances, but we must view them as concessions to mortal weakness. These accommodations eliminated, it becomes evident that man can never know God positively. Any adjective used to describe Him can do no more than point the contrast between His relationless Being and the dependence of finite things. *That* God is, Philo is fully persuaded; *what* He is, no man can ever tell. He is one and immutable, simple and immeasurable and eternal, just as man is *not*. "For he is unchangeable, requiring nothing else at all, so that all things belong to Him, but He, speaking strictly, belongs to nothing." This doctrine of the transcendence of Deity was an essential postulate of Philonic thought. For, seeing that He expels all the imperfections of the world, God is precisely in that condition of Being for which the whole creation then yearned. In a word, the dualism, so far from being a bar to salvation, was rather a condition without which the problem of salvation could neither be stated nor solved. Men stood in necessary relation to this Being, but, as yet, He stood in no relation whatever to them. Yet, men must return to God, but He abides so remote, in the realm of pure contemplation and completion, that He cannot approach them. Philo's familiarity with logical Gr thought debarred him from surmounting the difficulty after the manner of Jewish religion. An otiose reference to "God's choice," as distinct from His nature, could not suffice a mind trained in Hellenic methods. The question therefore was, How could mediation be effected?

(2) *God's relation to the world.*—At this point Philo's thought assumes a phase of great interest to readers of the NT. God, being above created things, is incomprehensible and immaterial. Accordingly, He cannot be connected with the world directly. Therefore He created it and sustains it by *intermediate* powers. These agencies were suggested to Philo by the Platonic Ideas. But he personalized them more or less and, as a characteristic addition, included them in the Logos. He substituted the term "Logos" for the Platonic term "Idea" on the basis of the Scripture phrase, "Word of God." The conception was influenced further by his Hellenistic psychological notion, that a word is a "shadow" of a deed. Accordingly, the Logos is the "shadow of God"—God being the "deed" whereby the "shadow" is cast. As a direct issue, the Logos presents two aspects. On the one side

it is internal and indwelling; on the other, it is external and mediating. The scope of this distinction is indicated very well by the epithets which Philo applies to each aspect respectively. The internal Logos is the "Firstborn," the "Second God," the "Mediator," the "Ransom," the "Image of God," "Member of the Trinity," "High Priest." The external Logos "abides in man," is the "Prophet," "Shepherd," "Ambassador," "Artist," "Elder," "Interpreter," "Shadow of God." The former represents Philo's conception of the unity of the Logos with God, the latter his provision for the manifestation of the Logos in created things. He thus tries to preserve the transcendence of God equally with His immanence. No doubt, in previous times, the mysteriousness of the Divine nature had impressed itself upon men with at least as much force as now. But with one of two consequences. Either the particular finites and the Deity were mixed in inextricable confusion, as by oriental pantheism, or God was banished from the world, as by the extreme developments within Gr dualism. Philo attempted to combine the two tendencies, and was able consequently to face the obvious contradiction between the idea of an absolute Being and the cloudy conception of a multiplicity of phenomena in which this Being ought to be present somehow, despite transcendence. He demands a God who, in His exaltation, shall be a worthy Deity; this is the Jew in him. But he also demands a definite relation between this God and His creation; this is the Greek and, in part, the Oriental, in him. Thanks to the former, he could not be satisfied with mere naturalism; thanks to the latter, no fable or picture could suffice. A real mediator was required, who would link the world and its heart's desire. But Philo could not surmount one difficulty peculiar to contemporary thought. He was unable to connect God directly with creation *and* preserve His purity unsullied. Hence the obscurity which surrounds his conception of the Logos, likewise his vacillation with respect to its personality. So we find the different intellectual forces which he inherited playing upon him—now one, now another. Sometimes the Platonic theory of Ideas dominates him; sometimes he leans to Stoicism, with its immanent world-reason; and here he even seems to foreshadow the doctrine of the Trinity; again, the ramifications of rabbinical lore cause him to bestow upon the Logos a priestly function or an atoning office. No single aspect achieves supremacy, although on the whole mystical Platonism may be said to predominate. Thus, "The world of Ideas has its place in the Divine Logos, just as the plan of a city is in the soul of the master-builder." Accordingly, God's thought may take its place in the world by being impressed upon things; yet, on account of its subjective nature, it must be apprehended subjectively, that is, by one who is capable of entering this sphere. The Logos thus seems to exist entirely in the same realm as Deity; thus it can mediate between Him and creation only if an element proper to Deity be discernible in mundane things. In other words, the Logos mediates between God and the world, but partakes of the Divine nature only. This, in any case, is the inner logic of Philo's view. It accounts for creation, but has no power to persuade man to overpass the limitations placed upon him by his bodily prison. Thus the question of the personality of the Logos is never cleared. In so far as Philo needs Logos to connect God with the world, he inclines to a doctrine of personality. In so far as he makes it the principle of all activities within the world, he inclines away from personality. In short, we have a "world-soul." And, as a consequence, there is an inherent tendency to reduce all finite being to illusion. Indeed, one might term the Logos a reply in some sort to Aristotle's question—which of the Platonic Ideas could connect the other Ideas with sensible things? Salvation is conceived as wrought out, not by a person, but by an abstract essence flowing from Deity, an essence that found due expression rather in the cosmic order than in a person. While, therefore, Philo thinks in a cultural perspective akin to that characteristic of the author of the Fourth Gospel, two vast differences sway his doctrine. On the one hand, it is speculative, not ethically personal. On the other hand, it fails completely to determine the nature of his mediator in itself, vacillating in a manner which shows how vague and fluid the conception really was.

(3) *Doctrine of man.*—This appears further in the doctrine of man. Following current interpretations of Plato, Philo makes man partake in the rational nature of God, but denies that he embodies the highest species of reason. That is, the ideal man and the man known to us in common experience are distinguished. The former is rational as God is. The latter is partly rational, partly irrational. The body vitiates the original angelic purity of the soul and, similarly, reason is alloyed. And yet, although the higher nature becomes more and more debased as the years lapse, a seed of Divinity is present, ready to burst forth. Thus man must crush the flesh and its desires. At this point we note the effect of the Stoic ideal of imperturbability. When he has attained this apathy, man can enjoy the life of contemplation. This, in its turn, culminates in ecstasy, when the human soul attains sudden and momentary union with the Divine. For a "fair moment" man escapes the thraldom of sense. Yet the doctrine remains intellectual even here. He "who escapes from his own *mind* flies to the *mind* of the universe, confessing that all the things of the human mind are vain and unreal, and attributing everything to God." Philo's anthropology therefore ends in contempt for this life, which is in no wise worth while, and in a counsel of perfection available only for a select *élite*. Accordingly, the conclusion of the whole matter is, that he never saw how the Divine and the human can be united, although he stated the factors of the problem with great clearness, and felt profoundly the urgency of a solution. His gospel was for the children of culture. He saw the eternal in the temporal, and hoped that good might lurk in evil. But he never understood that "love for a Divine Person" might be so diffused throughout a human soul as to render evil and unreality the means to the attainment of good and to the revelation of truth. The salvation he contemplated was *from* self, not *in* self. Hence, as he asserts himself, harmony with God "is an incomprehensible mystery to the multitude, and is to be imparted to the instructed only." Nor is this wonderful. For a God who is the reasonable "form" of the world; a "matter" which begins as an indistinguishable mass and ends as a "second principle"; and objects of sense rendered apparent by the operation of many curious intermediate forces, ranging from "angel-words" to the human soul, constitute a combination beyond the reach of any save the "initiate." More practicable is Philo's conception of the moral life—as a warfare of the soul against passion, pleasure and sensuality. Yet, even this contest is hopeless unless it be waged with the equipment of the "philosopher athlete." Escape from the "prison-house" of flesh would seem to be consequent only upon profound knowledge.

The probability is that Philo's works were written previous to his Rom embassy. They show how he tried to apply Gr philosophical conceptions to Jewish beliefs, history, and usages exclusively. The voluminous remains which have come down to us appear to belong to three commentaries on the Pent and the Mosaic Law.

6. Philo's Works

In all likelihood, they are portions of Philo's popular presentation, written for the instruction and information of educated Hellenistic circles rather than for the trained "initiate." The treatises most important for Philo's religio-philosophical views are as follows: *On the Creation of the World; On the Allegories of the Sacred Laws; On the Unchangeableness of God; On the Confusion of Languages; On the Migration of Abraham; On the Meeting for the Sake of Receiving Instruction; On the Life of the Wise Man Made Perfect by Instruction; The Unwritten Law; Abraham; On Special Laws; On Rewards and Punishments; That Every Man Who Is Virtuous Is Also Free; Concerning the World;* and the *Fragments*. Some 8 works attributed to Philo are in dispute. Most conspicuous of these is *Concerning the Contemplative Life*, with its ascetic view of morality, and its description of the ideal community of the Therapeutae.

LITERATURE.—E. Schürer, *A History of the Jewish People in the Time of Jesus Christ*, div II, vol III, pp. 321 f (Edinburgh, 1886); E. Schürer, "Philo" in *EB;* James Drummond, *Philo Judaeus, or, The Jewish-Alexandrian Philosophy in Its Development and Completion* (2 vols, London, 1888); R. M. Wenley, *Socrates and Christ: a Study in the Philosophy of Religion*, chs vii, viii (Edinburgh, 1889); H. Ewald, *The History of Israel*, VII, 194 f (London, 1885); A. Hausrath, *A History of NT Times*, div II, vol I, chs iv–vi (London, 1885); H. Graetz, *History of the Jews from the Earliest Times to the Present Day*, II, 183 f, 206 f (London, 1891); E. Caird, *The Evolution of Theology in the Gr Philosophers*, II, lects xx–xxi, xxvii (Glasgow, 1904); art. "Philo" in *Jew Enc;* Ernest F. Scott, *The Fourth Gospel, Its Purpose and Theology*, 54 f, 145 f (2d ed, Edinburgh, 1908); F. C. Conybeare, *Philo: About the Contemplative Life* (Oxford, 1895). An Eng. tr has been made by C. D. Yonge in the Bohn Library (London, G. Bell & Sons). The text cited usually is that of T. Mangey. The best modern text is that of Cohn and Wendland.

R. M. WENLEY

PHILOLOGUS, fi-lol'ō-gus (Φιλόλογος, *Philólogos*, "fond of learning," "learned"): The name of a Rom Christian to whom St. Paul sent greetings (Rom **16** 15). His name is coupled with that of Julia, who was probably his wife or sister. Philologus and those united with him in this salutation formed by themselves one of the "house churches" or groups in the Christian community. The name is found in inscriptions connected with the imperial household, with reference to one of which Bishop Lightfoot has the following note: "It has been supposed that the name Philologus was given by the master to the freedman mentioned in this inscription, as being appropriate to his office [Friedländer I, 89, 160]. . . . . If so, some light is thrown on the probable occupation of the Philologus of St. Paul" (*Phil*, 177, n. 1).

S. F. HUNTER

PHILOMETOR, fil-o-mē'tor. See PTOLEMY VI.

PHILOSOPHY, fi-los'ō-fi (φιλοσοφία, *philosophía*):

1. Definition and Scope
   (1) Intuitive Philosophy
   (2) Speculative Philosophy
2. Greek Philosophy
3. Philosophy in OT and Judaism
   (1) Of Nature
   (2) Of History
   (3) Post-exilic
   (4) Alexandrian
4. Philosophy in the NT
   (1) The Teaching of Jesus Christ
   (2) Apostolic Teaching
   (3) Attitude of NT Writers toward Philosophy

LITERATURE

Only found in Col **2** 8; lit. the love and pursuit of wisdom and knowledge. In its technical sense,

1. Definition and Scope

the term is now used for the conscious endeavor of thought, by speculative process, to interpret the whole of human experience, as a consistent and systematic unity, which would be the ultimate truth of all that may be known. The term is also used, in a wider sense, of all interpretations of experience, or parts of experience, however obtained, whether by revelation, intuition or unconscious speculation. No hard-and-fast line can be drawn between the two kinds of philosophy. Some of the ruling conceptions of speculation, such as God, spirit, order, causation, true and false, good and evil, were not discovered by reason, but given in experience.

(1) *Intuitive philosophy* is universal. The human mind has always and everywhere furnished itself with some kind of explanation of the universe. From the lowest animism and fetichism up to the higher religions, ideas are found which served men as explanations of those features of experience which attracted their attention. They were often regarded as given by vision, intuition or some other method of revelation. In the higher religions, the mind reflected upon these ideas, and elaborated them into systems of thought that bear some resemblance to the speculative theories of western thought. In China, both Confucianism and Taoism developed theories of human life and destiny that bear some resemblance to Stoicism. The religions of Assyria and Babylonia enshrined in their legends theories of the world and of man and his institutions. In India, men's belief in the Nature-gods gradually developed into pantheistic Brahmanism, which reduced the multiplicity of experience into one ultimate being, Brahma. But the desire for moral salvation and the sense of pain and evil produced a reaction, and led to the pessimistic and nihilistic philosophy of Buddhism. In Persia, the moral consciousness awoke earlier, and the attempt to systematize the multiplicity of polytheism issued in the dualistic philosophy of later Zoroastrianism. The whole realm of being was divided into two kingdoms, created and ruled by two lords: Ahura Mazda, the creator of light and life, law, order and goodness, and Añrō Mainyuš, the author of darkness, evil and death. Each was surrounded by a court of spiritual beings kindred to himself, his messengers and agents in the world (see PERSIAN RELIGION [ANCIENT]). Of all these religious philosophies, only those of Assyria and Babylonia, and of Persia, are likely to have come into any contact with Bib. thought. The former have some affinity with the accounts of creation and the flood in Gen; and the influence of the latter may be traced in the dualism and angelology and demonology of later Judaism, and again in the gnostic systems that grew up in the Christian church, and through both channels it was perpetuated, as a dualistic influence, in the lower strata of Christian thought down through the Middle Ages.

(2) *Speculative philosophy* belongs mainly to western thought. It arose in Greece about the beginning of the 6th cent. BC. It began with the problem of the general nature of being, or *ontology*. But it was soon forced to consider the conditions of knowing anything at all, or to *epistemology*. These two studies constitute *metaphysics*, a term often used as synonymous with philosophy in the stricter sense. Speculation about ideal truth again led to inquiries as to the ultimate nature of the kindred ideas of the good (*ethics*) and the beautiful (*aesthetics*). And as these ideas were related to society as well as to the individual, the Greeks developed theories of the ideal organization of society on the basis of the true, the good and the beautiful, or *politics* and *pedagogics*. The only branch of speculation to which the Greeks made no appreciable contribution was the *philosophy of religion*, which is a modern development.

The progress of philosophy in history divides itself naturally into three main periods: (*a*) *ancient*, from the 6th cent. BC to the 3d cent. AD, when it is almost exclusively Gr, with some practical adaptations of Gr thought by Rom writers; (*b*) *mediaeval*, from the 3d to the 16th cent., where some of the ruling conceptions of Gr thought were utilized for the systematization of Christian dogma, but speculation was mainly confined within the limits of ecclesiastical orthodoxy; there were, however, some independent Arabian and Jewish speculations; (*c*) *modern*, from the 16th cent. to the present time, in which thought becomes free again to speculate upon all the problems presented by experience, though it only realized its liberty fully in the hands of Locke, Hume and Kant.

2. Greek Philosophy

Gr philosophy was the only speculative system that could have had any influence upon Bib. thought. Its main development was contemporaneous with the later OT writers, but the two peoples were in every way so remote from one another that no interchange of ideas was probable.

During the last two centuries BC, Gr thought spread so widely that it came to dominate the cultured thought of the world into which Christianity entered, and it would have been strange if no trace of its influence were found in the NT. In the first stage of its development, from Thales to Socrates, it was concerned almost entirely with attempts to explain the nature of reality by reducing the phenomenal world into some one of its elements. Socrates changed its center of gravity, and definitely raised the problems of morality and knowledge to the position of first importance. His principles were developed by Plato into a complex and many-sided system which, more than any other, has influenced all subsequent thought. He united ultimate reality and the highest good into one supreme principle or idea which he called the Good, and also God. It was the essence, archetype and origin of all wisdom, goodness and beauty. It communicated itself as intermediary archetypal ideas to produce all individual things. So that the formative principles of all existence were moral and spiritual. But it had to make all things out of preëxisting matter, which is essentially evil, and which therefore was refractory and hostile to the Good. That is why it did not make a perfect world. Plato's system was therefore rent by an irreconcilable dualism of mind and body, spirit and matter, good and evil. And his mediating ideas could not bridge the gulf, because they belonged only to the side of the ideal. Aristotle was Plato's disciple, and he started from Plato's idealistic presuppositions, but endeavored to transcend his dualism. He thus applied himself to a closer and more accurate study of actual experience, and added much to the knowledge of the physical world. He organized and classified the methods and contents of knowledge and created the science of logic, which in the Christian Middle Ages became the chief instrument of the great systematic theologians of the church. He tried to bring Plato's ideas "down from heaven," and to represent them as the creative and formative principles within the world, which he conceived as a system of development, rising by spiritual gradations from the lower to the higher forms, and culminating in God, who is the uncaused cause of all things. But underneath all the forms still remained matter as an antithetical element, and Aristotle rather concealed than solved the dualism of Plato.

Meanwhile, the moral principles of Socrates were being developed with a more directly ethical interest, by the Cyrenaics and **Epicureans,** into a system of Hedonism, and, by the Cynics and **Stoics,** into a doctrine of intuitive right and duty, resting inconsistently upon a pantheistic and materialistic view of the universe. But the spiritual and ethical elements in Stoicism became only second to Platonism in the preparation of the Gr world for Christianity. During the last two and a half centuries BC, Gr philosophy showed signs of rapid decline. On the one hand, Pyrrho and his school propounded a thoroughgoing skepticism which denied the possibility of all knowledge whatsoever. On the other hand, the older schools, no longer served by creative minds, tended to merge their ideas into a common eclecticism which its teachers reduced into an empty and formal dogmatism. The most fruitful and fateful product of Gr thought in this period was its amalgamation with Jewish and oriental ideas in the great cosmopolitan centers of the Gr world. There are evidences that this process was going on in the cities of Asia, Syria and Egypt, but the only extensive account of it remaining is found in the works of Philo, the Jewish philosopher of Alexandria (see PHILO JUDÆUS). He tried to graft Plato's idealism upon Heb monotheism.

He starts with Plato's two principles, pure being or God, and preëxisting matter. In his endeavor to bridge the gulf between them, he interposed between God and the world the powers of God, goodness and justice; and to gather these into a final unity, he created his conception of the Logos of God. In the formation of this conception, he merged together the Platonic idea of the good, the Stoic world-reason, and a number of Jewish ideas, the glory, the word, the name, of God, the heavenly man and the great high priest, and personified the whole as the one mediator between God and the world. Christian thought laid hold of this idea, and employed it as its master-category for the interpretation of the person of Christ (see LOGOS).

3. In the OT and in Judaism

There is no speculative philosophy in the OT nor any certain trace of its influence. Its writers and actors never set themselves to pursue knowledge in the abstract and for its own sake. They always wrought for moral purposes. But moral activity proceeds on the intellectual presuppositions and interpretations of the experiences within which it acts. Hence we find in the OT accounts of the origin and course of nature, a philosophy of history and its institutions, and interpretations of men's moral and religious experiences. They all center in God, issue from His sovereign will, and express the realization of His purpose of righteousness in the world (see GOD).

(1) All nature originated in God's creative act (Gen **2**) or word (Gen **1**). In later literature the whole course and order of Nature, its beauty and bounty, as well as its wonders and terrors, are represented as the acts of God's will (Isa **40–45**; Pss **8 19, 29, 50, 65, 68, 104,** etc). But His action in Nature is always subordinated to His moral ends.

(2) Similarly, the course and events of the history of Israel and her neighbors are the acts of Jeh's will (Am **1**; **2**; Isa **41** 2; **43** 3; **45** 9.10.14). In the historical books of S and K, and still more of Ch, all the events of history are represented as the acts of God's moral government. In a more general way, the whole of history is set forth as a series of covenants that God, of His free grace, made with man (see COVENANT). The Noachic covenant fixed the order of Nature. The covenant with Abraham, Isaac and Jacob accounted for the origin and choice of Israel. The covenants with Moses and Aaron established the Law and the priesthood, and that with David, the kingship. And the hope of the future lies in the new covenant (Jer **31** 31–35). God's covenants were all acts of His sovereign and gracious will.

(3) In post-exilic times, new experiences, and perhaps new intellectual influences, drove the Jews to probe deeper into the problem of existence. They adhered to the cardinal principle of Heb thought, that God's sovereign will, working out His purpose of righteousness, was the first cause of all things (see RIGHTEOUSNESS). But they found it difficult to coördinate this belief with their other ideas, in two ways. Ethical monotheism tended to become an abstract deism which removed God altogether out of the world. And the catastrophes that befell the nation, in the exile and after, raised the problem of suffering and evil over against God's goodness and righteousness. Therefore in the Wisdom lit. we find some conscious speculation on these subjects (see WISDOM).

(*a*) The Book of Job discusses the problem of evil, and repudiates the idea that life and history are the process of God's rewards and punishments. (*b*) Eccl comes to the conclusion that all phenomenal experience is vanity. Yet its ultimate philosophy is not pessimistic, for it finds an abiding reality and hope in the fear of God and in the moral life (**12** 13.14). The same type of thought appears in Ecclus. Both books have been attributed to the circle of the **Sadducees.** Some would find in them traces of the influence of Epicureanism. (*c*) In Prov a more optimistic side prevails. Wisdom is gathered up into a conception or personification which is at once God's friend, His agent in creation, His vicegerent in the world, and man's instructress and guide (ch **8**). (*d*) The teaching of the **Pharisees** esp. reveals the tendency to dualism or deism in later Judaism; they interposed between God and the world various agents of mediation, the law, the word, the name, the glory of God and a host of angels, good and bad. They also fostered a new hope of the future, under the double form of the Messianic kingdom, and of resurrection and immortality. How far these tendencies were due to the influence of Pers dualism cannot here be considered. (*e*) **Essenism** represents another effort to get from the world to God by a crude kind of mysticism and asceticism, combined with an extensive angelology.

(4) Among the Hellenistic Jews in Alexandria, Aristobulus, the authors of Wisd and 4 Macc, and preëminently Philo, all deal with the two chief problems of Judaism, dualism and evil. But they approach them under the direct influence of Gr thought. The Heb idea of wisdom was merged into the Gr conception of the Logos, and so it becomes the mediator of God's thought and activity in the world.

4. In the NT

Philosophy appears in the NT as intuitive, speculative and eclectic. (1) Jesus Christ came to fulfil the law and the prophets, and, out of His filial consciousness of God, He propounded answers to the practical demands of His time. His doctrine of God the Father was a philosophy of Nature and life which transcended all dualism. In the kingdom of heaven, the good would ultimately prevail over the evil. The law of love expressed the ideal of conduct for man as individual, and in his relation to society and to God, the supreme and ultimate reality. This teaching was given in the form of revelation, without any trace of speculation.

(2) The apostolic writings built upon the teaching and person of Jesus Christ. Their ruling ideas are the doctrines which He taught and embodied. In Paul and John, they are realized as mystical experiences which are expressed in doctrines of universal love. But we may also discover in the apostolic writings at least three strands of speculative philosophy. (*a*) Paul employed arguments from natural theology, similar to those of the Stoics (Acts **14** 15–17; **17** 22–31; Rom **1** 19 ff), which involved the principles of the cosmological and teleological arguments. (*b*) John employs the Philonic term "Logos" to interpret the person of Christ in His universal relation to God, man and the world; and the main elements of Philo's scheme are clearly present in his doctrine, though here it is no abstract conception standing between God and man, but a living person uniting both (Jn **1** 1–18). Although the term "Logos" is not mentioned, in this sense, in Paul or He, the Philonic conception has been employed by both writers (Rom **5** 8; **8** 29; 1 Cor **15** 24.25; 2 Cor **5** 18.19; Phil **2** 6; Col **1** 15–17; **2** 9.10; He **1** 1–3.5.6). Paul also expresses his conception of Christ as the manifestation of God under the category of wisdom (1 Cor **1** 20; **2** 7; Eph **1** 8; Col **2** 3). (*c*) Both in Paul and He appear original speculations designed to interpret individual experience and human history as they culminate in Christ. Paul's interpretation consists of a series of parallel antitheses, flesh and spirit, sin and righteousness, law and grace, works and faith, Adam and Christ. But the author of He adopts the Platonic view that the world of history and phenomena is but the shadow or suggestion of the spiritual and eternal reality which lies behind it, and which partially expresses itself through it.

(3) In the one place in which the term philosophy appears in the NT (Col **2** 8), it seems to mean "subtle dialectics and profitless speculation . . . . combined with a mystic cosmogony and angelology" (Lightfoot, ad loc.), the first beginnings of Gnosticism in the Christian church. Paul warns his readers against it, as he also does the Corinthians against the "wisdom" of the Greeks (1 Cor **1** 19 ff; **2** 5.6). A similar tendency may be in view in the warning to Timothy against false doctrines (1 Tim **1** 4; **4** 3; 2 Tim **1** 14.16 ff). But with the true spirit of philosophy, as the pursuit of truth, and the endeavor to express more fully and clearly the nature of reality, the spirit and work of the NT writers were in complete accord.

LITERATURE.—Intros to philosophy by Külpe, Paulsen, Höffding, Watson and Mackenzie. Hists of Gr philosophy by Ritter and Preller, Burnet, and Zeller, and of general philosophy by Erdmann, Ueberweg, Windelband and Rogers; E. Caird, *The Evolution of Theology in the Gr Philosophies;* Hists of the Jews by Schürer, Graetz and Kent; OT Theologies by Schultz and Davidson; NT Theologies by Beyschlag and Weinel; Philo's works and treatises thereon by Dähne, Gfrörer and Drummond; Harnack, *What Is Christianity?* Bigg, *The Christian Platonists of Alexandria;* Lightfoot, *Col.*

T. REES

PHINEES, fin'ē-es (**Φινεές,** *Phineés,* B [Swete], **Φεινεές,** *Pheineés* [1 Esd **8** 2]):

(1) Phinehas, son of Eleazar, son of Aaron (1 Esd **5** 5; **8** 2.29; 2 Esd **1** 2; 1 Macc **2** 26; Sir **45** 23).

(2) The father of Achias and son of Heli (Eli), a descendant of (1), and one of Ezra's progenitors (2 Esd **1** 2); but this link is not found in Ezra's genealogy (1 Esd **8** 1 f), nor in Ezr **7** 1 ff; 1 Ch **6,** and its insertion in 2 Esd **1** 2 is a mistake, since Ezra's descent was from Eleazar, while this Phinees (Phinehas) was a descendant of Ithamar, the youngest son of Aaron.

(3) A Levite, the father of Eleazar (1 Esd **8** 63) = "Phinehas" of Ezr **8** 33. But it is just possible that the well-known Eleazar (1) is referred to here, and so not another and different Phinees.

(4) AV=RV "Phinoe" (1 Esd **5** 31).

S. ANGUS

PHINEHAS, fin'ē-as, -az, fin'ē-has, -haz (פִּינְחָס, *pīnᵉḥāṣ,* "mouth of brass"):

(1) Son of Eleazar and grandson of Aaron (Ex **6** 25; cf 1 Ch **6** 4; Ezr **7** 5, where he is seen to be an ancestor of Ezra). He took a leading part in cleansing Israel from whoredom at Shittim. He there punished the brazen licentiousness of Zimri, prince of Simeon, by slaying both him and the Midianite woman he had brought into camp (Nu **25** 6–18). This incident is referred to in Ps **106** 30.31 (cf 1 Macc **2** 26.54; Sir **45** 23.24). As priest he accompanied the expedition sent by Moses against Midian (Nu **31** 6). He was chief of the Korahite Levites (1 Ch **9** 20), and succeeded his father as high priest. While he was in that office the civil war with Benjamin occurred, and it was he who delivered the oracle's decision to fight Benjamin (Jgs **20** 28 ff). His faithful services secured to his house the succession of the priesthood (Nu **25** 11–13). He was sent as ambassador to inquire into the reported idolatry of Reuben, Gad and part of Manasseh (Josh **22** 13 ff.30–32). According to LXX he was buried with his father in Ephraim on the hill Gibeah Phinehas (see Josh **24** 33). His character was marked with strong moral indignation and fine integrity.

(2) The younger son of Eli (1 S **1** 3; 2 Esd **1** 2, "Phinees"). See HOPNI AND PHINEHAS.

(3) Father of a priest named Eleazar (Ezr **8** 33; cf ver 2; 1 Esd **8** 63, "Phinees"). HENRY WALLACE

PHINOE, fin'ō-ē (**Φινόε,** *Phinóe;* AV **Phinees**): Name of one of the families of temple-servants who went up from Babylon with Zerubbabel (1 Esd **5** 31) = "Paseah" of Ezr **2** 49; Neh **7** 51.

PHLEGON, flē'gon, fleg'on (**Φλέγων,** *Phlégōn*): The name of a Rom Christian to whom Paul sent greetings (Rom **16** 14). Of him nothing is known.

PHOEBE, fē'bē (**Φοίβη,** *Phoíbē;* AV **Phebe**): Described by St. Paul as (1) "our sister," (2) "who is a servant of the church that is at Cenchreae," (3) "a helper of many, and of mine own self" (Rom **16** 1.2). (1) "Our [Christian] sister": Paul calls the believing husband and wife "the brother or the sister" (1 Cor **7** 15), and also asks, "Have we no right to lead about a wife that is a sister?" (1 Cor **9** 5 m). The church was a family. (2) The Gr word tr[d] "servant" is *diákonos.* "Servant" is vague, and "deaconess" is too technical. In the later church there was an order of deaconesses for special work among women, owing to the peculiar circumstances of oriental life, but we have no reason to believe there was such an order at this early period. If Phoebe had voluntarily devoted herself "to minister unto the saints" by means of charity and hospitality, she would be called *diakonos.* (3) The Gr word *prostátis* tr[d] "helper" is better "patroness." The masc. is "the title of a citizen in Athens who took charge of the interests of clients and persons without civic rights" (Denney). Many of the early Christian communities had the appearance of clients under a patron, and probably the community of Cenchreae met in the house of Phoebe. She also devoted her influence and means to the assistance of "brethren" landing at that port. Paul was among those whom she benefited. Gifford thinks some special occasion is meant, and that Paul refers to this in Acts **18** 18. The vow "seems to point to a deliverance from danger or sickness" in which Phoebe may have attended on him.

It is generally assumed that this letter was taken to Rome by Phoebe, these verses introducing her to the Christian community. In commending her, Paul asks that the Rom Christians "receive her in the Lord," i.e. give her a Christian welcome, and that they "assist her in whatsoever matter she may have need" of them (Rom **16** 1.2).

S. F. HUNTER

PHOENICE, fē-nī'sē (**Φοῖνιξ,** *Phoínix*). See PHOENIX.

PHOENICIA, fē-nish'i-a, **PHOENICIANS,** fē-nish'anz:

1. The Land
2. The Colonies
3. The People
4. Arts and Manufactures
5. Commerce and Trade
6. Language and Culture
7. Religion
8. History

LITERATURE

The term "Phoenicia" is Gr (Φοινίκη, *Phoiníkē,* "land of dates, or palm trees," from *phoínix,* "the date-palm"). It occurs in the Bible only in Acts (**11** 19; **15** 3; **21** 2), the land being generally designated as the "coast" or "borders of Tyre and Sidon" (Mt **15** 21; Mk **7** 24.31; Lk **6** 17). In the OT we find it included in the land belonging to the Canaanites or to Sidon (Gen **10** 19; **49** 13; Josh **11** 8; 1 K **17** 9). The limits of P. were indefinite also. It is sometimes used by classic writers as including the coast line from Mt. Cassius on the N. to Gaza or beyond on the S., a distance of some 380 miles, or about 400 miles if we include the sweep of indentations and bays and the outstretching of the promontories. But in the stricter sense, it did not extend beyond Gabala (modern *Jebleh*) on the N., and Mt. Carmel on the S., or some 150 miles. The name was probably first applied to the region opposite Cyprus, from Gabala to Aradus and Marathus, where the date-palm was observed, and then, as it was found in still greater abundance farther S., it was applied to that region also. The palm tree is common on the coins of both Aradus and Tyre, and it still grows on the coast, though not in great abundance. The width of the land also was indefinite, not extending inland beyond the crest of the two ranges of mountains, the Bargylus (Nusairi Mountains) and the Lebanon, which run parallel to the coast and leave but little space between them and the sea for the greater portion of their length. It is doubtful whether the Phoenicians occupied the mountain tracts, but they must have dominated them on the western slopes, since they derived from them timber for their ships and temples. The width of the country probably did not exceed 25 or 30 miles at the most, and in many places it was much less, a very small territory, in fact, but one that played a distinguished rôle in ancient times.

1. The Land

There are few harbors on the whole coast, none in the modern sense, since what few bays and inlets there are afford but slight shelter to modern ships, but those of the ancients found sufficient protection in a number of places, esp. by means of artificial harbors, and the facility with which they could be drawn out upon the sandy beach in winter when navigation was suspended. The promontories are few and do not project far into the sea, such as *Theu-prosopon* S. of Tripolis, *Ras Beirût* and the broad projection S. of Tyre including *Ras el-'Abyadh* and *Ras en-Nakûra* and *Ras el-Musheirifeh* (see LADDER OF TYRE). The promontory of Carmel is rather more marked than the others, and forms quite an extensive bay, which extends to Acre. The promontory rises to a height of 500 ft. or more near the sea and to more than double that elevation in its course to the S.E.

Mt. Lebanon, which forms the background of P. for about 100 miles, is a most striking feature of the landscape. It rises to a height of 10,200 ft. in the highest point, E. of Tripolis, and to 8,500 in *Jebel Sunnin,* E. of Beirût, and the average elevation is from 5,000 to 6,000 ft. It is rent by deep gorges where the numerous streams have cut their way to the sea, furnishing most varied and picturesque scenery. It was originally heavily wooded with cedar, oak, and pine trees, which are still found in considerable numbers, but by far the larger part of the mountain has been denuded of forests, and the slopes have been extensively terraced for the cultivation of vines and fruit trees and the mulberry for silk culture. The plains along the coast are not extensive, but generally very fertile and bear abundant crops of wheat, barley and other cereals, where not given to the culture of the mulberry, orange, lemon, fig, apricot and other small fruits. In its greatest extent P. included the broad plain of Sharon and that of Acre, between Carmel and that city, and a portion of the region watered by the Kishon, but the plains of P., strictly speaking, are much more restricted. They are: the plain of Tyre, long but narrow, extending from *Ras el-'Abyadh* to *Sarepta;* the plain of Sidon extending from *Sarepta* to the Bostrenus (*Nahr el-'Auly*); the plain of Beirût (*Berytus*) between the extensive sand dunes along the shore and the rocky cape on the W. and the foot of Lebanon, 10 or 12 miles long but only one or two wide, containing one of the largest olive groves in Syria; the very small plain of Tripolis, including that city and its port; and, the most extensive of all, the plain of Marathus, extending from Arka to Aradus or even beyond, including the river Eleutherus (*Nahr el-Kebîr*). These plains furnished only a portion of the food needed by the inhabitants who were more or less dependent on their neighbors for it (1 K **5** 11; Acts **12** 20).

The rivers of P. are comparatively short and small; the Litany rises in the *Buka',* between Lebanon and Anti-Lebanon, and finds its way in a deep and narrow gorge between Lebanon and Mt. Hermon to the S., and finally turns westward and reaches the sea a few miles N. of Tyre, where it is called the *Ḳasimîyeh*. About 12 miles N. of Beirût is the Dog River (Lycus), a very short stream but noted for the famous pass at its mouth, where Egyp, Assyr and Bab kings engraved their monuments; and a few miles S. of *Jebail* (Gebal) is the Adonis (*Nahr Ibrahîm*), which comes down from *'Afḳa* (Apheca=Aphek, Josh **13** 4), noted for the rites of Venus and Adonis (see TAMMUZ); and the Eleutherus, already mentioned, which runs through the valley between Bargylus and Lebanon and provides the pass between these two mountains into the interior. The other rivers are very short, but furnish a perennial water-supply to the coast dwellers.

The products of the land, as well as the climate, are very varied on account of the difference in elevation of the tracts suitable to culture, ranging in temperature from the semi-tropical to Alpine. How far the ancients cultivated the mountain sides we do not know, but they certainly profited largely by the forests of cedar and pine, esp. the former, which was the most valuable for shipbuilding and architectural purposes, and was highly prized, not only by the Phoenicians, but by Egyptians, Assyrians and Babylonians, who transported it to their own countries for buildings. The mineral products are few, and the Phoenicians depended on their colonies and other lands for what they needed of these.

2. The Colonies

The narrowness of the land and the difficulty of expansion on account of the lofty mountain ranges and the hostility of the tribes of the interior led the Phoenicians to turn seaward for an outlet to their increasing population. We have only one instance of their attempt to colonize the Hinterland, and that ended in disaster (Jgs **18**). Hiram, king of Tyre, was not pleased with Solomon's gift of 20 cities in Galilee, probably not desiring to assume responsibility for their defence. The people early became mariners, and the dominion of the sea was more inviting to them, and they found room for expansion in the islands and on the coast of the Mediterranean, where they established colonies far and wide. Their first over-sea possessions were in Cyprus, the coasts of which they occupied in the 2d millennium BC, probably about 1500. On the southern coast they planted various colonies, such as Citium (Larnaca), Amathus, Curium and Paphos, and on the eastern, Salamis, Ammachosta and Soli, and, in the interior, Idalium and Golgi, besides other less important settlements. The evidences of the Phoen occupation of Cyprus are numerous. The southern portion of Asia Minor also attracted them at an early date, esp. the rich plains of Cilicia, and Tarsus became the most important of their colonies there. Its coins bear Phoen types and legends, among which Baal is conspicuous. Other points along the coast were occupied, and the island of Rhodes as well as certain ports on the south coast of Crete, and most of the islands of the Aegean. Their presence in Attica is vouched for by inscriptions, and legend connects Thebes with them in the person of Cadmus, the reputed son of Agenor, king of P. But it is doubtful whether they really colonized the mainland of Greece. They were more attracted by the lands farther to the W.

The greatest of their colonies was in Africa. They occupied Utica first, probably in the 12th cent. BC, and others in the same region until in the 9th cent. Great Carthage was founded, which was destined to become the richest and most powerful of all and the dreaded rival of Rome. All are familiar with the story of Elisa, or Dido, the reputed Tyrian queen who led her followers to the place and founded the city. The story is perhaps legendary, but that Carthage was a colony of Tyre there is no reason to doubt. Other colonists occupied portions of Sicily, such as Motya, Erix, Soli and Panormus (Palermo). They also crossed over to Sardinia and the Balearic Isles, and planted colonies on the south coast of Spain and the northwestern coast of Africa, within and beyond the straits of Gibraltar. Of their settlements in Spain Gades (Cades) and Tartessus were the most noted, the latter being probably the Tarshish of Scripture (1 K **10** 22). Malaca (Malaga) and Abdera, within the straits, were likewise important settlements, and there were others of less note.

The colonial enterprise of the Phoenicians was remarkable for the age, and was only surpassed in ancient times by the Greeks who came later, the former being the pioneers. The energy and daring of the Phoenicians in pushing out into unknown seas, with the imperfect means at their disposal, is evidence of the enterprise of this people. Their chief object, however, was trade. Their colonies were mostly factories for the exchange of their manufactured articles for the products of the lands they visited. They cared little about building up new states or for extending their civilization and molding barbarous tribes and imparting to them their culture. In this they were far surpassed by the Greeks whose colonies profoundly modified the peoples and lands with which they came in contact.

3. The People

The Phoenicians were the same as the Canaanites, under which name they are known in the OT, as well as Sidonians (Gen **10** 19; Nu **13** 29). They were of Sem stock, if we may judge by their language and characteristics. It is true that in Gen **10** 6 Canaan is called a son of Ham, but it is also true that the language of Canaan is identified with Heb (Isa **19** 18). If the early Phoenicians spoke a different tongue, they entirely lost it before their contact with the Hebrews. Their writings and all the references to them in ancient authorities show that their language was purely Sem. As to their origin and the time of their migration to the Syrian coast, it is more difficult to determine. Herodotus (i.2; vii.89) says that they lived at first on the Erythraean Sea, which is identified with the Pers Gulf, and modern authorities have not found evidence to refute the statement. It is quite certain that they were not the aborigines of the country, and must have come in with some of the various migrations from the E., which we know, from Egyp and Bab monuments, occurred in the 3d, perhaps in the 4th, millennium BC. Semites are found in Syria as early as the IVth Egyp Dynasty, about 3000 BC, and we may fairly conjecture that the Canaanites were in possession of the seacoast as early as 2500 BC. It is possible that they were among the Hyksos invaders of Egypt (Paton, *Syria and Pal*, 67).

That the Phoenicians took to the sea at a very early date and became the most skilful mariners of the ancient world is certain. Their enterprise in this direction is attested by classic writers, and the references to it in the OT are numerous. This was coupled with great industry and skill in the manufacture of the various articles which furnished the materials of their extended commerce. They exhibited a boldness and audacity in braving the perils of the sea in their little ships, which, for the age, demands our admiration. They were the first who dared to push out of sight of land in their voyages and sail beyond the Pillars of Hercules into the ocean. But in their commercial dealings they were often unscrupulous, and their greed of gain often led them to take unfair advantage of the barbarous races with whom they came in contact. The purchase of the land on which the citadel of Carthage was built may illustrate the opinion of the ancients regarding them, but we ought to remember that trickery and deceit are charged against them by their enemies, who alone have handed down accounts of them. The Heb prophets speak of their pride and vanity (Ezk **28** 17), and violence (ver 16), and Amos hints at a traffic in captives taken in war, but whether of Hebrews or not is not clear (Am **1** 9). Slaves were among the articles of merchandise in which they traded (Ezk **27** 13; Joel **3** 6), but this could hardly be charged against them as a great sin when slavery was universal. The chief reason for their being denounced by the prophets was their corrupt practices in worship and the baleful influence of the Baal and Astarte cult introduced by them into Israel through Ahab's marriage with Jezebel (1 K **16** 31–33). This evil influence was felt even after the captivity when the rites of the Phoen Tammuz were practised in Jerus (Ezk **8** 14). But the earlier relations of the Phoenicians with Israel in the days of David and Solomon were friendly and mutually beneficial. On the whole the judgment of history assigns to this people a high position for their enterprise and skill in carrying on their trade, and in being the pioneers of civilization in many of the Mediterranean lands, esp. by their introduction of alphabetical writing, which was by far the most valuable of all their contributions to the culture of the ancient world.

4. Arts and Manufactures

(1) The Phoenicians were celebrated for their textile fabrics of silk, wool, linen and cotton. The materials of the last three were obtained from Syria and Egypt, but the silk came from the Far East through Persia. The dyeing of these fabrics was by a process invented by the Phoenicians, and the luster and permanence of color were unequaled by the ancients and made the **Tyrian purple** famous throughout the world. The finer qualities of it were so precious that only the very wealthy, or kings and princes, could obtain it, and it became at last a synonym of royalty. This dye was obtained from the shell-fish which was abundant in the Mediterranean, esp. along the Phoen coast, species of the *Murex* and the *Buccinum.* The mode of manufacture is not definitely known and was probably kept a secret by the Phoenicians. At least they had a monopoly of the business.

(2) **Glass** was another well-known product of the country, and although not invented by the Phoenicians as formerly supposed, it was made in large quantities and exported to all countries about the sea. See GLASS.

(3) **Pottery** was also an article of manufacture and export, and some of the examples of their work found in Cyprus show considerable skill in the art of decoration as well as making. In this, however, they were far surpassed by the Greeks.

(4) **Bronze** was a specialty of the Phoenicians, and they were for centuries the leading producers, since they controlled the sources of supply of the copper and tin used in its manufacture. The remains of their bronze manufactures are numerous, such as arms for offence and defence, knives, toilet articles, axes, sickles, cups, paterae, and various other household utensils. Articles for artistic purposes are not of high value, although the pillars named Jachin and Boaz, the molten sea, the bases, lavers and other articles cast by Hiram of Tyre for the temple of Solomon must have exhibited considerable artistic merit. Their bronze was of good quality and was tempered so as to serve well for edged tools. The composition was about 9 parts copper to 1 of tin. They seem also to have made **iron** (2 Ch **2** 14), and some specimens have come down to us, but we cannot judge from their scarcity as to the extent of their manufactures in this metal, since most of the articles have perished by corrosion.

Aesthetic art among the Phoenicians was of low grade, as it was among the Semites generally, and where we find some works of moderate merit they undoubtedly manifest the influence of Gr art, such as those found in Cyprus by General Di Cesnola and others. In Phoenicia proper very little of artistic value has come to light that can be ascribed to native artists. In sculpture the style is stiff and conventional, much of it exceedingly rude, and lacks expression. The animal forms are generally grotesque, often absurd, reminding one of children's attempts at plastic art. The anthropoid sarcophagi discovered at Sidon were modeled after the Egyp, and the magnificent ones, of different design, from the same place, now in the Museum of Constantinople, were certainly the work of Gr artists of the age of Alexander the Great.

The architecture of the Phoenicians was characterized by massiveness, rather than elegance. The substructures of some of their temples and castles are cyclopean, like those of the temple at Jerus (1 K **7** 10), and other examples are found at Sidon, Gebal, Marathus and other places in Phoenicia itself. Their work seems lacking in symmetry and grace, showing a want of aesthetic taste.

5. Commerce and Trade

Trade was the very life of Phoenicia. The contracted limits of the land forbade any extensive agriculture, and the people were forced to get their living by other means. They applied themselves to industrial arts, and this led them to seek the means for distributing their wares. Trade was essential to them, and they sought outlets for it by sea and land. Their position was esp. favorable for commerce. In the very center of the ancient world, with the great rich and populous nations of antiquity at their back and on either side, they faced the young, vigorous and growing nations of the West, and they served them all as carriers and producers. Their caravans threaded all the well-beaten routes of the East, the deserts of Arabia and the mountain defiles of Armenia and Asia Minor, and their ships pushed boldly out to sea and explored the Mediterranean and the Euxine and did not hesitate to brave the unknown dangers of the Atlantic and perhaps even penetrated to the Baltic, emulating the mariners of a later day in their zeal for discovery and search for new avenues of trade. Could we find a detailed account of their voyages and discoveries, it would be a most interesting document, but we have little except what others have written about them, which, however, gives us a pretty fair idea of the extent of their commercial enterprise. The prophet Ezekiel has given us a remarkable catalogue of the wares of Tyre and of the countries with which she traded (Ezk **27**). There we have mention of nearly all the regions of Western Asia, Egypt, Greece and the islands, and Spain, indicated by the names of races, tribes and countries. The materials of their traffic include the most important known to the ancient world, the products of agriculture, such as wool, linen, oil, balm, spices, frankincense, wine, corn, etc; of metals, such as gold, silver, copper (brass), tin, iron, lead, etc; precious stones and the articles of manufacture, the "multitude of handiworks," which they were so skilful in producing. They traded in animals also, horses, mules, lambs, rams and goats, and, what is less to their credit, in the persons of men (ver 13). The range of their trade was much wider than is indicated by Ezekiel. We know they reached the Scilly Isles in Britain, and probably the Baltic, whither they went for amber, though this might have been brought overland to the Adriatic and received into their ships there. They passed along the western coast of Africa as far as Cape Non, and perhaps farther, for Herodotus tells us that Pharaoh-necoh dispatched a crew of Phoen sailors to circumnavigate Africa, which they accomplished in 3 years.

We know that they had a fleet in the Red Sea sailing from Elath or Ezion-geber (1 K **9** 26.27), and it is quite possible that they were allowed by some of the kings of Egypt to avail themselves of ports on the other branch of the Red Sea. They must have visited the eastern shore of Africa and perhaps struck across the Indian Ocean, after skirting the coast of Arabia, and thus carried on trade with India. The Ophir mentioned in connection with these voyages has not been definitely located, but was perhaps in Southern Arabia, though possibly in Southeast Africa (see GOLD).

The ships in which the Phoenicians made these voyages were small as compared with the great vessels of the present day, but the largest known in their age, as we may infer from the long voyages they made. Their superiority is testified to by classical writers. In the famous expedition of Xerxes to Greece the Phoen ships excelled all others in speed, and the king chose one of them when he embarked upon the sea (Herod. vii.100). These ships were impelled both by sails and oars, as we know from illustrations upon the coins (see COINS).

The ancients attributed the invention of the alphabet to the Phoenicians. This is now regarded as doubtful, and there are no reliable data for determining what people first analyzed speech to its ultimate elements, but to the Phoenicians belongs the merit of bringing the invention to the knowledge of the western world. It is quite certain that the alphabets of Western Asia and those of Europe were derived from the Phoen characters. This is what we should have expected from their wide commercial relations. The alphabetic writing was in fact one of their exports and was by far the most important of them all. The world owes a great debt to this people for this invaluable aid to literature, science and culture (see ALPHABET).

6. Language and Culture

The Phoen alphabet comprises 22 letters and is deficient in signs to indicate vowels, which were left to be supplied by the reader. This defect is common to the Sem alphabets, but was soon remedied when the Greeks adopted the Phoenician. Some of the letters have to serve for two sounds, such as the signs for *s* and *sh*, for *p* and *ph*, for *t* and *th;* besides, there is a redundant sign for the sound of *s*. Also the sounds of *y* and *w* are unrepresented.

The origin of the letters is probably to be found in the hieroglyphic signs for words and syllables used by the Egyptians and others, since the similarity of some of them to these signs is evident, but in some cases it is more likely that the Phoenicians adopted hieroglyphics of their own. Thus the first letter, *'āleph*, which means "ox," was evidently derived from the picture of an ox's head and then reduced to a conventional form.

The Phoen alphabet and language were common to the Canaanitish tribes and the Hebrews, as we know from the many inscriptions found in Western Asia. The M S testifies to their use E. of the Jordan, and the Siloam Inscription likewise for Israel, and the same characters have been found in North Syria. This would be natural, for people of these regions had become largely Sem by the 9th cent. BC, when we suppose that the Phoen alphabet was in general use.

It is strange that the Phoenicians, who had an alphabet so early, and made it so widely known to the world, made so little use of it for literature. The remains of their language are very scanty, mostly inscriptions, and these generally very brief. The longest ones in Phoen proper are those from Sidon, the most famous of which is that of Esmunazer, king of Sidon, comprising 298 words. Some few others, pertaining to the same dynasty, have been discovered in tombs and on the walls of the temple of Asmun, and show the Phoen character and style in its best form. Only two works of any length are known to us by tr or references in Gr authors. The first is the Phoen *History of Sanchoniathon*, of Beirût, which Philo of Byblus claims to have trd from the Phoen original. This, however, is doubted, and both the author and the history are suspected to be mythical. The other work is genuine; the short account of the voyage of a Carthaginian king beyond the Pillars of Hercules, called the Periplus of Hanno, is not without merit as a narrative, and indicates that the Carthaginian branch of the Phoen race, at least, may have had a lit. of some value, but it is unfortunately lost. We cannot suppose, however, that it was very extensive or very important, as more of it would then have been preserved. The conclusion is natural that the Phoenicians were so absorbed in commercial enterprise and the pursuit of wealth that they neglected the nobler uses of the invaluable instrument of culture they had found in alphabetic writing.

7. Religion

A very prominent rôle was assigned to religion in the life of the Phoenicians. As a Sem people, such a characteristic was but natural and they seem to have possessed it in large measure. Their religious ideas are important on account of the influence they had on the Hebrews, which is so apparent in the OT. The worship of the Canaanitish Baal and Ashtoreth, or Astarte, led the Israelites astray and produced most disastrous results.

There can be little doubt that the chief deities of the Phoenicians, as well as the forms of their cult, were derived from Babylonia, brought with them probably when they migrated to the W., but afterward modified by contact with Egypt and Greece. Some regard the earliest conception of the deity among the Semites to have been monotheism, and we find traces of this in the attributes ascribed by the Phoenicians to their chief god. He is Baal, "lord" or "master"; Baal-samin, "lord of heaven"; Eliun, "supreme," etc. These terms imply either one God or one who is supreme among the gods and their ruler. But this belief was changed before the Phoenicians came into contact with the Hebrews, and polytheism took its place, though their gods were less numerous than among most polytheistic races. One of the most corrupting tendencies we notice was the ascription of sexual characteristics to the chief deities of their pantheon, such as Baal and Ashtoreth, which led to licentious rites of the most abominable character.

Baal (Phoen בַּעַל, *ba'al*) was the chief deity and was universally worshipped, being usually designated by the locality in each place: Baal of Tyre or Baal-Tsur, Baal-Sidon, Baal-Tars (Tarsus), Baal-bek, etc. He was regarded as the god of the generative principle in Nature, and his statues were sometimes flanked by bulls. He was identified with Zeus, and he appears on the coins under the Gr type of Zeus, seated on a throne, holding an eagle in the outstretched right hand and a scepter in the left. Sometimes his head is encircled with rays showing him to be the sun-god.

Ashtoreth (Phoen עַשְׁתֹּרֶת, *'ashtōreth*) was the great Nature-goddess, the Magna Mater, queen of heaven (Jer **7** 18), and as Baal was the solar deity, so she was often represented under the lunar aspect, Ashteroth-karnaim, "Ashteroth of the two horns" (Gen **14** 5). Sometimes she is represented holding the dove, the symbol of fecundity, of which she was the goddess. She was commonly identified with Aphrodite or Venus. She, like Baal, had temples everywhere, and kings were sometimes her high priests, and her worship was too often accompanied with orgies of the most corrupt kind, as at Apheca (see ASHTORETH; TAMMUZ).

Among the other gods we may mention: **El,** or **Il** (אֵל, *'ēl*), originally the designation of the supreme God, but afterward a subordinate deity who became the special divinity of Byblus (Gebal), and was regarded by the Greeks as the same as Kronos. **Melkarth** (מלקרת, *melkarth*, "king of the city") originally was the same as Baal, representing one aspect of that god, but later a separate deity, the patron god of Tyre whose head appears on many of its coins, as well as his symbol, the club, since he was identified with Hercules. Herodotus describes his temple at Tyre to which he attributes great antiquity, 2,300 years before his time. **Dagon** (דָּגוֹן, *dāghōn*) seems to have been the tutelary deity of Aradus, his head appearing on the early autonomous coins of that city. He seems to have been regarded as the god of agriculture by the Phoenicians, rather than of fishing as generally supposed. **Adonis** (אָדוֹן, *'ādhōn*, "lord") was regarded as the son of Cinyras, a mythic king of Gebal and the husband of Ashtoreth. The myth of his death by the wild boar led to the peculiar rites celebrating it, instituted by the women of Gebal at Apheca and on the river named after him (see TAMMUZ). **Esmun** (אשמן, *'esmūn*) one of the sons of Siddik, the father of the Cabiri, was esp. honored at Sidon and Beirût. At Sidon a great temple was built in his honor, the ruins of which have been recently explored and various inscriptions found dedicating it to him. His name signifies "the eighth," i.e. the eighth son of Siddik, the others being the Cabiri, or Great Ones, who were regarded as presiding over ships and navigation, and as such were worshipped in many places, although their special seat was Beirût. Although they were called "Great" they are represented as dwarfs, and an image of one of them was placed on the prow, or stern, of each Phoen war galley. The goddess **Tanith** (תנת, *tanith*) occupied a lofty place in the pantheon, since in inscriptions she takes the precedence over Baal when the two names occur together. She was esp. honored at Carthage and to her most exalted names are given, such as "the parent of all"; "the highest of the gods"; "the mistress of the elements," etc. Besides some other gods of less note originally worshipped by the Phoenicians, they introduced some foreign deities into their pantheon. Thus **Poseidon** appears frequently on the coins of Beirût and became its patron deity in Rom times; **Isis** and her temple at Gebal are likewise represented on its coins, the **Dioscuri** or their symbols on those of Tripolis and Beirût, etc.

The corrupt nature of the Phoen worship has been referred to. It was also cruel, the custom of human sacrifices being common and carried to an extent unheard of among other peoples, such as the horrible sacrifice of 200 noble youths at Carthage when besieged by Agathocles. The sacrifice was by burning, the victim being placed in the arms of the statue of the god, heated for the purpose. In P. this god was Melḳarth, or Molech, and the custom is denounced in the OT (Lev **20** 2–5), but other gods were also honored in this way. The religious feeling of the Phoenicians was undoubtedly deep, but sadly corrupt and depraved.

8. History

The political history of P. is that of the towns and cities belonging to it. The country as a whole had no centralized government, but the chief towns exercised a sort of hegemony, at times, over some of the lesser ones. This was esp. the case with Sidon and Tyre, but every city had its king and its local government. The land is never referred to in ancient documents, but the people are designated by their cities. Thus we find in Gen **10** 17 f the mention of Sidon, the Arvadite, the Arkite, etc, and, in Josh **13** 4, the Gebalites and the Sidonians in connection with the land of the Canaanites. In the same way the inscriptions of Egypt, Babylonia and Assyria refer to the people of the different cities, but not to the land as a political unit, which it never was.

The cities first come into notice in the period of the Egyp domination, beginning in the 16th cent. BC under Thothmes III. This king subdued most of the Phoen cities, or received their submission, in his numerous campaigns to Syria, and the Egyp rule continued with more or less interruption until the decline of Egypt under the XXth Dynasty, or about 300 years. During this time Arvad seems to have exercised the hegemony in the N., and Sidon in the S., with Gebal controlling the middle region. The Am Tab reveal many facts concerning the condition of things while the Egyp power was declining in the latter part of the XVIIIth Dynasty, esp. in the reign of Amenhotep IV (Ikhnaton). The rise of the Amorite and Hittite power in the N. threatened these cities, which were under Egyp governors, and they called upon their suzerain for aid, which was not given, and they fell, one after another, into the hands of the enemy. Rameses II restored Egyp rule, but his successors of the XXth Dynasty could not maintain it, and the invasion of tribes from the W. and N., called the Peleset, or Philis, by land and sea, though repelled by Rameses III, continued to increase until the Egyp domination was broken, and the coast towns resumed their independence about the middle of the 12th cent. BC. Sidon came to the front as the chief city of P., and it is referred to by Joshua as "Great Sidon" (Josh **11** 8). Homer also mentions Sidon frequently, but makes no reference to Tyre. The latter city was certainly in existence in his day, but had not come to the front as the leading city in the mind of the Greeks. Yet it was a fortified city in the time of Joshua (**19** 29), and the king of Tyre is among the correspondents mentioned in the Am Tab. It seems to have taken precedence of Sidon when the latter was attacked by the Philis of Askelon, and the inhabitants were compelled to flee for safety to Tyre. At all events Tyre exercised the hegemony in P. by the time David came to the throne, and had probably obtained it a century or two before, and held it until P. became subject to Assyria in the 9th cent. BC. Asshur-nazir-pal first came into contact with P., which submitted to tribute, between 877 and 860 BC, and this subjection continued until the downfall of Assyria in the latter part of the 7th cent. BC. The subjection was nominal only for more than a century, the cities retaining their kings and managing their own affairs with no interference from the Assyrians as long as they paid the tribute. But with the advent of Tiglath-pileser in Syria, about 740 BC, conditions changed, and the Phoen towns were subjected to severe treatment, and some of the dynasts were driven from their cities and Assyr governors appointed in their places. Their oppression caused revolts, and Elulaeus of Tyre united Sidon and the cities to the S. in a league to resist the encroachments of Tiglath-pileser and his successor Shalmaneser IV, whom he successfully resisted, although the Assyrian gained over to his side Sidon, Acre, and some other towns and had the assistance of their fleets to make an attack upon the island city. The attack failed completely, and Shalmaneser left Elulaeus to his independence, which he maintained for a quarter of a century, regaining control of the towns that had fallen away and also of Cyprus. Sargon (722–705 BC) let P. alone, but Sennacherib (705–681) determined to punish the king of Tyre and prepared an army of 200,000 men for the war with P. Elulaeus was afraid and fled to Cyprus, but his towns dared to resist and Sennacherib had to reduce them one after another, but did not succeed in taking Tyre itself. He set over the conquered territory a certain Tubaal, probably a Phoen, who paid him tribute. He also took tribute from Gebal and Aradus, which indicates that all of P. was subject to him, as these two cities probably controlled all that was not under Tyre. In the reign of Esarhaddon (681–668) Sidon revolted under Abd-Melkarth, who was caught and beheaded, the city sacked, and the inhabitants either killed or carried into captivity, and it was repeopled by captives from the E. At a later date (672), when Esarhaddon was preparing to invade Egypt, Baal, the vassal king of Tyre, revolted and refused to aid him, but afterward submitted either to Esarhaddon or to his son Asshur-bani-pal and assisted the latter in his invasion of Egypt, 668 BC. Four years later, however, we find the Assyr king besieging Tyre and punishing Baal by making him give his daughter to be a member of the Assyrian's harem. Baal himself was left on his throne. The same fate was the lot of the king of Aradus, and Accho (Acre) was also punished.

The frequent rebellions of the Phoen towns show their love of independence and a sturdy resistance to oppression. They became freed from the yoke of Assyria probably about 630 BC, when the Medes attacked Nineveh and the Scythic hordes overran all Western Asia. The Phoen cities were fortified and did not suffer very much from the barbarian invasion, and, as Assyria was broken, they resumed their independence. In the struggle which followed between Egypt and Babylon for the mastery of Syria, P. fell, for a time, under the sway of Egypt, but was not oppressed, and her towns prospered, and it was in this period that Tyre attained great wealth and renown as reflected in the Book of Ezk. When Nebuchadnezzar laid siege to it, a resistance of 13 years showed its strength and resources, and although the town on the mainland was destroyed, it is doubtful whether the king of Babylon took the island city, but it must have submitted to pay tribute (585 BC). P. remained subject to Babylon until that empire fell into the hands of the Persians (538), and then accepted the yoke of the latter in the days of Cambyses, if not earlier, but the Pers king does not seem to have used force to gain the adherence of the Phoenicians. He needed their fleets to assist in the attack upon Egypt and secured them without difficulty. They aided him in the conquest of Egypt, but when he asked them to proceed against Carthage they refused, and he had to desist. The navy of P. was too necessary for him to run any risk of alienating it.

This navy was the strongest sea power of the Persians in all their coming wars with Greece. Without its assistance Darius and his successors could with difficulty have invaded that country or held in subjection the western coasts of Asia Minor. P. remained faithful to her Pers rulers about 150 years, but when the general revolt of the western satraps occurred in 362 BC, P. seems to have favored them, but no open rebellion broke out until 351, when Sidon, under her king Tabnit II (Tennes), boldly declared her independence and induced most of the Phoen cities to do the same. The Pers garrisons were massacred or driven out. Ochus, the king of Persia, marched with an army of 300,000 infantry and 30,000 horse to punish the rebels, and Tabnit, in cowardly alarm, betrayed Sidon into his hands, but the citizens set fire to the city and destroyed themselves rather than fall into the hands of Ochus, who, as treacherous as Tabnit, slew the traitor (see SIDON). The other cities then submitted, and P. remained subject to Persia until the time of Alexander the Great. When this conqueror invaded the dominions of Persia and had defeated Darius at Issus, 333 BC, he demanded the submission of the Phoen towns, and all yielded save Tyre. Alexander was obliged to lay siege to it, which cost him 7 months of the severest labor, such was the valor and skill of the Tyrians. The capture of Tyre is reckoned as one of the greatest exploits of this mighty conqueror who stained his record by his cruel treatment of the brave defenders. He massacred the male prisoners and sold the remainder of the inhabitants, to the number of 30,000, into slavery (see TYRE). After the death of Alexander the Phoen cities were subject to the Ptolemies of Egypt and the Seleucids of Syria, the latter finally obtaining control of all by the victory of Antiochus III over Scopas in 198 BC. From this time on P. formed a part of the Seleucid kingdom until it passed, together with Syria and Pal, into the hands of the Romans. Its cities became the home of many Greeks and its language became largely Gr, as inscriptions and coins testify. The Romans had also much to do in modifying the character of the people, and some towns, Berytus, esp., became largely Roman. P. can hardly be said to have had a separate existence after the Gr invasion.

LITERATURE.—Rawlinson, *Hist of Phoenicia;* Kenrick, *Phoenicia;* Movers, *Phönizier;* Breasted, *Hist of Egypt,* and *Ancient Records;* Budge, *Hist of Egypt;* Rawlinson, *Ancient Monarchies;* Rogers, *Babylonia and Assyria;* Bevan, *House of Seleucus;* Am Tab; Perrot and Chipiez, *Art in Phoenicia.*

H. PORTER

PHOENIX, fē'niks (**Φοίνιξ,** *Phoínix;* AV **Phenice**): A harbor in Crete (Acts **27** 12). The Alexandrian corn ship carrying St. Paul and the author of Acts, after it left Myra in Lycia, was prevented by adverse winds from holding a straight course to Italy, and sailed under the lee of Crete, off the promontory of Salmone (κατὰ Σαλμώνην, *katá Salmṓnēn*). The ship was then able to make her way along the S. shore of Crete to a harbor called Fair Havens (Καλοὶ Λιμένες, *Kaloí Liménes*), near a city Lasea (Λασαία, *Lasaía*). Thence, in spite of St. Paul's advice to winter in Fair Havens, it was decided to sail to Phoenix (εἰς Φοίνικα, λιμένα τῆς Κρήτης) βλέποντα κατὰ λίβα καὶ κατὰ χῶρον (*eis Phoínika, liména tḗs Krḗtēs*) *blépontα katá líba kaí katá chṓron*, a description which has been tr[d] in two ways: (1) "looking *toward* the S.W. wind and *toward* the N.W. wind, i.e. looking S.W. and N.W."; (2) "looking *down* the S.W. wind and *down* the N.W. wind, i.e. looking N.E. and S.E." On the way thither, they were struck by a wind from the N.E., called Euraquilo, and ran before it under the lee of an island, called Cauda or Clauda (Καῦδα, *Kaúda* [ℵ^c B 𝕷], Κλαῦδα, *Klaúda* [ℵ* A, etc]) in Acts **27** 7–17. It will be convenient to discuss those places together. The following account is based on Smith's elaborate study in his *Voyage and Shipwreck of St. Paul,* which has been followed by all later writers.

The ship, when it left Myra, was obviously making for Italy (Puteoli or Ostia) by the shortest route, round Cape Malea, but off Cnidus it encountered a N.W. wind and had to sail for shelter under the lee of Crete. **Salmone,** now called Cape Sidero, was the promontory which forms the N.E. corner of the island. Thence along the S. shore of Crete, as far as Cape Matala, a sailing ship is sheltered by the mountains from the violence of the N.W. wind; W. of Cape Matala, where the coast turns toward the N.W., there is no such shelter. **Fair Havens** must therefore be looked for to the E. of Cape Matala, and there is a harbor, lying 6 miles E. of Cape Matala, which is called Fair Havens by the modern Greek inhabitants of the island. There is no doubt that this is the harbor in which the Alexandrian ship took shelter. It is sheltered only from the N. and N.W. winds.

The ruins of a city which has been identified with **Lasea** have been found 5 miles E. from Fair Havens, and 12 miles S. of the important city of Gortyna. It has been suggested that St. Paul's desire to winter at Fair Havens (Acts **27** 10) may have been due to its proximity to Gortyna, and the opportunity which the latter city afforded for missionary work. There were many Jews in Gortyna. See CRETE.

From Fair Havens, against the advice of St. Paul, it was decided to sail to Phoenix, there to pass the winter. While the ship was on its way thither, it was struck by a violent N.E. wind from the mountains, called Euraquilo, and carried under the lee of an islet called **Cauda** or **Clauda.** When this happened, the ship was evidently crossing the Bay of Messariah, and from this point a N.E. wind must have carried her under the lee of an island now called Gaudho in Greek and Gozzo in Italian, situated about 23 miles S.W. of the center of the Gulf of Messariah. The modern name of the island shows that Cauda (Caudas in the *Notitiae Episcopatuum*), and not Clauda is the true ancient form.

The writer of Acts never saw **Phoenix,** which must have been a good harbor, as the nautical experts decided to winter there (Acts **27** 11). Now the only safe harbor on the S. coast of Crete in which a ship large enough to carry a cargo of corn and 268 souls could moor is the harbor beside Loutro, a village on the S. coast of Crete, directly N. of Cauda. All the ancient authorities agree in placing Phoenix in this neighborhood. The harbor at Loutro affords shelter from all winds, and its identification with Phoenix seems certain. But a serious difficulty arises on this view. The words describing the harbor of Phoenix ordinarily mean "looking toward the S.W. and the N.W.," but the harbor beside Loutro looks eastward. This led Bishop Wordsworth to identify Phoenix with an open roadstead on the western side of the isthmus on which Loutro stands. But this roadstead is not a suitable place for wintering in, and it is better *either* to take the words to mean, in sailor's language, "looking down the S.W. and N.W. winds"—a description which exactly fits the harbor at Loutro—or to assume that the reporter of the discussion referred to in Acts **27** 10–12 or the writer of Acts made a mistake in describing a place which he had never seen. An inscription belonging to the reign of Trajan found at Loutro shows that Egyp corn ships were wont to lie up there for the winter. W. M. CALDER

PHOROS, fō'ros (**Φορός,** *Phorós,* B [Swete], **Φαρές,** *Pharés* [1 Esd **8** 30, where AV **Pharez**]): Name of one of the families, part of whom went up from the exile with Zerubbabel (1 Esd **5** 9) and part with Ezra (**8** 30 RV) = "Parosh" of Ezr **2** 3; **8** 3, and some members of which had taken "strange wives" (1 Esd **9** 26).

PHRURAI, frū'rī, frū'rā-ī (**Φρουραί,** *Phrouraí;* al. in א and A, **Φρουραία,** *Phrouraía,* and **Φρουρίμ,** *Phrourím;* AV **Phurim**): In Ad Est **11** 1, "the ep. of Phrurai" means the preceding Book of Est. See PURIM.

PHRYGIA, frij'i-a (**Φρυγία,** *Phrugía*): A large ancient country of Central Asia Minor, very mountainous and with table-lands reaching 4,000 ft. in height. Its name is derived from Phryges, a tribe from Thrace, which in early times invaded the country and drove out or absorbed the earlier Asiatic inhabitants, among whom were the Hittites. Thus the Phrygians borrowed much of oriental civilization, esp. of art and mythology which they transferred to Europe. To define the boundaries of Phrygia would be exceedingly difficult, for as in the case of other Asia Minor countries, they were always vague and they shifted with nearly every age. The entire country abounds with ruins of former cities and with almost countless rock-hewn tombs, some of which are of very great antiquity. Among the most interesting of the rock sculptures are the beautiful tombs of the kings bearing the names Midas and Gordius, with which classical tradition has made us familiar. It seems that at one period the country may have extended to the Hellespont, even including Troy, but later the Phrygians were driven toward the interior. In Rom times, however, when Paul journeyed there, the country was divided into two parts, one of which was known as Galatian Phrygia, and the other as Asian Phrygia, because it was a part of the Rom province of Asia, but the line between them was never sharply drawn. The Asian Phrygia was the larger of the two divisions, including the greater part of the older country; Galatian Phrygia was small, extending along the Pisidian Mountains, but among its important cities were Antioch, Iconium and Apollonia. About 295 AD, when the province of Asia was no longer kept together, its different parts were known as Phrygia Prima and Phrygia Secunda. That part of Asia Minor is now ruled by a Turkish *wali* or governor whose residence is in Konia, the ancient Iconium. The population consists not only of Turks, but of Greeks, Armenians, Jews, Kurds and many small tribes of uncertain ancestry, and of peculiar customs and religious practices. The people live mostly in small villages which are scattered throughout the picturesque country. Sheep and goat raising are the leading industries; brigandage is common. According to Acts **2** 10, Jews from Phrygia went to Jerus, and in Acts **18** 23 we learn that many of them were influential and perhaps fanatical. According to Acts **16** 6, Paul traversed the country while on his way from Lystra to Iconium and Antioch in Galatian Phrygia. Twice he entered Phrygia in Asia, but on his 2d journey he was forbidden to preach there. Christianity was introduced into Phrygia by Paul and Barnabas, as we learn from Acts **13** 4; **16** 1–6; **18** 23, yet it did not spread there rapidly. Churches were later founded, perhaps by Timothy or by John, at Colossae, Laodicea and Hierapolis.

E. J. BANKS

PHURAH, fū'ra (פֻּרָה, *purāh,* "branch"). See PURAH.

PHUT, fut (פּוּט, *pūṭ*). See PUT.

PHUVAH, fū'va. See PUAH.

PHYGELUS, fī-jē'lus (**Φύγελλος,** *Phúgellos;* Tischendorf and WH, with others, read **Φύγελος,** *Phúgelos,* Phygellus or Phygelus [2 Tim **1** 15]; AV **Phygellus,** fi-jel'us): One of the Christians who deserted Paul at the time of his 2d imprisonment at Rome. Paul mentions him, along with Hermogenes, as being among those "that are in Asia," who turned away from him then. What is meant may be that Phygelus and Hermogenes, along with other native Christians from proconsular Asia, were in Rome when he was brought before the emperor's tribunal the second time, and that they had not merely taken no measures to stand by and support him, but that they had deserted him.

The meaning, however, may be that the turning away of Phygelus and Hermogenes from Paul took place, not in Rome, but in Asia itself.

The times during and immediately following the Neronic persecution were more dreadful than can easily be conceived, and the temptation was strong to forsake the Christian name, and to do so in a wholesale fashion. A great community like the Christian church in Ephesus or in Rome felt the terrible pressure of those times, when for a mere word—a word, however, denying the Lord who bought them—men were at once set free from persecution, from the loss of property or of home, and from death. 1 Pet records how the aftermath of the Neronic persecution had extended far indeed from Rome, where it had originated. Peter asks the Christians not to give way under "the fiery trial" which is trying them (1 Pet **4** 12), and those whom he thus addresses were the members of the church throughout Pontus, Galatia, Cappadocia, Asia and Bithynia (1 Pet **1** 1). The epp. to the seven churches in Asia in the Apocalypse also show how sorely persecution had raged throughout that province. See PERSECUTION.

But in addition to the temptation to deny Christ's name and to go back to heathenism or to Judaism, there was also another which pressed upon some of the churches, the temptation to repudiate the authority of Paul. Many passages in the NT show how the name of Paul was sometimes very lightly esteemed, and how his authority was repudiated, e.g. by persons in Corinth, and in the churches of Galatia.

What is said here is, that among the Christians of proconsular Asia, i.e. of Ephesus and the churches in the valley of the Cayster, there was a widespread defection from that loyalty to Paul which was to be expected from those who owed to him all that they possessed of the knowledge of Christ's salvation. "All that are in Asia turned away from me; of whom are Phygelus and Hermogenes." On the whole, all the necessary conditions of these words are satisfied by a reference to Rome and to Paul's environment there, and perhaps this is the more probable meaning. See HERMOGENES.

JOHN RUTHERFURD

PHYLACTERY, fi-lak'tēr-i (**φυλακτήριον,** *phulaktḗrion,* "guard"): This word is found only in Mt **23** 5 in Our Lord's denunciation of the Pharisees, who, in order that their works might "be seen of men," and in their zeal for the forms of religion, "make broad their phylacteries and enlarge the borders of their garments." The corresponding word in the OT, טוֹטָפֹת, *ṭōṭāphōth* (Kennedy in *HDB* suggests pointing as the segholate fem. sing.,

1. Bible References

ṭōṭepheth), is found in three passages (Ex **13** 16; Dt **6** 8; **11** 18), where it is trd "frontlets." This rendering, however, is not at all certain, and may have been read into the text from its later interpretation. In Ex **13** 9 the corresponding word to the *ṭōṭāphōth* of ver 16 is *zikkārōn*, "memorial" or "reminder"; and in the ‖ clauses of both verses the corresponding word is *'ōth*, "a sign" upon the hand, also used for the "sign" which Jeh appointed for Cain (Gen **4** 15). It may be rendered then as a mark or ornament or jewel, and used **figuratively** of Jeh's Law as an ornament or jewel to the forehead of the Israelite, a reference to the charm or amulet worn by the pagan. The word used in the Talm for the phylactery is תְּפִלָּה, *t^ephillāh*, "prayer," or "prayer-band" (pl. *t^ephillīn*), indicating its use theoretically as a reminder of the Law, although practically it might be esteemed as an automatic and ever-present charm against evil: an aid within toward the keeping of the Law, a guard without against the approach of evil; a degradation of an OT **figurative** and idealistic phrase to the materialistic and superstitious practices of the pagans.

2. Description

The phylactery was a leathern box, cube shaped, closed with an attached flap and bound to the person by a leather band. There were two kinds: (1) one to be bound to the inner side of the left arm, and near the elbow, so that with the bending of the arm it would rest over the heart, the knot

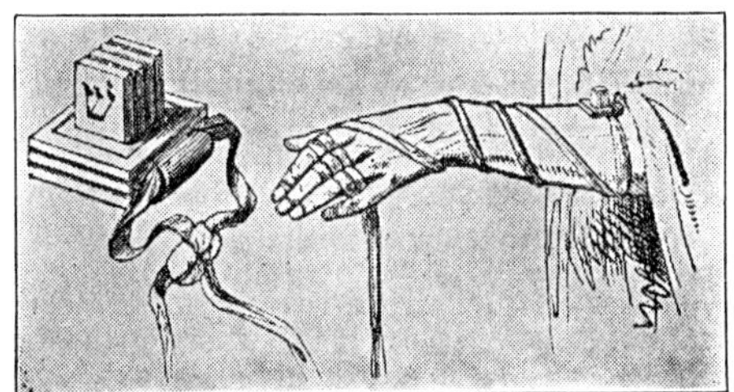

Phylacteries for Head and Arm.

fastening it to the arm being in the form of the letter *yōdh* (י), and the end of the string, or band, finally wound around the middle finger of the hand, "a sign upon thy hand" (Dt **6** 8). This box had one compartment containing one or all of the four passages given above. The writer in his youth found one of these in a comparatively remote locality, evidently lost by a Jewish peddler, which contained only the 2d text (Ex **13** 11–16) in unpointed Heb. (2) Another was to be bound in the center of the forehead, "between thine eyes" (Dt **6** 8), the knot of the band being in the form of the letter *dāleth* (ד), with the letter *shīn* (ש) upon each end of the box, which was divided into four compartments with one of the four passages in each. These two Heb letters, with the י of the arm-phylactery (see [1] above), formed the Divine name שַׁדַּי, *shadday*, "Almighty." Quite elaborate ceremonial accompanied the "laying" on of the phylacteries, that of the arm being bound on first, and that of the head next, quotations from Scripture or Talm being repeated at each stage of the binding. They were to be worn by every male over 13 years old at the time of morning prayer, except on Sabbaths and festal days, such days being in themselves sufficient reminders of "the commandment, the statutes, and the ordinances" of Jeh (Dt **6** 1).

3. Interpretation of OT Passages

The passages on which the wearing of the phylacteries is based are as follows: "It [i.e. the feast of unleavened bread] shall be for a sign unto thee upon thy hand, and for a memorial between thine eyes, that the law of Jeh may be in thy mouth" (Ex **13** 9); "And it [i.e. sacrifice of the firstborn] shall be for a sign upon thy hand, and for frontlets between thine eyes" (**13** 16); "thou shalt bind them [i.e. the words of Jeh] for a sign upon thy hand, and they shall be for frontlets between thine eyes" (Dt **6** 8); "therefore shall ye lay up these my words in your heart and in your soul; and ye shall bind them for a sign upon your hand, and they shall be for frontlets between your eyes" (**11** 18). It is evident that the words in Ex are beyond all question used **figuratively;** a careful reading of the verses in Dt in close relation to their contexts, in which are other figures of speech not to be taken literally, is sufficient proof of their purely figurative intention also. Only the formalism of later ages could distort these figures into the gross and materialistic practice of the phylactery. Just when this practice began cannot accurately be determined. While the Talm attempts to trace it back to the primitive, even Mosaic, times, it probably did not long antedate the birth of Christ. In conservative Jewish circles it has been maintained through the centuries, and at present is faithfully followed by orthodox Judaism. Every male, who at the age of 13 becomes a "son of the Law" (*bar miçwāh*), must wear the phylactery and perform the accompanying ceremonial.

In the NT passage (Mt **23** 5) Our Lord rebukes the Pharisees, who make more pronounced the un-Scriptural formalism and the crude literalism of the phylacteries by making them obtrusively large, as they also seek notoriety for their religiosity by the enlarged fringes, or "borders." See Fringes; Frontlets; Pharisees.

Literature.—The various comms. on Ex and Dt; tractate *T^ephillin;* the comprehensive art. by A. R. S. Kennedy in *HDB;* arts. in *EB* and *Jew Enc.*

Edward Mack

PHYLARCH, fī'lärk (φυλάρχης, *phulárchēs*): Given in AV of 2 Macc **8** 32 as a proper name "Philarches," but in RV "the phylarch of Timotheus's forces"; "probably the captain of an irregular auxiliary force" (RVm), rather than a cavalry officer.

PHYLARCHES, fī-lär'kēz (AV **Philarches**). See Phylarch.

PHYSICIAN, fi-zish'an (רֹפֵא, *rōphē'*; ἰατρός, *iatrós*): To the pious Jew at all times God was the healer (Dt **32** 39): "It was neither herb nor mollifying plaister that cured them, but thy word, O Lord, which healeth all things" (Wisd **16** 12). The first physicians mentioned in Scripture are those of Egypt. Long before the sojourn of the Hebrews in that land, Egypt had a priestly class of physicians (*snu*) and a god of healing (*Imḥtp*). From the ancient medical papyri which have been preserved, the largest of which is the Papyrus Ebers, we know that the medical knowledge of these physicians was purely empirical, largely magical and wholly unscientific. In spite of their ample opportunities they knew next to nothing of human anatomy, their descriptions of diseases are hopelessly crude, and three-fourths of the hundreds of prescriptions in the papyri are wholly inert. Even their art of embalming was so imperfect that few of their mummies would have remained in any other climate than that of Egypt. Physicians of this kind who were Joseph's servants embalmed Jacob (Gen **50** 2) and Joseph (ver 26). It was not until the foundation of the School of Alexandria, which was purely Greek, that Egypt became a place of medical education and research.

There is no evidence that at any time the priests of Israel were reputed to be the possessors of medical knowledge or tradition. In the ceremonial law they had explicit instructions as to the isolation of those suffering from skin eruptions, so that they might recognize certain obstinate and infectious forms which caused ceremonial uncleanness, but with this duty as sanitary police their function ended, and they used no means to cure these diseases. There is, as far as I know, no record or tradition of a priest-physician in Bible times. The records of cure by the prophets, esp. Elisha, are mostly recorded as miracles, not as cures by treatment. The salt which cured the noxious water at Jericho and the meal by which the poisonous gourds were rendered innoxious, like the manipulation of the Shunammite's son, can scarcely be regarded as adequate remedies. There is an implied reference to a healer of wounds in Ex **21** 19, as also in Isa **3** 7, and it is recorded in *Peṣāḥīm*, iv.9 that there was in existence in the time of the monarchy a book of cures, *ṣēpher rephū'ōth*, supposed to have been written by Solomon, but withdrawn from public use by Hezekiah. The first specific mention of Heb physicians is 2 Ch **16** 12, but Asa is obviously regarded by the Chronicler as reprehensible in trusting to their skill. In 2 K **8** 29 Joram, king of Israel, is said to have gone to Jezreel to be healed. Not far from this, across the Jordan, was Gilead, which possibly may also have been a place resorted to by those needing medical treatment, as indicated by Jeremiah's query: "Is there no balm in Gilead? is there no physician there?" (Jer **8** 22). Job, irritated by the platitudes of his friends, calls them physicians of no value (**13** 4).

In the NT Our Lord's saying, "They that are whole have no need of a physician," etc, shows that there were physicians in Galilee (Mt **9** 12; Mk **2** 17; Lk **5** 31), and in Nazareth He quotes what seems to have been a proverb: "Physician, heal thyself" (Lk **4** 23). There were physicians in Galilee who received fees from the woman of Caesarea Philippi who had the issue of blood (Mk **5** 26; Lk **8** 43). Of her there is a curious story told in Eusebius (VII, 18).

There are several Talmudic references to physicians; in *Sheḳālīm* **5** 1, it is said that there was a physician at the temple to attend to the priests. A physician was appointed in every city (*Giṭṭīn* **12***b*) who was required to have a license from the local authorities (*Bābhā' Bathrā'* **21***a*). The familiar passage in Ecclus **38** 1–15 RV in praise of the physician gives him but limited credit for his skill: "There is a time when in their very hands is the issue for good," and later, "He that sinneth before his Maker, Let him fall into the hands of the physician."

Luke, called "the beloved physician" in Col **4** 14, is said by Eusebius to have been a native of Antioch and a physician by profession. According to Origen he was the unnamed "brother whose praise in the gospel is spread through all the churches" (2 Cor **8** 18). There are evidences of his professional studies in the language of his writings, though of this probably more has been made by Hobart and others than it really merits. Had we not known of his profession it is doubtful whether it could have been conjectured from his choice of words. Sir W. Ramsay calls attention to the two words used of the healings at Melita in Acts **28** 8–10: for the cure of Publius' father the word used is *iásato*, but for the healing of those who came later it is *etherapeúonto*, which he renders "received medical treatment." From this he infers that Luke helped Paul with these (Ramsay, *Luke the Physician*. 1908). ALEX. MACALISTER

PI-BESETH, pī-bē'seth (פִּי־בֶסֶת, *pī-bheṣeth;* LXX **Βυβάστος**, *Bubástos;* Egyp *Pi-Básht*, "the house of Basht," the cat-headed goddess; the Egyp form is usually *Ha-Basht;* it is doubtful if the form *Pi-Basht* has yet been found): A city of ancient Egypt. The only occurrence of the name of this place in the OT is in Ezk **30** 17; where it is coupled with Aven, i.e. On (Heliopolis).

1. Location Pi-beseth was on the western bank of the Pelusiac branch of the Nile, about 40 miles N. of Memphis, about 15 miles N.E. of On. Herodotus found the city of Bubastis very beautiful in his day. The annual festival of the goddess, Basht, was celebrated here with revolting license, similar to that of the festival of Syyid el-Bedawer now kept in Ṭanṭa.

2. Exploration Pi-beseth was explored by Professor Naville under the Egyp Exploration Society in 1887–90. There were uncovered ruins of Egypt from the IVth Dynasty of the Old Empire, from the Middle Empire, an important Hyksos settlement, and ruins from the New Empire down to the end, and even from Rom times. The most unique discovery at Pi-beseth, one of the most unique in all Egypt, is the cemetery of cats. These cats, the animal sacred to Basht, were mummified at other places in Egypt, but at Pi-beseth they were burned and the ashes and bones gathered and buried in great pits lined with brick or hardened clay. Bones of the ichneumon were also found mixed with those of the cats in these pits (*Egypt Exploration Fund Report*, 1891).

M. G. KYLE

PICTURE, pik'ṭūr: This word (in the pl.) is found 3 t in AV, viz. Nu **33** 52; Isa **2** 16; Prov **25** 11. In Nu and Prov "pictures" represents the Heb word מַשְׂכִּית, *maskīth*, "showpiece," "figure." The context in Nu suggests that the "pictures" or "carved figures" (RV "figured stones") which the Israelites were to destroy were symbols of Can. worship and therefore foreign to the religion of Jeh. In Prov for AV "pictures of silver," ERV has "baskets [ARV "network"] of silver," but a more probable tr is "carvings of silver." "Pictures" stands for a slightly different word (but from the same root) in Isa, viz. שְׂכִיּוֹת, *sekhīyōth;* RV renders "imagery" (RVm "watchtowers"). The prophet probably alludes to carved figures (of gods in animal or human shapes) on the prows of vessels.

T. LEWIS

PIECE, pēs: In AV the word (sing. and pl.) represents a large number of different Heb words, many of which have more or less the same significance, e.g. piece of meat or flesh (Gen **15** 10; 2 S **6** 19; Ezk **24** 4); of bread or cake (1 S **2** 36; **30** 12; Jer **37** 21); of ground or land (2 S **23** 11); of wall (Neh **3** 11.19 ff); of an ear (Am **3** 12); of cloth or garment (1 K **11** 30); of millstone (Jgs **9** 53). It is used frequently in paraphrastic renderings of various Heb vbs.: "break," "tear," "cut," etc, in pieces (Gen **44** 28, etc).

In the NT "piece" renders ἐπίβλημα, *epíblēma*, "piece" or "patch of cloth" (Mt **9** 16; Mk **2** 21; Lk **5** 36). It is also found in paraphrastic renderings—broken in pieces (Mk **5** 4), pulled in pieces (Acts **23** 10). T. LEWIS

PIECE OF GOLD: The word "pieces" is supplied in 2 K **5** 5 (story of Naaman), "6,000 pieces of gold," where RVm more correctly suggests "shekels" (cf 1 K **10** 16). See MONEY.

PIECE OF MONEY: Two words are thus rendered in AV (קְשִׂיטָה, *ḳesīṭāh;* στατήρ, *statḗr*). RV gives only the first this rendering (Job **42** 11).

It is supposed to be from Arab. قسط, *ḳassaṭ*, "to divide equally by weight," and hence something weighed; a piece of silver weighed for money, and perhaps stamped with its weight. The stater is the well-known Gr weight and coin (Mt **17** 27 AV, m *stater*, RV "shekel"). In gold it was equal to about a guinea or five dollars, but in silver only to about 66 cts.

PIECE OF SILVER: Two words are thus rendered in the OT (רְצֵי־כֶסֶף, *raççē-khāşeph*, and קְשִׂיטָה, *ḳesīṭāh*) and two in the NT (ἀργύριον, *argúrion*, and δραχμή, *drachmḗ*). The first expression means pieces of silver broken off from bars or larger pieces (Ps **68** 30). The second is used for money in Josh **24** 32, and is so rendered in RV. The pieces were not coins, but perhaps bore a stamp. See MONEY. In other passages of the OT where pieces of silver are mentioned, the Heb has simply a numeral joined with *keşeph*, "silver," as in the account of the selling of Joseph (Gen **37** 28). In Isa **7** 23 the word **silverlings** means small pieces of silver, and they were no doubt shekels. In the NT the Gr ἀργύρια, *argúria* (Mt **26** 15; **27** 3–9), is tr[d] as pieces of silver, but probably means shekels. In Acts **19** 19 the same word occurs, but in this case the reference is probably to the denarius or drachma (cf Lk **15** 8 f). Thus the 30 pieces of Mt would be equal to about £4 or $20, and the 50,000 of Acts to about £2,000 or $10,000.

H. PORTER

PIETY, pī'e-ti: Only in 1 Tim **5** 4: "Let them learn first to show piety towards their own family," where "let them show piety" represents a single Gr vb. (εὐσεβέω, *eusebéō*), in its only other occurrence (Acts **17** 23) being rendered "worship." In Elizabethan Eng. "piety" (like the Lat *pietas*) could be used of devotion to one's parents (as still in the phrase "filial piety"), as well as of devotion to God. Hence there is no explicit statement here that filial devotion is one form of Divine worship.

PIGEON, pij'un (יוֹנָה, *yōnāh;* περιστερά, *peristerá;* Lat *pipire*): A bird of the family Columbidae. See DOVE. The Heb *yōnāh* seems to be tr[d] either pigeon or dove, yet almost every reference made to these birds proves that there were distinct branches of the family recognized, and one or the other or both are designated. On the other hand, some of the tr[s] read doves, where the remainder of the text makes it very clear that pigeons were the birds intended. The Lat *pipire* means "to cheep," and refers to the unusually clamorous young in the nest. The old birds coo, moan and wail as doves. The birds are almost 12 in. long, have full, plump bodies that are delicious food, and beautifully marked and shaded plumage. They feed principally on grain, seeds, small buds and fruit. Beyond question wild pigeons were the first birds domesticated and taught to home with man. They appeared in a state of such complete domestication, that they flew free, yet homed and bred in places provided by man at the time of the very first attempts at keeping records of history. At the time the earliest Bib. accounts were written, pigeons were so domesticated that in all known countries of the East they were reckoned when an estimate was made of a man's wealth.

Pigeons.

The rich provided large and expensive **cotes** of molded pottery for their birds, each section big enough for the home of one pair of birds, the regular **rows of openings** resembling lattice work, so that Isaiah refers to them as "windows" (**60** 8). LXX reads σὺν νοσσοῖς, *sún nossoís*, lit. "with young" or "fledglings" (see below). The middle classes modeled cotes of oven-baked clay, and the very poor cut holes in the walls, over the doors, and allowed the birds to enter and live with the family. In wild estate, rock and wood pigeons swarmed in countless numbers through rocky caves and caverns and over the plains of Gennesaret, the forests of Gilead and the woody slopes of Carmel. They remained throughout the season, breeding at all times. The doves were migratory, and were kept in confinement only as caged pets or to be held for sale for sacrifice. For these purposes, it appears that the dove was slightly preferred. When only one bird was to be used, a dove is always specified; where two, almost in every case the dove is mentioned first. Where one or the other will suffice, the dove seems to have been given preference. This may have been because it required greater effort to procure a dove, and so it was considered a greater sacrifice. Everyone having a home of any sort had pigeons they could use, or they could be taken wild at any time. The dove is first mentioned in Gen **15** 9: "And he said unto him, Take me a heifer three years old, and a she-goat three years old, and a ram three years old, and a turtle-dove, and a young pigeon."

It will be observed that the dove is mentioned first, and it is specified that the pigeon was to be young. It is probable that the people protected their domesticated pigeons by using the wild for sacrifice, whenever possible. Young birds could be taken from a nest at almost any time. The old birds, among the wild, were shy creatures and far more difficult to capture in nets or snares than doves that came close to cities and villages to live, and exhibited much less fear of man than the wild pigeons. The next reference is in Lev **5** 7: "And if his means suffice not for a lamb, then he shall bring his trespass-offering for that wherein he hath sinned, two turtle-doves, or two young pigeons, unto Jeh; one for a sin-offering, and the other for a burnt-offering." Here two birds of each kind were to be offered, if the person making the sacrifice could not afford a lamb. Again in Lev **12** 6: "And when the days of her purifying are fulfilled, for a son, or for a daughter, she shall bring a lamb a year old for a burnt-offering, and a young pigeon, or a turtle-dove, for a sin-offering, unto the door of the tent of meeting, unto the priest." Here is a rare instance where the text or the translators place the pigeon first.

"And on the eighth day he shall bring two turtle-doves, or two young pigeons, to the priest, to the door of the tent of meeting" (Nu **6** 10). In Cant **2** 14:

"O my dove, that art in the clefts of the rock,
In the covert of the steep place,
Let me see thy countenance,
Let me hear thy voice;
For sweet is thy voice, and thy countenance is
comely."

Here the text reads "dove," but the description of the location and the implication of the text prove the bird to have been a rock pigeon—a tender, loving thing, yet shy and timid, that peeps with eyes of bright concern over the rocks of its chosen home, down at the intruder. Isa **60** 8: "Who are these that fly as a cloud, and as the doves to their windows?" Here is another place where the wrong bird is used. Doves were wild and migratory. They had no "windows." But the tile pots massed in one diamond-shaped cote appeared at a little distance, like latticed windows. This should read "pigeons" instead of "doves." For the same reason see Jer **48** 28: "O ye inhabitants of Moab, leave the cities and dwell in the rock; and be like the dove that maketh her nest over the mouth of the abyss." Again the bird intended is the rock pigeon. Lk **2** 24: "A sacrifice according to that which is said in the law of the Lord, A pair of turtledoves, or two young pigeons." This describes the sacrifice offered in the temple by Mary following the birth of Jesus. GENE STRATTON-PORTER

PI-HAHIROTH, pī-ha-hī'roth (פִּי הַחִירוֹת, *pī-ha-ḥīrōth* [Ex **14** 2–9; Nu **33** 7–8]): Nothing is known of the meaning of the name Pi-H. Some attempts toward an Egyp etymology for it have been made, but without much success. Since the meaning of the name is unknown and no description of the place or its use is given, it is impossible to determine anything concerning the character of Pi-H., whether a city, a sanctuary, a fortress, or some natural feature of the landscape.

1. Meaning of Name

Neither Pi-H. nor any other place mentioned with it can be exactly located. A recent discovery of manuscripts in Egypt furnishes a mention of this place, but affords very little assistance in locating it, nothing comparable to the account in the Bible itself. If any one of the places mentioned in connection with the crossing of the Red Sea could be located approximately, all the others could, also, be similarly located by the description given in the account in Ex. The route beyond the Sea has been made out with almost positive certainty. A journey along the way is so convincing that hardly anything can shake the conviction which it produces. This identification of the route of the exodus beyond the Sea requires the place of the crossing to be within 3 days' journey of Marah, which puts it somewhere near the modern Suez. It may be anywhere within 10 miles of that point. This approximately locates all the other places mentioned in connection with the crossing: Migdol must be *Ras 'Ataḳah,* or some other high point in the mountains of the western deserts, where might be placed a watchtower. Pi-H. is between this point and the Sea and Baal-zephon near the opposite eastern shore. This puts Pi-H. at some point along the old shore line of the Sea within 10 miles of the site of modern Suez.

2. Location

M. G. KYLE

PILATE, ACTS OF. See following art., 4, and APOCRYPHAL GOSPELS.

PILATE, pī'lăt, pī'lat, **PONTIUS,** pon'shi-us (Πόντιος Πειλᾶτος, *Póntios Peilátos*):

1. Name and Office
2. Pilate's Procuratorship
3. Pilate and Jesus Christ
4. Pilate in Tradition and Legend
5. Character of Pilate

LITERATURE

The *nomen* Pontius indicates the stock from which Pilate was descended. It was one of the most famous of Samnite names; it was a Pontius who inflicted on a Rom army the disgrace of the Caudine Forks. The name is often met with in Rom history after the Samnites were conquered and absorbed. Lucius Pontius Aquila was a friend of Cicero and one of the assassins of Julius Caesar. The *cognomen* Pilatus indicates the *familia,* or branch of the *gens* Pontius, to which Pilate belonged. It has been derived from *pileus,* the cap worn by freedmen; this is improbable, as Pilate was of equestrian rank. It has also been derived from *pilum,* a spear. Probably the name was one that had descended to Pilate from his ancestors, and had long lost its meaning. The *praenomen* is nowhere mentioned. Pilate was 5th procurator of Judaea. The province of Judaea had formerly been the kingdom of Archelaus, and was formed when he was deposed (6 AD). Speaking roughly, it took in the southern half of Pal, including Samaria. Being an imperial province (i.e. under the direct control of the emperor), it was governed by a procurator (see PROCURATOR; PROVINCE). The procurator was the personal servant of the emperor, directly responsible to him, and was primarily concerned with finance. But the powers of procurators varied according to the appointment of the emperor. Pilate was a procurator *cum potestate,* i.e. he possessed civil, military, and criminal jurisdiction. The procurator of Judaea was in some way subordinate to the legate of Syria, but the exact character of the subordination is not known. As a rule a procurator must be of equestrian rank and a man of certain military experience. Under his rule, the Jews were allowed as much self-government as was consistent with the maintenance of imperial authority. The Sanhedrin was allowed to exercise judicial functions, but if they desired to inflict the penalty of death, the sentence had to be confirmed by the procurator.

1. Name and Office

We have no certain knowledge of Pilate except in connection with his time of rule in Judaea. We know nothing of his birth, his origin, or his earlier years. Tacitus, when speaking of the cruel punishments inflicted by Nero upon the Christians, tells us that Christ, from whom the name "Christian" was derived, was put to death when Tiberius was emperor by the procurator Pontius Pilate (*Annals* xv.44). Apart from this reference and what is told us in the NT, all our knowledge of him is derived from two Jewish writers, Jos the historian and Philo of Alexandria.

2. Pilate's Procuratorship

Pilate was procurator of Judaea, in succession to Gratus, and he held office for 10 years. Jos tells (*Ant,* XVIII, iv, 2) that he ruled for 10 years; that he was removed from office by Vitellius, the legate of Syria, and traveled in haste to Rome to defend himself before Tiberius against certain complaints. Before he reached Rome the emperor had passed away. Jos adds that Vitellius came in the year 36 AD to Judaea to be present at Jerus at the time of the Passover. It has been assumed by most authorities (so *HDB* and *EB*) that Pilate had departed before this visit of Vitellius. They accordingly date the procuratorship of Pilate as lasting from 26 to 36 AD. As against this view, von Dobschütz points out (*RE* s.v. "Pilate") that by this reckoning Pilate must have taken at least a year to get to Rome; for Tiberius died on March 16, 37 AD. Such delay is inconceivable in view of the circumstances; hence von Dobschütz rightly dates the period of his procuratorship 27–37 AD. The procurator of Judaea had no easy task, nor did Pilate make the task easier by his actions. He was not careful to conciliate the religious prejudices of the Jews, and at times this attitude of his led to violent collisions between ruler and ruled.

On one occasion, when the soldiers under his command came to Jerus, he caused them to bring with them their ensigns, upon which were the usual images of the emperor. The ensigns were brought in privily by night, but their presence was soon discovered. Immediately multitudes of excited Jews hastened to Caesarea to petition him for the removal of the obnoxious ensigns. For five days he refused to hear them, but on the sixth he took his place on the judgment seat, and when the Jews were admitted he had them surrounded with soldiers and threatened them with instant death unless they ceased to trouble him with the matter. The Jews thereupon flung themselves on the ground and bared their necks, declaring that they preferred death to the violation of their laws. Pilate, unwilling to slay so many, yielded the point and removed the ensigns (Jos, *Ant,* XVIII, iii, 1; *BJ,* II, ix, 2, 3).

At another time he used the sacred treasure of the temple, called corban (*ḳorbān*), to pay for bringing water into Jerus by an aqueduct. A crowd came together and clamored against him; but he had caused soldiers dressed as civilians to mingle with the multitude, and at a given signal they fell upon the rioters and beat them so severely with staves that the riot was quelled (Jos, *Ant,* XVIII, iii, 2; *BJ,* II, ix, 4).

Philo tells us (*Legatio ad Caium*, xxxviii) that on another occasion he dedicated some gilt shields in the palace of Herod in honor of the emperor. On these shields there was no representation of any forbidden thing, but simply an inscription of the name of the donor and of him in whose honor they were set up. The Jews petitioned him to have them removed; when he refused, they appealed to Tiberius, who sent an order that they should be removed to Caesarea.

Of the incident, mentioned in Lk **13** 1, of the Galileans whose blood Pilate mingled with their sacrifices, nothing further is known.

Jos (*Ant*, XVIII, iv, 1, 2) gives an account of the incident which led to Pilate's downfall. A religious pretender arose in Samaria who promised the Samaritans that if they would assemble at Mt. Gerizim, he would show them the sacred vessels which Moses had hidden there. A great multitude assembled in readiness to ascend the mountain, but before they could accomplish their aim they were attacked by Pilate's cavalry, and many of them were slain. The Samaritans thereupon sent an embassy to Vitellius, the legate of Syria, to accuse Pilate of the murder of those who had been slain. Vitellius, who desired to stand well with the Jews, deposed Pilate from office, appointed Marcellus in his place, and ordered Pilate to go to Rome and answer the charges made against him before the emperor. Pilate set out for Rome, but, before he could reach it, Tiberius had died; and it is probable that, in the confusion which followed, Pilate escaped the inquisition with which he was threatened. From this point onward history knows nothing more of Pilate.

The shortest and simplest account of Pilate's dealings with Jesus Christ is given in the Gospel of Mk.

3. Pilate and Jesus Christ

There we are told that Jesus was delivered to Pilate; that Pilate asked Him if He was the king of the Jews, receiving an affirmative answer; that, to Pilate's surprise, Jesus answered nothing to the accusations of the chief priests; that Pilate tried to release Jesus according to an ancient custom; that the multitude, in spite of the protest of Pilate, demanded the release of Barabbas, and cried out that Jesus should be crucified; that Pilate scourged Jesus and delivered Him to be crucified; and that Jesus, when He had been scourged and mocked, was led away to be crucified. Mk tells further how Joseph of Arimathaea begged of Pilate the body of Jesus. Pilate was surprised that Jesus died so quickly, and questioned the centurion about it. Pilate's surprise and question are peculiar to Mk. Being satisfied on this point, Pilate granted the body to Joseph. Mt adds the dream and message of Pilate's wife (**27** 19); it also tells how Pilate washed his hands before the people, disclaiming responsibility for the death of Jesus, and how the people accepted the responsibility (**27** 24 f); also how Pilate granted a guard for the tomb (**27** 62–66). Lk alone narrates the sending of Jesus to Herod (**23** 6–12), and reports Pilate's three times repeated asseveration that he found no fault in Jesus (**23** 4.14.22). Jn gives by far the fullest narrative, which forms a framework into which the more fragmentary accounts of the Synoptics can be fitted with perfect ease. Some critics, holding that Mk alone is trustworthy, dismiss the additional incidents given in Mt and Lk as apologetic amplifications; and many dismiss the narrative of Jn as wholly unworthy of credence. Such theories are based on preconceived opinions as to the date, authorship and reliability of the various Gospels. The reader who holds all the Gospels to be, in the main, authentic and trustworthy narratives will have no difficulty in perceiving that all four narratives, when taken together, present a story consistent in all its details and free from all difficulty. See GOSPELS. It should be noted that John evidently had special opportunities of obtaining exacter knowledge than that possessed by the others, as he was present at every stage of the trial; and that his narrative makes clear what is obscure in the accounts of the Synoptics.

The parts may be fitted together thus: Jesus is brought to Pilate (Mt **27** 2; Mk **15** 1; Lk **23** 1; Jn **18** 28). Pilate asks for a specific accusation (Jn **18** 29–32). Pilate enters the praetorium, questions Jesus about His alleged kingship, and receives the answer that He rules over the kingdom of truth, and over the hearts of men who acknowledge the truth. Pilate asks: "What is truth?" (reported briefly in Mt **27** 11; Mk **15** 2; Lk **23** 3, and with more detail Jn **18** 33–38). Pilate brings Him forth (this is the only detail that needs to be supplied in order to make the harmony complete, and in itself it is probable enough), and many accusations are made against Him, to which, to Pilate's surprise, He makes no reply (Mt **27** 12–14; Mk **15** 3–5). Pilate affirms His innocence, but the charges are repeated (Lk **23** 4 f). Pilate sends Him to Herod, who in mockery clothes Him in shining raiment, and sends Him back (Lk **23** 6–12). Pilate declares that neither Herod or himself can find any fault in Him, and offers to scourge Him and let Him go (Lk **23** 13–16; Jn **18** 38*b*). Pilate offers to release Jesus in accordance with an ancient custom (Mt **27** 15–18; Mk **15** 6–10; Jn **18** 39). Pilate's wife sends him a message warning him not to harm Jesus because she has suffered many things in a dream because of Him (Mt **27** 19). The people, persuaded thereto by the chief priests and elders, choose Barabbas, and, in spite of the repeated protests of Pilate, demand that Jesus shall be crucified (Mt **27** 20–23; Mk **15** 11–14; Lk **23** 18–23; Jn **18** 40). Pilate washes his hands before the people, and they take the guilt of the deed upon themselves and their children (Mt **27** 24 f). Pilate releases Barabbas and orders Jesus to be scourged (Mt **27** 26; Mk **15** 15; Lk **23** 24 f). Jesus is scourged and mocked, buffeted and spit upon (Mt **27** 27–31*a*; Mk **15** 16–20*a*; Jn **19** 1–3). Pilate again declares the innocence of Jesus, brings Him out, and says: "Behold the man!" The chief priests and officers cry out: "Crucify him!" They accuse Him of making Himself the Son of God. Pilate, becoming more afraid at this saying, once more interviews the prisoner in the praetorium. He again tries to release Him, but is accused of treachery to the emperor. Overborne by this, Pilate sits on the judgment seat (see GABBATHA), and says: "Behold, your King!" Again the cry goes up: "Away with him, crucify him!" Pilate says: "Shall I crucify your King?" The chief priests answered with a final renunciation of all that God had given them, saying: "We have no king but Caesar" (Jn **19** 4–15). Pilate sentences Jesus and gives Him up to be crucified, and He is led away (Mt **27** 31*b*; Mk **15** 20*b*; Lk **23** 26*a*; Jn **19** 16). Pilate writes a title for the cross, and refuses to alter it (Jn **19** 19–22). The Jews ask of Pilate that the legs of the three who were crucified might be broken (Jn **19** 31). Joseph of Arimathaea begs the body of Jesus from Pilate (Mt **27** 57.58*a*; Mk **15** 42 f; Lk **23** 50–52; Jn **19** 38*a*). Pilate is surprised that Jesus has died so soon, and questions the centurion (Mk **15** 44). He gives up to Joseph the body of Jesus (Mt **27** 58*b*; Mk **15** 45; Jn **19** 38*b*). The chief priests and the Pharisees obtain permission from Pilate to take precautions against any theft of the body of Jesus (Mt **27** 62–66).

Pilate is mentioned three times in Acts: in a speech of Peter (**3** 13), in a thanksgiving of the church (**4** 27), and in a speech of Paul (**13** 28). He is also mentioned in 1 Tim (**6** 13) as the one before whom Christ Jesus witnessed the good confession.

Eusebius, who lived in the 4th cent., tells us (*HE*, II) on the authority of certain Gr historians

4. Pilate in Tradition and Legend

that Pilate fell into such calamities that he committed suicide. Various apocryphal writings have come down to us, written from the 3d to the 5th cents., with others of a later date, in which legendary details are given about Pilate. In all these a favorable view is taken of his character; hence the Coptic church came to believe that he became a Christian, and enrolled him among the number of its saints. His wife, to whom tradition gives the name of Claudia Procula, or Procla, is said to have been a Jewish proselyte at the time of the death of Jesus, and afterward to have become a Christian. Her name is honored along with Pilate's in the Coptic church, and in the calendar of saints honored by the Gr church her name is found against the date October 27.

We find not unkindly references to Pilate in the recently discovered fragment of the Gospel of Peter, which was composed in the 2d cent. In the so-called Gospel of Nicodemus, which belongs to the 4th or 5th cent., we find in the first part, called the Acts of Pilate, a long account of the trial of Jesus. It tells how the standards in the hall of judgment bowed down before Jesus, in spite of the efforts of the standard-bearers, and others who attempted it, to hold them erect. It tells also how many of those who had been healed by Jesus bore testimony to Him at the trial (see Apocryphal Gospels). There has also come down to us, in various forms (e.g. in the Acts of Peter and Paul), a letter, supposed to be the report of Pilate to Tiberius, narrating the proceedings of the trial, and speaking of Jesus in the highest terms of praise. Eusebius, when he mentions this letter, avers that Tiberius, on perusing it, was incensed against the Jews who had sought the death of Jesus (*HE*, II, 2). Elsewhere (*HE*, IX, 5) he recounts that under Maximin forged Acts of Pilate, containing blasphemies against Christ, were circulated with consent of the emperor. None of these, if they ever existed, have come down to us. In the *Paradosis Pilati* we read that Caesar, being angry with Pilate for what he had done, brought him to Rome as a prisoner, and examined him. When the Christ was named, all the gods in the senate-chamber fell down and were broken. Caesar ordered war to be made on the Jews, and Pilate, after praying to Jesus, was beheaded. The head was taken away by an angel, and Procla, seeing this, died of joy. Another narrative, of late date, recounts that Pilate, at his trial, wore the seamless robe of Jesus; for this reason Caesar, though filled with anger, could not so much as say a harsh word to Pilate; but when the robe was taken off, he condemned Pilate to death. On hearing this, Pilate committed suicide. The body was sunk in the Tiber, but storms were raised by demons on account of this that it was taken up and sunk in the Rhone at Vienne. The same trouble recurred there, and the body was finally buried in the territory of Losania (Lausanne). Tradition connects Mt. Pilatus with his name, although it is probable that the derivation is from *pileatus*, i.e. the mountain with a cloud-cap.

5. The Character of Pilate

Philo (*Legatio ad Caium*, xxxviii) speaks of Pilate in terms of the severest condemnation. According to him, Pilate was a man of a very inflexible disposition, and very merciless as well as obstinate. Philo calls him a man of most ferocious passions, and speaks of his corruption, his acts of insolence, his rapine, his habit of insulting people, his cruelty, his continual murders of people untried and uncondemned, and his never-ending and most grievous inhumanity. This is very highly colored and probably much exaggerated; certainly the instances given do not bear out this description of the man. Much of what he says of Pilate is in direct opposition to what we learn of him in the Gospels. There he appears to us as a man who, in spite of many undoubted faults, tries hard to conduct the trial with fairness. Pilate had the ethics of his class, and obviously tried to act up to the standard which he had formed. There was in him, however, no deep moral basis of character, as is shown by the utter skepticism of his question, "What is truth?" When he found that the doing of strict justice threatened to endanger his position, he reluctantly and with a great deal of shame gave way to the demands of the Jews. He sent Jesus to the cross, but not before he had exhausted every expedient for saving Him, except the simple and straightforward one of dismissing the case. He had the haughtiness of the dominant race, and a profound contempt for the people over which he ruled. This contempt, as we have seen, continually brought him into trouble. He felt deeply humiliated at having to give way to those whom he utterly despised, and, in the manner of a small mind, revenged himself on them by calling Christ their king, and by refusing to alter the mocking inscription on the cross. It is certain that Pilate, in condemning Jesus, acted, and knew that he acted against his conscience. He knew what was right, but for selfish and cowardly reasons refused to do it. He was faced by a great moral emergency, and he failed. We rest on the judgment of Our Lord, that he was guilty, but not so guilty as the leaders of the chosen people.

Literature.—The Gospels; Philo, *Legatio ad Caium;* Jos, *Ant* and *BJ;* the *Annals* of Tacitus; Eusebius, *HE;* Walker, *Apocryphal Gospels, Acts, and Revelations* in the "Ante-Nicene Christian Library," and for the *Gospel according to Peter*, vol IX of the same series. Orr, *NT Apocryphal Writings* ("Temple Bible Series"), gives the text of the Gospel of Nicodemus and the Gospel of Peter. There is a great mass of literature on the subject, but there is no Eng. monograph on Pontius Pilate. In German there is G. A. Müller, *Pontius Pilatus der fünfte Prokurator von Judäa* (Stuttgart, 1888). See also the various articles on Pilate in books of reference on the NT, notably *RE* (von Dobschütz), *HDB* (G. T. Purves), *DCG* (A. Souter), and *EB* (W. J. Woodhouse). For the name of Pilate see arts. on "Pontius Pilatus et les Pontii" by Ollivier in *Rev. Bib.*, vol V. For the Apocryphal Gospels see art. on "Gospel of Nicodemus" in *HDB*, also art. "Apocryphal Gospels," in the supplementary volume of *HDB;* Orr, *NT Apocryphal Writings;* Zahn, *Geschichte des NT Kanons;* Harnack, *Altchristliche Litteraturgeschichte*. For the trial of Jesus see Lives of Christ by Keim, Edersheim, Stalker, Andrews and others; Taylor Innes, *Trial of Jesus Christ, a Legal Monograph*, 1899; and for the historical background, Schürer, *HJP*.

J. Macartney Wilson

PILDASH, pil′dash (פִּלְדָּשׁ, *pildāsh*, "steely"): Nephew of Abram (Gen **22** 22).

PILE, pīl (מְדוּרָה, *m*ᵉ*dhūrāh*, from *dūr*, "heap up"): Isa **30** 33, "The pile thereof is fire and much wood"; Ezk **24** 9.10, "I also will make the pile great. Heap on the wood, make the fire hot." Isa **30** 33 may be paraphrased, 'the pyre thereof is of much wood, burning fiercely.' See Topheth.

PILEHA, pil′ĕ-hä, pī′lē-hä. See Pilha.

PILGRIM, pil′grim, **PILGRIMAGE,** pil′grim-āj: "Pilgrim" in EV for παρεπίδημος, *parepídēmos* (He **11** 13; 1 Pet **2** 11). "Pilgrimage" for מָגוֹר, *māghōr* (Gen **47** 9 [RVm "sojournings"]; Ps **119** 54; and [AV] Ex **6** 4 [RV "sojournings"]). Both the Heb (see Ger) and Gr words contain the idea of foreign residence, but it is the residence and not travel that is implied. Consequently "pilgrim" is a poor tr, and "sojourner," "sojourning" should have been used throughout. In the NT passages heaven is thought of as the contrasted permanent dwelling-place, while the OT usages seem to be without a contrast definitely in mind.

PILHA, pil′hä (פִּלְחָא, *pilḥā'*, "ploughman"; AV **Pileha**): One of those who signed Nehemiah's covenant (Neh **10** 24).

PILL. See Peel.

PILLAR, pil′ar (מַצֵּבָה, *maççēbhāh*, עַמּוּד, *'ammūdh;* στῦλος, *stúlos*): In a good many cases RV substitutes "pillars" for AV "images" (*maççēbhōth*, Ex **34** 13; Dt **7** 5; 1 K **14** 23, etc). In Gen **19** 26, where "pillar of salt" is given, the word is *n*ᵉ*çībh;* in 1 S **2** 8 it is *māçūḳ;* while in most other single uses RVm gives variant renderings, as in Jgs **9** 6 (*muççābh*), RVm "garrison"; in 1 K **10** 12 (*miş'ādh*), RVm "'a railing,' Heb 'a prop'"; in 2 K **18** 16 (*'ōm*ᵉ*nōth*), RVm "doorposts." The *maççēbhōth* were (1) memorial pillars, as in the "pillars" of Jacob at Bethel (Gen **28** 18.22; cf **31** 13; **35** 14), in covenant with Laban (**31** 45 ff), at Rachel's grave (**35** 20); Absalom's pillar (2 S **18** 18). Such pillars were legitimate (the theory of a fetishistic character is ungrounded); it is predicted in Isa **19** 19 that such a pillar would be set up to Jeh at the border of Egypt. (2) Idolatrous pillars, in Canaanitish and other heathen worships. These were to be ruthlessly broken down (AV "images," see above; Ex **23** 24; **34** 13; Dt **7** 5, etc; cf Lev **26** 1). See Images. The other word, *'ammūdh*, is used of the pillar of cloud and fire (see below); of the pillars of the tabernacle and temple (see s.v.); of the two pillars Jachin and Boaz (q.v.); poetically of the "pillars" of heaven, of earth (Job **9** 6; **26** 11; Ps **75** 3; **99** 7), etc. In the few instances of the word in the NT, the use is **figurative.** James, Cephas and John "were reputed to be pillars" of the church at Jerus (Gal **2** 9); the church is "the pillar and ground of the truth" (1 Tim **3** 15); he that overcomes is made "a pillar" in the temple of God (Rev **3** 12); a strong angel had feet "as pillars of fire" (**10** 1).

Pillar of Cloud and Fire: The visible manifestation of the Divine presence in the journeyings of Israel at the time of the Exodus. Jeh, it is narrated, went before the people "by day in a pillar of cloud, to lead them the way, and by night in a pillar of fire, to give them light. . . . . The pillar of cloud by day, and the pillar of fire by night, departed not from before the people" (Ex **13** 21.22; cf **14** 19.24; Nu **14** 14). When the congregation was at rest, the cloud abode over the tabernacle (Ex **40** 36; Nu **9** 17; **14** 14). When Jeh wished to communicate His will to Moses, the pillar descended to the door of the Tent of Meeting (Ex **33** 9-11; Nu **12** 5; Dt **31** 15). These descriptions are not to be rationalistically explained; what is depicted is a true theophany. Criticism has sought to establish discrepancies between the allusions to the cloud in the JE and the P parts of the narrative, but these are not made out without straining; e.g. it is not the case that JE alone represents Jeh as speaking with Moses in the cloud at the *door* of the tabernacle. The same representation is found in Ex **29** 42.43, ascribed to P. An acute discussion of the alleged discrepancies may be seen in H. M. Wiener, *Essays in Pentateuchal Criticism*, 82 ff.

JAMES ORR

PILLAR OF SALT. See SLIME; LOT.

PILLAR, PLAIN OF THE. See PLAIN OF THE PILLAR.

PILLARS OF THE EARTH. See ASTRONOMY, III, 2.

PILLOW, pil'ō. See BOLSTER; CUSHION.

PILOT, pī'lot. See SHIPS AND BOATS.

PILTAI, pil'tī, pil-tā'ī (פִּלְטַי, *pilṭay*, probably "Jeh delivers"): One of the priests, described as "the chiefs of the fathers," in the days of Joiakim (Neh **12** 17).

PIN (יָתֵד, *yāthēdh*, from *yāthadh*, "to drive in a peg"[?]): A cylindrical piece of wood or metal (e.g. brass, Ex **27** 19) such as that used by weavers in beating up the woof in the loom (Jgs **16** 14, where Delilah fastened Samson's hair with the "pin"); or as a peg for hanging (Ezk **15** 3; cf Isa **22** 23 f; Ezr **9** 8); or as a tent-pin, such as those used in the tabernacle (Ex **27** 19; **35** 18; **38** 20. 31; **39** 40; Nu **3** 37; **4** 32; Jgs **4** 21, where AV translates "nail," RV "tent-pin"; cf **5** 26, where Heb has the same word, EV "nail"). The tent-pin, like that of today, was probably sharpened at one end (Jgs **4** 21) and so shaped at the other as to permit the attaching of the cords so frequently mentioned in the same connection (Ex **35** 18; **39** 40; Nu **3** 37; **4** 32; cf Isa **33** 20). From the acts of driving in the tent-pin (*ṭāka'*) and pulling it out (*nāsā'*) are derived the technical Heb terms for pitching a tent and for breaking camp. See also CRISPING PIN (Isa **3** 22, RV "satchels"); STAKE.

NATHAN ISAACS

PINE, pīn. See PINING SICKNESS.

PINE TREE, pīn trē: (1) עֵץ שֶׁמֶן, *'ēç shemen*, tr[d] RV "wild olive," AV "pine" (Neh **8** 15); RV "oil-tree," m "oleaster" (Isa **41** 19); "olive-wood" (1 K **6** 23.31-33). See OIL TREE. (2) תִּדְהָר, *tidhhār* (Isa **41** 19, m "plane"; **60** 13); πεύκη, *peúkē*, "fir." Lagarde, from similarity of *tidhhār* to the Syr *deddar*, usually the "elm," considers this the best tr. Symmachus also tr[d] *tidhhār* (Isa **41** 19) by πτελέα, *pteléa*, the "elm." The elm, *Ulmus campestris*, is rare in Pal and the Lebanon, though it is found today N. of Aleppo. Post (*HDB*, III, 592-93) considers that (1) should be tr[d] as "pine," which he describes as a "fat wood tree"; it is perhaps as probably a correct tr for (2), but great uncertainty remains. Two species of pine are plentiful in the

Pine Forest at Beirût.

Lebanon and flourish in most parts of Pal when given a chance. These are the stone pine, *Pinus pinea*, and the Aleppo pine, *P. halepensis;* all the highlands looking toward the sea are suited to their growth.

E. W. G. MASTERMAN

PINING, pīn'ing, **SICKNESS,** sik'nes: In the account of the epileptic boy in Mk **9** 18 it is said that "he pineth away." The vb. used here (ξηραίνω, *xēraínō*) means "to dry up," and is the same which is used of the withering of plants, but seldom used in this metaphorical sense. The Eng. word is from the AS *pinian* and is often found in the Elizabethan literature, occurring 13 t in Shakespeare. In the OT it is found in Lev **26** 39 (*bis*) and in Ezk **24** 23 and **33** 10. In RV it replaces "consume" in Ezk **4** 17. In all these passages it is the rendering of the Heb *māḳaḳ*, and means expressly being wasted on account of sin. In Lev **26** 16 "pine away" is used in RV to replace "cause sorrow of heart," and is the tr of the Heb *dūbh;* and in Dt **28** 65 "sorrow of mind" is also replaced in RV by "pining of soul," the word so rendered being *de'ābhōn*, which in these two passages is expressive of homesickness. In Isa **24** 16 the reduplicated exclamation, "my leanness," of AV is changed into "I pine away," the word being *rāzī*. The starving people in Lam **4** 9 are said to pine away, the word so tr[d] being *zūbh*. All these Heb words have a general meaning of to dry or to waste or wear away, or to be exhausted by morbid discharges.

Pining sickness in Isa **38** 12 AV is a mistranslation, the word so rendered, *dallāh*, meaning here the thrum by which the web is tied to the loom. The figure in the verse is that Hezekiah's life is being removed from the earth by his sickness as the web is removed from the loom by having the thrums cut, and being then rolled up. Both AVm and RVm have the correct reading, "from the thrum." LXX has ἐρίθου ἐγγιζούσης ἐκτεμεῖν, *eríthou eggizoúsēs ektemein*, and Vulg *dum adhuc ordirer, succidit me*. The other reading is due to another interpretation of the word which in a few passages, as Jer **52** 15, like its √ *dal*, means something small, poor, and decaying or weak, such as the lean kine of Pharaoh's dream (Gen **41** 19).

ALEX. MACALISTER

PINION, pin'yun (אֵבֶר, *'ēbher*, אֶבְרָה, *'ebhrāh*): RV has tr[d] these Heb words uniformly by "pinion," where AV uses either "wing" or "feathers," with which words they stand in parallelism in all passages. The shorter Heb word is found only once, in Jeh's parable to Ezekiel: "A great eagle with great wings and long pinions [AV "longwinged"], full of feathers, which had divers colors, came unto Lebanon, and took the top of the cedar" (Ezk **17** 3). The fem. form (*'ebhrāh*) is used of the wings of the dove (Ps **68** 13), of the ostrich (Job **39** 13) and of the eagle (Dt **32** 11). Once (Ps **91** 4) it stands in a **figurative** expression for the protective care of Jeh, which is bestowed on those that trust in Him.

H. L. E. LUERING

PINNACLE, pin'a-k'l (πτερύγιον, *pterúgion* [Mt **4** 5; Lk **4** 9, RVm "wing"]): "The pinnacle of the temple" is named as the place to which the devil took Jesus, and there tempted Him to cast Himself down. It is not known what precise elevated spot is meant, whether a part of the roof of the temple itself, or some high point in the adjacent buildings overlooking the deep ravine. It was more probably the latter.

PINON, pī'non (פִּינֹן, *pīnōn*, "darkness"): One of the "chiefs of Edom" (Gen **36** 41; 1 Ch **1** 52).

PIPE, pīp. See CANDLESTICK; LAMP; MUSIC.

PIRA, pī'ra (οἱ ἐκ Πειρᾶς, *hoi ek Peirás* [1 Esd **5** 19]): Thought to be a repetition of CAPHIRA (q.v.) earlier in the verse.

PIRAM, pī'ram (פִּרְאָם, *pir'ām*, "indomitable"): King of Jarmuth, one of the five Amorite kings who leagued themselves against Joshua's invasion (Josh **10** 3 ff).

PIRATHON, pir'a-thon, **PIRATHONITE**, pir'a-thon-īt (פִּרְעָתוֹן, *pir'āthōn*, פִּרְעָתוֹנִי, *pir'āthōnī*; B, Φαραθώμ, *Pharathōm*, A, Φρααθώμ, *Phraathōm*, Φαραθωνείτης, *Pharathuneitēs*): The home of Abdon the son of Hillel the Pirathonite (Jgs **12** 13 ff AV), where also he was buried, "in the land of Ephraim in the mount of the Amalekites." The latter name may have clung to a district which at some former time had been held by the Amalekites. From this town also came Benaiah, one of David's chief captains (2 S **23** 30; 1 Ch **11** 31; **27** 14). It is probably to be identified with *Fer'atā*, about 6 miles S.W. of *Nāblus*. A possible rival is *Fir'on*, 15 miles W. of *Nāblus*. G. A. Smith suggests a position at the head of *Wâdy Far'ah* (*HGHL*, 355). Moore thinks it may have been in Benjamin, Abdon being a Benjamite family (1 Ch **8** 23.30; **9** 36). It is just possible that the place may be identical with Pharathon, one of the towns fortified by Bacchides (1 Macc **9** 50).

W. EWING

PISGAH, piz'ga (הַפִּסְגָּה, *ha-pişgāh*; Φασγά, *Phasgá*, τὸ λελαξευμένον, *tó lelaxeuménon*, ἡ λαξευτή, *hē laxeutḗ*): This name, which has always the definite art., appears only in combination either with *rō'sh*, "head," "top," or *'ashdōth*, not tr[d] in AV save in Dt **4** 49, where it is rendered "springs," RV uniformly "slopes," RVm "springs."

Pisgah is identified with Nebo in Dt **34** 1; cf **3** 27. "The top of Pisgah, which looketh down upon the desert" marks a stage in the march of the host of Israel (Nu **21** 20). Hither Balak brought Balaam to the field of Zophim (**23** 14). Here Moses obtained his view of the Promised Land, and died. See NEBO. Many scholars (e.g. Buhl, *GAP*, 122; Gray, "Numbers," *ICC*, 291) take Pisgah as the name applying to the mountain range in which the Moab plateau terminates to the W., the "top" or "head" of Pisgah being the point in which the ridge running out westward from the main mass culminates. The summit commands a wide view, and looks down upon the desert. The identification is made surer by the name *Tal'at eṣ-Ṣufa* found here, which seems to correspond with the field of Zophim.

'Ashdōth is the constr. pl. of *'ashēdhāh* (sing. form not found), from *'eshedh*, "foundation," "bottom," "lower part" (slope); cf Assyr *ishdu*, "foundation." Some would derive it from Aram. *'ashadh*, "to pour," whence "fall" or "slope" (*OHL*, s.v.). Ashdoth-pisgah overlooked the Dead Sea from the E. (Dt **3** 17; **4** 49; Josh **12** 3; **13** 20). There can be no reasonable doubt that Ashdoth-pisgah signifies the steep slopes of the mountain descending into the contiguous valleys.

It is worthy of note that LXX does not uniformly render Pisgah by a proper name, but sometimes by a derivative of *laxeúō*, "to hew" or "to dress stone" (Nu **21** 20; **23** 14; Dt **3** 27; **4** 49). Jerome (*Onom*, s.v. *Asedoth*) gives *abscisum* as the Lat equivalent of *Fasga*. He derives Pisgah from *pāṣagh*, which, in new Heb, means "to split," "to cut off." This suggests a mountain the steep sides of which give it the appearance of having been "cut out." This description applies perfectly to *Jebel Nebā* as viewed from the Dead Sea.

W. EWING

PISHON, pī'shon (פִּישׁוֹן, *pīshōn*; AV **Pison**, pī'son): A river of EDEN (q.v.), said to compass the whole land of Havilah where there is gold, bdellium and onyx stone (Gen **2** 11), most probably identified with the Karun River which comes down from the mountains of Media and formerly emptied into the Pers Gulf.

PISIDIA, pi-sid'i-a (τὴν Πισιδίαν, *tēn Pisidían* [Acts **14** 24]; in Acts **13** 14, ℵ A B C give Ἀντιόχειαν τὴν Πισιδίαν, *Antiócheian tēn Pisidían*, "the Pisidian Antioch," the other MSS, Ἀντιόχειαν τῆς Πισιδίας, *Antiócheian tēs Pisidías*, "Antioch of Pisidia." The former, but not the latter, reading correctly describes the condition of affairs at the time when St. Paul traveled in the country; see below):

1. Situation and History

Pisidia, as a strict geographical term, was the name given to the huge block of mountain country stretching northward from the Taurus range where the latter overlooked the Pamphylian coast land, to the valleys which connected Apamea with Antioch, and Antioch with Iconium. It was bounded by Lycia on the W., by the Phrygian country on the N., and by Isauria on the E.; but there is no natural boundary between Pisidia and Isauria, and the frontier was never strictly drawn. The name is used in its geographical sense in the *Anabasis* of Xenophon, who informs us that the Pisidians were independent of the king of Persia at the end of the 5th cent. BC. Alexander the Great had difficulty in reducing the Pisidian cities, and throughout ancient history we find the Pisidian mountains described as the home of a turbulent and warlike people, given to robbery and pillage. The task of subjugating them was intrusted by the Romans to the Galatian king Amyntas, and, at his death in 25 BC, Pisidia passed with the rest of his possessions into the Rom province Galatia. Augustus now took seriously in hand the pacification of Pisidia and the Isaurian mountains on the E. Five military colonies were founded in Pisidia and the eastern mountains—Cremna, Comama, Olbasa, Parlais and Lystra—and all were connected by military roads with the main garrison city Antioch, which lay in Galatian Phrygia, near the northern border of

Pisidia. An inscription discovered in 1912 shows that Quirinius, who is mentioned in Lk **2** 2 as governor of Syria in the year of Christ's birth, was an honorary magistrate of the colony of Antioch; his connection with Antioch dates from his campaign against the Homonades—who had resisted and killed Amyntas—about 8 BC (see Ramsay in *Expos*, November, 1912, 385 ff, 406). The military system set up in Pisidia was based on that of Antioch, and from this fact, and from its proximity to Pisidia, Antioch derived its title "the Pisidian," which served to distinguish it from the other cities called Antioch. It is by a mistake arising from confusion with a later political arrangement that Antioch is designated "of Pisidia" in the majority of the MSS.

Pisidia remained part of the province Galatia till 74 AD, when the greater (southern) part of it was assigned to the new double province Lycia-Pamphylia, and the cities in this portion of Pisidia now ranked as Pamphylian. The northern part of Pisidia continued to belong to Galatia, until, in the time of Diocletian, the southern part of the province Galatia (including the cities of Antioch and Iconium), with parts of Lycaonia and Asia, were formed into a province called Pisidia, with Antioch as capital. Antioch was now for the first time correctly described as a city "of Pisidia," although there is reason to believe that the term "Pisidia" had already been extended northward in popular usage to include part at least of the Phrygian region of Galatia. This perhaps explains the reading "Antioch of Pisidia" in the Codex Bezae, whose readings usually reflect the conditions of the 2d cent. of our era in Asia Minor. This use of the term was of course political and administrative; Antioch continued to be a city of Phrygia in the ethnical sense and a recently discovered inscription proves that the Phrygian language was spoken in the neighborhood of Antioch as late as the 3d cent. of our era (see also Calder in *Journal of Rom Studies*, 1912, 84).

2. St. Paul in Pisidia

St. Paul crossed Pisidia on the journey from Perga to Antioch referred to in Acts **13** 14, and again on the return journey, Acts **14** 24. Of those journeys no details are recorded in Acts, but it has been suggested by Conybeare and Howson that the "perils of rivers" and "perils of robbers" mentioned by St. Paul in 2 Cor **11** 26 refer to his journeys across Pisidia, and Ramsay has pointed out in confirmation of this view that a considerable number of Pisidian inscriptions refer to the armed policemen and soldiers who kept the peace in this region, while others refer to a conflict with robbers, or to an escape from drowning in a river (*The Church in the Rom Empire*, 23 f; cf *Journal of Rom Studies*, 1912, 82 f). Adada, a city on St. Paul's route from Perga to Antioch, is called by the Turks *Kara Baulo;* "Baulo" is the Turkish pronunciation of "Paulos," and the name is doubtless reminiscent of an early tradition connecting the city with St. Paul. Pisidia had remained unaffected by Hellenic civilization, and the Rom occupation at the time of St. Paul was purely military. It is therefore unlikely that St. Paul preached in Pisidia. Except on the extreme N.W., none of the Christian inscriptions of Pisidia—in glaring contrast with those of Phrygia—date before the legal recognition of Christianity under Constantine.

Literature.—Murray, *Handbook of Asia Minor*, 150 ff; Ramsay, *The Church in the Rom Empire*, 18 ff; Lanckoronski, *Städte Pamphyliens und Pisidiens;* Sterrett, *Epigraphical Journey* and *Wolfe Expedition*. A few inscriptions containing Pisidian names with native inflections have been published by Ramsay in *Revue des universités du midi*, 1895, 353 ff.

W. M. Calder

PISON, pī'son. See Pishon.

PISPA, pis'pä (פִּסְפָּא, *piṣpā'*, "dispersion," AV **Pispah**): A son of Jether, an Asherite (1 Ch **7** 38).

PIT: The word translates different Heb words of which the most important are: (1) בּוֹר, *bōr*, "pit" or "cistern," made by digging (Gen **37** 20); hence "dungeon" (Jer **38** 6, m "pit"); (2) בְּאֵר, *be'ēr*, "pit" or "well" made by digging (Gen **21** 25); (3) שְׁאוֹל, *she'ōl*, generally rendered "hell" in AV (see Hell); (4) שַׁחַת, *shaḥath*, a pit in the ground to catch wild animals. (1), (2) and (4) above are used **metaphorically** of the pit of the "grave" or of "sheol" (Ps **28** 1; **30** 3; Job **33** 24). AV sometimes incorrectly renders (4) by "corruption." (5) פַּחַת, *paḥath*, "pit," literally (2 S **17** 9), and **figuratively** (Jer **48** 43). In the NT "pit" renders *βόθυνος*, *bóthunos* (Mt **15** 14), which means any kind of hole in the ground. In the corresponding passage Lk (**14** 5 AV) has *φρέαρ*, *phréar*, "well," the same as (2) above. For "bottomless pit" (Rev **9** 1, AV, etc) see Abyss.

T. Lewis

PITCH, pich: The tr of the noun כֹּפֶר, *kōpher*, and the vb. כָּפַר, *kāphar*, in Gen **6** 14 and of the noun זֶפֶת, *zepheth*, in Ex **2** 3; Isa **34** 9. In Gen **6** 14 the words are the ordinary forms for "covering," "cover," so that the tr "pitch" is largely guesswork, aided by the LXX, which reads *ἄσφαλτος*, *ásphaltos*, "bitumen," here, and by the fact that pitch is a usual "covering" for vessels. The meaning of *zepheth*, however, is fixed by the obvious Dead Sea imagery of Isa **34** 9–15—the streams and land of Edom are to become burning bitumen, like the sites of Sodom and Gomorrah. In Ex **2** 3 *zepheth* is combined with *ḥēmār*, which also means bitumen (Gen **14** 10; see Slime), and the distinction between the words (different consistencies of the same substance?) is not clear.

Burton Scott Easton

PITCHER, pich'ẽr (כַּד, *kadh;* **κεράμιον**, *kerámion*): The word is found chiefly in the OT in the story of Rebekah in Gen **24** 13 ff; but Gideon's men also had their lamps in pitchers (Jgs **7** 16.19). Eccl speaks of the pitcher broken at the fountain (**12** 6). The single use in the NT is in Mk **14** 13 ‖ Lk **22** 10. The pitcher was an earthenware vessel (cf Lam **4** 2, *nēbhel*), with one or two handles, used for carrying water, and commonly borne upon the head or shoulder (cf Gen **24**).

PITHOM, pī'thom (פִּתֹם, *pithōm;* Πειθώ, *Peithṓ* [Ex **1** 11]):

1. Meaning of Name

Champollion (Gesenius, *Lex.*, s.v.) considered this name to mean "a narrow place" in Coptic, but it is generally explained to be the Egyp *Pa-tum*, or "city of the setting sun." It was one of the cities built by the Hebrews (see Raamses), and according to Wessel was the *Thoum* of the Antonine Itinerary.

Brugsch (*Hist Egypt*, 1879, II, 343) says that it was identical with "Heracleopolis Parva, the capital of the Sethroitic nome in the age of the Greeks and Romans . . . . half-way on the great road from Pelusium to Tanis (Zoan), and this indication given on the authority of the itineraries furnishes the sole means of fixing its position." This is, however, disputed. Tum was worshipped at Thebes, at Zoan, and probably at Bubastis, while Heliopolis (Brugsch, *Geogr.*, I, 254) was also called *Pa-tum*.

There were apparently several places of the name; and Herodotus (ii.158) says that the Canal of Darius began a little above Bubastis, "near the Arabian city Patoumos," and reached the Red Sea.

(1) *Dr. Naville's theory.*—In 1885 Dr. E. Naville discovered a Rom milestone of Maximian and Severus, proving that the site of Heroopolis was at *Tell el Maḥûṭah* ("the walled mound") in *Wâdy Tumeilât*. The modern name he gives as *Tell el*

Maskhûtah, which was not that heard by the present writer in 1882. This identification had long been supposed probable. Excavations at

2. Situation the site laid bare strong walls and texts showing the worship of Tum. None was found to be older than the time of Rameses II—who, however, is well known to have defaced older inscriptions, and to have substituted his own name for that of earlier builders. A statue of later date, bearing the title "Recorder of Pithom," was also found at this same site. Dr. Naville concluded that this city must be the OT Pithom, and the region round it Succoth—the Egyp *T-k-u* (but see SUCCOTH). Brugsch, on the other hand, says that the old name of Heroopolis was *Ḳes* (see GOSHEN), which recalls the identification of the LXX (Gen **46** 28); and elsewhere (following Lepsius) he regards the same site as being "the *Pa-Khetam* of Rameses II" (see ETHAM), which Lepsius believed to be the OT Rameses (see RAAMSES) mentioned with Pithom (Brugsch, *Geogr.*, I, 302, 262). St. Silvia in 385 AD was shown the site of Pithom near Heroopolis, but farther E., and she distinguishes the two; but in her time, though Heroopolis was a village, the site of Pithom was probably conjectural. In the time of Minepthah, son of Rameses II (Brugsch, *Hist*, II, 128), we have a report that certain nomads from *Aduma* (or Edom) passed through "the *Khetam* [or fort] of Minepthah-Hotephima, which is situated in *T-k-u*, to the lakes [or canals] of the city *Pi-tum* of Minepthah-Hotephima, which are situated in the land of *T-k-u*, in order to feed themselves and to feed their herds."

(2) *Patoumos of Herodotus*.—These places seem to have been on the eastern border of Egypt, but may have been close to the Bitter Lakes or farther N. (see SUCCOTH), whereas *Tell el Mahûṭah* is about 12 miles W. of *Ism'ailieh*, and of Lake Timsaḥ. The definition of the Pithom thus noticed as being that of Minepthah suggests that there was more than one place so called, and the Patoumos of Herodotus seems to have been about 30 miles farther W. (near Zagazig and Bubastis) than the site of Heroopolis, which the LXX indentifies with Goshen and not with Pithom. The latter is not noticed as on the route of the Exodus, and is not identified in the OT with Succoth. In the present state of our knowledge of Egyp topography, the popular impression that the Exodus must have happened in the time of Minepthah, because Pithom was at Heroopolis and was not built till the time of Rameses II, must be regarded as very hazardous. See EXODUS. The Patoumos of Herodotus may well have been the site, and may still be discovered near the head of *Wâdy Tumeilât* or near Bubastis. C. R. CONDER

PITHOM, DISCOVERIES (Supplement, 1929)

I. DIFFICULTIES
II. RE-EXAMINATION
 1. Name
 2. Builder
 3. Character of Store Chambers
 4. Bricks and Mortar
 5. Bricks without Straw
 6. Name of Region
III. RECENT DISCOVERIES
 1. At Beisan
 2. At Kiriath-sepher

The great work of the veteran Egyptologist, Naville, mentioned above by Col. Conder, can now be fully reviewed and properly evaluated. Years of controversy, much research, and now very recently, important discoveries at *Beisan* in 1924–28 and at *Tell Beit-mirsim*, Kiriath-sepher, 1926–28, put the work of Naville in a light very different from that in which it was viewed by the great orientalist who prepared the article, PITHOM, in 1915.

*I. **Difficulties**.*—The rise of the difficulties concerning Naville's discovery at Pithom came in a strange way which, now that so many corroborations of Biblical history have been found by archaeologists, would not be possible in this year 1929. When Professor Naville published account of his discoveries in the *Egyp Exploration Fund Report* 1883 (cf also Edwards, *Pharaohs, Fellahs and Explorers* 41) and told the world that he had found the whole story of the building of the store cities by Israelite slaves, including the name of one of the cities, the character of the cities, the "brick and mortar," the strange story of the withdrawing of the supply of straw and even the name of the Pharaoh, there arose two outcries of incredulity, strangely alike, yet proceeding from very different sources. Some who did not believe that Biblical narratives could be corroborated, and perhaps had little desire to have them corroborated, began at once to discredit Naville's report. The backbone of their contention was that the building done by Rameses was but a rebuilding and that the Exodus had occurred long before, probably in the reign of Amenophis IV. On the other hand, people who thought they believed the Biblical story fully exclaimed, "Oh that is too exact a corroboration." Some people pray unctiously for a Pentacostal outpouring of the Holy Spirit, who, if the tongues of fire should appear, would run for the fire department!

*II. **Re-examination**.*—In 1908, while engaged in research and excavation in Egyp, I determined to make a careful re-examination of Naville's work at *Tell Maskhûtah*. An inquiry of the station master elicited the information that, if we crossed the canal and turned to the right, the ruins would be found on the desert at the south side of the canal. Some peasants met us of whom we made enquiry, "Is this ruin ahead of us on the desert *Tell Maskhûtah?*" They replied, "Yes." I objected that a scientific expedition must make a better start than that. For the Oriental loves to please, and especially in prospect of a *baksheesh*. Of the next group of farmers it was asked, "What is the name of this ruin in the distance?" The reply was "*Tell Maskhûtah*." Then we knew it was *Tell Maskhûtah;* we had asked no leading questions. This fundamental law of evidence is not strictly followed by all research workers. Some, who have gone to visit this ruin, *did not see it at all*, because guided to the wrong place. Some most promising researches in Bible lands have been vitiated by the asking of leading questions of Orientals.

The ruins here are extensive; about 1 mile east and west, a half mile wide at the east end and running to a point on the west. Most of this ruin is Greek and, later still, Roman; essentially interesting, but not germane to the subject under discussion. The ancient Egyp part of the ruins is a rectangular inclosure 210 yards by 220 yards on the southern edge of the ruins of the much larger Greek and Roman city. This Egyp fortress was surrounded by the usual Egyp wall now covered by the drifting sands of the desert, yet plainly discernible like fences in snowdrifts. In the N.E. corner of the inclosure appeared the gateway. Within was an open space, probably a parade ground. On the western side was a real fortification with solid brick foundation still intact. Along the south side was a temple in which was still to be seen the broken torso of an idol. On the right of this temple were the chambers which Naville reported to be the store chambers. They are without any intercommunication or any way of ingress, except from above; and were quite suitable for grain storerooms in accord with the still prevalent Egyp custom of making, not grain elevators toward heaven, but grain pits in the sand.

Concerning this ruin and Naville's report we will ask and answer some questions.

1. The Name

Ex (**1** 11) speaks of the building of "Pithom and Raamses." Naville was inclined to expect Raamses here, but when the gateway was found, the name of the city was upon it, *Pa Thum*, house of Thum, a god worshiped in this neighborhood. This name is the very exact equivalent of the Heb *Pīthōm*. Controversy has hardly concerned the name at all; the Bible says Israelites built Pithom and this was Pithom.

2. The Builder

Ex (**1** 11) tells us that Israelite slaves "built for Pharaoh store cities, Pithom and Raamses." The inscription over the gateway at Pithom was of Rameses the Great and stated categorically, "I built Pithom." That would seem to settle the question definitely, yet it is just here that the controversy starts. It is asserted, and correctly, that Rameses was the champion plagiarist among monarchs of all ages. He went up and down this Nile Valley and chiseled out the names of his predecessors and inserted his own upon their monuments. From this the positive conclusion is drawn that this inscription is historically worthless. But the case is not so; wherever Rameses inserted his name upon a monument erected by another, it is most easily detected, being either upon a lower level of the stone or upon an inserted slab of stone. *This inscription has never been tampered with.* It is objected that Rameses only rebuilt here, and that the building which Israelite slaves did here was a long time before. Yet the structure here, which, as we shall see, contains the whole story of the Israelite building, is of the peculiar bricks which Rameses made. We cannot believe that providence staged the whole affair again in later times to deceive us! If the Israelites built with Ramesside bricks, they did so *in the time of Rameses.* So Rameses was the Egyp builder and thus the great oppressor.

3. The Character

The Biblical account calls the cities "store cities," but makes no direct mention of what was stored there. Certainly the treasures of the court would be kept at the capital, Zoan, and not at a provincial fortress. This place was, as we have seen, a frontier city. Egypt was a military empire, and a frontier city in a military empire has usually one chief characteristic, a place to "store" supplies. In those days, when every man carried his weapon in his hand, or rode in his chariot, only provisions needed to be stored, and the principal food for the Oriental is grain. These grain chambers would be suitable "store" chambers for such supplies. Now Rameses in his inscription here says "I built Pithom at the mouth of the east." This is an idiomatic expression, but can have only one meaning, "where the land opens out to the east," i.e., a frontier city, and that in a military empire. Thus the Biblical statement and the inscription of Rameses are equivalent.

4. Brick and Mortar

The story in Ex (**1** 14) tells of "hard bondage in mortar and in brick." Up to the time of Naville's discovery, Egyptologists were obliged to say they knew nothing of walls laid in mortar in Egypt. Whatever might be their attitude toward Biblical statements in general, they knew nothing of bricks laid in mortar in Egypt. Yet, when Naville uncovered these store chambers he found and reported that the walls were *laid in mortar*. Examination of the walls very soon showed that his report in this also was absolutely correct. These walls are laid in good hard mortar, which, after twenty-six years exposure to the torrential rains of the winter season in the delta, still stood as perfect as the mortar in brick houses of the western world. And these walls have stood for more than 3000 years. Where Rameses' engineers got the idea of laying bricks in mortar is not certainly known, but probably in Palestine or Syria during Rameses' many raids in that part of the world. Since 1883 other walls have occasionally been found in Egypt in which bricks were laid in mortar.

5. Bricks without Straw

The long contest between Moses and Pharaoh commenced in the charge, by Pharaoh, that these were but labor troubles (Ex **5** 1–23), that the Israelite slaves had not enough work to do (Ex **5** 17) and that henceforth no straw would be given them, but that they must gather straw for themselves wherever they could find it (Ex **5** 11–12) and yet must deliver the daily tale of bricks (Ex **5** 5–9). Naville's report of this part of his discoveries at Pithom was the spectacular feature which aroused so much criticism among some and incredulity among others. A careful examination was to be made; so a hoe was borrowed from the neighboring village and an examination of the bricks in the lowest courses of the store chambers, now covered by drifting sand, was made. They were, indeed, made of Nile mud mixed with clean straw as Naville had reported. The rains so quickly sink into the sand and the hot sun dries the moisture and prevents the straw even on the surface of the brick from decay. It was still clear and bright. But this of itself does not constitute scientific evidence, for Egyptians usually laid bricks mixed with straw. Next the upper course of bricks in the walls was examined; and these were found to have been made of Nile mud with no binding material whatever, as Naville reported. But neither was this of itself scientific evidence, for Egyptians did sometimes lay bricks of mud in which no binding material was used. But now finally, if it should be found that the middle courses of bricks were made of mud mixed with stubble and rubbish collected by gleaning the grainfields, then we would have the most complete and satisfactory evidence. A place where the wall was broken down to the middle was found, a brick taken out and the mortar chipped from it. The evidence was startling; the mud for the bricks is put into the mold and some of the straw goes to the edge of the mold and so to the surface of the brick. When the bricks are laid in the sun to dry, the mud shrinks a bit and the straw on the surface is blown away by the wind, but leaves its impress. The mortar fills this impress and when now it is chipped away, leaves the impress of the straw like a die. In the bricks from the middle courses was the impress of straw pulled up by the roots, the impress of the thread-like roots being as clear as though cut by an engraver's tool. In one brick was found the impress of a weed with a root like a turkey-track. Bricks so made and appearing in the courses between the bricks made with good straw and bricks made with no straw at all is the most complete evidence and exact corroboration of the Ex story of the building of Pithom. Again Naville's report was correct.

6. Name of the region

According to the Biblical account the region was that of Succoth (Ex **12** 37; Gen **47** 11). Since Naville's work at Pithom, a tombstone of a priest has been found in this neighborhood, which says the priest ministered in the region of *Thūkū*. This is the Egyp equivalent of the Heb *Succoth*.

Thus every point in the Biblical story is exactly satisfied in the discoveries at *Tell Maskhûtah* and vicinity (cf Kyle, *Moses and the Monuments*, 154–61).

III. Recent Discoveries.—Some very recent discoveries have thrown strong additional light upon the discoveries in the region of *Tell Maskhûtah*, and have furnished independent corroborating evidence of the Biblical story, not only of the store cities, but also of the date of the Exodus and of the Pharaoh of the oppression (Ex **4** 19).

The University of Pennsylvania since 1922 has been excavating at the great mound of *Beisan*, the ancient Beth-shean. In Israelite times to David remains were found and then of the Philistine civilization of the time of Saul and of the Egyp suzerian of the Philistines of that time, Thothmes III, Amenophis III, and then Seti and especially Rameses the Great. A stela of Rameses was found on which among other events he mentions incidentally that he built the city of Raamses in Egypt and adds the most interesting information that he built it with Asiatic Semitic slaves. This statement taken in connection with the inscription over the gateway at Pithom, "I built Pithom," makes complete the parallel with the account in Ex (**1** 11) "And they built for Pharaoh store cities, Pithom and Raamses."

1. At Beisan

In the work at *Tell Beit-mirsim*, the ancient Kiriath-sepher, by Xenia Seminary in co-operation with the American School of Oriental Research at Jerusalem, 1926–28, some most important evidence concerning the events connected with the Exodus appeared incidentally, and are all the more cogent for that reason. A layer of ashes inside the east gate marked a great burning. Examination of all the layers of the ruins showed that all below the level of these ashes were Canaanite, all pottery, weapons and tools and of the various Bronze Ages, but there was nothing of the Iron Age. On the other hand, everything above that layer of ashes was Israelite; pottery, weapons and tools, and was invariably of the Iron Age. The Bronze Ages had completely passed away. Here was most positive evidence of three things: that there had been a conquest which had completely changed the civilization, that the conquest had been of the Canaanites by the Israelites, and that the conquest had been just at the time of the passing of the Bronze Age and the incoming of the Iron Age. This transition from the Bronze Age to the Iron Age is distinctly marked by another discovery, that by Sir Flinders Petrie's work at Gerar in 1928–29 (Petrie, *Gerar*). The Philistine iron furnaces at this place mark the incoming of the Iron Age at the time when the Philistines were in power in Palestine. Thus *a* conquest by Israelites, becomes *the* Conquest, at the beginning of the Iron Age in Palestine and fixes the date of the Exodus as about forty years earlier. This well accords with Rameses the Great as the Pharaoh of the oppression and the Builder of Pithom and Raamses. Will anyone say that the Iron Age and the power of the Philistines came in the time of Thothmes III? (See Exodus, Supplement, 1929).

2. At Kiriath-sepher

M. G. Kyle

PITHON, pī'thon (פִּיתוֹן, *pīthōn*): A grandson of Meribbaal, or Mephibosheth (1 Ch **8** 35; **9** 41).

PITIFUL, pit'i-fŏŏl: As found in Scripture, means "full of pity"; it is expressed by רַחֲמָנִי, *raḥămānī*, from *raḥămīm* (pl. of *raḥam*), "bowels," "compassion" (Lam **4** 10 AV, its only occurrence in the OT), "The hands of the pitiful women have sodden their own children." In Jas **5** 11, we have the beautiful saying, "The Lord is very pitiful [RV "full of pity"] and of tender mercy," where "very pitiful" is the tr of *polúsplagchnos*, lit. "of many bowels," a word which does not occur elsewhere; it might be tr[d] "large-hearted" or "tender-hearted." In Ecclus **2** 11, we have "The Lord is . . . . very pitiful" (*oiktírmōn*); *eúsplagchnos*, "well-hearted," "compassionate," "full of pity," occurs in 1 Pet **3** 8, "Love as brethren, be pitiful, be courteous," RV "loving as brethren, tenderhearted, humble-minded." The word is found in Pr Man **7**; XII P, Zeb **8** 2.

W. L. Walker

PITY, pit'i (חָמַל, *ḥāmal*, חוּס, *ḥūṣ*; ἐλεέω, *eleéō*): "Pity," probably contracted from "piety," is a tender feeling for others in misery or distress. It is allied to **compassion** (q.v.), but differs in respect of the object that causes the distress (or feeling). The feeling of pity is excited chiefly by the weakness, miserable or degraded condition of the object; compassion by his uncontrollable and inevitable misfortunes: "We *pity* a man of weak understanding who exposes his weakness; we *compassionate* the man who is reduced to a state of beggary and want" (Crabb, *English Synonymes*). Pity often becomes allied to contempt; "a pity" is something to be regretted. See Pitiful. In the OT "pity" is closely akin to "mercy." It is most frequently the tr of *ḥāmal*, "to pity," "to spare," e.g. in Nathan's parable of the poor man's one lamb, it is said that the rich man was worthy to die because he had "no pity" (2 S **12** 6).

In Jer **13** 14 we have, "I will not pity nor spare, nor have mercy," RV "compassion"; cf **21** 7; Lam **2** 2; Ezk **5** 11; **7** 4, in all of which passages "pity" stands in a negative connection; we have it positively attributed to God in Ezk **36** 21, "I had pity for mine holy name," RV "regard"; Joel **2** 18; *ḥūs*, probably meaning, primarily, "to cover," "protect," hence to pity, to spare, is tr[d] "pity" (Dt **7** 16; **13** 8; Ezk **16** 5, etc, all negative; Jon **4** 10, positive: "Thou hast had pity on the gourd [RV "regard for"] and should not I spare [RV "have regard for," *ḥūs*] Nineveh," etc); *ḥānan*, "to incline toward," "be gracious," "pity," is thrice rendered "pity" (Job **19** 21, "Have pity upon me, have pity upon me"; Prov **19** 17; **28** 8, "he that hath pity upon the poor"); *rāḥam*, "to feel warm," "to love," twice (Ps **103** 13, "like as a father pitieth his children"; Isa **13** 18, "no pity"); once in pl. *raḥămīm* (Am **1** 11); other words once so tr[d] are *ḥemlāh*, "pity" (Isa **63** 9); *ḥesedh*, "loving-kindness" (Job **6** 14, RV "kindness"); *maḥmāl*, "object of pity" (Ezk **24** 21); *nūdh*, "to move," "bemoan" (Ps **69** 20). In the NT "pity" occurs once only as the tr of *eleeō*, "to be kind," "tender" (Mt **18** 33, RV "mercy"). In 2 Macc **3** 21 we have (AV and RV) "pitied" in the obsolete sense of exciting pity, "Then it would have pitied [*eleeín*] a man to see the multitude," etc.

RV has "pity" for "mercy" (Prov **14** 21); "have pity on" for "spare" (Ps **72** 13); for "favour" (Ps **109** 12; **102** 13.14), "Have pity upon her dust." See Mercy; Compassion.

W. L. Walker

PLACE, plās: Normally for מָקוֹם, *mākōm*, OT, and τόπος, *tópos*, NT, but in AV "place" represents a great number of Heb and Gr words, often used with no difference in force (e.g. 2 Ch **35** 10.15). RV has made few changes, but occasionally has attempted to specialize the meaning (Gen **40** 13; Job **37** 8; Acts **8** 32; Jas **3** 11, etc).

PLACE, BROAD; HIGH. See City, II, 3, 2; High Place; Open Place.

PLAGUE, plāg (נֶגַע, *negha'*, מַכָּה, *makkāh*, מַגֵּפָה, *maggēphāh*; μάστιξ, *mástix*, πληγή, *plēgē*): This word which occurs more than 120 t is applied, like pestilence, to such sudden outbursts of disease as are regarded in the light of Divine visitations. It is used in the description of leprosy about 60 t in Lev **13** and **14**, as well as in Dt **24** 8. In the poetical, prophetic and eschatological books it occurs about 20 t in the general sense of a punitive disaster. The Gospel references (Mk **3** 10; **5** 29.34; Lk **7** 21) use the word as a synonym for disease.

The specific disease now named "plague" has been from the earliest historic times a frequent visitant to Pal and Egypt. Indeed in the S.E. between Gaza and Bubastis it has occurred so frequently that it may almost be regarded as endemic. The suddenness of its attack, the shortness of its incubation period and the rapidity of its course give it the characters which of old have been associated with manifestations of Divine anger. In the early days of an epidemic it is no infrequent occurrence that 60 per cent of those attacked die within three days. I have seen a case in which death took place ten hours after the first symptoms. In the filthy and insanitary houses of eastern towns, the disease spreads rapidly. In a recent epidemic in one village of 534 inhabitants 311 died within 21 days, and I once crossed the track of a party of pilgrims to Mecca of whom two-thirds died of plague on the road. Even with modern sanitary activity, it is very difficult to root it out, as our recent experiences in Hong Kong and India have shown.

Of the Bib. outbreaks that were not improbably bubonic plague, the first recorded is the slaughter of the firstborn in Egypt—the 10th plague. We have too little information to identify it (Ex **11** 1). The Philis, however, used the same name, *negha'*, for the Egyp plagues (1 S **4** 8) as is used in Ex. The next outbreak was at Kibroth-hataavah (Nu **11** 33). This was synchronous with the phenomenal flight of quails, and if these were, as is probable, driven by the wind from the plague-stricken Serbonian region, they were equally probably the carriers of the infection. Experience in both India and China has shown that animals of very diverse kinds can carry germs of the disease. A third visitation fell on the spies who brought back an evil report (Nu **14** 37). A fourth destroyed those who murmured at the destruction of Korah and his fellow-rebels (Nu **16** 47). These may have been recrudescences of the infection brought by the quails. The fifth outbreak was that which followed the gross religious and moral defection at Baal-peor (Nu **25** 8.9.18; **26** 1; **31** 16; Josh **22** 17; Ps **106** 29.30). Here the disease was probably conveyed by the Moabites.

A later epidemic, which was probably of bubonic plague, was that which avenged the capture of the ark (1 S **5** 6). We read of the tumors which were probably the glandular enlargements characteristic of this disease; also that at the time there was a plague of rats (**6** 5) —"mice," in our version, but the word is also used as the name of the rat. The cattle seem to have carried the plague to Beth-shemesh, as has been observed in more than one place in China (**6** 19). Concerning the three days' pestilence that followed David's census (2 S **24** 15; 1 Ch **21** 12), see Jos, *Ant*, VII, xiii, 3. The destruction of the army of Sennacherib may have been a sudden outbreak of plague (2 K **19** 35; Isa **37** 36). It is perhaps worthy of note that in Herodotus' account of the destruction of this army (ii.141) he refers to the incursion of swarms of mice.

One of the latest prophetic mentions of plague is Hos **13** 14, where the plague (*debher*, LXX *díkē*) of death and the destruction (*ḳāṭābh*, LXX *kéntron*) of the grave are mentioned. From this passage Paul quotes his apostrophe at the end of 1 Cor **15** 55, but the apostle correlates the sting (*kéntron*) with death, and changes the *díkē* into *níkos*.

ALEX. MACALISTER

PLAGUES, plāgz, **OF EGYPT** (נִפְלָאֹת, *niphlᵉ'ōth*, "wonders," from פָּלָא, *pālā'*, "to be separate," i.e. in a class by themselves; also called נֶגֶף, *negheph*, "plague," from נָגַף, *nāghaph*, "to smite" [Ex **9** 14], and נֶגַע, *negha'*, "a stroke," from נָגַע, *nāgha'*, "to touch" [Ex **11** 1; cf Josh **24** 10]):

Introduction

The Heb words are so used as to give the name "plagues" to all the "wonders" God did against Pharaoh. Thus it appears that the language in the account in Ex puts forward the wondrous character of these dealings of Jeh with Pharaoh. The account of the plagues is found in Ex **7** 8—**12** 31; Ps **78** 42–51; **105** 27–36. These poetical accounts of the plagues have a devotional purpose and do not give a full historical narrative. Ps **78** omits plagues 4, 6, 9; Ps **105** omits plagues 5 and 6. Both pss change the order of the plagues. Account of the preparation which led up to the plagues is found in the narrative of the burning bush (see BURNING BUSH), the meeting of Aaron with Moses, the gathering together of the elders of Israel for instruction and the preliminary wonders before Pharaoh (Ex **3, 4**). This preparation contemplated two things important to be kept in view in considering the plagues, namely, that the consummation of plagues was contemplated from the beginning (Ex **4** 22.23), and that the skepticism of Israel concerning Moses' authority and power was likewise anticipated (Ex **4** 1). It was thus manifestly not an age of miracles when the Israelites were expecting such "wonders" and ready to receive anything marvelous as a Divine interposition. This skepticism of Israel is a valuable asset for the credibility of the account of the "wonders." The immediate occasion of the plagues was the refusal of Pharaoh to let the people have liberty for sacrifice, together with the consequent hardening of Pharaoh's heart. No indication of any localizing of the plagues is given except in Ps **78** 12.43, where the "field of Zoan" is mentioned as the scene of the contest between Jeh and the Egyptians. But this is poetry, and the "field of Zoan" means simply the territory of the great capital Zoan. This expression might be localized in the Delta or it might extend to the whole of Egypt. Discussion of the plagues has brought out various classifications of them, some of which are philosophical, as that of Philo, others fanciful, as that of Origen. Arrangements of the order of the plagues for the purpose of moralizing are entirely useless for historical consideration of the plagues. The only order of any real value is the order of Nature, i.e. the order in which the plagues occurred, which will be found to be the order of the natural phenomena which were the embodiment of the plagues.

Much elaborate effort has been made to derive from the description of the plagues evidence for different documents in the narrative. It is pointed out that Moses (E) declared to Pharaoh that he would smite the waters (Ex **7** 17), and then the account, as it proceeds, tells us that Aaron smote the waters (**7** 19 20). But this is quite in accord with the preceding statement (**4** 16) that Aaron was to be the spokesman. Moses was to deal with God, Aaron with Pharaoh. Again it is noticed that some of the plagues are ascribed to the immediate agency of Jeh, some are represented as coming through the mediation of Moses, and still others through the mediation of Moses and Aaron. Certainly this may be an exact statement of facts, and, if the facts were just so, the record of the facts affords no evidence of different documents.

An examination of the account of the plagues as it stands will bring them before us in a most graphic and connected story.

I. The Natural Phenomena.—All the "wonders" represented anywhere in Scripture as done by the power of God are intimately associated with natural phenomena, and necessarily so. Human beings have no other way of perceiving external events than through those senses which only deal with natural phenomena. Accordingly, all theophanies and miraculous doings are embodied in natural events.

The presence of Jeh with the sacrifice by Abraham was manifested by the passing of a "smoking furnace and a burning lamp" between the pieces of the offerings (Gen **15** 17 AV). The majesty and power of God at Sinai were manifested in the "cloud" and the "brightness," the "voice" and the "sound of a trumpet" (He **12** 19). The Holy Spirit descended "as a dove" (Mt **3** 16). The Deity of Jesus was attested on the mountain by a "voice" (**17** 5). Jesus Himself was "God . . . . manifest in the flesh" (1 Tim **3** 16 AV). He was "found in fashion as a man" (Phil **2** 8). And all the miracles of Jesus were coupled with sensible phenomena: He spoke to the sea and it was calm; He touched the leper and he was clean; He called to Lazarus and he came forth.

Yet in all these natural events, the miraculous working of God was as clearly seen as the natural phenomena. It is thus to be expected that the "wonders" of God in the land of Pharaoh should also be associated with natural events as well as manifest miraculous elements. The "blood" in the river, the "frogs" hopping about on the land, the "lice," the "flies," the "murrain," the "boils," the "hail," the "locusts," the "darkness," and the "pestilence" are all named as natural phenomena. Long familiarity with the land of Egypt has made it perfectly plain to many intelligent people, also, that nearly, if not quite, all the plagues of Egypt are still in that land as natural phenomena, and occur, when they do occur, very exactly in the order in which we find them recorded in the narrative in Ex. But natural events in the plagues as in other "wonders" of God embodied miraculous doings.

1. Water Turned to Blood

The first of the plagues (דָּם, *dām*, from אָדַם, *'ādham*, "to be red" [Ex **7** 19–25]) was brought about by the smiting of the water with the rod in the hand of Aaron, and it consisted in the defilement of the water so that it became as "blood." The waters were polluted and the fish died. Even the water in vessels which had been taken from the river became corrupt. The people were forced to get water only from wells in which the river water was filtered through the sand. There are two Egyp seasons when, at times, the water resembles blood. At the full Nile the water is sometimes of a reddish color, but at that season the water is quite potable and the fish do not die. But a similar phenomenon is witnessed sometimes at the time of the lowest Nile just before the rise begins. Then also the water sometimes becomes defiled and very red, so polluted that the fish die (*Bib. Sacra*, 1905, 409). This latter time is evidently the time of the first plague. It would be some time in the month of May. The dreadful severity of the plague constituted the "wonder" in this first plague. The startling character of the plague is apparent when it is remembered that Egypt is the product of the Nile, the very soil being all brought down by it, and its irrigation being constantly dependent upon it. Because of this it became one of the earliest and greatest of the gods (Breasted, *Development of Religion and Thought in Egypt*, 3–47; "Hymn to the Nile," *Records of the Past*, New Series, III, 46–54). The magicians imitated this plague with their enchantments. Their success may have been by means of sleight of hand or other devices of magic, as may be seen in the East today, with claim of supernatural aid, and as used in western lands for entertainment, as mere cleverness. Or it may be, as has been suggested, that they counted upon the continuance of the plague for at least a time, and so took advantage of the materials the "wonder" had provided.

2. The Plague of Frogs

Frogs (צְפַרְדְּעִים, *çephardeʻīm*, probably "marsh-leapers" [Ex **8** 1–15]) are very abundant just after the high Nile when the waters begin to recede. Spawn in the mud is hatched by the sun, and the marshes are filled with myriads of these creatures. The frog was the hieroglyph for myriads. The frogs usually remain in the marshes, but in this case they came forth to the horror and disgust of the people. "Frogs in the houses, frogs in the beds, frogs baked with the food in the ovens, frogs in the kneading troughs worked up with the flour; frogs with their monotonous croak, frogs with their cold slimy skins, everywhere —from morning to night, from night to morning—frogs." The frog was also associated with Divinity, was the symbol of Heqt, a form of Hathor, and seems also at times to have been worshipped as divinity. This plague created such horror that thus early Pharaoh came to an agreement (**8** 8–10). A time was set for the disappearance of the frogs that he might know that "there is none like unto Jeh our God," but when the frogs were dead, Pharaoh hardened his heart (**8** 15). In this plague "the magicians did in like manner with their enchantments" (**8** 7). Frogs were plentiful, and it would not seem to be difficult to claim to have produced some of them.

3. The Plague of Lice

It is impossible to determine what particular troublesome insect pest of Egypt is meant by the 3d plague, whether body-lice or mosquitoes or sandflies or ticks or fleas (כִּנִּם, *kinnīm*, "gnats" [Ex **8** 16]). Those who have experience of these pests in Egypt are quite ready to accept any of them as adequate for the plague. Lice seem rather to be ruled out, unless different kinds of lice were sent, as there is no one kind that torments both man and beast. All the other insect pests appear in incredible numbers out of the "dust" when the pools have dried up after the receding of the waters. The assertion that the account of this plague is not complete, because it is not recorded that Pharaoh asked its removal or that Moses secured it, is amazing. Perhaps Pharaoh did not, in fact, ask its removal. There seems also at this time some difficulty in Moses having access to Pharaoh after this plague (**8** 20). Perhaps the plague was not removed at all. The Egyptians are disposed to think it was not! Certainly that season of the year spent in Egypt, not in a dahabiyeh on the Nile, but in a native village, will furnish very satisfying evidence that stinging and biting insects are a very real plague in Egypt yet. The magicians failed with their enchantments and acknowledged that Divine power was at work, and seem to have acknowledged that Jeh was supreme (**8** 19), but Pharaoh would not heed them.

4. The Plague of Flies

As the seasons pass on, after the recession of the waters, the flies (עָרֹב, *ʻārōbh*, "swarms," probably of flies [Ex **8** 20–32]) become more and more numerous until they are almost a plague every year. The increased severity of this plague, and the providential interference to separate between Israel and the Egyptians, drove Pharaoh and his people to such desperation that Pharaoh gave a half-promise of liberty for Israel to sacrifice "in the land." This called out the statement that they would sacrifice the "abomination of the Egyptians." This may have referred to the sacrifice of sheep, which were always held in more or less detestation by Egyptians, or it may have had reference to the sacrifice of heifers, the cow being the animal sacred to the goddess Hathor. The new element of separation between the Israelites and the Egyptians introduced into this plague was another step toward establishing the claims of Jeh to be the God of all the earth and to have taken Israel under His especial care.

5. The Plague of Murrain

In addition to the separation established between Israel and the Egyptians, a definite time is now set for the coming of the 5th plague. It is to be noticed also that diseases of cattle (דֶּבֶר, *debher*, "destruction" [Ex **9** 1–7]) and of men follow quickly after the plague of insects. This is in exact accord with the order of Nature as now thoroughly understood through the discovered relation of mosquitoes and flies to the spread of diseases. Rinderpest is still prevalent at times in Egypt, so that beef becomes very scarce in market and is sometimes almost impossible to obtain. It is a fact, also, that the prevalence of cattle plague, the presence of boils among men (see 6, below) and the appearance of bubonic plague are found to be closely associated together and in this order. The mention of camels as affected by this plague is interesting. It is doubtful if any clear indication of the presence of the camel in Egypt so early as this has yet been found among the monuments of Egypt. There is in the Louvre museum one small antiquity which seems to me to be intended for the camel. But Professor Maspero does not agree that it is so. It would seem likely that the Hyksos, who were Bedouin princes, princes of the desert, would have introduced the beasts of the desert into Egypt. If they did so, that may have been sufficient reason that the Egyptians would not picture it, as the Hyksos and all that was theirs were hated in Egypt.

6. The Plague of Boils

In the plague of boils (שְׁחִין, *sh^{e}ḥīn*, and אֲבַעְבֻּעֹת, *'ăbha'bu'ōth*, "boils" [Ex **9** 8–17]) ashes were used, probably in the same way and to the same end as the clay was used in opening the eyes of the blind man (Jn **9** 6), i.e. to attract attention and to fasten the mind of the observer upon what the Lord was doing. This plague in the order of its coming, immediately after the murrain, and in the description given of it and in the significant warning of the "pestilence" yet to come (Ex **9** 15), appears most likely to have been *pestis minor*, the milder form of bubonic plague. Virulent rinderpest among cattle in the East is regarded as the precursor of plague among men and is believed to be of the same nature. It may well be, as has been thought by some, that the great aversion of the ancient Egyptians to the contamination of the soil by decaying animals was from the danger thereby of starting an epidemic of plague among men (Dr. Merrins, *Bib. Sacra*, 1908, 422–23).

7. The Plague of Hail

Hail (בָּרָד, *bārādh*, "hail" [Ex **9** 18–35]) is rare in Egypt, but is not unknown. The writer has himself seen a very little, and has known of one instance when a considerable quantity of hail as large as small marbles fell. Lightning, also, is not as frequent in Egypt as in many semitropical countries, yet great electric storms sometimes occur. This plague is quite accurately dated in the seasons of the year (**9** 31.32). As the first plague was just before the rising of the Nile, so this one is evidently about 9 months later, when the new crops after the inundation were beginning to mature, January-February. This plague also marks another great step forward in the revelation of Jeh to Israel and to the Egyptians. First only His power was shown, then His wisdom in the timing of the plagues, and now His mercy appears in the warning to all godly-disposed Egyptians to save themselves, their herds and their servants by keeping all indoors (**9** 19–21). Pharaoh also now distinctly acknowledged Jeh (**9** 27).

8. The Plague of Locusts

The plague of locusts (אַרְבֶּה, *'arbeh*, "locust" [Ex **10** 1–20]) was threatened, and so frightened were the servants of Pharaoh that they persuaded him to try to make some agreement with Moses, but the attempt of Pharaoh still to limit in some way the going of Israel thwarted the plan (Ex **10** 7–10). Then devouring swarms of locusts came up over the land from the eastern desert between the Nile and the Red Sea. They devoured every green thing left by the hail. The desperate situation created by the locusts soon brought Pharaoh again to acknowledgment of Jeh (**10** 16). This was the greatest profession of repentance yet manifested by Pharaoh, but he soon showed that it was deceitful, and again he would not let the people go. When the wind had swept the locusts away, he hardened his heart once more.

9. The Plague of Darkness

The progress of the seasons has been quite marked from the first plague, just before the rising of the waters, on through the year until now the khamsin period (חֹשֶׁךְ, *ḥōshekh*, "darkness" from any cause [Ex **10** 21–29]) has come. When this dreadful scourge comes with its hot sand-laden breath, more impenetrable than a London fog, it is in very truth a "darkness which may be felt." The dreadful horror of this monster from the desert can hardly be exaggerated. Once again Pharaoh said "Go," but this time he wished to retain the flocks and herds, a hostage for the return of the people (**10** 24). Upon Moses' refusal to accept this condition, he threatened his life. Why had he not done so ere this? Why, indeed, did he let this man Moses come and go with such freedom, defying him and his people in the very palace? Probably Moses' former career in Egypt explains this. If, as is most probable, he had grown up at court with this Merenptah, and had been known as "the son of Pharaoh's daughter," heir to the throne and successor to Rameses II, instead of Merenptah, then this refugee had undoubtedly many friends still in Egypt who would make his death a danger to the reigning Pharaoh.

10. Death of the Firstborn

No intimation is given of the exact character of the death inflicted on the firstborn (בְּכוֹר, *b^{e}khōr*, "firstborn," "chief" or "best"; cf Job **18** 13; Isa **14** 30 [Ex **11—12** 36]) by the angel of the Lord, or its appearance. But it is already foretold as the "pestilence" (**9** 15). The *pestis major* or virulent bubonic plague corresponds most nearly in its natural phenomena to this plague. It culminates in a sudden and overwhelming virulence, takes the strongest and best, and then subsides with startling suddenness.

Thus it appears that probably all the plagues were based upon natural phenomena which still exist in Egypt in the same order, and, when they do occur, find place somewhere during the course of one year.

II. Miraculous Use of the Phenomena.—The miraculous elements in the plagues are no less distinctly manifest than the natural phenomena themselves.

1. Intensification

There was an intensification of the effect of the various plagues so much beyond all precedent as to impress everyone as being a special Divine manifestation, and it was so. There was national horror of the blood-like water, disgust at the frogs, intolerable torture by the stinging insects and flies, utter ruin of the farmers in the loss of the cattle, the beating down of the crops by the hail, and the devouring of every green thing by the locusts, the sufferings and dread of the inhabitants by reason of the boils, the frightful electric storm, the suffocating darkness and, finally, the crushing disaster of the death of the firstborn. All these calamities may be found in Egypt to the present day, but never any of them, not to say all of them, in such overwhelming severity. That all of them should come in one year and all with such devastation was plainly a Divine arrangement. Merely natural events do not arrange themselves so systematically. In this systematic severity were seen *miracles of power.*

2. Prediction

The prediction of the plagues and the fulfilment of the prediction at the exact time to a day, sometimes to an hour (as the cessation of the thunder and lightning): There was first a general prediction (Ex **3** 19.20; **7** 3; **9** 14.15) and an indication as the plagues went on that the climax would be pestilence (**9** 15). Then several of the plagues were specifically announced and a time was set for them; e.g. the flies (**8** 23), the murrain (**9** 5), the hail (**9** 18), the locusts (**10** 4), the death of the firstborn (**11** 4). In some cases a time for the removal of the plague was also specified: e.g. the frogs (**8** 10), the thunder and lightning (**9** 29). In every instance these predictions were exactly fulfilled. In some instances careful foresight might seem to supply in part this ability to predict. Perhaps it was by means of such foresight that the magicians "did so with their enchantments" for the first two plagues. The plague being in existence, foresight might safely predict that it would continue for a little time at least, so that, if the magicians sought for bloody water or called for frogs, they would seem to be successful. But the evidence which Jeh produced went beyond them, and, at the third plague, they were unable to do anything. These things postulate, on the part of Moses and Aaron, knowledge far beyond human ken. Not only magicians could not do so with their enchantments, but modern science and discoveries are no more able so to predict events. Even meteorological phenomena are only predicted within the limits of reasonable foresight. Such wonders as the plagues of Egypt can in no wise be explained as merely natural. The prediction was a *miracle of knowledge.*

3. Discrimination

The discrimination shown in the visitation by the plagues presents another miraculous element more significant and important than either the miracles of power or the miracles of knowledge. God put a difference between the Egyptians and the Israelites, beginning with the plague of flies and continuing, apparently, without exception, until the end. Such *miracles of moral purpose* admit of no possible explanation but the exercise of a holy will. Merely natural events make no such regular, systematic discriminations.

4. Orderliness

The orderliness and gradually increasing severity of the plagues with such arrangement as brought "judgment upon the gods of Egypt," vindicating Jeh as Ruler over all, and educating the people to know Jeh as Lord of all the earth, present an aspect of events distinctly non-natural. Such method reveals also a Divine mind at work.

5. Moral Purpose

Last of all and most important of all, the plagues were so arranged as to accomplish in particular a great Divine moral purpose in the revelation of God to the Israelites, to the Egyptians and to all the world. This is the distinctive mark of every real miracle. And this leads us directly to the consideration of the most important aspect of the plagues.

III. The Divine Moral Purpose.—This discrediting of the gods of Egypt is marked at every step of the progress of the plagues, and the accumulated effect of the repeated discrediting of the gods must have had, and, indeed, had, a great influence upon the Egyptians. The plagues did 'execute judgment against the gods of Egypt' (**12** 12), and the people and princes brought great pressure to bear upon Pharaoh to let the people go (**10** 7). The magicians who claimed to represent the gods of Egypt were defeated, Pharaoh himself, who was accounted divine, was humbled, the great god, the Nile, was polluted, frogs defiled the temples and, at last, the sun, the greatest god of Egypt, was blotted out in darkness.

1. Discrediting of the Gods of Egypt

2. Pharaoh Made to Know Jehovah Is Lord

Pharaoh was made to know that Jeh is Lord, and acknowledged it (**9** 27; **10** 16). To this end the issue was clearly drawn. Pharaoh challenged the right of Jeh to command him (**5** 2), and God required him then to "stand" to the trial until the evidence could be fully presented, in accordance with the fundamental principle that he who makes a charge is bound to stand to it until either he acknowledges its utter falsity or affords opportunity for full presentation of evidence. So we see God made Pharaoh to "stand" (**9** 16) (while the Bible, which speaks in the concrete language of life, calls it the hardening of Pharaoh's heart) until the case was tried out (cf Lamb, *Miracle of Science,* 126–49).

3. Revelation of God as Saviour

A more blessed and gracious moral purpose of the plagues was the revelation of God as the Saviour of the world. This began in the revelation at the burning bush, where God, in fire, appeared in the bush, yet the bush was not consumed, but saved. This revelation, thus given to the people, was further evidenced by the separation between Israel and the Egyptians; was made known even to the Egyptians by the warning before the plague of hail, that those Egyptians who had been impressed with the power of God might also learn that He is a God that will save those who give heed unto Him; and, at last, reached its startling climax when the angel of the Lord passed over the blood-marked door the night of the death of the firstborn and the institution of the Passover.

4. Divine Use of Evil

Last of all, the plagues had a great moral purpose in that they embodied the Divine use of evil in the experience of men in this world. As the experience of Job illustrates the use of evil in the life of the righteous, so the plagues of Egypt illustrate the same great problem of evil in the lot of the wicked. In the one case, as in the other, the wonders of God are so arranged as "to justify the ways of God to men."

The minutely accurate knowledge of life in Egypt displayed by this narrative in the Book of Ex is inconceivable in an age of so little and difficult intercommunication between nations, except by actual residence of the author in Egypt. This has an important bearing upon the time of the composition of this narrative, and so upon the question of its author.

Literature.—The literature of this subject is almost endless. It will suffice to refer the reader to all the general comms., and the special comms. on Ex, for discussion of doctrinal and critical questions. Two admirable recent discussions of the plagues, in English, are Lamb, *Miracle of Science,* and Merrins, "The Plagues of Egypt," in *Bibliotheca Sacra,* 1908, July and October.

M. G. Kyle

PLAIN, plān ([1] כִּכָּר, *kikkār,* "circle," "talent," or "round loaf"; [2] מִישׁוֹר, *mīshōr,* from יָשַׁר, *yāshar,* "to be level"; cf Arab. مَيْسُور, *maisûr,* "that which is easy"; [3] בִּקְעָה, *bikʿāh;* cf Arab. بَقْعَة, *bakʿat,* "a plot of ground," or "a wet meadow"; [4] עֲרָבָה, *'ărābhāh;* [5] שְׁפֵלָה, *shephēlāh;* [6] τόπος πεδινός, *tópos pedinós* [Lk **6** 17]; [7] אֵלוֹן, *'ēlōn;* cf אֵלָה, *'ēlāh,* and אַלּוֹן, *'allōn,* "oak" [Gen **35** 4.8, etc]; also אֵלָה, *'ēlāh,* "Elah" [1 S **17** 2]; [8] אָבֵל, *'ābhēl*): See NATURAL FEATURES.

(1) *Kikkār,* when meaning "plain" usually refers to the alluvial plain about Jericho near the north end of the Dead Sea: "Plain [RVm "circle"] of the Jordan" (Gen **13** 10.11; 1 K **7** 46; 2 Ch **4** 17); "Plain of the valley of Jericho" (Dt **34** 3); "cities of the Plain" (Gen **13** 12; **19** 29); "all the Plain" (Gen **19** 17.25); "by the way of the Plain" (2 S **18** 23); but "the plain round about Jerus" (Neh **12** 28). See CICCAR; CIRCLE.

(2) *Mīshōr,* EV "plain," RVm usually "tableland," clearly refers in most places to the highlands of Gilead and Moab, E. of the Jordan and the Dead Sea; e.g. Josh **13** 9, "the plain [RVm "table-land"] of Medeba."

(3) *Biḳ'āh* is more often trd "valley" (q.v.).

(4) *'Ărābhāh* is in RV often trd "the Arabah," denoting the whole Jordan-Dead-Sea-Arabah depression = Arab. *Ghaur* (Ghôr). In Dt **11** 30, AV has "champaign" (q.v.). The "plains of Moab" (Nu **22** 1; **26** 3.63; **31** 12; **33** 48.49.50; **35** 1; **36** 13; Dt **34** 1.8; Josh **13** 32) and "plains of Jericho" (Josh **4** 13; **5** 10; 2 K **25** 5; Jer **39** 5; **52** 8) are the low plain or *ghaur* N. of the Dead Sea. *'Ărābhāh* is here equivalent to *kikkār* (see above). Note the distinction between *mīshōr* used of the highlands, and *kikkār* and *'ărābhāh* used of the *ghaur.* See ARABAH.

(5) *Shephēlāh* is by RV throughout trd "lowland" (q.v.), and includes the western slopes of the Judaean hills and the maritime plain.

(6) *Topos pedinos* occurs only in Lk **6** 17.

(7) *'Ēlōn* is trd "plain" in AV: "plain of Moreh" (Gen **12** 6; Dt **11** 30); "plain [or plains] of Mamre" (Gen **13** 18; **14** 13; **18** 1); "plain of Zaanaim" (Jgs **4** 11); "plain of the pillar" (Jgs **9** 6); "plain of Meonenim" (Jgs **9** 37); "plain of Tabor" (1 S **10** 3). RV has throughout "oak," RVm "terebinth"; cf "oak" (Gen **35** 4.8, etc) and "vale of Elah" (1 S **17** 2.19; **21** 9).

(8) *'Ābhēl kerāmīm* (Jgs **11** 33) is in AV "the plain of the vineyards," RV "Abel-cheramim," RVm "the meadow of vineyards." Elsewhere in EV *'ābhēl* is "Abel" or "Abel-." See ABEL-CHERAMIM; MEADOW. ALFRED ELY DAY

PLAIN, plān, **PLAINLY,** plān'li: In Gen **25** 27, AV "plain" represents תָּם, *tam.* If a contrast between the vocations of Jacob and Esau is meant, RV ("quiet," m "harmless") may be right. But elsewhere (Job **1** 1; Ps **37** 37, etc) the word means "perfect," and so probably here; the failings of the great patriarch did not detract from the general estimate of him (Mt **8** 11). In Ezr **4** 18 "translated" (RVm) is better than "plainly read."

PLAIN, CITIES OF THE. See CITIES OF THE PLAIN.

PLAIN OF MOAB: In Dt **1** 1; **2** 8, "plain" is trd in RV "Arabah," and explained, "the deep valley running N. and S. of the Dead Sea." It was here that Moses delivered his last addresses. Usually the word is pl. (עַרְבוֹת, *'arebhōth*), the "plains" or steppes of Moab (Nu **22** 1, etc; Dt **34** 1.8). An interesting description is given in an article on "The Steppes of Moab" by Professor G. B. Gray in *Expos,* January, 1905. See MOAB.

PLAIN OF THE PILLAR (אֵלוֹן מֻצָּב, *'ēlōn muççābh;* B reads πρὸς τῇ βαλάνῳ τῇ εὑρετῇ τῆς στάσεως τῆς ἐν Σικίμοις, *prós tē balánō tē heuretē tēs stáseōs tēs en Sikimois;* A omits τῇ εὑρετῇ, and the second τῆς): With RVm we must read "terebinth of the pillar," the place where the men of Shechem and Beth-millo made Abimelech king (Jgs **9** 6). This was one of the sacred trees of which there seem to have been several near Shechem. See MEONENIM, OAK OF. "The pillar" may possibly have been the great stone which Joshua set up "under the oak that was by the sanctuary of Jeh" (Josh **24** 26). W. EWING

PLAIN OF THE VINEYARDS. See ABEL-CHERAMIM.

PLAISTER, plās'tẽr. See PLASTER.

PLAITING, plāt'ing, plat'ing (from OFr. *pleit,* from Lat *plicatum,* "fold"): An interweaving, braiding, knot; an elaborate gathering of the hair into knots; ἐμπλοκή, *emplokē,* "outward adorning of plaiting the hair" (1 Pet **3** 3). Compare "platted" (crown of thorns) (Mt **27** 29 ‖ Mk **15** 17; Jn **19** 2). See BRAIDED, BRAIDING.

PLANE, plān (Isa **44** 13). See TOOLS.

PLANE TREE, plān'trē (עַרְמוֹן, *'armōn;* πλάτανος, *plátanos* [Gen **30** 37], ἐλάτη, *elátē* ["pine" or "fir"] [Ezk **31** 8]; AV **chestnut**): *'Armōn* is supposed to be derived from √ עָרַם, *'āram,* meaning "to be bare" or "naked"; this is considered a suitable term for the plane, which sheds its bark annually. The chestnut of AV is not an indigenous tree, but the plane, *Planus orientalis,* is one of the finest trees in Pal, flourishing esp. by water courses (cf Ecclus **24** 14).

Plane (*Planus orientalis*).

PLANETS, plan'ets (מַזָּלוֹת, *mazzālōth*). See ASTROLOGY, II, 3.

PLANK, plaṇk: Thick beams or pieces of wood, for which several Heb words are used. RV changes "planks" (of fir) into "boards" in 1 K **6** 15, and in a few instances substitutes "planks" where AV has "boards" (Ex **27** 8; **38** 7, the altar; Ezk **27** 5). So in the NT in Acts **27** 44, for σανίς, *sanís.* See SHIPS AND BOATS, II, 2, (3).

PLANT, PLANTS. See BOTANY.

PLASTER, plas'tẽr (שִׂיד, *sīdh*): In Egypt, now as anciently, the buildings are plastered inside and out. The poor quality of the stone commonly used makes this necessary if a smooth attractive surface is desired. Among the poorer classes, clay mixed with straw is used. In Pal and Syria, where there is a rainy season, the coating on the outside walls, if of clay, must be frequently renewed. In Egypt burnt gypsum, and in Pal and Syria burnt limestone (lime) are the commonest materials for making mortar. For the first coat of plastering the lime is mixed with "fat" red sand or with the ash from the bathhouse fires, and the finishing coat is composed of white sand and slaked lime with or without chopped flax straw. The plaster on some of the ancient Egyp ruins seems to indicate that milk or some similar substance was added to the mortar to give a better surface.

The ancients preferred plastered surfaces for decorating, and even the finest granite was covered with stucco on which to paint or carve the decorations (Dt **27** 2; Dnl **5** 5). Columns were often first stuccoed and then painted.

The Arab. word for mortar is *ṭîn*, which really means "clay." The Heb שִׂיד, *sīdh*, lit. "to boil up," refers to the boiling of the water with which the lime is slaked, because of the heat generated during the slaking process. In Dnl **5** 5 occurs גִּיר, *gīr*, i.e. "burned in a kiln," which might mean either lime or gypsum. In Lev **14** 42 occurs טוּחַ, *ṭūₐḥ*, "to smear."

JAMES A. PATCH

PLASTER, plas'tẽr (מָרַח, *māraḥ*): Only used in Isa **38** 21 of the application of the cake of figs to the boil from which Hezekiah suffered. In Papyrus Ebers, figs are used as the ingredient in a plaster (xxxv, lxxix, lxxxiii). Dioscorides also recommends figs with other substances as a poultice in some skin diseases.

PLASTERING, plas'tẽr-ing. See CRAFTS, II, 15.

PLATE, plāt: A term seemingly not used in the Bible for a dish as it is so commonly used at present, but always for a tablet or sheet of metal. (1) צִיץ, *çīç* (Ex **28** 36; **39** 30; Lev **8** 9), a plate of gold on the front of the mitre of the high priest. The name seems to have been given because of the radiance of the object. (2) פַּח, *paḥ* (Ex **39** 3; Nu **16** 38), of plates or sheets of metal produced by hammering. (3) לוּחַ, *lūₐḥ*, used for tablets or tables of stone (Ex **24** 12, etc), but in 1 K **7** 36 for the metal plates on the bases of the lavers in the temple. The word סֶרֶן, *ṣeren*, is rendered "plate" in 1 K **7** 30 AV, manifestly incorrectly, RV "axle."

WALTER R. BETTERIDGE

PLATTER, plat'ẽr: (1) קְעָרָה, *ke'ārāh*, "a deep dish" (Nu **7** 13 f.84.85). In AV and ERV "charger," ARV "platter" (cf Ex **25** 29; **37** 16); LXX τρύβλιον, *trúblion*, and in the NT rendered "dish" (Mt **26** 23; Mk **14** 20). In Ezr **1** 9, ARV אֲגַרְטָל, *'ăghartāl*, rendered "platter," AV and ERV "chargers"; probably a deep dish or basin used in sacrificial slaughter. (2) παροψίς, *paropsís*, originally a side dish, for relishes, entrées, but of dishes for food, in general, esp. meats, fish, etc, used with ποτήριον, *potḗrion*, "cup" or "drinking vessel" (Mt **23** 25 f); also πίναξ, *pínax*, originally a large wooden dish or plate (Lk **11** 39); rendered "charger" in Mt **14** 8.11 AV, and Mk **6** 25.28 AV and ERV.

EDWARD BAGBY POLLARD

PLAY, plā. See GAMES.

PLEAD, plēd: In modern non-legal Eng. is a synonym of "pray" or "beseech," but in legal phraseology "plea," "plead," and "pleading" have a great variety of technical meanings, with "present a case before the court" as the idea common to all. All the uses of "plead" in EV are connected with this legal sense, so that outside of the set phrase "plead a cause" (1 S **24** 15, etc) there is hardly a use of the word in AV, ERV, or ARV that is clear modern Eng. The most obscure instances are due to AV's employment of "plead" to translate the Niphal of שָׁפַט, *shāphaṭ*. *Shāphaṭ* means "judge," so its Niphal means "bring one's self into a case to be judged," "enter into controversy with," and so "plead" in the legal sense. Hence "None pleadeth in truth" (Isa **59** 4) means "None of their lawsuits are honest." Accordingly, when God is said to "plead with" man (Isa **66** 16 AV, ERV, etc), the meaning is that God states His side of the case and not at all that He supplicates man to repent. And this statement by God is a judicial act that of course admits of no reply. Hence RV has changed "plead with" into "enter into judgment with" in Jer **2** 35, and ARV has carried this change into all the other passages (Jer **25** 31; Ezk **17** 20; **20** 35.36; **38** 22), with "execute judgment" in Isa **66** 16; Joel **3** 2. The same vb.-form occurs also in Isa **43** 26: "Let us plead together," where "Let us present our arguments on both sides" would be a fair paraphrase. Otherwise "plead" usually represents רִיב, *rībh*, for which RV gives "strive" in place of "plead" in Ps **35** 1, and "contend" in Job **13** 19; **23** 6 (ARV also in Jgs **6** 31.32; Isa **3** 13; Jer **2** 9; **12** 1; Hos **2** 2, retaining "plead" only in Isa **1** 17 and in the phrase "plead a cause"). יָכַח, *yākhaḥ*, is rendered "plead" in Job **19** 5 ("plead against me my reproach," where the meaning is "convict me of"), in Mic **6** 2 AV and ERV (ARV "contend"), and Job **16** 21 AV (RV "maintain the right"). "Plead" is used also for דִּין, *dīn*, in Jer **30** 13 and Prov **31** 9 AV (RV "minister justice to"), and Jer **5** 28 RV (AV "judge"; cf **22** 16, AV and RV "judge"). RV would have done vastly better if the use of "plead" had been avoided altogether.

Pleadings (i.e. "arguments") occurs in Job **13** 6 (for *rībh*), and "plea" (*dīn*, in a specific legal sense) in Dt **17** 8. AV uses "implead" in Acts **19** 38 for ἐγκαλέω, *egkaléō*, RV "accuse," lit. "call into court"; cf also "pleaded the cause" in 2 Macc **4** 44 (lit. "argued the case") and ver 47, RV "pleaded" (lit. "spoken," AV "told their cause").

BURTON SCOTT EASTON

PLEASURE, plezh'ūr (חֵפֶץ, *ḥēpheç*, רָצוֹן, *rāçōn*; εὐδοκία, *eudokía*, ἡδονή, *hēdonḗ*): "Pleasure" is the tr of various Heb words, chiefly of *ḥēpheç*, "inclination," hence "pleasure," "delight" (Job **21** 21, "What pleasure hath he in his house?" ARV "what careth he for"; **22** 3, "Is it any pleasure to the Almighty?"; Ps **111** 2; Eccl **5** 4; **12** 1; in Isa **44** 28; **46** 10; **48** 14; **53** 10, it has the sense of will or purpose, "He shall perform all my pleasure," etc); of *rāçōn*, "delight," "acceptance," "good will" (Ezr **10** 11; Neh **9** 37; Est **1** 8; Ps **51** 18; **103** 21, etc); *nephesh*, "soul," "desire," is tr[d] "pleasure" (Dt **23** 24; Ps **105** 22; Jer **34** 16).

In the NT "pleasure" is the tr of *eudokia*, "good thought or will," "good pleasure" (Lk **2** 14 RVm; Eph **1** 5.9; Phil **2** 13; 2 Thess **1** 11, RV "every desire of goodness," m "Gr 'good pleasure of goodness.' Cf Rom **10** 1").

"To take or have pleasure" is *eudokéō* (2 Cor **12** 10; 2 Thess **2** 12; He **10** 6.8.38); *eudokeō* is once tr[d] "good pleasure" (Lk **12** 32, "It is your father's good pleasure to give you the kingdom"); the neuter participle of *dokéō*, "to think," etc—meaning "it seems good to me"—*tó dokoún*, is tr[d] "pleasure" (He **12** 10, "after their pleasure," RV "as seemed good to them"); *hēdonē*, "sweetness," "pleasure," occurs in Lk **8** 14; Tit **3** 3; 2 Pet **2** 13 (referring to the lower pleasures of life); *thélēma*, "wish," "will" (Rev **4** 11, RV "because of thy will"); *cháris*, "favor" (Acts **24** 27; **25** 9, RV "favor"); *spataláō*, "to live voluptuously" (1 Tim **5** 6, RV "she that giveth herself to pleasure"); *suneudokéō*, "to think well with," "to take pleasure with others" (Rom **1** 32, RV "consent with"); *trupháō*, "to live luxuriously" (Jas **5** 5, RV "lived delicately").

The vb. "to pleasure" occurs in 2 Macc **2** 27 as the tr of *eucharistía*, RV "gratitude"; **12** 11, *ōphelḗsein*, RV "to help."

W. L. WALKER

PLEDGE, plej (vbs. חָבַל, *ḥābhal* [10 t], עָרַב, *'ārabh* [2 K **18** 23=Isa **36** 8]; nouns חֲבֹל, *ḥăbhōl* [Ezk **18** 12.16; **33** 15], חֲבֹלָה, *ḥăbhōlāh* [Ezk **18** 7], עֲרֻבָּה, *'ărubbāh* [1 S **17** 18], עֵרָבוֹן, *'ērābhōn* [Gen **38** 17.18.20]; also עֲבֹט, *'ăbhōṭ* [Dt **24** 10–13] and [RV only] עַבְטִיט, *'abhṭīṭ* [Hab **2** 6]): All these words have about the same meaning. (1) The "pledge" is, as in modern Eng., security given for future payment (Gen **38** 17–24) or conduct (Hab **2** 6, where the conquered nations have given guaranties of their subserviency to the Chaldaeans; AV's "thick clay" here rests on a misreading of the Heb). In 2 K **18** 23 (=Isa **36** 8) the "pledge" is a wager (so RVm). Rabshakeh mockingly dares Hezekiah to stake a "pledge" that he can produce 2,000 men for the defence of Jerus, although the mighty Assyr host has that number of horses alone. The general point of the obscure passage Prov **20** 16 (= **27** 13) is that he who guarantees strangers needs a guaranty himself. 1 S **17** 18 is uncertain and the text may be corrupt. If not, the "pledge" is some (prearranged?) token of the welfare of David's brethren. (2) Most of the occurrences of "pledge," however, deal with the debts of the very poor, who had no property that they could spare even temporarily. Consequently, the exaction of a pledge from such persons worked genuine hardship, and to take a pledge at all was a cruel act (Job **24** 3), although of course the dishonesty of withholding a pledge (Ezk **18** 7; **33** 15) was worse. Lowest in the scale was the creditor who took the garment the borrower was wearing (Am **2** 8; Job **22** 6; **24** 9 m), and special legislation controlled this practice. A garment (the outer "cloak"—see Dress—not worn while doing manual labor) so taken must be restored at night (Ex **22** 26; Dt **24** 12.13), for it was the usual covering of the sleeper. (Apparently, though, the creditor regained custody of it in the daytime until the debt was paid.) A widow's clothing, however, was entirely exempt (Dt **24** 17), as was the handmill used for bread-making (**24** 6). The lender had no right of entry into the borrower's house to obtain the pledge (**24** 10.11), but it is not said that he could not dictate what he would accept; indeed, the contrary is inconceivable. (3) ARV gives "pledge" for AV and ERV "faith" in 1 Tim **5** 12. See also Earnest.

Burton Scott Easton

PLEIADES, plī'a-dēz, plē'ya-dēz, plē'a-dēz. See Astrology, 10; Astronomy, II, 10.

PLEROMA, plĕ-rō'ma. See Fulness.

PLOW, plou (חָרַשׁ, *ḥārash;* ἀροτριόω, *arotrióō*): No implement of the Bible is more frequently illustrated today than the plow. This is partly because there is every reason to believe that the plows still used throughout Egypt, Pal, and Syria are counterparts of the ancient ones. The first plows were probably an adaptation of the ancient Egyp hoe, where the handle was lengthened in order that animals might be hitched to it. To make it easier to break up the ground, it was pointed, and handles were added by which it could be guided. The ancient plow probably varied in type in different sections of the country, as it does today. In one form a young tree of oak or other strong wood of a diameter of 3 or 4 in. is cut off just below a good-sized branch and again 15 or 20 in. above. The upper end of the severed trunk is pointed and forms **the share.** Between this and the side branch is fitted a brace. The branch is cut off 10 or 12 ft. from the trunk and forms the pole. A lighter stick, about 3 ft. long, projects upward from the share and forms the handle. The plow used in Syria is of slightly different construction. The handle and share are one continuous piece, so cut that there is a slight bend at the middle. The share is pointed and is used bare in the plains, or in more stony regions is shod with iron. The pole is of 2 pieces joined end to end. The thicker end of the pole is notched, so that it may be attached firmly to the share. The whole plow is so light that it can be easily carried on a man's shoulder. These plows literally *scratch* the soil, as the Heb word implies. They do not turn over the ground as the modern implement does. The plowman guides the plow with one hand, and

Syrian Plow, Yoke and Pick.

with the other sometimes goads the oxen, and at other times with the chisel end of his goad breaks away the lumps of earth or other material which impedes the progress of his plow. See Yoke.

In addition to the words which are found above, the following terms occur: עָבַד, *'ābhadh* (lit. "to serve"), "worked" or "plowed" (Dt **21** 4); פָּלַח, *pālaḥ* (lit. "to break open," Ps **141** 7).

One special law is mentioned in connection with plowing, namely that an ox and an ass should not be yoked together (Dt **22** 10), a prohibition which is utterly disregarded today. Principally oxen were used for plowing (Job **1** 14). Often several yokes of oxen followed each other plowing parallel furrows across the field, a sight still common on the plains of Syria (1 K **19** 19). Plowing was done by bond servants (Lk **17** 7; cf *'ābhadh,* Dt **21** 4). Plowing cannot be done before the rains (Jer **14** 4); on the other hand the soil is too sticky to plow in the winter time (Prov **20** 4). The law requiring one day of rest in every seven included plowing time (Ex **34** 21).

Figurative: "The plowers plowed upon my back" typified deep affliction (Ps **129** 3; cf **141** 7). "Plow iniquity" is urged in the sense of "plant iniquity." Doing evil was sure to bring evil consequences (Job **4** 8; cf Mic **3** 12). As surely as planting comes after plowing, so surely will Jeh carry out His decree of destruction (Isa **28** 23–25). "Judah shall plow," i.e. become enslaved (Hos **10** 11); cf "Foreigners shall be your plowmen" (Isa **61** 5). "Will one plow there with oxen?" (Am **6** 12), "neither plowing nor harvest" (Gen **45** 6) are figures of desolation. Zion plowed as a field, i.e. utterly destroyed (Jer **26** 18). The plowman shall overtake the reaper, i.e. the soil shall be so fertile as to require no rest—typical of great abundance (Am **9** 13). No opportunity to plow because of lack of rain is a desolate picture of drought (Jer **14** 4). As the plowman expects to share in the fruits of the harvest, so might an apostle expect his temporal needs to be provided for (1 Cor **9** 10). "If ye had not plowed with my heifer," i.e. used my wife, was Samson's reply to those who had secured the answer to his riddle from her (Jgs **14** 18). "Beat their swords into plowshares" (or hoes) (Isa **2** 4; Mic **4** 3) typified peace; "beat your plowshares into swords"—war (Joel **3** 10). "Having put his hand to the plow, and looking back," i.e. longing for evil things when one has set his face toward doing what is right, unfits a man for the kingdom of God (Lk **9** 62; cf Gen **19** 26; Phil **3** 13).

James A. Patch

PLUCKING, pluk′ing, **OFF THE HAIR.** See Hair, 7; Punishments.

PLUMB-LINE, plum′līn, **PLUMMET,** plum′et, plum′it. See Tools.

POCHERETH-HAZZEBAIM, pok′ĕ-reth, pō′kĕ-reth, pō-kē′reth, -ha-zĕ-bā′im (פֹּכֶרֶת הַצְּבָיִם, *pō-khereth haçç^{e}bhāyim* [Ezr **2** 57], or פ׳ הַצְּבָיִים, *p. ha-ç^{e}bhāyīm* [Neh **7** 59], "binder [fem.] of the gazelles"): Name of the head of a post-exilic family. The first word is a fem. participle Kal; cf *ķōheleth* ("preacher"), the Heb title of the Book of Eccl. *BDB* suggests that the fem. is that of office. AV has "Pochereth of Zebaim" in Ezr, but Ryle (*Cambridge Bible*, 235) notes that "of" is not in the 1611 ed.

POET, pō′et (ποιητής, *poiētēs*, "a maker"): Occurs in this sense only in Acts **17** 28, where St. Paul quotes from the general expression of Gr mythology. The quotation if intended to be exact is probably from Aratus, as the words of St. Paul in his speech at Athens precisely agree with the opening words of the *Phaenomena* by Aratus. A like but not identical expression is found in the *Hymn to Zeus* by Cleanthes. Aratus in his poem endeavors to posit Jupiter as the father and controller of all things, and worthy to be worshipped. In both his poem and that of Cleanthes, but esp. in the latter, there is a true and lofty note of spiritual devotion. St. Paul takes this praise and devotion offered by the Gr poets to their unknown or fictitious gods and bestows it upon the one true God whom he declared unto the people of Athens.

C. E. Schenk

POETRY, pō′et-ri, **HEBREW:**

I. Is There Poetry in the OT?
  Poetry Defined:
  1. In Matter Concrete and Imaginative
  2. In Form Emotional and Rhythmical
II. Neglect of Hebrew Poetry: Causes
III. Characteristics of Hebrew Poetry, External and Internal
  1. External or Formal Characteristics
    (1) Vocabulary
    (2) Grammar
    (3) Rhythm
    (4) Parallelism
    (5) Other Literary Devices
    (6) Units of Hebrew Poetry
    (7) Classification of Stichs or Verses
  2. Internal or Material Characteristics
    (1) Themes of Hebrew Poetry
    (2) Species of Hebrew Poetry
IV. Poetical Writings of the OT
  1. The Poetical Books in the Narrow Sense
  2. Customary Division of the Poetical Books
  3. Poetry in Non-poetical Books
Literature

By Heb poetry in the present article is meant that of the OT. There is practically no poetry in the NT, but in the OT Apoc Sir is largely poetical and Wisd only less so. Post-Bib. Heb poetry could not be discussed here.

I. Is There Poetry in the OT?—It is impossible to answer this question without first of all stating what poetry really is. The present writer submits the following as a correct definition: "Poetry is verbal composition, imaginative and concrete in matter, and emotional and rhythmic in form." This definition recognizes two aspects of poetry, the formal and the material. The substance of poetry must be concrete—it is philosophy that deals with the abstract; and it has to be the product more or less of the creative imagination. It is of the essence of poetry that, like music, it should be expressed in rhythmical but not necessarily in metrical form. Moreover, the language has to be such as will stir up the aesthetic emotions. Adopting this account of poetry as criticism, it may unhesitatingly be affirmed that the Heb Scriptures contain a goodly amount of genuine poetry; cf the Pss, Job, Cant, etc. It is strange but true that poetical is older than prose written composition. An examination of the literature of the ancient Indians, Babylonians, Hebrews, Greeks and Arabs makes this quite certain.

II. Neglect of Hebrew Poetry: Causes.—Notwithstanding the undoubted fact that poetry is largely represented in the Bible, it is noteworthy that this species of Bible literature was almost wholly ignored until the 18th cent. We may perhaps ascribe this fact mainly to two causes: (1) Since the Bible was regarded as preëminently, if not exclusively, a revelation of the Divine mind, attention was fixed upon *what* it contained, to the neglect of the literary form in which it was expressed. Indeed it was regarded as inconsistent with its lofty, Divine function to look upon it as literature at all, since in this last the appeal is made, at least to a large extent, to the aesthetic and therefore carnal man. The aim contemplated by Bible writers was practical—the communication of religious knowledge—not literary, and still less artistic. It was therefore regarded as inconsistent with such a high purpose that these writers should trouble themselves about literary embellishment or beautiful language, so long as the sense was clear and unambiguous. It was in this spirit and animated by this conception that toward the middle of the 19th cent. Isaac Taylor of Ongar (*The Spirit of Heb Poetry*, 1861, 56 ff) and Keil of Dorpat (*Intro to the OT*, 1881, I, 437) denied on a priori grounds the presence of epic and dramatic poetry in the Bible. How, they exclaimed, could God countenance the writing of fiction which is untruth—and the epic and the drama have both? Matthew Arnold rendered invaluable service to the cause of Bible science when he fulminated against theologians, Jewish and Christian, for making the Bible a mere collection of proof texts, an arsenal whence religious warriors might get weapons with which to belabor their opponents. "The language of the Bible is fluid . . . . and literary, not rigid, fixed, scientific" (Preface to 1st ed of *Literature and Dogma*). The Bible contains literature, poetical and prose, equal as literature to the best, as Matthew Arnold, Carlyle, and Froude (on Job) held. The neglect of this aspect of the Scriptures made theologians blind to the presence and therefore ignorant of the character of Bible poetry. (2) Another factor which led to the neglect of the poetical element in the OT is the undoubted fact that Bib. Heb poets were less conscious as poets than western poets, and thought much less of the external form in which they expressed themselves. Bible poetry lacks therefore such close adherence to formal rules as characterizes Gr, Arab. or Eng. poetry. The authors wrote as they felt and because they felt, and their strong emotions dictated the forms their words took, and not any objective standards set up by the schools. Heb poetry is destitute of meter in the strict sense, and also of rhyme, though this last occurs in some isolated cases (see below, III, 1, [4], *c* and *e*). No wonder then that western scholars, missing these marks of the poetry which they knew best, failed for so long to note the poetry which the OT contains.

III. Characteristics of Hebrew Poetry: External and Internal.—The definition of poetry accepted in I, above, implies that there are marks by which poetry can be distinguished from prose. This is equally true of Heb poetry, though this last lacks some of the features of the poetry of western nations.

(1) *Vocabulary.*—There are several Heb words which occur most frequently and in some cases exclusively in poetry. In the following list the corresponding prose

word is put in parenthesis: מִלָּה, *millāh*, "word" (=דָּבָר, *dābhār*); אֱנוֹשׁ, *'ĕnōsh*, "man" (= אִישׁ, *'īsh*); אֹרַח, *'ōraḥ*, "way" (= דֶּרֶךְ, *derekh*); חָזָה, *ḥāzāh*, "to see" (= רָאָה, *rā'āh*); the prepositions אֱלֵי, *'ĕlē*, "to," עֲדֵי, *'ădhē*, "unto," עֲלֵי, *'ălē*, "upon," and מִנִּי, *minnī*, "from," instead of the shorter forms —אֱל, *'ĕl*, עַד, *'adh*, עַל, *'al*, and מִן, *min*. The pronoun זוּ, *zū*, rare in prose, has in poetry the double function of a demonstrative and a relative pronoun in both genders. The negative בַּל, *bal*, is used for לֹא, *lō'*. For the inseparable prepositions *b*, *k*, *l* ("in," "as," "to") the separate forms *bemō*, *kemō* and *lemō* are employed.

1. External or Formal Characteristics

(2) *Grammar*.—(*a*) Accidence: The pronominal suffixes have peculiar forms in poetry. For *m*, *ām*, *em* ("their," "them") we find the longer forms *mō*, *āmō*, *ēmō*. For the pl. ending of nouns *n* (*īn*) takes the place of *m* (*īm*), as in Aram. (cf Job **4** 2; **12** 11), and frequently obsolete case endings are preserved, but their functions are wholly lost. Thus we have the old nominative ending *ō* in Ps **50** 10, etc; the old genitive ending *ī* in Isa **1** 21, and the accusative *āh* in Ps **3** 3.

(*b*) Syntax: The article, relative pronoun, accusative sing. *'ēth* and also the "*waw*-consecutive" are frequently omitted for the sake of the rhythm. There are several examples of the last in Ps **112** 12 ff. The construct state which by rule immediately precedes nouns has often a preposition after it. The jussive sometimes takes the place of the indicative, and the pl. of nouns occurs for the singular.

(3) *Rhythm*.—Rhythm (from ῥυθμός, *rhuthmós*) in literary composition denotes that recurrence of accented and unaccented syllables in a regular order which we have in poetry and rhetorical prose. Man is a rhythmic animal; he breathes rhythmically, and his blood circulates—outward and inward—rhythmically. It may be due to these reflex rhythms that the more men are swayed by feeling and the less by reflection and reasoning, the greater is the tendency to do things rhythmically. Man walks and dances and sings and poetizes by the repetition of what corresponds to metrical feet: action is followed by reaction. We meet with a kind of rhythm in elevated and passionate prose, like that of John Ruskin and other writers. Preachers when mastered by their theme unconsciously express themselves in what may be called rhythmic sentences. Though, however, rhythm may be present in prose, it is only in poetry as in music that it recurs at intervals more or less the same. In iambic poetry we get a repetition of a short and long syllable, as in the following lines:

"With ravished ears
The monarch hears,
Assumes the gods,
Affects the nods."
—Dryden.

(4) *Parallelism*.—What is so called is a case of logical rhythm as distinguished from rhythm that is merely verbal. But as this forms so important a feature of Bible poetry, it must be somewhat fully discussed. What since Bishop Lowth's day has been called parallelism may be described as the recurring of symmetrically constructed sentences, the several members of which usually correspond to one another. Lowth (d. 1787), in his epoch-making work on Heb poetry (*De Sacra poesi Hebraeorum prelectiones*, ET by G. Gregory), deals with what he (following Jebb) calls *Parallelismus membrorum* (ch x). And this was the first serious attempt to expound the subject, though Rabbi Asariah (Middle Ages), Ibn Ezra (d. 1167 AD), D. Kimḥi (d. 1232) and A. de Rossi (1514-1578) called attention to it. Christian Schoettgen (d. 1751) (see *Horae Hebraicae et Talmudicae*) anticipated much of what Lowth has written as to the nature, function and value of parallelism. The first to use the word itself in the technical sense was Jebb (*Sacred Lit.*, 1820). For the same thing Ewald used the expression *Sinnrhythmus*, i.e. sense rhythm, a not unsuitable designation.

(*a*) Kinds of parallelism: Lowth distinguished three principal species of parallelism, which he called synonymous, antithetic and synthetic.

(i) The synonymous: In this the same thing is repeated in different words, e.g. Ps **36** 5:

'Yahwe, (α) Thy lovingkindness [reaches] to the heavens,
(β) Thy faithfulness [reaches] to the clouds.'

Omitting "Yahwe," which belongs alike to both members, it will be seen that the rest of the two half-lines corresponds word for word: "thy lovingkindness" corresponding to "thy faithfulness," and "to the heavens" answering to "to the clouds" (cf Ps **15** 1; **24** 1-3; **25** 5; 1 S **18** 7; Isa **6** 4; **13** 7).

(ii) Antithetic parallelism: in which the second member of a line (or verse) gives the obverse side of the same thought, e.g. Prov **10** 1:

'A wise son gladdens his father,
But a foolish son grieves his mother'

(see Prov **11** 3; Ps **37** 9; cf Prov **10** 1 ff; Ps **20** 8; **30** 6; Isa **54** 7 ff). Sometimes there are more than two corresponding elements in the two members of the verse, as in Prov **29** 27; cf **10** 5; **16** 9; **27** 2.

(iii) Synthetic parallelism: called also constructive and epithetic. In this the second member adds something fresh to the first, or else explains it, e.g. Ps **19** 8 f:

'The precepts of Yahwe are right, rejoicing the heart:
The commandments of Yahwe are pure, enlightening the eyes.
The fear of Yahwe is clean, enduring for ever:
The judgments of Yahwe are true and righteous altogether.
More to be desired are they than gold, yea, than much fine gold;
Sweeter also than honey and the honeycomb'

(see Prov **1** 7; cf **3** 5.7; Ps **1** 3; **15** 4). In addition to the three principal species of parallelism noticed above, other forms have been traced and described.

(iv) Introverted parallelism (Jebb, *Sacred Lit.*, 53): in which the hemistichs of the parallel members are chiastically arranged, as in the scheme *ab ba*. Thus Prov **23** 15 f:

(*a*) 'My son, if thy heart be wise
(*b*) My heart shall be glad, even mine:
(*b*) Yea, my reins shall rejoice
(*a*) When thy lips speak right things'

(cf Prov **10** 4.12; **13** 24; **21** 17; Ps **51** 3).

(v) Palilogical parallelism: in which one or more words of the first member are repeated as an echo, or as the canon in music, in the second. Thus Nah **1** 2:

'Yahwe is a jealous God and avenges:
Yahwe avenges and is full of wrath;
Yahwe takes vengeance on his adversaries,
And he reserves wrath for his enemies'

(cf Jgs **5** 3.6 f.11 f.15 f.23.27; Ps **72** 2.12.17; **121**; **124**; **126**; Isa **2** 7; **24** 5; Hos **6** 4).

(vi) Climactic or comprehensive parallelism: In this the second line completes the first. Thus Ps **29** 1:

"Give unto Yahwe, O ye mighty ones,
Give unto Yahwe glory and strength"

(see Ex **15** 6; Ps **29** 8).

(vii) Rhythmical parallelism (De Wette, Franz Delitzsch): thus Ps **138** 4:

"All the kings of the earth shall give thee thanks . . . .
For they have heard the words of thy mouth."

See Prov **15** 3; cf **16** 7.10; **17** 13.15; **19** 20; **21** 23.25.

Perfect parallelism is that in which the number of words in each line is equal. When unequal, the parallelism is called imperfect. Ewald (see *Die poetischen Bücher des alten Bundes*, I, 57–92; *Die Dichter des alten Bundes*, I, 91 ff, 2d ed of the former) aimed at giving a complete list of the relations which can be expressed by parallelism, and he thought he had succeeded. But in fact every kind of relation which can be indicated in words may be expressed in two or more lines more or less parallel. On the alleged parallelism of strophes see below.

(*b*) Parallelism as an aid to exegesis and textual criticism: If in Lowth's words parallelism implies that "in two lines or members of the same period things for the most part shall answer to things, and words to words," we should expect obscure or unknown words to derive some light from words corresponding to them in parallel members or clauses. In not a few cases we are enabled by comparison of words to restore with considerable confidence an original reading now lost. The formula is in a general way as follows: *ab*: *cx*. We know what *a*, *b* and *c* mean, but are wholly in the dark as to the sense of *x*. The problem is to find out what *x* means. We have an illustration in Jgs **5** 28, which may be thus literally translated:

"Through the window she looked,
And Sisera's mother *x* through the *x*."

Here we have two unknown, each, however, corresponding to known terms. The Heb vb. accompanying "Sisera's mother" is וַתְּיַבֵּב, *watteyabbēbh*, EV "and . . . . cried." But no such vb. (*yābhabh*) is known, for the Talm, as usually, follows the traditional interpretation. We want a vb. with a meaning similar to "looked." If we read וַתַּבֵּט, *wattabbēṭ*, we have a form which could easily be corrupted into the word in the MT, which gives a suitable sense and moreover has the support of the Tgs of Onkelos and Jonathan, and even of the LXX (A and Luc.). What about the other Heb word untranslated above (אֶשְׁנָב, *'eshnābh*)? This occurs in but one other passage (Prov **7** 6), where it stands as in the present passage in parallelism with חַלּוֹן, *ḥallōn*, "window" (probably Prov **7** 6 is dependent). We get no help from etymology or in this case from the VSS, but parallelism had suggested to our translators the meaning "lattice," a kind of Eastern window, and something of the kind must be meant. The vb. *shānabh*, "to be cool," may possibly suggest the rendering "window," i.e. a hole in the wall to secure coolness in the house. Glass windows did not exist in Pal, and are rare even now. There are innumerable other examples in the OT of the use of parallelism in elucidating words which occur but once, or which are otherwise difficult to understand, and frequently a textual emendation is suggested which is otherwise supported.

(*c*) Prevalence and value of parallelism: Two statements anent parallelism in the OT may be safely made: (i) That it is not a characteristic of all OT poetry. Lowth who had so much to do with its discovery gave it naturally an exaggerated place in his scheme of Heb poetry, but it is lacking in the largest part of the poetry of the OT, and it is frequently met with in elevated and rhetorical prose. (ii) That it pervades other poetry than that of the OT. It occurs in Assyria (see A. Jeremias, *Die bab-assyr. Vorstellung vom Leben nach dem Tode*), in Egypt (Georg Ebers, *Nord u. Süd*, I), in Finnish, Ger. and Eng. Indeed, A. Wuttke (*Der deutsche Volks-Aberglaube der Gegenwart*, 1869, 157) and Eduard Norden (*Die antike Kunstprosa*, 1898, II, 813) maintain that parallelism is the most primitive form of the poetry of all nations. It must nevertheless be admitted that in the OT parallelism has in proportion a larger place than in any other literature and that the correspondence of the parts of the stichs or verses is closer.

(5) *Other literary devices.*—OT poetry has additional features which it shares with other oriental and with western poetry. Owing to lack of space these can be hardly more than enumerated.

(*a*) Alliteration: e.g. "Round and round the rugged rocks." We have good examples in the Heb of Ps **6** 8 and **27** 17. (*b*) Assonance: e.g. "dreamy seamy" (see for Bible examples the Heb of Gen **49** 17; Ex **14** 14; Dt **3** 2). (*c*) Rhyme: There are so few examples of this in the Heb Scriptures that no one can regard it as a feature in Heb poetry, though in Arab. and even in post-Bib. Heb poetry it plays a great part. We have Bib. instances in the Heb text of Gen **4** 23; Job **10** 8–11; **16** 12. (*d*) Acrostics: In some poems of the OT half-verses, verses, or groups of verses begin with the successive letters of the Heb alphabet. We have such alphabetical acrostics in Pss **9 f**, **34**, **37**; Prov **31** 10 ff; Lam **1–4**; cf ch **5**, where the number of verses agrees with that of the Heb alphabet, though the letters of that alphabet do not introduce the verses.

(*e*) Meter: The view of the present writer may be stated as follows: That the poetry of the Heb is not in the strict sense metrical, though the writers under the influence of strong emotion express themselves rhythmically, producing often the phenomena which came later to be codified under metrical rules. Thinking and reasoning and speaking preceded psychology, logic, and grammar, and similarly poetry preceded prosody. In the OT we are in the region of the *fact*, not of the law. Poets wrote under strong impulse, usually religious, and without recognizing any objective standard, though all the time they were supplying data for the rules of prosody. Those who think that OT poets had in their minds objective rules of meter have to make innumerable changes in the text. Instead of basing their theory on the original material, they bring their a priori theory and alter the text to suit it. It can be fearlessly said that there is not a single poem in the OT with the same number of syllables, or feet, or accents in the several stichs or hemistichs, unless we introduce violent changes into the MT, such as would be resented in classical and other ancient literature. It is important, before coming to any definite conclusion, to take into consideration the fact that the poetry of the OT belongs to periods separated by many centuries, from the Song of Deborah (Jgs **5**), the earliest Heb poem, down to the last hymns in the Psalter. In the oldest specimens of Heb poetry there is a naïve simplicity which excludes the idea of conscious art. In the latest the poet is much more conscious, and his poetry more artistic. It would be manifestly unfair to propound a theory of poetry based on the poetry of Keats and Tennyson and to apply it to the productions of Anglo-Saxon and Old Eng. poetry. Bound up in the one volume called the Bible there is a literature differing widely in age, aim and authorship, and it needs care in educing a conception of Heb poetry that will apply to all the examples in the OT. The later pss-acrostic, etc, many of them made up of bits of other pss, seem to have sprung from a more conscious effort at imitation. If, however, there were among the ancient Hebrews, as there was among the ancient Greeks, a code of prosody, it is strange that the Mish and Gemārā' should be wholly silent about it. And if some one system underlies our Heb Bible, it is strange that so many systems have been proposed. It should be remembered too that the oldest poetry of every people is non-metrical.

The following is a brief statement of the views advocated:

(i) Philo and Josephus, under the influence of Gr models and desiring to show that Heb was not inferior to pagan literature, taught that Heb poetry had meter, but they make no attempt to show what kind of meter this poetry possesses.

(ii) Calmet, Lowth and Carpzov held that though in the poetry of the Heb Bible as originally written and read there must have been metrical rules which the authors were conscious of following, yet, through the corruption of the text and our ignorance of the sounds and accentuation of primitive Heb, it is now impossible to ascertain what these metrical rules were.

(iii) In their scheme of Heb meter Bickell and Merx reckon syllables as is done in classical poetry, and they adopt the Syr law of accentuation, placing the tone on the penultimate. These writers make drastic changes in the text in order to bolster up their theories.

(iv) The dominant and by far the least objectionable theory is that advocated by Ley, Briggs, Duhm, Buhl, Grimme, Sievers, Rothstein and most modern scholars, that in Heb prosody the accented syllables were alone counted. If this principle is applied to Job, it will be found that most of the Bib. verses are distichs having two stichs, each with three main accents. See, for an illustration, Job **12** 16: עִמּוֹ עֹז וְתוּשִׁיָּה : לוֹ שֹׁגֵג וּמַשְׁגֶּה (*'immō' 'ōz wethūshiyāh*: *lō shōghēgh umashgeh'*: 'Strength and effectual working belong to [lit. "are with"] him, he that errs and he that causes to err'). Man's rhythmical instincts are quite sufficient to account for this phenomenon without assuming that the poet had in mind an objective standard. Those who adopt this last view and apply it rigidly make numerous textual changes. For an examination of the metrical systems of Hubert Grimme, who takes account of quantity as well as accent, and of Eduard Sievers who, though no Heb scholar, came to the conclusion after examining small parts of the Heb

Bible that Heb poetry is normally anapaestic, see W. H. Cobb, *Criticism of Systems of Heb Metre*, 152 ff, 169 ff. Herder, De Wette, Hupfeld, Keil, Nowack, Budde, Döller, and Toy reject all the systems of Heb meter hitherto proposed, though Budde has a leaning toward Ley's system.

(*f*) Budde's ķinah measure: Though Budde takes up in general a negative position in regard to Heb meter, he pleads strenuously for the existence of one specific meter with which his name is associated. This is what he calls the ķinah measure (from קִינָה, *ķīnāh*, "a lamentation"). In this each stich is said to consist of one hemistich with three beats or stress syllables and another having two such syllables, this being held to be the specific meter of the dirge (see Lam **1** 1, etc). Ley and Briggs call it "pentameter" because it is made up of five (3+2) feet (a foot in Heb prosody being equal to an accented syllable and the unaccented syllables combined with it). See Budde's full treatment of the subject in *ZATW*, 60, 152, "Das heb. Klagelied." It must, however, be borne in mind that even Herder (d. 1803) describes the use in elegies of what he calls, anticipating Ley and Briggs, the "pentameter" (see *Geist der ebräischen Poesie*, 1782, I, 32 f, ET *The Spirit of Heb Poetry*, 1833, I, 40). But the present writer submits the following criticisms: (i) Budde is inconsistent in rejecting all existing theories of meter and yet in retaining one of his own, which is really but part of the system advocated by Bellermann, Ley and Briggs. (ii) He says, following Herder, that it is the measure adopted by mourning women (Jer **9** 16), but we have extremely few examples of the latter, and his statement lacks proof. (iii) There are dirges in the OT not expressed in the ķinah measure. David's lament over Saul and Jonathan is more hexametric and tetrametric than pentametric, unless we proceed to make a new text (2 S **1** 19 ff). (iv) The ķinah measure is employed by Heb poets where the theme is joyous or indifferent; see Ps **119**, which is a didactic poem.

(6) *Units of Hebrew poetry*.—In western poetry the ultimate unit is usually the syllable, the foot (consisting of at least two syllables) coming next. Then we have the verse-line crowned by the stanza, and finally the poem.

According to the theory of Heb poetry adopted by the present writer, the following are the units, beginning with the simplest:

(*a*) The meter: This embraces the accented (tone) syllable together with the unaccented syllable preceding or succeeding it. This may be called a "rhythmic foot."

(*b*) The stich or verse: In Job and less regularly in Pss and Cant and in other parts of the OT (Nu **23** 19–24) the stich or verse consists commonly of three toned syllables and therefore three meters (see above for sense of "meter"). It is important to distinguish between this poetical sense of "verse" and the ordinary meaning—the subdivision of a Bible chapter. The stich in this sense appears in a separate line in some old MSS.

(*c*) Combinations of stichs (verses): In Heb poetry a stich hardly ever stands alone. We have practically always a distich (couplet, Job **18** 5), a tristich (triplet, Nu **6** 24–26), a tetrastich (Gen **24** 23), or the pentastich.

(*d*) Strophe: Kosters (*Stud. Krit.*, 1831, 40–114, "Die Strophen," etc) maintained that all poems in the Heb Scriptures are naturally divisible into strophes (stanzas) of similar, if not equal, length. Thus Ps **119** is arranged in strophes named after the letters of the Heb alphabet, each one containing eight Scripture verses, or sixteen metrical verses or stichs, most of the stichs having three meters or rhythmical feet. But though several Bib. poems are composed in strophes, many are not.

(*e*) Song: This (שִׁירָה, *shīrāh*) is made up of a series of verses and in some cases of strophes.

(*f*) Poem: We have examples of this (שִׁיר, *shīr*) in the books of Job and Cant which consist of a combination of the song.

(7) *Classification of stichs or verses*.—Stichs may be arranged as follows, according to the number of meters (or feet) which they contain: (*a*) the trimeter or tripod with three meters or feet; Bickell holds that in Job this measure is alone used; (*b*) the tetrameter or tetrapod, a stich with four meters or feet; (*c*) the pentameter or pentapod, which has five meters or feet: this is Budde's ķinah measure (see III, 1, [4]); (*d*) the hexameter or hexapod: this consists of six meters or feet, and is often hard to distinguish from two separate trimeters (or tripods).

2. Internal Characteristics of Hebrew Poetry

Our first and most original authority on the internal characteristics of Hebrew poetry is that great German theologian and man of letters, J. G. Herder, the pastor and friend of Goethe and Schiller at Weimar. In his *Vom Geist der ebräischen Poesie*, 1782 (*The Spirit of Poetry*, tr[d] by James Marsh, U.S.A., 1833), he discusses at length and with great freshness those internal aspects of the poetry of the OT (love of Nature, folklore, etc) which impressed him as a literary man. Reference may be made also to George Gilfillian's *Bards of the Bible*, 1851 (popular), and Isaac Taylor's *Spirit of Heb Poetry*. It is a strange but striking and significant coincidence that not one of these writers professed much if any knowledge of the Heb language. They studied the poetry of the OT mainly at least in translations, and were not therefore diverted from the literary and logical aspects of what is written by the minutiae of Heb grammar and textual criticism, though only a Heb scholar is able to enter into full possession of the rich treasures of Heb poetry.

(1) *Themes of Hebrew poetry*.—It is commonly said that the poetry of the ancient Hebrews is wholly religious. But this statement is not strictly correct. (*a*) The OT does not contain all the poetry composed or even written by the Hebrews in Bible times, but only such as the priests at the various sanctuaries preserved. We do not know of a literary caste among the Hebrews who concerned themselves with the preservation of the literature as such. (*b*) Within the Bible Canon itself there are numerous poems or snatches of poems reflecting the everyday life of the people. We have love songs (Cant), a wedding song (Ps **45**), a harvest song (Ps **65**), parts of ditties sung on discovering a new well (Nu **21** 17 f), on drinking wine, and there are references to war songs (Nu **21** 14; Josh **10** 13; 2 S **1** 18).

(2) *Species of poetry*.—Bib. poetry may be subsumed under the following heads: (*a*) folklore, (*b*) prophetical, (*c*) speculative, (*d*) lyrical.

(*a*) Folklore: "Poetry," said J. G. Hamann (d. 1788), "is the mother tongue of the human race." In both folk-music and folk-poetry, each the oldest of its class, the inspiration is immediate and spontaneous. We have examples of folk-songs in Gen **11** 1–9; **19** 24 f.

(*b*) Prophetic poetry: This poetry is the expression of the inspiration under which the seer wrote. One may compare the oracular utterances of diviners which are invariably poetical in form as well as in matter. But one has to bear in mind that the heathen diviner claimed to have his messages from jinns or other spirits, and the means he employed were as a rule omens of various kinds. The OT prophet professed to speak as he was immediately inspired by God (see DIVINATION, VIII). Duhm thinks that the genuine prophecies of Jeremiah are wholly poetical, the prose parts being interpolations. But the prophet is not merely or primarily a poet, though it cannot be doubted that a very large proportion of the prophecies of the OT are poetical in form and substance.

(*c*) Philosophical poetry: This expression is intended to include such poetry as is found in the Wisdom literature of the OT and the Apoc (see WISDOM LITERATURE). The so-called didactic poetry, that of the proverbs or parables (מָשָׁל, *māshāl*), also comes in here.

(*d*) Lyrical poetry: This includes the hymns of the Psalter, the love songs of Cant and the many other lyrics found in the historical and prophetical writings. In these lyrics all the emotions of the human soul are expressed.

Does the OT contain specimens of epic and dramatic poetry? The answer must depend on which definition of both is adopted.

(*a*) Epic poetry: The present writer would define an epic poem as a novel with its plot and development charged, however, with the passion and set out in the rhythmic form of poetry. There is no part of the OT which meets the requirements of this definition, certainly not the Creation, Fall and Deluge stories, which De Wette (*Beiträge*, 228 ff, Einleitung, 147) and R. G. Moulton (*Literary Study of the Bible*, ch ix) point to as true epics, and which Ewald (*Dichter des alten Bundes*, I, 87 ff) held rightly to have in them the stuff of epics, though not the form.

(*b*) Dramatic poetry: Defining dramatic poetry as that which can be acted on a stage, one may with confidence say that there is no example of this in the OT. Even the literary drama must have the general characteristics of that which is actable. Franz Delitzsch and other writers have pointed to Job and Cant as dramatic poems, but the definition adopted above excludes both.

IV. Poetical Writings of the OT.—According to the Massoretes or editors of our present Heb Bible, there are but three poetical books in the OT, Job, Prov, and Pss, known in Jewish circles by the mnemonic abbreviation אֱמֶת, *'ĕmeth*, the three consonants forming the initial letters of the Heb names of the above books. These three books have been supplied by the Massoretes with a special system of accents known as the poetical accents, and involving a method of intoning in the synagogue different from that followed when the prose books are read. But these accentual marks cannot be traced farther back than the 7th or 8th cent. of our era.

1. The Poetical Books in the Narrow Sense

It is customary to divide the poetical books of the OT into two classes, each containing three books: (1) those containing lyrical poetry (שִׁיר, *shīr*, or שִׁירָה, *shīrāh*), i.e. Pss, Cant, Lam; (2) those containing for the most part didactic poetry (מָשָׁל, *māshāl*), i.e. Job, Prov, Eccl.

2. Customary Division

There is a large amount of poetry in the OT outside the books usually classed as poetical: (*a*) poetry in the prophetical books (see above, III, 2); (*b*) poetry in the historical books including the Pent (see Michael Heilprin, *The Historical Poetry of the Hebrews*, 2 vols, 1879–80). We have examples in Gen **4** 23 f; **49**; Ex **15**; Nu **21** 14 f.27–30 (JE); **23** f (Balaam's songs); Dt **32** f (song and blessing of Moses); Josh **10** 12–14 (JE); Jgs **5** (Deborah's Song); **9** 8–15; 1 S **2** 1–10; 2 S **1**; **3** 33 f; **23** (=Ps **18**), etc.

3. Poetry in Non-poetical Books

Literature.—The most important books and articles on the subject have been mentioned in the course of the foregoing article. There is a full list of works dealing with Heb meter in W. H. Cobb, *Criticism of Systems of Heb Metre*, 19 ff. The first edition of Ewald's still valuable "Essay on Heb Poetry" prefixed to his comm. on the Pss was published in Eng. in the *Journal of Sacred Literature* (1848), 74 ff, 295 ff. In 1909 J. W. Rothstein issued a suggestive treatise on Heb rhythm (*Grundzüge des heb. Rhythmus . . . . nebst lyrischen Texten mit kritischem Kommentar*, 8vo +vi +398), reviewed by the present writer in *Review of Theol. and Philos.* (Edinburgh), October, 1911. *Early Religious Poetry of the Hebrews* by E. G. King (Cambridge University Press) contains a good, brief, popular statement of the subject, though it makes no pretense to originality. In *The Poets of the OT*, 1912, Professor A. R. Gordon gives an excellent popular account of the poetry and poetical literature of the OT.

T. Witton Davies

POETRY, NEW TESTAMENT: No one questions the presence of poetry of a high order in the OT. The study of the OT as the literature of the ancient Hebrews has been critically made, and the attention of even the ordinary reader of the Scriptures called to the beauty and wealth of its poetic passages. The message of the NT is so vitally spiritual and concerned with religion that but little attention has been paid to it as literature. Naturally it would be strange if the poetic inspiration which runs like a tide through the prophetic and post-exilic periods of the OT should altogether cease under the clearer spiritual dispensation of the NT. The fact is that it does not cease, but that under every fundamental rule for poetic utterance, save that of rhyme, the NT is seen to be rich in imaginative vision, in religion touched by emotion, and in poetic expression. The Gospels, the Pauline Epp., and the Ep. of Jas, all afford examples of lofty poetic utterance, while the message of Jesus is saturated with words which readily lend themselves to song. In fact it is thought by some that Jesus was no less careful of the form than of the content of His message, and that all the finer types of Heb poetry found in the OT can be matched from His sayings, even when tested by the same rules.

In the Gospels that of **St. Luke** gives us our best examples of poetry. "No sooner have we passed through the vestibule of his Gospel than we find ourselves within a circle of harmonies" (Burton, in *Expositor's Bible*). From the poetic utterances of Mary, Elisabeth, Zacharias, Simeon, and the Angels, the church gains her *Magnificat*, Beatitude, *Benedictus*, *Nunc Dimittis* and *Glorias*.

The utterances of **John the Baptist** are filled with a rugged desert vision and an expression which reveals a form of poesy in nowise to be mistaken for prose.

St. Paul presents many of his ideas in harmonious and beautiful forms. He knew the secular poets of his day, and has immortalized Cleanthes' Hymn to Zeus (Acts **17** 28). He also quotes from Epimenides and the Athenian dramatist Menander (1 Cor **15** 33). St. Paul knew the poetry of the Hebrews, and enriches his own message with many quotations from it. He was acquainted with the Christian hymnology of his own times, as is seen in Eph **5** 14 and 1 Tim **3** 16. He offers also original flashes of poetic inspiration and utterance, a good example of which is found in Rom **8** 31–37.

Who could doubt the poetic imagery of **St. James?** He might almost be called the poet of social justice and of patient waiting under affliction for the will of God to come to men.

When one comes to the words of **Jesus** he discovers that in a very true sense His speech answers to the requirements for Heb poetry. Examples of synonymous, antithetic, synthetic and causal parallelism are the rule rather than the exception in the utterances of Jesus. For the synonymous form see Mt **10** 24; for the antithetic see Lk **6** 41; for the synthetic and causal forms see Lk **9** 23 and Mt **6** 7. Not alone are these forms of Heb poetry found in the words of Jesus, but also the more involved and sustained poetic utterances (Lk **7** 31–32).

No one can question the deep emotional quality, the vivid imagination and spiritual idealism of Jesus. That the form of His speech is adequately set to poetic inspiration and conforms to the laws for Heb poetry has not been so freely acknowledged. Independently of the theory advanced in *Did Jesus Write His Own Gospel?* (William Pitt

MacVey), every student of the literature of the NT must be grateful for the chapter on "The Poems of Jesus."

Spirituality and poetry have a kinship, and the interpretation of any message is aided by the adequate knowledge of its form. When the NT has thus been carefully studied as literature, it will be seen, not only that Jesus was a poet, but that the entire NT, if not as rich as the OT in poetic passages, is sufficiently poetic to receive treatment as such in religious encyclopaedias. See also FAITHFUL SAYINGS; POETRY, HEBREW. C. E. SCHENK

POINTS, points: The word occurs in Eccl **5** 16, "In all points [עֻמָּה, *'ummāh*] as he came, so shall he go"—a man leaves the world in all regards as helpless as he entered it, no matter what he may have gained or accomplished during his life.

Also in He **4** 15, "In all points [κατὰ πάντα, *katá pánta*, "in all things," as in His human nature (**2** 14), so in His human experience (cf **2** 17.18)] tempted like as we are, yet without sin." He successfully resisted temptation at all points of His nature, in body, soul, and spirit. See TEMPTATION OF CHRIST. Westcott (in loc.) thinks that the reference is not so much to Christ issuing out of all His trials without the least stain of sin, as to "a limitation of His temptation. Man's temptations come in many cases from previous sin. Such temptations had necessarily no place in Christ. He was tempted as we are, sharing our nature, yet with this exception, that there was no sin in Him to become the spring of trial." Whichever interpretation is adopted there is profound insight into the things of the soul in joining sinlessness with fulness of experience of temptation. M. O. EVANS

POISON, poi'z'n (חֵמָה, *ḥēmāh*, רֹאשׁ, *rō'sh;* θυμός, *thumós*, ἰός, *iós*): Residents in Pal must, from the first, have been acquainted with venomous serpents. Six species of these are widely diffused in the land, and at least three of them are fairly common in places. Besides, there are scorpions, centipedes and the large spider, which are as much dreaded by the fellahîn as are the serpents, not to speak of the minor but very serious discomforts of mosquitoes, sandflies and ticks, some of which were credited with lethal powers. In Wisd **16** 9 RV we read that "the bites of locusts and flies did slay, and there was not found a healing for their life." There are also many poisonous plants, such as belladonna, henbane, thorn apple, and the opium poppy. None of these is mentioned in the Bible; the only names found there are the hemlock (*Conium maculatum*) of Hos **10** 4, the poisonous gourd (*Citrullus colocynthis*) of 2 K **4** 39, and the grapes of gall, probably the fruit of *Calotropis procera*, the apples of Sodom of Jos (*BJ*, IV, viii, 4). Some, however, believe that these are poppyheads. Poisonous waters are referred to at Marah (Ex **15** 23) and Jericho (2 K **2** 19). There are no direct records of any person dying of poison except in 2 Macc **10** 13, where the suicide of Ptolemy Macron is related. Our Lord's promise in the appendix to Mk **16** 18 shows, however, that poisons were known and might be administered by way of ordeal, as was the unknown "water of jealousy" (Nu **5** 17). In this connection the story in Eusebius (*HE*, III, 39) is interesting, that "Justus surnamed Barsabbas, though he drank a deadly poison, suffered no injury, through the grace of the Lord." The passages in which poisonous serpents are mentioned are Dt **32** 24, where serpents (RV "crawling things") of the dust, probably *Cerastes hasselquistii*, the little horned vipers, are mentioned, and in ver 33: "poison of serpents, and the cruel venom of asps." The asp may be the cobra *Naia haje*, not uncommon on the borders of the wilderness to the S. Ps **58** 4 mentions the poison of serpents. Ps **140** 3, "They have sharpened their tongue like a serpent; adders' poison is under their lips," indicates, what is still a common belief, that the forked tongue of the snake is the poison-bearer. This is referred to in Jas **3** 8. That it was the fang and not the tongue which carried the poison was known to Pliny (xi.62). This verse of Ps **140** is given in St. Paul's composite quotation in Rom **3** 13. There may be a reference to the giving of an intoxicant poison in Hab **2** 15, where RV reads "that addest thy venom." The prophets speak in several places of God's wrath as a cup of trembling (RV "staggering"), e.g. Isa **51** 17.22, probably suggested by the fact that *ḥēmāh* primarily means "fury" and is used in that sense in more than a hundred passages. In Zec **12** 2 Jerus is to be such a "cup of reeling unto all the peoples round about."

The *s^emāmith*, "lizard" (AV "spider"), mentioned in Prov **30** 28 (LXX *kalabōtēs*) was formerly regarded as poisonous and it is still much disliked by the fellahîn, as they believe that it makes mocking gestures mimicking them at their prayers. They are really not poisonous. It is doubtful whether the lizard mentioned by Agur is really this stellion; the description better fits the gecko.

ALEX. MACALISTER

POLE, pōl: Nu **21** 8.9 AV for נֵס, *nēṣ*, RV "standard."

POLICY, pol'i-si: Lit. "method of government," and so "ability to manage affairs." In a bad sense, "cunning," "craft," in Dnl **8** 25 (שֶׂכֶל, *sekhel*, "understanding"); in a good sense in 1 Macc **8** 4 (βουλή, *boulḗ*, "counsel"); also in AV 2 Macc **13** 18; **14** 29.31 (μέθοδος, *méthodos*, στρατήγημα, *stratḗgēma*, στρατηγέω, *stratēgéō*), where RV has "stratagem." **Policies** occurs in Jth **11** 8 AV for πανούργημα, *panoúrgēma*, lit. "readiness for anything," here in a good sense; RV "subtil devices."

POLISHED, pol'isht. See CORNER-STONE, (2).

POLL, pōl: The word (on the derivation of which see Skeat, *Concise Etym. Dict. of the Eng. Language*, 360) has been eliminated as a vb. in ARV. In AV and ERV it represents the Heb vbs. כָּסַם, *kāṣam*, lit. "to shear" (Ezk **44** 20), גָּזַז, *gāzaz*, lit. "to pull out," "to uproot," thence "to shear the sheep," **figuratively,** "to destroy an enemy" (Mic **1** 16), גָּלַח, *gālaḥ*, in Piel, lit. "to make bald or round-headed" (2 S **14** 26) and קָצַץ, *ḳāçaç*, "to cut off" (Jer **9** 26; **25** 23; **49** 32). The Heb noun is גֻּלְגֹּלֶת, *gulgōleth*. As will be seen from the above enumeration, the Heb vbs. differ considerably in etymology, while RV has not tried to distinguish. In Mic **1** 16 we have a reference to the oriental custom of cutting or tearing one's hair as a sign of mourning for one's relatives. "Make thee bald, and cut off thy hair [AV and ERV "poll thee," Heb *gāzaz*] for the children of thy delight: enlarge thy baldness as the eagle [m "vulture"]; for they are gone into captivity from thee." The priests, the sons of Zadok, are instructed to abstain from outward resemblance to heathen patterns of priesthood: "Neither shall they shave their heads, nor suffer their locks to grow long; they shall only cut off the hair [AV and ERV "poll," Heb *kāṣam*] of their heads" (Ezk **44** 20). The Piel form of *gālaḥ* is employed in the description of the annual hair-cutting of Absalom (2 S **14** 26). Thrice we find the vb. "to poll" as the tr of Heb *ḳāçaç*, where ARV materially improves the tr by adopting the marginal version of AV (Jer **9** 26; **25** 23; **49** 32). See HAIR.

The noun (*gulgōleth*, lit. "head") is tr[d] "poll" in the phrase "by the poll," "by their polls" (Nu **1** 2.18.20.22; **3** 47; 1 Ch **23** 3.24). The expression has its origin in the numbering of persons by their heads, in the same way in which we speak of head-tax, etc. H. L. E. LUERING

POLLUTION, po-lū'shun (גָּאַל, *gā'al*, "to pollute"; **ἀλίσγημα,** *alisgēma*, "contamination"): In Mal **1** 7, "Ye offer polluted bread," i.e. not actually unclean, but worthless, common (cf Ezr **2** 62), bread here being used metonymically for sacrificial offerings generally (cf Lev **21** 6; Mt **6** 11). The phrase in Acts **15** 20, "the pollutions of idols," is explained in ver 29 by "things sacrificed [AV "meats offered"] to idols."

POLLUX, pol'uks. See CASTOR AND POLLUX.

POLYGAMY, pŏ-lig'a-mi:

1. Meaning of the Term
2. Origin of Polygamy
3. OT and Polygamy
4. Polygamy Unnatural The Eunuch
5. Weakness of Polygamy

Polygamy has been and is the open blazon by the human race of sex vice. The very term is a misnomer. Since man became moralized he has apprehended that the proper marriage relation between the sexes is monogamy. Whatever may have been the practice, since man could ask himself, What is right? he has known that ἀπ' ἀρχῆς, *ap' archēs* ("from the beginning," Mt **19** 4), *au fond*, at bottom, marriage is the choice of one man and one woman of each other for a life family relation. La Rochefoucauld said: "Hypocrisy is a sort of homage which vice pays to virtue." There is hypocrisy beneath the word polygamy. It is an attempt to cover up by the term "plural marriage" what is not marriage and cannot be marriage. There is no particular need of defining what the condition is, so long as we can look upon it as a violation and negation of the marriage relation. The very use of the term from any language covering a like condition is attempt—

1. Meaning of the Term

> "To steal the livery of the court of heaven
> To serve the Devil in."

Polygamy is a general term and might mean a multiplicity of partners in the family relation by one of either sex. But it does not. Polygamy practically means exactly "polygyny" (γυνή, *gunē*), i.e. it describes a *many-wived man.* The correlative term "polyandry" describes the condition of a woman who has many men in family relation with herself. They are all husbands to her, as in polygamy all the women are wives to one man. But polyandry in historic times has had so little illustration that it may be dismissed as so exceptional as to be worthy of no further notice here.

Why polygamy has captured the whole position philologically covered by polygyny is readily apparent. The might of the physically strongest has dictated the situation. Man has on the average one-fourth more muscular force than woman. When it comes to wrong in sex relation, man has that advantage, and it has given him the field covered by the word "polygamy." There he is master and woman is the victim.

It is plainly evident that polygamy is primarily largely the outcome of tribal wars. When men had separated into clans and had taken up different places of abode, collisions would soon occur between them. What would happen in such cases would be what we know did happen in North America soon after its first settlement by Europeans, to wit, the destruction of the Hurons by the Iroquois. The great majority of the men were massacred; the women and children, driven to the abode of the conquerors, disappearing there mainly in concubinage and slavery. What shall be done with this surplus of women? Here again the might of the strongest comes to the front. The chief or the most heroic fighter would assert his right to choice of captives, and thus concubinage or what is the same thing—polygamy—would be set up. Successes in further wars come and add other women to be distributed. Of course to the sheik or king there soon comes the seraglio and the harem. Polygamous practices will come in in other ways. The prisoner of war becomes property and passes from hand to hand by gift or sale. So woman—the weaker party—endures what comes to her as slave, concubine. We have now no longer the "helpmeet" originally destined for man—"bone of my bones and flesh of my flesh"—for whom he would "leave his father and his mother" and to whose single self he would "cleave" for life (Gen **2** 18.24; Mt **19** 5.6). Monogamy, with its unity in labor, thought and feeling, with its immeasurable modifying influences of moral, ideal and spiritual cast, is gone. Woman is reduced to the position of ministrant to man's unmodified sensuality.

2. Origin of Polygamy

The complications introduced into morals by polygamy are not often considered. But the Bible sets them forth in plainness. The marriage of Abraham and Sarah seems to have been an original love match, and even to have preserved something of that character through life. Still we find Sarah under the influence of polygamous ideas, presenting Abraham with a concubine. Yet afterward, when she herself had a son, she induced Abraham to drive out into the wilderness this concubine and her son. Now Abraham was humane and kind, and it is said "The thing was very grievous in Abraham's sight" (Gen **21** 11). But he was in the toils of polygamy, and it brought him pain and retribution. A Divine direction may be hard to bear.

3. The OT and Polygamy

The conditions of Jacob's marriages were such that it is hard to say whether any of his children were of any other than of polygamous origin (Gen **35** 22–26). Where the family idea and affection went, in such mixed condition, is evidenced by the unblushing sale, for slavery in Egypt, of one of the brothers by the others (**37** 28).

David was a singer of sweet and noble songs and wanted to be a righteous man with his whole heart. Yet, probably in common with all the military leaders and kings of the earth of his day, he had a polygamous career. His retributions ran along an extended line. There was a case of incest and murder among his children (2 S **13**). The son in whom he had most hope and pride organized treason against his throne, and lost his life in the attempt. David left his kingdom to Solomon, of whom much might be said, but of whom this can be said—evidently originally a man bright, keen-witted, wise, yet in his old age he went to pieces by the wiles of the women with whom he had loaded his harem. Partly by his extravagance in his polygamous life, and partly in attempt to build temples in distant places for the religions represented by the inmates of his harem, he bankrupted his nation. As a consequence his kingdom was divided at his death, and there was never again a united Israel (1 K **11** 12). Polygamy may be justly charged with these untoward results.

It can be demonstrated scientifically, even mathematically, that polygamy is a moral wrong. Statistics show that births are substantially equally divided between the sexes. Excess seems slightly on the side of males. When this fact is considered and also the fact of the wide prevalence of polygamy, it would seem that polygamy (polygyny) is a greater crime against Nature than polyandry. To put out of view for a moment the wrong to woman in denying to her the rights and privileges of monogamous marriage, the interference with the rights of man to such marriage looms up in vast proportion. Every harem is the denial to men of the right to seek among its inmates wives according to the dictates of their own hearts.

4. Polygamy Unnatural

The eunuch.—But we are not done with the crime against man. Given a harem, and he who set it up has made, or there brought, the eunuch. The lord of the harem must be served by emasculated men. A search in history will reveal an amount of this wickedness that is past belief. The eunuch has been everywhere among all nations and peoples and tongues. They have not only been servitors to women in harems, but they have acquired such influence with their masters that they have sometimes even dictated the policy of government. They have been the secret cabinet that has had the last word in public affairs. They have sometimes held public positions and shown therein astonishing ability. Witness Narses, the brilliant general of the emperor Justinian. See EUNUCH.

5. Weakness of Polygamy

Gibbon noticed the fact that nations began to decline in power when their policies were dictated and managed by eunuchs. But that is taking a symptom for the disease. There are weaknesses behind that weakness. We have found woman in muscular strength equal to three-fourths of a man. If we claim nothing more for woman than that ratio through the whole scale of her potencies, what would be thought of a nation that should try to reduce that three-fourths of potency as nearly to zero as it could? This is what polygamy has done—reduced woman as nearly to a cipher as it could in all the departments of her being. She has been held to the lowest and most primitive industrial pursuits. She has been deprived of intellectual development. She has been debarred from society, permitted to look at it only through a home lattice, or, if abroad, through a swathed face. The harem of sheik or sultan has fixed the condition of woman in province or nation—set the bounds to her life. The highest office assigned her has been breeder of children, and for one-half of them—the daughters—she could have no possible hope or ambition (see WOMAN).

Where in such degradation is the "helpmeet" for man in all his problems? This condition is reflected back over man. What possible appeal can there be to him for thought and energy except to repeat the same dull round exhibited in his daily life? Polygamous nations have never been industrial inventors, have contributed little to science. They have usually ruined the fertility of the lands they have occupied. They have been heavily weighted with the lethargy of a system that appeals to nothing but the most primitive instincts and vices of man.

The monogamous have been the forceful nations. Rome conquered the world while she was monogamous, and lost control of it when she dropped to the moral level of the sex corruption of the peoples she had conquered. The Teuton trundled into and over Europe in ox-carts mounted on solid wood trucks. But his cart carried one wife, and now all polygamy is held under the trained guns of the Teuton.

There may seem to be two exceptions—the establishment of the Mogul empire in India and the subjugation of Western Asia and Eastern Europe by the Turk. That in both cases there was great success in war is granted. They were authorized by their religion to exhibit the frenzy of bloodshed and indulge in lust. Indeed, enjoyment of the latter was a bright hope for the life to come. But when they had possession of a country, and massacres and ravishing were over, what then? For what is mankind indebted to them?

A lyric.—A lyric has been put in the hand of the present writer by a friend who wrote it at the last date of the title. It is one of the lyrics of the centuries in its synthesis of history and in its insight into the forces physical, moral and immoral at work in the Mogul empire of India. Notice the dates. The text will show what took place between.

THE MOGUL 1525–1857

A war steed coursed out the wind-swept north,
Jarring the crags with hoofs of fire,
Snuffing far battle with nostril wide,
Neighing the joy of fierce desire.

The crisping herbage of arid plains
Had toughened his sinews like bands of steel;
The snow-fed waters of Zarafshan
Had nerved the might of a northern will.

The war steed grazed in the fertile meads,
Drinking the waters of indolent streams:
He rested at eve on bloom-dight beds,
Toyed with by maidens in the goldening gleams.

They charmed his ear with dalliant song:
They closed his eyes in witchery's glee:
They fed him the vineyards' wildering draught—
He slept in the breath of the lotus tree.

White bones lie strewn on the flowering mead,
In flesh-rank grass grown high and dark.
The carrion bird hath flown—hath died—
Riseth the war-horse? Neigheth? Hark!
—JOSIAH TORREY READE, Amherst, 1856.

The above lyric may be taken as the epitaph of any polygamous nation. The last words are significant—"Neigheth? Hark!" Would the old war steed arise? "Hark!" The Sepoy rebellion was on! We "harkened," but the rebellion went to pieces and an end was put to the Mogul empire. We have listened for half a century and heard no sound. We hear mutterings now, but the end will be as before—even if the "war-horse" riseth and is victorious. He will then again lie down in "flesh-rank grass grown high and dark," and the "carrion bird" will fly from his "white bones." Streams cannot rise higher than their fountains. The causes remaining, the same effects will follow. See DIVORCE; FAMILY; MARRIAGE.

C. CAVERNO

POMEGRANATE, pom′gran-āt, pom-gran′āt, pum′gran-āt (רִמּוֹן, *rimmōn* [tree and fruit]; the Heb name is similar to the Arab., Aram. and Ethiopic; ῥόα, *rhóa*): One of the most attractive and most characteristic of the fruit trees of Syria, probably indigenous to Persia, Afghanistan and the neighborhood of the Caucasus, but introduced to Pal in very ancient

1. A Tree Characteristic of Palestine

Pomegranate.

times. The spies brought specimens of figs and pomegranates, along with grapes, from the Vale of Eshcol (Nu **13** 23). Vines, figs and pomegranates are mentioned (Nu **20** 5) as fruits the Israelites missed in the wilderness; the promised land was to be one "of wheat and barley, and vines and fig-trees and pomegranates" (Dt **8** 8), a promise renewed in Hag **2** 19. In the lamentation in Joel **1** 11.12 we have the pomegranate, the palm tree and the apple tree represented as withered, "for joy is withered away from the sons of men."

2. The Fruit

The pomegranate tree, *Punica granatum* (N.O. *Granateae*) occurs usually as a shrub or small tree 10–15 ft. high, and is distinguished by its fresh green, oval leaves, which fall in winter, and its brilliant scarlet blossoms (cf Cant **7** 12). The beauty of an orchard of pomegranates is referred to in Cant **4** 13. The fruit which is ripe about September is apple-shaped, yellow-brown with a blush of red, and is surmounted by a crown-like hard calyx; on breaking the hard rind, the white or pinkish, translucent fruits are seen tightly packed together inside. The juicy seeds are sometimes sweet and sometimes somewhat acid, and need sugar for eating. The juice expressed from the seeds is made into a kind of syrup for flavoring drinks, and in ancient days was made into wine: "I would cause thee to drink of spiced wine, of the juice [m "sweet wine"] of my pomegranate" (Cant **8** 2). The beauty of a cut section of pomegranate—or one burst open naturally, when fully ripe—may have given rise to the comparison in Cant **4** 3; **6** 7: "Thy temples are like a piece of a pomegranate." The rind of the pomegranate contains a very high percentage of tannic acid, and is employed both as a medicine and for tanning, particularly in making genuine morocco leather.

Whether the pomegranate tree in Migron under which Saul is said (1 S **14** 2) to have abode with his 600 men was really a tree or a place, Rimmon, is doubtful. See RIMMON.

3. The Pomegranate in Art

A large number of references to the pomegranate are to the use of the form of the fruit in ornamentation, in which respect it appears among the Hebrews to have something of the position of the lotus bud as a decorative motive in Egypt. It was embroidered in many colors on the skirts of Aaron's garments, together with golden bells (Ex **28** 33 f; **39** 24–26; cf Ecclus **45** 9). Hiram of Tyre introduced the pomegranate into his brass work ornamentation in the temple: "So he made the pillars; and there were two rows round about upon the one network, to cover the capitals that were upon the top of the pillars" (m "So the Syr. The Heb has 'pomegranates' ") (1 K **7** 18). "And the pomegranates were two hundred, in rows round about upon the other capital" (ver 20; cf also ver 42; 2 K **25** 17; 2 Ch **3** 16; **4** 13).

E. W. G. MASTERMAN

POMMEL, pum'el (2 Ch **4** 12.13): RV reads "bowl" (q.v.).

POND. See CISTERN; POOL.

PONDER, pon'dẽr: Occurs in AV 5 t in the Book of Prov and nowhere else in the OT. In each case it means "to consider carefully," "to weigh mentally." In Prov **4** 26 and **5** 21, RV substitutes "make level." In Prov **5** 6, it drops out entirely in RV. In Prov **21** 2 and **24** 12, "weigh" is substituted for "ponder." The one NT passage is Lk **2** 19; here RV has "pondering" where AV has "and pondered."

PONTIUS, pon'shi-us, pon'ti-us. See PILATE.

PONTUS, pon'tus (**Πόντος**, *Pόntos*): Was an important province in the northeastern part of Asia Minor, lying along the south shore of the Black Sea. The name was geographical, not ethnical, in origin, and was first used to designate that part of Cappadocia which bordered on the "Pontus," as the Euxine was often termed. Pontus proper extended from the Halys River on the W. to the borders of Colchis on the E., its interior boundaries meeting those of Galatia, Cappadocia and Armenia. The chief rivers besides the Halys were the Iris, Lycus and Thermodon. The configuration of the

Rock Tombs at Amasia.

country included a beautiful but narrow, riparian margin, backed by a noble range of mountains parallel to the coast, while these in turn were broken by the streams that forced their way from the interior plains down to the sea; the valleys, narrower or wider, were fertile and productive, as were the wide plains of the interior such as the Chiliokomon and Phanaroea. The mountain slopes were originally clothed with heavy forests of beech, pine and oak of different species, and when the country was well afforested, the rainfall must have been better adequate than now to the needs of a luxuriant vegetation.

The first points in the earliest history of Pontus emerge from obscurity, much as the mountain peaks of its own noble ranges lift their heads above a fog bank. Thus we catch glimpses of Assyr culture at Sinope and Amisus, probably as far back as the 3d millennium BC. The period of Hittite domination in Asia Minor followed hard after, and there is increasing reason to suppose that the Hittites occupied certain leading city sites in Pontus, constructed the artificial mounds or tumuli that frequently meet the eyes of modern travelers, hewed out the rock tombs, and stamped their character upon the early conditions. The home of the Amazons, those warrior priestesses of the Hittites, was located on the banks of the Thermodon, and the mountains rising behind Terme are still called the "Amazon Range"; and the old legends live still in stories about the superior prowess of the modern women living there. See ARCHAEOLOGY OF ASIA MINOR.

As the Hittite power shrunk in extent and force, by the year 1000 BC bands of hardy Gr adventurers appeared from the W. sailing along the Euxine main in quest of lands to exploit and conquer and colonize. Cape Jason, which divides the modern mission fields of Trebizond and Marsovan, preserves the memory of the Argonauts and the Golden Fleece. Miletus, "greatest of the Ionic towns," sent out its colonists, swarm after swarm, up through the Bosphorus, and along the southern shore of the Black Sea. They occupied Sinope, the northernmost point of the peninsula with the best harbor and the most commanding situation. Sinope was in Paphlagonia, but politically as well as commercially enjoyed intimate relations with the Pontic cities. Settlers from Sinope, reinforced by others from Athens direct, pressed on and founded Amisus, the modern *Samsoun,* always an important commercial city. Another colony from Sinope founded Trebizond, near which Xenophon and the Ten Thousand reached the sea again after they had sounded the power of Persia and found it hollow at Cunaxa. Among the cities of the interior, picturesque Amasia in the gorge of the Iris River witnessed the birth of Strabo in the 1st cent. BC, and to the geographer Strabo, more than to any other man, is due our knowledge of Pontus in its early days. Zille, "built upon the mound of Semiramis," contained the sanctuary of Anaitis, where sacrifices were performed with more pomp than in any other place. Comana, near the modern *Tokat*, was a city famous for the worship of the great god Ma. Gr culture by degrees took root along the coast; it mixed with, and in turn was modified by, the character of the older native inhabitants.

When the Persians established their supremacy in Asia Minor with the overthrow of Lydia, 546 BC, Pontus was loosely joined to the great empire and was ruled by Pers satraps. Ariobarzanes, Mithradates and Pharnaces are the recurring names in this dynasty of satraps which acquired independence about 363 and maintained it during the Macedonian period. The man that first made Pontus famous in history was Mithradates VI, surnamed Eupator. Mithradates was a typical oriental despot, gifted, unscrupulous, commanding. Born at Sinope 136 BC and king at Amasia at the age of twelve, Mithradates was regarded by the Romans as "the most formidable enemy the Republic ever had to contend with." By conquest or alliance he widely extended his power, his chief ally being his son-in-law Dikran, or Tigranes, of Armenia, and then prepared for the impending struggle with Rome. The republic had acquired Pergamus in 133 BC and assumed control of Western Asia Minor. There were three Rom armies in different parts of the peninsula when war broke out, 88 BC. Mithradates attacked them separately and overthrew them all. He then planned and executed a general massacre of all the Romans in Asia Minor, and 80,000 persons were cut down. Sulla by patient effort restored the fortunes of Rome, and the first war ended in a drawn game; each party had taken the measure of its antagonist, but neither had been able to oust the other. The second war began in the year 74, with Lucullus as the Rom general. Lucullus took Amisus by siege, chased Mithradates to Cabira, modern *Niksar*, scattered his army and drove the oriental sultan out of his country. Subsequently on his return to Rome, Lucullus carried from Kerasoun the first cherries known to the western world. In the third war the hero on the Rom side was the masterful Pompey, appointed in 66 BC. As a result of this war, Mithradates was completely vanquished. His dominions were finally and permanently incorporated in the territories of the Rom republic. The aged king, breathing out wrath and forming impossible plans against his lifelong enemies, died in exile in the Crimea from poison administered by his own hand.

Most of Pontus was for administrative purposes united by the Romans with the province of Bithynia, though the eastern part subsisted as a separate kingdom under Polemon and his house, 36 BC to 63 AD, and the southwestern portion was incorporated with the province of Galatia.

It was during the Rom period that Christianity entered this province. There were Jews dwelling in Pontus, devout representatives of whom were in Jerus on the Day of Pentecost (Acts **2** 9). Paul's associates, Aquila and Priscilla, were originally from here (Acts **18** 2). The sojourners of the Dispersion are included in the address of the first Ep. of Peter together with the people of four other provinces in Asia Minor (1 Pet **1** 1). Local traditions connect the apostles Andrew and Thaddeus with evangelistic labors in this region. They are said to have followed the great artery of travel leading from Caesarea Mazaca to Sinope. Pliny, governor of Bithynia and Pontus 111–13 AD, found Christians under his authority in great numbers (see BITHYNIA), and Professor Ramsay argues that Pliny's famous letters, Nos. 96 and 97, written to the emperor Trajan on the subject of the treatment of Christians under his government (see PERSECUTION), were composed in view of conditions in Amisus (*Church in Rom Empire*, 224, 225).

The Rom empire in the East was gradually merged into the Byzantine, which is still known to the local inhabitants as the empire of "Roum," i.e. Rome. Pontus shared the vicissitudes of this rather unfortunate government until, in 1204, a branch of the Byzantine imperial family established in Pontus a separate small state with its capital at Trebizond. Here the house of the Grand Comneni, sheltered between the sea and the mountain ranges, maintained its tinsel sovereignty to and beyond the fall of Constantinople. In 1461 Trebizond was taken by Mohammed the Conqueror. since which date Pontus, with its conglomerate population of Turks, Armenians, Greeks and fragments of other races, has been a part of the Ottoman empire.

G. E. WHITE

POOL, pōōl, **POND,** pond, **RESERVOIR,** rez′ẽr-vwâr, rez′ẽr-vwär ([1] בְּרֵכָה, *berēkhāh*, "pool"; cf Arab. بِرْكَة, *birkat*, "pool"; cf בְּרָכָה, *berākhāh*, "blessing," and Arab. بَرَكَة, *barakat*, "blessing"; [2] אֲגַם, *'ăgham*, "pool," "marsh," "reeds"; cf Arab. أَجَم, *'ajam*, "thicket," "jungle"; [3] מִקְוָה, *miḳwāh*, "reservoir," AV "ditch" [Isa **22** 11]; [4] מִקְוֶה, *miḳweh*, "pond," AV "pool" [Ex **7** 19]; מִקְוֵה הַמַּיִם, *miḳwēh ha-mayim*, EV "gathering together of the waters" [Gen **1** 10]; מִקְוֵה־מַיִם, *miḳwēh-mayim*, "a gathering of water," AV "plenty of water" [Lev **11** 36]; [5] **κολυμβήθρα,** *kolumbēthra*, "pool," lit. "a place of diving," from **κολυμβάω,** *kolumbáō*, "to dive"): LAKES (q.v.) are very rare in Syria and Pal, but the dry climate, which is one reason for the fewness of lakes, impels the inhabitants to make artificial pools or reservoirs to collect the water of the rain or of springs for irrigation and also for drinking. The largest of these are made by damming water courses, in which water flows during the winter or at least after showers of rain. These may be enlarged or deepened by excavation. Good examples of this are found at *Dîbân* and *Mâdeba* in Moab. Smaller pools of rectangular shape and usually much wider than deep, having no connection with water courses, are built in towns to receive rain from the roofs or from the surface of the ground. These may be for common use like several large ones in Jerus, or may belong to particular houses. These are commonly excavated to some depth in the soil or rock, though the walls are likely to rise above the surface. Between these and cylindrical pits or cisterns no sharp line can be drawn.

The water of springs may be collected in large or small pools of masonry, as the pool of Siloam (Jn **9** 7). This is commonly done for irrigation when the spring is so small that the water would be lost by absorption or evaporation if it were attempted to convey it continuously to the fields. The pool (Arab. *birkat*) receives the trickle of water until it is full. The water is then let out in a large stream and conducted where it is needed. (In this way by patient labor a small trickling spring may support much vegetation.)

'Ăgham does not seem to be used of artificial pools, but rather of natural or accidental depressions containing water, as pools by the Nile (Ex **7** 19; **8** 5), or in the wilderness (Ps **107** 35; **114** 8; Isa **14** 23; **35** 7; **41** 18; **42** 15). In Isa **19** 10 the rendering of AV, "all that make sluices and ponds for fish," would be an exception to this statement, but RV has "all they that work for hire shall be grieved in soul." *Miḳweh* occurs with *'ăgham* in Ex **7** 19 of the ponds and pools by the Nile. *Berēkhāh* is used of "the pool of Gibeon" (2 S **2** 13), "the pool in Hebron" (2 S **4** 12), "the pool of Samaria" (1 K **22** 38), "the pools in Heshbon" (Cant **7** 4), "the pool of Shelah," AV "Shiloah" (Neh **3** 15); cf "the waters of Shiloah" (Isa **8** 6). We read in Eccl **2** 6, "I made me pools of water, to water therefrom the forest where trees were reared." There is mention of "the upper pool" (2 K **18** 17; Isa **7** 3; **36** 2), "the lower pool" (Isa **22** 9), "the king's pool" (Neh **2** 14). Isa **22** 11 has, "Ye made also a reservoir [*miḳwāh*] between the two walls for the water of the old pool [*berēkhāh*]." *Kolumbēthra* is used of the pool of Bethesda (Jn **5** 2.4.7) and of the pool of Siloam (Jn **9** 7.11). See also Cistern; Natural Features; *BJ*, V, iv, 2.

Alfred Ely Day

POOLS, pōōlz, **OF SOLOMON.** See Cistern; Pool.

POOR, pōōr (אֶבְיוֹן, *'ebhyōn*, דַּל, *dal*, עָנִי, *'ānī*, רוּשׁ, *rūsh*; πτωχός, *ptōchós*):

I. In the OT.—The poor have great prominence in the Bible; it is said, indeed, that there should be no poor among the Hebrews because Jeh should so greatly bless them (Dt **15** 4 RV and AVm); but this was only to be realized on certain conditions of obedience (ver 5), and in ver 11 it is said, "The poor will never cease out of the land"; but they were to see to it that none was left in destitution. The very foundation of the Heb religion was God's pity on a poor and oppressed people.

1. The Terms Employed

The words for "poor" are chiefly *'ebhyōn*, "desirous," "needy," "poor" (Ex **23** 6, etc); *dal*, "moving," "swaying," hence, weak, poor, lowly (Ex **23** 3, etc); *dallāh*, "poverty," "weakness" (2 K **25** 12, etc); *rūsh*, perhaps "to shake," "tremble," "to be poor," "impoverished" (1 S **18** 23, etc); *'ānī*, also *'ānāw*, "poor," "oppressed," from *'ānāh*, "to bend" or "bow down" (Ex **22** 25, etc); *'ănēh*, Aram. (Dnl **4** 27), *ḥēlekhāh*, "wretchedness" (Ps **10** 8.14 AV); *yārash*, "to make poor" (1 S **2** 7); *maḥṣōr*, "want" (Prov **21** 17); *miṣkēn*, "a needy one" (Eccl **4** 13; **9** 15*bis*.16).

2. Representations

(1) *Generally.*—God (Jeh and *'Ĕlōhīm*) is represented as having a special care for "the poor," which was illustrated in the deliverance of the nation from Egyp poverty and bondage and was never to be forgotten by them (Dt **24** 22); as punishing the oppressors of the poor and rewarding those who were kind to them; God Himself was the Protector and Saviour of the poor (Ex **22** 23): "If thou afflict them at all, and they cry at all unto me, I will surely hear their cry; and my wrath shall wax hot," etc (Dt **15** 9; **24** 15; 1 S **2** 8; Job **31** 16; Ps **9** 18; **12** 5; Prov **19** 17; Isa **25** 4; Eccl **5** 8, "one higher than the high regardeth," etc).

(2) *Liberality* to the poor is specially enjoined (Dt **15** 7 f), and they were to beware of self-deception and grudging in this (vs 9.10).

(3) *Special provisions* were made on behalf of the poor: (*a*) Every third year a tithe was to be given "unto the Levite, to the sojourner, to the fatherless and to the widow" that Jeh might bless them (Dt **14** 28.29; **26** 12 f); (*b*) the poor were to have the free use of all that grew spontaneously in field or vineyard during the Sabbatic year (Ex **23** 10 f; Lev **25** 5.6); (*c*) each year the gleanings of the fields and vineyards should belong to the poor, the corners of fields were to be left for them, and if a sheaf was forgotten it should remain (Lev **19** 9. 10; **23** 22; Dt **24** 19); (*d*) fruit and ripe grain in a field might be eaten by any hungry person, but none should be carried away (Dt **23** 24.25); (*e*) in the Feast of Weeks the poor were to participate (Dt **16** 9–12); (*f*) every seventh year there should be a "release" of debts (Dt **15** 1 f); in the seventh year of servitude the Heb bond-servant should go free (Ex **21** 2), or in the Jubilee, if that came first, on which occasion—the fiftieth year—property that had been sold returned to its owner or his family (Lev **25** 8–17); (*g*) they were to lend readily to the poor, and no interest or increase was to be taken from their brethren (Ex **22** 25; Lev **25** 35–37; Dt **15** 7 f); in Lev **25** 39, no poor Hebrew was to be made a bond-servant, and, if a hired servant, he was not to be ruled with rigor (ver 43); his hire was to be given him daily (Lev **19** 13; Dt **24** 15); no widow's raiment was to be taken in pledge (Dt **24** 17), nor the handmill, nor the upper millstone so essential for daily life (ver 6), a man's garment should be returned to him before sundown, and no house should be entered to seize or fetch any pledge (vs 10–13); breach of these laws should be *sin* and their observance *righteousness* (Dt **24** 13.15, etc; see Alms, Almsgiving); (*h*) justice was to be done to the poor (Ex **23** 6; Dt **27** 19, "Cursed be he that wresteth the justice due to the sojourner, fatherless, and widow"); (*i*) offerings were graduated according to means (Lev **5** 7; **12** 8).

(4) *Definite penalties* were not always attached to those laws, and the prophets and psalmists have many complaints of the unjust treatment and oppression of the poor, contrary to the will of God, and frequent exhortations to justice and a due regard for them (Ps **10** 2.9; **12** 5; **14** 6, etc; Isa **3** 14.15; Jer **2** 34; Ezk **16** 49, "the iniquity of . . . . Sodom"; **18** 12.17; **22** 29; Am **2** 7; **4** 1; Hab **3** 14; cf Job **20** 19; **24** 9.14, etc; Prov **14** 31).

(5) *The duty of caring for the poor* is frequently and strongly set forth and Divine promises attached to its fulfilment (Ps **41** 1; **72** 12 ff; Prov **17** 5; **22** 9; **28** 3.27; Isa **58** 7; Jer **22** 16; Ezk **18** 17; Dnl **4** 27; Zec **7** 10, etc; cf Job **29** 12.16; **30** 25; **31** 19; Ps **112** 9).

(6) *The day of the Divine manifestation*, the times of the Messiah, should bring deliverance and rejoicing to the poor (Ps **72** 12–15; Isa **11** 4, "With righteousness shall he judge the poor," etc; **14** 30; **29** 19; **61** 1 RVm).

(7) *The equality of rich and poor* before God and the *superiority* of the righteous poor to the ungodly rich, etc, are maintained (Prov **19** 1.22; **22** 1.2; Eccl **4** 13).

(8) Ways in which men can wilfully make themselves poor are mentioned (Prov **6** 11; **10** 4; **12** 24; **13** 4.18; **14** 23; **20** 13; **21** 5.17; **23** 21; **28** 19).

3. The Godly Poor

The chief words given above all mean *poor*, literally, but *'ānī* (rendered also "afflicted") may also denote Israel as a nation in its afflictions and low estate, e.g. Ps **68** 10; Isa **41** 17; **49** 13; **51** 21; **54** 11; in Zeph **3** 12, it is "the ideal Israel of the future." Dr. Driver remarks (art. "Poor," *HDB*) that such passages show that *'ānī* (as also its frequent parallel *'ebhyōn*, and, though somewhat less distinctly, *dal*) came gradually "to denote the *godly* poor, the suffering righteous, the persons who, whether 'bowed down' or 'needy' or 'reduced,' were the godly servants of Jeh." The humble poor became in fact distinguished as the line in which faithfulness to Jeh was maintained and spiritual religion developed. The less frequent word *'ānāw*, often tr[d] "meek," "humble," is regarded (see Driver in loc.) as having from the first a moral and religious significance. It is used of Moses (Nu **12** 3) and occurs in Ps **10** 12.17; **22** 26; **25** 9, etc; Prov **3** 34; **16** 19; Isa **29** 19; **32** 7; **61** 1; Am **2** 7; Zeph **2** 3.

II. In the NT.—In the NT *ptōchos*, "trembling," "poor," "beggar," is almost exclusively the word tr[d] "poor." It does not occur very frequently, but we see the same regard for the poor maintained as we have in the OT; besides, the new principle of *love* and the example of Him who "though he was rich, yet for your sakes . . . . became poor" (*ptōcheúō*, 2 Cor **8** 9) necessarily carry in them this regard even more fully than in the OT. Jesus announced His mission (Lk **4** 18) by quoting Isa **61** 1, "to preach good tidings [AV "the gospel"] to the poor" (or meek or humble); He gave as a proof of His Messiahship the fact that "the poor have the gospel [or good news of the Kingdom] preached to them" (Mt **11** 5; Lk **7** 22); according to Lk **6** 20, He pronounced a beatitude on the pious "poor" because the kingdom of God was theirs; in Mt **5** 3 it is "the poor in spirit" (the humble); we have the injunction to "give to the poor" (Mt **19** 21; Mk **10** 21; Lk **18** 22) who are "always with you" (Mt **26** 11; Mk **14** 7; Jn **12** 8), which does not mean that there must always be "the poor," but that, in contrast with Himself who was soon to leave them, the poor should remain and kindness could be shown to them at any time, which was His own practice (Jn **13** 29); we are enjoined to call not the rich or well-to-do to our entertainments, but the poor (Lk **14** 13; cf ver 21); Zacchaeus cited in his favor the fact that he gave 'half of his goods to the poor' (Lk **19** 8); special notice was taken by Jesus of the poor widow's contribution (Lk **21** 3). The first church showed its regard for the poor in the distribution of goods "according as any man had need" (Acts **2** 45; **4** 32; **6** 1); when the council at Jerus freed the Gentiles from the yoke of Judaism, they made it a condition, Paul says, "that we should remember the poor; which very thing I was also zealous to do" (Gal **2** 10); contributions were accordingly made "for the poor among the saints that are at Jerus" (Rom **15** 26), and it was in conveying such contributions that Paul got into the circumstances that led to his arrest. God's ability and will to provide for those who give to the poor is quoted from Ps **112** 9 (2 Cor **9** 9); James specially rebukes certain Christians of his day for their partiality for the rich and their dishonor of the poor (Jas **2** 5–9), and John asks how, in the man who "hath the world's goods, and beholdeth his brother in need, and shutteth up his compassion from him," the love of God can dwell (1 Jn **3** 17. 18).

Ptōchos is tr[d] "beggar" (Lk **16** 20.22) and "beggarly" (Gal **4** 9); *pénēs*, "one who works for his daily bread," "a poor man," is the word in 2 Cor **9** 9; the poor widow of Mk **12** 42 is described in Lk **21** 2 as *penichrós*, "very poor."

III. In the Apocrypha.—In the Apoc the poor are often mentioned; God's regard for them (Ecclus **21** 5 [*ptōchos*]; **35** 12.13); their oppression and wrongs (Wisd **2** 10 [*penēs*]; Ecclus **13** 3.19.23 [*ptōchos*]; Bar **6** 28); the duty of care for and of giving to the poor (Tob **4** 7 [*ptōchos*]; Ecclus **29** 8 [*tapeinós*].9 [*penēs*]; **34** 20–22); of justice and kindness to such (Ecclus **4** 1.5.8; **7** 32; **10** 23 [*ptōchos*]); "poor" in the sense of pitiable occurs in 2 Macc **4** 47 (*talaípōros*), RV "hapless."

IV. RV Changes.—For "the poor of this world" (Jas **2** 5) RV has "them that are poor as to the world"; for "The poor . . . . shall trust in it" (Isa **14** 32), "In her shall the afflicted . . . . take refuge"; instead of "Whereas also he that is born in his kingdom becometh poor" (Eccl **4** 14), "Yea, even in his kingdom he was born poor"; "poor" for "humble" (Ps **9** 12; **10** 12, m "meek"), for "lowly" (Prov **16** 19, m "meek").

W. L. WALKER

POPLAR, pop'lar (לִבְנֶה, *libhneh*, "whiteness"; **στυράκινος**, *sturákinos*, "storax" [Gen **30** 37], **λεύκη**, *leúkē*, "poplar" [Hos **4** 13] [*libhneh* is so similar to the Arab. *libna*, the storax, that the latter certainly has the first claim to be the true tr]): "Jacob took him rods of fresh poplar," m "storax tree" (Gen **30** 37). "They . . . . burn incense upon the hills, under oaks and poplars and terebinths, because the shadow thereof is good" (Hos **4** 13). In the latter reference the conjunction of the shrub, storax, with two great trees like the oak and terebinth—even though they all grow in the mountains—is strange. The storax cannot give a shade comparable with these trees. Had we other evidence of the storax being a sacred tree among the Hebrews, it might explain the difficulty.

The storax, *Styrax officinalis* (N.O. *Styraceae*), is a very common shrub in Pal which occasionally attains the height of 20 feet. The under surfaces of its oval leaves are covered with whitish hairs, and it has many beautiful pure-white flowers like orange blossoms—hence its name "whiteness."

The poplar, the traditional tr in Hos **4** 13, flourishes in many parts of Pal. The white poplar, *Populus alba*, Arab. *Haur*, is common everywhere; *Euphratica* occurs esp. in the Jordan valley; the black poplar, *P. nigra*, and the Lombardy poplar, *P. pyramidalis*—probably an importation—are both plentiful in the plain of Coele-Syria, around Damascus and along the river banks of Syria.

E. W. G. MASTERMAN

PORATHA, pō-rā'tha, por'a-tha (פּוֹרָתָא, *pōrāthā'*): One of the sons of Haman (Est **9** 8). The etymology is uncertain; perhaps from the Pers *purdata*, "given by fate."

PORCH, pōrch: Chiefly in the OT אוּלָם, *'ūlām*, used of the temples of Solomon and Ezekiel (see TEMPLE); once *miṣdᵉrōn*, a "vestibule," in Jgs **3** 23. In the NT, the word occurs in connection with the high priest's palace (Mt **26** 71, *pulṓn;* Mk **14** 68, *proaúlion*), and as the rendering of **στοά**, *stoá*, a "portico," in Jn **5** 2 (pool of Bethesda); and Jn **10** 23; Acts **3** 11; **5** 12. See PORCH, PORTICO, SOLOMON'S.

PORCH, PORTICO, pōr'ti-kō, **SOLOMON'S** (**ἡ στοὰ ἡ καλουμένη Σολομῶντος**, *hē stoá hē kalouménē Solomṓntos*): This important element of Herod's temple, preserving in its name a traditional connection with Solomon, is thrice referred to in the NT, viz. in Jn **10** 23; Acts **3** 11, "the porch that is called Solomon's"; and Acts **5** 12. In these passages the Gr word *stoa* is tr[d] "porch," but in RVm of Acts **3** 11 more correctly "portico." In architecture a "porch" is strictly an exterior structure forming a covered approach to the entrance of a building; a "portico" is an ambulatory, consisting of a roof supported by columns placed at regular intervals—a roofed colonnade. The portico bearing Solomon's name was that running along the eastern wall in the Court of the Gentiles of Herod's temple. It had double columns, while that on the S. known as the Royal Portico had four rows (cf Jos, *Ant*, XV, xi, 3; *BJ*, V, v, and see TEMPLE, HEROD'S). The portico was the scene of Christ's teaching at the Feast of the Dedication (Jn **10** 23), and was flocked to by the multitude after the healing of the lame man (Acts **3** 11). There the apostles preached and wrought other miracles (Acts **5** 12).

W. SHAW CALDECOTT

PORCIUS, pôr'shus (**FESTUS**). See FESTUS.

PORCUPINE, pôr'kū-pīn (קִפֹּד, *ḳippōdh* [Isa **14** 23; **34** 11; Zeph **2** 14], AV "bittern," RV "porcupine"; LXX ἐχῖνος, *echînos*, "hedgehog"; קִפּוֹז, *ḳippōz* [Isa **34** 15], AV "great owl," ERV "arrow-snake," ARV "dart-snake"; LXX *echinos;* cf Arab. قُنْفُد, *ḳunfud*, or قُنْفُذ, *ḳunfudh*, "hedgehog" or "porcupine." קִפֹּד, *ḳippōdh*, is referred to √ קָפַד, *ḳāphādh*, "to draw one's self together" or "to roll one's self up," while קִפּוֹז is referred to √ קָפַז, *ḳāphaz*, and √ קָפַץ, *ḳāphaç*, "to draw together in order to spring." The resemblance between all these words, including the Arab. قُنْفُذ, is obvious, and it is to be noted that LXX has *echinos* in all the places cited):

The Gr *echinos* is the hedgehog. The Arab. *ḳunfudh* is used in some localities for the hedgehog and in others for the porcupine, which is also called *nîs*. The hedgehog is also called *kibbâbat-ush-shauk*, or "ball of spines." These two animals are both found in Syria and Pal, and, while both have spines, they are very different animals, though often confounded. The hedgehog, *Erinaceus europeus*, is one of the *Insectivora*. It eats not only insects but also snakes and other small animals, as well as fruits and roots. It is about 10 in. long, covered with short spines, and rolls itself into a ball when attacked. It inhabits the countries bordering the Mediterranean. The porcupine, *Hystrix cristata*, is a rodent, about 26 in. long, having long spines. It is herbivorous. It backs rapidly at its foes, thrusting its sharp spines into their flesh, not shooting its spines, as is often stated. It inhabits most of Europe and Asia. It is very different from the Canadian porcupine, *Erethizon dorsatus*, as well as from the tree porcupines of Mexico and Central and South America.

As to the rendering "bittern" for *ḳippōdh* (Isa **14** 23; **34** 15; Zeph **2** 14), while the etymology favors "hedgehog," the context favors a bird, esp. in Isa **34** 11, though it cannot be said that in any of the passages the context makes "hedgehog" an impossible rendering.

In Isa **34** 15, for *ḳippōz*, most modern authorities (cf RV) have some sort of serpent, referring to the Arab. √ *ḳafaz*, "to spring." (See notes above on *ḳāphaz* and *ḳāphaç*.) In this passage also the context is not unfavorable to a bird (cf AV "great owl"). See Bittern; Owl; Serpent.

Alfred Ely Day

PORPHYRY, pôr′fi-ri (in Est **1** 6, RVm has "porphyry" [AVm "porphyre"] for בַּהַט, *bahaṭ*, EV "red [marble]"; LXX has σμαραγδίτης, *smaragdítēs*, which was a green stone): Porphyry is an igneous rock containing distinct crystals of feldspar in a feldspathic matrix. It may be purple or of other colors, as green. "Porphyry" is from πορφύρεος, *porphúreos*, "purple."

PORPOISE, pôr′pus (RVm has "porpoise-skin" for עוֹר תַּחַשׁ, *'ōr taḥash*, RV "sealskin," AV "badgers' skins" [Ex **25** 5; **26** 14; **35** 7.23; **36** 19; **39** 34; Nu **4** 6.8.10.11.12.14.25; Ezk **16** 10]): The word denotes leather used in the furnishings of the tabernacle (for shoes in Ezk **16** 10), and was probably the skin of the dugong, *Halichore dugong*, Arab. تُخَس, *tukhas*, which is found in the Red Sea. See Badger.

PORT, pōrt, **PORTER**, pōr′tẽr: "Port" in the sense of "gate" (of a city or building) is obsolete in modern Eng., and even in the AV is found only in Neh **2** 13. "Porter," as "gate-keeper," however, is still in some use, but "porter" now (but never in EV) generally means a burden-carrier. In the OT, except in 2 S **18** 26; 2 K **7** 10.11, the porter (שׁוֹעֵר, *shō'ēr*) is a sacred officer of the temple or tabernacle, belonging to a particular family of the Levites, with a share in the sacred dues (Neh **13** 5; **12** 47). The "porters" are mentioned only in Ch, Ezr and Neh, and Ch has an especial interest in them, relating that their duties were settled as far back as the time of David (1 Ch **26** 1–19), and that the office extended further to the first settlement of Pal and even to Moses' day (1 Ch **9** 17–26). The office was evidently one of some dignity, and the "chief-porters" (1 Ch **9** 26) were important persons. For some inscrutable reason RV renders *shō'ēr* by "doorkeeper" in 1 Ch **15**-**26**, but not elsewhere. See Doorkeeper.

Burton Scott Easton

PORTION, pōr′shun, **PART**: As far as a distinction between these words is possible in Eng., it lies in the fact that a "portion" is a "part" about whose destiny something is implied (Ps **142** 5, etc). The Heb has no two synonyms similarly related, and in consequence the use of the words in EV is settled either by rather arbitrary considerations (מְנָה, *m^enāh*, is always "portion" in RV, but is "part" in AV, Ex **29** 26; Lev **7** 33; **8** 29) or by the context, irrespective of the Heb word used. So "part" and "portion" both represent דָּבָר, *dābhār*, 1 K **6** 38; Neh **12** 47; פֶּה, *peh*, Zec **13** 8; Dt **21** 17; חֶבֶל, *ḥebhel*, Josh **17** 5 (RV); Ezk **47** 13; μέρος, *méros*, Lk **11** 36; **12** 46. And in the vast majority of cases in the OT both words represent simply some derivative of חָלַק, *ḥālaḳ*, normally the noun חֵלֶק, *ḥēleḳ*.

Burton Scott Easton

POSIDONIUS, pos-i-dō′ni-us (Πωσιδώνιος, *Pōsidṓnios*, al. Ποσιδόνιος, *Posidónios* and Ποσειδῶν, *Poseidṓn*): One of the three envoys sent by the Syrian general Nicanor to treat with the Jews under Judas during his invasion of Judaea, 161 BC (2 Macc **14** 19). In 1 Macc **7** 27 ff, proposals are sent by Nicanor to Judas, but no envoys are named, and it is there asserted in contradiction to 2 Macc that Judas broke off the negotiation because of the treacherous designs of Nicanor.

POSSESS, po-zes′, **POSSESSION**, po-zesh′un: "Possess" in modern Eng. means normally only "keep in one's possession." But in Elizabethan Eng. it means also "take into possession," and, in fact, the word in the OT always represents Heb vbs. with the latter as their primary meaning (יָרַשׁ, *yārash*, in nearly all cases, otherwise נָחַל, *nāḥal*, קָנָה, *ḳānāh*, אָחַז, *'āḥaz;* Aram. חֲסַן, *ḥăṣan*). Consequently, in almost every case "take possession of" could be substituted advantageously for "possess," but RV has not thought the change worth carrying through. In the Apoc and NT, however, the distinction has been made, AV's "possess" being retained for κατέχω, *katéchō*, in 1 Cor **7** 30; 2 Cor **6** 10, but the same tr for κτάομαι, *ktáomai*, is changed into "take us for a possession" (Jth **8** 22), "get" (Lk **18** 12), "win" (Lk **21** 19), and "possess himself of" (1 Thess **4** 4, a very obscure passage). In the noun **possession**, on the other hand, no such ambiguity exists, and attention need be called only to the following passages. In Dt **11** 6, AV has, "all the substance that was in their possession," Heb "all that subsisted at their feet," RV "every living thing that followed them." AV uses "possession" loosely in Acts **28** 7 for χωρίον, *chōríon*, RV "lands." περιποίησις, *peripoíēsis*, from *peripoiéō*, "cause to remain over," "gain," is rendered "God's own possession" in Eph **1** 14 RV (AV "possession") and 1 Pet **2** 9 (AV "peculiar," AVm "purchased"). "God's own" is a gloss but is implied in the context.

Burton Scott Easton

POSSESSION, DEMONIACAL, dē-mō-nī′a-kal (Mt **4** 24; **8** 16, etc). See Demon, Demoniac, Demonology.

POTTERY CHRONOLOGY OF PALESTINE
(1929)

BRONZE AGES

FIG 1.—EARLY BRONZE (BEFORE 2000 BC). BEFORE THE AGE OF THE PATRIARCHS

Types of Pottery: flat bottoms (all); ledge handles (3); tiny lug handles (2); high loop handles (4–6); projecting spouts (2); net designs and modified forms of such designs (2, 4); rich burnished slip of red ochre (5, 6).

FIG 2.—MIDDLE BRONZE (2000–1600 BC). EARLY PATRIARCHAL AGE

Types of Pottery: pear-shaped juglets with high loop handles and button base, generally black, with white incisions (1); similar juglets with flat bottoms (2); elongated vases with pointed base, generally covered with cream slip (3); graceful vessels with carinated bodies (4, 6); globular jugs with small mouths and loop handle on shoulder (5).

FIG 3.—LATE BRONZE (1600–1200 BC). LATE PATRIARCHAL AGE

Types of Pottery: small vessels, generally painted, with two tilted horizontal lug-handles (1); Mycaenean stirrup-vases, imported from Greece between fifteenth and thirteenth centuries (2); Cypro-Phoenician wine pitchers (3) and bilbils (for perfumes, 7), imported throughout Late Bronze Age; pilgrim flasks (5); miscellaneous painted vases (4, 6).

EARLY IRON AGE

FIG 4.—EARLY IRON I (1200–900 BC). PERIOD OF THE JUDGES AND UNITED MONARCHY

Types of Pottery: black burnished juglets for perfume (1–3); small bowls without ornamentation (4); pitchers with handle above mouth and filter-spout (5); burnished pitchers with pinched lip (6); libation chalices (7); pilgrim flasks (8).

FIG 5.—EARLY IRON II (900–600 BC). PERIOD OF DIVIDED MONARCHY

Types of Pottery: baby rattles of clay (1); black burnished perfume juglets (2); elongated vertically burnished juglets (3); small pitchers of various shapes (4); ring-burnished water decanters (5); ring-burnished plates and shallow bowls (6); squat one-handled juglets (7); deep two-handled cooking pots (8).

FIG 6.—EARLY IRON III (600–300 BC). POST-EXILIC AND EARLY HELLENISTIC

Types of Pottery: native vessels mostly very simple and practically never decorated (1–2, 4–7); imported Greek pottery in constantly increasing quantities, including especially lekythoi with red-figured drawings (3).

This POTTERY CHRONOLOGY is the criterion for the identification of Biblical History, when dug up in the excavations.

W. F. ALBRIGHT

(From the Lemon Bible Lands Museum, Presbyterian Seminary, Louisville, Kentucky, U. S. A.)

POST, pōst (רוּץ, *rūç,* "to run," רָצִים, *rāçīm,* "runners"): The "runners" formed the royal guard (1 S **22** 17; 1 K **14** 27; 2 K **11** 4.13; see GUARD). From them were chosen the couriers who carried royal letters and dispatches throughout the kingdom (2 Ch **30** 6.10; Est **3** 13.15; Jer **51** 31). In the Pers service they were mounted on the swiftest horses (Est **8** 10.14; cf Xenophon, *Cyrop.* viii.6.17; Herodotus viii.98). They had the right to command the service of either men or animals in order to expedite their progress (cf Mt **5** 41; Mk **15** 21, "compel," "impress").

Used in Job **9** 25 and AV Wisd **5** 9 (ἀγγελία, *aggelía,* RV "message") of the swift passage of time. See also HOUSE, II, 1, (4), (7). M. O. EVANS

POT, pot: A term used as the tr of a number of Heb and Gr words whose fundamental meaning seems to describe them as intended for the most part to hold liquid or semi-liquid substances, but the pots of Ex **27** 3 are intended to hold ashes. (1) סִיר, *sīr,* the most common word for "pot." It designates most frequently some household utensil, probably a pot or kettle for boiling. So 2 K **4** 38 ff; Ex **16** 3; Jer **1** 13 AV; Ezk **11** 3.7.11, "caldron"; **24** 3.6 AV; Mic **3** 3; Zec **14** 21, etc. It is also used as the name of some vessel of the sanctuary. So Ex **27** 3, where the context shows it was intended to hold ashes; 1 K **7** 45; 2 Ch **4** 16; 2 K **25** 14. In Ps **60** 8; **108** 9, it is a pot for washing. (2) פָּרוּר, *pārūr* (Nu **11** 8; 1 S **2** 14), a vessel for boiling; in Jgs **6** 19, a vessel for holding broth. (3) דּוּד, *dūdh,* rendered "pot" in Ps **81** 6 in AV, "basket" in RV; "pot" both AV and RV in Job **41** 20. (4) צִנְצֶנֶת, *çinçeneth* (Ex **16** 33), the jar in which the manna was placed. This jar or pot is mentioned in He **9** 4 under the name στάμνος, *stámnos.* (5) אָסוּךְ, *'āṣōn* (2 K **4** 2), some kind of jar for holding oil. (6) ξέστης, *xéstēs* (Mk **7** 4), some kind of household utensil. Mention may also be made of the word rendered "pot" in Lev **6** 28 AV, where RV renders more correctly by the general term "vessel"; for AV "pots" (Ps **68** 13) RV substitutes "sheepfolds." The root is uncertain. Those who render "sheepfolds" connect with the related root in Gen **49** 14; Jgs **5** 16. Others render "fireplaces" or "ash heaps." See also "range for pots" in Lev **11** 35; "pots," Jer **35** 5 AV, correctly "bowls" RV; "refining pots" in Prov **17** 3; **27** 21. See also FOOD.

WALTER R. BETTERIDGE

POTENTATE, pō'ten-tāt (δυνάστης, *dunástēs,* "mighty one," from δύναμαι, *dúnamai,* "to be able"): A person who possesses great power and authority. Only in 1 Tim **6** 15, "the blessed and only Potentate" (=God). The same Gr word is used of Zeus in Sophocles (*Ant.* 608), and of God in Apoc (e.g. Sir **46** 5; 2 Macc **15** 3.23). It is used of men in Lk **1** 52 (AV "the mighty," RV "princes") and Acts **8** 27 ("of great authority").

POTIPHAR, pot'i-far (פּוֹטִיפַר, *pōṭīphar;* cf Egyp *Potiphera* [Gen **39** 1 f]): A high Egyp official who became the master of Joseph. It is particularly mentioned that he was an Egyptian, i.e. one of the native Egyp officials at the Hyksos court.

POTI-PHERA, po-tif'e-ra (פּוֹטִי פֶרַע, *pōṭī phera';* Egyp *Padipara,* "the [one] given of the sun-god"; cf Heb Nathaniel, "the gift of God," Gen **41** 45.50; **46** 20): There is no certain evidence from Egypt that this name was in existence until the XXIId Dynasty, about 950 BC. But names of the Hyksos period, and, indeed, any kind of Hyksos inscriptions, are so scarce on account of the destruction of Hyksos monuments by the Egyptians of later times that the absence of such names is really no evidence on the subject. The fact that this name has not been discovered earlier than 950 BC does not give any warrant for the claim that the narrative is of a late date. M. G. KYLE

POTSHERD, pot'shûrd (חֶרֶשׂ, *ḥeres*): A piece of earthenware (Job **2** 8; Ps **22** 15; Isa **45** 9). RV renders the word in Prov **26** 23, "an earthen vessel," and in Job **41** 30 substitutes "sharp potsherds" for "sharp stones." Sir **22** 7 refers to the art of "gluing a potsherd [ὄστρακον, *óstrakon*] together." See HARSITH; OSTRACA.

POTSHERD GATE (Jer **19** 2). See HARSITH GATE.

POTTAGE, pot'āj. See FOOD, III.

POTTER, pot'ẽr, **POTTERY,** pot'ẽr-i:

1. Historical Development
2. Forms
3. Methods of Production
4. Uses
5. Biblical Terms
6. Archaeological Significance

LITERATURE

1. Historical Development

(1) *Prehistoric.*—The making of pottery ranks among the very oldest of the crafts. On the rocky plateaus of Upper Egypt, overlooking the Nile valley, are found the polished red earthenware pots of the prehistoric Egyptians. These are buried in shallow oval graves along with the cramped-up bodies of the dead and their chipped flint weapons and tools. These jars are the oldest examples of the potter's art. It is inconceivable that in the country of Babel, Egypt's great rival in civilization, the ceramic arts were less developed at the same period, but the difference in the nature of the country where the first Mesopotamian settlement probably existed makes it unlikely that relics of the prehistoric dwellers of that country will ever be recovered from under the débris of demolished cities and the underlying deposits of clay and silt.

(2) *Babylonia.*—The oldest examples of Bab ceramics date from the historical period, and consist of baked clay record tablets, bricks, drainage pipes, household shrines, as well as vessels for holding liquids, fruits and other stores. (See Perrot and Chipiez, *History of Art in Chaldaea and Assyria,* I, figs. 159, 160, II, figs. 163, 168.) Examples of pottery of this early period are shown in the accompanying figures. By the 9th to the 7th cent. BC the shaping of vessels of clay had become well developed. Fragments of pottery bearing the name of Esarhaddon establish the above dates.

(3) *Egypt.*—With the close of the neolithic period in Egypt and the beginning of the historical or dynastic period (4500–4000 BC) there was a decline in the pottery art. The workmanship and forms both became bad, and not until the IVth Dynasty was there any improvement. In the meantime the process of glazing had been discovered and the art of making beautiful glazed faïence became one of the most noted of the ancient Egyp crafts. The potter's wheel too was probably an invention of this date.

(4) *Palestine.*—The making of pottery in the land which later became the home of the children of Israel began long before this people possessed the land and even before the Phoenicians of the coast cities had extended their trade inland and brought the earthenware vessels of the Tyrian or Sidonian potters. As in Egypt and Babylonia, the first examples were hand-made without the aid of the wheel.

It is probable that Jewish potters learned their art from the Phoenicians. They at least copied Phoen and Mycenaean forms. During their wanderings the children of Israel were not likely to make much use of earthenware vessels, any more than the Arabs do today. Skins, gourds, wooden and metal vessels were less easily broken.

To illustrate this, a party, of which the writer was a member, took on a desert trip the earthenware water jars specially made for travel, preferring them to the skin bottles such as the Arab guides carried, for the bottles taint the water. At the end of six days only one out of eight earthenware jars was left. One accident or another had broken all the others.

When the Israelites became settled in their new surroundings they were probably not slow in adopting earthenware vessels, because of their advantages, and their pottery gradually developed distinctive though decadent types known as Jewish.

Toward the close of the Heb monarchy the pottery of the land again showed the effect of outside influences. The red and black figured ware of the Greeks was introduced, and still later the less artistic Rom types, and following these by several centuries came the crude glazed vessels of the Arab. or Saracenic period—forms which still persist.

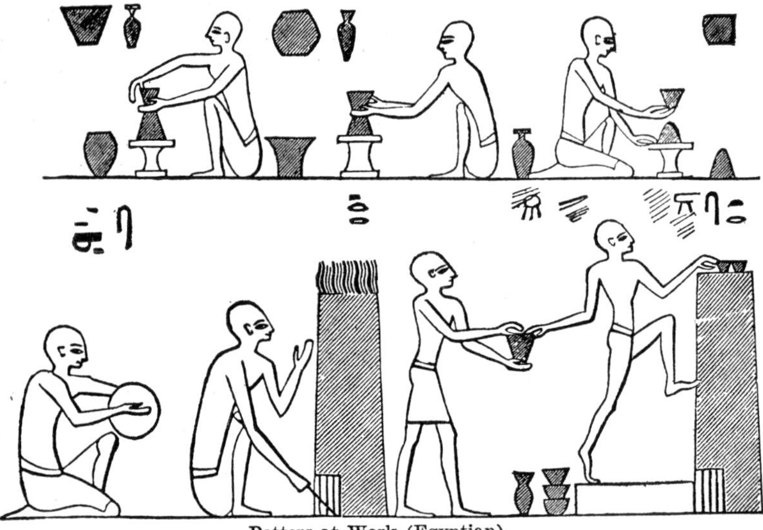

Potters at Work (Egyptian).

2. Forms

It is not within the limits of this article to describe in detail the characteristics of the pottery of the various periods. The accompanying illustrations taken from photographs of pottery in the Archaeological Museum of the Syrian Protestant College, Beirût, give a general idea of the forms. Any attempt at classification of Palestinian pottery must be considered more or less provisional, due to the uncertainty of origin of many forms. The classification of pre-Rom pottery here used is that adopted by Bliss and Macalister and based upon Dr. Petrie's studies.

(1) *Early pre-Israelite, called also "Amorite" (before 1500 BC)*.—Most of the vessels of this period are hand-made and often irregular in shape. A coarse clay, turning red or black when burned, characterizes many specimens. Some are brick red. Specimens with a polished or burnished surface are also found.

(2) *Late pre-Israelite or Phoenician (1500–1000 BC)*.—From this period on, the pottery is all wheel-turned. The clay is of a finer quality and burned to a brown or red. The ware is thin and light. Water jars with pointed instead of flat bases appear. Some are decorated with bands or lines of different colored meshes. Cypriote ware with its incised decorations was a like development of the period.

(3) *Jewish (1000–300 BC)*.—Foreign influence is lost. The types which survive degenerate. New forms are introduced. Ordinary coarse clay burning red is used. Cooking pots are most characteristic. Many examples bear Heb stamps, the exact meaning of which is uncertain.

(4) *Seleucidan*.—Foreign influence again appears. Gr and other types are imported and copied. Ribbed surfaces are introduced. The old type of burnishing disappears.

(5) *Roman and Saracenic*.—Degenerate forms persisting till the present time.

(6) *Present-day pottery*.

3. Methods of Production

The clay as found in the ground is not suitable for use. It is dug out and brought to the vicinity of the pottery (the "potter's field," Mt **27** 7) and allowed to weather for weeks. The dry material is then dumped into a cement-lined tank or wooden trough and covered with water. When the lumps have softened they are stirred in the water until all have disintegrated and a thin slimy mud or "slip" has been formed. In coast cities the potteries are all near the sea, as the sea-water is considered better for the "slipping" process. The slip is drawn off into settling tanks. All stones and lumps remain behind. When the clay has settled, the water is drawn off and the plastic material is worked by treading with the feet (cf Isa **41** 25; Wisd **15** 7). The clay used on the Syrian coast is usually a mixture of several earths, which the potters have learned by experience gives the right consistency. The prepared clay is finally packed away and allowed to stand another six months before using, during which time the quality, esp. the plasticity, is believed to improve.

Before the invention of the potter's wheel the clay was shaped into vessels by hand. In all of the countries previously mentioned the specimens representing the oldest work are all hand-made. Chopped straw was usually added to the clay of these early specimens. This material is omitted in the wheel-shaped objects. In a Mt. Lebanon village which is noted for its pottery the jars are still made by hand. Throughout the country the clay stoves are shaped by hand out of clay mixed with straw.

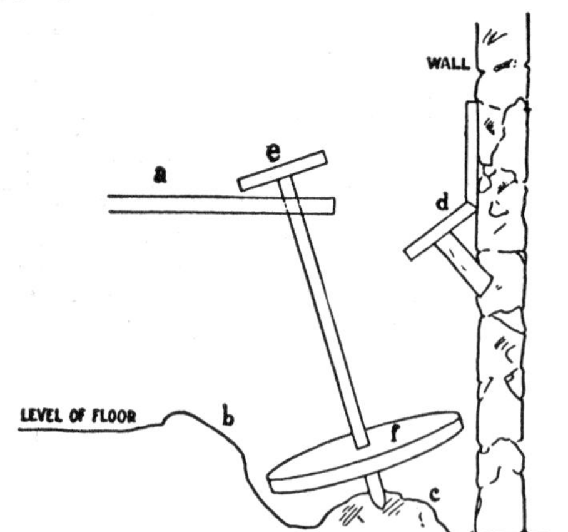

Potter's Wheel Still Used in Palestine and Syria.

a, table; *b*, footrest; *c*, socket for pivot of wheel; *d*, slanting seat against which potter "sits"; *e*, upper wheel on which jar is shaped; *f*, lower wheel "kicked" by potter.

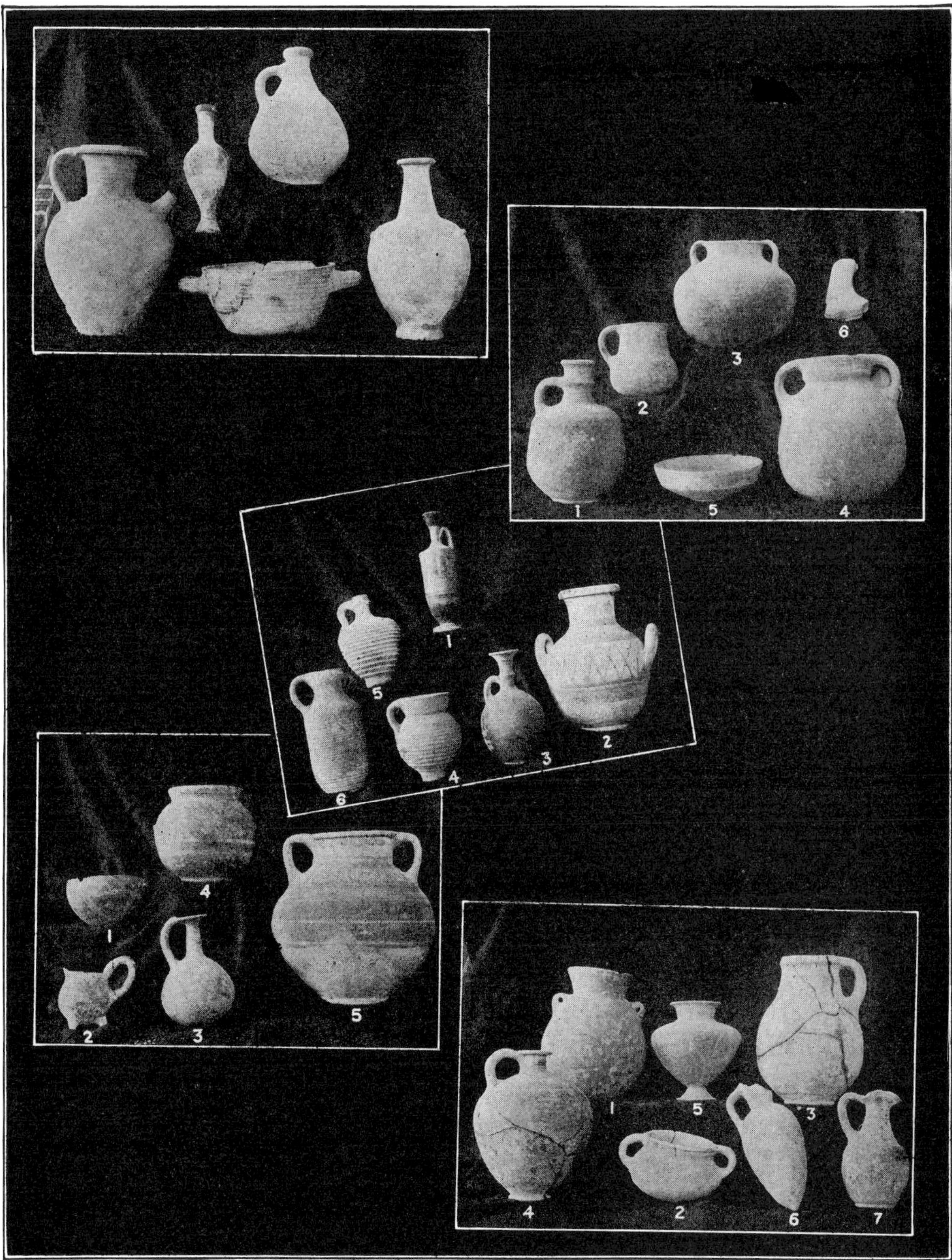

ANCIENT POTTERY

Seleucidan Period, 300 BC
Note appearance of "combing"

Jewish Period
Blackening on 3 due to use over fire

Greco-Roman Period
1, red and black figured, before 350 BC
2 and 3, Cyprian of 300 BC
4, 5 and 6, Roman pottery from Beirût
Note characteristic "combing"

Cypriote Pottery
1, 2 and 3, incised ware of pre-bronze period before 2000 BC
4 and 5, of Phoenician Period, 1500 BC

Pre-Israelite Period
1, hand-made throughout
1, 2 and 3, of early period or Amorite
4, 5, 6 and 7, of late period or Phoenician
4, 6 and 7 are burnished

The shaping of vessels is now done on **wheels,** the use of which dates back to earliest history. Probably the Egyptians were the first to use such a machine (IVth Dynasty). In their original form they were stone disks arranged to be turned by hand on a vertical axis. The wheel stood only a few inches above the ground, and the potter sat or squatted down on the ground before it as he shaped his object (see Wilkinson, *Ancient Egypt,* II, fig. 397). The wheels used in Pal and Syria today probably differ in no respect from those used in the potter's house visited by Jeremiah (Jer **18** 1–6). The wheel or, to be more exact, wheels (cf Jer **18** 3) are fitted on a square wooden or iron shaft about 3 ft. long. The lower disk is about 20 in. in diameter, and the upper one 8 in. or 12 in. The lower end of the shaft is pointed and fits into a stone socket or bearing in which it rotates. A second bearing just below the upper disk is so arranged that the shaft inclines slightly away from the potter. The potter leans against a slanting seat, bracing himself with one foot so that he will not slide off, and with the sole of his other foot he kicks the upper face of the lower wheel, thus making the whole machine rotate. The lower wheel is often of stone to give greater momentum. With a marvelous dexterity, which a novice tries in vain to imitate, he gives the pieces of clay any shape he desires.

After the vessel is shaped it is dried and finally fired in a furnace or kiln. The ancient Egyp kiln was much smaller than the one used today (Wilkinson, II, 192). Most of the kilns are of the crudest form of the "up-draught" variety, i.e. a large chamber with perforated bottom and a fireplace beneath. The fire passes up through the holes, around the jars packed in tiers in the chamber, and goes out at the top. An interesting survival of an early Gr form is still used in *Rachiyet-el-Fakhar* in Syria. In this same village the potters also use the lead dross, which comes from the parting of silver, for glazing their jars (cf Prov **26** 23).

In firing pottery there are always some jars which come out imperfect. In unpacking the kiln and storing the product others get broken. As a consequence the ground in the vicinity of a pottery is always strewn with **potsherds** (see also separate article). The ancient potteries can frequently be located by these sherds. The potter's field mentioned in Mt **27** 7.10 was probably a field near a pottery strewn with potsherds, thus making it useless for cultivation although useful to the potter as a place in which to weather his clay or to dry his pots before firing.

INTERIOR OF POTTERY.

4. Uses

Pottery was used anciently for storing liquids, such as wine or oil, fruits, grains, etc. The blackened bottoms of pots of the Jewish period show that they were used for cooking. Earthenware dishes were also used for boiling clothes. Every one of these uses still continues. To one living in Bible lands today it seems inconceivable that the Hebrews did not readily adopt, as some writers disclaim, the porous earthen water jars which they found already in use in their new country. Such jars were used for carrying live coals to start a fire, and not only for drawing water, as they are today, but for cooling it (Isa **30** 14). The evaporation of the water which oozes through the porous material cools down the contents of a jar, whereas a metal or leathern vessel would leave it tepid or tainted. They were also used for holding shoemaker's glue or wax; for filling up the cracks of a wall before plastering; ground up they are used as sand in mortar.

5. Biblical Terms

Only a few of the Heb words for vessels of different sorts, which in all probability were made of pottery, have been tr[d] by terms which indicate that fact. (For חֶרֶשׂ, *ḥeres*, and יָצַר, *yāçar*, see EARTHEN VESSELS; OSTRACA.)

כַּד, *kadh*, is tr[d] "pitcher" in Gen **24** 14 ff; Jgs **7** 16 ff; Eccl **12** 6 (cf κεράμιον, *kerámion*, Mk

14 13; Lk **22** 10); "jar" in 1 K **17** 12 (cf ὑδρία, *hudría*, Jn **4** 28). The *kadh* corresponded in size and use to the Arab. *jarrah* (cf Eng. deriv. "jar"). The *jarrah* is used for drawing and storing water and less frequently for holding other liquids or solids. It is used as an approximate standard of measure. For example, a man estimates the capacity of a cistern in *jirār* (pl. of *jarrah*).

בַּקְבֻּק, *baḳbuḳ*, "a bottle," usually leathern, but in Jer **19** 1.10 of pottery. This may have been like the Arab. إبريق, *ibrīḳ*, which causes a gurgling sound when liquid is turned from it. *Baḳbuḳ* is rendered "cruse" in 1 K **14** 3.

כְּלִי, *kelī*, "vessel," was of wood, metal or earthenware in Lev **6** 28; Ps **2** 9; **31** 12; Isa **30** 14; Jer **19** 11, etc; cf ὀστράκινος, *ostrákinos*, 2 Cor **4** 7, etc.

פַּךְ, *pakh*, is trd "vial" in 1 S **10** 1; 2 K **9** 1; see so-called pilgrim bottles.

כּוֹס, *kōṣ*, also קְשָׂה, *ḳāsāh*, "cup" or "bowl," trd "cup" in many passages, like Arab. كاس, *kā's*, which was formerly used for drinking instead of modern cups.

גְּבִיעַ, *gābhīa*, trd "bowl" in Jer **35** 5.

פָּרוּר, *pārūr*, trd "pots" in Nu **11** 8; cf Jgs **6** 19; 1 S **2** 14; cf χύτρα, *chútra*, which is similar to Arab. قدر, *kidr*, commonly used for cooking today.

עֶצֶב, *'eçebh*, "pot," Jer **22** 28 ARVm.

6. Archaeological Significance

The chemical changes wrought in clay by weathering and firing render it practically indestructible when exposed to the weather and to the action of moisture and the gaseous and solid compounds found in the soil. When the sun-baked brick walls of a Palestinian city crumbled, they buried, often intact, the earthenware vessels of the period. In the course of time, perhaps after decades or centuries, another city was built on the débris of the former. The brick walls required no digging for foundations, and so the substrata were left undisturbed. After long periods of time the destruction, by conquering armies or by neglect, of succeeding cities, produced mounds rising above the surrounding country, sometimes to a height of 60 or 100 ft. A typical example of such a mound is *Tell el-Ḥesy* (? Lachish). Dr. Flinders Petrie, as a result of the study of the various strata of this mound, has formed the basis of a classification of Palestinian pottery (see 2, above). With a knowledge of the forms of pottery of each period, the excavator has a guide, though not infallible, to the date of the ruins he finds. See also Crafts, II, 4.

Figurative: The shaping of clay into pottery typified the molding of the characters of individuals or nations by a master mind (Jer **18** 1–6; Isa **29** 16; **45** 9; **64** 8; Rom **9** 20 ff); commonplace (Lam **4** 2; 2 Tim **2** 20); frailness (Ps **2** 9; Isa **30** 14; Jer **19** 11; Dnl **2** 41; 2 Cor **4** 7; Rev **2** 27).

Literature.—Publications of *PEF*, esp. Bliss and Macalister, *Excavations in Pal; Excavations of Gezer;* Bliss, *A Mound of Many Cities;* Flinders Petrie, *Tell el-Ḥesy;* Bliss and Dickie, *Excavations at Jerus;* Perrot and Chipiez, *History of Art* (i) in Chaldaea and Assyria, (ii) Sardinia and Judaea, (iii) Cyprus and Phoenicia, (iv) Egypt; King and Hall, *Egypt and Western Asia in Light of Modern Discoveries;* S. Birch, *History of Ancient Pottery;* Wilkinson, *The Ancient Egyptians; PEFQ; EB; HDB.*

James A. Patch

POTTER'S, pot'ẽrz, **FIELD**. See Aceldama.

Exterior of Pottery.

POUND, pound (מָנֶה, *māneh;* **μνᾶ**, *mná*, **λίτρα**, *litra;* Lat *libra*): Pound does not correctly represent the Heb *māneh*, which was more than a pound (see Maneh). The *litra* of Jn **12** 3 and **19** 39 is the Rom pound (*libra*) of 4,950 grains, which is less than a pound troy, being about $10\frac{1}{3}$ oz. In a monetary sense (its use in Lk **19** 13–25) it is the *mna*, or *māneh*, which was either of silver or gold, the former, which is probably the one referred to by Luke, being equal to £6.17, or about $33; the latter £102.10 or $510. See Weights and Measures.

Figurative: "Pound," like "talent," is used in the NT for intellectual gifts and spiritual endowments, as in the passage given above.

H. Porter

POVERTY, pov'ẽr-ti:

1. OT References

This word, found but once in the OT (Gen **45** 11) outside of the Book of Prov in which it occurs 11 t (**6** 11; **10** 15; **11** 24 AV; **13** 18; **20** 13; **23** 21; **24** 34; **28** 19.22 AV; **30** 8; **31** 7), is a tr of יִוָּרֵשׁ, *yiwwārēsh*, "to be poor," "to come to poverty" (Gen **45** 11). Four different Heb words are used in the 11 references in Prov, all bearing the idea of being in need of the necessities of life, although a distinction is made between being in want and being in extreme want. Prov **18** 23 well illustrates the general meaning of "poverty" as found in this book: "The poor [רוּשׁ, *rūsh*, "to be impoverished," "destitute"] useth entreaties; but the rich answereth roughly."

"Poverty" occurs 3 t in the NT (2 Cor **8** 2.9;

Rev **2** 9) and is the tr of πτωχεία, *ptōcheia*, "to be reduced to a state of beggary or pauperism."

2. NT References The teaching of the Bible on this subject would, however, be incomplete unless all the references to the "poor" were considered in this connection. Indeed the word for "poverty" has its root in the word for "poor" (πτωχός, *ptōchós;* עָנִי, *'ānī*, or דַּל, *dal*). See Poor.

At least two degrees of poverty are recognized. The OT does not distinguish between them as clearly as does the NT.

3. Two Degrees of Poverty The NT, for example, by its use of two words for "poor" sets forth this distinction. In 2 Cor **9** 9, "he hath given to the poor," the word used is πένης, *pénēs*, which does not indicate extreme poverty, but simply a condition of living from hand to mouth, a bare and scant livelihood, such as that made by the widow who cast her two mites into the treasury (Lk **21** 2); while in such passages as 2 Cor **6** 10: "As poor, yet making many rich," and Lk **6** 20: "Blessed are ye poor" (πτωχοί, *ptōchoí*), a condition is indicated of abject beggary, pauperism, such as that in which we find Lazarus who was laid at the gate of the rich man's palace, begging even the crumbs which fell from the table of the rich man (Lk **16** 20. 21). It was into this latter condition that Christ voluntarily entered for our sakes: "For ye know the grace of our Lord Jesus Christ, that, though he was rich, yet for your sakes he became poor [a mendicant, a beggar], that ye through his poverty might become rich" (2 Cor **8** 9). Between 30 and 40 t in the NT this latter word is used.

The causes of poverty are failure of harvest and poor crops (Neh **5** 1-3); devastation caused by enemies sweeping through the land;

4. Causes of Poverty the oppression of the people by their own rulers (Isa **5** 8); excessive interest, usury (Neh **5** 1-5); persecution because of the faith (2 Cor **6, 8**). Widows and orphans by reason of their desolate condition were in a special sense subject to poverty. Gluttony brings poverty (Prov **23** 21), as does indolence (**28** 19).

God commanded His people to care for the poor. The exhortations to relieve poverty are numerous, esp. in the Pent. Those in poverty must be treated with kindness (Dt **15** 7-11); must be allowed to glean in the vineyards (Lev **19** 10); to reap the harvest (**23** 22; cf Ruth **2** 14-16); must not be neglected (Prov **28** 27); nor dealt with harshly (Am **8** 4-6); must be treated as equal before God (Prov **22** 2); are to share in our hospitality (Lk **14** 13.21). Indeed, the truth or falsity of a man's religion is to be tested, in some sense at least, by his relation to those in need (Jas **1** 27). The year of Jubilee was intended to be of great benefit to the poor by restoring to them any possessions which they, by reason of their poverty, had been compelled to deed over to their creditors (Lev **25** 25-54; Dt **15** 12-15). God required certain tithes from His people which were to be devoted to the helping of the poor and needy (Dt **14** 28; **26** 12.13). So in the NT the apostles lay special emphasis upon remembering the poor in the matter of offerings. Paul, esp., inculcated this duty upon the churches which he had founded (Rom **15** 26; Gal **2** 10). The attitude of the early Christian church toward its poor is amply illustrated in that first attempt at communism in Acts **2, 4**. James, in his Ep., stingingly reminds his readers of the fact that they had grossly neglected the important matter of caring for the poor (ch **2**). Indeed, so strong is he in his plea for the care of the poor that he claims that the man who wilfully neglects the needy thereby proves that the love of God has no place in his heart, and that he has consequently no real faith in God (vs 14-26). Christians are exhorted to abound in the grace of hospitality, which, of course, is nothing less than kindness to those in need (Rom **12** 13; 1 Tim **6** 18; 1 Jn **3** 17). See Poor.

The happiest mother and the noblest and holiest son that ever lived were among the poor. Jesus was born of poor parents, and had not where to lay His head (Mt **8** 20), no money with which to pay tribute (Mt **17** 27), no home to call His own (Jn **7** 53; cf **8** 1), and was buried in a borrowed grave (Mt **27** 57-61).

Figurative: Of course there is also a spiritual poverty indicated by the use of this word—a poverty in spiritual things: "Blessed are the poor in spirit." By this is meant, Blessed are they who feel that they have no self-righteousness, no worth of their own to present to Christ as a ground of their salvation, who feel their utter bankruptcy of spirit, who say "Nothing in my hand I bring." It is to this state of spirit that Christ refers in Rev **3** 17: "Because thou sayest, I am rich, and have gotten riches, and have need of nothing; and knowest not that thou art the wretched one and miserable and poor and blind and naked." William Evans

POWDERS, pou'dẽrz (אַבְקַת רֹכֵל, *'abh^eḳath rōkhēl*): The "powders of the merchant" in Cant **3** 6 were probably perfumes, as they are associated with myrrh and frankincense in the account of the festal procession of the litter of Solomon. They may have been some sweet-scented wood in powder, or else some form of incense.

POWER, pou'ẽr: This word, indicative of might, strength, force, is used in the OT to render very many Heb terms, the tr in numerous instances being varied in RV to words like "valor," "rule," "strength," "might," "dominion." The principal words for "power" in the NT are δύναμις, *dúnamis*, and ἐξουσία, *exousía*. In the latter case RV frequently changes to "authority" (Mk **3** 15; **6** 7; Eph **1** 21, etc) or "right" (Rom **9** 21; 1 Cor **9** 6; 2 Thess **3** 9, etc). Power is attributed preeminently to God (1 Ch **29** 11; Job **26** 14; Ps **66** 7; **145** 11; Rev **7** 12, etc). On this attribute of power of God, see Omnipotence. The supreme manifestation of the power, as of the wisdom and love of God, is in redemption (1 Cor **1** 18.24). The preaching of the gospel is accompanied by the power of the Holy Spirit (1 Cor **2** 4; 1 Thess **1** 5, etc). Miracles, as "mighty works," are denoted by the term "powers" (so Mt **11** 21.23 RVm, etc). The end of all time's developments is that God takes to Him His great power and reigns (Rev **11** 17). James Orr

POWER OF KEYS. See Keys, Power of.

PRÆTORIAN, prē-tō'ri-an, **GUARD:** "My bonds in Christ are manifest in all the palace, and in all other places" (Phil **1** 13 AV). This verse is tr[d] in RV, "My bonds became manifest in Christ throughout the whole prætorian guard, and to all the rest," and is noteworthy.

It has been usual to connect the words, "the soldier that guarded him," Acts **28** 16, with this statement

1. Prætorium in Phil—Usual View in Phil **1** 13, that the apostle's bonds were manifest in the whole prætorium, and to understand that the former was the cause of the latter; that the result of Paul's making the gospel known in his own hired house to those soldiers to one of whom he was chained by the wrist day and night, was that it became known in all the prætorian regiment that his bonds were endured for Christ's sake, that it was for conscience' sake that he was suffering wrongfully, that he was no wrongdoer but a prisoner of Jesus Christ. In this way the gospel would spread through the whole of the **prætorian guard** in that regiment's headquarters which were situated in a permanent camp established by Tiberius in Rome, outside the Colline Gate, at the N.E. of the city. This verse would also mean that the gospel had been proclaimed in the same way to those members of the prætorian guard who were on duty as the bodyguard of the emperor and who were lodged in one of the buildings which adjoined the emperor's palace on the Palatine Hill.

2. Lightfoot on Interpretations

Thus Lightfoot, discussing the meaning of the phrase "in the whole prætorium" (*Comm. on Phil*, 99 ff), reviews the different interpretations which have been given of the word, and shows (1) that no instance is to be found of its signifying Nero's palace on the Palatine Hill; (2) that there is no authority for the interpretation which would make it mean the prætorian barracks on the Palatine; (3) that neither is there any authority for making it mean the prætorian camp outside the walls of Rome. In Lightfoot's words (op. cit., 101), "All attempts to give a local sense to 'praetorium' thus fail for want of evidence." Lightfoot accordingly defends the interpretation, "the prætorian guard," and RV, above cited, follows him in this.

3. View of Mommsen and Ramsay

One of the meanings of "prætorium" is a council of war, the officers who met in the general's tent (see PRÆTORIUM). Lightfoot is very decided in interpreting "prætorium" to mean the prætorian regiment, the imperial guards, and he adds, "in this sense and in this alone can it be safely affirmed that the apostle would hear the word prætorium used daily," and that this sense is in all respects appropriate. But the other meaning, though not appropriate here, viz. a council of war composed of the officers and their general, is much nearer to that which is now accepted by such authorities as Mommsen and Sir W. M. Ramsay, who hold that in this passage "prætorium" means a council, not of war, however, but the council of judgment, the emperor's court of appeal in which he was assisted by his legal assessors (see Mommsen, *Berlin Akad. Sitzungsber.*, 1895, 501; Ramsay, *St. Paul the Traveller and the Rom Citizen*, 357; Workman, *Persecution in the Early Church*, 35). Over this court there presided the emperor or his delegate, the prefect of the prætorian guard, and associated with him were twenty assessors selected from the senators. Formerly their votes were taken by ballot, but Nero preferred to receive from each a written opinion and on the next day to deliver his judgment in person. Such, it is now believed, is the prætorium to which Paul refers.

The meaning, therefore, of the words, "My bonds in Christ are manifest in the whole prætorium," will be that when Paul wrote the Ep. to the Phil his first Rom trial was already so far advanced that he had been able to impress upon his judges, the twenty assessors and their president, the fact that he was no evildoer, but that the sole cause of his imprisonment was his loyalty to Christ. It was manifest to all the members of the emperor's court of appeal that Paul was enduring his long imprisonment, suffering wrongfully, but only for the sake of Jesus Christ.

4. Bearing on Paul's Captivity and Trial

The important bearing will be seen which this signification of "prætorium" in this passage has on the question of the order in which Eph, Phil, Col and Philem—the epp. of Paul's captivity in Rome—were written. On subjective evidence Lightfoot concludes that Phil is the earliest of them, basing his opinion largely on the resemblance which exists in many particulars between the thoughts and expressions in Phil and in the Ep. to the Rom, making Phil, as it were, a connecting link between Paul's earlier and his later epp. See Lightfoot, *Philippians*, 42 f; he writes: "These resemblances suggest as early a date for the Ep. to the Phil as circumstances will allow," earlier, that is, than Col and Eph. But Lightfoot's argument is set aside by the new light which has been thrown upon the real meaning of "prætorium." Sir W. M. Ramsay (*St. Paul the Traveller*, 357) writes: "The trial seems to have occurred toward the end of AD 61. Its earliest stages were over before Paul wrote to the Philippians, for he says, 'The things *which happened* unto me have fallen out rather unto the progress of the Good News; so that my bonds became manifest in Christ in the whole *Prætorium*, and to all the rest; and that most of the Brethren in the Lord, being confident in my bonds, are more abundantly bold to speak the word of God without fear.' This passage has been generally misconceived and connected with the period of imprisonment; and here again we are indebted to Mommsen for the proper interpretation. The *Prætorium* is the whole body of persons connected with the sitting in judgment, the supreme Imperial Court, doubtless in this case the Prefect or both Prefects of the Prætorian Guard, representing the emperor in his capacity as the fountain of justice, together with the assessors and high officers of the court. The expression of the chapter as a whole shows that the trial is partly finished, and the issue as yet is so favorable that the Brethren are emboldened by the success of Paul's courageous and free-spoken defence and the strong impression which he evidently produced on the court; but he himself, being entirely occupied with the trial, is for the moment prevented from preaching as he had been doing when he wrote to the Colossians and the Asian churches generally."

5. Bearing on Date of Epistle

Thus the correct meaning of "prætorium" enables us to fix the date of the Ep. to the Phil as having been written close to the end of Paul's first Rom imprisonment. That this inference is correct is confirmed by various other facts, such as his promise to visit that city, and the fact that in Phil **2** 20 f AV he says regarding Timothy, "I have no man likeminded, who will naturally care for your state. For all seek their own, not the things which are Jesus Christ's." We could not conceive of Paul writing like this if Mark, Tychicus, Aristarchus, and esp. if Luke had been with him then, and yet we know (Col **4** 7.10.14) that each and all of these companions of the apostle were with him in Rome when he wrote the Ep. to the Col. They had evidently, along with others, been sent on missions to Asia or other places, so that Paul now had only Timothy "likeminded" when he wrote to Philippi. See PAUL THE APOSTLE; PHILIPPIANS, EPISTLE TO THE.

All these facts and considerations confirm us in accepting the signification of "prætorium" as the emperor's supreme court of appeal, before which Paul when he wrote the Ep. to the Phil had so conducted his defence as to produce a most favorable impression, from which he inferred that he might soon be liberated from imprisonment. And his liberation, as the event proved, soon followed.

JOHN RUTHERFURD

PRÆTORIUM, prē-tō′ri-um (πραιτώριον, *praitṓrion*, Mt **27** 27 [AV "common hall"]; Mk **15** 16; Jn **18** 28.33; **19** 9 [in all m "palace," and in the last three AV "judgment hall"]; Acts **23** 35, [Herod's] "palace," m "Prætorium," AV "judgment hall"; Phil **1** 13, "prætorian guard" [m "Gr 'in the whole Prætorium,'" AV "palace," m "Cæsar's court"]):

1. Governor's Official Residence

The Prætorium was originally the headquarters of a Rom camp, but in the provinces the name became attached to the governor's official residence. In order to provide residences for their provincial governors, the Romans were accustomed to seize and appropriate the palaces which were formerly the homes of the princes or kings in conquered countries. Such a residence might sometimes be in a royal palace, as was probably the case in Caesarea, where the procurator used Herod's palace (Acts **23** 35).

2. In Gospels Herod's Palace

The Prætorium where Jesus was brought to trial has been traditionally located in the neighborhood of the present Turkish barracks where once stood the Antonia and where was stationed a large garrison (cf Acts **21** 32–35), but the statements of Jos make it almost certain that the headquarters of the procurator were at Herod's palace. This was a building whose magnificence Jos can hardly sufficiently appraise (*Wars*, I, xxi, 1; V, iv, 4). It was in this palace that "Florus, the procurator took up his quarters, and having placed his tribunal in front of it, held his sessions and the chief priests, influential persons and notables of the city appeared before the tribunal" (*Wars*, II, xiv, 8). Later on, "Florus . . . . brought such as were with him out of the king's palace, and would have compelled them to get as far as the citadel [Antonia]; but his attempt failed" (II, xv, 5). The word trd "palace" here is *aulḗ*, the same word as is trd "court" in Mk **15** 16, "the soldiers led him away within the court [*aulē*], which is the Prætorium." There is no need to suppose that Herod Antipas was in the same palace (Lk **23** 4 ff); it is more probable he went to the palace of the Hasmoneans which lay lower down on the eastern slope of this southwest hill, where at a later time Jos expressly states that Herod Agrippa II and his sister Bernice were living (*Wars*, II, xvi, 3).

The palace of Herod occupied the highest part of the southwest hill near the northwest angle of the ancient city, now traditionally called Zion, and the actual site of the Prætorium cannot have been far removed from the Turkish barracks near the so-called "Tower of David." It is interesting to note that the two stations of the Turkish garrison of Jerus today occupy the same spots as did the Rom garrison of Christ's time. It is needless to point out how greatly this view of the situation of the Prætorium must modify the traditional claims of the "Via Dolorosa," the whole course of which depends on the theory that the "Way of Sorrow" began at the Antonia, the Prætorium of late ecclesiastical tradition. See also GABBATHA.

3. Phil 1:13

With regard to the expression ἐν ὅλῳ τῷ πραιτωρίῳ, *en hólō tṓ praitōríō*, in Phil **1** 13, there is now a general consensus of opinion that "Prætorium" here means, not a place, but the imperial prætorian guard, ten thousand in number, which was instituted by Augustus. St. Paul was allowed to reside in his private house in the custody of a prætorian soldier. As these were doubtless constantly changed, it must have become "manifest" to the whole guard that his bonds were for the sake of Christ. See also preceding article.

E. W. G. MASTERMAN

PRAISE

1. Its Meaning

PRAISE, prāz (תְּהִלָּה, *tehillāh*, "psalm," "praise," תּוֹדָה, *tōdhāh*, "confession," "thanksgiving," שָׁבַח, *shābhaḥ*, "to praise," "glorify," זָמַר, *zāmar*, יָדָה, *yādhāh*, "to stretch out the hand," "confess"; **αἰνέω**, *ainéō*, **ἐπαινέω**, *epainéō*, **ἔπαινος**, *épainos*): The word comes from the Lat *pretium*, "price," or "value," and may be defined generally as an ascription of value or worth. Praise may be bestowed upon unworthy objects or from improper motives, but true praise consists in a sincere acknowledgment of a real conviction of worth. Its type may be seen in the representation given in the Apocalypse of the adoration of God and of the Lamb, which is inspired by a sense of their worthiness to be adored (Rev **4** 11; **5** 12).

2. With Man as Its Object

Man may be the object of praise, and may receive it either from God or from his fellow-men. In the former case (Rom **2** 29; 1 Cor **4** 5) the praise is inevitably just, as resting on a Divine estimate of worth; in the latter case its value depends upon the grounds and motives that lie behind it. There is a praise which is itself a condemnation (Lk **6** 26), an honor which seals the eyes in unbelief (Jn **5** 44), a careless use of the epithet "good" which is dishonoring to God (Lk **18** 19). This is the "praise of men" which Jesus warned His followers to shun as being incompatible with the "praise of God" (Mt **6** 1–4; cf Jn **12** 43; Gal **1** 10; 1 Thess **2** 6). On the other hand, there is a praise that is the instinctive homage of the soul to righteousness (Lk **23** 47), the acknowledgment given to well-doing by just government (Rom **13** 3; 1 Pet **2** 14), the tribute of the churches to distinguished Christian service (2 Cor **8** 18). Such praise, so far from being incompatible with the praise of God, is a reflection of it in human consciousness; and so Paul associates praise with virtue as an aid and incentive to holy living on which the mind should dwell (Phil **4** 8).

3. With God as Its Object

In the Bible it is God who is esp. brought before us as the object of praise. His whole creation praises Him, from the angels of heaven (Ps **103** 20; Rev **5** 11) to those lower existences that are unconscious or even inanimate (Ps **19** 1–4; **148** 1–10; Rev **5** 13). But it is with the praises offered to God by man, and with the human duty of praising God, that the Scriptures are principally concerned. In regard to this subject the following points may be noticed:

(1) *The grounds of praise.*—Sometimes God is praised for His inherent qualities. His majesty (Ps **104** 1) or holiness (Isa **6** 3) fills the mind, and He is "glorified as God" (Rom **1** 21) in view of what He essentially is. More frequently He is praised for His works in creation, providence, and redemption. References may be dispensed with here, for the evidence meets us on almost every page of the sacred literature from Gen to Rev, and the Book of Ps in particular, from beginning to end, is occupied with these themes. When God's operations under these aspects present themselves, not simply as general effects of His power and wisdom, but as expressions of His personal love to the individual, the nation, the church, His works become benefits, and praise passes into blessing and thanksgiving (Pss **34, 103**; Eph **1** 3; 1 Pet **1** 3).

(2) *The modes of praise.*—True praise of God, as distinguished from false praise (Isa **29** 13; Mt **15** 8), is first of all *an inward emotion*—a gladness and rejoicing of the heart (Ps **4** 7; **33** 21), a music of the soul and spirit (Ps **103** 1; Lk **1** 46 f) which no language can adequately express (Ps **106** 2; 2 Cor **9** 15). But utterance is natural to strong emotion, and *the mouth* instinctively strives to express the praises of the heart (Ps **51** 15 and *passim*). Many of the most moving passages in Scripture come from the inspiration of the spirit of praise awakened by the contemplation of the Divine majesty or power or wisdom or kindness, but above all by the revelation of redeeming love. Again, the spirit of praise is a social spirit calling for *social utterance*. The man who praises God desires to praise Him in the hearing of other men (Ps **40** 10), and desires also that their praises should be joined with his own (**34** 3). Further, the spirit of praise is *a spirit of song*. It may find expression in other ways—in sacrifice (Lev **7** 13), or testimony (Ps **66** 16), or prayer (Col **1** 3); but it finds its most natural and its fullest utterance in lyrical and musical forms. When God fills the heart with praise He puts a new song into the mouth (Ps **40** 3). The Book of Ps is the proof of this for the OT. And when we pass to the NT we find that, alike for angels and men, for the church on earth and the church in heaven, the higher moods of praise express themselves in bursts of song (Lk **2** 14; Eph **5** 19; Col **3** 16; Rev **5** 9; **14** 3; **15** 3). Finally, both in the OT and NT, the spirit of song gives birth to *ordered modes of public praise*. In their earlier expressions the praises of Israel were joyful outbursts in which song was mingled with shouting and dancing to a rude accompaniment of timbrels and trumpets (Ex **15** 20 ff; 2 S **6** 5.14 ff). In later times Israel had its sacred Psalter, its guilds of trained singers (Ezr **2** 41; Neh **7** 44), its skilled musicians (Pss **42, 49,** etc); and the praise that waited for God in Zion was full of the solemn beauty of holiness (Ps **29** 2; **96** 9). In the NT the Psalter is still a manual of social praise. The

"hymn" which Jesus sang with His disciples after the Last Supper (Mt **26** 30) would be a Hebrew psalm, probably from the Hallel (Pss **113–118**) which was used at the Passover service, and various references in the Epp. point to the continued employment of the ancient psalms in Christian worship (1 Cor **14** 26; Eph **5** 19; Col **3** 16; Jas **5** 13). But the Psalter of the Jewish church could not suffice to express the distinctive moods of Christian feeling. Original utterance of the spirit of Christian song was one of the manifestations of the gift of tongues (1 Cor **14** 15–17). Paul distinguishes hymns and spiritual songs from psalms (Eph **5** 19; Col **3** 16); and it was hymns that he and Silas sang at midnight in the prison of Philippi (Acts **16** 25 RV). But from hymns and songs that were the spontaneous utterance of individual feeling the development was natural, in NT as in OT times, to hymns that were sung in unison by a whole congregation; and in rhythmic passages like 1 Tim **3** 16; Rev **15** 3 f, we seem to have fragments of a primitive Christian hymnology, such as Pliny bears witness to for the early years of the 2d cent., when he informs Trajan that the Christians of Bithynia at their morning meetings sang a hymn in alternate strains to Christ as God (*Ep.* x.97). See PERSECUTION.

(3) *The duty of praise.*—Praise is everywhere represented in the Bible as a duty no less than a natural impulse and a delight. To fail in this duty is to withhold from God a glory that belongs to Him (Ps **50** 23; Rom **1** 20 f); it is to shut one's eyes to the signs of His presence (Isa **40** 26 ff), to be forgetful of His mercies (Dt **6** 12), and unthankful for His kindness (Lk **6** 35). If we are not to fall into these sins, but are to give to God the honor and glory and gratitude we owe Him, we must earnestly cultivate the spirit and habit of praise. From holy men of old we learn that this may be done by arousing the soul from its slothfulness and sluggishness (Ps **57** 8; **103** 1), by fixing the heart upon God (**57** 7; **108** 1), by meditation on His works and ways (**77** 11 ff), by recounting His benefits (**103** 2), above all, for those to whom He has spoken in His Son, by dwelling upon His unspeakable gift (2 Cor **9** 15; cf Rom **8** 31 ff; 1 Jn **3** 1). See also WORSHIP.

J. C. LAMBERT

PRAYER, prâr (δέησις, *deēsis*, προσευχή, *proseuchē*, ἔντευξις, *énteuxis;* for an excellent discussion of the meaning of these see Thayer's *Lexicon*, p. 126, s.v. δέησις; the chief vbs. are εὔχομαι, *eúchomai*, προσεύχομαι, *proseúchomai*, and δέομαι, *déomai*, esp. in Lk and Acts; αἰτέω, *aitéō*, "to ask a favor," distinguished from ἐρωτάω, *erōtáō*, "to ask a question," is found occasionally): In the Bible "prayer" is used in a simpler and a more complex, a narrower and a wider signification. In the former case it is supplication for benefits either for one's self (petition) or for others (intercession). In the latter it is an act of worship which covers all the attitudes of the soul in its approach to God. Supplication is at the heart of it, for prayer always springs out of a sense of need and a belief that God is a rewarder of them that diligently seek Him (He **11** 6). But adoration and confession and thanksgiving also find a place, so that the suppliant becomes a worshipper. It is unnecessary to distinguish all the various terms for prayer that are employed in the OT and the NT. But the fact should be noticed that in the Heb and Gr alike there are on the one hand words for prayer that denote a direct petition or short, sharp cry of the heart in its distress (Ps **30** 2; 2 Cor **12** 8), and on the other "prayers" like that of Hannah (1 S **2** 1–10), which is in reality a song of thanksgiving, or that of Paul, the prisoner of Jesus Christ, in which intercession is mingled with doxology (Eph **3** 14–21).

The history of prayer as it meets us here reflects various stages of experience and revelation. In the

1. In the OT

patriarchal period, when 'men began to call upon the name of the Lord' (Gen **4** 26; cf **12** 8; **21** 33), prayer is naïve, familiar and direct (**15** 2 ff; **17** 18; **18** 23 ff; **24** 12). It is evidently associated with sacrifice (**12** 8; **13** 4; **26** 25), the underlying idea probably being that the gift or offering would help to elicit the desired response. Analogous to this is Jacob's vow, itself a species of prayer, in which the granting of desired benefits becomes the condition of promised service and fidelity (**28** 20 ff). In *the preëxilic history* of Israel prayer still retains many of the primitive features of the patriarchal type (Ex **3** 4; Nu **11** 11–15; Jgs **6** 13 ff; **11** 30 f; 1 S **1** 11; 2 S **15** 8; Ps **66** 13 f). The Law has remarkably little to say on the subject, differing here from the later Judaism (see Schürer, *HJP*, II, i, 290, index-vol, p. 93; and cf Mt **6** 5 ff; **23** 14; Acts **3** 1; **16** 13); while it confirms the association of prayer with sacrifices, which now appear, however, not as gifts in anticipation of benefits to follow, but as expiations of guilt (Dt **21** 1–9) or thank offerings for past mercies (**26** 1–11). Moreover, the free, frank access of the private individual to God is more and more giving place to the mediation of the priest (**21** 5; **26** 3), the intercession of the prophet (Ex **32** 11–13; 1 S **7** 5–13; **12** 23), the ordered approach of tabernacle and temple services (Ex **40**; 1 K **8**). The prophet, it is true, approaches God immediately and freely—Moses (Ex **34** 34; Dt **34** 10) and David (2 S **7** 27) are to be numbered among the prophets—but he does so in virtue of his office, and on the ground esp. of his possession of the Spirit and his intercessory function (cf Ezk **2** 2; Jer **14** 15).

A new epoch in the history of prayer in Israel was brought about by the experiences of *the Exile.* Chastisement drove the nation to seek God more earnestly than before, and as the way of approach through the external forms of the temple and its sacrifices was now closed, the spiritual path of prayer was frequented with a new assiduity. The devotional habits of Ezra (Ezr **7** 27; **8** 23), Nehemiah (Neh **2** 4; **4** 4.9, etc) and Daniel (Dnl **6** 10) prove how large a place prayer came to hold in the individual life; while the utterances recorded in Ezr **9** 6–15; Neh **1** 5–11; **9** 5–38; Dnl **9** 4–19; Isa **63** 7—**64** 12 serve as illustrations of the language and spirit of the prayers of the Exile, and show esp. the prominence now given to confession of sin. In any survey of the OT teaching *the Psalms* occupy a place by themselves, both on account of the large period they cover in the history and because we are ignorant in most cases as to the particular circumstances of their origin. But speaking generally it may be said that here we see the loftiest flights attained by the spirit of prayer under the old dispensation—the intensest craving for pardon, purity and other spiritual blessings (**51, 130**), the most heartfelt longing for a living communion with God Himself (**42** 2; **63** 1; **84** 2).

Here it will be convenient to deal separately with the material furnished by the Gospel narratives of the life and teaching of Christ

2. In the NT

and that found in the remaining books. The distinctively Christian view of prayer comes to us from *the Christ of the Gospels.* We have to notice His own habits in the matter (Lk **3** 21; **6** 12; **9** 16.29; **22** 32.39–46; **23** 34–46; Mt **27** 46; Jn **17**), which for all who accept Him as the revealer of the Father and the final authority in religion immediately dissipate all theoretical objections to the value and efficacy of prayer. Next we have His general teaching on the subject in parables (Lk **11** 5–9; **18** 1–14) and incidental sayings (Mt **5** 44; **6** 5–8; **7** 7–11; **9** 38; **17** 21; **18** 19; **21** 22; **24** 20; **26** 41 and ||'s), which presents prayer, not as a mere energizing of the religious soul that is followed by beneficial spiritual reactions, but as the request of a child to a father (**6** 8; **7** 11), subject, indeed, to the father's will (**7** 11; cf **6** 10; **26** 39.42; 1 Jn **5** 14), but secure always of loving attention and response (Mt **7** 7–11; **21** 22). In thus teaching us to approach God as our Father, Jesus raised prayer to its highest plane, making it not less reverent than it was at its best in OT times, while far more intimate and trustful. In the LORD'S PRAYER (q.v.) He summed up His ordinary teaching on the subject in a concrete example which serves as a model and breviary of prayer (Mt **6** 9–13; Lk **11** 2–4). But according to the Fourth Gospel, this was not His final word upon the subject. On the night of the betrayal, and in full view of His death and resurrection and ascension to God's right hand, He told His disciples that prayer was henceforth to be addressed to the Father in the name of the Son, and that prayer thus offered was sure to be granted (Jn **16** 23.24.26). The differentia of Christian prayer thus consists in its being offered in the name of Christ; while the secret of its success lies on the one hand in the new access to the Father which Christ has secured for His people (**17** 19; cf He **4** 14–16; **10** 19–22), and on the other in the fact that prayer offered in the name of Christ will be prayer in harmony with the Father's will (**15** 7; cf 1 Jn **3** 22 f; **5** 13 f).

In *the Acts and Epp.* we see the apostolic church giving effect to Christ's teaching on prayer. It was in a praying atmosphere that the church was born (Acts **1** 14; cf **2** 1); and throughout its early history prayer continued to be its vital breath and native air (**2** 42; **3** 1; **6** 4.6 and *passim*). The Epp. abound in references to prayer. Those of Paul in particular contain frequent allusions to his own personal practice in the matter (Rom **1** 9; Eph **1** 16; Phil **1** 9; 1 Thess **1** 2, etc), and many exhortations to his readers to cultivate the praying habit (Rom **12** 12; Eph **6** 18; Phil **4** 6; 1 Thess **5** 17, etc). But the new and characteristic thing about Christian prayer as it meets us now is its connection with the Spirit. It has become a spiritual gift (1 Cor **14** 14–16); and even those who have not this gift in the exceptional charismatic sense may "pray in the Spirit" whenever they come to the throne of grace (Eph **6** 18; Jude ver 20). The gift of the Spirit, promised by Christ (Jn **14** 16 ff, etc), has raised prayer to its highest power by securing for it a Divine coöperation (Rom **8** 15.26; Gal **4** 6). Thus Christian prayer in its full NT meaning is prayer addressed to God as Father, in the name of Christ as Mediator, and through the enabling grace of the indwelling Spirit. See PRAYERS OF JESUS. J. C. LAMBERT

PRAYER, HOURS OF. See HOURS OF PRAYER.

PRAYER, LORD'S. See LORD'S PRAYER, THE.

PRAYER OF HABAKKUK. See HABAKKUK; BETH-HORON, BATTLE OF.

PRAYER OF JOSEPH. See JOSEPH, PRAYER OF.

PRAYER OF MANASSES. See MANASSES, PRAYER OF.

PRAYERS, prârz, **OF JESUS:**

1. The Lord's Prayer
2. Christ's Doctrine of Prayer
   Sacredness, Importunity, Conditions
3. Prayers Offered by Christ
   (1) The High-priestly Prayer
   (2) The Prayer in Gethsemane
   (3) The Prayers on the Cross
   (4) Prayer after the Resurrection
   (5) General Conclusions

In the history and doctrine of prayer, nothing is more important than the light shed upon the subject by the prayers of Jesus. These are to be studied in connection with His teaching concerning prayer found in the model of the Lord's Prayer, and general statements and hints to His disciples.

1. The Lord's Prayer

This model of prayer is given in two forms (Mt **6** 9–13; Lk **11** 2–4). The differences of form show that exactness of similarity in words is not essential. The prayer includes adoration, supplication for the Kingdom, for personal needs, for forgiveness, for deliverance from temptation and the ascription of glory. It is at once individual and universal; it sets the recognition of Divine things first, and yet clearly asserts the ethical and social relations of life. See LORD'S PRAYER, THE.

2. Christ's Doctrine of Prayer

That men should pray is taken for granted (Mt **6** 5). Its sacredness is involved in the command for privacy (Mt **6** 6); its importunity (Lk **11** 5–9; **18** 1–8); its necessary conditions of humility, absence of self-righteousness (Lk **18** 9–14), of display and repetition (Mt **6** 7); necessity of faith and a forgiving spirit (Mk **11** 24–26); of agreement in social prayer (Mt **18** 19); submission to the will of Christ, "in my name" (Jn **14** 13).

3. Prayers Offered by Christ

In Mt **11** 25.26 AV, Christ thanks God: "Thou hast hid these things from the wise and prudent, and hast revealed them unto babes. Even so, Father: for so it seemed good in thy sight." This language shows the essence of prayer to be not the mere expression of need and request for what is required, but resort to God. The prayer gives us insight into the deeper experience of the Son with the Father, and His perfect submission to the Father's will, with thanksgiving even for what might seem inexplicable. It thus illustrates the truth that the highest form of prayer is found in the serenity of the soul.

Mt **14** 23 narrates the retirement of the Lord to a "mountain apart to pray." No word of what the prayer was is given, but the record is suggestive. Following a day of severe toil and probably excitement, Jesus betakes Himself to prayer. The reality, the true humanity of the Christ, are here revealed. The former prayer may almost be regarded as that of the Son of God addressed to the Father in the sublime communion of the Godhead. This passage emphatically is a prayer-scene of the Son of Man. The association of this incident of prayer in Christ's life with the miracle of walking on the sea (an example of miracle in the person of the Lord Himself, and not performed on another) opens up an interesting question of the relation of the supernatural and the natural. Here perhaps lies an explanation of the true significance of the miraculous. The communion of the Lord with a supreme Father had filled the physical nature of Jesus with spiritual forces which extended the power of the spirit over the material world beyond the limits by which man is bound in his normal and sinful condition (see Lange, *Comm. on Mt;* Mt **15** 36; cf **14** 19). Christ's recognition of God as the Giver of food, in thanks at the meal, or "asking a blessing," should be noted as an example which in modern times is largely ignored or followed as a mere formality. But it is significant; it expresses that intense and all-compelling sense of the Divine which ever dwelt in Him; of which prayer is an expression, and which is evoked so naturally and becomingly at a social meal. In Mt **17** 21, Our Lord's reference to prayer as a necessary condition of miraculous power, in the light of Mk **7** 34, where "looking up to heaven, he sighed, and saith unto him [the deaf man], Ephphatha," may imply His own prayer in connection with the exercise of miraculous energy. This is apparently indicated in Jn **11** 41.42, although, as above, it is the expression of the intimate relation between Christ and the Father, which is the essence of prayer, and in which relation He ever exercised the fullest power of God Himself. Mt **19** 13 records that little children were brought to Him that He should put His hands on them *and pray*. That He prayed is not related, but ver 15 relates that He laid His hands on them and, presumably, with the imposition, prayed. The scene is most suggestive, in the light of Our Lord's words. In ver 14 and in Mt **26** 26 Our Lord blesses the bread or gives thanks at the institution of the Supper, and has set the mode of celebration universally adopted, even giving the term Eucharist ("giving of thanks") to the service.

(1) *The high-priestly prayer.*—This prayer (Jn **17**) is the special prayer of the Lord, and may be regarded as the sole example furnished by the evangelists of Our Lord's method of prayer. The thanksgiving in Mt **11** 25 is the only other instance of any extent in the report of the prayers of Jesus, but even that is brief compared to what is here furnished. The fulness of this prayer clearly shows that it was uttered in the hearing of the disciples. Their relation to it is remarkable. Auditors, they yet could not share in it. At the same time, it was a profound revelation to them both of the relation of the Master to God, and the character of the work which He had come to perform, and the part which they were to take in it. John gives us no hint as to the place in which it was spoken; **14** 31 indicates a departure from the upper room. But apparently the prayer was offered where the discourses of chs **15** and **16** were delivered. It has been suggested by Westcott that some spot in the temple courts was the scene of chs **15, 16** and **17.** It has been generally supposed that the ornament of the Golden Vine would naturally suggest the figure of the Vine and Branches which Our Lord employs. Jn **18 1** shows that the prayer was offered before the Lord and His disciples had passed over the brook Kidron. The determination of the exact spot is certainly impossible, except the probability that the words were spoken in the vicinity of the temple.

The first part of the prayer (Jn **17** 1–5) is an expression of profound communion between the Son and the Father, and the prayer that the Father should glorify the Son, but with the supreme end of the Father's own glory. The absolutely unique character of Christ's relation to God is the calm assertion of ver 4. Its consciousness of completeness in the work which He had received from God, impossible for the children of men, marks the supreme nature of the Son of God.

In the second part of the prayer (Jn **17** 6–19), Our Lord prays for His disciples, to whom He has revealed Himself and His relation to God (vs 7.8). He prays that they may be kept by the Father, and for their unity. Their separation from the world is declared (ver 14), and Our Lord prays that they may be kept from the evil that is in the world, which is alien from them as it is from Him.

In the third portion of the prayer Christ's relation to His ultimate followers is referred to. Their unity is sought, not an external unity, but the deep, spiritual unity found by the indwelling of Christ in them and God in Christ. The prayer closes by the declaration that Christ's knowledge of the Father is revealed to His people, and the end and crown of all is to be the indwelling of God's love in man by the dwelling of Christ in him.

This prayer is unique, not merely among the prayers of Our Lord, but also among the prayers of humanity. While it is distinctly a petition, it is at the same time a communion. In one or two places Our Lord expresses His will, thus setting Himself upon a level with God. The fact of this prayer of triumph in which every petition is virtually a declaration of the absolute certainty of its realization, immediately preceding the prayer of Gethsemane, is both difficult and suggestive. The anomaly is a powerful argument for the historic reality. The explanation of these contrasted moods is to be found in the depth of Our Lord's nature, and esp. in the complete consistency of His dual nature with the spheres to which each nature belongs. He is most Divine; He is most human. In the fulness of the reach of the prayer and its calm confidence, the believer may find a ceaseless and inexhaustible source of comfort and encouragement. Attention might be called to the remarkable forecast of the history and experience of the church which the prayer furnishes.

(2) *The prayer in Gethsemane.*—This is recorded by the three Synoptics (Mt **26** 36–44; Mk **14** 22–40; Lk **22** 39–46), and is probably referred to in He **5** 7. Brief though the prayer is, it exhibits most clearly recognition of God's infinite power, a clear object sought by the prayer, and perfect submission to God's will. All the elements of prayer, as it can be offered by man, are here except the prayer for forgiveness. It is to be noted that the prayer was three times repeated. This is not to be regarded as inconsistent with Our Lord's prohibition of repetition. It was vain repetition which was forbidden. The intensity of the prayer is expressed by its threefold utterance (cf Paul's prayer in regard to the thorn in 2 Cor **12** 8).

(3) *The prayers on the cross.*—In Mt **27** 46; Mk **15** 34, Christ uses the prayer of Ps **22** 1. In the moment of complete desolation, the Sufferer claimed His unbroken relationship with God. This is the victory of the atoning sacrifice. Lk **23** 34 records the prayer of intercession for those who crucified Him; in ver 46 is the calm committal of His spirit to the Father. Prayer here again assumes its highest form in the expression of recognition and trust. Thus the three prayers on the cross not only reveal the intimate relation of Our Lord to the Father, but they also illustrate prayer such as man may offer. They represent supplication, intercession, communion. Prayer thus expresses our relation to God, to others, to ourselves; our trust, our love, our need. In all things He was made like unto His brethren, except without sin (see POINTS). His prayers on the cross illustrate His high-priestly office. It rises at that intense crisis to its supreme manifestation and activity.

(4) *Prayer after the resurrection.*—It is to be observed that after His resurrection there is no record of any prayer offered by Christ. In the supper at Emmaus He "blessed" the bread (Lk **24** 30); and the ascension took place in the midst of blessing (Lk **24** 51), suggestive of the course of the church as ever beneath the benediction of the Lord, to be ended only at the final consummation. The act of eating the fish and honeycomb (Lk **24** 43) seems to have been unaccompanied by any act of specifically religious form. Mk, with characteristic regard to details, records Christ's "looking up to heaven" (Mk **6** 41; **7** 34); Jn **11** 41 refers to a similar act, and adds the Lord's words of thanksgiving that God had heard Him (see also Jn **17** 1). The gesture was usual in association with Christ's prayers; it is appropriate and suggestive. Lk narrates that Christ prayed at His baptism (Lk **3** 21); that He spent a night in prayer before choosing the Twelve (Lk **6** 12.13); that the transfiguration was preceded by

prayer (Lk **9** 29); and records the prayer in the garden (Lk **22** 41–45). The third evangelist thus in addition to the notes of Our Lord's prayers in retirement, which the other evangelists record, adds these instances of the special relation of prayer to events of critical importance.

(5) *General conclusions.*—The following conclusions as to prayer may be drawn from the records of Christ's prayers: (1) Prayer is the highest exercise of man's spiritual nature. (2) It is natural to the soul even in perfect accord with God. (3) It is not only the expression of need, the supply of which is sought of God, but by the example of Christ it is the highest expression of trust, submission and union with God. (4) It is to be used both in solitude and in society; it is personal and intercessory. (5) It may be accompanied by the plea of Christ's name, and for Christ's sake. These are the laws which should direct it; that is to say, it should be based upon the merit and the intercession of Christ, and should be addressed to God under the limitations of the Kingdom of the Lord and His purposes for good, both for the interest of the suppliant and others, under the conditions of the interest of the whole Kingdom.

Ll. D. Bevan

PREACHER, prēch′ẽr, **PREACHING,** prēch′ing (קֹהֶלֶת, *ḳōheleth,* "preacher" [Eccl **1** 1], בָּשַׂר, *bāsar,* "to bring or tell good tidings" [Ps **40** 9; Isa **61** 1], קָרָא, *ḳārā',* "to call," "proclaim" [Neh **6** 7; Jon **3** 2], קְרִיאָה, *ḳerī'āh,* "cry," "preaching" [Jon **3** 2]; **κήρυξ,** *kḗrux,* "crier," "herald" [1 Tim **2** 7], **κηρύσσω,** *kērússō,* "to cry or proclaim as a herald" [Mt **3** 1; Rom **10** 14], **εὐαγγελλίζω,** *euaggellízō,* "to announce good news" [Mt **11** 5]):

1. Definition
2. The Preacher's Limitations
3. A Man with a Message
4. Preaching a Necessary Agency
5. Biblical Terms and Their Meanings
6. The Hebrew Prophets
7. Christ as a Preacher
8. The Apostles as Preachers
9. Fundamental Postulates
   (1) Preach the Word
   (2) "We Are Ambassadors"

1. Definition

In the NT sense a preacher is a man who has the inner call from the Holy Ghost and the external call from the church, the witnessing body of Christ on earth, and has been duly set apart as an accredited and qualified teacher of the Christian religion. His vocation is that of addressing the popular mind and heart on religious truth, as that truth is set forth in the sacred Scripture, for the spiritual profit of the hearer as its end. The preacher, recognized as such by the church, speaks as a personal witness of God's saving truth, explaining it and applying it as the circumstances of the people and the time may require. The gravity and importance of this vocation, as set forth in the sacred Scriptures and amply illustrated in the history of the church, surpass those of any other calling among men. Luther said, "The devil does not mind the written word, but he is put to flight whenever it is preached aloud."

2. The Preacher's Limitations

The preacher, in the sense indicated above, is with all other Christians a sharer in the freedom that is in Christ. But as a recognized teacher and leader of the church, he is not an unattached and entirely unrestricted teacher. He is not to speak as his own, but as the mouthpiece of the church whose apprehension of the gospel he has voluntarily confessed. The faith of the church is, by his own assent, his faith, and her doctrine is his doctrine. He is not expected to give his own, as distinct from or opposed to the faith of the church in whose name he has been set apart to proclaim the gospel. Both the personal and the representative or official are united in him and his preaching.

3. A Man with a Message

His work is always to be related to the OT and NT. His sermon is under the creed of his church as the creed is under the word. The preacher is a man with a message, and the preacher who has no message of the particular kind indicated above is in no true sense a preacher. It has been well expressed in one of the valuable Yale series of lectures on the subject, "Every living preacher must receive his communication direct from God, and the constant purpose of his life must be to receive it uncorrupted and to deliver it without addition or subtraction." When he presents the message of his Divinely appointed ambassadorship in its integrity, he speaks with that peculiar kind of "authority" which has been pronounced "the first and indispensable requisite" in giving a message from God. He manifests thereby a "high celestial dogmatism," and "human weakness becomes immortal strength." The true preacher preaches from a Divine impulsion. He says with Paul, "Necessity is laid upon me; for woe is unto me, if I preach not the gospel" (1 Cor **9** 16; cf Jer **20** 9). He says with Peter, "Whether it is right in the sight of God to hearken unto you rather than unto God, judge ye: for we cannot but speak the things which we saw and heard" (Acts **4** 19.20). The message of the preacher is greater than the man, because it is from God. It largely makes the man who preaches it in its fulness and power. Whatever be his own gifts or whatever the alleged gift conferred in the laying on of hands, without the sense of the message he is not chosen of God to proclaim His word. Destitute of that, he does not have the sustaining impulse of his vocation to enlist his entire personality in his work and give him mastery over the minds and hearts of men.

4. Preaching a Necessary Agency

No agency of religion is older than preaching. It is as old as the Bible itself (2 Pet **2** 5). It is a necessary adjunct of a religion that is communicated to man by means of an objective and authoritative revelation, such as we have in the sacred Scriptures. It is an entirely natural agency of the forms of religion revealed in the OT and NT. It is strictly in harmony with those ideas that obtain in both testaments regarding the method of propagating the faith, set forth through the agency of holy men who spake as they were moved by the Holy Ghost. That faith is disseminated by means of teaching through argument, explanation, motive and exhortation. The agency for the spread of a religion of persuasion must be preaching.

5. Biblical Terms and Their Meanings

In the Bib. usage of the terms which have reference to the subject, preaching means the proclamation of religious truth. It is that continuous and public testimony which the church is always giving, through discourses, by men set apart for such work, to her own living faith as that faith is rooted in and sustained by the written word of God. In this sense "to call," "proclaim," "cry aloud" are used frequently of the prophetic message under the various aspects of denunciation, as in Jon **1** 2; of the relation of the Divine, as in Jer **11** 6, and of Messianic promise, as in Isa **61** 1. The term for "preaching" is also used to designate a political propagandism set forth by the prophet (Neh **6** 7). In two passages (Ps **68** 11, "publish"; Isa **61** 1) another word for preaching means "to declare good news." In the case of Jonah's preaching at Nineveh, the word used to designate what it was means strictly "proclamation" and corresponds to the NT word used to define Our Lord's "proclamation" as a herald of the advent of the Kingdom of God (Mt **4** 17), which in its initial stages particularly was closely associated with the preaching of John the Baptist (Mt **3** 1.2).

6. The Hebrew Prophets

Thus while preaching belongs esp. to Christianity, it has well-defined antecedents in the OT. Under both the old and the new dispensations the subject takes the church for granted and utters the testimony, not simply of a solitary believer, but of a Divinely founded society, whether it be of Jews or Christians. The older books in the Canon have in them the beginnings and some of the features of the preacher's office and of the high function of preaching. In them we find a special class of men set apart and separated unto that particular work, as we find in the Christian church, from its beginnings, the same Divinely instituted office. The Heb prophet had a message direct from God, which frequently came with supernatural knowledge in the power of prediction. The mission of the prophet, however, was not simply or chiefly to forecast the future, but to declare a present message from the Lord to the people. The prophet of the OT was the forerunner in office and the prototype of the ambassador of Christ. With the development of the synagogue as the center of Heb worship, application as well as interpretation of the Law became essential.

Moses, the most commanding figure in Heb history, was a prophet, and no messages in the OT are more imbued with power, sublimity and pathos than those uttered by the great lawgiver. He became the guide of Israel, not so much by his rod as by the word he delivered to the people. There are numerous indications that after Moses there was a continuous class of religious teachers whose work it was to instruct men and inspire the people, as is indicated in the cases of Joshua, in the history of Deborah and Barak, and in the days of solemn assembly which are inconceivable without men who spoke and other men who listened. In the time of Samuel there was a distinct advance made in the work of the prophets, and the prophetic office had become a fixed institution. There were schools of the prophets at Bethel, Jericho and Gilgal, the very seats of heathen idolatry. Under the OT dispensation the whole course of progress was toward presenting Divine truth in its simplicity and power, by bringing it to bear upon the popular mind and heart. One of the marks of the new era beginning with John the Baptist was a revival of prophetic preaching (Mt **11** 9), which again resumed its old character and meaning. See PROPHECY AND PROPHETS.

7. Christ as a Preacher

The words meaning "to proclaim as a herald" and "preaching," are frequent in the NT. The mission of Our Lord was essentially one of proclaiming good tidings concerning the Kingdom of God (Mt **4** 17). He at once, on His entrance upon His ministry, gave to preaching a spiritual depth and practical range which it never had before. At that time preaching had manifestly become a fixed part of the synagogue worship, and was made one of the chief instruments in the spread of the gospel. Our Lord constantly taught in the synagogue (Mt **4** 23; Mk **1** 21; Jn **6** 59). He thus read and interpreted and applied the Law and the Prophets (Mk **1** 39; Lk **4** 16). Christ's testimony about Himself was that He came "to bear witness to the truth." The spoken word became His great power in His life and ministry. Throughout His life Jesus was above all things a preacher of the truths of His kingdom. Telling men what He was in Himself, what in His relation to man and his salvation and what to God the Father, formed a large part of His public work.

8. The Apostles as Preachers

The preaching of the apostles was essentially prophetic in character, and bore testimony concerning the resurrection of Jesus and His early return to judgment (Acts **2** 24.32.36; 1 Cor **15** 15). The sermons of the apostles which are reported with much fulness are those of Peter on the Day of Pentecost (Acts **2**), his address in the house of Cornelius at Caesarea (Acts **10**), and the counsels of James to the brethren at Jerus, as to what ordinances should be imposed on gentile Christians. In the early church preachers were first of all witnesses to what Jesus had said and done, and to the significance to be attached to the great facts of the redemptive history. With the spread of the gospel and the passing of time, this office was taken up by others, esp. such as were endued with "the word of wisdom" and "of knowledge" (1 Cor **12** 8).

9. Fundamental Postulates

Upon the basis of what is taught in the word of God there are two fundamentally important postulates concerning preaching and the preacher.

(1) *Preach the word.*—The first note of preaching is that it be the word of God (2 Tim **4** 2). Out of the Bible must the life of every generation of Christians be fed. To Holy Scripture, therefore, ought the pulpit to abide faithful, for out of its treasures the preacher fulfils his double office of edifying believers and subjugating the world to Christ. There must always be an organic connection between the word in the text and the sermon.

(2) *"We are ambassadors."*—The work of preaching is the fulfilment of a Divinely instituted ambassadorship (2 Cor **5** 20). The gospel is put into the hands of men for a distinct purpose, and is to be administered in accordance with the plan of its author. The preacher is in a very distinct sense a trustee. "But even as we have been approved of God to be intrusted with the gospel, so we speak; not as pleasing men, but God who proveth our hearts" (1 Thess **2** 4). Those who have accepted the responsibility imposed upon them by this Divine commission are enjoined to exercise their office so as to warrant the approbation of Him who has appointed them to a specific work. The homiletic practice of taking the theme of every sermon from a passage of Holy Writ has been an almost invariable rule in the history of the church. It is the business of the preacher to present the truth embodied in the text in its integrity. In the exercise of his Divinely appointed ambassadorship he is to administer God's word revealed to Christian faith, not human opinions or speculations.

DAVID H. BAUSLIN

PRECEPT, prē'sept: A commandment, an authoritative rule for action; in the Scriptures generally a Divine injunction in which man's obligation is set forth (Lat *praeceptum*, fr. *praecipere*, "to instruct").

Four words are so rendered in AV: (1) מִצְוָה, *miçwāh*, very frequently (168 t) tr[d] "commandment," but 4 t "precept" (in RV only Jer **35** 18; Dnl **9** 5); (2) from the same root is צָו, *çāw*, or צַו, *çaw* (Isa **28** 10.13); (3) פִּקּוּדִים, *piḳḳūdhīm*, only in the Pss (21 t in Ps **119**, e.g. vs 4.15.27; also RV Ps **19** 8; **103** 18; **111** 7); (4) in the NT, ἐντολή, *entolḗ*, generally in AV tr[d] "commandment" (68 t), but twice "precept" (Mk **10** 5; He **9** 19; in both cases RV substitutes "commandment"). See COMMANDMENT.

D. MIALL EDWARDS

PRECIOUS, presh'us (stands for 17 different words, chief of which are יָקָר, *yāḳar;* τίμιος, *tímios*): (1) Generally in the literal sense, "of great price," "costly," "expensive," of material things (e.g. Prov **1** 13; Jer **20** 5; Mk **14** 3 AV), esp. of precious stones (2 S **12** 30; 2 Ch **3** 6; 1 Cor **3** 12 AV, etc). (2) Sometimes "of great *moral* [non-material] value." "Precious in the sight of Jeh is the death of his saints" (Ps **116** 15); "his precious and exceeding great promises" (2 Pet **1** 4); cf Ps **139** 17; 2 Pet **1** 1. The literal and the moral senses are both involved in the expression, "knowing that ye were redeemed, not with corruptible things, ... but with precious blood" (1 Pet **1**

18.19). "Preciousness" (τιμή, *timē*) occurs in 1 Pet **2** 7 ARV, ERV, for AV "precious."

D. Miall Edwards

PRECIOUS STONES. See Stones, Precious.

PRECIPITATION, prē-sip-i-tā'shun. See Punishments, III, (5).

PREDESTINATION, prē-des-ti-nā'shun (**πρόθεσις,** *próthesis,* **πρόγνωσις,** *prógnōsis,* **προορισμός,** *proörismós*):

1. Predestination as a Biblical Question
2. Importance of the Subject for Our Time
3. Nature of Predestination
4. The Doctrine in Scripture
5. Historic Rise and Development of the Doctrine
6. The Doctrine in the Middle Ages
7. Predestination in the Reformed Theology
8. Predestination in Lutheranism
9. The Arminian View
10. Wesleyanism on Predestination
11. Present Needs and Values of the Doctrine

Literature

1. As a Biblical Question

Predestination can be, and has sometimes been, regarded as a philosophical question rather than a Biblical one. It is with predestination as a Biblical question, however, that we are here mainly concerned. It is possible to urge, and it has been urged, that the philosophical question —whether all that occurs is foreordained—is not discussed and decided by Scripture. Theology, starting from God in its interpretation of all things, has arrived at universal foreordination by a species of deductive reasoning. But we must not argue the matter from any abstract principles, but deal with the actual facts as set forth in Scripture and as found, inductively, in the experience of man.

2. Its Fundamental Importance

It must first be asserted, however, in view of much loose modern thinking, that predestination is a category of religious thought of fundamental importance. No category of religious thought could go deeper, for it reaches down to the Infinite Will in relation to the universe of finite wills, and lays stress on will as the core of reality. The philosophy of our time may be said to have received, from the time of Schopenhauer, an impact toward will-emphasis, alike in respect of will in the universe and in man. But the relation of the Absolute Will to the universe, and to mankind, is precisely that with which we are concerned in predestination.

3. Nature of Predestination

Predestination is that aspect of foreordination whereby the salvation of the believer is taken to be effected in accordance with the will of God, who has called and elected him, in Christ, unto life eternal. The Divine plan of salvation must certainly be conceived under this aspect of individual reference. To understand and set forth the nature, and ethically justifiable character, of such a foreordaining to life eternal, is our purpose. For the doctrine has need to be purged of the historic inconsistencies, and fatal illogicalities, with which, in its older forms of presentation, it was often infected. This, esp., in order that the doctrine may appear as grounded in reason and righteousness, not in arbitrariness and almighty caprice.

4. The Doctrine in Scripture

To begin with, it must be said that there seems to be no evading the doctrine of an election by grace, as found both in the letter and the spirit of Scripture. The idea of predestination is set forth, with great power and clearness, in Rom **8** 29.30, and with its elements or parts articulated in natural and striking form. The idea recurs in Eph **1**, where it is finely said (vs 4.5) that God hath chosen us in Christ "before the foundation of the world," having predestinated or "foreordained us unto adoption as sons through Jesus Christ"; and where it is said, further, that our salvation imports "the mystery of his will, according to his good pleasure" (ver 9), which He purposed in Christ. This "eternal purpose" to save men through Christ is again referred to in Eph **3** 11. This helpful mode of viewing predestination as in Christ, and never outside Him, had a place in religious thought at the Reformation time, as the famous "Formula of Concord," to be referred to below, shows. The predestined certainty of God's gracious work in Christ was not meant to perplex men, but to encourage and reassure all who trust in His grace. In Rom **9** 14-25, the absolute sovereignty of God is put in a form whereby election is made to originate in the Divine will apart from all human merit, whether actual or foreseen. But from this assertion of God's free supremacy we can derive no concrete theodicy, or do more than infer that God is just and wise in His exercise of free grace, even when His doings are most perplexing to us.

5. Historic Rise and Development of the Doctrine

The needful thing is to understand, so far as may be, the nature of the coöperation that takes place between the Divine and the human factors or elements, which latter factors include natural capacity, disposition and development, working under grace. It must be carefully observed that nothing in Scripture points to any personal and inexorable predestination to reprobation, in any sense corresponding to the personal election to salvation just spoken of. A non-election there may be, of course, but not in any sense that annuls full personal responsibility for coming short of life everlasting. The appeal of Scripture from first to last is to men as free. Calvin's strange way of putting the matter was, "Man therefore falls, God's Providence so ordaining, but he falls by his own fault." This idea of reprobation was first introduced by Gottschalk, a monk of the 9th cent., long after the predestination doctrine had received its first full and positive exposition by Augustine. Augustine, following upon the indecision shown by the fathers in the first three centuries of the church, made the doctrine of a special predestination his foundation for special grace, in opposition to Pelagius. Augustine gave new prominence in his theory to the absolute will of God: he made Divine grace the only ground of man's salvation; it was to him the irresistible power working faith within the heart, and bringing freedom as its result. It was to him God's absolute predestination that determined who were believers. But Augustine held predestination as an inference from his conception of the Fall and of grace, rather than as a metaphysical principle.

6. The Doctrine in the Middle Ages

In the Middle Ages, Anselm, Peter Lombard, and Aquinas, followed the Augustinian views only to a certain extent. Aquinas admits that predestination implies a relation to grace, but holds that grace is not of the essence of predestination. Predestination is, to Aquinas, a part of Providence, and it presupposes election in the order of reason. Though Divine goodness in general be without election, Aquinas thinks the communication of a particular good cannot be without election. Predestination has, for him, its foundation in the goodness of God, which is its reason. Aquinas thinks predestination most surely takes effect, but not as from necessity; the effect takes place under the working of contingency. From such views we are recalled to the idea of a rigorous predestination, by Thomas Bradwardine and John Wyclif, in pre-Reformation times. We are thus brought up to the decretal system—so called from Calvin's making predestination consist of the eternal decree of God—which became, in its metaphysical principle, the fundamental position of the whole Reformed theology after the Reformation.

The theology of the Reformed church adopted the Calvinistic doctrine of the decree of predestination and election. Calvin, however, simply carried the Augustinian theory to its logical and necessary conclusion, and he was the first to adopt the doctrine as the cardinal point or primordial principle of a theological system. Zwingli, it must be remembered, was, even before Calvin, of consistent deterministic leanings, as part of his large speculative views, which were not without a tendency to universalism. Salvation was, to Calvin, the execution of a Divine decree, which was supposed to fix the extent and conditions of such salvation.

7. Predestination in the Reformed Theology

(1) *Calvin's definition.*—Reprobation was, for Calvin, involved in election, and Divine foreknowledge and foreordination were taken to be identical. Calvin's mode of defining predestination was as the eternal decree of God, by which He has decided with Himself what is to become of each and every individual. For all, he maintains, are not created in like condition; but eternal life is foreordained for some, eternal condemnation for others. Calvin confesses that this is a "horrible decree," and it is not surprising to find competent theologians in our time denying such a form of predestinarianism any place in the teachings of St. Paul, who never speaks of reprobation.

(2) *Theology advanced by Calvin.*—It is generally overlooked, however, that the theological advance registered by Calvin is to be seen by study of the views of the Middle Ages, and on to the Reformation, not by viewing Calvinism in our post-Reformation lights. It was love—"the fatherly love of God," as he terms it—the efficiency of saving love—which Calvin insisted upon, above all, in his teaching about God. But Calvin also heightened men's ideas as to the certitude of personal salvation. It is but fair to Calvin to remember—for superficial acquaintance with his teachings is far from rare—that he, in the strongest manner, maintained Divine sovereignty to be that of Divine wisdom, righteousness, and love, and expressly rejected the notion of absolute power as, in this connection, a heathenish idea. The Calvinistic doctrine was not absolute, but mediated in Christ, and conditioned upon faith.

Luther and the Lutheran church at first shared the doctrine of predestination and election, Luther in his treatment of free will reproducing the Augustinian form of the doctrine in a strict manner. The predestination of Luther and Melanchthon proceeded, not from their conception of God, but rather from the doctrine of sin and grace. Melanchthon was less disposed than Luther to press the doctrine of absolute predestination, and, in his "synergistic" tendencies, laid increasing stress on human freedom, until he at length rejected the doctrine of absolute predestination. He was blamed by strict Lutheranism for yielding too much to Pelagianism. But the Lutheran "Formula of Concord," prepared in 1577, was not a very logical and consistent presentation of the case, for, opposed at points to Augustinianism, it fell back, in the end, on election in the Augustinian spirit. Or, to put the matter in another form, the "Formula of Concord" may be said to have held with Augustinianism, but to have differed by maintaining a universal call along with a particular election, and it rejected the decree of reprobation. Later Lutheranism adopted a moderate form of the doctrine, wherein predestination was often identified with prescience. But Lutheranism ought not, in strictness, to be identified, as is sometimes done, with the Arminian theory. The Lutheran doctrine of predestination was further developed by Schleiermacher, who emphasized the efficiency of grace, while adopting its universality in the Lutheran sense.

8. Predestination in Lutheranism

Arminianism, in its earliest assertion, maintained simply universal grace and conditional election. But in the five Articles it formulated its opposition to Calvinism, although Arminius does not appear to have been more than moderately Calvinistic, as we would account it. Arminius gave grace supreme place, and made it, when welcome, pass into saving grace. He made election depend on faith, which latter is the condition of universal grace. Arminianism rejects the so-called common grace of the predestination theory, and its effectual grace for the elect, for, in the Arminian view, saving grace can in no case be missed save by resistance or neglect. Arminianism holds the awakened human will to coöperate with Divine grace, in such wise that it rests with the human will whether the Divine grace is really accepted or rejected. It is the claim of Arminianism to do more justice than Calvinism to faith and repentance, as conditions of personal salvation, and precedent thereto. The Arminian standpoint admits the foreknowledge of God, but denies foreordination, though it must seem difficult to reduce the foreknowledge of God to such a bare knowledge of the future. But it is, of course, freely to be granted that foreknowledge in God, simply as knowledge, does not carry any causal energy or efficiency with it. But it may still be doubted whether the prescience of God can be nothing more fruitful and creative than such a position implies, and whether its relation to predestination may not be a more necessary one. The theory seems to fail of giving satisfactory account of the Divine activity in its relation to human activity, in the sphere of grace. The shortcoming of Arminianism lies in its failing also to do justice to the spirit of Scripture with its emphatic assertion of the doctrine of God as the one absolute will, which, in its expression, is the sole originative power of the universe. See also PROVIDENCE.

9. The Arminian View

Wesleyanism, or Methodist Arminianism, maintains, like Calvinism, the will of God to be supreme. But it distinguishes between the desires and the determinations of God. It takes Divine foreknowledge to precede the Divine volitions. It makes God's prescience purely intuitional, and regards that which He knows as nowise necessitated by such knowledge, a conception of God which differentiates the Wesleyan type of thought from Calvinism. God is held to have left events in the moral sphere contingent, in an important sense, upon the human will. Hence human probation is based upon this position, as to man's free choice. Influence of God upon man's will is postulated, for its right guidance and direction, but not in any coercive sense, as Augustinianism seems to Wesleyanism to imply. Thus it is hoped to preserve just balance, and maintain proper responsibility, between the Divine and the human factors in this spiritual coöperation.

10. Wesleyanism on Predestination

When we come to the present needs and values of the predestination doctrine, we have to remark the primal need of a thoroughly ethicized conception of God. The past few decades have witnessed a lessened interest in this doctrine, largely because of the increasingly ethical conceptions of Deity.

11. Present Needs and Values of the Doctrine

That is to say, the doctrine of the sovereignty of God's will has ceased to be taken, as often in the older presentations, as mere almightiness, or arbitrary and resistless will. Calvin expressly taught that no cause or ground but God's unconditioned will was to be sought; but he feebly tried to save Divine will from sheer omnipotence by saying that God is law to Himself; and the notion of sovereignty continued to be presented in ways quite absolute and irresponsible. But God we now regard as the absolute and eternal reason, no less than the supreme will, and as both of these in the one indivisible and absolute personality. We have passed from an abstract predestinationism to maintain God in living and ethical relations to the world and to man. Such an ethical sovereignty we hold to be necessary, over against that lax humanitarian spirit, which, in its recoil from the older Calvinism, invests the Deity with no greater powers of moral determination than may be implied in His love, when viewed as a mere golden haze of good will. See ELECTION; FOREORDINATION.

LITERATURE.—The relative works of Augustine, Aquinas, Zwingli, Calvin, Luther, Melanchthon, Arminius, Wesley, Rothe, Dorner, Luthardt; W. Cunningham, *The Reformers, and the Theology of the Reformation*, 1862; James Orr, art. "Calvinism," in Hastings, *Enc of Religion and Ethics;* and the various Histories of Christian Doctrine.

JAMES LINDSAY

PREËMINENCE, prē-em'i-nens: Superiority, esp. in noble or excellent qualities. The word stands for: (1) מוֹתָר, *mōthār*, "what is over and above," "excellence"; "Man hath no preëminence above the beasts" (Eccl **3** 19); (2) πρωτεύω, *prōteúō*, "to be first"; "That in all things he [=Christ] might have the preëminence" (Col **1** 18); (3) ὁ φιλοπρωτεύων, *ho philoprōteúōn*, is trd "who loveth to have the preëminence," lit. "who loveth to be first" (of Diotrephes, 3 Jn ver 9).

PREFER, prē-fûr': Does not always have the general meaning "to choose before another." In Ps **137** 6, it does have this sense and the two VSS agree; in Est **2** 9, RV has "removed" where AV has "preferred"; in Dnl **6** 3, "distinguished" takes its place; in Jn **1** 15.30, "become" is substituted for "preferred"; in ver 27, "preferred" drops out entirely; in Rom **12** 10, the VSS agree.

PREPARATION, prep-a-rā'shun: The concordances indicate that the word "preparation" occurs only twice in the OT, once in 1 Ch **22** 5, where it is used in the ordinary sense "to make preparation," and once in Nah **2** 3, "in the day of his preparation," both of them translating the same Heb root and requiring no special elucidation. In Eph **6** 15 the apostle speaks of the equipment of the Christian as including the "feet shod with the preparation of the gospel of peace," which means, according to Thayer, "with the promptitude and alacrity which the gospel produces."

The word occurs with technical significance (**"the Preparation"**) in the gospel narratives of the crucifixion, translating the Gr παρασκευή, *paraskeuḗ* (Mt **27** 62; Mk **15** 42; Lk **23** 54; Jn **19** 14.31.42). It is used as a technical term indicating the day of the preparation for the Sabbath, that is, the evening of Friday. This is its use in Jos, *Ant*, XVI, vi, 2, and presumably in the Synoptics. Later its use seems to have been extended to denote regularly the 6th day (Friday) of each week. So in *Did.*, viii and the *Martyrdom of Polycarp*, vii.

The addition of the phrase τοῦ πάσχα, *toú páscha*, "of the passover," in Jn **19** 14, and of the phrase "for the day of that sabbath was a high day," in **19** 31, seems to indicate that the author of the Fourth Gospel regarded the Passover as occurring on the Sabbath in the year of the crucifixion. This is clearly the natural interpretation of the words of John's Gospel, and if it were not for the seeming contradiction to the narrative of the Synoptics it is very doubtful whether any other interpretation would ever have been put upon them. This question is discussed in the articles on the date of the crucifixion and the Lord's Supper, and it will be necessary only to allude to it here.

It is possible that the phrase the "Preparation of the passover" in Jn **19** 14 may mean it was the preparation day (Friday) of the Passover week (see Andrews, *Life of Our Lord*, 451 ff; and most recently Zahn, *Das Evangelium des Johannes*, 1908, 637 ff). This method of harmonizing seems to the present writer to be forced, and it therefore seems wiser to give to the words of Jn **19** 14 their natural interpretation, and to maintain that, according to the author of the Fourth Gospel, the Passover had not been celebrated at the time of the crucifixion. There seems to be reason to believe that the ordinary view that the Lord's Supper was instituted in connection with the Passover, based upon the narrative in Mark (**14** 12 ff), does not have the unanimous support of the Synoptic Gospels.

LITERATURE.—In addition to references in the body of the article, the comms., esp. Plummer, *Cambridge Bible*, "St. John," Appendix A; Allen, *ICC*, "St. Matthew," 270–74; Godet, *Comm. on the NT; Gospel of St. John*, ET, New York, 1886, II, 378, 379; and the significant articles on the interpretation of Lk **22** 15.16 by Burkitt and Brooke, *Journal of Theological Studies*, IX, 569 ff, and by Box, ib, X, 106.

WALTER R. BETTERIDGE

PRESBYTER, prez'bi-tẽr, pres'bi-tẽr (πρεσβύτερος, *presbúteros*), **PRESBYTERY,** prez'bi-ter-i, pres'bi-ter-i (πρεσβυτέριον, *presbutérion*):

1. Words Used in the NT

This latter word occurs in the NT once (1 Tim **4** 14), so rendered in both AV and RV. But the original Gr occurs also in Lk **22** 66, in RV trd "the assembly of the elders," in AV simply "the elders"; and in Acts **22** 5, trd in EV "the estate of the elders"; in both of which occurrences the word might more accurately be trd "the presbytery," just as it is in 1 Tim **4** 14. Besides these three occurrences of the neuter sing. *presbuterion*, the masc. pl. *presbúteroi*, always trd "elders," is often used to indicate the same organization or court as the former, being applied earlier in NT history to the Jewish Sanhedrin (Mt **27** 1; **28** 12; Lk **9** 22; Acts **4** 5.8), and later in the development of the church to its governing body, either in general (Acts **15** 2.4.6.22 f), or locally (Acts **14** 23; **16** 4; **20** 17; 1 Tim **5** 17; Tit **1** 5, etc). It is sometimes used of the body, or succession, of religious teachers and leaders of the nation's past (Mt **15** 2; He **11** 2). The word "presbyter" has been contracted by later ecclesiastical usage into the title "priest," although in the NT they are by no means identical, but on the contrary are often explicitly distinguished (Mk **14** 43; Acts **23** 14).

2. Based on Synagogue Plan

The local synagogue of the Jewish church was under the care and control of a body of representative men called "the elders" (Lk **7** 3). Naturally the Christian church, beginning at Jerus and formed on the lines of the synagogue, took over the eldership into its own organization (Acts **11** 30; **15** 2; 1 Pet **5** 1, etc); so also in all the cities in which the missionary activities of the apostles made church organization necessary, the local synagogues readily suggested and supplied a feasible plan for such organization (Acts **14** 23; Tit **1** 5). The mother-church at Jerus, formed after the pattern of the synagogue, might well have offered to the churches formed elsewhere under apostolic preaching the only conceivable plan. We do not know from the NT passages how these elders were selected; we must infer that they were elected by the membership of the churches, as under the synagogue plan; they were then installed into their office by apostles (Acts **14** 23), or by apostolic helpers (Tit **1** 5), or by "the presbytery" (1 Tim **4** 14), or by both together (2 Tim **1** 6; cf 1 Tim **4** 14). So early as the Pauline letters the office of presbyter seems already to have borne the distinction of two functions: teaching and ruling (1 Tim **5** 17; cf Acts **20** 17.28; 1 Thess **5** 12.13; 1 Pet **5** 2).

3. Principle Found in the NT

In the NT history and epp. it does not appear that the various churches of a district were already organized into an ecclesiastical body known as "the presbytery," having some basis of representation from the constituent churches. But the absence of such mention is far from being final proof that such district organizations did not exist; little dependence can be placed on mere negative arguments. Moreover, the council of apostles and elders in Jerus, to which Paul and Barnabas appealed (Acts **15**), is positive evidence of the principle of representation and central authority. The various district organizations would quickly follow as administrative and judicial needs demanded; such development came early in the growth of the church, so early that it is unmistakably present in the post-apostolic age.

In Rev the 24 elders occupy a conspicuous place in the ideal church (Rev **4** 4.10; **5** 6, etc), sitting for those they represent, as an exalted presbytery, close to the throne of the Eternal One. "The four and twenty elders occupying thrones (not seats) around the throne are to be regarded as representatives of the glorified church; and the number, twice twelve, seems to be obtained by combining the number of the patriarchs of the OT with that of the apostles of the NT" (Milligan on Rev **4** 4 in *Expositor's Bible*).

4. In the Presbyterian Church

Presbytery is the court, or representative body, in the Presbyterian Church next above the Session of the local church. The Session is composed of the ruling elders, elected by the membership of a particular church, with the minister as moderator or presiding officer. The Presbytery is composed of all the ordained ministers, or teaching elders, and one ruling elder from the Session of each church in a given district or community. To it now, as in NT times (1 Tim **4** 14), is committed the power of ordination; as also of installation and removal of ministers. It has supervision of the affairs which are general to the churches in its jurisdiction, and the power of review in all matters concerning the local churches (see *Form of Gov., Presb. Church in U.S.A.*, ch x). The Presbytery elects the representatives composing the General Assembly, which is the highest court of the Presbyterian Church.

5. In Architecture

In ecclesiastical architecture the presbytery is that part of the church structure which is set apart for the clergy, usually the space between altar and apse; sometimes used of the whole choir space, but ordinarily the word is more restricted in its meaning. See further, Bishop; Church; Elder; Government.

Edward Mack

PRESENCE, prez′ens: In the OT nearly always the rendition of פָּנִים, *pānīm*, "face" (Gen **3** 8; Ex **33** 14 f; Ps **95** 2; Isa **63** 9, etc); occasionally of עַיִן, *'ayin*, "eye" (Gen **23** 11; Dt **25** 9; Jer **28** 1.11, etc); and in 1 K **8** 22; Prov **14** 7, "the presence of" represents the prep. נֶגֶד, *neghedh*, "before"; cf also Aram. קֳדָם, *ḳŏdhām*, in Dnl **2** 27 AV (RV "before"). In Gr, "presence" has an exact equivalent in παρουσία, *parousía*, but this word is rendered "presence" only in 2 Cor **10** 10; Phil **2** 12; RV Phil **1** 26 (AV "coming"). Elsewhere *parousia* is rendered "coming," but always with "presence" in the m. Otherwise in the NT "presence" represents no particular word but is introduced where it seems to suit the context (cf e.g. Acts **3** 13 AV and **3** 19). See Parousia.

Burton Scott Easton

PRESENT, prez′ent. See Gift.

PRESENTLY, prez′ent-li: The strict meaning is of course "at the present moment," "instantly," and the modern force "after a short interval" is due simply to the procrastinating habits of mankind; hence RV modifications of the AV use of the word into "immediately" (Mt **21** 19), "even now" (Mt **26** 53), and "forthwith" (Phil **2** 23). In Prov **12** 16, the uncertainty of the meaning (m "openly," Heb "in the day") has led to the retention of the AV word.

PRESIDENT, prez′i-dent (סָרַךְ, *ṣārakh*): Used only in Dnl **6** 2–7. Probably a Pers derivative from *sar*, "head," and the Aram. equivalent for Heb *shōṭēr*. The meaning is self-evident and refers to the appointment of Daniel by Darius to be one of the three princes who had rule over the satraps of the empire.

PRESS, pres: As a vb. is used in RV as a tr of no less than 13 Gr and Heb words (rather more in AV). All the RV uses are modern. In AV may be noted Wisd **17** 11, "pressed with conscience" (RV "pressed hard by"); 2 Macc **14** 9, "pressed on every side" (RV "surrounded by foes"); Acts **18** 5, "pressed in the spirit" (RV "constrained by"). As a noun, AV uses "press" in Mk **2** 4 for ὄχλος, *óchlos*, "crowd" (so RV). For **wine press** see Vine; Wine.

PRESSFAT, pres′fat (Hag **2** 16 AV, ERV "winefat," ARV "winevat"). See Wine.

PRESUME, prē-zūm′, **PRESUMPTUOUS**, prē-zump′tū-us, **PRESUMPTUOUSLY**, prē-zump′tū-us-li: "To presume" ("to take or go beforehand") is to speak or act without warrant or proudly. In the OT the words are for the most part the tr of זוּד, *zūdh*, and זִיד, *zīdh*, "to boil up" (as water), and derivatives; hence to act proudly, to speak unauthorizedly, etc (Dt **18** 20.22, of the prophet; Ex **21** 14; Dt **1** 43; **17** 12.13; Ps **19** 13, "presumptuous sins" [*zēdh*, "proud"]; cf Ps **86** 14; **119** 21, etc; Prov **21** 24, etc). Other words are *mālē'*, "to fill," "to be full" (Est **7** 5, "presume"); *'āphal*, "to lift oneself up" (Nu **14** 44); *b^eyadh rāmāh*, "with a high hand" (Nu **15** 30, RV "with a high hand"); in 2 Pet **2** 10 *tolmētḗs*, "bold," "daring," is tr^d "presumptuous," RV "daring"; in 2 Macc **3** 24; **5** 15 we have *katatolmáō; thrasús*, is rendered "presumption" in 2 Macc **5** 18, RV "daring deed."

W. L. Walker

PREVENT, prē-vent′ (קָדַם, *ḳādham;* προφθάνω, *prophthánō*, φθάνω, *phthánō*): "Prevent" occurs in AV in the literal but obsolete sense of "to come or go before," "to anticipate," not in the sense of "to hinder." It is the tr of *ḳādham*, "to be sharp," "to be in front," "to be beforehand" (2 S **22** 6.19, RV "came upon"; Job **3** 12, RV "receive"; **30** 27, "are come upon"; **41** 11, "first given"; Ps **18** 5.18, "came upon"; **21** 3, ARV "meetest"; **59** 10, ARV "meet"; **79** 8, ARV "meet"; **88** 13, "come before"; **119** 147.148, ARV "anticipated"; Isa **21** 14, "did meet"; Am **9** 10, ARV "meet"). In the NT *prophthanō*, with same meaning, is tr^d "prevent" (Mt **17** 25, "Jesus prevented him," RV "spake first to him"); *phthanō* (1 Thess **4** 15, "shall not prevent," RV "shall in no wise precede"). "Prevent" in the above sense occurs in Wisd **6** 13, RV "forestalleth" (*phthanō*); **16** 28, "we must prevent the sun to give thee thanks," RV "rise before."

W. L. WALKER

PREY, prā (בַּז, *baz,* טֶרֶף, *ṭereph,* שָׁלָל, *shālāl*): "Prey" is frequent in the OT, chiefly as the tr of *baz,* "spoil," "plunder" (Nu **14** 3.31; Dt **1** 39; Isa **10** 6, etc); of *ṭereph,* "prey of wild beasts," "torn thing" (Gen **49** 9; Nu **23** 24; Job **4** 11, etc); of *malḳō*^{a}*h,* "a taking" (Nu **31** 11, etc; Isa **49** 24.25); of *shālāl,* "spoil" or "booty" (Jgs **5** 30 *bis;* **8** 24.25; Isa **10** 2, etc). *Mahēr-shālāl-ḥāsh-baz* (RVm "The spoil speedeth, the prey hasteth") was the symbolical name given to a son of Isaiah (Isa **8** 1.3). "Prey" does not occur in the NT, but is found in the Apoc: 1 Esd **8** 77, "for our sins . . . . were given up . . . . for a prey" (*pronomḗ*); Jth **9** 4; **16** 5; 1 Macc **7** 47; Ecclus **27** 10 (*thḗra*); Jth **5** 24 (*katábrōma*).

In RV *shālāl* is generally tr^{d} "spoil" (Jgs **5** 30; **8** 24.25; Isa **10** 2, etc), while, conversely, "prey" (noun and vb.) is occasionally substituted for "spoil," "booty" (Nu **31** 32, etc). See BOOTY; SPOIL.

W. L. WALKER

PRICE, prīs: Represents various words in the OT; τιμή, *timḗ,* is the usual Gr word for "price" in the NT. "Of great price" is πολύτιμος, *polútimos,* in Mt **13** 46, and πολυτελής, *polutelḗs,* in 1 Pet **3** 4. The vb. occurs in Zec **11** 13 AV and ERV as "prised." The spelling "prized" in ARV and some edd of AV is due to a confusion with "prize." For "price of a dog" (Dt **23** 18 AV) see DOG.

PRICK, prik: As a noun (=any slender pointed thing, a thorn, a sting) it translates two words: (1) שֵׂךְ, *sēkh,* a "thorn" or "prickle." Only in Nu **33** 55, "those that ye let remain of them be as pricks in your eyes," i.e. "shall be a source of painful trouble to you." (2) κέντρον, *kéntron,* "an iron goad" for urging on oxen and other beasts of burden: "It is hard for thee to kick against the pricks" (AV of Acts **9** 5, where RV omits the whole phrase, following the best MSS, including ℵABCE; AV of Acts **26** 14, where RV has "goad," m "Gr 'goads' "), i.e. to offer vain and perilous resistance. See GOAD. As a vb. (="to pierce with something sharply pointed," "to sting"), it occurs once in its literal sense: "a pricking brier" (Ezk **28** 24); and twice in a figurative sense: "I was pricked in my heart" (Ps **73** 21); "They were pricked in their heart" (Acts **2** 37, κατανύσσω, *katanússō,* Vulg *compungo;* cf Eng. word "compunction").

D. MIALL EDWARDS

PRIEST, prēst (כֹּהֵן, *kōhēn,* "priest," "prince," "minister"; ἱερεύς, *hiereús,* ἀρχιερεύς, *archiereús;* for ἱερεὺς μέγας, *hiereús mégas,* of He **10** 21, see Thayer's *Lexicon,* s.v. ἱερεύς):

A priest is one who is duly authorized to minister in sacred things, particularly to offer sacrifices at the altar, and who acts as mediator between men and God. In the NT the term is applied to priests of the Gentiles (Acts **14** 13), to those of the Jews (Mt **8** 4), to Christ (He **5** 5.6), and to Christians (1 Pet **2** 9; Rev **1** 6). The office of priest in Israel was of supreme importance and of high rank. The high priest stood next the monarch in influence and dignity. Aaron, the head of the priestly order, was closely associated with the great lawgiver, Moses, and shared with him in the government and guidance of the nation. It was in virtue of the priestly functions that the chosen people were brought into near relations with God and kept therein. Through the ministrations of the priesthood the people of Israel were instructed in the doctrine of sin and its expiation, in forgiveness and worship. In short, the priest was the indispensable source of religious knowledge for the people, and the channel through which spiritual life was communicated.

I. Nature of the Priestly Office.—The Scriptures furnish information touching this point. To them we at once turn. Priesthood implies choice. Not only was the office of Divine institution, but the priest himself was Divinely appointed thereto.

1. Implies Divine Choice

"For every high priest, being taken from among men, is appointed for men in things pertaining to God. . . . . And no man taketh the honor unto himself, but when he is called of God, even as was Aaron" (He **5** 1.4). The priest was not elected by the people, much less was he self-appointed. Divine selection severed him from those for whom he was to act. Even our Great High Priest, Jesus Christ, came not into the world unsent. He received His commission and His authority from the fountain of all sovereignty. At the opening of His earthly ministry He said, "He anointed me. . . . . He hath sent me" (Lk **4** 18). He came bearing heavenly credentials.

It implies the principle of representation. The institution of the office was God's gracious provision for a people at a distance from Him, who needed one to appear in the Divine presence in their behalf. The high priest was to act for men in things pertaining to God, "to make propitiation for the sins of the people" (He **2** 17).

2. Implies Representation

He was the mediator who ministered for the guilty. "The high priest represented the whole people. All Israelites were reckoned as being in him. The prerogative held by him belonged to the whole of them (Ex **19** 6), but on this account it was transferred to him because it was impossible that all Israelites should keep themselves holy as became the priests of Jeh" (Vitringa). That the high priest did represent the whole congregation appears, first, from his bearing the tribal names on his shoulders in the onyx stones, and, second, in the tribal names engraved in the twelve gems of the breastplate. The Divine explanation of this double representation of Israel in the dress of the high priest is, he "shall bear their names before Jeh upon his two shoulders for a memorial" (Ex **28** 12.19). Moreover, his committing heinous sin involved the people in his guilt: "If the anointed priest shall sin so as to bring guilt on the people" (Lev **4** 3). The LXX reads, "If the anointed priest shall sin so as to make the people sin." The anointed priest, of course, is the high priest. When he sinned the people sinned. His official action was reckoned as their action. The whole nation shared in the trespass of their representative. The converse appears to be just as true. What he did in his official capacity, as prescribed by the Lord, was reckoned as done by the whole congregation: "Every high priest . . . . is appointed for men" (He **5** 1).

It implies the offering of sacrifice. Nothing is clearer in Scripture than this priestly function. It was the chief duty of a priest to reconcile men to God by making atonement for their sins; and this he effected by means of sacrifice, blood-shedding (He **5** 1; **8** 3). He would be no priest who should have nothing to offer. It was the high priest who carried the blood of the sin offering into the Most Holy Place and who sprinkled it seven times on and before the mercy-seat, thus symbolically covering the sins of the people from the eyes of the Lord who dwelt between the cherubim (Ps **80** 1). It was he also who marked the same blood on the horns of the altar of burnt offering in the Court of the Tabernacle, and on those of the golden altar, that the red sign of propitiation might thus be lifted up in the sight of Jeh, the righteous Judge and Redeemer.

3. Implies Offering Sacrifice

It implies intercession. In the priestly ministry of Aaron and his sons this function is not so expressly set forth as are some of their other duties, but it is certainly included. For intercession is grounded in atonement. There can be no effective advocacy on behalf of the guilty until their guilt is righteously expiated. The sprinkling of the blood on the mercy-seat served to cover the guilt from the face of God, and at the same time it was an appeal to Him to pardon and accept His people. So we read that after Aaron had sprinkled the blood he came forth from the sanctuary and blessed Israel (Lev **9** 22–24; Nu **6** 22–27).

4. Implies Intercession

II. The Two Great Priests of the OT.—These were Melchizedek and Aaron. No others that ever bore the name or discharged the office rank with these, save, of course, the Lord Jesus Christ, of whom they were distinguished types. Of the two, Melchizedek was the greater. There are two reasons why they are to be considered chiefs: first, because they are first in their respective orders. Melchizedek was not only the head of his order, but he had no successor. The office began and terminated with him (He **7** 3). The ordinary priests and the Levites depended for their official existence on Aaron. Apart from him they would not be priests. Second, the priesthood of Christ was typified by both. The office is summed up and completed in Him. They were called and consecrated that they might be prophecies of Him who was to come and in whom all priesthood and offering and intercession would find its ample fulfilment. In the Ep. to the He the priesthood of both these men is combined and consummated in Christ. But let it be noted that while He is of the order of Melchizedek He exercises the office after the pattern of Aaron. He perfects all that Aaron did typically, because He is the true and the real Priest, while Aaron is but a figure.

Melchizedek and Aaron

III. Priestly Functions and Character.—These are minutely prescribed in the Law. In the institution of the office the Lord's words to Moses were, "Take thou unto thee Aaron thy brother, and his sons with him, from among the children of Israel, that he may minister unto me in the priest's office" (Ex **28** 1 AV). Their duties were strictly religious. They had no political power conferred upon them. Their services, their dependent position, and the way in which they were sustained, i.e. by the free gifts of the people, precluded them from exercising any undue influence in the affairs of the nation. It is true that in process of time the high office degenerated, and became a thing of barter and sale in the hands of unscrupulous and corrupt men, but as originally appointed the priesthood in Israel was not a caste, nor a hierarchy, nor a political factor, but a Divinely appointed medium of communication between God and the people.

1. A Strictly Religious Order

The Heb priests in no wise interfered with the conscience of men. The Heb worshipper of his own

Dress of Egyptian Priests.

free will laid his hand on the head of his sacrifice, and confessed his sins to God alone. His conscience was quite free and untrammeled.

2. Priestism Denied

There were certain duties which were peculiar to the high priest. He alone could wear the "garments for glory and for beauty." To him alone it pertained to enter the Most Holy Place and to sprinkle the blood of the sin offering on the mercy-seat. To him alone it pertained to represent the congregation before the Lord as mediator, and to receive the Divine communications. He was to be ceremonially pure and holy. He must be physically perfect. Any defect or deformity disqualified a member of the priestly family from performing the duties of the office (Lev **21** 17–21). The Law spoke with the utmost precision as to the domestic relations of the high priest. He could marry neither a widow, nor a divorced woman, nor one polluted, nor a harlot; only a virgin of his own people, a Hebrew of pure extraction, could become his wife (Lev **21** 14.15). Nor was he to come in contact with *death.* He must not rend his clothes, nor defile himself, even for his father or his mother (Lev **21** 10.11). His sons might defile themselves for their kin, but the

3. The High Priest's Qualifications

high priest must not. For he was the representative of *life*. Death did not exist for him, in so far as he was a priest. God is the Ever-Living, the Life-Giving; and His priest, who had "the crown of the anointing oil of his God upon him," had to do with life alone.

4. Symbolism of Aaron's Rod

Adolph Saphir believes there is deep significance in the miracle of Aaron's rod that budded and bare almonds (Nu **17**). It was a visible sign of the legitimacy of Aaron's priesthood and a confirmation of it, and a symbol of its vitality and fruitfulness. The twelve rods of the tribes were dead sticks of wood, and remained dead; Aaron's alone had life and produced blossoms and fruit. It was the emblem of his office which correlated itself with life, and had nothing to do with death.

IV. Consecration of Aaron and His Sons (***Ex 29; Lev 8***).—The process of the consecration is minutely described and is worthy of a more detailed and careful study than can here be given it. Only the more prominent features are noticed.

(1) Both the high priest and his sons were together washed with water (Ex **29** 4). But when this was done, the high priest parted company with his sons. (2) Next, Aaron was arrayed in the holy and beautiful garments, with the breastplate over his heart, and the holy crown on his head, the mitre, or turban, with its golden plate bearing the significant inscription, "Holy to Jehovah." This was Aaron's investiture of the high office. (3) He was then anointed with the precious oil. It is noteworthy that Moses *poured* the oil on his head. When he anointed the tabernacle and its furniture he *sprinkled* the oil, but in Aaron's case there was a profusion, an abundance in the anointing (Ps **133** 2). (4) After the anointing of the high priest the appointed sacrifices were offered (Ex **29** 10 ff). Up to this point in the ceremony Aaron was the principal figure, the sons having no part save in the bathing. But after the offerings had been made the sons became prominent participants in the ceremonies, sharing equally with the high priest therein.

1. Symbolism of Consecration

(5) The blood of the offering was applied to the person of father and sons alike (Ex **29** 20.21). On the tip of the right ear, on the thumb of the right hand, and on the great toe of the right foot was the consecrating blood-mark set.

The significance of this action should not escape the reader. The whole person and career of the priest were thus brought under power of the blood. He had a blood-stained ear that he might hear and obey the Divine injunctions, that he might understand the word of Jeh and interpret it to the people. His will was brought into subjection to the will of His Lord that he might be a faithful minister in things pertaining to God. He had a blood-stained hand that he might execute, rightly and efficiently, the services of the sanctuary and the duties of his great office. He had likewise a blood-stained foot that he might walk in the statutes and commandments of the Lord blameless, and tread the courts of the Lord's house as the obedient servant of the Most High. Sacrificial blood, the blood of atonement, is here, as everywhere else, the foundation for saints and sinners, for priests and ministers alike, in all their relations with God.

2. Type and Archetype

The priests of Israel were but dim shadows, obscure sketches and drafts of the one Great Priest of God, the Lord Jesus Christ. Without drawing out at length the parallelism between the type and the archetype, we may sum up in a few brief sentences the perfection found in the priestly character of Christ: (1) Christ as Priest is appointed of God (He **5** 5). (2) He is consecrated with an oath (He **7** 20–22). (3) He is sinless (He **7** 26). (4) His priesthood is unchangeable (He **7** 23.24). (5) His offering is perfect and final (He **9** 25–28; **10** 12). (6) His intercession is all-prevailing (He **7** 25). (7) As God and man in one Person He is a perfect Mediator (He **1, 2**). See CHRIST, OFFICES OF, V.

LITERATURE.—Smith, *DB*; *HDB*; P. Fairbairn, *Typology of Scripture*, II; Soltau, *Exposition of the Tabernacle; the Priestly Garments and the Priesthood;* Martin, *Atonement;* A. B. Davidson, *Hebrews;* Moorehead, *Mosaic Institutions.*

WILLIAM G. MOOREHEAD

PRIEST, CHRIST AS. See CHRIST, OFFICES OF.

PRIEST, HIGH (הַכֹּהֵן, *ha-kōhēn*, **ὁ ἱερεύς**, *ho hiereús;* הַכֹּהֵן הַמָּשִׁיחַ, *ha-kōhēn ha-māshī^{a}ḥ*, **ὁ ἱερεὺς ὁ χριστός**, *ho hiereús ho christós;* הַכֹּהֵן הַגָּדֹל, *ha-kōhēn ha-gādhōl*, **ὁ ἱερεὺς ὁ μέγας**, *ho hiereús ho mégas;* כֹּהֵן הָרֹאשׁ, *kōhēn hā-rō'sh*, **ὁ ἱερεὺς ἡγούμενος**, *ho hiereús hēgoúmenos;* NT **ἀρχιερεύς**, *archiereús*):

I. Institution of the High-Priesthood.—Temples with an elaborate ritual, a priesthood and a high priest were familiar to Moses. For a millennium or two before his time these had flourished in Egypt. Each temple had its priest or priests, the larger temples and centers having a high priest. For centuries the high priest of Amon at Thebes stood next to the king in power and influence. Many other high-priesthoods of less importance existed. Moses' father-in-law was priest of Midian, doubtless the chief or high priest. In founding a nation and establishing an ecclesiastical system, nothing would be more natural and proper for him than to institute a priestly system with a high priest at the head. The records give a fairly full account of the institution of the high-priesthood.

High Priest (Egyptian).

1. The Family

Aaron, the brother of Moses, was chosen first to fill the office. He was called "the priest" (*ha-kōhēn*) (Ex **31** 10). As the office was to be hereditary and to be preserved in perpetuity in the family of Aaron (Ex **29** 9.29), he is succeeded by his son Eleazar (Nu **20** 28; Dt **10** 6), and he in turn by his son Phinehas (Nu **25** 11). In his time the succession was fixed (Nu **25** 12.13). In Lev **4** 3.5.16; **6** 22 he is called "the anointed priest." Three times in the Pent he is spoken of as "great priest" or "high priest" (Lev **21** 10; Nu **35** 25.28). The first of these passages identifies him with the anointed priest.

2. The Consecration

The ceremonies by which he was installed in his office are recorded in Ex **29** 29 ff. Seven days of special solemnities were spent. The first consecration was by Moses; it is not said who performed the others. There was special washing and anointing with oil (Ps **133** 2). Each new high priest must wear the holy garments, as well as be specially anointed (Lev **21** 10). Every day a bullock for a sin offering must be offered for atonement; the altar also must be cleansed, atoned for, and anointed, the high priest offering a sacrifice or *minḥāh* for himself (Lev **6** 24 ff).

3. The Dress

Besides the regularly prescribed dress of the priests, the high priest must wear the robe of the ephod, the ephod, the breastplate and the mitre or headdress (Lev **8** 7–9). The robe of the ephod seems to have been a sleeveless tunic, made of blue, fringed with alternate bells and pomegranates (Ex **28** 31–35; **39** 22–26). The ephod seemed to be a variegated dress of the four colors of the sanctuary, blue, purple, scarlet and fine linen interwoven with gold (Ex **28** 6–8; **39** 2–5). This distinguishing ephod of the high priest was fastened at the shoulders by two clasps of *shōham* stone, upon each of which was engraved the names of six tribes of Israel (Ex **28** 9–14; **39** 6.7). Over the ephod and upon his breast he wore the breastplate, a four-cornered *ḥōshen* suspended by little chains. Set in this in four rows were twelve precious stones, having engraved upon them the names of the twelve tribes of Israel. This breastplate must have contained a pocket of some kind inside, for in it were deposited the Urim and Thummim, which seemed to be tangible objects of some kind (Ex **28** 15–30; **39** 8–21). The mitre or headdress was of fine linen, the plate of the crown of pure gold, and inscribed upon it the words, "Holy to Jehovah" (Ex **28** 36–38; **39** 30.31). When entering the Holy of Holies he must be dressed wholly in linen, but in his ordinary duties in the dress of the priests; only when acting as high priest he must wear his special robes. See PRIEST.

4. Duties of the High-Priesthood

In addition to his regular duties as a priest, the high priest was to enter the Holy of Holies on the Day of Atonement (Lev **16** 3.15.33.34). He must also officiate at the ceremony of the two goats, when one is sent into the wilderness to Azazel, and the other slain to make atonement for the sanctuary (Ex **30** 10; Lev **16** 8–10). He alone could make atonement for the sins of the people, the priests and his own house (Lev **4** 3 ff; **9** 8 ff; **16** 6; Nu **15** 25). He must offer the regular meal offering (Lev **6** 14.15). He must share with the priests in the caring for the lamp that burned continually (Ex **27** 21). He must assist in arranging the shewbread (Ex **25** 30). When he carried the breastplate with the names of the tribes inscribed thereon he acted as mediator between Israel and God (Ex **28** 29). He alone could consult the Urim and Thummim before Jeh, and according to his decision Israel must obey (Nu **27** 21).

5. Special Regulations

An office so important required certain special regulations. He must be free from every bodily defect (Lev **21** 16–23). He must marry only a virgin of Israel, not a widow, nor a divorced woman, nor a profane one (Lev **21** 14). He must not observe the external signs of mourning for any person, and not leave the sanctuary when news came of the death of even a father or mother (vs 10–12). He must not defile himself by contact with any dead body, even father or mother (ver 11); and is forbidden to let his hair grow long or rend his clothes as a sign of mourning (ver 10). If he should bring guilt upon the people, he must present a special offering (Lev **4** 3 ff). Sins affecting the priesthood in general must be expiated by the other priests as well as himself (Nu **18** 1). He must eat nothing that died of itself or was torn by beasts (Lev **22** 8). He must wash his feet and hands when he went to the tabernacle of the congregation and when he came near to the altar to minister (Ex **30** 19–21). At first Aaron was to burn incense on the golden altar every morning when he dressed the lamps and every evening when he lighted them (Ex **27** 21), but in later times the common priests performed this duty. He must abstain from holy things during his uncleanness (Lev **22** 1–3), or if he should become leprous (vs 4.7). He was to eat the people's meat offering with the inferior priests in the holy place (Lev **6** 16). He must assist in judging the leprosy in the human body and garments (Lev **13** 2–59), and in adjudicating legal questions (Dt **17** 12). When there was no Divinely inspired leader, the high priest was the chief ruler till the time of David and again after the captivity. See PRIEST; PRIESTHOOD.

6. The Emoluments

The emoluments were not much greater than those of the priests in general. He received no more inheritance among the tribes than any other Levite, but he and his family were maintained upon certain fees, dues and perquisites which they enjoyed from the common fund. In Nu **18** 28 the priests were to receive a tithe of the tithe paid in to the Levites. Jos says this was a common fund (*Ant*, IV, iv, 4), but the high priest was probably charged with the duty of distributing it. In general the family of the high priest was well-to-do, and in the later period became very wealthy. The high priest and his family were among the richest people of the land in the time of Christ, making enormous profits out of the sacrifices and temple business.

7. Importance of the Office

The importance of the high priest's office was manifest from the first. The high priest Eleazar is named in the first rank with Joshua, the prince of the tribes and successor of Moses (Nu **34** 17 f; Josh **14** 1). He with others officiated in the distribution of the spoils of the Midianites (Nu **31** 21.26). His sins were regarded as belonging to the people (Lev **4** 3.22). He acted with Moses in important matters (Nu **26** 1; **31** 29). The whole congregation must go or come according to his word (Nu **27** 20 ff). His death was a national event, for then the manslayer was free to leave the City of Refuge (Nu **35** 25.28). He had no secular authority, but was regarded generally as the leading religious authority. Later, he became also the leading secular as well as religious authority.

II. History of the High-Priesthood in Israel.—

1. In the OT

In general the present writer accepts the historical records of the OT as true and rejects the critical views of a fictitious or falsified history. Such views have only subjective reasons to support them and are based upon a naturalistic evolutionary view of the development of Israel's religion. As Moses was the founder of the high-priesthood in Israel he anticipated a perpetuation of the office throughout the history (Dt **26** 3). The high priest appears frequently. Eleazar officiated with Joshua in the division of the land among the twelve tribes (Josh **14** 1). The law of the manslayer shows that he was an important personage in the life of Israel (Josh **20** 6). He seemed to have the power to distribute the offices of the priests to those whom he would, and poor priests would appeal to him for positions (1 S **2** 36). The office seems to have remained in the family of Eleazar until the days of Eli, when, because of the wickedness of his sons, the family was destroyed and the position passed into the family of Ithamar (1 S **2** 31–36). A descendant of that family officiated at Nob in the times of Saul, whose name was Ahimelech (1 S **21** 2; **22** 11). His son, Abiathar, escaped from the slaughter, and later seems to have succeeded his father and to have been chief priest throughout David's reign (1 S **22** 20–23; **23** 9; **30** 7). Zadok seems to have had almost equal privilege (2 S **8** 17; 1 Ch **18** 16; **24** 6 almost certainly by copyist's error, transpose Abiathar and Ahimelech; Mk **2** 26 may be based on this reading. See ABIATHAR, etc). Because he joined the party of Adonijah rather than that of Solomon, Abiathar was deposed and banished to Anathoth, where he spent the rest of his days (1 K **2** 26.27). Zadok was put in his place (ver 35). He seems to have been a descendant of Eleazar. Under Jehoshaphat, Amariah was high priest (2 Ch **19** 11) and was the leading authority in all religious matters. In the time of Athaliah, during the minority of Joash and almost his entire reign Jehoiada was high priest and chief adviser. He seems to have been the most influential man in the kingdom for more than half a century (2 K **11** 4 ff; **12** 2–16; 2 Ch **24** *passim*). Azariah officiated in the days of Uzziah and Hezekiah (2 Ch **26** 20; **31** 10); Urijah in the reign of Ahaz (2 K **16** 10–16), and the latter priest seems to have been a friend of Isaiah (Isa **8** 2). Hilkiah held the office in the days of Josiah when the Book of the Law was discovered (2 K **22** 4 f; **23** 4; 2 Ch **34** 9); Zephaniah in the time of Jeremiah (Jer **29** 25 f); Seraiah in the days of Zedekiah, who was put to death at Riblah by Nebuchadnezzar (2 K **25** 18 f; Jer **52** 24). At the time, mention is made of a priest of the second rank (2 K **23** 4; **25** 18) and Zephaniah fills that office (Jer **52** 24). It is doubtful whether this is the same Zephaniah mentioned in Jer **29** 25. This "second priest" was doubtless a deputy, appointed to take the high priest's place in case anything should prevent his performing the duties of the office. Lists of high priests are given in 1 Ch **6** 1–15; **6** 50–53. The first of these gives the line from Levi to Jehozadak who was carried away in the captivity under Nebuchadnezzar. The second traces the line from Aaron to Ahimaaz, and is identical so far with the first list.

There could have been no place for the functions of the high priest during the captivity, but the family line was preserved and Joshua the son of Jehozadak was among those who first returned (Ezr **3** 2). From this time the high priest becomes more prominent. The monarchy is gone, the civil authority is in the hands of the Persians, the Jews are no longer independent, and hence the chief power tends to center in the high-priesthood. Joshua appears to stand equal with Zerubbabel (Hag **1** 1.12.14; **2** 2.4; Zec **3** 1.8; **4** 14; **6** 11–13).

He is distinctly known as high priest (*ha-kōhēn ha-gādhōl*). He takes a leading part in establishing the ecclesiastico-civil system, particularly the building of the temple. In the vision of Zechariah (Zec **3** 1–5) Satan accuses the high priest who is here the representative proper of the nation. The consummation of the Messianic age cannot be completed without the cooperation of the high priest who is crowned with Zerubbabel, and sits with him on the throne (Zec **6** 13). The prophet also describes Joshua and his friends as "men of the sign," alluding to the coming Messiah under whom the sin of the land was to be taken away in one day (Zec **3** 9 f). The promise is made to Joshua that if he will walk in Jeh's ways and keep His house, he shall judge Jeh's house, i.e. Israel, keep His court and have a place to walk among those who stand before Jeh (**3** 7). He is anointed equally with the prince of the royal line, for the two sons of oil (**4** 14) almost certainly refer to the royal Zerubbabel and priestly Joshua who are to be joint inspirers of Israel in rebuilding the temple.

This exaltation of the high priest is very different from the state of things pictured by Ezekiel (Ezk **40–42**). In that picture no place is left for a high priest; the prince seemed to be the chief personage in the ecclesiastical system. Ezekiel's vision was ideal, the actual restoration was very different, and the institutions and conditions of the past were carried out rather than the visions of the prophet. In the time of Nehemiah, Eliashib was high priest (Neh **3** 1.20). For abusing his office by using a temple chamber in the interests of his family he was reprimanded (**13** 4–9). The list of high priests from Jeshua to Jaddua is given in Neh **12** 10. According to Jos (*Ant*, XI, viii, 5) Jaddua was priest at the time of Alexander the Great (332 BC), but it is practically certain that it was Jaddua's grandson, Simon, who was then priest (see W. J. Beecher, *Reasonable Bib. Criticism*, ch xviii). Thus is preserved the unbroken line from Aaron to Jaddua, the office still being hereditary. No essential change can be found since the days of Ezra. The Book of Ch, compiled some time during this period, uses the three names, *ha-kōhēn, ha-kōhēn hā-rō'sh, ha-kōhēn ha-gādhōl*. The word *nāghīdh* ("prince") is also used, and he is called "the ruler of the house of God" (1 Ch **9** 11). This seems to imply considerable power invested in him. Usually the Chronicler in both Ch and Neh uses the term "the priest."

The line of Eleazar doubtless continued until the time of the Maccabees, when a decided change took place. The Syrian Antiochus deposed Onias III and put his brother Jason in his place (174 BC), who was soon displaced by Menelaus. About 153 BC Jonathan the Hasmonean was appointed by King Alexander, and thus the high-priesthood passed to the priestly family of Joiarib (1 Macc **10** 18–21). Whether the family of Joiarib was a branch of the Zadokites or not cannot be determined. After the appointment of Jonathan, the office became hereditary in the Hasmonean line, and continued thus until the time of Herod the Great. The latter set up and deposed high priests at his pleasure. The Romans did the same, and changed so frequently that the position became almost an annual appointment. Though many changes were thus made, the high priest was always chosen from certain priestly families. From this group of deposed priests arose a class known as "chief priests." The anointing prescribed in the law of Moses was not always carried out in later times, and in fact was generally omitted. The Mish speaks of high priests who were installed in office simply by clothing them with their special robes (Schürer, II, i, p. 217, note 24).

2. In the NT

In NT times the high priest was the chief civil and ecclesiastical dignitary among the Jews. He was chairman of the Sanhedrin, and head of the political relations with the Rom government. It is not clear just how far he participated in the ceremonies of the temple. No doubt he alone entered the Holy of Holies once a year on the Day of Atonement, and also offered the daily offerings during that week. What other part he took in the work was according to his pleasure. Jos says that he officiated at the Sabbath, the New Moon and yearly festivals. The daily *minḥāh* (Lev **6** 12 ff) which he was required to offer was not always offered by the high priest in person, but he was required to defray the expense of it. This was a duty which, according to Ezekiel's vision, was to be performed by the prince. The Jews had many contentions with the Romans as to who should keep the garments of the high priest. When Jerus fell into the hands of the Romans, the robe of state also fell into their hands.

In the time of Christ, Annas and Caiaphas were high priests (Lk **3** 2), though, as appears later in the Gospel, Caiaphas alone acted as such. Annas had probably been deposed, yet retained much of his influence among the priestly families. For particulars see ANNAS; CAIAPHAS; JESUS CHRIST. These two were also the chief conspirators against Jesus. As president of the council Caiaphas deliberately advised them to put Jesus to death to save the nation (Jn **11** 51). He was also chairman of the council which tried and condemned Jesus (Mt **26** 57.58.63.65; Mk **14** 53.60.61.63; Lk **22** 54; Jn **18** 12–14.19.24.28). They were also leaders in the persecution of the apostles and disciples after Pentecost (Acts **4** 6; **5** 17.21); Saul sought letters from the high priest to Damascus to give him authority to bring any Christians he might find there bound to Jerus (Acts **9** 2). He presided at the council which tried Paul (Acts **22** 5: **23** 4). See PAUL, THE APOSTLE.

In the Ep. to the He the doctrine of the priesthood of Jesus is fully and carefully elaborated. Jesus is here called the great High Priest, as well as priest. The opening words of the Ep. contain the essential thought: "when he had made purification of sins" (**1** 3). The title of high priest is first introduced in **2** 17, "a merciful and faithful high priest in things pertaining to God"; also in **3** 1, "the Apostle and High Priest of our confession." Having thus fairly introduced his great theme, the writer strikes the keynote of his great argument: "Having then a great high priest," etc (**4** 14.15). From **4** 14 to **7** 28 the argument deals with the high-priestly work of Jesus. His qualifications are not only those which distinguish all priesthood, but they are also unique. He is named after the order of Melchizedek. The general qualifications are: (1) He is appointed by God to His office (**5** 1). (2) He is well fitted for the office by His experiences and participation in human temptations (**5** 2–6; **2** 18). (3) He undergoes a Divine preparation (**5** 8.9). The special qualifications of His priesthood are: It is after the order of Melchizedek (**5** 10). This is an eternal one (**6** 20); royal or kingly (**7** 1–3); independent of birth or family (ver 3); it is timeless (ver 8); superior to that of Levi (vs 4–10); new and different from that of Aaron (vs 11.12). It is also indissoluble (ver 16); immutable (ver 21); inviolable (ver 24). Thus with all these general and special qualifications He is completely fitted for His work (**7** 26). That work consists in offering up Himself as a sacrifice for the sins of the people (ver 27); entering within the veil as a forerunner (**6** 20); presenting the sacrificial blood in heaven itself (**8** 3; **9** 7.24); thus obtaining eternal redemption (**9** 12); ratifying the new covenant (vs 15–22). The result of this high-priestly work is a cleansing from all sin (**9** 23); a possibility of full consecration to God and His service (**10** 10); an ultimate perfection (**10** 14); and full access to the throne of grace (**10** 21.22). See CHRIST, OFFICES OF; PRIEST; PRIESTHOOD IN THE NT.

LITERATURE.—Articles on the priesthood in general, with references to the high priest in *HDB*, *HCG*, *EB*, *Jew Enc*, Kitto, Smith, Fallows, Schaff-Herzog, etc; no article on "High Priest" only. For the history, Breasted, *History of Egypt;* Schürer, *History of the Jewish People in the Time of Jesus Christ*, II, i, 207–99; Jos, *Ant*, XV, XVIII, XX. For works on the priesthood from the radical viewpoint, see Graf, S. I. Curtiss, Jost, Graetz, Kautzsch, Budde, Baentsch, Benzinger, Büchler, Meyer, Wellhausen. For a more moderate position see Baudissin, *Die Geschichte des alttestamentlichen Priesterthums untersucht.* For a more conservative position see A. Van Hoonacker, *Le sacerdoce lévitique dans la loi et dans l'histoire des Hébreux.* On the high-priesthood subsequent to the return from Babylon, see B. Pick, *Lutheran Church Review*, 1898, I, 127–41; II, 370–74; III, 555–56; IV, 655–64; and the comms. on the passages cited.

JAMES JOSIAH REEVE

PRIESTHOOD, prēst'hŏŏd:

1. Priesthood an Office
2. In the OT
3. Hereditary Priesthood
4. In the NT
5. Conclusions

LITERATURE

All worship is based on priesthood, for the priestly office is an essential part of salvation. Christianity itself has its glorious Priest, the Lord Jesus Christ, and it is through His one supreme offering that we are brought into saved relations with God and enjoy fellowship with Him. The priesthood of Christ and its mighty effects in sacrifice and intercession on behalf of the people of God are the chief and fundamental theme of the Ep. to the He.

1. Priesthood an Office

Priesthood is a real office, definite and specific. It is needful to insist on this fact, for the noble word "priest" has been misappropriated and misapplied, so that its intrinsic import has been impaired. There is a certain literary slang indulged in by some who talk of the "priests of science," "priests of art," and similar absurdities. The idea of priesthood, if priesthood is to have any definite meaning, can have no place in literature or science or art or in anything of the kind. For it belongs to the realm of grace, presupposing as it does sin and the Divine purpose to remove it. Hugh Martin writes that he "would as soon think of transferring the language of geometry and of algebra to botany and talk of the hypothenuse of a flower and the square root of a tree, or the differential coefficient of a convolvulus, as to speak of the priesthood of nature or letters." Priesthood is an office, embracing very specific duties and functions.

2. In the OT

Priesthood in some form appears to have existed from the earliest times, even from the beginning of the history of our race. In patriarchal times the office was held and its duties were discharged by those who occupied some sort of headship, and particularly by the father or the chief of the family and of the tribe. Thus Noah in his capacity of priest and in behalf of his household "builded an altar unto Jeh, and took of every clean beast, and of every clean bird, and offered burnt-offerings on the altar" (Gen **8** 20). Abraham offered the ram "for a burnt-offering in the stead of his son" (Gen **22** 13). In like manner Job offered burnt offerings for his children, and likewise by Divine direction for the three "comforters" when the great trial had passed (Job **1** 5; **42** 8). In these and the like instances there was priestly action no less certainly than in that of Aaron or of any regularly appointed priest in Israel. Melchizedek was "priest of God Most High" (Gen **14** 18). Isaac "builded an altar there and called upon the name of Jeh" (Gen **26** 25), as did Jacob (Gen **33** 20). In these cases priestly acts were performed by the patriarchs in their capacity as fathers of the family or heads of clans. From the beginning, priesthood with its acts of expiation and of worship was thus recognized as a Divinely instituted office. But in pre-Mosaic times there was no special class of priests recognized.

3. Hereditary Priesthood

Regular priestly succession in a single family was established by Moses (Ex **28** 1–3). From this point of time onward the priesthood in Israel was confined to the family of Aaron. No hereditary priesthood seems to have prevailed in patriarchal times. According to the Ep. to the He, Melchizedek, a priest of the highest rank, had neither predecessor nor successor in his great office. By Divine direction Moses designated the Aaronic family as the priestly family in Israel, and he prescribed the garments they should wear, the sacrifices they should offer both for themselves and for the congregation, their maintenance, their domestic relations, and their conduct toward their fellow-Hebrews.

In the appointment of the priesthood there is no trace of Egyp influence. Yet we know that Joseph married the daughter of the priest of On (Gen **41** 50). But this fact had no bearing on the selection of Israel's priestly family. The Aaronic priesthood had nothing in common with that of Egypt; it claimed to be of Divine origin, and its duties, functions and powers in no way contradict the claim. The witness of an Egyp archaeologist (Dr. M. G. Kyle) may be here introduced touching one essential element in the duties of the priestly office, viz. sacrifice: "The entire absence from the offerings of old Egyp religion of any of the great Pentateuchal ideas of sacrifice, substitution, atonement, dedication, fellowship, and indeed of almost every essential idea of real sacrifice, as clearly established by recent very exhaustive examination of the offering scenes, makes for the element of revelation in the Mosaic system by delimiting the field of rationalistic speculation on the Egyp side. Egypt gave nothing to that system, for it had nothing to give." As much may be said respecting the priesthood; Israel took little or nothing of its powers and functions from Egyp sources.

Although the office was limited to the Aaronic family, nevertheless in certain exigencies and emergencies others beside the regular priest offered sacrifices to the Lord and were accepted by Him. Thus did Gideon in a time of great straits in Israel (Jgs **6** 24.26); thus the men of Beth-shemesh (1 S **6** 14.15); the prophet Samuel (1 S **7** 9); David (2 S **6** 13.17); Elijah (1 K **18** 23.32–38), etc. The chosen people appear to have felt free to offer sacrifices and to engage in priestly functions when occasion required, until the central sanctuary was established on Mt. Moriah. When the Temple was built and dedicated, priestly action was confined to Jerus and to the regular priestly household. When Pharisaism, with its rigid legalism, with its intolerable burdens, became dominant, all liberty of worship and spontaneous service largely disappeared. The religious life of Israel stiffened into a dreadful monotony.

4. In the NT

All priesthood reaches its climax in that of the Lord Jesus Christ. It is because of the perfection of His priesthood that the office as represented by Melchizedek and Aaron was effective, and fulfilled the end for which it was appointed. The one answers to the other as type and antitype, as prediction and fulfilment. Christ's priesthood is opened to us in the Ep. to the He (**2** 14–18; **4** 14–16; **5** 1–10; **7** 9.10.18). Two fundamental truths touching His priesthood are made very prominent in the Ep. to the He. These are its *order* and its *duties*. By the order is meant the rank or grade of the Priest, and by the duties the various functions of His ministry. Christ's order as Priest is that of Melchizedek, not at all that of Aaron; He **7** makes this fact perfectly clear. Like Melchizedek, and infinitely above Melchizedek, He is Priest, having no predecessor in the great office, and no successor; herein He stands absolutely alone, peerless and perfect forever. He executes the duties or functions of it after the pattern of Aaron, as He **9** clearly exhibits. These two priesthoods, Melchizedek's and Aaron's, are gloriously accomplished in the person and work of Jesus Christ.

The point is raised and discussed with some keenness in our day, Did Christ execute the office of priest during His sojourn on earth, or does He exercise the office only in heaven? A full discussion of this interesting subject would be inappropriate. However, let it be noted (1) that the Lord Jesus was appointed a Priest no less certainly than was Aaron (He **5** 4.5). In the words, "Thou art my Son, this day have I begotten thee," there appears to be a reference both to His incarnation (Lk **1** 32; He **1** 5) and also to His resurrection (Acts **13** 33). In He **2** 17 we are told that it "behooved him in all things to be made like unto his brethren, that he might become a merciful and faithful high priest in things pertaining to God, to make propitiation for the sins of the people." The assumption of human nature was needful that He might be such a priest. John the Baptist saw this truth, and said, "Behold the Lamb of God, that taketh away the sin of the world" (Jn **1** 29).

There was certainly priestly action in His death. Twice we are told that He "offered up himself" (He **7** 27), "For this he did once for all, when he offered up himself." This strong term, "offered," is sacrificial and points to His death as an offering made for the sins of the people. His own action in it must not be overlooked; it was He Himself who presented the offering; He was not, therefore, a struggling victim, a martyr, who could not escape the doom that came upon Him—nay, He voluntarily offered Himself.

In He **9** 14 we find these significant words: "How much more shall the blood of Christ, who through the eternal Spirit offered himself without blemish unto God, cleanse your conscience from dead works to serve the living God?" It was as Priest that He made this stupendous offering, and this He did when still on earth. He was at once both sacrifice and priest. Never was He more active than when He offered Himself to God.

It is worth while to remind ourselves that the words employed in Scripture to express the act of His dying are never used to denote the death of a creature, a man. Matthew has, He "yielded up [dismissed] his spirit" (Mt **27** 50). John has, He "gave up his spirit" (Jn **19** 30); Mk **15** 37 and Lk **23** 46 both have the same words: He "gave up the ghost." He died, not because He was mortal as we are, nor because He could not deliver Himself, but because He gave Himself for our sins that we might be forgiven and saved (Jn **10** 17.18). The voluntariness of His offering is the very essence of His priestly atonement. See CHRIST, OFFICES OF, V; PRIESTHOOD IN THE NT.

5. Conclusions

Priesthood springs out of the deepest need of the human soul. Men universally feel that somehow they have offended the Power to whom they are responsible, to whom they must give account of their deeds. They long to appease their offended Lord, and they believe that one who is authorized and qualified to act in their behalf may secure for them the abrogation of penalty and the pardon they seek. Hence priesthood connects itself most closely with sin, with guilt and its removal. The heart craves the intervention and intercession on their behalf of one who has liberty of access to God, and whose ministry is acceptable. In short, the priest is the representative of the sinner in things pertaining to God. He is the mediator whose office it is to meet and satisfy the claims of God upon those for whom he acts, and who secures the pardon and the favor which the offender must have, if he is to enjoy fellowship with God. And this, and more than this, we have in our Great High Priest, the Lord Jesus Christ.

LITERATURE.—P. Fairbairn, *Typology of Scripture*, II; Soltau, *Exposition of the Tabernacle, the Priestly Garments and the Priesthood;* Martin, *Atonement;* Moorehead, *Mosaic Institutions*, art. "Priest."

WILLIAM G. MOOREHEAD

PRIESTHOOD IN THE NT:

1. The Jewish Priesthood
2. The Priesthood and High-Priesthood of Jesus Christ
3. The Priesthood of Believers

In the NT ἱεράτευμα, *hieráteuma* (1 Pet **2** 5.9), "priesthood," is not found with reference to the Jewish priesthood, but ἱερεύς, *hiereús*, and ἀρχιερεύς, *archiereús*, "high priest," frequently occur.

1. The Jewish Priesthood

As until the fall of Jerus the activities of the priests were carried on in careful accordance with the prescriptions of the OT, there naturally is nothing new or striking in the numerous NT references to their work. Perhaps the information of the greatest interest is found in Lk **1** 5–9 to the effect that Zacharias was of the course of Abijah, the 8th of the 24 courses into which the priests were divided (cf 1 Ch **24** 7–18), and that in these courses the priests divided their work by lot. In the Gospels the *archiereis* are mentioned oftener than are the *hiereis*, the power of the priesthood seeming to have been absorbed by a sort of priestly aristocracy. As under the political pressure of that time the office of high priest could seldom be retained until the death of the holder, there might even be several living at the same time who had for a longer or shorter time held this office which made a man the head of the nation, not only ritually, but also politically, since the high priest was ex officio presiding officer of the Sanhedrin. Not only would these ex-high priests naturally retain the title belonging to their former dignity, but probably the name had come to include as well other members of the same families or of families of equal position, so that it seems that "chief priests" is a more exact tr of *archiereis* than high priests. In the sing., however, the reference of *archiereus* is usually, if not invariably, to the individual who at the time given was holding the unique office of high priest. The word *hiereus* is of course employed in its ordinary signification on the rare occasions when reference is made in the NT to corresponding ministers of other religions, as to the priest of Zeus (Acts **14** 13) and also to Melchizedek (He **7** 1).

2. The Priesthood and High-Priesthood of Jesus Christ

Only in He is the activity of Jesus set forth as priestly and high-priestly, but in this Ep. great emphasis is laid on these aspects of His work. Interpreters seldom distinguish between these two aspects of His work, and it is plain that sometimes at least the author himself made no effort sharply to distinguish them. But certain considerations make it probable that they were not really confused or combined in the mind of the author himself. For example, it is to be noted that the priesthood of Jesus is declared to be after the order of Melchizedek, and consequently radically unlike that of the Levitical priests. On the other hand, the Aaronic high-priesthood is regarded as having been analogous to that of Jesus, so that in spite of its inferiority, comparison is frequently made with it. It is readily seen that the work of the high priest, both because of his entry into the Most Holy Place and because he bore the names of the children of Israel in the breastplate of judgment for a memorial before Jeh continually, far more suitably than that of the ordinary priests typified the atoning and intercessory work of Jesus (Ex **28** 12.15).

Attempting then to treat separately the priestly and high-priestly functions of Jesus, we note that most of what is said of the priestly functions is involved in the declaration that He is a priest after the order of Melchizedek, and this thought is handled in He **7** in such a way as to make plain the superiority of a priesthood after the order of Melchizedek, and thus to confirm the superiority of Christianity over Judaism, the great theme of the book. Historically the blessing bestowed upon Abraham and the reception of tithes from him prove the superiority of Melchizedek to Levi, and still more to the priestly descendants of Levi (**7** 4–10).

Further, Jesus became priest not on the ground of a "carnal commandment," i.e. in an order based on descent and inheritance, but by "the power of an endless life" (**7** 16), of which fact Melchizedek reminds us, since Scripture is silent alike as to his birth and his death. Again, unlike the Levitical priests, Christ is inducted into His office by the oath of God (**7** 20.21; cf Ps **110** 4). Finally, while the priests of the Levitical line were hindered from permanence in office by their death, Jesus holds His priesthood untransmitted and untransmissible (**7** 23.24). This discussion of the priesthood of Christ "after the order of Melchizedek" occupies almost all of ch **7**, but at ver 26 His high-priesthood is suddenly introduced, and after that point, while His work is more than once contrasted with that of the temple priests (**8** 4.5; **9** 6; **10** 11 f), no further reference is in any way made to Melchizedek.

After having twice merely given the title of high priest to Jesus (**2** 17; **3** 1), the writer of the Ep. to the He at **4** 14 begins a statement of the resemblance between Jesus and the Jewish high priest, such "as was Aaron," finding the resemblance to reside (1) in His Divine appointment to His work (**5** 4.5), (2) in His experience of suffering (**5** 7.8; cf **4** 15; **5** 2), and (3) in His saving work suggested by the sacrificial activity of the ordinary high priest (**5** 9), which, however, it far transcends in value and effect. But (4) later the work of the high priest and that of Jesus are contrasted as to place where done, the high priest going into the second tabernacle, i.e. the Holy of Holies (**9** 7), while Christ passes through the greater and more perfect tabernacle, "heaven itself" (**9** 11.24). A similar contrast is (5) drawn between the sacrifices respectively offered, the ancient sacrifices being the blood of goats and calves (**9** 12), Christ's being "himself" (**9** 14), "his own blood" (**9** 12), "the blood of Christ, who through the eternal Spirit offered himself without blemish unto God" (**9** 14). The author also accepts and urges without argument or even explanation (6) the truly sacrificial character of this self-immolation of Jesus. Nor is this fact nullified by the emphasis which once is laid on doing God's will in an antithesis copied from the Ps (**10** 5–9; cf Ps **40** 6 ff), for here the contrast drawn is not between sacrifice on one side and obedience on the other, but rather between the sacrifice of animals dying involuntarily and wholly unconscious of the sacrificial significance of their death, and the offering of Himself on the part of Jesus in intelligent purpose to carry out the will of God, by which will the body of Jesus Christ is the only acceptable offering (**10** 10). Further the author urges (7) the actual effectiveness of Christ's work, his argument being that it would already have been repeatedly performed if this single offering had not been sufficient for all time, "once for all" (**7** 27; **9** 26). Finally is asserted (8) the intercessory work of Christ, which, though not explained, seems to be a figurative presentation of his idea that men are blessed because Christ died, i.e. that this was an indispensable condition of God's manifestation of His merciful love, and that the grace consequent on the death of Christ does not merely grow out of a fact, but that the Divine love and providence for believers are exercised, neither automatically or impersonally, but in virtue of a constant personal sympathy for varying temptations and needs, a sympathy intensified by the earthly experience, temptation, suffering of Him who had been and is, not only the Divine Son, but also the Son of Man. Thus the salvation of the believer is certain and complete, and the priestly and high-priestly work of Jesus reaches its consummation.

The priesthood of believers is an idea which finds formal expression less frequently in the NT than has been the case in Protestant theology. But it does not follow that there has been a corresponding divergence from the thought of the apostles. It only shows that a thought which according to apostolic conception was one of the invariable privileges of every Christian, and which found, if not constant, yet sufficiently clear expression in this figurative fashion, has come, in consequence of errors which have developed, to receive in the controversies of later centuries stronger emphasis than it did at first. It may well be noted first that this conception of the priesthood of believers, standing by itself, is in no way related to the various priestly activities which are also figuratively attributed to them. The writer of the Ep. to the He, who does not speak of the priesthood of believers, knowing no Christian priesthood but that of Jesus Himself, yet calls "praise," "to do good and to communicate," sacrifices (**13** 15.16). So Paul bids the Romans present their bodies "a living sacrifice" (Rom **12** 1), and Peter calls Christians "a holy priesthood, to offer up spiritual sacrifices" (1 Pet **2** 5). But this **figurative** usage is entirely distinct from the subject of the present paragraph. Also the conception of the Christian priesthood never in the NT attaches itself merely to the ministry of the Christian church, whatever may be held as to its orders or tasks. In no sense has the church or any church an official priesthood. Nor is it any part of the NT conception of the priesthood of believers that any individual should act in any respect for any other. Though the intercessory supplication of believers in behalf of other persons has of late often been represented as a priestly act, as being, indeed, that activity which is essential to any real priesthood of believers, the NT thought is quite different, and is to be thus conceived: In ancient times it was held that men in general could not have direct access to God, that any approach to Him must be mediated by some member of the class of priests, who alone could approach God, and who must accordingly be employed by other men to represent them before Him. This whole conception vanishes in the light of Christianity. By virtue of their relation to Christ all believers have direct approach to God, and consequently, as this right of approach was formerly a priestly privilege, priesthood may now be predicated of every Christian. That none needs another to intervene between his soul and God; that none can thus intervene for another; that every soul may and must stand for itself in personal relation with God—such are the simple elements of the NT doctrine of the priesthood of all believers. (Consult treatises on NT theology, and comms. on the Ep. to the Hebrews.)

3. The Priesthood of Believers

David Foster Estes

PRIESTS AND LEVITES (כֹּהֵן, *kōhēn*, "priest"; nothing is definitely known as to the origin of the word; לֵוִי, *lēwī*, "Levite," on which see Levi):

In some Minaean inscriptions found at El-'Olâ, dating back about 1200–800 BC (Hommel in Hilprecht, *Explorations in Bible Lands*, 719), certain "priests and priestesses of the god Wadd are designated by the term *lawî*, fem. *lawî'at*" (op. cit., 749). It is not known whether this is due to Israelitish influence.

I. Different Views of the History.—There are great divergences of opinion among modern writers as to the true course of history and the dating of the different documents. It will therefore be best to sketch these views in rough outline, and then give the evidence of the various authorities, together with the reasons that in each case arise naturally from the consideration of that evidence.

1. The Old View

The old belief was that the whole of the Pentateuchal laws were the work of Moses, that the account of the subsequent history given in the Books of Ch was correct, that Ezekiel's vision, if taken literally, could not be reconciled with the other known facts and was inexplicable, and that in the case of all other discrepancies harmonistic explanations should be adopted.

2. The Graf-Wellhausen View

The modern critical school have traversed every one of these doctrines. The Chronicler is declared to be in constant and irreconcilable conflict with the older authorities, harmonistic explanations are uniformly rejected, the Pent is denied to Moses and split up into a variety of sources of different ages, and Ezk gains a place of honor as representing a stage in a continuous and normal development. The subject is thus inextricably linked with the Pentateuchal problem, and reference must be made to the art. PENTATEUCH for an explanation of the supposed documents and a consideration of the analysis with its nomenclature. On the other hand the present article and the art. SANCTUARY (q.v.) explain and discuss the most widely held theory of the historical development into which the history of the supposed Pentateuchal sources has been fitted.

The dominant theory is that of Wellhausen. According to this, "Levite" was originally a term denoting professional skill, and the early Levites were not members of the tribe of Levi, but professional priests. Anybody could sacrifice. "For a simple altar no priest was required, but only for a house which contained a sacred image; this demanded watching and attendance" (Wellhausen, *Prolegomena*, 130). The whole Levitical Law was unknown and the distinction between priests and Levites unheard of. There were a few great sanctuaries and one influential priesthood, that of Shiloh (afterward at Nob). With the monarchy the priesthood became more important. The royal priests at Jerus grew in consequence and influence until they overshadowed all the others. Dt recognized the equal priestly right of all Levites, and Josiah's reformation placed the sons of Zadok, who were the priests of Jerus and not descendants of Aaron, in a position of decisive superiority. Then Ezk drew a new and previously unknown distinction between "the priests the Levites, the sons of Zadok" who are "keepers of the charge of the altar," and the other Levites who were made "keepers of the charge of the house" as a punishment for having ministered in the high places. The PC takes up this distinction and represents it as being of Mosaic origin, making of the sons of Zadok "sons of Aaron." "In this way arose as an illegal consequence of Josiah's reformation, the distinction between priests and Levites. With Ezk this distinction is still an innovation requiring justification and sanction; with the PC it is a 'statute forever,' although even yet not absolutely undisputed, as appears from the priestly version of the story of Korah's company. For all Judaism subsequent to Ezra, and so for Christian tradition, the PC in this matter also has been authoritative. Instead of the Deuteronomic formula 'the priests the Levites,' we henceforward have 'the priests and the Levites,' particularly in Ch" (op. cit., 147). From that time onward the priests and Levites are two sharply distinguished classes. It is an essential part of this theory that the Chronicler meant his work to be taken as literal history, correctly representing the true meaning of the completed law. See CRITICISM.

3. Mediating Views

There have been various attempts to construct less thoroughgoing theories on the same data. As a rule these views accept in some form the documentary theory of the Pent and seek to modify the Wellhausen theory in two directions, either by attributing earlier dates to one or more of the Pentateuchal documents—esp. to the PC—or else by assigning more weight to some of the statements of Ch (interpreted literally). Sometimes both these tendencies are combined. None of these views has met with any great measure of success in the attempt to make headway against the dominant Wellhausen theory, and it will be seen later that all alike make shipwreck on certain portions of the evidence.

4. An Alternative View

The independent investigations on which the present article is based have led the writer to a view that diverges in important particulars from any of these, and it is necessary to state it briefly before proceeding to the evidence. In one respect it differs from all the rival schemes, not merely in result, but also in method, for it takes account of versional evidence as to the state of the texts. Subject to this it accepts the Mosaic authenticity of all the Pentateuchal legislation and the clear and consentient testimony of the Law and the Prophets (i.e. of the two earlier and more authoritative portions of the Heb Canon), while regarding Ch as representing a later interpretation, not merely of the history, but also of the legal provisions. In outline the story of the priesthood is then as follows: Moses consecrated Aaron and his sons as the priests of the desert tabernacle. He purified the rest of the tribe of Levi as a body of sacred porters for the period of wanderings, but in the legislation of Nu he made no provision whatever for their performing any duties after the sanctuary obtained a permanent location. At the same time he gave a body of priestly teaching requiring for its administration in settled conditions a numerous and scattered body of priests, such as the house of Aaron alone could not have provided immediately after the entry into Canaan. To meet this, Dt—the last legislative work of Moses—contains provisions enlarging the rights and duties of the Levites and conferring on them a priestly position. The earlier distinction was thus largely obliterated, though the high-priestly dignity remained in the house of Aaron till the time of Solomon, when it was transferred from the house of Eli to that of Zadok, who, according to Ezekiel's testimony, was a Levite (but see below, IV, 1). So matters remained till the exile, when Ezekiel put forward a scheme which together with many ideal elements proposed reforms to insure the better application of the Mosaic principle of the distinction between holy and profane to greatly altered circumstances. Taking his inspiration from the wilderness legislation, he instituted a fresh division in the tribe of Levi, giving to the sons of Zadok a position similar to that once held by the sons of Aaron, and degrading all other Levites from the priesthood conferred on them by Dt to a lower rank. The duties now assigned to this class of "keepers of the charge of the house" were never even contemplated by Moses, but Ezekiel applies to them the old phrases of the Pent which he invests with a new significance. As a result of his influence, the distinction between priests and Levites makes its appearance in post-exilic times, though it had been unknown to all the writers of the second division of the Heb Canon. At the same time a meaning was read into the provisions of the Law which their original author could not have contemplated, and it was this interpretation which is presented (at any rate to some extent) in Ch, and has given us the current tradition. Many of the Chronicler's statements are, however, not meant to be taken literally, and could not have been so taken by his original public.

II. The Data of P in the Pentateuch.—To arrive at an objective conclusion it is necessary, in the first instance, to examine the facts without such bias as any view put forward by any other author, ancient or modern, sacred or profane, might impart. Every legislator is entitled to be judged on his own language, and where he has, so to speak, made his own dictionary, we are compelled to read his meaning into the terms used. The very first of the material references to the Levites drives this truth home. "But appoint thou the Levites over the tabernacle of the testimony, and over all the furniture thereof" (Nu **1** 50). It is necessary to consider whether such expressions are to be read in a wide or a narrow sense. We learn from **18** 3 that death would be the result of a Levite's touching any of these vessels, and it therefore appears that these words are meant to be construed narrowly. "They shall bear the tabernacle, and all the furniture thereof; and they shall minister unto it," are the next words (**1** 50); but yet we read later of the Kohathites who were to bear it that "they shall not touch the sanctuary, lest they die" (**4** 15). This shows that the service in question is strictly limited to a service of porterage *after* the articles have been wrapped up by Aaron and his sons. By no possibility could it include such a task as cleaning the vessels. It is then further directed that the Levites are to take down and set up the dwelling and camp round about it. All these are desert services and desert services only. Then we read that "the Levites shall keep the charge of the tabernacle [dwelling] of the testimony." This concludes the first material passage (Nu **1** 50–53). The other passages of Nu only amplify these directions; they never change them. But some phrases are used which must be more particularly considered.

1. The Levites

(1) *Technical phrases.*—We hear that the Levites are "to serve the service of the tent of meeting," and this looks as if it might refer to some general duties, but the context and the kindred passages always forbid this interpretation. Nu **7** 5 ff is an admirable instance. Six wagons are there assigned to the Levites for this service, two to the Gershonites and four to the Merarites. "But unto the sons of Kohath he gave none, because the service of the sanctuary belonged unto them; they bare it upon their shoulders." Here service is transport and nothing else. Again we read of the charge of the Levites in the tent of meeting, e.g. **4** 25 f. If we look to see what this was, we find that it consisted of transporting portions of the tent that had been packed up. The "in" of EV does not represent the meaning of the Hebrew fairly; for the context makes it clear that the legislator means "in respect to." "But they shall not go in to see the sanctuary even for a moment, lest they die" (**4** 20). In Eng. idiom we cannot speak of the transport of portions of a dismantled tent as service *in* that tent. One other expression requires notice, the phrase "keep the charge" which is distinguished in **8** 26 from "doing service." The exact meaning cannot be determined. It appears to denote something kindred to service, but of a less exacting nature, perhaps the camping round the tent and the guardianship of the articles on the march. We shall see hereafter by comparison with other books that in P it does not bear the same meaning as elsewhere.

(2) *Other legal provisions.*—The Levites were to act under the orders of Aaron and his sons, who were to assign to each man his individual functions (Nu **3, 4,** etc). They were to undergo a special rite of purification (Nu **8**), but not of consecration. They were taken in place of the firstborn (Nu **3**). The age for beginning service is given in ch **4** as 30 years, but in **8** 24 as 25, if the text be sound. The age for ceasing to serve was 50. In many passages the VSS suggest that a good many phrases are textually doubtful, and it is probable that when a critical text of the Pent is formed on scientific principles, a good many superfluous expressions will be found not to be original; but there is no reason to suppose that any real difference in the meaning of the passages would be revealed by such a text.

The story of Korah is easily misunderstood. It appears from Nu **16** 3 that his real object was to put himself on an equality with Moses and Aaron, and this is the "priesthood" referred to in ver 10. Nu **18** reinforces the earlier passages. It is noteworthy as showing that in the conception of the legislator the Levites were not to come near the vessels or the altar (ver 3). The penalty is death for both Levites and priests.

(3) *Contrast with Ezk and Ch.*—The impression as to the meaning of P which may be gathered from an examination of its statements is powerfully reinforced when they are tested by reference to Ezk and Ch. Ezk **44** 9–14 seems to demand of the Levites some service as gatekeepers, the slaying of burnt offering and sacrifice for the people and a keeping of "the charge of the house, for all the service thereof," which in the light of vs **7** f appears to mean in his terminology, not a service of transport, but an entry into the house and the performance of certain duties there. P, on the contrary, knows nothing of gatekeepers, regards the slaying of the burnt offering and sacrifice as the duty of the individual sacrificant (Lev **1, 3**), and—if, as Wellhausen thinks, it refers to the temple—it would have visited with death a Levite who was present in the places in which Ezk requires him to minister. Similarly with the Chronicler. For instance, he speaks of the Levites being 'for the service of the house . . . . in the courts and over the chambers, and over the cleansing of every holy thing' (1 Ch **23** 28), but P knows nothing of any chambers, would not have allowed the Levites to touch (much less clean) many of the holy things, and regarded service simply as porterage. In 1 Ch **23** 31 the Levites are to offer burnt offerings on certain occasions; in P their approach to the altar would have meant death both to themselves and the priests (Nu **18** 3). Other instances will be found in *PS*, 238 f.

(4) *What the foregoing proves.*—In view of these facts it is impossible to hold that the Levites in P represent a projection of the Levites of the second temple or any post-Mosaic age into the desert period. To P they are a body of sacred porters. The temple of course could not be carried about, and it cannot be held that in this respect the legislation mirrors later circumstances. "Secondly, the net result of such a scheme would be to create a body of Levites for use *during the period of wanderings and never thereafter.* As soon as the desert age was over the whole tribe would find their occupation gone. How can we conceive that any legislator deliberately sat down and invented such a scheme centuries

after the epoch to which it relates, well knowing that in so far as his scheme purported to be a narrative of events it was fictitious from beginning to end, and in so far as it might be regarded as a legislation applicable to his own or any future day, there was not a line in it that could conceivably be put into practice? If any theorist can be conceived as acting in this way, how are we to suppose that his work would meet with acceptance? . . . . Thirdly, P neither embodies the views of Ezk nor finds an accurate reflection in Ch. The facts are such as to enable us to say definitely that P is not in line with them. It is impossible to assume that he appointed the death penalty for certain acts if performed by Levites because he really wished the Levites to perform those acts" (*PS*, 241 f).

2. Aaron and His Sons

P also speaks of Aaron the priest and the sons of Aaron the priest. It is doubtful whether the expression "the sons of Aaron the priests," which occurs frequently in the MT, is ever original; the Massoretic expression is nowhere supported by all the authorities. "The phrase 'Aaron the high priest' is entirely unknown to P. Where the high priest's name is given the only qualifying apposition possible in his usage is 'the priest.'" Aaron and his sons, unlike the Levites, were consecrated, not merely purified.

At this point two features only of the legislation need be noticed: the inadequacy of the staff to post-conquest conditions and the signs of date. For example, the leprosy laws (Lev **13** f) postulate the presence of priests to inspect and isolate the patient. "Remembering that on the critical theory P assumes the capital at Jerus as self-evident, we must ask how such provisions were to work after the conquest. During the desert period nothing could have been simpler, but what was to happen when the Israelites dwelt all over Canaan from Beersheba to Dan?" (*PS*, 246). The difficulty is immensely increased if we postulate an exilic or post-exilic date, when the Jewish center of gravity was in Babylonia and there were large colonies in Egypt and elsewhere. And "What are we to say when we read of leprous garments (Lev **13** 47 ff)? Was a man to make the pilgrimage from Babylonia to Jerus to consult a priest about a doubtful garment? And what about the leper's offerings in ch **14**? Could they conceivably have been meant to apply to such circumstances?" (*PS*, 247). The case is no better with the law of leprous houses, which is expressed to apply to the post-conquest period (Lev **14** 33-53). The notification to the priest and his inspections require a priesthood scattered all over the country, i.e. a body far more numerous than the house of Aaron at the date of the conquest. Such instances could easily be multiplied from the legislation; one more only will be cited on account of its importance to the history of the priesthood. According to Lev, the individual sacrificant is to kill the victims and flay the burnt offerings. How could such procedure be applied to such sacrifices as those of Solomon (1 K **8** 63)? With the growth of luxury the sacrifices would necessarily become too large for such a ritual, and the wealthy would grow in refinement and object to performing such tasks personally. This suggests the reason for later abuses and for the modifications of Ezk and the representations of the Chronicler.

Result of the evidence.—Thus the evidence of P is unfavorable alike to the Wellhausen and the mediating views. The indications of date are consistently Mosaic, and it seems impossible to fit the laws into the framework of any other age without reading them in a sense that the legislator can be shown not to have contemplated. On the other hand P is a torso. It provides a large body of Levites who would have nothing to do after the conquest, and a *corpus* of legislation that could not have been administered in settled conditions by the house of Aaron alone.

III. The Other Portions of the Pentateuch.—In Ex **19** 22.24 we read of priests, but a note has come down to us that in the first of those verses Aquila had "elders," not "priests," and this appears to be the correct reading in both places, as is shown by the prominence of the elders in the early part of the chapter. In Hebrew the words differ by only two letters. It is said by Wellhausen that in Ex **33** 7-11 (E) Joshua has charge of the ark. This rests on a mistranslation of Ex **33** 7, which should be rendered (correcting EV), 'And Moses used to take *a* [or the] tent and pitch it *for himself* without the camp.' It is inconceivable that Moses should have taken the tent of the ark and removed it to a distance from the camp for his private use, leaving the ark bared and unguarded. Moreover, if he had done so, Joshua could not have been in charge of the ark, seeing that he was in this tent while the ark (*ex hypothesi*) remained in the camp. Nor had the ark yet been constructed. Nor was Joshua in fact a priest or the guardian of the ark in E: (1) in the Book of Josh E knows of priests who carry the ark and are quite distinct from Joshua (**3** ff); (2) in Dt **31** 14 (E) Joshua is not resident in the tent of meeting; (3) in E Aaron and Eleazar are priests (Dt **10** 6), and the Levitical priesthood is the only one recognized (Dt **33** 10); (4) there is no hint anywhere of Joshua's discharging any priestly duty whatsoever. The whole case rests on his presence in the tent in Ex **33** 7-11, and, as shown in the art. PENTATEUCH (q.v.), this passage should stand after Ex **13** 22.

Then it is said that in Ex **4** 14; Jgs **17** 7, "Levite" denotes profession, not ancestry. In the latter passage the youth whom Micah made a priest was of Levitical descent, being the grandson of Moses (Jgs **17** 13), and the case rests on the phrase, "of the family of Judah." Neither of the Septuagintal translations had this text (Field, *Hexapla*, ad loc.), which therefore cannot be supported, since it cannot be suggested that Moses belonged to the tribe of Judah. As to Ex **4** 14, the phrase "Aaron thy brother the Levite" is merely an adaptation of the more usual, "Aaron, son of Amram, the Levite," rendered necessary by the fact that his brother Moses is the person addressed. The Wellhausen theory here is shown to be untenable in *PS*, 250 and *RE*[3], XI, 418.

Ex **32** 26-29 foreshadows the sacred character of Levi, and Dt **10** 6 (E) knows the hereditary Aaronic priesthood. In D the most important passage is Dt **18** 6-8. In ver **7** three Septuagintal MSS omit the words "the Levites," and if this be a gloss, the whole historic sense of the passage is changed. It now contains an enactment that any Levite coming to the religious capital may minister there "as all his brethren do, who stand there," etc, i.e. like the descendants of Aaron. "The Levites" will then be the explanation of a glossator who was imbued with the latest post-exilic ideas, and thought that "his brethren" must mean those of his fellow-Levites who were not descended from Aaron. The passage is supplemented by **21** 5, giving to the Levites judicial rights, and **24** 8 assigning to them the duty of teaching the leprosy regulations. Together with **33** 10 (E), 'they shall teach thy judgments to Jacob and thy law to Israel: they shall put incense in thy nostrils and whole burnt-offering on thine altar,' these passages complete the provisions of P in giving to the Levites an occupation in place of their transport duties, and providing the necessary staff for administering the legislation when the Israelites were no longer massed together in a single camp, but scattered over the country. We shall see in the next section that this view of the meaning of the Law was taken by every writer of the second part of the Canon who touches on the subject. Everywhere we are confronted with the legitimacy of a Levitical priesthood; nowhere is there any mention of an exclusive Aaronic right. Smaller points which cannot be discussed here are examined in *PS*. It only remains to notice that these provisions fully explain the frequent Deuteronomic locution, "the priests the Levites." One other remark must be made. Though it is not expressly stated, we may assume that consecration would be necessary in the case of any Levite acting on the provisions of Dt **18** 6–8, and was not mentioned because in Heb antiquity it went without saying that every priest must be consecrated (cf Jgs **17**).

IV. From Moses to Malachi.—Josh adds but little to our information. In **18** 7 the priesthood is called the inheritance of the Levites, and it is singular that the Wellhausen critics attribute this to a priestly redactor, though such a writer should *ex hypothesi* have been jealous to withhold the priesthood from the Levites. It is very interesting to find that in Josh **3**, **4**, all the different critical documents speak in exactly the same terms of "the priests that bare the ark." The priestly writer ought, on the Wellhausen theory, to have said "the Levites." The expression "the priests the Levites" is found alternating with the expression "the priests." All this points to the construction put upon the provisions of the Law in the preceding section, and finds fresh confirmation in Jgs, where we see Micah rejoicing at having a Levite as a priest (**17** 13), thus showing that the sacred character of the tribe was recognized in the earliest post-Mosaic times. The lay sacrifices in this and the following books are explained under SANCTUARY; SACRIFICE (q.v.).

1. The Sources Other than Ezekiel

The period of the early kings shows us kings blessing the people (e.g. 2 S **6** 18). It is claimed that this is the priestly blessing, but without evidence, and there seems no more reason to see special priestly rights here than in David's blessing his household (2 S **6** 20), or the frequent blessings of the Bible (e.g. Gen *passim*, esp. "in thee will Israel bless," Gen **48** 20), while in 1 K **8** 55 ff we actually have the words of the blessing delivered on one of these occasions by Solomon, and it is quite unlike the blessing of the priests (Nu **6** 22 ff).

Textual criticism disposes of the supposed priesthood of certain non-Levitical persons. In 2 S **8** 18 the MT makes David's sons "priests," but this reading was unknown to the LXX, Symmachus and Theodotion (Field, ad loc.). The LXX has "aularchs," i.e. chamberlains. That this represents a different Hebrew word is proved by the Septuagintal list of 3 K **2** 46 (not extant in Heb), where we read that Benaiah, son of Jehoiada, was "over the aularchy and over the brick-making." It cannot be suggested that this represents an original Heb "over the priesthood and over the brick-making," and accordingly we must concede the existence of some secular court office which was rendered by this Gr phrase. Hitzig and Cheyne conjecture that סֹכְנִים, *sōkhenīm*, should be read for כֹּהֲנִים, *kōhănīm*. This word gives the sense required (see Isa **22** 15, RVm "steward"). In 2 S **20** 26 we read that Ira, הַיָּאִרִי, *ha yā'iri* ("the Jairite"), was a priest, but the Syr supported by Lucian and **23** 38 reads הַיִּתְרִי, *ha-yattiri* ("the Jattirite"). Jattir was a priestly city. In 1 K **4** 5 Nathan's son is described as 'priest friend of the king,' but LXX reads only "friend of the king" (cf esp. 1 Ch **27** 33 f; 2 S **15** 32), and at another period Nathan's son held the kindred secular office of king's counsellor (LXX 3 K **2** 46, a fact that is certainly unfavorable to the view that he ever held priestly office). There can therefore be no doubt that the word "priest," כֹּהֵן, *kōhēn*, has arisen through dittography of the preceding word נָתָן, *nāthān*, Nathan.

Various dealings with the ark in the age of Samuel require notice. As a boy Samuel himself is given into the service of Eli. It has been argued that he really officiated as a priest, though probably (if the Chronicler's data be rejected) not of Levitical descent. The answer is to be found in his age. Weaning sometimes took place at as late an age as three, and accordingly the boy may have been as much as four years old when he was taken to Shiloh (1 S **1** 24). His mother used to bring him a little cloak (1 S **2** 19) every year, and this notice also shows his extreme youth. In view of this it cannot seriously be contended that he performed any priestly service. He must have been a sort of page, and he performed some duties of a porter, opening the door-valves of the temple at Shiloh (1 S **3** 15).

(1) *The custody of the ark.*—When the ark was captured by the Philis, it was in the charge of priests. When David brought it to Jerus, it was again placed in priestly custody, but there is an interregnum of some 20 years (1 S **7** 2).

It must be remembered that whatever may have happened during this period of great national confusion, the practice of all the rest of history, extending over some 600 or 700 years, is uniform and would far outweigh any irregularities during so short and troubled a period.

(2) *On its return from the Philistines.*—The first difficulty arises on 1 S **6** 14.15. In the second of these verses the Levites come up after the Beth-shemites have finished, and, in Wellhausen's words, "proceed as if nothing had happened, lift the ark from the now no longer existent cart, and set it upon the stone on which the sacrifice is already burning" (*Prolegomena*, 128). It is therefore suggested that ver 15 is a gloss. But there is difficulty in ver 14 which tells of the breaking up of the cart, etc, without explaining what happened to the ark. The trouble may be met by a slight transposition thus: '14*a* And the cart came into the field, ... and stood there, and there was there a great stone: 15*a* and the Levites took down the ark, etc, and put them on the great stone: 14*b* and clave the wood of the cart,' etc, followed by 15*b*. This makes perfect sense.

(3) *In Abinadab's house.*—The second difficulty is made by 1 S **7** 1, where we read that the ark was brought to the house of Abinadab 'and Eleazar his son they sanctified to guard' it. Its old abode, the house at Shiloh, had apparently been destroyed (Jer **7** 12.14; **26** 6.9). There it enjoyed considerable importance, for Poels is unquestionably right in identifying the Gibeah of God (1 S **10** 5) with the Gibeah (hill) of the ark. Thus there was a high place there and a Phili garrison (cf 1 S **13** 3, where LXX and Tg have "Gibeah"). There remains the difficulty caused by the guardianship of Eleazar. Poels may be right in reading וְאֶת בְּנֵי אֶלְעָזָר, *we'eth benē 'el'āzār*, "and the sons of Eleazar," for וְאֶת אֶלְעָזָר בְּנוֹ, *we'eth 'el'āzār benō*, "and Eleazar his son"; but in the entire absence of information, alike as to Eleazar's functions and as to his tribe, nothing definite can be said. The narratives of the slaughter among the Beth-shemites and the fate of Uzzah make it certain that Eleazar's custody of the ark kept him at a respectful distance from it.

When David at the end of this period removed the ark, it was first taken in a cart. This proved fatal to Uzzah, and the ark was deposited in the house of Obed-edom the Gittite. The text of S knows nothing of any guardianship of the ark by Obed-edom. Probably he took very good care not to go near it in view of Uzzah's fate. Then it was transported to Jerus by bearers (2 S **6** 13)—presumably of Levitical descent. No further irregularities are urged.

More important is the change of priesthood; 1 S **2** 27–36 clearly threatens Eli, whose house had been chosen in Egypt, with a transference of the high-priesthood to another line. Careful comparison with 1 K **2** 27 makes it certain that the prophecy was fulfilled when Zadok was placed by Solomon in the place of Abiathar. Who was Zadok? According to Ch (1 Ch **6** 8.53; **24** 3; **27** 17) he was descended from Aaron through Eleazar, and this is accepted by Orr, Van Hoonacker and many others, who take Ch in a literal sense. According to Ezk he was a Levite (**40** 46, etc). It is noteworthy that throughout the prophetical books we always hear of the Levitical priesthood, not the Aaronic (see esp. 1 K **12** 31; Jer **33** 18–22; Mal **2**), and the "father's house" of 1 S **2** 27–36 that was chosen in Egypt could only be the house of

Aaron, not of Ithamar, if the passage is to be taken in its natural sense. On this view Zadok's appointment could only have fulfilled the prophecy if it terminated the Aaronic succession. It would seem therefore that the high-priesthood was transferred to a family of non-Aaronic Levites. For the alternative view see Zadok.

The prophet's speech in 1 S **2** 27–36 is also important for the light it throws on the organization of the priesthood. The high priest has in his gift a number of priestly offices with pecuniary and other emoluments. This postulates a far more advanced hierarchy than that of P.

The reference to "the priests and the Levites" in 1 K **8** 4 was unknown to the LXX, but in other passages the Books of K show further advances in hierarchical organization. There is not merely the high priest—generally like Aaron in P called "the priest," but sometimes the high priest—but also the second priest (2 K **25** 18; Jer **52** 24; 2 K **23** 4, according to the Tg), three keepers of the threshold (*ubi supra*, and 2 K **12** 10) and "elders of the priests" (2 K **19** 2; Isa **37** 2; perhaps also Jer **19** 1). See also Jer **20** 1 f; **29** 26 for priestly organization and jurisdiction in the temple precincts. All this contrasts strikingly with the simplicity of the Pentateuchal organization.

2. Ezekiel

Ezekiel is entirely in line with the other sources for this period, but he seeks to institute certain reforms. He writes, "Her priests have done violence to my law, and have profaned my holy things: they have made no distinction between the holy and the common, neither have they caused men to discern between the unclean and the clean," etc (Ezk **22** 26). If these words have any meaning they signify that he was acquainted with a law which followed the very words of Lev **10** and other passages of P, and was intended to reach the people through the teaching of the priests. In chs **40–48,** there is a vision of the future which stands in the closest relation to the Pent. Three views have been held of this. The old view was that Ezk could not be reconciled with the Pent at all, and that the difficulties presented were insoluble. Wellhausen and his followers maintain that the prophet is prior to P, and here introduces the distinction between priests and Levites for the first time. The third alternative is to hold that Ezekiel was familiar with P and drew from it the inspiration to make a fresh division among the Levites, giving the sons of Zadok a position similar to that occupied by the sons of Aaron in the wilderness period, and reënacting with slight modifications the legislation applicable to the sons of Aaron, this time applying it to the sons of Zadok. The crucial passage is **44** 6–16, from which it clearly appears that in Solomon's temple aliens had performed sundry tasks that should have been executed by more holy persons, and that Ezekiel proposes to degrade Levites who are not descended from Zadok to perform such tasks in the future as a punishment for their ministrations to idols in high places. Either of the two latter views would explain the close connection that evidently exists between the concluding chapters of Ezk and P, and, accordingly, in choosing between them, the reader must consider four main points: (1) Is P shown on the internal evidence to be early or late? Is it desert legislation, or is it accurately reflected in Ch? This point has already been discussed in part and is further treated in Pentateuch (q.v.). (2) Is the theory of the late composition of P psychologically and morally probable? On this see Pentateuch and *POT*, 292–99. (3) Is it the case that the earlier history attests the existence of institutions of P that are held by Wellhausen and his followers to be late—e.g. more national offerings than the critics allow? On this see *EPC*, 200 ff, and *passim; POT*, 305–15, and *passim; SBL* and *OP passim*, and art. Pentateuch. (4) Does Ezekiel himself show acquaintance with P (e.g. in **22** 26), or not? On this too see *SBL*, 96; *PS*, 281 f.

With regard to the non-mention of the high-priesthood and certain other institutions in Ezekiel's vision, the natural explanation is that in the case of these the prophet did not desire to institute any changes. It is to be noted that Ezekiel does not *codify and consolidate* all existing law. On the contrary, he is rather supplementing and reforming. In his ideal temple the prince is to provide the statutory national offerings (**45** 17), i.e. those of Nu **28, 29**. Apparently the king had provided these earlier (2 K **16** 13). But in addition to these there had grown up a "king's offering," and it is probably to this only that **45** 22 ff; **46** 2–15 relate. In **46** 13 LXX, Syr, Vulg, and some Heb MSS preserve the reading "he" for "thou."

V. Ezra, Nehemiah, Chronicles.—Whatever the course of the earlier history, there is general agreement that in these books a distinction between priests and Levites is established (see e.g. Neh **10** 37 f [38 f]; **12** 1 f). We also find singers and porters (Neh **13** 5, etc), Nethinim and the sons of Solomon's servants (Ezr **7** 7.24; **10** 23 f; Neh **10** 28 [29]; **11** 3, etc). It must not be assumed that these classes were new. The story of the Gibeonites (Josh **9**) gives us the origin of some of these grades, and the non-mention of them in many of the earlier books is easily explained by the character of those books. We know from such passages as Am **5** 23 that there were musical services in far earlier times (cf Neh **12** 42).

1. Estimates of the Chronicler

Ch presents an account of the earlier history of the priests and Levites that in many respects does not tally with the older sources. Many modern writers think that the author's views of the past were colored by the circumstances of his own day, and that he had a tendency to carry back later conditions to an earlier period. On the other hand it is impossible to deny fairly that he used some sources which have not been preserved to us elsewhere. Again, there is evidence to show that his work was not intended to be taken for history and would not have been so regarded by his contemporaries. Talmudical authorities held some such view as this. The historical value of his work has yet to be appraised in a more critical and impartial spirit than is exhibited in any of the current discussions. For the present purpose it is only possible to notice the effect of some of his statements, if interpreted literally. As there are passages where he has clearly substituted Levites for the less holy personages of the older sources (contrast e.g. 2 K **11** 4–12 with 2 Ch **23** 1–11), it may be that Levites have also been substituted by him for other persons in notices of which no other version has survived.

2. His Data

David and Solomon recognized the hierarchy. The former king instituted the musical services (1 Ch **6** 3 ff; **16** 4 ff; **25**). The Levites were divided into courses (1 Ch **23** 6) and were rendered liable to service from the age of twenty by his enactment (ver 27). There were also 24 courses or divisions of priests, 16 of the sons of Eleazar and 8 of the sons of Ithamar (ch **24**). The courses were divided by lot. In Neh **12** 1–7 we read of "chiefs of the priests," but these are only 22 in number, while vs 12–21 give us 21 in the time of Joiakim (ver 26). But not much importance can be attached to such lists, as names could easily fall out in transmission. According to 1 Ch **9** 26 the four chief porters were

Levites, and Levites were also over the things baked in pans and the shewbread (vs 31 f). This of course is not in accordance with the Law, but is found elsewhere in Ch. In 1 Ch **23** the Levites from 30 years old and upward number 38,000, of whom 24,000 oversee the work of the house of the Lord, 6,000 were officers and judges, 4,000 were doorkeepers and 4,000 were musicians. David altered the age of beginning service to 20, and an account of their functions is given in 1 Ch **23** 27–32 (see, further, Music). All these arrangements were confirmed and enforced by Solomon (2 Ch **8** 14 ff). There is often uncertainty as to whether the Chronicler identifies priests and Levites in particular cases or not, e.g. in 2 Ch **30** 27, "the priests the Levites" bless the people according to the ordinary text, but many authorities read "the priests and the Levites." Hezekiah appears to have undertaken some reorganization (2 Ch **29–31**), but the details are not clear. Jehoshaphat established in Jerus a court composed partly of Levites and priests (**19** 8–11). Previously he had sent priests and Levites and others to teach the Law in Judah (ch **17**). In **29** 34 it is clearly the duty of the priests to flay burnt offerings (contrast Lev **1**). It is impossible to draw any consistent picture from the Chronicler because he gives different data for different periods; it is doubtful whether he meant his statements to be taken as historical, e.g. in 1 Ch **25** we find Levites whose names Giddalti (="I have magnified"), etc, are really words forming part of a prayer, and it is difficult to believe that either the Chronicler or his public intended this chapter to be interpreted in any but a spiritual sense (see *PS*, 284–86).

In Ezr **2** 40 the number of Levites who returned with Zerubbabel is given as 74, as against 973 priests (ver 36), 128 singers (ver 41), 139 children of the porters (ver 42), 392 Nethinim and children of Solomon's servants (ver 58), and the figures are the same in Neh **7**, except that there the singers number 148 (ver 44) and the porters 138 (ver 45). When Ezra went up, he was at first joined by no Levites (**8** 15), but subsequently gathered 38 Levites and 220 Nethinim (vs 18–20). We get glimpses of the organization in Neh **12** 44–47 and **13** 10 ff. It appears that in this period genealogies were carefully scrutinized in the case of doubtful claims to priestly descent (Ezr **2** 61 ff; Neh **7** 63 ff). In Ezr **6** 19 ff the Levites are represented as killing the Passover.

Of these books no satisfactory account can be given in the present state of textual criticism and Bib. science generally. Some writers, e.g., hold that the Chronicler had before him a source to which the Levites were entirely unknown, others that he invented freely, others again that he reproduces trustworthy preëxilic information. The student has only an assortment of theories from which to choose. The bedrock fact is that the statements of these books, if taken in their natural meaning, convey an entirely different impression from the statements of the earlier books construed similarly. Modern research has not yet been seriously addressed to the question whether all the statements were really intended to be interpreted as mere history.

VI. Legal Provisions.—Aaron and his sons underwent consecration to fit them for their duties. Ex **28** f prescribes their garments and consecration (see Dress; Breastplate; Ephod; Robe; Coat; Mitre; Girdle; Urim and Thummim), and the account of the latter may be read in Lev **8** f. In individual sacrifices brought to the religious capital the priests performed the part of the ritual which related to the altar (sprinkling, burning, etc) (Lev **1–4**). See Sacrifice. A principal function was the duty of teaching the people the law of God (Lev **10** 11; **14** 54–57; Dt **24** 8; **33** 10; cf Ezk **44** 23; Hos **4** 1–6; Hag **2** 11 ff, and many passages in the Prophets).

The priests were subject to special laws designed to maintain their purity (Lev **21** f; cf Ezk **44**). The rules aim at preventing defilement through mourning (save in the case of ordinary priests for a near relation) and at preventing those who were physically unfitted from performing certain functions, and those who were for any reason unclean from approaching the holy things. See further Stranger. They performed several semi-judicial functions (Nu **5** 5 ff.11 ff, etc; see Judge). They also blessed the people (Nu **6** 22; cf Dt **10** 8, etc). See Blessing. On their dues see Sacrifice; Tithes; Firstlings; First-Fruits; Levitical Cities; Agrarian Laws; see further Chemarim; Nethinim; Sons of Solomon's Servants; Singers; Doorkeepers; Serving-Women; Judge.

Literature.—Wellhausen, *Prolegomena*, ch iv, for the Graf-Wellhausen view; Wiener, *PS*, 230–89, for the view taken above; S. I. Curtiss, *Levitical Priests*, for the conservative view. This writer afterward changed to the critical view. James Orr, *POT*; A. Van Hoonacker, *Le sacerdoce lévitique* (important); W. Baudissin, art. "Priests and Levites" in *HDB*, IV, for mediating views. The best account in Eng. of the details of the priestly duties is contained in Baudissin's art., where a further bibliography will be found.

Harold M. Wiener

PRIMOGENITURE, prī-mō-jen′i-tūr (בְּכוֹרָה, *bᵉkhōrāh*, from *bᵉkhōr*, "firstborn," from *bākhar*, "to act early"; **πρωτοτόκια**, *prōtotókia*):

1. Recognition of Doctrine

The right of the firstborn to inherit the headship of the family, carrying with it certain property rights and usually such titles as those of the high-priesthood or kingship. The writings of the Hebrews take for granted the recognition of a doctrine of primogeniture from the earliest times. In the most ancient genealogies a distinction is drawn between the firstborn and the other son (Gen **10** 15; **22** 21; **25** 13; **35** 23; **36** 15). In the bestowal of parental blessings in patriarchal times great importance was attached to preferring the firstborn (Gen **25** 31; **27** 29; **48** 13; **49** 3). The feud between Jacob and Esau (Gen **27** 1—**28** 21) grew out of the stealing of the firstborn's blessing by the younger brother. Joseph was displeased when, in his blessing, Jacob seemed to prefer Ephraim to Manasseh, his firstborn (Gen **48** 18). The father in such cases seems to have had the right to transfer the birthright from one son to another, from the days of Abraham in the case of Ishmael and Isaac, through those of Jacob in the matter of Reuben and Joseph and in the matter of Ephraim and Manasseh, down to the days of David in the selection of a successor to the kingship. Nevertheless the Mosaic code, which declared (rather than enacted) the law of primogeniture, prohibited the abuse of this parental privilege in the case of a younger son by a favorite wife (Dt **21** 16 f).

The manner of acknowledging the firstborn incidentally referred to in Dt is "by giving him a double

2. The Double Portion

portion of all that he hath" (Dt **21** 17), that is to say, double the share of each of the other brothers. Jewish tradition (*Bᵉkhō.* **46***a*, **47***b*, **51***a*, **51***b*; *Bābhā' Bathrā'* **122***a*, **122***b*, **123***a*, **124***a*, **142***b*) accepts and elaborates on this right of the firstborn son. Thus, it applies only to the firstborn and not the eldest surviving son; it does not apply to daughters; it has reference only to the paternal estate, and not to the inheritance left by a mother or other relative, nor to improvements or accessions made to an estate after the death of the father.

3. Reasons for the Custom

The object of the doctrine may be that the eldest son might be enabled to preside over the affairs of family with proper dignity, or that he might assume additional responsibilities, such as the support of unmarried sisters. Hence one's birthright could be waived or sold (Gen **25** 31. 34). On the other hand it may be based in the ultimate analysis on the primitive feeling of favoritism for the firstborn reflected in the disappointment of Jacob, when he speaks of Reuben as his firstborn, his might, and the beginning of his strength (*rē'shīth 'ōn*, Gen **49** 3; cf Dt **21** 17). This theory would be in accord with the right of the parent to transfer the right to a younger son. The suggestion of favoritism conveyed by the Heb *b*[e]*khōr* is manifested in its **figurative** use: of Israel (Ex **4** 22), of Ephraim (Jer **31** 9), of one dearly beloved (Zec **12** 10); (cf **figurative** usage in the NT: Rom **8** 29; He **12** 23; **1** 6; Rev **1** 5).

4. The Firstborn in Ancient Society; Sacrifice and Redemption

Light is thrown on the attitude of the ancient world toward the firstborn, and hence on the history of primogeniture, by the language used in connection with the plague of the firstborn: "from the first-born of Pharaoh that sitteth upon his throne, even unto the first-born of the maid-servant that is behind the mill" or "the captive that was in the dungeon." Apparently no more dreadful catastrophe for all classes of society could be thought of than this slaying of the firstborn (Ex **11** 5; **12** 29). The misguided fervor of the ancient Semites who offered their firstborn as the thing most dearly beloved as a sacrifice to their gods must be considered in this light, whether it appears among the Moabites, the Phoenicians or the Hebrews themselves (Jer **32** 35; Ezk **20** 26. 31; 2 Ch **28** 3). It is difficult to predicate a connection between the basis of the doctrine of primogeniture and that of the *Redemption of the Firstborn*, other than that both are ultimately based on the importance of a firstborn son and the fondness of his parents for him. It is interesting to note, however, that the tradition of redemption and the law of primogeniture are kept so distinct that, while the latter has reference only to the firstborn of a father, the former has reference only to the firstborn of a mother (*B*[e]*khō.*, viii.1, **46***a*; cf *peṭer reḥem*, "whatsoever openeth the womb," Ex **13** 2). In a polygamous society such as that presupposed in Dt **21** it is natural to suppose that the distinction between paternal and maternal primogeniture would be clearly before the minds of the people. See BIRTHRIGHT; FIRSTBORN.

NATHAN ISAACS

PRINCE, prins: This word occurs quite frequently in our Eng. Bible, mostly in the OT. While it is never used to denote royal parentage (cf 1 Ch **29** 24), it often indicates actual royal or ruling power, together with royal dignity and authority. As a rule, the name is given to human beings; in a few instances it is applied to God and Christ, the angels and the devil.

In Mt **2** 6 the word rendered "princes" might be tr[d] "princely cities"; at least, this seems to be implied. Here the term ἡγεμών, *hēgemōn*, "leader," "ruler," "prince," is used, undoubtedly to hint at the fact that Bethlehem was the native city of a great prince. In the other NT passages the word ἄρχων, *árchōn*, "a potentate," "a person in authority," "a magistrate," occurs most frequently (cf Mt **9** 34; **12** 24; **20** 25 [RV "ruler"]; Mk **3** 22; Jn **12** 31; **14** 30; **16** 11; **1** Cor **2** 6.8 AV; Eph **2** 2; Rev **1** 5 [RV "ruler"]). In most of these instances the term "prince" refers to the devil.

In Acts **3** 15; **5** 31, the word ἀρχηγός, *archēgós*, "leader," is employed referring to Christ as the author of life and salvation (cf He **12** 2, where the term *archēgos* is rendered "author" [RV] or "captain" [RVm]).

The OT contains a number of different words mostly rendered "prince" or "princes" in the EV.

(1) שַׂר, *sar:* In Josh **5** 14 the mysterious armed stranger seen by Joshua near Jericho calls himself the "prince of the host of Jeh": a high military title applied to a superhuman being. In Isa **9** 6, the name is given to the child representing the future Messiah. The term "Prince of Peace" denotes the eminent position and the peaceful reign of the Messianic king: the highest human title in its most ideal sense. Dnl **8** 11: here, again, as in Josh **5** 14, occurs the phrase "prince of the host." In Dnl **8** 25 "the prince of princes" refers to God Himself: the highest human title in its absolute sense applied to God. Dnl **10** 21: "Michael your prince." Michael the archangel is here called the prince of the Jewish people. He is the princely representative of God's people in the sight of God, a royal title suggesting high power and alliance with God in the great struggle going on between Him and the powers of darkness. Dnl **12** 1: here Michael is called "the great prince" who standeth for the children of Israel; supplementing Dnl **10** 21. In Dnl **10** 13: "the prince of the kingdom of Persia" (cf ver 20, "the prince of Persia," "the prince of Greece"), the expression is used in the same general sense as in Dnl **10** 21. Each individual nation is represented as guided by a spiritual being that may or may not be an ally of God in His combat with the devil. In the majority of cases, though, the term *sar* is applied (*a*) to men exercising royal or ruling power: Prov **8** 16: "By me princes [m "or rulers"] rule"; Isa **32** 1: "Behold, a king shall reign in righteousness, and princes shall rule in justice." Judicial power is included (cf Ex **2** 14: "Who made thee a prince and a judge over us?" and Ps **148** 11: "princes and all judges of the earth"). In some passages the word *sar*, having been rendered "prince," stands for "chief"; so Jgs **7** 25: "They took the two princes of Midian" (cf Jgs **8** 14; 1 S **29** 4; 2 S **10** 3, etc). (*b*) To royal officers of a high rank: Gen **12** 15: "the princes of Pharaoh" (cf 2 K **24** 14: "Jerus and all the princes"; 1 Ch **29** 24; 2 Ch **24** 23; Jer **36** 21; **52** 10; Hos **5** 10, etc). "Ambassadors" (Jer **36** 14); "governors" (1 K **20** 14: "By the young men [m "or, servants"] of the princes of the provinces"; cf Est **1** 3.14, "the seven princes"); "the chief of the eunuchs" (Dnl **1** 7); a "quartermaster" (Jer **51** 59: "Seraiah was chief chamberlain" [m "or, quartermaster"]). AV renders it "a quiet prince," i.e. a prince having rest, instead of procuring rest (שַׂר מְנוּחָה, *sar m*[e]*nūḥāh*, "a *sar* of rest"). In post-exilic times: Ezr **9** 1: "The princes drew near unto me." They were the political leaders of the people (cf Ezr **10** 8: "the princes and the elders"; Neh **9** 38: "our princes, our Levites, and our priests"; Neh **11** 1: "The princes of the people dwelt in Jerus"; Neh **12** 31: "the princes of Judah"). Of course, they were all subject to the authority of the Pers kings. (*c*) To the priesthood: 1 Ch **24** 5: "princes of the sanctuary, and princes of God" (cf Isa **43** 28). (*d*) On account of great achievements: 2 S **3** 38: "Know ye not that there is a prince and a great man fallen this day in Israel?"—an honorary title. Generally speaking, a prince is a wealthy man (cf Job **34** 19: "That respecteth not the persons of princes, nor regardeth the rich more than the poor"), and he is a prominent man embodying true, although mortal, manhood (cf Ps **82** 7: "Nevertheless ye shall die like men, and fall like one of the princes).

(2) נָשִׂיא, *nāsī'*: usually derived from נָשָׂא, *nāsā'*, "to lift," hence "exalted"; otherwise: a "speaker." (*a*) An honorary title (cf Gen **23** 6: "Thou art a prince of God among us." The distinction is conferred upon Abraham by the children of Heth). (*b*) A name given to the heads of the Israelitic tribes, families and fathers' houses: Nu **3** 24: "the prince of the fathers' house of the Gershonites" (cf vs 30. 35); **3** 32: "Eleazar . . . . shall be prince of the princes of the Levites, and have the oversight of them that keep the charge of the sanctuary"; Nu **4** 34: "the princes of the congregation." They seem to be identical with the "rulers of thousands, rulers of hundreds, rulers of fifties, and rulers of tens" (cf Ex **18** 21; Nu **16** 2). Nu **7** 2: "the princes of Israel, the heads of their fathers' houses . . . . the princes of the tribes" (cf **17** 2.6; **34** 18; Josh **22** 14; 1 Ch **4** 38). (*c*) Equivalent to chief or king: Gen **17** 20: "Twelve princes shall he beget" (cf **25** 16); Gen **34** 2: "Shechem the son of Hamor the Hivite, the prince of the land"; Nu **25** 18: "Cozbi, the daughter of the prince of Midian" (cf Josh **13** 21); 1 K **11** 34: "I will make him prince all the days of his life." This was said of Solomon, which shows the term equivalent to king. Of special interest is the use of the word *nāsī'* in Ezk. The name is given to the Jewish king (cf **12** 10: "This burden concerneth the prince in Jerus"). Then, again, it is applied to the future theocratic king (cf **34** 24; **37** 25, etc, and esp. chs **45, 46**). It is also used of foreign potentates and high officers (cf **26** 16: "the princes of the sea"; **28** 2: "the prince of Tyre"; **30** 13: "a prince from the land of Egypt"); **32** 29: "Edom, her kings and all her princes"; and, likewise, of high Jewish officers (**21** 12). (*d*) A title bestowed upon Sheshbazzar (Ezr **1** 8).

(3) נָדִיב, *nādhībh:* 1 S **2** 8: "To make them sit with princes" (cf Ps **113** 8). The original meaning of the term is willing or obliging; then generous ("liberal"; cf Prov **19** 6: "Many will entreat the favor of the liberal man"; yet, it might safely be rendered here "prince" [m]) or noble-minded; a gentleman, a nobleman, a person of rank, a prince. Job **12** 21: "He poureth contempt upon princes" (cf Ps **107** 40); Job **21** 28: "Where is the house of the prince? And where is the tent wherein the wicked dwelt?" The context here suggests the thought of a wicked prince, a tyrant. Ps **47** 9: "The princes of the peoples are gathered together" (cf Ps **118** 9; **146** 3; Prov **17** 7; **25** 7; Cant **7** 1).

(4) נָגִיד, *nāghīdh:* According to Gesenius, this term denotes originally either a high-minded person (cf the preceding word, *nādhībh*) or a speaker, a spokesman; then a prince, a king. 1 S **13** 14: "Jeh hath appointed him to be prince over his people" (cf 2 S **5** 2: "Thou shalt be prince [RVm "leader"] over Israel"; **6** 21; **7** 8; 1 K **1** 35; **14** 7; **16** 2; Job **29** 9; **31** 37; Ps **76** 12; Prov **28** 16; Ezk **28** 2: "prince of Tyre"; Dnl **9** 25: "the anointed one, the prince," AV the "Messiah the Prince"; Dnl **9** 26: "the prince that shall come" [the Rom emperor?]; **11** 22: "the prince of the covenant" [either a high priest or some Egyp king, Ptolemaeus Philometor?]).

(5), (6) רָזוֹן, *rāzōn*, and רֹזֵן, *rōzēn*, "a high official," "a prince," usually associated with the word "king" or "judge." Prov **14** 28: "In the multitude of people is the king's glory; but in the want of people is the destruction of the prince" (*rāzōn*); Jgs **5** 3: "Hear, O ye kings; give ear, O ye princes" (*rōzenīm*); Prov **8** 15: "By me kings reign, and princes [*rōzenīm*] decree justice" (cf **31** 4; Hab **1** 10); Isa **40** 23: "that bringeth princes [*rōzenīm*] to nothing; that maketh the judges of the earth as vanity."

(7) נָסִיךְ, *nāṣīkh*, derived from נָסַךְ, *nāṣakh*, "to install a king" (cf Ps **2** 6); hence a prince: Josh **13** 21: "the princes of Sihon" (cf Ps **83** 11); Ezk **32** 30: "the princes of the north"; Mic **5** 5: RV "principal men," RVm "princes among men"; Dnl **11** 8: RV "molten images," RVm "princes."

(8) קָצִין, *ḳāçīn*, "a judge," "a military leader," "a prince"; Dnl **11** 18: "A prince [RVm "captain"] shall cause the reproach . . . . to cease" (probably a Rom consul; a Rom general?).

(9) שָׁלִישׁ, *shālīsh:* The usual explanation, "one of the three men on a war-chariot" is highly improbable; Gesenius suggests that it is a loan-word, and renders it "hero." Ezk **23** 15: "All of them princes to look upon" ("picked men," Gesenius).

(10) חַשְׁמַנִּים, *ḥashmannīm:* Ps **68** 31: "Princes shall come out of Egypt." LXX renders it πρέσβεις, *présbeis*, "ambassadors," Vulg *legati*. But the meaning is uncertain. See also GOVERNOR, 1, (8).

WILLIAM BAUR

PRINCES, prin'sez, -siz, **THE SEVEN**. See PRINCE, (1), (*b*).

PRINCESS, prin'ses: The Heb term is שָׂרָה, *sārāh* (cf *sar*, prince, and "Sarah"); it means (1) a queen (Isa **49** 23, AV and RV both "queen"); (2) the consort of a king contrasted with his concubines (1 K **11** 3, "He had seven hundred wives, princesses, and three hundred concubines"); (3) the wife of a prince (Est **1** 18: the "princesses of Persia and Media"); (4) it is metaphorically used of the city of Jerus (Lam **1** 1).

PRINCIPAL, prin'si-pal: Appears in AV as a tr of nine Heb words (fewer in RV), in one case (Isa **28** 25) being used quite wrongly and in 2 K **25** 19 (Jer **52** 25); 1 Ch **24** 31 gives a wrong sense (all corrected in RV). In 1 K **4** 5, "principal officer" (ARV "chief minister") is an arbitrary tr of *kōhēn* to avoid "priest" (so ERV; cf 2 S **8** 18).

PRINCIPALITY, prin-si-pal'i-ti: In the OT the word occurs but once (Jer **13** 18, "your principalities shall come down"). Here AVm "head tires" is properly preferred by RV for מְרַאֲשׁוֹת, *mera-'ăshōth* (from רֹאשׁ, *rō'sh*, "head"), "head-parts."

In the NT "principality" occurs for ἀρχή, *archḗ*, "rule," generally in the pl., referring (*a*) to men in authority (Tit **3** 1, "Put them in mind to be subject [AV; "in subjection," RV] to principalities [AV; "rulers," RV], and powers" [AV; "to authorities," RV]); (*b*) to superhuman agencies, angelic or demonic (Rom **8** 38; Eph **3** 10; **6** 12; Col **1** 16; **2** 10.15). Paul was keenly sensible of the dualism of mind and body and of the law in his members warring against the law of his mind (Rom **7** 23), and of the temporary victory of the evil, residing in the flesh, over the good of the spirit (vs 14 ff). This dualism was objectified in Zoroastrianism, and among the Babylonians the several heavenly bodies were regarded as ruled by spirits, some good, some evil. The same belief, appropriated by the Jews during the captivity, appears also in Gr thought, as e.g. in Plato and later in the Stoics. The higher spheres, which hold the even tenor of their way, were in general regarded as ruled by good spirits; but in the sublunar sphere, to which the earth belongs, ill-regulated motions prevail, which must be due to evil spirits. The perversities of human conduct, in particular, thwarting, as was thought, the simple, intelligible Divine plan, were held to be subject to rebellious powers offering defiance to God. While Paul clearly recognized a hierarchy of such powers (Col **1** 16, "thrones or dominions or principalities or powers"), it is not certain that he had elaborated a system of *aeons* to serve the purposes of metaphysical theology and ethics, such as appears among the Gnostics, although they evidently believed they were developing his thought. In 1 Cor **2** 6 he repudiates the wisdom of this world (*aiôn*) and of the rulers of this world *aiôn*), and declares (Eph **6** 12) that the Christian has to contend with "the world-rulers of this darkness," and proclaims the triumph of Christ over "the principalities and the powers" in the forgiveness of sins (Col **2** 15). The same personification of such agencies or powers appears also in another passage, where the rendering of EV obscures it (Eph **1** 20.21: "when he raised him [Christ] from the dead, and made him to sit at his right hand in the heavenly places, far above all [read "every"] rule [RV; "principality," AV], and authority, and power, and dominion, and every name that is named not only in this world [*aiôn*], but also in that which is to come"). Not the least interesting passage is Eph **3** 10, where the church is said to be the means of revealing to "the principalities and the powers in the heavenly places" "the manifold wisdom of God." One naturally inquires what was the purpose of this revelation. Was it to effect a redemption and reconciliation of these demonic powers to God? To this question Paul supplies no answer. See ANGEL; SATAN. WILLIAM ARTHUR HEIDEL

PRINCIPLES, prin'si-p'lz: Found twice (He **5** 12; **6** 1). The Gr word (στοιχεῖον, *stoicheíon*) is also tr[d] in AV as "elements" and "rudiments." As rendered in He, its meaning is clearly related to the elementary knowledge of Christian truth or doctrine. See ELEMENTS; RUDIMENTS.

PRINT, print, **PRINTING,** prin'ting, **PRINTED,** prin'ted: Printing is the art of multiplying records —the "art of writing with many pens" (*Jew Enc*, XII, 295), or wholesale writing.

The art of making original records is writing. This, however, is a slow process. It involves tracing each letter and part of a letter through from beginning to end by the moving point of chisel, pen, or other instrument, and this process must be repeated with every copy. As soon, therefore, as occasion arose for frequently repeating the record, many ways were devised to save the labor of forming each symbol separately. All these ways involve making a character or a series of characters on a single surface and transferring as a whole to another surface. Neither "pressure," as some say, nor "ink," as others, is essential to the process, for printing from a photographic negative takes no pressure, and printing for the blind takes no ink. Any process which transfers a whole surface is printing.

The earliest use of printing seems to have been for painting the face or body with ownership, tribal, trophy, or ceremonial marks for worship, war, mourning, etc. This paint might be temporary or pricked in by the tattoo process. Tattooing itself is rather a writing than a printing process, but may be either, according as the color is laid on by drawing or by the "pintadera." The "pintadera" or "stamp used to impress patterns upon the skin" is best known from the Mexican and South American examples, but in recent years it has been found in deposits all over the Mediterranean region (North Italy, Austria, Hungary, Mycenae, Crete, Egypt) and in Borneo at least. Many of these specimens are from the Neolithic or Copper age. Both in South America and in Neolithic Liguria, some of these stamps were cylindrical and "were used like a printer's roller" (Mosso, *The Dawn of Mediterranean Civilization*, 254–61, with many illustrations, and Frobenius, *Childhood of Man*, fig. 31, "Dayak block for painting the body").

The injunction of Lev **19** 28, which is tr[d] "print," is commonly, and probably rightly, in view of the Heb word, supposed to refer to the permanent marks of tattooing which may or may not have been made by this printing process. Job **13** 27 AV, which speaks of printing upon the heels or soles of the feet, has been quite changed in RV, and, if the idea is one of printing at all, it refers rather to branding than stamping with color.

The use of the inkhorn in setting the mark upon the forehead (Ezk **9** 3.4.6) certainly points to marking with color rather than branding. See INKHORN. This may, of course, have been drawing rather than printing, but, on the other hand, the sealing of the servants of God on their foreheads (Rev **7** 4; **9** 4) necessarily means printing rather than drawing, and probably printing rather than branding, for the use of the seal with color had long been common. The marks of the beast upon the forehead and upon the hand in Rev **13, 14, 15, 16, 19** and **20,** more likely refer to branding, as the Gr word points more or less in this direction, while the stigmata of Gal **6** 17 may also point to branding. Branding was at all events also a common method of printing characters on the flesh in Bib. times (Isa **3** 24; perhaps Ex **21** 25; a branding on the forehead, CH § 127; branding of a slave §§ 226, 227). The reference in Jn **20** 25 is, of course, to the clearly visible marks or scars left by the nails in the hands. See MARK.

The use of seals is a true printing process, whether they are used with color, as they were both in Crete and Egypt almost from the beginning of history, or impressed on clay, wax, or other plastic substances. Mention of seals is frequent in the Bible (see SEAL). A new interest has been given to this aspect of the matter by the sealings discovered in Ahab's palace and other excavations throughout Pal, which are forming one of the most useful classes of modern inscriptions.

Both stamp and seal were used throughout the Middle Ages, the latter abundantly, and the stamp at least occasionally, for stamping the capital letters in Bib. and other MSS, as well as for various other purposes.

Modern printing begins with the carving of whole pages and books on blocks of wood (xylography), or metal plates for printing (chalcography). This method was quite early practised by the Chinese, and began to be common in Europe in the early 15th cent., most of the books printed by it having to do with Bib. topics (*Biblia pauperum*, etc).

It was only with the invention of movable type about the middle of the 15th cent. that the multiplying of books by writing began to come to an end. The printing with movable type is also closely associated with Bib. study, the Gutenberg Psalter and the Gutenberg Bible standing with most for the very beginning of modern printing.

For the printed edd of the Heb and Gr originals, and the various VSS, see arts. on TEXTUAL CRITICISM and allied topics in this encyclopaedia, with their literature. The art. on "Typography" in *Jew Enc* is of unusual excellence, and the general literature of printing given in *Enc Brit*, at the end of the first part of the art. on "Typography," is full and good. Compare also BOOK in this encyclopaedia and its literature, esp. Hortzschansky, supplementing the bibliography of *Enc Brit.* E. C. RICHARDSON

PRISCA, pris'ka, **PRISCILLA,** pri-sil'a. See AQUILA.

PRISON, priz″n, **PRISONER,** priz″n-ẽr, priz′nẽr (there are various Heb words which are rendered "prison" in AV, among them:

1. Hebrew Words

[1] סֹהַר, *ṣōhar*, "round house," "fortress" [8 t in Gen], [2] כֶּלֶא, *kele'*, "restraint," "confinement" [12 t: in historic books, Isa, Jer, with "house"], [3] מַטָּרָה, *maṭṭārāh*, "guard," "sentry" [13 t in Jer and Neh], [4] מַהְפֶּכֶת, *mah^aphekheth*, "distorting," i.e. stocks or pillory [4 t], [5] אֵסוּר, *'ēṣūr*, "bond," "fetters" [Eccl **4** 14; Jer **37** 15]; "ward" in AV is usually the rendering for מִשְׁמָר, *mishmār*):

2. In Early Times

The earliest occurrence of the word "prison" in AV is found in the narrative of Joseph's life in Egypt (J). The term used, viz. *ṣōhar*, means perhaps "round house" or "tower." It seems probable that among the Hebrews there were no special buildings erected as "jails" in the premonarchical period, and perhaps not before the post-exilic period, when the adoption of the civic institutions and customs of surrounding nations prevailed. In Egypt and Assyria, on the contrary, there were probably public buildings corresponding to our modern jails. Among the Hebrews, rooms in connection with the royal palace or the residence of prominent court officials would be used for the purpose.

3. Joseph in Egypt

According to one narrative (J) in Gen the prison in which Joseph was confined had a "keeper," while according to another narrative (E) the offending members of the royal household, viz. the royal butler and the royal baker, were placed "in ward" with the "captain of the guard" in charge, i.e. in some part of the royal palace. This is still more probable if, instead of "captain of the guard," we should translate "chief of the cooks," i.e. superintendent of the royal kitchen.

4. Causes of Imprisonment

It was often necessary to restrict the liberty of individuals who for various causes were a menace to those in authority, without inflicting any corporal punishment, e.g. Joseph's brethren were kept "in ward" three days (Gen **42** 19); Shimei was forbidden to pass beyond the boundary of Jerus (1 K **2** 36); the person who was caught gathering sticks on the Sabbath was put "in ward" pending his trial (Nu **15** 34). In the monarchical period, prophets who criticized the throne were put in prison, e.g. Micaiah by Ahab (1 K **22** 27), Hanani by Asa (2 Ch **16** 10). Hoshea, after his abortive effort to institute an alliance with So or Seve, king of Egypt, was shut up in prison by Shalmaneser (2 K **17** 4); cf also 2 K **25** 27 (Jehoiachin in Babylon); Jer **52** 11 (Zedekiah in Babylon).

5. Under the Monarchy

The Book of Jer throws considerable light on the prison system of Jerus in the later monarchical period. The prophet was put "*in the stocks* that were in the upper gate of Benjamin, which was in the house of Jeh" (**20** 2). Mere imprisonment was not adequate punishment for the prophet's announcement of Judah's doom; it was necessary to have recourse to the pillory. During the siege of Jerus Jeremiah was confined in the "court of the guard, which was in the king of Judah's house" (**32** 2, etc). The "court of the guard" was evidently the quarters of the sentry who guarded the royal palace. According to the narrative of ch **37**, the prophet was arrested on a charge of treachery and put in prison "in the house of Jonathan the scribe" (**37** 15). This verse does not necessarily mean that a private house was used as a prison. The words are capable of another interpretation, viz. that a building known as the "house of Jonathan the scribe" had been taken over by the authorities and converted into a jail. We read in the following verse that the house had a "dungeon" (lit. "house of the pit") and "cabins" or "cells."

6. The Treatment of Prisoners

The data are not sufficient to enable us to give any detailed description of the treatment of prisoners. This treatment varied according to the character of the offence which led to incarceration. Samson during the period of his imprisonment was compelled to do hard labor (Jgs **16** 21). Grinding was the occupation of women, and marked the depth of Samson's humiliation. Dangerous persons were subjected to various kinds of physical mutilation, e.g. Samson was deprived of his sight. This was a common practice in Assyria (2 K **25** 7). The thumbs and great toes of Adonibezek were cut off to render him incapable of further resistance (Jgs **1** 6).

Various forms of torture were in vogue. Hanani the seer was put into **the pillory** by Asa (for "in a prison house" we should render "in the stocks"; see RVm). In Jer **29** 26 for "prison," we should render "stocks" (so RV) or "pillory," and for "stocks," "collar" (as in RVm). AV renders a different Heb word by "stocks" in Job (**13** 27; **33** 11). There was a special prison **diet** (1 K **22** 27), as well as a prison **garb** (2 K **25** 29).

7. Other Hebrew Words

There are other Heb words rendered "prison" (sometimes incorrectly) in AV. In Ps **142** 7, the word which is tr^d "prison" means a "place of execution," and is derived from a root which denotes, for instance, the isolation of the leper (Lev **13** 5; cf Isa **24** 22; **42** 7). In Isa **53** 8 "oppression" not "prison" is the correct tr, while in Isa **61** 1 the Heb denotes "opening of the eyes," rather than "opening of the prison." Prisoners are promised "light after darkness, gleam after gloom."

8. In the NT

In the NT "prison" generally occurs for the Gr word φυλακή, *phulakḗ*, which corresponds to the Heb word מִשְׁמָר, *mishmār*, referred to above (Mt **5** 25; Mk **6** 17; Lk **3** 20; Acts **5** 19; 1 Pet **3** 19). In Rev **18** 2, AV renders this word by two different words, viz. "hold" and "cage"; RV employs "hold" in each case (RVm "prison"). In one passage "ward" is the rendering in AV (Acts **12** 10). In connection with the imprisonment of John the term used is δεσμωτήριον, *desmōtḗrion*, "place of bonds" or "fetters" (Mt **11** 2); the same word is used in the case of Peter and John (Acts **5** 21.23), and of Paul and Silas (Acts **16** 26). But the more common term is also found in these narratives. In Acts **12** 17 "prison" renders a Gr word which means "dwelling." In Acts **5** 18 AV, "prison" is the rendering for another Gr word, viz. τήρησις, *tḗrēsis*, "watching" or "ward" (RV "ward"). In Acts **4** 3, AV employs "hold" as the rendering for the same word. This would correspond to the modern "police station" or "lockup." See also PUNISHMENTS.

T. LEWIS

PRISON GARMENTS. See preceding article.

PRISON, SPIRITS IN: The phrase occurs in the much-disputed passage, 1 Pet **3** 18–20, where the apostle, exhorting Christians to endurance under suffering for well-doing, says: "Because Christ also suffered for sins once, the righteous for the unrighteous, that he might bring us to God; being put to death in the flesh, but made alive in the spirit; in which also he went and preached unto the spirits in prison, that aforetime were disobedient, when the longsuffering of God waited in the days of Noah, while the ark was a preparing, wherein few, that is, eight souls, were saved through water." It is plain that in this context "the spirits in prison" (τοῖς ἐν φυλακῇ πνεύμασιν, *toís en phulakḗ pneúmasin*) denote the generation who were disobedient in the days of Noah, while the words "spirits" and "in prison" refer to their present disembodied condition in a place of judgment in the unseen world (cf 2 Pet **2** 4-9). The crucial point in the passage lies in what is said of Christ's preaching to these spirits in prison. The interpretation which strikes one most naturally is that Christ, put to death in the flesh, and made alive again in the spirit, went in this spiritual (disembodied) state, and preached to these spirits, who once had been disobedient, but are viewed as now possibly receptive of His message. This is the idea of the passage taken by the majority of modern exegetes, and it finds support in what is said in 1 Pet **4** 6, "For unto this end was the gospel preached even to the dead, that they might be judged indeed according to men in the flesh, but live according to God in the spirit." On this basis is now often reared a mass of doctrine or conjecture respecting "second probation," "restoration," etc—in part going back to patristic times—for which the passage, even so taken, affords a very narrow foundation (see on this view, Plumptre, *The Spirits in Prison;* Dorner, *System of Christian Doctrine,* IV, 130-32; E. White, *Life in Christ,* ch xxii). It must be admitted, however, that, on closer examination, the above plausible explanation is compassed with many difficulties. A preaching of Christ in Hades is referred to in no other passage of Scripture, while Peter appears to be speaking to his readers of something with which they are familiar; it seems strange that these antediluvians should be singled out as the sole objects of this preaching in the spiritual world; the word "made alive" does not exegetically refer to a disembodied state, but to the resurrection of Christ in the body, etc. Another line of interpretation is therefore preferred by many, who take the words "in which also he went," to refer, not to a disembodied manifestation, but to the historical preaching to the antediluvian generation through Noah while they yet lived. In favor of this view is the fact that the apostle in **1** 11 regards the earlier prophetic preaching as a testifying of "the Spirit of Christ," that God's long-suffering with Noah's generation is described in Gen **6** 5, which Peter has doubtless in his mind, as a striving of God's Spirit, and that in 2 Pet **2** 5 there is another allusion to these events, and Noah is described as "a preacher of righteousness." The passage, 1 Pet **4** 6, may have the more general meaning that Christians who have died are at no disadvantage in the judgment as compared with those who shall be alive at the Parousia (cf 1 Thess **4** 15-18). (For an exposition of this view, with a full account of the interpretations and literature on the subject, cf Salmond's *Christian Doctrine of Immortality,* 4th ed, 364-87.) See also ESCHATOLOGY OF THE NT. JAMES ORR

PRIVY, priv'i, **PRIVILY,** priv'i-li: These words are obsolete in modern Eng. and are replaced by "secret," "secretly," rather than by the cognates "private," "privately." RV usually has not altered AV's use of the word, but in Ps **11** 2 has substituted "in darkness" and in Jgs **9** 31 uses "craftily," m "in Tormah" (see TORMAH). In Ezk **21** 14, AV "entereth into their privy chambers," "privy" is a gloss, omitted in RV. "To be privy to a thing" (1 K **2** 44; Acts **5** 2) is simply "to know" it; in Wisd **8** 4, RV has changed the phrase into "be initiated into."

PRIZE, prīz: Two Gr words are so rendered in EV: (1) βραβεῖον, *brabeíon,* the award to the victor in the Gr games, consisting of a garland of bay, olive, or pine; so called because it was given by the βραβεύς, *brabeús,* the adjudicator who assigned the prize at the games (Vulg *bravium,* from which *may* be derived the Eng. "brave" = originally gaily dressed, handsome). Used lit. in 1 Cor **9** 24, and **figuratively** of the heavenly reward for Christian character in Phil **3** 14. (2) ἁρπαγμός, *harpagmós,* in ERV of Phil **2** 6, "counted it not a prize to be on an equality with God." The termination -μος, *-mos,* would lead us to expect the active sense: "an act of grasping," "plundering" (AV "robbery"), which would imply that Christ did not deem it an act of usurpation to claim equality with God, for such equality was His inherent right. But the context demands a reference "not to the right which He *claimed,* but to the dignity which He *renounced*" (Lightfoot); hence the majority of modern expositors take the word in a passive sense (= ἅρπαγμα, *hárpagma*): "a thing to be seized, prized, retained at all costs as a booty" (ERV "a prize," ARV "a thing to be grasped"), implying that Christ did not regard equality with God as a thing to be clutched greedily, but waived His rights (see Lightfoot on Phil **2** 6). The vb. "to prize" occurs only in Zec **11** 13. See GRASP; HUMILIATION OF CHRIST; KENOSIS. D. MIALL EDWARDS

PROBATION, prō-bā'shun, **SECOND,** sek'und. See ESCHATOLOGY OF THE NT.

PROCHORUS, prok'ō-rus (Πρόχορος, *Próchoros*): One of "the seven" chosen by the Christian community in Jerus to superintend the dispensing of charity to the widows and other poor (Acts **6** 5). The name is Gr, and he may have been a Hellenist. According to tradition he became bishop of Nicomedia and died a martyr at Antioch.

PROCONSUL, prō-kon'sul (ἀνθύπατος, *anthúpatos* [Acts **13** 7; **18** 12]; AV **deputy**). See PROVINCE.

PROCURATOR, prok'ū-rā-tēr (ἐπίτροπος, *epítropos*): This word signified in a general sense a steward or bailiff of a private estate, or a financial agent with power of attorney, and the development of the special usage of the word to denote an imperial functionary or official is characteristic of the origin of many departments of administration under the Roman Empire which sprang from the emperor's household. At the time of Augustus, when the domestic quality of these offices had not been entirely lost, the procurators were mostly imperial freedmen. But after the systematic organization of the administration in the 2d cent., the title of procurator was reserved for functionaries of the equestrian class. In fact, the term is so intimately connected with the sphere of official activity of the Rom knights that the expressions "procuratorial career" and "equestrian career" are used synonymously (cf Hirschfeld, *Die kaiserlichen Verwaltungsbeamten bis auf Diocletian,* 410-65).

During the last century of the Republic, the class of knights (*equites*) embraced in general all citizens of wealth who were not magistrates or members of the senate. The Roscian Law (67 BC) established 400,000 sesterces (about $18,000 or £3,600) as the minimum census rating for membership in this class. The gold ring, tunic with narrow purple border, and privilege of sitting in the first 14 rows at the theater were the tokens of knighthood. Augustus added to these the public horse which was conferred henceforth by the emperor and recalled the original military significance of the order. From the time of Augustus the first three *decuriae* of jurors (*judices*), each containing 1,000 persons, were filled with knights.

Under the Republic the influence of the equestrian class was chiefly exerted in the financial transactions of the companies which farmed the variable revenues. The importance of the *publicani* was greatly reduced under the Empire, but the emperors recompensed the knights for this loss of opportunity by intrusting them with a great variety of administrative functions. Military service as prefect or tribune was the preliminary step in the official equestrian career. The highest positions held by members of the equestrian class were called prefectures, and included the prefecture of the guard, of Egypt, of the grain-supply, of the watchmen in Rome, and of the fleet. But between these extremes the title procurator was applied generally to the functionaries whose positions were of imperial origin.

The administration of the *fiscus* or imperial treasury at Rome and of the finances in the imperial provinces, as well as the collection of fiscal revenues in the senatorial provinces, was in the hands of procurators. They occupied many positions which, on account of their intimate relationship with the person of the monarch, could be safely intrusted only to those whose limited prestige precluded inordinate ambition (Friedlaender, *Sittengeschichte Roms*, 7th ed, Part I, 132–43). Finally, several provinces, where the conditions were unfavorable to the introduction of the ordinary administrative system and Rom public law, were governed as imperial domains by officials of the equestrian class as the emperor's representatives. In Egypt the title prefect (*praefectus*) was employed permanently as the appellation of the viceroy, and while the same term may have been used originally to denote the governors of this class generally, when their military outweighed their civil functions, yet the designation procurator became at an early date the term of common usage to designate them (Hirschfeld, 382).

Mauretania, Rhaetia, Noricum, Thrace, Cappadocia, Judaea and some smaller districts were all, for a time at least, governed by procurators (Tacitus *Hist.* i.11; Dio Cassius lvii.17).

The question concerning the original title of the Rom governors of Judaea has arisen because the NT employs the word *hēgemōn* (Mt **27** 2.11.14.15.21.27; **28** 14; Lk **3** 1; **20** 20; Acts **23** 24; **24** 1; **26** 30), which corresponds with the Lat term *praeses*, which might be considered synonymous with either procurator or *praefectus* (Hirschfeld, 384). There is no inscriptional evidence to establish the nomenclature of the rulers of Pal before the time of Vespasian, and Hirschfeld is of the opinion that a certain passage in Tacitus (*Ann.* xv.44) where Pilate is called *procurator* is not sufficient proof in view of this writer's carelessness in details of this sort. Josephus (*Ant*, XX, i, 2), however, employs *epitropos* (*procurator*) for the time of Claudius, and it is convenient to follow common usage and assume that this title was current from the first.

It was evidently the intention of Augustus that membership in the equestrian class should be a necessary qualification for the procurators who were appointed to govern provinces. But Claudius appointed a freedman, Antonius Felix, brother of the famous minister of finance, Pallas, as procurator of Judaea (Suetonius *Claud.* xxviii; Tacitus *Hist.* v.9). This remained, however, an isolated instance in the annals of Pal (Hirschfeld, 380), and it is probable, moreover, that Felix was raised to equestrian rank before the governorship was conferred upon him.

The following list of the procurators of Judaea is based on Marquardt (*Römische Staatsverwaltung*, I, 409, 412) and Schürer (*Geschichte des jüdischen Volkes*[4], I, 485–585):

Coponius (6 AD to c 10 AD)
M. Ambibulus (c 10–13)
Annius Rufus (c 13–15)
Valerius Gratus (c 15–26)
Pontius Pilatus (26–35)
Marcellus (probably 35–38)
Maryllus (38–44)
C. Cuspius Fadus (44–46)
Tiberius Alexander (46–48)
Ventidius Cumanus (48–52)
M. Antonius Felix (52–60 or 61)

NOTE.—Marquardt gives his name as Claudius Felix, supposing that he was a freedman of Claudius and therefore took his *nomen* (Suetonius *Claud.* xxviii; Victor, *epitome* iv, 8); but there is stronger evidence in support of the belief that Felix was a freedman of Antonia, Claudius' mother, like his brother Pallas (Tacitus *Ann.* xii.54; Jos, *Ant*, XVIII, vi, 4; XX, vii, 1, 2; XX, viii, 9; *BJ*, II, xii, 8), and accordingly had received the *praenomen* and *nomen* of Antonia's father (Jos, *Ant*, XVIII, vi, 6).

Portius Festus (61)
Albinus (62–64)
Gessius Florus (65–66)

See, further, GOVERNOR. GEORGE H. ALLEN

PROFANE, prō̇-fān′ (vb. חָלַל, *ḥālal*, adj. חָלָל, *ḥālāl*, חֹל, *ḥōl*; **βεβηλόω,** *bebēlóō*, **βέβηλος,** *bébēlos*): From *profanus*, "before [i.e. outside] the temple," therefore unholy, polluted, secular, is of frequent occurrence (vb. and adj.) in both the OT and the NT. It occurs as the tr of *ḥōl* in AV only in Ezk (**22** 26, RV "common"; **42** 20; **44** 23; **48** 15, RV "for common use"); as the tr of *ḥālāl* in Lev **21** 7.14, RVm "polluted"; and Ezk **21** 25, where, for AV "thou profane wicked prince of Israel," RV has "thou, O deadly wounded wicked one, the prince of Israel." "To profane" (*ḥālal*) is seen in Lev **18** 21; **19** 8; Neh **13** 17.18; Ps **89** 39; Isa **43** 28; Ezk **22** 8.26, etc. "Profaneness" in Jer **23** 15 (*ḥănuppāh*) is in ARV "ungodliness." In the NT "profane" occurs in the sense of unholy, godless, regardless of God and Divine things (1 Tim **1** 9; **4** 7; **6** 20; 2 Tim **2** 16; He **12** 16), and "to profane," or violate, in Mt **12** 5; Acts **24** 6. The vb. is frequent in Apoc in 1 Macc (**1** 43.45.63; **2** 34, etc; also in 2 Macc **8** 2; **10** 5; cf 2 Esd **15** 8; Jth **4** 3.12; 1 Macc **1** 48; 2 Macc **4** 13). In numerous cases RV substitutes "profane" for other words and phrases in AV, as for "to prostitute" (Lev **19** 29), "an hypocrite" (Isa **9** 17), "pollute" (Nu **18** 32; Ezk **7** 21), etc. W. L. WALKER

PROFESS, prō̇-fes′, **PROFESSION,** prō̇-fesh′un (נָגַד, *nāghadh*; **ὁμολογέω,** *homologéō*, **ὁμολογία,** *homología*): "Profess" means lit. "to own before," hence to make open or public announcement; it occurs only once in the OT as the tr of *nāghadh*, "to put before," often "to tell," "to show," "to declare" (Dt **26** 3); in the NT it is the tr of *homologeō*, "to speak or say together in common," "to assent," "to confess publicly" (Mt **7** 23, "Then will I profess unto them, I never knew you"; 1 Tim **6** 12, RV "didst confess the good confession"; Tit **1** 16, "They profess that they know God"); of *epaggéllomai*, "to announce one's self," "to make profession" (1 Tim **2** 10; **6** 21); of *pháskō*, "to say," "to assert" (Rom **1** 22). "Profession" is the tr of *homologia* (2 Cor **9** 13; 1 Tim **6** 12; He **3** 1, AV "the High Priest of our profession" [of our professed faith]; **4** 14; **10** 23; in each instance RV has "confession"). "Profess" occurs in AV of Ecclus **3** 25, but the verse is omitted by RV; m "Most authorities omit verse 25."

W. L. WALKER

PROGNOSTICATORS, prog-nos′ti-kā-tẽrz, **MONTHLY.** See ASTROLOGY, 6.

PROLOGUE, prō′log, prol′og (**πρόλογος,** *prólogos*, "foreword," "preface," "introduction"): The word occurs in the preface to Ecclus (Sir), and is commonly applied to Jn **1** 1–18. See ECCLESIASTICUS; JOHN, GOSPEL of.

PROLONG, prō-long′ (אָרַךְ, *'ārakh,* מָשַׁךְ, *māshakh*): "Prolong," "prolonged" are the tr[s] of *'ārakh,* "to stretch," "to make long" (Dt **4** 26, and frequently, "prolong days"; **4** 40, etc; Job **6** 11 AV; Prov **28** 16; Eccl **7** 15; **8** 13; Isa **53** 10); of *māshakh,* "to draw out" (Isa **13** 22; Ezk **12** 25.28 AV); of *yāṣaph,* "to add," "to increase" (Ps **61** 6; Prov **10** 27); of *nāṭāh,* "to stretch out," "to incline to" (Job **15** 29, "neither shall he prolong the perfection thereof upon the earth," ARV "neither shall their possessions be extended on the earth," m "their produce bend to the earth"; ERV reverses text and margin); of *'ar[e]khāh* (Aram.) (Dnl **7** 12, "Yet their lives were prolonged," AVm "A prolonging in life was given them"). "Prolong" occurs in Ecclus **29** 5, "prolong the time" (*parelkúō*); **38** 14, "prolong life," RV "maintenance of life" (*embíōsis*); **30** 22, "prolongeth his days," RV "length of days" (*makroēméreusis*); **37** 31, RV "shall prolong" (*prostíthēmi*).

W. L. WALKER

PROMISE, prom′is (most frequently in the OT דָּבָר, *dābhār,* "speaking," "speech," and דָּבַר, *dābhar,* "to speak," also אָמַר, *'āmar,* "to say," once in Ps **77** 8, *'ōmer,* "speech"; in the NT ἐπαγγελία, *epaggelía,* and the vbs. ἐπαγγέλλομαι, *epaggéllomai,* and compounds): Promise holds an important place in the Scriptures and in the development of the religion that culminated in Christ. The Bible is indeed full of "precious and exceeding great promises" (2 Pet **1** 4), although the word "promise" is not always used in connection with them. Of the more outstanding promises of the OT may be mentioned: (1) the *proto-evangelium* (Gen **3** 15); (2) the promise to Noah no more to curse the ground, etc (Gen **8** 21.22; **9** 1–17); (3) most influential, the promise to Abraham to make of him a great nation in whom all families of the earth should be blessed, to give to him and his seed the land of Canaan (Gen **12** 2.7, etc), often referred to in the OT (Ex **12** 25; Dt **1** 8.11; **6** 3; **9** 28, etc); (4) the promise to David to continue his house on the throne (2 S **7** 12.13.28; 1 K **2** 24, etc); (5) the promise of restoration of Israel, of the Messiah, of the new and everlasting kingdom, of the new covenant and outpouring of the Spirit (Isa **2** 2–5; **4** 2; **55** 5; **66** 13; Jer **31** 31–34; **32** 37–42; **33** 14; Ezk **36** 22–31; **37** 11 f; **39** 25 f, etc). In the NT these promises are founded on, and regarded as having their true fulfilment in, Christ and those who are His (2 Cor **1** 20; Eph **3** 6). The promise of the Spirit is spoken of by Jesus as "the promise of my Father" (Lk **24** 49; Acts **1** 4), and this was regarded as fulfilled at Pentecost. The promise of a Saviour of the seed of David is regarded as fulfilled in Christ (Acts **13** 23. 32, **26** 6; Rom **1** 2; **4** 13; **9** 4). Paul argues that the promise to Abraham that he should be "heir of the world," made to him before circumcision, is not confined to Israel, but is open to all who are children of Abraham by faith (Rom **4** 13–16; cf Gal **3** 16. 19.29). In like manner the writer to the Hebrews goes back to the original promises, giving them a spiritual and eternal significance (**4** 1; **6** 17; **11** 9, etc). The NT promises include manifold blessings and hopes, among them "life," "eternal life" (1 Tim **4** 8; **6** 19; 2 Tim **1** 1; Jas **1** 12), the "kingdom" (Jas **2** 5), Christ's "coming" (2 Pet **3** 9, etc), "new heavens and a new earth" (2 Pet **3** 13), etc. For "promise" and "promised" in AV, RV has frequently other terms, as "word" (Ps **105** 42), "spake," "spoken" (Dt **10** 9; Josh **9** 21; **22** 4; **23** 5.15, etc), "consented" (Lk **22** 6), etc. References to the promises occur repeatedly in the Apoc (Bar **2** 34; 2 Macc **2** 18; Wisd **12** 21; cf 2 Esd **3** 15; **5** 29).

W. L. WALKER

PROPER, prop′ẽr: For AV "proper" (child), in He **11** 23, RV substitutes "goodly"; in 1 Ch **29** 3; 1 Cor **7** 7, RV "own" is employed, and for the too emphatic "their proper tongue" in Acts **1** 19 "their language" is written. But none of the AV forms are really obsolete.

PROPER NAMES. See NAMES, PROPER.

PROPERTY, prop′ẽr-ti. See AGRARIAN LAWS; JUBILEE; POOR; PORTION; PRIMOGENITURE; WEALTH.

PROPHECY, prof′ĕ-si, prof′e-si, **PROPHETS,** prof′ets:

I. The Idea of Biblical Prophecy.—According to the uniform teaching of the Bible the prophet is a *speaker* of or for God. His words are not the production of his own spirit, but come from a higher source. For he is at the same time, also, a *seer,* who sees things that do not lie in the domain of natural sight, or who hears things which human ears do not ordinarily receive; cf 1 S **9** 9, where *nābhī',* "speaker," and *rō'eh,* "seer," are used as synonymous terms. Jer **23** 16 and Ezk **13** 2 f are particularly instructive in this regard. In these passages a sharp distinction is made between those persons who only claim to be prophets but who prophesy "out of their own heart," and the true prophets who declare the word which the Lord has spoken to them. In the latter case the contents of the prophecy have not originated in their own reflection or calculation; and just as little is this prophecy the product of their own feelings, fears or hopes, but, as something extraneous to man and independent of him, it has with a Divine certainty entered the soul of the prophet. The prophet has seen that which he prophesies, although he need not have seen it in the form of a real vision. He can also "see" words with his inner eyes (Isa **2** 1, and often). It is only another expression for this when it is frequently said that God has spoken to the prophet. In this case too it is not necessary that

1. The Seer and Speaker of God

there must have been a voice which he could hear phonetically through his natural ear. The main thing is that he must have been able sharply to distinguish the contents of this voice from his own heart, i.e. from his personal consciousness. Only in this way is he capable of speaking to the people in the name of God and able to publish his word as that of Jeh. In this case he is the speaker of Jeh (*nābhī'*), or the mouth of the Lord (cf Ezk **7** 1 with **4** 16). Under these conditions he then regards it as absolute compulsion to speak, just as a person must be filled with fear when he hears a lion roar nearby (Am **3** 8). The words burn in his soul until he utters them (Jer **20** 7.9).

2. Prophetical Inspiration

The Divine power, which comes over a human being and compels him to see or to hear things which otherwise would be hidden from him, is called by various terms expressive of inspiration. It is said that the Spirit of God has come over someone (Nu **24** 2); or has fallen upon him (Ezk **11** 5); or that the hand of Jeh has come over him and laid hold of him (2 K **3** 15; Ezk **1** 3; **3** 14.22, and often); or that the Holy Spirit has been put on him as a garment, i.e. has been incorporated in him (1 Ch **12** 18; 2 Ch **24** 20); or that the Spirit of revelation has permanently descended upon him (Nu **11** 25 f; 2 K **2** 15; Isa **11** 2; **61** 1); or that God has given this Spirit of His (Nu **11** 29; Isa **42** 1); or pours Him out upon man (Joel **2** 28 f [Heb **3** 1 f]). But this inspiration is not such that it suppresses the human consciousness of the recipient, so that he would receive the word of God in the state of sleep or trance. But rather the recipient is in possession of his full consciousness, and is able afterward to give a clear account of what happened. Nor is the individuality of the prophet eliminated by this Divine inspiration; unconsciously this individuality coöperates in the formal shaping of that which has been seen and heard. In accordance with the natural peculiarity of the prophet and with the contents of the message, the psychological condition of the recipient may be that of intense excitement or of calmness. As a rule the inspiration that takes possession of the prophets is evidenced also by an exalted and poetical language, which assumes a certain rhythmical character, but is not bound to a narrow and mechanical meter. It is, however, also possible that prophetical utterances find their expression in plain prose. The individual peculiarity of the prophet is a prime factor also in the form in which the revelation comes to him. In the one prophet we find a preponderance of visions; another prophet has no visions. But the visions of the future which he sees are given in the forms and the color which have been furnished by his own consciousness. All the more the form in which the prophet gives expression to his word of God is determined by his personal talents and gifts as also by his experiences.

3. The Dream

In a certain respect the dream can be cited as an analogous phenomenon, in which also the ideas that are slumbering in the soul uninvited put in their appearance without being controlled by consciousness and reason. On the other hand, prophecy differs specifically from dreams, first, because the genuine prophetical utterance is received when the prophet is clearly conscious, and, secondly, because such an utterance brings with it a much greater degree of certainty and a greater guaranty of its higher origin than is done even by a dream that seems to be prophetical. In Jer **23** 25 ff it is declared that these two are entirely dissimilar, and the relation between the two is compared to straw and wheat. The Moslem Arabs also put a much lower estimate on the visionary dream than on the prophetic vision in a waking condition.

4. Freedom of Inspiration

Because this Spirit of God acts with full freedom, He can select His organs at will from among every station, age or sex. The Spirit is not confined to any priestly class or organization. It indeed was the case at times, that a prophet gathered disciples around himself, who could themselves in turn also be seized by his spirit, although the transmission of this spirit was a difficult matter (2 K **2** 10). Yet genuine prophecies continued to be at all times a free gift of the sovereign God. Amos (**7** 14 f) appeals expressly to this fact, that he did not himself choose the prophet's calling nor was the pupil of a prophetic school, but that he had been directly called by Jeh from his daily occupation as a shepherd and workman. In the same way we indeed find prophets who belonged to the priestly order (Jeremiah, Ezekiel and others), but equally great is the number of those who certainly did not so belong. Further, age made no difference in the call to the prophetic office. Even in his earliest youth Samuel was called to be a prophet (1 S **3** 1 ff), and it did not avail Jeremiah anything when he excused himself because of his youth (Jer **1** 6). Then, too, a woman could be seized by this Spirit. From time to time prophetesses appeared, although the female sex is by no means so prominent here as it is in the sorcery of the heathen. See PROPHETESS. As an exceptional case the Spirit of God could lay hold even of a person who inwardly was entirely estranged from Him and could make an utterance through him (cf Saul, 1 S **10** 11; **19** 24; Balaam, Nu **23** f; Caiaphas, Jn **11** 51). As a rule, however, God has selected such prophetic organs for a longer service. These persons are called and dedicated for this purpose by Him through a special act (cf Moses Ex **3** 1 ff; 1 K **19** 16.19 ff; Isa **6**; Jer **1**; Ezk **1**). This moment was decisive for their whole lives and constituted their authorization as far as they themselves and others were concerned. Yet for each prophetic appearance these men receive a special enlightenment. The prophet does not at all times speak in an inspired state; cf Nathan (2 S **7** 3 ff), who afterward was compelled to take back a word which he had spoken on his own authority. Characteristic data on the mental state of the prophets in the reception and in the declaration of the Divine word are found in Jer **15** 16 f; **20** 7 ff. Originally Jeremiah felt it as a joy that Jeh spoke to him (cf Ezk **3** 3), but then he lost all pleasure in life and would have preferred not to have uttered this word, but he could not do as he desired.

5. Supernatural Visions of the Future

The attempt has often been made to explain prophecy as a natural product of purely human factors. Rationalistic theologians regarded the prophets as enthusiastic teachers of religion and morals, as warm patriots and politicians, to whom they ascribed nothing but a certain ability of guessing the future. But this was no explanation of the facts in the case. The prophets were themselves conscious of this, that they were not the intellectual authors of their higher knowledge. This consciousness is justified by the fact that they were in a condition to make known things which lay beyond their natural horizon and which were contrary to all probability. Those cases are particularly instructive in this respect which beyond a doubt were recorded by the prophets themselves. Ezekiel could indeed, on the basis of moral and religious reflections, reach the conviction that Zedekiah of Jerus would not escape his punishment for his political treachery and for his disobedience to the word of Jeh; but he could never from this source have reached the certainty that this king, as the prophet describes the case in **12** 8 ff, was to be taken captive while trying to escape from the besieged city and was then to be blinded and taken to Babylon. Just as little could he in Babylon know the exact day when the siege of Jerus began (**24** 2). If this prophet had learned of these things in a natural way and had afterward clothed them in the form of prophecy, he would have been guilty of a deception, something unthinkable in the case of so conscientious a preacher of morality. But such cases are frequently met with. Jeremiah predicts to Hananiah that he would die during the year (**28** 16), but it is not only such matters of detail that presuppose an extraordinary vision of the prophet. The whole way also in which Jeremiah predicts the destruction of Jerus as inevitable, in direct contrast to the hopes of the Jerusalemites and to the desires of his own heart, shows that he was speaking under Divine compulsion, which was more powerful than his own reflections and sympathies. On any other presupposition his conduct would have been reprehensible cowardice. The case of Isaiah is exactly the same. When he gives to Ahaz the word of God as a guaranty that the Syrians and the Ephraimites would not capture Jerus (**7** 4 ff), and when he promises Hezekiah that the Assyrians would not shoot an arrow into the city, but would return without having accomplished their purpose (**37** 22.33), these things were so much in contradiction to all the probabilities of the course events would take that he would have been a frivolous adventurer had he not received his information from higher sources. Doubtless it was just these predictions which established and upheld the influence of the prophets. Thus in the case of Amos it was his prediction of a great earthquake, which did occur two years later (**1** 1); in the case of Elijah, the prediction of the long dearth (1 K **17** 1); in the case of Elisha, the undertakings of the enemies (2 K **6** 12), and in other cases. It is indeed true that the contents of the prophetic discourses are not at all confined to the future. Everything that God has to announce to mankind, revelations concerning His will, admonitions, warnings, He is able to announce through the mouth of the prophet. But His determinations with reference to the future as a rule are connected with prophetical utterances of the latter kind. The prophets are watchmen, guardians of the people, who are to warn the nation, because they see the dangers and the judgments approaching, which must put in their appearance if the Divine will is disregarded. The prophets interpret also for the people that which is happening and that which has occurred, e.g. the defeats which they have suffered at the hands of their enemies, or the grasshopper plague (Joel), or a famine. They lay bare the inner reason for external occurrences and explain such events in their connection with the providential government of God. This gives to prophecy a powerful inner unity, notwithstanding the great differences of times and surrounding circumstances. It is prophecy which the Heb people must thank for their higher conception of history. This people know of a Highest Author of all things and of a positive end, which all things that transpire must serve. God's plan has for its purpose to bring about the complete supremacy of His will among the children of men.

In genuine prophecy, according to Bib. conceptions, the fulfilment constitutes an integral part.

6. The Fulfilment

This is set up by Dt **18** 21 f as a proof of the genuineness of a prophetic utterance. The prophetic word "falls to the ground" (1 S **3** 19) if it is not "raised up" (הֵקִים, *hēkīm*, "fulfil," for which we more rarely find מִלֵּא, *millē'*, but regularly in the NT πληροῦσθαι, *plēroústhai*, "being fulfilled") by the course of events. It would remain an empty word if it did not attain to its full content through its realization. In fact, in the word spoken by the prophet itself there dwells a Divine power, so that at the moment when he speaks the event takes place, even if it is not yet visible to man. This realization is also not infrequently represented symbolically by the prophet in confirmation of his prediction. Thus in a certain sense it is the prophet himself who through his word builds up and pulls down, plants and roots out (Jer **1** 10; **25** 15 ff). But the fulfilment can be judged by the contemporaries in the sense of Dt **18** 22 only when this fulfilment refers to the near future and when special emphasis is laid on external events. In these cases the prediction of certain events assumes the significance of a "sign" (cf Jer **28** 16; Isa **8** 1 ff; **37** 30, and elsewhere). In other cases it is only later generations who can judge of the correctness of a prediction or of a threat. In this way in Zec **1** 6 the fulfilment of a threat is declared, and in the NT often the fulfilment of a promise is after a long time pointed out. But it is not the case that a genuine prophecy must be fulfilled like an edict of fate. Such prophecy is not an inevitable decree of fate, but is a word of the living God to mankind, and therefore conditioned ethically, and God can, if repentance has followed, withdraw a threat (Jer **18** 2 ff; case of Jonah), or the punishment can be mitigated (1 K **21** 29). A prediction, too, Jeh can recall if the people prove unworthy (Jer **18** 9 f). A favorable or an unfavorable prediction can also be postponed, as far as its realization is concerned, to later times, if it belongs to the ultimate counsels of God, as e.g. the final judgment and deliverance on the last day. This counsel also may be realized successively. In this case the prophet already collects into one picture what is realized gradually in a longer historical development. The prophet in general spoke to his hearers in such a way as could be understood by them and could be impressed on them. It is therefore not correct to demand a fulfilment pedantically exact in the form of the historical garb of the prophecy. The main thing is that the Divine thought contained in the prophecy be entirely and completely realized. But not unfrequently the finger of God can be seen in the entirely literal fulfilment of certain prophecies. This is esp. the case in the NT in the appearance of the Son of Man, in whom all the rays of OT prophecy have found their common center.

II. Historical Development of the Prophetic Office.—It is a characteristic peculiarity of the religion of the OT that its very elementary beginnings are of a prophetical nature.

1. Abraham

The fathers, above all Abraham, but also Isaac and Jacob, are the recipients of visions and of Divine revelations. Esp. is this true of Abraham, who appeared to the foreigners, to whom he was neither kith or kin, to be indeed a prophet (*nābhī'*) (Gen **20** 7; cf Ps **105** 15), although in his case the command to preach the word was yet absent. Above all, the creative founder of the Israelitish national religion, Moses, is a prophet in the eminent sense of the word.

2. Moses

His influence among the people is owing neither to his official position, nor to any military prowess, but solely and alone to the one circumstance, that since his call at the burning bush God has spoken to him. This intercourse between God and Moses was ever of a particularly intimate character. While other men of God received certain individual messages only from time to time and through the mediation of dreams and visions, Jeh spoke directly and "face to face" with Moses (Nu **12** 6 ff; Dt **34** 10; cf Ex **33** 11). Moses was the permanent organ through whom Jeh brought about the Egyp plagues and through whom He explained what these meant to His people, as also through whom He led and ruled them. The voice of Moses too had to explain to them the Divine signs in the desert and communicate to them the commandments of God. The legislation of Moses shows that he was not only filled with the Spirit of God occasionally, but that he abode with God for longer periods of time and produced something that is a well-ordered whole. A production such as the Law is the result of a continuous association with God.

Since that time revelation through prophecy was probably never entirely wanting in Israel (Dt **18** 15). But this fountain did not always flow with the same fulness or clearness.

3. Period of the Judges

During the period of the Judges the Spirit of God urged the heroes who served Jeh rather to deeds than to words. Yet Deborah enjoyed a high rank as a prophetess, and for a long time pronounced decisions of justice in the name of the Lord before she, through her prophetical utterances, aroused the people to rise up against their oppressors. What is said in 1 S **3** 1 concerning the times of Eli can be applied to this whole period, namely that the word and vision of the prophet had become rare in the land. All the more epoch-making was the activity of Samuel, who while yet a boy received Divine revelations (1 S **3** 1 ff). He was by the whole people regarded as a "seer" whose prophecies were always fulfilled (**3** 19 f). The passage **9** 6 ff shows that the people expected of such a man of God that he should also as a clairvoyant come to the assistance of the people in the troubles of life. Such a professional clairvoyant, indeed, Samuel was not, as he was devoted entirely to the service of his God and of his people and obeyed the Divine Spirit, even in those cases when he was compelled to act contrary to his personal inclinations, as was the case when the kingdom was established in Israel (**8** 6 ff).

Since the days of Samuel we hear of schools of prophets, or "sons of prophets." These associations probably originated in this way, that an experienced prophet attracted to himself bands of youths, who sought to receive a measure of his spirit.

4. Schools of Prophets

These disciples of the prophets, together with their families, lived in colonies around the master. Possibly Samuel was the first who founded such a school of prophets. For in or near the city of Ramah we first find *nāyōth*, or colonies of such disciples (1 S **19** 18 f; **20** 1). Among these pupils is found to a much greater extent than among the teachers a certain ecstatic feature. They arouse their feelings through music and induce a frantic condition which also affects others in the same way, in which state they "prophesy" and, throwing off their garments, fall to the ground. In later times too we find traces of such ecstatic phenomena. Thus e.g. in Zec **13** 6; 1 K **20** 37.38, the "wounds" on the breast or on the forehead recall the self-mutilation of the priests of Baal (1 K **18** 28). The deeds, suggestive of what the dervishes of our own day do, probably were phenomena quite similar to the action of the prophets of the surrounding tribes. But that prophecy in Israel was not, as is now not infrequently claimed, merely a less crude form of the heathen prophetic institution, is proved by such men as Moses and Samuel, who even in their times represent something much higher. Also in the colonies of prophets there was assuredly not to be found merely an enthusiasm without the Spirit of God. Proof for this is Samuel, the spiritual father of this colony, as Elijah was for the later colonies of this kind. These places were rather the centers of a religious life, where communion with God was sought by prayer and meditation, and where the recollection of the great deeds of God in the past seemed to prepare for the reception of new revelations. From such centers of theocratic ideas and ideals without a doubt there came forth also corresponding influences that affected the people. Perhaps not only was sacred music cultivated at these places but also sacred traditions, which were handed down orally and in writing. Certain it is that at these colonies the religion of Jeh prevailed.

During the period of the kings prophetically inspired men frequently appeared, who demanded even of the kings that they should submit to their Divinely inspired word.

5. Period of the Kings

Saul, who refused such submission, perished as the result of this conflict. David owed much to the support of the prophets Samuel, Nathan, Gad (1 S **16** 1 ff; 2 S **7**; 2 Ch **29** 25, and elsewhere). But David also bowed in submission when these prophets rebuked him because of his transgression of the Divine commands (2 S **12, 24**). His son Solomon was educated by the prophet Nathan. But the destruction of his kingdom was predicted by the prophet Abijah, the Shilonite (1 K **11** 29 ff). Since Jeh, as the supreme Sovereign, has the right to enthrone or to dethrone kings, this is often done through the mouths of the prophets (cf 1 K **14** 7 ff; **16** 1 ff). After the division of the kingdom we find Shemaiah forbidding Rehoboam to begin a war with his brethren of Israel (1 K **12** 21; cf 2 Ch **11** 2 ff; cf another mission of the same prophet, 2 Ch **12** 5 ff). On the other hand in the Northern Kingdom the prophetic word is soon turned against the untheocratic rule of Jeroboam (1 K **13, 14**). It is in this very same Northern Kingdom that the prophets unfolded their full activity and generally in opposition to the secular rulers, although there was no lack of accommodating "prophets," who were willing to sanction everything that the king wanted. The opposition of the true prophets to these false representatives of prophecy is illustrated in the story of Micaiah, the son of Imlah (1 K **22**). But a still higher type of prophecy above the ordinary is found in Elijah, whose historic mission it was to fight to the finish the battle between the followers of Jeh and the worship of the Tyrian Baal. He was entirely a man of action; every one of his words is a deed on a grand scale (cf concerning Elijah and Elisha the art. Religion of Israel). His successor Elisha inherited from him not only his mantle, but also a double measure of his spiritual gifts. He exhibits the prophetic office more from its loving side. He is accustomed to visit the schools of prophets found scattered throughout the land, calls the faithful together around himself on the Sabbaths and the new moons (2 K **4** 23), and in this way establishes centers of a more spiritual culture than was common elsewhere among the people. We read that first-fruits were brought to him as to the priests (2 K **4** 42). But while the activity of Elijah was entirely in antagonism to the ruling house in the kingdom, this feature is not entirely lacking in the work of Elisha also. He has even been charged with wicked conspiracies against the dynasty of Omri and the king of Syria (2 K **8, 9**). His conduct in connection with these events can be excused only on the ground that he was really acting in the name of a higher Master. But in general it was possible for Elisha, after the radical change in public sentiment that had followed upon the work of Elijah, in later time to assume a more friendly attitude toward the government and the people. He often assisted the kings in their arduous contests with the Syrians (cf **6** 8 ff; **13** 14 ff). His deeds are generally of a benevolent character. In connection with these he exhibits to a remarkable degree the gift of prophetic foresight (2 K **4** 16; **5** 26; **6** 8 ff; **7** 1 ff; **8** 10.12; **9** 6 ff; **13** 19). Jonah, too, the son of Amittai, had at that time a favorable message for the Northern Kingdom (2 K **14** 25).

6. Amos, Hosea and the Literary Prophets

However, the flourishing condition of the kingdom under Jeroboam II had an unfavorable influence on its spiritual development. Soon Amos and Hosea were compelled to announce to this kingdom its impending destruction through a great world-power. These two prophets have left us books. To put prophetic utterances into written form had already been introduced before this. At any rate, many scholars are of the conviction that the prophecies of Obadiah and Joel belong to an earlier period, although others place them in the post-exilic period. In any case, the expectation of a day of settlement by Jeh with His people was already in the days of Amos common and current (**5** 18 ff). As the writing of individual prophecies (Isa **8** 1 f; **30** 8; Hab **2** 2 f) had for its purpose the preserving of these words in permanent authentic form and later to convince the reader of their wonderful fulfilment, thus too the writing down of larger collections of prophecies had for its purpose to intensify the power of the prophetic word and to secure this as a permanent possession of the people (Jer **30** 2; **36** 1 ff). Pupils of the prophets assisted them in this writing and in preserving their books (cf Jer **36** 4; Isa **8** 16).

7. Poetical Form of Prophecy

It is to this custom that we owe our knowledge of the very words of the utterances of many of the prophets of a later period. In addition to the larger books of Isa, Jer, Ezk, we have a number of smaller prophetical books, which have been united into the Book of the Twelve Prophets. These utterances as a rule exhibited an elevated form of language and are more or less poetical. However, in modern times some scholars are inclined to go too far in claiming that these addresses are given in a carefully systematized metrical form. Hebrew meter as such is a freer form of expression than is Arabic or Sanskrit meter, and this is all the more the case with the discourses of the prophets, which were not intended for musical rendering, and which are expressed in a rhythmically constructed rhetoric, which appears now in one and then in another form of melody, and often changes into prose.

8. Prophets in Judah

In the kingdom of Judah the status of the prophets was somewhat more favorable than it was in Ephraim. They were indeed forced in Jerus also to contend against the injustice on the part of the ruling classes and against immorality of all kinds. But in this kingdom there were at any rate from time to time found kings who walked more in the footsteps of David. Thus Asa followed the directions of the prophet Azariah (2 Ch **15** 1 ff). It is true that the prophet Hanani censured this king, but it was done for a different reason. Jehoshaphat also regularly consulted the prophets. Among those who had dealings with him Elisha is also mentioned (2 K **3** 14), as also some other prophets (cf 2 Ch **19** 2; **20** 14–37). The greatest among the prophets during the period of the Assyr invasions was Isaiah, who performed the duties of his office for more than 40 years, and under the kings Jotham, Ahaz, Hezekiah, and possibly too under Manasseh, through his word exercised a powerful influence upon the king and the nation. Although a preacher of judgments, he at critical times appeared also as a prophet of consolation. Nor did he despise external evidences of his prophetic office (cf **7** 11; **38** 22.8). His contemporary Micah is in full agreement with him, although he was not called to deal with the great of the land, with kings, or statesmen, as was the mission of Isaiah. Nahum, Zephaniah and Habakkuk belong rather to the period of transition from the Assyr to the Chaldaean periods. In the days of Josiah the prophetess Huldah had great influence in Jerus (2 K **22** 14). Much more important under this same king was the prophet Jeremiah, who was called by God for a great mission. This prophet during the siege and destruction of Jerus and after that time spoke as an unyielding yet deeply feeling exponent of God, and was compelled again and again to dash to the ground the false hopes of the patriots, whenever these arose. Not so firm was his contemporary and fellow-sufferer Uriah (Jer **26** 20).

9. In the Exile

In the time of the exile itself we find the period of the activity of Ezekiel. It was significant that this prophet became the recipient of Divine revelations while on Bab territory. His work was, in accordance with the condition of affairs, more that of a pastor and literary man. He seems also to have been a bodily sufferer. His abnormal conditions became symbolical signs of that which he had to proclaim. Deutero-Isaiah, too (Isa **40** ff), spoke during the Bab period, namely at its close, and prepared for the return. The peculiar prophecies of Daniel are also accorded to a prophet living during the exile, who occupied a distinguished position at the court of the heathen rulers, and whose apocalyptic utterances are of a kind different from the discourses of the other prophets, as they deal more with the political condition of the world and the drama of history, in so far as this tends toward the establishment of the supremacy of Jeh. These prophecies were collected in later times and did not receive their final and present form until the Gr period at the beginning of the 2d cent. BC.

10. After the Exile

After the return from Babylon the Jews were exhorted by Haggai and Zechariah to rebuild their temple (about 520 BC). At that time there were still to be found prophets who took a hostile attitude to the men of God. Thus Nehemiah (Neh **6** 6–14) was opposed by hostile prophets as also by a prophetess, Noadiah. In contrast with these, Malachi is at all times in accord with the canonical prophets, as he was an ardent advocate for the temple cultus of Jeh, not in the sense of a spiritless and senseless external worship, but as against the current indifference to Jeh. His style and his language, too, evidence a late age. The lyrical form has given way to the didactic. This is also probably the time when the present Book of Jonah was written, a didactic work treating of an older tradition.

11. Cessation of Prophecy

Malachi is regarded by the Jews as the last really canonical prophet. While doubtless there was not a total lack of prophetically endowed seers and speakers of God also in the closing centuries of the pre-Christian era, nevertheless the general conviction prevailed that the Spirit of God was no longer present, e.g. in the times of the Maccabees (cf 1 Macc **4** 46; **9** 27; **14** 41). It is true that certain modern critics ascribe some large sections of the Book of Isa, as well as of other prophets, even to a period as late as the Gr. But this is refuted by the fact mentioned in Ecclus (beginning of the 2d cent. BC) that in the writer's time the prophetical Canon appeared already as a closed collection. Dnl is not found in this collection, but the Book of the Twelve Minor Prophets is. It was during this period that apocalyptic literature began to flourish, many specimens of which are found among the Apoc and the Pseudepigrapha. These books consist of eschatological speculations, not the product of original inspiration, but emanating from the study of the prophetic word. The very name Pseudepigrapha shows that the author issued his work, not under his own name, but under the pseudonym of some man of God from older times, such as Enoch, Ezra, Moses, Isaiah, Jeremiah, Baruch, and others. This fact alone proves the secondary character of this class of literature. See APOCALYPTIC LITERATURE.

12. Prophecy in the NT

Malachi finds a successor in John the Baptist, whose coming the former had predicted. John is the greatest of the prophets, because he could directly point to Him who completed the old covenant and fulfilled its promises. All that we know in addition concerning the times of Jesus shows that the prophetical gift was yet thought of as possibly dwelling in many, but that prophecy was no longer the chief spiritual guide of the people (cf e.g. Jos, *Ant*, XIII, xi, 2; XV, x, 5, among the Essenes, or in the case of Hyrcanus, op. cit., XIII, x, 7). Jos himself claims to have had prophetic gifts at times (cf *BJ*, III, viii, 9). He is thinking in this connection chiefly of the prediction of some details. Such "prophets" and "prophetesses" are reported also in the NT. In Jesus Christ Himself the prophetic office reached its highest stage of development, as He stood in a more intimate relation than any other being to His Heavenly Father and spoke His word entirely and at all times. In the Christian congregation the office of prophecy is again found, differing from the proclamation of the gospel by the apostles, evangelists, and teachers. In the NT the terms προφήτης, *prophḗtēs*, προφητεία, *prophēteía*, προφητεύω, *prophēteúō*, signify speaking under the extraordinary influence of the Holy Ghost. Thus in Acts **11** 27 f (prophecy of a famine by Agabus); **21** 10 f (prediction of the sufferings of Paul); **13** 1 f (exhortation to mission work); **21** 9 ff (prophetical gift of the daughters of Philip). Paul himself also had this gift (Acts **16** 6 ff; **18** 9; **22** 17 ff; **27** 23 f). In the public services of tho church, prophecy occupied a prominent position (see esp. 1 Cor **14**). A prophetical book in a special sense is the Apocalypse of St. John. The gift of prophecy was claimed by many also in later times. But this gift ceased more and more, as the Christian church more and more developed on the historical basis of revelation as completed in Christ. Esp. in spiritually aroused eras in the history of the church, prophecy again puts in its appearance. It has never ceased altogether, but on account of its frequent misuse the gift has become discredited. Jesus Himself warned against false prophets, and during the apostolic times it was often found necessary to urge the importance of trying spirits (1 Jn **4** 1; 1 Cor **12** 10; **14** 29).

III. Historical Development of Prophecy.—The contents of prophecy are by no means merely predictions concerning the future. That

1. Contents of Prophecy

which is given by the Spirit to the prophet can refer to the past and to the present as well as to the future. However, that which is revealed to the prophet finds its inner unity in this, that it all aims to establish the supremacy of Jeh. Prophecy views also the detailed events in their relation to the Divine plan, and this latter has for its purpose the absolute establishment of the supremacy of Jeh in Israel and eventually on the entire earth. We are accustomed to call those utterances that predict this final purpose the Messianic prophecies. However, not only those that speak of the person of the Messiah belong to this class, but all that treat of the coming of the kingdom of God.

2. The Idea of the Messiah

The beginnings of the religion of Israel, as also the chief epoch in its development, emanated from prophetical revelations. The prophet Moses elevated the tribal religion into a national religion, and at the same time taught the people to regard the religion of the fathers more ethically, spiritually and vitally. Samuel crowned the earthly form of the concrete theocracy by introducing an "Anointed of Jeh" in whom the covenant relation between Jeh and Israel was concentrated personally. The Anointed of the Lord entered into a much more intimate relationship to Jeh as His Son or Servant than it was possible for the whole people of Israel to do, although as a people they were also called the servant or the son of God (cf Ps **2** 7 f; **110**). The Pss of David are a proof of this, that this high destiny of the kingdom was recognized. David himself became a prophet in those hymns in which he describes his own unique relation to Jeh. But the actual kings of history as a rule corresponded too imperfectly to this idea. For this reason the word "prophetic" already in David's time directs to the future, when this relationship shall be more perfectly realized (2 S **7** 12 ff; cf David's own words, 2 S **23** 4 ff). See MESSIAH.

3. Before the Exile

Solomon completed the external equipment of the theocracy by the erection of the temple. But it was just his reign that constituted the turning-point, from which time on the prophets begin to emphasize the judgment to come, i.e. the dissolution of the external existence of the kingdom of Jeh. Yet prophecy at all times does this in such a manner, that a kernel of the Divine establishment on Zion remains intact. The Divine establishment of the sanctuary and the kingdom cannot be destroyed; all that is necessary is that they be restored in greater purity and dignity. This can be seen also in Amos, who predicts that the fallen tabernacle of David shall be raised up again (Am **9** 11 ff), which shall then be followed by a condition of undisturbed blessing. The same is found in Hosea, who sees how all Israel is again united under "David" the king of the last times, when between God and the people, between heaven and earth, an unbroken covenant of love shall be made (Hos **2** 1 f.18 ff); and also in Isaiah, who predicts that during the time of the conquest and subjection of the country by the Gentiles a Son of David shall be born in a miraculous manner and attain supremacy (Isa **7** 14; **9** 2 ff; **11** 1 ff), and who speaks constantly of that Divine establishment on Zion (cf the quiet waters of Shiloah, **8** 6), the foundation stone that has been laid by Jeh (**28** 16, etc). Micah, his contemporary, does the same, and in an entirely similar manner predicts that the radical judgment of destruction which shall come over the temple and the royal palace shall be followed by the wondrous King of Peace from Bethlehem (**5** 1 ff). Possibly even at a somewhat earlier date Zec **9** 9 described this future ruler in similar terms. In general it is not probable that Isaiah and Micah were the first to speak so personally of this King. They seem to presuppose that their contemporaries were acquainted with this idea.

4. Analogous Ideas among Heathen Peoples

In recent times scholars have pointed to the fact that in the old Orient, among the Egyptians, the Babylonians and elsewhere, the expectation of a miraculously born King of the future, who was to bring to His own people and to all nations salvation and peace, was entertained at an early period. Yet so much is certain, that Isaiah and Micah did not base their hopes on the vague dreams of the gentile world, but upon the prophetic establishment of a Divine sanctuary and kingdom of Zion. The personal figure of this Son of David is not so much in the foreground in the other prophets down to the period of the exile. These prophets mention only casually the Good Shepherd, as e.g. Jer **23** 1 ff; **33** 12 ff; Ezk **34** 23 f. But after that time this Messianic expectation became a permanent element in the hopes of Israel.

In the meanwhile, prophecy had thrown much light on the ways of God, which prepare for His kingdom on earth. Even long before Amos (**5** 18 ff) the idea of a "day of Jeh," which was to be a day of revelation, on which God makes a settlement with the nations, must have been generally known, since Amos is already compelled to protest against the abuse of this expectation. But hand in hand with this settlement we find also and at all times the expectation of the exaltation and of the salvation of Israel. Yet the prophets have all emphasized that Israel and Judah must first be thoroughly purified by a judgment, before the land could, through God's grace, be glorified and richly blessed. The judgment which the preëxilic prophets are continually predicting is, however, only a means to an end. This judgment is not the final word of the Lord, as Amos, Hosea, Isaiah, Micah and Habakkuk constantly teach. They announce that return to Jeh and obedience to His commandments is the way to salvation (Hos **6** 1; Isa **1** 18; Jer **4** 1, and often). However, the prophets know that the people will not turn again to God, but that first the Jewish state must be entirely overthrown (Isa **6**). It is particularly deserving of notice, that believing trust in Jeh is regarded as the positive means for deliverance (Isa **7** 9; **30** 15; Hab **2** 4). It is through this that the "remnant" of the faithful, "the kernel" of the people, is saved. Also in the case of Jeremiah, whose work it was to predict the immediate destruction of Judah, there is not absent a kind of an esoteric book of consolation. His battle cry for the future is "Jeh our righteousness" (**23** 6; **33** 16). In his case we find a rich spiritualization of religion. The external customs, circumcision and the like, he declares, do no good, if the true state of the heart is lacking. Even the ark of the covenant is unnecessary and is discarded in the enlargement of the sanctuary. Ezekiel, who lays more stress on the external ordinances, nevertheless agrees with Jeremiah in this, that Jerus together with the temple must fall. Only after this destruction the prophet in his spirit builds the sanctuary again; notwithstanding the external character of his restoration, there is yet found in his picture a further development of its spiritual character. The ethical rights and the responsibility of the individual are strongly emphasized (chs **18, 33**). The land becomes transformed; the Gentiles are received into the covenant of God.

5. During the Exile

Isaiah (**40–66**), looking forward to the time of the Bab captivity, enriches prophecy in an extraordinary manner, through the figure of the true "Servant of Jeh," who in a peaceful way, through his words of instruction and esp. through his innocent sufferings and his vicarious deeds, converts Israel, the undeserving servant, and also wins over the gentile world to Jeh. It was not possible that the picture of a suffering man of God, who through his death as a martyr attains to exaltation, should be suggested to the Jews by the altogether different figure of a death and resurrection of a Bab god (Thammuz-Adonis!). Since the unjust persecutions of Joseph and David they were acquainted with the sufferings of the just, and Jeremiah's life as a prophet was a continuous martyrdom. But the writer of the second part of Isaiah had before his eyes a vision that far excelled all of these types in purity and in greatness to such a degree as did David's Son in Isa and Mic surpass His great ancestor. He brings to a completion the kingdom of God through teaching, suffering and death, and attains to the glory of rulership. In this way He unites the offices of prophet, priest and king.

6. After the Exile

After the exile prophecy continues its work. The Messianic expectations, too, are developed further by Haggai, and still more by Zechariah. Malachi announces the advent of the Day of Jeh, but expects before this a complete purification of the people of God. God Himself will come, and His angel will prepare the way for Him. The visions of Daniel picture the transformation of the world into a kingdom of God. The latter will mark the end of the history of the world. It comes from above; the earthly kingdoms are from below, and are pictured as beasts; the Ruler of the kingdom of God is a Son of man. The latter comes with the clouds of the heaven to take possession of His kingdom (Dnl **7** 13 ff). Then the judgment of the world will take place and include also each human being, who before this will bodily arise from the dead, in order to enter upon blessedness or condemnation. Here we find indicated a universal expansion of the kingdom of God extending over the whole world and all mankind.

7. Contemporaneous Character of Prophecy

If we survey this prophecy of the kingdom of God and its Divinely blessed Ruler, the Messiah, from a Christian standpoint, we find that a grand Divine unity connects its different elements. The form of this prophecy is indeed conditioned by the views and ideas of the time of utterance. The prophets were compelled to speak so that their hearers could understand them. Only gradually these limitations and forms become spiritualized, e.g. the kingdom of God is still pictured by the prophets as established around the local center of Zion. Mt. Zion is in a concrete manner exalted, in order to give expression to its importance, etc. It is the NT fulfilment that for the first time gives adequate form to Divine revelation. At least in the person of Jesus Christ this perfection is given, although the full unfolding of this kingdom is yet a matter of the future.

8. Partial Character of Prophecy

A second characteristic feature of prophecy is the partial nature of the individual prophetical utterances and prophetical pictures. One picture must be supplemented by the others, in order not to be misunderstood. Thus, e.g. according to Isa **11** 14; Zec **9** 13 ff, we might expect that the kingdom of God was to be established by force of arms. But the same prophets show in other utterances (Isa **9** 6 f; Zec **9** 9 f) that these warlike expressions are to be understood **figuratively,** since the Messianic King is more than all others a Prince of Peace.

9. Perspective Character of Prophecy

A third feature that deserves attention is the perspective character of prophecy. The prophet sees together and at once upon the surface of the pictures things which are to be fulfilled only successively and gradually. Thus, e.g., Isa (**40–66**) sees in the near future the return from captivity, and directly connected with this a miraculous glorification of the city of God. The return did as a matter of fact take place soon afterward, but the glorification of the city in which Jeh Himself had promised to dwell was yet in the distant future. The succeeding prophets, Haggai and Zechariah, predict that this consummation shall take place in the future.

Also in the predictions concerning the future made by Jesus and in the Apocalypse of St. John, these characteristics of prophecy, its contemporaneous and perspective and at times symbolical features, are not disregarded. The firm prophetic word is intended to give the congregation certain directive lines and distinctive work. But an adequate idea of what is to come the Christian church will become compelled to form for itself, when the fulfilment and completion shall have taken place.

IV. Analogous Phenomena among Gentiles.—The uniqueness of Bib. prophecy is grasped fully only when we try to find analogies among the gentile peoples. Here we find everywhere indeed the art of soothsaying, the headquarters for which was Babylon. But with this art the prophecy of the OT stands out in bold contrast (cf the prohibitions in Lev **19** 26.31; **20** 6.27; Dt **18** 10 ff, prohibitions that refer to necromancy for the purpose of discovering the future). This art was practised through a medium, a person who had an *'ōbh* (Bab *ubi*), i.e. a spirit that brought forth the dead in order to question them. The spirits were thought to speak in murmurings or piping sounds (Isa **8** 19), which could be imitated by the medium (ventriloquist). According to the Law, which forbade this under penalty of death, Saul had tried to destroy those who practised incantations, who generally were women (1 S **28** 9). This practice, however, continued to flourish. In addition, the Babylonians and other peoples had also a developed art of interpretation in order to find omens for the future. Esp. was the examination of intestines practised by them. The liver of sacrificial animals particularly was carefully examined, and, from this, predictions, good or bad, were inferred (cf Ezk **21** 21). See DIVINATION. This art passed over from the Babylonians to the seafaring Etruscans, and through these came to the Romans. But other phenomena also were by the different nations interpreted as prophetically significant and were by those skilled in this art interpreted accordingly. Among these were miscarriages by human beings and animals, the actions of hens, horses, the flight of birds, earthquakes, forms of the clouds, lightning, and the like. Further, mechanical contrivances were used, such as casting of lots, stones, sticks, etc.

1. Necromancy and Technical Witchcraft

More spiritual and popular was the interpretation of dreams. It also was the case that mediums intentionally would convert themselves into a semi-waking trance. In this way the suitable mediums attained to a certain kind of clairvoyance, found among various peoples. This approaches the condition of an ecstatically aroused pseudo-prophet, of whom mention is made above. In Greece, too, oracles were pronounced by the Pythian prophetess, who by vapors and the like was aroused to a practice of the mantic art. In Dodona it was the voice of the divinity in Nature, which they sought to read in the rustling of the trees and the murmuring of the water. How uncertain these sources were was well known to heathen antiquity. The ancients complain of the enigmatical character of the Sibylline utterances and the doubtful nature of what was said. See GREECE, RELIGION OF. In contrast to this, Israel knows that it possesses in prophecy a clear word (Nu **23** 23).

2. The Mantic Art

But the contents also of the Bib. prophecies are unique through their spiritual uniformity and greatness. The oracle at Delphi, too, at times showed a certain moral elevation and could be regarded as the conscience of the nation. But how insignificant and meager was that which it offered to those who questioned it, in comparison with the spontaneous utterances of the prophets of Israel! Also what has in recent times been said concerning the "prophetical texts" from ancient Egypt (Gressmann, *Texte und Bilder*, I, 20 ff) may indeed show some external similarity to the prophecies of Israel; but they lack the spiritual and religious depth and the strictly ethical dignity of the prophets of the Scriptures, as also the consistency with which these from century to century reveal the thoughts of God and make known with constantly increasing clearness their purposes and goal.

3. Contents of Extra-Biblical Oracles

LITERATURE.—Witsius, *De prophetis et prophetia*, 1731; Chr. A. Crusius, *Hypomnemata ad theologiam propheticam*, Part I, 1764; A. Knobel, *Der Prophetismus der Hebräer*, 1837; F. B. Koester, *Die Propheten des AT und NT*, 1838; B. Duhm, *Die Theologie der Propheten;* Kuenen, *The Prophets and Prophecy in Israel;* F. E. Koenig, *Der Offenbarungsbegriff des AT*, 1882; C. von Orelli, *Die alttestamentliche Weissagung von der Vollendung des Gottesreiches*, 1882; W. Robertson Smith, *The Prophets of Israel and Their Place in History*, 1882; E. Riehm, *Die messianische Weissagung*, ET, 1885; Delitzsch, *Messianic Prophecy*, 1891; A. T. Kirkpatrick, *The Doctrine of the Prophets*, 1892; G. Fr. Oehler, *Theologie des AT*, 1891; Ed. Koenig, *Das Berufungsbewusstsein der alttestamentlichen Propheten*, 1900; F. H. Woods, *The Hope of Israel*, 1896; R. Kraetzschmar, *Prophet und Seher im alten Israel*, 1902; A. B. Davidson, *OT Prophecy*, 1903; Eb. Schrader, *Die Keilinschriften und das AT*, 1902; C. von Orelli, *Allgemeine Religionsgeschichte;* M. Jastrow, *Die Religion Babyloniens und Assyriens*, 1903; Gressmann, *Ursprung der israelitisch-jüdischen Eschatologie*, 1905; W. J. Beecher, *The Prophets and the Promise*, 1905; C. S. Macfarland, *Jesus and the Prophets*, 1905; G. G. Findlay, *The Books of the Prophets in Their Historical Succession*, 1906–7; Gressmann, *Alt-orientalische Texte und Bilder zum AT*, 1909; Selwyn, *Christian Prophets*.

C. VON ORELLI

PROPHECY, GIFT OF. See SPIRITUAL GIFTS.

PROPHESYINGS, prof'ē-sī-ingz, **FALSE:** The distinction between the true and the false prophecy and prophets is very difficult to state. Broadly speaking, the false prophesying related itself to the national ideal independently of any spiritual quality, while the true prophesying ever kept uppermost the spiritual conception of the national life. Among those given to false prophesying were the ones who spoke after "the deceit of their own heart" (Jer **14** 13.14); those who without real prophetic gift borrowed a message and assumed the speech of prophecy (Jer **23** 28.31); and those who sought the prophet's rôle in order to gain the material gifts which came from the people to their prophets (Mic **3** 5). These, when discovered, were counted worthy of punishment and even death. There were, however, false prophesyings from men who honestly believed themselves to have a message from Jeh. These prophecies from self-deceived prophets often led the people astray. The dream of national greatness was substituted for the voice of Jeh. It was against such prophesying that the true prophets had to contend. The only test here was the spiritual character of the utterance, and this test demanded a certain moral or spiritual sense which the people did not always possess. Consequently, in times of moral darkness the false prophets, predicting smooth things for the nation, independent of repentance, consecration and the pursuit of spiritual ideals, were honored above the true prophets who emphasized the moral greatness of Jeh and the necessity of righteousness for the nation. In NT times false prophesying did much injury in the church. See PROPHECY.

C. E. SCHENK

PROPHET, THE OLD. See OLD PROPHET, THE.

PROPHETESS, prof'et-es (נְבִיאָה, *nebhī'āh;* προφῆτις, *prophḗtis*): Women were not excluded from the prophetic office in the OT, and were honored with the right of prophetic utterance in the

NT. It should be noted, however, that women like Miriam (Ex **15** 20), Deborah (Jgs **4** 4) and Huldah (2 K **22** 14) were not credited with the seer's insight into the future, but were called "prophetesses" because of the poetical inspiration of their speech. Among others mentioned as having the prophetic gift we find Hannah (1 S **2** 1), Anna (Lk **2** 36) and the four daughters of Philip (Acts **21** 8.9). See PROPHET. C. E. SCHENK

PROPITIATION, pro-pish-i-ā'shun: The word is Lat and brings into its Eng. use the atmosphere of heathen rites for winning the favor, or averting the anger, of the gods. In the OT it represents a number of Heb words—ten, including derivatives—which are sufficiently discussed under ATONEMENT (q.v.), of which propitiation is one aspect. It represents in LXX the Gr stems ἱλασκ-, *hilask-* (ἱλε-, *hile-*), and καταλλαγ-, *katallag-*, with derivatives; in the NT only the latter, and is rarely used. Propitiation needs to be studied in connection with reconciliation, which is used frequently in some of the most strategic sentences of the NT, esp. in the newer VSS. In He **2** 17, ERV and ARV have both changed "reconciliation" of AV to "propitiation," to make it correspond with the OT use in connection with the sacrifice on the DAY OF ATONEMENT (q.v.). Lk **18** 13 ("God, be thou merciful [m "be propitiated"] to me the sinner" [ARVm]); He **8** 12 (quoted from LXX); and Mt **16** 22 (an idiomatic asseveration like Eng. "mercy on us") will help in getting at the usage in the NT. In LXX *hilastērion* is the term for the "mercy-seat" or "lid of the ark" of the covenant which was sprinkled with blood on the Day of Atonement. It is employed in exactly this sense in He **9** 5, where later VSS have in m "the propitiatory."

1. Terms and Meaning

Elsewhere in the NT this form is found only in Rom **3** 25, and it is here that difficulty and difference are found extensively in interpreting. Greek fathers generally and prominent modern scholars understand Paul here to say that God appointed Christ Jesus to be the "mercy-seat" for sinners. The reference, while primarily to the Jewish ceremonial in tabernacle and temple, would not depend upon this reference for its comprehension, for the idea was general in religious thought, that some place and means had to be provided for securing friendly meeting with the Deity, offended by man's sin. In He particularly, as elsewhere generally, Jesus Christ is presented as priest and sacrifice. Many modern writers (cf Sanday and Headlam), therefore, object that to make Him the "mercy-seat" here complicates the figure still further, and so would understand *hilastērion* as "expiatory sacrifice." While this is not impossible, it is better to take the word in the usual sense of "mercy-seat." It is not necessary to complicate the illustration by bringing in the idea of priest at all here, since Paul does not do so; mercy-seat and sacrifice are both in Christ. ἱλασμός, *hilasmós*, is found in the NT only in 1 Jn **2** 2; **4** 10. Here the idea is active grace, or mercy, or friendliness. The teaching corresponds exactly with that in Rom. "Jesus Christ the righteous" is our "Advocate [m "Helper"] with the Father," because He is active mercy concerning (περί, *perí*) our sins and those of the whole world. Or (**4** 10), God "loved us, and sent his Son to be the propitiation for [active mercy concerning] our sins." This last passage is parallel with Rom **3** 25, the one dealing with the abstract theory, and so Christ is set forward as a "mercy-seat," the other dealing with experience of grace, and so Christ is the mercy of God in concrete expression.

The basal idea in Heb terms is that of covering what is offensive, so restoring friendship, or causing to be kindly disposed. The Gr terms lack the physical reference to covering but introduce the idea of friendliness where antagonism would be natural; hence graciousness. Naturally, therefore, the idea of expiation entered into the concept. It is esp. to be noted that all provisions for this friendly relation as between God and offending man find their initiation and provision in God and are under His direction, but involve the active response of man. All heathen and unworthy conceptions are removed from the Christian notion of propitiation by the fact that God Himself proposed, or "set forth," Christ as the "mercy-seat," and that this is the supreme expression of ultimate love. God had all the while been merciful, friendly, "passing over" man's sins with no apparently adequate, or just, ground for doing so. Now in the blood of Christ sin is condemned and expiated, and God is able to establish and maintain His character for righteousness, while He continues and extends His dealing in gracious love with sinners who exercise faith in Jesus. The propitiation originates with God, not to appease Himself, but to justify Himself in His uniform kindness to men deserving harshness. Cf also as to reconciliation, as in Rom **5** 1–11; 2 Cor **5** 18 ff. See also JOHANNINE THEOLOGY, V, 2.

2. Theological Implication

LITERATURE.—Besides the comms., the literature is the same as for ATONEMENT, to recent works on which add Stalker, *The Atonement;* Workman, *At Onement, or Reconciliation with God;* Moberly, in *Foundations, Christian Belief in Terms of Modern Thought.*

WILLIAM OWEN CARVER

PROPORTION, prō-pōr'shun: Occurs once in the sense of "space" as the tr of מַעַר, *ma'ar*, "void or open space" (1 K **7** 36, AVm "Heb 'nakedness,'" RV "space"); once in the obsolete sense of "form" as the tr of *'erekh*, "array," or "row" (Job **41** 12, RV "frame"); and once in the sense of "measure" as the tr of *analogía*, "proportion," "equality" (Rom **12** 6, "the proportion of faith," RV "the proportion of our faith"). "Proportionally" occurs in Wisd **13** 5, *analógōs*, RV "in like proportion," m "correspondently."

PROSELYTE, pros'ē-līt (προσήλυτος, *prosḗlutos*, from *prosérchomai*, "I approach"): Found 4 t in the NT. In the LXX it often occurs as the tr of גֵּר, *gēr*. The Heb vb. *gūr* means "to sojourn"; *gēr* accordingly means a stranger who has come to settle in the land, as distinguished on the one hand from *'ezrāḥ*, "a homeborn" or "native," and on the other from *nokhrī* or *ben-nēkhār*, which means a stranger who is only passing through the country. Yet it is to be noted that in 2 Ch **2** 17 those of the native tribes still living in the land as Amorites, Hittites, etc, are also called *gērīm*. In two places (Ex **12** 19; Isa **14** 1) LXX uses *g[e]iōras*, which is derived from *gīyōr*, the Aram. equivalent for *gēr*. LXX uses *pároikos* (the Gr equivalent for Heb *tōshābh*, "a settler") for *gēr* when Israel or the patriarchs are indicated (Gen **15** 13; **23** 4; Ex **2** 22; **18** 3; Dt **23** 7; 1 Ch **29** 15; Ps **39** 12; **119** 19; Jer **14** 8), and in a few other cases. In Talmudical lit. *gēr* always stands for proselyte in the NT sense, i.e. a Gentile who has been converted to Judaism. Onkelos, who was himself a proselyte, always translates the word in this way.

No difficulties were put in the way of those strangers who wished to settle down in the land of Israel. All strangers, the third generation of Egyptians and Edomites included, and only Ammonites and Moabites excluded, could enter "the congregation of God" without circumcision and without the obligation to keep the ceremonial law.

1. *Gēr* in the OT

'The stranger within the gate' was free to eat meat which was prohibited to the Israelite (Dt **14** 21). If, however, the stranger wished to take part in the Passover, a feast permeated with national ideals, he must be circumcised. The keeping of the Sabbath and other feasts was regarded rather as a privilege than as a duty (Ex **23** 12; Dt **16** 11.14); but according to Lev **16** 29 the *gēr* was obliged to keep the fast of Atonement. He was forbidden on pain of death to blaspheme (Lev **24** 16) or to offer children to Molech (Lev **20** 2). If he desired to bring a burnt offering, the same law applied to him as to the Israelites (Lev **17** 8; **22** 18). Though the law of circumcision was not forced upon the *gēr*, it seems that the Mosaic Law endeavored to bring him nearer to the cult of Israel, not from any proselytizing motives, but in order to preserve the theocracy from admixture of foreign elements, which would speedily have proved fatal to its existence.

Though the God of Israel, when He is thought of only as such, ceases to be God; though Israel was chosen *before* all nations *for* all nations; though Israel had been again and again reminded that the Messiah would bring a blessing to all nations; and though there were instances of pagans coming to believe in Jeh, yet it did not belong to the economy of OT religion to spread the knowledge of God directly among the Gentiles (the Book of Jon is an exception to this). There was certainly no active propagandism. Though we read in Neh **10** 28 of those who "separated themselves from the peoples of the lands unto the law of God" (cf Isa **56** 3, "the foreigner, that hath joined himself to Jeh"—the only and exact description of a proselyte proper in the OT), the spirit of exclusiveness prevailed; the doubtful elements were separated (Ezr **4** 3); mixed marriages were prohibited by the chiefs, and were afterward disapproved of by the people (Ezr **9**, **10**; Neh **13** 23 ff). Direct proselytism did not begin till about a century later.

2. Proselytizing

The preaching of the gospel was preceded and prepared for by the dispersion of the Jews, and a world-wide propagandism of Judaism. In the 5th cent. BC the Jews had a temple of their own at Syene. Alexander the Great settled 8,000 Jews in the Thebais, and Jews formed a third of the population of Alexandria. Large numbers were brought from Pal by Ptolemy I (320 BC), and they gradually spread from Egypt along the whole Mediterranean coast of Africa. After the persecution of Antiochus Epiphanes (170 BC) they scattered themselves in every direction, and, in the words of the Sibylline Oracles (c 160 BC), "crowded with their numbers every ocean and country." There was hardly a seaport or a commercial center in Asia Minor, Macedonia, Greece, or the Islands of the Ægean, in which Jewish communities were not to be found. Jos (*Ant*, XIV, vii, 2) quotes Strabo as saying: "It is hard to find a place in the habitable earth that hath not admitted this tribe of men, and is not possessed by them." Thus, in spite of the hatred and contempt which Judaism everywhere excited, its lofty, austere and spiritual religious aspirations and conceptions became known to the pagan world and exercised a profound attraction upon many souls that were deeply dissatisfied with contemporary religions. Judaism was at that period filled with missionary zeal and aspired to world-mastery. Many books on Judaism (e.g. the Sibylline Oracles) were written anonymously by Jews in order to influence pagan readers. The synagogue, which had become the center of Jewish worship, now opened its doors widely to the pagan world (cf Acts **15** 21), and many of the sermons delivered there were directly aimed at the conversion of pagans. The Jews began to feel that they were "a guide of the blind, a light of them that are in darkness" (Rom **2** 19).

Not only Jos (*CAp*, II; *BJ*, VII, iii, 3), but also Seneca (*Apud* Aug. *De Civit. Dei* vi.11), Dio Cassius (xxxvii.17), Tacitus (*Ann.* ii.85; *Hist.* v.5), Horace (*Sat.* i.4, 142), Juvenal (*Sat.* xiv.96 ff), and other Gr and Rom writers testify to the widespread effects of the proselytizing propaganda of the Jews.

Many gladly frequented the synagogues and kept some of the Jewish laws and customs. Among those were to be found the "men who feared God," spoken of in Acts. They were so called to distinguish them from full proselytes; and it was probably for this class that tablets of warning in the temple were inscribed in Gr and Lat.

Another class kept practically all the Jewish laws and customs, but were not circumcised. Some again, though not circumcised, had their children circumcised (Juvenal *Sat.* xiv.96 ff). Such Jewish customs as fasting, cleansings, abstaining from pork, lighting the candles on Friday evening, and keeping the Sabbath (Jos, *CAp*, II, 29, etc) were observed by these gentile sympathizers. Schürer holds that there were congregations of Greeks and Romans in Asia Minor, and probably in Rome, which, though they had no connection with the synagogue, formed themselves into gatherings after the pattern of the synagogue, and observed some of the Jewish customs.

Among the converts to Judaism there were probably few who were circumcised, and most of those who were circumcised submitted to the rite in order to marry Jewesses, or to enjoy the rights and privileges granted to the Jews by Syrian, Egyp and Rom rulers (Jos, *Ant*, XIV, vii, 2; XX, vii, 1; cf XVI, vii, 6). It would appear from Christ's words (Mt **23** 15, "one proselyte") that the number of full proselytes was not large. Hyrcanus forced the Edomites to adopt Judaism by circumcision (129 BC); and on other occasions the same policy of propagandism by force was followed. Jos tells an interesting story (*Ant*, XX, ii, 1) of the conversion of Queen Helena of Adiabene and her two sons. The conversion of the sons was due to the teaching of a merchant called Ananias, who did not insist on circumcision. Later, another Jew, Eliezer of Galilee, told the young princes that it was not enough to read the Law, but that they must keep it too, with the result that both were circumcised. From this it is evident that Jewish teachers of the gentile converts varied in the strictness of their teaching.

3. Proselytes in the NT

The word "proselyte" occurs 4 t in the NT; once in Mt (**23** 15), where Our Lord refers to the proselytizing zeal of the Pharisees, and to the pernicious influence which they exerted on their converts; and 3 t in Acts. Proselytes were present at Pentecost (Acts **2** 10); Nicolas, one of the deacons appointed by the primitive church at Jerus, was a proselyte (**6** 5); and after Paul had spoken in the synagogue at Antioch of Pisidia, many devout proselytes followed Paul and Barnabas (**13** 43). It is to be noted in this last case that the proselytes are called *sebómenoi*, a word generally reserved for another class. Certain people are spoken of in Acts as *phoboúmenoi tón theón*, "fearing God" (**10** 2.22.35; **13** 16.26), and as *sebómenoi tón theón*, "reverencing God," or simply *sebómenoi* (**13** 50; **16** 14; **17** 4.17; **18** 7). These seem (as against Bertholet and *EB*) to have been sympathizers with Judaism, who attended the worship of the synagogue, but were not circumcised. It was among this class that the gospel made its first converts among the Gentiles. Those who were fully proselytes were probably as fanatical opponents of Christianity as were the Jews.

4. Gēr in the Talmud

From the old strict Pharisaic-Palestinian point of view, circumcision, with the addition of baptism and the offering of sacrifice, was indispensable (so to Paul every circumcised person was a Jew; cf Gal **5** 3); and thus their converts had to submit to the whole burden of the Mosaic and traditional Law. The rabbinic distinction between *gēr tōshābh*, "a settler," and *gēr çedheḳ*, "a proselyte of righteousness," is, according to Schürer, only theoretical, and arose at a later date (*Bābhā' M*e*çī'ā'* **5** 6.9.12; *Makkōth* **2** 3; *N*e*ghā'īm* **3** 1, et al.).

While the *gēr çedheḳ* (or *gēr ha-b*e*rīth*, "proselyte of the covenant") was considered as being in every respect a "perfect Israelite," the *gēr tōshābh* (or *gēr sha'ar*, "proselyte of the gate"; cf Ex **20** 10) only professed his faith in the God of Israel, and bound himself to the observance of the 7 Noachic precepts, abstinence from blasphemy, idolatry, homicide, fornication, robbery, eating the flesh of an animal that had died a natural death, and disobedience to (Jewish) authority (*Ṣanh.* **56***a;* cf Acts **15** 20.29; **21** 25). He was considered more of a Gentile than a Jew.

Three things were required for the admission of a proselyte, circumcision, baptism, and the offering of sacrifice (*B*e*r.* **47***b; Y*e*bhām.* **45***b*, **46***a*, **48***b*, **76***a; 'Ābhōth* **57***a*, et al.). In the case of women only baptism and the offering of sacrifice were required; for that reason there were more women converts than men. Jos (*BJ*, II, xx, 2) tells how most of the women of Damascus were addicted to the Jewish religion. Doubt has been expressed as to the necessity of proselytes being baptized, since there is no mention of it by Paul or Philo or Jos, but it is probable that a Gentile, who was unclean, would not be admitted to the temple without being cleansed.

The proselyte was received in the following manner. He was first asked his reason for wishing to embrace Judaism. He was told that Israel was in a state of affliction; if he replied that he was aware of the fact and felt himself unworthy to share these afflictions, he was admitted. Then he received instruction in some of the "light" and "heavy" commandments, the rules concerning gleaning and tithes, and the penalties attached to the breach of the commandments. If he was willing to submit to all this, he was circumcised, and after his recovery he was immersed without delay. At this latter ceremony two "disciples of the wise" stood by to tell him more of the "light" and "heavy" commandments. When he came up after the immersion, those assembled addressed him saying: "Unto whom hast thou given thyself? Blessed art thou, thou hast given thyself to God; the world was created for the sake of Israel, and only Israelites are called the children of God. The afflictions, of which we spoke, we mentioned only to make thy reward the greater." After his baptism he was considered to be a new man, "a little child newly born" (*Y*e*bhām.* **22***a*, **47***a*, **48***b*, **97***b*); a new name was given him; either he was named "Abraham the son of Abraham," or the Scriptures were opened at hazard, and the first name that was read was given to him. Thenceforth he had to put behind him all his past; even his marriage ties and those of kinship no longer held good (cf *Y*e*bhām.* **22***a; Ṣanh.* **58***b*).

Although he was thus juridically considered a new man, and one whose praises were sung in the Talmudical literature, he was yet on the whole looked down on as inferior to a born Jew (*Ḳidd.* **4** 7; *Sh*e*bhū'ōth* **10** 9, et al.). Rabbi Chelbo said: "Proselytes are as injurious to Israel as a scab" (*Y*e*bhām.* **47***b; Ḳidd.* **70***b;* cf Phil **3** 5). See also STRANGER.

LITERATURE.—See articles on "Proselyte" and "*Gēr*" in *EB*, *HDB*, *Jew Enc*, and *RE;* Slevogt, *De proselytis Judaeorum*, 1651; A. Bertholet, *Die Stellung der Israeliten und der Juden zu den Fremden*, 1896; Schürer, *HJP*, 1898; Huidekoper, *Judaism at Rome*, 1887; Harnack, *Mission und Ausbreitung des Christentums*, 1906, ET; Allen, "On the Meaning of *prosēlutos* in the Septuagint," *Expos*, 1894; A. B. Davidson, "They That Fear the Lord," *Expos T*, III (1892), 491 ff.

PAUL LEVERTOFF

PROSEUCHE, prō-sū'kē, **PROSEUCHA**, prō-sū'ka (**προσευχή**, *proseuchē*): "A place in the open air where the Jews were wont to pray, outside of those cities where they had no synagogue," Acts **16** 13.16 (Thayer, *Lexicon of the NT*). See PHILIPPI.

PROSTITUTION, pros-ti-tū'shun. See CRIMES; HARLOT; PUNISHMENTS.

PROSTRATION, pros-trā'shun. See ATTITUDES.

PROTEVANGELIUM, pro-tē-van-jel'i-um, **OF JAMES.** See APOCRYPHAL GOSPELS, III, 1, (*a*).

PROVE, prōōv (בָּחַן, *bāḥan*, נָסָה, *nāṣāh;* **δοκιμάζω**, *dokimázō*, **πειράζω**, *peirázō*): Means (1) to test or try; (2) to establish, demonstrate; (3) to find by experience. It is for the most part in the first (original) sense that the word is found in Scripture. In the OT it is most frequently the tr of *nāṣāh*, primarily "to lift," hence to weigh (Gen **42** 15.16, etc). God is said to "prove" His people, i.e. to test or try them for their good (Gen **22** 1; Ex **15** 25; Dt **8** 16, etc). The Psalmist prays that God may prove him (Ps **26** 2). The word is frequently rendered "tempt." See TEMPT. The word *bāḥan*, primarily "to try by heat," has a similar meaning (Ps **17** 3, the heart, like metal, purified from dross; cf Job **23** 10; Ps **7** 9; Mal **3** 2, etc). In the NT the word most frequently rendered "prove" (sometimes "try") is *dokimazō* (Lk **14** 19; Rom **12** 2; 2 Cor **8** 8.22; **13** 5; Eph **5** 10; 1 Thess **5** 21). *Peirazō*, "to tempt," "to prove," used in both a good and a bad sense, frequently tr[d] "tempt" (q.v.), is rendered "prove" in Jn **6** 6, "This he said to prove him." Both Gr words occur frequently in Apoc (Wisd and Ecclus). RV has "prove" for "tempt" (Gen **22** 1); for "make" (Job **24** 25; Gal **2** 18); for "manifest" (Eccl **3** 18); for "examine" (1 Cor **11** 28); for "try" (1 Cor **3** 13; 1 Jn **4** 1), etc.

W. L. WALKER

PROVENDER, prov'en-dēr ([1] מִסְפּוֹא, *miṣpō'*, from obs. √ סָפָא, *ṣāphā'*, "to feed," fodder for cattle in general [Gen **24** 25.32; **42** 27; Jgs **19** 19.21]; [2] בְּלִיל, *b*e*līl*, from √ בָּלַל, *bālal*, "to mix": "Loweth the ox over his fodder?" [Job **6** 5]; בְּלִיל חָמִיץ, *b*e*līl ḥāmīç:* "The young asses that till the ground shall eat savory [Heb "salted"] provender" [Isa **30** 24]; this is fodder mixed with salt or aromatic herbs): The ordinary provender in Pal, besides fresh pasturage, is *tibn*, i.e. straw broken on the threshing floor, *kursenneh* (Vetch, *Vicia ervilia*), given esp. to camels and milch cows; bran, for fattening and esp. in cold weather; and, occasionally, hay made from the dried mixed grass and herbs which spring up luxuriously after the rains. The Circassian colonists E. of the Jordan are teaching their neighbors the value of this food, so long neglected. E. W. G. MASTERMAN

PROVERB, prov'ērb (מָשָׁל, *māshāl*, חִידָה, *ḥīdhāh;* **παραβολή**, *parabolē* [Lk **4** 23], **παροιμία**, *paroimia* [Jn **16** 25.29]):

By this term mainly, but sometimes by the term "parable" (e.g. Nu **23** 7.18; **24** 3.15; Job **27** 1; **29** 1), is tr^d the Heb word *māshāl* (מָשָׁל), which designates the formal unit or vehicle of didactic discourse. The *māshāl* was an enunciation of truth, self-evident and self-illustrative, in some pointed or concentrated form adapted to arrest attention, awaken responsive thought, and remain fixed in memory. Its scope was broader than that of our word "proverb," taking in subject-matter as well as form. The *māshāl* broadened indeed in the course of its history, until it became the characteristic idiom of Heb philosophy, as distinguished from the dialectic method of the Greeks. The Heb mind was not inductive but intuitive; it saw and asserted; and the word *māshāl* is the generic term for the form in which its assertion was embodied.

I. Folk Meaning and Use.—The *māshāl*, nearly in our sense of proverb, traces back to the heart and life of the common folk; it is a native form reflecting in a peculiarly intimate way the distinctive genius of the Heb people. As to the primitive sense of the word, it is usually traced to a root meaning "likeness," or "comparison," as if the first sense of it were of the principle of analogy underlying it; but this derivation is a guess. The word is just as likely to be connected with the vb. *māshal*, "to rule" or "master"; so by a natural secondary meaning to denote that statement which gives the decisive or final verdict, says the master word. The idea of *how* the thing is said, or by what phrasing, would be a later differentiation, coming in with literary refinement.

1. The Primitive Sense

The earliest cited proverb (1 S **10** 12, repeated with varied occasion, 1 S **19** 24) seems to have risen spontaneously from the people's observation. That Saul the son of Kish, whose very different temperament everybody knew, should be susceptible to the wild ecstasy of strolling prophets was an astonishing thing, as it were a discovery in psychology; "Therefore it became a proverb, Is Saul also among the prophets?" A few years later David, explaining his clemency in sparing the life of the king who has become his deadly foe, quotes from a folk fund of proverbs: 1 S **24** 13, "As saith the proverb of the ancients, Out of the wicked cometh forth wickedness; but my hand shall not be upon thee." The prophet Ezekiel quotes a proverb which evidently embodies a popular belief: "The days are prolonged, and every vision faileth"; which he corrects to, "The days are at hand, and the fulfilment of every vision" (Ezk **12** 22.23). Both Ezekiel and Jeremiah (Ezk **18** 2; Jer **31** 29) quote the same current proverb, "The fathers have eaten sour grapes, and the children's teeth are set on edge," in order to announce that the time has come for its discontinuance. These last two examples are very instructive. They show how the body of the people put the inwardness of their history into proverb form, as it were a portable lesson for the times; they show also how the prophets availed themselves of these floating sayings to point their own message. Ezekiel seems indeed to recognize the facility with which a situation may bring forth a proverb: Ezk **16** 44, "Every one that useth proverbs shall use this proverb against thee [lit. every one that *māshals* shall *māshal* against thee], saying, As is the mother, so is her daughter."

2. The Communal Origin

One element of the proverb, which a wide-awake people like the Hebrews would soon discover, was its adaptability for personal portrayal or satire, like a home thrust. Hence the popular use of the name *māshāl* came to connote its animus, generally of sarcasm or scorn. The taunting verse raised against Heshbon, Nu **21** 27–30, is attributed to them "that speak in proverbs" (*m^eshālīm*); and Isaiah's taunt in his burden of Babylon (Isa **14** 4–20) is composed in the proverb measure: "Thou shalt take up this parable [*māshāl*, AV "proverb"] against the king of Babylon." Answering to this prevailing animus of proverbs was a corresponding susceptibility to their sting and rankle; they were the kind of utterance that most surely found the national and individual self-consciousness. To be a proverb—to be in everybody's mouth as a subject of laughter, or as a synonym for some awful atrocity—was about the most dreadful thing that could befall them. To be "a reproach and a proverb, a taunt and a curse" (Jer **24** 9) was all one. That this should be the nation's fate was held as a threat over them by lawgiver and prophet (Dt **28** 37; 1 K **9** 7); and in adversities of experience, both individual and collective, the thing that was most keenly felt was to have become a byword (*māshāl*) (Ps **44** 14; **69** 11).

3. Animus of Proverbs

II. Literary Development of the Proverb.—The rank of proverb was by no means attributed to every popular saying, however the people might set store by it. If its application was merely local (e.g. 2 S **20** 18; Gen **22** 14) or temporary (note how Jeremiah and Ezekiel announce popular sayings as obsolete), it remained in its place and time. About the proverb, on the other hand, there was the sense of a value universal and permanent, fitting it for literary immortality. Nor was the proverb itself a run-wild thing, at the shaping of the crowd; from the beginning it was in the hands of "those who speak in *m^eshālīm*," whose business it was to put it into skilful wording. The popular proverb, however, and the literary proverb were and continued two different things. There came a time, in the literary development of Israel, when the value of the *māshāl* as a vehicle of instruction came to be recognized; from which time a systematic cultivation of this type of discourse began. That time, as seems most probable, was the reign of King Solomon, when in a special degree the people awoke to the life and industry and intercourse and wealth of the world around them. The king himself was 'large hearted' (1 K **4** 29), versatile, with literary tastes; "spake three thousand proverbs; and his songs were a thousand and five"; and his whole generation, both in Israel and surrounding nations, was engaged in a vigorous movement of thought and "wisdom" (see the whole passage, 1 K **4** 29–34). For the unit and vehicle of this new thought the old native form of the *māshāl* or proverb was chosen; it became the recognized medium of popular education and counsel, esp. of the young; and the *māshāl* itself was molded to the classic form, condensed, pointed, aphoristic, which we see best exemplified in the Book of Prov **10—22** 16—probably the earliest collection of this kind of literature. In this body of proverbs we see also that instead of retaining the unbalanced single assertion of the popular proverb, as it appears in 1 S **10** 12; **24** 13, these composers of literary proverbs borrowed the poetic parallelism, or couplet, which in two lines sets two statements over against each other by antithesis or repetition, and cultivated this to its most condensed and epigrammatic construction. Thus the *māshāl* took

1. Discovery of Literary Value

to itself a literary self-consciousness and became a work of art.

2. The Differentiation

Up to the time of this literary development a proverb was recognized simply as a proverb, with little sense of its various phases, except that there was a strong popular tendency to identify it with satire, and with less thought of the elements of its life and power. With the refinement of form, however, came a recognition of its inwardness. Under the generic term *māshāl*, certain elements were differentiated; not, however, as we are wont to distinguish—parable, fable, apologue, allegory—these remained undifferentiated. The most fundamental distinction of classes, perhaps, is given in Prov **1** 6: "To understand a proverb, and a figure, the words of the wise, and their dark sayings." Here it seems the word "proverb" (*māshāl*) and "words of the wise," paired off with each other, are the generic terms; the other two, the differentiating terms, name respectively the two fundamental directions of the *māshāl*, toward the clear and toward the enigmatic. Both are essential elements. The word tr[d] "figure" (מְלִיצָה, *m*[e]*līçāh*) is rather "interpretation," and seems to refer to the illuminative element of the *māshāl*, and this was mainly analogy. Natural objects, phases of experience, contrasts were drawn into the *māshāl* to furnish analogies for life; Solomon's use of plants and animals in his discourses (1 K **4** 33) was not by way of natural history, but as analogies to illustrate his *m*[e]*shālīm*. The word tr[d] "dark sayings" (חִידוֹת, *ḥīdhōth*) is the word elsewhere tr[d] "riddle" (Samson's riddle, for instance, was a *ḥīdhāh*, Jgs **14** 13.14), and refers to that quality of the proverb which, by challenging the hearer's acumen, gives it zest; it is due to an association of things so indirectly related that one must supply intermediate thoughts to resolve them. All of this of course goes to justify the proverb as a capital vehicle for instruction and counsel; it has the elements that appeal to attention, responsive thought, and memory, while on the other hand its basis of analogy makes it illuminative.

III. As Unit of a Strain of Literature.—Until it reached its classic perfection of phrasing, say during the time from Solomon to Hezekiah, the formal development of the proverb was concentrative; the single utterance disposed of its whole subject, as in a capsule. But the development of the *māshāl* form from the antithetic to the synonymous couplet gave rise to a proverb in which the explanatory member did not fully close the case; the subject craved further elucidation, and so a group of several couplets was sometimes necessary to present a case (cf e.g. about the sluggard, Prov **26** 13-16). From this group of proverbs the transition was easy to a continuous passage, in which the snappy parallelism of the proverb yields to the flow of poetry; see e.g. Prov **27** 23-27. This is due evidently to a more penetrative and analytic mode of thinking, which can no longer satisfy its statement of truth in a single illustration or maxim.

1. From Detachment to Continuity

2. The Conception of Wisdom

As the store of detached utterances on various phases of practical life accumulated and the task of collecting them was undertaken, it was seen that they had a common suffusion and bearing, that in fact they constituted a distinctive strain of literature. The field of this literature was broad, and recognized (see Prov **1** 1-5) as promotive of many intellectual virtues; but the inclusive name under which it was gathered was Wisdom (חָכְמָה, *ḥokhmāh*). Wisdom, deduced thus from a fund of maxims and analogies, became the Heb equivalent for philosophy. With the further history of it this article is not concerned, except to note that the *māshāl* or proverb form held itself free to expand into a continuous and extended discourse, or to hold itself in to the couplet form. As to illustrative quality, too, its scope was liberal enough to include a fully developed parable; see for instance Ezk **17** 1-10, where the prophet is bidden to "put forth a riddle, and speak a parable [lit. *māshal* a *māshāl*] unto the house of Israel."

3. In Later Time

The existence of so considerable a body of proverbs is a testimony to the Heb genius for sententious and weighty expression, a virtue of speech which was held in special esteem. From the uses of practical wisdom the *māshāl* form was borrowed by the later scribes and doctors of the law; we see it for instance in loose and artificial use in such books as *Pirḳē 'Ābhōth*, which gives the impression that the utterance so grandly represented in the Solomonic proverbs had become decadent. It is in another direction rather that the virtues of the *māshāl* reach their culmination. In the phrasal felicity and illustrative lucidity of Our Lord's discourses, and not less in His parables, employed that the multitude "may see and yet not see" (Mk **4** 12), we have the values of the ancient *māshāl* in their perfection, in a literary form so true to its object that we do not think of its artistry at all. See also GAMES, I, 6. JOHN FRANKLIN GENUNG

PROVERBS, prov'ẽrbz, BOOK OF:

The Scripture book which in both the Heb and the Gr arrangements of the OT Canon immediately succeeds the Pss. In the Heb Canon it stands second in the final or supplementary division called *k*[e]*thūbhīm* (LXX Παροιμίαι, *Paroimíai*), "writings"; placed there probably because it would be most natural to begin this section with standard collections nearest at hand, which of course would be psalms and proverbs. This book is an anthology of sayings or lessons of the sages on life, character, conduct; and as such embodies the distinctively educative strain of Heb literature.

I. The Book's Account of Itself.—At the beginning, intended apparently to cover the whole work, stands the title: "The proverbs of Solomon the son of David, king of Israel." It seemed good to the compilers, however, to repeat, or perhaps retain an older heading, "The proverbs of Solomon" at ch **10**, as if in some special sense the collection there beginning deserved it; and at ch **25** still another heading occurs: "These also are proverbs of Solomon, which the men of Hezekiah king of Judah copied out." All these ascribe the proverbs to Solomon; but the heading (**30** 1), "The words of Agur the son of Jakeh; the oracle," and the heading (**31** 1), "The words of king Lemuel; the oracle which his mother taught him," indicate

1. Title and Headings

that authorship other than that of Solomon is represented; while the mention of "the words of the wise" (**1** 6; **22** 17), as also the definite heading, "These also are sayings of the wise" (**24** 23), ascribe parts of the book to the sages in general. The book is confessedly a series of compilations made at different times; confessedly, also, to a considerable extent at least, the work of a number, perhaps a whole guild, of writers.

It is hazardous to argue either for or against a specific authorship; nor is it my intention to do so.

2. Authorship or Literary Species?

The question naturally arises, however, in what sense this book, with its composite structure so outspoken, can lay claim to being the work of Solomon. Does the title refer to actual personal authorship, or does it name a species and type of literature of which Solomon was the originator and inspirer—as if it meant to say "the Solomonic proverbs"? We may work toward the answer of this question by noting some literary facts.

Outside of the prophets only three of the OT books are provided in the original text with titles; and these three are all associated with Solomon—two of them, Prov and the Song of Songs, directly; the third, Eccl, by an assumed name, which, however, personates Solomon. This would seem to indicate in the composition of these books an unusual degree of literary finish and self-consciousness, a sense on the part of writers or compilers that literature as an art has its claims upon them. The subject-matter of the books, too, bears this out; they are, relatively speaking, the secular books of the Bible and do not assume Divine origin, as do law and prophecy. For the original impulse to such literary culture the history directs us to the reign of King Solomon; see 1 K **4** 29–34, where is portrayed, on the part of king and court, an intense intellectual activity for its own sake, the like of which occurs nowhere else in Scripture. The forms then esp. impressed upon the literature were the *māshāl* (proverb) and the song, in both of which the versatile young king was proficient; cf 1 K **4** 32. For the cultivation of the *māshāl* these men of letters availed themselves of a favorite native form, the popular proverb; but they gave to it a literary mold and finish which would thenceforth distinguish it as the Solomonic *māshāl* (see PROVERB). This then was the literary form in which from the time of Solomon onward the sages of the nation put their counsels of life, character, conduct; it became as distinctively the mold for this didactic strain of literature as was the heroic couplet for a similar strain in the age of Dryden and Pope.

It is reasonable therefore to understand this title of the Book of Prov as designating rather a literary species than a personal authorship; it names this anthology of Wisdom in its classically determined phrasing, and for age and authorship leaves a field spacious enough to cover the centuries of its currency. Perhaps also the proverb of this type was by the term "of Solomon" differentiated from *māshāls* of other types, as for instance those of Balaam and Job and Koheleth.

II. The Successive Compilations.—That the Book of Prov is composed of several collections made at different times is a fact that lies on the surface; as many as eight of these are clearly marked, and perhaps subdivisions might be made.

1. The Introductory Section

The book was not originally conceived as the development of a theme, or even as a unity; whatever unity it has was an afterthought. That it did come to stand, however, for one homogeneous body of truth, and to receive a name and a degree of articulation as such, will be maintained in a later section (see III, below). Meanwhile, we will take the sections in order and note some of the salient characteristics of each. The introductory section, chs **1–9,** has the marks of having been added later than most of the rest; and is introductory in the sense of concentrating the thought to the concept of Wisdom, and of recommending the spiritual attitude in which it is to be received. Its style—and in this it is distinguished from the rest of the book—is hortatory; it is addressed to "my son" (**1** 8 and often) or "my sons" (**4** 1; **5** 7; **7** 24; **8** 32), in the tone of a father or a sage, bringing stores of wisdom and experience to the young. The first six verses are prefatory, giving the purpose and use of the whole book. Then ver 7 lays down as the initial point, or spiritual bedrock of Wisdom, the fear of Jeh, a principle repeated toward the end of this introductory section (**9** 10), and evidently regarded as very vital to the whole Wisdom system; cf Job **28** 28; Ps **111** 10; Sir **1** 14. The effect of this prefatory and theme-propounding matter is to launch the collection of proverbs much after the manner of modern literary works, and the rest of the section bears this out fairly well. The most striking feature of the section, besides its general homiletic tone, is its personification of Wisdom. She is represented as calling to the sons of men and commending to them her ways (**1** 20–33; **8** 1–21.32–36); she condescends, for right and purity's sake, to enter into rivalry with the "strange woman," the temptress, not in secret, but in open and fearless dealing (**7** 6—**8** 9; **9** 1–6.13–18); and, in a supremely poetic passage (**8** 22–31), she describes her relation from the beginning with God and with the sons of men. It represents the value that the Heb mind came to set upon the human endowment of Wisdom. The Heb philosopher thought not in terms of logic and dialectics, but in symbol and personality; and to this high rank, almost like that of a goddess, his imagination has exalted the intellectual and spiritual powers of man. See WISDOM.

The section **10** 1—**22** 16, with the repeated heading "The proverbs of Solomon," seems to have been the original nucleus of the whole collection.

2. The Classic Nucleus

All the proverbs in this, the longest section of the book, are molded strictly to the couplet form (the one triplet, **19** 7, being only an apparent exception, due probably to the loss of a line), each proverb a parallelism in condensed phrasing, in which the second line gives either some contrast to or some amplification of the first. This was doubtless the classic art norm of the Solomonic *māshāl.*

The section seems to contain the product of that period of proverb-culture during which the sense of the model was a little rigid and severe, not venturing yet to limber up the form. Signs of a greater freedom, however, begin to appear, and possibly two strata of compilation are represented. In chs **10–15** the prevailing couplet is antithetic, which embodies the most self-closed circuit of the thought. Out of 184 proverbs only 19 do not contain some form of contrast, and 10 of these are in ch **15.** In **16—22** 16, on the other hand, the prevailing form is the so-called synonymous or amplified couplet, which leaves the thought-circuit more open to illustrative additions. Out of 191 proverbs only 18 are antithetic, and these contain contrasts of a more subtle and hidden suggestion. As to subject-matter, the whole section is miscellaneous; in the first half, however, where the antithesis prevails, are the great elemental distinctions of life, wisdom and folly, righteousness and wickedness, industry and laziness, wise speech and reticence, and the like; while in the second half there is a decided tendency to go farther afield for subtler and less obvious distinctions. In this way they seem to reflect a growing and refining literary development, the gradual shaping and accumulation of materials for a philosophy of life; as yet, however, not articulated or reduced to unity of principle.

In the short section **22** 17—**24** 22, the proverb literature seems for the first time to have become as it were self-conscious—to regard itself as a strain of wise counsel to be reckoned with for its educative value.

3. A Body of Solicited Counsel

The section is introduced by a preface (**22** 17–21), in which these "words of the wise" are recommended to some person or delegation, "that thou mayest carry back words of truth to them that send thee" (**22** 21). The counsels seem intended for persons in responsible position, perhaps attached to the court (cf **23** 1–3), who, as they are to deal officially with men and affairs, need the prudence, purity, and temperance which will fit them for their duties. As to form, the detached couplet appears only occasionally; the favorite form is the quatrain; but proverbs of a greater number of lines are freely used, and one, the counsel on wine drinking (**23** 29–35), runs to 17 lines. In tone and specific counsel the section has many resemblances to the introductory section (chs **1–9**), and provokes the conjecture that this latter section, as the introduction to a compiled body of Wisdom, was composed not long after it.

The little appendix (**24** 23–34) is headed, "These also are sayings of the wise." They refer to wise intercourse and ordered industry.

4. Some Left-over Precepts

The little poem on the sluggard (**24** 30–34), with its refrain (vs 33.34), is noteworthy as being apparently one stanza of a poem which is completed with the same refrain in the introductory section (**6** 6–11). The stanzas are of the same length and structure; and it would seem the latter named was either discovered later or composed as a supplement to the one in this section.

The long section (chs **25–29**) is headed, "These also are proverbs of Solomon, which the men of Hezekiah king of Judah copied out."

5. The Hezekian Collection

The collection claims to be only a compilation; but if, as already suggested, we understand the term "proverbs of Solomon" as equivalent to "Solomonic proverbs," referring rather to species than personal authorship, the compilation may have been made not merely from antiquity, but from the archives of the Wisdom guilds. If so, we have a clue to the state of the Wisdom literature in Hezekiah's time. The collection as a whole, unlike secs. 3 and 4, returns predominantly to the classic form of the couplet, but with a less degree of compression and epigram. There is a tendency to group numbers of proverbs on like subjects; note for instance the group on the king (**25** 2–7). The most striking feature of the collection is the prevalence of simile and analogy, and in general the strong figurative coloring, esp. in chs **25–27;** it reads like a new species of proverb when we note that in all the earlier Solomonic sections there are only two clearly defined similes (**10** 26; **11** 22). In chs **25–27** are several proverbs of three, four, or five lines, and at the end (**27** 23–27) a charming little poem of ten lines on husbandry. Chs **28, 29** are entirely of couplets, and the antithetic proverb reappears in a considerable number. As to subject-matter, the thought of this section makes a rather greater demand on the reader's culture and thinking powers, the analogies being less obvious, more subtle. It is decidedly the reflection of a more literary age than that of sec. 2.

Ch **30** is taken up with "the words of Agur the son of Jakeh," a person otherwise unknown, who disclaims expert knowledge of Wisdom

6. Words of Agur

lore (**30** 3), and avows an agnostic attitude toward theological speculations, yet shows a tender reverence before the name and unplumbed mystery of Jeh (vs 6.9.32). His words amount to a plea against a too adventurous, not to say presumptuous, spirit in the supposed findings of human Wisdom, and as such supply a useful makeweight to the mounting pride of the scholar. Yet over this peculiar plea is placed the word "Massa" (הַמַּשָּׂא, *ha-massā'*), "burden" or "oracle," the term used for prophetic disclosures; and the word for "said" ("the man said," נְאֻם הַגֶּבֶר, *n^e'um ha-gebher*) is the word elsewhere used for mystic or Divine utterance. This seems to mark a stage in the self-consciousness of Wisdom when it was felt that its utterances could be ranked by the side of prophecy as a revelation of truth (cf what Wisdom says of herself, **8** 14), and could claim the authoritative term "oracle." For the rest, apart from the humble reverence with which they are imbued, these words of Agur do not rise to a high level of spiritual thinking; they tend rather to the riddling element, or "dark sayings" (cf **1** 6). The form of his proverbs is peculiar, verging indeed on the artificial; he deals mostly in the so-called numerical proverb ("three things . . . . yea, four"), a style of utterance paralleled elsewhere only in **6** 16–19, but something of a favorite in the later cryptic sayings of the scribes, as may be seen in *Pirḳē 'Ābhōth.*

31 1–9 (possibly the whole chapter should be included) is headed, "The words of king Lemuel; the oracle which his mother taught him."

7. Words of King Lemuel

Here occurs again the mysterious word "oracle," which would seem to be open to the same interpretation as the one given in the previous paragraph, though some would make this otherwise unknown monarch a king of Massa, and refer to the name of one of the descendants of Ishmael (Gen **25** 14), presumably a tribal designation. The Heb sages from the beginning were in rivalry and fellowship with the sages of other nations (cf 1 K **4** 30.31); and in the Book of Job, the supreme reach of Wisdom utterance, all of the sages, Job included, are from countries outside of Pal. King Lemuel, if an actual personage, was not a Jew; and probably Agur was not. The words of Lemuel are a mother's plea to her royal son for chastity, temperance and justice, the kingly virtues. The form is the simple Heb parallelism, not detached couplets, but continuous.

The Book of Prov ends in a manner eminently worthy of its high standard of sanity and wisdom.

8. An Acrostic Eulogy of Woman

Without any heading (it may possibly belong to the "oracle" that the mother of Lemuel taught her son) the last 22 verses (**31** 10–31) constitute a single poem in praise of a worthy woman, extolling esp. her household virtues. In form these verses begin in the original with the successive 22 letters of the Heb alphabet; a favorite form of Heb verse, as may be seen (in the original) in several of the pss, notably Ps **119,** and in chs **1–4** of the Book of Lam.

III. Movement toward a Philosophy.—It has been much the fashion with modern critics to deny to the Hebrews a truly philosophic mind; this they say was rather the distinctive gift of the Greeks; while for their solution of the problem of life the Hebrews depended on direct revelation from above, which precluded that quasi-abeyance of concepts, that weighing of cosmic and human elements, involved in the commonly received notion of philosophy. This criticism takes account of only one side of the Heb mind. It is true they believed their life to be in direct contact with the will and word of Jeh, revealed to them in terms which could not be questioned; but in the findings and deliverance of their own intellectual powers, too, they had a reliance and confidence which merits the name of an authentic philosophy. But theirs was a philosophy not of speculative world-making, but of conduct and the practical management of life; and it was intuitive and analogical, not the result of dialectical reasoning. Hence its name wisdom, the solution itself, rather than philosophy, the love of wisdom, the search for solution. This Book of Prov, beginning with detached maxims on the elements of conduct, reveals in many suggestive ways the gradual emergence of a philosophy, a comprehensive wisdom, as it were, in the making; it is thus the pioneer book of that Heb Wisdom which we see developed to maturer things in the books of Job and Eccl. Some of its salient stages may here be traced.

1. Liberation of the *māshāl*

We may first note it, or the literary preparation for it, in the opening up of the *māshāl*, or proverb unit, toward added elements of illustration, explanation, amplitude, a development that begins to appear, in the oldest section (the classic nucleus, sec. 2) at about ch **16**. The primitive antithetic *māshāl* contrasted two aspects of truth in such a way as to leave the case closed; there was nothing for it but to go on to a new subject. This had the good effect of setting over against each other the great elemental antagonisms of life: righteousness and wickedness, obedience and lawlessness, teachableness and perversity, industry and laziness, prudence and presumption, reticence and prating, etc, and so far forth it was a masterly analysis of the essentials of individual and social conduct. As soon, however, as the synonymous and illustrative *māshāl* prevails, we are conscious of a limbering up and greater penetrativeness of the range of thought; it is open to subtler distinctions and remoter discoveries, and the analogies tend to employ the less direct relationships of cause and effect. This is increased as we go on, esp. by the greater call upon the imagination in the figurative tissue of the Hezekian section, and by the decidedly greater tendency to the riddling and paradox element. The *māshāl* increases in length and amplitude, both by the grouping of similar subjects and by the enlargement from the couplet to the quatrain and the developed poem. All this, while not yet a self-conscious philosophy, is a step on the way thereto.

2. Emergence of Basal Principles

One solid presupposition of the sages, like an axiom, was never called in question: namely, that righteousness and wisdom are identical, that wickedness of any sort is folly. This imparts at once a kind of prophetic coloring to the Wisdom precepts, well represented by the opening proverb in the original section (after the prefatory one about the wise son), "Treasures of wickedness profit nothing; but righteousness delivereth from death" (Prov **10** 2). Thus from the outset is furnished an uncompromising background on which the fascinating allurements of vice, the crooked ways of injustice and dishonesty, the sober habits of goodness and right dealing, show for what they are and what they tend to. The sages thus put themselves, too, in entire harmony with what is taught by priests and prophets; there is no quarrel with the law or the word; they simply supply the third strand in the threefold cord of instruction (cf Jer **18** 18). From this basal presumption other principles, scarcely less axiomatic, come in view: that the fount and spring of wise living is reverence, the fear of Jeh; that the ensuring frame of mind is teachableness, the precluding attitude perverseness; that it is the mark of wisdom, or righteousness, to be fearless and above board, of wickedness, which is folly, to be crooked and secretive. These principles recur constantly, not as a system, but in numerous aspects and applications in the practical business of life. For their sanctions they refer naïvely to the Heb ideal of rewards on the one hand—wealth, honor, long life, family (cf Prov **11** 31)—and of shame and loss and destruction on the other; but these are emphasized not as direct bestowments or inflictions from a personal Deity, rather as in the law of human nature. The law that evil works its own destruction, good brings its own reward, is forming itself in men's reason as one of the fundamental concepts out of which grew the Wisdom philosophy.

From times long before Solomon sagacity in counsel, and skill to put such counsel into maxim or parable, gave their possessor, whether man or woman, a natural leadership and repute in the local communities (cf 2 S **14** 2; **20** 16); and Solomon's exceptional endowment showed itself not merely in his literary tastes, but in his ability, much esteemed among Orientals, to determine the merits of cases brought before him for judgment (1 K **3** 16–28), and to answer puzzling questions (1 K **10** 1.6.7). It was from such estimate of men's intellectual powers, from the recognition of mental alertness, sagacity, grasp, in their application to the practical issues of life (cf Prov **1** 1–5), that the conception of Wisdom in its larger sense arose. As, however, the cultivation of such sagacity of utterance passed beyond the pastime of a royal court (cf 1 K **4** 29–34) into the hands of city elders and sages, it attained to greatly enhanced value; note how the influence of such a sage is idealized (Job **29** 7–25). The sages had a definite calling and mission of their own, more potent perhaps than belonged to priests and prophets; the frequent reference to the young and the "simple" or immature in the Book of Prov would indicate that they were virtually the schoolmasters and educators of the nation. As such, working as they did in a fellowship and collaboration with each other, the subject-matter with which they dealt would not remain as casual and miscellaneous maxims, but work toward a center and system of doctrine which could claim the distinction of an articulated philosophy of life, and all the more since it was so identified with the great Heb ideal of righteousness and truth. We have already noted how this sense of the dignity and value of their calling manifested itself in the body of precepts sent in response to solicitation (3 above), with its appendix (4 above) (Prov **22** 17—**24** 34). It was not long after this stage of Wisdom-culture, I think, that a very significant new word came into their vocabulary, the word *tūshīyāh* (תּוּשִׁיָּה, a puzzle to the translators, variously rendered "sound wisdom," "effectual working," and called by the lexicographers "a technical term of the Wisdom literature," *BDB*, s.v.). Its earliest appearance, and the only one except in the introductory section (Prov **18** 1), is where the man who separates himself from others' opinions and seeks his own desire is said to quarrel with all *tūshīyāh*. The word seems to designate Wisdom in its subjective aspect, as an authentic insight or intuition of truth, the human power to rise into the region of true revelation from below, as distinguished from the prophetic or legal word spoken directly from above. Outside of Prov and Job the word occurs only twice: once in Mic **6** 9, and once in Isa **28** 29, in which latter case the prophet has deliberately composed a passage (vs 23–29) in the characteristic *māshāl* idiom, and attributed that strain of insight to Jeh. Evidently there came a time in the culture of Wisdom when its utterances attained in men's estimate to a parity with utterances direct from the unseen; perhaps this explains why Agur's and Lemuel's words could be boldly ranked as oracles (see above, 6 and 7). At any rate, such a high distinction, an authority derived from intimacy with the creative work of Jeh (**8** 30.31), is ascribed to Wisdom (*ḥokhmāh*, חָכְמָה) in the introductory section; "counsel is mine," Wisdom is made to say, "and *tūshīyāh*" (**8** 14). Thus the Book of Prov reveals to us a philosophy, as it were, in the making and from scattered counsels attaining gradually to the summit where the human intellect could place its findings by the side of Divine oracles.

3. The Conception of Wisdom *(margin heading beside the preceding paragraph)*

IV. Considerations of Age and Literary Kinship.—To get at the history of the Book of Prov, several inquiries must be raised. When were the proverbs composed? The book, like the Book of Ps, is confessedly an anthology, containing various accumulations, and both by style and maturing thought bearing the marks of different ages. When were the successive compilations made? And, finally, when did the strain of literature here represented reach that point of self-conscious unity and coördination which justified its being reckoned with as a strain by itself and choosing the comprehensive name Wisdom? What makes these inquiries hard to answer is the fact that these proverbs are precepts for the common people, relating to ordinary affairs of the village, the market, and the field, and move in lines remote from politics and dynastic vicissitudes and wars. They are, to an extent far more penetrative and pervasive than law or prophecy, the educative literature on which the sturdy rank and file of the nation was nourished. 'Where there is no vision, the people let loose,' says a Hezekian proverb (Prov **29** 18); but so they are also when there is no abiding tonic of social convention and principle. Precisely this latter it is which this Book of Prov in a large degree reveals; and in course of time its value was so felt that, as we have seen, it could rank itself as an asset of life by the side of vision. It represents, in a word, the human movement toward self-directiveness and self-reliance, without supine dependence on ruler or public sentiment (cf Prov **29** 25.26). When and how was this sane and wholesome communal fiber developed?

When Solomon and his court made the *māshāl* an elegant fad, they builded better than they knew.

1. Under the Kings

They gave to the old native form of the proverb and parable, as reduced to epigrammatic mold and polish, the *éclat* of a popular literature. This was done orally at first (Solomon *spoke* his proverbs, 1 K **4** 32.33); but the recording of such carefully expressed utterances could not be long delayed; perhaps this brief *style coupé* was the most natural early exercise in the new transition from the unwieldly cuneiform to the use of papyrus and a more flexible alphabet, which probably came in with the monarchy. At any rate, here was the medium for a practical didactic literature, applied to the matters of daily life and intercourse to which in Solomon's time the nation was enthusiastically awake. There is no valid reason for denying to Solomon, or at least to his time, the initiation of the Solomonic *māshāl;* and if, as has been suggested, the name "proverbs of Solomon" designates rather literary species than personal authorship, the title of the whole book (**1** 1), as well as the headings of sections (**10** 1; **25** 1), may be given in entire good faith, whatever the specific time or personal authorship of the utterances. Nor is there anything either in recorded history or the likelihood of the case to make improbable that the activity of the "men of Hezekiah" means just what is said; these men of letters were adding this supplementary collection (Prov **25**–**29**) to a body of proverbs that already existed and were recognized as Solomon's. This would put the composition of the main body of the proverbs (chs **10**–**29**) prior to the reign of Hezekiah. They represent therefore the chief literary instruction available to the people in the long period of the Kings from Solomon onward, a period which otherwise was very meagerly supplied. The Mosaic Law, as we gather from the finding of the Law in the time of Josiah (2 K **22**), was at best a sequestered thing in the keeping—or neglect—of priests and judges; the prophetic word was a specific message for great national emergencies; the accumulations of sacred song were the property of the temple and the cultus; what then was there for the education of the people? There were indeed the folk-tales and catechetical legends of their heroic history; but there were also, most influential of all, these wise sayings of the sages, growing bodies of precept and parable, preserved in village centers, published in the open places by the gate (cf Job **29** 7), embodying the elements of a common-sense religion and citizenship, and representing views of life which were not only Hebrew, but to a great extent international among the neighbor kingdoms. Understood so, these Solomonic proverbs furnish incomparably the best reflection we have of the religious and social standards of the common people, during a period otherwise meagerly portrayed. And from it we can understand what a sterling fiber of character existed after all, and how well worth preserving for a unique mission in the world, in spite of the idolatrous corruptions that invaded the sanctuaries, the self-pleasing unconcern of the rulers and the pessimistic denunciations of the prophets.

For the point in the Heb literary history when these scattered Solomonic proverbs were recog-

2. The Concentrative Point

nized as a homogeneous strain of thought and the compilations were made and recommended as Wisdom, we can do no better, I think, than to name the age of Israel's literary prime, the age of Hezekiah. The "men of Hezekiah" did more than append their supplementary section (chs **25**–**29**); the words "these also" (גַּם־אֵלֶּה, *gam 'ēlleh*) in their heading imply it (see HEZEKIAH, THE MEN OF).

I apprehend the order and nature of their work somehow thus: Beginning with the classic nucleus (**10**—**22** 16) (see above, II, 2), which may have come to them in two subsections (chs **10**–**15**; **16**—**22** 16), they put these together as the proverbs most closely associated with Solomon, without much attempt at systematizing, substantially as these had accumulated through the ages in the rough order of their developing form and thought; compiling thus, in their zeal for the literary treasures of the past, the body of educational literature which lay nearest at hand, a body adapted especially, though not exclusively, to the instruction of the young and immature. This done, there next came to their knowledge a remarkable body of "words of the wise" (**22** 17—**24** 22), which had evidently been put together by request as a *vade mecum* for some persons in responsible position, and which were prefaced by a recommendation of them as "words of truth" designed to promote "trust in Jeh" (**22** 19–21)—which latter, as we know from Isaiah, was the great civic issue of Hezekiah's time. With this section naturally goes the little appendix of "sayings of the wise" (**24** 23–34), added probably at about the same time. These two sections, which seem to open the collection to matter beyond the distinctive Solomonic *māshāl*, are, beyond the rest of the book, in the tone of the introductory section (chs **1**–**9**), which latter, along with the Hezekian appendix (chs **25**–**29**), was added, partly as a new composition, partly as incorporating some additional findings (cf for instance the completion of the poem on the sluggard, **6** 6–11). Thus, by the addition of this introductory section, the Book of Prov was recognized as a unity, provided with a preface and initial proposition (**1** 1–6.7), and launched with such hortatory material as had already, on a smaller scale, introduced the third section. This part not only contains the praise of Wisdom as a human endowment, sharing in the mind and purpose of the Divine (**8** 22–31), but it has become aware also of the revelatory value of *tūshīyāh* (**2** 7; **3** 21; **8** 14), or chastened intuition (see above, III, 3), and dares to aspire, in its righteous teachableness, to the intimacy or secret friendship of Jeh (סוֹדוֹ, *sōdhō*, **3** 32). All this indicates the holy self-consciousness to which Wisdom has attained.

I see no cogent reason for postponing the substantial completion of the Book of Prov beyond the time of Hezekiah. The words of Agur and of King Lemuel, with the final acrostic poem, may be later additions; but their difference in tone and workmanship is just as likely to be due to the fact that they are admitted, in the liberal spirit of the compilers, from foreign stores of wisdom. For spiritual clarity and intensity they do not rise to the height of the native Heb consciousness; and they incline to an artificial structure which suggests that the writer's interest is divided between sincere *tūshīyāh* and literary skill. For the sake of like-minded neighbors, however, something may be forgiven.

It is too early in the history of Wisdom to regard this Book of Prov as an articulated and coördinated system. It is merely what it purports to be, a collected body of literature having a common bearing and purpose; a literature of reverent and intelligent self-culture, moving among the ordinary relations of life, and not assuming to embody any mystic disclosures of truth beyond the reach of human reason. As such, it has a vocabulary and range of ideas of its own, which distinguishes it from other strains of literature. This is seen in those passages outside of the Book of Prov which deliberately assume, for some specific purpose, the Wisdom dialect. In Isa **28** 23–29, the prophet, whom the perverse rulers have taunted with baby-talk (vs 9.10), appeals to them with the characteristic Wisdom call to attention (ver 23), and in illustrations drawn from husbandry proves to them that this also is from Jeh of hosts, 'who is transcendent in counsel, preëminent in *tūshīyāh*' (ver 29)—teaching them thus in their own vaunted idiom. In Mic **6** 9–15, similarly, calling in *tūshīyāh* to corroborate prophecy ("the voice of Jeh," קוֹל יהוה, *ḳōl Yahweh*, וְתוּשִׁיָּה, *w^ethūshīyāh*, **6** 9), the prophet speaks of the natural disasters that men ought to deduce from their abuse of trade relations, evidently appealing to them in their own favorite strain of thinking. Both these passages seem to reflect a time when the Wisdom dialect was prevalent and popular, and both are concerned to call in sound human intuition as an ally of prophecy. At the same time, as prophets have the right to do, they labor to give revelation the casting vote; the authentic disclosure of truth from Jeh is their objective, not the mere luxury of making clever observations on practical life. All this coincides, in the Wisdom sphere, with what in Isaiah's and Micah's time was the supreme issue of state, namely trust in Jeh, rather than in crooked human devices (cf Isa **28** 16; **29** 15); and it is noteworthy that this is the venture of Wisdom urged by the editors of Prov in their introductory exhortations (cf **22** 19; **3** 5–8). In other words, these editors are concerned with inducing a spiritual *attitude;* and so in their literary strain they make their book an adjunct in the movement toward spirituality which Isaiah is laboring to promote. As yet, however, its findings are still in the peremptory stage, stated as absolute and unqualified truths; it has not reached the sober testing of fact and interrogation of motive which it must encounter in order to become a seasoned philosophy of life. Its main pervading thesis—that righteousness in the fear of God *is* wisdom and bound for success, that wickedness is fatuity and bound for destruction—is eternally sound; but it must make itself good in a world where so many of the enterprises of life seem to come out the other way, and where there is so little appreciation of spiritual values. Nor is the time of skepticism and rigid test long in coming. Two psalms of this period (as I apprehend) (Pss **73** and **49**) concern themselves with the anomaly of the success of the wicked and the trials of the righteous; the latter pointedly adopting the Wisdom or *māshāl* style of utterance (Ps **49** 3.4), both laboring to induce a more inward and spiritual attitude toward the problem. It remains, however, for the Book of Job to take the momentous forward step of setting wisdom on the unshakable foundation of spiritual integrity, which it does by subjecting its findings to the rigid test of fact and its motives to a drastic Satanic sifting. It is thus in the Book of Job, followed later by the Book of Eccl, that the Wisdom strain of literature, initiated by the Proverbs of Solomon, finds its OT culmination.

3. Its Stage in Progressive Wisdom

JOHN FRANKLIN GENUNG

PROVIDENCE, prov′i-dens:

I. PROVIDENCE DEFINED
II. DIFFERENT SPHERES OF PROVIDENTIAL ACTIVITY DISTINGUISHED
III. BIBLICAL PRESENTATION OF THE DOCTRINE OF PROVIDENCE
1. The Doctrine of Providence in the OT
(1) The Pentateuch
(2) The Historical Books
(3) The Psalms
(4) The Wisdom Literature
(5) The Book of Job
(6) The Prophetical Writings
2. The Doctrine of Providence in the NT
(1) The Synoptic Gospels
(2) The Johannine Writings
(3) The Acts, and Other Historical Writings of the NT
(4) The Pauline Epistles
(5) The Petrine Epistles, and Other NT Writings
3. OT and NT Doctrines of Providence Compared
(1) The New Emphasis on the Fatherhood and Love of God
(2) The Place of Christ and the Holy Spirit in Providence
(3) The New Emphasis upon Moral and Spiritual Blessings
IV. DISCUSSION OF THE CONTENTS OF THE BIBLICAL DOCTRINE
1. Different Views of Providence Compared
(1) The Atheistic or Materialistic View
(2) The Pantheistic View
(3) The Deistic View
(4) The Theistic or Biblical View
(5) The Divine Immanence
2. The Divine Purpose and Final End of Providence
3. Special Providence
(1) Spiritual, Not Material, Good to Man the End Sought in Special Providence
(2) Special Providence and "Accidents"
(3) Special Providence as Related to Piety and Prayer
(4) Special Providence as Related to Human Coöperation
(5) General and Special Providence Both Equally Divine
4. Divine Providence and Human Free Will
(1) Divine Providence as Related to Willing Wills
(2) Divine Providence as Related to Sinful Free Will
5. Divine Providence as Related to Natural and Moral Evil
6. Evil Providentially Overruled for Good
7. Interpreting Providence
8. Conclusion
LITERATURE

I. Providence Defined.—The word "provide" (from Lat *providere*) means etymologically "to foresee." The corresponding Gr word, πρόνοια, *prónoia*, means "forethought." Forethought and foresight imply a future end, a goal, and a definite purpose and plan for attaining that end. The doctrine of final ends is a doctrine of final causes, and means that that which is last in realization and attainment is first in mind and thought. The most essential attribute of rational beings is that they act with reference to an end; that they act not only with thought but with forethought. As, therefore, it is characteristic of rational beings to make preparation for every event that is foreseen or anticipated, the word "providence" has come to be used less in its original etymological meaning of foresight than to signify that preparation, care and supervision which are necessary to secure a desired future result. While all rational beings exercise a providence proportioned to their powers, yet it is only when the word is used with reference to the Divine Being who is possessed of infinite knowledge and power that it takes on its real and true significance. The doctrine of Divine providence, therefore, has reference to that preservation, care and government which God exercises over all things that He has created, in order that they may accomplish the ends for which they were created.

"Providence is the most comprehensive term in the language of theology. It is the background of all the several departments of religious truth, a background mysterious in its commingled brightness and darkness. It penetrates and fills the whole compass of the relations of man with his Maker. It connects the unseen God with the visible creation, and the visible creation with the work of redemption, and redemption with personal salvation, and personal salvation with the end of all things. It carries our thoughts back to the supreme purpose which was in the beginning with God, and forward to the foreseen end and consummation of all things, while it includes between these the whole infinite variety of the dealings of God with man" (W. B. Pope, *Compendium of Christian Theology*, I, 456).

II. Different Spheres of Providential Activity Distinguished.—The created universe may be conveniently divided, with reference to Divine providence, into three departments: first, the inanimate or physical universe, which is conserved or governed by God according to certain uniform principles called the laws of Nature; secondly, animate existence, embracing the vegetable and animal world, over which God exercises that providential care which is necessary to sustain the life that He created; and thirdly, the rational world, composed of beings who, in addition to animate life, are possessed of reason and moral free agency, and are governed by God, not necessitatively, but through an appeal to reason, they having the power to obey or disobey the laws of God according to the decision of their own free wills. This widespread care and supervision which God exercises over His created universe is commonly designated as His general providence, which embraces alike the evil and the good, in addition to which there is a more special and particular providence which He exercises over and in behalf of the good, those whose wills are in harmony with the Divine will.

III. Biblical Presentation of the Doctrine of Providence.—The word "providence" is used only once in the Scriptures (Acts **24** 2), and here it refers, not to God, but to the forethought and work of man, in which sense it is now seldom used. (See also Rom **13** 14, where the same Gr word is tr[d] "provision.") While, however, the Bib. use of the word calls for little consideration, the doctrine indicated by the term "providence" is one of the most significant in the Christian system, and is either distinctly stated or plainly assumed by every Bib. writer. The OT Scriptures are best understood when interpreted as a progressive revelation of God's providential purpose for Israel and the world. Messianic expectations pervade the entire life and lit. of the Heb people, and the entire OT dispensation may not improperly be regarded as the moral training and providential preparation of the world, and esp. of the chosen people, for the coming Messiah. In the apocryphal "Book of Wisdom" the word "providence" is twice used (**14** 3; **17** 2) in reference to God's government of the world. Rabbinical Judaism, according to Jos, was much occupied with discussing the relation of Divine providence to human free will. The Sadducees, he tells us, held an extreme view of human freedom, while the Essenes were believers in absolute fate; the Pharisees, avoiding these extremes, believed in both the overruling providence of God and in the freedom and responsibility of man (*Ant*, XIII, v, 9; XVIII, i, 3; *BJ*, II, viii, 14). See PHARISEES. The NT begins with the announcement that the "kingdom of heaven is at hand," which declaration carries along with it the idea of a providential purpose and design running through the preceding dispensation that prepared for the Messiah's coming. But the work of Christ is set forth in the NT, not only as the culmination of a Divine providence that preceded it, but as the beginning of a new providential order, a definite and far-reaching plan, for the redemption of the world, a forethought and plan so comprehensive that it gives to the very idea of Divine providence a new, larger and richer meaning, both intensively and extensively, than it ever had before. The minutest want of the humblest individual and the largest interests of the world-wide kingdom of God are alike embraced within the scope of Divine providence as it is set forth by Christ and the apostles.

1. Divine Providence in the OT Scriptures

(1) *Providence in the Pentateuch.*—The opening sentence of the Scriptures, "In the beginning God created the heaven and the earth," is a noble and majestic affirmation of God's essential relationship to the origin of all things. It is followed by numerous utterances scattered throughout the sacred volume that declare that He who created also preserves and governs all that He created. But the Israelitish nation was from the beginning of its history, in the Heb conception, the special object of God's providence and care, though it was declared that Jeh's lordship and government extended over all the earth (Ex **8** 22). The Deuteronomist (**10** 14) uses language which implies that Divine possession of all things in heaven and earth carries along with it the idea of Divine providence and control; and he also regards Israel as Jeh's peculiar possession and special care (**32** 8).

This special providence that was over the elect nation as a whole was also minute and particular, in that special individuals were chosen to serve a providential purpose in the making of the nation, and were Divinely guided in the accomplishment of their providential mission. Thus Abraham's providential place in history is set forth in Neh **9** 7.8. Jacob acknowledges the same providential hand in his life (Gen **31** 42; **48** 15). The life of Joseph abounds in evidences of a Divine providence (Gen **45** 5.7; **50** 20). The whole life-history of Moses as it is found in the Pent is a study in the doctrine of Divine providence. Other lives as set forth in these early narratives may be less notable, but they are not less indebted to Divine providence for what they are and for what they accomplish for others. Indeed, as Professor Oehler remarks, "The whole Pentateuchal history of revelation is nothing but the activity of that Divine providence which, in order to the realization of the Divine aim, is at once directed to the whole, and at the same time proves itself efficacious in the direction of the life of separate men, and in the guiding of all circumstances" (*OT Theology*).

(2) *The historical books of the OT.*—In a sense all the books of the OT are historical in that they furnish material for writing a history of the people of Israel. See ISRAEL, HISTORY OF THE PEOPLE. The Pent, the Poetical Books, the Wisdom Lit., the Prophets, all furnish material for writing OT history; but there is still left a body of literature, including the books from Josh to Est, that may with peculiar fitness be designated as historical. These books are all, in an important sense, an interpretation and presentation of the facts of Heb history in their relation to Divine providence. The sacred historians undertake to give something of a Divine philosophy of history, to interpret in a religious way the facts of history, to point out the evils of individual and national sin and the rewards and blessings of righteousness, and to show God's ever-present and ever-guiding hand in human history—that He is not a silent spectator of human affairs, but the supreme moral Governor of the universe, to whom individuals and nations alike owe allegiance. To the Heb historian every event in the life of the nation has a moral significance, both because of its relation to God and because of its bearing on the providential mission and testing of Israel as the people of God. The Book of Jgs, which covers the "dark ages" of Bible history, and is an enigma to many in the study of God's hand in history, shows how far God must needs condescend at times in His use of imperfect and even sensual men through whom to reveal His will and accomplish His work in the world. While therefore He condescends to use as instruments of His providence such men as Samson and Jephthah, it is never

through these that He does His greatest work, but through an Abraham, a Joseph, a Moses, an Isaiah, through men of lofty moral character. And this is one of the most notable lessons of OT history if it be studied as a revelation of God's providential methods and instrumentalities. Among these historical writers none has given clearer and stronger expression to God's providential relation to the physical world as its preserver and to the moral world as its Divine Governor than the author of Nehemiah. "Thou, even thou, art Lord alone; thou hast made heaven, the heaven of heavens, with all their host, the earth, and all things that are therein, the seas, and all that is therein, and thou preservest them all. . . . . Yet thou in thy manifold mercies forsookest them not in the wilderness: the pillar of the cloud departed not from them by day, to lead them in the way; neither the pillar of fire by night, to shew them light, and the way wherein they should go. Thou gavest also thy good spirit to instruct them" (**9** 6.19.20 AV). His words reflect the views that were entertained by all the OT historians as to God's hand in the government and guidance of the nation. Heb history, because of the Divine promises and Divine providence, is ever moving forward toward the Messianic goal.

(3) *The Psalms.*—The poets are among the world's greatest religious teachers, and the theology of the best poets generally represents the highest and purest faith that is found among a people. Applying this truth to the Heb race, we may say that in the Pss and the Book of Job we reach the high-water mark of the OT revelation as to the doctrine of Divine providence. The Psalmist's God is not only the Creator and Preserver of all things, but is a prayer-hearing and prayer-answering God, a Being so full of tender mercy and loving-kindness that we cannot fail to identify Him with the God whom Christ taught us to call "our Father." Nowhere else in the entire Scriptures, except in the Sermon on the Mount, can we find such a full and clear exhibition of the minute and special providence of God over His faithful and believing children as in the Pss—notably such as Pss **91, 103, 104** and **139.** Ps **105** traces God's hand in providential and gracious guidance through every stage of Israel's wondrous history. Thanksgiving and praise for providential mercies and blessings abound in Pss **44, 66, 78, 85, 135.** While the relation of God's power and providence to the physical universe and to the material and temporal blessings of life is constantly asserted in the Pss, yet it is the connection of God's providence with man's ethical and spiritual nature, with righteousness and faith and love, that marks the highest characteristic of the Psalmist's revelation of the doctrine of providence. That righteousness and obedience are necessary conditions and accompaniments of Divine providence in its moral aspects and results is evidenced by numerous declarations of the psalmists (**1** 6; **31** 19.20; **74** 12; **84** 11; **91** 1; **125** 2). This thought finds happiest expression in Ps **37** 23 AV: "The steps of a good man are ordered of the Lord, and he delighteth in his way." The inspired poets make it plain that the purpose of Divine providence is not merely to meet temporal wants and bring earthly blessings, but to secure the moral good of individuals and nations.

(4) *The Wisdom Literature.*—The doctrine of providence finds ample and varied expression in the Wisdom Lit. of the OT, notably in the Book of Prov. The power that preserves and governs and guides is always recognized as inseparable from the power that creates and commands (Prov **3** 21–26; **16** 4). Divine providence does not work independently of man's free will; providential blessings are conditioned on character and conduct (Prov **26** 10 AV; **2** 7.8; **12** 2.21). There cannot be, in OT terms of faith, any stronger statement of the doctrine of Divine providence than that given by the Wise Men of Israel in the following utterances recorded in the Book of Prov: "In all thy ways acknowledge him, and he will direct thy paths" (**3** 6); "A man's heart deviseth his way, but Jeh directeth his steps" (**16** 9); "The lot is cast into the lap; but the whole disposing thereof is of Jeh" (**16** 33); "A man's goings are of Jeh" (**20** 24); "The king's heart is in the hand of Jeh as the watercourses: He turneth it whithersoever he will" (**21** 1); "The horse is prepared against the day of battle; but victory is of Jeh" (**21** 31). See also **3** 21–26; **12** 2.21. The conception of providence that is presented in the Book of Eccl seems to reflect the views of one who had had experience in sin and had come into close contact with many of life's ills. All things have their appointed time, but the realization of the providential purposes and ends of creaturely existence is, wherever human free agency is involved, always conditioned upon man's exercise of his free will. The God of providence rules and overrules, but He does not by His omnipotence overpower and override and destroy man's true freedom. Things that are do not reflect God's perfect providence, but rather His providence as affected by human free agency and as marred by man's sin (Eccl **3** 1–11). "I know that there is nothing better for them, than to rejoice, and to do good so long as they live. And also that every man should eat and drink, and enjoy good in all his labor, is the gift of God" (vs 12.13; see also ver 14); "The righteous, and the wise, and their works, are in the hand of God" (**9 1**); "The race is not to the swift, nor the battle to the strong" (**9** 11). The same conclusion that the author of Eccl reached as to how human life is affected by Divine providence and man's sin has found expression in the oft-quoted lines of the great poet:

> "There's a Divinity that shapes our ends,
> Rough-hew them how we will."

(5) *The Book of Job.*—The greatest of all the inspired contributions to the Wisdom Lit. of the OT, the Book of Job, demands special consideration. It is the one book in the Bible that is devoted wholly to a discussion of Divine providence. The perplexities of a thoughtful mind on the subject of Divine providence and its relation to human suffering have nowhere in the literature of the world found stronger and clearer expression than in this inspired drama which bears the name of its unique and marvelous hero, Job. Job represents not only a great sufferer, but an honest doubter: he dared to doubt the theology of his day, a theology which he had himself doubtless believed until experience, the best of all teachers, taught him its utter inadequacy to explain the deepest problems of human life and of Divine providence. The purpose of this book in the inspired volume seems to be to correct the prevailing theology of the day with regard to the subject of sin and suffering in their relation to Divine providence. There is no more deplorable and hurtful error that a false theology could teach than that all suffering in this world is a proof of sin and a measure of one's guilt (see AFFLICTION). It is hard enough for the innocent to suffer. To add to their suffering by teaching them that it is all because they are awful sinners, even though their hearts assure them that they are not, is to lay upon the innocent a burden too grievous to be borne. The value in the inspired Canon of a book written to reveal the error of such a misleading doctrine as this cannot easily be overestimated. The invaluable contribution which this book makes to the Bib. doctrine of providence is to be found, not in individual and detached sayings

striking and suggestive as some of these may be, but rather in the book as a whole. Statements concerning God's general providence abound in this inspired drama—such as these, for example: "Who knoweth not in all these, that the hand of Jeh hath wrought this, in whose hand is the soul of every living thing, and the breath of all mankind?" (Job **12** 9.10); "Who hath given him a charge over the earth? or who hath disposed the whole world? . . . . He shall break in pieces mighty men without number, and set others in their stead" (**34** 13.24 AV).

But the special contribution of the Book of Job to the doctrine of Divine providence, as already indicated, is to set forth its connection with the fact of sin and suffering. Perplexed souls in all ages have been asking: If God be all-powerful and all-good, why should there be any suffering in a world which He created and over which He rules? If He cannot prevent suffering, is He omnipotent? If He can, but will not prevent suffering, is He infinitely good? Does the book solve the mystery? We cannot claim that it does. But it does vindicate the character of God, the Creator, and of Job, the moral free agent under trial. It does show the place of suffering in a moral world where free agents are forming character; it does show that perfect moral character is made, not by Divine omnipotence, but by trial, and that physical suffering serves a moral end in God's providential government of men and nations. While the book does not clear the problem of mystery, it does show how on the dark background of a suffering world the luminous holiness of Divine and human character may be revealed. The picture of this suffering man of Uz, racked with bodily pains and irritated by the ill-spoken words of well-meaning friends, planting himself on the solid rock of his own conscious rectitude, and defying earth and hell to prove him guilty of wrong, and knowing that his Vindicator liveth and would come to his rescue—*that* is an inspired picture that will make every innocent sufferer who reads it stronger until the end of time. See also Job, Book of.

(6) *The prophetical writings.*—Nowhere in all literature is the existence and supremacy of a moral and providential order in the world more clearly recognized than in the writings of the OT prophets. These writings are best understood when interpreted as the moral messages and passionate appeals of men who were not only prophets and preachers of righteousness to their own times, but students and teachers of the moral philosophy of history for all time, seers, men of vision, who interpreted all events in the light of their bearing on this moral and providential order, in which Divine order the Israelitish nation had no small part, and over which Israel's God was sovereign, doing "according to his will in the army of heaven and among the inhabitants of earth." While each prophetic message takes its coloring from the political, social and moral conditions that called it forth, and therefore differs from every other message, the prophets are all one in their insistence upon the supremacy and Divine authority of this moral order, and in their looking forward to the coming of the Messiah and the setting up of the Messianic kingdom as the providential goal and consummation of the moral order. They all describe in varying degrees of light and shade a coming time when One born of their own oppressed and down-trodden race should come in power and glory, and set up a kingdom of righteousness and love in the earth, into which kingdom all nations shall be ultimately gathered; and of His kingdom there shall be no end. God's providential government of the nation was always and everywhere directed toward this Messianic goal. The language which an inspired writer puts into the mouth of Nebuchadnezzar, the heathen king, is an expression, not so much of the gentile conception of God and His government, as it is of the faith of a Heb prophet concerning God's relationship to men and nations: "He doeth according to his will in the army of heaven, and among the inhabitants of the earth; and none can stay his hand, or say unto him, What doest thou?" (Dnl **4** 35). The providential blessings which the prophets promise to the people, whether to individuals or to the nation, are never a matter of mere omnipotence or favoritism, but are inseparably connected with righteous conduct and holy character. The blessings promised are mainly spiritual, but whether spiritual or material, they are always conditioned on righteousness. The Book of Isa is esp. rich in passages that emphasize the place of moral conduct and character in God's providential government of the world, the supreme purpose and end of which are to establish a kingdom of righteousness in the earth (Isa **33** 13–16; **35** 8–10; **43** 2; **46** 4; **54** 14–17). Divine providence is both personal and national, and of each it is declared in varying terms of assurance that "Jeh will go before you; and the God of Israel will be your rearward" (**52** 12). Each of the major and minor prophets confirms and reënforces the teachings of this greatest and most truly representative of all the OT prophets.

2. Divine Providence in the NT

(1) *The Synoptic Gospels.*—The Synoptic Gospels furnish the richest possible material for a study of the doctrine of Divine providence. They recognize in the advent of Christ the fulfilment of a long line of Messianic prophecies and the culmination of providential purposes and plans that had been in the Divine mind from the beginning and awaited the fulness of time for their revelation in the Incarnation (Mt **1** 22; **2** 5.15; **3** 3). In His private and personal life of service and prayer Christ is a model of filial trust in the providence of the heavenly Father (Mt **11** 25; **26** 39; Mk **1** 35; **6** 46; Lk **3** 21; **11** 1). His private and public utterances abound in declarations concerning God's ever-watchful and loving care for all His creatures, but above all for those creatures who bear His own image; while His teachings concerning the Kingdom of God reveal a Divine providential plan for the world's redemption and education extending of necessity far into the future; and still beyond that, in His vision of Divine providence, comes a day of final judgment, of retribution and reward, followed by a new and eternal order of things, in which the destiny of every man will be determined by his conduct and character in this present life (see Our Lord's parables concerning the Kingdom: Mt **13** 24–50; Mk **4** 26 ff; Lk **14** 16 ff; also Mt **24** and **25**). The many familiar utterances of Our Lord, found in the Synoptic Gospels, contain the most essential and precious of all the NT revelations concerning the providence of the heavenly Father (Mt **5** 45; **6** 26–34; **10** 29–31; Lk **21** 16–18).

(2) *The Johannine writings.*—St. John's Gospel differs from the Synoptic Gospels in its mode of presenting the doctrine of providence chiefly in that it goes back to the mind and purpose of God in the very beginning (Jn **1** 1–5), whereas the Synoptic Gospels simply go back to the Messianic prophecies of the OT. Both the Gospel and the Epp. of John in their presentation of Divine providence place the greatest possible emphasis on Divine love and filial trust, the latter rising in many places to the point of positive assurance. The Book of Rev is a prophetic vision, in apocalyptic form, of God's providential purpose for the future, dealing not so much with individuals as with nations and with

the far-reaching movements of history extending through the centuries. God is revealed in St. John's writings, not as an omnipotent and arbitrary Sovereign, but as an all-loving Father, who not only cares for His children in this life but is building for them in the world to come a house of many mansions (Jn **14** 1-20).

(3) *The Book of Acts and other NT history.*—The historical portions of the NT, as contained in the Acts, and elsewhere, while not eliminating or depreciating the element of human freedom in individuals and nations, yet recognize in human life and history the ever-present and all-controlling mind of that God in whom, it is declared, "we live, and move, and have our being" (Acts **17** 28). The career of the first distinctive NT character begins with these words: "There came a man, sent from God, whose name was John" (Jn **1** 6). But not only John, the forerunner, but every other individual, according to the NT conceptions, is a man "sent from God." The apostles conceive themselves to be such; Stephen, the martyr, was such; Paul was such (Acts **22** 21). NT biography is a study in providentially guided lives, not omitting references to those who refuse to be so guided—for such is the power of human free agency, many who are "sent from God" refuse to go upon their Divinely appointed mission. The Day of Pentecost is the revelation of a new power in history—a revelation of the place and power which the Divine-human Christ and the Holy Spirit are to have henceforth in making history—in making the character of the men and the nations whose deeds are to make history. The most potent moral force in history is to be, from the day of Pentecost on, the ascended incarnate Christ, and He is to be all the more influential in the world after His ascension, when His work shall be done through the Holy Spirit. This is the historical view of providence as connected with the person of Christ, which the NT historians present, and which we, after 19 centuries of Christian history, are warranted in holding more confidently and firmly even than the Christians of the 1st cent. could hold it; for the Christian centuries have proved it true. What God is in Nature Christ is in history. All history is becoming Christian history, thus realizing the NT conception of Divine providence in and through Christ.

(4) *The Pauline writings.*—No character of whom we have any account in Christian literature was providentially prepared for his life-work and providentially guided in accomplishing that life-work more truly than was the apostle Paul. We find, therefore, as we would antecedently expect, that Paul's speeches and writings abound in proofs of his absolute faith in the overruling providence of an all-wise God. His doctrine of predestination and foreordination is best understood when interpreted, not as a Divine power predetermining human destiny and nullifying the human will, but as a conception of Divine providence as the eternal purpose of God to accomplish an end contemplated and foreseen from the beginning, viz. the redemption of the world and the creation in and through Christ of a new and holy humanity. Every one of the Pauline Epp. bears witness to the author's faith in a Divine providence that overrules and guides the life of every soul that works in harmony with the Divine will; but this providence is working to secure as its chief end, not material and temporal blessings, but the moral and spiritual good of those concerned. Paul's teachings concerning Divine providence as it concerns individuals and is conditioned on character may be found summed up in what is perhaps the most comprehensive single sentence concerning providence that was ever written: "And we know that all things work together for good to them that love God, to them who are the called according to his purpose" (Rom **8** 28 AV). Any true exposition of the NT doctrine of Divine providence that may be given can only be an unfolding of the content of this brief but comprehensive statement. The greatest of the Pauline Epp., that to the Rom, is a study in the divine philosophy of history, a revelation of God's providential purpose and plan concerning the salvation, not merely of individuals, but of the nations. These purposes, as Paul views them, whether they concern individuals or the entire race, are always associated with the mediatorial ministry of Christ: "For of him, and through him, and unto him, are all things. To him be the glory for ever" (Rom **11** 36).

(5) *The Petrine Epp. and other NT writings.*—The Epp. of Peter, James, and Jude, and the Ep. to the He, are all in entire accord with the teachings of the other NT writings already considered. St. Peter, who at first found it so hard to see how God's providential purpose in and for the Messiah could be realized if Christ should suffer and die, came later to see that the power and the glory of Christ and His all-conquering gospel are inseparably connected with the sufferings and death of the Messiah (1 Pet **1** 11.12). No statement concerning God's providence over the righteous can be clearer or stronger than the following utterance of Peter: "The eyes of the Lord are upon the righteous, And his ears unto their supplication. But the face of the Lord is upon them that do evil. And who is he that will harm you, if ye be zealous of that which is good?" (1 Pet **3** 12.13). The purpose and end of Divine providence as viewed in the Ep. of Jas are always ethical: as conduct and character are the end and crown of Christian effort, so they are the end and aim of Divine providence as it cooperates with men to make them perfect (Jas **1** 5. 17.27; **2** 5; **5** 7). The apologetic value of the Ep. to the He grows out of the strong proof it presents that Christ is the fulfilment, not only of the Messianic prophecies and expectations of Israel, but of the providential purposes and plans of that God who at sundry times and in divers manners had spoken in times past unto the fathers by a long line of prophets (He **1** 1.2; **11** 7-40; **13** 20.21). It would be difficult to crowd into one short chapter a more comprehensive study of the lessons of history that illustrate the workings and the retributions of the moral law under Divine providence than is found in the Ep. of Jude (see esp. vs 5.7.11. 14.15.24).

3. OT and NT Doctrines of Providence Compared

From this brief survey of the teachings of the OT and NT Scriptures concerning the doctrine of Divine providence, it will be seen that, while the NT reaffirms in most particulars the doctrine of Divine providence as set forth in the OT Scriptures, there are three particulars in which the points of emphasis are changed, and by which new and changed emphasis the doctrine is greatly enriched in the NT.

(1) *The fatherhood and love of God in providence.*—The God of providence in the OT is regarded as a Sovereign whose will is to be obeyed, and His leading attributes are omnipotence and holiness, whereas in the NT God is revealed as the heavenly Father, and His providence is set forth as the forethought and care of a father for his children. His leading attributes here are love and holiness—His very omnipotence is the omnipotence of love. To teach that God is not only a righteous Ruler to be feared and adored, but a tender and loving Father who is ever thinking of and caring for His children, is to make God lovable and turn His providence into an administration of Almighty love.

(2) *The place of Christ and the Holy Spirit in providence.*—The doctrine of providence in the NT is connected with the person of Christ and the administration of the Holy Spirit, in a manner that distinguishes it from the OT presentation of providence as the work of the one God who was there revealed in the simple unity of His nature without distinction of persons. If it be true, as some theologians have taught, that "God the Father plans, God the Son executes, and God the Holy Ghost applies," then it would follow that providence is the work exclusively of Christ and the Holy Spirit; but this theological formula, while it has suggestive value, cannot be accepted as an accurate statement of Bib. doctrine with reference to Divine providence. Christ constantly refers creation and providence to the Father. But He also said, "My Father worketh even until now, and I work" (Jn 5 17), and the NT writers attribute to Christ the work both of creation and providence. Thus Paul: "For by him were all things created, that are in heaven and that are in earth, visible and invisible, whether they be thrones, or dominions, or principalities, or powers: all things were created by him, and for him: and he is before all things, and by him all things consist" (Col 1 16.17 AV). Although this and other passages refer to Christ's relation to general providence, including the government of the physical universe, yet it is only when the Divine government is concerned with the redemption of a lost world and the establishment of the Kingdom of God in the hearts and lives of men, that the full extent of Christ's part in Divine providence can be realized. The saving and perfecting of men is the supreme purpose of providence, if it be viewed from the NT standpoint, which is that of Christ's mediatorial ministry.

(3) *The new emphasis upon moral and spiritual blessings.*—The NT not only subordinates the material and temporal aspects of providence to the spiritual and eternal more than does the OT, but Christ and the apostles, to an extent that finds no parallel in the OT, place the emphasis of their teaching concerning providence upon man's moral needs and eternal interests, and upon the Kingdom of God and His righteousness, the establishment of which in the hearts and lives of men is the one great object for which both the heavenly Father and His children are ceaselessly working. To be free from sin, to be holy in heart and useful in life, to love and obey God as a Father, to love and serve men as brothers—this is the ideal and the end for which, according to the NT, men should work and pray, and this is the end toward which God is working by His ceaseless coöperative providence.

IV. Discussion of the Contents of the Biblical Doctrine.—There are four distinct conceptions of providence as it concerns God's relation to the ongoing of the world and to man, the rational and moral free agent whom He has placed upon it, viz. the atheistic, the deistic, the pantheistic, and the theistic or Bib. view. See also God, I, 4. The last named view can best be understood only when stated in comparison and contrast with these opposing views.

1. Different Views of Providence

(1) *Atheism*, or materialism, stands at one extreme, affirming that there is no God, that the material universe is eternal, and that from material atoms, eternally endowed with certain properties, there have come, by a process of evolution, all existing forms of vegetable, animal and rational life. As materialism denies the existence of a personal Creator, it of course denies any and every doctrine of Divine providence.

(2) *Pantheism* stands at the other extreme from atheism, teaching that God is everything and everything is God. The created universe is "the living garment" of God—God is the soul of the world, the universe His existence form. But God is an infinite It, not a personal Being who can express His existence in terms of self-consciousness—I, Thou, He. Providence, according to pantheism, is simply the evolution of impersonal deity, differing from materialism only in the name which it gives to the infinite substance from which all things flow.

(3) *Deism* teaches that there is a God, and that He created the world, but created things do not need His presence and the exercise of His power in order to continue in existence and fulfil their functions. The material world is placed under immutable law; while man, the rational and moral free agent, is left to do as he wills. God sustains, according to deism, very much the same relation to the universe that the clock-maker does to his timepiece. Having made his clock, and wound it up, he does not interfere with it, and the longer it can run without the maker's intervention the greater the evidence of wisdom and skill on the part of the maker. God according to deism has never wrought a miracle nor made a supernatural revelation to man. The only religion that is possible to man is natural religion; he may reason from Nature up to Nature's God. The only value of prayer is its subjective influence; it helps us to answer our own prayers, to become and be what we are praying to be. If the Divine Being is a prayer-hearing God, He is at least not a prayer-answering God. The laws of Nature constitute God's general providence; but there is no other personal and special providence than this, according to deism. God, the deists affirm, is too great, too distant, too transcendent a Being to concern Himself with the details of creaturely existence.

(4) *The theistic or Biblical conception of providence* teaches that God is not only the Creator but the Preserver of the universe, and that the preservation of the universe, no less than its creation, implies and necessitates at every moment of time an omnipotent and omnipresent personal Being. This world is not "governed by the laws of Nature," as deism teaches, but it is "governed by God, according to the laws of Nature." "Law," in itself, is an impotent thing, except as it is the expression of a free will or person back of it; "the laws of Nature" are meaningless and impotent, except as they are an expression of the uniform mode, according to which God preserves and governs the world. It is customary to speak of the laws of Nature as if they were certain self-existent forces or powers governing the world. But shall we not rather say that there is no real cause except personal will—either the Divine will or created wills? If this be true, then it is inconsistent to say that God has committed the government of the physical universe to "secondary causes"—that is, to the laws of Nature—and that these laws are not immediately dependent upon Him for their efficiency. The omnipresent and ever-active God is the only real force and power and cause in the universe, except as created wills may be true and real causes within their limited bounds. This view of God's relation to the created universe serves to distinguish the Bib. doctrine of Divine providence from the teachings of materialists and deists, who eliminate entirely the Divine hand from the ongoing of the universe, and in its stead make a god of the "laws of Nature," and hence have no need for a Divine preserver. Bib. theism makes ample room for the presence of the supernatural and miraculous, but we must not be blind to a danger here, in that it is possible to make so much of the presence of God in the supernatural (revelation, inspiration, and miracle) as to overlook entirely His equally important and necessary presence in the natural—which would be to encourage a deistical conception of God's relation to the world by exaggerating His transcendence at the expense of His immanence. That is the true theistic doctrine of providence which, while not undervaluing the supernatural and miraculous, yet stedfastly maintains that God is none the less present in, and necessary to, what is termed the "natural."

(5) *The Divine Immanence.*—This idea of God's essential relation to the continuation of all things in existence is perhaps best expressed by the term "immanence." Creation emphasizes God's transcendence, while providence emphasizes His immanence. Pantheism affirms God's immanence, but denies His transcendence. Deism affirms His transcendence, but denies His immanence. Bib. theism teaches that God is both transcendent and immanent. By the term "transcendence," when applied to God, is meant that the Divine Being is a person, separate and distinct from Nature and above Nature—"Nature" being used here in its largest signification as including all created things. By the Divine Immanence is meant that God is in Nature as well as over Nature, and that the continuance of Nature is as directly and immediately dependent upon Him as the origin of Nature—indeed, by some, God's preservation of

the created universe is defined as an act of "continuous creation." By the Divine Immanence is meant something more than omnipresence, which term, in itself alone, does not affirm any causal relation between God and the thing to which He is present, whereas the term "immanence" does affirm such causal relation. By asserting the Divine Immanence, therefore, as the mode of God's providential efficiency, we affirm that all created things are dependent upon Him for continued existence, that the laws of Nature have no efficiency apart from their Creator and Preserver, that God is to be sought and seen in all forms and phases of creaturely existence, in the natural as well as the supernatural and miraculous, that He is not only omnipresent but always and everywhere active both in the natural and the spiritual world, and that without Him neither the material atom, nor the living organism, nor the rational soul could have any being. He not only created all things, but "by him all things consist," that is, by Him all things are preserved in being.

2. Purpose and Final End of Providence

What, then, let us ask, do the Scriptures teach as to the purpose and end of God's providential government of the world? Back of this question is another: What was the Divine motive and supreme thought in the creation of the universe, and what the final cause and end of all things in the mind and purpose of God? If we can think God's thoughts after Him and discover this "final cause" of creation, with even approximate accuracy, then we shall find a principle that will illuminate at least, if it does not fully explain, the methods and mysteries of providence. We venture to affirm that the controlling thought in the mind of God in establishing this order of things, of which we are a conscious part, was to create a race of beings who should find their highest happiness by being in the highest degree holy, and who should, in proportion as they attain their highest holiness and happiness, thereby in the highest degree glorify their Creator. The Creator's highest glory can be promoted only by such beings as are at once rational, moral, free, holy. There are unconscious, unthinking, unmoral forms of existence, but the motive and meaning of the universe is to be found, not in the lower, the physical and animal, but in the highest, in the rational and moral. The lower exists for the higher, the material and animal for the spiritual and moral. A being whose character is formed under the conditions and laws of intellectual and moral freedom is higher than any being can be that is what it is necessitatively, that is, by virtue of conditions over which it has no control. Character that is formed freely under God's government and guidance will glorify the Creator more than anything can which is made to be what it is wholly by Divine omnipotence. These things being true, it follows that God's providence in the world will be directed primarily and ceaselessly toward developing character in free moral agents, toward reducing sin to the minimum and developing the maximum of holiness, in every way and by every means compatible with perfect moral freedom in the creature.

The possibility of sin in a world of free agents and in a state of probation is unavoidable, but to say that sin is possible does not mean that it is necessary. See CHOICE; WILL. The final cause and end, the purpose and motive, of Divine providence, then, are not the temporal, material and earthly happiness of men, but the highest ultimate moral good of free beings whose highest happiness is secured through their highest holiness—which means first, their obedience to the holy will of God as their Father, and secondly, loving and self-sacrificing service to their fellow-men. This ever-present and all-dominating moral purpose of Divine providence determines its methods and explains, in part at least, what would otherwise be its mysteries. With this conception of Divine providence the general trend of Bib. thought is in entire accord. In the light of Christ's revelation of God as a holy and loving Father who regards all men as His children and whose chief concern is to develop holiness and love in those whom He loves, we may define Divine providence as Infinite Wisdom, using infinite power to accomplish the ends of infinite holiness and love. The originating and determining cause of Divine providence is, in the NT conception of it, always to be found in the love of God, while the final cause is the glory of the Father as realized in the holiness and happiness of His children.

3. Special Providence

By the doctrine of special providence, according to the best use of that term in theological literature, is meant as already indicated, that minute care and ever-watchful supervision which God exercises over His obedient and believing children in things, both small and great, which are designed to secure their ever-increasing holiness and usefulness. God's general providence is and must be special, in that it descends to particulars—to the minute details of creaturely existence—and is always and everywhere active. But the Scriptures teach that there is a more special care over and ordering of the lives of the spiritually good than pertains to the wicked, who have not the fear of God before their eyes. The following Scriptures set forth in unmistakable terms the doctrine of a special providence exercised by the heavenly Father over and in behalf of the righteous: "A man's goings are established of Jeh; and he delighteth in his way" (Ps **37** 23); "In all thy ways acknowledge him, and he will direct thy paths" (Prov **3** 6); "There shall no mischief happen to the righteous" (Prov **12** 21); "But seek ye first his kingdom, and his righteousness; and all these things shall be added unto you" (Mt **6** 33); "To them that love God all things work together for good" (Rom **8** 28). The following points seem to be plainly involved in any statement of the doctrine of special providence that can claim to be faithful to the teachings of the Scriptures:

(1) *Spiritual, not material, good to man the end sought in special providence.*—A mistaken and hurtful notion has long been prevalent to the effect that special providence is designed to secure the secular and earthly good, the material and temporal prosperity, of God's children. Nothing could be farther from the truth. Material blessings may indeed come as a special providence to the child of God (Mt **6** 33 et al.), but that "good" which all things work together to secure for them that love God is mainly spiritual good, and not financial, or social, or intellectual, or temporal good, except as these may secure ultimate spiritual good. Indeed, God's special providence may take away wealth and bring poverty in its stead in order to impart the "true riches." It may defeat rather than further one's worldly hopes and ambitions; may bring sickness rather than health, and even death instead of life—for sometimes a Christian can do more good by sickness or death than by health or continued life—and when that is the case, his sickness or death may well be interpreted as a special providence. "Every branch that beareth fruit, he purgeth it, that it may bring forth more fruit." Many of the OT promises do, it is true, seem to have special reference to material and temporal blessings, but we should remember that the best interpretation of these is to be found in the NT, where they are (as, for example, when quoted by Christ in the Temptation) interpreted as having mainly a spiritual significance. When Our Lord speaks of the very hairs of our heads being numbered, and declares that if a sparrow cannot fall to the ground without the Father's notice, surely we, who are of more value than many sparrows, cannot drift beyond His love and care, His words might be interpreted as teaching that God will save us from physical suffering and death; but such is not His meaning, for in the very same context He speaks of how they to whom He thus pledges His love and care shall be persecuted and hated for His name's sake, and how some of them shall be put to death; and yet His promise was true. God was with them in their physical sufferings, but the great blessing wherewith He blessed them was not physical, but moral and spiritual.

(2) *Special providence and "accidents."*—Another still more mistaken and hurtful notion concerning special providence is the association of it with, and the limitation of it largely to, what are called "accidents," those irregular and occasional occurrences which involve more than ordinary danger and risk to life. The popular notion of special providence associates it with a happy escape from visible dangers and serious injury, as when the house catches on fire, or the horses run away, or the train is

wrecked, or the ship encounters an awful storm, or one comes in contact with contagious disease or the terrible pestilence that walketh in darkness. A happy escape from injury and death on such an occasion is popularly designated as a "special providence," and this regardless of whether the individual thus escaping is a saint or a sinner. We cannot too strongly emphasize the fact that God's special providence is not a capricious, occasional, and irregular intervention of His love and power in behalf of His children, but involves ceaseless—yea infinite—thought and care for those that love Him, everywhere and in all the experiences of life.

(3) *Special providence as related to piety and prayer.*—God's special providence is conditioned upon piety and prayer, though it far transcends, in the blessings it brings, the specific requests of His children. While we may properly pray for things pertaining to our temporal and physical life with the assurance that God will answer such prayers in so far as He deems best, yet the Scriptures encourage us to make spiritual blessings the main object of our prayers. "Seek ye first his kingdom, and his righteousness," is the essence of the NT teaching on this subject; but we should not overlook the fact that this Divine injunction is both preceded and followed by the strongest assurances of the most minute and ceaseless provision for all our temporal and physical wants by the loving heavenly Father. "Therefore take no thought saying, What shall we eat? or, What shall we drink? or, Wherewithal shall we be clothed? . . . . For your heavenly Father knoweth that ye have need of all these things. But seek ye first the kingdom of God, and his righteousness; and all these things shall be added unto you," AV. In keeping with this Scripture, the poet has written:

"Make you His service your delight;
Your wants shall be His care."

But while it is true that God has promised to make our wants His care, we should remember that He has promised this only to that devout and godly number of pious, praying souls who "seek first the kingdom of God, and his righteousness." His general providence is alike to all, by which "he maketh his sun to rise on the evil and on the good, and sendeth rain on the just and on the unjust." But it is only "to them that love God" that it is promised that "all things work together for good"—and the proof of love is not in one's profession, but in his obedience and service.

(4) *Special providence as related to human coöperation.*—The words of Christ concerning the heavenly Father's watchful and loving providence do not mean that the children of God are not in any sense to take thought for food and raiment, and labor daily to obtain the necessities of life. Labor, both mental and physical, is as much a duty as prayer. The prayer, "Give us this day our daily bread," does not render it unnecessary that they who offer it should work for their own daily bread. Nothing could be more hurtful to healthful Christian activity than to interpret Our Lord's insistence, in the Sermon on the Mount and elsewhere, upon trust in the heavenly Father's watchful providence as a justification of thoughtlessness, idleness, and improvidence; seeing that its purpose is simply to warn us against that needless and hurtful anxiety about the future which is not only inconsistent with trust in God, but which is utterly destructive of man's best efforts in his own behalf.

(5) *General and special providence both equally Divine.*—While the Scriptures appear to us to make a real and true distinction between God's natural and His supernatural order, and between His general and His special providence, yet to truly pious and wisely discerning souls all is alike Divine, the natural as well the supernatural, general as well as special providence. So far as God's faithful and loving children are concerned, general and special providence blend into one. The only real and important distinction between the two is that made by the free wills of men, by virtue of which some are in loving accord with the Divine plans concerning them, and others are at enmity with God and oppose the purpose of His love concerning them. If all men were, and had always been, alike trustful and loving children of the heavenly Father, there would perhaps never have been any occasion for making a distinction between the general and the special providence of God. The only distinction we should have needed to recognize in that case would have been as to the varieties of Divine providence, in view of the fact that the all-loving Father would cause widely different events to happen to His different children. If anyone, therefore, is inclined to deny the distinction which we have here made between general and special providence, and prefers to affirm that there is but one general providential order over mankind in the world, that the distinction is in man and not in God's providence, his position cannot be seriously objected to, *provided* he does not thereby mean that the world is governed by impersonal and immutable laws, but will affirm with clearness and confidence that the world is governed by the all-loving, all-wise, omnipresent, and everywhere-active God. For, indeed, the only thing that is really "special" and out of order is the limitation which sin imposes upon the workings of Divine providence in so far as the self-will and opposition of men prevent the realization of the providential purposes of God concerning them. But, unfortunately, sin is now, and has long been, so prevalent and dominant in the world that we have come to regard God's providence as affected and limited by it, as that which is regular and general, and His more perfect and complete providence in behalf of and over the good as the exceptional and special. But whether we call Divine providence, as related to believers, "general" or "special," is of little consequence, provided we believe that "the steps of a good man are ordered by the Lord" (Ps **37** 23 AV), that "all things work together for [spiritual] good to them that love God," and that to those who, duly subordinating the temporal to the spiritual, seek "first the kingdom of God and his righteousness," all things needful "shall be added" by the heavenly Father.

The problem of Divine providence has its utmost significance, not in its bearing on the laws of physical nature, but in that phase of it which concerns God's dealings with moral agents, those creatures who may, and often do, act contrary to His will. God governs men as a father governs his children, as a king governs his free subjects; not as a machinist works his machine, or as a hypnotist controls his mesmerized victims. A father in his family and a sovereign in his realm may each do as he pleases within certain limits, and God infinitely more: "He doeth according to his will in the army of heaven, and among the inhabitants of the earth; and none can stay his hand, or say unto him, What doest thou?" (Dnl **4** 35). He setteth up one and putteth down another. Nevertheless, even God acts within limits; He limited Himself when He created free agents. As a mere matter of power God can predetermine man's volitions and necessitate his acts, but He can do so only by making of him a kind of rational machine, and destroying his true freedom. But Scripture, reason and consciousness all unite in teaching man that he is morally free, that he is an agent, and not something merely acted on. God's providential government of men, therefore, is based on their freedom as rational and moral beings, and consists in such an administration and guidance by the Holy Spirit of the affairs of men as shall encourage free moral agents to virtue, and discourage them from sin. God's providence must needs work upon and with two kinds of wills—willing wills and opposing wills.

4. Divine Providence and Human Free Will

(1) *Divine providence as related to willing wills.*—The apostle declares that God works in believers "both to will and to do of his good pleasure." If God's special providence over and in behalf of His children may involve an intervention of His Divine power within the realm of physical law, much more, it would seem, will it involve a similar intervention within the realm of the human mind and the human will. Spiritual guidance is one of the most precious privileges of believers, but it is difficult to conceive how the Holy Spirit can effectually guide a believer without finding some way of controlling his will and determining his volitions that is compatible with free agency. While most of man's thoughts, emotions and volitions are self-determined in their origin, being due to the free and natural workings of his own mind and heart and will, yet there are also thoughts,

emotions and volitions that are Divinely produced. Even a sinner under conviction of sin has thoughts and emotions that are produced by the Holy Ghost. Much more has the believer Divinely produced thoughts and feelings; and if Divinely produced thoughts and feelings, there may be, in like manner, it would seem, Divinely produced volitions. Does this seem irreconcilable with the fact of moral free agency? We think not; it is no more subversive of human free agency for God to influence effectively a man's volitions and secure a certain course of action than it is for one man effectively to influence another. No volition that is Divinely necessitated can be a free moral volition; for moral volitions are such as are put forth freely, in view of motives and moral ends. The element of necessity and compulsion would destroy all true freedom in, and moral accountability for, any particular volition, so that it could not be either virtuous or vicious. But—and here is the crucial point—when a man, by an act of his own will, freely commits the ordering of his life to God, and prays God to choose for him what is best, working in him both to will and to do, that act of self-commitment to God involves the very essence of moral freedom, and is the highest exercise of free agency. "Our wills are ours to make them Thine," the poet has truly said. In other words, the highest moral act of man's free will is the surrender of itself to the Divine will; and whatever control of man's will on God's part results from and follows this free act of self-surrender is entirely consistent with perfect moral freedom, even though it should involve Divinely produced volitions. Does a perplexed child cease to be free when in the exercise of his freedom he asks a wise and loving father to decide a matter for him, and be his guide in attaining a certain desired end? Surely not; and this intervention of parental wisdom and love is none the less effective if it should work, as far as possible, through the mind and will of the child, rather than allow the child to be entirely passive. So God works effectually through the mind and will of every soul who unreservedly commits himself to the Divine will—commits himself not once simply, but continually. God cannot under the Divinely appointed laws of freedom work in and through the sinner "both to will and to do," because the sinner's will is bent on evil, and hence opposed to the Divine will. God's will can work, not with, but only against, a sinful will; and if it should so work and necessitate his volitions, *that* would destroy his true freedom. But, if God should work in and through an obedient and acquiescent will that is seeking Divine guidance, *that* would be an exercise of Divine power in no way incompatible with the true moral freedom of men. Such is the influence, as we conceive it, of the Divine upon the human will in providence. God's providence works effectively only through willing wills.

(2) *Divine providence as related to sinful free will.*—But God's providence encounters opposing as well as willing wills. Not every unconverted man, however, represents an equally antagonistic will—there are different degrees of opposition. That God's gracious and special providence in behalf of an individual often antedates his forsaking sin and his acceptance of Christ as a personal Saviour is manifest to every student of Christian biography. Much of the best training that many a "chosen vessel" ever receives for his life-work turns out to be that unconscious providential preparation which he was receiving under a Father's guidance before he consciously consecrated himself to his Divine Master. "I girded thee, though thou hast not known me," said God to Cyrus—and on this text Horace Bushnell preached one of the greatest of modern sermons on Divine providence, taking as his theme, "Every man's life a plan of God." If this be true of a Christian man, that even before his conversion the Holy Spirit was seeking him, and even preparing him, as far as was then possible, for fulfilling the "plan of God" in his life, is it not in all probability equally true that the Holy Spirit and the good providence of God were working in behalf of other sinners who persisted to the end in rebellion against God? Such is the power of moral free agency with which God has endowed man that the created free agent can defeat the plan of Infinite Love concerning his life, and frustrate the workings of providence in his behalf (Jer **18**). Whether a free moral agent, then, shall allow God's providential plans to be wrought out for him or not, depends upon his own free will. It is said of the Divine Christ that He could not do many mighty works in a certain city because of their unbelief and opposition. In like manner Divine providence is conditioned and limited by a sinful free will.

5. Divine Providence as Related to Natural and Moral Evil

That the Bib. writers do not regard the existence of evil as a valid objection to Divine providence is evident to every student of the Scriptures. Indeed, it is in working good out of what the world accounts evil that Divine providence accomplishes many of its most salutary and beneficent ends in behalf of the good. That natural or physical evil (poverty, sickness, suffering, etc) is one of the mightiest agencies in the hands of God for restraining and correcting moral evil and for working out moral and spiritual good to fallen and sinful men, admits of easy demonstration. For the existence in the world of moral evil (sin), man, the moral free agent, is wholly responsible. God could prevent moral free agents from sinning only by not creating them, or else by placing their wills under irresistible Divine restraint and compulsion. But the latter method of controlling them would virtually destroy their real and true freedom; and if this were done, then not only all sin, but all virtue and holiness as attributes of free beings would be thereby rendered impossible in men; for only such beings can put forth free holy volitions as can put forth free sinful volitions. If man had never sinned, there would probably have never been such a large providential use of natural or physical evil as at present prevails; and this because of the fact that an unfallen and holy race of beings would not have needed the presence of natural evil to secure their highest moral development. But a fallen and sinful race does need such an agency to bring it back to God and to develop holy character and the highest moral service. It is not true that sin is now always or even generally the immediate cause of an individual's suffering physical evil, or that extraordinary suffering is a proof of extraordinary sin. "Master, who did sin," asked the disciples, "this man, or his parents, that he was born blind? Jesus answered, Neither hath this man sinned, nor his parents: but that the works of God should be made manifest in him" (Jn **9** 2.3 AV). Human suffering is for man's spiritual good and for the Divine glory, as shown in working good out of evil—this is the explanation which the Master gives as to why natural evil is permitted or sent by God. It is not only a powerful, but, in a world like ours, a necessary agency for the correction and cure of moral evil and for the spiritual development of fallen man. "Before I was afflicted I went astray; but now I observe thy word. . . . . It is good for me that I have been afflicted; that I may learn thy statutes" (Ps **119** 67.71); "Every branch that beareth fruit, he cleanseth it, that it may bear more fruit" (Jn **15** 2). The saintly and eminently useful men and women of history have, as a rule, had to undergo a severe discipline and to endure many and severe trials, and were made perfect only by their sufferings. Divine providence thus turns much of the world's natural and physical evil into moral good.

6. Evil Providentially Overruled for Good

Many of the things that befall the children of God are directly due to the sins of other men. That good men, even the very best of men, suffer many things at the hands of wicked men admits of no question; and yet these ills are among the "all things" which are declared by the apostle to work together for good to them that love God. The good that may ensue to good men from the evil conduct of the wicked is certainly not due to the intrinsic power in sin to work good to those against whom it is maliciously directed; it can only be due to the fact that God overrules it for the good of the innocent. "As for you," said Joseph, "ye meant evil against me; but God meant it for good" (Gen **50** 20); "The things which happened unto me," said Paul, "have fallen out rather unto the progress of the gospel" (Phil **1** 12). God, though foreknowing the evil that wicked men are planning to work against His children, may not prevent it; and this because He can and will overrule it for His glory and for their good, if they abide faithful. But, suppose a good man is not simply injured, but killed by the wicked, as in the case of the martyrs that died at the stake—does the principle still hold good? It does, we answer; the saint who dies in the discharge of duty and because of his fidelity to duty is not only assured, by all the promises of revelation, of a happy immortality, but he has the rare privilege of serving to advance the kingdom of God by his death as well as by his life. God's kingdom is advanced in manifold ways by the death of good men. Is not "the blood of the martyrs the seed of the church"? But we need here again to remark that it is not material and temporal, but moral and spiritual good, that God has guaranteed to His holy, loving and faithful children. If sin had an intrinsic power to work good, they would be right who maintain that "the end justifies the means, and one may do evil when good will come of it" (cf Rom **3** 8); and they also would be right who maintain that God is the author of evil, seeing that evil is, on that supposition, only disguised good—propositions which are thoroughly vicious and subversive of all that is good in man or God. The Scriptures, rightly interpreted, nowhere lend themselves to such false and misleading ethics (cf Isa **45** 7).

7. Interpreting Providence

To what extent may we, having studied God's providential methods as revealed in the Scriptures, in Nature, in human history, and in personal experience, venture to interpret providence as it applies to current events in our own lives and in the lives of others? Experience and observation will warn us both against haste and against too great confidence in our interpretations of providence. Hasty misinterpretations of providence in its bearing on present passing events frequently become fruitful sources of skepticism for the future. Some people are much given to interpreting providence. Certain ills or misfortunes come to a bad man; they are quick to assert that it is a Divine judgment sent upon him in view of his sin. Certain blessings come to a good man; they are sure the blessings are heaven-sent in view of his extraordinary piety. A whiskey merchant's store burns down: it is, say they, a Divine judgment, in view of his ill-gotten gains. But presently the property of an unquestionably pious and consecrated man is swept away by the flames: where now is the providence? The "oracles" fail to explain; and so they do in innumerable other cases: as, for example, when two men, a saint and a sinner, are prostrated on beds of sickness. The former, in spite of prayer and piety, continues to grow worse, and perhaps dies; while the other, without piety or prayer, is restored to health. God has not made us interpreters of His providences except for ourselves; and even much of that which we sincerely believe comes to us in a graciously providential manner we can well afford to keep as a sacred secret between ourselves and our God, seeing that God has not furnished us with any means of absolutely proving that what has happened to us might not have happened, under similar circumstances, even to sinful men. Many a Christian man comes to see that the ill that has happened to him—the loss of property, the terrible spell of sickness, and the like—things that, at the time, he would not interpret as providential—are among the best things that were ever sent upon him, in that they made him holier and more useful (cf Jn **13** 7).

"Blind unbelief is sure to err,
And scan His work in vain;
God is His own interpreter
And He will make it plain."

There are, however, many evident truths "writ large" on the pages of history, in the rise, decline and fall of kingdoms and nations, which he who runs may read. And to him who truly believes in the God and Father of Our Lord Jesus Christ and who will duly consider all the facts and lessons of life, in himself and others, in individuals and in nations, and not for a day merely but patiently as the years come and go, it will be made plain that "God's in His heaven—All's right with the world," and that all things work together for the spiritual good of those who love God and who prove their love for Him by serving their fellow-men.

8. Conclusion

We conclude, then, that there is, according to the Scriptures, an ever-watchful providence exercised by the heavenly Father over His faithful and loving children, which is ceaselessly working to secure their ever-increasing holiness and usefulness here, and their perfect happiness in a future state of existence. To prepare rational and immortal free agents through holiness and usefulness here for happiness hereafter is the aim and end of this all-embracing providence of God, which includes within its loving care every human being except such as exclude themselves therefrom by their own wilful and persistent sinning. And in the accomplishment of this end, what the world counts as the misfortunes and ills of life often contribute far more than what, in the estimation of men, are accounted the greatest earthly blessings. There is no providential highway to a state here that is free from life's ills, and that abounds in temporal and earthly blessings to the good. But there is a royal and holy highway, along which moves a providential pillar of cloud by day and a pillar of fire by night, leading the children of the covenant, through lives of loving service and sacrifice, to a holy land of promise, the goal of a gracious providence; and they who journey along this highway bear this seal: "The Lord knoweth them that are his: And, Let every one that nameth the name of Christ depart from iniquity" (2 Tim **2** 19 AV). They who bear this seal are the Divinely chosen instruments and agents of that larger and wider providence that is ever working to establish a perfect kingdom of righteousness in the whole earth, that kingdom of God, to inaugurate which, in its Messianic form, Our Lord became incarnate, and to consummate which, in its final and perfect form, He reigns from heaven and will continue to reign until, having "put all enemies under his feet," He shall "deliver up the kingdom to God, even the Father"—when the poet's vision shall be realized of

"That God who ever lives and loves;
One God, one law, one element,
And one far-off Divine event,
To which the whole creation moves."

Literature.—James Orr, *The Christian View of God and the World;* A. B. Bruce, *The Providential Order of the World;* James McCosh, *The Method of Divine Government;* James Hinton, *The Mystery of Pain;* John Telford, *Man's Partnership with Divine Providence;* W. N. Clarke, *The Christian Doctrine of God* and *An Outline of Christian Theology;* W. B. Pope, *Compendium of Christian Theology;* A. L. Lilley, *Adventus Regni;* Oehler, *Theology of the OT;* Wendt, *The Teaching of Jesus;* George B. Stevens, *The Pauline Theology;* E. P. Gould, *The Bib. Theology of the NT;* T. Jackson, *The Providence of God Viewed in the Light of the Holy Scripture;* H. M. Gwatkin, *The Knowledge of God; Lux Mundi: Preparation in History for Christ;* J. Flavell, *Divine Conduct, or the Mystery of Providence;* O. D. Watkins, *The Divine Providence;* Borden P. Bowne, *The Immanence of God.*

Wilbur F. Tillett

PROVINCE, prov′ins (מְדִינָה, *m^edhīnāh*, "jurisdiction"; ἐπαρχία, *eparchia* [EV province] [Acts **23** 34; **25** 1]):

1. Meaning of the Term
2. Roman Provincial Administration
   (1) First Period
   (2) Second Period
   (3) Third Period
3. Division of Provinces
4. Province of Judaea
5. Revenue

Literature

1. Meaning of the Term

Province (*provincia*) did not originally denote a territorial circumscription in Rom usage, since the employment of the word was much more ancient than any of the conquests of the Romans outside of Italy. In the most comprehensive official sense it signified a magistrate's sphere of administrative action, which in one instance might be the direction of jurisdiction at Rome, in another the management of military operations against a particular hostile community. When the *imperium* was conferred upon two consuls at the beginning of the Republic, and upon a praetor in 367 BC, and finally upon a second praetor in 241 BC, it became necessary in practice to define their individual competence which was unlimited in theory. When the Romans extended their control over lands situated outside of Italy, it became expedient to fix territorial limits to the exercise of authority by the magistrates who were regularly sent abroad, so that *provincia* signified henceforth in an abstract sense the rule of the governor, and in a concrete sense the specified region intrusted to his care; and with the development and consolidation of the Rom system of administration, the geographical meaning of the word became more and more significant.

The history of Rom provincial administration in the more definite sense commences in 227 BC, when four praetors were elected for the first time, of whom two were assigned to the government of the provinces. Three periods may be distinguished in the history of the system of provincial administration: (1) from 227 BC to Sulla, (2) from Sulla to Augustus, and (3) the Empire.

2. Roman Provincial Administration

(1) *First period.*—During the first period, provision was made for the government of the provinces by means of special praetors, or, in exceptional circumstances, by consuls, during their term of office. Accordingly, the number of praetors was increased from four in 227 BC to eight at the time of Sulla.

(2) *Second period.*—In accordance with the reforms of Sulla all the consuls and praetors remained at Rome during their year of office, and were intrusted with the administration of provinces a subsequent year with the title **proconsul** (*pro consule*) or **propraetor** (*pro praetore*). The proconsuls were sent to the more important provinces. The senate determined the distinction between consular and praetorian provinces and generally controlled the assignment of the provinces to the ex-magistrates. Julius Caesar increased the praetors to sixteen, but Augustus reduced them to twelve.

(3) *Third period.*—In 27 BC, Augustus as commander-in-chief of the Rom army definitely assumed the administration of all provinces which required the presence of military forces and left the other provinces to the control of the senate. There were then twelve imperial and ten senatorial provinces, but all provinces added after 27 BC came under imperial administration. The emperor administered his provinces through the agency of personal delegates, *legati Augusti* of senatorial, and *praefecti* or *procuratores* of equestrian, rank. The term of their service was not uniform, but continued usually for more than a single year. The senatorial administration was essentially a continuation of the post-Sullan, republican régime. The senatorial governors were called proconsuls generally, whether they were of consular or praetorian rank; but Africa and Asia alone were reserved for exconsuls, the eight remaining senatorial provinces being attributed to ex-praetors. The financial administration of each imperial province was intrusted to a procurator, that of each senatorial province to a quaestor.

The provinces were divided into smaller circumscriptions (*civitates*) for the purposes of local government. In the older provinces these districts corresponded generally with the urban communities which had been the units of sovereignty before the advent of the Romans. Under Rom rule they were divided into different classes on the basis of their dignity and prerogatives, as follows:

3. Division of Provinces

(1) *Coloniae:* Rom or Lat colonies established after the model of the Italian commonwealths.
(2) *Civitates foederatae:* Communities whose independence had been guaranteed by a formal treaty with Rome.
(3) *Civitates liberae:* Communities whose independence the Romans respected, although not bound to do so by a formal obligation.
(4) *Civitates stipendiariae:* Communities which had surrendered to the discretion of the Romans and to which limited powers of local government were granted by the conquerors as a matter of convenience.

The *civitates stipendiariae*, and in some cases the colonies, paid taxes to the Rom government, the greater part of which was in the form either of a certain proportion of the annual products of the soil, such as a fifth or tenth, or a fixed annual payment in money or kind.

4. Province of Judaea

Judaea became a part of the province of Syria in 63 BC, but was assigned in 40 BC as a kingdom to Herod the Great, whose sovereignty became effective three years later. The provincial régime was reëstablished in 6 AD, and was broken only during the years 41–44 AD, when Herod Agrippa was granted royal authority over the land (Jos, *Ant*, XIX, viii, 2). The Rom administration was in the hands of the procurators (see PROCURATORS) who resided at Caesarea (Jos, *BJ*, II, xv, 6; Acts **23** 23.33; **25** 1) in the palace of Herod the Great (Acts **23–35**). The procurators of Judaea were subject to the authority of the imperial governors of Syria, as is evident from the deposition of Pontius Pilate by Vitellius (Jos, *Ant*, XVIII, iv, 2; Tac. *Ann.* vi.32). The procurator was competent to exercise criminal jurisdiction over the provincials in cases involving a capital sentence (Jos, *BJ*, II, viii, 1), but he was bound to grant an appeal by Rom citizens for trial at Rome (Acts **25** 11). A death sentence by the Sanhedrin required the sanction of the procurator, as appears in the process against the Saviour. Under Rom rule cities like Caesarea, Sebaste, and Jerus became organs for local government, like the urban communities in other parts of the Empire.

5. Revenue

The revenue of Pal under Claudius is said to have been 12,000,000 denarii (about $2,400,000, or £500,000; cf Jos, *Ant*, XIX, viii, 2). In addition to the ground tax, the amount of which is not known, a variety of indirect contributions were collected on auctions, salt, highways, bridges, etc, which constituted, no doubt, the field of activity in which the publicans gained their unenviable reputation.

LITERATURE.—The reader may be directed to Marquardt, *Römische Staatsverwaltung*, I, 497–502, 517–57, for a general discussion of the Rom system of provincial administration, and to the same volume, pp. 405–12, for the provincial government of Pal.

GEORGE H. ALLEN

PROVOCATION, prov-ō-kā′shun, **PROVOKE**, prŏ-vōk′: "Provoke," lit. "to call forth," hence to excite or stir up, whether in a good or bad sense, appears frequently in the OT as the tr of Piel, or Hiph. of כָּעַס, *kā'aṣ* (noun, כַּעַס, *ka'aṣ*), in the sense of "to make angry" (Dt **4** 25; **9** 18; 1 K **14** 9.15, etc); sometimes of מָרָה, *mārāh* (Isa **3** 8), and of other words. In the NT we have παραζηλόω, *parazēlóō*, "to make jealous" (Rom **10** 19; **11** 11. 14); παροργίζω, *parorgízō*, "to make angry" (Eph **6** 4; cf Col **3** 21); with παραπικραίνω, *parapikraínō*, "to embitter" (He **3** 16; cf in 1 Esd **6** 15), and other Gr words. "Provocation" in He **3** 8.15 (quoting Ps **95** 8) is *parapikrasmós*, LXX for Heb *m^erībhāh*. An example of the good sense of the word is in He **10** 24, "Consider one another to provoke [lit. "to the provoking," here *paroxusmós*] unto love and good works."

For "provoke" RV has "despise" (Nu **14** 11; Dt **31** 20), "rebel against" (Ps **78** 40); for "provoked," "despised" (Nu **14** 23; **16** 30; Isa **1** 4), "moved" (Dt **32** 16; 1 Ch **21** 1), "rebelled against" (Ps **78** 56), "were rebellious" (**106** 33.43); for "provoking" (Ps **78** 17), "to rebel against"; for "provoked" (2 Cor **9** 2), "stirred up"; "provoked within" for "stirred in" (Acts **17** 16); "provoked" for "limited" (Ps **78** 41 m, "limited"); "provoketh" for "emboldeneth" (Job **16** 3); instead of "Provoke not your children to anger" (Col **3** 21), "Provoke not your children."

W. L. WALKER

PRUDENCE, prōō′dens, **PRUDENT**, prōō′dent: In the OT "prudence" is the tr of עָרְמָה, *'ormāh* (Prov **8** 12); also in AV of שֶׂכֶל, *sekhel* (2 Ch **2** 12, RV "discretion"); and "prudent" is the tr of עָרוּם, *'ārūm*, "subtle" (Prov **12** 16.23; **13** 16, etc; cf Gen **3** 1; Job **5** 12), and of בִּין, *bīn* (1 S **16** 18, RVm "skilful"; Prov **16** 21; **18** 15; Isa **5** 21; **10** 13, ARV "understanding," etc), with other words. In the NT "prudence" occurs once as the tr of φρόνησις, *phrónēsis* (Eph **1** 8); "prudent" is in AV the tr of συνετός, *sunetós*, changed in RV to "understanding" (Mt **11** 25; Acts **13** 7); in 1 Cor **1** 19, ARV has "the discerning," ERV retains "prudent." In its etymological sense of seeing beforehand (contraction of "providence"), "prudence" does not occur in the NT. As forethought, foresight, prudence was reckoned one of the cardinal virtues by the ancient ethical writers. See the remarks of Coleridge on its lower and higher character in his *Aids to Reflection*, Aphor. 29.

W. L. Walker

PRUNING-HOOK, prōōn'ing-hŏŏk. See Hook, (3); Vine.

PSALMS, sämz, **BOOK OF** (תְּהִלִּים, *tᵉhillīm*, "praises," סֵפֶר תְּהִלִּים, *ṣēpher tᵉhillīm*, "book of praises"; **Ψαλμοί**, *Psalmoi*, **Ψαλτήριον**, *Psaltērion*):

I. Introductory Topics.—The Heb title for the Psalter is *ṣēpher tᵉhillīm*, "book of praises." When we consider the fact that more than 20 of these poems have praise for their keynote, and that there are outbursts of thanksgiving in many others, the fitness of the Heb title dawns upon us. As Ker well says, "The book begins with benediction, and ends with praise —first, blessing to man, and then glory to God." Hymns of praise, though found in all parts of the Psalter, become far more numerous in Books IV and V, as if the volume of praise would gather itself up into a Hallelujah Chorus at the end.

1. Title

In the Gr version the book is entitled in some MSS *Psalmoi*, in others *Psaltērion*, whence come our Eng. titles "Psalms," and "Psalter." The Gr word *psalmos*, as well as the Heb *mizmōr*, both of which are used in the superscriptions prefixed to many of the separate pss, indicates a poem sung to the accompaniment of stringed instruments. The title *mizmōr* is found before 57 pss. The Psalter was the hymnal of the Jewish nation. To individual pss other titles are sometimes prefixed, such as *shīr*, "song"; *tᵉhillāh*, "praise"; *tᵉphillāh*, "prayer," etc. The Psalter was both prayerbook and hymnal to the Jewish people. It was also a manual for the nurture of the spiritual life in private as well as public worship.

2. Place in the Canon

The Pss were placed in the *kᵉthūbhīm* or "Writings," the third group of the Heb Scriptures. As the chief book of the *kᵉthūbhīm*, the Psalter appears first in the great majority of German MSS, though the Spanish MSS place Pss after Ch, and the Talm puts Ruth before Pss. There has never been any serious question as to the right of the Psalter to a place in the Canon of Scripture. The book is possibly more highly esteemed among Christians than by the Jews. If Christians were permitted to retain only one book in the OT, they would almost certainly choose Pss. By 100 BC, and probably at a much earlier date, the Book of Pss was completed and recognized as part of the *Hagiographa*, the 3d division of the Heb Bible.

3. The Number of Psalms

According to the Heb text, followed by modern VSS, there are 150 separate poems in the Psalter. The Gr version has an additional ps, in which David describes his victory over Goliath; but this is expressly said to be "outside the number." The LXX, followed by Vulg, combined Pss **9** and **10**, and also **114** and **115**, into a single ps. On the other hand, they divide Pss **116** and **147** each into two poems. Thus for the greater part of the Psalter the Heb enumeration is one number in advance of that in the Gr and Lat Bibles.

The existing division in the Heb text has been called in question at various points. Pss **42** and **43** are almost certainly one poem (see refrain in **42** 5.11; **43** 5); and it is probable that Pss **9** and **10** were originally one, as in LXX. On the other hand, it is thought by some that certain pss were composed of two originally separate poems. We may cite as examples Ps **19** 1–6.7–14; **24** 1–6.7–10; **27** 1–6.7–14; **36** 1–4.5–12. It is evident that such combinations of two different poems into one may have taken place, for we have an example in Ps **108**, which is composed of portions of two other pss (**57** 7–11; **60** 5–12).

4. Titles in the Hebrew Text

(1) *Value of the superscriptions.*—It is the fashion among advanced critics to waive the titles of the pss out of court as wholly worthless and misleading. This method is as thoroughly unscientific as the older procedure of defending the superscriptions as part of an inspired text. These titles are clearly very old, for the LXX, in the 2d cent. BC, did not understand many of them. The worst that can be said of the superscriptions is that they are guesses of Heb editors and scribes of a period long prior to the Gr version. As to many of the musical and liturgical titles, the best learning of Heb and Christian scholars is unable to recover the original meaning. The scribes who prefixed the titles had no conceivable reason for writing nonsense into their prayerbook and hymnal. These superscriptions and subscriptions all had a worthy meaning, when they were first placed beside individual pss. This indisputable fact of the great antiquity of these titles ought forever to make it impossible for scientific research to ignore them Grant, for the sake of argument, that not one of them came from the pen of the writers of the Pss, but only from editors and compilers of exilic or post-exilic days, it would still be reasonable to give attention to the views of ancient Heb scholars, before considering the conjectures of modern critics on questions of authorship and date. Sources of information, both oral and written, to which they had access, have long since perished. In estimating the value of their work, we have a right to use the best critical processes known to us; but it is unscientific to overlook the fact that their proximity to the time of the composition of the Pss gave them an advantage over the modern scholar. If it be said by objectors that these ancient scribes formed their conclusions by the study of the life of David as portrayed in the historical books of K and Ch, the reply is ready that several historical notices in the titles cannot be thus explained. Who was Cush? Who was Abimelech? (Pss **7** and **34**). A careful weighing of the facts concerning the superscriptions will make it seem highly improbable that the earliest of these titles does not reach back into preëxilic times. We almost certainly have in them the results of the labors of Heb scribes and compilers stretching over several centuries. Some of the titles may have been appended by the psalmists themselves.

We are far from claiming that the titles are always intelligible to us, or that, when understood, they are always correct. The process of constructing titles indicative of authorship had not ceased in the 2d cent. BC, the LXX adding many to pss that were anonymous in the Heb. The view expressed nearly 50 years ago by Perowne is eminently sane: "The inscriptions cannot always be relied on. They are sometimes genuine, and really represent the most ancient tradition. At other times, they are due to the caprice of later editors and collectors, the fruits of conjecture, or of dimmer and more uncertain traditions. In short, the inscriptions of the Pss are like the subscriptions to the Epp. of the NT. They are not of any necessary authority, and their value must be weighed and tested by the usual critical processes."

(2) *Thirtle's theory.*—J. W. Thirtle (*The Titles of the Pss*, 1904) advances the hypothesis that both superscriptions and subscriptions were incorporated in the Psalter, and that in the process of copying the Pss by hand, the distinction between the superscription of a given ps and the subscription of the one immediately preceding it was finally lost. When at length the different pss were separated from one another, as in printed edd, the subscriptions and superscriptions were all set forth as superscriptions. Thus it came about that the musical subscription of a given ps was prefixed to the literary superscription of the ps immediately following it. The prayer of Habakkuk (Hab **3**) was taken by Thirtle as a model or normal ps; and in this instance the superscription was literary, "A prayer of Habakkuk the prophet upon Shigiōnōth," while the subscription is musical, "For the Chief Musician, on my stringed instruments." The poem of Hezekiah in celebration of his recovery (Isa **38** 9–20) seems to support Thirtle's thesis, the superscription stating the authorship and the occasion that gave birth to the ps, while ver 20 hints at the musical instruments with which the ps was to be accompanied in public worship. If now the musical notes be separated from the notes of authorship and date that follow them, the musical notes being appended as subscriptions, while the literary notes are kept as real superscriptions, the outcome of the separation is in many instances a more intelligible *nexus* between title and poem. Thus the subscript to Ps **55**, "The dove of the distant terebinths," becomes a pictorial title of vs 6–8 of the ps. The application of the rule that the expression "for the Chief Musician" is always a subscript removes the difficulty in the title of Ps **88**. The superscription of Ps **88**, on Thirtle's hypothesis, becomes "Maschil of Heman the Ezrahite." Ps **87** thus has a subscript that repeats the statement of its superscription, but with an addition which harmonizes with the content of the poem. "Mahalath Leannoth," with a slight correction in vocalization, probably means "Dancings with Shoutings," and ver 7 of Ps **87** speaks of both singing and dancing. The tone of Ps **87** is exceedingly cheerful; but Ps **88** is the saddest in the entire Psalter. The application of Thirtle's hypothesis also leaves Ps **88** with a consistent literary title, whereas the usual title ascribes the ps first to the sons of Korah and then to Heman the Ezrahite.

(3) *Meaning of the Hebrew titles.*—Scholars have not been able to come to agreement as to the meaning and application of a goodly number of words and phrases found in the titles of the Pss. We append an alphabetical list, together with hints as to the probable meaning:

(*a*) *'Ayeleth ha-Shaḥar* (Ps **22**) means "the hind of the morning," or possibly "the help of the morning." Many think that the words were the opening line of some familiar song.

(*b*) *'Ălāmōth* (Ps **46**) means "maidens." The common view is that the ps was to be sung by soprano voices. Some speak of a female choir and compare 1 Ch **15** 20; Ps **68** 11.24 f. According to Thirtle, the title is a subscript to Ps **45**, which describes the marriage of a princess, a function at which it would be quite appropriate to have a female choir.

(*c*) *'Al-tashḥēth* (Pss **57–59**; **75**) means "destroy not," and is quite suitable as a subscript to Pss **56–58** and **74** (cf Dt **9** 26). Many think this the first word of a vintage song (cf Isa **65** 8).

(*d*) "Ascents, Song of" (Pss **120–134**): RV translates the title to 15 pss "A Song of Ascents," where AV has "A Song of Degrees." The most probable explanation of the meaning of the expression is that these 15 pss were sung by bands of pilgrims on their way to the yearly feasts in Jerus (Ps **122** 4). Pss **121–23**, **125**, **127**, **128** and **132–34** are well suited for use on such occasions (see, however, *Expos T*, XII, 62).

(*e*) "For the Chief Musician": 55 pss are dedicated to the precentor or choir leader of the temple. "To the Chief Musician" might mean that the precentor was the author of certain pss, or that there was a collection of hymns compiled by him for use in temple worship, or that certain pss were placed in his hands, with suggestions as to the character of the poems and the music which was to accompany them. It is quite likely that there was an official collection of pss for public worship in the custody of the choir master of the temple.

(*f*) "Dedication of the House" (Ps **30**): The title probably refers to the dedication of Jeh's house; whether in the days of David, in connection with the removal of the ark to Jerus, or in the days of Zerubbabel, or in the time of Judas Maccabaeus, it is impossible to say positively. If Ps **30** was used on any one of these widely separated occasions, that fact might account for the insertion of the caption, "a Song at the Dedication of the House."

(*g*) "Degrees": see "Ascents" above.

(*h*) *Gittīth* (Pss **8**, **81**, **84**) is commonly supposed to refer to an instrument invented in Gath or to a tune that was used in the Phili city. Thirtle emends slightly to *gittōth*, "wine presses," and connects Pss **7**, **80** and **83** with the Feast of Tabernacles.

(*i*) *Higgāyōn:* This word is not strictly a title, but occurs in connection with *Ṣelāh* in Ps **9** 16. RV translates the word in Ps **92** 3, "a solemn sound," and in Ps **19** 14, "meditation." It is probably a musical note equivalent to *largo*.

(*j*) *Y^{e}dhūthūn:* In the title of Ps **39**, Jeduthun might well be identical with the Chief Musician. In Pss **62** and **77** RV renders "after the manner of Jeduthun." We know from 1 Ch **16** 41; **25** 3 that JEDUTHUN (q.v.) was a choir leader in the days of David. He perhaps introduced a method of conducting the service of song which ever afterward was associated with his name.

(*k*) *Yōnath 'ēlem r^{e}ḥōḳīm* (Ps **56**): We have already called attention to the fact that as a subscript to Ps **55** "the dove of the distant terebinths," or "the silent dove of them that are afar off," would have a point of contact with Ps **55** 6–8.

(*l*) *Maḥălath* (Ps **53**), *Maḥălath l^e'annōth* (Ps **88**): Perhaps Thirtle's vocalization of the Heb consonants as *m^{e}ḥōlōth*, "dancings," is correct. As a subscript to Ps **87**, *m^{e}ḥōlōth* may refer to David's joy at the bringing of the ark to Zion (2 S **6** 14.15).

(*m*) *Maskīl* (Pss **32**, **42–45**, **52–55**, **74**, **78**, **88**, **89**, **142**): The exact meaning of this common term is not clear. Briggs suggests "a meditation," Thirtle and others "a ps of instruction," Kirkpatrick "a cunning ps." Some of the 13 pss bearing this title are plainly didactic, while others are scarcely to be classed as pss of instruction.

(*n*) *Mikhtām* (Pss **16**, **56–60**): Following the rabbinical guess, some translate "a golden poem." The exact meaning is unknown.

(*o*) *Mūth labbēn:* The title is generally supposed to refer to a composition entitled "Death of the Son." Possibly the melody to which this composition was sung was the tune to which Ps **9** (or **8**) was to be sung. Thirtle translates "The Death of the Champion," and regards it as a subscription to Ps **8**, in celebration of the victory over Goliath.

(*p*) *On "N^{e}ghīnōth"* occurs 6 t (Pss **4**, **6**, **54**, **55**, **67**, **76**), and means "with stringed instruments." *N^{e}ghīnath* (Ps **61**) may be a slightly defective writing for *N^{e}ghīnōth*. Perhaps stringed instruments alone were used with pss having this title. According to Thirtle's hypothesis, the title was originally a subscript to Pss **3**, **5**, **53**, **54**, **60**, **66**, **75**.

(*q*) *N^{e}ḥīlōth* (Ps **5**), possibly a subscript to Ps **4**, is supposed by some to refer to "wind instruments," possibly flutes.

(*r*) *Ṣelāh*, though not strictly a title, may well be discussed in connection with the superscriptions. It occurs 71 t in the Pss and 3 t in Hab. It is almost certainly a technical term whose meaning was well known to the precentor and the choir in the temple. The LXX always, Symmachus and Theodotion generally, render *diápsalma*, which probably denotes an instrumental interlude. The Tg Aquila and some other ancient VSS render "forever." Jerome, following Aquila, translates it "always." Many moderns derive *Ṣelāh* from a root meaning "to raise," and suppose it to be a sign to the musicians to strike up with a louder accompaniment. Possibly the singing ceased for a moment. A few think it is a liturgical direction to the congregation to "lift up" their voices in benediction. It is unwise to dogmatize as to the meaning of this very common word. See SELAH.

(*s*) *Sh^{e}mīnīth* (Pss **6**, **12**), meaning "the eighth," probably denotes the *male* choir, as distinguished from *'Ălāmōth*, the maidens' choir. That both terms are musical notes is evident from 1 Ch **15** 19–21.

(*t*) *Shiggāyōn* (Ps **7**) is probably a musical note. Some think it denotes "a dithyrambic poem in wild ecstatic wandering rhythms, with corresponding music."

(*u*) *Shōshannīm* (Pss **45**, **69**) means "lilies." *Shōshannīm 'ēdhūth* (Ps **80**) means "lilies, a testimony." *Shūshan 'ēdhūth* (Ps **60**) may be rendered "the lily of testimony." Thirtle represents these titles as subscripts to Pss **44**, **59**, **68**, **79**, and associates them with the spring festival, Passover. Others regard them as indicating the melody to which the various pss were to be sung.

(*v*) "Song of Loves" (Ps **45**) is appropriate as a literary title to a marriage song.

(4) *Testimony of the titles as to authorship.*—(*a*) Ps **90** is ascribed to Moses. (*b*) To David 73 pss are ascribed, chiefly in Books I and II. (*c*) Two are assigned to Solomon (Pss **72**, **127**). (*d*) 12 are ascribed to Asaph (Pss **50**, **73–83**). (*e*) 11 are assigned to the sons of Korah (Pss **42–49**, **84**, **85**, **87**). (*f*) Ps **88** is attributed to Heman the Ezrahite. (*g*) Ps **89** bears the name of Ethan the Ezrahite. In most cases it is plain that the editors meant to indicate the authors or writers of the pss. It is possible that the phrase "to David" may sometimes have been prefixed to certain pss, merely to indicate that they were found in a collection which contained Davidic pss. It is also possible that the titles "to Asaph" and "to the sons of Korah" may have originally meant that the pss thus designated belonged to a collection in the custody of these temple singers. Ps **72** may also be a prayer *for* Solomon rather than a ps *by* Solomon. At the same time, we must acknowledge, in the light of the titles describing the *occasion* of composition, that the most natural interpretation of the various superscriptions is that they indicate the supposed authors of the various poems to which they are

prefixed. Internal evidence shows conclusively that some of these titles are incorrect. Each superscription should be tested by a careful study of the ps to which it is appended.

(5) *Titles describing the occasion of writing.*—There are 13 of these, all bearing the name of David. (*a*) Pss **7, 59, 56, 34, 52, 57, 142, 54** are assigned to the period of his persecution by Saul. (*b*) During the period of his reign over all Israel, David is credited with Pss **18, 60, 51, 3** and **63**.

II. The Authorship and Age of the Pss.—Ps **90** is ascribed to Moses. It is the fashion now to deny that Moses wrote anything. A careful study of Ps **90** has brought to light nothing inconsistent with Mosaic authorship. The dignity, majesty and pathos of the poem are worthy of the great lawgiver and intercessor.

1. David as a Psalmist

(1) *The age of David offered fruitful soil for the growth of religious poetry.*—(*a*) The political and religious reforms of Samuel created a new sense of national unity, and kindled the fires of religious patriotism. (*b*) Music had a large place in the life of the prophetic guilds or schools of the prophets, and was used in public religious exercises (1 S **10** 5 f). (*c*) The victories of David and the internal expansion of the life of Israel would inevitably stimulate the poetic instinct of men of genius; cf the Elizabethan age and the Victorian era in Eng. literature. (*d*) The removal of the ark to the new capital and the organization of the Levitical choirs would stimulate poets to compose hymns of praise to Jeh (2 S **6**; 1 Ch **15, 16, 25**).

It is the fashion in certain critical circles to blot out the Mosaic era as unhistoric, all accounts of it being considered legendary or mythical. It is easy then to insist on the elimination of all the higher religious teaching attributed to Samuel. This leaves David "a rude king in a semi-barbaric age," or, as Cheyne puts it, "the versatile condottiere, chieftain, and king." It would seem more reasonable to accept as trustworthy the uniform tradition of Israel as to the great leaders, Moses, Samuel and David, than to rewrite Israel's history out of the tiny fragments of historical material that are accepted by skeptical critics as credible. It is often said that late writers read into their accounts of early heroes their own ideas of what would be fitting. James Robertson's remark in reply has great weight: "This habit of explaining the early as the backward projection of the late is always liable to the objection that it leaves the late itself without explanation" (*Poetry and Religion of the Pss*, 332).

(2) *David's qualifications for composing pss.*—(*a*) He was a skilful musician, with a sense of rhythm and an ear for pleasing sounds (1 S **16** 15–23). He seems to have invented new instruments of music (Am **6** 5). (*b*) He is recognized by critics of all schools as a poet of no mean ability. The genuineness of his elegy over Saul and Jonathan (2 S **1** 19–27) is commonly accepted; also his lament over Abner (**3** 33 f). In the elegy over Saul and Jonathan, David displays a magnanimity and tenderness that accord with the representations of S as to his treatment of Saul and of Jonathan. No mere rough border chieftain could have composed a poem full of the tenderest sentiment and the most exemplary attitude toward a persecutor. The moral elevation of the elegy has to be accounted for. If the author was a deeply religious man, a man enjoying the friendship of God, it is easy to account for the moral dignity of the poem. Surely it is only a step from the patriotism and magnanimity and devoted friendship of the elegy to the religious fervor of the Pss. Moreover, the poetic skill displayed in the elegy removes the possible objection that literary art in the days of David had not attained a development equal to the composition of poems such as the Pss. There is nothing more beautiful and artistic in the entire Psalter.

Radical critics saw the David of the Bible asunder. They contrast the rough border chieftain with the pious Psalmist. Though willing to believe every statement that reflects upon the moral character of David, they consider the references to David as a writer of hymns and the organizer of the temple choirs as the pious imaginings of late chroniclers. Robertson well says: "This habit of refusing to admit complexity in the capacities of Bib. characters is exceedingly hazardous and unsafe, when history is so full of instances of the combination in one person of qualities the most diverse. We not only have poets who can harp upon more than one string, but we have religious leaders who have united the most fervent piety with the exercise of poorly developed virtue, or the practice of very questionable policy. A critic, if he has not a single measure of large enough capacity for a historical character, should not think himself at liberty to measure him out in two half-bushels, making one man of each" (*Poetry and Religion of the Pss*, 332). Among kings, Charlemagne and Constantine the Great have been likened to David; and among poets, Robert Burns. There were contradictory elements in the moral characters of all these gifted men. Of Constantine it has been said that he "was by turns the docile believer and the cruel despot, devotee and murderer, patron saint and avenging demon." David was a many-sided man, with a character often at war with itself, a man with conflicting impulses, the flesh lusting against the spirit and the spirit against the flesh. Men of flesh and blood in the midst of life's temptations have no difficulty in understanding the David of the Bible.

(*c*) David was a man of deep feeling and of imperial imagination. Think of his love for Jonathan, his grateful appreciation of every exploit done in his behalf by his mighty men, his fondness for Absalom. His successful generalship would argue for imagination, as well as the vivid imagery of the elegy. (*d*) David was an enthusiastic worshipper of Jeh. All the records of his life agree in representing him as devoted to Israel's God. In the midst of life's dangers and disappointments, "David strengthened himself in Jeh his God" (1 S **30** 6). We should have been surprised had no trace of religious poetry come from his pen. It would be difficult to imagine Milton or Cowper or Tennyson as confining himself to secular poetry. "Comus," "John Gilpin," and the "Charge of the Light Brigade" did not exhaust their genius; nor did the elegy over Saul and Jonathan and the lament over Abner relieve David's soul of the poetry that clamored for expression. The known facts of his life and times prepare us for an outburst of psalmody under his leadership. (*e*) The varied experiences through which David passed were of a character to quicken any latent gifts for poetic expression.

James Robertson states this argument clearly, and yet with becoming caution: "The vicissitudes and situations in David's life presented in these narratives are of such a nature that, though we may not be able to say precisely that such and such a ps was composed at such and such a time and place, yet we may confidently say, Here is a man who has passed through certain experiences and borne himself in such wise that we are not surprised to hear that, being a poet, he composed this and the other pss. It is very doubtful whether we should tie down any lyric to a precise set of circumstances, the poet being like a painter, who, having found a fit landscape, sits down to transfer it to canvas. I do not think it likely that David, finding himself in some great perplexity or sorrow, called for writing materials in order to describe the situation or record his feelings. But I do think it probable that the vicissitudes through which he passed made such an impression on his sensitive heart, and became so inwrought into an emotional nature, that when he soothed himself in his retirement with his lyre, they came forth spontaneously in the form of a psalm or song or prayer, according as the recollection was sad or joyful, and as his singing mood moved him" (*Poetry and Religion of the Pss*, 343 f).

The Bib. writers, both early and late, agree in affirming that the Spirit of Jeh rested upon David, empowering him for service of the highest order (1 S **16** 13; 2 S **23** 1–3; Mt **22** 43; Acts **2** 29–31). The gift of prophetic inspiration was bestowed upon Israel's chief musician and poet.

(3) *External evidence for Davidic pss.*—(*a*) In the NT David is named as the author of certain pss. Thus Ps **110** is ascribed to David by Jesus in His debate with the Pharisees in the Temple (Mt **22** 41–45; Mk **12** 35–37; Lk **20** 41–44). Peter teaches that David prophesied concerning Judas (Acts **1** 16), and he also refers Pss **16** and **110** to

David (Acts **2** 25–34). The whole company of the disciples in prayer attribute Ps **2** to David (Acts **4** 25 f). Paul quotes Pss **32** and **69** as Davidic (Rom **4** 6–8; **11** 9 f). The author of He even refers Ps **95** to David, following the LXX (He **4** 7). From the last-named passage many scholars infer that any quotation from the Pss might be referred to David as the chief author of the Pss. Possibly this free and easy method of citation, without any attempt at rigorous critical accuracy, was in vogue in the 1st cent. AD. At the same time, it is evident that the view that David was the chief author of the Pss was accepted by the NT writers. (*b*) In 2 Macc **2** 13 (RV), in a letter purporting to have been written by the Jews of Pal to their brethren in Egypt, about 144 BC, occurs the following: "And the same things were related both in the public archives and in the records that concern Nehemiah; and how he, founding a library, gathered together the books about the kings and prophets, and the books of David, and letters of kings about sacred gifts." We do not know the exact date of 2 Macc, but it was almost certainly in the 1st cent. BC. The author regards David as the author of books in the sacred library gathered together by Nehemiah. (*c*) Jesus the Son of Sirach, who wrote not later than 180 BC, and possibly a good deal earlier, thus describes David's contribution to public worship: "In every work of his he gave thanks to the Holy One Most High with words of glory; with his whole heart he sang praise, and loved him that made him" (Ecclus **47** 8 f RV). David's fame as a psalmist and the organizer of choirs for the sanctuary was well known to Ben Sira at the beginning of the 2d cent. BC. (*d*) The author of Ch, writing not later than 300 BC, and probably much earlier, represents David as making provision for a service of song before the ark of God and in connection with its removal to the city of David (1 Ch **15, 16**). It seems to be imagined by some scholars that the Chronicler, whose historical accuracy is severely attacked by certain critics, is responsible for the idea that David was a great writer of hymns. On the contrary, he has less to say about David as a poet and psalmist than the author of S. Only in 2 Ch **29** 30 is there explicit mention of David as the author of praises to Jeh. The Chronicler speaks repeatedly of the instruments of David and of his organization of the choirs. And so in the kindred books of Ezr and Neh there is mention of the style of worship introduced by David (Ezr **3** 10; Neh **12** 24.36). The author of the Book of K refers repeatedly to David as a model king (1 K **11** 4; 2 K **14** 3; **20** 5 f, etc). He becomes a witness for the high reputation of David for uprightness and religious zeal. (*e*) Amos refers incidentally to David's great skill as an inventor of musical instruments (Am **6** 5). The same prophet is a witness to the fact that songs were sung in worship at Bethel to the accompaniment of harps or viols (Am **5** 23). (*f*) The earliest witness, or witnesses, if the narrative be composite, we find in 1 and 2 S. David is described as a wonderful musician and as one on whom the Spirit of Jeh rested mightily (1 S **16** 13–23). He is credited with the beautiful elegy over Saul and Jonathan (2 S **1** 17–27) and the brief lament over Abner (2 S **3** 33 f). He is said to have danced with joy before the ark, and to have brought it up to Jerus with shouting and with sound of trumpet (2 S **6** 12 ff). He is credited with the pious wish that he might build a temple for Jeh and the ark, and is said to have poured forth a prayer of thanksgiving to Jeh for the promise of a perpetual throne (2 S **7**). David dedicated to Jeh much wealth taken from his enemies (2 S **8** 11). Both the good and the bad in David's life and character are faithfully set forth in the vivid narrative.

We come next to two statements that would settle the question of David's pss, if critics would only accept them as the work of an author living within a generation or so of the time of David. Unfortunately 2 S **21–24** is regarded by most critical scholars as an appendix to the early narrative of David's career. There is no agreement as to the exact date of the composition of these chapters. Naturally the burden of proof is on the critic who tries to disintegrate a document, and suspicion of bias is inevitable, if by the disintegration he is able to escape the force of a disagreeable argument. Happily, we live in a free country, every man having a right to hold and to express his own opinion, for whatever it may be worth. It seems to the present writer that 2 S **21–24** may well have come from the pen of the early narrator who told the story of David's reign in such a masterly fashion. Even if these chapters were added by a later editor as an appendix, there is no sufficient reason for putting this writer so late as the exile. His statements cannot be set aside as unreliable, simply because they run counter to the current theory as to the date of the Pss. 2 S **22** purports to give the words of a song which David spake to Jeh, when he had been delivered from Saul and from all his enemies. Ps **18** is evidently a different recension of the same poem. The differences between 2 S **22** and Ps **18** are not much greater than the differences in the various edd of "Rock of Ages." Only the most advanced critics deny that David wrote this glorious song. 2 S **23** 1–7 must not be omitted, for here David claimed prophetic inspiration as the sweet Psalmist of Israel. This original and striking poem is worthy of the brilliant royal bard. (*g*) The titles of the Pss are external evidence of real value for determining the date and authorship of the Pss; and these ascribe 73 to David. A sweeping denial of all the forms of external evidence for Davidic pss ought to be buttressed by convincing arguments from internal evidence. Unverified conjectures will not answer.

(4) *Internal evidence for Davidic pss.*—The fact that many of the pss ascribed to David correspond in tone and temper and in historical allusions with incidents in his life, while not in itself convincing proof that David wrote them, certainly reënforces the external evidence in favor of Davidic pss. We must refer the reader to the commentaries of Delitzsch, Kirkpatrick, Perowne and others for the evidence discovered in individual pss. In many pss the evidence is strongly in favor of the superscriptions, in which David is named as the writer. See esp. Pss **18, 23, 32, 3.**

(5) *Number of Davidic pss.*—Opinion varies among conservative scholars all the way from 3 or 4 to 44 or 45. It has come to pass that a critic who acknowledges even Ps **18** to be David's is called conservative. In fact, the more radical critics regard a scholar as conservative if he assigns even a small group of pss to the period before the exile. We must not allow ourselves to be deterred from ascribing to David any ps that seems to us, on the basis of both external and internal evidence, to come from his pen. Delitzsch and Kirkpatrick are safer guides than Cheyne and Duhm. Maclaren also has made a close and sympathetic study of David's life and character, and accepts the results of sane criticism. W. T. Davison (*HDB*, IV) speaks out clearly and strongly for Davidic authorship of Pss **7, 11, 17, 18, 19** (first half), **24** and a few other pss or parts of pss, though he makes large concessions to the present tendency to bring down the pss to a later date. He stands firmly for a large body of preëxilic pss. Ewald assigned to David Pss **3, 4, 7, 8, 11, 18, 19, 24, 29, 32, 101**; also **60** 8–11 and **68** 14–19. Hitzig ascribed to David Pss **3–19**, with the exception of **5, 6** and **14**. If one follows the titles in the Heb text, except where internal evidence clearly contradicts the superscriptions, it will be easy to follow Delitzsch in attributing 44 or 45 pss to David.

2. Psalmody after David

(1) *Pss of Asaph* (***73–83****, also* ***50***).—The prophetic spirit throbs in most of the pss ascribed to Asaph (q.v.). God is pictured as a righteous Judge. He is also pictured as the Shepherd of Israel. Ps **73** holds fast to God's righteous rule of mankind, in spite of the prosperity of the wicked. Ps **50**, which is assigned by many to the time of Hosea and Isaiah, because of its powerful prophetic message, may well have come from Asaph, the contemporary of David and of Nathan. Some of the Asaph group, notably **74** and **79**, belong to the period of the exile or later. The family of Asaph continued for centuries to lead in the service of song (2 Ch **35** 15; Neh **7** 44). Inspired poets were raised up from age to age in the Asaph guild.

(2) *Pss of the sons of Korah* (***42–49, 84, 85, 87***).—This family of singers was prominent in the temple-worship in the days of David and afterward. Several of the most beautiful poems in the Psalter are ascribed to members of this guild (see Pss **42, 43, 45, 46, 49, 84**). We are not to think of these poems as having been composed by a committee of the sons of Korah; no doubt each poem had an individual author, who was willing to sink his personality in the ps he was composing. The privileges and blessings of social worship in the sanctuary are greatly magnified in this group of pss.

(3) *Pss of Solomon* (***72, 127***).—Even conservative critics are in doubt as to the Solomonic authorship of the two pss ascribed to him by the titles. Perhaps assurance is not attainable in the present state of inquiry. Delitzsch well says: "Under Solomon psalmody already began to decline; all the productions of the mind of that period bear the stamp of thoughtful contemplation rather than of direct feeling, for restless yearning for higher things had given place to sensuous enjoyment, national concentration to cosmopolitan expansion."

(4) *The era of Jehoshaphat.*—Delitzsch and others regard the period of Jehoshaphat as one of literary productivity. Possibly Pss **75** and **76** celebrate the deliverance from the great eastern invasion toward the close of Jehoshaphat's reign.

(5) *The era of Hezekiah.*—The latter half of the 8th cent. BC was one of literary vigor and expansion, esp. in Judah. Perhaps the great deliverance from Sennacherib's invasion is celebrated in Pss **46** and **48**.

(6) *The period of Jeremiah.*—Ehrt and some other scholars are inclined to attribute to Jeremiah a considerable number of pss. Among those which have been assigned to this prophet may be named Pss **31, 35, 38, 40, 55, 69, 71**. Those who deny the Davidic authorship of Ps **22** also assign this great poem to Jeremiah. Whether we are able to name definitely any pss of Jeremiah, it seems thoroughly reasonable that he should have been the author of certain of the plaintive poems in the Psalter.

(7) *During the exile.*—Ps **102** seems to have been composed during the exile. The poet pours out his complaint over the present distress, and reminds Jeh that it is time to have pity upon Zion. Ps **137** pictures the distress of the captives by the rivers of Babylon. The fire and fervor of the poem bespeak an author personally involved in the distress. No doubt other pss in our collection were composed during the captivity in Babylon.

(8) *Post-exilic pss.*—As specimens of the joyous hymns composed after the return from exile, we may name Pss **85** and **126**. Many of the liturgical hymns in the Psalter were no doubt prepared for use in the worship of the second temple. Certain recent critics have extended this class of hymns so as to include the greater part of the Psalter, but that is surely an extreme view. No doubt, the stirring times of Ezra and Nehemiah stimulated poets in Jerus to pour forth thanksgiving and praise to Israel's God. Ewald taught that the latest pss in our collection were composed at this time.

(9) *Are there Maccabean pss?*—Calvin assigned Pss **44, 74** and **79** to the Maccabean period. If there are Maccabean pss, Calvin has perhaps hit upon three of them. Hitzig assigns to the Maccabean period all the pss from **73** to **150**, together with a few pss in the earlier half of the Psalter. Among moderns, Duhm puts practically the whole Psalter in the period from 170 to 70 BC. Gesenius, Ewald, Hupfeld and Dillmann, four of the greatest names in OT criticism, oppose the view that the Psalter contains Maccabean pss. Most recent students admit the possibility of Maccabean pss. The question may well be left open for further investigation.

III. The Growth of the Psalter.—In the Heb text as well as in RV, the Pss are grouped into five books, as follows: Book I, Pss **1–41**; Book II, Pss **42–72**; Book III, Pss **73–89**; Book IV, Pss **90–106**; Book V, Pss **107–50**.

1. Division into Five Books

It is possible that this division into five books may have been already made before the Chronicler composed his history of Judah (cf 1 Ch **16** 36 with Ps **106** 48). At the end of Book II appears a subscript which is significant in the history of the Psalter. It is said in Ps **72** 20: "The prayers of David the son of Jesse are ended." It would seem from this note that the editor who appended it meant to say that in his collection he had included all the pss of David known to him. Singularly enough, the subscript is attached to a ps ascribed to Solomon. Pss **51–70**, however, lie near at hand, all of which are attributed to David. Ps **71** is anonymous, and Ps **72** might possibly be considered a prayer *for* Solomon. There is a further difficulty in the fact that the Second Book of Pss opens with nine poems ascribed to the sons of Korah and to Asaph. It is a very natural conjecture that these nine pss were at one time united with Pss **73–83**. With these removed, it would be possible to unite Pss **51–70** with Book I. Then the subscript to Ps **72** would be a fitting close to a roll made up of pss ascribed to David. It is impossible at this late date to trace fully and accurately the history of the formation of the Psalter.

2. Smaller Groups of Psalms

Within the Psalter there lie certain groups of pss which have in a measure retained the form in which they probably once circulated separately. Among these groups may be named the Psalms of Ascents (Pss **120–34**), the Asaph group (Pss **73–83**), the sons of Korah groups (Pss **42–49, 84–87**, except **86**), a *Mikhtām* group (Pss **56–60**), a group praising Jeh for His character and deeds (Pss **93–100**), to which Pss **90–92** form a fitting introduction. Pss **103–7** constitute another group of praise pss, and Pss **145–50** make a closing Hallelujah group.

The Psalter has had a long and varied history. No doubt the precentor of the temple choir had his own collection of hymns for public worship. Small groups of pss may have been issued also for private use in the home. As time went on, collections were made on different organizing principles. Sometimes hymns attributed to a given author were perhaps brought into a single group. Possibly pss of a certain type, such as *Maskīl* and *Mikhtām* pss, were gathered together in small collections. How these small groups were partly preserved and partly broken up, in the history of the formation of our present Psalter, will, perhaps, never be known.

IV. The Poetry of the Psalter.—For general discussion of the form of Heb poetry, see POETRY. In the Pss almost all known varieties of poetic parallelism are exemplified. Among moderns, C. A. Briggs has made extensive research into the poetical structure of the Pss. In summing up the result of his study of the various measures employed in the Pss, he classes 89 pss or parts of pss as trimeters, that is, the lines have three main accents; 22 pss or parts he regards as tetrameters, each of the lines having four accented syllables; 25 pss or portions are classed as pentameters, and an equal number as hexameters. He recognizes some variety of measure in certain pss. There is coming to be agreement among Heb scholars that the rhythm of Heb poetry is largely determined by the number of accented syllables to the line. Some critics insist rigorously on perfect regularity, and therefore are compelled to resort to conjectural emendation. See POETRY, HEBREW.

Nine pss are known as *alphabetical* poems, viz. Pss **9, 10, 25, 34, 37, 111, 112, 119, 145**. The most elaborate of these is Ps **119**, which is divided into 22 sections of 8 vs each. Each letter of the Heb alphabet occurs 8 t in succession as the initial letter of the verses in its section.

As to strophical structure or stanza formation, there is evidence in certain pss of such organization of the poems. The refrains with which strophes often close form an easy guide to the strophical divisions in certain pss, such as Pss **42, 43, 46, 107.** Among Eng. commentators, Briggs pays most attention to strophical structure. There is some evidence of antiphonal singing in connection with the Psalter. It is thought by some that Pss **20** and **21** were sung by responsive choirs. Pss **24** and **118** may each be antiphonal.

V. The Speaker in the Pss.—Smend, in *ZATW*, 1888, undertook to establish the thesis that the speaker in the Pss is not an individual, but a personification of the Jewish nation or church. At first he was inclined to recognize an individual speaker in Pss **3, 4, 62** and **73,** but one year later he interpreted these also as collective. Thus at one stroke individual religious experience is wiped out of the Psalter. A few scholars have accepted Smend's thesis; but the great majority of critics of every school have withheld their assent, and some of the best commentators have shown that the theory is wholly untenable.

Perhaps the best monograph on the subject, for the Ger. student, is one by Emil Balla, *Das Ich der Psalmen.* Balla's thesis is that the "I" pss, both in the Psalter and in the other books of the OT, are always to be understood as individual, with the exception of those in which from plain data in the text another interpretation of the "I" is necessary. Of 100 pss in which "I" occurs, Balla classes 80 as easy to interpret; in the remaining 20 there might be reasonable room for difference of opinion whether the ps was individual or collective.

Personification is largely used in all parts of the OT. There is no room for doubt that Ps **129,** though using "I," "my" and "me," is the language of Israel as a people. The same is true of Ps **124.** The author of Ps **126** likewise associates himself with his brethren. The author of Ps **122,** however, is evidently speaking for himself individually, when he says in ver 8, "For my brethren and companions' sakes, I will now say, Peace be within thee." The intelligent reader usually has no difficulty in deciding, after a careful reading of a ps, whether the "I" refers to an individual Israelite or to the congregation of Israel. Sane views on this subject are important, inasmuch as Smend's theory does violence to the strength and power of the individual religious experience of OT believers. In many portions of the OT, national duties are urged, and Israel is addressed as a whole. At the same time, it would be easy to exaggerate the relatively small place that individual religion occupies in the prophetic writings and in the Law. The Psalter absolutely refuses to be shut up in the molds of a rigid nationalism.

VI. The Gospel in the Pss.—Christians love the Psalter as much as the ancient Jew could possibly have done. On every page they discover elements of religious life and experience that are thoroughly Christian. In this respect the earlier dispensation came nearer to the perfection of Christian standards than in political and social organization. Along with the NT, the aged Christian saint desires a copy of the Pss. He passes easily from the Gospels to the Psalter and back again without the sense of shifting from one spiritual level to another. Religious experience was enjoyed and was portrayed by the ancient psalmists so well that no Christian book in the apostolic period was composed to displace the Psalter.

1. The Soul's Converse with God

(1) *The psalmists are always reverent in their approach to Deity.*—Jeh is infinitely holy (Ps **99** 3.5.9). Pss **95–100** are models of adoration and worship.

(2) *Thirsting for God.*—Pss **42** and **43,** which were originally one ps, voice the longing of the individual soul for God as no other human composition has been able to express it. Ps **63** is a worthy companion ps of yearning after God.

(3) *Praising God.*—More than 20 pss have for their keynote praise to God. See esp. Ps **8** 1.9; **57** 7–11; **71** 22–24; **95** 1–7. The first three vs of Pss **33, 34, 40, 92** and **105** reveal a rich vocabulary of praise for stammering human lips.

(4) *Joy in God's house.*—Pss **84** and **122** are classic hymns expressive of joy in public worship in the sanctuary. Religious patriotism has never received a more striking expression than is found in Ps **137** 5 f.

(5) *Practising the presence of God.*—In Pss **91** and **23** the worshipping saint delights his soul with the sense of God's protecting presence. The Shepherd, tender and true, is ever present to shield and to comfort. The shadow of the Almighty is over the saint who dwells in the secret place of the Most High.

(6) *God in Nature.*—The Psalmist did not go "through Nature up to Nature's God"; for he found God immanent in all things. He heard God's voice in the thunder; felt His breath in the twilight breeze; saw the gleam of His sword in the lightning's flash, and recognized His hand in every provision for the wants of man and the lower animals. See Ps **104,** "Hymn of Creation"; Ps **29,** "Jeh, the God of the storm"; and the first half of Ps **19,** "the heavens are telling."

(7) *Love for God's word.*—Ps **119** is the classic description of the beauty and power and helpfulness of the Word of God. The second half of Ps **19** is also a gem. Ps **119** was happily named by one of the older commentators "a holy alphabet for Zion's scholars." The Psalmist sings the glories of God's Word as a lamp to guide, as a spring of comfort, and as a fountain of hope.

(8) *God's care of all things.*—Faith in Divine Providence—both general and special—was a cardinal doctrine with the psalmists; yea more, the very heart of their religion. Ps **65** sings of God's goodness in sunshine and shower, which clothes the meadows with waving grain. The river of God is always full of water. Ps **121,** "Jeh thy Keeper," was read by David Livingstone at family worship on the morning when he left home to go out to Africa as a missionary.

(9) *God our refuge.*—The psalmists were fond of the figure of "taking refuge in God." Jeh was to them a rock of refuge, a stronghold, a high tower, an impregnable fortress. Pss **46, 61** and **62** exalt God as the refuge of His saints. His help is always easy to find. The might and wisdom of God do not overwhelm the inspired singers, but become a theme of devout and joyous contemplation.

Our Lord Jesus found in the Pss prophecies concerning Himself (Lk **24** 44–47).

2. The Messiah

(1) *The suffering Saviour.*—While hanging on the cross, the mind of Our Lord turned to the Psalter. He voiced the terrible anguish of His soul in the opening words of Ps **22,** and breathed out His spirit at the end with the trustful words of Ps **31** 5. He also invited the fulfilment of a Messianic prediction in Ps **69** 21 by saying, "I thirst." Isa and the Pss did not fail Him in the hour of His shame, when reproach broke His heart, and there was none to comfort Him. Only Isa **52** 13—**53** 12 surpasses Ps **22** as a picture of Calvary and an interpretation of the significance of the cross. Whether Ps **22** is a direct prophecy of Christ, or only a typically Messianic ps, is in dispute. Every sentence can be applied to Jesus without straining its meaning. If David or some other sufferer took up his harp to sing of his own sorrows, the Spirit of God guided him to describe those of a greater.

Rationalistic critics insist that to apply part of a ps to David and part to Christ introduces confusion. They ridicule the theory of a "double sense," and contend that the language refers to the Psalmist and to him alone, and that the application of certain vs to Our Lord Jesus is only by way of accommodation. This theory ignores the presence and activity of the Holy Spirit altogether; and when men talk of "psychological impossibilities," they may be talking nonsense; for who of us can understand fully the psychological experience of men while receiving revelations from God? The real author of inspired prophecies is the Holy Spirit. His meaning is that which the reverent interpreter most delights to find; and we have evidence that the OT writers did not fully comprehend their own predictions concerning Christ (1 Pet **1** 10–12). We ought not to be surprised that we should be unable to explain fully the method of the Holy Spirit's activity in guiding the thought of prophets and psalmists in their predictions of the sufferings of Christ and the glories that should follow them.

(2) *The conquering King.*—Pss **2** and **110** (with which Ps **72** may be compared) describe the Messiah as Jeh's Son, a mighty Conqueror, who shall overwhelm all foes and reign supported by Jeh. Some will oppose the Messiah, and so perish; others will enter His army as volunteers, and in the end will enjoy the fruits of victory. "It is better to sit on His throne than to be His footstool."

(3) *The growing kingdom.*—There is room in the earth for no god other than Jeh, the Creator and Redeemer of mankind. Pss **47, 67, 96–100** and **117** are proofs of the glorious missionary outlook of the Psalter. All nations are exhorted to forsake idols and worship Jeh. Ps **47** closes with a picture of the whole world united in the worship of the God of Israel. Ps **67** is a bugle call to all nations to unite in the worship of the true God. Pss **96–100** paint the character of Jeh as a basis of appeal to all nations to turn from idols and worship the God of Abraham. Pss **96** and **98** exalt His righteousness; Ps **97** His power and dominion; Ps **99** His holiness and His fidelity to Israel, while Ps **100** tells of His goodness. Idols will finally go down before a God worthy of men's reverence and love.

3. The Problem of Sin

The Psalter deals with man as a sinner. Seven of the best known poems in the collection are so charged with a sense of sin and of its deadly fruits that they have been known for centuries as the Penitential Pss (**6, 32, 38, 51, 102, 130, 143**). Besides these poems of penitence and confession, there are many passages elsewhere in the Psalter which depict the sinfulness of men. And yet there are assertions of personal innocence and righteousness in the Psalter that sound like the claims of self-righteous persons (**7** 3–9; **17** 1–5; **18** 20–24; **35** 11–17; **44** 17–22). The psalmists do not mean to affirm that they are sinless before God, but rather that they are righteous in comparison with their foes who are seeking to destroy them. Sometimes they plead for mercy in the same context. The honest exegete does not find the Pharisaic temper in these noble hymns, though he is quite willing to admit that the Christian cannot well employ some of the expressions concerning his own experiences. Jesus requires a humility deeper than that which was attained in OT times.

(1) *Confessing sin.*—(*a*) Individual confession: Pss **32** and **51** are notable examples of individual confession. The cries of the penitent in Ps **51** have been repeated by thousands on bended knee as the best expression of their own sense of sin and yearning for forgiveness. (*b*) National confession (see esp. **78, 95** and **106**). Ps **105** celebrates the praises of Jeh for His unfailing kindness to Israel; **106** tells the tale of Israel's repeated rebellion.

(2) *Seeking forgiveness.*—Ps **51** is the penitent's cry for mercy. Never did the soul of man plead more powerfully for forgiveness. God cannot despise a heart broken and crushed with the sense of sin and pleading like a lost child for home and mother.

(3) *Conquering sin.*—Ps **130** begins with a cry out of the depths and ends with a note of joy over redemption from sin. The plenteous redemption of which the poet speaks includes triumph over sin in one's heart and life. The cries of the OT saints for victory over sin were not unheeded (**139** 23 f; **19** 13; **119** 133). The author of Ps **84** truthfully depicts the life of Jeh's worshippers, "They go from strength to strength." Victory over sin is sure in the end.

4. Wrestling with Doubts

The ancient Hebrew seems to have had no temptation to atheism or pantheism. The author of Eccl felt the pull of agnosticism and materialism (Eccl **3** 19–21; **9** 2–10), but in the end he rejected both (**12** 7.13 f). The ancient Hebrew found in the world about him one difficulty which seemed almost insuperable. He believed in the wisdom and power and justice of God. How then could it be possible, in a world over which a wise and just God presides, that the wicked should prosper and the righteous suffer? This is the question which is hotly debated by Job and his three friends. A partial solution of the difficulty may be seen in Ps **37,** the theme of which is 'the brevity of godless prosperity, and the certainty that well-doing will lead to well-being.' A better solution is attained in Ps **73,** which depicts God's attitude toward the wicked and toward the righteous. The wicked will be suddenly overthrown, while the righteous will live forever in the enjoyment of communion with God. Not even death can sever him from God. The fleeting pleasures of proud scoffers pale into insignificance before the glories of everlasting fellowship with God.

5. Out of the Depths

(1) Out of the depths of persecution and slander the author of Ps **31** climbed into his refuge, as he exclaimed, "In the covert of thy presence wilt thou hide them from the plottings of man: Thou wilt keep them secretly in a pavilion from the strife of tongues." (2) Ps **77** is a stairway out of the depths of suspense and anxiety. The experience of the author well illustrates Maclaren's epigram, "If out of the depths we cry, we shall cry ourselves out of the depths." (3) The author of Ps **116** looked into the jaws of death. Perhaps no other ps has so much to say of physical death. The singer is filled with gratitude as he reviews the deadly peril from which Jeh has saved him. (4) Ps **88** is unique, because it is sad and plaintive from beginning to end. The singer has long cried for deliverance from bodily weakness and from loneliness. (5) Out of the depths of disaster and defeat the authors of Pss **60, 74, 79** and **89** cry to God. The Bab exile was a sore trial to patriotic Jews. They mourned over the destruction of their beautiful temple and the holy city in which their fathers had worshipped. The author of Ps **60** closes with hope and confidence (**60** 12).

6. Ethical Ideals

"Unquestionably in the Pss we reach the high-water mark of OT practical piety, the best that the OT can exhibit of heart-religion." (1) *What sort of man, then, would the Pss acclaim as good?*—Ps **1** opens with a vivid contrast between the righteous and the wicked. Ps **15** is the most complete description of a good man to be found in the Psalter. The picture is drawn in answer to the question, What sort of man will Jeh receive as an acceptable worshipper? The morality of the Bible is rooted in religion, and the religion of the Bible blossoms and bears fruit in the highest ethics known to man. Ps **131** makes humility a prime quality in real goodness. Ps **133** magnifies the spirit of brotherly love. The social virtues had a large place in the psalmists' ideals of goodness. Humility and brotherly love are a guaranty of peace in the home, the church and the nation. Ps **24** 4 is a compend of ethics in a single sentence.

(2) *The ethics of speech.*—Even a casual reading of the Pss must impress one with the fact that the psalmists felt very keenly the lies and slanders and boastings of the wicked. Stirred with righteous indignation, they call upon God to awake and confront the blatant foes of truth and righteousness (see esp. Pss **12, 52** and **120**).

(3) *Ministering to the needy.*—Bible readers are familiar with the ideal of the good man in Job **29** 12–16; **31** 13–22. Ps **82** is a plea for justice. Venal judges are one day to confront the great Judge. Men need fair play first. Perhaps there will then be no occasion for the exercise of almsgiving. Ps **41** is a plea for kindness. The Christian reader is reminded of the words of Jesus, "Blessed are the merciful: for they shall obtain mercy." The Ideal Ruler is both just and beneficent (Ps **72** 2.12–14).

To be a good lover one must know how to hate. The excitement of battle throbs in many of the Pss.

7. Praying against the Wicked

The enemies of righteousness are victorious and defiant. Their taunts drive the psalmists to importunate prayer. Jeh's honor is at stake and His cause in peril. More than 20 pss contain prayer for the defeat and overthrow of the wicked. Warlike imagery of the boldest kind is found in many of the imprecatory pss. To the Christian reader some of the curses pronounced against the wicked are startling and painful. Many are led to wonder how such imprecations ever found a place in the Bible. The most severe curses are found in Pss **35, 69** and **109**. Maclaren's words are well worth reading as an introduction to Ps **109**: "For no private injuries, or for those only in so far as the suffering singer is a member of the community which represents God's cause, does he ask the descent of God's vengeance, but for the insults and hurts inflicted on righteousness. The form of these maledictions belongs to a lower stage of revelation; the substance of them, considered as passionate desires for the destruction of evil, burning zeal for the triumph of truth, which is God's cause, and unquenchable faith that He is just, is a part of Christian perfection." Two remarks may be made, as suggestions to the student of the Psalter: (1) We ought to study the pss of imprecation in the light of their origin. They are poetry and not prose; and De Witt reminds us that the language of oriental poetry is that of exaggerated passion. Some of these imprecations pulse with the throb of actual battle. Swords are drawn, and blood is flowing. The champion of Jeh's people prays for the overthrow of His foes. The enemies cursed are men who break every moral law and defy God. The Psalmist identifies himself with Jeh's cause. "Do not I hate them, O Jeh, that hate thee? And am not I grieved with those that rise up against thee? I hate them with perfect hatred: They are become mine enemies" (Ps **139** 21 f). Thus the psalmists pray with God's glory in view. (2) We ought to use the imprecatory pss in the light of Our Lord's teaching. We cannot pronounce curses on our personal enemies. This heavenly artillery may be turned upon the saloon, the brothel and the gambling hell, though we must not forget to pray for the conversion of the persons who are engaged in these lines of business.

"If a man die, shall he live again?" What answer do the Pss give to Job's cry for light? There

8. The Future Life

are expressions in the Psalter which seem to forbid hope of a blessed immortality (Ps **6** 5; **30** 9; **39** 13; **115** 17). The psalmists are tempted to fear that fellowship with God would cease at death. Let this fact, however, be borne in mind, that not one of the poets or prophets of Israel settled down to a final denial of immortality. Some of them had moments of joyous assurance of a blessed life of fellowship with God in the world to come. Life everlasting in the presence of Jeh is the prospect with which the author of Ps **16** refreshes himself (**16** 8–11). The vision of God's face after the sleep of death is better than worldly prosperity (**17** 13–15). The author of Ps **73** wins rest for his distressed mind in the assurance of a fellowship with God that cannot be broken (**73** 23–26). God will finally take the singer to Himself. It has been well said that Ps **49** registers the high-water mark of OT faith in a future life. Death becomes the shepherd of the wicked who trusted in riches, while God redeems the righteous from the power of Sheol and takes the believing soul to Himself.

Literature.—One of the most elaborate and informing articles on the history of the exposition of the Pss is found in the Intro to Delitzsch's *Comm.* (pp. 64–87, ET). Among the Fathers, Jerome, Chrysostom and Augustine are most helpful. Among the Reformers, Calvin, the prince of expositors, is most valuable. Among modern commentators, Ewald and Delitzsch are scholarly and sane. Their comms. are accessible in Eng. tr. Hupfeld is strong in grammatical exegesis. Baethgen (1904) is very thorough. Among recent Eng. and American commentators, the most helpful are Perowne (6th ed. 1866), Maclaren in *Expositor's Bible* (1890–92), and Kirkpatrick in *Cambridge Bible* (1893–95). Briggs in *ICC* (1906) is learned; Davison, *New Century Bible*, is bright and attractive. Spurgeon, *Treasury of David*, is a valuable compilation, chiefly from the Puritan divines. Cheyne, *The Book of Pss* (1888) and *The Origin and Religious Contents of the Psalter* (1891), is quite radical in his critical views. Binnie, *The Pss: Their Origin, Teachings and Use* (1886), is a fine introduction to the Psalter. Robertson, *The Poetry and Religion of the Pss* (1898), constructs an able argument against recent radical views.

John Richard Sampey

PSALMS IN CHRISTIAN LITURGY (Supplement 1929).

Abbreviations: NPNF, Nicene and Post-Nicene Fathers; ANF, Ante-Nicene Fathers.

I. In the NT.—There is remarkable contrast evident between the OT and the NT on the score of the Psalms. The OT possesses a varied Psalter and enjoins its liturgical use (Ps **68** 4; **96** 2; 1 Ch **9** 33; **15** 27; **16** 9; **23** 30; **25** 1, 7). OT Psalms were rendered by as many as 4,000 musicians (1 Ch **23** 5), one of the largest choruses with orchestra on record. The NT contains no psalms designated for liturgical use, nor does it explicitly enjoin the OT Psalms for the Christian liturgy.

The OT Psalms were widely employed, but were not used exclusively in the early NT days. For

1. Not Exclusively Used

inspired NT Psalms were in evidence at Corinth (1 Cor **14** 26), "When ye come together, each one hath a psalm, hath a teaching, hath a revelation, hath a tongue, hath an interpretation." Together with the "revelation", etc., these psalms were the result of the charismata in the early Church and cannot, therefore, be identified with the OT Psalms. These NT Psalms have not been preserved, although various commentators hold that the poetic structure of certain NT passages may indicate that we have here echoes of such NT Psalms (Eph **5** 14; Phil **4** 8; He **12** 12, 13; 1 Tim **3** 16; Jas **1** 17).

Moreover, there is no evidence that, in Eph **5** 19 and Col **3** 16, "psalms and hymns and spiritual songs" refer exclusively to the Septuagintal superscriptions of the Psalter. For, on the one hand, the Septuagintal Psalter was entitled only *Psalmoi;* besides there were other superscriptions besides these three, like "writing," LXX: Ps **15** (**16**); "prayer," **16** (**17**); "instruction," **31** (**32**); "testimony," **79** (**80**); "praise," **90** (**91**); "alleluia," **104** (**105**); while "psalms and hymns and spiritual songs" was nowhere else a designation of the Psalter. And, on the other hand, each of these three terms has a broader meaning, going beyond the OT Psalter.

Now, furthermore, in view of the fact that there were Christian Psalms (1 Cor **14** 26), and songs (of Mary, Zechariah, the Angels, and Simeon) there is no reason to exclude such from the intent of Eph **5** 19 and Col **3** 16. Nor is it, on the other hand, reasonable to suppose that attempts to carry out the exhortation of the apostle would be limited to the use of NT Psalms, when Jewish Christians had the LXX Psalter in mind for ready quotation, or that such quotation would then go beyond the scope of the exhortation. Hence it is best to understand the expression "psalms and hymns and spiritual songs" as inclusive of both OT and NT Psalms; and as involving a conversational expression of the condition of being "filled with the Spirit" Eph **5** 18.

These two unique and famous passages have indirect liturgical importance, from also another point of view. Their contexts do not teach that Eph **5** 19 and Col **3** 16 relate to public worship, but to daily life, "And be not drunken with wine, wherein is riot, but be filled with the Spirit; *speaking one to another* in psalms and hymns and spiritual songs"; "*teaching and admonishing one another* with psalms and hymns and spiritual songs." Not meditation, nor public worship, but converse is the idea.

2. Not Liturgically Enjoined

The absence of this injunction is in keeping with the free state of the NT Church and leaves the principle defensible that the NT Church has not only the duty of recognizing the inherent authority of the OT Psalter, but also the liberty both of using metrical versions of the Psalter and of freely formulating hymns in harmony with God's revelation. On the other hand, if the Church has not the liberty of formulating spiritual songs for public worship, in the absence of an injunction to use the OT Psalter exclusively, then it also would not have the privilege of freely formulating sermons and liturgical prayers, but should use Scripture verbatim instead and even consistently banish metrical versions of the Psalter, using only direct translation, as in recitative.

However, though the NT is the dispensation of liberty, with respect to the Christian liturgy, involving only certain broad principles for the guidance of the Church, still it gives us the example of Christ and the Eleven singing the second half (Pss **115–118**) of the Hallel (Pss **113–118**) after the transition from the Passover to the Lord's Supper; and of the disciples at Jerusalem, "praising God" (Acts **2** 47); of Paul and Silas imprisoned at Philippi, where "at midnight they prayed and sang praises unto God" (Acts **16** 25); of James urging his readers, when cheerful, to "sing praise" (**5** 13); and of Paul similarly emphasizing the place of "psalms and hymns and spiritual songs" in the daily life of the Ephesians and Colossians: the NT inferentially suggests that the Church will do wisely nevertheless to retain a large place in its liturgy for the Psalter, as a precious inspired gift of God, for the use of the NT Church.

3. Their Basic Importance

II. Before the Reformation.—The service of the primitive Church was usually opened with the reading, or with the singing, of Psalms. Congregational singing, familiar among the Hebrews (Pss **68** 3; **100** 4; **111** 1; **132** 16; **150** 6; Jer **33** 11; Ezr **3** 11), continued in Apostolic times (Acts **2** 47) and in the primitive Church (Isidor. *Hispol. De Eccl. Offic.* 1.5).

1. Congregational Singing

In addition to the Psalms, the early Church possessed a few hymns, including the Logos, preserved by Clement of Alexandria, the Morning and Evening Hymns, *Gloria in Excelsis, Te Deum, Ter Sanctus,* all after the manner of Hebrew poetry (Euseb. *Hist. Eccl. Lib.* V, CXXVIII).

But considerable prominence was given to hymns by the Gnostic, Bardesanes, who composed a psalter of 150 psalms. However, the 59th canon of the Synod of Laodicea, 360 AD, enjoined that "No psalm composed by private individuals nor any uncanonical books may be read in the Church, but only . . . . the Canonical Books of the OT and NT" (*NPNF*, 2 Ser. XIV, 158).

2. Hymns Proscribed

In competition with pagan musical art, congregational singing began to wane. Basil states that he had "the Psalms rendered by skilled precentors after the manner of the triumphal Odes of Pindar, the congregation joining at the closing verse, with the accompaniment of lyres" (*Epist.* CCVII, 3; Eng. Translation in *NPNF*, 2 Ser. VIII, 24. Compare *Selah Higgaion* in Ps **9** and Peters *op cit*).

Psalmody thus came to be increasingly the monopoly of trained singers, and the 15th canon of the Council of Laodicea, 360 AD, proscribed that "no others shall sing in the Church save only the canonical singers, ... who go up into the ambo and sing from a book" (*NPNF*, 2 Ser. XIV, 132).

3. Choirs Exclusively

Antiphonal singing seems to have been introduced, in the East, by Ignatius at Antioch (Socrates, *Hist. Eccl.* VI, VIII). Basil describes its introduction into Cappadocia: "Divided into two parts, they sing antiphonally one with another, ... afterward they again commit the prelude of the strain to one and the rest take it up" (*NPNF*, 2 Ser. VIII, 247). But in the West, Ambrose is said by Eusebius to have introduced it into Milan, in order to provide rest for the singers, amid persecution. The Psalms, thus chanted, greatly influenced the youthful Augustine: "Their voices flowed in at my ears, truth was distilled into my heart, and the affection of piety overflowed in sweet tears of joy."

4. Ambrosian Chants

In harmony with the observations of Chrysostom, Jerome, and Augustine, that the Ambrosian Chants were, however, open to improvement, since their very complex music was "too intoxicating" for centering the attention upon the words, a further modification was introduced by means of the Gregorian Chants.

5. Gregorian Chants

III. During the Reformation and After.—The Reformation unsealed the Psalter, so that Christ's people might once more drink freely of this fountain of salvation. As formerly with the Albigenses, so during the Reformation, the Psalter gave joy, courage, and strength in days of trial and danger.

The Lutheran Reformation restored congregational singing. By 1524 Luther had versified Pss **12, 67,** and **130.** He gave still greater impetus to the movement by his hymns, though personally he was passionately fond of the Latin Psalter. The Jesuit Adam Contzen declared that "the hymns of Luther and the psalms of Beza slew more than their books" (*Politicorum Libri Decem,* Cologne, 1629).

1. Congregational Singing Restored

The Calvinistic Reformation regarded the Psalms as of basic, liturgical importance. In the preface of *La Forme de Prières et de Chantz Ecclesiastiques*, of 1545, Calvin wrote: "When we sing them, we are certain that God has put the words into our mouths, as if He himself sang within us to exalt His glory" (*Opera*, ed of Baum, VI 171). Furthermore, his Psalter embodied the principle of free formulation of liturgical materials by the Church, since it also contained a metrical version of the Apostolic Confession as well as of the Song of Simeon, the Ten Commandments, the Lord's Prayer and the *Salutatio Angelica*. In the first edition, 1539, containing 18 Psalms, Calvin collaborated with Marot, while after numerous larger editions Beza completed the version, in 1562, entitled *Les Pseaulmes mis en Rime Françoise*. It was translated into many languages.

2. Vernacular Metrical Versions

Official sanction was given to the Dutch translation of Datheen by the Reformed Synods of Dort, 1574 and 1618. This Psalter included metrical versions of the Songs of Zechariah, Mary, and Simeon; of the Ten Commandments; of the Apostolic Confession; and of a Prayer before the Sermon. In 1773, it was superseded by another version, used to this day.

In the State Church of England, Sternhold and Hopkins completed, in 1563, *The whole Boke of Psalms, collected into English metre*, followed by the New Version of Tate and Brady in 1696, and various hymnals. The Westminster Psalter of 1643, a revision of Rous's Version, long held sway in the Presbyterian churches of Scotland and England. Emphasizing the OT Psalter, John Knox would have the Church "hear that harmony and well tuned song of the Holy Spirit, speaking to our Fathers from the beginning." The United Presbyterian Church of 1858 employed Rous's Version; but in 1872 a new edition with many psalms from other sources came into use, followed by a Psalter revised on authority of the Assembly of 1884. Among the English Baptists appeared in 1857 the *Psalms and Hymns for Public, Social and Private Worship*.

Coming to America, the Congregationalists brought with them Ainsworth's version. In 1640 appeared *The Psalms in Metre, faithfully translated for the use and edification of the saints in public and private, especially in New England, The Bay Psalm Book*. In 1785 the Hymns of Watts were adopted, followed by many other hymnals. Until the American Revolution, the Presbyterian Church used Rous's Version, but in 1787 the Hymns of Watts were "allowed" by the Synod of Philadelphia, while in the Presbyterian Book of Praise of 1874 the use of the hymns largely displaced that of the Psalms. The Reformed Church used the Dutch Version of Datheen until the American Revolution. However, the New York consistory employed in 1767 an English translation of it, entitled *Psalms of David with the Ten Commandments, Creed, Lord's Prayer, in Metre, ... for the use of the Reformed Protestant Dutch Church of the City of New York*. In 1789, the Reformed Synod approved of adding 150 hymns to the Psalms; other hymnals have largely displaced the Psalms, except in the Dutch-speaking churches. The German Reformed derived Jorissen's Psalms and Hymns published at Marburg and Amsterdam from the Reformed churches in Germany.

The Protestant Episcopal Church in 1789 adopted the New Version of Tate and Brady and a few hymns. Though the Wesleys and Whitefield were in sympathy with psalmody, the Methodist Episcopal churches have given their impetus to hymns. The Baptists possess *The Psalmist*, by Stow and Smith, as well as certain hymnals.

But certain churches employ the Psalms largely or exclusively. The most prominent of these has been the United Presbyterian, using a Psalter adopted in 1912. But in 1926 a collection of hymns was added. This Psalter was accepted in 1914 by the Christian Reformed Church, which also uses the Dutch Psalter of 1773, besides the German edition of Jorissen and the *Ostfriesische Gesangbuch* by the Coetus. Other psalm-singing churches are the Associate Presbyterian Church of North America, the Associate Reformed Synod of the South, the Reformed Churches of the Netherlands, the Original Secession Church of Scotland, and the Reformed Presbyterian (Covenanters) of Scotland, Ireland, and America.

Furthermore, many protestant churches make a wide liturgical use of the Psalter in responsive reading, analogous to the *Responsoria* of the Latin and Greek Churches in which the Psalter has always a large place, and to the antiphonal chanting among the ancient Hebrews and in the Apostolic Church. The Psalter has contributed more to Christian liturgy than any other portion of the Bible, and this in every branch of the Christian Church. The large displacement of the Psalter by other matter of praise in the Protestant Churches during the last one hundred years has been due, not so much to lack of appreciation of the Psalms, as to the commercial enterprise of music publishers.

LITERATURE.—Cooper, *True Psalmody*, 1859; I. Taylor, *Spirit of Hebrew Poetry*, 1861; F. Dietrich, *De Usu Psalterii in ecclesia Syriaca*, 1862; N. Livingston, *Scottish Metrical Manual*, 1864; L. Schöberlein, *Schatz des Liturgischen Chor- und Gemeindegesangs*, 1865; F. Bovet, *Histoire du Psautier*, 1872; O. Douen, *Marot et le Psautier Huguenot*, 1878; Van Dyke, *Story of the Psalms*, 1921; J. Peters, *Psalms as Liturgies*, 1922; *Chr. Ref. Synodical Committee's Report*, 1930.

MARTIN J. WYNGAARDEN

PSALMS, IMPRECATORY, im'prē̆-ka-tō̆-ri, im-prē̆-kā'tē̃r-i. See PSALMS, VI, 7.

PSALTER, sôl'tẽr (PSALMS), OF SOLOMON. See APOCALYPTIC LITERATURE, III, 1; BETWEEN THE TESTAMENTS, IV, 1, (1), (*b*).

PSALTERY, sôl'tẽr-i. See MUSIC.

PSALTIEL, sôl'ti-el: Syr and RVm = "Phaltiel" of 2 Esd **5** 16.

PSEUDO-MATTHEW, sū'dō̆-math'ū, **GOSPEL OF.** See APOCRYPHAL GOSPELS, III, 1, (*b*).

PSYCHOLOGY, sī-kol'ō̆-ji:

1. Introduction: Scope of Biblical Psychology
2. Nature and Origin of the Soul
3. False Theories
4. Creationism and Traducianism
5. Trichotomy
6. Scriptural Terms
7. Pauline Expressions
8. Monism and Other Theories
9. The Fall of Man
10. Effects of the Fall
11. Death as a Problem
12. Immortality of the Soul

LITERATURE

1. Introduction: Scope of Biblical Psychology

The extravagant claims made by some writers for a fully developed system of Bib. psychology has brought the whole subject into disrepute. So much so, that Hofmann (*Schriftbeweis*) has boldly asserted that "a system of Bib. psychology has been got together without any justification for it in Scripture." At the outset, therefore, it must be borne in mind that the Bible does not present us with a systematized philosophy of man, but gives in popular form an account of human nature in all its various relationships. A reverent study of Scripture will undoubtedly lead to the recognition of a well-defined system of psychology, on which the whole scheme of redemption is based. Great truths regarding human nature are presupposed in and accepted by the OT and the NT; stress is there laid on other aspects of truth, unknown to writers outside of revelation, and presented to us, not in the language of the schools, but in that of practical life. Man is there described as fallen and degraded, but intended by God to be raised, redeemed, renewed. From this point of view Bib. psychology must be studied, and our aim should be "to bring out the views of Scripture regarding the nature, the life and life-destinies of the soul, as they are determined in the history of salvation" (Delitzsch, *Bibl. Psych.*, 15).

2. Nature and Origin of the Soul

As to the *origin* of the soul, Scripture is silent. It states very clearly that life was *inbreathed* into man by God (וַיִּפַּח, *wayyippaḥ;* LXX ἐνεφύσησεν, *enephúsēsen;* Vulg *inspiravit*). The human being thus inspired by God was thereby constituted a *nephesh ḥayyāh* ("living soul"), because the *nishmath ḥayyim* ("breath of lives") had been imparted to him (Gen **2** 7). Beyond this the first book of the Bible does not go. In later books the doctrine is taught with equal clearness. Thus in the Book of Job: "The Spirit of God hath made me, and the breath of the Almighty giveth me life" (Job **33** 4). The difference in expression should be carefully noted. The "living soul" (LXX *psuchḗ zṓsa*) is made to depend upon, as it has its origin in, the "breath of lives" (LXX *pnoḗ zōḗs*). The *neshāmāh* ("breath") is characteristic of man—though it is very rarely, if ever, attributed to animals; man is described as a being 'in whose nostrils is but a breath' (*neshāmāh*) (Isa **2** 22). That "breath" is 'God's breath in man' (Job **32** 8; **34** 14), or, as it is represented in Prov **20** 27, "The spirit of man [*nishmath*] is the lamp of Jeh." In the NT Paul evidently refers to this view of man's origin in the statement that "the first man Adam became a living soul. The last Adam . . . . a life-giving [quickening] spirit" (1 Cor **15** 45). This too agrees with what Christ has said: "It is the spirit that giveth life [quickeneth]" (Jn **6** 63), and with what Paul himself has stated elsewhere in the Ep. to the Rom (**8** 2): "The Spirit of life in Christ Jesus made me free from the law of sin and of death."

3. False Theories

Scripture therefore repudiates all doctrines of *emanation*, by which is meant a natural, forth-flowing life from God into the human sphere; it teaches a doctrine of *creation*, whereby it declares that the Almighty acts with deliberation and design, in free choice, and not of necessity. "Let us make man" is the sublime utterance of Divine wisdom and power. Nor does Scripture teach the *preëxistence* of the soul—a doctrine found in the extra-canonical, platonically inspired Book of Wisd (**8** 19.20), "For I was a child of parts, and a good soul fell to my lot; nay rather, being good, I came into a body undefiled." This doctrine was well known to Jewish writers, and was taught in Talm and *Ḳabbālāh.*

"All souls were, according to the Talm, created and kept in secret from the first moment of creation. As creatures of the highest sphere they are omniscient; but at the moment of birth in a human body an angel touches the lips of the child, so that he forgets whatever has been" (Emanuel Deutsch, *The Talmud*). The doctrine, however, must be a later importation into Jewish theology through Plato and Philo. It reminds us of Vergil (*Æneid* vi.713), who makes the souls—destined by the Fates to inhabit new bodies on earth—drink of the waters of Lethe (forgetfulness), so as to remove all remembrance of the joys of Elysium:

"The souls that throng the flood,
Are those to whom by Fate are other bodies owed;
In Lethe's lake they long oblivion taste
Of future life secure, forgetful of the past."

According to the *Ḳabbālāh*, souls are supposed to have an *ideal* as well as a *real* preëxistence: "*ideal* as emanations from the *sephirōth*, which are themselves emanations from the infinite *real*, as having been 'created' at a definite time" (cf Eric Bischoff, *De Kabbala*).

The doctrine with some modifications passed into the Christian church, was accepted by Justin Martyr, Theodoretus, Origen and others of the church Fathers, but became obsolete by the latter part of the 4th cent. (cf Shedd, *Hist of Christian Doctrine*, II, 9). It was formally condemned by a synod held at Constantinople in the 6th cent. In later times it was accepted in modified form by Kant, Schelling and others, and was specially defended by Julius Müller, who held that the soul had a timeless preëxistence and underwent a fall before the final act, whereby it was united in time to the body as its temporary home (*Ein ausserzeitlicher Urzustand und Urfall*). Reference is sometimes made to Jer **1** 5, where Jeh addresses His servant: "Before I formed thee in the belly I knew thee; and before thou camest forth out of the womb I sanctified thee; I have appointed thee a prophet unto the nations." But this text gives no warrant to the doctrine as taught by the writers mentioned. All that may be conceded is, what Delitzsch has termed "an ideal preëxistence," i.e. "a preëxistence, not only of man as such, but also of the individual and of all: a preëxistence in the Divine knowledge, which precedes the existence in the individual consciousness" (*Bibl. Psych.*, 46).

4. Creationism and Traducianism

A new question arises at this point, viz. Is the soul a special creation? Is it derived from the parents? Opinions are and have been divided on this point. Many have supported the theory of Creationism, by which is meant that in every instance where a new individual comes into being a soul is specially created by God, *de nihilo*, to inhabit the new-formed body. This view of the soul's birth found great favor in the early church. It was dominant in the East and was advocated in the West. "Jerome asserts that God *quotidie fabricatur animas*, and cites Scripture in proof" (Shedd, op. cit., II, 11). Scholastic theologians in the Middle Ages, Roman Catholic divines, Reformed orthodoxy upheld the theory. Though finding little support in Scripture, they appealed to such texts as the following: "He fashioneth their hearts alike" (Ps **33** 15 AV); Jeh "formeth the spirit of man within him" (Zec **12** 1); "The spirit returneth unto God who gave it" (Eccl **12** 7; cf Nu **16** 22; He **12** 9); "God, the God of the spirits of all flesh" (Nu **27** 16)—of which Delitzsch declared: "There can hardly be a more classical proof-text for creationism" (*Bibl. Psych.*, 137).

Traducianism again has found equal support in the Christian church. It declared that the parents were responsible, not merely for the bodies, but also for the souls of their offspring—*per traducem vel per propaginem* (i.e. by direct derivation, in the ordinary way of propagation). Tertullian was a strong supporter of this view: "The soul of man, like the shoot of a tree, is drawn out (*deducta*) into a physical progeny from Adam, the parent stock" (Shedd, *Hist of Doctrine*, II, 14). Jerome remarked that in his day it was adopted by *maxima pars occidentalium* ("the large majority of western theologians"). Leo the Great (d. 461) asserted that "the Catholic faith teaches that every man with reference to the substance of his soul as well as of his body is formed in the womb" (Shedd). Augustine, however, though doctrinally inclined to support the claims of Traducianists, kept an open mind on the subject: "You may blame, if you will, my hesitation," he wrote, "because I do not venture to affirm or deny that of which I am ignorant." And, perhaps, this is the safest attitude to assume; for there is little Scriptural warrant for either theory. Birth is a mystery which baffles investigation, and Scripture throws no light upon that mystery. Yet some who have discussed this subject have tried actually to calculate the very day on which the soul is created or infused into the body, as it is being formed in the mother's womb—in boys on the 40th day after pregnancy and in girls on the 80th. This indeed is the *reductio ad absurdum* of Creationism.

Whichever theory we accept, the difficulties are great either way. For if God *creates* a soul, that soul must be pure and sinless and stainless at birth. How then can it be said that man is "conceived" as well as "born in sin"? If the impure, sin-stained body contaminates the pure, unstained soul by contact, why cannot the stainless soul disinfect the contaminated body? And again, if every individual soul is a special creation by direct interposition of the Almighty, what becomes of the unity and solidarity of the race? Is its connection with Adam then purely one of physical or corporeal generation? Creationism cannot account for the birth of the soul. Nor can Traducianism. For it can account neither for the origin, nor for the hereditary taint of the soul. It lands us in a hopeless dilemma. In the one case we fall back upon Creationism with its difficulties; in the other, we plunge into a materialism which is equally fatal to the theory (cf Bavinck, *Gereformeerde Dogmatiek*, II, 626). Perhaps the words of Petrus Lombardus, though frequently misunderstood and misapplied, throw most light on the subject—a light, however, which is little more than "darkness visible"—*creando infundit eas Deus, et infundendo creat* ("in creating God infused [the soul]; and in infusing He creates"). The problem is and remains insoluble.

Passing allusion may be made to another very curious theory, to which reference is made by Martensen (*Christliche Ethik*, I, 107). It bears upon human individuality, as impressed not only upon the soul, but also upon the body. The soul and the body are represented as arising at the same moment, but the latter (not in regard to its physico-chemical composition, but in other respects) is the resultant of soul-influences, whatever these may be. The soul therefore exercises a formative influence upon the body, with which it is united. This theory is attributed by Martensen to G. E. Stahl, who died in Berlin in 1734, as physician to the royal family. We are here in a region where the way is barred—"a palpable obscure" without the light of day.

5. Trichotomy

The next important question which has occupied many minds is equally difficult of solution—the theory of *Tripartition*. Is man composed of "body" and "soul" (*dichotomy*) only, or is a third to be added to the two, so that "spirit" is another element in the constitution of human nature (*trichotomy*)? Either theory is supposed to be supported by Scripture, and both have had their defenders in all ages of the church. Where the tripartite division has found favor, soul and spirit have been distinguished from each other, as man's lower is distinguished from his higher nature; where dichotomy prevailed, soul and spirit were represented as manifestations of the same spiritual essence. Under the influence of Platonic philosophy, trichotomy found favor in the early church, but was discredited on account of the Apollinarian heresy. The threefold division of human nature into *sôma* ("body"), *psuchḗ* ("soul"), *pneúma* ("spirit") had been accepted by many when Apollinaris, bishop of Laodicea (d. 382), attempted to explain the mystery of Christ's person by teaching that the Logos (or second person of the Trinity) had taken the place of the rational soul in Christ, so that the person of Christ on earth consisted of the Divine Logos, a human body, and a soul (*psuchḗ*) as the link between the two.

For the *tripartite* division of human nature two texts are specially brought into the discussion: viz. 1 Thess **5** 23, "May your spirit and soul and body be preserved entire, without blame"—a text which is popularly interpreted as conveying that "soul" stands for "our powers natural—those we have by nature," and that by "spirit" is meant "that life in man which in his natural state can scarcely be said to exist at all, but which is to be called out into power and vitality by regeneration" (F. W. Robertson, *Sermons*). There is very little warrant in Scripture for such interpretation. "The language does not require a distinction of organs or substances, but may be accounted for by a vivid conception of *one substance in different relations* and under different aspects. The two terms are used to give exhaustive expression to the whole being and nature of man" (Davidson, *OT Theology*, 135). There is evidently no distinction of essence here—viz. of a *soul* distinct from the *spirit*, and a *body* distinct from either. In his "fervid desire for the complete and perfect sanctification of his disciples, the apostle accumulates these terms" in order to emphasize the doctrine of an entire renewal of the whole man by the working of the Holy Spirit. It has been pointed out (A. Kuyper, *Het werk v. d. Heiligen Geest*, III, 101)—and this must be carefully borne in mind—that "the apostle does not use the word *holomereís*, 'in all your parts,' and then summarize these parts in *body, soul* and *spirit*, but *holoteleís*, a word that has no reference to the parts, but to the *télos*, the end or aim. Calvin interprets 'soul' and 'spirit' here as referring to our rational and moral existence, as thinking, willing beings, both modes of operation of the one, undivided soul."

The next text to which an appeal is made is He **4** 12: "The word of God is living, and active, and sharper than any two-edged sword, and piercing even to the dividing of soul and spirit, of both joints and marrow, and quick to discern the thoughts and intents of the heart." Here *spirit, soul* and *heart* are brought into close correspondence, with *heart* evidently as the center of personality, manifesting itself in *soul* and *spirit*. The only question is, whether the dividing which takes place by the piercing word of God is one *within* the soul and spirit, causing a complete exposure of the inner man, a cutting asunder of all that composes his nature, or one *between* the soul and spirit, causing a division between them as separate parts of human nature. The probability lies with the first of these two contradictory views. The writer evidently meant that, as a sharp two-edged sword pierces to the very marrow in its sundering process, so the sword of the spirit cuts through all obstacles, pierces the very heart, lays bare what hitherto was hidden to all observers, even to the man himself, and "discerns" the "thoughts and intents," which in the unity of soul and spirit have hitherto been kept in the background. "The meaning is rather, that the word of God pierces and dissects both the soul and spirit, separates each into its parts, subtle though they may be, and analyzes their thoughts and intents" (Davidson, op. cit., 187). At any rate, to found a doctrine of Trichotomy on an isolated, variously interpreted text is dangerous in the extreme. The language of metaphor is not the language of literal speech; and here evidently we are in the region of metaphor.

The ground is now cleared for a fuller investigation of the meaning of these terms:

6. Scriptural Terms

(1) The terms are used interchangeably, though they are not synonymous. *Lēbhābh* ("heart"), *nephesh* ("soul"), *rū^a^h* ("spirit") are very closely connected in the OT. The *heart* is there represented as "the organ, the *spirit* as the principle, the *soul* as the subject of life" (Cremer, *Lexicon*). Hence we read that "out of it [the heart] are the issues of life" (Prov **4** 23). Dying is represented as the surrender of *soul* (Gen **35** 18; Job **11** 20), but also of *spirit* (Ps **31** 5; **146** 4). The dead are called *souls* (Rev **6** 9; **20** 4), and also *spirits* (He **12** 23; 1 Pet **3** 19). In the last mentioned text the "spirits in prison" are also called "souls." The living are described as "disturbed" or "grieved" in soul (Jgs **10** 16), "vexed" (Jgs **16** 16), "discouraged" (Nu **21** 4), "weary" (Zec **11** 8); but also as in "anguish of spirit" (Ex **6** 9), "impatient in spirit" (Job **21** 4, in the Heb), 'straitened in spirit' (Mic **2** 7). At death the "spirit" departs (Ps **146** 4, in the Heb), but also the "soul" (Gen **35** 18). As in the OT so in the NT, Our Lord "sighed," or "was troubled in the *spirit*" (Jn **13** 21); but we also read that His *soul* was "exceeding sorrowful," or troubled (Mt **26** 38; Jn **12** 27). See SPIRIT; SOUL; HEART.

(2) And yet there is a distinction, whatever the real nature of it may be. In Mary's *Magnificat*, e.g., we find the two combined in an interesting manner: "My soul doth magnify the Lord, and my

spirit hath rejoiced in God my Saviour" (Lk **1** 46.47), the one clause "referring to the personal emotions of Mary, to her feelings as a woman and a mother, all of which find an outlet in adoration," the second clause "appearing to indicate the moment when, in the profoundest depths of her being, by the touch of the Divine spirit, the promise of the angel was accomplished in her" (Godet, in loc.). A like contrast meets us in the story of Gethsemane. The Master was 'exceeding sorrowful in *soul*' (i.e. the emotional, sensitive center of His being was in deep sorrow), the disciples were 'willing in *spirit*,' but 'weak in the *flesh*' (Mt **26** 38.41). In the OT we find that when a man dies his "soul" departs, and when he is restored to life his "soul" returns (1 K **17** 22); but when consciousness or life-power returns to one not dead, "spirit" is used (Gen **45** 27; Jgs **15** 19; 1 S **30** 12; 1 K **10** 5). Even in popular language the distinction is recognized: we speak of so many "souls," not "spirits," as having perished.

(3) From all this it would appear that philosophic distinction or scientific accuracy of expression is not met with in Scripture. Man is there represented as a unity, and the various terms employed to indicate that unity in its diversity of activities or passivities do not necessarily imply the existence of different essences, or of separate organs, through which these are realized. Psychical action is sometimes ascribed to the body, as well as to the soul, for soul and body are inseparably united to each other. It is the possession of a soul which makes the body what it is; and on the other hand, a soul without a body is unthinkable. The resurrection of the body therefore is no mere figment of the creeds. The body is God's work (Job **10** 8), inseparable from the life of the soul. In the NT it is spoken of as "the house on earth" (*epígeios oikía*), the "tabernacle" or tent prepared for the occupant (*skēnos*) (1 Cor **12** 18; 2 Cor **4** 7; **5** 1). In the OT "we have such metaphorical expressions as 'houses of clay'; or, as in post-Bib. writings, 'earthly tabernacle.' In the latest, we have words which suggest a hollow, a framework, or a sheath, favoring the Gr idea of the body as the husk or clothing of the soul" (Laidlaw). Hence in Scripture, spirit and soul are interchangeably used with body for human nature in general, not as though indicating three separate entities, but as denoting a parallelism which brings out the full personality of man. Soul and body are threatened with destruction (Mt **10** 28); body without spirit is a corpse (Jas **2** 26); soul and spirit are interchangeably united: "Stand fast in one *spirit*, with one *soul* striving," etc (Phil **1** 27).

(4) Gathering all together, the Scriptural position seems to be as follows: The Divine Spirit is the source of all life, and its power is communicated in the physical, intellectual and moral sphere. That Spirit, as the *spiritus spirans*, the inspiring spirit, by its very breath makes man a living soul: "The spirit [or breath] of God is in my nostrils" (Job **27** 3); "Thou takest away their breath [*rūaḥ*, "spirit"], they die, and return to their dust" (Ps **104** 29). Hence God is called "God of the spirits of all flesh" (Nu **16** 22; **27** 16).

Soul, though identical with spirit, has shades of meaning which spirit has not; it stands for the individual. "Man is spirit, because he is dependent upon God. Man is soul, because, unlike the angels, he has a body, which links him to earth. He is *animal* as possessing *anima*, but he is a reasoning animal, which distinguishes him from the brute" (Bavinck, *Ger. Dogm.*, II, 628).

(5) In this connection stress may be laid upon some of Paul's expressions. He exhorts the Philippians to "stand fast in one spirit [*pneúma*], with one soul [*psuchē*] striving for the faith" (Phil **1** 27). He exhorts them to be "of the same mind" (*súmpsuchoi*, Phil **2** 2); he hopes to be "of good comfort" (*eupsuchō*, Phil **2** 19); he knows of 'no man likeminded, [*isópsuchon*], who [would] care truly for [their] state' (Phil **2** 20). Everywhere therefore we have "soul" in various combinations to indicate the mental attitude, which in the "fellowship of the Spirit" he would assume toward his readers, and his readers would adopt toward himself. There cannot be therefore that subtle distinction which men have found in the terms "spirit" and "soul," as though two separate essences were housed in one body. The text in Job (**33** 4), "The Spirit of God hath made me, and the breath of the Almighty giveth me life," is the key to the whole problem. The *spiritus spirans* becomes the *spiritus spiratus*—the inspiring spirit becomes in man the life which is expired, outbreathed by man, in both soul and spirit. "Soul," therefore, may well stand for the personal, living, animated being—the suffering, acting, thinking, reasoning, dying creature, "whose breath is in his nostrils." Christ gave His 'soul' (*psuchē*) for His sheep (Jn **10** 11). On the cross He Himself exclaimed: "Into thy hands I commend my *spirit*" (*pneuma*) (Lk **23** 46). Spirit may therefore indicate the all-embracing power, guiding the inward and the outward life—*principium illud internum ex quo fluunt actiones*, is Bengel's comment on Eph **2** 2 (cf Lk **9** 55 AV; **4** 36). Hence by an easy gradation it may stand for the abysmal depths of personality; while "soul" would express man's individuality in general. See SOUL; SPIRIT.

7. Pauline Expressions

Pauline phraseology has somewhat confused the issue; at any rate, new meanings, not obvious to the reader, have been assigned to various terms. Paul contrasts the *psychical* and the *pneumatic*, the man under the influence of the Divine *pneuma*, and the man as influenced by his own *psuchē*. The *psychical* man is man in his natural, unregenerate state, psychical in this connection being almost equivalent to carnal; while the *pneumatic* man would be the man guided and directed by the Spirit from on high. Nature and grace are contrasted in the two terms as the first and second Adam are contrasted in 1 Cor **15** 45—the first Adam being described as a living *psuchē* ("soul"), the second as a life-giving *pneuma* ("spirit"). Even so the *psychical* body is the body intended, fitted to bear the *psuchē*, while the *pneumatic* body is evidently the body capable of bearing the *pneuma*. Hence the one is corruptible and weak, the other incorruptible and full of power. The soul confined to the carnal body uses it as an organ, till it falls into decay and no longer lends itself to such use. The spirit, in constant fellowship with the Divine Spirit, communicates its energy to a body fitted to be the bearer of this renewed life, spiritualizes that organ, makes that body its docile instrument, enables the body to fulfil its wishes and thoughts, with inexhaustible power of action, "as we even now see the artist using his voice or his hand with marvelous freedom and thus foreshadowing the perfect spiritualizing of the body."

8. Monism and Other Theories

Other questions call for discussion here: they may be briefly touched upon. Scripture acknowledges a *dualism*, which recognizes the separate existence of soul *and* body. It rejects a *monism*, which makes man but "a doublefaced unity" (Bain); or considers mind and body as equally unreal, and as "aspects," "appearances," "sides" of one and the same reality (scientific monism). It knows nothing of mere *idealism*, which makes mind the only reality, of which matter is but a manifestation, nor of *materialism*, which considers matter as that which alone is substantial, while mind is a mere product of the brain (Haeckel). It does not support the theory of *harmonia praestabilita*—pre-established harmony, whereby

"Our birth is but a sleep and a forgetting,"

because soul and body were united in harmonious action before the individual was called into active being, body and soul acting in harmony after creation like two clocks accurately regulated, pointing to the same hour on the dial plate, though driven by different springs (Leibnitz). Scripture has no theory. It deals with facts and facts only in so far as they bear upon the history of man's sin and man's redemption. It throws no light on many problems raised by science or philosophy. It does not discuss origins—the origin of evil, of matter, of mind. "All is of God" is the Scriptural answer to many questions. Thus the relation of mind to body is and remains a mystery—as great as the relation between the forces in Nature, to which the names of light and electricity have been given. Science has attempted to explain that mystery and has failed. The words of Shenstone (*Cornhill Magazine*, 1907) may be applied to all psychical problems, outside of Holy Writ, which by him were applied to those scientific questions which remain unanswered in spite of all our efforts at solution: "We are still very far from knowing definitely that atoms are composed entirely of electrons or that electrons are nothing else than electric charges; and though electrons have been shown to exhibit electric inertia, it has not been proved that the inertia of atoms also is electrical." The mystery of matter is great; that of soul is greater still.

9. The Fall of Man

The next question which falls to be discussed is the influence of the *fall of man* upon his soul. Scripture is clear upon the point. Man's fall from a primeval state of innocence is there told in unambiguous terms, though the word itself is not found in the narrative, except perhaps in Rom **11** 11.12, where allusion is made to the fall (*paráptōma*) of Israel. With the *origin of evil* Scripture apparently does not concern itself, though it clearly states that man's sinful condition stands in direct connection with the transgression of Adam, as in Rom **5** 12, where the introduction of sin (*hamartía*) into the world (*kósmos*) is spoken of as the act of one man (s.c. Adam), *hamartia* being evidently taken as a power of evil working in the world of men. The OT allusion in Hos **6** 7 can hardly be referred to Adam's transgression; at any rate the reference is doubtful. AV renders the passage: "They *like men* have transgressed the covenant," though the revisers have tr[d]: "But they *like Adam* have transgressed the covenant." The German and Dutch VSS give the same interpretation to the verse: "like Adam." The LXX takes the term as an appellative (*hōs ánthrōpos*, "as man"), but the Vulg refers the transgression to Adam (*sicut Adam transgressi sunt*). The other allusions in the OT to this event are slight, as in Job **31** 33; Ezk **28** 13.15. In the NT, however, the references are much more frequent, esp. in the writings of John and of St. Paul (cf Jn **8** 44; 1 Jn **3** 8; 2 Cor **11** 3; 1 Tim **2** 14). The strong parallelism between Adam and Christ in Rom **5** 12–21, the obedience of the one bringing freedom, while that of the other brought woe, and the contrast in 1 Cor **15** 22 between Adam and Christ throw sufficient light on the question at issue.

Modern science, under the influence of the evolutionary hypothesis, has eliminated or at least has attempted to eliminate the factor of the Fall. That "fall" has been interpreted as a "rise," the "descent" is supposed to have been a real "ascent." Far down the ages, millenniums ago, "a miserable, half-starved, naked wretch, just emerged from the bestial condition, torn with fierce passions, and fighting his way among his compeers with low-browed cunning" (Orr, *Christian View of God*, 180) must have emerged somehow out of darkness into light. "We are no longer," says Professor J. A. Thomson, "as those who look back to a paradise in which man fell; we are as those 'who, rowing hard against the stream, see distant gates of Eden gleam, and do not dream it is a dream'" (*Bible of Nature*, 226). If science definitely teaches that man *has* arisen by slow, insensible gradations from the brute, and no further word may be said on the subject, then indeed the problem of human sin is utterly inexplicable. There can then be no agreement between the Bib. conception and the evolutionary theory as so presented. For primitive man's transgression would under such circumstances be but the natural expression of brute passion, to which the name of *sin* in the Christian sense can hardly be applied. But if for "minute" and "insensible" gradations in the evolutionary process be substituted the "mutations," "leaps" or "lifts," to which an increasing number of evolutionists are appealing; if primitive man be not pictured as a semi-animal, subject to brutish impulse and passion; if with man a new start was made, a "lift" occurred in the process of development under the guiding and directing influence of Almighty power, the problem assumes a different shape. A sinless creature, transgressing the moral law, is then not an unscientific assumption; conscience asserting itself as the voice Divine within the human soul is then not only possible, but actual and real, in the history of man's earliest progenitors. The Bib. narrative will after all remain as the most reasonable explanation of man's original condition and his terrible fall. In that narrative will be found enshrined the "shadowing tradition" of a real, historic event, which has influenced the human race through all the ages. Professor Driver, writing under the strong influence of the evolutionary theory, and accepting as "the law stamped upon the entire range of organic nature, progress, gradual advance from lower to higher, from the less perfect to the more perfect," has wisely remarked that "man *failed* in the trial to which he was exposed, that sin has entered into the world . . . . and that through the whole course of the race it has been attended by an element of moral disorder, and thus it has been marred, perverted, impeded or drawn back" (Driver, *Genesis*, 57). See FALL, THE.

10. Effects of the Fall

An equally serious question arises as to the *effects* of the fall of man. Shame, corruption, death is the answer given by the OT and NT. "In the day that thou eatest thereof thou shalt surely die" (Gen **2** 17) was the judgment pronounced upon man. By this was evidently meant "death" as a physical and as a spiritual fact. Man was doomed. The *posse non mori*, which according to older theologians was man's privilege, was lost and was succeeded by a punishment of which the *non posse non mori* was the doom, i.e. the possibility of immortal life was followed by the impossibility of not suffering death. Not as though immortality was absolutely lost; for with sin came decay, degeneration, death, not of the inbreathed spirit, but of the body into which the soul was breathed by God. But even the body is imperishable. It undergoes change, but not extinction. The resurrection-body has become a possibility through the atonement and resurrection of Christ. The tabernacle is removed, but renewed. The body is not a prison house, but a temple; not an adjunct but an integral part of the human being. The Bible teaches not only a resurrection-body, but a transformed body (Rom **12** 1). It speaks not only of a soul to be saved, but of a body to be redeemed. Scripture alone accounts for death and explains it.

11. Death as a Problem

With modern evolutionists death is an unsolved problem. Weissmann (*Essays on Heredity*) maintains on the one hand that "death is not an essential attitude of matter" (p. 159), and on the other, "it is only from the point of view of utility that we can understand the necessity of death" (p. 23), and again "death is to be looked upon as an occurrence which is advantageous to the species as a concession to the outer conditions of life, and not as an absolute necessity, essentially inherent in life." He even speaks of "the immortality of the protozoa," because "an immense number of the lower organisms" are not subject to death (ib, 26). Death therefore according to him has been "acquired secondarily as an adaptation," and must in a certain sense be unnatural. It is indeed "one of the most difficult problems in the whole range of physiology." If this be so, we may safely turn to Scripture for an explanation of the problem, which has a value peculiarly its own. "By man came death" is the authoritative declaration, because by man came sin. "In Adam all die," because through Adam came sin. Here we may safely leave the problem, because "by man" will come "resurrection from the dead." See DEATH.

But if the body is mortal, is the soul immortal? On this point the NT gives no uncertain sound, and though the doctrine be not as clearly expressed in the OT, yet even there kinship with God is man's guaranty for everlasting communion with Him (cf Ps **73**). Job longed for such fellowship, which to him and to the OT saints before and after him was life. In memorable words he gave utterance to the hope which was in him: 'I know that my Redeemer liveth . . . . and after my skin [read "body"] . . . . has been destroyed, yet from my flesh shall I see God; whom I shall see for myself, and mine eyes shall behold and not another' (Job **19** 25). Hosea, the mourner, is responsible for that sublime utterance, which in its NT form is recited at the graveside of those who die in the Lord: "I will ransom them from the power of Sheol; I will redeem them from death: O death, where are thy plagues? O Sheol, where is thy destruction?" (**13** 14). Reference may also be made to the words of Isaiah (**26** 19): "Thy dead shall live; my dead bodies shall arise. Awake and sing, ye that dwell in the dust." Still clearer is the note sounded by Daniel (**12** 2.3): "Many of them that sleep in the dust of the earth shall awake, some to everlasting life, and some to shame and everlasting contempt. And they that are wise shall shine as the brightness of the firmament; and they that turn many to righteousness as the stars for ever and ever." In one word, the OT saint based all his hope and fellowship on God. That hope strengthened his soul when he shuddered at the darkness of Sheol. "It overleaps Sheol in the vigor of his faith." In the Pss we find the same hope expressed on almost every page: "As for me, I shall behold thy face in righteousness; I shall be satisfied, when I awake, with beholding thy form" (AV "with thy likeness," Ps **17** 15); and again: "Thou wilt not leave my soul to Sheol; neither wilt thou suffer thy holy one to see corruption. . . . . In thy presence is fulness of joy; in thy right hand there are pleasures for evermore" (**16** 10.11). Whatever the ultimate verdict of science may be regarding the "utility" of death in regard to the human race, Scripture considers it abnormal, unnatural, a punishment, an infliction, the result of man's wrongdoing and his transgression of the law of God. But death in Holy Writ is not a hopeless separation of body and soul. The NT sounds a note even clearer than the OT; for Christ has brought "life and immortality to light." "*We know*," says Paul, "that we have a building from God," after the dissolution of our tabernacle (2 Cor **5** 1); and that is but the necessary corollary to Christ's great utterance: "I AM THE RESURRECTION, AND THE LIFE" (Jn **11** 25).

12. Immortality of the Soul

LITERATURE.—Beck, *Umriss der biblischen Seelenlehre*, ET; Hofmann, *Schriftbeweis;* Delitzsch, *System of Bib. Psychology;* Oehler, *OT Theology;* Wendt, *Die Begriffe Fleisch u. Geist*, etc; Dickson, *St. Paul's Use of the Flesh and Spirit;* Cremer, *Bibl.-theol. Wörterbuch*, etc; Herzog, *RE*, arts. "Geist" and "Seele"; Laidlaw, *Bible Doctrine of Man;* Orr, *God's Image in Man;* Davidson, *OT Theology*.

J. I. MARAIS

PTOLEMAIS, tol-ē-mā'is (**Πτολεμαΐς**, *Ptolemaïs*): Same as "Acco" in Jgs **1** 31. Ptolemais was the most prominent town on the Phoen seacoast in Maccabean times (1 Macc **5** 15.55; **10** 1.58.60; **12** 48), and is once mentioned in the NT in Acts **21** 7 as a seaport at which Paul landed for one day, visiting the "brethren" in the place. See ACCO; PHOENICIA.

PTOLEMY, tol'ē-mi (**Πτολεμαῖος**, *Ptolemaíos*, but usually called Ptolemy—"the Warlike"): The name Ptolemy is rather common from the days of Alexander the Great, but is best known as the dynastic name of the 13 (14) Macedonian kings of Egypt (323–43 BC) (as Pharaoh in the OT). Those of interest to the Bib. student are:

(1) **Ptolemy I**, surnamed Soter (Σωτήρ, *Sōtḗr*, "Savior"), called also Ptolemy Lagi, was born c 366 BC, the son of Lagus and Arsinoë, a concubine of Philip of Macedon. He was prominent among the officers of Alexander the Great, whom he accompanied in his eastern campaigns. On the death of Alexander, Ptolemy seized the satrapy of Egypt as his share (1 Macc **1** 6 ff). Now commenced the long hostilities between Egypt and Syria, Ptolemy on more than one occasion invading Syria. In 316 he joined in a war against Antigonus during which Coele-Syria and Phoenicia were lost, but in 312 regained from Demetrius the son of Antigonus. It was most probably in this year (312) that Ptolemy captured Jerus on a Sabbath day (Jos, *Ant*, XII, i, 1), and by force or persuasion induced many Jews to accompany him to Egypt as colonists or mercenaries. His kind treatment of them induced others to leave Syria for Egypt. In 306 Ptolemy was defeated in the great naval fight off Salamis in Cyprus by which Cyprus was lost to Egypt. About this date Ptolemy assumed the title of "king," following the example of the Syrian ruler. In 305–304 he defended the Rhodians against Demetrius Poliorcetes, forcing the latter to raise the siege —hence the title "Savior." In 285 BC Ptolemy abdicated in favor of his youngest son Philadelphus—the son of his favorite wife Berenice—and died in 283 BC. According to the usual interpretation this Philadelphus is "the king of the south" in Dnl **11** 5. This Ptolemy shares with his son and successor the honor of founding the famous Alexandrian Museum and Library.

(2) **Ptolemy II**, surnamed Philadelphus (Φιλάδελφος, *Philádelphos*, "Brother[sister?]-loving"), the youngest son of Ptolemy I; b. 309 BC in Cos; succeeded his father in 285 BC and d. 247. Like his father, he was actively engaged in two Syrian wars until peace was made about 250 BC, Berenice, the daughter of Philadelphus, being given in marriage to Antiochus II. This Ptolemy planted numerous colonies in Egypt, Syria and Pal, among which were several of the name of Arsinoë (his sister-wife), Philadelphia on the ruins of old Rabbah, Philotera south of the Sea of Galilee, and Ptolemais on the site of Acco. He devoted great attention to the internal administration of his kingdom, endowed the Museum and Alexandrian Library in which his father had taken much interest; in general he followed his father's example as a liberal patron of art, science and literature. According to one tradition it was Philadelphus who was instrumental in beginning the LXX tr (see SEPTUAGINT). At any rate, he was favorably disposed toward his Jewish subjects, and in his reign Jewish wisdom and Gr philosophy began to blend. Philadelphus is supposed to be "the king of the south" of Dnl **11** 6, whose daughter "shall come to the king of the north to make an agreement."

Octodrachm (Egyptian Talent) of Ptolemy II.

(3) **Ptolemy III**, surnamed Euergetes (Εὐεργέτης, *Euergétēs*, "Benefactor"), son of Philadelphus, whom he succeeded in 247 BC. In 246 he was provoked to a Syrian war to avenge the murder of his sister Berenice at Antioch; in the course of this campaign he met with remarkable success,

overran Syria, plundered Susa and Babylonia, penetrated to the shores of India and captured the important stronghold of Seleucia (1 Macc **11** 8). Euergetes was, however, prevented from reaping the fruits of his victories by being recalled by internal troubles in Egypt. He brought back with him from the East the Egyp gods that Cambyses had carried away 300 years before, thus earning from the Egyptians the title of "Benefactor." Two traditions obtain as to his death: the more probable is that of Polybius (ii.71), according to which he died a natural death (222 BC), or, according to another (Justin xxix.1), he was murdered by his son. Some regard this king as the Euergetes mentioned in the Prologue to Sir, but the reference must rather be to Euergetes II (Ptolemy VII). The "shoot" who "shall enter into the fortress of the king of the north" and prevail is Euergetes I (Dnl **11** 7–9), ver 8 referring to the act by which he won his title.

(4) **Ptolemy IV,** surnamed Philopator (Φιλοπάτωρ, *Philopátōr*, "Lover of his father"), or Tryphon (Τρύφων, *Trúphōn*), the eldest son of Euergetes whom he succeeded in 222 BC. Antiochus the Great of Syria declared war against Egypt about 219 BC, but, after conquering Coele-Syria and Phoenicia, he was defeated by Philopator at the battle of Raphia near Gaza (217 BC). On his victorious return to Alexandria, Philopator assumed a very anti-Jewish attitude, and indeed caused discontent generally among his subjects. In spite of the victory of Raphia, Egypt began to decline under his weakness. He was as dissolute as Nero, while his domestic tragedies are as dark as those of Herod the Great. He died in 205 BC. Dnl **11** 10–12 refers to the reign of Philopator. He was most probably the oppressor of 3 Macc.

(5) **Ptolemy V,** surnamed Epiphanes (Ἐπιφανής, *Epiphanḗs*, "Illustrious"). He was only 5 years old when his father Philopator died. Taking advantage of the king's minority, Antiochus the Great leagued with Philip of Macedon against Egypt. Philip took the Cyclades and some cities in Thrace, while Antiochus defeated the Egyp general Scopas at Paneas on the Jordan in 198 BC, and thus Pal passed to the Seleucid dynasty. The Romans now interfered to make Antiochus surrender his conquests. Not daring to disobey Rome, Antiochus compromised by making peace with Ptolemy and betrothing to him his daughter Cleopatra, who was to receive as her dower the revenues of the conquered provinces Coele-Syria, Pal and Phoenicia (Jos, *Ant*, XII, iv, 1; Polyb. xxviii.17), but the control of these provinces seems to have been retained by Antiochus. The marriage took place in 193 BC. After the dismissal of his faithful minister, Aristomenes, Epiphanes' character and reign deteriorated. At last he bestirred himself to recover the lost provinces from Seleucus, the successor of Antiochus, but was poisoned before his plans materialized, in 182 (181) BC (Jos, *Ant*, XII, iv, 11). Dnl **11** 14–17 is to be interpreted as referring to the relations between Ptolemy V and Antiochus III, "the Great."

(6) **Ptolemy VI,** surnamed Philometor (Φιλομήτωρ, *Philomḗtōr*, "Fond of his mother"), elder son of Ptolemy V whom he succeeded in 182 (181) BC. For the first 7 years of his reign his mother Cleopatra acted as queen-regent, and peace was maintained with Syria till 173 BC. Antiochus IV Epiphanes then invaded Egypt, defeated the Egyptians at Pelusium and secured the person of Philometor, whom he spared, hoping to employ him as a tool to gain the ascendancy over Egypt. Philometor's brother was now proclaimed king by the Alexandrians, with the title of Euergetes (II). When Antiochus retired, Philometor made peace with his brother, conceding him a share in the government (170 BC). This displeased Antiochus, who marched against Alexandria, but was stopped beneath the walls by a Rom embassy (168 BC), in obedience to which he withdrew. The brothers quarreled again, and Philometor, expelled by Euergetes, went to Rome to seek assistance (164 BC). The Romans seated him again on his throne, assigning Cyrenaica to Euergetes. The next quarrel was about Cyprus. Philometor this time secured his brother as a prisoner, but sent him back to his province. Philometor was later drawn into Syrian politics in the conflict between Alexander Balas and Demetrius. The Egyp king espoused the cause of the former, to whom he also betrothed his daughter Cleopatra. But on discovering Balas' treachery, he took away his daughter from him and gave her to his opponent, Demetrius Nikator, whom he now supported against Balas. Balas was defeated in a decisive battle on the Oenoparas and killed, but Ptolemy himself died in 146 BC from the effects of a fall from his horse in the battle (1 Macc **1** 18; **10** 51 ff; 2 Macc **1** 10; **4** 21). Dnl **11** 25–30 refers to the events of this reign. Philometor seems to have taken a friendly attitude toward the Jews. In his reign the Jewish temple of Leontopolis near Heliopolis was founded in 154 BC (Jos, *Ant*, XIII, iii, 1 f), and two Jewish generals, Onias and Dositheus, were at the head of his armies and had a large share in the government (Jos, *CAp*, II, 5). The Jewish-Alexandrine philosopher Aristobulus probably lived in this reign.

(7) (On the death of Philometor his young son was proclaimed king as **Ptolemy Eupator** ["of a noble father"], but after reigning but a few months was put to death by his uncle Euergetes II [Just. xxxviii.8]. His reign being so brief he need hardly be numbered among the Ptolemies.)

(8) **Ptolemy VII** (VIII), surnamed Euergetes (II) and called also Physcon (Φύσκων, *Phúskōn*, "Big-paunch"), became sole ruler in succession to his brother Philometor (or to his murdered nephew) in 146 BC, and reigned till 117 BC. His reign was characterized by cruelty, tyranny and vice, so that he was hated by his subjects, esp. by the people of Alexandria, who on one occasion expelled him during an insurrection. It is uncertain whether Physcon was an enemy and persecutor of the Jews or their patron. Some authorities refer the persecutions mentioned in 3 Macc to this reign, but most modern authorities are disposed to date them in the reign of the anti-Jewish Ptolemy IV Philopator. The statement, "in the 38th year of King Euergetes," in the Prologue to Sir refers to Physcon Euergetes II and = 132 BC, since he dated his reign from the year of joint kingship with his brother (170 BC).

The other Ptolemies of Egypt require no mention here.

The following are the apocryphal Ptolemies:

(1) **Ptolemy Macron.** See Macron.

(2) **Ptolemy,** son of Abubus, son-in-law of Simon the Maccabee. He treacherously assassinated Simon and two of his sons in the stronghold of Dok near Jericho, 135 BC (1 Macc **16** 15).

(3) **Ptolemy,** the father of Lysimachus (Apoc) (Ad Est **11** 1).

(4) **Ptolemy,** son of a Dositheus; he and his father were bearers of the "epistle of Phrurai" (Ad Est **11** 1).

Literature.—J. P. Mahaffy, *Empire of the Ptolemies*, is the best account for Eng. readers. A long list of Ptolemies will be found, e.g. in Smith's *Classical Dict.* The ancient authorities are Josephus, Polybius, Justin, Pausanias, Plutarch (*Cleom.*), Livy, Diodorus, Jerome (*Comm. to Dnl 11*).

S. Angus

PUAH, pū'a, **PUVAH,** pū'va:

(1) פּוּעָה, *pū'āh:* One of the Heb midwives whom the king of Egypt commanded to kill all male children of the Hebrews at birth. The midwives, fearing God, refused to obey, pretending that the children of the Heb women were usually born before they arrived. Their act is spoken of as being meritorious in the eyes of the Lord, who is said to have rewarded them by making "houses" for them (Ex **1** 15–20). In the Midhrash, Ex *Rabbā'*, Puah is identified with Miriam, and Shiphrah, the other midwife, with her mother Jochebed. According to another tradition Puah was a proselyte.

(2) פּוּאָה, *pū'āh,* in 1 Ch **7** 1; פֻּוָּה, *puwwāh,* in Gen **46** 13; Nu **26** 23; written also "Pua" AV, and "Puvah" RV: Second son of Issachar, ancestor of the Punites, enumerated in the desert census taken by Moses and Eleazar.

(3) פּוּאָה, *pū'āh:* Member of the tribe of Issachar, mentioned (Jgs **10** 1) as the son of Dodo and the father of Tola, the judge. ELLA DAVIS ISAACS

PUBLICAN, pub'li-kan. See TAX, TAXING.

PUBLIUS, pub'li-us (Πόπλιος, *Póplios,* from the Lat praenomen *Publius,* derived from *populus,* "popular"; according to Ramsay it is the Gr form of the Lat nomen *Popilius;* the Gr title meaning "first," applied to Publius in Acts **28** 7, was an official one, and has been found on an inscription from the island of Gaulus near Malta [cf Böckh, *CIG,* no. 5, 754]): Publius held office under the governor of Sicily. As the leading official in Malta, he was responsible for any Rom soldiers and their prisoners who might land there, but the account in Acts **28** 7 implies that he displayed more than ordinary solicitude for Paul and his shipwrecked company, for, according to the writer, he "received us, and lodged us three days courteously" (AV). The Apocryphal "Acts of St. Paul" (see APOCRYPHAL ACTS, B, I) states also that "he did for them many acts of great kindness and charity" (cf Budge, *Contendings of the Apostles,* II, 605). On this occasion Paul miraculously healed the father of Publius, who "lay sick of fever and dysentery" (Acts **28** 8). The exactitude of the medical terms here employed forms part of the evidence that the writer of Acts was a physician. Tradition relates that Publius was the first bishop of Malta and that he afterward became bishop of Athens. C. M. KERR

PUDENS, pū'denz, pū'dens (Πούδης, *Poúdēs,* lit. "bashful" [2 Tim **4** 21]): One of the Christians in Rome who remained loyal to Paul during his second and last imprisonment there, when most of the members of the church "forsook him."

1. Faithful to Paul

The pressure under which they acted must have been very great, as the apostle's final trial before the supreme court of the empire followed quickly after the Neronic persecution. Their defection from their loyalty to Paul must not be taken as implying that they had also proved untrue to Christ. At this time, however, there were some of the Christians who risked their earthly all, and their lives too, in order to prove their adherence to Paul, and Pudens was one of these.

2. Pudens and Claudia

Writing the last of all his letters, the Second Ep. to Tim, Paul sends greeting from "all the brethren" who were then with him. Among these he names Pudens. There are three other names associated by the apostle with that of Pudens: Eubulus, Linus and Claudia. There is an interesting conjecture regarding Pudens and Claudia, that they were husband and wife, and that Claudia was of British birth, a daughter of a British king, called Cogidunus. King Cogidunus was an ally of the Romans, and assumed the name of the emperor Tiberius Claudius, who was his patron. In this way his daughter would be named Claudia. But this identification of the British princess with the Claudia who sends salutation to Timothy is only a supposition; it lacks both evidence and proof. See CLAUDIA and *CH* (*St. P*), ch xxvii.

In modern Rome, however, the tourist is still shown a building which is called the house of Pudens, in the same way as "Paul's hired house" is also shown. The authenticity in both cases is lacking.

Pudens is not mentioned elsewhere in the NT. JOHN RUTHERFURD

PUHITES, pū'hīts (פּוּתִי, *pūthī*). See PUTHITES.

PUL, pul:

(1) An Assyr king (2 K **15** 19). See TIGLATH-PILESER.

(2) An African country and people (Isa **66** 19). See PUT.

PULPIT, po͝ol'pit: Neh **8** 4, "Ezra the scribe stood upon a *mighdōl* of wood." *Mighdōl* is one of the commonest words in the OT and means simply a high object—here a scaffolding or platform (βῆμα, *bēma,* 1 Esd **9** 42). "Tower" (so RVm) gives an entirely wrong picture.

PULSE, puls (זֵרֹעִים, *zērō'īm* [Dnl **1** 12 m, "herbs"], זֵרְעֹנִים, *zēr^e'ōnīm* [Dnl **1** 16]; cf זֵרוּעַ, *zērūa'*, "sowing seed" [Lev **11** 37], and זֵרוּעִים, *zērū'īm,* "things sown" [Isa **61** 11]): (1) In Dnl **1** 12.16, it must mean herbs or vegetables grown from seeds; a vegetable diet is what is implied. (2) In 2 S **17** 28, "pulse" after "parched" is not in the original, but is probably more correct than the tr in (1), as "pulse" usually implies leguminous plants, peas, beans, etc.

PUNISHMENT, pun'ish-ment, **EVERLASTING:**

I. Preliminary Assumptions.—(For "everlasting," where used in AV as the rendering of αἰώνιος, *aiōnios,* RV substitutes "eternal.") It is assumed in this art. that Scripture teaches the survival of the soul after death, the reality of retribution and of judgment to come, and a shorter or longer period of suffering for sin in the case of the unredeemed in the world beyond. Only a few words need be said, therefore, in preliminary remark on these assumptions.

1. Survival after Death

Whatever view may be taken of the development of the doctrine of immortality in the OT (see ESCHATOLOGY OF THE OT), it will scarcely be doubted that it is throughout assumed in the NT that the *souls of men,* good and bad, *survive death* (see IMMORTALITY). Two passages only need be referred to in proof: one, Christ's saying in Mt **10** 28: "Be not afraid of them that kill the body, but are not able to kill the soul; but rather fear him who is able to destroy both soul and body in hell"

(Gehenna); the other, the parable of the Rich Man and Lazarus in Lk **16** 19–31: Lazarus is carried by the angels to Abraham's bosom; the rich man lifts up his eyes in Hades, being in torments. The whole doctrine of the future judgment in the NT presupposes survival after death.

2. Retribution for Sin

Retribution for sin is a cardinal point in the teaching of both the OT and NT. The doctrine of judgment, again, in the NT, with Christ as judge, turns on this point. The following passages are decisive: Isa **3** 10.11; Mt **11** 22.24; **12** 41.42; Rom **2** 5.12; 2 Cor **5** 10; Gal **6** 7.8, etc (see RETRIBUTION).

3. Conscious Suffering in Future

The conscious endurance of punishment for sin in the future state is already implied in the preceding. The parable of the Rich Man speaks of it as following immediately on death in Hades; all the descriptions of the judgment imply pain and anguish as the result of condemnation (cf Rom **2** 5.12). This does not settle the nature or duration of the punishment; but it excludes the idea that physical death is the extinction of being, or that annihilation follows immediately upon death or judgment.

These things being assumed, the questions that remain are: Is the period of suffering for sin eternal, or is it terminable? May it be cut short by repentance or by annihilation? Is there any final solution of the discord it implies in the universe? It is maintained here that the punishment of sin, in the case of the finally impenitent, is everlasting.

II. Scriptural Support.—The doctrine that the punishment of sin is everlasting is sustained by many plain testimonies of Scripture.

1. OT and Jewish Conceptions

The doctrine of future punishment is not prominent in the OT, where rewards and punishments are chiefly connected with the present life. In a few passages (Ps **49** 14.15; **73** 18.19; cf Isa **24** 21.22; **66** 24), Dr. Charles thinks that "Sheol appears as the place of punishment of the wicked" (*Eschatology*, 73–76, 156). If so, there is no suggestion of escape from it. In Dnl **12** 2, some that sleep in the dust are represented as awaking to "shame and everlasting contempt" (the word for "everlasting" is the usual one, *'ōlām*). In the Jewish literature of the century before Christ, "Sheol is regarded," says Dr. Charles, "as the place of final eternal punishment, that is, it has become hell" (op. cit., 236; see ESCHATOLOGY OF THE OT).

2. NT Teaching

In the NT, the strongest language is used by Jesus and the apostolic writers on the certainty and severity of the punishment of sin in the future state, and always in a manner which suggests that the doom is final.

(1) "*Eternal.*"—The word "eternal" (*aiônios*) is repeatedly applied to the punishment of sin, or to the fire which is its symbol. A principal example is Mt **25** 41.46, "eternal fire," "eternal punishment" (*kólasis aiônios*). Here precisely the same word is applied to the punishment of the wicked as to the blessedness of the righteous. Other instances are Mt **18** 8; Jude ver 7; cf Rev **14** 11; **19** 3; **20** 10. In 2 Thess **1** 9, we have, "eternal destruction." The kindred word *aídios*, "everlasting," is in Jude ver 6 applied to the punishment of the fallen angels.

The reply made by Maurice (*Theological Essays*, 442 ff) that *aiōnios* in such passages denotes *quality*, not duration, cannot be sustained. Whatever else the term includes, it connotes duration. More pertinent is the criticism of other writers (e.g. Cox, *Salvator Mundi*, 96 ff; Farrar, *Eternal Hope*, Pref., xxxiv, pp. 78 ff, 197 ff; cf his *Mercy and Judgment*, *passim*) that *aiōnios* does not necessarily mean "eternal" (according to Cox it does not mean this at all), but is strictly "age-long," is therefore compatible with, if it does not directly suggest, a terminable period. Cox allows that the term is "saturated through and through with the element of time" (p. 100), but he denies its equivalence with "everlasting." The sense, no doubt, is to be determined by the context, but it can hardly be questioned that "the aeons of the aeons" and similar phrases are the practical NT equivalents for eternity, and that *aiōnios* in its application to God and to life ("eternal life") includes the idea of unending duration (cf Jn **10** 28.29 for express assertion of this). When, therefore, the term is applied in the same context to punishment and to life (Mt **25** 46), and no hint is given anywhere of limitation, the only reasonable exegesis is to take the word in its full sense of "eternal."

(2) *Equivalent expressions.*—The meaning "eternal" is confirmed by the use of equivalent expressions and of forms of speech which convey in the strongest manner the idea of finality. Such are the expressions, "the unquenchable fire," the "worm" that "dieth not" (Mt **3** 12; Mk **9** 43–48; cf Mt **13** 42.50), with those numerous references to "death," "destruction," "second death," on which the advocates of conditional immortality build their arguments for final extinction. Such is the dictum of Jesus: "He that obeyeth not the Son shall not see life, but the wrath of God abideth [remains] on him" (Jn **3** 36; the opposite of "life" is "perishing," ver 16); or that in Rev **22** 11, "He that is unrighteous, let him do unrighteousness still: and he that is filthy, let him be made filthy still." Finality is the note in all Christ's warnings —"the outer darkness" (Mt **8** 12; **22** 13); "The door was shut . . . . I know you not" (Mt **25** 10.12; cf **7** 23), as in those of the Epp. (e.g. He **2** 3; **6** 6.8; **10** 27.31; **12** 25.29). Jesus speaks of the blasphemy against the Spirit as a sin which shall not be forgiven, "neither in this world, nor in that which is to come" (Mt **12** 32; not as implying that other sins, unforgiven in this life, may be forgiven in the next), a passage which Mk gives in the remarkable form, "hath never forgiveness, but is guilty of an eternal sin" (Mk **3** 29). The Rich Man in Hades found an impassable gulf fixed between himself and Lazarus (Lk **16** 26). See GULF. It adds to the terribleness of these sayings that, as before remarked, there is nothing to put against them; no hint or indication of a termination of the doom. Why did Jesus not safeguard His words from misapprehension, if behind them there lay an assurance of restoration and mercy? One may ask with Oxenham, in a reply to Jukes, "whether if Christ had intended to teach the doctrine of eternal punishment, He could possibly have taught it in plainer terms."

(3) *The last judgment.*—The NT doctrine of the last judgment leads to the same conclusion. Two things seem plainly taught about this judgment: the first, that it proceeds on the matter of the present life—"the things done in the body" (Mt **25** 31–46; 2 Cor **5** 10; Rev **20** 12); and the second, that it is decisive in its issues. Not a single suggestion is given of a reversal of its decisions in any future age. Such silence is inexplicable if the Scriptures meant to teach what the opponents of this doctrine so confidently maintain.

3. Teaching of Analogy

In corroboration of this Scriptural view analogy might be pleaded. How constantly even in this life is the law illustrated of the tendency of character to fixity! The present is the season of grace (2 Cor **6** 2), yet what powers of resistance to God and goodness are seen to lie in human nature, and how effectually, often, does it harden itself under the influences that seem most fitted to break down its rebellion! What likelihood is there that eternity will alter this tendency, or make conversion more easy? Eternity can hardly be thought of as more really a scene of grace than time is for those to whom the gospel has already come. Its characteristic mark is said to be "judgment" (He **9** 27). Like the photographer's bath, may its effect not be to develop and fix existing character, rather than to change it? If so, the state in which judgment finds the soul may be presumed to be one that will remain.

III. Difficulties and Objections—Rival Hypotheses.—What, it will now be asked, of the tremendous difficulties which inhere in this doctrine, with their undeniable effect in alienating many generous minds from it and from Christianity? The lurid rhetorical picturings of the sufferings of the lost, too frequent in the teaching of the past, may be discounted; it is not necessary to go beyond the inexpressibly solemn words of Christ Himself and His apostles. But even with this limitation, does it not seem as if, by this doctrine, a reflection was cast on the righteousness and mercy of God in creating such multitudes of the human race, as, on any showing, are outside the pale of Christ's salvation—the countless generations of the heathen, with the masses even in Christian lands who have not received or do not obey the light—only to doom them to endless misery? Before attempting a positive answer, it is proper that a glance be taken at the rival theories put forth in alleviation of the difficulty.

1. Universal Salvation

The most comprehensive solution propounded is that of universal salvation—of a final restitution of all souls to God's favor and to blessedness. This tempting speculation—for it is no more—advocated by Origen in the early church, by Schleiermacher in the last century, has been urged by many writers in modern times. One of its best known advocates was Samuel Cox, in his book *Salvator Mundi*. It is noticeable that not a few who favor this theory (e.g. Maurice, Farrar) decline to commit themselves to it as more than a "hope," and admit the possibility of human souls continuing to resist God endlessly (Maurice, *Theological Essays*, 476; Farrar, *Eternal Hope*, Pref., xv, xvi; *Mercy and Judgment*, I, 485, "In this sense there may be for some souls an endless hell"). It must, however, be evident that, be the number greater or smaller—and who shall give assurance of its smallness?—if there are any such souls, the difficulty in principle remains, and the passages alleged as teaching universal restoration are equally contradicted. The deeper objection to this theory is that, springing, not from real knowledge, but from men's hopes and wishes, it has, as already shown, the tremendous stress of Scripture testimony against it; nor do the passages commonly adduced as favoring it really bear the weight put upon them. We read, e.g., of a "restoration of all things"—the same that Christ calls the *palingenesía*—but, in the same breath, we are told of those who will not hearken, and will be destroyed (Mt **19** 28; Acts **3** 21.23). We read of Christ drawing all men unto Him (Jn **12** 32); but we are not less clearly told that at His coming Christ will pronounce on some a tremendous condemnation (Mt **7** 23; **25** 41); we read of all things being gathered, or summed up, in Christ, of Christ subduing all things to Himself, etc; but representative exegetes like Meyer and Weiss show that it is far from Paul's view to teach an ultimate conversion or annihilation of the kingdom of evil (cf Meyer on 1 Cor **15** 21.28 and Eph **1** 10; Weiss, *Bib. Theol.*, II, 723, 107, 109, ET). We confess, however, that the strain of these last passages does seem to point in the direction of some ultimate unity, be it through subjugation, or in some other way, in which active opposition to God's kingdom is no longer to be reckoned with.

2. Annihilation

The view favored by another class is that of the annihilation of the finally impenitent. The type of doctrine called "conditional immortality" includes other elements which need not here be discussed (see IMMORTALITY). The annihilation theory takes different forms. So far as the annihilation is supposed to take place at death, it is contradicted by the Scriptures which support the soul's survival after death; so far as it is believed to take place after a longer or shorter period of conscious suffering (which is White's theory), it involves its advocates in difficulties with their own interpretations of "death," "destruction," "perishing," seeing that in Scripture this doom is uniformly represented as overtaking the ungodly at the day of judgment, and not at some indefinite period thereafter. The theory conflicts also with the idea of gradation of punishment, for which room has to be sought in the period of conscious suffering, and rests really on an unduly narrowed conception of the meaning of the Scriptural terms "life" and "death." Life is not bare existence, nor is "death" necessarily extinction of being. As said earlier, the language of many parts of Scripture implies the continued existence of the subjects of the Divine wrath.

3. Second Probation

It is significant that on the side alike of the advocates of restoration and of those of annihilation (e.g. E. White), refuge from the difficulties is frequently sought in the hypothesis of an extended probation and work of evangelization beyond death. This theory labors under the drawback that, in marked contrast with Scripture, it throws immensely the larger part of the work of salvation into the future state of being. It is, besides, apart from the dubious and limited support given to it by the passage on Christ's preaching to "the spirits in prison" (1 Pet **3** 19.20), destitute of Scriptural support. It has already been pointed out that the final judgment is uniformly represented as proceeding on the matter of this life. The theory is considered elsewhere (see ESCHATOLOGY OF THE NT, X).

IV. Nature, Conditions and Issues.—

1. Mystery of the Future

While dogmatisms like the above, which seem opposed to Scripture, are to be avoided, it is equally necessary to guard against dogmatisms of an opposite kind, as if eternity must not, in the nature of the case, have its undisclosed mysteries of which we here in time can frame no conception. The difficulties connected with the ultimate destinies of mankind are truly enormous, and no serious thinker will minimize them. Scripture does not warrant it in negative, any more than in positive, dogmatisms; with its uniformly practical aim, it does not seek to satisfy an idle curiosity (cf Lk **13** 23.24). Its language is bold, popular, figurative, intense; the essential idea is to be held fast, but what is said cannot be taken as a directory to all that is to transpire in the ages upon ages of an unending duration. God's methods of dealing with sin in the eternities may prove to be as much above our present thoughts as His dealings now are with men in grace. In His hands we must be content to leave it, only using such light as His immediate revelation yields.

2. Nature of Punishment

As respects the nature of the punishment of sin, it cannot be doubted that in its essence it is *spiritual*. Everything can be adopted here which is said by Maurice and others —"The eternal punishment is the punishment of being without the knowledge of God, who is love, and of Jesus Christ who has manifested it; even as eternal life is declared to be the having the knowledge of God and of Jesus Christ" (*Theological Essays*, 450). The supreme penalty of sin is unquestionably the loss of God's life and love—the *being* sinful. Environment, indeed, may be expected to correspond with character, but the hell is one the sinner essentially makes for himself, and, like the kingdom of God, is *within*. The fire, the worm, the stripes, that figure its severity, are not physical. Even should the *poena sensus* (were that conceivable) be utterly removed, the *poena damni* would eternally remain.

3. Range of Divine Mercy

It is a sound principle that, in His dealing with sin in the world to come, God's mercy will reach *as far as ever it can reach*. This follows from the whole Scriptural revelation of the character of God. What may be included in it, it is impossible for anyone to say. It should be noticed that those of whom it is said that they shall not see life, but the wrath of God abideth on them, are those who "obey not" the truth (Jn **3** 36)—who actively and consciously disregard and oppose it. But all do not belong to this class. It may be assumed that none will be lost who can in consistency with holiness and love be saved. The most germinal goodness, which is the implantation of His own Spirit, God will acknowledge and develop. The problem of undeveloped character may receive a solution we do not wot of with the entrance into the eternal light—not in change of character, but rather, as said before, in the revelation of character's inmost bent. In this sense, the entrance into eternity may be to many the revelation of a love and grace which had not been understood or appreciated as it should have been on earth, but with which it is in essential kinship. There are at least many shades and degrees of character, and God may be intrusted to take the most just, yet most merciful, account of all.

4. Gradation of Punishment

The fullest weight must further be given to what the Scripture so expressly says of gradation of punishment, even of the unsaved. It is not the case that the lot of all who fail of the eternal life in Christ is all of one grade. There are the "few stripes" and the "many stripes" (Lk **12** 47.48); those for whom it will be "more tolerable" than for others in the day of judgment (Mt **11** 20.24). Even "Sodom and her daughters" will be mercifully dealt with in comparison with others (Ezk **16** 48.49.53.55.61). There will be for everyone the most exact weighing of privilege, knowledge and opportunity. There is a vast area here for the Divine administration on which no light at all is afforded us.

5. God "All in All"

There remain those passages already alluded to which do seem to speak, not, indeed, of conversion or admission into the light and fellowship of Christ's kingdom, but still of a final subjugation of the powers of evil, to the extent, at least, of a cessation of active opposition to God's will, of some form of ultimate unification and acknowledgment of Christ as Lord. Such passages are Eph **1** 10; Phil **2** 9-11; above all, 1 Cor **15** 24-28. God, in this final vision, has become "all in all." Here, again, dogmatism is entirely out of place, but it is permissible to believe that these texts foreshadow such a final persuasion of God's righteousness in His judgment and of the futility of further rebellion as shall bring about an outward pacification and restoration of order in the universe disturbed by sin, though it can never repair that eternal loss accruing from exclusion from Christ's kingdom and glory.

Literature.—Against: Maurice, *Theological Essays*, "Eternal Life and Eternal Death"; S. Cox, *Salvator Mundi;* F. W. Farrar, *Eternal Hope; Mercy and Judgment;* A. Jukes, *The Second Death and the Restitution of All Things;* E. White, *Life in Christ;* H. Constable, *Duration and Nature of Future Punishment.* For: Pusey, *What Is of Faith as to Everlasting Punishment?* H. N. Oxenham, *Catholic Eschatology;* C. Clemance, *Future Punishment;* Edersheim, *Life and Times of Jesus, the Messiah*, Appendix, xix, "On Eternal Punishment, according to the Rabbis and the NT"; *The Future Life, A Defence of the Orthodox View, by the Most Eminent American Scholars*; S. D. F. Salmond, *The Christian Doctrine of Immortality*, Book VI; Orr, *Christian View of God*, lecture ix; Luthardt, *Saving Truths* (ET), lecture x. See also the various works on Dogmatic and Bib. Theology.

James Orr

PUNISHMENTS, pun'ish-ments (עָוֹן, *'āwōn*, "fault," "iniquity," "punishment for iniquity," "sin" [Gen **4** 13; Lev **26** 41; Job **19** 29; Ps **149** 7; Lam **4** 22; Ezk **14** 10 m; Am **1** 3.6.9.11.13; **2** 1.4.6], עֹנֶשׁ, *'ōnesh*, "tribute," "fine," "punishment" [Lam **3** 39], חֲטָאָה, *ḥăṭā'āh*, or חַטָּאת, *ḥaṭṭā'th*, "sin" and its retribution, "penalty," "expiation" [Zec **14** 19]; **κόλασις,** *kólasis*, "punishment," "torment" [Mt **25** 46], **ἐπιτιμία,** *epitimía*, "poll tax," hence "penalty" [2 Cor **2** 6], **τιμωρία,** *timōría*, "vindication," hence "penalty" [He **10** 29], **ἐκδίκησις,** *ekdíkēsis*, "vindication," "retribution" [1 Pet **2** 14 AV]): A court could inflict for a crime against the person, a sentence of (1) death in the form of stoning, burning, beheading, or strangling, etc; (2) exile to one of the cities of refuge in case of manslaughter (Nu **35**); or (3) stripes, not to exceed 40, in practice 39 or less (Dt **25** 3; 2 Cor **11** 24). Offences against property (theft, fraudulent conversion of deposit, embezzlement, robbery) were punished by exacting more than the value of the things taken (Lk **19** 8), the excess going to the injured party, thus differing from a fine, which goes into the treasury of the community. The housebreaker was liable to be slain with impunity (Ex **22** 2). A fine in the modern sense is unknown in the Scriptures, unless Lev **5** 6-19 be interpreted as referring to such.

1. History of the Hebrew Law concerning Punishment

The earliest theory of punishment seems to have been that of retaliation—"blood for blood"—and to some extent this principle appears even in the Law of Moses (Lev **24** 19.20; Mt **5** 38). Early in the history of the race, punishment was administered for sin and crime. Adam and Eve were driven from the Garden, and Cain, the first murderer, though not executed in retaliation for his deed, had a mark set on him. The words of Lamech (Gen **4** 24) indicate that death was regarded as the fitting punishment for murder, and the same thought apparently was in the minds of the brethren of Joseph (**42** 21). Judah, as head of his family, seems to have had power of life and death (**38** 24), and Abimelech threatens his people with the extreme punishment in case they injure or insult Isaac or his wife (**26** 11). Similar power is ascribed to Pharaoh (**41** 13).

2. The Mosaic Law concerning Punishment

Under the Law of Moses, the murderer was to be put to death without mercy. Even if he took refuge at the altar in a sanctuary or in an asylum city, he would not be immune from arrest and execution, and the same principle was applied in the case of an animal (Ex **21** 12.14.23.28.36 ||). But punishment under the Mosaic Law was not to be entailed or transmitted (Dt **24** 16), as was the case among the Chaldaeans (Dnl **6** 24) and the kings of Israel (1 K **21**; 2 K **9** 26).

It has been noted that capital punishment is extensively prescribed by the Mosaic Law, and undoubtedly the Law was carried out. This circumstance has been explained by reference to the fact that the nation consisted of newly emancipated slaves, and therefore required harsh measures to keep them in check.

Under the Mosaic Law, the offences that made one liable to the **punishment of death** were: (1) striking or reviling a parent (Ex **21** 15.17); (2) blasphemy (Lev **24** 14.16.23; 1 K **21** 10; Mt **26** 65.66); (3) Sabbath-breaking (Ex **31** 14; **35** 2; Nu **15** 32–36); (4) witchcraft and false pretension to prophecy (Ex **22** 18; Lev **20** 27; Dt **13** 5; **18** 20; 1 S **28** 9); (5) adultery (Lev **20** 10; Dt **22** 22); (6) unchastity: (*a*) before marriage, but detected afterward (Dt **22** 21), (*b*) in case of a woman with someone other than her betrothed (Dt **22** 23), (*c*) in a priest's daughter (Lev **21** 9); (7) rape (Dt **22** 25); (8) incestuous and unnatural connections (Ex **22** 19; Lev **20** 11.14. 16); (9) man-stealing (Ex **21** 16); (10) idolatry, actual or virtual, in any form (Lev **20** 2; Dt **13** 6; **17** 2–7); (11) false witness in capital cases (Dt **19** 16.19).

A large number of offences come under the law of punishment by **cutting off from the people,** the meaning of which expression has led to some controversy. It may signify excommunication or death, and occurs in connection with the following offences: (1) breach of morals, such as wilful sin in general (Nu **15** 30.31); incestuous or unclean connections (Lev **18** 29; **20** 9–21); (2) breach of covenant, brought about through uncircumcision (Gen **17** 14; Ex **4** 24), neglect of Passover (Nu **9** 13), Sabbath-breaking (Ex **31** 14), neglect of Atonement Day (Lev **23** 29), work done on the Atonement Day (Lev **23** 30), children offered to Molech (Lev **20** 3), witchcraft (Lev **20** 6), anointing an alien with holy oil (Ex **30** 33); (3) breach of ritual, committed by eating leavened bread during Passover (Ex **12** 15.19), eating fat of sacrifices (Lev **7** 25), eating blood (Lev **7** 27; **17** 14), eating sacrifices while unclean (Lev **7** 20.21; **22** 3.4. 9), offering too late (Lev **19** 8), making holy ointment for private use (Ex **30** 32.33), making perfume for private use (Ex **30** 38), general neglect of purification (Nu **19** 13.20), not bringing offering after slaying a beast for food (Lev **17** 9), slaying the animal at a place other than the tabernacle door (Lev **17** 4), touching holy things illegally (Nu **4** 15.18.20).

Of **capital punishments** that are properly regarded as of *Hebrew origin*, we note:

(1) *Stoning*, which was the ordinary mode of execution (Ex **19** 13; Lev **20** 27; Josh **7** 25; Lk **20** 6; Acts **7** 58; **14** 5). The witnesses, of whom there were at least two, were required to cast the first stone (Dt **13** 9 f; Jn **8** 7). If these failed to cause death, the bystanders proceeded to complete the sentence, whereupon the body was to be suspended until sunset (Dt **21** 23).

(2) *Hanging* is mentioned (Nu **25** 4; Dt **21** 22), probably not as a mode of execution, but rather of exposure after death. It may have been a Canaanitish punishment, since it was practised by the Gibeonites on the sons of Saul (2 S **21** 6.9).

(3) *Burning*, before the age of Moses, was the punishment of unchastity (Gen **38** 24). The Law prescribes it as a punishment in the case of a priest's daughter (Lev **21** 9), and in case of incest (Lev **20** 14), but it is also mentioned as following death by other means (Josh **7** 25), and some believe it was never used excepting after death. That it was sometimes used as a punishment on living persons among the heathen is shown by Dnl **3**.

(4) The *sword* or *spear* as an instrument of punishment is named in the Law (Ex **19** 13; **32** 27; Nu **25** 7 ff). It occurs frequently in monarchic and post-Bab times (Jgs **9** 5; 1 S **15** 33; 2 S **20** 22; 1 K **19** 1; Jer **26** 23; Mt **14** 8.10), but among these cases, there are some of assassination rather than of punishment.

(5) *Strangling* as a form of punishment has no Scripture authority, but according to tradition was frequently employed, and is said to have been performed by immersing the convict in clay or mud, and then strangling him by a cloth tied around the neck.

3. Punishments of Foreign Origin

Besides these, which are to be regarded as the ordinary capital punishments, we read of some that were either **of foreign introduction** or **of an irregular kind,** such as: (1) *crucifixion* (q.v.); (2) *drowning* (Mt **18** 6 ∥); (3) *sawing asunder* or *crushing* (2 S **12** 31; He **11** 37); (4) *torturing* (1 Ch **20** 3; He **11** 35); (5) *precipitation* (2 Ch **25** 12; Lk **4** 29); (6) *suffocation* (2 Macc **13** 4–8). The Persians are said to have filled a high tower a great way up with ashes, and then to have thrown the criminal into it, and continually stirred up the ashes by means of a wheel till he was suffocated (Rawlinson, *Ancient Monarchy*, III, 246). See also Herod, II, 100.

Secondary forms of punishment not heretofore mentioned are to be noted as follows:

(1) *Blinding* or *putting out of eyes* in the case of captives (Jgs **16** 21; 1 S **11** 2; 2 K **25** 7).

(2) *Chaining* by means of manacles or fetters of copper or iron, similar to our handcuffs fastened on the wrists and ankles and attached to each other by a chain (Jgs **16** 21; 2 S **3** 34; 2 K **25** 7); also alluded to in the life of Paul (Acts **28** 20; Eph **6** 20; 2 Tim **1** 16); and in the case of Peter (Acts **12** 6).

(3) *Confiscation of property* that had fallen under the ban, i.e. had been singled out for destruction by the special decree of Jeh, as in Nu **21** 2; Josh **6** 17; or had been reserved for the use of the army (Dt **2** 35; **20** 14; Josh **22** 8); or given over to the priesthood (Josh **6** 19). The term may be extended to include all things vowed or sanctified and those irrevocably devoted or consecrated to God (Lev **27** 21.28). The idea is applied with special emphasis to those things which, because of their uncleanness, must not be used by the Israelites, though, through their warfare with the heathen, they might have come into possession of them (Dt **7** 26; 1 S **15** 16–23).

(4) *Dashing in pieces* (Ps **2** 9; Isa **13** 18).

(5) *Divine visitation.* See Visitation.

(6) *Exposure to wild beasts* (Lev **26** 22; 1 S **17** 46; Dnl **6**).

(7) *Flaying* (Rawlinson, *Ancient Monarchy*, I, 478; *Nineveh and Babylon;* mentioned **figuratively** in Mic **3** 3).

(8) *Forfeiture* (Ezr **10** 8).

(9) *Gallows* in the modern sense probably were unknown to the ancients. Where the word occurs in Est (**5** 14; **6** 4; **7** 9.10; **9** 13.25), it probably refers to a beam or pole on which the body was impaled and then elevated to a height of 50 cubits as an object of warning to the people (see "Hanging").

Hanging.
Assyrian Sculptures (Brit. Mus.).

(10) *Imprisonment* is frequently referred to in both the OT and the NT, indicating that this was a common mode of punishment among both the Israelites and other nations (Gen **40** 3; **42** 17;

Lev **24** 12; Nu **15** 34; 1 K **22** 27; Jer **37** 15.21; Lk **3** 20; Acts **4** 3.10; **23** 10; and the Epp. of Paul). See PRISON.

(11) *Indignities.*—In this term may be included all those outbursts of vengeance or other evil dispositions that were practised in times or under circumstances when liberties with the prisoner were permitted on the part of bystanders or those who had charge beyond the execution of the judicial decree. Instances are found in the life of Christ (Mt **26** 59.67; Lk **22** 63 ff; Jn **18** 22); also in the life of Paul (Acts **23** 2).

(12) *Mutilation* (*Jgs* ***1*** *6.7; Ezk* ***23*** *25; 2 Macc* ***7***).—The Law was opposed to thus treating any Israelite, and Samuel, when referring to the arbitrary power of the future king (1 S **8** 10 ff), does not say that he would thus treat "their sons." It was a barbarous custom of the East (see EUNUCHS; POLYGAMY), evidently regarded, among the Hebrews, as a heinous practice (Dt **23** 1). The only act authorizing mutilation (except in *retaliation*) is mentioned in Dt **25** 11.

(13) *Plucking off the hair* is alluded to as a mode of punishment in Neh **13** 25; Isa **50** 6.

(14) *Prison garments* were in vogue to mark the convicts (Jer **52** 33).

(15) *Restitution* has been alluded to in the general introduction to this topic.

(16) *Retaliation* was recognized by Moses as a principle, but the application of it was left to the judge (Lev **24** 19–22). A fine example of it is found in the law of Dt **19** 19.

(17) *Scorpions, chastising with.*—Probably the use of thongs armed with pointed pieces of lead or other metal (1 K **12** 11; 2 Ch **10** 14). See SCORPIONS.

(18) *Scourging.* See separate article.

(19) *Slavery.* See separate article.

(20) *Stocks.* See PRISON.

FRANK E. HIRSCH

PUNITES, pū'nīts (פּוּנִי, *pūnī*, probably "dark"): Descendants of Puvah, of the tribe of Issachar (Nu **26** 23; cf Gen **46** 13; Jgs **10** 1; 1 Ch **7** 1).

PUNON, pū'non (פּוּנֹן, *pūnōn*): A desert camp of the Israelites, the second after leaving Mt. Hor (Nu **33** 42.43). Eusebius (*Onom* **299** 85; **123** 9) mentions an Idumaean village, N. of Petra, in the desert, where convicts were mining copper, called Phinōn or Phainōn. These are doubtless identical. See WANDERINGS OF ISRAEL.

PUR, pûr (Est **3** 7; **9** 26). See PURIM.

PURAH, pū'ra (פֻּרָה, *purāh*, "branch"): Gideon's "servant," lit. "young man," i.e. armor-bearer (Jgs **7** 10 f, AV "Phurah").

PURCHASE, pûr'chās: In modern Eng., "to acquire by payment," in Elizabethan Eng., "to acquire" by any means. In the OT, AV has used "purchase" to represent קָנָה, *ķānāh*, and its derivatives (vb. and noun), except in Lev **25** 33, where the word is גָּאַל, *gā'al* (RV "redeem"). In the NT the noun does not occur and the vb. is used for κτάομαι, *ktáomai*, in Acts **1** 18; **8** 20, and περιποιέω, *peripoiéō*, in Acts **20** 28; 1 Tim **3** 13. But none of these words connotes the payment of a price, so that RV has kept the word only in Acts **20** 28 (m "acquired"), changing it into "obtain" in Acts **1** 18; **8** 20, and "gain" in 1 Tim **3** 13. In the OT, RVm has "gotten" in Ex **15** 16 and ARV has (very properly) introduced the same word into the text of Ps **74** 2; **78** 54.

BURTON SCOTT EASTON

PURE, pūr, **PURELY,** pūr'li, **PURITY,** pū'ri-ti: This group of words has in the OT and the NT an almost exclusively ethical significance, though the word "pure" is of course used also in its literal sense of freedom from alloy or other alien matter (Ex **25** 11, etc). "Pure" in the OT represents many Heb words, most frequently טָהוֹר, *ṭāhōr;* "purely," occurs once only in AV, as the tr of בֹּר, *bōr*, properly "that which cleanses" (cf Job **9** 30, RVm "Heb 'cleanse my hands with lye,'" i.e. alkali for soap) in Isa **1** 25, RV "thoroughly [m "as with lye," AV "purely"] purge away thy dross"; "pureness" is the AV tr of the same word in Job **22** 30, RV "cleanness." In the NT "pure" is the tr chiefly of καθαρός, *katharós* (Mt **5** 8, "Blessed are the pure in heart," etc), but also of ἁγνός, *hagnós* (Phil **4** 8; 1 Tim **5** 22; Jas **3** 17; 1 Jn **3** 3—always in an ethical sense). A different word (*eilikrinḗs*) is used in 2 Pet **3** 1, RV "sincere." "Purity" (*hagneía*) occurs only in AV in 1 Tim **4** 12; **5** 2; in RV in 2 Cor **11** 3 (as the tr of *tḗs hagnótētos*). See CLEAN; PURITY.

W. L. WALKER

PURGE, pûrj: A number of words in both the OT and the NT are so rendered in AV and RV, although frequently in RV the older Eng. word "purge" is displaced by the more applicable modern terms "cleanse" and "purify," since the emphatic and medical senses of the word, as we now use it, are not justified by some of the Heb and Gr originals. In older Eng. the word was broader in meaning, today it is specific. Occurrences in AV, with the changes made in RV, are as follows:

1. In the OT

(1) טָהֵר, *ṭāhēr*, lit. "to be clean," used of the putting-away of idolatry from Judah by Josiah (2 Ch **34** 3.8), is tr[d] "purge" in all VSS, but, in Ezk **24** 13, ARV changes to "cleanse." (2) חָטָא, *ḥāṭā'*, lit. "to make a sin offering" (Ps **51** 7), is changed without improvement to "purify" in ARV, while "purge" is retained in ERV. (3) כָּפַר, *kāphar*, "to cover" or "to make atonement," occurs in Ps **65** 3; **79** 9; Ezk **43** 20.26; in the two passages in Pss, RV has "forgive" (the "expiate" of m is still better), and in Ezk the even more accurate "make atonement." In both (4) צָרַף, *çāraph*, "to refine" (Isa **1** 25), and (5) דּוּחַ, *dū[a]ḥ*, lit. "to rinse" (Isa **4** 4), "purge" is well retained in RV. (6) בָּרַר, *bārar*, lit. "to be shining," RV retains in Ezk **20** 38, but in Dnl **11** 35 changes to "purify." (7) זָקַק, *zāķaķ*, "to pour down" as molten metal (Mal **3** 3), also becomes "purify" in RV.

These occurrences are all in the figurative sense, and apply to sin, uncleanness, idolatry, etc. Most noteworthy is the ARV change of the familiar Ps **51** 7.

The Gr words rendered "purge" in AV of the Apoc and NT are καθαίρω, *kathaírō*, and καθαρίζω, *katharízō*,

2. In the NT

and their compounds and derivatives. In all passages except four, RV more properly translates "cleanse" (Mt **3** 12; Mk **7** 19; Lk **3** 17; Jn **15** 2; He **9** 14.22; **10** 2). In He **1** 3 "when he had by himself purged our sins" is changed to "had made purification of." But in the case of the vb. compounded with the preps. ἀπό, *apō*, and ἐκ, *ek*, i.e. *apokathaírō* and *ekkathaírō* (Job **12** 9; 1 Cor **5** 7; 2 Tim **2** 21), with strong signification to "cleanse *out*," RV properly retains "purge." Most worthy of note is the change of the familiar verse in Jn, "Every branch, that beareth fruit, he purgeth" to "Every branch . . . . he cleanseth" (**15** 2).

EDWARD MACK

PURIFICATION, pū-ri-fi-kā'shun. See PURGE; PURITY; UNCLEAN.

PURIM, pū'rim (פּוּרִים, *pūrīm*, "lots"; LXX **Φρουραί**, *Phrourai*), **PUR,** pûr: The name of a

Jewish festival celebrated on the 14th and 15th days of the month Adar, the final month of the Bib. year, corresponding to February-March. The origin of the festival is narrated in the Book of Est, and indeed is the motive of the book, as the time, reason and manner of its celebration are given in detail (Est **3** 7; **9** 24 ff). Reference also is made to it in apocryphal literature (Ad Est **10** 10–13; 2 Macc **15** 36) and in Jos (*Ant*, XI, vi, 13). No reference is made to this feast in the NT, as it was celebrated locally, and is therefore not to be connected with any of the festal pilgrimages to Jerus. For this reason the supposition of some that the feast of Jn **5** 1 was Purim is to be rejected, mention of it being immediately followed by the words, "And Jesus went up to Jerus."

1. Scripture References

For the complete account of the institution of Purim reference must be made to the Book of Est. Only a brief statement is possible here. Haman, son of Hammedatha the AGAGITE (q.v.; cf 1 S **15** 8.32), who had been made prime minister by King Ahasuerus (Xerxes), bitterly hated the Jews, some of whom, as Mordecai, were rising to prominence in the empire. After Queen Vashti had been put away from her royal position for cause (**1** 9–12), a Jewess named Esther, kinswoman and adopted daughter of Mordecai, was chosen to become the royal consort. This only increased the hatred of Haman, who in his jealous fury soon began to seek an opportune day to work his hate upon Mordecai and the whole Jewish people, and therefore resorted to the casting of the lots for the auspicious time: "They cast Pur, that is, the lot, before Haman from day to day, and from month to month, to the twelfth month, which is the month Adar" (**3** 7). Beginning with the 1st month, all the days and months were tried with unfavorable result, until the last. At Haman's request Ahasuerus caused his scribes to send into all the realm on the 13th day of the 1st month a decree that all Jews should be put to death on the 13th day of the 12th month (**3** 12 ff). As the narrative shows, the wisdom of Mordecai, Esther's heroism, and fasting and prayer availed to foil the dastardly scheme of Haman, who had already built the gallows on which his hated rival should be hanged. Haman was himself hanged on this gallows, while Mordecai was honored yet more (**7** 10; **8** 1.2). A second decree was issued on the 23d day of the 3d month that on the 13th day of the 12th month (**8** 9.12), the day appointed in the first decree for their extermination, the Jews should gather together and defend themselves against their foes. On that fateful day not only did the Jews successfully resist the malice of their enemies, but the public officials also, seeing that the royal favor was with the Jews, espoused their cause. In Shushan, the royal city, a second day, the 14th, was granted the Jews for vengeance on their foes (**9** 11–16). In view of so great a deliverance "Mordecai wrote these things . . . . unto all the Jews . . . . to enjoin them that they should keep the fourteenth day of the month Adar, and the fifteenth day of the same, yearly, as the days wherein the Jews had rest from their enemies" (**9** 20–22).

2. History of Institution

Already as early as the times of the Maccabees (2 Macc **15** 36), the festival was observed, the 14th day being called "Mordecai's day." Jos refers to it as continuously and widely observed down to his time: "For this cause the Jews still keep the forementioned days, and call them days of Purim" (*Ant*, XI, vi, 13). In succeeding centuries as the Jews have passed from one civilization or empire to another, so many causes have arisen to remind them of the persecutions of Haman as to make the festival of a triumph over such persecutions both attractive and most significant to them. Experiences in Syria, Egypt, Rome, Russia and elsewhere have not been lacking in suggestion of the original occasion of Purim. The 13th day has been observed by fasting in commemoration of Esther's prayer and fasting before she approached the king; in the evening, at the beginning of the 14th day, the Jews repair to the synagogues where the Book of Est, one of the *m^eghillōth*, is read with interpretations, execrations bursting out at the reading of Haman's name, accompanied by noise of rattles and stamping of feet, other persecutors and foes also sometimes coming in for a share of execration. The names of Mordecai and Esther receive blessings. On the following morning of the 14th synagogue services are again held, at which, in addition to the repetition of the Est reading, Ex **17** 8–16, which records the destruction of the Amalekites (cf Est **3** 1), is also read as the lesson from the Law, presents are given to the poor and to friends, and the rest of the day, as also the 15th, observed with feasting and rejoicing, even excesses being condoned in the exuberance of national spirit.

3. Manner of Observance

Many attempts have been made to trace the origin of Purim in pagan or cosmic festivals, but to the present time without success, without approach even to probability. Supposed connections with nature myths, national festivals, polytheistic legends have all found advocates. The word itself has suggested the possibility of identification with words of similar form or sound in other languages. But the ease of finding such similarities for any word casts doubt upon the reliability of any identification. (1) It has been traced to the Assyr *pûrû*, and identified with the Assyr New Year when officials entered upon their term of service. (2) The Bab *puhru*, new year festival, has also been claimed as the origin of Purim; Mordecai becomes Marduk, Esther is Ishtar, while Haman, Vashti and Zeresh are Median gods. (3) The most popular attempts at identification are in the Pers field, where *bahr*, "lot," is claimed as the source of Pur, or *purdighân*, "new year," or *farwardighan*, the feast of departed souls. (4) Origin also in a Gr bacchanalian occasion has been sought. (5) Others suggest origin in other Jewish experiences than that claimed by the Book of Est itself, such as a captivity in Edom, or a persecution under the Ptolemies in Egypt, or the victory of Judas Maccabaeus over Nicanor in 161 BC (1 Macc **7** 49). No one of all these theories has sufficient probability to secure for itself anything like general acceptance; the Book of Est remains as the most reasonable account; the difficulties met in it are not so great as those of the explanations sought in other languages and religions.

4. Theories of Origin

LITERATURE.—Bible dicts., esp. *HDB*, *EB* and *Jew Enc*; Paton, comm. on "Est" in *ICC*, particularly pp. 77–94.

EDWARD MACK

PURITY, pū'ri-ti: The Bible bears witness to the long struggle over and in man to secure physical, mental, and moral cleanliness. The various forms of purity have relation to each other.

We have a common proverb that "cleanliness is akin to godliness." Cleanliness and aesthetics are certainly nigh neighbors. But cleanliness and ethics do not dwell farther apart. When one realizes that by uncleanness of person or property he may endanger the health or life of family, or even of society about him—as in keeping conditions that develop typhoid fever—he begins to realize that there is a close tie between cleanliness and morals. "Ought" comes in on the sphere of cleanliness, and then the whole realm of ethics is open. So near are the departments of physical and ethical cleanliness that now if one hears the word "slum" without explanation, he cannot tell whether it relates to filth or sin.

The perception of this relationship is of very ancient date. Though it is Isaiah who says (**52** 11), "Cleanse yourselves, ye that bear the vessels of Jeh," and Mk **7** 3.4, "All the Jews, except they wash their hands diligently, eat not, holding the tradition of the elders; and when they come from the marketplace, except they bathe themselves, they eat not; and many other things there are, which they have received to hold, washings of cups, and pots, and brasen vessels," yet such statements are but summaries of directions distributed here and there throughout the whole Levitical Law. We can read therein what sounds like the hygienic orders of a general to his soldiers on the march, or like the rules of the board of health to preserve a city from pestilence. And these Levitical directions for cleanliness are connected inseparably with the worship of Jeh, as though physical purity were to that an essential. The Psalmist blends these two elements, the physical and the ethical, in the familiar question and answer (**24** 3-5), "Who shall ascend into the hill of Jeh? and who shall stand in his holy place? He that hath clean hands, and a pure heart; who hath not lifted up his soul unto falsehood, and hath not sworn deceitfully. He shall receive a blessing from Jeh, and righteousness from the God of his salvation."

The ceremonial cleansings called for by the Law had meaning and influence. They were interpretative of something spiritual—were a parable way of illustrating the necessity of purity of heart in order to gain acceptance with God. If in after-days the thing symbolized was forgotten in the symbol, that was owing to "blindness of mind." The darkness was not necessary.

But the main subject in respect to which we shall in this art. seek light on purity from the Bible will not be hygiene or aesthetics, but morals.

1. The Sex Relation

When we turn to that department we shall at once realize the fact that the sex relation is the most primitive and comprehensive of all the human relations.

The family.—The attitude of the Bible in respect to that relation is unmistakable. From the vision of the Garden of Eden to that of the New Jerusalem, the Bible rings true to the ideal of purity in family life and in the relations of the sexes to each other. This is remarkable, for it is a vast history over which its narrative sweeps, and in it every species of literature is represented. It sets forth the acts and views of a people in all the stages of civilization, from wandering nomads to dwellers in cities embellished by architecture and every device of man to set forth riches and splendor. It sets forth their crime, shame and sin, as well as their virtues, but its tone is approbative of the virtues and reprobative of the crime, shame and sin. In the Magna Charta of the Heb people—the Ten Commandments—there stands in equal rank with any other principle, "Thou shalt not commit adultery." The sanction of religion and law was thus given to the integrity and purity of family life. The minute regulations against marriage with relatives, and the severe punishments inflicted for disregard of the restrictions (Lev **18** and **20**), were a powerful force in the same direction. The adultery of married persons was to be punished by the death of both the parties (Lev **20** 10; Dt **22** 22).

Such laws may sometimes seem severe. Doubtless they are primitive and date from the time of nomadism. In primitive conditions, penalties for infraction of law are to be severe and swift. Pioneers the world over and through time, for very self-preservation's sake, could show little favor or tolerance to lawlessness. Be these laws severe, they show the intense earnestness of a people to have a pure family life in which children born should be genuine to it. These Levitical restrictions upon intermarriage with relatives fit the sense of propriety and right of civilized people, even to this day.

There is no question about the attitude of the prophets on purity. They were in harmony with the Law. They had no tolerance for

2. The Prophets

corrupt morals or manners leading to impurity or suggesting it. An illustration sometimes has the light of the sun in it. What it is that is illustrated is frequently best seen by looking at the illustration itself. The prophets were passionate monotheists. They wanted above all things that Israel should be true to Jeh and to Him alone. To the prophets, worship of other gods was treason to Jeh. One prophet after another, and over and over again, illustrates this highest of crimes by infidelity in the marriage relation. That shows in what estimate the family was held. To put any other in the place of Jeh was "to go a-whoring after other gods," or "to play the harlot." That shows as nothing else could how deep in the heart was sunk regard for pure family life. Infidelity was high treason there, or it never would have furnished language to describe high treason to God.

Prov **5** and **7** indicate the attitude of the book on purity. We may let the book make its own case.

3. The Proverbs

The wiles of "the strange woman" and the stupid folly and destruction of her victim are specially set forth in the chapters mentioned. In the last chapter of the book we have a portraiture of a "virtuous woman" in whom domesticity in purity has reached a high stage. "Let her own works praise her in the gates."

It is pleasant to turn from the tense severity of law, since it must deal largely with crime and sin, to the idealism of poetry. In the Pss and the

4. The Song of Songs

Prophets the relation of husband and wife, of bridegroom and bride, of lover and loved are always treated with tenderness and reverence. Here is familiar Scripture (Ps **19**): "The heavens declare the glory of God; and the firmament showeth his handiwork. . . . . In them hath he set a tabernacle for the sun, which is as a bridegroom coming out of his chamber, and rejoiceth as a strong man to run his course." That does not betray any lack of sympathy with the exuberant spirit of a lover. So Isa **62** 4.5: "For Jeh delighteth in thee, and thy land shall be married. For as a young man marrieth a virgin, so shall thy sons marry thee; and as the bridegroom rejoiceth over the bride, so shall thy God rejoice over thee." Language cannot more clearly disclose delight in the joy of those who are adjusting themselves under the "primal eldest" rule over sex: "Therefore shall a man leave his father and his mother, and shall cleave unto his wife: and they shall be one flesh" (Gen **2** 24).

It is sometimes thought strange that the Song of Songs should be in the Scripture Canon. But why should there be such doubt? It is but a more particular elaboration of what is boldly brought to notice in the quotations above. There is no more necessity of reading impurity into it than there is of reading it into the quotations above. The poem is illustrative of an experience as widely known as any in the life of the human race—an experience in which sin is no necessity. One must go out of his way who imputes sin to a single act or thought that comes to expression in the poem. The maiden is guileless and the lover is manly. The poem is said to be erotic. But the eros is idealized. It may be sensuous, but it is not sensual. It is not selfish. The passion of each finds expression in careful thoughtfulness for the other. It does not turn back to itself in coarse brute craving of lust for its own self-indulgence. The refrain of the poem is—

"I adjure you, O daughters of Jerusalem
. . . .
That ye stir not up, nor awake my love."
—Cant **2** 7; **3** 5; **8** 4.

The watchfulness is as tender as that for an infant. Where will the law lay its indictment of sin against such thoughts and feelings? The lovers are under the charm that has been and is to be from everlasting to everlasting with the human race upon the earth.

Christ at His strictest did not set Himself against the charm of love. He said it should be eternally single and true in spirit. The maiden in the song goes forth in the night, in the simplicity of her heart, to find her beloved (**3** 2 ff). In the same simplicity, Evangeline wandered all the night of her life to find the object of her affection,

From the same charm in the beginning came the faithfulness of Enoch Arden. Out of the love that springs from purity has come the integrity that has endured to the end. The exuberance of the charm, like every other spring of life and action, needs regulation, but the charm itself is not to be treated as sin.

5. Christ and Purity

Paul has said, "Ye are not under law, but under grace" (Rom **6** 14). But that depends upon the conditions to which it is applied. We may not be under the Levitical, ceremonial Law, but we are under the wide realm of ethical law always, even when we are under grace. What grace does is to idealize and spiritualize and make attractive and beautiful what before was perhaps hard, repellent statute and rule. Christ is sometimes thought to have relaxed the severity of "the reign of law." But six times even in the Sermon on the Mount He added to its strictness. Take the idea of the purity of the family as secured by its unity. Under the Mosaic legislation, certain not onerous forms of legal proceeding intervening, the termination of marriage might be said to be optional with the parties. All this liberty is swept away in one sentence: "I say unto you, Whosoever shall put away his wife, except for fornication, and shall marry another, committeth adultery" (Mt **19** 9). That is a law sentence. It was uttered in the realm of law. It was intended to have effect in law. No wonder, considering the liberty that had been allowed in the Law up to that time, that the disciples as soon as they got breath said, "If the case of a man is so with his wife, it is not expedient to marry." They knew that a new law for Christ's disciples was put over marriage. Even the exception confirmed His rule. If the exception is not allowed, polyandry or polygamy is established. No other sentence of human speech has done more for the purity of family life (see DIVORCE). But Christ did not stop with the utterance of law protective of purity physically; He went behind all acts and laid down law for the thoughts and intents of the heart: "But I say unto you, that every one that looketh on a woman to lust after her hath committed adultery with her already in his heart" (Mt **5** 28).

Sometimes it may be thought that there is a look of moral indifference about the way in which Jesus disposed of the woman's case who was taken in adultery (Jn **8** 1-11): "Did no man condemn thee? And she said, No man, Lord. And Jesus said, Neither do I condemn thee; go thy way; from henceforth sin no more." But it must first be remembered that it was not her case but that of her accusers that was immediately before the mind of Jesus. They brought her before Him to trap Him, but He turned and put them on trial. He made *their* moral condition the main issue. Hers was but an incident. But then, Jesus did not leave her without impressing on her mind that she was a sinner. The last words left ringing in her ears were, "Sin no more." And she was left, as all in sin are left, to wrestle out adjustment with the Holy Spirit who leaves no soul without conviction of "sin, righteousness and judgment." The words of Jesus no more than the words of anyone else can explain all things at once. They can cover a point in view, but much must always be left to the understanding that comes from known experience under the moral government of God.

The subsequent psychology of a sinner after the words of Scripture leave him is of deepest interest. Psychological action he must have had; what is it? The question arises, Had the prodigal son completed his repentance till he had asked the forgiveness of his mother and his elder brother? What is the subsequent psychology of a sinner as he disappears from our view? We can interpret here by what we know to be the operations of the Holy Spirit in the soul; just as we know a material object that disappears from view is still under the law of gravitation. Few who have thought on this subject have expressed the truth so well as Whittier in "Our Master," or in "John Underhill" in these words:

"And men took note of his gloomy air
The shame in his eye, the halt in his prayer,
The signs of a battle lost within,
The pain of a soul in the coils of sin.
. . . .
Into the desert alone rode he,
Alone with the Infinite Purity;
And bowing his soul to its tender rebuke,
As Peter did to the Master's look,
He measured his path with prayer of pain
For peace with God and nature again."

There is a recognition of the *burning with fire* that is infolded in the word "purity."

6. Paul

Paul is like his Master. He seeks for purity in this relation after marriage as well as before—purity of mind. In 1 Cor **7** we see how carefully and kindly Paul discoursed about all the complications in matters pertaining to sex. Then again, if Paul has exhorted wives to obedience to husbands, he has also called for equal self-surrender on the part of husbands (Eph **5** 22-32): "Husbands, love your wives, even as Christ also loved the church, and gave himself up for it." Can there be any self-surrender greater than that which Christ made? Here let attention rest on the fact that in his catalogue of the fruits of the Spirit (Gal **5** 22), if he has put "love" in the first place of emphasis among the nine, he has put "self-control" in the last.

We have only space for a glance at a few departments of action and thought to see what the world has gained in purity from the religion of the Bible. The age of chivalry ought to have a word put to its credit. The knights took the vow of chastity before the tribunals of the church. Take art—compare a Venus and a Madonna. Not only spirituality, but even intellectuality is wanting in a Venus. There is not a suggestion in a Venus that does not inhere in flesh and sense. Of what would she or could she speak if she were to open her mouth? To judge from her appearance, the utterance would be so "flat, stale and unprofitable" that even the charm of her physical beauty would disappear. In the Madonna you scarce see the physical. If she were to speak, her words would picture the peace and calm joy of a heavenly realm. If her countenance is suggestive of something far away, it is of something far above.

But art is not dead, and spiritual art did not die with the creation of the Madonna. Take St. Gaudens' "Puritan." Compare that with an Apollo. Again we have the contrast there is between a Madonna and a Venus. We have the physical and the aesthetic in an Apollo, but there is not a gleam of the intellectual. That Apollo thinks is not indicated, much less what he might be thinking about. There is not the faintest suggestion of the ethical. There is no intent and purpose in him. But in the Puritan there is intent and purpose. He means much. He is ethical. That determined bearing can only come from a spirit alive with the sense of *right*. When it comes to that, you will warrant that the Puritan carries more *physical* guns than the Apollo, and that if they were to clinch in a tug of wrestling Apollo would fall underneath. That ethical intent and purpose is *masterly*. You may look through a whole pantheon of Greek gods and meet not a trace of the force concentrated in the Puritan. He is forceful because right *makes* might. He is in the majority because he knows Who is with him. He is conscious of power because he has subdued the kingdom within. He has won the greatest of all victories—self-control.

C. CAVERNO

PURLOINING, pûr-loin'ing: Lit. "for far off," hence to carry away or steal; the word is the tr of νοσφίζομαι, *nosphízomai*, "to take away for one's self," "to secrete," "to steal," a word appropriate to those in the position of slaves in a master's service (Tit **2** 10, "not purloining").

PURPLE, pûr'p'l (אַרְגָּמָן, *'argāmān;* Chald אַרְגְּוָן, *'arg[e]wān* [2 Ch **2** 7]; cf Arab. أُرْجُوَان, *'urjuwân*, and Pers أَرْغَوَان, *'arghawân;* **πορφύρα,** *porphúra*, **πορφύρεος,** *porphúreos* [LXX and NT]):

Purple dye was manufactured by the Phoenicians from a marine mollusk, *Murex trunculus*. The shell was broken in order to give access to a small gland which was removed and crushed. The crushed gland gives a milky fluid that becomes red or purple on exposure to the air. Piles of these broken shells still remain on the coast at Sidon and Tyre. The purple gland is found in various species of *Murex* and also of *Purpura*.

Purple cloth was used in the furnishings of the tabernacle (Ex **25** 4, etc) and of Solomon's temple

(2 Ch **2** 14; **3** 14); in the palanquin of Solomon (Cant **3** 10); and in the hangings of the palace of Ahasuerus (Est **1** 6). The kings of Midian had purple raiment (Jgs **8** 26); the worthy woman of Prov **31** 22 has clothing of fine linen and purple. Mordecai was clothed with purple by Ahasuerus

Shells of *Murex trunculus* (the Broken Ones from a Large Shell Heap at Sidon).

(Est **8** 15); Jesus by the Rom soldiers (Mk **15** 17.20; Jn **19** 2.5). The rich man of Lk **16** 19 and the scarlet woman of Rev **18** 12.16 were arrayed in purple. In Cant **7** 5 the bride has hair like purple. Purple is in the merchandise of Babylon (Rev **18** 12). It is surprising that Ezekiel speaks of the Tyrians as obtaining purple from the isles of Elishah (Ezk **27** 7) and from Syria (Ezk **27** 16). See COLORS; DYE, DYEING.

ALFRED ELY DAY

PURPOSE, pûr'pus, **OF GOD** (**πρόθεσις,** *próthesis* [Rom **9** 11; Eph **1** 11]): The word "purpose" seems to be an equivalent of the word "decree" as used in regard to man's relation to eternity. More correctly stated, it softens the word "decree" and refers back to the cause of the decree as lodged in an intelligent design and forward to an aim consistent with the character of God. See FOREORDINATION; PREDESTINATION.

PURSE, pûrs. See BAG.

PURSLAIN, pûrs'lȧn, **JUICE,** jōōs, jūs. See JUICE.

PURTENANCE, pûr'tė̄-nans: With the significance of "belongings," this word occurs in AV of Ex **12** 9 as the tr of קֶרֶב, *ḳerebh*, "within," "inward," "roast . . . . with the purtenance thereof," RV "inwards" (cf Lev **1** 9; **3** 3, etc).

PUT, put (פּוּט, *pūṭ;* **Φούδ,** *Phoúd*, in Gen and Ch, variant for Gen **Φούτ,** *Phoút*, for Ch, **Φούθ,** *Phoúth*):

1. Renderings

In consequence of the identification at the time, the prophets have "Libya" (Λίβυες, *Líbues*), except Nah **3** 9, where the Gr renders the word as φυγή, *phugḗ*, "flight." The Vulg has "Phut," "Phuth," and in the Prophets "Libyes" and "Libya"; AV "Phut."

2. Son of Ham

In the "Table of Nations" Put is the third son of Ham (Gen **10** 6), the first and second being Cush and Misraim, and the fourth Canaan. Put is the only one of the sons of Ham who is not credited with descendants.

3. As Nationality

In the Prophets, warriors from Put are referred to, principally in connection with the forces of Egypt. They appear as shield-bearers (Jer **46** 9: "Cush and Put, that handle the shield; and the Ludim, that handle and bend the bow"). See also Ezk **30** 5, where the order in the Heb is Cush, Put and Lud. In Nah **3** 9 Put is the helper of No-amon (Thebes in Egypt), and in Ezk **27** 10 Put appears with Persia and Lydia (Lud) as being in the army of Tyre.

4. Identified with Punt

The common identification of Put is the Egyp *Punt* (or *Pwent*) proposed by Ebers. The assimilation of *n* to a following consonant is common in the Sem languages, and would occasion no difficulty if the vocalization be found to agree. The final *t* of Punt, however, seems to be the Egyp fem. ending, whereas the *ṭ* of Put is radical.

5. Somaliland and Yemen

Nevertheless, the district would seem to be rightly identified with the tract to the E. of Abyssinia (Somaliland), and as it is described as being on both sides of the sea (the Red Sea), Yemen would seem to be included. In connection with this, it is worthy of note that a fragment of a Bab tablet referring to Nebuchadrezzar's campaign in Egypt in his 37th year mentions, as though in the neighborhood, the city (here, apparently, standing for the district) of *Puṭu-yāman*—probably not "Ionian [Gr] Put" (Lesbos, according to Winckler), but "Put of Yemen." If this be in contradistinction to the district of Put (Punt) on the African mainland, the latter would be the *Pûṭu* referred to in the Pers inscription of Naqsh-i-Rustem, which mentions, among the tributary-countries, Kushiya, Putiya and Masiya, in Babylonian (*mât*) *Pûṭa*, [(*mât*) *K*]*ûšu*, (*mât*) *Massû*(?), "the land Put, the land Kush (Ethiopia), the land Massû(?)." The soldiers of Put in the army of Tyre may have been either from the African or the Yemenite Put, in which case there was no northern tract of that name, unless settlements had been made at any time from the original district. See W. Max Müller, *Asien und Europa*, Leipzig, 1893, 106 ff.

T. G. PINCHES

PUTEOLI, pū̆-tē'ō-lī (**Ποτίολοι,** *Potíoloi*, "sulphur springs" [Acts **28** 13, WH], the modern *Pozzuoli*): A maritime city of Campania, which occupied a central position on the northern shore of a recess in the Gulf of Naples, protected on the W. by the peninsula of Baiae and Cape Misenum. It was originally a colony of the neighboring Gr city Cumae.

The earliest event in the history of Puteoli which can be dated definitely was the repulse of Hannibal before its walls by a Rom garrison in 214 BC. The design of the Carthaginian to secure a seaport as base of supplies and communication was thus thwarted (Livy xxiv.7, 12, 13). A Rom colony was established here in 194 BC, and Puteoli thus became the first Rom port on the Gulf of Naples (Livy xxxiv.45; Strabo v.245; Velleius, i.15). Its subsequent remarkable prosperity and commercial activity are to be attributed to the safety of the harbor and the inhospitable character of the coast nearer Rome. For Puteoli became the chief seaport of the capital before the creation of an artificial harbor at Portus Augusti by Claudius, and before Trajan made the mouth of the Tiber the principal converging point for the over-sea carrying trade. The imports at Puteoli consisted mainly of Egyp grain and oriental wares, dispatched from Alexandria and other cities of the Levant (Cicero *Pro Rabirio* 40; Suetonius *Aug.* 98; Strabo xvii. 793; Cicero *Pro Caelio* 10). The eastern element in the population was very numerous (Petronius 81;

CIL, X, 1797). The harbor was rendered doubly safe by a mole, which is known to have been at least 418 yds. in length, consisting of massive piers connected by means of arches constructed in solid masonry (Strabo v.245). Extensive remains of this mole still exist. The shore line devoted to purposes of commerce (*emporium*) extended for a distance of about 1¼ miles westward from the mole. At the height of its prosperity under Claudius and Nero, the town is thought to have contained a population of nearly 100,000.

The region in which the town was situated is of volcanic formation, the name Puteoli being due to the odor of the sulphureous springs or to the wells of a volcanic nature which abound in the vicinity. The volcanic dust, called *pozzolana* today, was mixed with lime to form a cement of the greatest durability, which was proof against the influence of seawater.

Extensive remains of an amphitheater, whose axes measure 160 and 126 yds. across the space inclosed by the outer façade and 75 and 45 yds. within the arena, bear testimony to the former affluence of Puteoli.

The region about Puteoli together with Baiae became the favorite resort of the Rom nobility, and the foundations of many ancient villas are still visible, although partly covered by the sea. Cicero's villa in the territory of Puteoli (Cicero *Ad Fam.* v.15, 2; *Ad Att.* xiv.16, 1; 20, 1) was afterward selected as the place of burial of Hadrian (Spartianus *Had.* 25). The portion of the bay between Puteoli and Baiae was the scene of the attempt made at the instigation of Nero upon the life of his mother by means of a vessel so contrived that it was to break to pieces while conveying Agrippina toward her villa near the Lucrine Lake (Tacitus *Annals* xiv.8). See NERO.

The apostle Paul found a Christian community at Puteoli, when he arrived there on his way to Rome, and stopped 7 days with them (Acts **28** 13. 14). At that time the ordinary route to Rome, following the Via Appia from Capua, was 155 Rom, or about 142⅓ Eng., miles (Nissen, *Italische Landeskunde*, II, 739). Later, Domitian reduced the distance to 139 Rom miles (about 129 Eng.) by laying out the Via Domitia along the coast, joining the Via Appia at Sinuessa (*Geog. Raven.*, IV, 32; *Itin. Ant.*, 122; *Tab. Peut.*). GEORGE H. ALLEN

PUTHITES, pū'thīts (פּוּתִי, *pūthī*, "simple"; AV **Puhites**): One of the families of Kiriath-jearim, grandchildren of Caleb (1 Ch **2** 50.53).

PUTIEL, pū'ti-el (פּוּטִיאֵל, *pūṭī'ēl*, "contemned by El"): Father of the wife of Eleazar, Aaron's son, and thus grandfather of Phinehas, Eleazar's son (Ex **6** 25). See PHINEHAS, (3).

PUVAH, pū'va. See PUAH.

PYGARG, pī'gärg (דִּישֹׁן, *dīshōn;* LXX **πύγαργος**, *púgargos;* cf proper nouns, "Dishon" and "Dishan" [Gen **36** 21–30; 1 Ch **1** 38–42]; according to *BDB*, Hommel, *Säugethiere*, derives דִּישֹׁן from דּוּשׁ, *dūsh*, Arab. دَاسَ, *dâs*, "to tread," and cf Assyr *dashshu*, "mountain-goat"): *Dīshōn* as the name of an animal occurs only in Dt **14** 5 in the list of clean beasts. Both AV and RV have "pygarg," which is not the recognized name of any animal whatever. The LXX *pugargos* (from πυγή, *pugḗ*, "rump," and ἀργός, *argós*, "white") was used by Herodotus (iv.192) as the name of an antelope. A white rump is a very common feature of deer and antelopes, and is commonly explained as enabling the fleeing herd easily to keep in sight of its leaders. It has been used as a specific name of *Cervus pygargus*, the Tartarian roe, and *Bubalis pygargus*, a small South African antelope. The Arabic Bible has *ri'm*, "a white gazelle," a kindred word to *r*e*'ēm*, AV "unicorn," RV "wild-ox." Tristram, *NHB*, considers *dīshōn* to be the addax, *Antilope addax* or *Addax nasomaculatus*. There is excellent reason, however, for believing that the range of this African antelope does not extend into Pal, Sinai or Arabia. For a discussion of the animal names in Dt **14** 4.5, see ZOÖLOGY.

ALFRED ELY DAY

PYRAMID, pir'a-mid (**πυραμίς**, *puramís*): Pyramids are mentioned in connection with the splendid monument reared by Simon Maccabaeus in memory of his parents and brethren at Modin (1 Macc **13** 28; cf *Ant*, XIII, vi, 6). Jos describes them as "very surprising, both for their largeness and beauty." There is nothing to show how the pyramid allotted to each was distinguished, whether by difference in size or by inscriptions. It is remarkable that in Scripture there is no allusion to the giant structures in Egypt; but these may have supplied the suggestion to Simon's mind.

W. EWING

PYRRHUS, pir'us (**Πύρρος**, *Púrros*, "fiery-red"): The name is inserted in the text of RV in Acts **20** 4 as that of the father of SOPATER (q.v.).

PYTHON, pī'thon: Occurs only in Acts **16** 16, where RV reads, "a certain maid having a spirit of divination [m "a spirit, a Python"] met us." Πύθων, *Púthōn*, or Πυθώ, *Puthṓ*, is the oldest name of Delphi (or the country about Delphi), in which was situated the famous Delphic Oracle. Consequently "Pythian spirit" came to be the generic title of the supposed source of inspiration of diviners, including the slave-girl of the account in Acts. Exactly what facts underlie the narrative it is rather hard to say, but it is evident that the girl was sincere in her conviction that she spoke with Pythian inspiration. Probably she represents some hysterical type, of none too strong mentality, whose confused utterances were taken as coming from some supernatural power. Impressed by St. Paul's personality, she followed him about, and, when his command came, was in a state of mind that had prepared her to obey it. The narrative, incidentally, gives an interesting sidelight on a society in which a girl with hysteria had a greater commercial value than she had after her cure. See DIVINATION. BURTON SCOTT EASTON

Q

QOPH, kôf (ק, *ḳ*). See Ḳōph.

QUAIL, kwāl (שְׂלָו, *s^elāw;* **ὀρτυγομήτρα,** *ortugomētra;* Lat *Coturnix vulgaris*): A game bird of the family *Coturnix,* closely related to "partridges" (q.v.). Quail and partridges are near relatives, the partridge a little larger and of brighter color. Quail are like the gray, brown and tan of earth. Their plumage is cut and penciled by markings, and their flesh juicy and delicate food. Their habits are very similar. They nest on the ground and brood on from 12 to 20 eggs. The quail are more friendly

Quail.

birds and live in the open, brooding along roads and around fields. They have a longer, fuller wing than the partridge and can make stronger flight. In Pal they were migratory. They are first mentioned in Ex **16** 13: "And it came to pass at even, that the quails came up, and covered the camp: and in the morning the dew lay round about the camp." This describes a large flock in migration, so that they passed as a cloud. Nu **11** 31–33: "And there went forth a wind from Jeh, and brought quails from the sea, and let them fall by the camp, about a day's journey on this side, and a day's journey on the other side, round about the camp, and about two cubits above the face of the earth. And the people rose up all that day, and all the night, and all the next day, and gathered the quails: he that gathered least gathered ten homers: and they spread them all abroad for themselves round about the camp"; cf Ps **78** 26–30:

"He caused the east wind to blow in the heavens;
And by his power he guided the south wind.
He rained flesh also upon them as the dust,
And winged birds as the sand of the seas:
And he let it fall in the midst of their camp,
Round about their habitations.
So they did eat, and were well filled;
And he gave them their own desire."

Again the birds are mentioned in migration. Those that fell around the camp and the bread that was sent from heaven are described in Ps **105** 39–42. Commentators have had trouble with the above references. They cause the natural historian none —they are so in keeping with the location and the laws of Nature. First the Heb *s^elāw* means "to be fat." That would be precisely the condition of the quail after a winter of feeding in the S. The time was early spring, our April, and the quail were flocking from Africa and spreading in clouds—even to Europe. They were birds of earth, heavy feeders and of plump, full body. Migration was such an effort that when forced to cross a large body of water they always waited until the wind blew in the direction of their course, lest they tire and fall. Their average was about 16 birds to each nest. If half a brood escaped, they yet multiplied in such numbers as easily to form clouds in migration. Pliny writes of their coming into Italy in such numbers, and so exhausted with their long flight, that if they sighted a sailing vessel they settled upon it by hundreds and in such numbers as to sink it. Taking into consideration the diminutive vessels of that age and the myriads of birds, this does not appear incredible. Now compare these facts with the text. Israelites were encamped on the Sinai Peninsula. The birds were in migration. The quail followed the Red Sea until they reached the point of the peninsula where they selected the narrowest place, and when the wind was with them they crossed the water. Not far from the shore arose the smoke from the campfires of the Israelites. This bewildered them, and, weary from their journey, they began to settle in confused thousands over and around the camp. Then the Israelites arose and, with the ever-ready "throw sticks," killed a certain number for every soul of the camp and spread the bodies on the sand to dry, just as Herodotus (ii.77) records that the Egyptians always had done (see Rawlinson, *Herod,* II, for an illustration of catching and drying quail). Nature and natural history can account for this incident, with no need to call in the miraculous.

Gene Stratton-Porter

QUARREL, kwor′el: Originally (1) "a complaint" (cf "querulous"), or (2) "a cause of complaint," and so (3) "a contention." (1) In AV Mk **6** 19 (RV "set herself"; the colloquial "had it in for him" is an exact tr) and Col **3** 13 (*μομφή,* *momphē,* "complaint"; so RV). (2) In 2 K **5** 7 (אָנָה, *'ānāh,* "be opportune," RVm "an occasion"). (3) In AV Lev **26** 25 (loose tr of נָקָם, *nāḳām,* "vengeance"; so RV). Cf Sir **31** 29 AV (RV "conflict") and Prov **20** 3 RV (AV "meddling").

QUARRIES, kwor′iz (פְּסִילִים, *p^esīlīm* [Jgs **3** 19.26, "graven images"], שְׁבָרִים, *sh^ebhārīm* [Josh **7** 5, "Shebarim," RVm "the quarries"]):

P^esīlīm is elsewhere tr^d "graven images" (Dt **7** 5; Ps **78** 58; Isa **10** 10; Mic **5** 13, etc) and is a pl. form of *pesel,* "graven image" (Ex **20** 4, etc), from *pāsal,* "to carve." It occurs in the story of Ehud and Eglon and refers to images or hewn stones in the vicinity of Gilgal. *Sh^ebhārīm* is pl. of *shēbher,* "breach," "fracture," more often "destruction" (e.g. Prov **16** 18), from *shābhar,* "to break." The form *sh^ebhārīm* is also found in Job **41** 25, "consternation," AV "breakings." In Josh **7** 5 Shebarim is the point to which the Israelites were chased after their first attack upon Ai. See Shebarim.

Quarries in Pal are not usually very deep because there is plenty of good stone to be found at the surface. The quarryman seeks a thick stratum of firm limestone which has a favorable exposure. The vertical joint-planes divide the stratum into large blocks which the quarryman dislodges with the aid of crowbars. These great blocks he skilfully cleaves by inserting several wedges in a line in holes made by a pick, and driving the wedges in with a heavy hammer. In these days gunpowder is occasionally used, esp. when there are not favorable joint-planes producing blocks capable of being moved by the crowbar.

Another method, which is employed where stones of great size are wanted, is to carve the stones out of the rock by cutting channels around them with the pick. In the limestone quarries of *Ba'albek* and the granite quarries of *Aṣwân* at the first cataract of the Nile, enormous stones may be seen which were abandoned while in process of being removed by this method. The channels are wide enough to admit the body of the workman, and the marks of the picks on the sides of the channels are plainly visible. ALFRED ELY DAY

QUARTER, kwôr'tẽr: Lit., of course, "the fourth part," and so of the four "ends" (קָצָה, *ķāçāh*) in Jer **49** 36, and AV of the four "corners" (so RV, γωνία, *gōnía*) in Rev **20** 8. Hence, "any part" and in this sense used freely for various words by AV. RV has usually dropped "quarter," but unfortunately has retained it in Nu **34** 3; Josh **15** 5; **18** 14.15, and introduced it in Josh **18** 12.14.20 for פֵּאָה, *pē'āh*, usually rendered "side." The result is very obscure. Elsewhere in RV only in the phrase "from every quarter" (Gen **19** 4; Isa **56** 11; Mk **1** 45). Cf BORDER; COAST.

QUARTUS, kwôr'tus (**Κούαρτος,** *Koúartos*): A Christian in Corinth who with "Erastus the treasurer of the city" sent greetings to the Christian community in Rome (Rom **16** 23). He is known to Paul only as a Christian, "the brother."

QUATERNION, kwa-tûr'ni-un (**τετράδιον,** *tetrádion*): The name given to a company of four soldiers of Herod's army (Acts **12** 4). To four such companies St. Peter had been handed over, who would take their turn of acting as guard over the prisoner, each of the four watches of the night according to Rom reckoning, which Herod Agrippa I would follow. In the castle of Antonia St. Peter was thus closely secured, in order that Herod, who had already killed James, the brother of John, with the sword (**12** 2), might, after the solemnities of the Passover, make sure of his death likewise. On the night before his intended execution he was sleeping in his cell between two soldiers, "bound with two chains," his left hand chained to one and his right to the other. The other two soldiers of the quaternion mounted guard before the door, and are spoken of as "the first and the second guard" (ver 10) whom St. Peter and his angel guide had to pass on the way to liberty. The Gr word thus rendered is not found in LXX or anywhere else in the NT.

T. NICOL

STONE IN QUARRIES AT BA'ALBEK.

QUEEN, kwēn: The Bible applies this term: (1) To the wife of a king ("queen consort") (מַלְכָּה, *malkāh*). In the Book of Est it is the title given to Vashti (**1** 9) and Esther (**2** 22); cf Cant **6** 8 f. Another Heb word for queen consort is גְּבִירָה, *g^ebhīrāh*, lit. "mistress" (cf 1 K **11** 19, the wife of Pharaoh; 2 K **10** 13, "the children of the king and the children of the queen"). In Neh **2** 6 and Ps **45** 9 we find the expression שֵׁגַל, *shēghāl*, which some trace back to שָׁגַל, *shāghal*, "to ravish," a rather doubtful derivation. Still another term is שָׂרָה, *sārāh*, lit. "princess" (Isa **49** 23). The LXX sometimes uses the word βασίλισσα, *basílissa;* cf Ps **45** 9. (2) To a female ruler or sovereign ("queen regnant"). The only instances are those of the queen (*malkāh*) of Sheba (1 K **10** 1-13; cf 2 Ch **9** 1-12) and of Candace, the queen (*basilissa*) of the Ethiopians (Acts **8** 27). In Mt **12** 42 (cf Lk **11** 31) Christ refers to the queen of the south (βασίλισσα νότου, *basílissa nótou*), meaning, of course, the queen of Sheba. (3) To a heathen deity, מְלֶכֶת הַשָּׁמַיִם, *m^elekheth ha-shāmayim*, "the queen of heaven" (Jer **7** 18; **44** 17 ff). See QUEEN OF HEAVEN.

(4) **Metaphorically,** to the city of Babylon (Rome) (Rev **18** 7): an expression denoting sovereign contempt and imaginary dignity and power. WILLIAM BAUR

QUEEN MOTHER (גְּבִירָה, *g^ebhīrāh*, lit. "mistress," then a female ruler, and sometimes simply the wife of a king ["queen," 1 K **11** 19]; in Dnl **5** 10 the term מַלְכְּתָא, *malk^{e}thā'*, "queen," really means the mother of the king): It stands to reason that among a people whose rulers are polygamists the mother of the new king or chief at once becomes a person of great consequence. The records of the Books of K prove it. The *g^{e}bhīrāh*, or queen mother, occupied a position of high social and political importance; she took rank almost with the king. When Bath-sheba, the mother of Solomon, desired "to speak unto him for Adonijah," her son "rose up to meet her, and bowed himself unto her, and sat down on his throne, and caused a throne to be set for the king's mother; and she sat on his right hand" (1 K **2** 19). And again, in 2 K **24** 15, it is expressly stated that Nebuchadnezzar carried away the king's mother into captivity; Jeremiah calls her *g^{e}bhīrāh* (**29** 2). The king was Jehoiachin (Jeconiah, Jer **29** 2), and his mother's name was Nehushta (2 K **24** 8). This was the royal pair whose impending doom the prophet was told to forecast (Jer **13** 18). Here again the queen mother is mentioned with the king, thus emphasizing her exalted position. Now we understand why Asa removed Maacah his (grand?) mother from being queen (queen mother), as we are told in 1 K **15** 13 (cf 2 Ch **15** 16). She had used her powerful influence to further the cause of idolatry. In this connection Athaliah's *coup d'état* may be briefly mentioned. After the violent death of her son Ahaziah (2 K **9** 27), she usurped the royal power and reigned for some time in her own name (2 K **11** 3; cf 2 Ch **22** 12). This was, of course, a revolutionary undertaking, being a radical departure from the usual traditions.

And finally, the political importance of the *g^{e}bhīrāh* is illustrated by the fact that in the Books of K, with two exceptions, the names of the Jewish kings are recorded together with those of their respective mothers; they are as follows: Naamah, the Ammonitess, the mother of Rehoboam (1 K **14** 21; cf ver 31, and 2 Ch **12** 13); Maacah, the daughter of Abishalom (1 K **15** 2) or Absalom (2 Ch **11** 20), the mother of Abijah; Maacah, the daughter of Abishalom, the mother (grandmother?) of Asa (1 K **15** 10; cf 2 Ch **15** 16); Azubah, the daughter of Shilhi, the mother of Jehoshaphat (1 K **22** 42; cf 2 Ch **20** 31); Athaliah, the granddaughter of Omri, the mother of Ahaziah (2 K **8** 26; cf 2 Ch **22** 2); Zibiah of Beersheba, the mother of Jehoash (2 K **12** 1; cf 2 Ch **24** 1); Jehoaddin (Jehoaddan, 2 Ch **25** 1) of Jerus, the mother of Amaziah (2 K **14** 2); Jecoliah (Jechiliah, 2 Ch **26** 3) of Jerus, the mother of Azariah (2 K **15** 2) or Uzziah (2 K **15** 13.30, etc; cf 2 Ch **26** 3); Jerusha (Jerushah, 2 Ch **27** 1), the daughter of Zadok, the mother of Jotham (2 K **15** 33); Abi (Abijah, 2 Ch **29** 1), the daughter of Zechariah, the mother of Hezekiah (2 K **18** 2); Hephzibah, the mother of Manasseh (2 K **21** 1); Meshullemeth, the daughter of Haruz of Jotbah, the mother of Amon (2 K **21** 19); Jedidah, the daughter of Adaiah of Bozkath, the mother of Josiah (2 K **22** 1); Hamutal, the daughter of Jeremiah of Libnah, the mother of Jehoahaz (2 K **23** 31); Zebidah, the daughter of Pedaiah of Rumah, the mother of Jehoiakim (2 K **23** 36); Nehushta, the daughter of Elnathan of Jerus, the mother of Jehoiachin (2 K **24** 8); Hamutal (Hamital), the daughter of Jeremiah of Libnah, the mother of Zedekiah (2 K **24** 18). The exceptions are Jehoram and Ahaz.

William Baur

QUEEN OF HEAVEN (מְלֶכֶת הַשָּׁמַיִם, *m^{e}lekheth ha-shāmayim*, although there is another reading, מְלֶאכֶת, *m^{e}le'kheth*, "worship" or "goddess"): Occurs only in two passages: Jer **7** 18; **44** 17–19.25, where the prophet denounces the wrath of God upon the inhabitants of Judah and Jerus who have given themselves up to the worship of the host of heaven. This is no doubt a part of the astral worship which is found largely developed among the Jews in the later period of their history in Canaan. It is first mentioned in 2 K **17** 16 as practised by the men of the Northern Kingdom when Samaria had fallen and the ten tribes were being carried away into captivity. Moses is represented as warning the Israelites against the worship of the sun and moon and stars and all the host of heaven, practised by the people of Canaan (Dt **4** 19; **17** 3), and the existence of such worship among the Canaanites and neighboring nations is attested from an early period (cf Job **31** 26–28). The worship of the heavenly bodies was widely spread in the East and in Arabia; and the Bab pantheon was full of astral deities, where each divinity corresponded either to an astral phenomenon or to some circumstance or occurrence in Nature which is connected with the course of the stars (Jeremias, *The OT in the Light of the Ancient East*, I, 100). From the prophets we gather that before the exile the worship of the host of heaven had become established among all classes and in all the towns of Israel (Jer *ubi supra;* Ezk **8** 16). In that worship the queen of heaven had a conspicuous place; and if, as seems probable from the cakes which were offered, she is to be identified with the Assyr Ishtar and the Canaanite Astarte, the worship itself was of a grossly immoral and debasing character. That this Ishtar cult was of great antiquity and widely spread in ancient Babylonia may be seen from the symbols of it found in recent excavations (see *Nippur*, II, 236). How far the astral theorists like Winckler and Jeremias are entitled to link up with this worship the mourning for Josiah, the lamentations over Tammuz, the story of Jephthah's daughter, and even the narrative of the misfortunes and the exaltation of Joseph, is questionable. But that the people of Judah in the days before the exile had given themselves over to the worst and vilest forms of heathen worship and incurred the grievous displeasure of Jeh is made clear by the denunciation of the worship of the queen of heaven by Jeremiah.

T. Nicol

QUEEN OF SHEBA, shē'ba (1 K **10** 1–13; 2 Ch **9** 1–12, called in Mt **12** 42; Lk **11** 31, "the queen of the south" [βασίλισσα νότου, *basílissa nótou*]):

1. OT Accounts

The two OT accounts of the coming of the queen of Sheba (see Sheba) to Solomon differ slightly from one another, and, of the two, that in 1 K is the older. (1) The words "concerning the name of Jeh" (1 K **10** 1) are wanting in 2 Ch; while LXX in 1 K has "and the name of Jeh," apparently a correction of the MT. (2) For 1 K **10** 9, "because Jeh loved Israel for ever," 2 Ch **9** 8 has "because thy God loved Israel, to establish them for ever"; LXX in 1 K has "because Jeh loved Israel, to establish it for ever." (3) In the last verse of each account, we find another difference: 2 Ch **9** 12 says that Solomon gave to the queen all her desire, "besides that which she had brought unto the king," i.e. according to some, besides the equivalent of what she had brought to him; 1 K **10** 13 m has "besides that which he gave her according to the hand of king Solomon," i.e. besides gifts commensurate with his own wealth and power (*SBOT*), or besides gifts which he gave her *quâ* king.

2. The Narrative

The narrative tells of the queen of Sheba, on hearing of Solomon's great wisdom, coming to test him with perplexing questions or riddles (cf Jgs **14** 12). She brought presents to the king, and interviewed him: "And when the queen of Sheba had seen all the wisdom of Solomon, and the house that he had built" (i.e. the palace, not the temple) as well as its arrangements, "and his burnt-offering which he offered in the house of Jeh [so read and translate with RVm in 1 K **10** 5, and also in 2 Ch **9** 4]; there was no more spirit in her": the half of Solomon's wisdom had not been told her. "Happy," she said to him, "are thy wives [so read with LXX, Syr and Old Lat VSS], happy are these thy servants." She then exchanged gifts with him and returned to her own land.

The narrative is a complement of that in 1 K **3** 16–28, where the king's justice is exemplified; here his wisdom.

3. Employed by Jesus

The narrative is referred to by Jesus in Mt **12** 42; Lk **11** 31, where He refuses to accede to the request of the scribes and Pharisees for a sign from Him. He tells them that no sign will be given them except that of Jonah, whose sign was his preaching, one that proved sufficient to the Ninevites; and 'behold something greater than Jonah is here.' The men of Nineveh will be a living condemnation of them "in the judgment" (cf Lk **16** 31); and so will the "queen of the south" who came from the ends of the earth after hearing of Solomon's wisdom, 'and behold something greater than Solomon is here.' The only sign to be given is that of the wisdom of Jesus, a wisdom far greater than that of Solomon (see D. Smith, *Days of His Flesh*, 176 ff).

4. Eastern Literature

Eastern lit. has much to say about the queen of Sheba. The Arabs called her Bilḳis. Abyssinian legend declares that she came from Ethiopia, her name being Maḳeda, and that she had a son by Solomon. See Delitzsch, *Iris*, 116–27; *ZDMG*, X, 19 f; *J Pr T*, VI, 524 ff (1880). Gressmann (in *Schriften des AT*, II, 1, 203) has further references to Wilhelm Hertz, *Gesammelte Abhandlungen*, 1905, 413 ff; Bezold, *Kebra Nagast*, 1905, and also *ZDMG*, 60, 666 ff. For the Mohammedan story, see Koran xxvii, with notes in Sale's tr.

David Francis Roberts

QUENCH, kwench, kwensh: Where the word is used of fire or of thirst it has the usual meaning: "to allay," "to extinguish," "to suppress," "to cool." In the OT it is frequently applied to the affections and passions (see 2 K **22** 17; Cant **8** 7; Isa **42** 3; Jer **4** 4; **21** 12). Quenching the coal or the light of Israel may mean slaying a dear one or a brilliant leader. In the NT it is also used **figuratively,** as in Eph **6** 16 the shield of faith quenches the fiery darts of the evil one. In Mk **9** 48, σβέννυμι, *sbénnumi*, and its derivative are applied with reference to Gehenna (tr[d] "hell"). The same word is also used of resisting the gifts of the Holy Spirit in 1 Thess **5** 19.

G. H. Gerberding

QUESTION, kwes'chun: The noun for דָּבָר, *dābhār*, "word," in 1 K **10** 3 ‖ 2 Ch **9** 2, with "hard question" for חִידָה, *ḥīdhāh*, "dark saying," "riddle," in 1 K **10** 1 ‖ 2 Ch **9** 1. In the NT for ζήτημα, *zḗtēma*, the synonym ζήτησις, *zḗtēsis* (and 1 Tim **1** 4, ἐκζήτησις, *ekzḗtēsis*), being rendered "questionings" by RV (AV does not distinguish). In Mk **11** 29 for λόγος, *lógos*, "word" (so RVm). The vb. in the sense "ask a question" in 2 Ch **31** 9 for דָּרַשׁ, *dārash*, and Lk **2** 46; **23** 9 for ἐπερωτάω, *eperōtáō* (cf ARV, ERVm Jn **16** 23). Elsewhere the vb. is for συζητέω, *suzētéō*, "dispute" (Mk **1** 27, etc; cf Acts **6** 9; **9** 29). "Called in question," Acts **19** 40 AV, represents ἐγκαλέω, *egkaléō*, "call into court," but in **23** 6; **24** 21, "I am called in question" is for κρίνομαι, *krínomai*, "I am being judged."

Burton Scott Easton

QUICK, kwik, **QUICKEN,** kwik''n: Translates in AV four different words: (1) חָיָה, *ḥāyāh*, (2) מִחְיָה, *miḥyāh*, (3) רוּחַ, *rūaḥ*, and (4) ζάω, *záō*. Of these words (1) and (4) had simply the sense of life, and this idea was in 1611 adequately given by the word "quick," although this sense of the word has long been somewhat obscured. As the tr of *rūaḥ* (Isa **11** 3) "quick" as found in AV signified "acute." In this passage RV substitutes "delight" for "quick understanding." In Lev **13** 10.24 RV retains the rendering "quick," although originally the word *miḥyāh* must in some way have involved the conception of life, which no longer belongs to the Eng. word "quick." It is not clear exactly in what sense the flesh in the sore or scar was thought of as living, esp. as it was plainly regarded as in an unhealthy condition. Possibly the condition under consideration resembled what is sometimes idiomatically styled in Eng. "proud flesh," and was thought of as a peculiar manifestation of life.

To quicken also means a reviving, a refreshing, an increasing of life (Ps **71** 20; **85** 6; **119** 37.40. 88; Isa **57** 10). It often has reference to the resurrection from the dead (1 Cor **15** 36) and is so used in many places in AV. Where it refers to the giving of spiritual life ARV has changed it in every case (Eph **2** 1.5; Col **2** 13; cf Jn **5** 21).

David Foster Estes

QUICKSANDS, kwik'sandz. See Syrtis.

QUIET, kwī'et: Vb. or adj. only in EV, "quietness" being used for the noun. No special Heb or Gr words are represented, but in the OT usually for some form or derivative of שָׁקַט, *shāḳaṭ*, "be undisturbed" (Jgs **18** 7; cf Prov **1** 33, שָׁאַר, *shā'ar*, "to loll," "be at ease"; Eccl **9** 17, נַחַת, *naḥath*, "quiet," "be set on"). For "them that are quiet in the land" in Ps **35** 20, see Meek; Poor. For "quiet prince" in Jer **51** 59, RV substitutes "chief chamberlain," m "quartermaster." "Jacob was a quiet [תָּם, *tām*, "gentle"] man" (Gen **25** 27, AV "plain"). In the NT, it is the tr of ἡσυχάζω, *hēsucházō*, "to refrain from gossip or meddlesomeness": "that ye study to be quiet" (1 Thess **4** 11), and of ἡσύχιος, *hēsúchios*, "gentle": "a meek and quiet spirit" (1 Pet **3** 4; cf 1 Tim **2** 2).

M. O. Evans

QUINTUS MEMMIUS, kwin'tus mem'i-us. See Memmius, Quintus.

QUIRINIUS, kwi-rin'i-us. See Chronology of the NT, I, 1, (2); Luke, Gospel of, 5.

QUIT, kwit: Same derivation as "quiet," so that "to be quit" (Ex **21** 19.28; Josh **2** 20 AV) is "to be relieved of responsibility," נָקָה, *nāḳāh*, נָקִי, *nāḳī*, "guiltless" (so RV Josh **2** 20). Hence "to quit one's self" means "to be freed by discharging a duty." The phrase in EV, however, is a gloss, for in 1 S **4** 9 it is used for הָיָה, *hāyāh*, "to be," while in 1 Cor **16** 13 ἀνδρίζομαι, *andrízomai*, means "to behave like a man."

QUIVER, kwiv'ẽr (אַשְׁפָּה, *'ashpāh*, תְּלִי, *t^elī*; φαρέτρα, *pharétra* [Sir **26** 12]): A case or sheath for carrying arrows, a part of the ordinary equipment of the warrior, both foot-soldier and charioteer (Job **39** 23; Isa **22** 6), and also of the huntsman (Gen **27** 3). **Figuratively** of a group in passages where children (Ps **127** 5) or prophets of Jeh (Isa **49** 2) are spoken of as arrows. Arrows are called *b^enē 'ashpāh*, "sons of the quiver" (Lam **3** 13). By identifying the arrows with the death they produce, the quiver is likened to an open sepulcher (Jer **5** 16).

QUOTATIONS, kwō-tā'shunz, **NEW TESTAMENT:**

I. Introductory
Limitation of the Discussion

I. Introductory.—There are, all told, approximately 300 direct quotations from the OT in the NT. The presence of so many citations, each one of which involves an interpretation of the passage given a new context in quotation, opens many avenues of discussion and propounds many difficult and far-reaching problems. In every separate instance, in the long list of NT quotations, the principle of accommodation (see Accommodation) in some form is involved, and, consequently, the question of historical and exegetical accuracy is unavoidably raised. In the present article we shall concentrate attention upon that which is of far greater importance than the question whether the writer is incidentally correct, according to modern scientific principles, in any specific citation. This more important and vital issue we take to be the *general, guiding principles* adopted by the NT writers in their use of the book of the older covenant. A review of these principles, together with certain outstanding and typical instances in which these principles are used and applied, will form the substance of the discussion.

Limitation of the Discussion

II. Constructive Principles of NT Quotation.—In the first place, the NT writers regard the Christian religion as having its roots in the OT. From the call of Abraham to the founding and expansion of the Christian church the men of the NT recognize a single organic movement. In their use of the ancient oracles in new setting they constantly and confidently rely upon the unity of the two dispensations, that recorded in the OT and that in which they themselves were participants. Such a unity, taking for granted its existence, would remove to a degree the very distinction implied in the terms Old and New Testaments, and would involve a definite and organic relationship of all the books to each other. There are no longer two separate groups of books standing apart from each other and having bonds of union only within the group, but, on the contrary, two related sub-groups outwardly corresponding to contrasted phases of the historical movement, but inwardly conformed to the deep-lying principles which make the entire movement one. According to this idea the Book of Gen is as really related to the Gospel of Mt as it is to the Book of Ex. On the surface, and historically speaking, the Book of Gen leads immediately to the Book of Ex, which is its companion volume and complement, but go more deeply into Gen and just as really and just as directly it leads to Mt, which is also its fellow and complement. And so throughout. The unifying medium is, of course, the history which is one in that it involves the same organic principles applied to successive areas of human experience. The books of the Bible are, therefore, like any group of books on a common subject, phases of each other, contrasted and yet intimately cognate. In quoting from the OT the NT writers were simply obeying an impulse common to all thoughtful writers and accounting for all quotations, seeking for diversified expression of the same truths.

1. Unity of the Two Dispensations

The second great constructive principle of NT quotation, and manifestly in close harmony with the first one, is that the movement from Abraham to Christ was not only organically one, but that it was from the beginning planned and prepared for. The Bible is one because the history out of which it grew is one. The history is one because God is in the history and God is one. According to the writers of the NT in this history as a whole we have the unfolding of an all-embracing plan of God, stretching out into the remotest future and coming to its culmination in the person and the kingdom of the Messiah. They maintain also that this plan was disclosed in part beforehand, by way of anticipation and preparation, in order that men might intelligently coöperate with God in the fulfilment of His purpose. This is the idea involved in prophecy and its fulfilment, and in the closely related idea of promise and its realization. One mind, one will, and one central purpose are operating throughout the entire history which is, on the Divine side, the fulfilment of a plan complete in thought before it takes shape in events. On the basis of this conception, of the foreseen plan of God and its gradual revelation to men through messages of hope and warning set in the key of the great future and pointing the way thither, the greater part of the structure of NT quotation is reared.

2. Biblical Movement Planned from the Beginning

A third principle which really involves a combination of the other two and is prominently brought forward in the use of quotation for purposes of argument is the recognition and acceptance of the OT as authoritative, a real Word of God, in form occasional, but essentially applicable to all experiences, and hence good for all time. It is evident that the belief in the continued authority of the Scripture of the old covenant over the men of the new, rests upon the unity of the two dispensations and the acceptance of the same Divine mind and will as operating throughout all outward and historical changes. This is admirably expressed by Paul when he speaks of 'the mystery of his will, according to his good pleasure which he purposed in him unto an economy of the fulness of the periods, to sum up all things in Christ' (Eph **1** 9.10), and by the author of He when he says: 'God, having of old spoken unto the fathers in the prophets by various portions and in various ways, hath at the end of these days spoken unto us in his Son' (**1** 1.2).

3. The OT Accepted as Authoritative

The justification of these accepted principles of reference on the part of the NT writers lies beyond the scope of the present discussion. It is sufficient to emphasize the fact that any detailed discussion of NT quotations seriatim is meaningless and futile except upon the basis of an explicit and consistent determination of these antecedent questions. To the present writer the validity of these principles is beyond question. The denial of any one of the three involves one in difficulties of interpretation, both critical and historical, from which there is no escape. It is to be noted, therefore, that the establishment of the principles, in accordance with which the NT writers quote, carries with it in a general way the justification of their usage.

4. Issue Involved in Foregoing Principles of Reference

III. Typical Instances of NT Quotation.—With these constructive principles in mind we are prepared to pass in review typical instances in which general principles are embodied. At this point we shall be greatly assisted in the analysis and distribution of the complex material before us by giving careful heed to the formulas, more or less fixed and uniform, by which the writers introduce quotations and indicate their sense of the value and significance of that which is quoted. While these formulas exhibit certain verbal variations, they are practically reducible to three, which correspond with substantial accuracy to the three constructive principles already noted: the unity of the OT and NT; the prevision of the NT in the OT; the authority of the OT as the Word of God intended for all time.

1. Introductory Formulas

The unity of the two dispensations is asserted in all those passages introduced by a formula, in which fulfilment is asserted as a fact, and in which the operation of identical principles in two or more separate events in the field of history is implied. A suggestive example is in Mt **13** 14, where Our Lord asserts, in connection with the parable of the Sower, that in the unbelief of the people of His day "the prophecy of Isaiah" is fulfilled. The prophetic words here quoted (Isa **6** 9.10) are not predictive in any immediate sense, but are susceptible of repeated application and realization because of the general principle which they contain. They apply to the prophet's own day; they also apply—and in that sense are fulfilled—to the time of Jesus, and by a legitimate extension of meaning, to stubborn unbelief in any age (cf Jn **6** 45).

2. Unity of the Two Dispensations

Another passage in which the same formula is used in a very exceptional way clearly sets forth the fundamental principle upon which this usage rests. Jas **2** 23 asserts that the justification of Abraham in the offering of Isaac "fulfilled" the passage which affirms that his belief was counted to him for righteousness (Gen **15** 6). This passage is not predictive in any sense, nor is there in the narrative any hint of a connection between the passage and the episode on Mt. Moriah. This use of the formula of fulfilment by James involves the principle that any event which realizes the meaning and truth of a Scriptural statement fulfils it. A vast number of quotations in the NT come under this head. Persons, events, doctrines, illustrate and confirm, or embody and concretely realize, principles which are taught in the OT or implied in its history. We are warned by this passage and many others like it against a too rigid and literal interpretation of any formula implying fulfilment. While it may certainly be intended to imply literal prediction and an equally literal fulfilment, it may, on the contrary, be intended to intimate nothing more than a harmony of principle, fitting the passage to the person or event with which it is connected. In this connection it is to be remembered that a harmony of principle may extend all the way from a comparatively superficial illustrative resemblance to a profound assonance of thought. Not a few OT quotations were made for purposes of illustration and literary embellishment. Herein lies the significance of Matthew's use (**2** 17 f) of Jer **31** 15. A glance at this quoted passage indicates that it is a figurative and poetic expression in which Rachel (already for many years in her tomb) is represented as weeping for her exiled children and refusing to be comforted except by their return. There is no strictly predictive element in the passage, save only the promise of return, which is not used by Matthew. Its applicability to the massacre of the children of Bethlehem lies in its poetical appositeness, and there alone. Once again the voice of wailing motherhood is heard in Israel. The tender and beautiful imagery is applicable in this sense and is used with true insight, but with no intention of justifying a claim of prediction and fulfilment in the literal sense.

3. Prevision of Christianity in the OT

The prevision of events in the life of Jesus and in the history of Christianity is involved in all the quotations in which a *necessary* connection between the passage as predictive and the event is asserted, or in which a prophet is said to have been speaking or writing concerning the event or person in question. An examination of the OT without reference to its use in the NT seems to justify the conclusion that its bearing upon the future may be particularized under four heads, which in turn with sufficient accuracy and exhaustiveness will classify the pertinent NT quotations.

(1) The prophetic teaching of Israel embodied not only in the messages of the prophets, but also in laws, institutions, and rites, has a twofold dispensational application. Reference is made here only to those explicit references to a future era of especial blessing. For example, in Acts **2** 17 ff Peter interprets the Pentecostal experience in the terms of prophecy, referring to Joel (**2** 28 ff), who promises an outpouring of God's Spirit in a "great and notable day" of the Lord. The promise through Joel is an undeniable prediction (every promise is such), which in a measure would be fulfilled in any exceptional manifestation of God's Spirit among men. The only question which can possibly be raised in connection with Peter's use of this passage is whether the Pentecostal outpouring was the climactic realization of the promise: that is, the establishment of the era of blessing foretold by the prophet. Later in the same book (**3** 20–26) the same apostle sweeps the whole field of prophecy as centering in certain promises fulfilled in Christ and the Christian community.

He instances two, the prophet like Moses (Dt **18** 15) and the promised inclusive blessing through Abraham (Gen **12** 3). He also includes (Acts **3** 26) a hint of the Servant passages of Isa. This identification of the NT movement through two specific predictive promises is wholly justified by the prophetic character of Jesus, the range and richness of the blessings brought from Abraham through Him, and by the fact elsewhere emphasized that no other has measured up to the standard of the ideal servant. Negatively, it may be urged that if these promises were not fulfilled in Christ, history affords no possibility of discovering any fulfilment measurably adequate, either in the past or future. In He (**8** 8–12) reference is made to the promise of a new covenant in Jer (**31** 31 ff) as a justification for believing that the OT dispensation was not complete in itself and that in its very constitution it pointed forward to Christianity as its fulfilment. Combining this passage with that quoted above (Acts **2** 17 ff) taken from Joel, the strength of the case for this use of the OT is at once seen. Distinctively Jeremiah's "new covenant" was to be inward and gracious rather than outward and legal. The promise through Joel is an awakening of prophecy through the free outpouring of God's Spirit. The distinctive feature of the gospel is its idea of justification by faith, through grace revealed in Christ and imparted by the Holy Spirit given according to promise at Pentecost. The "new covenant" foretold by Jeremiah was established at Pentecost through the outpouring of the Spirit promised through Joel. To deny this as fulfilment is to nullify the meaning of Christian history and to erase both promises from the page of credible prophecy.

(2) Contemporary persons or institutions are sometimes interpreted, not in the terms of present actuality, but on the basis of the *ideal* not revealed or realized until the coming of Christ. One striking example of this method is to be found in the

so-called "Immanuel passage" (Mt **1** 23, quoting Isa **7** 14). Undoubtedly the message of the prophet to Ahaz had an immediate and contemporary significance. But, like many another notable prophetic message, it is set in the key of the Messianic King whose unworthy predecessor Ahaz was. "The Messiah comes, but the wilfulness of Ahaz has rendered His reign impossible" (G. A. Smith, "Isa," *Expositor's Bible,* I, 134).

In Acts **2** 24–36, passages representative of many others quoted, both the resurrection and ascension of Jesus are interpreted in the light of two quotations from the Pss (**16** 8 ff; **110** 1) as predetermined and therefore certain events in the plan and purpose of God. In both instances the argument is that the promises nominally made to David, or claimed by him, were couched in terms too vast to find fulfilment in his own experience, but were spoken of the greater King who was to come and in whose experience alone they were realized. In the former instance, a triumph over death was anticipated with assurance which not the Psalmist but only Christ attained; in the latter a royal ascendancy was promised that only Christ's ascension to the place of power could satisfy. An examination of the passages shows that Peter's interpretation is justified not merely by the wording of the promises, which point to a fulness of experience not realized by any OT man, but still more clearly by the descriptive titles which identify the person who is the subject of the experience. In the first instance he is spoken of as Jeh's "Holy One," in the second as "My Lord." The triumph over death which the speaker anticipates is grounded in a unity of purpose and will with God—a holiness which was ideal and still unrealized until Christ came. The logic of the ps is: God's "Holy One" must not see corruption. The logic of history is: Christ is God's Holy One and He did not see corruption. The principle that triumph over death is the logical issue of holiness found its justification and proof not directly in the experience of the singer who first glimpsed it as a truth, but in the career of Christ who first realized it as a fact.

Note.—The argument here is not affected if one accepts the variant reading "Holy Ones" for the preceding passage.

The second passage is particularly interesting because Our Lord Himself first pointed out its implications as to the place and work of the Messiah. Such a passage as this entire ps (**110**) would have been impossible had not the powers and responsibilities of the Davidic King been keyed from the beginning at the Messianic level. The logic here is the same as in Ps **16**. The Messianic kingdom over all nations awaited the coming of the true Messianic King. The long-delayed triumph followed hard upon the coming of the long-expected King (cf Ps **2** 1.2; Acts **13** 32–34).

The same principle is involved in Our Lord's use of the Servant passage (Isa **61** 1 ff) in His sermon at Nazareth. Here the issue as to Messianic prophecy is fairly joined at the center. It is central because it occurs in the Lord's own teaching and also because it concerns, not any external or incidental happenings in the life of Jesus, but the whole trend and movement of prophetic thought, together with the entire meaning and interpretation of His career.

Interpreted altogether apart from the NT, the passage has an unmistakable bearing upon the future. As one of the series concerned with the Servant (Isa **42** 1 ff), the quoted passage focuses attention upon the mission of Israel to the world, still to be carried out. "Ye are my witnesses, saith Jeh, and my servant whom I have chosen" (**43** 10), "Yet now hear, O Jacob my servant, and Israel, whom I have chosen" (**44** 1). It also involves the entire scope and meaning of the prophetic office through which Jeh's will was made known to Israel and through Israel to the world. Both these considerations sweep out into the prophet's future and both point unerringly to Christ as the historical fulfilment of Israel's mission and as the actual realization of the ideal and ministry of prophethood. The very ambiguity of the reference in this chapter (ch **61**), whether to the Servant or to the prophet, and the questions raised as to whether Israel idealized is referred to or some person or personification, serve to make more clear and unmistakable the central fact that only in Christ is the conception embodied in the entire series of passages altogether realized. It thus becomes for sober thought a distinct revelation and portraiture in advance of what Jesus was in His person and work.

(3) In the course of Israel's training to receive the Messiah, certain external items were given as bearing upon the identification of Him when He should come. We shall instance three items, closely related to each other, and each intensely interesting in itself. These three items are (*a*) His sonship to David (Acts **2** 30.31), (*b*) His birth from a Virgin (Mt **1** 22 f), (*c*) His birth at Bethlehem (Mt **2** 5). Objection is offered at once to the interpretation of these OT passages as predictive, and to the alleged fulfilments in the life of Jesus, on the ground mainly that being definite events (cf Mt **2** 15) they are not included within the legitimate scope of prediction; and, secondarily, that being items of this external kind it would be an easy matter to invent fulfilments. It may be granted at once that incidents of this kind could be indefinitely multiplied by fabricating coincidences, but the fact remains that, in the absence of any visible check upon invention, very few such instances are alleged by NT writers. Furthermore, there are suggestive variations between the events recorded and the natural interpretations of the OT passages connected with them; that is, the fulfilments arrive by such devious routes as to make it difficult to suppose them to be due to the imaginative stimulation of the passages. For example, the birth at Bethlehem was brought about by circumstances not at all to the liking of Jewish patriots, and was obscured to contemporaries by the previous and subsequent residence at Nazareth. The kinship of Jesus to the house of David was made adoptive (unless Mary was of that house) by the virgin birth. The interpretation of Isa **7** 14 as intimating a virgin birth was not compulsory to one familiar with the Heb text of the passage and would have been thought of in that connection only by one assured of the fact. The virgin birth (see Immanuel; Virgin Birth) is not an etymological but a providential commentary on Isa **7** 14. One other consideration of primary importance remains. In the one point where the identification of Jesus with the Messiah by His followers can be tested most severely, they are most completely triumphant. It would be comparatively easy to invent incidents suggested by OT prophecies, and to take dignities and titles wholesale from the same source—but given all these, to find one capable of realizing and fulfilling the expectations so aroused is the chief problem. Here fabrication is impossible. And here too the NT meets and answers the challenge of truth. In view of these considerations it is safe to assert that even in matters of historical detail the career of Jesus was foreseen and predicted. Such passages belong to the philosophy of preparation as a whole and should be studied in that connection.

(4) In certain instances the original passage and its reappearance in quotation indicate a process

which is continuous throughout all history. For example, the use of Zec **13** 7 (Mk **14** 27) suggests a deeper view of the connection between prophecy and history, immediate and more remote, than we are often aware of. On the face of them such passages as those concerning the Smitten Shepherd and the scattered sheep are predictions, and the life of Christ stands as fulfilment. It simply cannot be contended that such passages as these do not find fulfilment and explanation in the career of Jesus as nowhere else in the history. Nevertheless, the connection is far deeper than *mere* foresight of an isolated event and its occurrence. We may well say that, in a sense, the event is foreseen because it is already a fact. The allegory of the Smitten Shepherd is, as has well been said, "a summary of the history of Israel." But it is more than that. The relationship of God with Israel, which involved a dealing of Divine grace with men, their rejection of it and the consequent vicarious immolation of the Divine Friend and Shepherd, which came to its climax in the tragedy of the cross, was established in all essential factors in the early days. Therefore, Christ can say, as the outcome of the profoundest insight into the meaning of history, 'That which concerneth me hath fulfilment' (cf Lk **24** 44). He was more deeply concerned in the doings of an earlier time than being there foreseen. In a real sense, "the Lamb" was "slain from the foundation of the world" (Rev **13** 8). In this allegory of the rejected Shepherd and in the successive delineations of the Servant passages, we have the portrait of the Christ as He was—not merely as He was to be. In these quotations deep answers to deep. The only satisfactory interpretation of the tragedy of the cross is that in accordance with principles long operative in human history, "it must needs be." The only satisfactory interpretation of the passages cited is that they disclose the actual operation of the forces which in their culmination issued in the tragedy of the cross. This brings the passages in the original and in quotation into the framework of the same course of events. Peter in his sermon in Solomon's porch thus sums up the whole process: "But the things which God foreshowed by the mouth of all the prophets, that his Christ should suffer, he thus fulfilled" (Acts **3** 18).

The argumentative use of the OT involves exactly the same principles which have been dealt with in the foregoing discussion. These principles coalesce in the conception of the OT as authoritative.

4. Argumentative Quotations

(1) Throughout the NT, in the teaching of Our Lord Himself and in the apostolic writings, a clear-cut distinction is drawn between the temporary and permanent offices of the OT. It is recognized that in essential principles the OT is for all time, while in its outward form and in its actualization of underlying and essential truths it is preliminary and preparatory. There are different dispensations, but one economy. Whenever Our Lord uses the OT for purposes of argument (see Mt **4** 4.7; **12** 17 ff; **19** 18 f; Mk **10** 19; Lk **19** 46) it is on the basis of essential truth which is permanent and unchanging (Mt **5** 17–19). On the other hand, He never hesitates to annul that which had a merely temporary or preliminary value (Mt **5** 21.33.38; cf by way of contrast ver 27). He came not to destroy, but to fulfil, but fulfilment implies a new era—a new and higher stage in the delivery of truth.

(2) In like manner Paul and the other NT writers argue on the basis of an identity of principle which binds the two eras together. Paul contends for three great principles, the Messiahship of Jesus, justification by faith, the inclusion of the Gentiles in the plan of salvation (the doctrine of election is a detail of this last argument; see Rom **9** 7.9.12. 13.15.17). We shall consider typical examples of Paul's use of the OT in argumentation. Choice has been made of those which have provoked adverse criticism. Among these is the use of Gen **13** 15; **17** 8 in Gal **3** 16. This is a leading example of Paul's alleged "rabbinical" method: "He saith not, And to seeds, as of many; but as of one, And to thy seed, which is Christ." The Heb word "seed" as applied to offspring (זֶרַע, *zera'*) is singular. This, of course, means that a man's descendants are looked upon as organically one, inasmuch as they continue his life. The word would apply to any one of the family, but only by virtue of his belonging to the family. Etymologically Paul's argument would apply to Isaac as well as to Jesus—provided only the promise is looked upon as being fulfilled in him. But the promise which was fulfilled in Isaac, was fulfilled in a larger way in Israel as a whole, and was fulfilled in the largest way of all in Christ. The use of the sing. word indicates that Abraham's children were looked upon as one in him—they are also one in Christ. The true children of Abraham are such in Christ. Historically the argument is fully justified. "The personality of Christ is in some sense coextensive with the fulfilment of the promise to Abraham" (Beet). "Christ is the organ of fulfilment" (Meyer).

The classical passage in the discussion of justification based upon an OT quotation is Rom **1** 17, quoting Hab **2** 4. The quoted passage seems to fail the argument because the literal tr would appear to be that "the righteous shall live by their faithfulness." A deeper view, however, amply justifies the quotation; first, because the stedfastness demanded by the prophet is a persistent trust in God in view of the delay of the promised vision; second, the deepest principle common to the OT and NT is that stability of character has its root in trust in Jeh (Isa **28** 16; cf **26** 1–3). Nothing could be more foreign to the thought of the OT than that a man could be righteous without trust in God.

One further quotation argumentatively used by Paul may fitly close this section of our discussion. In Rom **11** 26.27 he quotes Isa **59** 20.21 as indicating the Divine purpose to include the Gentiles within the scope of salvation. This passage is doubly significant because it is attacked by Kuenen (*Prophets and Prophecy in Israel*) on the ground that it is uncritically taken from the LXX version which in this instance does not correctly represent the Heb text. It may be remarked that a large percentage of the NT quotations are taken from the LXX. (For estimates of the number see Johnson, *Quotations of the NT*, ch i.) This prevalent habit is amply justifiable by, and in large consideration of, the fact that the NT was written for the purpose of being read and understood by those to whom the LXX was often the only version available, and the familiarity of that version was ample compensation for any slight loss in verbal accuracy. The only reasonable qualification of this general statement is that we should call in question any deviation which is depended upon for a point in argument. Kuenen, the severest critic of the NT writers in this particular, alleges very few instances, and Professor Johnson has satisfactorily dealt with these in detail (as above). In the case immediately before us the deviations in the version used by Paul do not in the least modify, in the way of strengthening, the reference to the Gentiles (beginning in ver 19 and continuing throughout) which is the point upon which Paul is laying stress. It is not too much to say that Paul's argument would be unimpaired had he used the Heb text, upon which our RV rests (cf He **2** 6–8). In general, it may be premised that no stringent rule of verbal accuracy should be considered binding upon writers who address a popular audience beyond that which guards the substantial cogency of their argument. From the fair application of this reasonable rule the NT writers have nothing to fear.

For the most part the NT writers confine their quotations to the OT. In a single instance an extra-canonical saying of Jesus (Acts **20** 35), and, in at least two instances (Jude vs 9.14), non-canonical books are referred to. In addition to this Paul uses in the letter to Titus (**1** 12) and in his sermon at Athens (Acts **17** 28) lines from native poets to illustrate and enforce his discussion (see Poetry, New Testament). In these latter instances the difference in usage from his ordinary habit of quoting authoritative Scripture is sufficiently obvious. In the case of the saying attributed to Christ, it is enough to say that it is so obviously *Christlike* that we need not hesitate to accept it as genuine, while in the case of Jude nothing is made to depend upon the quotations except certain accepted Christian truths (see Plummer, *Expositor's Bible*, "James and Jude," 434 f).

5. Catena of Passages Illustrating Principles of Quotation

(1) *Based on unity of dispensations.*—Mt **2** 18; **13** 14; **27** 9; Mk **7** 6; Lk **4** 21; **20** 17; Jn **4** 37; **6** 45; **7** 38; **12** 14f; Acts **2** 31.39; **3** 25; **4** 25; **8** 23.32f; **13** 22.32.33.34; **28** 26.27; 1 Cor **15** 54.55; He **8** 8–12; Jas **2** 23.

(2) *Based on prevision.*—Mt **1** 22; **2** 5.15; **4** 14; **8** 17; **12** 17; **13** 35; **26** 31; Mk **14** 27; Lk **22** 37; Jn **7** 38.42; **12** 38.40.49; **13** 18; **15** 25; **19** 24.28.36; **20** 9; Acts **1** 20; **2** 25–28; **3** 25; **4** 11.25.26; **13** 32–34.

(3) *Based on authority of the OT.*—Mt **4** 4; **5** 38.43; **9** 13; **19** 4.18; **21** 13.16.42; **22** 24.31.32.43; Mk **4** 12; **7** 10; **10** 19; **11** 17; **12** 19; Lk **2** 22.23; **4** 10; **19** 46; Acts **15** 16.17; Rom **1** 17; **4** 3.7.8; **9** 25.26; **10** 5.6–8.11.13.16; **12** 19; **15** 21; 1 Cor **1** 19 (identity of principle).31; **15** 45; 2 Cor **4** 13; **6** 2.16; **8** 15; Gal **3** 6.8.10.11.12.13.16; **4** 27; Eph **4** 8; **6** 2; 1 Tim **5** 18.

See also CHRONICLES, BOOKS OF, 5, 7, 10.

LITERATURE.—The lit. is voluminous. Beside the standard comms. and dicts., the reader will do well to consult C. H. Toy, *Quotations in the NT*; Franklin Johnson, *Quotations of the NT*; *Cambridge Bib. Essays* ("Our Lord's Use of the OT" by McNeile); Westcott, *Intro to the Study of the NT*, Appendix A.

LOUIS MATTHEWS SWEET

R

RAAMA, rā′a-ma (רַעְמָא, *ra'mā'*): Thus spelled only in 1 Ch **1** 9; elsewhere "Raamah" (רַעְמָה, *ra'māh*). A son of Cush and father of Sheba and Dedan (Gen **10** 7=1 Ch **1** 9). In Ezekiel's lament over Tyre (Ezk **27** 22) the tribe of Raamah is mentioned along with Sheba as a mercantile people who provided the inhabitants of Tyre with spices, precious stones and gold. It has generally been identified with Regma, mentioned by Ptolemy and Steph. Byzantr. as a city in Southeastern Arabia on the shores of the Pers Gulf. The LXX ('Ρεγμά, *Rhegmá*) itself supposes this site. But the Arab. name of the city here indicated is spelled with a *g* and so gives rise to a phonological difficulty. A more probable identification has been found in the Sabaean *ra'māh* in Southwestern Arabia near *Me'īn* in the north of Marib. *Me'īn* was the capital of the old Minaean kingdom.

A. S. FULTON

RAAMIAH, rā-a-mī′a (רַעַמְיָה, *ra'amyāh;* B, **Ναamιά**, *Naamiá*, A, **'Ρεελμά**, *Rheelmá*): One of the leading men who returned with Zerubbabel from captivity (Neh **7** 7). In the corresponding passage in Ezr **2** 2, where the same list is named, a slight variation in form is given. "Reelaiah" is the name found in this passage. One is doubtless a corruption of the other. Both have the same root meaning.

RAAMSES, rȧ-am′sēz (Ex **1** 11), **RAMESES**, ram′ė-sēz (Gen **47** 11; Ex **12** 37; Nu **33** 3.5) (רַעְמְסֵס, *ra'meṣēṣ*, רַעַמְסֵס, *ra'amṣēṣ;* **'Ραμεσσῆ**, *Rhamessḗ;* Egyp *Ra-mes-su*, "Ra created him" [or "it"]): One

1. Meaning of "Store-Cities"

of the two "settlements" (*miṣkenōth*) built, or "built up," by the Hebrews for the Pharaoh, the other being Pithom, to which the LXX adds a third, namely, "On which is Heliopolis," a town near Cairo (Ex **1** 11). The Heb term *miṣkenōth* comes from a root meaning "to settle down" (Arab. *sakan*, "settlement," Assyr *sakanu* or *shakanu*, "to set"), but it is rendered "strong cities" in LXX, "treasure cities" in AV, and (incorrectly) "store-cities" in RV. The "land of Rameses," where Jacob and his sons settled, was apparently the "field of Zoan" (see ZOAN), thus lying in the Delta E. of the Bubastic branch of the Nile.

It is often assumed that no city called Rameses would have existed before the time of Rameses II, or the 14th cent. BC, though even before Rameses I the name occurs as that of a brother of Horemhib under the XVIIIth Dynasty. The usual tr "Child of Ra" is grammatically incorrect in Egyp, and as Ra was an ancient name for the "sun" it seems possible that a town may have borne the title "Ra created it" very early. The mention of Rameses in Gen (**47** 11) is often regarded as an anachronism, since no scholar has supposed that Jacob lived as late as the time of Rameses II. This would equally apply to the other notices, and at most would serve to mark the age of the passages in the Pent where Rameses is mentioned, but even this cannot be thought to be proved (see EXODUS). According to De Rougé (see Pierret, *Vocab. Hiéroglyph.*, 1875, 143) there were at least three towns in Lower Egypt that bore the name *Pa Rames-ses* ("city of Rameses"); but Brugsch supposes that the place mentioned in the OT was Zoan, to which Rameses II gave this name when making it his capital in the Delta. Dr. Budge takes the same view, while Dr. Naville and others suppose that the site of Raamses has still to be found.

2. Meaning of Name

There appears to have been no certain tradition preserving the site, for though St. Silvia (about 385 AD) was told that it lay 4 miles from the town of Arabia (see GOSHEN), she found no traces of such a place. Brugsch ("A New City of Rameses, 1876," *Aegyptische Zeitschrift*, 69) places one such city in the southern part of Memphis itself. Goodwin (*Rec. of Past*, Old Series, VI, 11) gives an Egyp letter describing the "city of Rameses-Miamun," which appears to be Zoan, since it was on the seacoast. It was a very prosperous city when this letter was written, and a *pa-khennu* or "palace city." It had canals full of fish, lakes swarming with birds, fields of lentils, melons, wheat, onions and sesame, gardens of vines, almonds and figs. Ships entered its harbor; the lotus and papyrus grew in its waters. The inhabitants greeted Rameses II with garlands of flowers. Besides wine and mead, of the "conqueror's city," beer was brought to the harbor from the Kati (in Cilicia), and oil from the "Lake Sagabi." The stela of Rameses II at Beisan records, among other things, that Rameses built the fortress Raamses and adds that he built it with Asiatic Semitic slaves. This accords with the inscription of Rameses at *Tell Maskhûta*, "I built Pithom." The description above given agrees with the OT account of the possession given by Joseph to his family "in the best of the land, in the land of Rameses."

3. Situation

C. R. CONDER

RABBAH, rab′a:

(1) (רַבָּה, *rabbāh;* 'Ραββά, *Rhabbá*, 'Ραββάθ, *Rhabbáth*, 'Ραββάν, *Rhabbán*. The full name is רַבַּת בְּנֵי עַמּוֹן, *rabbath benē 'ammōn;* ἡ ἄκρα τῶν υἱῶν 'Αμμών, *hē ákra tôn huiôn Ammôn*, 'Ραββάθ υἱῶν 'Αμμών, *Rhabbáth huiôn Ammôn*, "Rabbah of the children of Ammon"): This alone of the cities of the Ammonites is mentioned in Scripture, so we may take

it as the most important. It is first named in connection with the "bed" or sarcophagus of Og, king of Bashan, which was said to be found here (Dt **3** 11). It lay E. of the territory assigned to Gad (Josh **13** 25). Whatever may have been its history in the interval, it does not appear again in Scripture till the time of David. This monarch sent an embassy of sympathy to King Hanun when his father Nahash died. The kindness was met by wanton insult, which led to the outbreak of war. The Ammonites, strengthened by Aramaean allies, were defeated by the Israelites under Joab, and took refuge in Rabbah. After David's defeat of the Aramaeans at Helam a year later, the Ammonites were exposed alone to the full force of Israel, the ark of the covenant being carried with the troops. The country was ravaged and siege was laid to Rabbah. It was during this siege that Uriah the Hittite by David's orders was exposed "in the forefront of the hottest battle" (2 S **11** 15), where, treacherously deserted by his comrades, he was slain. How long the siege lasted we do not know; probably some years; but the end was in sight when Joab captured "the city of waters" (2 S **12** 27). This may mean that he had secured control of the water supply. In the preceding verse he calls it the "royal city." By the chivalry of his general, David was enabled in person to enjoy the honor of taking the city. Among the booty secured was the crown of Melcom, the god of the Ammonites. Such of the inhabitants as survived he treated with great severity (2 S **12** 26-31; 1 Ch **20** 1 ff).

Ruins at *'Ammān*—Façade of Theater.

In the utterances of the prophets against Ammon, Rabbah stands for the people, as their most important, or perhaps their only important, city (Jer **49** 2.3; Ezk **21** 20; **25** 5; Am **1** 14). Jer **49** 4 speaks of the "flowing valley"—a reference perhaps to the abundance of water and fruitfulness—and the treasures in which she gloried. Ezk **21** 21 represents the king of Babylon at "the head of the two ways" deciding by means of the divining arrows whether he should march against Jerus or against Rabbah. Amos seems to have been impressed with the palaces of Rabbah.

The city retained its importance in later times. It was captured by Ptolemy Philadelphus (285–247 BC), who called it Philadelphia. It was a member of the league of ten cities. Antiochus the Great captured it by means of treachery (Polyb. v.71). Jos (*BJ*, III, iii, 3) names it as lying E. of Peraea. In the 4th cent. AD, it ranked with Bostra and Gerasa as one of the great fortified cities of Coele-Syria (Ritter, *Erdkunde*, XV, ii, 1154 f). It became the seat of a bishop. Abulfeda (1321 AD) says that Rabbah was in ruins at the time of the Moslem conquest.

Rabbah is represented by the modern *'Ammān*, a ruined site with extensive remains, chiefly from Rom times, some 14 miles N.E. of Heshbon, and about 22 miles E. of the Jordan. It lies on the northern bank of *Wâdy 'Ammān*, a tributary of the upper Jabbok, in a well-watered and fruitful valley. Possibly the stream which rises here may be "the waters" referred to in 2 S **12** 27. Ancient Rabbah may have stood on the hill now occupied by the citadel, a position easy of defence because of its precipitous sides. The outer walls of the citadel appear to be very old; but it is quite impossible to say that anything Ammonite is now above ground. The citadel is connected by means of an underground passage with a large cistern or tank to the N., whence probably it drew its water-supply. This may be the passage mentioned in the account of the capture of the city by Antiochus.

Colonnade at *'Ammān*.

"It is," says Conder (*Heth and Moab*, 158), "one of the finest Rom towns in Syria, with baths, a theater, and an odeum, as well as several large private masonry tombs built in the valley probably in the 2d cent. The fortress on the hill, now surrounding a considerable temple, is also probably of this same date. The church with two chapels farther N., and perhaps some of the tombs, must belong to a later age, perhaps the 4th cent. The fine mosque and the fine Moslem building on the citadel hill cannot be earlier than the 7th, and are perhaps as late as the 11th cent.; and we have thus relics of every building epoch except the Crusading, of which there appears to be no indication."

The place is now occupied by Arabs and Circassians who profit by the riches of the soil. It is brought into contact with the outside world by means of the Damascus-Hejaz Railway, which has a station here; seat of Trans-Jordania government.

(2) (הָרַבָּה, *hā-rabbāh;* B, Σωθηβά, *Sōthēbá*, A, 'Ἀρεββά, *Arebbá*): An unidentified city of Judah named along with Kiriath-jearim (Josh **15** 60).

W. EWING

RABBI, rab'ī, rab'i (רַבִּי, *rabbī;* **ῥαββί,** *rhabbí,* or **ῥαββεί,** *rhabbeí*): A term used by the Jews of their religious teachers as a title of respect, from רַב, *rabh,* "great," so "my great one" (cf Lat *magister*), once of masters of slaves, but later of teachers (Mt **23** 7); therefore tr[d] by διδάσκαλος, *didáskalos,* "teacher" (Mt **23** 8; Jn **1** 38; cf ver 49). In AV frequently rendered "Master" (Mt **26** 25.49; Mk **9** 5; **11** 21; **14** 45; Jn **4** 31; **9** 2; **11** 8). John the Baptist (Jn **3** 26), as well as Christ, is addressed with the title (Jn **1** 49; **6** 25), both by disciples and others. Jesus forbade its use among His followers (Mt **23** 8). Later (Galilean) form of same, RABBONI (q.v.). For **Rabbinical literature** see TALMUD.

EDWARD BAGBY POLLARD

RABBITH, rab'ith (הָרַבִּית, *hā-rabbīth;* B, **Δαβειρών,** *Dabeirôn,* A, **'Ραββώθ,** *Rhabbôth*): A town in the territory of Issachar (Josh **19** 20) which is probably represented today by *Rāba,* a village in the southern part of the Gilboa range and N. of *Ibzāḳ*. The *hā* is, of course, the def. art.

RABBLE, rab''l: This word is not found in AV. RV has it once as the tr of ἀγοραῖος, *agoraíos* (lit. "lounger in the market place"), in Acts **17** 5, where it replaces "baser sort" of AV. It has the common meaning of an unruly, lawless set who are ready to join a mob.

RABBONI, rab-ō'nī, rab-o'ni (**ῥαββουνί,** *rhabbouní,* "my great master" [Mk **10** 51]; **ῥαββουνί** [WH **-νεί**], *rhabbouní* [*-neí*] [Jn **20** 16]). See RABBI.

RAB-MAG, rab'mag (רַב־מָג, *rabh-māgh;* LXX as proper noun, **'Ραβαμάθ,** *Rhabamáth*): The name of one of the Bab princes who were present at the destruction of Jerus by Nebuchadnezzar, during the reign of Zedekiah, king of Judah (Jer **39** 3.13). The word is a compound, the two parts seemingly being in apposition and signifying tautologically the same thing. The last syllable or section of the word, *māgh,* was the designation among the Medes, Persians and Babylonians for priests and wise men. Its original significance was "great" or "powerful"; Gr μέγας, *mégas,* Lat *magis, magnus.* The first syllable, *rabh,* expresses practically the same idea, that of greatness, or abundance in size, quantity, or power. Thus it might be interpreted the "all-wise" or "all-powerful" prince, the chief magician or physician. It is, therefore, a title and not a name, and is accordingly put in appositive relations to the proper name just preceding, as "Nergal-sharezer, the Rab-mag," tr[d] fully, "Nergal-sharezer the chief prince or magician." See NERGAL-SHAREZER.

In harmony with the commonly accepted view, the proper rendering of the text should be, "All the princes of the king of Babylon came in, and sat in the middle gate, to wit, Nergal-sharezer, Samgar-nebo, Sarsechim, [the] Rab-saris, Nergal-sharezer, [the] Rab-mag" (Jer **39** 3); and "so Nebuzaradan the captain of the guard sent, and Nebushazban, [the] Rab-saris, and Nergal-sharezer, [the] Rab-mag, and all the chief officers of the king of Babylon" (**39** 13).

WALTER G. CLIPPINGER

RAB-SARIS, rab'sa-ris (רַב־סָרִיס, *rabh-ṣārīṣ*): As with Rab-mag, which is not regarded as a name, but a title, so this is to be regarded as a descriptive title for the person whose name precedes it (see RAB-MAG). The first part, *rabh,* signifies "great" or "chief," the second, *ṣārīṣ,* is the title for eunuch or chamberlain. The tr then would be chief eunuch or the chief of the eunuchs (or chamberlains).

The oriental custom was for the king to surround himself with a number of eunuchs, who performed varied kinds of services, both menial and dignified. They usually had charge of his harem; sometimes they occupied court positions. Frequently they superintended the education of the youth. The term itself was sometimes used to designate persons in places of trust who were not emasculated. The above title describes the highest or chief in rank of these eunuchs. See EUNUCH.

The full title is used 3 t, once in connection with the titles of other important officers who were sent by the king of Assyria with a large army to demand the surrender of Jerus. The passage would be tr[d] properly, 'And the king of Assyria sent the Tartan and the Rab-saris (the chief eunuch) and the Rab-shakeh from Lachish to king Hezekiah' (2 K **18** 17). Again, it refers to a Babylonian whose real name was Sarsechim, who with the other Bab princes sat in the middle gate during the capture of Jerus. This event is described as having occurred in the 11th year of Zedekiah, king of Judah (Jer **39** 3). The third use is in connection with the name Nebushazban, who, with the other chief officers of the king of Babylon, sent and took Jeremiah out of the court of the guard and committed him to Gedaliah, who was to take him home to dwell with his own people (Jer **39** 13).

Thus it is seen that based upon this accepted theory the three titles would be in their connections as follows: (1) simply "the chief eunuch," (2) Sarsechim, the Rab-saris (or chief eunuch), and (3) Nebushazban, the Rab-saris (or chief eunuch). See also ASSYRIA, X.

WALTER G. CLIPPINGER

RABSHAKEH, rab'sha-ke, rab-shā'ke (רַבְשָׁקֵה, *rabhshāḳēh*): A compound word, the first part, *rabh,* indicating "head" or "chief" (see RAB-MAG; RAB-SARIS). The second part, which in the Aram., probably meant "cupbearer," had in this connection and elsewhere, according to later discoveries, an extended significance, and meant chief officer, i.e. chief of the heads or captains.

R. was one of the officers sent by Sennacherib, the king of Assyria, with the Tartan and the Rab-saris to demand the surrender of Jerus, which was under siege by the Assyr army (2 K **18** 17.19.26.27. 28.37; **19** 4.8; Isa **36** 2.4.11.12.13.22.; **37** 4.8). The three officers named went from Lachish to Jerus and appeared by the conduit of the upper pool. Having called upon King Hezekiah, his representatives Eliakim, the son of Hilkiah, Shebnah, the scribe, and Joah, the recorder, appeared. R. sent through them a message to the king in which he represented himself as the spokesman for the king of Assyria. He derided King Hezekiah in an insolent fashion in representing his trust in Egypt as a bruised reed which would pierce the hand. Likewise his confidence in Jeh was vain, for He also would be unable to deliver them. Then the officers of the king replied, requesting him to speak in the Syrian language which they understood, and not in the Jews' language which the people on the wall understood. This he refused to do, speaking still more loudly in order that they might hear and be persuaded. By bribery and appeal, by promise and by deception he exhorted them to turn traitor to Hezekiah and surrender to him. The people, however, true to the command of Hezekiah (2 K **18** 36), "held their peace, and answered him not a word." Afterward R. returned and "found the king of Assyria warring against Libnah" (2 K **19** 8). From this description it is inferred that R. was a man of considerable literary attainment, being able, in all probability, to speak in three languages. He had, in addition to his official power, dauntless courage, an insolent spirit and a characteristic oriental disregard for veracity.

WALTER G. CLIPPINGER

RACA, rā'ka, rā-kä' (ῥακά, *rhaká*, WH with codd. ℵ^c B E, etc; ῥαχά, *rhachá*, Tisch. with ℵ* D; Aram. רֵיקָא, *rēḳā'*, from רֵיק, *rēḳ*, "empty"): Vain or worthless fellow; a term of contempt used by the Jews in the time of Christ. In the Bible, it occurs in Mt **5** 22 only, but John Lightfoot gives a number of instances of the use of the word by Jewish writers (*Hor. Heb.*, ed by Gandell, Oxford, 1859, II, 108). Chrysostom (who was acquainted with Syr as spoken in the neighborhood of Antioch) says it was equivalent to the Gr σύ, *sú*, "thou," used contemptuously instead of a man's name. Jerome rendered it *inanis aut vacuus absque cerebro*. It is generally explained as expressing contempt for a man's intellectual capacity (="you simpleton!"), while μωρέ, *mōré* (tr^d "thou fool"), in the same verse is taken to refer to a man's moral and religious character (="you rascal!" "you impious fellow!"). Thus we have three stages of anger, with three corresponding grades of punishment: (1) the inner feeling of anger (ὀργιζόμενος, *orgizómenos*), to be punished by the local or provincial court (τῇ κρίσει, *tē krísei*, "the judgment"); (2) anger breaking forth into an expression of scorn (*Raca*), to be punished by the Sanhedrin (τῷ συνεδρίῳ, *tō sunedríō*, "the council"); (3) anger culminating in abusive and defamatory language (*Mōre*), to be punished by the fire of Gehenna. This view, of a double climax, which has been held by foremost Eng. and Ger. commentators, seems to give the passage symmetry and gradation. But it is rejected among others by T. K. Cheyne, who, following J. P. Peters, rearranges the text by transferring the clause "and whosoever shall say to his brother, Raca, shall be in danger of the council" to the end of the preceding verse (*EB*, IV, cols. 4001 f). There certainly does not seem to be trustworthy external evidence to prove that the terms "the judgment," "the council," "the Gehenna of fire" stand to each other in a relation of gradation, as lower and higher legal courts, or would be so understood by Christ's hearers. What is beyond dispute is that Christ condemns the use of disparaging and insulting epithets as a supreme offence against the law of humanity, which belongs to the same category as murder itself. It should be added, however, that it is the underlying feeling and not the verbal expression as such that constitutes the sin. Hence Our Lord can, without any real inconsistency, address two of His followers as "foolish men" (Lk **24** 25, ἀνόητοι, *anóētoi*, practically equivalent to *Raca*, as is also James's expression, "O vain man," Jas **2** 20).

D. MIALL EDWARDS

RACAL, rā'kal (רָכָל, *rākhāl*, "trader"): A place in Judah, enumerated among "the places where David himself and his men were wont to haunt," to the elders of which he sent a share of his spoils (1 S **30** 29). The LXX reading "Carmel" has been adopted, by many, because of the similarity of the words in Heb (רכל and כרמל) and because there was a Carmel in the neighborhood of Hebron (Josh **15** 55; 1 S **15** 12), which figures in the story of David's adventures when pursued by Saul (1 S **25**) in a manner that makes it improbable that he would overlook the place in his good fortune (AV "Rachal"). NATHAN ISAACS

RACE, rās (מֵרוֹץ, *mērōç;* ἀγών, *agṓn*, δρόμος, *drómos*). See GAMES, I, 2; II, 3.

RACES, rās'iz. See TABLE OF NATIONS.

RACHAB, rā'kab (Ῥαχάβ, *Rhacháb*): AV; Gr form of "Rahab" (thus Mt **1** 5 RV).

RACHAL, rā'kal. See RACAL.

RACHEL, rā'chel (רָחֵל, *rāḥēl*, "ewe"; Ῥαχήλ, *Rhachḗl* [Gen **29** 6; Jer **31** 15, AV "Rahel"]): An ancestress of Israel, wife of Jacob, mother of Joseph and Benjamin. Rachel was the younger daughter of Laban, the Aramaean, the brother of Jacob's mother; so Rachel and Jacob were cousins. They met for the first time upon the arrival of Jacob at Haran, when attracted by her beauty he immediately fell in love with her, winning her love by his chivalrous act related in Gen **29** 10 ff. According to the custom of the times Jacob contracted with Laban for her possession, agreeing to serve him 7 years as the stipulated price (**29** 17–20). But when the time had passed, Laban deceived Jacob by giving him Leah instead of Rachel. When Jacob protested, Laban gave him Rachel also, on condition that Jacob serve 7 years more (**29** 21–29). To her great dismay "Rachel was barren" (Gen **29** 30.31), while Leah had children. Rachel, envious of her sister, complained to Jacob, who reminded her that children are the gift of God. Then Rachel resorted to the expedient once employed by Sarah under similar circumstances (**16** 2 ff); she bade Jacob take her handmaid Bilhah, as a concubine, to "obtain children by her" (**30** 3). Dan and Naphtali were the offspring of this union. The evil of polygamy is apparent from the dismal rivalry arising between the two sisters, each seeking by means of children to win the heart of Jacob. In her eagerness to become a mother of children, Rachel bargained with Leah for the mandrakes, or love-apples of her son Reuben, but all to no avail (**30** 14). Finally God heard her prayer and granted her her heart's desire, and she gave birth to her firstborn, whom she named Joseph (**30** 22–24).

1. Biography

Some years after this, when Jacob fled from Laban with his wives, the episode of the theft of the teraphim of Laban by Rachel, related in **31** 19. 34.35, occurred. She hoped by securing the household gods of her father to bring prosperity to her own new household. Though she succeeded by her cunning in concealing them from Laban, Jacob later, upon discovering them, had them put away (**35** 2–4). In spite of all, she continued to be the favorite of Jacob, as is clearly evidenced by **33** 2, where we are told that he assigned to her the place of greatest safety, and by his preference for Joseph, her son. After the arrival in Canaan, while they were on the way from Beth-el to Ephrath, i.e. Bethlehem, Rachel gave birth to her second son, Benjamin, and died (**35** 16 ff).

2. Character

In a marked manner Rachel's character shows the traits of her family, cunning and covetousness, so evident in Laban, Rebekah and Jacob. Though a believer in the true God (**30** 6.8.22), she was yet given to the superstitions of her country, the worshipping of the teraphim, etc (**31** 19). The futility of her efforts in resorting to self-help and superstitious expedients, the love and stronger faith of her husband (**35** 2–4), were the providential means of purifying her character. Her memory lived on in Israel long after she died. In Ruth **4** 11, the names of Rachel and Leah occur in the nuptial benediction as the foundresses of the house of Israel.

Rachel's Tomb (מַצֶּבֶת קְבֻרַת רָחֵל, *maççebheth ḳᵉbhurath rāḥēl*): In Gen **35** 20 we read: "Jacob set up a pillar upon her grave: the same is the

Rachel's Tomb.

Pillar of Rachel's grave unto this day," i.e. the time of the writer. Though the pillar, i.e sepulchral monument, has long disappeared, the spot is marked until this day, and Christians, Jews and Mohammedans unite in honoring it. The present tomb, which, apparently, is not older than the 15th cent., is built in the style of the small-domed buildings raised by Moslems in honor of their saints. It is a rough structure of four square walls, each about 23 ft. long and 20 ft. high; the dome rising 10 ft. higher is used by Mohammedans for prayer, while on Fridays the Jews make supplication before the empty tomb within. It is doubtful, but probable, that it marks the exact spot where Rachel was buried. There are, apparently, two traditions as to the location of the place. The oldest tradition, based upon Gen **35** 16–20; **48** 7, points to a place one mile N. of Bethlehem and 4 miles from Jerus. Mt **2** 18 speaks for this place, since the evangelist, reporting the slaughter of the innocents of Bethlehem, represents Rachel as weeping for her children from her neighboring grave. But according to 1 S **10** 2 ff, which apparently represents another tradition, the place of Rachel's grave was on the "border of Benjamin," near Beth-el, about 10 miles N. of Jerus, at another unknown Ephrath. This location, some believe, is corroborated by Jer **31** 15, where the prophet, in relating the leading away of the people of Ramah, which was in Benjamin, into captivity, introduces Rachel the mother of that tribe as bewailing the fate of her descendants. Those that believe this northern location to be the place of Rachel's grave take the words, "the same is Beth-lehem," in Gen **35** 19; **48** 7, to be an incorrect gloss; but that is a mere assumption lacking sufficient proof.

Mr. Nathan Strauss, of New York City, has purchased the land surrounding Rachel's grave for the purpose of erecting a Jewish university in the Holy Land.

S. D. Press

RADDAI, rad'ā-ī, ra-dā'ī (רַדַּי, *radday*, "beating down"[?]): The 5th of the 7 sons of Jesse, father of David, according to 1 Ch **2** 14 (LXX Alex, "Rhaddaí"; Luc., "Rhedaí"; others, "Zaddaí").

RADIANT, rā'di-ant (נָהַר, *nāhar*, "to sparkle," i.e. [**fig.**] be cheerful; hence [from the *sheen* of a running stream], to flow, i.e. [**fig.**] assemble; flow [together], be lightened): ARV substitutes the active "radiant" for the passive "were lightened" in Ps **34** 5; Isa **60** 5 (ERV, AV "flow together"). As the earth and moon, both being dark, face a common sun and lighten each other, they are not only lightened, but radiant. So with the believers, "They looked unto him [Jeh], and were radiant." Thus *nāhar* combines the two ideas of *being lightened* and *flowing together*. This appears, also, in a different connection, in Isa **60** 5, "Then thou shalt see and be radiant." "It is liquid light—light that ripples and sparkles and runs across the face; . . . . the light which a face catches from sparkling water" (G. A. Smith, *Isaiah*, II, 430).

M. O. Evans

RAFT, raft. See Ships and Boats, II, 1, (2).

RAFTER, raf'tẽr (Cant **1** 17). See Gallery; House.

RAG: Pl. in Prov **23** 21, "Drowsiness will clothe a man with *rags*" (קְרָעִים, *ḳᵉrā'īm*, "torn garment"; cf 1 K **11** 30), and **figuratively** in Isa **64** 6 AV, "All our righteousnesses are as filthy *rags*," in the sense of "tattered clothing" (בֶּגֶד, *beghedh*, RV "garment"). In Jer **38** 11.12 ARV translates סְחָבָה, *ṣᵉḥābhāh*, as "rag" (AV, ERV "old cast clout"), while AV, ERV use "rotten *rag*" for מֶלַח, *melaḥ* (ARV "worn-out garment"). Both *ṣᵉḥābhāh* and *melaḥ* mean "worn out."

RAGAU, rā'gô (**Ῥαγαῦ** [WH], **Ῥαγαύ**, *Rhagaú*): AV; Gr form of "Reu" (thus RV) (Lk **3** 35).

RAGES, rā'jēz, **RAGAU**, rā'gô ("Rages," Tob **1** 14; **4** 1.20; **5** 5; **6** 9.12; **9** 2; "Ragau," Jth **1** 5.15; **Ῥαγαί**, *Rhagaí*, **Ῥάγα**, *Rhága*, **Ῥάγη**, *Rhágē*, **Ῥαγαύ**, *Rhagaú*; in Darius' Behistun Inscriptions, II, 71,72, *Ragā*, a province; in Avesta, *Vend.* I, 15, *Ragha*, city and province; perhaps, "the excellent"):

1. Location

In Eastern Media, one forced march from Caspian Gates, 11 days' journey from Ecbatana, 5½ miles S. of present *Ṭehrān;* the capital of the province of the same name, though by Ptolemy called Rhagiana.

2. History

(1) *Ancient.*—A very ancient city, the traditional birthplace of Zoroaster (Zarathuštra; Pahlavī *Vendidād*, *Zād sparad* XVI, 12, and *Dabistān i Maẕāhib*). In *Yasna* XIX, 18, of the Avesta, it is thus mentioned: "The Zoroastrian, four-chief-possessing Ragha, hers are the royal chiefs, both the house-chief, the village-chief, and the town-chief: Zoroaster is the fourth." In *Vend.* I, 15: "As the tenth, the best of both districts and cities, I, who am Ahura Mazda, did create Ragha, which possesses the three classes," i.e. fire-priests, charioteers, husbandmen. Later it was the religious center of magism. A large colony of captive Israelites settled there. Destroyed in Alexander's time, it was rebuilt by Seleucus Nicator (c 300 BC), who named it Europos. Later, Arsaces restored it and named it Arsacia.

(2) *Mediaeval.*—In the early Middle Ages Ragha, then called Rai, was a great literary and often political center with a large population. It was the birthplace of Hārūn'al Rashīd (763 AD). It was seized and plundered (1029 AD) by Sulṭān Maḥmūd, but became Ṭughril's capital. In the *Vis o Rāmin* (c 1048 AD) it is an important place, 10 days' journey across the Kavīr desert from Merv. It was a small provincial town in about 1200 AD. It was sacked by Mongols in 1220 AD and entirely destroyed under Ghāzān Khān c 1295. A Zoroastrian community lived there in 1278 AD, one of whom composed the *Zarātusht-Nāmah.*

(3) *Present condition.*—Near the ruins there now stands the village of *Shāh 'Abdu'l 'Aẓīm*, connected with *Ṭehrān* by the only railway in Persia (opened in 1888).

Literature.—Ptolemy, Diodorus Siculus, Pliny, Strabo; Ibnu'l Athīr, *Jâmi'u 't Tawārīkh, Tārīkh i*

Jahān-gushā Yāqūt; Justi, *Iranisches Namenbuch;* E. G. Browne, *Literary Hist of Persia;* modern travelers.

W. St. Clair Tisdall

RAGUEL, ra-gū'el (Ῥαγουήλ, *Rhagouḗl*): "The friend of God," of Ecbatana, the husband of Edna, father of Sarah, and father-in-law of Tobias (Tob **3** 7.17; **6** 10; **7** 2 f; **14** 12). In **7** 2 he is called cousin of Tobit, and in Tob **6** 10 AV he is erroneously represented as "cousin" of Tobias="kinsman" in RV. In En **20** 4 Raguel appears as one of the archangels, perhaps by confusion for Raphael (Tob **3** 17). Another form of the name is Reuel (q.v.).

RAGUEL, ra-gū'el, rag'ū-el (רְעוּאֵל, *r*e'*ū'ēl;* LXX *Rhagouḗl*): The Midianite *ḥōthēn*, i.e. either father-in-law or brother-in-law of Moses (Nu **10** 29 AV, RV "Reuel"), the father of Hobab, called a Kenite, who is likewise described as a *ḥōthēn* of Moses (Jgs **4** 11). See Relationships, Family. Moses' wife's father is called *r*e'*ū'ēl* in Ex **2** 18 where Lucian reads "Iothor" and EV "Reuel," which transliteration is adopted in RV in Nu **10** 29 also. In other passages the *ḥōthēn* of Moses is called "Jether" or "Jethro." Among the harmonizations suggested the following are worthy of consideration: (*a*) that all are names or perhaps titles of one man (Rashi); (*b*) that Reuel was the father of Hobab and Jethro, that Jethro was the father-in-law of Moses, and that the word "father" is used for grandfather in Ex **2** 18; (*c*) that Reuel was the father-in-law and Jethro and Hobab brothers-in-law; (*d*) that either Reuel or Hobab is to be identified with Jethro. None of these views is free from difficulty, nor is the view of those who would give Jethro as the name in E and Reuel as that in J and JE. See also Reuel.

Nathan Isaacs

RAHAB, rā'hab:

(1) (רָחָב, *rāḥābh*, "broad"; in Jos, *Ant,* V, i, 2, 7, Ῥάχαβ, *Rháchab;* He **11** 31 and Jas **2** 25, Ῥάαβ, *Rháab*): A *zōnāh*, that is either a "harlot," or, according to some, an "innkeeper" in Jericho (LXX πόρνη, *pórnē*, "harlot"). The two spies sent by Joshua from Shittim came into her house and lodged there (Josh **2** 1). She refused to betray them to the king of Jericho, and when he demanded them, she hid them on the roof of her house with stalks of flax that she had laid in order to dry. She pretended that they had escaped before the shutting of the gate, and threw their pursuers off their track. She then told the spies of the fear that the coming of the Israelites had caused in the minds of the Canaanites—"Our hearts did melt . . . . for Jeh your God, he is God in heaven above, and on earth beneath"—and asked that the men promise to spare her father, mother, brothers and sisters, and all that they had. They promised her to spare them provided they would remain in her house and provided she would keep their business secret. Thereupon she let them down by a cord through the window, her house being built upon the town wall, and gave them directions to make good their escape (Josh **2** 1–24). True to their promise, the Israelites under Joshua spared Rahab and her family (Josh **6** 16 ff AV); "And," says the author of Josh, "she dwelleth in Israel even unto this day." Her story appealed strongly to the imagination of the people of later times. He **11** 31 speaks of her as having been saved by faith; James, on the other hand, in demonstrating that a man is justified by works and not by faith only, curiously chooses the same example (Jas **2** 25). Jewish tradition has been kindly disposed toward Rahab; one hypothesis goes so far as to make her the wife of Joshua himself (*Jew Enc,* s.v.). Naturally then the other tr of *zōnāh*, deriving it from *zūn*, "to feed," instead of *zānāh*, "to be a harlot," has been preferred by some of the commentators.

(2) (Ῥάχαβ, *Rháchab*): Jos, *Ant,* V, 1, 2, 7, so spells the name of (1) (LXX and NT *contra*). The wife of Salmon and mother of Booz (Boaz) according to the genealogy in Mt **1** 5. Query, whether there was a tradition identifying (1) and (2); see Lightfoot, *Horae Heb* on Mt **1** 5.

(3) (רַהַב, *rahabh*, lit. "storm," "arrogance"): A mythical sea-monster, probably referred to in several passages where the word is tr[d] as a common noun "pride" (Job **9** 13), "the proud" (Job **26** 12; cf Ps **89** 10). It is used in parallelism with *tannīn*, "the dragon" (Isa **51** 9). It is most familiar as an emblem of Egypt, 'the boaster that sitteth still' (Isa **30** 7; Ps **87** 4; cf **89** 10). The Talm in *Bābhā' Bathrā'* speaks of *rahabh* as *sar ha-yām*, "master of the sea." See also Astronomy.

Nathan Isaacs

RAHAM, rā'ham (רַחַם, *raḥam*, "pity," "love"): Son of Shema, and father of Jorkeam (1 Ch **2** 44).

RAHEL, rā'hel (Jer **31** 15 AV). See Rachel.

RAID, rād (1 S **27** 10). See War, 3.

RAIL, rāl, **RAILING,** rāl'ing, **RAILER,** rāl'ẽr: To "rail" on (in modern usage "against") anyone is to use insolent or reproachful language toward one. It occurs in the OT as the tr of חָרַף, *ḥāraph* (2 Ch **32** 17, "letters to rail on Jeh"), and of עִיט, *'īṭ* (1 S **25** 14, of Nabal, "he railed at them," ERV "flew upon them," m "railed on"). In the NT "to rail" is the tr of βλασφημέω, *blasphēméō* (Mk **15** 29; Lk **23** 39; "railing," 1 Tim **6** 4; 2 Pet **2** 11; Jude ver 9). The word *loidoría*, rendered "railing" in 1 Pet **3** 9 AV, is in RV "reviling," and *loídoros*, "railer," in 1 Cor **5** 11 is in RV "reviler." See also Raca.

W. L. Walker

RAIMENT, rā'ment. See Dress.

RAIMENT, SOFT (μαλακός, *malakós*): In Mt **11** 8 EV, where Jesus, speaking of John the Baptist, asks "What went ye out to see? a man clothed in soft raiment?" where "raiment," though implied, is not expressed in the best text, but was probably added from Lk **7** 25 ‖. It is equivalent to "elegant clothing," such as courtiers wore, as shown by the words following, "Behold, they that wear soft raiment are in kings' houses." John had bravely refused to play courtier and had gone to prison for it. In the early days of Herod the Great some scribes who attached themselves to him laid aside their usual plain clothing and wore the gorgeous raiment of courtiers (Jost, in Plumptre).

Geo. B. Eager

RAIN, rān (מָטָר, *māṭār*, Arab. مَطَر, *maṭar*, "rain," גֶּשֶׁם, *geshem*, "heavy rain," מוֹרֶה, *mōreh*, "early rain," יוֹרֶה, *yōreh*, "former rain," מַלְקוֹשׁ, *malḳōsh*, "latter rain"; βρέχω, *bréchō*, ὑετός, *huetós*):

1. Water-Supply in Egypt and Palestine

In Egypt there is little or no rainfall, the water for vegetation being supplied in great abundance by the river Nile; but in Syria and Pal there are no large rivers, and the people have to depend entirely on the fall of rain for water for themselves, their animals and their fields. The children of Israel when in Egypt were promised by Jeh a land which "drinketh water of the rain of heaven" (Dt **11** 11). Springs and fountains are found in most of the valleys, but the flow of the springs depends directly on the fall of rain or snow in the mountains.

2. Importance of Rain in Season

The cultivation of the land in Pal is practically dry farming in most of the districts, but even then some water is necessary, so that there may be moisture in the soil. In the summer months there is no rain, so that the rains of the spring and fall seasons are absolutely essential for starting and maturing the crops. The lack of this rain in the proper time has often been the cause of complete failure of the harvest. A small difference in the amount of these seasonal rains makes a large difference in the possibility of growing various crops without irrigation. Ellsworth Huntington has insisted on this point with great care in his very important work, *Pal and Its Transformation.* The promise of prosperity is given in the assurance of "rain in due season" (Lev **26** 4 AV). The withholding of rain according to the prophecy of Elijah (1 K **17** 1) caused the mountain streams to dry up (1 K **17** 7), and certain famine ensued. A glimpse of the terrible suffering for lack of water at that time is given us. The people were uncertain of another meal (1 K **17** 12), and the animals were perishing (1 K **18** 5).

3. Amount of Rainfall

Pal and Syria are on the borderland between the sea and the desert, and besides are so mountainous, that they not only have a great range of rainfall in different years, but a great variation in different parts of the country.

The amount of rain on the western slopes is comparable with that in England and America, varying from 25 to 40 in. per annum, but it falls mostly in the four winter months, when the downpour is often very heavy, giving oftentimes from 12 to 16 in. in a month. On the eastern slopes it is much less, varying from 8 to 20 in. per annum. The highest amount falls in the mountains of Lebanon where it averages about 50 in. In Beirût the yearly average is 35.87 in. As we go S. from Syria, the amount decreases (Haifa 27.75, Jaffa 22.39, Gaza 17.61), while in the Sinaitic Peninsula there is little or none. Going from W. to E. the change is much more sudden, owing to the mountains which stop the clouds. In Damascus the average is less than 10 in. In Jerus the average for 50 years is 26.16 in., and the range is from 13.39 in 1870 to 41.62 in 1897. The yearly records as given by J. Glaisher and A. Datzi in *PEFQ* from 1861 to 1910, 50 years, are given in the accompanying table.

RAINFALL IN JERUSALEM IN INCHES

Year	Amount	Year	Amount	Year	Amount
1861....	27.30	1878...	32.21	1895...	23.25
1862....	21.86	1879...	18.04	1896...	32.90
1863....	26.54	1880...	32.11	1897...	41.62
1864....	15.51	1881...	16.50	1898...	28.66
1865....	18.19	1882...	26.72	1899...	22.43
1866....	18.55	1883...	31.92	1900...	21.20
1867....	29.42	1884...	23.96	1901...	17.42
1868....	29.10	1885...	29.47	1902...	25.51
1869....	18.61	1886...	31.69	1903...	18.04
1870....	13.39	1887...	29.81	1904...	34.48
1871....	23.57	1888...	37.79	1905...	34.22
1872....	22.26	1889...	13.56	1906...	28.14
1873....	22.72	1890...	35.51	1907...	27.22
1874....	29.75	1891...	34.72	1908...	31.87
1875....	27.01	1892...	31.23	1909...	21.13
1876....	14.41	1893...	30.54	1910...	24.64
1877....	26.00	1894...	35.38		

The amount of rainfall in ancient times was probably about the same as in present times, though it may have been distributed somewhat differently through the year, as suggested by Huntington. Conder maintains that the present amount would have been sufficient to support the ancient cities (*Tent-Work in Pal*). Trees are without doubt fewer now, but meteorologists agree that trees do not produce rain.

4. Dry and Rainy Seasons

The rainfall is largely on the western slopes of the mountains facing the sea, while on the eastern slopes there is very little. The moisture-laden air comes up from the sea with the west and southwest wind. When these currents strike the hills they are thrown higher up into the cooler strata, and the moisture condenses to form clouds and rain which increases on the higher levels. Having passed the ridge of the hills, the currents descend on the other side to warmer levels, where the moisture is easily held in the form of vapor so that no rain falls and few clouds are seen, except in the cold mid-winter months.

The summer months are practically rainless, with very few clouds appearing in the sky. From May 1 to the middle of October one can be sure of no rain; "The winter is past; the rain is over" (Cant **2** 11), so many sleep on the roofs of the houses or in tents of leaves and branches in the fields and vineyards throughout the summer. The continuous hot droughts make the people appreciate the springs and fountains of fresh running water and the cool shade of rock and tree.

The rainy season from October to May may be divided into three parts, the former, the winter, and the latter rains, and they are often referred to under these names in the OT.

The "former rains" are the showers of October and the first part of November. They soften the parched ground so that the winter grain may be sown before the heavy continuous rains set in. The main bulk of the rain falls in the months of December, January and February. Although in these months the rains are frequent and heavy, a dark, foggy day is seldom seen. The "latter rains" of April are the most highly appreciated, because they ripen the fruit and stay the drought of summer. They were considered a special blessing: Jeh "will come . . . . as the latter rain that watereth the earth" (Hos **6** 3); "They opened their mouth wide as for the latter rain" (Job **29** 23); and as a reason for worshipping Jeh who sent them, "Let us now fear Jeh our God, that giveth rain, both the former and the latter, in its season" (Jer **5** 24).

The rain storms always come from the sea with a west or southwest wind. The east wind is a hot wind and the "north wind driveth away rain" (Prov **25** 23 AV). "Fair weather cometh out of the north" (Job **37** 22 AV).

5. Biblical Uses

The Psalmist recognizes that the "showers that water the earth" (Ps **72** 6) are among the choicest blessings from the hand of Jeh: "The early rain covereth it with blessings" (Ps **84** 6). The severest punishment of Jeh was to withhold the rain, as in the time of Ahab and Elijah, when the usual rain did not fall for three years (1 K **17**); "the anger of Jeh be kindled against you, and he shut up the heavens, so that there shall be no rain, and the land shall not yield its fruit; and ye perish quickly" (Dt **11** 17). Too much rain is also a punishment, as witness the flood (Gen **7** 4) and the plague of rain and hail (Ezr **10** 9). Sending of rain was a reward for worship and obedience: "Jeh will open unto thee his good treasure, the heavens, to give the rain of thy land in its season, and to bless all the work of thy hand" (Dt **28** 12). Jeh controls the elements and commands the rain: "He made a decree for the rain" (Job **28** 26); "For he saith to the snow, Fall thou on the earth; likewise to the shower of rain" (Job **37** 6).

Literature.—*PEFQ;* meteorological observations from the Dead Sea, Jerus, Jaffa and Tiberias; various observers; *Zeitschrift des deutschen Palästina-Vereins;* H. Hilderscheid, *Die Niederschlagsverhältnisse Palästinas in alter and neuer Zeit;* C. R. Conder, *Tent-Work in Pal;* Edward Hull, *Mount Seir, Sinai and Western Pal;* Ellsworth Huntington, *Pal and Its Transformation;* bulletin of the Syrian Protestant College Observatory, *Meteorological Observations in Beirut and Syria.*

Alfred H. Joy

RAINBOW, rān'bō (קֶשֶׁת, *ḳesheth*, trd "a bow"; **ἶρις**, *íris*, "rainbow"): As most of the rainfall in Pal is in the form of short heavy showers it is often accompanied by the rainbow. Most beautiful double bows are often seen, and occasionally the moon is bright enough to produce the bow. It is rather remarkable that there are so few references to the rainbow in the Bible. The Heb *ḳesheth* is the ordinary word for a bow, there being no special word for rainbow.

The interpretation of the significance of the bow in the sky is given at the close of the story of the flood, where it is called "the token of the covenant" of Jeh with Noah that there should be no more flood: "I do set my bow in the cloud, ... and the waters shall no more become a flood to destroy all flesh" (Gen **9** 13.15). This addition to the story of the flood is not found in other mythical accounts. The foundation for the interpretation of the bow in this way seems to be that while His bow is hung in the sky God must be at peace with His people. The glory of God is likened to "the appearance of the bow that is in the cloud in the day of rain" (Ezk **1** 28). The rainbow forms a striking part of the vision in Rev **4** 3: "And there was a rainbow round about the throne." ALFRED H. JOY

RAISE, rāz: "To raise" in the OT is most frequently the tr of the Hiphil form of קוּם, *ḳūm*, "to cause to arise," e.g. raising up seed (Gen **38** 8), a prophet (Dt **18** 18), judges (Jgs **2** 16.18), etc; also of עוּר, *'ūr*, "to awake," "stir up" (Ezr **1** 5 AV; Isa **41** 2, etc), with other words. In the NT the chief words are *ἐγείρω*, *egeírō*, "to awaken," "arouse" (Mt **3** 9; Lk **1** 69; **3** 8, etc), frequently of raising the dead; and *ἀνίστημι*, *anístēmi* (Mt **22** 24; Jn **6** 39, etc; Acts **2** 24 [30 AV], etc), with compounds of the former. Among the RV changes may be noted, "to stir the fire" for "from raising" (Hos **7** 4); "raiseth high his gate" for "exalteth his gate" (Prov **17** 19); ARV, "can it be raised from the roots thereof" for "pluck it up by the roots thereof" (Ezk **17** 9 AV and ERV); "raised up" for "rise again" (Mt **20** 19; cf Mt **26** 32; Rom **8** 34; Col **3** 1). W. L. WALKER

RAISIN-CAKES, rā'z'n-kāks: RV gives this rendering for AV "foundations" in Isa **16** 7 (Heb *'ăshīshāh* from *'āshash*, "to found," "make firm," "press"). The trade in these would cease through the desolation of the vineyards. For AV "flagons of wine" in Hos **3** 1, RV gives "cakes of raisins," such as were offered to the gods of the land, the givers of the grape (cf Cant **2** 5). See next article.

RAISINS, rā'z'nz: (1) צִמּוּקִים, *çimmūḳīm*; *σταφίδες*, *staphídes*, trd "dried grapes," Nu **6** 3; mentioned in all other references as a portable food for a march or journey. Abigail supplied David with "a hundred clusters of raisins," among other things, in the wilderness of Paran (1 S **25** 18); David gave two clusters of raisins to a starving Egyp slave of the Amalekites at Besor (**30** 12); raisins formed part of the provision brought to David at Hebron for his army (1 Ch **12** 40); Ziba supplied David, when flying from Absalom, with a hundred clusters of raisins (2 S **16** 1). (2) אֲשִׁישָׁה, *'ăshīshāh*, something "pressed together," hence a "cake." In Hos **3** 1, mention is made of אֲשִׁישֵׁי עֲנָבִים, *'ăshīshē 'ănābhīm* (*πέμματα μετὰ σταφίδος*, *pémmata metá staphídos*), "cakes of raisins": "Jeh loveth the children of Israel, though they turn unto other gods, and love [m "or them that love"] cakes of raisins." These are supposed to have been cakes of dried, compressed grapes offered to false gods. Grätz considers that the Heb words are a corruption of *'ăshērīm* and *ḥammānīm* ("sun images"). Cf Isa **17** 8; **27** 9. In other passages "cakes" stands alone without "raisins," but the tr "cakes of raisins" is given in 2 S **6** 19; 1 Ch **16** 3; Cant **2** 5 (AV "flagons"); Isa **16** 7 m "foundations."

Raisins are today, as of old, prepared in considerable quantities in Pal, esp. at *es-Salt*, E. of the Jordan. The bunches of grapes are dipped in a strong solution of potash before being dried. E. W. G. MASTERMAN

RAKEM, rā'kem (רָקֶם, *rāḳem*, the pausal form of רֶקֶם, *reḳem*): The eponym of a clan of Machir (1 Ch **7** 16). See REKEM.

RAKKATH, rak'ath (רַקַּת, *raḳḳath*; B, **Ὠμαθαδακέθ**, *Ōmathadakéth*, A, **Ῥεκκάθ**, *Rhekkáth*): The Gr is obviously the result of confusing the two names Rakkath and Hammath, taking *r* in the former for *d*. Rakkath was one of the fortified cities in Naphtali (Josh **19** 35). It is named between Hammath and Chinnereth. Hammath is identified with the hot baths to the S. of Tiberias. There are traces of ancient fortifications here. The rabbis think that Tiberias was built on the site of Rakkath. Certain it is that Herod's town was built upon an ancient site, the graves of the old inhabitants being disturbed in digging the new foundations (Neubauer, *Géog. du Talm*, 208). W. EWING

RAKKON, rak'on (הָרַקּוֹן, *hā-raḳḳōn*; **Ἱεράκων**, *Hierákōn*). See ME-JARKON.

RAM, ram (רָם, *rām*, "high," "exalted"):

(1) An ancestor of David (Ruth **4** 19 ['Ἀρράν, *Arrán*]; Mt **1** 3.4 ['Ἀράμ, *Arám*]); in 1 Ch **2** 9 he is called the "brother," but in ver 25, the "son of Jerahmeel" (cf ver 27). Ram as the son of Hezron appears more likely than Ram the son of Jerahmeel, since, according to the narratives of 1 and **2** S, David cannot have been a Jerahmeelite.

(2) Name of Elihu's family (Job **32** 2). It is an open question as to whether Ram should be taken as a purely fictitious name, invented by the author of the Elihu speeches, or whether it is that of some obscure Arab tribe. In Gen **22** 21 Aram is a nephew of Buz (cf Elihu the Buzite), and the conjecture was at one time advanced that Ram was a contraction of Aram; but this theory is no longer held to be tenable. The suggestion that the initial *a* (א) has been changed by a scribal error into *h* (ה) is more acceptable. Rashi, the rabbinical commentator, takes the quaint position that Ram is identical with Abraham. HORACE J. WOLF

RAM, ram: (1) The ordinary word is אַיִל, *'ayil*, which is remarkably near to אַיָּל, *'ayyāl*, "deer" (cf Lat *caper*, *capra*, "goat," and *capreolus*, "wild goat" or "roe-buck"; also Gr *δορκάς*, *dorkás*, "roe-buck" or "gazelle"). (2) דְּכַר, *dekhār*, lit. "male" (Ezr **6** 9.17; **7** 17). (3) כַּר, *kar*, "battering ram" (Ezk **4** 2; **21** 22); elsewhere "lamb" (Dt **32** 14, etc). (4) עַתּוּד, *'attūdh*, properly "he-goat" ("ram," Gen **31** 10.12 AV). See SHEEP.

RAM, BATTERING. See SIEGE.

RAMA, rā'ma (**Ῥαμά**, *Rhamá*): AV; Gr form of RAMAH (q.v.) (Mt **2** 18).

RAMAH, rā'ma (הָרָמָה, *hā-rāmāh*, without the def. art. only in Neh **11** 33; Jer **31** 15): The name denotes height, from root רוּם, *rūm*, "to be high," and the towns to which it applied seem all to have stood on elevated sites.

(1) B, Ἀραήλ, *Araēl*, A, Ῥαμά, *Rhamá:* A fenced city in the lot assigned to Naphtali (Josh **19** 36). Only in this passage is the place referred to. It is probably identical with the modern *er-Rāmeh*, a large Christian village on the highway from *Ṣafed* to the coast, about 8 miles W.S.W. of that city. To the N. rises the mountain range which forms the southern boundary of Upper Galilee. In the valley to the S. there is much rich land cultivated by the villagers. The olives grown here are very fine, and fruitful vineyards cover many of the surrounding slopes. No remains of antiquity are to be seen above ground; but the site is one likely to have been occupied in ancient times.

(2) Ῥαμᾶ, *Rhamá:* A city that is mentioned only once, on the boundary of Asher (Josh **19** 29). The line of the boundary cannot be followed with certainty; but perhaps we may identify Ramah with the modern *Rāmiyeh*, a village situated on a hill which rises in the midst of a hollow, some 13 miles S.E. of Tyre, and 12 miles E. of the Ladder of Tyre. To the S.W. is a marshy lake which dries up in summer. Traces of antiquity are found in the cisterns, a large reservoir and many sarcophagi. To the W. is the high hill *Belāṭ*, with ancient ruins, and remains of a temple of which several columns are still *in situ*.

(3) B, Ῥαμά, *Rhamá*, A, Ἰαμά, *Iamá*, and other forms: A city in the territory of Benjamin named between Gibeon and Beeroth (Josh **18** 25). The Levite thought of it as a possible resting-place for himself and his concubine on their northward journey (Jgs **19** 13). The palm tree of Deborah was between this and Bethel (Jgs **4** 5). Baasha, king of Samaria, sought to fortify Ramah against Asa, king of Judah. The latter frustrated the attempt, and carried off the materials which Baasha had collected, and with them fortified against him Geba of Benjamin and Mizpah (1 K **15** 17; 2 Ch **16** 5). Here the captain of Nebuchadnezzar's guard released Jeremiah after he had been carried in bonds from Jerus (Jer **40** 1). It figures in Isaiah's picture of the Assyrians' approach (**10** 29). It is named by Hosea in connection with Gibeah (**5** 8), and is mentioned as being reoccupied after the exile (Ezr **2** 26; Neh **7** 30). It was near the traditional tomb of Rachel (Jer **31** 15; cf 1 S **10** 2; Mt **2** 18, AV "Rama").

From the passages cited we gather that Ramah lay some distance to the N. of Gibeah, and not far from Gibeon and Beeroth. The first is identified with *Tell el-Fūl*, about 3 miles N. of Jerus. Two miles farther N. is *er-Rām*. Gibeon (*el-Jīb*) is about 3 miles W. of *er-Rām*, and Beeroth (*el-Bīreh*) is about 4 miles to the N. *Onom* places Ramah 6 Rom miles N. of Jerus; while Jos (*Ant*, VIII, xii, 3) says it lay 40 furlongs from the city. All this points definitely to identification with *er-Rām*. The modern village crowns a high limestone hill to the S. of the road, a position of great strength. W. of the village is an ancient reservoir. In the hill are cisterns, and a good well to the S.

(4) Ἀραμαθαίμ, *Aramathaím:* The home of Elkanah and Hannah, and the birthplace of Samuel (1 S **1** 19; **2** 11, etc). In 1 S **1** 1 it is called "Ramathaim-zophim" (הָרָמָתַיִם צוֹפִים, *hā-rāmāthayim-çōphīm*). The phrase as it stands is grammatically incorrect, and suggests tampering with the text. It might possibly be tr[d] "Ramathaim of the Zuphites." It was in Mt. Ephraim, within accessible distance of Shiloh, whither Samuel's parents went up from year to year to worship and to sacrifice (**1** 3). From Ramah as a center Samuel went on circuit annually, to judge Israel, to Bethel, Gilgal and Mizpah (**7** 16 f). It is very probable that this is the city in which, guided by his servant, Saul first made the acquaintance of Samuel (**9** 6.10), where there was a high place (ver 12). Hither at all events came the elders of Israel with their demand that a king should be set over them (**8** 4 f). After his final break with Saul, Samuel retired in sorrow to Ramah (**15** 34 f). Here, in Naioth, David found asylum with Samuel from the mad king (**19** 18, etc), and hence he fled on his ill-starred visit to Nob (**20** 1). In his native city the dust of the dead Samuel was laid (**25** 1; **28** 3). In 1 Macc **11** 34 it is named as one of the three toparchies along with Aphaerema and Lydda, which were added to Judaea from the country of Samaria in 145 BC. *Onom* places it near Diospolis (Euseb.) in the district of Timnah (Jerome).

There are two serious rivals for the honor of representing the ancient Ramah. (*a*) *Beit Rīma*, a village occupying a height 13 miles E.N.E. of Lydda (Diospolis), 12 miles W. of Shiloh, and about the same distance N.W. of Bethel. This identification has the support of G. A. Smith (*HGHL*, 254), and Buhl (*GAP*, 170). (*b*) *Ramallah*, a large and prosperous village occupying a lofty position with ancient remains. It commands a wide prospect, esp. to the W. It lies about 8 miles N. of Jerus, 3 W. of Bethel, and 12 S.W. of Shiloh. The name meaning "the height" or "high place of God" may be reminiscent of the high place in the city where Saul found Samuel. In other respects it agrees very well with the Bib. data.

Claims have also been advanced on behalf of *Ramleh*, a village 2 miles S.W. of Lydda, in the plain of Sharon. This, however, is out of the question, as the place did not exist before Arab times. Others support identification with *Neby Samwīl*, which more probably represents the ancient MIZPAH (q.v.).

(5) **Ramah of the South,** AV "Ramath of the South": Ramath is the construct form of Ramah (Josh **19** 8) (רָאמַת נֶגֶב, *rā'math neghebh;* Βάμεθ κατὰ λίβα, *Bámeth katá líba*). A city in that part of the territory of Judah which was allotted to Simeon. It stands here in apposition to Baalath-beer, and is probably a second name for the same place. It seems to correspond also with "Ramoth [pl.] of the South" (1 S **30** 27), a place to which David sent a share of the spoil taken from the Amalekites. In this passage LXX retains the sing. form, *Rhamá nótou*. Identification has been suggested with *Ḳubbet el-Baul* about 37 miles S. of Hebron; and with *Kurnub* a little farther S. There is no substantial ground for either identification.

(6) B, Ῥεμμώθ, *Rhemmōth*, A, Ῥαμώθ, *Rhamōth:* Ramah in 2 K **8** 29; 2 Ch **22** 6, is a contraction of Ramoth-gilead. W. EWING

RAMATH, rā'math, **OF THE SOUTH** (Josh **19** 8 AV). See RAMAH, (5).

RAMATH-LEHI, rā'math-lē'hī (רָמַת לְחִי, *rāmath leḥī*, "the hill" or "height of Lehi"; **Ἀναίρεσις σιαγόνος**, *Anaíresis siagónos*): So the place is said to have been called where Samson threw away the jaw-bone of an ass, with which he had slain 1,000 Philis (Jgs **15** 17). LXX seems to have supposed that the name referred to the "heaving" or throwing up of the jaw-bone. The Heb, however, corresponds to the form used in other place-names, such as Ramath-mizpeh, and must be read as "Ramah of Lehi." The name Lehi may have been given because of some real or imagined likeness in the place to the shape of a jaw-bone (Jgs **15** 9.14.19). It may have been in *Wâdy es-Sarār*, not far from Zorah and Timnath; but the available data do not permit of certain identification. See JAW-BONE; LEHI. W. EWING

RAMATH-MIZPEH, rā'math-miz'pe (רָמַת הַמִּצְפֶּה, *rāmath ha-miçpeh;* B, **Ἀραβὼθ κατὰ τὴν Μασσηφᾶ,** *Arabōth katá tēn Massēphá,* A, **Ῥαμὼθ . . . . Μασφά,** *Rhamōth . . . . Maspha*): A place mentioned in Josh **13** 26 in a statement of the boundary of Gad, between Heshbon and Betonim. It may possibly be identical with MIZPAH, (1).

RAMATHAIM, rā-ma-thā'im (1 Macc **11** 34; AV **Ramathem,** ram'a-them). See RAMAH, (4).

RAMATHAIM-ZOPHIM, rā-ma-thā'im-zō'fim. See RAMAH, (4).

RAMATHITE, rā'math-īt (הָרָמָתִי, *hā-rāmāthī;* B, **ὁ ἐκ Ῥαήλ,** *ho ek Rhaēl,* A, **ὁ Ῥαμαθαῖος,** *ho Rhamathaíos*): So Shimei is called who was set by David over the vineyards (1 Ch **27** 27). There is nothing to show to which Ramah he belonged.

RAMESES, ram'ē-sēz, ra-mē'sēz. See RAAMSES.

RAMIAH, ra-mī'a (רַמְיָה, *ramyāh,* "Jeh hath loosened" or "Jeh is high"): One of the Israelites, of the sons of Parosh, mentioned in the register of those who had offended in the matter of foreign marriages (Ezr **10** 25). The form of the name in 1 Esd (**9** 26), "Hiermas," presupposes a Heb form *y^eremyāh* or possibly *yirm^eyāh*="Jeremiah."

RAMOTH, rā'moth:

(1) רְאמוֹת, *rā'mōth;* ἡ Ῥαμώθ, *hē Rhamōth:* A city in the territory of Issachar assigned to the Gershonite Levites (1 Ch **6** 73), mentioned between Daberath and Anem. It seems to correspond to "Remeth" in Josh **19** 21, and to "Jarmuth" in **21** 29, and is possibly identical with *er-Rāmeh* about 11 miles S.W. of *Jenīn.*

(2) **Ramoth of the South.** See RAMAH, (5).

(3) **Ramoth in Gilead.** See RAMOTH-GILEAD.

RAMOTH, rā'moth (רָמוֹת, *rāmōth,* Ḳ^erē for *y^erēmōth* [Ezr **10** 29 AV]; RVm K^ethībh makes the name similar to those in vs 26.27): One of the offenders in the matter of foreign marriages. ERV and ARV, adopting K^ethībh, read JEREMOTH (q.v.).

RAMOTH (Job **28** 18 AVm). See STONES, PRECIOUS.

RAMOTH-GILEAD, rā'moth-gil'ē-ad (רָמֹת גִּלְעָד, *rāmōth gil'ādh;* B, **Ῥεμμὰθ Γαλαάδ,** *Rhemmáth Galaád,* A, **Ῥαμμώθ,** *Rhammōth,* and other forms): A great and strong city E. of the Jordan in the territory of Gad, which played an important part in the wars of Israel. It is first mentioned in connection with the appointment of the Cities of Refuge (Dt **4** 43; Josh **20** 8). It was assigned to the Merarite Levites (Josh **21** 38; 1 Ch **6** 80). In these four passages it is called "Ramoth in Gilead" (ר' בַּגִּלְעָד, *rāmōth ba-gil'ādh*). This form is given wrongly by AV in 1 K **22** 3. In all other places the form "Ramoth-gilead" is used.

1. History

Here Ben-geber was placed in charge of one of Solomon's administrative districts (1 K **4** 13), which included Havvoth-jair and "the region of Argob, which is in Bashan." The city was taken from Omri by the Syrians under Ben-hadad I (*Ant,* VIII, xv, 3 ff), and even after the defeat of Ben-hadad at Aphek they remained masters of this fortress. In order to recover it for Israel Ahab invited Jehoshaphat of Judah to accompany him in a campaign. Despite the discouragement of Micaiah, the royal pair set out on the disastrous enterprise. In their attack on the city Ahab fought in disguise, but was mortally wounded by an arrow from a bow drawn "at a venture" (1 K **22** 1–40; 2 Ch **18**). The attempt was renewed by Ahab's son Joram; but his father's ill fortune followed him, and, heavily wounded, he retired for healing to Jezreel (2 K **8** 28 ff; 2 Ch **22** 5 f). During the king's absence from the camp at Ramoth-gilead Jehu was there anointed king of Israel by Elisha (2 K **9** 1 ff; 2 Ch **22** 7). He proved a swift instrument of vengeance against the doomed house of Ahab. According to Jos (*Ant,* IX, vi, 1) the city was taken before Joram's departure. This is confirmed by 2 K **9** 14 ff. The place is not mentioned again, unless, indeed, it be identical with "Mizpeh" in 1 Macc **5** 35.

It is just possible that Ramoth-gilead corresponds to MIZPAH, (1), and to RAMATH-MIZPEH.

2. Identification

The spot where Laban and Jacob parted is called both Galeed and Mizpah. Ramath may become Ramoth, as we see in the case of Ramah of the South.

Merrill identifies the city with *Jerash,* the splendid ruins of which lie in *Wâdy ed-Deir,* N. of the Jabbok. He quotes the Bab Talm (*Makkōth* **9***b*) as placing the Cities of Refuge in pairs, so that those on the E. of the Jordan are opposite those on the W. Shechem, being the middle one of the three W. of the Jordan, should have Ramoth-gilead nearly opposite to it on the E., and this would place its site at Gerasa, the modern *Jerash* (*HDB,* s.v.). But the words of the Talm must not be interpreted too strictly. It seems very probable that Golan lay far S. of a line drawn due E. from *Ḳedes* (Kedesh-naphtali). No remains have been discovered at *Jerash* older than Gr-Rom times, although the presence of a fine perennial spring makes occupation in antiquity probable. The place could be approached by chariots along *Wâdy 'Ajlūn,* and the country adjoining was not unsuitable for chariot evolutions.

Conder and others have suggested *Reimūn,* an ancient site to the W. of Jerash. The absence of any source of good water-supply is practically fatal to this identification. Buhl (*GAP,* 261 ff) favors *el-Jil'ād,* a ruined site on a hill S. of the Jabbok; see GILEAD, (1). Eusebius and Jerome (*Onom,* s.v.) contradict each other, the former placing Ramoth-gilead 15 miles W., and the latter 15 miles E. of Philadelphia. It is clear, however, that this is a mere slip on Jerome's part, as both say it is near the Jabbok. Many have identified it with *es-Salṭ,* which is indeed 15 miles W. of *'Ammān* (Philadelphia), but it is 10 miles S. of the Jabbok, and so can hardly be described as near that river. It is also no place for chariot warfare. The case against identification with Ramoth-gilead is conclusively stated by Rev. G. A. Cooke in Driver's *Dt,* xx.

In suggesting these sites sufficient attention has not been given to what is said in 1 K **4**. The authority of the king's officer in Ramoth-gilead extended over the land of Argob in Bashan, as well as over the towns of Jair in Gilead. A situation therefore to the N. of Mahanaim must be sought. Guthe would find it at *er-Remtheh,* on the pilgrim road, about 10 miles S. of *Mezērīb* (cf *HGHL,* 586 ff). Cheyne's suggestion of *Ṣalkhad,* away on the crest of the mountain of Bashan, is out of the question. Rev. Caleb Hauser (*PEFS,* 1906, 304 f) argues in favor of *Beit Rās,* over 11 miles S.E. of Gadara, a position commanding all Northern Gilead and as favorably situated as Jerash for chariot warfare and communication with the W. of Jordan.

"Here we have the heights of Northern Gilead. Ramoth, Capitolias, and *Beit Rās* are in their respective languages idiomatic equivalents. It is improbable that a large city like Capitolias should have superseded anything but a very important city of earlier times." We must be content to leave the question open meantime. W. EWING

RAMPART, ram'pärt (Lam **2** 8; Nah **3** 8). See FORTIFICATION.

RAM'S HORN. See MUSIC.

RAMS' SKINS: The skin of the sheep, roughly tanned with all the wool on, is the common winter jacket of the shepherd or peasant, the ram's being considered esp. desirable (cf He **11** 37). Hence the appropriateness of these skins in the covering of the tabernacle (Ex **25** 5, etc). See TABERNACLE; DYE, DYEING.

RANGE, rānj: "Range" and "rank" have the same derivation, and in the sense of a "row" (of men, etc) they were formerly interchangeable. "Range" with this meaning is found in 2 K **11** 8.15 AV ‖2 Ch **23** 14 (RV "rank"; שְׂדֵרָה, *sᵉdhērāh,* "row"). Hence "to range" is "to set in a line" (Jth **2** 16; 2 Macc **12** 20, *diatássō*) or "to move in a line" or, simply, "to roam," whence "a ranging bear" (Prov **28** 15; שָׁקַק, *shāḳaḳ,* "run to and fro"). A cooking "range" is a stove on which pots, etc, can be set in a row, but the *kīrayim* (כִּירַיִם) of Lev **11** 35 is a much more primitive affair, composed, probably, of two plates (*kīrayim* is a dual). In Job **39** 8 "range of the mountains" is good modern use, but יתור, *ythr,* should be pointed *yāthūr* (not *yᵉthūr* as in MT) and connected with *tūr,* "search." So translate "He searcheth out the mountains as his pasture." BURTON SCOTT EASTON

RANK, raṇk: (1) אֹרַח, *'ōraḥ,* used in Joel **2** 7 of the advance of the locust army which marched in perfect order and in straight lines, none crossing the other's track. (2) מַעֲרָכָה, *ma'ărākhāh,* "battle array" (1 Ch **12** 38 AV; cf 1 S **4** 16; **17** 22.48). See ARMY.

RANKS, raṇks (**πρασιά,** *prasiá,* "a square plot of ground," "a garden-bed"): "They sat down in ranks" (Mk **6** 40); the several reclining ranks formed, as it were, separate plots or "garden-beds."

RANSOM, ran'sum (the noun occurs in the Eng. Bible 12 t [Ex **21** 30 AV, פִּדְיוֹן, *pidhyōn;* **30** 12; Job **33** 24; **36** 18; Prov **6** 35; **13** 8; **21** 18; Isa **43** 3, כֹּפֶר, *kōpher;* Mt **20** 28; Mk **10** 45, **λύτρον,** *lútron;* 1 Tim **2** 6, **ἀντίλυτρον,** *antílutron*]; the verbal form occurs 4 t [Isa **35** 10; Hos **13** 14, פָּדָה, *pādhāh;* Isa **51** 10 AV; Jer **31** 11, גָּאַל, *gā'al;* these two Heb vbs. are generally rendered in other passages by the Eng. "redeem"]):

1. Usage by Christ
2. OT Usage—the Law
   - (1) General Cases
   - (2) Redemption Money—the Firstborn
   - (3) Connection with Sacrifice
   - (4) Typical Reference to the Messiah
3. The Pss and Job
4. Apostolic Teaching
5. To Whom Was the Ransom Paid?
   - (1) Not to Satan
   - (2) To Divine Justice
     - (*a*) Redemption by Price
     - (*b*) Redemption by Power

LITERATURE

The supremely important instance is the utterance of the Lord Jesus Christ as reported by Matthew and Mark (Mt **20** 28; Mk **10** 45), and in looking at it we shall be able, by way of illustration, to glance at the OT passages.

1. Usage by Christ

The context refers to the dispute among the disciples concerning position in the Kingdom, with their misconception of the true nature of Christ's Kingdom. Christ makes use of the occasion to set forth the great law of service as determining the place of honor in that Kingdom, and illustrates and enforces it by showing that its greatest exemplification is to be found in His own mission: "For the Son of man also came not to be ministered unto, but to minister" (Mk **10** 45). His ministry, however, was to pass into the great act of sacrifice, of which all other acts of self-sacrifice on the part of His people would be but a faint reflection—"and to give his life [soul] a ransom for many" (ib). He thus gives a very clear intimation of the purpose and meaning of His death; the clearest of all the intimations reported by the synoptists. The word He uses bears a well-established meaning, and is accurately rendered by our word "ransom," a price paid to secure the freedom of a slave or to set free from liabilities and charges, and generally the deliverance from calamity by paying the forfeit. The familiar vb. *lúō,* "to loose," "to set free," is the root, then *lútron,* that which secures the freedom, the payment or forfeit; thence come the cognate vb. *lutróō,* "to set free upon payment of a ransom," "to redeem"; *lútrōsis,* "the actual setting free," "the redemption," and *lutrōtḗs,* "the redeemer." The favorite NT word for "redemption" is the compound form, *apolútrōsis.*

The word *lutron* was common in Gr classical lit., constantly bearing the sense of "ransom price," and was frequently connected with ritual usage, with sacrifice and expiation.

2. OT Usage—the Law

But for the full explanation of Our Lord's great thought we have to look to the OT usage. The two leading Heb vbs. trᵈ in our version by "redeem," are generally rendered in the LXX by *lutroō,* and derivatives of these words conveying the idea of the actual price paid are trᵈ by this very word *lutron.*

(1) *General cases.*—In Ex **21** 30 we have the law concerning the case of the person killed by an ox; the ox was to be killed and the owner of it was also liable to death but the proviso was made, "If there be laid on him a sum of money, then he shall give for the ransom of his life whatsoever is laid upon him" (AV). The Heb for "sum of money" is *kōpher,* lit. "atonement" (RV "ransom"); the word for "ransom" (RV "redemption") is *pidhyōn* (from *pādhāh*); the LXX renders both by *lutron* (rather by the pl. form *lutra*). In Lev **25,** among the directions in relation to the Jubilee, we have the provision (ver 23) that the land was not to be sold "in perpetuity," but where any portion has been sold, opportunity is to be given for re-purchase: "Ye shall grant a *redemption* for the land" (ver 24). The Heb is *gᵉ'ullāh,* a derivative of *gā'al,* the LXX *lutra.* In vs 25.26, the case is mentioned of a man who through poverty has sold part of his land; if a near kinsman is able to redeem it he shall do so; if there is no one to act this brotherly part, and the man himself is able to redeem it, then a certain scale of price is arranged. In the Heb it is again *gā'al* that is used with the cognate *gō'ēl* for "kinsman." The last clause rendered in AV, "and himself be able to redeem it" (in RV "and he be waxed rich and find sufficient to redeem it"), is lit. "and his hand shall acquire and he find sufficient for its redemption"; LXX has the vb. *lutroō* in the first part, and renders the clause pretty literally, "and there be furnished to his hand and there be found with him the sufficient price [*lutra*] of it." In vs 51.52, in reference to the redemption of the Jew sold into slavery, we have twice in the Heb the word *gᵉ'ullāh,* rendered in Eng. accurately "the price of his redemption"; and by LXX with equal accuracy, in both cases, *lutra,* "the ransom-price." In Lev **27** 31 AV, the phrase "if a man will at all redeem aught of his tithes" is intended to represent the emphatic Heb idiom, "if a man redeeming will redeem," which is rendered by LXX *eán dé lutrōtai lútrō ánthrōpos.*

(2) *Redemption money—the firstborn.*—But perhaps the most important passage is the law concern-

ing the half-shekel to be paid by every Israelite from 20 years old and upward when a census was taken. It was to be the same for rich and poor, and it was called "atonement money," "to make atonement for their souls." In the opening words of the law, as given in Ex **30** 12 (AV), we read "Then shall they give every man a ransom for his soul unto the Lord"—the Heb *kōpher;* the LXX rendering is *lútra tês psuchês autoú*, "a ransom price for his soul." All the people were thus considered as doomed and needing atonement, and it is significant that this atonement money paid at the first census furnished the silver for the sockets of the tabernacle boards, intimating that the typical tabernacle was built upon atonement. The same thought, that the people's lives were forfeited, comes out in the provision for the consecration of the Levites, recorded in full in Nu **3** 40–51. The firstborn represented the people. God claimed all the firstborn as forfeited to Himself, teaching that Israel deserved the same punishment as the Egyptians, and was only spared by the grace of Jeh, and in virtue of the sprinkled blood. Now He takes to Himself for His services the Levites as the equivalent of the firstborn, and when it was found that the number of the firstborn exceeded the number of the Levites, equivalence was maintained by ransoming at a certain price the surplusage of the firstborn males. In the LXX account, *lutra* occurs 4 t, twice for the phrase "those to be redeemed," and twice for "redemption money." Thus the idea of ransom for the forfeited life became familiar to the people as educated by the typical system, and redemption expressed the sum total of their hopes for the future, however faulty might be their conception of the nature of that redemption.

(3) *Connection with sacrifice.*—It is also clear in the typical teaching that sacrifice and ransom were closely related. Even in classical Gr, as we have noted, the two conceptions were connected, and it is not surprising to find it so in the OT. *Kōpher*, we have seen, is lit. "atonement" and comes from *kāphar*, lit. "to cover," and thence by covering to make atonement, or to cover by making atonement; and so it is in the Piel form, the most common and technical Heb word for making atonement, or expiation, or propitiation, and is frequently rendered in the Gr by *hiláskomai*, often too by the compound *exiláskomai*. In Ex **21** 30, *kōpher*, we noted, is used interchangeably with *pidhyōn*, both being represented in the LXX by *lutra*, and so in Ex **30** 12; Nu **35** 31.32; the Heb *kōpher* is *lutra* in the Gr. In the latter place, where it is twice stated that no *satisfaction* shall be taken for the life of a murderer, the Heb is *kōpher*, LXX *lutra*, RV "ransom," AV "satisfaction."

(4) *Typical reference to the Messiah.*—Sacrifice was thus linked with ransom. Sacrifice was the Divinely appointed covering for sin. The ransom for the deliverance of the sinner was to be by sacrifice. Both the typical testimony of the Law and the prophetic testimony gave prominence to the thought of redemption. The Coming One was to be a Redeemer. Redemption was to be the great work of the Messiah. The people seem to have looked for the redemption of the soul to God alone through the observance of their appointed ritual, while redemption, in the more general sense of deliverance from all enemies and troubles, they linked with the advent of the Messiah. It required a spiritual vision to see that the two things would coincide, that the Messiah would effect redemption in all its phases and fulness by means of ransom, of sacrifice, of expiation.

Jesus appeared as the Messiah in whom all the old economy was to be fulfilled. He knew perfectly the meaning of the typical and prophetic testimony; and with that fully in view, knowing that His death was to fulfil the OT types and accomplish its brightest prophetic anticipations, He deliberately uses this term *lutron* to describe it (Mt **20** 28); in speaking of His death as a ransom, He also regarded it as a sacrifice, an expiatory offering. The strong preposition used intensifies the idea of ransom and expiation, even to the point of substitution. It is *antí*, "instead of," and the idea of exchange, equivalence, substitution cannot be removed from it. In Nu **3** 45, "Take the Levites *instead of* all the first-born," the LXX uses *anti*, which, like the Eng. "instead of," exactly represents the Heb *taḥath;* and all three convey most unmistakably the idea of substitution. And as the Levites were to be substituted for the firstborn, so for the surplus of the firstborn the "ransom money" was to be substituted, that idea, however, being clearly enough indicated by the use of the genitive. Indeed the simpler way of describing a ransom would be with the genitive, the ransom *of* many; or as our version renders, "a ransom *for* many"; but just because the ransom here is not simply a money payment, but is the actual sacrifice of the life, the substitution of His soul for many, He is appropriately said "to give his soul a ransom *instead of* many." The Kingdom of God which Christ proclaimed was so diverse in character from that which Salome and her sons anticipated that, so far from appearing in dazzling splendor, with distinguished places of power for eager aspirants, it was to be a spiritual home for redeemed sinners. Men held captive by sin needed to be ransomed that they might be free to become subjects of the Kingdom, and so the ransom work, the sufferings and death of Christ, must lie at the very foundation of that Kingdom. The need of ransom supposes life forfeited; the ransom paid secures life and liberty; the life which Christ gives comes through His ransoming death.

3. The Pss and Job

Besides the passages in the Pent which we have noted, special mention should be made of the two great passages which bear so closely upon the need of spiritual redemption, and come into line with this great utterance of Christ. Ps **49** 7.8, "None of them can by any means redeem [*pādhāh; lutroō*] his brother, nor give to God a ransom [*kōpher; exilasma*] for him (for the redemption of their life is costly, and it faileth for ever)." (The Heb gives *pidhyōn* for "redemption"; the Gr has "the price of the redemption of his soul.") No human power or skill, no forfeit in money or service or life can avail to ransom any soul from the doom entailed by sin. But in the same ps (ver 15) the triumphant hope is expressed, "But God will redeem [*pādhāh; lutroō*] my soul from the power of Sheol." In Job **33** 24, "Deliver him from going down to the pit, I have found a ransom": God is the speaker, and whatever may be the particular exegesis of the passage in its original application, it surely contains an anticipation of the gospel redemption. This Divine eureka is explained in the light of Christ's utterance; it finds its realization through the cross: "I have found a ransom," for "the Son of Man" has given "his soul a ransom for many."

4. Apostolic Teaching

This great utterance of the Saviour may well be considered as the germ of all the apostolic teaching concerning redemption, but it is not for us to show its unfolding beyond noting that in apostolic thought the redemption was always connected with the death, the sacrifice of Christ.

Thus Paul (Eph **1** 7), "In whom we have our redemption through his blood." Thus Peter (1 Pet **1** 18.19), "Ye were redeemed, not with corruptible things . . . . but with precious blood, as of a lamb without blemish and without spot, even the blood of Christ." So in He **9** 12 it is shown that Christ "through his own blood, entered in once for all into the holy place, having obtained eternal redemption"; and in the Apocalypse (Rev **5** 9) the song is, "Thou wast slain, and didst purchase unto God with thy blood men of every tribe," etc.

In all but the last of these passages there is an echo of the very word used by Christ, *apolutrōsis* and *lutrōsis*, both being connected with *lutron*. In 1 Tim **2** 5.6 Paul has a still closer verbal coincidence when he says, "Christ Jesus, who gave himself a ransom for all" (*antilutron*). The word used in the Apocalypse is *agorázō*, to buy in the open market, and is frequently used of the redeeming work of Christ (Rev **14** 3.4; 2 Pet **2** 1; 1 Cor **6** 20; **7** 23). In the two places where Paul uses it he adds the means of purchase: "Ye were bought with a price," which from his point of view would be equivalent to ransom. In the passage in Gal **3** 13; **4** 5, Paul uses the compound *exagorázō*, which is equivalent to "redeem, buy off, deliver by paying the price."

5. To Whom Was the Ransom Paid?

The question "Who receives the ransom?" is not directly raised in Scripture, but it is one that not unnaturally occurs to the mind, and theologians have answered it in varying ways.

(1) *Not to Satan.*—The idea entertained by some of the Fathers (Irenaeus, Origen) that the ransom was given to Satan, who is conceived of as having through the sin of man a righteous claim upon him, which Christ recognizes and meets, is grotesque, and not in any way countenanced by Scripture.

(2) *To Divine justice.*—But in repudiating it, there is no need to go so far as to deny that there is anything answering to a real ransoming transaction. All that we have said goes to show that, in no mere figure of speech, but in tremendous reality, Christ gave "his life a ransom," and if our mind demands an answer to the question to whom the ransom was paid, it does not seem at all unreasonable to think of the justice of God, or God in His character of Moral Governor, as requiring and receiving it. In all that Scripture asserts about propitiation, sacrifice, reconciliation in relation to the work of Christ, it is implied that there is wrath to be averted, someone to be appeased or satisfied, and while it may be enough simply to think of the effects of Christ's redeeming work in setting us free from the penal claims of the Law—the just doom of sin—it does not seem going beyond the spirit of Scripture to draw the logical inference that the ransom price was paid to the Guardian of that holy law, the Administrator of eternal justice. "Christ redeemed us from the curse of the law, having become a curse for us" (Gal **3** 13). This essential, fundamental phase of redemption is what theologians, with good Scripture warrant, have called redemption by blood, or by price, as distinguished from the practical outcome of the work of Christ in the life which is redemption by power.

(*a*) Redemption by price: As to Satan's claims, Christ by paying the ransom price, having secured the right to redeem, exercises His power on behalf of the believing sinner. He does not recognize the right of Satan. He is the "strong man" holding his captives lawfully, and Christ the "stronger than he" overcomes him and spoils him, and sets his captives free (Lk **11** 21.22). In one sense men may be said to have sold themselves to Satan, but they had no right to sell, nor he to buy, and Christ ignores that transaction and brings "to nought him that had the power of death, that is, the devil" (He **2** 14), and so is able to "deliver all them who through fear of death were all their lifetime subject to bondage" (He **2** 15).

(*b*) Redemption by power: Many of the OT passages about the redemption wrought on behalf of God's people illustrate this redemption by power, and the redemption by power is always founded on the redemption by price; the release follows the ransom. In the case of Israel, there was first the redemption by blood—the sprinkled blood of the Paschal Lamb which sheltered from the destroying angel (Ex **12**)—and then followed the redemption by power, when by strength of hand Jeh brought His people out from Egypt (Ex **13** 14), and in His mercy led forth the people which He had redeemed (Ex **15** 13).

So under the gospel when "he hath visited and wrought redemption for his people" (Lk **1** 68), He can "grant unto us that we being delivered out of the hand of our enemies should serve him without fear" (Lk **1** 74). It is because we have in Him our redemption through His blood that we can be delivered out of the power of darkness (Col **1** 13.14). See further, REDEEMER, REDEMPTION.

LITERATURE.—See works on NT Theology (Weiss, Schmid, Stevens, etc); arts. in *HDB; DCG*.

ARCHIBALD M'CAIG

RAPE, rāp. See CRIMES; PUNISHMENTS.

RAPHA, RAPHAH, rā'fa (רָפָא, *rāphā'*):

(1) In RVm these names are substituted for "the giant" in 1 Ch **20** 4.6.8 and in 2 S **21** 16.18.20.22. The latter passage states that certain champions of the Philis who were slain by David's warriors had been born to the *rāphāh* in Gath. The text is corrupt; Raphah is probably an eponym. Originally the name of one of the Philis who was of the body "Rephaites" stood in the text. The plural of this word, or at least a plural of this stem, is REPHAIM (q.v.).

(2) Raphah (AV "Rapha"), a descendant of Saul (1 Ch **8** 37). See REPHAIAH.

HORACE J. WOLF

RAPHAEL, raf'ȧ-el, rā'fȧ-el (רְפָאֵל, *r*ᵉ*phā'ēl*, from *rāphā' 'ēl*, "God has healed"; **Ῥαφαήλ**, *Rhaphaēl*): The name of the angel who, as Azarias, guides Tobias to ECBATANA and RAGES (q.v.). The purpose of his mission is, in accordance with his name, to cure Tobit of blindness, and to deliver Sarah, the daughter of Raguel, from the power of the evil spirit Asmodaeus (Tob **3** 8; **12** 14). Later, in addition, when he reveals himself (**12** 15), he declares that he is "one of the seven holy angels, which present the prayers of the saints, and go in before the glory of the Holy One." These seven angels are derived, according to Dr. Kohut, from the seven Am-shaspands (*Amesha-spentas*) of Zoroastrianism (cf Rev **4** 5). At the head of the elaborate angelology of the Enoch books there are "four presences," and Raphael is one of them (En **40** 9; **54** 6). In the first of these passages Raphael is the healer; in the second, he with Michael, Gabriel and Phanuel lead the wicked away to punishment. These four presences seem related to the four "living creatures" of Ezk (**1** 5) and of the Apocalypse (Rev **4** 6). While this is the general representation of Raphael's position in En, in **20** 3 he is named among the angels who "watch," whose number according to the Gr text is seven. Raphael shared in the function assigned to the archangels, in the *Oracula Sibyllina*, of leading souls to the judgment seat of God (II, 215, Alexandre's text). He occupies a prominent place in Jewish mediaeval writings; he with Michael and Gabriel cured Abraham (*Yōmā'* **37***a*); according to the book *Zōhar*, Raphael conveyed to Adam a book containing 72 kinds of wisdom in 670 writings. The painters of the Renaissance frequently depicted Raphael.

J. E. H. THOMSON

RAPHAIM, raf'ȧ-im, ra-fā'im (B omits; ℵ and A have **Ῥαφα[ε]ίν**, *Rhapha[e]in*): An ancestor of Judith (Jth **8** 1).

RAPHON, rā'fon (**Ῥαφειών**, *Rhapheiōn*): The place where in his campaign E. of Jordan Judas inflicted disastrous defeat on the host of Timotheus, the fugitives fleeing for refuge to the temple at Carnaim (1 Macc **5** 37 ff; *Ant*, XII, viii, 4). The same place is doubtless referred to by Pliny as "Raphana" (*NH*, v.16). It may possibly be represented by the modern *Rāfeh*, on the E. of the pilgrimage road, about 17 miles N. of *Ḍer'ah*, and 11 miles N.E. of

Tell el-'Ash'ary. It is a mile and a half N. of *Wâdy Kanawāt,* which would thus be the "brook" mentioned in the narrative. It is perhaps far enough away from Carnaim, if this is rightly placed at *Tell el-'Ash'ary.* W. EWING

RAPHU, rā'fū (רָפוּא, *rāphū',* "one healed"): The father of Palti, the spy selected from the tribe of Benjamin (Nu **13** 9).

RASSES, ras'ēz (א, **Ῥαασσείς,** *Rhaasseís,* A B, **Ῥασσείς,** *Rhasseís;* Vulg *Tharsis;* Old Lat *Thiras et Rasis*): The children of Rasses are mentioned with Put, Lud and the children of Ishmael as having been subdued by Holofernes (Jth **2** 23).

Their identity is a matter of conjecture only. Some think Vulg *Tharsis* (=Tarsus) is meant, others Rosh (Ezk **38** 2.3; **39** 1), others Rhosos, a mountain range and city S. from Anunus, on the Gulf of Issus. Most probably a district, not a town, is named, situated in the eastern part of Asia Minor.

S. F. HUNTER

RATHUMUS, ra-thū'mus (**Ῥάθυμος,** *Rháthumos*): One of those who joined in writing a letter to protest to Artaxerxes against the Jews (1 Esd **2** 16 ff). In **2** 17 he is styled "story-writer," RVm "recorder" (ὁ τὰ προσπίπτοντα sc. γράφων, *ho tá prospíptonta* [*gráphōn*]) = "Rehum the chancellor" of Ezr **4** 8, Rathumus being a Gr form of Rehum. In 1 Esd **2** 16 his title appears as an independent proper name, BEELTETHMUS (q.v.) (here AVm gives "Bahumus," a misprint), and in **2** 25 R. and Beeltethmus are given as distinct persons.

RAVEN, rā'v'n (עֹרֵב, *'ōrēbh;* **κόραξ,** *kórax;* Lat *Corvus corax*): A large family of the smaller birds of prey belonging to the genus *Corvus corax.* A bird of such universal distribution that it is known

Raven (*Corvus corax*).

from Iceland to Japan, all over Asia, Europe and Africa, but almost extinct and not of general distribution in our own country. In no land is it more numerous than in Pal. In general appearance it resembles the crow, but is much larger, being almost two feet long, of a glossy black, with whiskers around the beak, and rather stiff-pointed neck feathers. A bird exhibiting as much intelligence as any, and of a saucy, impudent disposition, it has been an object of interest from the beginning. It has been able to speak sentences of a few words when carefully taught, and by its uncanny acts has made itself a bird surrounded by superstition, myth, fable, and is connected with the religious rites of many nations. It is partially a carrion feeder, if offal or bodies are fresh; it also eats the young of other birds and very small animals and seeds, berries and fruit, having as varied a diet as any bird. It is noisy, with a loud, rough, emphatic cry, and its young are clamorous at feeding time.

Aristotle wrote that ravens drove their young from their location and forced them to care for themselves from the time they left the nest. This is doubtful. Bird habits and characteristics change only with slow ages of evolution. Our ravens of today are, to all intents, the same birds as those of Pal in the time of Moses, and ours follow the young afield for several days and feed them until the cawing, flapping youngsters appear larger than the parents. In Pliny's day, ravens had been taught to speak, and as an instance of their cunning he records that in time of drought a raven found a bucket containing a little water beside a sepulcher and raised it to drinking level by dropping in stones.

Pal has at least 8 different species of ravens. This bird was the first sent out by Noah in an effort to discover if the flood were abating (Gen **8** 6–8). Because it partially fed on carrion it was included among the abominations (see Lev **11** 15; Dt **14** 14). On **1** K **17** 4–6, see ELIJAH and the present writer's *Birds of the Bible,* 401–3. Among the marvels of creation and providence in Job **38** 41, we have this mention of the raven,

"Who provideth for the raven his prey,
When his young ones cry unto God,
And wander for lack of food?"

The answer to this question is in Ps **147** 9:

"He giveth to the beast his food,
And to the young ravens which cry."

Both these quotations point out the fact that the young are peculiarly noisy. In Prov **30** 17 it is indicated that the ravens, as well as eagles, vultures and hawks, found the eye of prey the vulnerable point, and so attacked it first. The Heb *'ōrēbh* means "black," and for this reason was applied to the raven, so the reference to the locks of the bridegroom in the Song of Solomon becomes clear (Cant **5** 11). The raven is one of the birds indicated to prey upon the ruins of Edom (Isa **34** 11). The last reference is found in Lk **12** 24: "Consider the ravens, that they sow not, neither reap; which have no store-chamber nor barn; and God feedeth them." This could have been said of any wild bird with equal truth. GENE STRATTON-PORTER

RAVEN, rav''n, **RAVIN,** rav'in: "Raven" (vb.) is from "rapine," "violent plundering," used for טָרַף, *ṭāraph,* in Gen **49** 27; Ps **22** 13; Ezk **22** 25.27, while "ravin" (noun) is the object ravened, in Nah **2** 12 the torn carcases (טְרֵפָה, *ṭ^erēphāh*). So a "ravenous bird" (Isa **46** 11; Ezk **39** 4) is a bird of prey (not a "hungry bird"), עַיִט, *'ayiṭ,* lit. "a screecher." "Ravenous beast" in Isa **35** 9 is for פָּרִיץ, *pārīç,* "violent one." In the NT ἅρπαξ, *hárpax,* "rapacious," is tr^d "ravening" in Mt **7** 15, while for the cognate ἁρπαγή, *harpagḗ* (Lk **11** 39), AV gives "ravening," RV "extortion."

RAZIS, rā'zis (**Ῥαζείς,** *Rhazeís*): "An elder of Jerus," "lover of his countrymen," and for his good will toward them called "father of the Jews," accused before the Syrian general Nicanor as an opponent of Hellenism. In order to escape falling into the hands of Nicanor's soldiers he committed suicide with the greatest determination in a rather revolting manner (2 Macc **14** 37 ff), in his death calling upon "the Lord of life" in the hope of a resurrection. His suicide—contrary to Jewish sentiment—was regarded with approbation by the author of 2 Macc (**14** 42.43).

RAZOR, rā'zẽr (תַּעַר, *ta'ar,* "knife" [Nu **6** 5; Ps **52** 2; Isa **7** 20; Ezk **5** 1], מוֹרָה, *mōrāh,* "razor" [Jgs **13** 5; **16** 17; 1 S **1** 11]). See BARBER; HAIR.

READING, rēd'ing (מִקְרָא, *miḳrā'; ἀνάγνωσις, anágnōsis*): As a noun occurs once in the OT (Neh **8** 8) and 3 t in the NT (Acts **13** 15; 2 Cor **3** 14; **1** Tim **4** 13), each time with reference to the public reading of the Divine Law. The vb. "to read" (קָרָא, *ḳārā'; ἀναγινώσκω, anaginōskō*) occurs frequently both in the OT and in the NT: (1) often in the sense of *reading aloud to others*, esp. of the public reading of God's Law or of prophecy, as by Moses (Ex **24** 7), Ezra (Neh **8** 3.18), Jesus in the synagogue at Nazareth (Lk **4** 16), of the regular reading of the Law and the Prophets in the synagogues (Acts **13** 27; **15** 21), and of the reading of apostolic epp. in the Christian church (Col **4** 16; **1** Thess **5** 27); (2) also in the sense of *reading to one's self*, whether the Divine word in Law or prophecy (Dt **17** 19; Acts **8** 28–30, etc), or such things as private letters (2 K **5** 7; **19** 14; Acts **23** 34, etc). D. MIALL EDWARDS

READY, red'i (מָהִיר, *māhīr*): Occurs twice in the sense of apt, skilful (Ezr **7** 6; Ps **45** 1). RV gives "ready" for "fit" (Prov **24** 27), for "asketh" (Mic **7** 3), for "prepared" (Mk **14** 15), for "not be negligent" (2 Pet **1** 12).

REAIAH, rē-ā'ya, rē-ī'a (רְאָיָה, *re'āyāh*, "Jeh has seen"; LXX B, **'Ραδά,** *Rhadá*, A, **'Ρειά,** *Rheiá*):

(1) The eponym of a Calebite family (1 Ch **4** 2). The word "Reaiah" should probably be substituted for "Haroeh" in 1 Ch **2** 52, but both forms may be corruptions.

(2) A Reubenite (1 Ch **5** 5, AV "Reaia"). See JOEL.

(3) The family name of a company of Nethinim (Ezr **2** 47; Neh **7** 50=1 Esd **5** 31).

REAPING, rēp'ing (קָצַר, *ḳāçar; θερίζω, therízō*): Reaping in ancient times, as at present, consisted in either pulling up the grain by the roots or cutting it with a sickle (see SICKLE), and then binding the

Reaping and Binding Sheaves.

stalks into bundles to be carried to the threshing-floor. If the Egyp sculptures are true to life, reaping was sometimes divided into two operations, the heads of grain and the stalks being reaped separately. In Pal and Syria both pulling and cutting are still practised, the former when the ground is stony and the spears scarce. Even where the sickle is used, much of the grain comes up by the roots, owing to the toughness of the dried stalks or the dullness of the sickle. The reaper sometimes wears pieces of cane on the fingers of the hand which gathers the grain in order to protect them from injury by the sharp grasses or the sickle. There were definite laws established by the Hebrews in regard to reaping (Lev **19** 9; **23** 10; **25** 5.11; Dt **16** 9). Samuel mentions the task of reaping the harvest as one of the requirements which would be made by the king for whom the people were clamoring (1 S **8** 12).

Figurative: The certainty of the consequences of good and evil doing were often typified by the sowing and the reaping of harvests (Job **4** 8; Prov **22** 8; Hos **8** 7; **10** 12.13; 2 Cor **9** 6; Gal **6** 7.8). "They that sow in tears shall reap in joy" is found in the liberated captives' song (Ps **126** 5). "He that regardeth the clouds shall not reap," i.e. a lack of faith in God's care will be punished (Eccl **11** 4); cf also the lesson of trust drawn from the birds (Mt **6** 26; Lk **12** 24). Sowing and not reaping the harvest is mentioned as a punishment for disobedience (Job **31** 8; Jer **12** 13; Mic **6** 15). Reaping where he sowed not, showed the injustice of the landlord (Mt **25** 26), as did also the withholding of the reapers' wages (Jas **5** 4). In God's Kingdom there is a division of labor: "He that soweth and he that reapeth may rejoice together" (Jn **4** 36–38). In John's vision he saw an angel reap the earth (Rev **14** 15.16). See AGRICULTURE; GLEANING. JAMES A. PATCH

REARWARD, rēr'wôrd (אָסַף, *'āṣaph*, "to gather," Nu **10** 25; Josh **6** 9 [AVm "gathering host"]; Isa **52** 12). See ARMY; DAN, TRIBE OF; WAR, 3.

REASON, rē'z'n, **REASONABLE,** rē'z'n-a-b'l, **REASONING,** rē'z'n-ing (יָכַח, *yākhaḥ*, etc; **λόγος,** *lógos*, **διαλογίζομαι, -ισμός,** *dialogízomai, -ismós*, etc): "Reason," with related terms, has a diversity of meanings, representing a large number of Heb and Gr words and phrases. In the sense of "cause" or "occasion" it stands in 1 K **9** 15 for *dābhār*, "a word" (RVm "account"), but in most cases renders prepositional forms as "from," "with," "because of," "for the sake of," etc. As the ground or argument for anything, it is the tr of *ta'am* (Prov **26** 16, RVm "answers discreetly"), of *yākhaḥ*, as in Isa **1** 18, "Come now, and let us reason together" (cf Job **13** 3; **15** 3); in 1 S **12** 7, the word is *shāphaṭ*, RV "that I may plead," etc. The principal Gr words for "reason," "reasoning," are those given above. The Christian believer is to be ready to give a reason (*logos*) for the hope that is in him (1 Pet **3** 15 AV). "Reason" as a human faculty or in the abstract sense appears in Apoc in Wisd **17** 12 (*logismós*); Ecclus **37** 16, "Let reason [*logos*] go before every enterprise," RV "be the beginning of every work." In Acts **18** 14, "reason would" is lit. *katá lógon*, "according to reason"; in Rom **12** 1, for "reasonable [*logikós*] service," RV has "spiritual," and in m "Gr 'belonging to the reason.'" In RV "reason," etc, occurs much oftener than in AV (cf Lev **17** 11; Dt **28** 47; Jgs **5** 22; Job **20** 2; **23** 7, etc; Lk **3** 15; **12** 17; Acts **17** 17, etc). W. L. WALKER

REBA, rē'ba (רֶבַע, *rebha'*, "fourth part"; LXX B, **'Ρόβε,** *Rhóbe*, A, **'Ρέβεκ,** *Rhébek*): One of the five chieftains of Midian who were slain by the Israelites, under Moses (Nu **31** 8; Josh **13** 21). Like his comrades, he is termed a "king" in Nu, but a "chief" or "prince" in Josh.

REBEKAH, rē-bek'a (רִבְקָה, *ribhḳāh;* LXX and NT **'Ρεβέκκα,** *Rhebékka*, whence the usual Eng. spelling **Rebecca**): Daughter of Bethuel and an unknown mother, granddaughter of Nahor and Milcah, sister of Laban, wife of Isaac, mother of Esau and Jacob.

Her name is usually explained from the Arab., رَبْقَة, *rabkat*, "a tie-rope for animals," or, rather, "a noose" in such a rope; its application would then by figure suggest the beauty (?) of her that bears it, by means of which men are snared or bound. The root is found in Heb only in the noun meaning "hitching-place" or "stall," in the familiar phrase "fatted calf" or "calf of the stall," and in view of the meaning of such names as Rachel and Eglah the name Rebekah might well mean (concrete for abstract, like רִקְמָה, *riḳmāh*, חֶמְדָּה, *ḥemdāh*, etc) a "tied-up calf" (or "lamb"?), one therefore peculiarly choice and fat.

Rebekah is first mentioned in the genealogy of the descendants of Nahor, brother of Abraham (Gen

22 20–24). In fact, the family is there carried down just so far as is necessary in order to introduce this woman, for whose subsequent appearance and rôle the genealogy is obviously intended as a preparation. All this branch of the family of Terah had remained in Aram when Abraham and Lot had migrated to Canaan, and it is at Haran, "the city of Nahor," that we first meet Rebekah, when in ch **24** she is made known to Abraham's servant at the well before the gate.

That idyllic narrative of the finding of a bride for Isaac is too familiar to need rehearsal and too simple to require comment. Besides, the substance both of that story and of the whole of Rebekah's career is treated in connection with the sketches of the other actors in the same scenes. Yet we note from the beginning the maiden's decision of character, which appears in every line of the narrative, and prepares the reader to find in subsequent chapters the positive, ambitious and energetic woman that she there shows herself.

Though the object of her husband's love (Gen **24** 67), Rebekah bore him no children for 20 years (**25** 20.26). Like Sarah, she too was barren, and it was only after that score of years and after the special intercession of Isaac that God at length granted her twin sons. "The purpose of God according to election," as Paul expresses the matter in Rom **9** 11, was the cause of that strange oracle to the wondering, inquiring parents, "The elder shall serve the younger" (Gen **25** 23).

Whether because of this oracle or for some other reason, it was that younger son, Jacob, who became the object of his mother's special love (Gen **25** 28). She it was who led him into the deception practised upon Isaac (Gen **27** 5–17), and she it was who devised the plan for extricating Jacob from the dangerous situation into which that deception had brought him (vs 42–46). When the absence of Jacob from home became essential to his personal safety, Rebekah proposed her own relations in Aram as the goal of his journey, and gave as motive the desirability of Jacob's marrying from among her kindred. Probably she did not realize that in sending her favorite son away on this journey she was sending him away from her forever. Yet such seems to have been the case. Though younger than Isaac, who was still living at an advanced age when Jacob returned to Canaan a quarter of a century later, Rebekah seems to have died during that term. We learn definitely only this, that she was buried in the cave of Machpelah near Hebron (Gen **49** 31).

Outside of Gen, Rebekah is alluded to in Scripture only in the passage from Rom (**9** 10–12) already cited. Her significance there is simply that of the wife of Isaac and the mother of two sons of such different character and destiny as Esau and Jacob. And her significance in Gen, apart from this, lies in her contribution to the family of Abraham of a pure strain from the same eastern stock, thus transmitting to the founders of Israel both an unmixed lineage and that tradition of separateness from Can. and other non-Heb elements which has proved the greatest factor in the ethnological marvel of the ages, the persistence of the Heb people.

J. Oscar Boyd

REBUKE, rē̇-būk′: As a vb. "rebuke" is in the OT the tr of גָּעַר, *gā'ar* and יָכַח, *yākhaḥ;* another word, *rībh*, in Neh **5** 7, is in RV tr[d] "contended with." "Rebuke" (noun) is most frequently the tr of *g[e]'ārāh;* also in AV of *ḥerpāh* (Isa **25** 8; Jer **15** 15, RV "reproach"), and of a few other words signifying reproach, etc. "Rebuker" (*mūṣār*, lit. "correction," "chastisement") in Hos **5** 2 has RVm "Heb 'rebuke.'" In the NT "to rebuke" is most often the tr of ἐπιτιμάω, *epitimáō* (Mt **8** 26; **16** 22; **17** 18 etc); also in AV of ἐλέγχω, *elégchō*, always in RV rendered "reprove" (1 Tim **5** 20; Tit **1** 13; **2** 15; He **12** 5; Rev **3** 19). Another word is *epiplḗttō* (once, 1 Tim **5** 1); "without rebuke" in Phil **2** 15 is in RV "without blemish." On the other hand, RV has "rebuke" for several words in AV, as for "reprove" (2 K **19** 4; Isa **37** 4), "reproof" (Job **26** 11; Prov **17** 10), "charged" (Mk **10** 48). In Isa **2** 4; Mic **4** 3, ERV has "reprove" for "rebuke," and in m "decide concerning," which is text in ARV. In Ecclus **11** 7 we have the wise counsel: "Understand first, and then rebuke" (*epitimaō*).

W. L. Walker

RECAH, rē′ka (רֵכָה, *rēkhāh;* B, Ῥηχάβ, *Rhēcháb*, A, Ῥηφά, *Rhēphá;* AV **Rechah**): In 1 Ch **4** 12 certain persons are described as "the men of Recah," but there is absolutely no information either about the place or its position.

RECEIPT, rē̇-sēt′, **OF CUSTOM.** See Custom.

RECEIVER, rē̇-sēv′ẽr: Found in AV (Isa **33** 18); but RV substitutes "he that weighed the tribute." The Heb is *shōḳēl*, which means "one who weighs," "a weigher."

RECHAB, rē′kab, **RECHABITES,** rek′a-bīts (רֵכָב, *rēkhābh*, רֵכָבִים, *rēkhābhīm*): Rechab is the name of two men of some prominence in the OT records:

(1) A Benjamite of the town of Beeroth, son of Rimmon (2 S **4** 2); he and his brother Baanah were "captains" of the military host of Ish-bosheth. On the death of Abner (2 S **3** 30) the two brothers treacherously entered Ish-bosheth's house, when at noon he was resting and helpless, beheaded him, and escaped with the head to David at Hebron (**4** 6–8). They expected to receive reward and honor from David for the foul deed, which left him without a rival for the throne of all Israel. But the just and noble-minded king ordered their immediate execution (**4** 9–12), as in the case of the Amalekite, who asserted that he had killed Saul (2 S **1**). For some reason the Beerothites left their own town and fled to Gittaim, another town in Benjamin, where they were still living when the Books of S were written (2 S **4** 3).

(2) The more prominent of the men bearing this name was a Kenite (q.v.), a descendant of Hammath (1 Ch **2** 55). A part of the Kenite tribe joined the Israelites during the wilderness wanderings (Nu **10** 29–32; Jgs **1** 16; **4** 17), becoming identified with the tribe of Judah, although Heber and Jael his wife were settled in Northern Pal (Jgs **4** 17). Rechab was the ancestor or founder of a family, or order, in Israel known as the **Rechabites,** who at various times were conspicuous in the religious life of the nation. The most notable member of this family was Jehonadab (2 K **10** 15 ff.23), or Jonadab, as he is called in Jer **35.** Jehonadab was a zealous Jeh-worshipper and took part with Jehu in the extirpation of Baal-worship and the house of Ahab. He set for his descendants a vow of asceticism: that they should drink no wine, nor plant fields or vineyards, nor build nor live in houses throughout their generations (Jer **35** 6.7). That must have been a singular feature in Palestinian life: the simple, nomadic life of this family from generation to generation in the midst of settled agricultural and industrial conditions! They followed this simple life in order to guard against the enervating tendencies of sensualism, and as a covenant of fidelity to Jeh, to whom they wholly devoted themselves when they joined themselves to Israel. Jeremiah used the **Rechabites,** who had been driven into Jerus by Nebuchadnezzar's investment of the land, as an object-lesson to covenant-

breaking Judah. The Rechabites, hungry and thirsty, refused wine when it was set before them, because of the command of their ancestor Jonadab (Jer **35** 8–10); but Judah refused to heed Jeh's commands or to keep His covenant (vs 14.15).

If the Rechab of Neh **3** 14 is the same as this Kenite, then his descendant Malchijah, who assisted Nehemiah in rebuilding the wall of Jerus, may have abandoned the vow of his ancestors, for he was "ruler of the district of Beth-haccherem" (i.e. "house of the vineyard").

EDWARD MACK

RECHAH, rē'ka (רֵכָה, *rēkhāh*). See RECAH.

RECLINING, rē-klīn'ing (Jn **13** 23). See MEALS, III; TRICLINIUM.

RECONCILE, rek'on-sīl, **RECONCILIATION,** rek-on-sil-i-ā'shun (**καταλλάσσω,** *katallássō*, **καταλλαγή,** *katallagḗ*, also the compound form **ἀποκαταλλάσσω,** *apokatallássō;* once the cognate **διαλλάσσομαι,** *diallássomai* is used in Mt **5** 24):

1. The Terms

(1) *NT usage.*—In the last case, Mt **5** 24, the word is not used in a doctrinal sense, though its use is very helpful in considering the force of the other terms. All the other instances are in Paul's Epp. (Rom **5** 10; 1 Cor **7** 11; 2 Cor **5** 18–20, the vb.; Rom **5** 11; **11** 15; 2 Cor **5** 18.19, the noun; Eph **2** 16; Col **1** 22, the compound). The word "reconcile" has a double meaning and usage, and the context must in each case determine how it is to be taken. The great doctrine is the reconciliation of God and men, but the question to be decided is whether it is God who is reconciled to men, or men who are reconciled to God, and different schools of theology emphasize one side or the other. The true view embraces both aspects. The word "to reconcile" means literally to exchange, to bring into a changed relationship. Some maintain that it is only a change in the sinner that is intended, a laying aside of his enmity, and coming into peaceful relations with God. But that manifestly does not exhaust the meaning, nor is it in the great Pauline passages the primary and dominant meaning.

(2) *The OT usage* does not materially help in the elucidation of the NT terms, for though the word occurs in a number of passages in AV, it is in RV generally changed to "atonement," which more accurately represents the Heb *kāphar,* which is generally rendered by "atonement," and by *hiláskomai* or *exiláskomai* in the Gr. (In one passage of the NT [He **2** 17], the phrase "to make reconciliation" represents the Gr *hilaskomai,* and is better rendered in RV by "to make propitiation.") The making atonement or propitiation is the basis of the reconciliation, the means of its accomplishment, and the fact that the translators of AV sometimes rendered *kāphar* by "reconcile" shows that they understood reconciliation to have the Godward aspect. Whatever may be said of the nature of the atonement or propitiation in the old dispensation, it was something contemplated as appeasing or satisfying, or at least in some way affecting God so as to make Him willing, or render it possible for Him, to enter into, or abide in, gracious relations with men. In one passage in the OT where "reconciliation" occurs (2 Ch **29** 24) it represents a different Heb word, but here RV has changed it into "sin-offering," which is in harmony with the general meaning and usage of the Heb.

(3) *Special passage in 1 S* **29** *4.*—There is yet another Heb word rendered "reconcile" in 1 S **29** 4, and inasmuch as this passage in the LXX has as the equivalent of the Heb the Gr word *diallássō*, it is of some importance in guiding to the NT meaning. On one occasion when the Philis gathered together to battle against Israel, David and his band of men accompanied Achish king of Gath to the muster-place. "The princes of the Philis" did not at all appreciate the presence of "these Hebrews," and although Achish testified in favor of David's fidelity, they were very indignant, and demanded that David and his men be sent back, "lest in the battle he become an adversary to us: for wherewith should this fellow reconcile himself unto his lord? should it not be with the heads of these men?" The Heb is *rāçāh,* which means "to be pleased with" or "to accept favorably," and the Hithpael form here used is "to make himself pleasing or acceptable," "to reconcile himself." But assuredly the Philistines' idea of David reconciling himself to Saul was not that he should lay aside his enmity against Saul, and so become friends with him. The enmity was on Saul's side, and the thought of the princes was that David by turning against them in the battle would gratify Saul, and lead him to lay aside his enmity against David.

(4) *Usage in the Apocrypha.*—It may be noted that in 2 Macc **5** 20, *katallagē* is used evidently of the Godward side: "And the place which was forsaken in the wrath of the Almighty was, at the reconciliation of the great Sovereign, restored again with all glory." The vb. occurs in 2 Macc **1** 5 when again the Godward side seems intended, though not perhaps so certainly: "May God . . . . hearken to your supplications, and be reconciled with you," and in **7** 33: "If for rebuke and chastening our living Lord has been angered a little while, yet shall he again be reconciled with his own servants," and **8** 29: "They besought the merciful Lord to be wholly reconciled with his servants." In these two, esp. the last, it is unquestionably the laying aside of the Divine displeasure that is meant.

Before passing on to look at the great utterances in the Epp., we may now look at the non-doctrinal passage referred to at the beginning. There is, indeed, another non-doctrinal instance in 1 Cor **7** 11, where the wife who has departed from her husband is enjoined either to "remain unmarried, or else be reconciled to her husband." But as it is indeterminate whether the wife or the husband is the offending party, and so which is the one to be influenced, the passage does not help us much. But Mt **5** 24 is a very illuminating passage. Here as in the passage from 1 S, the word used is *diallassō,* but it is practically identified in meaning with *katallassō.* The injunction is given by Christ to the one who is at variance with his brother, not to complete his offering until first he has been reconciled to his brother. But the whole statement shows that it is not a question of the one who is offering the gift laying aside his enmity against his brother, but the reverse. Christ says, "If therefore thou art offering thy gift at the altar, and there rememberest [not that thou hast a grudge against thy brother but] that thy brother hath aught against thee" —the brother was the offended one, he is the one to be brought round—"leave there thy gift before the altar, and go thy way, first be reconciled to thy brother, and then come and offer thy gift." Plainly it means that he should do something to remove his brother's displeasure and so bring about a reconciliation.

2. Non-doctrinal Passage—Mt 5:24

3. Doctrinal Passages

(1) *Rom* **5**.—Turning now to Rom **5**, how stands the matter? Paul has been speaking of the blessed results of justification; one of these results is the shedding abroad of the love of God in the heart. Then he dwells upon the manifestation of that love in the death of Christ, a love that was displayed to the loveless, and he argues that if in our sinful and unloving state we were embraced by the love of God, a fortiori that love will not be less now that it has already begun to take effect. If He loved us when we were under His condemnation sufficiently to give His Son to die for our salvation, much more shall His love bestow upon us the blessings secured by that death. "Much more then, being now justified by his blood, shall we be saved from the wrath of God through him" (**5** 9).

(*a*) The fact of Divine wrath: It is well to note, then, that there is "wrath" on the part of God against sin and sinners. One of the key-thoughts of the apostle in this ep. is that "the wrath of God is revealed from heaven against all ungodliness and unrighteousness of men" (**1** 18), and the coming day of judgment is "the day of wrath and revelation of the righteous judgment of God" (**2** 5). And because of this stern fact, the gospel is a revelation not only of love, but specifically "a righteousness of God" (**1** 17). And he shows that the essence of the gospel is found in the propitiatory death of the Lord Jesus Christ (**3** 24.25.26), through whom alone can men who have been "brought under the judgment of God" (**3** 19) find justification, salvation, deliverance from the wrath of God (**4** 25; **5** 1-6). Of course it is not necessary to add that the wrath of God is not to be thought of as having any unworthy or capricious element in it—it is the settled opposition of His holy nature against sin.

(*b*) Reconciliation, Godward, as well as manward: The apostle proceeds (ver 10): "For if, while we were enemies, we were reconciled to God through the death of his Son, much more, being reconciled, shall we be saved by his life." Now if, as many maintain, it is only the reconciliation on the manward side that is meant, that the manifested love led to the sinner laying aside his enmity, it would entirely reverse the apostle's argument. He is not arguing that if we have begun to love God we may reckon upon His doing so and so for us, but because He has done so much, we may expect Him to do more. The verse is parallel to the preceding, and the being reconciled is on the same plane as being justified; the being justified was God's action, and so is the reconciling. Justification delivers from "the wrath of God"; reconciliation takes effect upon enemies.

(*c*) The meaning of the word "enemies": The word "enemies" is important. By those who take the manward aspect of reconciliation as the only one, it is held that the word must be taken actively—those who hate God. But the passive meaning, "hatred of God," seems far the preferable, and is indeed demanded by the context. Paul uses the vb. *echthroí*, "enemies," in Rom **11** 28, in antithesis to "beloved" of God, and that is the consistent sense here. The enemies are those who are the objects of the wrath of the previous verse. And when we were thus hated of God, the objects of His just displeasure on account of our sin, "we were reconciled to God by the death of his Son." God laid aside His enmity, and in the propitiatory death of Christ showed Himself willing to receive us into His favor.

(*d*) The manward side: By this propitiation, therefore, the barrier was removed, and, God having assumed a gracious attitude toward the sinner, it is possible for the sinner now, influenced by His love, to come into a friendly relationship with God. And so in the second phrase, the two meanings, the Godward and the manward, may coalesce: "being reconciled, we shall be saved by his life." The reconciliation becomes mutual, for there is no kind of doubt that sinners are enemies to God in the active sense, and require to lay aside their hostility, and so be reconciled to Him. But the first step is with God, and the reconciliation which took place in the death of His Son could only be the Godward reconciliation, since at that time men were still uninfluenced by His love. But, perhaps, just because that first reconciliation is brought about through the Divine love which provides the propitiation, the apostle avoids saying "God is reconciled," but uses the more indirect form of speech. The manward aspect is emphasized in the next verse, although the Godward is not lost sight of: "We also rejoice in God through our Lord Jesus Christ, through whom we have now received the reconciliation" (**5** 11). It is therefore something that comes from God and does not proceed from man. God is the first mover; He makes the reconciliation as already indicated, and then the fruit of it is imputed to the believing sinner, and the very fact that our receiving the reconciliation, or being brought into a state of reconciliation, follows the being reconciled of ver 10, shows that the other is Divine reconciliation as the basis of the human.

(2) *2 Cor **5** 18-20*.—(*a*) The Godward aspect primary: In the same way the great passage in 2 Cor **5** 18-20 cannot be understood apart from the conception that there is a reconciliation on the Divine side. There is unquestionably reference to the human side of the matter as well, but, as in Rom, the Godward aspect is primary and dominating: "All things are of God, who reconciled us to himself through Christ, and gave unto us the ministry of reconciliation." It might be possible to argue from AV that this describes the process going on under gospel influences, men being brought into gracious relations with God, but the aorist of the Gr rightly rendered by RV, "who reconciled us to himself," points back to the historic time when the transaction took place. It cannot be simply the surrender of the sinner to God that is meant, though that comes as a consequence; it is a work that proceeds from God, is accomplished by God, and because of the accomplishment of that work it is possible for a ministry of reconciliation to be intrusted to men. To make this mean the human aspect of the reconciliation, it would be necessary unduly to confine it to the reconciliation of Paul and his fellow-workers, though even then it would be a straining of language, for there is the other historic act described, "and gave unto us the ministry of reconciliation." The plain meaning is that through Jesus Christ, God established the basis of agreement, removed the barrier to the sinner's approach to Himself, accomplished the work of propitiation, and, having done so, He intrusts His servants with the ministry of reconciliation, a ministry which, basing itself upon the great propitiatory, reconciling work of Christ, is directed toward men, seeking to remove their enmity, to influence them in their turn to be reconciled with God. This is more clearly set forth in the verse which follows, which in explaining the ministry of reconciliation says: "To wit, that God was in Christ reconciling the world unto himself, not reckoning unto them their trespasses." Here there can be no question that the historic Incarnation is meant, and the reconciling of the world can be nothing other than the objective work of atonement culminating in the cross. And in that transaction there can be no thought of the sinner laying aside his hostility to God; it is God in Christ so dealing with sin that the doom lying upon the guilty is canceled, the wrath is averted, propitiation is made.

(*b*) The manward side also prominent: God, in a word, enters into gracious relations with a world of sinners, becomes reconciled to man. This being done, gracious influences can be brought to bear upon man, the chief of which is the consideration of this stupendous fact of grace, that God has in Christ dealt with the question of sin. This is the substance of the "word of reconciliation" which is preached by the apostle. So he continues, "We are ambassadors therefore on behalf of Christ, as though God were entreating by us: we beseech you on behalf of Christ, be ye reconciled to God." Here is the human side. The great matter now is to get the sinner to lay aside his enmity, to respond to the gracious overtures of the gospel, to come into harmony with God. But that is only possible because the reconciliation in the Godward aspect has already been accomplished. If the first reconciliation, "the reconciliation of the world unto himself," had been the laying aside of human enmity, there could now be no point in the exhortation, "Be ye reconciled to God."

(3) *Eph 2 16.*—The two passages where the compound word occurs are in complete harmony with this interpretation. Eph **2** 16: "And might reconcile them both [Jew and Gentile] in one body unto God through the cross, having slain the enmity thereby," is the outcome of Christ "making peace" (**2** 15), and the reconciling work is effected through the cross, reconciliation both Godward and manward, and, having made peace, it is possible for Christ to come and preach peace to them that are far off—far off even though the reconciling work of the cross has been accomplished.

(4) *Col 1 20–22.*—So in Col **1** 20, "And through him to reconcile all things unto himself, having made peace through the blood of his cross; through him, I say, whether things upon the earth, or things in the heavens." Here the thought of the apostle trembles away into infinity, and there seems a parallel to the thought of He **9** 23, that according to the typical teaching even "the things in the heavens" in some way stood in need of cleansing. May it be that the work of Christ in some sense affected the angelic intelligence, making it possible for harmony to be restored between redeemed sinners and the perfect creation of God? In any case, the reconciling all things unto Himself is not the laying aside of the creaturely hostility, but the determining of the Divine attitude. Then comes the specific reference to the human side, "And you, being in time past alienated and enemies in your mind in your evil works, yet now hath he reconciled in the body of his flesh through death"; there, as in Rom, the two phases coalescing, God appearing gracious through the work of Christ, sinners coming into gracious relation with Him. "Having made peace through the blood of his cross," the ground of peace has been established. Christ has done something by His death which makes it possible to offer peace to men. God has laid aside His holy opposition to the sinner, and shows Himself willing to bring men into peace with Himself. He has found satisfaction in that great work of His Son, has been reconciled, and now calls upon men to be reconciled to Him—to receive the reconciliation. See Atonement; Propitiation; Wrath.

Literature.—See the works on NT Theology of Weiss, Schmid, Stevens, etc; Denney, *Death of Christ;* arts. on "Reconciliation" in *HDB, DCG*, etc.

Archibald M'Caig

RECORD, rek′ord, rek′ôrd: (1) The Eng. word, where it occurs in the OT and the NT in the sense of testimony, is tr[d] in RV "witness" (Dt **30** 19; **31** 28; Jn **1** 19.32; **8** 13.14; Rom **10** 2, etc). See Witness. But in Job **16** 19 for AV "my record," RV has "he that voucheth for me." (2) In Ezr **4** 15; **6** 2 (*dokhrān, dikhrōn*), and Est **6** 1 (*zikkārōn*), the word denotes Pers state chronicles; cf 1 Macc **14** 23; 2 Macc **2** 1.

RECORDER, rē-kôr′dẽr (מַזְכִּיר, *mazkīr;* RVm "chronicler"): A high functionary in the court of the Jewish kings, part of whose duty seems to have been to chronicle the events of the reign, but who also occupied a position corresponding with that of the modern vizier (2 S **8** 16; **20** 24; 1 Ch **18** 15, etc). His high rank is shown by the facts that, with other officers, he represented Hezekiah in speaking with Rabshakeh (2 K **18** 18), and, in the reign of Josiah, superintended the repairs of the temple (2 Ch **34** 8).

RECOVER, rē-kuv′ẽr: "Recover" has (1) the transitive meaning of "to retake" or "regain" (anything); and (2) the intransitive sense of "to regain health" or "become well." In Jth **14** 7 it means "restore to consciousness." In the former sense it is in the OT the tr of נָצַל, *nāçal*, "to snatch away" (Jgs **11** 26; 1 S **30** 8.22; in Hos **2** 9, RV "pluck away"); also of שׁוּב, *shūbh* (Kal and Hiph. 1 S **30** 19 AV; 2 S **8** 3, etc), and of various other words in single instances. In 2 K **5** 3.6.7.11, "to restore to health" is אָסַף, *'āṣaph*. In its intransitive sense "recover" is chiefly the tr of חָיָה, *ḥāyāh*, "to live," "revive" (2 K **1** 2, etc; Isa **38** 9.21). "Recover" appears only twice in AV of the NT; Mk **16** 18 (for *kalôs héxousin*) and 2 Tim **2** 26 (from *ananḗphō*, RVm "Gr 'return to soberness' "); but RV has "recover" for "do well" in Jn **11** 12 (*sōthḗsetai;* m "Gr 'be saved' "). "Recovering" (of sight) (*anáblepsis*) occurs in Lk **4** 18. W. L. Walker

RED. See Colors, (10).

RED DRAGON. See Revelation of John.

RED HEIFER. See Heifer, Red.

RED HORSE. See Horse, Red; Revelation of John.

RED SEA (יַם־סוּף, *yam-ṣūph* [Ex **10** 19 and often], but in many passages it is simply הַיָּם, *ha-yām*, "the sea"; LXX with 2 or 3 exceptions renders it by ἡ ἐρυθρὰ θάλασσα, *hē eruthrá thálassa*, "the Red Sea"; Lat geographers *Mare Rubrum*):

1. Name The Heb name *yam-ṣūph* has given rise to much controversy. *Yam* is the general word for sea, and when standing alone may refer to the Mediterranean, the Dead Sea, the Red Sea, or the Sea of Galilee. In several places it designates the river Nile or Euphrates. *Ṣūph* means a rush or seaweed such as abounds in the lower portions of the Nile and the upper portions of the Red Sea. It was in the *ṣūph* on the brink of the river that the ark of Moses was hidden (Ex **2** 3.5). But as this word does not in itself mean red, and as that is not the color of the bulrush, authorities are much divided as to the reason for this designation. Some have supposed that it was called red from the appearance of the mountains on the western coast, others from the red color given to the water by the presence of zoöphytes, or red coral, or some species of seaweed. Others still, with considerable probability, suppose that the name originated in the red or copper color of the inhabitants of the bordering Arabian peninsula. But the name *yam-ṣūph*, though applied to the whole sea, was esp. used with reference to the northern part, which is alone mentioned in the Bible, and to the two gulfs (Suez and Akabah) which border the Sinaitic Peninsula, esp. the Gulf of Suez.

2. Peculiarities The Red Sea has a length of 1,350 miles and an extreme breadth of 205 miles. It is remarkable that while it has no rivers flowing into it and the evaporation from its surface is enormous, it is not much salter than the ocean, from which it is inferred that there must be a constant influx of water from the Indian Ocean through the Straits of Bab-el-Mandeb, together with an outflow of the more saline water beneath the surface. The deepest portion measures 1,200 fathoms. Owing to the lower land levels which prevailed in recent geological times, the Gulf of Suez formerly extended across the lowland which separates it from the Bitter Lakes, a distance of 15 or 20 miles now traversed by the Suez Canal, which encountered no elevation more than 30 ft. above tide. In early historic times the Gulf ended at Ismailia at the head of Lake Timsah. North of this the land rises to a height of more than 50 ft. and for a long time furnished a road leading from Africa into Asia. At a somewhat earlier geological (middle and late Tertiary) period the depression of the land was such that this bridge was also submerged, so that the Red Sea and the Mediterranean were connected by a broad expanse of water which overflowed the whole surface of Lower Egypt.

The evidence of the more recent depression of the land surface in all Lower Egypt is unmistakable. Raised beaches containing shells and corals still living in the Red Sea are found at various levels up to more than 200 ft. above tide. One of the most interesting of these is to be seen near the summit of the "Crow's Nest," a half-mile S. of the great pyramids, where, near the summit of the eminence, and approximately 200 ft. above tide, on a level with the base of the pyramids, there is a clearly defined recent sea beach composed of water-worn pebbles from 1 in. to 1 or 2 ft. in diameter, the interstices of which are filled with small shells loosely cemented together. These are identified as belonging to a variable form, *Alectryonia cucullata* Born, which lives at the present time in the Red Sea. On the opposite side of the river, on the Mokattam Hills S. of Cairo, at an elevation of 220 ft. above tide, similar deposits are found containing numerous shells of recent date, while the rock face is penetrated by numerous borings of lithodomus mollusks (*Pholades rugosa* Broc.). Other evidences of the recent general depression of the land in this region come from various places on the eastern shores of the Mediterranean. According to Lartet at Ramleh, near Jaffa, a recent beach occurs more than 200 ft. above sea-level containing many shells of *Pectunculus violascens* Lamk, which is at the present time the most abundant mollusk on the shore of the adjoining Mediterranean. A similar beach has been described by Dr. Post at Lattakia, about 30 miles N. of Beirût; while others, according to Hull, occur upon the island of Cyprus. Further evidence of this depression is also seen in the fact that the isthmus between Suez and the Bitter Lakes is covered with recent deposits of Nile mud, holding modern Red Sea shells, showing that, at no very distant date, there was an overflow of the Nile through an eastern branch into this slightly depressed level. The line of this branch of the Nile overflow was in early times used for a canal, which has recently been opened to furnish fresh water to Suez, and the depression is followed by the railroad. According to Dawson, large surfaces of the desert N. of Suez, which are now above sea-level, contain buried in the sand "recent marine shells in such a state of preservation that not many centuries may have elapsed since they were in the bottom of the sea" (*Egypt and Syria*, 67).

3. OT References

The Red Sea is connected with the children of Israel chiefly through the crossing of it recorded in Ex (see 4, below); but there are a few references to it in later times. Solomon is said (1 K **9** 26) to have built a navy at "Ezion-geber, which is beside Eloth, on the shore of the Red Sea, in the land of Edom." This is at the head of the Gulf of Aḳabah, the eastern branch of the Red Sea. Here his ships were manned by Hiram king of Tyre with "shipmen that had knowledge of the sea" (ver 27). And (ver 28) "they came to Ophir, and fetched from thence gold." But Eloth was evidently lost to Israel when Edom successfully revolted in the time of Joram (2 K **8** 20). For a short time, however, it was restored to Judah by Amaziah (2 K **14** 22); but finally, during the reign of Ahaz, the Syrians, or more probably, according to another reading, the Edomites, recovered the place and permanently drove the Jews away. But in 1 K **22** 48 Jehoshaphat is said to have "made ships of Tarshish to go to Ophir for gold: but they went not; for the ships were broken at Ezion-geber"; while in 2 Ch **20** 36 Jehoshaphat is said to have joined with Ahaziah "to make ships to go to Tarshish; and they made the ships in Ezion-geber."

Unless there is some textual confusion here, "ships of Tarshish" is simply the name of the style of the ship, like "East Indiaman," and Tarshish in Ch may refer to some place in the East Indies. This is the more likely, since Solomon's "navy" that went to Tarshish once every 3 years came "bringing gold, and silver, ivory, and apes, and peacocks," which could hardly have come from any other place than India. See Ships and Boats, II, 1, (2).

4. Passage of, by Israelites

Until in recent times it was discovered that the Gulf of Suez formerly extended 30 miles northward to the site of the present Ismailia and the ancient Pithom, the scene of the Bib. miracle was placed at Suez, the present head of the Gulf. But there is at Suez no extent of shoal water sufficient for the east wind mentioned in Scripture (Ex **14** 21) to have opened a passage-way sufficiently wide to have permitted the host to have crossed over in a single night. The bar leading from Suez across, which is now sometimes forded, is too insignificant to have furnished a passage-way as Robinson supposed (*BR*³, I, 56–59). Besides, if the children of Israel were S. of the Bitter Lakes when there was no extension of the Gulf N. of its present limits, there would have been no need of a miracle to open the water, since there was abundant room for both them and Pharaoh's army to have gone around the northern end of the Gulf to reach the eastern shore, while S. of Suez the water is too deep for the wind anywhere to have opened a passage-way. But with an extension of the waters of the Gulf to the Bitter Lakes and Lake Timsah, rendered probable by the facts cited in the previous paragraph, the narrative at once so perfectly accords with the physical conditions involved as to become not only easily credible, but self-evidencing.

The children of Israel were at **Rameses** (Ex **12** 37) in the land of Goshen, a place which has not been certainly identified, but could not have been far from the modern *Zagazig* at the head of the Fresh Water Canal leading from the Nile to the Bitter Lakes. One day's journey eastward along *Wâdy Tumilat*, watered by this canal, brought them to **Succoth**, a station probably identical with *Thuket*, close upon the border line separating Egypt from Asia. Through the discoveries of Naville in 1883 this has been identified as Pithom, one of the store-cities built by Pharaoh during the period of Heb oppression (Ex **1** 11). Here Naville uncovered vast store pits for holding grain built during the reign of Rameses II and constructed according to the description given in Ex **1**: the lower portions of brick made with straw, the middle with stubble, and the top of simple clay without even stubble to hold the brick together (see Naville, "The Store-City Pithom and the Route of the Exodus," *Egyp Exploration Fund*, 1885; M. G. Kyle, "A Reëxamination of Naville's Works," *Records of the Past*, VIII, 1901, 304–7). The next day's journey brought them to **Etham** on the "edge of the wilderness" (Ex **13** 20; Nu **33** 6), probably in the vicinity of the modern Ismailia at the head of Lake Timsah. From this point the natural road to Pal would have been along the caravan route on the neck of land referred to above as now about 50 ft. above sea-level. Etham was about 30 miles S.E. of Zoan or Tanis, the headquarters at that time of Pharaoh, from which he was watching the movements of the host. If they should go on the direct road to Pal, his army could easily execute a flank movement and intercept them in the desert of Etham. But by Divine command (Ex **14** 2) Moses turned southward on the west side of the extension of the Red Sea and camped "before Pi-hahiroth, between Migdol and the sea, before Baal-zephon" (Ex **14** 2; Nu **33** 5–7). At this change of course Pharaoh was delighted, seeing that the children of Israel were "entangled in the land" and "the wilderness" had "shut them in." Instead of issuing a flank movement upon them, Pharaoh's army now followed them in the rear and "overtook them encamping by the sea, beside **Pi-hahiroth**," the location of which is essential to a proper understanding of the narrative which follows.

In ver 2 Pi-hahiroth is said to be "between Migdol and the sea, before Baal-zephon." Now though Migdol originally meant "watch-tower," it is hardly supposable that this can be its meaning here, otherwise the children of Israel would have been moving directly toward a fortified place. Most probably, therefore, **Migdol** was the tower-like mountain peak marking the northeast corner of *Jebel Geneffeh*, which runs parallel with the Bitter Lakes, only a short distance from their western border. **Baal-zephon** may equally well be some of the mountain peaks on the border of the Wilderness of Paran opposite *Cheloof*, midway between the Bitter Lakes and Suez. In the clear atmosphere of the region this line of mountains is distinctly visible throughout the whole distance from Ismailia to Suez. There would seem to be no objection to this supposition, since all authorities are in disagreement concerning its location. From the significance of the name it would seem to be the seat of some form of Baal worship, naturally a mountain. Brugsch would identify it with Mt. Cassius on the northern shore of Egypt. Naville (see Murray's *Illustrated Bible Dict.*, "Red Sea, Passage of") would connect it with the hill called *Tûssûm* E. of Lake Timsah, where there is a shrine at the present day visited every year about July 14 by thousands of pilgrims to celebrate a religious festival; but, as this is a Mohammedan festival, there seems no reason to connect it with any sanctuary of the Canaanites. Dawson favors the general location which we have assigned to Pi-hahiroth, but would place it beside the narrow southern portion of the Bitter Lakes.

Somewhere in this vicinity would be a most natural place for the children of Israel to halt, and there is no difficulty, such as Naville supposes, to their passing between *Jebel Geneffeh* and the Bitter Lakes; for the mountain does not come abruptly to the lake, but leaves ample space for the passage of a caravan, while the mountain on one side and the lake on the other would protect them from a flank movement by Pharaoh and limit his army to harassing the rear of the Israelitish host. Protected thus, the Israelites found a wide plain over which they could spread their camp, and if we suppose them to be as far S. as *Cheloof*, every condition would be found to suit the narrative which follows. Moses was told by the Lord that if he would order the children of Israel to go forward, the sea would be divided and the children of Israel could cross over on dry ground. And when, in compliance with the Divine command, Moses stretched out his hand over the sea, "Jeh caused the sea to go back by a strong east wind all the night, and made the sea dry land, and the waters were divided. And the children of Israel went into the midst of the sea upon the dry ground: and the waters were a wall unto them on their right hand, and on their left. And the Egyptians pursued, and went in after them into the midst of the sea, all Pharaoh's horses, his chariots, and his horsemen" (Ex **14** 21–30). But when the children of Israel were safely on the other side the waters returned and overwhelmed the entire host of Pharaoh. In the Song of Moses which follows, describing the event, it is said that the waters were piled up by the "blast of thy [God's] nostrils" (Ex **15** 8), and again, ver 10, "Thou didst blow with thy wind, the sea covered them." Thus 3 t the wind is mentioned as the means employed by God in opening the water. The competency of the wind temporarily to remove the water from the passage connecting the Gulf of Suez with the Bitter Lakes, provided it was only a few feet deep, is amply proved by facts of recent observation. Major General Tullock of the British army (*Proc. Victoria Inst.*, XXVIII, 267–80) reports having witnessed the driving off of the water from Lake Menzaleh by the wind to such an extent as to lower the level 6 ft., thus leaving small vessels over the shallow water stranded for a while in the muddy bottom. According to the report of the Suez Canal Co., the difference between the highest and the lowest water at Suez is 10 ft. 7 in., all of which must be due to the effect of the wind, since the tides do not affect the Red Sea. The power of the wind to affect water levels is strikingly witnessed upon Lake Erie in the United States, where according to the report of the Deep Waterways Commission for 1896 (165, 168) it appears that strong wind from the S.W. sometimes lowers the water at Toledo, Ohio, on the western end of the lake to the extent of more than 7 ft., at the same time causing it to rise at Buffalo at the eastern end a similar amount; while a change in the wind during the passage of a single storm reverses the effect, thus sometimes producing a change of level at either end of the lake of 14 ft. in the course of a single day. It would require far less than a tornado to lower the water at *Cheloof* sufficiently to lay bare the shallow channel which we have supposed at that time to separate Egypt from the Sinaitic Peninsula. See EXODUS, THE.

Several objections to this theory, however, have been urged which should not pass without notice. (1) Some have said that the children of Israel would have found an insuperable obstacle to their advance in the steep banks on either side of the supposed channel. But there were no steep banks to be encountered. A gentle sag leads down on one side to the center of the depression and a correspondingly gentle rise leads up on the other. (2) Much has also been made of the statement (Ex **14** 22) that "the waters were a wall unto them on their right hand, and on their left"; but when we consider the rhetorical use of this word "wall" it presents no difficulty. In Prov **18** 11 we are told that "The rich man's wealth is his strong city, And as a high wall in his own imagination." In Isa **26** 1 we are told that God will appoint salvation "for walls and bulwarks." Again Nahum (**3** 8) says of Egypt that her "rampart was the sea [m "the Nile"], and her wall was of the sea." The water upon either side of the opening served the purpose of a wall for protection. There was no chance for Pharaoh to intercept them by a flank movement. Nor is there need of paying further attention to the poetical expressions in the Song of Moses, where among other things it is said "that the deeps were congealed in the heart of the sea," and that the "earth [instead of the water] swallowed them." (3) Again it is objected that an east wind does not come from the right direction to produce the desired result. On the other hand it is an east wind only which could have freed the channel from water. A north wind would have blown the water from the Bitter Lakes southward, and owing to the quantity of water impounded would have increased the depth of the water in the narrow passage from the southern end of Suez. An east wind, however, would have pressed the water out from the channel both ways, and from the contour of the shore lines would be the only wind that could have done so. (4) Again, it is objected that this explanation destroys the miraculous character of the event. But it should be noted that little is said in the narrative about the miraculous. On the other hand, it is a straightforward statement of events, leaving their miraculous character to be inferred from their nature. On the explanation we have given the transaction it is what Robinson felicitously calls a mediate miracle, that is, a miracle in which the hand of God is seen in the use of natural forces which it would be impossible for man to command. If anyone should say that this was a mere coincidence, that the east wind blew at the precise time that Moses reached the place of crossing, the answer is that such a coincidence could have been brought about only by supernatural agency. There was at that time no weather bureau to foretell the approach of a storm. There are no tides on the Red Sea with regular ebb and flow. It was by a miracle of prophecy that Moses was emboldened to get his host into position to avail themselves of the temporary opportunity at exactly the right time. As to the relation of the Divine agency to the event, speculation is useless. The opening of the sea may have been a foreordained event in the course of Nature which God only foreknew, in which case the direct Divine agency was limited to those influences upon the human actors that led them to place themselves where they could take advantage of the natural opportunity. Or, there is no a priori difficulty in supposing that the east wind was directly aroused for this occasion; for man himself produces disturbances among the forces of Nature that are as far-reaching in their extent as would be a storm produced by direct Divine agency. But in this case the disturbance is at once seen to be beyond the powers of human agency to produce.

It remains to add an important word concerning the evidential value of this perfect adjustment of the narrative to the physical conditions involved. So perfect is this conformity of the narrative to the obscure physical conditions involved, which only recent investigations have made clear, that the account becomes self-evidencing. It is not within the power of man to invent a story so perfectly in accordance with the vast and complicated conditions involved. The argument is as strong as that for human design when a key is found to fit a Yale lock. This is not a general account which would fit into a variety of circumstances. There is only one place in all the world, and one set of conditions in all history, which would meet the requirements; and here they are all met. This is scientific demonstration. No higher proof can be found in the inductive sciences. The story is true. It has not been remodeled by the imagination, either of the original writers or of the transcribers. It is not the product of mythological fancy or of legendary accretion.

LITERATURE.—Dawson, *Egypt and Syria;* Hull, *Mt. Seir, Sinai and Western Pal;* Naville, "The Store-City Pithom and the Route of the Exodus," *Egyp Exploration Fund,* 1885; Kyle, "Bricks without Straw at Pithom: A Reëxamination of Naville's Works," *Records of the Past,* VIII, 1901, 304–7; Wright, *Scientific Confirmations of OT Hist,* 83–117.

GEORGE FREDERICK WRIGHT

REDEEMER, rē̇-dēm'ẽr, **REDEMPTION,** rē̇-demp'shun (פָּרַק, *pāraḳ,* "to tear loose," "to rescue," פָּדָה, *pādhāh,* גָּאַל, *gā'al;* **ἀγοράζω,** *agorázō,* referring to purchase, **λυτροῦμαι,** *lutroúmai,* from **λύτρον,** *lútron,* "a ransom"):

1. Gradual Moralizing of Idea of Redemption
2. Redemption as Life in Individual
3. Redemption as Social
4. Redemption as Process
5. Moral Implications in Scriptural Idea of Redeemer
6. Uniqueness of Son of God as Redeemer

LITERATURE

The idea of redemption in the OT takes its start from the thought of property (Lev **25** 26; Ruth **4** 4 ff). Money is paid according to law to buy back something which must be delivered or rescued (Nu **3** 51; Neh **5** 8). From this start the word "redemption" throughout the OT is used in the general sense of deliverance. God is the Redeemer of Israel in the sense that He is the Deliverer of Israel (Dt **9** 26; 2 S **7** 23; 1 Ch **17** 21; Isa **52** 3). The idea of deliverance includes deliverance from all forms of evil lot, from national misfortune (Isa **52** 9; **63** 9; cf Lk **2** 38), or from plague (Ps **78** 35.52), or from calamity of any sort (Gen **48** 16; Nu **25** 4.9). Of course, the general thought of the relation of Israel to God was that God had both a claim upon Israel (Dt **15** 15) and an obligation toward Israel (1 Ch **17** 21; Ps **25** 22). Israel belonged to Him, and it was by His own right that He could move into the life of Israel so as to redeem Israel. On the other hand, obligation was upon Him to redeem Israel.

In the NT the idea of redemption has more a suggestion of ransom. Men are held under the curse of the law (Gal **3** 13), or of sin itself (Rom **7** 23 f). The Redeemer purchases their deliverance by offering Himself as payment for their redemption (Eph **1** 7; 1 Pet **1** 18).

Throughout both the OT and the NT there is to be observed a gradual moralizing of the meaning of redemption. The same process of moralizing has continued throughout all the Christian ages. Starting with the idea of redemption price, conceived almost in material terms, religious thought has advanced to conceptions entirely moral and spiritual. Through the Scriptures, too, the idea of redemption becomes more specific with the progress of Christian revelation. In the beginning God is the Redeemer from distresses of all kinds. He redeems from calamity and from sorrows. This general idea, of course, persists throughout the revelation and enters largely into our thinking of today, but the growing moral discernment of the Bib. writers comes to attach more and more importance to sin as the chief disturber of man's welfare. We would not minimize the force of the Scriptural idea that God is the Deliverer from all misfortune to which man falls heir, but the Scriptural emphasis moves more and more to deliverance from sin. Paul states this deliverance as a deliverance from the law which brings sin out into expression, but we must not conceive his idea in any artificial fashion. He would have men delivered not only from the law, but also from the consequences of evil doing and from the spirit of evil itself (Rom **8** 2).

1. Gradual Moralizing of Idea

In trying to discern the meaning of redemption from sin, toward which the entire progress of Bib. and Christian thought points, we may well keep in mind the Master's words that He came that men might have life and might have it more abundantly (Jn **10** 10). The word "life" seems to be the final NT word as a statement of the purpose of Christ. God sent His Son to bring men to life. The word "life," however, is indefinite. Life means more at one period of the world's history than at another. It has the advantage, nevertheless, of always being entirely intelligible in its essential significance. Our aim must be to keep this essential significance in mind and at the same time to provide for an increasing fulness and enlargement of human capacity and endeavor. The aim of redemption can only be to bring men to the fullest use and enjoyment of their powers. This is really the conception implicit even in the earliest statements of redemption. The man redeemed by money payment comes out of the prison to the light of day, or he comes out of slavery into freedom, or he is restored to his home and friends. The man under the law is redeemed from the burden and curse of the law. Paul speaks of his experience under the law as the experience of one chained to a dead body (Rom **7** 24). Of course, relief from such bondage would mean life. In the more spiritual passages of the NT, the evil in men's hearts is like a blight which paralyzes their higher activities (Jn **8** 33–51).

2. Redemption as Life in Individual

In all redemption, as conceived of in Christian terms, there is a double element. There is first the deliverance as from a curse. Something binds a man or weights him down; redemption relieves him from this load. On the other hand, there is the positive movement of the soul thus relieved toward larger and fuller life. We have said that the Bib. emphasis is always upon deliverance from sin as the essential in redemption, but this deliverance is so essential that the life cannot progress in any of its normal activities until it is redeemed from evil. Accordingly in the Scriptural thought all manner of blessings follow deliverance. The man who seeks first the Kingdom of God and His righteousness finds all other things added unto him (Mt **6** 33). Material, intellectual and social blessings follow as matters of course from the redemption of the inner spirit from evil. The aim of redemption, to beget in men's hearts the will to do right, once fulfilled, leads men to seek successfully along all possible avenues for life. This, of course, does not mean that the redeemed life gives itself up to the cultivation of itself toward higher excellencies. It means that the redeemed life is delivered from every form of selfishness. In the unselfish seeking of life for others the redeemed life finds its own greatest achievement and happiness (Mt **16** 25).

Just as the idea of redemption concerned itself chiefly with the inner spirit, so also it concerns itself with the individual as the object of redemption. But as the redemption of the inner spirit leads to freedom in all realms of life, so also the redemption of the individual leads to large social transformations. It is impossible to strike out of the Scriptures the idea of a redeemed humanity. But humanity is not conceived of in general or class terms. The object of redemption is not humanity, or mankind, or the masses. The object of redemption is rather men set in relation to each other as members of a family. But it would do violence to the Scriptural conception to conceive of the individual's relations in any narrow or restricted fashion (1 Cor **12** 12–27).

3. Redemption as Social

An important enlargement of the idea of redemption in our own time has come as men have conceived of the redemption of individuals in their social relationships. Very often men have thought of redemption as a snatching of individuals from the perils of a world in itself absolutely wicked. Even the material environment of men has at times been regarded as containing something inherently evil. The thought of redemption which seems most in line with Scriptural interpretation would seem to be that which brings the material and social forces within reach of individual wills. Paul speaks of the whole creation groaning and travailing in pain waiting for the revelation of the sons of God (Rom **8** 22). This graphic figure sets before us the essentially Christian conception of the redemption of the forces in the midst of which men are placed. Those redeemed for the largest life, by the very force of their life, will seize all powers of this world to make them the servants of Divine purposes. The seer saw a great multitude which no man could number, of every kindred and nation and tongue, shouting the joys of salvation (Rev **7** 9), yet the implication nowhere appears that these were redeemed in any other fashion than by surrendering themselves to the forces of righteousness.

4. Redemption as Process

We have said that the aim of redemption is to bring men to the largest and fullest life. We have also said that "life" is a general term. To keep close to the Scriptural conceptions we would best say that the aim of redemption is to make men like Christ (Rom **8** 9). Otherwise, it might be possible to use the word "life" so as to imply that the riotous exercise of the faculties is what we mean by redemption. The idea of redemption, as a matter of fact, has been thus interpreted in various times in the history of Christian thinking. Life has been looked upon as sheer quantitative exuberance—the lower pleasures of sense being reckoned as about on the same plane with the higher. We can see the moral and spiritual anarchy which would thus be brought about. In Christ's words to His disciples He once used the expression, "Ye are clean because of the word which I have spoken unto you" (Jn **15** 3). In this particular context the idea does not seem to be that of an external washing. Christ seems rather to mean that His disciples are cleansed as a vineyard is cleansed by pruning away some of the branches that others may bear fruit. In other words, the redemption of life is to be interpreted so that stress is laid upon the qualitative rather than the quantitative. Christ indeed found place in His instructions and in His own life for the normal and healthy activities of human existence. He was not an ascetic; He went to feasts and to weddings, but His emphasis was always upon life conceived of in the highest terms. We can say then that the aim of redemption is to beget in men life like that in Christ.

5. Moral Implications in Scriptural Idea

Moreover, redemption must not be conceived of in such fashion as to do away with the need of response upon the part of the individual will. The literal suggestion of ransom has to do with paying a price for a man's deliverance, whether the man is willing to be delivered or not. Of course, the assumption in the mind of the Bib. writers was that any man in prison or in slavery or in sickness would be overjoyed at being redeemed; but in dealing with men whose lives are set toward sin we cannot always make this assumption. The dreadfulness of sin is largely in the love of sinning which sinning begets. Some thinkers have interpreted redemption to mean almost a seizing of men without regard to their own will. It is very easy to see how this conception arises. A man who himself hates sin may not stop to realize that some other men love sin. Redemption, to mean anything, must touch this inner attitude of will. We cannot then hold to any idea of redemption which brings men under a cleansing process without the assent of their own wills. If we keep ourselves alive to the growing moral discernment which moves through the Scriptures, we must lay stress always upon redemption as a moral process. Not only must we say that the aim of redemption is to make men like Christ, but we must say also that the method of redemption must be the method of Christ, the method of appealing to the moral will. There is no Scriptural warrant for the idea that men are redeemed by fiat. The most we can get from the words of Christ is a statement of the persistence of God in His search for the lost: '[He goeth] after that which is lost, until he finds it' (Lk **15** 4). Some would interpret these words to mean that the process of redemption continues until every man is brought into the kingdom. We cannot, in the light of the NT, limit the redeeming love of God; but we cannot, on the other hand, take passages from figurative expressions in such sense as to limit the freedom of men. The redemption must be conceived of as respecting the moral choices of men. In our thought of the Divine search for the control of inner human motive we must not stop short of the idea of men redeemed to the love of righteousness on its own account. This would do away with the plan of redeeming men by merely relieving them of the consequences of their sins. Out of a changed life, of course, there must come changed consequences. But the Scriptural teaching is that the emphasis in redemption is always moral, the turning to life because of what life is.

Having thus attempted to determine, at least in outline, the content of the Christian idea of redemption, it remains for us to point out some implications as to the work of the Redeemer. Throughout the entire teaching on redemption in the Scriptures, redemption is set before us primarily as God's own affair (Jn **3** 16). God redeems His people; He redeems them out of love for them. But the love of God is not to be conceived of as mere indulgence, partiality, or good-humored affection. The love of God rests down upon moral foundations. Throughout the Scriptures, therefore, we find implied often, if not always clearly stated, the idea that God is under obligations to redeem His people. The progress of later thinking has expanded this implication with sureness of moral discernment. We have come to see the obligations of power. The more powerful the man the heavier his obligations in the discharge of this power. This is a genuinely Christian conception, and this Christian conception we apply to the character of God, feeling confident that we are in line with Scriptural teaching. Hence we may put the obligations of God somewhat as follows: God is the most obligated being in the universe. If a man is under heavy obligations to use aright the power of controlling the forces already at work in the world, how much heavier must be the obligations on the Creator who started these forces! The obligation becomes appalling to our human thought when we think that creation includes the calling of human beings into existence and endowing them with the unsolicited boon of freedom. Men are not in the world of their own choice. Vast masses of them seem to be here as the outworking of impulses almost blind. The surroundings of men make it very easy for them to sin. The tendencies which at least seem to be innate are too often tragically inclined toward evil. Men seem, of themselves, utterly inadequate for their own redemption. If there is to be redemption it must come from God, and the Christian thought of a moral God would seem to include the obligation on the part of God to redeem those whom He has sent into the world. Christ has made clear forever the absolutely binding nature of moral considerations. If the obligation to redeem men meant everything to Christ, it must also mean everything to the God of Christ. So we feel in line with true Christian thinking in the doctrine that redemption comes first as a discharge of the obligations on the part of God Himself.

If we look for the common thought in all the Christian statements of God's part in redemption we find it in this: that in all these statements God is conceived of as doing all that He can do for the redemption of man. If in earlier times men conceived of the human race as under the dominion of Satan, and of Satan as robbed of his due by the deliverance of man and therefore entitled to some compensation, they also conceived of God Himself as paying the ransom to Satan. If they thought of God as a feudal lord whose dignity had been offended by sin, they thought of God as Himself paying the cost due to offended dignity. If their idea was that a substitute for sinners must be furnished, the idea included the thought of God as Himself providing a substitute. If they conceived of the universe as a vast system of moral laws—broken by sin—whose dignity must be upheld, they thought of God Himself as providing the means for maintaining the dignity of the laws. If they conceived of men as saved by a vast moral influence set at work, they thought of this influence as proceeding, not from man, but from God. The common thought in theories of redemption then, so far as concerns God's part, is that God Himself takes the initiative and does all He can in the discharge of the obligation upon Himself. Each phrasing of the doctrine of redemption is the attempt of an age of Christian thinking to say in its own way that God has done all that He can do for men.

6. Uniqueness of Son of God as Redeemer

It is from this standpoint that we must approach the part played by Christ in redemption. This is not the place for an attempt at formal statement, but some elements of Christian teaching are, at least in outline, at once clear. The question is, first, to provide some relation between God and Christ which will make the redemptive work of Christ really effective. Some have thought to find such a statement in the conception that Christ is a prophet. They would empty the expression, "Son of God," of any unique meaning; they would make Christ the Son of God in the same sense that any great prophet could be conceived of as a son of God. Of course, we would not minimize the teaching of the Scripture as to the full humanity of Christ, and yet we may be permitted to voice our belief that the representation of Christ as the Redeemer merely in the same sense in which a prophet is a redeemer does not do justice to the Scripture teaching; and we feel, too, that such a solution of the problem of Christ would be inadequate for the practical task of redemption. If Christ is just a prophet giving us His teaching we rejoice in the teaching, but we are confronted with the problem as to how to make the teaching effective. If it be urged that Christ is a prophet who in Himself realized the moral ideal, we feel constrained to reply that this really puts Christ at a vast distance from us. Such a doctrine of Christ's person would make Him the supreme religious genius, but the human genius stands apart from the ordinary mass of men. He may gather up into Himself and realize the ideals of men; He may voice the aspirations of men and realize those aspirations; but He may not be able to make men like unto Himself. Shakespeare is a consummate literary genius. He has said once and for all many things which the common man thinks or half thinks. When the common man comes upon a phrase of Shakespeare he feels that Shakespeare has said for all time the things which he would himself have said if he had been able. But the appreciation of Shakespeare does not make the ordinary man like Shakespeare; the appreciation of Christ has not proved successful in itself in making men like unto Christ.

If, on the contrary, without attempting formal theological construction, we put some real meaning into the idea of Christ as the Son of God and hold fast to a unique relationship between Christ and God which makes Christ the greatest gift that God can give us, we find indeed that Christ is lifted up to essentially Divine existence; but we find also that this divinity does not estrange Him from us. Redemption becomes feasible, not merely when we have a revelation of how far up man can go, but when we have also a revelation of how far down God can come. If we can think of God as having in some real way come into the world through His Son Jesus Christ, that revelation makes Christ the Lord who can lead us to redemption.

Such a conception furnishes the dynamic which we must have in any real process of redemption. We need not only the ideal, but we need power by which to reach the ideal. If we can feel that the universe is under the sway of a moral God, a God who is under obligations to bear the burdens of men, and who willingly assumes these obligations, we really feel that moral life at its fullest and best is the greatest fact in the universe. Moreover, we must be true to the Scriptures and lift the entire conception of redemption beyond the realm of conscience to the realm of the heart. What the conscience of God calls for, the love of God willingly discharges. The Cross of Christ becomes at once the revelation of the righteousness of God and the love of God. Power is thus put back of human conscience and human love to move forward toward redemption (Rom **8** 35–39).

The aim of the redemption in Christ then is to lift men out of death toward life. The mind is to be quickened by the revelation of the true ideals of human life. The conscience is to be reënforced by the revelation of the moral God who carries on all things in the interests of righteousness. The heart is to be stirred and won by the revelation of the love which sends an only begotten Son to the cross for our redemption. And we must take the work of Christ, not as a solitary incident or a mere historic event, but as a manifestation of the spirit which has been at work from the beginning and works forever. The Lamb was slain from the foundation of the world (Rev **13** 8); the spirit of God revealed in the cross of Christ is the same yesterday, today and forever. We have in the cross a revelation of holy love which, in a sense, overpowers and at the same time encourages. The cross is the revelation of the length to which God is willing to go in redemption rather than set aside one jot or tittle of His moral law. He will not redeem men except on terms which leave them men. He will not overwhelm them in any such manner as to do away with their power of free choice. He will show men His own feeling of holiness and love. In the name of a holy love which they can forever aspire after, but which they can never fully reach, men call to Him for forgiveness and that forgiveness men find forever available.

It remains to add one further item of Scriptural teaching, namely that redemption is a continuous process. If we may again use the word "life," which has been the key to this discussion, we may say that the aim of redemption is to make men progressively alive. There are not limits to the development of human powers touched by the redemptive processes of God. The cross is a revelation of Divine willingness to bear with men who are forever being redeemed. Of course, we speak of the redeemed man as redeemed once and for all. By this we mean that he is redeemed once and for all in being faced about and started in a right direction, but the progress toward full life may be faster or slower according to the man and the circumstances in the midst of which he is placed. Still the chief fact is the direction in which the man is moving. The revelation of God who aids in redemption is of the God who takes the direction as the chief fact rather than the length of the stride or the rate of the movement. Every man is expected to do his best. If he stumbles he is supposed to find his way to his feet; if he is moving slowly, he must attempt to move faster; if he is moving at a slower rate than he can attain, he must strive after the higher rate, but always the dynamic force is the revelation of the holy love of God.

The Scriptures honor the prophets in whatever land or time they appear. The Scriptures welcome goodness under any and all circumstances. They have a place for a "light that lighteneth every man that cometh into the world," but they still make it clear that the chief force in the redemption of men is the revelation of holy love in Jesus Christ. The redemption, we repeat, is never conceived of in artificial or mechanical terms. If any man hath not the spirit of Christ he does not belong to Christ (Rom **8** 9). The aim of redemption is to beget this spirit, and this spirit is life.

Literature.—H. C. Sheldon, *Systematic Theology;* Clarke, *Outline of Christian Theology;* Brown, *Christian Theology in Outline;* Mackintosh, *Doctrine of Person of Christ;* Bowne, *Studies in Christianity;* Tymms, *The Christian Atonement.*

Francis J. McConnell

REDNESS, red′nes, **OF EYES.** See Drunkenness, II.

REDOUND, rē-dound′ (from *re,* "back," and *undare,* "to surge as a wave"): To be sent back as a reaction, to overflow; occurs only as the tr of περισσεύω, *perisseúō,* "to be over and above," "to superabound" (frequent in the NT); in 2 Cor **4** 15, "might through the thanksgiving of many redound to the glory of God," RV "may cause the thanksgiving to abound."

REED, rēd: (1) אָחוּ, *'āḥū,* tr[d] "reed-grass" (Gen **41** 2.18; Job **8** 11m). See Flag. (2) אֵבֶה, *'ēbheh,* tr[d] "swift," m "reed" (Job **9** 26). The "ships of reed" are the light skiffs made of plaited reeds used on the Nile; cf "vessels of papyrus" (Isa **18** 2). (3) אֲגַמִּים, *'ăghammīm,* tr[d] "reeds," m "marshes," Heb "pools" (Jer **51** 32); elsewhere "pools" (Ex **7** 19; **8** 5; Isa **14** 23, etc). See Pools. (4) עָרוֹת, *'ārōth;* ἄχι, *áchi,* tr[d] "meadows," AV "paper reeds" (Isa **19** 7). See Meadows. (5) קָנֶה, *ḳāneh;* κάλαμος, *kálamos* (the Eng. "cane" comes from Heb via Lat and Gr *canna*), "stalk" (Gen **41** 5.22); "shaft" (Ex **37** 17, etc); "reed," or "reeds" (1 K **14** 15; 2 K **18** 21; Isa **36** 6; **42** 3; Ps **68** 30, AV "spearman"); "calamus" (Ex **30** 23; Cant **4** 14; Ezk **27** 19); "sweet cane," m "calamus" (Isa **43** 24; Jer **6** 20); "bone" (Job **31** 22); used of the cross-beam of a "balance" (Isa **46** 6); "a measuring reed" (Ezk **40** 3); "a staff of reed," i.e. a walking-stick (Isa **36** 6; Ezk **29** 6); the "branches" of a candlestick (Ex **37** 18). (6) κάλαμος, *kálamos,* "a reed shaken with the wind" (Mt **11** 7; Lk **7** 24); "a bruised reed" (Mt **12** 20); they put "a reed in his right hand" (Mt **27** 29.30); "They smote his head with a reed" (Mk **15** 19); "put it on a reed" (Mt **27** 48; Mk **15** 36); "a measuring reed" (Rev **11** 1; **21** 15.16); "a pen" (3 Jn ver 13).

It is clear that *ḳāneh* and its Gr equivalent *kalamos* mean many things. Some refer to different uses to which a reed is put, e.g. a cross-beam of a balance, a walking-stick, a measuring rod, and a pen (see above), but apart from this *ḳāneh* is a word used for at least two essentially different things: (1) an ordinary reed, and (2) some sweet-smelling substance.

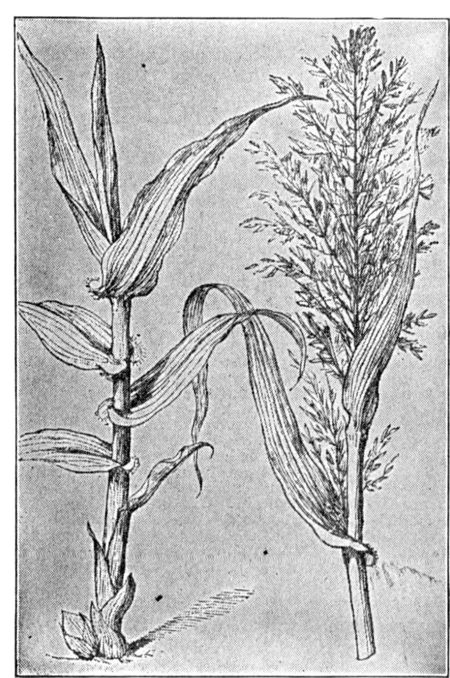

Reed (*Arundo donax*).

(1) The most common reed in Pal is the *Arundo donax* (N.O. *Gramineae*), known in Arab. as *ḳaṣab-farasi,* "Persian reed." It grows in immense quantities in the Jordan valley along the river and its tributaries and at the oases near the Dead Sea, notably around *'Ain Feshkhah* at the northwest corner. It is a lofty reed, often 20 ft. high, of a beautiful fresh green in summer when all else is dead and dry, and of a fine appearance from a distance in the spring months when it is in full bloom and the beautiful silky panicles crown the top of every reed. The "covert of the reed" (Job **40** 21) shelters a large amount of animal and bird life. This reed will answer to almost all the requirements of the above references.

(2) *Ḳāneh* is in Jer **6** 20 qualified קָנֶה הַטּוֹב, *ḳāneh ha-ṭōbh,* "sweet" or "pleasant cane," and in Ex **30** 23, קְנֵה בֹשֶׂם, *ḳ[e]nēh bhōsem,* "sweet calamus," or, better, a "cane of fragrance." Cant **4** 14; Isa **43** 24; Ezk **27** 19 all apparently refer to the same thing, though in these passages the *ḳāneh* is unqualified. It was an ingredient of the holy oil (Ex **30** 23); it was imported from a distance (Jer **6** 20;

Ezk **27** 19), and it was rare and costly (Isa **43** 24). It may have been the "scented calamus" (*Axorus calamus*) of Pliny (*NH*, xii.48), or some other aromatic scented reed or flag, or, as some think, some kind of aromatic bark. The sweetness refers to the scent, not the taste. See also BULRUSH; PAPYRUS. E. W. G. MASTERMAN

REED-GRASS (Gen **41** 2.18; Job **8** 11 m). See FLAG, (2); REED, (1).

REED, MEASURING, mezh'ûr-ing (קְנֵה הַמִּדָּה, *ḳ^enēh ha-middāh*): In Ezekiel's vision of the temple a "man" (an angel) appears with a "measuring reed" to measure the dimensions of the temple (Ezk **40** 3 ff; **42** 16 ff). The reed is described as 6 cubits long, "of a cubit and a handbreadth each," i.e. the cubit used was a handbreadth longer than the common cubit (see CUBIT; WEIGHTS AND MEASURES; TEMPLE). In the Apocalypse this idea of a measuring reed reappears for measuring the temple (Rev **11** 1) and the holy city (**21** 15.16, "a golden reed"). The thought conveyed is exactitude in the dimensions of these edifices, symbolic of the symmetry and perfection of God's church. JAMES ORR

REELAIAH, rē-el-ā'ya, rē-el-ī'a (רְעֵלָיָה, *r^e'ēl-yāh*): One of the 12 chiefs who returned with Zerubbabel (Ezr **2** 2 ‖ Neh **7** 7). In the passage in Neh the name is "Raamiah" (רַעַמְיָה, *ră'amyāh*), and in 1 Esd **5** 8 "Resaias." Which is the original, it is almost impossible to decide; "Reelaiah" seems preferable.

REELIAS, rē-el'i-as (A, Ῥεέλιας, *Rheélias* [Fritzsche], B, followed by Swete, Βορολείας, *Boroleías;* AV **Reelius**): One of the "leaders" with Zerubbabel in the return from exile (1 Esd **5** 8, m "Reelaiah"). It occupies the place of "Bigvai" in Ezr **2** 2; Neh **7** 7, but in form it must be the equivalent of "Reelaiah" of Ezr and "Raamiah" of Neh. It is perhaps a duplicate of "Resaias."

REESAIAS, rē-ē-sā'yas, rē-ē-sī'as: AV; RV RESAIAS (q.v.).

REFINER, rē-fīn'ēr, **REFINING,** rē-fīn'ing: Two Heb words have been tr^d "refine": (1) צָרַף, *çāraph*, lit. to "fuse" (Zec **13** 9; Isa **48** 10; Mal **3** 2.3, etc). The same word is rendered also "tried" (Ps **66** 10); "melt" (Jer **6** 29 AV); "purge" (Isa **1** 25). (2) זָקַק, *zāḳaḳ*, lit. to "strain" or "sift." In the case of silver and gold the term probably referred to some washing process in connection with refining, as in Mal **3** 3 both *çāraph* and *zāḳaḳ* are used (1 Ch **28** 18; **29** 4; Job **28** 1). The same word in Isa **25** 6 referred to the straining of wine. Gr πυρόω, *puróō*, in the passive, lit. "to be ignited," is tr^d "refined," in Rev **1** 15; **3** 18.

The ancient process of refining gold has already been described under METALLURGY (q.v.). Most of the Bible references are to the refining of silver (Prov **25** 4; Zec **13** 9; Isa **48** 10). The silver used by the ancients was probably obtained by smelting lead sulphide ore, rich in silver (argentiferous galena). After the ore had been reduced to a metallic condition, the lead was separated from the silver by blowing hot air over the surface of the melted metal. The lead was thus changed to lead oxide which, in a powdered condition, was driven away by the air blast.

Blowpipe and Small Furnace.—Thebes.

The resulting lead oxide, called in the Bible silver dross, was used for glazing pottery (Prov **26** 23), a use to which it is still put by Syrian potters. The description of refining in Ezk **22** 18–22 may indicate that a flux (cf "as with lye," Isa **1** 25 ARVm) was sometimes added to the melted metal to dissolve the oxides of copper, lead, tin and iron as they formed, thus leaving the silver pure. Crude processes similar to those described above are used in the Taurus Mountains today.

Figurative: In the various Bible references the refining of precious metals is used fig. to illustrate the kind of trial God's children are called upon to go through. If they are of the right metal the dross will finally be blown away, leaving pure, clear, shining silver. If of base metal they will be like the dross described in Jer **6** 29.30. The refiner may blow fiercely, but in vain, for nothing but lead dross appears. JAMES A. PATCH

REFORM, rē-fôrm' (יָסַר, *yāṣar*): The word in RV is found only in Lev **26** 23, in the phrase "ye will not be reformed." The meaning is, "to be instructed," or, more fully, "to let one's self be chastened," i.e. by God's discipline to learn the lessons of this chastening.

The Heb word is the same in a similar connection in Jer **6** 8, where it is rendered, "Be thou instructed," and in **31** 18, "I was chastised." Ps **2** 10 ("instructed"); Prov **29** 19 ("corrected") use the Heb term of admonition by the words of man.
AV also has "reform" in 2 Esd **8** 12; Wisd **9** 18.

REFORMATION, ref-or-mā'shun: The word is found only in He **9** 10, being the tr of διόρθωσις, *diórthōsis*, in its only occurrence. This Gr word means etymologically "making straight," and was used of restoring to the normally straight condition that which is crooked or bent. In this passage it means the rectification of conditions, setting things to rights, and is a description of the Messianic time.

REFRESH, rē-fresh', **REFRESHING,** rē-fresh'-ing: "Refresh" occurs a few times in the OT as the tr of נָפַשׁ, *nāphash*, "to take breath," figurative "to be refreshed" (Ex **23** 12; **31** 17; 2 S **16** 14); of רָוַח, *rāwaḥ*, "to have room" (1 S **16** 23; Job **32** 20, m "find relief," AVm "may breathe"); of סָעַד, *ṣā'adh*, "to support" (1 K **13** 7); and in the NT as the tr of ἀναπαύω, *anapaúō*, "to give rest" (1 Cor **16** 18; 2 Cor **7** 13; Philem vs 7.20; in compound middle, Rom **15** 32 AV); also of ἀναψύχω, *anapsúchō*, "to invigorate," "revive" (2 Tim **1** 16), and other words. "Refreshing" is in Isa **28** 12 *margē'āh*, "rest" or "quiet"; and in Acts **3** 19, ἀνάψυξις, *anápsuxis*, "seasons of refreshing," through the coming of Jesus, the Christ; cf 2 Esd **11** 46 and AV Sir **43** 22 (ἱλαρόω). W. L. WALKER

REFUGE, ref'ūj: A place of resort and safety. The principal words in the OT are מַחְסֶה, *maḥṣeh* (Ps **14** 6; **46** 1; **62** 7.8; Isa **4** 6, etc), and מָנוֹס, *mānōṣ* (2 S **22** 3; Ps **59** 16, etc), both applied chiefly to God as a "refuge" for His people. For AV "refuge" in Dt **33** 27, RV has "dwelling-place," and in Ps **9** 9, "high tower." Conversely, RV has "refuge" for AV "shelter" in Ps **61** 3, and "hope" in Jer **17** 17.

REFUGE, CITIES OF (עָרֵי הַמִּקְלָט, *'ārē ha-miḳlāṭ;* πόλεις τῶν φυγαδευτηρίων, *póleis tōn phugadeutēríōn* [cf 1 Macc **10** 28], and other forms): Six cities, three on each side of the Jordan, were set apart and placed in the hands of the Levites, to serve as places of asylum for such as might shed blood unwittingly. On the

1. Location

E. of the Jordan they were **Bezer** in the lot of Reuben, **Ramoth-gilead** in the tribe of Gad, and **Golan** in the territory of Manasseh. On the W. of the Jordan they were **Hebron** in Judah, **Shechem** in Mt. Ephraim, and **Kedesh** in Naphtali (Nu **35** 6.14; Josh **20** 2.7 ff; **21** 13.21.27.32.38; Bezer is named in ver 36, but not described as a City of Refuge). An account of these cities is given in separate arts. under their names. Dt **19** 2 speaks of *three* cities thus to be set apart, referring apparently to the land W. of the Jordan.

2. Purpose

From time immemorial in the East, if a man were slain the duty of avenging him has lain as a sacred obligation upon his nearest relative. In districts where more primitive conditions prevail, even to this day, the distinction between intentional and unintentional killing is not too strictly observed, and men are often done to death in revenge for what was the purest accident. To prevent such a thing where possible, and to provide for a right administration of justice, these cities were instituted. Open highways were to be maintained along which the manslayer might have an unobstructed course to the city gate.

3. Regulations

The regulations concerning the Cities of Refuge are found in Nu **35**; Dt **19** 1–13; Josh **20**. Briefly, everything was to be done to facilitate the flight of the manslayer, lest the avenger of blood, i.e. the nearest of kin, should pursue him with hot heart, and, overtaking him, should smite him mortally. On reaching the city he was to be received by the elders and his case heard. If this was satisfactory, they gave him asylum until a regular trial could be carried out. They took him, apparently, to the city or district from which he had fled, and there, among those who knew him, witnesses were examined. If it were proved that he was not a wilful slayer, that he had no grudge against the person killed, and had shown no sign of purpose to injure him, then he was declared innocent and conducted back to the city in which he had taken refuge, where he must stay until the death of the high priest. Then he was free to return home in safety. Until that event he must on no account go beyond the city boundaries. If he did, the avenger of blood might slay him without blame. On the other hand, if he were found guilty of deliberate murder, there was no more protection for him. He was handed over to the avenger of blood who, with his own hand, took the murderer's life. Blood-money, i.e. money paid in compensation for the murder, in settlement of the avenger's claim, was in no circumstances permitted; nor could the refugee be ransomed, so that he might "come again to dwell in the land" until the death of the high priest (Nu **35** 32), cf Kyle, *Problem of the Pentateuch* 59).

A similar right of refuge seems to have been recognized in Israel as attaching to the altar in the temple at Jerus (1 K **1** 50; **2** 28; cf Ex **21** 12 f). This may be compared with the right of asylum connected with the temples of the heathen. W. Ewing

REFUSE, rē̇-fūz′: Formerly used with the additional meaning "reject," and hence the change from AV to RV in 1 S **16** 7; Ezk **5** 6; 1 Tim **4** 4; 1 Pet **2** 7, etc.

REFUTE, rē̇-fūt′: Only in Jude ver 22, ARVm "And some *refute* while they dispute with you," where RV in the text reads "And on some have mercy, who are in doubt."

The Gr text of vs 22.23 is very uncertain, being given very differently in the various MSS. RV text follows the two oldest MSS, ℵ and B. Instead of ἐλεᾶτε, *eleáte*, "have mercy," the reading ἐλέγχετε, *elégchete*, "refute," "convict," has the powerful support of A C, the best cursives, Vulg, Memphitic, Armenian and Ethiopian VSS, and is placed in the text by Lachmann, Tischendorf and Tregelles (WH in list of "Suspected Readings" says: "Some primitive error probable: perhaps the first ἐλεᾶτε an interpolation"). Cf ver 15, where the same Gr word occurs in the same sense (AV "convince," RV "convict"); cf also 1 Tim **5** 20; Tit **1** 9, where the same idea of refuting the sinful occurs.

D. Miall Edwards

REGEM, rē′gem (רֶגֶם, *reghem*, "friend" [?]): A Calebite, the son of Jahdai (1 Ch **2** 47), mentioned as the eponym of a Calebite family or clan.

REGEM-MELECH, rē′gem-mē′lek, -mel′ek (רֶגֶם מֶלֶךְ, *reghem melekh*): One of a deputation sent to inquire concerning the propriety of continuing the commemoration of the destruction of the temple by holding a fast (Zec **7** 2). The text of the passage is in disorder. The name may mean "friend of the king"; hence some have sought to remove the difficulty by interpreting *reghem melekh* as a title, not a personal name, reading the clause, "They of Beth-el had sent Sharezer [q.v. (2)], the friend of the king."

REGENERATION, rē̇-jen-ẽr-ā′shun, rē-:

I. The Term Explained.—The theological term "regeneration" is the Lat tr of the Gr expression παλινγενεσία, *palingenesía*, occurring twice in the NT (Mt **19** 28; Tit **3** 5). The word is usually written παλιγγενεσία, *paliggenesía*, in classical Gr. Its meaning is different in the two passages, though an easy transition of thought is evident.

1. First Biblical Sense (Eschatological)

In Mt **19** 28 the word refers to the restoration of the world, in which sense it is synonymical to the expressions ἀποκατάστασις πάντων, *apokatástasis pántōn*, "restoration of all things" (Acts **3** 21; the vb. is found in Mt **17** 11, ἀποκαταστήσει πάντα, *apokatastḗsei pánta*, "shall restore all things"), and ἀνάψυξις, *anápsuxis*, "refreshing" (Acts **3** 19), which signifies a gradual transition of meaning to the second sense of the word under consideration. It is supposed that regeneration in this sense denotes the final stage of development of all creation, by which God's purposes regarding the same are fully realized, when "all things [are put] in subjection under his feet" (1 Cor **15** 27). This is a "regeneration in the proper meaning of the word, for it signifies a renovation of all visible things when the old is passed away, and heaven and earth are become new" (cf Rev **21** 1). To the Jew the regeneration thus prophesied was inseparably connected with the reign of the Messiah.

We find this word in the same or very similar senses in profane literature. It is used of the renewal of the world in Stoical philosophy. Jos (*Ant*, XI, iii, 9) speaks of the *anáktēsis kaí paliggenesía tḗs patrídos*, "a new foundation and regeneration of the fatherland," after the return from the Bab captivity. Philo (ed. Mangey, ii. 144) uses the word, speaking of the post-diluvial epoch of the earth, as of a new world, and Marcus Aurelius Antoninus (xi.1), of a periodical restoration of all things, laying stress upon the constant recurrence and uniformity of all happenings, which thought the Preacher expressed by "There is no new thing under the sun" (Eccl **1** 9). In most places, however, where the word occurs in philosophical writings, it is used of the "reincarnation" or "subsequent birth" of the individual, as in the Buddhistic and Pythagorean doctrine of the transmigration of souls (Plut., ed. Xylander, ii.998*c*; Clem. Alex., ed. Potter, 539) or else of a revival of life (Philo i.159). Cicero uses the word in his letters to Atticus (vi.6) metaphorically of his return from exile, as a new lease of life granted to him. See ESCHATOLOGY OF THE NT, IX.

2. Second Biblical Sense (Spiritual)

This sense is undoubtedly included in the full Bib. conception of the former meaning, for it is unthinkable that a regeneration in the eschatological sense can exist without a spiritual regeneration of humanity or the individual. It is, however, quite evident that this latter conception has arisen rather late, from an analysis of the former meaning. It is found in Tit **3** 5 which, without absolute certainty as to its meaning, is generally interpreted in agreement with the numerous nouns and vbs. which have given the dogmatical setting to the doctrine of regeneration in Christian theology. Clem. Alex. is the first to differentiate this meaning from the former by the addition of the adj. πνευματική, *pneumatikē*, "spiritual" (cf *anapsuxis*, Acts **3** 20; see REFRESHING). In this latter sense the word is typically Christian, though the OT contains many adumbrations of the spiritual process expressed thereby.

II. The Biblical Doctrine of Regeneration.—It is well known that in the earlier portions of the OT, and to a certain degree all through the OT, religion is looked at and spoken of more as a national possession, the benefits of which are largely visible and tangible blessings. The idea of regeneration here occurs therefore—though no technical expression has as yet been coined for the process—in the first meaning of the word elucidated above. Whether the Divine promises refer to the Messianic end of times, or are to be realized at an earlier date, they all refer to the nation of Israel as such, and to individuals only as far as they are partakers in the benefits bestowed upon the commonwealth. This is even true where the blessings prophesied are only spiritual, as in Isa **60** 21.22. The mass of the people of Israel are therefore as yet scarcely aware of the fact that the conditions on which these Divine promises are to be attained are more than ceremonial and ritual ones. Soon, however, great disasters, threatening to overthrow the national entity, and finally the captivity and dispersion which caused national functions to be almost, if not altogether, discontinued, assisted in the growth of a sense of individual or personal responsibility before God. The sin of Israel is recognized as the sin of the individual, which can be removed only by individual repentance and cleansing. This is best seen from the stirring appeals of the prophets of the exile, where frequently the necessity of a change of attitude toward Jeh is preached as a means to such regeneration. This cannot be understood otherwise than as a turning of the individual to the Lord. Here, too, no ceremony or sacrifice is sufficient, but an interposition of Divine grace, which is represented under the figure of a washing and sprinkling from all iniquity and sin (Isa **1** 18; Jer **13** 23). It is not possible now to follow in full the development of this idea of cleansing, but already in Isa **52** 15 the sprinkling of many nations is mentioned and is soon understood in the sense of the "baptism" which proselytes had to undergo before their reception into the covenant of Israel. It was the symbol of a radical cleansing like that of a "new-born babe," which was one of the designations of the proselyte (cf Ps **87** 5; see also the tractate *Y^ebhāmōth* **62***a*). Would it be surprising that Israel, which had been guilty of many sins of the Gentiles, needed a similar baptism and sprinkling? This is what Ezk **36** 25 suggests: "I will sprinkle clean water upon you, and ye shall be clean: from all your filthiness, and from all your idols, will I cleanse you." In other passages the cleansing and refining power of fire is alluded to (e.g. Mal **3** 2), and there is no doubt that John the Baptist found in such passages the ground for his practice of baptizing the Jews who came to him (Jn **1** 25–28 and ||'s).

1. In the OT

The turning of Israel to God was necessarily meant to be an inward change of attitude toward Him, in other words, the sprinkling with clean water, as an outward sign, was the emblem of a pure heart. It was Isaiah and Jeremiah who drew attention to this (Isa **57** 15; Jer **24** 7; **31** 33–35; **32** 38–40, *et passim*). Here again reference is made to individuals, not only to the people in general (Jer **31** 34). This promised regeneration, so lovingly offered by Jeh, is to be the token of a new covenant between God and His people (Jer **31** 31; Ezk **11** 19–21; **18** 31.32; **37** 23.24).

The renewing and cleansing here spoken of is in reality nothing else than what Dt **30** 6 had promised, a circumcision of the heart in contradistinction to the flesh, the token of the former (Abrahamic) covenant (of circumcision, Jer **4** 4). As God takes the initiative in making the covenant, the conviction takes root that human sin and depravity can be effectually eliminated only by the act of God Himself renewing and transforming the heart of man (Hos **14** 4). This we see from the testimony of some of Israel's best sons and daughters, who also knew that this grace was found in the way of repentance and humiliation before God. The classical expression of this conviction is found in the prayer of David: "Create in me a clean heart, O God; and renew a right [m "stedfast"] spirit within me. Cast me not away from thy presence; and take not thy holy Spirit from me. Restore unto me the joy of thy salvation; and uphold me with a willing spirit" (Ps **51** 10–12). Jeremiah puts the following words into the mouth of Ephraim: "Turn thou me, and I shall be turned" (Jer **31** 18). Clearer than any passages of the OT, John the Baptist, forerunner of Christ and last flaming torch of the time of the earlier covenant, spoke of the baptism, not of water, but of the Holy Spirit and of fire (Mt **3** 11; Lk **3** 16; Jn **1** 33), leading thus to the realization of OT foreshadowings which became possible by faith in Christ.

2. In the Teaching of Jesus

In the teaching of Jesus the need of regeneration has a prominent place, though nowhere are the reasons given. The OT had succeeded—and even the gentile conscience agreed with it—in convincing the people of this need. The clearest assertion of it and the explanation of the doctrine of regeneration is found in the conversation of Jesus with Nicodemus (Jn **3**). It is based upon (1) the observation that man, even the most punctilious in the observance of the Law, is dead and therefore unable to "live up" to the demands of God. Only He who gave life at the beginning can give the (spiritual) life necessary to do God's will. (2) Man has fallen from his virginal and Divinely appointed sphere, the realm of the spirit, the Kingdom of God, living now the perishing earthly life. Only by having a new spiritual nature imparted to him, by being "born anew" (Jn **3** 3, RVm "from above," Gr ἄνωθεν, *ánōthen*), by being "born of the Spirit" (**3** 6.8), can he live the spiritual life which God requires of man.

These words are a NT exegesis of Ezekiel's vision of the dead bones (**37** 1–10). It is the "breath from Jeh," the Spirit of God, who alone can give life to the spiritually dead.

But regeneration, according to Jesus, is more than life, it is also *purity*. As God is pure and sinless, none but the pure in heart can see God (Mt **5** 8). This was always recognized as impossible to mere human endeavor. Bildad the Shuhite declared, and his friends, each in his turn, expressed very similar thoughts (Job **4** 17; **14** 4): "How then can man be just with God? Or how can he be clean that is born of a woman? Behold, even the moon hath no brightness, and the stars are not pure in his sight: how much less man, that is a worm! and the son of man, that is a worm!" (**25** 4-6).

To change this lost condition, to impart this new life, Jesus claims as His God-appointed task: "The Son of man came to seek and to save that which was lost" (Lk **19** 10); "I came that they may have life, and may have it abundantly" (Jn **10** 10). This life is eternal, imperishable: "I give unto them eternal life; and they shall never perish, and no one shall snatch them out of my hand" (Jn **10** 28). This life is imparted by Jesus Himself: "It is the spirit that giveth life; the flesh profiteth nothing: the words that I have spoken unto you are spirit, and are life" (Jn **6** 63). This life can be received on the condition of faith in Christ or by coming to Him (Jn **14** 6). By faith power is received which enables the sinner to overcome sin, to "sin no more" (Jn **8** 11).

The parables of Jesus further illustrate this doctrine. The prodigal is declared to have been "dead" and to be "alive again" (Lk **15** 24). The new life from God is compared to a wedding garment in the parable of the Marriage of the King's Son (Mt **22** 11). The garment, the gift of the inviting king, had been refused by the unhappy guest, who, in consequence, was 'cast out into the outer darkness' (Mt **22** 13).

Finally, this regeneration, this new life, is explained as the knowledge of God and His Christ: "And this is life eternal, that they should know thee the only true God, and him whom thou didst send, even Jesus Christ" (Jn **17** 3). This seems to be an allusion to the passage in Hos (**4** 6): "My people are destroyed for lack of knowledge: because thou hast rejected knowledge, I will also reject thee, that thou shalt be no priest to me."

3. In Apostolic Teaching

It may be said in general that the teaching of the apostles on the subject of regeneration is a development of the teaching of Jesus on the lines of the adumbrations of the OT. Considering the differences in the personal character of these writers, it is remarkable that such concord of views should exist among them. **St. Paul,** indeed, lays more stress on the specific facts of justification and sanctification by faith than on the more comprehensive head of regeneration. Still the need of it is plainly stated by St. Paul. It is necessary to salvation for all men. "The body is dead because of sin" (Rom **8** 3-11; Eph **2** 1). The flesh is at enmity with God (Eph **2** 15); all mankind is "darkened in their understanding, alienated from the life of God" (**4** 18). Similar passages might be multiplied. Paul then distinctly teaches that thus is a new life in store for those who have been spiritually dead. To the Ephesians he writes: "And you did he make alive, when ye were dead through your trespasses and sins" (**2** 1), and later on: "God, being rich in mercy, ... made us alive together with Christ" (**2** 4.5). A spiritual resurrection has taken place. This regeneration causes a complete revolution in man. He has thereby passed from under the law of sin and death and has come under "the law of the Spirit of life in Christ Jesus" (Rom **8** 2). The change is so radical that it is possible now to speak of a "new creature" (2 Cor **5** 17; Gal **6** 15, m "new creation"), of a "new man, that after God hath been created in righteousness and holiness of truth" (Eph **4** 24), and of "the new man, that is being renewed unto knowledge after the image of him that created him" (Col **3** 10). All "old things are passed away; behold, they are become new" (2 Cor **5** 17).

St. Paul is equally explicit regarding the author of this change. The "Spirit of God," the "Spirit of Christ" has been given from above to be the source of all new life (Rom **8**); by Him we are proved to be the "sons" of God (Gal **4** 6); we have been adopted into the family of God (*υἱοθεσία, huiothesía,* Rom **8** 15; Gal **4** 5). Thus St. Paul speaks of the "second Adam," by whom the life of righteousness is initiated in us; just as the "first Adam" became the leader in transgression, He is "a life-giving spirit" (1 Cor **15** 45). St. Paul himself experienced this change, and henceforth exhibited the powers of the unseen world in his life of service. "It is no longer I that live," he exclaims, "but Christ liveth in me: and that life which I now live in the flesh I live in faith, the faith which is in the Son of God, who loved me, and gave himself up for me" (Gal **2** 20).

Regeneration is to St. Paul, no less than to Jesus, connected with the conception of purity and knowledge. We have already noted the second NT passage in which the word "regeneration" occurs (Tit **3** 5): "According to his mercy he saved us, through the washing [m "laver"] of regeneration and renewing of the Holy Spirit, which he poured out upon us richly, through Jesus Christ our Saviour." In 1 Cor **12** 13 such cleansing is called the baptism of the Spirit in agreement with the oft-repeated promise (Joel **2** 28 [in the Heb text **3** 1]; Mt **3** 11; Mk **1** 8; Lk **3** 16; Acts **1** 5; **11** 16). There is, of course, in these passages no reference to mere water-baptism, any more than in Ezk **36** 25. Water is but the *tertium comparationis.* As water cleanseth the outer body, so the spirit purifies the inner man (cf 1 Cor **6** 11; 1 Pet **3** 21).

The doctrine that regeneration redounds in true knowledge of Christ is seen from Eph **3** 15-19 and **4** 17-24, where the darkened understanding and ignorance of natural man are placed in contradistinction to the enlightenment of the new life (see also Col **3** 10). The church redeemed and regenerated is to be a special "possession," an "heritage" of the Lord (Eph **1** 11.14), and the whole creation is to participate in the final redemption and adoption (Rom **8** 21-23).

St. James finds less occasion to touch this subject than the other writers of the NT. His Ep. is rather ethical than dogmatical in tone, still his ethics are based on the dogmatical presuppositions which fully agree with the teaching of other apostles. Faith to him is the human response to God's desire to impart His nature to mankind, and therefore the indispensable means to be employed in securing the full benefits of the new life, i.e. the sin-conquering power (**1** 2-4), the spiritual enlightenment (**1** 5) and purity (**1** 27). There seems, however, to be little doubt that St. James directly refers to regeneration in the words: "Of his own will he brought us forth by the word of truth, that we should be a kind of firstfruits of his creatures" (**1** 18). It is supposed by some that these words, being addressed "to the twelve tribes which are of the Dispersion" (**1** 1), do not refer to individual regeneration, but to an election of Israel as a nation and so to a *Christian* Israel. In this case the aftermath would be the redemption of the Gentiles. I understand the expression "first-fruits" in the sense in which we have noticed St. Paul's final hope in Rom **8** 21-32, where the regeneration of the believing people of God (regardless of nationality) is the first stage in the regeneration or restoration of all creation. The "implanted [RVm "inborn"] word" (Jas **1** 21; cf 1 Pet **1** 23) stands parallel to the Pauline expression, "law of the Spirit" (Rom **8** 2).

St. Peter uses, in his sermon on the day of Pentecost, the words "refreshing" (Acts **3** 19) and "restoration of all things" (**3** 21) of the final completion of God's plans concerning the whole creation, and accordingly looks here at God's people as a whole. In a similar sense he says in his Second Ep., after mentioning "the day of God": "We look for new heavens and a new earth, wherein dwelleth righteousness" (2 Pet **3** 13). Still he alludes very plainly to the regeneration of individuals (1 Pet **1** 3.23). The idea of a second birth of the believers is clearly suggested in the expression, "newborn babes" (1 Pet **2** 2), and in the explicit statement of 1 Pet **1** 23: "having been begotten again, not of corruptible seed, but of incorruptible, through the word of God, which liveth and abideth." It is in this sense that the apostle calls God "Father" (**1** 17) and the believers "children of obedience" (**1** 14), i.e. obedient children, or children who ought to obey. We have seen above that the agent by which regeneration is wrought, the incorruptible seed of the word of God, finds a parallel in St. Paul's and St. James's theology. All these expressions go back probably to a word of the Master in Jn **15** 3. We are made partakers of the word by having received the spirit. This spirit (cf the Pauline "life-giving spirit," 1 Cor **15** 45), the "mind" of Christ (1 Pet **4** 1), is the power of the resurrected Christ active in the life of the believer. St. Peter refers to the same thought in 1 Pet **3** 15.21. By regeneration we become "an elect race, a royal priesthood, a holy nation, a people for God's own possession," in whom Divine virtues, "the excellencies of him who called you" (1 Pet **2** 9), are manifested. Here the apostle uses well-known OT expressions foreshadowing NT graces (Isa **61** 6; **66** 21; Ex **19** 6; Dt **7** 6), but he individualizes the process of regeneration in full agreement with the increased light which the teaching of Jesus has brought. The theology of St. Peter also points out the contact of regeneration with purity and holiness (1 Pet **1** 15.16) and true knowledge (**1** 14) or obedience (**1** 14; **3** 16). It is not surprising that the idea of purity should invite the OT parallel of "cleansing by water." The flood washed away the iniquity of the world "in the days of Noah," when "eight souls were saved through water: which also after a true likeness [RVm "in the antitype"] doth now save you, even baptism, not the putting away of the filth of the flesh, but the interrogation [RVm "inquiry," "appeal"] of a good conscience toward God, through the resurrection [-life] of Jesus Christ" (1 Pet **3** 20.21).

The teaching of **St. John** is very closely allied with that of Jesus, as we have already seen from the multitude of quotations we had to select from St. John's Gospel to illustrate the teaching of the Master. It is esp. interesting to note the cases where the apostle didactically elucidates certain of these pronouncements of Jesus. The most remarkable apostolic gloss or commentary on the subject is found in Jn **7** 39. Jesus had spoken of the change which faith in Him ("coming to him") would cause in the lives of His disciples; how Divine energies like "rivers of water" should issue forth from them; and the evangelist continues in explanation: "But this spake he of the Spirit, which they that believed on him were to receive: for the Spirit was not yet given; because Jesus was not yet glorified." This recognition of a special manifestation of Divine power, transcending the experience of OT believers, was based on the declaration of Christ, that He would send "another Comforter [RV "advocate," "helper," Gr *Paraclete*], that he may be with you for ever, even the Spirit of truth" (Jn **14** 16.17).

In his Epp. St. John shows that this Spirit bestows the elements of a Godlike character which makes us to be "sons of God," who before were "children of the devil" (1 Jn **3** 10.24; **4** 13, etc). This regeneration is "eternal life" (1 Jn **5** 13) and moral similarity with God, the very character of God in man. As "God is love," the children of God will love (1 Jn **5** 2). At the same time it is the life of God in man, also called fellowship with Christ, victorious life which overcomes the world (1 Jn **5** 4); it is purity (1 Jn **3** 3-6) and knowledge (1 Jn **2** 20).

The subject of regeneration lies outside of the scope of the **Ep. to the He,** so that we look in vain for a clear dogmatical statement of it. Still the ep. does in no place contradict the dogma, which, on the other hand, underlies many of the statements made. Christ, "the mediator of a better covenant, which hath been enacted upon better promises" (**8** 6), has made "purification of sins" (**1** 3). In contradistinction to the first covenant, in which the people approached God by means of outward forms and ordinances, the "new covenant" (**8** 13) brought an "eternal redemption" (**9** 12) by means of a Divine cleansing (**9** 14). Christ brings "many sons unto glory" and is "author of their salvation" (**2** 10). Immature Christians are spoken of (as were the proselytes of the OT) as babes, who were to grow to the stature, character and knowledge of "full-grown men" (**5** 13.14).

III. Later Development of the Doctrine.—Very soon the high spiritual meaning of regeneration was obscured by the development of priestcraft within the Christian church. When the initiation into the church was thought of as accomplished by the mediation of ministers thereto appointed, the ceremonies hereby employed became means to which magic powers were of necessity ascribed. This we see plainly in the view of baptismal regeneration, which, based upon half-understood passages of Scripture quoted above, was taught at an early date. While in the post-apostolic days we frequently find traces of a proper appreciation of an underlying spiritual value in baptism (cf *Didache*, vii) many of the expressions used are highly misleading. Thus Gregory Nazianzen (*Orations*, xi.2) calls baptism the second of the three births a child of God must experience (the first is the natural birth, the third the resurrection). This birth is "of the day, free, delivering from passions, taking away every veil of our nature or birth, i.e. everything hiding the Divine image in which we are created, and leading up to the life above" (Ullmann, *Gregor v. Nazienz*, 323). Cyril of Jerus (*Cat.*, xvii, c. 37) ascribes to baptism the power of absolution from sin and the power of endowment with heavenly virtues. According to Augustine baptism is essential to salvation, though the baptism of blood (martyrdom) may take the place of water-baptism, as in the case of the thief at the cross (Aug., *De Anima et Eius Origine*, i.11, c. 9; ii.14, c. 10; ii.16, c. 12). Leo the Great compares the spirit-filled water of baptism with the spirit-filled womb of the Virgin, in which the Holy Spirit engenders a sinless child of God (Serm. xxiv.3; xxv.5; see Hagenbach, *Dogmengeschichte*, § 137).

In general this is still the opinion of pronounced sacramentarians, while evangelical Christianity has gone back to the teaching of the NT.

IV. Present Significance.—Although a clear distinction is not always maintained between regeneration and other experiences of the spiritual life, we may summarize our belief in the following theses:

(1) Regeneration implies not merely an addition of certain gifts or graces, a strengthening of certain innate good qualities, but a radical change, which revolutionizes our whole being, contradicts and overcomes our old fallen nature, and places our spiritual center of gravity wholly outside of our own powers in the realm of God's causation.

(2) It is the will of God that all men be made partakers of this new life (1 Tim **2** 4) and, as it is clearly stated that some fall short of it (Jn **5** 40), it is plain that the fault thereof lies with man. God requires all men to repent and turn unto Him (Acts **17** 30) before He will or can effect regeneration. Conversion, consisting in repentance and faith in Christ, is therefore the human response to the offer of salvation which God makes. This response gives occasion to and is synchronous with the Divine act of renewal (regeneration). The Spirit of God enters into union with the believing, accept-

ing spirit of man. This is fellowship with Christ (Rom **8** 10; 1 Cor **6** 17; 2 Cor **5** 17; Col **3** 3).

(3) The process of regeneration is outside of our observation and beyond the scope of psychological analysis. It takes place in the sphere of subconsciousness. Recent psychological investigations have thrown a flood of light on the psychic states which precede, accompany and follow the work of the Holy Spirit. "He handles psychical powers; He works upon psychical energies and states; and this work of regeneration lies somewhere within the psychical field." The study of religious psychology is of highest value and greatest importance. The facts of Christian experience cannot be changed, nor do they lose in value by the most searching psychological scrutiny.

Psychological analysis does not eliminate the direct workings of the Holy Spirit. Nor can it disclose its process; the "underlying laboratory where are wrought radical remedial processes and structural changes in the psychical being as portrayed in explicit scriptural utterances: 'Create in me a clean heart' (Ps **51** 10); 'Ye must be born again' (Jn **3** 7 AV); 'If any man be in Christ, he is a new creature: old things are passed away; behold all things are become new' (2 Cor **5** 17 AV), is in the region of subconsciousness. To look in the region of consciousness for this Person or for His work is fruitless and an effort fraught with endless confusion. Christian psychology thus traces to its deep-lying retreat the Divine elaboration of the regenerated life. Here God works in the depths of the soul as silently and securely as if on the remotest world of the stellar universe" (H. E. Warner, *Psychology of the Christian Life*, 117).

(4) Regeneration manifests itself in the conscious soul by its effects on the will, the intelligence and the affections. At the same time regeneration supplies a new life-power of Divine origin, which enables the component parts of human nature to fulfil the law of God, to strive for the coming of God's kingdom, and to accept the teachings of God's spirit. Thus regenerate man is made conscious of the facts of justification and adoption. The former is a judicial act of God, which frees man from the law of sin and absolves him from the state of enmity against God; the latter an enduement with the Spirit, which is an earnest of his inheritance (Eph **1** 14). The Spirit of God, dwelling in man, witnesses to the state of sonship (Rom **8** 2.15.16; Gal **4** 6).

(5) Regeneration, being a new birth, is the starting-point of spiritual growth. The regenerated man needs nurture and training. He receives it not merely from outside experiences, but from an immanent power in himself, which is recognized as the power of the life of the indwelling Christ (Col **1** 26.27). Apart from the mediate dealings of God with man through word and sacraments, there is therefore an immediate communication of life from God to the regenerate.

(6) The truth which is mentioned as the agent by whom regeneration is made possible (Jn **8** 32; Jas **1** 18; 1 Pet **1** 23), is nothing else than the Divine Spirit, not only the spoken or written word of God, which may convince people of right or wrong, but which cannot enable the will of man to forsake the wrong and to do the right, but He who calls Himself the Truth (Jn **14** 6) and who has become the motive power of regenerated life (Gal **2** 20).

(7) Recent philosophy expressive of the reaction from the mechanical view of bare materialism, and also from the depreciation of personality as seen in socialism, has again brought into prominence the reality and need of personal life. Johannes Müller and Rudolf Eucken among others emphasize that a new life of the spirit, independent of outward conditions, is not only possible, but necessary for the attainment of the highest development. This new life is not a fruit of the free play of the tendencies and powers of natural life, but is in sharp conflict with them. Man as he is by nature stands in direct contrast to the demands of the spiritual life. Spiritual life, as Professor Eucken says, can be implanted in man by some superior power only and must constantly be sustained by superior life. It breaks through the order of causes and effects; it severs the continuity of the outer world; it makes impossible a rational joining together of realities; it prohibits a monistic view of the immediate condition of the world. This new life derives its power not from mere Nature; it is a manifestation of Divine life within us (*Hauptprobleme der Religionsphilosophie*, Leipzig, 1912, 17 ff; *Der Kampf um einen geistigen Lebensinhalt*, Leipzig, 1907; *Grundlinien einer neuen Lebensanschauung*, Leipzig, 1907; Johannes Müller, *Bausteine für persönliche Kultur*, 3 vols, München, 1908). Thus the latest development of idealistic philosophy corroborates in a remarkable way the Christian truth of regeneration. See also CONVERSION.

LITERATURE.—NT Theologies by Weiss, Beyschlag, Holtzmann, Schlatter, Feine, Stevens, Sheldon, Weinel. Textbooks on Systematic Theology: arts. "Bekehrung" by R. Seeberg; "Wiedergeburt" by O. Kirn in Hauck-Herzog *RE*[3]; "Regeneration" by J. V. Bartlett in *HDB*; "Conversion" by J. Strachan in *ERE*; George Jackson, *The Fact of Conversion*, London, 1908; Newton H. Marshall, *Conversion; or, the New Birth*, London, 1909; J. Herzog, *Der Begriff der Bekehrung*, Giessen, 1903; P. Feine, *Bekehrung im NT und in der Gegenwart*, Leipzig, 1908; P. Gennrich, *Die Lehre von der Wiedergeburt*, Leipzig, 1907. Psychological: W. James, *Varieties of Religious Experience*, 189–258; G. Stanley Hall, *Adolescence*, II, 281–362; G. A. Coe, *The Spiritual Life*, New York, 1900; E. D. Starbuck, *Psychology of Religion*, New York, 1911; G. B. Cutten, *Psychological Phenomena of Christianity*, London, 1909; H. E. Warner, *The Psychology of the Christian Life*, New York, 1910; H. W. Clark, *The Philosophy of Christian Experience*, London, 1906; Harold Begbie, *Broken Earthenware, or Twice-Born Men*, London, 1909; M. Scott Fletcher, *The Psychology of the NT*, London, 1912.

JOHN L. NUELSEN

REGENERATION, BAPTISMAL. See BAPTISMAL REGENERATION.

REGION, rē′jun: A "district," as in modern Eng. The word "region" is used by EV interchangeably with "country," "coasts," etc, for various Heb and Gr terms, but "region round about" is usually in AV and invariably in RV the tr of περίχωρος, *perichōros*, "surrounding country." For a possible technical use of "region" in Acts **16** 6 and RV **18** 23; see GALATIA.

REGISTER, rej′is-tẽr. See GENEALOGY; QUIRINIUS.

REHABIAH, rē-ha-bī′a (רְחַבְיָה, *r^eḥabhyāh*, רְחַבְיָהוּ, *r^eḥabhyāhū*, "Jeh is wide"): Son of Eliezer, and grandson of Moses. Eponym of a Levitical family (1 Ch **23** 17; **24** 21; **26** 25).

REHEARSE, rē̇-hûrs′ (שׂוּם, *sūm*, דָּבַר, *dābhar*, נָגַד, *nāghadh*, תָּנָה, *tānāh*; ἀναγγέλλω, *anaggéllō*): Usually means simply "to relate," "to tell," "to declare" (Ex **17** 14; Jgs **5** 11; 1 S **8** 21; **17** 31; Acts **14** 27); with "rehearse from the beginning" in Acts **11** 4 for ἄρχομαι, *árchomai*, "begin" (so RV). RV has preserved uniformity by translating *anaggellō* by "rehearse" also in Acts **15** 4, and has introduced "rehearse" as the tr of ἐξηγέομαι, *exēgéomai*, throughout (Lk **24** 35; Acts **10** 8; **15** 12.14; **21** 19), except in Jn **1** 18 ("declare"). Sir **19** 7, AV has "rehearse" for δευτερόω, *deuteróō*, "repeat" (so RV).

REHOB, rē′hob (רְחֹב, *r^eḥōbh*; **Ῥοώβ**, *Rhoōb*, **Ῥαάβ**, *Rhaáb*):

(1) Etymologically the word means "broad" and might be applied either to a road or a plain. Rehob is given (Nu **13** 21) as the northern limit

of Israel as reached by the spies. This agrees with the position assigned to Beth-rehob in the narrative of the settlement of the Danites (Jgs **18** 28). It is mentioned again along with the kingdom of Zobah in connection with the wars of Saul (1 S **14** 47 LXX Lag.), and as having been associated with Zobah and Maacah against David in the Ammonite war and as having been defeated by him (2 S **10** 6). Robinson sought to identify it with Hunin, but it hardly suits the references. Buhl (*GAP*, 240) following Thomson (*LB*, II, 547) seeks it at Paneas (modern *Bāniās*). This would suit all the requirements of the capital, Beth-rehob, which might then be the second Rehob, assigned as part of the territory of Sidon to the tribe Asher (Josh **19** 28.30; Jgs **18** 28). We must, however, assign to the kingdom of Rehob a territory extending from the settlements of the Danites to the "entering in of Hamath" or to Libo (modern *Leboue*), i.e. the Great Plain of Coele-Syria bounded by Lebanon and Anti-Lebanon and within the limits indicated.

(2) Two separate towns belonging to Asher (Josh **19** 28; **19** 30). One of them was given to the Gershonite Levites (Josh **21** 31), and one is mentioned as remaining in the hands of the Canaanites (Jgs **1** 31).

(3) Father of Hadadezer, king of Aram Zobah, who was overwhelmed by David at the Euphrates (2 S **8** 3.12).

(4) One of the Levites who sealed Nehemiah's covenant on the 24th Tishri, 444 BC (Neh **10** 11).

W. M. Christie

REHOBOAM, rē-hō-bō′am (רְחַבְעָם, *reḥabh‛ām*, "the people is enlarged," or perhaps "Am is wide"; **Ῥοβοάμ,** *Rhoboám;* "Roboam," Mt **1** 7 AV):

1. The Disruption of the Kingdom
2. Underlying Causes of Disruption
3. Shemaiah Forbids Civil War
4. Rehoboam's Prosperity
5. Shishak's Invasion
6. His Death

The son and successor of Solomon, the last king to claim the throne of old Israel and the first king of Judah after the division of the kingdom. He was born c 978 BC. His mother was Naamah, an Ammonitess. The account of his reign is contained in 1 K **14** 21–31; 2 Ch **10**–**12**. The incidents leading to the disruption of the kingdom are told in 1 K **11** 43—**12** 24; 2 Ch **9** 31—**11** 4.

R. was 41 years old (2 Ch **12** 13) when he began to reign (LXX 1 K **12** 24*a* says 16 years). He ascended the throne at Jerus immediately upon his father's death with apparently no opposition. North Israel, however, was dissatisfied, and the people demanded that the king meet them in popular assembly at Shechem, the leading city of Northern Israel. True, Israel was no longer, if ever, an elective monarchy. Nevertheless, the people claimed a constitutional privilege, based perhaps on the transaction of Samuel in the election of Saul (1 S **10** 25), to be a party to the conditions under which they would serve a new king and he become their ruler. David, in making Solomon his successor, had ignored this wise provision, and the people, having lost such a privilege by default, naturally deemed their negligence the cause of Solomon's burdensome taxes and forced labor. Consequently, they would be more jealous of their rights for the future, and R. accordingly would have to accede to their demand. Having come together at Shechem, the people agreed to accept R. as their king on condition that he would lighten the grievous service and burdensome taxes of his father. R. asked for three days' time in which to consider the request. Against the advice of men of riper judgment, who assured him that he might win the people by becoming their servant, he chose the counsel of the younger men, who were of his own age, to rule by sternness rather than by kindness, and returned the people a rough answer, saying: "My father made your yoke heavy, but I will add to your yoke: my father chastised you with whips, but I will chastise you with scorpions" (1 K **12** 14). R., however, misjudged the temper of the people, as well as his own ability. The people, led by Jeroboam, a leader more able than himself, were ready for rebellion, and so force lost the day where kindness might have won. The threat of the king was met by the Marseillaise of the people: "What portion have we in David? neither have we inheritance in the son of Jesse: to your tents, O Israel: now see to thine own house, David" (1 K **12** 16). Thus the ten tribes dethroned R., and elected Jeroboam, their champion and spokesman, their king (see Jeroboam). R., believing in his ability to carry out his threat (1 K **12** 14), sent Adoram, his taskmaster, who no doubt had quelled other disturbances, to subdue the populace, which, insulted by indignities and enraged by R.'s renewed insolence, stoned his messenger to death. Realizing, for the first time, the seriousness of the revolt, R. fled ignominiously back to Jerus, king only of Judah and of the adjacent territory of the tribe of Benjamin. The mistake of R. was the common mistake of despots. He presumed too much on privilege not earned by service, and on power for which he was not willing to render adequate compensation.

1. The Disruption of the Kingdom

It is a mistake, however, to see in the disruption the shattering of a kingdom that had long been a harmonious whole. From the earliest times the confederation of tribes was imperfectly cemented. They seldom united against their common foe. No mention is made of Judah in the list of tribes who fought with Deborah against Sisera. A chain of cities held by the Canaanites, stretching across the country from E. to W., kept the North and the South apart. Different physical characteristics produced different types of life in the two sections. Old jealousies repeatedly fanned into new flame intensified the divisions due to natural and artificial causes. David labored hard to break down the old antagonisms, but even in his reign Israel rebelled twice. Northern Israel had produced many of the strongest leaders of the nation, and it was not easy for them to submit to a ruler from the Judaean dynasty. Solomon, following David's policy of unification, drew the tribes closely together through the centralization of worship at Jerus and through the general splendor of his reign, but he, more than any other, finally widened the gulf between the North and the South, through his unjust discriminations, his heavy taxes, his forced labor and the general extravagances of his reign. The religion of Jeh was the only bond capable of holding the nation together. The apostasy of Solomon severed this bond. The prophets, with their profound knowledge of religious and political values, saw less danger to the true worship of Jeh in a divided kingdom than in a united nation ruled over by R., who had neither political sagacity nor an adequate conception of the greatness of the religion of Jeh. Accordingly, Ahijah openly encouraged the revolution, while Shemaiah gave it passive support.

2. Underlying Causes of Disruption

Immediately upon his return to Jerus, R. collected a large army of 180,000 men (reduced to 120,000 in LXX B), for the purpose of making war against Israel. The expedition, however, was forbidden by Shemaiah the prophet on the ground that they should not fight against their brethren, and that the division of the kingdom was from God. Notwithstanding the prohibition, we are informed that "there was war between Rehoboam and Jeroboam continually" (1 K **14** 30; 2 Ch **12** 15).

3. Shemaiah Forbids Civil War

R. next occupied himself in strengthening the territory which still remained to him by fortifying a number of cities (2 Ch **11** 5–12). These cities were on the roads to Egypt, or on the western hills of the Judaean Shephelah, and were doubtless fortified as a protection against Egypt. According to

4. Rehoboam's Prosperity

2 Ch **11** 13–17, Rehoboam's prosperity was augmented by an immigration of priests and Levites from Israel, who came to Jerus because of their opposition to the idolatrous worship instituted by Jeroboam. All who were loyal to Jeh in the Northern Kingdom are represented as following the example of the priests and Levites in going to Jerus, not simply to sacrifice, but to reside there permanently, thus strengthening R.'s kingdom. In view of the fact that R. added to the innovations of his father, erected pillars of Baal in Jerus long before they were common in Northern Israel, and that he permitted other heathen abominations and immoralities, it seems that the true worship of Jeh received little encouragement from the king himself. As a further evidence of his prosperity, Ch gives an account of R.'s family. Evidently he was of luxurious habit and followed his father in the possession of a considerable harem (2 Ch **11** 18–23). He is said to have had 18 wives and 60 concubines, (2 Ch **11** 21; LXX B and Jos, *Ant*, VIII, x, 1 give "30 concubines").

One of the direct results of the disruption of the kingdom was the invasion of Pal by Shishak, king

5. Shishak's Invasion

of Egypt, in the 5th year of R. Shishak is Sheshonk I, the first king of the XXIId or Bubastite Dynasty. He is the same ruler who granted hospitality to Jeroboam when he was obliged to flee from Solomon (1 K **11** 40). The LXX (1 K **12** 24*e*) informs us that Jeroboam married Ano, the sister of Shishak's wife, thus becoming brother-in-law to the king of Egypt. It is therefore easy to suppose that Jeroboam, finding himself in straits in holding his own against his rival, Rehoboam, called in the aid of his former protector. The results of this invasion, however, are inscribed on the temple at Karnak in Upper Egypt, where a list of some 180 (Curtis, "Chronicles," *ICC*) towns captured by Shishak is given. These belong to Northern Israel as well as Judah, showing that Shishak exacted tribute there as well as in Judah, which seems scarcely reconcilable with the view that he invaded Pal as Jeroboam's ally. However, the king of Israel, imploring the aid of Shishak against his rival, thereby made himself vassal to Egypt. This would suffice to make his towns figure at Karnak among the cities subjected in the course of the campaign. The Chronicler saw in Shishak an instrument in the hand of God for the punishment of R. and the people for the national apostasy. According to 2 Ch **12** 3, Shishak had a force of 1,200 chariots and 60,000 horsemen to which Jos adds 400,000 foot-soldiers, composed of Lubim, Sukkiim and Ethiopians. No resistance appears to have been offered to the advance of the invading army. Not even Jerus seems to have stood a siege. The palace and the temple were robbed of all their treasures, including the shields of gold which Solomon had made. For these R. later substituted shields of brass (vs 9.10). R. died at the age of fifty-eight, after having reigned in Jerus for 17

6. His Death

years. His son Abijah became his successor. He was buried in Jerus. Jos says that in disposition he was a proud and foolish man, and that he "despised the worship of God, till the people themselves imitated his wicked actions" (*Ant*, VIII, x, 2).

S. K. Mosiman

REHOBOTH, rē̆-hō'both, rē̆-hō'bōth (רְחֹבוֹת, *r^eḥōbhōth*, "broad places"; **Εὐρυχωρία**, *Euruchōría*): One of the wells dug by Isaac (Gen **26** 22). It is probably the Rubuta of the Am Tab (Petrie, nos. 256, 260; see also *Expos T*, XI, 239 [König], 377 [Sayce]), and it is almost certainly identical with the ruin *Ruḥaibeh*, 8 hours S.W. of Beersheba. Robinson (*BR*, I, 196–97) describes the ruins of the ancient city as thickly covering a "level tract of 10 to 12 acres in extent"; "many of the dwellings had each its cistern, cut in the solid rock"; "once this must have been a city of not less than 12,000 or 15,000 inhabitants. Now it is a perfect field of ruins, a scene of unutterable desolation, across which the passing stranger can with difficulty find his way." Huntington (*Pal and Its Transformation*, 124) describes considerable remains of a suburban population extending both to the N. and to the S. of this once important place.

E. W. G. Masterman

REHOBOTH BY THE RIVER (רְחֹבוֹת הַנָּהָר, *r^eḥōbhōth ha-nāhār;* B, **Ῥοωβὼθ** [**Ῥωβὼθ** in Ch] **ἡ παρὰ ποταμόν,** *Rhoōbôth* [*Rhōbôth*] *hē pará potamón*, A, **Ῥωβώθ,** *Rhōbôth*): This city is mentioned only as the residence of Shaul, one of the rulers of Edom (Gen **36** 37; 1 Ch **1** 48). There is nothing to guide us with certainty as to the situation of the city. *Onom* places it in Idumaea (Gebalene), but no trace of a name resembling this has been found in the district. "The river" usually means the Euphrates. If the city could have been so far from Edom, it might be identified with *Rahaba* on the W. of the river, 8 miles S. of its confluence with the *Khabūr*. Winckler thinks it might possibly be on the boundary between Pal and Egypt, "the river" being *Wâdy el-'Arīsh*, "the brook of Egypt" (Nu **34** 5; Josh **15** 4, etc).

W. Ewing

REHOBOTH-IR, r.-ûr, r.-ir (רְחֹבֹת עִיר, *r^eḥōbhōth 'īr*, "Rehoboth City"; LXX **ἡ Ῥοωβὼς** [**Ῥοωβὼθ**] **πόλις,** *hē Rhoōbôs* [*Rhoōbôth*] *pólis*, "the city Rhoōbōs, Rhoōbōth"): The

1. Probably Rêbit Ninua

second of the cities built by Asshur (RV by Nimrod) in Assyria (Gen **10** 11.12). Unlike the other three, the exact equivalent of this name is not found in Assyr lit. Fried. Delitzsch points out (*Wo lag das Paradies?* 260 f) that *r^eḥōbhōth* is the equivalent of the Assyr *rêbite*, "streets," and suggests that the site referred to may be the Rêbit Ninua, "streets of Nineveh," mentioned by Sargon of Assyria in connection with the peopling of Maganubba (Khorsabad or Dûr-Šarru-kīn; see Nineveh); and it was through this tract that Esar-haddon, his grandson, caused the heads of the kings of Kundi and Sidon to be carried in procession when he returned from his expedition to the Mediterranean.

Though the probabilities in favor of Rêbit Ninua are great, it is doubtful whether a suburb could

2. Or, Possibly, the Old Capital, Aššur

have been regarded as a foundation worthy of a primitive ruler, and that a very important city, Aššur, the old capital of Assyria, would rather be expected. One of the groups expressing its name is composed of the characters *Šag-uru*, or, dialectically, *Šab-eri*, the second element being the original of the Heb *'īr*. As the "center-city," Aššur may have been regarded as the city of broad spaces (*r^eḥōbhōth*)—its ruins are of considerable extent. The German explorers there have made many important discoveries of temples, temple-towers, palaces and streets, the most picturesque anciently being the twin tower-temples of Anu (the sky) and Adad (Hadad). The ruins lie on the Tigris, about 50 miles S. of Nineveh. It practically ceased to be the capital about the middle of the 8th cent. BC. See Nineveh.

T. G. Pinches

REHUM, rē'hum (רְחוּם, *r^eḥūm*, or רְחֻם, *r^eḥum*): (1) One of the twelve heads of the Jewish community returning from captivity with Zerubbabel (Ezr **2** 2; Neh **7** 7 [by a copyist's error "Nehum"]; **12** 3; 1 Esd **5** 8, "Roimus").

(2) A Pers officer of high rank (lit. "master of judgment, taste, reason") who with others wrote a letter against Jerus to King Artaxerxes (Ezr **4** 8.9.17.23).

(3) Son of Bani, a Levite, one of the wall-builders under Nehemiah (Neh **3** 17).

(4) One of the signers of the covenant in Neh **10** 25.

(5) In Neh **12** 3 (omitted in LXX) one Rehum is mentioned with those who went up with Zerubbabel. It is probable that we should read here "Harim" (חָרִם for רְחוּם of **12** 15).

W. N. Stearns

REI, rē'ī (רֵעִי, *rē'ī*, "friendly"; Ῥησεί, *Rhēseí*): Rei, Shimei and the **Gibbōrīm** who belonged to David are listed among those who did not join Adonijah in his attempt on the throne (1 K **1** 8). The name is very uncertain. Winckler (*Geschichte*, II, 247) identifies him with Ira, the Jairite, who was a "priest to David" (2 S **20** 26 RVm); he tries to prove that this Ira (or Jair) was a priest of Bethlehem. Stade (*GVI*, I, 293, n. 1) holds that Shimei and Rei were two officers of David's bodyguard. Jos (*Ant*, VII, xiv, 4) has ὁ Δαουίδου φίλος, *ho Daouídou phílos*, thus making Shimei a "friend," the courtier of 2 S **15** 37; **16** 16, and omitting Rei entirely. This would call for an original reading רֵעַ הַמֶּלֶךְ, *rēa' ha-melekh*, or רֵעֵה הַמֶּלֶךְ, *rē'ēh ha-melekh*, and is too wide a variant from the MT. Assuming that Rei belongs in the text, it is safe to conjecture that he was an officer of the royal guard.

Horace J. Wolf

REIGN, rān: The Heb word מַלְכוּת, *mal^ekhūth*, may be rendered "kinghood," "royal dignity," "kingdom," "government" ("reign"). The vb. is מָלַךְ, *mālakh*, "to be king" ("to reign as king"), "to become king," "to accede to the throne," "to assume royal power publicly" and, generally speaking, "to become powerful." In the NT ἡγεμονία, *hēgemonía*, βασιλεία, *basileía*, βασιλεύειν, *basileúein*. The word is used, either as a noun or as a vb., of Jeh (God), the Messiah (Christ) and men (kings, etc); then of such terms as sin, death, grace; of the woman in Rev and, conditionally, of the Christians; once, ironically, of the Corinthians. "Reign" as a noun referring to the time of reigning occurs in 1 K **6** 1 (Solomon); 2 K **24** 12 (Nebuchadnezzar); 1 Ch **4** 31 (David; cf 1 Ch **29** 30); 2 Ch **36** 20 ("until the reign of the kingdom of Persia"); Neh **12** 22 (Darius); Est **2** 16 (Ahasuerus); Lk **3** 1 (Tiberius Caesar). More often occurs the vb. "to reign," *mālakh*, *basileuein*. It is applied to: (1) Jeh at the close of the song of Moses (Ex **15** 18); "Jeh reigneth" (1 Ch **16** 31; cf Ps **93** 1; **96** 10; **99** 1; Rev **19** 6); "God reigneth over the nations" (Ps **47** 8); "Jeh of hosts will reign in mount Zion" (Isa **24** 23; cf Mic **4** 7); "Thy God reigneth" (Isa **52** 7); "Thou hast taken thy great power, and didst reign" (Rev **11** 17, meaning, probably, "thou didst assume thy might"); (2) the Messiah (Christ) as a just and righteous king (Jer **23** 5); an eternal king (Lk **1** 33; cf Rev **11** 15); punishing and subduing His enemies (Lk **19** 14.27; 1 Cor **15** 25).

(3) Men (kings, etc), in regard to the source of their power ("By me [i.e. the wisdom of God], kings reign" [Prov **8** 15]); respecting legitimate succession (2 Ch **23** 3); meaning "to have power or dominion" (Gen **37** 8 and Job **34** 30); in regard to an essential characteristic (Isa **32** 1); in connection with the covenant of Jeh with David (Jer **33** 21); then the word is used in 1 S **12** 12, where Samuel reminds the children of Israel of their demanding a king of him (cf ver 14); of Saul (1 S **13** 1; cf **11** 12); of Saul's son Ish-bosheth (2 S **2** 10); of David (2 S **5** 4 f; cf **3** 21); of Adonijah (1 K **1** 11.24; cf **2** 15); of Solomon (1 K **1** 13); quite frequently of the kings of Judah and Israel (in the Books of K and Ch); of the kings of Edom (Gen **36** 31); of Jabin, king of Canaan, in Hazor (Jgs **4** 2); of Abimelech, Jerubbaal's son, in Jotham's fable (Jgs **9** 8–15); of Hanun, king of the Ammonites (2 S **10** 1); of Rezon and his men in Damascus (1 K **11** 24); of Hazael and Ben-hadad, kings of Syria (2 K **8** 15 and **13** 24); of Esar-haddon, king of Assyria (2 K **19** 37); of Ahasuerus, king of Persia (Est **1** 1); of Archelaus (Mt **2** 22).

(4) In the NT the term *basileuein*, "to reign," is used to illustrate and emphasize the power of sin, death and grace (Rom **5** 14.17.21 and **6** 12). Sin, the vitiating mental factor, is to be looked upon as being constantly and resolutely bent on maintaining or regaining its hold upon man, its power being exercised and reinforced by the lusts of the body. Death, the logical outcome of sin, at once testifies to the power of sin and its inherent corruption, while grace is the restoring spiritual factor following up and combating everywhere and always the pernicious influence of sin. It strives to dethrone sin, and to establish itself in man as the only dominating force. (5) In describing the future glorious state of the believers, the NT uses the expression of those who endure (in faith; cf 2 Tim **2** 12); of those 'purchased unto God with the blood of the Lamb' (Rev **5** 10); of those partaking in the first resurrection (Rev **20** 6); of the servants of God, "they shall reign for ever and ever" (**22** 5); on the other hand, it teaches us not to anticipate the privileges of heaven, while our Christian life is anything but satisfactory (1 Cor **4** 8), and Rev **17** 18 shows us the terrible fate of the woman, the great city (the corrupt church), "which reigneth over the kings of the earth." See further King, Kingdom.

William Baur

REINS, rānz (כִּלְיָה, *kilyāh*; νεφρός, *nephrós*, words promiscuously tr^d "heart," "inward parts," "kidneys" or "reins." The latter word, which is derived from Lat *renes* through OFr. *reins*, has given place in modern Eng. to the word "kidneys" [see Skeat, *Concise Etymological Dictionary of the Eng. Language*, 398]. RV has, however, retained the older word, at least in the m, in all passages in which it is found in AV): According to Heb psychology the reins are the seat of the deepest emotions and affections of man, which God alone can fully know. Thus RV has substituted "heart" for "reins" in the text of Job **19** 27; Ps **7** 9; **16** 7; **26** 2; **73** 21; Prov **23** 16; Jer **11** 20; **12** 2; **17** 10; **20** 12; the tr "inward parts" is found but once (Ps **139** 13). In one passage AV has tr^d the Heb *ḥălāç* ("loins") with "reins" (Isa **11** 5), where the RV has rightly substituted "waist" (q.v.). The Gr word *nephros* (which is etymologically allied to the Middle Eng. *nere*, Ger. *Niere*; see Skeat, ibid, 231, s.v. "Kidney") is found in 1 Macc **2** 24; Rev **2** 23. See Kidneys.

H. L. E. Luering

REKEM, rē'kem (רֶקֶם, *reḳem*, "friendship"):

(1) One of the five kings of Midian slain by the Israelites under Moses (Nu **31** 8; Josh **13** 21 [B, Ῥόβοκ, *Rhóbok*, A, Ῥόκομ, *Rhókom*]). Like his companions, he is called a "king" in Nu, but a "prince" or "chieftain" in the passage in Josh. The two references are hardly related; both are based on an earlier tradition.

(2) Eponym of a Calebite family (1 Ch **2** 43 [Ῥέκομ, *Rhékom*]). Probably a town in Southern Judah. A town of this name is given as belonging to Benjamin (Josh **18** 27).

(3) A city of Benjamin, mentioned with Irpeel and Taralah (Josh **18** 27); the site is unknown. See also Rakem.

Horace J. Wolf

RELATIONSHIPS, rē̆-lā'shun-ships, **FAMILY:**

The family or domestic relations of the Bible include (1) those of consanguinity or blood relationship, (2) affinity or marriage relationship, and (3) legal convention. Those of consanguinity may be divided into lineal and collateral groups; the former are those of parents and children, grandparents and grandchildren, and ancestors and descendants in general; the latter are those of brothers and sisters, uncles and aunts in relation to nephews and nieces, cousins of various degrees, including mere tribesmen and even remoter kinsfolk. The relations of affinity include besides that of husband and wife or concubine, the relations among rival wives, and their children, those of father-in-law and mother-in-law in relation to son-in-law and daughter-in-law, and those of brothers-in-law and sisters-in-law. The domestic relations based on legal convention are either legal fictions or the results of agreement: among the former we must include those of foster-father or mother and foster-children; among the latter the relations between master and the various classes of servants and slaves held by the ancient Hebrews, those between host and guest, esp. where they became covenant brothers, and between the citizen and the stranger who had attached himself to him for his protection.

I. Consanguinity.—Genealogies were carefully kept by the ancient Hebrews (cf those of Gen, Nu, Ch, Ezr, Neh, Mt, Lk), not only because they formed the basis of a man's title to his property (Nu **27** 8–11; exceptional case, **36** 1–12), but also because on one's pedigree depended the right of his family to intermarry with the priestly caste. Descent was traced through the father; a man's closest association was therefore with his father's family, and he was ordinarily referred to as the son of his father, thus Isaac the son of Abraham (Gen **25** 19), Joshua the son of Nun, Caleb the son of Jephunneh (Nu **14** 6). Still there are instances of men named for their mothers (Joab the son of Zeruiah), and a man's relation with his mother's family was fully recognized in the laws forbidding incest. No lineal relatives were permitted to intermarry (Lev **18** 7.10). The relations of ancestors and descendants were considered so close that the ordinary terms of relationship between children and parents are used constantly in relation to grandparents and remoter ancestors. The wishes of a great-grandfather are respected long after his death as the wishes of a father (Jer **35** 16).

1. In General

The father (אָב, *'ābh;* πατήρ, *patḗr*) was the head of the family (*mishpāḥāh*) or household (*bayith*), which was a religious (1 S **20** 6.29; Ex **12** 3; Job **1** 5) as well as a social and political unit, consisting usually of a combination of families in the modern sense. As long as polygamy prevailed a family would include at least the several groups of children of the wives and concubines. The Bible represents the Heb father as commanding (Gen **50** 16; Jer **35** 6 ff; Prov **6** 20), instructing (Prov **1** 8; **4** 1), and rebuking (Gen **37** 10; Nu **12** 14); at the same time, as loving (Gen **25** 28; **37** 4; **44** 20), pitying (Ps **103** 13), and blessing his household (Gen **27** 41), rejoicing over its triumphs (Prov **10** 1; **15** 20), or grieving over its misfortunes (Gen **37** 35). The mother, too (אֵם, *'ēm;* μήτηρ, *mḗtēr*), naturally displays love and care (Gen **25** 28; Prov **4** 3; Isa **49** 15; **66** 13). To the Heb woman childlessness was considered the greatest of misfortunes (1 S **1** 10 ff, of Hannah; Gen **30** 23, of Rachel). Children were looked upon as a blessing from God (Ps **127** 3) and the defenders of the home (vs 4.5). In early life a child was more directly under the control of the mother than the father; the mother was its first teacher (Prov **1** 8). Thereafter the father was expected to direct the training of the son (בֵּן, *bēn;* υἱός, *huiós,* τέκνον, *téknon*) (Gen **18** 19; Ex **12** 26; **13** 8.14.15; Dt **6** 7), while the daughter (בַּת, *bath;* θυγάτηρ, *thugátēr*) probably remained with the mother until her marriage (Mic **7** 6). Both parents are looked upon in the Law as objects of honor (Ex **20** 12 ‖ Dt **5** 16 [the Fifth Commandment]; Ex **21** 15; Lev **20** 9; Dt **27** 16; Prov **20** 20; Ezk **22** 7; Mic **7** 6), obedience (Gen **28** 7; Lev **19** 3; Dt **21** 18 ff; Prov **1** 8; **30** 17) and love (1 K **19** 20; Prov **28** 24; **30** 11). The control of parents was so great as to include the right to sell daughters in marriage, but not, without restrictions, into slavery (Ex **21** 7–11; cf **22** 16 ff; Neh **5** 5), and never into a life of shame (Lev **19** 29); they could chastise children (Dt **8** 5; **21** 18; Prov **13** 24; cf Ecclus **30** 1–13), and in the early days even exerted the power of life and death over them (Gen **22**; Jgs **11** 39; Lev **18** 21; **20** 2–5; 2 K **23** 10; cf Mt **15** 4). This power, at least for sacrificial purposes, was entirely removed by the Law, and changed, even for punishment, in the case of a stubborn, rebellious, gluttonous and disobedient son to a mere right of complaint to the proper authorities (Dt **21** 18–21), who were to put him to death. Infanticide by exposure, such as was common among other ancient peoples, seems never to have been practised by the Hebrews. That the children were nevertheless the chattels of the parents seems to be attested from the fact that they could be seized for the debts of the father (2 K **4** 1). The father could annul the vows of his daughter (Nu **30** 3–5), and damages for wrongs done to her were paid to him, as in Eng. law "for loss of services" (Dt **22** 29). A widowed or divorced daughter could return to her father (Gen **38** 11; Lev **22** 13; Ruth **1** 15). At his death the mother would become the actual, if not the legal, head of the household (2 K **8** 1–6, the Shunammite woman; Tob **1** 8, Tobit's grandmother; cf the position of the mother of Jesus). This was esp. true of the queen mother (*gᵉbhīrāh*), whose name is usually given in the accounts of the kings of Judah (1 K **1** 11; **2** 19, where a throne at the king's right hand was set for the king's mother; **11** 26; **14** 21.31; **15** 2.10. 13; **22** 42; 2 K **8** 26; **10** 13; **14** 2; **15** 2.33; **18** 2; **21** 1.19; **22** 1; **23** 31.36; **24** 8.12.15.18; 2 Ch **22** 2; Jer **13** 18; **22** 26; see Queen Mother). While it is true that the position of the widowed mother depended to some extent on the will of her son (1 K **2** 18 ff), it must be remembered that the sense of filial duty was highly developed among all classes in Pal (Josh **2** 13.18; **6** 23; 1 S **22** 3; 2 S **19** 37; 1 K **19** 20). The rebellion of children marked the acme of social degeneration (Mic **7** 6; Prov **30** 11); on the other hand the "great day" according to Malachi (**4** 5 [Heb **3** 23]) is one of conciliation of parents and children.

2. Parents and Children

The terms "brother" (אָח, *'āḥ;* ἀδελφός, *adelphós*) and "sister" (אָחוֹת, *'aḥōth;* ἀδελφή, *adelphḗ*) apply to children of the same father and mother (Gen **4** 2), and also to children of one father (Gen

20 12) or of one mother (Gen **43** 7; Lev **18** 9; **20** 17). The brother as well as the father was the natural protector of the honor of his

3. Brothers and Sisters

sister; thus, the sons of Jacob speak of Dinah as "our daughter" (Gen **34** 17). Absalom feels more deeply aggrieved over the crime against Tamar than does David himself (2 S **13** 21). The brother's other duties toward a sister were very much like those of a father (Cant **8** 8). The Law strictly forbids the intermarriage of brother and sister, whether of the same father and mother or not, whether born at home or born abroad, as a "disgraceful thing" (*ḥeṣedh,* a different word from *ḥeṣedh,* "kindness" (Lev **18** 9.11; **20** 17). In earlier times marriage between half-brother and sister was allowable (Gen **20** 12; cf 2 S **13** 13). In fact, we are expressly told that the laws against incest were not obeyed by the Egyptians or the Canaanites (Lev **18** 3 ff; **20** 23). Brotherly sentiment was highly developed (Gen **24** 60; Josh **2** 13; Prov **17** 17; cf Lev **25** 35; Dt **15** 11 f; **25** 3); the dwelling of brothers together in unity is considered good and pleasant (Ps **133** 1). Brothers were ever ready to protect or avenge each other (2 S **3** 27). Indeed, it is part of the unwritten, common law, recognized though not necessarily approved in the Bible, that the brother or next of kin, the *gō'ēl,* is expected to avenge a death (Nu **35** 19 ff; Dt **19** 6; Josh **20** 3; 2 S **14** 11), and no punishment is meted out to prevent such self-help, unless it occurs in a refuge-city. A brother was also expected to ransom a captive or slave (Lev **25** 48; Ps **49** 7). Half-brothers were of course not so near as brothers of the full blood (cf Joseph and his brothers), and it is not surprising to find the sons of a wife despising and driving out the son of a harlot (Jgs **11** 1, Jephthah). The words "brother" and "sister" are used frequently of more distant relationships (see below) and **figuratively** of a friend.

The Heb דּוֹד, *dōdh* (Lev **10** 4, "uncles"; Nu **36** 11, "cousins"; 1 S **14** 50), coming from a primitive caressing word, possibly in-

4. Uncles, Aunts, Cousins, Kinsmen

dicating "dandle," "fondle," "love," means both "uncle" and "beloved." It is used of the father's and also of the mother's brother, and the corresponding fem. form (דּוֹדָה, *dōdhāh*) is used of the father's sister (Ex **6** 20; cf Nu **26** 59) and even of the father's brother's wife (Lev **18** 14; **20** 20). Intermarriage between nephew and aunt (i.e. father's sister, mother's sister, or father's brother's wife, or, in general, uncle's wife) was prohibited (Lev **18** 12.13.14; **20** 19.20), though nothing is said of intermarriage between uncle and niece nor between cousins (cf Nu **36** 11). On the relations between uncle and nephew compare the Bible accounts of Jacob and Laban, Abraham and Lot, David and Joab, etc. In a more general sense the word *dōdh* is used of kinsmen, Am **6** 10 (where the *dōdh,* "even he that burneth him" [*m^eṣār^ephō,*</sup> perhaps "maternal uncle"; *Jew Enc,* s.v. "Cremation"], takes charge of a dead body); *ben dōdh* is used of cousin (cf *ben 'āḥī 'immō,* "son of the brother of his mother," etc) and *bath dōdh* of a female cousin. For other relations of this and remoter degrees the word for brother is loosely used (e.g. of nephews, Gen **13** 8; **14** 14, etc; of tribesmen, Lev **21** 10; and of more distant relatives, Dt **2** 4.8; **23** 7).

II. Affinity.—The husband (אִישׁ, *'īsh;* cf בַּעַל, *ba'al,* Hos **2** 16; ἀνήρ, *anēr*), though in a sense leaving father and mother for his wife

1. Husband and Wife

(אִשָּׁה, *'ishshāh;* γυνή, *gunē*) (Gen **2** 24), under normal conditions remained a member of his father's family. If such passages as Gen **2** 24; **21** 10; **24** 5.67; **30** 3; **31** 31; Jgs **4** 17 ff; **5** 24 ff; **8** 19; **9** 3, indicate the existence in pre-Bib. times of a matriarchate, the allusions are at least too vague to justify the predication of its persistence in Bib. times. The wife was "taken" by her husband, or "given" by her father or, in the case of a servant, by her master or mistress (Gen **2** 22; **16** 3; **34** 9.21), and although the contract was between the men (Gen **29**; **34** 16; Ex **22** 16; Dt **22** 29; Ruth **4** 10) or the parents (Gen **21** 21; **24**), it is probable that the consent of the girl was usually asked (Gen **24** 58). Love between the young people was given due consideration (as in the case of Samson, Shechem, Jacob and Rachel [Gen **29** 18], David and Michal [1 S **18** 20]); at least it developed among married people, so that Hosea could compare the attitude of husband toward wife to that of Jeh toward Israel. As a matter of legal right, it is probable that throughout the Orient long before the events narrated in the Book of Est, every man did "bear rule in his own house" (Est **1** 22). In fact a precedent for the Pers decree has been traced as far back as the first human pair (Gen **3** 16). Nevertheless, we find many instances in which the wife seems to take the lead in the affairs of the household, as in the case of Samson's parents (Jgs **13** 23), of the Shunammite woman (2 K **4**), of Jael (Jgs **4** 18 ff; **5** 24 ff), of Achsah (Josh **15** 18 f; Jgs **1** 12 f), and in less pleasant matters of Jezebel (1 K **18** 4; **21**), Sapphira (Acts **5** 2), and Zeresh (Est **5** 14), who were at least consulted in the affairs of their several households. Abraham is even commanded by the voice of God, "In all that Sarah saith unto thee, hearken unto her voice" (Gen **21** 12). That most women were not so fortunate is probably best attested by the fact that at least in the earlier times the best of them had to resort to stratagem to accomplish their purposes (as in the cases of Rebekah [Gen **27** 6 ff], Rachel [Gen **31** 34], Leah [Gen **30** 16] and Abigail [1 S **25** 18 ff], and even to get information as to their husband's affairs [Sarah, Gen **18** 10; Rebekah, Gen **27** 5]). Perhaps their humbler sisters in later days accomplished their ends by being so contentious as to attract the notice of two proverb-collectors (Prov **21** 9; **25** 24). Though we have no instance of the exercise of the right of life and death over the wife by the husband, and though it is clear that the Heb husband had no power of sale (cf Ex **21** 8), it is frequently asserted on the basis of the one-sided divorce doctrine of the OT (Dt **24** 1), and on the basis of analogy with other ancient laws, as well as because the wife is spoken of in conjunction with property (Ex **20** 17) and because the husband exercised the right to annul the wife's vows (Nu **30** 6), that the wife occupied in the ordinary Heb home a very subordinate position. It must not be forgotten, however, that the husband owed duties to the wife (Ex **21** 10). It must also be borne in mind that great divergence existed at different times and places, and in different stations of society. Most of our OT evidence pertains to the wealthier classes. The two extremes of the women that are "at ease in Zion" (Isa **32** 9–20; cf Am **4** 1 ff; **6** 1 ff) and the busy "good wife" described in Prov **31** 10 ff are hardly exceeded in the most complex society today. The latter probably gives the fairer as well as the more wholesome picture of the functions of the wife in the home, and it is significant that her husband as well as her sons are expected to call her blessed (Prov **31** 28).

It is difficult to estimate the extent to which polygamy and concubinage were practised in ancient Pal, but it is clear that the former practice was discouraged even among kings (Dt **17** 17), and the latter, an outgrowth of slavery, was not held in high repute (cf Dt **21** 10–14). The position of a less-favored wife (Dt **21** 15, "hated") was naturally unpleasant, and her relations with other wives of her husband decidedly bitter—they were called each other's *çārōth*, lit. "vexers" (RV "rivals," Lev **18** 18; 1 S **1** 6, AV "adversary"; cf Ecclus **37** 11)—even when they were sisters (as in the case of Rachel and Leah, Gen **30** 1). Hence the Law forbade the marrying of two sisters (Lev **18** 18). On the other hand so strong was the desire of a Heb mother for children that the childless wife welcomed the children of a maidservant born to her husband as her own (Gen **30** 1–12, etc).

2. Father-in-Law, etc

In normal Heb society, for reasons already explained, the relations of a family with the husband's parents (חָם, *ḥām*, from חָמוֹת, *ḥāmōth*) were closer than those with the wife's parents (חֹתֵן, *ḥōthēn*, fem. חֹתֶנֶת, *ḥōtheneth;* πενθερός, -ά, *pentherós*, *-á*). Where under special conditions a man remained with his wife's tribe after marriage, as in the case of Jacob, serving out his *mōhar*, or Moses fleeing from the wrath of the Egyptians, or the sons of Elimelech sojourning in the land of Moab because of the famine in Pal, his identity with his own tribe was not destroyed, and at the first opportunity the natural impulse was to return to his own country. The bride, on the other hand, leaving her people, would become a member of her husband's family, with all the rights and duties of a daughter (Mic **7** 6). Thus Judah can order Tamar burned for violation of the obligations of a widow (Gen **38** 24). No doubt the position of the daughter-in-law varied in the Heb home between the extremes of those who vexed their parents-in-law unto the death (Gen **26** 35; **27** 46; **28** 8) and the one who said to her mother-in-law, "Jeh do so to me . . . . if aught but death part thee and me" (Ruth **1** 17). Parents-in-law and children-in-law were considered too closely related to intermarry (Lev **18** 15; **20** 12.14).

3. Brother-in-Law, etc

A woman's brother acting *in loco parentis* might perform all the offices of a father-in-law and possibly be called *ḥōthēn* (Gen **24** 50.55; **34** 11 ff). Naturally, brothers-in-law and sisters-in-law would be considered too closely related to intermarry (Lev **18** 16.18; **20** 21). Nevertheless the husband's brother (יָבָם, *yābhām*) was expected to marry the childless widow to establish the name of the deceased on his inheritance (Dt **25** 5–10). This custom dated back to Canaanitic practice (Gen **38** 8), and from the connection between marrying the childless widow and the redemption of land may be called a part of the land law of Pal (Ruth **4** 1–12; cf Jer **32** 6 ff). In practice the Levirate was probably considered more in the nature of a moral duty than a privilege (Dt **25** 7; Ruth **4** 6), and devolved not only on the brother, but on other members of a deceased husband's family in the order of the nearness of their relationship to him (Ruth **3** 12). In the Heb family brothers-in-law and sisters-in-law would form part of the same household. In this relation as in others we find both ideal friendship (David and Jonathan, 1 S **18** 3; 2 S **1** 26) and petty jealousies (in the matter of Moses' wife, Nu **12** 1).

III. Other Domestic Relations.—The Heb אֹמֵן, *'ōmēn*, fem. אֹמֶנֶת, *'ōmeneth* (participle of *'āman*), lit. "nourishing," is tr^d^ "nursing father" (Nu **11** 12; Isa **49** 23), "nursing mother" (Isa **49** 23), "nurse" (Ruth **4** 16; 2 S **4** 4), or simply as the equivalent of "bringing up" (2 K **10** 1.5; Est **2** 7).

1. Foster-Father

In the case of Esther and of Ahab's children, and possibly in the other instances referred to, the relation of foster-parents is suggested. The foster-children under such conditions obeyed the words of the foster-father as the words of a father (Est **2** 20). Michal is spoken of as the mother of Merab's two children (2 S **21** 8) because she reared them (*Sanhedhrīn* **19***b*). Adoption in the Rom sense was, however, hardly to be expected in a polygamous society where the childless father could remarry. Nevertheless, Jacob adopts Manasseh and Ephraim (Gen **48** 5), and thereby makes them the fathers of tribes. According to Jos, while Abraham was childless he adopted Lot (*Ant*, I, vii, 1), and the daughter of Pharaoh adopted Moses (*Ant*, II, ix, 7; cf Ex **2** 10). In NT times the notion of adoption was so familiar that Paul uses the word **figuratively** of conversion (υἱοθεσία, *huiothesía*, Rom **8** 15; **9** 4; Gal **4** 5; Eph **1** 5).

2. Master and Servants

The "family" as the word is used of ancient peoples included dependents. The Heb *mishpāḥāh* is connected with the word *shiphḥāh*, "maidservant," as the Lat *familia* is connected with *famulus*, "servant." For a discussion of the various classes of servants and slaves, Heb and foreign, male and female, see SLAVERY.

3. Host and Guest

When Lot protested against betraying his visitors to the men of Sodom, forasmuch as they had come under the shadow of his roof, and he even preferred to give his daughters to the mob rather than fail in his duties as a host (Gen **19** 8), he was acting on the ancient principle of guest-friendship (cf Gr *xenía*), which bound host and guest by sacred ties. In the light of this principle the act of Jael, who receives Sisera as a guest, and then betrays him, becomes startling and capable of explanation only on the basis of the intense hatred existing at the time, and justifiable, if at all, only on the theory that all is fair in war (Jgs **4** 18–21; **5** 24–27). The nomads of ancient times and even the post-exilic Hebrews, like the Arabs of today, were bound by a temporary covenant whenever there was "salt between them," that is, in the relation of host and guest (Ezr **4** 14; cf the expression "covenant of salt," 2 Ch **13** 5; Nu **18** 19). In the early Christian church breaking bread together served as a sort of a *b^e^rīth 'aḥīm*, or covenant of brothers. In large households such as those of a king, those that ate at the table were members of the household (2 S **9** 11, compared to sons; cf also 2 S **9** 7.10.13; **19** 28; 1 K **2** 7; **4** 27; **18** 19). See HOSPITALITY.

4. The Dependent Stranger

The *gēr* or stranger (as indicated by the expression "thy stranger" [Ex **20** 10; Lev **25** 6; Dt **5** 14; **29** 11; **31** 12; cf Dt **1** 16], Heb *gērō*, lit. "his stranger") attached himself to an influential Hebrew for protection. Thus we read of a "sojourner of the priest's" (Lev **22** 10, *tōshābh;* cf **25** 6) who was in many respects a dependent, but still to be distinguished from a servant (Lev **22** 11). The Mosaic Law commands that such strangers be treated with consideration (Ex **12** 49; **20** 10; **22** 21 ff; **23** 9; Lev **19** 33; Dt **1** 16; **10** 18; **14** 21, etc; Ps **146** 9) and even with love (Dt **16** 14; Lev **19** 34). See STRANGER.

NATHAN ISAACS AND ELLA DAVIS ISAACS

RELEASE, rē-lēs′: (1) The forgiveness of a debt (שְׁמִטָּה, *sh^e^miṭṭāh* [Dt **15** 1.2.9; **31** 10; see JUBILEE YEAR]), with vb. *shāmaṭ*, "to release," vs 2.3. (2) To exempt from taxation or military service (הֲנָחָה, *hănāḥāh*, "release," "rest" [Est **2** 18]). Some would render "granted a holiday." (3) To set a prisoner or slave at liberty (ἀπολύω, *apolúō*, "to let go free" [Mt **27** 15 ‖ Jn **19** 10], etc).

RELIGION, rē-lij′un: "Religion" and "religious" in Elizabethan Eng. were used frequently to denote the outward expression of worship. This is the force of θρησκεία, thrēskeía, tr[d] "religion" in Acts **26** 5; Jas **1** 26.27 (with adj. thrḗskos, "religious"), while the same noun in Col **2** 18 is rendered "worshipping" ("cult" would give the exact meaning). And in the same external sense "religion" is used by AV for λατρεία, latreía, "worship" (so RV), in 1 Macc **1** 43; **2** 19.22. Otherwise "Jews' religion" (or "religion of the Jews") appears in 2 Macc **8** 1; **14** 38 (RV *bis*); Gal **1** 13.14 (Ἰουδαϊσμός, *Ioudaïsmós*, "Judaism"); and "an alien religion" in 2 Macc **6** 24 (ἀλλοφυλισμός, *allophulismós*, "that belonging to another tribe"). The neglect of the external force of "religion" has led to much reckless misquoting of Jas **1** 26.27. Cf Acts **17** 22 and see SUPERSTITION. BURTON SCOTT EASTON

RELIGION, COMPARATIVE. See COMPARATIVE RELIGION.

RELIGION, SCIENCE OF. See COMPARATIVE RELIGION.

REMAINDER, rē-mān′dẽr (יָתַר, *yāthar*, "to be left," שְׁאֵרִית, *sh*e*'ērīth*, "remnant"): In 2 S **14** 7 "residue" would have been clearer (cf Ps **76** 10), but the changes of RV in Lev **6** 16; **7** 16.17 are pointless (contrast Ex **29** 34).

REMALIAH, rem-a-lī′a (רְמַלְיָהוּ, *r*e*malyāhū*, "whom Jeh has adorned"): The father of Pekah (2 K **15** 25 ff; Isa **7** 4 ff; **8** 6). The contemptuous allusion to Pekah as "the son of Remaliah" in Isa **7** 4 (similarly "the son of Kish," 1 S **10** 11) may be a slur on Remaliah's humble origin.

REMEMBER, rē-mem′bẽr, **REMEMBRANCE,** rē-mem′brans: "Remember" is mostly the tr, in the OT, of זָכַר, *zākhar*, and in the NT of μνάομαι, *mnáomai* (Mt **5** 23; **26** 75; Jn **2** 17, etc), and of μνημονεύω, *mnēmoneúō* (Mt **16** 9; Mk **8** 18; Lk **17** 32, etc), and "remembrance" the tr of derivatives of these (*zekher*, *anámnēsis*, etc). There are a few other words. "To remember" is used of God in remembering persons (Gen **8** 1; **19** 29, etc), His covenant (Gen **9** 15; Ex **2** 24; Ezk **16** 60, etc), in answering prayer (Jgs **16** 28; Neh **13** 14.22; Ps **20** 3, etc), and in other ways. Men are exhorted to "remember" God's dealings with them, His commandments (Dt **8** 2.18; Jgs **8** 34; 1 Ch **16** 12, etc), the Sabbath (Ex **20** 8), etc. A specially solemn command is that relating to the Lord's Supper in Lk **22** 19; 1 Cor **11** 24.25, "This do in remembrance of me." "Remembrancer" (writer of chronicles) occurs in AVm of 2 S **8** 16; **20** 24; 1 K **4** 3; 1 Ch **18** 15 (text "recorder," RVm "chronicler"). In Isa **62** 6, RV reads, "ye that are Jeh's remembrancers." RV has frequent changes on AV text, as "have marked" (1 S **15** 2); "make mention of" (Ps **20** 7; **77** 11; Cant **1** 4); "remember" for "be ye mindful of" (1 Ch **16** 15); "memorial" for "remembrance" (Isa **57** 8); in ARV, "to his holy memorial name" (Ps **30** 4; **97** 12, ERV "to his holy name," m "Heb 'memorial'"); in 2 Tim **1** 5, "having been reminded of" for AV "call to remembrance," etc. W. L. WALKER

REMETH, rē′meth, rem′eth (רֶמֶת, *remeth;* B, Ῥεμμάς, *Rhemmás*, A, Ῥαμάθ, *Rhamáth*): A place in the territory of Issachar named with En-gannim (Josh **19** 21). It is probably identical with Ramoth of 1 Ch **6** 73, and Jarmuth of Josh **21** 29. It is represented today by the village *er-Rāmeh*, situated on a hill which rises abruptly from the green plain about 11 miles S.W. of *Jenīn* (En-gannim). While the southern boundary of Issachar was, roughly, the southern edge of the plain of Esdraelon, the possessions of the tribes seem sometimes to have overlapped. See JARMUTH; RAMOTH.

REMISSION, rē-mish′un, **OF SINS** (ἄφεσις, *áphesis*, πάρεσις, *páresis*): The two Gr words, of which the latter occurs only in Rom **3** 25, were tr[d] by the same Eng. word in AV. In RV, *paresis* is tr[d] "passing over." It is contrasted with the other term as pretermission with remission. Remission is exemption from the consequences of an offence, forgiveness; pretermission is the suspension of the penalty (Philippi, Ellicott, Trench [*Synonyms*, XXXIII], Weiss; cf Acts **17** 30). Cremer (*Lexicon of NT Gr*) regards the meaning of the two words as identical, except that the one refers to the OT and the other to the NT. Sins are remitted when the offender is treated as though the offence had never been committed. Remission is restricted to the penalty, while forgiveness refers more particularly to the person, although it may be used also of the sin itself. Remission also is used of offences against God's law; forgiveness, against either Divine or human law. See ABSOLUTION; FORGIVENESS. H. E. JACOBS

REMMON, rem′on (רִמּוֹן, *rimmōn*, Josh **19** 7). See RIMMON.

REMMON-METHOAR, rem′on-meth′ō-är, rem′-on-mē-thō′är (רִמּוֹן הַמְּתֹאָר, *rimmōn ha-m*e*thō'ār* [Josh **19** 13]). See RIMMON, (3).

REMNANT, rem′nant: Remnant is the tr of יֶתֶר, *yether*, "what is left over" (Dt **3** 11; **28** 54; Josh **12** 4, etc); of שְׁאָר, *sh*e*'ār*, "the rest" (Ezr **3** 8 AV; Isa **10** 20.21.22; **11** 16, etc; Zeph **1** 4); more frequently of שְׁאֵרִית, *sh*e*'ērīth*, "residue," etc (2 K **19** 4.31; 2 Ch **34** 9; Ezr **9** 14; Isa **14** 30, etc). As the tr of the last-mentioned two words, "remnant" has a special significance in the prophecies of Isaiah, as denoting "a holy seed," or spiritual kernel, of the nation which should survive impending judgment and become the germ of the people of God, being blessed of God and made a blessing (cf Mic **2** 12; **4** 7; **5** 7.8; **7** 18; also Zeph **2** 7; **3** 13; Hag **1** 12.14; Zec **8** 6; Joel **2** 32). Paul, in Rom **9** 27, quotes from Isa **10** 22 f, "the remnant [*katáleimma*, "what is left over"] shall be saved"; cf also Rom **11** 5 (where the word is *leímma*) with 2 K **19** 4. Several other Heb words are less frequently tr[d] "remnant": *'āhar*, "after"; *yāthar*, "to be left over," etc; in the NT (AV) we have also *loipós*, "left," "remaining" (Mt **22** 6; Rev **11** 13, etc).

For "remnant" RV has "overhanging part" (Ex **26** 12), "rest" (Lev **14** 18, etc); on the other hand, gives "remnant" for "posterity" (Gen **45** 7), for "rest" (Josh **10** 20; 1 Ch **4** 43; Isa **10** 19), for "residue" (Hag **2** 2; Zec **8** 11), etc.

W. L. WALKER

REMPHAN, rem′fan. See REPHAN.

RENDING, ren′ding, **OF GARMENTS.** See BURIAL, IV; DRESS.

RENEW, rē-nū′: The word is used in various senses: (1) of material things, e.g. Ps **104** 30; here it means to give a new appearance, to refresh, to restore the face of the earth; (2) in 1 S **11** 14, to establish more firmly the kingdom by reinstalling King Saul; (3) in 2 Ch **15** 8, to rebuild or repair the broken altar; (4) in Lam **5** 21, "renew our days," restore the favors of former days; (5) in Isa **41** 1, 'let them gather together, or marshal their strongest arguments for answer'; (6) in Ps **103** 5;

Isa **40** 31, it refers to the restoring of spiritual strength; (7) in the NT it invariably refers to spiritual renewal, e.g. Rom **12** 2; 2 Cor **4** 16; Eph **4** 23; Col **3** 10; Tit **3** 5; He **6** 6; all derivatives of καινός, *kainós*, "new."

G. H. Gerberding

REPAIR, rē̇-pâr′ (מַחְסֶה, *maḥṣeh*, "refuge"): In Joel **3** 16, for AV "The Lord will be the hope of his people" AVm renders "place of repair," or, "harbour"=haven of repair. RV gives "refuge." Other words are חָזַק, *ḥāzaḳ*, "to strengthen," "harden," "fix" (2 K **12** 5 and often; Neh **3**); רָפָא, *rāphā'*, "to heal" (1 K **18** 30); עָמַד, *'āmadh*, "to cause to stand still" (Ezr **9** 9); חָיָה, *ḥāyāh*, "to revive" (1 Ch **11** 8); סָגַר, *ṣāghar*, "to close up" (1 K **11** 27).

In RV Apoc for ὑπορράπτω, *huporráptō*, "to patch up" (Sir **50** 1); ἐπισκευάζω, *episkeuázō*, "to get ready" (1 Macc **12** 37). In 1 Macc **14** 34 occurs "reparation" (modern Eng. "repairs") for ἐπανόρθωσις, *epanórthōsis*, "straightening up."

M. O. Evans

REPENTANCE, rē̇-pen′tans:

I. OT Terms
   1. To Repent—"to Pant," "to Sigh"
   2. To Repent—"to Turn" or "Return"
II. NT Terms
   1. Repent—"to Care," "Be Concerned"
   2. Repent—"to Change the Mind"
   3. Repent—"to Turn Over" or "Unto"
III. The Psychological Elements
   1. The Intellectual Element
   2. The Emotional Element
   3. The Volitional Element

Literature

To get an accurate idea of the precise NT meaning of this highly important word it is necessary to consider its approximate synonyms in the original Heb and Gr. The psychological elements of repentance should be considered in the light of the general teaching of Scripture.

I. OT Terms.—The Heb word נָחַם, *nāḥam*, is an onomatopoetic term which implies difficulty in breathing, hence "to pant," "to sigh," "to groan." Naturally it came to signify "to lament" or "to grieve," and when the emotion was produced by the desire of good for others, it merged into compassion and sympathy, and when incited by a consideration of one's own character and deeds it means "to rue," "to repent." To adapt language to our understanding, God is represented as repenting when delayed penalties are at last to be inflicted, or when threatened evils have been averted by genuine reformation (Gen **6** 6; Jon **3** 10). This word is tr[d] "repent" about 40 t in the OT, and in nearly all cases it refers to God. The principal idea is not personal relation to sin, either in its experience of grief or in turning from an evil course. Yet the results of sin are manifest in its use. God's heart is grieved at man's iniquity, and in love He bestows His grace, or in justice He terminates His mercy. It indicates the aroused emotions of God which prompt Him to a different course of dealing with the people. Similarly when used with reference to man, only in this case the consciousness of personal transgression is evident. This distinction in the application of the word is intended by such declarations as God "is not a man, that he should repent" (1 S **15** 29; Job **42** 6; Jer **8** 6).

1. Repent, "to Pant," "to Sigh"

The term שׁוּב, *shūbh*, is most generally employed to express the Scriptural idea of genuine repentance. It is used extensively by the prophets, and makes prominent the idea of a radical change in one's attitude toward sin and God. It implies a conscious, moral separation, and a personal decision to forsake sin and to enter into fellowship with God. It is employed extensively with reference to man's turning away from sin to righteousness (Dt **4** 30; Neh **1** 9; Ps **7** 12; Jer **3** 14). It quite often refers to God in His relation to man (Ex **32** 12; Josh **7** 26). It is employed to indicate the thorough spiritual change which God alone can effect (Ps **85** 4). When the term is tr[d] by "return" it has reference either to man, to God, or to God and man (1 S **7** 3; Ps **90** 13 [both terms, *nāḥam* and *shūbh*]; Isa **21** 12; **55** 7). Both terms are also sometimes employed when the twofold idea of grief and altered relation is expressed, and are tr[d] by "repent" and "return" (Ezk **14** 6; Hos **12** 6; Jon **3** 8).

2. Repent, "to Turn" or "Return"

II. NT Terms.—The term μεταμέλομαι, *metamélomai*, literally signifies to have a feeling or care, concern or regret; like *nāḥam*, it expresses the emotional aspect of repentance. The feeling indicated by the word may issue in genuine repentance, or it may degenerate into mere remorse (Mt **21** 29.32; **27** 3). Judas repented only in the sense of regret, remorse, and not in the sense of the abandonment of sin. The word is used with reference to Paul's feeling concerning a certain course of conduct, and with reference to God in His attitude toward His purposes of grace (2 Cor **7** 8 AV; He **7** 21).

1. Repent, "to Be Careful" or "Concerned With"

The word μετανοέω, *metanoéō*, expresses the true NT idea of the spiritual change implied in a sinner's return to God. The term signifies "to have another mind," to change the opinion or purpose with regard to sin. It is equivalent to the OT word "turn." Thus it is employed by John the Baptist, Jesus, and the apostles (Mt **3** 2; Mk **1** 15; Acts **2** 38). The idea expressed by the word is intimately associated with different aspects of spiritual transformation and of Christian life, with the process in which the agency of man is prominent, as faith (Acts **20** 21), and as conversion (Acts **3** 19); also with those experiences and blessings of which God alone is the author, as remission and forgiveness of sin (Lk **24** 47; Acts **5** 31). It is sometimes conjoined with baptism, which as an overt public act proclaims a changed relation to sin and God (Mk **1** 4; Lk **3** 3; Acts **13** 24; **19** 4). As a vital experience, repentance is to manifest its reality by producing good fruits appropriate to the new spiritual life (Mt **3** 8).

2. Repent, "to Change the Mind"

The word ἐπιστρέφω, *epistréphō*, is used to bring out more clearly the distinct change wrought in repentance. It is employed quite frequently in Acts to express the positive side of a change involved in NT repentance, or to indicate the return to God of which the turning from sin is the negative aspect. The two conceptions are inseparable and complementary. The word is used to express the spiritual transition from sin to God (Acts **9** 35; 1 Thess **1** 9); to strengthen the idea of faith (Acts **11** 21); and to complete and emphasize the change required by NT repentance (Acts **26** 20).

3. Repent, "to Turn Over" or "Upon," "Unto"

There is great difficulty in expressing the true idea of a change of thought with reference to sin when we translate the NT "repentance" into other languages. The Lat version renders it "exercise penitence" (*poenitentiam agere*). But "penitence" etymologically signifies pain, grief, distress, rather than a change of thought and purpose. Thus Lat Christianity has been corrupted by the pernicious error of presenting grief over sin rather than abandonment of sin as the primary idea of NT repentance. It was easy to make the transition from penitence to penance, consequently the Romanists represent Jesus and the apostles as urging people to do penance (*poenitentiam agite*). The Eng.

word "repent" is derived from the Lat *repoenitere*, and inherits the fault of the Lat, making grief the principal idea and keeping in the background, if not altogether out of sight, the fundamental NT conception of a change of mind with reference to sin. But the exhortations of the ancient prophets, of Jesus, and of the apostles show that the change of mind is the dominant idea of the words employed, while the accompanying grief and consequent reformation enter into one's experience from the very nature of the case.

III. The Psychological Elements.—Repentance is that change of a sinner's mind which leads him to turn from his evil ways and live.

1. The Intellectual Element

The change wrought in repentance is so deep and radical as to affect the whole spiritual nature and to involve the entire personality. The intellect must function, the emotions must be aroused, and the will must act. Psychology shows repentance to be profound, personal and all-pervasive. The intellectual element is manifest from the nature of man as an intelligent being, and from the demands of God who desires only rational service. Man must apprehend sin as unutterably heinous, the Divine law as perfect and inexorable, and himself as coming short or falling below the requirements of a holy God (Job **42** 5.6; Ps **51** 3; Rom **3** 20).

2. The Emotional Element

There may be a knowledge of sin without turning from it as an awful thing which dishonors God and ruins man. The change of view may lead only to a dread of punishment and not to the hatred and abandonment of sin (Ex **9** 27; Nu **22** 34; Josh **7** 20; 1 S **15** 24; Mt **27** 4). An emotional element is necessarily involved in repentance. While feeling is not the equivalent of repentance, it nevertheless may be a powerful impulse to a genuine turning from sin. A penitent cannot from the nature of the case be stolid and indifferent. The emotional attitude must be altered if NT repentance be experienced. There is a type of grief that issues in repentance and another which plunges into remorse. There is a godly sorrow and also a sorrow of the world. The former brings life; the latter, death (Mt **27** 3; Lk **18** 23; 2 Cor **7** 9.10). There must be a consciousness of sin in its effect on man and in its relation to God before there can be a hearty turning away from unrighteousness. The feeling naturally accompanying repentance implies a conviction of personal sin and sinfulness and an earnest appeal to God to forgive according to His mercy (Ps **51** 1.2.10–14).

3. The Volitional Element

The most prominent element in the psychology of repentance is the voluntary, or volitional. This aspect of the penitent's experience is expressed in the OT by "turn," or "return," and in the NT by "repent," or "turn." The words employed in the Heb and Gr place chief emphasis on the will, the change of mind, or of purpose, because a complete and sincere turning to God involves both the apprehension of the nature of sin and the consciousness of personal guilt (Jer **25** 5; Mk **1** 15; Acts **2** 38; 2 Cor **7** 9.10). The demand for repentance implies free will and individual responsibility. That men are called upon to repent there can be no doubt, and that God is represented as taking the initiative in repentance is equally clear. The solution of the problem belongs to the spiritual sphere. The psychical phenomena have their origin in the mysterious relations of the human and the Divine personalities. There can be no external substitute for the internal change. Sackcloth for the body and remorse for the soul are not to be confused with a determined abandonment of sin and return to God. Not material sacrifice, but a spiritual change, is the inexorable demand of God in both dispensations (Ps **51** 17; Isa **1** 11; Jer **6** 20; Hos **6** 6).

Repentance is only a condition of salvation and not its meritorious ground. The motives for repentance are chiefly found in the goodness of God, in Divine love, in the pleading desire to have sinners saved, in the inevitable consequences of sin, in the universal demands of the gospel, and in the hope of spiritual life and membership in the kingdom of heaven (Ezk **33** 11; Mk **1** 15; Lk **13** 1–5; Jn **3** 16; Acts **17** 30; Rom **2** 4; 1 Tim **2** 4). The first four beatitudes (Mt **5** 3–6) form a heavenly ladder by which penitent souls pass from the dominion of Satan into the Kingdom of God. A consciousness of spiritual poverty dethroning pride, a sense of personal unworthiness producing grief, a willingness to surrender to God in genuine humility, and a strong spiritual desire developing into hunger and thirst, enter into the experience of one who wholly abandons sin and heartily turns to Him who grants repentance unto life.

LITERATURE.—Various theological works and comms. Note esp. Strong, *Systematic Theology*, III, 832–36; Broadus on Mt 3 2, *American Comm.;* art. "Busse" (Penance), *PRE*.

BYRON H. DEMENT

REPETITIONS, rep-ē-tish′unz: In Mt **6** 7 only, "Use not vain repetitions," for βατταλογέω, *battalogéō* (so א B), a word found nowhere else and spelled variously in the MSS, *battologeō* in K L M, etc, *batologeō* in F G, *blattologeō* in D (probably influenced by the Lat *blatero*, "talk idly"); presumably connected with βατταρίζω, *battarízō*, "stammer," and perhaps formed under the influence of the Aram. *b*ᵉ*ṭā′*, "speak carelessly," or *bāṭēl*, "useless." Whether, however, *battalogeō* means the constant repetition of the same phrase or the mechanical recitation of a long series of obscure or meaningless formulas (if, indeed, a distinction between the acts was thought of) cannot be determined. Either practice is abundantly evidenced as a "heathen" custom of the day, and either can be classed as "much speaking." See PRAYER.

BURTON SCOTT EASTON

REPHAEL, rē′fā-el, ref′ā-el (רְפָאֵל, *r*ᵉ*phā′ēl*, "God has healed"; **Ῥαφαήλ**, *Rhaphaēl*): The eponym of a family of gatekeepers (1 Ch **26** 7). The name occurs in Tob and En ("Raphael"); it probably belongs to a group of late formations. See Gray, *HPN*, 225, 311.

REPHAH, rē′fa (רֶפַח, *rephaḥ* [the form is corrupt]; **Ῥάφη**, *Rháphē*): The eponym of an Ephraimite family (1 Ch **7** 25).

REPHAIAH, rē-fā′ya, rē-fī′a (רְפָיָה, *r*ᵉ*phāyāh*, probably "Jeh is healing"; LXX **Ῥαφαιά[s]**, *Rhaphaiá[s]*):

(1) In David's family, LXX also *Rhaphál* (1 Ch **3** 21).

(2) A captain of Simeon (1 Ch **4** 42).

(3) A grandson of Issachar, LXX also *Rhapharā́* (1 Ch **7** 2).

(4) A descendant of Saul (1 Ch **9** 43; in **8** 37 called "Raphah" [רָפָה]; LXX also *Rhaphaí*).

(5) One of the repairers of the wall under Nehemiah (Neh **3** 9).

REPHAIM, ref′ā-im, rē-fā′im (רְפָאִים, *r*ᵉ*phā′īm*, from רָפָא, *rāphā′*, "a terrible one," hence "giant," as in 1 Ch **20** 4, יְלִידֵי הָרָפָא, *y*ᵉ*līdhē hā-rāphā′*, "sons of the giant"; AV **Rephaims**): A race of aboriginal or early inhabitants E. of the Jordan in Ashteroth-karnaim (Gen **14** 5) and in the vale of Rephaim S.W. of Jerus (Josh **15** 8). They associated with other giant races, as the Emim and Anakim (Dt **2** 10.11) and the Zamzummim (ver 20). It is probable that they were all of the same stock, being given different names by the different tribes who came in contact with them. The same Heb word is rendered "the dead," or "the shades" in various passages (Job **26** 5 m; Ps **88** 10 m; Prov **2** 18 m; **9** 18 m; **21** 16 m; Isa **14** 9 m; **26** 14.19 m). In these instances the word is derived from רָפָה, *rāpheh*, "weak," "powerless," "a shadow" or "shade."

H. PORTER

REPHAIM, VALE OF (עֵמֶק רְפָאִים, *'ēmeḳ rephā'īm*; κοιλὰς Ῥαφαείμ, *koilás Rhaphaeím*, κοιλὰς τῶν Τιτάνων, *koilás tōn Titánōn*): This was a fertile vale (Isa **17** 5), to the S.W. of Jerus (Josh **15** 8; **18** 16; AV "Valley of the Giants"), on the border between Judah and Benjamin. Here David repeatedly defeated the invading Philis (2 S **5** 18. 22; **23** 13; 1 Ch **11** 15; **14** 9). It is located by Jos between Jerus and Bethlehem (*Ant*, VII, iv, i; xii, 4). It corresponds to the modern *el-Biḳa'*, which falls away to the S.W. from the lip of the valley of Hinnom. The name in ancient times may perhaps have covered a larger area, including practically all the land between Jerus and Bethlehem, where the head-waters of *Nahr Rubīn* are collected.

W. EWING

REPHAN, rē'fan: A name for Chiun, the planet Saturn. See ASTROLOGY, 7; CHIUN.

REPHIDIM, ref'i-dim (רְפִידִים, *rephīdhīm*, "rests"; Ῥαφιδίν, *Rhaphidín*): A station in the Wanderings, between the wilderness of Sin and the wilderness of Sinai (Ex **17** 1.8; **19** 2; Nu **33** 14). The host expected to find water here; to their distress the streams were dry, and water was miraculously provided. Palmer (*Desert of the Exodus*, 158 ff) states cogent reasons for identifying Rephidim with *Wâdy Feirān*. It is the most fertile part of the peninsula, well watered, with a palm grove stretching for miles along the valley. Palmer speaks of passing through the palm grove as a "most delightful" walk; "the tall, graceful trees afforded a delicious shade, fresh water ran at our feet, and, above all, bulbuls flitted from branch to branch uttering their sweet notes." His camp was pitched at "the mouth of *Wâdy 'Aleyât*, a large open space completely surrounded by steep, shelving mountains of gneiss, the fantastic cleavage of which added greatly to the beauty of the scene. Palms and tamarisks were dotted all around, and on every knoll and mountain slope were ruined houses, churches, and walls, the relics of the ancient monastic city of Paran. Behind our tents rose the majestic mass of Serbal, and beneath the rocky wall opposite ran a purling brook, only a few inches in depth, but still sufficiently cool, clear, and refreshing."

Such a place as this the Amalekites would naturally wish to preserve for themselves against an invading people. For these desert dwellers, indeed, the possession of this watered vale may well have been a matter of life and death.

If this identification is correct, then *Jebel Ṭaḥū-neh*, "Mount of the mill," a height that rises on the N. of the valley, may have been the hill from which Moses, with Aaron and Hur, viewed the battle.

W. EWING

REPROBATE, rep'rō-bāt: This word occurs in the Eng. Bible in the following passages: Jer **6** 30 (RV "refuse"); Rom **1** 28; 2 Cor **13** 5.6.7; 2 Tim **3** 8; Tit **1** 16. In all these cases the Gr has ἀδόκιμος, *adókimos*. The same Gr word, however, is found with other renderings in Isa **1** 22 ("dross"); Prov **25** 4 ("dross"); 1 Cor **9** 27 ("castaway," RV "rejected"). The primary meaning of *adokimos* is "not-received," "not-acknowledged." This is applied to precious metals or money, in the sense of "not-current," to which, however, the connotation "not-genuine" easily attaches itself. It is also applied to persons who do not or ought not to receive honor or recognition. This purely negative conception frequently passes over into the positive one of that which is or ought to be rejected, either by God or men. Of the above passages 1 Cor **9** 27 uses the word in this meaning. Probably Rom **1** 28, "God gave them up unto a reprobate mind," must be explained on the same principle: the *noús* of the idolatrous heathen is permitted by God to fall into such extreme forms of evil as to meet with the universal rejection and reprobation of men. Wettstein's interpretation, "an unfit mind," i.e. incapable of properly performing its function of moral discrimination, has no linguistic warrant, and obliterates the word-play between "they refused to have God in their knowledge [*ouk edokímasan*]," and "God gave them up to a reprobate [=unacknowledged, *adokimos*] mind." Even Tit **1** 16, "unto every good work reprobate," affords no instance of the meaning "unfit," but belongs to the following rubric.

The close phonetic resemblance and etymological affinity of *dokimos* to the vb. *dokimázō*, "to try," "test," has caused the notion of "being tested," "tried," and its opposite of "being found wanting in the test" to associate itself more or less distinctly with the adjs. *dokimos* and *adokimos*. Thus the more complex meaning results of that which is acknowledged or rejected, because it has approved or not approved itself in testing. This connotation is present in 2 Cor **13** 5.6.7; 2 Tim **3** 8; Tit **1** 16; He **6** 8. In the first two of these passages the word is used of Christians who ostensibly were in the true faith, but either hypothetically or actually are represented as having failed to meet the test. "Reprobate unto every good work" (Tit **1** 16) are they who by their life have disappointed the expectation of good works. The "reprobate [rejected] land" of He **6** 8 is land that by bearing thorns and thistles has failed to meet the test of the husbandman. It should be noticed, however, that *adokimos*, even in these cases, always retains the meaning of rejection because of failure in trial; cf in the last-named passage: "rejected and nigh unto cursing."

LITERATURE.—Cremer, *Biblisch-theologisches Wörterbuch der neutestamentlichen Gräcität*[10], 356-57.

GEERHARDUS VOS

REPROOF, rē-prōōf', **REPROVE**, rē-prōōv': "Reprove" in Elizabethan Eng. had a variety of meanings ("reject," "disprove," "convince," "rebuke"), with "put to the proof" (see 2 Tim **4** 2 RVm) as the force common to all, although in modern Eng. the word means only "rebuke" (with a connotation of deliberateness). AV uses the word chiefly (and RV exclusively, except in 2 Esd **12** 32; **14** 13; 2 Macc **4** 33) for יָכַח, *yākhaḥ*, and ἐλέγχω, *elégchō*, words that have very much the same ambiguities of meaning. Hence a fairly easy rendition into Eng. was possible, but the result included all the ambiguities of the original, and to modern readers such a passage as "But your reproof, what doth it reprove? Do ye think to reprove words" (Job **6** 25.26 ARV) is virtually incomprehensible. The meaning is, approximately: "What do your rebukes prove? Are you quibbling about words?" In Jn **16** 8 no single word in modern Eng. will translate *elegchō*, and "reprove" (AV), "convince" (AVm), and "convict" (RV) are all unsatisfactory. The sense is: "The Spirit will teach men the true meaning of these three words: sin, righteousness, judgment."

BURTON SCOTT EASTON

REPTILE, rep'til, -tīl: Vulg in Mic **7** 17 has *reptilis* for *zōḥălē*, "crawling things," ARV "worms of the earth," AVm "creeping things." See LEVIATHAN; LIZARD; SERPENT; TORTOISE.

REPUTATION, rep-ū-tā'shun: AV uses "reputation" where modern Eng. would use "repute," as connoting prominence rather than moral character. Hence RV's change to "repute" in Gal **2** 2 (for δοκέω, *dokéō*, "seem," perhaps with a slightly sarcastic touch). RV's alteration of "reputation" into "have in honor" (Acts **5** 34; Phil **2** 29) is to secure uniformity of tr for the derivatives of τιμή, *timḗ*, "honor," but RV retains "reputation" in Sus ver 64. AV's "made himself of no reputation" in Phil **2** 7 is a gloss. See KENOSIS. On Eccl **10** 1 see the commentaries.

REQUIRE, rē-kwīr': "Require" meant originally "seek after," whence "ask," and so (as in modern Eng.) "demand." All meanings are common in AV (e.g. 1 S **21** 8; Eccl **3** 15; Ezr **8** 22; 1 Cor **4** 2), and RV has made little change.

REREWARD, rēr'wôrd. See REARWARD.

RESAIAS, rē-sā'yas, rē-sī'as (Ῥησαίας, *Rhēsaías;* AV **Reesaias**): One of the "leaders" with Zerubbabel in the return (1 Esd **5** 8) = "Reelaiah" in Ezr **2** 2, "Raamiah" in Neh **7** 7. The name is apparently duplicated in **1** Esd **5** 8 in the form "Reelias."

RESEN, rē'sen (רֶסֶן, *reṣen;* LXX Δάσεν, *Dásen*, Δάσεμ, *Dásem*): The Gr forms show that the LXX translators had ד, *d*, for ר, *r*, but the reading of the MT is to be preferred. Resen—the last of the four cities mentioned in Gen **10** 11.12 as having been founded by Nimrod (AV by Asshur)—probably represents the Assyr pronunciation of the place-name *Rêš-êni*, "fountain-head." The only town so named in the inscriptions is one of 18 mentioned by Sennacherib in the Bavian inscription as places from which he dug canals connecting with the river Khosr—in fact, it was one of the sources of Nineveh's water supply. It probably lay too far N., however, to be the city here intended. Naturally the name "Resen" could exist in any place where there was a spring.

1. The Name and Its Native Equivalent

As the Bib. text requires a site lying between Nineveh and Calah (*Kouyunjik* and *Nimroud*), it is generally thought to be represented by the ruins at Selamiyeh, about 3 miles N. of the latter city. It is noteworthy that Xenophon (*Anab.* iii.4) mentions a "great" city called Larissa as occupying this position, and Bochart has suggested that it is the same place. He supposes that when the inhabitants were asked to what city the ruins belonged, they answered *la Resen*, "to Resen," which was reproduced by the Greeks as Larissa. Xenophon describes its walls as being 25 ft. wide, 100 ft. high, and 2 parasangs in circuit. Except for the stone plinth 20 ft. high, they were of brick. He speaks of a stone-built pyramid near the city—possibly the temple-tower at Nimroud. See CALAH; NINEVEH, 10. T. G. PINCHES

2. Possibly the Modern Selamiyeh

RESERVOIR, rez'ẽr-vwôr, -vwär (מִקְוָה, *miḳwāh;* AV **ditch** [Isa **22** 11]). See DITCH; CISTERN; POOL.

RESH, resh, rāsh (ר): The 20th letter of the Heb alphabet; transliterated in this Encyclopaedia as *r*. It came also to be used for the number 200. For name, etc, see ALPHABET.

RESHEPH, rē'-shef (רֶשֶׁף, *resheph*, "flame" or "fire-bolt"): Personal name found in Phoen as a divine name. In the OT the name of a descendant of Ephraim, the eponym of an Ephraimite family or clan (1 Ch **7** 25).

RESIDUE, rez'i-dū. See REMNANT.

RESPECT, rē-spekt', **OF PERSONS:** The phrase נָשָׂא פָּנִים, *nāsā' phānīm*, means lit. "lift up the face," and, among other trs, is rendered indifferently "accept" or "respect the person" in AV (contrast Prov **18** 5 and **24** 23). As applied to a (prostrate) suppliant, the phrase means "receive him with favor," and is so used in 1 S **25** 35; Mal **1** 8.9 (cf Gen **19** 21, etc). By a shift in force the phrase came to mean "accept the *person* instead of the *cause*" or "show partiality" (Job **13** 8.10 ARV), and is so used commonly. A literal tr into Gr gave λαμβάνω πρόσωπον, *lambánō prósōpon* (Sir **35** 13 [**32** 16]; Lk **20** 21; Gal **2** 6), with the noun προσωποληµψία, *prosōpolēmpsía*, "face-taking" (Rom **2** 11; Eph **6** 9; Col **3** 25; Jas **2** 1), rendered uniformly "respect of persons" in EV. A noun προσωπολήμπτης, *prosōpolḗmptēs*, "respecter of persons," and a vb. προσωποληµπτέω, *prosōpolēmptéō*, are found Acts **10** 34; Jas **2** 9. God's judgment rests solely on the character of the man and will be influenced by no worldly (Eph **6** 9) or national (Rom **2** 11) considerations. See also ACCEPT. BURTON SCOTT EASTON

REST (נוּחַ, *nūaḥ*, מְנוּחָה, *menūḥāh*, "cessation from motion," "peace," "quiet," etc; ἀνάπαυσις, *anápausis*, κατάπαυσις, *katápausis*): "Rest" in the above sense is of frequent occurrence, and is the tr of several words with various applications and shades of meaning, chiefly of the words given above. It is applied to God as ceasing from the work of creating on the 7th day (Gen **2** 2 f); as having His place of rest in the midst of His people in the temple (1 Ch **28** 2; Ps **132** 8.14); as resting in His love among His people (Zeph **3** 17, RVm "Heb, 'be silent' "). The 7th day was to be one of rest (Ex **16** 23; **31** 15; see SABBATH); the land also was to have its rest in the 7th year (Lev **25** 4 f). Jeh promised His people rest in the land He should give them; this they looked forward to and enjoyed (Dt **12** 9; Josh **11** 23). "To rest on" often means to come upon to abide, as of the Spirit of Jeh (Nu **11** 25 f; Isa **11** 2), of wisdom (Prov **14** 33), of anger (Eccl **7** 9). There is again the "rest" of the grave (Job **3** 13.17.18; Isa **57** 2; Dnl **12** 13). Rest is sometimes equivalent to trust, reliance (2 Ch **14** 11, RV "rely"). Hence rest in Jeh (Ps **37** 7, etc); "rest" in the spiritual sense is not, however, prominent in the OT. In the NT Christ's great offer is rest to the soul (Mt **11** 28). In He **4** 1 ff, it is argued from God's having promised His people a "rest"—a promise not realized in Canaan (ver 8)—that there remains for the people of God "a Sabbath rest" (*sabbatismós*, ver 9). For "rest" RV has "solemn rest" (Ex **16** 23; **31** 15, etc), "resting-place" (Ps **132** 8.14; Isa **11** 10), "peace" (Acts **9** 31), "relief" (2 Cor **2** 13; **7** 5), etc. See also REMNANT. W. L. WALKER

RESTITUTION, res-ti-tū'shun, **RESTORATION.** See PUNISHMENTS.

RESTORATION, res-tō-rā'shun: The idea of a restoration of the world had its origin in the preaching of the OT prophets. Their faith in the unique position and mission of Israel as the chosen people of God inspired in them the conviction that the destruction of the nation would eventually be followed by a restoration under conditions that would insure the realization of the original Divine purpose. When the restoration came and passed without fulfilment of this hope, the Messianic era was projected into the future. By the time of Jesus the conception became more or less spiritualized, and the anticipation of a new order in which the consequences of sin would no longer appear was a prominent feature of the Messianic conception. In the teaching of Jesus and the apostles such a restoration is taken for granted as a matter of course.

In Mt **17** 11 (cf Mk **9** 12), the moral and spiritual regeneration preached by John the Baptist is described as a restoration and viewed as a fulfilment of Mal **4** 6. It is to be observed, however, that the work of John could be characterized as a restoration only in the sense of an inception of the regeneration that was to be completed by Jesus. In Mt **19** 28 Jesus speaks of a regeneration (παλιγγενεσία, *palingenesía*) of the world in terms that ascribe to the saints a state of special felicity. Perhaps the most pointed expression of the idea of a restoration as a special event or crisis is found in the address of Peter (Acts **3** 21), where the restoration is described as an ἀποκατάστασις πάντων, *apokatástasis pántōn*, and is viewed as a fulfilment of prophecy.

In all the passages cited the restoration is assumed as a matter with which the hearers are familiar, and consequently its nature is not unfolded. The evidence is, therefore, too limited to justify any attempt to outline its special features. Under such circumstances there is grave danger of reading into the language of the Scriptures one's own conception of what the restoration is to embody. We are probably expressing the full warrant of the Scripture when we say that the reconstruction mentioned in these passages contemplates the restoration of man, under the reign of Christ, to a life in which the consequences of sin are no longer present, and that this reconstruction is to include in some measure a regeneration of both the physical and the spiritual world.

Whether the benefits of the restoration are to accrue to all men is also left undefined in the Scriptures. In the passages already cited only the disciples of Christ appear in the field of vision. Certain sayings of Jesus are sometimes regarded as favorable to the more inclusive view. In Jn **12** 32 Jesus speaks of drawing all men to Himself, but here, as in Jn **3** 14.15, it is to be observed that while Christ's sacrifice includes all men in its scope, its benefits will doubtless accrue to those only who respond willingly to His drawing power. The saying of Caiaphas (Jn **11** 52) is irrelevant, for the phrase, "the children of God that are scattered abroad," probably refers only to the worthy Jews of the dispersion. Neither can the statements of Paul (Rom **11** 32; 1 Cor **15** 22; Eph **1** 9.10; Col **1** 20; 1 Tim **2** 4; **4** 10; Tit **2** 11) be pressed in favor of the restorationist view. They affirm only that God's plan makes provision for the redemption of all, and that His saving will is universal. But men have wills of their own, and whether they share in the benefits of the salvation provided depends on their availing themselves of its privileges. The doctrine of the restoration of all can hardly be deduced from the NT. See also PUNISHMENT, EVERLASTING.

RUSSELL BENJAMIN MILLER

RESURRECTION, rez-u-rek'shun (in the NT **ἀνάστασις**, *anástasis*, with vbs. **ἀνίστημι**, *anístēmi*, "stand up," and **ἐγείρω**, *egeírō*, "raise." There is no technical term in the OT, but in Isa **26** 19 are found the vbs. חָיָה, *ḥāyāh*, "live," קוּם, *ḳūm*, "rise," קִיץ, *ḳīç*, "awake"):

I. ISRAEL AND IMMORTALITY
   1. Nationalism
   2. Speculation
   3. Religious Danger
   4. Belief in Immortality
   5. Resurrection
   6. Greek Concepts
II. RESURRECTION IN THE OT AND INTERMEDIATE LITERATURE
   1. The OT
   2. The Righteous
   3. The Unrighteous
   4. Complete Denial
III. TEACHING OF CHRIST
   1. Mk **12** 18–27
   2. In General
IV. THE APOSTOLIC DOCTRINE
   1. References
   2. Pauline Doctrine
   3. Continuity
   4. 2 Cor **5**
V. SUMMARY
   1. NT Data
   2. Interpretation
LITERATURE

I. Israel and Immortality.—It is very remarkable that a doctrine of life after death as an essential part of religion was of very late development in Israel, although this doctrine, often highly elaborated, was commonly held among the surrounding nations. The chief cause of this lateness was that Israel's religion centered predominantly in the ideal of a holy *nation*. Consequently the individual was a secondary object of consideration, and the future of the man who died before the national promises were fulfilled either was merged in the future of his descendants or else was disregarded altogether.

1. Nationalism

Much speculation about life after death evidently existed, but it was not in direct connection with the nation's religion. Therefore the OT data are scanty and point, as might be expected, to non-homogeneous concepts. Still, certain ideas are clear. The living individual was composed of "flesh" and *nephesh*, or *rū^{a}ḥ* (a trichotomy appears to be post-Bib., despite 1 Thess **5** 23; see PSYCHOLOGY). In the individual *nephesh* and *rū^{a}ḥ* seem to be fairly synonymous words, meaning primarily "breath," as the animating principle of the flesh (so for the lower animals in Ps **104** 29.30). But *nephesh* came to be used to denote the "inner man" or "self" (Dt **12** 20, etc; see HEART), and so in EV is usually rendered "soul." But there are only a very few cases where *nephesh* is used for the seat of the personality after death (Ps **30** 3; cf **16** 10; Isa **38** 17; Job **33** 18, etc), and nearly all of such passages seem quite late. Indeed, in some 13 cases the *nephesh* of a dead man is unmistakably his *corpse* (Lev **19** 28; Nu **5** 2; Hag **2** 13, etc). It seems the question of what survives death was hardly raised; whatever existed then was thought of as something quite new. On the one hand the dead man could be called a "god" (1 S **28** 13), a term perhaps related to ancestor-worship. But more commonly the dead are thought of as "shades," *r^{e}phā'īm* (Job **26** 5 m, etc), weak copies of the original man in all regards (Ezk **32** 25). But, whatever existence such "shades" might have, they had passed out of relation to Jeh, whom the "dead praise not" (Ps **115** 17.18; Isa **38** 18.19), and there was no religious interest in them.

2. Speculation

Indeed, any interest taken in them was likely to be anti-religious, as connected with necromancy, etc (Dt **14** 1; **26** 14; Isa **8** 19; Ps **106** 28, etc; see SORCERY), or as connected with foreign religions. Here, probably, the very fact that the surrounding nations taught immortality was a strong reason for Israel's refusing to consider it. That Egypt held an elaborate doctrine of individual judgment at death, or that Persia taught the resur-

3. Religious Danger

rection of the body, would actually tend to render these doctrines suspicious, and it was not until the danger of syncretism seemed past that such beliefs could be considered on their own merits. Hence it is not surprising that the prophets virtually disregard the idea or that Eccl denies any immortality doctrine categorically.

4. Belief in Immortality

None the less, with a fuller knowledge of God, wider experience, and deeper reflection, the doctrine was bound to come. But it came slowly. Individualism reaches explicit statement in Ezk **14, 18, 33** (cf Dt **24** 16; Jer **31** 29.30), but the national point of view still made the rewards and punishments of the individual matters of this world only (Ezk **14** 14; Ps **37,** etc), a doctrine that had surprising vitality and that is found as late as Sir (**1** 13; **11** 26). But as this does not square with the facts of life (Job), a doctrine of immortality, already hinted at (II, 1, below), was inevitable. It appears in full force in the post-Maccabean period, but why just then is hard to say; perhaps because it was then that there had been witnessed the spectacle of martyrdoms on a large scale (1 Macc **1** 60-64).

5. Resurrection

Resurrection of the body was the form immortality took, in accord with the religious premises. As the saint was to find his happiness in the nation, he must be restored to the nation; and the older views did not point toward pure soul-immortality. The "shades" led a wretched existence at the best; and St. Paul himself shudders at the thought of "nakedness" (2 Cor **5** 3). The *nephesh* and *rūaḥ* were uncertain quantities, and even the NT has no consistent terminology for the immortal part of man ("soul," Rev **6** 9; **20** 4; "spirit," He **12** 23; 1 Pet **3** 19; St. Paul avoids any term in 1 Cor **15,** and in 2 Cor **5** says: "I"). In the Talm a common view is that the old bodies will receive new souls (*Ber. R.* **2** 7; **6** 7; *Vayy. R.* **12** 2; **15** 1, etc; cf Sib Or **4** 187).

6. Greek Concepts

Where direct Gr influence, however, can be predicated, pure soul-immortality is found (cf Wisd **8** 19.20; **9** 15 [but Wisd's true teaching is very uncertain]; En **102** 4—**105; 108;** Slav En; 4 Macc; Jos, and esp. Philo). According to Jos (*BJ*, II, viii, 11) the Essenes held this doctrine, but as Jos graecizes the Pharisaic resurrection into Pythagorean soul-migration (II, viii, 14; contrast *Ant*, XVIII, i, 3), his evidence is doubtful. Note, moreover, how Lk **6** 9; **9** 25; **12** 4.5 has reworded Mk **3** 4; **8** 36; Mt **10** 28 for Gr readers. In a vague way even Palestinian Judaism had something of the same concepts (2 Esd **7** 88; 2 Cor **4** 16; **12** 2), while it is commonly held that the souls in the intermediate state can enjoy happiness, a statement first appearing in En **22** (Jub **23** 31 is hardly serious).

II. Resurrection in the OT and Intermediate Literature.—For the reasons given above, references in the OT to the resurrection doctrine are few. Probably it is to be found in Ps **17** 15; **16** 11; **49** 15; **73** 24, and in each case with increased probability, but for exact discussions the student must consult the comms. Of course no exact dating of these Ps passages is possible. With still higher probability the doctrine is expressed in Job **14** 13-15; **19** 25-29, but again alternative explanations are just possible, and, again, Job is a notoriously hard book to date (see JOB, BOOK OF). The two certain passages are Isa **26** 19 m and Dnl **12** 2. In the former (to be dated about 332 [?]) it is promised that the "dew of light" shall fall on the earth and so the (righteous) dead shall revive. But this resurrection is confined to Pal and does not include the unrighteous. For Dnl **12** 2 see below.

1. The OT

2. The Righteous

Indeed, resurrection for the righteous only was thought of much more naturally than a general resurrection. And still more naturally a resurrection of martyrs was thought of, such simply receiving back what they had given up for God. So in En **90** 33 (prior to 107 BC) and 2 Macc **7** 9.11. 23; **14** 46 (only martyrs are mentioned in 2 Macc); cf Rev **20** 4. But of course the idea once given could not be restricted to martyrs only, and the intermediate lit. contains so many references to the resurrection of the righteous as to debar citation. Early passages are En **91** 10 (*perhaps* pre-Maccabean); XII P, Test. Judah **25** 4 (before 107). A very curious passage is En **25** 6, where the risen saints merely live longer than did their fathers, i.e. resurrection does *not* imply immortality. This passage seems to be unique.

3. The Unrighteous

For a resurrection of unrighteous men (Dnl **12** 2; En **22** 11; XII P, Test. Benj. **10** 7.8, Armenian text —in none of these cases a *general* resurrection), a motive is given in En **22** 13: for such men the mere condition of Sheol is not punishment enough. For a general resurrection the motive is always the final judgment, so that all human history may be summed up in one supreme act. The idea is not very common, and XII P, Test. Benj. **10** 7.8 (Gr text); Bar **50** 2; En **51** 1; Sib Or **4** 178-90; Life of Adam (Gr) **10,** and 2 Esd **5** 45; **7** 32; **14** 35 about account for all the unequivocal passages. It is not found in the earliest part of the Talm. XII P, Test. Benj. **10** 7.8 (Gr) has *two* resurrections.

4. Complete Denial

Finally, much of the lit. knows no immortality at all. Eccl, Sir and 1 Macc are the most familiar examples, but there are many others. It is esp. interesting that the very spiritual author of 2 Esd did not think it worth while to modify the categorical denial in the source used in **13** 20. Of course, the Jewish party that persisted most in a denial of any resurrection was the Sadducees (Mt **22** 23 and ||'s; Acts **23** 8), with an extreme conservatism often found among aristocrats.

III. Teaching of Christ.—The question is discussed explicitly in the familiar passage Mk **12** 18-27 || Mt **22** 23-33 || Lk **20** 27-38.

1. Mk 12: 18-27

The Sadducees assumed that resurrection implies simply a resuscitation to a resumption of human functions, including the *physical* side of marriage. Their error lay in the low idea of God. For the Scriptures teach a God whose ability and willingness to care for His creatures are so unlimited that the destiny He has prepared for them is caricatured if conceived in any terms but the absolutely highest. Hence there follows not only the truth of the resurrection, but a resurrection to a state as far above the sexual sphere as that of the angels. (The possibility of mutual *recognition* by husband and wife is irrelevant, nor is it even said that the resurrection bodies are asexual.) Luke (**20** 36) adds the explanation that, as there are to be no deaths, marriage (in its relation to births) will not exist. It may be thought that Christ's argument would support equally well the immortality of the soul only, and, as a matter of fact, the same argument is used for the latter doctrine in 4 Macc **7** 18.19; **16** 25. But in Jerus and under the given circumstances this is quite impossible. And, moreover, it would seem that any such dualism would be a violation of Christ's teaching as to God's care.

However, the argument seems to touch only the resurrection of the righteous, esp. in the form given in Lk (cf Lk **14** 14). (But that Luke thought of so limiting the resurrection is disproved by Acts **24** 15.) Similarly in Mt **8** 11 ‖ Lk **13** 28; Mk **13** 27 ‖ Mt **24** 31. But, as a feature in the Judgment, the resurrection of all men is taught. Then the men of Sodom, Tyre, Nineveh appear (Mt **11** 22.24; **12** 41.42 ‖ Lk **10** 14; **11** 32), and those cast into Gehenna are represented as having a body (Mk **9** 43–47; Mt **5** 29.30; **10** 28; **18** 8.9). And at the great final assize (Mt **25** 31–46) all men appear. In the Fourth Gospel a similar distinction is made (**6** 39.40.44.54; **11** 25), the resurrection of the righteous, based on their union with God through Christ and their present possession of this union, and (in **5** 28.29) the general resurrection to judgment. Whether these passages imply two resurrections or emphasize only the extreme difference in conditions at the one cannot be determined.

2. In General

The passages in 4 Macc referred to above read: "They who care for piety with their whole heart, they alone are able to conquer the impulses of the flesh, believing that like our patriarchs Abraham, Isaac, Jacob, they do not die to God but live to God" (**7** 18.19); and "They knew that dying for God they would live to God, even as Abraham and Isaac and Jacob and all the patriarchs" (**16** 25). It is distinctly possible that Our Lord's words may have been known to the author of 4 Macc, although the possibility that Christ approved and broadened the tenets of some spiritually-minded few is not to be disregarded. More possible is it that 4 Macc influenced Luke's Gr phraseology. See MACCABEES, BOOK OF, IV.

IV. The Apostolic Doctrine.—For the apostles, Christ's victory over death took the resurrection doctrine out of the realm of speculative eschatology. Henceforth it is a fact of experience, basic for Christianity. Direct references in the NT are found in Acts **4** 2; **17** 18.32; **23** 6; **24** 15.21; Rom **4** 17; **5** 17; **6** 5.8; **8** 11; **11** 15; 1 Cor **6** 14; **15**; 2 Cor **1** 9; **4** 14; **5** 1–10; Phil **3** 10. 11.21; Col **1** 18; 1 Thess **4** 13–18; 2 Tim **2** 18; He **6** 2; **11** 19.35; Rev **20** 4.5 (martyrs only); **20** 12.13. Of these only Acts **24** 15; Rev **20** 12. 13, refer to a *general* resurrection with absolute unambiguity, but the doctrine is certainly contained in others and in 2 Tim **4** 1 besides.

1. References

A theology of the resurrection is given fully by St. Paul. Basic is the conception of the union of the believer with Christ, so that our resurrection follows from His (esp. Rom **6** 5–11; Phil **3** 10.11). Every deliverance from danger is a foretaste of the resurrection (2 Cor **4** 10.11). Indeed so certain is it, that it may be spoken of as accomplished (Eph **2** 6). From another standpoint, the resurrection is simply part of God's general redemption of Nature at the consummation (Rom **8** 11. 18–25). As the believer then passes into a condition of glory, his body must be altered for the new conditions (1 Cor **15** 50; Phil **3** 21); it becomes a "spiritual" body, belonging to the realm of the spirit (*not* "spiritual" in opposition to "material"). Nature shows us how different "bodies" can be—from the "body" of the sun to the bodies of the lowest animals the kind depends merely on the creative will of God (1 Cor **15** 38–41). Nor is the idea of a change in the body of the same thing unfamiliar: look at the difference in the "body" of a grain of wheat at its sowing and after it is grown! (ver 37). Just so, I am "sown" or sent into the world (probably not "buried") with one kind of body, but my resurrection will see me with a body adapted to my life with Christ and God (vs 42–44). If I am still alive at the Parousia, this new body shall be clothed upon my present body (vs 53.54; 2 Cor **5** 2–4), otherwise I shall be raised in it (ver 52). This body exists already in the heavens (2 Cor **5** 1.2), and when it is clothed upon me the natural functions of the present body will be abolished (1 Cor **6** 13). Yet a motive for refraining from impurity is to keep undefiled the body that is to rise (1 Cor **6** 13.14).

2. Pauline Doctrine

The relation of the matter in the present body to that in the resurrection body was a question St. Paul never raised. In 1 Cor **6** 13.14 it appears that he thought of the body as something more than the sum of its organs, for the organs perish, but the body is raised. Nor does he discuss the eventual fate of the dead body. The imagery of 1 Thess **4** 16.17; 1 Cor **15** 52 is that of leaving the graves, and in the case of Christ's resurrection, the type of ours, that which was buried was that which was raised (1 Cor **15** 4). Perhaps the thought is that the touch of the resurrection body destroys all things in the old body that are unadapted to the new state; perhaps there is an idea that the essence of the old body is what we might call "non-material," so that decay simply anticipates the work the resurrection will do. At all events, such reflections are "beyond what is written."

3. Continuity

A partial parallel to the idea of the resurrection body being already in heaven is found in Slav En **22** 8.9, where the *soul* receives clothing laid up for it (cf Asc Isa **7** 22.23 and *possibly* Rev **6** 11). But Christ also speaks of a reward being already in heaven (Mt **5** 12). A more important question is the time of the clothing in 2 Cor **5** 1–5. A group of scholars (Heinrici, Schmiedel, Holtzmann, Clemen, Charles, etc) consider that St. Paul has here changed his views from those of 1 Cor; that he now considers the resurrection body to be assumed immediately at death, and they translate vs 2.3 "'we groan [at the burdens of life], longing to be clothed upon with our habitation which is from heaven': because, when we shall be clothed with it, we shall have no more nakedness to experience" (Weizsäcker's tr of the NT). But 2 Cor would have been a most awkward place to announce a change of views, for it was written in part as a defence against inconsistency (**1** 17, etc). The willingness to be absent from the body (**5** 8) loses all its point if another and better body is to be given at once. The grammatical reasons for the interpretation above (best stated by Heinrici) are very weak. And the tr given reads into the verse something that simply is not there. Consequently it is far better to follow the older interpretation of Meyer (B. Weiss, Bousset, Lietzmann, Bachmann, Menzies, etc; Bachmann is esp. good) and the obvious sense of the passage: St. Paul dreads being left naked by death, but finds immediate consolation at the thought of being with Christ, and eventual consolation at the thought of the body to be received at the Parousia. (In Phil **1** 21–24 this dread is overcome.)

4. 2 Cor, Ch 5

Of a resurrection of the wicked, St. Paul has little to say. The doctrine seems clearly stated in 2 Cor **5** 10 (and in 2 Tim **4** 1, unless the Pauline authorship of 2 Tim is denied). But St. Paul is willing to treat the fate of the unrighteous with silence.

V. Summary.—The points in the NT doctrine of the resurrection of the righteous, then, seem to be these: The personality of the believer survives after death and is with Christ. But it is lacking in something that will be supplied at the consummation, when a body will be given in which there is nothing to hinder perfect intercourse with God. The connection of this body with the present body is not discussed, except for saying that some connection exists, with the necessity of a transformation for those alive at the end. In this state nothing remains

1. NT Data

that is inconsistent with the height to which man is raised, and in particular sexual relations (Mk **12** 25) and the processes of nutrition (1 Cor **6** 13) cease. For this end the whole power of God is available. And it is insured by the perfect trust the believer may put in God and by the resurrection of Christ, with whom the believer has become intimately united. The unrighteous are raised for the final vindication of God's dealings in history. *Two* resurrections are found in Rev **20** 5.13 and quite possibly in 1 Thess **4** 16; 1 Cor **15** 23.24. Hence the phrase **first resurrection;** see LAST JUDGMENT.

2. Interpretation

Into the "blanks" of this scheme the believer is naturally entitled to insert such matter as may seem to him best compatible with his other concepts of Christianity and of philosophy. As is so often the case with passages in the Bible, the student marvels at the way the sacred writers were restrained from committing Christianity to metaphysical schemes that growth in human knowledge might afterward show to be false. But the theologian must take care to distinguish between the revealed facts and the interpretation given them in any system that he constructs to make the doctrine conform to the ideas of his own time or circle—a distinction too often forgotten in the past and sometimes with lamentable results. Esp. is it well to remember that such a phrase as "a purely spiritual immortality" rests on a metaphysical dualism that is today obsolete, and that such a phrase is hardly less naïve than the expectation that the resurrection body will contain identically the material of the present body. We are still quite in the dark as to the relations of what we call "soul" and "body," and so, naturally, it is quite impossible to dogmatize. A. Meyer in his *RGG* art. ("Auferstehung, dogmatisch") has some interesting suggestions. For an idealistic metaphysic, where soul and body are only two forms of God's thought, the resurrection offers no difficulties. If the body be regarded as the web of forces that proceed from the soul, the resurrection would take the form of the return of those forces to their center at the consummation. If "body" be considered to embrace the totality of effects that proceed from the individual, at the end the individual will find in these effects the exact expression of himself (Fechner's theory). Or resurrection may be considered as the end of evolution—the reunion in God of all that has been differentiated and so evolved and enriched. Such lines must be followed cautiously, but may be found to lead to results of great value.

In recent years the attention of scholars has been directed to the problem of how far the teachings of other religions assisted the Jews in attaining a resurrection doctrine. Practically only the Pers system comes into question, and here the facts seem to be these: A belief among the Persians in the resurrection of the body is attested for the pre-Christian period by the fragments of Theopompus (4th cent. BC), preserved by Diogenes Laertius and Aeneas of Gaza. That this doctrine was taught by Zoroaster himself is not capable of exact proof, but is probable. But on the precise details we are in great uncertainty. In the Avesta the doctrine is not found in the oldest part (the *Gathas*), but is mentioned in the 19th *Yasht*, a document that has certainly undergone post-Christian redaction of an extent that is not determinable. The fullest Pers source is the *Bundahesh* (30), written in the 9th Christian cent. It certainly contains much very ancient matter, but the age of any given passage in it is always a problem. Consequently the sources must be used with great caution. It may be noted that late Judaism certainly was affected to some degree by the Pers religion (see Tob, esp.), but there are so many native Jewish elements that were leading to a resurrection doctrine that familiarity with the Pers belief could have been an assistance only. Esp. is it to be noted that the great acceptance of the doctrine lies in the post-Maccabean period, when direct Pers influence is hardly to be thought of. See ZOROASTRIANISM.

LITERATURE.—The older works suffer from a defective understanding of the presuppositions, but Salmond, *Christian Doctrine of Immortality*, is always useful. Brown, *The Christian Hope*, 1912, is excellent and contains a full bibliography. Charles, *Eschatology*, and art. "Eschatology" in *EB* are invaluable, but must be used critically by the thorough student, for the opinions are often individualistic. Wotherspoon's art. "Resurrection" in *DCG* is good; Bernard's in *HDB* is not so good. On 1 Cor, Findlay or (better) Edwards; on 2 Cor Menzies. In German the NT Theologies of Weiss, Holtzmann, Feine; Schaeder's "Auferstehung" in *PRE*[3]. On 1 Cor, Heinrici and J. Weiss in Meyer (eds 8 and 9); on 2 Cor, Bachmann in the Zahn series. On both Cor epp. Bousset in the *Schriften des NT* of J. Weiss (the work of an expert in eschatology), and Lietzmann in his *Handbuch*. See BODY; ESCHATOLOGY (OT and NT); FLESH; SOUL; SPIRIT.

BURTON SCOTT EASTON

RESURRECTION, GOSPEL OF THE. See APOCRYPHAL GOSPELS.

RESURRECTION OF JESUS CHRIST, THE:

The Resurrection has always been felt to be vital in connection with Christianity. As a consequence, opponents have almost always concentrated their attacks, and Christians have centered their defence, upon it. It is therefore of the utmost importance to give attention to the subject, as it appears in the NT. There are several converging lines of evidence, and none can be overlooked. Each must have its place and weight. The issues at stake are so serious that nothing must be omitted.

1. First Proof: The Life of Jesus

The first proof is the life of Jesus Christ Himself. It is always a disappointment when a life which commenced well finishes badly. We have this feeling even in fiction; instinct demands that a story should end well. Much more is this true of Jesus Christ. A perfect life characterized by Divine claims ends in its prime in a cruel and shameful death. Is that a fitting close? Surely death could not end everything after such a noble career. The Gospels give the resurrection as the completion of the picture of Jesus Christ. There is no real doubt that Christ anticipated His own resurrection. At first He used only vague terms, such as, "Destroy this Temple, and in three days I will raise it up." But later on He spoke plainly, and whenever He mentioned His death, He added, "The Son of man . . . . must be raised the third day." These references are too numerous to be overlooked, and, in spite of difficulties of detail, they are, in any proper treatment of the Gospels, an integral part of the claim made for Himself by Jesus Christ (Mt **12** 38–40; **16** 21; **17** 9.23; **20** 19; **27** 63; Mk **8** 31; **9** 9.31; **10** 34; **14** 58; Lk **9** 22; **18** 33; Jn **2** 19–21). His veracity is at stake if He did not rise. Surely the word of such a One must be given due credence. We are therefore compelled to face the fact that the resurrection of which the Gospels speak is the resurrection of no ordinary man, but of *Jesus*—that is of One whose life and character had been unique, and for whose shameful death no proper explanation was conceivable (Denney, *Jesus and the Gospel*, 122 f). Is it possible that, in view of His perfect truthfulness of word and deed, there should be such an anti-climax as is involved in a denial of His assurance that He would rise again (C. H. Robinson, *Studies in the Resurrection*, 30)? Consider, too, the death of Christ in the light of His perfect life. If that death was the close of a life so beautiful, so remarkable, so Godlike, we are faced with an insoluble mystery—the permanent triumph of wrong over right, and the impossibility of believing in truth or justice in the world (C. H. Robinson, op. cit., 36). So the resurrection is not to be regarded as an isolated event, a fact in the history of Christ separated from all else. It must be taken in close connection with what precedes. The true solution of the problem is to be found in that estimate of Christ which "most entirely fits in with the totality of the facts" (Orr, *The Resurrection of Jesus*, 14).

Another line of proof is the fact of the empty grave and the disappearance of the body. That Jesus died and was buried, and that on the third morning the tomb was empty, is not now seriously challenged. The theory of a swoon and a recovery in the tomb is impossible, and to it Strauss "practically gives its deathblow" (Orr, op. cit., 43).

2. Second Proof: The Empty Grave

At Christ's burial a stone was rolled before the tomb, the tomb was sealed, and a guard was placed before it. Yet on the third morning the body had disappeared, and the tomb was empty. There are only two alternatives. His body must have been taken out of the grave by human hands or else by superhuman power. If the hands were human, they must have been those of His friends or of His foes. If His friends had wished to take out His body, the question at once arises whether they *could* have done so in the face of the stone, the seal and the guard. If His foes had contemplated this action, the question arises whether they *would* seriously have considered it. It is extremely improbable that any effort should have been made to remove the body out of the reach of the disciples. Why should His enemies do the very thing that would be most likely to spread the report of His resurrection? As Chrysostom said, "If the body had been stolen, they could not have stolen it naked, because of the delay in stripping it of the burial clothes and the trouble caused by the drugs adhering to it" (quoted in Day, *Evidence for the Resurrection*, 35). Besides, the position of the grave-clothes proves the impossibility of the theft of the body (see Gr of Jn **20** 6.7; **11** 44; Grimley, *Temple of Humanity*, 69, 70; Latham, *The Risen Master; Expos T*, XIII, 293 f; XIV, 510). How, too, is it possible to account for the failure of the Jews to disprove the resurrection? Not more than seven weeks afterward Peter preached in that city the fact that Jesus had been raised. What would have been easier or more conclusive than for the Jews to have produced the dead body and silenced Peter forever? "The silence of the Jews is as significant as the speech of the Christians" (Fairbairn, *Studies in the Life of Christ*, 357).

The fact of the empty tomb with the disappearance of the body remains a problem to be faced. It is now admitted that the evidence for the empty tomb is adequate, and that it was part of the primitive belief (*Foundations*, 134, 154). It is important to realize the force of this admission, because it is a testimony to St. Paul's use of the term "third day" (see below) and to the Christian observance of the first day of the week. And yet in spite of this we are told that a belief in the empty tomb is impossible. By some writers the idea of resurrection is interpreted to mean the revival of Christ's spiritual influence on the disciples, which had been brought to a close by His death. It is thought that the essential idea and value of Christ's resurrection can be conserved, even while the belief in His bodily rising from the grave is surrendered (Orr, *The Resurrection of Jesus*, 23). But how can we believe in the resurrection while we regard the basis of the primitive belief in it as a mistake, not to say a fraud? The disciples found the tomb empty, and on the strength of this they believed He had risen. How can the belief be true if the foundation be false? Besides, the various forms of the vision-theory are now gradually but surely being regarded as inadequate and impossible. They involve the change of almost every fact in the Gospel history, and the invention of new scenes and conditions of which the Gospels know nothing (Orr, op. cit., 222). It has never been satisfactorily shown why the disciples should have had this abundant experience of visions; nor why they should have had it so soon after the death of Christ and within a strictly limited period; nor why it suddenly ceased. The disciples were familiar with the apparition of a spirit, like Samuel's, and with the resuscitation of a body, like Lazarus', but what they had not experienced or imagined was the fact of a spiritual body, the combination of body and spirit in an entirely novel way. So the old theory of a vision is now virtually set aside, and for it is substituted the theory of a real spiritual manifestation of the risen Christ. The question at once arises whether this is not prompted by an unconscious but real desire to get rid of anything like a physical resurrection. Whatever may be true of unbelievers, this is an impossible position for those who believe Christ is alive.

Even though we may be ready to admit the reality of telepathic communication, it is impossible to argue that this is equivalent to the idea of resurrection. Psychical research has not proceeded far enough as yet to warrant arguments being built on it, though in any case it is difficult, if not impossible, to obtain material from this quarter which will answer to the conditions of the physical resurrection recorded in the NT. "The survival of the soul is not resurrection." "Whoever heard of a spirit being buried?" (Orr, *The Resurrection of Jesus*, 229).

In view of the records of the Gospels and the general testimony of the NT, it is impossible to be "agnostic" as to what happened at the grave of Jesus, even though we are quite sure that He who died now lives and reigns. It is sometimes said that faith is not bound up with holding a particular view of the relations of Christ's present glory with the body that was once in Joseph's tomb, that faith is to be exercised in the exalted Lord, and that belief in a resuscitation of the human body is no vital part of it. It is no doubt true that faith today is to be exercised solely in the exalted and glorified Lord, but faith must ultimately rest on fact, and it is difficult to understand how Christian faith can really be "agnostic" with regard to the facts about the empty tomb and the risen body, which are so prominent in the NT, and which form an essential part of the apostolic witness. The attempt to set faith and historical evidence in opposition to each other, which is so marked a characteristic of much modern thought, will never satisfy general Christian intelligence, and if there is to be any real belief in the historical character of the NT, it is impossible to be "agnostic" about facts that are writ so large on the face of the records. When once the evidence for the empty tomb is allowed to be adequate, the impossibility of any other explanation than that indicated in the NT is at once seen. The evidence must be accounted for and adequately explained. And so we come again to the insuperable barrier of the empty tomb, which, together with the apostolic witness, stands impregnable against all the attacks of visional and apparitional theories. It is becoming more evident that these theories are entirely inadequate to account for the records in the Gospels, as well as for the place and power of those Gospels in the early church and in all subsequent ages. The force of the evidence for the empty grave and the disappearance of the body is clearly seen by the explanations suggested by various modern writers (those of Oscar Holtzmann, K. Lake, and A. Meyer can be seen in Orr, *The Resurrection of Jesus*, ch viii, and that of Reville in C. H. Robinson, *Studies in the Resurrection of Christ*, 69; see also art. by Streeter in *Foundations*). Not one of them is tenable without doing violence to the Gospel story, and also without putting forth new theories which are not only improbable in themselves, but are without a shred of real historical or literary evidence. The one outstanding fact which baffles all these writers is the empty grave.

Others suggest that resurrection means a real objective appearance of the risen Christ without implying any physical reanimation, that "the resurrection of Christ was an objective reality, but was not a physical resuscitation" (C. H. Robinson, *Studies in the Resurrection of Christ*, 12). But the difficulty here is as to the meaning of the term "*re*surrection." If it means a *return* from the dead, a rising *again* (*re-*), must there not have been some identity between that which was put in the tomb and the "objective reality" which appeared to the disciples? Wherein lies the essential difference between an objective vision and an objective appearance? If we believe the apostolic testimony to the empty tomb, why may we not accept their evidence to the actual resurrection? They evidently recognized their Master, and this recognition must have been due to some familiarity with His bodily appearance. No difficulty of conceiving of the resurrection of mankind hereafter must be allowed to set aside the plain facts of the record about Christ. It is, of course, quite clear that the resurrection body of Jesus was not exactly the same as when it was put in the tomb, but it is equally clear that there was definite identity as well as definite dissimilarity, and both elements must be faced and accounted for. There need be no insuperable difficulty if we believe that in the very nature of things Christ's resurrection must be unique, and, since the life and work of Jesus Christ transcend our experience (as they certainly should do), we must not expect to bring them within the limitations of natural law and human history. How the resurrection body was sustained is a problem quite outside our ken, though the reference to "flesh and *bones*," compared with St. Paul's words about "flesh and *blood*" not being able to enter the kingdom of God, may suggest that while the resurrection body was not constituted upon a natural basis through blood, yet that it possessed "all things appertaining to the perfection of man's nature" (Church of England Article IV). We may not be able to solve the problem, but we must hold fast to all the facts, and these may be summed up by saying that the body was the same though different, different though the same. The true description of the resurrection seems to be that "it was an objective reality, but that it was not merely a physical resuscitation." We are therefore brought back to a consideration of the facts recorded in the Gospels as to the empty tomb and the disappearance of the body, and we only ask for an explanation which will take into consideration all the facts recorded, and will do no violence to any part of the evidence. To predicate a new resurrection body in which Christ appeared to His disciples does not explain how in three days' time the body which had been placed in the tomb was disposed of. Does not this theory demand a new miracle of its own (Kennett, *Interpreter*, V, 271)?

3. Third Proof: Transformation of the Disciples

The next line of proof to be considered is the transformation of the disciples caused by the resurrection. They had seen their Master die, and through that death they lost all hope. Yet hope returned three days after. On the day of the crucifixion they were filled with sadness; on the first day of the week with gladness. At the crucifixion they were hopeless; on the first day of the week their hearts glowed with certainty. When the message of the resurrection first came they were incredulous and hard to be convinced, but when once they became assured they never doubted again. What could account for the astonishing change in these men in so short a time? The mere removal of the body from the grave could never have transformed their spirits and characters. Three days are not enough for a legend to spring up which should so affect them. Time is needed for a process of legendary growth. There is nothing more striking in the history of primitive Christianity than this marvelous change wrought in the disciples by a belief in the resurrection of their Master. It is a psychological fact that demands a full explanation. The disciples were prepared to believe in the appearance of a spirit, but they never contemplated the possibility of a resurrection (see Mk **16** 11). Men do not imagine what they do not believe, and the women's intention to embalm a corpse shows they did not expect His resurrection. Besides, a hallucination involving five hundred people at once, and repeated several times during forty days, is unthinkable.

4. Fourth Proof: Existence of the Primitive Church

From this fact of the transformation of personal life in so incredibly short a space of time, we proceed to the next line of proof, the existence of the primitive church. "There is no doubt that the church of the apostles believed in the resurrection of their Lord" (Burkitt, *The Gospel History and Its Transmission*, 74). It is now admitted on all hands that the church of Christ came into existence as the result of a belief in the resurrection of Christ. When we consider its commencement, as recorded in the Book of the Acts of the Apostles, we see two simple and incontrovertible facts: (1) the Christian society was gathered together by preaching; (2) the substance of the preaching was the resurrection of Jesus Christ. Jesus Christ was put to death on a cross, and would therefore be rejected by Jews as accursed of God (Dt **21** 23). Yet multitudes of Jews were led to worship Him (Acts **2** 41), and a great company of priests to obey Him (Acts **6** 7). The only explanation of these facts is God's act of resurrection (Acts **2** 36), for nothing short of it could have led to the Jewish acceptance of Jesus Christ as their Messiah. The apostolic church is thus a result of a belief in the resurrection of Jesus Christ. The early chapters of Acts bear the marks of primitive documents, and their evidence is unmistakable. It is impossible to allege that the early church did not know its own history, that myths and legends quickly grew up and were eagerly received, and that the writers of the Gospels had no conscience for principle, but manipulated their material at will, for any modern church could easily give an account of its history for the past fifty years or more (Orr, *The Resurrection of Jesus*, 144). And it is simply absurd to think that the earliest church had no such capability. In reality there was nothing vague or intangible about the testimony borne by the apostles and other members of the church. "As the church is too holy for a foundation of rottenness, so she is too real for a foundation of mist" (Archbishop Alexander, *The Great Question*, 10).

5. Fifth Proof: The Witness of St. Paul

One man in the apostolic church must, however, be singled out as a special witness to the resurrection. The conversion and work of Saul of Tarsus is our next line of proof. Attention is first called to the evidence of his life and writings to the resurrection of Jesus Christ. Some years ago an article appeared (E. Medley, *Expos*, V, iv, 359), inquiring as to the conception of Christ which would be suggested to a heathen inquirer by a perusal of Paul's earliest extant writing (1 Thess). One point at least would stand out clearly—that Jesus Christ was killed (**2** 15; **4** 14) and was raised from the dead (**4** 14). As this Ep. is usually dated about 51 AD—that is, only about 22 years after the resurrection—and as the same Ep. plainly attributes to Jesus Christ the functions of God in relation to men (**1** 1.6; **2** 14; **3** 11), we can readily see the force of this testimony to the resurrection. Then a few years later, in an ep. which is universally accepted as one of St. Paul's, we have a much fuller reference to the event. In the well-known chapter (1 Cor **15**) where he is concerned to prove (not Christ's resurrection, but) the resurrection of Christians, he naturally adduces Christ's resurrection as his greatest evidence, and so gives a list of the various appearances of Christ, ending with one to himself, which he puts on an exact level with the others:

"Last of all he was seen of me also." Now it is essential to give special attention to the nature and particularity of this testimony. "I delivered unto you first of all that which also I received: that Christ died for our sins according to the scriptures; and that he was buried; and that he hath been raised on the third day according to the scriptures" (1 Cor **15** 3 f). This, as it has often been pointed out, is our earliest authority for the appearances of Christ after the resurrection, and dates from within 30 years of the event itself. But there is much more than this: "He affirms that within 5 years of the crucifixion of Jesus he was taught that 'Christ died for our sins according to the Scriptures; and that he was buried, and that he rose again the third day according to the Scriptures'" (Kennett, *Interpreter*, V, 267). And if we seek to appreciate the full bearing of this act and testimony we have a right to draw the same conclusion: "That within a very few years of the time of the crucifixion of Jesus, the evidence for the resurrection of Jesus was, in the mind of at least one man of education, absolutely irrefutable" (Kennett, op. cit., V, 267).

Besides, we find this narrative includes one small but significant statement which at once recalls a very definite feature of the Gospel tradition—the mention of "the third day." A reference to the passage in the Gospels where Jesus Christ spoke of His resurrection will show how prominent and persistent was this note of time. Why, then, should St. Paul have introduced it in his statement? Was it part of the teaching which he had "received"? What is the significance of this plain emphasis on the *date* of the resurrection? Is it not that it bears absolute testimony to the empty tomb? From all this it may be argued that St. Paul believed the story of the empty tomb at a date when the recollection was fresh, when he could examine it for himself, when he could make the fullest possible inquiry of others, and when the fears and opposition of enemies would have made it impossible for the adherents of Jesus Christ to make any statement that was not absolutely true. "Surely common sense requires us to believe that that for which he so suffered was in his eyes established beyond the possibility of doubt" (Kennett, op. cit., V, 271).

In view, therefore, of St. Paul's personal testimony to his own conversion, his interviews with those who had seen Jesus Christ on earth before and after His resurrection, and the prominence given to the resurrection in the apostle's own teaching, we may challenge attention afresh to this evidence for the resurrection. It is well known that Lord Lyttelton and his friend Gilbert West left Oxford University at the close of one academic year, each determining to give attention respectively during the long vacation to the conversion of St. Paul and the resurrection of Christ, in order to prove the baselessness of both. They met again in the autumn and compared experiences. Lord Lyttelton had become convinced of the truth of St. Paul's conversion, and Gilbert West of the resurrection of Jesus Christ. If, therefore, Paul's 25 years of suffering and service for Christ were a reality, his conversion was true, for everything he did began with that sudden change. And if his conversion was true, Jesus Christ rose from the dead, for everything Paul was and did he attributed to the sight of the risen Christ.

6. Sixth Proof: The Gospel Record

The next line of proof of the resurrection is the record in the Gospels of the appearances of the risen Christ, and it is the *last* in order to be considered. By some writers it is put first, but this is in forgetfulness of the dates when the Gospels were written. The resurrection was believed in by the Christian church for a number of years before our Gospels were written, and it is therefore impossible for these records to be our primary and most important evidence. We must get behind them if we are to appreciate fully the force and variety of the evidence. It is for this reason that, following the proper logical order, we have reserved to the last our consideration of the appearances of the risen Christ as given in the Gospels. The point is one of great importance (Denney, *Jesus and the Gospel*, 111).

Now, with this made clear, we proceed to consider the evidence afforded by the records of the post-resurrection appearances of Christ. Modern criticism of the Gospels during recent years has tended to adopt the view that Mk is the earliest, and that Mt and Lk are dependent on it. This is said to be "the one solid result" (W. C. Allen, "St. Matthew," *ICC*, Preface, vii; Burkitt, *The Gospel History*, 37) of the literary criticism of the Gospels. If this is so, the question of the records of the resurrection becomes involved in the difficult problem about the supposed lost ending of Mk, which, according to modern criticism, would thus close without any record of an appearance of the risen Christ. On this point, however, two things may be said at the present juncture: (1) There are some indications that the entire question of the criticism of the Gospels is to be reopened (Ramsay, *St. Luke the Physician*, ch ii; see also Orr, *The Resurrection of Jesus*, 63 ff). (2) Even if the current theory be accepted, it would not seriously weaken the intrinsic force of the evidence for the resurrection, because, after all, Mark does not invent or "doctor" his material, but embodies the common apostolic tradition of his time (Orr, *The Resurrection of Jesus*, 62).

We may, therefore, meanwhile examine the record of the appearances without finding them essentially affected by any particular theory of the origin and relations of the Gospels. There are two sets of appearances, one in Jerus and the other in Galilee, and their number, and the amplitude and weight of their testimony should be carefully estimated. While we are precluded by our space from examining each appearance minutely, and indeed it is unnecessary for our purpose to do so, it is impossible to avoid calling attention to two of them. No one can read the story of the walk to Emmaus (Lk **24**), or of the visit of Peter and John to the tomb (Jn **20**), without observing the striking marks of reality and personal testimony in the accounts. As to the former incident: "It carries with it, as great literary critics have pointed out, the deepest inward evidences of its own literal truthfulness. For it so narrates the intercourse of 'a risen God' with commonplace men as to set natural and supernatural side by side in perfect harmony. And to do this has always been the difficulty, the despair of imagination. The alternative has been put reasonably thus: St. Luke was either a greater poet, a more creative genius, than Shakespeare, or—he did not create the record. He had an advantage over Shakespeare. The ghost in Hamlet was an effort of laborious imagination. The risen Christ on the road was a fact supreme, and the Evangelist did but tell it as it was" (Bishop Moule, *Meditations for the Church's Year*, 108). Other writers whose attitude to the Gospel records is very different bear the same testimony to the impression of truth and reality made upon them by the Emmaus narrative (A. Meyer and K. Lake, quoted in Orr, *The Resurrection of Jesus*, 176 f).

It is well known that there are difficulties connected with the number and order of these appearances, but they are probably due largely to the summary character of the story, and certainly are not sufficient to invalidate the uniform testimony to the two facts: (1) the empty grave, (2) the appearances of Christ on the third day. These are the main facts of the combined witness (Orr, op. cit., 212).

The very difficulties which have been observed in the Gospels for nearly nineteen centuries are a testimony to a conviction of the truth of the narratives on the part of the whole Christian church. The church has not been afraid to leave these records as they are because of the facts that they embody and express. If there had been no difficulties men might have said that everything had been artificially arranged, whereas the differences bear testimony to the reality of the event recorded. The fact that we possess these two sets of appearances—one in Jerus and one in Galilee—is really an argument in favor of their credibility, for if it had been recorded that Christ appeared in Galilee only, or Jerus only, it is not unlikely that the account might have been rejected for lack of support. It is well known that records of eyewitnesses often vary in details, while there is no question as to the events themselves. The various books recording the story of the Indian mutiny, or the surrender of Napoleon III at Sedan are cases in point, and Sir William Ramsay has shown the entire compatibility of certainty as to the main fact with great uncertainty as to precise details (Ramsay, *St. Paul the Traveller*, 29). We believe, therefore, that a careful examination of these appearances will afford evidence of a chain of circumstances extending from the empty grave to the day of the ascension.

When we examine carefully all these converging lines of evidence and endeavor to give weight to all the facts of the case, it seems impossible to escape from the problem of a physical miracle. That the prima facie view of the evidence afforded by the NT suggests a miracle and that the apostles really believed in a true physical resurrection are surely beyond all question. And yet very much of present-day thought refuses to accept the miraculous. The scientific doctrine of the uniformity and continuity of Nature bars the way, so that from the outset it is concluded that miracles are impossible. We are either not allowed to believe (see Orr, *The Resurrection of Jesus*, 44), or else we are told that we are not required to believe (C. H. Robinson, *Studies in the Resurrection of Christ*, ch ii), in the reanimation of a dead body. If we take this view, "there is no need, really, for investigation of evidence: the question is decided before the evidence is looked at" (Orr, op. cit., 46).

7. Summary and Conclusion

We challenge the tenableness of this position. It proves too much. We are not at all concerned by the charge of believing in the abnormal or unusual. New things have happened from the beginning of the present natural order, and the Christian faith teaches that Christ Himself was a "new thing," and that His coming as "God manifest in the flesh" was something absolutely unique. If we are not allowed to believe in any Divine intervention which we may call supernatural or miraculous, it is impossible to account for the Person of Christ at all. "A Sinless Personality would be a miracle in time." Arising out of this, Christianity itself was unique, inaugurating a new era in human affairs. No Christian, therefore, can have any difficulty in accepting the abnormal, the unusual, the miraculous. If it be said that no amount of evidence can establish a fact which is miraculous, we have still to account for the moral miracles which are really involved and associated with the resurrection, esp. the deception of the disciples, who could have found out the truth of the case; a deception, too, that has proved so great a blessing to the world. Surely to those who hold a true theistic view of the world this a priori view is impossible. Are we to refuse to allow to God at least as much liberty as we possess ourselves? Is it really thinkable that God has less spontaneity of action than we have? *We* may like or dislike, give or withhold, will or not will, but the course of Nature must flow on unbrokenly. Surely God cannot be conceived of as having given such a constitution to the universe as limits His power to intervene if necessary and for sufficient purpose with the work of His own hands. Not only are all things *of* Him, but all things are *through* Him, and *to* Him. The resurrection means the presence of miracle, and "there is no evading the issue with which this confronts us" (Orr, *The Resurrection of Jesus*, 53). Unless, therefore, we are prepared to accept the possibility of the miraculous, all explanation of the NT evidence is a pure waste of time.

Of recent years attempts have been made to account for the resurrection by means of ideas derived from Bab and other Eastern sources. It is argued that mythology provides the key to the problem, that not only analogy but derivation is to be found. But apart from the remarkable variety of conclusions of Bab archaeologists there is nothing in the way of historical proof worthy of the name. The whole idea is arbitrary and baseless, and prejudiced by the attitude to the supernatural. There is literally no link of connection between these oriental cults and the Jewish and Christian beliefs in the resurrection.

And so we return to a consideration of the various lines of proof. Taking them singly, they must be admitted to be strong, but taking them altogether, the argument is cumulative and sufficient. Every effect must have its adequate cause, and the only proper explanation of Christianity today is the resurrection of Christ. Thomas Arnold of Rugby, no mean judge of historical evidence, said that the resurrection was the "best-attested fact in human history." Christianity welcomes all possible sifting, testing, and use by those who honestly desire to arrive at the truth, and if they will give proper attention to all the facts and factors involved, we believe they will come to the conclusion expressed years ago by the Archbishop of Armagh, that the resurrection is the rock from which all the hammers of criticism have never chipped a single fragment (*The Great Question*, 24).

8. Theology of the Resurrection

The theology of the resurrection is very important and calls for special attention. Indeed, the prominence given to it in the NT affords a strong confirmation of the fact itself, for it seems incredible that such varied and important truths should not rest on historic fact. The doctrine may briefly be summarized: (1) *evidential:* the resurrection is the proof of the atoning character of the death of Christ, and of His Deity and Divine exaltation (Rom **1** 4); (2) *evangelistic:* the primitive gospel included testimony to the resurrection as one of its characteristic features, thereby proving to the hearers the assurance of the Divine redemption (1 Cor **15** 1–4; Rom **4** 25); (3) *spiritual:* the resurrection is regarded as the source and standard of the holiness of the believer. Every aspect of the Christian life from the beginning to the end is somehow associated therewith (Rom **6**); (4) *eschatological:* the resurrection is the guaranty and model of the believer's resurrection (1 Cor **15**). As the bodies of the saints arose (Mt **27** 52), so ours are to be quickened (Rom **8** 11), and made like Christ's glorified body (Phil **3** 21), thereby becoming spiritual bodies (1 Cor **15** 44), that is, bodies ruled by their spirits and yet bodies. These points offer only the barest outline of the fulness of NT teaching concerning the doctrine of the resurrection of Christ.

LITERATURE.—Orr, *The Resurrection of Jesus*, 1908; W. J. Sparrow Simpson, *The Resurrection and Modern Thought;* Westcott, *The Historic Faith* and *The Gospel of the Resurrection*. Very full literary references in Bowen, *The Resurrection in the NT*, 1911, which, although negative in its own conclusions, contains a valuable refutation of many negative arguments.

W. H. GRIFFITH THOMAS

RETAIN, rḗ-tān′: Several Heb words are thus tr^{d}: חָזַק, *ḥāzaḳ*, "to hold fast" (Jgs **7** 8; **19** 4; Job **2** 9 AV [RV "hold fast"]; Mic **7** 18); עָצַר, *'āçar*, "to shut up" (only in Dnl **10** 8.16; **11** 6); תָּמַךְ, *tāmakh*, "to hold" (Prov **3** 18; **4** 4; **11** 16 AV [RV "obtain"]); in one case *kālā'* (Eccl **8** 8). In the NT κρατέω, *kratéō*, is used in Jn **20** 23 of the "retaining" of sins by the apostles (see RETENTION OF SINS); in Rom **1** 28, RV has "refused to have," m "Gr, 'did not approve,'" for AV "did not like to retain" (*échō*); and in Philem ver 13, substitutes "fain have kept" for "retained" (*katéchō*). Sir **41** 16 has "retain" for *diaphulássō*, "keep."

RETALIATION, rḗ-tal-i-ā′shun, rē-. See LAW IN THE NT; PUNISHMENTS; RETRIBUTION.

RETENTION, rḗ-ten′shun, **OF SINS** (κρατέω, *kratéō*, "to lay fast hold of" [Jn **20** 23]): The opposite of "the remission of sins." Where there was no evidence of repentance and faith, the community of believers were unauthorized to give assurance of forgiveness, and, therefore, could only warn that the guilt of sin was retained, and that the sinner remained beneath God's judgment.

While such retention has its place in connection with all preaching of the gospel, since the offers of grace are conditional, it is esp. exercised, like the absolution, in the personal dealing of a pastor with a communicant, preparatory to the reception of the Lord's Supper. As the absolution is properly an assurance of individual forgiveness, so the retention is an assurance of individual non-forgiveness. That the retention is exercised by the ministry, not as an order, but as the representatives of the congregation of believers to which Christ gave the power of the keys, is shown by Alford, *Gr Test.*, on above passage. See also Melanchthon, *Appendix* to the "Schmalkald Articles."

H. E. JACOBS

RETRIBUTION, ret-ri-bū'shun:

1. NT Terms
2. A Revelation of Wrath as Well as Grace
3. Witness of Natural Theology
4. Retribution the Natural Consequence of Sin
5. Also the Positive Infliction of Divine Wrath
6. Instances of Use of *orgḗ* and *thumós*
7. Instances of Use of Greek Words for "Vengeance"
8. Words Meaning "Chastisement" Not Used of the Impenitent
9. Judgment Implies Retribution
10. Moral Sense Demands Vindication of God's Righteousness
11. Scripture Indicates Certainty of Vindication

LITERATURE

The word as applied to the Divine administration is not used in Scripture, but undoubtedly the idea is commonly enough expressed. The words which come nearest to it are ὀργή, *orgḗ*, and θυμός, *thumós*, wrath attributed to God; ἐκδικέω, *ekdikéō*, ἐκδίκησις, *ekdíkēsis*, ἔκδικος, *ékdikos*, and δίκη, *díkē*, all giving the idea of vengeance; κόλασις, *kólasis*, and τιμωρία, *timōría*, "punishment"; besides κρίνω, *krínō*, and its derivatives, words expressive of judgment.

1. NT Terms

Rom **2** is full of the thought of retribution. The apostle, in vs 5.6, comes very near to using the word itself, and gives indeed a good description of the thing: the day of wrath and revelation of the righteous judgment of God, "who will render to every man according to his works." It is well in approaching the subject to remind ourselves that there is undoubtedly, as the apostle says, a *Revelation of wrath.* We are so accustomed to think of the gracious revelation which the gospel brings us, and to approach the subject of the doom of the impenitent under the influence of the kindly sentiments engendered thereby, and with a view of God's gracious character as revealed in salvation, that we are apt to overlook somewhat the sterner facts of sin, and to misconceive the Divine attitude toward the impenitent sinner. It is certainly well that we should let the grace of the gospel have full influence upon all our thinking, but we must beware of being too fully engrossed with one phase of the Divine character. It is an infirmity of human nature that we find it difficult to let two seemingly conflicting conceptions find a place in our thought. We are apt to surrender ourselves to the sway of one or the other of them according to the pressure of the moment.

2. A Revelation of Wrath as Well as Grace

Putting ourselves back into the position of those who have only the light of natural theology, we find that all deductions from the perfections of God, as revealed in His works, combined with a consideration of man's sin and want of harmony with the Holy One, lead to the conclusion announced by the apostle: "The wrath of God is revealed from heaven against all ungodliness and unrighteousness of men" (Rom **1** 18). Wrath implies punishment, punishment is decreed, punishment is denounced. The word of God but confirms the verdict which conscience forecasts. Nature teaches that punishment, retribution, must follow sin. Within the sphere of physical law this is clearly exemplified. No breach of the so-called laws of Nature is tolerated. Strictly speaking, the laws of Nature cannot be broken, but let a man fail to keep in harmony with them, and the natural consequences will be trouble, punishment, retribution. Harmony with law is blessing; collision with law is loss. Thus law in Nature "worketh wrath" to the neglecters of it. Punishment necessarily results. So we may well expect that in the higher sphere, God's moral laws cannot be neglected or violated with impunity, and Scripture fully justifies the expectation and shows that sin must be punished. All things considered, the fact of punishment for sinners need not surprise; the fact of pardon is the surprising thing. The surprise of pardon has ceased to surprise us because we are so familiar with the thought. We know the "how" of it because of the revelation of grace. Grace, however, saves on certain conditions, and there is no such thing known in Scripture as indiscriminate, necessary, universal grace. It is only from the Bible that we know of the salvation by grace. That same revelation shows that the grace does not come to all, in the sense of saving all; though, of course, it may be considered as presented to all. Those who are not touched and saved by grace remain shut up in their sins. They are, and must be, in the nature of the case, left to the consequences of their sins, with the added guilt of rejecting the offered grace. "Except ye believe that I am he," said Incarnate Grace, "ye shall die in your sins" (Jn **8** 24).

3. Witness of Natural Theology

Another conclusion we may draw from the general Scriptural representation is that the future retribution is one aspect of the *natural consequence of sin*, yet it is also in another aspect the *positive infliction of Divine wrath.* It is shown to be the natural outcome of sin in such passages as "Whatsoever a man soweth, that shall he also reap" (Gal **6** 7); "He that soweth unto his own flesh shall of the flesh reap corruption" (Gal **6** 8). It is not without suggestiveness that the Heb word *'āwōn* means both iniquity and punishment, and when Cain said "My punishment is greater than I can bear" (Gen **4** 13), he really said "My iniquity is greater than I can bear"; his iniquity became his punishment. A due consideration of this thought goes a long way toward meeting many of the objections brought against the doctrine of future punishment.

4. Retribution the Natural Consequence of Sin

The other statement, however, remains true and must be emphasized, that there is an *actual infliction of Divine wrath.* All the great statements about the Divine judgment imply this, and while it is wrong not to take account of the natural working out of sin in its terrible consequences, it is equally wrong, perhaps more so, to refuse to recognize this positive Divine infliction of punishment. This, indeed, is the outstanding feature of retribution as it assumes form in Scripture. Even the natural consequences of sin, rightly viewed, are part of the Divine infliction, since God, in the nature of things, has conjoined sin and its consequences, and part of the positive infliction is the judicial shutting up of the sinner to the consequences of his sin. So in the case of Cain, his iniquity became his punishment, inasmuch as God sentenced him to bear the consequences of that iniquity. On the other hand, we might say that even the terribly positive outpourings of God's wrath upon the sinner are the natural consequences of sin, since sin in its very

5. Also the Positive Infliction of Divine Wrath

nature calls down the Divine displeasure. Indeed, these two phases of future punishment are so very closely connected that a right view of the matter compels us to keep both before us, and no full explanation of the punishment is possible when either phase is ignored.

6. Instances of Use of *orgḗ* and *thumós*

The terms in Scripture applied to the doom of sinners all imply Divine displeasure, punitive action, retribution. The two outstanding Gr words for "wrath," *orgē* and *thumos*, are both freely applied to God. *Orgē* indicates settled displeasure, whereas *thumos* is rather the blazing out of the anger. The former is, as we should expect, more frequently applied to God, and, of course, all that is capricious and reprehensible in human wrath must be eliminated from the word as used of God. It indicates the settled opposition of His holy nature against sin. It was an affection found in the sinless Saviour Himself, for "he looked round about on them with anger" (Mk **3** 5). In the Baptist's warning "to flee from the wrath to come" (Mt **3** 7; Lk **3** 7), it is unquestionably the wrath of God that is meant, the manifestation of that being further described as the burning of the chaff with unquenchable fire (Mt **3** 12). In Jn **3** 36 it is said of the unbeliever that "the wrath of God" abideth on him. In Rom it is used at least 9 t in reference to God, first in Rom **1** 18, the great passage we have already quoted about "the wrath of God revealed from heaven." The connection is a suggestive one and is often overlooked. In the passage Paul has quite a chain of reasons; he is ready to preach the gospel at Rome *for* he is not ashamed of the gospel; he is not ashamed of the gospel *for* it is the power of God unto salvation; it is the "power of God" *for* therein is revealed the righteousness of God by faith; and this salvation by faith is a necessity "*for* the wrath of God is revealed," etc. Thus the Divine wrath on account of sin is the dark background of the gospel message. Had there been no such just wrath upon men, there had been no need for the Divine salvation. The despising of God's goodness by the impenitent means a treasuring up of "wrath in the day of wrath and revelation of the righteous judgment of God" (Rom **2** 3–5). God "visiteth with wrath" (**3** 5).

In Rom **4** 15 the apostle shows that "the law worketh wrath" (i.e. brings down the Divine displeasure), while in **5** 9 he shows that believers are saved from wrath—undoubted wrath of God. The other two instances are in **9** 22. Men are "by nature children of wrath" (Eph **2** 3); surely not "wrathful children," but liable to the wrath of God, and because of evil deeds cometh "the wrath of God upon the sons of disobedience" (Eph **5** 6; Col **3** 6). Christ "delivereth us from the wrath to come" (1 Thess **1** 10); wrath has come upon the opposing Jews (**2** 16); but believers are not appointed unto wrath (**5** 9). With all these specific passages in view, to say nothing of the general teaching of the apostle on the question of coming judgment and punishment, it is utterly impossible to eliminate the idea of the Divine displeasure against sinners, and His consequent retributive action toward them. Even Ritschl, who absolutely denies the great principle of retribution, of positive displeasure, admits that Paul teaches it; hence the only way for him out of the difficulty is to reject Paul's teaching as unauthoritative. Other references to the "wrath of God" are in He **3** 11; **4** 3; and 6 passages in the Apocalypse—Rev **6** 16 f; **11** 18; **14** 10; **16** 19; **19** 15. Two of these refer to the "wrath of the Lamb," one of the most terrible phrases in the whole of the NT. *Thumos* is only used in the Apocalypse concerning God (Rev **14** 10–19; **15** 1–7; **16** 1–19; **19** 15). In each case it refers to the manifestation, the blazing forth of the wrath; in the last two passages it is used in combination with *orgē*, and is rendered "fierceness," the fierceness of His wrath.

7. Greek Use of Words for "Vengeance"

Ekdikeō, which means to avenge, is twice used of God (Rev **6** 10; **19** 2); and *ekdikēsis*, "vengeance," 6 t (Lk **18** 7 ff; Rom **12** 19; 2 Thess **1** 8; He **10** 30). In the first two instances it is used by Jesus concerning the Divine action; *ekdikos*, "avenger," occurs once in application to God (1 Thess **4** 6); *dikē*, "judgment" or "vengeance" is twice used of God (2 Thess **1** 9; Jude ver 7). The use of these terms shows that the punishment inflicted on sinful men is strictly punishment of the vindicatory sort, the vindication of outraged justice, the infliction of deserved penalty. Very significant is the passage in 2 Thess **1** 6, "It is a righteous thing with God to recompense affliction to them that afflict you." There is no question of bettering the offender.

8. Words Meaning "Chastisement" Not Used of the Impenitent

It is very remarkable that the terms in Gr which would carry the meaning of punishment for the good of the offender are never used in the NT of the infliction which comes upon the impenitent; these are *paideía* and *paideúō*, and they are frequently used of the "chastisement" of believers, but not of the impenitent. It is often claimed that the word *kolasis* used in Mt **25** 46 carries the meaning of chastisement for the improvement of the offender, but although Aristotle, in comparing it with *timōria*, may seem to suggest that it is meant for the improvement of the offender (what he really says is that it is *toú páschontos héneka*, "on account of the one suffering it," "has the punished one in view," whereas *timōria* is *toú poioúntos*, "on account of the one inflicting" "that he may be satisfied"), the usage even in classical Gr is predominantly against making the supposed distinction. Both words are used interchangeably by the leading classical authors, including Aristotle himself, and *kolasis* is continually employed where no thought of betterment can be in question, while all admit that in Hellenistic Gr the distinction is not maintained, and in any case *timōria* is also used of the punishment of the sinner (He **10** 29).

9. Judgment Implies Retribution

All the representations of the coming day of judgment tell of the fact of retribution, and Christ Himself distinctly asserts it. Apart from His great eschatological discourses, concerning which criticism still hesitates and stammers, we have the solemn close of the Sermon on the Mount, and the pregnant statement of Mt **16** 27, "The Son of man shall come in the glory of his Father with his angels; and then shall he render unto every man according to his deeds," and all the apostolic teaching upon the solemn theme is but the unfolding of the same great thought.

10. Moral Sense Demands Vindication of God's Righteousness

The conception of God as a perfect moral governor demands that His righteousness shall be fully vindicated. Looking at the course of history as it unfolds itself before us, we cannot fail to be struck with the anomalies which are presented. Righteousness does not always triumph, goodness is often put to shame, wickedness appears to be profitable, and wicked men often prosper while good men are under a cloud. Sometimes signal Divine interpositions proclaim that God is indeed on the side of righteousness, but too often it seems as if He were unmindful, and men are tempted to ask the old question, "How doth God know? And is there knowledge in the Most High?" (Ps **73** 11), while the righteous say in their distress, "Jeh, how long shall the wicked, how long shall the wicked triumph?" (Ps **94** 3). The moral sense cries out for some Divine vindication, and the Scriptures, in harmony with this feeling, indicate that the final judgment will bring such vindication.

In the OT it is frequently presented as the solution of the baffling problems which beset the ethical sphere, as for instance in that fine utterance of religious philosophy in Ps **73**; the Psalmist has before him all the puzzling elements of the problem; the prosperity, the insolent and aggressive prosperity of the wicked, the non-success, the oppression, the misery of the righteous; he is well-nigh overwhelmed by the contemplation, and nearly loses his footing on the eternal verities, until he carries the whole problem into the light of God's presence and revelation, and then he understands that the *end* will bring the true solution.

11. Scripture Indicates Certainty of Vindication

So too the somber ruminations of the Preacher upon the contradictions and anomalies and mysteries of human life, "under the sun," close in the reflection which throws its searchlight upon all the blackness: "This is the end of the matter: . . . . Fear God, and keep his commandments; for this is the whole duty of man. For God will bring every work into judgment, with every hidden thing, whether it be good, or whether it be evil" (Eccl **12** 13 f). In the light of the same truth, the apostles labored, believing that when the Lord comes He "will both bring to light the hidden things of darkness, and make manifest the counsels of the hearts" (1 Cor **4** 5). The more fully the subject is considered, the more we must feel that for the vindication of righteousness, the justification of the Divine procedure, the rectification of wrongs, the explanation of mysteries, the reward and triumph of the righteous and the confession and punishment of the wicked, a great final, retributive judgment is Scriptural, reasonable, necessary.

LITERATURE.—See arts. on PUNISHMENT, EVERLASTING; JUDGMENT; SHEOL, etc, and works cited there.

ARCHIBALD M'CAIG

REU, rē'ū, rōō (רְעוּ, r^e'ū; **Ῥαγαύ**, *Rhagaú*): A son of Peleg, a descendant of Shem (Gen **11** 18 ff; 1 Ch **1** 25; Lk **3** 35).

REUBEN, rōō'ben, rū'ben (רְאוּבֵן, r^e'ūbhēn; **Ῥουβήν**, *Rhoubḗn*): The eldest son of Jacob, born to him by Leah in Paddan-aram (Gen **29** 32). This verse seems to suggest two derivations of the name. As it stands in MT it means "behold a son"; but the reason given for so calling him is "The Lord hath looked upon my affliction," which in Heb is *rā'āh* b^e*'onyī*, lit. "He hath seen my affliction." Of his boyhood we have only the story of the mandrakes (Gen **30** 14). As the firstborn he should really have been leader among his father's sons. His birthright was forfeited by a deed of peculiar infamy (**35** 22), and as far as we know his tribe never took the lead in Israel. It is named first, indeed, in Nu **1** 5.20, but thereafter it falls to the fourth place, Judah taking the first (**2** 10, etc). To Reuben's intervention Joseph owed his escape from the fate proposed by his other brethren (Gen **37** 29). Some have thought Reuben designed to set him free, from a desire to rehabilitate himself with his father. But there is no need to deny to Reuben certain noble and chivalrous qualities. Jacob seems to have appreciated these, and, perhaps, therefore all the more deeply lamented the lapse that spoiled his life (Gen **49** 3 f). It was Reuben who felt that their perils and anxieties in Egypt were a fit recompense for the unbrotherly conduct (**42** 22). To assure his father of Benjamin's safe return from Egypt, whither Joseph required him to be taken, Reuben was ready to pledge his own two sons (ver 37). Four sons born to him in Canaan went down with Reuben at the descent of Israel into Egypt (**46** 8 f).

1. Jacob's Eldest Son

The incidents recorded are regarded by a certain school of OT scholars as the vague and fragmentary traditions of the tribe, wrought into the form of a biography of the supposed ancestor of the tribe. This interpretation raises more difficulties than it solves, and depends for coherence upon too many assumptions and conjectures. The narrative as it stands is quite intelligible and self-consistent. There is no good reason to doubt that, as far as it goes, it is an authentic record of the life of Jacob's son.

At the first census in the wilderness Reuben numbered 46,500 men of war (Nu **1** 21); at the second they had fallen to 43,730; see NUMBERS. The standard of the camp of Reuben was on the south side of the tabernacle; and with him were Simeon and Gad; the total number of fighting men in this division being 151,450. Tg Pseudojon says that the standard was a deer, with the legend "Hear O Israel, the Lord thy God is one Lord." On the march this division took the second place (Nu **2** 10 ff). The prince of the tribe was Elizur ben Shedeur, whose oblation is described in **7** 30 ff. The Reubenite among the spies was Shammua ben Zaccur (**13** 4). It is possible that the conspiracy against Moses, organized by the Reubenites Dathan and Abiram, with the assistance of Korah the Levite (Nu **16**), was an attempt on the part of the tribe to assert its rights as representing the firstborn. It is significant that the children of Korah did not perish (**26** 11). May not the influence of this incident on Moses' mind be traced in his "blessing," wishing for the continuance of the tribe, indeed, but not in great strength (Dt **33** 6)? This was a true forecast of the tribal history.

2. Tribal History

When the high plateau E. of the Dead Sea and the Jordan fell into the hands of the Israelite invaders, these spacious pastoral uplands irresistibly attracted the great flock-masters of Reuben and Gad, two tribes destined to be neighbors during succeeding centuries. At their earnest request Moses allowed them their tribal possessions here subject to one condition, which they loyally accepted. They should not "sit here," and so discourage their brethren who went to war beyond the Jordan. They should provide for the security of their cattle, fortify cities to protect their little ones and their wives from the inhabitants of the land, and their men of war should go before the host in the campaign of conquest until the children of Israel should have inherited every man his inheritance (Nu **32** 1–27). Of the actual part they took in that warfare there is no record, but perhaps "the stone of Bohan the son of Reuben" (Josh **15** 6; **18** 17) marked some memorable deed of valor by a member of the tribe. At the end of the campaign the men of Reuben, having earned the gratitude of the western tribes, enriched by their share of the spoils of the enemy, returned with honor to their new home. Along with their brethren of Gad they felt the dangers attaching to their position of isolation, cut off from the rest of their people by the great cleft of the Jordan valley. They reared therefore the massive altar of Ed in the valley, so that in the very throat of that instrument of severance there might be a perpetual witness to themselves and to their children of the essential unity of Israel. The western tribes misunderstood the action and, dreading religious schism, gathered in force to stamp it out. Explanations followed which were entirely satisfactory, and a threatening danger was averted (Josh **22**). But the instincts of the eastern tribes were right, as subsequent history was to prove. The Jordan valley was but one of many causes of sundering. The whole circumstances and conditions of life on the E. differed widely from those on the W. of the river, pastoral pursuits and life in the open being contrasted with agricultural and city life.

The land given by Moses to the tribe of Reuben reached from the Arnon, *Wâdy el-Mōjib*, in the S., to the border of Gad in the N. In Nu **32** 34 cities of Gad are named which lay far S., Aroer being on the very lip of the Arnon; but these are probably to be taken as an enclave in the territory of Reuben. From Josh **13** 15 ff it is clear that the northern border ran from some point N. of the Dead Sea in a direction E.N.E., passing to the N. of Heshbon. The Dead Sea formed the western boundary, and it marched with the desert on the E. No doubt many districts changed hands in the course of the history. At the invasion of Tiglath-pileser, e.g., we read that Aroer was in the hands of the Reubenites, "and eastward . . . . even unto the entrance of the wilderness from the river Euphrates" (1 Ch **5** 8 f). Bezer the city of refuge lay in Reuben's territory (Josh **20** 8, etc). A general description of the country will be found under MOAB; while the cities of Reuben are dealt with in separate articles.

Reuben and Gad, occupying contiguous districts, and even, as we have seen, to some extent overlapping, are closely associated in the history. Neither took part in the glorious struggle against Sisera (Jgs **5** 15 ff). Already apparently the sundering influences were taking effect. They are not excepted, however, from "all the tribes of Israel" who sent contingents for the war against Benjamin (Jgs **20** 10; **21** 5), and the reference in **5** 15 seems to show that Reuben might have done great things had he been disposed. The tribe therefore was still powerful, but perhaps absorbed by anxieties as to its relations with neighboring peoples. In guarding their numerous flocks against attack from the S., and sudden incursions from the desert, a warlike spirit and martial prowess were developed. They were "valiant men, men able to bear buckler and sword, and to shoot with bow, and skilful in war" (1 Ch **5** 18). They overwhelmed the Hagrites with Jetur and Naphish and Nodab, and greatly enriched themselves with the spoil. In recording the raid the Chronicler pays a compliment to their religious loyalty: "They cried to God in the battle, and he was entreated of them, because they put their trust in him" (**5** 19 ff). Along with Gad and Manasseh they sent a contingent of 120,000 men "with all manner of instruments of war for the battle, ... men of war, that could order the battle array," men who "came with a perfect heart to Hebron, to make David king" (**12** 37 f). Among David's mighty men was Adina, "a chief of the Reubenites, and thirty with him" (**11** 42). In the 40th year of David's reign overseers were set over the Reubenites "for every matter pertaining to God, and for the affairs of the king" (**26** 32). Perhaps in spite of the help given to David the Reubenites had never quite got over their old loyalty to the house of Saul. At any rate, when disruption came they joined the Northern Kingdom (1 K **11** 31).

The subsequent history of the tribe is left in much obscurity. Exposed as they were to hostile influences of Moab and the East, and cut off from fellowship with their brethren in worship, in their isolation they probably found the descent into idolatry all too easy, and the once powerful tribe sank into comparative insignificance. Of the immediate causes of this decline we have no knowledge. Moab established its authority over the land that had belonged to Reuben; and Mesha, in his inscription (M S), while he speaks of Gad, does not think Reuben worthy of mention. They had probably become largely absorbed in the northern tribe. They are named as suffering in the invasion of Hazael during the reign of Jehu (2 K **10** 32 f). That "they trespassed against the God of their fathers, and played the harlot after the gods of the peoples of the land" is given as the reason for the fate that befell them at the hands of Pul, king of Assyria, who carried them away, "and brought them unto Halah, and Habor, and Hara, and to the river of Gozan" (1 Ch **5** 25 f).

The resemblance of Reuben's case to that of Simeon is striking, for Simeon also appears to have been practically absorbed in the tribe of Judah. The prestige that should have been Reuben's in virtue of his birthright is said to have passed to Joseph (1 Ch **5** 1). And the place of Reuben and Simeon in Israel is taken by the sons of Joseph, a fact referred to in the blessing of Jacob (Gen **48** 5).

Ezekiel finds a place for Reuben in his picture of restored Israel (**48** 6). He appears also—in this case preceded by Judah only—in Rev **7** 5.

W. EWING

REUBENITES, rōō'ben-īts (הָרְאוּבֵנִי, *hā-re'ū-bhēnī;* **δῆμοι Ῥουβήν,** *dēmoi Rhoubēn*): Members of the tribe of Reuben (Nu **26** 7, etc). Adina, one of David's mighty men, was a Reubenite (1 Ch **11** 42).

REUEL, rōō'el (רְעוּאֵל, *re'ū'ēl*, "God is his friend"; LXX **Ῥαγουήλ,** *Rhagouēl*):

(1) In the genealogical system Reuel is both a son of Esau by Basemath (Gen **36** 4.10.13.17; 1 Ch **1** 35.37) and the father of the father-in-law of Moses, Hobab (Nu **10** 29). In the account of the marriage of Zipporah to Moses (Ex **2** 16–21) Jethro seems to be called Reuel (cf HOBAB). The various names of Jethro perplexed the Talmudists, too; some held that his real name was "Hobab," and that Reuel was his father. Reuel is probably a clan name (Gray, "Nu," *ICC*), and Hobab is a member of the clan ("son") of Reuel (Nu **10** 29 AV reads "Raguel").

(2) The father of Eliasaph, the prince of Gad (Nu **2** 14), called (by some copyist's mistake) "Deuel" in **1** 14; **7** 42.47; **10** 20. LXX has uniformly *Rhagouēl.*

(3) A Benjamite (1 Ch **9** 8).

HORACE J. WOLF

REUMAH, rōō'ma (רְאוּמָה, *re'ūmāh*): The concubine of Nahor (Gen **22** 24).

REVELATION, rev-ē-lā'shun:

I. THE NATURE OF REVELATION
   1. The Religion of the Bible the Only Supernatural Religion
   2. General and Special Revelation
      (1) Revelation in Eden
      (2) Revelation among the Heathen
II. THE PROCESS OF REVELATION
   1. Place of Revelation among the Redemptive Acts of God
   2. Stages of Material Development
III. THE MODES OF REVELATION
   1. The Several Modes of Revelation
   2. Equal Supernaturalness of the Several Modes
   3. The Prophet God's Mouthpiece
   4. Visionary Form of Prophecy
   5. "Passivity" of Prophets
   6. Revelation by Inspiration
   7. Complete Revelation of God in Christ
IV. BIBLICAL TERMINOLOGY
   1. The Ordinary Forms
   2. "Word of the Lord" and "Torah"
   3. "The Scriptures"
LITERATURE

I. The Nature of Revelation.—The religion of the Bible is a frankly supernatural religion. By this is not meant merely that, according to it, all men, as creatures, live, move and have their being in God. It is meant that, according to it, God has intervened extraordinarily, in the course of the sinful world's development, for the salvation of men otherwise lost. In Eden the Lord God had been present with sinless man in such a sense as to form a distinct element in his social

1. The Religion of the Bible the Only Supernatural Religion

environment (Gen **3** 8). This intimate association was broken up by the Fall. But God did not therefore withdraw Himself from concernment with men. Rather, He began at once a series of interventions in human history by means of which man might be rescued from his sin and, despite it, brought to the end destined for him. These interventions involved the segregation of a people for Himself, by whom God should be known, and whose distinction should be that God should be "nigh unto them" as He was not to other nations (Dt **4** 7; Ps **145** 18). But this people was not permitted to imagine that it owed its segregation to anything in itself fitted to attract or determine the Divine preference; no consciousness was more poignant in Israel than that Jeh had chosen it, not it Him, and that Jeh's choice of it rested solely on His gracious will. Nor was this people permitted to imagine that it was for its own sake alone that it had been singled out to be the sole recipient of the knowledge of Jeh; it was made clear from the beginning that God's mysteriously gracious dealing with it had as its ultimate end the blessing of the whole world (Gen **12** 2.3; **17** 4.5.6.16; **18** 18; **22** 18; cf Rom **4** 13), the bringing together again of the divided families of the earth under the glorious reign of Jeh, and the reversal of the curse under which the whole world lay for its sin (Gen **12** 3). Meanwhile, however, Jeh was known only in Israel. To Israel God showed His word and made known His statutes and judgments, and after this fashion He dealt with no other nation; and therefore none other knew His judgments (Ps **147** 19 f). Accordingly, when the hope of Israel (who was also the desire of all nations) came, His own lips unhesitatingly declared that the salvation He brought, though of universal application, was "from the Jews" (Jn **4** 22). And the nations to which this salvation had not been made known are declared by the chief agent in its proclamation to them to be, meanwhile, "far off," "having no hope" and "without God in the world" (Eph **2** 12), because they were aliens from the commonwealth of Israel and strangers from the covenant of the promise.

The religion of the Bible thus announces itself, not as the product of men's search after God, if haply they may feel after Him and find Him, but as the creation in men of the gracious God, forming a people for Himself, that they may show forth His praise. In other words, the religion of the Bible presents itself as distinctively a revealed religion. Or rather, to speak more exactly, it announces itself as the revealed religion, as the only revealed religion; and sets itself as such over against all other religions, which are represented as all products, in a sense in which it is not, of the art and device of man.

It is not, however, implied in this exclusive claim to revelation—which is made by the religion of the Bible in all the stages of its history—that the living God, who made the heaven and the earth and the sea and all that in them is, has left Himself without witness among the peoples of the world (Acts **14** 17). It is asserted indeed, that in the process of His redemptive work, God suffered for a season all the nations to walk in their own ways; but it is added that to none of them has He failed to do good, and to give from heaven rains and fruitful seasons, filling their hearts with food and gladness. And not only is He represented as thus constantly showing Himself in His providence not far from any one of them, thus wooing them to seek Him if haply they might feel after Him and find Him (Acts **17** 27), but as from the foundation of the world openly manifesting Himself to them in the works of His hands, in which His everlasting power and Divinity are clearly seen (Rom **1** 20). That men at large have not retained Him in their knowledge, or served Him as they ought, is not due therefore to failure on His part to keep open the way to knowledge of Him, but to the darkening of their senseless hearts by sin and to the vanity of their sin-deflected reasonings (Rom **1** 21 ff), by means of which they have supplanted the truth of God by a lie and have come to worship and serve the creature rather than the ever-blessed Creator. It is, indeed, precisely because in their sin they have thus held down the truth in unrighteousness and have refused to have God in their knowledge (so it is intimated); and because, moreover, in their sin, the revelation God gives of Himself in His works of creation and providence no longer suffices for men's needs, that God has intervened supernaturally in the course of history to form a people for Himself, through whom at length all the world should be blessed.

It is quite obvious that there are brought before us in these several representations two species or stages of revelation, which should be discriminated to avoid confusion.

2. General and Special Revelation

There is the revelation which God continuously makes to all men: by it His power and Divinity are made known. And there is the revelation which He makes exclusively to His chosen people: through it His saving grace is made known. Both species or stages of revelation are insisted upon throughout the Scriptures. They are, for example, brought significantly together in such a declaration as we find in Ps **19**: "The heavens declare the glory of God .... their line is gone out through all the earth" (vs 1.4); "The law of Jeh is perfect, restoring the soul" (ver 7). The Psalmist takes his beginning here from the praise of the glory of God, the Creator of all that is, which has been written upon the very heavens, that none may fail to see it. From this he rises, however, quickly to the more full-throated praise of the mercy of Jeh, the covenant God, who has visited His people with saving instruction. Upon this higher revelation there is finally based a prayer for salvation from sin, which ends in a great threefold acclamation, instinct with adoring gratitude: "O Jeh, my rock, and my redeemer" (ver 14). "'The heavens,'" comments Lord Bacon, "indeed tell of the glory of God, but not of His will according to which the poet prays to be pardoned and sanctified." In so commenting, Lord Bacon touches the exact point of distinction between the two species or stages of revelation. The one is adapted to man as man; the other to man as sinner; and since man, on becoming sinner, has not ceased to be man, but has only acquired new needs requiring additional provisions to bring him to the end of his existence, so the revelation directed to man as sinner does not supersede that given to man as man, but supplements it with these new provisions for his attainment, in his new condition of blindness, helplessness and guilt induced by sin, of the end of his being.

These two species or stages of revelation have been commonly distinguished from one another by the distinctive names of natural and supernatural revelation, or general and special revelation, or natural and soteriological revelation. Each of these modes of discriminating them has its particular fitness and describes a real difference between the two in nature, reach or purpose. The one is communicated through the media of natural phenomena, occurring in the course of Nature or of history; the other implies an intervention in the natural course of things and is not merely in source but in mode supernatural. The one is addressed generally to all intelligent creatures, and is therefore accessible to all men; the other is addressed to a special class of sinners, to whom God would make known His salvation. The one has in view to meet and supply the natural need of creatures for knowledge of their God; the other to rescue broken and deformed sinners from their sin and its consequences. But, though thus distinguished from one another, it is important that the two species or stages of revelation should not be set in opposition to one another, or the closeness of their mutual relations or the constancy of their interaction be obscured. They constitute together a unitary whole, and each is incomplete without the other. In its most general idea, revelation is rooted in creation and the relations with His intelligent creatures into which God has brought Himself by giving them being. Its object is to realize the end of man's creation, to be attained only through knowledge of God and perfect and unbroken communion with Him. On the entrance of sin into the world, destroying this communion with God and obscuring the knowledge of Him derived from Nature, another mode of revelation was necessitated, having also another content, adapted to the new relation to God and the new conditions of intellect, heart and will brought about by sin. It must not be supposed, however, that this new mode of revelation was an *ex post facto* expedient, introduced to meet an unforeseen contingency. The actual course of human development was in the nature of the case the expected and the intended course of human development, for which man was created; and revelation, therefore, in its double form was the Divine purpose for man from the beginning, and constitutes a unitary provision for the realization of the end of his creation in the actual circumstances in which he exists. We may distinguish in this unitary revelation the two elements by the coöperation of which the effect is produced; but we should bear in mind that only by their coöperation is the effect produced. Without special revelation, general revelation would be for sinful men incomplete and ineffective, and could issue, as in point of fact it has issued wherever it alone has been accessible, only in leaving them without excuse (Rom **1** 20). Without general revelation, special revelation would lack that basis in the fundamental knowledge of God as the mighty and wise, righteous and good maker and ruler of all things, apart from which the further revelation of this great God's interventions in the world for the salvation of sinners could not be either intelligible, credible or operative.

(1) *Revelation in Eden.*—Only in Eden has general revelation been adequate to the needs of man. Not being a sinner, man in Eden had no need of that grace of God itself by which sinners are restored to communion with Him, or of the special revelation of this grace of God to sinners to enable them to live with God. And not being a sinner, man in Eden, as he contemplated the works of God, saw God in the unclouded mirror of his mind with a clarity of vision, and lived with Him in the untroubled depths of his heart with a trustful intimacy of association, inconceivable to sinners. Nevertheless, the revelation of God in Eden was not merely "natural." Not only does the prohibition of the forbidden fruit involve a positive commandment (Gen **2** 16), but the whole history implies an immediacy of intercourse with God which cannot easily be set to the credit of the picturesque art of the narrative, or be fully accounted for by the vividness of the perception of God in His works proper to sinless creatures. The impression is strong that what is meant to be conveyed to us is that man dwelt with God in Eden, and enjoyed with Him immediate and not merely mediate communion. In that case, we may understand that if man had not fallen, he would have continued to enjoy immediate intercourse with God, and that the cessation of this immediate intercourse is due to sin. It is not then the supernaturalness of special revelation which is rooted in sin, but, if we may be allowed the expression, the specialness of supernatural revelation. Had man not fallen, heaven would have continued to lie about him through all his history, as it lay about his infancy; every man would have enjoyed direct vision of God and immediate speech with Him. Man having fallen, the cherubim and the flame of a sword, turning every way, keep the path; and God breaks His way in a round-about fashion into man's darkened heart to reveal there His redemptive love. By slow steps and gradual stages He at once works out His saving purpose and molds the world for its reception, choosing a people for Himself and training it through long and weary ages, until at last when the fulness of time has come, He bares His arm and sends out the proclamation of His great salvation to all the earth.

(2) *Revelation among the heathen.*—Certainly, from the gate of Eden onward, God's general revelation ceased to be, in the strict sense, supernatural. It is, of course, not meant that God deserted His world and left it to fester in its iniquity. His providence still ruled over all, leading steadily onward to the goal for which man had been created, and of the attainment of which in God's own good time and way the very continuance of men's existence, under God's providential government, was a pledge. And His Spirit still everywhere wrought upon the hearts of men, stirring up all their powers (though created in the image of God, marred and impaired by sin) to their best activities, and to such splendid effect in every department of human achievement as to command the admiration of all ages, and in the highest region of all, that of conduct, to call out from an apostle the encomium that though they had no law they did by nature (observe the word "nature") the things of the law. All this, however, remains within the limits of Nature, that is to say, within the sphere of operation of Divinely directed and assisted second causes. It illustrates merely the heights to which the powers of man may attain under the guidance of providence and the influences of what we have learned to call God's "common grace." Nowhere, throughout the whole ethnic domain, are the conceptions of God and His ways put within the reach of man, through God's revelation of Himself in the works of creation and providence, transcended; nowhere is the slightest knowledge betrayed of anything concerning God and His purposes, which could be known only by its being supernaturally told to men. Of the entire body of "saving truth," for example, which is the burden of what we call "special revelation," the whole heathen world remained in total ignorance. And even its hold on the general truths of religion, not being vitalized by supernatural enforcements, grew weak, and its knowledge of the very nature of God decayed, until it ran out to the dreadful issue which Paul sketches for us in that inspired philosophy of religion which he incorporates in the latter part of the first chapter of the Ep. to the Rom.

Behind even the ethnic development, there lay, of course, the supernatural intercourse of man with God which had obtained before the entrance of sin into the world, and the supernatural revelations at the gate of Eden (Gen **3** 8), and at the second origin of the human race, the Flood (Gen **8** 21.22; **9** 1–17). How long the tradition of this primitive revelation lingered in nooks and corners of the heathen world, conditioning and vitalizing the natural revelation of God always accessible, we have no means of estimating. Neither is it easy to measure the effect of God's special revelation of Himself to His people upon men outside the bounds of, indeed, but coming into contact with, this chosen people, or sharing with them a common natural inheritance. Lot and Ishmael and Esau can scarcely have been wholly ignorant of the word of God which came to Abraham and Isaac and Jacob; nor could the Egyptians from whose hands God wrested His people with a mighty arm fail to learn something of Jeh, any more than the mixed multitudes who witnessed the ministry of Christ could fail to infer something from His gracious walk and mighty works. It is natural to infer that no nation which was intimately associated with Israel's life could remain entirely unaffected by Israel's revelation. But whatever impressions were thus conveyed reached apparently individuals only: the heathen which surrounded Israel, even those most closely affiliated with Israel, remained heathen; they had no revelation. In the sporadic instances when God visited an alien with a supernatural communication—such as the dreams sent to Abimelech (Gen **20**) and to Pharaoh (Gen **40, 41**) and to Nebuchadnezzar (Dnl **2** 1 ff) and to the soldier in the camp of Midian (Jgs **7** 13)—it was in the interests, not of the heathen world, but of the chosen people that they were sent; and these instances derive their significance wholly from this fact. There remain, no doubt, the mysterious figure of Melchizedek, perhaps also of Jethro, and the strange apparition of Balaam, who also, however, appear in the sacred narrative only in connection with the history of God's dealings with His people and in their interest. Their unexplained appearance cannot in any event avail to modify the general fact that the life of the heathen peoples lay outside the supernatural revelation of God. The heathen were suffered to walk in their own ways (Acts **14** 16).

II. The Process of Revelation.—Meanwhile, however, God had not forgotten them, but was preparing salvation for them also through the supernatural revelation of His grace that He was making to His people. According to the Bib. representation, in the midst of and working confluently with the revelation which He has always been giving of Himself on the plane of Nature, God was making also from the very fall of man a further revelation of Himself on the plane of grace. In contrast with His general, natural revelation, in which all men by virtue of their very nature as men share, this special, supernatural revelation was granted at first only to individuals, then progressively to a family, a tribe, a nation, a race, until, when the fulness of time was come, it was made the possession of the whole world. It may be difficult to obtain from Scripture a clear account of why God chose thus to give this revelation of His grace only progressively; or, to be more explicit, through the process of a historical development. Such is, however, the ordinary mode of the Divine working: it is so that God made the worlds, it is so that He creates the human race itself, the recipient of this revelation, it is so that He builds up His kingdom in the world and in the individual soul, which only gradually comes whether to the knowledge of God or to the fruition of His salvation. As to the fact, the Scriptures are explicit, tracing for us, or rather embodying in their own growth, the record of the steady advance of this gracious revelation through definite stages from its first faint beginnings to its glorious completion in Jesus Christ.

1. Place of Revelation among the Redemptive Acts of God

So express is its relation to the development of the kingdom of God itself, or rather to that great series of Divine operations which are directed to the building up of the kingdom of God in the world, that it is sometimes confounded with them or thought of as simply their reflection in the contemplating mind of man. Thus it is not infrequently said that revelation, meaning this special redemptive revelation, has been communicated in deeds, not in words; and it is occasionally elaborately argued that the sole manner in which God has revealed Himself as the Saviour of sinners is just by performing those mighty acts by which sinners are saved. This is not, however, the Bib. representation. Revelation is, of course, often made through the instrumentality of deeds; and the series of His great redemptive acts by which He saves the world constitutes the preëminent revelation of the grace of God—so far as these redemptive acts are open to observation and are perceived in their significance. But revelation, after all, is the correlate of understanding and has as its proximate end just the production of knowledge, though not, of course, knowledge for its own sake, but for the sake of salvation. The series of the redemptive acts of God, accordingly, can properly be designated "revelation" only when and so far as they are contemplated as adapted and designed to produce knowledge of God and His purpose and methods of grace. No bare series of unexplained acts can be thought, however, adapted to produce knowledge, esp. if these acts be, as in this case, of a highly transcendental character. Nor can this particular series of acts be thought to have as its main design the production of knowledge; its main design is rather to save man. No doubt the production of knowledge of the Divine grace is one of the means by which this main design of the redemptive acts of God is attained. But this only renders it the more necessary that the proximate result of producing knowledge should not fail; and it is doubtless for this reason that the series of redemptive acts of God has not been left to explain itself, but the explanatory word has been added to it. Revelation thus appears, however, not as the mere reflection of the redeeming acts of God in the minds of men, but as a factor in the redeeming work of God, a component part of the series of His redeeming acts, without which that series would be incomplete and so far inoperative for its main end. Thus the Scriptures represent it, not confounding revelation with the series of the redemptive acts of God, but placing it among the redemptive acts of God and giving it a function as a substantive element in the operations by which the merciful God saves sinful men. It is therefore not made even a mere constant accompaniment of the redemptive acts of God, giving their explanation that they may be understood. It occupies a far more independent place among them than this, and as frequently precedes them to prepare their way as it accompanies or follows them to interpret their meaning. It is, in one word, itself a redemptive act of God and by no means the least important in the series of His redemptive acts.

This might, indeed, have been inferred from its very nature, and from the nature of the salvation which was being wrought out by these redemptive acts of God. One of the most grievous of the effects of sin is the deformation of the image of God reflected in the human mind, and there can be no recovery from sin which does not bring with it the correction of this deformation and the reflection in the soul of man of the whole glory of the Lord God Almighty. Man is an intelligent being; his superiority over the brute is found, among other things, precisely in the direction of all his life by his intelligence; and his blessedness is rooted in the true knowledge of his God—for this is life eternal, that we should know the only true God and Him whom He has sent. Dealing with man as an intelligent being, God the Lord has saved him by means of a revelation, by which he has been brought into an ever more and more adequate knowledge of God, and been led ever more and more to do his part in working out his own salvation with fear and trembling as he perceived with ever more and more clearness how God is working it out for him through mighty deeds of grace.

2. Stages of Material Development

This is not the place to trace, even in outline, from the material point of view, the development of God's redemptive revelation from its first beginnings, in the promise given to Abraham—or rather in what has been called the Protevangelium at the gate of Eden—to its completion in the advent and work of Christ and the teaching of His apostles; a steadily advancing development, which, as it lies spread out to view in the pages of Scripture, takes to those who look at it from the consummation backward, the appearance of the shadow cast athwart preceding ages by the great figure of Christ. Even from the formal point of view, however, there has been pointed out a progressive advance in the method of revelation, consonant with its advance in content, or rather with the advancing stages of the building up of the kingdom of God, to subserve which is the whole object of revelation. Three distinct steps in revelation have been discriminated from this point of view. They are distinguished precisely by the increasing independence of revelation of the deeds constituting the series of the redemptive acts of God, in which, nevertheless, all revelation is a substantial element. Discriminations like this must not be taken too absolutely; and in the present instance the chronological sequence cannot be pressed. But, with much interlacing, three generally successive stages of revelation may be recognized, producing periods at least characteristically of what we may somewhat conventionally call theophany, prophecy and inspiration. What may be somewhat indefinitely marked off as the Patriarchal age is characteristically "the period of Outward Manifestations, and Symbols, and Theophanies": during it "God spoke to men through their senses, in physical phenomena, as the burning bush, the cloudy pillar, or in sensuous forms, as men, angels, etc. . . . . In the Prophetic age, on the contrary, the prevailing mode of revelation was by means of inward prophetic inspiration": God spoke to men characteristically by the movements of the Holy Spirit in their hearts. "Prevailingly, at any rate from Samuel downwards, the supernatural revelation was a revelation in the hearts of the foremost thinkers of the people, or, as we call it, prophetic inspiration, without the aid of external sensuous symbols of God" (A. B. Davidson, *OT Prophecy*, 1903, p. 148; cf pp. 12–14, 145 ff). This internal method of revelation reaches its culmination in the NT period, which is preëminently the age of the Spirit. What is esp. characteristic of this age is revelation through the medium of the written word, what may be called apostolic as distinguished from prophetic inspiration. The revealing Spirit speaks through chosen men as His organs, but through these organs in such a fashion that the most intimate processes of their souls become the instruments by means of which He speaks His mind. Thus at all events there are brought clearly before us three well-marked modes of revelation, which we may perhaps designate respectively, not with perfect discrimination, it is true, but not misleadingly, (1) external manifestation, (2) internal suggestion, and (3) concursive operation.

III. Modes of Revelation.—Theophany may be taken as the typical form of "external manifestation"; but by its side may be ranged all of those mighty works by which God makes Himself known, including express miracles, no doubt, but along with them every supernatural intervention in the affairs of men, by means of which a better understanding is communicated of what God is or what are His purposes of grace to a sinful race. Under "internal suggestion" may be subsumed all the characteristic phenomena of what is most properly spoken of as "prophecy": visions and dreams, which, according to a fundamental passage (Nu **12** 6), constitute the typical forms of prophecy, and with them the whole "prophetic word," which shares its essential characteristic with visions and dreams, since it comes not by the will of man but from God. By "concursive operation" may be meant that form of revelation illustrated in an inspired psalm or epistle or history, in which no human activity—not even the control of the will—is superseded, but the Holy Spirit works in, with and through them all in such a manner as to communicate to the product qualities distinctly superhuman. There is no age in the history of the religion of the Bible, from that of Moses to that of Christ and His apostles, in which all these modes of revelation do not find place. One or another may seem particularly characteristic of this age or of that; but they all occur in every age. And they occur side by side, broadly speaking, on the same level. No discrimination is drawn between them in point of worthiness as modes of revelation, and much less in point of purity in the revelations communicated through them. The circumstance that God spoke to Moses, not by dream or vision but mouth to mouth, is, indeed, adverted to (Nu **12** 8) as a proof of the peculiar favor shown to Moses and even of the superior dignity of Moses above other organs of revelation: God admitted him to an intimacy of intercourse which He did not accord to others. But though Moses was thus distinguished above all others in the dealings of God with him, no distinction is drawn between the revelations given through him and those given through other organs of revelation in point either of Divinity or of authority. And beyond this we have no Scriptural warrant to go on in contrasting one mode of revelation with another. Dreams may seem to us little fitted to serve as vehicles of Divine communications. But there is no suggestion in Scripture that revelations through dreams stand on a lower plane than any others; and we should not fail to remember that the essential characteristics of revelations through dreams are shared by all forms of revelation in which (whether we should call them visions or not) the images or ideas which fill, or pass in procession through, the consciousness are determined by some other power than the recipient's own will. It may seem natural to suppose that revelations rise in rank in proportion to the fulness of the engagement of the mental activity of the recipient in their reception. But we should bear in mind that the intellectual or spiritual quality of a revelation is not derived from the recipient but from its Divine Giver. The fundamental fact in all revelation is that it is from God. This is what gives unity to the whole process of revelation, given though it may be in divers portions and in divers manners and distributed though it may be through the ages in accordance with the mere will of God, or as it may have suited His developing purpose—this and its unitary end, which is ever the building up of the kingdom of God. In whatever diversity of forms, by means of whatever variety of modes, in whatever distinguishable stages it is given, it is ever the revelation of the One God, and it is ever the one consistently developing redemptive revelation of God.

1. Modes of Revelation

2. Equal Supernaturalness of the Several Modes

On a prima facie view it may indeed seem likely that a difference in the quality of their supernaturalness would inevitably obtain between revelations given through such divergent modes. The completely supernatural character of revelations given in theophanies is obvious. He who will not allow that God speaks to man, to make known His gracious purposes toward him, has no other recourse here than to pronounce the stories legendary. The objectivity of the mode of communication which is adopted is intense, and it is thrown up to observation with the greatest emphasis. Into the natural life of man God intrudes in a purely supernatural manner, bearing a purely supernatural communication. In these communications we are given accordingly just a series of "naked messages of God." But not even in the Patriarchal age were all revelations given in theophanies or objective appearances. There were dreams, and visions, and revelations without explicit intimation in the narrative of how they were communicated. And when we pass on in the history, we do not, indeed, leave behind us theophanies and objective appearances. It is not only made the very characteristic of Moses, the greatest figure in the whole history of revelation except only that of Christ, that he knew God face to face (Dt **34** 10), and God spoke to him mouth to mouth, even manifestly, and not in dark speeches (Nu **12** 8); but throughout the whole history of revelation down to the appearance of Jesus to Paul on the road to Damascus, God has shown Himself visibly to His servants whenever it has seemed good to Him to do so and has spoken with them in objective speech. Nevertheless, it is expressly made the characteristic of the Prophetic age that God makes Himself known to His servants "in a vision," "in a dream" (Nu **12** 6). And although, throughout its entire duration, God, in fulfilment of His promise (Dt

18 18), put His words in the mouths of His prophets and gave them His commandments to speak, yet it would seem inherent in the very employment of men as instruments of revelation that the words of God given through them are spoken by human mouths; and the purity of their supernaturalness may seem so far obscured. And when it is not merely the mouths of men with which God thus serves Himself in the delivery of His messages, but their minds and hearts as well—the play of their religious feelings, or the processes of their logical reasoning, or the tenacity of their memories, as, say, in a psalm or in an epistle, or a history—the supernatural element in the communication may easily seem to retire still farther into the background. It can scarcely be a matter of surprise, therefore, that question has been raised as to the relation of the natural and the supernatural in such revelations, and, in many current manners of thinking and speaking of them, the completeness of their supernaturalness has been limited and curtailed in the interests of the natural instrumentalities employed. The plausibility of such reasoning renders it the more necessary that we should observe the unvarying emphasis which the Scriptures place upon the absolute supernaturalness of revelation in all its modes alike. In the view of the Scriptures, the completely supernatural character of revelation is in no way lessened by the circumstance that it has been given through the instrumentality of men. They affirm, indeed, with the greatest possible emphasis that the Divine word delivered through men is the pure word of God, diluted with no human admixture whatever.

3. The Prophet God's Mouthpiece

We have already been led to note that even on the occasion when Moses is exalted above all other organs of revelation (Nu **12** 6 ff), in point of dignity and favor, no suggestion whatever is made of any inferiority, in either the directness or the purity of their supernaturalness, attaching to other organs of revelation. There might never afterward arise a prophet in Israel like unto Moses, whom the Lord knew face to face (Dt **34** 10). But each of the whole series of prophets raised up by Jeh that the people might always know His will was to be like Moses in speaking to the people only what Jeh commanded them (Dt **18** 15.18.20). In this great promise, securing to Israel the succession of prophets, there is also included a declaration of precisely how Jeh would communicate His messages not so much to them as through them. "I will raise them up a prophet from among their brethren, like unto thee," we read (Dt **18** 18), *"and I will put my words in his mouth*, and he shall speak unto them all that I shall command him." The process of revelation through the prophets was a process by which Jeh put His words in the mouths of the prophets, and the prophets spoke precisely these words and no others. So the prophets themselves ever asserted. "Then Jeh put forth his hand, and touched my mouth," explains Jeremiah in his account of how he received his prophecies, "and Jeh said unto me, Behold, I have put my words in thy mouth" (Jer **1** 9; cf **5** 14; Isa **51** 16; **59** 21; Nu **22** 35; **23** 5. 12.16). Accordingly, the words "with which" they spoke were not their own but the Lord's: "And he said unto me," records Ezekiel, "Son of man, go, get thee unto the house of Israel, and speak with my words unto them" (Ezk **3** 4). It is a process of nothing other than "dictation" which is thus described (2 S **14** 3.19), though, of course, the question may remain open of the exact processes by which this dictation is accomplished. The fundamental passage which brings the central fact before us in the most vivid manner is, no doubt, the account of the commissioning of Moses and Aaron given in Ex **4** 10–17; **7** 1–7. Here, in the most express words, Jeh declares that He who made the mouth can be with it to teach it what to speak, and announces the precise function of a prophet to be that he is "a mouth of God," who speaks not his own but God's words. Accordingly, the Heb name for "prophet" (*nābhī'*), whatever may be its etymology, means throughout the Scriptures just "spokesman," though not "spokesman" in general, but spokesman by way of eminence, that is, God's spokesman; and the characteristic formula by which a prophetic declaration is announced is: "The word of Jeh came to me," or the brief "saith Jeh" (נְאֻם יהוה, *n^e'um Yahweh*). In no case does a prophet put his words forward as his own words. That he is a prophet at all is due not to choice on his own part, but to a call of God, obeyed often with reluctance; and he prophesies or forbears to prophesy, not according to his own will but as the Lord opens and shuts his mouth (Ezk **3** 26 f) and creates for him the fruit of the lips (Isa **57** 19; cf **6** 7; **50** 4). In contrast with the false prophets, he strenuously asserts that he does not speak out of his own heart ("heart" in Bib. language includes the whole inner man), but all that he proclaims is the pure word of Jeh.

4. Prophecy in Vision-Form

The fundamental passage does not quite leave the matter, however, with this general declaration. It describes the characteristic manner in which Jeh communicates His messages to His prophets as through the medium of visions and dreams. Neither visions in the technical sense of that word, nor dreams, appear, however, to have been the customary mode of revelation to the prophets, the record of whose revelations has come down to us. But, on the other hand, there are numerous indications in the record that the universal mode of revelation to them was one which was in some sense a vision, and can be classed only in the category distinctively so called.

The whole nomenclature of prophecy presupposes, indeed, its vision-form. Prophecy is distinctively a word, and what is delivered by the prophets is proclaimed as the "word of Jeh." That it should be announced by the formula, "Thus saith the Lord," is, therefore, only what we expect; and we are prepared for such a description of its process as: "The Lord Jeh . . . . wakeneth mine ear to hear," He "hath opened mine ear" (Isa **50** 4.5). But this is not the way of speaking of their messages which is most usual in the prophets. Rather is the whole body of prophecy cursorily presented as a thing seen. Isaiah places at the head of his book: "The vision of Isaiah . . . . which he saw" (cf Isa **29** 10.11; Ob ver 1); and then proceeds to set at the head of subordinate sections the remarkable words, "The word that Isaiah . . . . saw" (**2** 1); "the burden [m "oracle"] . . . . which Isaiah . . . . did see" (**13** 1). Similarly there stand at the head of other prophecies: "the words of Amos . . . . which he saw" (Am **1** 1); "the word of Jeh that came to Micah . . . . which he saw" (Mic **1** 1); "the oracle which Habakkuk the prophet did see" (Hab **1** 1 m); and elsewhere such language occurs as this: "the word that Jeh hath showed me" (Jer **38** 21); "the prophets have seen . . . . oracles" (Lam **2** 14); "the word of Jeh came . . . . and I looked, and, behold" (Ezk **1** 3.4); "Woe unto the foolish prophets, that follow their own spirit, and have seen nothing" (Ezk **13** 3); "I . . . . will look forth to see what he will speak with me, ... Jeh . . . . said, Write the vision" (Hab **2** 1 f). It is an inadequate explanation of such language to suppose it merely a relic of a time when vision was more predominantly the form of revelation. There is no proof that vision in the technical sense ever was more predominantly the form of revelation than in the days of the great writing prophets; and such language as we have quoted too obviously represents the living point of view of the prophets to admit of the supposition that it was merely conventional on their lips. The prophets, in a word, represent the Divine communications which they received as given to them in some sense in visions.

It is possible, no doubt, to exaggerate the significance of this. It is an exaggeration, for example, to insist that therefore all the Divine communications made to the prophets must have come to them in external appearances and objective speech, addressed to and received by means of the bodily eye and ear. This would be to break down the distinction between manifestation and revelation, and to assimilate the mode of prophetic revelation to that granted to Moses, though these are expressly distinguished (Nu **12** 6–8). It is also an exaggeration to insist that therefore the prophetic state must be conceived as that of strict ecstasy, involving the complete abeyance of all mental life on the part of the prophet (*amentia*), and possibly also accompanying physical effects. It is quite clear from the records which the prophets themselves give us of their revelations that their intelligence was alert in all stages of their reception of them. The purpose of both these extreme views is the good one of doing full justice to the objectivity of the revelations vouchsafed to the prophets. If these revelations took place entirely externally to the prophet, who merely stood off and contemplated them, or if they were implanted in the prophets by a process so violent as not only to supersede their mental activity but, for the time being, to annihilate it, it would be quite clear that they came from a source other than the prophets' own minds. It is undoubtedly the fundamental contention of the prophets that the revelations given through them are not their own but wholly God's. The significant language we have just quoted from Ezk **13** 3: "Woe unto the foolish prophets, that follow their own spirit, and have seen nothing," is a typical utterance of their sense of the complete objectivity of their messages. What distinguishes the false prophets is precisely that they "prophesy out of their own heart" (Ezk **13** 2-17), or, to draw the antithesis sharply, that "they speak a vision of their own heart, and not out of the mouth of Jeh" (Jer **23** 16.26; **14** 14). But these extreme views fail to do justice, the one to the equally important fact that the word of God, given through the prophets, comes as the pure and unmixed word of God not merely to, but from, the prophets; and the other to the equally obvious fact that the intelligence of the prophets is alert throughout the whole process of the reception and delivery of the revelation made through them (see INSPIRATION; PROPHECY).

That which gives to prophecy as a mode of revelation its place in the category of visions, strictly so called, and dreams is that it shares with them the distinguishing characteristic which determines the class. In them all alike the movements of the mind are determined by something extraneous to the subject's will, or rather, since we are speaking of supernaturally given dreams and visions, extraneous to the totality of the subject's own psychoses. A power not himself takes possession of his consciousness and determines it according to its will. That power, in the case of the prophets, was fully recognized and energetically asserted to be Jeh Himself or, to be more specific, the Spirit of Jeh (1 S **10** 6.10; Neh **9** 30; Zec **7** 12; Joel **2** 28.29). The prophets were therefore 'men of the Spirit' (Hos **9** 7). What constituted them prophets was that the Spirit was put upon them (Isa **42** 1) or poured out on them (Joel **2** 28.29), and they were consequently filled with the Spirit (Mic **3** 8), or, in another but equivalent locution, that "the hand" of the Lord, or "the power of the hand" of the Lord, was upon them (2 K **3** 15; Ezk **1** 3; **3** 14.22; **33** 22; **37** 1; **40** 1), that is to say, they were under the Divine control. This control is represented as complete and compelling, so that, under it, the prophet becomes not the "mover," but the "moved" in the formation of his message. The apostle Peter very purely reflects the prophetic consciousness in his well-known declaration: 'No prophecy of scripture comes of private interpretation; for prophecy was never brought by the will of man; but it was as borne by the Holy Spirit that men spoke from God' (2 Pet **1** 20.21).

5. "Passivity" of the Prophets

What this language of Peter emphasizes—and what is emphasized in the whole account which the prophets give of their own consciousness—is, to speak plainly, the passivity of the prophets with respect to the revelation given through them. This is the significance of the phrase: 'it was as borne by the Holy Spirit that men spoke from God.' To be "borne" (φέρειν, *phĕrein*) is not the same as to be led (ἄγειν, *ágein*), much less to be guided or directed (ὁδηγεῖν, *hodēgeín*): he that is "borne" contributes nothing to the movement induced, but is the object to be moved. The term "passivity" is, perhaps, however, liable to some misapprehension, and should not be overstrained. It is not intended to deny that the intelligence of the prophets was active in the reception of their message; it was by means of their active intelligence that their message was received: their intelligence was the instrument of revelation. It is intended to deny only that their intelligence was active in the production of their message: that it was creatively as distinguished from receptively active. For reception itself is a kind of activity. What the prophets are solicitous that their readers shall understand is that they are in no sense co-authors with God of their messages. Their messages are given them, given them entire, and given them precisely as they are given out by them. God speaks through them: they are not merely His messengers, but "His mouth." But at the same time their intelligence is active in the reception, retention and announcing of their messages, contributing nothing to them but presenting fit instruments for the communication of them—instruments capable of understanding, responding profoundly to and zealously proclaiming them.

There is, no doubt, a not unnatural hesitancy abroad in thinking of the prophets as exhibiting only such merely receptive activities. In the interests of their personalities, we are asked not to represent God as dealing mechanically with them, pouring His revelations into their souls to be simply received as in so many buckets, or violently wresting their minds from their own proper action that He may do His own thinking with them. Must we not rather suppose, we are asked, that all revelations must be "psychologically mediated," must be given "after the mode of moral mediation," and must be made first of all their recipients' "own spiritual possession"? And is not, in point of fact, the personality of each prophet clearly traceable in his message, and that to such an extent as to compel us to recognize him as in a true sense its real author? The plausibility of such questionings should not be permitted to obscure the fact that the mode of the communication of the prophetic messages which is suggested by them is directly contradicted by the prophets' own representations of their relations to the revealing Spirit. In the prophets' own view they were just instruments through whom God gave revelations which came from them, not as their own product, but as the pure word of Jeh. Neither should the plausibility of such questionings blind us to their speciousness. They exploit subordinate considerations, which are not without their validity in their own place and under their own limiting conditions, as if they were the determining or even the sole considerations in the case, and in neglect of the really determining considerations. God is Himself the author of the instruments He employs for the communication of His messages to men and has framed them into precisely the instruments He desired for the exact communication of His message. There is just ground for the expectation that He will use all the instruments He employs according to their natures; intelligent beings therefore as intelligent beings, moral agents as moral agents. But there is no just ground for asserting that God is incapable of employing the intelligent beings He has Himself created and formed to His will, to proclaim His messages purely as He gives them to them; or of making truly the possession of rational minds conceptions which they have themselves had no part in creating. And there is no ground for imagining that God is unable to frame His own message in the language of the organs of His revelation without its thereby ceasing to be, because expressed in a fashion natural to these organs, therefore purely His message. One would suppose it to lie in the very nature of the case that if the Lord makes any revelation to men, He would do it in the language of men; or, to individualize more explicitly, in the language of the man He employs as the organ of His revelation; and that naturally means, not the language of his nation or circle merely, but his own particular language, inclusive of all that gives individuality to his self-expression. We may speak of this, if we will, as "the accommodation of the revealing God to the several prophetic individualities." But we should avoid thinking of it externally and therefore mechanically, as if the revealing Spirit artificially phrased the message which He gives through each prophet in the particular forms of speech proper to the individuality of each, so as to create the illusion that the message comes out of the heart of the prophet himself. Precisely what the prophets affirm is that their messages do not come out of their own hearts and do not represent the workings of their own spirits. Nor is there any illusion in the phenomenon we are contemplating; and it is a much more intimate, and, we may add, a much more interesting phenomenon than an external "accommodation" of speech to individual habitudes. It includes, on the one hand, the "accommodation" of the prophet, through his total preparation, to the speech in which the revelation to be given through him is to be clothed; and on the other involves little more than the consistent carrying into detail of the broad principle that God uses the instruments He employs in accordance with their natures.

No doubt, on adequate occasion, the very stones might cry out by the power of God, and dumb beasts speak, and mysterious voices sound forth from the void; and there have not been lacking instances in which men have been compelled by the same power to speak what they would not, and in languages whose very sounds were strange to their ears. But ordinarily when God the Lord would speak to men He avails Himself of the services of a human tongue with which to speak, and He employs this tongue according to its nature as a tongue and according to the particular nature of the tongue which He employs. It is vain to say that the message delivered through the instrumentality of this tongue is conditioned at least in its form by the tongue by which it is spoken, if not, indeed, limited, curtailed, in some degree determined even in its matter, by it. Not only was it God the Lord who made the tongue, and who made this particular tongue with all its peculiarities, not without regard to the message He would deliver through it; but His control of it is perfect and complete, and it is as absurd to say that He cannot speak His message by it purely without that message suffering change from the peculiarities of its tone and modes of enunciation, as it would be to say that no new truth can be announced in any language because the elements of speech by the combination of which the truth in question is announced are already in existence with their fixed range of connotation. The marks of the several individualities imprinted on the messages of the prophets, in other words, are only a part of the general fact that these messages are couched in human language, and in no way beyond that general fact affect their purity as direct communications from God.

6. Revelation by Inspiration

A new set of problems is raised by the mode of revelation which we have called "concursive operation." This mode of revelation differs from prophecy, properly so called, precisely by the employment in it, as is not done in prophecy, of the total personality of the organ of revelation, as a factor. It has been common to speak of the mode of the Spirit's action in this form of revelation, therefore, as an assistance, a superintendence, a direction, a control, the meaning being that the effect aimed at—the discovery and enunciation of Divine truth—is attained through the action of the human powers—historical research, logical reasoning, ethical thought, religious aspiration—acting not by themselves, however, but under the prevailing assistance, superintendence, direction, control of the Divine Spirit. This manner of speaking has the advantage of setting this mode of revelation sharply in contrast with prophetic revelation, as involving merely a determining, and not, as in prophetic revelation, a supercessive action of the revealing Spirit. We are warned, however, against pressing this discrimination too far by the inclusion of the whole body of Scripture in such passages as 2 Pet **1** 20 f in the category of prophecy, and the assignment of their origin not to a mere "leading" but to the "bearing" of the Holy Spirit. In any event such terms as assistance, superintendence, direction, control, inadequately express the nature of the Spirit's action in revelation by "concursive operation." The Spirit is not to be conceived as standing outside of the human powers employed for the effect in view, ready to supplement any inadequacies they may show and to supply any defects they may manifest, but as working confluently in, with and by them, elevating them, directing them, controlling them, energizing them, so that, as His instruments, they rise above themselves and under His inspiration do His work and reach His aim. The product, therefore, which is attained by their means is His product through them. It is this fact which gives to the process the right to be called actively, and to the product the right to be called passively, a revelation. Although the circumstance that what is done is done by and through the action of human powers keeps the product in form and quality in a true sense human, yet the confluent operation of the Holy Spirit throughout the whole process raises the result above what could by any possibility be achieved by mere human powers and constitutes it expressly a supernatural product. The human traits are traceable throughout its whole extent, but at bottom it is a Divine gift, and the language of Paul is the most proper mode of speech that could be applied to it: "Which things also we speak, not in words which man's wisdom teacheth, but which the Spirit teacheth" (1 Cor **2** 13); "The things which I write unto you . . . . are the commandment of the Lord" (1 Cor **14** 37). See INSPIRATION.

7. Complete Revelation of God in Christ

It is supposed that all the forms of special or redemptive revelation which underlie and give its content to the religion of the Bible may without violence be subsumed under one or another of these three modes —external manifestation, internal suggestion, and concursive operation. All, that is, except the culminating revelation, not through, but in, Jesus Christ. As in His person, in which dwells all the fulness of the Godhead bodily, He rises above all classification and is *sui generis;* so the revelation accumulated in Him stands outside all the divers portions and divers manners in which otherwise revelation has been given and sums up in itself all that has been or can be made known of God and of His redemption. He does not so much make a revelation of God as Himself is the revelation of God; He does not merely disclose God's purpose of redemption, He is unto us wisdom from God, and righteousness and sanctification and redemption. The theophanies are but faint shadows in comparison with His manifestation of God in the flesh. The prophets could prophesy only as the Spirit of Christ which was in them testified, revealing to them as to servants one or another of the secrets of the Lord Jeh; from Him as His Son, Jeh has no secrets, but whatsoever the Father knows that the Son knows also. Whatever truth men have been made partakers of by the Spirit of truth is His (for all things whatsoever the Father hath are His) and is taken by the Spirit of truth and declared to men that He may be glorified. Nevertheless, though all revelation is thus summed up in Him, we should not fail to note very carefully that it would also be all sealed up in Him—so little is revelation conveyed by fact alone, without the word—had it not been thus taken by the Spirit of truth and declared unto men. The entirety of the NT is but the explanatory word accompanying and giving its effect to the fact of Christ. And when this fact was in all its meaning made the possession of men, revelation was completed and in that sense ceased. Jesus Christ is no less the end of revelation than He is the end of the law.

IV. Biblical Terminology.—There is not much additional to be learned concerning the nature and processes of revelation, from the terms currently employed in Scripture to express the idea.

1. The Ordinary Forms

These terms are ordinarily the common words for disclosing, making known, making manifest, applied with more or less heightened significance to supernatural acts or effects in kind. In the Eng. Bible (AV) the vb. "reveal" occurs about 51 t, of which 22 are in the OT and 29 in the NT. In the OT the word is always the rendering of a

Heb term גָּלָה, *gālāh*, or its Aram. equivalent גְּלָה, *g^e^lāh*, the root meaning of which appears to be "nakedness." When applied to revelation, it seems to hint at the removal of obstacles to perception or the uncovering of objects to perception. In the NT the word "reveal" is always (with the single exception of Lk **2** 35) the rendering of a Gr term ἀποκαλύπτω, *apokalúptō* (but in 2 Thess **1** 7; 1 Pet **4** 13 the corresponding noun ἀποκάλυψις, *apokálupsis*), which has a very similar basal significance with its Heb parallel. As this Heb word formed no substantive in this sense, the noun "revelation" does not occur in the Eng. OT, the idea being expressed, however, by other Heb terms variously rendered. It occurs in the Eng. NT, on the other hand, about a dozen times, and always as the rendering of the substantive corresponding to the vb. rendered "reveal" (*apokalupsis*). On the face of the Eng. Bible, the terms "reveal," "revelation" bear therefore uniformly the general sense of "disclose," "disclosure." The idea is found in the Bible, however, much more frequently than the terms "reveal," "revelation" in EV. Indeed, the Heb and Gr terms exclusively so rendered occur more frequently in this sense than in this rendering in the Eng. Bib. And by their side there stand various other terms which express in one way or another the general conception.

In the NT the vb. φανερόω, *phaneróō*, with the general sense of making manifest, manifesting, is the most common of these. It differs from *apokaluptō* as the more general and external term from the more special and inward. Other terms also are occasionally used: ἐπιφάνεια, *epipháneia*, "manifestation" (2 Thess **2** 8; 1 Tim **6** 14; 2 Tim **1** 10; **4** 1; Tit **2** 13; cf ἐπιφαίνω, *epiphaínō*, Tit **2** 11; **3** 4); δεικνύω, *deiknúō* (Rev **1** 1; **17** 1; **22** 1.6.8; cf Acts **9** 16; 1 Tim **4** 15); ἐξηγέομαι, *exēgéomai* (Jn **1** 18), of which, however, only one perhaps—χρηματίζω, *chrēmatízō* (Mt **2** 12.22; Lk **2** 20; Acts **10** 22; He **8** 5; **11** 7; **12** 25); χρηματισμός, *chrēmatismós* (Rom **11** 4)—calls for particular notice as in a special way, according to its usage, expressing the idea of a Divine communication.

In the OT, the common Heb vb. for "seeing" (רָאָה, *rā'āh*) is used in its appropriate stems, with God as the subject, for "appearing," "showing": "the Lord appeared unto . . . ."; "the word which the Lord showed me." And from this vb. not only is an active substantive formed which supplied the more ancient designation of the official organ of revelation: רֹאֶה, *rō'eh*, "seer"; but also objective substantives, מַרְאָה, *mar'āh*, and מַרְאֶה, *mar'eh*, which were used to designate the thing seen in a revelation—the "vision." By the side of these terms there were others in use, derived from a root which supplies to the Aram. its common word for "seeing," but in Heb has a somewhat more pregnant meaning, חָזָה, *ḥāzāh*. Its active derivative, חֹזֶה, *ḥōzeh*, was a designation of a prophet which remained in occasional use, alternating with the more customary נָבִיא, *nābhī'*, long after רֹאֶה, *rō'eh*, had become practically obsolete; and its passive derivatives *ḥāzōn*, *ḥizzāyōn*, *ḥāzūth*, *maḥăzeh* provided the ordinary terms for the substance of the revelation or "vision." The distinction between the two sets of terms, derived respectively from *rā'āh* and *ḥāzāh*, while not to be unduly pressed, seems to lie in the direction that the former suggests external manifestations and the latter internal revelations. The *rō'eh* is he to whom Divine manifestations, the *ḥōzeh* he to whom Divine communications, have been vouchsafed; the *mar'eh* is an appearance, the *ḥāzōn* and its companions a vision. It may be of interest to observe that *mar'āh* is the term employed in Nu **12** 6, while it is *ḥāzōn* which commonly occurs in the headings of the written prophecies to indicate their revelatory character. From this it may possibly be inferred that in the former passage it is the mode, in the latter the contents of the revelation that is emphasized. Perhaps a like distinction may be traced between the *ḥāzōn* of Dnl **8** 15 and the *mar'eh* of the next verse. The ordinary vb. for "knowing," יָדַע, *yādha'*, expressing in its causative stems the idea of making known, informing, is also very naturally employed, with God as its subject, in the sense of revealing, and that, in accordance with the natural sense of the word, with a tendency to pregnancy of implication, of revealing effectively, of not merely uncovering to observation, but making to know. Accordingly, it is paralleled not merely with גָּלָה, *gālāh* (Ps **98** 2: 'The Lord hath *made known* his salvation; his righteousness hath he *displayed* in the sight of the nation'), but also with such terms as לָמַד, *lāmadh* (Ps **25** 4: '*Make known* to me thy ways, O Lord: *teach* me thy paths'). This vb. *yādha'* forms no substantive in the sense of "revelation" (cf דַּעַת, *da'ath*, Nu **24** 16; Ps **19** 3).

The most common vehicles of the idea of "revelation" in the OT are, however, two expressions which are yet to be mentioned. These are the phrase, "word of Jeh," and the term commonly but inadequately rendered in the EV by "law." The former (*d^e^bhar Yahweh*, varied to *d^e^bhar 'Ĕlōhīm* or *d^e^bhar hā-'Ĕlōhīm;* cf *n^e^'um Yahweh*, *massā' Yahweh*) occurs scores of times and is at once the simplest and the most colorless designation of a Divine communication. By the latter (*tōrāh*), the proper meaning of which is "instruction," a strong implication of authoritativeness is conveyed; and, in this sense, it becomes what may be called the technical designation of a specifically Divine communication. The two are not infrequently brought together, as in Isa **1** 10: "Hear the word of Jeh, ye rulers of Sodom; give ear unto the law [m "teaching"] of our God, ye people of Gomorrah"; or Isa **2** 3 m; Mic **4** 2: "For out of Zion shall go forth the law [m "instruction"], and the word of Jeh from Jerus." Both terms are used for any Divine communication of whatever extent; and both came to be employed to express the entire body of Divine revelation, conceived as a unitary whole. In this comprehensive usage, the emphasis of the one came to fall more on the graciousness, and of the other more on the authoritativeness of this body of Divine revelation; and both passed into the NT with these implications. "The word of God," or simply "the word," comes thus to mean in the NT just the gospel, "the word of the proclamation of redemption, that is, all that which God has to say to man, and causes to be said" looking to his salvation. It expresses, in a word, precisely what we technically speak of as God's redemptive revelation. "The law," on the other hand, means in this NT use, just the whole body of the authoritative instruction which God has given men. It expresses, in other words, what we commonly speak of as God's supernatural revelation. The two things, of course, are the same: God's authoritative revelation is His gracious revelation; God's redemptive revelation is His supernatural revelation. The two terms merely look at the one aggregate of revelation from two aspects, and each emphasizes its own aspect of this one aggregated revelation.

2. "Word of Jehovah" and "Torah"

Now, this aggregated revelation lay before the men of the NT in a written form, and it was impossible to speak freely of it without consciousness of and at least occasional reference to its written form. Accordingly we hear of a Word of God that is written (Jn **15** 25; 1 Cor **15** 54), and the Divine Word is naturally contrasted with mere tradition, as if its written form were of its very idea (Mk **7** 10); indeed, the written body of revelation—with an emphasis on its written form—is designated expressly 'the prophetic word' (2 Pet **1** 19). More distinctly still, "the Law" comes to be thought of as a written, not exactly, code, but body of Divinely authoritative instructions. The phrase, "It is written in your law" (Jn **10** 34; **15** 25; Rom **3** 19; 1 Cor **14** 21), acquires the precise sense of, "It is set forth in your authoritative Scriptures, all the content of which is 'law,' that is, Divine instruction." Thus "the Word of God," "the Law," came to mean just the written body of revelation, what we call, and what the NT writers called, in the same high sense which we give the term, "the Scriptures." These "Scriptures" are thus identified with the revelation of God, conceived as a well-defined *corpus*, and two conceptions rise before us which have had a determining part to play in the history of Christianity—the conception of an authoritative Canon of Scripture, and the conception of this Canon of Scripture as just the Word of God written. The former conception was thrown into prominence in opposition to the gnostic heresies in the earliest age of the church, and gave rise to a richly varied mode of speech concerning the Scriptures, emphasizing their authority in legal language, which goes back to and rests on the Bib. usage of "Law." The latter it was left to the Reformation to do justice to in its struggle against, on the one side, the Romish depression of the Scriptures in favor of the traditions of the church, and on the other side the Enthusiasts' supercession of them in the interests of the "inner Word." When Tertullian, on the one hand, speaks of the Scriptures as an "Instrument," a legal document, his terminology has an express warrant in the Scriptures' own usage of *tōrāh*, "law," to designate their entire content. And when John Gerhard argues that "between the Word of God and Sacred Scripture, taken in a material sense, there is no real difference," he is only declaring plainly what is definitely implied in the NT use of "the Word of God" with the written revelation in mind. What is important to recognize is that the Scriptures themselves represent the Scriptures as not merely containing here and there the record of revelations—"words of God," *tōrōth*—given by God, but as themselves, in all their extent, a revelation, an authoritative body of gracious instructions from God; or, since they alone, of all the revelations which God may have given, are extant—rather as the Revelation, the only "Word of God" accessible to men, in all their parts "law," that is, authoritative instruction from God.

3. "The Scriptures"

LITERATURE.—Herman Witsius, "De Prophetis et Prophetia" in *Miscell. Sacr.*, I, Leiden, 1736, 1–318; G. F. Oehler, *Theology of the OT*, ET, Edinburgh, 1874, I, part I (and the appropriate sections in other Bib. Theologies); H. Bavinck, *Gereformeerde Dogmatiek*[2], I, Kampen, 1906, 290–406 (and the appropriate sections in other dogmatic treatises); H. Voigt, *Fundamentaldogmatik*, Gotha, 1874, 173 ff; A. Kuyper, *Encyclopaedia of Sacred Theology*, ET, New York, 1898, div. III, ch ii; A. E. Krauss, *Die Lehre von der Offenbarung*, Gotha, 1868; C. F. Fritzsche, *De revelationis notione biblica*, Leipzig, 1828; E. W. Hengstenberg, *The Christology of the OT*, ET[2], Edinburgh, 1868, IV, Appendix 6, pp. 396–444; E. König, *Der Offenbarungsbegriff des AT*, Leipzig, 1882; A. B. Davidson, *OT Prophecy*, 1903; W. J. Beecher, *The Prophets and the Promise*, New York, 1905; James Orr, *The Christian View of God and the World*, 1893, as per Index, "Revelation," and *Revelation and Inspiration*, London and New York, 1910. Also: T. Christlieb, *Modern Doubt and Christian Belief*, ET, New York, 1874; G. P. Fisher, *The Nature and Method of Revelation*, New York, 1890; C. M. Mead, *Supernatural Revelation*, 1889; J. Quirmbach, *Die Lehre des h. Paulus von der natürlichen Gotteserkenntnis*, etc, Freiburg, 1906.

BENJAMIN B. WARFIELD

REVELATION OF JOHN:

The last book of the NT. It professes to be the record of prophetic visions given by Jesus Christ to John, while the latter was a prisoner, "for the word of God and the testimony of Jesus" (**1** 9), in PATMOS (q.v.), a small rocky island in the Aegean, about 15 miles W. of Ephesus. Its precursor in the OT is the Book of Dnl, with the symbolic visions and mystical numbers of which it stands in close affinity. The peculiar form of the book, its relation to other "apocalyptic" writings, and to the Fourth Gospel, likewise attributed to John, the interpretation of its symbols, with controverted questions of its date, of worship, unity, relations to contemporary history, etc, have made it one of the most difficult books in the NT to explain satisfactorily.

I. Title and General Character of Book.—"Revelation" answers to ἀποκάλυψις, *apokálupsis*, in ver 1. The oldest form of the title would seem to be simply, "Apocalypse of John," the appended words "the Divine" (θεολόγος, *theológos*, i.e. "theologian") not being older than the 4th cent. (cf the title given to Gregory of Nazianzus, "Gregory the theologian"). The book belongs to the class of works commonly named "apocalyptic," as containing visions and revelations of the future, frequently in symbolical form (e.g. the Book of En, the Apocalypse of Bar, the Apocalypse of Ezr; see APOCALYPTIC LITERATURE), but it is doubtful if the word here bears this technical sense. The tendency at present is to group the NT Apocalypse with these others, and attribute to it the same kind of origin as theirs, viz. in the unbridled play of religious phantasy, clothing itself in unreal visional form.

1. Title

But there is a wide distinction. These other works are pseudonymous—fictitious; on the face of them products of imagination; betraying that this is their origin in their crude, confused, unedifying character. The Apocalypse bears on it the name of its author—an apostle of Jesus Christ (see below); claims to rest on real visions; rings with the accent of sincerity; is orderly, serious, sublime, purposeful, in its conceptions; deals with the most solemn and momentous of themes. On the modern Nero-theory, to which most recent expositors give adherence, it is a farrago of baseless phantasies, no one of which came true. On its own claim it is a product of true prophecy (**1** 3; **22** 18 f), and has or will have sure fulfilment. Parallels here and there are sought between it and the Book of En or the Apocalypse of Ezr. As a rule the resemblances arise from the fact that these works draw from the same store of the ideas and imagery of the OT. It is there the key is chiefly to be sought to the symbolism of John. The Apocalypse is steeped in the thoughts, the images, even the language of the OT (cf the illustrations in Lightfoot, *Gal*, 361, where it

2. Uniqueness and Reality of Visions

is remarked: "The whole book is saturated with illustrations from the OT. It speaks not the language of Paul, but of Isaiah and Ezekiel and Daniel"). These remarks will receive elucidation in what follows.

II. Canonicity and Authority.—The two questions of canonicity and authorship are closely connected.

1. Patristic Testimony

Eusebius states that opinion in his day was divided on the book, and he himself wavers between placing it among the disputed books or ranking it with the acknôwledged (*homologoúmena*). "Among these," he says, "if such a view seem correct, we must place the Apocalypse of John" (*HE*, III, 25). That it was rightly so placed appears from a survey of the evidence. The first to refer to the book expressly is Justin Martyr (c 140 AD), who speaks of it as the work of "a certain man, whose name was John, one of the apostles of Christ" (*Dial*, 81). Irenaeus (c 180 AD) repeatedly and decisively declares that the Apocalypse was written by John, a disciple of the Lord (*Adv. Haer.*, iv.20, 11; 30, 4; v.26, 1; 35, 2, etc), and comments on the number 666 (v.30, 1). In his case there can be no doubt that the apostle John is meant. Andreas of Cappadocia (5th cent.) in a *Comm. on the Apocalypse* states that Papias (c 130 AD) bore witness to its credibility, and cites a comment by him on Rev **12** 7–9. The book is quoted in the Ep. on the martyrs of Vienne and Lyons (177 AD); had a commentary written on it by Melito of Sardis (c 170 AD), one of the churches of the Apocalypse (Euseb., *HE*, IV, 26); was used by Theophilus of Antioch (c 168 AD) and by Apollonius (c 210 AD; *HE*, V, 25)—in these cases being cited as the Apocalypse of John. It is included as John's in the Canon of Muratori (c 200 AD). The Johannine authorship (apostolic) is abundantly attested by Tertullian (c 200 AD; *Adv. Mar.*, iii.14, 24, etc); by Hippolytus (c 240 AD), who wrote a work upon it; by Clement of Alexandria (c 200 AD); by Origen (c 230 AD), and other writers. Doubt about the authorship of the book is first heard of in the obscure sect of the Alogi (end of 2d cent.), who, with Caius, a Rom presbyter (c 205 AD), attributed it to Cerinthus. More serious was the criticism of Dionysius of Alexandria (c 250 AD), who, on internal grounds, held that the Fourth Gospel and the Apocalypse could not have come from the same pen (Euseb., *HE*, VII, 25). He granted, however, that it was the work of a holy and inspired man—another John. The result was that, while "in the Western church," as Bousset grants, "the Apocalypse was accepted unanimously from the first" (*EB*, I, 193), a certain doubt attached to it for a time in sections of the Gr and Syrian churches. It is not found in the Pesh, and a citation from it in Ephraim the Syrian († 373) seems not to be genuine. Cyril of Jerus (c 386 AD) omits it from his list, and it is unmentioned by the Antiochian writers (Chrysostom, Theodore of Mopsuestia, Theodoret). The Canon attributed to the Council of Laodicea (c 360 AD) does not name it, but it is doubtful whether this document is not of later date (cf Westcott; also Bousset, *Die Offenb. Joh.*, 28). On the other hand, the book is acknowledged by Methodius, Pamphilus, Athanasius, Gregory of Nyssa, Cyril Alex., Epiphanius, etc.

The testimony to the canonicity, and also to the Johannine authorship, of the Apocalypse is thus exceptionally strong.

2. Testimony of Book Itself

In full accordance with it is the claim of the book itself. It proclaims itself to be the work of John (**1** 1.4.9; **22** 8), who does not, indeed, name himself an apostle, yet, in his inspired character, position of authority in the Asian churches, and selection as the medium of these revelations, can hardly be thought of as other than the well-known John of the Gospels and of consentient church tradition. The alternative view, first suggested as a possibility by Eusebius, now largely favored by modern writers, is that the John intended is the "presbyter John" of a well-known passage cited by Eusebius from Papias (*HE*, III, 39). Without entering into the intricate questions connected with this "presbyter John"—whether he was really a distinct person from the apostle (Zahn and others dispute it), or whether, if he was, he resided at Ephesus (see John, Gospel of)—it is enough here to say that the reason already given, viz: the importance and place of authority of the author of the Apocalypse in the Asian churches, and the emphatic testimony above cited connecting him with the apostle, forbid the attribution of the book to a writer wholly unknown to church tradition, save for this casual reference to him in Papias. Had the assumed presbyter really been the author, he could not have dropped so completely out of the knowledge of the church, and had his place taken all but immediately by the apostle.

One cause of the hesitancy regarding the Apocalypse in early circles was dislike of its millenarianism; but the chief reason, set forth with much critical skill by Dionysius of Alexandria (Euseb., *HE*, VII, 25), was the undoubted contrast in character and style between this work and the Fourth Gospel, likewise claiming to be from the pen of John.

3. Objections to Johannine Authorship —Relation to Fourth Gospel

Two works so diverse in character—the Gospel calm, spiritual, mystical, abounding in characteristic expressions as "life," "light," "love," etc, written in idiomatic Gr; the Apocalypse abrupt, mysterious, material in its imagery, inexact and barbarous in its idioms, sometimes employing solecisms—could not, it was argued, proceed from the same author. Not much, beyond amplification of detail, has been added to the force of the arguments of Dionysius. There were three possibilities—either first, admitting the Johannine authorship of the Apocalypse, to assail the genuineness of the Gospel—this was the method of the school of Baur; or, second, accepting the Gospel, to seek a different author for the Apocalypse—John the presbyter, or another: thus not a few reverent scholars (Bleek, Neander, etc); or, third, with most moderns, to deny the Johannine authorship of both Gospel and Apocalypse, with a leaning to the "presbyter" as the author of the latter (Harnack, Bousset, Moffatt, etc). Singularly there has been of late in the advanced school itself a movement in the direction of recognizing that this difficulty of style is less formidable than it looks—that, in fact, beneath the surface difference, there is a strong body of resemblances pointing to a close relationship of Gospel and Apocalypse. This had long been argued by the older writers (Godet, Luthardt, Alford, Salmon, etc), but it is now more freely acknowledged. As instances among many may be noted the use of the term "Logos" (**19** 13), the image of the "Lamb," figures like "water of life," words and phrases as "true," "he that overcometh," "keep the commandments," etc. A striking coincidence is the form of quotation of Zec **12** 10 in Jn **19** 37 and Rev **1** 7. If the Gr in parts shows a certain abruptness and roughness, it is plainly evidenced by the use of the correct constructions in other passages that this is not due to want of knowledge of the language. "The very rules which he breaks in one place he observes in others" (Salmon). There are, besides, subtle affinities in the Gr usage of the two books, and some of the very irregularities complained of are found in the Gospel (for ample details consult Bousset, op.

cit.; Godet, *Comm. on Jn*, I, 267–70, ET; Alford, *Gr Test.*, IV, 224–28; Salmon, *Intro to the NT*, 233–43, 2d ed; the last-named writer says: "I have produced instances enough to establish decisively that there is the closest possible affinity between the Revelation and the other Johannine books"). Great differences in character and style no doubt still remain. Some, to leave room for these, favor an early date for the Apocalypse (68–69 BC; on this below); the trend of opinion, however, now seems, as will be shown, to be moving back to the traditional date in the reign of Domitian, in which case the Gospel will be the earlier, and the Apocalypse the later work. This, likewise, seems to yield the better explanation. The tremendous experiences of Patmos, bursting through all ordinary and calmer states of consciousness, must have produced startling changes in thought and style of composition. The "rapt seer" will not speak and write like the self-collected, calmly brooding evangelist.

III. Date and Unity of the Book.—Eusebius, in summing up the tradition of the Church on this subject, assigns John's exile to Patmos, and consequently the composition of the Apocalypse, to the latter part of the reign of Domitian (81–96 AD). Irenaeus (c 180 AD) says of the book, "For it was seen, not a long time ago, but almost in our own generation, at the end of the reign of Domitian" (*Adv. Haer.*, v.30, 3). This testimony is confirmed by Clement of Alexandria (who speaks of "the tyrant"), Origen, and later writers. Epiphanius (4th cent.), indeed, puts (*Haer.*, li.12, 233) the exile to Patmos in the reign of Claudius (41–54 AD); but as, in the same sentence, he speaks of the apostle as 90 years of age, it is plain there is a strange blunder in the name of the emperor. The former date answers to the conditions of the book (decadence of the churches; widespread and severe persecution), and to the predilection of Domitian for this mode of banishment (cf Tacitus *Hist.* i.2; Euseb., *HE*, III, 18).

1. Traditional Date under Domitian

This, accordingly, may be regarded as the traditional date of composition of the Apocalypse, though good writers, influenced partly by the desire to give time for the later composition of the Gospel, have signified a preference for an earlier date (e.g. Westcott, Salmon). It is by no means to be assumed, however, that the Apocalypse is the earlier production. The tendency of recent criticism, it will be seen immediately, is to revert to the traditional date (Bousset, etc); but for a decade or two, through the prevalence of what may be called the "Nero-theory" of the book, the pendulum swung strongly in favor of its composition shortly after the death of Nero, and before the destruction of Jerus (held to be shown to be still standing by ch **11**), i.e. about 68–69 AD. This date was even held to be demonstrated beyond all question. Reuss may be taken as an example. According to him (*Christian Theology of the Apostolic Age*, I, 369 ff, ET), apart from the ridiculous preconceptions of theologians, the Apocalypse is "the most simple, most transparent book that prophet ever penned." "There is no other apostolical writing the chronology of which can be more exactly fixed." "It was written before the destruction of Jerus, under the emperor Galba—that is to say, in the second half of the year 68 of our era." He proceeds to discuss "the irrefutable proofs" of this. The proof, in brief, is found in the beast (not introduced till ch **13**) with seven heads, one of which has been mortally wounded, but is for the present healed (**13** 3). "This is the Rom empire, with its first 7 emperors, one of whom is killed, but is to live again as Antichrist" (cf **17** 10 f). The key to the whole book is said to be given in **13** 18, where the number of the beast is declared to be 666. Applying the method of numerical values (the Jewish *Gematria*), this number is found to correspond with the name "Nero Caesar" in Heb letters (omitting the *yōdh*). Nero then is the 5th head that is to live again; an interpretation confirmed by rumors prevalent at that time that Nero was not really dead, but only hidden, and was soon to return to claim his throne. As if to make assurance doubly sure, it is found that by dropping the final *n* in "Neron," the number becomes 616—a number which Irenaeus in his comments on the subject (v.30.1) tells us was actually found in some ancient copies. The meaning therefore is thought to be clear. Writing under the emperor Galba, the 6th emperor (reckoning from Augustus), the author anticipates, after a short reign of a 7th emperor (**17** 10), the return of the Antichrist Nero—an 8th, but of the 7, with whom is to come the end. Jerus is to be miraculously preserved (ch **11**), but Rome is to perish. This is to happen within the space of 3½ years. "The final catastrophe, which was to destroy the city and empire, was to take place in three years and a half. . . . . The writer knows . . . . that Rome will in three years and a half perish finally, never to rise again." It does not matter for this theory that not one of the things predicted happened—that every anticipation was falsified. Nero did not return; Jerus was not saved; Rome did not perish; 3½ years did not see the end of all things. Yet the Christian church, though the failure of every one of these predictions had been decisively demonstrated, received the book as of Divine inspiration, apparently without the least idea that such things had been intended (see the form of the theory in Renan, with a keen criticism in Salmon's *Intro to the NT*, lect xiv).

2. The Nero-Theory

What is to be said with reference to this "Nero-theory" belongs to subsequent sections: meanwhile it is to be observed that, while portions of the theory are retained, significant changes have since taken place in the view entertained of the book as a whole, and with this of the date to be assigned to it. First, after 1882, came a flood of disintegrating hypotheses, based on the idea that the Apocalypse was not a unity, but was either a working up of one or more Jewish apocalypses by Christian hands, or at least incorporated fragments of such apocalypses (Völter, Vischer, Weizsäcker, Weyland, Pfleiderer, Spitta, etc). Harnack lent his influential support to the form of this theory advocated by Vischer, and for a time the idea had vogue. Very soon, however, it fell into discredit through its own excesses (for details on the different views, see Bousset, or Moffat's *Intro to the NT*, 489 ff), and through increasing appreciation of the internal evidence for the unity of the book. Gunkel, in his *Schöpfung und Chaos* (1895), started another line of criticism in his derivation of the conceptions of the book, not from Jewish apocalypse, but from Bab mythology. He assailed with sharp criticism the "contemporary history" school of interpretation (the "Nero-theory" above), and declared its "bankruptcy." The number of the beast, with him, found its solution, not in Nero, but in the Heb name for the primeval chaos. This theory, too, has failed in general acceptance, though elements in it are adopted by most recent interpreters. The modified view most in favor now is that the Apocalypse is, indeed, the work of a Christian writer of the end of the 1st cent., but embodies certain sections borrowed from Jewish apocalypse (as **7** 1–8, the 144,000; ch **11,** measuring of the temple and the two witnesses; esp. ch **12,** the woman and red dragon—

3. Composite Hypotheses —Babylonian Theory

this, in turn, reminiscent of Bab mythology). These supposed Jewish sections are, however, without real support in anything that is known, and the symbolism admits as easily of a Christian interpretation as any other part of the book. We are left, therefore, as before, with the book as a unity, and the tide of opinion flows back to the age of Domitian as the time of its origin. Moffatt (connecting it mistakenly, as it seems to us, with Domitian's emphasis on the imperial cultus, but giving also other reasons) goes so far as to say that "any earlier date for the book is hardly possible" (*Expos Gr Test.*, V, 317). The list of authorities for the Domitianic date may be seen in Moffatt, *Intro*, 508.

IV. Plan and Analysis of the Book.—The method of the book may thus be indicated. After an introduction, and letters to the seven churches (chs **1–3**), the properly prophetic part of the book commences with a vision of heaven (chs **4, 5**), following upon which are two series of visions of the future, parallel, it would appear, to each other—the first, the 7 seals, and under the 7th seal, the 7 trumpets (chs **6–11**, with interludes in ch **7** and again in **10**; **11** 1–12); the second, the woman and her child (ch **12**), the 2 beasts (ch **13**), and, after new interludes (ch **14**), the bowls and 7 last plagues (chs **15, 16**). The expansion of the last judgments is given in separate pictures (the scarlet woman, doom of Babylon, Har-Magedon, chs **17-19**); then come the closing scenes of the millennium, the last apostasy, resurrection and judgment (ch **20**), followed by the new heavens and new earth, with the descending new Jerus (chs **21, 22**). The theme of the book is the conflict of Christ and His church with anti-Christian powers (the devil, the beast, the false prophet, **16** 13), and the ultimate and decisive defeat of the latter; its keynote is in the words, "Come, Lord Jesus" (**22** 20; cf **1** 7); but it is to be noticed, as characteristic of the book, that while this "coming" is represented as, in a manner, ever near, the end, as the crisis approaches, is again always postponed by a fresh development of events. Thus, under the 6th seal, the end seems reached (**6** 12–17), but a pause ensues (ch **7**), and on the opening of the seventh seal, a new series begins with the trumpets (**8** 2 ff). Similarly, at the sounding of the 6th trumpet, the end seems at hand (**9** 12–21), but a new pause is introduced before the last sounding takes place (**11** 15 ff). Then is announced the final victory, but as yet only in summary. A new series of visions begins, opening into large perspectives, till, after fresh interludes, and the pouring out of 6 of the bowls of judgment, Har-Magedon itself is reached; but though, at the outpouring of the 7th bowl, it is proclaimed, "It is done" (**16** 17), the end is again held over till these final judgments are shown in detail. At length, surely, in ch **19**, with the appearance of the white horseman—"The Word of God" (ver 13)—and the decisive overthrow of all his adversaries (vs 18–21), the climax is touched; but just then, to our surprise, intervenes the announcement of the binding of Satan for 1,000 years, and the reign of Jesus and His saints upon the earth (the interpretation is not here discussed), followed by a fresh apostasy, and the general resurrection and judgment (ch **20**). Precise time-measures evidently fail in dealing with a book so constructed: the 3½ years of the Nero-interpreters sink into insignificance in its crowded panorama of events. The symbolic numbers that chiefly rule in the book are "seven," the number of completeness (7 spirits, seals, trumpets, bowls, heads of beasts); "ten," the number of worldly power (10 horns); "four," the earthly number (4 living creatures, corners of earth, winds, etc); 3½ years—42 months—"time, and times, and half a time" (**12** 14) = 1,260 days, the period, borrowed from Dnl (**7** 25; **12** 7), of anti-Christian ascendency.

1. General Scope

2. Detailed Analysis

The following is a more detailed analysis:

I. Introduction
- 1. Title and Address (**1** 1–8)
- 2. Vision of Jesus and Message to the Seven Churches of the Province of Asia (vs 9–20)
- 3. The Letters to the Seven Churches (chs **2, 3**)
  - (1) Ephesus (**2** 1–7)
  - (2) Smyrna (vs 8–11)
  - (3) Pergamos (vs 12–17)
  - (4) Thyatira (vs 18–29)
  - (5) Sardis (**3** 1–6)
  - (6) Philadelphia (vs 7–13)
  - (7) Laodicea (vs 14–22)

II. The Things to Come. First Series of Visions: The Seals and Trumpets
- 1. The Vision of Heaven
  - (1) Adoration of the Creator (ch **4**)
  - (2) The 7-Sealed Book; Adoration of God and the Lamb (ch **5**)
- 2. Opening of Six Seals (ch **6**)
  - (1) The White Horse (vs 1.2)
  - (2) The Red Horse (vs 3.4)
  - (3) The Black Horse (vs 5.6)
  - (4) The Pale Horse (vs 7.8)
  - (5) Souls under the Altar (vs 9–11)
  - (6) The Wrath of the Lamb (vs 12–17)
- 3. Interludes (ch **7**)
  - (1) Sealing of 144,000 on Earth (vs 1–8)
  - (2) Triumphant Multitude in Heaven (vs 9–17)
- 4. Opening of Seventh Seal: under This Seven Trumpets, of Which Six Now Sounded (chs **8, 9**)
  - (1) Hail and Fire on Earth (**8** 7)
  - (2) Burning Mountain in Sea (vs 8.9)
  - (3) Burning Star on Rivers and Fountains (vs 10.11)
  - (4) One-third Sun, Moon, and Stars Darkened (ver 12). "Woe"—Trumpets (ver 13)
  - (5) The Fallen Star-Locusts (**9** 1–11)
  - (6) Angels Loosed from Euphrates—the Horseman (vs 12–21)
- 5. Interludes—
  - (1) Angel with Little Book (ch **10**)
  - (2) Measuring of Temple and Altar—the Two Witnesses (**11** 1–13)
- 6. Seventh Trumpet Sounded—Final Victory (vs 14–19)

III. Second Series of Visions: The Woman and the Red Dragon; the Two Beasts; the Bowls and Last Plagues
- 1. The Woman and Child; the Red Dragon and His Persecutions (ch **12**)
- 2. The Beast from the Sea, Seven-headed, Ten-horned (**13** 1–10); the Two-horned Beast (vs 11–18)
- 3. Interludes (ch **14**)
  - (1) The Lamb on Mt. Zion; the 144,000 (vs 1–5)
  - (2) The Angel with "an Eternal Gospel" (vs 6.7)
  - (3) Second Angel—(Anticipatory) Proclamation of Fall of Babylon (ver 8)
  - (4) Third Angel—Doom of Worshippers of the Beast (vs 9–12)
  - (5) Blessedness of the Dead in the Lord (ver 13)
  - (6) The Son of Man and the Great Vintage (vs 14–20)
- 4. The Seven Last Plagues—the Angels and Their Bowls: the Preparation in Heaven (ch **15**)—the Outpouring (ch **16**)
  - (1) On Earth (**16** 2)
  - (2) On Sea (ver 3)
  - (3) On Rivers and Fountains (vs 4–7)
  - (4) On Sun (vs 8.9)
  - (5) On Seat of Beast (vs 10.11)
  - (6) On Euphrates —Har-Magedon (vs 12–16)
  - (7) In the Air—Victory and Fall of Babylon (vs 17–21)

IV. Expansion of Last Judgments (chs **17–19**)
- 1. The Scarlet Woman on Beast—Her Judgment (ch **17**)
- 2. Doom of Babylon and Lament over Her (ch **18**)
- 3. Interlude—Announcement of Marriage of the Lamb (**19** 1–10)
- 4. Rider on White Horse ("The Word of God") and His Armies—Last Battle and Doom of Beast, False Prophet, and Their Followers (vs 11–21)

V. The Millennium—New Heavens and New Earth (chs **20–22**)
- 1. Satan Bound; First Resurrection and Reign of Saints for 1,000 Years (**20** 1–6)
- 2. Loosing of Satan and Final Conflict—Doom of Adversaries and of the Devil (vs 7–10)
- 3. General Resurrection and Last Judgment (vs 11–15)

4. New Heavens and New Earth
   (1) The New Jerus from Heaven (**21** 1-9)
   (2) Description of the City (vs 10-27)
   (3) Blessedness of Its Citizens (**22** 1-7)
   (4) Epilogue (vs 8-21)

V. Principles of Interpretation.—As a book intended for the consolation of the church under present and future afflictions, the Apocalypse is meant by its author to be understood (**1** 3; **22** 7). He must have been aware, however, that, while its general scope might be apprehended, mystery must rest upon many of its symbols, till the time of their actual fulfilment. The book relates to "things which must shortly come to pass" (**1** 1)—in their beginnings at least—and the divers interpretations since put upon its prophecies are the best evidence of the difficulties attaching to them. Schemes of interpretation have generally been grouped into *praeterist* (the prophecies being regarded as already fulfilled), *futurist* (the fulfilment being thrown wholly into the future), and the *historical* (the fulfilment being looked for in the continuous history of the church from John's day till the end). (1) The older praeterist view may be taken as represented by Moses Stuart, who finds the fulfilment of chs **6-11** in the destruction of Jerus (*Comm.*, 520 ff), and of chs **13-19** in the reign of Nero (690 ff). Even he, however, has to interpret the chapter on the last things of the future. (2) The futurist view connects the whole with the times of the second advent and the millennium. The beast is an individual who shall then appear as Antichrist. This rejects the plain intimations of the book that the events predicted lay, in their beginnings at least, immediately in the future of the writer. (3) The historical view connects the various symbols with definite occurrences—as the invasions which overthrew the Rom Empire (the first 4 trumpets), the Saracens (first woe-trumpet), the Turks (second woe-trumpet), the papacy (the beast, ch **13**; the scarlet woman, ch **17**), etc. A day-year principle is applied to the periods (1,260 days—1,260 years). As representatives of this view may be mentioned Mede, Vitringa, Sir Isaac Newton, Elliott in *Horae Apocalypticae*, A. Barnes.

1. General Scheme of Interpretation

These older schemes are largely put out of date by the newer theories, already alluded to, in which the Apocalypse is explained out of contemporary conditions, the legend of the returning Nero, Jewish apocalypse, and Bab mythology. These are praeterist theories also, but differ from the older in that in them all real prophecy is denied. A mainstay of such theories is the declaration of the book that the events announced are close at hand (**1** 1.3; **22** 20). When, however, it is remembered that, on any view, this nearness includes a period of 1,000 years before the judgment and descent of the new Jerus, it will be felt that it will not do to give these expressions too restricted a temporal significance. The horizon is wider. The coming of Christ is ever near—ever approaching—yet it is not to be tied down to "times and seasons"; it is more of the nature of a process and has anticipatory exemplifications in many crises and providential events forecasting the end (see above). The "coming," e.g. to the church at Ephesus (**2** 5), or to the church at Pergamos (**2** 16)—contingent events—can hardly exhaust the full meaning of the Parousia. The Nero-theory demands a date at latest under Galba, but that date we have seen to be generally abandoned. Those who place it under Vespasian (omitting three short reigns) sacrifice the advantage of dating the book before the destruction of Jerus, and have to fall back on a supposititious Jewish fragment in ch **11**, which those who incorporated it must have known had never been fulfilled. The attempt to give a "contemporary historical" interpretation to the symbols of the successive churches, as Gunkel has acutely shown, completely breaks down in practice, while Gunkel's own attempt at a Bab explanation will be judged by most to be overstrained. "Dragon" in the OT and elsewhere may be associated with widespread oriental ideas, but the definite symbolism of the Apocalypse in ch **12** has no provable connection with Bab myths. There is the widest disagreement in the theories of "composite" origin (from Jewish apocalypse). What seems simple and demonstrable to one has no plausibility to others. A form of "Nero Caesar," indeed, yields the mystic 666, but so do 1,000 other names—almost any name, with proper manipulation (cf Salmon, lect xiv). Lastly, the returning-Nero legend yields no satisfactory explanation of the language in **13** 3.12.14; **17** 11. The theory is that these words allude to the belief that Nero would return from the dead and become Antichrist (see above). Tacitus attests that there were vague rumors that Nero had not really died (*Hist.* ii.8), and later a pretender arose in Parthia taking advantage of this feeling (Suet. *Nero.* 57). The idea of Nero returning from the dead is categorically stated in Sib Or **5** 363-70 (c 120 AD); cf Sib Or **4** 119-22 (c 80 AD). Augustine mentions the idea (*City of God*, xx.19, 3), but without connection with the Apocalypse. By Domitian's time, however, it was perfectly certain that Nero had not returned, and there was no longer, on this interpretation, any appositeness in speaking of a "head" the "deathstroke" of which was healed (**13** 3), which became the "eighth head" of **17** 11—if, indeed, the apostle could be conceived capable of being influenced by such vagaries. The events predicted lay, evidently, still in the future. It may be added that neither Irenaeus, nor any early interpreter, seems to have heard of the connection of 666 with "Nero." Irenaeus himself suggests the solution *Lateinos* (cf Salmon, ut supra).

2. The Newer Theories

It is not proposed here to attempt the lines of a positive interpretation. If it is once recognized that the Apocalypse is a book of true prophecy, that its symbols stand for something real, and that its perspective is not to be limited to a brief period like 3½ years, the way is opened, not, indeed, for a reading into it of a series of precise historical occurrences, but still for doing justice to the truth which lies at the basis of the historical interpretation, viz. that there are here prefigured the great crises in the age-long conflict of Christ and His church with pagan and anti-Christian adversaries. Events and tendencies may be grouped, or under different forms may relate to the same subject (e.g. the 144,000 sealed on earth—a spiritual Israel—in **7** 1-8, and the triumphant multitude in heaven, vs 9-17); successions of events may be foreshortened; different pictures may overlap; but, shining through the symbols, great truths and facts which have historical realization appear. There is no need for supposing that, in a drama of this range, the "heads" of the beast of chs **13** and **17** (behind whom is the Dragon-enemy, Satan, of ch **12**) stand, in contrariety to the analogy of Dnl, for seven individual emperors, and that "the image of the beast," which has life given to it and "speaks" (**13** 14.15), is the statue of the emperor; or that such tremendous events as the fall of the Rom Empire, or the rise of the papacy—with which, however, must be combined all ecclesiastical anti-Christianism—or the false prophecy of later intellectual anti-Christianism have no place in the symbolism of the book. Sane, reverent thought will suggest many lines of correspondence with the

3. The Book a True Prophecy

course of God's providence, which may serve to illuminate its dark places. More than this need not be said here.

VI. Theology of the Book.—On this it is hardly necessary to dwell, for expositors are now well agreed that in its great doctrines of God, Christ, man, sin, redemption, the teaching of the Apocalypse does not vary essentially from the great types in the Epp. The assonances with John's mode of thinking have already been alluded to. It is granted by all writers that the Christology is as high as anywhere in the NT. "It ought unhesitatingly to be acknowledged," says Reuss, "that Christ is placed in the Apocalypse on a par with God" (op. cit., I, 397–98; cf Rev **1** 4.17; **2** 8; **5** 12–14; **22** 13, etc). Not less striking are the correspondences with the teaching of Paul and of Peter on redemption through the blood of Christ (**1** 5; **5** 9; **7** 14; **14** 4, etc). The perverted conception of the school of Baur that we have in the book an anti-Pauline manifesto (thus also Pfleiderer; cf *Hibbert Lectures*, 178), is now practically dead (see the criticism of it by Reuss, op. cit., I, 308–12). The point in which its eschatology differs from that of the rest of the NT is in its introduction of the millennium before the final resurrection and judgment. This enlarges, but does not necessarily contradict, the earlier stage of thought.

LITERATURE.—Moses Stuart, *Comm. on Apocalypse;* Alford, *Gr Test.*, IV, "The Revelation"; S. Davidson, *Intro to the NT* (3d ed), 176 ff; G. Salmon, *Intro to the NT* (2d ed), lects xiii, xiv; Elliott, *Horae Apocalypticae*, with lit. there mentioned; Farrar, *Early Days of Christianity*, ch xxviii; Milligan, *Discussions on the Apocalypse;* H. Gunkel, *Schöpfung und Chaos;* W. Bousset, *Die Offenbarung Johannis*, and art. "Apocalypse" in *EB*, I; C. Anderson Scott, "Revelation" in *Century Bible;* J. Moffatt, *Intro to Lit. of the NT* (with notices of lit.); also "Revelation" in *Expositor's Bible;* Trench, *Epp. to the Seven Churches;* W. M. Ramsay, *Letters to the Seven Churches*; H. B. Swete, *The Apocalypse of St. John.*

JAMES ORR

REVELLINGS, rev′el-ingz (κῶμος, *kṓmos*): The word is found both in AV and in RV in Wisd **14** 23 (RV "revels," orgiastic heathen worship is in point); 2 Macc **6** 4; Gal **5** 21; 1 Pet **4** 3. In Gal **5** 21 it is classed with fornication, uncleanness, lasciviousness, etc, as one of the works of the flesh. In 1 Pet **4** 3 it is spoken of the Gentiles and is classed with drunkenness and carousings and such like. In Rom **13** 13 RV has "revelling" instead of AV "rioting," and in 2 Pet **2** 13, "revel" replaces "riot." Similarly in Am **6** 7, "revelry" replaces "banquet." The obvious meaning of the word is excessive and boisterous intemperance and lustful indulgence. G. H. GERBERDING

REVENGE, rē-venj′, **REVENGER**, rē-venj′ẽr: The same Heb and Gr words are used to express the idea of "to avenge" and "to revenge" (נָקַם, *nāḳam*, or derivative; ἐκδικέω, *ekdikéō*, or derivative). In Eng. these words are synonymous in that they are both used to express the infliction of punishment upon the wrongdoer, but "to take revenge" may also imply a spiteful, wrong or malignant spirit. In the latter case RV preserves "revenge" (cf Jer **20** 10; Ezk **25** 15; **25** 17 is an anthropomorphism), but, wherever it is synonymous with "avenge," this word is used (cf Nu **31** 2.3; Ps **79** 10; Nah **1** 2; Jth **13** 20; Rom **13** 4; 2 Cor **7** 11; **10** 6 RV; AV has "revenge" in all these cases). In Dt **32** 42, AV "revenge" is a wrong tr. Read with RV "from the head of the leaders of the enemy" or RVm "the hairy head of the enemy." Cf AVENGE, AVENGER; BLOOD; GOEL. A. L. BRESLICH

REVENUE, rev′ē-nū: (1) אַפְּתֹם, *'appᵉthōm*, "revenue or income" (Ezr **4** 13 AV); (2) תְּבוּאָה, *tᵉbhū'āh*, "increase," "revenue" (Prov **8** 19; **15** 6; Isa **23** 3; Jer **12** 13); πρόσοδος, *prósodos*, "income" (2 Macc **3** 3; **4** 8 [RV "fund"]; **9** 16).

REVERENCE, rev′ẽr-ens: In the OT, "reverence" occurs as the tr of two Heb words, *yārē'* and *shāḥāh*. The root idea of the former is "fear." It is used to express the attitude toward God Himself, as in Ps **89** 7 AV; or toward His sanctuary, as in Lev **19** 30; **26** 2. So the group of ideas there would be "fear," "awe," "reverence." The root idea of the second is "falling down," as prostration of the body. It is used to express the bearing toward another who is considered superior, as in 2 S **9** 6 AV; 1 K **1** 31 AV; Est **3** 2.5. The group of ideas here, therefore, is "honor," "obeisance," "reverence."

In the NT "reverence" occurs as the tr of three Gr words, *aidṓs*, *phobéomai*, and *entrépomai*. In the first, the idea is "modesty" (He **12** 28; cf 1 Tim **2** 9). In the second, "fear" (Eph **5** 33 AV), though here it is used to set forth the attitude of proper subjection on the part of a wife toward her husband (cf 1 Pet **3** 2.5). In the third, the idea is that of the "self-valuation of inferiority," and so sets forth an attitude toward another of doing him honor (Mt **21** 37; Mk **12** 6; Lk **20** 13; He **12** 9).

In the Apoc *entrepomai* occurs in Wisd **2** 10; Sir **4** 22. In addition, *proskunéō*, "make obeisance," occurs in Jth **10** 23; **14** 7; *thaumázō*, "wonder," Sir **7** 29, and *aischúnomai*, "be ashamed," Bar **4** 15.

Reverend occurs in the OT in Ps **111** 9, of the name of God (*yārē'*), and in the Apoc in 2 Macc **15** 12, "a man reverend [*aidḗmōn*, "modest"] in bearing," and in the NT RV has **"reverent** in demeanor" (*hieroprepḗs*) in Tit **2** 3 and "reverend" in Phil **4** 8 m (*semnós*). E. J. FORRESTER

REVILE, rē-vīl′. See CRIMES; PUNISHMENTS.

REVIVE, rē-vīv′, **REVIVING**, rē-vīv′ing: "To revive" is the tr of חָיָה, *ḥāyāh*, "to live," "cause to live," used of restoration to life (Gen **45** 27; Jgs **15** 19, etc); of rebuilding (Neh **4** 2); of restoration to well-being (Ps **85** 6 [RV "quicken"]; **138** 7; Isa **57** 15; Hos **6** 2; **14** 7); of Jeh's gracious work for His people (Hab **3** 2, "revive thy work in the midst of the years," etc); "reviving" is the tr of מִחְיָה, *miḥyāh*, "preservation," or "means of life" (Ezr **9** 8.9). "Revive" occurs in the NT as the tr of ἀναζάω, *anazáō*, "to live again" (Rom **7** 9, and **14** 9, AV "Christ both died, and rose, and revived," RV [omitting "and rose"] "Christ died and lived again," *záō*).

In 1 Macc **13** 7 RV we have "And the spirit of the people revived," ἀναζωπυρέω, *anazōpuréō*, "to stir or kindle up as a fire," the same word as in 2 Tim **1** 6, RV "stir up the gift of God, which is in thee," m "Gr 'stir into flame.'"

In view of the frequent modern use of "revive" and "revival," it is worthy of notice that it is to Timothy himself the exhortation is addressed. We too often merely *pray* for "revivals," forgetting that it is for *us* to "stir into flame" the gift of the Spirit which we have already received of God. It is *ours* from Him, but we let it lie dormant, as a slumbering ember merely.

W. L. WALKER

REWARD, rē-wôrd′: In modern Eng. (except when influenced by the Bib. forms) a "reward" is something given in recognition of a good act. In EV, however, "reward" is used quite generally for anything given, and the term covers the recompense of evil (Ps **91** 8), wages (1 Tim **5** 18 AV), bribes (Mic **7** 3), and gifts (Jer **40** 5 AV). RV has specialized the meaning in a number of cases (Ps **94** 2; Ezk **16** 34; Jer **40** 5, etc), but not systematically.

REZEPH, rē′zef (רֶצֶף, *reçeph;* B, **Ῥάφεις**, *Rháphei*s, **Ῥάφες**, *Rháphes*, A, **τὴν Ῥάφεθ**, *tēn Rhápheth* [2 K **19** 12], BQ^mg **Ῥάφεθ**, **א**Q^c **Ῥάφες**, A, **Ῥάφεις** [Isa **37** 12]; Vulg *Roseph* [2 K **19** 12], *Reseph* [Isa **37** 12]): One of the places referred to by Sennacherib's Rabshakeh when delivering that king's message to Hezekiah demanding the surrender of Jerus. The names which precede are Gozan and Haran; and "the children of Eden that were in Telassar" follows.

1. Forms of the Name

It is now represented by *Ruṣafa*, E. of Tipsah and N.E. of Hamath, and is regarded as the Ῥησάφα, (*Rhēsápha*) of Ptolemy (v.15). It was for some time under Assyr dominion, and appears in a geographical list (2 R 53, 37*a*) preceded by Arrapḫa (Arrapachitis) and Ḫalaḫḫu (Halah), and followed by Tamnunu, under the form of Raṣappa (elsewhere Raṣapi).

2. Now Called *Ruṣafa*

From the Eponym Canons, Ninip-kibsi-uṣur was, it appears, prefect in 839 BC, Uraš-ereš from 804 to 775 BC, Sin-šallimanni in 747, and Bêl-êmuranni in 737 BC. Judging from their names, all these were Assyrians, but a seemingly native governor, Abda'u (or Abda'i), possibly later than the foregoing, is mentioned in a list of officials (K. 9921). Yaḫuṭu was šanû (deputy-governor?) of Rezeph in 673 BC. Its mention in the Assyr geographical lists implies that Rezeph was an important trade-center in OT times.

3. Its Assyrian Governors

T. G. Pinches

REZIA, rē-zī′a. See Rizia.

REZIN, rē′zin (רְצִין, *reçīn;* **Ῥαασσών**, *Rhaassṓn*): The last of the kings of Syria who reigned in Damascus (2 K **15** 37; **16** 5–10; Isa **7** 1; **8** 4–7). Along with Pekah, the son of Remaliah, who reigned 20 years over Israel in Samaria, he joined in the Syro-Ephraimitic war against Ahaz, the king of Judah. Together they laid siege to Jerus, but were unsuccessful in the effort to take it (2 K **16** 5; Isa **7** 1). It was to calm the fears, and to restore the fainting spirits of the men of Judah, that Isaiah was commissioned by the Lord to assure them that the schemes of "these two tails of smoking firebrands" (Isa **7** 4) were destined to miscarry. It was then, too, that the sign was given of the virgin who should conceive, and bear a son, and should call his name Immanuel. Rezin had to content himself on this campaign to the S. with the capture of Elath from the men of Judah and its restoration to the men of Edom, from whom it had been taken and made a seaport by Solomon (2 K **16** 6, where it is agreed that "Syria" and "Syrians" should be read "Edom" and "Edomites," which in the Heb script are easy to be mistaken for one another, and are in fact often mistaken). Rezin, however, had a more formidable enemy to encounter on his return to Damascus. Ahaz, like kings of Judah before and after him, placed his reliance more on the arm of flesh than on the true King of his people, and appealed to Tiglath-pileser III, of Assyria, for help. Ahaz deliberately sacrificed the independence of his country in the terms of his offer of submission to the Assyrian: "I am thy servant and thy son" (2 K **16** 7). Tiglath-pileser had already carried his arms to the W. and ravaged the northern border of Israel; and now he crossed the Euphrates and hastened to Damascus, slaying Rezin and carrying his people captive to Kir (2 K **16** 9). In the copious Annals of Tiglath-pileser, Rezin figures with the designation Raṣunu(ni), but the tablet recording his death, found and read by Sir Henry Rawlinson, has been irrecoverably lost, and only the fact of its existence and loss remains (Schrader, *COT*, I, 252, 257). With the death of Rezin the kingdom of Damascus and Syria came to an end.

Rezin, Sons of: Mentioned among the Nethinim (Ezr **2** 48), who returned to Jerus with Zerubbabel from captivity (cf Neh **7** 50).

Literature.—Schrader, *COT*, as above; Driver, *Authority*, 99 ff.

T. Nicol

REZON, rē′zon (רְזוֹן, *rezōn;* **Ῥάζων**, *Rházōn*): Son of Eliadah, and a subject of Hadadezer, king of Zobah (1 K **11** 23). The name appears to be given as חֶזְיוֹן, *ḥezyōn;* Ἀζείν, *Hazeín* (1 K **15** 18; see Hezion), where he is the father of Tabrimmon, whose son Ben-hadad I is known through his league with Asa, king of Judah. When David conquered Zobah, Rezon renounced his allegiance to Hadadezer and became powerful as an independent chief, capturing Damascus and setting up as king. Along with Hadad, the noted Edomite patriot, he became a thorn in the side of Solomon, the one making himself obnoxious in the S., the other in the N., of the kingdom of Israel, both being animated with a bitter hatred of the common foe. It is said of Rezon that he "reigned over Syria" (1 K **11** 25), and if the surmise adopted by many scholars is correct that he is the same as Hezion (1 K **15** 18), then he was really the founder of the dynasty of Syrian kings so well known in the history of this period of Israel; and the line would run: Rezon, Tabrimmon, Ben-hadad I, and Ben-hadad II.

Literature.—Burney on 1 K 11 23 and 15 18 in *Notes on Heb Text of Books of Kings;* Winckler, *Alttest. Untersuchungen*, 60 ff.

T. Nicol

RHEGIUM, rē′ji-um: This city (Ῥήγιον, *Rhēgion* [Acts **28** 13], the modern Reggio di Calabria) was a town situated on the east side of the Sicilian Straits, about 6 miles S. of a point opposite Messana (Messina). Originally a colony of Chalcidian Greeks, the place enjoyed great prosperity in the 5th cent. BC, but was captured and destroyed by Dionysius, tyrant of Syracuse, in 387 BC, when all the surviving inhabitants were sold into slavery (Diodorus xiv.106–8, 111, 112). The city never entirely recovered from this blow, although it was partially restored by the younger Dionysius. On the occasion of the invasion of Italy by Pyrrhus, the people of Rhegium had recourse to an alliance with Rome (280 BC) and received 4,000 Campanian troops within their walls, who turned out to be very unruly guests. For, in imitation of a similar band of mercenaries across the strait in Messana, they massacred the male inhabitants and reduced the women to slavery (Polybius i.7; Orosius iv.3). They were not punished by the Romans until 270 BC, when the town was restored to those of its former inhabitants who still survived. The people of Rhegium were faithful to their alliance with Rome during the Second Punic War (Livy xxiii.30; xxiv.1; xxvi.12; xxix.6). At the time of the Social War they were incorporated with the Rom state, Rhegium becoming a municipality (Cicero *Verr.* v.60; *Pro Archia*, 3).

The ship in which Paul sailed from Melita to Puteoli encountered unfavorable winds after leaving Syracuse, and reached Rhegium by means of tacking. It waited at Rhegium a day for a south wind which bore it to Puteoli (Acts **28** 13), about 180 miles distant, where it probably arrived in about 26 hours.

George H. Allen

RHESA, rē′sa (Ῥησά, *Rhēsá*): A son of Zerubbabel in the genealogy of Jesus according to St. Luke (Lk **3** 27).

RHINOCEROS, rī-nos'ĕr-os: This word is found in AVm to Isa **34** 7 ("rhinocerots") for רְאֵמִים, *re'ēmīm*, AV "unicorns," RV "wild-oxen." The word is quite inappropriate to the passage, which refers to the land of Edom. The one-horned rhinoceros, *Rhinoceros unicornis*, is confined to India. Other rhinoceroses are found in India and in equatorial Africa, but it is hardly to be presumed that these animals were meant by the Heb writers. See UNICORN.

RHODA, rō'da (Ῥόδη, *Rhódē*, "rose"): A maid in the house of Mary the mother of John Mark. She came to answer when Peter knocked at Mary's door after his miraculous release from prison. On recognizing his voice, she so forgot herself with joy that she neglected to open the door, but ran in to tell the others the glad news. They would not believe her, thinking she was mad; and when she persisted in her statement they said it must be his angel. The Jewish belief was that each man had a guardian angel assigned to him. Peter continued knocking, and was ultimately admitted (Acts **12** 12 ff).

S. F. HUNTER

RHODES, rōdz (Ῥόδος, *Rhódos*): An island (and city) in the Aegean Sea, W. of Caria, rough and rocky in parts, but well watered and productive, though at present not extensively cultivated. Almost one-third of the island is now covered with trees in spite of earlier deforestation. The highest mountains attain an altitude of nearly 4,000 ft. The older names were Ophiusa, Asteria, Trinacria, Corymbia. The capital in antiquity was Rhodes, at the northeastern extremity, a strongly fortified city provided with a double harbor. Near the entrance of the harbor stood one of the seven wonders of the ancient world—a colossal bronze statue dedicated to Helios. This colossus, made by Chares about 290 BC, at a cost of 300 talents ($300,000), towered to the height of 104 ft.

In the popular mind—both before and after Shakespeare represented Caesar as bestriding the world like a colossus—this gigantic figure is conceived as an image of a human being of monstrous size with legs spread wide apart, at the entrance of the inner harbor, so huge that the largest ship with sails spread could move in under it; but the account on which this conception is based seems to have no foundation.

The statue was destroyed in 223 BC by an earthquake. It was restored by the Romans. In 672 AD the Saracens sold the ruins to a Jew. The quantity of metal was so great that it would fill the cars of a modern freight train (900 camel loads).

The most ancient cities of Rhodes were Ialysus, Ochyroma, and Lindus. The oldest inhabitants were immigrants from Crete. Later came the Carians. But no real advance in civilization was made before the immigration of the Dorians under Tlepolemus, one of the Heraclidae, and (after the Trojan war) Aethaemanes. Lindus, Ialysus and Camirus formed with Cos, Cnidus and Halicarnassus the so-called Dorian Hexapolis (Six Cities), the center of which was the temple of the Triopian Apollo on the coast of Caria. Rhodes now founded many colonies—in Spain (Rhode), in Italy (Parthenope, Salapia, Sirus, Sybaris), in Sicily (Gela), in Asia Minor (Soli), in Cilicia (Gagae), and in Lycia (Corydalla). The island attained no political greatness until the three chief cities formed a confederation and founded the new capital (Rhodes) in 408 BC. In the beginning of the Peloponnesian war, Rhodes sided with the Athenians, but, after 19 years of loyalty to Athens, went over to the Spartans (412 BC). In 394, when Conon appeared with his fleet before the city, the island fell into the hands of the Athenians again. A garrison was stationed at Rhodes by Alexander the Great. After his death this garrison was driven out by the Rhodians. It is at this time that the really great period of the island's history begins. The inhabitants bravely defended their capital against Demetrius Poliorcetes in 304 BC—the same Demetrius who two years before had won a naval victory and had coins stamped with a "Victory" that is the counterpart of the "Winged Vic-

Coin of Rhodes.

tory" which commands the unbounded admiration of the modern world—and extended their dominion over a strip of the Carian coast, as well as over several of the neighboring islands, and for the first time in the history of the world established an international maritime and commercial law. The arts and sciences now began to flourish in the fair island in the southeastern Aegean. Aeschines, the famous orator of Athens, fled to Rhodes after his defeat by Demosthenes, and founded a school of oratory, which was attended by many Romans. Rhodes became the faithful ally of Rome after the defeat of Antiochus in 189 BC. As a reward for her loyalty she received Caria. In 168, however, only a small portion of this territory remained under Rhodian sway (Peraea, or the Chersonesus). In 42 BC the island was devastated by Cassius. Later it was made a part of the Rom province of Asia (44 AD). Strabo says that he knows no city so splendid in harbor, walls and streets. When the Rom power declined, Rhodes fell into the hands of Caliph Moawijah, but later was taken by the Greeks, from whom at a later date the Genoese wrested the island. In 1249 John Cantacuzenus attempted to recover Rhodes, but in vain. Finally, however, success crowned the efforts of the Greeks under Theodoros Protosebastos. In 1310 the Knights of St. John, who had been driven from Pal, made Rhodes their home. After the subjugation of the island by Sultan Soliman in 1522 the Knights of St. John removed to Malta, and Rhodes has remained uninterruptedly a possession of the Sublime Porte down to the recent war between Turkey and the Balkan allies, forming, with the other islands, the province of the "Islands of the White Sea" (Archipelago). It has a Christian governor whose seat, though mostly at Rhodes, is sometimes at Chios. The population of the island has greatly diminished by emigration. In 1890 the total number of inhabitants was 30,000 (20,000 Greeks, 7,000 Mohammedans, 1,500 Jews). The chief products of Rhodes are wheat, oil, wine, figs and tropical fruits. A very important industry is the exportation of sponges. The purity of the air and the mildness of the climate make Rhodes a most delightful place to live in during the fall, winter and early spring. The city, built in the shape of an amphitheater, has a magnificent view toward the sea. It contains several churches made out of old mosques. The once famous harbor is now almost filled with sand. The inhabitants number nearly 12,000 (all Turks and Jews). Rhodes is mentioned in the NT only as a point where Paul touched on his voyage southward from the Hellespont to Caesarea (Acts **21** 1); but in 1 Macc **15** 23 we are informed that it was one of the states to which the Romans sent letters in behalf of the Jews.

LITERATURE.—Berg, *Die Insel Rhodes* (Braunschweig, 1860–62); Schneiderwirth, *Geschichte der Insel Rhodes* (Heiligenstadt, 1868); Guérin, *L'île de Rhodes*, 2d ed, Paris, 1880; Biliotti and Cottrel, *L'île de Rhodes* (Paris, 1881); Torr, *Rhodes in Ancient Times* (Cambridge, 1885) and *Rhodes in Modern Times* (1887).

J. E. HARRY

RHODOCUS, rod'ō-kus (Ῥόδοκος, *Rhódokos*): A Jewish traitor who disclosed the plans of Judas to Antiochus (Eupator) (2 Macc **13** 21) 162 BC. Of his fate nothing more is known.

RIB (צֵלָע, *çēlā'*, צַלְעָה, *çal'āh;* Aram. עֲלַע, *'ăla'*): The Heb words designate the "side," "flank," thence the "ribs." They are found thus tr[d] only in connection with the creation of Eve: "He [Jeh] took one of his [Adam's] ribs, and closed up the flesh instead thereof: and the rib, which Jeh God had taken from the man, made he [m "builded he into"] a woman" (Gen **2** 21.22). The Aram. word is only found in Dnl **7** 5.

Twice the RV uses the word "rib" in a figurative sense of two beams or rafters built into the ark of the covenant and the altar of incense, on which the golden rings were fastened, which served to carry ark and altar by means of staves (Ex **30** 4; **37** 27).

A curious mistr has crept into AV, which here follows Jewish commentators or etymologists, in four passages in 2 S (**2** 23; **3** 27; **4** 6; **20** 10), where the "fifth rib" is mentioned as the place of the body under which spears or swords are thrust, so as to cause lethal wounds. The Heb word *hōmesh*, which indeed means "fifth," is here a noun, derived from a root meaning "to be staunch," "stalwart," "stout," "fleshy," "obese" (cf חָמֻשׁ, *ḥāmush*, "armed," "equipped soldier"; Arab. الخميس, *el khamīs* [*el ḥamīs*], "the army," which, however, Arab. lexicographers explain as meaning "fivefold," viz. vanguard, right and left wing, center and rear guard). The word is to be tr[d] "abdomen," "belly." RV renders correctly "into the body."

H. L. E. LUERING

RIBAI, rī'bā-ī, rī'bī (רִיבַי, *rībhay;* LXX Ῥειβά, *Rheibá*, with variants): A Benjamite, the father of ITTAI (q.v.), one of David's "mighty men" (2 S **23** 29 ‖ 1 Ch **11** 31).

RIBBAND, rib'and, rib'an (פָּתִיל, *pāthīl* [Nu **15** 38 AV]). See COLOR, (2); CORD, (4).

RIBLAH, rib'la (רִבְלָה, *ribhlāh;* Ῥεβλαθά, *Reblathá*, with variants):

(1) Riblah in the land of Hamath first appears in history in 608 BC. Here Pharaoh-necoh, after defeating Josiah at Megiddo and destroying Kadytis or Kadesh on the Orontes, fixed his headquarters, and while in camp he deposed Jehoahaz and cast him into chains, fixed the tribute of Judah, and appointed Jehoiakim king (2 K **23** 31–35). In 588 BC Nebuchadnezzar, at war with Egypt and the Syrian states, also established his headquarters at Riblah, and from it he directed the subjugation of Jerus. When it fell, Zedekiah was carried prisoner to Riblah, and there, after his sons and his nobles had been slain in his presence, his eyes were put out, and he was taken as a prisoner to Babylon (2 K **25** 6.20; Jer **39** 5–7; **52** 8–11). Riblah then disappears from history, but the site exists today in the village of *Ribleh*, 35 miles N.E. of Baalbek, and the situation is the finest that could have been chosen by the Egyp or Bab kings for their headquarters in Syria. An army camped there had abundance of water in the control of the copious springs that go to form the Orontes. The Egyptians coming from the S. had behind them the command of the rich corn and forage lands of Coele-Syria, while the Bab army from the N. was equally fortunate in the rich plains extending to Hamath and the Euphrates. Lebanon, close by, with its forests, its hunting grounds and its snows, ministered to the needs and luxuries of the leaders. Riblah commanded the great trade and war route between Egypt and Mesopotamia, and, besides, it was at the dividing-point of many minor routes. It was in a position to attack with facility Phoenicia, Damascus or Pal, or to defend itself against attack from those places, while a few miles to the S. the mountains on each side close in forming a pass where a mighty host might easily be resisted by a few. In every way Riblah was the strategical point between North and South Syria. Riblah should probably be read for Diblah in Ezk **6** 14, while in Nu **34** 11 it does not really appear. See (2).

(2) A place named as on the ideal *eastern* boundary of Israel in Nu **34** 11, but omitted in Ezk **47** 15–18. The MT reads "Hariblah"; but the LXX probably preserves the true vocalization, according to which we should tr "to Harbel." It is said to be to the east of *'Ain*, and that, as the designation of a district, can only mean *Merj 'Ayun*, so that we should seek it in the neighborhood of Hermon, one of whose spurs Furrer found to be named *Jebel 'Arbel.*

W. M. CHRISTIE

RICHES, rich'ez, rich'iz: Used to render the following Heb and Gr words: (1) *'Ōsher*, which should, perhaps, be considered the most general word, as it is the most often used (Gen **31** 16; Eccl **4** 8; Jer **9** 23). It looks at riches simply as riches, without regard to any particular feature. Alongside this would go the Gr πλοῦτος, *ploútos* (Mt **13** 22; Eph **2** 7). (2) *Ḥōṣen* (Prov **27** 24; Jer **20** 5), *n[e]khāṣīm* and *r[e]khūsh* (Gen **36** 7; Dnl **11** 13.24 AV) look at riches as things accumulated, collected, amassed. (3) *Hōn* looks upon riches as earnings, the fruit of toil (Ps **119** 14; Prov **8** 18; Ezk **27** 27). (4) *Hāmōn* regards riches in the aspect of being much, this coming from the original idea of noise, through the idea of a multitude as making the noise, the idea of many, or much, being in multitude (Ps **37** 16 AV). (5) *Ḥayil* regards riches as power (Ps **62** 10; Isa **8** 4; **10** 14). (6) *Yithrāh* means "running over," and so presents riches as abundance (Jer **48** 36 AV). Along with this may be placed *shū[a]'*, which has the idea of breadth, and so of abundance (Job **36** 19 AV). (7) *Ḳinyān* regards riches as a creation, something made (Ps **104** 24; cf m); (8) χρῆμα (*chrēma*) looks at riches as useful (Mk **10** 23 f ‖). Like the NT, the Apoc uses only *ploutos* and *chrēma.*

Material riches are regarded by the Scriptures as neither good nor bad in themselves, but only according as they are properly or improperly used. They are transitory (Prov **27** 24); they are not to be trusted in (Mk **10** 23; Lk **18** 24; 1 Tim **6** 17); they are not to be gloried in (Jer **9** 23); the heart is not to be set on them (Ps **62** 10); but they are made by God (Ps **104** 24), and come from God (1 Ch **29** 12); and they are the crown of the wise (Prov **14** 24). Material riches are used to body forth for us the most precious and glorious realities of the spiritual realm. See, e.g., Rom **9** 23; **11** 33; Eph **2** 7; Phil **4** 19; Col **1** 27. Cf MAMMON; TREASURE; WEALTH.

E. J. FORRESTER

RID, rid, **RIDDANCE**, rid'ans: "Rid" originally meant "rescue" (AV Gen **37** 22; Ex **6** 6; Ps **82** 4; **144** 7.11), whence the meaning "remove" or "clean out" (Lev **26** 6 AV, with "riddance" in Lev **23** 22; Zeph **1** 18). The word occurs in ARV and in ERV in Ex **6** 6.

RIDDLE, rid″l (חִידָה, *ḥīdhāh;* **αἴνιγμα,** *aínigma*). See GAMES.

RIE, rī (AV, Ex **9** 32; Isa **28** 25). See SPELT.

RIGHT, rīt (יָשָׁר, *yāshār,* מִשְׁפָּט, *mishpāṭ;* **δίκαιος,** *díkaios,* **εὐθύς,** *euthús*): Many Heb words are trd "right," with different shades of meaning. Of these the two noted are the most important: *yāshār,* with the sense of being straight, direct, as "right in the sight" of Jeh (Ex **15** 26; Dt **12** 25, etc), in one's own eyes (Jgs **17** 6), "right words" (Job **6** 25 AV, *yōsher*), "right paths" (Prov **4** 11 AV); and *mishpāṭ,* "judgment," "cause," etc, a forensic term, as "Shall not the Judge of all the earth do right?" (Gen **18** 25). In Job **34** 17, RV has "justice" (ver 6, "right"), etc. The words *çedheḳ, çedhāḳāh,* ordinarily trd "righteousness," are in a few cases rendered "right" (2 S **19** 28; Neh **2** 20; Ps **9** 4; **17** 1; **119** 75; Ezk **18** 5, etc). In the NT the chief word is *dikaios,* primarily "even," "equal" (Mt **20** 4; Lk **12** 57, etc); more generally the word is rendered "just" and "righteous." *Euthus,* used by LXX for *yāshār* (1 S **12** 23; Hos **14** 9), occurs a few times (Acts **8** 21; **13** 10; 2 Pet **2** 15); so *orthôs,* "straight," "upright" (Lk **10** 28).

"Right-hand" or "side" represents Heb *yāmīn* and kindred forms (Gen **48** 13.14.17; Ex **15** 6, etc); the Gr, in this sense, is *dexiós* (Mt **6** 3; **20** 21, etc).

RV, among other changes, has "right" for AV "judgment" in Job **27** 2; **34** 5, and for "right" in AV substitutes "straight" in Ezr **8** 21, "skilful" in Eccl **4** 4, m "successful," etc. In Jn **1** 12 RV reads, "the right to become children of God" for AV "the power" (*exousía*); in Mt **20** 7.15 "right" is omitted, with the larger part of the verse. In 2 Tim **2** 15 "rightly dividing" (*orthotoméō*) is changed to "handling aright," with m "holding a straight course in the word of truth. *Or,* rightly dividing the word of truth." W. L. WALKER

RIGHTEOUSNESS, rī′chus-nes (צַדִּיק, *çaddīḳ,* adj., "righteous," or occasionally "just"; צֶדֶק, *çedheḳ,* noun, occasionally = "righteousness," occasionally = "justice"; **δίκαιος,** *díkaios,* adj., **δικαιοσύνη,** *dikaiosúnē,* noun, from **δίκη,** *díkē,* whose first meaning seems to have been "custom"; the general use suggested conformity to a standard: righteousness, "the state of him who is such as he ought to be" [Thayer]):

1. Double Aspect of Righteousness: Changing and Permanent
2. Social Customs and Righteousness
3. Changing Conception of Character of God: Obligations of Power
4. Righteousness as Inner
5. Righteousness as Social
6. Righteousness as Expanding in Content with Growth in Ideals of Human Worth

LITERATURE

In Christian thought the idea of righteousness contains both a permanent and a changing element.

1. Double Aspect of Righteousness

The fixed element is the will to do right; the changing factor is the conception of what may be right at different times and under different circumstances. Throughout the entire course of Christian revelation we discern the emphasis on the first factor. To be sure, in the days of later Pharisaism righteousness came to be so much a matter of externals that the inner intent was often lost sight of altogether (Mt **23** 23); but, on the whole and in the main, Christian thought in all ages has recognized as the central element in righteousness the intention to be and do right. This common spirit binds together the first worshippers of God and the latest. Present-day conceptions of what is right differ by vast distances from the conceptions of the earlier Hebrews, but the intentions of the first worshippers are as discernible as are those of the doers of righteousness in the present day.

There seems but little reason to doubt that the content of the idea of righteousness was determined

2. Social Customs and Righteousness

in the first instance by the customs of social groups. There are some, of course, who would have us believe that what we experience as inner moral sanction is nothing but the fear of consequences which come through disobeying the will of the social group, or the feeling of pleasure which results as we know we have acted in accordance with the social demands. At least some thinkers would have us believe that this is all there was in moral feeling in the beginning. If a social group was to survive it must lay upon its individual members the heaviest exactions. Back of the performance of religious rites was the fear of the group that the god of the group would be displeased if certain honors were not rendered to him. Merely to escape the penalties of an angry deity the group demanded ceremonial religious observances. From the basis of fear thus wrought into the individuals of the group have come all our loftier movements toward righteousness.

It is not necessary to deny the measure of truth there may be in this account. To point out its inadequacy, however, a better statement would be that from the beginning the social group utilized the native moral feeling of the individual for the defence of the group. The moral feeling, by which we mean a sense of the difference between right and wrong, would seem to be a part of the native furnishing of the mind. It is very likely that in the beginning this moral feeling was directed toward the performance of the rites which the group looked upon as important (see ALMS).

As we read the earlier parts of the OT we are struck by the fact that much of the early Heb morality was of this group kind. The righteous man was the man who performed the rites which had been handed down from the beginning (Dt **6** 25). The meaning of some of these rites is lost in obscurity, but from a very early period the characteristic of Heb righteousness is that it moves in the direction of what we should call today the enlargement of humanity. There seemed to be at work, not merely the forces which make for the preservation of the group, not merely the desire to please the God of the Hebrews for the sake of the material favors which He might render the Hebrews, but the factors which make for the betterment of humanity as such. As we examine the laws of the Hebrews, even at so late a time as the completion of the formal Codes, we are indeed struck by traces of primitive survivals (Nu **5** 11–31). There are some injunctions whose purpose we cannot well understand. But, on the other hand, the vast mass of the legislation had to do with really human considerations. There are rules concerning sanitation (Lev **13**), both as it touches the life of the group and of the individual; laws whose mastery begets emphasis, not merely upon external consequences, but upon the inner result in the life of the individual (Ps **51** 3); and prohibitions which would indicate that morality, at least in its plainer decencies, had come to be valued on its own account. If we were to seek for some clue to the development of the moral life of the Hebrews we might well find it in this emphasis upon the growing demands of human life as such. A suggestive writer has pointed out that the apparently meaningless commandment, "Thou shalt not boil a kid in its mother's milk" (Ex **23** 19), has back of it a real human purpose, that there are some things which in themselves are revolting apart from any external consequences (see also Lev **18**).

An index of the growth of the moral life of the people is to be found in the changing conception of the character of God. We need not enter into the question as to just where on the moral plane the idea of the God of the Hebrews started, but from the very beginning we see clearly that the Hebrews believed in their God as one passionately devoted to the right (Gen **18** 25). It may well be that at the start the God of the Hebrews was largely a God of War, but it is to be noticed that His enmity was against the peoples who had little regard for the larger human considerations. It has often been pointed out that one proof of the inspiration of the Scriptures is to be found in their moral superiority to the Scriptures of the peoples around about the Hebrews. If the Heb writers used material which was common property of Chaldaeans, Babylonians, and other peoples, they nevertheless used these materials with a moral difference. They breathed into them a moral life which forever separates them from the Scriptures of other peoples. The marvel also of Heb history is that in the midst of revoltingly immoral surroundings the Hebrews grew to such ideals of human worth. The source of these ideals is to be found in their thought of God. Of course, in moral progress there is a reciprocal effect; the thought of God affects the thought of human life and the thought of human life affects the thought of God; but the Hebrews no sooner came to a fresh moral insight than they made their moral discovery a part of the character of God. From the beginning, we repeat, the God of the Hebrews was a God directed in His moral wrath against all manner of abominations, aberrations and abnormalities. The purpose of God, according to the Hebrews, was to make a people "separated" in the sense that they were to be free from anything which would detract from a full moral life (Lev **20** 22).

3. Changing Conception of Character of God

We can trace the more important steps in the growth of the Heb ideal. First, there was an increasingly clear discernment that certain things are to be ruled out at once as immoral. The primitive decencies upon which individual and social life depended were discerned at an early period (cf passages in Lev cited above). Along with this it must be admitted there was a slower approach to some ideals which we today consider important, the ideals of the marriage relations for example (Dt **24** 1.2). Then there was a growing sense of what constitutes moral obligation in the discharge of responsibilities upon the part of men toward their fellows (Isa **5** 8.23). There was increasing realization also of what God, as a moral Being, is obligated to do. The hope of salvation of nations and individuals rests at once upon the righteousness of God.

By the time of Isaiah the righteousness of God has come to include the obligations of power (Isa **63** 1). God will save His people, not merely because He has promised to save them, but because He must save them (**42** 6). The *must* is moral. If the people of Israel show themselves unworthy, God must punish them; but if a remnant, even a small remnant, show themselves faithful, God must show His favor toward them. Moral worth is not conceived of as something that is to be paid for by external rewards, but if God is moral He must not treat the righteous and the unrighteous alike. This conception of what God must do as an obligated Being influences profoundly the Heb interpretation of the entire course of history (**10** 20.21).

Upon this ideal of moral obligation there grows later the thought of the virtue of vicarious suffering (ch **53**). The sufferings of the good man and of God for those who do not in themselves deserve such sufferings (for them) are a mark of a still higher righteousness (see HOSEA, BOOK OF). The movement of the Scriptures is all the way from the thought of a God who gives battle for the right to the thought of a God who receives in Himself the heaviest shocks of that battle that others may have opportunity for moral life.

These various lines of moral development come, of course, to their crown in the NT in the life and death of Christ as set before us in the Gospels and interpreted by the apostles. Jesus stated certain moral axioms so clearly that the world never will escape their power. He said some things once and for all, and He did some things once and for all; that is to say, in His life and death He set on high the righteousness of God as at once moral obligation and self-sacrificing love (Jn **3** 16) and with such effectiveness that the world has not escaped and cannot escape this righteous influence (Jn **12** 32). Moreover, the course of apostolic and subsequent history has shown that Christ put a winning and compelling power into the idea of righteousness that it would otherwise have lacked (Rom **8** 31.32).

The ideas at work throughout the course of Heb and Christian history are, of course, at work today.

4. Righteousness as Inner

Christianity deepens the sense of obligation to do right. It makes the moral spirit essential. Then it utilizes every force working for the increase of human happiness to set on high the meaning of righteousness. Jesus spoke of Himself as "life," and declared that He came that men might have life and have it more abundantly (Jn **10** 10). The keeping of the commandments plays, of course, a large part in the unfolding of the life of the righteous Christian, but the keeping of the commandments is not to be conceived of in artificial or mechanical fashion (Lk **10** 25–37). With the passage of the centuries some commandments once conceived of as essential drop into the secondary place, and other commandments take the controlling position. In Christian development increasing place is given for certain swift insights of the moral spirit. We believe that some things are righteous because they at once appeal to us as righteous. Again, some other things seem righteous because their consequences are beneficial, both for society and for the individual. Whatever makes for the largest life is in the direction of righteousness. In interpreting life, however, we must remember the essentially Christian conception that man does not live through outer consequences alone. In all thought of consequences the chief place has to be given to inner consequences. By the surrender of outward happiness and outward success a man may attain inner success. The spirit of the cross is still the path to the highest righteousness.

The distinctive note in emphasis upon righteousness in our own day is the stress laid upon social service. This does not mean that Christianity is to lose sight of the worth of the individual in himself. We have come pretty clearly to see that the individual is the only moral end in himself. Righteousness is to have as its aim the upbuilding of individual lives. The commandments of the righteous life are not for the sake of society as a thing in itself. Society is nothing apart from the individuals that compose it; but we are coming to see that individuals have larger relationships than we had once imagined and greater responsibilities than we had dreamed of. The influence of the individual touches others at more points than we had formerly realized. We have at times con-

5. Righteousness as Social

demned the system of things as being responsible for much human misery which we now see can be traced to the agency of individuals. The employer, the day-laborer, the professional man, the public servant, all these have large responsibilities for the life of those around. The unrighteous individual has a power of contaminating other individuals, and his deadliness we have just begun to understand. All this is receiving new emphasis in our present-day preaching of righteousness. While our social relations are not ends in themselves, they are mighty means for reaching individuals in large numbers. The Christian conception of redeemed humanity is not that of society as an organism existing on its own account, but that of individuals knit very closely together in their social relationships and touching one another for good in these relationships (1 Cor **1** 2; Rev **7** 9.10). If we were to try to point out the line in which the Christian doctrine of righteousness is to move more and more through the years, we should have to emphasize this element of obligation to society. This does not mean that a new gospel is to supersede the old or even place itself alongside the old. It does mean that the righteousness of God and the teaching of Christ and the cross, which are as ever the center of Christianity, are to find fresh force in the thought of the righteousness of the Christian as binding itself, not merely by commandments to do the will of God in society, but by the inner spirit to live the life of God out into society.

6. Expanding in Content

In all our thought of righteousness it must be borne in mind that there is nothing in Christian revelation which will tell us what righteousness calls for in every particular circumstance. The differences between earlier and later practical standards of conduct and the differences between differing standards in different circumstances have led to much confusion in the realm of Christian thinking. We can keep our bearing, however, by remembering the double element in righteousness which we mentioned in the beginning; on the one hand, the will to do right, and, on the other, the difficulty of determining in a particular circumstance just what the right is. The larger Christian conceptions always have an element of fluidity, or, rather, an element of expansiveness. For example, it is clearly a Christian obligation to treat all men with a spirit of good will or with a spirit of Christian love. But what does love call for in a particular case? We can only answer the question by saying that love seeks for whatever is best, both for him who receives and for him who gives. This may lead to one course of conduct in one situation and to quite a different course in another. We must, however, keep before us always the aim of the largest life for all persons whom we can reach. Christian righteousness today is even more insistent upon material things, such as sanitary arrangements, than was the Code of Moses. The obligation to use the latest knowledge for the hygienic welfare is just as binding now as then, but "the latest knowledge" is a changing term. Material progress, education, spiritual instruction, are all influences which really make for full life.

Not only is present-day righteousness social and growing; it is also concerned, to a large degree, with the thought of the world which now is. Righteousness has too often been conceived of merely as the means of preparing for the life of some future Kingdom of Heaven. Present-day emphasis has not ceased to think of the life beyond this, but the life beyond this can best be met and faced by those who have been in the full sense righteous in the life that now is. There is here no break in true Christian continuity. The seers who have understood Christianity best always have insisted that to the fullest degree the present world must be redeemed by the life-giving forces of Christianity. We still insist that all idea of earthly righteousness takes its start from heavenly righteousness, or, rather, that the righteousness of man is to be based upon his conception of the righteousness of God. Present-day thinking concerns itself largely with the idea of the Immanence of God. God is in this present world. This does not mean that there may not be other worlds, or are not other worlds, and that God is not also in those worlds; but the immediate revelation of God to us is in our present world. Our present world then must be the sphere in which the righteousness of God and of man is to be set forth. God is conscience, and God is love. The present sphere is to be used for the manifestation of His holy love. The chief channel through which that holy love is to manifest itself is the conscience and love of the Christian believer. But even these terms are not to be used in the abstract. There is an abstract conscientiousness which leads to barren living: the life gets out of touch with things that are real. There is an experience of love which exhausts itself in well-wishing. Both conscience and love are to be kept close to the earth by emphasis upon the actual realities of the world in which we live.

Literature.—G. B. Stevens, *The Christian Doctrine of Salvation;* A. E. Garvie, *Handbook of Christian Apologetics;* Borden P. Bowne, *Principles of Ethics;* Newman Smyth, *Christian Ethics;* A. B. Bruce, *The Kingdom of God;* W. N. Clarke, *The Ideal of Jesus;* H. C. King, *The Ethics of Jesus.*

Francis J. McConnell

RIMMON, rim'on:

(1) The rock Rimmon (סֶלַע רִמּוֹן, *ṣela' rimmōn; ἡ πέτρα Ῥεμμών, hē pétra Rhemmṓn*): The place of refuge of the 600 surviving Benjamites of Gibeah (*Jeba'*) who "turned and fled toward the wilderness unto the rock of Rimmon, and abode in the rock of Rimmon four months" (Jgs **20** 45.47; **21** 13). Robinson's identification (*RB*, I, 440) has been very generally accepted. He found a conical and very prominent hill some 6 miles N.N.E. of *Jeba'* upon which stands a village called *Rummōn.* This site was known to Eusebius and Jerome (*OS* **146** 6; **287** 98), who describe it as 15 Rom miles from Jerus. Another view, which would locate the place of refuge of the Benjamites in the *Mughāret el jai,* a large cavern on the south of the *Wâdy Suweinît,* near *Jeba'*, is strongly advocated by Rawnsley and Birch (see *PEF*, III, 137–48). The latter connects this again with 1 S **14** 2, where Saul, accompanied by his 600, "abode in the uttermost part of Gibeah" under the pomegranate tree (Rimmon).

(2) (רִמּוֹן, *rimmōn; Ἐρεμμών, Eremmṓn,* or *Ῥεμμώθ, Rhemmṓth*): A city in the Negeb, near the border of Edom, ascribed to Judah (Josh **15** 32) and to Simeon (**19** 7; 1 Ch **4** 32, AV "Remmon"). In Zec **14** 10 it is mentioned as the extreme S. of Judah—"from Geba to Rimmon, S. of Jerus." In the earlier references Rimmon occurs in close association with *'Ain* (a spring), and in Neh **11** 29, what is apparently the same place, *'Ain Rimmon,* is called *En-rimmon* (q.v.).

(3) (רִמּוֹן, *rimmōn* [Josh **19** 13], רִמּוֹנָה, *rimmōnāh,* in some Heb MSS דִּמְנָה, *dimnāh* [see Dimnah] [Josh **21** 35], and רִמּוֹנוֹ, *rimmōnō* [1 Ch **6** 77]): In AV we have "Remmon-methoar" in Josh **19** 13, but RV translates the latter as "which stretcheth." This was a city on the border of Zebulun (Josh **19** 13) allotted to the Levites (Josh **21** 35, "Dimnah"; 1 Ch **6** 77). The site is now the little village of *Rummāneh* on a low ridge S. of the western end of the marshy plain *el Baṭṭauf* in Galilee; there are many rock-cut tombs and cisterns. It is about 4 miles

N. of *el Mesh-hed*, usually considered to be the site of Gath-hepher. See *PEF*, I, 363, Sh VI.

E. W. G. Masterman

RIMMON (רִמּוֹן, *rimmōn*, "pomegranate"; see Rimmon-perez):

(1) A Syrian god. Naaman the Syrian leper after being cured is troubled over the fact that he will still have to bow down in the house of the Syrian god, Rimmon, when his master goes into the house to worship leaning on his hand (2 K **5** 18). Elisha answers him ambiguously: "Go in peace." Judging from Naaman's position and this incident, R. must have been one of the leading gods of the Syrians worshipped in Damascus. He has been identified with Rammânu, the Assyr god of wind, rain and storm. The name appears in the Syrian personal names Hadadrimmon and Tab-rimmon (q.v.) and its meaning is dubious (*ramâmu*, "to thunder" [?])

(2) A Benjamite of Beeroth, whose sons Baanah and Rechab assassinated Ish-bosheth (2 S **4** 2.5.9).

Nathan Isaacs

RIMMON-PEREZ, r.-pē'rez (רִמֹּן פֶּרֶץ, *rimmōn pereç;* AV **Rimmon-parez**): A desert camp of the Israelites (Nu **33** 19 f), unidentified. Gesenius translates *rimmōn* as "pomegranate," the place deriving its name from the abundance of pomegranates. But Conder derives it from *rāmam*, "to be high," and translates it "cloven height." See Wanderings of Israel.

RIMMON, ROCK OF. See Rimmon, (1).

RIMMONAH, rim-mō'na, **RIMMONO,** rim-mō'no. See Rimmon, (3).

RING (AS *Hring*, "ring"): The word renders (ARV) two Heb words (in AV and ERV three) and two Gr words. טַבַּעַת, *ṭabba'ath*, the principal Heb word, is from טָבַע, *ṭābha'*, "sink," either because the ring is something "cast" or molded, or, more prob-

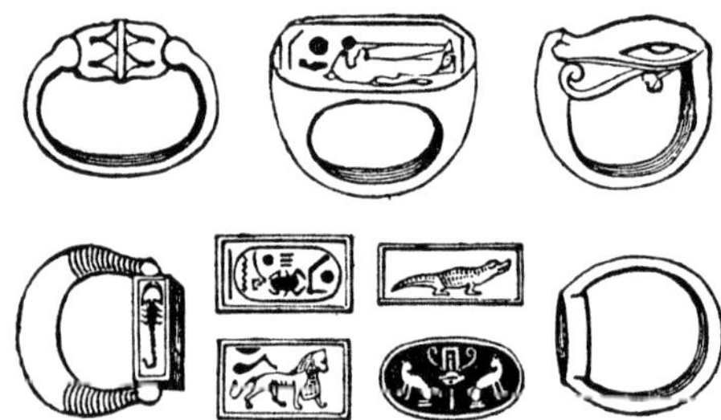

Egyptian Signet Rings and Impressions Made from Them.

ably, since the principal use of the ring was as a seal, because it "sank" into the wax or clay that received the impression. In Ex, *ṭabba'ath*, "ring," is a detail of furniture or equipment, as the rings of the ark through which the staves were thrust (Ex **25** 12, etc), rings for curtains, in the high priest's ephod (Ex **28** 28; **39** 21), etc. Its other use was perhaps the original, to describe the article of personal adornment worn on the finger, apparently in the OT always a **signet-ring,** and as such an indispensable article of masculine attire. Such a ring Pharaoh gave Joseph as a symbol of authority (Gen **41** 42); and Ahasuerus gave Haman (Est **3** 10); with it the royal missive was sealed (Est **3** 12; **8** 8 *bis*. 10). It was also a feminine ornament in Isaiah's list of the fashionable feminine paraphernalia, "the rings and the nose-jewels" (quite likely rings also) (Isa **3** 21). Either as ornaments or for their intrinsic value, or both, rings were used as gifts for sacred purposes from both men and women: "brooches, and ear-rings, and signet-rings" (m "nose-rings") (Ex **35** 22); "bracelets, rings [ARV "signet-rings"], ear-rings" (Nu **31** 50 AV). חוֹתָם, *ḥōthām*, "signet," mentioned in Gen **38** 18.25; Ex **28** 11. 21.36; Ex **39** 6.14.30; Jer **22** 24; Hag **2** 23, etc, was probably usually a seal ring, but in Gen **38** and elsewhere the seal may have been swung on wire, and suspended by a cord from the neck. It was not only an identification, but served as a stamp for signature. גָּלִיל, *gālīl*, "circle" (cf "Galilee," "Circle" of the Gentiles), rendered "ring" in Est **1** 6; Cant **5** 14, may rather mean "cylinder" or "rod" of metal. **Earring** (q.v.) in AV is from totally different words: נֶזֶם, *nezem*, whose etymology is unknown, עָגִיל, *'āghīl*, "round," or לַחַשׁ, *laḥash*, "amulet"; so RV. The "rings" of the wheels in Ezk **1** 18 (AV) are גַּב, *gabh*, "curved," and mean "rims" (ARV), "felloes." Egyptians esp. wore a great profusion of rings, principally of silver or gold, engraved with scarabaei, or other devices. In the NT the ring, δακτύλιος, *daktúlios*, "finger-ring," is a token of means, position, standing: "put a ring on his hand" (Lk **15** 22). Perhaps also it included the right to give orders in his father's name. To be χρυσοδακτύλιος, *chrusodaktúlios*, "golden-ringed," perhaps with more than one, indicated wealth and social rank: "a man with a gold ring" (Jas **2** 2). See also Earring; Signet; Seal.

Philip Wendell Crannell

RINGLEADER, ring'lēd-ẽr: In Acts **24** 5 the tr of πρωτοστάτης, *prōtostátēs*, "one who stands first." Not an opprobrious word in the Gr.

RINGSTREAKED, ring'strēkt (AV and ERV **ringstraked**): Gen **30** 35.39.40; **31** 8 (*bis*).10.12 for עָקֹד, *'āḳōdh*. In the context of **30** 35, etc, *'āḳōdh* certainly denotes defective coloring of some sort, but the exact meaning of the word is uncertain. The tr "ringstreaked" ("marked with circular bands") comes from connecting the word with the √ *'ḳd*, "to bind" (Gen **22** 9), but this connection is dubious.

RINNAH, rin'a (רִנָּה, *rinnāh*, "praise to God"; LXX B, **'Ανά,** *Aná*, A, **'Ραννών,** *Rhannôn*): A Judahite, according to MT a son of Shimon (1 Ch **4** 20). But LXX makes him a son of Hanan (B, *Phaná*, A, *Anán*) by reading "ben" in the next name (Ben-hanan) as "son of."

RIOT, rī'ut: Properly, "unrestrained behavior" of any sort, but in modern Eng, usually connoting mob action, although such phrases as a "riotous banquet" are still in common use. AV uses the word in the first sense, and it is retained by RV in Lk **15** 13; Tit **1** 6; 1 Pet **4** 4 for ἀσώτως, *asōtōs*, ἀσωτία, *asōtía*, "having no hope of safety," "profligate." In Prov **23** 20; **28** 7 RV has preferred "gluttonous," "glutton," in Rom **13** 13, "revelling," and in 2 Pet **2** 13, "revel."

Burton Scott Easton

RIPHATH, rī'fath (רִיפַת, *rīphath*): A son of Gomer, the eldest son of Japhet (Gen **10** 3; 1 Ch **1** 6, where MT and RV read Diphath [q.v.]). Jos (*Ant*, I, vi, 1) identifies the Ripheans with the Paphlagonians, through whose country on the Black Sea ran the river "Rhebas" (Pliny, *NH*, vi.4).

RISING, rīz'ing (שְׂאֵת, *s^e'ēth*, "a tumor," "swelling" [Lev **13** 2.10, etc]). See Leprosy.

RISSAH, ris'a (רִסָּה, *riṣṣāh*, "dew"): A camp of the Israelites in the wilderness wanderings between

Libnah and Kehelathah (Nu **33** 21 f). See WANDERINGS OF ISRAEL.

RITHMAH, rith'ma (רִתְמָה, *rithmāh*, "broom"): A desert camp of the Israelites (Nu **33** 18.19). The name refers to the white desert broom. See WANDERINGS OF ISRAEL.

RIVER, riv'ẽr:

(1) The usual word is נָהָר, *nāhār* (Aram. נְהַר, *nᵉhar* [Ezr **4** 10, etc]), used of the rivers of Eden (Gen **2** 10–14), often of the Euphrates (Gen **15** 18, etc), of Abana and Pharpar (2 K **5** 12), the river of Gozan (2 K **17** 6), the river Chebar (Ezk **1** 1), the rivers (canals ?) of Babylon (Ps **137** 1), the rivers of Ethiopia (Isa **18** 1; Zeph **3** 10). Cf نَهْر, *nahr*, the common Arab. word for "river."

(2) יְאוֹר, *yᵉ'ōr*, according to *BDB* from Egyp *'iotr*, *'io'r*, "watercourse," often of the Nile (Ex **1** 22, etc). In Isa **19** 6, for יְאֹרֵי מָצוֹר, *yᵉ'ōrē māçōr*, AV "brooks of defence," RV has "streams of Egypt." In Isa **19** 7[3].8, for *yᵉ'ōr*, AV "brooks," and Zec **10** 11, AV "river," RV has "Nile." In Job **28** 10, AV "He cutteth out rivers among the rocks," RV has "channels," RVm "passages."

(3) There are nearly 100 references to נַחַל, *naḥal*. In about half of these AV has "brook" and in about half "river." RV has more often "brook" or "valley." But RV has river in "whatsoever hath fins and scales in the waters, in the seas, and in the rivers" (Lev **11** 9); "the river Jabbok" (Dt **2** 37; Josh **12** 2); the stream issuing from the temple (Ezk **47** 5–12). RV has "brook of Egypt," i.e. *el-'Arîsh* (Nu **34** 5; Josh **15** 47; 1 K **8** 65; 2 K **24** 7; 2 Ch **7** 8; Am **6** 14, "of the Arabah"); "brook [AV "river"] of Kanah" (Josh **16** 8); "valley [AV "river"] of the Arnon" (Dt **2** 24). EV has "valley": of Gerar (Gen **26** 17), of Zered (Nu **21** 12), but "brook Zered" (Dt **2** 13), of Eschol (Nu **32** 9), of Sorek (Jgs **16** 4), of Shittim (Joel **3** 18). EV has "brook": Besor (1 S **30** 10), Kidron (2 S **15** 23), Gaash (2 S **23** 30), Cherith (1 K **17** 3); also the fem. נַחֲלָה, *naḥălāh*, "brook [AV "river"] of Egypt" (Ezk **47** 19; **48** 28). The torrent-valley (*wâdy*) is often meant.

(4) פֶּלֶג, *pelegh*, with fem. פְּלַגָּה, *pᵉlaggāh*, AV "river," is in RV tr[d] "stream," except EV "river of God" (Ps **65** 9); "streams of water" (Ps **1** 3; Prov **5** 16; Isa **32** 2; Lam **3** 48); "streams of honey" (Job **20** 17); "streams of oil" (Job **29** 6).

(5) אָפִיק, *'āphīḳ*, AV "river," except EV "water brooks" (Ps **42** 1), is in RV "watercourses" (Ezk **6** 3; **31** 12; **32** 6; **34** 13; **35** 8; **36** 4.6), "water-brooks" (Cant **5** 12; Joel **1** 20).

(6) יוּבַל, *yūbhal*, EV "river" (Jer **17** 8). אֻבָל, *'ubhāl*, and אוּבָל, *'ūbhāl*, EV "river" (Dnl **8** 2.3.6).

(7) ποταμός, *potamós*: of the Jordan (Mk **1** 5); Euphrates (Rev **9** 14); "rivers of living water" (Jn **7** 38); "river of water of life" (Rev **22** 1). So always in Gr for "river" in RV Apoc (1 Esd **4** 23, etc). See BROOK; STREAM; VALLEY.

ALFRED ELY DAY

RIVER OF EGYPT. See BROOK OF EGYPT.

RIVER, THE (GREAT). See EUPHRATES.

RIVERS OF EDEN. See EDEN (1).

RIZIA, riz'i-a (רִצְיָא, *riçyā'*): An Asherite (1 Ch **7** 39).

RIZPAH, riz'pä (רִצְפָּה, *riçpāh*, "hot stone"; Jos, Ῥαισφά, *Rhaisphá*): In 2 S **3** 7 the subject of a coarse slander. 2 S **21** contains the pathetic story of Rizpah's faithful watch over the bodies of her dead sons Mephibosheth and Armoni (vs 10.11). Did this story suggest Tennyson's "Rizpah"? A three years' famine had made David anxious, and in seeking a reason for the affliction he concluded that it lay in Saul's unavenged conduct to the Gibeonites (ver 2). To appease Jeh he gave up to the Gibeonites the two sons of Saul, Mephibosheth and Armoni, as well as Saul's 5 grandsons (whether by Michal or Merab; see MERAB). These seven were hanged at Gibeah. Rizpah watched 5 months over their exposed bodies, but meanwhile the famine did not abate. Word was brought to David of Rizpah's act (vs 10.11), and it is possible that her action suggested to David his next step in expiation. At any rate, he remembered the uncared-for bones of Jonathan and Saul lying in ignominy at Jabesh-gilead, whither they had been carried by stealth after the Philis had kept them hung in the streets of Beth-shan for some time. The bones were recovered and apparently mingled with the bones Rizpah had guarded, and they were together buried in the family grave at Zelah. We are told that then "God was entreated for the land" (ver 14).

HENRY WALLACE

ROAD, rōd **(INROAD)** AV (1 S **27** 10; cf **23** 27). See RAID.

ROAD (WAY). See ROMAN EMPIRE AND CHRISTIANITY, II, 6; WAY.

ROAST, rōst. See FOOD.

ROBBER, rob'ẽr, **ROBBERY,** rob'ẽr-ĭ: "Robber" represents no particular Heb word in the OT, but in the Apoc and the NT is always a tr of λῃστής, *lēstḗs* (see THIEF). In AV Job **5** 5; **18** 9, "robber" stands for the doubtful word צַמִּים, *çammīm*, RV "hungry" in **5** 5 and "snare" in **18** 9. The meaning is uncertain, and perhaps *çᵉmē'īm*, "thirsty," should be read in both places. Ps **62** 10, "Become not vain in robbery," means "put not your trust in riches dishonestly gained." RV's changes of AV in Prov **21** 7; Dnl **11** 14; Nah **3** 1 are obvious. In Phil **2** 6 AV reads "thought it not robbery to be equal with God." ERV has "a prize," while ERVm and ARV read "a thing to be grasped," ARV rewording "counted not the being on an equality with God a thing to be grasped." The Gr here is ἁρπαγμός, *harpagmós*, a word derived from *harpázō*, "to ravish away," "carry off," "plunder" (cf "harpy"). Properly speaking, the termination *-mos* should give the derived noun an active sense, "the act of plundering," whence AV's "robbery." The verse would then mean "who thought that being on an equality with God did not consist in grasping," and this tr gives good sense in the context and has some excellent scholarly support. But a passive significance is frequently found despite a *-mos* termination, giving to *harpagmos* the sense of "thing grasped," as in RV. Usually Eng. commentators take "grasped" as meaning "clung to"—"did not think equality with God should be clung to tenaciously"—but "to cling to" seems unknown as a tr of *harpazō*. Hence render "a thing to be grasped at"—"did not seek equality with God by selfish methods but by humbling himself." It is to be noticed, naturally, that St. Paul is thinking of "equality with God" simply in the sense of "receiving explicit adoration from men" (vs 10.11), and that the metaphysical relation of the Son to the Father is not at all in point. See also GRASP.

BURTON SCOTT EASTON

ROBBERS OF TEMPLES (ἱερόσυλοι, *hierósuloi*, "guilty of sacrilege"): A term used by the town clerk of Ephesus (Acts **19** 37, AV "robbers of churches"). As the temple of Diana had a great treasure-chamber, the offence might not be unknown among them; cf Rom **2** 22.

In 2 Macc **4** 42 AV the epithet "church-robber" (RV "author of the sacrilege") is applied to LYSIMACHUS (q.v.).

ROBE, rōb. See DRESS, 1, (3).

ROBOAM, rō-bō'am (Ῥοβοάμ, *Rhobodm*). AV; Gr form of "Rehoboam" (thus RV) (Mt **1** 7); successor of Solomon.

ROCK, rok ([1] סֶלַע, *ṣela'*; [2] צוּר, *çūr;* [3] חַלָּמִישׁ, *ḥallāmīsh,* "flint"; cf Arab. خَلَنْبُوس, *khalanbûs,* "flint"; [4] כֵּפִים, *kēphīm* [Job **30** 6; Jer **4** 29]; cf Κηφᾶς, *Kēphás,* "Cephas" = Πέτρος, *Pétros,* "Peter" [Jn **1** 42 AV and RVm]; [5] πέτρα, *pétra*):

1. Names

Çūr and *ṣela'* are the words most often found, and there is no well-defined distinction between them. They are frequently coupled together in the parallelism which is characteristic of the Heb writers: e.g.

"Be thou to me a strong rock [*çūr*],
A house of defence to save me.
For thou art my rock [*ṣela'*] and my fortress" (Ps **31** 2.3).
"He clave rocks [*çūr*] in the wilderness,
And gave them drink abundantly as out of the depths.
He brought streams also out of the rock [*ṣela'*],
And caused waters to run down like rivers" (Ps **78** 15.16).

It is plain here that the two words are used for the sake of variety, without any clear difference of meaning. Even *ḥallāmīsh* (tr[d] "flint") is used in the same way with *çūr* in Ps **114** 8:

"Who turned the rock [*çūr*] into a pool of water,
The flint [*ḥallāmīsh*] into a fountain of waters."

2. Figurative

(1) Some of the most striking and beautiful imagery of the Bible is based upon the rocks. They are a symbol of God: "Jeh is my rock, and my fortress" (2 S **22** 2; Ps **18** 2; **71** 3); "God, the rock of my salvation" (2 S **22** 47; cf Ps **62** 2.7; **89** 26); "my God the rock of my refuge" (Ps **94** 22); "the rock of thy strength" (Isa **17** 10); "Lead me to the rock that is higher than I" (Ps **61** 2); repeatedly in the song of Moses (Dt **32** 3.1.18.30.31; cf 2 S **22** 32). Paul applies the rock smitten in the wilderness (Ex **17** 6; Nu **20** 11) to Christ as the source of living water for spiritual refreshment (1 Cor **10** 4).

(2) The rocks are a refuge, both figuratively and literally (Jer **48** 28; Cant **2** 14); "The rocks are a refuge for the conies" (Ps **104** 18). Many a traveler in Pal has felt the refreshment of "the shade of a great rock in a weary land" (Isa **32** 2). A very different idea is expressed in Isa **8** 14, "And he shall be for a sanctuary; but for a stone of stumbling and for a rock of offence" (cf Rom **9** 33; 1 Pet **2** 8).

(3) The rock is a symbol of hardness (Jer **5** 3; cf Isa **50** 7). Therefore the breaking of the rock exemplifies the power of God (Jer **23** 29; cf 1 K **19** 11). The rock is also a symbol of that which endures, "Oh that they . . . . were graven in the rock for ever!" (Job **19** 23.24). A rock was an appropriate place for offering a sacrifice (Jgs **6** 20; **13** 19). The central feature of the Mosque of '*Umar* in Jerus is *Ḳubbat-uṣ-Ṣakhrat,* the "dome of the rock." The rock or *ṣakhrat* under the dome is thought to be the site of Solomon's altar of burnt offering, and further is thought to be the site of the threshing-floor of Araunah the Jebusite which David purchased to build an altar to Jeh.

3. Kinds of Rock

(1) The principal rock of Pal and Syria is limestone of which there are many varieties, differing in color, texture, hardness and degrees of impurity, some of the limestone having considerable admixtures of clay or sand. Some of the harder kinds are very dense and break with a conchoidal fracture similar to the fracture of flint. In rocks which have for ages been exposed to atmospheric agencies, erosion has produced striking and highly picturesque forms. Nodules and layers of flint are of frequent occurrence in the limestone.

(2) Limestone is the only rock of Western Pal, with the exception of some local outpourings of basaltic rock and with the further exception of a light-brown, porous, partly calcareous sandstone, which is found at intervals along the coast. This last is a superficial deposit of Quaternary or recent age, and is of aeolian origin. That is, it consists of dune sands which have solidified under the influence of atmospheric agencies. This is very exceptional, nearly all stratified rocks having originated as beds of sand or mud in the bottom of the sea.

(3) In Sinai, Edom, Moab, Lebanon and Anti-Lebanon is found the Nubian sandstone, a silicious sandstone which, at least in the N., is of middle or lower Cretaceous age. In the S., the lower strata of this formation seem to be paleozoic. Most of it is not sufficiently coherent to make good building stone, though some of its strata are very firm and are even used for millstones. In some places it is so incoherent or friable that it is easily dug with the pick, the grains falling apart and forming sand that can be used in mortar. In color the Nubian sandstone is on the whole dark reddish brown, but locally it shows great variation, from white through yellow and red to black. In places it also has tints of blue. The celebrated rock tombs and temples of Petra are carved in this stone.

(4) Extensive areas of the northern part of Eastern Pal are covered with igneous rock. In the *Jaulân* S.E. of Mt. Hermon, this has been for ages exposed to the atmosphere and has formed superficially a rich dark soil. Further S.E. is the *Leja'* (Arab. "refuge"), a wild tract covered with a deposit of lava which is geologically recent, and which, while probably earlier than man, is still but little affected by the atmosphere. It is with difficulty traversed and frequently furnishes an asylum to outlaws. See CRAG; FLINT; GEOLOGY; LIME.

ALFRED ELY DAY

ROCK OF AGES. See AGES, ROCK OF; ISAIAH, VII.

ROCK-BADGER, r.-baj'ẽr: This term is found in RVm for "coney," שָׁפָן, *shāphān* (Lev **11** 5; cf Dt **14** 7; Ps **104** 18; Prov **30** 26). It is a tr of *klip das,* the name given by the Boers to the Cape hyrax or coney. See CONEY.

ROD (מַקֵּל, *maḳḳēl,* מַטֶּה, *maṭṭeh,* שֵׁבֶט, *shēbheṭ,* ῥάβδος, *rhábdos*): Little distinction can be drawn between the Heb words used for "rod" and "staff." *Maḳḳēl* is the word used in Gen **30** 37 ff for the twigs of poplar put by Jacob before his sheep, and in Jer **1** 11 of the "rod of an almond-tree." *Maṭṭeh* is used of a rod in the hand, as the "rods" of Moses and of Aaron (Ex **4** 2 ff; **7** 9 ff, etc). *Shēbheṭ* is used, but sometimes also *maṭṭeh,* of the rod used for correction (Ex **21** 20; 2 S **7** 14; Prov **10** 13; **13** 24; Isa **10** 5, etc). In Ps **23** 4 ("Thy rod and thy staff, they comfort me"), however, *shēbheṭ* is the shepherd's rod, figurative of Divine guidance and care. In Ezk **21** 10.13, the word stands for the royal scepter. In the NT "rod" is used of a rod of correction (1 Cor **4** 21), Aaron's rod (He **9** 4), a ruler's rod "of iron" (severity, as in Rev **2** 27; **12** 5; **19** 15), a measuring rod (Rev **11** 1). See also ARMOR, ARMS.

JAMES ORR

RODANIM, rod'a-nim: The reading of MT in 1 Ch **1** 7 for the DODANIM (q.v.) of Gen **10** 4, corresponding to the Ῥόδιοι, *Rhódioi* of LXX in both passages. The Rodanim are generally identified as inhabitants of the island of RHODES (q.v.), well known to the ancient Phoenicians (Homer's *Iliad*).

ROE, rō, **ROEBUCK,** rō'buk: AV has "roe" and "roebuck" for צְבִי, *ç^ebhī*, צְבִיָּה, *ç^ebhīyāh*. RV usually substitutes "gazelle" in the text (Dt **12** 15, etc) or m (Prov **6** 5, etc), but retains "roe" in 2 S **2** 18; 1 Ch **12** 8; Cant **3** 5; **7** 3. So RV has "gazelle" for AV "roe" in Sir **27** 20 (*dorkás*). RV has

Gazelle (*Antilope dorcas*).

"roe-buck" for יַחְמוּר, *yaḥmūr* (Dt **14** 5; 1 K **4** 23), where AV has "fallow deer." In the opinion of the writer, אַיָּל, *'ayyāl*, EV "hart," should be tr^d "roe-buck," *yaḥmūr* "fallow deer," and *ç^ebhī* "gazelle." See DEER; GAZELLE. ALFRED ELY DAY

ROGELIM, rō'gē-lim, rŏ-gē'lim (רֹגְלִים, *rōgh^elīm*; Ῥωγελλείμ, *Rhōgelleím*): The place whence came Barzillai the Gileadite to succor David in his flight from Absalom (2 S **17** 27; **19** 31). It probably lay near the path followed by David, but it is not identified.

ROHGAH, rō'ga (K^ethībh רוֹהֲגָה, *rōhăghāh*, K^erē רָהְגָה, *rohgāh*): A name in the genealogy of Asher (1 Ch **7** 34).

ROIMUS, rō'i-mus (Ῥόειμος, *Rhóeimos*, A, Ῥομέλιος, *Rhomélios*): One of the leaders with Zerubbabel in the return (1 Esd **5** 8) = "Rehum" in Ezr **2** 2, of which it is the Gr form = "Nehum" in Neh **7** 7.

ROLL, rōl (**SCROLL**): The usual form of book in Bib. times. It had been in use in Egypt for perhaps 2,000 years at the time when, according to the Pent, the earliest Bib. books were written in this form. The Bab tablet seems to have been the prevailing form in Pal up to about 1350 BC, but by 1100 BC, at least, the roll had been in established use for some time as far N. as Byblos. Two Heb words, *gillāyōn, m^eghillāh*, one Aram., *ç^ephar*, and one Gr word, *biblion*, are so tr^d in AV. *Ç^ephar* (Ezr **6** 1, RV "archives," m "books"), with the corresponding Heb form *çephēr*, is the generic word for any whole work large or small, but as a book form (Isa **34** 4) it may mean "roll," and, according to Blau (pp. 37, 45, etc), it never does mean anything else. Both the other words seem to be connected with *gālal*, "roll," which is the technical term for opening or closing a book The *m^eghillath çephēr* (Jer **36** 2) means the unwritten roll, or the roll considered in its material form as contrasted with the work. *M^eghillāh*, which is found in Ezr **6** 2 (EV "roll"), Jer (often), Ezk (often) and Zec, is a somewhat late word, and came to mean a small roll (but with a complete work) as distinguished from a book, corresponding thus to the modern distinction of pamphlet and book or document and book. The word *gillāyōn* is tr^d in RV as "tablet," and is universally regarded as meaning (Isa **8** 1) some smooth surface, corresponding to the same word in Isa **3** 23 which is rendered "hand-mirror." But "cylinder-seal" would possibly fit the sense in both cases; this being hung round the neck as an ornament in one case and inscribed with a personal name in the other.

Egyptian Roll and Case.

Biblion is regarded by the Bible translators as equivalent to *m^eghillāh* in the sense of small roll. It is in fact 4 t in the LXX of Jer **36** used as the tr for *m^eghillāh*, but very much oftener it is the tr for *çephēr*, for which in fact it is the correct technical equivalent (Birt, *Buchrolle*, 21). Indeed the "small book" (Thayer, *Lex.*, 101) is hardly consistent with the ideas of the heavens as a scroll, of the Lamb's Book of Life, or of the vast quantity of books of Jn **21** 25, although in Lk **4** 17 it may perhaps correspond closely with *m^eghillāh* in the sense of a complete roll and work, which is at the same time a whole part of a larger work. Its use in Rev **6** 14 is reminiscent of Isa **34** 4 ("scroll"), and is conclusive for the roll form. It is indeed always technically a roll and never codex or tablet.

It is not likely that Isaiah and St. John (here and in his Gospel, **21** 25) refer directly to the Bab idea that the heavens are a series of written tablets or to the rabbinic saying that "if all the oceans were ink, all reeds pens, the heavens and earth sheets to write upon, and all men writers, still it would not suffice for writing out the teachings of my Masters" (Blau, op. cit., 34). Nevertheless, the "whole Cosmos" does suggest "the heavens and earth" as sheets to write on, and under all there does perhaps lurk a conception of the broad expanse of heaven as a roll for writing upon.

LITERATURE.—Birt, *Die Buchrolle in der Kunst*, Leipzig, 1907; *Jew Enc*, XI, 126–34, "Scroll of the Law"; Blau, *Studien z. althebr. Buchwesen*, Strassburg, 1902, 37–66, etc, and the literature under the art. "Writing," esp. Gardthausen, 134–54.

E. C. RICHARDSON

ROLLER, rōl'ēr: AV and ERV in Ezk **30** 21 for חִתּוּל, *ḥittūl*, "bandage" (so ARV). "Roller" was formerly a technical term in surgery for a wide bandage.

ROLLING, ** rōl'ing, **THING: Isa **17** 13, AV "like a rolling thing before the whirlwind," a noncommittal tr of גַּלְגַּל, *galgal*, "revolving thing," "wheel" (Eccl **12** 6). RV "like the whirling dust before the storm" is probably right. But see CHAFF; DUST; STUBBLE.

ROMAMTI-EZER, rŏ-mam-ti-ē'zēr, rŏ-mam-tī-ē'zēr (רֹמַמְתִּי עֶזֶר, *rōmamtī 'ezer*, "highest help"): Son of Heman, appointed chief of the 24th division of singers in David's time (1 Ch **25** 4.31). See JOSHBEKASHAH.

ROMAN, rō'man, **ROMANS,** rō'manz. See ROME, III, 2; CITIZENSHIP.

ROMAN ARMY. See ARMY, ROMAN.

ROMAN EMPIRE, em'pīr, **AND CHRISTIANITY:**

I. Outline of Roman Empire.—The founding of the Rom empire was the grandest political achievement ever accomplished. The conquests of Alexander the Great, Charlemagne and Napoleon seem small compared with the durable structure reared by Julius and his successor, Augustus. In one sense Julius Caesar—the most wonderful man that Rome or any other country produced—was the founder of the *empire,* and Augustus the founder of the *principate.* But the Rom empire was the culmination of a long process of political, constitutional, and social growth which gives a lasting interest to Rom history. The Rom empire was the only possible solution of a 700 years' struggle, and Rom history is the story of the conflict of class with class, patrician against plebeian, *populus* against *plebs,* the antagonism of oligarchy and democracy, plutocracy against neglected masses. It is the account of the triumphant march of democracy and popular government against an exclusive governing caste. Against heavy odds the plebeians asserted their rights till they secured at least a measure of social, political and legal equality with their superiors (see ROME, I, 2–4). But in the long conflict both parties degenerated until neither militant democracy nor despotic oligarchy could hold the balance with justice. Democracy had won in the uphill fight, but lost itself and was obliged to accept a common master with aristocracy. It was of no small importance for Christianity that the Rom empire—practically synonymous with the *orbis terrarum*—had been converging both from internal and external causes toward a one-man government, the political counterpart of a universal religion with *one* God and Saviour.

1. Roman Empire a Result

(1) *Julius Caesar.*—For a couple of generations political leaders had foreseen the coming of supreme power and had tried to grasp it. But it was Julius Caesar who best succeeded in exploiting democracy for his own aggrandizement. He proved the potent factor of the first triumvirate (60 BC); his consulship (59) was truly kingly. In 49 BC he crossed the Rubicon and declared war upon his country, but in the same year was appointed Dictator and thus made *his* enemies the enemies of his country. He vanquished the Pompeians—senatorial and republican—at Pharsalia in 48 BC, Thapsus in 46 BC, and Munda in 45 BC. Between 46 and the Ides of March 44 no emperor before Diocletian was more imperial. He was recognized officially as "demigod"; temples were dedicated to his "clemency." He encouraged the people to abdicate to him their privileges of self-government and right of election, became chief (*princeps*) of the senate and high priest (*pontifex maximus*), so that he could manipulate even the will of the gods to his own purposes. His plans were equally great and beneficent. He saw the necessity of blending the heterogeneous populations into one people and extending Rom citizenship. His outlook was larger and more favorable to the coming of Christianity than that of his successor, Augustus. The latter learned from the fate of Caesar that he had advanced too rapidly along the imperial path. It taught Augustus caution.

(2) *Augustus.*—Octavian (Augustus) proved the potent factor of the second triumvirate. The field of Actium on September 2, 31 BC, decided the fate of the old Rom republic. The commonwealth sank in exhaustion after the protracted civil and internecine strife. It was a case of the survival of the fittest. It was a great crisis in human history, and a great man was at hand for the occasion. Octavian realized that supreme power was the only possible solution. On his return to Rome he began to do over again what Caesar had done—gather into his own hands the reins of government. He succeeded with more caution and shrewdness, and became the *founder of the Rom empire,* which formally began on January 16, 27 BC, and was signalized by the bestowal of the title AUGUSTUS (q.v.). Under republican forms he ruled as emperor, controlling legislation, administration and the armies. His policy was on the whole adhered to by the Julio-Claudian line, the last of which was Nero (d. 68 AD).

(3) *Flavian Dynasty.*—In 68 AD a new "secret of empire" was discovered, viz. that the principate was not hereditary in one line and that emperors could be nominated by the armies. After the bloody civil wars of 68, "the year of the four emperors," Vespasian founded the IId Dynasty, and dynastic succession was for the present again adopted. With the Flavians begins a new epoch in Rom history of pronounced importance for Christianity. The exclusive Rom ideas are on the wane. Vespasian was of plebeian and Sabine rank and thus non-Rom, the first of many non-Rom emperors. His ideas were provincial rather than Rom, and favorable to the amalgamation of classes, and the leveling process now steadily setting in. Though he accepted the Augustan "diarchy," he began to curtail the powers of the senate. His son Titus died young (79–81). Domitian's reign marks a new epoch in imperialism: his autocratic spirit stands half-way between the Augustan principate and the absolute monarchy of Diocletian. Domitian, the last of the "twelve Caesars" (Suetonius), was assassinated September 18, 96 AD. The soldiers amid civil war had elected the last dynasty. This time the senate asserted itself and nominated a brief series of emperors—on the whole the best that wore the purple.

(4) *Adoptive or Antonine emperors.*—The Antonine is another distinct era marked by humane government, recognition of the rights of the provinces and an enlargement of the ideas of universalism. Under Trajan the empire was extended; a series of frontier blockades was established—a confession that Rome could advance no farther. Under Hadrian a policy of retreat began; henceforth Rome is never again on the aggressive but always on the defensive against restless barbarians. Unmistakable signs of weakness and decay set in under

Antoninus Pius and Marcus Aurelius. This, the best and happiest period of Rom imperial government, was the beginning of the end. In this era we detect a growing centralization of authority; the senate practically becomes a tool of the emperor. A distinct civil service was established which culminated in bureaucracy under Hadrian.

(5) *Changing dynasties, 193–284 AD.*—On the death of Commodus, whose reign 180–93 AD stands by itself, the empire was put up for sale by the soldiery and knocked down to the highest bidder. The military basis of the empire was emphasized—which was indeed essential in this period of barbaric aggressiveness to postpone the fall of the empire until its providential mission was accomplished. A rapid succession of rulers follows, almost each new ruler bringing a new dynasty. Those disintegrating forces set in which developed so rapidly from the reign of Diocletian. The *pax Romana* had passed; civil commotion accentuated the dangers from invading barbarians. Plague and famine depopulated rich provinces. Rome itself drops into the background and the provincial spirit asserts itself proportionally. The year 212 AD is memorable for the edict of Caracalla converting all the free population into Rom citizens.

(6) *From Diocletian till partition.*—In the next period absolute monarchy of pure oriental type was established by Diocletian, one of the ablest of Rom rulers. He inaugurated the principle of division and subdivision of imperial power. The inevitable separation of East and West, with the growing prominence of the East, becomes apparent. Rome and Italy are reduced to the rank of provinces, and new courts are opened by the two Augusti and two Caesars. Diocletian's division of power led to civil strife, until Constantine once more united the whole empire under his sway. The center of gravity now shifted from West to East by the foundation of Constantinople. The empire was again parceled out to the sons of Constantine, one of whom, Constantius, succeeded in again reuniting it (350 AD). In 364 it was again divided, Valentinian receiving the West and Valens the East.

(7) *Final partition.*—On the death of Theodosius I (395), West and East fell to his sons Honorius and Arcadius, never again to be united. The western half rapidly degenerated before barbaric hordes and weakling rulers. The western provinces and Africa were overrun by conquering barbarians who set up independent kingdoms on Rom soil. Burgundians and Visigoths settled in Gaul; the latter established a kingdom in Spain. The Vandals under Genseric settled first in Southern Spain, then crossed to Africa and reduced it. Goths burst over Rom frontiers, settled in Illyria and invaded Italy. Alaric and his Goths spared Rome in 408 for a ransom; in 409 he appeared again and set up Attalus as king of the Romans, and finally in 410 he captured and sacked the city. It was again sacked by the Vandals under Genseric in 462, and, lastly, fell before Odoacer and his Germans in 476; he announced to the world that the empire of the West had ceased. The empire of the East continued at Constantinople the greatest political power through a chequered history down to the capture of the city in 1214 and its final capture by the Turks in 1453, when its spiritual and intellectual treasures were opened to western lands and proved of untold blessing in preparing the way for the Reformation of the 16th cent. The East conquered the West intellectually and spiritually. In the East was born the religion of humanity.

2. Coming of Monarchy

(1) *Exhaustion of parties.*—The Rom world had for two generations been steadily drifting toward monarchy, and at least one generation before the empire was set up clear minds saw the inevitable necessity of one-man government or supreme power, and each political leader made it his ambition to grasp it. The civil wars ceased for a century with the death of Antony. But the struggles of Tiberius Gracchus and Scipio Aemilianus, Caius Gracchus and Opimius, Drusus and Philippus, Marius and Sulla, Pompey and Caesar, and lastly Octavian and Antony had exhausted the state, and this exhaustion of political parties opened the way for monarchy. In fact it was a necessity for the welfare of the commonwealth that one should be elevated who could fairly hold the balance between oligarchy and the commons and duly recognize the claims of all parties. Even Cato Uticensis—the incarnation of republican ideas—admitted it would be better to choose a master than wait for a tyrant. The bloody wars could find no solution except the survival of the fittest. Moreover, the free political institutions of Rome had become useless and could no longer work under the armed oppression of factions. If any form of government, only supreme power would prove effectual amid an enfeebled, unpopular senate, corrupt and idle commons, and ambitious individuals.

(2) *Inability of either aristocracy or democracy to hold equilibrium.*—Events had proved that a narrow exclusive aristocracy was incapable of good government because of its utterly selfish policy and disregard for the rights of all lower orders. It had learned to burke liberty by political murders. Neither was the heterogeneous population of later Rome disciplined to obey or to initiate just government when it had seized power. This anarchy within the body politic opened an easy way to usurpation by individuals. No republic and no form of free popular government could live under such conditions. Caesar said of the republic that it was "a name without any substance," and Curio declared it to be a "vain chimera." The law courts shared in the general corruption. The *judicia* became the bone of contention between the senate and the knights as the best instrument for party interests, and enabled the holders (*a*) to receive large bribes, (*b*) to protect their own order when guilty of the most flagrant injustice, and (*c*) to oppress other orders. Justice for all, and esp. for conquered peoples, was impossible. Elective assemblies refused to perform their proper functions because of extravagant bribery or the presence of candidates in arms. In fact, the people were willing to forego the prerogative of election and accept candidates at the nomination of a despotic authority. The whole people had become incapable of self-government and were willing—almost glad—to be relieved of the necessity.

(3) *Precedents.*—Besides, precedents for one-man government, or the concentration of supreme power in one hand, were not wanting, and had been rapidly multiplying in Rom history as it drew nearer to the end of the republic. Numerous protracted commands and special commissions had accustomed the state to the novelty of obedience without participation in administration. The 7 consulships of Marius, the 4 of Cinna, the 3 extraordinary commissions of Pompey and his *sole* consulship, the dictatorship of Sulla *without time limit*, the two 5-year-period military commands of Caesar, his repeated dictatorships the last of which was to extend for 10 years—all these were pointing directly toward Caesarism.

(4) *Withdrawal from public life: individualism.*—On another side the way was opened to supreme power by the increasing tendency for some of the noblest and best minds to withdraw from public life to the seclusion of the heart life and thus leave the field open for demagogic ambition. After the conquests of Alexander the Great, philosophy abandoned the civic, political or city-state point of view and became moral and individual. Stoicism adopted the lofty spiritual teachings of Plato and combined them with the idea of the brotherhood of humanity. It also preached that man must work out his salvation, not in public political life, but in the secret agonies of his own soul. This religion took hold of the noblest Rom souls who were conscious of the weariness of life and felt the desire for spiritual fellowship and comfort. The pendulum in human systems of thought generally swings to the opposite extreme, and these serious souls abandoned public life for private speculation and meditation. Those who did remain at the helm of affairs—like the younger Cato—were often too much idealists, living in the past or in an ideal Platonic republic, and proved very unequal to the practical demagogues who lived much in the present with a keen eye to the future. Also a considerable number of the moderate party, who in better days would have furnished leaders to the state, disgusted with the universal corruption, saddened by the hopeless state of social strife and disquieted by uncertainty as to the issue of victory for either contending party, held aloof and must have wished for and welcomed a paramount authority to give stability to social life. Monarchy was in the air, as proved by the sentiments of the two pseudo-Sallustian letters, the author of which calls upon Caesar to restore government and reorganize the state, for if Rome perish the whole world must perish with her.

(5) *Industrial.*—To another considerable class monarchy must have been welcome—the industrial and middle class who were striving for competence and were engaged in trade and commerce. Civil wars and the strife of parties must have greatly hindered their activity. They cast their lot neither with the optimates nor with the idle commonalty. They desired only a stable condition of government under which they could uninterruptedly carry on their trades.

(6) *Military.*—Military conditions favored supreme power. Not only had the lengthened commands familiarized the general with his legions and given him time to seduce the soldiery to his own cause, but the soldiery too had been petted and spoiled like the spoon-fed populace. The old republican safeguards against ambition had been removed. The ranks of the armies had also been swollen with large numbers of provincials and non-Romans who had no special sentiment about republican forms. We have seen the military power growing more and more prominent. The only way of averting a military despotism supported and prompted by the soldiers was to set up a monarchy, holding all the military, legislative and administrative functions of the state in due proportion. This was superior to a merely nominal republic always cringing under fear of military leaders.

(7) *Imperial interests.*—Lastly, the aggression and conquests of the republic had brought about a state of affairs demanding an empire. The East and the West had been subdued; many provinces and heterogeneous populations were living under the Rom eagle. These provinces could not permanently be plundered and oppressed as under the republican senate. The *jus civile* of Rome must learn also the *jus naturale* and *jus gentium*. An exclusive selfish senatorial clique was incapable of doing justice to the conquered peoples. One supreme ruler over all classes raised above personal

ambition could best meet their grievances. The senate had ruled with a rod of iron; the provinces could not possibly be worse under any form of government. Besides, monarchy was more congenial to the provincials than a republic which they could not comprehend.

(8) *Influence of Orient.*—The Orientals had long been used to living under imperial and absolute forms of government and would welcome such a form among their new conquerors. Besides, residence in the Orient had affected Rom military leaders with the thirst after absolute power. And no other form was possible when the old city-state system broke down, and as yet federal government had not been dreamed of. Another consideration: the vast and dissimilar masses of population living within the Rom dominions could more easily be held together under a king or emperor than by a series of ever-changing administrations, just as the Austro-Hungarian and the British empires are probably held together better under the present monarchies than would be possible under a republican system. This survey may make clear the permanent interest in Rom history for all students of human history. The Rom empire was established indeed in the fulness of the times for its citizens and for Christianity.

II. Preparation of the Roman Empire for Christianity.—About the middle of the reign of Augustus a Jewish child was born who was destined to rule an empire more extensive and lasting than that of the Caesars. It is a striking fact that almost synchronous with the planting of the Rom empire Christianity appeared in the world. Although on a superficial glance the Rom empire may seem the greatest enemy of early Christianity, and at times a bitter persecutor, yet it was in many ways the grandest preparation and in some ways the best ally of Christianity. It ushered in politically the fulness of the times. The Caesars—whatever they may have been or done—prepared the way of the Lord. A brief account must here be given of some of the services which the Rom empire rendered to humanity and esp. to the kingdom of God.

1. *Pax Romana* and Unification of the World

The first universal blessing conferred by the empire was the famous *pax Romana* ("Rom peace"). The world had not been at peace since the days of Alexander the Great. The quarrels of the Diadochi, and the aggression of the Rom republic had kept the nations in a state of constant turmoil. A universal peace was first established with the beginning of the reign of Augustus and the closing of the temple of Janus. In all the countries round the Mediterranean and from distant Britain to the Euphrates the world was at rest. Rome had made an end of her own civil wars and had put a stop to wars among the nations. Though her wars were often iniquitous and unjustifiable, and she conquered like a barbarian, she ruled her conquests like a humane statesman. The quarrels of the Diadochi which caused so much turmoil in the East were ended, the territory of the Lagids, Attalids, Seleucids and Antigonids having passed under the sway of Rome. The empire united Greeks, Romans and Jews all under one government. Rome thus blended the nations and prepared them for Christianity. Now for the first time we may speak of *the world* as universal humanity, the *orbis terrarum*, ἡ οἰκουμένη, *hē oikoumenē* (Lk **2** 1), the *genus humanum*. These terms represented humanity as living under a uniform system of government. All were members of one earthly state; the Rom empire was their *communis omnium patria*.

2. Cosmopolitanism

This state of affairs contributed largely to the spread of cosmopolitanism which had set in with the Macedonian conqueror. Under the Rom empire all national barriers were removed; the great cities—Rome, Alexandria, Antioch, etc—became meeting-places of all races and languages. The Romans were everywhere carrying their laws and civilization; Greeks settled in thousands at all important centers as professors, merchants, physicians, or acrobats; Orientals were to be found in large numbers with their gods and mysteries in Rome, "the epitome of the world." In the Rom armies soldiers from all quarters of the empire became companions. And many thousands of slaves of fine education and high culture contributed much to cosmopolitanism. Being in many cases far superior in culture to their masters, they became their teachers. And in every city of importance, East or West, large bodies of the Jewish Diaspora were settled.

3. Eclecticism

This cosmopolitanism gave great impetus to a corresponding eclecticism of thought. Nothing could have been more favorable to Christianity than this intermixture of all races and mutual exchange of thought. Each people discovered how much it had in common with its neighbors. From the days of the Diadochi, Stoicism had been preaching the gospel of a civic and ethical brotherhood of humanity. In the fusion of different philosophic systems the emphasis had shifted from the city-state or political or national to the moral and human point of view. All men were thus reduced to equality before the One; only virtue and vice were the differentiating factors. Men were akin with the Divine—at least the wise and good—so that one poet could say, "We are His offspring."

Stoicism did a noble service in preparation for Christianity by preaching universalism along the path of individualism. It also furnished comfort and strength to countless thousands of weary human lives and ministered spiritual support and calm resignation at many a heathen deathbed. It may be declared to be the first system of religious thought—for it was a religion more than a philosophy—which made a serious study of the diseases of the human soul. We know of course its weakness and imperfections, that it was an aristocratic creed appealing only to the elect of mortals, that it had little message for the fallen and lower classes, that it was cold and stern, that it lacked—as Seneca felt—the inspiration of an ideal life. But with all its failures it proved a worthy pedagogue to a religion which brought a larger message than that of Greece. It afforded the spiritual and moral counterpart to the larger human society of which the Rom empire was the political and visible symbol. Hitherto a good citizen had been a good man. Now a good man is a good citizen, and that not of a narrow city-state, but of the world. Stoicism also proved the interpreter and mouthpiece to the Rom empire of the higher moral and spiritual qualities of Gr civilization; it diffused the best convictions of Greece about God and man, selecting those elements that were universal and of lasting human value (see Stoics).

The mind of the Rom empire was further prepared for Christianity by the Jewish Diaspora. Greeks learned from Jews and Jews from Greeks and the Romans from both. The unification effected by Rom Law and administration greatly aided the Diaspora. Jewish settlements became still more numerous and powerful both in the East and West. Those Jews bringing from the homeland the spiritual monotheism of their race combined it with Gr philosophy which had been setting steadily for monotheism. With the Jews the exclusively national element was subordinated to the more human and universal, the ceremonial to the religious. They even adopted the world-language of that day—Greek—and had their sacred Scriptures tr[d] into this language in which they carried on an active proselytism. The Rom spirit was at first essentially narrow and exclusive. But even the Romans soon fell beneath the spell of this cosmopolitanism and eclecticism. As their conquests increased, their mind was correspondingly widened. They adopted the policy of Alexander—sparing the gods of the conquered and admitting them into the responsibility of guarding Rome; they assimilated them with their own Pantheon or identified them with Rom gods. In this way naturally the religious ideas of conquered races more highly civilized than the conquerors laid hold on Rom minds (see Dispersion).

Another inestimable service rendered to humanity and Christianity was the protection which the Rom power afforded the Gr civilization.

4. Protection for Greek Culture

We must remember that the Romans were at first only conquering barbarians who had little respect for culture, but idealized power. Already they had wiped out two ancient and superior civilizations—that of Carthage without leaving a trace, and that of Etruria, traces of which have been discovered in modern times. It is hard to conceive what a scourge Rome would have proved to the world had she not fallen under the influence of the superior culture and philosophy of Greece. Had the Rom Mars not been educated by Pallas Athene the Romans would have proved Vandals and Tartars in blotting out civilization and arresting human progress. The Greeks, on the other hand, could conquer more by their preëminence in everything that pertains to the intellectual life of man than they could hold by the sword. A practical and political power was needed to protect Gr speculation. But the Romans after causing much devastation were gradually educated and civilized and have contributed to the uplifting and enlightenment of subsequent civilizations by both preserving and opening to the world the spiritual qualities of Greece. The kinship of man with the Divine, learned from Socrates and Plato, went forth on its wide evangel. This Gr civilization, philosophy and theology trained many of the great theologians and leaders of the Christian church, so that Clement of Alexandria said that Gr philosophy and Jewish law had proved schoolmasters to bring the world to Christ. Paul, who prevented Christianity from remaining a Jewish sect and proclaimed its universalism, learned much from Gr—esp. from Stoic—thought. It is also significant that the early Christian missionaries apparently went only where the Gr language was known, which was the case in all centers of Rom administration.

The state of the Rom empire linguistically was in the highest degree favorable to the spread of Christianity.

5. Linguistically

The Gr republics by their enterprise, superior genius and commercial abilities extended their dialects over the Aegean Islands, the coasts of Asia Minor, Sicily and Magna Graecia. The preëminence of Attic culture and literature favored by the short-lived Athenian empire raised this dialect to a standard among the Gr peoples. But the other dialects long persisted. Out of this babel of Gr dialects there finally arose a normal *koinḗ* or "common language." By the conquests of Alexander and the Hellenistic sympathies of the Diadochi this common Gr language became the *lingua franca* of antiquity. Gr was known in Northern India, at the Parthian court, and on the distant shores of the Euxine (Black Sea). The native land of the gospel was surrounded on all sides by Gr civilization. Gr culture and language penetrated into the midst of the obstinate home-keeping Palestinian Jews. Though Gr was not the mother-tongue of Our Lord, He understood Gr and apparently could speak it when occasion required—Aram. being the language of His heart and of His public teachings. The history of the Maccabean struggle affords ample evidence of the extent to which Gr culture, and with it the Gr language, were familiar to the Jews. There were in later days Hellenistic bodies of devout Jews in Jerus itself. Gr was recognized by the Jews as the universal language: the inscription on the wall of the outer temple court forbidding Gentiles under pain of death to enter was in Gr. The *koinē* became the language even of religion—where a foreign tongue is least likely to be used—of the large Jewish Diaspora. They perceived the advantages of Gr as the language of commerce—the Jews' occupation—of culture and of proselytizing. They threw open their sacred Scriptures in the LXX and other VSS to the Gr-Rom world, adapting the tr in many respects to the requirements of Gr readers. "The Bible whose God was *Yahweh* was the Bible of one people: the Bible whose God was κύριος [*kúrios*, "Lord"] was the Bible of humanity." When the Romans came upon the scene, they found this language so widely known and so deeply rooted they could not hope to supplant it. Indeed they did not try—except in Sicily and Magna Graecia—to suppress Gr, but rather gladly accepted it as the one common means of intercourse among the peoples of their eastern dominions (see LANGUAGE OF THE NT).

Though Latin was of course the official language of the conquerors, the decrees of governors generally appeared with a Gr tr, so that they might be "understanded of the people," and Gr overcame Lat, as English drove out the French of the Norman invaders. Lat poets and historians more than once complained that *Graecia capta ferum victorem cepit* ("conquered Greece vanquished its stern conqueror"). With the spread of Lat there were two world-languages side by side for the whole Rom empire, but Gr was prevailingly the language of the eastern half of the Rom empire which was the first soil for Christian churches and the first half of the empire to be Christianized. Later when Christianity was able to extend her activity to the West, she found Lat ready as the common means of intercourse. That Rome respected Gr is greatly to her credit and much to the advantage of Christianity. For Christianity, when it began to aim at universalism, dropped its native Aramaic. The gospel in order to become a world-evangel was tr[d] into Gr. The early Christian missionaries did not learn the languages or *patois* of the Rom empire, but confined themselves to centers of Gr culture. Paul wrote in Gr to the church in Rome itself, of which Gr was the language. And while Christianity was spreading through the Gr East under the unification of Rom administration, the Romans were Romanizing and leveling the West for Lat Christianity (see LATIN). In the West it may be noted that the first foothold of the Christian religion was in Gr—witness the church in Gaul.

In material ways too Rome opened the way for Christianity by building the great highways for the gospel.

6. Materially

The great system of roads that knit the then civilized world together served not only the legions and the imperial escorts, but were of equal service to the early missionaries, and when churches began to spring up over the empire, these roads greatly facilitated that church organization and brotherhood which strengthened the church to overcome the empire. With the dawn of the *pax Romana* all these roads became alive once more with a galaxy of caravans and traders. Commerce revived and was carried on under circumstances more favorable than any that obtained till the past century. Men exchanged not only material things, but also spiritual things. Many of these early traders and artisans were Christians, and while they bought and sold the things that perish, they did not lose an opportunity of spreading the gospel. For an empire which embraced the Mediterranean shores, the sea was an important means of intercommunication; and the Mediterranean routes were safer for commerce and travel at that period than during any previous one. Pompey the Great had driven the pirates off the sea, and with the fall of Sextus Pompey no hostile maritime forces remained. The ships which plied in countless numbers from point to point of this great inland sea offered splendid advantages and opportunity for early Christian missionary enthusiasm.

7. Tolerance

The large measure of freedom permitted by Rom authorities to the religions of all nations greatly favored the growth of infant Christianity. The Rom empire was never in principle a persecutor with a permanent court of inquisition. Strange cults from the East and Egypt flourished in the capital, and except when they became a danger to public morality or to the peace of society they were allowed to spread unchecked under the eyes of the police. See below on non-Rom religions.

8. Pattern for a Universal Church

Further, the Rom empire afforded Christianity a material and outward symbol for its spiritual ambition. It enlarged the vision of the church. Only a citizen (Paul) of such a world-empire could dream of a religion for all humanity. If the Rom sword could so conquer and unify the *orbis terrarum*, the militant church should be provoked to attempt nothing less in the religious sphere. It also furnished many a suggestion to the early organizers of the new community, until the Christian church became the spiritual counterpart of the Rom empire. The Christians appropriated many a weapon from the arsenal of the enemy and learned from them aggressiveness, the value of thorough organization and of military methods.

9. Roman Jurisprudence

Rom law in its origins was characterized by the narrowest exclusiveness, and the first formal Rom code was on Gr patterns, yet the Romans here as in so many other respects improved upon what they had borrowed and became masters of jurisprudence in the antique world. As their empire and conceptions expanded, they remodeled their laws to embrace all their subjects. One of the greatest boons conferred by Rome upon the antique world was a uniform system of good laws—the source of much of our European jurisprudence. The Rom law played an equally important rôle with the Jewish in molding and disciplining for Christianity. It taught men to obey and to respect authority, and proved an effective leveling and civilizing power in the empire. The universal law of Rome was the pedagogue for the universal law of the gospel. See ROMAN LAW.

10. Negative Preparation

The Romans could offer their subjects good laws, uniform government and military protection, but not a satisfactory religion. A universal empire called for a universal religion, which Christianity alone could offer. Finally, not only by what Rome had accomplished but by what she proved incapable of accomplishing, the way of the Lord was made ready and a people prepared for His coming. It was a terrible crisis in the civilization and religion of antiquity. The old national religions and systems of belief had proved unable to soothe the increasing imperious moral and spiritual demands of man's nature. A moral bankruptcy was immanent. The old Rom religion of abstract virtues had gone down in formalism; it was too cold for human hearts. Man could no longer find the field of his moral activity in the religion of the state; he was no longer merely an atom in society performing religious rites, not for his own soul, but for the good of the commonwealth. Personality had been slowly emerging, and the new schools of philosophy called man away from the state to seek peace with God in the solitude of his own soul first of all. But even the best of these schools found the crying need of a positive, not a negative religion, the need for a perfect ideal life as a dynamic over ordinary human lives. Thus was felt an imperious demand for a new revelation, for a fresh vision or knowledge of God. In earlier days men had believed that God had revealed Himself to primitive wise men or heroes of their race, and that subsequent generations must accept with faith what these earlier seers, who stood nearer God, as Cicero said, had been pleased to teach of the Divine. But soon this stock of knowledge became exhausted. Plato, after soaring to the highest point of poetic and philosophic thought about the Divine, admitted the need of a demon or superman to tell us the secrets of eternity. With the early Rom empire began a period of tremendous religious unrest. Men tried philosophy, magic, astrology, foreign rites, to find a sure place of rest. This accounts for the rapid and extensive diffusion of oriental mysteries which promised to the initiated communion with God here, a "better hope" in death, and satisfied the craving for immortality beyond time. These were the more serious souls who would gladly accept the consolations of Jesus. Others, losing all faith in any form of religion, gave themselves up to blank despair and accepted Epicureanism with its gospel of annihilation and its *carpe diem* morals. This system had a terrible fascination for those who had lost themselves; it is presented in its most attractive form in the verses of Lucretius—the Omar Khayyám of Lat literature. Others again, unable to find God, surrendered themselves to cheerless skepticism. The sore need of the new gospel of life and immortality will be borne in upon the mind of those who read the Gr and Rom sepulchral inscriptions. And even Seneca, who was almost a Christian in some respects, speaks of immortality as a "beautiful dream" (*bellum somnium*), though tribulation later gave a clearer vision of the "city of God." Servius Sulpicius, writing to Cicero a letter of consolation on the death of his much-missed Tullia, had only a sad "if" to offer about the future (Cic. *Fam.* iv.5). Nowhere does the unbelief and pessimism of pre-Christian days among the higher classes strike one more forcibly than in the famous discussion recorded by Sallust (*Bel. Cat.* li f) as to the punishment of the Catilinarian conspirators. Caesar, who held the Rom high-priesthood and the highest authority on the religion of the state, proposes life imprisonment, as death would only bring annihilation and rest to these villains—no hereafter, no reward or punishment (*eam cuncta mortalium mala dissolvere; ultra neque curae neque gaudio locum esse*). Cato next speaks—the most religious man of his generation—in terms which cast no rebuke upon Caesar's Epicureanism and materialism (ib, 52). Cicero (*In Cat.* iv.4) is content to leave immortality an open question. The philosophers of Athens mocked Paul on Mars' Hill when he spoke of a resurrection. Such was the attitude of the educated classes of the Gr-Rom world at the dawn of Christianity, though it cannot be denied that there was also a strong desire for continued existence. The other classes were either perfunctorily performing the rites of a dead national religion or were seeking, some, excitement or aesthetic worship or even scope for their baser passions, some, peace and promise for the future, in the eastern mysteries. The distinction between moral and physical evil was coming to the surface, and hence a consciousness of sin. Religion and ethics had not yet been united. "The throne of the human mind" was declared vacant, and Christianity was at hand as the best claimant. In fact, the Gr-Rom mind had been expanding to receive the pure teachings of Jesus.

III. Attitude of the Roman Empire to Religions.—

1. Roman or State Religion

The history of Rom religion reveals a continuous penetration of Italian, Etruscan, Gr, Egyp and oriental worship and rites, until the old Rom religion became almost unrecognizable, and even the antiquarian learning of a Varro could scarcely discover the original meaning or use of

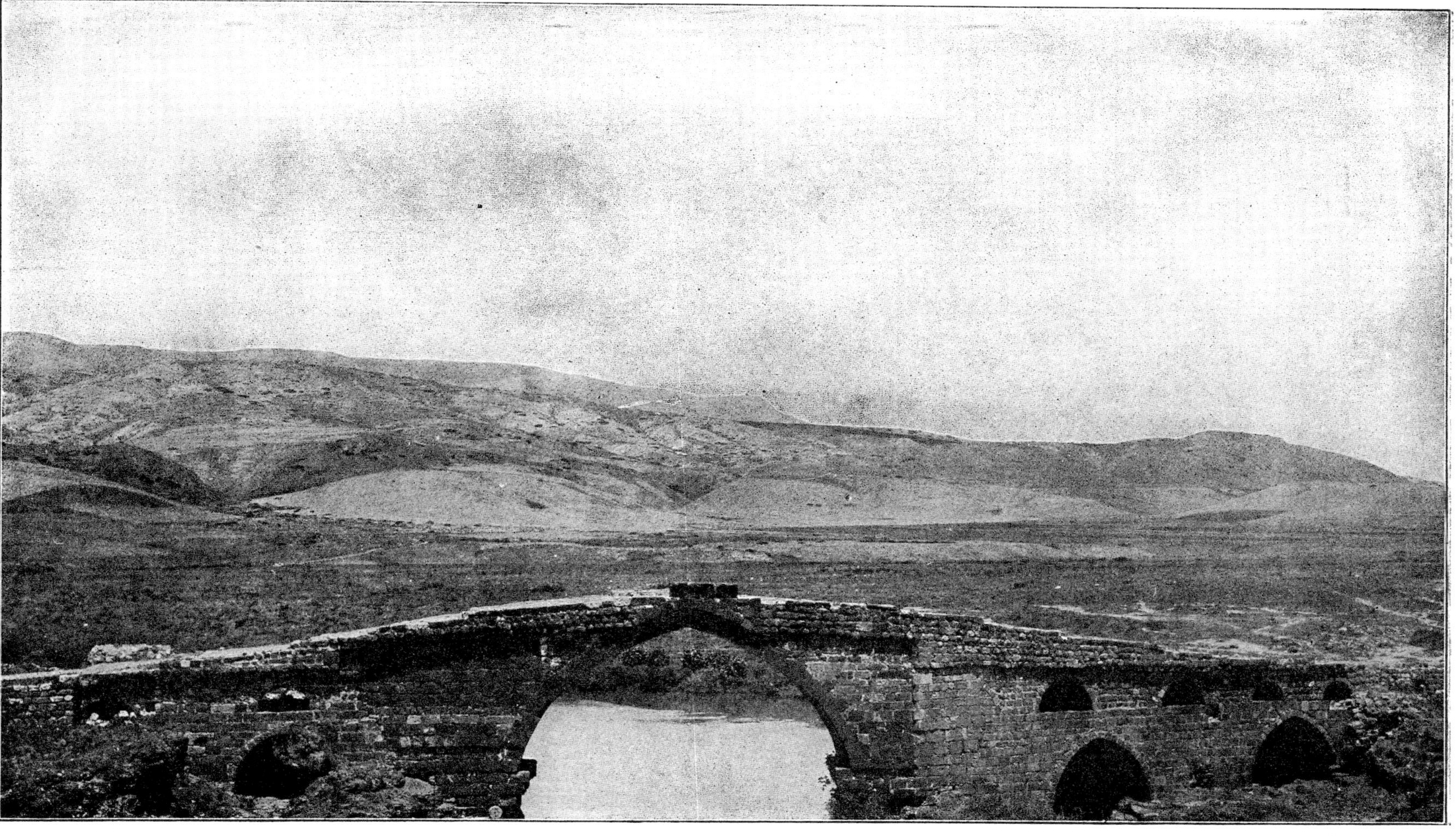

OLD JISR EL-MUJAMIA, ROMAN BRIDGE ACROSS UPPER JORDAN

many Rom deities. The Rom elements or modes of worship progressively retreated until they and the foreign rites with which they were overlaid gave way before the might of Christianity. As Rome expanded, her religious demands increased. During the regal period Rom religion was that of a simple agricultural community. In the period between the *Regifugium* and the Second Punic War Rom religion became more complicated and the Rom Pantheon was largely increased by importations from Etruria, Latium and Magna Graecia. The mysterious religion of Etruria first impressed the Rom mind, and from this quarter probably came the Trinity of the Capitol (Jupiter, Juno, Minerva) previously introduced into Etruria from Gr sources, thus showing that the Romans were not the first in Italy to be influenced by the religion of Greece. New modes of worship, non-Rom in spirit, also came in from the Etruscans and foreign elements of Gr mythology. Latium also made its contribution, the worship of Diana coming from Aricia and also a Lat Jupiter. Two Lat cults penetrated even within the Rom *pomoerium*—that of Hercules and Castor, with deities of Gr origin. The Gr settlements in Southern Italy (Magna Graecia) were generous in their contributions and opened the way for the later invasion of Gr deities. The Sibylline Books were early imported from Cumae as sacred scriptures for the Romans. In 493 BC during a famine a temple was built to the Gr trinity Demeter, Dionysus, and Persephone, under the Lat names of Ceres, Liber, and Libera—the beginning of distrust in the primitive Rom *numina* and of that practice, so oft repeated in Rom history, of introducing new and foreign gods at periods of great distress. In 433 Apollo came from the same region. Mercury and Asclepius followed in 293 BC, and in 249 BC Dis and Proserpina were brought from Tarentum. Other non-Rom modes of approach to deity were introduced. Rome had been in this period very broad-minded in her policy of meeting the growing religious needs of her community, but she had not so far gone beyond Italy. A taste had also developed for dramatic and more aesthetic forms of worship. The period of the Second Punic War was a crisis in Rom religious life, and the faith of the Romans waned before growing unbelief. Both the educated classes and the populace abandoned the old Rom religion, the former sank into skepticism, the latter into superstition; the former put philosophy in the place of religion, the latter the more sensuous cults of the Orient. The Romans went abroad again to borrow deities—this time to Greece, Asia and Egypt. Gr deities were introduced wholesale, and readily assimilated to or identified with Rom deities (see Rome, III, 1). In 191 BC Hebe entered as Juventas, in 179 Artemis as Diana, in 138 Ares as Mars. But the home of religion—the Orient—proved more helpful. In 204 BC Cybele was introduced from Pessinus to Rome, known also as the Great Mother (*magna mater*)—a fatal and final blow to old Rom religion and an impetus to the wilder and more orgiastic cults and mysterious glamor which captivated the common mind. Bacchus with his gross immorality soon followed. Sulla introduced Mâ from Phrygia as the counterpart of the Rom Bellona, and Egypt gave Isis. In the wars of Pompey against the pirates Mithra was brought to Rome—the greatest rival of Christianity. Religion now began to pass into the hands of politicians and at the close of the republic was almost entirely in their hands. Worship degenerated into formalism, and formalism culminated in disuse. Under the empire philosophic systems continued still more to replace religion, and oriental rites spread apace. The religious revival of Augustus was an effort to breathe life into the dry bones. His plan was only partly religious, and partly political—to establish an imperial and popular religion of which he was the head and centering round his person. He discovered the necessity of an imperial religion. In the East kings had long before been regarded as divine by their subjects. Alexander the Great, like a wise politician, intended to use this as one bond of union for his wide dominions. The same habit extended among the Diadochian kings, esp. in Egypt and Syria. When Augustus had brought peace to the world, the Orient was ready to hail him as a god. Out of this was evolved the cult of the reigning emperor and of Roma personified. This worship gave religious unity to the empire, while at the same time magnifying the emperor. But the effort was in vain: the old Rom religion was dead, and the spiritual needs of the empire continued to be met more and more by philosophy and the mysteries which promised immortality. The cult of the *Genius* of the emperor soon lost all reality. Vespasian himself on his deathbed jested at the idea of his becoming a god. The emperor-worship declined steadily, and in the 3d and 4th cents. oriental worships were supreme. The religion of the Rom empire soon became of that cosmopolitan and eclectic type so characteristic of the new era.

2. *Religiones licitae* and *religiones illicitae*

The non-Rom religions were divided into *religiones licitae* ("licensed worships") and *religiones illicitae* ("unlicensed"). The Romans at different times, on account of earthquakes, pestilences, famine or military disasters, introduced non-Rom cults as means of appeasing the *numina.* This generally meant that the cults in question could be performed with impunity by their foreign adherents. It legalized the *collegia* necessary for these worships from which Rom citizens were by law excluded. But, generally speaking, any people settling at Rome was permitted the liberty of its own native worship in so far as the exercise of it did not interfere with the peace of the state or corrupt the morals of society. On one occasion (186 BC), by a decree of the senate, a severe inquisition was instituted against the Bacchanalian rites which had caused flagrant immorality among the adherents. But Rome was never a systematic persecutor. These foreign rites and superstitions, though often forbidden and their professed adherents driven from the city, always returned stronger than ever. Rom citizens soon discovered the fascination of oriental and Gr mysteries, and devoted themselves to foreign gods while maintaining the necessary formalism toward the religion of the state. Very often too Rom citizens would be presidents of these religious brotherhoods. It should not be forgotten that the original moral elements had fallen out of Rom religion, and that it had become simply a political and military religion for the welfare of the state, not for the salvation of the individual. The individual must conform to certain prescribed rites in order to avert calamity from the state. This done, the state demanded no more, and left him a large measure of freedom in seeking excitement or aesthetic pleasure in the warm and more social foreign mysteries. Thus, while the Romans retained the distinction of *religiones licitae* and *illicitae,* they seldom used severity against the latter. Many unlicensed cults were never disturbed. In fact, the very idea of empire rendered toleration of non-Rom religions a necessity. Practically, though not theoretically, the empire abandoned the idea of *religiones illicitae,* while it retained it upon the statute-book to use in case of such an emergency as the Christian religion involved. Not only the government was tolerant, but the different varieties of religions were tolerant and on good terms with each other. The same man might be initiated into the mysteries of half a dozen divinities. The same man might even be priest of two or more gods. Some had not the slightest objection to worshipping Christ along with Mithra, Isis and Adonis. Men were growing conscious of the oneness of the Divine, and credited their neighbors with worshipping the One Unknown under different names and forms. Hadrian is said to have meditated the erection of temples throughout the empire to the Unknown God.

(1) *Judaism a "religio licita."*—An interesting and, for the history of Christianity, important example of a *religio licita* is Judaism. No more exclusive and obstinate people could have been found upon whom to bestow the favor. Yet from the days of Julius Caesar the imperial policy toward the Jew and his religion was uniformly favorable, with the brief exception of the mad attempt of Gaius. The government often protected them against the hatred of the populace. Up to 70 AD they were allowed freely to send their yearly contribution to the temple; they were even allowed self-governing privileges and legislative powers among themselves, and thus formed an exclusive community in the midst of Rom society. Even the disastrous war of 68–70 AD and the fall of Jerus did not bring persecution upon the Jew, though most of these self-governing and self-legislating powers were withdrawn and the Jews were compelled to pay a poll-tax to the temple of the Capitoline Jupiter. Still their religion remained licensed, tolerated, protected. They were excused from duties impossible for their religion, such as military service. This tolerance of the Jewish religion was of incalculable importance to infant Christianity which at first professed to be no more than a reformed and expanded Judaism.

(2) *Why Christianity alone was proscribed.*—The question next arises: If such was the universally mild and tolerant policy of the empire to find room for all gods and cults, and to respect the beliefs of all the subject peoples, how comes the anomaly that Christianity alone was proscribed and persecuted? Christianity was indeed a *religio illicita*, not having been accepted by the government as a *religio licita*, like Judaism. But this is no answer. There were other unlicensed religions which grew apace in the empire. Neither was it simply because Christianity was aggressive and given to proselytism and dared to appear even in the imperial household: Mithraism and Isism were militant and aggressive, and yet were tolerated. Nor was it simply because of popular hatred, for the Christian was not hated above the Jew. Other reasons must explain the anomaly.

(3) *Two empires: cause of conflict.*—The fact was that two empires were born about the same time so like and yet so unlike as to render a conflict and struggle to the death inevitable. The Christians were unequivocal in asserting that the society for which they were waiting and laboring was a "kingdom."

(*a*) Confusion of spiritual and temporal: They thought not merely in national or racial but in ecumenical terms. The Romans could not understand a kingdom of God upon earth, but confused Christian ambition with political. It was soon discovered that Christianity came not to save but to destroy and disintegrate the empire. Early Christian enthusiasm made the term "kingdom" very provoking to pagan patriotism, for many, looking for the *Parousia* of their Lord, were themselves misled into thinking of the new society as a kingdom soon to be set up upon the earth with Christ as king. Gradually, of course, Christians became enlightened upon this point, but the harm had been done. Both the Rom empire and Christianity were aiming at a social organization to embrace the *genus humanum*. But though these two empires were so alike in several points and the one had done so much to prepare the way for the other, yet the *contrast* was too great to allow conciliation. Christianity would not lose the atom in the mass; it aimed at universalism along the path of individualism—giving new value to human personality.

(*b*) Unique claims of Christianity: It seemed also to provoke Rom pride by its absurd claims. It preached that the world was to be destroyed by fire to make way for new heavens and a new earth, that the Eternal City (Rome) was doomed to fall, that a king would come from heaven whom Christians were to obey, that amid the coming desolations the Christians should remain tranquil.

(*c*) Novelty of Christianity: Again after Christianity came from underneath the aegis of Judaism, it must have taken the government somewhat by surprise as a new and unlicensed religion which had grown strong under a misnomer. It was the newest and latest religion of the empire; it came suddenly, as it were, upon the stage with no past. It was not apparent to the Rom mind that Christianity had been spreading for a generation under the tolerance granted to Judaism (*sub umbraculo licitae Judaeorum religionis:* Tert.), the latter of which was "protected by its antiquity," as Tacitus said. The Romans were of a conservative nature and disliked innovations. The greatest statesman of the Augustan era, Maecenas, advised the emperor to extend no tolerance to *new religions* as subversive of monarchy (Dio Cassius lii.36). A new faith appearing suddenly with a large clientèle might be dangerous to the public peace (*multitudo ingens:* Tac. *Ann.* xv.44; πολὺ πλῆθος: Clem. Rom.; Cor **1** 6).

(*d*) Intolerance and exclusiveness of Christian religion and society: In one marked way Christians contravened the tolerant eclective spirit of the empire—the intolerance and absoluteness of their religion and the exclusiveness of their society. All other religions of the empire admitted compromise and eclecticism, were willing to dwell rather on the points of contact with their neighbors than on the contrast. But Christianity admitted no compromise, was intolerant to all other systems. It must be admitted that in this way it was rather unfair to other cults which offered comfort and spiritual support to thousands of the human race before the dawn of Christianity. But we shall not blame, when we recognize that for its own life and mission it was necessary to show itself at first intolerant. Many heathen would gladly accept Christ along with Mithra and Isis and Serapis. But Christianity demanded complete separation. The Jesus cult could tolerate no rival: it claimed to be absolute, and worshippers of Jesus must be separate from the world. The Christian church was absolute in its demands; would not rank with, but above, all worships. This spirit was of course at enmity with that of the day which enabled rival cults to co-exist with the greatest indifference. Add to this the exclusive state of Christian society. No pious heathen who had purified his soul by asceticism and the sacraments of antiquity could be admitted into membership unless he renounced things dear to him and of some spiritual value. In every detail of public life this exclusive spirit made itself felt. Christians met at night and held secret assemblies in which they were reputed to perpetrate the most scandalous crimes. Thyestean banquets, Oedipean incest, child murder, were among the charges provoked by their exclusiveness.

(*e*) *Obstinatio:* Add to this also the sullen obstinacy with which Christians met the demands of imperial power—a feature very offensive to Rom governors. Their religion would be left them undisturbed if they would only render formal obedience to the religion of the state. Rom clemency and respect for law were baffled before Christian obstinacy. The martyr's courage appeared as sheer fanaticism. The pious Aurelius refers but once to Christianity, and in the words ψιλὴ παράταξις, *psilḗ parátaxis*, "sheer obstinacy," and Aristides apparently refers to Christianity as αὐθάδεια, *authádeia*, "stubbornness." See PERSECUTIONS, 18.

(*f*) Aggressiveness against pagan faith: But the Christians were not content with an uncompromising withdrawal from the practices of heathen worship: they also actively assailed the pagan cultus. To the Christians they became doctrines of demons.

The imperial cult and worship of the *Genius* of the emperor were very unholy in their sight. Hence they fell under the charges of disloyalty to the emperor and might be proved guilty of *majestas*. They held in contempt the doctrine that the greatness of Rome was due to her reverence for the gods; the Christians were *atheists* from the pagan point of view. And as religion was a political concern for the welfare of the state, atheism was likely to call down the wrath of divinity to the subversion of the state.

(*g*) *Christianos ad leones:* Very soon when disasters began to fall thickly upon the Rom empire, the blame was laid upon the Christians. In early days Rome had often sought to appease the gods by

Coliseum.

introducing external cults; at other times oriental cults were expelled in the interests of public morality. Now in times of disaster Christians became the scapegoats. If famine, drought, pestilence, earthquake or any other public calamity threatened, the cry was raised "the Christians to the lions" (see NERO; PERSECUTIONS, 12). This view of Christianity as subversive of the empire survived the fall of Rome before Alaric. The heathen forgot—as the apologists showed—that Rome had been visited by the greatest calamities before the Christian era and that the Christians were the most self-sacrificing in periods of public distress, lending succor to pagan and Christian alike.

(*h*) *Odium generis humani:* All prejudices against Christianity were summed up in *odium generis humani*, "hatred for the human race" or society, which was reciprocated by "hatred of the human race toward them." The Christians were bitterly hated, not only by the populace, but by the upper educated classes. Most of the early adherents belonged to the slave, freedman and artisan classes, "not many wise, not many noble." Few were Rom citizens. We have mentioned the crimes which popular prejudice attributed to this hated sect. They were in mockery styled *Christiani* by the Antiochians (a name which they at first resented), and *Nazarenes* by the Jews. No nicknames were too vile to attach to them—*Asinarii* (the sect that worshipped the ass's head), *Sarmenticii* or *Semaxii*. Rom writers cannot find epithets strong enough. Tacitus reckons the Christian faith among the "atrocious and abominable things" (*atrocia aut pudenda*) which flooded Rome, and further designates it *superstitio exitiabilis* ("baneful superstition," *Ann.* xv.44), Suetonius (*Ner.* 16) as novel and malefic (*novae ac maleficae*), and the gentle Pliny (*Ep.* 97) as vile and indecent (*prava immodica*). Well might Justus say the Christians were "hated and reviled by the whole human race." This opprobrium was accentuated by the attacks of philosophy upon Christianity. When the attention of philosophers was drawn to the new religion, it was only to scorn it. This attitude of heathen philosophy is best understood in reading Celsus and the Christian apologists.

(4) *The Roman empire not the only disturbing factor.*—Philosophy long maintained its aloofness from the religion of a crucified Galilean: the "wise" were the last to enter the kingdom of God. When later Christianity had established itself as a permanent force in human thought, philosophy deigned to consider its claims. But it was too late; the new faith was already on the offensive. Philosophy discovered its own weakness and began to reform itself by aiming at being both a philosophy and a religion. This is particularly the case in neo-Platonism (in Plotinus) in which reason breaks down before revelation and mysticism. Another force disturbing the peace of the Christian church was the enemy within the fold. Large numbers of heathen had entered the *ecclesia* bringing with them their oriental or Gr ideas, just as Jewish Christians brought their Judaism with them. This led to grave heresies, each system of thought distorting in its own way the orthodox faith. Later another ally joined the forces against Christianity—reformed paganism led by an injured priesthood. At first the cause of Christianity was greatly aided by the fact that there was no exclusive and jealous priesthood at the head of the Gr-Rom religion, as in the Jewish and oriental religions. There was thus no dogma and no class interested in maintaining a dogma. Religious persecution is invariably instituted by the priesthood, but in the Rom world it was not till late in the day when the temples and sacrifices were falling into desuetude that we find a priesthood as a body in opposition. Thus the Rom imperial power stood not alone in antagonism to Christianity, but was abetted and often provoked to action by (*a*) popular hate, (*b*) philosophy, (*c*) pagan priesthood, (*d*) heresies within the church.

IV. Relations between the Roman Empire and Christianity.—We have here to explain how the attitude of the Rom empire, at first friendly or indifferent, developed into one of fierce conflict, the different stages in the policy—if we can speak of any uniform policy—of the Rom government toward Christianity, the charges or mode of procedure on which Christians were condemned, and when and how the profession of Christianity (*nomen ipsum*) became a crime. We shall see the Rom empire progressively weakening and Christianity gaining ground. For the sake of clearness we shall divide the Rom empire into six periods, the first from the commencement of the Christian era till the last of the Julio-Claudian dynasty.

1. Beginning of Christianity till Death of Nero, 68 AD

At first the presence of the Christian faith was unknown to Rom authorities. It appeared first merely as a reformed and more spiritual Judaism; its earliest preachers and adherents alike never dreamed of severing from the synagogue. Christians were only another of the Jewish sects to which a Jew might belong while adhering to Mosaism and Judaism. But soon this friendly relation became strained on account of the expanding views of some of the Christian preachers, and from the introduction of gentile proselytes. The first persecutions for the infant church came entirely from exclusive Judaism, and it was the Jews who first accused Christians before the Rom courts. Even so, the Rom government not only refused to turn persecutor, but even protected the new faith both against Jewish accusations and against the violence of the populace (Acts **21** 31 f). And the Christian missionaries—esp. Paul—soon recognized in the Rom empire an ally and a power for good. Writing to the Romans Paul counsels them to submit in obedience to the powers that be, as "ordained of God." His favorable impression must have been greatly enhanced by his mild captivity at Rome and his acquittal by Nero on the first trial. The Rom soldiers had come to his rescue in Jerus to save his life from the fanaticism of his own coreligionists. Toward the accusations of the Jews against their rivals the Romans were either indifferent, as Gallio the proconsul of Achaia, who "cared for none of those things" (Acts **18** 12 ff), or recognized the innocence of the accused, as did both Felix (Acts **24** 1 ff) and Porcius Festus (**25** 14 ff). Thus the Romans persisted in looking upon Christians as a sect of the Jews. But the Jews took another step in formulating a charge of disloyalty (begun before Pilate) against the new sect as acting "contrary to the decrees of Caesar, saying that there is another king, one Jesus" (Acts **17** 7; cf **25** 8). Christianity was disowned thus early by Judaism and cast upon its own resources. The increasing numbers of Christians would confirm to the Rom government the independence of Christianity. And the trial of a Rom citizen, Paul, at Rome would further enlighten the authorities.

The first heathen persecution of Christianity resulted from no definite policy, no apprehension of danger to the body politic, and no definite charges, but from an accidental spark which kindled the conflagration of Rome (July, 64 AD). Up to this time no emperor had taken much notice of Christianity. It was only in the middle of the reign of Augustus that Jesus was born. In the reign of Tiberius belong Jesus' public ministry, crucifixion and resurrection; but his reign closed too early (37 AD) to allow any prominence to the new faith, though this emperor was credited with proposing to the senate a decree to receive Christ into the Rom pantheon—legend of course. Under the brief principate of the mad Gaius (37–41 AD) the "new way" was not yet divorced from the parent faith. Gaius caused a diversion in favor of the Christians by his persecution of the Jews and the command to set up his own statue in the temple. In the next reign (Claudius, 41–54 AD) the Jews were again harshly treated, and thousands were banished from Rome (*Judaeos impulsore Chresto assidue tumultuantes Roma expulit:* Suet. *Claud.* 25). Some would see in this an action against the Christians by interpreting the words as meaning riots between Jews and Christians, in consequence of which some Christians were banished as Jews, but Dio Cassius (lx.6) implies that it was a police regulation to restrain the spread of Jewish worship. It was in the reign of Nero, after the fire of 64 AD, that the first hostile step was taken by the government against the Christians, earliest account of which is given by Tacitus (*Ann.* xv.44). Nero's reckless career had given rise to the rumor that he was the incendiary, that he wished to see the old city burned in order to rebuild it on more magnificent plans. See NERO. Though he did everything possible to arrest the flames, even exposing his own life, took every means of alleviating the destitution of the sufferers, and ordered such religious rites as might appease the wrath of the gods, the suspicion still clung to him.

"Accordingly in order to dissipate the rumor, he put forward as guilty [*subdidit reos*] and inflicted the most cruel punishments on those who were hated for their abominations [*flagitia*] and called *Christians* by the populace. The originator of that name, Christus, had been executed by the procurator Pontius Pilatus in the reign of Tiberius, and the baneful superstition [*exitiabilis superstitio*] put down for the time being broke out again, not only throughout Judaea, the home of this evil, but also in the City [Rome] where all atrocious and shameful [*atrocia aut pudenda*] things converge and are welcomed. Those therefore who confessed [i.e. to being Christians] were first arrested, and then by the information gained from them a large number [*multitudo ingens*] were implicated [*coniuncti* is the MS reading, not *conuicti*], not so much on the charge of incendiarism as for hatred of mankind [*odio humani generis*]. The victims perished amid mockery [text here uncertain]; some clothed in the skins of wild beasts were torn to pieces by dogs; others impaled on crosses in order to be set on fire to afford light by night after daylight had died. . . . . Whence [after these cruelties] commiseration began to be felt for them, though guilty and deserving the severest penalties [*quamquam adversus sontes et novissima exempla meritos*], for men felt their destruction was not from considerations of public welfare but to gratify the cruelty of one person [Nero]."

This passage—the earliest classical account of the crucifixion and the only mention of Pilate in a heathen author—offers some difficulties which require to be glanced at. It is held by some that Tacitus contradicts himself by writing *subdidit reos* at the beginning and *sontes* at the end, but *sontes* does not mean guilty of incendiarism, but guilty from the point of view of the populace and deserving severe punishment for other supposed *flagitia*, not for arson. It is thus quite clear that Tacitus regards the Christians as innocent, though he had not the slightest kindly feeling toward them. *Qui fatebantur* means most naturally, "those who confessed to being Christians," though Arnold argues that *confiteri* or *profiteri* would be the correct word for professing a religion. But this would contradict both the sense and the other evidences of the context; for if *fatebantur* could mean "confessed to arson," then the whole body of Christians should have been arrested, and, further, this would have diverted suspicion from Nero, which was not the case according to Tacitus. Some Christians boldly asserted their religion, others no doubt, as in Bithynia, recanted before tribulation. By *indicio eorum* Ramsay (*Christianity in the Rom Empire,* 233) understands "on the information elicited at their trial," i.e. from information gathered by the inquisitors in the course of the proceedings. This incidental information implicated a large number of others, hence Ramsay prefers the MS reading *coniuncti* to the correction *conuicti*. This is in order to explain the difficulty seemingly raised, viz. that the noblest Christians who boldly confessed their Christianity would seek to implicate brethren. But it is not impossible that *some* of these bold spirits did condescend to give the names of their coreligionists to the Rom courts. Hence Hardy (*Christianity and the Rom Government,* 67) prefers the more usual rendering of *indicio eorum* as "on information received from them." This may have occurred either (1) through torture, or (2) for promised immunity, or (3) on account of local jealousies. The early Christian communities were not perfect; party strife often ran high as at Corinth. And in a church like that of Rome composed of Jewish and pagan elements and undoubtedly more cosmopolitan than Corinth, a bitter sectarian spirit is easy to understand. This as a probable explanation is much strengthened and rendered almost certain by the words of Clement of Rome, who, writing to the church at Corinth (ch vi) *from Rome only a generation after the persecution,* and thus familiar with the internal history of the Rom *ecclesia,* twice asserts that a πολὺ πλῆθος (*polú plēthos* =Tac. *multitudo ingens*) of the Rom Christians suffered διὰ ζῆλος (*diá zēlos*), "through jealousy or strife." The most natural and obvious meaning is "mutual or sectarian jealousy." But those who do not like this fact explain it as "by the jealousy of the Jews." Nothing is more easily refuted, for had it been the jealousy of the Jews Clement would not have hesitated one moment to say so. Those who are familiar with the Christian literature of that age know that the Christians were none too sensitive toward Jewish feelings. But the very fact that it was *not* the Jews made Clement rather modestly omit details the memory of which was probably still bearing fruit, even in his day. Once more *correpti,* usually rendered "arrested," is taken by Hardy as "put upon their trial." He argues that this is more in accord with Tacitean usage. A "huge multitude" need not cause us to distrust Tacitus. It is a relative term; it was a considerable number to be so inhumanly butchered. There is some hesitation as to whether *odio humani generis* is objective or subjective genitive: "hatred of the Christians toward the human race" or "hatred of the human race toward the Christians." Grammatically of course it may be either, but that it is the former there can be no doubt: it was of the nature of a charge against Christians (Ramsay). See PERSECUTION.

Some have impugned the veracity of Tacitus in this very important passage, asserting that he had read back the feelings and state of affairs of his own day (half a century later) into this early Neronian period. This early appearance of Christianity as a distinct religion and its "huge multitude" seem impossible to some. Schiller has accordingly suggested that it was the Jews who as a body at Rome were persecuted, that the Christians being not yet distinct from Jews shared in the persecutions and suffered, not as Christians, but as Jews. But Tacitus is too trustworthy a historian to be guilty of such a confusion; besides, as proconsul in Asia he must have been more or less familiar with the origin of the Christian party. Also Poppaea was at this time mistress of Nero's affections and sufficiently influential with him to stay such a cruel persecution against those to whom she had a leaning and who claimed her as a proselyte. Again, the Jewish faith was *certe licita* and a recognized worship of the empire.

The next question is, Why were the *Christians alone* selected for persecution? That they were so singled out we know, but exactly for what reason is hard to say with certainty. A number of reasons no doubt contributed. (1) Farrar (*Early Days*, ch iv) sees "in the proselytism of Poppaea, guided by Jewish malice, the only adequate explanation of the first Christian persecution," and Lightfoot is of the same opinion, but this by itself is inadequate, though the Jews would be glad of an opportunity of taking revenge on their aggressive opponents. (2) Christians *had* already become in the eyes of the Rom authorities a distinct sect, either from the reports of the eastern provincial governors, where Christianity was making most headway, or from the attention attracted by Paul's first trial. They were thus the newest religious sect, and as such would serve as victims to appease deity and the populace. (3) Even if *ingens multitudo* be rhetorical, the Christians were no doubt considerably numerous in Rome. Their aggressiveness and active proselytism made their numbers even more formidable. (4) They were uncompromising in their expression of their beliefs; they looked for a consummation of the earth by fire and were also eagerly expecting the *Parousia* of their king to reconstitute society. These tenets together with their calm faith amid the despair of others would easily cast suspicion upon them. (5) For whatever reason, they had earned the opprobrium of the populace. "The hatred for the Jews passed over to hatred for the Christians" (Mommsen). A people whom the populace so detested must have fallen under the surveillance of the city police administration. (6) A large proportion of the Christian community at Rome would be non-Rom and so deserve no recognition of Rom privileges. These reasons together may or may not explain the singling-out of the Christians. At any rate they were chosen as scapegoats to serve Nero and his minion Tigellinus. The origin of the first persecution was thus purely accidental—in order to remove suspicion from Nero. It was not owing to any already formulated policy, neither through apprehension of any danger to the state, nor because the Christians were guilty of any crimes, though it gave an opportunity of investigation and accumulation of evidence. But accidental as this persecution was in origin, its consequences were of far-reaching importance. There are three principal views as to the date of the policy of proscription of the new faith by the Rom government: (1) the old view that persecution for the name, i.e. for the mere profession of Christianity, began under Trajan in 112 AD—a view now almost universally abandoned; (2) that of Ramsay (*Christianity in the Rom Empire*, 242 ff, and three arts. in *Expos*, 1893), who holds that this development from punishment for definite crimes (*flagitia*) to proscription "for the name" took place between 68 and 96 AD, and (3) that of Hardy (*Christianity and the Rom Government*, 77), Mommsen (*Expos*, 1893, 1-7) and Sanday (ib, 1894, 406 ff)—and adopted by the writer of this article—that the trial of the Christians under Nero resulted in the declaration of the mere profession of Christianity as a crime punishable by death. Tacitus apparently represents the persecution of the Christians as accidental and isolated and of brief duration (l.c.), while Suetonius (*Ner.* 16) mentions the punishment of Christians in a list of permanent police regulations for the maintenance of good order, into which it would be inconsistent to introduce an isolated case of procedure against the "baneful superstition" (Ramsay, op. cit., p. 230). But these two accounts are not contradictory, Tacitus giving the initial stage and Suetonius "a brief statement of the permanent administrative principle into which Nero's action ultimately resolved itself" (ib, 232). Nero's police administration, then, pursued as a permanent policy what was begun merely to avert suspicion from Nero. But as yet, according to Ramsay, Christians were not condemned *as Christians*, but on account of certain *flagitia* attaching to the profession and because the Rom police authorities had learned enough about the Christians to regard them as hostile to society. A trial still must be held and condemnation pronounced "in respect not of the name but of serious offences naturally connected with the name," viz. first incendiarism, which broke down, and secondly hostility to civilized society and charges of magic. The others agree so far with Ramsay as describing the first stages, but assert that *odium humani generis* was not of the nature of a definite charge, but disaffection to the social and political arrangements of the empire. At the outset a trial was needed, but soon as a consequence the trial could be dispensed with, the Christians being "recognized as a society whose principle might be summarized as *odium generis humani*." A trial became unnecessary; the religion itself involved the crimes, and as a religion it was henceforth proscribed. The surveillance over them and their punishment was left to the police administration which could step in at any time with severe measures or remain remiss, according as exigencies demanded. Christianity was henceforth a *religio illicita*. The Rom government was never a systematic persecutor. The persecution or non-persecution of Christianity depended henceforth on the mood of the reigning emperor, the character of his administration, the activity of provincial governors, the state of popular feeling against the new faith, and other local circumstances. There is no early evidence that the Neronian persecution extended beyond Rome, though of course the "example set by the emperor necessarily guided the action of all Rom officials." The stormy close of Nero's reign and the tumultuous days till the accession of Vespasian created a diversion in favor of Christianity. Orosius (*Hist.* vii.7) is too late an authority for a general persecution (*per omnes provincias pari persecutione excruciari imperavit; ipsum nomen exstirpare conatus . . . .*). Besides, Paul after his acquittal seems to have prosecuted his missionary activity without any extraordinary hindrances, till he came to Rome the second time. This Neronian persecution is important for the history of Christianity: Nero commenced the principle of punishing Christians, and thus made a precedent for future rulers. Trouble first began in the world-capital; the next stage will be found in the East; and another in Africa and the West. But as yet persecution was only local. Nero was the first of the Rom persecutors who, like Herod Agrippa, came to a miserable end—a fact much dwelt upon by Lactantius and other Christian writers.

2. The Flavian Period, 68–96 AD

In the Flavian period no uniform imperial *policy* against Christianity can be discovered. According to Ramsay the Flavians developed the practice set by Nero from punishment of Christians for definite crimes to proscription of the name. But, as we have seen, the Neronian persecution settled the future attitude of the Rom state toward the new faith. The Flavians could not avoid following the precedent set by Nero. Christianity was spreading—esp. in the East and at Rome. We have no account of any persecution under Vespasian (though Hilary erroneously speaks of him as a persecutor along with Nero and Decius) and Titus, but it does not follow that none such took place. As the whole matter was left to the police administration, severity would be spasmodic and called forth by local circumstances. The fall of Jerus must have had profound influence both on Judaism and on Christianity. For the former it did what the fall of Rome under Goths, Vandals, and Germans did for the old Rom religion—it weakened the idea of a national God bound up with a political religion. The cleft between Judaism and its rival would now become greater. Christianity was relieved from the overpowering influence of a national center, and those Jews who now recognized the futility of political dreams would more readily join the Christian faith. Not only the distinction but the opposition and hostility would now be more apparent to outsiders, though Vespasian imposed the poll-tax on Jewish Christians and Jews alike. No memory of harshness against Christianity under Vespasian has survived. Ramsay (op. cit., 257) would interpret a mutilated passage of Suetonius (*Vesp.* 15) as implying Vespasian's reluctance to carry out *justa supplicia* against Christians.

Titus, "the darling of the human race," is not recorded as a persecutor, but his opinion of Judaism and Christianity as stated in the council of war before Jerus in 70 AD and recorded by Sulpicius Severus (*Chron.* ii.30, 6) is interesting as an approval of the policy adopted by Nero. Severus' authority is undoubtedly Tacitus (Bernays and Mommsen). The authenticity of the speech as contradicting the account of Jos has been impugned; at any rate it represents the point of view of Tacitus. Titus then advocates the destruction of the temple in order that the religion of the Jews and the Christians may be more thoroughly extirpated (*quo plenius Judaeorum et Christianorum religio tolleretur*), since these religions though opposed to each other were of the same origin, the Christians having sprung from the Jews. If the root was removed the stem would readily perish (*radice sublata, stirpem facile perituram*). We know, however, of no active measures of Titus against either party, his short reign perhaps allowing no time for such.

It is Domitian who stands out prominently as the persecutor of this period, as Nero of the first period. His procedure against Christians was not an isolated act, but part of a general policy under which others suffered. His reign was a return to ancient principles. He attempted to reform morals, suppress luxury and vice, banish immoral oriental rites, actors, astrologers and philosophers. It was in his attempt to revive the national religion that he came in conflict with the universal religion. His own cousin, Flavius Clemens, was condemned apparently for Christianity (atheism), and his wife, Domitilla, was banished. The profession of Christianity was not sufficient for the condemnation of Rom citizens of high standing; hence the charges of atheism or *majestas* were put forward. Refusal to comply with the religion of the national gods could be brought under the latter. But for ordinary Rom citizens and for provincials the profession of Christianity merited death. No definite edict or general proscription was enacted; only the principle instituted by Nero was allowed to be carried out. There was, as Mommsen remarks, a standing proscription of Christians as of brigands, but harsh procedure against both was spasmodic and depended on the caprice or character of provincial governors. Domitian took one definite step against Christianity in establishing an easy test by which to detect those who were Christians and so facilitate inquiries. This test was the demand to worship the *Genius* of the emperor. This too was only part of Domitian's general policy of asserting his own *dominus et deus* title and emphasizing the imperial cult as a bond of political union. The Apocalypse reflects the sufferings of the church in this reign.

3. The Antonine Period, 96–192 AD

(1) *Nerva and Trajan.*—On the death of Domitian peace was restored to the Christian church which lasted throughout the brief reign of Nerva (96–98) and the first 13 years of Trajan. It is a curious fact that some of the best of the Rom emperors (Trajan, Marcus Aurelius, Decius and Diocletian) were harsh to the Christians, while some of the worst (as Commodus, Caracalla, Heliogabalus) left them in peace (see PERSECUTION, 17). Christianity had been rapidly spreading in the interval of tranquillity. Pliny became governor of Bithynia in 111 AD and found, esp. in the eastern part of his province, the temples almost deserted. Some Christians were brought before him and *on established precedents* were ordered to be executed for their religion. But Pliny soon discovered that many of both sexes and all ages, provincials and Rom citizens, were involved. The Rom citizens he sent to Rome for trial; but being of a humane disposition he shrank from carrying out the wholesale execution required by a consistent policy.

He wrote to Trajan telling him what he had already done, rather covertly suggesting tolerant measures. Should no distinction be made between old and young? Should pardon not be extended to those who recanted and worshipped the emperor's image and cursed Christ? Should mere profession (*nomen ipsum*) be a capital offence if no crimes could be proven, or should the crimes rather be punished that were associated with the faith (*an flagitia cohaerentia nomini*)? He then explains his procedure: he gave those who were accused an abundant opportunity of recanting; those who persisted in this faith were executed. He considered their "stubbornness and inflexible obstinacy" (*pertinaciam certe et inflexibilem obstinationem*) as in itself deserving punishment. But the administration having once interfered found plenty to do. An anonymous list of many names was handed in, most of whom, however, denied being Christians. Informers then put forward others who likewise denied belonging to the faith. Pliny was convinced their meetings were harmless, and on examination of two deaconesses under torture discovered nothing but a perverse extravagant superstition (*sup. pravam immodicam*). Trajan replied that no universal and definite rule could be laid down, apparently confirming the correctness of Pliny's action and perhaps disappointing Pliny in not yielding to his humane suggestions. Nevertheless, the emperor made three important concessions: (1) the Christians were not to be sought out by the police authorities, but if they were accused and convicted they must be punished; (2) anonymous information against them was not to be accepted; (3) even those suspected of *flagitia* in the past were to be pardoned on proving they were not Christians or on renouncing Christianity. Some regard this rescript of Trajan as the first official and legal authorization to proscribe Christianity; but we have already seen that Christianity *as such* was proscribed as a result of the Neronian investigations. Besides, there is not the slightest trace of any new principle of severity, either in the letters of Pliny or in the rescript of Trajan. The persecution of Christianity had been "permanent" like that of highwaymen, but not systematic or general. Neither was Trajan's rescript an edict of toleration, though on the whole it was favorable to the Christians in minimizing the dangers to which they were exposed. The question was as yet purely one of administration.

Trajan initiated no procedure against Christians —in fact rather discouraged any, asking his lieutenant to close his eyes to offenders—and Pliny consulted him in the hope of obtaining milder treatment for the Christians by putting in question form what he really wished to be approved. Trajan's rescript "marks the end of the old system of uncompromising hostility" (see PERSECUTION, 15).

(2) *Hadrian.*—The reign of Hadrian (117–38) was a period of toleration for the Christians. He was no bigot, but tolerant and eclective, inquiring into all religions and initiated into several mysteries and willing to leave religion an open question. In Asia, where Christianity was making most progress,

a state of terrorism was imminent if *delatores* were encouraged against Christians making a profession of *delatio* (giving information). As we saw in the letter of Pliny, even non-Christians were accused, and any professing Christian could be threatened by these informers in order to secure a bribe for proceeding no farther. Licinius Silvanus Granianus, like Pliny, found himself involved in difficulties and wrote to Hadrian for advice. Hadrian's rescript in reply is addressed to Granianus' successor, Minucius Fundanus, the proconsul of Asia, about 124 AD. The genuineness of this important document, though impugned by Overbeck, Keim and Lipsius, is vouched for by Mommsen, Hardy, Lightfoot and Ramsay. Indeed, it is much easier accounted for as authentic than as a forgery, for who but the broad-minded Hadrian could have written such a rescript? Apparently the questions put by the proconsul must have been of a similar nature to those extant of Pliny. The answer of Hadrian is a decided step in favor of Christianity and goes beyond that of Trajan: (1) information is not to be passed over (*a*) lest the innocent suffer (as was the case under Pliny), and (*b*) lest informers should make a trade of lodging accusations; (2) provincials accusing Christians must give proof that the accused have committed something illegal; (3) mere petitions and acclamations against the Christians are not to be admitted; (4) a prosecutor on failing to make good his case is to be punished. These terms would greatly increase the risk for informers and lessen the dangers for Christians. That the name is a crime is not admitted, neither is this established principle rescinded. It is quite possible that Hadrian's rescript "gave a certain stimulus toward the employment of the more definite and regular legal procedure."

(3) *Antoninus Pius* (*138–61*).—The liberal policy of Trajan and Hadrian was continued by Antoninus, though persecution occurred in his reign in which Ptolemaeus and Lucius were executed at Rome and Polycarp at Smyrna. But he decidedly confirmed Hadrian's policy of protecting the Christians uncondemned against mob violence in his letters to Larissae, Athens, Thessalonica and to "all the Hellenes." As at Smyrna, his "rescript was in advance of public feeling," and so was disregarded. Anonymous delation was also repressed.

(4) *Marcus Aurelius* (*161–80*).—Under Aurelius a strong reaction set in affecting the Christians, caused partly by the frontier disasters and devastating pestilence and partly by Aurelius' policy of returning to ancient principles and reviving the Rom national religion. In this reign we find persecution extending to the West (Gaul) and to Africa—a step toward the general persecutions of the next century. Though no actual change was made by Aurelius, the leniency of the last three reigns is absent. No general edict or definite rescript of persecution was issued; the numerous martyrdoms recorded in this reign are partly due to the fuller accounts and the rise of a Christian literature. Christianity in itself still constituted a crime, and the obstinacy (παράταξις, *parátaxis*) of Christians in itself deserved punishment. Aurelius seems to have actually rebuked the severity of the Rom governor at Lugdunum, and to have further discouraged the trade of informers against Christians. Tertullian actually styles him as *debellator Christianorum* ("protector of Christians"). We find as yet therefore no systematic or serious attempt to extirpate the new faith. The central government "was all this time without a permanent or steady policy toward the Christians. It had not yet made up its mind" (Hardy).

Under the rule of Commodus (180–92) Christians again enjoyed a respite. The net result of the collisions between the new faith and the government in this period is somewhat differently estimated by Ramsay and by Hardy. The latter thinks (*Christianity and Rom Government*, 156 f) that Ramsay "has to some extent antedated the existence of anything like a policy of proscription," due to antedating the time when Christianity was regarded as a serious political danger. Hardy thinks that the Christian organization was never suspected as more than an abstract danger during the first two centuries. Had Rome taken the view that Christianity in its organization was a real danger and an *imperium in imperio*, she must have started a systematic exterminating policy during a period when Christianity could have least withstood it. When the empire did—as in the 3d cent.—apprehend the practical danger and took the severest general measures, Christianity was already too strong to be harmed, and we shall find the empire henceforth each time worsted and finally offering terms.

4. Changing Dynasties, 192–284 AD

In the next period the insecurity of the throne, when in less than 100 years about a score of candidates wore the purple and almost each new emperor began a new dynasty, enabled Christianity to spread practically untroubled. Further diversions in its favor were created by those fierce barbarian wars and by the necessity of renewed vigilance at the frontier posts. The Christians' aloofness from political strife and their acquiescence in each new dynasty brought them generally into no collision with new rulers. Further, the fact that many of these emperors were non-Rom provincials, or foreigners who had no special attachment to the old Rom faith, and were eclectic in their religious views, was of much importance to the new eastern faith. Moreover, some of the emperors proved not only not hostile to Christianity, but positively friendly. In this period we find no severe (except perhaps that of Decius) and certainly no protracted persecution. The Christian church herself was organized on the principle of the imperial government, and made herself thus strong and united, so that when the storm did come she remained unshaken. In 202 Severus started a cruel persecution in Africa and Egypt, but peace was restored by the savage Caracalla (*lacte Christiano educatus:* Tert.). Heliogabalus assisted Christianity indirectly (1) by the degradation of Rom religion, and (2) by tolerance. According to one writer he proposed to fuse Christianity, Judaism and Samaritanism into one religion. Alexander Severus was equally tolerant and syncretic, setting up in his private chapel images of Orpheus, Apollonius, Abraham, and Christ, and engraving the golden rule on his palace walls and public buildings. He was even credited with the intention of erecting a temple to Christ. Local persecution broke out under Maximin the Thracian. The first general persecution was that of Decius, in which two features deserve notice: (1) that death was not the immediate result of Christian profession, but every means was employed to induce Christians to recant; (2) Rom authorities already cognizant of the dangers of Christian organization directed their efforts esp. against the officers of the church. Gallus continued this policy, and Valerian, after first stopping persecution, tried to check the spread of the worship by banishing bishops and closing churches, and later enacted the death penalty. Gallienus promulgated what was virtually the first edict of toleration, forbade persecution and restored the Christian endowments. Christianity now entered upon a period of 40 years' tranquillity: as outward dangers decreased, less desirable converts came within her gates and her adherents were overtaken in a flood of worldliness, stayed only by the persecution of Diocletian.

Like some other persecutors, Diocletian was one of the ablest Rom rulers. He was not disposed to proceed against the Christians, but was finally driven to harsh measures by his son-in-law Galerius. The first edict, February 24, 303, was not intended to exterminate Christianity, but to check its growth and weaken its political influence, and was directed principally against Bibles, Christian assemblies and churches. The second was against church organization. A third granted freedom to those who recanted, but sought to compel the submission of recalcitrants by tortures —a partial confession of failure on the part of the imperial government. Bloodshed was avoided and the death penalty omitted. But a fourth edict issued by Maximin prescribed the death penalty and required the act of sacrifice to the gods. In the same year (304) Diocletian, convinced of the uselessness of these measures, stayed the death penalty. The change of policy on the part of the emperor and his abdication next year were virtually a confession that the Galilean had conquered. After the persecution had raged 8 years (or 10, if we include local persecutions after 311), Galerius, overtaken by a loathsome disease, issued from Nicomedia with Constantine and Licinius the first general edict of toleration, April 30, 311. Christianity had thus in this period proved a state within a state; it was finally acknowledged as a *religio licita*, though not yet on equality with paganism.

5. Diocletian till First General Edict of Toleration, 284–311 AD

In the next period the first religious wars began, and Christianity was first placed on an equal footing with its rival, then above it, and finally it became the state religion of both West and East. As soon as Christianity had gained tolerance it immediately became an intolerant, bitter persecutor, both of its old rival and of heresy. Constantine, having defeated Maxentius at the Milvian Bridge (October 27, 312), became sole ruler of the West, and, in conjunction with his eastern colleague Licinius, issued the famous edict of toleration from Milan, March 30, 313, by which all religions were granted equal tolerance, and Christianity was thus placed on an equal footing with heathenism. Constantine's favors toward the Christian faith were largely political; he wished simply to be on the winning side. With each fresh success he inclined more toward Christianity, though his whole life was a compromise. His dream was to weld pagan and Christian into one society under the same laws; he in no way prohibited paganism. With the founding of Constantinople Christianity became practically the state religion—an alliance with baneful consequences for Christianity. It now began to stifle the liberty of conscience for which it had suffered so much, and orthodoxy began its long reign of intolerance. The sons of Constantine inherited their father's cruel nature with his nominal Christianity. Constantine had left the old and the new religions on equal footing: his sons began the work of exterminating paganism by violence. Constantius when sole emperor, inheriting none of his father's compromise or caution, and prompted by women and bishops, published edicts demanding the closing of the temples and prohibiting sacrifices. Wise provincial administrators hesitated to carry out these premature measures. Christianity was now in the ascendancy and on the aggressive. It not only persecuted paganism, but the dominant Christian party proscribed its rival—this time heterodoxy banishing orthodoxy. The violence and intolerance of the sons of Constantine justified the mild reaction under Julian the Apostate—the most humane member of the Constantine family. He made a "romantic" effort to reëstablish the old religion, and while proclaiming tolerance for Christianity, he endeavored to weaken it by heaping ridicule upon its doctrines, rescinding the privileges of the clergy, prohibiting the church from receiving many bequests, removing Christians from public positions and forbidding the teaching of classics in Christian schools lest Christian tongues should become better fitted to meet heathen arguments, and lastly by adding renewed splendor to pagan service as a counter-attraction. But the moral power of Christianity triumphed. Dying on a battle-field, where he fought the Persians, he is said (but not on good authority) to have exclaimed, "Thou hast conquered, O Galilean" (νενίκηκας Γαλιλαῖε, *neníkēkas Galilaîe*). For a brief period after his death there was religious neutrality. Gratian—at the instigation of Ambrose—departed from this neutrality, removed the statue of Victory from the senate-house, refused the title and robes of *pontifex maximus*, prohibited bloody sacrifices, and dealt a severe blow to the old faith by withdrawing some of the treasury grants, thereby making it dependent on the voluntary system. Theodosius I, or the Great, adopted a strenuous religious policy against both heresy and paganism. His intolerance must be attributed to Ambrose—a bigot in whose eyes Jews, heretics and pagans alike had no rights. Systematic proscription of paganism began. In 381 Theodosius denied the right of making a will to apostates from Christianity, in 383 the right of inheritance, in 391 heathen public worship was interdicted, in 392 several acts of both private and public heathen worship were forbidden, and greater penalties were attached to the performance of sacrifice. Christian vandalism became rampant; all kinds of violence and confiscation were resorted to, monks or priests often leading the populace. For the present the West did not suffer so severely from fanatic iconoclasm. Under the sons of Theodosius the suppression of paganism was steadily pursued. Honorius in the West excluded (408 AD) pagans from civil and military offices; in a later edict (423) the very existence of paganism is doubted (*paganos . . . . quamquam iam nullos esse credamus*). That heathenism was still an attraction is proved by the repeated laws against apostasy. Under Valentinian III (423–55) and Theodosius II, laws were enacted for the destruction of temples or their conversion into Christian churches. In the western empire heathenism was persecuted till the end, and its final overthrow was hastened by the extinction of the western empire (476). In the East Justinian closed the heathen schools of philosophy at Athens (529 AD), and in a despotic spirit prohibited even heathen worship in private under pain of death.

6. First General Edict of Toleration till Fall of Western Empire, 311–476 AD

V. Victory of Christianity and Conversion of the Roman Empire.—Christianity was now acknowledged as the religion of both East and West. It had also grown strong enough to convert the barbarians who overran the West. It restrained and educated them under the lead of the papacy, so that its conquests now extended beyond the Rom empire.

Merivale (preface to *Conversion of Rom Empire*) attributes the conversion of the Rom empire to four causes: (1) the external evidence of apparent fulfilment of prophecy and the evidence of miracles, (2) internal evidence as satisfying the spiritual wants of the empire and offering a Redeemer, (3) the example of the pure lives and heroic deaths of the early Christians, and (4) the success which attended the Christian cause under Constantine. Gibbon (ch xv of *Decline and Fall*) seeks to account for the phenomenal success of Christianity in the empire by (1) the zeal and enthusiasm of the early Christians, (2) the belief of Christianity in immortality with both future rewards and future retributions, (3) miracles, (4) the high ethical code and pure morals of professing Christians, and (5) strong ecclesiastical organization on imperial patterns. But neither of these lists of causes seems to account satisfactorily for the progress and success of the religion of Jesus.

This was due in the first place to negative causes

—the moral and spiritual bankruptcy of the antique world, the internal rottenness and decay of heathen systems. All ancient national religions had failed and were abandoned alike by philosophers and the masses, and no universal religion for humanity was offered except by Christianity. Worship had degenerated into pure formalism which brought no comfort to the heart. An imperious demand for revelation was felt which no philosophy or natural religion could satisfy.

1. Negative Causes

But it was to positive causes chiefly that the success of the new religion was due, among which were the zeal, enthusiasm, and moral earnestness of the Christian faith. Its sterling qualities were best shown in persecution and the heroic deaths of its adherents. Paganism, even with the alliance of the civil power and the prestige of its romantic past, could not withstand persecution. And when heathenism was thrown back on the voluntary system, it could not prosper as Christianity did with its ideals of self-sacrifice. The earnestness of early Christianity was raised to its highest power by its belief in a near second coming of the Lord and the end of the aeon. The means of propagation greatly helped the spread of Christianity, the principal means being the exemplary lives of its professors. It opposed moral and spiritual power to political. Besides, Christianity when once studied by the thinkers of the ancient world was found to be in accord with the highest principles of reason and Nature. But "the chief cause of its success was the congruity of its teaching with the spiritual nature of mankind" (Lecky). There was a deep-seated earnestness in a large section of the ancient world to whom Christianity offered the peace, comfort and strength desired. It was possessed also of an immense advantage over all competing religions of the Rom empire in being adapted to all classes and conditions and to all changes. There was nothing local or national about it; it gave the grandest expression to the contemporary ideal of brotherhood. Its respect for woman and its attraction for this sex gained it many converts who brought honor to it; in this respect it was far superior to its greatest rival, Mithraism. In an age of vast social change and much social distress it appealed to the suffering by its active self-denial for the happiness of others. As an ethical code it was equal and superior to the noblest contemporary systems. One incalculable advantage it could show above all religions and philosophies—the charm and power of an ideal perfect life, in which the highest manhood was held forth as an incentive to nobler living. The person of Jesus was an ideal and moral dynamic for both philosopher and the common man, far above any abstract virtue. "It was because it was true to the moral sentiments of the age, because it represented faithfully the supreme type of excellence to which men were then tending, because it corresponded with their religious wants, aims and emotions, because the whole spiritual being could then expand and expatiate under its influence that it planted its roots so deeply in the hearts of men" (Lecky, *Hist of European Morals*, ch iii). Add to all this the favorable circumstances mentioned under "Preparation for Christianity," above (II), and we can understand how the Rom empire became the kingdom of Christ.

2. Positive Causes

LITERATURE.—*Ancient sources* include Tacitus, Suetonius, Josephus, Pliny's *Letters*, x.97–98 (in Hardy's ed), Dio Cassius (in Xiphilin), the apologists, Church Fathers, Inscriptions, etc.

Modern sources are too numerous to mention in full, but those most helpful to the student are: Gibbon, *Decline and Fall of the Rom Empire;* Merivale, *Hist of the Romans under the Empire; The Fall of the Rom Republic*, 1856; *Conversion of the Rom Empire*, 1865; Milman, *Hist of Christianity; Hist of Lat Christianity;* Ramsay, *The Church in the Rom Empire; Expos*, IV, viii, pp. 8 ff, 110 ff, 282 ff; E. G. Hardy, *Christianity and the Rom Government*, 1894; D. Duff, *The Early Church: a Hist of Christianity in the First Six Centuries*, Edinburgh, 1891; J. J. Blunt, *A Hist of the Christian Church during the First Three Centuries*, 1861; Harnack, *Mission and Expansion of Christianity*, 1907; Mommsen, "Der Religionsfrevel nach röm. Recht," in *Hist. Zeit*, 1890, LXIV (important); *Provinces of the Rom Empire; Expos*, 1893, pp. 6 ff; G. Boissier, *La religion romaine d' Auguste aux Antonins; La fin du paganisme;* Wissowa, *Religion u. Kultus der Römer;* Gerb. Uhlhorn, *Conflict of Christianity with Heathenism*, ET by Smyth and Ropes, 1879; B. Aubé, *Histoire des persécutions de l'église jusqu'à la fin des Antonins*, 1875; Schaff, *Hist of the Christian Church* (with useful bibliographies of both ancient and modern authorities); Orr, *Neglected Factors in Early Church Hist;* Keim, *Rom u. Christentum;* Deissmann, *Light from the Ancient East*, ET, London, 1910; Wendland, *Die hellenistisch-römische Kultur*², 1912; F. Overbeck, "Gesetze der röm. Kaiser gegen die Christen," in his *Studien*, 1875; C. F. Arnold, *Die Neronische Christenverfolgung; Stud. zur Gesch. der Plinianischen Christenverfolgung;* Westcott, "The Two Empires," in comm. to *Epp. of St. John*, 250–82; Friedländer, *Sittengeschichte Roms;* Lightfoot. *Apostolic Fathers;* Lecky, *Hist of European Morals*, ch iii, "The Conversion of Rome."

S. ANGUS

ROMAN LAW:

In the present art. we shall treat (I) Rom Private Law and (II) Criminal Law only, reserving a consideration of the development of the principles of constitutional law for the art. on ROME, since it is so closely interwoven with the political history of the state.

It will be necessary to confine the discussion of private law to its external history, without attempting to deal with the substance of the law itself. In the treatment of criminal law attention will be directed chiefly to the constitutional guaranties which were intended to protect Rom citizens against arbitrary and unjust punishments, these being one of the most important privileges of Rom citizenship (see CITIZENSHIP).

Rom law found its original source in the family as a corporation. The proprietary rights of the *pater familias* as representative of this primitive unit of organization are a fundamental element in private law, and the scope of the criminal jurisdiction of the state was limited by the power of life and death which was exercised by the head of the family over those who were under his authority, by virtue of which their transgressions were tried before the domestic tribunal.

It is likewise of fundamental importance to recall the fact that before the earliest period in the history of Rom law of which we have positive information, there must have been a time when a large number of different classes of crime were punished by the priests as sacrilege, in accordance with divine law (*fas*), by putting the offender to death as a sacrifice to the offended deity, while restitution for private violence or injustice was left to private initiative to seek. For a law of the Twelve Tables that the person guilty of cutting another's grain by night should be hanged, as an offering to Ceres, is a survival of the older religious character of condemnation to death, and the right to kill the nocturnal thief and the adulterer caught in the act may be cited as survivals of primitive private vengeance. The secular conception of crime as an offence against the welfare of the state gradually superseded the older conception, while private law arose when the community did away with the disorder incident to the exercise of self-help in attempting to secure justice, by insisting that the parties to a disagreement should submit their claims to an arbitrator.

I. Roman Private Law.—Rom private law was at first a body of unwritten usages handed down by tradition in the patrician families.

1. The Twelve Tables

The demand of the plebeians for the publication of the law resulted in the adoption of the famous Twelve Tables (449 BC), which was looked upon by later authorities as the source of all public and private law (*quae nunc quoque in hoc immenso aliarum super alias acervatarum legum cumulo fons omnis publici privatique est iuris:* Livy iii.34, 6), although it was not a scientific or comprehensive code of all the legal institutions of the time. This primitive system of law was made to expand to meet the growing requirements of the republican community chiefly by means of interpretation and the *jus honorarium*, which corresponds to equity.

The function of interpretation may be defined by mentioning the principal elements in civil procedure.

2. Civil Procedure

The *praetor*, or magistrate, listened to the claims of the litigants and prepared an outline of the disputed issues, called a *formula*, which was submitted to the *judex*, or arbitrator, a jury, as it were, consisting of one man, who decided the questions of fact involved in the case. Neither *praetor* nor *judex* had special legal training. The court had recourse, therefore, for legal enlightenment to those who had gained distinction as authorities on the law, and the opinions, or *responsa*, of these scholars (*jurisprudentes*) formed a valuable commentary on the legal institutions of the time. In this way a body of rules was amassed by interpretative adaptation which the authors of the Twelve Tables would never have recognized.

Jus honorarium derived its name from the circumstance that it rested upon the authority of magistrates (*honor* = magistracy). In

3. *Jus honorarium*

this respect and because it was composed of orders issued for the purpose of affording relief in cases for which the existing law did not make adequate provision, this second agency for legal expansion may be compared with English equity. These orders issued by the praetors had legal force during the tenure of their office only; but those the expediency of which had been established by this period of trial were generally reissued by succeeding magistrates from year to year, so that in time a large, but uniform body of rules, subject to annual renewal, formed the greater part of the edict which was issued by the praetors before entering upon their term of office. By these means Rom law maintained a proper balance between elasticity and rigidity.

After the institution of the *praetor peregrinus* (241 BC), who heard cases in which one or both of the parties were foreigners, a series of

4. The *praetor peregrinus*

similar edicts proceeded from those who were chosen to this tribunal. The annual edicts of the *praetor peregrinus* became an important means for broadening Rom law, for the strangers who appeared in the court of this magistrate were mostly Greeks from Southern Italy, so that the principles of law which were gradually formulated as a basis for proceedings were largely an embodiment of the spirit of Gr law.

Direct legislation superseded the other sources of law under the empire, taking the form, occasionally, of bills ratified by the people (*leges*), but usually of enactments of the senate (*senatus consulta*), or imperial ordinances. The

5. Imperial Ordinances

latter, which eventually prevailed to the exclusion of all other types, may be classified as *edicta*, which were issued by the emperor on the analogy of the similar orders of the republican magistrates, *decreta*, or decisions of the imperial tribunal, which had force as precedents, and *rescripta*, which were replies by the emperor to requests for the interpretation of the law. All these acts of imperial legislation were known as *constitutiones*.

In the 2d cent. Salvius Julianus was commissioned to invest the praetorian edict with definite form. The Institutes of Gaius ap-

6. Golden Age of Juristic Literature

pearing about the same time became a model for subsequent textbooks on jurisprudence (*Gaii institutionum commentarii quattuor*, discovered by Niebuhr in 1816 at Verona in a palimpsest). This was the Golden Age of juristic literature. A succession of able thinkers, among whom Papinian, Paulus, Ulpian, Modestinus, and Gaius hold foremost rank (cf Codex Theodosianus 1, 4, 3), applied to the incoherent mass of legal material the methods of scientific investigation, developing a system of Rom law and establishing a science of jurisprudence.

The period of the later empire was characterized by various attempts at codification which culminated in the final treatment of the body

7. Codification in the Later Empire

of Rom law under Justinian. The work of the board of eminent jurists to whom this vast undertaking was intrusted was published in three parts: (1) the *Code*, which contains a selection of the imperial enactments since Hadrian in twelve books, (2) the *Digest* or *Pandects*, which is composed of extracts from the juristic literature in fifty books, and (3) the *Institutes*, which is a textbook in four books. In this form mainly Rom private law has come down to modern times, and has become, in the words of an eminent authority (Bryce, *Studies in History and Jurisprudence*, Oxford, 1901), next to the Christian religion, the most plentiful source of the rules governing actual conduct throughout Western Europe.

II. Roman Criminal Law.—In the royal period criminal jurisdiction, in so far as it was a function of secular administration, belonged by

1. Jurisdiction in the Royal Period

right to the king. The titles *quaestores parricidii* and *duumviri perduellionis*, belonging to officials to whom the royal authority in these matters was occasionally delegated, indicate the nature of the earliest crimes brought under secular jurisdiction. The royal prerogative passed to the republican magistrates, and embraced, besides the right to punish crimes, the power to compel obedience to their own decrees (*coercitio*) by means of various penalties.

But the right of the people to final jurisdiction in cases involving the life or civil status of citizens was estab-

2. Right of Appeal

lished by an enactment (*lex Valeria*) which is said to have been proposed by one of the first consuls (509 BC), and which granted the right of appeal to the assembly (*provocatio*) against the execution of a capital or other serious penalty pronounced by a magistrate (Cicero *De Re Publica* ii.31, 54; Livy ii.8, 2; Dionysius v.19). This right of appeal was reinforced or extended by subsequent enactments (*leges Valeriae*) in 449 and 299 BC. It was valid against penalties imposed by virtue of the coercive power of the magistrates as well as those based upon a regular criminal charge. Generally the magistrates made no provisional sentence of their own, but brought their charges directly before the people.

(1) *Penalties.*—The death penalty was practically abrogated in republican times by allowing the accused

the alternative of voluntary exile. The Romans rarely employed imprisonment as a punishment. The imposition of fines above a certain amount was made subject to the right of appeal. At first the dictator possessed absolute power of life and death over the citizens, but this authority was limited, probably about 300 BC (Livy xxvii.6, 5), by being made subject to the right of appeal.

(2) *The Porcian law.*—The right of appeal to the people was valid within the city and as far as the first milestone; and although it was never extended beyond this limit, yet its protection was virtually secured for all Rom citizens, wherever they might be, by the provision of the Porcian law (of unknown date), which established their right to trial at Rome. In consequence of this a distinction of great importance was created in criminal procedure in the provinces, since Rom citizens were sent to Rome for trial in all serious cases, while other persons were subject to the criminal jurisdiction of the municipalities, except when the governor summoned them before his own tribunal.

of 70 BC provided for the equal representation of all three classes of the people in the courts. There were then about 1,080 names on the list of available jurors, of whom 75 seem to have been chosen for each trial (Cicero *In Pisonem* 40). Caesar abolished the plebeian jurors (Suetonius *Caesar* 41). Augustus restored the representatives of the third class (Suetonius *Aug.* 32), but confined their action to civil cases of minor importance. He likewise excused the members of the senate from service as jurors.

The system of criminal courts (*quaestiones perpetuae*) diminished in importance under the empire and finally disappeared toward the close of the 2d cent. Their place was taken by the senate under the presidency of a consul, the emperor, and eventually by imperial officials by delegated authority from the emperor. In the first case the

ROMAN FORUM.

3. Popular Jurisdiction Curtailed

The exercise of popular jurisdiction in criminal matters was gradually curtailed by the establishment of permanent courts (*quaestiones perpetuae*) by virtue of laws by which the people delegated their authority to judge certain classes of cases. The first of these courts was authorized in 149 BC for the trial of charges of extortion brought against provincial governors. Compensation was the main purpose of accusers in bringing charges before this and later permanent courts, and for this reason, perhaps, the procedure was similar to that which was employed in civil cases. A praetor presided over the tribunal; a number of *judices* took the place of the single juror. The laws by which Sulla reorganized the systems of criminal jurisdiction provided for seven courts dealing individually with extortion, treason, peculation, corrupt electioneering practices, murder, fraud, and assault.

4. Jurors

The *judices*, or jurors, were originally chosen from the senate. A law proposed by C. Gracchus transferred membership in all the juries to the equestrian class. Sulla replenished the senate by admitting about 300 members of the equestrian class, and then restored to it the exclusive control of the juries. But a judicial law

senate stood in somewhat the same relation to the presiding consul as the jurors in the permanent courts to the praetor. But the emperor and imperial officials decided without the help of a jury, so that after the 3d cent., when the judicial competence of the senate was gradually lost, trial by jury ceased to exist.

5. Disappearance of Criminal Courts

An important innovation in the judicial system of the empire was the principle of appeal from the decision of lower courts to higher tribunals. For the emperors and eventually their delegates, chiefly the *praefectus urbi* and *praefectus praetorio*, heard appeals from Rom and Italian magistrates and provincial governors.

6. Right of Trial at Rome

Under the early empire, provincial governors were generally under obligation to grant the demand of Rom citizens for the privilege of trial at Rome (*Digest* xlviii.6, 7), although there appear to have been some exceptions to this rule (Pliny, *Epist.* ii.11; *Digest* xlviii.8, 16). Lysias, tribune of the cohort at Jerus, sent St. Paul as prisoner to Caesarea, the capital of the province, so that Felix the procurator might determine what was to be done in his case, inasmuch as he was a Rom citizen (Acts **23** 27), and two years later St. Paul asserted his privilege of being tried at Rome by the emperor for the same reason (**25** 11.21).

Rom citizens who were sent to Rome might be brought either before the senate or emperor, but cognizance of these cases by the imperial tribunal was more usual, and finally supplanted entirely that of the senate, the formula of appeal becoming proverbial: *cives Romanus sum, provoco ad Caesarem* (*Kaísara epikaloúmai:* Acts **25** 11).

As Rom citizenship became more and more widely extended throughout the empire its relative value diminished, and it is obvious that many of the special privileges, such as the right of trial at Rome, which were attached to it in the earlier period must have been gradually lost. It became customary for the emperors to delegate their power of final jurisdiction over the lives of citizens (*ius gladii*) to the provincial governors, and finally, after Rom citizenship had been conferred upon the inhabitants of the empire generally by Caracalla, the right of appeal to Rome remained the privilege of certain classes only, such as senators, municipal decurions (*Digest* xlviii.19, 27), officers of equestrian rank in the army, and centurions (Dio Cassius lii.22, 33).

LITERATURE.—Greenidge, *The Legal Procedure of Cicero's Time*, Oxford, 1901; Krüger, *Geschichte der Quellen u. Litteratur des römischen Rechts*, Leipzig, 1888; Mommsen, *Römisches Strafrecht*, Leipzig, 1899; Roby, *Rom Private Law in the Times of Cicero and of the Antonines*, Cambridge, 1902; Sohm, *The Institutes of Rom Law*, trd by J. C. Ledlie, Oxford, 1892.

GEORGE H. ALLEN

ROMAN RELIGION. See ROMAN EMPIRE AND CHRISTIANITY, III; ROME, IV.

ROMANS, EPISTLE TO THE:

This is the greatest, in every sense, of the apostolic letters of St. Paul; in scale, in scope, and in its wonderful combination of doctrinal, ethical and administrative wisdom and power. In some respects the later Epp., Eph and Col, lead us to even higher and deeper *arcana* of revelation, and they, like Rom, combine with the exposition of truth a luminous doctrine of duty. But the range of Rom is larger in both directions, and presents us also with noble and far-reaching discussions of Christian polity, instructions in spiritual utterance and the like, to which those Epp. present no parallel, and which only the Corinthian Epp. rival.

No suspicion on the head of the genuineness of the Ep. exists which needs serious consideration.

1. Genuineness

Signs of the influence of the Ep. can be traced, at least very probably, in the NT itself; in 1 Pet, and, as some think, in Jas. But in our opinion Jas was the earlier writing, and Lightfoot has given strong grounds for the belief that the paragraph on faith and justification (Jas **2**) has no reference to perversions of Pauline teaching, but deals with rabbinism. Clement of Rome repeatedly quotes Rom, and so do Ignatius, Polycarp, Justin. Marcion includes it in his list of Pauline Epp., and it is safe to say in general Rom "has been recognized in the Christian church as long as any collection of St. Paul's Epp. has been extant" (A. Robertson, in *HDB*, s.v.). But above all other evidences it testifies to itself. The fabrication of such a writing, with its close and complex thought, its power and marked originality of treatment, its noble *morale*, and its spiritual elevation and ardor, is nothing short of a moral impossibility. A mighty mind and equally great heart live in every page, and a soul exquisitely sensitive and always intent upon truth and holiness. Literary personation is an art which has come to anything like maturity only in modern times, certainly not before the Renaissance. In a fully developed form it is hardly earlier than the 19th cent. And even now who can point to a consciously personated authorship going along with high moral principle and purpose?

The question remains, however, whether, accepting the Ep. in block as Pauline, we have it, as to

2. Integrity

details, just as it left the author's hands. Particularly, some phenomena of the text of the last two chapters invite the inquiry. We may—in our opinion we must—grant those chapters to be Pauline. They breathe St. Paul in every sentence. But do they read precisely like part of a *letter to Rome?* For example, we have a series of names (**16** 1-15), representing a large circle of personally known and loved friends of the writer, a much longer list than any other in the Epp., and all presumably—on the theory that the passage is integral to the Ep.—residents at Rome. May not such a paragraph have somehow crept in, after date, from another writing? Might not a message to Philippian, Thessalonian or Ephesian friends, dwellers in places where St. Paul had already established many intimacies, have fallen out of its place and found lodgment by mistake at the close of this letter to Rome? It seems enough to reply by one brief statement of fact. We possess some 300 MSS of Rom, and not one of these, so far as it is uninjured, fails to give the Ep. complete, all the chapters as we have them, and in the present order (with one exception, that of the final doxology). It is observable meanwhile that the difficulty of supposing St. Paul to have had a large group of friends living at Rome, before his own arrival there, is not serious. To and from Rome, through the whole empire, there was a perpetual circulation of population. Suppose Aquila and Priscilla (e.g.) to have recently returned (Acts **18** 2) to Rome from Ephesus, and suppose similar migrations from Greece or from Asia Minor to have taken place within recent years; we can then readily account for the greetings of Rom **16**.

Lightfoot has brought it out in an interesting way (see his *Philippians*, on **4** 22) that many of the names (e.g. Amplias, Urbanus, Tryphena) in Rom **16** are found *at Rome*, in inscriptions of the early imperial age, in cemeteries where members of the widely scattered "household of Caesar" were interred. This at least suggests the abundant possibility that the converts and friends belonging to the "household" who, a very few years later, perhaps not more than three, were around him at Rome when he wrote to Philippi (Phil **4** 22), and sent their *special* greeting ("chiefly they") to the Philippians, were formerly residents at Philippi, or elsewhere in Macedonia, and had moved thence to the capital not long before the apostle wrote to the Romans. A. Robertson (ut supra) comes to the conclusion, after a careful review of recent theories, "that the case for transferring this section . . . . from its actual connection to a lost Ep. to Ephesus is not made out."

Two points of detail in the criticism of the text of Rom may be noted. One is that the words "at

Rome" (**1** 7.15) are omitted in a very few MSS, in a way to remind us of the interesting phenomenon of the omission of "at Ephesus" (Eph **1** 1 m). But the evidence for this omission being original is entirely inadequate. The fact may perhaps be accounted for by a possible circulation of Rom among other mission churches as an Ep. of universal interest. This would be much more likely if the MSS and other authorities in which the last two chapters are missing were identical with those which omit "at Rome," but this is not the case.

The other and larger detail is that the great final doxology (**16** 25–27) is placed by many cursives at the end of ch **14,** and is omitted entirely by three MSS and by Marcion. The leading uncials and a large preponderance of ancient evidence place it where we have it. It is quite possible that St. Paul may have *reissued* Rom after a time, and may only then have added the doxology, which has a certain resemblance in manner to his later (captivity) style. But it is at least likely that dogmatic objections led Marcion to delete it, and that his action accounts for the other phenomena which seem to witness against its place at the finale.

It is worth noting that Hort, a singularly fearless, while sober student, defends without reserve the entirety of the Ep. as we have it, or practically so. See his essay printed in Lightfoot's *Bib. Studies.*

3. Proximate Date

We can fix the proximate date with fair certainty within reasonable limits. We gather from **15** 19 that St. Paul, when he wrote, was in the act of closing his work in the East and was looking definitely westward. But he was first about (**15** 25.26) to revisit Jerus with his collection, mainly made in Macedonia and Achaia, for the "poor saints." Placing these allusions side by side with the references in 1 and 2 Cor to the collection and its conveyance, and again with the narrative of Acts, we may date Rom very nearly at the same time as 2 Cor, just before the visit to Jerus narrated in Acts **20,** etc. The year may be fixed with great probability as 58 AD. This estimate follows the lines of Lightfoot's chronology, which Robertson (ut supra) supports. More recent schemes would move the date back to 56 AD.

"The reader's attention is invited to this date. Broadly speaking, it was about 30 years at the most after the Crucifixion. Let anyone in middle life reflect on the freshness in memory of events, whether public or private, which 30 years ago made any marked impression on his mind. Let him consider how concrete and vivid still are the prominent personages of 30 years ago, many of whom of course are still with us. And let him transfer this thought to the 1st cent., and to the time of our Ep. Let him remember that we have at least this one great Christian writing composed, for certain, within such easy reach of the very lifetime of Jesus Christ when His contemporary friends were still, in numbers, alive and active. Then let him open the Ep. afresh, and read, as if for the first time, its estimate of Jesus Christ—a Figure then of no legendary past, with its halo, but of the all but present day. Let him note that this transcendent estimate comes to us conveyed in the vehicle not of poetry and rhetoric, but of a treatise pregnant with masterly argument and admirable practical wisdom, tolerant and comprehensive. And we think that the reader will feel that the result of his meditations on date and circumstances is reassuring as to the solidity of the historic basis of the Christian faith" (from the present writer's introduction to the Ep. in the *Temple Bible;* see also his *Light from the First Days: Short Studies in 1 Thess*).

4. Place of Writing

With confidence we may name Corinth as the place of writing. St. Paul was at the time in some "city" (**16** 23). He was staying with one Gaius, or Caius (ib), and we find in 1 Cor **1** 14 a Gaius, closely connected with St. Paul, and a Corinthian. He commends to the Romans the deaconess Phoebe, attached to "the church at Cenchreae" (**16** 1), presumably a place near that from which he was writing; and Cenchreae was the southern part of Corinth.

5. Destination

The first advent of Christianity to Rome is unrecorded, and we know very little of its early progress. Visiting Romans (ἐπιδημοῦντες, *epidēmoúntes*), both Jews and proselytes, appear at Pentecost (Acts **2** 10), and no doubt some of these returned home believers. In Acts **18** 2 we have Aquila and Priscilla, Jews, evidently Christians, "lately come from Italy," and probably from Rome. But we know practically nothing else of the story previous to this Ep., which is addressed to a mission church obviously important and already spiritually advanced. On the other hand (a curious paradox in view of the historical development of Rom Christianity), there is no allusion in the Ep. to church organization. The Christian ministry (apart from St. Paul's own apostleship) is not even mentioned. It may fairly be said to be incredible that if the legend of St. Peter's long episcopate were historical, no allusion whatever to his work, influence and authority should be made. It is at least extremely difficult to prove that he was even present in Rome till shortly before his martyrdom, and the very ancient belief that *Peter and Paul* founded the Rom church is more likely to have had its origin in their martyrdoms there than in St. Peter's having in any sense shared in the early evangelization of the city.

As to Rome itself, we may picture it at the date of the Ep. as containing, with its suburbs, a closely massed population of perhaps 800,000 people; a motley host of many races, with a strong oriental element, among which the Jews were present as a marked influence, despised and sometimes dreaded, but always attracting curiosity.

6. Language

The Ep. was written in Gr, the "common dialect," the Gr of universal intercourse of that age. One naturally asks, why not in Lat, when the message was addressed to the supreme Lat city? The large majority of Christian converts beyond doubt came from the lower middle and lowest classes, not least from the slave class. These strata of society were supplied greatly from immigrants, much as in parts of East London now aliens make the main population. Not Lat but Gr, the then *lingua franca* of the Mediterranean, would be the daily speech of these people. It is remarkable that all the early Rom bishops bear Gr names. And some 40 years after the date of this Ep. we find Clement of Rome writing in Gr to the Corinthians, and later again, early in the 2d cent., Ignatius writing in Gr to the Romans.

7. Occasion

We cannot specify the occasion of writing for certain. No hint appears of any acute crisis in the mission (as when 1 Cor, 2 Cor, Gal, or Col were written). Nor would personal reminiscences influence the writer, for he had not yet seen Rome. We can only suggest some possibilities as follows:

(1) A good opportunity for safe communication was offered by the deaconess Phoebe's proposed visit to the metropolis. She doubtless asked St. Paul for a commendatory letter, and this may have suggested an extended message to the church.

(2) St. Paul's thoughts had long gone toward Rome. See Acts **19** 21: "*I must* see Rome," words which seem perhaps to imply some Divine intimation (cf **23** 11). And his own life-course would fall in with such a supernatural call. He had always aimed at large centers; and now his great work in the central places of the Levant was closing; he had worked at Ephesus, Thessalonica, Corinth; he was at last to think of the supreme center of all. Rome must always have had a dominant interest for the "Apostle of the Nations," and any suggestion that his Lord's will tended that way would intensify it to the highest degree.

(3) The form of the Ep. may throw further light on the occasion. The document falls, on the whole, into three parts. First we have chs **1–8** inclusive, a prolonged

exposition of the contrasted and related phenomena of sin and salvation, with special initial references to the cases of Jew and non-Jew respectively. Then come chs **9–11**, which deal with the Jewish rejection of the Jewish Messiah, developing into a prophetic revelation of the future of Israel in the grace of God. Lastly we have chs **12–16**. Some account of the writer's plans, and his salutations to friends, requests for prayer, etc, form the close of this section. But it is mainly a statement of Christian duty in common life, personal, civil, religious. Under the latter head we have a noble treatment of problems raised by varying opinions, particularly on religious observances, among the converts, Jew and Gentile.

Such phenomena cast a possible light on the occasion of writing. The Rom mission was on one side, by its locality and surroundings, eminently gentile. On the other, there was, as we have seen, a strong Judaic element in Rom life, particularly in its lower strata, and no doubt around the Jewish community proper there had grown up a large community of "worshippers" (σεβόμενοι, *sebómenoi*) or, as we commonly call them, "proselytes" ("adherents," in the language of modern missionary enterprise), people who, without receiving circumcision, attended Jewish worship and shared largely in Jewish beliefs and ideals. Among these proselytes, we may believe, the earliest evangelists at Rome found a favorable field, and the mission church as St. Paul knew of it contained accordingly not only two definite classes, converts from paganism, converts from native Judaism, but very many in whose minds both traditions were working at once. To such converts the problems raised by Judaism, both without and within the church, would come home with a constant intimacy and force, and their case may well have been present in a special degree in the apostle's mind alike in the early passages (chs **1–3**) of the Ep. and in such later parts as chs **2–11, 14, 15**. On the one hand they would greatly need guidance on the significance of the past of Israel and on the destiny of the chosen race in the future. Moreover, discussions in such circles over the way of salvation would suggest to the great missionary his exposition of man's reconciliation with a holy God and of His secrets for purity and obedience in an unholy world. And meanwhile the ever-recurring problems raised by ceremonial rules in common daily life—problems of days and seasons, and of forbidden food—would, for such disciples, need wise and equitable treatment.

(4) Was it not with this position before him, known to him through the many means of communication between Rome and Corinth, that St. Paul cast his letter into this form? And did not the realization of the central greatness of Rome suggest its ample scale? The result was a writing which shows everywhere his sense of the presence of the Judaic problem. Here he meets it by a statement, massive and tender, of "heaven's easy, artless, unencumbered plan" of redemption, grace, and glory, a plan which on its other side is the very mystery of the love of God, which statement is now and forever a primary treasure of the Christian faith. And then again he lays down for the too eager champions of the new "liberty" a law of loving tolerance toward slower and narrower views which is equally our permanent spiritual possession, bearing a significance far-reaching and benign.

(5) It has been held by some great students, notably Lightfoot and Hort, that *the main* purpose of Rom was to reconcile the opposing "schools" in the church, and that its exposition of the salvation of the individual is secondary only. The present writer cannot take this view. Read the Ep. from its spiritual center, so to speak, and is not the perspective very different? The apostle is always conscious of the collective aspect of the Christian life, an aspect vital to its full health. But is he not giving his deepest thought, animated by his own experience of conviction and conversion, to *the sinful man's* relation to eternal law, to redeeming grace, and to a coming glory? It is the question of personal salvation which with St. Paul seems to us to live and move always in the depth of his argument, even when Christian polity and policy is the immediate theme.

8. Some Characteristics

Excepting only Eph (the problem of the authorship of which is insoluble, and we put that great document here aside), Rom is, of all St. Paul has written, least a letter and most a treatise. He is seen, as we read, to approach religious problems of the highest order in a free but reasoned succession; problems of the darkness and of the light, of sin and grace, fall and restoration, doom and remission, faith and obedience, suffering and glory, transcendent hope and humblest duty, now in their relation to the soul, now so as to develop the holy collectivity of the common life. The Rom converts are always first in view, but such is the writer, such his handling, that the results are for the universal church and for every believer of all time. Yet all the while (and it is in this a splendid example of that *epistolary method* of revelation which is one of the glories of the NT) it is never for a moment the *mere* treatise, however great. The writer is always vividly personal, and conscious of persons. The Ep. is indeed a masterpiece of doctrine, but also always "the unforced, unartificial utterance of a friend to friends."

9. Main Teachings of the Epistle

Approaching the Ep. as a treatise rather than a letter (with the considerable reserves just stated), we indicate briefly some of its main doctrinal deliverances. Obviously, *in limine*, it is not set before us as a complete system either of theology or of morals; to obtain a full view of a Pauline dogma and ethics we must certainly place Eph and Col, not to speak of passages from Thess, beside Rom. But it makes by far the nearest approach to doctrinal completeness among the Epp.

(1) *The doctrine of man.*—In great measure this resolves itself into the doctrine of man as a sinner, as being guilty in face of an absolutely holy and absolutely imperative law, whether announced by abnormal revelation, as to the Jew, or through nature and conscience only, as to the Gentile. At the back of this presentation lies the full recognition that man is cognizant, as a spiritual being, of the eternal difference of right and wrong, and of the witness of creation to personal "eternal power and Godhead" as its cause, and that he is responsible in an awe-inspiring way for his unfaithfulness to such cognitions. He is a being great enough to be in personal moral relation with God, and able to realize his ideal only in true relation with Him; therefore a being whose sin and guilt have an unfathomable evil in them. So is he bound by his own failure that he cannot restore himself; God alone, in sovereign mercy, provides for his pardon by the propitiation of Christ, and for his restoration by union with Christ in the life given by the Holy Spirit. Such is man, once restored, once become "a saint" (a being hallowed), a "son of God" by adoption and grace, that his final glorification will be the signal (in some sense the cause?) of a transfiguration of the whole finite universe. Meanwhile, man is a being actually in the midst of a life of duty and trial, a member of civil society, with obligations to its order. He lives not in a God-forsaken world, belonging only to another and evil power. His new life, the "mind of the Spirit" in him, is to show itself in a conduct and character good for the state and for society at large, as well as for the "brotherhood."

(2) *The doctrine of God.*—True to the revelation of the OT, St. Paul presents God as absolute in will and power, so that He is not only the sole author of nature but the eternal and ultimately sole cause of goodness in man. To Him in the last resort all is due, not only the provision of atonement but the power and will to embrace it. The great passages which set before us a "fore-defining" (πρoόρισις, *proórisis*, "predestination") and election of the saints are all evidently inspired by this motive, the jealous resolve to trace to the one true Cause all motions and actions of good. The apostle seems e.g. almost to risk affirming a sovereign causation of the opposite, of unbelief and its sequel. But patient study will find that it is not so. God is not said to "fit for ruin" the "vessels of wrath." Their woeful end is overruled to His glory, but nowhere is it taken to be caused by Him. All along the writer's intense purpose is to constrain the *actual believer* to see *the whole* causation of his salvation in the will and power of Him whose inmost character is revealed in the supreme fact that, "for us all," "he spared not his Son."

(3) *The doctrine of the Son of God.*—The Ep. affords materials for a magnificently large Christology. The relation of the Son to creation is indeed not expounded in terms (as in Col), but it is implied in the language of ch **8,** where the inter-relation of our redemption and the transfiguration of Nature is dealt with. We have the Lord's manhood fully recognized, while His Godhead (as we read in **9** 5; so too Robertson, ut supra) is stated in terms, and it is most certainly implied in the language and tone of e.g. the close of ch **8.** Who but a bearer of the Supreme Nature could satisfy the conception indicated in such words as those of **8** 32.35–39, coming as they do from a Heb monotheist of intense convictions? Meantime this transcendent Person has so put Himself in relation with us, as the willing worker of the Father's purpose of love, that He is the sacrifice of peace for us (ch **3**), our "propitiatory" One (ἱλαστήριον, *hilastḗrion*, is now known to be an adj.), such that (whatever the mystery, which leaves the fact no less certain) the man who believes on Him, i.e. (as ch **4** fully demonstrates) relies on Him, gives himself over to His mercy, is not only forgiven but "justified," "justified by faith." And "justification" is more than forgiveness; it is not merely the remission of a penalty but a welcome to the offender, pronounced to be lawfully at peace with the eternal holiness and love. See Justification; Propitiation.

In closest connection with this message of justification is the teaching regarding union with the Christ who has procured the justification. This is rather assumed than expounded in Rom (we have the exposition more explicitly in Eph, Col, and Gal), but the assumption is present wherever the pregnant phrase "in Christ" is used. Union is, for St. Paul, the central doctrine of all, giving life and relation to the whole range. As Lightfoot has well said (*Sermons in St. Paul's*, no. 16), he is the apostle not primarily of justification, or of liberty, great as these truths are with him, but of union with Christ. It is through union that justification is ours; the merits of the Head are *for the member.* It is through union that spiritual liberty and power are ours; the Spirit of life is from the Head to *the member.* Held by grace in this profound and multiplex connection, where life, love and law are interlaced, the Christian is entitled to an assurance full of joy that nothing shall separate him, soul and (ultimately) body, from his once sacrificed and now risen and triumphant Lord.

(4) *The doctrine of the Spirit of God.*—No writing of the NT but St. John's Gospel is so full upon this great theme as Rom. Ch **8** may be said to be the *locus classicus* in the Epp. for the work of the Holy Ghost in the believer. By implication it reveals personality as well as power (see esp. ver 26). Note particularly the place of this great passage, in which revelation and profoundest conditions run continually into each other. It follows ch **7,** in which the apostle depicts, in terms of his own profound and typical experience, the struggles of conscience and will over the awful problem of the "bondage" of indwelling sin. If we interpret the passage aright, the case supposed is that of a regenerate man, who, however, attempts the struggle against inward evil armed, as to consciousness, with his own faculties merely, and finds the struggle insupportable. Then comes in the Divine solution, the promised Spirit of life and liberty, welcomed and put into use by the man who has found his own resources vain. "In Christ Jesus," in union with Him, he "by the Spirit does to death the practices of the body," and rises through conscious liberty into an exulting hope of "the liberty of the glory of the sons of God"—not so, however, as to know nothing of "groaning within himself," while yet in the body; but it is a groan which leaves intact the sense of sonship and Divine love, and the expectation of a final completeness of redemption.

(5) *The doctrine of duty.*—While the Ep. is eminently a message of salvation, it is also, in vital connection with this, a treasury of principle and precept for the life of duty. It does indeed lay down the sovereign freedom of our acceptance for Christ's sake *alone,* and so absolutely that (**6** 1.2.15) the writer anticipates the inference (by foes, or by mistaken friends), "Let us continue in sin." But the answer comes instantly, and mainly through the doctrine of union. Our pardon is not an isolated fact. Secured only by Christ's sacrifice, received only by the faith which receives Him as our all, it is *ipso facto* never received alone but with all His other gifts, for it becomes ours as we receive, not merely one truth about Him, but Him. Therefore, we receive His Life as our true life; and it is morally unthinkable that we can receive this and express it in sin. This assumed, the Ep. (ch **12** and onward) lays down with much detail and in admirable application large ranges of the law of duty, civil, social, personal, embracing duties to the state, loyalty to its laws, payment of its taxes, recognition of the sacredness of political order, even ministered by pagans; and also duties to society and the church, including a large and loving tolerance even in religious matters, and a response to every call of the law of unselfish love. However we can or cannot adjust mentally the two sides, that of a supremely free salvation and that of an inexorable responsibility, there the two sides are, in the Pauline message. And reason and faith combine to assure us that both sides are eternally true, "antinomies" whose harmony will be explained hereafter in a higher life, but which are to be lived out here concurrently by the true disciple, assured of their ultimate oneness of source in the eternal love.

(6) *The doctrine of Israel.*—Very briefly we touch on this department of the message of Rom, mainly to point out that the problem of Israel's unbelief nowhere else in St. Paul appears as so heavy a load on his heart, and that on the other hand we nowhere else have anything like the light he claims to throw (ch **11**) on Israel's future. Here, if anywhere, he appears as the predictive prophet, charged with the statement of a "mystery," and with the announcement of its issues. The promises to Israel have never failed, nor are they canceled. At the worst, they have always been inherited by a chosen remnant, Israel within Israel. And a time is coming when, in a profound connection with Messianic blessing on the Gentiles, "all Israel shall be saved,"

with a salvation which shall in turn be new life to the world outside Israel. Throughout the passage St. Paul speaks, not as one who "will not give up a hope," but as having had revealed to him a vast and definite prospect, in the Divine purpose.

It is not possible in our present space to work out other lines of the message of Rom. Perhaps enough has been done to stimulate the reader's own inquiries.

LITERATURE.—Of the Fathers, Chrysostom and Augustine are preëminent as interpreters of Rom: Chrysostom in his expository *Homilies*, models of eloquent and illuminating discourse, full of "sanctified common sense," while not perfectly appreciative of the inmost doctrinal characteristics; Augustine, not in any continuous comm., but in his anti-Pelagian writings, which show the sympathetic intensity of his study of the doctrine of the Ep., not so much on justification as on grace and the will. Of the Reformers, Calvin is eminently the great commentator, almost modern in his constant aim to ascertain the sacred writer's meaning by open-eyed inference direct from the words. On Rom he is at his best; and it is remarkable that on certain leading passages where grace is the theme he is much less rigidly "Calvinistic" than some of his followers. In modern times, the not learned but masterly exposition of Robert Haldane (c 1830) claims mention, and the eloquent and highly suggestive expository lectures (about the same date) of Thomas Chalmers. H. A. W. Meyer (5th ed, 1872, ET 1873–74) among the Germans is excellent for carefulness and insight; Godet (1879, ET 1881) equally so among French-writing divines; of late English interpreters I. A. Beet (1877, many revisions), Sanday and Headlam (1895, in the "International" series) and E. H. Gifford (admirable for scholarship and exposition; his work was printed first in the *Speaker's* [*Bible*] *Comm.*, 1881, now separately) claim particular mention. J. Denney writes on Rom in *The Expositor's Gr Test.* (1900).

Luther's lectures on Rom, delivered in 1516–17 and long supposed lost, have been recovered and were published by J. Ficker in 1908. Among modern German commentators, the most important is B. Weiss in the later revisions of the Meyer series (9th ed, 1899), while a very elaborate comm. has been produced by Zahn in his own series (1910). Briefer are the works of Lipsius (*Hand-Kommentar*, 2d ed, 1892, very scholarly and suggestive); Lietzmann (*Handbuch zum NT*, interest chiefly linguistic), and Jülicher (in J. Weiss, *Schriften des NTs*, 2d ed, 1908, an intensely able piece of popular exposition).

A. E. Garvie has written a brilliant little comm. in the "[New] Century" series (no date); that of R. St. John Parry in the *Cambridge Gr Test.*, 1913, is more popular, despite its use of the Gr text. F. B. Westcott's *St. Paul and Justification*, 1913, contains a close grammatical study with an excellent paraphrase.

The writer may be allowed to name his short comm. (1879) in the *Cambridge Bible for Schools* and a fuller one, in a more homiletic style, in the *Expositor's Bible*, 1894.

HANDLEY DUNELM

ROME, rōm:

Rome (Lat and Ital. *Roma;* Ῥώμη, *Rhṓmē*): The capital of the Rom republic and empire, later the center of Lat Christendom, and since 1871 capital of the kingdom of Italy, is situated mainly on the left bank of the Tiber about 15 miles from the Mediterranean Sea in 41° 53′ 54″ N. lat. and 12° 0′ 12″ long. E. of Greenwich.

It would be impossible in the limited space assigned to this article to give even a comprehensive outline of the ancient history of the Eternal City. It will suit the general purpose of the work to consider the relations of the Rom government and society with the Jews and Christians, and, in addition, to present a rapid survey of the earlier development of Rom institutions and power, so as to provide the necessary historical setting for the appreciation of the more essential subjects.

I. Development of the Republican Constitution.—The traditional chronology for the earliest period of Rom history is altogether unreliable, partly because the Gauls, in ravaging the city in 390 BC, destroyed the monuments which might have offered faithful testimony of the earlier period (Livy vi.1). It is known that there was a settlement on the site of Rome before the traditional date of the founding (753 BC).

1. Original Roman State

The original Rom state was the product of the coalition of a number of adjacent clan-communities, whose names were perpetuated in the Rom *gentes*, or groups of imaginary kindred, a historical survival which had lost all significance in the period of authentic history. The chieftains of the associated clans composed the primitive senate or council of elders, which exercised sovereign authority. But as is customary in the development of human society a military or monarchical régime succeeded the looser patriarchal or sacerdotal organs of authority. This second stage may be identified with the legendary rule of the Tarquins, which was probably a period of Etruscan domination. The confederacy of clans was welded into a homogeneous political entity, and society was organized for civic ends, upon a timocratic basis. The forum was drained and became a social, industrial and political center, and the Capitoline temple of Jupiter, Juno, and Minerva (Etruscan pseudo-Hellenic deities) was erected as a common shrine for all the people. But above all the Romans are indebted to these foreign kings for a training in discipline and obedience which was exemplified in the later conception of magisterial authority signified by the term *imperium.*

The prerogatives of the kings passed over to the consuls. The reduction of the tenure of power to a single year and the institution of the principle of colleagueship were the earliest checks to the abuse of unlimited authority. But the true cornerstone of Rom liberty was thought to be the *lex Valeria*, which provided that no citizen should be put to death by a magistrate without being allowed the right of appeal to the decision of the assembly of the people.

A period of more than 150 years after the establishment of the republic was consumed chiefly by the struggle between the two classes or orders, the patricians and plebeians.

2. Struggle between Patricians and Plebeians

The former were the descendants of the original clans and constituted the *populus*, or body-politic, in a more particular sense. The plebeians were descendants of former slaves and dependents, or of strangers who had been attracted to Rome by the obvious advantages for industry and trade. They enjoyed the franchise as members of the military assembly (*comitia centuriata*), but had no share in the magistracies or other civic honors and emoluments, and were excluded from the knowledge of the civil law which was handed down in the patrician families as an oral tradition.

The first step in the progress of the plebeians toward political equality was taken when they wrested from the patricians the privilege of choosing representatives from among themselves, the tribunes, whose function of bearing aid to oppressed plebeians was rendered effective by the right of veto (*intercessio*), by virtue of which any act of a magistrate could be arrested. The codification of the law in the Twelve Tables was a distinct advantage to the lower classes, because the evils which they had suffered were largely due to a harsh and abusive interpretation of legal institutions, the nature of which had been obscure (see ROMAN LAW). The abrogation, directly thereafter, of the prohibition of intermarriage between the classes resulted in their gradual intermingling.

3. Senate and Magistrates

The kings had reduced the senate to the position of a mere advising body. But under the republican régime it recovered in fact the authority of which it was deprived in theory. The controlling power of the senate is the most significant feature of the republican government, although it was recognized by no statute or other constitutional document. It was due in part to the diminution of the power of the magistrates, and in part to the manner in which the senators were chosen. The lessening of the authority of the magistrates was the result of the increase in their number, which led not only to the curtailment of the actual prerogative of each, but also to the contraction of their aggregate independent influence. The augmentation of the number of magistrates was made necessary by the territorial expansion of the state and the elaboration of administration. But it was partly the result of plebeian agitation. The events of 367 BC may serve as a suitable example to illustrate the action of these influences. For when the plebeians carried by storm the citadel of patrician exclusiveness in gaining admission to the consulship, the highest regular magistracy, the necessity for another magistrate with general competency afforded an opportunity for making a compensating concession to the patricians, and the praetorship was created, to which at first members of the old aristocracy were alone eligible. Under the fully developed constitution the regular magistracies were five in number, consulship, praetorship, aedileship, tribunate, and quaestorship, all of which were filled by annual elections.

Mention has been made of the manner of choosing the members of the senate as a factor in the development of the authority of the supreme council. At first the highest executive officers of the state exercised the right of selecting new members to maintain the senators at the normal number of three hundred. Later this function was transferred to the censors who were elected at intervals of five years. But custom and later statute ordained that the most distinguished citizens should be chosen, and in the Rom community the highest standard of distinction was service to the state, in other words, the holding of public magistracies. It followed, therefore, that the senate was in reality an assembly of all living ex-magistrates. The senate included, moreover, all the political wisdom and experience of the community, and so great was its prestige for these reasons, that, although the expression of its opinion (*senatus consultum*) was endowed by law with no compelling force, it inevitably guided the conduct of the consulting magistrate, who was practically its minister, rather than its president.

When the plebeians gained admission to the magistracies, the patriciate lost its political significance. But only the wealthier plebeian families were able to profit by this extension of privilege, inasmuch as a political career required freedom from gainful pursuits and also personal influence. These plebeian families readily coalesced with the patricians and formed a new aristocracy, which is called the *nobilitas* for the sake of distinction. It rested ultimately upon the foundation of wealth. The dignity conferred by the holding of public magistracies was its title to distinction. The senate was its organ. Rome was never a true democracy except in theory. During the whole period embraced between the final levelling of the old distinctions based upon blood (287 BC) and the beginning of the period of revolution (133 BC), the magistracies were occupied almost exclusively by the representatives of the comparatively limited number of families which constituted the aristocracy. These alone entered the senate through the doorway of the magistracies, and the data would almost justify us in asserting that the republican and senatorial government were substantially and chronologically identical.

The seeds of the political and social revolution were sown during the Second Punic War and the period which followed it. The prorogation of military authority established a dangerous precedent in violation of the spirit of the republic, so that Pub. Cornelius Scipio was really the forerunner of Marius, Julius Caesar, and Augustus. The stream of gold which found its way from the provinces to Rome was a bait to attract the cupidity of the less scrupulous senators, and led to the growth of the worst kind of professionalism in politics. The middle class of small farmers decayed for various reasons; the allurement of service in the rich but effete countries of the Orient attracted many. The cheapness of slaves made independent farming unprofitable and led to the increase in large estates; the cultivation of grain was partly displaced by that of the vine and olive, which were less suited to the habits and ability of the older class of farmers.

The more immediate cause of the revolution was the inability of the senate as a whole to control the conduct of its more radical or violent members. For as political ambition became more ardent with the increase in the material prizes to be gained, aspiring leaders turned their attention to the people, and sought to attain the fulfilment of their purposes by popular legislation setting at nought the concurrence of the senate, which custom had consecrated as a requisite preliminary for popular action. The loss of initiative by the senate meant the subversion of senatorial government. The senate possessed in the veto power of the tribunes a weapon for coercing unruly magistrates, for one of the ten tribunes could always be induced to interpose his veto to prohibit the passage of popular legislation. But this weapon was broken when Tib. Gracchus declared in 133 BC that a tribune who opposed the wishes of the people was no longer their representative, and sustained this assertion.

4. Underlying Principles

It would be foreign to the purpose of the present article to trace the vicissitudes of the civil strife of the last century of the republic. A few words will suffice to suggest the general principles which lay beneath the surface of political and social phenomena. Attention has been called to the ominous development of the influence of military commanders and the increasing emphasis of popular favor. These were the most important tendencies throughout this period, and the coalition of the two was fatal to the supremacy of the senatorial government. Marius after winning unparalleled military glory formed a political alliance with Glaucia and Saturninus, the leaders of the popular faction in the city in 100 BC. This was a turning-point in the course of the revolution. But the importance of the sword soon outweighed that of the populace in the combination which was thus constituted. In the civil wars of Marius and Sulla constitutional questions were decided for the first time by superiority of military strength exclusively. Repeated appeals to brute force dulled the perception for constitutional restraints and the rights of minorities. The senate had already displayed signs of partial paralysis at the time of the Gracchi. How rapidly its debility must have increased as the sword cut off its most stalwart members! Its power expired in the proscriptions, or organized murder of political opponents. The popular party was nominally triumphant, but in theory the Rom state was still an urban commonwealth with a single political center. The franchise could be exercised only at Rome. It followed from this that the actual political assemblies were made up largely of the worthless element which was so numerous in the city, whose irrational instincts were guided and controlled by shrewd political leaders, particularly those who united in themselves military ability and the wiles of the demagogue. Sulla, Crassus, Julius Caesar, Antony, and lastly Octavian were in effect the ancient counterpart of the modern political "boss." When such men realized their ultimate power and inevitable rivalry, the ensuing struggle for supremacy and for the survival of the fittest formed the necessary process of elimination leading naturally to the establishment of the monarchy, which was in this case the rule of the last survivor. When Octavian received the title Augustus and the proconsular power (27 BC), the transformation was accomplished.

LITERATURE.—The standard work on Rom political institutions is Mommsen and Marquardt, *Handbuch der klassischen Altertümer*. Abbott, *Rom Political Institutions*, Boston and London, 1901, offers a useful summary treatment of the subject.

II. Extension of Roman Sovereignty.—See ROMAN EMPIRE AND CHRISTIANITY, I.

LITERATURE.—Only the most important general works on Rom history can be mentioned: Ihne, *Römische Geschichte* (2d ed), Leipzig, 1893–96, ET, Longmans, London, 1871–82; Mommsen, *History of Rome*, ET by Dickson, New York, 1874; Niebuhr, *History of Rome*, ET by Hare and Thirlwall, Cambridge, 1831–32; Pais, *Storia di Roma*, Turin, 1898–99; Ferrero, *Greatness and Decline of Rome*, ET by Zimmern, New York, 1909.

III. The Imperial Government.—Augustus displayed considerable tact in blending his own mastery in the state with the old institutions of the republican constitution. His authority, legally, rested mainly upon the tribunician power, which he had probably received as early as 36 BC, but which was established on a better basis in 23 BC, and the proconsular prerogative (*imperium proconsulare*), conferred in 27 BC. By virtue of the first he was empowered to summon the senate or assemblies and could veto the action of almost any magistrate. The second title of authority conferred upon him the command of the military forces of the state and consequently the administration of the provinces where troops were stationed, besides a general supervision over the government of the other provinces. It follows that a distinction was made (27 BC) between the imperial provinces which were administered by the emperor's representatives (*legati Augusti pro praetore*) and the senatorial provinces where the republican machinery of administration was retained. The governors of the latter were called generally proconsuls (see PROVINCE). Mention is made of two proconsuls in the NT, Gallio in Achaia (Acts **18** 12) and Sergius Paulus in Cyprus (**13** 7). It is instructive to compare the lenient and common-sense attitude of these trained Rom aristocrats with that of the turbulent local mobs who dealt with St. Paul in Asia Minor, Judaea, or Greece (Tucker, *Life in the Rom World of Nero and St. Paul*, New York, 1910, 95).

1. Imperial Authority

Rom citizens were still divided into three classes socially, senatorial, equestrian, and plebeian, and the whole system of government harmonized with this triple division. The senatorial class was composed of descendants of senators and those upon whom the emperors conferred the *latus clavus*, or privilege of wearing the tunic with broad purple border, the sign of membership in this order. The quaestorship was still the door of admission to the senate. The qualifications for membership in the senate were the possession of senatorial rank and property of the value of not less than 1,000,000 sesterces ($45,000; £9,000). Tiberius transferred the election of magistrates from the people to the senate, which was already practically a closed body. Under the empire *senatus consulta* received the force of law. Likewise the senate acquired judicial functions, sitting as a court of justice for trying important criminal cases and hearing appeals in civil cases from the senatorial provinces. The equestrian class was made up of those who possessed property of the value of 400,000 sesterces or more, and the privilege of wearing the narrow purple band on the tunic. With the knights the emperors filled many important financial and administrative positions in Italy and the provinces which were under their control.

2. Three Classes of Citizens

IV. Roman Religion.—(1) The Rom religion was originally more consistent than the Gr, because the deities as conceived by the unimaginative Lat genius were entirely without human character. They were the influences or forces which directed the visible phenomena of the physical world, whose favor was necessary to the material prosperity of mankind. It would be incongruous to assume the existence of a system of theological doctrines in the primitive period. Ethical considerations entered to only a limited extent into the attitude of the Romans toward their gods. Religion partook of the nature of a contract by which men pledged themselves to the scrupulous observance of certain sacrifices and other ceremonies, and in return deemed themselves entitled to expect the active support of the gods in bringing their projects to a fortunate conclusion. The Romans were naturally polytheists as a result of their conception of divinity. Since before the dawn of science there was no semblance of unity in the natural world, there could be no unity in heaven. There must be a controlling spirit over every important object or class of objects, every person, and every process of nature. The gods, therefore, were more numerous than mankind itself.

1. Deities

(2) At an early period the government became distinctly secular. The priests were the servants of the community for preserving the venerable aggregation of formulae and ceremonies, many of which lost at an early period such spirit as they once possessed. The magistrates were the true representatives of the community in its relationship with the deities both in seeking the divine will in the auspices and in performing the more important sacrifices.

(3) The Romans at first did not make statues of their gods. This was partly due to lack of skill, but mainly to the vagueness of their conceptions of the higher beings. Symbols sufficed to signify their existence, a spear, for instance, standing for Mars. The process of reducing the gods to human form was inaugurated when they came into contact with the Etruscans and Greeks. The Tarquins summoned Etruscan artisans and artists to Rome, who made from terra cotta cultus statues and a pediment group for the Capitoline temple.

The types of the Gr deities had already been definitely established when the Hellenic influence in molding Rom culture became predominant. When the form of the Gr gods became familiar to the Romans in works of sculpture, they gradually supplanted those Rom deities with which they were nominally identified as a result of a real or fancied resemblance. See GREECE, RELIGION IN.

(4) The importation of new gods was a comparatively

easy matter. Polytheism is by its nature tolerant because of its indefiniteness. The Romans could no more presume to have exhaustive knowledge of the gods than they could pretend to possess a comprehensive acquaintance with the universe. The number of their gods increased of necessity as human consciousness of natural phenomena expanded. Besides, it was customary to invite the gods of conquered cities to transfer their abode

Pantheon.

to Rome and favor the Romans in their undertakings. But the most productive source for religious expansion was the Sibylline Books. See Apocalyptic Literature, V. This oracular work was brought to Rome from Cumae, a center of the cult of Apollo. It was consulted at times of crisis with a view to discover what special ceremonies would secure adequate divine aid. The forms of worship recommended by the Sibylline Books were exclusively Gr. As early as the 5th cent. BC the cult of Apollo was introduced at Rome. Heracles and the Dioscuri found their way thither about the same time. Later Italian Diana was merged with Artemis, and the group of Ceres, Liber, and Libera were identified with foreign Demeter, Dionysus, and Persephone. Thus Rom religion became progressively Hellenized. By the close of the Second Punic War the greater gods of Greece had all found a home by the Tiber, and the myriad of petty local deities who found no counterpart in the celestial beings of Mt. Olympus fell into oblivion. Their memory was retained by the antiquarian lore of the priests alone (see Roman Empire and Christianity, III, 1).

2. Religious Decay

Rom religion received with the engrafted branches of Gr religion the germs of rapid decay, for its Hellenization made Rom religion peculiarly susceptible to the attack of philosophy. The cultivated class in Gr society was already permeated with skepticism. The philosophers made the gods appear ridiculous. Gr philosophy gained a firm foothold in Rome in the 2d cent. BC, and it became customary a little later to look upon Athens as a sort of university town where the sons of the aristocracy should be sent for the completion of their education in the schools of the philosophers. Thus at the termination of the republican era religious faith had departed from the upper classes largely, and during the turmoil of the civil wars even the external ceremonies were often abandoned and many temples fell into ruins. There had never been any intimate connection between formal religion and conduct, except when the faith of the gods was invoked to insure the fulfilment of sworn promises.

Augustus tried in every way to restore the old religion, rebuilding no fewer than 82 temples which lay in ruins at Rome. A revival of religious faith did occur under the empire, although its spirit was largely alien to that which had been displayed in the performance of the official cult. The people remained superstitious, even when the cultivated classes adopted a skeptical philosophy. The formal religion of the state no longer appealed to them, since it offered nothing to the emotions or hopes. On the other hand the sacramental, mysterious character of oriental religions inevitably attracted them. This is the reason why the religions of Egypt and Syria spread over the empire and exercised an immeasurable influence in the moral life of the people. The partial success of Judaism and the ultimate triumph of Christianity may be ascribed in part to the same causes.

In concluding we should bear in mind that the state dictated no system of theology, that the empire in the beginning presented the spectacle of a sort of religious chaos where all national cults were guaranteed protection, that Rom polytheism was naturally tolerant, and that the only form of religion which the state could not endure was one which was equivalent to an attack upon the system of polytheism as a whole, since this would imperil the welfare of the community by depriving the deities of the offerings and other services in return for which their favor could be expected.

Literature.—Marquardt, *Römische Staatsverwaltung*, III, 3, "Das Sacralwesen"; Wissowa, *Religion u. Kultus der Römer*, Munich, 1902; Boissier, *La religion romaine*, Paris, 1884.

V. Rome and the Jews.—Judaea became a part of the province of Syria in 63 BC (Jos, *BJ*, vii, 7),

1. Judaea under Roman Procurators and Governors

and Hyrcanus, brother of the last king, remained as high priest (*archiereús kaí ethnárchēs;* Jos, *Ant*, XIV, iv, 4) invested with judicial as well as sacerdotal functions. But Antony and Octavius gave Pal (40 BC) as a kingdom to Herod, surnamed the Great, although his rule did not become effective until 3 years later. His sovereignty was upheld by a Rom legion stationed at Jerus (Jos, *Ant*, XV, iii, 7), and he was obliged to pay tribute to the Rom government and provide auxiliaries for the Rom army (Appian, *Bell. Civ.*, v.75). Herod built Caesarea in honor of Augustus (Jos, *Ant*, XV, ix, 6), and the Rom procurators later made it the seat of government. At his death in 4 BC the kingdom was divided between his three surviving sons, the largest portion falling to Archelaus, who ruled Judaea, Samaria and Idumaea with the title *ethnarchēs* (Jos, *Ant*, XVII, xi, 4) until 6 AD, when he was deposed and his realm reduced to the position of a province. The administration by Rom procurators (see Procurator), which was now established, was interrupted during the period 41–44 AD, when royal authority was exercised by Herod Agrippa, grandson of Herod the Great, over the lands which had been embraced in the kingdom of his grandfather (Jos, *Ant*, XIX, viii, 2), and, after 53 AD, Agrippa II ruled a considerable part of Pal (Jos, *Ant*, XX, vii, 1; viii, 4).

After the fall of Jerus and the termination of the great revolt in 70 AD, Pal remained a separate province. Henceforth a legion (*legio X Fretensis*) was added to the military forces stationed in the land, which was encamped at the ruins of Jerus. Consequently, imperial governors of praetorian rank (*legati Augusti pro praetore*) took the place of the former procurators (Jos, *BJ*, VII, i, 2, 3; Dio Cassius lv.23).

Several treaties are recorded between the Romans and Jews as early as the time of the Maccabees (Jos, *Ant*, XII, x, 6; XIII, ix, 2; viii, 5), and Jews are known to have been at Rome as early as 138 BC. They became very numerous in the capital after the return of Pompey who brought back many captives (see Libertines). Cicero speaks of multitudes of Jews at Rome in 58 BC (*Pro Flacco* 28), and Caesar was very friendly toward them (Suetonius *Caesar* 84). Held in favor by Augustus, they recovered the privilege of collecting sums to send to the temple (Philo *Legatio ad Caium* 40). Agrippa offered 100 oxen in the temple when visiting Herod (Jos, *Ant*, XVI, ii, 1), and Augustus established a daily offering of a bull and two lambs. Upon the whole the Rom government displayed noticeable consideration for the religious scruples of the Jews. They were exempted from military service and the duty of appearing in court on the Sabbath. Yet Tiberius repressed Jewish rites in Rome in 19 AD (Suetonius *Tiberius* 36) and Claudius expelled the Jews from the city in 49 AD (Suetonius *Claudius* 25); but in both instances repression was not of long duration.

2. Jewish Proselytism

The Jews made themselves notorious in Rome in propagating their religion by means of proselytizing (Horace *Satires* i.4, 142; i.9, 69; Juvenal xiv.96; Tacitus *Hist.* v. 5), and the literature of the Augustan age contains several references to the observation of the Sabbath (Tibullus i.3; Ovid *Ars amatoria* i.67, 415; *Remedium amoris* 219). Proselytes from among the Gentiles were not always required to observe all the prescriptions of the Law. The proselytes of the Gate (*sebómenoi*), as they were called, renounced idolatry and serious moral abuses and abstained from the blood and meat of suffocated animals. Among such proselytes may be included the centurion of Capernaum (Lk **7** 5), the centurion Cornelius (Acts **10** 1), and the empress Poppaea (Jos, *Ant*, XX, viii, 11; Tacitus *Ann.* xvi.6).

On "proselytes of the Gate," *GJV*[4], III, 177, very properly corrects the error in *HJP*. These "Gate" people were not proselytes at all; they refused to take the final step that carried them into Judaism—viz. circumcision (Ramsay, *Expos*, 1896, p. 200; Harnack, *Expansion of Christianity*, I, 11; see DEVOUT; PROSELYTES).

Notwithstanding the diffusion of Judaism by means of proselytism, the Jews themselves lived for the most part in isolation in the poorest parts of the city or suburbs, across the Tiber, near the Circus Maximus, or outside the Porta Capena. Inscriptions show that there were seven communities, each with its synagogue and council of elders presided over by a gerusiarch. Five cemeteries have been discovered with many Gr, a few Lat, but no Heb inscriptions.

LITERATURE.—Ewald, *The Hist of Israel*, ET by Smith, London, 1885; Renan, *Hist of the People of Israel*, ET, Boston, 1896; Schürer, *The Jewish People in the Time of Jesus Christ*, ET by MacPherson, New York.

VI. Rome and the Christians.—

1. Introduction of Christianity

The date of the introduction of Christianity into Rome cannot be determined. A Christian community existed at the time of the arrival of St. Paul (Acts **28** 15), to which he had addressed his Ep. a few years before (58 AD). It is commonly thought that the statement regarding the expulsion of the Jews from Rome under Claudius on account of the commotion excited among them by the agitation of Chrestus (Suetonius *Claudius* 25: *Iudaeos impulsore Chresto assidue tumultuantis Roma expulit*), probably in 49 AD, is proof of the diffusion of Christian teaching in Rome, on the ground that Chrestus is a colloquial, or mistaken, form of Christus. It has been suggested that the Christian faith was brought to the capital of the empire by some of the Romans who were converted at the time of Pentecost (Acts **2** 10.41). It would be out of place to discuss here the grounds for the traditional belief that St. Peter was twice in Rome, once before 50 AD and again subsequent to the arrival of St. Paul, and that together the two apostles established the church there. Our present concern is with the attitude of the government and society toward Christianity, when once established. It may suffice, therefore, to remind the reader that St. Paul was permitted to preach freely while nominally in custody (Phil **1** 13), and that as early as 64 AD the Christians were very numerous (Tacitus *Ann.* xv.44: *multitudo ingens*).

2. Tolerance and Proscription

At first the Christians were not distinguished from the Jews, but shared in the toleration, or even protection, which was usually conceded to Judaism as the national religion of one of the peoples embraced within the empire. Christianity was not legally proscribed until after its distinction from Judaism was clearly perceived. Two questions demand our attention: (1) When was Christianity recognized as distinct from Judaism? (2) When was the profession of Christianity declared a crime? These problems are of fundamental importance in the history of the church under the Rom empire.

(1) If we may accept the passage in Suetonius cited above (*Claudius* 25) as testimony on the vicissitudes of Christianity, we infer that at that time the Christians were confused with the Jews. The account of Pomponia Graecina, who was committed to the jurisdiction of her husband (Tacitus *Ann.* xiii.32) for adherence to a foreign belief (*superstitionis externae rea*), is frequently cited as proof that as early as 57 AD Christianity had secured a convert in the aristocracy. The characterization of the evidence in this case by the contemporary authority from whom Tacitus has gleaned this incident would apply appropriately to the adherence to Judaism or several oriental religions from the point of view of Romans of that time; for Pomponia had lived in a very austere manner since 44 AD. Since there is some other evidence that Pomponia was a Christian, the indefinite account of the accusation against her as mentioned by Tacitus is partial proof that Christianity had not as yet been commonly recognized as a distinct religion (Marucchi, *Éléments d'archéologie chrétienne* I, 13). At the time of the great conflagration in 64 AD the populace knew of the Christians, and Nero charged them collectively with a plot to destroy the city (Tacitus *Ann.* xv.44). The recognition of the distinctive character of Christianity had already taken place at this time. This was probably due in large measure to the circumstances of St. Paul's sojourn and trial in Rome and to the unprecedented number of converts made at that time. The empress Poppaea, who was probably an adherent of Judaism (Jos, *Ant*, XX, viii), may have enlightened the imperial court regarding the heresy of the Christians and their separation from the parent stock.

(2) In attempting to determine approximately the time at which Christianity was placed under the official ban of the imperial government, it will be convenient to adopt as starting-points certain incontestable dates between which the act of prosecution must have been issued. It is clear that at the time of the great conflagration (64 AD), the profession of Christianity was not a ground for criminal action. St. Paul had just been set at liberty by decree of the imperial court (cf 2 Tim **4** 17). Moreover, the charge against the Christians was a plot to burn the city, not adherence to a proscribed religion, and they were condemned, as it appears, for an attitude of hostility toward the human race (Tacitus *Ann.* xv. 44). While governor of Bithynia (c 112 AD), Pliny the younger addressed Trajan in a celebrated letter (x.96) asking advice to guide his conduct in the trial of many persons who were accused as Christians, and inquiring particularly whether Christianity in itself was culpable, or only the faults which usually accompanied adherence to the new faith. The reply of the emperor makes quite plain the fundamental guilt at that time of adherence to Christianity, and it supposes a law already existing against it (x.97). It follows, therefore, that the law against Christianity which was the legal basis for persecution must have been issued between the conflagration in 64 AD and Pliny's administration of Bithynia.

We cannot define the time of this important act of legislation more closely with absolute certainty, although evidence is not wanting for the support of theories of more or less apparent probability. Tradition ascribes a general persecution to the reign of Domitian, which would imply that Christianity was already a forbidden religion at that time. Allusions in Rev (as **6** 9), the references to recent calamities in Rome by St. Clement in his letter to the Corinthians (1 *Ad Cor.*), the condemnation of Acilius Glabrio (Dio Cassius lxvii.13), a man of consular rank, together with the emperor's cousin Flavius Clemens (Dio Cassius, xiii) and Flavia Domitilla and many others on the charge of atheism and Jewish customs (95 AD), are cited as evidence for this persecution. The fact that a number of persons in Bithynia abandoned Christianity 20 years before the judicial investigation of Pliny (Pliny x. 96) is of some importance as corroborative evidence.

But there are grounds worthy of consideration for carrying the point of departure back of Domitian. The letter of St. Peter from Babylon (Rome ?) to the Christians in Asia Minor implies an impending persecution (1 Pet **4** 12–16). This was probably in the closing years of the reign of Nero. Allard cleverly observes (*Histoire des persécutions*, 61) that the mention of the Neronian persecution of the Christians apart from the description of the great fire in the work of Suetonius (*Ner.* 16), amid a number of acts of legislation, is evidence of a general enactment, which must have been adopted at the time of, or soon after, the proceedings which were instituted on the basis of the charge of arson. Upon the whole the theory that the policy of the imperial government was definitely established under Nero carries with it considerable probability (cf Sulpitius Severus, *Chron.*, ii.41).

Although the original enactment has been lost the correspondence of Pliny and Trajan enables us to formulate the imperial policy in dealing with the Christians during the 2d cent. Adherence to Christianity was in itself culpable. But proceedings were not to be undertaken by magistrates on their own initiative; they were to proceed only from charges brought by voluntary accusers legally responsible for establishing the proof of their assertions. Informal and anonymous information must be rejected. Penitence shown in abjuring Christianity absolved the accused from the legal penalty of former guilt. The act of adoring the gods and the living emperor before their statues was sufficient proof of non-adherence to Christianity or of repentance.

3. Persecution

The attitude of the imperial authorities in the 3d cent. was less coherent. The problem became more complicated as Christianity grew. Persecution was directed more esp. against the church as an organization, since it was believed to exert a dangerous power. About 202 AD, Septimius Severus issued a decree forbidding specifically conversion to Judaism or Christianity (Spartianus, *Severus*, 17), in which he departed from the method of procedure prescribed by Trajan (*conquirendi non sunt*), and commissioned the magistrates to proceed directly against suspected converts. At this time the Christians organized funerary associations for the possession of their cemeteries, substituting corporative for individual ownership, and it would appear that under Alexander Severus they openly held places of worship in Rome (Lampridius, *Alexander Severus*, 22, 49). The emperor Philip (244–49) is thought to have been a Christian at heart (Eusebius, *HE*, VI, 34). A period of comparative calm was interrupted by the persecution under Decius (250–51 AD), when the act of sacrifice was required as proof of non-adherence to Christianity. Several certificates testifying to the due performance of this rite have been preserved.

Under Valerian (257 AD) the Christian organizations were declared illegal and the cemeteries were sequestrated. But an edict in 260 AD restored this property (Eusebius, VII, 13). A short persecution under Aurelian (274 AD) broke the long period of calm which extended to the first edict of persecution of Diocletian (February 24, 303). The Christians seem to have gained a sort of prescriptive claim to exist, for Diocletian did not at first consider them guilty of a capital crime. He sought to crush their organization by ordering the cessation of assemblies, the destruction of churches and sacred books, and abjuration under pain of political and social degradation. (Lactantius, *De Morte Persecutorum*, x.11, 12, 13; Eusebius, VIII, 2; IX, 10). Later he ordered the arrest of all the clergy, who were to be put to death unless they renounced the faith (Eusebius, VIII, 6). Finally the requirement of an act of conformity in sacrificing to the gods was made general. This final persecution, continuing in an irregular way with varying degrees of severity, terminated with the defeat of Maxentius by Constantine (October 29, 312). The Edict of Milan issued by Constantine and Licinius the following year established toleration, the restoration of ecclesiastical property and the peace of the church. See ROMAN EMPIRE AND CHRISTIANITY, III, IV, V.

LITERATURE.—Allard, *Histoire des persécutions*, Paris, 1903; *Le christianisme et l'empire romain*, Paris, 1903; Duchesne, *Histoire ancienne de l'église*, Paris, 1907 (ET); Marucchi, *Éléments d'archéologie chrétienne*, Paris, 1899–1902; Hardy, *Christianity and the Rom Government*, London, 1894; Renan, *L'église chrétienne*, Paris, 1879; Ramsay, *The Church in the Rom Empire*, London, 1893.

GEORGE H. ALLEN

ROOF, rōōf. See HOUSE.

ROOF-CHAMBER. See HOUSE.

ROOM, rōōm. See HOUSE.

ROOT, rōōt (שֹׁרֶשׁ, *shōresh*; ῥίζα, *rhiza*): Frequently mentioned in the OT and NT, but almost always in a figurative sense, e.g. "root of the righteous" (Prov **12** 3.12); "root that beareth gall" (Dt **29** 18); "Their root shall be as rottenness" (Isa **5** 24); "root of bitterness" (He **12** 15). Also of peoples: "they whose root is in Amalek" (Jgs **5** 14); of Assyria (Ezk **31** 7); "Ephraim is smitten, their root is dried up" (Hos **9** 16); "Judah shall again take root downward" (2 K **19** 30; cf Isa **27** 6; **37** 31); the root of Jesse (Isa **11** 10; Rom **15** 12); root of David (Rev **5** 5; **22** 16).

ROOT OF DAVID. See DAVID, ROOT OF.

ROOT OF JESSE (שֹׁרֶשׁ יִשַׁי, *shōresh yishay* [Isa **11** 10]; ῥίζα τοῦ Ἰεσσαί, *rhiza toú Iessaí* [Rom **15** 12]): The Heb and Gr words are practically the same in meaning. "Root" means descendant, branch of the family or stock. The Messianic king was to be of the family of Jesse the father of David. In Rom **15** 12 Paul quotes the LXX of Isa **11** 10. Jesus is a branch or descendant of the family of Jesse, as well as of David. See also DAVID, ROOT OF.

ROPE, rōp: Used in the OT for חֶבֶל, *ḥebhel*, "that which binds" (2 S **17** 13, etc), and for עֲבֹת, *'ăbhōth*, "that which is woven" (Jgs **15** 13, etc). In neither word is any specified thickness or strength connoted, and *ḥebhel* is tr[d] equally well by "line" (2 S **8** 2, etc) or "cord" (Josh **2** 15, etc), and *'ăbhōth* by "cord" (Ps **118** 27, etc), as best suits the context. Similarly in the NT the word σχοινίον, *schoinion*, lit. "made of rushes," can mean the rope by which a boat is fastened (Acts **27** 32) or small cords suitable for a whip (Jn **2** 15). The usual material for ropes was certainly flax (hemp), but the Egyptians, and so possibly the Hebrews, at times made ropes of leathern thongs. See CORD; LINE; SHIPS AND BOATS, III, 2.

BURTON SCOTT EASTON

ROSE, rōz: (1) (חֲבַצֶּלֶת, *ḥăbhaççeleth*; ἄνθος, *ánthos*, "a flower" [Cant **2** 1], κρίνον, *krínon*, "a lily" [Isa **35** 1]): By general consent EV is wrong: in Cant **2** 1 m reads "Heb *hăbazzeleth*, the autumn crocus," and in Isa **35** 1, m reads "*or* autumn crocus." This is the *Colchicum autumnale* (N.O. *Liliaceae*). A Tg on Cant **2** 1 explains the Heb word as "narcissus," a very common plant in the plains and mountains of Pal and a great favorite with the natives. Two species, *N. tazetta* and *N. serolinus* (N.O. *Amaryllideae*), occur, the latter being the finer; they are autumn plants. All authorities agree that the so-called "rose" was some kind of bulbed plant. (2) (ῥόδον, *rhódon*, "the rose," mentioned in Ecclus **24** 14; **39** 13; **50** 8; Wisd **2** 8; 2 Esd **2** 19): There is no reason why the rose, of which several varieties are common in Pal, should not be meant. Tristram favors the rhododendron. The expression, "rose plants in Jericho," in Ecclus **24** 14 has nothing whatever to do with what is now sold there as a "rose of Jericho," a dwarf annual plant, *Anastatica hierochuntina* (N.O. *Cruciferae*), which dries up and can be made to reëxpand by placing the root in water.

E. W. G. MASTERMAN

ROSH, rosh, rōsh (רֹאשׁ, *rō'sh*): A son or grandson of Benjamin (Gen **46** 21).

ROSH (רֹאשׁ, *rō'sh*; Ῥώς, *Rhṓs*, var. [Q[mg]] κεφαλῆς, *kephalḗs*; Vulg *capitis*): This name occurs in the prophecies against Gog in Ezk **38** 2.3 and **39** 1, where AV has "Gog, the land of Magog, the chief prince of Meshech and Tubal." This tr is due to *rō'sh* being the common Heb word for "head" or "chief" (cf the Gr variant and the Vulg), and is regarded as incorrect, that of the RV,

1. Rosh and Its Renderings

"Gog, of the land of Magog, the prince of Rosh, Meshech and Tubal," being preferred.

2. Identification with Russia

The identification of Rosh is not without its difficulties. Gesenius regarded it as indicating the Russians, who are mentioned in Byzantine writers of the 10th cent. under the name of Ῥῶς, *Rhōs*. He adds that they are also noticed by Ibn Fosslan (same period), under the name of Rûs, as a people dwelling on the river Rha (Volga). Apart from the improbability that the dominion of Gog extended to this district, it would be needful to know at what date the Rûs of the Volga arrived there.

3. Probably the Assyrian Râšu

Notwithstanding objections on account of its eastern position, in all probability Fried. Delitzsch's identification of Rosh with the *mât Râši*, "land of Râsh" of the Assyr inscriptions, is the best. Sargon of Assyria (c 710 BC) conquered the countries "from the land of Râšu on the border of Elam as far as the river of Egypt," and this country is further described in his Khorsabad Inscription, 18, as "the land of Râšu, of the boundary of Elam, which is beside the Tigris." Assyria having disappeared from among the nations when Ezekiel wrote his prophecies, Babylonia was probably the only power with which "Gog of the land of Magog" would have had to reckon, but it may well be doubted whether the Bab king would have allowed him to exercise power in the district of Râšu, except as a very faithful vassal. It may here be noted that the Heb spelling of Rosh presupposes an earlier pronunciation as *Râsh*, a form agreeing closely with that used by the Assyrians. See Fried. Delitzsch, *Wo lag das Paradies?* 325.

T. G. PINCHES

ROT, rot, **ROTTENNESS**, rot''n-nes (vb. רָקֵב, *rāḳēbh*, noun *rāḳābh* [*riḳḳābhōn*, Job **41** 27], with מַק, *maḳ*, "decay" [Isa **5** 24], and עָבַשׁ, *'ābhash*, "shrivel" [so Joel **1** 17 RVm]): "Rottenness of the bones" (Prov **12** 4; **14** 30; Hab **3** 16) is ulceration (*caries*) of the bones, used as an example of an intensely painful disease. AV, in addition, has "rot" in Nu **5** 21.22.27, where RV has "fall away" (נָפַל, *nāphal*), but a euphemistic paraphrase is in point (see the comms.). In Jer **38** 11.12 AV has "old rotten rags" for מְלָח, *melaḥ*, "rag" (RV "worn-out garments," a tr that specializes too far).

ROTE, rōt: RVm gives "learned *by rote*" in Isa **29** 13 for AV "taught," which indicates that the service of Jeh was merely formal.

ROWER, rō'ẽr, **ROWING**, rō'ing. See SHIPS AND BOATS, III, 1.

ROYAL, roi'al: Either belonging to a king (kingdom) or having kingly power, dignity, authority, etc. In Heb, the word is expressed by using different nouns in the gen. case (the "construct state"). They are: (1) *melekh*, "king": "Asher . . . . shall yield royal dainties," lit. choice morsels of the king, meaning fit for a king (Gen **49** 20); "besides that which Solomon gave her of his royal bounty," lit. which he gave her according to the hand (the wealth) of King Solomon (1 K **10** 13; cf RVm); "a royal statute," lit. statute of a *malkā'*, which is the emphatic Aram. term for *melekh*, "king" (Dnl **6** 7); (2) *mamlākhāh*, "the power and dignity of a king," "Gibeon . . . . one of the royal cities," i.e. a capital city with a king of her own (Josh **10** 2; cf 1 S **27** 5); "all the seed royal," lit. the seed of the kingdom (2 K **11** 1; cf 2 Ch **22** 10); (3) *malkhūth*, "kinghood," "kingdom": "royal majesty," lit. majesty of kinghood (1 Ch **29** 25); quite frequently in the Book of Est; royal wine (**1** 7); crown (**1** 11; cf **2** 17; **6** 8); commandment (**1** 19); "her royal estate," lit. her kinghood (**1** 19); house royal (**2** 16; cf **5** 1); royal apparel (**5** 1; cf **6** 8. 15); throne (**5** 1); (4) *melūkhāh*, "kingdom," "kingly power and dignity": "royal city," lit. the city of the kingdom, meaning here that part of the city (Rabbah) in which the royal palace was situated (2 S **12** 26); "royal diadem," lit. turban of kinghood (Isa **62** 3); (5) in Jer **43** 10 we find the word *shaphrīr;* its meaning is uncertain: "royal pavilion" (RV and AV), "glittering" (RVm), "scepter," "a carpet covering a throne."

The NT uses the word for *basilikós*, "belonging to a king": "royal apparel" (Acts **12** 21); "the royal law," something like "the golden rule," being foremost because including all others (Jas **2** 8), and for *basíleios* (being vested with kingly power and honor), "royal priesthood," the Heb rendering would be *mamlekheth kōhănīm*, "a kingdom of priests," i.e. a kingdom whose citizens are priests, emphasizing the two facts that the true Christians have free access to the grace of God and that they enjoy the liberties and privileges of His kingdom (1 Pet **2** 9).

WILLIAM BAUR

ROYAL CITY. See ROYAL, (2), (4).

RUBY, rōō'bi. See STONES, PRECIOUS.

RUDDER, rud'ẽr, **RUDDER-BANDS.** See SHIPS AND BOATS, III, 2, (3).

RUDDY, rud'i (אַדְמוֹנִי, *'adhmōnī* [1 S **16** 12; **17** 42; Gen **25** 25 RVm], אָדֹם, *'ādhōm* [Cant **5** 10]; vbs. אָדַם, *'ādham* [Lam **4** 7], and ἐρυθριάω, *eruthriáō*, "to blush" [Ad Est **15** 5]): "Ruddy" is the form taken by the adj. "red" when used as a term of praise of the human skin, and this is its use in the Bible (the Heb and Gr words are all usual words for "red" or "to be red"). The dark-skinned Hebrews found great beauty in a clear complexion.

RUDE, rōōd: Not "impolite" in EV (except perhaps 2 Macc **12** 14), but "untrained," "ignorant"; cf the modern phrase, "a rude drawing." So Sir **8** 4 (ἀπαίδευτος, *apaídeutos*) and 2 Cor **11** 6 (ἰδιώτης, *idiōtēs*, 'though I lack technical training in rhetoric'); cf AV and RVm Sir **21** 24.

RUDIMENTS, rōō'di-ments (στοιχεῖα, *stoicheía*, pl. of στοιχεῖον, *stoicheîon* [Gal **4** 3.9; Col **2** 8.20; He **5** 12; 2 Pet **3** 10.12]): This word occurs 7 t in the NT, and AV translates it in three different ways. In the two passages in Gal, and in the two in 2 Pet, it is rendered "elements." In the two passages in Col, it is tr[d] "rudiments." In He it is rendered "first principles."

1. Etymological Meaning

The etymological meaning of the word is, that which belongs to a row or rank, hence any first thing, an element, first principle. It denotes, specially (1) the letters of the alphabet, the spoken sounds, as the elements of speech; (2) the material elements of the universe, the physical atoms of which the world is composed; (3) the heavenly bodies; (4) the elements, rudiments, fundamental principles of any art, science or discipline; cf the phrase, "the a, b, c."

(1) The NT use of the word, where it always occurs in the pl., is as follows: In 2 Pet **3** 10.12, "*The elements* shall be dissolved with fervent heat," that is, the physical elements of the world and of the heavens are to be consumed, or subjected to change,

by means of fire. In He **5** 12, AV "Ye have need that one teach you again which be *the first principles* of the oracles of God." This means that the Heb Christians had not made the advance expected, in grace and in the knowledge of God, but were in need of instruction in the elementary truths of the Christian faith.

2. Use of Term in the NT

(2) The Pauline use of the term is in Gal and Col; see references as above. In Gal **4** 3.9 AV Paul writes, "When we were children, [we] were in bondage under *the elements* of the world"; "How turn ye again to the weak and beggarly *elements*, whereunto ye desire again to be in bondage?" The apostle here means the ceremonial precepts of the worship of the Jews. These requirements involved much and protracted difficulty in their observance; they were "a yoke . . . . which neither our fathers nor we were able to bear" (Acts **15** 10). Yet the Galatian converts were turning back again to these legal ordinances, and desired to be in bondage to them. These elements were "of the world," they had reference to material and not to spiritual things, they were formal and sensuous. They were "weak," for they had no power to rescue man from condemnation, and they could not save him from sin. They were "beggarly," for they brought no endowment of the heavenly riches. By these epithets Paul signifies that rites, ordinances, sacrifices, observance of days and seasons belonged to the elementary stages of the Jewish religion, which had now attained its end and purpose in the coming of Christ and His work. These things were necessary at the time they were Divinely instituted, but the time had come when they were no longer required. They contained and conveyed an elementary knowledge, and were intended, from the first, to lead to an advance in the moral and spiritual life, which is now revealed in Christ.

It has been thought by some that what is meant by "elements" or "rudiments" in Gal and Col is the physical elements, presided over by angels, and that this is in some way connected with the worship of angels, to which Paul refers in Col **2** 18. The Jews believed that there were angels of fire and of the wind, and of the other physical elements. The apostle therefore wished to show the foolishness of the worship of angels and of the heavenly bodies which they were supposed to control.

This latter meaning of the term is a possible, but not a probable one. The interpretation, already first given, which understands "elements" to mean the ordinances of Jewish legalism, is most in harmony with the gospel and with the teaching of Paul. "This is probably the correct interpretation, both as simpler in itself and as suiting the context better. St. Paul seems to be dwelling still on the rudimentary character of the law, as fitted for an earlier stage in the world's history" (Lightfoot, Comm. on *Gal*, 167).

In Col **2** 8 AV Paul writes, "Beware lest any man spoil you . . . . after the *rudiments* of the world, and not after Christ"; and in ver 20, AV "Wherefore if ye be dead with Christ from the *rudiments* of the world, why . . . . are ye subject to ordinances?" The meaning of the term here is the elements of religious training, the ceremonial precepts of the Jewish Law. In Col and Gal the meaning is that the systems of the false teachers, both in Colossae and in Galatia, laid stress on Jewish ritual, ceremonial law and ascetic observances—things of this world, belonging to the visible sphere, things elementary, and intended, so far as the Jewish Law is concerned, simply as a preparation for the coming of Christ. Such were the rudiments of the world, so far as their source was Jewish. On their heathen side they were still more decidedly anti-Christian. Both of these tendencies, Jewish and heathen, were "not according to Christ." For Christ Himself who atoned for sin, and who now lives and reigns, delivers believers from all such methods, as well as from the need of them. JOHN RUTHERFURD

RUE, ro͞o (πήγανον, *pḗganon*): One of the plants mentioned in Lk **11** 42 as subject to tithe: in the ‖ passage, Mt **23** 23, anise and cummin are mentioned. *Ruta graveolens* (N.O. *Rutaceae*) is the officinal rue, and a very similar species, *R. chalepensis*, is indigenous. Rue is a small shrub growing 2 to 4 ft. high with a heavy odor, disagreeable to Westerners, but a favorite with Orientals. A sprig of rue is often fixed on a child's cap or clothes as a kind of charm.

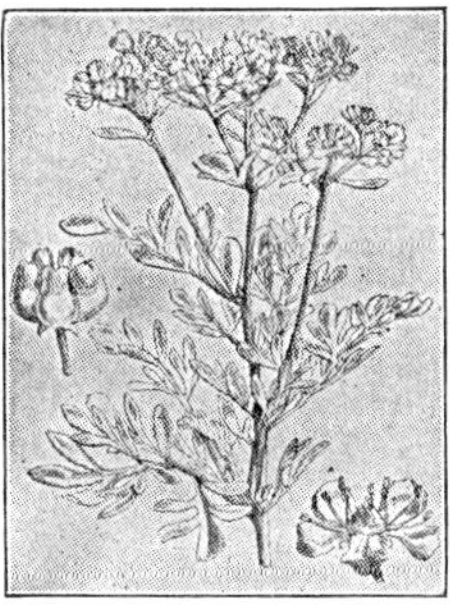

Rue (*Ruta graveolens*).

RUFUS, ro͞o′fus (Ῥοῦφος, *Rhoúphos*): The name is mentioned twice: (1) Simon of Cyrene, who was compelled to bear the cross of Jesus, is "the father of Alexander and Rufus" (Mk **15** 21); (2) Paul sends greetings to Rom Christians, "Rufus the chosen in the Lord, and his mother and mine" (Rom **16** 13). Rufus was well known among those for whom Mark primarily wrote his Gospel, and according to tradition this was the Christian community at Rome. There seems no reason to doubt, therefore, that the Rufus of Mark and the Rufus of Paul are the same person. The name, meaning "red," "reddish," was, however, one of the commonest of slave names; the identification of these two is therefore merely a conjecture. The Rufus whom Paul greets is "the chosen in the Lord," i.e. "that choice Christian" (Denney). Since all Christians are "chosen," this title must express some distinction. The mother of Rufus had played the mother's part to Paul on some occasion of which we are ignorant, hence the phrase "his mother and mine" (cf Mk **10** 30). S. F. HUNTER

RUG, rug: Alternative rendering of a word (שְׂמִיכָה, *s*ᵉ*mīkhāh*) in Jgs **4** 18 RV, "mantle" AV. The tr is doubtful; *OHL* gives "rug or thick coverlet [?]."

RUHAMAH, ro͞o-hā′ma, ro͞o-hā′ma: See LO-RUHAMAH, the symbolical name of Hosea's daughter (Hos **1** 6.8).

RUIN, ro͞o′in (הֲרִיסָה, *hărīṣāh*, etc; ῥῆγμα, *rhēgma*): "Ruin," the tr of *hărīṣāh* (Am **9** 11; cf Acts **15** 16, where RV Gr text, *tá katestramména*), and of a number of other Heb words: in Lk **6** 49 *rhēgma*, "breakage," is used both in a literal sense (Isa **23** 13; **25** 2, of fallen buildings; Ezk **27** 27; **31** 13, of a state or people; Lk **6** 49, of a house, etc) and with a moral significance (Prov **26** 28). RVm correctly renders *mikhshōl* in Ezk **18** 30 "stumblingblock" (AV "ruin"), and RV in **21** 15 "stumblings" (AV "ruins"). RV has "ruins" for AV "desolations" in Ezr **9** 9, m "waste places"; Ps **74** 3; "in their ruins" for "with their mattocks" (2 Ch **34** 6, m "'with their axes.' The Heb is obscure"); "midst of the ruin" for "desolation" (Job **30** 14); "their ruin" for "their wickedness" (Prov **21** 12). "Ruinous" is the tr of *mappālāh* (Isa **17** 1) and of *nāçāh* (2 K **19** 25; Isa **37** 26). W. L. WALKER

RULER, ro͞ol′ẽr:

(1) מֹשֵׁל, *mōshēl*, "ruler," "prince," "master" (tyrant), applied to Joseph in Egypt (Gen **45** 8; cf Ps **105** 21); to the Philis (Jgs **15** 11); to David's descendants, the future kings of Israel (2 Ch **7**

1. In the OT

18; cf Jer **33** 26); to Pharaoh (Ps **105** 20); to a wicked prince, a tyrant (Prov **28** 15; cf Isa **14** 5; **49** 7); to the theocratic king, the Messiah (Mic **5** 2); it is often used in general (Prov **6** 7; **23** 1; **29** 12; Eccl **10** 4; Isa **16** 1, etc).

(2) נָגִיד, *nāghīdh*, "leader," "noble" (nobles), "prince." In a number of instances RV renders it "prince," where AV has ruler (1 S **25** 30; 2 S **6** 21; 1 K **1** 35, etc). It is used of Azrikam having charge of the palace of King Ahaz (2 Ch **28** 7, "governor" of the house, AV); of Azariah (Seraiah, Neh **11** 11), who is called the "ruler of the house of God" (1 Ch **9** 11; cf 2 Ch **31** 13); he was the leader of a division or group of priests. In 2 Ch **35** 8 the names of three others are given (Hilkiah, Zechariah and Jehiel).

(3) נָשִׂיא, *nāsī'*, "prince" (so Nu **13** 2, AV "ruler"); generally speaking, the *nāsī'* is one of the public authorities (Ex **22** 28); the rulers of the congregation (Ex **16** 22; cf **34** 31); "The rulers brought the onyx stones" (Ex **35** 27), as it was to be expected from men of their social standing and financial ability: "when a ruler [the head of a tribe or tribal division] sinneth" (Lev **4** 22).

(4) סָגָן, *ṣāghān*, the representative of a king or a prince; a vice-regent; a governor; then, in the times of Ezra and Nehemiah, a leader or principal of the people of Jerus under the general supervision of these two men. The EV renders it "ruler" (Ezk **23** 12.23), "deputy" (Jer **51** 23.28.57), and, in most cases, "ruler" with "deputy" in m (Ezr **9** 2; Neh **2** 16; **4** 14.19; **5** 7.17; **7** 5; **12** 40; **13** 11; Isa **41** 25; Ezk **23** 6) always used in pl.

(5) קָצִין, *ḳāṣīn*, "a judge" or "magistrate" (Isa **1** 10; **3** 6.7; **22** 3; Mic **3** 1.9); "a military chief" (Josh **10** 24).

(6) רֹדֶה, *rōdheh*, one having dominion: "There is little Benjamin their ruler" (Ps **68** 27); the meaning is obscure; still we may point to the facts that Saul, the first one to conquer the heathen (1 S **14** 47 f), came of this the smallest of all the tribes, and that within its boundaries the temple of Jeh was erected.

(7) רוֹזֵן, *rōzēn*, a "dignitary," a "prince." "The kings of the earth set themselves, and the rulers take counsel together, against Jeh" (Ps **2** 2); in the NT the word is rendered *árchontes* (Acts **4** 26).

(8) שַׂר, *sar*, "chief," "head"; prince, king; a nobleman having judicial or other power; a royal officer. RV renders it frequently "prince": "rulers over my cattle" ("head-shepherds," Gen **47** 6); "rulers of thousands, rulers of hundreds," etc (Ex **18** 21); they had to be men of good character because they were endowed with judicial power (ver 22); in Dt **1** 15 the rendering of EV is "captains," etc; they were military leaders. "Zebul the ruler of the city" (of Shechem, Jgs **9** 30), meaning "governor" (cf 1 K **22** 26; 2 K **23** 8); "rulers [or captains; cf 1 K **16** 9] of his [Solomon's] chariots" (1 K **9** 22); the rulers of Jezreel (2 K **10** 1) were, presumably, the ruler of the palace of the king and the ruler of the city of Samaria (cf ver 5). It is difficult to explain why they should be called the rulers of Jezreel; both LXX and Vulg omit the word; "the rulers of the substance which was king David's" (1 Ch **27** 31) overseers of the royal domain; "The rulers were behind all the house of Judah" (Neh **4** 16), the officers were ready to assume active command in case of an attack.

(9), (10) שִׁלְטוֹן, *shilṭōn*, "a commander," "an officer": "the rulers of the provinces" (Dnl **3** 2 f); שַׁלִּיט, *shallīṭ*, "a person in power," "a potentate" (Dnl **2** 10); there seems to be little doubt that the Aram. term is used as an adj. (cf RVm); in Dnl **5** 7 occurs the vb. *sh^e^laṭ*, "to have dominion," "he shall rule as the third in rank" (cf vs 16.29).

(11) מָגֵן, *māghēn*, "shield": "Her rulers [shields] dearly love shame" (Hos **4** 18). Perhaps we ought to read (with LXX) *migg^e^'ōnām*, "their glory," and to translate it "they love shame more than their glory"; they would rather have a good (!) time than a good name.

2. In the Apoc

(1) ἄρχων, *árchōn*, used of the "rulers" of the Spartans (1 Macc **14** 20) and, in a general sense, of the priest Mattathias (1 Macc **2** 17). AV has the word also in a general sense in Sir **41** 18 (RV "mighty man").

(2) ἡγούμενος, *hēgoúmenos*, "one leading the way." A quite general term, Sir **10** 2 (ruler of a city); **17** 17 (of gentile nations); **46** 18 (of the Tyrians). Also **2** 17 AV (RV "he that ruleth"), and **32** 1 RV ("ruler *of a feast*," AV "master").

(3) οἱ μεγιστάνες, *hoi megistánes*, a rare word found only in the pl., for "rulers of the congregation" (Sir **33** 18). The same word in Mk **6** 21 is tr^d^ "lords."

(4) 2 Macc **4** 27 AV for ἐπάρχος, *epárchos* (RV "governor").

(5) AV inserts the word without Gr equivalent in 1 Macc **6** 14; **11** 57; 2 Macc **13** 2.

3. In the NT

(1) ἄρχων, *árchōn*, "a person in authority," "a magistrate," "a judge," "a prince"; a councillor, a member of the supreme council of the Jews; a man of influence. "There came a ruler" (Mt **9** 18), meaning a ruler of the synagogue (cf Mk **5** 22; Lk **8** 41); see (2) below; "one of the rulers of the Pharisees" (Lk **14** 1), perhaps a member of the Jewish council belonging, at the same time, to the Pharisees, or, more probably, one of the leading Pharisees; "the chief priests and the rulers" (Lk **23** 13.35; **24** 20; cf Jn **3** 1; **7** 26.48; **12** 42; Acts **3** 17; **4** 5.8; **13** 27; **14** 5); the rulers were, with the chief priests and the scribes, members of the Sanhedrin, either of two councils of the Jews (the Great and the Lesser); they were lay-members (elders); "before the rulers" (Acts **16** 19), the police magistrates (*praetores*, "praetors") of the city of Philippi; "Thou shalt not speak evil of a ruler of thy people" (Acts **23** 5; cf Ex **22** 28, *nāsī'*; see 1, [3] above), a magistrate, a person in authority (cf Acts **7** 27.35; Rom **13** 3, the public authorities); "the rulers of this world" (1 Cor **2** 6.8), persons being mentally superior to their fellow-men, and so having great influence in shaping their opinions and directing their actions.

(2) ἀρχισυνάγωγος, *archisunágōgos*, "ruler of the synagogue." He was the presiding officer of a board of elders, who had charge of the synagogue. Sometimes they, also, were given the same name (cf "one of the rulers of the synagogue," Mk **5** 22.35; Lk **8** 41.49; in Mt **9** 18 Jairus is simply called *archōn*); the ruler mentioned in Lk **13** 14 was, of course, the president of the board (cf Acts **18** 17, Sosthenes), while in Acts **13** 15 the phrase "rulers of the synagogue" simply signifies the board. It was a deliberative body, but at the same time responsible for the maintenance of good order in the synagogue and the orthodoxy of its members; having, therefore, disciplinary power, they were authorized to reprimand, and even to excommunicate, the guilty ones (cf Jn **9** 22; **12** 42; **16** 2).

(3) ἀρχιτρίκλινος, *architríklinos*, the ruler ("steward," RVm) of the feast (Jn **2** 8.9). See separate article.

(4) κοσμοκράτωρ, *kosmokrátōr*, a "world-ruler" (Eph **6** 12). The angels of the devil (Mt **25** 41; **12** 45) or Satan, the prince of this world (Jn **12** 31), participate in his power; they are his tools, their sphere of action being "this darkness," i.e. the morally corrupt state of our present existence.

(5) πολιτάρχης, *politárchēs*, the prefect of a city (Acts **17** 6.8). Luke being the only one of the Bib. authors to hand down to us this word, it is a

noteworthy fact that, in relatively modern times, a Gr inscription was discovered containing this very word and, moreover, having reference to the city of Thessalonica (*AJT*, 1898, II, 598–643). Here it was where Paul and Silas preached the gospel so successfully that the Jews, "being moved with jealousy," caused Jason and certain brethren to be dragged before the rulers of the city (*epí toús politárchas*). These magistrates suffered themselves to be made the tools of the unscrupulous Jews by demanding and getting security from Jason and the rest.

William Baur

RULER OF THE FEAST (ἀρχιτρίκλινος, *architríklinos;* AV **governor**): The word occurs in the NT in the account of the wedding feast in Cana of Galilee (Jn **2** 8.9). According to Ecclus (**32** 1) it was customary to appoint a "master of the ceremonies" from among the invited guests. It was his duty to determine the places of the guests, to see that the ordinary rules of etiquette were observed, etc, and generally to supervise the arrangements. RVm "steward" is possible if the "governor of the feast" meant the "head waiter" (Merx renders "head servant of the feast"), and not one of the guests appointed for the purpose. But the context is in favor of the view that the person in question was one of the prominent guests—an intimate friend or relative of the host. See Ruler, 2, (2). T. Lewis

RULER OF THE SYNAGOGUE. See Ruler, 3, (1), (2).

RULERS OF THE CITY. See Ruler, 1, (8), 2, (2), 3, (5).

RUMAH, rōō′ma (רוּמָה, *rūmāh;* B, Ῥουμά, *Rhoumá*, A, Ῥυμά, *Rhumá*): To this place belonged Pedaiah whose daughter Zebudah (RV "Zebidah") entered the harem of Josiah, king of Judah, and became the mother of Jehoiakim (2 K **23** 36). Jos (*Ant*, X, v, 2) calls the place Abouma, but this is an obvious clerical error for Arouma. This suggests a possible identification with Arumah (Jgs **9** 41), which lay not far from Shechem. Another possible identification is with the Rumah mentioned by Jos (*BJ*, III, vii, 21) in Galilee (cf Neubauer, *Géog. du Talm*, 203), which may be identical with the modern *Khirbet Rūmeh*, about 3 miles N. of *Ṣeffūriyeh*. Some, however, would identify Rumah with Dumah of Josh **15** 52, where the substitution of *r* for *d* is supported by the LXX (*Rheuma*), possibly represented by the modern *Dōmeh*, about 13 miles S.E. of *Beit Jibrīn*. This of course was in the territory of Judah, and no question of *jus connubium* is involved, such as might arise in the case of a Galilean site. W. Ewing

RUMP, rump: AV uses this word as tr of אַלְיָה, *'alyāh* (Ex **29** 22; Lev **3** 9; **7** 3; **8** 25; **9** 19), where RV correctly renders "fat tail." Reference is here had to the broad tail of the Syrian sheep, which occasionally weighs as much as 20 lbs., and is considered one of the daintiest portions of mutton. It was one of those portions of the peace and trespass offering which were not eaten by the priest or the sacrificer, but which with other choice portions were waved before the Lord and wholly burnt on the altar as a sweet savor unto Jeh.

RUNAGATE, run′a-gāt: A runaway: "The runagates continue in scarceness" (Ps **68** 6, Prayer Book Version, RV "The rebellious dwell in a parched land").

RUNNER, run′ẽr. See Games.

RUSH: (1) (גֹּמֶא, *gōme';* πάπυρος, *pápuros*, "bulrushes," m "papyrus" [Ex **2** 3]; "rush," m "papyrus" [Job **8** 11]; "papyrus," AV "rush" [Isa **18** 2]; "rushes" [**35** 7]): This is almost certainly the famous papyrus, *Cyperus papyrus* (N.O. *Cyperaceae*), known in Arab. as *babīr* (whence comes our word "paper"). This plant, the finest of the sedges, flourishes plentifully in Upper Egypt; in Pal there is a great mass of it growing in the marsh to the N. of Lake Huleh, and it also occurs on the Lake of Galilee and the Jordan. Light boats of plaited papyrus have been used on the Nile from ancient times and are mentioned by many writers (cf Ex **2** 3; Isa **18** 2).

(2) (אַגְמוֹן, *'aghmōn*, "rope," m "Heb 'a rope of rushes,'" AV "hook" [Job **41** 2]; "[burning] rushes," AV "caldron" [Job **41** 20]; "rush," AV "bulrush" [Isa **58** 5]; "rush" in Isa **9** 14; **19** 15, used of the humble and lowly folk as contrasted with the "palm branch," the highest class): The word *'aghmōn* comes from אֲגַם, *'ăgham*, meaning a marsh (see Pools), being transferred from the place of the things growing there. The word doubtless includes not only the rushes—of which there are several kinds in Pal—but also members of the sedge family, the *Cyperaceae*. See also Reed.

E. W. G. Masterman

RUST, rust (חֶלְאָה, *ḥel'āh;* βρῶσις, *brōsis*): Strictly speaking rust is the red oxide of iron formed by the corrosion of that metal, but by extension it has come to mean corrosion produced on any metal. *Ḥel'āh* is trd "rust" in Ezk **24** 11.12. This rendering is probably based on ver 11. Copper caldrons are still used in Bible lands. Such vessels must be constantly watched when on the fire to guard against the possibility of their becoming dry. If this should happen the contents, whatever they may be, and the vessel itself will be injured. The copper of the caldron oxidizes and scales off in black or brownish scales, or rust. *lós, iós*, was used in Gr to denote the corroding of metals. In Jas **5** 3 occurs, "Your gold and your silver are rusted; and their rust . . . . shall eat your flesh as fire." The writers must have had in mind the actions of chemicals upon these metals which formed some such compound as the caustic silver nitrate.

Brōsis, lit. "eating," which occurs in Mt **6** 19. 20, may refer to the diseases which attack such vegetation as wheat, grapes, cucumbers, etc. In no country is the saying "where moth and rust consume" (Mt **6** 19) more true than in Syria. Any metal subject to corrosion seems to rust faster in that country than anywhere else. There are also many rusting fungi which the people have not learned to destroy and which do much damage to the crops. See also Scum. James A. Patch

RUTH, rōōth (רוּת, *rūth;* Ῥούθ, *Rhoúth*): The name Ruth is found in the OT only in the book which is so entitled. It is a contraction for *re'ūth* (רְעוּת), perhaps signifying "comrade," "companion" (fem.; cf Ex **11** 2, "every woman of her neighbor"). *OHL*, 946, explains the word as an abstract noun = "friendship." The Book of Ruth details the history of the one decisive episode owing to which Ruth became an ancestress of David and of the royal house of Judah. From this point of view its peculiar interest lies in the close friendship or alliance between Israel and Moab, which rendered such a connection possible. Not improbably also there is an allusion to this in the name itself.

The history lies in the period of the Judges (**1** 1), at the close of a great famine in the land of Israel.

1. History

Elimelech, a native of Bethlehem, had, with his wife Naomi and two sons, taken refuge in Moab from the famine. There, after an interval of time which is not more precisely defined, he died (**1** 3), and his two sons, having married women of Moab, in the course of a further ten years also died, and left Orpah and Ruth widows (**1** 5). Naomi then decided to return to Pal, and her two daughters-in-law accompanied her on her way (**1** 7). Orpah, however, turned back and only Ruth remained with Naomi, journeying with her to Bethlehem, where they arrived "in the beginning of barley harvest" (**1** 22). The piety and fidelity of Ruth are thus early exhibited in the course of the narrative, in that she refused to abandon her mother-in-law, although thrice exhorted to do so by Naomi herself, on account of her own great age and the better prospects for Ruth in her own country. Orpah yielded to persuasion, and returned to Moab, but Ruth remained with Naomi.

At Bethlehem Ruth employed herself in gleaning in the field during the harvest and was noticed by Boaz, the owner of the field, a near kinsman of her father-in-law Elimelech. Boaz gave her permission to glean as long as the harvest continued; and told her that he had heard of her filial conduct toward her mother-in-law. Moreover, he directed the reapers to make intentional provision for her by dropping in her way grain from their bundles (**2** 15 f). She was thus able to return to Naomi in the evening with a whole ephah of barley (ver 17). In answer to questioning she explained that her success in gleaning was due to the good-will of Boaz, and the orders that he had given. She remained accordingly and gleaned with his maidens throughout the barley and wheat harvest, making her home with her mother-in-law (**2** 23). Naomi was anxious for the remarriage of Ruth, both for her sake and to secure compliance with the usage and law of Israel; and sent her to Boaz to recall to him his duty as near kinsman of her late husband Elimelech (**3** 1 f). Boaz acknowledged the claim and promised to take Ruth in marriage, failing fulfilment of the legal duty of another whose relationship was nearer than that of Boaz himself (**3** 8–13). Naomi was confident that Boaz would fulfil his promise, and advised Ruth to wait in patience.

Boaz then adopted the customary and legal measures to obtain a decision. He summoned the near kinsman before ten elders at the gate of the city, related to him the circumstances of Naomi's return, with her desire that Ruth should be married and settled with her father-in-law's land as her marriage-portion, and called upon him to declare his intentions. The near kinsman, whose name and degree of relationship are not stated, declared his inability to undertake the charge, which he renounced in legal form in favor of Boaz according to ancient custom in Israel (**4** 6 ff). Boaz accepted the charge thus transferred to him, the elders and bystanders bearing witness and pronouncing a formal blessing upon the union of Boaz and Ruth (**4** 9–12). Upon the birth of a son in due course the women of the city congratulated Naomi, in that the continuance of her family and house was now assured, and the latter became the child's nurse. The name of Obed was given to the boy; and Obed through his son Jesse became the grandfather of David (cf Mt **1** 5.6; Lk **3** 31.32).

2. Interest and Importance of the Narrative

Thus the life and history of Ruth are important in the eyes of the narrator because she forms a link in the ancestry of the greatest king of Israel. From a more modern point of view the narrative is a simple idyllic history, showing how the faithful loving service of Ruth to her mother-in-law met with its due reward in the restored happiness of a peaceful and prosperous home-life for herself. Incidentally are illustrated also ancient marriage customs of Israel, which in the time of the writer had long since become obsolete. The narrative is brief and told without affectation of style, and on that account will never lose its interest. It has preserved moreover the memory of an incident, the national significance of which may have passed away, but to which value will always be attached for its simplicity and natural grace.

For the literature, see Ruth, Book of.

A. S. Geden

RUTH, BOOK OF: The place which the Book of Ruth occupies in the order of the books of the Eng. Bible is not that of the Heb Canon. There it is one of the five *meghillōth* or Rolls, which were ordered to be read in the synagogue on 5 special occasions or festivals during the year.

1. Order in the Canon

In printed edd of the OT the *meghillōth* are usually arranged in the order: Cant, Ruth, Lam, Eccl, Est. Ruth occupied the second position because the book was appointed to be read at the Feast of Weeks which was the second of the 5 special days. In Heb MSS, however, the order varies considerably. In Spanish MSS generally, and in one at least of the Ger. school cited by Dr. Ginsburg (*Intro to the Heb Bible*, London, 1897, 4), Ruth precedes Cant; and in the former Eccl is placed before Lam. The *meghillōth* constitute the second portion of the *kethūbhīm* or Hagiographa, the third great division of the books of the Heb Scriptures. The Talm, however, dissociates Ruth altogether from the remaining *meghillōth*, and places it first among the Hagiographa, before the Book of Pss. By the Gr translators the book was removed from the position which it held in the Heb Canon, and because it described events contemporaneous with the Judges, was attached as a kind of appendix to the latter work. This sequence was adopted in the Vulg, and so has passed into all modern Bibles.

2. Authorship and Purpose

The book is written without name of author, and there is no direct indication of its date. Its aim is to record an event of interest and importance in the family history of David, and incidentally to illustrate ancient custom and marriage law. There is no ground for supposing, as has been suggested, that the writer had a polemical purpose in view, and desired to show that the strict and stern action taken by Ezra and Nehemiah after the return in forbidding mixed marriages was not justified by precedent. The narrative is simple and direct, and the preservation of the tradition which it records of the descent of Israel's royal house from a Moabite ancestress was probably due in the first instance to oral communication for some considerable time before it was committed to writing. The Book of 1 S also indicates a close relation between David and Moab, when during the period of his outlawry the future king confided his father and mother to the care of the king of Moab (1 S **22** 3 f), and so far supports the truth of the tradition which is embodied in the Book of Ruth.

3. Date of Composition

With regard to the date at which the narrative was committed to writing, it is evident from the position of the Book of Ruth in the Heb Canon that the date of its composition is subsequent to the close of the great period of the "earlier prophets." Otherwise it would have found a natural place, as was assigned to it in the Gr Bible, together with the Book of Jgs and other historical writings, in the second division of the Heb Scriptures. In the opening words of the book also, "It came to pass in the days when the judges judged" (Ruth **1** 1), the writer appears to look back to the period of the Judges as to a comparatively distant epoch. The character of the diction is pure and chaste; but has been supposed in certain details, as in the presence of so-called Aramaisms, to betray a late origin. The reference to the observance of marriage customs and their sanctions "in former time in Israel" (**4** 7) does not necessarily imply that the composition of Ruth was later than that of Dt, in which the laws and rights of the succession are enjoined, or that the writer of the former work was acquainted with the latter in its existing form. Slight differences of detail in the procedure would seem to suggest the contrary. On the other hand, the motive of the book in the exhibition of the ancestry of David's house would have lost its significance and *raison d'être* with the death or disappearance of the last ruler of David's line in the early period of the return from Babylon (cf Zec **4** 9). The most probable date therefore for the composition of the book would be in the later days of the exile, or immediately after the return. There is no clue to the authorship. The last four verses, giving the genealogy from Perez to David (cf 1 Ch **2** 4–15; Mt **1** 3–6; Lk **3** 31–33), are generally recognized as a later addition.

4. Ethical Teaching

The ethical value of the Book of Ruth is considerable, as setting forth an example of stedfast filial piety. The action of Ruth in refusing to desert her mother-in-law and persevering in accompanying her to her own land meets with its due reward in the prosperity and happiness which become hers, and in the honor which she receives as ancestress of the royal house of David. The writer desires to show in the person and example of Ruth that a sincere and generous regard for the claims of duty and affection leads to prosperity and honor; and at the same time that the principles and recompense of righteous dealing are not dependent upon race, but are as valid for a Moabitess as for a Jew. There is no distinctive doctrine taught in the book. It is primarily historical, recording a decisive incident in the origin of David's house; and in the second place ethical, indicating and enforcing in a well-known example the advantage and importance of right dealing and the observance of the dictates of filial duty. For detailed contents see preceding article.

LITERATURE.—Eng. comms. upon the Book of Ruth are naturally not numerous. Cf G. W. Thatcher, "Judges and Ruth," in [*New*] *Century Bible;* R. A. Watson, in *Expositor's Bible;* the most recent critical comm. is by L. B. Wolfenson in *AJSL*, XXVII (July, 1911), 285 ff, who defends the early date of the book. See also the relevant arts. in *Jew Enc*, *HDB*, *EB*, and Driver, *LOT*, 6, 454 ff.

A. S. GEDEN

RYE, rī. See SPELT.

S

SABACHTHANI, sä-bäk′thä-nē. See ELI, ELI, LAMA SABACHTHANI.

SABACO, sab′a-ko, **SABAKON,** sab′a-kon. See So.

SABAEANS, sa-bē′anz (שְׁבָאִים, *shebhā'īm* [Joel **3** 8 AV], סְבָאִים, *ṣebhā'īm;* Σαβαείμ, *Sabaeim*, Σεβαείμ, *Sebaeim* [Isa **45** 14]; סוֹבָאִים, read *ṣābhā'īm*, but rendered as though from *ṣābhā'*, "to imbibe," hence "drunkards"; οἰνωμένοι, *oinōménoi*, "wine-drunken" [Ezk **23** 42 AV]): "Sabaeans" is also the tr of the name of the country itself (שְׁבָא, *shebhā'*) in Job **1** 15; **6** 19. This last, which is the root of *shebhā'īm*, is regarded by Arabists as coming from that root with the meaning of "to take captive," though *seba'a*, "he raided" (cf Job **1** 15), has also been suggested.

1. Forms of the Word

2. Two Different Races

As Sheba is said in Gen **10** 7; **10** 28; and **25** 3 respectively to have been (1) a son of Raamah, the 4th son of Cush; (2) the 10th son of Joktan, son of Eber; (3) the 1st son of Jokshan, 2d son of Abraham and Keturah, at least two nationalities of this name are implied. The former were identified by Jos (*Ant*, II, x, 2) with the tall people of Saba in Upper Egypt, described by him as a city of Ethiopia, which Moses, when in the service of the Egyptians, besieged and captured.

3. Semitic Sabaeans and Their Commerce

It is the Sem Sabaeans, however, who are the best known, and the two genealogies attributed to them (Joktan-Eber and Jokshan-Abraham) seem to imply two settlements in the land regarded as that of their origin. As Ezekiel (**27** 23) mentions Haran (Hirran), Canneh (Kannah), and Eden (Aden) as being connected with Sheba, and these three places are known to have been in Southern Arabia, their Sem parentage is undoubted. The Sabaeans are described as being exporters of gold (Isa **60** 6; Ps **72** 15), precious stones (Ezk **27** 23), perfumes (Jer **6** 20; Isa and Ezk), and if the rendering "Sabaeans" for Joel **3** (**4**) 8 be correct, the Sebaim, "a nation far off," dealt in slaves. See SEBA; SHEBA; TABLE OF NATIONS.

T. G. PINCHES

SABANNEUS, sab-a-nē′us (B, Σαβανναιοῦς, *Sabannaioús*, A, Βανναιοῦς, *Bannaioús;* AV **Bannaia,** following the Aldine): One of the sons of Asom who had married "strange wives" (1 Esd **9** 33) = "Zabad" in Ezr **10** 33.

SABANNUS, sa-ban′nus (Σάβαννος, *Sábannos;* AV **Sabban**): The father of Moeth, one of the Levites to whom the silver and gold were delivered (1 Esd **8** 63). "Moeth the son of Sabannus" stands in the position of "Noadiah the son of Binnui," in Ezr **8** 33.

SABAOTH, sab′ā-oth, sa-bā′oth. See GOD, NAMES OF, III, 8; LORD OF HOSTS.

SABAT, sā′bat: AV = RV SAPHAT, (2) (q.v.).

SABATEUS, sab-a-tē′us (A, Σαββαταίας, *Sabbataías*, B, 'Αβταῖος, *Abtaíos;* AV **Sabateas**): One of the Levites who "taught the law of the Lord" to the multitude (1 Esd **9** 48) = "Shabbethai" in Neh **8** 7.

SABATHUS, sab′a-thus (Σάβαθος, *Sábathos;* AV **Sabatus**): An Israelite who put away his "strange wife" (1 Esd **9** 28) = "Zabad" in Ezr **10** 27.

SABATUS, sab′a-tus: AV = RV SABATHUS (q.v.).

SABBAN, sab′an: AV = RV SABANNUS (q.v.).

SABBATEUS, sab-a-tē′us (Σαββαταῖος, *Sabbataíos;* AV **Sabbatheus**): One of the three (or rather two, for "Levis" = Levite) "assessors" in the investigation held concerning "foreign wives" (1 Esd **9** 14) = "Shabbethai the Levite" in Ezr **10** 15. He is probably the "Sabateus," one of the Levites who expounded the Law (1 Esd **9** 48), and so = the "Shabbethai" in Neh **8** 7.

SABBATH, sab′ath (שַׁבָּת, *shabbāth*, שַׁבָּתוֹן, *shabbāthōn;* σάββατον, *sábbaton*, τὰ σάββατα, *tá sábbata;* the √ *shābhath* in Heb means "to desist," "cease," "rest"):

I. ORIGIN OF THE SABBATH
  1. The Biblical Account
  2. Critical Theories

The Sabbath was the day on which man was to leave off his secular labors and keep a day holy to Jeh.

I. Origin of the Sabbath.—The sketch of creation in Gen **1** 1—**2** 3 closes with an impressive account of the hallowing of the 7th day, because on it God rested from all the work which He had made creatively. The word "Sabbath" does not occur in the story; but it is recognized by critics of every school that the author (P) means to describe the Sabbath as primeval. In Ex **20** 8–11 (ascribed to JE) the reason assigned for keeping the 7th day as a holy Sabbath is the fact that Jeh rested after the six days of creative activity. Ex **31** 17 employs a bold figure, and describes Jeh as refreshing Himself ("catching His breath") after six days of work. The statement that God set apart the 7th day for holy purposes in honor of His own rest after six days of creative activity is boldly challenged by many modern scholars as merely the pious figment of a priestly imagination of the exile. There are so few hints of a weekly Sabbath before Moses, who is comparatively a modern character, that argumentation is almost excluded, and each student will approach the question with the bias of his whole intellectual and spiritual history. There is no distinct mention of the Sabbath in Gen, though a 7-day period is referred to several times (Gen **7** 4.10; **8** 10.12; **29** 27 f). The first express mention of the Sabbath is found in Ex **16** 21–30, in connection with the giving of the manna. Jeh taught the people in the wilderness to observe the 7th day as a Sabbath of rest by sending no manna on that day, a double supply being given on the 6th day of the week. Here we have to do with a weekly Sabbath as a day of rest from ordinary secular labor. A little later the Ten Words were spoken by Jeh from Sinai in the hearing of all the people, and were afterward written on the two tables of stone (Ex **20** 1–17; **34** 1–5.27 f). The Fourth Commandment enjoins upon Israel the observance of the 7th day of the week as a holy day on which no work shall be done by man or beast. Children and servants are to desist from all work, and even the stranger within the gates is required to keep the day holy. The reason assigned is that Jeh rested on the 7th day and blessed it and hallowed it. There is no hint that the restrictions were meant to guard against the wrath of a jealous and angry deity. The Sabbath was meant to be a blessing to man and not a burden. After the sin in connection with the golden calf Jeh rehearses the chief duties required of Israel, and again announces the law of the Sabbath (Ex **34** 21, ascribed to J). In the Levitical legislation there is frequent mention of the Sabbath (Ex **31** 13–16; **35** 2 f; Lev **19** 3.30; **23** 3.38). A wilful Sabbath-breaker was put to death (Nu **15** 32–36). In the Deuteronomic legislation there is equal recognition of the importance and value of the Sabbath (Dt **5** 12–15). Here the reason assigned for the observance of the Sabbath is philanthropic and humanitarian; "that thy man-servant and thy maid-servant may rest as well as thou." It is thus manifest that all the Pentateuchal codes, whether proceeding from Moses alone or from many hands in widely different centuries, equally recognize the Sabbath as one of the characteristic institutions of Israel's religious and social life. If we cannot point to any observance of the weekly Sabbath prior to Moses, we can at least be sure that this was one of the institutions which he gave to Israel. From the days of Moses until now the holy Sabbath has been kept by devout Israelites.

1. The Biblical Account

2. Critical Theories

"The older theories of the origin of the Jewish Sabbath (connecting it with Egypt, with the day of Saturn, or in general with the seven planets) have now been almost entirely abandoned [see Astronomy, I, 5]. The disposition at present is to regard the day as originally a lunar festival, similar to a Bab custom (Schrader, *Stud. u. Krit.*, 1874), the rather as the cuneiform documents appear to contain a term *šabattu* or *šabattum*, identical in form and meaning with the Heb word *šabbāthōn*." Thus wrote Professor C. H. Toy in 1899 (*JBL*, XVIII, 190). In a syllabary (II R, 32, 16*a*, *b*) *šabattum* is said to be equivalent to *ûm nûḫ libbi*, the natural tr of which seemed to be "day of rest of the heart." Schrader, Sayce and others so understood the phrase, and naturally looked upon *šabattum* as equivalent to the Heb Sabbath. But Jensen and others have shown that the phrase should be rendered "day of the appeasement of the mind" (of an offended deity). The reference is to a day of atonement or pacification rather than a day of rest, a day in which one must be careful not to arouse the anger of the god who was supposed to preside over that particular day. Now the term *šabattum* has been found only 5 or 6 t in the Bab inscriptions and in none of them is it connected with the 7th day of a week. There was, however, a sort of institution among the superstitious Babylonians that has been compared with the Heb Sabbath. In certain months of the year (Elul, Marcheshvan) the 7th, 14th, 19th, 21st and 28th days were set down as favorable days, or unfavorable days, that is, as days in which the king, the priest and the physician must be careful not to stir up the anger of the deity. On these days the king was not to eat food prepared by fire, not to put on royal dress, not to ride in his chariot, etc. As to the 19th day, it is thought that it was included among the unlucky days because it was the 49th (7 times 7) from the 1st of the preceding month. As there were 30 days in the month, it is evident that we are not dealing with a recurring 7th day in the week, as is the case with the Heb Sabbath. Moreover, no proof has been adduced that the term *šabattum* was ever applied to these *dies nefasti* or unlucky days. Hence the assertions of some Assyriologists with regard to the Bab origin of the Sabbath must be taken with several grains of salt. Notice must be taken of an ingenious and able paper by Professor M. Jastrow, which was read before the Eleventh International Congress of Orientalists in Paris in 1897, in which the learned author attempts to show that the Heb Sabbath was originally a day of propitiation like the Bab *šabattum* (*AJT*, II, 312–52). He argues that the restrictive measures in the Heb laws for the observance of the Sabbath arose from the original conception of the Sabbath as an unfavorable day, a day in which the anger of Jeh might flash forth against men. Although Jastrow has supported his thesis with many arguments that are cogent, yet the reverent student of the Scriptures will find it difficult to resist the impression that the OT writers without exception thought of the Sabbath not as an unfavorable or unlucky day but rather as a day set apart for the benefit of man. Whatever may have been the attitude of the early Hebrews toward the day which was to become a characteristic institution of Judaism in all ages and in all lands, the organs of revelation throughout the OT enforce the observance of the Sabbath by arguments which lay emphasis upon its beneficent and humanitarian aspects.

We must call attention to Meinhold's ingenious hypothesis as to the origin of the Sabbath. In 1894

Theophilus G. Pinches discovered a tablet in which the term *shapattu* is applied to the 15th day of the month. Meinhold argues that *shabattu* in Bab denotes the day of the full moon. Dr. Skinner thus describes Meinhold's theory: "He points to the close association of new-moon and Sabbath in nearly all the preëxilic references (Am **8** 5; Hos **2** 11; Isa **1** 13; 2 K **4** 23 f); and concludes that in early Israel, as in Babylonia, the Sabbath was the full-moon festival and nothing else. The institution of the weekly Sabbath he traces to a desire to compensate for the loss of the old lunar festivals, when these were abrogated by the Deuteronomic reformation. This innovation he attributes to Ezekiel; but steps toward it are found in the introduction of a weekly day of rest during harvest only (on the ground of Dt **16** 8 f; cf Ex **34** 21), and in the establishment of the sabbatical year (Lev **25**), which he considers to be older than the weekly Sabbath" (*ICC* on Gen, p. 39). Dr. Skinner well says that Meinhold's theory involves great improbabilities. It is not certain that the Babylonians applied the term *šabattu* to the 15th day of the month because it was the day of the full moon; and it is by no means certain that the early prophets in Israel identified Sabbath with the festival of the full moon.

The wealth of learning and ingenuity expended in the search for the origin of the Sabbath has up to the present yielded small returns.

II. History of the Sabbath after Moses.—The early prophets and historians occasionally make mention of the Sabbath. It is sometimes named in connection with the festival of the new moon (2 K **4** 23; Am **8** 5; Hos **2** 11; Isa **1** 13; Ezk **46** 3). The prophets found fault with the worship on the Sabbath, because it was not spiritual nor prompted by love and gratitude. The Sabbath is exalted by the great prophets who faced the crisis of the Bab exile as one of the most valuable institutions in Israel's life. Great promises are attached to faithful observance of the holy day, and confession is made of Israel's unfaithfulness in profaning the Sabbath (Jer **17** 21–27; Isa **56** 2.4; **58** 13; Ezk **20** 12–24). In the Pers period Nehemiah struggled earnestly to make the people of Jerus observe the law of the Sabbath (Neh **10** 31; **13** 15–22).

1. In the OT

With the development of the synagogue the Sabbath became a day of worship and of study of the Law, as well as a day of cessation from all secular employment. That the pious in Israel carefully observed the Sabbath is clear from the conduct of the Maccabees and their followers, who at first declined to resist the onslaught made by their enemies on the Sabbath (1 Macc **2** 29–38); but necessity drove the faithful to defend themselves against hostile attack on the Sabbath (1 Macc **2** 39–41). It was during the period between Ezra and the Christian era that the spirit of Jewish legalism flourished. Innumerable restrictions and rules were formulated for the conduct of life under the Law. Great principles were lost to sight in the mass of petty details. Two entire treatises of the Mish, *Shabbāth* and *'Ērūbhīn*, are devoted to the details of Sabbath observance. The subject is touched upon in other parts of the Mish; and in the Gemara there are extended discussions, with citations of the often divergent opinions of the rabbis. In the Mish (*Shabbāth*, vii.2) there are 39 classes of prohibited actions with regard to the Sabbath, and there is much hair-splitting in working out the details. The beginnings of this elaborate definition of actions permitted and actions forbidden are to be found in the centuries immediately preceding the Christian era. The movement was at flood tide during Our Lord's earthly ministry and continued for centuries afterward, in spite of His frequent and vigorous protests.

2. In the Inter-Testamental Period

Apart from His claim to be the Messiah, there is no subject on which Our Lord came into such sharp conflict with the religious leaders of the Jews as in the matter of Sabbath observance. He set Himself squarely against the current rabbinic restrictions as contrary to the spirit of the original law of the Sabbath. The rabbis seemed to think that the Sabbath was an end in itself, an institution to which the pious Israelite must subject all his personal interests; in other words, that man was made for the Sabbath: man might suffer hardship, but the institution must be preserved inviolate. Jesus, on the contrary, taught that the Sabbath was made for man's benefit. If there should arise a conflict between man's needs and the letter of the Law, man's higher interests and needs must take precedence over the law of the Sabbath (Mt **12** 1–14; Mk **2** 23—**3** 6; Lk **6** 1–11; also Jn **5** 1–18; Lk **13** 10–17; **14** 1–6). There is no reason to think that Jesus meant to discredit the Sabbath as an institution. It was His custom to attend worship in the synagogue on the Sabbath (Lk **4** 16). The humane element in the rest day at the end of every week must have appealed to His sympathetic nature. It was the one precept of the Decalogue that was predominantly ceremonial, though it had distinct sociological and moral value. As an institution for the benefit of toiling men and animals, Jesus held the Sabbath in high regard. As the Messiah, He was not subject to its restrictions; He could at any moment assert His lordship over the Sabbath (Mk **2** 28). The institution was not on a par with the great moral precepts, which are unchangeable. It is worthy of note that, while Jesus pushed the moral precepts of the Decalogue into the inner realm of thought and desire, thus making the requirement more difficult and the law more exacting, He fought for a more liberal and lenient interpretation of the law of the Sabbath. Rigorous sabbatarians must look elsewhere for a champion of their views.

3. Jesus and the Sabbath

The early Christians kept the 7th day as a Sabbath, much after the fashion of other Jews. Gradually the 1st day of the week came to be recognized as the day on which the followers of Jesus would meet for worship. The resurrection of Our Lord on that day made it for Christians the most joyous day of all the week. When Gentiles were admitted into the church, the question at once arose whether they should be required to keep the Law of Moses. It is the glory of Paul that he fought for and won freedom for his gentile fellow-Christians. It is significant of the attitude of the apostles that the decrees of the Council at Jerus made no mention of Sabbath observance in the requirements laid upon gentile Christians (Acts **15** 28 f). Paul boldly contended that believers in Jesus, whether Jew or Gentile, were set free from the burdens of the Mosaic Law. Even circumcision counted for nothing, now that men were saved by believing in Jesus (Gal **5** 6). Christian liberty as proclaimed by Paul included all days and seasons. A man could observe special days or not, just as his own judgment and conscience might dictate (Rom **14** 5 f); but in all such matters one ought to be careful not to put a stumbling-block in a brother's way (Rom **14** 13 ff). That Paul contended for personal freedom in respect of the Sabbath is made quite clear in Col **2** 16 f, where he groups together dietary laws, feast days, new moons and sabbaths. The early Christians brought over into their mode of observing the Lord's Day the best elements of the Jewish Sabbath, without its onerous restrictions. See further LORD'S DAY; ETHICS OF JESUS, I, 3, (1).

4. Paul and the Sabbath

LITERATURE.—J. A. Hessey, *Sunday, Its Origin, History, and Present Obligation* (Bampton Lects for 1860); Zahn, *Geschichte des Sonntags*, 1878; Davis, *Genesis and Semitic Tradition*, 1894, 23–35; Jastrow, "The Original Character of the Heb Sabbath," *AJT*, II, 1898, 312–52; Toy, "The Earliest Form of the Sabbath," *JBL*, XVIII,

1899, 190–94; W. Lotz, *Questionum de historia Sabbati libri duo*, 1883; Nowack, *Hebr. Arch.*, II, 1894, 140 ff; Driver, *HDB*, IV, 1902, 317–23; *ICC*, on "Gen," 1911, 35–39; Dillmann, *Ex u. Lev*³, 1897, 212–16; Edersheim, *Life and Times of Jesus the Messiah*, II, 1883, 51–62, 777–87; Broadus, *Comm. on Mt*, 256–61; *EB*, IV, 1903, 4173–80; Gunkel, *Gen*³, 1910, 114–16; Meinhold, *Sabbat u. Woche im AT*, 1905; Beer, *Schabbath*, 1908.

JOHN RICHARD SAMPEY

SEVENTH-DAY ADVENTIST POSITION

The views entertained by Seventh-Day Adventists concerning the nature and obligation of the Sabbath may conveniently be presented under three general divisions: (1) what the Bible says concerning the Sabbath; (2) what history says concerning the Sabbath; (3) the significance of the Sabbath.

1. What the Bible Says concerning the Sabbath

(1) *OT teaching.*—In their views concerning the institution and primal obligation of the Sabbath, Seventh-Day Adventists are in harmony with the views held by the early representatives of nearly all the evangelical denominations. The Sabbath is coeval with the finishing of creation, and the main facts connected with establishing it are recorded in Gen **2** 2.3. The blessing here placed upon the seventh day distinguishes it from the other days of the week, and the day thus blessed was "sanctified" (AV, RV "hallowed") and set apart for man.

That the Sabbath thus instituted was well known throughout the Patriarchal age is clearly established both by direct evidence and by necessary inference.

"If we had no other passage than this of Gen **2** 3, there would be no difficulty in deducing from it a precept for the universal observance of a Sabbath, or seventh day, to be devoted to God as holy time by all of that race for whom the earth and all things therein were specially prepared. The first men must have known it. The words, 'He hallowed it,' can have no meaning otherwise. They would be a blank unless in reference to some who were required to keep it holy" (Lange's *Comm.* on Gen **2** 3, I, 197).

"And the day arrived when Moses went to Goshen to see his brethren, that he saw the children of Israel in their burdens and hard labor, and Moses was grieved on their account. And Moses returned to Egypt and came to the house of Pharaoh, and came before the king, and Moses bowed down before the king. And Moses said unto Pharaoh, I pray thee, my lord, I have come to seek a small request from thee, turn not away my face empty; and Pharaoh said unto him, Speak. And Moses said unto Pharaoh, Let there be given unto thy servants the children of Israel who are in Goshen, one day to rest therein from their labor. And the king answered Moses and said, Behold I have lifted up thy face in this thing to grant thy request. And Pharaoh ordered a proclamation to be issued throughout Egypt and Goshen, saying, To you, all the children of Israel, thus says the king, for six days you shall do your work and labor, but on the seventh day you shall rest, and shall not perform any work; thus shall you do in all the days, as the king and Moses the son of Bathia have commanded. And Moses rejoiced at this thing which the king had granted to him, and all the children of Israel did as Moses ordered them. For this thing was from the Lord to the children of Israel, for the Lord had begun to remember the children of Israel to save them for the sake of their fathers. And the Lord was with Moses, and his fame went throughout Egypt. And Moses became great in the eyes of all the Egyptians, and in the eyes of all the children of Israel, seeking good for his people Israel, and speaking words of peace regarding them to the king" (*Book of Jashar* 70:41–51, published by Noah & Gould, New York, 1840).

"Hence you can see that the Sabbath was before the Law of Moses came, and has existed from the beginning of the world. Esp. have the devout, who have preserved the true faith, met together and called upon God on this day" (Luther's Works, XXXV, p. 330).

"Why should God begin two thousand years after (the creation of the world) to give men a Sabbath upon the reason of His rest from the creation of it, if He had never called man to that commemoration before? And it is certain that the Sabbath was observed at the falling of the manna before the giving of the Law; and let any considering Christian judge . . . . (1) whether the not falling of manna, or the rest of God after the creation, was like to be the original reason of the Sabbath; (2) and whether, if it had been the first, it would not have been said, Remember to keep holy the Sabbath day; for on six days the manna fell, and not on the seventh; rather than 'for in six days God created heaven and earth, etc. and rested the seventh day.' And it is casually added, 'Wherefore the Lord blessed the Sabbath day, and hallowed it.' Nay, consider whether this annexed reason intimates not that the day on this ground being hallowed before, therefore it was that God sent not down the manna on that day, and that He prohibited the people from seeking it" (Richard Baxter, *Practical Works*, III, 774, ed 1707).

That the Sabbath was known to those who came out of Egypt, even before the giving of the Law at Sinai, is shown from the experience with the manna, as recorded in Ex **16** 22–30. The double portion on the sixth day, and its preservation, was the constantly recurring miracle which reminded the people of their obligation to observe the Sabbath, and that the Sabbath was a definite day, the seventh day. To the people, first wondering at this remarkable occurrence, Moses said, "This is that which the Lord hath said, To morrow is the rest of the holy sabbath unto the Lord" (ver 23 AV). And to some who went out to gather manna on the seventh day, the Lord administered this rebuke: "How long refuse ye to keep my commandments and my laws?" (ver 28). All this shows that the Sabbath law was well understood, and that the failure to observe it rendered the people justly subject to Divine reproof.

At Sinai, the Sabbath which was instituted at creation, and had been observed during the intervening centuries, was embodied in that formal statement of man's duties usually designated as the "Ten Commandments." It is treated as an institution already well known and the command is, "Remember the sabbath day, to keep it holy" (Ex **20** 8). In the 4th commandment the basis of the Sabbath is revealed. It is a memorial of the Creator's rest at the close of those six days in which He made "heaven and earth, the sea, and all that in them is." For this reason "Jeh blessed the sabbath day, and hallowed it." This blessing was not placed upon the day at Sinai, but in the beginning, when "God blessed the seventh day, and hallowed it" (Gen **2** 3).

From the very nature of the basis of the Sabbath, as set forth in this commandment, both the institution itself and the definite day of the Sabbath are of a permanent nature. So long as it is true that God created heaven and earth, and all things therein, so long will the Sabbath remain as a memorial of that work; and so long as it is true that this creative work was completed in six days, and that God Himself rested on the seventh day, and was refreshed in the enjoyment of His completed work, so long will it be true that the memorial of that work can properly be celebrated only upon the seventh day of the week.

During all the period from the deliverance out of Egypt to the captivity in Babylon, the people of God were distinguished from the nations about them by the worship of the only true God, and the observance of His holy day. The proper observance of the true Sabbath would preserve them from idolatry, being a constant reminder of the one God, the Creator of all things. Even when Jerus was suffering from the attacks of the Babylonians, God assured His people, through the prophet Jeremiah, that if they would hallow the Sabbath day, great should be their prosperity, and the city should remain forever (Jer **17** 18). This shows that the spiritual observance of the Sabbath was the supreme test of their right relation to God. In those prophecies of Isaiah, which deal primarily with the restoration from Babylon, remarkable promises were made to those who would observe the Sabbath, as recorded in Isa **56** 1–7.

(2) *NT teaching.*—From the record found in the four Gospels, it is plain that the Jews during all the previous centuries had preserved a knowledge both of the Sabbath institution and of the definite day.

It is equally plain that they had made the Sabbath burdensome by their own rigorous exactions concerning it. And Christ, the Lord of the Sabbath, both by example and by precept, brushed aside these traditions of men that He might reveal the Sabbath of the commandment as God gave it—a blessing and not a burden. A careful reading of the testimony of the evangelists will show that Christ taught the observance of the commandments of God, rather than the traditions of men, and that the charge of Sabbath-breaking was brought against Him for no other reason than that He refused to allow the requirements of man to change the Sabbath, blessed of God, into a merely human institution, grievous in its nature, and enforced upon the people with many and troublesome restrictions.

All are agreed that Christ and His disciples observed the seventh-day Sabbath previous to the crucifixion. That His followers had received no intimation of any proposed change at His death, is evident from the recorded fact that on the day when He was in the tomb they rested, "on the sabbath . . . . according to the commandment" (Lk **23** 56); and that they treated the following day, the first day of the week, the same as of old, is further evident, as upon that day they came unto the sepulcher for the purpose of anointing the body of Jesus. In the Book of Acts, which gives a brief history of the work of the disciples in proclaiming the gospel of a risen Saviour, no other Sabbath is recognized than the seventh day, and this is mentioned in the most natural way as the proper designation of a well-known institution (Acts **13** 14.27.42; **16** 13; **18** 4).

In Our Lord's great prophecy, in which He foretold the experience of the church between the first and the second advent, He recognized the seventh-day Sabbath as an existing institution at the time of the destruction of Jerus (70 AD), when He instructed His disciples, "Pray ye that your flight be not in the winter, neither on a sabbath" (Mt **24** 20). Such instruction given in these words, and at that time, would have been confusing in the extreme, had there been any such thing contemplated as the overthrow of the Sabbath law at the crucifixion, and the substitution of another day upon an entirely different basis.

That the original Sabbath is to be observed, not only during the present order of things, but also after the restoration when, according to the vision of the revelator, a new heaven and a new earth will take the place of the heaven and the earth that now are, is clearly intimated in the words of the Lord through the prophet Isaiah: "For as the new heavens and the new earth, which I will make, shall remain before me, saith Jeh, so shall your seed and your name remain. And it shall come to pass, that from one new moon to another, and from one sabbath to another, shall all flesh come to worship before me, saith Jeh" (Isa **66** 22.23).

Seventh-Day Adventists regard the effort to establish the observance of another day than the seventh by using such texts as Jn **20** 19.26; Acts **20** 7; 1 Cor **16** 1.2; Rev **1** 10 as being merely an afterthought, an effort to find warrant for an observance established upon other than Bib. authority. During the last two or three centuries there has been a movement for the restoration of the original seventh-day Sabbath, not as a Jewish, but as a Christian, institution. This work, commenced and carried forward by the Seventh-Day Baptists, has been taken up and pushed with renewed vigor by the Seventh-Day Adventists during the present generation, and the Bible teaching concerning the true Sabbath is now being presented in nearly every country, both civilized and uncivilized, on the face of the earth.

2. What History Says about the Sabbath

(1) *Josephus.*—This summary of history must necessarily be brief, and it will be impossible, for lack of space, to quote authorities. From the testimony of Jos it is clear that the Jews, as a nation, continued to observe the seventh-day Sabbath until their overthrow, when Jerus was captured by Titus, 70 AD. As colonies, and individuals, scattered over the face of the earth, the Jews have preserved a knowledge of the original Sabbath, and the definite day, until the present time. They constitute a living testimony for the benefit of all who desire to know the truth of this matter.

(2) *Church history.*—According to church history the seventh-day Sabbath was observed by the early church, and no other day was observed as a Sabbath during the first two or three centuries (see *HDB*, IV, 322 *b*).

In the oft-repeated letter of Pliny, the Rom governor of Bithynia, to the emperor Trajan, written about 112 AD, there occurs the expression, "a certain stated day," which is usually assumed to mean Sunday. With reference to this matter W. B. Taylor, in *Historical Comms.*, ch i, sec. 47, makes the following statement: "As the Sabbath day appears to have been quite as commonly observed at this date as the sun's day (if not even more so), it is just as probable that this 'stated day' referred to by Pliny was the 7th day as that it was the 1st day; though the latter is generally taken for granted." "Sunday was distinguished as a day of joy by the circumstances that men did not fast upon it, and that they prayed standing up and not kneeling, as Christ had now been raised from the dead. The festival of Sunday, like all other festivals, was always only a human ordinance, and it was far from the intentions of the apostles to establish a Divine command in this respect, far from them, and from the early apostolic church, to transfer the laws of the Sabbath to Sunday. Perhaps at the end of the 2d cent., a false application of this kind had begun to take place; for men appear by that time to have considered laboring on Sunday as a sin" (Tertullian *De Orat.*, c. 23). This quotation is taken from Rose's *Neander*, London, 1831, I, 33 f, and is the correct tr from Neander's first Ger. ed, Hamburg, 1826, I, pt. 2, p. 339. Neander has in his 2d ed, 1842, omitted the second sentence, in which he expressly stated that Sunday was only a human ordinance, but he has added nothing to the contrary. "The Christians in the ancient church very soon distinguished the first day of the week, Sunday; however, not as a Sabbath, but as an assembly day of the church, to study the Word of God together and to celebrate the ordinances one with another: without a shadow of doubt this took place as early as the first part of the 2d cent." (*Geschichte des Sonntags*, 60).

Gradually, however, the first day of the week came into prominence as an added day, but finally by civil and ecclesiastical authority as a required observance. The first legislation on this subject was the famous law of Constantine, enacted 321 AD. The acts of various councils during the 4th and 5th cents. established the observance of the first day of the week by ecclesiastical authority, and in the great apostasy which followed, the rival day obtained the ascendancy. During the centuries which followed, however, there were always witnesses for the true Sabbath, although under great persecution. And thus in various lands, the knowledge of the true Sabbath has been preserved.

3. The Significance of the Sabbath

In the creation of the heavens and the earth the foundation of the gospel was laid. At the close of His created work, "God saw everything that he had made, and, behold, it was very good" (Gen **1** 31). The Sabbath was both the sign and the memorial of that creative power which is able to make all things good. But man, made in the image of God, lost that image through sin. In the gospel, provision is made for the restoration of the image of God in the soul of man. The Creator is the Redeemer and redemption is the new creation. As the Sabbath was the sign of that creative power which wrought in Christ, the Word, in the making of the heaven and the earth and all things therein, so it is the sign of that same creative power working through the same eternal Word for the restoration of all things. "Wherefore if any man is in Christ, there is a new creation: the old things are passed away; behold, they are become new" (2 Cor **5** 17 m). "For neither is circumcision anything, nor uncircumcision, but a new creation" (Gal **6** 15 m). "For we are his workmanship, created in Christ Jesus for good works, which God afore prepared that we should walk in them" (Eph **2** 10).

A concrete illustration of this gospel meaning of the Sabbath is found in the deliverance of Israel from Egypt. The same creative power which wrought in the beginning was exercised in the signs and miracles which preceded their deliverance, and in those miracles, such as the opening of the Red Sea, the giving of the manna, and the water from the rock, which attended the journeyings of the Israelites. In consequence of these manifestations of creative power in their behalf, the children of Israel were instructed to remember in their observance of the Sabbath that they were bondmen in the land of Egypt. Israel's deliverance from Egypt is the type of every man's deliverance from sin; and the instruction to Israel concerning the Sabbath shows its true significance in the gospel of salvation from sin, and the new creation in the image of God.

Furthermore, the seventh-day Sabbath is the sign of both the divinity and the deity of Christ. God only can create. He through whom this work is wrought must be one with God. To this the Scriptures testify: "In the beginning was the Word, ... and the Word was God. . . . . All things were made through him; and without him was not anything made that hath been made." But this same Word which was with God, and was God, "became flesh, and dwelt among us" (Jn **1** 1.3.14). This is the eternal Son, "in whom we have our redemption through his blood, the forgiveness of our trespasses, according to the riches of his grace" (Eph **1** 7). To the Christian the Sabbath, which was the sign and memorial of that Divine power which wrought through the eternal Word in the creation of the heaven and the earth, becomes the sign of the same power working through the same eternal Son to accomplish the new creation, and is thus the sign of both the divinity and the deity of Christ.

Inasmuch as the redemptive work finds its chiefest expression in the cross of Christ, the Sabbath, which is the sign of that redemptive work, becomes the sign of the cross.

Seventh-Day Adventists teach and practise the observance of the Sabbath, not because they believe in salvation through man's effort to keep the law of God, but because they believe in that salvation which alone can be accomplished by the creative power of God working through the eternal Son to create believers anew in Christ Jesus.

Seventh-Day Adventists believe, and teach, that the observance of any other day than the seventh as the Sabbath is the sign of that predicted apostasy in which the man of sin would be revealed who would exalt himself above all that is called God, or that is worshipped.

Seventh-Day Adventists believe, and teach, that the observance of the true Sabbath in this generation is a part of that gospel work which is to make ready a people prepared for the Lord.

W. W. PRESCOTT

SABBATH-BREAKING, s.-brāk'ing. See CRIMES; PUNISHMENTS.

SABBATH, COURT OF THE. See COVERED WAY.

SABBATH, DAY BEFORE THE. See DAY BEFORE THE SABBATH.

SABBATH DAY'S JOURNEY, jûr'ni (**σαββάτου ὁδός**, *sabbátou hodós*): Used only in Acts **1** 12, where it designates the distance from Jerus to the Mount of Olives, to which Jesus led His disciples on the day of His ascension. The expression comes from rabbinical usage to indicate the distance a Jew might travel on the Sabbath without transgressing the Law, the command against working on that day being interpreted as including travel (see Ex **16** 27–30). The limit set by the rabbis to the Sabbath day's journey was 2,000 cubits from one's house or domicile, which was derived from the statement found in Josh **3** 4 that this was the distance between the ark and the people on their march, this being assumed to be the distance between the tents of the people and the tabernacle during the sojourn in the wilderness. Hence it must have been allowable to travel thus far to attend the worship of the tabernacle. We do not know when this assumption in regard to the Sabbath day's journey was made, but it seems to have been in force in the time of Christ. The distance of the Mount of Olives from Jerus is stated in Jos (*Ant*, XX, viii, 6) to have been five stadia or furlongs and in *BJ*, V, ii, 3, six stadia, the discrepancy being explained by supposing a different point of departure. This would make the distance of the Sabbath day's journey from 1,000 to 1,200 yds., the first agreeing very closely with the 2,000 cubits. The rabbis, however, invented a way of increasing this distance without technically infringing the Law, by depositing some food at the 2,000-cubit limit, before the Sabbath, and declaring that spot a temporary domicile. They might then proceed 2,000 cubits from this point without transgressing the Law.

And in some cases even this intricacy of preparation was unnecessary. If, for instance, the approach of the Sabbath found one on his journey, the traveler might select some tree or some stone wall at a distance of 2,000 paces and mentally declare this to be his residence for the Sabbath, in which case he was permitted to go the 2,000 paces to the selected tree or wall and also 2,000 paces beyond, but in such a case he must do the work thoroughly and must say: "Let my Sabbath residence be at the trunk of that tree," for if he merely said: "Let my Sabbath residence be under that tree," this would not be sufficient, because the expression would be too general and indefinite (Tract. *'Ērūbhīn* **4** 7).

Other schemes for extending the distance have been devised, such as regarding the quarter of the town in which one dwells, or the whole town itself, as the domicile, thus allowing one to proceed from any part of the town to a point 2,000 cubits beyond its utmost limits. This was most probably the case with walled towns, at least, and boundary stones have been found in the vicinity of Gaza with inscriptions supposed to mark these limits. The 2,000-cubit limits around the Levitical cities (Nu **35** 5) may have suggested the limit of the Sabbath day's journey also. The term came to be used as a designation of distance which must have been more or less definite.

H. PORTER

SABBATH, MORROW AFTER THE. See MORROW AFTER THE SABBATH.

SABBATH, SECOND AFTER THE FIRST (**σάββατον δευτερόπρωτον**, *sábbaton deuteróprōton* [Lk **6** 1], lit. "the second-first sabbath," of RVm): We will mention only a few of the explanations elicited by this expression. (1) It was the first Sabbath in the second year of a 7-year cycle comprising the period from one Sabbatic year to the other; (2) the first Sabbath after the second day of Passover, i.e. the first of the seven Sabbaths the Hebrews were to "count unto" themselves from "the morrow after the sabbath" (the day after Easter) until Pentecost (Lev **23** 15); (3) the first Sabbath in the Jewish ecclesiastical year (about the middle of March), the first Sabbath in the civil year (about the middle of September) being counted as the "first-first" Sabbath; (4) the term *deuteróprōtos*, is a monstrous combination of the words *deúteros*, "second," and *prōtos*, "first," attributable to unskilful attempts at textual emendation on the part of copyists. This supposition would, of course, render unnecessary all other efforts to unravel the knotty problem, and, as a matter of fact, *deuteróprōtos* is omitted by many MSS (including א and B). To those not feeling inclined to accept this solution we would suggest the first of the above-named explanations as the most natural and probable one.

WILLIAM BAUR

SABBATHEUS, sab-a-thē'us: AV=RV SABBATEUS (q.v.).

SABBATHS, sab'aths, **OF YEARS** (שַׁבְּתֹת שָׁנִים, *shabbᵉthōth shānīm;* **ἀναπαύσεις ἐτῶν**, *anapaúseis etôn* [Lev **25** 8]): The seven sabbatic years preceding the Year of Jubilee. See SABBATICAL YEAR; JUBILEE YEAR; ASTRONOMY, I, 5.

SABBATICAL, sa-bat'ik-al, **YEAR** (שְׁנַת שַׁבָּתוֹן, *shᵉnath shabbāthōn;* **ἐνιαυτὸς ἀναπαύσεως**, *eniautós anapaúseōs*, "a year of solemn rest"; or שַׁבַּת שַׁבָּתוֹן, *shabbath shabbāthōn;* **σάββατα ἀνάπαυσις**, *sábbata anápausis*, "a sabbath of solemn rest" [Lev **25** 4];

or שְׁנַת הַשְּׁמִטָּה, *shᵉnath ha-shᵉmiṭṭāh;* ἔτος τῆς ἀφέσεως, *étos tḗs aphéseōs*, "the year of release" [Dt 15 9; 31 10]): We find the first rudiments of this institution in the so-called Covenant Book (Ex **21**-**23**). Its connection with the day of rest (Sabbath) is obvious, although it strikes us as somewhat remarkable that in Ex **23** 10-12 the regulation regarding the 7th year should precede the statute respecting the 7th day. Still it seems natural that after the allusion in ver 9, "Ye were sojourners in the land of Egypt," the Covenant Book should put in a good word for the poor in Israel (ver 11: "Let it rest and lie fallow, that the poor of thy people may eat"). Even the beasts of the field are remembered (cf Jon **4** 11).

1. Primary Intention

We must, therefore, conclude that in this early period of the history of Israel the regulation regarding the 7th year was primarily intended for the relief of the poor and for the awakening of a sense of responsibility in the hearts of those better provided with the means of subsistence. It would be wrong, however, to deny its Sabbatic character, for the text says expressly, "But in the 7th year thou shalt let it rest" (lit. "thou shalt release it"), implying that the land was entitled to a rest because it needed it; it must be released for a time in order to gain fresh strength and insure its future fertility. Two motives, then, present themselves most clearly, one of a social, the other of an economic character, and both are rooted in God's dealings with Israel (cf Ex **21** 1).

2. Mosaic Legislation Humane

Another evidence of the humane spirit pervading the Mosaic Law may be found in Ex **21** 2-6 where, in the case of a Heb slave, the length of his servitude is limited to six years. The connection with the idea of the Sabbath is evident, but we fail to detect here any reference to the Sabbatical year. It is clear that the 7th year in which a slave might be set free need not necessarily coincide with the Sabbatical year, though it might, of course. The same is true of Dt **15** 12-18; it has nothing to do with the Sabbatical year. On the other hand it is reasonable to assume that the "release" mentioned in Dt **15** 1-3 took place in the Sabbatical year; in other words, its scope had been enlarged in later years so as to include the release from pecuniary obligation, i.e. the remission of debts or, at least, their temporary suspension. This means that the children of Israel were now developing from a purely agricultural people to a commercial nation. Still the same spirit of compassion for the poor and those struggling for a living asserts itself as in the earlier period, and it goes without saying that the old regulation concerning the release of the land in the 7th year was still in force (cf ver 2: "because Jeh's release hath been proclaimed").

According to ver 1, this proclamation occurred at the end of every 7 years, or, rather, during the 7th year; for we must be careful not to strain the expression "at the end" (cf ver 9, where the 7th year is called "the year of release"; it is quite natural to identify this 7th year with the Sabbatical year).

Moreover, we are now almost compelled to assert that the Sabbatical year by this time had become an institution observed simultaneously all over the country. From the wording of the regulation regarding the 7th year in the Covenant Book we are not certain about this in those early times. But now it is different. "Jeh's release hath been proclaimed."

3. General Observance

It was a solemn and general proclamation, the date of which was very likely the day of atonement in the 7th month (the Sabbatical month). The celebration of the Feast of Tabernacles (booths) began five days later and it lasted from the 15th day to the 21st of the 7th month (Tisri). In the Sabbatical year, at that time, the Law was read "before all Israel in their hearing," a fact which tends to prove that the Sabbatical year had become a matter of general and simultaneous observance (cf Dt **31** 10-13). Another lesson may be deduced from this passage: it gives us a hint respecting the use to which the people may have put their leisure time during the 12 months of Sabbatical rest; it may have been a period of religious and probably other instruction.

In Lev **25** 1-7 the central idea of the Sabbatical year is unfolded. Although it has been said we should be careful not to look for too much of the ideal and dogmatic in the institutions of the children of Israel, yet we must never lose sight of the religious and educational character even of their ancient legislation.

4. Central Idea

One central thought is brought home to them, viz. God is the owner of the soil, and through His grace only the chosen people have come into its possession. Their time, i.e. they themselves, belong to Him: this is the deepest meaning of the day of rest; their land, i.e. their means of subsistence, belong to Him: this reveals to us the innermost significance of the year of rest. It was Jeh's pleasure to call the children of Israel into life, and if they live and work and prosper, they are indebted to His unmerited loving-kindness. They should, therefore, put their absolute trust in Him, never doubt His word or His power, always obey Him and so always receive His unbounded blessings.

If we thus put all the emphasis on the religious character of the Sabbatical year, we are in keeping with the idea permeating the OT, namely that the children of Israel are the chosen people of Jeh. All their agricultural, social, commercial and political relations were to be built upon their Divine calling and shaped according to God's sovereign will.

But did they live up to it? Or, to limit the question to our subject: Did they really observe the Sabbatical year? There are those who hold that the law regarding the Sabbatical year was not observed before the captivity. In order to prove this assertion they point to Lev **26** 34 f.43; also to 2 Ch **36** 21. But all we can gather from these passages is the palpable conclusion that the law regarding the Sabbatical year had not been strictly obeyed, a deficiency which may mar the effect of any law.

The possibility of observing the precept respecting the Sabbatical year is demonstrated by the post-exilic history of the Jewish people. Nehemiah registers the solemn fact that the reëstablished nation entered into a covenant to keep the law and to maintain the temple worship (Neh **9** 38; **10** 32 ff). In ver 31 of the last-named chapter he alludes to the 7th year, "that we would forego the 7th year, and the exaction of every debt." We are not sure of the exact meaning of this short allusion; it may refer to the Sabbatical rest of the land and the suspension of debts.

For a certainty we know that the Sabbatical year was observed by the Jews at the time of Alexander the Great. When he was petitioned by the Samaritans "that he would remit the tribute of the 7th year to them, because they did not sow therein, he asked who they were that made such a petition"; he was told they were Hebrews, etc (Jos, *Ant*, XI, viii, 6).

During Maccabean and Asmonean times the law regarding the Sabbatical year was strictly observed, although it frequently weakened the cause of the Jews (1 Macc **6** 49.53; Jos, *Ant*, XIII, viii, 1; cf *BJ*, I, ii, 4; *Ant*, XIV, x, 6; XV, i, 2). Again we may find references to the Sabbatical year in Jos, *Ant*, XIV, xvi, 2, etc; Tac. *Hist.* v.4, etc, all of which testifies to the observance of the Sabbatical year in the Herodian era. The words of Tacitus show the proud Roman's estimate of the Jewish character and customs: "For the 7th day they are said to have prescribed rest because this day ended their labors; then, in addition, being allured by their lack of energy, they also spend the 7th year in laziness." See also ASTRONOMY, I, 5, (3), (4); JUBILEE YEAR.

WILLIAM BAUR

SABBEUS, sa-bē'us (**Σαββαίας,** *Sabbaías*): In 1 Esd **9** 32, the same as "Shemaiah" in Ezr **10** 31.

SABI, sā'bī:

(1) A, Σαβεί, *Sabeí*, B, Τωβείς, *Tōbeís*, Fritzsche; AV **Sami**): Eponym of a family of porters who returned with Zerubbabel (1 Esd **5** 28) = "Shobai" in Ezr **2** 42; Neh **7** 45.

(2) AV = RV Sabie (q.v.).

SABIAS, sa-bī'as (**Σαβίας,** *Sabías*, Fritzsche, **'Ασαβίας,** *Asabías;* AV **Assabias**): One of the six "captains over thousands" who supplied the Levites with much cattle for Josiah's Passover (1 Esd **1** 9) = "Hashabiah" in 2 Ch **35** 9.

SABIE, sā'bi-ē (**Σαβειή,** *Sabeiḗ*, or **Σαβιή,** *Sabiḗ;* AV **Sabi**): In 1 Esd **5** 34 both AV and RV, following A, read "the sons of Phacareth, *the sons of* Sabie" (AV "Sabi") for the "Pochereth-hazzebaim" of Ezr **2** 57; Neh **7** 59. B reads correctly as one proper name: "Phacareth Sabie."

SABTA, or SABTAH, sab'ta (סַבְתָּא, *ṣabhtā'*, סַבְתָּה, *ṣabhtāh*): Third son of Cush (Gen **10** 7 = 1 Ch **1** 9). A place Sabta is probably to be looked for in South Arabia. Arab geographers give no exact equivalent of the name. Al Bekri (i.65) quotes a line of early poetry in which Dhu 'l Sabta is mentioned, and the context might indicate a situation in Yemamah; but the word is possibly not a proper name. It is usually identified with Saubatha (Ptol., vi.7, 38) or with the Sabota of Pliny (vi.32; xii.32), an old mercantile city in South Arabia celebrated for its trade in frankincense and, according to Ptolemy, possessing 60 temples. It is said also to have been the territory of a king Elisarus, whose name presents a striking resemblance to Dhu 'l-Adhār, one of the "Tubbas" or Himyarite kings of Yemen. Another conjecture is the Saphtha of Ptolemy (vi.7, 30) near the Arabian shore of the Pers Gulf.

A. S. Fulton

SABTECA, sab'tē-ka (סַבְתְּכָא, *ṣabhtekhā'; **Σαβακαθά,*** *Sabakathá*, **Σεβεθαχά,** *Sebethachá;* AV **Sabtechah**): The 5th named of the sons of Cush in the genealogy of Gen **10** 5-7. In 1 Ch **1** 8.9 AV reads "Sabtecha," RV "Sabteca." Many conjectures have been made as to the place here indicated. Recently Glazer (*Skizze*, II, 252) has revived the suggestion of Bochart that it is to be identified with Samydake in Carmania on the E. of the Pers Gulf. This seems to rest on nothing more than superficial resemblance of the names; but the phonetic changes involved are difficult. Others have thought of various places in Arabia, toward the Pers Gulf; but the data necessary for any satisfactory decision are not now available.

W. Ewing

SACAR, sā'kär (שָׂכָר, *sākhār*):

(1) Father of Ahiam, a follower of David (1 Ch **11** 35, B, 'Αχάρ, *Achár*, A, Σαχάρ, *Sachár* = "Sharar" of 2 S **23** 33; Sharar is favored as the original reading).

(2) Eponym of a family of gatekeepers (1 Ch **26** 4).

SACKBUT, sak'but. See Music, III, 1, (*f*).

SACKCLOTH, sak'klōth. See Burial.

SACRAMENTS, sak'ra-ments: The word "sacrament" comes from the Lat *sacramentum*, which in the classical period of the language was used in two chief senses: (1) as a legal term to denote the sum of money deposited by two parties to a suit which was forfeited by the loser and appropriated to sacred uses; (2) as a military term to designate the oath of obedience taken by newly enlisted soldiers. Whether referring to an oath of obedience or to something set apart for a sacred purpose, it is evident that *sacramentum* would readily lend itself to describe such ordinances as Baptism and the Lord's Supper. In the Gr NT, however, there is no word nor even any general idea corresponding to "sacrament," nor does the earliest history of Christianity afford any trace of the application of the term to certain rites of the church. Pliny (c 112 AD) describes the Christians of Bithynia as "binding themselves by a *sacramentum* to commit no kind of crime" (*Epp.* x.97), but scholars are now pretty generally agreed that Pliny here uses the word in its old Rom sense of an oath or solemn obligation, so that its occurrence in this passage is nothing more than an interesting coincidence.

1. The Term

It is in the writings of Tertullian (end of 2d and beginning of 3d cent.) that we find the first evidence of the adoption of the word as a technical term to designate Baptism, the Eucharist, and other rites of the Christian church. This Christian adoption of *sacramentum* may have been partly occasioned by the evident analogies which the word suggests with Baptism and the Eucharist; but what appears to have chiefly determined its history in this direction was the fact that in the Old Lat VSS (as afterward in the Vulg) it had been employed to translate the Gr μυστήριον, *mustḗrion*, "a mystery" (e.g. Eph **5** 32; 1 Tim **3** 16; Rev **1** 20; **17** 7)—an association of ideas which was greatly fostered in the early church by the rapidly growing tendency to an assimilation of Christian worship with the mystery-practices of the Gr-Rom world.

2. Nature and Number

Though esp. employed to denote Baptism and the Eucharist, the name "sacraments" was for long used so loosely and vaguely that it was applied to facts and doctrines of Christianity as well as to its symbolic rites. Augustine's definition of a sacrament as "the visible form of an invisible grace" so far limited its application. But we see how widely even a definition like this might be stretched when we find Hugo of St. Victor (12th cent.) enumerating as many as 30 sacraments that had been recognized in the church. The Council of Trent was more exact when it declared that visible forms are sacraments only when they *represent* an invisible grace and become its channels, and when it sought further to delimit the sacramental area by reënacting (1547) a decision of the Council of Florence (1439), in which for the first time the authority of the church was given to a suggestion of Peter Lombard (12th cent.) and other schoolmen that the number of the sacraments should be fixed at seven, viz. Baptism, Confirmation, the Eucharist, Penance, Extreme Unction, Orders, and Matrimony—a suggestion which was supported by certain fanciful analogies designed to show that seven was a sacred number.

The divergence of the Protestant churches from this definition and scheme was based on the fact that these proceeded on no settled principles. The notion that there are seven sacraments has no NT authority, and must be described as purely arbitrary; while the definition of a sacrament is still so vague that anything but an arbitrary selection of particulars is impossible. It is perfectly arbitrary, for example, to place Baptism and the Lord's Supper, which were instituted by Christ as ordinances of the church, in the same category with marriage, which rests not on His appointment but on a natural relationship between the sexes that is as old as the human race. While, therefore, the Reformers retained the term "sacrament" as a convenient one to express the general idea that has to be drawn from the characteristics of the rites classed together under this name, they found the distinguishing marks of sacraments (1) in their institution by Christ, (2) in their being enjoined by Him upon His followers, (3) in their being bound up with His word and revelation in such a way that they become "the expressions of Divine thoughts, the visible symbols of Divine acts." And as Baptism and the Lord's Supper are the only two rites for which such marks can be claimed, it follows that there are only two NT sacraments. Their unique place in the original revelation justifies us in separating them from all other rites and ceremonies that may have arisen in the history of the church, since it raises them to the dignity of forming an integral part of the historical gospel. A justification for their being classed together under a common name may be found, again, in the way in which they are associated in the NT (Acts **2** 41.42; 1 Cor **10** 1–4) and also in the analogy which Paul traces between Baptism and the Lord's Supper on the one hand, and Circumcision and the Passover—the two most distinctive rites of the Old Covenant—on the other (Col **2** 11; 1 Cor **5** 7; **11** 26).

3. Institution by Christ

The assumption made above, that both Baptism and the Lord's Supper owe their origin as sacraments of the church to their definite appointment by Christ Himself, has been strongly challenged by some modern critics.

(1) In regard to **Baptism** it has been argued that as Mk **16** 15 f occurs in a passage (vs 9–20) which textual criticism has shown to have formed no part of the original Gospel, Mt **28** 19, standing by itself, is too slender a foundation to support the belief that the ordinance rests upon an injunction of Jesus, more esp. as its statements are inconsistent with the results of historical criticism. These results, it is affirmed, prove that all the narratives of the Forty Days are legendary, that Mt **28** 19 in particular only canonizes a later ecclesiastical situation, that its universalism is contrary to the facts of early Christian history, and its Trinitarian formula "foreign to the mouth of Jesus" (see Harnack, *History of Dogma*, I, 79, and the references there given). It is evident, however, that some of these objections rest upon anti-supernatural presuppositions that really beg the question at issue, and others on conclusions for which real premises are wanting. Over against them all we have to set the positive and weighty fact that from the earliest days of Christianity Baptism appears as the rite of initiation into the fellowship of the church (Acts **2** 38.41, *et passim*), and that even Paul, with all his freedom of thought and spiritual interpretation of the gospel, never questioned its necessity (cf Rom **6** 3 ff; 1 Cor **12** 13; Eph **4** 5). On any other supposition than that of its appointment by Our Lord Himself it is difficult to conceive how within the brief space of years between the death of Jesus and the apostle's earliest references to the subject, the ordinance should not only have originated but have established itself in so absolute a manner for Jewish and gentile Christians alike.

(2) In the case of the **Lord's Supper** the challenge of its institution by Christ rests mainly upon the fact that the saying, "This do in remembrance of me," is absent from the Mk-Mt text, and is found only in the Supper-narratives of Paul (1 Cor **11** 24.25) and his disciple Luke (Lk **22** 19). Upon this circumstance large structures of critical hypothesis have been reared. It has been affirmed that in the upper room Jesus was only holding a farewell supper with His disciples, and that it never occurred to Him to institute a feast of commemoration. It has further been maintained that the views of Jesus regarding the speedy consummation of His kingdom make it impossible that He should have dreamed of instituting a sacrament to commemorate His death. The significance of the feast was eschatological merely; it was a pledge of a glorious future hour in the perfected kingdom of God (see Mt **26** 29 and parallels). And the theory has even been advanced that the institution of this sacrament as an ordinance of the church designed to commemorate Christ's death was due to the initiative of Paul, who is supposed to have been influenced in this direction by what he had seen in Corinth and elsewhere of the mystery-practices of the Gr world.

All these hypothetical fabrics fall, of course, to the ground if the underlying assumption that Jesus never said, "This do in remembrance of me," is shown to be unwarrantable. And it is unwarrantable to assume that a saying of Jesus which is vouched for by Paul and Luke cannot be authentic because it does not occur in the corresponding narratives of Matthew and Mark. In these narratives, which are highly compressed in any case, the first two evangelists would seem to have confined themselves to setting down those sayings which formed the essential moments of the Supper and gave its symbolic contents. The command of its repetition they may have regarded as sufficiently embodied and expressed in the universal practice of the church from the earliest days. For as to that practice there is no question (Acts **2** 42.46; **20** 7; 1 Cor **10** 16; **11** 26), and just as little that it rested upon the *belief* that Christ had enjoined it. "Every assumption of its having originated in the church from the recollection of intercourse with Jesus at table, and the necessity felt for recalling His death, is precluded" (Weizsäcker, *Apostolic Age*, II, 279). That the simple historical supper of Jesus with His disciples in the upper room was converted by Paul into an institution for the gentile and Jewish churches alike is altogether inconceivable. The primitive church had its bitter controversies, but there is no trace of any controversy as to the origin and institutional character of the Lord's Supper.

4. Efficacy

In the NT the sacraments are presented as means of grace. Forgiveness (Acts **2** 38), cleansing (Eph **5** 25 f), spiritual quickening (Col **2** 12) are associated with Baptism; the Lord's Supper is declared to be a participation in the body and blood of Christ (1 Cor **10** 16). So far all Christians are agreed; but wide divergence shows itself thereafter. According to the doctrine of the Rom church, sacraments are efficacious *ex opere operato*, i.e. in virtue of a power inherent in themselves as outward acts whereby they communicate saving benefits to those who receive them without opposing any obstacle. The Reformed doctrine, on the other hand, teaches that their efficacy lies not in themselves as outward acts, but in the blessing of Christ and the operation of His Spirit, and that it is conditioned by faith in the recipient. The traditional Lutheran doctrine agrees with the Reformed in affirming that faith is necessary as the condition of saving benefits in the use of the sacraments, but resembles the Rom teaching in ascribing the efficacy of Baptism and the Lord's Supper, not to the attendant working of the Holy Spirit, but to a real inherent and objective virtue resident in them—a virtue, however, which does not lie (as the Rom church says) in the mere elements and actions of the sacraments, but in the power of the Divine word which they embody. See BAPTISM; LORD'S SUPPER.

LITERATURE.—Candlish, *The Christian Sacraments;* Lambert, *The Sacraments in the NT;* Bartlet, *Apostolic Age*, 495 ff; Hodge, *Systematic Theology*, III, ch xx.

J. C. LAMBERT

SACRIFICE, sak'ri-fīs, sak'ri-fīz:

IN THE OLD TESTAMENT

I. TERMS AND DEFINITIONS
II. ORIGIN AND NATURE OF SACRIFICES
  1. Theory of a Divine Revelation
  2. Theories of a Human Origin
    (1) The Gift-Theory
    (2) The Magic Theory
    (3) The Table-Bond Theory
    (4) The Sacramental Communion Theory
    (5) The Homage Theory
    (6) The Piacular Theory
    (7) Originating in Religious Instincts
III. CLASSIFICATION OF SACRIFICES
  1. Maimonides
  2. W. R. Smith and Others
  3. Oehler
  4. Paterson and Others
  5. H. M. Wiener
IV. SACRIFICES IN THE PRE-MOSAIC AGE
  1. In Egypt
  2. In Babylonia
  3. Among Arabians and Syrians, etc
  4. The Offerings of Cain and Abel
  5. Of Noah
  6. Of Abraham
  7. Of Job
  8. Of Isaac
  9. Of Jacob
  10. Of Israel in Egypt
  11. Of Jethro
  12. Summary and Conclusions
V. THE MOSAIC SACRIFICIAL SYSTEM
  1. The Covenant Sacrifice
  2. The Common Altars
  3. The Consecration of Aaron and His Sons
  4. Before the Golden Calf
  5. The Law of the Burnt Offering
    (1) Ritual for the Offerer
    (2) Ritual for the Priest
    (3) General Laws for the Priest
    (4) Laws in Deuteronomy
  6. The Law of the Meal Offering
    (1) Ritual for the Offerer
    (2) Ritual for the Priest
    (3) General Laws for the Priest
  7. The Law of the Peace Offering
    (1) Ritual for the Offerer
    (2) Ritual for the Priest
    (3) General Laws for the Priest
  8. The Law of the Sin Offering
    (1) At the Consecration of Aaron
    (2) Laws
      (a) The Occasion and Meaning
      (b) Ritual for the Offerer
      (c) Ritual for the Priest
      (d) General Laws for the Priest
      (e) Special Uses of the Sin Offering
        (i) Consecration of Aaron and His Sons
        (ii) Purifications from Uncleanness
        (iii) On the Day of Atonement
        (iv) Other Special Instances
  9. The Guilt Offering
    (1) The Ritual
    (2) Special Laws: Leper, Nazirite, etc
  10. The Wave Offering
  11. The Heave Offering
  12. Drink Offerings
  13. Primitive Nature of the Cultus
VI. SACRIFICES IN THE HISTORY OF ISRAEL
  1. The Situation at Moses' Death
  2. In the Time of Joshua
  3. The Period of the Judges
  4. Times of Samuel and Saul
  5. Days of David and Solomon
  6. In the Northern Kingdom
  7. In the Southern Kingdom to the Exile
  8. In the Exilic and Post-exilic Periods
  9. At Elephantine
  10. Human Sacrifices
  11. Certain Heathen Sacrifices
VII. THE PROPHETS AND SACRIFICES
VIII. SACRIFICE IN THE "WRITINGS"
  1. Proverbs
  2. The Psalms
IX. THE IDEA AND EFFICACY OF SACRIFICES
  1. A Gift of Food to the Deity
  2. Expression of Adoration and Devotion, etc
  3. Means of Purification from Uncleanness
  4. Means of Consecration to Divine Service
  5. Means of Establishing a Community of Life
  6. View of Ritschl
  7. The Sacramental View
  8. Symbol or Expression of Prayer
  9. View of Kautzsch
  10. Vicarious Expiation Theory; Objections
  11. Typology of Sacrifice
LITERATURE

I. Terms and Definitions.—זֶבַח, *zebhaḥ*, "sacrifice"; עֹלָה, *'ōlāh*, "burnt offering"; חֲטָאָה, *ḥăṭā'āh*, חַטָּאת, *ḥaṭṭā'th*, "sin offering"; אָשָׁם, *'āshām*, "guilt" or "trespass offering"; שֶׁלֶם, *shelem*, שְׁלָמִים, *shelāmīm*, "peace offerings"; מִנְחָה, *minḥāh*, "offering," "present"; זֶבַח שְׁלָמִים, *zebhaḥ shelāmīm*, "sacrifice of peace offerings"; זֶבַח הַתּוֹדָה, *zebhaḥ ha-tōdhāh*, "thank offerings"; זֶבַח נְדָבָה, *zebhaḥ nedhābhāh*, "free-will offerings"; זֶבַח נֶדֶר, *zebhaḥ nedher*, "votive offerings"; תְּנוּפָה, *tenūphāh*, "wave offering"; תְּרוּמָה, *terūmāh*, "heave offering"; קָרְבָּן, *ḳorbān*, "oblation," "gift"; אִשֶּׁה, *'ishsheh*, "fire offering"; נֶסֶךְ, *neṣekh*, "drink offering"; כָּלִיל, *kālīl*, "whole burnt offering"; חַג, *ḥagh*, "feast"; לְבוֹנָה, *lebhōnāh*, "frankincense"; קְטוֹרָה, *ḳeṭōrāh*, קְטֹרֶת, *ḳeṭōreth*, "odor," "incense"; מֶלַח, *melaḥ*, "salt"; שֶׁמֶן, *shemen*, "oil":

Zebhaḥ: a "slaughtered animal," a "sacrifice," general term for animals used in sacrifice, including burnt offerings, peace offerings, thank offerings, and all sacrifices offered to the Deity and eaten at the festivals. More particularly it refers to the flesh eaten by the worshippers after the fat parts had been burned on the altar and the priest had received his portion.

'Ōlāh: a "burnt offering," sometimes whole burnt offering. Derived from the vb. *'ālāh*, "to go up." It may mean "that which goes up to the altar" (Knobel, Wellhausen, Nowack, etc), or "that which goes up in smoke to the sky" (Bähr, Delitzsch, Dillmann, etc); sometimes used synonymously with *kālīl* (q.v.). The term applies to beast or fowl when entirely consumed upon the altar, the hide of the beast being taken by the priest. This was perhaps the most solemn of the sacrifices, and symbolized worship in the full sense, i.e. adoration, devotion, dedication, supplication, and at times expiation.

Ḥăṭā'āh, ḥaṭṭā'th: a "sin offering," a special kind, first mentioned in the Mosaic legislation. It is essentially expiatory, intended to restore covenant relations with the Deity. The special features were: (1) the blood must be sprinkled before the sanctuary, put upon the horns of the altar of incense and poured out at the base of the altar of burnt offering; (2) the flesh was holy, not to be touched by worshipper, but eaten by the priest only. The special ritual of the Day of Atonement centers around the sin offering.

'Ashām: "guilt offering," "trespass offering" (AV; in Isa **53** 10, AV and RV "an offering for sin," ARVm "trespass offering"). A special kind of sin offering introduced in the Mosaic Law and concerned with offences against God and man that could be estimated by a money value and thus covered by compensation or restitution accompanying the offering. A ram of different degrees of value, and worth at least two shekels, was the usual victim, and it must be accompanied by full restitution with an additional fifth of the value of the damage. The leper and Nazirite could offer he-lambs. The guilt toward God was expiated by the blood poured out, and the guilt toward men by the restitution and fine. The calling of the Servant an *'āshām* (Isa **53** 10) shows the value attached to this offering.

Shelem, shelāmīm: "peace offering," generally used in the pl., *shelāmīm*, only once *shĕlem* (Am **5** 22). These were sacrifices of friendship expressing or promoting peaceful relations with the Deity, and almost invariably accompanied by a meal or feast, an occasion of great joy. They are sometimes called *zebhāḥīm*, sometimes *zebhaḥ shelāmīm*, and were of different kinds, such as *zebhaḥ ha-tōdhāh*, "thank offerings," which expressed the gratitude of the giver because of some blessings, *zebhaḥ nedhābhāh*, "free-will offerings," bestowed on the Deity out of a full heart, and *zebhaḥ nedher*, "votive offerings," which were offered in fulfilment of a vow.

Minḥāh: "meal offering" (RV), "meat offering" (AV), a gift or presentation, at first applied to both bloody and unbloody offerings (Gen **4** 5), but in Moses' time confined to cereals, whether raw or roasted, ground to flour or baked and mixed with oil and frankincense. These cereals were the produce of man's labor with the soil, not fruits, etc, and thus represented the necessities and results of life, if not life itself. They were the invariable accompaniment of animal sacrifices, and in one instance could be substituted for them (see SIN OFFERING). The term *minḥāh* describes a gift or token of friendship (Isa **39** 1), an act of homage (1 S **10** 27; 1 K **10** 25), tribute (Jgs **3** 15.17 f), propitiation to a friend wronged (Gen **32** 13.18 [Heb **14** 19]), to procure favor or assistance (Gen **43** 11 ff; Hos **10** 6).

Tenūphāh: "wave offering," usually the breast, the priest's share of the peace offerings, which was waved before the altar by both offerer and priest together (the exact motion is not certain), symbolic of its presentation to Deity and given back by Him to the offerer to be used in the priests' service.

T^{e}rūmāh: "heave offering," something lifted up, or, properly, separated from the rest and given to the service of the Deity. Usually the right shoulder or thigh was thus separated for the priest. The term is applied to products of the soil, or portion of land separated unto the Divine service, etc.

Ḳorbān: "an oblation," or "offering"; another generic term for all kinds of offerings, animal, vegetable, or even gold and silver. Derived from the vb. *ḳārabh,* "to draw near," it signifies what is drawn or brought near and given to God.

'Ishsheh: "fire offering," applied to offerings made by fire and usually bloody offerings, but at times to the *minḥāh,* the sacred bread and frankincense placed on the tables as a memorial, part of which was burned with the frankincense, the bulk, however, going to the priest. The gift was thus presented through fire to the Deity as a sort of etherealized food.

Nesekh: "drink offering," or "libation," a liquid offering of wine, rarely water, sometimes of oil, and usually accompanying the *'ōlāh,* but often with the peace offerings.

Kālīl: "whole burnt offering," the entire animal being burned upon the altar. Sometimes used synonymously with *'ōlāh.* A technical term among the Carthaginians.

Ḥagh: a "feast," used metaphorically for a sacrificial feast because the meat of the sacrifices constituted the material of the feast.

L^{e}bhōnāh: "frankincense," "incense," used in combination with the meal offerings and burnt offerings and burned also upon the altar in the holy place. See INCENSE.

Ḳ^{e}ṭōrāh, ḳ^{e}ṭōreth: "smoke," "odor of sacrifice," or incense ascending as a sweet savor and supposed to be pleasing and acceptable to God.

Melaḥ: "salt," used in all sacrifices because of its purifying and preserving qualities.

Shemen: "oil," generally olive oil, used with the meal offerings of cakes and wafers, etc.

Sacrifice is thus a complex and comprehensive term. In its simplest form it may be defined as "a gift to God." It is a presentation to Deity of some material object, the possession of the offerer, as an act of worship. It may be to attain, restore, maintain or to celebrate friendly relations with the Deity. It is religion in action—in early times, almost the whole of religion—an inseparable accompaniment to all religious exercises. Few or many motives may actuate it. It may be wholly piacular and expiatory, or an offering of food as a gift to God; it may be practically a bribe, or a prayer, an expression of dependence, obligation and thanksgiving. It may express repentance, faith, adoration, or all of these combined. It was the one and only way of approach to God. Theophrastus defines it as expressing homage, gratitude and need. Hubert and Mauss define it as "a religious act which by the consecration of the victim modifies the moral state of the sacrificer, or of certain material objects which he has in view, i.e., either confers sanctity or removes it and its analogue, impiety."

II. Origin and Nature of Sacrifices.—The beginnings of sacrifice are hidden in the mysteries of prehistoric life. The earliest narrative in Gen records the fact, but gives no account of the origin and primary idea. The custom is sanctioned by the sacred writings, and later on the long-established custom was adopted and systematized in the Mosaic Law. The practice was almost universal. The Vedas have their elaborate rituals. Some Sem peoples, Greeks, Romans, Africans, and Indians of Mexico offered human sacrifices. It is unknown in Australia, but even there something akin to it exists, for some natives offer a portion of a kind of honey, others offer a pebble or a spear to their god. For this practically universal habit of the race, several solutions are offered.

One view maintains that God Himself initiated the rite by Divine order at the beginnings of human history. Such a theory implies a monotheistic faith on the part of primitive man. This theory was strongly held by many of the Reformed theologians, and was based mainly on the narrative in Gen **4** 4 f. Abel offered an acceptable sacrifice, and, according to He **11** 4, this was because of his faith. Faber makes a strong plea as follows: Since faith was what made the sacrifice acceptable to God, this faith must have been based upon a positive enactment of God in the past. Without this Divine positive enactment to guarantee its truthfulness, faith, in Abel, would have been superstition. In other words, faith, in order to be truly based and properly directed, must have a revelation from God, a positive expression of the Divine will. Fairbairn, in his *Typology,* goes further and holds that the skins wherewith Adam and Eve were clothed were from animals which had been slain in sacrifices. This is entirely without support in the narrative. The theory of a Divine order cannot be maintained on the basis of the Bib. narrative. Moreover, it involves certain assumptions regarding the nature of faith and revelation which are not generally held in this age. A revelation is not necessarily a positive Divine command, an external thing, and faith may be just as real and true without such a revelation as with it. That there may have been such a revelation cannot be denied, but it is not a necessary or probable explanation.

1. Theory of a Divine Revelation

2. Theories of a Human Origin

(1) *The gift-theory.*—By this it is held that sacrifices were originally presents to the deity which the offerer took for granted would be received with pleasure and even gratitude. Good relations would thus be established with the god and favors would be secured. Such motives, while certainly true among many heathen people, were obviously based upon low conceptions of the deity. They were either Nature-spirits, ancestral ghosts or fetiches which needed what was given, and of course the god was placed under obligations and his favor obtained. Or, the god may have been conceived of as a ruler, a king or chief, as was the custom in the East.

Cicero vouches for such a view when he says: "Let not the impious dare to appease the gods with gifts. Let them hearken to Plato, who warns them that there can be no doubt what God's disposition to them will be, since even a good man will refuse to accept presents from the wicked" (*HDB,* IV, 331*a*). This view of sacrifice prevails in classical literature. Spencer therefore thinks it is self-evident that this was the idea of primitive man. Tylor and Herbert Spencer also find the origin of sacrifices in the idea of a gift, whether to the deity or to dead ancestors, food being placed for them, and this afterward comes to be regarded as a sacrifice. Such a view gives no account of the peculiar value attached to the blood, or to the burnt offerings. It may account for some heathen systems of sacrifice, but can help in no degree in understanding the Bib. sacrifices.

(2) *The magic theory.*—There are two slightly variant forms of this: (*a*) that of R. C. Thompson (*Sem Magic, Its Origins and Developments,* 175–218), who holds that a sacrificial animal serves as a substitute victim offered to a demon whose activity has brought the offerer into trouble; the aim of the priest is to entice or drive the malignant spirit out of the sick or sinful man into the sacrificial victim where it can be isolated or destroyed; (*b*) that of L. Marillier, who holds that sacrifice in its origin is essentially a magical rite. The liberation of a magical force by the effusion of the victim's blood will bend the god to the will of the man. From this arose under the "cult of the dead" the gift-theory of sacrifice. Men sought to ally themselves with the god in particular by purifying a victim and effecting communion with the god by the application of the blood to the altar, or by the sacrifice of the animal and the contact of the sacrificer with its blood. Such theories give no account of the burnt offerings, meal offerings and sin offerings, disconnect them entirely from any sense of sin or estrangement from God, and divest them of all piacular value. They may account for certain depraved and heathen systems, but not for the Biblical.

(3) *The table-bond theory.*—Ably advocated by Wellhausen and W. R. Smith, this view holds that sacrifices were meals which the worshippers and the god shared, partaking of the same food and thus establishing a firmer bond of fellowship between them. Sykes (*Nature of*

Sacrifices, 75) first advocated this, holding that the efficacy of sacrifices "is the fact that eating and drinking were the known and ordinary symbols of friendship and were the usual rites in engaging in covenants and leagues." Thus sacrifices are more than gifts; they are deeds of hospitality which knit god and worshipper together. W. R. Smith has expounded the idea into the notion that the common meal unites physically those who partake of it. Though this view may contain an element of truth in regard to certain Arabian customs, it does not help much to account for Bible sacrifices. As A. B. Davidson says, "It fails utterly to account for the burnt offering, which was one of the earliest, most solemn and at times the most important of all the sacrifices."

(4) *The sacramental communion theory.*—This is a modification of the table-bond theory. The basis of it is the totemistic idea of reverencing an animal which is believed to share with man the Divine nature. On certain solemn occasions this animal would be sacrificed to furnish a feast. At this meal, according to men's savage notions, they literally "ate the god," and thus incorporated into themselves the physical, the intellectual and the moral qualities which characterized the animal. If the Divine life dwelt in certain animals, then a part of that precious life would be distributed among all the people (*RS*², 313). In some cases the blood is drunk by the worshippers, thus imbibing the life. Sometimes, as in the case of the sacred camel, they devoured the quivering flesh before the animal was really dead, and the entire carcase was eaten up before morning.

The brilliant work of W. R. Smith has not been universally accepted. L. Marillier has criticized it along several lines. It is by no means certain that totemism prevailed so largely among Semites and there is no evidence of its existence in Israel. Also, if an original bond of friendship existed between the god and the kin, there is no need to maintain it by such sacrificial rites. There is no clear instance of this having been done. If on the other hand there was no common bond between the god and the people but that of a common meal, it does not appear that the god is a totem god. There is no reason why the animal should have been a totem. In any case, this idea of sacrifice could hardly have been anything but a slow growth, and consequently not the origin of sacrifice. Hubert and Mauss also point out that W. R. Smith is far from having established the historical or the logical connection between the common meal and the other kinds of sacrifices. Under *piacula* he confuses purification, propitiation and expiations. His attempts to show that purifications of magical character are late and not sacrificial do not succeed. Smith's theory is mainly the sacramental, though he does recognize the honorific and piacular element. The theory may be applicable to some of the heathen or savage feasts of the Arabs, but not to the practices of the Hebrews (see *Enc Brit*, XXIII, 981).

(5) *The homage theory.*—This has been advocated by Warburton and F. D. Maurice. The idea is that sacrifices were originally an expression of homage and dependence. Man naturally felt impelled to seek closer communion with God, not so much from a sense of guilt as from a sense of dependence and a desire to show homage and obedience. In giving expression to this, primitive man had recourse to acts rather than words and thoughts. Thus sacrifice was an acted prayer, rather than a prayer in words. It was an expression of his longings and aspirations, his reverence and submission. There is much truth in this view; the elements of prayer—dependence and submission—enter into some sacrifices, the burnt offerings in particular; but it does not account for all kinds of offerings.

(6) *The piacular theory.*—This holds that sacrifices are fundamentally expiatory or atoning, and the death of the beast is a vicarious expiation of the sins of the offerer. Hubert and Mauss admit that in all sacrifices there are some ideas of purchase or substitution, though these may not have issued from some primitive form. The unifying principle in all sacrifices is that the Divine is put in communication with the profane by the intermediary—the victim—which may be piacular or honorific. It is thus a messenger, a means of divination, a means of alimenting the eternal life of the species, a source of magical energy which the rite diffuses over objects in its neighborhood. Westermarck (*Origin of Moral Ideas*) makes the original idea in sacrifice a *piaculum*, a substitute for the offerer.

This view is the most simple, the most natural, and the only one that can explain certain sacrifices. Man felt himself under liability to punishment or death. The animal was his, it had life, it was of value, and perchance the god would accept that life in place of his. He felt that it would be accepted, and thus the animal was sacrificed. The offerer in a sense gives up part of himself. The beast must be his own; no sacrifice can be made of another person's property (2 S **24** 24*a*). The true spirit of sacrifice appears in a willingness to acknowledge God's right to what is best and dearest (Gen **12**).

Objection is raised to this by A. B. Davidson (*OT Theology*), Paterson (*HDB*, IV, 331) and others, on the ground that such an origin represents too advanced a stage of ethical thought and reflection for primitive man. We question seriously whether this be an advanced stage of moral reflection. On the contrary, it represents a very simple and primitive stage. The feeling that sin of some kind is never absent from human life, and that its true penalty is death, has been inseparable from the human heart's sense of sin. What could be more simple and natural than to take an innocent animal and offer it in place of himself, hoping that the Deity would accept it instead? Nor is there much force in Professor Paterson's objection that sacrifices were preponderantly joyous in character and therefore could not be offered as an expiation. This joyous character belongs to such sacrifices as peace offerings and thank offerings, but does not belong to the *'ōlāh* and others. In most cases the joyous feast *followed* the killing of the animal by which the expiation was accomplished, and the feast was joyous *because* atonement had been made. In fact, many sacrifices were of the most solemn character and represented the deepest and most serious emotions of the heart.

(7) *Originating in religious instincts.*—Neither the theory of an objective Divine revelation, nor of a human origin will account for the universality and variety of sacrifices. The truth lies in a proper combination of the two. The notion of offering a gift to the Deity arose out of the religious instincts of the human heart, which in an early period had a consciousness of something wrong between itself and God, and that this something would mean death sooner or later. Added to these true instincts was the Omnipresent Spirit to guide men in giving expression. What could be more simple and primitive than to offer something possessing life? Of course the notion originated in simple and childlike ideas of God, and its real motive was not to gratify God by sharing a meal with Him, or to gain His favor by a bribe, but to present Him with something that represented a part of the offerer which might be accepted in his stead. Thus sacrifices became the leading features of the religious life of primitive man. Naturally other ideas would be added, such as a gift of food by fire to the Deity, the peace offerings, etc, to celebrate the friendly relations with God, the thank offerings, the sin offerings, etc, all of which naturally and logically developed from the primitive idea. It might be expected that there would be many corruptions and

abuses, that the sense of sin would be obscured or lost among some peoples, and the idea of sacrifice correspondingly degraded. Such has been the case, and as well might we try to understand man at his best by studying the aboriginal tribes of Africa and Australia, or the inmates of asylums and penitentiaries, as to attempt to understand the Bible ideas in sacrifices by studying the cults of those heathen and savage tribes of Semites, etc.

III. Classification of Sacrifices.—Maimonides was among the first to classify them, and he divided them into two kinds: (1) Those on behalf of the whole congregation, fixed by statute, time, number and ritual being specified. This would include burnt, meal and peace offerings with their accompaniments. (2) Those on behalf of the individual, whether by virtue of his connection with the community or as a private person. These would be burnt, sin and guilt offerings with their accompaniments.

1. Maimonides

Others, such as W. R. Smith, classify them as: (1) honorific, or designed to render homage, devotion, or adoration, such as burnt, meal and peace offerings; (2) piacular, designed to expiate or make atonement for the errors of the people, i.e. burnt, sin and guilt offerings; (3) communistic, intended to establish the bond between the god and the worshipper, such as peace offerings.

2. W. R. Smith and Others

Oehler divides them into two classes, viz.: (1) those which assume that the covenant relation is undisturbed, such as peace offerings; (2) those intended to do away with any disturbance in the relation and to set it right, such as burnt, sin and guilt offerings.

3. Oehler

Professor Paterson and others divide them into three: (1) animal sacrifices, burnt, peace, sin and guilt offerings; (2) vegetable sacrifices, meal offerings, shewbread, etc; (3) liquid and incense offerings; wine, oil, water, etc.

4. Paterson

H. M. Wiener offers a more suggestive and scientific division (*Essays on Pentateuchal Criticism*, 200 f): (1) customary lay offerings, such as had from time immemorial been offered on rude altars of earth or stone, without priest, used and regulated by Moses and in more or less general use until the exile, viz. burnt, meal and peace offerings; (2) statutory individual offerings, introduced by Moses, offered by laymen with priestly assistance and at the religious capital, i.e. burnt, peace, meal, sin and guilt offerings; (3) statutory national offerings introduced by Moses and offered by the priest at the religious capital, viz. burnt, meal, peace and sin offerings.

5. Wiener

IV. Sacrifices in the Pre-Mosaic Age.—Out of the obscure period of origins emerged the dimly lighted period of ancient history. Everywhere sacrifices existed and sometimes abounded as an essential part of religion. The spade of the archaeologist, and the researches of scholars help us understand the pre-Mosaic period.

In Egypt—probably from the beginning of the 4th millennium BC—there were sacrifices and sacrificial systems. Temples at Abydos, Thebes, On, etc, were great priestly centers with high priests, lower priests, rituals and sacrifices in abundance. Animals, birds, meal, wine and beer, incense and flowers were offered, for both the dead and the gods, chiefly supplies, sometimes expiatory. The sacrifices were not burned and human beings were not offered (Kyle, *Recueil de Traveaux*, XXVII). In these offerings there were many resemblances to the Heb gifts, and many significant exceptions. Moses would be somewhat familiar with these practices though not with the details of the ritual. He would appreciate the unifying power of a national religious center. It is inconceivable that in such an age a national leader and organizer like Moses would not take special care to institute such a system.

1. In Egypt

In Babylonia, from the year 3000 BC or thereabouts, according to E. Meyer (*Geschichte des Alterthums*), there were many centers of worship such as Eridu, Nippur, Agade, Erech, Ur, Nisin, Larsa, Sippar, etc. These and others continued for centuries with elaborate systems of worship, sacrifices, temples, priesthoods, etc. Considerably over 100 temples and sanctuaries are mentioned on inscriptions, and several hundreds in the lit. and tablets, so that Babylonia was studded with temples and edifices for the gods. At all these, sacrifices were constantly offered—animal and vegetable. A long list of the offerings of King Gudea includes oxen, sheep, goats, lambs, fish, birds (i.e. eagles and doves), dates, milk, greens (Jastrow, in *HDB*, V, 580 f, s.v.). The sacrifices provided an income for the priests, as did the Mosaic system at a later time. It had long passed the stage when it was supposed to furnish a meal for the god. A sacrifice always accompanied a consultation with a priest, and was really an assessment for the services rendered. It was not a voluntary offering or ritualistic observance. The priests on their own behalf offered a daily sacrifice, as in the Mosaic Law, and likewise on special occasions, to insure the good will of the gods they served. It seems certain that in some of the larger centers of worship animals were offered up twice a day, morning and evening. At these sacrifices certain portions were consumed on the altar, the rest belonging to the priest. The similarity of much of this to the Mosaic institutions is obvious. That the culture and civilization of Babylon was known to Egypt and Israel with other nations is shown clearly by the Am Tab. Special sacrifices on special occasions were offered in Babylonia as in Israel. As Jastrow says, "In the Heb codes, both as regards the purely legal portions and those sections dealing with religious ritual, Bab methods of legal procedure and of ritual developed in Bab temples must be taken into consideration as determining factors." We do not doubt that Moses made use of many elements found in the Egyp and Bab systems, and added to or subtracted from or purified as occasion required. As sacrificial systems and ritual had been in use more than a millennium before Moses, there is absolutely no need to suppose that Israel's ritual was a thousand years in developing, and was completed after the exile. To do so is to turn history upside down.

2. In Babylonia

Among the nomads and tribes of Arabia and Syria, sacrifices had been common for millenniums before Moses. The researches of Wellhausen and W. R. Smith are valuable here, whatever one may think of their theories. The offerings were usually from the flocks and herds, sometimes from the spoils taken in war which had been appropriated as their own. The occasions were many and various, and the ritual was very simple. A rude altar of earth or stone, or one stone, a sacred spot, the offerer killing the victim and burning all, or perhaps certain parts and eating the remainder with the clan or family, constituted the customary details. Sometimes wild animals were offered. Babylonians, Phoenicians and Arabs offered gazelles, but the Hebrews did not. Arabs would sometimes sacrifice a captive youth, while the Carthaginians chose some of the fairest of the captives for offerings by night. Assyr kings sometimes sacrificed captive kings. The Canaanites and others constantly sacrificed children, esp. the firstborn.

3. Nomads and Tribes of Arabia and Syria

The account of the offerings of Cain and Abel (Gen **4** 4 f) shows that the ceremony dates from almost the beginnings of the human race. The custom of offering the firstlings and first-fruits had already begun. Arabian tribes later had a similar custom. Cain's offering was cereal and is called *minḥāh*, "a gift" or "presentation." The same term is applied to Abel's. There is no hint that the bloody sacrifice was *in itself* better than the unbloody one, but it is shown that sacrifice without a right attitude of heart is not acceptable to God. This same truth is emphasized by the prophets and others, and is needed in this day as much as then. In this case the altars would be of the common kind and no priest was needed. The sacrifices were an act of worship, adoration, dependence, prayer and possibly propitiation.

4. Cain and Abel

The sacrifices of Noah followed and celebrated the epochal and awe-inspiring event of leaving the ark and beginning life anew. He offered burnt offerings of all the clean animals (Gen **8** 20 ff). On such a solemn occasion only an *‛ōlāh* would suffice. The custom of using domestic animals had arisen at this time. The sacrifices expressed adoration, recognition of God's power and sovereignty, and a gift to please Him, for it is said He smelled a sweet savor and was pleased. It was an odor of satisfaction or restfulness. Whether or not the idea of expiation was included is difficult to prove.

5. Noah

Abraham lived at a time when sacrifices and religion were virtually identical. No mention is made of his offering at Ur or Ḥaran, but on his arrival at Shechem he erected an altar (Gen **12** 7). At Beth-el also (ver 8), and on his return from Egypt he worshipped there (Gen **13** 4). Such sacrifices expressed adora-

6. Abraham

tion and prayer and probably propitiation. They constituted worship, which is a complex exercise. At Hebron he built an altar (Gen **13** 18), officiating always as his own priest. In **15** 4 ff he offers a "covenant" sacrifice, when the animals were slain, divided, the parts set opposite each other, and prepared for the appearance of the other party to the covenant. The exact idea in the killing of these animals may be difficult to find, but the effect is to give the occasion great solemnity and the highest religious sanction. What was done with the carcases afterward is not told. That animals were slain for food with no thought of sacrifice is shown by the narrative in ch **18,** where Abraham had a calf slain for the meal. This is opposed to one of the chief tenets of the Wellhausen school, which maintains that all slaughtering of animals was sacrificial until the 7th cent. BC. In ch **22** Abraham attempts to offer up Isaac as a burnt offering, as was probably the custom of his neighbors. That he attempted it shows that the practice was not shocking to his ethical nature. It tested the strength of his devotion to God, shows the right spirit in sacrifices, and teaches for all time that God does not desire human sacrifice—a beast will do. What God does want is the obedient heart. Abraham continued his worship at Beer-sheba (Gen **21** 33).

7. Book of Job

Whatever may be the date of the writing of the Book of Job, the saint himself is represented as living in the Patriarchal age. He constantly offered sacrifices on behalf of his children (**1** 5), "sanctifying" them. His purpose no doubt was to atone for possible sin. The sacrifices were mainly expiatory. This is true also of the sacrifices of his friends (**42** 7–9).

8. Isaac

Isaac seems to have had a permanent altar at Beer-sheba and to have regularly offered sacrifices. Adoration, expiation and supplication would constitute his chief motives (Gen **26** 25).

9. Jacob

Jacob's first recorded sacrifice was the pouring of the oil upon the stone at Beth-el (Gen **28** 18). This was consecration or dedication in recognition of the awe-inspiring presence of the Deity. After his covenant with Laban he offered sacrifices (*zᵉbhāḥim*) and they ate bread (Gen **31** 54). At Shechem, Jacob erected an altar (Gen **33** 20). At Beth-el (**35** 7) and at Beer-sheba he offered sacrifices to Isaac's God (**46** 1).

10. Israel in Egypt

While the Israelites were in Egypt they would be accustomed to spring sacrifices and spring feasts, for these had been common among the Arabs and Syrians, etc, for centuries. Nabataean inscriptions testify to this. Egyp sacrifices have been mentioned (see above). At these spring festivals it was probably customary to offer the firstlings of the flocks (cf Ex **13** 15). At the harvest festivals sacrificial feasts were celebrated. It was to some such feast Moses said Israel as a people wished to go in the wilderness (Ex **3** 18; **5** 3 ff; **7** 16). Pharaoh understood and asked who was to go (Ex **10** 8). Moses demanded flocks and herds for the feast (**10** 9). Pharaoh would keep the flocks, etc (**10** 24), but Moses said they must offer sacrifices and burnt offerings (**10** 25 f).

The sacrifice of the Passover soon occurs (Ex **12** 3–11). That the Hebrews had been accustomed to sacrifice their own firstborn at this season has no support and is altogether improbable (Frazer, *Golden Bough*³, pt. III, 175 f). The whole ceremony is very primitive and has retained its primitiveness to the end. The choosing of the lamb or kid, the killing at a certain time, the family gathered in the home, the carcase roasted whole, eaten that night, and the remainder, if any, burned, while the feasters had staff in hand, etc, all this was continued. The blood in this case protected from the Deity, and the whole ceremony was "holy" and only for the circumcised. Frazer in his *Golden Bough* gives a very different interpretation.

11. Jethro

As a priest of Midian Jethro was an expert in sacrificing. On meeting Moses and the people he offered both *'ōlāh* and *zᵉbhāḥim* and made a feast (Ex **18** 12).

12. Summary and Conclusions

From the above it is evident that sacrifices were almost the substance of religion in that ancient world. From hilltops and temples innumerable, the smoke of sacrifices was constantly rising heavenward. Burnt offerings and peace offerings were well known. Moses, in establishing a religion, must have a sacrificial system. He had abundance of materials to choose from, and under Divine guidance would adopt such rules and regulations as the pedagogic plans and purposes of God would require in preparing for better things.

V. The Mosaic Sacrificial System.—The fundamental function of Moses' work was to establish the covenant between Israel and God.

1. The Covenant Sacrifice

This important transaction took place at Sinai and was accompanied by solemn sacrifices. The foundation principle was *obedience,* not sacrifices (Ex **19** 4–8). No mention is made of these at the time, as they were incidental—mere by-laws to the constitution. The center of gravity in Israel's religion is now shifted from sacrifices to obedience and loyalty to Jeh. Sacrifices were helps to that end and without obedience were worthless. This is in exact accordance with Jer **7** 21 ff. God did not speak unto the fathers at this time about sacrifices; He did speak about obedience.

The covenant having been made, the terms and conditions are laid down by Moses and accepted by the people (Ex **24** 3). The Decalogue and Covenant Code are given, an altar is built, burnt and peace offerings of oxen are slain by young men servants of Moses, not by priests, and blood is sprinkled on the altar (**24** 4 ff). The blood would symbolize the community of life between Jeh and Israel, and consecrated the altar. The Law was read, the pledge again given, and Moses sprinkled the representatives of the people, consecrating them also (**24** 7 f). Ascending the mount, they had a vision of God, held a feast before Him, showing the joys and privileges of the new relationship. The striking feature of these ceremonies is the use of the blood. It is expiatory and consecrating, it is life offered to God, it consecrates the altar and the people: they are now acceptable to God and dare approach Him and feast with Him. There is no idea of God's drinking the blood. The entire ritual is far removed from the crass features of common Sem worship.

2. The Common Altars

In the Covenant Code, which the people accepted, the customary altars are not abolished, but regulated (Ex **20** 24 ff). This law expressly applies to the time when they shall be settled in Canaan. 'In the whole place where I cause my name to be remembered,' etc (ver 24 m). No need to change the reading to "in every place where I cause," etc, as the Wellhausen school does for obvious reasons. All the land was eligible. On such rude altars sacrifices were allowed. This same law is implied in Dt **16** 21, a passage either ignored or explained away by the Wellhausen school (see Wiener, *Essays in Pentateuchal Criticism,* 200 f). Moses commanded Joshua in accordance with it (Dt **27** 5 ff). Joshua, Gideon, Jephthah, Samuel,

Saul, David, Elijah and many others used such altars. There were altars at Shechem (Josh **24** 1.26), Mizpah in Gilead (Jgs **11** 11), Gilgal (1 S **13** 9). High places were chiefly used until the times of Hezekiah and Josiah, when they were abolished because of their corruptions, etc. All such altars were perfectly legitimate and in fact necessary, until there was a central capital and sanctuary in Jerus. The customary burnt and peace offerings with the worshipper officiating were the chief factors. Heathen sacrifices and the use of heathen altars were strictly forbidden (Ex **22** 20 [Heb 19]; **34** 15).

3. The Consecration of Aaron and His Sons

The altar used at the consecration of Aaron and his sons was a "horned" or official altar, the central one. The offerings were a bullock, two rams, unleavened bread, etc (Ex **29** 1–4), and were brought to the door of the sanctuary. The ritual consisted of Aaron laying his hand on the bullock's head, designating it as his substitute (**29** 10), killing it before the tent of meeting (ver 11), smearing some blood on the horns of the altar, and pouring the rest at its base (ver 12). The blood consecrated the altar, the life was given as atonement for sins, the fat parts were burned upon the altar as food for God, and the flesh and remainder were burned without the camp (vs 13.14). This is a sin offering—*ḥaṭṭā'th*—the first time the term is used. Probably introduced by Moses, it was intended to be piacular and to "cover" possible sin. One ram was next slain, blood was sprinkled round about the altar, flesh was cut in pieces, washed and piled on the altar, then burned as an offering by fire (*'ishsheh*) unto God as a burnt offering, an odor of a sweet savor (vs 15–18). The naïve and primitive nature of this idea is apparent. The other ram, the ram of consecration, is slain, blood is smeared on Aaron's right ear, thumb and great toe; in the case of his sons likewise. The blood is sprinkled on the altar round about; some upon the garments of Aaron and his sons (vs 19–21). Certain parts are waved before Jeh along with the bread, and are then burned upon the altar (vs 22–25). The breast is offered as a wave offering (*t^enūphāh*), and the right thigh or shoulder as a heave offering (*t^erūmāh*). These portions here first mentioned were the priests' portion for all time to come, although this particular one went to Moses, since he officiated (vs 26–30). The flesh must be boiled in a holy place, and must be eaten by Aaron and his sons only, and at the sanctuary. What was left till morning must be burned (vs 31–34). Consecrated to a holy service it was dangerous for anyone else to touch it, or the Divine wrath would flame forth. The same ceremony on each of the seven days atoned for, cleansed and consecrated the altar to the service of Jeh, and it was most holy (vs 35–37). The altar of incense is ordered (Ex **30** 1), and Aaron is to put the blood of the sin offering once a year upon its horns to consecrate it.

4. Sacrifices before the Golden Calf

When the golden calf was made an altar was erected, burnt and peace offerings were presented. From the latter a feast was made, the people followed the usual habits at such festivals, went to excess and joined in revelry. Moses' ear quickly detected the nature of the sounds. The covenant was now broken and no sacrifice was available for this sin. Vengeance was executed on 3,000 Israelites. Moses mightily interceded with God. A moral reaction was begun; new tables of the Law were made with more stringent laws against idols and idol worship (Ex **32** 1–35).

At the setting-up of the tabernacle burnt and meal offerings were sacrificed (Ex **40** 29). The law of the burnt offering is found in Lev **1**.

5. Law of the Burnt Offering (*'ōlāh*)

Common altars and customary burnt offerings needed no minute regulations, but this ritual was intended primarily for the priest, and was taught to the people as needed. They were for the statutory individual and national offering upon the "horned" altar before the sanctuary. Already the daily burnt offerings of the priests had been provided for (Ex **29** 38–42). The burnt offering is here called *ḳorbān*, "oblation."

(1) *The ritual for the offerer* (*Lev **1** 3–17*).—This may have been from the herd or flock or fowls, brought to the tent of meeting; hands were laid (heavily) upon its head designating it as the offerer's substitute, it was killed, flayed and cut in pieces. If of the flock, it was to be killed on the north side of the altar; if a fowl, the priest must kill it.

(2) *The ritual for the priest* (*Lev **1** 3–17*).—If a bullock or of the flock, the priest was to sprinkle the blood round about the altar, put on the fire, lay the wood and pieces of the carcase, wash the inwards, legs, etc, and burn it all as a sweet savor to God. If a fowl, he must wring the neck, drain out the blood on the side of the altar, cast the crop, filth, etc, among the ashes, rend the wings without dividing the bird and burn the carcase on the altar.

(3) *General laws for the priest.*—The burnt offering must be continued every morning and every evening (Ex **29** 38 f; Nu **28** 3–8). At the fulfilment of his vow the Nazirite must present it before God and offer it upon the altar through the priest (Nu **6** 14. 16): on the Sabbath, two lambs (Nu **28** 9); on the first of the month, two bullocks, one ram and seven lambs (Nu **28** 11); on the day of first-fruits, the same (Nu **28** 27); on the 1st day of the 7th month, one bullock, one ram, seven lambs (Nu **29** 8); on the 15th day, 13 bullocks, two rams, 14 lambs, the number of bullocks diminishing daily until the 7th day, when seven bullocks, two rams, 14 lambs were offered (Nu **29** 12–34); on the 22nd day of this month one bullock, one ram and seven lambs were offered (Nu **29** 35.36). Non-Israelites were permitted to offer the *'ōlāh*, but no other sacrifices (Lev **17** 8; **22** 18.25).

(4) *Laws in Dt* (***12** 6.13.14.27; **27** 6*).—Anticipating a central sanctuary in the future, the lawgiver counsels the people to bring their offerings there (**12** 6.11); they must be careful not to offer them in any place (ver 13), but must patronize the central sanctuary (ver 14). In the meantime common altars and customary sacrifices were allowable and generally necessary (**16** 21; **27** 6).

6. Law of the Meal Offering (*minḥāh*)

The term "meal offering" is here confined to offerings of flour or meal, etc (AV "meat-offering"), and was first used at the consecration of Aaron and his sons (Ex **29** 41). These must not be offered on the altar of incense (Ex **30** 9); were used at the completion of the tabernacle (**40** 29); and always with the morning and evening burnt offerings.

(1) *The ritual for the offerer* (*Lev **2** 1–16*).—It must be of fine flour, with oil and frankincense added, and brought to the priest; if *baked in the oven*, unleavened cakes mingled with oil, or wafers and oil; if of the *baking pan*, fine flour mingled with oil parted into pieces and oil thereon; if of the *frying pan*, the same ingredients. Leaven and honey must never be used as they quickly become corrupt. Every offering must be seasoned with salt. If of the first-fruits (*bikkūrīm*), it should consist of corn in the ear, parched with oil and frankincense upon it.

(2) *The ritual for the priest* (*Lev **2** 1–16*).—This required him to take out a handful with the oil and frankincense thereon and burn it as a memorial upon the altar. The remainder was holy and belonged to the priest. Of the cakes, after bringing them to the altar, he was to take a portion, burn it and appropriate the remainder; the same with the first-fruits.

(3) *General laws for the priest* (*Lev **6** 14–18 [Heb 7–11], etc*).—He might eat his portion without leaven in the holy place. At his anointing Aaron offered his own oblation of fine flour—$\frac{1}{10}$ of an ephah, one-half in the morning and one-half in the evening. If baked, it must be with oil. This meal offering must all be burnt; none could be eaten. With the sin and guilt offerings every meal offering baked in any way belongs to the priest (Lev **7** 9.10; **10** 12; Nu **18** 9). The meal offerings accompanied the other offerings on all important occasions, such as the consecration of Aaron (Lev **9** 4.17); cleansing of a leper (Lev **14** 10.20.21.31); feast of first-fruits

(Lev **23** 13); Pentecost (Lev **23** 16); set feasts (Lev **23** 37). Special charge was given to Eleazar to care for the continual meal offerings (Nu **4** 16). The Nazirite must offer it (Nu **6** 15.17). When the tribes presented their offerings, meal offerings were always included (Nu **7** 13.19, etc); when the Levites were set apart (Nu **8** 8); with vows of freewill offerings (Nu **15** 4.6); with the sin offerings (**15** 24); at all the several seasons (Nu **28** 5—**29** 39). A special form was the "showbread" (bread of memorial). Twelve loaves were to be placed in two rows or heaps of six each on a pure table in the holy place, with frankincense on each pile or row. These were to remain for one week and then to be eaten by the priests. They were an offering of food by fire, though probably only the frankincense was actually burned (Lev **24** 5 f).

7. Law of the Peace Offering

The peace offerings indicated right relations with God, expressing good-fellowship, gratitude and obligation. The common altars were fitted for their use (Ex **20** 24), as feasts had been thus celebrated from time immemorial. At the feast before God on the Mount, peace offerings provided the food (Ex **24** 5); also before the golden bull (Ex **32** 6). The wave and heave offerings were portions of these.

(1) *The ritual for the offerer* (*Lev* **3** *1–17*).—The offering might be a bullock, a lamb, or a goat, either male or female, latitude being allowed in this case. The ritual was the same as in the case of the burnt offering (see above).

(2) *The ritual for the priest* (*Lev* **3** *1–17*).—Blood must be sprinkled on the altar round about, the caul, the liver and the kidneys must be taken away and the fat parts burned on the altar; the fat tail of the lamb must also be burned. These portions were offerings of food by fire to the Deity. The ritual for a goat was the same as for a bullock.

(3) *General laws for the priest* (*Lev* **6** *12* [*Heb 5*]; **7** *1 ff*).—The fat was to be burned on the altar of burnt offering. If it was a thank offering (*zebhaḥ ha-tōdhāh*), it must have unleavened cakes with oil, cakes mingled with oil and fine flour soaked. Cakes of leavened bread might be offered, and one cake was to be a heave offering to the priest. The flesh was to be eaten that day, none was to be left till morning (Lev **22** 30). If it was a votive offering (*zebhaḥ nedher*) or a freewill offering (*zebhaḥ n^edhābhāh*), it might be eaten on the first and second days, but not on the third day; it should then be an abomination (Lev **7** 18 f). If eaten then by anyone, that person was to be cut off from the community. Of all peace offerings the wave-breast and heave-thigh belong to the priest (Lev **7** 29–34), the remainder was to be eaten by the worshippers. At Aaron's consecration an ox and a ram were the peace offerings (Lev **9** 4. 18.22). The priest's portion was to be eaten in a clean place by the priest's family (Lev **10** 14). When Israel should have a central sanctuary, all were to be brought there (Lev **17** 4.5). When they had no central place, the common altars would suffice. All peace offerings must be made in an acceptable manner (Lev **19** 5). Votive offerings must be perfect (Lev **22** 18–22), but certain imperfections are allowable in freewill offerings (ver 23). At Pentecost two he-lambs of the first year could be offered as peace offerings (Lev **23** 19). The Nazirite at the end of his separation must offer one ram for a peace offering with unleavened bread (Nu **6** 14.17), and the hair shaved from his head must be burned under the peace offerings (**6** 18). This hair was regarded as a thing having life and offered as a sacrifice by other nations. The various tribes brought peace offerings (ch **7**, *passim*), and at the feast of trumpets the people were to rejoice and blow trumpets over the peace offerings (**10** 10). Some further regulations are given (**15** 9 f).

8. The Sin Offering

The sin offering was a sacrifice of a special kind, doubtless peculiar to Israel and first mentioned at the consecration of Aaron and his sons. It is not then spoken of as an innovation. It was of special value as an expiatory sacrifice.

(1) *Use at the consecration of Aaron and his sons* (*Ex* **29** *10 ff*).—A bullock was killed before the altar, some blood was put upon the horns of the altar by Moses, the rest was poured out at the base. The fat of the inwards was burned upon the altar, the flesh and skin were burned without the camp. Every day during the consecration this was done (Ex **29** 36).

(2) *The law of the sin offering* (*Lev* **4** *1–35;* **6** *24–30, etc*).—(*a*) The occasion and meaning: Specifically to atone for unwitting sins, sins of error (*sh^eghāghāh*), mistakes or rash acts, unknown at the time, but afterward made known. There were gradations of these for several classes of offenders: the anointed priest (vs 3–12), the whole congregation (vs 13–21), a ruler (vs 22–26), one of the common people (vs 27–35), forswearing (**5** 1), touching an unclean thing (ver 2) or the uncleanness of man (ver 3), or rashly swearing in ignorance (ver 4). For conscious and wilful violations of the Law, no atonement was possible, with some exceptions, for which provision was made in the guilt offerings (see below).

(*b*) The ritual for the offerer (Lev **4** 1–5.13, etc): The anointed priest must offer a bullock at the tent of meeting, lay his hands upon it and slay it before Jeh. The congregation was also required to bring a young bullock before the tent of meeting, the elders were to lay hands upon it and slay it before Jeh. The ruler must bring a he-goat and do the same. One of the common people might bring a she-goat or lamb and present it in the same manner. If too poor for these, two turtledoves or young pigeons, one for a sin offering and one for a burnt offering, would suffice. If too poor for these, the tenth part of an ephah of fine flour without oil or frankincense would suffice.

(*c*) The ritual for the priest (Lev **4** 1–5.13, etc): He must bring the bullock's blood to the tent of meeting, dip his finger into it and sprinkle blood 7 t before the veil of the sanctuary, and put some on the horns of the altar of incense, but most of the blood must be poured out at the base of the altar. The fat must be burned upon the altar, all the rest of the carcase must be carried to a clean place without the camp and burned. In the case of the whole congregation, the ritual is the same. In the case of a ruler, the blood is to be put upon the horns of the altar of burnt offering, not the altar of incense. In the case of one of the common people, the ritual is similar to that of the ruler. In both the latter cases the carcase belonged to the priest. If a bird, the priest must wring off its head, sprinkle some blood on the side of the altar and pour the rest at the base. Nothing is said of the disposal of the carcase. If of fine flour, the priest must take out a handful and burn it upon the altar, keeping the remainder for himself. The use of fine flour for an expiatory sacrifice is evidently exceptional and intended to be so. Though life was not given, yet a necessity of life—that which represented life—was offered.

(*d*) General laws for the priest (Lev **6** 24–30): The sin offering was to be slain in the same place as the burnt offering. It was most holy, and the priest alone might eat what was left of the ram, pigeon or flour, in the holy place. Whatever touched it was to be holy, any garment sprinkled with the blood must be washed in a holy place, earthen vessels used must be broken, and brazen vessels thoroughly scoured and rinsed.

(*e*) Special uses of the sin offering: (i) The consecration of Aaron and his sons (Lev **8** 2.14.15) was similar to that of Lev **4** 11.12, only Moses was to kill the offering and put the blood on the horns of the altar. On the 8th day a bull-calf was offered (**9** 2), and the congregation offered a he-goat (ver 3). In this case Aaron performed the ceremony, as in Lev **4** 11.12. Moses complained that they had not eaten the flesh of the calf and goat in the sanctuary, since that was requisite when the blood was not brought into the sanctuary (Lev **10** 16–20).

(ii) Purifications from uncleannesses required after childbirth a young pigeon or turtledove (Lev **12**

6-8). The leper must bring a guilt offering (a special kind of sin offering), a he-lamb (Lev **14** 12-14.19); if too poor for a lamb, a turtledove or young pigeon (vs 22.31). Special use of the blood is required (ver 25). In uncleanness from issues a sin offering of a turtledove or young pigeon must be offered by the priest (Lev **15** 15.30).

(iii) On the Day of Atonement (Lev **16** 1-28) Aaron must take a bullock for himself and house, two he-goats for the people, present the goats at the sanctuary, cast losts, one for Jeh, as a sin offering, the other for Azazel, to be sent into the wilderness. The bullock was killed, sweet incense was burned within the rail, blood was sprinkled on the mercy-seat and before it 7 times. The one he-goat was killed and a similar ceremony was performed. Blood must be put on the horns of the altar and sprinkled 7 t about it. The other goat was presented, hands were laid on it, the sins of all confessed and put upon the goat, and it was sent into the wilderness. The carcase of the bullock and he-goat were burned without the camp. At the feast of first-fruits a he-goat was offered (Lev **23** 19).

(iv) Other special instances were: in the case of defilement, the Nazirite must offer a turtledove or young pigeon on the 8th day after contraction (Nu **6** 10 ff); when the days of the separation were fulfilled a ewe-lamb with the other offerings (ver 14) was to be offered; the twelve tribes included in each case a he-goat for sin offering (**7** 16 ff); at the consecration of the Levites a young bullock (**8** 8.12). For unwitting sins of the congregation a he-goat was to be offered (**15** 24.25). If one person erred, a she-goat was permitted (ver 27). A sin offering was required at the feast of the new moon (**28** 15), at the Passover (ver 22), at Pentecost (ver 30), on the 1st day of the 7th month (**29** 5), and on the 10th, 15th-22d days (vs 10-38). The ceremony of the red heifer (**19** 1-10.17) was a special sin offering for purification purposes only. It was of ancient and primitive origin. The young cow was brought without the camp and was slain before the priest's face, blood was sprinkled 7 t before the sanctuary, the entire carcase with cedar wood, hyssop and scarlet was burned, the ashes gathered and laid without the camp in a clean place to be kept for the water of impurity. It was to purify after contact with the dead. In the case of the unknown homicide (Dt **21** 1-9) a young unbroken heifer was brought to a running stream, its neck was broken, the elders washed their hands over the heifer in the presence of the priests, declaring their innocence. Thus the bloodshed was expiated. The action was a judicial one, but essentially vicarious and expiatory and had doubtless a primitive origin.

9. The Guilt Offering

The guilt offering (AV "trespass offering") (Lev **5** 14—**6** 7) was a special kind of sin offering, always of a private character and accompanied by a fine. It expressed expiation and restitution. The classes of sin requiring a guilt offering with reparation in money are: (1) a trespass in the holy things done unwittingly; (2) anything which the Law forbade depriving God or the priest of their due; (3) dealing falsely with a neighbor in a deposit, or pledge, or robbery, or oppression; (4) swearing falsely regarding anything lost; (5) seduction of a betrothed bondmaid (Lev **19** 20-22). The first two of these are unwitting sins, the others cannot be. The clear statement is made in another place that sins done with a "high hand," i.e. in rebellion against the covenant and its provisions, can have no sacrifice (Nu **15** 30). Is this a contradiction, or a later development when it was found that the more stringent law would not work? (See J. M. P. Smith, et al., *Atonement,* 47 f.) Neither conclusion is probable. These conscious sins are of a kind that will admit of full reparation because against rights of property or in money matters. The sin offering makes atonement toward God, the restitution with the additional one-fifth makes full reparation to man. No such reparation can be made with such sins described as committed with a "high hand." In the case of seduction, rights of property are violated (cf Nu **5** 5-8; Dt **22** 29).

(1) *The ritual* (*Lev* **5** *14*—**6** *7*).—A ram proportionate in value to the offence and worth at least two shekels is required. The ritual is probably the same as that of the sin offering, though no mention is made of the laying on of hands, and the blood is not brought into the sanctuary, but sprinkled about the base of the altar, the fat and inside parts being burned, and the flesh eaten by the priests in a holy place.

(2) *Special statutes.*—The leper, when cleansed, on the 8th day must bring a guilt offering of two he-lambs and one ewe-lamb; the priest must wave one he-lamb before Jeh, kill it, and smear blood on the right ear, thumb and toe of the leper. The guilt offering belongs to the priest (Lev **14** 12-20). If the leper were too poor for two lambs, one sufficed, with a corresponding meal offering, or one turtledove and a young pigeon (vs 21.22). The Nazirite, if defiled during his period of separation, must bring a he-lamb for a guilt offering (Nu **6** 12). All guilt offerings were the priests' and most holy (**18** 9).

10. Wave Offerings

The wave offerings were parts of the peace offerings, and the custom was seemingly initiated at the consecration of Aaron and his sons (Ex **29** 24-27), when the breast and bread were waved before Jeh. Lev **7** 30.34 fixes the law. It must be brought from the peace offerings of the offerer himself. At Aaron's consecration Moses put the breast, etc, on Aaron's hands and waved them before Jeh (Lev **8** 27). On the 8th day Aaron did the waving (Lev **9** 21). The priests were to eat it in a clean place (Lev **10** 14 f). The leper's he-lamb was to be waved by the priest, before being offered (Lev **14** 12); the lamb of the guilt offering also (**14** 24). At the feast of first-fruits the sheaf must be waved before Jeh (Lev **23** 10.11.15); two loaves also (vs 17.20). Of the Nazirite the priest took the boiled shoulder, a cake and a wafer, put them on the Nazirite's hand and waved them before Jeh (Nu **6** 19 f).

11. Heave Offerings

Heave offerings also are parts of the peace offerings, and refer particularly to what is lifted up, or separated unto the service of Jeh. They are first mentioned at the consecration of Aaron (Ex **29** 27.28). The offering consisted of the right shoulder or thigh and was the fixed due of the priest (Lev **7** 32.34). One cake of the peace offering must be heaved (Lev **7** 14). The offering must be eaten in a clean place (Lev **7** 14) by the priest's family only (Lev **10** 14.15). Of the Nazirite's offering the heave thigh also went to the priest (Nu **6** 20). When the Israelites should come into the promised land to eat bread, they must offer a heave offering of the dough, a cake (Nu **15** 19.20.21). The law is repeated in Nu **18** 8.11.19, and the Levites are to receive a tithe of the heave offerings of the people (ver 24). They were in turn to offer up a tithe of this to the priests (vs 26-32). A portion of the spoil of Midian was a heave offering (**31** 29.41). Dt commands that all heave offerings be brought to the central sanctuary and eaten there (**12** 6.11).

12. Drink Offerings or Libations

Jacob poured oil on the stone he had set up (Gen **28** 18) in honor of the Deity and consecrated the spot. Jacob later (Gen **35** 14) set up a pillar where God had revealed Himself and poured drink offerings and oil upon it. Probably wine was used. Drink offerings accompanied many of the sacrifices (Ex **29** 40.41). None could be poured upon the altar of incense (Ex **30** 9). At all set feasts the drink offerings must be presented (Lev **23** 13.18.37). The Nazirite was not exempt (Nu **6** 15.17). Wine and oil must accompany all votive and freewill offerings (**15** 4.5.7.10.24); the continual burnt offering (**28** 7.8); sabbaths (vs 9.10) and all the other set feasts (vs 14-31; **29** 6-39, *passim*). That drink offerings were common among the heathen is shown by Dt **32** 38.

The cultus is thoroughly in keeping with and adapted to the age, and yet an ideal system in many respects. The ethical side is in the background, the external has the emphasis. No sacrifices will avail for a breach of the covenant between God and the people. The people thoroughly believed in the efficacy of the blood. It secured atonement and forgiveness. Their religious life found expression in the sacrifices.

13. Primitive Nature of the Cultus

God was fed and pleased by the offerings by fire. Many of the customs are ancient and crude, so that it is difficult to imagine how such a primitive system could have been arranged and accepted afterward by the people who had the lofty ethical teachings of the prophets in their hands.

VI. Sacrifices in the History of Israel.—The tribes were outwardly consolidated, and a religious system was provided. Some of it was for the rulers, much for the people and much for the priests alone. The various laws were given in portions and afterward compiled. No one expected them to be observed until the nation had a capital and central sanctuary. Even then not every detail was always possible. They were not observed to any extent in the wilderness (Am **5** 25), as it was impracticable. Even circumcision was neglected until the wanderers crossed the Jordan (Josh **5** 2). The body of the system was not in full practice for 300 or 400 years. The ritual, as far as it could be observed, served as an educational agency, producing in the minds of the worshippers proper conceptions of the holiness of God, the sinfulness of man, and the proper spirit in approaching God.

1. The Situation at Moses' Death

Lay or common altars were in accordance with Ex **20** 24; Dt **16** 21; **27** 7. In the days of Joshua, the Passover was celebrated (Josh **5** 10 f). At Ebal an altar was erected, burnt and peace offerings were presented (Josh **8** 30–32). The tabernacle was set up at Shiloh with a horned altar doubtless (Josh **18** 1), and the cultus was observed to some extent. Concerning the altar on the east side of the Jordan, see ALTAR.

2. In the Time of Joshua

Canaanitish altars were abundant with their corrupt and licentious cults of the Nature gods. Israelites with their common altars would naturally use the high places, when possible. The stationary altars of the Canaanites were of course unlawful. The inevitable tendency would be to imitate the worship of the Canaanites. They were rebuked and threatened for this, and, weeping, offered sacrifices at Bochim (Jgs **2** 1–5). Gideon rebuilt an altar of Jeh and offered a bullock as a burnt offering (**6** 25.26). The kid prepared for the angel was not first a sacrifice, but its acceptance as a gift was indicated by its being burned (**6** 19 f). Jephthah offered up his daughter as a burnt offering, believing such a sacrifice well-pleasing to Jeh (**11** 31.39). Manoah and his wife prepared a kid for a burnt offering, a meal offering accompanying it (**13** 16 f). At the time of the civil war with Benjamin the ark and statutory altar seemed to be at Beth-el, where they offered burnt and peace offerings (**20** 26). The feasts at Shiloh imply at least peace offerings (**21** 19).

3. In the Period of the Judges

Common lay altars and customary sacrifices were still much in use. The official altar with the statutory individual and national offerings appears to be at Shiloh. Elkanah sacrifices and feasts there yearly (1 S **1** 3 f). Such feasts were joyous and tended to excesses, as drunkenness seemed common (**1** 13 f). All Israel came thither (**2** 14); the priests claimed their portion, seizing it in an unlawful manner before the fat had been burned, or the flesh had been boiled (**2** 13–17). This shows that such ritual as was prescribed in Lev was practised and considered by the people the only lawful custom. Was it in writing? Why not? Guilt offerings were made by the Philis when smitten by tumors (**6** 3.4.8.17). There were five golden mice and five golden tumors. Crude as were their ideas of a guilt offering, their actions show familiarity with the concept. Burnt offerings were used on special occasions and in great crises, such as receiving the ark (**6** 14 f), going to war (**7** 9 f; **13** 9–12), victory (**11** 15), etc. Saul met Samuel at a sacrificial feast in a small city (**9** 12.13) on a high place. At Gilgal there were burnt and peace offerings (**10** 8; **15** 15.21). Saul offered burnt offerings himself (**13** 9–12), but his fault was not in offering them himself, but in his haste and disobedience toward Samuel. "To obey is better than sacrifice," etc, says Samuel (**15** 22), recognizing the fundamental principle of the covenant and realizing that ceremonies are in themselves worthless without the right spirit. The same truth is reiterated by the prophets later. To prevent the eating of flesh with the blood Saul built a special altar (**14** 32–35). Family and clan sacrifices and feasts were evidently common (**16** 2–5).

4. In the Times of Samuel and Saul

The common altars and those on the high places were still in use. The central sanctuary at Shiloh had been removed, first apparently to Gilgal, then to Nob, and later to Gibeon. David's and Saul's families kept the feast of the new moon, when peace offerings would be sacrificed (1 S **20** 5.24–29). The sanctuary at Nob had the shewbread upon the table (**21** 4 ff) according to Ex **25** 30. When the ark was brought up to Jerus, burnt and peace offerings were offered according to the Law (2 S **6** 17.18; 1 Ch **16** 2.40). Ahithophel offered private sacrifices at Shiloh (2 S **15** 12). David offered up burnt, meal and peace offerings when purchasing the threshing-floor of Araunah (1 Ch **21** 23–26). The statutory horned altar at this time was at Gibeon (2 Ch **1** 6; 1 Ch **21** 29), but was soon removed to Jerus (1 Ch **22** 1). In the organized sanctuary and ritual, Levites were appointed for attendance on the shewbread, meal offerings, burnt offerings, morning and evening sacrifices, sabbaths, new moons and set feasts (**23** 28–31), attempting to carry out the Levitical laws as far as possible. At the dedication of the temple Solomon offered burnt, meal and peace offerings in enormous quantities (1 K **8** 63; 2 Ch **7** 4–7); also burnt and peace offerings with incense triennially (1 K **9** 25). The ritual at the regular seasons, daily, sabbaths, new moons, set feasts, etc, was observed according to the Levitical Law (2 Ch **2** 4; **8** 13). Was it written?

5. In the Days of David and Solomon

The golden calf worship was carried on at Dan and Beth-el, with priests, altars and ritual (1 K **12** 27 f). The high places were in use, but very corrupt (**13** 2 ff). A common altar was in use on Mt. Carmel (**18** 30.32). Many others were known as Jeh's altars (**19** 10). The system was in full swing in Amos' time (Am **4** 4.5) at Beth-el and Gilgal and probably at Beer-sheba (**5** 5). Amos bitterly satirizes the hollow, insincere worship, but does not condemn the common altars and sacrifices, as these were legitimate. With Hosea the situation is worse, the cultus has been "canonized," priests have been fed on the sin or sin offerings of the people, and the kingdom soon perished because of its corruption.

6. In the Northern Kingdom

The high places were still in use and not denounced yet by the prophets (1 K **3** 2; 2 K **14** 4; **15** 4.35). Worship was not fully centralized, though tending in that direction. In the days of Abijah the temple cult was in full operation according to Moses' Law (2 Ch **13** 10 f). Asa removed many strange altars and high places because of their corruption (**14** 3), but not all (**15** 17; **20** 33). In the days of Jehoiada priests and Levites were on duty according to Moses (**23** 18; **24** 14*b;* 2 K **12** 4–16). Sin and guilt offerings were in sufficient numbers to be mentioned, but the money went to the priests. Kautzsch (*HDB*, V) and Paterson (*HDB*, IV), with others, think these offerings were only fines and altogether different from those of Lev **4**, **5**. Such a statement is wholly gratuitous. The guilt offerings must be accompanied by fines, but not necessarily the sin offerings. The passage speaks of both as perfectly familiar and of long standing, but details are lacking and there can be no certainty in the matter, except that it proves nothing regarding a ritual of sin and guilt offerings existent or non-existent at that time. Kautzsch's and Paterson's motives are obvious. Having reversed the history and put the ritual law late, they must needs make adjustments in the records to have them agree. In the days of Ahaz, the regular offerings were observed for priests, kings and people (2 K **16** 13–15). Hezekiah destroyed many high places (**18** 4). When repairing the temple, many sin offerings were presented to expiate the terrible sins of the previous reigns and the desecration of the temple (2 Ch **29** 21–24); and so, also, burnt offerings (vs 27 f), peace and thank offerings, etc, in large number (vs 31–35; cf Isa **1** 10–17). The Passover was celebrated with peace offerings (2 Ch **30** 1.2.15.22), oblations and tithes (**31** 12); courses of Levites were established (**31** 2), and the king's portion (ver 3). All the common altars were abolished as far as possible, and worship centralized in Jerus (**32** 12). Reversed by Manasseh (**33** 3 f), the high places were again used (ver 17). Josiah purged Jerus (**34** 3), and on the discovery of the Book of the Law, with its rule regarding a central sanctuary, that law was rigidly enforced (**35** 6–14). The reformation under Josiah did not change the hearts of the people, and the rule followed in spite of all the efforts of Jeremiah and other prophets.

7. In the Southern Kingdom to the Exile

That the cultus was entirely suspended in Jerus from 586 to 536 BC seems certain. There is no support for G. F. Moore's statement (*EB*, IV) that an altar was soon rebuilt and sacrificing was carried on with scarcely a break. On the return of the exiles an altar was soon built and the continual burnt offerings began (Ezr **3** 2 f), and likewise at the Feast of Tabernacles, new moons and set feasts (vs 4–7). Darius decreed that the Israelites should be given what was needed for the sacrifices (**6** 9 f). The band under Ezra offered many sin offerings on their return (**8** 35). At the dedication of the temple many burnt and sin offerings were made for all the tribes (**6** 17). Those who had married foreign wives offered guilt offerings (**10** 19). The firman of Artaxerxes provided money for bullocks, rams, lambs, with meal and drink offerings (**7** 17). Under Nehemiah and after the formal acceptance of the Law, a more complete effort was made to observe it. The shewbread, continual burnt and meal offerings, sabbaths, new moons, set feasts, sin offerings, first-fruits, firstlings, first-fruits of dough, heave offerings of all trees, wine and oil, etc, were carefully attended to (Neh **10** 33–37) and were in full force later (**13** 5.9). There is no hint of innovation, only a thoroughgoing attempt to observe laws that had been somewhat neglected.

8. In the Exilic and Post-exilic Periods

At the time of Nehemiah and probably two or three centuries previous, there existed a temple on the island of Elephantine in the Nile. It was built by a Jewish military colony, and a system of sacrifices was observed. Just how far they copied the laws of Moses, and what were their ideas of a central sanctuary are uncertain.

9. A Temple and Sacrifices at Elephantine

Several Sem tribes or nations practised human sacrifices. It was common among the Canaanites, as is shown by the excavations at Gezer, Taanach, etc. They seemed to offer children in sacrifice at the laying of cornerstones of houses and other such occasions. Among the Carthaginians, Phoenicians, Greeks and Romans human sacrifices were all too common. The custom was not unknown to the Israelites. Abraham felt called upon to offer up Isaac, but was stopped in the act, and a lesson was given for all time. The abominable practice is forbidden by Moses (Lev **18** 21), where it is spoken of as a passing through the fire to Moloch, referring to Moabitish and Ammonitish practices. Anyone practising it was to be stoned (Lev **20** 2–5; Dt **12** 31; **18** 10). The rash vow of Jephthah resulted in the immolation of his daughter, but the incident is recorded as something extraordinary (Jgs **11** 31 f). The execution of Zebah and Zalmunna is a case of blood revenge, not sacrifice (**8** 18 ff). Nor is the slaughter of Agag in any sense a sacrifice (1 S **15** 32 f). The death of Saul's sons because of his breach of covenant with the Gibeonites was an expiatory sacrifice, to atone for the father's perfidy (2 S **21** 9). The Moabite king in desperation offered up his firstborn and heir to appease the anger of Chemosh, and the effect was startling to the Israelites (2 K **3** 27). Ahaz practised the abomination in times of trouble (**16** 3). Such sacrifices were intended to secure favor with the Deity or appease His wrath. Hiel's firstborn and youngest sons were probably sacrificed at the rebuilding or fortifying of Jericho (1 K **16** 34; cf Josh **6** 26). Manasseh practised the custom (2 K **21** 6), but it was stopped by Josiah (**23** 10). Micah's words were probably applicable to those times of Ahaz or Manasseh, when they thought to obtain God's favor by costly gifts apart from ethical conditions (Mic **6** 6–8). Isaiah refers to a heathen custom practised by Israel of slaying the children in secret places (Isa **57** 5), and Jeremiah represents it as practised in his time (Jer **7** 31; **19** 5). Ezekiel denounces the same practice (Ezk **16** 20.21; **23** 37).

10. Human Sacrifices in Israel's History

Heathen sacrifices are hinted at in the later books, such as swine, a mouse, a horse, a dog (Isa **65** 4; **66** 3.17; Ezk **8** 10; 2 K **23** 11). All such animals were unclean to the Hebrews, and the practice had its roots in some form of primitive totemism which survived in those heathen cults. They were little practised among the Israelites. See TOTEMISM.

11. Certain Heathen Sacrifices

VII. The Prophets and Sacrifices.—The prophets were reformers, not innovators. Their emphasis was on the ethical, rather than the ritual. They based their teachings on the fundamentals of the covenant, not the incidentals. They accepted sacrifices as part of the religious life, but would give them their right place. They accepted the law regarding common altars, and Samuel, David and Elijah used these altars. They also endorsed the movement toward a central sanctuary, but it is the abuse of the cult that they condemned, rather than its use. They combated the heathenish idea that all God needed was gifts, lavish gifts, and would condone any sin if only they bestowed abundance of gifts. They demanded an inward religion, morality, justice, righteousness, in short, an ethical religion. They preached an ethical God, rather than the profane, debasing and almost blasphemous idea of God which prevailed in their times. They reminded the people of the covenant at Sinai, the foundation principle of which was obedience and loyalty to Jeh. If Joel be early, the cult is in full practice, as he deplores the cutting-off of the meal offering, or *minḥāh*, and the *neṣekh* or drink offering, through the devastation of the locusts. He does not mention the burnt offerings, etc, as these would not be cut off by the locusts (Joel **1** 7.13; **2** 14). Joel emphasized the need for a genuine repentance, telling them to rend their hearts and not their garments (**2** 13).

Amos condemns the cultus at Beth-el and Gilgal, and sarcastically bids them go on transgressing (**4** 4.5), mentions burnt, peace, thank and freewill offerings (**4** 4 f; **5** 22), reminds them of the fact that they did not offer sacrifices in the wilderness (**5** 25), but demands rather righteousness and justice. There is nothing here against the Mosaic origin of the laws.

In **Hosea's** time the hollow externalism of the cult had become worse, while vice, falsehood, murder, oppression, etc, were rampant. He utters an epoch-making sentence when he says, "I desire mercy, and not sacrifice," etc (**6** 6). This is no sweeping renunciation of sacrifices, as such; it is only putting the emphasis in the right place. Such sacrifices as Hosea speaks of were worse than worthless. It is somewhat extravagant for Kautzsch to say, "It is perfectly futile to read out of **6** 6 anything else than a categorical rejection of sacrifices." Hosea recognizes their place in religion, and deplores the loss during exile (**3** 4). The corrupt cults he condemns (**4** 13 f), for they are as bad as the Canaanitish cults (**4** 9). Jeh will spurn them (**8** 13; **9** 4). The defection of the nation began early (**11** 2), and they have multiplied altars (**12** 11; **13** 2). He predicts the time when they shall render as bullocks the "calves" of their lips (**14** 2 AV).

Micah is as emphatic. The sacrifices were more costly in his day, in order the more surely to purchase the favor of the Deity. Human sacrifices were in vogue, but Micah says God requires them "to do justly, and to love kindness, and to walk humbly with thy God" (**6** 8). This does not in the least affect sacrifices of the right kind and with the right spirit.

Isaiah faces the same situation. There are multitudes of sacrifices, burnt offerings, blood of bullocks and goats, oblations, sweet incense, beasts, etc, but no justice, morality, love, truth or goodness. Thus their sacrifices, etc, are an abomination, though right in themselves (**1** 11–17; **61** 8). The same is true of all pious performances today. It is probable that Isaiah worshipped in the temple (**6** 1.6). In his eschatological vision there is freedom to offer sacrifices in Egypt (**19** 19.21). The people are to worship in the holy mountain (**27** 13). Ariel must let the feasts come around (**29** 1).

Jeremiah maintains the same attitude. Your "frankincense from Sheba, and the sweet cane," burnt offerings and sacrifices are not pleasing to God (**6** 20; **14** 12). They made the temple a den of robbers, in the streets they baked cakes to the Queen of heaven, etc. He speaks sarcastically, saying, "Add your burnt-offerings unto your sacrifices, and eat ye flesh. For I spake not unto your fathers .... concerning .... sacrifices: but .... commanded .... saying, Hearken unto my voice," etc (**7** 21–23). This was literally true, as we have seen above; the covenant was not based on sacrifices but on obedience. Such a statement does not deny the institution of sacrifices for those within the covenant who are obedient. It is no "subterfuge," as Kautzsch calls it, "to say that the prophets never polemize against sacrifice *per se*, but only against offerings presented hypocritically, without repentance and a right disposition, with blood-stained hands; against the *opera operata* of the carnally-minded, half-heathen mass of the people." This is exactly what they do, and they are in perfect harmony with the covenant constitution and with their own ethical and spiritual functions. Kautzsch can make such an extravagant assertion only by ignoring the fact that Jeremiah himself in predicting the future age of righteousness and blessedness makes sacrifice an important factor (**33** 11.18). Picturing possible prosperity and glory, Jeremiah speaks of burnt and meal offerings, frankincense, thank offerings, etc, being brought into the house of Jeh (**17** 26). (We are aware of the harsh and arbitrary transference of this passage to a later time.)

Ezekiel is called by Kautzsch "the founder of the Levitical system." He is said to have preserved the fragment of the ritual that was broken up in the exile. But his references to the burnt, sin and trespass offerings presuppose familiarity with them (**40** 38–42).

He assigns the north and south chambers for the meal, sin and trespass offerings (**42** 13). The cleansing of the altar requires a bullock and he-goat for a sin offering, with burnt and peace offerings with a ritual similar to Lev **8** 1 f (Ezk **43** 18–27). The Levites are to be ministers and slay burnt offerings and sacrifice for the people (**44** 11). The priest must offer his sin offering before he ministers in the sanctuary (**44** 27). They are to eat the meal, sin, and trespass offerings as in **44** 29. In ch **45**, the people are to give the wheat, barley, oil and lambs for meal, burnt and peace offerings, while the prince shall give the meal, burnt and drink offerings for the feasts, the new moons, sabbaths and appointed feasts. He is to prepare them to make atonement (**45** 13–17). In cleansing the sanctuary the Levitical ritual is followed with added details (**45** 18–20). The Passover requires the burnt, sin and meal offerings with an extra amount of cereal. The priests prepare the prince's burnt and peace offerings (**46** 2–4.6.9–12) for the sabbaths, new moons, etc. The daily burnt offerings (vs 13–15) must have a sixth instead of a tenth part of an ephah, as in Lev **1**. The sin and guilt offerings are to be boiled in a certain place, and the meal offering baked (vs 20.26). Ezk varies from the Levitical Law in the quantity of the meal offering, picturing the ritual in a more ideal situation than Moses. The people are all righteous, with new hearts, the Spirit in them enabling them to keep the Law (**36** 26 f), and yet he institutes an elaborate ritual of purification for them. Does this seem to indicate that the prophets would abolish sacrifices entirely? It is strange reasoning which makes the prophets denounce the whole sacrificial system, when one of the greatest among them seeks to conserve an elaborate cult for the blessed age in the future.

In the second part of Isa, God declares that He has not been honored by the people with burnt and meal offerings, etc., and that He has not burdened them with such offerings, but that He is wearied with their sins (**43** 23 f). Those foreigners who respect the covenant shall offer acceptable sacrifices (**56** 7) in the blessed age to come. The Servant of Jeh is to be a guilt offering (**53** 10) to expiate the sins of Israel. Sacrifice is here for the first time lifted out of the animal to the human sphere, thus forging the link between the OT and the NT. In the glorious age to come there are to be priests and Levites, new moons, sabbaths and worship in Jerus (**66** 21.23).

Daniel speaks of the meal offering being caused to cease in the midst of the week (**9** 27).

Zechariah pictures the golden age to come when all nations shall go up to Jerus to keep the Feast of Tabernacles, which implies sacrifices. Pots are used, and all the worshippers shall use them in the ritual (**14** 16–21).

In **Malachi's** age the ritual was in practice, but grossly abused. They offered polluted bread (**1** 7), blind, lame and sick animals (**1** 13 f). Jeh has the same attitude toward these as toward those in the times of Amos, Hosea, and Isaiah (Mal **1** 10 f). The Gentiles offer better ones (**1** 11). The Israelites covered the altar of Jeh with tears by their hypocritical, non-ethical actions (**2** 13). They robbed God in withholding tithes and heave offerings (**3** 8). It is the abuse of the cult that is denounced here, as in all the other Prophets.

A special use of the term "sacrifice" is made by **Zephaniah** (**1** 7 f), applying it to the destruction of Israel by Jeh. Bozrah and Edom are to be victims (Isa **34** 6); also Gog and Magog (Ezk **39** 17.19).

In summing up the general attitude of the prophets toward sacrifices, even G. F. Moore in *EB* admits: "It is not probable that the prophets distinctly entertained the idea of a religion without a cultus, a purely spiritual worship. Sacrifice may well have seemed to them the natural expression of homage and gratitude." He might have added, "and of atonement for sin, and full fellowship with God."

VIII. Sacrifice in the "Writings."—Dates are very uncertain here. The Pss and Prov extend from David and Solomon into the Pers period.

The sages take the same attitude as the prophets. They enjoin the sacrifice of first-fruits (Prov **3** 9).

1. In the Proverbs

A feast usually follows a sacrifice of peace offerings (**7** 14). The trespass offering (?) has no meaning to fools (**14** 9), and the sacrifices of the wicked are an abomination to God (**15** 8; **21** 27). Righteousness and justice are more acceptable to Jeh than sacrifices (**21** 3), yet to them sacrifices are a regular part of worship. *Ḳōheleth* speaks of sacrifices as quite the custom, and deprecates the offerings of fools (Eccl **5** 1; **9** 2).

2. In the Psalms

The Psalmist admonishes the faithful to offer the sacrifices of righteousness, i.e. sacrifices offered in the right spirit (**4** 5). The drink offerings of idolaters are well known (**16** 4). Prayer is made for the acceptance of sacrifices (**20** 3). It is a coveted privilege to offer them (**27** 6; **84** 1–4). The true relation between sacrifice and obedience is expressed in **40** 6–8. As in Jer **7** 21 f, the emphasis is laid on obedience, without which sacrifices are worthless and repugnant to God. They are not the important thing in Israel's religion, for that religion *could* exist without them as in the wilderness and exile. The teaching corresponds exactly with that of the prophets and is probably late. Ps **50** is even more emphatic. The Psalmist knows that sacrifices are in the covenant regulations (ver 5), but repudiates the idea of giving anything to God or of feeding Him (vs 12.13). Everything belongs to Him, He is not hungry, He would scorn the idea of drinking the blood of goats, etc. The idea of the cultus being of any real value to God is scouted. Yet in the next verse the reader is admonished to offer sacrifices of thanksgiving and pay vows (ver 14). The sacrifices that express worship, penitence, prayer, thanksgiving and faith are acceptable. The penitent Psalmist speaks in similar terms. Sacrifices as such are no delight to God, the real sacrifice is a broken heart (**51** 16 f). When the heart is right, then, as an expression of true-heartedness, devotion, repentance and faith, burnt offerings are highly acceptable (ver 19). Another Psalmist promises a freewill offering to God (**54** 6; **66** 13.15). Sacrifices of thanksgiving are advised (**96** 8; **107** 22; **118** 27) and promised (**116** 17). Prayer is likened to the evening sacrifice (**141** 2).

IX. The Idea and Efficacy of Sacrifices.—That the Hebrews thoroughly believed in the efficacy of sacrifices is without doubt. What ideas they entertained regarding them is not so clear. No single theory can account for all the facts. The unbloody sacrifices were regarded as food for the Deity, or a pleasant odor, in one instance, taking the place of a bloody offering (see above). The bloody offerings present some difficulties, and hence many different views.

1. A Gift of Food to the Deity

Included under the head of gifts of food to the Deity would be the meal and peace offerings, in so far as they were consumed by fire, the burnt offerings and the shewbread, etc. They were fire-food, the fire-distilled essence or etherealized food for God which gave Him pleasure and disposed Him favorably toward the offerer. They were intended either to appease wrath, to win favor, or to express thanks and gratitude for favors experienced. The earlier and more naïve idea was probably to win the favor of the Deity by a gift. Later, other ideas were expressed in the offerings.

2. Expression of Adoration and Devotion

The burnt offering best gave expression to the sentiments of adoration and devotion, though they may not be excluded from the meal and peace offerings. In other words, sacrifice meant worship, which is a complex exercise of the soul. Such was Abraham's attempted sacrifice of Isaac. The daily burnt offerings were intended to represent an unbroken course of adoration and devotion, to keep the right relations with the Deity. On particular occasions, special offerings were made to insure this relation which was specially needed at that time.

3. A Means of Purification from Uncleanness

The burnt and sin offerings were the principal kinds used for the purpose of purification; water being used in case of uncleanness from contact with the dead. There were three classes of uncleanness: (1) those inseparable from the sex functions of men and women; (2) those resulting from contact with a corpse; (3) the case of recovery from leprosy. Purification ceremonies were the condition of such persons enjoying the social and religious life of the community. Why they should require a sin offering when most of them occurred in the regular course of nature and could not be guarded against, can be understood only as we consider that these offences were the effects of sin, or the weaknesses of the fleshly nature, due to sin. Such uncleannesses made the subject unfit for society, and that unfitness was an offence to God and required a piacular offering.

4. A Means of Consecration to the Divine Service

Consecration was of men and things. The ceremonies at the sealing of the covenant and the consecration of the Levites and of Aaron and his sons have been mentioned. The altar and furniture of the tabernacle were consecrated by the blood of the sin offering. This blood being the means of expiation, it cleansed from all defilement caused by human hands, etc. The sprinkling and smearing of the blood consecrated them to the service of God. The blood being holy, it sanctified all it touched (cf Ezk **45** 19 f).

5. To Establish a Community of Life between Worshipper and God

In other words, it is a kind of sacral communion. The blood is the sacred cement between man and God. This is possible only because it contains the life and is appropriated by God as a symbol of the communion into which He enters with the offerer. This blood "covers" all sin and defilement in man, permits him to enter God's presence and attests the communion with Him. This is the view of Schultz, and partly that of Kautzsch, in regard to earlier ideas of sacrifice. Such a view may have been held by certain peoples in primitive times, but it does not do justice to the Levitical system.

6. View of Ritschl

The view of Ritschl is that sacrifices served as a form of self-protection from God whose presence meant destruction to a weak creature. Thus sacrifices have no moral value and no relation to sin and defilement. They have relation only to man's creaturely weakness which is in danger of destruction as it approaches the presence of God. God's presence necessarily meant death to the creature without reference to his holiness, etc. Such a view banishes all real sense of sin, all ethical values, and furnishes no proper motives. It gives a false idea of the character of God, and is entirely out of accord with the sacred record.

7. Sacrifice a Sacrament

That sacrifices were really a sacrament has been advocated by many. According to some theologians, the sacrifices were *signs* of spiritual realities, not only representing but sealing and applying spiritual blessings, and their efficacy was proportionate to the faith of the offerer. By some Roman Catholic theologians it is held that the Passover was esp. of a sacramental character, corresponding to the Eucharist. The purificatory rites corresponded to penance and the consecrating sacrifices to the sacrament of ordination. Bähr says that the acceptance of the sacrifice by Jeh and His gift of sanctification to the worshippers give to the sacrifice the character of a sacramental act. Cave also speaks of them as having a sacramental significance, while refuting the position of Bähr. Though there may be a slight element of truth in some of these ideas, it is not the idea expressed in the cultus, and seems to read into the ritual the theology of the theologians themselves. This view is closely allied to a phase of the following view (see Paterson, *HDB*, IV).

8. A Symbol or Expression of Prayer

That it is a symbol or expression of prayer is held by Maurice and to some extent by Schultz. Thus the sacrifices are supposed to be symbols of the religious sentiment, which are the conditions of acceptance with God. The victim serves as an index of what is in the worshipper's heart, and its virtue is exhausted when it is presented to God. Thus it may express spiritual aspiration or supplication, hatred of sin and surrender to God with confession and supplication. Bähr holds that a valuable and unblemished victim is selected as symbolical of the excellence and purity to which the offerer aspires, the death is necessary to procure life which may be offered to God, and the sprinkling of the blood is the presentation to God of the life still resident in the blood. Schultz thinks that the sin offering was distinctively purifying. "Hence the real ground of purification is that God accepts the sacrifice and thereby enters into communion with the sinner, granting him actual pardon, and that man in *this offering* enjoined by God as the embodied prayer of a penitent expresses his confession, his regrets and his petition for forgiveness." While there is an element of truth in this, and it is particularly applicable to the burnt offering, it does not embrace all the facts. It represents the views of the prophets and psalmists more than that of the Levitical code.

9. View of Kautzsch

Kautzsch holds that the efficacy of sacrifices consists in this: "God has connected the accomplishment of atonement with the obedient discharge of the sacrificial prescriptions; whoever fulfils these and gets the priest to perform the atoning usages, is forgiven. The ritual, esp. the presenting of the blood, is the indispensable condition of atonement, but it is not synonymous. Forgiveness of sin flows from the grace of God as taught by the prophets, only with them it is unnecessary, but with the PC it is necessary." Thus Kautzsch teaches a fundamental contradiction between the prophets and the Law, which is utterly wrong and is made necessary by first turning the history upside down and making the PC a hideous anachronism. He says, "That the process of atonement is connected with the presenting of blood, explains itself naturally as a powerful after-influence of primitive sacrificial usages, in which the presenting of blood had a different meaning. It is a symbolic (not real) satisfaction, as through the animal's life symbolic expression is given to the fact that the sinner's life is forfeited to God. But the main idea is that God has *commanded* it" (*HDB*, V, 721*a*). The half-truths in these statements will be obvious to most readers.

10. Vicarious Expiation Theory

The theory that sacrifices were a vicarious expiation of sin and defilement, by a victim whose life is forfeited instead of the sinner's, is the only one that will complete the Levitical idea of sacrifices. This of course applies esp. to the sin offering. While there is an element of truth in the gift-theory, the prayer and sacramental theories and others, including that of Kautzsch, the idea of a vicarious suffering is necessary to complete the conception. Oehler recognizes the force of the prayer-theory, but advances to the idea that in sacrifices man places the life of a pure, innocent, sacrificial animal between himself and God, because he is unable to approach God on account of his sinfulness and impurity. Thus it becomes a *kōpher* for him, to cover his sin. This is not a punishment inflicted on the animal, although in the case of uncertain homicide it is (Dt **21** 1–9). The law does not lay the emphasis upon the slaughter, but on the shedding of the blood and the sprinkling of it on certain articles. The slaughter is of course presupposed. The altar is not regarded as a place of execution, it is the means for "covering" the sins of the covenant people, a gracious ordinance of God and well-pleasing to Him. But the gift can please God only as the gift of one who has given himself up to Him; therefore the ritual must represent this self-surrender, the life of the clean and guiltless animal in place of the impure and sinful soul of the offerer, and this pure soul, coming in between the offerer and the Holy God, lets Him see at the altar a pure life by which the impure life is covered. In the same way the pure element serves to cover the pollutions of the sanctuary and the altar, etc. Its meaning is specific, it is the self-sacrifice of the offerer vicariously accomplished. This self-sacrifice necessarily involves suffering and punishment, which is inflicted on the beast to which the guilt and sin are imputed, not imparted (see Oehler, *OT Theol.*, 278 f).

Objections have been raised by Dillmann, Kautzsch and others on the ground that it could not have been vicarious because sacrifices were not allowed for sins which *merited death*, but only for venial transgressions (Nu **15** 30). Certainly, but the entire sacrificial system was for those who were in the covenant, who did not commit sins that merited death, and was never intended as a *penal* substitute, because the sins of those in the covenant were not of a penal nature. The sacrifices were "to cover" the *sin* and *defilement* of the offerer, not the deserved death-penalty of one who broke the covenant. Again, they object, a cereal offering may atone, and this excludes a penal substitute. But sacrifices were *not strictly penal*, and the cereal was distinctly an exception in case of the very poor, and the exception proves the rule. In any case it represented the self-sacrifice of the offerer, and that was the important thing. Further, the victim was slain by the offerer and not by the priest, whereas it should have been put to death by God's representative. This carries no weight whatever, as the essential thing was a sacrifice, and priests were not necessary for that. A more serious objection is that in the case of penal substitution, by which the sin and guilt are transferred to the animal, the flesh of that animal is regarded as most holy and to be eaten by the priests only, whereas it would necessarily be regarded as laden with guilt and curse, and hence polluted and unfit for use. This is a pure assumption. In the first place, the substitution was not strictly *penal*, and, secondly, there is no hint that actual pollution is conveyed to the flesh of the animal or to the blood. Even if it were so, the shedding of the blood would expiate the sin and guilt, wipe out the pollution, and the flesh would be in no way affected. On the contrary, the flesh, having been the vehicle for the blood which has accomplished such a sacred and meritorious service, would necessarily be regarded as most holy. All the animal would be holy, rather than polluted, since it had performed such a holy service. Kautzsch's objection thus appears puerile. The ritual of the Day of Atonement presents all these features. It is distinctly stated that the high priest confesses the iniquities of the children of Israel over the scapegoat, and that the goat carries this guilt away to the desert. Its blood is not shed, it is wholly unclean, and the man leading it away is unclean. This is undeniably a vicarious act. In the case of the other goat, a sin offering, the sin and guilt are imputed to it, but the life is taken and thus the expiation is made and the flesh of the victim used in such a holy service is most holy.

That this view of a vicarious expiation was generally accepted is evident on every hand. There was no need of a theoretical explanation in the cultus; it was self-evident; as Holtzmann says, "the most external indeed, but also the simplest and most generally intelligible and the readiest answer to the nature of expiation" (*NT Theol.*, I, 68). This view is amply corroborated by the researches of S. I. Curtiss in his *Primitive Sem Religion of Today*. By searching questions he found that the fundamental idea of bloody sacrifices was that the victim took the place of the man, redeemed him, or atoned for him as a substitute. The "bursting forth of the blood" was the essential thing (see pp. 218 f).

11. Typology of Sacrifice

The typology of sacrifice has been much discussed. There can be no question that, from the standpoint of the NT, many of the sacrifices were typical. They prefigured, and designedly so, the great sacrifice of Christ. Thus they could not really take away sin; they were in that sense unreal. But the question is, were they typical to the people of Israel? Did Moses and the priests and prophets and people understand that they were merely figures, adumbrations of the true Sacrifice to come, which alone could take away sin? Did they understand that their Messiah was to be sacrificed, His blood shed, to make an atonement for them, and render their Divinely given means of atonement all unreal? The answer must be an emphatic "No." There is no hint that their minds were directed to think of the Coming One as their *sacrifice*, foreshadowed by their offerings. That was the one thing the nation could not and would not understand, and to this day the cross is their chief stumbling-block. The statement that the Servant is to be a guilt offering (Isa **53** 10) is the nearest approach to it, but this is far from saying that the whole sacrificial system was understood as foreshadowing that event. The great prophets all speak of a sacrificial system in full vogue in the Messianic age.

We prefer to regard the sacrificial system as a great religious educational system, adapted to the capacity of the people at that age, intended to develop right conceptions of sin, proper appreciation of the holiness of God, correct ideas of how to approach God, a familiarity with the idea of sacrifice as the fundamental thing in redemption, life, and service to God and man.

LITERATURE.—Only a selection is attempted: arts. in *Enc Brit*, 11th ed; *EB* (G. F. Moore); *HDB* (Paterson); *RE* and *Sch-Herz* (Orelli); *Jew Enc;* McClintock and Strong, etc; Murray's *Bible Dict.; Standard BD*, etc. Kautzsch, Jastrow and Wiedermann in *HDB;* art. on "Comparative Religion" in *Sch-Herz;* OT Theologies of Oehler, Dillmann, Smend, Schultz, Davidson, Koenig, etc.

On sacrifices in general: Wellhausen, *Reste des arabischen Heidenthums;* W. R. Smith, *Religion of the Semites;* J. G. Frazer, *Golden Bough*, II, III; E. B. Tylor, *Primitive Culture;* E. Westermarck, *Origin of Moral Ideas;* H. Hubert et Mauss, *Année sociologique*, II; L. Marillier, *Revue de l'histoire des religions*, XXXVI, 208; S. I. Curtiss, *Primitive Sem Religion of Today.*

Biblical sacrifices: F. Bähr, *Symbolik des Mosäischen Kultus;* J. H. Kurtz, *Der alttestamentliche Opfercultus;* A. Stewart, *The Mosaic Sacrifices;* J. G. Murphy, *Sacrifice as Set Forth in Scripture;* A. Cave, *Scriptural Doctrine of Sacrifice;* F. Maurice, *The Doctrine of Sacrifice;* J. M. P. Smith, *Bib. Doctrine of Atonement.* See also: Schultz, *AJT*, 1900, 257 ff; Smöller, *Studien und Kritiken*, 1891; Wiener, *Essays in Pentateuchal Criticism; Pentateuchal Studies;* Driver, *ERE*, VI.

J. J. REEVE

IN THE NEW TESTAMENT

I. Terms of Sacrifice Epitomized.—The word "offering" (προσφορά, *prosphorá*) describes the death of Christ, once in Paul (Eph **5** 2); 5 t in He (**10** 5.8.10.14.18). The vb. προσφέρω, *prosphérō*, "to offer," is also used, 15 t in He (**5** 1.3; **8** 3².3.4; **9** 7.14.25.28; **10** 1.8.11.12; **11** 4). The noun *prosphora* occurs 15 t in LXX, usually as the tr of מִנְחָה, *minḥāh*, "sacrifice." This noun in the NT refers to OT sacrifices in Acts **7** 42; **21** 26; to the offering of money in Acts **24** 17; Rom **15** 16. The vb. ἀναφέρω, *anaphérō*, also occurs 3 t in He (**7** 27; **9** 28; **13** 15); also in 1 Pet **2** 5.

The word "sacrifice" (θυσία. *thusía*, translates in LXX 8 Heb words for various kinds of sacrifice, occurring about 350 t) refers to Christ's death, once in Paul (Eph **5** 2) and 5 t in He (**5** 1; **9** 23.26; **10** 12.26). It refers several times to OT sacrifice and 5 t to Christian living or giving (Phil **2** 17; **4** 18; He **13** 15.16; 1 Pet **2** 5). The vb. "to sacrifice" (θύω, *thúō*) is used once by Paul to describe Christ's death (1 Cor **5** 7).

The blood (αἷμα, *haíma*) of Christ is said to secure redemption or salvation, 6 t in Paul (Rom **3** 25; **5** 9; 1 Cor **10** 16; Eph **1** 7; **2** 13; Col **1** 20); 3 t in He (**9** 12.14; **10** 19; cf also **10** 29); 2 t in 1 Pet (**1** 2.19) and 5 t in the Johannine writings (1 Jn **1** 7; **5** 6².8; Rev **1** 5). Unmistakably this figure of the blood refers to Christ's sacrificial death. "In any case the phrase ἐν τῷ αὐτοῦ αἵματι [*en tō̃ autoú haímati*, 'in his blood,' Rom **3** 25] carries with it the idea of sacrificial blood-shedding" (Sanday, *Comm. on Ep. to Rom*, 91).

Λύτρον (*lútron*, "ransom," the price paid for redeeming, occurring in LXX 19 t, meaning the price paid for redeeming the servant [Lev **25** 51.52]; ransom for first-born [Nu **3** 46]; ransom for the life of the owner of the goring ox [Ex **21** 30, etc]) occurs in the NT only twice (Mt **20** 28; Mk **10** 45). This word is used by Jesus to signify the culmination of His sacrificial life in His sacrificial death.

'Αντίλυτρον (*antílutron*, "ransom," a word not found in LXX, stronger in meaning than the preceding word) occurs only once in the NT (1 Tim **2** 6).

'Απολύτρωσις (*apolútrōsis*, "redemption," in Ex **21** 8, meaning the ransom paid by a father to redeem his daughter from a cruel master) signifies (1) deliverance from sin by Christ's death, 5 t in Paul (Rom **3** 24; 1 Cor **1** 30; Eph **1** 7.14; Col **1** 14); once in He (**9** 15); (2) general deliverance, twice (Lk **21** 28; He **11** 35); (3) the Christian's final deliverance, physical and spiritual (Rom **8** 23; Eph **4** 30). The simple word λύτρωσις (*lútrōsis*, "redemption," 10 t in LXX as the tr of 5 Heb words) occurs once for spiritual deliverance (He **9** 12).

'Εξαγοράζω (*exagorázō*, "redeem," only once in LXX, Dnl **2** 8) in the NT means (1) to deliver from the curse of the law, twice by Paul (Gal **3** 13; **4** 5); (2) to use time wisely, twice by Paul (Eph **5** 16; Col **4** 5). The simple vb. ἀγοράζω (*agorázō*, meaning in Lev **27** 19 to redeem land) occurs twice in Paul (1 Cor **6** 20; **7** 23) and means "to redeem" (in a spiritual sense).

Καταλλαγή (*katallagḗ*, "reconciliation," only twice in LXX) means the relation to God into which men are brought by Christ's death, 4 t by Paul (Rom **5** 11; **11** 15; 2 Cor **5** 18.19).

Καταλλάσσειν (*katallássein*, "to reconcile," 4 t in LXX [3 in 2 Macc]) means to bring men into the state of reconciliation with God, 5 t in Paul (Rom **5** 10 *bis;* 2 Cor **5** 18.19.20).

The words with the propitiatory idea occur as follows: ἱλάσκομαι (*hiláskomai*, "to propitiate," 12 t in LXX, trd "to forgive") occurs twice (Lk **18** 13; He **2** 17); ἱλασμός (*hilasmós*, 9 t in LXX, Nu **5** 8; Ps **129** [**130**] 4, etc; "atonement," "forgiveness") occurs twice in 1 Jn (**2** 2; **4** 10); ἱλαστήριον (*hilastḗrion*, 24 t in LXX, translates "mercy-seat," where God was gracious and spake to man) translates in the NT "propitiation" (Rom **3** 25), "mercy-seat" (He **9** 5).

Christ is called "the Lamb," ἀμνός, *amnós*, twice by the Baptist (Jn **1** 29.36); once by Philip applied to Christ from Isa **53** 7 (Acts **8** 32); and once by Peter (1 Pet **1** 19); ἀρνίον, *arníon*, 28 t in Rev (**5** 6.8.12.13; **6** 1.16; **7** 9.10.14; **19** 7.9; **21** 9.14.22.23.27; **22** 1.3).

The cross (σταυρός, *staurós*) is used by Paul 10 t to describe the sacrificial death of Christ (1 Cor **1** 17.18; Gal **5** 11; **6** 12.14; Eph **2** 16; Phil **2** 8; **3** 18; 1 Cor **1** 20; **2** 14) and once by the author of He (**12** 2). Jesus also 5 t used the figure of the cross to define the life of sacrifice demanded of His disciples and to make His own cross the symbol of sacrifice (Mt **10** 38; **16** 24; Mk **8** 34; Lk **9** 23; **14** 27, with contexts; cf Jn **3** 14; **12** 32, etc).

Though it is not our province in this article to discuss the origin and history of sacrifice in the ethnic religions, it must be noted that sacrifice has been a chief element in almost every religion (Jainism and Buddhism being the principal exceptions). The bloody sacrifice, where the idea of propitiation is prominent, is well-nigh universal in the ethnic religions, being found among even the most enlightened peoples like the Greeks and Romans (see art. "Expiation and Atonement" in *ERE*). Whether or not the system of animal sacrifices would have ceased, not only in Judaism but also in all the ethnic religions, had not Jesus lived and taught and died, is a question of pure speculation. It must be conceded that the sect of the Jews (Essenes) attaining to the highest ethical standard and living the most unselfish lives of brotherhood and benevolence did not believe in animal sacrifices. But they exerted small influence over the Jewish nation as compared with the Pharisees. It is also to be noted that the prophets Amos, Hosea, Micah and Isaiah exalted the ethical far above the ceremonial; even denounced the sacrifice of animals if not accompanied by personal devotion to righteousness (Am **5** 21 ff; Hos **6** 6; Mic **6** 6 ff; Isa **1** 11 ff). The Stoic and Platonic philosophers also attacked the system of animal sacrifices. But these exceptions only accentuate the historical fact that man's sense of the necessity of sacrifice to Deity is well-nigh universal. Only the sacrifice of Christ and the destruction of Jerus caused a cessation of the daily, weekly, monthly and annual sacrifices among the Jews, and only the knowledge of Christ's sacrifice of Himself will finally destroy the last vestige of animal sacrifice.

II. Attitude of Jesus and NT Writers to the OT Sacrificial System.—Jesus never attacks the sacrificial system. He even takes for granted that the Jews should offer sacrifices (Mt **5** 24). More than that, He accepted the whole sacrificial system, a part of the OT scheme, as of Divine origin, and so He commanded the cleansed leper to offer the sacrifice prescribed in the Mosaic code (Mt **8** 4). There is no record that Jesus Himself ever worshipped by offering the regular sacrifices. But He worshipped in the temple, never attacking the sacrificial system as He did the oral law (Mk **7** 6 ff). On the other hand, Jesus undermined the sacrificial system by teaching that the ethical transcends the ceremonial, not only as a general principle, but also in the act of worship (Mt **5** 23.24). He endorses Hosea's fine ethical epigram, 'God will have mercy and not sacrifice' (Mt **9** 13; **12** 7). He also commends as near the kingdom the scribe who put love to God and man above sacrifice (Mk **12** 33). But Jesus teaches not merely the inferiority of sacrifice to the moral law, but also the discontinuance of sacrifice as a system, when He said, "This is my blood of the covenant, which is poured out for many" (Mk **14** 24; Mt **26** 28; Lk **22** 20). Not only is the ethical superior to the ceremonial, but His sacrifice of Himself is as superior to the sacrifices of the old system as the new covenant is superior to the old.

1. Jesus' Attitude

Paul's estimate of the Jewish sacrifices is easily seen, although he does not often refer to them. Once only (Acts **21** 26) after his conversion does he offer the Jewish sacrifice, and then as a matter of expediency for winning the Judaistic wing of Christianity to his universal gospel of grace. He regarded the sacrifices of the OT as types of the true sacrifice which Christ made (1 Cor **5** 7).

2. Paul's Attitude

The author of the Ep. to the He discusses the OT sacrifices more fully than other NT writers. He regards the bloody sacrifices as superior to the unbloody and the yearly sacrifice on the Day of Atonement by the high priest as the climax of the OT system. The high priest under the old covenant was the type of Christ under the new. The sacrifices of the old covenant could not take away sin, or produce moral transformation, because of the frailties of men (**10** 1–11), shown by the necessity of repeating the offerings (**5** 2), and because God had appointed another high priest, His Son, to supplant those of the old covenant (**5** 5; **7** 1–28). The heart of this author's teaching is that animal sacrifices cannot possibly atone for sin or produce moral transformation, since they are Divinely appointed only as a type or shadow of the one great sacrifice by Christ (**8** 7; **10** 1).

3. Attitude of the Author of Hebrews

To sum up, the NT writers, as well as Jesus, regarded the OT sacrificial system as of Divine origin and so obligatory in its day, but imperfect and only a type of Christ's sacrifice, and so to be supplanted by His perfect sacrifice.

III. The Sacrificial Idea in the NT.—The one central idea of NT writers is that the sacrifice made by Christ on the cross is the final perfect sacrifice for the atonement of sin and the salvation of men, a sacrifice typified in the various sacrifices of the OT, which are in turn abrogated by the operation of the final sacrifice. Only James and Jude among NT writers are silent as to the sacrifice of Christ, and they write for practical purposes only.

The Baptist, it is true, presents Jesus as the coming Judge in the Synoptic Gospels, but in Jn **1** 29.36 he refers to Him as "the Lamb of God," in the former passage adding "that taketh away the sin of the world." Westcott (*Comm. on St. John*, 20) says: "The title as applied to Christ . . . . conveys the ideas of vicarious suffering, of patient submission, of sacrifice, of redemption, etc." There is scarcely any doubt that the Baptist looked upon the Christ as the one who came to make the great sacrifice for man's sins. Professor Burton (*Bib. Ideas of Atonement*, Burton, Smith and Smith, 107) says that John sees Christ "suffering under the load of human sin."

1. Teaching of John the Baptist

There are recorded in the Synoptic Gospels two unmistakable references by Jesus to His death as a sacrifice (Mk **10** 45 ‖ Mt **20** 28; Mk **14** 24 ‖ Mt **26** 28 ‖ Lk **22** 20; cf 1 Cor **11** 25). In the former He declares He came to give His "life a ransom." Thayer (*Gr-Eng. Lex. of the NT*) says this word means "the price paid for redeeming." Hence the idea in ransom must be of sacrificial significance. But if there could be any doubt as to the sacrificial import of this passage, there is a clear case of the sacrificial idea in Mk **14** 24. Practically all writers of the NT theology, Wendt, Weiss, Stevens, Sheldon and others, hold that Jesus considered the death as the ratification sacrifice of the new covenant, just as the sacrifice offered at Sinai ratified the old covenant (Ex **24** 3–8). Ritschl and Beyschlag deny that this passage is sacrificial. But according to most exegetes, Jesus in this reference regarded His death as a sacrifice. The nature of the sacrifice, as Jesus estimated it, is in doubt and is to be discussed later. What we are pressing here is the fact that Jesus regarded His death as a sacrifice. We have to concede the meagerness of material on the sacrificial idea of His death as taught by Jesus. Yet these two references are unquestioned by literary and historical critics. They both occur in Mk, the primitive Gospel (the oldest Gospel record of Jesus' teachings). The first occurs in two of the Synoptists, the second in all three of them. Luke omits the first for reasons peculiar to his purpose. According to Lk **24** 25, Jesus regarded His sufferings and death as the fulfilment of the OT Scriptures.

2. Teaching of Jesus

Though the head apostle does not in the early chapters of Acts refer to Christ as the sacrifice for sin, he does imply as much in **2** 36 (He is Lord and Christ in spite of His crucifixion); **3** 18.19 (He fulfilled the prophecies by suffering, and by means of repentance sins are to be blotted out); **4** 10–12 (only in His name is salvation) and in **5** 30.31 (through whose death Israel received

3. Teaching of Peter

remission of sins). In his First Ep. (**1** 18.19) he expressly declares that we are redeemed by the blood of the spotless Christ, thus giving the sacrificial significance to His death. The same is implied in **1** 2; **3** 18.

4. Paul's Teaching

Paul ascribes saving efficacy to the blood of Christ in Rom **3** 25; **5** 9; 1 Cor **10** 16; Eph **1** 7; **2** 13; Col **1** 20. He identifies Christ with a sin offering in Rom **8** 3, and perhaps also in 2 Cor **5** 21, and with the paschal lamb in 1 Cor **5** 7. In other passages he implies that the death of Christ secured redemption, forgiveness of sins, justification and adoption (Rom **3** 24–26; **5** 10.11; **8** 15.17, etc).

5. Teaching of Hebrews

The argument of the author of He to prove the finality of Christianity is that Christ is superior to the Aaronic high priest, being a royal, eternal high priest, after the order of Melchizedek, and offering Himself as the final sacrifice for sin, and for the moral transformation of men (**4** 14; **10** 18).

6. Johannine Teaching

In the First Ep. of Jn (**1** 7; **2** 2; **5** 6.8) propitiation for sin and cleansing from sin are ascribed to the blood of Christ. In Rev **1** 5 John ascribes deliverance (not washing or cleansing, according to best MSS) from sin, to the blood of Christ. Several times he calls Christ the Lamb, making the sacrificial idea prominent. Once he speaks of Him as the Lamb slain from the foundation of the world (**13** 8).

To sum up, all the NT writers, except James and Jude, refer to Christ's death as the great sacrifice for sin. Jesus Himself regarded His death as such. In the various types of NT teaching Christ's death is presented (1) as the covenant sacrifice (Mk **14** 24 ‖ Mt **26** 28 ‖ Lk **22** 20; He **9** 15–22); (2) as the sin offering (Rom **8** 3; 2 Cor **5** 21; He **13** 11; 1 Pet **3** 18); (3) as the offering of the paschal lamb (1 Cor **5** 7); (4) as the sacrifice of the Day of Atonement (He **2** 17; **9** 12 ff).

IV. Relation of Christ's Sacrifice to Man's Salvation.—The saving benefits specified in the NT as resulting from the sacrificial death of Christ are as follows:

1. Redemption or Deliverance from Curse of Sin

Redemption or deliverance from the curse of sin: This must be the implication in Jesus' words, "The Son of man also came . . . . to give his life a ransom for many" (Mk **10** 45 ‖ Mt **20** 28). Man is a captive in sin, the Father sends His Son to pay the ransom price for the deliverance of the captive, and the Son's death is the price paid. Paul also uses the words "redeemed" and "redemption" in the same sense. In the great letters he asserts that we are "justified freely by his grace through the redemption that is in Christ Jesus: whom God set forth to be a propitiation . . . . in his blood" (Rom **3** 24.25). Here the apostle traces justification back to redemption as the means for securing it, and redemption back to the "blood" (Christ's death) as the cause of its procurement. That is, Christ's death secures redemption and redemption procures justification. In Gal (**3** 13), he speaks of being redeemed "from the curse of the law." The law involved man in a curse because he could not keep it. This curse is the penalty of the broken law which the transgressor must bear, unless deliverance from said penalty is somehow secured. Paul represents Christ by His death as securing for sinners deliverance from this curse of the broken law (cf Gal **4** 5 for the same thought, though the word "curse" is not used). Paul also emphasizes the same teaching in the Captivity Epp.: "In whom we have our redemption through his blood, the forgiveness of our trespasses" (Eph **1** 7; cf Col **1** 14). In the pastoral letters (1 Tim **2** 6) he teaches that Christ gave "himself a ransom for all." This is the only NT passage in which occurs the strong word *antilutron* for "ransom." In his old age the apostle feels more positively than ever before that Christ's death is the ransom price of man's deliverance from sin.

The author of He asserts that Christ by the sacrifice of Himself "obtained eternal redemption" for man (**9** 12). John says that Christ "loosed [λύω, *lúō*] us from our sins by his blood" (Rev **1** 5). This idea in John is akin to that of redemption or deliverance by ransom. Peter teaches the same truth in 1 Pet **1** 19. So, we see, Jesus and all the NT writers regard Christ's sacrifice as the procuring cause of human redemption.

2. Reconciliation

The idea of reconciliation involves a personal difference between two parties. There is estrangement between God and man. Reconciliation is the restoration of favor between the two parties. Jesus does not utter any direct message on reconciliation, but implies God's repugnance at man's sin and strained relations between God and the unrepentant sinner (see Lk **18** 13). He puts into the mouth of the praying tax-gatherer the words, 'God be propitious to me' (see Thayer, *Gr-Eng. Lex.*, *hilaskomai*), but Jesus nowhere asserts that His death secures the reconciliation of God to the sinner. Paul, however, does. "For if, while we were enemies, we were reconciled to God through the death of his Son," etc (Rom **5** 10). There can be no doubt from this passage that Paul thought of the death of Christ as the procuring cause of reconciliation. In Eph **2** 13.14.18 Paul makes the cross of Christ the means of reconciliation between the hostile races of men. Paul reaches the climax in his conception of the reconciliation wrought by the cross of Christ when he asserts the unifying results of Christ's death to be cosmic in extent (Eph **1** 10).

The author of He also implies that Christ's death secures reconciliation when he regards this death as the ratification of the "better covenant" (**8** 6 ff), and when he plays on the double meaning of the word διαθήκη (*diathḗkē*, **9** 15 ff), now "covenant" and now "will," "testament." The death of Christ is necessary to secure the ratification of the new covenant which brings God and man into new relations (**8** 12). In **2** 17 the author uses a word implying propitiation as wrought by the death of Christ. So the doctrine of reconciliation is also in the Ep. to the He. John teaches reconciliation with God through Christ our Advocate, but does not expressly connect it with His death as the procuring cause (1 Jn **2** 1.2). Peter is likewise silent on this point.

3. Remission of Sins

Reconciliation implies that God can forgive; yea, has forgiven. Jesus and the NT writers declare the death of Christ to be the basis of God's forgiveness. Jesus in instituting the memorial supper said, "This is my blood of the covenant, which is poured out for many unto remission of sins" (Mt **26** 28). It is true Mk and Lk do not record this last phrase, "unto remission of sins." But there is no intimation that this phrase is the result of Matthew's theologizing on the purpose of Christ's death (see Wendt, *Teaching of Jesus*, II, 239 ff, who claims this phrase is not from Jesus; also Allen in "Mt," *ICC*, in loc.). But Paul leaves no doubt as to the connection between man's forgiveness by God and Christ's sacrifice for him. This idea is rooted in the great passage on justification (Rom **3** 21—**5** 21; see esp. **4** 7); is positively declared in Eph **1** 7; Col **1** 14. The author of He teaches that the shedding of Christ's blood under the new covenant is as necessary to secure forgiveness as the shedding of animal's blood under the old. John also implies that forgiveness is based on the blood (1 Jn **1** 7–9).

True reconciliation and forgiveness include the canceling of the offender's guilt. Jesus has no direct word on the cancellation of guilt. Paul closes his argument for the universality of human sin by asserting that "all the world may be brought under the judgment of God" (AV "guilty before God," Rom **3** 19). Thayer (*Gr-Eng. Lex.*, in loc.) says this word "guilty" means "owing satisfaction to God" (liable to punishment by God). But in Rom **8** 1.3 Paul exclaims, "There is therefore now no condemnation to them that are in Christ Jesus . . . . God, sending his own Son in the likeness of sinful flesh and for sin" (ERV and ARVm "as an offering for sin"). The guilt, or exposure of the sinner to God's wrath and so to punishment, is removed by the sin offering which Christ made. This idea is implied by the author of He (**2** 15), but is not expressed in Peter and John.

4. The Cancellation of Guilt

Right standing with God is also implied in the preceding idea. Forgiving sin and canceling guilt are the negative, bringing into right standing with God the positive, aspects of the same transaction. "Him who knew no sin he made to be sin [i.e. the sin offering; so Augustine and other Fathers, Ewald, Ritschl; see Meyer, *Comm.*, in loc., who denies this meaning] on our behalf; that we might become the righteousness of God in him" (2 Cor **5** 21). In this passage Paul makes justification the Divine purpose of the sacrificial death of Christ. This thought is elaborated by the apostle in Gal and Rom, but is not expressed by Jesus, or in He, in Pet or in Jn.

5. Justification or Right Standing with God

Jesus does not connect our cleansing or sanctification with His death, but with His word (Jn **17** 17). The subst. "cleansing" (καθαρισμός, *katharismós*) is not used by Paul, and the vb. "to cleanse" (καθαρίζω, *katharízō*) occurs only twice in his later letters (Eph **5** 26; Tit **2** 14). He does use the idea of sanctification, and in Rom **6–8** teaches that sanctification is a logical consequence of justification which is secured by Christ's sacrificial death. In Phil **3** 10.11, he views Christ's death and resurrection as the dynamic of transformation in the new life. The author of He (**1** 3; **9** 14.22.23; **10** 2), following his OT figures, uses the idea of cleansing for the whole process of putting away sin, from atonement to sanctification (see Westcott, *Comm.*, in loc.). He makes Christ's death the procuring cause of the cleansing. John does the same (1 Jn **1** 7; Rev **7** 14).

6. Cleansing or Sanctification

Divine sonship of the believer is also traced by Paul to the sacrificial death of Christ (Rom **8** 17), though this thought is not found in other NT writers.

7. Sonship

So, we sum up, the whole process of salvation, from reconciliation with God to the adoption of the saved sinner into heaven's household, is ascribed, to some extent by Jesus, largely by Paul the theologian of the NT, and, in varying degrees, by other NT writers, to the sacrificial death of Christ. Even Holtzmann (*Neutest. Theol.*, II, 111) admits "It is upon the moment of death that the grounding of salvation is exclusively concentrated."

V. How Christ's Sacrifice Procures Salvation.— It must be conceded that the NT writers, much less Jesus, did not discuss this subject from the philosophical point of view. Jesus never philosophizes except incidentally. Paul, the author of He, and John had a philosophy underlying their theology, the first and second dealing most with the sacrificial work of Christ, the last with His person. But Paul and the author of He did not write their letters to produce a philosophical system explaining *how* Christ's sacrificial death can and does procure man's salvation.

By some it is claimed that the word "ransom" (Mk **10** 45) gives us the key to the philosophy of the atonement as presented by Jesus Himself. But the rules of exegesis are against this supposition. Jesus in the context is teaching His disciples that sacrificial service is greatness. To illustrate the truth He refers to His own example of coming to "minister, and to give his life a ransom for many." That is, Jesus is enforcing a practical principle and not elaborating a theoretical truth. Moreover, the word "ransom" is used metaphorically, and the laws of exegesis forbid us to press the literal meaning of a figure. The figure suggests captivity in sin and deliverance by payment of a price (the death of Christ). But Jesus does not tell us *how* His sacrificial death can and does pay the price for man's redemption from sin. The word "ransom" does give the clue to the development of the vicarious sacrifice elaborated later by Paul. Ritschl (*Rechtfertigung und Versöhnung*, II, 85) does not do the word "ransom" justice when he claims that it merely reproduces the meaning of the Heb כֹּפֶר, *kōpher*, "covering as a protection," and that Christ's death, like a covering, delivers us by stimulating us to lead the life of sacrificial service as Christ did. Wendt (*Lehre Jesu*, II, 237; *Teaching of Jesus*, II, 226 f) admits the "ransom"-idea in the word, but says Christ delivers us from bondage to suffering and death, not by His death, but by His teaching which is illustrated by His sacrificial death. Beyschlag (*Neutest. Theol.*, I, 153) thinks Christ's death delivers us from worldly ambitions and such sins by showing us the example of Jesus in sacrifice. Weiss (*Bib. Theol. of the NT*, I, 101–3) thinks Christ's "surrender of His life . . . . avails *as* a ransom which He gives instead of the many" who were not able to pay the price themselves. He also adds, "The saying regarding the ransom lays emphasis upon the God-pleasing performance of Jesus which secures the salvation," etc.

1. Jesus' Teaching

Nor does Jesus' saying at the Last Supper, "This is my blood of the covenant" (Mk **14** 24) give us unmistakable evidence of *how* His death saves men. It does teach that sinners on entering the kingdom come into a new covenant relation with God which implies forgiveness of sin and fellowship with God, and that, as the covenant sacrifices at Mt. Sinai (Ex **24** 3–8) ratified the legal covenant between God and His people, so the death of Christ as a covenant sacrifice ratifies the covenant of grace between God and lost sinners, by virtue of which covenant God on His part forgives the penitent sinner, and the surrendering sinner on his part presents himself to God for the life of sacrifice. But this statement fails to tell us *how* God can forgive sin on the basis of a covenant thus ratified by Christ's death. Does it mean substitution, that as the animal whose blood ratified the covenant was slain instead of the people, so Christ was slain in the place of sinners? Or does it suggest the immutability of the covenant on the basis of the animal's (and so Christ's) representing both God and man, and killing signifying loss of life or will to change the covenant (so Westcott, *Comm. on He*, 301)? It could scarcely mean that Christ's sacrifice was the offering of a perfect, acceptable life to God (Wendt, op. cit., II, 237), or that Christ's death is viewed merely as the common meal sacrifice, that God and His people thus enter into a kind of union and communion (so some evolutionists in the study of comparative religion; see Menzies, *Hist of Religion*, 416 ff).

Ritschl and many modern scholars are disposed to reject all philosophy in religion. They say, "Back to Christ." Paul was only a human interpreter of Jesus. But he was a Divinely-guided interpreter, and we need his first-hand interpretations of Jesus. What has he to say as to how Christ's death saves men?

2. Paul's Teaching

(1) *The words expressing the idea of redemption.*— See above on the terms of sacrifice. The classical passage containing the idea of redemption is Rom **3** 24–26: "Being justified freely by his grace through the redemption that is in Christ Jesus: whom God set forth *to be* a propitiation, through faith, in his blood, to show his righteousness because of the passing over of the sins done aforetime, in the forbearance of God; for the showing, *I say*, of his righteousness at this present season: that he might himself be just, and the justifier of him that hath faith in Jesus." A fair interpretation of this passage gives us the following propositions: (*a*) The believer obtains right standing with God by means of, through the channel of (see Thayer, *Gr-Eng. Lex.*, Διά, A, III, 2), redemption which is in Christ. (*b*) This redemption in Christ involves, or is based upon, the Divinely-purposed propitiation which Christ made

in His death. (*c*) The design of God in making such a propitiation was the exhibition of His righteousness; i.e., the vindication of that side of His character which demands the punishment of sin, which had not been shown in former generations when His forbearance passed over men's sins. See Sanday, *Comm. on Rom*, in loc. The classical passage containing the other word to redeem (ἐξαγοράζω, *exagorázō*) is Gal **3** 13: "Christ redeemed us from the curse of the law, having become a curse for us," etc. Professor E. D. Burton (*AJT*, October, 1907) thinks: (*a*) Law here means "law legalistically understood." (*b*) The "curse" was the verdict of the law of pure legalism, "a disclosure to man of his actual status before God on a basis of merit." (*c*) The redemption meant is that Christ "brought to an end the régime of law . . . . rather than deliverance of individuals through release from penalty." He bases this argument largely on the use of ἡμᾶς, *hēmás*, "us," meaning Jews in antithesis with τὰ ἔθνη, *tá éthnē*, the Gentiles (ver 14). Everett (*The Gospel of Paul*) thinks that Christ was cursed in that He was "crucified" (the *manner* not the *fact* of His death being the curse); that is, as Everett sees it, Christ became ceremonially unclean, and so free from the law. So does His follower by being crucified with Christ become ceremonially unclean and so free from the law. The passage seems to give us the following propositions: (*a*) Man under law (whether the revealed law of the OT or the moral law) is under a "curse," that is, liable to the penalty which the broken law demands. (*b*) Christ by His death on the cross became a "curse for us." (*c*) By means of Christ thus becoming a "curse for us" He delivered us, "not the Jews as a nation, but all of us, Jews and Gentiles, who believed," from the curse incurred by the breaking of the law. Professor Burton admits that the participle γενόμενος, *genómenos*, "becoming," may be a "participle of means" (art. cited above, 643), and so we have "Christ redeemed us from the curse of the law *by becoming* a curse for us." The passage at least suggests, if it does not declare, that Christ saves us by *vicariously* enduring the penalty to which we were exposed.

(2) *The idea of reconciliation.*—Paul uses the phrase "wrath of God" (Rom **1** 18, etc) to express the attitude of God toward sin, an attitude of displeasure and of grief, of revulsion of holy character which demands the punishment of sin. On the other hand, God loves the sinner; love is the prompting cause of redemption through Christ (Rom **5** 8; **8** 32). That is, wrath is love grieving and righteousness revolting because of sin, and both phases may act simultaneously (Simon, *Redemption of Man*, 216, to the contrary). So Paul says, "God was in Christ reconciling the world unto himself, not reckoning unto them their trespasses" (2 Cor **5** 19). Now this word "reconcile" (*katallassein*) means in the active, "to receive into favor," in the passive, "to be restored to favor" (Thayer). See also *Rev. and Expos*, October, 1909, 600 ff, where Professor Estes shows, from Sophocles, Xenophon, Josephus, LXX and passages in the NT like Mt **5** 24, that the word must mean a change in the attitude of God toward men and not merely a change of men toward God. Practically the same is taught by Meyer (*Comm. on 2 Cor*); Lipsius (*Handcomm. zum NT*); Sanday (*Comm. on Rom*); Denney (*Exeget. Gr Test. on Rom*); Lietzmann (*Handbuch zum NT*); Holtzmann (*Neutest. Theol.*); Weiss (*Rel. of the NT*); Pfleiderer (*Paulinism*); Stevens (*Christian Doctrine of Salvation*), and in nearly all the great comms. on Rom and 2 Cor, and by all the writers on NT theology except Beyschlag. See also Reconciliation; Retribution.

(3) *The idea of propitiation.*—Only once (Rom **3** 25) does Paul use the word "propitiation." As we saw in (1) above, the redemption in Christ is based upon the propitiation which Christ made in His death. Thayer (*Gr-Eng. Lex.*, in loc.) says the noun signifies "a means of appeasing, expiating, a propitiation, an expiatory sacrifice." He thinks it has this meaning in Rom **3** 25, but refers it to the "mercy-seat" in He **9** 5. Sanday (*Comm. on Rom*, 88) regards *hilastērion* as an adj. meaning "propitiatory." De Wette, Fritzsche, Meyer, Lipsius and many others take it in this sense; Gifford, Vaughan, Liddon, Ritschl think it means "mercy-seat" here as in He. But with either meaning the blood of Christ is viewed as securing the mercy of God. Propitiation of God is made by the blood of Christ, and because of that men have access to the mercy-seat where shines the glory of God in His forgiveness of man's sins. See Romans, Epistle to the, 9, (3).

(4) *The prepositions* ὑπέρ, *hupér, and* ἀντί, *antí.*—Paul never uses *anti* ("for," "instead of," "in place of," so Thayer) to express what Christ's sacrifice does for the sinner, but *huper* ("for one's safety or advantage," primarily, but also "in the place of," "instead of," so Thayer). See Rom **5** 8; **8** 32; **14** 15; 1 Cor **11** 24; 2 Cor **5** 15; Gal **3** 13; Eph **5** 2.25; 1 Thess **5** 10; 1 Tim **2** 6; Tit **2** 14. It is to be noted that in 1 Tim **2** 6 Paul uses *antilutron*, "ransom," compounded with the preposition *anti*, but follows it with *huper*, which may suggest that *huper* is here used in the sense of *anti*, "in the place of."

Summing up Paul's teaching as to how Christ's sacrifice saves: (*a*) The propitiatory sacrifice does not "soften God, or assuage the anger of God" (as Bushnell claims the advocates of the satisfaction theories assert, *Vicarious Sacrifice*, 486). God is already willing to save men, His love makes the propitiatory sacrifice (Rom **5** 8). God's love makes the sacrifice, not the sacrifice His willingness to save. (*b*) But man by breaking God's law had come under the curse, the penalty of the broken law (Gal **3** 13), and so was under God's wrath (Rom **1** 18), i.e. man's sin exposed him to punishment, while at the same time God's love for the sinner was grieved. (*c*) Christ by His sacrificial death made it possible for God to show His righteousness and love at the same time; i.e. that He did punish sin, but did love the sinner and wish to save him (Rom **3** 25.26; **5** 8). (*d*) Christ, who was sinless, suffered *vicariously* for sinful men. His death was not due to His sins but those of men (2 Cor **5** 21). (*e*) His death, followed by His resurrection which marked Him off as the sinless Son of God, and so appointed the Saviour of men (Rom **1** 4), was designed by God to bring men into right relation with God (Rom **3** 26*b*; 2 Cor **5** 21*b*). So, we may say, Paul explained the relation of Christ's death to the sinner's spiritual life by thinking of a transfer of the sinner's "curse" to Christ, which He bore on the cross, and of God's righteousness through Christ (Phil **3** 9) to the sinner by faith in Christ. But we must not press this vicarious idea too far into a system of philosophy of the atonement and claim that the system is the teaching of Paul. The quantitative, commercial idea of transfer is not in Paul's mind. The language of redemption, propitiation, ransom, is largely figurative. We must feel the spiritual truth of a qualitative transfer of sin from man to Christ and of righteousness from Christ to man, and rest the matter there, so far as Paul's teaching goes. Beyond this our conclusions as to substitution as the method of atonement are results of philosophizing on Paul's teaching.

3. Teaching of Hebrews

The author of He adds nothing to Paul's teaching respecting the method whereby Christ's sacrifice operates in saving men. His purpose to produce an apology showing forth the superior efficacy of Christ's high-priestly sacrifice over that of the Aaronic priesthood fixes his first thought on the *efficacy* of the sacrifice rather than on its mode of operation. He does use the words "redemption" (**9** 12; cf ver 15), "propitiate" (**2** 17), and emphasizes the opening up of the heavenly holy of holies by the high-priestly sacrifice of Christ (the way of access to the very presence of God by Christ's death, **10** 19.20), which gives us data for forming a system based on a real propitiation for sin and reconciliation of God similar to the Pauline teaching formulated above.

4. Petrine and Johannine Teaching

Peter asserts that Christ suffered vicariously (1 Pet **2** 22–24), who, although He "did no sin," "his own self bare our sins in his body upon the tree"; who "suffered for sins once, the righteous for [*huper*, not *anti*] the unrighteous" (1 Pet **3** 18). But Peter goes no farther than Paul (perhaps not so far) in elaborating *how* Jesus' vicarious suffering saves the sinner. The Johannine writings contain the propitiatory idea (1 Jn **2** 2; **4** 10), although John writes to emphasize the *incarnation* and not the *work* of the Incarnate One (Jn **1** 1–18; 1 Jn **4** 2.3).

To sum up the NT teachings on the *mode* or operation: Jesus asserts His vicarious suffering (Mk **10** 45; cf Jn **10** 11) and hints at the mode of its operation by using the "ransom" figure. Paul, Peter and John teach that Christ's sacrifice was vicarious, and all but Peter suggest the idea of propitiation as to the mode of its operation. There is no direct discussion of what propitiation means.

VI. Rationale of the Efficacy of Christ's Sacrifice.—Jesus emphasizes His voluntary spirit in making the sacrifice. "The Son of man also came . . . . to give his life a ransom." The sacrifice was voluntary, not compulsory. God did not force Him to lay down His life; He chose to do so (cf Jn **10** 11). But Jesus gives us no philosophy on this or any other element in His sacrifice as being the ground of its efficacy.

1. Jesus' Teaching

Paul also emphasizes the voluntary gift of Christ (Gal **2** 20), but he urges rather the dignity of Him who makes the sacrifice as a ground of its efficacy. It is the sacrifice of God's Son, shown to be such in His resurrection (Rom **1** 4; **4** 25*b*). It was no ordinary man but the sinless Son who gave "himself" (Gal **2** 20). It was not merely a dying Christ but the Son who rose again "in power" (Rom **1** 4), who secures our "justification" (Rom **4** 25*b*; 1 Cor **15** 3.4.17*b*). Paul also emphasizes the sinless life and character of Jesus as a ground of efficacy in Christ's sacrifice, "who knew no sin" in His life experience (2 Cor **5** 21*a*).

2. Paul's Teaching

The author of He, most of all NT writers, elaborates the grounds of efficacy in Christ's sacrifice. (1) It was a *personal* not an *animal* sacrifice (**9** 12–14; **9** 26, "sacrifice of himself"; **10** 4). (2) It was the sacrifice of the *Son* of God (**3** 5). (3) It was a *royal* person who made the sacrifice (**6** 20*b*; **7** 1, "after the order of Melchizedek . . . . king of Salem"). (4) It was a *sinless* person (**7** 26.27; **9** 14; **10** 10.12). Westcott, *Comm. on He*, 298, well says, "It becomes necessary, therefore, in order to gain a complete view of the Sacrifice of Christ, to combine with the crowning act upon the Cross His fulfilment of the will of God from first to last, the Sacrifice of Life with the Sacrifice of Death." (5) It was an *eternal* person (**6** 20, "for ever"; **7** 16, "after the power of an endless [m "indissoluble"] life"). The author of He reaches the climax of his argument for the superior efficacy of Christ's sacrifice when he represents Him as entering the holy of holies in the very presence of God to complete the offering for man's sin (**8** 1.2; **9** 11.12.24).

3. The Teaching in Hebrews

Peter and John do not discuss the ground of efficacy, and so add nothing to our conclusions above. The efficacy of the sacrifice is suggested by describing the glory of the person (1 Pet **1** 19; **2** 22.23; 1 Jn **1** 7*b*; **2** 2).

To sum up our conclusion as to the efficacy of Christ's sacrifice: Jesus and the leading NT writers intimate that the efficacy of His sacrifice centers in His personality. Jesus, Peter and John do not discuss the subject directly. Paul, though discussing it more extensively, does not do so fully, but the author of He centers and culminates his argument for the finality of Christianity, in the superior efficacy of Christ's sacrifice, which is grounded in His personality, Divine, royal, sinless, eternal (see Ménégoz, *Théol. de l'Ep. aux Hébreux*). It is easy to see, from the position taken by the author of He, how Anselm in *Cur Deus Homo* developed his theory of satisfaction, according to which the Divinity in Christ gave His atoning sacrifice its priceless worth in God's eyes.

VII. The Human Conditions of Application.—The sacrificial death of Christ is universal in its objective potentiality, according to Jesus (Lk **24** 47, "unto all the nations"); according to Paul (Rom **1** 5; **5** 18; **11** 32; 2 Cor **5** 14.15; Gal **3** 14); according to the author of He (**2** 9, "taste of death for every man"); according to John (1 Jn **2** 2, "propitiation . . . . for the whole world").

1. Universal in Objective Potentiality

But the objective redemption to be efficacious must be subjectively applied. The blood of Christ is the universally efficacious remedy for the sin-sick souls of men, but each man must make the subjective application. How is the application made? And the threefold answer is, by repentance, by faith, and by obedience.

2. Efficacious When Subjectively Applied

(1) *By repentance.*—The Baptist and Jesus emphasized repentance (change of mind first of all, then change of relation and of life) as the condition of entrance into the kingdom and of enjoyment of the Messianic salvation (Mt **3** 2; Mk **1** 15). Peter preached repentance at Pentecost and immediately after as a means of obtaining forgiveness (Acts **2** 38; **3** 19, etc). Paul, although emphasizing faith, also stressed repentance as an element in the human condition of salvation (Acts **20** 21; Rom **2** 4, etc). John (Rev **2**, **3**, *passim*) emphasizes repentance, though not stressing it as a means of receiving the benefits of redemption.

(2) *By faith.*—Jesus connected faith with repentance (Mk **1** 15) as the condition of receiving the Messianic salvation. Paul makes faith the all-inclusive means of applying the work of Christ. The gospel is "the power of God unto salvation to every one that believeth" (Rom **1** 16); "whom God set forth to be a propitiation, through faith" (**3** 25); "faith [not works] is reckoned for righteousness" (**4** 5); "justified by faith" (**5** 1). In Gal, the letters to the Cor, in the Captivity and the Pastoral Epp. he emphasizes faith as the sole condition of receiving salvation. But what kind of faith is it that appropriates the saving benefit of Christ's death? Not historical or intellectual but "heart" faith (Rom **10** 10). To Paul "heart" meant the seat or essence of the whole personality, and so faith which applies the redemption in Christ is the personal commitment of one's self to Christ as Saviour and Lord (2 Cor **5** 15). See Thayer, *Gr-Eng. Lex.*, πιστεύω, *pisteúō*, 1, *b*, *γ*, for a particular discussion of the meaning of faith in this sense. The author of He discusses esp. faith as a conquering power, but also implies that it is the condition of entrance upon the life of spiritual rest and fellowship (chs **3** and **4**, *passim*). Peter (1 Pet **1** 9) and John (1 Jn **3** 23; **4** 16; **5** 1.5, etc) also regard faith as a means of applying the saving benefits of Christ's death.

(3) *By obedience in sacrificial service.*—Jesus said, "If any man would come after me, let him deny himself, and take up his cross, and follow me" (Mk **8** 34). Here He lays down two elements in the conditions of discipleship, denying one's self and taking up his cross. The former means the renunciation of self as the center of thought, faith, hope and life. The latter means the life of sacrifice. Jesus was stressing this truth when He uttered that incomparable saying, "The Son of man came not to be ministered unto, but to minister, and to give his life a ransom for many" (Mk **10** 45 ‖ Mt **20** 28). Paul also emphasizes this phase of the human condition of salvation when he shows how sanctification grows spontaneously out of justification (Rom **6** 8) and when he says that what "avails" is "faith working through love" (Gal **5** 6). The author of He says, "He became unto all them that obey him the author [Gr αἴτιος, *aítios*, "cause"] of eternal salvation" (**5** 9). Peter and John, the latter esp., emphasize the keeping of His commandments, the life of service, as the means of appropriating to the fullest the saving benefits of Christ's death. The theologians in classrooms and preachers in the pulpits have failed to emphasize this aspect of "saving faith" as did Jesus, Paul, the author of He, and John. In the NT salvation is a process as well as an instantaneous act on the part of God, and the process is carried on by means of obedience, the life of service, which appropriates by faith the dynamic of Christ's sacrifice.

VIII. The Christian's Life the Life of Sacrifice.—This discussion of the faith that "obeys" leads to the consideration of that climactic thought of NT writers, namely, that the Christian's life is sacrificial living based on Christ's sacrifice for him. We note in outline the following:

The Christian's life of sacrifice is the logical consequence of Christ's sacrificial death. The Christ who sacrificed Himself for the believer is now continuing the sacrifice in the believer's life

(Gal **2** 20; Phil **1** 21). Paul was crucified when Christ was crucified (in a bold mystic figure), and the life of Christ which sacrificed itself on the cross and perpetuates itself in resurrection power now operates as a mighty dynamic for the apostle's moral and spiritual transformation (Phil **3** 10.11). It is to be noted, Jesus also emphasized this kind of living, though not so expressly connecting the believer's sacrificial life with His sacrificial death (see Mk **8** 34 f).

1. Consequence of Christ's Sacrifice

2. Christ's Death the Appeal for Christian's Sacrifice

Christ's sacrificial death becomes the persuasive appeal for the Christian's sacrificial life, "Because we thus judge, that one died for all, therefore all died; and he died for all, that they that live should no longer live unto themselves, but unto him who for their sakes died and rose again" (2 Cor **5** 14.15). Because He died for us we should live for Him. But what is the appeal which Christ's sacrificial death makes to the saved sinner? "The love of Christ constraineth us" (2 Cor **5** 14). Christ's death on the cross exhibits His love, unspeakable, unthinkable love, for it was love for His "enemies" (Rom **5** 10), and that matchless love kindles love in the forgiven sinner's heart. He is willing to do anything, even to die, for his Saviour who died for him (Acts **21** 13; Phil **1** 29.30). It is a greater privilege for the saved sinner to suffer for Christ than it is to believe on Him. Peter (1 Pet **3** 17.18), the author of He (**12; 13** 13) and John (1 Jn **3** 16; **4** 16–19) emphasize this truth.

3. Necessary to Fill Out Christ's Sacrifice

The Christian's sacrifice is necessary to fill out Christ's sacrifice. "Now I rejoice in my sufferings for your sake, and fill up on my part that which is lacking of the afflictions of Christ in my flesh for his body's sake, which is the church" (Col **1** 24). Roman Catholic exegetes have made the apostle teach that the sufferings of the saints, along with Christ's sufferings, have atoning efficacy. But Paul nowhere intimates that his sufferings avail for putting away sins. We may hold with Weiss (*Comm. on the NT*) that Paul longed to experience in his life the perfect sacrificial spirit as Christ did; or with Alford (in loc.) that he wished to suffer his part of Christ's sufferings to be endured by him through His church; or, as it seems to us, he longed to make effective by his ministry of sacrificial service to as many others as possible the sacrificial death of Christ. Christ's sacrifice avails in saving men only when Christians sacrifice their lives in making known this sacrifice of Christ.

4. Content of the Christian's Sacrifice

(1) The Christian is to present his personality (Rom **15** 16). Paul commends the Macedonians for "first" giving "their own selves to the Lord" (2 Cor **8** 5). (2) Christians must present their "bodies a living sacrifice, holy, acceptable to God" (Rom **12** 1). In the old system of sacrifices the animals were offered as dead; Christians are to offer their bodies, all their members with their powers, to God a "living sacrifice," i.e. a sacrifice which operates in lives of holiness and service (see also Rom **6** 13.19). (3) Christians must offer their money or earthly possessions to God. Paul speaks of the gift from the church at Philippi as "a sacrifice acceptable, well-pleasing to God" (Phil **4** 18). This gift was to the apostle a beautiful expression of the sacrificial spirit imparted to them because they had the "mind" of Christ who "emptied himself, ... becoming obedient even unto death, yea, the death of the cross" (**2** 5–8). The author of He (**13** 16) exhorts his readers, "But to do good and to communicate forget not: for with such sacrifices God is well pleased." (4) The general exercise of all our gifts and graces is viewed by Peter as sacrificial living (1 Pet **2** 5): "Ye also, as living stones, are built up a spiritual house, to be a holy priesthood, to offer up spiritual sacrifices," etc. All Christians are priests and daily offer up their burnt offerings acceptable to God, if they 'suffer as Christians' (1 Pet **2** 20; **3** 18) in the exercise of their graces and powers.

But how do these sacrifices of the Christian affect him and God? The NT writers never hint that our sacrifices propitiate God, or so win His favor that He will or can on account of our sacrifices forgive our sins. They are "well-pleasing" to Him, a "sweet odor"; that is, they win His approval of our lives thus lived according to the standard which Christ gives us. Their influence on us is the increase of our spiritual efficiency and power and finally a greater capacity for enjoying spiritual blessings in heaven (1 Cor **3** 14).

5. The Supper as a Sacrifice

Some scholars (Roman Catholic, Episcopalian, etc) regard the memorial supper as a kind of sacrifice which the Christian offers in worship. Neither Jesus, Paul, the author of He, Peter, or John, ever hints that in eating the bread and drinking the wine the Christian offers a sacrifice to God in Christ. Paul teaches that in partaking of the Supper we "proclaim the Lord's death till he come" (1 Cor **11** 26). That is, instead of offering a sacrifice ourselves to God, in partaking of the Supper we proclaim the offering of Christ's sacrifice for us. Milligan argues that as Christ in heaven perpetually offers Himself for us, so we on earth, in the Supper, offer ourselves to Him (*Heavenly Priesthood*, 266). Even Cave (*Spiritual Doctrine of Sacrifice*, 439) maintains, "In a certain loose sense the Lord's Supper may be called a sacrifice." See the above books for the argument supporting this position.

To sum up our conclusions on sacrifice in the NT:

(1) Jesus and NT writers regard the OT sacrificial system as from God, but imperfect, the various sacrifices serving only as types of the one great sacrifice which Christ made.

(2) All the writers, except James and Jude, with Jesus, emphasize the sacrificial idea, Jesus less, giving only two hints of His sacrificial death (in the Synoptic Gospels), the author of He putting the climactic emphasis on Christ's sacrifice as the sacrifice of atonement.

(3) As to the relation of Christ's sacrifice to man's salvation, the latter is the achievement of the former, so expressed only twice by Jesus, but emphatically so declared by Paul, the author of He, Peter, and John (Paul and He laying most emphasis on this point).

(4) As to *how* Christ's sacrifice saves men, Jesus, the author of He, Peter and John suggest the idea of propitiation, while Paul emphatically teaches that man is under a curse, exposed to the displeasure of God, and that Christ's sacrifice secured the reconciliation of God by vindicating His righteousness in punishing sin and His love in saving sinners. Jesus and the leading NT writers agree that Christ saves men through His vicarious suffering.

(5) As to the rational basis of efficacy in Christ's sacrifice, there is no direct discussion in the NT except by the author of He who grounds its final, eternal efficacy in Christ's personality, Divine, royal, sinless and eternal.

(6) As to the conditions of applying Christ's sacrifice, repentance and faith, which lives and fruits in obedience and sacrificial living, are recognized by Jesus and all the leading NT writers as the means of appropriating the benefits of Christ's sacrifice.

(7) By Jesus, Paul, the author of He, Peter and John the Christian life is viewed as the life of sacrifice. Christ's death is at once the cause, motive,

measure, and the dynamic of the Christian's sacrificial life.

LITERATURE.—In addition to the great comms.—*ICC*, Allen on "Mt," Gould on "Mk," Sanday-Headlam on "Rom"; Westcott on the *Gospel and Epp. of John*, and on the *Hebrews;* Davidson, Delitzsch and Meyer on *He;* Meyer on *2 Cor;* Lightfoot and Abbott on *Col;* and the standard authors of the *Bib. Theol. of the NT*, Weiss, Beyschlag, Bovon, Stevens, Sheldon—see the following special works: Cave, *Scriptural Doctrine of Sacrifice*, Edinburgh, 1890; Simon, *Redemption of Man*, 1886; G. Milligan, *The Theology of the Ep. to the He*, Edinburgh, 1899; Milligan, *The Ascension and Heavenly Priesthood of Our Lord*, London, 1908; W. P. Du Bose, *High-Priesthood and Sacrifice;* Everett, *The Gospel of Paul*, Boston, 1893; Burton, Smith, and Smith, *Bib. Ideas of Atonement*, Chicago, 1909; Denney, *The Death of Christ: Its Place and Interpretation in the NT*, London, 1902; Denney, *The Atonement and the Modern Mind*, London, 1903; Ritschl, *Rechtfertigung und Versöhnung* (*Justification and Reconciliation*), Bonn, 1895–1902, ET, 1900; Ménégoz, *Théol. de l'Ep. aux Hébreux;* art. "Blood," *ERE*, by H. Wheeler Robinson; art. "Communion with Deity," ib, by Nathan Söderblom; art. "Communion with Deity" (Christian), ib, by Darwell Stone and D. C. Simpson; art. "Expiation and Atonement," ib, by W. A. Brown (Christian viewpoint), S. R. Driver (Heb), H. Loewe (Jewish); art. "Redemption from the Curse of the Law," in *AJT*, October, 1907, by Professor E. D. Burton; art. "Some Thoughts as to the Effects of the Death of Christ," in *Rev. and Expos*, October, 1909.

C. B. WILLIAMS

SACRIFICE, HUMAN, hū'man: As an expression of religious devotion, human sacrifice has been widespread at certain stages of the race's development. The tribes of Western Asia were deeply affected by the practice, probably prior to the settlement of the Hebrews in Pal, and it continued at least down to the 5th cent. BC. At times of great calamity, anxiety and danger, parents sacrificed their children as the greatest and most costly offering which they could make to propitiate the anger of the gods and thus secure their favor and help. There is no intimation in the Bible that enemies or captives were sacrificed; only the offering of children by their parents is mentioned. The belief that this offering possessed supreme value is seen in Mic **6** 6 f, where the sacrifice of the firstborn is the climax of a series of offerings which, in a rising scale of values, are suggested as a means of propitiating the angry Jeh. A striking example of the rite as actually practised is seen in 2 K **3** 27, where Mesha the king of Moab (made famous by the Moabite Stone), under the stress of a terrible siege, offered his eldest son, the heir-apparent to the throne, as a burnt offering upon the wall of Kir-hareseth. As a matter of fact this horrid act seems to have had the effect of driving off the allies.

Human sacrifice was ordinarily resorted to, no doubt, only in times of great distress, but it seems to have been practised among the old Canaanitish tribes with some frequency (Dt **12** 31). The Israelites are said to have borrowed it from their Can. neighbors (2 K **16** 3; 2 Ch **28** 3), and as a matter of fact human sacrifices were never offered to Jeh, but only to various gods of the land. The god who was most frequently worshipped in this way was Moloch or Molech, the god of the Ammonites (2 K **23** 10; Lev **18** 21; **20** 2), but from Jeremiah we learn that the Phoen god Baal was, at least in the later period of the history, also associated with Molech in receiving this worship (Jer **19** 5; **32** 35).

As in the case of the Canaanites, the only specific cases of human sacrifice mentioned among the Israelites are those of the royal princes, sons of Ahaz and Manasseh, the two kings of Judah who were most deeply affected by the surrounding heathen practices and who, at the same time, fell into great national distress (2 K **16** 3; 2 Ch **28** 3; 2 K **21** 6; 2 Ch **33** 6). But it is clear from many general statements that the custom was widespread among the masses of the people as well. It is forbidden in the Mosaic legislation (Lev **18** 21; **20** 2–5; Dt **18** 10); it is said in 2 K **17** 17 that the sacrifice of sons *and daughters* was one of the causes of the captivity of the ten tribes. Jeremiah charges the people of the Southern Kingdom with doing the same thing (Jer **7** 31; **19** 5; **32** 35); with these general statements agree Isa **57** 5; Ezk **16** 2 f; **20** 31; **23** 37; Ps **106** 37 f. A study of these passages makes it certain that in the period immediately before the captivity of Judah, human sacrifice was by no means confined to the royal family, but was rather common among the people. Daughters as well as sons were sacrificed. It is mentioned only once in connection with the Northern Kingdom, and then only in the summary of the causes of their captivity (2 K **17** 17), but the Southern Kingdom in its later years was evidently deeply affected. There were various places where the bloody rite was celebrated (Jer **19** 5), but the special high place, apparently built for the purpose, was in the Valley of Tophet or Hinnom (*gē-hinnōm*, Gehenna) near Jerus (2 Ch **28** 3; **33** 6). This great high place, built for the special purpose of human sacrifice (Jer **7** 31; **32** 35), was defiled by the good king Josiah in the hope of eradicating the cruel practice (2 K **23** 10).

The Bib. writers without exception look upon the practice with horror as the supreme point of national and religious apostasy, and a chief cause of national disaster. They usually term the rite "passing through fire," probably being unwilling to use the sacred term "sacrifice" in reference to such a revolting custom. There is no evidence of a continuance of the practice in captivity nor after the return. It is said, however, that the heathen Sepharvites, settled by the Assyr kings in the depopulated territory of the Northern Kingdom, "burnt their children in the fire to Adrammelech and Anammelech, the gods of Sepharvaim" (2 K **17** 31). The practice is not heard of again, and probably rapidly died out. The restored Israelites were not affected by it. Cf SACRIFICE (OT), VI, 10.

WILLIAM JOSEPH MCGLOTHLIN

SACRILEGE, sak'ri-lej: For "commit sacrilege" in Rom **2** 22 (AV and ERVm), RV has "rob temples," which more exactly expresses the meaning of the vb. (*hierosuléō;* cf Acts **19** 37, "robbers of temples" [q.v.]). The noun occurs in 2 Macc **4** 39 (AV and RV) for the corresponding form *hierosúlēma*.

SADAMIAS, sad-a-mī'as: AV=RV SALEMAS (q.v.).

SADAS, sā'das: AV=RV ASTAD (q.v.).

SADDEUS, sa-dē'us: AV=RV LODDEUS (q.v.).

SADDLE, sad''l: As noun (מֶרְכָּב, *merkābh*, "a riding seat") the word occurs in Lev **15** 9 (m "carriage"); ordinarily it is used as a vb. (חָבַשׁ, *ḥābhash*, lit. to "bind up" or "gird about"), to saddle an ass (Gen **22** 3; Nu **22** 21; Jgs **19** 10, etc).

SADDUCEES, sad'ū-sēz (צַדּוּקִים, *çaddūḳīm;* Σαδδουκαῖοι, *Saddoukaioi*):

I. INTRODUCTORY
1. Name: Rival Etymologies. Probably from Zadok the High Priest
2. Authorities: NT, Josephus, Talmud (primary), Church Fathers (secondary)

II. ORIGIN AND HISTORY
1. Early Notices in Josephus: Alleged Relation to Differences between Prophets and Priests
2. Tendencies of Sadducees toward Hellenism as Causing Rise of *ḥăṣidhim*
3. Favored by Alex. Jannaeus: Put in the Background by Alexandra Salome
4. From a Political, Become Also a Religious Party
5. NT Time—Dread of Roman Interference if Messianic Claim Recognized
6. Sadducees Antagonistic to the Apostles: Pharisees More Favorable
7. Fall of Sadducean Party at Outbreak of Jewish War

This prominent Jewish sect, though not so numerous as their opponents, the Pharisees, by their wealth and the priestly descent of many of them had an influence which fully balanced that of their more popular rivals. They were a political party, of priestly and aristocratic tendency, as against the more religious and democratic Pharisees.

I. Introductory.—The Talm form suggests derivation from the name of their founder, but the form in NT and Jos would imply connection with the vb. "to be righteous." The probability is, that the name is derived from some person named "Zadok." The most prominent Zadok in history was the Davidic high priest (2 S **8** 17; **15** 24; 1 K **1** 35), from whom all succeeding high priests claimed to descend. It is in harmony with this, that in the NT the Sadducees are the party to whom the high priests belonged. On the authority of *'Ābhōth d^e-Rabbī Nāthān* (c 1000 AD), another Zadok is asserted to be he from whom the Sadducees received their name. He was a disciple of Antigonus of Socho (c 250 BC) who taught that love to God should be absolutely disinterested (*Pirḳē 'Ābhōth*, i.3). *'Ābhōth d^e-Rabbī Nāthān's* account of the derivation of the Sadduceanism from this teaching is purely an imaginary deduction (Charles Taylor, *Sayings of the Jewish Fathers*^{2}, 112). The majority of authoritative writers prefer to derive the name from Zadok, the colleague of Abiathar, the contemporary of David.

1. Name: Rival Etymologies

Our main authorities for the teaching of the Sadducees are the NT and Jos. According to the former, the Sadducees denied the resurrection of the body, and did not believe in angels or spirits (Mt **22** 23; Acts **23** 8). More can be learned from Jos, but his evidence is to be received with caution, as he was a Pharisee and, moreover, had the idea that the Sadducees were to be paralleled with the Epicureans. The Talm is late. Before even the Mishna was committed to writing (c 200 AD) the Sadducees had ceased to exist; before the Gemara was completed (c 700 AD) every valid tradition of their opinions must have vanished. Further, the Talm is Pharisaic. The Fathers, Origen, Hippolytus, Epiphanius and Jerome, have derived their information from late Pharisaic sources.

2. Authorities

II. Origin and History.—Jos describes the Sadducees along with the contemporary sects, the Pharisees and the Essenes (Jos, *Ant*, XIII, v, 9; X, vi, 2; XVIII, i, 4, 5; *BJ*, II, viii, 14). His earliest notice of them is after his account of the treaties of Jonathan with the Romans and the Lacedemonians. He indicates his belief that the parties were ancient; but if so, they must have formerly had other names. It has been suggested that the earlier form of the conflict between the Sadducees and Pharisees was opposition between the priests and the prophets. This, however, is not tenable; in the Southern Kingdom there was no such opposition; whatever the state of matters in the Northern Kingdom, it could have had no influence on opinion in Judaea and Galilee in the time of Our Lord. By others the rivalry is supposed to be inherited from that between the scribes and the priests, but Ezra, the earliest scribe, in the later sense of the term, was a priest with strong sacerdotal sympathies.

1. Early Notices in Josephus

Probably the priestly party only gradually crystallized into the sect of the Sadducees. After the return from the exile, the high priest drew to himself all powers, civil and religious. To the Pers authorities he was as the king of the Jews. The high priest and those about him were the persons who had to do with the heathen supreme government and the heathen nationalities around; this association would tend to lessen their religious fervor, and, by reaction, this roused the zeal of a section of the people for the law. With the Gr domination the power of the high priests at home was increased, but they became still more subservient to their heathen masters, and were the leaders in the Hellenizing movement. They took no part in the Maccabean struggle, which was mainly supported by their opponents the *ḥăṣīdhīm*, as they were called (the Hasidaeans of 1 Macc **2** 42, etc). When the *ḥăṣīdhīm*, having lost sympathy with the Maccabeans, sought to reconcile themselves to the priestly party, Alcimus, the legitimate high priest, by his treachery and cruelty soon renewed the breach. The Hasmoneans then were confirmed in the high-priesthood, but were only lukewarmly supported by the *ḥăṣīdhīm*.

2. Tendencies toward Hellenism

The division between the Hasmoneans and the *ḥăṣīdhīm*, or, as they were now called, Pharisees, culminated in the insult offered by Eleazar to John Hyrcanus, the Hasmonean high priest (Jos, *Ant*, XIII, x, 5). Alexander Jannaeus, the son of Hyrcanus, became a violent partisan of the Sadducees, and crucified large numbers of the Pharisees. Toward the end of his life he fell out of sympathy with the Sadducees, and on his deathbed recommended his wife Alexandra Salome, who as guardian to his sons succeeded him, to favor the Pharisees, which she did. In the conflict between her two sons, John Hyrcanus II and Aristobulus II, the Sadducees took the side of Aristobulus, the younger and abler brother. So long as the contest was between Jews, the Sadducean candidate prevailed. When the Romans were called in, they gave the advantage to Hyrcanus.

3. Favored by Jannaeus; Put in Background by Alexandra Salome

Thrown into the background by the overthrow of their candidate for the high-priesthood, they soon regained their influence. They allied themselves with the Herodians who had supported Hyrcanus, but were subservient to Rome. Though they were not theological at first, they became so, to defend their policy against the attacks of the Pharisees. A historic parallel may be found in the Cavaliers of the reign of Charles I, as over against the Puritans.

4. Become a Religious Party

The Sadducees at first regarded the struggle between Our Lord and the Pharisees as a matter with which they had no concern. It was not until Our Lord claimed to be the Messiah, and the excitement of the people consequent on this proved likely to draw the attention of the Rom authorities, that they intervened. Should Tiberius learn that there was widespread among the Jews the belief in the coming of a Jewish king who was to rule the world, and that one had appeared who claimed to be this Messiah, very soon would the

5. Fear Roman Interference if Jesus' Messianic Claims Are Recognized

quasi-independence enjoyed by the Jews be taken from them, and with this the influence of the Sadducees would depart. An oligarchy is proverbially sensitive to anything that threatens its stability; a priesthood is unmeasured in its vindictiveness; and the Sadducees were a priestly oligarchy. Hence it is not wonderful that only the death of Jesus would satisfy them.

6. Continue Antagonistic to Apostles after Christ's Departure

After the resurrection, the Pharisees became less hostile to the followers of Christ; but the Sadducees maintained their attitude of suspicion and hatred (Acts **4** 1). Although a Pharisee, it was as agent of the Sadducean high priest that Paul persecuted the believers. The Sadducees gained complete ascendency in the Sanhedrin, and later, under the leadership of Annas, or as he is sometimes called by Jos, Ananus, the high priest, they put James the brother of Our Lord to death (Jos, *Ant*, XX, ix, 1) with many others, presumably Christians. The Pharisees were against these proceedings; and even sent messengers to meet Albinus who was coming to succeed Festus as governor to entreat him to remove Annas from the high-priesthood.

7. Fall of Sadducean Party

With the outbreak of the Jewish war, the Sadducees with their allies the Herodians were driven into the background by the Zealots, John of Gischala and Simon ben Gioras. Annas and Joshua, also called high priest by Jos, were both put to death by the Zealots and their Idumaean allies (Jos, *BJ*, IV, v, 2). With the destruction of the temple and the fall of the Jewish state the Sadducean party disappeared.

III. Doctrines of the Sadducees.—As the sacerdotal party, the Sadducees laid great stress on the ceremonial of sacrifice, and rejected the changes introduced by their opponents unless these found support in the words of the Law.

1. Ceremonial Exactness

2. Disbelief in Spiritual World and Resurrection

The most prominent doctrine of the Sadducees was the denial of the immortality of the soul and of the resurrection of the body. The Pharisees believed that Moses had delivered these doctrines to the elders, and that they had in turn handed them on to their successors. The Sadducees rejected all these traditions. From Acts (**23** 8) we learn that they believed in neither "angel or spirit." As appearances of angels are mentioned in the Law, it is difficult to harmonize their reverence for the Law with this denial. They may have regarded these angelophanies as theophanies. Jos distinctly asserts (*Ant*, XVIII, i, 4) that the Sadducees believe that the soul dies with the body. They deny, he says, Divine providence (*BJ*, II, viii, 14). Their theology might be called "religion within the limits of mere sensation."

3. Alleged Belief in Canonicity of Pentateuch Alone

The Fathers, Hippolytus, Origen and Jerome, credit the Sadducees with regarding the Pent as alone canonical (Hipp., *Haer.*, ix.24; Orig., *Contra Celsum*, i.49; on Mt **22** 24–31; Jer on Mt **22** 31.32). This idea may be due to a false identification of the views of the Sadducees with those of the Samaritans. Had they rejected all the rest of Scripture, it is hardly possible that Jos would have failed to notice this. The Talm does not mention this among their errors. It is certain that they gave more importance to the Pent than to any other of the books of Scripture. Hence Our Lord, in the passage commented on by Origen and Jerome, appeals to the Law rather than to the Prophets or the Pss. It follows from the little value they put upon the Prophets that they had no sympathy with the Messianic hopes of the Pharisees.

4. Relation to Epicureanism

It need hardly be said that there was no real connection between Sadduceanism and the doctrines of Epicurus. There was a superficial resemblance which was purely accidental. Their favor for Hellenism would give a color to this identification.

IV. Character of the Sadducees.—Jos says that while the Pharisees have amiable manners and cultivate concord among all, the Sadducees are "very boorish" (*BJ*, II, viii, 14). This want of manners is not a characteristic usually associated with an aristocracy, or with supple diplomats, yet it suits what we find in the NT. The cruel horseplay indulged in when Our Lord was tried before the irregular meeting of the Sanhedrin (Mt **26** 67.68), the shout of Ananias at the trial of Paul before the same tribunal to "smite him on the mouth," show them to be rough and overbearing. What Jos relates of the conduct of Annas (or Ananus) in regard to James, above referred to, agrees with this. Jos, however, does not always speak in such condemnatory terms of Ananus—in *BJ* (IV, v, 2) he calls him "a man venerable and most just." Only the violence which, as Jos relates in the chapter immediately preceding that from which we have quoted, Ananus resorted to against the Zealots better suits the earlier verdict of Jos than the later. As to their general character Jos mentions that when the Sadducees became magistrates they conformed their judgments to Pharisaic opinion, otherwise they would not have been tolerated (*Ant*, XVIII, i, 4).

1. Characterized as Rough and Boorish

2. Talmudic Accounts

As noted above, the Talm account is untrustworthy, late and Pharisaic. The Gemara from which most of the references are taken was not committed to writing till 7 centuries after Christ—when the traditions concerning the Sadducees, such as had survived, had filtered through 20 generations of Pharisaism. Despite this lengthened time and suspicious medium, there may be some truth in the representations of the Talmudic rabbin. In *Peṣāḥīm* **57***a* it is said, "Woe's me on account of the house of Beothus, woe's me on account of their spears; woe's me on account of the house of Hanun [Annas], woe's me on account of their serpent brood; woe's me on account of the house of Kathros, woe's me on account of their pen; woe's me on account of the house of Ishmael ben Phabi; woe's me on account of their fists. They are high priests and their sons are treasurers of the temple, and their sons-in-law, assistant treasurers; and their servants beat the people with sticks." As these are Sadducean names, this passage exhibits Pharisaic tradition as to the habits of the Sadducees.

3. Relation to Temple and Its Worship

The Sadducean high priests made Hophni and Phinehas too much their models. Annas and his sons had booths in the courts of the temple for the sale of sacrificial requisites, tables for money-changers, as ordinary coins had to be changed into the shekels of the sanctuary. From all these the priests of the high-priestly caste derived profit at the expense of desecrating the temple (Edersheim, *Life and Times of Jesus*, I, 371 ff). They did not, as did the Pharisees, pay spiritual religion the homage of hypocrisy; they were frankly irreligious. While officials of religion, they were devoid of its spirit. This, however, represents their last stage.

4. Sadducean Literature

The favor for the memory of John Hyrcanus shown by the writer of 1 Macc (**16** 23.24) renders probable Geiger's opinion that the author was a Sadducee. He shows the party in its best form: his outlook on life is eminently sane, and his history is trustworthy. He has sympathy with the patriotism of the Hasidaeans, but none with the religious scruples which led them to desert Judas Maccabaeus. That the writer of Ecclus from his silence as to the national expectation of a Messiah and the hope of a future life was also a Sadducee, is almost certain.

V. The Relation of the Sadducees to Jesus.—As the doctrines and practices of the Sadducees were quite alien from the teaching of Our

1. Less Denounced by Jesus Than the Pharisees

Lord and the conduct He enjoined, it is a problem why He did not denounce them more frequently than He did. Indeed He never denounces the Sadducees save along with their opponents the Pharisees; whereas He frequently denounces the Pharisees alone. As His position, both doctrinal and practical, was much nearer that of the Pharisees, it was necessary that He should clearly mark Himself off from them. There was not the same danger of His position being confused with that of the Sadducees. Jos informs us that the Sadducees had influence with the rich; Jesus drew His adherents chiefly from the poor, from whom also the Pharisees drew. The latter opposed Him all the more that He was sapping their source of strength; hence He had to defend Himself against them. Further, the Gospels mainly recount Our Lord's ministry in Galilee, whereas the Sadducees were chiefly to be found in Jerus and its neighborhood; hence there may have been severe denunciations of the Sadducees that have not come down to us.

2. Attitude toward Jesus

The Sadducees probably regarded Jesus as a harmless fanatic who by His denunciations was weakening the influence of the Pharisees. Only when His claim to be the Messiah brought Him within the sphere of practical politics did they desire to intervene. When they did determine to come into conflict with Jesus, they promptly decreed His arrest and death; only the arrest was to be secret, "lest a tumult arise among the people" (Mt **26** 5). In their direct encounter with Our Lord in regard to the resurrection (Mt **22** 25 ff; Mk **12** 20 ff; Lk **20** 29 ff), there is an element of contempt implied in the illustration which they bring, as if till almost the end they failed to take Him seriously. For Literature see PHARISEES.

J. E. H. THOMSON

SADDUK, sad'uk (A [Fritzsche], **Σάδδουκος,** *Sáddoukos,* B, **Σαδδούλουκος,** *Saddoúloukos;* AV Sadduc): The high priest, an ancestor of Ezra (1 Esd **8** 2) = "Zadok" in Ezr **7** 2 = "Sadoc" in 2 Esd **1** 1.

SADOC, sā'dok:

(1) (Lat *Sadoch*): An ancestor of Ezra (2 Esd **1** 1) = "Zadok" in Ezr **7** 2 = "Sadduk" in 1 Esd **8** 2.

(2) (Σαδώκ, *Sadōk*): A descendant of Zerubbabel and ancestor of Jesus (Mt **1** 14).

SAFFRON, saf'run (כַּרְכֹּם, *karkōm;* **κρόκος,** *krókos*): Identical with the Arab. *kurkum,* the same as *za'farān,* "saffron." The source of the true saffron is *Crocus sativus* (N.O. *Indaceae*), a plant cultivated in Pal; there are 8 wild varieties in all of which, as in the cultivated species, the orange-colored styles and stigmas yield the yellow dye, saffron. Cant **4** 14 probably refers to the *C. sativus.* There is a kind of bastard saffron plant, the *Carthamus tinctorius* (N.O. *Compositae*), of which the orange-colored flowers yield a dye like saffron.

E. W. G. MASTERMAN

SAIL, sāl, **SAILOR,** sāl'ẽr. See SHIPS AND BOATS, II, 2, (3); III, 2.

SAINTS, sānts: In AV 3 words are thus rendered: (1) קָדוֹשׁ, *ḳādhōsh* (in Dnl the same root occurs several times in its Aram. form, קַדִּישׁ, *ḳadhīsh*); (2) חָסִיד, *ḥāṣīdh,* and (3) ἅγιοι, *hágioi.* Of these words (2) has in general the meaning of righteousness or goodness, while (1) and (3) have the meaning of consecration and Divine claim and ownership. They are not primarily words of character, like *ḥāṣīdh,* but express a relation to God as being set apart for His own. Wherever *ḳādhōsh* refers to angels, the rendering "holy one" or "holy ones" has been substituted in RV for AV "saint" or "saints," which is the case also in Ps **106** 16 m (cf **34** 9), and in 1 S **2** 9, as the tr of *ḥāṣīdh.*

While *hagioi* occurs more frequently in the NT than does *ḳādhōsh* in the OT, yet both are applied with practical uniformity to the company of God's

Saffron (*Crocus sativus*).

people rather than to any individual. Perhaps the rendering "saints" cannot be improved, but it is necessary for the ordinary reader constantly to guard against the idea that NT saintship was in any way a result of personal character, and consequently that it implied approval of moral attainment already made. Such a rendering as "consecrate ones," for example, would bring out more clearly the relation to God which is involved, but, besides the fact that it is not a happy tr, it might lead to other errors, for it is not easy to remember that consecration—the setting apart of the individual as one of the company whom God has in a peculiar way as His own—springs not from man, but from God Himself, and that consequently it is in no way something optional, and admits of no degrees of progress, but, on the contrary, is from the beginning absolute duty. It should also be noted that while, as has been said, to be a saint is not directly and primarily to be good but to be set apart by God as His own, yet the godly and holy character ought inevitably and immediately to result. When God consecrates and claims moral beings for Himself and His service, He demands that they should go on to be fit for and worthy of the relation in which He has placed them, and so we read of certain actions as performed "worthily of the saints" (Rom **16** 2) and as such "as becometh saints" (Eph **5** 3). The thought of the holy character of the "saints," which is now so common as almost completely to obscure the real thought of the NT writers, already lay in their thinking very close to their conception of saintship as consecration by God to be His own. DAVID FOSTER ESTES

SALA, SALAH, sā'la (שֶׁלַח, *shelaḥ*, "a missile," "petition"; **Σαλά**, *Salá*): A son of Arpachshad (AV Gen **10** 24; **11** 13 ff; 1 Ch **1** 18.24). Lk **3** 35.36 follows LXX of Gen **10** 24; **11** 12=SHELAH (q.v.).

SALAMIEL, sa-lā'mi-el (B A, **Σαλαμιήλ**, *Salamiēl*, ℵ, **Σαμαμιήλ**, *Samamiēl*): An ancestor of Judith (Jth **8** 1)=AV "Samael"="Shelumiel."

SALAMIS, sal'a-mis (**Σαλαμίς**, *Salamís*): A town on the east coast of Cyprus, situated some 3 miles to the N. of the mediaeval and modern *Famagusta*. It lay near the river Pediaeus, at the eastern extremity of the great plain of the Mesoréa, which runs far into the interior of the island toward *Nicosia* (Lefkosia), the present capital. It possessed a good harbor and was the most populous and flourishing town of Cyprus in the Hellenic and Rom periods, carrying on a vigorous trade with the ports of Cilicia and Syria. Its population was mixed, consisting of Gr and Phoen elements. The former, however, gave its tone and color to the city, and the chief cult and temple were those of Salaminian Zeus.

1. Site

Tradition represented Salamis as founded soon after the fall of Troy by Teucer, the prince of Gr archers according to the narrative of the *Iliad*, who named it after his home, the island of Salamis off the Attic coast. In the 6th cent. BC it figures as an important Hellenic city, ruled by a line of kings reputed to be descended from Teucer and strengthened by an alliance with Cyrene (Herod. iv.162). Gorgus, who was on the throne in 498 BC, refused to join the Ionic revolt against Persia, but the townsmen, led by his brother Onesilus, took up arms in the struggle for freedom. A crushing defeat, however, inflicted under the walls of Salamis, restored the island to its Pers overlords, who reinstated Gorgus as a vassal prince (Herod. v.103 ff). In 449 a Gr fleet under Athenian leadership defeated the Phoen navy, which was in the service of Persia, off Salamis; but the Athenian withdrawal which followed the battle led to a decided anti-Hellenic reaction, until the able and vigorous rule of the Salaminian prince Euagoras, who was a warm friend of the Athenians (Isocrates, *Euag.*) and a successful champion of Hellenism. In 306 a second great naval battle was fought off Salamis, in which Demetrius Poliorcetes defeated the forces of Ptolemy I (Soter), king of Egypt. But 11 years later the town came into Ptolemy's hands and, with the rest of the island, remained an appanage of the Egyp kingdom until the incorporation of Cyprus in the Rom Empire (58 BC).

2. Early History

When Barnabas and Paul, accompanied by John Mark, set out on their 1st missionary journey, they sailed from Seleucia, the seaport of Antioch, and landed at Salamis, about 130 miles distant, as the harbor nearest to the Syrian coast. There they preached the gospel in the "synagogues of the Jews" (Acts **13** 5); the phrase is worth noting as pointing to the existence of several synagogues and thus of a large Jewish community in Salamis. Of work among the Gentiles we hear nothing, nor is any indication given either of the duration of the apostles' visit or of the success of their mission; but it would seem that after a short stay they proceeded "through the whole island" (Acts **13** 6 RV) to Paphos. The words seem to imply that they visited all, or at least most, of the towns in which there were Jewish communities. Paul did not return to Salamis, but Barnabas doubtless went there on his 2d missionary journey (Acts **15** 39), and tradition states that he was martyred there in Nero's reign, on the site marked by the monastery named after him.

3. Visit of the Apostles

In 116 AD the Jews in Cyprus rose in revolt and massacred 240,000 Greeks and Romans. The rising was crushed with the utmost severity by Hadrian. Salamis was almost depopulated, and its destruction was afterward consummated by earthquakes in 332 and 342 AD. It was rebuilt, though on a much smaller scale, by the emperor Constantius II (337–61 AD) under the name Constantia, and became the metropolitan see of the island. The most famous of its bishops was Epiphanius, the staunch opponent of heresy, who held the see from 367 to 403. In 647 the city was finally destroyed by the Saracens. Considerable remains of ancient buildings still remain on the site; an account of the excavations carried on there in 1890 by Messrs. J. A. R. Munro and H. A. Tubbs under the auspices of the Cyprus Exploration Fund will be found in the *Journal of Hellenic Studies*, XII, 59–198.

4. Later History

M. N. TOD

SALASADAI, sal-a-sad'ā-ī (A, **Σαλασαδαί**, *Salasadaí*, B, **Σαρασαδαί**, *Sarasadaí*, ℵ, **Σαρισαδαί**, *Sarisadaí*): An ancestor of Judith (Jth **8** 1).

SALATHIEL, sa-lā'thi-el:

(1) (Σαλαθιήλ, *Salathiēl*): AV; Gr form of "Shealtiel" (thus RV). The father of Zerubbabel (1 Esd **5** 5.48.56; **6** 2; Mt **1** 12; Lk **3** 27).

(2) RV: Another name of Esdras (2 Esd **3** 1, "Salathiel").

SALE, sāl (מִמְכָּר, *mimkār*): The word is used: (1) in the sense of the transaction (Lev **25** 50); (2) in the sense of the limit of time involved in the transaction (Lev **25** 27); (3) in the sense of the price paid in the transaction (Dt **18** 8), though it may be the same as (1) above.

SALECAH, sal'ē-ka, **SALCAH, SALCHAH**, sal'-ka (סַלְכָה, *ṣalᵉkhāh;* B, **Σεκχαί**, *Sekchaí*, **'Αχά**, *Achá*, **Σελά**, *Selá*, A, **'Ελχά**, *Elchá*, **'Ασελχά**, *Aselchá*, **Σελχά**, *Selchá*): This place first appears in Dt **3** 10 as marking the eastern boundary of Bashan. It is named as one of the cities in which Og, king of Bashan, ruled (Josh **12** 5). It must certainly have been included in the portion given to the half-tribe of Manasseh, "all the kingdom of Og king of Bashan," although it is not named among the cities that fell to him (Josh **13** 29 ff). At a later time we are told that Gad dwelt over against the Reubenites in the land of Bashan unto Salecah (1 Ch **5** 11). The boundaries of the tribes probably changed from time to time.

The ancient city is represented by the modern *Ṣalkhad*, a city in a high and strong position at the southern end of *Jebel ed-Drūze* (the Mountain of Bashan). On a volcanic hill rising some 300 ft. above the town, in what must have been the crater, stands the castle. The view from the battlements, as the present writer can testify, is one of the finest E. of the Jordan, including the rich hollow of the *Ḥaurān*, Mt. Hermon, and all the intervening country to the mountains of Samaria, with vast reaches of the desert to the S. and to the E. The old Rom roads are still clearly seen running without curve or deviation across the country to Bozrah and *Ḍerʿah*, away to the S.E. over the desert to *Ḳalʿat el-ʾAzraḳ*, and eastward to the Pers Gulf. The castle was probably built by the Romans. Restored by the Arabs, it was a place of strength in Crusading times. It has now fallen on evil days. The modern town, containing many ancient houses, lies mainly on the slopes S.E. of the castle. The inhabitants are Druzes, somewhat noted for turbulence. In the recent rising of the Druzes (1911) the place suffered heavily from bombardment by the Turks. For water-supply it is entirely dependent on cisterns filled during the rainy season.

W. EWING

SALEM, sā'lem (שָׁלֵם, *shālēm;* **Σαλήμ,** *Salēm*): The name of the city of which Melchizedek was king (Gen **14** 18; He **7** 1.2; cf Ps **76** 2). To all appearance it lay near "the Vale of Shaveh," described as "the King's Vale." The general opinion among the Jews was that Salem was the same as Jerus, as stated by Jos (*Ant,* I, x, 2), who adds (VII, iii, 2) that it was known as Solyma (Σόλυμα, *Sóluma,* variants, according to Whiston, *Salem* and *Hierosolyma*) in the time of Abraham. It was also reported that the city and its temple were called Solyma by Homer, and he adds that the name in Heb means "security." This identification with Jerus was accepted by Onkelos and all the Tgs, as well as by the early Christians. The Samaritans have always identified Salem with *Salim,* E. of *Nablūs,* but Jewish and Christian tradition is more likely to be correct, supported, as it is, by Ps **76** 2.

1. Identification and Meaning

The testimony of the Am Tab is apparently negative. Knudtzon's no. 287 mentions "the land" and "the lands of Urusalim," twice with the prefix for "city"; no. 289 likewise has this prefix twice; and no. 290 refers to "the city" or "a city of the land Urusalim called *Bît-Ninip*" (*Beth-Anušat* [?]). As there is no prefix of any kind before the element *salim,* it is not probable that this is the name of either a man (the city's founder) or a god (like the Assyr *Šulmanu*). The form in Sennacherib's inscriptions (cf Taylor Cylinder, III, 50), *Ursalimmu,* gives the whole as a single word in the nominative, the double *m* implying that the *i* was long. As the Assyrians pronounced *s* as *sh,* it is likely that the Urusalimites did the same, hence the Heb *y^erûshālaim,* with *sh.* See JERUSALEM.

2. Testimony of Tell el-Amarna Tablets

T. G. PINCHES

SALEM (**Σάλημος,** *Sálēmos;* AV **Salum**): An ancestor of Ezra (1 Esd **8** 1) = "Shallum" in Ezr **7** 2 = "Salemas" in 2 Esd **1** **1.**

SALEMAS, sal'ē-mas, sa-lē'mas (Lat *Salame;* AV **Sadamias**): An ancestor of Ezra (2 Esd **1** 1) = "Shallum" in Ezr **7** 2; called also "Salem" in 1 Esd **8** 1.

SALIM, sā'lim (**Σαλείμ,** *Saleím*): A place evidently well known, since the position of Aenon, the springs where John was baptizing, was defined by reference to it: they were "near to Salim" (Jn **3** 23). It must be sought on the W. of the Jordan, as will be seen from comparison of Jn **1** 28; **3** 26; **10** 40. Many identifications have been proposed: e.g. that of Alford with Shilhim and Ain in the S. of Judah; that of Büsching with *'Ain Kārim,* and that of Barclay, who would place Salim in *Wâdy Suleim* near *'Anāta,* making Aenon the springs in *Wâdy Fār'ah.* These are all ruled out by their distance from the district where John is known to have been at work. If there were no other objection to that suggested by Conder (*Tent Work,* 49 f) following Robinson (*BR,* III, 333) with *Sālim* in the plain E. of *Nāblus,* Aenon being *'Ainūn* in *Wâdy Fār'ah,* it would be sufficient to say that this is in the very heart of Samaria, and therefore impossible. In any case the position of Aenon, 6 miles distant, with a high ridge intervening, would hardly be defined by the village of *Sālim,* with the important city of Shechem quite as near, and more easily accessible. *Onom* places Aenon 8 Rom miles S. of Scythopolis (*Beisān*), near Salumias (*Sālim*) and the Jordan. This points to *Tell Ridhghah,* on the northern side of which is a shrine known locally as *Sheikh Selīm.* Not far off, by the ruins of *Umm el-'Amdān,* there are seven copious fountains which might well be called Aenon, "place of springs."

There is reason to believe that this district did not belong to Samaria, but was included in the lands of Scythopolis, which was an important member of the league of ten cities.

W. EWING

SALIMOTH, sal'i-moth (B, **Σαλειμώθ,** *Saleimôth,* A, **'Ασσαλιμώθ,** *'Assalimôth;* the latter is due to a wrong division of syllables; AV **Assalimoth**): The same as "Shelomith" (Ezr **8** 10). S., the son of Josaphias, of the family of Banias, and with him 130 men went up to Jerus with Ezra (1 Esd **8** 36).

SALLAI, sal'ā-ī, sal'ī (סַלַּי, *ṣallay;* **Σαλώμ,** *Salôm,* A, **Σαλώ,** *Salô,* with variants):

(1) Eponym of a Benjamite family which settled at Jerus after the return, descendants of "Sallu" (1 Ch **9** 7; Neh **11** 7.8); the pedigrees of Sallu differ decidedly in the two passages. Curtis (*ICC*) suggests that "son of Hodaviah, the son of Hassenuah" (Ch) is a corruption or derivation of "Judah the son of Hassenuah" (Neh).

(2) Name of a priestly family (Neh **12** 20), called "Sallu" in ver **7.**

SALLU, sal'ū. See SALLAI.

SALLUMUS, sa-lū'mus, sal'ū-mus (**Σάλλουμος,** *Sálloumos*): One of the porters who had taken "strange wives" (1 Esd **9** 25) = "Shallum" in Ezr **10** 24; called also "Salum" in 1 Esd **5** 28.

SALMA, sal'ma. See SALMON.

SALMAI, sal'mī, sal'mā-ī (שַׁלְמַי, *salmay;* AV **Shalmai** [AV in Neh **7** 48 is "Shalmai" = Ezr **2** 46]; RV "Salmai"): The eponym of a family of Nethinim, called "Shamlai" in Ezr **2** 46 (K^erē, שַׁמְלַי, *shamlay,* K^ethībh, שַׁלְמַי, *shalmay,* followed by AV text, "Shalmai"; B, Σαμαάν, *Samaán,* A, Σελαμί, *Selamí;* Neh **7** 48, B, Σαλεμεί, *Salemeí,* A, Σελμεί, *Selmeí,* א, Σαμαεί, *Samaeí*). The name suggests a foreign reign. In 1 Esd **5** 30 the corresponding name is "Subai."

SALMANASAR, sal-ma-nā'sar (2 Esd **13** 40) = SHALMANESER (q.v.).

SALMON, sal'mon, **SALMA** (שַׂלְמוֹן, *salmōn,* "investiture" [Ruth **4** 21], שַׂלְמָה, *salmāh,* "clothing" [Ruth **4** 20], שַׂלְמָא, *salmā'* [1 Ch **2** 11.51.54]; **Σαλμών,** *Salmôn*):

(1) The father of Boaz the husband of Ruth, and thus the grandfather of Jesse, David's father (Ruth **4** 20.21). He is mentioned in both the genealogies of Jesus (Mt **1** 4.5; Lk **3** 32). From Mt **1** 5 we learn that he married Rahab, by whom he begat Boaz.

(2) In **1** Ch **2** 51 ff, we read of a Salma, "the father of Beth-lehem," a son of Caleb the son of Hur. He is also said to be the father of "the Netophathites, Atroth-beth-joab, and half of the Manahathites, the Zorites," and several "families of scribes." See also ZALMON.

S. F. HUNTER

SALMONE, sal-mō'nē (**Σαλμώνη,** *Salmônē*): Acts **27** 7. See PHOENIX.

SALOAS, sal'ō-as (**Σαλόας,** *Salóas;* AV **Talsus** after Lat *Thalsas*): In 1 Esd **9** 22, for "Elasah" of Ezr **10** 22.

SALOM, sā'lom (**Σαλώμ,** *Salōm*):

(1) The father of Helkias (Bar **1** 7). Gr form of "Shallum."

(2) AV=RV "Salu" (1 Macc **2** 26).

SALOME, sa-lō'mē (**Σαλώμη,** *Salṓmē*):

(1) One of the holy women who companied with Jesus in Galilee, and ministered to Him (Mk **15** 40.41). She was present at the crucifixion (**15** 40), and was among those who came to the tomb of Jesus on the resurrection morning (**16** 1.2). Comparison with Mt **27** 56 clearly identifies her with the wife of Zebedee. It is she, therefore, whose ambitious request for her sons James and John is recorded in Mt **20** 20–24; Mk **10** 35–40. From Jn **19** 25 many infer that she was a sister of Mary, the mother of Jesus (thus Meyer, Luthardt, Alford); others (as Godet) dispute the inference.

(2) Salome was the name of the daughter of Herodias who danced before Herod, and obtained as reward the head of John the Baptist (Mt **14** 3–11; Mk **6** 17–28; cf Jos, *Ant*, XVIII, v, 4). She is not named in the Gospels. James Orr

SALT, sôlt (מֶלַח, *melaḥ;* **ἅλας,** *hálas,* **ἅλς,** *háls*): Common salt is considered by most authorities as an essential ingredient of our food. Most people intentionally season their cooking with more or less salt for the sake of palatability. Others depend upon the small quantities which naturally exist in water and many foods to furnish the necessary amount of salt for the body. Either too much salt or the lack of it creates undesirable disturbance in the animal system. Men and animals alike instinctively seek for this substance to supplement or improve their regular diet. The ancients appreciated the value of salt for seasoning food (Job **6** 6). So necessary was it that they dignified it by making it a requisite part of sacrifices (Lev **2** 13; Ezr **6** 9; **7** 22; Ezk **43** 24; Mk **9** 49). In Nu **18** 19; 2 Ch **13** 5, a "covenant of salt" is mentioned (cf Mk **9** 49). This custom of pledging friendship or confirming a compact by eating food containing salt is still retained among Arab.-speaking people. The Arab. word for "salt" and for a "compact" or "treaty" is the same. Doughty in his travels in Arabia appealed more than once to the superstitious belief of the Arabs in the "salt covenant," to save his life. Once an Arab has received in his tent even his worst enemy and has eaten salt (food) with him, he is bound to protect his guest as long as he remains. See Covenant of Salt.

The chief source of salt in Pal is from the extensive deposits near the "sea of salt" (see Dead Sea), where there are literally mountains and valleys of salt (2 S **8** 13; 2 K **14** 7; 1 Ch **18** 12; 2 Ch **25** 11). On the seacoast the inhabitants frequently gather the sea salt. They fill the rock crevices with sea water and leave it for the hot summer sun to evaporate. After evaporation the salt crystals can be collected. As salt-gathering is a government monopoly in Turkey, the government sends men to pollute the salt which is being surreptitiously crystallized, so as to make it unfit for eating. Another extensive supply comes from the salt lakes in the Syrian desert E. of Damascus and toward Palmyra. All native salt is more or less bitter, due to the presence of other salts such as magnesium sulphate.

Salt was used not only as a food, but as an antiseptic in medicine. Newborn babes were bathed and salted (Ezk **16** 4), a custom still prevailing. The Arabs of the desert consider it so necessary, that in the absence of salt they bathe their infants in camels' urine. Elisha is said to have healed the waters of Jericho by casting a cruse of salt into the spring (2 K **2** 20 f). Abimelech sowed the ruins of Shechem with salt to prevent a new city from arising in its place (Jgs **9** 45). Lot's wife turned to a pillar of salt (Gen **19** 26).

Figurative: Salt is emblematic of loyalty and friendship (see above). A person who has once joined in a "salt covenant" with God and then breaks it is fit only to be cast out (cf Mt **5** 13; Mk **9** 50). Saltness typified barrenness (Dt **29** 23; Jer **17** 6). James compares the absurdity of the same mouth giving forth blessings and cursings to the impossibility of a fountain yielding both sweet and salt water (Jas **3** 11 f). James A. Patch

SALT, CITY OF (עִיר הַמֶּלַח, *'īr ha-melaḥ;* A, **αἱ πόλ[ε]ις ἁλῶν,** *hai pól[e]is halōn*): One of the six cities in the wilderness of Judah mentioned between Nibshan and Engedi (Josh **15** 62). The site is very uncertain. The large and important *Tell el-Milḥ* (i.e. "the salt hill"), on the route from Hebron to Akaba, is possible.

SALT, COVENANT OF. See Covenant of Salt.

SALT, PILLAR OF. See Lot; Salt; Siddim; Slime.

SALT SEA. See Dead Sea.

SALT, VALLEY OF (גֵּיא הַמֶּלַח, *gē' ha-melaḥ*): The scene of battles, firstly, between David or his lieutenant Abishai and the Edomites (2 S **8** 13; 1 Ch **18** 12; Ps **60,** title), and later between Amaziah and these same foes (2 K **14** 7; 2 Ch **25** 11). It is tempting to connect this "Valley of Salt" with *es Sebkhah,* the marshy, salt-impregnated plain which extends from the southern end of the Dead Sea to the foot of the cliffs, but in its present condition it is an almost impossible place for a battle of any sort. The ground is so soft and spongy that a wide détour around the edges has to be made by those wishing to get from one side to the other. It is, too, highly probable that in earlier times the whole of this low-lying area was covered by the waters of the Dead Sea. It is far more natural to identify *gē' ha-melaḥ* with the *Wâdy el-Milḥ* ("Valley of Salt"), one of the three valleys which unite at Beersheba to form the *Wâdy eṣ-Ṣeba'*. These valleys, *el-Milḥ* and *eṣ-Ṣeba'*, together make a natural frontier to Canaan.

E. W. G. Masterman

SALT-WORT, sôlt'wûrt (מַלּוּחַ, *mallūaḥ,* a word connected with *melaḥ,* "salt," trd in LXX **ἅλιμος,** *hálimos;* AV **mallows**): The *halimos* of the Greeks is the sea orache, *Atriplex halimus,* a silvery whitish shrub which flourishes upon the shores of the Dead Sea alongside the *rutm* (see Juniper). Its leaves are oval and somewhat like those of an olive. They have a sour flavor and would never be eaten when better food was obtainable (Job **30** 4). The tr "mallows" is due to the apparent similarity of the Heb *mallūaḥ* to the Gr *μαλάχη, maláchē,* which is the Lat *malva* and Eng. "mallow." Certain species of *malva* known in Arab., as خبّازة, *khubbâzeh,* are very commonly eaten by the poor of Pal.

E. W. G. Masterman

SALU, sā'lū (סָלוּא, *ṣālū';* LXX B, **Σαλμών,** *Salmōn,* A, **Σαλώ,** *Salō;* AV has "Salom" in 1 Macc **2** 26): A prince and the head of a house of the tribe of Simeon and the father of Zimri who was slain by Phinehas along with the Midianitish woman whom he had brought to the camp of Israel (Nu **25** 14; 1 Macc **2** 26).

SALUM, sā'lum (Σαλούμ, *Saloúm*):
(1) The head of one of the families of porters (1 Esd **5** 28; om. in B) = "Shallum" in Ezr **2** 42; **10** 24; Neh **7** 45 = "Sallumus" in 1 Esd **9** 25.
(2) 1 Esd **8** 1 AV = RV "Salem."

SALUTATION, sal-ū-tā'shun (ἀσπασμός, *aspasmós*): A greeting which might be given in person, orally (Lk **1** 29.41.44), or in writing, usually at the close of a letter (1 Cor **16** 21; Col **4** 18; 2 Thess **3** 17; cf use of χαίρειν, *chaírein*, "greeting," "joy" in Jas **1** 1). The Pharisaic Jews loved salutations in public places (Mt **23** 7; Mk **12** 38, AV "greeting," RV "salutation"; Lk **11** 43; **20** 46). Often these salutations were very elaborate, involving much time in prostrations, embracings, etc. When Jesus therefore sent out the Seventy, He forbade salutation by the way (Lk **10** 4), though He ordinarily encouraged proper civilities of this sort (Mt **5** 47; **10** 12). Edward Bagby Pollard

SALVATION, sal-vā'shun:

In EV the words "salvation," "save," are not technical theological terms, but denote simply "deliverance," in almost any sense the latter word can have. In systematic theology, however, "salvation" denotes the whole process by which man is delivered from all that would prevent his attaining to the highest good that God has prepared for him. Or, by a transferred sense, "salvation" denotes the actual enjoyment of that good. So, while these technical senses are often associated with the Gr or Heb words tr[d] "save," etc, yet they are still more often used in connection with other words or represented only by the general sense of a passage. And so a collection of the original terms for "save," etc, is of value only for the student doing minute detailed work, while it is the purpose of the present article to present a general view of the Bib. doctrine of salvation.

I. In the OT.—(1) As long as revelation had not raised the veil that separates this life from the next, the Israelite thought of his highest good as long life in a prosperous Pal, as described most typically in Dt **28** 1–14. But a definite religious idea was present also, for the "land of milk and honey," even under angelic protection, was worthless without access to God (Ex **33** 1–4), to know whom gives happiness (Isa **11** 9; Hab **2** 14; Jer **31** 34). Such a concept is normal for most of the OT, but there are several significant enlargements of it. That Israel should receive God's characteristic of righteousness is a part of the ideal (Isa **1** 26; **4** 3.4; **32** 1–8; **33** 24; Jer **31** 33.34; Ezk **36** 25. 26; Zec **8**; Dnl **9** 24; Ps **51** 10–12). Good was found in the extension of Israel's good to the surrounding nations (Mic **4** 1–4; Isa **2** 2–4; **45** 5.6; Zec **2** 11; **8** 22.23; Isa **60**; **66** 19–21; Zec **14** 16.17, etc), even to the extension of the legitimate sacrificial worship to the soil of Egypt (Isa **19** 19–22). Pal was insufficient for the enjoyment of God's gifts, and a new heaven and a new earth were to be received (Isa **65** 17; **66** 22), and a share in the glories was not to be denied even to the dead (Isa **26** 19; Dnl **12** 2). And, among the people so glorified, God would dwell in person (Isa **60** 19. 20; Zec **2** 10–12). (2) Salvation, then, means deliverance from all that interferes with the enjoyment of these blessings. So it takes countless forms—deliverance from natural plagues, from internal dissensions, from external enemies, or from the subjugation of conquerors (the exile, particularly). As far as enemies constitute the threatening danger, the prayer for deliverance is often based on their evil character (Ps **101,** etc). But for the individual all these evils are summed up in the word "death," which was thought to terminate all relation to God and all possibility of enjoying His blessings (Ps **115** 17; Isa **38** 18, etc). And so "death" became established as the antinomy to "salvation," and in this sense the word has persisted, although the equation "loss of salvation = physical death" has long been transcended. But death and its attendant evils are worked by God's wrath, and so it is from this wrath that salvation is sought (Josh **7** 26, etc). And thus, naturally, salvation is from everything that raises that wrath, above all from sin (Ezk **36** 25.26, etc).

1. General

2. Individualism

(1) At first the "unit of salvation" was the nation (less prominently the family), i.e. a man though righteous could lose salvation through the faults of others. A father could bring a curse on his children (2 S **21** 1–14), a king on his subjects (2 S **24**), or an unknown sinner could bring guilt on an entire community (Dt **21** 1–9). (On the other hand, ten righteous would have saved Sodom [Gen **18** 32].) And the principle of personal responsibility was grasped but slowly. It is enunciated partly in Dt **24** 16 (cf Jer **31** 29.30), definitely in Ezk **14** 12–20; **18**; **33** 1–20, and fairly consistently in the Pss. But even Ezekiel still held that five-and-twenty could defile the whole nation (**8** 16), and he had not the premises for resolving the problem—that temporal disasters need not mean the loss of salvation. (2) But even when it was realized that a man lost salvation through his own fault, the converse did not follow. Salvation came, not by the man's mere merit, but because the man belonged to a nation peculiarly chosen by God. God had made a covenant with Israel and His fidelity insured salvation: the salvation comes from God because of His promise or (in other words) because of His name. Indeed, the great failing of the people was to trust too blindly to this promise, an attitude denounced continually by the prophets throughout (from, say, Am **3** 2 to Mt **3** 9). And yet even the prophets admit a real truth in the attitude, for, despite Israel's sins, eventual salvation is certain. Ezk **20** states this baldly: there has been nothing good in Israel and there is nothing good in her at the prophet's own day, but, notwithstanding, God will give her restoration (cf Isa **8** 17.18; Jer **32** 6–15, etc).

Hence, of the human conditions, whole-hearted trust in God is the most important. (*Belief* in God is, of course, never argued in the Bible.)

3. Faith

Inconsistent with such trust are, for instance, seeking aid from other nations (Isa **30** 1–5), putting reliance in human skill (2 Ch **16** 12), or forsaking Pal through fear (Jer **42**). In Isa **26** 20 entire passivity is demanded, and in 2 K **13** 19 lukewarmness in executing an apparently meaningless command is rebuked.

4. Moral Law

(1) Next in importance is the attainment of a moral standard, expressed normally in the various codes of the Law. But fulfilment of the letter of the commandment was by no means all that was required. For instance, the Law permitted the selling of a debtor into slavery (Dt **15** 12), but the reckless use of the creditor's right is sharply condemned (Neh **5** 1–13). The prophets are never weary of giving short formulae that will exclude such supra-legalism and reduce conduct to a pure motive: "Hate the evil, and love the good, and establish justice in the gate" (Am **5** 15); "To do justly, and to love kindness, and to walk humbly with thy God" (Mic **6** 8). And the chief emphasis on the Law as *written* is found in the later books, esp. Ps **119** (cf Ps **147** 20). (2) Certain breaches of the Law had no pardon, but were visited with death at once, even despite repentance and confession (Josh **7**). But for the most part it is promised that repentance will remove the guilt of the sin if the sin be forsaken (Ezk **18**) or, in the case of a sin that would not be repeated, if contrition be felt (2 S **12**). Suffering played a part in salvation by bringing knowledge of sin to the conscience, the exile being the most important example (Ezk **36** 31). But almost always it is assumed that the possibility of keeping the Law is in man's own power, Dt **30** 11–14 stating this explicitly, while the Wisdom Books equate virtue with learning. Consequently, an immense advance was made when man felt the need of God's help to keep the Law, the need of the inscription of the Laws on the *heart* (Jer **31** 31–34). So an outlook was opened to a future in which God would *make* the nation righteous (see references in 1, above).

5. Sacrifices

(1) The acceptance of repentance as expiating past sins was an act of God's mercy. And so His mercy instituted other and additional means of expiation, most notably that of the sacrifices. But a *theology* of sacrifice is conspicuously absent from the whole OT, for Lev **17** 11 is too incidental and too obscure to be any exception. The Christian (or very late Jewish) interpretations of the ritual laws lack all solidity of exegetical foundation, despite their one-time prevalence. Nor is the study of origins of much help for the meaning attached to the rites by the Jews in *historic* times. General ideas of offering, of self-denial, of propitiation of wrath, and of entering into communion with God assuredly existed. But in the advanced stages of the religion there is no evidence that sacrifices were thought to produce their effect because of any of these things, but solely because God had commanded the sacrifices. (2) Most sins required a sacrifice as part of the act of repentance, although in case of injury done the neighbor, only after reparation had been made. It is not quite true that for conscious sins no sacrifices were appointed, for in Lev **5** 1; **6** 1–3, sins are included that could not be committed through mere negligence. And so such rules as Nu **15** 30.31 must not be construed too rigorously. (3) Sacrifices as means of salvation are taught chiefly by Ezk, while at the rebuilding of the temple (Hag, Zec) and the depression that followed (Mal), they were much in the foreground, but the preëxilic prophets have little to say about their positive value (Jer **7** 22 is the nadir). Indeed, in preëxilic times the danger was the exaltation of sacrifice at the expense of morality, esp. with the peace offering, which could be turned into a drunken revel (Am **5** 21–24; Isa **22** 13; cf Prov **7** 14). Attempts were made to "strengthen" the sacrifices to Jeh by the use of ethnic rites (Hos **4** 14; Isa **65** 1–5), even with the extreme of human sacrifice (Jer **7** 31; Ezk **20** 26). But insistence on the strict centralization of worship and increasing emphasis laid on the sin and trespass offerings did away with the worst of the abuses. And many of the Pss, esp. **66, 118,** give beautiful evidence of the devotion that could be nourished by the sacrificial rites.

6. Ritual Law

Of the other means of salvation the ritual law (not always sharply distinguishable from the moral law) bulks rather large in the legislation, but is not prominent in the prophets. Requisite to salvation was the abstention from certain acts, articles of food, etc, such abstinence seeming to lie at the background of the term "holiness." But a ritual breach was often a matter of moral duty (burying the dead, etc), and, for such breaches, ritual means of purification are provided and the matter dropped. Evidently such things lay rather on the circumference of the religion, even to Ezekiel, with his anxious zeal against the least defilement. The highest ritual point is touched by Zec **14** 20.21, where all of Jerus is so holy that not a pot would be unfit to use in the temple (cf Jer **31** 38–40). Yet, even with this perfect holiness, sacrifices would still have a place as a means by which the holiness could be increased. Indeed, this more "positive" view of sacrifices was doubtless present from the first.

II. Intermediate Literature.—(1) The great change, compared with the earlier period, is that the idea of God had become more transcendent. But this did not necessarily mean an increase in religious value, for there was a corresponding tendency to take God out of relation to the world by an intellectualizing process. This, when combined with the persistence of the older concept of salvation in this life only, resulted in an emptying of the religious instinct and in indifferentism. This tendency is well represented in Eccl, more acutely in Sir, and in NT times it dominated the thought of the Sadducees. On the other hand the expansion of the idea of salvation to correspond with the higher conception of God broke through the limitations of this life and created the new literary form of apocalyptics, represented in the OT esp. by Zec **9–14;** Isa **24–27,** and above all by Dnl. And in the intermediate literature all shades of thought between the two extremes are represented. But too much emphasis can hardly be laid on the fact that this intermediate teaching is in many regards simply faithful to the OT. Almost anything that can be found in the OT—with the important exception of the note of joyousness of Dt, etc—can be found again here. (2) Of the conceptions of the highest good the lowest is the Epicureanism of Sir. The highest is probably that of 2 Esd **7** 91–98 RV: "To behold the face of him whom in their lifetime they served," the last touch of materialism being eliminated. Indeed, real materialism is notably absent in the period, even En **10** 17–19 being less exuberant than the fancies of such early Christian writers as Papias. Individualism is generally taken for granted, but that the opposite opinion was by no means dormant, even at a late period, is shown by Mt **3** 9. The idea of a special privilege of Israel, however, of course pervades all the literature, Sib Or **5** and Jub being the most exclusive books and the XII Tests. the most broad-hearted. In place of national privilege, though, is sometimes found the

1. General

still less edifying feature of party privilege (Ps Sol; En **94-105**), the most offensive case being the assertion of En **90** 6-9 that the (inactive) Israel will be saved by the exertions of the "little lamb" Pharisees, before whom every knee shall bow in the Messianic kingdom.

2. The Law

(1) The conceptions of the moral demands for salvation at times reach a very high level, esp. in the XII Tests. (making every allowance for Christian interpolations). "The spirit of love worketh together with the law of God in long-suffering unto the salvation of men" (Test. Gad **4** 7) is hardly unworthy of St. Paul, and even Jub can say, "Let each love his brother in mercy and justice, and let none wish the other evil" (**36** 8). But the great tendency is to view God's law merely as a series of written statutes, making no demands except those gained from a rigid construing of the letter. In Lk **10** 29, "Who is my neighbor?" is a real question—if he is not my *neighbor* I need not love him! So duties not literally commanded were settled by utilitarian motives, as outside the domain of religion, and the unhealthy phenomenon of works of supererogation made its appearance (Lk **17** 10). The writer of Wisd can feel smugly assured of salvation, because idolatry had been abstained from (**15** 4; contrast St. Paul's polemic in Rom **2**). And discussions about "greatest commandments" caused character in its relation to religion to be forgotten. (2) As God's commands were viewed as statutes the distinction between the moral and the ritual was lost, and the ritual law attained enormous and familiar proportions. The beautiful story of Judith is designed chiefly to teach abstinence from ritually unclean food. And the most extreme case is in Jub **6** 34-38—all of Israel's woes come from keeping the feasts by the actual moon instead of by a correct (theoretical) moon (!). (3) Where self-complacency ceased and a strong moral sense was present, despair makes its appearance with extraordinary frequency. The period is the period of penitential prayers, with an undercurrent of doubt as to how far mercy can be expected (Three vs 3-22; Pr Man; Bar **3** 1-8, etc). "What profit is it unto us, if there be promised us an immortal time, whereas we have done the works that bring death?" (2 Esd **7** 119 RV). The vast majority of men are lost (**9** 16) and must be forgotten (**8** 55), and Ezra can trust for his own salvation only by a special revelation (**7** 77 RV). So, evidently, St. Paul's pre-Christian experience was no unique occurrence. (4) Important for the NT background is the extreme lack of prominence of the sacrifices. They are never given a theological interpretation (except in Philo, where they cease to be sacrifices). Indeed, in Sir **35** they are explicitly said to be devotions for the righteous only, apparently prized only as an inheritance from the past and "because of the commandment" (Sir **35** 5; yet cf **38** 11). When the temple was destroyed and the sacrifices ceased, Judaism went on its way almost unaffected, showing that the sacrifices meant nothing essential to the people. And, even in earlier times, the Essenes rejected sacrifices altogether, without losing thereby their recognition as Jews.

III. The Teaching of Christ.—

1. The Baptist

The Baptist proclaimed authoritatively the near advent of the kingdom of God, preceded by a Messianic judgment that would bring fire for the wicked and the Holy Spirit for the righteous. Simple but incisive moral teaching and warning against trusting in national privileges, with baptism as an outward token of repentance, were to prepare men to face this judgment securely. But we have no data to determine how much farther (if any) the Baptist conceived his teaching to lead.

2. Kingdom of God

It was in the full heat of this eschatological revival that the Baptist had fanned, that Christ began to teach, and He also began with the eschatological phrase, "The kingdom of God is at hand." Consequently His teaching must have been taken at once in an eschatological sense, and it is rather futile to attempt to limit such implications to passages where modern eschatological phrases are used unambiguously. "The kingdom of God is at hand" had the inseparable connotation "Judgment is at hand," and in this context, "Repent ye" (Mk **1** 15) must mean "lest ye be judged." Hence, Our Lord's teaching about salvation had primarily a future content: positively, admission into the kingdom of God, and negatively, deliverance from the preceding judgment. So the kingdom of God is the "highest good" of Christ's teaching but, with His usual reserve, He has little to say about its externals. Man's nature is to be perfectly adapted to his spiritual environment (see RESURRECTION), and man is to be with Christ (Lk **22** 30) and the patriarchs (Mt **8** 11). But otherwise—and again as usual—the current descriptions are used without comment, even when they rest on rather materialistic imagery (Lk **22** 16.30). Whatever the kingdom is, however, its meaning is most certainly not exhausted by a mere reformation of the present order of material things.

3. Present and Future

But the fate of man at judgment depends on what man is before judgment, so that the practical problem is salvation from the conditions that will bring judgment; i.e. present and future salvation are inseparably connected, and any attempt to make rigid distinctions between the two results in logomachies. Occasionally even Christ speaks of the kingdom of God as present, in the sense that citizens of the future kingdom are living already on this earth (Mt **11** 11; Lk **17** 21[?]; the meaning of the latter verse is very dubious). Such men are "saved" already (Lk **19** 9; **7** 50[?]), i.e. such men were delivered from the bad moral condition that was so extended that Satan could be said to hold sway over the world (Lk **10** 18; **11** 21).

4. Individualism

That the individual was the unit in this deliverance needs no emphasis. Still, the Divine privilege of the Jews was a reality and Christ's normal work was limited to them (Mt **10** 5; **15** 26, etc). He admitted even that the position of the Jewish religious leaders rested on a real basis (Mt **23** 3). But the "good tidings" were so framed that their extension to all men would have been inevitable, even had there not been an explicit command of Christ in this regard. On the other hand, while the message involved in every case strict individual choice, yet the individual who accepted it entered into social relations with the others who had so chosen. So salvation involved admission to a community of service (Mk **9** 35, etc). And in the latter part of Christ's ministry, He withdrew from the bulk of His disciples to devote Himself to the training of an inner circle of Twelve, an act explicable only on the assumption that these were to be the leaders of the others after He was taken away. Such passages as Mt **16** 18; **18** 17 merely corroborate this.

5. Moral Progress

Of the conditions for the individual, the primary (belief in God being taken for granted) was a correct moral ideal. Exclusion from salvation came from the Pharisaic casuistry which had invented limits to righteousness. Ex **20** 13 had never contemplated permitting angry thoughts if actual murder was avoided, and so on. In contrast is set the idea of character, of the single eye (Mt **6** 22), of the pure heart (**5** 8). Only so can the spiritual house be built on a rock foundation. But the mere ideal is not enough; persistent effort toward it and a certain amount of progress are demanded imperatively. Only those who have learned to forgive can ask for forgiveness (Mt **6** 12; **18** 35). They who omit natural works of mercy have no share in the kingdom (**25** 31–46), for even idle words will be taken into account (**12** 36), and the most precious possession that interferes with moral progress is to be sacrificed ruthlessly (**18** 8.9, etc). Men are known by their fruits (**7** 20); it is he that doeth the will of the Father that shall enter into the kingdom (**7** 21), and the final ideal—which is likewise the goal—is becoming a son of the Father in moral likeness (**5** 45). That this progress is due to God's aid is so intimately a part of Christ's teaching on the entire dependence of the soul on God that it receives little explicit mention, but Christ refers even His own miracles to the Father's power (Lk **11** 20).

Moral effort, through God's aid, is an indispensable condition for salvation. But complete success in the moral struggle is not at all a condition, in the sense that moral perfection is required. For Christ's disciples, to whom the kingdom is promised (Lk **12** 32), the palsied man who receives remission of sins (Mk **2** 5), Zacchaeus who is said to have received salvation (Lk **19** 9), were far from being models of sinlessness. The element in the character that Christ teaches as making up for the lack of moral perfection is becoming "as a little child" (cf Mk **10** 15). Now the point here is not credulousness (for belief is not under discussion), nor is it meekness (for children are notoriously *not* meek). And it most certainly is not the pure passivity of the newly born infant, for it is gratuitous to assume that only such infants were meant even in Lk **18** 15, while in Mt **18** 2 (where the child comes in answer to a call) this interpretation is excluded. Now, in the wider teaching of Christ the meaning is made clear enough. Salvation is for the poor in spirit, for those who hunger and thirst after righteousness, for the prodigal knowing his wretchedness. It is for the penitent publican, while the self-satisfied Pharisee is rejected. A sense of need and a desire that God will give are the characteristics. A child does not argue that it has earned its father's benefits but looks to him in a feeling of dependence, with a readiness to do his bidding. So it is the soul that desires all of righteousness, strives toward it, knows that it falls short, and trusts in its Father for the rest, that is the savable soul.

6. Forgiveness

Christ speaks of the pardon of the publican (Lk **18** 9 ff) and of the prodigal welcomed by the Father (Lk **15** 20), both without intermediary. And it is perhaps not necessary to assume that all of those finding the strait gate (Mt **7** 14) were explicitly among Christ's disciples. But would Christ have admitted that anyone who had come to know Him and refused to obey Him would have been saved? To ask this question is to answer it in the negative (Mk **9** 40 is irrelevant). Real knowledge of the Father is possible only through the unique knowledge of the Son (Lk **10** 21.22), and lack of faith in the Son forfeits all blessings (Mk **6** 5.6; **9** 23). Faith in Him brings instant forgiveness of sins (Mk **2** 5), and love directed to Him is an indisputable sign that forgiveness has taken place (Lk **7** 47). But Christ thought of Himself as Messiah and, if the term "Messiah" is not to be emptied of its meaning, this made Him judge of the world (such verses as Mk **8** 38 are hardly needed for direct evidence). And, since for Christ's consciousness an earthly judgeship is unthinkable, a transcendental judgeship is the sole alternative, corroborated by the use of the title Son of Man. But passage from simple humanity to the transcendental glory of the Son-of-Man Messiah involved a change hardly expressible except by death and resurrection. And the expectation of death was in Christ's mind from the first, as is seen by Mk **2** 18.19 (even without ver 20). That He could have viewed His death as void of significance for human salvation is simply inconceivable, and the ascription of Mk **10** 45 to Pauline influence is in defiance of the facts. Nor is it credible that Christ conceived that in the interval between His death and His Parousia He would be out of relation to His own. To Him the unseen world was in the closest relation to the visible world, and His passage into glory would strengthen, not weaken, His power. So there is a complete justification of Mk **14** 22–25: to Christ His death had a significance that could be paralleled only by the death of the Covenant victim in Ex **24** 6–8, for by it an entirely new relation was established between God and man.

7. Person of Christ

(1) Salvation from *physical* evil was a very real part, however subordinate, of Christ's teaching (Mk **1** 34, etc). (2) Ascetic practices as a necessary element in salvation can hardly claim Christ's authority. It is too often forgotten that the Twelve were not Christ's only disciples. Certainly not all of the hundred and twenty of Acts **1** 15 (cf ver 21), nor of the five hundred of 1 Cor **15** 6, were converted after the Passion. And they all certainly could not have left their homes to travel with Christ. So the demands made in the special case of the Twelve (still less in such an extremely special case as Mk **10** 21) in no way represent Christ's normal practice, whatever readiness for self-sacrifice may have been asked of all. So the representations of Christ as ruthlessly exacting all from everyone are quite unwarranted by the facts. And it is well to remember that it is Mt **11** 19 that contains the term of reproach that His adversaries gave Him.

8. Notes

IV. St. Paul.—Instead of laying primal stress on St. Paul's peculiar contributions to soteriology, it will be preferable to start from such Pauline passages as simply continue the explicit teaching of Christ. For it is largely due to the common reversal of this method that the present acute "Jesus-Paulus" controversy exists.

1. General

That St. Paul expected the near advent of the kingdom of God with a judgment preceding, and that salvation meant to him primarily deliverance from this judgment, need not be argued. And, accordingly, emphasis is thrown sometimes on the future deliverance and sometimes on the present conditions for the deliverance (contrast Rom **5** 9 and **8** 24), but the *practical* problem is the latter. More explicitly than in Christ's recorded teaching the nature and the blessings of the kingdom are described (see Kingdom of God), but the additional matter is without particular religious import. A certain privilege of the Jews appears (Rom **3** 1–8; **9–11**), but the practical content of the privilege seems to be eschatological only (**11** 26). Individual conversion is of course taken for granted, but the life after that becomes highly corporate (see Church).

2. Moral Progress

(1) The moral ideal is distinctly that of character. St. Paul, indeed, is frequently obliged to give directions as to details, but the detailed directions are referred constantly to the underlying principle, Rom **14** or 1 Cor **8** being excellent examples of this, while "love is the fulfilment of the law" (Rom **13** 10) is the summary. (2) Persistent moral effort is indispensable, and the new life absolutely must bring forth fruit to God (Rom **6** 4; **13** 12; Gal **5** 24; Col **3** 5; Eph **2** 3; **4** 17.22–32;

Tit **2** 11–14). Only by good conduct can one please God (1 Thess **4** 1), and the works of even Christians are to be subjected to a searching test (1 Cor **3** 13; **4** 5; 2 Cor **5** 10) in a judgment not to be faced without the most earnest striving (1 Cor **10** 12; Phil **2** 12), not even by St. Paul himself (1 Cor **9** 27; Phil **3** 12–14). And the possibility of condemnation because of a lack of *moral* attainment must not be permitted to leave the mind (1 Cor **3** 17; Gal **5** 21; cf Rom **8** 12.13; **11** 20; 1 Cor **10** 12; Gal **6** 7–9). Consequently, growth in *actual* righteousness is as vital in St. Paul's soteriology as it is in that teaching of Christ: Christians have "put off the old man with his doings" (Col **3** 9).

That this growth is God's work is, however, a point where St. Paul has expanded Christ's quiet assumption rather elaborately. In particular, what Christ had made the source of His own supernatural power —the Holy Spirit—is specified as the source of the power of the Christian's ordinary life, as well as of the more special endowments (see Spiritual Gifts). In the Spirit the Christian has received the blessing promised to Abraham (Gal **3** 14); by it the deeds of the body can be put to death and all virtues flow into the soul (Gal **5** 16–26), if a man walks according to it (1 Cor **6** 19.20; 1 Thess **4** 8). The palmary passage is Rom **7–8**. In ch **7** St. Paul looks back with a shudder on his pre-Christian helplessness (it is naturally the extreme of exegetical perversity to argue that he dreaded not the sin itself but only God's penalty on sin). But the Spirit gives strength to put to death the deeds of the body (**8** 13), to disregard the things of the flesh (**8** 5), and to fulfil the ordinance of the Law (**8** 4). Such moral power is the test of Christianity: as many as are led by the Spirit of God, these are the sons of God (**8** 14).

3. The Spirit

This doctrine of the Spirit is simply that what Christ did on earth would be carried on with increased intensity after the Passion. That this work could be thought of out of relation to Christ, or that Christ Himself could have so thought of it (see above, III, 7) is incredible. So the exalted Christ appears as the source of moral and spiritual power (St. Paul speaks even more of Christ's resurrection than of the Passion), the two sources (Christ and the Spirit) being very closely combined in 2 Cor **3** 17; Rom **8** 9; Gal **4** 6. Our old man has been crucified, so putting an end to the bondage of sin, and we can prevent sin from reigning in our mortal bodies, for our burial into Christ's death was to enable us to walk in newness of life (Rom **6** 2–14). The resurrection is a source of power, and through Christ's strength all things can be done (Phil **4** 13.20). Christ is the real center of the believer's personality (Gal **2** 20); the man has become a new creature (2 Cor **5** 17; cf Col **2** 20; **3** 3); we were joined to another that we might bring forth fruit to God (Rom **7** 4). And by contact with the glory of the Lord we are transformed into the same image (2 Cor **3** 18), the end being conformation to the image of the Son (Rom **8** 30).

4. Mystical Union

(1) This growth in actual holiness, then, is fundamental with St. Paul: "If any man hath not the Spirit of Christ, he is none of his" (Rom **8** 9). And the acquisition of strength through union with Christ is vitally connected with the remission of sins. In Rom **7** 1–6 (cf Col **2** 11.12), the mystical union with Christ makes His death ours (cf Col **3** 3) and so removes us from the Law (cf Rom **10** 4; 1 Cor **15** 56), which has no relation to the dead. And by the life-giving power of this union the strength of sin is broken (Rom **6** 6). (2) The condition in man that makes forgiveness possible St. Paul calls "faith"—a very complicated term. Its chief use, however, is in opposition to "works" (most clearly in Rom **9** 30—**10** 13). The Jews' "pursuit after righteousness"—the attempt to wring salvation from God as wages earned—was vain (Rom **10** 13), and in contrast is the appeal to God, the conscious relinquishment of all claim (**4** 5). The soul looks trustingly for salvation to its Father, precisely the attitude of the "children" in the teaching of Christ. But no more than in the teaching of Christ is faith a purely passive virtue, for man must be "obedient" to it (Rom **1** 5; **10** 16; 1 Thess **2** 13). And for the necessary presence of love in faith cf 1 Cor **13** 2; Gal **5** 6; Eph **3** 17.

5. Forgiveness

Because of faith—specifically, faith in Christ (except Rom **4**; Gal **3** 6)—God does not visit the penalties of sins on believers, but treats them as if they were righteous (Rom **5** 1, etc). But this is not because of a quality in the believer or in the faith, but because of an act that preceded any act of Christian faith, the death of Christ (not the cross, specifically, for St. Paul does not argue from the cross in all of Rom). Through this death God's mercy could be extended safely, while before this the exercise of that mercy had proved disastrous (Rom **3** 25.26). And this death was a sacrifice (Rom **3** 25, etc). And it is certain that St. Paul conceived of this sacrifice as existing quite independently of its effect on any human being. But he has given us no data for a really complete sacrificial doctrine, a statement sufficiently proved by the hopeless variance of the interpretations that have been propounded. And that St. Paul ever constructed a theory of the operation of sacrifices must be doubted. There is none in the contemporary Jewish literature, there is none in the OT, and there is none in the rest of the NT, not even in He. Apparently the rites were so familiar that sacrificial terminology was ready to hand and was used without particular reflection and without attempting to give it precise theological content. This is borne out by the ease with which in Rom **3** 24.25 St. Paul passes from a ransom (redemption) illustration to a (quite discordant) propitiation illustration. For further discussion see Atonement; Justification. Here it is enough to say that to make a juridical theory constructed from Pauline implications and illustrations central in Christianity is to do exactly what St. Paul did not do.

6. Atonement

Summing up, there is a double line of thought in St. Paul: the remission of penalties through the atoning death of Christ and the destruction of the power of sin through strength flowing from Christ, the human element in both cases being faith. The question of the order of the steps is futile, for "to have faith," "to be in Christ," and "to have the Spirit" are convertible terms, i.e. in doctrinal phraseology, the beginnings of sanctification are simultaneous with justification. Attempts to unify the two lines of thought into a single theory cannot claim purely Bib. support. The "ethical" theory, which in its best form makes God's pardon depend on the fact that the sinner will be made holy (at least in the next world), introduces the fewest extraneous elements, but it says something that St. Paul does not say. On the other hand one may feel that considering St. Paul as a whole—to say nothing of the rest of the NT—the pure justification doctrine has bulked a little too large in our dogmatics. God's pardon for sin is an immensely important matter, but still more important is the new power of holiness.

7. Summary

8. Notes

(1) Baptism presents another obstacle to a strict unifying of Pauline theology. A very much stronger sacramentarianism is admitted in St. Paul today than would have been accepted a generation ago, and such passages as Rom **6** 1–7; Gal **3** 27; Col **2** 12 make it certain that he regarded baptism as conferring very real spiritual powers. But that he made a mechanical distinction between the blessings given then and those given at some other time must be doubted. (2) Salvation from the flesh (Rom **7** 24) involves no metaphysical dualism, as "flesh" is the whole of the lower nature from which the power to holiness saves a man (**8** 13). Indeed, the body itself is an object of salvation (Rom **8** 11; and see Resurrection). (3) Quite in the background lies the idea of salvation from physical evil (2 Cor **1** 10, etc). Such evils are real evils (1 Cor **11** 30), but in God's hands they may become pure blessings (Rom **5** 3; 2 Cor **12** 7). (4) Salvation from sin *after* conversion is due to God's judging the man in terms of the acquired supernatural nature (Rom **8** 14, etc). Yet certain sins may destroy the union with Christ altogether (1 Cor **3** 17, etc), while others bring God's chastening judgment (1 Cor **11** 30–32). Or proper chastisement may be inflicted by St. Paul himself (1 Cor **5** 1–5; 1 Tim **1** 20) or by the congregation (Gal **6** 1; 2 Thess **3** 10–15; 2 Cor **2** 6).

V. Rest of NT: Summary.—(1) St. John had the task of presenting Christ to Gentiles, who were as unfamiliar with the technical meaning of such phrases as "kingdom of God" or "Son of Man" as is the world today, and to Gentiles who had instead a series of concepts unknown in Pal. So a "translation of spiritual values" became necessary if the gospel were to make an immediate appeal, a translation accomplished so successfully that the Fourth Gospel has always been the most popular. The Synoptists, esp. the extremely literal St. Mark, imperatively demand a historical commentary, while St. John has successfully avoided this necessity. (2) The "kingdom of God," as a phrase (**3** 3.5; cf **18** 36), is replaced by "eternal life." This life is given in this world to the accepter of Christ's teaching (**5** 24; **6** 47), but its full realization will be in the "many mansions" of the Father's house (**14** 2), where the believer will be with Christ (**17** 24). A judgment of all men will precede the establishment of this glorified state (**5** 28.29), but the believer may face the judgment with equanimity (**5** 24). So the believer is delivered from a state of things so bad as expressible as a world under Satan's rule (**12** 31; **14** 30; **16** 11), a world in darkness (**3** 19), in ignorance of God (**17** 25), and in sin (**8** 21), all expressible in the one word "death" (**5** 24). (3) The Jews had real privilege in the reception of Christ's message (**1** 11; **4** 22, etc), but the extension of the good tidings to all men was inevitable (**12** 23.32, etc). Belief in Christ is wholly a personal matter, but the believers enter a community of service (**13** 14), with the unity of the Father and Son as their ideal (**17** 21). (4) The nature of the moral ideal, reduced to the single word "love" (**13** 34; **15** 12), is assumed as known and identified with "Christ's words" (**5** 24; **6** 63, etc), and the necessity of progress toward it as sharply pointed as in the Synoptists. The sinner is the servant of sin (**8** 34), a total change of character is needed (**3** 6), and the blessing is only on him who does Christ's commandments (**13** 17). This "doing" is the proof of love toward Christ (**14** 15. 21); only by bearing fruit and more fruit can discipleship be maintained (**15** 1–6; cf **14** 24), and, indeed, by bearing fruit men actually become Christ's disciples (**15** 8, Gr). The knowledge of Christ and of God that is eternal life (**17** 3) comes only through moral effort (**7** 17). In St. John the contrasts are colored so vividly that it would almost appear as if perfection were demanded. But he does not present even the apostles as models of sanctity (**13** 38; **16** 32), and self-righteousness is condemned without compromise; the crowning sin is to say, "We see" (**9** 41). It is the Son who frees from sin (**8** 36), delivers from darkness (**8** 12; **12** 46), and gives eternal life (**11** 25.26; cf **3** 16; **5** 24; **6** 47). This emphasis on the Divine side of the process is probably the reason for the omission of the terms "repent," "repentance," from the Gospel in favor of "faith" (**6** 29, esp.), but this "faith" involves in turn human effort, for, without "abiding," faith is useless (**8** 30.31). (5) An advance on the Synoptists is found in the number of times Christ speaks of His death (**3** 14.15; **10** 11.15; **12** 24.32; **17** 19) and in the greater emphasis laid on it, but no more than in the Synoptists is there any explanation of how the Atonement became effectual. A real advance consists in the prospect of Christ's work after His death, when, through the Paraclete (**7** 38.39; **14** 16 ff), a hitherto unknown spiritual power would become available for the world. And spiritual power is due not only to a union of will with Christ but to mystical union with Him (**15** 1–9). See above, III, 7, for the relation of these thoughts to the synoptic teaching.

1. St. John

2. Hebrews

(1) The emphasis of He is of course on the sacrificial work of Christ, but the Ep. makes practically no contribution to the theology of sacrifice. The argument is this: The OT sacrifices certainly had an efficacy; Christ's sacrifice fulfilled their types perfectly, therefore it had a perfect efficacy (**9** 13.14). This must have been a tremendously potent argument for He's own purpose, but it is of very little help to the modern theologian. (2) More than in St. Paul is emphasized the human training of Christ for His high-priestly work. Since He laid hold of the seed of Abraham (**2** 16), He learned by experience all that man had to suffer (**2** 17; **4** 15; **5** 8, etc). In He the essence of the sacrifice lies not in the death but in what we call the ascension—the presentation of the blood in the heavenly tabernacle (**9** 11–14; see the comms.). That the death was specifically on the cross (**12** 2 only) belonged to the stage of training and had no especial significance in the sacrificial scheme. Christ's intercession for us in heaven receives more emphasis than in the rest of the NT (**7** 25).

3. St. Peter

The one other distinct contribution to NT soteriology is made in 1 Pet's evaluation of the vicarious suffering of the "Servant" of Isa **53**. What Christ did through His sufferings we may do in some degree through our sufferings; as His pains helped not only living mankind, but even departed sinners, so we may face persecution more happily with the thought that our pains are benefiting other men (**3** 16–20). It is hardly possible that St. Peter thought of this comparison as conveying an exhaustive description of the Atonement (cf **1** 19), but that the comparison should be made at all is significant.

4. Summary

(1) Salvation is both a present and a future matter for us. The full realization of all that God has in store will not be ours until the end of human history (if, indeed, there will not be opened infinite possibilities of eternal growth), but the enjoyment of these blessings depends on conditions fulfilled in us and by us now. But a foretaste of the blessings of forgiveness of sins and growth in holiness is given on this earth. The pardon depends on the fact of God's mercy through the death of Christ—a fact for religious experience but probably incapable of expression as a complete philosophical dogma.

But strength comes from God through the glorified Christ (or through the Spirit), this vital union with God being a Christian fundamental. These two lines are in large degree independent, and the selection of the proportions profitable to a given soul is the task of the pastor. (2) That human effort is an essential in salvation is not to be denied in the face of all the NT evidence, esp. St. Paul taken as a whole. And yet no one with the faintest conception of what religion means would think of coming before God to claim merit. Here the purely intellectual discussions of the subject and its psychological course in the soul run in different channels, and "anti-synergistic" arguments are really based on attempts to petrify psychological experience into terms of pure dogma. (3) Still more true is this of attempts to describe mathematically the steps in salvation—the *ordo salutis* of the older dogmatics—for this differs with different souls. In particular, NT data are lacking for the development of the individual born of Christian parents in a Christian country. (4) Further, the social side of salvation is an essentially Christian doctrine and cannot be detached from the corporate life of the Christian church. Salvation from temporal evils is equally, if secondarily, Christian. Nationalism in salvation is at present much in the background. But it is as true today as it was in ancient Israel that the sins of a nation tend to harm the souls of even those who have not participated actively in those sins.

LITERATURE.—The literature of salvation is virtually the literature of theology (see under separate arts., ATONEMENT; JUSTIFICATION; SANCTIFICATION; PERSON OF CHRIST; JOHANNINE THEOLOGY; PAULINE THEOLOGY, etc), but a few recent works may be mentioned. Indispensable are the works of Stevens, *The Christian Doctrine of Salvation* and *The Pauline Theology*. Garvie's *Romans* in the "New Century" series should be used as a supplement to any other comm. on Rom. The juridical theory has as its best defence in Eng. Denney's *The Death of Christ*. The ethical theory is best presented in the works of Du Bose, *The Gospel in the Gospels*, *The Gospel according to St. Paul*, and *High-Priesthood and Sacrifice* (Sanday's *Expos* reviews of the two former, reprinted in *The Life of Christ in Recent Research*, should be read in any case).

BURTON SCOTT EASTON

SAMAEL, sam'ā-el: AV=RV SALAMIEL (q.v.).

SAMAIAS, sa-mā'yas (Σαμαίας, *Samaías*):

(1) One of the "captains over thousands" prominent at the Passover of Josiah (1 Esd **1** 9) = "Shemaiah" in 2 Ch **35** 9.

(2) One of the heads of families of the sons of Adonikam who returned with Ezra (1 Esd **8** 39) = "Shemaiah" in Ezr **8** 13.

(3) One of the "men of understanding" whom Ezra commissioned to obtain from Loddeus, the captain, men to execute the priest's office (1 Esd **8** 44) = "Shemaiah" in Ezr **8** 16 (AV **Mamaias**).

(4) AV=RV "Shemaiah the great," a kinsman of Tobit and father of Ananias and Jonathan (Tob **5** 13).

S. ANGUS

SAMARIA, sa-mā'ri-a, **CITY OF** (שֹׁמְרוֹן, *shōmerōn;* Σαμάρεια, *Samáreia,* Σεμερών, *Semerôn,* and other forms):

(1) Shechem was the first capital of the Northern Kingdom (1 K **12** 25). Jeroboam seems later to have removed the royal residence to Tirzah (**14** 17). After the brief reigns of Elah and Zimri came that of Omri, who reigned 6 years in Tirzah, then he purchased the hill of Samaria and built a city there, which was thenceforward the metropolis of the kingdom of Israel (**16** 24). Here the hill and the city are said to have been named after Shemer, the original owner of the land. There is nothing intrinsically improbable in this. It might naturally be derived from *shāmar*, and the name in the sense of "outlook" would fitly apply to a city in such a commanding position. The residence, it was also the burying-place, of the kings of Israel (1 K **16** 28; **22** 37; 2 K **10** 35; **13** 9.13; **14** 16).

Toward the western edge of the Ephraimite uplands there is a broad fertile hollow called *Wâdy esh-Sha'īr*, "valley of barley." From the midst of it rises an oblong hill to a height of over 300 ft., with a level top. The sides are steep, esp. to the S. The greatest length is from E. to W. The surrounding mountains on three sides are much higher, and are well clad with olives and vineyards. To the W. the hills are lower, and from the crest a wide view is obtained over the Plain of Sharon, with the yellow ribbon of sand that marks the coast line, and the white foam on the tumbling billows; while away beyond stretch the blue waters of the Mediterranean. On the eastern end of the hill, surrounded by olive and cactus, is the modern village of *Sebasṭiyeh*, under which a low neck of land connects the hill with the eastern slopes. The position

Ruins in Samaria.

is one of great charm and beauty; and in days of ancient warfare it was one of remarkable strength. While it was overlooked from three sides, the battlements crowning the steep slopes were too far off to be reached by missiles from the only artillery known in those times—the sling and the catapult. For besiegers to attempt an assault at arms was only to court disaster. The methods adopted by her enemies show that they relied on famine to do their work for them (2 K **6** 24 f, etc). Omri displayed excellent taste and good judgment in the choice he made.

The city wall can be traced in almost its entire length. Recent excavations conducted by American archaeologists have uncovered the foundations of Omri's palace, with remains of the work of Ahab and of Herod (probably here was Ahab's ivory palace), on the western end of the hill, while on the western slope the gigantic gateway, flanked by massive towers, has been exposed to view.

Under the influence of Jezebel, Samaria naturally became a center of idolatrous worship. Ahab "reared up an altar for Baal in the house of Baal, which he had built in Samaria. And Ahab made the Asherah" (1 K **16** 32 f). Jehoram his son put away the pillar of Baal (2 K **3** 2), and within the temple Jehu made an end at once of the instruments of idolatry and of the priests (**10** 19 f). There are many prophetic references to the enormities practised here, and to their inevitable consequences (Isa **8** 4; **9** 9; **10** 9; **28** 1 ff; **36** 19; Jer **23** 13; Ezk **23** 4; Hos **7** 1; **13** 16; Am **3** 12; Mic **1** 6, etc).

Under pressure of Damascus Omri conceded to the

Syrians the right to "make streets in Samaria" (1 K **20** 34).

Ben-hadad II besieged the city, but suffered ignominious defeat (**20** 1–21; Jos, *Ant,* VIII, xiv, 1 f). Persistent attempts by the Syrians to reach the city in the time of Jehoram were frustrated by Elisha (2 K **6** 8 ff; Jos, *Ant,* IX, iv, 3). At length, however, Ben-hadad again invested the city, and the besieged were reduced to dire straits, in which, urged by famine, scenes of awful horror were enacted (2 K **6** 24 ff). A mysterious panic seized the Syrians. Their deserted camp was discovered by despairing lepers who carried the good news to the famished citizens of the plenty to be found there. Probably in the throat of the great western gateway occurred the crush in which the incredulous captain was trampled to death (ch **7**; Jos, *Ant,* IX, iv, 5).

Here the 70 sons of Ahab were slain by Jehu in the general destruction of the house of Ahab (2 K **10** 1 ff). In Samaria, the Chronicler tells us, Ahaziah in vain hid from Jehu (2 Ch **22** 9; cf 2 K **9** 27). Pekah brought hither much spoil from Jerus and many captives, whom, at the instance of the prophet Oded, he released (2 Ch **28** 8 ff). The siege of Samaria was begun by Shalmaneser in the 7th year of Hoshea, and the city was finally taken by Sargon II at the end of 3 years, 722 BC (2 K **17** 5 f; **18** 9 f; *Ant,* IX, xiv, 1). This marked the downfall of the Northern Kingdom, the people being transported by the conqueror. That this was not done in a thoroughgoing way is evident from the fact recorded in the inscriptions that two years later the country had to be subdued again. Colonists were brought from other parts to take the places of the exiles (2 K **17** 24; Ezr **4** 10). Alexander the Great took the city in 331 BC, killed many of the inhabitants, and settled others in Shechem, replacing them with a colony of Syro-Macedonians. He gave the adjoining country to the Jews (*CAp,* II, 4). The city suffered at the hands of Ptolemy Lagi and Demetrius Poliorcetes, but it was still a place of strength (Jos, *Ant,* XIII, x, 2) when John Hyrcanus came against it in 120 BC. It was taken after a year's siege, and the victor tried to destroy the city utterly. His turning of the water into trenches to undermine the foundations could only refer to the suburbs under the hill. From the only two sources, *'Ain Hārūn* and *'Ain Kefr Rīma,* to the E. of the town, the water could not rise to the hill. The "many fountains of water" which Benjamin of Tudela says he saw on the top, from which water enough could be got to fill the trenches, are certainly not to be seen today; and they have left no trace behind them. The city was rebuilt by Pompey and, having again fallen under misfortune, was restored by Gabinius (Jos, *Ant,* XIV, iv, 4; v, 3; *BJ,* I, vii, 7; viii, 4). To Herod it owed the chief splendor of its later days. He extended, strengthened and adorned it on a scale of great magnificence, calling it Sebaste (=Augusta) in honor of the emperor, a name which survives in the modern *Sebasṭiyeh.* A temple also was dedicated to Caesar. Its site is probably marked by the impressive flight of steps, with the pedestal on which stood the gigantic statue of Augustus, which recent excavations have revealed. The statue, somewhat mutilated, is also to be seen. Another of Herod's temples W. of the present village was cleared out by the same explorers. The remains of the great double-columned street, which ran round the upper terrace of the hill, bear further testimony to the splendor of this great builder's work (Jos, *Ant,* XV, vii, 3; viii, 5; *BJ,* I, xxi, 2). It was here that Herod killed perhaps the only human being whom he ever really loved, his wife Mariamne. Here also his sons perished by his hand (Jos, *Ant,* XV, vii, 5–7; XVI, iii, 1–3; xi, 7).

It is commonly thought that this city was the scene of Philip's preaching and the events that followed recorded in Acts **8**, but the absence of the def. art. in ver 5 makes this doubtful. A Rom colony was settled here by Septimius Severus. From that time little is known of the history of the city; nor do we know to what the final castastrophe was due. It became the seat of a bishopric and was represented in the councils of Nicaea, Constantinople and Chalcedon. Its bishop attended the Synod of Jerus in 536 AD.

The Harvard excavations found the lower walls of the palace of Ahab. Abundant fragments of ivory scattered in the neighborhood probably indicate that this was the ivory palace of that king.

(2) *ἡ Σαμάρεια, hē Samáreia:* A town mentioned in 1 Macc **5** 66 as on the route followed by Judas from the district of Hebron to the land of the Philis. The name is probably a clerical error. The margin reads Marisa, and probably the place intended is Mareshah, the site of which is at *Tell Sandaḥannah,* about a mile S. of *Beit Jibrīn.* W. Ewing

SAMARIA, COUNTRY OF (שֹׁמְרוֹן, *shōmᵉrōn;* **ἡ Σαμαρεῖτις χώρα,** *hē Samareítis chōra*): The name of the city was transferred to the country of which it was the capital, so that Samaria became synonymous with the Northern Kingdom (1 K **13** 32; Jer **31** 5, etc). The extent of territory covered by this appellation varied greatly at different periods. At first it included the land held by Israel E. of the Jordan, Galilee and Mt. Ephraim, with the northern part of Benjamin. It was shorn of the eastern portion by the conquest of Tiglath-pileser (1 Ch **5** 26). Judah probably soon absorbed the territory of Dan in the S. In NT times Samaria had shrunk to still smaller dimensions. Then the country W. of the Jordan was divided into three portions: Judaea in the S., Galilee in the N., and Samaria in the middle. The boundaries are given in general terms by Jos (*BJ,* III, iii, 1, 4, 5). The southern edge of the Plain of Esdraelon and the lands of Scythopolis, the city of the Decapolis W. of the Jordan, formed the northern boundary. It reached S. as far as the toparchy of Acrabatta (modern *'Aḳrabeh*), while on the border between Samaria and Judaea lay the villages of Annath and Borceos, the modern *Khirbet 'Aina* and *Berḳīt,* about 15 miles S. of *Nāblus.* The Jordan of course formed the eastern boundary. On the W. the coast plain as far as Acre belonged to Judaea. The country thus indicated was much more open to approach than the high plateau of Judah with its steep rocky edges and difficult passes. The road from the N. indeed was comparatively easy of defence, following pretty closely the line of the watershed. But the gradual descent of the land to the W. with long, wide valleys, offered inviting avenues from the plain. The great trade routes, that to the fords of Jordan and the E., passing through the cleft in the mountains at Shechem, and those connecting Egypt with the N. and the N.E., traversed Samarian territory, and brought her into constant intercourse with surrounding peoples. The influence of the heathen religions to which she was thus exposed made a swift impression upon her, leading to the corruptions of faith and life that heralded her doom (Jer **23** 13; Hos **7** 1 ff, etc). The Assyrians came as the scourge of God (2 K **17** 5–23). Their attack centered on the capital. Shalmaneser began the siege, and after three years the city fell to Sargon II, his successor. With the fall of Samaria the kingdom came to an end. Following the usual Assyr policy, great numbers of the inhabitants were deported from the conquered country, and their places taken by men brought from "Babylon, and from Cuthah, and from Avva, and from Hamath and Sepharvaim," cities which had already bowed to the Assyr power (ver 24).

It appears from the Assyr inscriptions that the number carried away was 27,290. The number afterward deported from Judah was 200,000, and then the poorest of the land were left to be vinedressers and husbandmen (2 K **25** 12). It is evident that a similar policy must have been followed in Samaria, as 27,290 could certainly not include the whole population of the cities and the country. But it would include the higher classes, and esp. the priests from whom the victors would have most to fear. The population therefore after the conquest contained a large proportion of Israelites. It was no doubt among these that Josiah exercised his reforming energy (2 K **23** 19 f; 2 Ch **34** 6 f). Here also must have been that "remnant of Israel," Manasseh and Ephraim, who contributed for the repair of the house of God (ver 9). These people, left without their religious guides, mingling with the heathen who had brought their gods and, presumably, their priests with them, were apt to be turned from the purity of their faith. A further importation of pagan settlers took place under Esar-haddon and Osnappar (Ezr **4** 9.10). The latter is to be identified with Assur-bani-pal. What the proportions of the different elements in the population were, there is now no means of knowing. That there was some intermarriage is probable; but having regard to racial exclusiveness, we may suppose that it was not common. When the Jews deny to them any relation to Israel, and call them Cuthaeans, as if they were the descendants purely of the heathen settlers, the facts just mentioned should be borne in mind.

After the Assyr conquest we are told that the people suffered from lions (2 K **17** 25). Jos (*Ant*, IX, xiv, 3) says "a plague seized upon them." In accordance with the ideas of the time, the strangers thought this due to the anger of the tutelary deity of the land, because they worshipped other gods in his territory, while neglecting him. Ignorant of his special ritual ("manner"), they petitioned the Assyr king, who sent one (Jos says "some") of the priests who had been carried away to teach them "how they should fear the Lord." How much is implied in this "fearing of the Lord" is not clear. They continued at the same time to serve their own gods. There is nothing to show that the Israelites among them fell into their idolatries. The interest of these in the temple at Jerus, the use of which they may now have shared with the Jews, is proved by 2 Ch **34** 9. In another place we are told that four score men "from Shechem, from Shiloh, and from Samaria," evidently Israelites, were going up with their offerings to the house of the Lord (Jer **41** 5). Once the people of the country are called Samaritans (2 K **17** 29). Elsewhere this name has a purely religious significance. See SAMARITANS.

Of the history of Samaria under Assyr and Bab rulers we know nothing. It reappears at the return of the Jews under Pers auspices. The Jews refused the proffered assistance of the Samaritans in rebuilding the temple and the walls of Jerus (Ezr **4** 1.3). Highly offended, the latter sought to frustrate the purpose of the Jews (vs 4 ff; Neh **4** 7 ff; 1 Esd **2** 16 ff). That the Samaritans were accustomed to worship in Jerus is perhaps implied by one phrase in the letter sent to the Pers king: "The Jews that came up from thee are come *to us* unto Jerus" (Ezr **4** 12). Perhaps also they may be referred to in **6** 21. Idolatry is not alleged against the "adversaries." We can hardly err if we ascribe the refusal in some degree to the old antagonism between the N. and the S., between Ephraim and Judah. Whatever the cause, it led to a wider estrangement and a deeper bitterness. For the history of the people and their temple on Gerizim, see SAMARITANS.

Samaria, with Pal, fell to Alexander after the battle of Issus. Antiochus the Great gave it to Ptolemy Epiphanes, as the dowry of his daughter Cleopatra (Jos, *Ant*, XII, iv, 1). John Hyrcanus reduced and desolated the country (Jos, *BJ*, I, ii, 6 f). After varying fortunes Samaria became part of the kingdom of Herod, at whose death it was given to Archelaus (Jos, *Ant*, XVII, xi, 4; *BJ*, II, vi, 3). When Archelaus was banished it was joined to the Rom province of Syria (Jos, *Ant*, XVII, xiii, 5; *BJ*, II, viii, 1).

Samaria is a country beautifully diversified with mountain and hill, valley and plain. The olive grows plentifully, and other fruit trees abound. There is much excellent soil, and fine crops of barley and wheat are reaped annually. The vine also is largely cultivated on the hill slopes. Remains of ancient forests are found in parts. As Jos said, it is not naturally watered by many rivers, but derives its chief moisture from rain water, of which there is no lack (*BJ*, III, iii, 4). He speaks also of the excellent grass, by reason of which the cows yield more milk than those in any other place.

There is a good road connecting *Nāblus* with Jaffa; and by a road not quite so good, it is now possible to drive a carriage from Jerus to Nazareth, passing through Samaria. W. EWING

SAMARITAN, sa-mar′i-tan, **PENTATEUCH, THE.** See PENTATEUCH, THE SAMARITAN.

SAMARITANS, sa-mar′i-tanz (שֹׁמְרֹנִים, *shōmᵉ-rōnīm;* **Σαμαρεῖται,** *Samareítai,* NT **Σαμαρίτης** [sing.], *Samarítēs*): The name "Samaritans" in 2 K **17** 29 clearly applies to the Israelitish inhabitants of the Northern Kingdom. In subsequent history it denotes a people of mixed origin, composed of the peoples brought by the conqueror from Babylon and elsewhere to take the places of the expatriated Israelites and those who were left in the land (722 BC). Sargon claims to have carried away only 27,290 of the inhabitants (*KIB*, II, 55). Doubtless these were, as in the case of Judah, the chief men, men of wealth and influence, including all the priests, the humbler classes being left to till the land, tend the vineyards, etc. Hezekiah, who came to the throne of Judah probably in 715 BC, could still appeal to the tribes of Ephraim, Manasseh, Issachar, Asher and Zebulun (2 Ch **30** 5.10.11. 18 ff); and the presence of these tribesmen is implied in the narrative of Josiah's reformation (**34** 6 f). Although the number of the colonists was increased by Esar-haddon and Osnappar (Assur-bani-pal, Ezr **4** 2.9 f), the population, it is reasonable to suppose, continued prevailingly Israelite; otherwise their religion would not so easily have won the leading place. The colonists thought it necessary for their own safety to acknowledge Jeh, in whose land they dwelt, as one among the gods to be feared (2 K **17** 24 ff). In the intermixture that followed "their own gods" seem to have fallen on evil days; and when the Samaritans asked permission to share in building the temple under Zerubbabel, they claimed, apparently with a good conscience, to serve God and to sacrifice to Him as the Jews did (Ezr **4** 1 f). Whatever justification there was for this claim, their proffered friendship was turned to deadly hostility by the blunt refusal of their request. The old enmity between north and south no doubt intensified the quarrel, and the antagonism of Jew and Samaritan, in its bitterness, was destined to pass into a proverb. The Samaritans set themselves, with great temporary success, to frustrate the work in which they were not permitted to share (Ezr **4** 4 ff: Neh **4** 7 ff. etc).

From the strict administration of the Law in Jerus malcontents found their way to the freer atmosphere of Samaria. Among these renegades was Manasseh, brother of the high priest, who had married a daughter of Sanballat, the Pers governor of Samaria. According to Jos, Sanballat, with the sanction of Alexander the Great, built a temple for the Samaritans on Mt. Gerizim, of which Manasseh became high priest (*Ant*, XI, vii, 2; viii, 2 ff). Jos, however, places Manasseh a century too late. He was a contemporary of Ezra and Nehemiah (Neh **13** 28).

When it suited their purpose the Samaritans claimed relationship with the Jews, asserting that their roll of the Pent was the only authentic copy (see PENTATEUCH, THE SAMARITAN); they were equally ready to deny all connection in times of stress, and even to dedicate their temple to a heathen deity (Jos, *Ant*, XII, v, 5). In 128 BC, John Hyrcanus destroyed the temple (XIII, ix, 1). In the time of Christ the Samaritans were ruled by procurators under the Rom governor of Syria. Lapse of years brought no lessening of the hatred between Jews and Samaritans (*Ant*, XX, vi, 1). To avoid insult and injury at the hands of the latter, Jews from Galilee were accustomed to reach the feasts at Jerus by way of Peraea. "Thou art a Samaritan, and hast a demon" was an expression of opprobrium (Jn **8** 48). Although Jesus forbade the Twelve to go into any city of the Samaritans (Mt **10** 5), the parable of the Good Samaritan shows that His love overleaped the boundaries of national hatred (Lk **10** 30 ff; cf **17** 16; Jn **4** 9).

During the Jewish war Cerealis treated the Samaritans with great severity. On one occasion (67 AD) he slaughtered 11,600 on Mt. Gerizim. For some centuries they were found in considerable numbers throughout the empire, east and west, with their synagogues. They were noted as "bankers" and money-changers. For their anti-Christian attitude and conduct Justinian inflicted terrible vengeance on them. From this the race seems never to have recovered. Gradually dwindling, they now form a small community in *Nāblus* of not more than 200 souls. Their great treasure is their ancient copy of the Law. See SAMARIA.

LITERATURE.—The best account of the Samaritans is Mills, *Nāblus and the Modern Samaritans* (Murray, London); cf Montgomery, *The Samaritans* (1907). A good recent description by Rev. J. E. H. Thomson, D.D., of the Passover celebrated annually on Mt. Gerizim will be found in *PEFS*, 1902, 82 ff.

W. EWING

SAMATUS, sam'a-tus (**Σάματος**, *Sámatos*): One of the sons of Ezora who put away their "strange wives" (1 Esd **9** 34). It is difficult to say which, if any, name it represents in ‖ Ezr **10** 34 ff, where no "sons of Ezora" are inserted between "sons of Bani" and "sons of Nebo": probably Shallum (ver 42), but possibly Shemariah (ver 41).

SAMECH, sam'ek (ס, *ṣamekh*): The 15th letter of the Heb alphabet; transliterated in this Encyclopaedia as *ṣ*. It came to be used for the number 60. For name, etc, see ALPHABET.

SAMEIUS, sa-mē'yus: AV=RV SAMEUS (q.v.).

SAMELLIUS, sa-mel'i-us (B, **Σαμέλλιος**, *Saméllios*, A, **Σεβέλλιος**, *Sebéllios*, al **Σεμέλλιος**, *Seméllios;* AV Semellius): "S. the scribe," one of those who wrote a letter of protest to Artaxerxes against the building of Jerus by the returned exiles (1 Esd **2** 16.17.25.30) = "Shimshai" in Ezr **4** 8.

SAMEUS, sa-mē'us (A and Fritzsche, **Σαμαῖος**, *Samaíos*, B, **Θαμαῖος**, *Thamaíos;* AV **Sameius**): One of the sons of Emmer who put away their "strange wives" (1 Esd **9** 21) = "Shemaiah" (RVm "Maaseiah") of the sons of Harim in Ezr **10** 21.

SAMGAR-NEBO, sam-gär-nē'bō (סַמְגַּר נְבוֹ, *ṣamgar nᵉbhō*, a Bab name): An officer of Nebuchadnezzar, king of Babylon, who, according to the MT of Jer **39** 3, took his seat with other nobles in the middle gate of Jerus after the Chaldaean army had taken the city. Schrader (*COT*, ii, 109) holds that the name is a Hebraized form of the Assyr *Sumgirnabu* ("be gracious, Nebo"), but Giesebrecht (*Comm.*, 211) conjectures for Samgar a corruption of Sar-mag (*sar-magh*), equivalent to Rab-mag (*rab-magh*), which implies virtual dittography. The number of variant readings exhibited by the LXX seems to confirm the belief that the text is corrupt. Nebo (*nabu*) is there joined with the following Sarsechim to agree with Nebushazban of ver 13. If the name Samgar-nebo is correct, the first Nergal-sharezer should perhaps be dropped; we would then read: "Samgar-nebo the Sarsechim, Nebushazban the Rab-saris [cf ver 13] and Nergal-sharezer the Rab-mag" (Sayce). See RAB-MAG; RAB-SARIS.

HORACE J. WOLF

SAMI, sā'mī: AV=RV SABI (q.v.).

SAMIS, sā'mis: AV=RV SOMEIS (q.v.).

SAMLAH, sam'la (שַׂמְלָה, *samlāh;* **Σαλαμά**, *Salamá*): One of the kings of Edom, of the city of Masrekah. He reigned before the Israelites had kings (Gen **36** 36.37; 1 Ch **1** 47.48). The fact that the city is mentioned in connection with the name of the king suggests that Edom was a confederacy at this time and the chief city was the metropolis of the whole country.

SAMMUS, sam'us (A, **Σαμμοῦς**, *Sammoús*, B, **Σαμμού**, *Sammoú*): One of those who stood on Ezra's right hand as he expounded the Law (1 Esd **9** 43) = "Shema" in Neh **8** 4.

SAMOS, sā'mos (**Σάμος**, *Sámos*, "height," "mountain" [see Strabo 346, 457]): One of the most famous of the Ionian islands, third in size among the group which includes Lesbos, CHIOS (q.v.) and Cos (q.v.). It is situated at the mouth of the bay of Ephesus, between the cities of EPHESUS and MILETUS (q.v.), and separated from the mainland of Ionia by the narrow strait where the Greeks met and conquered the Pers fleet in the battle of Mycale, 479 BC (Herod. ix.100 ff). The surface of the island is very rugged and mountainous, Mt. Kerki (modern name) rising to a height of 4,700 ft., and it was due to this that the island received its name (see above; see also SAMOTHRACE).

Samos was renowned in antiquity as one of the noted centers of Ionian luxury, and reached its zenith of prosperity under the rule of the famous tyrant Polycrates (533–522 BC), who made himself master of the Aegean Sea. He carried on trade with Egypt, and his intercourse with that country, his friendship with Amasis, the famous "ring" story and the revolting manner of the death of Polycrates are all told in one of the most interesting stories of Herodotus (Herod. iii.39 ff).

In 84 BC, the island was joined to the province of Asia, and in 17 BC it became a *civitas libera*, through the favor of Augustus (Dio Cass. liv.9; Pliny, *NH*, v.37). Both Marcus Agrippa and Herod visited the island; and according to Jos (*Ant*, XVI, ii, 2; *BJ*, I, xxi, 11) "bestowed a great many benefits" on it. In the Apoc, Samos is mentioned among the places to which Lucius, consul of the Romans, wrote, asking their good will toward the Jews (1 Macc **15** 23).

In the NT, Paul touched here, after passing Chios (q.v.), on his return from his third missionary journey (Acts **20** 15). In *TR*, we find in this passage *καὶ μείναντες ἐν Τρωγυλλίῳ, kaí meínantes en Trōgulliō* ("and having remained in Trogyllium"). This reading is wanting in the oldest MSS, and may be a sort of gloss, or explanation, due to the technical use of *parabállein*, "to touch land" (cf Jos, *Ant*, XVIII, vi, 4), and not necessarily "to make a landing." Trogyllium lay on the mainland opposite Samos, at the end of the ridge of Mycale. Still there is no particular reason why this reading should be supported, esp. as it is not found in the earliest of authorities. Soden's 1913 text, however, retains the reading in brackets.

Literature.—Tozer, *Islands of the Aegean* (1890). Herodotus and Pausanias have rather full accounts of Samos, and *Enc Brit* (11th ed) gives a good bibliography of works both ancient and modern.

Arthur J. Kinsella

SAMOTHRACE, sam'ō-thrās (**Σαμοθρᾴκη**, *Samothrákē*, "the Thracian Samos"; AV **Samothracia**, sam-ō-thrā'sha; the island was formerly Dardania; for change of name see Pausanias vii.4,3; Strabo x.457, and for a full discussion Conze, Hauser and Benndorf, *Neue Untersuchungen auf S.*, 1880): An island in the Aegean Sea, S. of Thrace opposite the mouth of the Hebrus River, and N.W. of Troas. The island is mountainous, as the name indicates (see Samos), and towers above Imbros when viewed from the Trojan coast. The summit is about a mile high. It is mentioned in the *Iliad* (xiii.12) as the seat of Poseidon and referred to by Virgil *Aeneid* vii.208.

The island was always famous for sanctity, and the seat of a cult of the Cabeiri, which Herodotus (ii.51) says was derived from the Pelasgian inhabitants (see also Aristophanes, *Pax* 277). The mysteries connected with the worship of these gods later rivaled the famous mysteries of Eleusis, and both Philip of Macedon and Olympias his wife were initiated here (Plut. *Alex.* 3).

Probably because of its sacred character the island did not figure to any extent in history, but in the expedition of Xerxes in 480 BC, one ship at least of the Samothracian contingent is mentioned as conspicuous in the battle of Salamis.

The famous "Victory of Samothrace" (now in the Louvre) was set up here by Demetrius Poliorcetes c 300 BC, and was discovered in 1863. Since that time (1873–75), the Austrian government carried on extensive excavations (see Conze, Hauser and Benndorf, op. cit.).

In the NT the island is mentioned in Acts **16** 11. From Troas, Paul made a straight run to Samothrace, and the next day sailed to Neapolis (q.v.) on the Thracian coast, the port of Philippi (q.v.). At the northern end of S. was a town where the ship could anchor for the night, and on the return journey (Acts **20** 6) a landing may have been made, but no details are given. Pliny characterizes the island as being most difficult for anchorage, but because of the hazards of sailing by night, the ancient navigators always anchored somewhere if possible.

Literature.—See under Samos.

Arthur J. Kinsella

SAMPSAMES, samp'sa-mēz (**Σαμψάμης**, *Sampsámēs*): A place mentioned in 1 Macc **15** 23, usually identified with Samsun, on the coast of the Black Sea. Vulg, with RVm, has "Lampsacus."

SAMSON, sam'sun (שִׁמְשׁוֹן, *shimshōn*, derived probably from שֶׁמֶשׁ, *shemesh*, "sun," with the diminutive ending וֹן-, *-ōn*, meaning "little sun" or "sunny," or perhaps "sun-man"; **Σαμψών**, *Sampsṓn;* Lat and Eng. Samson): His home was near Beth-shemesh, which means "house of the sun." Compare the similar formation שִׁמְשַׁי, *shimshay* (Ezr **4** 8.9.17.23).

1. Name

2. Character

Samson was a judge, perhaps the last before Samuel. He was a Nazirite of the tribe of Dan (Jgs **13** 5); a man of prodigious strength, a giant and a gymnast—the Heb Hercules, a strange champion for Jeh! He intensely hated the Philis who had oppressed Israel some 40 years (**13** 1), and was willing to fight them alone. He seems to have been actuated by little less than personal vengeance, yet in the NT he is named among the heroes of faith (He **11** 32), and was in no ordinary sense an OT worthy. He was good-natured, sarcastic, full of humor, and fought with his wits as well as with his fists. Milton has graphically portrayed his character in his dramatic poem *Samson Agonistes* (1671), on which Handel built his oratorio *Samson* (1743).

3. Story of His Life

The story of S.'s life is unique among the biographies of the OT. It is related in Jgs **13–16.** Like Isaac, Samuel and John the Baptist, he was a child of prayer (**13** 8.12). To Manoah's wife the angel of Jeh appeared twice (**13** 3.9), directing that the child which should be born to them should be a Nazirite from the womb, and that he would "*begin* to save Israel out of the hand of the Philis" (**13** 5.7.14). The spirit of Jeh first began to move him in Mahaneh-dan, between Zorah and Eshtaol (**13** 25). On his arriving at manhood, five remarkable circumstances are recorded of him.

(1) His marriage with a Phili woman of Timnah (ch **14**). His parents objected to the alliance (**14** 3), but S.'s motive in marrying her was that he "sought an occasion against the Philis." At the wedding feast S. propounded to his guests a riddle, wagering that if they guessed its answer he would give them 30 changes of raiment. Dr. Moore felicitously renders the text of the riddle thus:

> 'Out of the eater came something to eat,
> And out of the strong came something sweet' (**14** 14).

The Philis threatened the life of his bride, and she in turn wrung from S. the answer; whereupon he retorted (in Dr. Moore's version):

> 'If with my heifer ye did not plough,
> Ye had not found out my riddle, I trow' (**14** 18).

Accordingly, in revenge, S. went down to Ashkelon, slew some 30 men, and paid his debt; he even went home without his wife, and her father to save her from shame gave her to S.'s "best man" (**14** 20). It has been suggested by W. R. Smith (*Kinship and Marriage in Early Arabia*, 70–76) that S. did not from the first intend to take his bride to his home, his marriage being what is known among the Arabs as a *çadīkat*, or gift marriage, by which is meant that the husband becomes a part of the wife's tribe. This assumes that the social relations of the Hebrews at that time were matriarchate, the wife remaining with her family, of which custom there are other traces in the OT, the husband merely visiting the wife from time to time. But this is not so obvious in S.'s case in view of his pique (**14** 19), and esp. in view of his parents' objection to his marrying outside of Israel (**14** 3). Not knowing that his bride had been given by her father to his friend, S. went down to Timnah to visit her, with a kid; when he discovered, however, that he had been taken advantage of, he went out and caught 300 jackals, and putting firebrands between every two tails, he burned up the grain fields and olive yards of the Philis. The Philis, however, showed they could play with fire, too, and burned his wife and her father. Thereupon, S.

smote the Philis in revenge, "hip and thigh" (**15** 1–8).

(2) When he escaped to Etam, an almost vertical rock cliff in Judah (by some identified with *'Araq Ismain*) not far from Zorah, S.'s home, the Philis invaded Judah, encamped at Lehi above Etam, and demanded the surrender of their arch-enemy. The men of Judah were willing to hand S. over to the Philis, and accordingly went down to the cliff Etam, bound S. and brought him up where the Philis were encamped (**15** 9–13). When S. came to Lehi the Philis shouted as they met him, whereupon the spirit of Jeh came mightily upon him, so that he broke loose from the two new ropes with which the 3,000 men of Judah had bound him, and seizing a fresh jawbone of an ass he smote with it 1,000 men of the Philis, boasting as he did so in pun-like poetry, 'With the jawbone of an ass, m-ass upon m-ass'; or, as Dr. Moore translates the passage, 'With the bone of an ass, I ass-ailed my ass-ailants' (**15** 16). At the same time, S. reverently gave Jeh the glory of his victory (**15** 18). S. being thirsty, Jeh provided water for him at a place called En-hakkore, or "Partridge Spring," or "the Spring of the Caller"—another name for partridge (**15** 17–19).

(3) S. next went down to Gaza, to the very stronghold of the Philis, their chief city. There he saw a harlot, and, his passions not being under control, he went in unto her. It was soon noised about that S., the Heb giant, was in the city. Accordingly, the Philis laid wait for him. But S. arose at midnight and laid hold of the doors of the gate and their two posts, and carried them a full quarter of a mile up to the top of the mountain that looketh toward Hebron (**16** 1–3).

(4) From Gaza S. betook himself to the valley of Sorek where he fell in love with another Phili woman, named Delilah, through whose machinations he lost his spiritual power. The Phili lords bribed her with a very large sum to deliver him into their hands. Three times S. deceived her as to the secret of his strength, but at last he explains that he is a Nazirite, and that his hair, which has never been shorn, is the secret of his wonderful power. J. G. Frazer (*Golden Bough*, III, 390 ff) has shown that the belief that some mysterious power resides in the hair is still widespread among savage peoples, e.g. the Fiji Islanders. Thus S. fell. By disclosing to Delilah this secret, he broke his covenant vow, and the Spirit of God departed from him (**16** 4–20). The Philis laid hold on him, put out his eyes, brought him down to Gaza, bound him with fetters, and forced him to grind in the prison house. Grinding was women's work! It is at this point that Milton catches the picture and writes,

"Eyeless in Gaza, at the mill with slaves."

Howbeit, the hair of his head began to grow again; but his eyes did not! (**16** 21.22).

(5) The final incident recorded of S. is in connection with a great sacrificial feast which the Phili lords gave in honor of Dagon, their god. In their joyous celebration they sang in rustic rhythm:

'Our god has given us into our hand
The foe of our land,
Whom even our most powerful band
Was never able to withstand' (**16** 24).

This song was accompanied probably, as Mr. Macalister suggests, by hand-clapping (*Gezer*, 129). When they became still more merry, they called for S. to play the buffoon, and by his pranks to entertain the assembled multitude. The house of Dagon was full of people; about 3,000 were upon the roof beholding as S. made sport. With the new growth of his hair his strength had returned to him. The dismantled giant longed to be avenged on his adversaries for at least *one* of his two eyes (**16** 28). He prayed, and Jeh heard his prayer. Guided by his attendant, he took hold of the wooden posts of the two middle pillars upon which the portico of the house rested, and slipping them off their pedestals, the house fell upon the lords and upon all the people that were therein. "So the dead that he slew at his death were more than they that he slew in his life" (**16** 29.30). His kinsmen came and carried him up and buried him near his boyhood home, between Zorah and Eshtaol, in the family burying-ground of his father. "And he judged Israel twenty years" (**16** 31).

4. Historical Value

The story of Samson is a faithful mirror of his times: "Every man did that which was right in his own eyes" (**17** 6; **21** 25). There was no king in those days, i.e. no central government. Each tribe was separately occupied driving out their individual enemies. For 40 years the Philis had oppressed S.'s tribal compatriots. Their suzerainty was also recognized by Judah (**14** 4; **15** 11). S. was the hero of his tribe. The general historicity of his story cannot be impeached on the mere ground of improbability. His deeds were those which would most naturally be expected from a giant, filled with a sense of justice. He received the local popularity which a man of extraordinary prowess would naturally be given. All peoples glory in their heroes. The theory that the record in Jgs **13–16** is based upon some "solar myth" is now generally abandoned. That there are incidents in his career which are difficult to explain, is freely granted. For example, that he killed a lion (**14** 6) is not without a parallel; David and Benaiah did the same (1 S **17** 34–36; 2 S **23** 20). God always inspires a man in the line of his natural endowments. That God miraculously supplied his thirst (**15** 19) is no more marvelous than what God did for Hagar in the wilderness (Gen **21** 19). That S. carried off the doors of the gate of Gaza and their two posts, bar and all, must not confound us till we know more definitely their size and the distance from Gaza of the hill to which he carried them. The fact that he pulled down the roof on which there were 3,000 men and women is not at all impossible, as Mr. Macalister has shown. If we suppose that there was an immense portico to the temple of Dagon, as is quite possible, which was supported by two main pillars of wood resting on bases of stone, like the cedar pillars of Solomon's house (1 K **7** 2), all that S., therefore, necessarily did, was to push the wooden beams so that their feet would slide over the stone base on which they rested, and the whole portico would collapse. Moreover, it is not said that the whole of the 3,000 on the roof were destroyed (**16** 30). Many of those in the temple proper probably perished in the number (R. A. S. Macalister, *Bible Side-Lights from the Mound of Gezer*, 1906, 127–38).

5. Religious Value

Not a few important and suggestive lessons are deducible from the hero's life: (1) S. was the object of parental solicitude from even before his birth. One of the most suggestive and beautiful prayers in the OT is that of Manoah for guidance in the training of his yet unborn child (**13** 8). Whatever our estimate of his personality is, S. was closely linked to the covenant. (2) He was endowed with the Spirit of Jeh—the spirit of personal patriotism, the spirit of vengeance upon a foe of 40 years' standing (**13** 1.25; **14** 6 19; **15** 14). (3) He also prayed, and Jeh answered him, though in judgment (**16** 30). But he was prodigal of his strength. S. had spiritual power and performed feats which an ordinary man would hardly perform. But he was unconscious of his high vocation. In a moment of weakness he yielded to Delilah and divulged the secret of his strength. He was careless of his personal endowment. He did not realize that physical endowments no less than spiritual are gifts from God, and that to retain them we must be obedient. (4) He was passionate and therefore weak. The animal of his nature was never curbed, but rather ran unchained and free. He was given to sudden fury. S. was a wild, self-willed man. Passion ruled. He could not resist the blandishments of women. In short, he was an overgrown schoolboy, without self-mastery. (5) He accordingly wrought no permanent deliverance for Israel; he lacked the spirit of coöperation. He undertook a task far too great for even a giant single-handed. Yet, it must be allowed that S. paved the way for Saul and David. He *began* the deliverance of Israel from the Philis. He must, therefore, be judged according to his times. In his days there was unrestrained individual independence on every side, each one doing as he pleased. S. differed from his contemporaries in that he was a hero of faith (He **11** 32). He was a Nazirite, and therefore dedicated to God. He was given to revenge, yet he was ready to sacrifice himself in order that his own and his people's enemies might be overthrown. He was willing to lay down his own life for the sake of his fellow-tribesmen—not to save his enemies, however, but to kill them. (Cf Mt **5** 43 f; Rom **5** 10.)

LITERATURE.—(1) Comms. on Jgs, notably those by G. F. Moore, *ICC*, 1895; Budde, *Kurzer Handkommentar*, 1897; Nowack, *Handkommentar*, 1900; E. L. Curtis, *The Bible for Home and School*, 1913; Bachmann, 1868; Keil, 1862; Farrar in *Ellicott's Comm.*; Watson, *Expositor's Bible*. (2) Arts. on "Samson" in the various Bible Dicts. and Encs; in particular those by Budde, *HDB*; C. W. Emmet, in 1-vol *HDB*; S. A. Cook, *New Enc Brit*; Davis, *Dict. of the Bible*.

GEORGE L. ROBINSON

SAMUEL, sam'ū-el (שְׁמוּאֵל, *shᵉmū'ēl*; Σαμουήλ, *Samouēl*): The word "Samuel" signifies "name of God," or "his name is El" (God). Other interpretations of the name that have been offered are almost certainly mistaken. The play upon the name in 1 S **1** 20 is not intended of course to be an explanation of its meaning, but is similar to the play upon the name Moses in Ex **2** 10 and frequently elsewhere in similar instances. Thus by the addition of a few letters *shᵉmū'ēl* becomes *shā'ūl mē'ēl* (שָׁאוּל מֵאֵל, שמואל), "asked of God," and recalls to the mother of Samuel the circumstances of the Divine gift to her of a son. Outside of the 1st Book of S the name of the great judge and prophet is found in Jer **15** 1; Ps **99** 6 and in 1 and 2 Ch. The reference in Jer seems intended to convey the same impression that is given by the narrative of 1 S, that in some sense Samuel had come to be regarded as a second Moses, upon whom the mantle of the latter had fallen, and who had been once again the deliverer and guide of the people at a great national crisis.

1. Sources and Character of the History

The narrative of the events of the life of Samuel appears to be derived from more than one source (see SAMUEL, BOOKS OF). The narrator had before him and made use of biographies and traditions, which he combined into a single consecutive history. The completed picture of the prophet's position and character which is thus presented is on the whole harmonious and consistent, and gives a very high impression of his piety and loyalty to Jeh, and of the wide influence for good which he exerted. There are divergences apparent in detail and standpoint between the sources or traditions, some of which may probably be due merely to misunderstanding of the true nature of the events recorded, or to the failure of the modern reader rightly to appreciate the exact circumstances and time. The greater part of the narrative of the life of Samuel, however, appears to have a single origin.

2. Life

In the portion of the general history of Israel contained in 1 S are narrated the circumstances of the future prophet's birth (ch **1**); of his childhood and of the custom of his parents to make annual visits to the sanctuary at Shiloh (**2** 11.18–21.26); of his vision, and the universal recognition of him as a prophet enjoying the special favor of Jeh (**3—4** 1). The narrative is then interrupted to describe the conflicts with the Philis, the fate of Eli and his sons, and the capture of the ark of God. It is only after the return of the ark, and apparently at the close of the 20 years during which it was retained at Kiriath-jearim, that Samuel again comes forward publicly, exhorting the people to repentance and promising them deliverance from the Philis. A summary narrative is then given of the summoning of a national council at Mizpah, at which Samuel "judged the children of Israel," and offered sacrifice to the Lord, and of Jeh's response in a great thunderstorm, which led to the defeat and panic-stricken flight of the Philis. Then follows the narrative of the erection of a commemorative stone or pillar, Eben-ezer, "the stone of help," and the recovery of the Israelite cities which the Philis had captured (**7** 5–14). The narrator adds that the Philis came no more within the border of Israel all the days of Samuel (**7** 13); perhaps with an intentional reference to the troubles and disasters of which this people was the cause in the time of Saul. A brief general statement is appended of Samuel's practice as a judge of going on annual circuit through the land, and of his home at Ramah (**7** 15–17).

No indication is given of the length of time occupied by these events. At their close, however, Samuel was an old man, and his sons who had been appointed judges in his place or to help him in his office proved themselves unworthy (**8** 1–3). The elders of the people therefore came to Samuel demanding the appointment of a king who should be his successor, and should judge in his stead. The request was regarded by the prophet as an act of disloyalty to Jeh, but his protest was overruled by Divine direction, and at Samuel's bidding the people dispersed (**8** 4–22).

At this point the course of the narrative is again interrupted to describe the family and origin of Saul, his personal appearance, and the search for the lost asses of his father (**9** 1–5); his meeting with Samuel in a city in the land of Zuph, in or on the border of the territory of Benjamin (Zuph is the name of an ancestor of Elkanah, the father of Samuel, in 1 S **1** 1), a meeting of which Samuel had received Divine pre-intimation (**9** 15 f); the honorable place given to Saul at the feast; his anointing by Samuel as ruler of Israel, together with the announcement of three "signs," which should be to Saul assurances of the reality of his appointment and destiny; the spirit of prophecy which took possession of the future king, whereby is explained a proverbial saying which classed Saul among the prophets; and his silence with regard to what had passed between himself and Samuel on the subject of the kingdom (**9** 6—**10** 16).

It is usually, and probably rightly, believed that the narrative of these last incidents is derived from a different source from that of the preceding chapters. Slight differences of inconsistency or disagreement lie on the surface. Samuel's home is not at Ramah, but a nameless city in the land of Zuph, where he is priest of the high place, with a local but, as far as the narrative goes, not a national influence or reputation; and it is anticipated that he will require the customary present at the hands of his visitors (**9** 6–8). He is described, moreover, not as a judge, nor does he discharge judicial functions, but expressly as a "seer," a name said to be an earlier title equivalent to the later "prophet" (**9** 9.11.19). Apart, however, from the apparently different position which Samuel occupies, the tone and style of the narrative is altogether distinct from that of the preceding chapters. It suggests, both in its form and in the religious conceptions which are assumed or implied, an older and less elaborated tradition than that which has found expression in the greater part of the book; and it seems to regard events as it were from a more primitive standpoint than the highly religious and monotheistic view of the later accounts. Its value as a witness to history is not impaired, but perhaps rather enhanced by its separate and independent position. The writer or compiler of 1 S has inserted it as a whole in his completed narrative at the point which he judged most suitable. To the same source should possibly be assigned the announcement of Saul's rejection in **13** 8–15*a*.

The course of the narrative is resumed at **10** 17 ff,

where, in a second national assembly at Mizpah, Saul is selected by lot and accepted by the people as king (**10** 17–24); after which the people dispersed, and Saul returned to his home at Gibeah (vs 25–27). At a solemn assembly at Gilgal, at which the kingship is again formally conferred upon Saul, Samuel delivered a farewell address to his fellow-countrymen. A thunderstorm terrified the people; they were reassured, however, by Samuel with promises of the protection and favor of Jeh, if they continued to fear and serve Him (**11** 14—**12** 25). Later the rejection of Saul for disobedience and presumption is announced by Samuel (**13** 8–15*a*). The commission to destroy Amalek is delivered to Saul by Samuel; and the rejection of the king is again pronounced because of his failure to carry out the command. Agag is then slain by Samuel with his own hand; and, the latter having returned to his home at Ramah, the narrator adds that he remained there in seclusion until the day of his death, "mourning" for Saul, but refusing to meet him again (ch **15**). Finally the death and burial of Samuel at Ramah, together with the lamentation of the people for him, are briefly recorded in **25** 1, and referred to again in **28** 3.

Two incidents of Samuel's life remain, in which he is brought into relation with the future king David. No indication of date or circumstance is given except that the first incident apparently follows immediately upon the second and final rejection of Saul as recorded in ch **15**. In **16** 1–13 is narrated the commission of Samuel to anoint a successor to Saul, and his fulfilment of the commission by the choice of David the son of Jesse, the Bethlehemite. And, in a later chapter (**19** 18–24), a second occasion is named on which the compelling spirit of prophecy came upon Saul, and again the proverbial saying, "Is Saul also among the prophets?" is quoted (**19** 24; cf **10** 11.12), and is apparently regarded as taking its origin from this event.

The anointing of David by Samuel is a natural sequel to his anointing of Saul, when the latter has been rejected and his authority and rights as king have ceased. There is nothing to determine absolutely whether the narrative is derived from the same source as the greater part of the preceding history. Slight differences of style and the apparent presuppositions of the writer have led most scholars to the conclusion that it has a distinct and separate origin. If so, the compiler of the Books of S drew upon a third source for his narrative of the life of the seer, a source which there is no reason to regard as other than equally authentic and reliable. With the second incident related in **19** 18–24, the case is different. It is hardly probable that so striking a proverb was suggested and passed into currency independently on two distinct occasions. It seems evident that here two independent sources or authorities were used, which gave hardly reconcilable accounts of the origin of a well-known saying, in one of which it has been mistakenly attributed to a similar but not identical occurrence in the life of Saul. In the final composition of the book both accounts were then inserted, without notice being taken of the inconsistency which was apparent between them.

Yet later in the history Samuel is represented as appearing to Saul in a vision at Endor on the eve of his death (**28** 11–20). The witch also sees the prophet and is stricken with fear. He is described as in appearance an old man "covered with a robe" (ver 14). In characteristically grave and measured tones he repeats the sentence of death against the king for his disobedience to Jeh, and announces its execution on the morrow; Saul's sons also will die with him (ver 19), and the whole nation will be involved in the penalty and suffering, as they all had a part in the sin.

The high place which Samuel occupies in the thought of the writers and in the tradition and esteem of the people is manifest throughout the history. The different sources from which the narrative is derived are at one in this, although perhaps not to an equal degree. He is the last and greatest of the judges, the first of the prophets, and inaugurates under Divine direction the Israelite kingdom and the Davidic line. It is not without reason, therefore, that he has been regarded as in dignity and importance occupying the position of a second Moses in relation to the people. In his exhortations and warnings the Deuteronomic discourses of Moses are reflected and repeated. He delivers the nation from the hand of the Philis, as Moses from Pharaoh and the Egyptians, and opens up for them a new national era of progress and order under the rule of the kings whom they have desired. Thus, like Moses, he closes the old order, and establishes the people with brighter prospects upon more assured foundations of national prosperity and greatness. In nobility of character and utterance also, and in fidelity to Jeh, Samuel is not unworthy to be placed by the side of the older lawgiver. The record of his life is not marred by any act or word which would appear unworthy of his office or prerogative. And the few references to him in the later literature (Ps **99** 6; Jer **15** 1; 1 Ch **6** 28; **9** 22; **11** 3; **26** 28; **29** 29; 2 Ch **35** 18) show how high was the estimation in which his name and memory were held by his fellow-countrymen in subsequent ages.

3. Character and Influence of Samuel

Literature.—The literature is given in the art. Samuel, Books of (q.v.).

A. S. Geden

SAMUEL, BOOKS OF:

I. Place in the Canon.—In the Heb Canon and enumeration of the sacred books of the OT, the two Books of S were reckoned as one, and formed the third division of the Earlier Prophets (נְבִיאִים רִאשֹׁנִים, *nᵉbhī'īm rī'shōnīm*). The one book bore the title "Samuel" (שְׁמוּאֵל, *shᵉmū'ēl*), not because Samuel was believed to be the author, but because his life and acts formed the main theme of the book, or at least of its earlier part. Nor was the Book of S separated by any real division in subject-matter or continuity of style from the Book of K, which in the original formed a single book, not two as in the Eng. and other modern VSS. The history was carried forward without interruption; and the record of the life of David, begun in S, was completed in K. This continuity in the narrative of Israelite history was made more prominent in the LXX, where the four books were comprised under one title and were known as the four "Books of the Kingdoms" (βίβλοι βασιλειῶν, *bíbloi basileiȭn*). This name was probably due to the translators or scholars of Alexandria. The division into four books, but not the Gr title, was then adopted in the Lat tr, where, however, the influence of Jerome secured the restoration of the Heb names, 1 and 2 S, and 1 and 2 K (*Regum*). Jerome's example was universally followed, and the fourfold division with the Heb titles found a place in all subsequent VSS of the OT Scriptures. Ultimately the distinction of S and K each into two books was received also into printed editions of the Heb Bible. This was done for the first time in the *editio princeps* of the Rabbinic Bible, printed at Venice in 1516–17 AD.

II. Contents and Period of the History.—The narrative of the two Books of S covers a period of about a hundred years, from the close of the unsettled era of the Judges to the establishment and consolidation of the kingdom under David. It is therefore a record of the changes, national and constitutional, which accompanied this growth and development of the national life, at the close of which the Israelites found themselves a united people under the rule of a king to whom all owed allegiance, controlled and guided by more or less definitely established institutions and laws. This may be described as the general purpose and main theme of the books, to trace the advance of the people under Divine guidance to a state of settled prosperity and union in the promised land, and to give prominence to the theocratic rule which was the essential condition of Israel's life as the people of God under all the changing forms of early government. The narrative therefore centers itself around the lives of the three men, Samuel, Saul and David, who were chiefly instrumental in the establishment of the monarchy, and to whom it was due more than to any others that Israel emerged from the depressed and disunited state in which the tribes had remained during the period of the rule of the Judges, and came into possession of a combined and effective national life. If the formal separation therefore into two books be disregarded, the history of Israel as it is narrated in "Samuel" is most naturally divided into three parts, which are followed by an appendix recording words and incidents which for some reason had not found a place in the general narrative:

A. The life and rule of Samuel (1 S **1–15**) (death 1 S **25** 1).
B. The life, reign and death of Saul (1 S **16**—2 S **1**).
C. The reign and acts of David to the suppression of the two rebellions of Absalom and Sheba (2 S **2–20**).
D. Appendix; other incidents in the reign of David, the names of his chief warriors and his Song or Psalm of Praise (2 S **21–24**).

III. Summary and Analysis.—To present a brief and clear analysis of these Books of S is not altogether easy. For as in the Pent and the earlier historical Books of Josh and Jgs, repetitions and apparently duplicate accounts of the same event are found, which interfere with the chronological development of the narrative. Even the main divisions, as stated above, to a certain extent overlap.

1. Life of Samuel (1 S 1–15)

(1) Visit of Hannah to Shiloh, and promise of the birth of a son (1 S **1** 1–19); birth and weaning of Samuel, and presentation to Eli at Shiloh (**1** 19–28).

(2) Hannah's song or prayer (**2** 1–10); ministry of Samuel to Eli the priest (**2** 11.18–21.26); the evil practices of the sons of Eli and warning to Eli of the consequences to his house (**2** 12–17.22–25. 27–36).

(3) Samuel's vision at the sanctuary and his induction to the prophetic office (**3** 1—**4** 1).

(4) Defeat of the Israelites by the Philis, capture of the ark of God, death of the two sons of Eli and of Eli himself (ch **4**).

(5) Discomfiture of Dagon before the ark of God at Ashdod; return of the ark to Beth-shemesh, with expiatory offerings of golden tumors and golden mice; its twenty years' sojourn at Kiriath-jearim (**5** 1—**7** 4).

(6) Assembly of Israel under Samuel at Mizpah, and victory over the Philis (**7** 5–14); Samuel established as judge over all Israel (vs 15–17).

(7) Samuel's sons appointed to be judges and the consequent demand of the people for a king; Samuel's warning concerning the character of the king for whom they asked (ch **8**).

(8) Saul's search for the lost asses of his father and meeting with Samuel (ch **9**).

(9) Saul is anointed by Samuel to be ruler over the people of Israel, and receives the gift of prophecy (**10** 1–16); second assembly of the people under Samuel at Mizpah, and election of Saul to be king (vs 17–27).

(10) Victory of Saul over the Ammonites and deliverance of Jabesh-gilead (**11** 1–13); Saul made king in Gilgal (vs 14.15).

(11) Samuel's address to the people in Gilgal, defending his own life and action, and exhorting them to fear and serve the Lord (ch **12**).

(12) Saul at Gilgal offers the burnt offering in Samuel's absence; gathering of the Philis to battle at Michmash; the Israelites' lack of weapons of iron (ch **13**).

(13) Jonathan's surprise of the Phili army, and their sudden panic (**14** 1–23); Saul's vow, unwittingly broken by Jonathan, whom the people deliver from the fatal consequences (vs 24–45); victories of Saul over his enemies on every side (vs 46–52).

(14) War against Amalek, and Saul's disobedience to the Divine command to exterminate the Amalekites (ch **15**).

2. Reign and Death of Saul (1 S 16—2 S 1)

(1) Anointing of David as Saul's successor (**16** 1–13); his summons to the court of Saul to act as minstrel before the king (vs 14–23).

(2) David and Goliath (ch **17**).

(3) The love of David and Jonathan (**18** 1–4); the former's advancement and fame, the jealousy of Saul, and his attempt to kill David (**18** 5–16.29.30); David's marriage to the daughter of Saul (vs 17–28).

(4) Saul's renewed jealousy of David and second attempt to kill him (**19** 1–17); David's escape to Ramah, whither the king followed (vs 18–24).

(5) Jonathan's warning to David of his father's resolve and their parting (ch **20**).

(6) David at Nob (**21** 1–9); and with Achish of Gath (vs 10–15).

(7) David's band of outlaws at Adullam (**22** 1.2); his provision for the safety of his father and mother in Moab (vs 3–5); vengeance of Saul on those who had helped David (vs 6–23).

(8) Repeated attempts of Saul to take David (chs **23**, **24**).

(9) Death of Samuel (**25** 1); Abigail becomes David's wife, after the death of her husband Nabal (vs 2–44).

(10) Saul's further pursuit of David (ch **26**).

(11) David's sojourn with Achish of Gath (**27** 1—**28** 2.29); Saul and the witch of Endor (**28** 3–25).

(12) David's pursuit of the Amalekites who had raided Ziklag, and victory (ch **30**).

(13) Battle between the Philis and Israel in Mt. Gilboa and death of Saul (ch **31**).

(14) News of Saul's death brought to David at Ziklag (2 S **1** 1–16); David's lamentation over Saul and Jonathan (vs 17–27).

3. Reign of David (2 S 2–20)

(1) David's seven and a half years' reign over Judah in Hebron (2 S **2** 1—**5** 3).

(*a*) Consecration of David as king in Hebron (**2** 1–4*a*); message to the men of Jabesh-gilead (**2** 4*b*–7); Ish-bosheth made king over Northern Israel (vs 8–11); defeat of Abner and death of Asahel (vs 12–32).

(*b*) Increase of the fame and prosperity of David, and the names of his sons (**3** 1–5); Abner's submission to David, and treacherous murder of the former by Joab (vs 6–39).

(*c*) Murder of Ish-bosheth and David's vengeance upon his murderers (**4** 1–3.5–12); notice of the escape of Mephibosheth, when Saul and Jonathan were slain at Jezreel (ver 4).

(*d*) David accepted as king over all Israel (**5** 1–3).

(2) Reign of David in Jerus over united Israel (**5** 4—**20** 26).

(*a*) Taking of Jerus and victories over the Philis (**5** 4–25).

(*b*) Return of the ark to the city of David (ch **6**).

(*c*) David's purpose to build a temple for the Lord (**7** 1–3); the Divine answer by the prophet Nathan, and the king's prayer (vs 4–29).

(*d*) Victories over the Philis, Syrians, and other peoples (ch **8**).

(*e*) David's reception of Mephibosheth (ch **9**).

(*f*) Defeat of the Ammonites and Syrians by the men of Israel under the command of Joab (**10** 1—**11** 1).

(*g*) David and Uriah, the latter's death in battle, and David's marriage with Bath-sheba (**11** 2–27).

(*h*) Nathan's parable and David's conviction of sin (**12** 1–15*a*); the king's grief and intercession for his sick son (vs 15*b*–25); siege and capture of Rabbah, the Ammonite capital (vs 26–31).

(*i*) Amnon and Tamar (**13** 1–22); Absalom's revenge and murder of Amnon (vs 23–36); flight of Absalom (vs 37–39).

(*j*) Return of Absalom to Jerus (**14** 1–24); his beauty, and reconciliation with the king (vs 25–33).

(*k*) Absalom's method of ingratiating himself with the people (**15** 1–6); his revolt and the flight of the king from Jerus (vs 7–31); meeting with Hushai (vs 32–37*a*); Absalom in Jerus (ver 37*b*).

(*l*) David's meeting with Ziba (**16** 1–4), and Shimei (vs 5 14); counsel of Ahitophel and Hushai (**16** 15—**17** 14); the news carried to David (vs 15–22); death of Ahitophel (ver 23).

(*m*) David at Mahanaim (**17** 24–29).

(*n*) The revolt subdued, death of Absalom, and reception by David of the tidings (**18** 1—**19** 8*a*).

(*o*) Return of the king to Jerus, and meetings with Shimei, Mephibosheth, and Barzillai the Gileadite (**19** 8*b*–43).

(p) Revolt of Sheba the Benjamite, and its suppression by Joab with the death of Amasa (**20** 1.2.4–22); the king's treatment of the concubines left at Jerus (ver 3); the names of his officers (vs 23–26).

4. Appendix (2 S 21–24)

(1) Seven male descendants of Saul put to death at the instance of the Gibeonites (**21** 1–14); incidents of wars with the Philis (vs 15–22).

(2) David's song of thanksgiving and praise (ch **22**).

(3) The "last words" of David (**23** 1–7); names and exploits of David's "mighty men" (vs 8–39).

(4) The king's numbering of the people, the resulting plague, and the dedication of the threshing-floor of Araunah the Jebusite (ch **24**).

IV. Sources of the History.—The natural inference from the character and contents of the Books of S, as thus reviewed, is that the writer has made use of authorities, "sources" or "documents," from which he has compiled a narrative of the events which it was his desire to place on record. The same characteristics are noticeable here which are found in parts of the Pent and of the Books of Josh and Jgs, that in some instances duplicate or parallel accounts are given of one and the same event, which seems to be regarded from different points of view and is narrated in a style which is more or less divergent from that of the companion record. Examples of this so-called duplication are more frequent in the earlier parts of the books than in the later. There are presented, for instance, two accounts of Saul's election as king, and an act of disobedience is twice followed, apparently quite independently, by the sentence of rejection. Independent also and hardly consistent narratives are given of David's introduction to Saul (1 S **16** 14–23; **17** 31 ff.55 ff); and the two accounts of the manner of the king's death can be imperfectly reconciled only on the hypothesis that the young Amalekite told a false tale to David in order to magnify his own part in the matter. In these and other instances little or no attempt seems to be made to harmonize conflicting accounts, or to reconcile apparent discrepancies. In good faith the writer set down the records as he found them, making extracts or quotations from his authorities on the several events as they occurred, and thus building up his own history on the basis of the freest possible use of the materials and language of those who had preceded him.

However alien such a method of composition may appear to modern thought and usage in the West, it is characteristic of all early oriental writing. It would be almost impossible to find in any eastern literature a work of any length or importance which was not thus silently indebted to its predecessors, had incorporated their utterances, and had itself in turn suffered interpolation at the hands of later editors and transcribers. Accordingly, early Heb historical literature also, while unique in its spirit, conformed in its methods to the practice of the age and country in which it was composed. It would have been strange if it had been otherwise.

Two Main and Independent Sources

Apart from the appendix and minor additions, of which Hannah's song or psalm in 1 S **2** is one, the main portion of the book is derived from two independent sources, which themselves in all probability formed part of a larger whole, a more or less consecutive history or histories of Israel. These sources may, however, have been, as others think, rather of a biographical nature, presenting and enforcing the teaching of the acts and experience of the great leaders and rulers of the nation. The parallelism and duplication of the narrative is perhaps most evident in the history of Saul. The broad lines of distinction between the two may be defined without much difficulty or uncertainty. The greater part of the first eight chapters of 1 S is in all probability derived from the later of these two sources, to which is to be assigned more or less completely chs **10–12, 15, 17–19, 21–25, 28** and 2 S **1–7**. The earlier source has contributed 1 S **9** with parts of chs **10, 11, 13, 14, 16, 20** and considerable portions of chs **22, 23, 26–27, 29–31**, 2 S **1** (in part), **2–6, 9–20**. Some details have probably been derived from other sources, and additions made by the editor or editors. This general determination of sources rests upon a difference of standpoint and religious conception, and upon slighter varieties of style which are neither so pronounced nor so readily distinguished as in the books of the Pent. It is reasonable also to bear in mind that a close and exact division or line of demarcation in every detail is not to be expected.

V. Character and Date of Sources.—Attempts which have been made to determine the date of these two sources, or to identify them with one or other of the principal authorities from which the historical narratives of the Pent are derived, have not been convincing. In the judgment of some, however, the later of the two sources should be regarded as a continuation of the narrative or document known as E, and the earlier be assigned to J. The style of the latter has much in common with the style of J, and is clear, vigorous and poetical; the religious conceptions also that are embodied and taught are of a simple and early type. The later writing has been supposed to give indications of the influence of the prophetic teaching of the 8th cent. The indications, however, are not sufficiently decisive to enable a final judgment to be formed. If it is borne in mind that J and E represent rather schools of teaching and thought than individual writers, the characteristics of the two sources of the Books of S would not be out of harmony with the view that from these two schools respectively were derived the materials out of which the history was compiled. The "sources" would then, according to the usual view, belong to the 9th and 8th cents. before the Christian era; and to a period not more than a century or a century and a half later should be assigned the final compilation and completion of the book as it is contained in the Heb Canon of Scripture.

VI. Greek Versions.—For an exact estimate and understanding of the history and text of the Books of S account must further be taken of the Gr version or versions. In the LXX there is great divergence from the Heb Massoretic text, and it is probable that in the course of transmission the Gr has been exposed to corruption to a very considerable extent. At least two recensions of the Gr text are in existence, represented by the Vatican and Alexandrian MSS respectively, of which the latter is nearer to the Heb original, and has apparently been conformed to it at a later period with a view to removing discrepancies; and this process has naturally impaired its value as a witness to the primary shape of the Gr text itself. There are therefore three existing types of the text of S; the Massoretic Heb and B and A in the Greek. The original form of the LXX, if it could be recovered, would represent a text anterior to the Massoretic recension, differing from, but not necessarily superior to, the latter. For the restoration of the Gr text, the Old Lat, where it is available, affords valuable help. It is evident then that in any given instance the agreement of these three types or recensions of the text is the strongest possible witness to the originality and authenticity of a reading; but that the weight attaching to the testimony of A will not in general, on account of the history of its text, be equivalent to that of either of the other two.

VII. Ethical and Religious Teaching.—The religious teaching and thought of the two Books of S it is not difficult to summarize. The books are in form a historical record of events; but they are at the same time and more particularly a history conceived with a definite purpose, and made to subserve a definite moral and religious aim. It is not a narrative of events solely, or the preservation of historical detail, that the writer has in view, but rather to elucidate and enforce from Israel's experience the significance of the Divine and moral government of the nation. The duty of king and people alike is to obey Jeh, to render strict and willing deference to His commands, and on this path of obedience alone will national independence and prosperity be secured. With the strongest emphasis, and with uncompromising severity, sin even in the highest places is condemned; and an ideal of righteousness is set forth in language and with an earnestness which recalls the exhortations of Dt. Thus the same is true of the Books of S as is manifest in the preceding books of the canonical OT: they are composed with a didactic aim. The experience of the past is made to afford lessons of warning and encouragement for the present. To the writer or writers—the history of the development and upbuilding of the Israelite kingdom is pregnant with a deeper meaning than lies on the surface, and this meaning he endeavors to make plain to his readers through the record. The issues of the events and the events themselves are under the guidance and control of Jeh, who always condemns and punishes wrong, but approves and rewards righteousness. Thus the narrative is history utilized to convey moral truth. And its value is to be estimated, not primarily as recording the great deeds of the past, but as conveying ethical teaching; that by means of the history with all its glamor and interest the people may be recalled to a sense of their high duty toward God, and be warned of the inevitable consequences of disobedience to Him.

LITERATURE.—Upon all points of introduction, criticism and interpretation, the comms. afford abundant and satisfactory guidance. The principal Eng. comms. are by H. P. Smith in *ICC*, Edinburgh, 1899, and S. R. Driver, *Notes on the Heb Text of the Books of S*, 2d ed, Oxford, 1913; A. R. S. Kennedy, "Samuel," *New Century Bible*, New York, Frowde, 1905; in German by R. Budde, 1902, W. Nowack, 1902, A. Klostermann, 1887. See also the arts. "Samuel" in *HDB*, *EB* and *Jew Enc*.

A. S. GEDEN

SANAAS, san'ā-as (A and Fritzsche, **Σανάας**, *Sanáas*, B, **Σαμά**, *Samá;* AV **Annaas**): The sons of Sanaas returned in large numbers with Zerubbabel (1 Esd **5** 23) = "Senaah" in Ezr **2** 35; Neh **7** 38. The numbers vary in each case (Esd, 3,330 or 3,301; Ezr, 3,630; Neh, 3,930).

SANABASSAR, san-a-bas'ar (in 1 Esd **2** 12.15), **SANABASSARUS**, san-a-bas'a-rus (in **6** 18.10; a name appearing in many variations, A always reading **Σαναβάσσαρος**, *Sanabássaros*, B, **Σαναμασσάρῳ**, *Sanamassárō*, in **2** 12[11] [RVm *Samanassar*], **Σαμανασσάρου**, *Samanassárou*, in **2** 15[14], but **Σαβανασσάρῳ**, *Sabanassárō*, in **6** 18[17] [RVm] and **Σαναβάσσαρος**, *Sanabássaros*, in **6** 20 [19]): He was "governor of Judaea" under Cyrus, conveyed the holy vessels of the temple from Babylon to Jerus and "laid the foundations of the house of the Lord" for the first time since its destruction (1 Esd **2** 12. 15; **6** 18–20) = "SHESHBAZZAR [q.v.] the prince of Judah" (Ezr **1** 8).

Some identify him with Zerubbabel as AVm in 1 Esd **6** 18: "Z., which is also S. the ruler." This view appears to be favored by the order of the words here, where, in case of two persons, one might expect "S. the ruler" to come first. Zerubbabel appears as "governor of Judaea" also in 1 Esd **6** 27–29. Ezr **3** 10 speaks of the foundation of the temple under Zerubbabel and **5** 16 as under Sheshbazzar. There is further the analogy of 1 Esd **5** 40, where Nehemias and Attharias refer to the same person. Against this identification: Zerubbabel is not styled ruler or governor either in Neh or Ezr, but in Hag **1** 14; **2** 2.21 he is *peḥāh* or governor of Judah; no explanation is given of the double name, as in the case of e.g. Daniel, Belteshazzar; the language of Ezr **5** 14 f seems to refer to work commenced under a different person than Zerubbabel. Nor is there any reason against supposing a first return under Sheshbazzar (Sanabassar) and a foundation of the temple previous to the time of Zerubbabel—an undertaking into which the Jews did not enter heartily, perhaps because Sanabassar may have been a foreigner (though it is uncertain whether he was a Babylonian, a Persian, or a Jew). A later proposal is to identify Sanabassar with Shenazzar, the uncle of Zerubbabel in 1 Ch **3** 18. But either of these identifications must remain doubtful. See SHENAZZAR; ZERUBBABEL.

S. ANGUS

SANASIB, san'a-sib (Fritzsche, **Σανασίβ**, *Sanasíb*, but B and Swete, **Σαναβείς**, *Sanabeís*, A, **'Ανασείβ**, *Anaseíb*): Found only in 1 Esd **5** 24, where the sons of Jeddu, the son of Jesus, are a priestly family returning "among the sons of Sanasib." The name is not found in the ‖ Ezr **2** 36; Neh **7** 39, and is perhaps preserved in the Vulg "Eliasib."

SANBALLAT, san-bal'at (סַנְבַלַּט, *ṣanᵉbhallaṭ;* Gr and Vulg *Sanaballát*, Pesh *Samballat*): Sanballat the Horonite was, if the appellation which follows his name indicates his origin, a Moabite of Horonaim, a city of Moab mentioned in Isa **15** 5; Jer **48** 2.5.34; Jos, *Ant*, XIII, xxiii; XIV, ii. He is named along with Tobiah, the Ammonite slave (Neh **4** 1), and Geshem the Arabian (Neh **6** 1) as the leading opponent of the Jews at the time when Nehemiah undertook to rebuild the walls of Jerus (Neh **2** 10; **4** 1; **6** 1). He was related by marriage to the son of Eliashib, the high priest at the time of the annulment of the mixed marriages forbidden by the Law (Neh **13** 28).

Renewed interest has been awakened in Sanballat from the fact that he is mentioned in the papyri I and II of Sachau (*Die aramäischen Papyrusurkunden aus Elephantine*, Berlin, 1908, and in his later work, *Aramäische Papyrus und Ostraka*, Leipzig, 1911; cf Staerk's convenient ed in *Lietzmanns Kleine Texte*, No. 32, 1908) as having been the governor (*paḥath*) of Samaria some time before the 17th year of Darius (Nothus), i.e. 408–407 BC, when Bagohi was governor of Judah. His two sons, Delaiah and Shelemiah, received a letter from Jedoniah and his companions the priests who were in Yeb (Elephantine) in Upper Egypt. This letter contained information concerning the state of affairs in the Jewish colony of Yeb, esp. concerning the destruction of the temple or synagogue (*agora*) which had been erected at that place.

The address of this letter reads as follows: "To our lord Bagohi, the governor of Judaea, his servants Jedoniah and his companions, the priests in the fortress of Yeb [Elephantine]. May the God of Heaven inquire much at every time after the peace of our lord and put thee in favor before Darius the king," etc. The conclusion of the letter reads thus: "Now, thy servants, Jedoniah and his companions and the Jews, all citizens of Yeb, say thus: If it seems good to our lord, mayest thou think on the rebuilding of that temple [the *agora* which had been destroyed by the Egyptians]. Since it has not been permitted us to rebuild it, do thou look on the receivers of thy benefactions and favors here in Egypt. Let a letter with regard to the rebuilding of the temple of the God Jaho in the fortress of Yeb, as it was formerly built, be sent from thee. In thy name will they offer the meal offerings, the incense, and the burnt offerings upon the altar of the God Jaho; and we shall always pray for thee, we and our wives and our children and all the Jews found here, until the temple has been rebuilt. And it will be to thee a meritorious work [*çᵉdhāḳāh*] in the sight of Jaho, the God of Heaven, greater than the meritorious work of a man who offers to him a burnt offering and a sacrifice of a value equal to the value of 1,000 talents of silver. And as to the gold [probably that which was sent by the Jews to Bagohi as a baksheesh] we have sent word and given knowledge. Also, we have in our name communicated in a letter all [these] matters unto Delaiah and Shelemiah, the sons of Sanballat, governor of Samaria. Also, from all that has been done to us, Arsham [the satrap of Egypt] has learned nothing.

The 20th of Marcheshvan in the 17th year of Darius the king."

Sanballat is the Bab Sin-uballit, "may Sin give him life," a name occurring a number of times in the contract tablets from the time of Nebuchadnezzar, Nabonidus, and Darius Hystaspis. (See Tallquist, *Neubabylonisches Namenbuch*, 183.)

R. DICK WILSON

SANCTIFICATION, saṇk-ti-fi-kā'shun:

Etymology
I. THE FORMAL SENSE
 1. In the OT
 2. In the NT
II. THE ETHICAL SENSE
 1. Transformation of Formal to Ethical Idea
 2. Our Relation to God as Personal: NT Idea
 3. Sanctification as God's Gift
 4. Questions of Time and Method
 5. An Element in All Christian Life
 6. Follows from Fellowship with God
 7. Is It Instantaneous and Entire?
 8. Sanctification as Man's Task
LITERATURE

Etymology

The root is found in the OT in the Heb vb. קָדַשׁ, *ḳādhash*, in the NT in the Gr vb. ἁγιάζω, *hagiázō*. The noun "sanctification" (ἁγιασμός, *hagiasmós*) does not occur in the OT and is found but 10 t in the NT, but the roots noted above appear in a group of important words which are of very frequent occurrence. These words are "holy," "hallow," "hallowed," "holiness," "consecrate," "saint," "sanctify," "sanctification." It must be borne in mind that these words are all tr[s] of the same root, and that therefore no one of them can be treated adequately without reference to the others. All have undergone a certain development. Broadly stated, this has been from the formal, or ritual, to the ethical, and these different meanings must be carefully distinguished.

I. The Formal Sense.—By sanctification is ordinarily meant that hallowing of the Christian believer by which he is freed from sin and enabled to realize the will of God in his life. This is not, however, the first or common meaning in the Scriptures. To sanctify means commonly to make holy, that is, to separate from the world and consecrate to God.

To understand this primary meaning we must go back to the word "holy" in the OT. That is holy which belongs to Jeh. There is nothing implied here as to moral character. It may refer to days and seasons, to places, to objects used for worship, or to persons. Exactly the same usage is shown with the word "sanctify." To sanctify anything is to declare it as belonging to God. "Sanctify unto me all the first-born .... it is mine" (Ex **13** 2; cf Nu **3** 13; **8** 17). It applies thus to all that is connected with worship, to the Levites (Nu **3** 12), the priests and the tent of meeting (Ex **29** 44), the altar and all that touches it (Ex **29** 36 f), and the offering (Ex **29** 27; cf 2 Macc **2** 18; Ecclus **7** 31). The feast and holy days are to be sanctified, that is, set apart from ordinary business as belonging to Jeh (the Sabbath, Neh **13** 19–22; a fast, Joel **1** 14). So the nation as a whole is sanctified when Jeh acknowledges it and receives it as His own, "a kingdom of priests, and a holy nation" (Ex **19** 5.6). A man may thus sanctify his house or his field (Lev **27** 14.16), but not the firstling of the flock, for this is already Jeh's (Lev **27** 26).

1. In the OT

It is this formal usage without moral implication that explains such a passage as Gen **38** 21. The word tr[d] "prostitute" here is from the same √ *ḳādhash*, meaning lit., as elsewhere, the sanctified or consecrated one (*ḳ[e]dhēshāh*; see margin and cf Dt **23** 18; 1 K **14** 24; Hos **4** 14). It is the hierodule, the familiar figure of the old pagan temple, the sacred slave consecrated to the temple and the deity for immoral purposes. The practice is protested against in Israel (Dt **23** 17 f), but the use of the term illustrates clearly the absence of anything essentially ethical in its primary meaning (cf also 2 K **10** 20, "And Jehu said, Sanctify a solemn assembly for Baal. And they proclaimed it"; cf Joel **1** 14).

Very suggestive is the transitive use of the word in the phrase, "to sanctify Jeh." To understand this we must note the use of the word "holy" as applied to Jeh in the OT. Its meaning is not primarily ethical. Jeh's holiness is His supremacy, His sovereignty, His glory, His essential being as God. To say the Holy One is simply to say God. Jeh's holiness is seen in His might, His manifested glory; it is that before which peoples tremble, which makes the nations dread (Ex **15** 11–18; cf 1 S **6** 20; Ps **68** 35; **89** 7; **99** 2.3). Significant is the way in which "jealous" and "holy" are almost identified (Josh **24** 19; Ezk **38** 23). It is God asserting His supremacy, His unique claim. To sanctify Jeh, therefore, to make Him holy, is to assert or acknowledge or bring forth His being as God, His supreme power and glory, His sovereign claim. Ezekiel brings this out most clearly. Jeh has been profaned in the eyes of the nations through Israel's defeat and captivity. True, it was because of Israel's sins, but the nations thought it was because of Jeh's weakness. The ethical is not wanting in these passages. The people are to be separated from their sins and given a new heart (Ezk **36** 25. 26.33). But the word "sanctify" is not used for this. It is applied to Jeh, and it means the assertion of Jeh's power in Israel's triumph and the conquest of her foes (**20** 41; **28** 25; **36** 23; **38** 16; **39** 27). The sanctification of Jeh is thus the assertion of His being and power as God, just as the sanctification of a person or object is the assertion of Jeh's right and claim in the same.

The story of the waters of Meribah illustrates the same meaning. Moses' failure to sanctify Jeh is his failure to declare Jeh's glory and power in the miracle of the waters (Nu **20** 12.13; **27** 14; Dt **32** 51). The story of Nadab and Abihu points the same way. Here "I will be sanctified" is the same as "I will be glorified" (Lev **10** 1–3). Not essentially different is the usage in Isa **5** 16: "Jeh of hosts is exalted in justice, and God the Holy One is sanctified in righteousness." Holiness again is the exaltedness of God, His supremacy, which is seen here in the judgment (justice, righteousness) meted out to the disobedient people (cf the recurrent refrain of **5** 25; **9** 12.17.21; **10** 4; see JUSTICE; JUSTICE OF GOD). Isa **8** 13; **29** 23 suggest the same idea by the way in which they relate "sanctify" to fear and awe. One NT passage brings us the same meaning (1 Pet **3** 15): "Sanctify in your hearts Christ as Lord," that is, exalt Him as supreme.

In a few NT passages the OT ritual sense reappears, as when Jesus speaks of the temple sanctifying the gold, and the altar the gift (Mt **23** 17.19; cf also He **9** 13; 1 Tim **4** 5). The prevailing meaning is that which we found in the OT. To sanctify is to consecrate or set apart. We may first take the few passages in the Fourth Gospel. As applied to Jesus in **10** 36; **17** 19, sanctify cannot mean to make holy in the ethical sense. As the whole context shows, it means to consecrate for His mission in the world. The reference to the disciples, "that they themselves also may be sanctified in truth," has both meanings: that they may be set apart (for Jesus sends them, as the Father sends Him), and that they may be made holy in truth.

2. In the NT

This same meaning of consecration, or separation, appears when we study the word **saint,** which is the same as "sanctified one." Aside from its use in the Pss, the word is found mainly in the NT. Outside the Gospels, where the term "disciples" is used, it is the common word to designate the followers of Jesus, occurring some 56 t. By "saint" is not meant the morally perfect, but the one who belongs to Christ, just as the sanctified priest or offering belonged to Jeh. Thus Paul can salute the disciples at Corinth as saints and a little later rebuke them as carnal and babes, as those among whom are jealousy and strife, who walk after the manner of men (1 Cor **1** 2; **3** 1–3). In the same way the phrase "the sanctified" or "those that are sanctified" is used to designate the believers. By "the inheritance among all them that are sanctified" is meant the heritage of the Christian believer (Acts **20** 32; **26** 18; cf 1 Cor **1** 2; **6** 11; Eph **1** 18; Col **1** 12). This is the meaning in He, which speaks of the believer as being sanctified by the blood of Christ. In **10** 29 the writer speaks of one who has fallen away, who "hath counted the blood of the covenant wherewith he was sanctified an unholy thing." Evidently it is not the inner and personal holiness of this apostate that is referred to, esp. in view of the tense, but that he had been separated unto God by this sacrificial blood and had then counted the holy offering a common thing. The contrast is between sacred and common, not between moral perfection and sin (cf **10** 10; **13** 12). The formal meaning appears again in 1 Cor **7** 12–14, where the unbelieving husband is said to be sanctified by the wife, and vice versa. It is not moral character that is meant here, but a certain separation from the profane and unclean and a certain relation to God. This is made plain by the reference to the children: "Else were your children unclean; but now are they holy." The formal sense is less certain in other instances where we have the thought of sanctification in or by the Holy Spirit or in Christ; as in Rom **15** 16, "being sanctified by the Holy Spirit"; 1 Cor **1** 2, to "them that are sanctified in Christ Jesus"; 1 Pet **1** 2, "in sanctification of the Spirit." Paul's doctrine of the Spirit as the new life in us seems to enter in here, and yet the reference to 1 Cor suggests that the primary meaning is still that of setting apart, the relating to God.

II. The Ethical Sense.—We have been considering so far what has been called the formal meaning of the word; but the chief interest of Christian thought lies in the ethical idea, sanctification considered as the active deed or process by which the life is made holy.

Our first question is, How does the idea of belonging to God become the idea of transformation of life and character? The change is, indeed, nothing less than a part of the whole movement for which the entire Scriptures stand as a monument. The ethical is not wanting at the beginning, but the supremacy of the moral and spiritual over against the formal, the ritual, the ceremonial, the national, is the clear direction in which the movement as a whole tends. Now the pivot of this movement is the conception of God. As the thought of God grows more ethical, more spiritual, it molds and changes all other conceptions. Thus what it means to belong to God (holiness, sanctification) depends upon the nature of the God to whom man belongs. The hierodules of Corinth are women of shame because of the nature of the goddess to whose temple they belong. The prophets caught a vision of Jeh, not jealous for His prerogative, not craving the honor of punctilious and proper ceremonial, but with a gracious love for His people and a passion for righteousness. Their great message is: This now is Jeh; hear what it means to belong to such a God and to serve Him. "What unto me is the multitude of your sacrifices? . . . . Wash you, make you clean; . . . . seek justice, relieve the oppressed" (Isa **1** 11.16.17). "When Israel was a child, then I loved him. . . . . I desire goodness, and not sacrifice; and the knowledge of God more than burnt-offerings" (Hos **11** 1; **6** 6).

1. Transformation of Formal to Ethical Idea

In this way the formal idea that we have been considering becomes charged with moral meaning. To belong to God, to be His servant, His son, is no mere external matter. Jesus' teaching as to sonship is in point here. The word "sanctification" does not occur in the Synoptic Gospels at all, but "sonship" with the Jews expressed this same relation of belonging. For them it meant a certain obedience on the one hand, a privilege on the other. Jesus declares that belonging to God means likeness to Him, sonship is sharing His spirit of loving good will (Mt **5** 43–48). Brother and sister for Jesus are those who do God's will (Mk **3** 35). Paul takes up the same thought, but joins it definitely to the words "saint" and "sanctify." The religious means the ethical, those "that are sanctified" are "called to be saints" (1 Cor **1** 2). The significant latter phrase is the same as in Rom **1** 1, "Paul . . . . called to be an apostle." In this light we read Eph **4** 1, "Walk worthily of the calling wherewith ye were called." Cf 1 Thess **2** 12; Phil **1** 27. And the end of this calling is that we are "foreordained to be conformed to the image of his Son" (Rom **8** 29). We must not limit ourselves to the words "saint" or "sanctify" to get this teaching with Paul. It is his constant and compelling moral appeal: You belong to Christ; live with Him, live unto Him (Col **3** 1–4; 1 Thess **5** 10). It is no formal belonging, no external surrender. It is the yielding of the life in its passions and purposes, in its deepest affections and highest powers, to be ruled by a new spirit (Eph **4** 13.20.23.24.32; cf Rom **12** 1).

But we do not get the full meaning of this thought of sanctification as consecration, or belonging, until we grasp the NT thought of our relation to God as personal. The danger has always been that this consecration should be thought of in a negative or passive way. Now the Christian's surrender is not to an outer authority but to an inner, living fellowship. The sanctified life is thus a life of personal fellowship lived out with the Father in the spirit of Christ in loving trust and obedient service. This positive and vital meaning of sanctification dominates Paul's thought. He speaks of living unto God, of living to the Lord, and, most expressively of all, of being alive unto God (Rom **14** 8; cf **6** 13; Gal **2** 19). So completely is his life filled by this fellowship that he can say, "It is no longer I that live, but Christ liveth in me" (Gal **2** 20). But there is no quietism here. It is a very rich and active life, this life of fellowship to which we are surrendered. It is a life of sonship in trust and love, with the spirit that enables us to say, "Abba, Father" (Rom **8** 15; Gal **4** 6). It is a life of unconquerable kindness and good will (Mt **5** 43–48). It is a life of "faith working through love" (Gal **5** 6), it is having the mind of Christ (Phil **2** 5). The sanctified life, then, is the life so fully surrendered to fellowship with Christ day by day that inner spirit and outward expression are ruled by His spirit.

2. Relation to God Personal: NT Idea

We come now to that aspect which is central for Christian interest, sanctification as the making holy of life, not by our act, but by God's deed and by God's gift. If holiness represents the state of heart and life in conformity with God's will, then sanctification is the deed or process by which that state is wrought. And this deed we are to consider now as the work of God. Jesus prays that the Father may sanctify His disciples in truth (Jn **17** 17). So Paul prays for the Thessalonians (1 Thess **5** 23), and declares that Christ is to sanctify His church (cf Rom **6** 22; 2 Thess **2** 13; 2 Tim **2** 21; 1 Pet **1** 2). Here sanctification means to make clean or holy in the ethical sense, though the idea of consecration is not necessarily lacking. But aside from special passages, we must take into account the whole NT teaching, according to which every part of the Christian life is the gift of God and wrought by His Spirit. "It is God that worketh in you both to will and to work" (Phil **2** 13; cf Rom **8** 2–4.9.14.16–26; Gal **5** 22 f). Significant is the use of the words "creature" ("creation," see margin) and "workmanship" with Paul (2 Cor **5** 17; Gal **6** 15; Eph **2** 10; **4** 24). The new life is God's second work of creation.

3. Sanctification as God's Gift

When we ask, however, when and how this work is wrought, there is no such clear answer. What we have is on the one hand uncompromising ideal and demand, and on the other absolute confidence in God. By adding to these two the evident fact that the Christian believers seen in the NT are far from the attainment of such Christian perfection, some writers have assumed to have the foundation here for the doctrine that the state of complete holiness of life is a special experience in the Christian life wrought in a definite moment of time. It is well to realize that no NT passages give a specific answer to these questions of time and method, and that our conclusions must be drawn from the general teaching of the NT as to the Christian life.

4. Questions of Time and Method

First, it must be noted that in the NT view sanctification in the ethical sense is an essential element and inevitable result of all Christian life and experience. Looked at from the religious point of view, it follows from the doctrine of regeneration. Regeneration is the implanting of a new life in man. So far as that is a new life from God it is *ipso facto* holy. The doctrine of the Holy Spirit teaches the same (see HOLY SPIRIT).

5. An Element in All Christian Life

There is no Christian life from the very beginning that is not the work of the Spirit. "No man can [even] say, Jesus is Lord, but in the . . . . Spirit" (1 Cor **12** 3). But this Spirit is the Holy Spirit, whether with Paul we say Spirit of Christ or Spirit of God (Rom **8** 9). His presence, therefore, in so far forth means holiness of life. From the ethical standpoint the same thing is constantly declared. Jesus builds here upon the prophets: no religion without righteousness; clean hands, pure hearts, deeds of mercy are not mere conditions of worship, but joined to humble hearts are themselves the worship that God desires (Am **5** 21–25; Mic **6** 6–8). Jesus deepened the conception, but did not change it, and Paul was true to this succession. "If any man hath not the Spirit of Christ, he is none of his. And if Christ is in you, ... the spirit is life because of righteousness" (Rom **8** 9.10). There is nothing in Paul's teaching to suggest that sanctification is the special event of a unique experience, or that there are two kinds or qualities of sanctification. All Christian living meant for him clean, pure, right living, and that was sanctification. The simple, practical way in which he attacks the bane of sexual impurity in his pagan congregations shows this. "This is the will of God, even your sanctification, that ye abstain from fornication; that each one of you know how to possess himself of his own vessel in sanctification and honor. For God called us not for uncleanness, but in sanctification" (1 Thess **4** 3.4.7). The strength of Paul's teaching, indeed, lies here in this combination of moral earnestness with absolute dependence upon God.

The second general conclusion that we draw from the NT teaching as to the Christian life is this: the sanctification which is a part of all Christian living follows from the very nature of that life as fellowship with God. Fundamental here is the fact that the Christian life is personal, that nothing belongs in it which cannot be stated in personal terms.

6. Follows from Fellowship with God

It is a life with God in which He graciously gives Himself to us, and which we live out with Him and with our brothers in the spirit of Christ, which is His Spirit. The two great facts as to this fellowship are, that it is God's gift, and that its fruit is holiness. First, it is God's gift. What God gives us is nothing less than Himself. The gift is not primarily forgiveness, nor victory over sin, nor peace of soul, nor hope of heaven. It is fellowship with Him, which includes all of these and without which none of these can be. Secondly, the fruit of this fellowship is holiness. The real hallowing of our life can come in no other way. For Christian holiness is personal, not something formal or ritual, and its source and power can be nothing lower than the personal. Such is the fellowship into which God graciously lifts the believer. Whatever its mystical aspects, that fellowship is not magical or sacramental. It is ethical through and through. Its condition on our side is ethical. For Christian faith is the moral surrender of our life to Him in whom truth and right come to us with authority to command. The meaning of that surrender is ethical; it is opening the life to definite moral realities and powers, to love, meekness, gentleness, humility, reverence, purity, the passion for righteousness, to that which words cannot analyze but which we know as the Spirit of Christ. Such a fellowship is the supreme moral force for the molding of life. An intimate human fellowship is an analogue of this, and we know with what power it works on life and character. It cannot, however, set forth either the intimacy or the power of this supreme and final relation where our Friend is not another but is our real self. So much we know: this fellowship means a new spirit in us, a renewed and daily renewing life.

It is noteworthy that Paul has no hard-and-fast forms for this life. The reality was too rich and great, and his example should teach us caution in the insistence upon theological forms which may serve to compress the truth instead of expressing it. Here are some of his expressions for this life in us: to "have the mind of Christ" (1 Cor **2** 16; Phil **2** 5), "the Spirit of Christ" (Rom **8** 9), "Christ is in you" (Rom **8** 10), "the spirit which is from God" (1 Cor **2** 12), "the Spirit of God" (1 Cor **3** 16), "the Holy Spirit" (1 Cor **6** 19), "the Spirit of the Lord" (2 Cor **3** 17), "the Lord the Spirit" (2 Cor **3** 18). But in all this one fact stands out, this life is personal, a new spirit in us, and that spirit is one that we have in personal fellowship with God; it is His Spirit. Especially significant is the way in which Paul relates this new life to Christ. We have already noted that Paul uses indifferently "Spirit of God" and "Spirit of Christ," and that in the same passage (Rom **8** 9). Paul's great contribution to the doctrine of the Holy Spirit lies here. As he states it in 2 Cor **3** 17: "Now the Lord is the Spirit." With that the whole conception of the Spirit gains moral content and personal character. The Spirit is personal, not some thing, nor some strange and magical power. The Spirit is ethical; there is a definite moral quality which is expressed when we say Christ. He has the Spirit who has the qualities of Christ. Thus the presence of the Spirit is not evidenced in the unusual, the miraculous, the ecstatic utterance of the enthusiast, or some strange deed of power, but in the workaday qualities of kindness, goodness, love, loyalty, patience, self-restraint (Gal **5** 22 f). With this identification of the Spirit and the Christ in mind, we can better understand the passages in which Paul brings out the relation of Christ to the sanctification of the believer. He is the goal (Rom **8** 29). We are to grow up in Him (Eph **4** 15). He is to be formed in us (Gal **4** 19). We are to behold Him and be changed into His image (2 Cor **3** 17 f). This deepens into Paul's thought of the mystical relation with Christ. The Christian dies to sin with Him that he may live with Him a new life. Christ is now his real life. He dwells in Christ, Christ dwells in him. He has Christ's thoughts, His mind. See Rom **6** 3–11; **8** 9.10; 1 Cor **2** 16; **15** 22; Gal **2** 20.

This vital and positive conception of the sanctification of the believer must be asserted against some popular interpretations. The symbols of fire and water, as suggesting cleansing, have sometimes been made the basis for a whole superstructure of doctrine. (For the former, note Isa **6** 6 f; Lk **3** 16; Acts **2** 3; for the latter, Acts **2** 38; **22** 16; 1 Cor **6** 11; Eph **5** 26; Tit **3** 5; He **10** 22; Rev **1** 5; **7** 14.) There is a twofold danger here, from which these writers have not escaped. The symbols suggest cleansing, and their over-emphasis has meant first a negative and narrow idea of sanctification as primarily separation from sin or defilement. This is a falling back to certain OT levels. Secondly, these material symbols have been literalized, and the result has been a sort of mechanical or magical conception of the work of the Spirit. But the soul is not a substance for mechanical action, however sublimated. It is personal life that is to be hallowed, thought, affections, motives, desires, will, and only a personal agent through personal fellowship can work this end.

The clear recognition of the personal and vital character of sanctification will help us with another problem.

7. Is It Instantaneous and Entire?

If the holy life be God's requirement and at the same time His deed, why should not this sanctification be instantaneous and entire? And does not Paul imply this, not merely in his demands but in his prayer for the Thessalonians, that God may establish their hearts in holiness, that He may sanctify them wholly and preserve spirit and soul and body entire, without blame at the coming of Our Lord Jesus Christ (1 Thess **3** 13; **5** 23)?

In answer to this we must first discriminate between the ideal and the empirical with Paul. Like John (1 Jn **1** 6; **3** 9), Paul insists that the life of Christ and the life of sin cannot go on together, and he knows no qualified obedience, no graduated standard. He brings the highest Christian demand to the poorest of his pagan converts. Nor have we any finer proof of his faith than this uncompromising idealism. On the other hand, how could he ask less than this? God cannot require less than the highest, but it is another question how the ideal is to be achieved. In the realm of the ideal it is always either . . . . or. In the realm of life there is another category. The question is not simply, Is this man sinner or saint? It is rather, What is he becoming? This matter of becoming is the really vital issue. Is this man turned the right way with all his power? Is his life wholly open to the Divine fellowship? Not the degree of achievement, but the right attitude toward the ideal, is decisive. Paul does not stop to resolve paradoxes, but practically he reckons with this idea. Side by side with his prayer for the Thessalonians are his admonitions to growth and progress (1 Thess **3** 12; **5** 14). Neither the absolute demand or the promise of grace gives us the right to conclude how the consummation shall take place.

That conclusion we can reach only as we go back again to the fundamental principle of the personal character of the Christian life and the relation thus given between the ethical and the religious. All Christian life is gift and task alike. "Work out your own salvation . . . . for it is God who worketh in you" (Phil **2** 12 f). All is from God; we can only live what God gives. But there is a converse to this: only as we live it out can God give to us the life. This appears in Paul's teaching as to sanctification. It is not only God's gift, but our task. "This is the will of God, even your sanctification" (1 Thess **4** 3). "Having therefore these promises . . . . let us cleanse ourselves from all defilement of flesh and spirit, perfecting holiness [*hagiōsúnē*] in the fear of God" (2 Cor **7** 1). Significant is Paul's use of the word "walk." We are to "walk in newness of life," "by [or in] the Spirit," "in love," and "in Christ Jesus the Lord" (Rom **6** 4; Gal **5** 16; Eph **5** 2; Col **2** 6). The gift in each case becomes the task, and indeed becomes real and effective only in this activity. It is only as we walk by the Spirit that this becomes powerful in overcoming the lusts of the flesh (Gal **5** 16; cf **5** 25). But the ethical is the task that ends only with life. If God gives only as we live, then He cannot give all at once. Sanctification is then the matter of a life and not of a moment. The life may be consecrated in a moment, the right relation to God assumed and the man stand in saving fellowship with Him. The life is thus made holy in principle. But the real making holy is coextensive with the whole life of man. It is nothing less than the constant in-forming of the life of the inner spirit and outer deed with the Spirit of Christ until we, "speaking truth in love, may grow up in all things into him, who is the head" (Eph **4** 15). (Read also Rom **6**; that the Christian is dead to sin is not some fixed static fact, but is true only as he refuses the lower and yields his members to a higher obedience. Note that in 1 Cor **5** 7 Paul in the same verse declares "ye are unleavened," and then exhorts "Purge out the old leaven, that ye may be a new lump"; cf also 1 Thess **5** 5–10.)

8. Sanctification as Man's Task

We may sum up as follows: The word "sanctify" is used with two broad meanings: (1) The first is to devote, to consecrate to God, to recognize as holy, that is, as belonging to God. This is the regular OT usage and is most common in the NT. The prophets showed that this belonging to Jeh demanded righteousness. The NT deepens this into a whole-hearted surrender to the fellowship of God and to the rule of His Spirit. (2) Though the word itself appears in but few passages with this sense, the NT is full of the thought of the making holy of the Christian's life by the Spirit of God in that fellowship into which God lifts us by His grace and in which He gives Himself to us. This sanctifying, or hallowing, is not mechanical or magical. It is wrought out by God's Spirit in a daily fellowship to which man gives himself in aspiration and trust and obedience, receiving with open heart, living out in obedient life. It is not negative, the mere separation from sin, but the progressive hallowing of a life that grows constantly in capacity, as in character, into the stature of full manhood as it is in Christ. And from this its very nature it is not momentary, but the deed and the privilege of a whole life. See also HOLY SPIRIT and the following article.

LITERATURE.—The popular and special works are usually too undiscriminating and unhistorical to be of value for the Bib. study. An exception is Beet, *Holiness Symbolic and Real*. Full Bib. material in Cremer, *Bib. Theol. Lex.*, but treated from special points of view. See Systematic Theologies, OT Theologies (cf esp. Smend), and NT Theologies (cf esp. Holtzmann).

HARRIS FRANKLIN RALL

WESLEYAN DOCTRINE

1. Doctrine Stated
2. Objections Answered
3. Importance for the Preacher
4. Hymnology
5. Its Glorious Results
6. Wesley's Personal Testimony

1. Doctrine Stated

Christian perfection, through entire sanctification, by faith, here and now, was one of the doctrines by which John Wesley gave great offence to his clerical brethren in the Anglican church. From the beginning of his work in 1739, till 1760, he was formulating this doctrine. At the last date there suddenly arose a large number of witnesses among his followers. Many of these he questioned with Baconian skill, the result being a confirmation of his theories on various points.

In public address he used the terms "Christian Perfection," "Perfect Love," and "Holiness," as synonymous, though there are differences between them when examined critically. With St. Paul he taught that all regenerate persons are saints, i.e. holy ones, as the word "saint," from Lat *sanctus*, through the Norman-Fr., signifies (1 Cor **1** 2; 2 Cor **1** 1). His theory is that in the normal Christian the principle of holiness, beginning with the new birth, gradually expands and strengthens as the believer grows in grace and in the knowledge of the truth, till, by a final, all-surrendering act of faith in Christ, it reaches an instantaneous completion through the act of the Holy Spirit, the sanctifier: 2 Cor **7** 1, "perfecting holiness," etc; Eph **4** 13, AV "Till we all come . . . . unto a perfect man," etc. Thus sanctification is gradual, but entire sanctification is instantaneous (Rom **6** 6, "our old man was crucified," etc, a sudden death; Gal **2** 20, "I have been crucified with Christ; and it is no longer I that live"). In 1 Thess **5** 23, the word "sanctify" is a Gr aorist tense, signifying an act and not a process, as also in Jn **17** 19, "that they . . . . may be sanctified in truth," or truly. (See Meyer's note.) Many Christians experience this change on their deathbeds. If death suddenly ends the life of a growing Christian before he is wholly sanctified, the Holy Spirit perfects the work. Wesley's advice to the preachers of this evangelical perfection was to draw and not to drive, and never to quote any threatenings of God's word against God's children. The declaration, "Without sanctification no man shall see the Lord" (He **12** 14), does not apply to the saints, "the holy ones."

Wesley's perfection of love is not perfection of degree, but of kind. Pure love is perfect love. The gradual growth toward perfect purity of love is beautifully expressed in Monod's hymn,

"O the bitter shame and sorrow!"
The first response to the Saviour's call is,
"All of self, and none of Thee."
But after a view of Christ on the cross, the answer is faintly,
"Some of self, and some of Thee."
Then, after a period of growing love, the cry is,
"Less of self, and more of Thee."
After another period, the final cry is,
"None of self, and all of Thee!"
an aspiration for pure love, without any selfishness.

The attainment of this grace is certified by the total cessation of all servile fear (1 Jn **4** 18). Wesley added to this the witness of the Spirit, for which his only proof-text is 1 Cor **2** 12.

2. Objections Answered

(1) Paul, in Phil **3** 12, declares that he is not "made perfect": (*a*) in ver 15, he declares that he *is* perfect; (*b*) "made perfect" is a term, borrowed from the ancient games, signifying a finished course. This is one of the meanings of *teleióō*, as seen also in Lk **13** 32 m, "The third day I end my course." Paul no more disclaims spiritual perfection in these words than does Christ before "the third day." Paul claims in ver 15, by the use of an adj., that he is perfect. In ver 12 Paul claims that he is not perfect as a victor, because the race is not ended. In ver 15 he claims that he is perfect as a racer.

(2) Paul says (1 Cor **15** 31), "I die daily." This does not refer to death to sin, as some say that it does, but to his daily danger of being killed for preaching Christ, as in Rom **8** 36, "we are killed all the day long."

(3) 1 Jn **1** 8: "If we say that we have no sin," etc. (*a*) If this includes Christians, it contradicts John himself in the very next verse, and in **3** 9, "Whosoever is begotten of God doeth no sin," and Jn **8** 36, "If . . . . the Son shall make you free," etc, and in all those texts in the NT declaring sins forgiven.

(*b*) Bishop Westcott says that the expression, "to have sin," is distinguished from "to sin," as the sinful principle is distinguished from the sinful act in itself. It includes the idea of personal guilt. Westcott asserts that John refers to the Gnostics, who taught that moral evil exists only in matter, and never touches spirit, which is always holy; and, therefore, though guilty of all manner of vice, their spirits had no need of atonement, because they were untouched by sin, which existed only in their bodies, as it does in all matter. When told that this made the body of Christ sinful, they denied the reality of His body, saying that it was only a phantom. Hence, in the very first verse of this Ep., John writes evidently against the gnostic error, quoting three of the five senses to prove the reality of Christ's humanity. (By all means, see "The Epp. of St. John," *Cambridge Bible for Schools*, etc, 17–21.)

3. Required for the Highest Success of the Preacher

The relation of this doctrine to the Methodist Episcopal church in the United States is seen in the following questions, which have been affirmatively answered in public by all its preachers on their admission to the Conferences: "Are you going on to perfection?"; "Do you expect to be made perfect in love in this life?"; "Are you earnestly striving after it?"

4. Hymnology

The hymns of the Wesleys, still universally sung, are filled with this doctrine, in which occur such expressions as:

"Take away our bent to sinning," . . . .
"Let us find that second rest," . . . .
"Make and keep me pure within," . . . .
"'Tis done! Thou dost this moment save,
With full salvation bless." . . . .

5. Its Glorious Results

To the preaching of Christian perfection Wesley ascribed the success of his work in the conversion, religious training and intellectual education of the masses of Great Britain. It furnished him a multitude of consecrated workers, many of them lay preachers, who labored in nearly every hamlet, and who carried the gospel into all the British colonies, including America. It is declared by secular historians that this great evangelical movement, in which the doctrine of entire sanctification was so prominent, saved England from a disastrous revolution, like that which drenched France with the blood of its royal family and its nobility, in the last decade of the 18th cent. It is certain that the great Christian and humanitarian work of William Booth, originally a Methodist, was inspired by this doctrine which he constantly preached. This enabled his followers in the early years of the Salvation Army to endure the persecutions which befell them at that time.

6. Personal Testimony

On March 6, 1760, Wesley enters in his Journal the following testimony of one Elizabeth Longmore: "'I felt my soul was all love. I was so stayed on God as I never felt before, and knew that I loved Him with all my heart. . . . . And the witness that God had saved me from all my sins grew clearer every hour. . . . . I have never since found my heart wander from God.' Now this is what I always did, and do now, mean by perfection. And this I believe many have attained, on the same evidence that I believe many are justified."

We have Wesley's only recorded testimony to his own justification in these words (May 24, 1738): "I felt my heart strangely warmed . . . . and an assurance was given me that He had taken away my sins," etc.

DANIEL STEELE

SANCTITY, saṇk'ti-ti, **LEGISLATION,** lej-is-lā'shun, **OF.** See ASTRONOMY, I, 5, (6).

SANCTUARY, saṇk'ṭū-ȧ-ri, saṇk'ṭū-a-ri (מִקְדָּשׁ, *miḳdāsh*, מִקְּדָשׁ, *miḳḳ^edhāsh*, קֹדֶשׁ, *ḳōdhesh*, "holy place"; **ἅγιον,** *hágion*):

1. Nature of Article
2. The Graf-Wellhausen Hypothesis
   The Three Stages
3. Difficulties of the Theory
   (1) Slaughter Not Necessarily Sacrificial
   (2) Sacrifice and Theophany
   (3) Alleged Plurality of Sanctuaries
   (4) The Altar of God's House
   (5) Local Altars in Deuteronomy
4. The Alternative View
   (1) Lay Sacrifice
   (2) Three Pilgrimage Festivals
5. The Elephantine Papyri
   The Elephantine Temple

LITERATURE

1. Nature of the Article

The present art. is designed to supplement the arts. on ALTARS; HIGH PLACE; PENTATEUCH; TABERNACLE; TEMPLE, by giving an outline of certain rival views of the course of law and history as regards the place of worship. The subject has a special importance because it was made the turning-point of Wellhausen's discussion of the development of Israel's literature, history and religion. He himself writes: "I differ from Graf chiefly in this, that I always go back to the centralization of the cultus, and deduce from it the particular divergences. My whole position is contained in my first chapter" (*Prolegomena*, 368). For the purposes of this discussion it is necessary to use the symbols JE, D, H, and P, which are explained in the art. PENTATEUCH.

It is said that there are three distinct stages of law and history.

(1) *In the first stage* all slaughter of domestic animals for food purposes was sacrificial, and every layman could sacrifice locally at an altar of earth or unhewn stones. The law of JE is contained in Ex

20 24-26, providing for the making of an altar of earth or stones, and emphasis is laid on the words "in every place ["in all the place" is grammatically an equally possible rendering] where I record my name I will come unto thee and I will bless thee." This, it is claimed, permits a plurality of sanctuaries. Illustrations are provided by the history. The patriarchs move about the country freely and build altars at various places. Later sacrifices or altars are mentioned in connection with Jethro (Ex **18** 12), Moses (**17** 15, etc), Joshua (Josh **8** 30), Gideon (Jgs **6** 26 etc), Manoah (**13** 19), Samuel (1 S **7** 17, etc), Elijah (1 K **18** 32), to take but a few instances. Perhaps the most instructive case is that of Saul after the battle of Michmash. Observing that the people were eating meat with blood, he caused a large stone to be rolled to him, and we are expressly told that this was the first altar that he built to the Lord (1 S **14** 35). While some of these examples might be accounted for by theophanies or other special circumstances, they are too numerous when taken together for such an explanation to suffice. In many instances they represent the conduct of the most authoritative and religious leaders of the age, e.g. Samuel, and it must be presumed that such men knew and acted upon the Law of their own day. Hence the history and the Law of Ex **20** are in unison in permitting a multiplicity of sanctuaries. Wellhausen adds: "Altars as a rule are not built by the patriarchs according to their own private judgment wheresoever they please; on the contrary, a theophany calls attention to, or, at least afterward, confirms, the holiness of the place" (op. cit., 31).

2. The Graf-Wellhausen Hypothesis

(2) *The second stage* is presented by Dt in the Law and Josiah's reformation in the history. Undoubtedly Dt **12** permits local non-sacrificial slaughter for the purposes of food, and enjoins the destruction of heathen places of worship, insisting with great vehemence on the central sanctuary. The narrative of Josiah's reformation in 2 K **23** tallies with these principles.

(3) *The third great body of law* (P) does not deal with the question (save in one passage, Lev **17**). In Dt "the unity of the cultus is *commanded;* in the PC it is *presupposed*. . . . . What follows from this forms the question before us. To my thinking, this: that the PC rests upon the result which is only the aim of Dt" (*Prolegomena*, 35). Accordingly, it is later than the latter book and dates from about the time of Ezra. As to Lev **17** 1-9, this belongs to H, an older collection of laws than P, and is taken up in the latter. Its intention was "to secure the exclusive legitimation of the one lawful place of sacrifice. . . . . Plainly the common man did not quite understand the newly drawn and previously quite unknown distinction between the religious and the profane act" (*Prolegomena*, 50). Accordingly, this legislator strove to meet the difficulty by the new enactment. See Criticism (**The Graf-Wellhausen Hypothesis**).

3. Difficulties of the Theory

(1) *Slaughter not necessarily sacrificial.*—The general substratum afforded by the documentary theory falls within the scope of the art. Pentateuch. The present discussion is limited to the legal and historical outline traced above. The view that all slaughter of domestic animals was sacrificial till the time of Josiah is rebutted by the evidence of the early books. The following examples should be noted: in Gen **18** 7 a calf is slain without any trace of a sacrifice, and in **27** 9-14 (Jacob's substitute for venison) no altar or religious rite can fairly be postulated. In 1 S **28** 24 the slaughter is performed by a *woman,* so that here again sacrifice is out of the question. If Gideon performed a sacrifice when he "made ready a kid" (Jgs **6** 19) or when he killed an animal for the broth of which the narrative speaks, the animals in question must have been sacrificed twice over, once when they were killed and again when the food was consumed by flames. Special importance attaches to Ex **22** 1 (Heb **21** 37), for there the JE legislation itself speaks of slaughter by cattle thieves as a natural and probable occurrence, and it can surely not have regarded this as a sacrificial act. Other instances are to be found in Gen **43** 16; 1 S **25** 11; 1 K **19** 21. In 1 S **8** 13 the word tr[d] "cooks" means lit. "women slaughterers." All these instances are prior to the date assigned to Dt. With respect to Lev **17** 1-7 also, the theory is unworkable. At any time in King Josiah's reign or after, it would have been utterly impossible to limit all slaughter of animals for the whole race wherever resident to one single spot. This part of the theory therefore breaks down.

(2) *Sacrifice and theophany.*—The view that the altars were erected at places that were peculiarly holy, or at any rate were subsequently sanctified by a theophany, is also untenable. In the Patriarchal age we may refer to Gen **4** 26, where the calling on God implies sacrifice but not theophanies, Abram at Beth-el (**12** 8) and Mamre (**13** 18), and Jacob's sacrifices (**31** 54; **33** 20). Compare later Samuel's altar at Ramah, Adonijah's sacrifice at En-rogel (1 K **1**), Naaman's earth (2 K **5**), David's clan's sacrifice (1 S **20** 6.29). It is impossible to postulate theophanies for the sacrifices of every clan in the country, and it becomes necessary to translate Ex **20** 24 "in *all* the place" (see *supra* 2, [1]) and to understand "the place" as the territory of Israel.

(3) *Alleged plurality of sanctuaries.*—The hypothesis of a multiplicity of sanctuaries in JE and the history also leaves out of view many most important facts. The truth is that the word "sanctuary" is ambiguous and misleading. A plurality of altars of earth or stone is not a plurality of sanctuaries. The early legislation knows a "house of Jeh" in addition to the primitive altars (Ex **23** 19; **34** 26; cf the parts of Josh **9** 23.27 assigned to J). No eyewitness could mistake a house for an altar, or vice versa.

(4) *The altar of God's house.*—Moreover a curious little bit of evidence shows that the "house" had quite a different kind of altar. In 1 K **1** 50 f; **2** 28 ff, we hear of the *horns* of the altar (cf Am **3** 14). Neither earth nor *unhewn* stones (as required by the Law of Ex **20**) could provide such horns, and the historical instances of the altars of the patriarchs, religious leaders, etc, to which reference has been made, show that they had no horns. Accordingly we are thrown back on the description of the great altar of burnt offering in Ex **27** and must assume that an altar of this type was to be found before the ark before Solomon built his Temple. Thus the altar of the House of God was quite different from the customary lay altar, and when we read of "mine altar" as a refuge in Ex **21** 14, we must refer it to the former, as is shown by the passages just cited. In addition to the early legislation and the historical passages cited as recognizing a House of God with a horned altar, we see such a house in Shiloh where Eli and his sons of the house of Aaron (1 S **2** 27) ministered. Thus the data of both JE and the history show us a House of God with a horned altar side by side with the multiplicity of stone or earthen altars, but give us no hint of a plurality of legitimate houses or shrines or sanctuaries.

(5) *Local altars in Deuteronomy.*—Dt also recognizes a number of local altars in **16** 21 (see *ICC*, ad

loc.) and so does D_2 in Josh **8** 30 ff. There is no place for any of these passages in the Wellhausen theory; but again we find one house side by side with many lay altars.

(1) *Lay sacrifice.*—The alternative view seeks to account for the whole of the facts noted above. In bald outline it is as follows: In pre-Mosaic times customary sacrifices had been freely offered by laymen at altars of earth or stone which were not "sanctuaries," but places that could be used for the nonce and then abandoned. Slaughter, as shown by the instances cited, was not necessarily sacrificial. Moses did not forbid or discourage the custom he found. On the contrary, he regulated it in Ex **20** 24–26; Dt **16** 21 f to prevent possible abuses. But he also superimposed two other kinds of sacrifice—certain new offerings to be brought by individuals to the religious capital and the national offerings of Nu **28, 29** and other passages. If P assumes the religious capital as axiomatic, the reason is that this portion of the Law consists of teaching intrusted to the priests, embracing the procedure to be followed in these two classes of offerings, and does not refer at all to the procedure at customary lay sacrifices, which was regulated by immemorial custom. Dt thunders not against the lay altars—which are never even mentioned in this connection—but against the Canaanitish high places. Dt **12** contemplates only the new individual offerings. The permission of lay slaughter for food was due to the fact that the infidelity of the Israelites in the wilderness (Lev **17** 5–7) had led to the universal prohibition of lay slaughter for the period of the wanderings only, though it appears to be continued by Dt for those who lived near the House of God (see **12** 21, limited to the case "if the place . . . . be too far from thee").

4. The Alternative View

(2) *Three pilgrimage festivals in JE.*—The JE legislation itself recognizes the three pilgrimage festivals of the House of God (Ex **34** 22 f). One of these festivals is called "the feast of weeks, even of the *bikkūrīm* [a kind of first-fruits] of wheat harvest," and as **23** 19 and **34** 26 require these *bikkūrīm* to be brought to the House of God and not to a lay altar, it follows that the pilgrimages are as firmly established here as in Dt. Thus we find a House (with a horned altar) served by priests and lay altars of earth or stone side by side in law and history till the exile swept them all away, and by breaking the continuity of tradition and practice paved the way for a new and artificial interpretation of the Law that was far removed from the intent of the lawgiver.

The Elephantine temple.—Papyri have recently been found at Elephantine which show us a Jewish community in Egypt which in 405 BC possessed a local temple. On the Wellhausen hypothesis it is usual to assume that P and Dt were still unknown and not recognized as authoritative in this community at that date, although the Deuteronomic law of the central sanctuary goes back at least to 621. It is difficult to understand how a law that had been recognized as Divine by Jeremiah and others could still have been unknown or destitute of authority. On the alternative view this phenomenon will have been the result of an interpretation of the Law to suit the needs of an age some 800 years subsequent to the death of Moses in circumstances he never contemplated. The Pent apparently permits sacrifice only in the land of Israel: in the altered circumstances the choice lay between interpreting the Law in this way or abandoning public worship altogether; for the synagogue with its non-sacrificial form of public worship had not yet been invented. All old legislations have to be construed in this way to meet changing circumstances, and this example contains nothing exceptional or surprising.

5. The Elephantine Papyri

LITERATURE.—J. Wellhausen, *Prolegomena to the History of Israel*, ch i, for the critical hypothesis; H. M. Wiener, *EPC*, ch vi, *PS passim* for the alternative view; *POT*, 173 ff.

HAROLD M. WIENER

SAND (חוֹל, *ḥōl;* ἄμμος, *ámmos;* a variant of the more usual ψάμμος, *psámmos;* cf ἄμαθος, *ámathos,* ψάμαθος, *psámathos*):

Sand is principally produced by the grinding action of waves. This is accompanied by chemical solution, with the result that the more soluble constituents of the rock diminish in amount or disappear and the sands tend to become more or less purely silicious, silica or quartz being a common constituent of rocks and very insoluble. The rocks of Pal are so largely composed of limestone that the shore and dune sands are unusually calcareous, containing from 10 to 20 per cent of calcium carbonate. This is subject to solution and redeposition as a cement between the sand grains, binding them together to form the porous sandstone of the seashore, which is easily worked and is much used in building. See ROCK, III, (2).

Figurative: (1) Used most often as a symbol of countless multitude; esp. of the children of Israel (Gen **22** 17; **32** 12; 2 S **17** 11; 1 K **4** 20; Isa **10** 22; **48** 19; Jer **33** 32; Hos **1** 10; Rom **9** 27; He **11** 12); also of the enemies of Israel (Josh **11** 4; Jgs **7** 12; 1 S **13** 5; cf Rev **20** 8). Joseph laid up grain as the sand of the sea (Gen **41** 49); God gave Solomon wisdom and understanding and largeness of heart as the sand that is on the seashore (1 K **4** 29); Job says "I shall multiply my days as the sand" (Job **29** 18); the multitude of quails provided for the Israelites in the desert is compared to the sand (Ps **78** 27); the Psalmist says of the thoughts of God, "They are more in number than the sand" (Ps **139** 18); Jeremiah, speaking of the desolation of Jerus, says that the number of widows is as the sand (Jer **15** 8). (2) Sand is also a symbol of weight (Job **6** 3; Prov **27** 3), and (3) of instability (Mt **7** 26).

It is a question what is meant by "the hidden treasures of the sand" in Dt **33** 19.

ALFRED ELY DAY

SAND FLIES, sand'flīz (כִּנִּם, *kinnim* [Ex **8** 16 m; Wisd **19** 10 m]): EV "lice." See FLEA; GNAT; INSECTS; LICE.

SAND, GLOWING, glō'ing. See MIRAGE.

SAND-LIZARD, sand'liz-ard (חֹמֶט, *ḥōmeṭ;* LXX σαῦρα, *saúra,* "lizard"; AV snail): *Ḥōmeṭ* is 7th in the list of unclean "creeping things" in Lev **11** 29.30, and occurs nowhere else. It is probably a skink or some species of *Lacerta.* See LIZARD; SNAIL.

SANDAL, san'dal. See DRESS, 6; SHOE; SHOE-LATCHET.

SANHEDRIN, san'hē-drin (סַנְהֶדְרִין, *ṣanhedhrīn,* the Talmudic transcription of the Gr συνέδριον, *sunédrion*): The Sanhedrin was, at and before the time of Christ, the name for the highest Jewish tribunal, of 71 members, in Jerus, and also for the lower tribunals, of 23 members, of which Jerus had two (*Tōṣephtā' Ḥăghīghāh* **11** 9; *Ṣanh.* **1** 6; **11** 2). It is derived from *sún,* "together," and *hédra,* "seat." In Gr and Rom literature the senates of Sparta, Carthage, and even Rome, are so called (cf Pausan. iii.11, 2; Polyb. iii.22; Dion Cassius xl.49). In Jos we meet with the word for the first time in connection with the governor Gabinius (57–55 BC), who divided the whole of Pal into 5 *sunédria* (*Ant,* XIV, v, 4), or *súnodoi* (*BJ,* I, viii, 5); and with the term *sunedrion* for the high council in Jerus first in *Ant,* XIV,

1. Name

ix, 3–5, in connection with Herod, who, when a youth, had to appear before the *sunedrion* at Jerus to answer for his doings in Galilee. But before that date the word appears in the LXX version of Proverbs (c 130 BC), esp. in **22** 10; **31** 23, as an equivalent for the Mishnaic *bēth-dīn*="judgment-chamber."

In the NT the word sometimes, esp. when used in the pl. (Mt **10** 17; Mk **13** 9; cf *Ṣanh.* **1** 5), means simply "court of justice," i.e. any judicatory (Mt **5** 22). But in most cases it is used to designate the supreme Jewish Court of Justice in Jerus, in which the process against Our Lord was carried on, and before which the apostles (esp. Peter and John, Stephen, and Paul) had to justify themselves (Mt **26** 59; Mk **14** 55; **15** 1; Lk **22** 66; Jn **11** 47; Acts **4** 15; **5** 21 ff; **6** 12 ff; **22** 30; **23** 1 ff; **24** 20). Sometimes *presbutérion* (Lk **22** 66; Acts **22** 5) and *gerousía* (Acts **5** 21) are substituted for *sunedrion*. See SENATE.

In the Jewish tradition-literature the term "Sanhedrin" alternates with *kenīshtā'*, "meeting-place" (*Meghillath Ta'ănīth* **10,** compiled in the 1st cent. AD), and *bēth-dīn*, "court of justice" (*Ṣanh.* **11** 2.4). As, according to Jewish tradition, there were two kinds of *sunedria*, viz. the supreme *sunedrion* in Jerus of 71 members, and lesser *sunedria* of 23 members, which were appointed by the supreme one, we find often the term *ṣanhedhrīn gedhōlāh*, "the great Sanhedrin," or *bēth-dīn ha-gādhōl*, "the great court of justice" (*Middōth* **5** 4; *Ṣanh.* **1** 6), or *ṣanhedhrīn gedhōlāh ha-yōshebheth be-lishekhath ha-gāzīth*, "the great Sanhedrin which sits in the hall of hewn stone."

There is lack of positive historical information as to the origin of the Sanhedrin. According to Jewish tradition (cf *Ṣanh.* **1** 6) it was constituted by Moses (Nu **11** 16–24) and was reorganized by Ezra immediately after the return from exile (cf the Tg to Cant **6** 1). But there is no historical evidence to show that previous to the Gr period there existed an organized aristocratic governing tribunal among the Jews. Its beginning is to be placed at the period in which Asia was convulsed by Alexander the Great and his successors.

2. Origin and History

The Hellenistic kings conceded a great amount of internal freedom to municipal communities, and Pal was then practically under home rule, and was governed by an aristocratic council of Elders (1 Macc **12** 6; 2 Macc **1** 10; **4** 44; **11** 27; 3 Macc **1** 8; cf Jos, *Ant*, XII, iii, 4; XIII, v, 8; *Meghillath Ta'ănīth* **10**), the head of which was the hereditary high priest. The court was called *Gerousia*, which in Gr always signifies an aristocratic body (see Westermann in Pauly's *RE*, III, 49). Subsequently this developed into the Sanhedrin.

During the Rom period (except for about 10 years at the time of Gabinius, who applied to Judaea the Rom system of government; cf Marquardt, *Römische Staatsverwaltung*, I, 501), the Sanhedrin's influence was most powerful, the internal government of the country being practically in its hands (*Ant*, XX, x), and it was religiously recognized even among the Diaspora (cf Acts **9** 2; **22** 5; **26** 12). According to Schürer (*HJP*, div II, vol 1, 171; *GJV*4, 236) the civil authority of the Sanhedrin, from the time of Archelaus, Herod the Great's son, was probably restricted to Judaea proper, and for that reason, he thinks, it had no judicial authority over Our Lord so long as He remained in Galilee (but see G. A. Smith, *Jerus*, I, 416).

The Sanhedrin was abolished after the destruction of Jerus (70 AD). The *bēth-dīn* (court of judgment) in Jabneh (68–80), in Usah (80–116), in Shafran (140–63), in Sepphoris (163–93), in Tiberias (193–220), though regarded in the Talm (cf *Rō'sh ha-shānāh* **31***a*) as having been the direct continuation of the Sanhedrin, had an essentially different character; it was merely an assembly of scribes, whose decisions had only a theoretical importance (cf *Ṣōṭāh* **9** 11).

3. Constitution

The Great Sanhedrin in Jerus was formed (Mt **26** 3.57.59; Mk **14** 53; **15** 1; Lk **22** 66; Acts **4** 5 f; **5** 21; **22** 30) of high priests (i.e. the acting high priest, those who had been high priests, and members of the privileged families from which the high priests were taken), elders (tribal and family heads of the people and priesthood), and scribes (i.e. legal assessors), Pharisees and Sadducees alike (cf Acts **4** 1 ff; **5** 17.34; **23** 6). In Mk **15** 43; Lk **23** 50, Joseph of Arimathaea is called *bouleutḗs*, "councillor," i.e. member of the Sanhedrin.

According to Jos and the NT, the acting high priest was as such always head and president (Mt **26** 3.57; Acts **5** 17 ff; **7** 1; **9** 1 f; **22** 5; **23** 2; **24** 1; *Ant*, IV, viii, 17; XX, x). Caiaphas is president at the trial of Our Lord, and at Paul's trial Ananias is president. On the other hand, according to the Talm (esp. *Ḥăghīghāh* **2** 2), the Sanhedrin is represented as a juridical tribunal of scribes, in which one scribe acted as *nāsī'*, "prince," i.e. president, and another as *'abh-bēth-dīn*, father of the judgment-chamber, i.e. vice-president. So far, it has not been found possible to reconcile these conflicting descriptions (see "Literature," below).

Ṣanh. **4** 3 mentions the *ṣōpherē-ha-dayānīm*, "notaries," one of whom registered the reasons for acquittal, and the other the reasons for condemnation. In the NT we read of *hupērétai*, "constables" (Mt **5** 25) and of the "servants of the high priest" (Mt **26** 51; Mk **14** 47; Jn **18** 10), whom Jos describes as "enlisted from the rudest and most restless characters" (*Ant*, XX, viii, 8; ix, 2). Jos speaks of the "public whip," Matthew mentions "tormentors" (**18** 34), Luke speaks of "spies" (**20** 20).

The whole history of post-exilic Judaism circles round the high priests, and the priestly aristocracy always played the leading part in the Sanhedrin (cf *Ṣanh.* **4** 2). But the more the Pharisees grew in importance, the more were they represented in the Sanhedrin. In the time of Salome they were so powerful that "the queen ruled only in name, but the Pharisees in reality" (*Ant*, XIII, xvi, 2). So in the time of Christ, the Sanhedrin was formally led by the Sadducean high priests, but practically ruled by the Pharisees (*Ant*, XVIII, i, 4).

4. Jurisdiction

In the time of Christ the Great Sanhedrin at Jerus enjoyed a very high measure of independence. It exercised not only civil jurisdiction, according to Jewish law, but also, in some degree, criminal. It had administrative authority and could order arrests by its own officers of justice (Mt **26** 47; Mk **14** 43; Acts **4** 3; **5** 17 f; **9** 2; cf *Ṣanh.* **1** 5). It was empowered to judge cases which did not involve capital punishment, which latter required the confirmation of the Rom procurator (Jn **18** 31; cf *Jerus Ṣanh.* **1** 1; **7** 2 [p. 24]; Jos, *Ant*, XX, ix, 1). But, as a rule, the procurator arranged his judgment in accordance with the demands of the Sanhedrin.

For one offence the Sanhedrin could put to death, on their own authority, even a Rom citizen, namely, in the case of a Gentile passing the fence which divided the inner court of the Temple from that of the Gentiles (*BJ*, VI, ii, 4; *Middōth* **11** 3; cf Acts **21** 28). The only case of capital punishment in connection with the Sanhedrin in the NT is that of Our Lord. The stoning of Stephen (Acts **7** 54 ff) was probably the illegal act of an enraged multitude.

5. Place and Time of Meeting

The Talmudic tradition names "the hall of hewn stone," which, according to *Middōth* **5** 4, was on the south side of the great court, as the seat of the Great Sanhedrin (*Pē'āh* **2** 6; *'Ēdhuyōth* **7** 4, et al.). But the last sittings of the Sanhedrin were held in the city outside the Temple area (*Ṣanh.* **41***a; Shabbāth* **15***a; Rō'sh ha-shānāh* **31***a; 'Ăbhōdhāh zārāh* **8***c*). Jos also mentions the place where the *bouleutaí*, "the councillors," met as the *boulḗ*, outside the Temple (*BJ*, V, iv, 2), and most probably he refers to these last sittings.

According to the *Tōṣephtā' Ṣanh.* **7** 1, the Sanhedrin held its sittings from the time of the offering of the daily morning sacrifice till that of the evening sacrifice. There were no sittings on Sabbaths or feast days.

6. Procedure

The members of the Sanhedrin were arranged in a semicircle, so that they could see each other (*Ṣanh.* **4** 3; *Tōṣephtā'* **8** 1). The two notaries stood before them, whose duty it was to record the votes (see 3, above). The prisoner had to appear in humble attitude and dressed in mourning (*Ant*, XIV, ix, 4). A sentence of capital punishment could not be passed on the day of the trial. The decision of the judges had to be examined on the following day (*Ṣanh.* **4** 1), except in the case of a person who misled the people, who could be tried and condemned the same day or in the night (*Tōṣephtā' Ṣanh.* **10**). Because of this, cases which involved capital punishment were not tried on a Friday or on any day before a feast. A herald preceded the condemned one as he was led to the place of execution, and cried out: "N. the son of N. has been found guilty of death, etc. If anyone knows anything to clear him, let him come forward and declare it" (*Ṣanh.* **6** 1). Near the place of execution the condemned man was asked to confess his guilt in order that he might partake in the world to come (ib; cf Lk **23** 41–43).

Literature.—Our knowledge about the Sanhedrin is based on three sources: the NT, Jos, and the Jewish tradition-literature (esp. Mish *Ṣanhedhrīn* and *Makkōth*, best ed, Strack, with Ger. tr, *Schriften des Institutum Judaicum in Berlin*, N. 38, Leipzig, 1910). See art. Talmud.

Consult the following histories of the Jewish people: Ewald, Herzfeld, Grätz, but esp. Schürer's excellent *HJP*, much more fully in *GJV*[4]; also G. A. Smith, *Jerus.* Special treatises on Sanhedrin: D. Hoffmann, *Der oberste Gerichtshof in der Stadt des Heiligtums*, Berlin, 1878, where the author tries to defend the Jewish traditional view as to the antiquity of the Sanhedrin; J. Reifmann, *Ṣanhedhrīn* (in Heb), Berditschew, 1888; A. Kuenen, *On the Composition of the Sanhedrin*, in Dutch, tr[d] into Ger. by Budde, *Gesammelte Abhandlungen*, etc, 49–81, Freiburg, 1894; Jelski, *Die innere Einrichtung des grossen Synedrions zu Jerusalem*, Breslau, 1894, who tries to reconcile the Talmudical statements about the composition of the Sanhedrin with those of Jos and the NT (esp. in connection with the question of president) by showing that in the Mish (except *Ḥăghīghāh* **11** 2) *nāsī'* always stands for the political president, the high priest, and *'abh-bēth-dīn* for the scribal *head* of the Sanhedrin, and not for the vice-president; A. Büchler, *Das Synedrium in Jerusalem und das grosse Beth-din in der Quaderkammer des jerusalemischen Tempels*, Vienna, 1902, a very interesting but not convincing work, where the author, in order to reconcile the two different sets of sources, tries to prove that the great Sanhedrin of the Talm is not identical with the Sanhedrin of Jos and the NT, but that there were two Sanhedrins in Jerus, the one of the NT and Jos being a *political* one, the other a *religious* one. He also thinks that Christ was seized, not by the Sanhedrin, but by the temple authorities.

See also W. Bacher's art. in *HDB* (excellent for sifting the Talmudic sources); Dr. Lauterbach's art. in *Jew Enc* (accepts fully Büchler's view); H. Strack's art. in *Sch-Herz* (concise and exact).

Paul Levertoff

SANSANNAH, san-san'a (סַנְסַנָּה, *ṣanṣannāh;* **Σανσάννα**, *Sansánna*, or **Σεθεννάκ**, *Sethennák*): One of the uttermost cities in the Negeb of Judah (Josh **15** 31), identical with Hazar-susah (Josh **19** 5), one of the cities of Simeon, and almost certainly the same as Hazar-susim (1 Ch **4** 31). It cannot be said to have been identified with any certainty, though *Simsim*, "a good-sized village with well and pool, surrounded by gardens and having a grove of olives to the north," has been suggested (*PEF*, III, 260, Sh XX).

SAPH, saf (סַף, *ṣaph;* B, **Σάφ**, *Sáph*, A, **Σεφέ**, *Sephé*): A Philistine, one of the four champions of the race of Rapha ("giant") who was slain by Sibbecai, one of David's heroes (2 S **21** 18; 1 Ch **20** 4). It is supposed by some that he was the son of the giant Goliath, but this is not proved. In 1 Ch **20** 4, the same person is called "Sippai."

SAPHAT, sā'fat:

(1) A and Fritzsche, Σαφάτ, *Saphát;* omitted in B (and Swete); B[ab mg] 'Ασάφ, *Asáph:* The eponym of a family which returned with Zerubbabel (1 Esd **5** 9) = "Shephatiah" in Ezr **2** 4; Neh **7** 9.

(2) A, Σαφάτ, *Saphát;* B, Swete, and Fritzsche, Σαφάγ, *Sapház;* AV **Sabat:** One of the families of "the sons of the servants of Solomon" who returned with Zerubbabel (1 Esd **5** 34); wanting in the ‖ Ezr **2** 57; Neh **7** 59.

SAPHATIAS, saf-a-tī'as (**Σαφατίας**, *Saphatías*, B, **Σοφοτίας**, *Sophotías;* omitted in A): Name of a family of returning exiles (1 Esd **8** 34) = "Shephatiah" in Ezr **8** 8. If Saphatias (1 Esd **8** 34) = Saphat (**5** 9), as would appear, then part of the family went up with Zerubbabel and part with Ezra.

SAPHETH, sā'feth: AV = RV Saphuthi (q.v.).

SAPHIR, sā'fēr (שָׁפִיר, *shāphīr*). See Shaphir.

SAPHUTHI, saf'ū-thī, sa-fū'thi (A and Fritzsche, **Σαφυθί**, *Saphuthí*, B [and Swete], **Σαφυεί**, *Saphueí;* AV **Sapheth**): Name of one of the families of "the sons of the servants of Solomon" (1 Esd **5** 33) = "Shephatiah" in Ezr **2** 57; Neh **7** 59.

SAPPHIRA, sa-fī'ra (שַׁפִּירָא, *shappīrā';* Aram. for either "beautiful" or "sapphire"; **Σαπφείρα**, *Sappheíra*): Wife of Ananias (Acts **5** 1–10). See Ananias, (1).

SAPPHIRE, saf'īr. See Stones, Precious.

SARABIAS, sar-a-bī'as (**Σαραβίας**, *Sarabías*): One of the Levites who taught and expounded the Law for Ezra (1 Esd **9** 48) = "Sherebiah" in Neh **8** 7, probably identical with the "Asebebias" in 1 Esd **8** 47 (Ezr **8** 18).

SARAH, sā'ra, **SARAI**, sā'rī:

(1) In Gen **17** 15 the woman who up to that time has been known as Sarai (שָׂרַי, *sāray;* Σάρα, *Sára*) receives by Divine command the name Sarah (שָׂרָה, *sārāh;* Σάρρα, *Sárra*). (This last form in Gr preserves the ancient doubling of the *r*, lost in the Heb and the Eng. forms.)

The former name appears to be derived from the same root as Israel, if, indeed, Gen **32** 28 is intended as an etymology of Israel. "She that strives," a contentious person, is a name that might be given to a child at birth (cf Hos **12** 3.4, of Jacob), or later when the child's character developed; in Gen **16** 6 and **21** 10 a contentious character appears. Yet comparison with the history of her husband's name (see Abraham) warns us not to operate solely upon the basis of the Heb language. Sarai was the name this woman brought with her from Mesopotamia. On the other hand there can be little doubt that the name Sarah, which she received when her son was promised, means "princess," for it is the fem. form of the extremely common title *sar*, used by the Semites to designate a ruler of greater or lesser rank.

In the verse following the one where this name is conferred, it is declared of Sarah that "kings of peoples shall be of her" (Gen **17** 16).

We are introduced to Sarai in Gen **11** 29. She is here mentioned as the wife that Abraham "took," while still in Ur of the Chaldees, that is, while among his kindred. It is immediately added that "Sarai was barren; she had no child." By this simple remark in the overture of his narrative, the writer sounds the *motif* that is to be developed in all the sequel. When the migration to Haran occurs, Sarai is named along with Abram and Lot as accompanying Terah. It has been held that the author (or authors) of ch **11** knew nothing of the relationship announced in **20** 12. But there can be no proof of such ignorance, even on the assumption of diversity of authorship in the two passages.

Sarai's career as described in ch **11** was not dependent on her being the daughter of Terah. Terah had other descendants who did not accompany him. Her movements were determined by her being Abram's wife. It appears, however, that she was a daughter of Terah by a different mother from the mother of Abram. The language of **20** 12 would indeed admit of her being Abram's niece, but the fact that there was but 10 years' difference between his age and hers (Gen **17** 17) renders this hypothesis less probable. Marriage with half-sisters seems to have been not uncommon in antiquity (even in the OT cf 2 S **13** 13).

This double relationship suggested to Abraham the expedient that he twice used when he lacked faith in God to protect his life and in cowardice sought his own safety at the price of his wife's honor. The first of these occasions was in the earlier period of their wanderings (ch **12**). From Canaan they went down into Egypt. Sarai, though above 60 years of age according to the chronology of the sacred historian, made the impression on the Egyptians by her beauty that Abraham had anticipated, and the result was her transfer to the royal palace. But this was in direct contravention of the purpose of God for His own kingdom. The earthly majesty of Pharaoh had to bow before the Divine majesty, which plagued him and secured the stranger's exodus, thus foreshadowing those later plagues and that later exodus when Abraham's and Sarah's seed "spoiled the Egyptians."

We meet Sarah next in the narrative of the birth of Ishmael and of Isaac. Though 14 years separated the two births, they are closely associated in the story because of their logical continuity. Sarah's barrenness persisted. She was now far past middle life, even on a patriarchal scale of longevity, and there appeared no hope of her ever bearing that child who should inherit the promise of God. She therefore adopts the expedient of being "builded by" her personal slave, Hagar the Egyp (see Gen **16** 2 m). That is, according to contemporary law and custom as witnessed by the CH (see ABRAHAM, IV, 2), a son born of this woman would be the freeborn son and heir of Abraham and Sarah.

Such was in fact the position of Ishmael later. But the insolence of the maid aroused the vindictive jealousy of the mistress and led to a painful scene of unjustified expulsion. Hagar, however, returned at God's behest, humbled herself before Sarah, and bore Ishmael in his own father's house. Here he remained the sole and rightful heir, until the miracle of Isaac's birth disappointed all human expectations and resulted in the ultimate expulsion of Hagar and her son.

The change of name from Sarai to Sarah when Isaac was promised has already been noted. Sarah's laughter of incredulity when she hears the promise is of course associated with the origin of the name of Isaac, but it serves also to emphasize the miraculous character of his birth, coming as it does after his parents are both so "well stricken in age" as to make parenthood seem an absurdity.

Before the birth of this child of promise, however, Sarah is again exposed, through the cowardice of her husband, to dishonor and ruin. Abimelech, king of Gerar, desiring to be allied by marriage with a man of Abraham's power, sends for Sarah, whom he knows only as Abraham's sister, and for the second time she takes her place in the harem of a prince. But the Divine promise is not to be thwarted, even by persistent human weakness and sin. In a dream God reveals to Abimelech the true state of the case, and Sarah is restored to her husband with an indemnity. Thereupon the long-delayed son is born, the jealous mother secures the expulsion of Hagar and Ishmael, and her career comes to a close at the age of 127, at Hebron, long time her home. The grief and devotion of Abraham are broadly displayed in ch **23**, in which he seeks and obtains a burying-place for his wife. She is thus the first to be interred in that cave of the field of Machpelah, which was to be the common resting-place of the fathers and mothers of the future Israel.

The character of Sarah is of mingled light and shade. On the one hand we have seen that lapse from faith which resulted in the birth of Ishmael, and that lack of self-control and charity which resulted in a quarrel with Abraham, an act of injustice to Hagar, and the disinheriting of Ishmael. Yet on the other hand we see in Sarah, as the NT writers point out (He **11** 11; 1 Pet **3** 6), one who through a long life of companionship with Abraham shared his hope in God, his faith in the promises, and his power to become God's agent for achieving what was humanly impossible. In fact, to Sarah is ascribed a sort of spiritual maternity, correlative with Abraham's position as "father of the faithful"; for all women are declared to be the (spiritual) daughters of Sarah, who like her are adorned in "the hidden man of the heart," and who are "doers of good" and "fearers of no terror" (1 Pet l.c., literally rendered). That in spite of her outbreak about Hagar and Ishmael she was in general "in subjection to her husband" and of "a meek and quiet spirit," appears from her husband's genuine grief at her decease, and still more clearly from her son's prolonged mourning for her (Gen **24** 67; cf **17** 17 and **23** 1 with **25** 20). And He who maketh even the wrath of man to praise Him used even Sarah's jealous anger to accomplish His purpose that "the son of the freewoman," Isaac, "born through promise," should alone inherit that promise (Gal **4** 22–31).

Apart from the three NT passages already cited, Sarah is alluded to only in Isa **51** 2 ("Sarah that bare you," as the mother of the nation), in Rom **4** 19 ("the deadness of Sarah's womb"), and in Rom **9** 9, where God's promise in Gen **18** 10 is quoted. Yet her existence and her history are of course presupposed wherever allusion is made to the stories of Abraham and of Isaac.

To many modern critics Sarah supplies, by her name, a welcome argument in support of the mythical view of Abraham. She has been held to be the local *numen* to whom the cave near Hebron was sacred; or the deity whose consort was worshipped in Arabia under the title Dusares, i.e. Husband-of-Sarah; or, the female associate of Sin the moon-god, worshipped at Haran. On these views the student will do well to consult Baethgen, *Beiträge*, 94, 157, and, for the most recent point of view, Gressmann's art., "Sage und Geschichte in den Patriarchenerzählungen," *ZATW*, 1910, and Eerdmans, *Alttestamentliche Studien*, II, 13.

(2) The daughter of Raguel, and wife of Tobias (Tob **3** 7.17, etc). See TOBIT, BOOK OF.

J. OSCAR BOYD

SARAIAS, sa-rā'yas, sa-rī'as (**Σαραίας**, *Saraías*, Lat *Sareus*):

(1) = Seraiah, the high priest in the reign of Zedekiah (1 Esd **5** 5, cf 1 Ch **6** 14).

(2) Sareus the father of Ezra (2 Esd **1** 1) = "Seraiah" in Ezr **7** 1, sometimes identified with

Saraias under (1). He is probably identical with the "Azaraias" of 1 Esd **8** 1.

(3) AV=RV "Azaraias" (1 Esd **8** 1).

SARAMEL, sar'a-mel: AV=RV Asaramel (q.v.).

SARAPH, sā'raf, sä'raf (שָׂרָף, *sāraph*, "noble one"; cf שָׂרַף, *sārāph*, "burn," "shine"): A descendant of Judah through Shelah (1 Ch **4** 22).

SARCHEDONUS, sär-ked'ō-nus (B א, **Σαχερδονός,** *Sacherdonós*, A, **Σαχερδάν,** *Sacherdán*, but **Σαχερδονοσός,** *Sacherdonosós* in Tob **1** 22): An incorrect spelling, both in AV and RV, for Sacherdonus in Tob **1** 21 f, another form of Esar-haddon.

SARDEUS, sär-dē'us: AV=RV Zardeus (q.v.).

SARDIN(E), sär'din, sär'dīn, **SARDIUS.** See Stones, Precious.

SARDIS, sär'dis (**Σάρδεις,** *Sárdeis*): Sardis is of special interest to the student of Herodotus and Xenophon, for there Artaphernes, the brother of Darius, lived, and from there Xerxes invaded Greece and Cyrus marched against his brother Artaxerxes; it is also of interest to the student of early Christian history as the home of one of the Seven Churches of Rev (**1** 11; **3** 1 ff). It was moreover one of the oldest and most important cities of Asia Minor, and until 549 BC, the capital of the kingdom of Lydia. It stood on the northern slope of Mt. Tmolus; its acropolis occupied one of the spurs of the mountain. At the base flowed the river Pactolus which served as a moat, rendering the city practically impregnable. Through the failure to watch, however, the acropolis had been successfully scaled in 549 BC by a Median soldier, and in 218 by a Cretan (cf Rev **3** 2.3). Because of its strength during the Pers period, the satraps here made their homes. However, the city was burned by the Ionians in 501 BC, but it was quickly rebuilt and regained its importance. In 334 BC it surrendered to Alexander the Great who gave it independence, but its period of independence was brief, for 12 years later in 322 BC it was taken by Antigonus. In 301 BC, it fell into the possession of the Seleucidan kings who made it the residence of their governor. It became free again in 190 BC, when it formed a part of the empire of Pergamos, and later of the Rom province of Asia. In 17 AD, when it was destroyed by an earthquake, the Rom emperor Tiberius remitted the taxes of the people and rebuilt the city, and in his honor the citizens of that and of neighboring towns erected a large monument, but Sardis never recovered its former importance (cf Rev **3** 12). Again in 295 AD, after the Rom province of Asia was broken up, Sardis became the capital of Lydia, and during the early Christian age it was the home of a bishop. The city continued to flourish until 1402, when it was so completely destroyed by Tamerlane that it was never rebuilt. Among the ruins there now stands a small village called *Sert*, a corruption of its ancient name. The ruins may be reached by rail from Smyrna, on the way to Philadelphia.

The ancient city was noted for its fruits and wool, and for its temple of the goddess Cybele, whose worship resembled that of Diana of Ephesus. Its wealth was also partly due to the gold which was found in the sand of the river Pactolus, and it was here that gold and silver coins were first struck. During the Rom period its coins formed a beautiful series, and are found in abundance by the peasants who till the surrounding fields. The ruins of the buildings which stood at the base of the hill have now been nearly buried by the dirt washed down from above. The hill upon which the acropolis stood measures 950 ft. high: the triple walls still surround it. The more imposing of the ruins are on the lower slope of the hill, and among them the temple of Cybele is the most interesting, yet only two of its many stone columns are still standing. Equally imposing is the necropolis of the city, which is at a distance of two hours' ride from *Sert*, S. of the Gygaean lake. The modern name of the necropolis is *Bin Tepe* or Thousand Mounds, because of the large group of great mounds in which the kings and nobles were buried. Many of the mounds were long ago excavated and plundered.

Coin of Sardis.

We quote the following from the *Missionary Herald* (Boston, Mass., August, 1911, pp. 361–62):

Dr. C. C. Tracy, of Marsovan, has made a visit to ancient Sardis and observed the work of his countryman, Professor Butler, of Princeton University, who is uncovering the ruins of that famous city of the past. Already rich "finds" have been made; among them portions of a temple of Artemis, indicating a building of the same stupendous character as those at Ephesus and Baalbec, and a necropolis from whose tombs were unearthed three thousand relics, including utensils, ornaments of gold and precious stones, mirrors, etc. What chiefly impressed Dr. Tracy was the significance of those "Seven Churches of Asia," of which Sardis held one. "When I think of the myriads of various nationality and advanced civilization for whose evangelization these churches were responsible, the messages to the Christian communities occupying the splendid strategic centers fill me with awe. While established amid the splendors of civilization, they were set as candlesticks in the midst of gross spiritual darkness. Did they fulfil their mission?"

One of Dr. Butler's recoveries is the marble throne of the Bishop of Sardis; looking upon it the message to Sardis recurs to mind. A fact of current history quickened the visitor's appreciation of the word to "the angel" of that church. "Yonder among the mountains overhanging Sardis there is a robber gang led by the notorious Chakirjali. He rules in the mountains; no government force can take him. Again and again he swoops down like an eagle out of the sky, in one quarter of the region or another. From time immemorial these mountains have been the haunts of robbers; very likely it was so when Rev was written, 'I will come upon thee as a thief.' In each case the message was addressed to 'the angel of the church.' Over every church in the world there is a spirit hovering, as it were—a spirit representing that church and by whose name it can be addressed. The messages are as vital as they were at the first. 'He that hath an ear, let him hear what the Spirit saith unto the churches.' "

E. J. Banks

SARDITE, sär'dīt. See Sered.

SARDIUS, sär'di-us. See Stones, Precious.

SARDONYX, sär'dō-niks. See Stones, Precious.

SAREPTA, sa-rep'ta (**Σάρεπτα,** *Sárepta*): The name in Lk **4** 26 AV, following the Gr, of the Phoen town to which Elijah was sent in the time of the great famine, in order to save the lives of a widow and her son (1 K **17** 9.10). RV adopts the form of the name based upon the Heb, and as found in the OT: Zarephath (q.v.).

SARID, sā'rid (שָׂרִיד, *sārīdh;* B, **'Εσεδεκγωλά,** *Esedekgōlá*, **Σεδδούκ,** *Seddoúk*, A, **Σαρθίδ,** *Sarthíd*, **Σαρίδ,** *Saríd*): A place on the southern border of Zebulun to the W. of Chisloth-tabor (Josh **19** 10.12). It is mentioned but not identified in *Onom*. Probably we should read "Sadid," and in that case may with Conder locate it at *Tell Shaddū*, an artificial mound with some modern ruins and good springs.

which stands on the plain, about 5 miles W. of *Iksāl*.

SARGON, sär′gon (722–705 BC): The name of this ruler is written סַרְגוֹן, *ṣargōn*, in the OT, *Shar-ukîn* in the cuneiform inscriptions, 'Αρνά, *Arná*, in the LXX, and 'Αρκεανος, *Arkeanos*, in the Ptolemaic Canon. Sargon is mentioned but once by name in the OT (Isa **20** 1), when he sent his Tartan (*turtannu*) against Ashdod, but he is referred to in 2 K **17** 6 as "the king of Assyria" who carried Israel into captivity.

Shalmaneser V had laid siege to Samaria and besieged it three years. But shortly before or very soon after its capitulation, Sargon, perhaps being responsible for the king's death, overthrew the dynasty, and in his annals credited himself with the capture of the city and the deportation of its inhabitants. Whether he assumed the name of the famous ancient founder of the Accad dynasty is not known.

Sargon at the beginning of his reign was confronted with a serious situation in Babylon. Merodach-baladan of Kaldû, who paid tribute to previous rulers, on the change of dynasty had himself

Sargon in His War Chariot.

proclaimed king, New Year's Day, 721 BC. At Dur-ilu, Sargon fought with the forces of Merodach-baladan and his ally Khumbanigash of Elam, but although he claimed a victory the result was apparently indecisive. Rebellions followed in other parts of the kingdom.

In 720 Ilu-bi'di (or Yau-bi'di), king of Hamath, formed a coalition against Sargon with Hanno of Gaza, Sib'u of Egypt, and with the cities Arpad, Ṣimirra, Damascus and Samaria. He claims that Sib'u fled, and that he captured and flayed Ilu-bi'di, burned Ḳarḳar, and carried Hanno captive to Assyria. After destroying Rapihu, he carried away 9,033 inhabitants to Assyria.

In the following year Ararat was invaded and the Hittite Carchemish fell before his armies. The territory of Rusas, king of Ararat, as well as a part of Melitene became Assyr provinces.

In 710 Sargon directed his attention to Merodach-baladan, who no longer enjoyed the support of Elam, and whose rule over Babylon had not been popular with his subjects. He was driven out from Babylon and also from his former capital Bît-Yakîn, and Sargon had himself crowned as the *shakkanak* of Babylon.

In 706 the new city called Dûr-Sharrukîn was dedicated as his residence. A year later he was murdered. It was during his reign that the height of Assyr ascendancy had been reached.

A. T. Clay

SARON, sā′ron (Σάρων, *Sárōn*): AV; Gr form of Sharon (Acts **9** 35).

SAROTHIE, sa-rō′thi-ē (A, Σαρωθιέ, *Sarōthiē*, B and Swete, Σαρωθεί, *Sarōthei*): Name of a family of "the sons of the servants of Solomon" who returned with Zerubbabel (1 Esd **5** 34); it is wanting in the ‖ lists in Ezr **2** 57; Neh **7** 59.

SARSECHIM, sär′sē-kim, sär-sē′kim (שַׂרְסְכִים, *sarṣ^ekhīm*): A prince of Nebuchadnezzar, present at the taking of Jerus by Nebuchadnezzar in the 11th year of Zedekiah (Jer **39** 3). The VSS with their various readings—"Nabousachar," "Nabousarach," "Sarsacheim"—point to a corrupt text. The best emendation is the reading "N^ebhōshazibhon" (= *Nabûšêzib-anni*, "Nebo delivers me"); this is based on the reading in Jer **39** 13.

SARUCH, sā′ruk (Σαρούχ, *Saroúch*, Σερούχ, *Seroúch*): AV; Gr form of Serug (thus Lk **3** 35 RV).

SATAN, sā′tan (שָׂטָן, *sāṭān*, "adversary," from the vb. שָׂטַן, *sāṭan*, "to lie in wait" [as adversary]; Σατᾶν, *Satán*, Σατανᾶς, *Satanás*, "adversary," διάβολος, *diábolos*, "devil," "adversary" or "accuser," κατήγωρ, *katēgōr* [altogether unclassical and un-Greek] [used once in Rev **12** 10], "accuser"):

I. Definition
II. Scriptural Facts concerning Satan
 1. Names of Satan
 2. Character of Satan
 3. Works of Satan
 4. History of Satan
III. General Considerations
 1. Scripture Doctrine of Satan Not Systematized
 2. Satan and God
 3. Satan Essentially Limited
 4. Conclusions
Literature

I. Definition.—A created but superhuman, personal, evil, world-power, represented in Scripture as the adversary both of God and men.

II. Scriptural Facts concerning Satan.—The most important of these are the Heb and Gr equivalents noticed above. These words are used in the general sense justified by their etymological significance. It is applied even to Jeh Himself (Nu **22** 22.32; cf 1 S **29** 4; 2 S **19** 22; Ps **109** 6, etc).

1. Names of Satan

The word "Satan" is used 24 t in the OT. In Job (**1** 6 f) and Zec (**3** 1 f) it has the prefixed definite article. In all cases but one when the art. is omitted it is used in a general sense. This one exception is 1 Ch **21** 1 (cf 2 S **24** 1), where the word is generally conceded to be used as a proper name. This meaning is fixed in NT times. We are thus enabled to note in the term "Satan" (and Devil) the growth of a word from a general term to an appellation and later to a proper name. All the other names of Satan save only these two are descriptive titles. In addition to these two principal names a number of others deserve specific enumeration. Tempter (Mt **4** 5; 1 Thess **3** 5); Beelzebub (Mt **12** 24); Enemy (Mt **13** 39); Evil One (Mt **13** 19.38; 1 Jn **2** 13.14; **3** 12, and particularly **5** 18); Belial (2 Cor **6** 15); Adversary (ἀντίδικος, *antídikos*), (1 Pet **5** 8); Deceiver (lit. "the one who deceives") (Rev **12** 9); Dragon (Great) (Rev **12** 3); Father of Lies (Jn **8** 44); Murderer (Jn **8** 44); Sinner (1 Jn **3** 8)—these are isolated references occurring from 1 to 3 t each. In the vast majority of passages (70 out of 83) either Satan or Devil is used.

Satan is consistently represented in the NT as the enemy both of God and man. The popular notion is that Satan is the enemy of man and active in misleading and cursing humanity because of his intense hatred and opposition to God.

2. Character of Satan

Mt **13** 39 would seem to point in this direction, but if one were to venture an opinion in a region where there are not enough facts to warrant a conviction, it would be that the general tenor of Scripture indicates quite the contrary, namely, that Satan's jealousy and hatred of men has led him into antagonism to God and, consequently, to goodness. The fundamental moral description of Satan is given by Our Lord when He describes Satan as the "evil *one*" (Mt **13** 19.38; cf Isa's description of Jeh as the "Holy One," **1** 4 and often); that is, the one whose nature and will are given to evil. Moral evil is his controlling attribute. It is evident that this description could not be applied to Satan as originally created. Ethical evil cannot be concreated. It is the creation of each free will for itself. We are not told in definite terms how Satan became the evil one, but certainly it could be by no other process than a fall, whereby, in the mystery of free personality, an evil will takes the place of a good one.

3. Works of Satan

The world-wide and age-long works of Satan are to be traced to one predominant motive. He hates both God and man and does all that in him lies to defeat God's plan of grace and to establish and maintain a kingdom of evil, in the seduction and ruin of mankind. The balance and sanity of the Bible is nowhere more strikingly exhibited than in its treatment of the work of Satan. Not only is the Bible entirely free from the extravagances of popular Satanology, which is full of absurd stories concerning the appearances, tricks, and transformations of Satan among men, but it exhibits a dependable accuracy and consistency of statement which is most reassuring. Almost nothing is said concerning Satanic agency other than wicked men who mislead other men. In the controversy with His opponents concerning exorcism (Mk **3** 22 f and ||'s) Our Lord rebuts their slanderous assertion that He is in league with Satan by the simple proposition that Satan does not work against himself. But in so saying He does far more than refute this slander. He definitely aligns the Bible against the popular idea that a man may make a definite and conscious personal alliance with Satan for any purpose whatever. The agent of Satan is always a victim. Also the hint contained in this discussion that Satan has a kingdom, together with a few other not very definite allusions, are all that we have to go upon in this direction. Nor are we taught anywhere that Satan is able to any extent to introduce disorder into the physical universe or directly operate in the lives of men. It is true that in Lk **13** 16 Our Lord speaks of the woman who was bowed over as one "whom Satan has bound, lo, these eighteen years," and that in 2 Cor **12** 7 Paul speaks of his infirmity as a "messenger of Satan sent to buffet him." Paul also speaks (1 Thess **2** 18) of Satan's hindering him from visiting the church at Thessalonica. A careful study of these related passages (together with the prologue of Job) will reveal the fact that Satan's direct agency in the physical world is very limited. Satan may be said to be implicated in all the disasters and woes of human life, in so far as they are more or less directly contingent upon sin (see particularly He **2** 14). On the contrary, it is perfectly evident that Satan's power consists principally in his ability to deceive. It is interesting and characteristic that according to the Bible Satan is fundamentally a liar and his kingdom is a kingdom founded upon lies and deceit. The doctrine of Satan therefore corresponds in every important particular to the general Bib. emphasis upon truth. "The truth shall make you free" (Jn **8** 32)—this is the way of deliverance from the power of Satan.

Now it would seem that to make Satan preëminently the *deceiver* would make man an innocent victim and thus relax the moral issue. But according to the Bible man is *particeps criminis* in the process of his own deception. He is deceived only because he ceases to love the truth and comes first to love and then to believe a lie (2 Cor **1** 10). This really goes to the very bottom of the problem of temptation. Men are not tempted by evil, *per se*, but by a good which can be obtained only at the cost of doing wrong. The whole power of sin, at least in its beginnings, consists in the sway of the fundamental falsehood that any good is really attainable by wrongdoing. Since temptation consists in this attack upon the moral sense, man is constitutionally guarded against deceit, and is morally culpable in allowing himself to be deceived. The temptation of Our Lord Himself throws the clearest possible light upon the methods ascribed to Satan. The temptation was addressed to Christ's consciousness of Divine sonship; it was a deceitful attack emphasizing the good, minimizing or covering up the evil; indeed, twisting evil into good. It was a deliberate, malignant attempt to obscure the truth and induce to evil through the acceptance of falsehood. The attack broke against a loyalty to truth which made self-deceit, and consequently deceit from without, impossible. The lie was punctured by the truth and the temptation lost its power (see TEMPTATION OF CHRIST). This incident reveals one of the methods of Satan—by immediate suggestion as in the case of Judas (Lk **22** 3; Jn **13** 2.27). Sometimes, however, and, perhaps, most frequently, Satan's devices (2 Cor **2** 11) include human agents. Those who are given over to evil and who persuade others to evil are children and servants of Satan (see Mt **16** 23; Mk **8** 33; Lk **4** 8; Jn **6** 70; **8** 44; Acts **13** 10; 1 Jn **3** 8). Satan also works through persons and institutions supposed to be on the side of right but really evil. Here the same ever-present and active falseness and deceit are exhibited. When he is called "the god of this world" (2 Cor **4** 4) it would seem to be intimated that he has the power to clothe himself in apparently Divine attributes. He also makes himself an angel of light by presenting advocates of falsehood in the guise of apostles of truth (2 Cor **11** 13.15; 1 Jn **4** 1; 2 Thess **2** 9; Rev **12** 9; **19** 20). In the combination of passages here brought together, it is clearly indicated that Satan is the instigator and fomenter of that spirit of lawlessness which exhibits itself as hatred both of truth and right, and which has operated so widely and so disastrously in human life.

4. History of Satan

The history of Satan, including that phase of it which remains to be realized, can be set forth only along the most general lines. He belongs to the angelic order of beings. He is by nature one of the sons of Elohim (Job **1** 6). He has fallen, and by virtue of his personal forcefulness has become the leader of the anarchic forces of wickedness. As a free being he has merged his life in evil and has become altogether and hopelessly evil. As a being of high intelligence he has gained great power and has exercised a wide sway over other beings. As a created being the utmost range of his power lies within the compass of that which is permitted. It is, therefore, hedged in by the providential government of God and essentially limited. The Bib. emphasis upon the element of falsehood in the career of Satan might be taken to imply that his kingdom may be less in extent than appears. At any rate, it is confined to the cosmic sphere and to a limited portion of time. It is also doomed. In the closely related passages 2 Pet **2** 4 and Jude ver 6 it is affirmed that God cast the angels, when they sinned, down to Tartarus and committed them to pits of darkness, to be reserved unto judgment. This both refers to the constant Divine control of these insurgent forces and also points to their final and utter destruction. The putting of Satan in bonds is evidently both constant and progressive. The essential limitation of the empire of evil and its ultimate overthrow are foreshadowed in the Book of Job (chs **38–41**), where Jeh's power extends even to the symbolized spirit of evil.

According to synoptic tradition, Our Lord in the crisis of temptation immediately following the baptism (Mt **4** and ||) met and for the time conquered Satan as His own personal adversary. This preliminary contest did not close the matter, but was the earnest of a complete victory. According to Lk (**10** 18), when the Seventy returned from their mission flushed with victory over the powers of evil, Jesus said: 'I saw Satan fall [not "fallen"; see Plummer, "Lk," *ICC*, in loc.] as lightning from heaven.' In every triumph over the powers of evil Christ beheld in vision the downfall of Satan. In connection with the coming of the Hellenists who wished to see Him, Jesus asserted (Jn **12** 31), "Now is the judgment of this world: now shall the prince of this world be cast out." In view of His approaching passion He says again (Jn **14** 30), "The prince of the world cometh: and he hath nothing in me." Once again in connection with the promised advent of the Spirit, Jesus asserted (Jn **16** 11) that the Spirit would convict the world of judgment, "because the prince of this world hath been judged." In He (**2** 14.15) it is said that Christ took upon Himself human nature in order "that through death he might bring to nought him that had the power of death, that is, the devil." In 1 Jn **3** 8 it is said, "To this end was the Son of God manifested, that he might destroy the works of the devil." In Rev **12** 9 it is asserted, in connection with Christ's ascension, that Satan was cast down to the earth and his angels with him. According to the passage immediately following (**12** 10–12), this casting down was not complete or final in the sense of extinguishing his activities altogether, but it involves the potential and certain triumph of God and His saints and the equally certain defeat of Satan. In 1 Jn **2** 13 the young men are addressed as those who "have overcome the evil one." In Rev **20** the field of the future is covered in the assertion that Satan is "bound a thousand years"; then loosed "for a little time," and then finally "cast into the lake of fire."

A comparison of these passages will convince the careful student that while we cannot construct a definite chronological program for the career of Satan, we are clear in the chief points. He is limited, judged, condemned, imprisoned, reserved for judgment from the beginning. The outcome is certain though the process may be tedious and slow. The victory of Christ is the defeat of Satan; first, for Himself as Leader and Saviour of men (Jn **14** 30); then, for believers (Lk **22** 31; Acts **26** 18; Rom **16** 20; Jas **4** 7; 1 Jn **2** 13; **5** 4.18); and, finally, for the whole world (Rev **20** 10). The work of Christ has already destroyed the empire of Satan.

III. General Considerations.—There are, no doubt, serious difficulties in the way of accepting the doctrine of a personal, superhuman, evil power as Satan is described to be. It is doubtful, however, whether these difficulties may not be due, at least in part, to a misunderstanding of the doctrine and certain of its implications. In addition, it must be acknowledged, that whatever difficulties there may be in the teaching, they are exaggerated and, at the same time, not fairly met by the vague and irrational skepticism which denies without investigation. There are difficulties involved in any view of the world. To say the least, some problems are met by the view of a superhuman, evil world-power. In this section certain general considerations are urged with a view to lessening difficulties keenly felt by some minds. Necessarily, certain items gathered in the foregoing section are here emphasized again.

1. Scripture Doctrine of Satan Not Systematized

The Scriptural doctrine of Satan is nowhere systematically developed. For materials in this field we are shut up to scattered and incidental references. These passages, which even in the aggregate are not numerous, tell us what we need to know concerning the nature, history, kingdom and works of Satan, but offer scant satisfaction to the merely speculative temper. The comparative lack of development in this field is due partly to the fact that the Bib. writers are primarily interested in God, and only secondarily in the powers of darkness; and partly to the fact that in the Bible doctrine waits upon fact. Hence the malign and sinister figure of the Adversary is gradually outlined against the light of God's holiness as progressively revealed in the providential world-process which centers in Christ. It is a significant fact that the statements concerning Satan become numerous and definite only in the NT. The daylight of the Christian revelation was necessary in order to uncover the lurking foe, dimly disclosed but by no means fully known in the earlier revelation. The disclosure of Satan is, in form at least, historical, not dogmatic.

2. Satan and God

In the second place, the relationship of Satan to God, already emphasized, must be kept constantly in mind. The doctrine of Satan merges in the general doctrine concerning angels (see ANGELS). It has often been pointed out that the personal characteristics of angels are very little insisted upon. They are known chiefly by their functions: merged, on the one hand, in their own offices, and, on the other, in the activities of God Himself.

In the OT Satan is not represented as a fallen and malignant spirit, but as a servant of Jeh, performing a Divine function and having his place in the heavenly train. In the || accounts of David's numbering of Israel (1 S **24** 1; 1 Ch **21** 1) the tempting of David is attributed both to Jeh and Satan. The reason for this is either that 'the temptation of men is also a part of his providence,' or that in the interval between the documents the personality of the tempter has more clearly emerged. In this case the account in Ch would nearly approximate the NT teaching. In the Book of Job (**1** 6), however, Satan is among the Sons of God and his assaults upon Job are Divinely permitted. In Zec (**3** 1.2) Satan is also a servant of Jeh. In both these passages there is the hint of opposition between Jeh and Satan. In the former instance Satan assails unsuccessfully the character of one whom Jeh honors; while in the latter Jeh explicitly rebukes Satan for his attitude toward Israel (see G. A. Smith, *BTP*, II, 316 f). The unveiling of Satan as a rebellious world-power is reserved for the NT, and with this fuller teaching the symbolic treatment of temptation in Gen is to be connected. There is a sound pedagogical reason, from the viewpoint of revelation, for this earlier withholding of the whole truth concerning Satan. In the early stages of religious thinking it would seem to be difficult, if not impossible, to hold the sovereignty of God without attributing to His agency those evils in the world which are more or less directly connected with judgment and punishment (cf Isa **45** 7; Am **3** 6). The OT sufficiently emphasizes man's responsibility for his own evil deeds, but superhuman evil is brought upon him from above. "When wilful souls have to be misled, the spirit who does so, as in Ahab's case, comes from above" (G. A. Smith, op. cit., 317). The progressive revelation of God's character and purpose, which more and more imperatively demands that the origin of moral evil, and consequently natural evil, must be traced to the created will in opposition to the Divine, leads to the ultimate declaration that Satan is a morally fallen being to whose conquest the Divine Power in history is pledged. There is, also, the distinct possibility that in the significant transition from the Satan of the OT to that of the NT we have the outlines of a biography and an indication of the way by which the angels fell.

3. Satan Essentially Limited

A third general consideration, based upon data given in the earlier section, should be urged in the same connection. In the NT delineation of Satan, his limitations are clearly set forth. He is superhuman, but not in any sense Divine. His activities are cosmic, but not universal or transcendent. He is a created being. His power is definitely circumscribed. He is doomed to final destruction as a world-power. His entire career is that of a secondary and dependent being who is permitted a certain limited scope of power—a *time-lease* of activity (Lk **4** 6).

4. Conclusions

These three general considerations have been grouped in this way because they dispose of three objections which are current against the doctrine of Satan.

(1) The first is, that it is mythological in origin. That it is not dogmatic is a priori evidence against this hypothesis. Mythology is primitive dogma. There is no evidence of a theodicy or philosophy of evil in the Bib. treatment of Satan. Moreover, while the Scriptural doctrine is unsystematic in form, it is rigidly limited in scope and everywhere essentially consistent. Even in the Apocalypse, where naturally more scope is allowed to the imagination, the same essential ideas appear. The doctrine of Satan corresponds, item for item, to the intellectual saneness and ethical earnestness of the Bib. world-view as a whole. It is, therefore, not mythological. The restraint of chastened imagination, not the extravagance of mythological fancy, is in evidence throughout the entire Bib. treatment of the subject. Even the use of terms current in mythology (as perhaps Gen **3** 1.13.14; Rev **12** 7–9; cf 1 Pet **5** 8) does not imply more than a literary clothing of Satan in attributes commonly ascribed to malignant and disorderly forces.

(2) The second objection is that the doctrine is due to the influence of Pers dualism (see PERSIAN RELIGION; ZOROASTRIANISM). The answer to this is plain, on the basis of facts already adduced. The Bib. doctrine of Satan is not dualistic. Satan's empire had a beginning, it will have a definite and permanent end. Satan is God's great enemy in the cosmic sphere, but he is God's creation, exists by Divine will, and his power is relatively no more commensurate with God's than that of men. Satan awaits his doom. Weiss says (concerning the NT representation of conflict between God and the powers of evil): "There lies in this no Manichaean dualism, ... but only the deepest experience of the work of redemption as the definite destruction of the power from which all sin in the world of men proceeds" (*Bib. Theol. NT*, ET, II, 272; cf G. A. Smith, op. cit., II, 318).

(3) The third objection is practically the same as the second, but addressed directly to the doctrine itself, apart from the question of its origin, namely, that it destroys the unity of God. The answer to this also is a simple negative. To some minds the reality of created wills is dualistic and therefore untenable. But a true doctrine of unity makes room for other wills than God's—namely of those beings upon whom God has bestowed freedom. Herein stands the doctrine of sin and Satan. The doctrine of Satan no more militates against the unity of God than the idea, so necessary to morality and religion alike, of other created wills set in opposition to God's. Just as the conception of Satan merges, in one direction, in the general doctrine of angels, so, in the other, it blends with the broad and difficult subject of evil (cf "Satan," *HDB*, IV, 412*a*).

LITERATURE.—All standard works on Bib. Theology, as well as Dicts., etc, treat with more or less thoroughness the doctrine of Satan. The German theologians of the more evangelical type, such as Weiss, Lange, Martensen (Danish), Dorner, while exhibiting a tendency toward excessive speculation, discern the deeper aspects of the doctrine. Of monographs known to the writer none are to be recommended without qualification. It is a subject on which the Bible is its own best interpreter.

LOUIS MATTHEWS SWEET

SATAN, DEPTHS OF (**τὰ βαθέα τοῦ Σατανᾶ,** *tá bathéa toú Sataná*): Found in Rev **2** 24, and has reference to false teaching at Thyatira. It is a question (that perhaps may not be decided) whether *tou Satana*, "of Satan," represents the claim of the false teachers, or is thrown in by the Lord. Did those false teachers claim to know "the depths" of Satan? Or was it that they claimed to know "the depths" of Deity, and the Lord said it was rather "the depths of Satan"? In either case the antithesis to "depths of Satan" is "depths of God," as referred to in Rom **11** 33; 1 Cor **2** 10.

E. J. FORRESTER

SATAN, SYNAGOGUE OF: The expression occurs neither in the Heb nor in the Gr of the OT, nor in Apoc. Three passages in the OT and one in Apoc suggest the idea conveyed in the expression. In Nu **14** 27.35, Jeh expresses His wrath against "the evil congregation" (LXX *συναγωγὴ πονηρά, sunagōgḗ ponērá*) which He threatens to consume in the wilderness. In Ps **21** (**22**) 16, we find, "A company of evil doers [LXX *συναγωγὴ πονηρευομένων, sunagōgḗ ponēreuoménōn*] have inclosed me." In Sir **16** 6, we read, "In the congregation of sinners [LXX *συναγωγῇ ἁμαρτωλῶν, sunagōgḗ hamartōlṓn*] shall a fire be kindled."

Only in the NT occurs the phrase "synagogue of Satan," and here only twice (Rev **2** 9; **3** 9). Three observations are evident as to who constituted "the synagogue of Satan" in Smyrna and Philadelphia. (1) They claimed to be Jews, i.e. they were descendants of Abraham, and so laid claim to the blessings promised by Jeh to him and his seed. (2) But they are not regarded by John as real Jews, i.e. they are not the genuine Israel of God (the same conclusion as Paul reached in Rom **2** 28). (3) They are persecutors of the Christians in Smyrna. The Lord "knows their blasphemy," their sharp denunciations of Christ and Christians. They claim to be the true people of God, but really they are "the synagogue of Satan." The gen. *Σατανᾶ, Sataná*, is probably the possessive gen. These Jewish persecutors, instead of being God's people, are the "assembly of Satan," i.e. Satan's people.

In Polyc., *Mar.* xvii.2 (c 155 AD) the Jews of Smyrna were still persecutors of Christians and were conspicuous in demanding and planning the martyrdom of Polycarp the bishop of Smyrna, the same city in which the revelator calls persecuting Jews "the assembly of Satan."

In the 2d cent., in an inscription (*CIJ*, 3148) describing the classes of population in Smyrna, we find the expression *οἱ ποτὲ Ἰουδαῖοι, hoi poté Ioudaíoi*, which Mommsen thinks means "Jews who had abandoned their religion," but which Ramsay says "probably means those who formerly were the nation of the Jews, but have lost the legal standing of a separate people."

LITERATURE.—Ramsay, *The Seven Churches of Asia*, ch xii; Swete, *The Apocalypse of St. John*, 31, 32; Polycarp, *Mar.* xiii ff.17.2; Mommsen, *Historische Zeitschrift*, XXXVII, 417.

CHARLES B. WILLIAMS

SATCHEL, sach'el. See BAG.

SATHRABUZANES, sath-ra-bū'za-nēz, sath-ra-bū-zā'nēz (**Σαθραβουζάνης,** *Sathrabouzánēs*): In 1 Esd **6** 3.7.27="Shethar-bozenai" in Ezr **5** 3.6; **6** 6.13.

SATISFACTION, sat-is-fak′shun: Occurs twice in AV (Nu **35** 31.32) as a rendering of the Heb *kōpher* (RV "ransom"). It means a price paid as compensation for a life, and the passage cited is a prohibition against accepting such, in case of murder, or for the return of the manslayer. Such compensation was permitted in ancient justice among many peoples. Cf ποινή, *poinḗ*, which Liddell and Scott define as "properly quit-money for blood spilt, the fine paid by the slayer to the kinsman of the slain, as *a ransom* from all consequences." The same custom prevailed among Teutonic peoples, as seen in the Ger. *Wergeld* and Old Eng. *wergild*. The Heb laws of the OT permit it only in the case of a man or woman gored to death by an ox (Ex **21** 30–32).

BENJAMIN RENO DOWNER

SATRAPS, sā′traps, sat′raps (אֲחַשְׁדַּרְפְּנִים, *'ăḥashdarp*^{e}*nīm*, Ezr **8** 36; Est **3** 12; **8** 9; **9** 3, AV "lieutenants"; Dnl **3** 2.3.27; **6** 1 ff, AV "princes"): The viceroys or vassal rulers to whom was intrusted the government of the provinces in the Pers empire. The word answers to the Old Pers *khshathrapāvan*, "protectors of the realm."

SATYR, sat′ẽr, sā′tẽr (שָׂעִיר, *sā'īr*, lit. "he-goat"; cf שָׂעִר, *sā'ir*, "hairy" [Gen **27** 11, of Esau], and Arab. شَعْر, *sha'r*, "hair"; pl. שְׂעִירִים, *s*^{e}*'īrīm*): For *s*^{e}*'īrīm* in Lev **17** 7 and 2 Ch **11** 15, AV has "devils," RV "he-goats," ERVm "satyrs," LXX τοῖς ματαίοις, *toís mataíois*, "vain things." For *s*^{e}*'īrīm* in Isa **13** 21, AV and ERV have "satyrs," ERVm "he-goats," ARV "wild goats," LXX δαιμόνια, *daimónia*, "demons." For *sā'īr* in Isa **34** 14, AV and ERV have "satyr," ERVm "he-goat," ARV "wild goat." LXX has ἕτερος πρὸς τὸν ἕτερον, *héteros prós tón héteron*, "one to another," referring to *daimonia*, which here stands for *çīyīm*, "wild beasts of the desert."

The text of ARV in these passages is as follows: Lev **17** 7, "And they shall no more sacrifice their sacrifices unto the he-goats, after which they play the harlot"; 2 Ch **11** 15, "And he [Jeroboam] appointed him priests for the high places, and for the he-goats, and for the calves which he had made"; Isa **13** 21 f (of Babylon), "But wild beasts of the desert [*çīyīm*] shall lie there; and their houses shall be full of doleful creatures [*'ōḥīm*]; and ostriches [*b*^{e}*nōth ya'ănāh*] shall dwell there, and wild goats [*s*^{e}*'īrīm*] shall dance there. And wolves [*'īyīm*] shall cry in their castles, and jackals [*tannīm*] in the pleasant palaces"; Isa **34** 11.13.14.15 (of Edom), "But the pelican [*ḳā'āth*] and the porcupine [*ḳippōdh*] shall possess it; and the owl [*yanshōph*] and the raven [*'ōrēbh*] shall dwell therein: . . . . and it shall be a habitation of jackals [*tannīm*], a court for ostriches [*b*^{e}*nōth ya'ănāh*]. And the wild beasts of the desert [*çīyīm*] shall meet with the wolves [*'īyīm*], and the wild goat [*sā'īr*] shall cry to his fellow; yea, the night monster [*līlīth*] shall settle there. . . . . There shall the dart-snake [*ḳippōz*] make her nest . . . . there shall the kites [*dayyōth*] be gathered, every one with her mate."

The question is whether *sā'īr* and *s*^{e}*'īrīm* in these passages stand for real or for fabulous animals. In Lev **17** 7 and 2 Ch **11** 15, it is clear that they are objects of worship, but that still leaves open the question of their nature, though it may to many minds make "devils" or "demons" or "satyrs" seem preferable to "he-goats." In Isa **13** 20 we read, "neither shall the Arabian pitch tent there; neither shall shepherds make their flocks to lie down there." This may very likely have influenced the American Committee of Revisers to use "wild goat" in Isa **13** 21 and **34** 14 instead of the "he-goat" of the other passages. In ARV, no fabulous creatures (except perhaps "night-monster") are mentioned here, but LXX employs *daimonia*, "demons," in Isa **13** 21 for *s*^{e}*'īrīm* and in **34** 14 for *çīyīm*; ὀνοκένταυροι, *onokéntauroi*, from ὄνος, *ónos*, "ass," and κένταυρος, *kéntauros*, "centaur," in Isa **13** 22 and **34** 14 for *'īyīm*, and again in **34** 14 for *līlīth*; σειρῆνες, *seirēnes*, "sirens," in Isa **13** 21 for *b*^{e}*nōth ya'ănāh*, and in **34** 13 for *tannīm*. We must bear in mind the uncertainty regarding the identity of *çīyīm*, *'īyīm*, *'ōḥīm* and *tannīm*, as well as of some of the other names, and we must recall the tales that are hung about the name *līlīth* (AV "screech owl," AVm and RV "night-monster," RVm "Lilith"). While *sā'īr* is almost alone among these words in having ordinarily a well-understood meaning, i.e. "he-goat," there is good reason for considering that here it is used in an exceptional sense. The tr "satyr" has certainly much to be said for it. See GOAT; JACKAL.

ALFRED ELY DAY

SAUL, sôl (שָׁאוּל, *shā'ūl*; Σαούλ, *Saoúl*):

(1) The first king of Israel.

I. EARLY HISTORY
1. Name and Meaning
2. Genealogy
3. Home and Station
4. Sources for Life
5. Election as King
6. Reasons for It

II. REIGN AND FALL
1. His First Action
2. Army Reorganized
3. Battle of Michmash
4. Defeats the Amalekites
5. Deposition Pronounced
6. David Introduced to Saul
7. Two Accounts
8. Saul's Envy of David
9. Attempts to Get Rid of Him
10. David Spares Saul
11. Saul's Divided Energies
12. Consults a Necromancer
13. Battle of Gilboa
14. Double Accounts
15. Saul's Posterity

III. CHARACTER
1. Book of Chronicles
2. Saul's Failings
3. His Virtue
4. David's Elegy

I. Early History.—The name Saul is usually regarded as simply the passive participle of the vb. "to ask," and so meaning "asked" (cf 1 S **8** 4 ff), but the gentilic adj *shā'ūlī* (Nu **26** 13) would point to its having also an intensive connotation, "the one asked importunately," or perhaps, "the one asking insistently," "the beggar."

1. Name and Meaning

Saul was the son of Kish, a Benjamite. His genealogical tree is given in 1 S **9** 1 (cf LXX **10** 21). In 1 S **9** 1 his grandfather is Abiel, but in 1 Ch **8** 33; **9** 39, Ner, who appears as his paternal uncle in 1 S **14** 50.51.

2. Genealogy

The last verse contains a very curious scribal error, a *yodh* having slipped out of one word in it into another. It states that both Abner and Ner were sons of Abiel. These apparent inconsistencies are to be explained by the fact that in Heb, as in Arab., "son" is often used in the sense of grandson. Also, with the facility of divorce then prevalent, by "brother" and "sister" we must in most cases understand half-brother and half-sister. Moreover, Saul's mother might have been the wife at different times of Kish and of his brother Ner (cf 1 S **20** 30). This was quite common, and in some cases compulsory (Dt **25** 5–9).

Saul's home was at GIBEAH (q.v.), which is also called Gibeah of Saul, i.e. Saul's Hill (1 S **11** 4; cf also **10** 5, God's Hill, or simply The Hill, **10** 10; Hos **5** 8, etc), or the Hill of Benjamin or of the Benjamites (1 S **13** 15; 2 S **23** 29). It is usually identified with *Tell el-Fûl*. This conspicuous small *tell*, 3 miles north of Jerusalem, was excavated in 1922 by Dr. W. F. Albright. The simplicity of things was in harmony with the humble early life of Saul and justifies the self-depreciation which he expressed upon being chosen to be king (1 S **9** 21).

3. Home and Station

The very brief record of the history of the times found in 1 S and 2 S is not easily understood. The historians of the time were analysts who set down various episodes briefly and independently.

4. Sources for Life The attempt to understand these as a continuous narrative after the fashion of modern histories is not successful, if, indeed, it be a reasonable attempt.

Especially is this true of the account of the anointing of Saul as king. There is undoubtedly a

5. Election as King double line of events rather than a duplication of narratives: God was directing Samuel (1 S **9** 10–16); on the other hand foreign oppression made the elders of the people feel the need of a more centralized government (1 S **8**; **10** 17–27; **12**). In addition there had been the practice of Samuel as Judge. There were, during the whole history of the Judges, three provinces of judgships, a north district, an east district, and a southwest district. And the historian in the Book of Judges goes around these in regular succession four times. Then Samuel judged in each of the three districts in circuit "to Bethel and Gilgal and Mizpah and judged Israel in all those places," and also at Ramah his home town in the center. He was centralizing the government (1 S **7** 15–17).

This practice of Samuel undoubtedly was a molding influence on the desire of the people for a king.

6. Reasons for it Then three reasons additional appear in the narrative for placing a king at the head of the government of the nation; the unworthy character of Samuel's sons and his apparent desire to make the judgship hereditary (1 S **8** 1 ff), the long standing and terrible oppression by the Philistines (1 S **9** 16), and latterly an invasion by Ammonites (1 S **12** 12).

II. Reign and Fall.—The election of Saul at Mizpah was conducted in the presence of the chief-

1. His First Action tains of the clans; it is not to be supposed that the whole nation was present. As soon as it was over, the electors went home, and Saul also returned to his father's farm and, like Cincinnatus, once more followed the plough. "Within about a month," however (**10** 27 LXX, for MT "But he held his peace"), the summons came. A message from the citizens of JABESH-GILEAD (q.v.) was sent round the tribes appealing for help against the Ammonites under Nahash. They, of course, knew nothing about what had taken place at Mizpah, and it was only by chance that their messengers arrived at Gibeah when they did. Saul rose to the occasion, and immediately after he was acclaimed king by the whole body of the people (ch **11**). This double election, first by the chiefs and then by the people, is quite a regular proceeding.

This first success encouraged Saul to enter upon what was to be the mission of his life, namely, the

2. Army Reorganized throwing off of the Phili suzerainty. From the first he had had the boldest spirits upon his side (**10** 26 LXX, RVm); he was now able to form a standing army of 3,000 men, under the command of himself and his son JONATHAN (q.v.). The Philis, the last remnant of the Minoan race, had the advantage of the possession of iron weapons. It was, in fact, they who introduced iron into Pal from Crete—the Israelites knowing only bronze, and having even been deprived of weapons of the softer metals. They seem to have armed themselves—with the exception of the king and his son—with mattocks and ploughshares (**13** 19 ff).

The first encounter was the attack upon the Phili post at Michmash (1 S **13, 14**). The text of the narrative is uncertain, but the following outline is clear. On hearing that the Hebrews had revolted (**13** 3 LXX), the Philis gathered in great force, including 3,000 chariots (**13** 5 LXX; MT has 30,000) at Michmash. In dismay, Saul's troops deserted (vs 6 f), until he was left with only 600 (**14** 2).

3. Battle of Michmash In spite of this, Jonathan precipitated hostilities by a reckless attack upon one of the outposts. This was so successful that the whole Phili army was seized with panic, and the onset of Saul and the desertion of their Heb slaves completed their discomfiture. Saul followed up his victory by making predatory excursions on every side (**14** 47).

Saul's next expedition was against the Amalekites under Agag, who were likewise completely defeated.

4. Defeats the Amalekites The fight was carried out with all the remorselessness common to tribal warfare. Warning was sent to the friendly Kenites to withdraw out of danger; then the hostile tribe was slaughtered to a man, their chief alone being spared for the time being. Even the women and children were not taken as slaves, but were all killed (1 S **15**).

It is not clear what was the precise attitude of Samuel toward Saul. As the undoubted head of

5. Deposition Pronounced the theocracy he naturally objected to his powers being curtailed by the loss of the civil power (**8** 6). Even after the elections of Saul, Samuel claimed to be the ecclesiastical head of the state. He seems to have objected to Saul's offering the sacrifice before battle (**13** 10 ff), and to have considered him merely as his lieutenant (**15** 3) who could be dismissed for disobedience (**15** 14 ff). Here again some think to see two accounts woven together, because Saul in one place is presented as weary waiting (1 S **13** 8) and in the other is guilty of disobedience (1 S **15** 3 ff). There is no contradiction, or inconsistency, or even discrepancy here; in the one instance, Saul is trying to excuse himself; in the other his wrongdoing is denounced.

For a time, how long is not certainly known, Samuel mourned for Saul and allowed him to go on

6. David introduced to Saul unhindered in the exercise of his kingly office. The time has been estimated at about fifteen years; it seems doubtful, if it could have been so long. Then we read (1 S **16** 1), "And the Lord said unto Samuel, 'How long wilt thou mourn over Saul seeing I have rejected him from reigning over Israel? fill thine horn with oil, and go, I will send thee to Jesse, the Bethlehemite: for I have provided me a king among his sons.'" Samuel feared to go on this errand, for Saul would undoubtedly regard his act as treasonable. So God sent the prophet secretly to annoint David (1 S **16** 2–5). Saul did not at once accept his deposition, but he lost heart. And then his servants introduced to him a musician who played until his spirits revived (**16** 14 ff; cf 2 K **3** 15).

In the providence of God (cf I, 5), this same minstrel was the very person whom Samuel had secretly

7. Two Accounts anointed to supplant Saul. According to what looks like another account, however, it was his encounter with Goliath which led to the introduction of David to Saul (**17** 1 ff; see DAVID). In spite of all that has been said to the contrary, the two narratives are not incompatible, since we are not told the order of the events nor over how many years these events were spread. The theory of duplicate narratives rests upon the assumption that all statements made by the *dramatis personae* in the Bible are to be taken at their face value. If chs **16** and **17** had formed part of a play of Shakespeare, they would have been considered a fine example of his genius. Treatises would have been written to explain why Saul did not recognize David, and why Abner denied all knowledge of him. LXX, however, omits **17** 12–31.41.50.55—**18** **5**.

8. Saul's Envy of David

Whether Saul actually discovered that David had been anointed by Samuel or not, he soon saw in him his rival and inevitable successor, and he would hardly have been human if he had not felt envious of him. His dislike of David had two motives. The first was jealousy, because the women preferred the military genius of David to his own (**18** 7 f). His consequent attempt upon the life of David (vs 8–11) is omitted in LXX. Not least was the love of his own daughter for David (**18** 20; in ver 28 read with LXX "all Israel"). The second cause was his natural objection to see his son Jonathan supplanted in his rights to the throne, an objection which was aggravated by the devotion of that son to his own rival (**20** 30; see also David; Jonathan).

9. Attempts to Get Rid of Him

Saul could not believe that David could remain loyal to him (**24** 9); at the first favorable opportunity he would turn upon him, hurl him from the throne, and exterminate his whole house. In these circumstances, it was his first interest to get rid of him. His first attempt to do so (omitting with LXX **18** 8*b*–11) was to encourage him to make raids on the Philis in the hope that these might kill him (**18** 21 ff); his next, assassination by one of his servants (**19** 1), and then by his own hand (**19** 9 f). When David was compelled to fly, the quarrel turned to civil war. The superstitious fear of hurting the chosen of Jeh had given place to blind rage. Those who sheltered the fugitive, even priests, were slaughtered (**22** 17 ff). From one spot to another David was hunted, as he says, like a partridge (**26** 20).

10. David Spares Saul

It is generally maintained that here also we have duplicate accounts; for example, that there are two accounts of David taking refuge with Achish, king of Gath, and two of his sparing Saul's life. The latter are contained in chs **24** and **26**, but the points of resemblance are slight. Three thousand (**24** 2; **26** 2) was the number of Saul's picked men (cf **13** 2). David uses the simile of "a flea" in **24** 14, but in **26** 20 for "a flea" LXX has "my soul," which is no doubt original. The few other expressions would occur naturally in any narrative with the same contents.

11. Saul's Divided Energies

Obviously Saul's divided energies could not hold out long; he could not put down the imaginary rebellion within, and at the same time keep at bay the foreign foe. No sooner had he got the fugitive within his grasp than he was called away by an inroad of the Philis (**23** 27 f); but after his life had been twice spared, he seemed to realize at last that the latter were the real enemy, and he threw his whole strength into one desperate effort for existence.

12. Consults a Necromancer

Saul himself saw that his case was desperate, and that in fact the game was up. As a forlorn hope he determined to seek occult advice. He could no longer use the official means of divination (**28** 6), and was obliged to have recourse to a necromancer, one of a class whom he himself had taken means to suppress (**28** 3). The result of the séance confirmed his worst fears and filled his soul with despair (**28** 7 ff).

13. Battle of Gilboa

It says much for Saul that, hopeless as he was, he engaged in one last forlorn struggle with the enemy. The Philis had gathered in great force at Shunem. Saul drew up his army on the opposing hill of Gilboa. Between the two forces lay a valley (cf **14** 4). The result was what had been foreseen. The Israelites, no doubt greatly reduced in numbers (contrast **11** 8), were completely defeated, and Saul and his sons slain. Their armor was placed in the temple of Ashtaroth, and their bodies hung on the wall of Bethshan, but Saul's head was set in the temple of Dagon (1 Ch **10** 10). The citizens of Jabesh-gilead, out of ancient gratitude, rescued the bodies and, in un-Semitic wise, burned them and buried the bones.

It is one of the marvels of recent excavation that at *Beisan*, the ancient Beth-shean (1922–28) upon reaching the layer of débris indicated by the pottery to be of the time of the early monarchy of Israel, the temple of Ashtaroth was laid bare; possession of Beth-shean by the Philistines is clearly shown and also that the Philistines were but tools of the Egyptians. Thus Beth-shean remained in Egyptian control until the rise of the dynasty of David.

14. Double accounts

Here again attempts have been made to find two accounts, setting 1 S **31** 4 over against 2 S **1** 2 ff. Really there is no discrepancy, and we have no means of knowing whether the Amalekite who was seeking a reward, was telling the truth or not.

15. Saul's Posterity

With Saul the first Israelite dynasty began and ended. The names of his sons are given in 1 S **14** 49 as Jonathan, Ishvi and Malchishua. Ishvi or Ishyo (LXX) is Eshbaal, called in 2 S **2** 8 Ish-bosheth (q.v.). 1 Ch **8** 33 adds Abinadab. Jonathan left a long line of descendants famous, like himself, as archers (1 Ch **8** 34 ff). The rest of Saul's posterity apparently died out. Malchishua and Abinadab were slain at Gilboa (1 S **31** 6; 1 Ch **10** 2), and Ish-bosheth was assassinated shortly after (2 S **4** 2 ff). Saul had also two natural sons by Rizpah who were put to death by David in accordance with a superstitious custom, as also were the five sons of Saul's daughter Merab (2 S **21** 8, not Michal; cf 1 S **18** 19). Saul's other daughter Michal apparently had no children. Saul had, it seems, other wives, who were taken into the harem of David in accordance with the practice of the times (2 S **12** 8), but of them and their descendants we know nothing.

III. Character.—Saul's life and character are disposed of in a somewhat summary fashion by the Chronicler (1 Ch **10**, esp. vs. 13.14).

1. Book of Chronicles

"So Saul died for his transgression which he committed against the Lord, even against the word of the Lord which he kept not, and also for asking council of one that had a familiar spirit, to inquire of it; and inquired not of the Lord."

2. Saul's Failings

Like everyone else, Saul had his virtues and his failings. His chief weakness seems to have been want of decision of character. He was easily swayed by events and by people. The praises of David (1 S **18** 7 f) at once set his jealousy on fire. His persecution of David was largely due to the instigation of mischievous courtiers (**24** 9). Upon remonstrance his repentance was as deep as it was short-lived (**24** 16; **26** 21). His impulsiveness was such that he did not know where to stop. His interdict (**14** 24 ff) was quite as uncalled for as his religious zeal (**15** 9) was out of place. He was always at one extreme. His hatred of David was only equal to his affection for him at first (**18** 2). His pusillanimity led him to commit crimes which his own judgment would have forbidden (**22** 17). Like most beaten persons, he became suspicious of everyone (**22** 7 f), and, like those who are easily led, he soon found his evil genius (**22** 9.18.22). Saul's inability to act alone appears from the fact that he never engaged in single combat, so far as we know. Before he could act at all his fury or his pity had to be roused to boiling-point (**11** 6). His mind was peculiarly subject to external influences, so that he was now a respectable man of the world, now a prophet (**10** 11; **19** 24).

3. His Virtues

On the other hand, Saul possessed many high qualities. His dread of office (**10** 22) was only equaled by the coolness with which he accepted it (**11** 5). To the first call to action he responded with promptitude (**11** 6 ff). His timely aid excited the lasting gratitude of the citizens of Jabesh-gilead (**31** 11 ff). If we remember that Saul was openly disowned by Samuel (**15** 30), and believed himself cast off by Jeh, we cannot but admire the way in which he fought on to the last. Moreover, the fact that he retained not only his own sons, but a sufficient body of fighting men to engage a large army of Philis, shows that there must have been something in him to excite confidence and loyalty.

4. David's Elegy

There is, however, no question as to the honorable and noble qualities of Saul. The chief were his prowess in war and his generosity in peace. They have been set down by the man who knew him best in what are among the most authentic verses in the Bible (2 S **1** 19 ff).

(2) Saul of Tarsus. See PAUL.

THOMAS HUNTER WEIR

SAVARAN, sav′a-ran: AV=RV AVARAN (q.v.).

SAVE, sāv: In the sense "except," the word came into Eng. through the Fr. (*sauf*) and is fairly common (38 t, in addition to "saving," AV Eccl **5** 11; Am **9** 8; Mt **5** 32; Lk **4** 27; Rev **2** 17). It represents no particular Heb or Gr terms but is employed wherever it seems useful. It is still in good (slightly archaic) use, and RV has few modifications (Dt **15** 4 AV; Ps **18** 31*b*, etc), but ERV has dropped "saving" in Lk **4** 27 and Rev **2** 17 and ARV also in Eccl **5** 11; Am **9** 8, retaining it only in Mt **5** 32.

SAVIAS, sa-vī′as (**Σαουΐα,** *Saouía*): In 1 Esd **8** 2, for Uzzi, an ancestor of Ezra, in Ezr **7** 4.

SAVIOUR, sāv′yẽr: (1) While that "God is the deliverer of his people" is the concept on which, virtually, the whole OT is based (see SALVATION), yet the Hebrews seem never to have felt the need of a title for God that would sum up this aspect of His relation to man. Nearest to our word "Saviour" is a participial form (מוֹשִׁיעַ, *mōshīaʿ*) from the vb. יָשַׁע, *yāshāʿ* (Qal not used; "save" in Hiphil), but even this participle is not frequently applied to God (some 13 t of which 7 are in Isa **43**-**63**). (2) In the NT, however, the case is different, and Σωτήρ, *Sōtḗr*, is used in as technical a way as is our "Saviour." But the distribution of the 24 occurrences of the word is significant, for two-thirds of them are found in the later books of the NT—10 in the Pastorals, 5 in 2 Pet, and one each in Jn, 1 Jn, and Jude—while the other instances are Lk **1** 47; **2** 11; Acts **5** 31; **13** 23; Eph **5** 23; Phil **3** 20. And there are no occurrences in Mt, Mk, or the earlier Pauline Epp. The data are clear enough. As might be expected, the fact that the OT used no technical word for Saviour meant that neither did the earliest Christianity use any such word. Doubtless for Our Lord "Messiah" was felt to convey the meaning. But in Gr-speaking Christianity, "Christ," the tr of Messiah, soon became treated as a proper name, and a new word was needed. (3) *Sōtēr* expressed the exact meaning and had already been set apart in the language of the day as a *religious* term, having become one of the most popular Divine titles in use. Indeed, it was felt to be a most inappropriate word to apply to a human being. Cicero, for instance, arraigns Verres for using it: "Soter . . . . How much does this imply? So much that it cannot be expressed in one word in Latin" (*Verr.* ii.2, 63, § 154). So the adoption of *Sōtēr* by Christianity was most natural, the word seemed ready-made. (4) That the NT writers derived the word from its contemporary use is shown, besides, by its occurrence in combination with such terms as "manifestation" (*epipháneia*, 2 Tim **1** 10; Tit **2** 13), "love toward man" (*philanthrōpía*, Tit **3** 4), "captain" (*archēgós*, Acts **5** 31; cf He **2** 10), etc. These terms are found in the Gr sources many times in exactly the same combinations with *Sōtēr*. (5) In the NT *Sōtēr* is uniformly reserved for Christ, except in Lk **1** 47; Jude ver 25, and the Pastorals. In 1 Tim (**1** 1; **2** 3; **4** 10) it is applied only to the Father, in 2 Tim (**1** 10, only) it is applied to Christ, while in Tit there seems to be a deliberate alternation: of the Father in **1** 3; **2** 10; **3** 4; of Christ in **1** 4; **2** 13; **3** 6.

LITERATURE.—P. Wendland, "Σωτήρ," *ZNTW*, V, 335-53, 1904; J. Weiss, "Heiland," in *RGG*, II, 1910; H. Lietzmann, *Der Weltheiland*, 1909. Much detailed information is available in various parts of Deissmann, *Light from the Ancient East*, 1910.

BURTON SCOTT EASTON

SAVOR, sā′vẽr (רֵיחַ, *rēaḥ;* **ὀσμή,** *osmḗ*): (1) The primary meaning of the word is "taste," "flavor" (from Lat *sapor*, "taste"). So in Mt **5** 13; Lk **14** 34, "if the salt have lost its savor" (*μωρανθῇ*, *mōranthḗ*, "become tasteless," "insipid," so as to lose its characteristic preserving virtue). (2) But generally it has the meaning of "smell," "odor": (*a*) once of evil odor: "Its stench shall come up, and its ill savor shall come up" (Joel **2** 20); (*b*) elsewhere in the sense of pleasant smell. In the OT, with the exception of Ex **5** 21 and AV Cant **1** 3 (RV "fragrance"), it is always accompanied by the adj. "sweet." It stands for the smell of sacrifices and oblations, in agreement with the ancient anthropomorphic idea that God smells and is pleased with the fragrance of sacrifices (e.g. "Jeh smelled the sweet savor," Gen **8** 21; "to make a sweet savor unto Jeh," Nu **15** 3; and frequently). In the NT, "savor" in the sense of smell is used **metaphorically:** (*a*) once the metaphor is borrowed from the incense which attends the victor's triumphal procession; God is said to make manifest through His apostles "the savor of his knowledge in every place" as He "leadeth" them "in triumph in Christ" (2 Cor **2** 14; see TRIUMPH). (*b*) Elsewhere the metaphor is borrowed from the fragrant smell of the sacrifices. The apostles "are a sweet savor of Christ unto God" (2 Cor **2** 15), i.e. they are, as it were, a sweet odor for God to smell, an odor which is pleasing to God, even though its effect upon men varies (to some it is a "savor from death unto death," i.e. such as is emitted by death and itself causes death; to others it is "a savor from life unto life," ver 16). By the same sacrificial metaphor, Christ's offering of Himself to God is said to be "for a sweet smelling savor" (Eph **5** 2 AV, RV "for an odor of a sweet smell"; the same phrase is used in Phil **4** 18 of acts of kindness to Paul, which were "a sacrifice acceptable, well-pleasing to God"). (3) Once it is used in the **figurative** sense of reputation: "Ye have made our savor to be abhorred [lit. "our smell to stink"] in the eyes of Pharaoh" (Ex **5** 21). Cf the Eng. phrase, "to be in bad odor."

The vb. "to savor" means: (1) intransitively, to taste or smell of, to partake of the quality of something, as in the Preface of AV, "to savour more of curiosity than wisdome," or (2) transitively, to perceive by the taste or smell, to discern: "thou savourest not the things that be of God" (AV Mt **16** 23; Mk **8** 33, RV "mindest"; *φρονεῖς, phroneîs;* Vulg *sapis*). The adj. "savory" occurs only in Gen **27** 4.7.9.14.17.31 ("savory food") and RV Isa **30** 24 (m "salted").

D. MIALL EDWARDS

SAW, sô. See Tools.

SAWING ASUNDER, sô′ing a-sun′dẽr. See Punishments.

SAYEST, sā′est: "Thou sayest" (Mt **27** 11; Mk **15** 2; Lk **22** 70, "Ye say"; Jn **18** 37), i.e. rightly; "Thou hast said" (Mt **26** 25.64), = "Yes"; a rabbinical idiom never found in the OT. Mark (**14** 62) renders by "I am." All these passages WHm punctuate interrogatively (cf *K^{e}thūbhōth*, f. 103 *b*).

SAYINGS, sā′ingz, **DARK.** See Dark Sayings.

SAYINGS, FAITHFUL. See Faithful Sayings.

SAYINGS OF JESUS. See Logia.

SAYINGS, UNWRITTEN, un-rit″n. See Agrapha.

SCAB, skab, **SCABBED,** skab′ed, skabd (יַלֶּפֶת, *yallepheth*, מִסְפַּחַת, *mispahath*, סַפַּחַת, *ṣappaḥath*, vb. שִׂפַּח, *sippaḥ; σημασία, sēmasía*, **λειχήν**, *leichḗn*): These are generic terms for any skin disease in which there are patches of hard crusts on the surface. The commonest of these are the forms now named eczema, herpes and, perhaps, psoriasis, all of which are common in Bible lands. Milder cases in which the disease was localized and in small patches (the *sēmasia* of LXX) did not render the bearer unclean, and they were to be distinguished by the priest (Lev **13** 2.6) from the more virulent and spreading eruptions which (ver 7) were regarded as causes of ceremonial uncleanness. These severer forms are the *leichēn* of LXX mentioned in Lev **21** 20, which disqualified any son of Aaron from serving as a priest, and when affecting an animal rendered it unfit to be offered as a burnt offering (Lev **22** 22). Hippocrates speaks of these cases as obstinate and persistent, and Galen believed that they might degenerate into leprosy; hence the terms in which Aeschylus speaks of it (*Choephori* 281). Celsus, however, recognized that *leichēn* was a papular eruption, not a true scab. The name *yallepheth* seems to have been given to it on account of the firmness of attachment of the scabs, while the term *miṣpaḥath* refers to its tendency to spread and cover the surface. A cognate word in Ezk **13** 18 is the name of a large *ṭallith* or prayer veil used by the false prophetesses in Israel (tr^d "kerchief"). Scabs were esp. disfiguring on the head, and this infliction was threatened as a punishment on the daughters of Zion for their wanton haughtiness (Isa **3** 17). In Middle Eng., "scab" is used for itch or mange, and as a term of opprobrium, as in Greene, *Bacon and Bungay*, 35, 1591.

Alex. Macalister

SCABBARD, skab′ard, **SHEATH,** shēth. See Armor, III, 5; War, 9.

SCAFFOLD, skaf′old (כִּיּוֹר, *kiyyōr*): The Eng. word is used once of Solomon's "brazen scaffold" on which he knelt at the dedication of the temple (2 Ch **6** 13).

SCALE, skāl. See Siege, 4, (*e*); Weights and Measures.

SCALES, skālz ([1] קַשְׂקֶשֶׂת, *ḳasḳeseth*, "fish-scales"; [2] מְגִנָּה, *m^{e}ghinnāh*, מָגֵן, *māghēn*, "scales of the crocodile"; [3] **λεπίς**, *lepís*, with vb. **λεπίζω**, *lepízō*, "scale away" [Tob **3** 17; **11** 13]): (1) The first Heb word *ḳasḳeseth* means the imbricated scales of fish, which together with the dorsal fin were a distinguishing mark of all fish allowed as food to the Israelite (Lev **11** 9 ff; Dt **14** 9 f). In the **figurative** sense the word is used of a coat of mail (1 S **17** 5.38). (2) *M^{e}ghinnāh* from *māghēn*, lit. "a buckler" or "small shield" (2 Ch **23** 9; Jer **46** 3), is used in the description of the crocodile (see Leviathan) for the horny scales or scutes imbedded in the skin, not imbricated upon it (Job **41** 15 [Heb ver 7]). (3) The Gr *lepis*, which in classical language has a much wider range of meaning than the above Heb words ("rind," "husk," "shell," "fish-scale," "scale of snake," "flake of metal and of snow," etc), is found in the NT description of St. Paul's recovery from temporary blindness, "And straightway there fell from his eyes as it were scales, and he received his sight" (Acts **9** 18). There is nothing in the words of the sacred text which compels us to think of literal scales. (In Tob, however, a literal flaking-off of foreign substance is meant.) We have here rather a description of the sensation which terminated the three days' period of blindness which the apostle suffered after his meeting with the risen Lord on the road to Damascus. The apostle himself does not use this expression in his own graphic description of the same experience: "In that very hour I looked upon him" (**22** 13). The phrase has, however, come into Eng., for we speak of "scales falling from one's eyes" when we mean a sudden illumination or remembrance or a dissipation of harassing doubt.

In Isa **40** 12; RV Prov **16** 11 for פֶּלֶס, *peleṣ*, in the sense of "instrument for weighing." See Balance.

H. L. E. Luering

SCALL, skôl (נֶתֶק, *netheḳ;* **θραῦσμα**, *thraúsma*): This only occurs in Lev **13** and **14** where it is used 14 t to describe bald or scaly patches of eruption on the skin. Such patches are generally the result of the action of parasitic organisms. The common form known now as scalled head is produced by a microscopic plant, *Achōrion schoenleinii*. In Old and Middle Eng., scall was used for scabbiness of the head (Chaucer and Spenser). See also Skeat, *Concise Etymol. Dict. of Eng. Language*.

SCAPE-GOAT, skāp′gōt. See Azazel.

SCARLET, skär′let. See Colors; Dyeing.

SCARLET (WORM) (תּוֹלַעַת שָׁנִי, *tōla'ath shānī* [Ex **25** 4, etc]): *Cermes vermilio*, a scale insect from which a red dye is obtained. See Color; Dyeing; Worm.

SCATTERED ABROAD, skat′ẽrd a-brôd′. See Dispersion.

SCENT, sent: (1) In Hos **14** 7, "The scent [m "his memorial"] thereof shall be as the wine of Lebanon." "Scent" is used for זֵכֶר, *zekher* (so MT, but the pointing is uncertain), properly "memorial," whence RVm. The Eng. tr comes through the LXX which took *zkr* as "offering of sweet savor," and so "sweet savor." For the "wine of Lebanon" see Wine. If this tr is not right, the alternative is "memorial" in the sense of "renown." (2) Job **14** 9; Jer **48** 11 for רֵיחַ, *rē^{a}ḥ*, "odor." "Scent" of the water in Job **14** 9 is poetic for "contact with." (3) Wisd **11** 18 AV has "filthy scents of scattered smoke," where "scent" is used in the obsolete sense of "disagreeable odor." The tr is, however, very loose, and "scents" is a gloss; RV "noisome smoke."

Burton Scott Easton

SCEPTRE, SCEPTER, sep′tẽr (שֵׁבֶט, *shēbheṭ*, שַׁרְבִיט, *sharbhīṭ*, expanded form in Est **4** 11; **5** 2; **8** 4; **ῥάβδος**, *rhábdos* [Ad Est **15** 11; He **1** 8], σκῆπτρος, *skēptros*): A rod or mace used by a sovereign as a symbol of royal authority. The Heb *shēbheṭ* is the ordinary word for rod or club, and is used of an ordinary rod (cf 2 S **7** 14), of the shepherd's crook (Ps **23** 4), scribe's baton or marshal's staff (Jgs **5** 14), as well as of the symbol of royalty. Its symbolism may be connected with the use of the *shēbheṭ* for protection (2 S **23** 21; Ps **23** 4) or for punishment (Isa **10** 24; **30** 31). It is used with reference to the royal line descended from Judah (Gen **49** 10), and **figuratively** of sovereignty in general and possibly of conquest (Nu **24** 17, in Israel; Isa **14** 5, in Babylonia; Am **1** 5.8, in Syria, among Philis; Zec **10** 11, in Egypt), the disappearance or cutting off of him that holdeth the scepter being tantamount to loss of national independence. The kingship of Jeh is spoken of as a scepter (Ps **45** 6 [Heb ver 7] quoted in He **1** 8). The manner of using the scepter by an oriental monarch is suggested in the act of Ahasuerus, who holds it out to Esther as a mark of favor. The subject touches the top of it, perhaps simply as an act of homage or possibly to indicate a desire to be heard. The scepter of Ahasuerus is spoken of as "golden" (Est **5** 2), but it is probable that scepters were ordinarily made of straight branches (*maṭeh*) of certain kinds of vines (Ezk **19** 11.14).

It is sometimes difficult to determine whether the word *shēbheṭ* is used in figurative passages in the sense of scepter or merely in the ordinary sense of staff (e.g. Ps **125** 3, AV "rod," RV and ARV "sceptre" [of the wicked]; Ps **2** 9, "rod of iron"; Prov **22** 8, "rod of his wrath"). Another word, *m^eḥōḳēḳ*, lit. "prescribing" (person or thing), formerly tr^d uniformly "lawgiver," is now generally taken, on the basis of parallelism, to mean "sceptre" in four poetic passages (Gen **49** 10, "ruler's staff" to avoid repetition; Nu **21** 18; Ps **60** 7; **108** 8).

NATHAN ISAACS

SCEVA, sē'va (Σκευᾶ, *Skeuá*): A Jew, a chief priest, resident in Ephesus, whose seven sons were exorcists (Acts **19** 14 ff). Ewald regards the name as being Heb *sh^ekhabhyāh*. He was not an officiating priest, as there were only synagogues in Asia Minor. He may have belonged to a high-priestly family, or perhaps at one time he had been at the head of one of the 24 courses in the temple.

In the narrative the construction is loose. There were seven sons (ver 14), and it would appear (ver 16) that in this particular case all were present. But (ver 16) the demon-possessed man overpowered "both of them." *TR* gets over the difficulty by omitting "both," but ℵABD, so Tisch., WH, Soden, and best critics, retain the difficult reading. The explanation is that ver 14 states the custom: "who did this" being *hoi toúto poioúntes*, "who used to do this." Vs 15 and 16 state a particular case in which two took part, but the incident is introduced in a careless manner.

Ewald would translate *amphotérōn* as "in both sides," but this is impossible. Baur understood "disciples" for "sons." *D* and *Syr* have an interesting expansion which Blass considers original (ver 14): "Among whom also the sons [*Syr* 'seven'] of a certain Sceva, a priest, wished to do the same, [who] were in the custom of exorcising such. And entering into the demon-possessed man they began to call upon the Name, saying, 'We charge you by Jesus whom Paul preaches to come out.' "

S. F. HUNTER

SCHISM, siz'm (σχίσμα, *schísma*): Only in 1 Cor **12** 25. The same Gr word, lit. "a split," is tr^d "rent" in Mt **9** 16; Mk **2** 21; and "division" in Jn **7** 43; **9** 16; **10** 19. It designates "a separation," not from, but within, the church, interfering with the harmonious coördination and coöperation of the members described in the preceding verses (1 Cor **12** 18 ff). The ecclesiastical meaning is that of a break from a church organization, that may or may not be connected with a doctrinal dissent.

SCHOOL, skōōl (σχολή, *scholē*). See TYRANNUS.

SCHOOLMASTER, skōōl'mas-tēr: Gal **3** 24 f AV reads: "The law was our schoolmaster to bring us unto Christ, that we might be justified by faith. But after that faith is come, we are no longer under a schoolmaster." "Schoolmaster" is a tr of παιδαγωγός, *paidagōgós*, lit. "child-leader." This *paidagōgos* was not a teacher but a slave, to whom in wealthy families the general oversight of a boy was committed. It was his duty to accompany his charge to and from school, never to lose sight of him in public, to prevent association with objectionable companions, to inculcate moral lessons at every opportunity, etc. He was a familiar figure in the streets, and the (sour) "face of a *paidagōgos*" and "to follow one like a *paidagōgos*" were proverbial expressions. Naturally, to the average boy the *paidagōgos* must have represented the incorporation of everything objectionable. Hence St. Paul's figure may be paraphrased: "The law was a *paidagōgos*, necessary but irksome, to direct us until the time of Christ. Then was the time of our spiritual coming-of-age, so that the control of the *paidagōgos* ceased." The word *paidagōgos* was taken over into Aram. at an early date, and St. Paul's language, which is hardly that of a mere adult observer, suggests that he had had personal experience with the institution. Wealthy and intensely orthodox Jewish parents living in a gentile city may well have adopted such a precaution for the protection of their children.

No Eng. word renders *paidagōgos* adequately. "Schoolmaster" is quite wrong, but RV's "tutor" (cf 1 Cor **4** 15) is little better in modern Eng.

BURTON SCOTT EASTON

SCHOOLS OF THE PROPHETS. See EDUCATION; PROPHETS.

SCIENCE, sī'ens: This word as found in AV means simply "knowledge." "Science" occurs in AV only in two places, Dnl **1** 4, "children . . . understanding science" (יֹדְעֵי דַעַת, *yōdh^eʿē dhaʿath*, "those who understand science"). The meaning of the term here is "knowledge," "wisdom." The only other occurrence of "science" is in the NT (1 Tim **6** 20, "avoiding . . . . oppositions of science falsely so called," τῆς ψευδωνύμου γνώσεως, *tēs pseudōnúmou gnṓseōs*, "the falsely called *gnōsis*"). "Science" is the tr of the Gr *gnōsis*, which in the NT is usually rendered "knowledge." The science here referred to was a higher knowledge of Christian and Divine things, which false teachers alleged that they possessed, and of which they boasted. It was an incipient form of Gnosticism, and it prevailed to a considerable extent in the churches of proconsular Asia, e.g. in Colossae and Ephesus. Timothy is put on his guard against the teaching of this *gnōsis* falsely so called, for it set itself in opposition to the gospel. See GNOSTICISM.

"Science" in the modern sense of the word, as the discovery and orderly classification and exposition of the phenomena and of the laws of Nature, is not found either in the OT or the NT unless the passage in Dnl be interpreted as meaning the scientific knowledge which the learned men of Babylon possessed of mathematics and astronomy, etc. See also Acts **7** 22. To the Heb mind all natural phenomena meant the working of the hand of God in the world, directly and immediately, without the intervention of any secondary laws.

JOHN RUTHERFURD

SCIMITAR, sim'i-tar, -tẽr (**ἀκινάκη,** *akinákē*): Formerly given as "fauchion" in AV Jth **13** 6; **16** 9, the weapon which Judith took down from the rail of the bed at Holofernes' head, and with which she severed his head from his body.

SCOFF, skof, **SCOFFER,** skof'ẽr: The vb. indicates the manifestation of contempt by insulting words or actions; it combines bitterness with ridicule. It is much more frequent in RV than in AV, replacing "scorn" of the latter in Ps **1** 1; Prov **1** 22, etc. "Scorn" refers rather to an inner emotion based on a sense of superiority; "scoff," to the outward expression of this emotion.

SCORN, skôrn: Fox Talbot connects this Eng. word with the Danish *skarn*, "dirt," "ordure," "mud," "mire." As distinguished from such words as "mock," "deride," "scoff," all of which refer specifically to the various ways in which scorn finds outward expression, scorn itself denotes a subjective state or reaction.

Further, this state or reaction is not simple but complex. It includes a sense of superiority, resentment, and aversion. This reaction occurs when one is confronted with a person or a proposition that by challenging certain things for itself evokes a vivid sense of one's own superiority and awakens mingled resentment, repulsion and contempt by the hollowness of its claims and its intrinsic inferiority or worse. Scorn is a hotter, fiercer emotion than disdain or contempt. It is obvious that *scorn* may—indeed, it not uncommonly does—arise in connection with an ungrounded, arrogant sense of self-esteem.

The word, outside of the phrase "laugh to scorn," is found only in the OT, and then only 4 t (Est **3** 6; AV Ps **44** 13; **79** 4; Hab **1** 10), and it represents three different Heb words for none of which it is a suitable rendering. The two words "thought scorn" in Est **3** 6 represent but one in Heb, viz. *bāzāh*, for which "disdain" would be a nearer equivalent. In Hab **1** 10 AV the word trd "scorn" is *miṣḥāḳ*, "an object of laughter," "laughing-stock." In Ps **44** 13; **79** 4 the Heb word is *la'agh* from a root, probably meaning "to stutter," "stammer," for which "mocking" is a better Eng. equivalent. In AV Job **34** 7; Ps **123** 4, *la'agh* is rendered "scorning" (the rendering given in Prov **1** 22 to *lāçōn*, a word from a totally different root and one much more nearly approximating the fundamental idea of the Eng. word "scorn." In Prov **29** 8 and Isa **28** 14 *lāçōn* is rendered "scornful").

As a vb. the word is the tr given to *lā'agh*, "to mock" (2 K **19** 21 ‖ Isa **37** 22; Job **22** 19; Neh **2** 19; Ps **22** 7, "all laugh to scorn"); *ḳālas* = "to scoff" (Ezk **16** 31, m "Gr *scoffeth*," but text still "scorneth"); for the noun *çeḥōḳ*, "laughter" (Ezk **23** 32); *sāḥaḳ* = "to laugh," "laugh at" (Job **39** 7.18; 2 Ch **30** 10), with the noun *seḥōḳ*, "laugh to scorn" (RV "laughing-stock," Job **12** 4); *lūç* = "to scoff" (as used in ethical and religious connections) (Job **16** 20; Prov **3** 34; **9** 12, all "scoff" in RV); in Prov **19** 28 RV, not happily, "mock at." RV is warranted in substituting "scoff" for "scorn" because the context indicates some form of outward expression of the scorn.

RV always (except Job **12** 4; Sir **6** 4; 1 Macc **10** 70) retains "laugh to scorn" (2 K **19** 21; 2 Ch **30** 10; Neh **2** 19; Job **22** 19; Ps **22** 7; Isa **37** 22; Ezk **16** 31; **23** 32; 2 Esd **2** 21; Jth **12** 12; Wisd **4** 18; Sir **7** 11; **13** 7; **20** 17; Mt **9** 24; Mk **5** 40; Lk **8** 53). The vb. in Apoc and the NT is usually καταγελάω, *katageláō*, but in Wisd **4** 1 ἐκγελάω, *ekgeláō;* in Sir **13** 7 καταμωκάομαι, *katamōkáomai;* and in 2 Esd **2** 21 *inrideo*. In addition "scorn" is retained in Est **3** 6; Job **39** 7.18; 2 Esd **8** 56 (*contemno*). In Prov **19** 28 "scorn" is changed to "mock at," but elsewhere invariably to "scoff."

Scorner is the tr of the participle of *lūç*, and once of the participle of *lāçaç*. For "scorner" RV everywhere substitutes—properly—"scoffer." Outside of Prov (and Hos **7** 5) the word is to be found only in Ps **1** 2. The force of the word has been well indicated by Cheyne, who says that the "scorner [scoffer] is one who despises that which is holy and avoids the company of the noble 'wise men,' but yet in his own vain way seeks for truth; his character is marked by arrogance as that of the wise is characterized by devout caution."

W. M. McPheeters

SCORPION, skôr'pi-un (עַקְרָב, *'aḳrābh;* cf Arab. عَقْرَب, *'aḳrab*, "scorpion"; מַעֲלֵה עַקְרַבִּים, *ma'ălēh 'aḳrabbīm*, "the ascent of Akrabbim"; **σκορπίος,** *skorpíos*. Note that the Gr and Heb may be akin; cf, omitting the vowels, *'krb* and *skrp*: In Dt **8** 15, we have, "who led thee through the great and terrible wilderness, wherein were fiery serpents [*nāḥāsh sārāph*] and scorpions [*'aḳrābh*]." Rehoboam (1 K **12** 11.14; 2 Ch **10** 11.14) says, "My father chastised you with whips, but I will chastise you with scorpions." Ezekiel is told to prophesy to the children of Israel (**2** 6), and "Be not afraid of them, neither be afraid of their words, though briers and thorns are with thee, and thou dost dwell among scorpions." "The ascent of Akrabbim," the north end of *Wâdi-ul-'Arabah*, S. of the Dead Sea, is mentioned as a boundary 3 t (Nu **34** 4; Josh **15** 3; Jgs **1** 36). Jesus says to the Seventy (Lk **10** 19), "Behold, I have given you authority to tread upon serpents and scorpions," and again in Lk **11** 12 He says, "Or if he shall ask an egg, will he give him a scorpion?"

Note that we have here three doublets, the loaf and the stone, the fish and the serpent, and the egg and the scorpion, whereas in the passage in Mt (**7** 9 f) we have only the loaf and stone and the fish and serpent. *EB* (s.v. "Scorpion") ingeniously seeks to bring Lk into nearer agreement with Mt by omitting from Lk the second doublet, i.e. the fish and the serpent, instancing several texts as authority for the omission, and reading ὄψον, *ópson*, "fish," for ᾠόν, *ōón*, "egg."

In Rev **9** 2–10 there come out of the smoke of the abyss winged creatures ("locusts," ἀκρίδες, *akrídes*) like war-horses with crowns of gold, with the faces of men, hair of women, teeth of lions, breastplates of iron, and with stinging tails like scorpions. In Ecclus **26** 7 it is said of an evil wife, "He that taketh hold of her is as one that graspeth a scorpion." In 1 Macc **6** 51 we find mention of "pieces [σκορπίδια, *skorpídia*, diminutive of *skorpios*] to cast darts." In Plutarch *skorpios* is used in the same sense (Liddell and Scott, s.v. σκορπιος).

In the passage cited from Dt, and probably also in the name "ascent of Akrabbim," we find references to the abundance of scorpions, esp. in the warmer parts of the country. Though there is a Gr proverb, "Look for a scorpion under every stone," few would agree with the categorical statement of Tristram (*NHB*) that "every third stone is sure to conceal one." Nevertheless, campers and people sleeping on the ground need to exercise care in order to avoid their stings, which, though often exceedingly painful for several hours, are seldom fatal.

Scorpion.

Scorpions are not properly insects, but belong with spiders, mites and ticks to the *Arachnidae*. The scorpions of Pal are usually 2 or 3 in. long. The short cephalothorax bears a powerful pair of jaws, two long limbs terminating with pincers, which make the creature look like a small crayfish or lobster, and four pairs of legs. The rest of the body consists of the abdomen, a broad part continuous with the cephalothorax, and a slender part forming the long tail which terminates with the sting. The tail is usually carried curved over the back and is used for stinging the prey into insensibility. Scorpions feed mostly on insects for which they lie in wait. The scorpion family is remarkable for having existed with very little change from the Silurian age to the present time.

It does not seem necessary to consider that the

words of Rehoboam (1 K **12** 11, etc) refer to a whip that was called a scorpion, but rather that as the sting of a scorpion is worse than the lash of a whip, so his treatment would be harsher than his father's.

Alfred Ely Day

SCORPIONS, skôr′pi-unz, **CHASTISING WITH.** See Punishments, 3, (17); Scorpion.

SCOURGE, skûrj, **SCOURGING,** skûr′jing (**μάστιξ,** *mástix,* **μαστιγόω,** *mastigóō;* in Acts **22** 25 **μαστίζω,** *mastízō,* in Mk **15** 15 ‖ Mt **27** 26 **φραγελλόω,** *phragellóō*): A Rom implement for severe bodily punishment. Horace calls it *horribile flagellum.* It consisted of a handle, to which several cords or leather thongs were affixed, which were weighted with jagged pieces of bone or metal, to make the blow more painful and effective. It is comparable, in its horrid effects, only with the Russian knout. The victim was tied to a post (Acts **22** 25) and the blows were applied to the back and loins, sometimes even, in the wanton cruelty of the executioner, to the face and the bowels. In the tense position of the body, the effect can easily be imagined. So hideous was the punishment that the victim usually fainted and not rarely died under it. Eusebius draws a horribly realistic picture of the torture of scourging (*HE,* IV, 15). By its application secrets and confessions were wrung from the victim (Acts **22** 24). It usually preceded capital punishment (Livy xxxiii.36). It was illegal to apply the *flagellum* to a Rom citizen (Acts **22** 25), since the Porcian and Sempronian laws, 248 and 123 BC, although these laws were not rarely broken in the provinces (Tac. *Hist.* iv.27; Cic. *Verr.* v.6, 62; Jos, *BJ,* II, xiv, 9). As among the Russians today, the number of blows was not usually fixed, the severity of the punishment depending entirely on the commanding officer. In the punishment of Jesus, we are reminded of the words of Ps **129** 3. Among the Jews the punishment of flagellation was well known since the Egyp days, as the monuments abundantly testify. The word "scourge" is used in Lev **19** 20, but ARV translates "punished," the original word *biḳḳōreth* expressing the idea of investigation. Dt **25** 3 fixed the mode of a Jewish flogging and limits the number of blows to 40. Apparently the flogging was administered by a rod. The Syrians reintroduced true scourging into Jewish life, when Antiochus Epiphanes forced them by means of it to eat swine's flesh (2 Macc **6** 30; **7** 1). Later it was legalized by Jewish law and became customary (Mt **10** 17; **23** 34; Acts **22** 19; **26** 11), but the traditional limitation of the number of blows was still preserved. Says Paul in his "foolish boasting": "in stripes above measure," "of the Jews five times received I forty stripes save one," distinguishing it from the "beatings with rods," thrice repeated (2 Cor **11** 23–25).

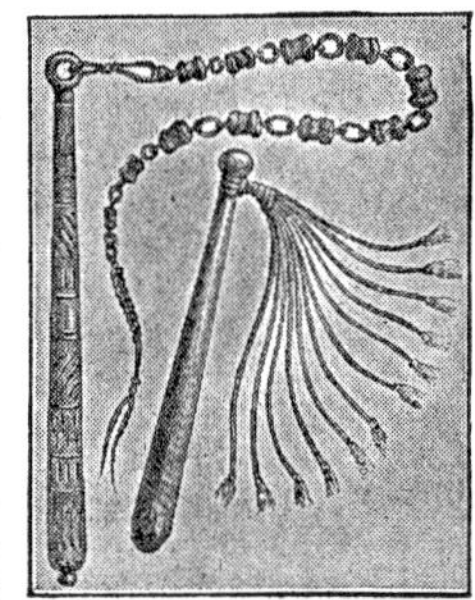
Roman Scourges.

The other OT references (Job **5** 21; **9** 23; Isa **10** 26; **28** 15.18 [שׁוֹט, *shōt*]; Josh **23** 13 [שֹׁטֵט, *shōṭēṭ*]) are **figurative** for "affliction." Notice the curious mixture of metaphors in the phrase "overflowing scourge" (Isa **28** 15.18).

Henry E. Dosker

SCRABBLE, skrab′'l: Occurs only in 1 S **21** 13, as the tr of תָּוָה, *tāwāh:* "David . . . . feigned himself mad and scrabbled on the doors of the gate." "To scrabble" (modern Eng. "scrawl") is here to make unmeaning marks; *tāwāh* means "to make a mark" from *tāw,* "a mark," esp. as a cross (Ezk **9** 4), a signature (Job **31** 35, see RV), the name of the letter ת, originally made in the form of a cross; RVm has "made marks"; but LXX has *tumpanízō,* "to beat as a drum," which the Vulg, Ewald, Driver and others follow ("beat upon" or "drummed on the doors of the city," which seems more probable).

SCREECH, skrēch, **OWL.** See Night-Monster.

SCRIBES, skrībz: The existence of law leads necessarily to a profession whose business is the study and knowledge of the law; at any rate, if the law is extensive and complicated. At the time of Ezra and probably for some time after, this was chiefly the business of the priests. Ezra was both priest and scholar (סֹפֵר, *ṣōphēr*). It was chiefly in the interest of the priestly cult that the most important part of the Pent was written. The priests were therefore also in the first instance the scholars and the guardians of the Law; but in the course of time this was changed. The more highly esteemed the Law became in the eyes of the people, the more its study and interpretation became a life-work by itself, and thus there developed a class of scholars who, though not priests, devoted themselves assiduously to the Law. These became known as the scribes, that is, the professional students of the Law. During the Hellenistic period, the priests, esp. those of the upper class, became tainted with the Hellenism of the age and frequently turned their attention to paganistic culture, thus neglecting the Law of their fathers more or less and arousing the scribes to opposition. Thus the scribes and not the priests were now the zealous defenders of the Law, and hence were the true teachers of the people. At the time of Christ, this distinction was complete. The scribes formed a solid profession which held undisputed sway over the thought of the people. In the NT they are usually called γραμματεῖς, *grammateís,* i.e. "students of the Scriptures," "scholars," corresponding to the Heb סֹפְרִים, *ṣōpherīm* = *homines literati,* those who make a profession of literary studies, which, in this case, of course, meant chiefly the Law. Besides this general designation, we also find the specific word νομικοί, *nomikoí,* i.e. "students of the Law," "lawyers" (Mt **22** 35; Lk **7** 30; **10** 25; **11** 45.52; **14** 3); and in so far as they not only know the Law but also teach it they are called νομοδιδάσκαλοι, *nomodidáskaloi,* "doctors of the Law" (Lk **5** 17; Acts **5** 34).

The extraordinary honors bestowed on these scholars on the part of the people are expressed in their honorary titles. Most common was the appellative "rabbi" = "my lord" (Mt **23** 7 and otherwise). This word of polite address gradually became a title. The word "rabboni" (Mk **10** 51; Jn **20** 16) is an extensive form, and was employed by the disciples to give expression to their veneration of Christ. In the Gr NT "rabbi" is trd as κύριε, *kúrie* (Mt **8** 2.6.8.21.25 and otherwise), or διδάσκαλε, *didáskale* (Mt **8** 19 and otherwise), in Lk by ἐπιστάτα, *epistáta* (Lk **5** 5; **8** 24.45; **9** 33.49; **17** 13). Besides these, we find πατήρ, *patḗr,* "father," and καθηγήτης, *kathēgḗtēs,* "teacher" (Mt **23** 9 f).

From their students the rabbis demanded honors even surpassing those bestowed on parents. "Let the honor of thy friend border on the honor of thy teacher, and the honor of thy teacher on the fear of God" (*'Ābhōth* **4** 12). "The honor of thy teacher must surpass the honor bestowed on thy father; for son and father are both in duty bound to honor the teacher" (*Kerīthōth* **6** 9). Everywhere the rabbis demanded the position of first rank (Mt **23** 6 f; Mk **12** 38 f; Lk **11** 43; **20** 46). Their dress equaled that of the nobility. They wore στολαί, *stolaí,* "tunics," and these were the mark of the upper class.

Since the scribes were lawyers (see LAWYER), much of their time was occupied in teaching and in judicial functions, and both these activities must be pursued gratuitously. Rabbi Zadok said: "Make the knowledge of the Law neither a crown in which to glory nor a spade with which to dig." Hillel used to say: "He who employs the crown [of the Law] for external purposes shall dwindle." That the judge should not receive presents or bribes was written in the Law (Ex **23** 8; Dt **16** 19); hence the Mish said: "If anyone accept pay for rendering judgment, his judgment is null and void." The rabbis were therefore obliged to make their living by other means. Some undoubtedly had inherited wealth; others pursued a handicraft besides their study of the Law. Rabbi Gamaliel II emphatically advised the pursuit of a business in addition to the pursuit of the Law. It is well known that the apostle Paul kept up his handicraft even after he had become a preacher of the gospel (Acts **18** 3; **20** 34; 1 Cor **4** 12; **9** 6; 2 Cor **11** 7; 1 Thess **2** 9; 2 Thess **3** 8), and the same is reported of many rabbis. But in every instance the pursuit of the Law is represented as the worthier, and warning is given not to overestimate the value of the ordinary avocation. It was a saying of Hillel: "He that devotes himself to trade will not become wise." The principle of gratuity was probably carried out in practice only in connection with the judicial activity of the scribes; hardly in connection with their work as teachers. Even the Gospels, in spite of the admonition that the disciples should give without pay because they had received without pay (Mt **10** 8), nevertheless also state that the workman is worthy of his hire (Mt **10** 10; Lk **10** 7); and Paul (1 Cor **9** 14) states it as his just due that he receive his livelihood from those to whom he preaches the gospel, even though he makes use of this right only in exceptional cases (1 Cor **9** 3–18; 2 Cor **11** 8.9; Gal **6** 6; Phil **4** 10.18). Since this appears to have been the thought of the times, we are undoubtedly justified in assuming that the Jewish teachers of the Law also demanded pay for their services. Indeed, the admonitions above referred to, not to make instruction in the Law the object of self-interest, lead to the conclusion that gratuity was not the rule; and in Christ's philippics against the scribes and Pharisees He makes special mention of their greed (Mk **12** 40; Lk **16** 14; **20** 47). Hence, even though they ostensibly gave instruction in the Law gratuitously, they must have practised methods by which they indirectly secured their fees.

Naturally the place of chief influence for the scribes up to the year 70 AD was Judaea. But not only there were they to be found. Wherever the zeal for the law of the fathers was a perceptible force, they were indispensable; hence we find them also in Galilee (Lk **5** 17) and in the Diaspora. In the Jewish epitaphs in Rome, dating from the latter days of the empire, *grammateis* are frequently mentioned; and the Bab scribes of the 5th and 6th cents. were the authors of the most monumental work of rabbinical Judaism—the Talmud.

Since the separation of the Pharisaic and the Sadducean tendencies in Judaism, the scribes generally belonged to the Pharisaic class; for this latter is none other than the party which recognized the interpretations or "traditions" which the scribes in the course of time had developed out of the body of the written Law and enforced upon the people as the binding rule of life. Since, however, "scribes" are merely "students of the Law," there must also have been scribes of the Sadducee type; for it is not to be imagined that this party, which recognized only the written Law as binding, should not have had some opposing students in the other class. Indeed, various passages of the NT which speak of the "scribes of the Pharisees" (Mk **2** 16; Lk **5** 30; Acts **23** 9) indicate that there were also "scribes of the Sadducees."

Under the reign and leadership of the scribes, it became the ambition of every Israelite to know more or less of the Law. The aim of education in family, school and synagogue was to make the entire people a people of the Law. Even the common laborer should know what was written in the Law; and not only know it, but also do it. His entire life should be governed according to the norm of the Law, and, on the whole, this purpose was realized in a high degree. Jos avers: "Even though we be robbed of our riches and our cities and our other goods, the Law remains our possession forever. And no Jew can be so far removed from the land of his fathers nor will he fear a hostile commander to such a degree that he would not fear his Law more than his commander." So loyal were the majority of the Jews toward their Law that they would gladly endure the tortures of the rack and even death for it. This frame of mind was due almost wholly to the systematic and persistent instruction of the scribes.

The motive underlying this enthusiasm for the Law was the belief in Divine retribution in the strictest judicial sense. The prophetic idea of a covenant which God had made with His select people was interpreted purely in the judicial sense. The covenant was a contract through which both parties were mutually bound. The people are bound to observe the Divine Law literally and conscientiously; and, in return for this, God is in duty bound to render the promised reward in proportion to the services rendered. This applies to the people as a whole as well as to the individual. Services and reward must always stand in mutual relation to each other. He who renders great services may expect from the justice of God that he will receive great returns as his portion, while, on the other hand, every transgression also must be followed by its corresponding punishment.

The results corresponded to the motives. Just as the motives in the main were superficial, so the results were an exceedingly shallow view of religious and moral life. Religion was reduced to legal formalism. All religious and moral life was dragged down to the level of law, and this must necessarily lead to the following results: (1) The individual is governed by a norm, the application of which could have only evil results when applied in this realm. Law has the purpose of regulating the relations of men to each other according to certain standards. Its object is not the individual, but only the body of society. In the law, the individual must find the proper rule for his conduct toward society as an organism. This is a matter of obligation and of government on the part of society. But religion is not a matter of government; where it is found, it is a matter of freedom, of choice, and of conduct. (2) By reducing the practice of religion to the form of law, all acts are placed on a par with each other. The motives are no longer taken into consideration, but only the deed itself. (3) From this it follows that the highest ethical attainment was the formal satisfaction of the Law, which naturally led to finical literalism. (4) Finally, moral life must, under such circumstances, lose its unity and be split up into manifold precepts and duties. Law always affords opportunity for casuistry, and it was the development of this in the guidance of the Jewish religious life through the "precepts of the elders" which called forth Christ's repeated denunciation of the work of the scribes.

FRANK E. HIRSCH

SCRIP, skrip: A word connected with "scrap," and meaning a "bag," either as made from a "scrap" (of skin) or as holding "scraps" (of food, etc). AV has "scrip" in 1 S **17** 40 and 6 t in NT; ERV has "wallet" in the NT, but retains "scrip" in 1 S **17** 40; ARV has "wallet" throughout. See BAG.

SCRIPTURE, skrip'tūr (ἡ γραφή, *hē graphḗ*, pl. αἱ γραφαί, *hai graphai*): The word means "writing." In the OT it occurs in AV only once, "the scripture of truth," in Dnl **10** 21, where it is more correctly rendered in RV, "the writing of truth." The reference is not to Holy Scripture, but to the book in which are inscribed God's purposes. In the NT, "scripture" and "scriptures" stand regularly for the OT sacred books regarded as "inspired" (2 Tim **3** 16), "the oracles of God" (Rom **3** 2). Cf on this usage Mt **21** 42; **22** 29; Mk **12** 10; Lk **4** 21; **24** 27.32.45; Jn **5** 39; **10** 35; Acts **8** 32; **17** 2.11; Rom **15** 4; **16** 26, etc; in Rom **1** 2, "holy scriptures." See BIBLE. The expression "holy scriptures" in 2 Tim **3** 15 AV represents different words (*hierá grámmata*) and is properly rendered in RV "sacred writings." In 2 Pet **3** 16, the term "scriptures" is extended to the Epp. of Paul. In Jas **4** 5, the words occur: "Think ye that the scripture speaketh in vain? Doth the spirit which he made to dwell in us long unto envying?" The passage is probably rather a summary of Scripture teaching than intended as a direct quotation. Others (e.g. Westcott) think the word is used in a wide sense of a Christian hymn. JAMES ORR

SCRIPTURES, skrip'tūrz, **SEARCH THE.** See SEARCH THE SCRIPTURES.

SCROLL, skrōl. See ROLL.

SCUM, skum (חֶלְאָה, *ḥel'āh;* LXX ἰός, *iós*, "poison" or "verdigris"; cf Plato *Rep.* 609*a*): The word is only found in Ezk **24** 6.11.12, where RV translates it "rust." The fact, however, that the caldron is of brass and therefore not liable to rust, and the astonishment expressed that the fire did not remove it (ver 12), would seem to point to the preferability of the tr "scum," the residue of dirt adhering to the caldron from previous use.

SCURVY, skûr'vi (גָּרָב, *gārābh;* ψώρα ἀγρία, *psṓra agría* [Lev **21** 20; **22** 22]): This word is used to denote an itchy, scaly disease of the scalp, probably any of the parasitic diseases which are known as *tinea, porrigo* or *impetigo*. These cases have no relation whatever to the disease now known as *scorbutus* or scurvy. The name was probably derived from its scaliness, and the old Gr physicians believed these diseases to be peculiarly intractable.

The name "Gareb" is used in Jer **31** 39 as the place-name of a hill at or near the southeastern corner of Jerus, probably from the bare roughness of the surface of its slope at the southern end of the *Wâdy er-Rabābi*. Another hill of this name is mentioned near Shiloh in the Talm, and the name is given to one of David's warriors (2 S **23** 38).

Scurvy etymologically means any condition of scaliness of skin which can be scraped off, such as dandruff. ALEX. MACALISTER

SCYTHIANS, sith'i-anz (οἱ Σκύθαι, *hoi Skúthai*): The word does not occur in the Heb of the OT, but LXX of Jgs **1** 27 inserts Σκυθῶν πόλις, *Skuthōn pólis* (Scythopolis), in explanation, as being the same as Beth-shean. The same occurs in Apoc (Jth **3** 10; 1 Macc **12** 29), and the S. as a people in 2 Macc **4** 47, and the adj. in 3 Macc **7** 5. The people are also mentioned in the NT (Col **3** 11), where, as in Macc, the fact that they were barbarians is implied. This is clearly set forth in classical writers, and the description of them given by Herodotus in book iv of his history represents a race of savages, inhabiting a region of rather indefinite boundaries, north of the Black and Caspian seas and the Caucasus Mountains. They were nomads who neither plowed nor sowed (iv.19), moving about in wagons and carrying their dwellings with them (ib, 46); they had the most filthy habits and never washed in water (ib, 75); they drank the blood of the first enemy killed in battle, and made napkins of the scalps and drinking bowls of the skulls of the slain (ib, 64–65). Their deities were many of them identified with those of the Greeks, but the most characteristic rite was the worship of the naked sword (ib, 62), and they sacrificed every hundredth man taken in war to this deity. War was their chief business, and they were a terrible scourge to the nations of Western Asia. They broke through the barrier of the Caucasus in 632 BC and swept down like a swarm of locusts upon Media and Assyria, turning the fruitful fields into a desert; pushing across Mesopotamia, they ravaged Syria and were about to invade Egypt when Psammitichus I, who was besieging Ashdod, bought them off by rich gifts, but they remained in Western Asia for 28 years, according to Herodotus. It is supposed that a company of them settled in Beth-shean, and from this circumstance it received the name **Scythopolis.** Various branches of the race appeared at different times, among the most noted of which were the PARTHIANS (q.v.). H. PORTER

SCYTHOPOLIS, sī-thop'ō-lis, si-thop'ō-lis. See BETH-SHEAN.

SEA, sē (יָם, *yām;* θάλασσα, *thálassa;* in Acts **27** 5 πέλαγος, *pélagos*): The Mediterranean is called *ha-yām ha-gādhōl*, "the great sea" (Nu **34** 6; Josh **1** 4; Ezk **47** 10, etc); *ha-yām hā-'aḥărōn*, "the hinder," or "western sea" (Dt **11** 24; **34** 2; Joel **2** 20; Zec **14** 8); *yām pelishtīm*, "the sea of the Philis" (Ex **23** 31); AV translates *yām yāphō'* in Ezr **3** 7 by "sea of Joppa," perhaps rightly.

The Dead Sea is called *yām ha-melaḥ*, "the Salt Sea" (Nu **34** 3; Dt **3** 17; Josh **3** 16, etc); *ha-yām ha-ḳadhmōnī*, "the east sea" (Ezk **47** 18; Joel **2** 20; Zec **14** 8); *yām hā-'ărābhāh*, "the sea of the Arabah" (Dt **3** 17; Josh **3** 16; **12** 3; 2 K **14** 25).

The Red Sea is called *yām ṣūph*, lit. "sea of weeds" (Ex **10** 19; Nu **14** 25; Dt **1** 1; Josh **2** 10; Jgs **11** 16; 1 K **9** 26; Neh **9** 9; Ps **106** 7; Jer **49** 21, etc); ἐρυθρὰ θάλασσα, *eruthrá thálassa*, lit. "red sea" (Wisd **19** 7; Acts **7** 36; He **11** 29); *yām miçrayim*, "the Egyp sea" (Isa **11** 15).

Yām is used of the Nile in Nah **3** 8 and probably also in Isa **19** 5, as in modern Arab. *baḥr*, "sea," is used of the Nile and its affluents. *Yām* is often used for "west" or "westward," as "look from the place where thou art, ... westward" (Gen **13** 14); "western border" (Nu **34** 6). *Yām* is used for "sea" in general (Ex **20** 11); also for "molten sea" of the temple (1 K **7** 23).

The Sea of Galilee is called *kinnereth*, "Chinnereth" (Nu **34** 11); *kinărōth*, "Chinneroth" (Josh **11** 2); *kinnerōth*, "Chinneroth" (1 K **15** 20); *yām kinnereth*, "the sea of Chinnereth" (Nu **34** 11; Josh **13** 27); *yām kinnerōth*, "the sea of Chinneroth" (Josh **12** 3); ἡ λίμνη Γεννησαρέτ, *hē límnē Gennēsarét*, "the lake of Gennesaret" (Lk **5** 1); and τὸ ὕδωρ Γεννησάρ, *tó húdōr Gennēsár*, "the water of Gennesar" (1 Macc **11** 67), from late Heb גִּנֵּסַר, *ginēṣar*, or גְּנֵיסַר, *genēṣar;* ἡ θάλασσα τῆς Γαλιλαίας, *hē thálassa tēs Galilaías*, "the sea of Galilee" (Mt **4** 18; **15** 29; Mk **1** 16; **7** 31; Jn **6** 1); ἡ θάλασσα τῆς Τιβεριάδος, *hē thálassa tēs Tiberiádos*, "the sea of Tiberias" (Jn **21** 1; cf Jn **6** 1).

In Jer **48** 32 we have *yām ya'zēr*, "the sea of Jazer." Jazer is a site E. of the Jordan, not satisfactorily identified (Nu **21** 32; **32** 1.3.35; Josh **13** 25; **21** 39; 2 S **24** 5; 1 Ch **6** 81; **26** 31; Isa **16** 8.9). See SEA OF JAZER.

In *midhbar yām*, "the wilderness of the sea" (Isa **21** 1), there may perhaps be a reference to the Pers Gulf. ALFRED ELY DAY

SEA, ADRIATIC, ā-dri-at'ic, ad-ri-at'ik. See ADRIA.

SEA, BRAZEN, brā'z'n. See SEA, THE MOLTEN.

SEA, DEAD; EASTERN, ēs'tērn. See DEAD SEA.

SEA, FORMER, fôr'mēr. See DEAD SEA; FORMER.

SEA, HINDER, hīn'dēr; **UTMOST,** ut'mōst; **UTTERMOST,** ut'ēr-mōst; **WESTERN,** wes'tērn. See MEDITERRANEAN SEA.

SEA, MEDITERRANEAN. See MEDITERRANEAN SEA.

SEA-MEW, sē'mū (שַׁחַף, *shaḥaph;* λάρος, *láros;* Lat *Larus canus*): The sea-gull. Used by modern translators in the list of abominations in the place of the cuckoo (Lev **11** 16; Dt **14** 15). It is very probable that the sea-gull comes closer to the bird intended than the CUCKOO (q.v.). The sea-gull is a "slender" bird, but not "lean" as the root *shaḥaph* implies. However, with its stretch of wing and restless flight it gives this impression. Gulls are common all along the Mediterranean coast and around the Sea of Galilee. They are thought to have more intelligence than the average bird, and to share with some eagles, hawks, vultures and the raven the knowledge that if they find a mollusk they cannot break they can carry it aloft and drop it on the rocks. Only a wise bird learns this. Most feathered creatures pick at an unyielding surface a few times and then seek food elsewhere. There are two reasons why these birds went on the abomination lists. To a steady diet of fish they add carrion. Then they are birds of such nervous energy, so exhaustless in flight, so daring in flying directly into the face of fierce winds, that the Moslems believed them to be tenanted with the souls of the damned. Moses was reared and educated among the Egyptians, and the laws he formulated often are tinged by traces of his early life. History fails to record any instance of a man reared in Egypt who permitted the killing of a gull, ibis, or hoopoe. GENE STRATTON-PORTER

SEA-MONSTER, sē'mon-stēr: Gen **1** 21 (תַּנִּינִם, *tannīnīm*), "sea monsters," AV "whales," LXX τὰ κήτη, *tá kḗtē*, "sea-monsters," "huge fish," or "whales." Job **7** 12 (תַּנִּין, *tannīn*), "sea-monster," AV "whale," LXX δράκων, *drákōn*, "dragon." Ps **74** 13 (תַּנִּינִים, *tannīnīm*), ARV and ERVm "sea-monsters," AV and ERV "dragons," AVm "whales," LXX δράκοντες, *drákontes*, "dragons." Ps **148** 7 (תַּנִּינִים, *tannīnīm*), "sea-monsters," AV and ERV "dragons," ERVm "sea-monsters" or "water-spouts," LXX *drakontes*, "dragons." Lam **4** 3 (תַּנִּין, *tannīn*), "jackals," AV "sea monsters," AVm "sea calves," LXX *drakontes*. Mt **12** 40 (referring to Jonah) (κῆτος, *kḗtos*), EV "whale," RVm "sea-monster." In the Apoc RV changes AV "whale" (*kētos*) into "sea-monster" in Sir **43** 25 but not in Three ver 57. See DRAGON; JACKAL; WHALE. ALFRED ELY DAY

SEA OF CHINNERETH, kin'ĕ-reth. See GALILEE, SEA OF.

SEA OF GALILEE. See GALILEE, SEA OF.

SEA OF GLASS. See GLASS, SEA OF.

SEA OF JAZER (יָם יַעְזֵר, *yām ya'zēr*): This is a scribal error (Jer **48** 32), *yām* ("sea") being accidentally imported from the preceding clause. See JAZER; SEA.

SEA OF JOPPA. See MEDITERRANEAN SEA.

SEA OF LOT. See DEAD SEA; LAKE.

SEA OF SODOM (SODOMITISH, sod-om-īt'-ish). See DEAD SEA.

SEA OF THE ARABAH. See DEAD SEA.

SEA OF THE PHILISTINES. See MEDITERRANEAN SEA.

SEA OF THE PLAIN (ARABAH, ar'a-ba). See DEAD SEA.

SEA OF TIBERIAS, tī-bē'ri-as. See GALILEE, SEA OF.

SEA, RED. See RED SEA.

SEA, SALT. See DEAD SEA.

SEA, THE. See MEDITERRANEAN SEA; SEA, THE GREAT.

SEA, THE GREAT (הַיָּם הַגָּדוֹל, *ha-yām ha-gādhōl*): This is the name given to the Mediterranean, which formed the western boundary of Pal (Nu **34** 6 f; Josh **15** 12. 47; Ezk **47** 19 f; **48** 28). It is also called "the hinder sea" (Heb *ha-yām hā-'aḥărōn*), i.e. the western sea (Dt **11** 24; **34** 2; Joel **2** 20; Zec **14** 8), and "the sea of the Philis" (Ex **23** 31), which, of course, applies esp. to the part washing the shore of Philistia, from Jaffa southward. Generally, when the word "sea" is used, and no other is definitely indicated, the Mediterranean is intended (Gen **49** 13; Nu **13** 29, etc). It was the largest sheet of water with which the Hebrews had any acquaintance. Its gleaming mirror, stretching away to the sunset, could be seen from many an inland height.

1. Names of the Sea

It bulked large in the minds of the landsmen—for Israel produced few mariners—impressing itself upon their speech, so that "seaward" was the common term for "westward" (Ex **26** 22; Josh **5** 1, etc). Its mystery and wonder, the raging of the storm, and the sound of "sorrow on the sea," borne to their upland ears, infected them with a strange dread of its wide waters, to which the seer of Patmos gave the last Scriptural expression in his vision of the new earth, where "the sea is no more" (Rev **21** 1).

2. Israel and the Sea

Along the coast lay the tribal territories assigned to Asher, Zebulun, Manasseh, Dan and Judah. Many of the cities along the shore they failed to possess, however, and much of the land. The coast line offered little facility for the making of harbors. The one seaport of which in ancient times the Hebrews seem to have made much use was Joppa—the modern *Jaffa* (2 Ch **2** 16, etc). From this place, probably, argosies of Solomon turned their prows westward. Here, at least,

3. The Coast Line

"ships of Tarshish" were wont to set out upon their adventurous voyages (Jon **1** 3). The ships on this sea figure in the beautiful vision of Isaiah (**60** 8 f). See Acco; Joppa.

The boy Jesus, from the heights above Nazareth, must often have looked on the waters of the great

4. The Sea in the NT

sea, as they broke in foam on the curving shore, from the roots of Carmel to the point at Acre. Once only in His journeyings, so far as we know, did He approach the sea, namely on His ever-memorable visit to the "borders of Tyre and Sidon" (Mt **15** 21; Mk **7** 24). The sea, in all its moods, was well known to the great apostle of the Gentiles. The three shipwrecks, which he suffered (2 Cor **11** 25), were doubtless due to the power of its angry billows over the frail craft of those old days. See Paul.

The land owes much to the great sea. During the hot months of summer, a soft breeze from

5. Debt of Palestine to the Sea

the water springs up at dawn, fanning all the seaward face of the Central Range. At sunset the chilled air slips down the slopes and the higher strata drift toward the uplands, charged with priceless moisture, giving rise to the refreshing dews which make the Palestinian morning so sweet. See, further, Mediterranean Sea. W. Ewing

SEA, THE MOLTEN, mōl'tʼn, **or BRAZEN** (יָם מוּצָק, *yām mūçāḳ*, יָם הַנְּחֹשֶׁת, *yām ha-nᵉḥōsheth*): This was a large brazen (bronze) reservoir for water which stood in the court of Solomon's Temple between the altar and the temple porch, toward the S. (1 K **7** 23–26; 2 Ch **4** 2–5.10). The bronze from which it was made is stated in 1 Ch **18** 8 to have been taken by David from the cities Tibhath and Cun. It replaced the laver of the tabernacle, and, like that, was used for storing the water in which the priests washed their hands and their feet (cf Ex **30** 18; **38** 8). It rested on 12 brazen (bronze) oxen, facing in four groups the four quarters of heaven. For particulars of shape, size and ornamentation, see Temple. The "sea" served its purpose till the time of Ahaz, who took away the brazen oxen, and placed the sea upon a pavement (2 K **16** 17) It is recorded that the oxen were afterward taken to Babylon (Jer **52** 20). The sea itself shared the same fate, being first broken to pieces (2 K **25** 13.16).

W. Shaw Caldecott

SEA, WESTERN, wes'tẽrn. See Mediterranean Sea.

SEAH, sē'ä (סְאָה, *ṣᵉʼāh*): A dry measure equal to about one and one-half pecks. See Weights and Measures.

SEAL, sēl (subst. חוֹתָם, *ḥōthām*, "seal," "signet," טַבַּעַת, *ṭabbaʻath*, "signet-ring"; Aram. עִזְקָא, *ʻizḳāʼ*; **σφραγίς,** *sphragís*; vb. חָתַם, *ḥātham* [Aram. חֲתַם, *ḥătham*]; **σφραγίζω,** *sphragízō*, **κατασφραγίζομαι,** *katasphragízomai*, "to seal"):

I. Literal Sense.—A seal is an instrument of stone, metal or other hard substance (sometimes set in a ring), on which is engraved some device or figure, and is used for making an impression on some soft substance, as clay or wax, affixed to a document or other object, in token of authenticity.

The use of seals goes back to a very remote antiquity, esp. in Egypt, Babylonia and Assyria. Herodotus (i.195) records the Bab custom of wearing signets. In Babylonia the seal generally took the form of a cylinder cut in crystal or some hard stone, which was bored through from end to end and a cord passed through it. The design, often accompanied by the owner's name, was engraved on the curved part. The signet was then suspended

1. Prevalence in Antiquity

by the cord round the neck or waist (cf RV "cord" in Gen **38** 18; "upon thy heart . . . . upon thine arm," i.e. one seal hanging down from the neck and another round the waist; Cant **8** 6). In Egypt, too, as in Babylonia, the cylinder was the earliest form used for the purpose of a seal;

Ancient Seals from Originals in the British Museum.

1. Signet cylinder. 2. Signet cylinder of Sennacherib. 3. Seal of chalcedony with Phoenician inscription. 4. Seal of sapphire chalcedony, with Assyrian inscription. 5. Seal of chalcedony, with Persian inscription. 6. Seal in form of a duck with head resting on the back. 7. Clay impression from seal of Esar-haddon, from Kouyunjik. 8. Clay impression from seal, device, ear of wheat, from Kouyunjik. 9. Clay impression from seal, device, a scorpion, from Kouyunjik.

but this form was in Egypt gradually superseded by the scarab (=beetle-shaped) as the prevailing type. Other forms, such as the cone-shaped, were also in use. From the earliest period of civilization the **finger-ring** on which some distinguishing badge was engraved was in use as a convenient way of carrying the signet, the earliest extant rings being those found in Egyp tombs. Other ancient peoples, such as the Phoenicians, also used seals. From the East the custom passed into Greece and other western countries. Devices of a variety of sorts were in use at Rome, both by the emperors and by private individuals. In ancient times, almost every variety of precious stones was used for seals, as well as cheaper material, such as limestone or terra-cotta. In the West wax came early into use as the material for receiving the impression of the seal, but in the ancient East clay was the medium used (cf Job **38** 14). Pigment and ink also came into use.

That the Israelites were acquainted with the use in Egypt of signets set in rings is seen in the statement that Pharaoh delivered to Joseph

2. Seals among the Hebrews

his royal signet as a token of deputed authority (Gen **41** 41 f). They were also acquainted with the use of seals among the Persians and Medes (Est **3** 12; **8** 8.10; Dnl **6** 17). The Hebrews themselves used them at an early period, the first recorded instance being Gen **38** 18.25, where the patriarch Judah is said to have pledged his word to Tamar by leaving her his signet, cord and staff. We have evidence of engraved signets being in important use among them in early times in the description of the two stones on the high priest's ephod (Ex **28** 11; **39** 6), of his golden plate (Ex **28** 36; **39** 30), and breastplate (**39** 14). Ben-Sirach mentions as a distinct occupation the work of engraving on signets

(Sir **38** 27). From the case of Judah and the common usage in other countries, we may infer that every Hebrew of any standing wore a seal. In the case of the signet ring, it was usual to wear it on one of the fingers of the right hand (Jer **22** 24). The Hebrews do not seem to have developed an original type of signets. The seals so far discovered in Pal go to prove that the predominating type was the Egyptian, and to a less degree the Babylonian.

3. Uses of Sealing

(1) One of the most important uses of sealing in antiquity was *to give a proof of authenticity and authority to letters, royal commands,* etc. It served the purposes of a modern signature at a time when the art of writing was known to only a few. Thus Jezebel "wrote letters in Ahab's name, and sealed them with his seal" (1 K **21** 8); the written commands of Ahasuerus were "sealed with the king's ring," "for the writing which is written in the king's name, and sealed with the king's ring, may no man reverse" (Est **8** 8.10; **3** 12). (2) Allied to this is the *formal ratification of a transaction or covenant.* Jeremiah sealed the deeds of the field which he bought from Hanamel (Jer **32** 10–14; cf ver 44); Nehemiah and many others affixed their seal to the written covenant between God and His people (Neh **9** 38; **10** 1 ff). (3) An additional use was *the preservation of books in security.* A roll or other document intended for preservation was sealed up before it was deposited in a place of safety (Jer **32** 14; cf the "book . . . . close sealed with seven seals," Rev **5** 1). In sealing the roll, it was wrapped round with flaxen thread or string, then a lump of clay was attached to it impressed with a seal. The seal would have to be broken by an authorized person before the book could be read (Rev **5** 2.5.9; **6** 1.3, etc). (4) *Sealing was a badge of deputed authority and power,* as when a king handed over his signet ring to one of his officers (Gen **41** 42; Est **3** 10; **8** 2; 1 Macc **6** 15). (5) *Closed doors were often sealed* to prevent the entrance of any unauthorized person. So the door of the lion's den (Dnl **6** 17; cf Bel ver 14). Herodotus mentions the custom of sealing tombs (ii.121). So we read of the chief priests and Pharisees sealing the stone at the mouth of Our Lord's tomb in order to "make the sepulchre sure" against the intrusion of the disciples (Mt **27** 66). Cf the sealing of the abyss to prevent Satan's escape (Rev **20** 3). A door was sealed by stretching a cord over the stone which blocked the entrance, spreading clay or wax on the cord, and then impressing it with a seal. (6) To any other object might a seal be affixed, as *an official mark of ownership;* e.g. a large number of clay stoppers of wine jars are still preserved, on which seal impressions of the cylinder type were stamped, by rolling the cylinder along the surface of the clay when it was still soft (cf Job **38** 14).

Sealed Stone at Entrance to a Tomb.

II. Metaphorical Use of the Term.—The word "seal," both subst. and vb., is often used **figuratively** for the act or token of authentication, confirmation, proof, security or possession. Sin is said not to be forgotten by God, but treasured and stored up with Him against the sinner, under a seal (Dt **32** 34; Job **14** 17). A lover's signet is the emblem of love as an inalienable possession (Cant **8** 6); an unresponsive maiden is "a spring shut up, a fountain sealed" (Cant **4** 12). The seal is sometimes a metaphor for *secrecy.* That which is beyond the comprehension of the uninitiated is said to be as "a book that is sealed" (Isa **29** 11 f; cf the book with seven seals, Rev **5** 1 ff). Daniel is bidden to "shut up the words" of his prophecy "and seal the book, even to the time of the end," i.e. to keep his prophecy a secret till it shall be revealed (Dnl **12** 4.9; cf Rev **10** 4). Elsewhere it stands for the ratification of prophecy (Dnl **9** 24). The exact meaning of the figure is sometimes ambiguous (as in Job **33** 16; Ezk **28** 12). In the NT the main ideas in the figure are those of authentication, ratification, and security. The believer in Christ is said to "set his seal to this, that God is true" (Jn **3** 33), i.e. to attest the veracity of God, to stamp it with the believer's own endorsement and confirmation. The Father has sealed the Son, i.e. authenticated Him as the bestower of life-giving bread (Jn **6** 27). The circumcision of Abraham was a "sign" and "seal," an outward ratification, of the righteousness of faith which he had already received while uncircumcised (Rom **4** 11; cf the prayer offered at the circumcision of a child, "Blessed be He who sanctified His beloved from the womb, and put His ordinance upon his flesh, and *sealed* His offering with the *sign* of a holy covenant"; also Tg Cant **38**: "The *seal* of circumcision is in your flesh as it was sealed in the flesh of Abraham"). Paul describes his act in making over to the saints at Jerus the contribution of the Gentiles as having "sealed to them this fruit" (Rom **15** 28); the meaning of the phrase is doubtful, but the figure seems to be based on sealing as ratifying a commercial transaction, expressing Paul's intention formally to hand over to them the fruit (of his own labors, or of spiritual blessings which through him the Gentiles had enjoyed), and to mark it as their own property. Paul's converts are the "seal," the authentic confirmation, of his apostleship (1 Cor **9** 2). God by His Spirit indicates who are His, as the owner sets his seal on his property; and just as documents are sealed up until the proper time for opening them, so Christians are sealed up by the Holy Spirit "unto the day of redemption" (Eph **1** 13; **4** 30; 2 Cor **1** 22). Ownership, security and authentication are implied in the words, "The firm foundation of God standeth, having this seal, The Lord knoweth them that are his" (2 Tim **2** 19). The seal of God on the foreheads of His servants (Rev **7** 2–4) marks them off as His own, and guarantees their eternal security, whereas those that "have not the seal of God on their foreheads" (Rev **9** 4) have no such guaranty.

On the analogy of the rite of circumcision (see above), the term "seal" (*sphragis*) was at a very early period applied to Christian baptism. But there is no sufficient ground for referring such passages as Eph **1** 13; **4** 30; 2 Cor **1** 22 to the rite of baptism (as some do). The use of the metaphor in connection with baptism came after NT times (early instances are given in Gebhardt and Lightfoot on 2 Clem **7** 6). Harnack and Hatch maintain that the name "seal" for baptism was taken from the Gr mysteries, but Anrich and Sanday-Headlam hold that it was borrowed from the Jewish view of circumcision as a seal. See MYSTERY.

D. MIALL EDWARDS

SEALED, sēld, **FOUNTAIN:** These words, applied to the bride (Cant **4** 12), find their explanation under SEAL (q.v.). Anything that was to be authoritatively protected was sealed. Where water was one of the most precious things, as in the East, fountains and wells were often sealed (Gen **29** 3; Prov **5** 15–18).

SEALSKIN, sēl′skin: The rendering of RV (Ex **25** 5; Ezk **16** 10) for עוֹר תַּחַשׁ, *ʽōr taḥash,* RVm "porpoise-skin," AV "badgers' skin." A seal, *Monachus albiventer,* is found in the Mediterranean, though not in the Red Sea, but it is likely that *taḥash* means the dugong, which is found in the Red Sea. See BADGER; PORPOISE.

SEAM, sēm, **SEAMLESS,** sēm'les: The coat or inner garment (χιτών, *chitṓn*) of Jesus is described in Jn **19** 23 as "without seam" (ἄρραφος, *árrhaphos*), i.e. woven in one piece.

SEAR, sēr: In 1 Tim **4** 2 for καυστηριάζω, *kaustēriázō*, "burn with a hot iron" (cf "cauterize"), AV "having their conscience seared with a hot iron," and RVm. "Seared" in this connection means "made insensible," like the surface of a deep burn after healing. The vb., however, probably means "brand" (so RV). "Criminals are branded on their forehead, so that all men may know their infamy. The consciences of certain men are branded just as truly, so that there is an inward consciousness of hypocrisy." See the comms.

SEARCH, sûrch: Some peculiar senses are: (1) In the books of Moses, esp. in Nu, "searching out the land" means to spy out (רַגֵּל, *raggēl*), to investigate carefully, to examine with a view to giving a full and accurate report on. (2) When applied to the Scriptures, as in Ezr **4** 15.19 (בַּקֵּר, *baḳḳēr*); Jn **5** 39; 1 Pet **1** 11 (ἐραυνάω, *eraunáō*), it means to examine, to study out the meaning. In Acts **17** 11, RV substitutes "examining" for the "searched" of AV. See SEARCHINGS. (3) "Search out" often means to study critically, to investigate carefully, e.g. Job **8** 8; **29** 16; Eccl **1** 13; Lam **3** 40; Mt **2** 8; 1 Cor **2** 10; 1 Pet **1** 10. (4) When the word is applied to God's searching the heart or spirit, it means His opening up, laying bare, disclosing what was hidden, e.g. 1 Ch **28** 9; Ps **44** 21; **139** 1; Prov **20** 27; Jer **17** 10; Rom **8** 27.

G. H. GERBERDING

SEARCH THE SCRIPTURES: The sentence beginning with ἐραυνᾶτε, *eraunáte*, in Jn **5** 39 AV has been almost universally regarded as meaning "Search the scriptures, for in them ye think ye have eternal life." But one cannot read as far as δοκεῖτε, *dokeíte*, "ye think," without feeling that there is something wrong with the ordinary version. This vb. is at least a disturbing element in the current of thought (if not superfluous), and only when the first vb. is taken as an indicative does the meaning of the writer become clear. The utterance is not a command, but a declaration: "Ye search the scriptures, because ye think that in them," etc. Robert Barclay as early as 1675, in his *Apology for the True Christian Divinity* (91 ff), refers to two scholars before him who had handed down the correct tradition: "Moreover, that place may be taken in the indicative mood, Ye search the Scriptures; which interpretation the Gr word will bear, and so Pasor tr[d] it: which by the reproof following seemeth also to be the more genuine interpretation, as Cyrillus long ago hath observed." So Dr. Edwin A. Abbott, in his *Johannine Grammar* (London, 1906, §2439 [i]). See also *Transactions American Philological Association*, 1901, 64 f. J. E. HARRY

SEARCHINGS, sûr'chingz (חִקְרֵי[לֵב], *ḥiḳrē* [*lēbh*], from *ḥāḳar*, to "search," "explore," "examine thoroughly"): In the song of Deborah the Reubenites are taunted because their great resolves of heart, *ḥiḳeḳē lēbh*, led to nothing but great "searchings" of heart, *ḥiḳrē lēbh*, and no activity other than to remain among their flocks (Jgs **5** 15 f). The first of the two Heb expressions so emphatically contrasted (though questioned by commentators on the authority of 5 MSS as a corruption of the second) can with reasonable certainty be interpreted "acts prescribed by one's understanding" (cf the expressions *ḥăkham lēbh*, *nᵉbhōn lēbh*, in which the heart is looked upon as the seat of the understanding). The second expression may mean either irresolution or hesitation based on selfish motives, as the heart was also considered the seat of the feelings, or answerability to God (cf Jer **17** 10; Prov **25** 3); this rendering would explain the form *liphᵉlaghōth* in Jgs **5** 16, lit. '*for* the water courses of Reuben, great the searchings of heart!'

NATHAN ISAACS

SEASONS, sē'z'nz (summer: קַיִץ, *ḳayiç*, Chald קַיִט, *ḳayiṭ* [Dnl **2** 35]; θέρος, *théros;* winter: סְתָו, *ṣᵉthāw* [Cant **2** 11], חֹרֶף, *ḥōreph;* χειμών, *cheimṓn*): The four seasons in Pal are not so marked as in more northern countries, summer gradually fading into winter and winter into summer. The range of temperature is not great. In the Bible we have no reference to spring or autumn; the only seasons mentioned are "summer and winter" (Gen **8** 22; Ps **74** 17; Zec **14** 8).

Winter is the season of rain lasting from November to May. "The winter is past; the rain is over" (Cant **2** 11). See RAIN. The temperature at sea-level in Pal reaches freezing-point occasionally, but seldom is less than 40° F. On the hills and mountains it is colder, depending on the height. The people have no means of heating their houses, and suffer much with the cold. They wrap up their necks and heads and keep inside the houses out of the wind as much as possible. "The sluggard will not plow by reason of the winter" (Prov **20** 4). Jesus in speaking of the destruction of Jerus says, "Pray ye that your flight be not in the winter" (Mt **24** 20). Paul asks Timothy to "come before winter" (2 Tim **4** 21) as navigation closed then and travel was virtually impossible.

Summer is very hot and rainless. "[When] the fig tree . . . . putteth forth its leaves, ye know that the summer is nigh" (Mk **13** 28); "The harvest is past, the summer is ended" (Jer **8** 20). It is the season of harvesting and threshing (Dnl **2** 35). "He that gathereth in summer is a wise son" (Prov **10** 5). See COLD; HEAT; ASTRONOMY, I, 5.

ALFRED H. JOY

SEAT, sēt: This word is used to translate the Heb words מוֹשָׁב, *mōshābh*, שֶׁבֶת, *shebheth*, כִּסֵּא, *kiṣṣē'*, and תְּכוּנָה, *tᵉkhūnāh*, once (Job **23** 3). It translates the Gr word καθέδρα, *kathédra* (Mt **21** 12; **23** 2; Mk **11** 15), and "chief seat" translates the compound word πρωτοκαθεδρία, *prōtokathedría* (Mt **23** 6; Mk **12** 39; Lk **20** 46). In AV it translates θρόνος, *thrónos* (Lk **1** 52; Rev **2** 13; **4** 4; **11** 16; **13** 2; **16** 10), which RV renders "throne." It denotes a place or thing upon which one sits, as a chair, or stool (1 S **20** 18; Jgs **3** 20). It is used also of the exalted position occupied by men of marked rank or influence, either in good or evil (Mt **23** 2; Ps **1** 1). JESSE L. COTTON

SEATS, sēts, **CHIEF.** See CHIEF SEATS.

SEBA, sē'ba (סְבָא, *ṣᵉbhā';* Σαβά, *Sabá* [Gen **10** 7; 1 Ch **1** 9]; Gr ib, but B has Σαβάν, *Sabán*):

1. Forms of Name, and Parentage of Seba

The first son of Cush, his brothers being Havilah, Sabtah, Raamah, and Sabtecha. In Ps **72** 10 and Isa **43** 3 (where the Gr has Σοήνη, *Soḗnē*), Seba is mentioned with Egypt and Ethiopia, and must therefore have been a southern people. In Isa **45** 14 we meet with the gentilic form, סְבָאִים, *ṣᵉbhā'īm* (Σαβαείμ, *Sabaeím*), rendered "Sabaeans," who are described as "men of stature" (i.e. tall), and were to come over to Cyrus in chains, and acknowledge that God was in him—their merchandise, and that of the Ethiopians, and the labor of Egypt, were to be his.

Their country is regarded as being, most likely, the district of Saba, N. of Adulis, on the west coast of the Red Sea. There is just a possibility that the Sabi River, stretching from the coast to the Zambesi and the Limpopo, which was utilized as a waterway by the states in that region, though, through silting, not suitable now, may contain a trace of the name, and perhaps testifies to still more southern extensions of the power and influence of the Sebaim. (See Th. Bent, *The Ruined Cities of Mashonaland*, 1892.) The ruins of this tract are regarded as being the work of others than the black natives of the country. Dillmann, however, suggests (on Gen **10** 7) that the people of Seba were another branch of the Cushites E. of Napatha by the Arabian Sea, of which Strabo (xvi. 4, 8, 10) and Ptolemy (iv.7, 7 f) give information. See SHEBA and *HDB*, s.v.

2. Position of the Nation

T. G. PINCHES

SEBAM, sē′bam (שְׂבָם, *s[e]bhām;* Σεβαμά, *Sebamá;* AV **Shebam**): A town in the upland pasture land given to the tribes of Reuben and Gad. It is named along with Heshbon, Elealeh and Nebo (Nu **32** 3). It is probably the same place as Sibmah (AV "Shibmah") in ver 38 (so also Josh **13** 19). In the time of Isaiah and Jeremiah it was a Moabite town, but there is no record of how or when it was taken from Israel. It appears to have been famous for the luxuriance of its vines and for its summer fruits (Isa **16** 8 f; Jer **48** 32). *Onom* calls it a city of Moab in the land of Gilead which fell to the tribe of Reuben. Jerome (*Comm. in Isa* **5**) says it was about 500 paces from Heshbon, and he describes it as one of the strong places of that region. It may be represented by the modern *Sīmia*, which stands on the south side of *Wâdy Ḥesbān*, about 2 miles from *Ḥesbān*. The ancient ruins are considerable, with large sarcophagi; and in the neighboring rock wine presses are cut (*PEFM*, "Eastern Pal," 221 f). W. EWING

SEBAT, se-bät′, sē′bat (Zec **1** 7). See SHEBAT.

SECACAH, sē-kā′ka, sek′a-kä (סְכָכָה, *ṣ[e]khākhāh;* B, Αἰχιοζά, *Aichiozá*, A, Σοχοχά, *Sochochá*): One of the six cities "in the wilderness of Judah" (Josh **15** 61), that is in the uncultivated lands to the W. of the Dead Sea, where a scanty pasturage is still obtained by wandering Bedouin tribes. There are many signs in this district of more settled habitation in ancient times, but the name Secacah is lost. Conder proposed *Kh. ed Diḳḳeh* (also called *Kh. es Siḳḳeh*), "the ruin of the path," some 2 miles S. of Bethany. Though an ancient site, it is too near the inhabited area; the name, too, is uncertain (*PEF*, III, 111, Sh XVII). E. W. G. MASTERMAN

SECHENIAS, sek-ē-nī′as:

(1) (A, Σεχενίας, *Sechenias;* omitted in B and Swete): 1 Esd **8** 29 = "Shecaniah" in Ezr **8** 3; the arrangement in Ezr is different.

(2) (A, *Sechenias*, but B and Swete, Ἐιεχονίας, *Eiechonías*): Name of a person who went up at the head of a family in the return with Ezra (1 Esd **8** 32) = "Shecaniah" in Ezr **8** 5.

SECHU, sē′kū (שֵׂכוּ, *sēkhū*). See SECU.

SECOND COMING, sek′und kum′ing. See PAROUSIA; ESCHATOLOGY OF THE NT, V.

SECOND DEATH. See DEATH; ESCHATOLOGY OF THE NT, X, (6).

SECOND SABBATH. See SABBATH, SECOND.

SECONDARILY, sek′un-da-ri-li: AV for δεύτερον, *deúteron* (1 Cor **12** 28). Probably without distinction from "secondly" (so RV, and so AV also for *deuteron* in Sir **23** 23). Still AV may have wished to emphasize that the prophets have a lower *rank* than the apostles.

SECRET, sē′kret: In Ezk **7** 22, EV has "secret place" for צָפַן, *çāphan*, "hide," "treasure." A correct tr is, "They shall profane my *cherished* place" (Jerus), and there is no reference to the Holy of Holies. The other uses of "secret" in RV are obvious, but RV's corrections of AV in Jgs **13** 18; 1 S **5** 9; Job **15** 11 should be noted.

SECT, sekt (αἵρεσις, *haíresis*): "Sect" (Lat *secta*, from *sequi*, "to follow") is in the NT the tr of *hairesis*, from *hairéō*, "to take," "to choose"; also tr[d] "heresy," not *heresy* in the later ecclesiastical sense, but a school or party, a sect, without any bad meaning attached to it. The word is applied to schools of philosophy; to the Pharisees and Sadducees among the Jews who adhered to a common religious faith and worship; and to the Christians. It is tr[d] "sect" (Acts **5** 17, of the Sadducees; **15** 5, of the Pharisees; **24** 5, of the Nazarenes; **26** 5, of the Pharisees; **28** 22, of the Christians); also RV **24** 14 (AV and ERVm "heresy"), "After the Way which they call a sect, so serve I the God of our fathers" (just as the Pharisees were "a sect"); it is tr[d] "heresies" (1 Cor **11** 19, m "sects," ARV "factions," m "Gr 'heresies' "; ERV reverses the ARV text and margin; Gal **5** 20, ARV "parties," m "heresies"; ERV reverses text and margin; 2 Pet **2** 1, "damnable heresies," RV "destructive heresies," m "sects of perdition"); the "sect" in itself might be harmless; it was the teaching or principles which should be followed by those sects that would make them "destructive." *Hairesis* occurs in 1 Macc **8** 30 ("They shall do it at their *pleasure*," i.e. "choice"); cf LXX Lev **22** 18.21. See HERESY. W. L. WALKER

SECU, sē′kū (שֵׂכוּ, *sēkhū;* B, ἐν τῷ Σεφεί, *en tō̃ Sepheí*, A, ἐν Σοκχώ, *en Sokchṓ;* AV **Sechu**): This name occurs only in the account of David's visit to Samuel (1 S **19** 22). Saul, we are told, went to "Ramah, and came to the great well that is in Secu," where he inquired after Samuel and David. It evidently lay between the residence of Saul at Gibeah and Ramah. It is impossible to come to any sure conclusion regarding it. Conder suggested its identification with *Khirbet Suweikeh*, which lies to the S. of *Bīreh*. This is possible, but perhaps we should read with LXX B, "He came to the cistern of the threshing-floor that is on the bare hill" (*en tō Sephei*). The threshing-floors in the East are naturally on high exposed ground where this is possible, and often form part of the area whence water in the rainy season is conducted to cisterns. This might have been a place actually within the city of Ramah. W. EWING

SECUNDUS, sē-kun′dus (WH, Σέκουνδος, *Sékoundos*, *TR*, Σεκοῦνδος, *Sekoúndos*): A Thessalonian who was among those who accompanied Paul from Greece to Asia (Acts **20** 4). They had preceded Paul and waited for him at Troas. If he were one of the representatives of the churches in Macedonia and Greece, intrusted with their contributions to Jerus (Acts **24** 17; 2 Cor **8** 23), he probably accompanied Paul as far as Jerus. The name is found in a list of politarchs on a Thessalonian inscription.

SECURE, sē-kūr′, **SECURITY,** sē-kū′ri-ti: The word *bāṭaḥ* and its derivatives in Heb point to security, either real or imaginary. Thus we read of a host that "was secure" (Jgs **8** 11) and of those "that provoke God [and] are secure" (Job **12** 6); but also of a security that rests in hope and is safe (Job **11** 18). The NT words ποιέω ἀμερίμνους, *poiéō amerímnous*, used in Mt **28** 14 [AV "secure you"], guarantee the safety of the soldiers, who witnessed against themselves, in the telling of the story of the disappearance of the body of Christ.

Securely is used in the sense of "trustful," "not anticipating danger" (Prov **3** 29; Mic **2** 8; Ecclus **4** 15).

The word ἱκανόν, *hikanón*, tr[d] **security** (Acts **17** 9), may stand either for a guaranty of good behavior exacted from, or for some form of punishment inflicted on, Jason and his followers by the rulers of Thessalonica. HENRY E. DOSKER

SEDECIAS, sed-ē-sī'as: AV=RV SEDEKIAS (q.v.).

SEDEKIAS, sed-ē-kī'as:

(1) (B A, Σεδεκίας, *Sedekías;* AV **Zedechias**): 1 Esd **1** 46 (44) = Zedekiah king of Judah; also in Bar **1** 8 where AV reads "Sedecias."

(2) In Bar **1** 1 (AV "Sedecias"), an ancestor of Baruch, "the son of Asadias," sometimes (but incorrectly) identified with the false prophet "Zedekiah the son of Maaseiah" (Jer **29** 21).

SEDITION, sē-dish'un: The tr in Ezr **4** 15.19 for אֶשְׁתַּדּוּר, *'eshtaddūr*, "struggling," "revolt"; in 2 Esd **15** 16 for *inconstabilitio*, "instability," with "be seditious" for στασιάζω, *stasiázō*, "rise in rebellion" in 2 Macc **14** 6. In addition, AV has "sedition" for στάσις, *stásis*, "standing up," "revolt" (RV "insurrection") in Lk **23** 19.25; Acts **24** 5, with διχοστασία, *dichostasía*, "a standing asunder" (RV "division") in Gal **5** 20. As "sedition" does not include open violence against a government, the word should not have been used in any of the above cases.

SEDUCE, sē-dūs', **SEDUCER,** sē-dūs'ẽr (Hiphil of טָעָה, *ṭā'āh*, or תָּעָה, *tā'āh*, "to err"; of פָּתָה, *pāthāh*, "to be simple"; πλανάω, *planáō*, ἀποπλανάω, *apoplanáō*, "to lead astray"): (1) The word "seduce" is only used in the Bible in its general meaning of "to lead astray," "to cause to err," as from the paths of truth, duty or religion. It occurs in AV and RV Ezk **13** 10; 2 K **21** 9; 1 Tim **4** 1; Rev **2** 20; in AV only, Prov **12** 26 (RV "causeth to err"); Isa **19** 13 (RV "caused to go astray"); Mk **13** 22; 1 Jn **2** 26 (RV "lead astray"). The noun "seducer" (2 Tim **3** 13 AV, γόης, *góēs*) is correctly changed in RV into "impostor." (2) It is not found in its specific sense of "to entice a female to surrender her chastity." Yet the crime itself is referred to and condemned.

Three cases are to be distinguished: (*a*) The seduction of an unbetrothed virgin: In this case the seducer according to JE (Ex **22** 16 f) is to be compelled to take the virgin as his wife, if the father consents, and to pay the latter the usual purchase price, the amount of which is not defined. In the Deuteronomic Code (Dt **22** 28) the amount is fixed at 50 shekels, and the seducer forfeits the right of divorce. (*b*) The seduction of a betrothed virgin: This case (Dt **22** 23–27; not referred to in the other codes) is treated as virtually one of adultery, the virgin being regarded as pledged to her future husband as fully as if she were formally married to him; the penalty therefore is the same as for adultery, viz. death for both parties (except in the case where the girl can reasonably be acquitted of blame, in which case the man only is put to death). (*c*) The seduction of a betrothed bondmaid (mentioned only in Lev **19** 20–22): Here there is no infliction of death, because the girl was not free; but the seducer shall make a trespass offering, besides paying the fine. See CRIMES; PUNISHMENTS.

D. MIALL EDWARDS

SEE, sē: In addition to the ordinary sense of perceiving by the eye, we have (1) חָזָה, *ḥāzāh*, "to see" (in vision): "Words of Amos . . . . which he *saw* concerning Israel" (Am **1** 1). The revelation was made to his inward eye. "The word of Jeh . . . . which he [Micah] *saw* concerning Samaria" (Mic **1** 1), describing what he saw in prophetic vision (cf Hab **1** 1); see REVELATION, III, 4; (2) ὁράω, *horáō*, "to take heed": "*See* thou say nothing" (Mk **1** 44); (3) εἶδον, *eídon*, "to know," "to note with the mind": "Jesus *saw* that he answered discreetly" (Mk **12** 34); (4) θεωρέω, *theōréō*, "to view," "to have knowledge or experience of": "He shall never *see* death" (Jn **8** 51). M. O. EVANS

SEED, sēd (OT always for זֶרַע, *zera'*, Aram. [Dnl **2** 43] זְרַע *zᵉra'*, except in Joel **1** 17 for פְּרֻדוֹת, *pᵉrudhōth* [pl. RV "seeds," AV "seed"], and Lev **19** 19 [AV "mingled seed"] and Dt **22** 9 [AV "divers seeds"] for כִּלְאַיִם, *kil'ayim*, lit. "two kinds," RV "two kinds of seed." Invariably in Gr Apoc and usually in the NT for σπέρμα, *spérma*, but Mk **4** 26.27; Lk **8** 5.11; 2 Cor **9** 10 for σπόρος, *spóros*, and 1 Pet **1** 23 for σπορά, *sporá*): (1) For "seed" in its literal sense see AGRICULTURE. Of interest is the method of measuring land by means of the amount of seed that could be sown on it (Lev **27** 16). The prohibition against using two kinds of seed in the same field (Lev **19** 19; Dt **22** 9) undoubtedly rests on the fact that the practice had some connection with Canaanitish worship, making the whole crop "consecrated" (*taboo*). Jer **31** 27 uses "seed of man" and "seed of beast" as a figure for the means by which God will increase the prosperity of Israel (i.e. "seed yielding men"). (2) For the transferred physiological application of the word to human beings (Lev **15** 16, etc) see CLEAN; UNCLEAN. The conception of Christians as "born" or "begotten" of God (see REGENERATION) gave rise to the figure in 1 Pet **1** 23; 1 Jn **3** 9. If the imagery is to be stressed, the Holy Spirit is meant. In 1 Jn **3** 9 a doctrine of certain Gnostics is opposed. They taught that by learning certain formulas and by submitting to certain rites, union with God and salvation could be attained without holiness of life. St. John's reply is that union with a righteous God is meaningless without righteousness as an ideal, even though shortcomings exist in practice (1 Jn **1** 8). (3) From the physiological use of "seed" the transition to the sense of "offspring" was easy, and the word may mean "children" (Lev **18** 21, etc) or even a single child (Gen **4** 25; 1 S **1** 11 RVm). Usually, however, it means the whole posterity (Gen **3** 15, etc); cf "seed royal" (2 K **11** 1, etc), and "Abraham's seed" (2 Ch **20** 7, etc) or "the holy seed" (Ezr **9** 2; Isa **6** 13; 1 Esd **8** 70; cf Jer **2** 21) as designations of Israel. So "to show one's seed" (Ezr **2** 59; Neh **7** 61) is to display one's genealogy, and "one's seed" may be simply one's nation, conceived of as a single family (Est **10** 3). From this general sense there developed a still looser use of "seed" as meaning simply "men" (Mal **2** 15; Isa **1** 4; **57** 4; Wisd **10** 15; **12** 11, etc).

In Gal **3** 16 St. Paul draws a distinction between "seeds" and "seed" that has for its purpose a proof that the promises to Abraham were realized in Christ and not in Israel. The distinction, however, overstresses the language of the OT, which never pluralizes *zera'* when meaning "descendants" (pl. only in 1 S **8** 15; cf Rom **4** 18; **9** 7). But in an argument against rabbinical adversaries St. Paul was obliged to use rabbinical methods (cf Gal **4** 25). For modern purposes it is probably best to treat such an exegetical method as belonging simply to the (now superseded) science of the times. BURTON SCOTT EASTON

SEER, sē′ẽr, sēr: The word in EV represents two Heb words, רֹאֶה, *rō'eh* (1 S **9** 9.11.18.19; 2 S **15** 27; 1 Ch **9** 22, etc), and חֹזֶה, *ḥōzeh* (2 S **24** 11; 2 K **17** 13; 1 Ch **21** 9; **25** 5; **29** 29, etc). The former designation is from the ordinary vb. "to see"; the latter is connected with the vb. used of prophetic vision. It appears from 1 S **9** 9 that "seer" (*rō'eh*) was the older name for those who, after the rise of the more regular orders, were called "prophets." It is not just, however, to speak of the "seers" or "prophets" of Samuel's time as on the level of mere fortune-tellers. What insight or vision they possessed is traced to God's Spirit. Samuel was the *rō'eh* by preëminence, and the name is little used after his time. Individuals who bear the title "seer" (*ḥōzeh*) are mentioned in connection with the kings and as historiographers (2 S **24** 11; 1 Ch **21** 9; **25** 5; **29** 29; 2 Ch **9** 29; **12** 15; **19** 2, etc), and distinction is sometimes made between "prophets" and "seers" (2 K **17** 13; 1 Ch **29** 29, etc). Hävernick thinks that "seer" denotes one who does not belong to the regular prophetic order (*Intro to OT*, 50 ff, ET), but it is not easy to fix a precise distinction. See PROPHET, PROPHECY. JAMES ORR

SEETHE, sēth: Old Eng. for "boil"; past tense, "sod" (Gen **25** 29), past participle, "sodden" (Lam **4** 10). See Ex **23** 19 AV.

SEGUB, sē′gub (שְׂגוּב, *seghūbh* [Kerē], שְׂגִיב, *seghībh* [Kethībh]; B, **Ζεγούβ**, *Zegoúb*, A, **Σεγούβ**, *Segoúb*):

(1) The youngest son of Hiel, the rebuilder of Jericho (1 K **16** 34). The death of Segub is probably connected with the primitive custom of laying foundations with blood, as, indeed, skulls were found built in with the brickwork when the tower of Bel at Nippur was excavated. See GEZER. If the death of the two sons was based on the custom just mentioned, the circumstance was deliberately obscured in the present account. The death of Segub may have been due to an accident in the setting up of the gates. In any event, tradition finally yoked the death of Hiel's oldest and youngest sons with a curse said to have been pronounced by Joshua on the man that should venture to rebuild Jericho (Josh **6** 26).

(2) Son of Hezron and father of Jair (1 Ch **2** 21). HORACE J. WOLF

SEIR, sē′ir:

(1) (הַר שֵׂעִיר, *har sē'īr*, "Mt. Seir" [Gen **14** 6, etc], אֶרֶץ שֵׂעִיר, *'ereç sē'īr* [Gen **32** 3, etc]; *τὸ ὄρος Σηείρ*, *tó óros Seéir*, *γῆ Σηείρ*, *gḗ Seéir*): In Gen **32** 3 "the land of Seir" is equated with "the field of Edom." The Mount and the Land of Seir are alternative appellations of the mountainous tract which runs along the eastern side of the Arabah, occupied by the descendants of Esau, who succeeded the ancient Horites (Gen **14** 6; **36** 20), "cave-dwellers," in possession. For a description of the land see EDOM.

(2) (הַר שֵׂעִיר, *har sē'īr;* B, *'Ασσάρ*, *Assár*, A, *Σηείρ*, *Seéir*): A landmark on the boundary of Judah (Josh **15** 10), not far from Kiriath-jearim and Chesalon. The name means "shaggy," and probably here denoted a wooded height. It may be that part of the range which runs N.E. from *Sārīs* by *Ḳaryat el-'Anab* and *Biddu* to the plateau of *el-Jīb*. Traces of an ancient forest are still to be seen here. W. EWING

SEIRAH, sḗ-ī′ra, sē′i-ra (הַשְּׂעִירָה, *ha-se'īrāh;* B, **Σετειρωθά**, *Seteirōthá*, A, **Σεειρῶθα**, *Seeirṓtha;* AV Seirath): The place to which Ehud escaped after his assassination of Eglon, king of Moab (Jgs **3** 26). The name is from the same root as the foregoing, and probably applied to some shaggy forest. The quarries by which he passed are said to have been by Gilgal (ver 19), but there is nothing to guide us to an identification. *Onom* gives the name, but no indication of the site.

SEIRATH, sḗ-ī′rath, sē′i-rath. See SEIRAH.

SELA, sē′la (סֶלַע, *ṣela'*, הַסֶּלַע, *ha-ṣela'* [with the art.]; **πέτρα**, *pétra*, **ἡ πέτρα**, *hē pétra;* AV **Selah** [2 K **14** 7]): EV renders this as the name of a city in 2 K **14** 7; Isa **16** 1. In Jgs **1** 36; 2 Ch **25** 12; and Ob ver 3, it translates lit. "rock"; but RVm in each case "Sela." It is impossible to assume with Hull (*HDB*, s.v.) that this name, when it appears in Scripture, always refers to the capital of Edom, the great city in *Wâdy Mūsa*. In Jgs **1** 36 its association with the Ascent of Akrabbim shuts us up to a position toward the southwestern end of the Dead Sea. Probably in that case it does not denote a city, but some prominent crag. Moore ("Judges," *ICC*, 56), following Buhl, would identify it with *eṣ-Ṣâfieh*, "a bare and dazzlingly white sandstone promontory 1,000 ft. high, E. of the mud flats of *es-Sebkah*, and 2 miles S. of the Dead Sea." A more probable identification is a high cliff which commands the road leading from *Wâdy el-Milḥ*, "valley of Salt," to Edom, over the pass of Akrabbim. This was a position of strategic importance, and if fortified would be of great strength. (In this passage "Edomites" must be read for "Amorites.") The victory of Amaziah was won in the Valley of Salt. He would naturally turn his arms at once against this stronghold (2 K **14** 7); and it may well be the rock from the top of which he hurled his prisoners (2 Ch **25** 12). He called it Jokteel, a name the meaning of which is obscure. Possibly it is the same as Jekuthiel (1 Ch **4** 18), and may mean "preservation of God" (*OHL*, s.v.). No trace of this name has been found. The narratives in which the place is mentioned put identification with Petra out of the question.

"The rock" (RVm "Sela") in Ob ver 3, in the phrase "thou that dwellest in the clefts of the rock," is only a vivid and picturesque description of Mt. Edom. "The purple mountains into which the wild sons of Esau clambered run out from Syria upon the desert, some hundred miles by twenty, of porphyry and red sandstone. They are said to be the finest rock scenery in the world. 'Salvator Rosa never conceived so savage and so suitable a haunt for banditti.' . . . . The interior is reached by defiles so narrow that two horsemen may scarcely ride abreast, and the sun is shut out by the overhanging rocks. . . . . Little else than wild fowls' nests are the villages: human eyries perched on high shelves or hidden away in caves at the ends of the deep gorges" (G. A. Smith, *The Book of the Twelve Prophets*, II, 178 f).

In Isa **16** 1; **42** 11 RV, perhaps we have a reference to the great city of Petra. Jos (*Ant*, IV, vii, 1) tells us that among the kings of the Midianites who fell before Moses was one Rekem, king of Rekem (*akre*, or *rekeme*), the city deriving its name from its founder. This he says was the Arab. name; the Greeks called it Petra. *Onom* says Petra is a city of Arabia in the land of Edom. It is called Jechthoel; but the Syrians call it Rekem. Jokteel, as we have seen, must be sought elsewhere. There can be no doubt that Jos intended the city in *Wâdy Mūsa*. Its OT name was Bozrah (Am **1** 12, etc). Wetzstein (*Excursus in Delitzsch's Isa*³, 696 ff) hazards the conjecture that the complete ancient name was *Bozrat has-Sela*, "Bozrah of the Rock."

This "rose-red city half as old as Time"

was for long difficult of access, and the attempt to visit it was fraught with danger. In recent years, however, it has been seen by many tourists and exploring parties. Of the descriptions written the best is undoubtedly that of Professor Dalman of Jerus (*Petra und seine Felsheiligtümer*, Leipzig, 1908). An excellent account of this wonderful city, brightly and interestingly written, will be found in Libbey and Hoskins' book (*The Jordan Valley and Petra*, New York and London, 1905; see also *National Geographic Magazine*, May, 1907, Washington, D.C.). The ruins lie along the sides of a spacious hollow surrounded by the many-hued cliffs of Edom, just before they sink into the Arabah on the W. It is near the base of *Jebel Harūn*, about 50 miles

Entrance to the *Sīk*.

from the Dead Sea, and just N. of the watershed between that sea and the Gulf of Akaba. The valley owes its modern name, *Wâdy Mūsa*, "Valley of Moses," to its connection with Moses in Mohammedan legends. While not wholly inaccessible from other directions, the two usual approaches are that from the S.W. by a rough path, partly artificial, and that from the E. The latter is by far the more important. The valley closes to the E., the only opening being through a deep and narrow defile, called the *Sīk*, "shaft," about a mile in length. In the bottom of the *Sīk* flows westward the stream that rises at *'Ain Mūsa*. E. of the cleft is the village of *Elji*, an ancient site, corresponding to Gaia of *Onom*. Passing this village, the road threads its way along the shadowy winding gorge, overhung by lofty cliffs. When the valley is reached, a sight of extraordinary beauty and impressiveness opens to the beholder. The temples, the tombs, the theater, etc, hewn with great skill and infinite pains from the living rock, have defied to an astonishing degree the tooth of time, many of the carvings being as fresh as if they had been cut yesterday. An idea of the scale on which the work was done may be gathered from the size of the theater, which furnished accommodation for no fewer than 3,000 spectators.

Such a position could not have been overlooked in ancient times; and we are safe to assume that a city of importance must always have existed here. It is under the Nabataeans, however, that Petra begins to play a prominent part in history. This people took possession about the end of the 4th cent. BC, and continued their sway until overcome by Hadrian, who gave his own name to the city—Hadriana. This name, however, soon disappeared. Under the Romans Petra saw the days of her greatest splendor.

According to old tradition St. Paul visited Petra when he went into Arabia (Gal **1** 17). Of this there is no certainty; but Christianity was early introduced, and the city became the seat of a bishopric. Under the Nabataeans she was the center of the great caravan trade of that time. The merchandise of the East was brought hither; and hence set out the caravans for the South, the West, and the North. The great highway across the desert to the Pers Gulf was practically in her hands. The fall of the Nabataean power gave Palmyra her chance; and her supremacy in the commerce of Northern Arabia dates from that time. Petra shared in the declining fortunes of Rome; and her death blow was dealt by the conquering Moslems, who desolated Arabia Petraea in 629–32 AD. The place now furnishes a retreat for a few poor Bedawy families. W. Ewing

SELA-HAMMAHLEKOTH, sē-la-ha-mä'lē-koth, -kōth (סֶלַע הַמַּחְלְקוֹת, *ṣela' ha-maḥlekōth;* **πέτρα ἡ μερισθεῖσα,** *pétra hē meristheísa*): "The rock of divisions (*or*, escape)" (1 S **23** 28m). "Saul . . . . pursued after David in the wilderness of Maon. And Saul went on this side of the mountain, and David and his men on that side of the mountain: and David made haste to get away for fear of Saul" (1 S **23** 25.26). The name seems to survive in *Wâdy Malāki*, "the great gorge which breaks down between Carmel and Maon eastward, with vertical cliffs" (*PEF*, III, 314, Sh XXI).

SELAH, sē'la. See Music, II, 1.

SELED, sē'led (סֶלֶד, *ṣeledh*): A Jerahmeelite (1 Ch **2** 30 *bis*).

SELEMIA, sel-ē-mī'a: One of the swift scribes whose services Ezra was commanded to secure (2 Esd **14** 24). The name is probably identical with Selemias of 1 Esd **9** 34 (q.v.).

SELEMIAS, sel-ē-mī'as (**Σελεμίας,** *Selemías*): One of those who put away their "strange wives" (1 Esd **9** 34) = "Shelemiah" in Ezr **10** 39, and probably identical with "Selemia" in 2 Esd **14** 24.

SELEUCIA, sē-lū'shi-a (**Σελευκία,** *Seleukía*): The seaport of Antioch from which it is 16 miles distant. It is situated 5 miles N. of the mouth of the Orontes, in the northwestern corner of a fruitful plain at the base of Mt. Rhosus or Pieria, the modern *Jebel Mūsa*, a spur of the Amanus Range. Built by Seleucus Nicator (d. 280 BC) it was one of the Syrian Tetrapolis, the others being Apameia, Laodicea and Antioch. The city was protected

GENERAL VIEW OF PETRA

by nature on the mountain side, and, being strongly fortified on the S. and W., was considered invulnerable and the key to Syria (Strabo 751; Polyb. v.58). It was taken, however, by Ptolemy Euergetes (1 Macc **11** 8) and remained in his family till 219 BC, when it was recovered for the Seleucids by Antiochus the Great, who then richly adorned it. Captured again by Ptolemy Philometor in 146 BC, it remained for a short time in the hands of the Egyptians. Pompey made it a free city in 64 BC in return for its energy in resisting Tigranes (Pliny, *NH*, v.18), and it was then greatly improved by the Romans, so that in the 1st cent. AD it was in a most flourishing condition.

On their first missionary journey Paul and Barnabas passed through it (Acts **13** 4; **14** 26), and though it is not named in Acts **15** 30.39, this route is again implied; while it is excluded in Acts **15** 3.

The ruins are very extensive and cover the whole space within the line of the old walls, which shows a circuit of four miles. The position of the Old Town, the Upper City and the suburbs may still be identified, as also that of the Antioch Gate, the Market Gate and the King's Gate, which last leads to the Upper City. There are rock-cut tombs, broken statuary and sarcophagi at the base of the Upper City, a position which probably represents the burial place of the Seleucids. The outline of a circus or amphitheater can also be traced, while the inner harbor is in perfect condition and full of water. It is 2,000 ft. long by 1,200 ft. broad, and covers 47 acres, being oval or pear-shaped. The passage seaward, now silted up, was protected by two strong piers or moles, which are locally named after Barnabas and Paul. The most remarkable of the remains, however, is the great water canal behind the city, which the emperor Constantius cut through the solid rock in 338 AD. It is 3,074 ft. long, has an average breadth of 20 ft., and is in some places 120 ft. deep. Two portions of 102 and 293 ft. in length are tunneled. The object of the work was clearly to carry the mountain torrent direct to the sea, and so protect the city from the risk of flood during the wet season.

Church synods occasionally met in Seleucia in the early centuries, but it gradually sank into decay, and long before the advent of Islam it had lost all its significance. W. M. Christie

SELEUCIDAE, sḗ-lū′si-dē. See Seleucus.

SELEUCUS, sḗ-lū′kus (**Σέλευκος,** *Séleukos*):

(1) Seleucus I (Nicator, "The Conqueror"), the founder of the Seleucidae or House of Seleucus, was an officer in the grand and thoroughly equipped army, which was perhaps the most important part of the inheritance that came to Alexander the Great from his father, Philip of Macedon. He took part in Alexander's Asiatic conquests, and on the division of these on Alexander's death he obtained the satrapy of Babylonia. By later conquests and under the name of king, which he assumed in the year 306, he became ruler of Syria and the greater part of Asia Minor. His rule extended from 312 to 280 BC, the year of his death; at least the Seleucid era which seems to be referred to in 1 Macc **1** 16 is reckoned from Seleucus I, 312 BC to 65 BC, when Pompey reduced the kingdom of Syria to a Rom province. He followed generally the policy of Alexander in spreading Gr civilization. He founded Antioch and its port Seleucia, and is said by Jos (*Ant*, XII, iii, 1) to have conferred civic privileges upon the Jews. The reference in Dnl **11** 5 is usually understood to be to this ruler.

(2) Seleucus II (Callinicus, "The Gloriously Triumphant"), who reigned from 246 to 226 BC, was the son of Antiochus Soter and is "the king of the north" in Dnl **11** 7–9, who was expelled from his kingdom by Ptolemy Euergetes.

(3) Seleucus III (Ceraunus, "Thunderbolt"), son of Seleucus II, was assassinated in a campaign which he undertook into Asia Minor. He had a short reign of rather more than 2 years (226–223 BC) and is referred to in Dnl **11** 10.

(4) Seleucus IV (Philopator, "Fond of his Father") was the son and successor of Antiochus the Great and reigned from 187 to 175 BC. He is called "King of Asia" (2 Macc **3** 3), a title claimed by the Seleucidae even after their serious losses in Asia Minor (see 1 Macc **8** 6; **11** 13; **12** 39; **13** 32). He was present at the decisive battle of Magnesia (190 BC). He was murdered by Heliodorus (q.v.), one of his own courtiers whom he had sent to plunder the Temple (2 Macc **3** 1–40; Dnl **11** 20).

For the connection of the above-named Seleucidae with the "ten horns" of Dnl **7** 24, the commentators must be consulted.

Seleucus V (125–124 BC) and Seleucus VI (95–93 BC) have no connection with the sacred narrative. J. Hutchison

SELF-CONTROL, self-kon-trōl′ (**ἐγκράτεια,** *egkráteia*): Rendered in AV "temperance" (cf Lat *temperatio* and *continentia*), but more accurately "self-control," as in RV (Acts **24** 25; Gal **5** 23; 2 Pet **1** 6); adj. of same, *ἐγκρατής*, *egkratḗs*, "self-controlled" (Tit **1** 8 RV); cf vb. forms in 1 Cor **7** 9, "have . . . . continency"; **9** 25, the athlete "exerciseth self-control." Self-control is therefore repeatedly set forth in the NT as among the important Christian virtues.

SELF-RIGHTEOUSNESS, self-rī′chus-nes: A term that has come to designate moral living as a way of salvation; or as a ground for neglecting the redemptive work of Jesus Christ. The thought is present in the teaching of Jesus, who spoke one parable particularly to such as reckoned themselves to be righteous (Lk **18** 9 ff). The Pharisees quite generally resented the idea of Jesus that all men needed repentance and they most of all. They regarded themselves as righteous and looked with contempt on "sinners." Paul in all his writings, esp. Rom **3**; Gal **3**; Eph **2**; Phil **3**, contrasts the righteousness that is God's gift to men of faith in Jesus Christ, with righteousness that is "of the law" and "in the flesh." By this latter he means formal conformity to legal requirements in the strength of unregenerate human nature. He is careful to maintain (cf Rom **7**) that the Law is never really kept by one's own power. On the other hand, in full agreement with Jesus, Paul looks to genuine righteousness in living as the demand and achievement of salvation based on faith. God's gift here consists in the capacity progressively to realize righteousness in life (cf Rom **8** 1 ff). See also Sanctification. William Owen Carver

SELF-SURRENDER, self-su-ren′dẽr: The struggle between the natural human impulses of self-seeking, self-defence and the like, on the one hand, and the more altruistic impulse toward self-denial, self-surrender, on the other, is as old as the race. All religions imply some conception of surrender of self to deity, ranging in ethical quality from a heathen fanaticism which impels to complete physical exhaustion or rapture, superinduced by more or less mechanical means, to the high spiritual quality of self-sacrifice to the divinest aims and achievements. The Scriptures represent self-surrender as among the noblest of human virtues.

I. In the OT.—In the OT self-surrender is taught in the early account of the first pair. Each was to be given to the other (Gen **2** 24; **3** 16*b*) and both were to be surrendered to God in perfect obedience (**3** 1–15). The faithful ones, throughout the Bible narratives, were characterized by self-surrender. Abraham abandons friends and native country to go to a land unknown to him, because God called him to do so (**12** 1). He would give up all his cherished hopes in his only son Isaac, at the voice of God (**22** 1–18). Moses, at the call of Jeh, surrenders self, and undertakes the deliverance of his fellow-Hebrews (Ex **3** 1—**4** 13; cf He **11** 25). He would be blotted out of God's book, if only the people might be spared destruction (Ex **32** 32).

1. Illustrious Examples

The whole Levitical system of sacrifice may be said to imply the doctrine of self-surrender. The nation itself was a people set apart to Jeh, a holy people, a surrendered nation (Ex **19** 5.6; **22** 31; Lev **20** 7; Dt **7** 6; **14** 2). The whole burnt offering implied the complete surrender of the worshipper to God (Lev **1**). The ceremony for the consecration of priests emphasized the same fundamental doctrine (Lev **8**); so also the law as to the surrender of the firstborn child (Ex **13** 13 ff; **22** 29).

2. The Levitical System

In the Divine call to the prophets and in their life-work self-surrender is prominent. The seer, as such, must be receptive to the Divine impress, and as mouthpiece of God, he must speak not his own words, but God's: "Thus saith the Lord." He was to be a "man of God," a "man of the spirit." 'The hand of the Lord was upon me' (Ezk **1** 3; **3** 14) implies complete Divine mastery. Isaiah must submit to the Divine purification of his lips, and hearken to the inquiry, "Who will go for us?" with the surrendered response, "Here am I; send me" (Isa **6** 8). Jeremiah must yield his protestations of weakness and inability to the Divine wisdom and the promise of endowment from above (Jer **1** 1–10). Ezekiel surrenders to the dangerous and difficult task of becoming messenger to a rebellious house (Ezk **2** 1—**3** 3). Jonah, after flight from duty, at last surrenders to the Divine will and goes to the Ninevites (Jon **3** 3).

3. The Prophets

On the return of the faithful remnant from captivity, self-giving for the sake of Israel's faith was dominant, the people enduring great hardships for the future of the nation and the accomplishment of Jeh's purposes. This is the spirit of the great Messianic passage, Isa **53** 7: "He was oppressed, yet when he was afflicted he opened not his mouth; as a lamb that is led to the slaughter, and as a sheep that before its shearers is dumb, so he opened not his mouth." Nehemiah surrendered position in Shushan to help reëstablish the returned exiles in Jerus (Neh **2** 5). Esther was ready to surrender her life in pleading for the safety of her people (Est **4** 16).

4. Post-exilic Examples

II. In the NT.—In the NT self-surrender is still more clearly set forth. Christ's teachings and example as presented in the Gospels, give to it special emphasis. It is a prime requisite for becoming His disciple (Mt **10** 38 f; **16** 24; Lk **9** 23.24. 59 f; **14** 27.33; cf Mt **19** 27; Mk **8** 34). When certain of the disciples were called they left all and followed (Mt **4** 20; **9** 9; Mk **2** 14; Lk **5** 27 f). His followers must so completely surrender self, as that father, mother, kindred, and one's own life must be, as it were, hated for His sake (Lk **14** 26). The rich young ruler must renounce self as an end and give his own life to the service of men (Mt **19** 21; Mk **10** 21; cf Lk **12** 33). But this surrender of self was never a loss of personality; it was the finding of the true self-hood (Mk **8** 35; Mt **10** 39). Our Lord not only taught self-surrender, but practised it. As a child, He subjected Himself to His parents (Lk **2** 51). Self-surrender marked His baptism and temptation (Mt **3** 15; **4** 1 ff). It is shown in His life of physical privation (**8** 20). He had come not to do His own will, but the Father's (Jn **4** 34; **5** 30; **6** 38). He refuses to use force for His own deliverance (Mt **26** 53; Jn **18** 11). In His person God's will, not His own, must be done (Mt **26** 29; Lk **22** 42); and to the Father He at last surrendered His spirit (Lk **23** 46). So that while He was no ascetic, and did not demand asceticism of His followers, He "emptied himself . . . . becoming obedient even unto death, yea, the death of the cross" (Phil **2** 7 f; see KENOSIS).

1. Christ's Teaching and Example

The early disciples practised the virtue of self-surrender. Counting none of their possessions their own, they gave to the good of all (Acts **2** 44.45; **4** 34.35.37). Stephen and others threw themselves into their witnessing with the perfect abandon of the martyr; and Stephen's successor, Paul, counted not his life dear unto himself that he might finish the Divinely appointed course (**20** 22–24).

2. Acts of Apostles

The Epp. are permeated with the doctrine of self-surrender. The Pauline Epp. are particularly full of it. The Christian life is conceived of as a dying to self and to the world—a dying with Christ, a crucifixion of the old man, that a new man may live (Gal **2** 20; **6** 14; Col **2** 20; **3** 3; Rom **6** 6), so that no longer the man lives but Christ lives in him (Gal **2** 20; Phil **1** 21). The Christian is no longer his own but Christ's (1 Cor **6** 19.20). He is to be a living sacrifice (Rom **12** 1); to die daily (1 Cor **15** 31). As a corollary to surrender to God, the Christian must surrender himself to the welfare of his neighbor, just as Christ pleased not Himself (Rom **15** 3); also to leaders (1 Cor **16** 16), and to earthly rulers (Rom **13** 1).

3. Epistles of Paul

In the Epp. of Peter self-surrender is taught more than once. Those who were once like sheep astray now submit to the guidance of the Shepherd of souls (1 Pet **2** 25). The Christian is to humble himself under the mighty hand of God (**5** 6); the younger to be subject to the elder (**5** 5); and all to civil ordinances for the Lord's sake (**2** 13).

4. Epistles of Peter

So also in other Epp. The Christian is to subject himself to God (Jas **4** 7; He **12** 9).

EDWARD BAGBY POLLARD

SELF-WILL, self-wil′ (רָצוֹן, *rāçōn;* αὐθάδης, *authádēs*): Found once in the OT (Gen **49** 6, "In their self-will they hocked an ox") in the death song of Jacob (see HOCK). The idea is found twice in the NT in the sense of "pleasing oneself": "not self-willed, not soon angry" (Tit **1** 7); and "daring, self-willed, they tremble not to rail at dignities" (2 Pet **2** 10). In all these texts it stands for a false pride, for obstinacy, for "a pertinacious adherence to one's will or wish, esp. in opposition to the dictates of wisdom or propriety or the wishes of others."

HENRY E. DOSKER

SELL, SELLER, sel′ẽr. See TRADE; LYDIA.

SELVEDGE, sel′vej (קָצָה, *ḳāçāh*): The word occurs only in the description of the tabernacle (Ex **26** 4; **36** 11). It has reference to the ten curtains which overhung the boards of the sanctuary. Five of these formed one set and five another.

These were "coupled" at the center by 50 loops of blue connected by "clasps" (q.v.) with 50 others on the opposite side. The "selvedge" (self-edge) is the extremity of the curtain in which the loops were.

SEM, sem (Σήμ, *Sēm*): AV from the Gr form of Shem; thus RV (Lk **3** 36).

SEMACHIAH, sem-a-kī'a (סְמַכְיָהוּ, *ṣ^emakhyāhū*, "Jeh has sustained"): A Korahite family of gatekeepers (1 Ch **26** 7). Perhaps the same name should be substituted for "Ismachiah" in 2 Ch **31** 13 (see *HPN*, 291, 295).

SEMEI, sem'ē-ī:

(1) (A, Σεμεί, *Semei*, B, Σεμεεί, *Semeei*): One of those who put away their "strange wives" (1 Esd **9** 33) = "Shimei" "of the sons of Hashum" in Ezr **10** 33.

(2) AV = RV "Semeias" (Ad Est **11** 2).

(3) AV form of RV "Semein" (Lk **3** 26).

SEMEIAS, sē-mē-ī'as (א A, **Σεμείας,** *Semeias;* B, **Σεμεείας,** *Semeeias;* AV **Semei**): An ancestor of Mordecai (Ad Est **11** 2) = "Shimei" (Est **2** 5).

SEMEIN, sē-mē'in (א B, **Σεμεείν,** *Semeein*, A, **Σεμεεί,** *Semeei*, *TR*, **Σεμεΐ,** *Semeï*; AV **Semei**): An ancestor of Jesus in Lk's genealogy (Lk **3** 26).

SEMEIS, sem'ē-is (A and Fritzsche, **Σεμεῖς,** *Semeis;* B, **Σενσεῖς,** *Senseis*; AV **Semis**): One of the Levites who put away their "strange wives" (1 Esd **9** 23) = "Shimei" in Ezr **10** 23.

SEMELLIUS, sē-mel'i-us: AV = RV SAMELLIUS (q.v.).

SEMIS, sē'mis: AV = RV SEMEIS (q.v.).

SEMITES, sem'īts, **SEMITIC,** sem-it'ik, **RELIGION:**

1. Biblical References

The words "Semites," "Semitic," do not occur in the Bible, but are derived from the name of Noah's oldest son, Shem (Gen **5** 32; **6** 10; **9** 18.23 ff; **10** 1.21 f; **11** 10 f; 1 Ch **1**). Formerly the designation was limited to those who are mentioned in Gen **10, 11** as Shem's descendants, most of whom can be traced historically and geographically; but more recently the title has been expanded to apply to others who are not specified in the Bible as Semites, and indeed are plainly called Hamitic, e.g. the Babylonians (Gen **10** 10) and the Phoenicians and Canaanites (vs 15–19). The grounds for the inclusion of these Bib. Hamites among the Semites are chiefly linguistic, although political, commercial and religious affinities are also considered. History and the study of comparative philology, however, suggest the inadequacy of a linguistic argument.

2. The Five Sons of Shem

The sons of Shem are given as Elam, Asshur, Arpachshad, Lud and Aram (Gen **10** 22). All except the third have been readily identified, Elam as the historic nation in the highlands E. of the Tigris, between Media and Persia; Asshur as the Assyrians; Lud as the Lydians of Asia Minor; and Aram as the Syrians both E. and W. of the Euphrates. The greatest uncertainty is in the identification of Arpachshad, the most prolific ancestor of the Semites, esp. of those of Bib. and more recent importance. From him descended the Hebrews and the Arab tribes, probably also some East African colonies (Gen **10** 24–30; **11** 12–26). The form of his name (אַרְפַּכְשַׁד, *'arpakhshadh*) has given endless trouble to ethnographers. McCurdy divides into two words, *Arpach* or *Arpath*, unidentified, and *kesedh*, the sing. of *kasdīm*, i.e. the Chaldaeans; Schrader also holds to the Chaldaean interpretation, and the Chaldaeans themselves traced their descent from Arpachshad (Jos, *Ant*, I, vi, 4); it has been suggested also to interpret as the "border of the Chaldaeans" (*BDB;* Dillmann, in loc.). But the historic, ordinary and most satisfactory identification is with *Arrapachitis*, N.E. of Assyria at the headwaters of the Upper Zab in the Armenian highlands (so Ptolemy, classical geographers, Gesenius, Delitzsch). Delitzsch calls attention to the Armenian termination *shadh* (*Comm. on Gen*, in loc.).

3. Original Home of the Semites

If we accept, then, this identification of Arpachshad as the most northeasterly of the five Sem families (Gen **10** 22), we are still faced by the problem of the primitive home and racial origin of the Semites. Various theories of course have been proposed; fancy and surmise have ranged from Africa to Central Asia. (1) The most common, almost generally accepted, theory places their beginnings in Arabia because of the conservative and primitive Semitic of the Arabic language, the desert characteristics of the various branches of the race, and the historic movements of Sem tribes northward and westward from Arabia. But this theory does not account for some of the most significant facts: e.g. that the Sem developments of Arabia are the last, not the first, in time, as must have been the case if Arabia was the cradle of the race. This theory does not explain the Sem origin of the Elamites, except by denial; much less does it account for the location of Arpachshad still farther north. It is not difficult to understand a racial movement from the mountains of the N.E. into the lowlands of the South and West. But how primitive Arabs could have migrated uphill, as it were, to settle in the Median and Armenian hills is a much more difficult proposition. (2) We must return to the historic and the more natural location of the ancient Sem home on the hillsides and in the fertile valleys of Armenia. Thence the eldest branch migrated in prehistoric times southward to become historic Elam; Lud moved westward into Asia Minor; Asshur found his way down the Tigris to become the sturdy pastoral people of the middle Mesopotamian plateau until the invasion of the Bab colonists and civilization; Aram found a home in Upper Mesopotamia; while Arpachshad, remaining longer in the original home, gave his name to at least a part of it. There in the fertile valleys among the high hills the ancient Semites developed their distinctively tribal life, emphasizing the beauty and close relationship of Nature, the sacredness of the family, the moral obligation, and faith in a personal God of whom they thought as a member of the tribe or friend of the family. The confinement of the mountain valleys is just as adequate an explanation of the Sem traits as the isolation of the oasis. So from the purer life of their highland home, where had been developed the distinctive and virile elements which were to impress the Sem faith on the history of mankind, increasing multitudes of Semites poured over the mountain barriers into the broader levels of the plains. As their own mountain springs and torrents sought a way to the sea down the Tigris and Euphrates beds, so the Sem tribes followed the same natural ways into their future homes: Elam, Babylonia, Assyria, Mesopotamia, Arabia, Pal. Those who settled Arabia sent further migrations into Africa, as well as rebounding into the desert west of the Euphrates, Syria and Pal. Thus Western Asia became the arena of Sem life, whose influences also reached Egypt and, through Phoenicia, the far-away West-Mediterranean.

4. Confusion with Other Races

While we may properly call Western and Southwestern Asia the home of the Sem peoples, there still remains the difficulty of separating them definitely from the other races among whom they lived. The historic Babylonians, e.g., were Sem; yet they dispossessed an earlier non-Sem people, and were themselves frequently invaded by other races, such as the Hittites, and even the Egyptians. It is not certain therefore which gods, customs, laws, etc, of the Babylonians were Sem, and not adopted from those whom they superseded.

Assyria was racially purely Sem, but her laws, customs, literature, and many of her gods were acquired from Babylonia; to such an extent was this true that we are indebted to the library of the Assyr Asshurbanipal for much that we know of Bab religion, literature and history. In Syria also the same mixed conditions prevailed, for through Syria by the fords of the Euphrates lay the highway of the nations, and Hittite and Mitannian at times shared the land with her, and left their influence. Possibly in Arabia Sem blood ran purest, but even in Arabia there were tribes from other races; and the table of the nations in Gen divides that land among the descendants of both Ham and Shem (see TABLE OF NATIONS). Last of all, in Pal, from the very beginning of its historic period, we find an intermingling and confusion of races and religions such as no other Sem center presents. A Hamitic people gave one of its common names to the country—Canaan, while the pagan and late-coming Philistine gave the most used name—Palestine. The archaic remains of Horite, Avite and Hivite are being uncovered by exploration; these races survived in places, no doubt, long after the Sem invasion, contributing their quota to the customs and religious practices of the land. The Hittite also was in the land, holding outposts from his northern empire, even in the extreme south of Pal. If the blue eyes and fair complexions of the Amorites pictured on Egyp monuments are true representations, we may believe that the gigantic Aryans of the North had their portion also in Pal.

5. Reliability of Gen 10

It is customary now in Bib. ethnology to disregard the classification of Gen **10,** and to group all the nations of Pal as Sem, esp. the Canaanite and the Phoenician along with the Hebrew. McCurdy in the *Standard BD* treats the various gods and religious customs of Pal as though they were all Sem, although uniformly these are represented in the OT as perversions and enormities of alien races which the Hebrews were commanded to extirpate. The adoption of them would be, and was, inimical to their own ancestral faith. Because the Hebrews took over eventually the language of the Phoenician, appropriated his art and conveniences, did traffic in his ships, and in Ahab's reign adopted his Baal and Astarte, we are not warranted at all in rushing to the conclusion that the Phoenicians represented a primitive Sem type. Racial identification by linguistic argument is always precarious, as history clearly shows. One might as well say that Latin and the gospel were Saxon. There are indications that the customs and even the early language of the Hebrews were different from those of the people whom they subdued and dispossessed. Such is the consistent tradition of their race, the Bible always emphasizing the irreconcilable difference between their ancestral faith and the practices of the people of Canaan. We may conclude that the reasons for disregarding the classification of Gen with reference to the Semites and neighboring races are not final. Out from that fruitful womb of nations, the Caucasus, the Semites, one branch of the Caucasian peoples, went southwestward—as their cousins the Hamites went earlier toward the South and as their younger relatives, the Aryans, were to go northward and westward—with marked racial traits and a pronounced religious development, to play a leading part in the life of man.

6. Semitic Languages

The phrase **Sem Languages** is used of a group of languages which have marked features in common, which also set them off from other languages. But we must avoid the unnecessary inference that nations using the same or kindred languages are of the same ancestry. There are other explanations of linguistic affinity than racial, as the Indians of Mexico may speak Spanish, and the Germans of Milwaukee, English. So also neighboring or intermingled nations may just as naturally have used branches of the Sem language stock. However, it is true that the nations which were truly Sem used languages which are strikingly akin. These have been grouped as (1) Eastern Sem, including Bab and Assyr; (2) Northern, including Syriac and Aramaic; (3) Western, including Canaanite, or Phoenician, and Hebrew, and (4) Southern, including Arabic, Sabaean and Ethiopic (cf Geden, *Intro to the Heb Bible,* 14–28). The distinctive features of this family of languages are (1) the tri-literal root, (2) the consonantal writing, vowel indications being unnecessary so long as the language was spoken, (3) the meager use of moods and tenses in verbal inflection, every action being graphically viewed as belonging to one of two stages in time: completed or incomplete, (4) the paucity of parts of speech, verb and noun covering nearly all the relations of words, (5) the frequent use of internal change in the inflection of words, e.g. the doubling of a consonant or the change of a vowel, and (6) the use of certain letters, called "serviles," as prefixes or suffixes in inflection; these are parts of pronouns or the worn-down residua of nouns and particles. The *manner* of writing was not uniform in these languages, Bab and Assyr being ideographic and syllabic, and written from left to right, while Aram., Heb and Arab. were alphabetic and written from right to left. The primitive forms and inflections of the group are best preserved in the Arab. by reason of the conservatism of the desert peoples, and in the Assyr by the sudden destruction of that empire and the burial of the records of that language in a comparatively pure state, to be brought back to light by 19th-cent. exploration. All the characteristics given above are clearly manifest in the Heb of the OT.

7. Semitic Religion

In the study of **Sem Religion** there are two tendencies toward error: (1) the Western pragmatical and unsympathetic overtaxing of oriental Nature-symbols and vividly imaginative speech. Because the Semite used the figure of the rock (Dt **32** 4.18.30) in describing God, or poetically conceived of the storm-cloud as Jeh's chariot (Ps **104** 3), we must not be led into believing that his religion was a savage animism, or that Jeh of Israel was only the Zeus of the Greeks. How should an imaginative child of Nature speak of the unseen Spiritual Power, except in the richest analogies of Nature? (2) The second error is the tendency to treat the accretions acquired by contact with other nations as of the essence of Sem religion, e.g. the golden calf following the Egyp bondage, and the sexual abominations of the Can. Baal and Astarte.

The primitive and distinctive beliefs of the Sem peoples lie still in great uncertainty because of the long association with other peoples, whose practices they readily took over, and because of the lack of records of the primitive periods of Sem development, their origin and dispersion among the nations being prehistoric. Our sources of information are the Bab and Assyr tablets and monuments, the Egyp inscriptions, Phoen history, Arabian traditions and inscriptions, and principally the OT Scriptures. We can never know perhaps how much the pure Semitism of Babylonians and Assyrians was diverted and corrupted by the developed civilization which they invaded and appropriated; Egypt was only indirectly affected by Sem life; Sem development in Arabia was the latest in all the group, besides which the monuments and *reste* of Arabian antiquity which have come down to us are comparatively few; and the Phoen development was corrupted by the sensuality of the ancient Canaanitish cults, while the Bible of the Hebrews emphatically differentiated from the unwholesome religions of Pal their own faith, which was ancestral, revealed and pure. Was that Bible faith the primitive Sem cult? At least we must take the Heb tradition at its face value, finding in it the prominent features of an ancestral faith, preserved through one branch of the Sem group. We are met frequently in these Heb records by the claim that the religion they present is not a new development, nor a thing apart from the origin of their race, but rather the preservation of an ancient worship, Abraham, Moses and the prophets appearing not as originators, but reformers, or revivers, who sought to keep their people true to an inherited religion. Its elemental features are the following:

(1) *It was pronouncedly theistic;* not that other religions do not affirm a god; but the theism of the Semites was such as to give their religion a unique place among all others. To say the least, it had the germ of or the tendency toward monotheism, if we have not sufficient evidence to affirm its monotheism, and to rate the later polytheistic representations of Babylonia and Assyria as local perversions. If the old view that Sem religion was essentially monotheistic be incapable of proof, it is true that the necessary development of their concept of God must ultimately arrive at monotheism. This came to verification in Abram the Hebrew, Jesus the Messiah (Jn **4** 21–24) and Mohammed the false prophet. A city-state exclusively, a nation predominantly, worshipped one god, often through some Nature-symbol, as sun or star or element. With the coming of world-conquest, intercourse and vision, the one god of the city or the chief god of the nation became universalized. The ignorant and materialistic Hebrew might localize the God of Israel in a city or on a hilltop; but to the spiritual mind of Amos or in the universal vision of Isaiah He was Jeh, Lord of all the earth.

(2) Closely related to this high conception of Deity was the apparently contradictory but really *potent idea of the Deity as a personality.* The Semite did not grossly materialize his God as did the savage, nor vainly abstract and etherealize Him and so eliminate Him from the experience of man as did the Greek; but to him God universal was also God personal and intimate. The Hebrew ran the risk of conditioning the spirituality of God in order to maintain His real personality. Possibly this has been the most potent element in Sem religion; God was not far from every one of them. He came into the closest relations as father or friend. He was the companion of king and priest. The affairs of the nation were under His immediate care; He went to war with armies, was a partner in harvest rejoicings; the home was His abode. This conception of Deity carried with it the necessary implication of revelation (Am **3** 8). The office, message and power of the Heb prophet were also the logical consequence of knowing God as a Person.

(3) *Its peculiar view of Nature* was another feature of Sem religion. God was everywhere and always present in Nature; consequently its symbolism was the natural and ready expression of His nature and presence. Simile, parable and Nature-marvels cover the pages and tablets of their records. Unfortunately this poetic conception of Nature quickly enough afforded a ready path in which wayward feet and carnal minds might travel toward Nature-worship with all of its formalism and its degrading excesses. This feature of Sem religion offers an interesting commentary on their philosophy. With them the doctrine of Second Causes received no emphasis; God worked directly in Nature, which became to them therefore the continuous arena of signs and marvels. The thunder was His voice, the sunshine reflected the light of His countenance, the winds were His messengers. And so through this imaginative view of the world the Semite dwelt in an enchanted realm of the miraculous.

(4) The Semite believed in *a God who is a moral being.* Such a faith in the nature of it was certain to influence profoundly their own moral development, making for them a racial character which has been distinctive and persistent through the changes of millenniums. By it also they have impressed other nations and religions, with which they have had contact. The CH is an expression of the moral issues of theism. The Law and the Prophets of Israel arose out of the conviction of God's righteousness and of the moral order of His universe (Ex **19** 5.6; Isa **1** 16–20). The Decalogue is a confession of faith in the unseen God; the Law of Holiness (Lev **17–26**) is equally a moral code.

While these elements are not absent altogether from other ancient religions, they are pronouncedly characteristic of the Sem to the extent that they have given to it its permanent form, its large development, and its primacy among the religions of the human race. To *know* God, to hear His eternal tread in Nature, to clothe Him with light as with a garment, to establish His throne in righteousness, to perceive that holiness is the all-pervading atmosphere of His presence—such convictions were bound to affect the life and progress of a race, and to consecrate them as a nation of priests for all mankind.

LITERATURE.—For discussion of the details of Sem peoples and religions reference must be made to the particular articles, such as ARPACHSHAD; EBER; ABRAHAM; HAMMURABI; ASSYRIA; BABYLONIA; BAAL; ASHTORETH; ASHERIM; MOLOCH; CHEMOSH; CHIUN; ISRAEL, RELIGION OF, etc. The lit. on the subject is vast, interesting and far from conclusive. Few of the Bible Dicts. have arts. on this particular subject; reference should be made to those in the *Standard* and in the *HDB*, vol V, both by McCurdy; "Semites" in *Catholic Enc* skims the surface; arts. in *International Enc* are good. In OT Theologies, Davidson, pp. 249–52; Schultz, ch iii of vol I; Riehm, *Alttestamentliche Theologie;* Delitzsch, *Psychology of the OT.* For language see *Wright's Comparative Grammar of Sem Languages.* For history and religion: Maspero's three vols; McCurdy, *HPM;* Hommel, *Ancient Heb Tradition*, and *Sem Völker u. Sprache;* Jastrow, *Comparative Sem Religion;* Friedr. Delitzsch, *Babel u. Bibel;* W. R. Smith, *Religion of the Semites.*

EDWARD MACK

SENAAH, sē-nā'a, sen'ā-a (סְנָאָה, *ṣ^enā'āh;* B, **Σαανά,** *Saaná,* **Σαναάτ,** *Sananát,* A, **Σαναvá,** *Sananá,* **Σενναά,** *Sennaá,* **'Ασάν,** *Hasán*): The children of Senaah are mentioned as having formed part of the company returning from the captivity with Zerubbabel (Ezr **2** 35; Neh **7** 38). The numbers vary as given by Ezr (3,630) and Neh (3,930), while 1 Esd **5** 23 puts them at 3,330. In the last place the name is Sanaas, AV "Annaas" (B, Σαμά, *Samá,* A, Σανάας, *Sanáas*). In Neh **3** 3 the name occurs with the def. art., *ha-senaah.* The people may be identical with the Benjamite clan Hassenuah (1 Ch **9** 7). *Onom* speaks of Magdalsenna, a village about 7 miles N. of Jericho, which may be the place intended; but the site is not known.

W. EWING

SENATE, sen'āt, **SENATOR,** sen'a-tēr: In Ps **105** 22, "teach his senators [RV "elders"] wisdom." The Heb is זָקֵן, *zāḳēn,* "elder" (LXX πρεσβύτεροι, *presbúteroi*). In Acts **5** 21, "called the council together and all the senate of the children of Israel." The Gr γερουσία, *gerousía,* is here evidently used as a more precise equivalent of the foregoing "council" (συνέδριον, *sunédrion*), to which it is added by καί, *kaí,* explicative. Reference is had to the Sanhedrin. See SANHEDRIN. This term *gerousia* occurs in LXX Ex **3** 16, etc, and in 1 Macc **12** 6; 2 Macc **1** 10; **4** 44 of the supreme council of the Jews (see GOVERNMENT). In 1 Macc **8** 15; **12** 3, *βουλευτήριον*, *bouleutērion*, is used of the Rom senate, which is said to consist of 320 members meeting daily, consulting always for the people, to the end that they may be well governed. These statements are not quite accurate, since the senate consisted normally of 300 members, and met not daily, but on call of the magistrates. Originally, like the *gerousia* of the Jews, the representatives of families and clans (*gentes*), the senators were subsequently the ex-magistrates, supplemented, to complete the tale of members, by representatives of patrician (in time also of plebeian) families selected by the censor. The tenure was ordinarily for life, though it might be terminated for cause by the censor. Although constitutionally the senate was only an advisory body, its advice (*senatus consultum, auctoritas*) in fact became in time a mandate which few dared to disregard. During the republican period the senate practically ruled Rome; under the empire it tended more and more to become the creature and subservient tool of the emperors. WILLIAM ARTHUR HEIDEL

SENEH, sē'ne (סֶנֶה, *ṣeneh; Σεννά, Senná*): This was the name attaching to the southern of the two great cliffs between which ran the gorge of Michmash (1 S **14** 4). The name means "acacia," and may have been given to it from the thorn bushes growing upon it. Jos (*BJ*, V, ii, 1) mentions the "plain of thorns" near Gabathsaul. We may hear an echo of the old name in that of *Wâdy Suweinīṭ*, "valley of the little thorn tree," the name by which the gorge is known today. The cliff must have stood on the right side of the *wâdy*; see BOZEZ. Conder gives an excellent description of the place in *Tent Work in Pal*, II, 112-14. W. EWING

SENIR, sē'nir (שְׂנִיר, *s*ᵉ*nīr; Σανείρ, Saneír*): This was the Amorite name of Mt. Hermon, according to Dt **3** 9 (AV "Shenir"). But in 1 Ch **5** 23; Cant **4** 8, we have Senir *and* Hermon named as distinct mountains. It seems probable, however, that Senir applied to a definite part of the Anti-Lebanon or Hermon range. An inscription of Shalmaneser tells us that Hazael, king of Damascus, fortified Mt. Senir over against Mt. Lebanon. So in Ezk **27** 5, Senir, whence the Tyrians got planks of fir trees, is set over against Lebanon, where cedars were obtained. The Arab geographers give the name *Jebel Sanīr* to the part of the Anti-Lebanon range which lies between Damascus and Homs (Yakut, c 1225 AD, quoted by Guy le Strange in *Pal under the Moslems*, 79. He also quotes Mas'udi, 943 AD, to the effect that Baalbek is in the district of Senir, 295). W. EWING

SENNACHERIB, se-nak'ẽr-ib (סַנְחֵרִיב, *ṣanḥērībh; Σενναχηρείμ, Sennachēreím*, Assyr *Sin-akhi-erba*, "the moon-god Sin has increased the brothers"): Sennacherib (704-682 BC) ascended the throne of Assyria after the death of his father Sargon. Appreciating the fact that Babylon would be difficult to control, instead of endeavoring to conciliate the people he ignored them. The Babylonians, being indignant, crowned a man of humble origin, Marduk-zâkir-shum by name. He ruled only a month, having been driven out by the irrepressible Merodach-baladan, who again appeared on the scene.

In order to fortify himself against Assyria the latter sent an embassy to Hezekiah, apparently for the purpose of inspiring the W. to rebel against Assyria (2 K **20** 12-19).

Sennacherib in his first campaign marched into Babylonia. He found Merodach-baladan intrenched at Kish, about 9 miles from Babylon, and defeated him; after which he entered the gates of Babylon, which had been thrown open to him. He placed a Babylonian, named Bêl-ibni, on the throne.

This campaign was followed by an invasion of the country of the Cassites and Iasubigalleans. In his third campaign he directed his attention to the W., where the people had become restless under the Assyr yoke. Hezekiah had been victorious over the Philis (2 K **18** 8). In preparation to withstand a siege, Hezekiah had built a conduit to bring water within the city walls (2 K **20** 20). Although strongly opposed by the prophet Isaiah, gifts were sent to Egypt, whence assistance was promised (Isa **30** 1-4). Apparently also the Phoenicians and Philis, who had been sore pressed by Assyria, had made provision to resist Assyria. The first move was at Ekron, where the Assyr governor Padi was put into chains and sent to Hezekiah at Jerus.

Sennacherib, in 701, moved against the cities in the W. He ravaged the environs of Tyre, but made no attempt to take the city, as he was without a naval force. After Elulaeus the king of Sidon fled, the city surrendered without a battle, and Ethbaal was appointed king. Numerous cities at once sent presents to the king of Assyria. Ashkelon and other cities were taken. The forces of Egypt were routed at Eltekeh, and Ekron was destroyed. He claims to have conquered 46 strongholds of Hezekiah's territory, but he did not capture Jerus, for concerning the king he said, in his annals, "himself like a bird in a cage in Jerus, his royal city, I penned him." He states, also, how he reduced his territory, and how Hezekiah sent to him 30 talents of gold and 800 talents of silver, besides hostages.

The Bib. account of this invasion is found in 2 K **18** 13—**19** 37; Isa **36, 37**. The Assyr account differs considerably from it; but at the same time it corroborates it in many details. One of the striking parallels is the exact amount of gold which Hezekiah sent to the Assyr king (see *Expos T*, XII, 225,405; XIII, 326).

In the following year Sennacherib returned to Babylonia to put down a rebellion by Bêl-ibni and Merodach-baladan. The former was sent to Assyria, and the latter soon afterward died. Ashur-nâdin-shum, the son of Sennacherib, was then crowned king of Babylon. A campaign into Cilicia and Cappadocia followed.

In 694 Sennacherib attacked the Elamites, who were in league with the Babylonians. In revenge, the Elamites invaded Babylonia and carried off Ashur-nâdin-shum to Elam, and made Nergal-ushêzib king of Babylon. He was later captured and in turn carried off to Assyria. In 691 Sennacherib again directed his attention to the S., and at Khalutê fought with the combined forces. Two years later he took Babylon, and razed it to the ground.

In 681 Sennacherib was murdered by his two sons (2 K **19** 37; see SHAREZER). Esar-haddon their younger brother, who was at the time conducting a campaign against Ararat, was declared king in his stead. A. T. CLAY

SENSES, sen'siz: The tr of *αἰσθητήριον, aisthētērion* (He **5** 14, "those who by reason of use have their senses exercised to discern good and evil"). The word means, primarily, the seat of the senses, the region of feeling; in the LXX of Jer **4** 19, it represents the Heb *ḳīr*, "the walls of the heart" (see RV), and is used to denote the *internal* sense or faculty of perceiving and judging, which in He **5**

14 is regarded as becoming perfected by use or exercise (cf Eph **4** 12 f; 1 Tim **4** 7; 2 Pet **3** 18).

In 2 Esd **10** 36 we have "Or is my sense deceived, or my soul in a dream?" Lat *sensus*, here "mind" rather than "sense." W. L. WALKER

SENSUAL, sen'shōō-al (ψυχικός, *psuchikós*, "animal," "natural"): Bib. psychology has no Eng. equivalent for this Gr original. Man subject to the lower appetites is σαρκικός, *sarkikós*, "fleshly"; in the communion of his spirit with God he is πνευματικός, *pneumatikós*, "spiritual." Between the two is the ψυχή, *psuchē*, "soul," the center of his personal being. This *ego* or "I" in each man is bound to the spirit, the higher nature; and to the body or lower nature.

The soul (*psuchē*) as the seat of the senses, desires, affections, appetites, passions, i.e. the lower animal nature common to man with the beasts, was distinguished in the Pythagorean and Platonic philosophy from the higher rational nature (*noús*, *pneúma*).

The subjection of the soul to the animal nature is man's debasement, to the spirit indwelt of God is his exaltation. The Eng. equivalent for *psuchikos*, "psychic," does not express this debasement. In the NT "sensual" indicates man's subjection to self and self-interest, whether animal or intellectual—the selfish man in whom the spirit is degraded into subordination to the debased *psuchē*, "soul." This debasement may be (1) *intellectual*, "not wisdom . . . . from above, but . . . . earthly, sensual" (Jas **3** 15); (2) *carnal* (and of course *moral*), "sensual, having not the Spirit" (Jude ver 19). It ranges all the way from sensuous self-indulgence to gross immorality. In the utter subjection of the spirit to sense it is the utter exclusion of God from the life. Hence "the *natural* [*psuchikos*] man receiveth not the things of the Spirit of God" (1 Cor **2** 14). The term is equivalent to "the mind of the flesh" (Rom **8** 7) which "is not subject to the law of God." See PSYCHOLOGY. DWIGHT M. PRATT

SENT (שָׁלַח, *shālaḥ*; ἀποστέλλω, *apostéllō*): "Sent" in the OT is the tr of *shālaḥ*, "to send" (of presents, messengers, etc, Gen **32** 18; **44** 3; Jgs **6** 14; 1 K **14** 6; Est **3** 13; Prov **17** 11; Jer **49** 14; Ezk **3** 5; **23** 40; Dnl **10** 11; Ob ver 1); of *shelāḥ*, Aram. (Ezr **7** 14; Dnl **5** 24); of *shillūḥīm*, "sending" (Ex **18** 2); in the NT of *apostellō*, "to send off" or "away," "to send forth" (Jn **9** 7, "the pool of Siloam [which is by interpretation, Sent]"); cf Lk **13** 4; Neh **3** 15, "the pool of Siloah," RV "Shelah"; Isa **8** 6, "the waters of Shiloah that go softly," where LXX has *Silōam* for Heb *shilōaḥ*, "a sending," which, rather than "Sent," is the original meaning—a sending forth of waters. See SILOAM. "Sent" is also the tr of *apóstolos*, "one sent forth" (the original of the familiar word "apostle"); in Jn **13** 16, "one that is sent" (m "Gr 'an apostle'"); cf He **1** 14. W. L. WALKER

SENTENCE, sen'tens: Eight Heb and three Gr words are thus trd in AV. Sometimes it points to a mystery (Dnl **5** 12; **8** 23); then again to the contents of the Law (Dt **17** 11); then again to the idea of judgment (Ps **17** 2) or of a judicial sentence (2 Cor **1** 9; Lk **23** 24), or of judicial advice (Acts **15** 19, ARV "judgment").

SENUAH, sē-nū'a, sen'ū-a (סְנוּאָה, *senū'āh*): In AV "A Benjamite" (Neh **11** 9); RV has "Hassenuah," transliterating the def. art. AV is to be preferred (cf 1 Ch **9** 7).

SEORIM, sē-ō'rim, sē-ôr'im (שְׂעֹרִים, *se'ōrīm*): The name borne by one of the (post-exilic) priestly courses (1 Ch **24** 8).

SEPARATE, sep'a-rāt: The tr of a number of Heb and Gr words, בָּדַל, *bādhal* (Lev **20** 24, etc), and ἀφορίζω, *aphorízō* (Mt **25** 32, etc), being the most common. "To separate" and "to consecrate" were originally not distinguished (e.g. Nu **6** 2 m), and probably the majority of the uses of "separate" in EV connote "to set apart for God." But precisely the same term that is used in this sense may also denote the exact opposite (e.g. the use of *nāzar* in Ezk **14** 7 and Zec **7** 3). See HOLY; NAZIRITE; SAINT.

SEPARATION, sep-a-rā'shun: In the Pent the word *niddah* specially points to a state of ceremonial uncleanness (Lev **12** 2.5; **15** 20 ff; Nu **6** 4 ff; **12** 13; **19** 21). For a description of the "water of purification," used for cleansing what was ceremonially unclean (Nu **19**), see HEIFER, RED; UNCLEANNESS. For "separation" in the sense of *nēzer*, see NAZIRITE.

SEPHAR, sē'fär: Only in Gen **10** 30 (סְפָרָה, *ṣephārāh*, "toward Sephar"), as the eastern limit of the territory of the sons of Yoktan (Joktan). From the similarity between the names of most of Yoktan's sons and the names of South Arabian towns or districts, it can hardly be doubted that Sephar is represented by the Arab. *Ẓafār*. The appropriateness of the site seems to outweigh the discrepancy between Arab. *ẓ* and Heb *ṣ*. But two important towns in South Arabia bear this name. The one lies a little to the S. of *Ṣan'ā'*. According to tradition it was founded by Shammir, one of the Sabaean kings, and for a long time served as the royal seat of the Tubbas. The other *Ẓafār* stands on the coast in the district of *Shiḥr*, E. of *Ḥaḍramaut*. The latter is probably to be accepted as the Bib. site. A. S. FULTON

SEPHARAD, sē-fā'rad, sef'a-rad (סְפָרַד, *ṣephāradh*): Mentioned in Ob ver 20 as the place of captivity of certain "captives of Jerus," but no clear indication is given of locality. Many conjectures have been made. The Tg of Jonathan identifies with Spain; hence the Spanish Jews are called Sephardim. Others (Pusey, etc) have connected it with the "Çparda" of the Behistun Inscription, and some have even identified it with "Sardis." The now generally accepted view is that which connects it with the "Saparda" of the Assyr inscriptions, though whether this is to be located to the E. of Assyria or in Northern Asia Minor is not clear. See Schrader, *Cuneiform Inscriptions*, II, 145–46; Sayce, *HCM*, 482–84; arts. in *DB*, *HDB*, *EB*, etc. JAMES ORR

SEPHARVAIM, sef-är-vā'im, sē-fär-vā'im (סְפַרְוַיִם, *sepharwayim*; Σεφφαρουάιμ, *Sephpharouáim*, Σεπφαρουάιμ, *Seppharouáim*, Σεπφαρούν, *Seppharoún*, Σεπφαρουμάιν, *Seppharoumáin*, Ἐπφαρουάιμ, *Eppharouáim*, Σεπφαρείμ, *Seppharéim*, the first two being the forms in MSS A and B respectively, of the passages in K, and the last two in Isa): This city, mentioned in 2 K **17** 24; **18** 34; **19** 13; Isa **36** 19; **37** 13, is generally identified with the *Sip(p)ar* of the Assyr-Bab inscriptions (*Zimbir* in Sumerian), on the Euphrates, about 16 miles S.W. of Bagdad. It was one of the two great seats of the worship of the Bab sun-god Šamaš, and also of the goddesses Ištar and Anunit, and seems to have had two principal districts, Sippar of Šamaš, and Sippar of Anunit, which, if the identification were correct, would account for the dual termination *-ayim*, in Heb. This site is the modern *'Abu-Habbah*, which was first excavated by the late Hormuzd Rassam in

1. Formerly Identified with the Two Babylonian Sippars

1881, and has furnished an enormous number of inscriptions, some of them of the highest importance.

2. Difficulties of That Identification

Besides the fact that the deities of the two cities, Sippar and Sepharvaim, are not the same, it is to be noted that in 2 K **19** 13 the king of Sepharvaim is referred to, and, as far as is known, the Bab Sippar never had a king of its own, nor had Akkad, with which it is in part identified, for at least 1,200 years before Sennacherib. The fact that Babylon and Cuthah head the list of cities mentioned is no indication that Sepharvaim was a Bab town—the composition of the list, indeed, points the other way, for the name comes after Ava and Hamath, implying that it lay in Syria.

3. Another Suggestion

Joseph Halévy therefore suggests (*ZA*, II, 401 ff) that it should be identified with the Sibraim of Ezk **47** 16, between Damascus and Hamath (the dual implying a frontier town), and the same as the *Šabara'in* of the Bab Chronicle, there referred to as having been captured by Shalmaneser. As, however, Šabara'in may be read Šamara'in, it is more likely to have been the Heb *Shōmᵉrōn* (Samaria), as pointed out by Fried. Delitzsch.

Literature.—See Schrader, *COT*, I, 71 f; Kittel on *K*; Dillmann-Kittel on *Isa*, ad loc.; *HDB*, s.v.

T. G. Pinches

SEPHARVITES, sē'fär-vīts, sė-fär'vīts (סְפַרְוִים, *ṣᵉpharwīm*): In 2 K **17** 31, the inhabitants of Sepharvaim (q.v.), planted by the king of Assyria in Samaria. They continued there to burn their children to their native gods.

SEPPHORIS, sef'ō-ris: A city of Galilee, taken by Josephus (*Vita*, IX, lxvii, 71) and later destroyed by the son of Varus (*Ant*, XVII, x, 9).

SEPTUAGINT, sep'tū-a-jint:

I. Importance.—The Gr VS of the OT commonly known as the Septuagint holds a unique place among translations. Its importance is many-sided. Its chief value lies in the fact that it is a VS of a Heb text earlier by about a millennium than the earliest dated Heb MS extant (916 AD), a VS, in particular, prior to the formal rabbinical revision of the Heb which took place early in the 2d cent. AD. It supplies the materials for the reconstruction of an older form of the Heb than the MT reproduced in our modern Bibles. It is, moreover, a pioneering work; there was probably no precedent in the world's history for a series of translations from one language into another on so extensive a scale. It was the first attempt to reproduce the Heb Scriptures in another tongue. It is one of the outstanding results of the breaking-down of international barriers by the conquests of Alexander the Great and the dissemination of the Gr language, which were fraught with such vital consequences for the history of religion. The cosmopolitan city which he founded in the Delta witnessed the first attempt to bridge the gulf between Jewish and Gr thought. The Jewish commercial settlers at Alexandria, forced by circumstances to abandon their language, clung tenaciously to their faith; and the tr of the Scriptures into their adopted language, produced to meet their own needs, had the further result of introducing the outside world to a knowledge of their history and religion. Then came the most momentous event in its history, the starting-point of a new life; the tr was taken over from the Jews by the Christian church. It was the Bible of most writers of the NT. Not only are the majority of their express citations from Scripture borrowed from it, but their writings contain numerous reminiscences of its language. Its words are household words to them. It laid for them the foundations of a new religious terminology. It was a potent weapon for missionary work, and, when VSS of the Scriptures into other languages became necessary, it was in most cases the LXX and not the Heb from which they were made. Preëminent among these daughter VSS was the Old Lat which preceded the Vulg. Jerome's VS, for the most part a direct tr from the Heb, was in portions a mere revision of the Old Lat; our Prayer-book VS of the Psalter preserves peculiarities of the LXX, transmitted through the medium of the Old Lat. The LXX was also the Bible of the early Gr Fathers, and helped to mold dogma; it furnished proof-texts to both parties in the Arian controversy. Its language gives it another strong claim to recognition. Uncouth and unclassical as much of it appears, we now know that this is not wholly due to the hampering effects of translation. "Biblical Greek," once considered a distinct species, is now a rather discredited term. The hundreds of contemporary papyrus records (letters, business and legal documents, etc) recently discovered in Egypt illustrate much of the vocabulary and grammar and go to show that many so-called "Hebraisms" were in truth integral parts of the *koinē*, or "common language," i.e. the international form of Gr which, since the time of Alexander, replaced the old dialects, and of which the spoken Gr of today is the lineal descendant. The VS was made for the populace and written in large measure in the language of their everyday life.

II. Name.—The name "Septuagint" is an abbreviation of *Interpretatio secundum* (or *juxta*) *Septuaginta seniores* (or *viros*), i.e. the Gr tr of the OT of which the first instalment was, according to the Alexandrian legend (see III, below), contributed by 70 (or 72) elders sent from Jerus to Alexandria for the purpose at the request of Ptolemy II. The legend in its oldest form restricts their labors to the Pent, but they were afterward credited with the tr of the whole Bible, and before the 4th cent. it had become customary to apply the title to the whole collection: Aug., *De Civ. Dei*, xviii.42, "quorum interpretatio ut Septuaginta vocetur iam obtinuit consuetudo" ("whose tr is now by custom called the Septuagint"). The MSS refer to them under the abbreviation οἱ ο′, *hoi o′* ("the seventy"), or οἱ οβ′, *hoi ob′* ("the seventy-two"). The "Septuagint" and the abbreviated form "LXX" have been the usual designations hitherto, but, as these are based on a now discredited legend, they are coming to be replaced by "the OT in Greek," or "the Alexandrian version" with the abbreviation 𝔊.

III. Traditional Origin.—The traditional account of the tr of the Pent is contained in the so-called letter of Aristeas (edd Gr text, P. Wendland, Teubner series, 1900, and Thackeray in the App. to Swete's *Intro to the OT in Gr*, 1900, etc; Wendland's sections cited below appear in Swete's *Intro*, ed 2; ET by Thackeray, Macmillan, 1904, reprinted from *JQR*, XV, 337, and by H. T. Andrews in Charles's *Apocrypha and Pseudepigrapha of the OT*, II, 83–122, Oxford, 1913).

1. Letter of Aristeas

The writer professes to be a high official at the court of Ptolemy Philadelphus (285–247 BC), a Greek interested in Jewish antiquities. Addressing his brother Philocrates he describes an embassy to Jerus on which he has recently been sent with another courtier Andreas. According to his narrative, Demetrius of Phalerum, a prominent figure in later Athenian history, who here appears as the royal librarian at Alexandria, convinced the king of the importance of securing for his library a tr of the Jewish Law. The king at the same time, to propitiate the nation from whom he was asking a favor, consented, on the suggestion of Aristeas, to liberate all Jewish slaves in Egypt. Copies follow of the letters which passed between Ptolemy and Eleazar, the high priest at Jerus. Ptolemy requests Eleazar to select and dispatch to Alexandria 72 elders, proficient in the Law, 6 from each tribe, to undertake the tr, the importance of the task requiring the services of a large number to secure an accurate VS. Eleazar complies with the request and the names of the selected translators are appended to his letter.

There follow: (1) a detailed description of votive offerings sent by Ptolemy for the temple; (2) a sketch of Jerus, the temple and its services, and the geography of Pal, doubtless reflecting in part the impressions of an eyewitness and giving a unique picture of the Jewish capital in the Ptolemaic era; (3) an exposition by Eleazar of portions of the Law.

The translators arrive at Alexandria, bringing a copy of the Law written in letters of gold on rolls of skins, and are honorably received by Ptolemy. A seven days' banquet follows, at which the king tests the proficiency of each in turn with hard questions. Three days later Demetrius conducts them across the mole known as the Heptastadion to the island of Pharos, where, with all necessaries provided for their convenience, they complete their task, as by a miracle, in 72 days; we are expressly told that their work was the result of collaboration and comparison. The completed VS was read by Demetrius to the Jewish community, who received it with enthusiasm and begged that a copy might be intrusted to their leaders; a solemn curse was pronounced on any who should venture to add to or subtract from or make any alteration in the tr. The whole VS was then read aloud to the king who expressed his admiration and his surprise that Gr writers had remained in ignorance of its contents; he directed that the books should be preserved with scrupulous care.

2. Evidence of Aristobulus and Philo

To set beside this account we have two pre-Christian allusions in Jewish writings. Aristobulus, addressing a Ptolemy who has been identified as Philometor (182–146 BC), repeats the statement that the Pent was tr^{d} under Philadelphus at the instance of Demetrius Phalereus (Euseb., *Praep. Ev.*, XIII, 12.664*b*); but the genuineness of the passage is doubtful. If it is accepted, it appears that some of the main features of the story were believed at Alexandria within a century of the date assigned by "Aristeas" to the tr. Philo (*Vit. Moys*, ii.5 ff) repeats the story of the sending of the translators by Eleazar at the request of Philadelphus, adding that in his day the completion of the undertaking was celebrated by an annual festival on the isle of Pharos. It is improbable that an artificial production like the Aristeas letter should have occasioned such an anniversary; Philo's evidence seems therefore to rest in part on an independent tradition. His account in one particular paves the way for later accretions; he hints at the inspiration of the translators and the miraculous agreement of their separate VSS: "They prophesied like men possessed, not one in one way and one in another, but all producing the same words and phrases as though some unseen prompter were at the ears of each." At the end of the 1st cent. AD Jos includes in his *Antiquities* (XII, ii, 1 ff) large portions of the letter, which he paraphrases, but does not embellish.

3. Later Accretions

Christian writers accepted the story without suspicion and amplified it. A *catena* of their evidence is given in an Appendix to Wendland's ed. The following are their principal additions to the narrative, all clearly baseless fabrications.

(1) The translators worked independently, in separate cells, and produced identical versions, Ptolemy proposing this test of their trustworthiness. So Irenaeus, Clement of Alexandria, Augustine, the *Chronicon Paschale* and the *Cohortatio ad Graecos* (wrongly attributed to Justin); the author of the last work asserts that he had seen the cells and heard the tradition on the spot. (2) A modification of this legend says that the translators worked in pairs in 36 cells. So Epiphanius (d. 403 AD), and later G. Syncellus, Julius Pollux and Zonaras. Epiphanius' account is the most detailed. The translators were locked up in sky-lighted cells in pairs with attendants and shorthand writers; each pair was intrusted with one book, the books were then circulated, and 36 identical VSS of the whole Bible, canonical and apocryphal books, were produced; Ptolemy wrote two letters, one asking for the original Scriptures, the second for translators. (3) This story of the two embassies appears already in the 2d cent. AD, in Justin's *Apology*, and (4) the extension of the translators' work to the Prophets or the whole Bible recurs in the two Cyrils and in Chrysostom. (5) The miraculous agreement of the translators proved them to be no less inspired than the authors (Irenaeus, etc; cf Philo). (6) As regards date, Clement of Alexandria quotes an alternative tradition referring the VS back to the time of the first Ptolemy (322–285 BC); while Chrysostom brings it down to "a hundred or more years [elsewhere "not many years"] before the coming of Christ." Justin absurdly states that Ptolemy's embassy was sent to King Herod; the *Chronicon Paschale* calls the high priest of the time Onias Simon, brother of Eleazar.

Jerome was the first to hold these later inventions up to ridicule, contrasting them with the older and more sober narrative. They indicate a growing oral tradition in Jewish circles at Alexandria. The origin of the legend of the miraculous consensus of the 70 translators has been reasonably sought in a passage in Ex **24** LXX to which Epiphanius expressly refers. We there read of 70 elders of Israel, not heard of again, who with Aaron, Nadab and Abihu form a link between Moses and the people. After reciting the Book of the Covenant Moses ascends to the top of the mount; the 70, however, ascend but a little way and are bidden to worship from afar: according to the LXX text "They saw the place where the God of Israel stood . . . . and of the elect of Israel not one perished" (ver 11), i.e. they were privileged to escape the usual effect of a vision of the Deity (Ex **33** 20). But the vb. used for "perish" (*diaphōnein*) was uncommon in this sense; "not one disagreed" would be the obvious meaning; hence apparently the legend of the agreement of the translators, the later intermediaries between Moses and Israel of the Dispersion. When the translations were recited, "no difference was discoverable," says Epiphanius, using the same vb. Cave-dwellings in the island of Pharos probably account for the legend of the cells. A curious phenomenon has recently suggested that there is an element of truth in one item of Epiphanius' obviously incredible narrative, viz. the working of the translators in pairs. The Gr books of Jer and Ezk fall into two nearly equal parts, apparently the work of separate translators (see VIII, 1, [2], below); while in Ex, Lev and Pss orthographical details indicate a similar division of the books for clerical purposes. There was, it seems, a primitive custom of transcribing each book on 2 separate rolls, and in the case of Jer and Ezk the practice goes back to the time of tr (*JTS*, IV, 245 ff, 398 ff; IX, 88 ff).

Beside the later extravagances, the story of Aristeas appears comparatively rational. Yet it has long been recognized that much of it is unhistorical, in particular the professed date and nationality of the writer. Its claims to authenticity were demolished by Dr. Hody two centuries ago (*De bibliorum textibus originalibus*, Oxon., 1705). Clearly the writer is not a Greek, but a Jew, whose aim is to glorify his race and to disseminate information about their sacred books. Yet the story is not wholly to be rejected, though it is difficult to disentangle truth from fiction. On one side his veracity has since Hody's time been established; his court titles, technical terms, epistolary formulae, etc, reappear in Egyp papyri and inscriptions, and all his references to Alexandrian life and customs are probably equally trustworthy (§§ 28, 109 ff, measures to counteract the ill effects upon agriculture of migration from country to town; § 167, treatment of informers [cf § 25]; § 175 reception of foreign embassies [cf § 182]). The import of this discovery has, however, since its announcement by Lombroso (*Recherches sur l'économie politique de l'Égypte*, Turin, 1870), been somewhat modified by the new-found papyri which show that Aristeas' titles and formulae are those of the later, not the earlier, Ptolemaic age.

4. Criticism of the Aristeas Story

The letter was used by Jos and probably known to Philo. How much earlier is it? Schürer (*HJP*, II, iii, 309 f [*GJV*[4], III, 608–16]), relying on (1) the questionable Aristobulus passage, (2) the picture drawn of Pal as if still under Ptolemaic rule, from which it passed to the Seleucids c 200 BC, argued that the work could not be later than that date. But it is hard to believe that a fictitious story (as he regards it to be) could have gained credence within little more than half a century of the period to which it relates, and Wendland rightly rejects so ancient an origin. The following indications suggest a date about 100–80 BC.

5. Date

(1) Many of Aristeas' formulae, etc (see above), only came into use in the 2d cent. BC (Strack, *Rhein. Mus.*, LV, 168 ff; Thackeray, *Aristeas*, ET, pp. 3, 12). (2) The later Maccabean age or the end of the 2d cent. BC is suggested by some of the translators' names (Wendland, xxvi), and (3) by the independent position of the high priest. (4) Some of Ptolemy's questions indicate a tottering dynasty (§ 187, etc). (5) The writer occasionally forgets his rôle and distinguishes between his own time and that of Philadelphus (§§ 28, 182). (6) He appears to borrow his name from a Jewish historian of the 2d cent. BC and to wish to pass off the latter's history as his own (§ 6). (7) He is guilty of historical inaccuracies concerning Demetrius, etc. (8) The prologue to the Gr Ecclus (after 132 BC) ignores and contradicts the Aristeas story, whereas Aristeas possibly used this prologue (Wendland, xxvii; cf Hart, *Ecclus in Greek*, 1909). (9) The imprecation upon any who should alter the tr (§ 311) points to divergences of text which the writer desired to check; cf § 57, where he seems to insist on the correctness of the LXX text of Ex **25** 22, "gold of pure gold," as against the Heb. (10) Allusions to current criticisms of the Pent (§§ 128, 144) presuppose a familiarity with it on the part of non-Jewish readers only explicable if the LXX had long been current. (11) Yet details in the Gr orthography preclude a date much later than 100 BC.

The probable amount of truth in the story is ably discussed by Swete (*Intro*, 16–22). The following statements in the letter may be accepted: (1) The tr was produced at Alexandria, as is conclusively proved by Egyp influence on its language. (2) The Pent was trd first and, in view of the homogeneity of style, as a whole. (3) The Gr Pent goes back to the first half of the 3d cent. BC; the style is akin to that of the 3d-cent. papyri, and the Gr Gen was used by the Hellenist Demetrius toward the end of the cent. (4) The Heb rolls were brought from Jerus. (5) Possibly Philadelphus, the patron of literature, with his religious impartiality, may have countenanced the work. But the assertion that it owed its inception wholly to him and his librarian is incredible; it is known from other sources that Demetrius Phalereus did not fill the office of librarian under that monarch. The language is that of the people, not a literary style suitable to a work produced under royal patronage. The importation of Palestinian translators is likewise fictitious. Dr. Swete acutely observes that Aristeas, in stating that the tr was read to and welcomed by the Jewish community before being presented to the king, unconsciously reveals its true origin. It was no doubt produced to meet their own needs by the large Jewish colony at Alexandria. A demand that the Law should be read in the synagogues in a tongue "understanded of the people" was the originating impulse.

6. Credibility

IV. Evidence of Prologue to Sirach.—The interesting, though in places tantalizingly obscure, prologue to Ecclus throws light on the progress made with the tr of the remaining Scriptures before the end of the 2d cent. BC.

The translator dates his settlement in Egypt, during which he produced his VS of his grandfather's work, as "the 38th year *under* Euergetes the king." The words have been the subject of controversy, but, with the majority of critics, we may interpret this to mean the 38th year of Euergetes II, reckoning from the beginning (170 BC) of his joint reign with Philometor, i.e. 132 BC. Euergetes I reigned for 25 years only. Others, in view of the superfluous preposition, suppose that the age of the translator is intended, but the cumbrous form of expression is not unparalleled. A recent explanation of the date (Hart, *Ecclus in Gr*) as the 38th year of *Philadelphus* which was also the 1st year of Euergetes I (i.e. 247 BC) is more ingenious than convincing.

The prologue implies the existence of a Gr VS of the Law, the Prophets and "the rest of the books." The translator, craving his readers' indulgence for the imperfections of his own work, due to the difficulty of reproducing Heb in Gr, adds that others have experienced the same difficulties: "The Law itself and the prophecies and the rest of the books have no small difference when spoken in their original language." From these words we may understand that at the time of writing (132–100 BC) Alexandrian Jews possessed Gr VSS of a large part (probably not the whole) of "the Prophets," and of some of "the Writings" or Hagiographa. For some internal evidence as to the order in which the several books were trd see VIII, below.

V. Transmission of the LXX Text.—The main value of the LXX is its witness to an older Heb text than our own. But before we can reconstruct this Heb text we need to have a pure Gr text before us, and this we are at present far from possessing. The Gr text has had a long and complex history of its own. Used for centuries by both Jews and Christians it underwent corruption and interpolation, and, notwithstanding the multitude of materials for its restoration, the original text has yet to be recovered. We are much more certain of the *ipsissima verba* of the NT writers than of the original Alexandrian VS of the OT. This does not apply to all portions alike. The Gr Pent, e.g., has survived in a relatively pure form. But everywhere we have to be on our guard against interpolations, sometimes extending to whole paragraphs. Not a verse is without its array of variant readings. An indication of the amount of "mixture" which has taken place is afforded by the numerous "doublets" or alternative renderings of a single Heb word or phrase which appear side by side in the transmitted text.

1. Early Corruption of Text

Textual corruption began early, before the Christian era. We have seen indications of this in the letter of Aristeas (III, 5, [9] above). Traces of corruption appear in Philo (e.g. his comment, in *Quis Rer. Div. Her*. 56, on Gen **15** 15, shows that already in his day *tapheis*, "buried," had become *trapheis*, "nurtured," as in all our MSS); doublets already exist. Similarly in the NT the author of He quotes (**12** 15) a corrupt form of the Gr of Dt **29** 18.

2. Official Revision of Hebrew Text c 100 AD

But it was not until the beginning of the 2d cent. AD that the divergence between the Gr and the Palestinian Heb text reached an acute stage. One cause of this was the revision of the Heb text which took place about this time. No actual record of this revision exists, but it is beyond doubt that it originated in the rabbinical school, of which Rabbi Akiba was the chief representative, and which had its center at Jamnia in the years following the destruction of Jerus. The Jewish doctors, their temple in ruins, concentrated their attention on the settlement of the text of the Scriptures which remained to them. This school of eminent critics, precursors of the Massoretes, besides settling outstanding questions concerning the Canon, laid down strict rules for Bib. interpretation, and in all probability established an official text.

3. Adoption of LXX by Christians

But another cause widened still farther the distance between the texts of Jerus and Alexandria. This was the adoption of the LXX by the Christian church. When Christians began to cite the Alexandrian VS in proof of their doctrines, the Jews began to question its accuracy. Hence mutual recriminations which are reflected in the pages of Justin's *Dialogue with Trypho*. "They dare to assert," says Justin (*Dial*., 68), "that the interpretation produced by your seventy elders under Ptolemy of Egypt is in some points inaccurate." A crucial instance cited by the Jews was the rendering "virgin" in Isa **7** 14, where they claimed with justice that "young woman" would be more accurate. Justin retaliates by charging the Jews with deliberate excision of passages favorable to Christianity.

4. Alternative 2d-Century Greek Versions

That such accusations should be made in those critical years was inevitable, yet there is no evidence of any material interpolations having been introduced by either party. But the Alexandrian VS, in view of the revised text and the new and stricter canons of interpretation, was felt by the Jews to be inadequate, and a group of new translations of Scripture in the 2d cent. AD supplied the demand. We possess considerable fragments of the work of three of these translators, viz. Aquila, Symmachus and Theodotion, besides scanty remnants of further anonymous VSS.

5. Aquila

The earliest of "the three" was Aquila, a proselyte to Judaism, and, like his NT namesake, a native of Pontus. He flourished, according to Epiphanius (whose account of these later translators in his *De mens. et pond*. is not wholly trustworthy), under Hadrian (117–38 AD) and was related to that emperor; there is no probability in Epiphanius' further statement that Hadrian intrusted to Aquila the superintendence of the building of Aelia Capitolina on the site of Jerus, that there he was converted to Christianity by Christian exiles returning from Pella, but that refusing to abandon astrology he was excommunicated, and in revenge turned Jew and was actuated by a bias against Christianity in his VS of the OT. What is certain is that he was a pupil of the new rabbinical school, in particular of Rabbi Akiba (95–135 AD), and that his VS was an attempt to reproduce exactly the revised official text. The result was an extraordinary production, unparalleled in Gr lit., if it can be classed under that category at all. No jot or tittle of the Heb might be neglected; uniformity in the tr of each Heb word must be preserved and the etymological kinship of different Heb words represented. Such were some of his leading principles. The opening words of his tr (Gen **1** 1) may be rendered: "In heading founded God with the heavens and with the earth." "Heading" or "summary" was selected because the Heb word for "beginning" was a derivative of "head." "With" represents an untranslatable word (*'ēth*) prefixed to the accusative case, but indistinguishable from the preposition "with." The Divine Name (the tetragrammaton) was not tr[d], but written in archaic Heb characters. "A slave to the letter," as Origen calls him, his work has aptly been described by a modern writer as "a colossal crib" (Burkitt, *JQR*, October, 1896, 207 ff). Yet it was a success. In Origen's time it was used by all Jews ignorant of Heb, and continued in use for several centuries; Justinian expressly sanctioned its use in the synagogues (*Nov*., 146). Its lack of style and violation of the laws of grammar were not due to ignorance of Gr, of which the writer shows, in vocabulary at least, a considerable command. Its importance lay and lies (so far as it is preserved) in its exact reproduction of the rabbinical text of the 2d cent. AD; it may be regarded as the beginning of the scientific study of the Heb Scriptures. Though "a bold attempt to displace the LXX," it cannot be charged with being intentionally antagonistic to Christianity. Of the original work, previously known only from extracts in MSS, some palimpsest fragments were recovered from the Cairo Genizah in 1897 and edited by F. C. Burkitt (*Fragments of the Books of Kings*, 1897) and by C. Taylor (*Sayings of the Jewish Fathers*[2], 1897; *Heb-Gr Cairo Genizah Palimpsests*, 1900). The student of Swete's *OT* will trace Aquila's unmistakable style in the footnotes to the Books of S and K; the older and shorter B text in those books has constantly been supplemented in the A text from Aquila. A longer specimen of his work occurs in the Gr Eccl, which has no claim to be regarded as "Septuagint"; Jerome refers to a second ed of Aquila's VS, and the Gr Eccl is perhaps his first ed of that book, made on the basis of an unrevised Heb text (McNeile, *Intro to Eccl*, Cambridge, 1904, App. I). The suggested identification of Aquila with Onkelos, author of the Tg of that name, has not been generally accepted.

6. Theodotion

Epiphanius' account of the dates and history of Theodotion and Symmachus is untrustworthy. He seems to have reversed their order, probably misled by the order of the tr[s] in the columns of the Hexapla (see below). He also apparently confused Aquila and Theodotion in calling the latter a native of Pontus. As regards date, Theodotion, critics are agreed, preceded Symmachus and probably flourished under M. Aurelius (161–80), whereas Symmachus lived under Commodus (180–92); Irenaeus mentions only the VSS of Aquila and Theodotion, and that of Symmachus had in his day either not been produced or at least not widely circulated. According to the more credible account of Irenaeus, Theodotion was an Ephesian and a convert to Judaism. His VS constantly agrees with the LXX and was rather a revision of it, to bring it into accord with the current Heb text, than an independent work. The supplementing of *lacunae* in the LXX (due partly to the fact that the older VS of some books did not aim at completeness) gave scope for greater originality. These *lacunae* were greatest in Job and his VS of that book was much longer than the LXX. The text of Job printed in Swete's ed is a patchwork of old and new; the careful reader may detect the Theodotion portions by transliterations and other peculiarities. Long extracts from Theodotion are preserved in cod. Q in Jer. As regards the additional matter contained in LXX, Theodotion was inconsistent; he admitted, e.g., the additions to Dnl (Sus, Bel and the Three), but did not apparently admit the non-canonical books as a whole. The church adopted his Dnl in place of the inadequate LXX VS, which has survived in only one Gr MS; but the date when the change took place is unknown and the early history of the two Gr texts is obscure. Theodotion's renderings have been found in writings before his time (including the NT), and it is reasonably conjectured that even before the 2d cent. AD the LXX text had been discarded and that Theodotion's VS is but a working over of an older alternative VS. Theodotion is free from the barbarisms of Aquila, but is addicted to transliteration, i.e. the reproduction of Heb words in Gr letters. His reasons for this habit are not always clear; ignorance of Heb will not account for all (cf VIII, 1, [5], below).

7. Symmachus and Others

Beside the two VSS produced by, and primarily intended for, Jews was a third, presumably to meet the needs of a Jewish Christian sect who were dissatisfied with the LXX. Symmachus, its author, was, according to the more trustworthy account, an Ebionite, who also wrote a comm. on Mt, a copy of which was given to Origen by Juliana, a lady who received it from its author (Euseb., *HE*, VI, 17). Epiphanius' description of him as a Samaritan convert to Judaism may be rejected. The date of his work, as above stated, was probably the reign of Commodus (180–92 AD). In one respect the VS resembled Aquila's, in its faithful adherence to the *sense* of the current Heb text; its style, however, which was flowing and literary, was a revolt against Aquila's monstrosities. It seems to have been a recasting of Aquila's VS, with free use of both LXX and Theodotion. It carried farther a tendency apparent in the LXX to refine away the anthropomorphisms of the OT.

Of three other MSS discovered by Origen (one at Nicopolis in Greece, one at Jericho) and known from their position in the Hexapla as *Quinta*, *Sexta*, and *Septima*, little is known. There is no reason to suppose that they embraced the whole OT. *Quinta* is characterized by Field as the most elegant of the Gr VSS. F. C. Burkitt has discussed "the so-called *Quinta* of 4 Kings" in *PSBA*, June, 1902. The Christian origin of *Sexta* betrays itself in Hab **3** 13 ("Thou wentest forth to save thy people for the sake of [or "by"] Jesus thy anointed One").

These later VSS play a large part in the history of the text of the LXX. This is due to the labors

8. Origen and the Hexapla

of the greatest LXX scholar of antiquity, the celebrated Origen of Alexandria, whose active life covers the first half of the 3d cent. Origen frankly recognized, and wished Christians to recognize, the merits of the later VSS, and the divergences between the LXX and the current Heb. He determined to provide the church with the materials for ascertaining the true text and meaning of the OT. With this object he set himself to learn Heb—a feat probably unprecedented among non-Jewish Christians of that time—and to collect the later VSS. The idea of using these VSS to amend the LXX seemed to him an inspiration: "By the gift of God we found a remedy for the divergence in the copies of the OT, namely to use the other editions as a criterion" (*Comm.* on Mt **15** 14). The *magnum opus* in which he embodied the results of his labors was known as the *Hexapla* or "six-column" edition. This stupendous work has not survived; a fragment was discovered toward the end of the 19th cent. in the Ambrosian Library at Milan (Swete, *Intro*, 61 ff) and another among the Cairo Genizah palimpsests (ed C. Taylor, Cambridge, 1900). The material was arranged in six parallel columns containing (1) the current Heb text, (2) the same in Gr letters, (3) the VS of Aquila, (4) that of Symmachus, (5) that of the LXX, (6) that of Theodotion. The text was broken up into short clauses; not more than two words, usually one only, stood in the first column. The order of the columns doubtless represents the degree of conformity to the Heb; Aquila's, as the most faithful, heads the VSS, and Symmachus' is on the whole a revision of Aquila as Theodotion's is of the LXX. But Origen was not content with merely collating the VSS; his aim was to revise the LXX and the 5th column exhibited his revised text. The basis of it was the current Alexandrian text of the 3d cent. AD; this was supplemented or corrected where necessary by the other VSS. Origen, however, deprecated alteration of a text which had received ecclesiastical sanction, without some indication of its extent, and the construction of the 5th column presented difficulties. There were (1) numerous cases of words or paragraphs contained in the LXX but not in the Heb, which could not be wholly rejected, (2) cases of omission from the LXX of words in the Heb, (3) cases of paraphrase and minor divergences, (4) variations in the order of words or chapters. Origen here had recourse to a system of critical signs, invented and employed by the grammarian Aristarchus (3d cent. BC) in his ed of Homer. Passages of the first class were left in the text, but had prefixed to them an *obelus*, a sign of which the original form was a "spit" or "spear," but figuring in LXX MSS as a horizontal line usually with a dot above and a dot below (÷); other varieties are —, ┬, ∽; the sign in Aristarchus indicated censure, in the Hexapla the doubtful authority of the words which followed. The close of the obelized passage was marked by the *metobelus*, a colon (:), or, in the Syr VSS, a mallet (Y). Passages missing in the LXX were supplied from one of the other VSS (Aquila or Theodotion), the beginning of the extract being marked by an asterisk (※)—a sign used by Aristarchus to express special approval—the close, by the *metobelus*. Where LXX and Heb widely diverged, Origen occasionally gave two VSS, that of a later translator under an asterisk, that of LXX obelized. Divergence in order was met by transposition, the Heb order being followed; in Prov, however, the two texts kept their respective order, the discrepancy being indicated by a combination of signs. Minor supposed or real corruptions in the Gr were tacitly corrected. Origen produced a minor edition, the *Tetrapla*, without the first two columns of the larger work. The *Heptapla* and *Octapla*, occasionally mentioned, appear to be alternative names given to the Hexapla at points where the number of columns was increased to receive other fragmentary VSS. This gigantic work, which according to a reasonable estimate must have filled 5,000 leaves, was probably never copied *in extenso*. The original was preserved for some centuries in the library of Pamphilus at Caesarea; there it was studied by Jerome, and thither came owners of Bib. MSS to collate their copies with it, as we learn from some interesting notes in our uncial MSS (e.g. a 7th-cent. note appended to Est in cod. ℵ). The Library probably perished c 638 AD, when Caesarea fell into the hands of the Saracens.

But, though the whole work was too vast to be copied, it was a simple task to copy the 5th column.

9. Hexaplaric MSS

This task was performed, partly in prison, by Pamphilus, a martyr in the Diocletian persecution, and his friend Eusebius, the great bishop of Caesarea. Copies of the "Hexaplaric" LXX, i.e. Origen's doctored text with the critical signs and perhaps occasional notes, were, through the initiative of these two, widely circulated in Pal in the 4th cent. Naturally, however, the signs became unintelligible in a text detached from the parallel columns which explained them; scribes neglected them, and copies of the doctored text, lacking the precautionary symbols, were multiplied. This carelessness has wrought great confusion; Origen is, through others' fault, indirectly responsible for the production of MSS in which the current LXX text and the later VSS are hopelessly mixed. No MSS give the Hexaplaric text as a whole, and it is preserved in a relatively pure form in very few: the uncials G and M (Pent and some historical books), the cursives 86 and 88 (Prophets). Other so-called Hexaplaric MSS, notably cod. Q (Marchalianus: Proph.) preserve fragments of the 5th and of the other columns of the Hexapla. (For the Syro-Hexaplar see below, VI, 1.) Yet, even did we possess the 5th column entire, with the complete apparatus of signs, we should not have "the original LXX," but merely, after removing the asterisked passages, a text current in the 3d cent. The fact has to be emphasized that Origen's gigantic work was framed on erroneous principles. He assumed (1) the purity of the current Heb text, (2) the corruption of the current LXX text where it deviated from the Heb. The modern critic recognizes that the LXX on the whole presents the older text, the divergences of which from the Heb are largely attributable to an official revision of the latter early in the Christian era. He recognizes also that in some books (e.g. Job) the old Gr VS was only a *partial* one. To reconstruct the original text he must therefore have recourse to other auxiliaries beside Origen.

10. Recensions Known to Jerome

Such assistance is partly furnished by two other recensions made in the century after Origen. Jerome (*Praef. in Paralipp.*; cf *Adv. Ruf.*, ii.27) states that in the 4th cent. three recensions circulated in different parts of the Christian world: "Alexandria and Egypt in their Septuagint acclaim Hesychius as their authority, the region from Constantinople to Antioch approves the copies of Lucian the martyr, the intermediate Palestinian provinces read the MSS which were promulgated by Eusebius and Pamphilus on the basis of Origen's labors, and the whole world is divided between these three varieties of text."

11. Hesychian Recension

Hesychius is probably to be identified with the martyr bishop mentioned by Eusebius (*HE*, VIII, 13) along with another scholar martyr, Phileas bishop of Thmuis, and it is thought that these two were engaged in prison in revising the Egyp text at the time when Pamphilus and Eusebius were employed on a similar task under similar conditions. How far existing MSS preserve the Hesychian recension is uncertain; agreement of their text with that of Egyp VSS and Fathers (Cyril in particular) is the criterion. For the Prophets Ceriani has identified cod. Q and its kin as Hesychian. For the Octateuch N. McLean (*JTS*, II, 306) finds the Hesychian text in a group of cursives, 44, 74, 76, 84, 106, 134, etc. But the first instalments of the larger Cambridge LXX raise the question whether cod. B (Vaticanus) may not itself be Hesychian; its text is more closely allied to that of Cyril Alex. than to any other patristic text, and the consensus of these two witnesses against the rest is sometimes (Ex **32** 14) curiously striking. In the Psalter also Rahlfs (*Septuaginta-Studien*, 2. Heft, 1907, 235) traces the Hesychian text in B and partially in S (Sinait.). Cf von Soden's theory for the NT and see TEXT AND MSS OF THE NT.

12. Lucianic Recension

The Lucianic recension was the work of another martyr, Lucian of Antioch (d. 311–12), probably with the collaboration of the Hebraist Dorotheus. There are, as Hort has shown, reasons for associating Lucian with a "Syrian" revision of the NT in the 4th cent., which became the dominant type of text. That he produced a Syrian recension of the Gr OT is expressly stated by Jerome, and we are moreover able with considerable certainty to identify the extant MSS which exhibit it. The identification, due to Field and Lagarde, rests on these grounds: (1) certain verses in 2 K are in the Arab. Syro-Hexaplar marked with the letter L, and a note explains that the letter indicates Lucianic readings; (2) the readings so marked occur in the cursives 19, 82, 93, 108, 118; (3) these MSS in the historical books agree with the LXX citations of the Antiochene Fathers Chrysostom and Theodoret. This clue enabled Lagarde to construct a Lucianic text of the historical books (*Librorum Vet. Test. canonic. pars prior*, Göttingen, 1883); his death prevented the completion of the work. Lagarde's edition is vitiated by the fact that he does not quote the readings of the individual MSS composing the group, and it can be regarded only as an approximate reconstruction of "Lucian." It is evident, however, that the Lucianic LXX possessed much the same qualities as the Syrian revision of the NT; lucidity and completeness were the main objects. It is a "full" text, the outcome of a desire to include, so far as possible, all recorded matter; "doublets" are consequently numerous. While this "conflation" of texts detracts from its value, the Lucianic revision gains importance from the fact that the sources from which it gleaned include an element of great antiquity which needs to be disengaged; where it unites with the Old Lat VS against all other authorities its evidence is invaluable.

VI. Reconstruction of LXX Text; Versions, Manuscripts and Printed Editions.—The task of restoring the original text is beset with difficulties. The materials (MSS, VSS, patristic citations) are abundant, but none has escaped "mixture," and the principles for reconstruction are not yet securely established (Swete, *Intro*, I, iv–vi; III, vi).

1. Ancient Versions Made from the LXX

Among the chief aids to restoration are the daughter VSS made from the LXX, and above all the Old Lat (pre-Hieronymian) VS, for the earliest (African) Old Lat VS dates from the 2d cent. AD, i.e. before Origen, and contains a text from which the asterisked passages in Hexaplaric MSS are absent; it thus "brings us the best independent proof we have that the Hexaplar signs introduced by Origen can be relied on for the reconstruction of the LXX" (Burkitt). The Old Lat also enables us to recognize the ancient element in the Lucianic recension. But the Lat evidence itself is by no means unanimous. Augustine (*De Doctr. Christ.*, ii.16) speaks of the infinite variety of Lat VSS, though they may ultimately prove all to fall into two main families, African and European. Peter Sabatier's collection of patristic quotations from the Old Lat is still useful, though needing verification by recent editions of the Fathers. Of Old Lat MSS one of the most important is the cod. Lugdunensis, edited by U. Robert (*Pentateuchi e cod. Lugd. versio Lat. antiquissima*, Paris, 1881; *Heptateuchi partis post. versio Lat. antiq. e cod. Lugd.*, Lyons, 1900). The student should consult also Burkitt's ed of *The Rules of Tyconius* ("Texts and Studies," III, 1, Cambridge, 1894) and *The Old Latin and the Itala* (ib, IV, 3, 1896).

Jerome's Vulgate is mainly a direct tr from the Heb, but the Vulg Psalter, the so-called Gallican, is one of Jerome's two revisions of the Old Lat, not his later VS from the Heb, and some details in our Prayer-book Psalter are ultimately derived through the Vulg Psalter from the LXX. Parts of the Apoc (Wisd, Ecclus, Bar, 1 and 2 Macc) are also pure Old Lat, untouched by Jerome.

The early date (2d cent. AD) once claimed for the Egyp or Coptic VSS (Bohairic, i.e. in the dialect of Lower Egypt, Sahidic or Upper Egyp, and Middle Egyp) has not been confirmed by later researches, at least as regards the first-named, which is probably not earlier than the 3d or 4th cent. AD. Rahlfs (*Sept.-Studien*, II, 1907) identifies the Bohairic Psalter as the Hesychian recension. The Sahidic VS of Job has fortunately preserved the shorter text lacking the later insertions from Theodotion (Lagarde, *Mittheilungen*, 1884, 204); this does not conclusively prove that it is pre-Origenic; it may be merely a Hexaplaric text with the asterisked passages omitted (Burkitt, *EB*, IV, 5027). The influence of the Hexapla is traceable elsewhere in this VS.

The Ethiopic VS was made in the main from the Gr and in part at least from an early text; Rahlfs (*Sept Stud.*, I, 1904) considers its text of S-K, with that of cod. B, to be pre-Origenic.

The Vulg or Peshiṭta Syriac VS was made from the Heb, though partly influenced by the LXX. But another Syr VS is of primary importance for the LXX text, viz. that of Paul, bishop of Tella (Constantine in Mesopotamia), executed at Alexandria in 616–17 and known as the Syro-Hexaplar. This is a bald Syr VS of the LXX column of the Hexapla, containing the Hexaplar signs. A MS of the poetical and prophetical books is in the Ambrosian Library at Milan and has been edited by Ceriani (*Monumenta sacra et profana*, 1874); fragments of the historical books are also extant (Lagarde and Rahlfs, *Bibliothecae Syriacae*, Göttingen, 1892). This VS supplements the Gr Hexaplaric MSS and is the principal authority for Origen's text. For the original VS of Dnl, which has survived in only one late MS, the

Syro-Hexaplar supplies a second and older authority of great value.

The Armenian VS (ascribed to the 5th cent.) also owes its value to its extreme literalness; its text of the Octateuch is largely Hexaplaric.

A bare mention must suffice of the Arabic VS (of which the prophetical and poetical books, Job excluded, were rendered from the LXX); the fragments of the Gothic VS (made from the Lucianic recension), and the Slavonic (partly from LXX, also Lucianic) and the Georgian VSS.

2. Manuscripts

For a full description of the Gr MSS see Swete, *Intro*, I, ch v. They are divided according to their script (capitals or minuscules) into uncials and cursives, the former ranging from the 4th cent. (four papyrus scraps go back to the 3d cent.; Nestle in *PRE*, XXIII, 208) to the 10th cent. AD, the latter from the 9th to the 16th cent. AD. Complete Bibles are few; the majority contain groups of books only, such as the Pent, Octateuch (Gen-Ruth), the later historical books, the Psalter, the 3 or 5 "Solomonic" books, the Prophets (major, minor or both). Uncials are commonly denoted by capital letters (in the ed of Holmes and Parsons by Roman figures); cursives, of which over 300 are known, by Arabic figures; in the larger Cambridge LXX the selected cursives are denoted by small Roman letters.

The following are the chief uncials containing, or which once contained, the whole Bible: B (Vaticanus, at Rome, 4th cent. AD), adopted as the standard text in all recent edd; S or ℵ (Sinaiticus, at St. Petersburg and Leipzig, 4th cent. AD), discovered by Tischendorf in 1844 and subsequent years in St. Catherine's Convent, Mt. Sinai; A (Alexandrinus, British Museum, probably 5th cent. AD); C (Ephraemi rescriptus, Paris, probably 5th cent.), a palimpsest, the older Bib. matter underlying a mediaeval Gr text of works of Ephrem the Syrian. For the Octateuch and historical books: D (Cottonianus, Brit. Mus., probably 5th or 6th cent.), fragments of an illuminated Gen, the bulk of which perished in a fire at Ashburnham House in 1731, but earlier collations of Grabe and others are extant, which for the lost portions are cited in the Cambridge texts as *D* (*Dsil*, i.e. *silet Grabius*, denotes an inference from Grabe's silence that the MS did not contain a variant); F (Ambrosianus, Milan, 4th to 5th cent.), fragments of the Octateuch; G (Sarravianus, fragments at Leyden, Paris and St. Petersburg, 4th to 5th cent.), important as containing an Origenic text with the Hexaplar signs; L (Purpureus Vindobonensis, Vienna, 5th to 6th cent.), fragments of an illuminated MS Genesis on purple vellum; M (Coislinianus, Paris, 7th cent.), important on account of its marginal Hexaplaric matter. For the Prophets, Q (Marchalianus, Rome, 6th cent.) is valuable, both for its text, which is "Hesychian" (see above), and for its abundant marginal Hexaplaric matter. A curious mixture of uncial and cursive writing occurs in E (Bodleianus, probably 10th cent.), fragments of the historical books (to 3 R **16** 28) preserved at Oxford, Cambridge (1 leaf), St. Petersburg and London; Tischendorf, who brought the MS from the East, retained the tell-tale Cambridge leaf, on which the transition from uncial to cursive script occurs, until his death. The long-concealed fact that the scattered fragments were part of a single MS came to light through Swete's identification of the Cambridge leaf as a continuation of the Bodleian fragment. Many of the cursives still await investigation, as do also the lectionaries. The latter, though the MSS are mainly late, should repay study. The use of the LXX for lectionary purposes was inherited by the church from the synagogue, and the course of lessons may partly represent an old system; light may also be expected from them on the local distribution of various types of text.

3. Printed Texts

Of the printed text the first four editions were (1) the Complutensian Polyglot of Cardinal Ximenes, 1514–17, comprising the Gr, Heb and Vulg texts, the last in the middle place of honor being compared to Jesus in the midst between the two thieves (!). The Gr was based on MSS from the Vatican and one from Venice; it exhibits on the whole the Lucianic recension, as the Hesychian is by a curious coincidence represented in (2) the Aldine ed of 1518, based on Venetian MSS. (3) The monumental Sixtine ed, published at Rome in 1586 under the auspices of Pope Sixtus V and frequently reprinted, was mainly based on the cod. Vaticanus, the superiority of which text is justly recognized in the interesting preface (printed in Swete's *Intro*). (4) The Eng. ed (Oxford, 1707–20) begun by Grabe (d. 1712) was based on the cod. Alexandrinus, with aid from other MSS, and had the peculiarity that he employed Origen's critical signs and different sizes of type to show the divergence between the Gr and the Heb. Of more recent edd three are preëminent. (5) The great Oxford ed of Holmes and Parsons (Oxford, 1798–1827, 5 vols, folio) was the first attempt to bring together in a gigantic *apparatus criticus* all the evidence of uncial and cursive MSS (upward of 300), VSS and early citations from Philo and Jos onward. As a monumental storehouse of materials "H. and P." will not be wholly superseded by the latest ed now (1913) in preparation. (6) The serviceable Cambridge "manual," ed of Swete (1st ed 1887–94, ed 3, 1901–7, 3 vols, 8vo), is in the hands of all serious LXX students. The text is that of B, or (where B fails) of A, and the apparatus contains the readings of the principal uncial MSS. New materials discovered since the ed of H. and P., esp. cod. S, are employed, and greater accuracy in the presentation of the other evidence has been made possible by photography. The fact that the text here printed is but a provisional one is sometimes overlooked. Swete's ed was designed as a precursor to (7) the larger Cambridge LXX, of which three instalments embracing the Pent have (1913) appeared (*The OT in Gr*, ed A. E. Brooke and N. McLean, Cambridge, 1911 pt. III, Nu and Dt). The text is a reprint of Swete's except that from Ex onward a few alterations of errors in the primary MS have been corrected, a delicate task in which the editors have rejected a few old readings without sufficient regard to the peculiarities of Hellenistic Gr. The importance of the work lies in its apparatus, which presents the readings of *all* the uncials, VSS and early citations, and those of a careful representative selection of the cursives. The materials of H and P are brought up to date and presented in a more reliable and convenient form. Besides these there is (8) Lagarde's reconstruction of the Lucianic recension of the historical books, which, as stated, must be used with caution (see above).

4. Reconstruction of Original Text

The task of reconstructing the oldest text is still unaccomplished. Materials have accumulated, and much preliminary "spade-work" has been done, by Lagarde in particular (see his "axioms" in Swete, *Intro*, 484 ff) and more recently by Nestle and Rahlfs; but the principles which the editor must follow are not yet finally determined. The extent to which "mixture" has affected the documents is the stumbling-block. Clearly no single MS presents the oldest text. That of cod. B, as in the NT, is on the whole the purest. In the 4 books of "Reigns" (1 S–2 K), e.g., it has escaped the grosser interpolations found in most MSS, and Rahlfs (*Sept.-Studien*, I, 1904) regards its text as pre-Origenic. It is, however, of unequal value and by no means an infallible guide; in Jgs, e.g., its text is undoubtedly late, no earlier than the 4th cent. AD, according to one authority (Moore, "Jgs," *ICC*). In relation to two of the 4th-cent. recensions its text is neutral, neither predominantly Lucianic nor Hexaplaric; but it has been regarded by some authorities as Hesychian. Possibly the recension made in the country which produced the LXX adhered more closely than others to the primitive text; some "Hesychian" features in the B text may prove to be original. Still even its purest portions contain marks of editorial revision and patent corruptions. Cod. A presents a quite different type of text, approximating to that of the MT. In the books of "Reigns" it is practically a Hexaplaric text without the critical signs, the additional matter being mainly derived from Aquila. Yet that it contains an ancient element is shown by the large support given to its readings by the NT and early Christian writers. Individual MSS must give place to groups. In order to reconstruct the texts current before Origen's time, it is necessary to isolate the groups containing the three 4th-cent. recensions, and to eliminate from the recensions thus recovered all Hexaplaric matter and such changes as appear to have been introduced by the authors of those recensions. Other groups brought to light by the larger Cambridge text have also to be taken into account. The attempt to penetrate into the earlier stages of the history is the hardest task. The Old Lat VS is here the surest guide; it has preserved readings which have disappeared from all Gr MSS, and affords a criterion as to the relative antiquity of the Gr variants. The evidence of early Christian and Jewish citations is also valuable. Ultimately, after elimination of all readings proved to be "recensional" or late, the decision between outstanding variants must depend on internal evidence. These variants will fall into two classes: (1) those merely affecting the Gr text, by far the larger number and presenting less difficulty; (2) those which imply a different Heb text. In adjudicating on the latter Lagarde's main axioms have to be borne in mind, that a free tr is to be preferred to a slavishly literal one, and a tr presupposing another Heb original to one based on the MT.

VII. Number, Titles and Order of Books.—In addition to the Heb canonical books, the LXX includes all the books in the Eng. Apoc except 2 Esd (Pr Man only finds a place among the canticles appended in some MSS to the Ps) besides a 3d and 4th book of Macc. Swete further includes in his text as an appendix of Gr books on the borderland of canonicity the Ps of Sol (found in some cursives and mentioned in the list in cod. A), the Gr fragments of the Book of En and the ecclesiastical canticles above mentioned. Early Christian writers in quoting freely from these additional books as Scripture doubtless perpetuate a tradition inherited from the Jews of Alexandria. Most of the books being original

1. Contents

Gr compositions were *ipso facto* excluded from a place in the Heb Canon. Greater latitude as regards canonicity prevailed at Alexandria; the Pent occupied a place apart, but as regards later books no very sharp line of demarcation between "canonical" and "uncanonical" appears to have been drawn.

2. Titles

Palestinian Jews employed the first word or words of each book of the Pent to serve as its title; Gen e.g. was denoted "in the beginning," Ex "[And these are the] names"; a few of the later books have similar titles. It is to the LXX, through the medium of the Lat VSS, that we owe the familiar descriptive titles, mostly suggested by phrases in the Gr VS. In some books there are traces of rival titles in the Ptolemaic age. Exodus ("outgoing") is also called *Exagōgē* ("leading out") by Philo and by the Hellenist Ezekiel who gave that name to his drama on the deliverance from Egypt. Philo has also alternative names for Dt—*Epinomis* ("after-law") borrowed from the title of a pseudo-Platonic treatise, and for Jgs "the Book of Judgments." The last title resembles the Alexandrian name for the books of S and K, viz. the four Books of Kingdoms or rather Reigns; the name may have been given in the first place to a partial VS including only the reigns of the first few monarchs. Jerome's influence in this case restored the old Heb names as also in Ch (=Heb "Words of Days," "Diaries"), which in LXX is entitled Paraleipomena, "omissions," as being a supplement to the Books of Reigns.

3. Bipartition of Books

Another innovation, due apparently to the Gr translators or later editors, was the breaking up of some of the long historical narratives into volumes of more manageable compass. In the Heb MSS, S, K, Ch, Ezr-Neh form respectively one book apiece. In the LXX the first three of these collections are subdivided into two volumes as in modern Bibles; an acquaintance with the other arrangement is, however, indicated in cod. B by the insertion at the end of 1 R, 3 R, 1 Ch of the first sentence of the succeeding book, a reminder to the reader that a continuation is to follow. Ezr-Neh, the Gr VS (2 Esd) being made under the influence of Palestinian tradition, remains undivided. Originally Ch-Ezr-Neh formed a unit, as was apparently still the case when the oldest Gr VS (1 Esd) was made.

4. Grouping and Order of Books

In the arrangement of books there is a radical departure from Palestinian practice. There were three main unalterable divisions in the Heb Bible, representing three stages in the formation of the Canon: Law, Prophets ("Former," i.e. Josh, Jgs, S, K, and "Latter") and "Writings." This arrangement was known at Alexandria at the end of the 2d cent. BC (Sir, prol.) but was not followed. The "Writings" were a miscellaneous collection of history and poetry with one prophetical book (Dnl). Alexandrian scholars introduced a more literary and symmetrical system, bringing together the books of each class and arranging them with some regard to the supposed chronological order of their authors. The Law, long before the Gr tr, had secured a position of supreme sanctity; this group was left undisturbed, it kept its precedence and the individual books their order (Lev and Nu, however, exchange places in a few lists). The other two groups are broken up. Ruth is removed from the "Writings" and attached to Jgs. Ch and Ezr-Neh are similarly transferred to the end of the historical group. This group, from chronological considerations, is followed by the poetical and other "Writings," the Prophets coming last (so in B, etc; in S A prophets precede poets). The internal order of the Gr Hagiographa, which includes quasi-historical (Est, Tob, Jth) and Wisdom books, is variable. Dnl now first finds a place among the Prophets. The 12 minor prophets usually precede the major (S and Western authorities give the Four precedence), and the order of the first half of their company is shuffled, apparently on chronological grounds, Hos being followed by Am, Mic, Joel, Ob, Jon. Jer has his train of satellites, Bar, Lam (transferred from the "Writings") and Ep. Jer; Sus and Bel consort with and form integral parts of Dnl. Variation in the order of books is partly attributable to the practice of writing each book on a separate papyrus roll, kept in a cylindrical case; rolls containing kindred matter would tend to be placed in the same case, but there would be no fixed order for these separate items until the copying of large groups in book-form came into vogue (Swete, *Intro*, 225 f, 229 f).

VIII. Characteristics of the Version and Its Component Parts.—Notwithstanding the uncertain state of the text, some general characteristics of the VS are patent. It is clear that, like the Heb itself, it is not a single book, but a library. It is a series of VSS and Gr compositions covering well-nigh 400 years, since it includes a few productions of the 2d cent. AD; the bulk of the trs, however, fall within the first half of the period (Sir, prol.).

1. Grouping of LXX Books on Internal Evidence

The trs may be grouped and their chronological order approximately determined from certain characteristics of their style. (1) We may inquire how a Heb word or phrase is rendered in different parts of the work. Diversity of renderings is not an infallible proof that different hands have been employed, since invariable uniformity in tr is difficult of attainment and indeed was not the aim of the Pent translators, who seem rather to have studied variety of expression. If, however, a Heb word is consistently rendered by one Gr word in one portion and by another elsewhere, and if each of the two portions has other features peculiar to itself, it becomes highly probable that the two portions are the work of different schools. Among "test-words" which yield results of this kind are "servant" in "Moses the servant of the Lord," "Hosts" in "Lord of Hosts," "Philistines" (Swete, *Intro*, 317 f; Thackeray, *Grammar of the OT*, 7 ff). (2) We may compare the Gr with that of dated documents of the Ptolemaic age. The trs were written in the *koinē* or "common" Gr, most of them in the vernacular variety of it, during a period when this new cosmopolitan language was in the making; the abundant dated papyri enable us to trace some stages in its evolution. The Petrie and Hibeh papyri of the 3d cent. BC afford the closest parallels to the Gr Pent. The following century witnessed a considerable development or "degeneracy" in the language, of which traces may be found in the Gr of the prophetical books. Beside the vernacular Gr was the literary language of the "Atticistic" school which persistently struggled, with indifferent success, to recover the literary flavor of the old Gr masterpieces. This style is represented in the LXX by most of the original Gr writings and by the paraphrases of some of the "Writings." (3) We may compare the Gr books as *translations*, noting in which books license is allowed and which adhere strictly to the Heb. The general movement is in the direction of greater literalism; the later books show an increasing reverence for the letter of Scripture, resulting in the production of pedantically literal VSS; the tendency culminated in the 2d cent. AD in the barbarisms of Aquila. Some of the "Writings" were freely handled, because they had not yet obtained canonical rank at the time of tr. Investigation on these lines goes to show that *the order of the tr was approximately that of the Heb Canon.* The Gr Hexateuch may be placed in the 3d cent. BC, the Prophets mainly in the 2d cent. BC, the "Writings" mainly in the 2d and 1st cents. BC.

(1) *The Hexateuch.*—The Gr Pent should undoubtedly be regarded as a unit: the Aristeas story may so far be credited. It is distinguished by a uniformly high level of the "common" vernacular style, combined with faithfulness to the Heb, rarely lapsing into literalism. It set the standard which later translators tried to imitate. The text was more securely established in this portion and substantial variant readings are comparatively few. The latter part of Ex is an exception; the Heb had

here not reached its final form in the 3d cent. BC, and there is some reason for thinking that the VS is not the work of the translator of the first half. In Dt a few new features in vocabulary appear (e.g. *ekklēsía;* see Hort, *Christian Ecclesia,* 4 ff). The Gr VS of Jos forms a link between the Pent and the later historical books. The text was not yet fixed, and variants are more abundant than in the Pent. The earliest VS, probably of selections only, appears from certain common features to have been nearly coeval with that of the Law.

(2) *The "Latter" Prophets.*—There is little doubt that the next books to be tr[d] were the Prophets in the narrower sense, and that Isa came first. The style of the Gr Isa has a close similarity, not wholly attributable to imitation, to that of the Pent: a certain freedom of treatment connects it with the earlier tr period: it was known to the author of Wisd (Isa **3** 10 with Ottley's n.). The tr shows "obvious signs of incompetence" (Swete), but the task was an exacting one. The local Egyp coloring in the tr is interesting (R. R. Ottley, *Book of Isa according to the LXX,* 2 vols, Gr text of A, tr and notes, Cambridge, 1904–6, with review in *JTS,* X, 299). Jer, Ezk and the Minor Prophets were probably tr[d] *en bloc* or nearly so. The Palestinian Canon had now been enlarged by a second group of Scriptures and this stimulated a desire among Alexandrian Jews to possess the entire collection of the Prophets in Gr. The undertaking seems to have been a formal and quasi-official one, not a haphazard growth. For it has been ascertained that Jer and Ezk were divided for tr purposes into two nearly equal parts; a change in the Gr style occurs at the junctures. In Jer the break occurs in ch **29** (LXX order); the clearest criterion of the two styles is the twofold rendering of "Thus saith the Lord." The last ch (**52**) is probably a later addition in the Gr. The translator of the second half of Jer also tr[d] the first half of Bar (**1** 1—**3** 8); he was incompetent and his work, if our text may be relied on, affords flagrant examples of Gr words being selected to render Heb words which he did not understand merely because of their similar sound. Ezk is similarly divided, but here the translator of the first half (chs **1–27**) undertook the difficult last quarter as well (chs **40–48**), the remainder being left to a second worker. An outstanding test is afforded by the renderings of the refrain, "They shall know that I am the Lord." The Gr VS of "the twelve" shows no trace of a similar division; in its style it is closely akin to the first half of Ezk and is perhaps by the same hand (*JTS,* IV, 245, 398, 578). But this official VS of the Prophets had probably been preceded by VSS of short passages selected to be read on the festivals in the synagogues. *Lectionary requirements occasioned the earliest VSS of the Prophets,* possibly of the Pent as well. Two indications of this have been traced. There exists in four MSS a Gr VS of the Psalm of Habakkuk (Hab **3**), a chapter which has been a Jewish lesson for Pentecost from the earliest times, independent of and apparently older than the LXX and made for synagogue use. Similarly in Ezk LXX there is a section of sixteen verses (**36** 24–38) with a style quite distinct from that of its context. This passage was also an early Christian lesson for Pentecost, and its lectionary use was inherited from Judaism. Here the LXX translators seem to have incorporated the older VS, whereas in Hab **3** they rejected it (*JTS,* XII, 191; IV, 407).

(3) *Partial version of the "Former" Prophets (1–3 R).*—The Gr style indicates that the history of the monarchy was not all tr[d] at once. Ulfilas is said to have omitted these books from the Gothic VS as likely to inflame the military temper of his race; for another reason the Gr translators were at first content with a partial VS. They omitted as unedifying the more disastrous portions, David's sin with the subsequent calamities of his reign and the later history of the divided monarchy culminating in the captivity. Probably the earliest VSS embraced only (1) 1 R, (2) 2 R **1** 1—**11** 1 (David's early reign), (3) 3 R **2** 12—**21** 13 (Solomon and the beginning of the divided monarchy); the third book of "Reigns" opened with the accession of Solomon (as in Lucian's text), not at the point where 1 K opens. These earlier portions are written in a freer style than the rest of the Gr "Reigns," and the Heb original differed widely in places from that tr[d] in the Eng. Bible (*JTS,* VIII, 262).

(4) *The "Writings."*—The Hagiographa at the end of the 2d cent. BC were regarded as national lit. (Sir, prol. "the other books of our fathers"), but not as canonical. The translators did not scruple to treat these with great freedom, undeterred by the prohibition against alteration of Scripture (Dt **4** 2; **12** 32). Free paraphrases of extracts were produced, sometimes with legendary additions. A partial VS of Job (one-sixth being omitted) was among the first; Aristeas, the historian of the 2d cent. BC, seems to have been acquainted with it (Freudenthal, *Hellenistische Studien,* 1875, 136 ff). The translator was a student of the Gr poets; his VS was probably produced for the general reader, not for the synagogues. Hatch's theory (*Essays in Bib. Gr,* 1889, 214) that his Heb text was shorter than ours and was expanded later is untenable; avoidance of anthropomorphisms explains some omissions, the reason for others is obscure. The first Gr narrative of the return from exile (1 Esd) was probably a similar VS of extracts only from Ch-Ezr-Neh, grouped round a fable of non-Jewish origin, the story of the 3 youths at the court of Darius. The work is a fragment, the end being lost, and it has been contended by some critics that the VS once embraced the whole of Ch-Ezr-Neh (C. C. Torrey, *Ezra Studies,* Chicago, 1910). The Gr is obviously earlier than Esd B and is of great value for the reconstruction of the Heb. The same translator appears from peculiarities of diction to have produced the earliest VS of Dnl, treating it with similar freedom and incorporating extraneous matter (the Three Children, Sus, Bel). The maximum of interpolation is reached in Est, where the Gr additions make up two-thirds of the story. The Gr Prov (probably 1st cent. BC) includes many maxims not in the Heb; some of these appear to be derived from a lost Heb collection, others are of purely Gr origin. This translator also knew and imitated the Gr classics; the numerous fragments of iambic and hexameter verse in the tr cannot be accidental (*JTS,* XIII, 46). The Psalter is the one tr in this category in which liberties have not been taken; in Ps **13** [**14**] 3 the extracts from other parts of Pss and from Isa included in the B text must be an interpolation possibly made before St. Paul's time (Rom **3** 13 ff), or else taken from Rom. The little Ps **151** in LXX, described in the title as an "autograph" work of David and as "outside the number," is clearly a late Gr production, perhaps an appendix added after the VS was complete.

(5) *The latest LXX translations.*—The latest VSS included in the LXX are the productions of the Jewish translators of the 2d cent. AD; some books may be rather earlier, the work of pioneers in the new school which advocated strict adherence to the Heb. The books of "Reigns" were now completed, by Theodotion, perhaps, or by one of his school; the later portions (2 R **11** 2—3 R **2** 11, David's downfall, and 3 R **22**—4 R end, the downfall of the monarchy) are by one hand, as shown by pecu-

liarities in style, e.g. "I am have with child" (2 R **11** 5) = "I am with child," a use which is due to a desire to distinguish the longer form of the pronoun *'ānōkhī* ("I," also used for "I am") from the shorter *'ănī*. A complete VS of Jgs was now probably first made. In two cases the old paraphrastic VSS were replaced. Theodotion's Dnl, as above stated, superseded in the Christian church the older VS. A new and complete VS of Ch-Ezr-Neh was made (Esd B), though the older VS retained its place in the Gr Bible on account of the interesting legend imbedded in it; the new VS is here again possibly the work of Theodotion; the numerous transliterations are characteristic of him (Torrey, *Ezra Studies;* the theory had previously been advanced by Sir H. Howorth). In the Gr Eccl we have a specimen of Aquila's style (see McNeile's ed, Cambridge, 1904). Canticles is another late VS.

2. General Characteristics

A marked feature of the whole tr is the scrupulous avoidance of anthropomorphisms and phrases derogatory to the Divine transcendence. Thus Ex **4** 16, "Thou shalt be to him in things pertaining to God" (Heb "for" or "as God"); **15** 3, "The Lord is a breaker of battles" (Heb "a Man of war"); **24** 10, "They saw the place where the God of Israel stood" (Heb "they saw the God of Israel"); ver 11, "Of the elect of Israel not one perished and they were seen in the place of God" (Heb "Upon the nobles . . . . He laid not His hand, and they beheld God"). The comparison of God to a rock was consistently paraphrased as idolatrous, as was sometimes the comparison to the sun from fear of sun-worship (Ps **83** [**84**] 12, "The Lord loves mercy and truth" for Heb "The Lord is a sun and shield"). "The sons of God" (Gen **6** 2) becomes "the angels of God." For minor liberties, e.g. slight amplifications, interpretation of difficult words, substitution of Gr for Heb coinage, tr of place-names, see Swete, *Intro*, 323 ff. Blunders in tr are not uncommon, but the difficulties which these pioneers had to face must be remembered, esp. the paleographical character of the Heb originals. These were written on flimsy papyrus rolls, in a script probably in a transitional stage between the archaic and the later square characters; the words were not separated, and there were no vowel-points; two of the radicals (*wāw* and *yōdh*) were also frequently omitted. Add to this the absence at Alexandria, for parts at least of the Scriptures, of any sound tradition as to the meaning. On the other hand the vocalization adopted by the translators, e.g. in the proper names, is of great value in the history of early Sem pronunciation. It must further be remembered that the Sem language most familiar to them was not Heb but Aram., and some mistakes are due to Aram. or even Arab. colloquialisms (Swete, *Intro*, 319).

IX. Salient Differences between Greek and Hebrew Texts.—Differences indicating a Heb original other than the MT affect either the sequence or the subject-matter (cf Swete, *Intro*, 231 ff).

1. Sequence

The most extensive discrepancies in arrangement of materials occur in (1) Ex **35—39,** the construction of the Tabernacle and the ornaments of its ministers, (2) 3 R **4–11,** Solomon's reign, (3) Jer (last half), (4) Prov (end). (1) In Ex the LXX gives precedence to the priests' ornaments, which in the Heb follow the account of the Tabernacle, and omits altogether the altar of incense. The whole section describing the execution of the instructions given in the previous chapters in almost identical words is one of the latest portions of the Pent and the text had clearly not been finally fixed in the 3d cent. BC; the section was perhaps absent from the oldest Gr VS. In Ex **20** 13–15 cod. B arranges three of the commandments in the Alexandrian order (7, 8, 6), attested in Philo and in the NT. (2) Deliberate rearrangement has taken place in the history of Solomon, and the LXX unquestionably preserves the older text. The narrative of the building of the Temple, like that of the Tabernacle, contains some of the clearest examples of editorial revision in the MT (Wellhausen, *Hist of Israel*, 67, 280, etc). At the end of 3 R LXX places chs **20** and **21** in their proper order; MT reverses this, interposing the Naboth story in the connected account of the Syr wars and justifying the change by a short preface. (3) In Jer the chapter numbers differ from the middle of ch **25** to the end of ch **51,** the historical appendix (ch **52**) concluding both texts. This is due to the different position assigned to a group of prophecies against the nations: LXX places them in the center, MT at the end. The items in this group are also rearranged. The diversity in order is earlier than the Gr tr; see *JTS*, IV, 245. (4) The order of some groups of maxims at the end of Prov was not finally fixed at the time of the Gr tr; like Jeremiah's prophecies against the nations, these little groups seem to have circulated as late as the 2d or 1st cent. BC as separate pamphlets. The Ps numbers from **10** to **147** differ by one in LXX and MT, owing to discrepancies in the lines of demarcation between individual pss.

2. Subject-Matter

Excluding the end of Ex, striking examples of divergence in the Pent are few. LXX alone preserves Cain's words to his brother, "Let us go into the field" (Gen **4** 8). The close of Moses' song appears in an expanded form in LXX (Dt **32** 43). Similarly Hannah's song in 1 R **2** (? originally a warrior's triumph-song) has been rendered more appropriate to the occasion by the substitution in ver 8*c* of words about the answer to prayer, and enlarged by the insertion of a passage from Jer; the changes in both songs may be connected with their early use as canticles. In Josh the larger amount of divergence suggests that this book did not share the peculiar sanctity of the Law. But the books of "Reigns" present the widest differences and the fullest scope for the textual critic. The LXX here proves the existence of two independent accounts of certain events. Sometimes it incorporates both, while the MT rejects one of them; thus LXX gives (3 R **2** 35*a* ff.46*a* ff) a connected summary of events in Solomon's personal history; most of which appear elsewhere in a detached form, **12** 24*a–z* is a second account of the dismemberment of the kingdom; **16** 28*a-h* a second summary of Jehoshaphat's reign (cf **22** 41 ff); 4 R **1** 18*a* another summary of Joram's reign (cf **3** 1 ff). Conversely in 1 R **17–18,** MT has apparently preserved two contradictory accounts of events in David's early history, while LXX presents a shorter and consistent narrative (Swete, *Intro*, 245 f). An "addition" in LXX of the highest interest appears in 3 R **8** 53*b*, where a stanza is put into the mouth of Solomon at the Temple dedication, taken from "the Song-book" (probably the Book of Jashar); the MT gives the stanza in an edited form earlier in the chapter (**8** 12 f); for the reconstruction of the original Heb see *JTS*, X, 439; XI, 518. The last line proves to be a title, "For the Sabbath—On Alamoth" (i.e. for sopranos), showing that the song was set to music for liturgical purposes. In Jer, besides transpositions, the two texts differ widely in the way of excess and defect; the verdict of critics is mainly in favor of the priority of the LXX (Streane, *Double Text of Jer*, 1896). For divergences in the "Writings" see VIII, above; for additional titles to the Pss see Swete, *Intro*, 250 f.

Literature.—The most important works have been mentioned in the body of the article. See, further, the very full lists in Swete's *Intro* and the bibliographies by Nestle in *PRE*³, III, 1–24, and XXIII, 207–10 (1913); *HDB*, IV, 453–54.

H. St. J. Thackeray

SEPULCHRE, sep'ul-kẽr (2 Ch **21** 20; **32** 33; Jn **19** 41 f; Acts **2** 29, etc). See Burial; Jerusalem, VIII.

SERAH, sē'ra (שֶׂרַח, *seraḥ*, "abundance"): Daughter of Asher (Gen **46** 17; Nu **26** 46, AV "Sarah"; 1 Ch **7** 30).

SERAIAH, sḗ-rā'ya, sḗ-rī'a (שְׂרָיָהוּ, *s*ᵉ*rāyāhū*, "Jeh hath prevailed"; LXX **Σαραίας**, *Saraías*, or **Σαραία**, *Saraía*):

(1) Secretary of David (2 S **8** 17); in 2 S **20** 25 he is called Sheva; in 1 K **4** 3 the name appears as Shisha. This last or Shasha would be restored elsewhere by some critics; others prefer the form Shavsha, which is found in 1 Ch **18** 16.

(2) A high priest in the reign of Zedekiah; executed with other prominent captives at Riblah by order of Nebuchadnezzar (2 K **25** 18.21; Jer **52** 24.27). Mentioned in the list of high priests (1 Ch **6** 14). Ezra claims descent from him (Ezr **7** 1[3]). See Azaraias; Saraias.

(3) The son of Tanhumeth the Netophathite, and one of the heroic band of men who saved themselves from the fury of Nebuchadnezzar when he stormed Jerus. They repaired to Gedaliah, the son of Ahikam, but killed him on account of his allegiance to the Chaldaeans (2 K **25** 23.25).

(4) Son of Kenaz, and younger brother of Othniel, and father of Joab, the chief of Ge-harashim (1 Ch **4** 13.14).

(5) Grandfather of Jehu, of the tribe of Simeon (1 Ch **4** 35).

(6) A priest, the third in the list of those who returned from Babylon to Jerus with Zerubbabel (Ezr **2** 2; Neh **7** 7, here called Azariah; **12** 1), and third also (if the same person is meant) in the record of those who sealed the covenant binding all Jews not to take foreign wives (Neh **10** 2). As the son of Hilkiah, and consequently a direct descendant of the priestly family, he became governor of the temple when it was rebuilt (Neh **11** 11). He is mentioned (under the name Azariah) also in 1 Ch **9** 11. Neh **12** 2 adds that "in the days of Joiakim" the head of Seraiah's house was Meraiah.

(7) Son of Azriel, one of those whom Jehoiakim commanded to imprison Jeremiah and Baruch, the son of Neriah (Jer **36** 26).

(8) The son of Neriah, who went into exile with Zedekiah. He was also called *Sar M*ᵉ*nūḥāh* ("prince of repose"). The Tg renders *Sar M*ᵉ*nūḥāh* by *Rabh Tīḳrabhtā'*, "prince of battle," and LXX by ἄρχων δώρων, *árchōn dṓrōn*, "prince of gifts," reading *Minḥah* for *M*ᵉ*nūḥāh*. At the request of Jeremiah he carried with him in his exile the passages containing the prophet's warning of the fall of Babylon, written in a book which he was bidden to bind to a stone and cast into the Euphrates, to symbolize the fall of Babylon (Jer **51** 59–64).

Horace J. Wolf

SERAPHIM, ser'a-fim (שְׂרָפִים, *s*ᵉ*rāphīm*): A pl. word occurring only in Isa **6** 2 ff—Isaiah's vision of Jeh. The origin of the term in Heb is uncertain. *Sārāph* in Nu **21** 6; Isa **14** 29, etc, signifies a fiery serpent. A Bab name for the fire-god, Nergal, was *Sharrapu*. In Egypt there have been found eagle-lion-shaped figures guarding a grave, to which is applied the name *seref*. The equivalent Eng. term is "griffin."

It is probable enough that popular mythology connected fire with the attendants of the deity in various ways among different peoples, and that burning lies at the base of the idea in all these suggested etymologies. It remains, however, that in Isaiah's use there is nothing of the popular legend or superstition. These seraphim are august beings whose forms are not at all fully described. They had faces, feet, hands and wings. The six wings, in three pairs, covered their faces and feet in humility and reverence, and were used for sustaining them in their positions about the throne of Jeh. One of them is the agent for burning (with a coal off the altar, not with his own power or person) the sin from the lips of the prophet.

Seraphim are in Jewish theology connected with *cherubim* and *ophanim* as the three highest orders of attendants on Jeh, and are superior to the angels who are messengers sent on various errands. As the cherubim in popular fancy were represented by the storm-clouds, so the seraphim were by the serpentine flashes of the lightning; but none of this appears in Isaiah's vision.

In the NT the only possible equivalent is in "the living ones" ("beasts" of AV) in Rev **4**, **5**, etc. Here, as in Isa, they appear nearest Jeh's throne, supreme in praise of His holiness.

William Owen Carver

SERAR, sē'rär (**Σεράρ**, *Serár;* AV Aserer): Name of one of the families which returned with Zerubbabel (1 Esd **5** 32) = "Sisera" of Ezr **2** 53; Neh **7** 55.

SERED, sē'red (סֶרֶד, *ṣeredh*): Son of Zebulun (Gen **46** 14; Nu **26** 26).

SERGIUS PAULUS, sûr'ji-us pô'lus. See Paulus, Sergius.

SERJEANTS, sär'jents, -jants (**ῥαβδοῦχοι**, *rhabdoúchoi*): In Acts **16** 35.38 the word (lit. "holders of rods," corresponding to Rom "lictors," thus RVm) is used of the officers in attendance on the Philippian magistrates, whose duty it was to execute orders in scourging, etc, in this case in setting prisoners free. Paul and Silas, however, as Romans, refused thus to be "privily" dismissed.

SERMON, sûr'mun, **ON THE MOUNT, THE:**

I. Parallel Accounts
II. Historicity of the Discourse
III. Time and Occasion
IV. Scene
V. The Hearers
VI. The Message: Summary
  1. Analysis
  2. Argument: The Kingdom of God (Heaven)
    (1) Characteristics of the Subjects
    (2) Vocation of the Subjects
    (3) Relation of New Righteousness to Mosaic Law
      (a) The Relation Defined
      (b) The Relation Illustrated
    (4) Motives and Principles of Conduct
      (a) In Worship
      (b) In Life's Purpose
      (c) In Social Relations
    (5) Hortatory Conclusion
      (a) The Narrow Way
      (b) The Tests of Character
VII. Principles
Literature

The Sermon on the Mount is the title commonly given to the collection of sayings recorded in Mt **5–7** and in Lk **6** 20–49. The latter is sometimes called the Sermon on the Plain from the fact that it is said to have been delivered on a level space somewhere on the descent of the mountain. The Sermon appears to be an epitome of the teachings of Jesus concerning the kingdom of heaven, its subjects and their life. For this reason it has always held the first place of attention and esteem among the sayings of Jesus. See Sermon on the Plain.

I. Parallel Accounts.—As indicated above, the Sermon is reported by both Matthew and Luke.

A comparison of the two accounts reveals certain striking differences. A total of 47 verses of the account in Mt have no parallel in Lk, while but 4½ verses of the latter are wanting in the former. On the other hand, many of the sayings in Mt that are lacking in the Sermon of Lk, amounting in all to 34 verses, appear elsewhere distributed throughout the Lukan narrative and in some instances connected with different incidents and circumstances.

These facts give rise to some interesting literary and historical questions: Do the two accounts represent two distinct discourses dealing with the same general theme but spoken on different occasions, or are they simply different reports of the same discourse? If it be held that the Sermon was delivered but once, which of the accounts represents more closely the original address? Is the discourse in Mt homogeneous or does it include sayings originally spoken on other occasions and early incorporated in the Sermon in the gospel tradition?

II. Historicity of the Discourse.—There have been and are today scholars who regard the sermons recorded in Mt and Lk as collections of sayings spoken on different occasions, and maintain that they do not represent any connected discourse ever delivered by Jesus. In their view the Sermon is either a free compilation by the evangelists or a product of apostolic teaching and oral tradition.

The prevailing opinion among NT scholars is, however, that the gospel accounts represent a genuine historical discourse. The Sermon as recorded in Mt bears such marks of inner unity of theme and exposition as to give the appearance of genuineness. That Jesus should deliver a discourse of this kind accords with all the circumstances and with the purpose of His ministry. Besides, we know that in His teaching He was accustomed to speak to the multitudes at length, and we should expect Him to give early in His ministry some formal exposition of the kingdom, the burden of His first preaching. That such a summary of one of His most important discourses should have been preserved is altogether probable.

On the other hand, it may be conceded that the accounts need not necessarily be regarded as full or exact reports of the discourse but possibly and probably rather summaries of its theme and substance. Our Lord was accustomed to teach at length, but this discourse could easily be delivered in a few minutes. Again, while His popular teaching was marked by a unique wealth of illustration the Sermon is largely gnomic in form. This gnomic style and the paucity of the usual concrete and illustrative elements suggest the probability of condensation in transmission. Moreover, it is hardly probable that such an address of Jesus would be recorded at the time of its delivery or would be remembered in detail.

There is evidence that the account in Mt **5–7** contains some sayings not included in the original discourse. This view is confirmed by the fact that a number of the sayings are given in Luke's Gospel in settings that appear more original. It is easy to believe that related sayings spoken on other occasions may have become associated with the Sermon in apostolic teaching and thus handed down with it, but if the discourse were well known in a specific form, such as that recorded in Mt, it is hardly conceivable that Luke or anyone else would break it up and distribute the fragments or associate them with other incidents, as some of the sayings recorded in both Gospels are found associated in Lk.

III. Time and Occasion.—Both Matthew and Luke agree in assigning the delivery of the Sermon to the first half of the Galilean ministry. The former apparently places it a little earlier than the latter, in whose account it follows immediately after the appointment of the twelve apostles. While the time cannot be accurately determined, the position assigned by the Gospels is approximately correct and is supported by the internal evidence. Portions of the Sermon imply that the opposition of the religious teachers was already in evidence, but it clearly belongs to the first year of Our Lord's ministry before that opposition had become serious. On the other hand, the occasion was sufficiently late for the popularity of the new Teacher to have reached its climax. In the early Galilean ministry Jesus confined His teaching to the synagogues, but later, when the great crowds pressed about Him, He resorted to open-air preaching after the manner of the Sermon. Along with the growth in His popularity there is observed a change in the character of His teaching. His earlier message may be summed up in the formula, "Repent ye; for the kingdom of heaven is at hand" (Mt **4** 17). Later, both in His public discourses and in His more intimate conferences with His disciples, He was occupied with the principles of the kingdom. The Sermon on the Mount belongs to this later type of teaching and fits naturally into the circumstances to which it has been assigned. Luke probably gives the true historical occasion, i.e. the appointment of the Twelve.

IV. Scene.—According to the evangelists, the scene of the delivery of the Sermon was one of the mountains or foothills surrounding the Galilean plain. Probably one of the hills lying N.W. of Capernaum is meant, for shortly after the Sermon we find Jesus and His disciples entering that city. There are no data justifying a closer identification of the place. There is a tradition dating from the time of the Crusades that identifies the mount of the Sermon with *Ḳarn Ḥaṭṭîn*, a two-peaked hill on the road from Tiberias to Nazareth, but there are no means of confirming this late tradition and the identification is rather improbable.

V. The Hearers.—The Sermon was evidently addressed, primarily, to the disciples of Jesus. This is the apparent meaning of the account of both evangelists. According to Matthew, Jesus, "seeing the multitudes, ... went up into the mountain: and when he had sat down, his disciples came unto him: and he opened his mouth and taught them." The separation from the multitudes and the direction of His words to the disciples seem clear, and the distinction appears intentional on the part of the writer. However, it must be observed that in the closing comments on the Sermon the presence of the multitudes is implied. In Luke's account the distinction is less marked. Here the order of events is: the night of prayer in the mountain, the choice of the twelve apostles, the descent with them into the presence of the multitude of His disciples and a great number of people from Judaea, Jerus and the coast country, the healing of great numbers, and, finally, the address. While the continued presence of the multitudes is implied, the plain meaning of the words, "And he lifted up his eyes on his disciples, and said," is that his address was intended esp. for the latter. This view is borne out by the address itself as recorded in both accounts. Observe the use of the second person in the reference to suffering, poverty and persecution for the sake of the Son of Man. Further the sayings concerning the "salt of the earth" and "the light of the world" could hardly have been addressed to any but His disciples. The term disciple, however, was doubtless employed in the broader sense by both evangelists. This is clearly the case in Matthew's account, according to which the Twelve had not yet been appointed.

VI. The Message: A Summary.—It is hardly proper to speak of the Sermon on the Mount as a digest of the teaching of Jesus, for it does not include any reference to some very important subjects discussed by Our Lord on other occasions in the course of His ministry. It is, however, the most comprehensive and important collection or summary of His sayings that is preserved to us in the gospel record. For this reason the Sermon properly holds in Christian thought the first place of esteem among all the NT messages. As an exposition of the ideal life and the program of the new society which Jesus proposed to create, its interpretation is of the deepest interest and the profoundest concern.

1. Analysis

It may assist the student of the Sermon in arriving at a clear appreciation of the argument and the salient features of the discourse if the whole is first viewed in outline. There is some difference of opinion among scholars as to certain features of the analysis, and consequently various outlines have been presented by different writers. Those of C. W. Votaw in *HDB*, Canon Gore in *The Sermon on the Mount*, and H. C. King in *The Ethics of Jesus* are worthy of special mention. The following analysis of the Sermon as recorded by Matthew is given as the basis of the present discussion.

It is not implied that there was any such formal plan before the mind of Jesus as He spoke, but it is believed that the outline presents a faithful syllabus of the argument of the Sermon as preserved to us.

THEME: THE KINGDOM OF GOD (HEAVEN), ITS SUBJECTS AND ITS RIGHTEOUSNESS (**5** 3—**7** 27).

I. The subjects of the kingdom (**5** 3–16).
 1. The qualities of character essential to happiness and influence (vs 3–12).
 2. The vocation of the subjects (vs 13–16).
II. The relation of the new righteousness to the Mosaic Law (**5** 17–48).
 1. The relation defined as that of continuance in a higher fulfilment (vs 17–20).
 2. The higher fulfilment of the new righteousness illustrated by a comparison of its principles with the Mosaic Law as currently taught and practised (vs 21–48).
  (1) The higher law of brotherhood judges ill-will as murder (vs 21–26).
  (2) The higher law of purity condemns lust as adultery (vs 27–32).
  (3) The higher law of truth forbids oaths as unnecessary and evil (vs 33–37).
  (4) The higher law of rights substitutes self-restraint and generosity for retaliation and resistance (vs 38–42).
  (5) The higher law of love demands universal good will of a supernatural quality like that of the Father (vs 43–48).
III. The new righteousness. Its motives as applied to religious, practical and social duties, or the principles of conduct (**6** 1—**7** 12).
 1. Reverence toward the Father essential in all acts of worship (**6** 1–18).
  (1) In all duties (ver 1).
  (2) In almsgiving (vs 2–4).
  (3) In prayer (vs 5–15).
  (4) In fasting (vs 16–18).
 2. Loyalty toward the Father fundamental in all activities (**6** 19–34).
  (1) In treasure-seeking (vs 19–24).
  (2) In trustful devotion to the kingdom and the Father's righteousness (vs 25–34).
 3. Love toward the Father dynamic in all social relations (**7** 1–12).
  (1) Critical estimate of self instead of censorious judgment of others (vs 1–5).
  (2) Discrimination in the communication of spiritual values (ver 6).
  (3) Kindness toward others in all things like the Father's kindness toward all His children (vs 7–12).
IV. Hortatory conclusion (**7** 13–27).
 1. The two gates and the two ways (vs 13–14).
 2. The tests of character (vs 15–27).

2. Argument: The Kingdom of God (Heaven)

(1) *Characteristics of the subjects* (***5** 3–12*).—The Sermon opens with the familiar Beatitudes. Unlike many reformers, Jesus begins the exposition of His program with a promise of happiness, with a blessing rather than a curse. He thus connects His program directly with the hopes of His hearers, for the central features in the current Messianic conception were deliverance and happiness. But the conditions of happiness proposed were in strong contrast with those in the popular thought. Happiness does not consist, says Jesus, in what one possesses, in lands and houses, in social position, in intellectual attainments, but in the wealth of the inner life, in moral strength, in self-control, in spiritual insight, in the character one is able to form within himself and in the service he is able to render to his fellow-men. Happiness, then, like character, is a by-product of right living. It is presented as the fruit, not as the object of endeavor.

It is interesting to note that character is the secret of happiness both for the individual and for society. There are two groups of Beatitudes. The first four deal with personal qualities: humility, penitence, self-control, desire for righteousness. These are the sources of inner peace. The second group deals with social qualities; mercifulness toward others, purity of heart or reverence for personality, peace-making or solicitude for others, self-sacrificing loyalty to righteousness. These are the sources of social rest. The blessings of the kingdom are social as well as individual.

(2) *Vocation of the subjects* (***5** 13–16*).—Men of the qualities described in the Beatitudes are called "the salt of the earth," "the light of the world." Their happiness is not, then, in themselves or for themselves alone. Their mission is the hope of the kingdom. Salt is a preservative element; light is a life-giving one; but the world is not eager to be preserved or willing to receive life. Therefore such men must expect opposition and persecution, but they are not on that account to withdraw from the world. On the contrary, by the leaven of character and the light of example they are to help others in the appreciation and the attainment of the ideal life. By their character and deeds they are to make their influence a force for good in the lives of men. In this sense the men of the kingdom are the salt of the earth, the light of the world. See BEATITUDES.

(3) *The relation of the new righteousness to the Mosaic Law* (***5** 17–48*).—(*a*) Relation defined (**5** 17–20): The qualities of character thus set before the citizens of the kingdom were so surprising and revolutionary as to suggest the inquiry: What is the relation of the new teaching to the Mosaic Law? This Jesus defines as continuance and fulfilment. His hearers are not to think that He has come to destroy the law. On the contrary, He has come to conserve and fulfil. The old law is imperfect, but God does not despair of what is imperfect. Men and institutions are judged, not by the level of present attainment, but by character and direction. The law moves in the right direction and is so valuable that those who violate even its least precepts have a very low place in the kingdom.

The new righteousness then does not set aside the law or offer an easier religion, but one that is more exacting. The kingdom is concerned, not so much with ceremonies and external rules, as with motives and with social virtues, with self-control, purity, honesty and generosity. So much higher are the new standards of righteousness that Jesus is constrained to warn His hearers that to secure even a place in the kingdom, their righteousness must exceed that of the scribes and Pharisees.

(*b*) The relation illustrated (**5** 21–48): In illustration of the deeper meaning of the new righteousness and its relation to the Mosaic Law, Jesus proceeds to deal in detail with the precepts of the old moral law, deepening it as He proceeds into the higher law of the kingdom. In each instance the standard of judgment is raised and the individual precepts are deepened into spiritual principles that call for perfect fulfilment. In considering specific precepts no account is taken of overt acts, for in the new righteousness they are impossible. All acts are treated as expressions of the inner life. The law is carried back to the impulse and the will to sin, and these are judged as in the old law the completed acts were judged. Therefore all anger and lust in the heart are strictly enjoined. Likewise every word is raised to a sacredness equal with that of the most solemn religious vow or oath. Finally, the instinct to avenge is entirely forbidden, and universal love like that of the Father is made the fundamental law of the new social life. Thus Jesus does not abrogate any law but interprets its precepts in terms that call for a deeper and more perfect fulfilment.

(4) *Motives and principles of conduct* (***6** 1—**7** 12*).—The relation of His teaching to the law defined, Jesus proceeds to explain the motives and principles of conduct as applied to religious and social duties.

(*a*) In worship (**6** 1–18): In the section **6** 1—**7** 12 there is one central thought. All righteousness looks toward God. He is at once the source and the aim of life. Therefore worship aims alone at Divine praise. If acts of worship are performed before men to be seen of them there is no reward for them before the Father. In this Jesus is passing no slight on public worship. He Himself instituted the Lord's Supper and authorized the continuance of the rite of baptism. Such acts have their proper value. His censure is aimed at the love of ostentation so often associated with them. The root of ostentation is selfishness, and selfishness has no part in the new righteousness. Any selfish desire for the approval of men thwarts the purpose of all worship. The object of almsgiving, of prayer or of fasting is the expression of brotherly love, communion with God or spiritual enrichment. The possibility of any of these is excluded by the presence of the desire for the approval of men. It is not merely a Divine fiat but one of the deeper laws of life which decrees that the only possible reward for acts of worship performed from such false motives is the cheap approval of men as well as the impoverishment of the inner life.

(*b*) In life's purpose (**6** 19–34): The same principle holds, says Jesus, in the matter of life's purpose. There is only one treasure worthy of man's search, only one object worthy of his highest endeavor, and that is the kingdom of God and His righteousness. Besides, there can be no division of aim. God will be first and only. Material blessings must not be set before duty to Him or to men. With any lower aim the new righteousness would be no better than that of the Gentiles. And such a demand is reasonable, for God's gracious providence is ample guaranty that He will supply all things needful for the accomplishment of the purposes He has planned for our lives. So in our vocations as in our worship, God is the supreme and effectual motive.

(*c*) In social relations (**7** 1–12): Then again because God is our Father and the supreme object of desire for all men, great reverence is due toward others. Considerate helpfulness must replace the censorious spirit. For the same reason men will have too great reverence for spiritual values to cast them carelessly before the unworthy. Moreover, because God is so gracious and ready to bestow the best gifts freely upon His children, the men of the kingdom are under profound obligation to observe the higher law of brotherhood expressed in the Golden Rule: "All things . . . . whatsoever ye would that men should do unto you, even so do ye also unto them." Thus in the perfect law of the Fatherhood of God and the brotherhood of men the new righteousness makes perfect the Law and the Prophets.

(5) *Hortatory conclusion* (***7** 13–27*).—(*a*) The narrow way (**7** 13–14): In the hortatory conclusion (**7** 13–27), Jesus first of all warns His hearers that the way into the kingdom is a narrow one. It might seem that it ought to be different; that the way to destruction should be narrow and difficult, and the way to life broad and easy, but it is not so. The way to all worthy achievement is the narrow way of self-control, self-sacrifice and infinite pains. Such is the way to the righteousness of the kingdom, the supreme object of human endeavor. "Narrow is the gate, and straitened the way, that leadeth unto life."

(*b*) The tests of character (**7** 15–27): The test of the higher fulfilment is fruit. By their fruits alone the subjects of the kingdom will be known. In the presence of the Father there is no room for those who bring nothing but the leaves of empty professions. The kingdom is for those alone who do His will. The test of righteousness is illustrated in conclusion by the beautiful parable of the Two Builders. The difference between the two is essentially one of character. It is largely a question of fundamental honesty. The one is superficial and thinks only of that which is visible to the eye and builds only for himself and for the present. The other is honest enough to build well where only God can see, to build for others and for all time. Thus he builds also for himself. The character of the builder is revealed by the building.

VII. Principles.—The Sermon on the Mount is neither an impractical ideal nor a set of fixed legal regulations. It is, instead, a statement of the principles of life essential in a normal society. Such a society is possible in so far as men attain the character and live the life expressed in these principles. Their correct interpretation is therefore important.

Many of the sayings of the Sermon are metaphorical or proverbial statements, and are not to be understood in a literal or legal sense. In them Jesus was illustrating principles in concrete terms. Their interpretation literally as legal enactments is contrary to the intention and spirit of Jesus. So interpreted, the Sermon becomes in part a visionary and impractical ideal. But rather the principles behind the concrete instances are to be sought and applied anew to the life of the present as Jesus applied them to the life of His own time.

The following are some of the leading ideas and principles underlying and expressed in the Sermon:

(1) Character is the secret of happiness and strength. Men of the qualities described in the Beatitudes are called "blessed." Happiness consists, not in external blessings, but in the inner poise of a normal life. The virtues of the Beatitudes are also the elements of strength. Humility, self-control, purity and loyalty are the genuine qualities of real strength. Men of such qualities are to inherit the earth because they are the only ones strong enough to possess and use it.

(2) Righteousness is grounded in the inner life. Character is not something imposed from without but a life that unfolds from within. The hope of a perfect morality and a genuine fulfilment of the law lies in the creation of a sound inner life. Therefore the worth of all religious acts and all personal and social conduct is judged by the quality of the inner motives.

(3) The inner life is a unity. The spiritual nature is all of a piece, so that a moral slump at one point imperils the whole life. Consequently a rigid and exacting spiritual asceticism, even to the extent of extreme major surgery, is sometimes expedient and necessary. "If thy right eye causeth thee to stumble, pluck it out, and cast it from thee: for it is profitable for thee that one of thy members should perish, and not thy whole body be cast into Gehenna" (Mt **5** 29m).

(4) Universal love is the fundamental social law. It is the dynamic principle of true character and right conduct. In this respect, at least, the perfection of the Father is set as the standard for men. Kindliness in disposition, in word and in act is an obligation binding on all. We may not feel alike toward all, but our wills must be set to do good even to our enemies. In this the supernatural quality of the Christian life may be known.

(5) The Sermon sets the fact of God the Father at the center of life. Character and life exist in and for fellowship with the Father. All worship and conduct look toward God. His service is the supreme duty, His perfection the standard of character, His goodness the ground of universal love. Given this fact, all the essentials of religion and life follow as a matter of course. God is Father, all men are brothers. God is Father, all duties are sacred. God is Father, infinite love is at the heart of the world and life is of infinite worth.

(6) Fulfilment is the final test of life. The blossoms of promises must ripen into the fruit of abiding character. The leaves of empty professions have no value in the eyes of the Father. Deeds and character are the only things that abide, and endurance is the final test. The life of perfect fulfilment is the life anchored on the rock of ages. See further Ethics; Ethics of Jesus; Kingdom of God.

Literature.—The standard comms. and Lives of Christ. Among the most important encyclopaedic arts. are those of C. W. Votaw in *HDB*, James Moffatt in *EB* and W. F. Adeney in *DCG*. The following are a few of the most helpful separate volumes on the subject: A. Tholuck, *Exposition of Christ's Sermon on the Mount;* Canon Gore, *The Sermon on the Mount;* B. W. Bacon, *The Sermon on the Mount;* W. B. Carpenter, *The Great Charter of Christ;* Hubert Foston, *The Beatitudes and the Contrasts;* cf H. C. King, *The Ethics of Jesus*, and Stalker, *The Ethic of Jesus.* The following periodical arts. are worthy of notice: Franklin Johnson, "The Plan of the Sermon on the Mount," *Homiletic Review*, XXIV, 360; A. H. Hall, "The Gospel in the Sermon on the Mount," *Bib. Sac.*, XLVIII, 322; The Bishop of Peterborough (W. C. Magee), "The State and the Sermon on the Mount," *Fortnightly Review*, LIII, 32; J. G. Pyle, "The Sermon on the Mount," *Putnam's Magazine*, VII, 285.

Russell Benjamin Miller

SERMON ON THE PLAIN, THE: This title is sometimes given to the discourse recorded in Lk **6** 20–49, because according to the Gospel (ver 17) it was delivered on a plain at the foot of the mountain. In many respects this address resembles the one recorded in Mt **5–7**, but in general the two are so different as to make it uncertain whether they are different reports of the same discourse or reports of different addresses given on different occasions. See Sermon on the Mount.

1. The Occasion

In contrast with the Sermon on the Mount which is assigned a place early in the Galilean ministry, and prior to the appointment of the Twelve, that event is represented as the occasion of this discourse. If the two accounts are reports of the same address the setting of Lk is probably the historical one.

2. Contents

The Sermon of Lk includes a little less than one-third of the matter recorded in the Sermon on the Mount. The Lukan discourse includes only a portion of the Beatitudes, with a set of four "woes," a rather brief section on the social duties, and the concluding parable of the Two Houses.

3. Message

The Gospel of Lk has been called the social Gospel because of its sympathy with the poor and its emphasis on the duty of kindliness of spirit. This social interest is esp. prominent in the Sermon. Here the Beatitudes deal with social differences. In Mt they refer to spiritual conditions. Here Jesus speaks of those who hunger now, probably meaning bodily hunger. In Mt the reference is to hunger and thirst after righteousness. In Mt the invectives are addressed against the self-satisfied religious teachers and their religious formalism. Here the rich and their unsocial spirit are the subject of the woes. This social interest is further emphasized by the fact that in addition to this social bearing of the Beatitudes, Lk's discourse omits the remainder of the Sermon on the Mount, except those portions that deal with social relations, such as those on the Golden Rule, the duty of universal love, the equality of servant and master, and the obligation of a charitable spirit. Russell Benjamin Miller

SERON, sē′ron (Σήρων, *Sērōn*): "The commander of the host of Syria" of Antiochus Epiphanes, who was defeated at Beth-horon by Judas in 166 BC (1 Macc **3** 13 ff). Not a Gr name; "perhaps it represents the Phoen Hiram" (Rawlinson, ad loc.).

SERPENT, sûr′pent: Serpents are not particularly abundant in Pal, but they are often mentioned in the Bible. In the Heb there are 11 names. The NT has four Gr names and LXX employs two of these and three others as well as several compound expressions, such as ὄφις πετάμενος, *óphis petámenos*, "flying serpent," ὄφις θανατῶν, *óphis thanatṓn*, "deadly serpent," and ὄφις δάκνων, *óphis dáknōn*, "biting" or "stinging serpent." Notwithstanding this large vocabulary, it is impossible to identify satisfactorily a single species. Nearly every reference states or implies poisonous qualities, and in no case is there so much as a hint that a snake may be harmless, except in several expressions referring to the millennium, where their harmlessness is not natural but miraculous. In Arab. there is a score or more of names of serpents, but very few of them are employed at all definitely. It may be too much to say that the inhabitants of Syria and Pal consider all snakes to be poisonous, but they do not clearly distinguish the non-poisonous ones, and there are several common and well-known species which are universally believed to be poisonous, though actually harmless. Of nearly 25 species which are certainly known to be found in Syria and Pal, four are deadly poisonous, five are somewhat poisonous, and the rest are absolutely harmless. With the exception of *ḳippōz*, "dart-snake" (Isa **34** 15), which is probably the name of a bird and not of a snake, every one of the Heb and Gr names occurs in passages where poisonous character is expressed or implied. The deadly poisonous snakes have large perforated poison fangs situated in the front of the upper jaw, an efficient apparatus like a hypodermic syringe for conveying the poison into the depths of the wound. In the somewhat poisonous snakes, the poison fangs are less favorably situated, being farther back, nearly under the eye. Moreover, they are smaller and are merely grooved on the anterior aspect instead of being perforated. All snakes, except a few which are nearly or quite toothless, have numerous small recurved teeth for holding and helping to swallow the prey, which is usually taken into the stomach while living, the peculiar structure of the jaws and the absence of a breastbone enabling snakes to swallow animals which exceed the ordinary size of their own bodies.

1. General

2. Serpents of Pal and Syria

The following list includes all the serpents which are certainly known to exist in Pal and Syria, omitting the names of several which have been reported but whose occurrence does not seem to be sufficiently confirmed. The range of each species is given.

(1) *Harmless serpents.*—*Typhlops vermicularis* Merr., Greece and Southwestern Asia; *T. simoni* Bttgr., Pal; *Eryx jaculus* L., Greece, North Africa, Central and Southwestern Asia; *Tropidonotus tessellatus* Laur., Central and Southeastern Europe, Central and Southwestern Asia; *Zamenis gemonensis* Laur., Central and Southeastern Europe, Gr islands, Southwestern Asia; *Z. dahlii* Fitz., Southeastern Europe, Southwestern Asia, Lower Egypt, *Z. rhodorhachis* Jan., Egypt, Southwestern Asia, India; *Z. ravergieri* Menatr., Southwestern Asia: *Z. nummifer* Renss., Egypt, Syria, Pal, Cyprus, Asia Minor; *Oligodon melanocephalus* Jan., Syria, Pal, Sinai, Lower Egypt; *Contia decemlineata* D. and B., Syria, Pal; *C. collaris* Menetr., Gr islands, Cyprus, Asia Minor, Syria, Pal; *C. rothi* Jan., Syria, Pal; *C. coronella* Schleg., Syria, Pal.

(2) *Somewhat poisonous serpents.*—*Tarbophis savignyi* Blgr., Syria, Pal, Egypt; *T. fallax* Fleischm., Balkan Peninsula, Gr islands, Cyprus, Asia Minor, Syria, Pal; *Coelopeltis monspessulana* Herm., Mediterranean countries, Caucasus, Persia; *Psammophis schokari* Forsk., North Africa, Southwestern Asia; *Micrelaps muelleri* Bttgr., Syria, Pal.

(3) *Deadly poisonous serpents.*—*Vipera ammodytes* L., Southeastern Europe, Asia Minor, Syria; *Vipera lebetina* L., North Africa, Gr islands, Southwestern Asia; *Cerastes cornutus* Forsk., Egypt, Sinai, Arabia; *Echis coloratus* Gthr., Southern Pal, Arabia, Socotra.

To this list should be added the scheltopusik, a large snake-like, limbless lizard, *Ophiosaurus apus*, inhabiting Southeastern Europe, Asia Minor, Persia, Syria and Pal, which while perfectly harmless is commonly classed with vipers.

Of all these the commonest is *Zamenis nummifer*, Arab. عَقْدُ آلْجَوْز, *'aḳd-ul-jauz*, "string of walnuts," a fierce but non-poisonous snake which attains the length of a meter. Its ground color is pale yellow and it has a dorsal series of distinct diamond-shaped dark spots. Alternating with spots of the dorsal row are on each side two lateral rows of less distinct dark spots. It is everywhere considered to be fatal. Another common snake is *Zamenis gemonensis*, Arab. حَنَش, *ḥanash*, which attains the length of two meters. It is usually black and much resembles the American black snake, *Zamenis constrictor.* Like all species of *Zamenis,* these are harmless. Other common harmless snakes are *Zamenis dahlii, Tropidonotus tessellatus* which is often found in pools and streams, *Contia collaris, Oligodon melanocephalus,* a small, nearly toothless snake with the crown of the head coal black.

Among the somewhat poisonous snakes, a very common one is *Coelopeltis monspessulana,* Arab. الحَيَّة البَرْشَة, *al-haiyat ul-barshat,* which is about two meters long, as large as the black snake. It is uniformly reddish brown above, paler below. Another is *Psammophis schokari,* Arab. النَشَّاب, *an-nashshâb,* "the arrow." It is about a meter long, slender, and white with dark stripes. Many marvelous and utterly improbable tales are told of its jumping powers, as for instance that it can shoot through the air for more than a hundred feet and penetrate a tree like a rifle bullet.

The commonest of the deadly poisonous snakes is *Vipera lebetina,* which attains the length of a meter, has a thick body, a short tail, a broad head and a narrow neck. It is spotted somewhat as *Zamenis nummifer,* but the spots are less regular and distinct and the ground color is grey rather than yellow. It does not seem to have a distinct name. *Cerastes cornutus,* having two small horns, which are modified scales, over the eyes, is a small but dangerous viper, and is found in the south. Not only are the species of poisonous serpents fewer than the non-poisonous species, but the individuals also appear to be less numerous. The vast majority of the snakes which are encountered are harmless.

3. Names

As stated above, all of the Heb and Gr names except *ḳippōz,* which occurs only in Isa **34** 15, are used of snakes actually or supposedly poisonous. This absence of discrimination between poisonous and non-poisonous kinds makes determination of the species difficult. Further, but few of the Heb names are from roots whose meanings are clear, and there is little evident relation to Arab. names.

(1) The commonest Heb word is נָחָשׁ, *nāḥāsh,* which occurs 31 t and seems to be a generic word for serpent. While not always clearly indicating a venomous serpent, it frequently does: e.g. Ps **58** 4; **140** 3; Prov **23** 32; Eccl **10** 8.11; Isa **14** 29; Jer **8** 17; Am **5** 19. According to *BDB* it is perhaps from an onomatopoetic √, נָחַשׁ, *nāḥash,* "to hiss." It may be akin to the Arab. حَنَش, *ḥanash,* which means "snake" in general, or esp. the black snake. Cf Ir-nahash (1 Ch **4** 12); Nahash (*a*) (1 S **11** 1; 2 S **10** 2), (*b*) (2 S **17** 27), (*c*) (2 S **17** 25); also נְחֹשֶׁת, *neḥōsheth,* "copper" or "brass"; and נְחֻשְׁתָּן, *neḥushtān,* "Nehushtan," the brazen serpent (2 K **18** 4). But *BDB* derives the last two words from a different root.

(2) שָׂרָף, *sārāph,* apparently from שָׂרַף, *sāraph,* "to burn," is used of the fiery serpents of the wilderness. In Nu **21** 8, it occurs in the sing.: "Make thee a fiery serpent, and set it upon a standard." In ver 6 we have הַנְּחָשִׁים הַשְּׂרָפִים, *ha-neḥāshīm ha-serāphīm,* "fiery serpents"; in Dt **8** 15 the same in the sing.: נָחָשׁ שָׂרָף, *nāḥāsh sārāph,* also trd "fiery serpents"; in Isa **14** 29; **30** 6 we have שָׂרָף מְעוֹפֵף, *sārāph me'ōphēph,* "fiery flying serpent." The same word in the pl. שְׂרָפִים, *serāphīm,* is trd "seraphim" in Isa **6** 2.6.

(3) תַּנִּין, *tannīn,* elsewhere "dragon" or "sea-monster" (q.v.), is used of the serpents into which the rods of Aaron and the magicians were transformed (Ex **7** 9.10.12), these serpents being designated by *nāḥāsh* in Ex **4** 3; **7** 15. *Tannīn* is rendered "serpent" (AV "dragon") in Dt **32** 33, "Their wine is the poison of serpents," and Ps **91** 13, "The young lion and the serpent shalt thou trample under foot." On the other hand, *nāḥāsh* seems in three passages to refer to a mythical creature or dragon: "His hand hath pierced the swift serpent" (Job **26** 13); "In that day Jeh . . . . will punish leviathan the swift serpent and leviathan the crooked serpent" (Isa **27** 1); ". . . . though they be hid from my sight in the bottom of the sea, thence will I command the serpent, and it shall bite them" (Am **9** 3).

(4) זֹחֲלֵי, *zōḥălē,* is trd "crawling things" in Dt **32** 24 (AV "serpents") and in Mic **7** 17 (AV "worms").

(5) עַכְשׁוּב, *'akhshūbh,* occurs only in Ps **140** 3, where it is trd "adder" (LXX ἀσπίς, *aspís,* Vulg *aspis*), "adders' poison is under their lips." It has been suggested (*BDB*) that the reading should be עַכָּבִישׁ, *'akkābhīsh,* "spider" (q.v.). The ‖ word in the previous line is *nāḥāsh.*

(6) פֶּתֶן, *pethen,* like most of the other names a word of uncertain etymology, occurs 6 t and it is trd "asp," except in Ps **91** 13, "Thou shalt tread upon the lion and adder." According to Liddell and Scott, *aspis* is the name of the Egyp cobra, *Naia haje* L., which is not included in (2) above, because it does not certainly appear to have been found in Pal. The name "adder" is applied to various snakes all of which may perhaps be supposed to be poisonous but some of which are actually harmless. *Aspis* occurs in Rom **3** 13 in a paraphrase of Ps **140** 3 (see [5] above); it occurs frequently, though not uniformly, in LXX for (2), (5), (6), (7), (8) and (10).

(7) צֶפַע, *çepha',* occurs only in Isa **14** 29 where it is trd "adder" (AV "cockatrice," ERV "basilisk," LXX ἔκγονα ἀσπίδων, *ékgona aspídōn,* Vulg *regulus*). The √ צָפַע, *çāpha',* of (7) and (8) may be an onomatopoetic word meaning "to hiss" (*BDB*).

(8) צִפְעֹנִי, or צִפְעוֹנִי, *çiph'ōnī,* occurs in Prov **23** 32, "At the last it biteth like a serpent [*nāḥāsh*], and stingeth like an adder" (*çiph'ōnī*). In Isa **11** 8; **59** 5, and Jer **8** 17, ARV has "adder," while AV has "cockatrice" and ERV has "basilisk."

(9) שְׁפִיפֹן, *shephīphōn,* occurs only in Gen **49** 17:

> "Dan shall be a serpent [*nāḥāsh*] in the way,
> An adder [*shephīphōn*] in the path,
> That biteth the horse's heels,
> So that his rider falleth backward."

This has been thought to be *Cerastes cornutus,* on the authority of Tristram (*NHB*), who says that lying in the path it will attack the passer-by, while most snakes will glide away at the approach of a person or large animal. He adds that his horse was much frightened at seeing one of these serpents coiled up in a camel's footprint. The word is perhaps akin to the Arab. سِفّ, *siff,* or سُفّ, *suff,* which denotes a spotted and deadly snake.

Adder.

(10) אֶפְעֶה, *'eph'eh,* is found in Job **20** 16; Isa **30** 6; **59** 5, and in EV is uniformly trd "viper." It is the same as the Arab. أفعى, *'af'a,* which is usually trd "viper," though the writer has never found anyone who could tell to what snake the name belongs. In Arab. as in Heb a poisonous snake is always understood.

(11) קִפּוֹז, *ḳippōz,* ARV "dart-snake," ERV "arrowsnake," AV "great owl," only in Isa **34** 15, "There shall the dart-snake make her nest, and lay, and hatch, and gather under her shade; yea, there shall the kites be gathered, every one with her

mate." This is the concluding verse in a vivid picture of the desolation of Edom. The renderings "dart-snake" and "arrowsnake" rest on the authority of Bochert, but LXX has ἐχῖνος, *echínos*, "hedgehog," and Vulg *ericeus*, "hedgehog." The rendering of AV "great owl" seems preferable to the others, because the words "make her nest, and lay, and hatch, and gather under her shade" are as a whole quite inapplicable to a mammal or to a reptile. The derivation from קָפַז, *ḳāphaz* (cf Arab. قَفَزَ, *ḳāfaz*), "to spring," "to dart," suits, it is true, a snake, and not a hedgehog, but may also suit an owl. Finally, the next word in Isa **34** 15 is "kites," דַּיּוֹת, *dayyōth;* cf Arab. حِدَأَة, *ḥida'at.* See BITTERN; OWL; PORCUPINE.

(12) ὄφις, *óphis*, a general term for "serpent," occurs in numerous passages of the NT and LXX, and is fairly equivalent to *nāḥāsh.*

(13) ἀσπίς, *aspís*, occurs in the NT only in Rom **3** 13 ‖ to Ps **140** 3. See under (5) *'akhshūbh* and (6) *pethen.* It is found in LXX for these words, and also for *'eph'eh* (Isa **30** 6).

(14) ἔχιδνα, *échidna*, occurs in Acts **28** 3, "A viper came out . . . . and fastened on his [Paul's] hand," and 4 t in the expression "offspring [AV "generation"] of vipers," γεννήματα ἐχιδνῶν, *gennḗmata echidnṓn* (Mt **3** 7; **12** 34; **23** 33; Lk **3** 7). The allied (masc.?) form ἔχις, *échis*, occurs in Sir **39** 30, RV "adder."

(15) ἑρπετόν, *herpetón*, "creeping thing," AV "serpent," is found in Jas **3** 7.

That the different Heb and Gr names are used without clear distinction is seen from several examples of the employment of two different names in ‖ expressions:

"Their poison is like the poison of a serpent [*nāḥāsh*];
They are like the deaf adder [*pethen*] that stoppeth her ear" (Ps **58** 4).
"They have sharpened their tongue like a serpent [*nāḥāsh*];
Adders' [*'akhshūbh*] poison is under their lips" (Ps **140** 3).
"For, behold, I will send serpents [*neḥāshīm*], adders [*çiph'ōnīm*], among you, which will not be charmed; and they shall bite you, saith Jeh" (Jer **8** 17).
"They shall lick the dust like a serpent [*nāḥāsh*]; like crawling things of the earth [*zōḥălē 'ereç*] they shall come trembling out of their close places" (Mic **7** 17).
"He shall suck the poison of asps [*pethen*]: The viper's [*'eph'eh*] tongue shall slay him" (Job **20** 16).
"Their wine is the poison of serpents [*tannīnīm*], and the cruel venom of asps [*pethānīm*]" (Dt **32** 33).
"And the sucking child shall play on the hole of the asp [*pethen*], and the weaned child shall put his hand on the adder's [*çiph'ōnī*] den" (Isa **11** 8).

See also (8) and (9) above.

4. Figurative

Most of the Bib. references to serpents are of a figurative nature, and they usually imply poisonous qualities. The wicked (Ps **58** 4), the persecutor (Ps **140** 3), and the enemy (Jer **8** 17) are likened to venomous serpents. The effects of wine are compared to the bites of serpents (Prov **23** 32). Satan is a serpent (Gen **3**; Rev **12** 9; **20** 2). The term "offspring of vipers" is applied by John the Baptist to the Pharisees and Sadducees (Mt **3** 7) or to the multitudes (Lk **3** 7) who came to hear him; and by Jesus to the scribes and Pharisees (Mt **12** 34; **23** 33). Dan is a "serpent in the way . . . . that biteth the horse's heels" (Gen **49** 17). Serpents are among the terrors of the wilderness (Dt **8** 15; Isa **30** 6). Among the signs accompanying believers is that "they shall take up serpents" (Mk **16** 18; cf Acts **28** 5). It is said of him that trusts in Jeh:

"Thou shalt tread upon the lion and adder:
The young lion and the serpent shalt thou trample under foot" (Ps **91** 13).

In the millennium, "the sucking child shall play on the hole of the asp, and the weaned child shall put his hand on the adder's den" (Isa **11** 8). The serpent is subtle (Gen **3** 1; 2 Cor **11** 3); wise (Mt **10** 16); accursed (Gen **3** 14); eats dust (Gen **3** 14; Isa **65** 25; Mic **7** 17). The adder is deaf (Ps **58** 4). The serpent lurks in unexpected places (Gen **49** 17; Eccl **10** 8; Am **5** 19). Serpents may be charmed (Ps **58** 5; Eccl **10** 11; Jer **8** 17). Among four wonderful things is "the way of a serpent upon a rock" (Prov **30** 19). ALFRED ELY DAY

SERPENT, BRAZEN, brā'z'n. See NEHUSHTAN.

SERPENT-CHARMING, -chärm'ing: Allusion to this art, widely practised by the ancients (see references in *DB*, s.v.; esp. Bochart, *Hieron.*, III, 161, 164, etc), as by modern Orientals, is found in Ps **58** 5; Eccl **10** 11; Jer **8** 17; Sir **12** 13, perhaps in Jas **3** 7. The skill displayed in taming snakes, often without removing the poison fangs, is very surprising. Bruce, Davy and other travelers give striking illustrations. See esp. the interesting account of serpent-charming in Hengstenberg's *Egypt and the Books of Moses*, ET, 100–104.

SERPENT, CROOKED, krōōk'ed: With reference to the constellation round the North Pole, in Job **26** 13, RV "the swift serpent," m "fleeing"; and Isa **27** 1, RVm "winding." In the first part of the latter passage, AV "piercing serpent" is changed in RV to "swift serpent," m "gliding" or "fleeing." See ASTRONOMY, II, 1.

SERPENT, FIERY. See SERPENT, 3, (2).

SERPENT WORSHIP, wûr'ship: Traces of this superstition are thought by certain critics to be discoverable in the religion of Israel. Stade mentions that W. R. Smith supposed the serpent to be the totem of the house of David (*Geschichte*, I, 465). H. P. Smith says: "We know of a Serpent's Stone near Jerus, which was the site of a sanctuary (1 K **1** 9), and this sanctuary was dedicated to Jeh" (*Hist of OT*, 239, 240). Special reliance is placed on the narrative of the brazen serpent, which Hezekiah is recorded to have destroyed as leading to idolatry (2 K **18** 4). "In that case," says H. P. Smith, "we must treat the Nehushtan as a veritable idol of the house of Israel, which had been worshipped in the temple from the time of its erection. Serpent worship is so widespread that we should be surprised not to find traces of it in Israel" (ut supra). In the same line, see G. B. Gray, *Nu*, 275–76. The fancifulness of these deductions is obvious. See NEHUSHTAN. JAMES ORR

SERUG, sē'rug (שְׂרוּג, *serūgh;* Σερούχ, *Seroúch*): Son of Reu and great-grandfather of Abraham (Gen **11** 20 ff; 1 Ch **1** 26; Lk **3** 35).

SERVANT, sûr'vant (עֶבֶד, *'ebhedh;* δοῦλος, *doúlos*): A very common word with a variety of meanings, all implying a greater or less degree of inferiority and want of freedom: (1) The most frequent usage is as the equivalent of "slave" (q.v.), with its various shades in position (Gen **9** 25; **24** 9; Ex **21** 5; Mt **10** 24; Lk **17** 7, and often); but also a hired workman where "hired servant" translates Heb and Gr expressions which differ from the above. (2) An attendant in the service of someone, as Joshua was the "servant," RV "minister," of Moses (Nu **11** 28). (3) As a term of respectful self-depreciation referring to one's self, "thy servant" or "your servant" is used in place of the personal pronoun of the first person: (*a*) in the presence of superiors (Gen

19 2; **32** 18, and often); (*b*) in addressing the Supreme Being (1 S **3** 9; Ps **19** 11; **27** 9; Lk **2** 29, and often). (4) Officials of every grade are called the "servants" of kings, princes, etc (1 S **29** 3; 2 S **16** 1; 1 K **11** 26; Prov **14** 35, and often). (5) The position of a king in relation to his people (1 K **12** 7). (6) One who is distinguished as obedient and faithful to God or Christ (Josh **1** 2; 2 K **8** 19; Dnl **6** 20; Col **4** 12; 2 Tim **2** 24). (7) One who is enslaved by sin (Jn **8** 34).

William Joseph McGlothlin

SERVANT OF JEHOVAH (THE LORD):

1. Historical Situation
2. The Authorship of Isa Chs **40–66**
3. The Prophet of the Exile
4. The Unity of Chs **40–66**
5. Principal Ideas of Chs **40–66**
6. The Servant-Passages
   (1) Date of the Servant-Passages
   (2) Discussion of the Passages
   (3) Whom Did the Prophet Mean by the Servant?
   (4) The Psychology of the Prophecy
7. Place of the Servant-Passages in OT Prophecy
8. Large Messianic Significance of the Servant-Passages

1. Historical Situation

A century and a half had passed since the great days of Isaiah in Jerus. The world had vastly changed during those long decades when politicians had planned, armies surged back and forth, and tribes and nations had lost or won in the struggle for existence, place and power. The center of the world had changed—for Assyria had gone to its long home, and the city claiming preeminence was not Nineveh but Babylon.

Nowhere perhaps had time laid a heavier hand than on the city of Jerus and the country of Judah. For city and land had come to desolation, and the inhabitants of the country had become familiar with the strange sights and sounds of Babylonia, whither they had been carried by their conquerors. Many had found graves in the land of the exile, and new generations had arisen who had no memory of the hill country of their fathers. It is the situation of these captive Jews in Babylonia which is reflected and they who are addressed at the waning of the long night of captivity by the stirring message recorded in Isa chs **40–66** (leaving out of account here disputed passages in chs **40–66**).

2. Authorship of Isa Chs 40–66

The more one studies the problem of the authorship of these chapters, the more unlikely does it seem that their author penned them 150 years before the time with which they are vitally connected. It is obviously impossible to treat that problem in a detailed way here, but one may sum up the arguments by saying that in theological ideas, in style, and use of words they show such differences from the assured productions of Isaiah's pen as to point to a different authorship. And the great argument, the argument which carries the most weight to the author of this article, is that these late chapters are written from the *standpoint* of the exile. The exile is assumed in what is said. These chapters do not prophesy the exile, do not say it is to come; they all the time speak as though it *had come*. The message is not that an exile is to be, but beginning with the fact that the exile *already is*, it foretells deliverance. Now of course it is conceivable that God might inspire a man to put himself forward 150 years, and with a message to people who were to live then, assuming their circumstances as a background of what he said, but it is improbable to the last degree. To put it in plain, almost gruff, English, it is not the way God did things. The prophet's message was always primarily a message to his own age. Then there is no claim in the chapters themselves that Isaiah was their author. And having once been placed so that it was supposed they were by Isaiah—placed so through causes we do not know—the fact that in speaking of passages from these chapters NT authors referred to them by a name the people would recognize, is not a valid argument that they meant to teach anything as to their authorship. The problem had not arisen in NT times. Isa, chs **40–66,** as Professor Davidson has suggested, has a parallel in the Book of Job, each the production of a great mind, each from an author we do not know (cf Isaiah).

3. The Prophet of the Exile

Out of the deep gloom of the exile—when the Jew was a man without a country, when it seemed as if the nation's sins had murdered hope—out of this time comes the voice most full of gladness and abounding hope of all the voices from the OT life. In the midst of the proud, confident civilization of Babylonia, with its teeming wealth and exhaustless splendor, came a man who dared to speak for Jeh—a man of such power to see reality that to him Babylonia was already doomed, and he could summon the people to prepare for God's deliverance.

4. The Unity of Chs 40–66

In recent criticism, esp. in Germany, there has been a strong tendency to assign the last chapters of this section to a different author from the first. The background it is claimed is not Bab; the sins rebuked are the sins of the people when at home in Judaea, and in at least one passage the temple at Jerus seems to be standing. That these chapters present difficulties need not be disputed, but it seems to me that again and again in them one can find the hand of Second Isa. Then undoubtedly the author quotes from previous prophecies which we can recognize, and the suggestion that some of the difficult passages may be quotations from other older prophecies which are not preserved to us, I think an exceedingly good one. The quotation of such passages in view of the prospect of return, and the prophet's feeling of the need of the people, would seem to me not at all unnatural. If a later hand is responsible for some utterances in the latter part of the section, it seems to me fairly clear that most of it is from the hand of the great unknown prophet of the exile.

The questions regarding the Servant-passages as affecting the unity of the book will be treated later.

5. Principal Ideas of Chs 40–66

The first part of this section vividly contrasts Jeh and the idols worshipped with such splendor and ceremony. All the resources of irony and satire are used to give point and effect to the contrast. Cyrus the Median conqueror is already on the horizon, and he is declared to be God's instrument in the deliverance. The idols are described in process of manufacture; they are addressed in scornful apostrophe, they are seen carried away helpless. On the other side Jeh, with illimitable foresight and indomitable strength, knows and reveals the future. They know and reveal nothing. He brings to pass what He has planned. They do nothing. Not only the idols but Babylonia itself is made the victim of satire—and the prophet hurls a taunt song at the proud but impotent city.

Israel—the people of Jeh—the elect of God—is given the prophet's message. The past is called up as a witness to Jeh's dealings. His righteousness—His faithfulness to His people—shall not fail. They are unworthy, but out of His own bounty salvation is provided. And with joy of this salvation from exile and from sin the book rings and rings. The Zion of the restored Israel is pictured with all the play of color and richness of imagery at the prophet's command. And this restored Israel is to have a world-mission. Its light is to fall upon all lands. It is to minister salvation to all races of men.

But back of and under these pictures of great hope is the prophet's sense of his people's sin and their struggle with it. In the latter part of the book, esp. chs **59** and **64** this comes out clearly. And the mood of these chapters expresses the feeling out of which some of the deep things of the Servant-passages came. There is no need to insist that the chapters as they stand are in the order in which they were written. We know from other prophecies that this was not always true. But even if a man were convinced that the chapters now occurring after the Servant-passages were all written after them, he could still hold, and I think would be justified in holding, that in places in those chapters the reader finds the record of a state of the prophet's mind before the writing of those passages. The former view would be, I think, the preferable one. At any rate the point of view is logically that out of which some of the deep things in the Servant-passages came.

In profoundness of meaning the climax of the book is reached in these passages where the deliverance from exile and the deliverance from sin are connected with one great figure—the Servant of Jeh.

6. The Servant-Passages

The word "servant," as applied to servants of God, is not an unfamiliar one to readers of the OT. It is applied to different individuals and by Jeremiah to the nation (cf Jer **30** 10; **46** 27); but its message is on the whole so distinct and complete in Second Isa that we can study it without any further reference to previous usage.

The "servant" first appears in Isa **41** 8. Here the reference is undoubtedly to Israel, chosen and called of God and to be upheld by Him. Here Israel is promised victory over its enemies. In vivid picture their destruction and Israel's future trust and glory in God are portrayed.

There are several incidental references to Israel as Jeh's servant: created by Jeh and not to be forgotten (**41** 8); Cyrus is said to be called for the sake of His servant Jacob (**45** 4); Jeh is said to have redeemed His servant Jacob (**48** 20).

In **44** 26 "servant" seems to be used with the meaning of prophet. It is said of Jeh that He "confirmeth the word of his servant, and performeth the counsel of his messengers."

In **42** 19 we find the failure and inadequacy of Israel presented in the words, "Who is blind, but my servant? or deaf, as my messenger that I send?" This passage is an explanation of the exile. Israel proved unworthy and sinned, hence its punishment, but even in the exile the lesson had not been taken to heart.

In **43** 8 ff Jeh summons Israel the servant, who in spite of blindness and deafness yet is His witness. It has at least seen enough to be able to witness for Him in the presence of the heathen.

In **44** 1-5, leaving the unworthiness of the actual Israel, there comes what seems to me a summons in the name of the possible, the ideal. The underlying thought is a call to the high future which God has ready to give.

This covers the reference to the servant outside the great Servant-passages to which we now come. There are four of these: **42** 1-9; **49** 1-9*a*; **50** 4-11; **52** 13—**53** 12. **61** 1-4 perhaps represents words of the Servant, but may refer to words of the prophet, and, as at any rate it adds no new features to the picture of the Servant already given in the passages undoubtedly referring to him, we will not discuss it.

(1) *Date of the Servant-passages.*—Ewald long ago suggested that the last of the Servant-passages must have been borrowed from an earlier composition, which he assigned to the age of Manasseh. "If we find in the study of the passage reason for its vividness, we shall not need to seek its origin in the description of some past martyrdom."

Duhm quoted by Cheyne thinks the Servant-passages post-exilic. The gentleness and quiet activity of the Servant for one thing, according to Duhm, suggest the age of the scribes, rather than that of the exile. But might not an age of suffering be a time to learn the lesson of gentleness? According to Skinner, Duhm thinks the passages were inserted almost haphazard, but Skinner also refers to Kosters, showing that the passages cannot be lifted without carrying some of the succeeding verses with them. This is particularly significant in view of the recent popularity of other theories which deny the Servant-passages to the hand and time of Second Isa. The theory that these passages form by themselves a poem or a set of poems which have been inserted here can boast of distinguished names.

There does not seem much to commend it, however. As to the argument from difference as to rhythm, there is disagreement, and the data are probably not of a sort to warrant much significance being applied to it either way. The fact that the passages are not always a part of a connected movement of thought would play great havoc if made a universal principle of discrimination as to authorship in the prophecies of the OT. If we succeed in giving the fundamental ideas of the passages a place in relation to the thought of Deutero-Isa, an argument for which cogency might be claimed will be dissipated. But even at its best this argument would not be conclusive. To deny certain ideas to an author simply because he has not expressed them in a certain bit of writing acknowledged to him is perilous business. A message of hope surely does not preclude an appreciation of the dark things.

The truth of the matter is that even by great scholars the temptation to a criticism of knight-errantry is not always resisted. And I think we shall not make any mistake in believing that this is the case with the attempt to throw doubt upon the Deutero-Isaianic authorship of the Servant-passages.

(2) *Discussion of the passages.*—**42** 1-9: In these verses Jeh Himself is the speaker, describing the Servant as His chosen, in whom His soul delights, upon whom He has put His spirit. He is to bring justice to the Gentiles. His methods are to be quiet and gentle, and the very forlorn hope of goodness He will not quench. He is to set justice in the earth, and remote countries are described as waiting for His law. Then comes a declaration by the prophet that Jeh, the Creator of all, is the speaker of words declaring the Servant's call in righteousness to be a covenant for the people, a light to the Gentiles, a helper to those in need—the blind and imprisoned. Jeh's glory is not to be given to another, nor His praise to graven images. Former prophecies have come to pass. New things He now declares. One's attention needs to be called to the distinction of the Servant from Israel in this passage. He is to be a covenant of the people: according to Delitzsch, "he in whom and through whom Jeh makes a new covenant with His people in place of the old one that has been broken."

49 1-9*a*; Here the Servant himself speaks, telling of his calling from the beginning of his life, of the might of his word, of his shelter in God, of a time of discouragement in which he thought his labor in vain, followed by insistence on his trust in God. Then Jeh promises him a larger mission than the restoration of Israel, viz. to be a light to the Gentiles. Jeh speaks of the Servant as one despised, yet to be triumphant so that he will be honored by kings and princes. He is to lead his people forth at their restoration, "to make them inherit the desolate heritages; saying to them that are bound, Go forth; to them that are in darkness, Show yourselves."

Clearly the Servant is distinct from the people Israel in this passage. Yet in ver 3 he is addressed as Israel. The word Israel here may be a gloss, which would solve the difficulty, or the Servant may be addressed as Israel because he gathers up in himself the meaning of the ideal Israel. If it is true that the prophet gradually passed from the conception of Israel as a nation to a person through whom its true destiny would be realized, this last suggestion would gain in probability.

One notices here the emphasis on the might of the Servant, and in this passage we come to understand that he is to pass through a time of ignominy. The phrase "a servant of rulers" is a difficult one, which would be clear if the prophet conceived of him as one of the exiles, and typically representing them. The Servant's mission in this passage seems quite bound up with the restoration.

50 4-11: In the first part of this passage the Servant is not mentioned directly, but it seems clear that he is speaking. He is taught of God continually, that he may bring a message to the weary. He has opened his ear so that he may fully understand Jeh's message. The Servant now describes his sufferings as coming to him because of his obedience. He was not rebellious and did not turn back from his mission. Flint-like he set his face and with confidence in God met the shame which came upon him. After language vivid with a sense of ignominy his assured consciousness of victory and faith in God are expressed.

In vs 10–11, according to Delitzsch, Jeh speaks, first encouraging those who listen to the Servant, then addressing those who despise his word. Cheyne thinks the Servant mentioned in ver 10 may be the prophet, but I prefer Delitzsch's view.

52 13—**53** 12: The present division of **52** 13—**53** 12 is unfortunate, for obviously it is all of a piece and ought to stand together in one chapter.

In **52** 13–15 Jeh speaks of the humiliation and later of the exaltation of the Servant. He shall deal wisely—the idea here including the success resulting from wisdom—and shall be exalted. Words are piled upon each other here to express his exaltation. But the appearance of the Servant is such as to suggest the very opposite of his dignity, which will astonish nations and kings when they come to understand it.

Entering upon ch **53** we find the people of Israel speaking confessing their former unbelief, and giving as a reason the repulsive aspect of the Servant—despised, sad, sick with a visage to make men turn from him. He is described as though he had been a leper. They thought all this had come upon him as a stroke from God, but they now see how he went even to death, not for his own transgression but for theirs. Their peace and healing came through his suffering and death. They have been sinful and erring; the result of it all God has caused to light upon him.

They look back in wonder at the way he bore his sufferings—like a lamb led to the slaughter; with a false judicial procedure he was led away, no one considering his death, or its relation to them. His grave even was an evidence of ignominy.

Beginning at ver 10 the people cease speaking, according to Delitzsch, and the prophecy becomes the organ of God who acknowledges His Servant. The reference to a trespass offering in ver 10 is remarkable. Nowhere else is prophecy so connected with the sacrificial system (A.B. Davidson). It pleased God to bruise the Servant—his soul having been made a trespass offering; the time of humiliation over, the time of exaltation will come.

By his knowledge we are told—here a momentary reversion to the time of humiliation taking place—by his knowledge he shall justify many and bear their iniquities. Then comes the exaltation—dividing of spoils and greatness—the phrases suggesting kingly glory: all this is to be his because of his suffering. The great fact of ch **53** is vicarious suffering.

(3) *Whom did the prophet mean by the Servant?*—(*a*) Obviously not all of Israel always, for the Servant is distinguished from Israel. (*b*) Not the godly remnant, for he is distinguished from them. Then the godly remnant does not attain to any such proportions as to fit the description of ch **53**. (*c*) And one cannot accept the theory that the prophetic order is intended. The whole order is not great enough to exhaust the meaning of one of a half-dozen of the greatest lines in ch **53**.

Professor A. B. Davidson's *OT Prophecy* contains a brilliant and exceedingly able discussion of the question which he approaches from the standpoint of Bib. rather than simply exegetical theology. His fundamental position is that in the prophet's outlook the restoration is the consummation. In his mind the Servant and his work cannot come after the restoration. The Servant, if a real person, must be one whose work lies in the past or the present, as there is not room in the future for him, for the restoration which is at the door brings felicity, and after that no sufferings of the Servant are conceivable. But there is no actual person in the past and none in the present who could be the Servant. Hence the Servant cannot be to the prophet's mind a real person (see Coniah).

Of course Davidson relates the result to his larger conception of prophecy in such a way as to secure the Messianic significance of the passages in relation to their fulfilment in Our Lord. The ideas they contain are realized in Him.

But coming back to the prophet's mind—if the Servant was not a person to him, what significance did he have? The answer according to Davidson is, He is a great personification of the ideal Israel. "He is Israel according to its idea." To quote more fully, "The prophet has created out of the Divine determinations imposed on Israel, election, creation and forming, endowment with the word or spirit of Jeh, and the Divine purpose in these operations, an ideal Being, an inner Israel in the heart of the phenomenal or actual Israel, an indestructible Being having these Divine attributes or endowments, present in the outward Israel in all ages, powerful and effectual because really composed, if I can say so, of Divine forces, who cannot fail in God's purpose, and who as an inner power within Israel by his operation causes all Israel to become a true servant" (cf Davidson, *OT Prophecy*, 435–36).

Now it seems to me that Davidson is more effective in his destructive than in his constructive work. One must confess that he presents real difficulties in the way of holding to a personal Servant as the prophet's conception. But on the other hand when he tries to replace that by a more adequate conception, I do not think he conspicuously succeeds.

The greatest of the Servant-passages (it seems to me) presents more than can be successfully dealt with under the conception of the Servant as the ideal Israel. The very great emphasis on vicarious suffering in ch **53** simply is not answered by the theory. Words would not leap with such a flame of reality in describing the suffering of a personification. The sense of sin back of the passage is not a thing whose problem could be solved by a glittering figure of speech. There it surges—the movement of an aroused conscience—and the answer to it could never be anything less than a real deed by a real person. My own feeling is that if language can express anything it expresses the fact that the prophet had a real personal Servant in view.

But what of the difficulties Davidson suggests? Even if the answer were not easy to find, one could rest on the *total impression* the passages make. One cannot vaporize a passage for the sake of placing it in an environment in which one believes it belongs. As Cheyne in other days said, "In the sublimest descriptions of the Servant I am unable to resist the impression that we have the presentment of an individual, and venture to think that our general view of the Servant ought to be ruled by those passages in which the enthusiasm of the author is at its height."

The first thing we need to remember in dealing with the difficulties Davidson has brought forth is the *timelessness of prophecy*, and the resulting fact that *every* prophet saw the future as if lying just on the horizon of his own time. As prophets saw the *day of Jeh* as if at hand, so it seems to me Deutero-Isaiah saw the Servant: each really afar off, yet each really seen in the colors of the present. Then we must remember that the prophets did not relate all their conceptions. They stated truths whose meaning and articulation they did not understand. They were not philosophers with a Hegelian hunger for a total view of life, and when we try to read them from this standpoint we misjudge them. Then we must remember that the prophet may here have been lifted to a height of prophetic receptiveness where he received and uttered what went beyond the limits of his own understanding. To be sure there was a point of contact, but I see no objection to the thought that in a place of unique significance and importance like this, God might use a man to utter words which reached far beyond the limits of his own understanding. In this connection some words of Professor Hermann Schultz are worth quoting: "If it is true anywhere in the history of poetry and prophecy, it is true here that the writer being full of the spirit has said more than he himself meant to say and more than he himself understood."

(4) *The psychology of the prophecy.*—This does not mean that something may not be said about the connection of the Servant-passages with the prophet's own thought. Using Delitzsch's illustration, we can see how from regarding all Israel as the servant the prophet could narrow down to the godly part of Israel as experience taught him the faithlessness of many, and it ought not to be impossible for us to see how all that Israel really meant at its best could have focused itself in his thought upon one person. Despite Davidson's objection, I can see nothing artificial about this movement in the prophet's mind. There was probably more progression in his thought than Professor Davidson is willing to allow. If it is asked, Where was the person to whom the prophet could ascribe such greatness, conceiving as he did that he was to come at once? surely a similar question would be fair in relation to Isaiah's Messiah. The truth is that even on the threshold of the restoration there was time for a great one suddenly to arise. As John the Baptist on the Jordan watched for the coming One whom he knew not, yet who was *alive*, so the great prophet of the exile may have watched even day by day for the coming Servant whose work had been revealed to him.

But deep in the psychology of the prophecy is the sense of sin out of which these passages came and indications of which I think are found in the latter part of the book. The great guilt-laden past lay terribly behind the prophet, and as he mused over the sufferings of the righteous, perhaps esp. drawn to the heart-rent Jeremiah, the thought of redemptive suffering may have dawned upon him. And if in its light, and with a personal sense of sin drawn from what experiences we know not, he grapples with the problem, can we not understand, can we not see that God might flash upon him the great conception of a sin-bearer?

7. Place of the Servant-Passages in OT Prophecy

At last the idea of vicarious suffering had been connected with the deep things of the nation's life, and henceforward was a part of its heritage. To the profoundest souls it would be a part of the nation's forward look. The priestly idea had been deepened and filled with new moral meaning. The Servant was a prophet too—so priest and prophet met in one. And I think Cheyne was right when he suggested that in the Servant's exaltation in ch **53**, the idea of the Servant is brought nearer to that of king than we sometimes think. So in suggestion, at least, prophet, priest and king meet in the great figure of the suffering Servant.

A new rich stream had entered into prophecy, full of power to fertilize whatever shores of thought it touched. In the thoughts of these passages prophecy seemed pressing with impatient eagerness to its goal, and though centuries were to pass before that goal was reached, its promise is seen here, full of assurance and of knowledge of the kind of goal it is to be.

8. Larger Messianic Significance of the Servant-Passages

But whatever our view of the meaning of the prophet, we must agree (cf Mt **8** 17; **12** 18–21; **26** 67; Jn **12** 41, et al.) that the conception he so boldly and powerfully put upon his canvas had its realization, its fulfilment in the One who spoke to the world from the cross on Calvary. And in its darkly glorious shadow the Christian with all the sadness and joy and wonder of it, with a sense of its solving all his problems and meeting the deepest needs and outreaches of his life, can feel a strange companionship with the exilic prophet whose yearning for a sin-bearer and belief in His coming call across the long and slowly moving years. In the light and penetration of that hour he may be trusted to know what the prophet meant. Professor Delitzsch well said of that passage, "Every word is as it were written under the cross at Golgotha."

LYNN HAROLD HOUGH

SERVANTS, SOLOMON'S. See SOLOMON'S SERVANTS.

SERVICE, sûr′vis: Six Heb, two Aram. and four Gr words are so rendered.

1. In the OT

In the OT the word most used for "service" is (1) *'ăbhōdhāh,* from *'ābhadh,* which is the general word, meaning "to work" and so "to serve," "to till," also "to enslave." The noun means "bondage," "labor," "ministering," "service," "tillage," "work," "use." The word is used in describing work in the fields (Ex **1** 14, et al.), work in the tabernacle (Ex **27** 19, et al.), sanctuary service (Nu **7** 9), service of Jeh (Nu **8** 11), Levitical or priestly service (Nu **8** 22), kingly service (1 Ch **26** 30), etc. Reference is made to instruments, wood vessels, cattle, herbs, shekels for the service in the house of Jeh. (2) *'Ābhadh* itself is tr[d] "service" in Nu **8** 15; **18** 23; Jer **22** 13. (3) *Serādh* means "stitching," i.e. piercing with a needle; it occurs only 4 t, and in each case in RV instead of "service" is tr[d] "finely wrought garments" (Ex **31** 10; **35** 19; **39** 1.41). (4) *Shārath* means primarily "to attend" as a servant or worshipper, and to contribute to or render service, wait on, and thence service; occurs only 3 t (Ex **35** 19; **39** 1.41 AV) and in ARV is rendered "for ministering." (5) *Çābhā'* is found 7 t, used in the same connection each time, and refers to those numbered for service in the tent of meeting. Its primary root meaning refers to service for war, campaign, hardship (Nu **4** 30.35.39.43; **8** 24). (6) *Yādh* means lit. an "open hand," indicating direction, power, and so ministry as in 1 Ch **6** 31, where David appoints certain ones to have direction of the music, tr[d] in 1 Ch **29** 5, RV not service, but "himself." (7) *'Ăbhīdhāh* means "business," "labor," "affairs"; Ezr **6** 18 is the only place where it is found. (8) *Polḥān,* from root meaning "to worship," "minister to," and so in Ezr **7** 19 vessels given for service.

2. In the NT

The following are the uses in the NT: (1) *Diakonía,* from root meaning "to run on errands," and so attendance, aid as a servant, ministry, relief, and hence service; cf Eng. word "deacon"; Paul: "that I might minister unto you" (2 Cor **11** 8); also found in Rom **15** 31 ("ministration") and Rev **2** 19 ("ministry"). (2) *Douleúō,* lit. "to be a slave," in bondage, service (Gal **4** 8, "bondage"; Eph **6** 7, "service"; 1 Tim **6** 2, "serve"). (3) *Latreía,* from root meaning "to render religious homage," menial service to God, and so worship (Jn **16** 2, "service"; Rom **9** 4, "service"; Rom **12** 1, "spiritual service"; He **9** 1, "service"; **9** 6, "services"). (4) *Leitourgía,* from root "to perform religious or charitable functions," worship, relieve, obey, minister, and hence a public function, priestly or charitable (liturgy) (2 Cor **9** 12, "service"; also in Phil **2** 17.30). See SERVANT.

WILLIAM EDWARD RAFFETY

SERVITUDE, sûr′vi-tūd. See SERVANT; SLAVE.

SESIS, sē′sis (B, **Σεσεΐς,** *Seseís,* A, **Σεσσεΐς,** *Sesseís*): One who put away his foreign wife (1 Esd **9** 34) = "Shashai" in Ezr **10** 40.

SESTHEL, ses′thel (**Σεσθήλ,** *Sesthḗl*): One of the sons of Addi who put away their foreign wives (1 Esd **9** 31) = "Bezalel" in Ezr **10** 30.

SET: Few words in the Eng. language have such a rich variety of meaning and are used in so rich a variety of idiomatic expression as the word "set." A glance at any of the great dicts. will convince anyone of the truth of this statement. The *Standard Dictionary* devotes three and a half columns to the word. In its primary meaning it there denotes 22 distinct things, in its secondary meaning 17 more, while 18 distinct phrases are given in which it is used, in some cases again in a variety of meanings. It is indeed a word calculated to drive a foreigner to despair. Some 70 Heb and about 30 Gr words in the original tongues of the Holy Scriptures have been rendered by the word "set," in AV and also in RV. A careful comparative study of the original and of tr^s in other tongues will at once indicate that a lack of discrimination is evident on the part of the Eng. translators in the frequent use of the word "set."

Thus in Cant **5** 14, "hands are as rings of gold set with beryl," the Heb word is מָלֵא, *mālē'*, "to be filled," "full." Vulg translates *plenae,* the Dutch *gevuld,* the Ger. *voll;* Prov **8** 27, "when he set a circle," Heb חָקַק, *ḥāḳaḳ,* "to describe," "decree," Vulg *vallabat,* Dutch *beschreef;* Ezr **4** 10, "set in the city of Samaria," Aram. יְתִב, *yethibh,* "to cause to sit down," "to cause to dwell," Vulg *habitare eas fecit,* Dutch *doen wonen;* Ps **2** 6, "Yet have I set my king upon my holy hill," Heb נָסַךְ, *nāṣakh,* "to pour out," "to anoint," Dutch *gezalfd;* Isa **19** 2, AV "I will set the Egyptians against the Egyptians," Heb סָכַךְ, *ṣākhakh,* "to disturb," "to confuse," Vulg *concurrere faciam,* Dutch *verwarren,* Ger. *an einander setzen;* Rev **3** 8, "I have set before thee a door," Gr δίδωμι, *dídōmi,* "to give," Vulg *dedi coram te,* Dutch *gegeven,* Ger. *gegeben;* Acts **19** 27, AV "Our craft is in danger to be set at nought," Gr ἔρχομαι, *érchomai,* "to come," Vulg *periclitabitur,* Dutch *in verachting komen;* Lk **4** 18, "to set at liberty them," Gr ἀποστέλλω, *apostéllō,* "to send away," Dutch *heen te zenden in vrijheid;* Acts **13** 9, AV "Saul . . . . set his eyes on him," Gr ἀτενίζω, *atenízō,* "to stare fixedly," Vulg *intuens in eum,* Dutch *de oogen op hem houdende.* These are but a few examples chosen at random where our Eng. translators have rendered Heb and Gr words by "set," where a more literal tr, in equally good idiomatic language, was possible. The word "set" is the causative of "sit," and indicates primarily a power of self-support, in opposition to the idea of the word "lay."

(1) In its primary meaning the word "set" is used in our Eng. Bible in many senses: (*a*) *Foundation:* Cant **5** 15, "His legs are as pillars of marble set upon." (*b*) *Direction:* Ezk **21** 16, "whithersoever thy face is set." (*c*) *Appointed time:* Acts **12** 21, "upon a set day." (*d*) *Fixed place:* 2 Ch **20** 17, "Set yourselves, stand ye still, and see"; 2 S **6** 17; Mt **4** 5. (*e*) *Cause to sit:* 1 S **2** 8, AV "to set them among princes"; 2 Ch **23** 20; Ps **68** 6. (*f*) *Appointment:* Ezr **7** 25, AV "set magistrates and judges"; Gen **41** 41; 1 S **12** 13; Ps **2** 6; Dnl **1** 11. (*g*) *To lift up:* Gen **31** 17, "set his sons and his wives upon." (*h*) *Appointed place:* Gen **1** 17, "God set them in the firmament." (*i*) *Cause to stand:* Gen **47** 7, "Joseph brought in Jacob . . . . and set him before Pharaoh"; Nu **8** 13; 2 Ch **29** 25. (*j*) *Sitting:* Mt **5** 1, AV "when he was set"; He **8** 1 AV. (*k*) *Location:* Mt **5** 14, "a city set on a hill." These by no means exhaust the meaning which the word, in its primary sense, has in our Eng. Bible.

(2) In a secondary or tropical sense it is used with equal frequency, usually with various prepositions. Thus (*a*) *To attack:* Jgs **9** 33, AV "and set upon the city." (*b*) *To imprint:* Gen **4** 15, AV "The Lord set a mark upon Cain." (*c*) *To direct to:* 1 K **2** 15, "And that all Israel set their faces on me." (*d*) *To place:* 1 K **20** 12, Ben-hadad shouted one word to his allies: "Set," i.e. set the armies in array, the battering-rams and engines of attack in their place. (*e*) *To incline toward:* Ezk **40** 4, "Set thy heart upon all that I shall show." (*f*) *To trust in:* Ps **62** 10, "If riches increase, set not your heart thereon." (*g*) *To place before:* Ps **90** 8, "Thou hast set our iniquities before"; Ps **141** 3, "Set a watch, O Jeh, before my mouth." (*h*) *To go down:* of the setting of the sun (Mk **1** 32; Lk **4** 40). (*i*) *To be proud:* Mal **3** 15, AV "They that work wickedness are set up." (*j*) *To fill in:* Ex **35** 9, "stones to be set, for the ephod." (*k*) *To plant:* Mk **12** 1, "set a hedge about it." (*l*) *To mock:* Lk **23** 11, "Herod . . . . set him at nought." (*m*) *To honor:* 1 S **18** 30, "so that his name was much set by." (*n*) *To start:* Acts **21** 2, "We went aboard, and set sail." As may be seen the word is used in an endless variety of meanings. HENRY E. DOSKER

SETH, seth, **SHETH,** sheth (שֵׁת, *shēth;* **Σήθ,** *Sḗth*):

(1) The son born to Adam and Eve after the death of Abel (Gen **4** 25 f; **5** 3 ff; 1 Ch **1** 1; Sir **49** 16; Lk **3** 38). In Gen **4** 25 the derivation of the name is given. Eve "called his name Seth: For, said she, God hath appointed [*shāth*] me another seed instead of Abel." In 1 Ch **1** 1 AV, the form is "Sheth"; elsewhere in AV and in RV throughout the form is "Seth."

(2) AV "the children of Sheth," RV "the sons of tumult." According to AV rendering, the name of an unknown race mentioned in Balaam's parable (Nu **24** 17). S. F. HUNTER

SETHUR, sē′thur (סְתוּר, *ṣethūr;* **Σαθούρ,** *Sathoúr*): An Asherite spy (Nu **13** 13 [14]).

SETTING, set′ing (מִלֻּאָה, *millu'āh,* lit. "a filling"): The word is used in the description of the manufacture of the breastplate of judgment (Ex **28** 17). The instruction runs: "Thou shalt set in it settings of stones," viz. four rows of precious stones. The same word is rendered "inclosings" in ver 20, and in **39** 13 AV.

SETTLE, set′'l (עֲזָרָה, *'ăzārāh*): For this word in Ezk **43** 14.17.20; **45** 19, ARV and ERVm substitute more correctly "ledge." See TEMPLE.

SETTLE: The Heb language has 8 words which are thus tr^d: *yāshabh, nāḥath, 'āmadh, shāḳaṭ, ṭābha',* *nāçabh, māḳōm, ḳāphā'.* Now the meaning is to settle down, to cause to occur (Ezk **36** 11 AV; 1 Ch **17** 14); then it denotes fixedness (2 K **8** 11; Ps **119** 89; Prov **8** 25); again it points to a condition of absolute quiescence, as the settlings on the lees (Jer **48** 11); and in still another place it means packing solidly together (Ps **65** 10). In the NT the words ἑδραῖος, *hedraíos,* θεμελιόω, *themelióō,* and τίθημι, *títhēmi,* have been tr^d "settle." RV in 1 Pet **5** 10 has tr^d "establish," and the context unquestionably points to the idea of a fixed establishment in the faith. In Lk **21** 14 the word tr^d "settle" evidently points to a fixed determination. HENRY E. DOSKER

SEVEN, sev′'n (שֶׁבַע, *shebha';* **ἑπτά,** *heptá*). See NUMBER.

SEVEN CHURCHES. See CHURCHES, SEVEN.

SEVEN STARS. See ASTRONOMY.

SEVENEH, sē-ven'e, se-vē'ne (סְוֵנֵה, *ṣ^ewēnēh*): For AV "the tower of Syene," in Ezk **29** 10; **30** 6, RV reads, "the tower of Seveneh," with note m, "or, from Migdol to Syene." Seveneh is the town at the First Cataract in Egypt, now known as Assuan. Fresh interest has recently been given to it by the Elephantine discoveries bearing on the ancient Jewish colony and temple of Jeh in that place in the 5th cent. BC. See ARAMAIC; EGYPT; PAPYRI; SANCTUARY, 4, etc.

SEVENTH, sev''nth, **DAY.** See SABBATH.

SEVENTY, sev''n-ti (שִׁבְעִים, *shibh'īm;* **ἑβδομή-κοντα,** *hebdomēkonta*). See NUMBER.

SEVENTY DISCIPLES: The account of the designation and mission of these is found only in Lk **10**. Some have therefore sought to maintain that we have here only a confused variant of the appointment of the Twelve; but this is impossible in the light of Luke's account of the Twelve in ch **9**.

The documents vary as between the numbers seventy and seventy-two, so that it is impossible to determine which is the correct reading; and internal evidence does not help at all in this case. There is nothing in the function or circumstances to indicate any reason for the specific number.

Commentators have sought parallels in the seventy elders chosen to assist Moses (Nu **11**) and suppose that Jesus was incidentally indicating Himself as the "prophet like unto Moses" whom God would raise up.

Again, the Jews popularly reckoned the "number of the nations of the earth" at seventy (cf Gen **10**), and some have supposed Jesus to be thus indicating that His gospel is universal. Attention is called to the fact that the Seventy are not forbidden to go to Gentiles and that their commission probably included Peraea, where many Gentiles were to be found. Some, again, have supposed that Jesus had in mind the Jewish Sanhedrin, composed of seventy (or seventy-two), and that the appointment of a like number to extend the work of His kingdom was a parabolic recognition that as the Jews were officially rejecting Him, so He was rejecting them as agents for the work of the kingdom. It is impossible to speak with any certainty as to any of these suggestions. It is to be noted that there is the same confusion between the numbers seventy and seventy-two in all four instances, as also in the tradition as to the number of translators of the LXX.

Inasmuch as no further mention is made of these workers, it is to be understood that they were appointed for a temporary ministry. Tradition names several of them and identifies them with disciples active after Pentecost. While it is probable that some of these were witnesses later, the tradition is worthless in details. The mission of these and the reason assigned for their appointment are essentially the same as in the case of the Twelve. Jesus is now completing His last popular campaign in preaching and introducing the kingdom of heaven. The employing of these in this service is in line with the permanent ideal of Christianity, which makes no distinction between the "laymen" and the "clergy" in responsibility and service. Jesus was perhaps employing all whose experience and sympathy made them fit for work in the harvest that was so plenteous while the laborers were few. He found seventy such now as He would find a hundred and twenty such after His ascension (Acts **1** 15). WILLIAM OWEN CARVER

SEVENTY WEEKS: The "seventy weeks" of the prophecy in Dnl **9** 24–27 have long been a subject of controversy in the critical schools. The conflicting views may be seen very fully in Dr. Driver's *Dnl*, 94 ff, 143 ff, and Dr. Pusey's *Daniel the Prophet*, lects II, III, IV. On both sides it is agreed that the "weeks" in this prophecy are to be interpreted as "weeks of years," i.e. the 70 weeks represent 490 years. This period, commencing with "the going forth of the commandments to restore and build Jerus" (ver 25), is divided into three parts, 7 weeks (49 years), 62 weeks (434 years), and one week (7 years). The 69 weeks extend to the appearance of "an anointed one [Heb "Messiah"], the prince" (ver 25), who, after the 62 weeks, shall be "cut off" (ver 26), apparently in the "midst" of the 70th week (ver 27). On the traditional view (see Pusey), the 69 weeks (483 years) mark the interval from the decree to rebuild Jerus till the appearance of Christ; and if, with Pusey, the decree in question be taken to be that of the 7th year of Artaxerxes (457–56 BC; the mission of Ezra; cf Ezr **7** 8 ff), confirmed and extended in the 20th year of the same king (mission of Nehemiah; cf Neh **2** 1 ff), the 483 years run out about 27–28 AD, when Our Lord's public ministry began. On the other hand, the view which supposes that the Book of Dnl belongs wholly to the Maccabean age, and does not here contain genuine prediction, is under the necessity of making the 490 years terminate with the reign of Antiochus Epiphanes (171–164 BC), and this, it is admitted, cannot be done. To give time the violent expedient is adopted of dating the commencement of the 70 weeks from the prophecy of Jeremiah of the 70 years' captivity, or of the rebuilding of Jerus (606 or 587 BC), i.e. *before* the captivity had begun. Even this, as Dr. Driver admits (p. 146), leaves us in 171 BC, some 67 years short of the duration of the 62 weeks, and a huge blunder of the writer of Dnl has to be assumed. The divergent reckonings are legion, and are mutually contradictory (see table in Pusey, p. 217). To invalidate the older view Dr. Driver avails himself of the altered renderings of vs 25 and 27 in ERV. It is to be noted, however, that ARV does not follow ERV in these changes. Thus, whereas ERV reads in ver 25, "Unto the anointed one, the prince, shall be seven weeks: and threescore and two weeks, it shall be built again," and accordingly takes "the anointed one" of ver 26 to be a distinct person, ARV (as also ERVm) reads, as in AV, "shall be seven weeks, and threescore and two weeks." Again, where ERV reads in ver 27 "For the half of the week he shall cause the sacrifice and the oblation to cease," ARV (and ERVm) has as formerly, "In the midst of the week he shall cause" etc (conversely, in ver 25 ARVm gives the ERV rendering). The question cannot be discussed here, but it is believed that the traditional interpretation may yet claim acceptance from those who do not accept the postulates of the newer critical writers. See DANIEL; JUBILEES, BOOK OF.

JAMES ORR

SEVENTY YEARS: The period assigned by Jeremiah for the duration of the Jewish exile in Babylon (Jer **25** 11.12; **29** 10; cf 2 Ch **36** 21 f; Ezr **1** 1; Dnl **9** 2). If the period be reckoned from the date of the first deportation in the 4th year of Jehoiakim (2 K **24** 1; 2 Ch **36** 6 ff; Dnl **1** 1 by another reckoning calls it the 3d year), i.e. 606 BC, till the decree of Cyrus, 536 BC, the prediction was fulfilled to a year. See CAPTIVITY.

SEVER, sev'ẽr: The three Heb words *bādhal*, *pālāh* and *pāradh* are thus tr[d]. The idea conveyed is that of setting apart (Lev **20** 26 AV) or of setting someone or something apart in a miraculous way (Ex **8** 22; **9** 4 AV, ERV), or, again, of simple separation on one's own volition (Jgs **4** 11 AV, ERV). The Gr word ἀφορίζω, *aphorízō* (Mt **13** 49) stands for final judicial segregation.

SEVERAL, sev'ẽr-al, **SEVERALLY,** sev'ẽr-al-i: The Heb words *ḥophshūth* and *ḥophshīth*, tr[d] "several" in AV, ERV, 2 K **15** 5; 2 Ch **26** 21, are in both cases tr[d] "separate" in ARV, and indicate ceremonial uncleanness and consequent severance on account of leprosy. In the parable of the Talents (Mt **25** 15) and also in 1 Cor **12** 11 the word ἴδιος, *idios*, is tr[d] "several," "severally." In both cases it points to the individuality of the recipients of the gift bestowed.

SHAALABBIN, shā-a-lab'in (שַׁעַלַבִּין, *sha'ălab-bīn;* B, **Σαλαβείν,** *Salabein*, A, **Σαλαμείν,** *Salamein*): A town in the territory of Dan named between Ir-shemesh and Aijalon (Josh **19** 42). It seems to be identical with SHAALBIM.

SHAALBIM, shā-al'bim (שַׁעַלְבִים, *sha'albīm;* B, **Βηθαλαμεί,** *Bēthalameí*, A, **Σαλαβείμ,** *Salabeim*, in Josh BA, **Θαλαβείμ,** *Thalabeim*): When the Amorites had forced the children of Dan into the mountain they came and dwelt in Mt. Heres, Aijalon and Shaalbim, where, it appears, they were made tributary to the house of Joseph (Jgs **1** 35). In the time of Solomon it was included in the administrative district presided over by Ben-deker, along with Makaz, Beth-shemesh and Elon-beth-hanan (1 K **4** 9). Beth-shemesh is the same as Ir-shemesh (Josh **19** 42). Shaalbim is probably only another name of **Shaalabbin.** One of David's mighty men is called Eliahba the **Shaalbonite.** This presumes the existence of a town called Shaalbon (2 S **23** 32; 1 Ch **11** 33), which again is probably identical with Shaalbim. *Onom* identifies it with Salaba, a large village in the district of Sebaste (Samaria), which apparently Eusebius and Jerome thought to be in the territory of Dan. It seems, however, too far to the N. Jerome in his comm. on Ezk **48** speaks of the towers of Aijalon and Selebi and Emmaus. Conder would identify Selebi with *Selbīṭ*, 3 miles N.W. of Aijalon (*Yālo*), and 8 miles N. of Beth-shemesh. This would suit for Shaalbim, as far as position is concerned; but it is difficult to account for the heavy *ṭ* in the name, if derived from Shaalbim.

W. EWING

SHAALBONITE, shā-al-bō'nīt, shā-al'bō-nīt (הַשַּׁעַלְבֹנִי, *ha-sha'albōnī;* **ὁ Σαλαβωνείτης,** *ho Salabōneítēs* [2 S **23** 32], B, **ὁ 'Ομεί,** *ho Homeí*, A, **ὁ Σαλαβωνί,** *ho Salabōni*): Eliahba, one of David's heroes, a native of Shaalbon. See SHAALBIM.

SHAALIM, shā'a-lim, **LAND OF** (אֶרֶץ שַׁעֲלִים, *'ereç sha'ălīm;* B, **τῆς γῆς 'Εασακέμ,** *tēs gēs Easakém*, A, **τῆς γῆς Σααλείμ,** *tēs gēs Saaleím;* AV **Shalim**): Saul in search of his father's asses passed through Mt. Ephraim and the land of Shalishah, then through the land of Shaalim and the land of *y^emīnī*. This last name EV renders "Benjamin" (1 S **9** 4). The whole passage is so obscure that no certain conclusions can be reached. The search party may have proceeded northward from Gibeah, through the uplands of Ephraim, turning then westward, then southward, and finally eastward. We should thus look for the land of Shalishah and the land of Shaalim on the west side of the mountain range: and the latter may have been on the slopes to the E. of Lydda. Possibly we ought here to read "Shaalbim," instead of "Shaalim." W. EWING

SHAAPH, shā'af (שַׁעַף, *sha'aph*):

(1) A son of Jahdai (1 Ch **2** 47).

(2) The son of Maachah, a concubine of Caleb, the brother of Jerahmeel. Shaaph is called the "father," or founder, of the city Madmannah (1 Ch **2** 48 f).

SHAARAIM, shā-a-rā'im (שַׁעֲרַיִם, *sha'ărayim*, "two gates"; **Σακαρείμ,** *Sakareím;* AV **Sharaim**):

(1) A city in the Shephelah or "lowland" of Judah mentioned (Josh **15** 36) in close association with Socoh and Azekah; the vanquished army of the Philis passed a Shaaraim in their flight from Socoh toward Gath and Ekron (1 S **17** 52). It is possible that in this latter reference the "two gates" may refer—as LXX implies—to the two Phili strongholds themselves. Shaaraim has been identified with *Tell Zakarīya* (see however AZEKAH) and with *Kh. Sa'īreh* (*PEF*, III, 124, Sh XVII), an old site W. of *Beit 'Atāb*. Both proposals are hazardous.

(2) One of the towns of Simeon (1 Ch **4** 31), called (Josh **19** 6) "Sharuhen" and, as one of the uttermost cities of Judah, called (Josh **15** 32) "Shilhim." This town was in Southwestern Pal and is very probably identical with the fortress Sharhana, a place of some importance on the road from Gaza to Egypt. Aahmes (XVIIIth Dynasty) besieged and captured this city in the 5th year of his reign in his pursuit of the flying Hyksos (Petrie, *Hist*, II, 22, 35), and a century later Tahutmes III, in the 23d year of his reign, took the city of Sharuhen on his way to the siege and capture of Megiddo (Petrie, *Hist*, II, 104). On philological grounds *Tell esh-Sheri'ah*, 12 miles N.W. of Beersheba, a large ruin, has been proposed, but it does not suit at all the Egyp data (*PEF*, III, 399, Sh XXIV).

E. W. G. MASTERMAN

SHAASHGAZ, shā-ash'gaz (שַׁעַשְׁגַּז, *sha'ash-gāz;* LXX reads **Γαί,** *Gai*, the same name it gives to the official referred to in Est **2** 8.15; the name may go back to the Old Bactrian word *Sāsakshant*, "one anxious to learn" [Scheft]; most commentators suggest no explanation): A chamberlain of Ahasuerus, king of Persia; as keeper of "the second house of women," he had Esther under his charge (ver 14).

SHABBETHAI, shab'ĕ-thī (שַׁבְּתַי, *shabb^ethay*, "one born on the Sabbath"; B, **Σαβαθαί,** *Sabathaí*, A, **Καββαθαί,** *Kabbathaí* = "Sabbateus" of 1 Esd **9** 14): A Levite who opposed (?) Ezra's suggestion that the men who had married foreign wives put them aside (Ezr **10** 15). Kuenen, however, renders the phrase עָמְדוּ עַל זֹאת, *'ām^edhū 'al zō'th*, of which Asahiel and Jahaziah are the subjects, to mean "stand over," "have charge of," rather than "stand against," "oppose" (*Gesammelte Abhandlungen*, 247 f); this would make Shabbethai, who was in accord with the two men mentioned above, an ally rather than an opponent of Ezra. We incline toward Kuenen's interpretation in view of the position attained by Shabbethai under Nehemiah—one he would have been unlikely to attain had he been hostile to Ezra. He is mentioned among those appointed to explain the Law (Neh **8** 7), and as one of the chiefs of the Levites who had the oversight of "the outward business of the house of God" (Neh **11** 16). HORACE J. WOLF

SHACHIA, sha-kī'a, shak'i-a (שָׂכְיָה, *sākh^eyāh* [so Baer, Ginsberg]; some edd read שָׂכְיָא, *sākh^eyā'*, or שַׂכְיָא, *sakh^eyā';* also שָׁכְיָה, *shākh^eyāh*, and שָׁבְיָה, *shābh^eyāh*. This last reading is favored by the Syrian and the LXX [B, **Σαβιά,** *Sabia*, A, **Σεβιά,** *Sebiá*, but Luc., **Σεχιά,** *Sechiá*]; the forms in *kh* (כ) instead of *bh* (ב) have the support of the Vulg, *Sechia*, "Yahweh has forgotten"[?]): A name in a genealogy of Benjamin (1 Ch **8** 10).

SHADDAI, shad'ā-ī, shad'ī. See GOD, NAMES OF, II, 8.

SHADE, shād, **SHADOW,** shad'ō, **SHADOWING,** shad'ō-ing (צֵל, *çēl;* **σκιά,** *skiá*): A shadow is any obscuration of the light and heat with the form of the intervening object, obscurely projected, constantly changing and passing away. "Shadow" is used lit. of a roof (Gen **19** 8), of mountains (Jgs **9** 36), of trees (Jgs **9** 15, etc), of wings (Ps **17** 8, etc), of a cloud (Isa **25** 5), of a great rock (Isa **32** 2), of a man (Peter, Acts **5** 15), of the shadow on the dial (2 K **20** 9, etc), of Jonah's gourd (Jon **4** 5 f). It is used also **figuratively** (1) of shelter and protection (of man, Gen **19** 8; Cant **2** 3; Isa **16** 3, etc; of God, Ps **36** 7; **91** 1; Isa **4** 6, etc); (2) of anything fleeting or transient, as of the days of man's life on earth (1 Ch **29** 15; Job **8** 9; Ps **109** 23); (3) with the idea of obscurity or imperfection (in He **8** 5; **10** 1, of the Law; cf Col **2** 17); (4) of darkness, gloom; see SHADOW OF DEATH. In Jas **1** 17, we have in AV, "the Father of lights, with whom is no variableness, neither shadow of turning" (*aposkíasma*), RV "shadow that is cast by turning"; the reference is to the unchangeableness of God as contrasted with the changes of the heavenly bodies. RV has "of the rustling of wings" for "shadowing with wings" in Isa **18** 1; ARV has "shade" for "shadow" in various places (Jgs **9** 15; Job **40** 22; Isa **4** 6, etc). In Job **40** 21.22, for "shady trees" RV has "lotus-trees." W. L. WALKER

SHADOW OF DEATH (צַלְמָוֶת, *çalmāweth*): The Heb word trd "shadow of death" is used poetically for thick darkness (Job **3** 5), as descriptive of Sheol (Job **10** 21 f; **12** 22; **38** 17); **figuratively** of deep distress (Job **12** 22; **16** 16; **24** 17 *bis;* **28** 3; **34** 22 [in the last three passages ARV has "thick darkness" and "thick gloom"]; Ps **23** 4, RVm "deep darkness [and so elsewhere]"; **44** 19; **107** 10.14; Isa **9** 2; Jer **2** 6; **13** 16; Am **5** 8; Mt **4** 16; Lk **1** 79, *skiá thanátou*). The Heb word is perhaps composed of *çēl*, "shadow," and *māweth*, "death," and the idea of "the valley of the shadow of death" was most probably derived from the deep ravines, darkened by over-hanging briars, etc, through which the shepherd had sometimes to lead or drive his sheep to new and better pastures. W. L. WALKER

SHADRACH, shā'drak: The Bab name of one of the so-called Heb children. Shadrach is probably the Sumerian form of the Bab Kudurru-Aki, "servant of Sin." It has been suggested by Meinhold that we should read Merodach instead of Shadrach. Since there were no vowels in the original Heb or Aram., and since *sh* and *m* as well as *r* and *d* are much alike in the old alphabet in which Dnl was written, this change is quite possible.

Shadrach and his two companions were trained along with Daniel at the court of Nebuchadnezzar, who had carried all four captive in the expedition against Jerus in the 3d year of Jehoiakim (Dnl **1** 1). They all refused to eat of the food provided by Ashpenaz, the master who had been set over them by the king, but preferred to eat pulse (Dnl **1** 12). The effect was much to their advantage, as they appeared fairer and fatter in flesh than those who ate of the king's meat. At the end of the appointed time they passed satisfactory examinations, both as to their physical appearance and their intellectual acquirements, so that none were found like them among all with whom the king communed, and they stood before the king (see Dnl **1**).

When Daniel heard that the wise men of Babylon were to be slain because they could not tell the dream of Nebuchadnezzar, after he had gained a respite from the king, he made the thing known to his three companions that they might unite with him in prayer to the God of heaven that they all might not perish with the rest of the wise men of Babylon. After God had heard their prayer and the dream was made known to the king by Daniel, Nebuchadnezzar, at Daniel's request, set Shadrach, Meshach and Abed-nego over the affairs of the province of Babylon (Dnl **2**). With Meshach and Abed-nego, Shadrach was cast into a fiery furnace, but escaped unhurt (Dnl **3**). See ABED-NEGO; HANANIAH; SONG OF THREE CHILDREN.

R. DICK WILSON

SHADY, TREES (Job **40** 21 f). See LOTUS TREES.

SHAFT, shaft: Isa **49** 2 for חֵץ, *ḥēç*, "an arrow"; also Ex **25** 31; **37** 17; Nu **8** 4 AV for a part of the candlestick of the tabernacle somewhat vaguely designated by the word יָרֵךְ, *yārēkh*, "thigh." The context in the first 2 verses shows that the upright stem or "shaft" is intended, but in Nu **8** 4 a different context has caused RV to substitute "base." See also ARCHERY; ARMOR, ARMS.

SHAGEE, shā'gē (שָׁגֵא, *shāghē';* B, **Σωλά**, *Sōlá*, A, **Σαγή**, *Sagḗ;* AV **Shage**): The father of Jonathan, one of David's heroes (1 Ch **11** 34).

SHAHARAIM, shā-ha-rā'im (שַׁחֲרַיִם, *shaḥărayim;* B, **Σααρήλ**, *Saarḗl*, A, **Σααρήμ**, *Saarḗm*): A Benjamite name (1 Ch **8** 8). The passage is corrupt beyond only the most tentative emendation. "Sharaim" has no connection with the foregoing text. One of the suggested restorations of vs 8.9 reads: "And Shaharaim begat in the field of Moab, after he had driven them [i.e. the Moabites] out, from Hodesh his wife, Jobab," etc (Curtis, *ICC*).

SHAHAZUMAH, shā-ha-zōō'ma, sha-haz'ŏŏ-ma (שַׁחֲצוּמָה, *shaḥăçūmāh;* B, **Σαλεὶμ κατὰ θάλασσαν**, *Saleím katá thálassan*, A, **Σασειμάθ**, *Saseimáth;* AV **Shahazimah**, sha-haz'i-mah): A town in the territory of Issachar on the boundary which ran from Tabor to the Jordan (Josh **19** 22). The site, which has not yet been recovered, must be sought, probably, to the S.E. of the mountain.

SHALEM, shā'lem (שָׁלֵם, *shālēm;* **εἰς Σαλήμ**, *eis Salḗm*): The word as a place-name occurs only in Gen **33** 18. With Luther, following LXX, Pesh and Vulg, AV reads "And Jacob came to Shalem, a city of Shechem." RV with the Tgs Onkelos and pseudo-Jonathan, the Sam codex and the Arab., reads, "came in peace to the city of Shechem." There is a heavy balance of opinion among scholars in favor of the latter reading. It is certainly a remarkable fact, supporting AV, that about 4 miles E. of Shechem (*Nāblus*), there is a village bearing the name *Sālem*. If AV is right, this must represent the city referred to; and E. of *Sālem* would transpire the events recorded in Gen **44**. Against this is the old tradition locating Jacob's well and Joseph's tomb near to Shechem. *Onom* gets over the difficulty by identifying Shalem with Shechem.

W. EWING

SHALIM, shā'lim. See SHAALIM.

SHALISHAH, sha-lī'sha, shal'i-shä, **LAND OF** (אֶרֶץ־שָׁלִשָׁה, *'ereç shālishāh;* B, **ἡ γῆ Σελχά**, *hē gē Selchá*, A, **ἡ γῆ Σαλισσά**, *hē gē Salissá*): If the general indication of the route followed by Saul, given under SHAALIM, is correct, the land of Shalishah (1 S **9** 4) will lie to the N.E. of Lydda on the western slope of the range. Baal-shalishah would most likely be in the district, and may indeed have given its name to it. If Conder is right in identifying this city with *Khirbet Kefr Thilth*, about 19 miles N.E. of Jaffa, it meets well enough the general indication given above. *Onom* knows the name, but gives no guidance as to where the district is.

Baal-shalishah it places in the Thamnite region, 15 miles N. of Diospolis (Lydda). No boundaries can be laid down, but probability points to this neighborhood. W. EWING

SHALLECHETH, shal'ē-keth, sha-lē'keth, **THE GATE** (שַׁעַר שַׁלֶּכֶת, *sha'ar shallekheth,* i.e. as in m, "Casting forth"): A gate of the temple "at the causeway that goeth up" (1 Ch **26** 16)—probably an ascent from the Tyropœon Valley to the W. of the temple. It has been supposed on account of the meaning of the name that the ashes and offal of the temple were cast forth there, but this is very unlikely—they were thrown into the Kidron valley to the E. or S.E. The LXX has *παστοφορίον, pastophorion,* which seems to point to a building with chambers; in consonance with this Cheyne reads in the Heb לִשְׁכוֹת, *lishkōth,* "[of] the chambers." E. W. G. MASTERMAN

SHALLUM, shal'um (שַׁלּוּם, *shallūm,* שַׁלֻּם, *shallum;* various forms in LXX): This is the name of not less than 12 Heb persons:

(1) The youngest son of Naphtali (1 Ch **7** 13). He is also called "Shillem" in Gen **46** 24; Nu **26** 49.

(2) A descendant of Simeon, the son of Shaul and the father of Mibsam (1 Ch **4** 25). He lived in 1618 BC.

(3) The son of Sismai "son" of Shesham of the tribe of Judah (1 Ch **2** 40.41). He lived in 1300 BC.

(4) A son of Kore, a porter of the sanctuary during the reign of David (1 Ch **9** 17.19.31; Ezr **2** 42; Neh **7** 45). The name is also written "Meshullam" in Neh **12** 25, "Salum" in 1 Esd **5** 28, "Meshelemiah" in 1 Ch **26** 1.2.9, and "Shelemiah" in 1 Ch **26** 14. He lived about 1050 BC.

(5) A son of Zadok and father of Hilkiah, a high priest and ancestor of Ezra the scribe (1 Ch **6** 12.13; Ezr **7** 2). In the works of Jos he is called "Sallumus"; in 1 Esd **8** 1, "Salem," and in 2 Esd **1** 1, "Salemas."

(6) The 15th king of Israel. See following article.

(7) A son of Bani, a priest who had taken a heathen wife and was compelled by Ezra the scribe to put her away (Ezr **10** 42; omitted in 1 Esd **9** 34).

(8) The father of Jehizkiah, an Ephraimite in the time of Ahaz king of Israel (2 Ch **28** 12).

(9) The husband of the prophetess Huldah (2 K **22** 14; 2 Ch **34** 22). He was the keeper of the sacred wardrobe and was probably the uncle of Jeremiah the prophet (Jer **32** 7; cf Jer **35** 4).

(10) King of Judah and son of Josiah (Jer **22** 11; 1 Ch **3** 15), better known by the name Jehoahaz II. This name he received when he ascended the throne of the kingdom of Judah (2 Ch **36** 1).

(11) A Levite who was a porter at the time of Ezra (Ezr **10** 24; "Sallumus" in 1 Esd **9** 25).

(12) A ruler over a part of Jerus and a son of Hallohesh. He with his daughters aided in building the walls of Jerus in the time of Nehemiah (Neh **3** 12). S. L. UMBACH

SHALLUM (שַׁלּוּם, *shallūm,* שַׁלֻּם, *shallum,* "the requited one" [2 K **15** 10–15]): The 15th king of Israel, and successor of Zechariah, whom he publicly assassinated in the 7th month of his reign. Nothing more is known of Shallum than that he was a son of Jabesh, which may indicate that he was a Gileadite from beyond Jordan. He is said to have made "a conspiracy" against Zechariah, so was not alone in his crime. The conspirators, however, had but a short-lived success, as, when Shallum had "reigned for the space of a month in Samaria," Menahem, then at Tirzah, one of the minor capitals of the kingdom, went up to Samaria, slew him and took his place.

It was probably at this time that Syria threw off the yoke of tribute to Israel (see JEROBOAM II), as when next we meet with that kingdom, it is under its own king and in alliance with Samaria (2 K **16** 5).

The 10 years of rule given to Menahem (2 K **15** 17) may be taken to include the few months of military violence under Zechariah and Shallum, and cover the full years 758–750, with portions of years before and after counted as whole ones. The unsuccessful usurpation of Shallum may therefore be put in 758 BC (some date lower). W. SHAW CALDECOTT

SHALLUN, shal'un (שַׁלּוּן, *shallūn,* not in LXX): Another form of Shallum, the son of Col-hozeh. He was the ruler of the district of Mizpah. He assisted Nehemiah in building the wall of Jerus and in repairing the gate by the Pool of Siloah at the King's Gardens (Neh **3** 15).

SHALMAI, shal'mī, shal'mā-ī: AV form in Ezr **2** 46 for "Shamlai"; Neh **7** 48 "Salmai" (q.v.).

SHALMAN, shal'man (שַׁלְמַן, *shalmān*): A name of uncertain meaning, found only once in the OT (Hos **10** 14), in connection with a place-name, equally obscure, "as Shalman destroyed Beth-arbel." Shalman is most commonly interpreted as a contracted form of Shalmaneser, the name of several Assyr kings. If this explanation is correct, the king referred to cannot be identified. Some have thought of Shalmaneser IV, who is said to have undertaken expeditions against the West in 775 and in 773–772. Others have proposed Shalmaneser V, who attacked Samaria in 725. This, however, is improbable, because the activity of Hosea ceased before Shalmaneser V became king. Shalman has also been identified with Salamanu, a king of Moab in the days of Hosea, who paid tribute to Tiglath-pileser V of Assyria; and with Shalmah, a North Arabian tribe that invaded the Negeb. The identification of BETH-ARBEL (q.v.) is equally uncertain. From the reference it would seem that the event in question was well known and, therefore, probably one of recent date and considerable importance, but our present historical knowledge does not enable us to connect any of the persons named with the destruction of any of the localities suggested for Beth-arbel. The ancient tr[s] offer no solution; they too seem to have been in the dark. F. C. EISELEN

SHALMANESER, shal-ma-nē'zēr (שַׁלְמַנְאֶסֶר, *shalman'eṣer;* LXX **Σαμεννάσαρ,** *Samennásar,* **Σαλμανάσαρ,** *Salmanásar*): The name of several Assyr kings. See ASSYRIA; ASSYRIAN CAPTIVITY. It is Shalmaneser IV who is mentioned in the Bib. history (2 K **17** 3; **18** 9). He succeeded Tiglath-pileser on the throne in 727 BC, but whether he was a son of his predecessor, or a usurper, is not apparent. His reign was short, and, as no annals of it have come to light, we have only the accounts contained in 2 K for his history. In the passages referred to above, we learn that Hoshea, king of Israel, who had become his vassal, refused to continue the payment of tribute, relying upon help from So, king of Egypt. No help, however, came from Egypt, and Hoshea had to face the chastising forces of his suzerain with his own unaided resources, the result being that he was taken prisoner outside Samaria and most likely carried away to Nineveh. The Bib. narrative goes on to say that the king of Assyria came up throughout all the land, and went up to Samaria and besieged it 3 years. There is reason to believe that, as the siege of Samaria was proceeding, Shalmaneser retired to Nineveh and died, for, when the city was taken in 722 BC, it is Sargon who claims, in his copious annals, to have captured it and carried its inhabitants into captivity. It is just possible that Shalman (Hos **10** 14) is a contraction for Shalmaneser, but the identity of Shalman and of Beth-arbel named in the same passage is not sufficiently made out.

LITERATURE.—Schrader, *COT*, I, 258 ff; McCurdy, *HPM*, I, 387 ff.

T. NICOL

SHAMA, shā′ma (שָׁמָע, *shāmā'*): One of David's heroes (1 Ch **11** 44).

SHAMAI, sham′ă-ī. See SALMAI.

SHAMARIAH, sham-a-rī′a, sha-mär′ya. See SHEMARIAH.

SHAMBLES, sham′b'lz (μάκελλον, *mákellon*): A slaughter-house; then a butcher's stall, meat-market. The word is once used in the NT in 1 Cor **10** 25.

SHAME, shām (בּוֹשׁ, *bōsh*, "to be ashamed," בֹּשֶׁת, *bōsheth*, "shame," קָלוֹן, *ḳālōn;* αἰσχύνη, *aischúnē*, "ignominy," ἀτιμία, *atimía*, "dishonor," and other words): An oft-recurring word in Scripture almost uniformly bound up with a sense of sin and guilt. It is **figuratively** set forth as a wild beast (Jer **3** 24), a Nessus-garment (**3** 25), a blight (**20** 18), a sin against one's own soul (Hab **2** 10), and twice as the condensed symbol of Heb abomination—Baal (Jer **11** 13 m; Hos **9** 10 m; see ISH-BOSHETH). It is bracketed with defeat (Isa **30** 3), reproach (Ps **69** 7; Isa **54** 4; Mic **2** 6), confusion (Isa **6** 7), nakedness (Isa **47** 3; Mic **1** 11), everlasting contempt (Dnl **12** 2), folly (Prov **18** 13), cruelty (Isa **50** 6; He **12** 2), poverty (Prov **13** 18), nothingness (Prov **9** 7 AV), unseemliness (1 Cor **11** 6; **14** 35 AV; Eph **5** 12), and "them that go down to the pit" (Ezk **32** 25). In the first Bib. reference to this emotion, "shame" appears as "the correlative of sin and guilt" (Delitzsch, *New Comm. on Gen* and *Bib. Psychology*). Shamelessness is characteristic of abandoned wickedness (Phil **3** 19; Jude ver 13, m "Gr 'shames' "). Manifestly, then, shame is a concomitant of the Divine judgment upon sin; the very worst that a Hebrew could wish for an enemy was that he might be clothed with shame (Ps **109** 29), that the judgment of God might rest upon him visibly.

Naturally, to the Hebrew, shame was the portion of those who were idolaters, who were faithless to Jeh or who were unfriendly to themselves—the elect people of Jeh. Shame is to come upon Moab because Moab held Israel in derision (Jer **48** 39.27), and upon Edom "for violence against his brother Jacob" (Ob ver 10). But also, and impartially, shame is the portion of faithless Israelites who deny Jeh and follow after strange gods (Ezk **7** 18; Mic **7** 10; Hos **10** 6, and often). But shame, too, comes upon those who exalt themselves against God, who trust in earthly power and the show of material strength (2 Ch **32** 21; Isa **30** 3); and upon those who make a mock of righteousness (Job **8** 22; Ps **35** 26; **132** 18). With a fine sense of ethical distinctions the Bib. writers recognize that in confessing to a sense of shame there is hope for better things. Only in the most desperate cases is there no sense of shame (Hos **4** 18; Zeph **3** 5; Phil **3** 19; Jude ver 13); in pardon God is said to remove shame (Isa **54** 4 *bis;* **61** 7).

On conditions beyond the grave the Bib. revelation is exceedingly reticent, but here and there are hints that shame waits upon the wicked here and hereafter. Such an expression as that in Dnl (**12** 2) cannot be ignored, and though the writing itself may belong to a late period and a somewhat sophisticated theological development, the idea is but a reflection of the earlier and more elementary period, when the voice of crime and cruelty went up from earth to be heard in the audience chamber of God (Gen **4** 11; **6** 13). In the NT there is similar reticence but also similar implications. It cannot be much amiss to say that in the mind of the Bib. writers sin was a shameful thing; that part of the punishment for sin was a consciousness of guilt in the sense of shame; and that from this consciousness of guilt there was no deliverance while the sin was unconfessed and unforgiven. "Many of them that sleep in the dust of the earth shall awake, some to everlasting life and some to shame and everlasting contempt." From one's own past there is no deliverance, save through contrition of spirit and the grace and forgiveness of God. While the sense of shame persists, or, in other words, while the moral constitution of man's nature remains as it is, there will never be wanting an avenger of sin.

CHARLES M. STUART

SHAMED, shā′med. See SHEMED.

SHAMEFACEDNESS, shām′fāst-nes, shām-fās′ed-nes. See SHAMEFASTNESS.

SHAMEFASTNESS, shām′fast-nes: The original AV tr of αἰδώς, *aidṓs*, in Sir **41** 16 and 1 Tim **2** 9. Perhaps half a century later the spelling "shamefacedness" supplanted the better form, and continues in the ordinary editions of the King James Version. RV, however, rightly restores "shamefastness."

SHAMER, shā′mẽr. See SHEMER.

SHAMGAR, sham′gär (שַׁמְגַּר, *shamgar*): One of the judges, son of Anath (*'ănāth*), in whose days, which preceded the time of Deborah (Jgs **5** 6.7) and followed those of Ehud, Israel's subjugation was so complete that "the highways were unoccupied, and the travelers walked through byways." The government had become thoroughly disorganized, and apparently, as in the days of Deborah, the people were entirely unprepared for war. Shamgar's improvised weapon with which he helped to "save Israel" is spoken of as an ox-goad. With this he smote of the Philis 600 men. This is the first mention of the Philis as troublesome neighbors of the Israelites (Jgs **3** 31). According to a tradition represented in Jos (*Ant*, V, iv, 3), Shamgar died in the year he became judge.

1. Biblical Account

Several writers have challenged the Bib. account on the following grounds: that in Jgs **5** no mention is made of any deliverance; that the name "Shamgar" resembles the name of a Hittite king and the name "Anath" that of a Syrian goddess; that the deed recorded in Jgs **3** 31 is analogous to that of Samson (Jgs **15** 15), and that of Shammah, son of Agee (2 S **23** 11 f); and lastly, that in a group of Gr MSS and other VSS this verse is inserted after the account of Samson's exploits. None of these is necessarily inconsistent with the traditional account. Nevertheless, they have been used as a basis not only for overthrowing the tradition, but also for constructive theories such as that which makes Shamgar a foreign oppressor and not a judge, and even the father of Sisera. There is, of course, no limit to which this kind of interesting speculation cannot lead.

2. Critical Hypotheses

(For a complete account of these views see Moore, "Jgs," in *ICC*, 1895, 104 f, and same author in *Journal of the American Oriental Society*, XIX, **2**, 159–60.) Ella Davis Isaacs

SHAMHUTH, sham′huth. See Shammuah, IV.

SHAMIR, shā′mēr (שָׁמִיר, *shāmīr;* **Σαμείρ,** *Sameír*):

(1) Mentioned along with Jattir and Socoh (Josh **15** 48) as one of the cities of Judah in the hill country. Possibly it is *Kh.* (or *Umm*) *Sōmerah*, 2,000 ft. above sea-level, a site with ancient walls, caves, cisterns and tombs not far W. of Debîr (*edh Dhatherîyeh*) and 2 miles N. of Anab (*'Anab*) (*PEF*, III, 262, 286, Sh XX).

(2) A place in the hill country of Ephraim (Jgs **10** 1) from which came "Tola, the son of Pual, a man of Issachar," who judged Israel 23 years; he died and was buried there. It is an attractive theory (Schwartz) which would identify the place with the semi-fortified and strongly-placed town of *Sanûr* on the road from *Nāblus* to *Jenîn*. A local chieftain in the early part of the last century fortified *Sanûr* and from there dominated the whole district. That *Sanûr* could hardly have been within the bounds of Issachar is an objection, but not necessarily a fatal one. It is noticeable that LXX A has Σαμάρεια, *Samáreia*, for Shamir (*PEF*, II, Sh XI). E. W. G. Masterman

SHAMIR (שָׁמִיר, *shāmīr;* **Σαμήρ,** *Samḗr*): A Kohathite, son of Micah (1 Ch **24** 24).

SHAMLAI, sham′lā-ī, sham′lī. See Salmai.

SHAMMA, sham′a (שַׁמָּא, *shammā';* B, **Σεμά,** *Semá*, A, **Σαμμά,** *Sammá*): An Asherite (1 Ch **7** 37).

SHAMMAH, sham′a (שַׁמָּה, *shammāh*):

(1) The son of Reuel, the son of Esau, a tribal chief of Edom (Gen **36** 13.17; 1 Ch **1** 37, Σομέ, *Somé*).

(2) The third son of Jesse and brother of David. Together with his two other brothers he fought under Saul in the campaign against the Philis and was with the army in the valley of Elah when David slew Goliath (1 S **17** 13 ff). One redactor states that he was a witness of the anointing of David by Samuel (1 S **16** 1–13). He was the father of Jonadab, the friend of Amnon (2 S **13** 3 ff), and that Jonathan whose victory over a Phili giant is narrated in 2 S **21** 20 ff was also his son. His name is rendered as "Shammah" (1 S **16** 9; **17** 13), "Shimeah" (2 S **13** 3.32), "Shimei" (2 S **21** 21), and "Shimea" (1 Ch **2** 13; **20** 7).

(3) The son of Agee, a Hararite, one of the "three mighty men" of David (2 S **23** 11, LXX Σαμαιά, *Samaiá*), who held the field against the Philis. The ‖ passage (1 Ch **11** 10 ff) ascribes this deed to Eleazar, the son of Dodo. The succeeding incident (2 S **23** 13 ff), viz. the famous act of three of David's heroes who risked their lives to bring their leader water from the well of Bethlehem, has frequently been credited to Shammah and two other members of "the three"; but the three warriors are plainly said (ver 13) to belong to "the thirty"; ver 33 should read "Jonathan, son of Shammah, the Hararite." Jonathan, one of David's "thirty," was a son of Shammah; the word "son" has been accidentally omitted (Driver, Budde, Kittel, etc). The ‖ passage (1 Ch **11** 34) has "son of Shagee," which is probably a misreading for "son of Agee." Lucian's version, "son of Shammah," is most plausible. "Shimei the son of Ela" (1 K **4** 18) should also appear in this passage if Lucian's reading of "Ela" for "Agee" (2 S **23** 11) be correct.

(4) A Harodite (2 S **23** 25.33), i.e. probably a native of *'Ain-ḥarod* (*'Ain Jalūd*, Jgs **7** 1; see Harod). One of "the thirty" and captain of Solomon's 5th monthly course. In the ‖ lists (1 Ch **11** 27) he is called "the Harorite" (this last being a scribal error for Harodite) and "Shamhuth the Izrahite" (1 Ch **27** 8). Horace J. Wolf

SHAMMAI, sham′ā-ī, sham′ī (שַׁמַּי, *shammay*):

(1) A Jerahmeelite (1 Ch **2** 28.32).

(2) The son of Rekem and father of Maon (1 Ch **2** 44 ff).

(3) A Judahite (1 Ch **4** 17).

SHAMMOTH, sham′oth, sham′ōth. See Shammah, (4).

SHAMMUA, SHAMMUAH, sha-mū′a, sham′ū-a (שַׁמּוּעַ, *shammūa'*):

(1) The Reubenite spy (Nu **13** 4, Σαμουήλ, *Samouḗl*, and other forms).

(2) One of David's sons (2 S **5** 14; 1 Ch **14** 4, Σαμμοῦς, *Sammoús*). In 1 Ch **3** 5 he is called "Shimea."

(3) A Levite (Neh **11** 17); he is called "Shemaiah" in 1 Ch **9** 16.

(4) The head of a priestly family (Neh **12** 18); a contemporary of Joiakim.

SHAMSHERAI, sham′shē-rī, sham-shē-rā′ī (שַׁמְשְׁרַי, *shamsheray*): A Benjamite (1 Ch **8** 26).

SHAPE, shāp: In AV the tr of εἶδος, *eidos*, "form," "appearance" (Lk **3** 22; Jn **5** 37), and of ὁμοίωμα, *homoíōma*, "likeness," "resemblance" (Rev **9** 7). The meaning of these words is not so much "tangible shape," in which sense we use the word in modern Eng., but rather "aspect," "appearance," the looks of a thing or a person. This is even the case where the word is joined with the adj. σωματικός, *sōmatikós*, "bodily," as in the passage Lk **3** 22, "The Holy Spirit descended in a bodily form [i.e. "in a corporeal appearance," AV "in a bodily shape"], as a dove, upon him." The second passage also refers to the "appearance" of God, and cannot therefore be regarded as material shape: "Ye have neither heard his voice at any time, nor seen his form" (AV "shape") (Jn **5** 37). As has been seen from the above quotations, RV, which retains the tr "shape" for *homoiōma*, has trd *eidos* with "form," which also serves to render several other Gr synonyms, such as μορφή, *morphḗ* (Mk **16** 12; Phil **2** 6 f), μόρφωσις, *mórphōsis* (Rom **2** 20; 2 Tim **3** 5), τύπος, *túpos* (RVm "pattern," Rom **6** 17), and ὑποτύπωσις, *hupotúpōsis* (RV "pattern," 2 Tim **1** 13). In AV Wisd **18** 1 "shape" translates *morphē*, RV "form."

H. L. E. Luering

SHAPHAM, shā′fam (שָׁפָם, *shāphām;* **Σαφάμ,** *Saphám*, **Σαβάτ,** *Sabát*): Name of a Gadite chief, who had the second place in command of his tribe (1 Ch **5** 12). So far as the fragmentary genealogies are intelligible, they seem to indicate that Shapham and his chief, Joel, lived in the time of Saul and shared in the war against the Hagrites (1 Ch **5** 7–10.18–22), but it is to be noted that these lists were first recorded between the years 750 and 740 BC, just before the eastern tribes were carried into captivity.

SHAPHAN, shā′fan (שָׁפָן, *shāphān*, "rock-badger," EV "coney"; **Σαφφάν,** *Saphphán*): An old totem clan name (so W. R. Smith; cf, however, art. Totemism; Gray, *HPN*, 103 ff, and Jacob's *Studies in Bib. Archaeology*, 84 ff).

(1) Son of Azaliah and scribe of King Josiah. He received from Hilkiah the Book of the Law

which had been found in the Temple (2 K **22** 3 ff; 2 Ch **34** 8–28). It was from Shaphan's lips that Josiah heard the Law read. Shaphan was also one of those sent by the king to the prophetess Huldah (2 K **22**; 2 Ch **34**). He was undoubtedly one of the staunchest supporters of Josiah in his work of reform. He was the father of Ahikam (2 K **22** 12; 2 Ch **34** 20; Jer **26** 24), who befriended and protected the prophet Jeremiah. Another son, Elasah, was one of the two men intrusted by Jeremiah with his letter to the captives in Babylon (Jer **29** 3). A third son, Gemariah, vainly tried to prevent King Jehoiakim from burning "the roll" (Jer **36** 10.11.12.25). The Micaiah of Jer **36** 11.12, and Gedaliah, the governor of Judaea after the captivity of 586 BC, were his grandsons (Jer **39** 14).

(2) Perhaps the father of Jaazaniah, one of the 70 men whom Ezekiel saw, in his vision of the Temple, sacrificing to idols (Ezk **8** 11).

HORACE J. WOLF

SHAPHAT, shā'fat (שָׁפָט, *shāphāṭ*):

(1) The Simeonite spy (Nu **13** 5, Σαφάτ, *Saphát*).

(2) The father of the prophet Elisha (1 K **19** 16; 2 K **3** 11, LXX *Sapháth*).

(3) A name in the royal genealogy of Judah (1 Ch **3** 22).

(4) A Gadite (1 Ch **5** 12).

(5) One of David's herdsmen (1 Ch **27** 29).

SHAPHER, shā'fẽr. See SHEPHER.

SHAPHIR, shā'fẽr (שָׁפִיר, *shāphīr*, "glittering"; **καλῶς**, *kalōs;* AV **Saphir**): One of a group of towns mentioned in Mic **1** 10–15. From the association with Gath, Achzib (of Judah) and Mareshah, it would seem that the places mentioned were in Southwestern Pal. According to *Onom*, there was a Σαφείρ, *Sapheír*, "in the hill country" (from a confusion with Shamir [Josh **15** 48], where LXX A has *Sapheír*) between Eleutheropolis and Ascalon. The name probably survives in that of three villages called *es-Sûāfir*, in the plain, some 3½ miles S.E. of Ashdod (*PEF*, II, 413, Sh XV). Cheyne (*EB*, col. 4282) suggests the white "glittering" hill *Tell eṣ-Ṣāfi*, at the entrance to the *Wâdy eṣ-Sunṭ*, which was known to the Crusaders as *Blanchegarde*, but this site seems a more probable one for GATH (q.v.).

E. W. G. MASTERMAN

SHARAI, sha-rā'ī, shā'rī (שָׁרַי, *shāray*): One of the sons of Bani who had married foreign wives (Ezr **10** 40).

SHARAIM, sha-rā'im. See SHAARAIM.

SHARAR, shā'rar. See SACAR.

SHARE, shār. See PLOW.

SHAREZER, sha-rē'zẽr (שַׁרְאֶצֶר, *sar'eçer*, 'שׁ, *shar'eçer*): Corresponds to the Assyr *Shar-uṣur*, "protect the king"; found otherwise, not as a complete name, but as elements in personal names, e.g. *Bel-shar-uṣur*, "may Bel protect the king," which is the equivalent of Belshazzar (Dnl **5** 1). The name is borne by two persons in the OT:

(1) The son of Sennacherib, king of Assyria, who with ADRAMMELECH (q.v.) murdered his father (2 K **19** 37; Isa **37** 38). The Bab Chronicle says concerning Sennacherib's death: "On the 20th day of Tebet Sennacherib, king of Assyria, was slain by his son in a revolt." This differs from the OT account in that it speaks of only one murderer, and does not give his name. How the two accounts can be harmonized is still uncertain. Hitzig, (*Kritik*, 194 ff), following Abydenus, as quoted by Eusebius, completed the name of Sennacherib's son, so as to read Nergal-sharezer = *Nergal-shar-uṣur* (Jer **39** 3.13), and this is accepted by many modern scholars. Johns thinks that Sharezer (*shar'eçer* or *sar'eçer*) may be a corruption from *Shar-etir-Ashur*, the name of a son of Sennacherib (1-vol *HDB*, s.v.). The question cannot be definitely settled.

(2) A contemporary of the prophet Zechariah, mentioned in connection with the sending of a delegation to the spiritual heads of the community to inquire concerning the propriety of continuing the fasts: "They of Beth-el had sent Sharezer and Regem-melech" (Zec **7** 2). This tr creates a difficulty in connection with the succeeding words, lit. "and *his* men." The Revisers place in the margin as an alternative rendering, "They of Beth-el, even Sharezer . . . . had sent." Sharezer sounds peculiar in apposition to "they of Beth-el"; hence some have thought, esp. since Sharezer seems incomplete, that in the two words Beth-el and Sharezer we have a corruption of what was originally a single proper name, perhaps Bel-sharezer = *Bel-shar-uṣur* = Belshazzar. The present text, no matter how tr[d], presents difficulties. See REGEM-MELECH.

F. C. EISELEN

SHARON, shâr'un (הַשָּׁרוֹן, *ha-shārōn*, with the def. art. possibly meaning "the plain"; **τὸ πεδίον**, *tó pedíon*, **ὁ δρυμός**, *ho drumós*, **ὁ Σαρών**, *ho Sarṓn*):

(1) This name is attached to the strip of fairly level land which runs between the mountains and the shore of the Mediterranean, stretching from *Nahr Rubīn* in the S. to Mt. Carmel in the N. There are considerable rolling hills; but, compared with the mountains to the E., it is quite properly described as a plain. The soil is a deep rich loam, which is favorable to the growth of cereals. The orange, the vine and the olive grow to great perfection. When the many-colored flowers are in bloom it is a scene of rare beauty.

Of the streams in the plain four carry the bulk of the water from the western slopes of the mountains to the sea. They are also perennial, being fed by fountains. *Nahr el-'Aujeh* enters the sea to the N. of Jaffa; *Nahr Iskanderūneh* 7 miles, and *Nahr el-Mefjir* fully 2 miles S. of Caesarea; and *Nahr ez-Zerḳā*, the "Crocodile River," 2½ miles N. of Caesarea. *Nahr el-Fālik* runs its short course about 12 miles N. of *Nahr el-'Aujeh*. Water is plentiful, and at almost any point it may be obtained by digging. Deep, finely built wells near some of the villages are among the most precious legacies left by the Crusaders. The breadth of the plain varies from 8 to 12 miles, being broadest in the S. There are traces of a great forest in the northern part, which accounts for the use of the term *drumos*. Jos (*Ant*, XIV, xiii, 3) speaks of "the woods" (*hoi drumoi*) and Strabo (xvi) of "a great wood." There is still a considerable oak wood in this district. The "excellency" of Carmel and Sharon (Isa **35** 2) is probably an allusion to the luxuriant oak forests. As in ancient times, great breadths are given up to the pasturing of cattle. Over David's herds that fed in Sharon was Shitrai the Sharonite (1 Ch **27** 29). In the day of Israel's restoration "Sharon shall be a fold of flocks" (Isa **65** 10). Jerome speaks of the fine cattle fed in the pastures of Sharon, and also sings the praises of its wine (*Comm. on Isa* **33** and **65**). Toward the S. no doubt there was more cultivation then than there is at the present day. The Ger. colony to the N. of Jaffa, preserving in its name, *Sarōna*, the old Gr name of the plain, and several Jewish colonies are proving the wonderful productiveness of the soil. The orange groves of Jaffa are far-famed.

"The rose of Sharon" (Cant **2** 1) is a mistranslation: *ḥăbhaççeleth* is not a "rose," but the white narcissus, which in season abounds in the plain.

Sharon is mentioned in the NT only in Acts **9** 35.

(2) A district E. of the Jordan, occupied by the tribe of Gad (1 Ch **5** 16; here the name is without the art.). Kittel ("Ch," *SBOT*) suggests that this is a corruption from "Sirion," which again is synonymous with Hermon. He would therefore identify Sharon with the pasture lands of Hermon. Others think that the *mīshōr* or table-land of Gilead is intended.

(3) In Josh **12** 18 we should perhaps read "the king of Aphek in Sharon." See LASHARON. The order seems to point to some place N.E. of Tabor. Perhaps this is to be identified with the Sarona of *Onom* in the district between Tabor and Tiberias. If so, the name may be preserved in that of *Sarōna* on the plateau to the S.W. of Tiberias.

W. EWING

Canaanitish descent. The patronymic **Shaulites** is found in Nu **26** 13.

(3) An ancestor of Samuel (1 Ch **6** 24 [Heb **9**]); in ver 36 he is called "Joel."

SHAVEH, shā've, **VALE OF** (עֵמֶק שָׁוֵה, *'ēmeḳ shāwēh*). See KING'S VALE.

SHAVEH-KIRIATHAIM, shā've-kir-ya-thā'im (שָׁוֵה קִרְיָתַיִם, *shāweh ḳiryāthayim;* ἐν Σαυὴ τῇ πόλει, *en Sauē tē pólei*): Here Chedorlaomer is said to have defeated the Emim (Gen **14** 5). RVm reads "the plain of Kiriathaim." If this rendering is right, we must look for the place in the neighborhood of Kiriathaim of Moab (Jer **48** 1, etc), which is probably represented today by *el-Ḳareiyāt*, about 7 miles to the N. of Dibon.

PLAIN OF SHARON.

SHARONITE, shār'un-īt (הַשָּׁרֹנִי, *ha-shārōnī;* ὁ Σαρωνείτης, *ho Sarōneítēs*): Applied in Scripture only to Shitrai (1 Ch **27** 29). See SHARON.

SHARUHEN, sha-rōō'hen (שָׁרוּחֶן, *shārūḥen;* οἱ ἀγροὶ αὐτῶν, *hoi agroi autōn*): One of the cities in the territory of Judah assigned to Simeon (Josh **19** 6). In **15** 32 it is called "Shilhim," and in 1 Ch **4** 31, "Shaaraim" (q.v.).

SHASHAI, shā'shī (שָׁשַׁי, *shāshay;* Σεσεί, *Seseí*): One of the sons of Bani who had married foreign wives (Ezr **10** 40) = "Sesis" in 1 Esd **9** 34.

SHASHAK, shā'shak (שָׁשַׁק, *shāshaḳ*): Eponym of a Benjamite family (1 Ch **8** 14.25).

SHAUL, shā'ul, **SHAULITES,** shā'ul-īts (שָׁאוּל, *shā'ūl;* Σαούλ, *Saoúl*):

(1) A king of Edom (Gen **36** 37 ff = 1 Ch **1** 48 ff).

(2) A son of Simeon (Gen **46** 10; Ex **6** 15; Nu **26** 13; 1 Ch **4** 24). The clan was of notoriously impure stock, and, therefore, Shaul is called "the son of a Canaanitish woman" (Gen **46** 10; Ex **6** 15); the clan was of mixed Israelitish and

SHAVING, shāv'ing (in Job **1** 20, גָּזַז, *gāzaz*, usually גָּלַח, *gālaḥ;* in Acts **21** 24, ξυράω, *xuráō*): Customs as to shaving differ in different countries, and in ancient and modern times. Among the Egyptians it was customary to shave the whole body (cf Gen **41** 14). With the Israelites, shaving the head was a sign of mourning (Dt **21** 12; Job **1** 20); ordinarily the hair was allowed to grow long, and was only cut at intervals (cf Absalom, 2 S **14** 26). Nazirites were forbidden to use a razor, but when their vow was expired, or if they were defiled, they were to shave the whole head (Nu **6** 5.9.18 ff; cf Acts **21** 24). The shaving of the beard was not permitted to the Israelites; they were prohibited from shaving off even "the corner of their beard" (Lev **21** 5). It was an unpardonable insult when Hanun, king of the Ammonites, cut off the half of the beards of the Israelites whom David had sent to him (2 S **10** 4; 1 Ch **19** 4).

Shaving "with a razor that is hired" is Isaiah's graphic figure to denote the complete devastation of Judah by the Assyr army (Isa **7** 20).

JAMES ORR

SHAVSHA, shav'sha (שַׁוְשָׁא, *shawshā';* in 2 S **20** 25, Kᵉthībh, שׁיא, *shᵉyā'*, Ḳᵉrē, שְׁוָא, *shᵉwā'*, EV "Sheva," are refuted by LXX; in 2 S **8** 15–18, in other respects identical with Ch, "Seraiah" is found; LXX varies greatly in all passages; it is the general consensus that Shavsha is correct): State secretary or scribe during the reign of David (1 Ch **18** 16; 2 S **20** 25). He was the first occupant of this office, which was created by David. It is significant that his father's name is omitted in the very exact list of David's officers of state (1 Ch **18** 14–17 ‖ 2 S **8** 15–18); this fact, coupled with the foreign sound of his name, points to his being an "alien"; the assumption that the state secretary handled correspondence with other countries may explain David's choice of a foreigner for this post. Shavsha's two sons, Elihoreph and Ahijah, were secretaries of state under Solomon; they are called "sons of **Shisha**" (1 K **4** 3), "Shisha" probably being a variant of "Shavsha."

HORACE J. WOLF

SHAWL, shôl: RV substitutes "shawls" for AV "wimples" in Isa **3** 22. See DRESS.

SHEAF, shēf, **SHEAVES,** shēvz (אֲלֻמָּה, *'ălummāh,* עֹמֶר, *'ōmer,* עָמִיר, *'āmīr*): When the grain is reaped, it is laid in handfuls back of the reaper to be gathered by children or those who cannot stand the harder work of reaping (Ps **129** 7). The handfuls are bound into large sheaves, two of which are laden at a time on a donkey (cf Neh **13** 15). In some districts carts are used (cf Am **2** 13). The sheaves are piled about the threshing-floors until threshing time, which may be several weeks after harvest. It is an impressive sight to see the huge stacks of sheaves piled about the threshing-floors, the piles often covering an area greater than the nearby villages (see AGRICULTURE). The ancient Egyptians bound their grain into small sheaves, forming the bundles with care so that the heads were equally distributed between the two ends (see Wilkinson, *Ancient Egyptians,* 1878, II, 424; cf Joseph's dream, Gen **37** 5–8). The sheaves mentioned in Lev **32** 10–12.15 must have been handfuls. It is a custom in parts of Syria for the gatherers of the sheaves to run toward a passing horseman and wave a handful of grain, shouting *kemshi, kemshi* (lit. "handful"). They want the horseman to feed the grain to his horse. In OT times forgotten sheaves had to be left for the sojourner (Dt **24** 19); cf the kindness shown to Ruth by the reapers of Boaz (Ruth **2** 7.15).

Figurative: "Being hungry they carry the sheaves" is a picture of torment similar to that of the hungry horse urged to go by the bundle of hay tied before him (Job **24** 10). The joyful sight of the sheaves of an abundant harvest was used by the Psalmist to typify the joy of the returning captives (Ps **126** 6).

JAMES A. PATCH

SHEAL, shē'al (שְׁאָל, *sh^e'āl,* "request"): One of the Israelites of the sons of Bani who had taken foreign wives (Ezr **10** 29, LXX *Salouiá,* LXX Luc., *Assaél;* 1 Esd **9** 30, "Jasaelus").

SHEALTIEL, shē-ol'ti-el (שְׁאַלְתִּיאֵל, *sh^e'altī'ēl,* but in Hag **1** 12.14; **2** 2, שַׁלְתִּיאֵל, *shaltī'ēl;* LXX and the NT always **Σαλαθιήλ,** *Salathiēl,* hence "Salathiel" of 1 Esd **5** 5.48.56; **6** 2; AV of Mt **1** 12; Lk **3** 27): Father of Zerubbabel (Ezr **3** 2.8; **5** 2; Neh **12** 1; Hag **1** 1.12.14; **2** 2.23). But, according to 1 Ch **3** 17, Shealtiel was the oldest son of King Jeconiah; in ver 19 the MT makes Pedaiah, a brother of Shealtiel, the father of Zerubbabel (cf Curtis, *ICC*).

SHEAR, shēr. See SHEEP; SHEEP TENDING.

SHEARIAH, shē-a-rī'a, shē-är'ya (שְׁעַרְיָה, *sh^e'aryāh;* **Σαραιά,** *Saraiá*): A descendant of Saul (1 Ch **8** 38; **9** 44).

SHEARING, **shēr'ing, **HOUSE (בֵּית עֵקֶד הָרֹעִים, *bēth 'ēkedh hā-rō'īm,* "house of binding of the shepherds"; B, **Βαιθάκαθ** [A, **Βαιθάκαδ**] **τῶν ποιμένων,** *Baithákath* [*Baithákad*] *tōn poimenōn*): Here, in the course of his extinction of the house of Ahab, Jehu met and destroyed 42 men, "the brethren of Ahaziah king of Judah" (2 K **10** 12–14). *Onom* takes the phrase as a proper name, Bethacath, and locates the village 15 miles from Legio in the plain. This seems to point to identification with *Beit Kād,* about 3 miles E. of *Jenīn.*

SHEAR-JASHUB, shē-är-jā'shub or jash'ub (שְׁאָר יָשׁוּב, *sh^e'ār yāshūbh,* "a remnant shall return"; LXX *ho kataleiphtheìs Iasoúb*): The son of Isaiah, who accompanied him when he set out to meet Ahaz (Isa **7** 3). The name like that of other children of prophets (cf "Immanuel," "Maher-shalal-hash-baz," "Lo-ruhamah," etc) is symbolic of a message which the prophet wishes to emphasize. Thus Isaiah uses the very words *sh^e'ār yāshūbh* to express his oft-repeated statement that a remnant of Israel will return to Jeh (Isa **10** 21).

SHEATH, shēth. See SWORD.

SHEBA, shē'ba (שְׁבָא, *sh^ebhā';* **Σαβά,** *Sabá*): (1) Sheba and Dedan are the two sons of Raamah son of Cush (Gen **10** 7). (2) Sheba and Dedan are the two sons of Jokshan the son of Abraham and Keturah (**25** 3). (3) Sheba is a son of Joktan son of Eber who was a descendant of Shem (**10** 28).

From the above statements it would appear that Sheba was the name of an Arab tribe, and consequently of Sem descent. The fact that Sheba and Dedan are represented as Cushite (Gen **10** 7) would point to a migration of part of these tribes to Ethiopia, and similarly their derivation from Abraham (**25** 3) would indicate that some families were located in Syria. In point of fact Sheba was a South-Arabian or Joktanite tribe (Gen **10** 28), and his own name and that of some of his brothers (e.g. Hazarmaveth = Hadhramaut) are place-names in Southern Arabia.

The Sabaeans or people of Saba or Sheba, are referred to as traders in gold and spices, and as inhabiting a country remote from Pal (1 K **10** 1 f; Isa **60** 6; Jer **6** 20; Ezk **27** 22; Ps **72** 15; Mt **12** 42), also as slave-traders (Joel **3** 8), or even desert-rangers (Job **1** 15; **6** 19; cf *CIS* **84** 3).

By the Arab genealogists Saba is represented as great-grandson of Ḳaḥṭân (= Joktan) and ancestor of all the South-Arabian tribes. He is the father of Ḥimyar and Kahlân. He is said to have been named Saba because he was the first to take prisoners (*shābhāh*) in war. He founded the capital of Saba and built its citadel Marib (Mariaba), famous for its mighty barrage.

1. History

The authentic history of the Sabaeans, so far as known, and the topography of their country are derived from South-Arabian inscriptions, which began to be discovered about the middle of the last century, and from coins dating from about 150 BC to 150 AD, the first collection of which was published in 1880, and from the South-Arabian geographer Hamdānī, who was later made known to European scholars. One of the Sabaean kings is mentioned on Assyr inscriptions of the year 715 BC; and he is apparently not the earliest. The native monuments are scattered over the period extending from before that time until the 6th cent. AD, when the

Sabaean state came to an end, being most numerous about the commencement of our era. Saba was the name of the nation of which Marib was the usual capital. The Sabaeans at first shared the sovereignty of South Arabia with Ḥimyar and one or two other nations, but gradually absorbed the territories of these some time after the Christian era. The form of government seems to have been that of a republic or oligarchy, the chief magistracy going by a kind of rotation, and more than one "king" holding office simultaneously (similarly Dt **4** 47 and often in the OT). The people seem to have been divided into patricians and plebeians, the former of whom had the right to build castles and to share in the government.

2. Religion

A number of deities are mentioned on the inscriptions, two chief being Il-Maḳḳih and Ta'lab. Others are Athtar (masc. form of the Bib. *'ashtārōth*), Rammon (the Bib. Rimmon), the Sun, and others. The Sun and Athtar were further defined by the addition of the name of a place or tribe, just as Baal in the OT. Worship took the form of gifts to the temples, of sacrifices, esp. incense, of pilgrimages and prayers. Ceremonial ablution, and abstinence from certain things, as well as formal dedication of the worshipper and his household and goods to the deity, were also religious acts. In return the deity took charge of his worshipper's castle, wells, and belongings, and supplied him with cereals, vegetables and fruits, as well as granted him male issue.

3. Civilization

(1) The chief occupations of the Sabaeans were raiding and trade. The chief products of their country are enumerated in Isa **60** 6, which agrees with the Assyr inscriptions. The most important of all commodities was incense, and it is significant that the same word which in the other Sem languages means "gold," in Sabaean means "perfume" (and also "gold"). To judge, however, from the number of times they are mentioned upon the inscriptions, agriculture bulked much more largely in the thoughts of the Sabaean than commerce, and was of equal importance with religion.

(2) The high position occupied by women among the Sabaeans is reflected in the story of the Queen of Sheba and Solomon. In almost all respects women appear to have been considered the equal of men, and to have discharged the same civil, religious and even military functions. Polygamy does not seem to have been practised. The Sabaean inscriptions do not go back far enough to throw any light upon the queen who was contemporary with Solomon, and the Arab. identification of her with Bilḳīs is merely due to the latter being the only Sabaean queen known to them. Bilḳīs must have lived several centuries later than the Heb monarch.

(3) The alphabet used in the Sabaean inscriptions is considered by Professor Margoliouth to be the original Sem alphabet, from which the others are derived. In other respects Sabaean art seems to be dependent on that of Assyria, Persia and Greece. The coins are Gr and Rom in style, while the system of weights employed is Persian. See further SABAEANS.

LITERATURE.—Rödiger and Osiander in *ZDMG*, vols XX and XXI; Halévy in *Journal Asiatique*, Série 6, vol IX; *CIS*, pt. IV, ed by J. and H. Derenbourg; Ḥamdānī, ed by D. H. Müller, 1891; Mordtmann, *Himyarische Inschriften*, 1893; Hommel, *Südarabische Chrestomathie*, 1893; Glaser, *Abyssinien in Arabien*, 1895; D. H. Müller, *Südarabische Alterthümer*, 1899; Derenbourg, *Les monuments sabéens*, 1899. On the coins, Schlumberger, *Le trésor de San'a*, 1880; Mordtmann in *Wiener numismatische Zeitschrift*, 1880.

THOMAS HUNTER WEIR

SHEBA, shē'ba (שֶׁבַע, *shebha'*; Σάβεε, *Sábee*, or Σάμαα, *Sámaa*): The name of one of the towns allotted to Simeon (Josh **19** 2). AV mentions it as an independent town, but as it is not mentioned at all in the parallel list (1 Ch **4** 28), and is omitted in Josh **19** 2 in some MSS, it is probable that RV is correct in its tr "Beer-sheba *or* Sheba." Only in this way can the total of towns in this group be made 13 (Josh **19** 6). If it is a separate name, it is probably the same as SHEMA (q.v.).

E. W. G. MASTERMAN

SHEBA, QUEEN OF. See QUEEN OF SHEBA.

SHEBAH, shē'ba. See SHIBAH.

SHEBAM, shē'bam. See SEBAM.

SHEBANIAH, sheb-a-nī'a, shĕ-ban'ya (שְׁבַנְיָה, *shᵉbhanyāh*, in 1 Ch **15** 24, *shᵉbhanyāhū*):

(1) Name of a Levite or a Levitical family that participated in the religious rites that followed the reading of the Law (Neh **9** 4). The name is given in Neh **10** 10 among those that sealed the covenant.

(2) A priest or Levite who took part in the sealing of the covenant (Neh **10** 4; **12** 14). See SHECANIAH.

(3) Another Levite who sealed the covenant (Neh **10** 12).

(4) A priest in the time of David (1 Ch **15** 24).

SHEBARIM, sheb'a-rim, shĕ-bā'rim (הַשְּׁבָרִים, *ha-shᵉbhārīm*; συνέτριψαν, *sunétripsan*): After the repulse of the first attack on their city the men of Ai chased the Israelites "even unto Shebarim" (Josh **7** 5). RVm reads "the quarries"; so Keil, Steuernagel, etc. LXX reads "until they were broken," i.e. until the rout was complete. The direction of the flight was of course from Ai toward Gilgal in the Jordan valley. No trace of such a name has yet been found.

SHEBAT, she-bät' (שְׁבָט, *shᵉbhāṭ*): The 11th month of the Jewish year (Zec **1** 7), corresponding to February. See CALENDAR.

SHEBER, shē'bēr (שֶׁבֶר, *shebher*; B, Σάβερ, *Sáber*, A, Σέβερ, *Séber*): A son of Caleb by his concubine Maacah (1 Ch **2** 48).

SHEBNA, sheb'na (שֶׁבְנָא, *shebhnā'*; Σόμνας, *Sómnas*; but שֶׁבְנָה, *shebhnāh*, in 2 K **18** 18.26; meaning uncertain [2 K **18** 18.26.37 and **19** 2=Isa **36** 3.11.22 and **37** 2; Isa **22** 15]):

1. Position in Isa 22

In Isa **22** 15 Shebna is referred to as he "who is over the house," or household, apparently that of the king. The phrase is tr^d "steward of the house" in RV of Gen **43** 16.19; **44** 1, and occurs also in **39** 4, "overseer"; **44** 4. It is used of an officer of the Northern Kingdom in 1 K **16** 9; **18** 3; 2 K **10** 5. This officer is distinguished from him "that was over the city" in 2 K **10** 5, and it is said in 2 K **15** 5 that after his father Azariah was stricken with leprosy, "Jotham, the king's son, was over the household, judging all the people of the land." Again Isa **22** 15 speaks of "this *ṣōkhēn*," a phrase that must apply to Shebna if the prophecy refers to him. This word is the participle of a vb. meaning "to be of use or service," so "to benefit" in Job **15** 3; **22** 2; **34** 9. The fem. participle is employed of Abishag in 1 K **1** 2.4, where AVm translates "cherisher"; *BDB* renders it "servitor" or "steward" in Isa **22** 15. It occurs also as a Can. gloss in the Am Tab (Winckler no. 237.9). The *ṣōkhēn* was evidently a high officer: Shebna had splendid chariots (ver 18), but what the office exactly was is not certain. The other reference to Shebna in the title of the prophecy would lead one to conclude that it denoted him "who was over the household," i.e. governor of the palace, probably, or major-domo. The word *ṣōkhēn* is thus a general title; others deny this, maintaining that it would then occur more frequently.

In 2 K **18** f=Isa **36** f we find too a Shebna mentioned among the officers of Hezekiah. There he is called the *ṣōphēr*, "scribe" or "secretary," i.e. a minister of state of some kind, whereas Eliakim is he "who is over the household." Is then the Shebna of Isa **22** the same as this officer? It is of course possible that two men of the same name should hold high office about the same time. We find a Joah (ben Asaph) "recorder" under Hezekiah (2 K **18** 18) and a Joah (ben Joahaz) having the very same position under Josiah a century later (2 Ch **34** 8). But such a coincidence is rare. Had there been two high officers of state bearing this name, it is most probable that they would somehow have been distinguished one from the other. Shebna's name is thought to be Aram., thus pointing to a foreign descent, but G. B. Gray, "Isa," *ICC*, 373 ff, denies this. We can perhaps safely infer that he was a parvenu from the fact that he was hewing himself a sepulcher in Jerus, apparently among those of the Heb nobility, whereas a native would have an ancestral burial-place in the land.

2. Shebna in 2 K 18 f

However, in 2 K, Shebna is the scribe and not the governor of the palace. How is this to be explained? The answer is in Isaiah's prophecy.

The prophecy of Isa **22** divides itself into 3 sections. The words "against [not as RV "unto"] Shebna who is over the house," or palace, are properly the title of the prophecy, and should come therefore at the very beginning of ver 15.

3. Isa 22: 15 ff

(1) Vs 15–18 form one whole. In ver 16 the words "hewing him out a sepulchre," etc, should be placed immediately before the rest of the verse as ver 16*a* with the rest of the section is in the second person. We thus read (vs 15–17): 'Against Shebna who was over the house. Thus saith the Lord, Jeh of hosts, Go unto this steward [RVm] that is hewing him out a sepulchre on high, graving a habitation for himself in the rock, [and say] What doest thou here and whom hast thou here that thou hast hewed thee out here a sepulchre? Behold, Jeh of hosts, ...' etc. G. H. Box (*Isa*) would further transpose some parts of vs 17 f. Shebna is to be tossed like a ball into "a land wide of sides," i.e. a broad extensive land. He is addressed as a disgrace to the house of his royal master. The prophet's language is that of personal invective, and one asks what had made him so indignant. Some (e.g. Dillmann, Delitzsch) suggest that Shebna was the leader of a pro-Egyp party, while others (e.g. Cheyne) believe that the party was pro-Assyr (cf Isa **8** 5–8*a*). The actual date of the prophecy can only be inferred.

(2) Isa **22** 19–23 contains a prophecy which states that Eliakim is to be given someone's post, apparently that of Shebna, if this section be by Isaiah; ver 23, however, is held by many to be a gloss. These verses are not so vehement in tone as the previous ones. Some maintain that the section is not by Isaiah (Duhm, Marti). It can, however, be Isaianic, only later in date than vs 15 ff, being possibly meant to modify the former utterance. The palace governor is to lose his office and to be succeeded by Eliakim, who is seen to hold that post in 2 K **18** f (see Eliakim).

(3) Vs 24 f are additions to the two utterances by a later hand; they predict the ruin of some such official as Eliakim owing to his own family.

There is nothing a priori against believing that these three sections are entirely independent one of another, but there seems to be some connection between (1) and (2), and again between (2) and (3).

4. Date of the Prophecy

Now the question that has to be solved is that of the relation of Isa **22** 15 ff with 2 K **18** f=Isa **36** f, where are given the events of 701 BC. We have the following facts: (*a*) Shebna is scribe in 701, and Eliakim is governor of the palace; (*b*) Shebna is governor of the palace in Isa **22** 15, and is to be deposed; (*c*) if Isa **22** 18–22 be by Isaiah, Eliakim was to succeed Shebna in that post. Omitting for the moment everything but (*a*) and (*b*), the only solution that is to any extent satisfactory is that Isa **22** 15–18 is to be dated previous to 701 BC. This is the view preferred by G. B. Gray, op. cit. And this is the most satisfactory theory if we take (2) above into consideration. The prophecy then contained in (1) had not been as yet fulfilled in 701, but (2) had come to pass; Shebna was no longer governor of the palace, but held the position of scribe. Exile might still be in store for him.

Another explanation is put forward by K. Fullerton in *AJT*, IX, 621–42 (1905) and criticized by E. König in X, 675–86 (1906). Fullerton rejects vs 24 f as not due to Isaiah, and maintains that Isa **22** 15–18 was spoken by the prophet early in the reign of Manasseh, i.e. later than 2 K **18** f, "not so much as a prophecy, a simple prediction, as an attempt to drive Shebna from office. . . . . It must be admitted that Isaiah probably did *not* succeed. The reactionary party seems to have remained in control during the reign of Manasseh. . . . . Fortunately, the moral significance of Isaiah does not depend on the fulfilment of this or that specific prediction. We are dealing not with a walking oracle, but with a great character and a noble life" (p. 639). He then infers from the massacres of Manasseh (2 K **21** 16) "that a conspiracy had been formed against him by the prophetic party which proposed to place Eliakim on the throne" (p. 640). Isaiah he thinks would not "resort to such violent measures," and so the character of Isaiah makes it questionable whether he was the author of vs 20–23. This part would then be due to the prophetic party "who went a step farther than their great leader would approve." This view assumes too much, (*a*) that the terms in vs 20–23 refer to kingly power; (*b*) that Eliakim was of Davidic descent, unless we have a man of non-Davidic origin aiming at the throne, which is again a thing unheard of in Judah; and (*c*) that there was such a plot in the reign of Manasseh, of which we have no proof.

David Francis Roberts

SHEBUEL, shē̇-bū'el, sheb'ū̇-el (שְׁבוּאֵל, *shebhū'ēl;* **Σουβαήλ,** *Soubaḗl*):

(1) A son of Gershom and grandson of Moses (1 Ch **23** 16). He was "ruler over the treasures" (**26** 24). In **24** 20 he is called "Shubael," which is probably the original form of the name (see Gray, *HPN*, 310).

(2) A son of Heman (1 Ch **25** 4), called in ver 20 "Shubael" (LXX as in ver 4).

SHECANIAH, SHECHANIAH, shek-a-nī'a, shē̇-kan'ya (שְׁכַנְיָה, *shekhanyāh* [in 1 Ch **24** 11; 2 Ch **31** 15, *shekhanyāhū*]; B, **Ἰσχανιά,** *Ischaniá,* **Σεκενιά,** *Sekeniá*):

(1) A descendant of Zerubbabel (1 Ch **3** 21.22). This is the same Shecaniah mentioned in Ezr **8** 3.

(2) "The sons of Shecaniah," so the MT of Ezr **8** 5 reads, were among those who returned with Ezra, but a name appears to have been lost from the text, and we should probably read "of the sons of Zattu, Shecaniah the son of Jahaziel" (cf 1 Esd **8** 32, "of the sons of Zathoes, Sechenias the son of Jezelus").

(3) Chief of the tenth course of priests (1 Ch **24** 11).

(4) A priest in the reign of Hezekiah (2 Ch **31** 15).

(5) A contemporary of Ezra who supported him in his opposition to foreign marriages (Ezr **10** 2).

(6) The father of Shemaiah, "the keeper of the east gate" (Neh **3** 29).

(7) The father-in-law of Tobiah the Ammonite (Neh **6** 18).

(8) The eponym of a family which returned with Zerubbabel (Neh **12** 3). It is the same name which, by an interchange of (ב) *bh* and (כ) *kh*, appears as Shebaniah (see SHEBANIAH, [2]) in Neh **10** 4.12.14. HORACE J. WOLF

SHECHEM, shē'kem (שְׁכֶם, *sh^ekhem*, "shoulder"; **Συχέμ**, *Suchém*, **ἡ Σίκιμα**, *hē Síkima*, **τὰ Σίκιμα**, *tá Síkima*, etc; AV gives "Sichem" in Gen **12** 6; and "Sychem" in Acts **7** 16):

1. Historical

This place is first mentioned in connection with Abraham's journey from Haran. At the oak of Moreh in the vicinity he reared his first altar to the Lord in Pal (Gen **12** 6 f). It was doubtless by this oak that Jacob, on his return from Paddan-aram, buried "the strange [ARV "foreign"] gods" (**35** 4). Hither he had come after his meeting with Esau (**33** 18). *Onom* here identifies Shechem with Shalem; but see SHALEM. To the E. of the city Jacob pitched his tent in a "parcel of ground" which he had bought from Hamor, Shechem's father (ver 19). Here also he raised an altar and called it El-Elohe-Israel, "God, the God of Israel" (ver 20). Then follows the story of Dinah's defilement by Shechem, son of the city's chief; and of the treacherous and terrible vengeance exacted by Simeon and Levi (ch **34**). To the rich pasture land near Shechem Joseph came to seek his brethren (**37** 12 ff). It is mentioned as lying to the W. of Michmethath (*el-Makhneh*) on the boundary of Manasseh (Josh **17** 7). It was in the territory of Ephraim; it was made a city of refuge, and assigned to the Kohathite Levites (**20** 7; **21** 21). Near the city the Law was promulgated (Dt **27** 11; Josh **8** 33). When his end was approaching Joshua gathered the tribes of Israel here and addressed to them his final words of counsel and exhortation (ch **24**). Under the oak in the neighboring sanctuary he set up the stone of witness (ver 26). The war of conquest being done, Joseph's bones were buried in the parcel of ground which Jacob had bought, and which fell to the lot of Joseph's descendants (ver 33). Abimelech, whose mother was a native of the city, persuaded the men of Shechem to make him king (Jgs **9** 1-6), evidently seeking a certain consecration from association with "the oak of the pillar that was in Shechem." Jotham's parable was spoken from the cliff of Gerizim overhanging the town (vs 7 ff). After a reign of three years Abimelech was rejected by the people. He captured the city, razed it to the foundations, and sowed it with salt. It was then the seat of Can. idolatry, the temple of Baal-berith being here (Jgs **9** 4.46). In the time of the kings we find that the city was once more a gathering-place of the nation. It was evidently the center, esp. for the northern tribes; and hither Rehoboam came in the hope of getting his succession to the throne confirmed (1 K **12** 1; 2 Ch **10** 1). At the disruption Jeroboam fortified the city and made it his residence (ver 25; *Ant*, VIII, viii, 4). The capital of the Northern Kingdom was moved, however, first to Tirzah and then to Samaria, and Shechem declined in political importance. Indeed it is not named again in the

NĀBLUS AND MT. EBAL.

history of the monarchy. Apparently there were Israelites in it after the captivity, some of whom on their way to the house of the Lord at Jerus met a tragic fate at the hands of Ishmael ben Nethaniah (Jer **41** 5 ff). It became the central city of the Samaritans, whose shrine was built on Mt. Gerizim (Sir **50** 26; *Ant*, XI, viii, 6; XII, i, 1; XIII, iii, 4). Shechem was captured by John Hyrcanus in 132 BC (*Ant*, XIII, ix, 1; *BJ*, I, ii, 6). It appears in the NT only in the speech of Stephen (Acts **7** 16, AV "Sychem"). Some (e.g. Smith, *DB*, s.v.) would identify it with Sychar of Jn **4** 5; but see SYCHAR. Under the Romans it became Flavia Neapolis. In later times it was the seat of a bishopric; the names of five occupants of the see are known.

2. Location and Physical Features

There is no doubt as to the situation of ancient Shechem. It lay in the pass which cuts through Mts. Ephraim, Ebal and Gerizim, guarding it on the N. and S. respectively. Along this line runs the great road which from time immemorial has formed the easiest and the quickest means of communication between the E. of the Jordan and the sea. It must have been a place of strength from antiquity. The name seems to occur in Travels of a Mohar (Max Müller, *Asien u. Europa*, 394), "Mountain of Sahama" probably referring to Ebal or Gerizim. The ancient city may have lain somewhat farther E. than the modern *Nāblus*, in which the Rom name Neapolis survives. The situation is one of great beauty. Near the village and spring *Balata* important excavations were made by Sellin in 1926 and have been continued in '27 and '28. They probably represent the ancient Shechem. The great Hittite gate was found. Also what is believed to be the temple of Baal-berith (Jgs **8** 33; **9** 4). The "filling" in front of the gate of the temple revealed the meaning of the puzzling Heb word "*millō*" literally a "filling" outside the wall to keep the enemy off (Jgs **9** 6). A similar "filling," or revêtment, outside the great wall was found at Kiriath-sepher (*Bibliotheca Sacra*, Oct 26, 390). To the E. of the city, in a recess at the base of Gerizim, is the sanctuary known as *Rijāl el-'Amūd*, lit. "men of the column" or "pillar," where some would locate the ancient "oak of Moreh" or "of the pillar." Others would find it in a little village farther E. with a fine spring, called *Balāṭa*, a name which may be connected with *ballūṭ*, "oak." Still farther to the E. and near the base of Ebal is the traditional tomb of Joseph, a little white-domed building beside a luxuriant orchard. On the slope of the mountain beyond is the village of *'Askar;* see SYCHAR. To the S. of the vale is the traditional Well of Jacob; see JACOB'S WELL. To the S.W. of the city is a small mosque on the spot where Jacob is said to have mourned over the blood-stained coat of Joseph. In the neighboring minaret is a stone whereon the Ten Commandments are engraved in Samaritan characters. The main center of interest in the town is the synagogue of the Samaritans, with their ancient MS of the Pent.

3. Modern Shechem

The modern town contains about 20,000 inhabitants, the great body of them being Moslems. There are some 700 or 800 Christians, chiefly belonging to the Gr Orthodox church. The Samaritans do not total more than 200. The place is still the market for a wide district, both E. and W. of Jordan. A considerable trade is done in cotton and wool. Soap is manufactured in large quantities, oil for this purpose being plentifully supplied by the olive groves. Tanning and the manufacture of leather goods are also carried on. In old times the slopes of Ebal were covered with vineyards; but these formed a source of temptation to the "faithful." They were therefore removed by authority, and their place taken by the prickly pears mentioned above.

W. EWING

SHECHEMITES, shē'kem-īts (הַשִּׁכְמִי, *ha-shikhmī;* **Συχεμεί**, *Suchemeí*): The descendants of Shechem the son of Gilead, a clan of Eastern Manasseh (Nu **26** 31; Josh **17** 2).

SHED, SHEDDING: The three Heb words, *nāghar, sīm* or *sūm* and *shāphakh*, trd "shed" in many OT passages, always mean a "pouring out," and in nearly every case point to the effusion of blood (Gen **9** 6; Nu **35** 33; Dt **21** 7; 2 S **20** 10; 1 Ch **22** 8; Prov **1** 16, etc). The Gr words ἐκχέω, *ekchéō*, and ἐκχύνω, *ekchúnō*, have precisely the same specific meaning (Mt **23** 35; **26** 28; Mk **14** 24; Lk **11** 50; He **9** 22; Rev **16** 6). Sometimes they are tropically used in reference to the outpouring of the Holy Spirit (Acts **2** 33 AV; Tit **3** 6), and to the outpouring of the love of God in the believer's heart (Rom **5** 5).

HENRY E. DOSKER

SHEDEUR, shed'ē-ur, shē-dē'ur (שְׁדֵיאוּר, *shedhē'ūr*, "daybreak"; B, **Σεδιούρ**, *Sedioúr*, **'Εδιούρ**, *Edioúr*): The father of Elizur, the chief of Reuben (Nu **1** 5; **2** 10; **7** 30). Fr. Delitzsch correctly conceives the name as an Assyr compound, *šad uri*, "daybreak." Cf, however, Gray, *HPN*, 169, 197, who emends the text to read *Shaddai 'Ūr*, "Shaddai is flame."

1. Names

SHEEP, shēp: The usual Heb word is צֹאן, *çō'n*, which is often trd "flock," e.g. "Abel . . . . brought of the firstlings of his flock" (Gen **4** 4); "butter of the herd, and milk of the flock" (Dt **32** 14). AV and ERV have "milk of sheep." Cf Arab. ضَأْن, *ḍa'n*. The Gr word is πρόβατον, *próbaton*. For other names, see notes under CATTLE; EWE; LAMB; RAM.

2. Zoölogy

The origin of domestic sheep is unknown. There are 11 wild species, the majority of which are found in Asia, and it is conceivable that they may have spread from the highlands of Central Asia to the other portions of their habitat. In North America is found the "bighorn," which is very closely related to a Kamschatkan species. One species, the *urial* or *sha*, is found in India. The Barbary sheep, *Ovis tragelaphus*, also known as the *aoudad* or *arui*, inhabits the Atlas Mountains of Northwest Africa. It is thought by Tristram to be *zemer*, EV "chamois" of Dt **14** 5, but there is no good evidence that this animal ranges eastward into Bible lands. Geographically nearest is the Armenian wild sheep, *Ovis gmelini*, of Asia Minor and Persia. The Cyprian wild sheep may be only a variety of the last, and the *mouflon* of Corsica and Sardinia is an allied species. It is not easy to draw the line between wild sheep and wild goats. Among the more obvious distinctions are the chin beard and strong odor of male goats. The pelage of all wild sheep consists of hair, not wool, and this indeed is true of some domestic sheep as the fat-rumped short-tailed sheep of Abyssinia and Central Asia. The young lambs of this breed have short curly wool which is the astrachan of commerce. Sheep are geologically recent, their bones and teeth not being found in earlier deposits than the pleiocene or pleistocene. They were, however, among the first of domesticated animals.

3. Sheep of Palestine

The sheep of Syria and Pal are characterized by the possession of an enormous fat tail which weighs many pounds and is known in Arab. as أَلْيَة, *'alyat*, or commonly لِيَّة, *līyat*. This is the אַלְיָה, *'alyāh*, "fat tail" (AV "rump") (Ex **29** 22; Lev **3** 9; **7** 3; **8** 25; **9** 19), which was burned in sacrifice. This is at the present day esteemed a great delicacy. Sheep are kept in large numbers by the Bedawin, but a large portion of the supply of mutton for the cities is from the sheep of Armenia and Kurdistan, of which great droves are brought down to the coast in easy stages. Among the Moslems every well-to-do family sacrifices a sheep at the feast of *al-'aḍḥa'*, the 10th day of the month *dhû-l-ḥijjat*, 40 days after the end of *ramaḍân*, the month of fasting. In Lebanon every peasant family during the summer fattens a young ram, which is

Broad-tailed Sheep.

literally crammed by one of the women of the household, who keeps the creature's jaw moving with one hand while with the other she stuffs its mouth with vine or mulberry leaves. Every afternoon she washes it at the village fountain. When slaughtered in the fall it is called مَعْلُوف, *ma'lûf*, "fed," and is very fat and the flesh very tender. Some of the meat and fat are eaten at once, but the greater part, fat and lean, is cut up fine, cooked together in a large vessel with pepper and salt, and stored in an earthen jar. This, the so-called قَوْرَمَة, *ḳauramat*, is used as needed through the winter.

In the mountains the sheep are gathered at night into folds, which may be caves or inclosures of rough stones. Fierce dogs assist the shepherd in warding off the attacks of wolves, and remain at the fold through the day to guard the slight bedding and simple utensils. In going to pasture the sheep are not driven but are led, following the shepherd as he walks before them and calls to them. "When he hath put forth all his own, he goeth before them, and the sheep follow him: for they know his voice" (Jn **10** 4).

4. OT References

The sheepfolds of Reuben on the plain of Gilead are referred to in Nu **32** 16 and Jgs **5** 16. A cave is mentioned in 1 S **24** 3 in connection with the pursuit of David by Saul. The shepherd origin of David is referred to in Ps **78** 70:

"He chose David also his servant,
And took him from the sheepfolds."

Cf also 2 S **7** 8 and 1 Ch **17** 7.

The shearing of the sheep was a large operation and evidently became a sort of festival. Absalom invited the king's sons to his sheep-shearing in Baal-hazor in order that he might find an opportunity to put Amnon to death while his heart was "merry with wine" (2 S **13** 23–29). The character of the occasion is evident also from the indignation of David at Nabal when the latter refused to provide entertainment at his sheep-shearing for David's young men who had previously protected the flocks of Nabal (1 S **25** 2–13). There is also mention of the sheep-shearing of Judah (Gen **38** 12) and of Laban (Gen **31** 19), on which occasion Jacob stole away with his wives and children and his flocks.

Sheep were the most important sacrificial animals, a ram or a young male being often specified. Ewes are mentioned in Lev **3** 6; **4** 32; **5** 6; **14** 10; **22** 28; Nu **6** 14.

In the Books of Ch we find statements of enormous numbers of animals consumed in sacrifice: "And king Solomon offered a sacrifice of twenty and two thousand oxen, and a hundred and twenty thousand sheep" (2 Ch **7** 5); "And they sacrificed unto Jeh in that day [in the reign of Asa] . . . . seven hundred oxen and seven thousand sheep" (2 Ch **15** 11); at the cleansing of the temple by Hezekiah "the consecrated things were six hundred oxen and three thousand sheep. But the priests were too few, so that they could not flay all the burnt-offerings: wherefore their brethren the Levites did help them" (2 Ch **29** 33 f); and "Hezekiah king of Judah did give to the assembly for offerings a thousand bullocks and seven thousand sheep; and the princes gave to the assembly a thousand bullocks and ten thousand sheep" (2 Ch **30** 24). In the account of the war of the sons of Reuben and their allies with the Hagrites, we read: "And they took away their cattle; of their camels fifty thousand, and of sheep two hundred and fifty thousand, and of asses two thousand, and of men a hundred thousand" (1 Ch **5** 21). Mesha king of Moab is called a "sheep-master," and we read that "he rendered unto the king of Israel the wool of a hundred thousand lambs, and of a hundred thousand rams" (2 K **3** 4).

5. Figurative

Christ is represented as the Lamb of God (Isa **53** 7; Jn **1** 29; Rev **5** 6). Some of the most beautiful passages in the Bible represent God as a shepherd: "From thence is the shepherd, the stone of Israel" (Gen **49** 24); "Jeh is my shepherd; I shall not want" (Ps **23** 1; cf Isa **40** 11; Ezk **34** 12–16). Jesus said "I am the good shepherd; and I know mine own, and mine own know me . . . . and I lay down my life for the sheep" (Jn **10** 14 f). The people without leaders are likened to sheep without a shepherd (Nu **27** 17; 1 K **22** 17; 2 Ch **18** 16; Ezk **34** 5). Jesus at the Last Supper applies to Himself the words of Zec **13** 7; "I will smite the shepherd, and the sheep of the flock shall be scattered abroad" (Mt **26** 31; Mk **14** 27). The enemies of Jeh are compared to the fat of the sacrifice that is consumed away in smoke (Ps **37** 20). God's people are "the sheep of his pasture" (Ps **79** 13; **95** 7; **100** 3). In sinning they become like lost sheep (Isa **53** 6; Jer **50** 6; Ezk **34** 6; Lk **15** 3 ff). In the mouth of Nathan the poor man's one little ewe lamb is a vivid image of the treasure of which the king David has robbed Uriah the Hittite (2 S **12** 3). In Cant **6** 6, the teeth of the bride are likened to a flock of ewes. It is prophesied that "the wolf shall dwell with the lamb" (Isa **11** 6) and that "the wolf and the lamb shall feed together" (Isa **65** 25). Jesus says to His disciples, "I send you forth as sheep in the midst of wolves" (Mt **10** 16; cf Lk **10** 3). In the parable of the Good Shepherd we read: "He that is a hireling, and not a shepherd, whose own the sheep are not, beholdeth the wolf coming, and leaveth the sheep, and fleeth" (Jn **10** 12).

ALFRED ELY DAY

SHEEPCOTE, shēp'kot, shēp'kōt, **SHEEPFOLD,** shēp'fōld (גְּדֵרָה, *gᵉdhērāh*, מִכְלָה, *mikhlāh*, מִשְׁפְּתַיִם, *mishpᵉthayim*, נָוֶה, *nāweh;* αὐλή, *aulḗ*): At night the sheep are driven into a sheepfold if they are in a district where there is danger from robbers or wild beasts. These folds are simple walled inclosures (Nu **32** 16; Jgs **5** 16; 2 Ch **32** 28; Ps **78** 70; Zeph **2** 6; Jn **10** 1). On the top of the wall is heaped thorny brushwood as a further safeguard. Sometimes there is a covered hut in the corner for the shepherd. Where there is no danger the sheep huddle together in the open until daylight, while the shepherd watches over them (Gen **31** 39; Lk **2** 8). In the winter time caves are sought after (1 S **24** 3; Zeph **2** 6). The antiquity of the use of some of the caves for this purpose is indicated by the thick deposit of potassium nitrate formed from the decomposition of the sheep dung.

JAMES A. PATCH

SHEEP GATE (שַׁעַר הַצֹּאן, *sha'ar ha-çō'n* [Neh **3** 1.32; **12** 39]): One of the gates of Jerus, probably near the northeast corner. See JERUSALEM. For the "sheep gate" of Jn **5** 2, see BETHESDA; SHEEP MARKET.

SHEEP MARKET (Jn **5** 2, RV "sheep gate"): The Gr (ἡ προβατική, *hē probatikē*) means simply something that pertains to sheep. See BETHESDA; SHEEP GATE.

SHEEP-MASTER (נֹקֵד, *nōkēdh*, "herdsman," 2 K **3** 4). See SHEEP-SHEARING.

SHEEP-SHEARING, shēp′shēr-ing: The sheep-shearing is done in the springtime, either by the owners (Gen **31** 19; **38** 13; Dt **15** 19; 1 S **25** 2.4) or by regular "shearers" (גָּזַז, *gāzaz*) (1 S **25** 7.11; Isa **53** 7). There were special houses for this work in OT times (2 K **10** 12.14). The shearing was carefully done so as to keep the fleece whole (Jgs **6** 37). The sheep of a flock are not branded but spotted. Lime or some dyestuff is painted in one or more spots on the wool of the back as a distinguishing mark. In 2 K **3** 4, Mesha, the chief or sheikh of Moab, was a sheep-master, lit. "a sheep spotter." JAMES A. PATCH

SHEEPSKIN, shēp′skin. See BOTTLE; DRESS; RAMS' SKINS, etc.

SHEEP TENDING, ten′ding: The Scriptural allusions to pastoral life and the similes drawn from that life are the most familiar and revered in the Bible. Among the first verses that a child learns is "The Lord is my shepherd, I shall not want" (Ps **23** 1 AV, ERV). What follower of the Master does not love to dwell on the words of the "Good Shepherd" chapter in the Gospel of John (Jn **10**)? Jesus must have drawn a sympathetic response when He referred to the relationship of sheep to shepherd, a relationship familiar to all His hearers and doubtless shared by some of them with their flocks. As a rule the modern traveler in the Holy Land meets with disappointment if he comes expecting to see things as they were depicted in the Bible. An exception to this is the pastoral life, which has not changed one whit since Abraham and his descendants fed their flocks on the rich plateaus E. of the Jordan or on the mountains of Pal and Syria. One may count among his most prized experiences the days and nights spent under the spell of Syrian shepherd life. JAMES A. PATCH

SHEERAH, shē′ē-ra (שֶׁאֱרָה, *she'ĕrāh;* A, **Σααρά**, *Saará*, B omits): A daughter of Ephraim, who, according to the MT of 1 Ch **7** 24 (AV "Sherah"), built the two Beth-horons and Uzzen-sheerah. The verse has been suspected because elsewhere in the OT the founders of cities are men. Uzzen-sheerah as a place is unidentified; Conder suggests as the site *Bēt Sīrā*, a village 2 miles S.W. of the Lower Beth-horon (*Mem* **3** 16).

SHEET, shēt. See DRESS; cf Acts **10** 11, "as it were a great *sheet*" (ὀθόνη, *othónē*).

SHEHARIAH, shē-ha-rī′a (שְׁחַרְיָה, *shᵉharyāh*): A Benjamite (1 Ch **8** 26).

SHEKEL, shek′'l, shek′el, shē′kel, shē′kul (שֶׁקֶל, *shekel*): A weight and a coin. The Heb shekel was the 50th part of a mina, and as a weight about 224 grains, and as money (silver) was worth about 2*s.* 9*d.*, or 66 cents. No gold shekel has been found, and hence it is inferred that such a coin was not used; but as a certain amount of gold, by weight, it is mentioned in 2 Ch **3** 9 and is probably intended to be supplied in 2 K **5** 5. The gold shekel was 1/60 of the heavy Bab mina and weighed about 252 grains. In value it was about equal to £2 1*s.* 0*d.*, or $10. See MONEY; WEIGHTS AND MEASURES. In RV of Mt **17** 27 "shekel" replaces "piece of money" of AV, the tr of στατήρ, *statḗr*. See STATER. H. PORTER

SHEKEL OF THE KING'S WEIGHT, or ROYAL SHEKEL (אֶבֶן הַמֶּלֶךְ, *'ebhen ha-melekh*, "stone [i.e. weight] of the king"): The shekel by which Absalom's hair was weighed (2 S **14** 26), probably the light shekel of 130 grains. See WEIGHTS AND MEASURES.

SHEKEL OF THE SANCTUARY, or SACRED SHEKEL (שֶׁקֶל הַקֹּדֶשׁ, *shekel ha-kōdhesh* [Nu **7** *passim*]): The same as the silver shekel mentioned under SHEKEL (q.v.), except in Ex **38** 24, where it is used in measuring gold. The term is used for offerings made for sacred purposes.

SHEKINAH, shē-kī′na (שְׁכִינָה, *shᵉkhīnāh*, "that which dwells," from the vb. שָׁכֵן, *shākhēn*, or שָׁכַן, *shākhan*, "to dwell," "reside"): This word is not found in the Bible, but there are allusions to it in Isa **60** 2; Mt **17** 5; Lk **2** 9; Rom **9** 4. It is first found in the Tgs. See GLORY.

SHELAH, shē′la (שֵׁלָה, *shēlāh;* **Σάλα,** *Sála*):

(1) The youngest son of Judah and the daughter of Shua the Canaanite (Gen **38** 5.11.14.26; **46** 12; Nu **26** 20 [16]; 1 Ch **2** 3; **4** 21). He gave his name to the family of the Shelanites (Nu **26** 20 [16]). Probably "the Shelanite" should be substituted for "the Shilonite" of Neh **11** 5; 1 Ch **9** 5.

(2) (שֶׁלַח, *shelaḥ*): The son or (LXX) grandson of Arpachshad and father of Eber (Gen **10** 24; **11** 13 [12].14.15; 1 Ch **1** 18.24; Lk **3** 35).

(3) Neh **3** 15="Shiloah" of Isa **8** 6. See SILOAM.

SHELANITES, shē′lan-īts, shē-lā′nīts. See SHELAH.

SHELEMIAH, shel-ē-mī′a, shē-lem′ya (שֶׁלֶמְיָה, *shelemyāh;* B, **Σελεμιά,** *Selemiá*, A, **Σελεμίας,** *Selemías*):

(1) One of the sons of Bani who married foreign wives in the time of Ezra (Ezr **10** 39), called "Selemias" in 1 Esd **9** 34.

(2) Father of Hananiah who restored part of the wall of Jerus (Neh **3** 30) (B, Τελεμιά, *Telemiá*, א, Τελεμίας, *Telemías*).

(3) A priest who was appointed one of the treasurers to distribute the Levitical tithes by Nehemiah (Neh **13** 13).

(4) The father of Jehucal (or Jucal) in the reign of Zedekiah (Jer **37** 3; **38** 1; in the second passage the name is *Shelemyāhū*).

(5) The father of Irijah, the captain of the ward, who arrested Jeremiah as a deserter to the Chaldaeans (Jer **37** 13).

(6) 1 Ch **26** 14. See MESHELEMIAH.

(7) Another of the sons of Bani who married foreign wives in the time of Ezra (Ezr **10** 41). It is of interest to note that the order of names in this passage—Sharai, Azarel, and Shelemiah—is almost identical with the names in Jer **36** 26, viz. Seraiah, Azriel, Shelemiah.

(8) Ancestor of Jehudi (Jer **36** 14).

(9) (LXX omits.) Son of Abdeel, one of the men sent by Jehoiakim to seize Baruch and Jeremiah after Baruch had read the "roll" in the king's presence (Jer **36** 26). HORACE J. WOLF

SHELEPH, shē'lef (שָׁלֶף, *shāleph,* in pause; LXX **Σάλεφ,** *Sáleph*): Son of Joktan (Gen **10** 26; 1 Ch **1** 20). Sheleph is the name of a Yemenite tribe or district, named on Sabaean inscriptions and also by Arabian geographers, located in Southern Arabia.

SHELESH, shē'lesh (שֶׁלֶשׁ, *shēlesh;* B, **Σεμή,** *Semḗ,* A, **Σελλής,** *Sellḗs,* Luc., **Σέλεμ,** *Sélem*): An Asherite, son of Helem (1 Ch **7** 35).

SHELOMI, shē-lō'mī, shel'ō-mī (שְׁלֹמִי, *sh^elōmī*): An Asherite (Nu **34** 27).

SHELOMITH, shē-lō'mith, shel'ō-mith (שְׁלֹמִית, *sh^elōmīth;* in Ezr **8** 10, שְׁלוֹמִית, *sh^elōmīth*):

(1) The mother of the man who was stoned for blasphemy (Lev **24** 11) (BAF, Σαλωμείθ, *Salōmeíth,* Luc., Σαλμίθ, *Salmíth*).

(2) Daughter of Zerubbabel (1 Ch **3** 19) (B, Σαλωμεθεί, *Salōmetheí,* A, Σαλωμεθί, *Salōmethí,* Luc., Σαλωμίθ, *Salōmíth*).

(3) One of the "sons of Izhar" (1 Ch **23** 18) (B, Σαλωμώθ, *Salōmṓth,* A, Σαλουμώθ, *Saloumṓth,* Luc., Σαλωμίθ, *Salōmíth*), called "Shelomoth" in **24** 22.

(4) The name of a family whose representatives returned with Ezra (Ezr **8** 10) (B, Σαλειμούθ, *Saleimoúth,* Luc., Σαλιμώθ, *Salimṓth*). The MT here should read, "and the sons of Bani; Shelomith, son of Josiphiah"; and in 1 Esd **8** 36, "of the sons of Banias, Salimoth, son of Josaphias."

Horace J. Wolf

SHELOMOTH, shē-lō'moth, shel'ō-moth, -mōth (שְׁלֹמוֹת, *sh^elōmōth*):

(1) An Izharite (1 Ch **24** 22, BA, Σαλωμώθ, *Salōmṓth,* Luc., Σαλωμίθ, *Salōmíth* = "Shelomith" of **23** 18).

(2) A Levite descended from Eliezer ben Moses (1 Ch **26** 25, Ḳ^erē שְׁלֹמִית, *sh^elōmīth;* **26** 28).

(3) A Gershonite (1 Ch **23** 9, Ḳ^erē שְׁלֹמִית; B, Ἀλωθείμ, *Alōtheím,* A, Σαλωμείθ, *Salōmeíth*).

SHELUMIEL, shē-lū'mi-el (שְׁלֻמִיאֵל, *sh^elumī'ēl;* both the punctuation and interpretation are in doubt. MT punctuates the first element as a passive participle; the use of the participle in compounds is common in Assyr but rare in Heb [cf Gray, *HPN,* 200]. The meaning of the present form, if it be correct, is "at peace with God" [Hommel, *AHT,* 200, "my friend is God"]. LXX reads **Σαλαμιήλ,** *Salamiḗl*): Prince of the tribe of Simeon (Nu **1** 6; **2** 12; **7** 36.41; **10** 19). The genealogy of Judith (**8** 1) is carried back to this Shelumiel or Shelamiel, called there "Salamiel."

Horace J. Wolf

SHEM, shem (שֵׁם, *shēm;* **Σήμ,** *Sḗm*): The eldest son of Noah, from whom the Jews, as well as the Semitic ("Shemitic") nations in general have descended.

1. Position in Noah's Family: His Name

When giving the names of Noah's three sons, Shem is always mentioned first (Gen **9** 18; **10** 1, etc); and though "the elder" in "Shem the brother of Japheth the elder" (**10** 21 m) is explained as referring to Shem, this is not the rendering of Onkelos. His five sons peopled the greater part of West Asia's finest tracts, from Elam on the E. to the Mediterranean on the W. Though generally regarded as meaning "dusky" (cf the Assyr-Bab *sâmu*—also Ham—possibly= "black," Japheth, "fair"), it is considered possible that Shem may be the usual Heb word for "name" (*shēm*), given him because he was the firstborn—a parallel to the Assyr-Bab usage, in which "son," "name" (*šumu*) are synonyms (*W. A. Inscriptions,* V, pl. 23, ll. 29–32*abc*).

Shem, who is called "the father of all the children of Eber," was born when Noah had attained the age of 500 years (Gen **5** 32).

2. History, and the Nations Descended from Him

Though married at the time of the Flood, Shem was then childless. Aided by Japheth, he covered the nakedness of their father, which Ham, the youngest brother, had revealed to them; but unlike the last, Shem and Japheth, in their filial piety, approached their father walking backward, in order not to look upon him. Two years after the Flood, Shem being then 100 years old, his son Arpachshad was born (Gen **11** 10), and was followed by further sons and daughters during the remaining 500 years which preceded Shem's death. Noah's prophetic blessing, on awakening from his wine, may be regarded as having been fulfilled in his descendants, who occupied Syria (Aram), Pal (Canaan), Chaldaea (Arpachshad), Assyria (Asshur), part of Persia (Elam), and Arabia (Joktan). In the first three of these, as well as in Elam, Canaanites had settled (if not in the other districts mentioned), but Shemites ruled, at some time or other, over the Canaanites, and Canaan thus became "his servant" (Gen **9** 25. 26). The tablets found in Cappadocia seem to show that Shemites (Assyrians) had settled in that district also, but this was apparently an unimportant colony. Though designated sons of Shem, some of his descendants (e.g. the Elamites) did not speak a Semitic language, while other nationalities, not his descendants (e.g. the Canaanites), did. See Ham; Japheth; Table of Nations.

T. G. Pinches

SHEMA, shē'ma (שְׁמַע, *sh^emā';* **Σαμαά,** *Samaá*): A city of Judah in the Negeb (Josh **15** 26). If, as some think, identical with Sheba (q.v.) of Josh **19** 2, then the latter must have been inserted here from Josh **15** 26. It is noticeable that the root letters (שמע) were those from which Simeon is derived Shema is probably identical with Jeshua (Neh **11** 26). The place was clearly far S., and it may be *Kh. Sa'wah,* a ruin upon a prominent hilltop between *Kh. 'Attīr* and *Kh. el-Milḥ.* There is a wall around the ruins, of large blocks of conglomerate flint (*PEF,* III, 409, Sh XXV).

E. W. G. Masterman

SHEMA (שֶׁמַע, *shema'*):

(1) A Reubenite (1 Ch **5** 8, BA, Σάμα, *Sáma,* Luc., Σεμεεί, *Semeeí*). See Shimei.

(2) One of the heads of "fathers' houses" in Aijalon, who put to flight the inhabitants of Gath (1 Ch **8** 13, BA, Σάμα, *Sáma,* Luc., Σαμαά, *Samaá*); in ver 21 he is called "Shimei." The statement is very obscure and the whole incident is probably due to some marginal note.

(3) One of those who stood at Ezra's right during the reading of the Law (Neh **8** 4, Σαμαίας, *Samaías*). He is called "Sammus" in 1 Esd **9** 43.

Horace J. Wolf

SHEMAAH, shē-mā'a, shem'ā-a (הַשְּׁמָעָה, *ha-sh^emā'āh;* B, **Ἀμά,** *Amá,* A, **Σαμαά,** *Samaá,* Luc., **Ἀσμά,** *Asmá*): A Benjamite, who was the father, according to the MT, of Ahiezer and Joash; but according to the LXX υἱός, *huiós* = בֵּן (*ben*) instead of בְּנֵי (*b^enē*) of Joash alone (1 Ch **12** 3). The original text may have read בֶּן יְהשָׁמָע, *ben y^ehōshāmā'* (cf הוֹשָׁמָע, *hōshāmā',* of **3** 18); then a dittography of the following ה (*h*) caused the error (Curtis, *ICC*).

SHEMAIAH, shē-mā'ya, shē-mī'a (שְׁמַעְיָה, *sh^ema'yāh* [in 2 Ch **11** 2; **17** 8; **31** 15; **35** 9; Jer **26** 20; **29** 24; **36** 12, *sh^ema'yāhū*], "Jahveh hears"):

The name is most frequently borne by priests, Levites and prophets.

(1) B, Σαμμαίας, *Sammaías*, A, Σαμαίας, *Samaías* (2 Ch **12** 5.7). A prophet who, together with Ahijah, protested against Rehoboam's contemplated war against the ten revolted tribes (1 K **12** 22–24 = 2 Ch **11** 2–4). He declared that the rebellion had Divine sanction. The second Gr account knows nothing of Ahijah in this connection and introduces Shemaiah at the gathering at Shechem where both Jeroboam and Rehoboam were present; it narrates that on this occasion Shemaiah (not Ahijah) rent his garment and gave ten parts to Jeroboam to signify the ten tribes over which he was to become king. (This version, however, is not taken very seriously, because of its numerous inconsistencies.) Shemaiah also prophesied at the invasion of Judah by Shishak (2 Ch **12** 5–7). His message was to the effect that as the princes of Israel had humbled themselves, God's wrath against their idolatrous practices would not be poured out upon Jerus by the hand of Shishak (2 Ch **13** 7). He is mentioned as the author of a history of Rehoboam (2 Ch **12** 15).

(2) Son of Shecaniah (1 Ch **3** 22, Σαμαιά, *Samaiá*), a descendant of Zerubbabel. This is also the name of one of the men who helped to repair the wall (Neh **3** 29, Σεμεΐα, *Semeía* [א] [cf Curtis, *ICC*, in vs 17–24 of 1 Ch **3**]).

(3) A Simeonite (1 Ch **4** 37, B, Συμεών, *Sumeṓn*, A, Σαμαίας, *Samaías*), identical, perhaps, with the Shimei of 1 Ch **4** 26.27.

(4) A Reubenite (1 Ch **5** 4, B, Σεμεεί, *Semeeí*, A, Σεμεΐν, *Semeín*), called Shema in ver 8.

(5) A Merarite Levite (1 Ch **9** 14; Neh **11** 15, Σαμαιά, *Samaiá*), one of those who dwelt in Jerus.

(6) A Levite of the family of Jeduthun, father of Obadiah or Abda (1 Ch **9** 16, B, Σαμειά, *Sameiá*, A, Σαμίας, *Samías*, called "Shammua" in Neh **11** 17).

(7) Head of the Levitical Kohathite clan of Elizaphan in the time of David (1 Ch **15** 8, B, Σαμαίας, *Samaías*, A, Σεμαιά, *Semaiá*, א, Σαμέας, *Saméas;* ver 11, B, Σαμίας, *Samías*, A, Σεμείας, *Semeías*, א, Σαμαί, *Samaí*). He may be the same person as (8).

(8) The scribe (1 Ch **24** 6), the son of Nethanel, who registered the names of the priestly courses.

(9) A Korahite Levite, eldest son of Obed-edom (1 Ch **26** 4.6, B, Σαμαίας, *Samaías*, A, Σαμείας, *Sameías;* ver 7, B, Σαμαί, *Samaí*, A, Σεμεΐα, *Semeía*).

(10) A Levite (2 Ch **17** 8, B, Σαμούας, *Samoúas*, A, Σαμουίας, *Samouías*). One of the commission appointed by Jehoshaphat to teach the book of the Law in Judah. The names of the commissioners as a whole belong to a period later than the 9th cent. (Gray, *HPN*, 231).

(11) One of the men "over the free-will offerings of God" (2 Ch **31** 15, Σεμεεί, *Semeeí*).

(12) A Levite of the family of Jeduthun in the reign of Hezekiah (2 Ch **29** 14), one of those who assisted in the purification of the Temple.

(13) A chief of the Levites (2 Ch **35** 9), called "Samaias" in LXX and 1 Esd **1** 9.

(14) A "chief man" under Ezra (Ezr **8** 16), called "Maasmas" and "Samaias" in 1 Esd **8** 43. 44.

(15) A member of the family of Adonikam (Ezr **8** 13, B, Σαμαία, *Samaía*, A, Σαμαειά, *Samaeiá;* "Samaias" in 1 Esd **8** 39).

(16) A priest of the family of Harim who married a foreign wife (Ezr **10** 21), called "Sameus" in 1 Esd **9** 21.

(17) A layman of the family of Harim who married a foreign wife (Ezr **10** 31), called "Sabbeus" in 1 Esd **9** 32.

(18) A prophet (Neh **6** 10–14, B, Σεμεεί, *Semeeí*, A, Σεμεί, *Semeí*), employed by Sanballat and Tobiah to frighten Nehemiah and hinder the rebuilding of the wall.

(19) One of the 24 courses of priests, 16th under Zerubbabel (Neh **12** 6, א A, Σεμείας, *Semeías*), 15th under Joiakim (Neh **12** 18, א A, Σεμεΐα, *Semeía*), and 21st under Nehemiah (Neh **10** 8, Σαμαιά, *Samaiá*), mentioned in connection with the dedication of the wall.

(20) A priest, descendant of Asaph (Neh **12** 35).

(21) A singer (or clan) participating in the dedication of the wall (Neh **12** 36).

(22) Father of the prophet Urijah (Jer **26** 20, B A, Σαμαίας, *Samaías*, א, Μασέας, *Maséas*).

(23) A false prophet who was upbraided by Jeremiah (**29** 24–32) for attempting to hinder his work. He is styled "the Nehelamite" and was among those carried into captivity with Jehoiachin. In opposition to Jeremiah, he predicted a speedy ending to the captivity. Jeremiah foretold the complete destruction of Shemaiah's family.

(24) Father of Delaiah, who was a prince in the reign of Zedekiah (Jer **36** 12).

(25) "The great," kinsman of Tobias (Tob **5** 13).

Horace J. Wolf

SHEMARIAH, shem-a-rī'a, shē-mär'ya (שְׁמַרְיָה, *shemaryāh* and שְׁמַרְיָהוּ, *shemaryāhū*, "whom Jahveh guards"):

(1) A Benjamite warrior who joined David at Ziklag (1 Ch **12** 5, B, Σαμμαραιά, *Sammaraiá*, א A, Σαμαριά, *Samariá*, Luc., Σαμαρίας, *Samarías*).

(2) A son of Rehoboam (2 Ch **11** 19).

(3) One of the sons of Harim who had married foreign wives (Ezr **10** 32, B, Σαμαρειά, *Samareiá*, Luc., Σαμαρίας, *Samarías*, א A, Σεμαριά, *Semariá*).

(4) One of the sons of Bani who had married foreign wives (Ezr **10** 41, A, Σαμαρείας, *Samareías*, B, Σαμαρειά, *Samareiá*, Luc., Σαμαρίας, *Samarías*).

Horace J. Wolf

SHEMEBER, shem-ē'bẽr, shem'ē-bẽr (שֶׁמְאֵבֶר, *shem'ēbher*): The king of Zeboiim (Gen **14** 2). See Shinab.

SHEMED, shē'med. See Shemer, (4).

SHEMER, shē'mẽr (שֶׁמֶר, *shemer;* Σέμηρ, *Sémēr*, Luc., Σέμμηρ, *Sémmēr*):

(1) The owner of the hill which Omri bought and which became the site of Samaria (1 K **16** 24, שֹׁמְרוֹן, *shōmerōn*). Shemer may be an ancient clan name. The fact, however, that the mountain was called Shomeron when Omri bought it makes one doubt that the city of Samaria was named after Shemer; the passage is questionable. The real etymology of Samaria roots it in "watch mountain" (see Stade, *Zeitschrift*, 165 f).

(2) A Merarite (1 Ch **6** 46 [31], Σέμμηρ, *Sémmēr*).

(3) An Asherite (1 Ch **7** 34, A and Luc., Σώμηρ, *Sṓmēr*), called "Shomer" in ver 32.

(4) A Benjamite (1 Ch **8** 12, B, Σήμηρ, *Sḗmēr;* A, Σέμμηρ, *Sémmēr*, Luc., Σαμαιήλ, *Samaiḗl*); RV "Shemed," AV "Shamed."

The Heb MSS differ; some read "Shemer," others "Shemedh."

Horace J. Wolf

SHEMIDA, SHEMIDAH, shē-mī'da, **SHEMIDAITES**, shē-mī'da-īts (שְׁמִידָע, *shemīdhā'*): A Gileadite clan belonging to Manasseh (Nu **26** 32; Josh **17** 2, B, Συμαρείμ, *Sumareím*, A, Σεμιραέ, *Semiraé*, Luc., Σαμιδάε, *Samidáe;* 1 Ch **7** 19, AV "Shemidah," after whom the Shemidaites [Nu **26** 32] were called).

SHEMINITH, shem'i-nith. See Music; Psalms.

SHEMIRAMOTH, shē̆-mir′a-moth, shē̆-mī′ra-mōth, shem-i-rā′mōth (שְׁמִירָמוֹת, *shemīrāmōth;* in 2 Ch **17** 8, Kethībh שמרימות; Σεμειραμώθ, *Semeiramṓth*): The name of a Levitical family. In 1 Ch **15** 18.20; **16** 5 Shemiramoth is listed among the names of David's choirs; in 2 Ch **17** 8 the same name is given among the Levites delegated by Jehoshaphat to teach the Law in the cities of Judah. According to Schrader (*KAT* [2], 366) the name is to be identified with the Assyr Sammuramat; the latter occurs as a woman's name on the monuments, more esp. on the statues of Nebo from Nimrod. Another suggestion is that Shemiramoth was originally a place-name meaning "image of Shemiram" (=name of Ram or "the Exalted One").

HORACE J. WOLF

SHEMITES, shem′īts. See SEMITES.

SHEMUEL, shē̆-mū′el, shem′ū-el (שְׁמוּאֵל, *shemū′ēl,* "name of God" [?] [1 Ch **6** 33 (18)]; RV Samuel, the prophet [see SAMUEL]; cf Gray, *HPN,* 200, n. 3):

(1) The Simeonite appointed to assist in the division of the land (Nu **34** 20). The MT should be emended to שְׁלֻמִיאֵל, *shelumī′ēl,* to correspond with the form found in **1** 6; **2** 12; **7** 36.41; **10** 19. LXX has uniformly Σαλαμιήλ, *Salamiēl.*

(2) Grandson of Issachar (1 Ch **7** 2) (B, Ἰσαμουήλ, *Isamouēl,* A and Luc., Σαμουήλ, *Samouēl*).

SHEN, shen (הַשֵּׁן, *ha-shēn,* "the tooth" or "peak"; τῆς παλαιᾶς, *tēs palaiás*): A place named only in 1 S **7** 12 to indicate the position of the stone set up by Samuel in connection with the victory over the Philis, "between Mizpah and Shen." LXX evidently read *yāshān,* "old." Probably we should here read *yeshānāh,* as in 2 Ch **13** 19 (*OHL,* s.v.). Then it may be represented by *'Ain Sīnia,* to the N. of *Beitīn.*

SHENAZAR, shē̆-nā′zar: AV=RV SHENAZZAR (q.v.).

SHENAZZAR, shē̆-naz′är (שֶׁנְאַצַּר, *shen′aççar*): A son of Jeconiah (Jehoiachin) and uncle of Zerubbabel (1 Ch **3** 18, BA, Σάνεσαρ, *Sánesar,* Luc., Σάνασαρ, *Sánasar,* Vulg *Sennaser, Senneser*). It is highly probable that Sheshbazzar (Ezr **1** 8.11), "the prince of Judah," and Shenazzar are identical (so Meyer, Rothstein, etc). The name is difficult; some suggest a corruption of שורשבלאצר, *shūshbalaççar,* and as equivalent to Sin-usur, "Sin [the moon-god] protect."

SHENIR, shē′nēr (שְׂנִיר, *senīr,* שְׁנִיר, *shenīr*): Only found in Cant **4** 8 (MT). See SENIR.

SHEOL, shē′ōl (שְׁאוֹל, *she′ōl*):

1. The Name
2. The Abode of the Dead
   (1) Not a State of Unconsciousness
   (2) Not Removed from God's Jurisdiction
   (3) Relation to Immortality
3. Post-canonical Period

1. The Name This word is often trd in AV "grave" (e.g. Gen **37** 35; 1 S **2** 6; Job **7** 9; **14** 13; Ps **6** 5; **49** 14; Isa **14** 11, etc) or "hell" (e.g. Dt **32** 22; Ps **9** 17; **18** 5; Isa **14** 9; Am **9** 2, etc); in 3 places by "pit" (Nu **16** 30.33; Job **17** 16). It means really the unseen world, the state or abode of the dead, and is the equivalent of the Gr *Háidēs,* by which word it is trd in LXX. The Eng. Revisers have acted somewhat inconsistently in leaving "grave" or "pit" in the historical books and putting "Sheol" in the margin, while substituting "Sheol" in the poetical writings, and putting "grave" in the margin ("hell" is retained in Isa **14**). Cf their "Preface." The American Revisers more properly use "Sheol" throughout. The etymology of the word is uncertain. A favorite derivation is from *shā'al,* "to ask" (cf Prov **1** 12; **27** 20; **30** 15.16; Isa **5** 14; Hab **2** 5); others prefer the √ *shā'al,* "to be hollow." The Babylonians are said to have a similar word *Sualu,* though this is questioned by some.

Into Sheol, when life is ended, the dead are gathered in their tribes and families. Hence the

2. Abode of the Dead expression frequently occurring in the Pent, "to be gathered to one's people," "to go to one's fathers," etc (Gen **15** 15; **25** 8.17; **49** 33; Nu **20** 24.28; **31** 2; Dt **32** 50; **34** 5). It is figured as an *underworld* (Isa **44** 23; Ezk **26** 20, etc), and is described by other terms, as "the pit" (Job **33** 24; Ps **28** 1; **30** 3; Prov **1** 12; Isa **38** 18, etc), ABADDON (q.v.) or Destruction (Job **26** 6; **28** 22; Prov **15** 11), the place of "silence" (Ps **94** 17; **115** 17), "the land of darkness and the shadow of death" (Job **10** 21 f). It is, as the antithesis of the living condition, the synonym for everything that is gloomy, inert, insubstantial (the abode of *Rephaim,* "shades," Job **26** 5; Prov **2** 18; **21** 16; Isa **14** 9; **26** 14). It is a "land of forgetfulness," where God's "wonders" are unknown (Ps **88** 10–12). There is no remembrance or praise of God (Ps **6** 5; **88** 12; **115** 17, etc). In its darkness, stillness, powerlessness, lack of knowledge and inactivity, it is a true abode of death (see DEATH); hence is regarded by the living with shrinking, horror and dismay (Ps **39** 13; Isa **38** 17–19), though to the weary and troubled it may present the aspect of a welcome rest or sleep (Job **3** 17–22; **14** 12 f). The Gr idea of Hades was not dissimilar.

(1) *Not a state of unconsciousness.*—Yet it would be a mistake to infer, because of these strong and sometimes poetically heightened contrasts to the world of the living, that Sheol was conceived of as absolutely a place without consciousness, or some dim remembrance of the world above. This is not the case. Necromancy rested on the idea that there was some communication between the world above and the world below (Dt **18** 11); a Samuel could be summoned from the dead (1 S **28** 11–15); Sheol from beneath was stirred at the descent of the king of Babylon (Isa **14** 9 ff). The state is rather that of slumbrous semi-consciousness and enfeebled existence from which in a partial way the spirit might temporarily be aroused. Such conceptions, it need hardly be said, did not rest on revelation, but were rather the natural ideas formed of the future state, in contrast with life in the body, in the absence of revelation.

(2) *Not removed from God's jurisdiction.*—It would be yet more erroneous to speak with Dr. Charles (*Eschatology,* 35 ff) of Sheol as a region "quite independent of Yahwe, and outside the sphere of His rule." "Sheol is naked before God," says Job, "and Abaddon hath no covering" (**26** 6). "If I make my bed in Sheol," says the Psalmist, "behold thou art there" (Ps **139** 8). The wrath of Jeh burns unto the lowest Sheol (Dt **32** 22). As a rule there is little sense of moral distinctions in the OT representations of Sheol, yet possibly these are not altogether wanting (on the above and others points in the theology of Sheol, see ESCHATOLOGY OF THE OT).

(3) *Relation to immortality.*—To apprehend fully the OT conception of Sheol one must view it in its relation to the idea of death as something unnatural and abnormal for man; a result of sin. The believer's hope for the future, so far as this had place, was not prolonged existence in Sheol, but deliverance from it and restoration to new life in

God's presence (Job **14** 13–15; **19** 25–27; Ps **16** 10.11; **17** 15; **49** 15; **73** 24–26; see IMMORTALITY; ESCHATOLOGY OF THE OT; RESURRECTION). Dr. Charles probably goes too far in thinking of Sheol in Pss **49** and **73** as "the future abode of the wicked only; heaven as that of the righteous" (op. cit., 74); but different destinies are clearly indicated.

3. Post-canonical Period

There is no doubt, at all events, that in the post-canonical Jewish lit. (Apoc and apocalyptic) a very considerable development is manifest in the idea of Sheol. Distinction between good and bad in Israel is emphasized; Sheol becomes for certain classes an intermediate state between death and resurrection; for the wicked and for Gentiles it is nearly a synonym for Gehenna (hell). For the various views, with relevant lit. on the whole subject, see ESCHATOLOGY OF THE NT; also DEATH; HADES; HELL, etc. JAMES ORR

SHEPHAM, shē'fam (שְׁפָם, *sh^ephām;* Σεπφάμαρ, *Sepphámar*): A place, probably a hill town, on the ideal eastern boundary of Israel, named in Nu **34** 10, but omitted in Ezk **47** 15–18. It lay between Hazar-enan and Harbel (MT "Hariblah"), which must have been in the neighborhood of Hermon. The word means a "naked" place, and doubtless indicates one of the barer midway ridges of Anti-Lebanon. It was probably the native place of Zabdi the Shiphmite, who was David's chief vine-gardener (1 Ch **27** 27).

SHEPHATIAH, shef-a-tī'a, shĕ-fat'ya (שְׁפַטְיָה, *sh^ephaṭyāh,* "Jeh has judged"):

(1) A son of David, by Abital (2 S **3** 4; 1 Ch **3** 3).

(2) A Benjamite, father of Meshullam, of Jerus (1 Ch **9** 8).

(3) A Benjamite, who joined David at Ziklag (1 Ch **12** 5).

(4) A prince of the Simeonites in the time of David (1 Ch **27** 16).

(5) A son of King Jehoshaphat (2 Ch **21** 2).

(6) A family, 372 of whom returned with Zerubbabel (Ezr **2** 4; Neh **7** 9); 80 more males of this family, with their head, returned with Ezra (Ezr **8** 8).

(7) A servant of Solomon, 392 of whose descendants returned with Zerubbabel (Ezr **2** 57 f; Neh **7** 59 f); "Saphat" in 1 Esd **5** 9 and "Saphatias" in 1 Esd **8** 34.

(8) A Perezzite (Judahite), some of whose descendants dwelt at Jerus in the time of Nehemiah (Neh **11** 4).

(9) A son of Mattan, a contemporary of Jeremiah (Jer **38** 1). JAMES ORR

SHEPHELAH, shef-ē'lä (הַשְּׁפֵלָה, *ha-sh^ephēlāh;* σεφηλά, *sephēlá,* σαφηλά, *saphēlá*):

1. Name and References

The word denotes "lowland," and is variously rendered in AV. It is "vale" in Dt **1** 7; Josh **10** 40; 1 K **10** 27; 2 Ch **1** 15; Jer **33** 13; "valley" in Josh **9** 1; **11** 2.16; **12** 8; **15** 33; Jgs **1** 9; Jer **32** 44; "low plain" in 1 Ch **27** 28; 2 Ch **9** 27; "plain" in Jer **17** 26; Ob ver 19; Zec **7** 7; and "low country" in 2 Ch **28** 18. RV renders uniformly "lowland." As the word always occurs with the definite art., indicating a distinct district, it might have been well to retain it without tr. The boundaries of the district are clearly marked and include much broken country; the hills being low compared with the mountains to the E., but much higher than the plain that runs to the shore. If a tr was to be made, perhaps "lowlands" would have been the best, as applied to the "Low-lands" of Scotland, "which likewise are not entirely plain, but have their groups and ranges of hills" (*HGHL*, 203). In the wide sense the Shephelah included the territory originally given to the tribe of Dan, and also a considerable part of Western and Southwestern Judaea. At an early day the tribes of Dan and Simeon were practically absorbed by Judah, and hence we find in Josh **15** many cities in the Shephelah which belonged to that tribe (*LB*, I, 211).

2. Districts and Features

(1) The sites of many ancient cities named in the Shephelah have been identified. They all lie within the strip of hill country that runs along the western base of the mountains of Judah, terminating in the N. at the Valley of Aijalon. Once indeed the name appears to apply to the low hills N. of this (Josh **11** 16, 'the mount of Israel and its Shephelah'). Every other reference applies only to the S.

Principal G. A. Smith has pointed out the difference between the district to the N. and that to the S. of Aijalon (*HGHL*, 203 ff). "North of Ajalon the low hills which run out on Sharon are connected with the high mountains behind them. You ascend to the latter from Sharon either by long sloping ridges, such as that which today carries the telegraph wire and the high road from Jaffa to *Nāblus;* or else you climb up terraces, such as the succession of ranges closely built upon one another by which the country rises from Lydda to Bethel. That is, the low hills west of Samaria are (to use the Heb phrase) *'ăshēdhōth,* or slopes of the central range, and not a separate group. But S. of Ajalon the low hills do not so hang upon the Central Range, but are separated from the mountains of Judah by a series of valleys, both wide and narrow, which run all the way from Ajalon to near Beersheba; and it is only when the low hills are thus flung off the Central Range into an independent group, separating Judaea from Philistia, that the name Shephelah seems to be applied to them."

(2) On the E. of the Shephelah, then, taking the name in this more limited sense, rises the steep wall of the mountain, into which access is gained only by narrow and difficult defiles. The hills of the Shephelah are from 500 to 800 ft. high, with nothing over 1,500. The formation is soft limestone. In the valleys and upland plains there is much excellent land which supports a fairly good population still. Wheat, barley and olives are the chief products. But ancient wine presses cut in the rocks testify to the culture of the vine in old times. The district is almost entirely dependent on the rain for its water-supply. This is collected in great cisterns, partly natural. The rocks are in many places honeycombed with caves.

The western boundary is not so definite as that on the E. Some have held that it included the Phili plain. This contention draws support from the mention of the Phili cities immediately after those of Judah, which are said to be in the Shephelah (Josh **15** 45 ff; these verses can hardly be ruled out as of a later date). On the other hand the Philis are said to have invaded the cities of the Shephelah (2 Ch **28** 18), which implies that it was outside their country. In later times the Talm (Jerus *Sh^ebhī'īth* **9** 2) distinguishes the Mountain, the Shephelah, and the Plain. See, however, discussion in Buhl (*GAP*, 104, n.; and G. A. Smith, *Expos*, 1896, 404 ff).

3. The Five Valleys

The Shephelah is crossed by five wide valleys which furnish easy access from the plain. These are of importance chiefly because from each of them a way, crossing the "foss," enters one of the defiles by which alone armies could approach the uplands of Judaea. The hills of Judaea are much steeper on the east than on the west, where they fall toward Philistia in long-rolling hills, forming the Shephelah.

(1) The most noteworthy of these is the Vale of Aijalon. It winds its way first in a northeasterly direction, past the Beth-horons, then, turning to the S.E., it reaches

the plateau at *el-Jīb*, the ancient Gibeon, fully 5 miles N.W. of Jerus. This is the easiest of all the avenues leading from the plain to the heights, and it is the one along which the tides of battle most frequently rolled from the days of Joshua (Josh **10** 12) to those of the Maccabees (1 Macc **3** 16 ff, etc). It occupies also a prominent place in the records of the Crusades.

(2) *Wâdy eṣ-Ṣurār*, the Valley of Sorek, crosses the Shephelah S. of Gezer, and pursues a tortuous course past Beth-shemesh and Kiriath-jearim to the plateau S.W. of Jerus. This is the line followed by the Jaffa-Jerus Railway.

(3) *Wâdy es-Sunṭ* runs eastward from the N. of *Tell eṣ-Ṣâfieh* (Gath) up the Vale of Elah to its confluence with *Wâdy es-Ṣur* which comes in from the S. near *Khirbet Shuweikeh* (Socoh); and from that point, as *Wâdy el-Jindy*, pursues its way S. of Timnah to the uplands W. of Bethlehem.

(4) *Wâdy el-'Afranj* crosses the plain from Ashdod (Esdud), passes *Beit Jibrīn* (Eleutheropolis), and winds up through the mountains toward Hebron.

(5) *Wâdy el-Ḥesy*, from the sea about 7 miles N. of Gaza, runs eastward with many windings, passes to the N. of Lachish, and finds its way to the plateau some 6 miles S.W. of Hebron.

From the Shephelah thus opened the gateways by which Judaea and Jerus might be assailed: and the course of these avenues determined the course of much of the history. It is evident that the Shephelah lay open to attack from both sides, and for centuries it was the debatable land between Israel and the Philis. The ark for a time sojourned in this region (1 S **5** 6 f). In this district is laid the scene of Samson's exploits (Jgs **14–16**). The scene of David's memorable victory over the giant was in the *Wâdy eṣ-Sunṭ*, between Socoh and Azekah (1 S **17** 1). David found refuge here in the cave of Adullam (1 S **22** 1). For picturesque and vivid accounts of the Shephelah and of the part it played in history see Smith, *HGHL*, 201 ff; A. Henderson, *Palestine, Its Historical Geography*, 1894. W. Ewing

SHEPHER, shē′fẽr (שֶׁפֶר, *shepher*, "beauty"): A mount near which the Israelites encamped (Nu **33** 23 f). See Wanderings of Israel.

SHEPHERD, shep′ẽrd (רֹעֶה, *rō'eh*, רֹעִי, *rō'ī*; **ποιμήν**, *poimēn*, "a feeder"): The sheep owner frequently tends the flocks himself (Gen **4** 4; **30** 40; cf Ezk **34** 12), but more often he delegates the work to his children (Gen **29** 9; 1 S **16** 19; **17** 15) or relatives (Gen **31** 6). In such cases the sheep have good care because the keepers have a personal interest in the well-being of the animals, but when they are attended by a hireling (1 S **17** 20) the flocks may be neglected or abused (Isa **56** 10.11; Ezk **34** 8.10; Zec **11** 15.17; Jn **10** 12). The chief care of the shepherd is to see that the sheep find plenty to eat and drink. The flocks are not fed in pens or folds, but, summer and winter, must depend upon foraging for their sustenance (Ps **23** 2). In the winter of 1910–11 an unprecedented storm ravaged Northern Syria. It was accompanied by a snowfall of more than 3 ft., which covered the ground for weeks. During that time, hundreds of thousands of sheep and goats perished, not so much from the cold as from the fact that they could get no food. Goats hunt out the best feeding-grounds, but sheep are more helpless and have to be led to their food (cf Nu **27** 16.17); nor do they possess the instinct of many other animals for finding their way home (cf Ezk **34** 6–8). Flocks should be watered at least once a day. Where there are springs or streams this is an easy matter. Frequently the nearest water is hours away. One needs to travel in the dry places in Syria or Pal, and then enter the watered valleys like those in Edom where the flocks are constantly being led for water, to appreciate the Psalmist's words, "He leadeth me beside still waters." Sometimes water can be obtained by digging shallow wells (Gen **26** 18–22. 25.32). The shepherd frequently carries with him a pail from which the sheep can drink when the water is not accessible to them. On the mountain tops the melting snows supply the needed water. In other districts it is drawn from deep wells (Gen **29** 2; Jn **4** 6). The usual time for watering is at noon, at which time the flocks are led to the watering-places (Gen **29** 2.3). After drinking, the animals lie down or huddle together in the shade of a rock while the shepherd sleeps. At the first sound of his call, which is usually a peculiar guttural sound, hard to imitate, the flock follow off to new

Shepherd and Sheep.

feeding-grounds. Even should two shepherds call their flocks at the same time and the sheep be intermingled, they never mistake their own master's voice (Jn **10** 3–5).

The shepherd's equipment is a simple one. His chief garment is a cloak woven from wool or made from sheepskins. This is sleeveless, and so made that it hangs like a cloak on his shoulders. When he sleeps he curls up under it, head and all. During the summer a lighter, short-sleeved *'aba* or coat is worn. He carries a **staff** or **club** (see STAFF), and a characteristic attitude is to make a rest for his arms by placing his staff on his shoulders against the back of his neck. When an esp. productive spot is found, the shepherd may pass the time, while the animals are grazing, by playing on his pipe (Jgs **5** 16). He sometimes carries a **sling** (קֶלַע, *ḳela'*) of goat's hair (1 S **17** 40). His chief belongings are kept in a skin pouch or bag (כְּלִי, *k^elī*) (1 S **17** 40). This bag is usually a whole tawed skin turned wrong side out, with the legs tied up and the neck forming the opening. He is usually aided in the keeping and the defending of the sheep by a dog (Job **30** 1). In Syria the Kurdish dogs make the best protectors of the sheep, as, unlike the cowardly city dogs, they are fearless and will drive away the wild beasts. The shepherd is often called upon to aid the dogs in defending the sheep (Gen **31** 39; 1 S **17** 34.35; Isa **31** 4; Jer **5** 6; Am **3** 12).

Figurative: The frequent use of the word "shepherd" to indicate a spiritual overseer is familiar to Bible readers (Ps **23** 1; **80** 1; Eccl **12** 11; Isa **40** 4; **63** 14; Jer **31** 10; Ezk **34** 23; **37** 24; Jn **21** 15–17; Eph **4** 11; 1 Pet **5** 1–4). We still use the term "pastor," lit. "a shepherd." Leaders in temporal affairs were also called shepherds (Gen **47** 17 m; Isa **44** 28; **63** 11). "Sheep without a shepherd" typified individuals or nations who had forgotten Jeh (Nu **27** 17; 1 K **22** 17; 2 Ch **18** 16; Ezk **34** 5.8; Zec **10** 2; Mt **9** 36; Mk **6** 34). Jesus is spoken of as the good shepherd (Jn **10** 14); chief shepherd (1 Pet **5** 4); great shepherd (He **13** 20); the one shepherd (Jn **10** 16). "He will feed his flock like a shepherd, he will gather the lambs in his arm, and carry them in his bosom, and will gently lead those that have their young" (Isa **40** 11) is a picture drawn from pastoral life of Jeh's care over His children. A strong sympathy for helpless animals, though sometimes misdirected, is a marked characteristic of the people of Bible lands. The birth of offspring in a flock often occurs far off on the mountain side. The shepherd solicitously guards the mother during her helpless moments and picks up the lamb and carries it to the fold. For the few days, until it is able to walk, he may carry it in his arms or in the loose folds of his coat above his girdle. See also SHEEP. JAMES A. PATCH

SHEPHI, shē'fī, **SHEPHO,** shē'fō (שְׁפִי, *sh^ephī;* B, **Σώβ,** *Sṓb,* A, **Σωφάρ,** *Sōphár,* Luc., **Σαπφεί,** *Sappheí* [1 Ch **1** 40]; or **Shepho,** שְׁפוֹ, *sh^ephō;* A, **Σώφ,** *Sṓph,* Luc., **Σωφάν,** *Sōphán* [Gen **36** 23]): A Horite chief.

SHEPHUPHAM, SHEPHUPHAN, shē-fū'fam or -fan (שְׁפוּפָם, *sh^ephūphām;* B A, **Σωφάν,** *Sōphán,* Luc., **Σοφάν,** *Sophán* [Nu **26** 39 (43)]; or **Shephuphan,** שְׁפוּפָן, *sh^ephūphān;* B, **Σωφαρφάκ,** *Sōpharphák,* A, **Σωφάν,** *Sōphán,* Luc., **Σεπφάμ,** *Sepphám* [1 Ch **8** 5], "a kind of serpent," Gray, *HPN,* 95): Eponym of a Benjamite family. The name occurs in Gen **46** 21 as "Muppim" and in 1 Ch **7** 12.15; **26** 16 as "Shuppim." It is almost impossible to arrive at the original form; the gentilic "Shuphamites" appears in Nu **26** 39 (43).

SHERAH, shē'ra. See SHEERAH.

SHERD, shûrd. See POTSHERD.

SHEREBIAH, sher-ē-bī'a, shē-reb'ya (שֵׁרֵבְיָה, *shērēbhyah,* "God has sent burning heat"[?]; the form is doubtful): A post-exilic priest and family. Sherebiah, who joined Ezra at the river Ahava (Ezr **8** 18; LXX omits), and had charge, along with eleven others, of the silver and gold and vessels for the Temple (ver 24, B A, Σαραιά, *Saraiá,* Luc., Σαραβίας, *Sarabías*). He aided in the exposition of the Law (Neh **8** 7), was among those who made public confession (**9** 4) and sealed the covenant (**10** 12 [13]). His name also appears in **12** 8.24. In every passage listed above except **10** 12 (13), B A read Σαραβία, *Sarabía,* Luc., Σαραβίας, *Sarabías.* In 1 Esd **8** 47 the name appears as "Asebebia," RV "Asebebias"; in ver 54, "Esebrias," RV "Eserebias," and 1 Esd **9** 48, "Sarabias." Many of the companion-names on the lists are plainly ethnic (Cheyne). HORACE J. WOLF

SHERESH, shē'resh (שֶׁרֶשׁ, *shāresh;* B, **Σοῦρος,** *Soúros,* A, **Σόρος,** *Sóros,* Luc., **Φάρες,** *Pháres,* **Φόρος,** *Phóros*): A Machirite name in a genealogy of Manasseh (1 Ch **7** 16).

SHEREZER, she-rē'zēr (Zec **7** 2 AV). See SHAREZER.

SHERGHAT, shûr'gat, sher'gat, **or ASSHUR, or ASSUR:** The name of **the first capital city of Assyria** is known by the Arabs as *Ḳala'at Sherghat,* or the Fortress of Sherghat. Its ancient name was Asshur or Assur (Gen **10** 11 m). From it was derived the name of the country, Assyria, and of the people, Assyrians. The date of the founding of the city is not known. Apparently about 2000 BC a colony of Babylonians migrated northward along the Tigris River and settled upon the right shore about halfway between the Upper and Lower Zab, or halfway between the modern cities of Mosul and Bagdad. Assur, the local deity of the place, became the national god of Assyria. It is uncertain whether the deity gave the name to the city, or the city to the deity, but probably an early shrine of Assur stood there, and the people, building their city about it, became known as the Assyrians. At first the city was a Bab dependency, governed by priests from Babylonia. In time, as the city acquired a political significance, the power of the priesthood declined; allegiance to Babylonia ceased, and the Assyr empire came into existence. About 1200 BC the political power had so increased that a new capital, Nimrud (Calah) was built to the N. near the junction of the Upper Zab with the Tigris. In 722 BC the capital was transferred by Sargon to his new city, Dur-Sharrukin, and in 705 BC Sennacherib enlarged Nineveh, and it remained the capital city till the fall of the empire in 606 BC. Assur, however, as the seat of the national deity, never ceased to be the chief religious center.

The mounds of Assur are among the largest in Mesopotamia. They rise abruptly from the Tigris, which they follow for about half a mile, and extend a quarter of a mile inland. In the surrounding plain are other mounds, marking the sites of temples, and indicating that a part of the city was without the walls. At the northern end the mounds are surmounted by a high conical peak, which represents the tower or *ziggurat* of the temple of Assur.

Of the early excavators Layard and Rassam examined the ruins, but the fanaticism of the surrounding Arabs prevented extensive **excavations.** In 1904 Dr. W. Andrae, for the Deutsche Orientgesellschaft, began the systematic excavations which have been continued by Dr. P. Maresch for ten years. Discoveries of the greatest importance have been made. The city was found to have been surrounded on the land side by **a double wall.** The space between the walls, several rods in width, was occupied by houses, possibly the homes of the soldiers. The base of the outer wall was of stone; above it were mud bricks strengthened at intervals with courses of burned bricks. Along the outer upper edge was a parapet, protected by battlements. From the floor of the parapet small holes were bored vertically downward, so that the soldiers, without exposing themselves, might discharge their arrows at the enemy close to the base of the wall. Many of the holes are still visible. The wall was pierced with several gateways; the names "Gate of Assur," "Gate of the Tigris," "Gate of the Sun God" have survived. At the sides of the gateways were small chambers for the guards, and from them passageways led to the parapet above. The gates were reached by bridges which spanned the moat. Along the river side the city was protected by a high steep embankment, which was built partly of limestone, but chiefly of square bricks laid in bitumen.

Loopholes through Which Arrows Were Shot.

The temple of Assur at the northern end of the city has been thoroughly excavated. With its outer and inner court and tower it conformed in its general plan to the older Bab temples. Several of the **palaces** of the early kings were discovered, but the best-preserved of the palaces was one which the excavators have called the residence of the mayor. It stood near the western edge of the city on the main street which ran from the western gate to the Tigris. It consisted of two courts surrounded by chambers. Grooves in the paved floor conducted fresh water to the kitchen, the baths and the chambers, and round tiles beneath the floor carried away the waste water to the arched city sewer and to the Tigris. To the rear of the mayor's house was a crowded residential quarter. The streets were very narrow and winding. The houses were exceedingly small; in some of them one could not lie at full length upon the floor. Among their ruins appeared little but stone mortars and broken pottery and other essential household implements.

Near the southern end of the city a most remarkable discovery was made. About a hundred **monoliths,** from 4 to 8 ft. high, were found still standing erect. On the side of each one, near the top, was an inscription of several lines, dedicating the stone to some individual who had been of great service to the state. They were not tombstones; apparently they had been erected during the lifetime of the people whom they honored. Of the greatest interest was one which bore the name of Sammuramat or **Semiramis,** the once supposed mythical queen of Nineveh. Its tr reads: "The column of Sa-am-mu-ra-mat, the palace wife of Samsi-Adad,

Monuments in Assur Discovered by the Germans.

king of the world, king of Assyria, the mother of Adad-Nirari, king of the world, king of Assyria, the . . . . of Shalmaneser, king of the four regions." The inscription not only makes Semiramis a historical character, but places her among the foremost rulers of Assyria.

The tombs of the kings and nobles were found deep in the ruins in the very center of the city. They were rectangular structures of cut stone, covered above with a rounded arch of burned bricks. In some cases the massive stone doors still turned in their sockets. The roofs of many of them had fallen in; others, which were intact, were filled with dust. From the tombs a vast amount of silver, gold and copper jewelry and stone beads and ornaments were recovered.

One of the **chief temples** of the city stood at a short distance without the eastern wall. Nothing but its foundations remain. However, the temple was surrounded by a park, traces of which still exist. The soil of the surrounding plain is a hard clay, incapable of supporting vegetable life. Into the clay large holes, several feet in diameter, were dug and filled with loam. Long lines of the holes may still be traced, each marking the spot where a tree, probably the date palm, stood in the temple park.

A modern cemetery on the summit of the main mound is still used by the neighboring Arabs, and therefore it will likely prevent the complete excavation of this oldest of the capital cities of Assyria. See further ASSYRIA. E. J. BANKS

SHERIFF, sher′if (Aram. תִּפְתָּיֵא, *tiphtāyē′*, "judicial," "a lawyer," "a sheriff" [Dnl **3** 2 f]): Probably a "lawyer" or "jurist" whose business it was to decide points of law. At best, however, the tr "sheriff" is but a conjecture.

SHESHACH, shē′shak (שֵׁשַׁךְ, *shēshakh*, as if "humiliation"; cf שָׁכַךְ, *shākhakh*, "to crouch"): The general explanation is that this is "a cypher-form of 'Bābel' (Babylon)" which is the word given as equivalent to "Sheshach" by the Tg (Jer **25** 26; **51** 41; LXX omits in both passages). By the device known as Atbaš (אתבש), i.e. disguising a name by substituting the last letter of the alphabet for the first, the letter next to the last for the second, etc, ששך is substituted for בָּבֶל, *bābhel*. This theory has not failed of opposition. Delitzsch holds that "Sheshach" represents *Šiš-kû-KI* of an old Bab regal register, which may have stood for a part of the city of Babylon. (For a refutation of this interpretation see Schrader, *KAT*², 415; *COT*, II, 108 f.) Lauth, too, takes "Sheshach" to be a Hebraization of *Šiška*, a Bab district. Winckler and Sayce read *Uru-azagga*. Finally, Cheyne and a number of critics hold that the word has crept into the text, being "a conceit of later editors." See further JEREMIAH, 6. HORACE J. WOLF

SHESHBAZZAR, shesh-baz'ar (שֵׁשְׁבַּצַּר, *sheshbaççar*, or 'שֵׁ, *shēshbaççar*): Sheshbazzar is the Heb or Aram. form of the Bab *Shamash-aba-uṣur*, or *Shamash-bana-uṣur:* "Oh Shamash, protect the father." It is possible that the full name was *Shamash-ban-zeri-Babili-uṣur*, "Oh Shamash, protect the father [builder] of the seed of Babylon." (See Zerubbabel, and compare the Bab names *Ashur-bana-uṣur*, *Ban-ziri*, *Nabu-ban-ziri*, *Shamash-ban-apli*, *Shamash-apil-uṣur*, *Shamash-ban-aḫi*, and others in Tallquist's *Neubabylonisches Namenbuch*, and the Aram. names on nos. 35, 44, 36, and 45 of Clay's *Aramaic Dockets*.) If this latter was the full name, there would be little doubt that Sheshbazzar may have been the same person as Zerubbabel, since the former is called in Ezr **5** 14 the governor of Judah, and the latter is called by the same title in Hag **1** 1.14; **2** 2.21. It is more probable, however, that Sheshbazzar and Zerubbabel were different persons, and that Sheshbazzar was governor of Judah in the time of Cyrus and Zerubbabel in that of Darius. It is possible that Sheshbazzar came to Jerus in the time of Cyrus and laid the foundations, and that Zerubbabel came later in the time of Darius Hystaspis and completed the building of the temple (cf Ezr **2** 68; **4** 2; Hag **1** 14).

According to Ezr **1** 8 Sheshbazzar was the prince (Hannasi) of Judah into whose hands Cyrus put the vessels of the house of the Lord which Nebuchadnezzar had brought forth out of Jerus and had put in the house of his gods. It is further said in ver 11 that Sheshbazzar brought these vessels with them of the captivity which he brought up from Babylon to Jerus. In Ezr **5** 14 f it is said that these vessels had been delivered by Cyrus unto one whose name was Sheshbazzar, whom he had made governor (*peḥāh*), and that Sheshbazzar came and laid the foundations of the house of God which was in Jerus. See SANABASSAR. R. DICK WILSON

SHESHAI, shē'shī (שֵׁשַׁי, *shēshay*): One of the sons of Anak, perhaps an old Hebronite clan name. (Sayce combines the name with *Šasu*, √ שסה, the Egyp name for the Syrian Bedouins.) The clan lived in Hebron at the time of the conquest and was expelled by Caleb (Nu **13** 22, B, Σεσσεί, *Sesseí*, A, Σεμεί, *Semeí;* Josh **15** 14, B, Σουσεί, *Souseí*, A, Σουσαί, *Sousaí;* Jgs **1** 10, B, Σεσσεί, *Sesseí*, A, Γεθθί, *Geththí*).

SHESHAN, shē'shan (שֵׁשָׁן, *shēshān;* **Σωσάν**, *Sōsán*): A Jerahmeelite whose daughter married his servant Jarha (1 Ch **2** 31.34.35). The genealogical list which follows embraces some very early names (cf Curtis, *ICC*, ad loc.).

SHETH. See SETH.

SHETHAR, shē'thär (שֵׁתָר, *shēthar;* B and Luc., **Σαρσαθαῖος**, *Sarsathaíos*, A, **Σαρέσθεος**, *Saréstheos*): One of the "seven princes" at the court of Ahasuerus (Est **1** 14); these princes "sat first in the kingdom" and had the right of entrance to the king's presence at any time, except when he was in the company of one of his wives. (According to Marquart, *Fund.*, 69, Shethar comes from שרשתר, with which the Pers *šiyātis*, "joy," is to be compared.) The word has never really been satisfactorily explained; it is presumably Pers.

SHETHAR-BOZENAI, shē'thär-boz'ē-nī, **SHETHAR-BOZNAI**, shē'thär-boz'nī, -boz'nā-ī, (שְׁתַר בּוֹזְנַי, *shᵉthar bōznay*, meaning uncertain): The name of a Pers (?) official mentioned with Tattenai in connection with the correspondence with Darius relative to the rebuilding of the Temple (Ezr **5** 3.6; **6** 6.12; B, Σαθαρβουζάν, *Satharbouzán*, A, Σαθαρβουζαναί, *Satharbouzanaí*, in **5** 3; **6** 13; Σαθαρβουζανής, *Satharbouzanḗs*, in **5** 6; Σαθαρβουζανέ, *Satharbouzané*, in **6** 6; Luc., throughout, Θαρβουζαναῖος, *Tharbouzanaíos*), called in 1 Esd **6** 3.7.27; **7** 1 "Shathrabuzanes."

Among the conjectures as to the meaning and derivation of the name, the following may be mentioned: (1) Shethar-boznai may be a corruption of מְתַרְבּוֹזְנַי, *mᵉtharbōznay* = Μιθροβουζάνης, *Mithrobouzánēs*, Old Pers *Mithrobauzana*—i.e. "Mithra is deliverer." (2) שֵׁתַר is identical with the Old Pers *Çithra* ("seed," "brilliance"); names have been found that are confounded with this word. (3) שְׁתַר בּוֹזְנַי may be a title, but שְׂתַר, *sᵉthar*, must then be read for שְׁתַר, *shᵉthar*. (4) שתר בזני is equivalent to the Old Pers *Sêthrabûzana*, "empire-delivering"; cf *EB*, art. "Shethar-boznai," and *BDB*. HORACE J. WOLF

SHEVA, shē'va (שְׁוָא, *shᵉwā';* B, **Σαού**, *Saoú*, A, **Σαούλ**, *Saoúl*, Luc., **Σουέ**, *Soué*):

(1) A son of Caleb by his concubine Maacah (1 Ch **2** 49).

(2) See SHAVSHAH.

SHEW, SHOW, shō: "Show" (so always ARV) is simply a modernized spelling of "shew" (so always in AV and generally in ERV), and it should be carefully noted that "shew" is never pronounced "shoo," not even in the combination "shewbread"; cf "sew."

In AV "shew" as a vb. is the tr of a very large number of terms in the original. This number is reduced considerably by RV (esp. in the NT), but most of these changes are to secure uniformity of rendition, rather than to correct obscurities. The proper sense of the vb., of course, is "to cause a person to see" (Gen **12** 1, etc) or "to cause a thing [or "person"] to be seen" (Dt **4** 35; Jgs **4** 22, etc). "Seeing," naturally, can be taken as intellectual or moral (Jer **38** 21; Ps **16** 11, etc), and can even be used for "hearing" (Isa **43** 9, etc; contrast RV 1 S **9** 27). Hence "shew" can be used as a general tr for the most various phrases, as "be shewed" for γίνομαι, *gínomai*, "come to pass" (Acts **4** 22, RV "be wrought"); "shew forth themselves" for ἐνεργέω, *energéō*, "be active" (Mt **14** 2, RV "work"); "shew" for ποιέω, *poiéō*, "do" (Acts **7** 36, RV "having wrought"); for διηγέομαι, *diēgéomai*, "relate" (Lk **8** 39, RV "declare"); for δηλόω, *dēlóō*, "make clear" (2 Pet **1** 14, RV "signify"), etc. In Cant **2** 9 AV (ERV) "shewing himself" and ARV (ERVm) "glanceth" both miss the poetry of the original: "His eyes shine in through the lattice" (*çûç*, "blossom," "sparkle").

AV's uses of the noun "shew" usually connote appearance in contrast to reality. So Lk **20** 47, "for a shew" (πρόφασις, *próphasis*, "apparent cause," RV "pretence"); Col **2** 23, "shew of wisdom" (so RV, λόγος, *lógos*, "word," "repute"); Gal **6** 12, "make a fair shew" (so RV, εὐπροσωπέω, *euprosōpéō*, "have a fair face"); Ps **39** 6, "vain shew" (so ARV צֶלֶם, *çelem*, "image," RVm "shadow"). However, in Sir **43** 1 (ὅραμα, *hórama*, "spectacle" [so RV]) and in Col **2** 15 (δειγματίζω, *deigmatízō*, "to display") "shew" = "spectacle."

In Isa **3** 9 "the shew of their countenance" is a bad tr for "their respect of persons" (so RVm for *hakkārath p^enēhem*). The "shewing" of the Baptist "unto Israel" (Lk **1** 80 AV, ERV) is of course his appearing to begin his ministry.

BURTON SCOTT EASTON

SHEWBREAD, shō'bred, **THE** (לֶחֶם הַפָּנִים, *leḥem ha-pānīm*, "bread of the presence"; ἡ πρόθεσις τῶν ἄρτων, *hē próthesis tōn ártōn* [He **9** 2]; ARV "showbread." See SHEW):

1. The Term

The marginal reading of Ex **25** 30; **35** 13, RV "Presence-bread," exactly gives the meaning of the Heb. In 2 Ch **2** 4 it is spoken of as the "continual showbread," because it was to be before Jeh "alway" (Ex **25** 30).

2. Mosaic Regulations

Later Judaism has much to say as to the number and size of the loaves, more properly thin cakes, which bore this name, together with many minute regulations as to the placing of the loaves, the covering of them with frankincense, and other ritualistic vapidities. All that the Mosaic legislation required was that, once in every week, there should be twelve cakes of unleavened bread, each containing about four-fifths of a peck of fine flour, placed in two piles upon a pure table with frankincense beside each pile and changed every Sabbath day (Lev **24** 5–9). From the description of the table upon which the flat cakes were to lie (Ex **25** 23–30; **37** 10–16), it held a series of golden vessels comprising dishes, spoons, flagons and bowls. As it is unlikely that empty cups were set before Jeh—they being described as "the vessels which were upon the table"—we may conclude that the table held presentation offerings of "grain and wine and oil," the three chief products of the land (Dt **7** 13). The "dishes" were probably the salvers on which the thin cakes were piled, six on each. The "flagons" would contain wine, and the bowls (made with spouts, "to pour withal"), the oil; while the "spoons" held the frankincense, which was burned as a memorial, "even an offering made by fire unto Jeh." The cakes themselves were eaten by the priests on every Sabbath day, as being among the "most holy" sacrifices. Each of the synoptists refers to the incident of David and his companions having eaten of the shewbread (*hoi ártoi tḗs prothéseōs*), as told in 1 S **21** 4–6 (Mt **12** 4; Mk **2** 26; Lk **6** 4).

3. On Journeyings

At such times as the removal of the tabernacle took place, the separate appointments of the table of incense were not parted from it, but were carried with it—dishes, spoons, bowls, and cups (Nu **4** 7). These, like the other furniture, were borne by the Kohathite Levites, but a few articles of lighter weight were in the personal care of the high priest. These comprised the oil for the candlestick, the sweet incense, the holy oil of consecration, and the meal for the continual bread offering (Nu **4** 7.8.16). Small quantities of these alone would be borne from place to place, such as would be needed with the least delay to refurnish the vessels of the sanctuary on every reërection of the tent of meeting.

4. Significance

With this view of the nature, we have a natural and adequate sense of the meanings and importance of the shewbread, in the economy of the temple ritual and service. It was a continual reminder to the worshippers of the truth that man does not live by bread alone, emphasized by the fact that these most holy offerings were afterward eaten. It was the OT version of the prayer, "Give us this day our daily bread"; and in the fact that the holy table was never for a moment left without some loaves lying on it, we have the symbol of man's continued and unbroken dependence upon God. Even during the travels of the table of shewbread with the tabernacle, the "continual bread" was required to be in its place thereon (Nu **4** 7).

It has been usual to say that "frankincense in golden urns stood beside the twelve loaves" (*EB*, IV, col. 4212). But this is a mere repetition of a Jewish legend, as spoons were the recognized holders of the frankincense to be burned (cf Nu **7** 14 ff). Such spoons formed a part of the equipment of the shewbread table, and on the removal of the week-old cakes the spoons were carried forth and the frankincense in them burned on the great altar on the Sabbath day. If this were done while the grain and wine and oil were being consumed, it would derive additional significance, as betokening the gratitude and adoration of the representative recipients of the bounties of Nature, just as the daily burning of incense in the holy place betokened the worship and adoration of the praying multitudes without the temple (Lk **1** 10). See SHEWBREAD, TABLE OF.

W. SHAW CALDECOTT

SHEWBREAD, TABLE OF (שֻׁלְחָן, *shulḥān* [Ex **25** 25–30, etc]; ἡ τράπεζα καὶ ἡ πρόθεσις τῶν ἄρτων, *hē trápeza kaí hē próthesis tōn ártōn* [He **9** 2]): For construction, see TABERNACLE; TEMPLE. A rude representation of the table is given on the Arch of Titus in Rome. The bas-relief was measured by Professor Boni in 1905, and the height and width of the represented tables were found to be 48 cms., or nearly 19 in. The table represented is, of course, that of Herod's temple, taken at the fall of Jerus in 70 AD. See the author's art. on "The Temple Spoils" in *PEFS*, 1906, 306 ff.

The table of shewbread is to be distinguished from the altar of incense. It has become the fashion of the newer criticism to deny the existence of the altar of incense in preëxilic times, and to explain the allusion to it in 1 K **6** 20 as the table of shewbread (so in Ezk **41** 22). The other references (1 K **6** 22; **7** 48; **9** 25) are dismissed as interpolations. The procedure is radically vicious. The table of shewbread is not an "altar," though the altar is once spoken of as a "table" (Ezk **41** 22). There was only one altar of incense (1 K **6** 20), but (in 2 Ch **4** 8) ten tables of shewbread. See SHEWBREAD.

W. SHAW CALDECOTT

SHIBAH, shī'ba (שִׁבְעָה, *shibh'āh*, "seven"; ὅρκος, *hórkos;* Swete reads Φρέαρ ὅρκου, *Phréar hórkou*, lit. "well of oath"; AV **Shebah**): The name of the original well of Beer-sheba according to Gen **26** 33. See BEER-SHEBA.

SHIBBOLETH, shib'ō-leth (שִׁבֹּלֶת, *shibbōleth*): A test of speech applied by the men of Gilead to the Ephraimites, who wished to cross the Jordan, after defeat. If they pronounced the word *ṣibbōlēth*, their dialectic variety of speech betrayed them (Jgs **12** 6). The word probably has the sense of "stream" or "flood" (cf Ps **69** 2).

SHIBMAH, shib'ma (שִׂבְמָה, *sibhmāh*). See SIBMAH.

SHICRON, shik'ron (שִׁכְּרוֹן, *shikk^erōn*). See SHIKKERON.

SHIELD, shēld. See ARMOR, IV, 1.

SHIGGAION, shi-gā'yon, shi-gī'on (שִׁגָּיוֹן, *shiggāyōn*): Occurs in the title of Ps **7**, and, in the pl., in the verse introducing Habakkuk's prayer (Hab **3** 1). Derived from a vb. meaning "to wander," it is generally taken to mean a dithyramb, or rhapsody.

This is not supported by the Gr VSS, but they are evidently quite at a loss. See PSALMS, BOOK OF.

SHIHON, shī'hon (שִׁיאוֹן, *shī'ōn*). See SHION.

SHIHOR, shī'hôr (שִׁיחוֹר, *shīḥōr*, also written without י and ו in Heb and incorrectly "Sihor" in Eng.): A stream of water mentioned in connection with Egypt. Joshua (**13** 3) speaks of the "Shihor, which is before Egypt," a stream which commentators have thought to be "the brook of Egypt," the stream which separated Egypt from Pal, now called *Wâdy el-'Arish*. Jeremiah (**2** 18 AV) says, "What hast thou to do in the way to Egypt, to drink the waters of Sihor?" Commentators have thought Shihor in this case to be a name for the Nile. Both interpretations cannot be correct. Whatever the name S. means, at least it did not denote a movable river. It must be the same stream in both these passages, and no identification of the stream can be correct that does not satisfy both of them. Professor Naville has recently shown conclusively (*Proc. Soc. Bib. Arch.*, January, 1913) that neither of these interpretations is strictly correct, and has made clear the Bib. references to S. In the northeasternmost province of ancient Egypt, *Khentabt* ("Fronting on the East"), was a canal, a fresh-water stream drawn off from the Nile, called in the Egyp language *Shi-t-Hor*, i.e. "the Horus Canal" (the *-t-* is an Egyp fem. ending). There have been many changes in the branches and canals from the Nile in the Delta, and this one with many others has been lost altogether; but there is a tradition among the Bedouin of *Wâdy el-'Arish* to this day that once a branch of the Nile came over to that point. This *Shi-t-Hor*, "Stream of Horus," makes perfectly clear and harmonious the different references of Scripture to S. It was "before Egypt," as Josh describes it, and it was the first sweet water of Egypt which the traveler from Pal in those days was able to obtain, as the words of Jeremiah indicate. "To drink the waters of S." meant to reach the supply of the fresh water of the Nile at the border of the desert. The two other references to S. (1 Ch **13** 5; Isa **23** 3) are perfectly satisfied by this identification. The "seed of S." (Isa **23** 3 AV) would be grain from Egypt by way of the Shihor. M. G. KYLE

SHIHOR-LIBNATH, shī'hôr-lib'nath (שִׁיחוֹר לִבְנָת, *shīḥōr libhnāth;* B, τῷ Σειὼν καὶ Λαβανάθ, *tō Seiōn kai Labanáth*, A, Σειώρ κτλ., *Seiṓr*, etc): A place named on the boundary of Asher (Josh **19** 26). It seems to mark with Carmel the western limit, and may have been on the S. of that mountain. Pesh, Syr, and *Onom* take this as two distinct names attaching to cities in this region. So far, however, no trace of either name has been found in the course of very careful exploration. More probably Shihor was the name of a river, "Libnath" distinguishing it from the Nile, which was called Shihor of Egypt. It may have been called Shihor because, like the Nile, it contained crocodiles. The boundary of Asher included Dor (*Ṭanṭūrah*), so the river may be sought S. of that town. Crocodiles are said still to be found in the Kishon; but this river runs N. of Carmel. The Crocodeilon of Ptolemy (V. xv.5; xvi.2) and Pliny (v.19), which the latter makes the southern boundary of Phoenicia, may possibly be *Nahr ez-Zerḳā*, which enters the sea about 5 miles S. of *Ṭanṭūrah*. Here also it is said the crocodile is sometimes seen. Perhaps therefore we may identify this stream with Shihor-libnath. W. EWING

SHIKKERON, shik'ẽr-on (שִׁכְּרוֹן, *shikkᵉrōn;* AV Shicron): A place mentioned in Josh **15** 11 as being on the northern border of Judah, between Ekron and Baalah, Jabneel being beyond, toward the sea. The site is unknown, but Rev. C. Hauser (*PEFS*, 1907, 289) suggests *Tell es-Sellakeh*, N.W. of *'Akir*, remarking that if this were the site the boundary would follow a natural course over the mountain to Jabneel.

SHILHI, shil'hī (שִׁלְחִי, *shilḥī*): Father of Jehoshaphat's mother (1 K **22** 42=2 Ch **20** 31; BA in 2 Ch, Σαλεί, *Saleí*, B in 1 K, Σεμεεί, *Semeeí*, A in 1 K, Σαλαλά, *Salalá*, Luc. in both, Σελεεί, *Seleeí*). Cheyne (*EB*, art. "Shilhi") ventures the supposition that "Shilhi" is a misreading for "Shilhim" (Josh **15** 32), and is therefore the name of a place rather than that of a person; he holds it to be the name of the birthplace of Azubah, the king's mother.

SHILHIM, shil'him (שִׁלְחִים, *shilḥīm* [Josh **15** 32]): See SHAARAIM, (2). Possibly Azubah the mother of Jehoshaphat, who is called "the daughter of Shilhi" (1 K **22** 42; 2 Ch **20** 31), was a native of Shilhim.

SHILLEM, shil'em, **SHILLEMITES**, shil'em-īts (שִׁלֵּם, *shillēm*, הַשִּׁלֵּמִי, *ha-shillēmī*): Shillem is found in Gen **46** 24, a son of Naphtali; Shillemites, his descendants, are mentioned in Nu **26** 49; SHALLUM (q.v.) is found in 1 Ch **7** 13.

SHILOAH, shi-lō'a, shī-lō'a (Isa **8** 6). See SILOAM.

SHILOH, shī'lō (שִׁילֹה, *shīlōh*): The prophecy in Gen **49** 10, "The sceptre shall not depart from Judah, ... until Shiloh come," etc, has been the subject of very diverse interpretations. RVm gives as alternative renderings, " 'Till he come to Shiloh having the obedience of the peoples' Or, acc. to Syr, 'Till he come whose it is,' etc." (1) From the earliest times the passage has been regarded as Messianic, but the rendering in the text, which takes "Shiloh" as a proper name, bearing a meaning such as "peaceful" (cf Isa **9** 6, "Prince of Peace"), labors under the difficulty that Shiloh is not found elsewhere as a personal name in the OT, nor is it easy to extract from it the meaning desired. Further, the word was not personally applied to the Messiah in any of the ancient VSS, which rather assume a different reading (see below). Apart from a purely fanciful passage in the Talm (cf Driver, *Gen*, 413), this application does not appear earlier than the version of Seb. Münster in the 16th cent. (1534). (2) The rendering, "till he come to Shiloh," where Shiloh is taken as the name of a place, not a person, is plausible, but is felt to yield no suitable sense in the context. It is, therefore, now also set aside by most recent scholars. (3) The 3d rendering, which regards Shiloh as representing the Heb שֶׁלֹּה (*shellōh*)=שֶׁלֹּה for אֲשֶׁר לוֹ, *'ăsher lō*, "whose [it is]," has in its favor the fact that this is evidently the reading presupposed in the LXX, the Pesh, and the Jewish Tgs, and seems to be alluded to in Ezk **21** 27, "until he come whose right it is." In this view the passage has still a Messianic reference, though critics argue that it must then be regarded as late in origin. Other interpretations need not detain us. See for details the full discussions in Hengstenberg's *Christology*, I, 54 ff, ET, the comms. of Delitzsch, Driver, and Skinner, on Gen (esp. Excursus II in Driver), and the arts. in the various Bible dicts.; see also PROPHECY. JAMES ORR

SHILOH (the most usual form is שִׁלֹה, *shīlōh*, but it appears 8 t as שִׁלוֹ, *shīlō*, and 3 t as

שִׁילֹו; Σηλώ, *Sēlō*, Σηλώμ, *Sēlōm*): A town in the lot of Ephraim where Israel assembled under Joshua at the close of the war of conquest (Josh **18** 1). Here territory was allotted to the seven tribes who had not yet received their portions. A commission was sent out to "describe the land into seven portions"; this having been done, the inheritances were assigned by lot. Here also were assigned to the Levites their cities in the territories of the various tribes (chs **18–21**). From Shiloh Reuben and Gad departed for their homes E. of the Jordan; and here the tribes gathered for war against these two, having misunderstood their building of the great altar in the Jordan valley (ch **22**). From Jgs **18** 31 we learn that in the period of the Judges the house of God was in Shiloh; but when the sanctuary was moved thither from Gilgal there is no indication. The maids of Shiloh were captured by the Benjamites on the occasion of a feast, while dancing in the vineyards; this having been planned by the other tribes to provide the Benjamites with wives without involving themselves in responsibility (**21** 21 ff). While the house of the Lord remained here it was a place of pilgrimage (1 S **1** 3). To Shiloh Samuel was brought and consecrated to God's service (ver 24). The sanctuary was presided over by Eli and his wicked sons; and through Samuel the doom of their house was announced. The capture of the ark by the Philis, the fall of Hophni and Phinehas, and the death of the aged priest and his daughter-in-law followed with startling rapidity (chs **3,4**). The sanctuary in Shiloh is called a "temple" (**1** 9; **3** 3) with doorpost and doors (**1** 9; **3** 15). It was therefore a more durable structure than the old tent. See TABERNACLE; TEMPLE. It would appear to have been destroyed, probably by the Philis; and we find the priests of Eli's house at Nob, where they were massacred at Saul's order (**22** 11 ff). The disaster that befell Shiloh, while we have no record of its actual occurrence, made a deep impression on the popular mind, so that the prophets could use it as an effective illustration (Ps **78** 60; Jer **7** 12.14; **26** 6). Here the blind old prophet Ahijah was appealed to in vain by Jeroboam's wife on behalf of her son (1 K **14** 2.4), and it was still occupied in Jeremiah's time (**41** 5).

The position of Shiloh is indicated in Jgs **21** 19, as "on the north of Beth-el, on the east side of the highway that goeth up from Beth-el to Shechem, and on the south of Lebonah." This is very explicit, and points definitely to *Seilūn*, a ruined site on a hill at the N.E. of a little plain, about 9 miles N. of *Beitīn* (Bethel), and 3 miles S.E. of *Khān el-Lubbān* (Lebonah), to the E. of the highway to Shechem (*Nāblus*). The path to *Seilūn* leaves the main road at *Sinjil*, going eastward to *Turmus 'Aya*, then northward across the plain. A deep valley runs to the N. of the site, cutting it off from the adjoining hills, in the sides of which are rock-hewn tombs. A good spring rises higher up the valley. There are now no vineyards in the district; but indications of their ancient culture are found in the terraced slopes around.

Excavations here were conducted in '22 by a Danish expedition under the direction of Dr. O. A. Schmidt. No Canaanite strata were found; the earliest is early Israelite. Shiloh does not appear to have been occupied at all until the tabernacle was pitched there soon after the conquest of Palestine by the Israelites. The results of these excavations agree remarkably well with the Biblical indications (*Bull. American School of Oriental Research*, Feb '23). Further excavations are in progress at this site in 1929. REVISED BY M. G. K.

W. EWING

SHILONITE, shī'lō-nīt (שִׁילֹנִי, *shīlōni* [2 Ch **9** 29], שִׁילֹנִי, *shīlōnī* [**10** 15; Neh **11** 5], שִׁלֹנִי; Σηλωνεί, *Sēlōneí*, Σηλωνείτης, *Sēlōneítēs*): This denotes an inhabitant of Shiloh, and applies (1) to Ahijah the prophet (1 K **11** 29, etc); and (2) to a family of the children of Judah, who, after the exile, made their home in Jerus (1 Ch **9** 5; Neh **11** 5, AV "Shiloni").

SHILSHAH, shil'shä (שִׁלְשָׁה, *shilshāh;* B A, **Σαλεισά**, *Saleisá*, Luc., **Σελεμσάν**, *Selemsán*): An Asherite (1 Ch **7** 37).

SHIMEA, shim'ē-a (שִׁמְעָא, *shim'ā'*): See SHAMMUA and SHAMMAH.

(1) Brother of David (see SHAMMAH).

(2) Son of David (1 Ch **3** 5, B, Σάμαν, *Sáman;* but in 2 S **5** 14; 1 Ch **14** 4, "Shammua").

(3) A Merarite Levite (1 Ch **6** 30, B, Σομέα, *Soméa*, A, Σαμά, *Samá*, Luc., Σαμαάδ, *Samaá*).

(4) A Gershonite Levite (1 Ch **6** 39 [24], Σεμαά, *Semaá*).

SHIMEAH, shim'ē-a (שִׁמְאָה, *shim'āh;* B, **Σεμαά**, *Semaá*, A, **Σαμεά**, *Sameá*, Luc., **Σαμαά**, *Samaá*): A descendant of Jehiel, the "father" of Gibeon (1 Ch **8** 32); in 1 Ch **9** 38 he is called "Shimeam" (B א, Luc., Σαμαά, *Samaá*, A, Σαμά, *Samá;* see *JQR*, XI, 110–13, §§10–12).

SHIMEAM, shim'ē-am. See SHIMEAH.

SHIMEATH, shim'ē-ath (שִׁמְעָת, *shim'āth*, or שִׁמְעַת, *shim'ath;* LXX in 2 K, **'Ιεμουάθ**, *Iemouáth*, B in 2 Ch, **Σαμά**, *Samá*, A, **Σαμάθ**, *Samáth*, Luc., **Σαμαάθ**, *Samaáth*): Father of Jozacar (2 K **12** 21 [22]), one of the murderers of Joash, king of Judah. According to 2 Ch **24** 26 Shimeath is an Ammonitess and the mother, not the father, of Jozacar. Many textual emendations have been suggested (cf *HDB*, art. "Shimeath"), but they are unnecessary, as the Chronicler's revised version of the incident in K was a deliberate one. The Chronicler was a sturdy opponent of intermarriage, and in the story of the assassination of King Joash he saw an opportunity to strike a blow against the hated practice. In the older account in K the names of the conspirators are given as "Jozakar the son of שִׁמְעָת [*shim'āth*], and Jehozabad the son of שֹׁמֵר [*shemer*]." The two names are both masc.; but the final ת of the former looked to the Chronicler like the fem. ending and offered him his opportunity. In his account, the one of the two murderers (dastardly villains, even though the king had merited death) was "the son of שִׁמְעַת [*shim'ath*], the *Ammonitess*," and the other was "the son of שִׁמְרִית [*shimrīth*], the *Moabitess*" (cf Torrey, *Ezra Studies*, 212 ff).

HORACE J. WOLF.

SHIMEATHITES, shim'ē-ath-īts (שִׁמְעָתִים, *shim'āthīm;* B A, **Σαμαθιείμ**, *Samathieím*, Luc., **Σαμαθείν**, *Samathein*): A subdivision of the tribe of Caleb (1 Ch **2** 55). In the three families mentioned in this passage Jerome saw three distinct classes of religious functionaries: Vulg *canentes atque resonantes et in tabernaculis commorantes*. The Tg has a similar explanation, except that the "Sucathites" are those "covered" with a spirit of prophecy. Bertheau (*Handbuch zum AT*) accepts Jerome's explanation, except that he regards the first class as gate-keepers (Aram. תְּרַע, *t'ra'* = Heb שַׁעַר, *sha'ar*). Wellhausen (*DGJ*, 30 f) finds underlying the three names תְּרְעָה, *tir'āh*, a technical term for sacred music-making, שִׁמְעָה, *shim'āh*, the Halacha or sacred tradition. Buhl (*HWB*[11]) derives Shimeathites and Sucathites from unknown places. Keil interprets as descendants from the unknown Shemei (cf Curtis, *ICC*). The passage is hopelessly obscure. HORACE J. WOLF

SHIMEI, shim'ē-ī (שִׁמְעִי, *shim'ī*, possibly "hear me [El]" or "[Jah]"; **Σεμεεί,** *Semeeí*, **Σεμεί,** *Semeí*): A name of frequent occurrence throughout the OT records, sometimes varying slightly in form in EV. AV has "Shimi" in Ex **6** 17; "Shimhi" in 1 Ch **8** 21; "Shimeah" in 2 S **21** 21. RV has "Shimeites" in Zec **12** 13, where AV has "Shimei," and Nu **3** 21 for AV "Shimites." EV has "Shema" in 1 Ch **8** 13.21 m for the "Shimei" of ver 21. In all others of the many occurrences in AV and RV the form is "Shimei."

(1) A family name among the Levites before and after the exile, at least five of whom bore it: (*a*) Son of Gershon and grandson of Levi (Ex **6** 17; Nu **3** 18; 1 Ch **6** 17; **23** 7.10). The text of 1 Ch **6** and **23** is corrupt, making difficult the tracing of the various genealogies and the identification of the several Shimeis. Evidently that of **23** 9 is a scribe's error for one of the four sons of Ladan or Libni, whose names are given in the preceding verse. (*b*) An ancestor of Asaph the musician (1 Ch **6** 42), possibly the same as (*a*) above, Jahath the son of S. (cf **23** 10) being by a copyist's error transposed so as to read as if he were the father of S. (*c*) A descendant of the Merarite branch of the Levites (1 Ch **6** 29). (*d*) One of the 288 trained singers in the service of the sanctuary under Asaph (1 Ch **25** 17). (*e*) One of the Levites who helped to cleanse the Temple in Hezekiah's reformation (2 Ch **29** 14). He was a descendant of Heman the musician. Hezekiah afterward appointed him with Conaniah to have chief oversight of "the oblations and the tithes and the dedicated things" which were brought into the chambers of Jeh's house prepared for them (2 Ch **31** 11.12). (*f*) A Levite who under Ezra put away his foreign wife (Ezr **10** 23), "Semeis" in 1 Esd **9** 23.

(2) The best-known Bible character of this name is the Benjamite, of the family of Saul (2 S **16** 5–12; **19** 16–20; 1 K **2** 8.9.36–46), who met David at Bahurim as he was fleeing from Absalom, and in bitter and cowardly fashion cursed and attacked the hard-pressed king. Apparently David's flight to the Jordan led through a narrow ravine, on one side of which, or on the ridge above, stood Shimei in safety as he cast stones at David and his men, cursing as he threw (2 S **16** 5.6). His hatred of David who had displaced his royal kinsman Saul had smouldered long in his mean heart; and now the flame bursts out, as the aged and apparently helpless king flees before his own son. S. seizes the long-coveted opportunity to pour out the acid hate of his heart. But when David's faithful companions would cross the ravine to make quick work of S., the noble king forbade them with these remarkable words: "Behold, my son, who came forth from my bowels, seeketh my life: how much more may this Benjamite now do it? let him alone, and let him curse; for Jeh hath bidden him. It may be that Jeh . . . . will requite me good for his cursing" (2 S **16** 11.12). After Absalom's overthrow, as the king was returning victorious and vindicated, S. met him at the Jordan with most abject confession and with vows of allegiance (2 S **19** 16–23).

The king spared his life; but shortly before his death charged his son Solomon to see that due punishment should come to Shimei for his sins: "Thou shalt bring his hoar head down to Sheol with blood" (1 K **2** 9). When he came to the throne Solomon summoned Shimei and bade him build a house in Jerus, to which he should come and from which he must not go out on pain of death (1 K **2** 36–38). Feeling secure after some years, Shimei left his home in Jerus to recapture some escaped slaves (vs 39–41), and in consequence he was promptly dispatched by that gruesome avenger of blood, the royal executioner, "Benaiah the son of Jehoiada," who "fell upon him," as he had upon Adonijah and Joab, "so that he died" (ver 46).

(3) Another Benjamite, mentioned with Rei as an officer in the king's bodyguard, who was faithful to David in the rebellion of Adonijah (1 K **1** 8). Jos reads Rei as a common noun, describing S. as "the friend of David." He is to be identified with the son of Elah (1 K **4** 18), whom Solomon, probably because of his fidelity, named as one of the 12 chief commissary officers appointed over all Israel, "who provided victuals for the king and his household."

(4) A man of some prominence in the tribe of Benjamin (1 Ch **8** 21), whose home was in Aijalon, where he was a "head of fathers' houses" (ver 13); but his descendants lived in Jerus (ver 28). In AV he is called "Shimhi"; in ver 13 he is called "Shema."

(5) Another Benjamite, an ancestor of Mordecai (Est **2** 5), "Semeias" in Ad Est **11** 2.

(6) A brother of David (2 S **21** 21, AV "Shimeah"); in 1 S **16** 9 he is called "Shammah"; cf "Shimeah," "Shimea."

(7) A man of Judah, called "the Ramathite," who was "over the vineyards" in David's reign (1 Ch **27** 27).

(8) A Simeonite living in the time of David (1 Ch **4** 26.27), whose chief claim to distinction was that he was father of 16 sons and 6 daughters. The descendants of such a numerous progeny, not being able to maintain themselves in their ancestral home in Beer-sheba, in the days of Hezekiah fell upon Gerar, and dispossessed "the sons of Ham" (ver 39 LXX), and upon Mt. Seir, driving out the Amalekites (ver 43).

(9) A man of Reuben, son of Gog (1 Ch **5** 4).

(10), (11) Two men of "Israel," i.e. not priests or Levites, one "of the sons of Hashum" (Ezr **10** 33), the other "of the sons of Bani" (**10** 38), who put away their foreign wives at Ezra's command, in 1 Esd called respectively "Semei" (**9** 33) and "Someis" (**9** 34).

(12) A brother of Zerubbabel (1 Ch **3** 19).

The **Shimeites** were descendants of Shimei, grandson of Levi; cf (1) (*a*) above (Nu **3** 21; Zec **12** 13). EDWARD MACK

SHIMEON, shim'ē-on (שִׁמְעוֹן, *shim'ōn;* elsewhere "Simeon"): One of the sons of Harim who had married foreign wives (Ezr **10** 31; BA, Σεμεών, *Semeōn*, Luc., Συμεών, *Sumeōn* = 1 Esd **9** 32, "Simon Chosameus").

SHIMHI, shim'hī. See SHIMEI.

SHIMI, shim'ī, shī'mī, **SHIMITES,** shim'īts. See SHIMEI.

SHIMMA, shim'a. See SHAMMAH.

SHIMON, shī'mon (שִׁימוֹן, *shīmōn;* B, **Σεμιών,** *Semiōn*, A, **Σεμειών,** *Semeiōn*, Luc., **Σαμί,** *Samí*): A name in the Judahite genealogy (1 Ch **4** 20).

SHIMRATH, shim'rath (שִׁמְרָת, *shimrāth;* **Σαμαράθ,** *Samaráth*): The last of nine sons of Shimei of the tribe of Benjamin (1 Ch **8** 21).

SHIMRI, shim'rī (שִׁמְרִי, *shimrī;* various forms in LXX): There are four Hebrews mentioned in the Bible who bear this name:

(1) A Simeonite, a son of Shemaiah and father of Jedaiah, a chief of his tribe (1 Ch **4** 37).

(2) The father of Jediael, a bodyguard of King David (1 Ch **11** 45).

(3) A son of Hosah, a Levite. He was appointed by David to be doorkeeper in the house of the Lord. He was made chief of the tribe, although not the firstborn of his family (1 Ch **26** 10).

(4) One of the sons of Elizaphan, a Levite. He assisted in purifying the temple in the time of Hezekiah (2 Ch **29** 13). S. L. UMBACH

SHIMRITH, shim'rith (שִׁמְרִית, *shimrīth*, "guard," fem.): A Moabitess, the mother of Jehozabad, one of those that conspired against King Joash (2 Ch **24** 26). Elsewhere (2 K **12** 21) Jehozabad is described as the son of SHOMER (q.v.), the same name without the fem. ending.

SHIMRON, shim'ron (שִׁמְרוֹן, *shimrōn*, "watch"): The 4th son of Issachar (Gen **46** 13; Nu **26** 24; 1 Ch **7** 1), and ancestor of the **Shimronites** (Nu **26** 24).

SHIMRON (שִׁמְרוֹן, *shimrōn;* B, **Συμοών,** *Sumoōn*, A, **Σομερών,** *Somerōn* and other forms): A town whose king was tributary to Jabin king of Hazor, and who joined in the attempt to resist the invasion under Joshua (Josh **11** 1). It was in the territory allotted to Zebulun (**19** 15). No sure identification is yet possible. LXX and Talm both omit the *r* from the name; and Neubauer would identify it with Simonias (*Vita*, 24), the Simonia of the Talm, which is now represented by *Semūniyeh*, a village about 5 miles W. of Nazareth, on the edge of the plain (*Géog. du Talm*). *Beit Laḥm*, named by Jos along with it, is a short distance to the N.W. *Es-Semeirīyeh*, about 3 miles N. of Acre, has also been suggested; but it is perhaps too far to the W. W. EWING

SHIMRON-MERON, shim'ron-mē'ron (שִׁמְרוֹן מְרֹאון, *shimrōn m*[e]*r'ōn;* **Συμοών . . . . Μαμρώθ,** *Sumoōn . . . . Mamrōth*, A, **Σαμρών . . . . Φασγά . . . . Μαρών,** *Samrōn . . . . Phasgá . . . . Marōn*): A royal city of the Canaanites, the king of which was slain by Joshua (**12** 20). Here the name is followed by that of Achshaph, which also follows the name of Shimron in **11** 1. This suggests that the two are in reality one, and that Shimron-meron may only be the full name. A royal Can. city, Samsimuruna, is mentioned in the inscriptions of Sennacherib, Esar-haddon and Assur-bani-pal, which Schrader (*KAT*[2], 163) would identify with this, and thinks it may now be represented by *es-Semeirīyeh*. See SHIMRON. W. EWING

SHIMSHAI, shim'shī, shim'shā-ī (שִׁמְשַׁי, *shimshay;* B, **Σαμασά,** *Samasá*, **Σαμαέ,** *Samaé*, **Σαμεαίς,** *Sameaís*, **Σαμεσά,** *Samesá*, A, **Σαμσαί,** *Samsaí*, Luc., **Σαμαίας,** *Samaías*, throughout; in 1 Esd **2** 17 he is called "Semellius," RV "Samellius"; a number of explanations of this name have been offered, but no one has been generally favored. One conjecture traces it to an Old Iranian caritative שׁשׁמי conformed to שׁמשׁ; another prefers the Old Bactrian *simēzhi=simaēzhi;* cf *BDB*, s.v. The name looks as though it were derived from שֶׁמֶשׁ, *shemesh*, "the sun"): A state secretary who, with REHUM (q.v.) and others, wrote to Artaxerxes to persuade him to prohibit the rebuilding of the temple (Ezr **4** 8.9.17.23). HORACE J. WOLF

SHIN, shēn, **SIN**, sēn (שׁ, שׂ): The 21st letter of the Heb alphabet; transliterated in this Encyclopaedia as *sh*, *s*. It came also to be used for the number 300. For name, etc, see ALPHABET.

SHINAB, shī'nab (שִׁנְאָב, *shin'ābh*, Sam. שִׁנְאָר, *shin'ār;* **Σενναάρ,** *Sennaár*): King of ADMAH (q.v.). He is mentioned with Shemeber, king of Zeboiim; he was attacked by Chedorlaomer and his allies (Gen **14** 2). The reading is very uncertain. If the incident narrated is founded on fact, Shinab may be identical with Sanibu, an Ammonite king in the time of Tiglath-pileser III (so Fr. Delitzsch, *Wo lag das Paradies?* 294); or the name may be equated by the Assyr *Sin-šar-uṣur* (cf "Shenazzar"), and Shemeber with the Assyr *Sumu-abi* (Sayce, *Expos T*, VIII, 463). Jewish exegesis gives a sinister explanation of all four names (ver 2). The Midr (*B*[e]*r. Rab.* **42**) explains Shinab as שׁוֹאֵב מָמוֹן, *shō'ēbh māmmōn*, "one who draws money [wherever he can]." It is of interest to note that the names fall into two alliterative pairs and that each king's name contains exactly as many letters as that of his city. On the whole, however, the list leaves an impression of artificiality; as the names are not repeated in ver 8, it is highly probable that they are later additions to the text. HORACE J. WOLF

SHINAR, shī'när (שִׁנְעָר, *shin'ar;* **Σεναάρ, Σεν[ν]αάρ,** *Sen[n]aár*):

1. Identification
2. Possible Babylonian Form of the Name
3. Sumerian and Other Equivalents
4. The Syriac *Sen'ar*
5. The Primitive Tongue of Shinar
6. Comparison with the Semitic Idiom
7. The Testimony of the Sculptures, etc, to the Race
8. The Sumerians Probably in Shinar before the Semites
9. The States of Shinar: Sippar; Kêš; Babylon; Nippur; Adab; Šurippak; Umma; Erech; Lagaš; Larsa; Ur; Eridu; the Land of the Sea; Nisin, Isin, or Karrak; Upê or Upia (Opis); Other Well-known Cities
10. Shinar and Its Climate
11. Sculpture in Shinar
12. The First Nation to Use Writing in Western Asia
13. The System Employed, with an Example

1. Identification

The name given, in the earliest Heb records, to Babylonia, later called Babel, or the land of Babel (*bābhel*, *'ereç bābhel*). In Gen **10** 10 it is the district wherein lay Babel, Erech, Accad, and Calneh, cities which were the "beginning" of Nimrod's kingdom. In **11** 2 Shinar is described as the land of the plain where migrants from the E. settled, and founded Babel, the city, and its great tower.

2. Possible Babylonian Form

Though sometimes identified with the Bab *Šumer*, the connection of Shinar with that name is doubtful. The principal difficulty lies in the fact that what might be regarded as the non-dialectical form *šingar* (which would alone furnish a satisfactory basis of comparison) is not found, and would, if existent, only apply to the southern portion of Babylonia. The northern tract was called Akkad, after the name of its capital city (see ACCAD). The Gr form *Sen(n)aar* shows that, at the time the LXX tr was made, there was no tradition that the *'ayin* was guttural, as the supposed Bab forms would lead us to expect. As the Bib. form *Shinar* indicates the whole of Babylonia, it corresponds with the native (Sumerian) *Kingi-Ura*, rendered "Šumer and Akkad," from which, by changing *K* into *Sh* (found in Sumerian), Shinar may have been derived, but this explanation is not free from difficulties.

3. Sumerian and Other Equivalents

This twofold designation, *Kingi-Ura*, is that which is commonly used in the inscriptions of the earlier kings, though it cannot then have indicated always the whole country, but only such parts of it as acknowledged their overlordship. Later on the corresponding term seems to have been *Kar-Duniaš* ("the territory of the god Duniaš," to all appearance a term introduced by the Kassite rulers). Nabonassar and his successors seem to have contented themselves with the title "king of Babylon," rule in the city implying also the dominion over the whole country. Often, however, the equivalent term for Babylonia is *E^hi*, probably an abbreviation of *Êridu*, and here standing for the land belonging to that sacred city—"the good city," a type of Paradise, Babylonia being, in fact, situated upon the *êdinu*, or "plain" (see Eden).

All these comparisons tend to show that the Bab equivalent of Shinar is not any of the above, and as yet has not, in fact, been found. This is also implied by the fact, that *Sen'ar* was used in Syr for the country around Bagdad, and anciently included (it may be supposed) the plain upon which the ruins of Babylon stand. *Sen'ar* was therefore in all probability an ancient Bab designation of the tract, now lost, but regarded by the Hebrews as synonymous with Babylonia.

4. The Syriac *Sen'ar*

From the inscriptions it would seem that the primitive language of Shinar was not Semitic, but the agglutinative idiom now named Sumerian—a tongue long regarded as Turanian, and having, it is thought, Turko-Chinese affinities—*gal*, "to be," Turkish *ol-mak; ama* (*ana*), "mother," Turkish *ana; abba*, "old man," Turkish *baba*, "father"; (*h*)*ê*, "house," Turkish *ev*, etc. The Chinese affinities seem less close, but the following may be quoted: *a*(*y*)*a*, "father," Chinese *ye* (Amoy *iâ*); *ge*, "night," Chinese *ye; gu*, "to speak," Chinese *yü; shu*, "hand," Chinese *sheù; kin*, "business," Chinese *kūng*, "work"; etc. Chinese and Turkish, however, have had time to pass through many changes since Sumerian was current in Shinar. Many words of the Sumerian language were borrowed by the Sem Babylonians, and a few (like *hēkal*, "temple," Sem [*h*]*êgal*, "great house") entered the other Sem languages.

5. Primitive Tongue of Shinar

Halévy's contention, that Sumerian is simply "an allography" for the expression of Sem Bab, seems to be untenable, as they differ not only in words, but also in grammar; moreover, Sumerian had a dialect, called by the natives "woman's tongue." For the rest, the principal differences between Sumerian and Sem Bab are: (1) post-positional suffixes instead of prepositions; (2) verbs with long strings of prefixes and infixes to express the persons and regimens, instead of a prefix and a suffix; (3) compound words, both nouns and verbs, are common instead of being exceedingly rare. Sumerian seems to have borrowed several words from Sem Bab.

6. Comparison with Semitic Idiom

Not only the language, but also the sculptures which they have left, point to the probability that the earlier inhabitants of Shinar belonged to a different race from the later. The Semites of Babylonia were to all appearance thick-set and muscular, but the Sumerians, notwithstanding the stumpy figures which their statues and bas-reliefs show, seem to have been slim—in any case, their warriors, in the better bas-reliefs, as well as the figures of the god Nin-Girsu (formerly known as "the god with the firestick"), and the engraved cylinders, have this type. Moreover, the sculptures and cylinder-seals show that certain classes—priests or the like—were clean shaven, in marked contrast to Sem usage elsewhere. Their deities, however, always had hair and beard, implying that they came from a different, though possibly related, stock. These deities were very numerous, and it is noteworthy that, though those with Sumerian names may be counted by hundreds, those with Sem names are only to be reckoned by tens.

7. Testimony of the Sculptures, etc

Though there is no certain indication which race entered Shinar first, it is to be noted that Nimrod, presumably Shinar's first king and the founder of its great cities, was a son of Cush (Gen **10** 8), and the name of Shinar seems to have existed before the foundation of Babel (Babylon) and its tower (Gen **11** 2). In the native sculptures, moreover, the non-Sem type precedes the Sem; and in the inscriptions the non-Sem idiom precedes that of the Sem tr. Everything points, therefore, to the Sumerians having been in Babylonia before the Sem inhabitants.

8. Sumerians Probably Preceded Semites in Shinar

At the earliest period to which our records refer the Sumerians of Shinar were divided into a number of small states, of which the following may be regarded as the principal:

9. States of Shinar

(1) *Sippar* or *Sippar-Aruru* (*-Ya' ruru*), possibly including Accad (Gen **10** 10), some distance S.W. of Bagdad. It is the modern *'Abu-habbah*, "father of grain." Though it seems to have fallen early under the dominion of the Semites, it was at first Sumerian, as its native name, *Zimbir*, and the ideographic writing thereof show. According to Berosus, who calls it *Pantabiblion*, one of its earliest kings was *Amelon* or *Amillarus*, who reigned 13 *sari*, or 46,800 years. Later on came *Evedoreschus*, the native *Enwe-dur-an-ki*, renowned as a priest favored by the gods. His descendants, if of pure race, inherited the divine grace which he enjoyed It is said to have been in *Sippara* (*Sippar*) that *Ut-napištim*, the Bab Noah, buried the records before entering the ark.

(2) About 18 miles N. of Babylon lay *Kêš*, now *Oheimer*—a foundation which seems to have preceded Babylon as the capital of Shinar. Its early queen, *Azag-Bau*, is said to have been the wife of a wine-merchant and to have reigned 100 years.

(3) *Babylon*, for which see Babel; Babylon. As one of its early kings, Berosus mentions *Alorus*, "the shepherd of the people," as having reigned for 10 *sari*, or 36,000 years. The state of Babylon probably included Cuthah (*Tel Ibrahim*), which once had kings of its own, and possessed a special legend of the Creation. Belonging to Babylon, also, was the renowned city Borsippa, now *Birs*, or the *Birs Nimroud*, the traditional site of the Tower of Babel (see Babel, Tower of).

(4) Some distance S.E. of Babylon lay *Nippur* or *Niffur*, now *Niffer* (*Noufar*), identified by the rabbis with the "Calneh" of Gen **10** 10. It was a place of considerable importance, and the seat of the worship of Enlil and Ninlil, later, also, of their son Ninip and his spouse (see Calneh). The American excavations on this site have thrown a flood of light upon almost every branch of Assyriological research.

(5) *Adab*, now called *Bismaya*, the city of *Maḫ*, the goddess of reproduction. One of the earliest rulers of Adab was seemingly called *Lugal-dalu*, of whom a fine statue, discovered by the American explorers, exists. It was apparently renowned as a necropolis.

(6) S. and a little W. of Adab was *Šurippak*, now *Fara*. This was the birthplace of the Bab Noah, *Ut-napištim*, son of *Opartes* (*Umbara-Tutu*), a Chaldaean of Larancha. The coming of the Flood was revealed to *Ut-napištim* here.

(7) Practically E. of *Fara* lay *Umma* or *Gišuḫ* (or *Giuḫ*), now *Jokha*. This city was apparently of considerable importance, and the traditional rival of *Lagaš*.

(8) S. of *Fara* lay *Unuga*, Sem *Uruk*, the Bib. Erech (q.v.), now *Warka*. Its most celebrated king, after *Gilgameš*, was *Lugal-zaggi-si*, one of the opponents of the rulers of *Lagaš*.

(9) Some distance E. of *Warka* was the territory of *Lagaš*, now *Tel-loh*—a little state, rather in-

accessible, but of considerable importance to the antiquarian, which is a testimonial to the advance in civilization which it had made. Its kings and viceroys were among the most renowned, though apparently unknown outside their own domains. The most celebrated were the reformer *Uru-ka-gina* and viceroy *Gudêa*, to whom many erections in the city were due. (See *Gudêa's* remarkable statue in the Louvre.)

(10) Somewhat to the S.E. of *Warka* lay *Larsa*, the "Ellasar" of Gen **14** 1 (q.v.). This center of learning maintained its independence even after the other states had been absorbed by Ḫammurabi and his dynasty into the Bab empire.

(11) To the S.E. of *Warka* and *Senqara* lies the site of the ancient Ur of the Chaldees (q.v.) now *Mugheir*. It was renowned for its temple to the moon, and for the kings known as the dynasty of Ur: *Sur-Engur*, *Dungi*, *Bûr-Sin*, *Gimil-Sin*, and *Ibi-Sin*.

(12) S. of the Ur lay *Êridu*, or, in full, *Guru-duga*, "the good city," wherein, apparently, lay the earthly Paradise. This is identified with the present *'Abu-shahrein*, and was the seat of *Ea* or *Enki*, god of the sea and of fertilizing streams. According to the tradition, it was there that the "dark vine" grew—a type, seemingly, of the tree of life. The later kings of Babylon sometimes bear the title "king of Êridu," as though rulers of the domain of Paradise.

(13) *The Land of the Sea* (that bordering on the Pers Gulf), in which, seemingly, the Chaldaeans afterward settled, seems to have played an important part in the early history of Shinar. Berosus speaks of its king *Ammenon*, who reigned 12 *sari*, or 43,200 years, and in whose time the *Musarus Oannes*, or Annedotus, arose out of the Pers Gulf. Like others referred to in the legends which Berosus refers to, he was half-man and half-fish. It is thought that these incidents, though evidently mythical, point to the introduction of civilization into Babylonia, from this point. See also Jonah; Jonah, The Book of.

(14) *Nisin*, *Isin*, or *Karrak*, seat of the worship of *Nin-Karraga*, was also an important state governed by its own kings.

(15) *Upê* or *Upia*, the Gr *Opis*, apparently obtained renown at a very early date, its kings being given in the great chronological list before those of *Kiš*.

(16) *Other well-known cities*, possibly state-capitals, were *Larak*, Gr *Laranche; Amarda*, one of the centers of the worship of *Nergal; Ašnunna*, a province E. of the present Bagdad; *Dilmu*, now *Dailem; Nuru*, *Ennigi*, and *Kakra*, seemingly centers of the worship of Hadad; *Tilmun*, at the head of the Pers Gulf, and including the island of *Bahrein;* the province of *Sabu; Šešeb* or *Bagdadu*, possibly the modern Bagdad; and several others.

10. Shinar and Its Climate

Whether the country was in the same seemingly uncared-for state anciently as at present is unknown; but one cannot help admiring the courage of the original immigrants into such a district, for example, as that of *Lagaš*. This, which belongs to the southern region, is very inaccessible on account of the watercourses and marshes. Like the whole of Shinar in general, it is more or less dried up in summer, and unhealthy for Europeans. The alterations in the waterways, owing to changes in the irrigation-channels, must then, as now, have hindered communication. Sharp cold, with frost, succeeds the heat of summer, and from time to time sand-storms sweep across the plain. Notwithstanding the destruction sometimes wrought, the floods were always welcomed in consequence of the fruitfulness which followed, and which was such as to make Babylonia one of the most fertile tracts known.

11. Sculpture in Shinar

The reference to the Sumerian sculptures in (**7**) above will have shown that the inhabitants of the Plain of Shinar possessed an art of no mean order and of some antiquity, even at the time when it first presents itself to our notice. It is true that many specimens are crude and uncouth, but this is probably due to the sculptors having been, often enough, the slaves of their material. Their stones were frequently more or less pebble-shaped, and they had neither the skill nor the tools to reduce them to better proportions—moreover, reduction of bulk would have meant a diminution of their importance. The broad, squat figures which they produced, however, gave them bad models for their bas-reliefs, and it was long ere this defect was removed, notwithstanding the superior work produced by their seal-engravers during and after the 4th millennium BC.

12. First to Use Writing in Western Asia

But in all probability special renown will always be attached to the non-Semitic inhabitants of Shinar as the inventors, or at least the earliest users known to us, of the cuneiform script. It may be objected that the system which they introduced was cumbersome and imperfect, but they knew of nothing simpler, and modern Chinese, with which their script has been compared, is far less practical. Briefly, the system may be described as syllabic for the prefixes and suffixes, and ideographic for the roots. To show this the following transcribed example will probably suffice:

13. System Employed

Ê nu-DU URU nu-DIM, A house was not built, a city was not constructed;
URU nu-DIM ADAM nu-mun-GAR, A city was not constructed, a community he had not founded;
ABZU nu-DU GURUDUGA nu-DIM, The abyss was not built, Êridu was not constructed;
Ê AZAGA DINGIRene KI-DURA-bi nu-DIM, The holy house of the gods, its seat was not constructed;
Šu-NIGIN KURKURAgi AABBAama, The whole of the lands was sea.

The nominal and verbal roots of the above extract from the bilingual account of the Creation are in capitals, and the pronominal prefixes and suffixes, with a couple of lengthenings which determine the pronunciations of the nouns, in small letters. This will not only give an idea of the poetical form of the Sumerian legend of the Creation by Merodach and Aruru, but also show how short and concise, as a language, was the speech of Shinar, before Sem supremacy. T. G. Pinches

SHINE, shīn: The Heb words *'āhal*, *'ōr*, *hālal*, *zāhar*, *zāraḥ*, *yāpha'*, *nāghāh*, *'āshath* and *ḳāran* are all tr[d] "shine." All indicate either the direct or indirect diffusion of beams of light. In a direct and literal sense the word "shine" is used of the heavenly bodies, or of candles, and fire (Job **18** 5; **25** 5 AV; **29** 3; **31** 26; 2 K **3** 22). In a figurative sense it is used of reflected light or brightness, in any sense (Ex **34** 29 f.35; Isa **60** 1; Ezk **43** 2; Dnl **12** 3). God as the sun of righteousness is thus depicted in Ps **50** 2. The NT words *astráptō*, *augázō*, *lámpō* and *phaínō* are tr[d] "shine." Thus literally it is said of the lightning that it shines (Mt **24** 27 AV; Lk **17** 24); the word is tropically applied to the life of faith or to men prominent in the kingdom of God (Mt **5** 16; Jn **5** 35; 2 Cor **4** 6; Phil **2** 15; 2 Pet **1** 19); to the glory of God (Lk **2** 9); to angelic appearances (Lk **24** 4; Acts **12** 7), or to Christ as He appeared to John on Patmos (Rev **1** 16). Henry E. Dosker

SHION, shī'on (שִׁיאֹן, *shī'ōn;* B, **Σιωνά,** *Siōná,* A, **Σειάν,** *Seián*): A town in the territory of Issachar, named with Shunem, Hapharaim and Anaharath (Josh **19** 19). It is possibly identical with *Khirbet Sha'īn,* near *'Ain esh-Sha'īn,* c 4 miles N.W. of Mt. Tabor.

SHIPHI, shī'fī (שִׁפְעִי, *shiph'ī;* B, **Σαφάλ,** *Saphál,* A, **Σεφείν,** *Sephein,* Luc., **Σωφεί,** *Sōphei*): A Simeonite prince (1 Ch **4** 37 [36]).

SHIPHMITE, shif'mīt. See Shepham; Siphmoth.

SHIPHRAH, shif'ra (שִׁפְרָה, *shiphrāh,* "fairness," "beauty"; LXX **Σεπφωρά,** *Sepphōrá,* the rendering also of צִפֹּרָה, *çippōrāh,* in Ex **2** 21): The name of one of the Heb midwives (Ex **1** 15). See also Zipporah.

SHIPHTAN, shif'tan (שִׁפְטָן, *shiphṭān;* B, **Σαβαθά,** *Sabathá,* A, **Σαβαθάν,** *Sabathán,* F, **Σαφατάν,** *Saphatán,* Luc., [Σ]**εφαθά,** [*S*]*ephathá*): An Ephraimite prince (Nu **34** 24).

SHIPMASTER, ship'mas-tēr. See Ships and Boats; Phoenix.

SHIPMEN, ship'men. See Ships and Boats, II, 2, (3); III, 2.

SHIPS AND BOATS:

In the OT the following words are found:

(1) The word most commonly used in Heb for "a ship" is אֳנִיָּה, *'ŏnīyāh* (Prov **30** 19; Jon **1** 3.4), of which the pl. *'ŏnīyōth* is found most frequently (Jgs **5** 17; 1 K **22** 48 f, and many other places).

The collective term for "a navy of ships" is אֳנִי, *'ŏnī* (1 K **9** 26 f; **10** 22, *'ŏnī Tharshīsh,* "a navy [of ships] of Tarshish"; but Isa **33** 21, *'ŏnī shayit,* a "galley with oars").

(2) צִי, *çī* (Nu **24** 24; Ezk **30** 9; Isa **33** 21), *çī 'addīr,* "gallant ship"; Dnl **11** 30, *çiyīm Kittīm,* "ships of Kittim."

(3) סְפִינָה, *s^ephīnāh,* "innermost parts of the ship" RV, "sides of the ship" AV (Jon **1** 5, the only place where the word is found).

In Apoc πλοῖον, *ploíon,* is the usual word (Wisd **14** 1; Ecclus **33** 2, etc), tr^d "vessel" in Wisd **14** 1, but "ship" elsewhere. For "ship" Wisd **5** 10 has ναῦς, *naús.* "Boat" in 2 Macc **12** 3.6 is for σκάφος, *skáphos,* and "navy" in 1 Macc **1** 17; 2 Macc **12** 9; **14** 1 for στόλος, *stólos.* In Wisd **14** 6 Noah's ark is called a σχεδία, *schedía,* a "clumsy ship" (the literal tr "raft" in RV is impossible).

In the NT there are four words in use: (1) ναῦς, *naús* (Acts **27** 41, the only place where it occurs, designating the large sea-going vessel in which St. Paul suffered shipwreck). (2) πλοιάριον, *ploiárion,* "a little boat" (Mk **3** 9 and two other places, Jn **6** 22 ff; **21** 8). (3) πλοῖον, *ploíon,* "boat" (Mt **4** 21.22 and many other places in the Gospels—the ordinary fishing-boat of the Sea of Galilee rendered "boat" uniformly in RV instead of "ship" AV), "ship" (Acts **20** 13, and all other places where the ship carrying St. Paul is mentioned, except **27** 41, as above). In Jas **3** 4; Rev **8** 9; **18** 17 ff, it is rendered "ship." (4) σκάφη, *skáphē,* "boat" (Acts **27** 16.30.32, where it means the small boat of the ship in which St. Paul was being conveyed as a prisoner to Rome).

Cognate expressions are: "shipmen," אַנְשֵׁי אֳנִיּוֹת, *'anshē 'ŏnīyōth* (1 K **9** 27); ναῦται, *naútai* (Acts **27** 27.30 AV, "sailors" RV); "mariners," מַלָּחִים, *mallāḥīm* (Jon **1** 15; Ezk **27** 9.27.29), שָׁטִים, *shāṭīm* (Ezk **27** 8 AV, "rowers" RV; **27** 26, AV and RV); "pilot," חֹבֵל, *ḥōbhēl* (Jon **1** 6; Ezk **27** 8.27.28.29); "sailing," "voyage," πλοῦς, *ploús* (Acts **21** 7; **27** 9.10, RV "voyage" in all verses).

I. The Hebrews and the Sea.—The Hebrews were a pastoral and agricultural people, and had no inducements to follow a seafaring life. They were possessed of a considerable seaboard along the Mediterranean, but the character of their coast gave little encouragement to navigation. The coast line of the land of Israel from Carmel southward had no bays and no estuaries or river-mouths to offer shelter from storm or to be havens of ships. Solomon landed his timber and other materials for the Temple at Joppa, and tradition has handed down what is called "Solomon's Harbor" there. The builders of the second temple also got timber from Lebanon and conveyed it to Joppa. It was Simon Maccabaeus, however, who built its harbor, and the harbor at Joppa was "the first and only harbor of the Jews" (G. A. Smith, *HGHL,* 136). Caesarea in NT times was a place of shipping and possessed a harbor which Jos declared to be greater than the Piraeus, but it was Herodian and more Gr and Rom than Jewish. It was mostly inhabited by Greeks (Jos, *BJ,* III, ix, 1). Now Caesarea has disappeared; and Joppa has only an open roadstead where vessels lie without shelter, and receive and discharge cargo and passengers by means of boats plying between them and the shore. It was in other directions that Israel made acquaintance with the activities of the sea. Of internal navigation, beyond the fishing-boats on the Sea of Galilee which belong exclusively to the NT, the ferry boat on the Jordan (2 S **19** 18, עֲבָרָה, *'ăbhārāh*) alone receives notice, and even that is not perfectly clear (RVm "convoy," but a "ford" is doubtless meant). It is from Tyre and Egypt and even Assyria and Babylonia, rather than from their own waters, that the Heb prophets and psalmists drew their pictures of seafaring life.

II. Ships in the OT and Apoc.—(1) *In early times.*—In the early books of the OT there are references connecting certain of the tribes, and these northern tribes, with the activities of the sea. In the "Blessing of Jacob" and in the "Blessing of Moses" Zebulun and Issachar are so connected (Gen **49** 13; Dt **33** 19); and in Deborah's Song, which is acknowledged to be a very early fragment of Heb lit., Dan and Asher are also spoken of as connected with the life and work of the sea (Jgs **5** 17). The Oracle of Balaam (Nu **24** 24) looks forward to a day when a fleet from Kittim should take the sea for the destruction of Assyria. "Ships of Kittim" are mentioned in Dnl (**11** 30). Kittim is referred to in the three greater Prophets (Isa **23** 1.12; Jer **2** 10; Ezk **27** 6). The land of Kittim is Cyprus, and in the references in Isaiah it is associated with Tyre and the ships of Tarshish.

1. Among the Hebrews

(2) *During the monarchy.*—It is not till the time of the monarchy that the Hebrews begin to figure as a commercial people. Already in the time of David commercial relations had been established between Israel and Tyre (2 S **5** 11 f). The friendly coöperation was continued by Solomon, who availed himself not only of the cedar and the fir at Hiram's command on Lebanon, but also of the skilled service of Hiram's men to bring the timber from the mountains to the sea. Hiram also undertook to make the cedar and the fir into rafts (1 K **5** 9, דֹּבְרוֹת, *dōbh^erōth,* AV "floats"; 2 Ch **2** 16, רַפְסֹדוֹת, *raphṣōdhōth,* "flotes" AV, "floats" RV) to go by sea and to deliver them to Solomon's men

at the place appointed, which the Chronicler tells us was Joppa. From this coöperation in the building of the Temple there grew up a larger connection in the pursuit of sea-borne commerce. It was at Ezion-geber near to Eloth on the Red Sea, in the land of Edom which David had conquered, that Solomon built his fleet, "a navy of ships" (1 K **9** 26–28). Hiram joined Solomon in these enterprises which had their center on the Red Sea, and thus the Phoenicians had water communication with the coasts of Arabia and Africa, and even of India. The same partnership existed for the commerce of the West. "For the king [Solomon] had at sea a navy of Tarshish with the navy of Hiram: once every three years came the navy of Tarshish, bringing gold, and silver, ivory, and apes, and peacocks" (1 K **10** 22).

Tarshish is the name of the Phoen colony on the river Tartessus, called also Baetis, the modern Guadalquivir. It was the farthest limit of the western world as known to the Hebrews. Attempts have been made to identify it with Tarsus of Cilicia, but they are not convincing. It is conceived of in Heb lit. as remote (Isa **66** 19; Jon **1** 3; **4** 2), as rich (Ps **72** 10; Jer **10** 9), as powerful in commerce (Ezk **38** 13). Ships of Tarshish were no doubt ships actually built for the Tarshish trade (2 Ch **20** 36 f; Jon **1** 3), but the expression became a general designation for large sea-going vessels to any quarter. Ships of Tarshish made a deep impression upon the imagination of the Heb people. The Psalmist takes it as a proof of the power of Jeh that He breaks the ships of Tarshish with an east wind (Ps **48** 7). Isaiah includes them among the great and lofty objects of power and glory which the terror of the Lord would certainly overtake (Isa **2** 16). Ezekiel regards them as the caravans that bore the merchandise of the mistress of the sea (**27** 25). It is in ships of Tarshish that the prophet of the Return sees the exiles borne in crowds to Jerus as their natural home (Isa **60** 9).

From Solomon's time onward the kings of Judah retained their hold upon Eloth (1 K **22** 48 f; 2 Ch **20** 35–37) till it was seized by the Syrians in the days of Ahaz (2 K **16** 6).

(3) *In later times.*—As Solomon had the coöperation of Hiram in securing material and craftsmen for the building of the first Temple, so Joshua and Zerubbabel by the favor of Cyrus obtained timber from Lebanon, and masons and carpenters from Sidon and Tyre for the building of the second. Again, cedar trees were brought from Lebanon by sea to Joppa, and thence conveyed to Jerus (Ezr **3** 7).

From Joppa Jonah fled to avoid compliance with God's command to go to Nineveh and preach repentance there (Jon **1** 1 ff). He found a ship bound for Tarshish as far toward the W. as Nineveh to the E. The fare (*sākhār*) paid by him as a passenger, the hold of the ship in which he stowed himself away (*ṣ^ephīnāh*), the crew (*mallāḥīm*), the captain or shipmaster (*rabh ha-ḥōbhēl*), the storm, the angry sea, the terrified mariners and their cry to their gods, and the casting of Jonah overboard to appease the raging waters—all make a lifelike picture.

It was in the time of Simon, the last survivor of the Maccabean brothers, that Joppa became a seaport with a harbor for shipping—"Amid all his glory

Making a Papyrus Boat.
(From Tomb at the Pyramids.)

he took Joppa for a haven, and made it an entrance for the isles of the sea" (1 Macc **14** 5). When Simon reared his monument over the sepulcher of his father and brothers at Modin, he set up seven pyramids with pillars, upon which were carved figures of ships to be "seen of all that sail on the sea" (1 Macc **13** 29). About this period we hear of ships in naval warfare. When Antiochus IV Epiphanes planned his expedition against Egypt, he had with other armaments "a great navy," presumably ships of war (1 Macc **1** 17); and at a later time Antiochus VII speaks expressly of "ships of war" (1 Macc **15** 3).

Assyrian Armed Galley in Motion.
(Sculpture from Koyunjik. Brit. Mus.)

2. Among Neighboring Nations

(1) *Egypt.*—The Egyptians, like other nations of antiquity, had a great horror of the open sea, although they were expert enough in managing their craft upon the Nile. Pharaoh-necoh built up a powerful navy to serve him both in commerce and in war. See PHARAOH-NECOH.

Of explicit references to Egyp ships in the OT there are but few. Isaiah speaks of "vessels of papyrus upon the waters" of the Upper Nile, on board of which are the messengers of Cush or Ethiopia returning to tell the tidings of the overthrow of Assyria to the inhabitants of those remote lands (**18** 2 AV has "bulrushes" instead of "papyrus"). Ezekiel also, foretelling the overthrow of Egypt, speaks of messengers traveling with the news on swift Nile boats to strike terror into the hearts of the "careless Ethiopians" (**30** 9). When Job compares his days to "the swift ships" ("the ships of reed" RVm), the allusion is most likely to Egypt's, these being skiffs with a wooden keel and the rest of bulrushes, sufficient to carry one person, or at most two, and light, to travel swiftly (**9** 26).

(2) *Assyria and Babylonia.*—The Assyrians and Babylonians were mainly an inland people, but their rivers gave them considerable scope for navigation. The Assyr monuments contain representations of naval engagements and of operations on the seacoast. When Isaiah pictures Jeh as a better defence of Judah than the rivers and streams of Assyria and Egypt are to their people he says, "There Jeh will be with us in majesty, a place of broad rivers and streams, wherein shall go no galley with oars [*'ŏnī shayiṭ*], neither shall gallant ship [*çī 'addīr*] pass thereby. . . . . Thy *tacklings* [ropes, cables] are loosed; they could not strengthen the foot of their mast, they could not spread the sail" (**33** 21.23). Speaking of Jeh's wonders to be performed toward His people after Babylon had been overthrown, the prophet declares: "Thus saith Jeh, your Redeemer, the Holy One of Israel: For your sake I have sent to Babylon, and I will bring down all of them as fugitives, even the Chaldeans, in the ships of their rejoicing" (**43** 14). In this case, however, the ships are not war ships, but more probably merchant ships, or ships for pleasure, sailing in the Euphrates.

(3) *Phoenicia.*—It was from the Phoenicians that the Mediterranean peoples learned seamanship and skill in navigation. It is fitting, therefore, that in his dirge over the downfall of the mistress of the sea, Ezekiel should represent Tyre as a gallant ship, well built, well furnished, and well manned, broken by the seas in the depths of the waters, fallen into the heart of the seas in the day of her ruin. Ezekiel's description (ch **27**, with Davidson's notes) brings together more of the features of the ship of antiquity than any other that has come down to us. Her builders have made her perfect in beauty with **planks** of fir or cypress, **mast** of cedar, **oars** of the oak of Bashan, **benches** or deck of ivory inlaid with boxwood, **sail** of fine linen with broidered work from Egypt, and **an awning** of blue and purple

from the coastlands of Elishah (possibly Sicily). She is manned with **oarsmen** of Sidon and Arvad, **pilots** of the wise men of Tyre, **calkers** from Gebal to stop up the cracks and seams in her timbers, **mariners** and **men of war** from other lands who enhanced her beauty by hanging up the shield and helmet within her. She is freighted with the most varied **cargo,** the produce of the lands around, her customers, or as they are called, her **traffickers,** being Tarshish in the far W., Sheba and Arabia in the S., Haran and Asshur in the E., Javan, which is Greece, and Togarmah, which is Armenia, in the N.

One or two of the particulars of this description may be commented upon. (*a*) As regards **rigging,** the Phoen ships of the time of Ezekiel, as seen in Assyr representations, had one **mast** with one **yard** and carried a **square sail.** Egyp ships on the Red Sea about the time of the Exodus, from reliefs of the XIXth Dynasty, had one mast and two yards, and carried also one large square sail. The masts and yards were made of fir, or of pine, and the sails of linen, but the fiber of papyrus was employed as well as flax in the manufacture of sail-cloth. The sail had also to serve "for an **ensign**" (*lenēs*, Ezk **27** 7). "The flag proper," says Davidson (ad loc.), "seems not to have been used in ancient navigation; its purpose was served by the sail, as for example at the battle of Actium the ship of Antony was distinguished by its purple sail."

(*b*) As regards the **crew,** in the two-banked Phoen ship the **rowers** of the first bank work their oars over the gunwale, and those of the second through portholes lower down, so that each may have free play for his oar. The **calkers** were those who filled up seams or cracks in the timbers with tow and covered them over with tar or wax, after the manner of the instruction given to Noah regarding the Ark: "Thou . . . . shalt pitch it within and without with pitch" (Gen **6** 14).

(*c*) As regards **cargo,** it is to be noted that "the persons of men," that is, slaves, formed an article of merchandise in which Javan, Tubal, and Meshech, countries to the N., traded with Tyre.

3. General References

Of general references to shipping and seafaring life there are comparatively few in the OT. In his great series of Nature-pictures in Ps **104,** the Psalmist finds a place for the sea and ships (vs 25 ff), and in Ps **107** there is a picture of the storm overtaking them that go down to the sea in ships, and of the deliverance that comes to them when God "bringeth them into their desired haven" (vs 23 ff). In the Book of Prov the ideal woman who brings her food from far is like "the merchant ships" (**31** 14). In the same book the drunkard, because of his unnatural insensibility to danger, is likened to a man "that lieth down in the midst of the sea, or as he that lieth upon the top of a mast" (**23** 34); and among the inscrutable things of the world the writer includes "the way of a ship in the midst of the sea" (**30** 19). In Wisd, human life is described "as a ship passing through the billowy water, whereof, when it is gone by, there is no trace to be found, neither pathway of its keel in the billows" (**5** 10). The same book notes it as a striking example of the case of a divine and beneficent Providence that "men intrust their lives to a little piece of wood, and passing through the surge on a raft are brought safe to land" (**14** 1-5). The Jews like the Egyptians and the Assyrians had a natural shrinking from the sea, and Ecclesiasticus interprets their feeling when he says: "They that sail on the sea tell of the danger thereof; and when we hear it with our ears, we marvel" (**43** 24).

III. Ships in the NT.—It is the fishing-boats of the Sea of Galilee which exclusively occupy attention in the Gospels. In the time of Our Lord's ministry in Galilee the shores of the Sea were densely peopled, and there must have been many boats engaged in the fishing industry. Bethsaida at the northern end of the Lake and Tarichaea at the southern end were great centers of the trade. The boats were probably of a size and build similar to the few employed on the Lake today, which are between 20 and 30 ft. in length and 7 ft. in breadth. The word "launch," of putting a boat or a ship into the sea, has disappeared from RV, except in Lk **8** 22, where it is more appropriate to an inland lake. They were propelled by oars, but no doubt also made use of the sail when the wind was favorable (Lk **8** 23), though the pictures which we have in the Gospels are mostly of the boatmen toiling in rowing in the teeth of a gale (Mk **6** 48), and struggling with the threatening waves (Mt **14** 24). In the boat on which Jesus and the disciples were crossing the Lake after the feeding of the 5,000, Jesus was in the stern "asleep on the cushion" (Mk **4** 38, AV "a pillow"; Gr *proskephálaion*, "headrest"). More than once Jesus made special use of a boat. As He was by the seashore a great concourse of people from all parts made it desirable that "a small boat" (*ploiarion*) should be in attendance off the shore to receive Him in case of need, though He does not seem to have required it (Mk **3** 9). On another occasion, when the crowds were still greater, He went into a boat and sat "in the sea" with the multitude on the sloping beach before Him (Mk **4** 1; Lk **5** 3). This boat is said in St. Luke's narrative to have been Simon's, and it seems from references to it as "the boat" on other occasions to have been generally at the disposal of Jesus.

1. In the Gospels

It is St. Paul's voyages which yield us the knowledge that we possess from Bib. sources of ships in NT times. They are recorded for us in the Acts by St. Luke, who, as Sir William Ramsay puts it, had the true Gr feeling for the sea (*St. Paul the Traveller*, 21). In St. Luke's writings there are many nautical terms, peculiar to him, used with great exactitude and precision.

2. In the Acts of the Apostles

When St. Paul had appealed to Caesar and was proceeding to Rome in charge of Julius, the centurion, along with other prisoners, a ship of Adramyttium, a coasting vessel, carried the party from

Roman Ship from Tomb at Pompeii.

Caesarea along the Syrian coast, northward of Cyprus, past Cilicia and Pamphylia, to Myra of Lycia. There the centurion found a ship of Alexandria sailing for Italy, one of the great corn fleet carrying grain from Egypt for the multitudes of Rome. (After the capture of Jerus the emperor Titus returned to Italy in such a vessel, touching at Rhegium and landing at Puteoli.) The size of the vessel is indicated by the fact that there were 276 persons on board, crew and passengers all told (Acts **27** 37). St. Luke has made no note of the name of this or of the previous vessels in which St. Paul had voyaged. Of the presumably larger vessel, also an Alexandrian corn ship bound for Rome, which had wintered in Melita, and which afterward took on board the shipwrecked party

(Acts **28** 11), "the sign" (παράσημον, *parásēmon*) is given, and she is called "The Twin Brothers." The expression shows that it was in painting or relief; a figurehead, with the Twin Brothers represented, would be given by ἐπίσημον, *epísēmon.* The **cargo** (φορτίον, *phortíon*, Acts **27** 10, AV and RV "lading") in this case was wheat (**27** 38), but another word is used, γόμος, *gómos*, by St. Luke of a ship's load of varied wares (Acts **21** 3; cf Rev **18** 11 ff).

Of those engaged in handling the ship we find (ver 11) the **master** (κυβερνήτης, *kubernḗtēs*), the **owner** (ναύκληρος, *naúklēros*, although this expression seems not quite consistent with the ownership of a corn ship of the imperial service, and Ramsay's distinction between the words, making the former "sailing-master" and the latter "captain," may be better), the **sailors** (ver 30, who treacherously sought to lower the ship's boat on the pretence of laying out anchors from the "foreship" or prow, and to get away from the doomed vessel).

Of operations belonging to the navigation of the vessel in the storm there were (1) the taking on board of the ship's boat and securing it with **ropes** (ver 16, in which operation St. Luke seems to have taken part; cf ver 32), (2) the undergirding of the ship (ver 17, using **helps**, that is taking measures of relief and adopting the expedient, only resorted to in extremities, of passing cables under the keel of the ship to keep the hull together and to preserve the timbers from starting), (3) the lowering of the gear (ver 17, reducing sail, taking down the mainsail and the main yard), (4) throwing freight overboard and later casting out the tackling of the ship (ver 19), (5) taking soundings (ver 28), (6) letting go four anchors from the stern (ver 29, stern-anchoring being very unusual, but a necessity in the circumstances), (7) further lightening the ship by throwing the wheat into the sea (ver 38), (8) cutting the anchor cables, unlashing the rudders, hoisting up the foresail to the wind, and holding straight for the beach (ver 40).

Coin of Antoninus Pius, Showing Anchor.

Of the parts of the ship's **equipment** there are mentioned "the sounding lead" (βολίς, *bolís*, though it is the vb. which is here used), "the anchors" (ἄγκυραι, *ágkurai*, of which every ship carried several, and which at successive periods have been made of stone, iron, lead and perhaps other metals, each having two flukes and being held by a cable or a chain), "the rudders" (πηδάλια, *pēdália*, of which every ship had two for steering, which in this case had been lifted out of the water and secured by "bands" to the side of the ship and unlashed when the critical moment came), "the foresail" (ἀρτέμων, *artémōn*, not the mainsail, but the small sail at the bow of the vessel which at the right moment was hoisted to the wind to run her ashore), and "the boat" (σκάφη, *skáphē*, which had been in tow in the wake of the vessel, according to custom still prevalent in those seas—coasting-vessels being sometimes becalmed, when the crew get into the small boat and take the ship in tow, using the oars to get her round a promontory or into a position more favorable for the wind). The season for navigation in those seas in ancient times was from April to October. During the winter the vessels were laid up, or remained in the shelter of some suitable haven. The reason for this was not simply the tempestuous character of the weather, but the obscuration of the heavens which prevented observations being taken for the steering of the ship (Acts **27** 20).

3. In Other Books

In 2 Cor **11** 25 St. Paul mentions among sufferings he had endured for Christ's sake that thrice he had suffered shipwreck, and that he had been "a night and a day in the deep," implying that he had been in danger of his life clinging to a spar, or borne upon a hurriedly constructed raft. It may be a reminiscence of the sea when St. Paul in the very earliest of his Epp. (1 Thess **4** 16), speaking of the coming of the Lord, says "The Lord himself shall descend from heaven, with a shout" (ἐν κελεύσματι, *en keleúsmati*), where the picture is that of the κελευστής, *keleustḗs*, giving the time to the rowers on board a ship. Although ὑπηρέτης, *hupērétēs*, was "an underrower" and ὑπηρεσία, *hupēresía*, "the crew of a ship," as contrasted with κυβερνήτης, *kubernḗtēs*, "the sailing-master," the derived meaning of "servant" or "officer" has lost in the NT all trace of its origin (Mt **5** 25; Lk **1** 2 and many passages; cf στέλλειν, *stéllein*, and συστέλλειν, *sustéllein*, where the idea of "furling" or "shifting a sail" is entirely lost: 1 Cor **7** 29; 2 Cor **8** 20).

Figurative: In He the hope of the gospel is figured as "an anchor . . . . sure and stedfast, and entering into that which is within the veil" (**6** 19, esp. with Ebrard's note in Alford, ad loc.). St. James, showing the power of little things, adduces the ships, large though they be, and driven by fierce winds, turned about by a very small "rudder" (πηδάλιον, *pēdálion*), as "the impulse of the steersman willeth" (Jas **3** 4). In Rev there is a representation of the fall of Babylon in language reminiscent of the fall of Tyre (Ezk **27**), in which lamentations arise from the merchants of the earth who can no more buy her varied merchandise (τόν γόμον, *tón gómon*, "cargo" RVm), and shipmasters and passengers and seafaring people look in terror and grief upon the smoke of her burning (Rev **18** 12–18).

Literature.—The usual books on Gr and Rom antiquities furnish descriptions and illustrations. Works on the monuments like Layard, *Nineveh*, II, 379 ff; Maspero, *Ancient Egypt and Assyria;* Ball, *Light from the East*, and Reissner, *Cairo Museum Catalogue*, "Models of Ships and Boats," 1913, contain descriptions and figured representations which are instructive. On shipping and navigation in classical antiquity Smith of Jordanhill, *Voyage and Shipwreck of St. Paul*, is still the standard authority.

T. Nicol

SHISHA, shī'sha (שִׁישָׁא, *shīshā'*): One of Solomon's officers of state (1 K **4** 3).

SHISHAK, shī'shak (שִׁישַׁק, *shīshak* [1 K **14** 25]; Σουσακείμ, *Sousakeím*): Sheshonk or Sheshenq I,

1. Shishak, 952–930 BC

as he is called on the monuments, the founder of the XXIId Dynasty, was in all probability of Libyan origin. It is possible that his claim to the throne was that of the sword, but it is more likely that he acquired it by marriage with a princess of the dynasty preceding. On the death of Pasebkhanu II, the last of the kings of the XXIst Dynasty, 952 BC, Shishak ascended the throne, with an efficient army and a well-filled treasury at his command. He was a warlike prince and cherished dreams of Asiatic dominion.

2. Patron of Jeroboam

He had not long been seated on the throne when Jeroboam the son of Nebat, of the tribe of Ephraim, whom Solomon had promoted but afterward had cause to suspect, fled from the displeasure of his sovereign to the court of Shishak (1 K **11** 26 ff). There Jeroboam remained till the death of Solomon, when he returned to Canaan, and, on Rehoboam's returning an unsatisfactory answer to the people's demands for relief from their burdens, headed the revolt of the Ten Tribes, over whom he was chosen king with his capital at Shechem (1 K **12** 25 ff). Whether there was not in the XXIst Dynasty some kind of suzerainty of Egypt over Pal, when Solomon married Pharaoh's daughter and received with her Gezer as a dowry, seems not to be clearly established.

It is, however, natural that Jeroboam's patron in the day of adversity should take sides with him against Rehoboam, now that the kingdom was divided. Active support of Jeroboam would be in the line of his dreams of an eastern empire.

So it came to pass that in the 5th year of Rehoboam, Shishak came up against Jerus with 1,200 chariots, and 60,000 horsemen, and people without number out of Egypt, the Libyans, Sukkiim, and Ethiopians, and took the fenced cities of Judah, and came to Jerus. At the preaching of the prophet

3. Syrian Campaign

Figure of the God Amon Holding Captive the Cities of Judah for Shishak.
One of the Heads of the Cities, Jud-ha-malek (Jehud of the King, Josh **19** 45), Which is the Third behind the Knee of the God Amon.

Shemaiah, Rehoboam and his people repented, and Jerus was saved from destruction, though not from plunder nor from servitude, for he became Shishak's servant (2 Ch **12** 8). Shishak took away the treasures of the house of the Lord and the treasures of the king's house, carrying off among the most precious of the spoils all the shields of gold which Solomon had made (1 K **14** 25 ff; 2 Ch **12** 1–9). From the Scripture narrative it does not appear that there was any occupation of Pal by the Egyp forces on this occasion.

4. Shishak's Record at Karnak

There is, however, a remarkable contemporary record of the campaign engraved on the south wall of the Temple of Amon at Karnak by Shishak himself. Not only is the expedition recorded, but there is a list of districts and towns of Pal granted to his victories by Amon-Ra and the goddess of Thebes engraved there. A number of towns mentioned in the Book of Josh have been identified; and among the names of the list are Rabbath, Taanach, Gibeon, Mahanaim, Beth-horon and other towns both of Israel and Judah. That names of places in the Northern Kingdom are mentioned in the list does not imply that Shishak had directed his armies against Jeroboam and plundered his territories. It was the custom in antiquity for a victorious monarch to include among conquered cities any place that paid tribute or was under subjection, whether captured in war or not; and it was sufficient reason for Shishak to include these Israelite places that Jeroboam, as seems probable, had invited him to come to his aid. Among the names in the list was "Jud-ha-malek"—Yudhmalk on the monuments—which was at first believed to represent the king of Judah, with a figure which passed for Rehoboam. Being, however, a place-name, it is now recognized to be the town Yehudah, belonging to the king. On the death of Shishak his successor assumed a nominal suzeraînty over the land of Canaan.

Literature.—Flinders Petrie, *History of Egypt*, III, 227 ff; Maspero, *Struggle of the Nations*, 772 ff; Nicol, *Recent Archaeology and the Bible*, 222–25.

T. Nicol

SHITRAI, shit′rī, shit-rā′ī, shit′rȧ-ī (שִׁטְרַי, *shiṭray*): A Sharonite, David's chief shepherd (1 Ch **27** 29).

SHITTAH, shit′a, **TREE** (שִׁטָּה, *shiṭṭāh;* LXX **ξύλον ἄσηπτον**, *xúlon ásēpton;* RV ACACIA TREE [Isa **41** 19]); **SHITTIM WOOD** (עֲצֵי שִׁטִּים, *'ăçē shiṭṭīm;* RV ACACIA WOOD [Ex **25** 5.10.13; **26** 15.26; **27** 1.6; Dt **10** 3]): The word was originally *shinṭah*, derived from the Arab. *sanṭ*, now a name confined to one species of acacia, *Acacia nilotica* (N.O. *Leguminosae*), but possibly was once a more inclusive term. The *A. nilotica* is at present confined to the Sinaitic peninsula and to Egypt. Closely allied species, the *A. tortilis* and *A. seyal*, both classed together under the Arab. name *sayyāl*, are plentiful in the valleys about the Dead Sea from Engedi southward. Those who have ridden from *'Ain Jidy* to *Jebel Usdum* will never forget these most striking features of the landscape. They are most picturesque trees with their gnarled trunks, sometimes 2 ft. thick, their twisted, thorny branches, which often give the whole tree an umbrella-like form, and their fine bipinnate leaves with minute leaflets. The curiously twisted pods and the masses of gum arabic which exude in many parts are also peculiar features. The trees yield a valuable, hard, close-grained timber, not readily attacked by insects.

E. W. G. Masterman

SHITTIM, shit′im (הַשִּׁטִּים, *ha-shiṭṭīm*, "the acacias"; **Σαττείν**, *Sattein*):

(1) This marked the last camping-ground of Israel before they crossed the Jordan to begin the conquest of Western Pal. Here it was that the people fell into the snare set for them by the satanic counsel of Balaam, who thus brought upon them greater evil than all his prohibited curses could have done (Nu **25** 1 ff; **31** 16). In Nu **33** 49 it is called **Abel-shittim**. It was from Shittim that Joshua sent the spies to view out the land and Jericho (Josh **2** 1); and from this point the host moved forward to the river (**3** 1). The place is mentioned by Micah in a passage of some difficulty (**6** 5): after "what Balaam the son of Beor answered," perhaps some such phrase as "remember what I did" has fallen out. This would then be a reference to the display of Divine power in arresting the flow of Jordan until the host had safely crossed. Jos places the camp "near Jordan where the city Abila now stands, a place full of palm trees" (*Ant*, IV, viii, 1). *Onom* says Shittim was near to Mt. Peor (Fogor). It may possibly be identical with *Khirbet el-Kefrain*, about 6 miles S. of the Jordan, on the lip of *Wâdy Seisebān*, where there are many acacias.

(2) In Joel **3** 18 we read of the **valley of Shittim** which is to be watered by a fountain coming forth of the house of the Lord. It must therefore be sought on the W. of the Jordan. The waters from the Jerus district are carried to the Dead Sea down the *Wâdy* which continues the Brook Kidron: *Wâdy en-Nār*. The acacia is found plentifully in the lower reaches of this valley, which may possibly be intended by the prophet.

W. Ewing

SHIZA, shī′za (שִׁיזָא, *shīzā';* **Σαιζά**, *Saizá*): A Reubenite, one of David's leading warriors (1 Ch **11** 42).

SHOA, shō′a (שׁוֹעַ, *shōa'; **Σουέ**, Soué*): A people named in Ezk **23** 23 in association with Babylonians, Chaldaeans and Assyrians. Schrader identifies with the *Sutū* of the inscriptions (E. of the Tigris).

SHOBAB, shō'bab (שׁוֹבָב, *shōbhābh;* **Σωβάβ,** *Sōbáb*):

(1) One of the sons of David (2 S **5** 14; **1** Ch **3** 5; **14** 4).

(2) A son of Caleb (1 Ch **2** 18).

SHOBACH, shō'bak (שׁוֹבַךְ, *shōbhakh;* **Σωβάκ,** *Sōbák*): Captain of the Syrian host (2 S **10** 16.18); but "Shophach" (שׁוֹפַךְ, *shōphakh*) in 1 Ch **19** 16.18.

SHOBAI, shō'bī, shō-bā'ī, shō'bā-ī (שֹׁבָי, *shōbhāy;* B, **'Αβαού,** *Abaoú,* A, Luc., **Σωβαί,** *Sōbaí*): The head of one of the families which returned from the Bab captivity (Ezr **2** 42; Neh **7** 45).

SHOBAL, shō'bal (שׁוֹבָל, *shōbhāl,* "overflowing"; **Σωβάλ,** *Sōbál,* with variants):

(1) An Edomite name mentioned in connection with Lotan, Zibeon and Anah, as that of a "son" of Seir (Gen **36** 20), the father of a clan (ver 23), and a Horite "duke" (*'allūph*) (ver 29; 1 Ch **1** 38. 40).

(2) A Calebite, the father (possibly of the inhabitants) of Kiriath-jearim (1 Ch **2** 50.52).

(3) A Judahite, perhaps to be identified with (2) above (1 Ch **4** 1 f).

SHOBEK, shō'bek (שׁוֹבֵק, *shōbhēḳ;* **Σωβήκ,** *Sōbēk*): One of those who sealed the covenant under Nehemiah after the Bab captivity (Neh **10** 24).

SHOBI, shō'bī (שֹׁבִי, *shōbhī;* **Οὐεσβεί,** *Ouesbei*): One of those who remained faithful to David during the rebellion of Absalom (2 S **17** 27).

SHOCHOH, shō'kō (שׂוֹכֹה, *sōkhōh,* B, **Σοκχώθ,** *Sokchōth,* A, **'Οκχώ,** *Okchō*): This in 1 S **17** 1 AV is a variant of Socoh (q.v.).

SHOE, shōō, **SHOE-LATCHET,** shōō'lach-et (נַעַל, *na'al,* lit. "that which is fastened," with denominative vb. נָעַל, *nā'al,* "to provide with

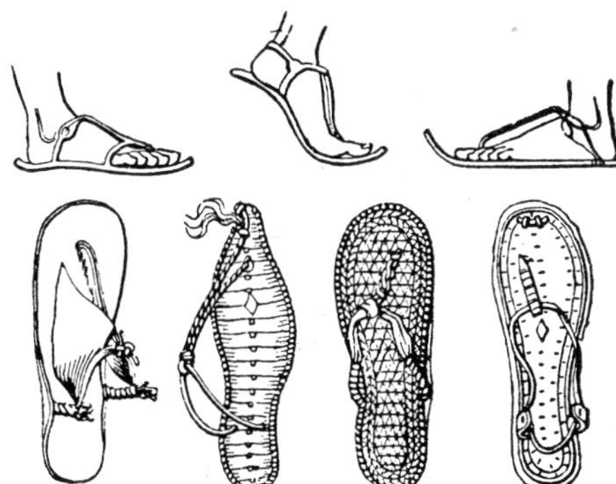

Egyptian Sandals.

shoes" [2 Ch **28** 15; Ezk **16** 10]; **ὑπόδημα,** *hupódēma* [Sir **46** 19; Mt **3** 11, etc], from the vb. **ὑποδέω,** *hupodéō* [Mk **6** 9; Eph **6** 15], "to bind under," **σανδάλιον,** *sandálion,* "sandal" [Jth **10** 4; **16** 9; Mk **6** 9; Acts **12** 8]; AV, RVm also have "shoe" for מִנְעָל, *min'āl,* "bar" [so RV text] in Dt **33** 25; the "latchet" is either שְׂרוֹךְ, *s*ᵉ*rōkh,* "twisted thing" [Gen **14** 23; Isa **5** 27], or **ἱμάς,** *himás,* "leather thong" [Mk **1** 7; Lk **3** 16; Jn **1** 27]): The *na'al* was a simple piece of leather tied on the foot with the *s*ᵉ*rōkh,* so easy of construction that its low cost was proverbial (Am **2** 6; **8** 6; Sir **46** 19; cf Gen **14** 23), and to be without it was a sign of extreme poverty (2 Ch **28** 15; Isa **20** 2). Women, however, might have ornamental sandals (Cant **7** 1; Jth **16** 9), and Ezekiel names "sealskin" (**16** 10) as a particularly luxurious material, but the omission of sandals from the list of Isa **3** 18–23 shows that they were not commonly made articles of great expense. The *hupodēma* was likewise properly a sandal, but the word was also used to denote a shoe that covered the foot. The contrast between *hupodēma* in Mt **10** 10 and *sandalion* in Mk **6** 9 seems to show that this meaning is not unknown in the NT, the "shoe" being regarded as an article of luxury (cf Lk **15** 22). But in Mt **3** 11 and ‖'s, only the sandal can be meant.

Sandals were not worn indoors, so that putting them on was a sign of readiness for activity (Ex **12** 11; Acts **12** 8; Eph **6** 15), the more wealthy having them brought (Mt **3** 11) and fastened (Mk **1** 7 and ‖'s) by slaves. When one entered a house they were removed; all the more, naturally, on entering a sanctuary (Ex **3** 5; Josh **5** 15; Acts **7** 33). Mourners, however, did not wear them even out of doors, as a sign of grief (Ezk **24** 17.23), perhaps for the same reason that other duties of the toilet were neglected (2 S **12** 20, etc). A single long journey wore out a pair of sandals (Josh **9** 5.13), and the preservation of "the latchet of their shoes" from being broken (Isa **5** 27) would require almost miraculous help.

Ruth **4** 7 f states as a "custom in former times in Israel," that when any bargain was closed "a man drew off his shoe, and gave it to his neighbor." This was of course simply a special form of earnest-money, used in all transactions. In Dt **25** 9 f the custom appears in a different light. If a man refused to perform his duty to his deceased brother's wife, the elders of the city were to remove his shoe and disgrace him publicly, "And his name shall be called in Israel, The house of him that hath his shoe loosed." The removal of the shoe is apparently connected with the rite in Ruth **4** 7 as a renunciation of the man's privilege. But the general custom seems to have become obsolete, for the removal of the shoe is now a reproach.

The meaning of Ps **60** 8 ‖ **108** 9, "Upon [m "unto"] Edom will I cast my shoe," is uncertain. עַל, *'al,* may mean either "upon" or "unto." If the former, some (otherwise unsubstantiated) custom of asserting ownership of land may be meant. If the latter, the meaning is "Edom I will treat as a slave," to whom the shoes are cast on entering a house.

Burton Scott Easton

SHOHAM, shō'ham (שֹׁהַם, *shōham,* "onyx"; B, **'Ισοάμ,** *Isoám,* A, **'Ισσοάμ,** *Issoám*): One of the sons of Merari (1 Ch **24** 27).

SHOMER, shō'mẽr (שׁוֹמֵר, *shōmēr*):

(1) The father of one of the conspirators who killed Joash (2 K **12** 21). See Shimeath.

(2) One of the sons of Heber of the tribe of Asher (1 Ch **7** 32). See Shemer.

SHOPHACH, shō'fak. See Shobach.

SHOPHAN, shō'fan (שׁוֹפָן, *shōphān*). See Atroth-Shophan.

SHORE, shōr: (1) חוֹף, *ḥōph,* always of the Mediterranean, variously trᵈ "haven," "beach," "shore," "sea-shore," "coast," "sea coast" (Gen **49** 13; Dt **1** 7; Josh **9** 1; Jgs **5** 17; Jer **47** 7; Ezk **25** 16). (2) שָׂפָה, *sāphāh,* lit. "lip"; cf Arab. شَفَة, *shafat,* "lip"; of the sand upon the seashore, a figure of multitude (Gen **22** 17; Ex **14** 30; Josh **11** 4; Jgs **7** 12; 1 S **13** 5; 1 K **4** 29); the shore of the Red Sea or Gulf of *'Aḳabah* by Ezion-geber (1 K **9** 26; 2 Ch **8** 17); the brink of the River Nile (Gen **41** 3.17); the edge (AV "brink") of the valley of Arnon (Dt **2** 36). (3) קָצֶה, *ḳāçeh*, lit. "end," "extremity," the uttermost part (AV "shore") of the Salt Sea (Josh **15** 2); קְצֵה הָאָרֶץ, *ḳeçēh hā-'āreç*, "the end of the earth" (Ps **46** 9); cf Arab. اقاصي الارض, *'aḳâṣî-l-'arḍ*, "the uttermost parts of the earth." (4) χεῖλος, *cheîlos*, lit. "lip," "as the sand which is by the seashore" (He **11** 12). (5) αἰγιαλός, *aigialós*, the beach (AV "shore") of the Sea of Galilee (Mt **13** 2.48; Jn **21** 4); of the Mediterranean (Acts **21** 5; **27** 39.40). (6) ἆσσον παρελέγοντο τὴν Κρήτην, *ásson parelégonto tḗn Krḗtēn*, doubtful reading, "sailed along Crete, close in shore" (AV "sailed along by Crete") (Acts **27** 13). See COAST; HAVEN; SAND.

ALFRED ELY DAY

SHORTEN, shôr't'n: The Heb word *ḳāçar* and the Gr *kolobóō* lit. indicate abbreviation of time or space (Ps **89** 45; Prov **10** 27; Ezk **42** 5); **figuratively** they point to limitation of power or of suffering (Nu **11** 23; Isa **50** 2; **59** 1; Mt **24** 22; Mk **13** 20).

SHOSHANNIM EDUTH, shō-shan'im ē'duth. See SONG; PSALMS.

SHOULDER, shōl'dēr (שְׁכֶם, *shekhem*, כָּתֵף, *kāthēph*, זְרֹעַ or זְרוֹעַ, *zerōa'*, זְרֹעָה or זְרוֹעָה, *zerō'āh*, שׁוֹק, *shōḳ*; ὦμος, *ōmos*, βραχίων, *brachiōn* [Sir **7** 31 only]): The meanings of the Heb words are rather varied. The first (*shekhem*) has perhaps the widest application. It is used for the part of the body on which heavy loads are carried (Gen **21** 14; **24** 15.45; Ex **12** 34; Josh **4** 5; Jgs **9** 48). King Saul's impressive personality is thus described: "There was not among the children of Israel a goodlier person than he: from his shoulders and upward he was higher than any of the people" (1 S **9** 2; **10** 23). To carry loads on the shoulder or to have "a staff on the shoulder" is expressive of subjection and servitude, yea, of oppression and cruel punishment, and the removal of such burdens or of the rod of the oppressor connotes delivery and freedom (Isa **9** 4; **14** 25).

Figuratively: The shoulders also bear responsibility and power. Thus it is said of King Messiah, that "the government shall be upon his shoulder" (Isa **9** 6) and "the key of the house of David will I lay upon his shoulder; and he shall open, and none shall shut; and he shall shut, and none shall open" (**22** 22). Job declares that he will refute all accusations of unlawful conduct made against him, in the words: "Oh . . . . that I had the indictment which mine adversary hath written! Surely I would carry it upon my shoulder" (Job **31** 35 f).

The Heb word *kāthēph* comes very close in meaning to the above, though it is occasionally used in the sense of arm- and shoulder-piece of a garment. Like Heb *shekhem*, it is used to describe the part of the body accustomed to carry loads. On it the Levites carried the implements of the sanctuary (Nu **7** 9; 1 Ch **15** 15; 2 Ch **35** 3). Oriental mothers and fathers carried their children on the shoulder astride (Isa **49** 22; cf **60** 4); thus also the little bundle of the poor is borne (Ezk **12** 6.7.12). The loaded shoulder is likely to be "worn" or chafed under the burden (**29** 18). In the two passages of the NT in which we find the Gr equivalent of shoulder (*ōmos*, fairly common in Apoc), it corresponds most closely with this use (Mt **23** 4; Lk **15** 5). Of the shoulders of animals the word *kāthēph* is used in Ezk **34** 21 (of sheep, where, however, men are intended) and in Isa **30** 6 (of asses).

Stubborn opposition and unwillingness is expressed by "withdrew the shoulder" (Neh **9** 29), or "pulled away the shoulder" (Zec **7** 11), where the marginal rendering is "they gave [or "turned"] a stubborn shoulder." Contrast "bow the shoulder," i.e. "submit" (Bar **2** 21). Cf "stiffnecked"; see NECK. Somewhat difficult for the understanding of Occidentals is the poetical passage in the blessing of Moses: "Of Benjamin he said, The beloved of Jeh shall dwell in safety by him; he covereth him all the day long, and he dwelleth between his shoulders" (Dt **33** 12). The "shoulders" refer here to the mountain saddles and proclivities of the territory of Benjamin between which Jerus, the beloved of Jeh, which belonged to Judah, lay nestling close upon the confines of the neighboring tribe, or even built in part on ground belonging to Benjamin.

Much less frequently than the above-mentioned words, we find *zerōa'*, *zerō'āh*, which is used of the "boiled shoulder of the ram" which was a wave offering at the consecration of a Nazirite (Nu **6** 19) and of one of the priestly portions of the sacrifice (Dt **18** 3). In Sir **7** 31 this portion is called *brachiōn*, properly "arm," but both AV and RV translate "shoulder." Regarding the wave and heave offerings see SACRIFICE. AV frequently translates Heb *shōḳ*, lit. "leg," "thigh" (q.v.) by "shoulder," which RV occasionally retains in the margin (e.g. Nu **6** 20).

H. L. E. LUERING

SHOULDER-BLADE, shōl'dēr-blād (שִׁכְמָה, *shikhmāh*): "Then let my shoulder [*kāthēph*] fall from the shoulder-blade [*shikhmāh*], and mine arm [*zerōa'*] be broken from the bone [*ḳāneh*]" (Job **31** 22). The Heb word is the fem. form of *shekhem* (see SHOULDER). It is found only in this passage.

SHOULDER-PIECE, shōl'dēr-pēs (כָּתֵף, *kāthēph*): The word designates the two straps or pieces of cloth which passed from the back of the ephod (see EPHOD) of the high priest over the shoulder and were fastened at the front. These shoulder-pieces seem to have been made of a precious texture of linen (or byssos) with threads of gold, blue, purple and scarlet, to which two onyx (or beryl) stones were attached bearing the names of six tribes of Israel each. These are called the "stones of memorial" (Ex **39** 18). On these straps there were also fastened the plaited or woven bands ("wreathed chains") from which, by means of two golden rings, the breastplate was suspended. It is by no means clear from the descriptions (Ex **28** 7.12.25; **39** 4.7.18.20) how we have to imagine the form and attachment of these shoulder-pieces. It has been thought that the ephod might be of Egyp origin, which is not very probable, though V. Ancessi, *Annales de philosophie chrétienne*, 1872, 45 ff, reproduces some representations from the great work of Lepsius, *Denkmäler*, where costly royal garments have two shoulder straps, like the ephod. Usually Egyp garments have no shoulder strap, or at most one. H. L. E. LUERING

SHOVEL, shuv''l: (1) רַחַת, *rahath*, is a wooden shovel used on the threshing-floor for winnowing the grain (Isa **30** 24). (2) יָע, *yā'*, is used in various passages to indicate some instrument employed to carry away ashes from the altar (Ex **27** 3; **38** 3; Nu **4** 14; 1 K **7** 40.45; 2 K **25** 14; 2 Ch **4** 11.16; Jer **52** 18). It was very likely a small shovel like those used in connection with modern fireplaces for cleaning away the ashes (cf Heb *yā'āh*, "to sweep away") or for carrying live coals to start a new fire. (3) יָתֵד, *yāthēdh* (Dt **23** 13 RVm).

JAMES A. PATCH

SHOW, shō. See SHEW.

SHOWBREAD, shō'bred. See SHEWBREAD.

SHOWBREAD, TABLE OF. See SHEWBREAD, TABLE OF.

SHOWER, shou'ēr: (1) רְבִיבִים, *r*ᵉ*bhībhīm*, a pl. form apparently denoting gentle rain, usually used **figuratively,** as in Dt **32** 2; Ps **72** 6; Mic **5** 7. (2) גֶּשֶׁם, *geshem*, used of gentle rain in Job **37** 6: "shower of rain," AV "small rain"; used of the flood in Gen **7** 12. **Figuratively,** of blessing, "showers of blessing" (Ezk **34** 26); of destruction: "There shall be an overflowing shower in mine anger, and great hailstones in wrath to consume it" (Ezk **13** 13). (3) זֶרֶם, *zerem*, usually storm or tempest (cf Isa **4** 6; **28** 2): "They are wet with the showers of the mountain" (Job **24** 8). (4) ὄμβρος, *ómbros* (Lk **12** 54). Rain is unknown in Pal in the long summer of 5 or 6 months. A few showers usually fall in September, succeeded by fine weather for some weeks before the beginning of the heavy and long-continued winter rains.

ALFRED ELY DAY

SHRINE, shrīn (**ναός,** *naós*): In Acts **19** 24 small models of temples for Diana.

SHROUD, shroud (חֹרֶשׁ, *ḥōresh*, "bough"): Winding-sheet for the dead. See BURIAL. Used in AV, ERV Ezk **31** 3 in the rare old sense of "shelter," "covering." ARV has "a forest-like shade" (חֹרֶשׁ, *ḥōresh*, "wood," "wooded height") (Isa **17** 9, etc). Cf Milton, *Comus*, 147.

SHRUB, shrub (שִׂיחַ, *sī*ᵃ*ḥ* [Gen **21** 15]). See BUSH, (2).

SHUA, SHUAH, shōō'a:

(1) (שׁוּעַ, *shū*ᵃ*'*, "prosperity"): A Canaanite whose daughter Judah took to wife (Gen **38** 2.12; 1 Ch **2** 3; see BATH-SHUA).

(2) (שׁוּעָא, *shū'ā'*, "prosperity"): Daughter of Heber, an Asherite (1 Ch **7** 32).

(3) (שׁוּחַ, *shū*ᵃ*ḥ*, "depression"): A son of Keturah by Abraham (Gen **25** 2; 1 Ch **1** 32), and his posterity. See BILDAD.

(4) A brother of Caleb (1 Ch **4** 11). See SHUHAH.

SHUAL, shōō'al (שׁוּעָל, *shū'āl*): An Asherite (1 Ch **7** 36).

SHUAL, LAND OF (אֶרֶץ שׁוּעָל, *'ereç shū'āl*; **ἡ Σωγάλ,** *hē Sōgál*): From their encampment at Michmash the Philis sent out marauding bands, one going westward toward Beth-horon, another eastward, "the way of the border that looketh down upon the valley of Zeboim." The pass to the S. was held against them by Israel. The third party therefore went northward, turning "unto the way that leadeth to Ophrah, unto the land of Shual" (1 S **13** 17 f). Ophrah is probably identical with *eṭ-Ṭaiyibeh*, a village which lies some 5 miles E. of *Beitīn* (Bethel). It is in this district therefore that the land of Shual must be sought, but no definite identification is possible. W. EWING

SHUBAEL, shōō'bā-el, shōō-bā'el (שׁוּבָאֵל, *shūbhā'ēl*):

(1) A Levite, son of Amram (1 Ch **24** 20); one of the leaders of song in the temple (1 Ch **25** 20). See SHEBUEL; Gray, *HPN*, 310.

(2) A son of Heman (1 Ch **25** 4). See SHEBUEL.

SHUHAH, shōō'ha (שׁוּחָה, *shūḥāh*, "depression"); A brother of Caleb (1 Ch **4** 11).

SHUHAM, shōō'ham (שׁוּחָם, *shūḥām*): Son of Dan, ancestor of the **Shuhamites** (Nu **26** 42 f). In Gen **46** 23 called "Hushim."

SHUHITE, shōō'hīt (שׁוּחִי, *shūḥī*): Cognomen of Bildad, one of Job's friends (Job **2** 11; **8** 1; **18** 1; **25** 1; **42** 9). The place referred to cannot be definitely located. See BILDAD; SHUAH.

SHULAMMITE, shōō'la-mīt (Cant **6** 13, AV "Shulamite"). See SHUNAMMITE.

SHUMATHITES, shōō'math-īts (שֻׁמָתִי, *shumā-thī*): One of the families of Kiriath-jearim (1 Ch **2** 53).

SHUNAMMITE, shōō'na-mīt (שֻׁנַמִּית, *shunam-mīth*, שׁוּנַמִּית, *shūnammīth*; B, **Σωμανεῖτις,** *Sōma-neîtis*, A, **Σουμανιτῆς,** *Soumanitḗs*): Applied to natives of Shunem.

(1) Abishag, who was brought to minister to the aged king David, love for whom led Adonijah to his doom (1 K **1** 3.15; **2** 17, etc).

(2) The woman, name unknown, whose son Elisha raised from the dead (2 K **4** 12, etc). Later when apparently she had become a widow, after seven years' absence on account of famine, in the land of the Philis, she returned to find her property in the hands of others. Elisha's intervention secured its restoration (**8** 1–6).

(3) The Shulammite (Cant **6** 13). In this name there is the exchange of *l* for *n* which is common.

W. EWING

SHUNEM, shōō'nem (שׁוּנֵם, *shūnēm*; B, **Σουνάν,** *Sounán*, A, **Σουνάμ,** *Sounám*): A town in the territory of Issachar named with Jezreel and Chesulloth (Josh **19** 18). Before the battle of Gilboa the Philis pitched their camp here. They and the army of Saul, stationed on Gilboa, were in full view of each other (1 S **28** 4). It was the scene of the touching story recorded in 2 K **4** 8–37, in which the prophet Elisha raises to life the son of his Shunammite benefactress. *Onom* describes it as a village called Sulem, 5 Rom miles S. of Mt. Tabor. This points to the modern *Sōlam*, a village surrounded by cactus hedges and orchards on the lower southwestern slope of *Jebel ed-Duḥy* ("Hill of Moreh"). It commands an uninterrupted view across the plain of Esdraelon to Mt. Carmel, which is about 15 miles distant. It also looks far across the valley of Jezreel to the slopes of Gilboa on the S. It therefore meets satisfactorily the conditions of Josh and 1 S. A question has, however, been raised as to its identity with the Shunem of 2 K **4**. Elisha's home was in Samaria. Apparently Carmel was one of his favorite haunts. If he passed Shunem "continually" (ver 9), going to and coming from the mountain, it involved a very long détour if this were the village visited. It would seem more natural to identify the Shunem of Elisha with the Sanim of *Onom*, which is said to be in the territory of Sebaste (Samaria), in the region of Akrabatta: or perhaps with *Sālim*, fully a mile N. of Taanach, as nearer the line of travel between Samaria and Carmel.

There is, however, nothing to show that Elisha's visits to Shunem were paid on his journeys between Samaria and Carmel. It may have been his custom to visit certain cities on circuit, on business calling for his personal attention, e.g. in connection with the "schools of the prophets." Materials do not exist on which any certain conclusion can rest. Both *Sōlam* and *Sālim* are on the edge of the splendid grain fields of Esdraelon (2 K **4** 18).

W. EWING

SHUNI, shōō′nī, **SHUNITES,** shōō′nīts (שׁוּנִי, *shūnī*): One of the sons of Gad and his descendants (Gen **46** 16; Nu **26** 15).

SHUPHAM, shōō′fam, **SHUPHAMITES,** shōō′-fam-īts. See SHEPHUPHAM.

SHUPPIM, shup′im (שֻׁפִּים, *shuppīm*):
(1) One of the descendants of Benjamin (1 Ch **7** 12.15).
(2) One of the porters in the temple (1 Ch **26** 16). See MUPPIM; SHEPHUPHAM.

SHUR, shûr, shōōr (שׁוּר, *shūr;* Σούρ, *Soúr*): The name of a desert E. of the Gulf of Suez. The word means a "wall," and may probably refer to the mountain wall of the *Tîh* plateau as visible from the shore plains. In Gen **16** 7 Hagar at Kadesh (*'Ain Ḳadîs*) (see ver 14) is said to have been "in the way to Shur." Abraham also lived "between Kadesh and Shur" (Gen **20** 1). The position of Shur is defined (Gen **25** 18) as being "opposite Egypt on the way to Assyria." After crossing the Red Sea (Ex **15** 4) the Hebrews entered the desert of Shur (ver 22), which extended southward a distance of three days' journey. It is again noticed (1 S **15** 7) as being opposite Egypt, and (**27** 8) as near Egypt. There is thus no doubt of its situation, on the E. of the Red Sea, and of the Bitter Lakes.

Brugsch, however, proposed to regard Shur ("the wall") as equivalent to the Egyp *anbu* ("wall"), the name of a fortification of some kind apparently near *Ḳanṭarah* (see MIGDOL [2]), probably barring the entrance to Egypt on the road from Pelusium to Zoan. The extent of this "wall" is unknown, but Brugsch connects it with the wall mentioned by Diodorus Siculus (i.4) who wrote about 8 BC, and who attributed it to Sesostris (probably Rameses II) who defended "the east side of Egypt against the irruptions of the Syrians and Arabians, by a wall drawn from Pelusium through the deserts as far as to Heliopolis, for a space of 1,500 furlongs." Heliopolis lies 90 miles (not 188) S.W. of Pelusium: this wall, if it existed at all, would have run on the edge of the desert which extends N. of *Wâdy Tumeilât* from *Ḳanṭarah* to *Tell el-Kebîr;* but this line, on the borders of Goshen, is evidently much too far W. to have any connection with the desert of Shur E. of the Gulf of Suez. See Budge, *Hist. Egypt*, 90; Brugsch, *Egypt under the Pharaohs*, abridged edition, 320.

C. R. CONDER

SHUSHAN, shōō′shan (שׁוּשַׁן, *shūshan;* Σουσάν, *Sousán*, Σοῦσα, *Soúsa*): This city, the *Šušu* or *Šušan* of the Babylonians, and the native

1. Position, Etymology and Forms of Its Name

(Elamite) *Šušun*, is the modern *Shush* (*Sus*) in Southwestern Persia, a series of ruin-mounds on the banks of the river Kerkha. The ancient etymologies ("city of lilies" or "of horses") are probably worthless, as an etymology in the language of the place would rather be expected. Sayce therefore connects the name with *šašša*, meaning "former," and pointing to some such meaning as "the old" city. It is frequently mentioned in the Bab inscriptions of the 3d millennium BC, and is expressed by the characters for the goddess Ištar and for "cedar," implying that it was regarded as the place of the "divine grove" (see 5, below). In later days, the Assyrians substituted for the second character, that having the value of *šeš*, possibly indicating its pronunciation. Radau (*Early Bab History*, 236) identifies *Shushan* (Susa) with the *Šâša* of the Bab king Kuri-galzu (14th cent. BC, if the first of the name), who dedicates to the Bab goddess Ninlil an inscription of a certain Siatu, who had, at an earlier date, dedicated it to Ištar for the life of the Bab king Dungi (c 2500 BC).

The surface still covered with ruins is about 2,000 hectares (4,940 acres), though this is but a fraction compared with the ancient extent of the city, which is estimated to have been between 12,000 and 15,000 hectares (29,640–37,000 acres). Though considerable, the extent of Susa was small compared with Nineveh and Babylon.

2. The Ruins

The ruins are divided by the French explorers into four tracts: (1) The Citadel-mound (W.), of the Achaemenian period (5th cent. BC), c 1,476 by 820 ft., dominating the plain (height c 124 ft.). (2) The Royal City on the E. of the Citadel, composed of two parts: the Apadana (N.E.), and a nearly triangular tract extending to the E. and the S. This contains the remains of the palace of Darius and his successors, and occupies rather more than 123 acres. The palace proper and the throne-room were separated from the rest of the official buildings. (3) The City, occupied by artisans, merchants, etc. (4) The district on the right bank, similarly inhabited. This anciently extended into all the lower plain, between the Shaour and the Kerkha. Besides these, there were many isolated ruins, and the suburbs contained a number of villages and separate constructions.

3. The "Royal City," "The Citadel," and the Ruins Therein

Most of the constructions at Susa are of the Pers period. In the northern part of the Royal City lie the remains of the Apadana, the only great monument of which remains were found on the level. The principal portion consisted of a great hall of columns, known as the throne-room of Artaxerxes Mnemon. It replaced an earlier structure by Darius, which was destroyed by fire in the time of Artaxerxes I. The columns apparently had capitals of the style common in Persia—the foreparts of two bulls kneeling back to back. In the Citadel a palace built by Xerxes seems to have existed, the base of one of his columns having been found there. Bricks bearing the inscriptions of early Elamite kings, and the foundations of older walls, testify to the antiquity of the occupation of this part. According to the explorers, this was the portion of the city reserved for the temples.

The number of important antiquities found on the site is considerable. Among the finds may be mentioned the triumphal stele of Narâm-

4. The Monuments Discovered

Sin, king of Agadé (3d–4th millennium BC); the statuettes of the Bab king Dungi (c 2360 BC); the reliefs and inscriptions of the Elamite king Ba(?)-ša-Šušinak (c 2340 BC); the obelisk inscribed with the laws of Ḫammurabi of Babylon; the bronze bas-relief of the Elamite king Sutruk-Naḫḫunte (c 1120 BC), who carried off from Babylonia the stelae of Narâm-Sin and Ḫammurabi above mentioned, together with numerous other Bab monuments; the stele of Adda-ḫamiti-In-Šušnak, of a much later date, together with numerous other objects of art and inscriptions—a most precious archaeological find.

Shushan passed through many serious crises, one of the severest being its capture and destruction by the armies of the Assyr king Aššur-

5. Aššur-bani-âpli's Description of the City

bani-âpli about 640 BC. According to his account, the *ziqqurat* or temple-tower of Susa was built of enameled brick imitating lapis-lazuli, and was adorned with pinnacles of bright bronze. The god of the city was Šušinak, who dwelt in a secret place, and none ever saw the form of his divinity. Lagamaru (Laomer) and five other of the city's deities were adored only by kings, and their images, with those of 12 more (worshipped by the people), were carried off as spoil to Assyria. Winged bulls and genii adorned Susa's temples, and figures of wild bulls protected the entrances to their shrines. Other noteworthy things were the sacred groves into which no stranger was allowed to enter, and the burial-places of the Elamite kings. After recovering from the blow inflicted by the Assyrians, Shushan ultimately regained its old importance, and, as the summer residence of the Pers kings, became the home of Ahasuerus and Queen Esther (Neh **1** 1; Est **1** 2.5; **2** 3; **3** 15; **9** 11 ff; Dnl **8** 2; Ad Est **11** 3).

LITERATURE.—See Perrot et Chipiez, *Histoire de l'art dans l'antiquité*, vol V, Perse, 1890; de Morgan, *Délégation en Perse* (*Mémoires*), 1900, etc; *Histoire et travaux de la délégation en Perse*, 1905; art. "Elamites" in Hastings *ERE*; art. ELAM in this work.

T. G. PINCHES

SHUSHAN EDUTH, shōō'shan ē'duth. See SONG; PSALMS.

SHUSHANCHITES, shōō-shan'kīts (שׁוּשַׁנְכָיֵא, *shūshānᵉkhāyē'* [Aram.]; B, **Σουσυναχαῖοι,** *Sousunachaioi;* AV **Susanchites**): Colonists in Samaria whose original home was in Shushan (Ezr **4** 9).

SHUTHALHITES, shōō-thal'hīts, shōō'thal-hīts. See SHUTHELAH.

SHUTHELAH, shōō-thē'la, shōō'thē-la, **SHUTHELAHITES,** shōō-thē'la-hīts, shōō'thē-la-hīts (שֻׁתַלְחִי, *shuthalḥī*): A son of Ephraim (Nu **26** 35.36; cf 1 Ch **7** 20.21), and his descendants. See GENEALOGY.

SHUTTLE, shut''l. See WEAVING.

SIA, sī'a, **SIAHA,** sī'a-ha (סִיעָא, *ṣī'ā'*): One of the remnant which returned from captivity (Neh **7** 47; Ezr **2** 44).

SIBBECAI, SIBBECHAI, sib'ē-kī, sib-ē-kā'ī (סִבְּכַי, *ṣibbᵉkhay*): One of the valiant men in David's army (2 S **21** 18; 1 Ch **11** 29; **20** 4; **27** 11).

SIBBOLETH, sib'ō-leth (סִבֹּלֶת, *ṣibbōleth*). See SHIBBOLETH.

SIBMAH, sib'ma. See SEBAM.

SIBRAIM, sib-rā'im, sib'ra-im (סִבְרַיִם, *ṣibhrayim;* B, **Σεβράμ,** *Sebrám*, A, **Σεφράμ,** *Sephrám*): A place named as on the boundary of Pal in Ezekiel's ideal delineation, "between the border of Damascus and the border of Hamath" (Ezk **47** 16). It may possibly be represented by the modern *Khirbet Sanbariyeh* on the west bank of *Nahr el-Ḥasbāny*, about 3 miles S.E. of *'Abil.*

SIBYLLINE ORACLES, sib'i-līn, -lin or'a-k'lz. See APOCALYPTIC LITERATURE, B, V.

SICARII, si-kā'ri-ī. See ASSASSINS.

SICHEM, sī'kem (שְׁכֶם, *shᵉkhem*). AV in Gen **12** 6. See SHECHEM.

SICK, sik, **SICKNESS,** sik'nes (חָלָה, *ḥālāh* [Gen **48** 1, etc], חֳלִי, *ḥŏlī* [Dt **28** 61, etc], תַּחֲלֻא, *taḥălu'* [Dt **29** 21, etc], מַחֲלָה, *maḥălāh* [Ex **23** 25, etc], דָּוֶה, *dāweh* [Lev **15** 33, etc], אָנַשׁ, *'ānash* [2 S **12** 15, etc]; **ἀσθενέω,** *asthenéō* [Mt **10** 8, etc; cf 2 Macc **9** 22], **κακῶς ἔχων,** *kakṓs échōn* [Lk **7** 2], **κακῶς ἔχοντας,** *kakṓs échontas* [Mt **4** 24, etc], **ἄρρωστος,** *árrhōstos* [Sir **7** 35; Mt **14** 14, etc], **ἀρρώστημα,** *arrhṓstēma* [Sir **10** 10, etc], with various cognates, **κάμνω,** *kámnō* [Jas **5** 15]; Lat *morbus* [2 Esd **8** 31]): Compared with the number of deaths recorded in the historical books of the Bible the instances in which diseases are mentioned are few. "Sick" and "sickness" (including "disease," etc) are the trs of 6 Heb and 9 Gr words and occur 56 t in the OT and 57 t in the NT. The number of references in the latter is significant as showing how much the healing of the sick was characteristic of the Lord's ministry. The diseases specified are varied. Of infantile sickness there is an instance in Bath-sheba's child (2 S **12** 15), whose disease is termed *'ānash*, not improbably *trismus nascentium*, a common disease in Pal. Among adolescents there are recorded the unspecified sickness of Abijah (1 K **14** 1), of the widow's son at Zarephath (1 K **17** 17), the sunstroke of the Shunammite's son (2 K **4** 19), the epileptic boy (Mt **17** 15), Jaïrus' daughter (Mt **9** 18), and the nobleman's son (Jn **4** 46). At the other extreme of life Jacob's death was preceded by sickness (Gen **48** 1). Sickness resulted from accident (Ahaziah, 2 K **1** 2), wounds (Joram, 2 K **8** 29), from the violence of passion (Amnon, 2 S **13** 2), or mental emotion (Dnl **8** 27); see also in this connection Cant **2** 5; **5** 8. Sickness the result of drunkenness is mentioned (Hos **7** 5), and as a consequence of famine (Jer **14** 18) or violence (Mic **6** 13). *Dāweh* or periodic sickness is referred to (Lev **15** 33; **20** 18), and an extreme case is that of Lk **8** 43.

In some examples the nature of the disease is specified, as Asa's disease in his feet (1 K **15** 23), for which he sought the aid of physicians in vain (2 Ch **16** 12). Hezekiah and Job suffered from sore boils, Jehoram from some severe dysenteric attack (2 Ch **21** 19), as did Antiochus Epiphanes (2 Macc **9** 5). Probably the sudden and fatal disease of Herod was similar, as in both cases there is reference to the presence of worms (cf Acts **12** 23 and 2 Macc **9** 9). The disease of Publius' father was also dysentery (Acts **28** 8). Other diseases specified are paralysis (Mt **8** 6; **9** 2), and fever (Mt **8** 14). Not improbably the sudden illness of the young Egyptian at Ziklag (1 S **30** 11), and the illness of Ben-hadad which weakened him so that he could not resist the violence of Hazael, were also the common Pal fever (2 K **8** 15) of whose symptoms and effects there is a graphic description in Ps **38**. Unspecified fatal illnesses were those of Elisha (2 K **13** 14), Lazarus (Jn **11** 1), Tabitha (Acts **9** 37). In the language of the Bible, leprosy is spoken of as a defilement to be cleansed, rather than as a disease to be cured.

The proverb concerning the sick quoted by the Lord at Capernaum (Mk **2** 17) has come down to us in several forms in apocryphal and rabbinical writings (*Bābhā' Ḳammā'* **26** 13; *Ṣanhedhrīn* **176**), but is nowhere so terse as in the form in which He expresses it. The Lord performed His healing of the sick by His word or touch, and one of the most emphatic charges which He gave to His disciples when sending them out was to heal the sick. One of the methods used by them, the anointing with oil, is mentioned in Mk **6** 13 and enjoined by James (**5** 15). In later times the anointing which was at first used as a remedial agent became a ceremonial in preparation for death, one of the seven sacraments of the Rom church (Aquinas, *Summa Theologia* suppl. ad P iii. 29).

The duty of visiting the sick is referred to in Ezk **34** 4.16, and by the Lord in the description of the Judgment scene (Mt **25** 36.43). It is inculcated in several of the rabbinical tracts. "He that visits the sick lengthens his life, he who refrains shortens it," says Rabbi Ishanan in *Nᵉdhārīm* **29**. In *Shulḥan 'Ārūkh, Yōreh Dē'āh* there is a chapter devoted to this duty, which is regarded as incumbent on the Jew, even though the sick person be a Gentile (*Giṭṭīn* **61***a*). The church's duty to the sick, so long neglected, has, within the last century, been recognized in the mission field, and has proved, in heathen lands, to be the most important of all pioneer agressive methods.

While we find that the apostles freely exercised their gifts of healing, it is noteworthy that we read of the sickness of two of St. Paul's companions, Epaphroditus (Phil **2** 26) and Trophimus (2 Tim **4** 20), for whose recovery he seems to have used no other means than prayer. See also DISEASE.

ALEX. MACALISTER

SICKLE, sik″l (חֶרְמֵשׁ, *ḥermēsh* [Dt **16** 9; **23** 25], מַגָּל, *maggāl;* cf Arab. *minjal* [Jer **50** 16; Joel **3** 13]; **δρέπανον,** *drépanon* [Mk **4** 29; Rev **14** 14–19]): Although the ancients pulled much of their grain by hand, we know that they also used sickles. The form of this instrument varied, as is evidenced by the Egyp sculptures. The earliest sickle was probably of wood, shaped like the modern scythe, although much smaller, with the cutting edge made of sharp flints set into the wood. Sickle flints were found at *Tel el-Ḥesy*. Crescent-shaped iron sickles were found in the same mound. In Pal and Syria the sickle varies in size. It is usually made wholly of iron or steel and shaped much like the instrument used in western lands. The smaller-sized sickles are used both for pruning and for reaping.

JAMES A. PATCH

SICYON, sish′i-on (**Σικυών,** *Sikuôn,* **Συκυών,** *Sukuôn,* **Συκιών,** *Sukiôn*): Mentioned in 1 Macc **15** 23 in the list of countries and cities to which Lucius the Rom consul (probably Lucius Calpurnius Piso, 139 BC) wrote, asking them to be friendly to the Jews. The Jewish dispersion had already taken place, and Jews were living in most of the seaports and cities of Asia Minor, Greece and Egypt (cf Sib Or **3** 271, c 140 BC, and Philo).

Sicyon was situated 18 miles W. of Corinth on the south side of the Gulf of Corinth. Its antiquity and ancient importance are seen by its coins still extant, dating from the 5th cent. Though not as important as Corinth in its sea trade, the burning of that city in 143 BC, and the favor shown to Sicyon by the Rom authorities in adding to its territory and assigning to it the direction of the Isthmian games, increased its wealth and influence for a time.

S. F. HUNTER

SIDDIM, sid′im, **VALE OF** (עֵמֶק הַשִּׂדִּים, *'ēmeḳ ha-siddīm;* LXX **ἡ φάραγξ** [or **κοιλὰς**] **ἡ ἁλυκή,** *hē pháragx* [*koilás*] *hē halukḗ*): The place mentioned in Gen **14** 3–8 as being the scene of encounter between Chedorlaomer and his allies with the kings of Sodom, Gomorrah, Admah, Zeboiim and Zoar. In ver 3 it is identified with the Salt Sea, and in ver 10 it is said to have been full of slime pits ("bitumen").

According to the traditional view, the Vale of Siddim was at the southern end of the Dead Sea. But in recent years a number of eminent authorities have maintained that it was at the northern end of the Dead Sea, in the vicinity of Jericho. Their argument has mainly been drawn from incidental references in the scene (Gen **13** 1–13) describing the parting of Lot and Abram, and again in the account of Moses' vision from Pisgah (Dt **34** 3).

In the account of Abram and Lot, it is said that from Bethel they saw "all the Plain of the Jordan, that it was well watered everywhere, before Jeh destroyed Sodom and Gomorrah." The word here tr[d] "plain" means "circle," and well describes the view which one has of the plain about Jericho from Bethel as he looks down the valley past Ai. But it seems to go beyond the text to assume that the Vale of Siddim was within that circle of vision, for it is said in Gen **13** 12 simply that Lot dwelt "in the cities of the Plain, and moved his tent as far as Sodom." In the vision of Moses, likewise, we have a very general and condensed description, in which it is said that he was shown "the Plain of the valley of Jericho, the city of palm-trees, unto Zoar," which, as we learn from Gen **19** 22, was not far from the Vale of Siddim. It is true that from the traditional site of Pisgah the south end of the Dead Sea could not be seen. But we are by no means sure that the traditional site of Pisgah is the true one, or that the import of this language should be restricted to the points which are actually within range of vision.

The tendency at the present time is to return to the traditional view that the Vale of Siddim was at the south end of the Dead Sea. This is supported by the fact that *Jebel Usdum,* the salt mountain at the southwest corner of the Dead Sea, still bears the name of Sodom, *Usdum* being simply another form of the word. A still stronger argument, however, is drawn from the general topographical and geological conditions. In the first place, Zoar, to which Lot is said to have fled, was not far away. The most natural site for it is near the mouth of the *Wâdy Kerak,* which comes down from Moab into the southern end of the Dead Sea (see ZOAR); and this city was ever afterward spoken of as a Moabite city, which would not have been the case if it had been at the north end of the sea. It is notable in Josh **13** 15–21, where the cities given to Reuben are enumerated, that, though the slopes of Pisgah are mentioned, Zoar is not mentioned.

In Gen **14,** where the battle between Amraphel and his allies with Sodom and the other cities of the plain is described, the south end of the Dead Sea comes in logical order in the progress of their campaign, and special mention is made of the slime or bitumen pits which occurred in the valley, and evidently played an important part in the outcome of the battle.

At the south end of the Dead Sea there is an extensive circle or plain which is better supplied with water for irrigation than is the region about Jericho, and which, on the supposition of slight geological changes, may have been extremely fertile in ancient times; while there are many indications of such fertility in the ruins that have been described by travelers about the mouth of the *Kerak* and other localities nearby. The description, therefore, of the fertility of the region in the Vale of Siddim may well have applied to this region at the time of Lot's entrance into it.

There are very persistent traditions that great topographical changes took place around the south end of the Dead Sea in connection with the destruction of Sodom and Gomorrah, while the opinion has been universally prevalent among the earlier historical writers that the site of Sodom and Gomorrah is beneath the waters of the Dead Sea.

Geological investigations, so far from disproving these traditions, render them altogether possible and credible. There is a remarkable contrast between the depths of the north end of the Dead Sea and of the south end. Near the north end the depth descends to 1,300 ft., whereas for many miles out from the south end it is very shallow, so that at low water a ford exists, and is occasionally used, from the north end of the salt mountain across to *el-Lisân.*

The precipitous salt cliffs of *Jebel Usdum* which border the southwest corner of the Dead Sea would indicate that, in comparatively recent times, there had been abrupt subsidence of a good many feet in the bottom of the Dead Sea at that end.

Such subsidences of limited areas and in connection with earthquakes are by no means uncommon. In 1819 an area of 2,000 sq. miles about the delta of the Indus sank beneath the level of the sea, so that the tops of the houses were barely seen above the water. A smaller area in the delta of the Selenga River sank during the last century beneath the waters of Lake Baikal. Professor R. S. Tarr of Cornell University has recently described the effect of an earthquake on the shores of Alaska, in which there was a change of level of 47 ft.

More probably (see ARABAH; DEAD SEA) there has been a rise in the waters of the Dead Sea since Abraham's time, caused by the encroachment upon the original area of evaporation by the deltas which have been pushed into the main part of the depression by the Jordan, and various smaller streams descending from the highlands on either side. In consequence of these encroachments, the equilibrium between precipitation and evaporation could be maintained only by a rise in the water causing it to spread over the shallow shelf at the south end, thus covering a large part of the Vale of Siddim with the shoal water now found between *el-Lisân* and *Jebel Usdum.* GEORGE FREDERICK WRIGHT

SIDE, sī'dē (Σίδη, *Sidē*): An ancient town of Pamphylia, occupying a triangular promontory on the coast. It was one of the towns to which a letter favorable to the Jews was sent by the Rom consul Lucius (1 Macc **15** 23). The town seems to have been of considerable antiquity, for it had existed long before it fell into the possession of Alexander the Great, and for a time it was the metropolis of Pamphylia. Off the coast the fleet of Antiochus was defeated by the Rhodians. During the 1st cent. Side was noted as one of the chief ports of pirates who disposed of much of their booty there. The ruins of the city, which are now very extensive, bear the name *Eski Adalia,* but among them there are no occupied houses. The two harbors protected by a sea wall may still be traced, but they are now filled with sand. The wall on the land side of the city was provided with a gate which was protected with round towers; the walls themselves are of Gr-Rom type. Within the walls the more important of the remains are three theaters near the harbors, and streets with covered porticoes leading from the city gate to the harbors. Without the walls, the street leading to the city gate is lined with sarcophagi, and among the shrubbery of the neighboring fields are traces of many buildings and of an aqueduct. E. J. BANKS

SIDES, sīdz (יַרְכָה, *yarᵉkhāh,* "thigh," "flank"): RV substitutes "innermost parts" for AV "sides" in Jon **1** 5; cf 1 S **24** 3.

SIDON, sī'don (צִידוֹן, *çīdhōn*): The eldest son of Canaan (Gen **10** 15).

SIDON, sī'don (צִידוֹן, *çīdhōn;* Σιδών, *Sidōn;* AV **Sidon** and **Zidon;** RV SIDON only): One of the oldest Phoen cities, situated on a narrow plain between the range of Lebanon and the sea, in lat. 33° 34′ nearly. The plain is well watered and fertile, about 10 miles long, extending from a little N. of Sarepta to the Bostrenus (*Nahr el-'Auly*). The ancient city was situated near the northern end of the plain, surrounded with a strong wall. It possessed two harbors, the northern one about 500 yds. long by 200 wide, well protected by little islets and a breakwater, and a southern about 600 by 400 yds., surrounded on three sides by land, but open to the W., and thus exposed in bad weather. The date of the founding of the city is unknown, but we find it mentioned in the Am Tab in the 14th cent. BC, and in Gen **10** 19 it is the chief city of the Canaanites, and Joshua (Josh **11** 8) calls it Great S. It led all the Phoen cities in its early development of maritime affairs, its sailors being the first to launch out into the open sea out of sight of land and to sail by night, guiding themselves by the stars. They were the first to come into contact with the Greeks and we find the mention of them several times in Homer, while other Phoen towns are not noticed. S. became early distinguished for its manufactures and the skill of its artisans, such as beautiful metal-work in silver and bronze and textile fabrics embroidered and dyed with the famous purple dye which became known as Tyrian, but which was earlier produced at S. Notices of these choice articles are found in Homer, both in the *Iliad* and the *Odyssey.* S. had a monarchical form of government, as did all the Phoen towns, but it also held a sort of hegemony over those to the S. as far as the limit of Phoenicia. It likewise made one attempt to establish an inland colony at Laish or Dan, near the headwaters of the Jordan, but this ended in disaster (Jgs **18** 7.27.28). The attempt was not renewed, but many colonies were established over-sea. Citium, in Cyprus, was one of the earliest.

1. Location and Distinction

2. Historical

(1) The independence of S. was lost when the kings of the XVIIIth and XIXth Dynasties of Egypt added Pal and Syria to their dominions (1580–1205 BC). The kings of S. were allowed to remain on the throne as long as they paid tribute, and perhaps still exercised authority over the towns that had before been subject to them. When the power of Egypt declined under Amenhotep IV (1375–1358), the king of S. seems to have thrown off the yoke, as appears from the Am Tab. Rib-addi of Gebal writes to the king of Egypt that Zimrida, king of S., had joined the enemy, but Zimrida himself claims, in the letters he wrote, to be loyal, declaring that the town belonging to him had been taken by the Khabiri (Tab. 147). S., with the other towns, eventually became independent of Egypt, and she retained the hegemony of the southern towns and perhaps added Dor, claimed by the Philis, to her dominion. This may have been the reason for the war that took place about the middle of the 12th cent. BC, in which the Philis took and plundered S., whose inhabitants fled to Tyre and gave the latter a great impetus. S., however, recovered from the disaster and became powerful again. The Book of Jgs claims that Israel was oppressed by S. (**10** 12), but it is probable S. stands here for Phoenicia in general, as being the chief town.

(2) S. submitted to the Assyr kings as did the Phoen cities generally, but revolted against Sennacherib and again under Esar-haddon. The latter destroyed a large part of the city and carried off most of the inhabitants, replacing them by captives from Babylon and Elam, and renamed it Ir-Esar-haddon ("City of Esar-haddon"). The settlers readily mingled with the Phoenicians, and S. rose to power again when Assyria fell, was besieged by Nebuchadnezzar at the time of his siege of Jerus and Tyre, and was taken, having lost about half of its inhabitants by plague. The fall of Babylon gave another short period of independence, but the Persians gained control without difficulty, and S. was prominent in the Pers period as the leading naval power among the Phoenicians who aided their suzerain in his attacks upon Greece. In 351 BC, S. rebelled under Tabnit II (Tennes), and called in the aid of Gr mercenaries to the number of 10,000; but Ochus, the Pers king, marched against him with a force of 300,000 infantry and 30,000 horse, which so frightened Tabnit that he betrayed the city to save his own life. But the citizens, learning of the treachery, first burned their fleet and then their houses, perishing with their wives and children rather than fall into the hands of Ochus, who butchered all whom he seized, Tabnit among them. It is said that 40,000 perished in the flames. A list of the kings of S. in the Pers period has been recovered from the inscriptions and the coins, but the dates of their reigns are not accurately known. The dynasty of the known kings begins with Esmunazar I, followed by Tabnit I, Amastoreth; Esmunazar II, Strato I (Bodastart), Tabnit II (Tennes) and Strato II. Inscriptions from the temple of Esmun recently discovered give the name of a Bodastart and a son Yatonmelik, but whether the first is one of the Stratos above mentioned or a third is uncertain; also whether the son ever reigned or not. As Bodastart calls himself the grandson of Esmun-

azar, he is probably Strato I who reigned about 374–363 BC, and hence his grandfather, Esmunazar I, must have reigned in 400 BC or earlier. Strato II was on the throne when Alexander took possession of Phoenicia and made no resistance to him, and even aided him in the siege of Tyre, which shows that S.

Coin of Sidon.

had recovered after the terrible disaster it suffered in the time of Ochus. It perhaps looked upon the advance of Alexander with content as its avenger. The destruction of Tyre increased the importance of S., and after the death of Alexander it became attached to the kingdom of the Ptolemies and remained so until the victory of Antiochus III over Scopas (198 BC), when it passed to the Seleucids and from them to the Romans, who granted it a degree of autonomy with native magistrates and a council, and it was allowed to coin money in bronze.

S. comes into view several times in the NT; first when Christ passed into the borders of Tyre and S. and healed the daughter of the Syrophoenician woman (Mk **7** 24–30); also when Herod Agrippa I received a delegation from Tyre and S. at Caesarea (Acts **12** 20), where it appears to have been outside his jurisdiction. St. Paul, on his way to Rome, was permitted to visit some friends at S. (Acts **27** 3). See also Mt **11** 21 f and Mk **3** 8.

3. NT Mention

It was noted for its school of philosophy under Augustus and Tiberius, its inhabitants being largely Greek; and when Berytus was destroyed by an earthquake in 551, its great law school was removed to S. It was not of great importance during the Crusades, being far surpassed by Acre, and in modern times it is a small town of some 15,000.

LITERATURE.—See PHOENICIA.

H. PORTER

SIDONIANS, sī-dō'ni-anz: Natives or inhabitants of Sidon (Dt **3** 9; Josh **13** 4.6; Jgs **3** 3; 1 K **5** 6).

SIEGE, sēj (מָצוֹר, *māçōr* [Dt **28** 52.53; 1 K **15** 27; 2 K **25** 2; Isa **29** 3; Ezk **4** 2]; "to be besieged," "to suffer siege," *ba-māçōr bō'* [Dt **20** 19; 2 K **24** 10; **25** 2]):

1. In Early Hebrew History
2. In the Monarchy
3. Preliminaries to Siege
4. Siege Operations: Attack
   (1) Investment of City
   (2) Line of Circumvallation
   (3) Mound, or Earthworks
   (4) Battering-Rams
   (5) Storming of Walls and Rushing of Breach
5. Siege Operations: Defence
6. Raising of Siege
7. Horrors of Siege and Capture
8. Siege in the NT

LITERATURE

1. In Early Hebrew History

In early Heb history, siege operations are not described and can have been little known. Although the Israelites had acquired a certain degree of military discipline in the wilderness, when they entered Canaan they had no experience of the operations of a siege and were without the engines of war necessary for the purpose. Jericho, with its strongly fortified wall, was indeed formally invested—it "was straitly shut up because of the children of Israel: none went out, and none came in" (Josh **6** 1)—but it fell into their hands without a siege. Other cities seem to have yielded after pitched battles, or to have been taken by assault. Many of the Canaanite fortresses, like Gezer (2 S **5** 25; Josh **16** 10), Taanach and Megiddo (Jgs **1** 27), remained unreduced. Jerus was captured by the men of Judah (Jgs **1** 8), but the fort of Jebus remained unconquered till the time of David (2 S **5** 6).

2. In the Monarchy

In the days of the monarchy more is heard of siege operations. At the siege of Rabbath-Ammon Joab seems to have deprived the city of its water-supply and rendered it untenable (2 S **11** 1; **12** 27). At Abel of Beth-maacah siege operations are described in which Joab distinguished himself (2 S **20** 15). David and Solomon, and, after the disruption of the kingdom, Rehoboam and Jeroboam built fortresses which ere long became the scene of siege operations. The war between Judah and Israel in the days of Nadab, Baasha, and Elah was, for the most part, a war of sieges. It was while besieging Gibbethon that Nadab, the son of Jeroboam, was slain by Baasha (1 K **15** 27), and, 27 years after, while the army of Israel was still investing the same place, the soldiery chose their commander Omri to be king over Israel (1 K **16** 16). From the Egyptians, the Syrians, the Assyrians, and the Chaldaeans, with whom they came into relations in later times as allies or as enemies, the people of the Southern and of the Northern Kingdoms learned much regarding the art, both of attack and of defence of fortified places.

3. Preliminaries to Siege

It was an instruction of the Deuteronomic Law that before a city was invested for a long siege, it should be summoned to capitulate (Dt **20** 10; cf 2 S **20** 18; 2 K **18** 17 ff). If the offer of peace be declined, then the siege is to be proceeded with, and if the city be captured, all the male population is to be put to death, and the women and children reserved as a prey for the captors. To this humane reservation the cities of the Canaanites were to be an exception: their inhabitants were to be wholly exterminated (Dt **20** 16–18).

The same law prescribed that there should be no unnecessary destruction of fruit trees in the prosecution of a long siege. Trees not yielding fruit for human sustenance might be cut down: "And thou shalt build bulwarks [*māçōr*, "siegeworks"] against the city that maketh war with thee, until it fall" (Dt **20** 19.20). This instruction to have regard to the fruit trees around a hostile city seems to have been more honored in the breach than in the observance, even in Israel. When the allied kings of Israel, Judah, and Edom were invading Moab and had instruction to "smite every fortified city," the prophet Elisha bade them also "fell every good tree, and stop all fountains of water, and mar every good piece of land with stones" (2 K **3** 19.25). When the assault of Jerus by the Chaldaeans was imminent, Jeh commanded the cutting down of the trees (Jer **6** 6). In Arabian warfare, we are told, the destruction of the enemy's palm groves was a favorite exploit (Robertson Smith, *OTJC*², 369), and the Assyrians when they captured a city had no compunction in destroying its plantations (Inscription of Shalmaneser II on Black Obelisk).

4. Siege Operations: Attack

From passages in the Prophets, upon which much light has been thrown by the ancient monuments of Assyria and Chaldaea, we gain a very clear idea of the siege works directed against a city by Assyr or Chaldaean invaders. The siege of Lachish (2 K **18** 13.14; Isa **36** 1.2) by Sennacherib is the subject of a series of magnificent reliefs from the mound of Koyunjik (Layard, *Monuments of Nineveh*, II, plates 20, 21, 22). The downfall of Nineveh as predicted in Nahum's prophecy lets us see the siege operations proceeding with striking realism (see *Der Untergang Niniveh*s by A. Jeremias and Colonel Billerbeck). Nowhere, however, are the incidents of a siege—the gathering of hostile forces, the slaughter of peaceful inhabitants in the country around, the raising of siege-works, the setting of engines of war against the walls, the demolition of the towers, the breach in the principal wall, the rush of men and the clatter of horses' hoofs through the streets, the slaughter, the pillage, the destruction of walls and houses—more fully and faithfully recorded than by Ezekiel when predicting the capture of Tyre by Nebuchadrezzar (Ezk **26** 7-12). The siege of Tyre lasted 13 years, and Ezekiel tells how every head was made bald and every shoulder worn by the hard service of the besiegers (Ezk **29** 18). There were various ways in which an invading army might deal with a fortified city so as to secure its possession. Terms might be offered to secure a capitulation (1 K **20** 1 ff; 2 K **18** 14 ff). An attempt might be made to reduce the city by starvation (2 K **6** 24 ff; 2 K **17** 5 ff). The city might be invested and captured by assault and storm, as Lachish was by Sennacherib (2 K **18** 13; **19** 8; see Layard, op cit., II, plates 20-24). The chief operations of the besiegers were as follows: (1) There was *the investment* of the city by the besieging army. It was sometimes necessary to establish a fortified camp, like that of Sennacherib at Lachish to guard against sorties by the defenders. Of the siege of Jerus we read that Nebuchadrezzar came, "he and all his army, against Jerus, and encamped against it" (Jer **52** 4; cf 2 K **25** 1). From the commencement of the siege, slingers and archers were posted where they could keep the defenders engaged; and it is to this that reference is made when Jeremiah says: "Call together the archers against Babylon, all them that bend the bow; encamp against her round about; let none thereof escape" (Jer **50** 29).

(2) There was next the drawing of *a line of circumvallation* (*dāyēḳ*) with detached forts round about the walls. These forts were towers manned by archers, or they were used as stations from which to discharge missiles (Jer **52** 4; Ezk **17** 17). In this connection the word "munition" in AV and ERV (*măçōr*) in Nah **1** 1 disappears in ARV and is replaced by "fortress."

(3) Following upon this was *the mound* (*ṣōl^elāh*), or earthworks, built up to the height of the walls, so as to command the streets of the city, and strike terror into the besieged. From the mound thus erected the besiegers were able to batter the upper and weaker part of the city wall (2 S **20** 15; Isa **37** 33; Jer **6** 6; Ezk **4** 2; Dnl **11** 15; Lam **4** 18). If, however, the town, or fortress, was built upon an eminence, an inclined plane reaching to the height of the eminence might be formed of earth or stones, or trees, and the besiegers would be able to bring their engines to the foot of the walls. This road was even covered with bricks, forming a kind of paved way, up which the ponderous machines could be drawn without difficulty. To such roads there are references in Scripture (Job **19** 12; Isa **29** 3, "siege works"; cf Layard, *Nineveh and Its Remains,* II, 366 f). In the case of Tyre this mound, or way of approach, was a dam thrown across the narrow strait to obtain access to the walls (Ezk **26** 8). Very often, too, there was a trench, sometimes filled with water, at the foot of the wall, which had to be dealt with previous to an assault.

(4) The earthworks having been thrown up, and approaches to the walls secured, it was possible to set and to work *the battering-rams* (*kārīm*) which were to be employed in breaching the walls (Ezk **4** 2), or in bursting open the gates (Ezk **21** 22). The battering-rams were of different kinds. On Assyr monuments they are found joined to movable towers holding warriors and armed men, or, in other cases, joined to a stationary tower constructed on the spot. When the men who are detailed to work the ram get it into play, with its heavy beams of planks fastened together and the great mass of

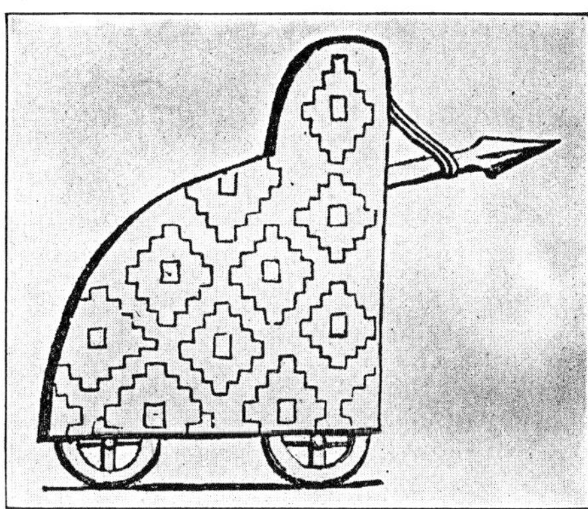

Battering-Ram.

metal forming its head, they can hardly fail to make an impression, and gradually, by the constantly repeated shocks, a breach is opened and the besiegers are able to rush in and bear down the defenders. It is to the shelter furnished by these towers that the prophet Nahum refers (**2** 5) when he says, "The mantelet is prepared," and that Isaiah points when he declares that the king of Assyria "shall not come unto this city, nor shoot an arrow there, neither shall he come before it with shield [*māghēn*], nor cast up a mound against it" (Isa **37** 33). Ezekiel has the same figure when, describing the siege of Tyre by Nebuchadrezzar, he declares that he shall "cast up a mound" against her, and "raise up the buckler," the **buckler** (*çinnāh*) being like the Rom *testudo*, or roof of shields, under cover of which the besiegers carried on operations (Ezk **26** 8; Colonel Billerbeck [op. cit., 178] is doubtful whether this device was known to the Assyrians). Under the shelter of their movable towers the besiegers could push forward mines, an operation known as part of siegecraft from a high antiquity (see 2 S **20** 15, where ARVm and ERVm give "undermined" as an alternative to "battered"; tunneling was well known in antiquity, as the Siloam tunnel shows).

(5) The culminating operation would be *the storming of the walls, the rushing of the breach. Scaling-ladders* were employed to cross the encircling trench or ditch (Prov **21** 22); and Joel in his powerful description of the army of locusts which had devastated the land says that they "climb the wall like men of war" (Joel **2** 7). Attempts were made to set fire to the gates and to break them open with axes (Jgs **9** 52; cf Neh **1** 3; **2** 3; Ezk **26** 9). Jeremiah tells of *the breach* that was made in the city when Jerus was captured (Jer **39** 2). The breaches in the wall of Samaria are referred to by Amos (**4** 3), who pictures the women rushing forth headlong like a herd of kine with hooks and fishhooks in their nostrils.

While the besiegers employed this variety of means of attack, the besieged were equally ingenious and active in maintaining the defence.

5. Siege Operations: Defence

All sorts of obstructions were placed in the way of the besieging army. Springs and cisterns likely to afford supplies of water to the invaders were carefully covered up, or drained off into the city. Where possible, trenches were filled with water to make them impassable. As the siege-works of the enemy approached the main wall, it was usual to build inner fortifications, and for this purpose houses were pulled down to provide the needful space and also to supply building materials (Isa **22** 10). Slingers placed upon the walls hurled stones upon the advancing enemy, and archers from loopholes and protected battlements discharged arrows against the warriors in their movable towers. Sorties were made to damage the siege-works of the enemy and to prevent the battering-rams from being placed in position. To counteract the assaults of the battering-rams, sacks of chaff were let down like a ship's fender in front of the place where the engine operated—a contrivance countered again by poles with scythes upon them which cut off the sacks (Jos, *BJ*, III, vii, 20). So, too, the defenders, by dropping a doubled chain or rope from the battlements, caught the ram and broke the force of its blows. Attempts were made to destroy the ram also by fire. In the great bas-relief of the siege of Lachish an inhabitant is seen hurling a lighted torch from the wall; and it was a common device to pour boiling water or oil from the wall upon the assailants. Missiles, too, were thrown with deadly effect from the battlements by the defenders, and it was by a piece of a millstone thrown by a woman that Abimelech met his death at Thebez (Jgs **9** 53). While Uzziah of Judah furnished his soldiers with shields and spears and helmets and coats of mail and bows and slingstones, he also "made in Jerus engines, invented by skilful men, to be on the towers and upon the battlements, wherewith to shoot arrows and great stones" (2 Ch **26** 15). The Jews had, for the defence of Jerus against the army of Titus, engines which they had taken from the Twelfth Legion at Beth-horon which seem to have

Catapult for Hurling Missiles.

had a range of 1,200 ft. Many ingenious devices are described by Jos as employed by himself when conducting the defence of Jotapata in Galilee against Vespasian and the forces of Rome (*BJ*, III, vii).

6. Raising of the Siege

When Nahash king of the Ammonites laid siege to Jabesh-gilead in the opening days of the reign of Saul, the terms of peace offered to the inhabitants were so humiliating and cruel that they sought a respite of seven days and appealed to Saul in their distress. When the newly chosen king heard of their desperate condition he assembled a great army, scattered the Ammonites, and raised the siege of Jabesh-gilead, thus earning the lasting gratitude of the inhabitants (1 S **11**; cf 1 S **31** 12. 13). When Zedekiah of Judah found himself besieged in Jerus by the Chaldaean army under Nebuzaradan, he sent intelligence to Pharaoh Hophra who crossed the frontier with his army to attack the Chaldaeans and obliged them to desist from the siege. The Chaldaeans withdrew for the moment from the walls of Jerus and offered battle to Pharaoh Hophra and his host, but the courage of the Egyp king failed him and he retired in haste without encountering the Chaldaeans in a pitched battle. The siege was prosecuted to the bitter end, and Jerus was captured and completely overthrown (2 K **25** 1; Jer **37** 3–10; Ezk **17** 17).

7. Horrors of Siege and Capture

In the ancient law of Israel "siege" is classed with drought and pestilence and exile as punishments with which Jeh would visit His people for their disobedience (Dt **28** 49–57). Of the horrors there described they had again and again bitter experience. At the siege of Samaria by Ben-hadad II, so terrible were the straits to which the besieged

Rock of Masada.

were reduced that they cooked and ate their own children (2 K **6** 28). In the siege of Jerus by the Chaldaeans, which ended in the overthrow of the city and the destruction of the Temple, the sufferings of the inhabitants from hunger and disease were incredible (2 K **25** 3; Jer **32** 24; Lam **2** 20; **4** 8–10). The horrors of siege have, perhaps, reached their climax in the account given by Jos of the tragedy of Masada. To escape capture by the Romans, ten men were chosen by lot from among the occupants of the fortress, 960 in number, including combatants and non-combatants, men, women and children, to slay the rest. From these ten one was similarly chosen to slay the survivors, and he, having accomplished his awful task, ran his sword into his own body (Jos, *BJ*, VII, ix, 1). While all the inhabitants of a city under siege suffered the famine of bread and the thirst for water, the combatants ran the risk of impalement and other forms of torture to which prisoners in Assyr and Chaldaean and Rom warfare were subjected.

The horrors attending the siege of a city were only surpassed by the barbarities perpetrated at its *capture*. The emptying of a city by its capture is likened to the hurling of a stone from a sling (Jer **10** 17.18). Deportation of the whole of the inhabitants often followed (2 K **17** 6; **24** 14). Not only were the inhabitants of the captured city deported, but their gods were carried off with them and the idols broken in pieces. This is predicted or recorded of Babylon (Isa **21** 9; **46** 1; Jer **50** 2), of Egypt (Jer **43** 12), of Samaria (Hos **10** 6). Indiscriminate slaughter followed the entrance of the assailants, and the city was usually given over to the flames (Jer **39** 8.9; Lam **4** 18). "Cities without number," says Shalmaneser II in one of his inscriptions, "I wrecked, razed, burned with fire." Houses were destroyed and women dishonored (Zec **14** 2). When Darius took Babylon, he impaled three thousand prisoners (Herod. iii.159). The Scythians scalped and flayed their enemies and used their skins for horse trappings (ib, iv.64). The Assyr sculptures show prisoners subjected to horrible tortures, or carried away into slavery. The captured Zedekiah had his eyes put out after he had seen his own sons cruelly put to death (2 K **25** 7). It is only employing the imagery familiar to Assyr warfare when Isaiah represents Jeh as saying to Sennacherib: "Therefore will I put my hook in thy nose, and my bridle in thy lips, and I will turn thee back by the way by which thou camest" (Isa **37** 29). Anticipating the savage barbarities that would follow the capture of Samaria by the Assyrians, Hosea foresees the infants being dashed to pieces and the women with child being ripped up (Hos **10** 14; **13** 16; cf Am **1** 13). The prophet Nahum predicting the overthrow of Nineveh recalls how at the capture of No-amon (Egyp Thebes) by the Assyr conqueror, Ashurbanipal, "her young children also were dashed in pieces at the head of all the streets; and they cast lots for her honorable men, and all her great men were bound in chains" (Nah **3** 10).

8. Siege in the NT

The only explicit reference to siege operations in the NT is Our Lord's prediction of the complete destruction of Jerus when He wept over its coming doom: "For the days shall come upon thee, when thine enemies shall cast up a bank [χάραξ, *chárax*, AV, quite incorrectly, "trench"] about thee, and compass thee round, and keep thee in on every side, and shall dash thee to the ground, and thy children within thee; and they shall not leave in thee one stone upon another" (Lk **19** 43.44). The order and particulars of the siege are in accordance with the accounts of siege operations in the OT. How completely the prediction was fulfilled we see from Jos (*BJ*, V, vi, 10).

Figurative: In St. Paul's Epp. there are figures taken from siege operations. In 2 Cor **10** 4 we have "the casting down of strongholds," where the Gr word καθαίρεσις, *kathaíresis*, from καθαιρεῖν, *kathaireín*, is the regular word used in LXX for the reduction of a fortress (Prov **21** 22; Lam **2** 2; 1 Macc **5** 65). In Eph **6** 16 there is allusion to siege-works, for the subtle temptations of Satan are set forth as the flaming darts hurled by the besiegers of a fortress which the Christian soldier is to quench with the shield of faith.

LITERATURE.—Nowack, *Hebräische Archaeologie*, 71; Benzinger, "Kriegswesen" in *Herzog*[3]; Billerbeck and A. Jeremias, *Der Untergang Ninivehs*; Billerbeck, *Der Festungsbau im alten Orient*.

T. NICOL

SIEVE, siv, **SIFT**. See AGRICULTURE; THRESHING.

SIGLOS, sig′los (σίγλος, *síglos*): A Pers silver coin, twenty of which went to the gold DARIC (q.v.).

SIGN, sīn (אוֹת, *'ōth*, "a sign," "mark," מוֹפֵת, *mōphēth*, "wonder"; σημεῖον, *sēmeíon*, "a sign," "signal," "mark"): A mark by which persons or things are distinguished and made known. In Scripture used generally of an address to the senses to attest the existence of supersensible and therefore Divine power. Thus the plagues of Egypt were "signs" of Divine displeasure against the Egyptians (Ex **4** 8 ff; Josh **24** 17, and often); and the miracles of Jesus were "signs" to attest His unique relationship with God (Mt **12** 38; Jn **2** 18; Acts **2** 22). Naturally, therefore, both in the OT and the NT, "signs" are assimilated to the miraculous, and prevailingly associated with immediate Divine interference. The popular belief in this manner of communication between the visible and the invisible worlds has always been, and is now, widespread. So-called "natural" explanations, however ingenious or cogent, fail with the great majority of people to explain anything. Wesley and Spurgeon were as firm believers in the validity of such methods of intercourse between man and God as were Moses and Gideon, Peter and John.

The faith that walks by signs is not by any means to be lightly esteemed. It has been allied with the highest nobility of character and with the most signal achievement. Moses accepted the leadership of his people in response to a succession of signs: e.g. the burning bush, the rod which became a serpent, the leprous hand, etc (Ex **3** and **4**); so, too, did Gideon, who was not above making proof of God in the sign of the fleece of wool (Jgs **6** 36–40). In the training of the Twelve, Jesus did not disdain the use of signs (Lk **5** 1–11, and often); and the visions by which Peter and Paul were led to the evangelization of the Gentiles were interpreted by them as signs of the Divine purpose (Acts **10** and **16**).

The sacramental use of the sign dates from the earliest period, and the character of the sign is as diverse as the occasion. The rainbow furnishes radiant suggestion of God's overarching love and assurance that the waters shall no more become a flood to destroy the earth (Gen **9** 13; cf **4** 15); the Feast of Unleavened Bread is a reminder of God's care in bringing His people out of bondage (Ex **13** 3); the Sabbath is an oft-recurring proclamation of God's gracious thought for the well-being of man (Ex **31** 13; Ezk **20** 12); the brazen serpent, an early foreshadowing of the cross, perpetuates the imperishable promise of forgiveness and redemption (Nu **21** 9); circumcision is made the seal of the special covenant under which Israel became a people set apart (Gen **17** 11); baptism, the Christian equivalent of circumcision, becomes the sign and seal of the dedicated life and the mark of those avowedly seeking to share in the blessedness of the Kingdom of God (Lk **3** 12–14; Acts **2** 41, and often); bread and wine, a symbol of the spiritual manna by which soul and body are preserved unto everlasting life, is the hallowed memorial of the Lord's death until His coming again (Lk **22** 14–20; 1 Cor **11** 23–28). Most common of all were the local altars and mounds consecrated in simple and sincere fashion to a belief in God's ruling and overruling providence (Josh **4** 1–10).

Signs were offered in proof of the Divine commission of prophet (Isa **20** 3) and apostle (2 Cor **12** 12), and of the Messiah Himself (Jn **20** 30; Acts **2** 22); and they were submitted in demonstration of the Divine character of their message (2 K **20** 9; Isa **38** 1; Acts **3** 1–16). By anticipation the child to be born of a young woman (Isa **7** 10–16; cf Lk **2** 12) is to certify the prophet's pledge of a deliverer for a captive people. See IMMANUEL.

With increase of faith the necessity for signs will gradually decrease. Jesus hints at this (Jn **4** 48), as does also Paul (1 Cor **1** 22). Nevertheless "signs," in the sense of displays of miraculous powers, are to accompany the faith of believers (Mk **16** 17 f), usher in and forthwith characterize the dispensation of the Holy Spirit, and mark the consummation of the ages (Rev **15** 1). See also MIRACLE.

For **"sign" of a ship** (παράσημος, *parásēmos*, "ensign," Acts **28** 11) see DIOSCURI; SHIPS AND BOATS, III, 2.

CHARLES M. STUART

SIGNET, sig′net. See SEAL.

SIGNS, NUMERICAL, nū-mer′i-kal. See NUMBER.

SIGNS OF THE HEAVENS. See ASTRONOMY, I, 4.

SIHON, sī'hon (סִיחוֹן, *ṣīḥōn*): King of the Amorites, who vainly opposed Israel on their journey from Egypt to Pal, and who is frequently mentioned in the historical books and in the Pss because of his prominence and as a warning for those who rise against Jeh and His people (Nu **21** 21, and often; Dt **1** 4; **31** 4; Josh **2** 10; Jgs **11** 19.20.21; 1 K **4** 19; Neh **9** 22; Ps **135** 11; **136** 19; Jer **48** 45).

SIHOR, sī'hôr. See SHIHOR.

SIHOR-LIBNATH, sī'hôr-lib'nath. See SHIHOR-LIBNATH.

SILAS, sī'las (**Σίλας,** *Sílas*, probably contraction for **Σιλουανός,** *Silouanós;* the Heb equivalents suggested are שָׁלִישׁ, *shālīsh*, "Tertius," or שֶׁלַח, *shelaḥ* [Gen **10** 24] [Knowling], or שְׁאוּל, *shā'ūl*="asked" [Zahn]): The Silas of Acts is generally identified with the **Silvanus** of the Epp. His identification with Titus has also been suggested, based on 2 Cor **1** 19; **8** 23, but this is very improbable (cf Knowling, *Expositor's Gr Test.*, II, 326). Silas, who was probably a Rom citizen (cf Acts **16** 37), accompanied Paul during the greater part of his 2d missionary journey (Acts **15–18**). At the meeting of the Christian community under James at Jerus, which decided that circumcision should not be obligatory in the case of gentile believers, Silas and Judas Barsabas were appointed along with Paul and Barnabas to convey to the churches in Antioch and Syria and Cilicia the ep. informing them of this decision. As "leading men among the brethren" at Jerus, and therefore more officially representative of the Jerus church than Paul and Barnabas, Silas and Judas were further commissioned to confirm the contents of the letter by "word of mouth." On arrival at Antioch, the ep. was delivered, and Judas and Silas, "being themselves also prophets, exhorted the brethren with many words, and confirmed them." Their mission being thus completed, the four were "dismissed in peace from the brethren unto those that had sent them forth" (RV), or "unto the apostles" (AV) (Acts **15** 22–33).

Different readings now render the immediate movements of Silas somewhat obscure; ver 33 would imply that he returned to Jerus. But some texts proceed in ver 34, "Notwithstanding it pleased Silas to abide there still," and others add "and Judas alone proceeded." Of this, the first half is accepted by AV. The principal texts however reject the whole verse and are followed in this by RV. It is held by some that he remained in Antioch till chosen by Paul (ver 40). Others maintain that he returned to Jerus where John Mark then was (cf Acts **13** 13); and that either during the interval of "some days" (Acts **15** 36), when the events described in Gal **2** 11 ff took place (Wendt), he returned to Antioch along with Peter, or that he and John Mark were summoned thither by Paul and Barnabas, subsequent to their dispute regarding Mark. (For fuller discussion, see Knowling, *Expositor's Gr Test.*, II, 330, 332–35.)

Upon Barnabas' separation from Paul, Silas was chosen by Paul in his place, and the two missionaries, "after being commended by the brethren [at Antioch] to the grace of the Lord," proceeded on their journey (Acts **15** 33m–40). Passing through Syria, Cilicia, Galatia, Phrygia and Mysia, where they delivered the decree of the Jerus council and strengthened the churches, and were joined by Timothy, they eventually reached Troas (Acts **15** 41—**16** 8). Indications are given that at this city Luke also became one of their party (cf also the apocryphal "Acts of St. Paul," where this is definitely stated; Budge, *Contendings of the Apostles*, II, 544).

Upon the call of the Macedonian, the missionary band set sail for Greece, and after touching at Samothrace, they landed at Neapolis (Acts **16** 9–11). At Philippi, Lydia, a seller of purple, was converted, and with her they made their abode; but the exorcism of an evil spirit from a sorceress brought upon Silas and Paul the enmity of her masters, whose source of gain was thus destroyed. On being charged before the magistrates with causing a breach of the peace and preaching false doctrine, their garments were rent off them and they were scourged and imprisoned. In no way dismayed, they prayed and sang hymns to God, and an earthquake in the middle of the night secured them a miraculous release. The magistrates, on learning that the two prisoners whom they had so maltreated were Rom citizens, came in person and besought them to depart out of the city (Acts **16** 12–39). After a short visit to the house of Lydia, where they held an interview with the brethren, they departed for Thessalonica, leaving Luke behind (cf Knowling, op. cit., 354–55). There they made many converts, esp. among the Greeks, but upon the house of Jason, their host, being attacked by hostile Jews, they were compelled to escape by night to Berœa (**16** 40—**17** 10). There they received a better hearing from the Jews, but the enmity of the Thessalonian Jews still pursued them, and Paul was conducted for safety to Athens, Silas and Timothy being left behind. On his arrival, he dispatched an urgent message back to Berœa for Silas and Timothy to rejoin him at that city (**17** 11–15). The narrative of Acts implies, however, that Paul had left Athens and had reached Corinth before he was overtaken by his two followers (**18** 5). Knowling (op. cit., 363-64) suggests that they may have actually met at Athens, and that Timothy was then sent to Thessalonica (cf 1 Thess **3** 1.2), and Silas to Philippi (cf Phil **4** 15), and that the three came together again at Corinth. The arrival of Silas and Timothy at that city is probably referred to in 2 Cor **11** 9. It is implied in Acts **18** 18 that Silas did not leave Corinth at the same time as Paul, but no further definite reference is made to him in the narrative of the 2d missionary journey.

Assuming his identity with Silvanus, he is mentioned along with Paul and Timothy in 2 Cor **1** 19 as having preached Christ among the Corinthians (cf Acts **18** 5). In 1 Thess **1** 1, and 2 Thess **1** 1, the same three send greetings to the church at Thessalonica (cf Acts **17** 1–9). In 1 Pet **5** 12 he is mentioned as a "faithful brother" and the bearer of that letter to the churches of the Dispersion (cf on this last Knowling, op. cit., 331–32). The theory which assigns He to the authorship of Silas is untenable.

C. M. KERR

SILENCE, sī'lens: Five Heb roots, with various derivatives, and two Gr words are thus tr[d]. The word is used lit. for dumbness, interrupted speech, as in Lam **2** 10; Ps **32** 3; Eccl **3** 7; Am **5** 13; Acts **15** 12; 1 Cor **14** 28; 1 Tim **2** 11.12 AV (ARV "quietness"); Rev **8** 1, or figuratively of the unanswered prayers of the believer (Ps **83** 1; **35** 22; Jer **8** 14); of awe in the presence of the Divine majesty (Isa **41** 1; Zec **2** 13), or of death (1 S **2** 9; Ps **94** 17; **115** 17).

SILK, SILKWORM, silk'wûrm ([1] מֶשִׁי, *meshī* [Ezk **16** 10.13], perhaps from √ מָשָׁה, *māshāh*, "to draw," "to extract"; cf Arab. مسى, *masa'*, of same meaning; LXX **τρίχαπτον,** *tríchapton*, "woven of hair"; [2] **σηρικόν,** *sērikon* [Rev **18** 12]; [3] שֵׁשׁ, *shēsh;* cf Arab. شاش, *shâsh*, a thin cotton material; [4] בּוּץ, *būç;* cf Arab. أبيض, *'abyaḍ*, "white" from √ باض, *bâḍ;* [5] **βύσσος,** *bússos*, "fine linen," later used of cotton and silk): The only undoubted reference to silk in the Bible is the passage cited from Rev, where it is mentioned among the merchandise of Babylon. *Sērikon*, "silk," is from *Sēr*, the Gr name of China, whence silk was first obtained. The equivalent Lat *sericum* occurs frequently in classical

Silkworm.
1. Moth. 2. Chrysalis. 3. Cocoon.

authors, and is found in the Vulg (Est **8** 15) for *būç*, "fine linen." For *būç*, *bussos*, and *shēsh* EV has nearly always "fine linen," but for *shēsh* in Prov **31** 22, AV has "silk," and in Gen **41** 42 and Ex **25** 4, AVm has "silk" and RVm has "cotton." See LINEN; FINE.

There can be little doubt of the correctness of EV "silk" for *meshī* in Ezk **16** 10, "I girded thee about with fine linen [*shēsh*], and covered thee with silk [*meshī*]," and in the similar passage, Ezk **16** 13.

Silk is produced by all *Lepidoptera*, butterflies and moths, but it is of great economic importance only in the Chinese silkworm, *Bombyx mori*, whose larva, a yellowish-white caterpillar from 2 to 3 in. long, feeds on the leaves of the mulberry (*Morus*). A pair of large glands on the two sides of the stomach secrete a viscous fluid, which is conveyed by ducts to an orifice under the mouth. On issuing into the air, the fine stream is hardened into the silk fiber, which the caterpillar spins into a cocoon. Within the cocoon the caterpillar is presently transformed into the chrysalis or pupa. The cocoons from which silk is to be spun are subjected to heat which kills the pupae and prevents them from being transformed into the perfect insects or moths, which would otherwise damage the cocoons as they made their exit.

The raising of silkworms, and the spinning and weaving of silk are now important industries in Syria, though the insect was unknown in Bible times. It was introduced to the Mediterranean region from China a few centuries after Christ. Coarse silk is produced from the Chinese oak silk-moth, *Saturnia pernyi*, and from the Japanese oak silk-moth, *Saturnia yama-mai*. The largest moth of Syria and Pal is *Saturnia pyri*, from which silk has also been spun, but not commercially. See, further, WEAVING.

ALFRED ELY DAY

SILLA, sil′a (סִלָּא, *ṣillā′*; B, **Γαλλά**, *Gallá*, A, **Γααλλάδ**, *Gaallád*): Joash was assassinated by his servants "at the house of Millo, on the way that goeth down to Silla" (2 K **12** 20). Wherever Beth-millo stood, Silla was evidently in the valley below it; but nothing is known of what it was or where it stood.

SILOAM, si-lō′am, sī-lō′am, **SILOAH**, si-lō′a, **SHELAH**, shē′la, **SHILOAH**, shi-lō′a: (1) מֵי הַשִּׁלֹחַ, *mē ha-shilōaḥ* (*shilōaḥ* or *shillōaḥ* is a passive form and means "sent" or "conducted"), "the waters of [the] Shiloah" (Isa **8** 6). (2) בְּרֵכַת הַשֶּׁלַח, *berēkhath ha-shelaḥ*, "the pool of [the] Shelah" (AV "Siloah") (Neh **3** 15). (3) τὴν κολυμβήθραν τοῦ (or τὸν) Σιλωάμ, *tḗn kolumbḗthran toú* (*tón*) *Silōám*, "the pool of Siloam" (Jn **9** 7). (4) ὁ πύργος ἐν τῷ Σιλωάμ, *ho púrgos en tō̃ Silōám*, "the tower in Siloam" (Lk **13** 4).

Although the name is chiefly used in the OT and Jos as the name of certain "waters," the surviving name today, *Silwān*, is that of a fairly prosperous village which extends along the steep east side of the Kidron valley from a little N. of the "Virgin's Fountain" as far as *Bīr Eyyūb*. The greater part of the village, the older and better built section, belongs to Moslem *fellahin* who cultivate the well-watered gardens in the valley and on the hill slopes opposite, but a southern part has recently been built in an extremely primitive manner by *Yemen* Jews, immigrants from South Arabia, and still farther S., in the commencement of the *Wâdy en Nâr*, is the wretched settlement of the lepers.

1. The Modern *Silwān*

How long the site of *Silwān* has been occupied it is impossible to say. The village is mentioned in the 10th cent. by the Arab writer Muḳaddasi. The numerous rock cuttings, steps, houses, caves, etc, some of which have at times served as chapels, show that the site has been much inhabited in the past, and at one period at least by hermits. The mention of "those eighteen, upon whom the **tower in Siloam** fell, and killed them" (Lk **13** 4) certainly suggests that there was a settlement there in NT times, although some writers consider that this may have reference to some tower on the city walls near the Pool of Siloam.

2. The Siloam Aqueduct

Opposite to the main part of *Silwān* is the "Virgin's Fount," ancient GIHON (q.v.), whose waters are practically monopolized by the villagers. It is the waters of this spring which are referred to in Isa **8** 5.6: "Forasmuch as this people have refused the waters of Shiloah that go softly, ... now therefore, behold, the Lord bringeth up upon them the waters of the River."

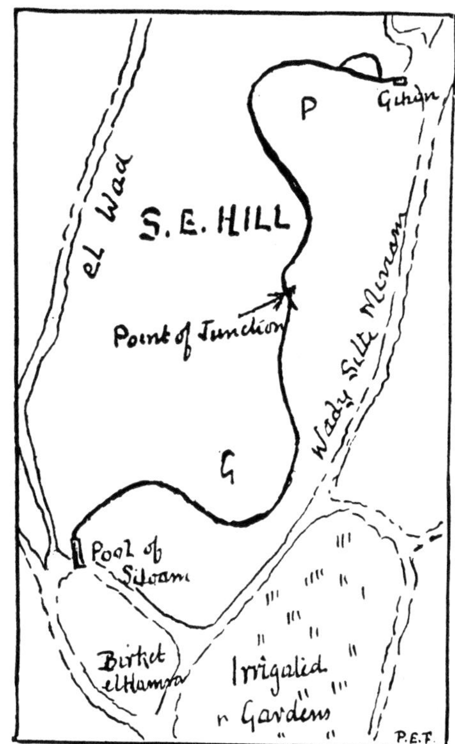

Serpentine Course of Siloam Aqueduct.

The contrast between the little stream flowing from the Gihon and the great Euphrates is used as a figure of the vast difference between the *apparent* strength of the little kingdom of Judah and the House of David on the one hand, and the might of "Rezin and Remaliah's son" and "all his glory." Although it is quite probable that in those days there was an open streamlet in the valley, yet the meaning of Shiloah, "sent" or "conducted," rather implies some kind of artificial channel, and there is also archaeological evidence that some at least of the waters of Gihon were even at that time conducted by a rock-cut aqueduct along the side of the Kidron valley (see JERUSALEM, VII, 5). It was not, however, till the days of Hezekiah that the great tunnel aqueduct, Siloam's most famous work, was made (2 K **20** 20): "Hezekiah also stopped the upper spring of the waters of Gihon, and brought them straight down on the west side of the City of David" (2 Ch **32** 30); "They stopped all the fountains, and the brook [*naḥal*] that flowed through the midst of the land, saying, Why should the kings of Assyria come, and find much water?" (2 Ch **32** 4; Ecclus **48** 17). Probably the exit of the water at Gihon was entirely covered up and the water flowed through the 1,700 ft. of tunnel and merged in the pool made for it (now known as the *Birket Silwān*) near the mouth of the Tyropœon valley. This extraordinary winding aqueduct along which the waters of the "Virgin's Fount" still flow is described in JERUSALEM, VII, 4 (q.v.). The lower end of this tunnel which now emerges under a modern arch has long been known as *'Ain Silwān*, the "Fountain of Siloam," and indeed, until the rediscovery of the tunnel connecting this with the Virgin's Fount (a fact known to some in the 13th cent., but by no means generally known until the last century), it was thought this was simply a spring. So many springs all over Pal issue from artificial tunnels—it is indeed the rule in Judaea—that the mistake is natural. Jos gives no hint that he knew of so great a work as this of Hezekiah's, and in the 5th cent. a church was erected, probably by the empress Eudoxia, at this spot, with the high altar over the sacred "spring." The only pilgrim who mentions this church is Antonius Martyr (c 570), and after its destruction, probably by the Persians in 614, it was entirely lost sight of until excavated by Messrs. Bliss and Dickie. It is a church of extraordinary architectural features; the floor of the center aisle is still visible.

3. The "Pool of Siloam"

The water from the Siloam aqueduct, emerging at *'Ain Silwān*, flows today into a narrow shallow pool, approached by a steep flight of modern steps; from the southern extremity of this pool the water crosses under the modern road by means of an aqueduct, and after traversing a deeply cut rock channel below the scarped cliffs on the north side of *el-Wâd*, it crosses under the main road up the Kidron and enters a number of channels of irrigation distributed among the gardens of the people of *Silwān*. The water here, as at its origin, is brackish and impregnated with sewage.

The modern *Birket es-Silwān* is but a poor survivor of the fine pool which once was here. Bliss showed by his excavations at the site that once there was a great rock-cut pool, 71 ft. N. and S., by 75 ft. E. and W., which may, in part at least, have been the work of Hezekiah (2 K **20** 20), approached by a splendid flight of steps along its west side. The pool was surrounded by an arcade 12 ft. wide and 22½ ft. high, and was divided by a central arcade, to make in all probability a pool for men and another for women. These buildings were probably Herodian, if not earlier, and therefore this, we may reasonably picture, was the condition of the pool at the time of the incident in Jn **9** 7, when Jesus sent the blind man to "wash in the pool of Siloam."

This pool is also probably the **Pool of Shelah** described in Neh **3** 15 as lying between the Fountain Gate and the King's Garden. It may also be the "king's pool" of Neh **2** 14. If we were in any doubt regarding the position of the pool of Siloam, the explicit statement of Jos (*BJ*, V, iv, 1) that the fountain of Siloam, which he says was a plentiful spring of sweet water, was at the mouth of the Tyropœon would make us sure.

4. The Birket el Ḥamra

A little below this pool, at the very mouth of *el-Wâd*, is a dry pool, now a vegetable garden, known as *Birket el Ḥamra* ("the red pool"). For many years the sewage of Jerus found its way to this spot, but when in 1904 an ancient city sewer was rediscovered (see *PEFS*, 1904, 392–94), the sewage was diverted and the site was sold to the Gr convent which surrounded it with a wall. Although this is no longer a pool, there is no doubt but that hereabouts there existed a pool because the great and massive dam which Bliss excavated here (see JERUSALEM, VI, 5) had clearly been made originally to support a large body of water. It is commonly supposed that the original pool here was older than the *Birket Silwān*, having been fed by an aqueduct which was constructed from Gihon along the side of the Kidron valley before Hezekiah's great tunnel. If this is correct (and excavations are needed here to confirm this theory), then this may be the "lower pool" referred to in Isa **22** 9, the waters of which Hezekiah "stopped," and perhaps, too, that described in the same passage as the "old pool."

5. The Siloam Aqueduct

The earliest known Heb inscription of any length was accidentally discovered near the lower end of the Siloam aqueduct in 1880, and reported by Dr. Schick. It was inscribed upon a rock-smoothed surface about 27 in. square, some 15 ft. from the mouth of the aqueduct; it was about 3 ft. above the bottom of the channel on the east side. The inscription consisted of six lines in archaic Heb, and has been trd by Professor Sayce as follows:

(1) Behold the excavation. Now this [is] the history of the tunnel: while the excavators were still lifting up

(2) The pick toward each other, and while there were yet three cubits [to be broken through] . . . . the voice of the one called

(3) To his neighbor, for there was an [?] *excess* in the rock on the right. They rose up . . . . they struck on the west of the

(4) Excavation; the excavators struck, each to meet the other, pick to pick. And there flowed

(5) The waters from their outlet to the pool for a thousand, two hundred cubits; and [?]

(6) Of a cubit, was the height of the rock over the head of the excavators . . . .

It is only a roughly scratched inscription of the nature of a graffito; the flowing nature of the writing is fully explained by Dr. Reissner's recent discovery of ostraca at Samaria written with pen and ink. It is not an official inscription, and consequently there is no kingly name and no date, but the prevalent view that it was made by the work people who carried out Hezekiah's great work (2 K **20** 20) is now further confirmed by the character of the Heb in the ostraca which Reissner dates as of the time of Ahab.

Unfortunately this priceless monument of antiquity was violently removed from its place by some miscreants. The fragments have been collected and are now pieced together in the Constantinople museum. Fortunately several excellent "squeezes" as well as transcriptions were made before the inscription was broken up, so that the damage done is to be regretted rather on sentimental than on literary grounds. E. W. G. MASTERMAN

SILOAM, TOWER IN. See JERUSALEM; SILOAM.

SILVANUS, sil-vā'nus (**Σιλουανός,** *Silouanós* [2 Cor **1** 19]). See SILAS.

SILVER, sil'vẽr (כֶּסֶף, *keṣeph;* **ἀργύριον,** *argúrion,* **ἄργυρος,** *árguros*): Silver was known in the earliest historic times. Specimens of early Egyp and Bab silver work testify to the skill of the ancient silversmiths. In Pal, silver objects have been found antedating the occupation of the land **by**

the Hebrews. This metal was used for making all kinds of ornamental objects. In the mound of Gezer were found bowls, vases, ladles, hairpins, rings and bracelets of silver. The rings and settings for scarabs or seals were commonly of this metal. The first mention of silver in the Bible is in Gen **13** 2, where it says that Abraham was rich in cattle, in silver and gold. At that time it was commonly used in exchange in the form of bars or other shapes. Coins of that metal were of a much later date (Gen **20** 16; **23** 15; **24** 53; **37** 28, etc). Booty was collected in silver (Josh **6** 19); tribute was paid in the same (1 K **15** 19). It was also used for jewelry (Gen **44** 2). The Children of Israel systematically despoiled the Egyptians of their silver before the exodus (Ex **3** 22; **11** 2; **12** 35, etc). Ex **20** 23 implies that idols were made of it. It was largely used in the fittings of the tabernacle (Ex **26** ff) and later of the temple (2 Ch **2** ff).

It is likely that the ancient supply of silver came from the mountains of Asia Minor where it is still found in abundance associated with lead as argentiferous galena, and with copper sulphide. The Turkish government mines this silver on shares with the natives. The Sinaitic peninsula probably also furnished some silver. Later Phoen ships brought quantities of it from Greece and Spain. The Arabian sources are doubtful (2 Ch **9** 14). Although silver does not tarnish readily in the air, it does corrode badly in the limestone soil of Pal and Syria. This probably partly accounts for the small number of objects of this metal found. On the site of the ancient jewelers' shops of Tyre the writer found objects of gold, bronze, lead, iron, but none of silver.

Figurative: Silver to be as stones in Jerus (1 K **10** 27) typified great abundance (cf Job **3** 15; **22** 25; **27** 16; also Isa **60** 17; Zec **9** 3). The trying of men's hearts was compared to the refining of silver (Ps **66** 10; Isa **48** 10). Jeh's words were as pure as silver refined seven times (Ps **12** 6). The gaining of understanding is better than the gaining of silver (Prov **3** 14; cf **8** 19; **10** 20; **16** 16; **22** 1; **25** 11). Silver become dross denoted deterioration (Isa **1** 22; Jer **6** 30). Breast and arms of silver was interpreted by Daniel to mean the inferior kingdom to follow Nebuchadnezzar's (Dnl **2** 32. 39).

In the NT, reference should be made esp. to Acts **19** 24; Jas **5** 3; Rev **18** 12. JAMES A. PATCH

SILVERLING, sil'vẽr-ling (אֶלֶף כֶּסֶף, *'eleph keṣeph* [Isa **7** 23]): 'A thousand of silver' means a thousand shekels. See PIECE OF SILVER.

SILVERSMITH, sil'vẽr-smith (**ἀργυροκόπος,** *argurokópos*): Mentioned only once (Acts **19** 24), where reference is made to Demetrius, a leading member of the silversmiths' guild of Ephesus.

SIMALCUE, sī-mal-kū'ē: AV = RV IMALCUE (q.v.).

SIMEON, sim'ē-on (שִׁמְעוֹן, *shim'ōn;* **Συμεών,** *Sumeōn;* the Heb root is from שָׁמַע, *shāma'*, "to hear" [Gen **29** 33]; some modern scholars [Hitzig, W. R. Smith, Stade, etc] derive it from Arab. *sima'*, "the offspring of the hyena and female wolf"): In Gen **29** 33; **30** 18–21; **35** 23, Simeon is given as full brother to Reuben, Levi, Judah, Issachar and Zebulun, the son of Leah; and in Gen **34** 25; **49** 5 as the brother of Levi and Dinah. He was left as a hostage in Egypt by orders of Joseph (Gen **42** 24; **43** 23).

In the "blessing" of the dying Jacob, Simeon and Levi are linked together:

1. The Patriarch: Biblical Data

"Simeon and Levi are brethren;
Weapons of violence are their swords.
O my soul, come not thou into their council;
Unto their assembly, my glory, be not thou united;
For in their anger they slew a man,
And in their self-will they hocked an ox.
Cursed be their anger, for it was fierce;
And their wrath, for it was cruel:
I will divide them in Jacob,
And scatter them in Israel" (Gen **49** 5–7).

Whatever view may be taken of the events of Gen **34** 25 (and some would see in it "a tradition of the settlement of Jacob which belongs to a cycle quite independent of the descent into Egypt and the Exodus" [see S. A. Cook, *Enc Brit*, art. "Simeon"]), it is clear that we have here a reference to it and the suggestion that the subsequent history of the tribe, and its eventual absorption in Judah, was the result of violence. In the same way the priestly Levites became distributed throughout the other tribes without any tribal inheritance of their own (Dt **18** 1; Josh **13** 14). From the mention (Gen **46** 10; Ex **6** 15) of Shaul as being the son of a Canaanite woman, it may be supposed that the tribe was a mixed one.

In the "blessing of Moses" (Dt **33**) Simeon is not mentioned at all in the Heb text, although in some MSS of LXX the latter half of ver 6 is made to apply to him: "Let Simeon be a small company." The history of the tribe is scanty and raises many problems. Of the many theories advanced to meet them it cannot be said that any one answers all difficulties.

2. The Tribe in Scripture

In the wilderness of Sinai the Simeonites camped beside the Reubenites (Nu **2** 12; **10** 19); it was Zimri, a member of one of the leading families of this tribe, who was slain by Phinehas in the affair of Baal-peor (Nu **25** 14). The statistics in Nu **1** 22 f, where the Simeonites are given as 59,300, compared with the 2d census (Nu **26** 14), where the numbers are 22,200, indicate a diminishing tribe. Some have connected this with the sin of Zimri.

At the recital of the law at Mt. Gerizim, Simeon is mentioned first among those that were to respond to the blessings (Dt **27** 12). In the conquest of Canaan "Judah said unto Simeon his brother, Come up with me into my lot, that we may fight against the Canaanites; and I likewise will go with thee into thy lot. So Simeon went with him" (Jgs **1** 3; cf ver 17). (Many scholars find in Gen **34** a tribal attempt on the part of the Simeonites to gain possession of Shechem; if this is so, Judah did not assist, and the utter failure may have been a cause of Simeon's subsequent dependence upon, and final absorption in, Judah.) In Jgs **4** and **5** Simeon is never mentioned. In the settlement of the land there is no account of how Simeon established himself in his territory (except the scanty reference in Jgs **1** 3), but "their inheritance was in the midst of the inheritance of the children of Judah" (Josh **19** 1); this is accounted for (ver 9), "for the portion of the children of Judah was too much for them." Nevertheless we find there the very cities which are apportioned to Simeon, allotted to Judah (Josh **15** 21–32; cf Neh **11** 26–29). It is suggested (in 1 Ch **4** 31) that the independent possession of these cities ceased in the time of David. David sent spoil to several Simeonite towns (1 S **30** 26 f), and in 1 Ch **12** 25 it is recorded that 7,100 Simeonite warriors came to David in Hebron. In 1 Ch **27** 16 we have mention of a ruler of the Simeonites, Shephatiah, son of Maacah.

In 1 Ch **4** 39 f mention is made of certain isolated exploits of Simeonites at GEDOR (q.v.), against the MEUNIM (q.v.), and at MT. SEIR (q.v.). Later references associate certain Simeonites with the Northern Kingdom (2 Ch **15** 9; **34** 6), and tradition has come to view them as one of the ten tribes (cf Ezk **48** 24.25.33; Rev **7** 7), although all the history of them we have is bound up with Judah and the Southern Kingdom. There is no mention of the return of any Simeonites after the captivity; their cities fall to Judah (Neh **11** 26 f).

3. References in Egyp and Assyr Inscriptions

It has been supposed by many authorities that the name *Shim'an* occurs in the list of places plundered by Thothmes III (see Petrie, *Hist*, II, 104; also Hommel, *AHT*, 268; Sayce, *Early Heb Traditions*, 392). In the 7th cent. we have a doubtful reference in an inscription of Esar-haddon relating his Egyp campaign when a city *Ap-ku* is mentioned as in the country of *Sa-me-n(a)*, which may possibly be a reference to Simeon. The survival of the name so late, if true, is strange, in the light of what we gather from the Bible about the tribe. (For discussion of both of these inscriptions, with references to the lit., see *EB*, coll. 4528–30.)

4. The Territory of Simeon

The cities of Simeon as given in Josh **19** 2–6 and 1 Ch **4** 28.31 are (the names in parentheses are variations in the latter reference): Beer-sheba, Moladah, Hazar-shual, Balah (Bilhah), Azem (AV) (Ezem), Eltolad (Tolad), Bethuel, Hormah, Ziklag, Beth-marcaboth, Hazar-susah (Hazar Susim), Beth-lebaoth (Beth-biri), Sharuhen (Shaaraim) (Etam), Ain Rimmon, Ether (Tochen), Ashan—in all, 16 cities in Josh and 17 in 1 Ch. Ashan (1 Ch **6** 59) is the only one assigned to the priests. It is written wrongly as "Ain" in Josh **21** 16. All the above cities, with certain variations in form, and with the exception of Etam in 1 Ch **4** 32, which is probably a mistake, occur in the list of the cities of Judah (Josh **15** 26–32.42). Ziklag is mentioned (1 S **27** 6) as being the private property of the kings of Judah from the days of David, who received it from Achish, king of Gath.

For the situation of these cities, so far as is known, see separate arts. under their names. It is clear that they were all situated in the southwestern part of Pal, and that Simeon had no definite territorial boundaries, but isolated cities, with their villages, among those of the people of Judah.

E. W. G. MASTERMAN

SIMEON (שִׁמְעוֹן, *shim'ōn;* **Συμεών,** *Sumeṓn*):
(1) The 2d son of Jacob by Leah (see separate art.).
(2) Great-grandfather of Judas Maccabaeus (1 Macc **2** 1).
(3) A man in Jerus described as "righteous and devout, looking for the consolation of Israel." When the infant Jesus was brought into the Temple, he took Him into his arms and blessed God in words which are famous as the *Nunc dimittis*. Simeon bestowed his blessing on the wondering father and mother (Lk **2** 25.34). Legend has made him the son of Hillel and father of Gamaliel I, but this has no historical basis.
(4) An ancestor of Jesus (Lk **3** 30); RV "Symeon."
(5) RV "Symeon": one of the prophets and teachers in the Christian community at Antioch. He is also called Niger, which was the gentile name he had assumed, Symeon being Heb. He was among those who set apart Paul and Barnabas for their missionary work (Acts **13** 1.2). Nothing more is known of him.
(6) RV "Symeon": the Heb name of Simon Peter (Acts **15** 14). S. F. HUNTER

SIMEON (NIGER, nī'jẽr): AV in Acts **13** 1, RV "Symeon" (q.v.).

SIMEONITES, sim'ē-on-īts. See SIMEON.

SIMILITUDE, si-mil'i-tūd: In AV means either "an exact facsimile" (Ps **106** 20 AV, RV "likeness"; Rom **5** 14, etc), or else "the form itself" (Nu **12** 8; Dt **4** 12.15.16 for *t^emūnāh,* "form" [so RV]); cf LIKENESS. ERV has retained the word in 2 Ch **4** 3; Dnl **10** 16 (ARV "likeness"), while ERV and ARV have used "similitudes" in Hos **12** 10 (דָּמָה, *dāmāh,* "be like"). The meaning is "I have inspired the prophets to speak parables."

SIMON (**Σίμων,** *Simōn,* Gr form of SIMEON [q.v.]): The persons of the name of Simon mentioned in the Apocrypha are:

(1) Simon the Maccabean (Hasmonean), surnamed THASSI (q.v.), the 2d son of Mattathias and elder brother of Judas Maccabaeus. On his deathbed, Mattathias commended Simon as a "man of counsel" to be a "father" to his brethren (1 Macc **2** 65), and a "man of counsel" he proved himself. But it was not till after the death of Judas and the capture of Jonathan that he played the chief rôle. Dispatched by Judas with a force to the relief of the Jews in Galilee he fought with great success (**5** 17 ff; Jos, *Ant*, XII, viii, 1 f). We find him next taking revenge along with Jonathan on the "children of Jambri" (1 Macc **9** 33 ff), and coöperating in the successful campaign around Bethbasi against Bacchides (c 156 BC) (**9** 62 ff), and in the campaign against Apollonius (**10** 74 ff). In the conflict between Tryphon and Demetrius II, Simon was appointed by Antiochus VI "captain from the Ladder of Tyre unto the borders of Egypt" (**11** 59). After the capture of Jonathan at Ptolemais by Tryphon, Simon became acknowledged leader of his party. He thwarted Tryphon in his attempts upon Jerus, in revenge for which the latter murdered Jonathan (**13** 23). Simon then took the side of Demetrius on condition of immunity for Judaea, and so 'in the 170th year' (143–142 BC) 'the yoke of the heathen was taken away from Israel' (**13** 41). Simon applied himself to rebuild the strongholds of Judaea, reduced Gazara, captured the Acra (citadel) and made Joppa a seaport. He showed his wisdom most of all in his internal administration: "He sought the good of his country"; commerce and agriculture revived; lawlessness was suppressed, and "the land had rest all the days of Simon" (**14** 4 ff). His power was acknowledged by Sparta and Rome (**14** 16 ff). In 141 BC he was appointed by the nation leader, high priest and captain "for ever, until there should arise a faithful prophet" (**14** 41 ff), and thus the Hasmonean dynasty was founded. A new chronological era began with the first year of his administration, and he minted his own coins. A few years later Simon again meddled in Syrian politics (139 BC), this time at the entreaty of Antiochus VII (Sidetes) in his contest against Tryphon; when, however, Antiochus was assured of success, he refused the help of Simon and sent Cendebaeus against Judaea. Judas and John, sons of Simon, defeated the invaders near Modin (137–136 BC). In 135 BC Simon met his death by treachery. Ptolemy the son of Abubus, Simon's own son-in-law, determined to secure supreme power for himself and, in order to accomplish this, to assassinate the whole family of Simon. He accordingly invited Simon and his sons to a banquet in the stronghold of Dok near Jericho, where he treacherously murdered Simon with his two sons Mattathias and Judas. The other son, John Hyrcanus, governor of Gazara, received intimation of the plot and saved himself to become

the head of the Hasmonean dynasty. "The significance of Simon's administration consists in this, that he completed the work of Jonathan and left the Jewish people absolutely independent of Syria" (Schürer). See MACCABAEUS, II, 4.

(2) Simon I, the high priest, son of Onias I, whom he succeeded c 300 BC. He was one of the last of the Great Synagogue, and to him is attributed the saying, "On three things the world depends—the Law, worship and the showing of kindness." According to Jos (*Ant*, XII, ii, 5) this Simon was called "the Just" (ὁ δίκαιος, *ho díkaios*), "on account of his piety and his benevolent disposition toward his countrymen."

Many authorities (Herzfeld, Derenbourg, Stanley, Cheyne) assert that Jos is wrong in attaching this epithet to Simon I instead of Simon II, and Schürer is not certain on this question. But the Talm passage which Derenbourg cites means the opposite of what he takes it, viz. it is intended to show how splendid and holy were the days of Simeon (*ha-çaddīk*) compared with the later days. Besides, Jos is more likely to have known the truth on this matter than these later authorities. The same uncertainty obtains as to whether the eulogium in Sir **50** 1 ff of "the great priest" refers to Simon I or Simon II. Schürer and others refer it to Simon II. It is more likely to refer to the Simon who was famous as "the Just," and consequently to Simon I. Besides we know of no achievements of Simon II to entitle him to such praise. The building operations mentioned would suit the time of Simon I better, as Ptolemy captured Jerus and probably caused considerable destruction. The Talm states that this Simon (and not Jaddua) met Alexander the Great.

(3) Simon II, high priest, son of Onias II and grandson of Simon I and father of Onias III, flourished about the end of the 3d cent. BC, and was succeeded by his son Onias III c 198 BC. Jos says that this Simon in the conflict of the sons of Joseph sided with the elder sons against Hyrcanus the younger. Schürer (probably incorrectly) thinks he is the Simon praised in Sir **50** 1 ff. See (2) above (3 Macc **2** 1; Jos, *Ant*, XII, iv, 10).

(4) Simon, a Benjamite, guardian of the temple, who, having quarreled with the high priest Onias III, informed Apollonius of the untold sums of money in the temple treasury. Apollonius laid the matter before the king Seleucus IV, who sent Heliodorus to remove the money. An apparition prevented Heliodorus from accomplishing his task (2 Macc **3** 4 ff). It is further recorded, that Simon continued his opposition to Onias. He is spoken of as brother of the renegade Menelaus (**4** 23). Of his end we know nothing.

(5) Simon Chosameus (B [and Swete], Χοσάμαος, *Chosámaos*, A, Χοσομαῖος, *Chosomaíos*), one of the sons of Annas who had married "strange wives" (1 Esd **9** 32). Simon apparently="Shimeon" (*shim'ōn*) of the sons of Harim (Ezr **10** 31); Chosameus is probably a corruption standing in the place of, but not resembling, any of the three names: Benjamin, Malluch, Shemaraiah, which Esd omits from the Ezr list. S. ANGUS

SIMON, sī'mon (**Σίμων**, *Símōn*):

(1) Simon Peter. See PETER (SIMON).

(2) Another of the Twelve, Simon "the Cananaean" (Mt **10** 4; Mk **3** 18), "the Zealot" (Lk **6** 15; Acts **1** 13). See CANANAEAN.

(3) One of the brethren of Jesus (Mt **13** 55; Mk **6** 3). See BRETHREN OF THE LORD.

(4) "The leper" in Bethany, in whose house a woman poured a cruse of precious ointment over the head of Jesus (Mt **26** 6; Mk **14** 3). He had perhaps been healed by Jesus; in that case his ungracious behavior was not consistent with due gratitude. However he was healed, the title referred to his condition in the past, as lepers were ostracized by law.

(5) A Pharisee in whose house a woman, "a sinner," wet the feet of Jesus with her tears, and anointed them with ointment (Lk **7** 36 ff). By some he is identified with (4), this being regarded as Luke's version of the incident recorded in Mt **26** and Mk **14**. Others as strongly deny this view. For discussion see MARY, IV.

(6) A man of Cyrene, who was compelled to carry the cross of Jesus (Mt **27** 32; Mk **15** 21; Lk **23** 26). Mark calls him "the father of Alexander and Rufus," well-known members of the church at (probably) Rome (cf Acts **19** 33; Rom **16** 13). See CYRENIAN.

(7) The father of Judas Iscariot (Jn **6** 71; **12** 4 AV, RV omits; **13** 2.26).

(8) Simon Magus (Acts **8** 9 ff). See separate article.

(9) Simon, the tanner, with whom Peter lodged at Joppa. His house was by the seaside outside the city wall, because of its ceremonial uncleanness to a Jew, and also for reasons of sanitation (Acts **9** 43). S. F. HUNTER

SIMON MAGUS, mā'gus (**Σίμων**, *Símōn*, Gr form of Heb שִׁמְעוֹן, *shim'ōn;* Gesenius gives the meaning of the Heb word as "hearing with acceptance"; it is formed from √ שָׁמַע, *shāma'*, "to hear"):

1. Simon, a Magician
2. Simon and the Apostles
   (1) Simon and Philip
   (2) Simon and Peter and John
3. The Magicians and the Gospel
4. Testimony of Early Christian Writers
5. Sources of Legendary History
6. Traditions of His Death
7. The Simoniani
8. Was Simon the Originator of Gnosticism?

1. Simon, a Magician

The name or term "Magus" is not given to him in the NT, but is justly used to designate or particularize him on account of the incident recorded in Acts **8** 9–24, for though the word "Magus" does not occur, yet in ver 9 the present participle *mageúōn* is used, and is tr^d, both in AV and in RV, "used sorcery." Simon accordingly was a sorcerer, he "bewitched the people of Samaria" (AV). In ver 11 it is also said that "of long time he had amazed" them "with his sorceries" (*magíais*). The claim, given out by himself, was that he "was some great one"; and this claim was acknowledged by the Samaritans, for previous to the introduction of the gospel into Samaria, "they all gave heed [to him], from the least to the greatest, saying, This man is that power of God which is called Great" (ver 10).

2. Simon and the Apostles

(1) It so happened, however, that Philip the deacon and evangelist went down from Jerus to Samaria, and "proclaimed unto them the Christ" (ver 5); and as the result of the proclamation of the gospel, many were gathered into the Christian church. Many miracles also were performed by Philip, sick persons cured, and demons cast out; and Simon fell under the influence of all these things, both of the preaching and of "the signs." So great was the impression now made upon Simon that he "believed" (ver 13). This means, at least, that he saw that Philip was able in the name of Jesus Christ to display powers greater than anything he himself was acquainted with: Philip's power was greater by far than Simon's. He therefore came forward as one of the new converts, and was baptized. After his baptism he continued with Philip. The signs which accompanied the introduction of the gospel into this city did not cease, and Simon seeing them "was amazed." The word denoting Simon's amazement at the "signs" wrought by Philip is the same as that used to express how the people of Samaria had been

amazed at Simon's sorceries. It is an indication of the nature of the faith which he possessed in the gospel—wondering amazement at a new phenomenon not yet understood, not repentance or trust in Christ.

(2) News having reached Jerus of the events which had occurred in Samaria, the apostles sent Peter and John to establish the work there. These two apostles prayed for the converts that they might receive the Holy Ghost, which they had not yet received. And when they had laid their hands upon the converts, the Spirit was given to them. At this early period in the history of the church the Holy Ghost was bestowed in a visible manner which showed itself in such miraculous gifts as are described in Acts **2**. Simon saw what had taken place, and then, instead of joining the company of those who had truly repented and trusted Christ, he came forward with the same amazement as he had previously shown, and offered money to Peter and John, if they would impart to him the power of giving the Holy Ghost to others. Peter instantly rebuked this bold and ungodly request, and did so with such sternness as to cause Simon to ask that the judgment threatened by the apostle might not fall upon him.

Such is the unenviable history of Simon Magus, as it is recorded in the NT. Later centuries have shown their estimation of the heinousness of Simon's sin by employing his name to indicate the crime of buying or selling a spiritual office for a price in money—"simony."

3. The Magicians and the Gospel

It is not strange to find the gospel brought into direct conflict with magicians, for in the 1st and 2d cents. there were a multitude of such persons who pretended to possess supernatural powers by which they endeavored to deceive men. They flattered the sinful inclinations of the human heart, and fell in with men's current ways of thinking, and required no self-renunciation at all. For these reasons the magicians found a ready belief on the part of many. The emperor Tiberius, in his later years, had a host of magicians in constant attendance upon him. Elymas, with whom Paul came in contact in Cyprus "was with the deputy of the country, Sergius Paulus, a prudent man" (Acts **13** 7 AV). Elymas was one of those magicians, and he endeavored to turn away the deputy from the faith. Luke expressly calls this man "magus," Elymas the magus (Acts **13** 6.8 m).

The influence of such persons presented an obstacle to the progress of the Christian faith, which had to force its way through the delusions with which these sorcerers had surrounded the hearts of those whom they deceived. When the gospel came in contact with these magicians and with their works, it was necessary that there should be striking facts, works of supernatural power strongly appealing to men's outward senses, in order to bring them out of the bewilderment and deception in which they were involved, and to make them able to receive the impression of spiritual truth. Such miracles were wrought both in Cyprus and in Samaria, the spheres of influence of the magicians Elymas and Simon. These Divine works first arrested men's attention, and then dispelled the delusive influence of the sorcerers.

4. Testimony of Early Writers

(1) The history of Simon Magus does not close with what is narrated in the Acts, for the early Christian writers have much to say in regard to him.

Justin Martyr, himself a Samaritan, states that Simon Magus was a "Samaritan from the village called Gittōn." Justin also relates that, in the time of Claudius Caesar, Simon was worshipped as a god at Rome on account of his magical powers, and that a statue had been erected to him, on the island in the river Tiber, with the inscription *Simoni Deo Sancto*, that is, "To Simon the sacred god." Curiously enough, in the year 1574, a stone which appears to have served as a pedestal of a statue, was dug up in the Tiber at the spot described by Justin; and on it were inscribed the words *Semoni Sanco Deo Fidio Sacrum*, that is, the stone then discovered was dedicated to the god Semo Sancus, the Sabine Hercules. This antiquarian find makes it probable that Justin was mistaken in what he said about a statue having been erected in honor of Simon Magus. "It is incredible that the folly should ever be carried to such an extent as that a statue should be erected, and the senate should pass a decree enrolling Simon Magus among the *deos Romanos*" (Neander, *Church History*, II, 123). The inscription found in 1574 shows the source of the error into which Justin had fallen.

There are many stories told by some of the early Christian writers regarding Simon Magus, but they are full of legend and fable: some of them are improbable in the extreme and border on the impossible.

(2) Jerome, who professes to quote from writings of Simon, represents him as employing these words in reference to himself, "I am the Word of God, I am the Comforter, I am Almighty, I am all there is of God" (Mansel, *The Gnostic Heresies*, 82). Irenaeus (Mansel, ib, 82) writes regarding him: "Simon, having purchased a certain woman named Helena, who had been a prostitute in the city of Tyre, carried her about with him, and said that she was the first conception of his mind, the mother of all things, by whom, in the beginning, he conceived the thought of making the angels and archangels; for that this conception proceeded forth from him, and knowing her father's wishes, she descended to the lower world, and produced the angels and powers; by whom also he said that this world was made. But after she had produced them, she was detained by them through envy, since they were unwilling to be considered the offspring of any other being; for he himself was entirely unknown by them; but his conception was detained by those powers and angels which were put forth from her, and suffered every insult from them that she might not return upward to her father; and this went so far that she was even confined within a human body, and for ages passed into other female bodies, as if from one vessel into another. He said also that she was that Helen, on whose account the Trojan war was fought . . . . and that after passing from one body to another, and constantly meeting with insult, at last she became a public prostitute, and that this was the lost sheep. On this account he himself came, that he might first of all reclaim her and free her from her chains, and then give salvation to men through the knowledge of himself. For since the angels ruled the world badly, because one of them desired the chief place, he had come down for the restoration of all things, and had descended, being changed in figure, and made like to principalities and powers and angels, so that he appeared among men as a man, and was thought to have suffered in Judaea, though he did not suffer. . . . . Furthermore he said that the prophets uttered their prophecies under the inspiration of those angels who framed the world; for which reason they who rest their hope on him and his Helena no longer cared for them, but as free men could act as they pleased, for that men are saved by his [i.e. Simon's] grace, and not according to their own just works, for that no acts were just by nature, but by accident, according to the rules established by the angels, who made the world, and who attempt by these precepts to bring men into bondage. For this reason he promised that the world should be released, and those who are his set at liberty from the government of those who made the world."

5. Sources of Legendary History

The chief sources of the legendary history of Simon Magus are the collection of writings known as *The Clementines* (see LITERATURE, SUB-APOSTOLIC; PETER, FIRST EPISTLE OF; PETER, SECOND EPISTLE OF). What is there said of him is, that he studied at Alexandria, and that he had been, along with the heresiarch Dositheus, a disciple of John the Baptist. He became also a disciple of Dositheus, and afterward his successor. *The Clementines* comprise (1) *The Homilies*, (2) *The Recognitions*, and (3) *The Epitome*. These three are cognate works, and in part are identical. The date of *The Homilies* may be placed about 160 AD. The contents comprise a supposed letter from the apostle Peter to the apostle James, along with other matter. Then follow the homilies, of which there are twenty. These record the supposed travels of Clement, a Rom citizen. Clement meets with Barnabas and with Peter. Then there is narrated a discussion between Peter and Simon Magus. This disputation lasts for three days, Simon maintaining that there are two gods, and that the God of the OT is an imperfect being. Simon Magus withdraws to Tyre and then to Sidon. Peter follows Simon from place to place, counteracting his sorceries, and instructing the people. At Laodicea a second disputation takes place between the apostle and Simon on the same subjects.

The Homilies are not a Christian protest against Gnosticism, but merely that of one gnostic school or sect against another, the Ebionite against the Marcionite. The Deity of Christ is denied, and He is regarded as one of the Jewish prophets.

In the legends Simon is represented as constantly opposing Peter, who ultimately discredits and vanquishes him. These legends occur in more forms than one, the earlier form selecting Antioch as the place where Simon was discomfited by the apostle and where he also died, while the later tradition chooses Rome for these events.

6. Traditions of His Death

One tradition tells how the magician ordered his followers to bury him in a grave, promising that if this were done, he would rise again on the third day. They did as he wished and buried him; but this was the end of him, for he did not rise again.

Simon is said to have met his death at Rome, after an encounter with the apostle Peter. During this his final controversy with the apostle, Simon had raised himself in the air by the help of evil spirits, and in answer to the prayer of Peter and Paul he was dashed to the ground and killed.

According to another form of this tradition, Simon proposed to give the Rom emperor a proof of his power by flying off to God. He succeeded, it is said, in flying for a certain distance over Rome, but in answer to the prayer of Peter he fell and broke one of his legs. This tradition accounts for his end by saying that the people stoned him to death.

7. The Simoniani

The Simoniani, the Simonians or followers of Simon, were an eclectic sect, who seem, at one time, to have adopted tenets and opinions derived from paganism, at another, from Judaism and the beliefs of the Samaritans, and at another still, from Christianity. Sometimes they seem to have been ascetics; at others they are wild scoffers at moral law. They regarded Simon Magus as their Christ, or at least as a form of manifestation of the redeeming Christ, who had manifested Himself also in Jesus. The Simonians were one of the minor gnostic sects and were carried far away both from the doctrine and from the ethical spirit of the Christian faith.

Origen denies that the followers of Simon were Christians in any sense. The words of Origen are, "It escapes the notice of Celsus that the Simonians do not in any way acknowledge Jesus as the Son of God, but they call Simon the Power of God." In the time of Origen the followers of Simon had dwindled in number to such a degree that he writes, "I do not think it possible to find that all the followers of Simon in the whole world are more than thirty: and perhaps I have said more than there really are" (*Contr. Cels.*, i.57, quoted by Alford, *Gr NT*, Acts **8** 9).

8. Was Simon the Originator of Gnosticism?

Irenaeus also has much to say regarding Simon and his followers. He makes the legendary Simon identical with the magician of Acts **8**, makes him also the first in the list which he gives of heretics, and also says that it was from him that Gnosticism sprang. The account which he gives of the Simonians shows that by the time when Irenaeus lived, their system had developed into Gnosticism; but this fact does not justify Irenaeus in the assertion that Simon of Acts **8** is the originator of the gnostic system. The early Christian writers took this view, and regarded Simon Magus as the founder of Gnosticism. Perhaps they were right, "but from the very little authentic information we possess, it is impossible to ascertain how far he was identified with their tenets" (Alford, *NT*, II, 86). In the midst of the various legends regarding Simon, it may be that there is a substratum of fact, of such a nature that future investigation and discovery will justify these early Christian writers in their judgment, and will show that Simon Magus is not to be overlooked as one of the sources from which Gnosticism sprang. The exact origin of Gnosticism is certainly difficult to trace, but there is little or no indication that it arose from the incidents narrated in Acts **8**. It cannot be denied that a connection is possible, and may have existed between the two, that is between Simon Magus and some of the gnostic heresies; but the facts of history show widespread tendencies at work, during and even before the Apostolic age, which amply account for the rise of Gnosticism. These are found e.g. in the Alexandrian philosophy, and in the tenets of the false teachers at Colossae and in other places. These philosophical and theosophical ideas commingled with the influences of Zoroastrianism from Persia, and of Buddhism from India, and these tendencies and influences, taken in conjunction, were the sources of the various heresies known by the name of Gnosticism. See GNOSTICISM.

JOHN RUTHERFURD

SIMON PETER. See PETER, SIMON.

SIMON THE CANAANITE, OR CANANAEAN, OR ZEALOT (**Σίμων Καναναῖος**, *Símōn Kananaíos;* קַנָּאִי, *kannā'ī,* "the Jealous [or Zealous] One"): One of the Twelve Apostles. This Simon was also named "the Canaanite" (Mt **10** 4; Mk **3** 18 AV) or "the Cananaean" (Mt **10** 4; Mk **3** 18 RV) or "Zelotes" (Lk **6** 15; Acts **1** 13 AV) or "the Zealot" (Lk **6** 15; Acts **1** 13 RV).

According to the "Gospel of the Ebionites" or "Gospel of the Twelve Apostles" (of the 2d cent. and mentioned by Origen) Simon received his call to the apostleship along with Andrew and Peter, the sons of Zebedee, Thaddaeus and Judas Iscariot at the Sea of Tiberias (cf Mt **4** 18–22; see also Hennecke, *Neutestamentliche Apokryphen,* 24–27).

Although Simon, like the majority of the apostles, was probably a Galilean, the designation "Cananaean" is regarded as of political rather than of geographical significance (cf St. Luke's rendering). The Zealots were a faction, headed by Judas of Galilee, who "in the days of the enrolment" (cf Acts **5** 37; Lk **2** 1.2) bitterly opposed the threatened increase of taxation at the census of Quirinius, and would have hastened by the sword the fulfilment of Messianic prophecy.

Simon has been identified with Simon the brother of Jesus (Mk **6** 3; Mt **13** 55), but there also are reasons in favor of identifying him with Nathanael.

Thus (1) all the arguments adduced in favor of the Bartholomew-Nathanael identification (see NATHANAEL) can equally be applied to that of Simon-Nathanael, except the second. But the second is of no account, since the Philip-Bartholomew connection in the Synoptists occurs merely in the apostolic lists, while in St. John it is narrative. Further, in the Synoptists, Philip is connected in the narrative, not with Bartholomew but with Andrew.

(2) The identity is definitely stated in the *Genealogies of the Twelve Apostles* (see NATHANAEL). Further, the "Preaching of Simon, son of Cleopas" (cf Budge, II, 70 ff) has the heading "The preaching of the blessed St. Simon, the son of Cleopas, who was surnamed Judas, which is interpreted Nathanael, who became bishop of Jerus after James the brother of Our Lord." Eusebius (*HE,* III, xi, 32; IV, xxii) also refers to a Simon who succeeded James as bishop of Jerus and suffered martyrdom under Trajan; and Hegesippus, whom Eusebius professes to quote, calls this Simon a son of Cleopas.

(3) The invitation of Philip to Nathanael (cf Jn **1** 45) was one which would naturally be addressed to a follower of the Zealots, who based their cause on the fulfilment of Messianic prophecy.

(4) As Alphaeus, the father of James, is generally regarded as the same as Clopas or Cleopas (see JAMES, SON OF ALPHAEUS), this identification of the above Simon Nathanael, son of Cleopas, with Simon Zelotes would shed light on the reason of the juxtaposition of James son of Alphaeus and Simon Zelotes in the apostolic lists of St. Luke and Acts, i.e. they were brothers.

C. M. KERR

SIMPLE, sim′p'l: In the OT the uniform tr of the Heb word *pethī* (root *pāthāh*, "be open"). Like the Eng. word "simple" (etymologically "of one fold"), the Heb *pethī* is used sometimes in a good sense, i.e. "open-minded" (Ps **19** 7; **116** 6; **119** 130, possibly in all three cases the sense is *neutral* rather than *positively good*), and sometimes in a bad sense (Prov **7** 7, ‖ to "destitute of understanding"; **8** 5, ‖ to "fools" [blockheads]; **14** 15, opposed to prudent). The fundamental idea of *pethī* seems to be *open* to influence, i.e. easily influenced. That one open to influence should as a rule be classed with the irreligious is one of many instances in which language is an unwilling witness to the miasmatic moral atmosphere in which we live. The line between moral weakness and moral turpitude, between negative goodness (if indeed such a thing be conceivable) and positive badness, is soon passed.

In the NT the word "simple" is found only in Rom **16** 18.19 AV. In the first of these passages it is used to translate *ákakos* (RV "innocent"). In He **7** 26 AV the same word is rendered "harmless," the rendering of RV in this instance being "guileless." This would suit Rom **16** 18 better than "innocent." Guilelessness is not a synonym for gullibility; but the guileless are frequently the prey of designing men. In Rom **16** 19 the word tr[d] "simple" is *akéraios*, lit. "unmixed," "sincere" (Trench and Godet; Young, erroneously "hornless" and so "harmless"). "Uncontaminated" seems to be the idea of the apostle. He would have those to whom he wrote "wise as regards good" and not ignorant as regards evil—for that would be impossible, even if desirable—but without that kind of knowledge of evil that comes from engaging in it, as we say, mixing themselves up with it, unalloyed with evil.

W. M. MCPHEETERS

SIMPLICITY, sim-plis′i-ti (פְּתַיּוּת, *pᵉthayyūth*; **ἁπλότης,** *haplótēs*): The words in the OT commonly tr[d] "simplicity" are *pethī*, "simple" (Prov **1** 22), *pᵉthayyūth*, "simplicity" (**9** 13 m), *tōm*, "completeness," "integrity" (2 S **15** 11), "They went in their simplicity." In the NT, *haplotēs*, "singleness of mind," "simplicity," occurs in Rom **12** 8, "He that giveth let him do it with simplicity," RV "liberality," m "Gr 'singleness'"; 2 Cor **1** 12, "in simplicity and godly sincerity," RV (with corrected text) "in holiness and sincerity of God"; **11** 3, "the simplicity that is in Christ," RV (with corrected text) "the simplicity and the purity that is toward Christ"; cf Eph **6** 5; Col **3** 22, where the tr is "singleness." In Wisd **1** 1 we have, "Think ye of the Lord with a good mind [AV "heart"], and in singleness [AV "simplicity"] of heart seek ye him" (*haplotēs*). Our Lord also speaks (Mt **6** 22; Lk **11** 34) of the "*single* eye" (*haploús*), and James (**1** 5) applies *haplōs*, "simply," "directly," without after-thought [AV and RV "liberally"] to *God*, who had been described by Plato (*Rep.* ii.382 *E*) as being perfectly simple (*haplous*) and true, both in word and deed. In such "simplicity"—openness, sincerity, freedom from double-mindedness—man most resembles God and is most open to His visitation and blessing.

W. L. WALKER

SIMRI, sim′rī. See SHIMRI.

SIN חַטָּאת, *ḥaṭṭā'th*, "a missing"; פֶּשַׁע, *peshᶜ*, "rebellion, transgression"; עָוֹן, *ᶜwōn*, "perversion"; רַע, *rᶜ*, "evil" in disposition; רֶשַׁע, *reshᶜ*, "impiety"; ἁμαρτία, *hamartía*, "a missing the mark"; παράβασις, *parábasis*, "transgression"; ἀδικία, *adikía*, "unrighteousness"; ἀσέβεια, *asébeia*, "impiety"; ἀνομία, *anomía*, "contempt and violation of law"; πονηρία, *ponēría*, "depravity"; ἐπιθυμία, *epithumía*, "desire for what is forbidden, lust).

1. Elements of Definition
2. Definition
3. Effects of Sin
4. Story of the Fall
5. Sin and Freedom
6. Original Nature
7. Judgment of Actual Sin
8. Inwardness of True Morality and Religion
9. Power and Development of Sin
10. Heredity
11. Social Heredity
12. Atonement
13. "In Christ"
14. Conversion
15. Sanctification
16. Forgiveness

LITERATURE

There is variety of description of sin in the Bible, rather than formal definition, hence the various elements must be gathered together. Sin is voluntary, ethical (Gen **3** 2–6; Rom **1** 18, 28) hence never necessarily inherent in man's physical or finite nature. The merely ethical conception of voluntary transgression of law is in the Bible not only taken up into the larger religious conception of a wrong attitude toward God's specific commands (Gen **3** 3) and his law (Rom **3** 19, 20), but is applied to the refusal to be guided in life by the restraining and directing influence of the knowledge of God's power (Rom **1** 18, 28), of his nature (Jn **3** 19), and of his love revealed in his Son (Jn **3** 36). Such a knowledge of God comes to all men from their own nature (Rom **2** 14, 15), from creation (Rom **1** 20), and from the Spirit of God (Jn **1** 9; Gen **6** 3; Acts **7** 51; **14** 17). Transgression of known law, then, is sin; but so is wrong attitude, wrong desires, wrong "set" of the will or self (*peshᶜ*, *asebeia*, rebellion; *ᶜwōn*, *adikía*, perversion; *rᶜ*, *reshᶜ*, ruin, confusion: *apostasia*, *epithumía*; 1 Jn **3** 4; Mt **5** 22, 28; Rom **7** 8 ff; **5** 21). Sin is thus unbelief (He **3** 12, 19), the centering of the self upon something, or some one, less than God himself (Gen **3** 6; Rom **1** 28; **8** 7).

1. Elements of Definition

Sin is any attitude of indifference, unbelief, or disobedience to the will of God revealed in conscience, law, or gospel—whether this attitude express itself in thought, word, deed, or settled disposition and conduct.

2. Definition

According to the Bible, sin has direct effect under the immanent laws of creation, and also brings on men the retributive action of God. Under psychological law sin involves the whole self in perverting man from his highest possibilities, darkening the mind, inflaming the passions, and hardening the will against God and all good (Rom **1** 21–32; Gal **5** 19 ff). Under the law of heredity sin transmits evil tendency and guilt to the sinner's offspring (Ps **51** 5, 6; Eph **2** 3). The first sin thus involved the race, and sin always tends to be self-propagating, intensively and extensively. See HEREDITY; TRADITION. Sin also brings upon the sinner the direct punishment of God here (Ps **51** 11; Rom **1** 28; **6** 23), and hereafter (Rom **2** 8, 9). On these facts are built up the various systems of theology, with their differing conceptions of sin and of imputation of the first sin and of final judgment and rewards.

3. Effects of Sin

Probably all students admit that the story of the

4. Story of the Fall

fall (Gen **3** 1–6) is psychologically a wonderful account of how sin begins. There is voluntary disobedience of an explicit command of God their creator and friend—the disobedience not being in any sense a necessity of their nature or state. It is suggested to our first parents that the prohibition is not clearly understood; that the threatened punishment is not certain; that a privilege is arbitrarily and selfishly denied them; the appeal is made to an appetite innocent in itself. The imagination of the woman is stirred by the prospect of promised enjoyment and power; desire is aroused; then the deed follows as choice. All of this is amazingly true to actual experience of temptation and sin. There are elements of the story specially worthy of notice. In a sense it is a moral test, but more truly a religious test; the trial was whether they would believe God and trust him. The prohibition tested whether they would make God the center and goal of their lives, or whether they would center their lives about their own purposes—the inevitable religious test we all face soon or late. Note, too, that the sin is first inner, the fall is first in imagination and affection and thought, then in deed. The sin must be seen against the facts that they knew God and his explicit command; and against the fact that God's love did not leave them, but sought them after the sinful deed. The test therefore was necessary alike to the nature of man and the purpose of God—to wit, man's self-realization in right relation to God. The narrative, moreover, is presented not only as psychologically true, but as actual fact, as the historical beginning of sin, and is so held in the rest of the Bible (Jn **8** 44; Rom **5** 12 ff; 1 Cor **15** 21, 22). On the face of it the narrative is not mythological or allegorical. But there are symbolical elements in it; to wit, "the serpent," his subtlety, his conversation, his change of form. The fact of man's creation as good, his living so for a time, his fall, and the historical beginning of sin all seem clearly taught, the exact significance of the details being an exegetical problem.

5. Sin and Freedom

A discussion of sin and its effects inevitably raises the question of sin and freedom. In the case of Adam and Eve, there is no difficulty in the Bible view, since they are represented as free from sinful bias, and freely choosing. Paul teaches that through the man's sin death passed to all men "for that all sinned" (Rom **5** 12), and also that the natural man cannot keep the law (Rom **8** 3–8); he insists that all are "by nature children of wrath" (Eph **2** 3), and that only by the Spirit, and by being "in Christ," can we "fulfill the ordinance of the law." Yet Paul is insistent that sin is resistance of God and refusal to walk in the light (Rom **1** 21, 28, 32), even while he insists that the law is hopeless as a way of salvation (Rom **3** 20), and is a source of transgression (Rom **5** 20). In like manner we find Jesus insisting that sin is free, conscious choice (Lk **15** 13; Jn **15** 22; **9** 41; **8** 11), at the same time that he insists there must be an entire change of the ruling affections of the natural man by regeneration (Jn **3** 3, 6; Mt **7** 18; **12** 33). To this fact of universal, inherited evil tendency in man—and imputed guilt, see IMPUTATION III, **1**—must be added the fact on which is based the theological doctrine of common grace, that God by his Spirit curbs the ravages of sin in the individual and in society, so that all men have conscience, a sense of divine law, of God and of civic virtue (Gen **6** 3; Jn **1** 9; Acts **7** 51; **14** 17; Rom **1** 14, 15). These facts together present the Bible doctrine of the natural man as born with a corrupt nature, which is itself sinful, born guilty, yet never left by the Spirit without light. Every one who comes to years of discretion is free in the sense that he is self-determined, self-determined to evil. See REGENERATION.

6. Original Nature

What exactly is the inborn nature of the child is today at the end of the first quarter of the twentieth century one of the most widely and earnestly discussed questions. On the whole results are in line with Bible teachings as set forth above. All agree on inherited evil capacity (as well as good), the possibility of subconscious evil "set" of the self, the necessity of "moralizing" the child, inevitable struggle to hold moral positions, community moral solidarity, the danger of utter moral perversion, the emotional, passional control of life. Competent Christian educators seem agreed that inborn evil tendencies cannot be controlled in education save by supernatural "grace," and that the best Christian education can hope to be is an instrument to keep the child in relation to this divine power (cf Jerusalem Meeting International Missionary Council, *Religious Education*, Vol. II, pp. 3–89; Clark: *Psychology of Religious Awakening*, Macmillan, 1929, p. 95; Betts, *New Program of Religious Education*, pp. 39, 40).

7. Judgment of Actual Sin

The Bible makes very clear that individual, personal sin is to be judged according to the individual's personal light, and that in the matters he knows to be evil the individual must make his fight. This is very clear in Jesus (Jn **15** 22; Mt **11** 20 ff), and in Paul (Acts **17** 30; Rom **14** 5; 1 Cor **8** 7; 1 Tim **1** 13). This does not mean that the sinner fully knows the bitterness of sin before it is committed; sin committed, under the reproach of conscience, under the fear of God's anger, in view of some of its dreadful consequences, is very different from sin in contemplation. This fact that the individual's sin is to be judged by the light that he has means only that the Bible correctly reckons with the fact that conscience, so far as it comprises material judgments on actual facts, is largely mediated by social heredity and community standards. This is the reason why men of other times and other lands, like the Bible characters, must be judged by the light of their times as to the degree of their personal guilt or merit.

8. Inwardness of True Morality and Religion

The Bible shows wonderful progress from observance of indifferent forms to the true inwardness of morality and religion. The end of the process of revelation that began with matters in some sense little above taboo is the high and noble religion of the spirit as stated by Micah (**6** 8), Paul (Rom **8** 4; 1 Cor **10** 31; Gal **5** 22 ff), and Jesus in the Sermon on the Mount.

(1) *Mosaic code.* There are elements of the code, like food taboos and forms of sacrifice, that have no moral significance in themselves. It must not be forgotten that, like the Edenic prohibition, these were of religious significance only by raising the question of obedience to Jehovah. The code therefore presupposes religious instruction, and symbolism to be developed, and thus leaves room for growth into the spirit of true religion and morality. According to the Bible the code was never without such interpretation.

(2) *Prophets.* The mission of the prophets was to educate the people in religion. They were therefore to become incarnate consciences and embodiments of true religion. Increasingly therefore is the emphasis placed on the moral meaning and spiritual intention of the forms. With Elijah and Elisha it may seem at times almost to be a matter of old forms and the national worship—though there is much more of real morality and religion in their messages, if one look for them—but the end of the movement is in Isaiah's "Is not this the fact that I have chosen:

to loose the bonds of wickedness. . . . ." (Isa **58**). So insistent is this prophetic emphasis on the true meaning of religion and morality as the real purpose of the commandments and ceremonies imposed upon the Jewish people (Hos **6**; Micah **6**), that some have inferred from it that the prophets were antagonistic to the law and all its forms. It would be far truer to say that the prophets were so well taught of God the nature of morality and religion as the real purpose of law and form and promise that they became opposed to the law and sacrifice as mere forms without the true spirit. This tendency to be content with forms and external observances remains to this day the persistent vitiation of codes and liturgies. Needing form to express spirit, we lose the spirit and keep the form, and so destroy our purpose and fall into worse sins.

(3) *Paul.* The law has thus one of two effects on sinful human nature. It leads to superficiality and externalism, and thus to increased worse sin in the sight of God; or else, taken earnestly, it leads to utter despair of one's own rightness. In Paul it took this second trend. "Advancing in the Jew's religion beyond many of his own age among his countrymen, being more exceedingly zealous for the traditions of his fathers (Gal **1** 14)," he nevertheless found that the law was his despair, inasmuch as it forbade not only wrong deeds but wrong desire (Rom **7**); he found that the law revealed his carnal nature, that it became an instrument to work death in him. So he saw in law a means of God to make the trespass abound (Rom **5** 20); and thus the law became a "tutor to bring us to Christ (Gal **3** 24)" that we might all "die unto the law in order to live unto God" (Gal **2** 19). Legalism as a means of salvation is dead; he knows the true inwardness of the law and the heart of true religion in being "under law to Christ (1 Cor **9** 20 ff)," and so the law is kept in the real sense (Rom **8** 2) "the law of the Spirit of life in Christ Jesus."

(4) *Jesus.* In his views Paul shows how completely he had absorbed the spirit of Jesus. Jesus honors the law—no jot or tittle of it shall be abolished, it can only be fulfilled (Mt **5** 17). But Jesus knows the only way to keep the law is from the heart and in spirit; the attitude, the desire, the purpose is all. Adultery, murder, and revenge are sin, of course; but causing these acts and the real source of sin that must be healed are lust and anger and the vengeful spirit. Purity, therefore, and love, and a forgiving spirit—these are the keeping of the law. Indeed, in going on to the principle "Ye shall therefore be perfect as your Father is perfect" (Mt **5** 48) Jesus takes the same position later so well enunciated by Paul, that, as sin is never only ethical, but a matter of wrong attitude toward God and man, so morality and religion in reality are a matter of right spiritual attitude toward God and man (Mt **22** 35; Lk **18** 22). Every expression or codification, therefore, of moral law is imperfect, partial, an unsuccessful attempt to embody the true spirit (Rom **7** 6; 2 Cor **3** 6). Yet there is to be no disparagement of law: civil and moral codes are always necessary as guides, even though they can never express or create the true spirit of the citizen, the good man, or the Christian.

This powerlessness of mere law is due to the fact that sin is itself power and has its own law of development.

9. Power and Development

Sin is not an entity—neither a material nor a spiritual substance. Sin is a quality of personal beings, which they ought not to have, substituted for a quality they ought to have. Sin is therefore privative, not negative. Man as person should know God's will, love God, and choose to obey—that is virtue and religion. Sin is not merely absence of this which ought to be; it is substituting for this another knowledge, another love, and another choice. The law of human personality is inter-relation of intellect, sensibility, and will, in the unity of the self, and the tendency to fixity of acts and moods into fixed attitudes of character. As the good man grows into truer knowledge, purer love, and settled habit of right-doing, so the evil man grows into false knowledge, into love of the foul, and hatred of the fair, into settled habits of doing wrong. The power of sin, then, is first of all the power of the law of personality perverted. This is clearly taught in Scripture. Paul makes clear that sinners become "vain in their reasonings, their senseless heart is darkened, they become fools" (Rom **1** 22, 23); then follows the perversion of love and the kindling of lusts (vv 24–27), and the "reprobate" mind settled in doing all manner of evil (vs 28 ff); until finally there is the state "darkened in their understanding, alienated from God, ... past feeling, given up to lasciviousness, working all uncleanness with greediness" (Eph **4** 17 ff). Such is the Biblical conception of the power of sin. All of this has been made much clearer for our understanding by present-day psychology as shown, e.g., in the psychology of association and habit as developed by Prof. William James (cf Steven, *Psychology of the Christian Soul*, ch iv) and in the later psychology with its emphasis on emotion, desire, the subconscious set of character, and the power of the subconscious complex. The effect of sin is thus to prevent the achievement of personality, making the individual the plaything of lust and impulses and solicitation from without, involving the disintegration of the self; or else sin's effect is to concentrate the powers of the individual about some strong ambition contrary to God, producing a powerful personality hating God and loving evil.

One would expect a power so blasting to the individual to have bad effect on his offspring. Yet the Bible has practically nothing to say on

10. Heredity

heredity in its psychological or biological sense. The one great fact is asserted, that through the one sin of the first Adam all "flesh" is sinful, i.e., the natural man; beyond that it knows nothing of transmitted sinful tendencies due to special sins of the parents. See HEREDITY. Present science on the whole bears out this view. It knows of children born subnormal in mental power, with emotional instability or deadness and some with far stronger appetites than others; little progress, however, has been made in connecting this with special characteristics in the life of the parents. Some individuals inherit insanity; but this seems a matter of certain blood strains, or families, and difficult to connect in any way with special sins in parents.

The Bible makes much more of what we today call the social heredity of sin, that is, the transmission of sin to others through example, teach-

11. Social Heredity

ing, suggestion in all its forms, group opinions, tastes, standards, institutions—in a word, communication in its full sociological meaning. The Bible is packed full of warnings against association with evil persons; the power of evil example; the deadliness of wrong customs and social usages; the power of the leaven of wrong doctrine and teaching. No literature ever stressed more strongly the duty of training up children in godly families, of instructing them in truth and training them by example and in the actual performance of right deeds. The whole trend of its exhortation is to gather the godly into families and groups with their own thought and standards, usages and devotions, and to separate them from every possible association with evil. The pictures it gives of Sodom, of the world before the flood, of the world of the Canaanites that were to be destroyed before tribes settled in the promised land; or of the society of the Roman world as Paul saw it; these all are in full accord not only with truth, but with what modern sociology has learned about social law. This terrible fact of the fell power of sin, through this totality of influence by all recognized laws of social heredity, throws light on both the command to destroy the Canaanites, and on the exhortations in various form to Christians to live as a separate people. The Bible indeed gathers up this total power of evil through social heredity and social groups under the term "the world," "the mass of men alienated from God and hostile to Christ, the whole circle of earthly goods, endowments, riches, pleasures, which although hollow, frail and fleeting, stir desire, seduce from God, and are obstacles to the cause of Christ" (Thayer, *Gr-Engl Lex. of NT*, 6, 7). In this sense, "the world," is very common in the Gospel of Jn, the Epistles of John, and in the other NT epistles (cf Jn **7** 7; 1 Jn **2** 15–17; 1 Cor **1** 21; Gal **6** 14; Jas **1** 27). Here, too, as in the case of the power of sin in individual life, these social laws are not of themselves evil, any more than are the laws of individual development. They are social laws of God inherent in society, turned against God and man by the perversion of sin. In the Christian community, these very laws are to be a blessing to further the "kingdom of God." A Christian sociology seeks to utilize these laws for God's purpose, hence the idea of a Christian family, Christian community, Christian education, literature, art, industry, etc. It is in accord with the OT to look upon the evils of society as in some sense the sin of the individual, due to the solidarity of humanity (Dan **9** 5 ff, see ACHAN and ACCOUNTABILITY 3), though there is correction of a wrong use of this principle (Dt **24** 16), and the assertion that the individual shall be dealt with according to his own record (Ezk **18**). This principle is in accord with the tendencies of sociologists to divide and distribute responsibility between the individual and the group, and leave the individual accountable for his own character.

12. Atonement

The correct conception of sin is necessary, if we are to grasp at all the Biblical idea of how man is to be delivered. Life for man and for society is to be found in the right relation to God (Jn **17** 3). Sin is a break with God, rejection of his loving purpose for the creature, wrong relation to fellow-man, opposition to the law God has given his creation, perversion of man's own powers and laws of development, involving moral and spiritual death. At best it is thoughtless content with a low moral level of self-indulgence, which has implicit at the heart of it self-deification despite God and brother man. Hence the Biblical idea that God himself must take away the guilt, and become the first mover in bringing man back into harmony with himself; hence the idea of ATONEMENT, JUSTIFICATION, REDEMPTION, which see. Hence also the Biblical idea of a burden laid on the conscience, so that only by pardon can a man get peace, and the right to forget (Rom **5** 1). Indeed, the whole conception of salvation, whether as changed status before God, or as complete inner change in the sinner at the beginning, or in the continuance, of his new life, is conceived of through this conception of the actual nature and tendency of sin.

13. "In Christ"

The whole process of saving the sinner, originating in the love of God (Jn **3** 16), centers in Christ. His life, particularly his death, produces atonement and RECONCILIATION (q.v.) of God's wrath against the sinner, and of the sinner's fear of God (Rom **5** 1–11); brings the new knowledge of God to minds darkened by sin (Jn **1** 18); imposes on the will the new motives that cause repentance, faith, and love (Gal **2** 19, 20; Rom **5** 11); supplies continuous stimuli for the new life to turn from sin (Rom **8** 12 ff); and gives power and guidance through the Spirit (Rom **8** 5, 26). Indeed, it is Christ living, dying, risen to live forevermore, who supplies the Spirit that by regeneration makes possible the new life in its beginning, continuance, and consummation (Mt **3** 11; Acts **2** 33; Rom **6** 4–14). It is therefore "in Christ," that is, through being united with him, that sin is overcome in the individual (Rom **8** 2; 2 Cor **5** 17; Eph **2** 10; Col **3** 4), and from union with him results the union and fellowship of believers in the kingdom (1 Cor **10** 17; 1 Jn **1** 3).

14. Conversion

In the reception and experience of salvation by the individual, the nature of sin makes necessary the experience of conversion, involving repentance and faith, so much exploited by the psychology of religion. In all who reach years of discretion, it is a conscious change of the whole self, from an auto-centered to not merely a hetero-centered, but to a Christ-centered life, involving a change in material judgments, standards, affections, and attitude; all of which is very clear in all Biblical words describing this subjective change (see CONVICT, REPENTANCE, CONVERSION, FAITH). Conviction means new light on our own life in view of God's judgment; repentance means acceptance of this judgment, so that we have a "new mind" on the matter, with concern and grief; conversion means a turning away from sin, but also a turning to God; faith means reliance and trust and love. This is exactly the change of attitude of the total self which is a reversal of what sin makes a man. No doubt the degree of emotional upheaval depends on the individual's past aberration, and on the standards, socially mediated, of what is considered proper conversion; but the Biblical view considers it a conscious crisis, a break with sin. For that reason the Bible presents repentance and conversion as duty, making appeal to the whole self. The law and the gospel are recognized as instruments in conversion. The real cause is God himself (Jn **1** 13), and the real object to which man turns is Christ Jesus (1 Pet **1** 8; Rom **3** 22).

15. Sanctification

The personal nature both of sin and salvation make necessary not only the experience of conversion but also the nature of SANCTIFICATION (q.v. specially II, 2, 3, 8). As changed status, as inner cleansing, as power and guidance through indwelling Spirit, sanctification is God's gift. As a personal experience it is possession of an ideal, and constant striving to attain a life wholly in conformity with God's will. It involves personal use of all the means of spiritual growth God has given. Christians are to grow in grace and knowledge (2 Pet **3** 18), they are to continue in prayer (Rom **12** 12), they are not to neglect assembling together (He **10** 25); they are to walk in newness of life by the Spirit (Rom **6** 4; Gal **5** 16; Eph **5** 2), they are to put to death the deeds of the body (Rom **8** 13) cleansing themselves from all defilement of the flesh and spirit, perfecting holiness in the fear of God (2 Cor **7** 1); all their gifts are to be put to the service of Christ and of the brethren, writes Paul in outlining an ideal of perfect conduct which is to be the goal of their efforts and study. He shows that the Bible presents the redeemed and saved life as the complete antithesis of sin (Rom **12** 1, 2).

16. Forgiveness

Sin and its forgiveness, the recovery of the forgiven sinner and the sanctification of the new humanity in Christ Jesus is thus the supreme work of redemption. Inasmuch as God is holy and governs the world in holiness; inasmuch as He has impressed

His law upon His creation and upon the nature of man; inasmuch as He must be true to Himself in His holiness as well as in His love of man, forgiveness must not be regarded as a simple matter of overlooking the past, as it is sometimes represented. Overcoming of sin required nothing less than atonement by the gift of the Son of God; and is not accomplished until through the Spirit man becomes a new creature, with a right attitude of faith and love and obedience to God. See further, ETHICS, III; ETHICS OF JESUS I, 2; GUILT; PAULINE THEOLOGY; JOHANNINE THEOLOGY, etc.

LITERATURE.—Tennant, *Origen and Propagation of Sin; The Concept of Sin; Sources of the Doctrine of the Fall and Original Sin;* Orr, *Sin as a Present Day Problem; Christian View of God and the World,* lects. VIII, IX; Denny, *Christian Doctrine of Reconciliation;* Bavinck, *Gereformeerde Dogmatiek,* vol III; *Bijbelsche en Religieuze Psychologie.*

JOHN E. KUIZENGA

SIN, sin (סִין, *ṣīn,* "clay or mud"; **Συήνη,** *Suēnē,* A, **Τάνις,** *Tánis*): A city of Egypt mentioned only in Ezk **30** 15.16. This seems to be a pure Sem name. The ancient Egyp name, if the place ever had one such, is unknown. Pelusium (Gr Πελούσιον, *Peloúsion*) also meant "the clayey or muddy town." The Pelusiac mouth of the Nile was "the muddy mouth," and the modern Arab. name of this mouth has the same significance. These facts make it practically certain that the Vulg is correct in identifying S. with Pelusium. But although Pelusium appears very frequently in ancient history, its exact location is still not entirely certain. The list of cities mentioned in Ezk in connection with S. furnishes no clue to its location. From other historical notices it seems to have been a frontier city. Rameses II built a wall from S. to Heliopolis, probably by the aid of Heb slaves (Diodorus Siculus; cf Budge, *Hist of Egypt,* V, 90), to protect the eastern frontier. S. was a meeting-place of Egypt with her enemies who came to attack her, many great battles being fought at or near this place. Sennacherib and Cambyses both fought Egypt near Pelusium (Herod. ii.141; iii.10–13). Antiochus IV defeated the Egyptians here (Budge, VIII, 25), and the Romans under Gabinius defeated the Egyptians in the same neighborhood. Pelusium was also accessible from the sea, or was very near a seaport, for Pompey after the disaster at Pharsalia fled into Egypt, sailing for Pelusium. These historical notices of Pelusium make its usual identification with the ruins near *el-Kantara,* a station on the Suez Canal 29 miles S. of Port Said, most probable. "S., the stronghold of Egypt," in the words of Ezk (**30** 15), would thus refer to its inaccessibility because of swamps which served as impassable moats. The wall on the S. and the sea on the N. also protected it on either flank.

M. G. KYLE

SIN AGAINST THE HOLY GHOST (SPIRIT). See BLASPHEMY.

SIN, MAN OF. See MAN OF SIN.

SIN MONEY. See SACRIFICE IN THE OT.

SIN OFFERING. See SACRIFICE.

SIN, WILDERNESS OF. See WANDERINGS OF ISRAEL.

SINA, sī′na: In Acts **7** 38 AV, RV "Sinai" (q.v.).

SINAI, sī′nī, sī′nā̇-ī (סִינַי, *ṣīnay;* A, **Σινά,** *Siná,* B, **Σεινά,** *Seiná*): The name comes probably from a root meaning "to shine," which occurs in Syr, and which in Bab is found in the name *sinu* for "the moon." The old explanation, "clayey," is inappropriate to any place in the Sinaitic desert, though it might apply to Sin (Ezk **30** 15.16) or Pelusium; even there, however, the applicability is doubtful. The desert of Sin (Ex **16** 1; **17** 1; Nu **33** 11 f) lay between Sinai and the Gulf of Suez, and may have been named from the "glare" of its white chalk. But at Sinai "the glory of Jeh was

1. The Name

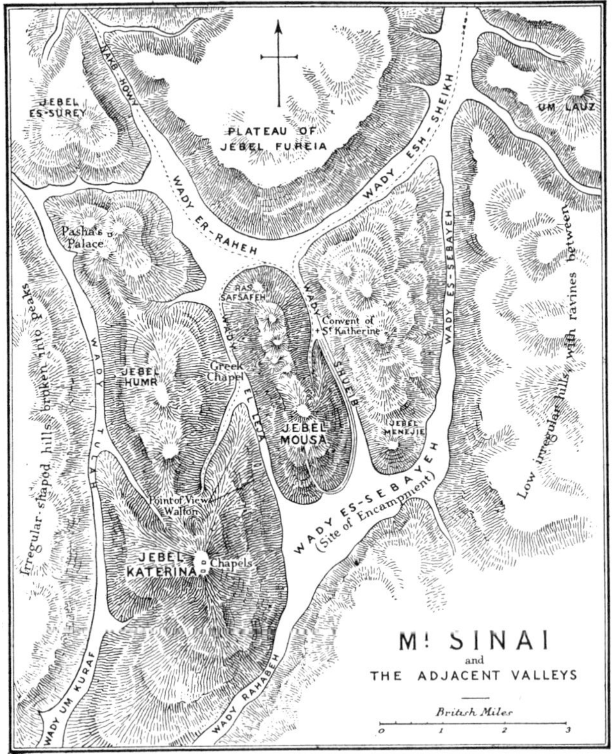

like devouring fire on the top of the mount in the eyes of the children of Israel" (Ex **24** 17); and, indeed, the glory of the Lord still dyes the crags of *Jebel Mûsa* (the "mountain of Moses") with fiery red, reflected from its red granite and pink gneiss rocks, long after the shadows have fallen on the plain beneath. Sinai is mentioned, as a desert and a mountain, in 35 passages of the OT. In 17 passages the same desert and mountain are called "Horeb," or "the waste." This term is chiefly used in Dt, though Sinai also occurs (Dt **33** 2). In the other books of the Pent, Sinai is the usual name, though Horeb also occurs (Ex **3** 1; **17** 6; **33** 6), applying both to the "Mount of God" and to the desert of Rephidim, some 20 miles to the N.W.

2. Traditional Site

The indications of position, in various passages of the Pent, favor the identification with the traditional site, which has become generally accepted by all those explorers who have carefully considered the subject, though two other theories may need notice. Moses fled to the land of Midian (or "empty land"), which lay E. of the Sinaitic peninsula

VIEW FROM THE TOP OF MOUNT SINAI

(Nu **22** 4.7; **25, 31**), and when he wandered with his flocks to Horeb (Ex **3** 1) he is said to have reached the west side of the desert. In another note (Dt **1** 2) we read that the distance was "eleven days' journey from Horeb by the way of Mount Seir unto Kadesh-barnea" or Petra (see WANDERINGS OF ISRAEL), the distance being about 145 miles, or 14 miles of daily march, though Israel—with its flocks, women and children—made 16 marches between these points. Sinai again is described as being distant from Egypt "three days' journey into the wilderness" (Ex **5** 3), the actual route being 117 miles, which Israel accomplished in 10 journeys. But, for Arabs not encumbered with families and herds, this distance could still be covered by an average march of 39 miles daily, on riding camels, or even, if necessary, on foot.

3. Identification with *Jebel Mûsa*

These distances will not, however, allow of our placing Sinai farther E. than *Jebel Mûsa*. Lofty mountains, in all parts of the world, have always been sacred and regarded as the mysterious abode of God; and Jos says that Sinai is "the highest of all the mountains thereabout," and again is "the highest of all the mountains that are in that country, and is not only very difficult to be ascended by men, on account of its vast altitude, but because of the sharpness of its precipices: nay, indeed, it cannot be looked at without pain of the eyes, and besides this it was terrible and inaccessible, on account of the rumor that passed about, that God dwelt there" (*Ant*, II, xii, 1; III, v, 1). Evidently in his time Sinai was supposed to be one of the peaks of the great granitic block called *et Ṭûr*—a term applying to any lofty mountain. This block has its highest peak in *Jebel Kâtarîn* (so named from a legend of St. Catherine of Egypt), rising 8,550 ft. above the sea. N.E. of this is *Jebel Mûsa* (7,370 ft.), which, though less high, is more conspicuous because of the open plain called *er Râḥah* ("the wide") to its N.W. This plain is about 4 miles long and has a width of over a mile, so that it forms, as Dr. E. Robinson (*Bib. Res.*, 1838, I, 89) seems to have been the first to note, a natural camp at the foot of the mountain, large enough for the probable numbers (see EXODUS, 3) of Israel.

Jebel Mûsa has two main tops, that to the S.E. being crowned by a chapel. The other, divided by gorges into three precipitous crags, has the Convent to its N., and is called *Râs-es-Ṣafṣâfeh*, or "the willow top." N. of the Convent is the lower top of *Jebel ed Deir* ("mountain of the monastery").

Râs-es-Ṣafṣâfeh.

4. Description of *Jebel Mûsa*

These heights were accurately determined by Royal Engineer surveyors in 1868 (Sir C. Wilson, *Ordnance Survey of Sinai*); and, though it is impossible to say which of the peaks Moses ascended, yet they are all much higher than any mountains in the Sinaitic desert, or in Midian. The highest tops in the *Tîh* desert to the N. are not much over 4,000 ft. Those in Midian, E. of Elath, rise only to 4,200 ft. Even *Jebel Serbâl*, 20 miles W. of Sinai—a ridge with many crags, running 3 miles in length—is at its highest only 6,730 ft. above the sea. Horeb is not recorded to have been visited by any of the Hebrews after Moses, excepting by Elijah (1 K **19** 8) in a time of storm. In favor of the traditional site it may also be observed that clouds suddenly formed, or lasting for days (Ex **24** 15 f), are apt to cap very lofty mountains. The Hebrews reached Sinai about the end of May (Ex **19** 1) and, on the 3d day, "there were thunders and lightnings, and a thick cloud upon the mount" (ver 16). Such storms occur as a rule in the Sinaitic desert only in December and January, but thunderstorms are not unknown in Pal even in May.

A constant tradition fixing the site is traceable back to the 4th cent. AD. Eusebius and Jerome (*Onom*, s.v. "Choreb") place Horeb near Paran, which in their time was placed (*Onom*, s.v. "Raphidim") in *Wâdy Feirân*. Anchorites lived at Paran, and at Sinai at least as early as 365 AD, and

5. Patristic Evidence

Convent Garden, Sinai.

are noticed in 373 AD, and often later (Robinson, *Bib. Res.*, 1838, I, 122–28); the monastery was first built for them by Justinian in 527 AD and his chapel still exists. Cosmas (*Topogr. Christ.*), in the same reign, says that Rephidim was then called Pharan, and (distinguishing Horeb from Sinai, as Eusebius also does) he places it "about 6 miles from Pharan," and "near Sinai." These various considerations may suffice to show that the tradition as to Horeb is at least as old as the time of Jos, and that it agrees with all the indications given in the OT.

6. Lepsius' Theory

Lepsius, it is true (*Letters from Egypt*, 1842–44), denying the existence of any unbroken tradition, and relying on his understanding of Cosmas, supposed Sinai to be the *Jebel Serbâl* above mentioned, which lies immediately S. of *Wâdy Feirân*. His main argument was that, visiting Sinai in March, he considered that the vicinity did not present sufficient water for Israel (Appendix B, 303–18). But, on this point, it is sufficient to give the opinion of the late Rev. F. W. Holland, based on the experience of four visits, in 1861, 1865, 1867–68.

He says (*Recovery of Jerus*, 524):

"With regard to water-supply there is no other spot in the whole Peninsula which is nearly so well supplied as the neighborhood of *Jebel Mûsa*. Four streams of running water are found there: one in *Wâdy Leja;* a second in *Wâdy et Ṭl'ah* which waters a succession of gardens extending more than 3 miles in length, and forms pools in which I have often had a swim; a third stream rises to the N. of the watershed of the plain of *er Râḥah* and runs W. into *Wâdy et Ṭl'ah;* and a fourth is formed by the drainage from the mountains of *Umm 'Alawy*, to the E. of *Wâdy Sebaiyeh* and finds its way into that valley by a narrow ravine opposite *Jebel ed Deir*. In addition to these streams there are numerous wells and springs, affording excellent water throughout the whole of the granitic district. I have seldom found it necessary to carry water when making a mountain excursion, and the intermediate neighborhood of *Jebel Mûsa* would, I think, bear comparison with many mountain districts in Scotland with regard to its supply of water. There is also no other district in the Peninsula which affords such excellent pasturage."

This is important, as Israel encamped near Sinai from the end of May till April of the next year. There is also a well on the lower slope of *Jebel Mûsa* itself, where the ascent begins.

7. Greene's Theory

Another theory, put forward by Mr. Baker Greene (*The Heb Migration from Egypt*), though accepted by Dr. Sayce (*Higher Cricitism*, 1894, 268), appears likewise to be entirely untenable. Mr. Greene supposed Elim (Ex **15** 27) to be Elath (Dt **2** 8), now *'Ailah* at the head of the Gulf of *'Akâbah;* and that Sinai therefore was some unknown mountain in Midian. But in this case Israel would in 4 days (see Ex **15** 22.23.27) have traveled a distance of 200 miles to reach Elim, which cannot but be regarded as quite impossible for the Hebrews when accompanied by women, children, flocks and herds.

C. R. Conder

SINCERE, sin-sēr′, **SINCERITY,** sin-ser′i-ti (תָּמִים, *tāmīm;* **ἀφθαρσία,** *aphtharsía,* **εἰλικρίνεια,** *eilikríneia*): "Sincerity" occurs once in the OT as the tr of *tāmīm*, "complete," "entire," "sincere," etc (Josh **24** 14); the same word is tr[d] "sincerity" (Jgs **9** 16.19, RV "uprightly"). Four different words are rendered "sincere," "sincerely," "sincerity," in the NT: *ádolos*, "without guile," "unadulterated," "desire the sincere milk of the word" (1 Pet **2** 2 AV, RV "the spiritual," ARVm "Gr, 'belonging to the reason'; cf Rom **12** 1," ERVm "reasonable"), "milk which is without guile," with no other purpose but to nourish and benefit the soul (Alford); *hagnôs*, "without blame," "pure," "preach Christ . . . . not sincerely" (Phil **1** 17); *aphtharsia*, "without corruption" (Eph **6** 24, AV "that love our Lord Jesus Christ in sincerity," ARV "with a love incorruptible," m "'in incorruption.' See Rom **2** 7," ERV "uncorruptness"; Tit **2** 7, AV "shewing uncorruptness . . . . sincerity," RV "uncorruptness"); *gnḗsios*, "not spurious" (2 Cor **8** 8); *eilikrinḗs*, lit., judged of in the sunlight, hence, "clear," "manifest" (Phil **1** 10); *eilikrineia*, with same meaning, is tr[d] "sincerity" (1 Cor **5** 8; 2 Cor **1** 12; **2** 17).

RV has "sincere" for "pure" (2 Pet **3** 1), "sincerely" for "clearly" (Job **33** 3).

In Wisd **7** 25 we have *eilikrinēs* in the description of Wisdom as a "pure influence," RV "clear effluence."

W. L. Walker

SINEW, sin′ū (גִּיד, *gīdh* [Job **10** 11, etc]): The tendons and sinews of the body are uniformly (7 t) thus called. "Therefore the children of Israel eat not the sinew of the hip which is upon the hollow of the thigh, unto this day: because he touched the hollow of Jacob's thigh in the sinew of the hip" (Gen **32** 32). In the poetical description of Behemoth (hippopotamus) it is said: "He moveth his tail like a cedar: the sinews of his thighs are knit together" (Job **40** 17). The prophet Ezekiel saw in his vision (**37** 6.8) that the dry bones were gathered together, that they were covered with sinews, flesh and skin, and that they were revived by the spirit of the Lord. In **figurative** language the neck of the obstinate is compared to an "iron sinew" (Isa **48** 4). AV "my sinews take no rest" (*w*[e]*'ōr*[e]*ḳay lō' yishkābhūn*, Job **30** 17) has been corrected by RV into "the pains that gnaw me take no rest," but the earlier version has been retained in the margin.

H. L. E. Luering

SINGERS, sing′ẽrz, **SINGING,** sing′ing: Singing seems to have become a regular profession at a quite early date among the Hebrews. David had his troupe of "singing men and singing women" at Jerus (2 S **19** 35), and no doubt Solomon added to their numbers. Isa **23** 16 suggests that it was not uncommon for foreign female minstrels of questionable character to be heard making "sweet melody," singing songs along the streets and highways of Judaea. Nor was the worship of the temple left to the usually incompetent and inconstant leadership of amateur choristers. The elaborate regulations drawn up for the constitution of the temple orchestra and chorus are referred to under MUSIC (q.v.). It has been inferred from Ezr **2** 65 that women were included among the temple singers, but this is erroneous, as the musicians there mentioned were of the class employed at banquets, festivals, etc. The temple choir consisted exclusively of Levites, one essential qualification of an active member of that order being a good voice.

Of the vocal method of the Hebrews we know nothing. Wellhausen imagines that he can detect one of the singers, in the portrayal of an Assyr band, compressing his throat in order to produce a vibrato; and it is quite possible that in other respects as well as this, ancient and modern oriental vocalization resembled each other. But that is about all that can be said.

On the other hand, we cannot repeat too often that we are quite unable to identify any intervals, scales, or tunes as having been used in ancient Israel. Even those who hold that the early church took the Gregorian "tones" from the synagogue, confess that it was "certainly not without considerable modifications." And, of course, there was not the slightest affinity between the Heb and the Anglican chant. See MUSIC; PRAISE; SONG; TEMPLE.

JAMES MILLAR

SINGLE, siṇ'g'l, **EYE:** Mt **6** 22 f ‖ Lk **11** 34: "If therefore thine eye be single, thy whole body shall be full of light. But if thine eye be evil, thy whole body shall be full of darkness." "Single" and "evil" here represent ἁπλοῦς, *haploús*, and πονηρός, *ponērós*. *Ponēros* elsewhere in the NT means "wicked"; *haplous* occurs only here in the NT, but is very common in ordinary Gr and always has the meaning "simple." But in view of the context, most commentators take *haplous* here as meaning "normal," "healthy," and *ponēros* as "diseased," so rendering "Just as physical enlightenment depends on the condition of the eye, so does spiritual enlightenment depend on the condition of the heart." This is natural enough, but it is not satisfactory, as it gives to *haplous* a unique sense and to *ponēros* a sense unique in the 73 NT examples of the word. Moreover, the same expression, "evil eye," is found also in Mt **20** 15; Mk **7** 22, where it means "jealousy" or "covetousness." With *ponēros*="covetous," *haplous* would="generous"; and this rendition gives excellent sense in Mt, where the further context deals with love of money. Yet in Lk it is meaningless, where the context is of a different sort, a fact perhaps indicating that Lk has placed the saying in a bad context. Or the Gr tr of Christ's words used by Matthew and Luke may have taken the moral terms *haplous* and *ponēros* to translate physical terms ("healthy" and "diseased"?) employed in the original Aramaic. The Sinaitic Syr version of Lk **11** 36 may perhaps contain a trace of an older rendering. See Jülicher, *Die Gleichnisreden Jesu,* II, 98–108.

BURTON SCOTT EASTON

SINGULAR, siṇ'gū-lar: "Pertaining to the single person," "individual," and so sometimes "unusual," "remarkable." So Wisd **14** 18, AV "the singular diligence of the artificer" (φιλοτιμία, *philotimía*, "love of honor," RV "ambition"). In Lev **27** 2 by "when a man shall make a singular vow" AV seems to have understood a "personal" or "private" vow. RV has "accomplish a vow," with m "make a special vow." Cf the same phrase (*yaphlī'* [*y*ᵉ*phallē'*] *nedher*) used of the Nazirite vow in Nu **6** 2.

SINIM, sī'nim, sin'im, **LAND OF** (אֶרֶץ סִינִים, *'ereç şīnīm;* γῆ Περσῶν, *gē Persōn*): The name occurs in Isaiah's prophecy of the return of the people from distant lands: "Lo, these shall come from far; and, lo, these from the north and from the west; and these from the land of Sinim" (**49** 12). The land is clearly far off, and it must be sought either in the S. or in the E. LXX points to an eastern country. Many scholars have favored identification with China, the classical Sinae. It seems improbable that Jews had already found their way to China; but from very early times trade relations were established with the Far East by way of Arabia and the Pers Gulf; and the name may have been used by the prophet simply as suggesting extreme remoteness. Against this view are Dillmann (*Comm. on Isa*), Duhm, Cheyne and others. Some have suggested places in the S.: e.g. Sin (Pelusium, Ezk **30** 15) and Syene (Cheyne, *Intro to Isa*, 275). But these seem to be too near. In harmony with his reconstruction of Bib. history, Cheyne finally concludes that the reference here is to the return from a captivity in North Arabia (*EB*, s.v.). While no certain decision is possible, probability points to the E., and China cannot be quite ruled out. See art. "China," *Enc Brit*[11], 188*b*.

W. EWING

SINITES, sī'nīts (סִינִי, *şīnī*): A Canaanite people mentioned in Gen **10** 17; 1 Ch **1** 15. The identification is uncertain. Jerome mentions a ruined city Şin, near Arka, at the foot of Lebanon.

SINLESSNESS, sin'les-nes: The 15th Anglican article ("Of Christ Alone without Sin") may be quoted as a true summary of Scripture teaching on sinlessness: "Christ in the truth of our nature was made like unto us in all things, sin only excepted, from which He was clearly [*prorsus*] void, both in His flesh and in His spirit. . . . . Sin, as Saint John saith, was not in Him. But all we the rest, though baptized, and born again in Christ, yet offend in many things; and, if we say we have no sin, we deceive ourselves."

Here the sinlessness of the Incarnate Son is affirmed. It needs no elaborate argument to show that this is the affirmation of Scripture. It is not only, as we are reminded above, definitely taught there. Yet more is it implied in the mysterious (and morally miraculous) phenomenon of the Lord's evidently *total immunity from the sense of sin*, His freedom from inward discord or imperfection, from the slightest discontent with self. It is not too much to say that this representation is self-evidential of its truth to fact. Had it been the invention of worshipping disciples, we may say with confidence that they (supposed thus capable of "free handling") would have been certain to betray some moral aberrations in their portraiture of their Master. They must have failed to put before us the profound ethical paradox of a person who, on the one hand, enjoins penitence and (with a tenderness infinitely deep) loves the penitent, and, on the other hand, is never for a moment penitent Himself, and who all the while has proved, from the first, a supreme moral and spiritual magnet, "drawing all men to him." Meanwhile the Scripture represents the sinlessness of the Incarnate Lord as no mere automatic or effortless condition. He is sensitive to temptation, to a degree which makes it agony. His sinlessness, as to actual experience (we are not here considering the matter *sub specie aeternitatis*), lies in the perfect fidelity to the Father of a will, exercised under human conditions, filled absolutely with the Holy Spirit, willingly received.

1. Christ Sinless

On the other hand, "we the rest," contemplated as true believers, are warned by the general teaching of Scripture never to affirm sinlessness as our condition. There are passages (e.g. 1 Jn **3** 9; **5** 1 f) which affirm of the regenerate man that he "sinneth not." But it seems obvious to remark that such words, taken without context and balance, would prove too much; they would make the smallest sense of sin a tremendous evidence against the person's regeneration at all. It would seem that such words practically mean that sin and the regenerate *character* are diametrical opposites, so that sinning is *out of character*, not in the man as such, but in the Christian as such. And the practical result is an unconquerable aversion and opposition in the regenerate will toward all known sin, and a readiness as sensitive as possible for confession of failure. Meanwhile such passages as 1 Jn are, to the unbiased reader, an urgent warning of the peril of affirming our perfect purity of will and character. But then, on the other hand, Scripture abounds in both precepts and promises bearing on the fact that in Christ and by the power of His Spirit, received by faith into a watchful soul, our weakness can be so lifted and transformed that a moral purification and emancipation is possible for the weakest Christian which, compared with the best efforts of unregenerate nature, is a "more than conquest" over evil (see e.g. 2 Cor **12** 9.10; Gal **2** 20; Eph **6** 16; Jude ver 24). See further FLESH; SPIRIT.

2. Saints Not Sinless

HANDLEY DUNELM

SINNER, sin′ẽr (חַטָּא, *ḥaṭṭā'*; ἁμαρτωλός, *hamartōlós*, "devoted to sin," "erring one"): In the NT, in addition to its ordinary significance of one that sins (Lk **5** 8; **13** 2; Rom **5** 8.19; 1 Tim **1** 15; He **7** 26), the term is applied to those who lived in disregard of ceremonial prescription (Mt **9** 10.11; Mk **2** 15 ff; Lk **5** 30; Gal **2** 15); to those stained with certain definite vices or crimes, as the publicans (Lk **15** 2; **18** 13; **19** 7); to the heathen (Mt **26** 45; Gal **2** 15; cf Tob **13** 6; 1 Macc **1** 34; 2 Macc **2** 48. 62); to the preëminently sinful (Mk **8** 38; Jn **9** 24. 31; Gal **2** 17; 1 Tim **1** 9; Jude ver 15). It was the Jewish term for a woman of ill-fame (Lk **7** 37; cf Mt **21** 32, where it is stated that such had come even to John's baptism also). For the general Bib. conception of the term, see SIN. M. O. EVANS

SION, sī′un (שִׂיאֹן, *sī'ōn*; Σηών, *Sēōn*):

(1) A name given to Mt. Hermon in Dt **4** 48. The name may mean "protuberance" or "peak," and may have denoted the lofty snow-covered horn of the mountain as seen from the S. It may, however, be a scribal error for Sirion, the name by which the mountain was known to the Zidonians. Syr takes it in this sense, which, however, may be a correction of the Heb. It is possible that this name, like Senir, may have applied to some distinct part of the Hermon Range.

(2) Mt. Sion; see ZION.

SIPHMOTH, sif′moth, sif′mōth (שִׂפְמוֹת, *siphmōth* [Ginsburg], שִׂפֲמוֹת, *shiphămōth* [Baer]; Σαφεί, *Saphei*): One of the cities to which David sent presents from Ziklag (1 S **30** 28). It occurs between Aroer and Eshtemoa, so it must have been somewhere in Southern Judah. The site has not been recovered. Zabdi the Shiphmite (1 Ch **27** 27) may quite probably have been a native of this place.

SIPPAI, sip′ī, si-pā′ī. See SAPH.

SIR, sûr: In the OT this word in Gen **43** 20 AV (*'ădhōn*) is changed in RV into "my lord." In the NT the word sometimes represents ἀνήρ, *anḗr*, as in Acts **7** 26; **14** 15; **19** 25, etc; more frequently κύριος, *kúrios*, "lord," as in Mt **13** 27; **21** 30; **27** 36; Jn **4** 11.15.19.49 (RVm "lord"); **20** 15. In Rev **7** 14, RV renders "my lord."

SIRACH, sī′rak (**BOOK OF**), or **The Wisdom of Jesus the Son of Sirach:**

Sirach is the largest and most comprehensive example of Wisdom Literature (see WISDOM LITERATURE), and it has also the distinction of being the oldest book in the Apoc, being indeed older than at least two books (Dnl, Est) which have found a place in the Canon alike of the Eastern and Western churches.

I. Name.—The Heb copy of the book which Jerome knew bore, according to his explicit testimony (see his preface to his version of *Libri Sol.*), the same title as the canonical Prov, i.e. מְשָׁלִים, *m^eshālīm*, "Proverbs" (*Parabolae* is Jerome's word). It is quoted in rabbinical lit. by the sing. of this name, מָשָׁל, *māshāl*=Aram. מַתְלָא, *mathlā'*, but in the Talm it is cited by the author's name, "Ben Sira" (בֶּן סִירָא, *ben ṣīrā'*). The Heb fragments found in recent years have no title attached to them. In the Gr MSS the heading is Σοφία Ἰησοῦ υἱοῦ Σιράχ (or Σειράχ), *Sophía Iēsoú huioú Sirách* (*Seirách*), "The Wisdom of Jesus, son of Sirach" (so א A); or simply Σοφία Σειράχ, *Sophía Seirách* (B), "The Wisdom of Sirach." The Fathers called it either (as Euseb., etc) ἡ πανάρετος σοφία, *hē panáretos sophía*, "the all virtuous wisdom," or simply ἡ πανάρετος, *hē panáretos*, "the all virtuous (one)," or (Clement of Alex.) παιδαγωγός, *paidagōgós*, "teacher." The first Heb and the several Gr titles describe the subject-matter, one Heb title (*ben ṣīrā'*) the author. But the Lat name *Ecclesiasticus* was given the book because it was one of the books allowed to be read in the *Ecclesia*, or church, for edification (*libri ecclesiastici*), though not one of the books of the Canon (*libri canonici*) which could be quoted in proof or disproof of doctrine. The present book is called *Ecclesiasticus* by way of preëminence since the time of Cyprian (*Testimon.* 2, etc). The Syr (Pesh) title as given in the London Polyglot is "The Book of Jesus the son of Simon *'Āṣīrā'* [אָסִירָא], called also the Book of the Wisdom of Bar [=Heb *ben*, "son of"] *'Āṣīrā'*." There can be no doubt that Asira (sometimes tr[d] "bound") is but a corrupted form of Sira. For other explanations see Ryssel in Kautzsch, *AT Apoc*, 234.

Lagarde in his corrected text prefixes the title, "The Wisdom of Bar [=Heb *ben*, "son of"] Sira." How is it that the Heb סִירָא, *ṣīrā'*, has in the Gr become *Sirach* (or *Seirach*)? How are we to explain the final *ch* in the Gr? The present writer thinks it is due to an attempt to represent in writing the guttural sound of the final letter *'aleph* in the Heb name as in the Gr 'Ακελδαμάχ, *Akeldamách*, for the Aram. חֲקַל דְּמָא, *ḥăḳal dᵉmā'* (Acts **1** 19). Dalman, however (*Aram. Gramm.*, 161, n. 6), followed by Ryssel, holds that the final *ch* is simply a sign that the word is indeclinable; cf 'Ιωσήχ, *Iōsēch* (Lk **3** 26), for Heb יוֹסֵי, *yōṣē*.

II. Canonicity.—Though older than both Dnl and Est, this book was never admitted into the Jewish Canon. There are numerous quotations from it, however, in Talmudic and rabbinic lit. (see a list in Zunz, *Die Gottesdienstlichen Vorträge*², 101 f; Delitzsch, *Zur Geschichte der jüd. Poësie*, 204 f; Schechter, *JQR*, III, 682–706; Cowley and Neubauer, *The Original Heb of a Portion of Ecclus*, xix–xxx). It is not referred to explicitly in Scripture, yet it is always cited by Jewish and Christian writers with respect and perhaps sometimes as Scripture. It forms a part of the Vulg of the Tridentine Council and therefore of the Romanist Canon, but the Protestant churches have never recognized it as canonical, though the bulk of modern Protestant scholars set a much higher value upon it than they do upon many books in the Protestant Canon (Ch, Est, etc). It was accepted as of canonical rank by Augustine and by the Councils of Hippo (393) and Carthage (397, 419), yet it is omitted from the lists of accepted books given by Melito (c 180 AD), Origen, in the *Apost. Canons* and in the list of the Councils of Laodicea (341 and 381). Jerome writes in *Libri Sol.*: "Let the church read these two books [Wisd and Sir] for the instruction of the people, not for establishing the authority of the dogmas of the church." It suffered in the respect of many because it was not usually connected with a great name; cf the so-called "Proverbs of Solomon." Sir is cited or referred to frequently in the Ep. of Jas (Jas **1** 2–4—cf Sir **2** 1–5; Jas **1** 5—cf Sir **1** 26; **41** 22; **51** 13 f; Jas **1** 8 ["double minded"]—cf Sir **1** 28, etc). The book is often cited in the works of the Fathers (Clem. Alex., Origen, Augustine, etc) and also in the Apos Const with the formula that introduces Scripture passages: "The Scripture says," etc. The Reformers valued Sir highly, and parts of it have been incorporated into the Anglican Prayer-book.

III. Contents.—It is quite impossible in the book as it stands to trace any one scheme of thought, for the author's mind moves lightly from topic to topic, recurring frequently to the same theme and repeating not seldom the same idea. It is, however, too much to say with Sonntag (*De Jesu Siracidae*, etc) that the book is a farrago of sayings with no connection, or with Berthold that the "work is but a rhapsody," for the whole is informed and controlled by one master thought, the supreme value to every-one of Wisdom. By this last the writer means the Jewish religion as conceived by enlightened Jews toward the beginning of the 2d cent. BC, and as reflected in the Law of Moses (see **24** 23–34), and in a less degree in the books of the Prophets and in the other writings (see Prologue). The book follows the lines of the canonical Book of Prov, and is made up of short pithy sayings with occasional longer discussions, largely collected but in part composed, and all informed and governed by the dominant note of the book: true Wisdom, the chief end of man. Most of the book is poetical in form, and even in the prose parts the parallelism of Heb poetry is found. Many unsuccessful attempts have been made to trace a definite continuous line of reasoning in the book, but the vital differences in the schemes propounded suggest what an examination of the book itself confirms, that the compiler and author put his materials together with little or no regard to logical connection, though he never loses sight of his main theme—Wisdom the chief thing.

Eichhorn (*Einleitung*, 50 ff) divides the book into three parts (chs **1–23**; **24—42** 14; **42** 15—**50** 24), and maintains that at first each of these was a separate work, united subsequently by the author. Julian divides the work into three, Scholz into twelve, Fritzsche (*Einleitung*, xxxii) and Ryssel (op. cit., 240) into seven, Edersheim (op. cit., 19 f) and R. G. Moulton (*Modern Reader's Bible: Ecclus*, xvi ff) into five portions, and many other arrangements have been proposed and defended as by Ewald, Holzmann, Bissell, Zöckler, etc. That there are small independent sections, essayettes, poems, etc, was seen by the early scribes to whom the LXX in its present form was largely due, for they have prefixed headings to the sections beginning with the following verses: **18** 30 ("Temperance of Soul"); **20** 27 ("Proverbs"); **23** 7 ("Discipline of the Mouth"); **24** 1 ("The Praise of Wisdom"); **30** 1 ("Concerning Children"); **30** 14 ("Concerning Health"); **30** 16 ("Concerning Foods"; this is absent from many MSS, though retained by Swete who, however, omits the preceding heading); **30** 24 (EV **33** 24, "Concerning Servants"); **35** (EV **32** 1, "Concerning Rulers"); **44** 1 ("Praise of the Fathers"); **51** 1 ("The Prayer of Jesus, Son of Sirach"). Probably the whole book possessed such headings at one time, and it is quite possible that they originated in the need to guide readers after the book had become one of the chief church reading-books (so W. J. Deane in *Expos*, II, vi, 327). These headings are given in Eng. in AV proper (in the margin), though in modern reprints, as also in RV, they are unfortunately omitted. The whole book has been arranged in headed sections by H. J. Holzmann (Bunsen's *Bibelwerk*, IX, 392 ff) and by R. G. Moulton (op. cit.).

IV. Teaching.—In general it may be said that the principles enunciated in this book agree with those of the Wisdom school of Palestinian Judaism about 200 BC, though there is not a word in the book about a Messianic hope or the setting up of a Messianic kingdom. None of the views characteristic of Alexandrian Judaism and absent from the teaching of Palestinian Judaism are to be found in this book, though some of them at least are represented in Wisd (see WISDOM OF SOLOMON, VI; TEACHING). Gfrörer (*Milo und die jüd.-alex. Philo.*, II, 18 ff) and Dähne (*Gesch. der jüd.-alex. rel. Phil.*, II, 141 ff) hold that the book contains many Alexandrian expressions and numerous statements peculiar to the Alexandrian philosophy. But apart from some late interpolations, mostly Christian, what these Ger. scholars say is untrue, as Drummond (*Philo Judaeus*, I, 144 ff), Deane (*Expos*, II, v, 334 ff) and others have shown. The outstanding features of Alexandrianism are the allegorical interpretation of the Scriptures, its conception of the ecstatic vision of God, its doctrine of mediating powers between man and God and its adoption of purely Gr ideas. None of these can be traced in Sir. The Hebrews never developed a theoretical or speculative theology or philosophy; all their thinking gathered about life and conduct; the duties that men owed to God and to one another; the hopes that they cherished and the fears by which they were animated. This is the only philosophy which the Bible and the so-called Apoc teach, and it is seen at its highest point in the so-called WISDOM LITERATURE (q.v.). The main lines of the teaching of Sir may be set out as follows, under the three heads of religion, morals, and manners.

1. Religion

(1) *God.*—The view of God given in this book agrees generally with that put forth by the later writers of the OT from the exile (Second Isa, Job, etc) onward, though the God of this book lacks the love and tenderness of the Jeh of the OT prophets. God is present everywhere (**16** 17–23); He created the world as an ordered whole (**16** 26–30) and made man intelligent and supreme over all flesh. The expressions used are no doubt modeled on Gen **1**, and it may fairly be inferred that creation out of nothing is meant. Wisd, on the other hand, teaches the Alexandrian doctrine that matter (ὕλη, *húlē*) is eternal and that the Creator's work consisted of fashioning, adapting and beautifying. The world is a creature of God, not (as in Philo, etc)

an emanation from Him. Yet is He compassionate and forgiving (**17** 24 ff). His works are past finding out (**18** 2 ff); but His compassion is upon all flesh (**18** 13), i.e. upon all that accept His chastening and seek to do His will (**18** 14). In **43** 27 God is said to be "the all" (τὸ πᾶν, *tó pán*), which simply means that He pervades and is the ground of everything. It is not Alexandrian pantheism that is taught. Gfrörer and others take a contrary view.

(2) *Revelation.*—In harmony with other products of the "Wise Men," Sir sets chief value upon natural religion, that revealed in the instincts, reason and conscience of man as well as by the sun, moon, stars, etc. Yet Sir gives far more prominence than Prov to the idea that the Divine Will is specially made known in the Law of Moses (**24** 23; **45** 1–4). We do not meet once with the word "law" in Eccl, nor law in the technical sense (Law of Moses) in either Job, Wisd or Prov. In the last-named it is simply one of many synonyms denoting "Wisdom." In Sir the word occurs over 20 t, not, however, always, even when the expression "Law of Moses" is used, in the sense of the "five books" (Pent). It generally includes in its connotation also "the prophecies and the rest of the books" (Prologue); see **32** (LXX **35**) 24; **33** (LXX **36**) 1-3.

(3) *Sin.*—Sin is due to the wrong exercise of man's free will. Men can, if they like, keep the commandments, and when they break from them they are themselves alone to be blamed (**15** 14–17). Yet it was through a woman (Eve) that sin entered the world and death by sin (**25** 24; cf 1 Tim **2** 14). See Rom **5** 12 where "one man," strictly "human being" (ver 14, "Adam"), is made the first cause of sin. But nowhere in Sir is the doctrine of original sin taught.

(4) *Predestination.*—Notwithstanding the prominence given to "free will" (see [3], above), Sir teaches the doctrine of predestination, for God has determined that some men should be high and some low, some blessed and others cursed (**33** 10 ff).

(5) *Satan.*—The word "Satan" (Σατανᾶς, *Satanás*) in **21** 27 (it occurs nowhere else in the Apoc) denotes one's own wicked heart, as the parallelism shows.

(6) *Salvation.*—There is *no salvation* except by way of good works on man's part (**14** 16 f) and forgiveness on God's (**17** 24–32). The only atonement is through one's own good works (**5** 5 f), honoring parents (**32** 14 f), almsgiving, etc (**3** 30; **17** 19 ff). There is no objective atonement ("expiation," lit. "propitiation"; the Gr vb. ἐξιλάσκομαι, *exiláskomai*, is the great LXX word for the Heb כִּפֶּר, *kipper*, "to atone").

(7) *Sacrifice.*—The sacrifice of the wicked is an abomination to God (**34** 18 ff), though He Himself appointed sacrifices and first-fruits (**45** 20 f), and when the righteous offer sacrifices to God they are accepted and remembered in the time to come (**35** 1–12).

(8) *Feasts.*—Festivals as well as seasons are ordained by God to be observed by man (**33** [LXX **36**] 8 f; cf Gen **1** 14).

(9) *Prayer.*—The duty of prayer is often pointed out (**37** 15, etc), the necessary preparation defined (**17** 25; **18** 20.23), and its successful issue promised (**35** 17). There must be no vain repetitions (**7** 14; cf Mt **6** 7), nor should there be any faintheartedness in the matter (**5** 10; cf Jas **1** 6). Men are to pray in sickness (**38** 9), but all the same the physician should be consulted and his advice followed (**38** 1 f.12 ff).

(10) *Angelology.*—Sir nowhere clearly expresses his belief in angels or uses language which implies such a belief. For "an angel [ὁ ἄγγελος, *ho ággelos*] destroyed them" the Heb of the original passage (2 K **19** 35) has מַגֵּפָה, *maggēphāh*, "plague," and so the Syr, though the LXX (followed by the Vulg) has "angel."

(11) *Eschatology.*—Nowhere in this book is the doctrine of a future life taught, and the whole teaching of the book leaves no place for such a doctrine. Men will be indeed rewarded or punished according to their conduct, but in this world (see **2** 10 f; **9** 12; **11** 26 f). The retribution is, however, not confined to the individuals in their lifetime; it extends to their children and involves their own glorious or inglorious name after death (see **11** 28; **40** 15; **41** 6; **44** 11–13). The passage concerning Gehenna (**7** 17) is undoubtedly spurious and is lacking in the Syr, Ethiopic, etc. Since the book is silent as to a future life, it is of necessity silent on the question of a resurrection. Nothing is hinted as to a life beyond the grave, even in **41** 1–4, where the author deprecates the fear of death. In these matters Sir agrees with the Pent and the prophetic and poetical books of the OT (Pss, Job, etc), none of which give any intimation of a life beyond the grave. Little or nothing is said of the Messianic hope which must have been entertained largely by Palestinian Jews living in the author's time, though in **36** (LXX **33**) 1–17 the writer prays for the restoration of Israel and Jerus, i.e. R. H. Charles thinks (*Eschatology*, etc, 65), for the bringing in of the Messianic kingdom.

(12) *Sirach's doctrine of Wisdom.*—For a general discussion of the rise and development of the conception of Wisdom in the OT and in the Apoc see WISDOM LITERATURE. A brief statement as to what the word implies in Sir is all that can here be attempted. It is in chs **1** and **24** that Ben Sira's doctrine is chiefly contained.

Wisdom is from God: He created it and it must therefore have a separate existence. Yet it is dependent on Him. It is omnipresent, though it dwells in a peculiar sense with all flesh. The root and beginning of Wisdom, its fulness and crown, are the fear of God (**1** 14.16.18.21); so that only the obedient and pious possess it (**1** 10.26); indeed Wisdom is identified with the fear of the Lord and the observance of the Law (**19** 20); it is even made one with the Law of Moses (**24** 23), i.e. it consists of practical principles, of precepts regulating the life. In this doctrine we have a combination of universalism, principles of reason and Jewish particularism as the teaching of the revealed Law. We have the first in **24** 3–21; the second in **24** 23–34. Have we in this chapter, as in Prov, nothing outside the teaching of Palestinian Judaism? Gfrörer (op. cit., II, 18 ff) denies this, maintaining that the whole of ch **24** was written by an Alexandrian Jew and adopted unchanged by Ben Sira. But what is there in this chapter which an orthodox, well-informed Palestinian Jew of Ben Sira's time might not well have written? It is quite another question whether this whole conception of Wisdom in the so-called Wisdom books is not due, in some measure, to Gr, though not Alexandrian, influence, unless indeed the Gr influence came by way of Alexandria. In the philosophy of Socrates, and in a less exclusive sense in that of Plato and Aristotle, the good man is the wise one. Cheyne (*Job and Sol*, 190) goes probably too far when he says, "By Gr philosophy Sirach, as far as we can see, was wholly uninfluenced."

2. Morals

The ethical principle of Sir is Hedonism or individual utilitarianism, as is that of Prov and the OT generally, though in the Pss and in the prophetical writings gratitude to God for the love He has shown and the kind acts He has performed is the basis of endless appeals and vows. Moreover, the individual point of view is reached only in the late parts of the OT. In the older OT books, as in Plato, etc, it is the state that constitutes the unit, not the individual human being. The rewards and penalties of conduct, good and bad, belong to this present world. See what is said in (11) "Eschatology," above; see also **2** 7 f; **11** 17; **16** 6 f; **40** 13 f, etc.

The hedonistic principle is carried so far that we are urged to help the good because they are most likely to prove serviceable to us (**12** 2); to aid our fellow-man in distress, so that in his days of prosperity he may be our friend (**22** 23); contrast the teaching of Jesus Christ (Lk **6** 30–36). Friends are to be bemoaned for appearance' sake (**38** 17). Yet many of the precepts are lofty. We are exhorted to show kindness and forbearance to the poor and to give help to our fellow-man (**29** 8.20); to give alms (**12** 3); speak kindly (**18** 15–18); masters should treat servants as brethren, nay as they would themselves be treated (**7** 20–22; **33** 30 f); parents should give heed to the proper training of their children (**3** 2; **7** 23; **30** 1–13); and children ought to respect and obey their parents (**3** 1–16). It is men's duty to defend the truth and to fight for it. So shall the Lord fight for them (**4** 25.28). Pride is denounced (**10** 2 ff), and humility (**3** 18), as well as forgiveness (**28** 2), commended.

3. Manners

Sir is as much a code of etiquette as one of ethics, the motive being almost invariably the individual's own good. Far more attention is given to "manners" in Sir than in Prov, owing to the fact that a more complex and artificial state of society had arisen in Pal. When one is invited to a banquet he is not to show greed or to be too forward in helping himself to the good things provided. He is to be the first to leave and not to be insatiable (**31** 12–18). Moderation in eating is necessary for health as well as for appearance' sake (**31** 19–22). Mourning for the dead is a social propriety, and it should on that account be carefully carried out, since failure to do this brings bad repute (**38** 16 f). It is quite wrong to stand in front of people's doors, peeping and listening: only fools do this (**21** 23 f). Music and wine are praised: nay even a "concert of music" and a "banquet of wine" are good in their season and in moderation (**32** [LXX **35**] 5 f). The author has not a high opinion of woman (**25** 13). A man is to be on his strict guard against singing and dancing girls and harlots, and adultery is an evil to be feared and avoided (**36** 18–26). From a woman sin began, and it is through her that we all die (**25** 4). Yet no one has used more eulogistic terms in praising the good wife than Ben Sira (**26** 1 ff), or in extolling the happiness of the home when the husband and wife "walk together in agreement" (**25** 1).

4. Counsels of Prudence

Never lend money to a man more powerful than thyself or thou wilt probably lose it (**8** 12). It is unwise to become surety for another (**29** 18; **8** 13), yet for a good man one would become surety (**29** 14) and he would even lend to him (**29** 1 ff). It should be remembered that in those times lending and becoming financially liable were acts of kindness, pure and simple: the Jewish Law forbade the taking of interest in any form (see *Century Bible*, "Ezra," etc, 198). "A slip on a pavement is better than a slip with the tongue," so guard thy mouth (**20** 18); "He that is wise in words shall advance himself; and one that is prudent will please great men" (**20** 27). The writer has the pride of his class, for he thinks the common untrained mind, that of the ploughman, carpenter and the like, has little capacity for dealing with problems of the intellect (**38** 24–34).

V. Literary Form.—The bulk of the book is poetical in form, abounding in that parallelism which characterizes Heb poetry, though it is less antithetic and regular than in Prov. No definite meter has been discovered, though Bickell, Margoliouth and others maintain the contrary (see POETRY, HEBREW). Even in the prose parts parallelism is found. The only strophic arrangement is that suggested by similarity of subject-matter.

Bickell (*Zeitschr. für katholische Theol.*, 1882) trd **51** 1–20 back into Heb and tried to prove that it is an alphabetic acrostic ps, and Taylor supports this view by an examination of the lately discovered fragments of the Heb text (see *The Wisdom of Ben Sira*, etc, by S. Schechter and C. Taylor, lxxix ff). After **51** 12 of the Gr and other VSS the Heb has a ps of 15 verses closely resembling Ps **136**; but the Heb VS of **51** 1–20 does not favor Bickell's view, nor does the ps, found only in the Heb, lend much support to what either Bickell or Taylor says. Space precludes detailed proofs.

VI. Author.—The proper name of the author was Jesus (*Jeshua*, Gr *Iēsous*[?]), the family name being "Ben Sira." The full name would be therefore "Jesus Ben Sira." In the Talm and other Jewish writings he is known as "Ben Sira," lit. "son [or descendant?] of Sira." Who Sira was is unknown. No other book in the Apoc gives the name of its author as the Prologue to Sir does.

1. Jesus, Son of Sirach

In the best Gr MSS (B ℵ A) of **50** 27, the author's name appears as Ἰησοῦς υἱὸς Σειρὰχ Ἐλεαζάρ ὁ Ἱεροσολυμείτης, *Iēsoús huiós Seirách Eleazár ho Hierosolumeítēs*, "Jesus the son of Sirach [son of] Eleazar the Jerusalemite." For the last two words ℵ has by a copyist's error, ὁ ἱερεὺς ὁ Σολυμείτης, *ho hiereús ho Solumeítēs*, "the Solomon-like priest." The Heb text of **50** 27 and **51** 30 gives the following genealogy: Simeon son of Jesus, son of Eleazar, son of Sira, making the author the grandson and not the son of Sira, and so he is called by Saadia; see *HDB* (Nestle) and *EB*, II, 1165 (Toy). We know nothing of Ben Sira beyond what can be gathered from the book itself. He was a resident in Pal (**24** 10 f), an orthodox Jew, well read in at least Jewish lit., a shrewd observer of life, with a philosophical bent, though true to the national faith. He had traveled far and seen much (**34** 11 f). His interests were too general and his outlook too wide to allow of his being either a priest or a scribe.

2. Other Views

Many suppositions have been put forward as to the author's identity.

(1) That the author was a priest: so in cod. ℵ (**50** 27). In **7** 29–31 he speaks much of the priesthood, and there are numerous references to sacrifices in the book. In **45** 6–26 he has a long poem in praise of Aaron and his high-priesthood. Yet on the whole Ben Sira does not write as a priest.

(2) That he was a high priest: so Syncellus (*Chron*, ed Dindf., **1** 525) through a misunderstanding of a passage in Eusebius. But the teaching and temper of the book make this supposition more improbable than the last.

(3) That he was a physician: an inference drawn from **38** 1 f.12 ff and other references to the professional healer of the body (**10** 10). But this is a very small foundation on which to build so great an edifice.

(4) That he was one of the 72 translators (LXX): so Lapide (*Comm.*), Calmet, Goldhager, a wholly unsupported hypothesis.

(5) No one of course believes that Solomon wrote the book, though many of the early Fathers held that he was the author of the five Wisdom Books, Prov, Eccl, Cant, Sir and Wisd.

VII. Unity and Integrity.—There is, on the whole, such a uniformity in the style and teaching of the book that most scholars agree in ascribing the whole book (except the Prologue, which is the work of the translator) to Ben Sira. This does not mean that he composed every line; he must have adopted current sayings, written and oral, and this will account for the apparent contradictions, as about becoming surety (**29** 14), and refusing to become surety (**8** 13; **29** 18); words in praise (**25** 1; **26** 1 ff) and condemnation of women (**25** 4.13; **36** 18–26); the varying estimates of life (**36** 16–35;

40 1–11), etc. But in these seeming opposites we have probably no more than complementary principles, the whole making up the complete truth. Nothing is more manifest in the book than the all-pervading thought of one dominant mind. Some have denied the genuineness of ch **51**, but the evidence is at least indecisive. There is nothing in this chapter inconsistent with the rest of the book.

In the recently discovered fragments of Heb text there is a ps between vs 12 and 13 of the Gr and EV which seems a copy of Ps **136**. It is absent from the VSS and its genuineness is doubtful. But in both the Heb and Gr texts there are undoubted additions and omissions. There are, in the Gr, frequent glosses by Christian editors or copyists and other changes (by the translators?) in the direction of Alexandrian Judaism; see *Speaker's Apoc* and other comms. for details.

VIII. Date.—In the book itself there is one mark of definite date (**50** 1), and in the Prologue there is another. Unfortunately both are ambiguous. In the Prologue the translator, whose grandfather or ancestor (Gr πάππος, *páppos*) wrote the book (the younger Siracides, as he is called), says that he reached Egypt, where he found and tr[d] this book in the reign of Euergetes, king of Egypt. But there were two Egyp kings called Euergetes, viz. Ptolemy Euergetes, or Euergetes I (247–222 BC), and Ptolemy VII Physcon, or Euergetes II (218–198 BC). Sir **50** 1 mentions, among the great men whom he praises, Simon the high priest, son of Onias, who is named last in the list and lived probably near the time of the elder Siracides. But there were two high priests called Simon and each of them was a son of Onias, viz. Simon I, son of Onias I (c 310–290 BC), and Simon II, son of Onias II (c 218–198 BC). Scholars differ as to which Euergetes is meant in the Prologue and which Simon in **50** 1.

The conclusions to which the evidence has brought the present writer are these: (1) that Simon I (d. 290 BC) is the high priest meant; (2) that Ptolemy VII Physcon (218–198 BC) is the Euergetes meant.

1. Most Probable Views

(1) In favor of the first proposition are the following:

(*a*) The book must have been written some time after the death of Simon, for in the meantime an artificial fame had gathered around the name, and the very allusion to him as a hero of the past makes it clear that he had been long dead. Assuming that Simon had died in 290 BC, as seems likely, it is a reasonable conclusion that the original Heb work was composed somewhat later than 250 BC. If Simon II is the man intended, the book could hardly have been composed before 150 BC, an impossible date; see below.

(*b*) In the list of great men in chs **44–50** the praises of Simon (**50** 1 ff) are sung after those of Nehemiah (**49** 13), suggesting that the space of time between them was not very great.

(*c*) The "Simon the Just" of Jos was certainly Simon I, he being so called, this Jewish historian says (*Ant*, XII, ii, 5), on account of his piety and kindness.

(*d*) It is probable that the "Simon the Just" of the Mish (*'Ābh* i.2) is also Simon I, though this is not certain. It is said of him that he was one of the last members of the great synagogue and in the Talm he is the hero of many glorifying legends. The so-called great synagogue never really existed, but the date assigned to it in Jewish tradition shows that it is Simon I that is thought of.

(*e*) In the Syr VS (Pesh) **50** 23 reads thus: "Let it [peace] be established with Simon the Just," etc. Some MSS have "Simon the Kind." This text may of course be wrong, but Graetz and Edersheim support it. This is the exact title given to Simon I by Jos (op. cit.), the Mish and by Jewish tradition generally.

(*f*) The only references to Simon II in Jewish history and tradition depict him in an unfavorable light. In 2 Macc **3** he is the betrayer of the temple to the Syrians. Even if the incident of the above chapter were unhistorical, there must have been some basis for the legend. Jos (*Ant*, XII, iv, 10 f) makes him side with the sons of Tobias against Hyrcanus, son of Joseph, the wrong side from the orthodox Jewish point of view.

(*g*) The high priest Simon is said (**50** 1–13) to have repaired the temple and fortified the city. Edersheim says that the temple and city stood in need of what is here described in the time of Simon I, but not in the time of Simon II, for Ptolemy I (247–222 BC) in his wars with Demetrius destroyed many fortifications in Pal to prevent their falling into the hands of the enemy, among which Acco, Joppa, Gaza are named, and it is natural to think that the capital and its sanctuary were included. This is, however, but a priori reasoning, and Derenbourg argues that Simon II must be meant, since according to Jos (*Ant*, XII, iii, 3) Antiochus the Great (223–187 BC) wrote a letter in which he undertakes that the city and temple of Jerus shall be fully restored. This is not, however, to say that Simon II or anyone else did, at that time, restore either.

(*h*) Of the numerous errors in the Gr text some at least seem due to the fact that the VS in that language was made so long after the composition of the original Heb that the sense of several Heb words had become lost among the Alexandrian Jews. If we assume that the Simon of ch **50** was Simon I (d. 290 BC), so that the Heb work was composed about 250 BC; if we further assume that the Euergetes of the Prologue was Ptolemy VII (d. 198 BC), there is a reasonable space of time to allow the sense of the Heb to be lost in many instances (see Halévy, *Rev. Sem.*, July, 1899). It must be admitted that there is no decisive evidence on one side or the other, but the balance weighs in favor of Simon I in the opinion of the present writer.

(2) That the Euergetes of the Prologue in whose reign the translation was made must have been Ptolemy VII Physcon, Euergetes II, seems proved by the translator's statement that he came to Egypt in the 38th year, ἐπὶ τοῦ Εὐεργέτου βασιλέως, *epí toú Euergétou basiléōs*, i.e. almost certainly of the reign of Euergetes, for what reason could the younger Siracides have for giving his own age? Now Euergetes I reigned but 25 years, but Euergetes II (Physcon) reigned in all 54 years, from 170 to 145 BC as regent with his father, and from 145 to 116 BC as sole monarch. If we accept this interpretation of the above words, the question is settled. Westcott, however (*DB*, 1863, I, 479, n. *c*), says "the words can only mean that the translator in his 38th year came to Egypt during the reign of Euergetes." The other rendering adopted by Eichhorn is, he adds, "absolutely set at variance with the grammatical structure of the sentence." In the second ed of *DB* (1893) this note has become expunged, and the article as edited by D. S. Margoliouth (I, 841) teaches the contrary view, which is now accepted by nearly all scholars (Schürer, etc). We may therefore assume that the original Heb book was composed about 240–200 BC, or some 50 or more years after the death of Simon I, and that the translation was made about 130 BC, for the younger Siracides came to Egypt in 132 BC, and he gives us to understand in the Prologue that he tr[d] the Heb work of his grandfather almost immediately after reaching that country. If Simon II (d. 198 BC) is meant in ch **50**, we are compelled to assume a date for the original work of about 150 BC in order to allow time for the growth of the halo of legend which had gathered about Simon. The trans-

lation must, in that case, have been completed some 20 years after the composition of the Heb, a conclusion which the evidence opposes. The teaching of the book belongs to 200 BC, or slightly earlier. The doctrine of the resurrection taught in Dnl (165 BC) is ignored in Sir, as it has not yet become a Jewish doctrine.

2. Brief Statement of Other Views

(1) That the Euergetes of the Prologue and the Simon of ch 50 are in both cases the first so called. So Hug, Scholz, Welt, Keil, Edersheim (*Speaker's Apoc*) and many others. The book was accordingly written after 290 BC, perhaps in 250 BC, or later, and the translation was made some time after 220 BC, say 200 BC.

(2) That Euergetes II (d. 116 BC) and Simon II (d. 198 BC) are the two persons referred to. So Eichhorn, De Wette, Ewald, Franz Delitzsch, Hitzig, Schürer.

(3) Hitzig (*Psalms*, 1836, II, 118) made the original work a product of the Maccabean period—an impossible supposition, for the book says nothing at all about the Maccabees. Moreover, the priestly house of Zadok is praised in this book (chs **50**, etc); it was held in little respect during the time of the Maccabean wars, owing to the sympathy it showed toward the Hellenizing party.

IX. Original Languages.—Even before the discovery of the substantial fragments of what is probably the original Heb text of this book, nearly all scholars had reached the conclusion that Sir was composed in Heb.

1. Composed in Hebrew

(1) The fact of a Heb original is definitely stated in the Prologue. (2) Jerome (*Praef. in vers. libri Sol.*) says that he had seen the Heb original—the same text probably that underlies the fragments recently published, though we cannot be sure of this. (3) Citations apparently from the same Heb text are made not seldom in Talmudic and rabbinical literature. (4) There are some word-plays in the book which in the Gr are lost, but which reappear in the discovered Heb text, e.g. (**43** 8) ὁ μὴν κατὰ τὸ ὄνομα αὐτῆς ἐστιν αὐξανομένη (read ἀνανεομένη), *ho mēn katá tó ónoma autēs estin auxanoménē* (read *ananeoménē*), "the month is called after her name," חדש כשמו הוא מתחדש, *ḥōdhesh kish^emō hū' mithḥadhēsh*, "the *moon* according to its name *renews itself*"; the Heb words for "moon" and "renews itself" come from one root, as if we said in English—what of course is not English—"the moon moons itself." There are other cases where mistakes and omissions in the Gr are explained by a reference to the newly found Heb text.

The strongly supported conjecture of former years that the book was composed in Heb was turned into a practical certainty through the discovery, by Dr. S. Schechter and others in 1896 and after, of the fragments of a (probably *the*) Heb text called now A B C and D. These contain much over half the whole book, and that the text in them, nearly always identical when the same passages are given in more than one, is the original one, is exceedingly likely, to say the least.

2. Margoliouth's View

D. S. Margoliouth (*Origin of the Original Heb of Ecclus*, 1899) has tried to prove that the Heb text of the fragments is a tr of a Pers VS which is itself derived from Gr and Syr. The proofs he offers have not convinced scholars.

(1) He refers to words in Heb which in that language are senseless, and he endeavors to show that they are disguised Pers words. As a matter of fact, in such cases the copyist has gone wholly wrong or the word is undecipherable.

(2) There do appear to be Pers glosses, but they are no part of the original text, and there can be no reasonable doubt that they are due to a Pers reader or copyist.

(3) There are many cases in which the Heb can be proved to be a better and older text than the Gr or Syr (see König, *Expos T*, XI, 170 ff).

(4) As regards the character of the language, it may be said that in syntax it agrees in the main with the classical Heb of the OT, but its vocabulary links it with the latest OT books. Thus we have the use of the "*waw*-consecutive" with the imperfect (**43** 23; **44** 9.23; **45** 2 f, etc) and with the perfect (**42** 1.8.11), though the use of the simple *waw* with both tenses occurs also. This mixed usage is exactly what meets us in the latest part of the OT (Eccl, Est, etc). As regards vocabulary, the word חֵפֶץ, *ḥēpheç*, has the sense of "thing," "matter," in **20** 9, as in Eccl **3** 1; **5** 7; **8** 6. In general it may be said that the Heb is that of early post-Bib. times. Margoliouth holds that the extant Heb VS is no older than the 11th cent., which is impossible. His mistake is due to confounding the age of the MSS with that of the VS they contain.

(5) It is nevertheless admitted that in some cases the Syr or the Gr or both together preserve an older and correcter text than the Heb, but this because the latter has sometimes been miscopied and intentionally changed.

(6) The numerous Hebraisms in the Gr VS which in the Heb have their original expression point to the same conclusion—that this Heb text is the original form of the book.

Margoliouth has been answered by Smend (*TLZ*, 1889, col. 506), König (*Expos T*, X, XI, 1899–1900), Nöldeke (*ZATW*, XX, 81–94), and by many others. Bickell (*Zeitschrift für katholische Theol.*, III, 387 ff) holds also that the Heb Sir extant is a tr from the Gr or Syr or both.

X. Versions.—The LXX tr was made from the Heb direct; it is fairly correct, though in all the extant MSS the text is very corrupt in several places.

1. Greek

(1) The book occurs in the uncials B ℵ C and part of A fairly free from glosses, though abounding in obvious errors. (2) The text is found in a much purer form in cod. V and also in ℵ[ca] and part of A. All extant Gr MSS except the late cursive 248 seem to go back to one original MS, since in all of them the two sections **30** 25—**33** 15 and **33** 16—**36** 11 have changed places, so that **33** 16—**36** 11 follows **30** 24 and **30** 25—**33** 15 comes after **36** 11. Most scholars accept the explanation of Fritzsche (*Exeg. Handbuch zu den Apok*, V, 21 f) that the two leaves on which these two parts (of similar size) were written got mixed, the wrong one being put first. On the other hand, the cursive 248 (14th cent.) has these sections in their proper order, and the same is true of the Syr (Pesh), Lat and Armenian VSS and of the Gr VS of the Complutensian Polyglot (which follows throughout 248 and not the uncials) and EV which is made from this Polyglot. The superiority of 248 to the older MS (B ℵ A C V) is seen in other parts of the Gr text. In the other Gr MSS, **3** 25 is omitted, as it is by Edersheim and most commentators before the discovery of the Heb text. But this last supports 248 in retaining the verse, and it is now generally kept. In **43** 23 "islands" is properly read by 248, Vulg, Syr, 23 and the Heb, but older Gr MSS read "Jesus," making nonsense ("And Jesus planted her" [αὐτήν, *autēn*] for "he planted islands therein"). The other MSS have a text which yields no sense in **43** 26: EV "By reason of him his end hath success." The Gr of 248 and the Heb give this sense: "The angel is equipped for his task," etc.

2. Syriac

The Syr (Pesh) VS is now almost universally acknowledged to have been made from the Heb, of which, on the whole, it is a faithful rendering. In some places, however, it agrees with the LXX against the Heb, probably under the influence of the inaccurate idea that the Gr text is the original one. In this VS the two sections **30** 25—**33** 5 and **33** 16—**36** 11 are in proper order, as in the Heb, a fresh proof that the Syr is not tr[d] from the Gr.

The Vulg agrees with the Old Lat which follows the LXX closely. Lapide, Sabatier and Bengel tried to prove that the Vulg was based on the lost original Heb, but the evidence they supply falls far short of proof, and recently discovered Heb fragments show that they were wrong. The two sections transposed in the LXX (except 248) are also transposed in the Lat, showing that the latter is based on the Gr text. The Lat text of both Sir and Wisd according to the cod. Amiant is given by Lagarde in his *Mittheilungen*, I, 243–84. This closely follows the Gr text.

3. Latin

AV follows the cursives and often repeats their errors. RV is based, for the most part, on the uncials and thus often departs from the Heb. **3** 19 is retained by AV but omitted by RV. For the latter clause of the verse ("mysteries are revealed unto the meek"), AV is supported by cod. 248, the Syr and the Heb. Both EV should be corrected by the Heb in **7** 26 and **38** 1. 15.

4. English

For fuller details concerning VSS see *Speaker's Apoc*, II, 23–32 (Edersheim); Kautzsch, *Die Apok. des AT*, I, 242 ff (Ryssel), and the art. by Nestle in *HDB*, IV, 544 ff.

Literature.—In addition to books mentioned under Apoc and in the course of the present art., note the following:

(1) The text of the Heb fragments: For accounts of the discovery and decipherments of these see *HDB*, IV, 546 f (Nestle); *Bible Polyglotte* (F. Vigoureux), V, 4 ff; Schürer, *GJV*[4], III, 221 ff. The text of the Heb as yet known is conveniently printed in the following: H. L. Strack, *Die Sprüche Jesus*, etc (with notes and glossary), Leipzig, 1903; Isaac Levi, *The Heb Text of Ecclesiasticus* (with notes and glossary), Leiden, 1906; Rudolf Smend, *Die Weisheit des Jesus Sirach, Heb und Deutsch* (with notes and glossary), Berlin, 1906. The Heb appears also in the *Bible Polyglotte*, ed F. Vigoureux, with the LXX, Vulg and a French translation in ‖ columns. (No other Polyglot has appeared since the discovery of the Heb.) There are ‖ texts in Heb, Syr, Gr and Eng., and also useful notes and tables in *The Original Heb of Sir* ***39** 15—**49** 11*, by Cowles and Neubauer, Oxford, 1897. Still later and fuller is *The Wisdom of Ben Sira* in Heb and Eng., with notes on the Heb by Schechter and Taylor, Cambridge, 1899.

(2) Commentaries: The works of Fritzsche (1859), who neglects the evidence of the Syr and ignores the Heb idioms in the book, and of Bissell (1880) and Edersheim (1888) appeared before the discovery of the Heb fragments. The last-named shows both learning and ingenuity in tracking the Heb idioms and in explaining difficulties by means of Heb. The following comms. take full note of the Heb text as far as discovered: Israel Levi, *L'Ecclésiastique ou la sagesse de Jésus fils de Sira: traduit et commenté*, Paris, 1898, 1901; Ryssel in *Kautzsch's Apok. des AT*, I, 280–475, exceedingly valuable, esp. for the text and introduction, but he takes account of the Heb fragments published by Cowley and Neubauer only in this book. To complete his treatment of the Heb parts published after he wrote, see further articles by him in *Stud. u. Krit.*, 1900–1–2; Knabenbaur, *Commentarius in Ecclesiasticum*, Paris, 1902; Peters, *Der jüngst wieder aufgefundene hebräische Text des Buches Ecclesiasticus*, 1902 (cf the notice by Smend, *TLZ*, 1903, 72–77); Smend, *Die Weisheit des Jesus Sirach erklärt*, 1906 (full discussion of the book in the newest light; cf notice by Jülicher in *TLZ*, 1908, 323–29). The New Oxford Apoc (Intro and Notes), ed by R. H. Charles (1913), contains a full Intro and Comm. J. H. A. Hart has published separately a critical edition of cod. 248, in which he collates the principal authorities, MS and printed.

Of the Dict. articles those in *HDB* (Nestle, strong in the critical, but weak and defective on the historical and exegetical side); *EB* (C. H. Toy, sound and well balanced); see also *Jew Enc* (Israel Levi) and *Enc Brit* (W. Baxendale). For detailed register of the literature see *HDB* (Nestle); *Jew Enc*, "Sirach" (Israel Levi); and esp. Schürer, *GJV*[4], III, 219 ff.

T. Witton Davies

SIRACH, THE ALPHABET OF: Usually called **The Alphabet of Ben Sira.** The compilation so designated consists of two lists of proverbs, 22 in Aram. and 22 in Heb, arranged in each case as alphabet acrostics. Each of these proverbs is followed by a haggadic comm., with legends and tales, many of them indecent. Some of the proverbs in the Alphabets are probably genuine compositions by Ben Sira and are quoted as such in the Talm, but in their present form the Alphabets are at least as late as the 11th cent. AD.

Literature.—The only complete copy of the text known is in the British Museum, the copy in the Bodleian being defective. Steinschneider has published a reprint of this last with critical notes (*Alphabeticum Syracidis*, Berlin, 1854). Cowley and Neubauer (*The Original Heb of a Portion of Ecclus*), besides giving a general account of this work, add a tr into Eng. of the Aram. proverbs. In his brief but excellent articles in *Jew Enc* (*Ben Sira, The Alphabet of*), Dr. Louis Ginzberg (New York) also gives a tr of the 22 Aram. proverbs with useful remarks after each. The work has been tr[d] into Lat, Yiddish (often), Judaeo-Spanish, Fr. and Ger., but never, so far, completely into English.

T. Witton Davies

SIRAH, sī'ra, **WELL OF** (בּוֹר הַסִּרָה, *bōr ha-ṣirāh*, "the pit," "well" or "cistern of Sarah"): The spot from which Abner was enticed back to Hebron to his death (2 S **3** 26). Jos (*Ant*, VII, i, 5) calls it Βη(ρ)σιρά, *Bē(r)sirá*, implying that it was a "well." It is possible that this spot is now *'Ain Sārah*, a spring which flows into a little tank near the west side of the road about a mile out of ancient Hebron, on the way to Jerus. There is, however, a curious cistern with steps known as *Ḥamam Sarah* ("Sarah's bath") near *Ramet el-Khalîl*, which is also possibly the site (*PEF*, 314, Sh XXI).

SIRION, sir'i-on (שִׂרְיוֹן, *siryōn;* **Σανιώρ,** *Saniôr*): The name of Mt. Hermon among the Phoenicians (Dt **3** 9). It is given as "Shirion" in Ps **29** 6 (Heb "breastplate" or "body armor"). Here it is named with Lebanon. Sirion therefore probably did not denote a particular part of the Hermon Range, as did Senir, but may have been suggested by the conformation of the range itself, as seen from the heights above the Phoen coast.

SISAMAI, sis'a-mī. See Sismai.

SISERA, sis'ẽr-a (סִיסְרָא, *ṣīṣ[e]rā'*, of doubtful meaning; **Σ[ε]ισάρα,** *S[e]isára*):

(1) Given in Jgs **4** as the captain of the army of Jabin, king of Hazor. The accounts given of the battle of Sisera with Barak, as found in Jgs **4** and **5**, have important points of difference. The first is a prose, the second a poetic narrative. In the first only Naphtali and Zebulun are mentioned as being under the command of Barak; in the second 6 tribes are given as being under his command. In Jgs **4** Sisera is known as the captain of Jabin's forces, while in Jgs **5** he seems to have been an independent leader. There is also a difference as to the scene of the battle and as to the manner in which Sisera met his death at the hand of Jael. Because of these points of difference, added to the fact that this is the only account, in these early times, where a king did not lead his own forces, it is thought by many that there is here the combination of two traditions dealing with different and distinct events.

Sisera resided in Harosheth of the Gentiles, a place identified with *el-Ḥārithīyeh*, on the right bank of the Kishon and commanding the way from the Central Plain to the sea. Taking the versions in the two chapters of Jgs as being the account of a single campaign, we find Deborah urging Barak to combine the forces of Israel to wage war with Sisera as the representative of Jabin, the king of Hazor. The scene of the battle was on the plain at the foot of the slopes of Mt. Tabor (**4** 12–14), or at the foot of the Carmel heights (**5** 19). The attack of Barak and Deborah was so furious, animated as it was by the hatred of Sisera and the Canaanites, that the hosts of Sisera were put to rout, and Sisera, deserting his troops, fled on foot to the N.E. He took refuge in the tent of Heber, near Kedesh, and here met death at the hands of Jael, the wife of Heber (see JAEL). Sisera's name had long produced fear in Israel because of his oppression of the people, his vast army and his 900 chariots of iron. His overthrow was the cause of much rejoicing and was celebrated by the song in which Deborah led the people. See DEBORAH.

It is interesting to note that the great rabbi Aḳiba, who fought so valiantly in the Jewish war for independence as standard bearer to Bar-cocheba, was descended from the ancient warlike Sisera of Harosheth.

(2) In Ezr **2** 53 and Neh **7** 55 the name Sisera, after a long interval, reappears in a family of the Nethinim. There is no evidence that the latter Sisera is connected by family descent with the former.

C. E. SCHENK

SISINNES, si-sin'ēz (Σισίννης, *Sisínnēs*): "The eparch [governor] of Syria and Phoenicia" under Darius Hystaspis (1 Esd **6** 3.7.27; **7** 1) c 520 BC= "Tattenai the governor beyond the river" in Ezr **5** 3.6; **6** 6.13. He took a prominent part in the efforts to prevent the rebuilding of the temple.

SISMAI, sis'mī (סִסְמַי, *ṣiṣmay;* AV **Sisamai**): A Judahite, of the descendants of the daughter of Sheshan and Jarha, his Egyp servant (1 Ch **2** 40). Commentators have compared the name to ססם, *ṣṣm*, a Phoen god (cf Rudolph Kittel, *Comm.* ad loc.; *BDB*, s.v.).

SISTER, sis'tẽr (אָחוֹת, *'āḥōth*): Used repeatedly in the OT of a female (1) having the same parents as another; or (2) having one parent in common, with another, half-sister (Gen **20** 12; Lev **18** 9), and also (3) of a female belonging to the same family or clan as another, so a kinswoman (Gen **24** 60; Job **42 11**); (4) also of a woman of the same country (Nu **25** 18). (5) **Figuratively,** the two kingdoms, Israel and Judah, are sisters (Ezk **23** 7 ff). (6) Confederate cities are conceived of as sisters (Ezk **16** 45 ff). (7) *'Aḥōth* is used of objects which go in pairs, as curtains, each 'coupled to its sister' (Ex **26** 3.6), and of wings in pairs (Ezk **1** 9; **3** 13); (8) of virtues or conditions, with which one is closely related: "Say unto wisdom, thou art my sister" (Prov **7** 4; cf Job **17** 14); (9) of a lover concerning his spouse, as a term of endearment (Cant **4** 9 f; **5** 1 f; **8** 8).

In the NT, ἀδελφή, *adelphḗ*, used (1) in sense of physical or blood kinship (Mt **12** 50; **13** 56; **19** 29; Lk **10** 39 f; **14** 26; Jn **11** 1 ff; **19** 25; Acts **23** 16); (2) of fellow-members in Christ: "Phoebe, our sister" (Rom **16** 1; see also 1 Cor **7** 15; 1 Tim **5** 1; Jas **2** 15); (3) possibly, of a church, "thy elect sister" (2 Jn ver 13). See RELATIONSHIPS, FAMILY.

EDWARD BAGBY POLLARD

SISTER'S SON: AV translates rightly (1) בֶּן־אֲחוֹתוֹ, *ben-'ăḥōthō* (Gen **29** 13); and (2) υἱὸς τῆς ἀδελφῆς, *huiós tḗs adelphḗs* (Acts **23** 16), and wrongly, (3) ἀνεψιός, *anepsiós* (Col **4** 10), where, without doubt, the real meaning is "cousin," as in RV. See RELATIONSHIPS, FAMILY.

SITH, sith: An Anglo-Saxon word meaning "afterward," "since" (Ezk **35** 6 AV and ERV, ARV "since").

SITHRI, sith'rī (סִתְרִי, *ṣithrī*): A grandson of Kohath (Ex **6** 22).

SITNAH, sit'na (שִׂטְנָה, *siṭnāh*, "hatred," "hostility"; ἐχθρία, *echthría*): The name of the second of the two wells dug by the herdsmen of Isaac, the cause of further "enmity" with the herdsmen of Gerer (Gen **26** 21, m "That is, *Enmity*"). The site is unknown, but Palmer (*PEFS*, 1871) finds an echo of the name in *Shuṭnet er Ruḥeibeh*, the name of a small valley near *Ruḥeibeh*. See REHOBOTH.

SITTING, sit'ing (יָשַׁב, *yāshabh*, "to sit down or still," דָּגַר, *dāghar*, "to brood," "hatch"; καθέζομαι, *kathézomai*, "to sit down," ἀνάκειμαι, *anákeimai*, "to lie back," "recline"): The favorite position of the Orientals (Mal **3** 3; Mt **9** 9; **26** 55 [cf **5** 1; Lk **4** 20; **5** 3]; Mk **14** 18; Lk **18** 35; Jn **2** 14, etc).

"In Pal people *sit* at all kinds of work; the carpenter saws, planes, and hews with his hand-adze, sitting upon the ground or upon the plank he is planing. The washer-woman sits by the tub, and, in a word, no one stands where it is possible to sit. . . . . On the low shop-counters the turbaned salesmen squat in the midst of the gay wares" (*LB*, II, 144, 275; III, 72, 75).

Figurative: (1) To sit *with* denotes intimate fellowship (Ps **1** 1; **26** 5; Lk **13** 29; Rev **3** 21); (2) to sit *in the dust* indicates poverty and contempt (Isa **47** 1), *in darkness*, ignorance (Mt **4** 16) and trouble (Mic **7** 8); (3) to sit *on thrones* denotes authority, judgment, and glory (Mt **19** 28).

M. O. EVANS

SIVAN, sē-vän', sī'van (סִיוָן, *ṣīwān*): The third month of the Jewish year, corresponding to June (Est **8** 9). See CALENDAR.

SIXTY, siks'ti (שִׁשִּׁים, *shishshīm;* ἑξήκοντα, *hexḗkonta*). See NUMBER.

SKILL, skil, **SKILFUL**, skil'fo͝ol (forms of יָדַע, *yādha'* [2 Ch **2** 14, etc], בִּין, *bīn* [1 Ch **15** 22], שָׂכַל, *sākhal* [Dnl **1** 4, etc], לָמַד, *lāmadh* [1 Ch **5** 18], חָכָם, *ḥākham* [1 Ch **28** 21], חָרַשׁ, *ḥārash* [Ezk **21** 31], יָטַב, *yāṭabh* [Ps **33** 3]; in Apoc ἐμπειρία, *empeiría* [Wisd **13** 13], ἐπιστήμη, *epistḗmē* [Sir **1** 19; **38** 3.6]; advb. εὐμαθῶς, *eumathṓs* [Wisd **13** 11]): As a vb. "to skill," meaning to have understanding or to be dexterous, common in Elizabethan Eng. and in AV and ERV (1 K **5** 6; 2 Ch **2** 7 f; **34** 12), is obsolete. ARV substitutes such expressions as "knoweth how" (1 K **5** 6) and "were skilful with" (2 Ch **34** 12). As a noun the word is used in the sense of "knowledge" (Eccl **9** 11), "insight" (Dnl **1** 17), and "wisdom" (1 Ch **28** 21). The adj. **skilful** is used in corresponding senses, esp. in ARV, where it takes the place of "cunning" (Ex **26** 31; **31** 4; **35** 33.35; **38** 23; 2 Ch **2** 7.13.14; Cant **7** 1; Isa **40** 20; Jer **10** 9) and of "curious" (Ex **35** 32), where the Heb *ḥāshabh* suggests planning or devising, and thus what we should call "original" work. Both ERV and ARV use the word in place of "eloquent" (Isa **3** 3), "right" (Eccl **4** 4) and "cunning" (1 Ch **25** 7). In the first of these instances the Heb word means "understanding"; in the second, it refers to the manner of doing a thing, and in the third, to the training that makes one "skilled." RV uses the word "skilled" of those that "took the war upon them" (Nu **31** 27 AV). **Skilfulness** (Ps **78** 72) is used with reference to the hands, not only in their work, but also in guiding (as, e.g., a pilot). To play well (Heb *hēṭībhū naggēn*) is rendered "play skilfully" (Ps **33** 3). "Unskilful" is used with reference to the uninitiated in the sense of "inexperienced" (He **5** 13, ἄπειρος, *ápeiros*).

NATHAN ISAACS

SKIN (עוֹר, *'ōr*, גֶּלֶד, *geledh*, "human skin" [Job **16** 15], בָּשָׂר, *bāsār*, "flesh," in the sense of "nakedness" [Ps **102** 5 AV]; δέρμα, *dérma*):

Literal: The word *'ōr* designates the skin of both men and animals, the latter both raw and in tanned condition: "Jeh God made for Adam and for his wife coats of skins [*'ōr*], and clothed them" (Gen **3** 21); "She put the skins [*'ōr*] of the kids of the goats upon his hands, and upon the smooth of his neck" (**27** 16); "Can the Ethiopian change his skin, or the leopard his spots?" (Jer **13** 23). The Heb *geledh* is found in the sense of human skin: "I have sewed sackcloth upon my skin, and have laid my horn in the dust" (Job **16** 15).

Figurative: 'To escape by the skin of the teeth' is equivalent to a narrow escape (Job **19** 20). Satan says in his calumny of Job: "Skin for skin, yea, all that a man hath will he give for his life" (**2** 4). The idea here is, that a man will endure or do the worst, even as it were the flaying of his body, to save his life. The RV has replaced "skin" as the tr of Heb *bāsār* by "flesh": "My bones cleave to my flesh" (Ps **102** 5). "The bars of his skin" is a poetical expression for "the members of his body" in Job **18** 13 m, where the text interprets rather than translates the original.

Skins served for purposes of clothing from an early date (Gen **3** 21). In later days they were the raiment of prophets and hermits (Zec **13** 4; He **11** 37). LXX translates אַדֶּרֶת, *'addereth*, "the mantle" of Elijah (1 K **19** 13.19; 2 K **2** 8.13 f), with μηλωτή, *mēlōtē*, i.e. "sheepskin," the word in He being derived from these passages. It is not unlikely that the raiment of John the Baptist made "of camel's hair" and the "leathern girdle about his loins" are identical with the rough garb of OT prophets. The skins of cattle were largely employed for technical uses; "rams' skins and badgers' skins" are esp. mentioned in the construction of the tabernacle as material for the waterproof covering of the roof (Ex **25** 5; Nu **4** 8.10 ff).

RV, rejecting the tr "badgers' skins," substitutes "sealskins" and adds "porpoise skins" in the margin. There is little doubt that the rendering of the AV is indeed incorrect. The Heb name of the animal (*taḥash*) is the same as the Arab. تُخَس, *tūḥas*, which means the dolphin and the "sea-cow" or halicore of the Red Sea, of which genus there are two species even now extant (*H. tabernaculi* Russ. and *H. Helprichii* Ehr.). It is probable that the Jews included various marine animals, seals, porpoises, dolphins and halicores, under the same expression. See SEALSKIN.

In Ezk **16** 10 we find these skins mentioned as material for elegant shoes, and the Arabs of the Red Sea littoral use the same material in the manufacture of sandals. A quaint use was made of skins in the making of skin bottles, the *ḳurbeh* or *ḳirbeh* of modern Arabia. We find a great variety of Heb expressions, which possibly designated special varieties, all of which were rendered ἀσκός, *askós*, in LXX and the NT (חֵמֶת, *ḥēmeth*, נֹאד, נאוד, *nō'dh*, נֹאדָה, *nō'dhāh*, נֶבֶל, *nebhel*, נֵבֶל, *nēbhel*, בַּקְבֻּק, *baḳbuḳ*, אוֹב, *'ōbh*). RV has rendered the Gr *askos* in the NT by "wineskin" (Mt **9** 17; Mk **2** 22; Lk **5** 37) with the marginal addition "that is, *skins used as bottles*." These skin bottles were made of the skins of goats, sheep, oxen or buffaloes; the former had more or less the shape of the animals, the holes of the extremities being closed by tying or sewing, and the neck of the skin being closed by a tap or a plug, while the larger ones were sewn together in various shapes. As a rule only the inside of the skin was tanned, the skin turned inside out, and the fluid or semi-fluid filled in, e.g. water, milk, butter, cheese. The hairy inside was not considered as in any way injurious to the contents. Only in the case of wine- and oil-skins was it thought advantageous to tan the skins inside and out.

H. L. E. LUERING

SKIRT, skûrt: (1) כָּנָף, *kānāph*, "wing," "extremity" (Ruth **3** 9, etc), is the usual word. But in 1 S **24** 4 ff perhaps "corner" is the best tr. (2) שׁוּל, *shūl*, "loose hanging" (Ex **28** 33, etc; in AV often rendered "hem"). (3) פֶּה, *peh*, "mouth," "opening" (Ps **133** 2, "the precious oil . . . . that came down upon the skirt"). But the "opening" is that for the head, so that RVm "collar" is the correct tr. "Skirt" is frequently used in a euphemistic sense, for which the comms. must be consulted. See DRESS; TRAIN.

SKULL, skul (גֻּלְגֹּלֶת, *gulgōleth;* κρανίον, *kraníon*): The Heb word, which is well known to Bible readers in its Aram.-Gr form "Golgotha," expresses the more or less globular shape of the human skull, being derived from a root meaning "to roll." It is often tr[d] in EV by "head," "poll," etc. In the meaning "skull" it is found twice (Jgs **9** 53; 2 K **9** 35). In the NT the word is found only in connection with GOLGOTHA (q.v.), "the place of a skull" (Mt **27** 33; Mk **15** 22; Jn **19** 17), or "the skull" (Lk **23** 33).

SKY, skī (שַׁחַק, *shaḥak*, "fine dust" or "cloud," apparently from √ שָׁחַק, *shāḥak*, "to rub," "to pulverize"; Sam שְׁחָקִיָּה, *sheḥāḳayyāh* instead of Heb שָׁמַיִם, *shāmayim*; سحق, *saḥk* = "cloud," "small dust"):

1. In the OT

RV has "skies" for AV "clouds" in Job **35** 5; **36** 28; **37** 21; Ps **36** 5; **57** 10; **68** 34; **78** 23; **108** 4; Prov **3** 20; **8** 28, in which passages *BDB* supports the rendering of AV. In Ps **89** 6.37 RV has "sky" for AV "heaven." EV has "sky" in Dt **33** 26; 2 S **22** 12; Job **37** 18; Ps **18** 11; **77** 17; Isa **45** 8; Jer **51** 9. The word occurs mainly in poetical passages.

2. In the NT

In the NT οὐρανός, *ouranós*, is tr[d] "heaven" (AV "sky") in connection with the weather in Mt **16** 2.3; Lk **12** 56. In He **11** 12 we find "the stars of heaven" ("the sky") as a figure of multitude. The conception, however, that the visible "sky" is but the dome-like floor of a higher world often makes it hard to tell whether "heaven" in certain passages may or may not be identified with the sky. See HEAVEN; COSMOGONY.

ALFRED ELY DAY

SLANDER, slan'dẽr (subst., דִּבָּה, *dibbāh*, "slander"; διάβολος, *diábolos*, "slanderer"; vb. רָגַל, *rāghal*, "to slink about" as a talebearer, לָשַׁן, *lāshan*, "to use the tongue," "to slander"; διαβάλλω, *diabállō*, "to calumniate," "to slander"; and other words): Slander (etymologically a doublet of "scandal," from OFr. *esclandre*, Lat *scandalum*, "stumbling-block") is an accusation maliciously uttered, with the purpose or effect of damaging the reputation of another. As a rule it is a false charge (cf Mt **5** 11); but it may be a truth circulated insidiously and with a hostile purpose (e.g. Dnl **3** 8, "brought accusation against," where LXX has *diaballō*, "slander"; Lk **16** 1, the same Gr word). Warnings, condemnations and complaints in reference to this sin are very frequent, both in the OT and NT. Mischievous "tale-bearing" or "whispering" is condemned (Lev **19** 16; Ezk **22** 9). There are repeated warnings against evil-speaking (as in Ps **34** 13; Prov **15** 28; Eph **4** 31; Col **3** 8; Jas **4** 11; 1 Pet **3** 10), which is the cause of so much strife between man and man (Prov **16** 27–30), and which recoils on the speaker himself to his destruction (Ps **101** 5; **140** 11). Esp. is false witness, which is "slander carried into a court of justice," to be condemned and punished (Ex **20** 16;

Dt **19** 16–21; cf Prov **12** 17; **14** 5.25; **19** 5; **21** 28; **24** 28). Special cases of slander more than usually mean are when a wife's chastity is falsely impeached by her husband (Dt **22** 13–19), and when one slanders a servant to his master (Prov **30** 10). Even a land may be slandered as well as persons (Nu **14** 36). Slanderers and backbiters are mentioned in some of Paul's darkest catalogues of evildoers (Rom **1** 29.30; 2 Cor **12** 20; 2 Tim **3** 3). To refrain from slander is an important qualification for citizenship in the theocracy (Ps **15** 1.3; **24** 3.4) and for a place in the Christian church (1 Tim **3** 11; Tit **2** 3). Jesus Himself was the victim of slanders (Mt **11** 19) and of false testimony (Mt **27** 63). The apostles, too, came in for a full share of it (e.g. Acts **24** 5 f; **28** 22; 2 Cor **6** 8). In the case of Paul, even his central doctrine of justification was "slanderously reported" as if it encouraged immorality (Rom **3** 8). The devil (="the calumniator") is represented as the great accuser of God's people (Rev **12** 10), the slanderer *par excellence* (cf Job **1** 9–11; Zec **3** 1). See also CRIMES; PUNISHMENTS.

D. MIALL EDWARDS

SLAUGHTER, slô'tẽr, **OF THE INNOCENTS.** See INNOCENTS, MASSACRE OF.

SLAUGHTER, VALLEY OF: In Jer **7** 32; **19** 6, a name given to the valley of Hinnom. See HINNOM, VALLEY OF; JERUSALEM, III, 2.

SLAVE, slāv, **SLAVERY,** slāv'ẽr-i:

1. Acquiring of Slaves
2. Hebrews as War Captives
3. Freedom of Slaves
4. Rights of Slaves
5. Rights of Slave Masters
6. The NT Conception

LITERATURE

The origin of the term "slave" is traced to the Ger. *sklave*, meaning a captive of the Slavonic race who had been forced into servitude (cf Slav); Fr. *esclave*, Dutch *slaaf*, Swedish *slaf*, Spanish *esclavo*. The word "slave" occurs only in Jer **2** 14 and in Rev **18** 13, where it is suggested by the context and not expressed in the original languages (Heb *yelīdh bayith*, "one born in the house"; Gr *sôma*, "body"). However, the Heb word עֶבֶד, *'ebhedh*, in the OT and the Gr word δοῦλος, *doúlos*, in the NT more properly might have been trd "slave" instead of "servant" or "bondservant," understanding though that the slavery of Judaism was not the cruel system of Greece, Rome and later nations. The prime thought is *service;* the servant may render *free service*, the slave, *obligatory, restricted service.*

Scripture statement rather than philological study must form the basis of this article. We shall notice how slaves could be secured, sold and redeemed; also their rights and their masters' rights, confining the study to OT Scripture, noting in conclusion the NT conception. The word "slave" in this art. refers to the Heb slave unless otherwise designated.

Slaves might be acquired in the following ways, viz.:

1. Acquiring of Slaves

(1) *Bought.*—There are many instances of buying slaves (Lev **25** 39 ff). Heb slavery broke into the ranks of every human relationship: a father could sell his daughter (Ex **21** 7; Neh **5** 5); a widow's children might be sold to pay their father's debt (2 K **4** 1); a man could sell himself (Lev **25** 39.47); a woman could sell herself (Dt **15** 12.13.17), etc. Prices paid were somewhat indefinite. According to Ex **21** 32 thirty shekels was a standard price, but Lev **27** 3–7 gives a scale of from 3 to 50 shekels according to age and sex, with a provision for an appeal to the priest in case of uncertainty (ver 8). Twenty shekels is the price set for a young man (ver 5), and this corresponds with the sum paid for Joseph (Gen **37** 28).

But in 2 Macc **8** 11 the price on the average is 90 for a talent, i.e. 40 shekels each. The ransom of an entire talent for a single man (1 K **20** 39) means that unusual value (far more than that of a slave) was set on this particular captive.

There were certain limitations on the right of sale (Ex **21** 7 ff).

(2) *Exchange.*—Slaves, i.e. non-Heb slaves, might be traded for other slaves, cattle, or provisions.

(3) *Satisfaction of debt.*—It is probable that a debtor, reduced to extremity, could offer himself in payment of his debt (Lev **25** 39), though this was forbidden in the *Tōrath Kōhănīm;* cf *'Ōçar Yisrā'ēl*, vii.292*b*. That a creditor could sell into slavery a debtor or any of his family, or make them his own slaves, has some foundation in the statement of the poor widow whose pathetic cry reached the ears of the prophet Elisha: "Thy servant my husband is dead; . . . . and the creditor is come to take unto him my two children to be bondmen" (2 K **4** 1).

(4) *Gift.*—The non-Heb slave, and possibly the Heb slave, could be acquired as a gift (Gen **29** 24).

(5) *Inheritance.*—Children could inherit non-Heb slaves as their own possessions (Lev **25** 46).

(6) *Voluntary surrender.*—In the case of a slave's release in the seventh year there was allowed a willing choice of indefinite slavery. The ceremony at such a time is interesting: "Then his master shall bring him unto the judges [m], and shall bring him to the door, or unto the door-post; and his master shall bore his ear through with an awl; and he shall serve him for ever" (Ex **21** 6). A pierced ear probably meant obedience to the master's voice. History, however, does not record a single instance in which such a case occurred.

(7) *Arrest.*—"If the thief be found breaking in, ... he shall make restitution: if he have nothing, then he shall be sold for his theft" (Ex **22** 2.3).

(8) *Birth.*—The children of slaves, born within the master's house of a wife given to the slave there, became slaves, and could be held, even if the father went free (Ex **21** 4; cf Lev **25** 54).

(9) *Capture in war.*—Thousands of men, women and children were taken in war as captives and reduced, sometimes, to most menial slavery. Such slavery, however, was more humane than wholesale butchery according to the customs of earlier times (Nu **31** 7–35). Males were usually slain and females kept for slavery and concubinage (Dt **21** 10.11.14). Captive slaves and bought slaves, "from nations round about," forced moral ruin into Israel's early civilization. See SIEGE, 3.

The two principal sources of slave supply were poverty in peace and plunder in war.

2. Hebrews as War Captives

The Hebrews themselves were held as captive slaves at various times by (1) Phoenicians (the greatest slave traders of ancient times), (2) Philis, (3) Syrians (2 K **5** 2 ff), (4) Egyptians, and (5) Romans. There must have been thousands subjected to severest slavery. See also EGYPT; ISRAEL; PHARAOH; SERVANT, etc.

The freedom of slaves was possible in the following ways:

3. Freedom of Slaves

(1) *By redemption.*—Manumission by redemption was common among the Hebrews. The slave's freedom might be bought, the price depending on (*a*) the nearness to the seventh year or the Jubilee year, (*b*) the first purchase price, and (*c*) personal considerations as to age and ability of the one in bondage. A slave could be redeemed as follows:

(*a*) by himself, (*b*) by his uncle, (*c*) by his nephew or cousin, (*d*) or by any near relative (Lev **25** 48–55). The price depended on certain conditions as indicated above.

(2) *By the lapse of time.*—The seventh year of service brought release from bondage. "If thou buy a Heb servant [m "bondman"], six years he shall serve: and in the seventh he shall go out free for nothing" (Ex **21** 2–4).

(3) *By the law of the Jubilee year.*—The year of Jubilee was the great year when slaves were no longer slaves but free. "He shall serve with thee unto the year of jubilee: then shall he go out from thee, he and his children . . . . return unto his own family, and unto the possession of his fathers" (Lev **25** 40 f).

(4) *By injury.*—A servant whose master maimed him (or her), in particular by causing the loss of an eye or even a tooth, was thereby freed (Ex **21** 26f).

(5) *By escape.*—(Dt **23** 15 f; 1 K **2** 39). See "Code of Ḥammurabi" in *HDB* (extra vol, p. 600) and cf Philem vs 12 ff.

(6) *By indifference.*—In case of a certain kind of female slave, the neglect or displeasure of her master in itself gave her the right to freedom (Ex **21** 7–11; Dt **21** 14).

(7) *By restitution.*—A caught thief, having become a bondsman, after making full restitution by his service as a slave, was set at liberty (Ex **22** 1–4).

(8) *By the master's death.*—"And Abram said, ... I go childless, and he that shall be possessor of my house is Eliezer of Damascus . . . . and, lo, one born in my house is mine heir" (Gen **15** 2 f). This passage has been mistakenly supposed to indicate that a master without children might give freedom to a slave by constituting the slave an heir to his possessions. But on the contrary, Abram seems to contemplate with horror the possibility that Eliezer will take possession of his goods in the absence of an heir. In view of the fact that adoption, the *adrogatio* of the Rom law, was unknown both to Bib. and Talmudic law (see *Jew Enc*, s.v.), the statement in Gen **15** 2 does not seem to indicate any such custom as the adoption of slaves. If any method of emancipation is here suggested, it is by the death of the master without heir, a method thoroughly discussed in the Talm (*mīthath hā-'ādhōn*).

(9) *By direct command of Jeh.*—"The word that came unto Jeremiah from Jeh, ... that every man should let his man-servant, and . . . . his maid-servant, that is a Hebrew or a Hebrewess, go free; that none should make bondmen of them . . . . they obeyed, and let them go" (Jer **34** 8–10).

The nine methods here enumerated may be classified thus:

A. By operation of law:
 1. By lapse of time.
  (*a*) After serving six years or other contractual period. See (2) above.
  (*b*) Upon the approach of the Jubilee year. See (3) above.
 2. By death of the master without heirs. See (8) above.

B. By act of the parties:
 1. By an act of the master.
  (*a*) Voluntary manumission, including (9) above.
  (*b*) Indifference in certain cases. See (6) above.
  (*c*) Maiming servant. See (4) above.
 2. By act of the servant.
  (*a*) Redemption. See (1) above.
  (*b*) Restitution. See (7) above.
  (*c*) Escape. See (5) above.
 3. By act of a third party.
  Redemption—(1) above.

As noted in the beginning of this article, the Heb slaves fared far better than the Grecian, Rom and other slaves of later years. In general, the treatment they received and the rights they could claim made their lot reasonably good. Of course a slave was a slave, and there were masters who disobeyed God and even abused their "brothers in bonds." As usual the unfortunate female slave got the full measure of inhuman cruelty. Certain rights were discretionary, it is true, but many Heb slaves enjoyed valuable individual and social privileges. As far as Scripture statements throw light on this subject, the slaves of OT times might claim the following rights, viz.:

4. Rights of Slaves

(1) *Freedom.*—Freedom might be gained in any one of the above-mentioned ways or at the master's will. The non-Hebrew could be held as a slave in perpetuity (Lev **25** 44–46).

(2) *Good treatment.*—"Thou shalt not rule over him [Heb slave] with rigor, but shalt fear thy God. . . . . Ye shall not rule, one over another, with rigor" (Lev **25** 43.46). The non-Hebrew seemed to be left unprotected.

(3) *Justice.*—An ancient writer raises the query of fairness to slaves. "If I have despised the cause of my man-servant or of my maid-servant, when they contended with me; what then shall I do when God riseth up?" (Job **31** 13 f). No doubt the true Heb master was considerate of the rights of his slaves. The very fact, however, that the Heb master could punish a Heb slave, "to within an inch of his life," gave ready opportunity for sham justice. "And if a man smite his servant, or his maid ["bondman or bondwoman"], with a rod, and he die under his hand; he shall surely be punished. Notwithstanding, if he continue a day or two, he shall not be punished; for he is his money" (Ex **21** 20 f).

(4) *Family.*—The slave before his release might have his wife and children (Ex **21** 5).

(5) *Voluntary slavery.*—Even when the seventh year came, the slave had a right to pledge himself, with awl-pierced ear, to perpetual service for his master (Ex **21** 5 f; Dt **15** 16). The traditional interpretation of "for ever" in these passages is "until the next Jubilee year" (cf *Ḳiddūshīn* **21**).

(6) *Money or property.*—Some cases at least indicate that slaves could have money of their own. Thus, if a poor slave "waxed rich" he could redeem himself (Lev **25** 49). Cf 1 S **9** 5–10, where, however, the Heb throughout calls the "servant" *na'ar*, "a youth," never *'ebhedh*.

(7) *Children.*—If married when free, the slave could take wife and children with him when freedom came, but if he was married after becoming a slave, his wife and children must remain in possession of his master. This law led him often into perpetual slavery (Ex **21** 3 f).

(8) *Elevation.*—A chance to rise was allowable in some instances, e.g. Eliezer, a foreign slave in a Heb household, and Joseph, a Heb slave in a foreign household. Each rose to a place of honor and usefulness (Gen **15** 2; **39** 4).

(9) *Religious worship.*—After being circumcised, slaves were allowed to participate in the paschal sacrifice (Ex **12** 44) and other religious occasions (Dt **12** 12).

(10) *Gifts.*—Upon obtaining freedom, slaves, at the discretion of masters, were given supplies of cattle, grain and wine (Dt **15** 13 f).

5. Rights of Slave Masters

The rights of a slave master may briefly be stated as follows: (1) to hold as chattel possession his non-Heb slaves (Lev **25** 45); (2) to leave such slaves as an inheritance for his children (Lev **25** 46); (3) to hold as his own property the wife and children of all slaves who were unmarried at the time they became slaves (Ex **21** 4); (4) to pursue and recover runaway slaves (1 K **2** 39–41); (5) to grant freedom at any time to any slave. This is implied rather than stated. Emancipation other than at the Sabbatical and Jubilee years was evidently the right of masters; (6) to circumcise slaves, both Jew and Gentile, within his own household (Gen **17** 13.23.27); (7) to sell, give away, or trade slaves (Gen **29** 24. According to *Tōrath Kōhănīm* a Heb servant could be sold only under certain restrictions. See **1,** [1]); (8) to chastise male and female slaves, though not unto death (Ex **21** 20); (9) to marry a slave himself, or give his female slaves in marriage to others (1 Ch **2** 35); (10) to marry a daughter to a slave (1 Ch **2** 34 f); (11) to purchase slaves in foreign markets (Lev **25** 44); (12) to keep, though not as a slave, the runaway slave from a foreign master (Dt **23** 15.16. See **3,** [5]); (13) to enslave or sell a caught thief (Gen **44** 8–33; Ex **22** 3); (14) to hold, in perpetuity, non-Heb slaves (Lev **25** 46); (15) to seek advice of slaves (1 S **25** 14 ff; but the reference here is open to doubt. See **4,** [6]); (16) to demand service (Gen **14** 14; **24**).

Throughout OT times the rights of both slaves and masters varied, but in general the above may be called the accepted code. In later times Zedekiah covenanted with the Hebrews never again to enslave their own brothers, but they broke the covenant (Jer **34** 8).

6. NT Conception

There were slaves during NT times. The church issued no edict sweeping away this custom of the old Judaism, but the gospel of Christ with its warm, penetrating love-message mitigated the harshness of ancient times and melted cruelty into kindness. The equality, justice and love of Christ's teachings changed the whole attitude of man to man and master to servant. This spirit of brotherhood quickened the conscience of the age, leaped the walls of Judaism, and penetrated the remotest regions. The great apostle proclaimed this truth: "There can be neither Jew nor Greek, there can be neither bond nor free, ... ye all are one man in Christ Jesus" (Gal **3** 28). The Christian slaves and masters are both exhorted in Paul's letters to live godly lives and make Christ-like their relations one to the other—obedience to masters and forbearance with slaves. "Bondservants [m], be obedient unto . . . . your masters, ... as bondservants [m] of Christ . . . . And, ye masters, ... forbear threatening: . . . . their Master and yours is in heaven, and there is no respect of persons with him" (Eph **6** 5–9).

Christ was a reformer, but not an anarchist. His gospel was dynamic but not dynamitic. It was leaven, electric with power, but permeated with love. Christ's life and teaching were against Judaistic slavery, Rom slavery and any form of human slavery. The love of His gospel and the light of His life were destined, in time, to make human emancipation earth-wide and human brotherhood as universal as His own benign presence.

LITERATURE.—Nowack, *Heb Arch.;* Ewald, *Alterthümer*, III, 280–88; Grünfeld, *Die Stellung des Sklaven bei den Juden, nach bibl. und talmud. Quellen*, 1886; Mielziner, *Die Verhältnisse der Sklaven bei den alten Hebräern*, 1859; Mandl, *Das Sklavenrecht des AT*, 1886; Kahn, *L'esclavage dans la Bible et le Talmud*, 1867; Sayce, *Social Life among the Assyrians and Babylonians;* Lane, *Manners and Customs of Modern Egyptians*, 205; *Arabian Nights*, I, 64 ff; Thomson, *LB;* McCurdy, *HPM*, 1894; Trumbull, *Studies in Oriental Social Life*, 1894. There is a wealth of material in the Talmudic tractate *Ḳiddūshīn* (pp. 17–22).

WILLIAM EDWARD RAFFETY

SLAYING, slā'ing (by spear, dart, or sword). See PUNISHMENTS.

SLEEP, slēp: Represents many words in Heb and Gr. For the noun the most common are שֵׁנָה, *shēnāh*, and ὕπνος, *húpnos;* for the vb., יָשֵׁן, *yāshēn*, שָׁכַב, *shākhabh*, and καθεύδω, *katheúdō*. The figurative uses for death (Dt **31** 16, etc) and sluggishness (Eph **5** 14, etc) are very obvious. See DREAMS.

SLEEP, DEEP (תַּרְדֵּמָה, *tardēmāh*, vb. רָדַם, *rādham*, from a root meaning "to be deaf"): The vb. *rādham* has no further meaning than "to be fast asleep" (Jgs **4** 21; Jon **1** 5), but AV used "deep sleep" as a tr only in Dnl **8** 18; **10** 9, where a sleep supernaturally caused (a "trance") is meant (cf "dead sleep" in Ps **76** 6). RV's insertion of "deep sleep" in place of AV's "fast asleep" in Jgs **4** 21 is consequently unfortunate. The noun *tardēmāh* has the same meaning of "trance" in Gen **2** 21; **15** 12; 1 S **26** 12; Job **4** 13; **33** 15, but in Prov **19** 15; Isa **29** 10, it is used **figuratively** of torpor. In Acts **20** 9 (*húpnos bathús*), heavy natural sleep is meant.

BURTON SCOTT EASTON

SLEEVES, slēvz (Gen **37** 3 m). See DRESS.

SLEIGHT, slīt: No connection with "slight," but from the same root as "sly" and so = "cunning." So in Eph **4** 14, "sleight of men," for κυβεία, *kubeía*, "dice-playing" (cf "cube"), "gamblers' tricks," "trickery."

SLIME, slīm, **SLIME PITS,** slīm'pits (חֵמָר, *ḥēmār;* LXX **ἄσφαλτος,** *ásphaltos;* Vulg *bitumen;* RVm "bitumen"; cf Arab. حُمَّر, *ḥummar*, "bitumen"; and cf חֹמֶר, *ḥōmer*, "clay," "mortar"): In the account of the ark in Gen **6** 14, כֹּפֶר, *kōpher* (LXX ἄσφαλτος, *ásphaltos;* Vulg *bitumen;* cf Arab. كُفْر, *kufr*, "pitch") does not necessarily denote vegetable pitch, but may well mean bitumen. The same may be said of זֶפֶת, *zepheth*, "pitch" (cf Arab. زِفْت, *zift*, "pitch"), in Ex **2** 3 and Isa **34** 9. The word "slime" occurs in the following passages: "And they had brick for stone, and slime had they for mortar" (Gen **11** 3); "Now the vale of Siddim was full of slime pits" (Gen **14** 10, m "bitumen pits"); "She took for him an ark of bulrushes, and daubed it with slime and with pitch" (Ex **2** 3).

Bitumen is a hydrocarbon allied to petroleum and natural gas. It is a lustrous black solid, breaking with a conchoidal fracture, burning with a yellow flame, and melting when ignited. It is probably derived from natural gas and petroleum by a process of oxidation and evaporation, and its occurrence may be taken as a sign that other hydrocarbons are or have been present in the strata. It is found in small lumps and larger masses in the cretaceous limestone on the west side of the Dead Sea, and there is reason to believe that considerable quantities of it rise to the surface of the Dead Sea during earthquakes. In ancient times it was exported to Egypt to be used in embalming mummies. Important mines of it exist at *Ḥâsbeiya* near Mt. Hermon and in North Syria. Springs of liquid bituminous matter exist in Mesopotamia, where according to Herodotus and other classical writers it was used as mortar with sun-dried bricks. Various conjectures have been made as to the part played by bitumen in the destruction of Sodom and Gomorrah. Diodorus Siculus calls the Dead Sea λίμνη ἀσφαλτῖτις, *límnē asphaltítis*, "lake of asphalt." See SIDDIM; CITIES OF THE PLAIN.

ALFRED ELY DAY

SLING. See ARMOR, III, 2.

SLIP: As meaning "a cutting from a plant," it is still good Eng. In this sense in Isa **17** 10 for

זְמוֹרָה, *zemōrāh*, "branch," "twig." For the phrase "slip of the tongue" cf Sir **14** 1; **19** 16; **20** 18; **21** 7; **25** 8.

SLOPES, slōps. See Ashdoth-pisgah.

SLOW, slō: Chiefly for אֶרֶךְ, *'erekh*, lit. "long," in the phrase "slow to anger" (Neh **9** 17, etc). In Ex **4** 10; Lk **24** 25; Jas **1** 19, for כָּבֵד, *kābhēdh; βραδύς, bradús*, both meaning "heavy," "sluggish," while Sir **7** 35 uses "be slow" for ὀκνέω, *oknéō*, "hesitate." In addition, AV uses "slow" for ἀργός, *árgos*, "inactive," in Wisd **15** 15, "slow to go" (RV "helpless for walking"), and in Tit **1** 12, "slow bellies" (RV "idle gluttons"). In Sir **51** 24, AV has "be slow" for ὑστερέω, *husteréō*, "be lacking" (so RV).

SLUGGARD, slug'ard: Found only in the OT, and there only in Prov. It is the rendering given the word *'āçēl* everywhere in RV, but in AV only in Prov **6** 6.9; **10** 26; **13** 4; **20** 4; **26** 16 (elsewhere AV translates by "slothful"). The root meaning of *'āçēl* is "to be sluggish," "stupid." The Eng. word "slug" is said to be "allied to slack" (Webster).

SLUICE, slōōs (שֶׂכֶר, *sekher*, lit. "hire"): In Isa **19** 10, AV reads, "all that make sluices and ponds for fish." RV entirely alters the tr of the whole verse. It reads, "And the pillars of Egypt shall be broken in pieces; all they that work for hire [m "that make dams"] shall be grieved in soul."

SMELL, smel (Heb and Aram. רֵיחַ, *rē*[a]*ḥ*, as noun, "savor," "scent"; רוּחַ, *rū*[a]*ḥ*, as vb., lit. "to breathe," "to inhale," thence "to smell"; **ὀσμή,** *osmḗ*, the "smell," "savor," **εὐωδία,** *euōdía*, "sweet smell," "fragrance," **ὄσφρησις,** *ósphrēsis*, "the sense of smell"; vb. **ὀσφραίνομαι,** *osphraínomai*): "And he came near, and kissed him: and he smelled [*wayyāraḥ*] the smell [*rē*[a]*ḥ*] of his raiment, and blessed him, and said, See, the smell [*rē*[a]*ḥ*] of my son is as the smell [*rē*[a]*ḥ*] of a field which Jeh hath blessed" (Gen **27** 27). Idols are described as "gods, the work of men's hands, wood and stone, which neither see, nor hear, nor eat, nor smell" (Dt **4** 28). Acceptable sacrifices and pious conduct are called a "sweet smell" or "savor" (Ex **29** 18; Eph **5** 2; Phil **4** 18), well-pleasing to God. The godless life, which dishonors God, is hateful to Him: "I will not smell the savor of your sweet odors" (Lev **26** 31). The phrase, "being in bad odor with a person," can be traced to Bib. language: "Ye have made our savor to be abhorred in the eyes of Pharaoh, and in the eyes of his servants" (Ex **5** 21). Thus "smell" is occasionally equivalent with "quality," "character": "His [Moab's] taste remaineth in him, and his scent is not changed" (Jer **48** 11). Character or quality is the most infallible test, the most manifest advertisement of a thing or a person; thus we find the following very instructive passage: "[God] maketh manifest through us the savor [*osmē*] of his knowledge in every place. For we are a sweet savor [*euōdia*] of Christ unto God, in [better: "among"] them that are saved, and in [better: "among"] them that perish; to the one a savor [*osmē*] from death unto death; to the other a savor [*osmē*] from life unto life" (2 Cor **2** 14–16). See Triumph. In the passage Isa **3** 24, AV "sweet smell" (בֶּשֶׂם, *besem*, "balsam plant") has been changed to "sweet spices" in RV.

H. L. E. Luering

SMITH, smith. See Crafts, 10; Tubal-cain.

SMITING BY THE SUN. See Sun Smiting.

SMOKE, smōk: Used figuratively of the Divine jealousy (Dt **29** 20) and anger (Ps **74** 1); symbolic of the glory of the Divine holiness (Isa **4** 5; **6** 4; Rev **15** 8).

SMYRNA, smûr'na (**Σμύρνα,** *Smúrna*): Smyrna, a large ancient city on the western coast of Asia Minor, at the head of a gulf which reaches 30 miles inland, was originally peopled by the Asiatics known as the Lelages. The city seems to have been taken from the Lelages by the Aeolian Greeks about 1100 BC; there

1. Ancient

Ancient Aqueduct at Smyrna.

still remain traces of the cyclopean masonry of that early time. In 688 BC it passed into the possession of the Ionian Greeks and was made one of the cities of the Ionian confederacy, but in 627 BC it was taken by the Lydians. During the years 301 to 281 BC, Lysimachus entirely rebuilt it on a new site to the S.W. of the earlier cities, and surrounded it by a wall. Standing, as it did, upon a good harbor, at the head of one of the chief highways to the interior, it early became a great trading-center and the chief port for the export trade. In Rom times, Smyrna was considered the most brilliant city of Asia Minor, successfully rivaling Pergamos and Ephesus. Its streets were wide and paved. Its system of coinage was old, and now about the city coins of every period are found. It was celebrated for its schools of science and medicine, and for its handsome buildings. Among them was the Homerium, for Smyrna was one of several places which claimed to be the birthplace of the poet. On the slope of Mt. Pagus was a theater which seated 20,000 spectators. In the year 23 AD a temple was built in honor of Tiberius and his mother Julia, and the Golden Street, connecting the temples of Zeus and Cybele, is said to have been the best in any ancient city. Smyrna early became a Christian city, for there was one of the Seven Churches of the Book of Rev (**2** 8–11). There Polycarp, the bishop of Smyrna, was martyred, though without the sanction of the Rom government. It seems that the Jews of Smyrna were more antagonistic than were the Romans to the spread of Christianity, for it is said that even on Saturday, their sacred day, they brought wood for the fire in which Polycarp was burned. His grave is still shown in a cemetery there. Like many other cities of Asia Minor, Smyrna suffered frequently, esp. during the years 178–80 AD, from earthquakes, but it always escaped entire destruction. During the Middle Ages the city was the scene of many struggles, the most fierce of which was directed by Timur against the Christians. Tradition relates that there he built a tower, using as stones the heads of a thousand captives which he put to death, yet Smyrna was the last of the Christian cities to hold out against the Mohammedans; in 1424 it fell into the hands of the Turks. It was the discovery of America and the resulting discovery of a sea route to India which ruined the Smyrna trade.

2. Modern

Modern Smyrna is still the largest city in Asia Minor, with a population of about 250,000, of whom half are Greek and less than one-fourth are Mohammedans. Its modern name, *Ismir,* is but a Turkish corruption of the ancient name. Even under the Turkish government the city is progressive, and is the capital of the Aidin vilayet, and therefore the home of a governor. Several railroads follow the courses of the ancient routes into the distant interior. In its harbor ships from all parts of the world may be seen. The ancient harbor of Paul's time has been filled in, and there the modern bazaars stand. The old stadium has been destroyed to make room for modern buildings, and a large part of the ancient city lies buried beneath the modern houses and the 40 mosques of which the city boasts. The better of the modern buildings, belonging to the government and occupied by the foreign consuls, stand along the modern quay. Traces of the ancient walls are still to be found. W. of Mt. Pagus is the Ephesian gate, and the Black-gate, as the Turks call it, is near the railroad station. The castle upon Mt. Pagus, 460 ft. above the sea, dates from Byzantine times. The prosperity of Smyrna is due, not only to the harbor and the port of entry to the interior, but partly to the perfect climate of spring and autumn—the winters are cold and the summers are hot; and also to the fertility of the surrounding country. Figs, grapes, valonia, opium, sponges, cotton and liquorice root are among the chief articles of trade. See also CHURCHES, SEVEN.

E. J. BANKS

SNAIL, snāl ([1] חֹמֶט, *ḥōmeṭ,* RV "sand-lizard," LXX σαῦρα, *saúra,* "lizard" [Lev **11** 30]; [2] שַׁבְּלוּל, *shabbᵉlūl,* LXX κηρός, *kērós,* "wax" [Ps **58** 8]): (1) *Ḥōmeṭ* is 7th in the list of unclean "creeping things" in Lev **11** 30, and occurs nowhere else. "Snail" is not warranted by LXX or Vulg. RV has "sand-lizard." It may be the skink or a species of *Lacerta.* See LIZARD. (2) *Shabbᵉlūl* is trd "snail" in Ps **58** 8: "Let them be as a snail which melteth and passeth away." Mandelkern gives *limax,* "slug." Gesenius derives *shabbᵉlūl* from *bālal,* "to pour"; cf Arab. *balla,* "to wet," instancing λεῖμαξ, *leímax,* "snail," or "slug," from λείβω, *leíbō,* "to pour." While LXX has *kēros,* "wax," Talm (*Mōʻēdh Ḳāṭān* **6***b*) supports "snail." The ordinary explanation of the passage, which is not very satisfying, is that the snail leaves a trail of mucus (i.e. it melts) as it moves along. This does not in any way cause the snail to waste away, because its glands are continually manufacturing fresh mucus. Two large species of snail, *Helix aspersa* and *Helix pomatia,* are collected and eaten, boiled, by the Christians of Syria and Pal, esp. in Lent. The Jews and Moslems declare them to be unclean and do not eat them.

ALFRED ELY DAY

SNARE, snâr (פַּח, *paḥ;* παγίς, *pagís,* but βρόχος, *bróchos,* in 1 Cor **7** 35): Over half a dozen Heb words are used to indicate different methods of taking birds and animals, of which the snare (פַּח, *paḥ*) is mentioned oftener than any other. It was a noose of hair for small birds, of wire for larger birds or smaller animals. The snares were set in a favorable location and grain scattered to attract the attention of feathered creatures. They accepted the bribe of good feeding and walked into the snare, not suspecting danger. For this reason the snare became particularly applicable in describing a tempting bribe offered by men to lead their fellows into trouble, and the list of references is a long one, all of the same nature. See Ex **10** 7; 1 S **18** 21; **28** 9; Ps **11** 6; **18** 5, "snares of death"; used symbolically of anything that may kill: **91** 3; **124** 7; **140** 5; **141** 9; Prov **7** 23; **13** 14; **18** 7; **20** 25; **22** 25; **29** 25; Eccl **9** 12. "But this is a people robbed and plundered; they are all of them snared in holes, and they are hid in prison-houses: they are for a prey, and none delivereth; for a spoil, and none saith, Restore" (Isa **42** 22). Here it is specified that the snare was in a hole so covered as to conceal it. Jer **18** 22 clearly indicates that the digging of a pit to take prey was customary, and also the hiding of the snare for the feet. North American Indians in setting a snare usually figure on catching the bird around the neck. Jer **50** 24, "I have laid a snare for thee"; Hos **9** 8, "A fowler's snare is in all his ways"; Am **3** 5 seems to indicate that the snare was set for the feet; Lk **21** 34, "But take heed to yourselves, lest haply . . . . that day come on you suddenly as a snare"; Rom **11** 9, "Let their table be made a snare, and a trap"; 1 Cor **7** 35, "not that I may cast a snare upon you"; 1 Tim **3** 7, "the snare of the devil"; also **6** 9, "But they that are minded to be rich fall into a temptation and a snare and many foolish and hurtful lusts, such as drown men in destruction and perdition." See GIN; NET; TRAP.

GENE STRATTON-PORTER

SNEEZE, snēz (זוֹרֵר, *zōrēr,* Pōʻēl-form זָרַר, *zārar*): "The child sneezed seven times, and the child opened his eyes" (2 K **4** 35). "Sneezing," better "snorting," is found in the description of Leviathan (the crocodile): "His sneezings [עֲטִישָׁה, *ʻăṭīshāh*] flash forth light, and his eyes are like the eyelids of the morning" (Job **41** 18 [Heb 10]). See NEESING.

SNOW, snō (שֶׁלֶג, *shelegh,* תְּלַג, *tᵉlagh* [Dnl **7** 9]; χιών, *chiṓn*): (1) Snow is not uncommon in the winter in Jerus, but it never reaches any depth and in many winters it is not seen at all. It usually disappears, for the most part, as soon as the sun appears, though it may "hide itself" for a time in the gorge cut by a stream (Job **6** 16). On lower levels than Jerus there is never sufficient to cover the ground, though often there are some flakes seen in the air. Even at sea-level there is occasionally a sufficient fall of hail to cover the ground. A very exceptional snowfall is related in 1 Macc **13** 22 at Adora (near Hebron). It was heavy enough to prevent the movement of troops. (2) The tops of the mountains of Lebanon are white with snow for most of the year, and snow may be found in large banks in the valleys and the northern slopes at any time in the summer. Mt. Hermon, 9,200 ft. high, has long streaks of snow in the valleys all the summer. (3) The snow of the mountains is the source of the water of the springs which last throughout the drought of summer. In case the snow fails there is sure to be a lack of water in the fountains: "Shall the snow of Lebanon fail . . . . or shall the cold waters that flow down from afar be dried up?" (Jer **18** 14). (4) Large quantities of snow are stored in caves in the mountains in winter and are brought down to the cities in summer to be used in place of ice for cooling drinks and refrigerating purposes.

(5) God's power over the elements of Nature is often brought out in the OT: "For he saith to the snow, Fall thou on the earth" (Job **37** 6); but man cannot fathom the works of God: "Hast thou entered the treasuries of the snow?" (Job **38** 22). "The snowy day" (1 Ch **11** 22; 2 S **23** 20) and the "fear of snow" (Prov **31** 21) are **figurative** uses describing winter and cold. "Snow in sum-

mer" (Prov **26** 1) would be most out of place, yet it might be most refreshing to the tired workmen in the time of harvest.

(6) Snow is the symbol of purity and cleanness, giving us some of our most beautiful passages of Scripture: "Wash me and I shall be whiter than snow" (Ps **51** 7); "Though your sins be as scarlet, they shall be as white as snow" (Isa **1** 18). Carrying the figure farther, snow-water might be expected to have a special value for cleansing: "If I wash myself with snow-water" (Job **9** 30). The most common use in Scripture is to denote whiteness in color and implying purity as well: "His raiment was white as snow" (Dnl **7** 9; Mt **28** 3; Mk **9** 3; Rev **1** 14).

(7) The whiteness of leprosy is compared to snow (Ex **4** 6; Nu **12** 10; 2 K **5** 27).

Alfred H. Joy

SNUFFERS, snuf'ẽrz, **SNUFFDISHES,** snuf'-dish-ez (מְלְקָחַיִם, *melḳāḥayim*, מַחְתּוֹת, *maḥtōth*): These two utensils are thrice mentioned in connection with the wilderness tabernacle (Ex **25** 38; **37** 23; Nu **4** 9). ARV prefers to read "snuffers and snuffdishes" in place of "tongs and snuffdishes" (cf 2 Ch **4** 22), the connection between the two utensils being indicated by the fact that both are said to belong to the seven lamps, and were to be made out of the talent of gold which was specified as the weight of the whole (Ex **25** 37–39).

The seven-branched candlestick which stood in the holy place of both tabernacle and temple was surmounted, in each of its arms, by a removable lamp in which olive oil was burnt. From the requirement of keeping these lights brilliantly burning throughout each night of the year, arose the need for snuffers and snuffdishes. By the former, the burnt portions of the wick were removed; in the latter they were deposited previous to removal. The lamps may have required to be trimmed as often as every half-hour. For this purpose a priest would enter the outer chamber "accomplishing the services" (He **9** 6).

In the time of Solomon's Temple another word than *melḳāḥayim* was used to describe this utensil. It is מְזַמְּרוֹת, *m^e zamm^e rōth*, from a vb. meaning "to prune" or "trim," and is found in 1 K **7** 50; 2 K **12** 13; **25** 14; 2 Ch **4** 22; Jer **52** 18. In 4 of these passages, the Eng. text reads, "the snuffers and the basins"; the 5th is merely a summary of things taken to Babylon (2 K **25** 14). In this constant later association of "basins" and "snuffers" it is seen that the basins referred to were used for the reception of the cast-off portions of the wicks of the seven lamps, and took the place of the snuffdishes of an earlier age. See Tongs.

W. Shaw Caldecott

SO, sō (סוֹא, *ṣō'*, although the Heb might be pointed סֶוֶא, *ṣewe'*; Assyr *Sib'u;* LXX **Σηγώρ**, *Sēgôr*, **Σωά**, *Sōá;* Manetho, **Σεύεχος**, *Seúechos;* Lat *Sevechus;* Herod. [ii. 137 ff], **Σαβακῶν**, *Sabakōn*): In all probability the "Sabaeo" of Herodotus, the Shabaka, who founded the Ethiopian dynasty, the XXVth of Egyp kings. His date is given as 715–707 BC (Flinders Petrie, *History of Egypt*, III, 281 ff), but we may suppose that before his accession to the throne he was entitled to be designated king, as being actually regent. To this So, Hoshea, king of Israel, made an appeal for assistance to enable him to throw off the yoke of the Assyr Shalmaneser IV (2 K **17** 3 ff). But Hoshea's submission to So brought him no advantage, for Shalmaneser came up throughout all the land and laid siege to Samaria. Not long after the fall of Samaria, So ventured upon an eastern campaign, and was defeated by Sargon, the successor of Shalmaneser, in the battle of Raphia in 720 BC.

Literature.—Flinders Petrie, *History of Egypt*, III, 281 ff; McCurdy, *HPM*, I, 422; Schrader, *COT*, I, 261.

T. Nicol

SOAP, sōp (בֹּרִית, *bōrīth;* AV **sope**): *Bōrīth* is a derivative of בֹּר, *bōr*, "purity," hence something which cleanses or makes pure. Soap in the modern sense, as referring to a salt of a fatty acid, for example, that produced by treating olive oil with caustic soda, was probably unknown in OT times. Even today there are districts in the interior of Syria where soap is never used. Cooking utensils, clothes, even the body are cleansed with ashes. The ashes of the household fires are carefully saved for this purpose. The cleansing material referred to in Jer **2** 22 (cf LXX ad loc., where *bōrīth* is rendered by **πoία**, *poía*="grass") and Mal **3** 2 was probably the vegetable lye called in Arab. *el ḳali* (the origin of Eng. *alkali*). This material, which is a mixture of crude sodium and potassium carbonates, is sold in the market in the form of greyish lumps. It is produced by burning the desert plants and adding enough water to the ashes to agglomerate them. Before the discovery of Leblanc's process large quantities of *ḳali* were exported from Syria to Europe.

For washing clothes the women sprinkle the powdered *ḳali* over the wet garments and then place them on a flat stone and pound them with a wooden paddle. For washing the body, oil is first smeared over the skin and then *ḳali* rubbed on and the whole slimy mixture rinsed off with water. *Ḳali* was also used anciently as a flux in refining precious metals (cf Mal **3** 2). At the present time many Syrian soap-makers prefer the *ḳali* to the imported caustic soda for soap-making.

In Sus (ver 17) is a curious reference to "washing balls" (*smēgmata*).

James A. Patch

SOBER, sō'bẽr, **SOBRIETY,** sō-brī'ē-ti, **SOBERNESS,** sō'bẽr-nes (Gr adj. *sōphrōn*, and its related nouns, *sōphrosúnē*, *sōphronismós;* vbs. *sōphronéō* and *sōphronízō;* advb. *sōphrónōs*, "of sound mind," "self-possessed," "without excesses of any kind," "moderate and discreet"): In Mk **5** 15; Lk **8** 35, "sane," said of one out of whom demons had just been cast. In the Pastoral Epp., this virtue is esp. commended to certain classes, because of extravagances characterizing particular periods of life, that had to be guarded against, viz. to aged men, with reference to the querulousness of old age (Tit **2** 2); to young men, with reference to their sanguine views of life, and their tendency to disregard consequences (Tit **2** 6); enjoined upon young women, with reference to extravagance in dress and speech (Tit **2** 5; 1 Tim **2** 9); and, in a similar manner, commended to ministers, because of the importance of their judgment and conduct, as teachers and exemplars (1 Tim **3** 2). "Words of soberness" (Acts **26** 25) are contrasted with the "mania," "madness," that Festus had just declared to be the explanation of Paul's eloquence (ver 24).

In a few passages, the Gr vb. *nḗphō* and its derivative adj. *nēphálios* are used in the same sense. The word originally had a physical meaning, as opposed to drunkenness, and is thus used in 1 Thess **5** 6.8, as the foundation of the deeper meaning. Used **metaphorically** also in the Pastoral Epp. and 1 Pet, as sometimes in the classics, for "cool," "unimpassioned." Ellicott, on 1 Tim **3** 2.11, distinguishes between the two words by regarding *sōphrōn* "as pointing to the outward exhibition of the inward virtue" implied in *nēphalios*.

H. E. Jacobs

SOCHO, sō'kō: Occurs in 1 Ch **4** 18, RV "Soco." See Socoh.